LET'S GO

www.letsgo.com

EUROPE

researcher-writers
Sophia Angelis
Asa Bush
Ama Francis
Beatrice Franklin
Nelson Greaves
Vanda Gyuris
Christa Hartsock
Jocelyn Karlan
Michal Labik
Rachel Lipson
Joshua McTaggart
Ned Monahan
Benjamin Naddaff-Hafrey
Taylor Nickel
Julia Rooney
Ansley Dawn Rubinstein
Elyssa Spitzer
Grace Sun
Joe Tobias
Alex Tomko
Xin (Cindy) Wang
Mark Warren
Elizabeth Weinbloom
William N. White

editors
Sarah Berlow
Teresa Cotsirilos
Meagan Michelson
Bronwen Beseda O'Herin
Jonathan Rossi

research managers
Anna E. Boch
Joseph B. Gaspard
Chris Kingston
Colleen O'Brien
Matthew Whitaker

managing editor
Daniel C. Barbero

staff writers
Sophia Angelis
Sophie Arlow
Elias Berger
Juan Cantu
Dwight Livingstone Curtis
Simone Gonzalez
Rachel Granetz
Ryan E. Heffrin
Meghan Houser
Adrienne Y. Lee
Dorothy McLeod
Taylor Nickel
Alexandra Perloff-Giles
Ansley Dawn Rubinstein
Maya Shwayder
William N. White
Sara Joe Wolansky
Qichen Zhang

CONTENTS

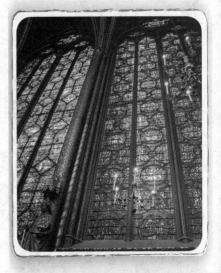

Europe Overview

RESEARCHER-WRITERS

SOPHIA ANGELIS. Freshman phenom Sophie tore through northeast Germany, holding her own on a team of Harvard grads. While last-minute German lessons helped Sophie navigate small villages and big cities alike, her outdoorsy California spirit and photographic eye are what truly helped her discover the country.

ASA BUSH. This *Let's Go* veteran kept us laughing with his witty writing and quirky photos from Scotland and Ireland. From a tour of the Jameson Irish Whiskey Factory to "Bloomsday" celebrations with fellow James Joyce fanatics, Asa's eye for excitement found him plenty of kindred—and distilled—spirits during his stay in Dublin.

AMA FRANCIS. Ama is from the lovely, but little known, island of Dominica. A Caribbean childhood in the Caribbean left Ama with fabulous French skills, a love for the beach, and a taste for mangoes. Her time in France was spent researching, drinking bottles of rose wine, and getting into a steady (or dependent) relationship with pain au chocolat.

BEATRICE FRANKLIN. A walk through the Red Light District was like a stroll through a tulip field after Beatrice's last gig as an RW for *Let's Go Thailand*. She dug out her one orange sundress to celebrate Oranje success at the World Cup and turned a well-trained eye toward everything from the diviest hostel to the smartest smartshop.

NELSON GREAVES. On the few occasions that Nelson was able to suppress his attraction to Czech women and addiction to Eastern European cuisine, he pumped out copy that left his editors in stitches. Come the fall, the recent Harvard grad will move south of his hometown of Fresno, California, to start writing the screenplays for all of your favorite TV shows.

VANDA GYURIS. This *Let's Go* veteran planned her research around the World Cup schedule, watching each match with lively local septuagenarians. With her Harvard degree in hand, Vanda is off to China to teach English—but she'll undoubtedly take frequent vacations to Portugal to showcase her badass California surfing skills.

CHRISTA HARTSOCK. Christa's love affair with Barcelona began with her extensive research on the city's urban planning for her senior thesis. An art and architecture scholar, she was powerless to resist the likes of Gaudí's Manzana de Discordia. After her immaculate research was finished, Christa embarked on an epic biking trip to Amsterdam, where she snored loud enough to wake up the whole town.

JOCELYN KARLAN. After spending part of last summer stranded on top of a mountain in Ecuador, Jocey chalks up her time with *Let's Go* as a success. A student of psychology, Jocey may have used hypnosis to charm the locals—or maybe she's just incredibly amiable. sHer editors think it's the latter; Jocey's enthusiasm to research every nook and cranny (and cave) in Andalusia made her indispensable.

MICHAL LABIK. Michal was really looking forward to wearing a fez in Istanbul, but was saddened to hear that the Ottoman Empire wouldn't be reinstated in time. However, he made do with cavorting in the bazaars, eating more kebab than he thought possible, and being hit on in a gay hammam. Though as Michal likes to say, being hit on is always better than being hit.

RACHEL LIPSON. Britain's confusing accents and dreary weather couldn't put a damper on this New York native and first-time *Let's Go* RW. Whether chatting with Vikings or pretending to be an Oxford student, Rachel showed an incredible thirst for adventure (and cider!) as she traveled all across England.

JOSHUA MCTAGGART. Josh has a surprisingly good British accent. We promise, it has nothing to do with the fact that he grew up just outside Bristol, UK. Researching the Loire Valley as well as Brussels, Bruges, and parts of the Netherlands, Josh certainly got his fill of castles. He'd like to be a spy (channeling James Bond, much?), though he sampled wine, not martinis, throughout his travels.

NED MONAHAN. Born Edward Monahan III, Ned is truly Boston's boy. A hip-hop enthusiast with a habit of befriending strangers on the street, Ned once spent a summer working on a champagne vineyard in France. When he returned to France to work for *Let's Go*, he knew he'd be in for a whole new experience (and certainly one with a very different final product).

BENJAMIN NADDAFF-HAFREY. Though some travel to London for prestige and tradition, this feisty freshman came to the British capital with a different mission: to get into his first bar fight. Lucky for us, Ben decided to play it safe while he single-handedly navigated London, even as World Cup mania brought out the hooligan in every Englishman.

TAYLOR NICKEL. From the shores of SoCal to the French Riviera 20-year-old Taylor has already traveled to over 50 countries. When he wasn't researching the best hostels in Marseille, he was working the tables at a casino in Monte Carlo or riding a scooter from Saint-Tropez to Cannes. His winning smile and enviable tan make it hard for anybody, from hotel managers to customs officials, to say no to.

JULIA ROONEY. This veteran of *Let's Go Italy 2009* demonstrated a prodigious knowledge of Italian culture that put her editors—and probably even a few locals—to shame. From trying (and failing) to sketch Marcus Aurelius's foot to devouring dangerous amounts of Roman gelato, Julia kept her cool with perfect prose and perfetto italiano.

ANSLEY DAWN RUBINSTEIN. With the help of her ever-present cup of coffee, this *Let's Go* veteran and recent Harvard grad reenergized our coverage of Vienna. Bound for stardom as a dancer and actress, Ansley will undoubtedly enjoy fame in Hollywood, but she dreams of eventually returning to her previous *Let's Go* haunts—Australia and the Greek Islands.

ELYSSA SPITZER. The quintessential straight shooter, Elyssa didn't put up with BS. No sub-par orange juice or cigarette-burned bed was going to slip into her listings. If this ball-busting research weren't enough to make her an champ, Elyssa's always pleasant calls and hilarious stories about old, pants-less Greek dudes made her editors love her.

GRACE SUN. Grace explored the heart of Spain—Madrid—and mastered the inner workings of its atria (discotecas) and ventricles (endless tapas bars). Starting off her route with a nasty case of bronchitis did nothing to dampen Grace's spirits—and neither did encountering a bunkmate doing meth in southern Portugal. Grace's willingness to try new things (except meth) made her research shine.

JOE TOBIAS. Hailing from the Great White North, Joe is a mountain man with a poet's soul. When he isn't writing sonnets, he can be found somewhere in the wilderness of the Northeastern US. His travels for *Let's Go* took him to Morocco and southwestern France, allowing him to master snake charming and wine tasting.

ALEX TOMKO. Refusing to be worn down by Venice's antiquated structure, Alex somehow found time to train for a triathlon between afternoons visiting palatial hotels and nights wandering the streets in search of the perfect bar in Dorsoduro.

XIN (CINDY) WANG. Fresh off a stint as an RW for *Let's Go Boston*, this Geneva (Illinois!) native strapped on a backpack and hopped a plane for her next *Let's Go* adventure. Even a recently earned Harvard degree won't keep Cindy resting on her laurels; after researching musical traditions in China next year, she's off to Berkeley for grad school.

MARK WARREN. Traipsing along the Camino in northern Spain and scooting south into Portugal, Mark circumnavigated nearly half of the Iberian Peninsula. This modern-day Magellan's route was a whirlwind of port wine, seafood, and learning that Portuguese is really not that similar to Spanish.

ELIZABETH WEINBLOOM. After the Dark Ages of grad school, Elizabeth went to Italy for *Let's Go* seeking her own Renaissance—and found it in the hallowed galleries of the Uffizi. After stressful encounters with Tuscan train schedules and angry San Gimignano nuns, Elizabeth resisted the temptation to settle down in Lucca and instead completed her route like a champ.

WILLIAM N. WHITE. An experienced sailor, William proved himself no ordinary **boat** nerd, displaying additional talents as a hiker, pizza critic, and—of course—star RW. While the beach bums around him soaked up the sun in Monterosso, William spent his time bringing subtle wit and a travel-savvy perspective to his research.

DISCOVER

EUROPE

Sick of your parents' stories about "When I was in Europe..." to show that they were, in fact, cool? Well, it's time to shut them up forever with your own, because there's a reason that this continent has been the stomping ground of students for generations, with castles and gory stories to match. It has the whole gamut of architectural periods and incredible renovations, brogues and rolling r's, and residents who drink alcohol like water. It has some of the best art and culture concentrated into a continent that's less than half of the size of the United States. And you're always in the good company of fellow travelers, both young and old, out on adventures like you. Europe is a trendy place to visit, but nothing about it is cliche (unless you reenact *Notting Hill* or *Eurotrip*). In addition, the once dangerous or less popular places in Europe have blossomed into student havens with exciting venues and deals and steals. Think out of the box, and make your trip to Europe an experience that far surpasses anything your mom or pops ever bragged about.

when to go

Summer is the busiest time to travel in Europe. Fun festivals in the summer can jack up prices, but who wants to miss the *Fête de la Musique* or Avignon's Festival, each bursting with local flavor and communal joviality. Late spring and early autumn mean fewer tourists and cheaper airfare. Winter travel is a unique experience, giving adventurers the chance to ski in northern Italy, Germany, and basically any place with great mountain ranges. But this also means some hotels, restaurants, and sights have limited hours or are on vacation—from you.

what to do

MY HOSTEL OR YOURS?

While your exchange rate in Mexico might be better than the one you'll get in Europe (though even that's improving), there are lots of places where students can stay without breaking the bank. Hostels are a great option, particularly in more affordable places like the Netherlands, Portugal, and Eastern Europe.

- **CITRUS SUNSHINE:** Naxos's dirt cheap hostel options give you the chance to live more like a Greek god at the Archway of Apollo, and the island's own *citron* liquor is worth a sip or more (p. 581).

- **AVENTURA HOSTEL:** Be prepared for your own adventure when you stay in one of the best hostels in Budapest, known especially for the amazing tourists it attracts (p. 613).

- **OOPS!:** The only thing you won't be saying when you step into Paris' first boutique hostel (p. 275).

- **ALESSANDRO PALACE:** This authentically decorated hostel in Rome will make you feel like royalty, especially with the free pizza (p. 692).

top five places to ☉see dead people

5. STEPHANSDOM AND GRABEN: A great view upstairs, a catacomb of Viennese plague skeletons downstairs (p. 23).

4. WESTMINSTER ABBEY: Bow down (figuratively) to Elizabeth I and quote sonnets (in your head) at the "Poet's Corner" (p. 104)

3. PÈRE LACHAISE CEMETERY: Pay homage to Oscar Wilde, Georges Bizet, Honoré de Balzac, Maria Callas, and Max Ernst, in Paris (p. 301).

2. WESTERKERK CHURCH: See if you can find Rembrandt's burying place in Amsterdam—even if the sanctuary's keepers don't know where he's hiding. (p. 906)

1. ST. PETER'S BASILICA: Try not to be too creeped out by the mummified popes on display in Vatican City (p. 703).

WHERE THE WATER IS WINE

Sometimes even the lowliest grub tastes better in Europe. Pizza and ice cream become an art form in Italy; cheese, bread, and mayonnaise do the same in France. Beer gardens and rolling vineyards mean alcohol flows liberally, and with the delightful European embrace of the table wine, you don't have to spend much to drink well and often.

- **PIVOVARSKÝ DŮM:** Beyond the funny-sounding name, this microbrewery does Prague proud (p. 236).
- **SIRIUS KLUB:** Try a concoction at one of Budapest's celebrated tea houses (p. 627).
- **BERTHILLON:** You may feel a little bit like Blaire Waldorf, but eating ice cream on Île St-Louis is worth the price (p. 303).

VENI, VIDI, VICI

You've got the ruins of Ancient Rome, the art and architecture of the Middle Ages and Renaissance, masterpieces of the Impressionists, and reminders of Europe's oft-troubled political and religious history. Sounds corny, but it's true: traveling in Europe brings the snooze fests of history class (the papacy, German unification, Protestant Reformation, World War II—to name a few) to life.

- **COLOSSEUM:** It's got a bloody history, but you'll be bloody impressed (p. 695).
- **MUSEO NACIONAL DEL PRADO:** Only one-tenth of the museum's collection is displayed at any time. Go there and realize what that means (p. 987).
- **VERSAILLES:** The Sun King had it pretty sweet—at least for awhile (p. 325).
- **CHECKPOINT CHARLIE:** Check it out and learn more about the Cold War and its impact on the people caught in-between (p. 458).
- **BLUE MOSQUE:** It's incredible. And blue, if you didn't guess (p. 1145).

BEYOND TOURISM

Rebuild castles in France and Germany, intern at NATO, work abroad as an au pair. All of these options are at your finger tips.

- **WORLD WIDE OPPORTUNITIES ON ORGANIC FARMS:** Channel your inner dirty hippie and work on Europe's organic farms (p. 1200).
- **STUDY ABROAD:** Whether you're a Shakespearean or a biologist, you're bound to find a titillating program at one of England, Ireland, or Scotland's premiere universities. Get your Econ on at London School of Economics (p. 1196), or be "supervised" in one of Cambridge's (p. 1196) small tutorials.
- **SNACKST DU INGELSCH?** Don't understand what that means? You will after an intensive German language program (p. 1197).

suggested itineraries

BEST OF WESTERN EUROPE (2 MONTHS)

There's a good, if hackneyed, reason that this is possibly the most student-traveled part of the world. It's awesome. Go there. Do it all.

1. LONDON: People whine about the weather and the icky British food, but Buckingham Palace and the Tate Modern more than compensate.

2. PARIS: The Louvre and the whiffs from *boulangeries* will have you singing *La Vie en Rose* in no time.

3. MADRID: Churros y chocolate in Plaza Mayor after a night of partying? Win.

4. LISBON: Sip *vinho do porto* while gazing at the sunset over the Rio Tejo.

5. BARCELONA: Gaudí's *La Sagrada Família*, the world's most visited (and unfinished) construction site, will make you admire what the man's completed projects were like.

6. NICE: Enjoy some of the best of the Riviera along with floods of American tourists.

7. FLORENCE: Drool at David. Or just respectfully admire.

8. ROME: All roads may not lead to it anymore, but the Colosseum is still incredible.

9. VENICE: You don't have to ride a gondola to enjoy the nooks and crannies of this lagoon island.

10. MILAN: Fashionistas will rejoice at this Italian metropolis.

11. MUNICH: Beer lovers should make it here for Oktoberfest. Just sayin'.

12. PRAGUE: Křižík's Fountain and its light show with dancing will have you reeling.

13. BERLIN: Travel west to east to see the differences that remain in the city even after the Cold War.

14. AMSTERDAM: Yes, marijuana is legal here, but there is so much more here than drugs and tulips.

15. BRUSSELS: Look beyond the waffles, if you can bear it, and explore, even if it's only to try the chocolate and the beer.

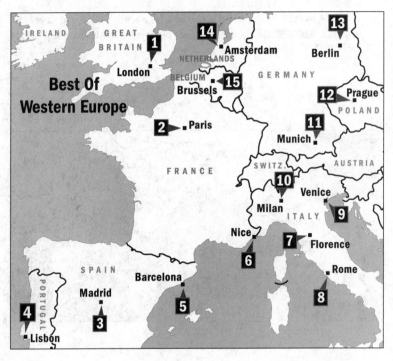

DEBEACHERY (6 WEEKS)

Another reason to go to Europe—the beaches are incredible (if infested with people), the people beautiful (most of the time), the food fantastic (beware of overpriced tourist traps), and the drinks free-flowing (at a price).

1. SEVILLA: Think bullfighting, flamenco, and tapas. Then add beaches to the mix and you've got perfection.

2. GIBRALTAR: Also called The Rock, this entrance to the Mediterranean has the name of a wrestler but the beauty of a Miss Universe contestant.

3. VALENCIA: The city's white beaches and architectural masterpieces are less crowded than some Spanish cities, but the energy is all there.

4. IBIZA: Extravagance is the name of the game here, with music from the discos lining the gorgeous beaches.

5. BARCELONA: This city was once home to Picasso and Miró, and its art scene still breaks modern ground.

6. NICE: The unofficial capital of the Riviera will have you partying like never before.

7. CINQUE TERRE: Hikers gazing at the sea from the cliffs will love the escapades over Cinque Terre's five villages.

8. BAY OF NAPLES: Augustus fell in love with this place in 29 BCE, and so will you.

9. GREEK ISLANDS: Go island-hopping and discover the individual personalities of the Aegean islands.

CELTS VS. ENGLISH VS. FRENCH (1 MONTH)

Forget the Lakers; these three really mean business and their attractions vie for your attention. Hop across waters to see all that this part of the pool has to offer.

1. LONDON: Conquered by the Romans in 43BCE, London is now one of the hottest metropolises in Europe (scratch that—the world).

2. STONEHENGE: Colossal stones and swaying grass will bring you to over five millennia in the past, when people made this monument for who knows what.

3. EDINBURGH: The Celts made this home, then the Romans took over. Notice a pattern?

4. BELFAST: Since the Bronze Age, Belfast's history has been riddled with conflict and rivalries, making for a fascinating destination.

5. DUBLIN: This Celtic-pride city is still a force to be reckoned with. Make your own journey of Joycean proportions.

6. BRITTANY: Cross the Channel and explore the Celtic side of France.

7. PARIS: Enter into the city of romance and bloody revolutions that the British love to hate—and still end up loving anyway.

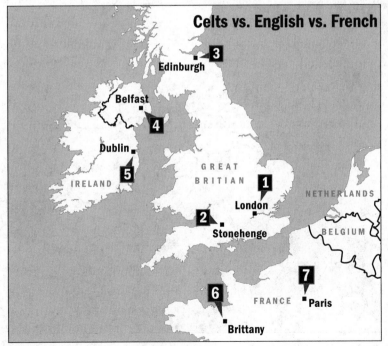

Celts vs. English vs. French

ORIENT YOURSELVES (3-4 WEEKS)

Imagine you're Hercule Poirot (or someone with a less ridiculous waxed mustache) on the Orient Express and solve your own mysteries on this epic trip.

1. PARIS: Begin your trip in the city of culture and snobbery. Only fashionably, of course.

2. STRASBOURG: Strasbourg's history epitomizes the Franco-German rivalry.

3. MUNICH: The capital of Bavaria, this Eastern German city knows a thing or two about keeping people happy. The key? Beer.

4. PRAGUE: Eastern Europe would have a much more appreciative audience if everyone visited Prague Castle.

5. BUDAPEST: Hungary's famous hospitality and thermal baths will make you glad you decided to go further east on your adventures.

6. ISTANBUL: It doesn't get more Oriental in Europe than Istanbul's Blue Mosque.

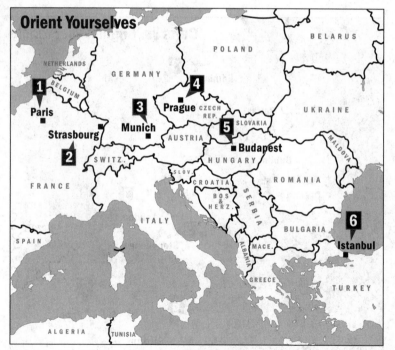

Orient Yourselves

BEST PLACE TO CONTRACT EARLY-ONSET DIABETES: Germany's Schoko-laden Museum (p. 475), where gold fountains spurt out samples of sweet, sweet, chocolate goodness.

BEST PLACE TO ASK FOR AN EARLY DEATH: Adrenaline junkies unite during the Running of the Bulls in Pamplona (p. 1073).

BEST PLACE TO STOMP IN YOUR NEW AIR FORCE ONES: The Temple of Athena Nike (p. 554).

BEST PAPARAZZI MOMENT: In front of the Mona Lisa at the Louvre, if you can manage to glimpse her lack of eyebrows with the tourist paparazzi all over (p. 283).

BEST PLACE TO BE AN EENIE-MEENIE MYNIE MO LOVER: Topkapi Palace's Harem (p. 1145). You get the picture.

how to use this book

CHAPTERS

Conquering the great continent that is █Europe is no easy task. Yes, dear reader, there are many mysteries in this Old World. That is why you have come to us. We will be your Virgil, teaching you the art of budget travel. The next few pages, the travel coverage chapters—the meat of any *Let's Go* book—begin with Austria, where you can enact your own Alpine adventure, à la *The Sound of Music*. From there, we trek on over to Belgium whose mascot is a little peeing boy called the Manneken Pis. Next, we jetset over to Britain, where Shakespeare and cider abound, before touring through the Czech Republic and the dirt-cheap eats of its capital city, Prague. Then France makes its move, catching our eye (and heart) with Parisian lights. Our journey continues to Germany, where Berlin takes the roughest and arguably most curious travelers. Explore the thermal baths in Hungary and the beer factories in Ireland. Experience the unique wonders of Italy and the Netherlands. Share some ancestral history in Portugal and Spain, and conjure up some more history in Turkey.

But that's not all, folks. We also have a few extra chapters for you to peruse:

CHAPTER	DESCRIPTION
Discover Europe	Discover tells you what to do, when to do it, and where to go for it. The absolute coolest things about any destination get highlighted in this chapter at the front of all *Let's Go* books.
Essentials	Essentials contains the practical info you need before, during, and after your trip—visas, regional transportation, health and safety, phrasebooks, and more.
Beyond Tourism	As students ourselves, we at *Let's Go* encourage studying abroad, or going beyond tourism more generally, every chance we get. This chapter lists ideas for how to study, volunteer, or work abroad with other young travelers in Europe to get more out of your trip.

LISTINGS

Listings—a.k.a. reviews of individual establishments—constitute a majority of *Let's Go* coverage. Our Researcher-Writers list establishments in order from **best to worst value**—not necessarily quality. (Obviously a five-star hotel is nicer than a hostel, but it would probably be ranked lower because it's not as good a value.) Listings pack in a lot of information, but it's easy to digest if you know how they're constructed:

ESTABLISHMENT NAME 💳💵♿🚫📶🍸❄⛅▼ type of establishment [1]
Address ☎phone number 💻website
Editorial review goes here.
🔀 Directions to the establishment. ℹ Other practical information about the establishment, like age restrictions at a club or whether breakfast is included at a hostel. $ Prices for goods or services. ⏰ Hours or schedules.

ICONS

First things first: places and things that we absolutely love, sappily cherish, generally obsess over, and wholeheartedly endorse are denoted by the all-empowering 👍**Let's Go thumbs-up.** In addition, the icons scattered throughout a listing (as you saw in the sample above) can tell you a lot about an establishment. The following icons answer a series of yes-no questions about a place:

💳	Credit cards accepted	💵	Cash only	♿	Wheelchair-accessible
🚫	Not wheelchair-accessible	📶	Internet access available	🍸	Alcohol served
❄	Air-conditioned	⛅	Outdoor seating available	▼	GLBT or GLBT-friendly

The rest are visual cues to help you navigate each listing:

☎	Phone numbers	💻	Websites	🔀	Directions
ℹ	Other hard info	$	Prices	⏰	Hours

OTHER USEFUL STUFF

Area codes for each destination appear opposite the name of the city and are denoted by the ☎ icon.

PRICE DIVERSITY

A final set of icons corresponds to what we call our "price diversity" scale, which approximates how much money you can expect to spend at a given establishment. For **accommodations,** we base our range on the cheapest price for which a single traveler can stay for one night. For **food,** we estimate the average amount one traveler will spend in one sitting. The table below tells you what you'll *typically* find in Europe at the corresponding price range, but keep in mind that no system can allow for the quirks of individual establishments.

ACCOMMODATIONS	WHAT YOU'RE LIKELY TO FIND
❶	Campgrounds and dorm rooms, both in hostels and actual universities. Expect bunk beds and a communal bath. You may have to provide or rent towels and sheets. Be ready for things to go bump in the night.
❷	Upper-end hostels or lower-end hotels. You may have a private bathroom, or there may be a sink in your room and a communal shower in the hall.
❸	A small room with a private bath. Should have decent amenities, such as phone and TV. Breakfast may be included.
❹	Should have bigger rooms than a ❸, with more amenities or in a more convenient location. Breakfast probably included.
❺	Large hotels or upscale chains. If it's a ❺ and it doesn't have the perks you want (and more), you've paid too much.

FOOD	WHAT YOU'RE LIKELY TO FIND
❶	Street food, *gelateria*, milk bar, corner crêperie, or a fast-food joint, but also university cafeterieas and bakeries. Soups, gyros, kebab, and simple dishes in minimalist surroundings. Usually takeout, but you may have the option of sitting down.
❷	Sandwiches, *bocadillos*, appetizers at a bar, or low-priced entrees and tapas. Most trattorie or ethnic eateries are a ❷. Either takeout or a sit-down meal (sometimes with servers!), but only slightly more fashionable decor.
❸	Mid-priced entrees, seafood, and exotic pasta dishes. Many traditional and hunting-lodge-decor establishments. More upscale ethnic eateries. Since you'll have the luxury of a waiter, tip will set you back a little extra.
❹	A somewhat fancy restaurant. Entrees tend to be heartier or more elaborate, but you're really paying for decor and ambience. Few restaurants in this range have a dress code, but some may look down on T-shirts and sandals.
❺	Your meal might cost more than your room, but there's a reason—it's something fabulous, famous, or both. Slacks and dress shirts may be expected. Offers foreign-sounding food and a decent wine list. Don't order a PB and J!

discover europe

AUSTRIA

Austria's pristine metropolises and exquisite forests and mountains have inspired artists for centuries—now let it do the same for you. Vienna, the city of painters and psychoanalysis, composers and coronations, gives Paris a run for its money. Even if you came for the kitschy Mozart action figures, stay for life in a city like no other. After days of wandering, shout, "so long, farewell, auf wiedersehen, goodbye." Relieve your over-cultured soul with forests, picturesque castles, and unbeatable backdrops of the Danube River and the majestic Alps, all thanks to some of the best organized train systems in the world. Have no fear of getting lost (you might even enjoy it), and delve right into Austria.

greatest hits

- **THE HIGH GROUNDS.** Wander around Schloß Schönbrunn (p. 29)—an imperial summer residence with a French garden that harkens to Versailles.
- **DRINK LIKE A FISH.** Sip some of the strongest cocktails of your life at First Floor (p. 36), where a modern fish aquarium runs the length of the bar.
- **PLEASE DON'T STOP THE MUSIC.** Gorge on food, drink, and free music at Donauinsel Fest, held every June on Danube Island (p. 41).
- **ONE-NIGHT STAND.** Buy a €5 standing-room ticket to Mozart's *Don Giovanni* at the gorgeous Staatsoper (p. 40).

Austria (Österreich)

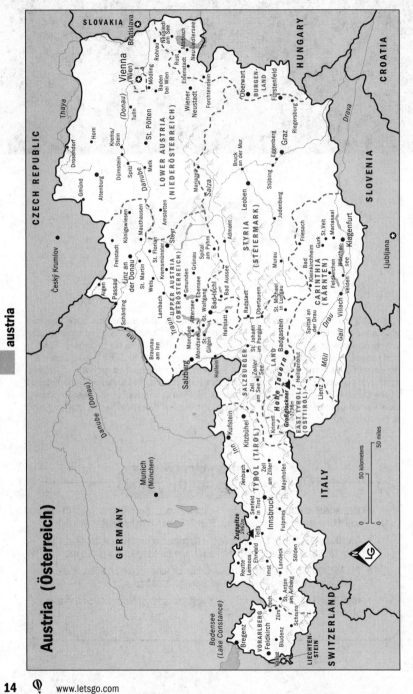

vienna ☎431

Vienna is a city where you can live in both the past and the present. While half of the city floats majestically along in the 17th and 18th centuries, the other half zooms into the 21st, creating a fusion of time and space that will transport you from one age to the next in a blink of an eye.

First and foremost, Vienna is a city of the arts. After all, it seems that every classical music genius lived and worked in Vienna; Mozart, Beethoven, Schubert, Strauss, Brahms, and Haydn all came to Vienna at some point in their lives. Walk by an apartment building in the Inner Stadt, and you will probably hear a violin coming from within. Or just walk down a major street and lose track counting theaters with nightly music, theater, and dance performances. Famous thinkers like Sigmund Freud met to pore over controversial ideas, while artists like Hundertwasser, Klimt, and Schiele painted so many masterpieces that Vienna has enough museums to last a lifetime, and in just a few days you can barely scratch the surface.

The cobbled streets of Vienna's Inner Stadt conjure an Old World romance that is still reflected in the people's love for tradition—where else in the world do people waltz en masse on New Year's Eve? Yet, for its upcoming generation, Vienna offers the modern shopping, dining, and nightlife of any cosmopolitan city—clubs cluster under the brick train track archways, and small cocktail bars craft drinks as an art form. Walk through Belvedere and see modern art sculptures or to drink wine overlooking vineyards and the Danube—the old and the new, the city and the country—all of it is within reach.

ORIENTATION

Inner City

Vienna's Inner Stadt is the city's heart and soul, and if you are only visiting for a few days, you will undoubtedly spend most of your time here. Named a UNESCO World Heritage Site in 2001, this historical area measures a mere 1.4 sq. mi.—it's hard to believe so much is crammed into such a small space. At the center of the district is the grand, gothic **Stephansdom** at Stephanspl., from which the district's main arteries extend— **Rotenturmstrasse** leads toward the Danube canal and the nightlife of the "Bermuda Triangle," while in the opposite direction, the shopping thoroughfare of **Karntner Strasse** paves the path toward the Opera House. The grandest of all is **Graben** with its historic facades (ignore the McDonald's golden arches and the H&M signs),

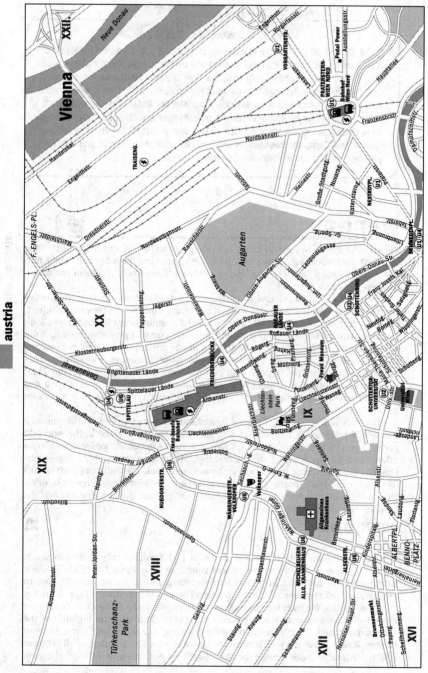

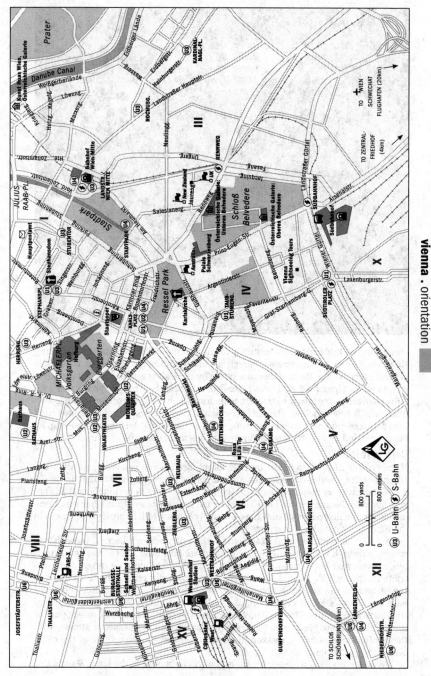

connecting to **Kohlmarkt** and eventually leading to the **Hofburg Palace,** the Hapsburg Empire's former headquarters. Though a museum, church, or palace is literally around every corner, the real pleasure of the Inner Stadt is getting lost in its winding streets of Baroque, medieval, and Jugendstil architecture. You will pass cafes with patrons overflowing into the streets, and then suddenly find yourself in a quiet grassy plaza with a few benches. The clickety-clack of horse shoes on cobblestones can't help but transport you to another time, even if the tourist hustlers dressed up as Mozart remind you every now and again that it is in fact the 21st century.

Core Districts

If the crowds of tourists in the Inner Stadt are driving you camera-crazy, the Core Districts offer a series of lesser known, but just as interesting, sights that are really not as far away as they may seem on the map. These districts (numbers II-IX) are also home to the majority of local Viennese and city inhabitants and offer a modern-day flavor and diversity that may have originally seemed to fall through the cracks in the Inner Stadt cobblestone streets.

Across the Danube canal to the east is the gritty second district, **Leopoldstadt,** which, although home to the overly photographed Prater Reisenrad and Augarten, is otherwise rather un-picturesque. In a C-shape around the Inner Stadt, districts III through IX fan out in a counter-clockwise direction. The third district, **Landstrasse,** to the south, is home to the sweeping grounds of Schloß Belvedere with the famous Klimt collection, and color-crazy, quirky Kunsthaus Wien and Hundertwasser Haus. The fourth, **Weiden,** and the fifth, **Margareten,** offer some of the greatest palate pleasures; the tasty **Naschmarkt** and **Gumpendorfer Strasse,** with their collections of cafes, restaurants, and coffeehouses, have some of the city's best dining experiences.

If you are booking a hostel, it's likely you will be staying in the sixth, **Mariahilf,** or the seventh, **Neubau.** Mariahilf is named after the city's longest shopping throroughfare, Mariahilferstr., with more H&M branches than can be counted on two hands as well as many other international chain stores, ice-cream shops, and shoe stores. The seventh district stretches west from the Museum Quartier and is refreshingly non-mainstream next to Mariahilf. Many of the city's young artisans have set up high-end boutiques with creative clothing and jewelry, the nightlife is vibrant, and the former red-light district of Spittelberg offers some cobblestoned character to the area. Behind the Rathaus (City Hall), the eighth district of **Josefstadt** is a comparatively quiet residential area, with the exception of the nightlife hot spot along the **Gürtel** (the Belt Road). Here, the bars are built into the structure of the Stadtbahn, where the U6 runs, creating a funky underground vibe where DJs spin and the drinking never ends. **Alsergrund,** the ninth district, is mainly home to the university campus and a wealthier enclave. The spectacular spires of **Votivkirche** accompany some more notable museums, including the **Lichenstein.**

Outer Districts

The Outer Districts (numbers X and up) encircle the core districts starting from the south in a clockwise direction and include far fewer sights and way more locals. Welcome to suburbia, baby. The southernmost districts, **Simmering (XI), Favoriten (X),** and **Meidling (XII)** are not terribly interesting and are generally avoided by tourists, with the exception of the Zentralfriedhof. Locals consider these blue-collar neighborhoods the underbelly of the city, and this may be the only area with the potential for danger.

By far the most popular draw for tourists in the Outer Districts are the grounds and imperial rooms of **Schloβ Schonbrunn** in the 13th, one of the most spectacular sights in the whole city. In the 14th, Otto Wagner's **Kirche am Steinhof** glistens among a backdrop of green hillside in one of the city's wealthier districts, Hietzing.

Just beyond the Gürtel in the 15th and 16th, a number of additional hostels lie along and around the top portion of Mariahilferstr., around Westbahhof. With the exception of the commercial Mariahilferstr., this area tends to feel either industrial or strictly residential, and even dining options become more limited. The 15th, **Rudolfsheim-Funfhaus,** houses much of the immigrant population, including Turks and Serbs.

A gem of the Outer Districts is **Dobling (XIX)** and, in particular, the *heurigers* (wine taverns) of **Grinzing,** where you can spend an evening dining (and drinking) and arrive back in the city happily tipsy. Over the past few years, this has become a popular stop for tourists wishing to get a bit of the countryside, and so at times there is the inevitable eyesore of the coach tour buses. If you can Photoshop those out of your mental picture, Grinzing is a pleasure, with quiet tree-lined streets and cobbled plazas. There are still many fine dining options and *heurigers* without the tourist souvenirs; be sure to find one with a spectacular view out into the vineyards and over the Danube.

ACCOMMODATIONS

Inner City

There are no budget accommodations in the Inner City. Be prepared to spend your life savings here.

ALMA BOUTIQUE HOTEL ♿ 📶 🍸 ❄ HOTEL [5]

Hafnersteig 7 ☎1 533 296 10 🖥www.hotel-alma.com

All 26 rooms at the Alma have been newly renovated into sleek, modern singles and doubles with private baths. The decorations are "Viennese Art Noveau," tasteful splashes of red and large designs in gold manage to be professional and not cross the line into tacky. From the flatscreen TVs and Wi-Fi to biscuits on your pillow, this hotel offers all the comforts of home and more.

🚇 U1 or U4: Schwedenpl.; Tram #1 or 2. ℹ Breakfast included. $ Singles €87-122; doubles €127-188. 🕐 Reception 24hr.

PENSION PERTSCHY
💳♿📶 PENSION, HOTEL ❺

Habsburgergasse 5 ☎1 53 44 90 🖥www.pertschy.com

This pension is the closest you'll come to living in an imperial-style room at a reasonable price. The singles and doubles (some of which can actually accommodate three or four people) are traditionally decorated with gold-trimmed cabinets and hanging chandeliers. Size varies greatly, so consider booking a superior or deluxe double room if you want extra legroom.

🚇 U1 or U3: Stephanspl. ℹ Breakfast included. $ Singles €79-122; doubles €119-188. Extra bed €23-38. ⏰ Reception 24hr.

HOTEL POST
💳♿📶 HOTEL ❺

Fleischmarkt 24 ☎1 51 58 30 🖥www.hotel-post-wien.at

Mere steps away from the bustling Schwedenpl. and all the other Inner Stadt sights, these rooms are a great price for the location, especially in comparison to the other first district hotels. The hotel was recently refurbished, and the rooms feel clean, though the decor leaves something to be desired.

🚇 U1 or U4: Schwedenpl.; Tram #1 or 2. ℹ Breakfast included. $ Singles €42-51, with bath €73-87; doubles €68-79/100-130; triples €87-103/120-157. ⏰ Reception 24hr.

Core Districts

👍 BELIEVE-IT-OR-NOT HOSTEL
🧺🚭📶 HOSTEL ❸

Myrthengasse 10, Apt. 14 ☎676 55 000 55 🖥www.believe-it-or-not-vienna.at

Don't let the entrance fool you—this hostel has more spunk, character, and free stuff than you will believe. As an apartment that has been converted into a hostel, Believe-It-Or-Not has a full living room and kitchen for use, and the rooms of only four or eight beds are styled like a ski lodge. Spiral stairs lead up to the top bunks in the four-person rooms. Be sure to sign your name in gold or silver on the black furniture in the foyer—it's the guestbook!

🚇 Bus #48A. $ 8-bed dorms with shared bath €24; 4-bed dorms with private bathroom €28. ⏰ Reception 8am-noon, 24hr. availability over intercom.

WESTEND CITY HOSTEL
🧺♿📶🔔 HOSTEL ❷

Fuegergasse 3 ☎1 597 67 29 🖥www.westendhostel.at

Westend City Hostel will welcome you to Vienna with a helpful English-speaking staff and a variety of room types to choose from. Every room is different, though most have a table and chairs and all have an ensuite toilet and shower. All kinds of amenities are available...even alarm clocks for rent.

🚇 U3 or U6: Westbahnhof. ℹ Breakfast, linens, and Wi-Fi included. $ 4- to 12-bed dorms €20.50-27; singles €52-70; doubles €31-44. Rates increase during summer and holidays. ⏰ Reception 24hr.

PENSION KRAML
🧺🚭🔔 PENSION ❹

Brauergasse 5 ☎1 587 85 88 🖥www.pensionkraml.at

This family-run pension is the epitome of hospitality. All of the rooms are sparkling clean, spacious, and plush with wall-to-wall carpeting. Some have shared bath but still have a sink in the room. This prime real estate includes a buffet breakfast, and is definitely worth the extra moolah if you can afford it.

🚇 U3: Zieglergasse or U4: Pilgramgasse. ℹ Breakfast and Wi-Fi included. $ Singles €35; doubles €56-66, with bath €76-87; triples €78/76-87; family apartment (3-5 people) €99-135. ⏰ Reception 24hr.

HAPPY HOSTEL
💳🚭📶🔔 APARTMENTS, HOSTEL ❷

Kurzgasse 2 ☎1 208 26 18 🖥www.happyhostel.at

Renting out one of Happy Hostel's apartments will certainly make you and your group of travelers happy. The apartments have kitchens and ensuite baths as well as spacious living areas with TVs and couches. In a newer building across the street, the limited dorm rooms are more standard with bunk beds, shared bathrooms, and wooden floors.

➡ U3 or U6: Westbahnhof. ℹ Internet access included. $ 3- to 6-bed dorms €15-23, with kitchen and bath €18-27; singles €33-36; doubles €44-52/54-72; apartments €42-48 per person. ⏰ Reception 24hr.

JUGENDHERBERGE MYRTHENGASSE 💳⊗📶⛅ HOSTEL ❷

Myrthengasse 7 ☎1 523 63 16 💻www.hihostels.com

Highly popular with HI regulars, the 3- to 4-bed dorms in this hostel book up quickly in the busy summer months. The linoleum-floor rooms are not particularly homey, but they do have a private showers (toilets in the halls) and are kept extremely clean. Lockers, great lounge spaces, and an outdoor courtyard complete this dependable hostel, and there is a hearty daily dinner offered for €6.

➡ Bus 48A. ℹ Reservations recommended in summer months. HI card required. $ Dorms €16.50-17.50; doubles €19.50-20.50. ⏰ Reception 24hr.

PANDA HOSTEL ⊘♿ HOSTEL ❶

Kaiserstr. 77, 3rd fl. ☎1 522 25 55 💻www.panda-vienna.at

Located on the third floor of an apartment building, Panda Hostel feels like staying in a large apartment with dormmates. The rooms have high ceilings (with really tall bunk beds), but they are spacious and have tables, chairs, or couches for extra seating. The small kitchen has no stove, so don't anticipate high-quality cooking, but there is a refrigerator and microwave.

➡ Bus 48 A. Tram #5. ℹ 2-night min. stay. $ 5- to 7-bed dorms €15. ⏰ Reception 8am-2pm. Check-in until 11pm. Lockout 10am-2pm.

BAG AND MAP APARTMENT GUESTHOUSE ⊘♿📶 APARTMENT ❷

Wimbergasse 31 ☎1 957 69 34 💻www.bagandmap.com

Hidden on a quiet residential street, Bag and Map Apartment Guesthouse is on the top floor of an old, traditional building. Many of the rooms are apartment style, including a convenient private kitchen for cooking. While this is not for travelers who want to meet their neighbors or make new hostel friends, you will certainly be comfortable here.

➡ U6: Burrgasse. Tram #18. ℹ All rooms and apartments have private bathrooms. Ring bell for reception. $ Doubles €52-58; triples €69-78.

Outer Districts

👍 HOSTEL RUTHENSTEINER 💳⊗📶🍸⛅ HOSTEL ❷

Robert Hamerlinggasse 24 ☎1 89 342 02 or ☎1 89 327 96 💻www.hostelruthensteiner.com

With its quiet flowered courtyard, countryside-style living room, and even a bar made out of solid cherry-wood, this hostel will undoubtedly feel like home. The rooms have a rustic feel, with wood-plank doors and prints from famous Vienna artists like Klimt and Hundertwasser on the walls, and many also are off the balcony overlooking the courtyard. To add to its character and charm, there is a free book exchange and musical instruments for guest use.

➡ U3 or U6: Westbahnhof. Walk down Mariahilferstr. away from the train station and take a left on Haidmannsgasse. Your 1st right will be Robert Hamerlinggasse, and you will see a sign for the hostel. ℹ Wi-Fi and lockers included. Book exchange and musical instruments available. Credit card surcharge 3%. $ 8-bed dorms €15-20; 3- to 5-bed dorms €17-22. Doubles €25-27, with bath €28-30. ⏰ Reception 24hr.

WOMBATS CITY HOSTEL—THE LOUNGE 💳♿📶🍸 HOSTEL ❷

Mariahilferstr. 137 ☎1 897 23 36 💻www.wombats.eu

Just 50m from Westbahnhof, Wombat's newest Vienna hostel is young, social, and in the know. The receptionists will gladly assist you in getting settled in your bunk, where your magnetic key card also automatically locks your locker, so you don't have to worry about a clunky padlock. The rooms are all ensuite and immaculate—a few years ago, the Lounge was elected as the cleanest hostel worldwide. From 6pm onward, meet new friends and grab cheap drinks in the womBar downstairs.

🚇 U3 or U6: Westbahnhof. ℹ Wi-Fi, lockers, and luggage storage included. Breakfast €4. $ 4- to 6-bed dorms €16-29; doubles €29-39. ⏰ Reception 24hr.

HOSTEL SCHLOßHERBERGE 💳⊗⛅ HOSTEL [2]

Savoyenstr. 2 ☎1 481 0300 🖥www.hostel.at

Located on the outskirts of the District XVI on the grounds of an old palace, this hostel is certainly not your average city hostel. Heck, it's practically in the woods, as you will see when you take the bus to the top of the hill, after also riding the U-Bahn. The large grassy space overlooks the city, with plenty of room for sunbathing, a volleyball net, and even a minigolf course. The rooms are all ensuite, with bunks and locker space. Keep your fingers crossed that you end up in one of the first-floor rooms with the doors that open directly onto the lawn with the spectacular view.

🚇 U3: Ottakring. From the stop, take Bus 46A or 146A: Schloß Wilhelminenberg ℹ Breakfast, parking and Wi-Fi included. Notify reception if you plan to arrive after 10pm. $ 4-bed dorms €19-27; 3-bed dorms €22-32.50. Singles €50-60; doubles €57-73.

DO STEP INN 💳⊗📶⛅ PENSION, HOSTEL [3]

Felberstr. 20 ☎699 19 23 27 69 🖥www.dostepinn.at

Many of these double and triple rooms have beds with frames (no bunks!), lending this pension the professionalism of a hotel. The rooms are all ensuite and have sparkling new wood flooring, yet, possibly to some inconvenience, you must rent by the room, not by the bed. The common spaces and kitchens are adorned with colorful mosaics and potted plants that emphasize the old-style building and spiral staircase. While the locale is not ideal, the walk to more bustling streets is not too strenuous.

🚇 U3 or U6: Westbahnhof. Exit from the upper platform, turn left on Felberstr. ℹ Luggage storage, lockers, and Wi-Fi included. Credit card surcharge 4%. $ Singles €35-39, with bath €45-49.50; doubles €44-48.40/52-70; triples €51-55.50/66-75; quads €60-66/75.60-76.60. ⏰ Reception open daily 8am-9pm. Ring bell for entrance.

WOMBATS CITY HOSTEL—THE BASE 💳♿📶🍸⛅ HOSTEL [2]

Grangasse 6 ☎1 897 23 36 🖥www.wombats.eu

The original Wombats hostel in Vienna is a few blocks off Mariahilferstr., and is not quite as shiny and spunky as its younger sibling. The bright blue building feels a bit grittier, with darker masculine tones and slightly smaller rooms, though the cleanliness standard is still A+. The Base has all the same perks as the Lounge (Wi-Fi, ensuite rooms, etc.), and as an added bonus, there is a terrace bar to enjoy drinks outside on warm summer nights.

🚇 U3 or U6: Westbahnhof. Follow Mariahilferstr. until no. 152, then turn right into Rosinagasse. Take your second left. ℹ Wi-Fi in common spaces, lockers, and luggage storage included. Breakfast €3.50. $ 4- to 6-bed dorms €14-29; doubles €50-78; triples €60-87. ⏰ Reception 24hr.

HOSTEL HUTTELDORF 💳♿⛅ HOSTEL [2]

Schloßberggasse 8 ☎1 877 02 63 🖥www.hostel.at

Located off the western end of the U4 line, Hostel Hutteldorf is not for party animals who plan on having late nights (unless, of course, you are a party animal that will keep going until the Ubahn opens the next morning at 5am). The majority of the four- to six-bed rooms are located in the high-rise building that has views of the city and the hills, and it's worth booking ahead to reserve this rather than being stuck in the 20-bed dorm (which is, strangely enough, the same price as the 6 bed-dorm). The hostel highlight is the large grassy backyard lawn surrounded by trees—great for a lazy afternoon of sleeping and sunbathing.

U4: Hutteldorf. Exit to Hadikgasse, then follow the signs to the hostel. i Wi-Fi, luggage storage, lockers, and breakfast included. $ 6- or 20-bed dorms €13-22; 4-bed dorms €16-27; 3-bed dorms €17.50-30. Singles €28-50; doubles €40-72. Reception 24hr.

A AND O WIEN HOSTEL 1

Lerchenfelder Gürtel 9-11 ☎1 49 30 480 39 00 www.aohostels.com

The Vienna branch of A and O's hostel chain is located on the busy Gürtel road, closer to the outskirts of the city. Inside, don't expect coziness; the rooms are basic with metal-framed bunks and lockers in a tall high-rise building. Luckily, the large windows offer plenty of light and air. Despite the lack of homey decor, A and O does offer all the other necessities such as Wi-Fi, luggage storage, easy bike rental, and plenty of brochures to guide you around the city.

U6: Burggasse Stadthalle. i Breakfast €4. $ 8- to 10-bed dorms from €12, with bath from €13; 4- to 6-bed dorms from €13/15; doubles with bath €25; singles with bath €39. Reception 24hr.

HOTEL HADRIGAN HOTEL 3

Maroltingergasse 68 ☎1 604 00 00 www.hadrigan.com

Just as long as you are not expecting the Marriott, the facilities of this budget hotel should suit your stay in the city just fine. The rooms are cleaner and fresher than the common spaces, with new coats of paint and simple decorations for a homey feel. Ignore the faux-oriental rugs in the hallways and the dim lighting and focus on the clean sheets and comfy pillows.

U3: Ottakring. $ Singles €40-64; doubles €44-69; family rooms (3-4 beds) €64-99. Reception 24hr.

HOTEL GEBLERGASSE HOTEL 3

Geblergasse 21 ☎1 406 33 66 www.geblergasse.com

While the lobby and common spaces have seen better years, the newly renovated rooms are surprisingly crisp, clean, and very white—white sheets, white walls, white curtains. The location is a toss-up: there is a sex shop around the corner, but it's also within close distance to public transportation and you will not be bothered by noise or traffic at night.

U6: Alser Str. i Free Wi-Fi, safe and TV in room. All rooms ensuite. $ Singles €34-89; doubles €49-99; family rooms (3-6 beds) €79-139. Parking €9 per day. Rates vary greatly, so check website. Reception 24hr.

PENSION ELIZABETH PENSION, APARTMENTS 2

Holochergasse 17 ☎1 983 56 34

These apartment-style rooms are quite off the beaten track; you are literally staying in extra rooms in a residential apartment building a good 10 blocks beyond Westbahnhof. Instead of any cohesive decor scheme, rugs, refrigerators, leftover beds, and mismatched dining furniture seem haphazardly thrown together to furnish these sometimes cramped or oddly shaped spaces. There won't be the opportunity to meet other travelers here because the rooms are entirely self-sufficient, and at most you will share a kitchenette or bathroom with one other room.

U3 or U6: Westbahnhof. Exit from the upper platform, then turn left on Felberstr. Turn right on Holochergasse (it will be after the 2nd bridge on your left). i Rooms must be rented by the room, not bed. Ring bell. $ 2- to 6-bed rooms €19.50-29 per person.

SIGHTS

Inner City

STEPHANSDOM CHURCH

Stephanspl. ☎1 515 52 35 26 www.stephanskirche.at

Monolithic by day and ethereal by night, this Gothic masterpiece is one of

Vienna's must-see sights. Its massive towers and colorful tiled roof depicting the Hapsburg crown punctuate the city skyline, dwarfing the plaza and people below. Inside, the high-vaulted ceilings and arches offer a somber darkness, broken only by the rustling of tourists and their cameras. You can enter the cathedral at the back for free, while the €3 ticket will get you up close to the nave and stone-carved pulpit.

⇄ U1 or U3: Stephanspl. $ Church admission €3, with audioguide €4.90. Catacomb tour €4.50, children €1.50. Tower and bell €4.50/1.50. All-inclusive ticket €14.50, students €12. ⏰ Church open M-Sa 6am-10pm, Su 7am-10pm. Bell and tower open daily 8:15am-4:30pm. Tours M-Sa 9-11:30am and 1-4:30pm, Su 1-4:30pm.

👍 ALBERTINA — 🎫♿🍸🛍 MUSEUM, STATE ROOMS

Albertinapl. 1 — ☎1 534 830 💻www.albertina.at

A ticket to the Albertina grants you access to all the impressive museum floors in addition to a series of plush state rooms (which are, dare we say, nicer than the main Hofburg complex, and far less crowded). The permanent art collection on the top floor encompasses all the modern art greats, including Degas, Picasso, Miro, and Kandinsky, to name just a few. The remaining exhibits rotate every few months, and temporary exhibits on Picasso, Michaelangelo's drawings, and South African artist William Kentridge will be presented through early 2011.

⇄ U1 or U3: Stephanspl. Or U1, U2, or U4: Karlspl. $ Adults €9.50. Seniors and Vienna card holders €8, under 19 free. Audioguide €4. ⏰ Open M-Tu 10am-6pm, W 10am-9pm, Th-Su 10am-6pm.

👍 NATIONALBIBLIOTHEK/STATE HALL — 🎫♿ LIBRARY

Josefpl. 1 — ☎1 534 10394 💻www.onb.ac.at

Bookworms should not miss this stunning Baroque library, one of the most beautiful historical libraries in the world. Commissioned by Emperor Charles VI, the library has double-story nutwood bookcases, marble statues, rose-and-cream marble floors and pillars, and pastel ceiling frescoes that stretch to every corner. Today, the library holds over 200,000 volumes that can still be accessed in the adjacent reading room and also has two temporary displays per year that focus on some bookish theme; the exhibit at the time of research explored "Intercultural Dialogue in Old Writings" and displayed magnificent manuscripts in Hebrew, Arabic, Greek, and Latin. Warning: you might have to get a neck massage afterward from all the craning to look up.

⇄ U1, U2, or U4: Karlspl. Or U3: Herrengasse. $ €7, students €4.50. ⏰ Open Tu-W 10am-6pm, Th 10am-9pm, F-Su 10am-6pm.

HOFBURG PALACE — 🎫♿🍸 MUSEUM, IMPERIAL APARTMENTS

Heldenpl. — ☎1 533 75 70 💻www.hofburg-wien.at

A visit inside the Hofburg consists of three parts: the Imperial Silver Collection, a museum about Empress Elisabeth, and the Imperial Apartments where Franz Joseph and Elisabeth lived. The Silver Collection is an extensive display of cutlery, plates, bowls, and centerpieces—gold, silver, porcelain—in every shape, size, and design imaginable. In this portion of the museum, the audioguide is particularly helpful (and concise) at guiding visitors through what would otherwise be one packed display case after the next. The Sisi Museum then delves into the life of Empress Elisabeth Sisi, from her childhood to tragic death, with artifacts and stunning replicas of her gowns and jewels. Finally, the Imperial Apartments, the most interesting part of the Palace, you can see where Franz worked, slept, and ate and even where Elisabeth bathed.

⇄ U3: Herrengasse. Or, U2 or U3: Volkstheater, then Tram #1 or 2. ℹ Audioguide free with entrance ticket. $ Tickets for each sight €10, students €9, ages 6-18 €6. Sisi Ticket (entrance to all 3 Hofburg venues plus the Furniture Collection and Schonbrunn Palace) €22.50, students €20,

ages 6-18 €13.50, family (2 adults, 3 children) €47. Tours €2.50, children €1. ⏰ Open daily July-Aug 9am-6pm; Sept-June 9am-5:30pm.

KUNSTHISTORISCHES MUSEUM ♿ MUSEUM

Maria Theresien-Pl. ☎1 525 240 💻www.khm.at

This stunning building houses the city's most extensive and impressive collection of work, including art from the 15th to 19th centuries, Greek and Roman antiquities, one of the five largest coin cabinets in the world), and halls of Egyptian and Near Eastern works. Start at the picture galleries so you don't run out of steam, and pace yourself—Room X, devoted to Bruegel's works, is worth spending some time in. Don't miss the Rembrandt self-portraits and Canaletto's cityscapes, the latter of which elegantly show how much the city has changed.

🚇 U2 or U3: Volkstheater, Tram #1, 2, D. $ Adults €12, with Vienna card €11, students under 27 €9, under 19 free. ⏰ Open Tu-W 10am-6pm, Th 10am-9pm, F-Su 10am-6pm.

STADTPARK ♿ PARK

Main entrance from Johannesgasse

Nestled into the Ringstr., this large green space filled with benches, walkways, and statues of musicians (10 points for spotting the gilded Johann Strauss) beckons to all on summer afternoons. Enter through the stone collonades, then wander until you find the perfect spot for reading or a picnic. Drool from afar at Vienna's most acclaimed restaurant, Steierereck, where a meal will set you back over €100, and avoid the Kursalon, whose nightly dinner-music deals ooze tourist tackiness.

🚇 U4: Stadtpark or U3: Stubentor, Tram #1 or 2. $ Free. ⏰ Open 24hr.

SECESSION EXHIBITION HALL

Friedrichstr. 12 ☎587 53 07 💻www.secession.at

This square building with a golden laurel-leaf dome will certainly catch your eye as you wander through the Naschmarkt and Karlspl. area. The inside spaces are used for rotating art exhibits (check the current program online), but most people go just to see the basement room housing Gustav Klimt's *Beethoven Frieze.* Said to be an interpretation of Beethoven's *Ninth Symphony*, it depicts mankind's search for happiness on three walls of the rectangular room.

🚇 U1, U2, or U4: Karlspl. $ €5 (groups of 8 or more €4 per person), students and seniors €4 (groups of 8 or more €2.50 per person). Tours €1.50. ⏰ Open Tu-W 10am-6pm, Th 10am-8pm, F-Su 10am-6pm.

FRANZISKANEKIRCHE ♿ CHURCH

Franziskanerpl. ☎1 512 45 78 💻www.franziskaner.at

In a chill, charming, and cobblestoned plaza slightly hidden from tourist hordes at Stephanzpl., Franzikanerkirche is worth a quick visit and photo op. While the interior has two rows of ornate wooden pews, the church is perhaps best experienced from the outside. Sit in the square at the outdoor seating of Kleines Cafe and relish in the pale blue exterior and pretty fountain.

🚇 U1 or U3: Stephanspl. $ Free. Church guide booklet €4.70. ⏰ Open daily 6:30am-5:30pm.

HAUS DER MUSIK ♿ MUSEUM

Seilerstätte 30 ☎1 513 48 50 💻www.hdm.at

The four floors of this interactive world of music could take 5hr. to fully explore. The journey begins with information about Vienna's premier philharmonic orchestra, where you can watch (in HD) the previous year's New Year's Eve concert. In the Sonosphere (second floor), sound becomes the focus, as you learn about what we hear and how we hear it through electronic computer and headset stations. The third floor of "Great Composers" has cleverly arranged displays on the lives and work of the many musical geniuses who worked in Vienna. There is a free audio tour, but it is more of a joy to read the English placards with Beethoven, Mozart, or Haydn playing in the background. The final Futuresphere offers interactive sound games that kids will love.

U1, U2, or U4: Karlspl. $ €10, students €8.50, ages 3-12 €5.50. Combined ticket with Mozarthaus €15, children €7. Open daily 10am-10pm.

MAK (MUSEUM FUR ANGEWANDTE KUNST) MUSEUM

Stubenring 5 ☎1 711 360 www.mak.at

Antique junkies and architecture aficionados will love this museum's brightly colored walls and hanging glass cases filled with everything from Venetian glassware and lace to architectural models of 20th- and 21st-century buildings. Klimt's *Stoclet Frieze* is one of the few paintings in a museum otherwise devoted entirely to applied arts. The MAK also boasts one of the most famous and comprehensive collections of oriental carpets in the world.

U3: Stubentor, Tram #1 or 2. $ €8, students €5.50. Children and under 19 free. Family €11. Free for all Sa. Tours €2. Open Tu 10am-midnight, W-Su 10am-6pm. English tours Su noon.

BURGGARTEN PARK

Entrance on Burgring

Because of the prime location amidst the Inner Stadt sights, this green space is most frequented by tourists sitting on benches and eating gelato. There is a Mozart statue with flowers in the shape of a treble clef, though you will have to sneak past the scalpers selling concert tickets to snap your photo. Stroll behind the Hofburg or drink coffee in the majestic Palmenhaus restaurant overlooking the park.

U1, U2, or U4: Karlspl.; Tram #1, 2, D. $ Free. Open daily dawn-dusk.

MOZARTHAUS 🎫♿ MUSEUM

Domgasse 5 ☎1 512 17 91 💻www.mozarthausvienna.at

This apartment is the only surviving Mozart house, and was where the musical genius composed *The Marriage of Figaro* at the height of his wealth and fame. The first floor of the museum speculates how Mozart lived during his time there, and much of the building and surrounding streets remain as they were. The second and third floors focus on his life history and music, but unfortunately many of the displays don't do the composer or his music justice. You might also find yourself wishing the audio tour had more of his music and less commentary.

🚇 U1 or U3: Stephanspl. From the stop, walk down Singerstr. and turn left on Blutgasse. ℹ Audio tour in English included with ticket price. $ €9, students and seniors €7. Combined ticket with Haus der Musik €15, children €7. ⏰ Open daily 10am-7pm.

PETERSKIRCHE 🚫 CHURCH

Peterspl. ☎1 533 64 33 💻www.peterskirche.at

Established by the Fraternity of the Holy Trinity and supported by the Opus Dei (Da Vinci Code, anyone?), Peterskirche's turquoise dome glows eerily, especially when illuminated at night. The soft beige-rose marble walls balance out the otherwise ornate interior and are accented by the royal purple curtains on the confessionals.

🚇 U1 or U3: Stephanspl. From the stop, head down Graben on the left. $ Free. ⏰ Open M-F 7am-8pm, Sa-Su 9am-9pm. Free organ concerts M-F 3pm, Sa-Su 8pm.

JÜDISCHES MUSEUM (JEWISH MUSEUM) 🎫♿ HISTORY MUSEUM

Dorotheergasse 11 ☎1 535 04 31 💻www.jmv.at

While the Jewish Museum has a wide collection of prayer books, scrolls, Torah curtains, and other artifacts—many of which are quite beautiful—the lengthy historical explanations might be a bit dry for those who aren't obsessed with the past. The viewable storage area on the top floor has an impressive number of objects collected over the years from synagogues, prayer houses, and private homes.

🚇 U1 or U3: Stephanspl. From the stop, walk down Graben, then turn left on Dorotheergasse. $ €6.50, students €4. ⏰ Open M-F 10am-6pm, Su 10am-6pm.

NATURHISTORISCHES MUSEUM 🎫♿☀ NATURAL HISTORY MUSEUM

Burgring 7 ☎1 521 77 💻www.nhm-wien.ac.at

Across from the Kunsthistorisches Museum, in an identically beautiful building, this natural-history museum has two floors that take the visitor on a journey from the beginning of the world and its lifeforms up until modern day. Fossils, mineral collections, and plenty of preserved amphibians floating in glass jars await, as do some impressively large skeletons of dinosaurs and whales. The breathtaking gem collection in Room IV is the most valuable gem collection on the continent, and includes a topaz weighing 250 lb.

🚇 U2 or U3: Volkstheater, Tram #1 or 2; bus 2A, 48A. $ €10, students €5, seniors €8, under 19 free. Guided tours €2.50. Scientific tours €6.50. ⏰ Open M 9am-6:30pm, W 9am-9pm, Th-Su 9am-6:30pm. Tours to roof Su 3pm.

Core Districts

☑ BELVEDERE 🎫♿❄☀ MUSEUM, PALACE GARDENS

Prinz Eugen Str. 27 (Upper), Rennweg 6 (Lower) ☎1 795 570 💻www.belvedere.at

The sweeping grounds of Schloß Belvedere house two magnificent museums, with Vienna's best-known work of art, Gustav Klimt's *The Kiss.* Oberes (Upper) Belvedere houses the Klimt collection as well as a magnificent spread of Beidermeier, Neoclassic, Medieval, and Baroque art arranged over three floors around the grand Marble Hall. From Oberes Belvedere, take a leisurely stroll through the gardens to Unteres (Lower) Belvedere, taking in the manicured hedges, fountains, and the views of Stephansdom and the city in the distance. Unteres Belvedere has rotating exhibits, one in the palace and another (usually contemporary) in the

Orangery, accessed though the Marble Gallery and the Golden Room. There is a quiet, private garden in front of the Orangery with views back up to Oberes Belvedere and magnificent arrays of exotic flowers in the summer. On your way out, the multiple museum shops offer Klimt-printed everything—even teddy bears.

Tram #D, O, or 71. $ Unteres (Lower) Belvedere €9.50, seniors €7.50, students €7, under 18 free. Combined tickets (Unteres and Oberes) €14/11/10/free. 🕐 Upper open daily 10am-6pm. Lower open M-Tu 10am-6pm, W 10am-9pm, Th-Su 10am-6pm.

KUNST HAUS WIEN — MUSEUM

Untere Weißgerberstr. 13 ☎1 712 04 91 www.kunsthauswien.com

From an early age, school teachers noticed Friedensreich Hundertwaßer's "unusual sense of color and form," currently apparent in the building of the Kunst Haus Wien and all of his works within. The floor and pipes curve, the stairs are stacked with bright tiles and bits of mirror, and the house is filled with live "tree tenants," making the KunstHaus a cartoonish, magical land. The first two floors of the museum contain Hundertwaßer's spectacular works, with titles including *Stokes, Splotches, and Heads* and *Who Has Eaten All My Windows?* while the third floor is used for rotating exhibits.

U1 or U4: Schwedenpl. From the stop, Tram #1: Radetzkypl. $ €9, ages 11-18 €4.50, children under 10 free. M (except holidays) €4.50. Combination ticket (Kunsthaus and temporary exhibitions) €12, ages 11-18 €6. 🕐 Open daily 10am-7pm.

KARLSKIRCHE — CHURCH

Karlspl. ☎1 504 61 87 www.karlskirche.at

One of Vienna's most stunning churches, Karlskirche's gleaming turquoise dome and two elaborately engraved columns reflect in the circular pool in Karlspl. Inside, the cream and pink marble is softly elegant. Take the glass elevator 35 meters up to admire the frescoes from mere feet away. You can also climb additional stairs up into the dome for (slightly obscured) views of the entire city.

U1, U2, or U4: Karlspl. $ €6, students €4, under 11 free. Groups of 6 or more €5 per person. Audio tour €2. 🕐 Open M-Sa 9am-12:30pm and 1-6pm, Su noon-5:45pm.

LEOPOLD MUSEUM — ART MUSEUM

Museumspl. 1 ☎1 525 700 www.leopoldmuseum.org

The Leopold collection has recently been rearranged to guide the viewer through the art, architecture, and design elements of "Vienna 1900." The glistening white walls and large airy rooms provide a cheery setting to view some of the comparitively dark (and depressing) works of Egon Schiele, on whom the collection has a particular focus. There are also works by other prominent Austrian artists, such as Gustav Klimt, Kolo Moser, and Oskar Kokoschka.

U2: Museumsquartier. Or U2 or U3: Volkstheater. $ €11, students €7, seniors €8, family (2 adults, 3 children) €23. 🕐 Open M, W 10am-6pm, Th 10am-9pm, F-Su 10am-6pm.

PRATER AND WEINER REISENRAD — AMUSEMENT PARK

Riesenradpl. ☎1 729 54 30 www.wienerreisenrad.at

The Prater is home to Vienna's symbolic ferris wheel, the Wiener Reisenrad, which you will have undoubtedly seen on numerous postcards (if not in a certain James Bond film, you die-hard fans). While a corner of the park is devoted to over 250 amusement rides and games and plenty of ice cream stands, the rest is pure, peaceful green space that was formerly an imperial hunting ground. On the weekends, a walk or run through the expanse is a common activity for the local Viennese.

U1 or U2: Praterstern. $ Park free. Each ride has individual prices. Wiener Reisenrad €8.50, students and Vienna cardholders €7.50, ages 3-14 €3.50, under 3 free. 🕐 Each ride has its own hours. Check the website for rotating schedule.

ST. MARXER FRIEDHOF

&♿ CEMETERY

III, Leberstr. 6-8 ☎1 4000 80 42

Even bringing along a friend or visiting in the middle of the day won't prevent this spooky cemetery from feeling like a real-life horror film. The gravestones are overgrown with weeds, and the grass comes up to your knees in this ghost town. St. Marxer's claim to fame is as the real resting place of Amadeus Mozart, which is easily spotted as the only manicured tomb in the entire place.

✦ Tram #71: St. Marx. Bus 74A. *i* A map of the tombs is located at the entrance. ⓢ Free. ◪ Open daily 7am-dusk.

MUMOK (MUSEUM MODERNER KUNST STIFTUNG LUDWIG WIEN)

♥⊗❀♿ MUSEUM

Museumspl. 1 ☎525 00 1400 ◼www.mumok.at

This modern art museum seems to be hit or miss depending on the current exhibits that rotate every two to three months. The events range from displays of prominent modern art to more obscure installations that experiment with interesting themes such as light, movement, or space. The museum space itself is a grey, square warehouse with glass elevators to swiftly guide you through the museum's five floors.

✦ U2 or U3: Volkstheater. Or U2: Museumsquartier. ⓢ €9, seniors and Vienna cardholders €7, students under 27 free, students over 27 €6.50, families €14, annual pass €33. ◪ Open M-W 10am-6pm, Th 10am-9pm, F-Su 10am-6pm.

AUGARTEN

&♿ RECREATION

Entrance on Obere Augartenstr.

Although slightly secluded from the rest of District II, this green space is immensely popular with families and almost overrun with squealing children on the weekends. Tall trees line gravel paths that lead to the park's slightly frightening (and somewhat hideous) Flakturm, tall cement bunkers built during WWII.

✦ Tram #21. ⓢ Free. ◪ Open daily dawn-dusk.

Outer Districts

▨ SCHLOß SCHÖNBRUNN

♥&♿ PALACE, GARDENS, IMPERIAL APARTMENTS

Schönbrunner Schloßstr. 47 ☎1 811 130 ◼www.schoenbrunn.at

Schonbrunn Palace's gardens rival many a famous French palace garden (ahem, Versailles). The main avenue stretches from the palace to the Fountain of Neptune, behind which the arched structure of the Gloriette stands majestically on a hill. The Gloriette was built to commemorate the return of Prague to Habsburg rule in 1775 and the view of the palace, gardens, and city from here is breathtaking. The palace itself has an extensive set of imperial rooms, the most impressive of which you can view on the Imperial Tour (although the Great Gallery is unfortunately under restoration until 2012). If you have the time and a few extra euros to spare, the Grand Tour has some of the most ornate, albeit smaller, rooms, including the Millions Room, the palace's most valuable room due to the rare rosewood wall paneling.

✦ U4, Tram #10 or 58, or Bus 10A: Schonbrunn. ⓢ Admission to gardens and grounds free. Imperial Tour (22 rooms) €9.50, children €6.60, students €8.50, Vienna cardholders €9.50. Grand Tour (40 rooms) €13, students and Vienna cardholders €11.40, children €9. Grand Tour with guide €14.40/13/10. ◪ Open daily Apr-June 8:30am-5pm; July-Aug 8:30am-6pm; Sept-Oct 8:30am-5pm; Nov-Mar 8:30am-4:30pm.

KIRCHE AM STEINHOF

⊜⊗ CHURCH

Baumgartner Höhe 1 ☎1 910 601 12 04

Kirche am Steinhof, built by Otto Wagner, is a shining (literally) example of

Viennese Art Nouveau architecture. The copper dome is blindingly bright against the otherwise green hillside where the church resides. The surrounding parkland was formerly a Nazi psychiatry center that played a horrific role in the Nazi euthanasia experiments, but today the whole complex is part of the Otto Wagner Hospital. Four angels stand guard at the entrance to the church, while ornate mosaics, creamy white walls, and stained-glass windows illuminate the interior.

✈ *U3: Ottakring. From the stop, take 48A: Psychiatrisches Zentrum.* Ⓢ *Tours (50min.) €6, students and children €4, under 15 free. Art Nouveau tour (1½hr.) €10, ages 15-18 €7, students €6.* ✪ *Viewing Sa 4-5pm. Mass Su and holidays 9am. Tours Sa 3pm. Art Nouveau tour runs Apr-Sept every F at 3:30pm.*

ZENTRALFRIEDHOF
                      ♿☺ CEMETERY

Simmeringer Haupstr. 234   ☎1 760 410 ▣www.friedhoefewien.at

Stone cherubim, crosses, and pillars decorate over 2.5 million tombs in Vienna's Central Cemetery. From the main entrance (Gate II), a straight walk down the central aisle will bring you to the most famous inhabitants, including Beethoven, Brahms, Schubert, and Wolf in section 32A, as well as a fake tomb for Mozart (the real one is in St. Marx). In front of the large Dr. Karl Lueger Kirche, the central church, the presidents of the Second Republic are buried in the manicured Presidentsgruft. Gate 1 of the cemetery leads to the large and unfortunately neglected area of Jewish memorials.

✈ *Tram #71: Zentralfriedhof; the 2nd Zentralfriedhof stop is the main entrance.* Ⓢ *Free. Cars €2.20.* ✪ *Open daily May-Aug 7am-8pm; Sept 7am-7pm; Oct 7am-6pm; Nov-Feb 8am-5pm; Mar 7am-6pm; Apr 7am-7pm.*

FOOD
                            ◖

Inner City

▨ KLEINES CAFE
                ●⊗❤☺ CAFE ❷

Franziskanerpl. 3

Kleines Cafe might just be the smallest coffeehouse in the whole city, but you know what they say—small coffee house, big heart. Or is it big feet, big... nevermind. The cappuccinos are piled high with a top hat (not just cap) of foam, and beers and wine are also a popular choice. The outdoor seating in Franziskanerpl. is a delight during the summer, and the cozy, leather interior feels expanded with the clever use of mirrors.

✈ *U1 or U3: Stephanspl.* Ⓢ *Coffee €2-4. Entrees €5.50-10.* ✪ *Open M-Sa 10am-2am, Su 1pm-2am.*

IMERVOLL
              ●⊗❤☺ VIENNESE ❸

Weihburggasse 17   ☎513 52 88

Imervoll is one of the best places to go in the Inner Stadt for traditional Viennese cuisine that's more authentic (and flavorful) than just a schnitzel. The constantly changing menu is a handwritten paper on the glass wall of the entrance, boasting dishes like *Rindsgulasch (beef stew with dumplings and paprika; €9.40)* and *Gebratene Bachforelle (fried trout with onion and salad; €11.70).* In warm weather, customers flock to the outdoor seating in Franziskanerpl., leaving the simple yellow interior quite empty.

✈ *U1 or U3: Stephanspl.* Ⓢ *Entrees €8-17.50. Appetizers and salads €6.50-14.50.* ✪ *Open daily noon-midnight.*

FIGLMÜLLER
              ✈♿❤ VIENNESE ❸

Wollzeile 5   ☎512 617 77 ▣www.figlmueller.at

For a *weiner schnitzel* bigger than your head, Figlmüller is undoubtedly the place to come. This family-run restaurant has become well known for its massive schnitzels (*€13*), so tourists abound, though a table or two of locals still emerge. The recommended side potato salad and greens (*€3.80*) is the ideal schnitzel companion and should not be overlooked. Come hungry, leave with a food baby.

✠ *U1 or U3: Stephanspl.* *i* *Additional location at Backerstr. 6. English menu available.* Ⓢ *Entrees €10-15.* 🕐 *Open daily 11am-10:30pm.*

TRZESNIEWSKI ⊛ὸ♨Ψ SANDWICHES ❶

Dorotheerg 1 ☎1 512 32 91

From Polish origins to a Vienna institution, Trzesniewski (try saying that three times fast) offers mini open-faced sandwiches on brown bread *(€1)*. The intriguing flavors, including wild paprika (quite spicy!) and mushroom and egg are definitely for those willing to step out of a PB-and-J comfort zone. Other ingredients include onion, tunafish, and cucumber, and many are vegetarian.

✠ *U1 or U3: Stephanspl. From the stop, walk down Graben, and look for the signs on your left about 3 blocks down.* Ⓢ *Brotchen €1.* 🕐 *Open M-F 8:30am-7:30pm, Sa 9am-5pm.*

EISSALON TUCHLAUBEN ⊛ὸ☒ GELATO, DESSERT ❷

Tuchlauben 15 ☎1 533 25 53 🖵www.eissalon-tuchlauben.at

So creamy, so delicious, and easily the best gelato in the entire city. Look for the bright orange overhangs and the orange cups to match. Sit down at the outdoor patio to indulge in a large sundae or take out a cup or cone for a cheap, sweet thrill. The hazelnut is not to be missed.

✠ *U1 or U3: Stephanspl.* Ⓢ *Cups and cones €1.70-4.* 🕐 *Open M-F 10am-11:30pm, Sa 11am-11:30pm.*

ÖSTERREICHER IM MAK ♥ὸΨ☒ CAFE, BAR ❸

Stubenring 5 ☎1 714 01 21 🖵www.oesterreicherimmak.at

Serving up modern and traditional Viennese cuisine, Österreicher im MAK has all the appropriate design elements to rival its neighboring museum (yes, the MAK)—a large hanging chandelier made entirely of wine glasses and a combination of oddly shaped high and low bar tables, which admittedly look cooler than they feel. During lunch, if the weather is good, most people enjoy the outdoor patio and take advantage of the bargain daily lunch special *(€6.40)*.

✠ *U3 to Stubentor; Tram #1 or 2.* Ⓢ *Coffee €3-5. Entrees €9-20. Wine by the glass €7-10, by the bottle €20-30.* 🕐 *Open daily 9:30am-1am.*

CAFE DIGLAS ⊛ὸΨ☒ CAFE ❷

Wollzeile 10 ☎1 512 57 65 🖵www.diglas.at

The popularity of this plush *kaffeehaus* has grown over the years, evident now by the menu offered in every language imaginable. While the crystal chandeliers, velvet booths, and marble tables may feel like a step back in time, the prices do not, so don't rush home and put on your corset just yet. A coffee and dessert alone can set you back close to €10.

✠ *U1 or U3: Stephanspl.* Ⓢ *Teas €3.30. Breakfast €4.20-9.20. Entrees €7.50-15.50. Apple strudel €4.50.* 🕐 *Open daily 7am-midnight.*

LIMES ♥ὸΨ☒ MEDITERRANEAN ❸

Hoher Markt 10 ☎1 905 800 🖵www.restaurant-limes.at

Limes serves up fresh salads, pastas and other Mediterranean fare in an "urban chic" interior or out on the patio at the edge of Hoher Markt. Inside, the bar's high white stools seem to contradict the dining room's low, green couches and candelabras; luckily they are separated by wispy strands of green fabric. Decor aside, the food is downright tasty.

✠ *U1 or U3: Stephanspl. Or U1 or U4: Schwedenpl.* *i* *Credit card min. €15.* Ⓢ *Entrees €6.50-20.50.* 🕐 *Open M-Sa 9am-midnight.*

1516 BREWING COMPANY ♥ὸΨ☒ PUB ❷

Schwarzenbergstr. 2 ☎961 15 16 🖵www.1516brewingcompany.com

If you want some familiar-looking food (read: classic American grub), 1516 has large portions of burgers, soups, and salads in a pub-style restaurant and bar.

Its tap beer brewed on the premises is the drink of choice, and the large slab of barbecued baby-back ribs served with potatoes and salad *(€13)* is large enough to share.

U1, U2, or U4: Karlpl. $ Entrees €8-13. Sandwiches and burgers €5.50-9.20. Open M-Th 10am-2am, F 10am-3am, Sa 11am-3am, Su 11am-2am. Kitchen open until 2am.

ZANONI AND ZANONI GELATO, DESSERT ❶

Lugeck 7 ☎512 79 79 www.zanoni.co.at

On a hot summer's night, Zanoni and Zanoni is just the thing to make all your gelato dreams come true. With an impressive list of choices, you may as well opt for the large cone with three flavors *(€2.50)* and make your selection easier. If we put these flavors in a milkshake, it would definitely bring all the boys to the yard.

U1 or U3: Stephanspl. U1 or U4: Schwedenpl. [i] Another location at Burging 1. $ Small cone (2 flavors) €2. Large cone (3 flavors) €2.50. Open daily 7:30am-midnight.

AIDA CAFE, CONFECTIONERY ❶

Singerstr. 1 ☎089 898 82 10 www.aida.at

Undoubtedly you will stumble across the coffee and confectionery shop Aida at one of its multiple branches all over the city. You can't miss it; the decor is bubble-gum pink chairs and neon pink signs, for crying out loud. While the melange *(€3)* is a bit on the small side, the Stephanspl. location overlooks the plaza and church, and it's satisfying to sit in the chairs instead of being blinded by them from afar.

U1 or U3: Stephanspl. $ Coffee €1.80-3. Strudel and torten slices €1.30-3. Sundaes and ice cream €4.30-5. Open M-Sa 7am-8pm, Su 9am-8pm.

Core Districts

NASCHMARKT MARKET ❷

Wienzeile

This open-air market is the best way to begin a day of sightseeing in the city, as the market feels like a sight itself! Endless stalls of olives, stuffed peppers, dried fruits and nuts, cheeses, meats, vegetables and fruit sell their wares, and on Saturdays, there is a flea market. Running parallel to the stands, sit-down restaurants and cafes offer coffee and more professionally assembled meals, from sandwiches to seafood.

U1, U2, or U4: Karlspl. $ Prices vary by stall. Market stalls open M-F 6am-7:30pm, Sa 6am-5pm. Flea market open Sa 6:30am-4pm.

RA'MIEN VIETNAMESE ❷

Gumpendorfer Str. 9 ☎1 585 47 98 www.ramien.at

You will be worshipping your large bowl of *pho* noodles, *lo mein*, or rice by the end of your meal and craving *gyoza* dumplings *(€7)* for days afterward. The rice bowls, such as the one with duck, Thai basil, and chili *(€8.50)*, come with a small salad and slice of fruit.

U2: Museumsquartier. [i] Credit cards min. €10. $ Entrees €7-14. Open Tu-Su 11am-11pm.

ZUM ROTEN ELEFANTEN VIENNESE, FRENCH, CAFE ❸

Gumpendorferstr. 3 ☎1 966 80 08 www.zumrotenelefanten.at

The cream-colored walls and dark wooden chairs give this cafe an artsy yet sophisticated flair that is emphasized by the patrons, who sip their coffee particularly daintily. The French-inspired cuisine is flawless, and the lunch menu is an extremely good value. Look for the sign with just the picture of a red elephant.

U1, U2, U4; Tram #1, 2, or D: Karlspl. $ Lunch €8. 2-course dinner €19. Open M-F 11:30am-2:30pm and 6pm-midnight, Sa 6pm-midnight.

GASTHAUS WICKERL
💳♿🍸☀ VIENNESE [2]

Porzellangasse 24A ☎1 317 74 89

This cozy, traditional *beisel* (pub) has everything from the wooden tables and chairs to the beers on tap. The food is delicious, especially the *Karnter Nudeln* (Viennese dumplings) topped with diced tomatoes and with side salad *(€9.10)*, though if you're really sticking to "tradition," you could always go with the *weiner schnitzel (€9.50)* instead.

🚌 Tram #D. $ Salads €5-7. Entrees €7-14. ⏰ Open M-F 9am-midnight, Sa 10am-midnight.

DER WIENER DEEWAN
🚫💳🚫♿☀ PAKISTANI, HALAL [1]

Liechtensteinstr. 10 ☎925 1185 💻www.deewan.at

This well-loved Pakistani buffet lives by the motto, "eat what you want, pay what you wish." The booths with high ceilings and funky painted walls are always packed (and the university is nearby), so come on off hours to ensure you get a table. The buffet always offers meat and vegetarian dishes, and all of the food is halal.

🚌 U2: Schottentor. Or Bus #40A: Bergasse. $ You decide! ⏰ Open M-Sa 11am-11pm.

HALLE
💳♿🍸☀ CAFE [2]

Museumspl. 1 ☎523 70 01 💻www.motto.at

One of the trendy outdoor cafes in the middle of Museumsquartier, Halle's breakfasts *(€5.50-9.40)* will set your day on the right track. The lunch special changes daily *(eggs and omelettes, crossiants, and extra large cafe lattes; €7.20-8.50)*, and there is a bar and drink menu for when the sun goes down. If the weather is right, take advantage of the tables on the patio overlooking the bustle of the MQ courtyard.

🚌 U2: Museumsquartier. Alternatively, U2 or U3: Volkstheater. $ Entrees €7-10. Sandwiches €8. Cafe latte €3.50. ⏰ Open daily 10am-2am.

YAK AND YETI
💳♿🍸☀ NEPALESE [2]

Hofmühlgasse 21 ☎1 595 54 52 💻www.yakundyeti.at

Take your taste buds on a journey east for some traditional Nepalese cuisine. Thursdays is "Momo Day" so you can sample all the sauces and fillings in an all-you-can-eat *momo* (Himalayan dumpling) buffet *(€12)*. Or, on Tuesdays, eat *Dal Bhaat* (a rice, lentil, meat, and veggie meal) with your fingers in the traditional style *(all you can eat; €10)*.

🚌 U4: Pilgramgasse. Or bus #13A: Esterhazygasse. $ Appetizers €3-4.25. Entrees €5.50-18. Desserts €3.50-4.50. ⏰ Open M-F 11:30am-2:30pm and 6-10:30pm, Sa 11:30am-10:30pm.

UBL
🚫💳♿🍸☀ VIENNESE [3]

Presgasse 26 ☎1 587 64 37

Just down the street from the Naschmarkt, this Viennese *beisel* holds its own culinary clout in the city dining arena. The traditional Austrian dishes, often with slight influences from other cuisines, have garnered much acclaim and won awards. Enjoy your *schweinsbraten*, *schnitzel*, or *semmelknodel* on the surprisingly peaceful, although narrow, terrace, barricaded from the street by tall, thick trees.

🚌 U4 or bus #59A: Kettenbruckengasse. $ Entrees €8.50-16. ⏰ Open daily noon-2pm and 6-10pm.

ZU DEN 2 LIESERLN
🚫💳♿🍸☀ VIENNESE [2]

Burggasse ☎1 523 32 82 💻www.2lieserln.at

So many *schnitzels*, so little time. This traditional *beisel* certainly offers the Viennese *weiner schnitzel* (pork with a side potato salad), but there is also a fascinating selection of schnitzel specials to choose from—"Cordon Bleu" and "Puszta" are among the list. Enjoy your *schnitzel* in a warm, wood-paneled interior or a pleasant outdoor seating area with large sweeping trees.

🚌 Bus #48A. $ Weiner schnitzels €8.50-13. ⏰ Open daily 11am-11pm.

LUCKY NOODLES ♿ 🍸 ASIAN ❶

Mariahilferstr. 77

If you are in the mood for fast and easy takeout, you can't go wrong with a steaming box of Lucky Noodles, either with vegetables, chicken, or both. No fance or schmance, just noodles, and the steady stream of people means the noodles are always fresh. Add your own sauces, and even use chopsticks.

🚇 U3: Zieglergasse. $ Noodles €2.50-3.50. ⏰ Open daily 10:30am-11:30pm.

FRESCO GRILL 🍸 MEXICAN ❷

Liechtensteinstr.10 ☎660 467 89 83 💻www.frescogrill.at

This is Vienna's version of a Tex-Mex joint—minimal decor, maximum burritos. The ingredients are tasty, fresh, and not as greasy as you would expect, so you can indulge guilt-free. Quesadillas, taco salads, chips and salsa, and beer are all on the menu.

🚇 U2: Schottentor. ℹ 30min. free Wi-Fi access for customers. Can create student account for a 5% discount. $ Burritos €4.60-6.60. ⏰ Open M-F noon-9pm.

NICE RICE VEGETARIAN, INDIAN ❷

Mariahilfer Str. 45, im Raimundhof 49 ☎1 586 28 39 💻www.raimundhof.at/nicerice/

Down a cobblestone alley filled with boutiques and cafes, this cheery restaurant offers Indian-inspired all-vegetarian meals. Entrees include basmati rice with hummus and tofu *(€8.50)* or Indian samosas with salad and yogurt sauce *(€9.30)*. The outdoor seats are perfect for mango-lassi-sipping *(€2.80)* and people-watching *(priceless)*.

🚇 U3: Neubaugasse or U2: Museumsquartier. The restaurant is down an alleyway off Mariahilfer Str. $ Entrees €4-15. ⏰ Open M-Sa 10am-7pm.

ELEPHANT CASTLE ♿ 🍸 INDIAN, CAFE ❶

Neubaugasse 45 ☎0699 920 84 59 💻www.elefantcastle.at

Walk into this tiny cafe and mistake it for someone's kitchen. The Indian-inspired food is made in front of you with a healthy homemade flair. The mango chutney is particularly tasty (in anything!), while the curry dishes are heartier than the simple and slightly small sandwiches.

🚇 U3: Neubaugasse $ Sandwiches €3.50-5.50. Curries €6.50-8.50. ⏰ Open M-F 11:30am-3:30pm.

Outer Districts

HEURIGER HIRT ♿ 🍸 WINE TAVERN ❷

Eisernenhandgasse 165 ☎1 318 9641 💻www.zurschildkrot.com

The slightly strenuous trek to reach this hillside *heuriger* (wine tavern) is completely worth the experience of sipping spritzer and looking over the sweeping views of the vineyards, lush hillsides, and the tiny town of Kahlenbergerdorf alongside the Danube. There is no fancy decor, just peeling picnic tables and some hanging lanterns, and you will likely be the only English-speaker there. The self-serve menu changes daily, and you can walk into the kitchen and point at what you want. Bring your own water—there is no drinking water available, only wine!

🚇 Bus #239: Verein Kahlenbergerdorf. From the stop, walk through the small town to your left and up Eisernenhandgasse at the back. It's about a 15min. walk up the hill. ℹ The place is popular with locals, so if you plan to come around 7:30 or 8pm, make a reservation. Pay as you go. $ Meat portions €3-6. Salad portion €2-4. Slices of bread or garnishes €0.40 each. ⏰ Open Apr-Oct M-F 3pm-late, Sa-Su noon-late; Nov-Mar F-Su noon-late.

CAFE DOMMAYER ♿ 🍸 VIENNESE ❷

Auhofstr. 2 ☎1 877 546 50 💻www.dommayer.at

This traditional coffeehouse has one of the most elegant courtyards in the city—sweeping green and white striped umbrellas shade high hedges, as though made for ladies sipping on tea with pinkies up. The waiters in white button-down shirts, black vests, and in some cases black bowties offer additional elegance, yet somehow the atmosphere is friendly, not stuffy. Take a book, order a coffee and dessert, and spend a few hours.

⚑ *U4: Hietzing.* Ⓢ *Coffee €2.30-6. Entrees €4.80-12. Desserts €2.40-3.50.* ⏲ *Open daily 7am-10pm.*

FRANCESCO
❤♿♀⚏ ITALIAN, BIERGARTEN ❸

Grinzinger Str. 50 ☎1 369 23 11 ▥www.francesco.at

After all the *schwein* and *suppen*, some Italian cuisine is just what the doctor (or chef) ordered. Francesco serves pizzas, pastas, risottos; and at quite reasonable prices, as well as some pricier meat and fish dishes. The large open courtyard is shaded by a canopy of green, while inside the feel is rustic Viennese, with exposed brick, dark wooden tables in cozy booths with low ceilings, and even gold-framed paintings and some statues scattered throughout. Italian food in a Viennese hunting lodge... makes total sense.

⚑ *Bus #38A.* Ⓢ *Entrees €6.50-24.* ⏲ *Open daily 11:30am-midnight.*

KENT
❤♿♀⚏ TURKISH ❷

Brunnengasse 67 ☎1 405 91 73 ▥www.kentrestaurant.at

Kent likes to advertise itself as the "best Turkish food in the world," and it might not be too far off the mark—it's at least the best Turkish food in Austria. At this more casual cafe location (they also have branches in districts X and XV), you can see all the food in trays before you order—see whether the stuffed eggplant or *moussaka* catches your eye. There are also plenty of meat dishes from the grill, salads, and dips.

⚑ *U6: Josefstadter Str.* Ⓢ *Entrees €5-11.* ⏲ *Open M-Sa 6am-2am.*

MAYER AM PFARRPLATZ
❤♿♀⚏ WINE TAVERN ❸

Eroicagasse 4 ☎1 370 12 87 ▥www.pfarrplatz.at

This *heuriger* is tourist-friendly without being overly touristy. In other words, there are a few souvenirs for sale but no tourist buses at its tiny plaza location. The long courtyard is filled with wooden tables and flowers, while indoors the restaurant could be your grandma's living room—flowered drapes matching flowered hanging lamps, muted green and rose tones, and even portraits of old ladies on the walls. Order a meal off the menu or frequent the buffet, where you put together your own meal and pay by portion.

⚑ *Bus #38A.* Ⓢ *Menu and buffet style offerings from €10.* ⏲ *Open M-F 4pm-midnight, Sa-Su 11am-midnight.*

STRANDGASTHAUS BIRNER'S
❀⊚♀⚏ VIENNESE ❷

An der Oberen Alten Donau 47 ☎1 271 53 36

Along the edge of the Obere Alte Donau, the sliver of the Donau that runs through district XXI, Strandgasthaus Birner's is a favorite among locals enjoying the water and sunny weather. Three tiers of seating look out over couples boating and children splashing on the other side and are decorated with bright tablecloths and umbrellas, flowers, vines, and potted plants. Birner's serves traditional Viennese dishes, but the best is an *eis kaffee (cold coffee with ice cream; €4.20)* after a day in the sun.

⚑ *U6: Neue Donau.* Ⓢ *Entrees €5.50-14.50.* ⏲ *Open daily 9am-11pm.*

SAIGON
❀♿♀ VIETNAMESE ❷

Neulerchenfelderstr. 37 ☎1 408 74 36 ▥www.saigon.at

This Vietnamese restaurant is the real deal—from the crispy, light egg rolls with dipping sauce and mint leaves to the large bowls of noodle soup *(pho.)* The dishes are artistically arranged and garnished with cucumber and tomato slices and a flower-shaped radish, and luckily the meals taste as good as they look. Saigon also has a quick-meal stall in Brunnengasse market (in front of no. 40), with cheap boxes of noodles, rice, and meat for a meal on the go *(€2.50-5)*.

🚇 U6: Josefstatter Str. $ Entrees €7.20-15. ⏰ Open daily 11:30am-11pm.

FIGL'S 💳♿🍸🌳 VIENNESE, BIERGARTEN [3]

Grinzinger Str. 55 ☎1 320 42 57 💻www.figls.at

This Viennese restaurant at the entrance to Grinzing offers traditional cuisine in a modern restaurant setting rather than a touristy *heuriger* get-up. The refined decor offers crisp wooden tables and booths, as well as a curved wooden bar around a large brass fireplace. The leafy courtyard offers private sections in a gentle slope out back, while the menu is a blend of traditional Austrian dishes as well as a Caesar salad *(€12)* or burger *(€9.50)*.

🚇 Bus #38A. $ Entrees €7.50-23. ⏰ Open daily 11:30am-midnight. Lunch menu served M-F 11:30am-4pm.

NIGHTLIFE

Inner City

👍 FIRST FLOOR 💳🚭🍸 BAR

Seitenstettengasse 5 ☎533 78 66

This is one of Vienna's classic bars in district I, with paneling and molding from the 1930s mixed with a modern fish aquarium running the length of the bar. Although the fish are on "permanent holiday," as one bartender put it, the jazzy music and smoky velvet of this bar's interior gives it plenty of good ambience. On an off night the friendly bartenders might even let you mix your own pisco sour.

🚇 U1 or U4: Schwedenpl. $ Mixed drinks €6-9. ⏰ Open M-F 5pm-3am, Sa-Su 7pm-3am.

FLEX 🚬♿🍸🌳 CLUB, BAR

Am Donaukanal ☎1 533 75 25 💻www.flex.at

Located in a gritty, unused subway tunnel, Flex boasts the best sound system in the city as well as the most famous name. (In 2003, the magazine *Spex* voted Flex the best club in the German-speaking world.) Though 2003 is actually quite a while ago, people still flood this alternative venue. Come in break it down on the club's dance floor which is attached to cafe's Danube banks (where you can also easily bring your own booze... score!).

🚇 U2 or U4: Schottenring; Tram #1 or 31: Schottenring. $ Free entrance to Flex Cafe. Club cover €4-12. ⏰ Open daily 6pm-4am.

VOLKSGARTEN DISCO ♿🍸🌳 CLUB, BAR

Burgring 1, Volksgarten ☎1 532 42 41 💻www.volksgarten.at

Located on the edge of the Volksgarten green space, this popular club has been a part of the Vienna nightlife scene for almost as long as the 180-year-old building. Okay, not really, but in club-years, definitely so. The mix of indoor and outdoor space is adorned with plants, kidney-bean shaped tables, and colorful benches. The music ranges from R and B to reggae, and there's always plenty of dancing.

🚇 U2 or U3: Volkstheater. $ Cover free-€20, depending on event. ⏰ Open F-Sa 11pm-late; sometimes open during the week for special events.

DICK MACK'S 🚬♿🍸 IRISH PUB

Marc-Aurel-Str. 7 ☎1 676 706 81 24 💻www.paddysco.at/dickmack

Just beyond Schwedenpl.'s Bermuda Triangle and its pricey beers, Dick Mack's is the Irish pub that all the local university students swear by. The decor is nothing special (it's a typical pub), but the beers are cheap, cheap, cheap. You won't be sorry you began the night here when you leave happily intoxicated and likewise happily not broke.

🚇 *U1 or U4: Schwedenpl.* 💲 *Beer €2. Mixed drinks €2.80.* 🕙 *Open M-Sa 8pm-4am.*

ONYX

●♿♥ BAR

Stephanspl. 12 ☎1 535 39 69 🖥www.doco.com

The floor-to-ceiling windows of this sixth-floor bar in Haas Haus give unparalleled views of Stephansdom. It feels as though you could literally reach out and touch the roof. The view is to die for and so are the pricey drinks, especially the Frozen Blackberry with vodka and lemon, which mainly draw Vienna's young business crowd to the bar's sleek couches and stools.

🚇 *U1 or U3: Stephanspl.* 💲 *Mixed drinks €9-14.* 🕙 *Open daily 9am-2am.*

PLANTER'S CLUB

●♿♥♨ BAR

Zelinkagasse 4 ☎1 533 33 93 15 🖥www.plantersclub.com

Low leather chairs, small coffee tables, and palm fronds adorn this colonial-style bar with deep wood accents and soft green and yellow lights. Be prepared to stay a while because the cocktail menu is at least 20 pages, and each one seems to be tastier than the last. There are over 450 single malt whiskeys alone. The place gets crowded around 10pm, so come early to snag a seat. The neighboring restaurant of the same name also comes highly recommended.

🚇 *U2 or U4: Schottenring.* 💲 *Mixed drinks €7-15.* 🕙 *Open daily 5pm-4am.*

Core Districts

◪ STRANDBAR HERRMANN

●♿♥♨ BAR, BEACH CLUB

Herrmannpark 🖥www.strandbarherrmann.at

This canal-side venue is as close to a beach bar as it gets in Vienna. Parts of the ground have been covered with sand, and there are plenty of deck chairs for sunbathing during the day (although swimming in the canal is generally not recommended). By night, beers are passed around, and there is plenty of live or mixed music to set the scene.

🚇 *U1 or U4: Schwedenpl., exit to Urania. Or U3, Tram #1, 2, or 2A: Stubentor.* 💲 *Beer €3.30-4.80.* 🕙 *Open daily 10am-2am.*

CHELSEA

●♿♥♨ BAR, CLUB, MUSIC VENUE

Lerchenfelder Gürtel/Stadtbahnbogen 29-30 ☎1 407 93 09 🖥www.chelsea.co.at

Back when the area was a red-light district, Chelsea opened in the Stadtbahnbogen, soon to revolutionize the Gürtel nightlife scene. The exterior lacks the glass facades that many of the newer Gürtel venues boast (look for the brick walls covered in posters instead), but that suits Chelsea's down-to-earth plain quality that gives it a pub vibe. With rock, Britpop, and funk blaring, the people are always ready to party. Come early because it gets packed.

🚇 *U6, Tram #46, or Bus #48A: Thaliastr.* 💲 *Cover free-€12.* 🕙 *Open daily 6pm-4am.*

BABU

●⊗♥♨ BAR, CLUB

Stadtbahnbögen 181-184 ☎699 1 175 40 72 🖥www.babu.at

This large restaurant, bar, and club expands over four archways of the Gürtel underneath the train tracks. Inside, it's all glass and air, with a split-level design and crisp white seats. From the top floor, you can look out the windows onto the Gürtel, while below in the bar a gussied-up crowd schmoozes and sips cocktails.

🚇 *U6: Nußdorfer Str.* 🕙 *Open daily 6pm-late.*

PRATERSAUNA

●♿♥♨ CLUB

Waldsteingartenstr. 135 ☎1 72 919 27 🖥www.pratersauna.tv

One of the newest clubs in Vienna's "in" scene, Pratersauna is a former sauna converted into a club. A deck and lawn with chairs encircle the pool, which looks temptingly lit up on warm summer evenings, but unfortunately it's not open when the club is in full swing. (And yes, they will kick you out if you try to swim. Also, Let's Go does not recommend swimming under the influence.) The alternative, warehouse-style dance floors reflect the minimalist music that is generally played and is too monotone for anyone who's looking for a dance beat. The high entrance price is mostly due to hype; spend willingly but don't be surprised if you are a bit underwhelmed. Oh yeah, and it generally doesn't get packed until after 2am.

U2: Messe. Or Tram #1: Prater Hauptallee. $ Cover free-€15. Beers €3.80. Mixed drinks €7-9. ⏰ Open W-Sa 9pm-late. Pool open W until 4am.

B72 BAR, MUSIC VENUE

Hernalser Gürtel, Stadtbahnbogen 72 ☎1 409 21 28 www.b72.at

Part of the growing Gürtel nightlife scene (under the railway arches), this small venue regularly hosts national and international DJs and bands, though it's particularly known within the Austrian alternative music world. The venue is cleverly split over two floors—on the ground level, the two bars and stage reside, while on the first level, there are tables and chairs with views down onto the stage.

U6 or Tram #43: Alser Str. $ Cover free-€15. ⏰ Open daily 8pm-4am.

Q [KJU:] BAR, CLUB

Währinger Gürtel, Stadtbahnbogen 142-144 ☎1 804 50 55 www.kju-bar.at

Frequented by a young, party-going crowd, Q [kju:] is another club venue on the Gürtel nightlife scene, with a rowdy, dance-happy clientele. The red walls with gold and leather accents are adorned with hanging mirrors that make the dance floor seem larger (and also provide a convenient means of checking out your latest dance moves). If you don't feel like shakin' your booty, observe the sunken dance floor from a booth alongside it.

U6: Währinger Str., Volksoper. ⏰ Open daily 8pm-4am.

PRATERDOME CLUB

Riesenradpl.7 ☎1 908 119 29 00 www.praterdome.at

The largest club in Austria, Praterdome fulfills every disco-goer's fantasy... within reason, of course. There are four dance floors playing every type of music imaginable and 12 bars to serve you up drinks. While the laser lights and neon colors are cool, the clientele often thinks they are a bit too cool (in other words, trashy). Mentally prepare yourself for a large night out and bring a very very large group of friends—it's likely you will lose a few in this massive party complex.

U1: Praterstern. $ Cover free-€10. ⏰ Open Th-Sa 9 or 10pm-late.

ALL IN BAR, MUSIC VENUE

Währinger Gürtel, Stadtbahnbögen 90-91 ☎1 236 52 89 www.allinbar.com

One of the more recent arrivals on the Gürtel nightlife scene, All In boasts a sleek design that blends the exposed brick of the subway arches with modern glass shelves and geometric furniture. There is a dance floor as well as a long bar with high square stools—dress up a bit and order one of the delicious, fruity cocktails. The music ranges from oldies to jazz to hip hop, so check the website for upcoming events.

U6 or Tram #43: Alser Str. $ Cover free-€8. ⏰ Open Tu-Sa 9pm-4am, Su 10am-8pm.

Outer Districts

U4 DANCE CLUB

Schonbrunner Str. 222 ☎1 817 11 92 www.u-4.at

U4 is a club legend in Vienna—everyone has their own story and impression of the place, but all will undoubtedly name-drop that Nirvana once played there. In its dark underground locale, U4 has two dance floors with different music, and the program changes every night. Its far-out location in the district XII eliminates the possibility of club-hopping easily, so everyone commits to the night, oftentimes taking the first U-Bahn train home in the morning.

🚇 U4: Meidlinger Hauptstr. The club is directly behing the station on Schonbrunner Str. ⏰ Open M-Sa 10pm-5-6am.

ARTS AND CULTURE ♫

Theater

TANZQUARTIER WIEN 🎟♿ CORE

Museumspl. 1 ☎1 581 35 91 💻www.tqw.at

With an ambitious schedule of new shows every weekend, Tanzquartier Wien has become a premier dance space for contemporary and modern-style dance. Much of it is experimental, and the shows range from one-woman acts to ensemble pieces performed in the studio spaces or the neighboring Kunsthalle theater.

🚇 U2: Musemspl. Or U2 or U3: Volkstheater. In Museumsquartier, walk beyond the Leopold Museum and turn right. Ⓢ Tickets €11, students €7.50. Open dance classes (professional level) €9. ⏰ Box office and info office open M-Sa 9am-8pm.

THEATER AN DER WIEN 🎟♿ CORE

Linke Wienzeile 6 ☎1 588 85 💻www.theater-wien.at

One of Vienna's youngest opera houses (it opened in 2006), Theater an der Wien becomes *the* opera destination in July and August when its shows keep running even though the normal opera season stops. A new show usually premieres each month.

🚇 U1, U2, or U4: Karlspl. Ⓢ Tickets €12-160. Student rush operas €15, concerts €10. Standing-room tickets €7. ⏰ Box office open daily 10am-7pm. Student-rush tickets are available 30min. before curtain at the box office. Standing room (based on availability) can be purchased 1hr. before showtime.

VIENNA'S ENGLISH THEATER 🎟 CORE

Josefsgasse 12 ☎1 402 126 00 💻www.englishtheatre.at

Vienna's English Theater was established in 1963 as a summer theater for tourists, but its popularity enabled it to expand into the traditional theater season (and now it doesn't even run shows during the summer months). In 2004, it was awarded the Nestroy Prize for 40 years of achievement, with appearances by the likes of Judi Dench and Leslie Nielsen and European premieres of plays by David Auburn and Edward Albee.

🚇 U2 and U3: Volkstheater. Or Tram #1 or D: Parliament; Tram #2: Rathaus; or Bus #13A: Piaristengasse. Ⓢ Tickets €22-42. Students and under 18 20% off. Standby tickets €9. ⏰ Box office open Jan-May and Sept-Dec M-F 10am-7:30pm, Sa and holidays 5-7:30pm; on non-performance days Jan-May and Sept-Dec M-F 10am-5pm. Limited number of standby tickets are available 15min. before curtain.

Film

ENGLISH CINEMA HAYDN ⊗ CORE

Mariahilfer Str. 57 ☎1 587 22 62 💻www.haydnkino.at

If you're on the lookout for some good ol' American pop culture, this cinema is one of the few in the city that presents English-language films without subtitles. All the major motion pictures you've heard of and, surprisingly, not too behind the US in terms of release dates (i.e., you will probably find a few that you haven't seen already).

🚇 U3: Neubaugasse. Ⓢ Tickets €5.90-8.50, depending on length of film and day of the week. ⏰ Box office opens 15min. before 1st show and closes 15min. after beginning of last show.

BURG KINO 🍴♿ INNER

Opernring 19 ☎1 587 8406 🖥www.burgkino.at

A centrally located theater that shows a mix of mainstream and indie. There are two screens—one reserved for a popular Hollywood movie or cartoon (screened in the original version), while the other, smaller screen offers a rotation of less prominent indie flicks (although still fairly recent and also in the original English versions).

🚇 U1, U2, U4, Tram #1, 2, or D: Karlspl. $ Tickets M-Th €5, F-Su €6. ⏰ Box office opens 30min. before 1st showing.

ARTIS INTERNATIONAL 🍴♿ INNER

Schultergasse 5 ☎1 535 65 70 🖥www.cineplexx.at

This old Inner Stadt cinema shows only recent Hollywood flicks in English and generally without subtitles. There is even an occasional 3D offering. Some movie-goers balk that the screens are too small, especially compared to the uber large, stadium style theaters we are now used to.

🚇 U1 or U3: Stephanspl. Or U3: Herrengasse. $ Tickets €6-10. ⏰ Opens 15-30min. before 1st showing.

Music

STAATSOPER (STATE OPERA) 💳 INNER

Opernring 2 ☎1 514 44 22 50 🖥www.wiener-staatsoper.at

For many visitors, seeing an opera in the gorgeous Staatsoper is a highlight of a trip to Vienna. Hindemith's *Cadillac*, Mozart's *Don Giovanni* and *Le nozze di Figaro*, Janácek's *Kátja Kabanová*, Händel's *Alcina*, and Donizetti's *Anna Bolena* are just six of the more recent new productions. Opera season runs Sept-June, but during the summer months, operas are shown on a 50 sq. m screen on the plaza in front of the Opera House for free.

🚇 U1, U2, U4, Trams 1, 2, D, J, 62, 65: Karlspl. $ Tickets €3-250. Standing-room tickets €2.50-5. Tours €6.50, seniors €5.50, students and children €3.50. ⏰ Box office (Operngasse 2 ☎514 44 78 10) open M-F 8am-6pm, Sa-Su 9am-noon. Tours of the Opera House vary based on show schedule, but usually 1-3 per day in the afternoon at 2, 3, and 4pm; check website ahead of time. Tickets include entrance to Opera Museum (except on M). Standing-room tickets are available 80min. before curtains.

WIENER PHILHARMONIC ORCHESTRA INNER

Ticket and Ball Office, Kärntner Ring 12 ☎1 505 65 25 🖥www.wienerphilharmoniker.at

The Wiener Philharmonic Orchestra embodies the musical spirit of Vienna. Strauss, Mahler, Bruckner, and Wagner are some of the famous names that have been associated with the orchestra over the years, which is perhaps why season subscriptions often sell out years in advance. Tickets for their annual New Year's Eve concert performed in the Musikverein has to be lotteried due to such high demand, but they perform at many other venues and times throughout the city.

🚇 U1, U2, U4, Tram #1, 2, or D: Karlspl. $ Prices vary. ⏰ Box office open M-F 9:30am-3:30pm, and 1hr. before the subscription concerts and end-of-year concerts.

WIENER STADHALLE 💳♿🍸 OUTER

Vogelweidpl. 14 ☎1 98 100 🖥www.stadthalle.com

The Stadthalle presents the greatest variety of music, entertainment, and artistic acts of any Vienna venue, as well as some sports and even kid's musicals. Although it's lacking Old World opera house charm (the building resembles a spaceship), it has seen big-name musicians including Guns N' Roses and the Red Hot Chili Peppers.

🚇 U6: Burgasse. $ Ticket prices vary based on event. ⏰ Box office (between Hall D and Hall F) open M-Sa 10am-8pm.

Festivals

Here are some of the best festivals to partake in when in Vienna.

DONAUINSEL FEST (DANUBE ISLAND FESTIVAL) DANUBE ISLAND

Danube Island 🖥www.donauinselfest.at

This three-day festival is one of the most popular outdoor events in Europe, taking place on the Danube Island and welcoming over 2 million attendees. Free concerts galore with every genre of music imaginable, plenty of food and drink (sometimes too much!), and even a section with amusement park rides and games.

U1: Donauinsel or U6: Handelskai. $ Concerts and music free. Food, drink, and rides vary. ⏰ A weekend in June.

VIENNALE INNER

Siebensterngasse 2 ☎1 526 59 47 🖥www.viennale.at

The Viennale prides itself on showcasing Austrian and international films for young audiences, focusing on documentary films, international shorts, and experimental works. Every year, the festival screens over 300 films and receives over 90,000 visitors and audience members, including about 700 accredited guests from the film industry. Many of the screenings include discussions with the filmmakers, and there are other events such as concerts, book presentations, and cultural exhibitions throughout.

Cinemas throughout the Inner Stadt. ⏰ Festival runs every Oct.

RAINBOW PARADE INNER, CORE

Ringstr. ☎1 216 66 04 🖥www.regenbogenparade.at

Only begun in 1996, the gay pride parade has now become one of Vienna's largest events, sweeping the Ringstr. with the rainbow flags, outrageous outfits and body paint, and lots and lots of glitter. The parade culminates in a free concert with multiple acts, food and drink stands on the streets, and a generally exuberant atmosphere that might seem unexpected in this otherwise traditional city. Be on the lookout for the blow-up, rainbow-colored balloons shaped like male genitalia.

U4: Stadtpark. From Stadtpark to Schwarzenbergerpl. $ Parade and concert free. ⏰ Early in July.

SHOPPING

Clothing

MOTMOT CORE

Kirchengasse 36 ☎1 924 27 19 🖥www.motmotshop.com

T-shirts, T-shirts, T-shirts in every color and style imaginable and with hilarious designs and idioms. If you like surprises, buy a sale bag, which has a mysterious selection of shirts in a brown bag for a fixed, cheap price (male or female is indicated). Other fun accessories like buttons and belts are also available.

Tram #49. $ T-shirts €25-50. Buttons €1. ⏰ Open Tu-F noon-7pm, Sa noon-5pm.

BE A GOOD GIRL ♿ CORE

Westbahnstr. 5A ☎1 524 47 28 🖥www.beagoodgirl.at

While part of this shop is a hair salon (chic, obviously), the other half has funky bags, wallets, fedoras, and sneakers for sale. There is also an interesting selection of books and notebooks, one of which has Vienna city grids on the pages in the place of regular lines or graph paper.

Tram #49. ⏰ Open Tu-F 10am-7pm, Sa 10am-4pm.

ART POINT ♿ CORE

Westbahnstr. 3 ☎1 522 04 25 🖥www.artpoint.eu

This store epitomizes the creativity of up-and-coming European designers, whose clothing is sometimes more like a work of art than particularly practical. Art Point is best known for their "two sleeves and one collar," which is as it sounds: two dress shirt sleeves attached to a dress-shirt collar, then wrapped around and tied like a scarf. They come in every pattern imaginable and are made for men and women.

➔ Tram #49. $ 2 sleeves and 1 collar €85. 🕐 Open M-F 11am-7pm, Sa 11am-5pm.

Music

SCOUT RECORDS
💳♿ CORE

Capistrangasse 3

Stepping into this record store is like venturing into a music-collector's basement. Wall shelves, filing bins, and even cardboard boxes are all packed to the brim with CDs, DVDs, and records. There is a large selection of jazz as well as rock, metal, and classical. Be prepared to spend some time getting lost in the music.

➔ U3: Neubaugasse. $ CDs from €3. Vinyl records up to €40. 🕐 Open M-F 2-7pm, Sa 10am-5pm.

SUBSTANCE
💳♿ CORE

Westbahnstr. 16 ☎1 523 67 57 💻www.substance-store.com

The pristine rows of CDs and vinyl records are shiny and expensive, making this music store the place to buy new music. The collection is extensive, though the focus is on indie, electronica, and alternative.

➔ U3 or Tram #49: Neubaugasse. 🕐 Open M-F 11am-7:30pm, Sa 10am-6pm.

AUDIAMO
💳♿ OUTER

Kaiserstr. 70 ☎1 699 95 31 90 💻www.audiamo.com

It's not too often you can find books on tape when traveling abroad, and in English no less! Audiamo has crime, romance, thriller, biography, fiction, and children's books on tape, as well as some CDs and DVDs for your listening and viewing pleasure. Look for the British flags on the boxes that indicate English-language selections. There is also a pleasant cafe in the shop with coffee and snacks.

➔ U6 or Tram #5: Burggasse. 🕐 Open M-F 9am-7pm, Sa 10am-5pm.

austria

Books

👍 SHAKESPEARE AND COMPANY BOOKSELLERS
💳♿ CORE

Sterngasse 2 ☎1 535 50 35 💻www.shakespeare.co.at

This store's motto is "Let yourself be found by a book," and there really is no better place to do just that. Located in a nook in one of the oldest parts of the Inner Stadt, Shakespeare and Co. has large English selections of travel literature, fiction, and history books arranged on wooden bookshelves that stretch from floor to ceiling. It often holds book readings and other events open to the public.

➔ U1 or U4: Schwedenpl. $ Used books from €3. New books from €8. 🕐 Open 6 days a week 9am-9pm; call ahead for weekly schedule.

THE BRITISH BOOKSHOP
💳♿❄ CORE

Weihburggasse 24 ☎1 512 19 450 💻www.britishbookshop.at

Just when you just thought you would never find the perfect vacation read, The British Bookshop is overflowing with more selection than you know what to do with. Choose from fiction, travel (👍**Let's Go** included!), classics, crime, romance, and even business books. Don't miss the sale bin hidden behind the bulletin board next to the cash register.

➔ U3, Tram #1 or 2: Stubentor. $ Paperback novels €9-12. 🕐 Open M-F 9:30am-6:30pm, Sa 9:30-6pm.

KUNSTHALLE WIEN SHOP
💳♿ CORE

Museumspl. 1 ☎1 524 02 20 💻www.kunsthallewien.at/en/shop

The kooky knick-knacks assembled here will certainly entertain. Because who doesn't need a massive chocolate-bar shaped calculator or kama sutra dice? Pick up hilarious postcards *(€1.20-3.50)* to send home or a new eraser for "Really Big Mistakes."

🚇 U2: Musemspl. Alternatively U2 or U3: Volkstheater. In Museumsquartier, the shop is beneath the stairs of the MUMOK. ⏰ Open daily 11am-7pm.

LIFE BOOKS/"BÜCHER FUR'S LEBEN" 💳♿ CORE

Capistrangasse 5 ☎1 587 94 60 💻www.lifebooks.at

This bookstore has got its motto right, offering all the "life books" you could need, though unfortunately the majority are in German. There is a selection in English that consists of mainstream novels and bestsellers, and the English-speaking staff is happy to recommend their favorites.

🚇 U3: Neubaugasse. From the stop, the bookstore is off Mariahilfer Str. $ English books €8-11. ⏰ Open M-F 10am-6pm, Sa 10am-4pm.

ESSENTIALS

Practicalities

- **TOURIST OFFICES:** The Vienna Card, opera and theater tickets, and other brochures are available. *(☎1 24 555 💻www.vienna.info 🚇 Located in the Inner Stadt, Albertinapl. across from the Albertina museum, behind the Opera House. $ Hotel reservations €2.90. ⏰ Open daily 9am-7pm.)*
- **EMBASSIES: Australia** *(IV, Mattiellistr. 2-4. ☎1 506 740 💻www.australian-embassy.at ⏰ Open M-F 8:30am-4:30pm.)*, **Canada** *(I, Laurenzerberg 2 ☎1 531 38 30 00 💻www.kanada.at ⏰ Open M-F 8:30am-12:30pm and 1:30-3:30pm.)*, **UK** *(III, Jauresgasse 12 ☎1 716 130 💻www.britishembassy.at ⏰ Open M-F 9am-1pm and 2-5pm.)*, and **US** *(IX, Boltzmanngasse 16 ☎1 313 390 💻www.usembassy.at ⏰ Open M-F 8-11:30am.)*.
- **INTERNET CAFES: künstlerhauskino wien – internetcafé** *(Karlspl. 5. ☎587 96 63 19 $ €1.60 per 30min. ⏰ Open daily 11am-9pm.)* and **Surfland.c@fe** *(Krugerstr. 10 ☎512 77 01 $ €6 per hr. Photocopy €0.50. Color copy €1. Printing €0.30 per page. ⏰ Open daily Apr-Oct 10am-11pm; Nov-Mar 10am-10pm.)*.
- **POST OFFICE:** The main office *(Hauptpotamt)* is located in the Inner Stadt. *(Fleishmarkt 19 ☎0577 677 10 10 ℹ Other branches are located throughout the city; look for the yellow signs and post boxes. ⏰ Open M-F 7am-10pm, Sa-Su 9am-10pm.)*
- **POSTAL CODES:** 1010 (Inner Stadt) through 1023 (District XXIII).

Emergency!

- **POLICE:** *(☎133)*
- **AMBULANCE:** *(☎144)*
- **FIRE:** *(☎122)*
- **PHYSICIAN:** *(☎141)* **Physicians Hotline for Visitors:** *(☎513 9595 ⏰ 24hr.)*
- **EMERGENCY DENTAL:** *(☎512 20 78 ⏰ Service on nights and weekends.)*
- **PHARMACY:** *(☎15 50 ⏰ Open on nights and weekends.)*

Getting There

By Plane

Vienna is centrally located in Europe and as a result is quite easy to reach via plane. **Vienna-Schwechat Airport** *(Wien-Schwechat Flughafen. ☎7007 222 33 💻www.viennaairport.at)* is home to **Austrian Airlines** *(💻www.austrian.com)*, which runs non-stop flights from most major cities in Europe to Vienna multiple times a day. Other airlines that fly to Vienna include **British Airways** *(🖳www.britishairways.com)*, **easyJet** *(🖳www.easyjet.com)*, **Aer Lingus** *(🖳www.aerlingus.com)*, **Lufthansa** *(🖳www.lufthansa.com)*, **KLM** *(🖳www.klm.com)*, **Air France** *(🖳www.airfrance.com)*, and **United Airlines** *(🖳www.united.com)*.

One of the least stressful ways to reach the city center after a long flight is with the **City Airport Train** *(CAT, 🖳www.cityairporttrain.com)*. It brings you to **Wien Mitte** in a mere 16min., from which you can then connect to the U4 underground line at Landstr. The CAT runs every half hour. *(⏰ From the airport to the city daily 5:38am-11:38pm. From the city to the airport daily 6:05am-12:05am. $ One-way €9, round-trip €16; with a Vienna Card €7.50/15. On board tickets cost €12. Children under 14 ride free.)*

In addition to the CAT, the **Schellbahn** *(S-7 or S-8)* runs into the city as well, though it's a bit trickier. The trains going to the city should read "Wien Mitte," "Wien Nord," or "Florisdorf," while the train to the airport should have a "Flughafen" or "Wolfsthal" sign. *($ One-way tickets (2 zones) €4.40, bought in advance €3.60. With the Vienna card €2.20/1.80.)*

Airport Express Buses also shuttle between various places in the city center and the airport and take about 20min. *(🖳www.postbus.at ☎1 7007 323 00, 517 17 $ One-way €6, children €3, Vienna Cardholders €5. Round trip €11/5.50/10. ⏰Every 30min., 5am-midnight.)*

By Train

There are a number of train stations located throughout the city that serve as major hubs for both local and international trains.

Sudbahnhof

If you are wondering where the Sudbahnhof went, in short, it's gone. But don't freak out just yet. Since 2009, the Sudbahnhof has been under construction, and a shining new **Vienna Central Station** will take the place of this defunct station. The VCS is scheduled for completion in 2013. During construction, the eastern portion of Sudbahnhof (Ostbahn) will remain running, serving eastern bound trains to destinations like Bratislava.

Westbahnhof

The Westbahnhof is also undergoing construction and large portions are closed until 2011, but all the normal destinations are still active. This includes trains to other parts of **Austria** (Innsbruck, Salzburg) as well as international destinations including **Hungary** (Budapest), **Germany** (Munich, Hamburg, Berlin), and **Switzerland** (Zurich). The airport buses and taxis ranks still drop off and pick up in from the station, and you can easily connect to the U3 or U6 underground lines as well as Tram #lines 5, 6, 9, 18, 52, and 58. Westbahnhof also still has ticket windows and machines, an ÖBB Travel Centre, luggage storage, shops, cafes, and an information point in operation.

Wien Meidling

In Vienna's District XII, Wien Meidling lies at the end of Meidlinger Haupstr. and serves international destinations in the **Czech Republic, Poland,** and **Germany.** It has taken over all the local arrivals and departures that previously used the Sudbahnhof and also connects to the U6 Station Philadelphiabrücke, Tram #62, Bus lines 7A, 7B, 8A, 9A, 15A, 59A, and 62A, and S-bahn lines S1, S2, S3, S4, S5, S6, S9, and S15. Wien Meidling has taxi stands, luggage lockers, ticket machines, an ÖBB Travel Centre, and an information desk.

Wien Mitte

The City Airport Train arrives at Wien Mitte, where you can easily connect to the U3 and U4 underground lines and multiple S-bahn lines.

Getting Around

If you are staying in the city, a car is definitely not needed. Save the parking money and buy yourself a drink.

By Wiener Linien

The public transportation system in Vienna—the Wiener Linien (*💻www.wienerlinien.at*)—is extensive, reliable, and safe. It consists of the **U-Bahn** (underground), **trams** (above ground), and **buses.** The **Vienna Card** *(available in hotels and at the tourist information center on Albertinapl. and the airport for €18.50),* gives you 72hr. of unlimited transportation access within the city as well as over 200 discounts on other sights. Other useful transportation tickets include the 24hr. season ticket *($ €5.70),* the 48hr. season ticket *($ €10),* the 72hr. season ticket *($ €13.60),* and monthly *($ €49.50).* A single ride costs €1.80. For the U-Bahn, buy your ticket at the multilingual machines and validate it (stamp it) at the little blue boxes before reaching the platforms. Single tickets for trams and buses can be purchased on board for €2.20, coins only. The five U-Bahn lines run on weekdays from 5am to midnight, while the buses and trams end a bit earlier. Check the Wiener Linien website for exact schedules of specific lines. In September 2010, the U-Bahn lines started to run all night on Fridays and Saturdays in addition to the night buses that already reach a large portion of the city.

By Taxi

Because the public transportation system is so extensive, taxis are not entirely necessary, but they come in handy when the Nightbus is elusive. Some taxi numbers include ☎4000 011 11, ☎4000 010 00 (Inner Stadt), ☎601 60, ☎401 00, and ☎313 00, although the best bet is to pick one on the street. (All accredited taxis in the city are known to be reliable.) In the Inner Stadt, taxis cluster on **Rotenturmstrasse** and **Schwedenplatz** near the nightlife, but they also wait outside other well-known clubs in the core and outer districts. Taxis have set rates for the airport, and there are some that are exclusively airport taxis: **C and K** *(☎444 44)* and **Airportdriver** *(☎22 8 22)* run €35-48, depending on the number of passengers. An Austria-wide taxi number is ☎1718.

By Bike

Because of Vienna's manageable size, bikes are extremely common in the warmer spring and summer months, and there are safe bikepaths (over 1100km total) throughout the city. **Citybike** is a public bike-rental system with over 60 stands located around the city, usually close to public transportation hubs. To rent a CityBike, tourists need the CityBike Tourist card (unless you somehow have a MasterCard or Visa associated with an Austrian bank). **Royal Tours** *(Herrengasse 1-3)* and **Pedal Power** *(Ausstellunstr. 3)* offer the cards for €2 per day, but it's worth asking your hostel or hotel as well. *($ From €4 per hr.)*

By Suburban Train

The suburban train network **(Austrian Federal Railways, ÖBB)** is also extensive and provides swift and easy access to the surrounding towns and countryside. These trains require different tickets than the inner-city public transport, but all the stations have the multilingual machines or ticket counters. Single rides start at €1.80 for nearby towns, such as **Mödling**.

klosterneuburg ☎2243

According to legend, **Klosterneuburg Monastery** was built when Margrave Leopold III found his wife's wedding veil that she had lost nine years earlier. It was hanging from an elderberry tree somewhere between the Vienna Woods and the Danube, and at that moment, the Virgin Mary appeared and commanded Leopold to construct a monastery in her honor. Thus the magnificent Abbey came into being. Over 900-years-old, Klosterneubug Abbey is at the heart of the small city of Klosterneuburg, located 10km up the **Danube** from Vienna. Around it, a selection of streets with shops and cafes have a small-town flavor; there are just enough large grocery stores to prevent the town from feeling as archaic as the abbey. Access to the town is easy via public transportation, making Klosterneuburg a popular daytrip from Vienna.

ORIENTATION

Wiener Str. is the main highway toward the town center, along which the bus #239 drives and the City Train runs parallel. On this street, with the city behind you, the **Essl Museum** will come up first on the right, and the **abbey** will be further ahead on the left. In the town center, Wiener Str. turns into **Neidermarkt,** where multiple bus stops and tourist information center can be found around a small plaza. Neidermarkt then curves left uphill and turns into Stadtpl., another main artery with the city's shops and cafes. Bus #239 runs along Stadtpl. toward **Maria Gugging,** a neighboring town about 8km further into the Vienna countryside.

SIGHTS

KLOSTERNEUBURG ABBEY
💰♿🍸☀ CHURCH, WINERY

Stiftspl. 1, 3400 Klosterneuburg ☎2243 44 12 12 💻www.stift-klosterneuburg.at

The most frequented sight in the town of Klosterneuburg, the abbey houses an elaborate church, the **Verdun Altar,** and Austria's oldest and largest winery below. If you have some hours to spare, it's a good deal to invest in the Stiftsticket, which will allow you to tour-hop the whole day.

*✈ It's the huge monastery with 2 towers. **i** The Sacred Tour including the Church and Verdun Altar is the only tour offered in English. The self-guided "Imperial Tour" through the imperial rooms has English explanations. $ Tours €5-9, students €4-6. Stiftsticket tour €14/10. ⏰ Open daily 9am-6pm. Sacred Tour Sa and Su 2pm.*

ESSL MUSEUM
💰♿☀ ART MUSEUM

An der Donau - Au 1, 3400 Klosterneuburg ☎2243 37 05 01 50 💻www.essl.museum

Agnes and Karlhienz Essl have collected over 7,000 works of art during their lifetimes, and it is their primary wish to share and educate others about the world of contemporary art (hence the free shuttle bus and free entry for students). The Essls are highly involved in the organization of the permanent collection as well as the program of visiting artists (all of whom they have met while traveling). In 2011, look forward to two special exhibits featuring up-and-coming artists from India and from New York.

✈ A free shuttle bus (25min.) leaves from Vienna at Albertinapl. 2 at 10am, noon, 2, and 4pm. Return shuttle buses to the city leave the museum at 11am, 1, 3, and 6pm. $ Students, retirees, and unemployed free. Adults €5. Family €9. W 6-9pm free. ⏰ Open Tu 10am-6pm, W 10am-9pm, Th-Su 10am-6pm.

MUSEUM GUGGING
💰♿ MUSEUM, GALLERY

Am Campus 2, 3400 Maria Gugging ☎2243 870 87 💻www.gugging.at

Museum Gugging was established as a showcase for the artwork of the neighboring Haus de Kunstler, where mentally ill patients are given a voice through artistic expression. Their work—mostly drawing and painting—has revolutionized the field of "Art Brut," popularizing artists such as Johann Hauser. The upstairs museum is paired with the downstairs Galerie Gugging, where visitors can purchase selected artworks.

✈ U4: Heiligenstadt or bus #239: ART/Brut Center Gugging. Follow the signs for the museum and gallery up the really big hill. $ €7, seniors €5.50, students €5, family €14, children under 6 free. ⏰ Open Tu-Su Jan-May and Sept-Dec 10am-5pm; June-Aug 10am-6pm.

FOOD

HOTEL ANKER
💰♿🍸☀ RESTOBAR [2]

Niedermarkt 5, 3400 Klosterneuburg ☎2243 32 13 40 💻www.hotel-anker.at

Hotel Anker offers meat, potatoes, and beer at more reasonable prices than the few other sit-down restaurants located in town. Many locals enjoy Hotel Anker as a regular smoking and drinking establishment, so don't expect white tablecloths and crystal wine glasses. The staff will kindly offer you an English menu and satisfyingly greasy french fries.

Behind the bus stop, across from the train tracks in Klosterneuburg. [$] Entrees €6.50-13. Open daily 10am-11pm.

ESSENTIALS

Practicalities

Everything you need is on the main street, **Stadtplatz,** or **Niedermarkt,** where the train and buses drop off. Along Stadtpl., there are a number of 24hr. **ATMs** (*bankomats*) and full-service branches of Bank Austria and Este Bank. **Grocery stores** (Spar, Billa), **pharmacies** (Bipa, dm), cafes and specialty shops are all located along Stadtpl.

- **TOURIST OFFICES:** The tourist office can give you maps and information on rooms. *(Niedermarkt 4 ☎2243 320 38).*

Getting There

If you are planning on visiting the **Essl Museum** in Klosterneuburg, take advantage of the free shuttle to and from the museum. From the Essl Museum, you can walk down the street to Klosterneuburg town center or take the bus #239 one stop. If you are not planning on visiting the Essl, Klosterneuburg is also easily accessible by public transportation. Take the U4 to Heiligenstadt, then pick up bus #239 toward Klosterneuburg/Maria Gugging. The **City Train** *(S40)* also runs to the town and drops off right near the bus stops in the town center.

mödling ☎2258

A small town on the edge of the **Vienna Woods** (*Weinerwald*), Mödling offers a peaceful atmosphere from which to taking hiking trips or explorations of nature. In reality, the neighboring towns like Hitnerbruhl and Heiligenkruez have more desirable sights, including the underground lake of Seegrotte and the picturesque Cistercian Abbey against a backdrop of green mountains. Mödling itself is a low-key town, with pleasant pedestrian streets ideal for an afternoon walk—or a wedding?! According to statistics, Mödling is the marriage capital of Lower Austria, with over 1200 ceremonies each year. If you are ridin' solo, Mödling is better known as the summer destination of Beethoven, who wrote Missa Solemnis at the **Hafner House** at Haupstr. 79. There are a few other museums in town, as well as the swimming pools of **Stadtbad** at Badstr. 25, but these constitute more of a children's water park than a relaxing spa, so it's best to get out into the surrounding wilderness.

ORIENTATION

Exiting right from the Mödling train station, a left at the first intersection with lights will put you on **Hauptstrasse,** the town's main thoroughfare with restaurants, shops, banks, and supermarkets. A walk up Haupstr. (with the building numbers increasing) will bring you through **Jospeh Deutsch Platz** and **Freiheitsplatz** to the network of pedestrian streets and the **Hauptplatz,** where the tourist information office is found.

SIGHTS

SEEGROTTE UNDERGROUND LAKE, CAVE

Grutschgasse 2a ☎2236 263 64 www.seegrotte.at

Set in the Vienna Woods, the former gypsum mine is now Europe's largest underground lake, and attracts more than 200,000 visitors annually (including lots of school groups). The mine experienced its most prominent 15 minutes of fame as the filming location for the 1993 movie, *The Three Musketeers;* parts of the set are still intact to prove it, including a viking-style boat. The caves and lake are only accessible via a tour, which takes you through the mines and on a boatride around the lake. The mines are nine degrees Celsius, so be sure to bring a jacket.

⇟ Bus #364 or #365: Hinterbruhl Seegrotte. From the stop, continue along the street in the same direction as the bus, then make your 1st right at the Seegrotte cafe. You will see tour buses and the Seegrotte entrance will be down the street in front of you. $ €9, children 4-14 €6, children under 4 free. Family (2 adults and 2 children) €24. Group rates (20+ people) available. Blanket rental €0.50. ⏰ Open Apr-Oct M-Su 8:30am-5pm; Nov-Mar M-F 9am-3pm, Sa-Su 9am-3:30pm. English tours usually at noon.

STIFT HEILIGENKREUZ ♿ ABBEY, CHURCH

Zisterzienserabtei Stift Heiligenkreuz ☎2258 870 31 38 💻www.stift-heiligenkreuz.at

While the grounds and courtyards are free to explore, it's worth taking the tour to see inside this Abbey, currently home to over 80 monks. The tour journeys through the cloister, reading corridor, chapels, chapterhouse, fountain house, and sacristy, culminating in the magnificent Abbey Church which has garnered much attention for its unique blend of Romanesque and Gothic styles. In the sacristy, be sure to look closely at the inlaid woodwork of the cabinets, handcrafted by two monks over the course of 20 years.

*⇟ Bus #364 or #365. **i** The Abbey is only accessible via tour. $ €7, students €3.50, seniors €6, family card €13. ⏰ Open Mar-Oct daily 9-11:30am and 1:30-5pm, Nov-Feb daily 9-11:30am and 1:30-4pm. Tours M-Sa 10am, 11am, 2pm, 3pm, and 4pm, Su 11am, 2pm, 3pm, and 4pm. Tours in German unless there's a large percentage of English-speakers, but helpful information cards are otherwise provided.*

FOOD

There are not many good food options in this city. One good way of feeding yourself is to go to one of the supermarkets, such as **Spar** *(across from the train station, on Haupstr.)* or **Billa** *(Elizabeth Str. ⏰ Most shops close M-F 6pm, Sa around noon, and closed on Su.).*

KLOSTERGASTHOF STIFT HEILIGENKREUZ ♿ INTERNATIONAL ❸

Stift Heiligenkreuz ☎2258 870 30

As the only restaurant near the abbey, tourists make up the majority of the customers, with higher prices to match. However, the meals are large, hearty, and quite flavorful with a range of meat and vegetarian options from a simple salmon steak with rice and vegetables *(€13.60)* to an Indian curry with grilled turkey and rice *(€10.10)*. Vegetarian entrees include fried cauliflower with tartar and salad *(€7.60)*. The pleasant courtyard with fountain and spreading trees is delightful.

⇟ Bus #364 or #365: Stift Heiligenkreuz. $ Entrees €7.60-18. ⏰ Open daily 9am-9pm.

ESSENTIALS

Practicalities

- **TOURIST OFFICE:** *(in the center of town, off the Hauptpl. at K. Elizabeth Str. 2 ☎2236 267 27 💻www.moedling.at ⏰ Open M-F 9am-12:30 and 1:30pm-5pm.)*
- **PHARMACY:** *(In Friheitspl. Look for the large green cross. ⏰ Open M-F 8am-6pm, Sa 8am-noon.)*
- **POLICE STATION:** *(Joseph Deutsch Pl., off Hauptstr.)*
- **BANKS: Oberbank, Ertse,** and **Volksbank** are scattered along Haupstr. and in the pedestrian streets.

Getting There

Getting to the town of Mödling is incredibly simple. **S-bahn** trains (Vienna's suburban train network) run every 5-10min. from Wien Meidling *(accessible from the U6 Philadelphiabrucke stop)* to Mödling. The journey takes 20min. and a one-way ticket costs €1.80. In Mödling, a less extensive bus network connects to the surrounding towns, including **Hinterbruhl** and **Heiligenkreuz.** Bus #364 and #365 run to both these towns and stop close to, if not at, the main sights there such as the **Seegrotte** and **Stift Heiligenkreuz.** Each one-way journey costs €1.80. Buses run 1-2 times per hour, and up to 4 times per hour around 11am and noon. Check the schedules ahead of time to plan your day most efficiently.

tulln an der donau ☎2272

As the district capital of Lower Austria, Tulln an der Donau (Tulln on the Danube) feels much like a normal city with regular citizens going about their business, all with the flowing Danube as a picturesque backdrop. While the city has a modern feel with plenty of commercial shops and restaurants, there are remnants of the old **Roman equestrian camp** mixed in, such as the oldest structure in town—the **Salzturm**—and the **Roman walls,** now preserved in an underground glass enclosure. The two churches, **St. Stephans** and **Minorite Church,** add their spires to the skyline, while the small **Schiele Museum** and **Roman Museum** give the city more cultural clout. Tulln provides plenty of simple pleasures for a day away from the big city, including fountains, statues, promenades, and gardens. Come for a sunny day and you might find yourself anxiously awaiting to return.

ORIENTATION

From the **Tulln Stadt** train station, a short walk up Bahnhofstr., with the station directly behind you, brings you to **Rathausplatz** and the neighboring **Hauptplatz** with benches, cafes, banks, and a fountain. From the Hauptpl., a number of streets lead toward the **Danube Promenade** along the water, and to a number of the town's notable fountains and sights. From the Hauptpl., Lederergasse brings you to **Minoritenplatz.**

SIGHTS

DANUBE PROMENADE — PROMENADE

along the Danube

Tulln's waterfront location is part of the town's draw, so it's worth walking or biking along the promenade and taking in a few of the sights. Starting from the western end, you can find artist Hundertwasser's boat *Regentag* ("Rainy Day") docked at the Schiffstation. Following the walkway, you will then see the **Nibelungen Denkmal** (fountain) which depicts the meeting of Kriemhild and Etzel in Tulln in the German epic *Nibelungenlied.* Passing the **Donaubuhne** where concerts are regularly held, you will see the **Salzturm** (Salt Tower), which was used as a flank tower when Tulln was a Roman equestrian camp. Short as the walk may be, spending time on the promenade is a highlight of Tulln.

From the train station, walk down Bahnhofstr., through the Hauptpl., straight to the Danube. $ *Free.*

EGON SCHIELE MUSEUM — MUSEUM

Donaulande 28 ☎2272 645 70 www.gonschiele.museum.com

This small, three-story museum is located in the former county jail of Tulln, Egon Schiele's birthtown. The prison rooms are adapted to display over 60 original works—mostly drawings, water colors, and oil paintings—many of which were done early in his lifetime. The first floor also gives history on Schiele's childhood between Tulln, Krems, and Klosterneuburg; be sure to ask for the handy English translation cards.

➡ Along the Danube Promenade; look for signs. $ €5, students €3, seniors €3.50. ⏰ Open Apr-Oct Tu-Su 10am-noon and 1pm-5pm.

DIE GARTEN 💳♿🍸 GARDENS

Am Wasserpark 1 ☎2272 681 88 💻www.diegartentulln.at

Opened in 2008, this permanent garden show displays over 50 individually-designed and constructed gardens, some dedicated to pleasure and beauty while others addressing specific structural or ecological issues. Explore the "Japanese garden," "wellness garden," "rosarium," or "farmer's garden," to name just a few. Each garden has an English description and explanation, and many have benches and chairs on which to relax and fully absorb your surroundings. Nearby, there is a treetop path that takes you 30 meters above the garden for a bird's-eye view.

➡ Walk along the Danube Promenade with the water to your right. Follow the signs. $ €11, students and seniors €9, children under 17 €6, children under 6 free, groups (20+) €7.50 per person. Season passes available. ⏰ Open Apr-Oct M-Su 9am-6pm.

FOOD

One option for food is to eat cheap at a local grocery like **Zielpunkt grocery.** *(Hauptpl. 24 ⏰ Open M-F 7:30am-7pm, Sa 7:30am-6pm.)*

GASTHAUS "ZUM GOLDENEN SCHIFF" 💳♿🍸 VIENNESE [2]

Weiner Str. 10 ☎2272 626 71

This *gasthaus* has a classic wood-paneled interior, simple white and blue checkered tablecloths, and a cozy, no-frills atmosphere. All the classic Viennese dishes are on order, including *gebackene scholle (€11.50), wiener schnitzel (€9.50), zweibelrostbraten (€12.50),* as well as a selection of soups and side dishes.

➡ From Bahnhofstr., cross through Rathauspl., then make your first right on to Weiner Str. The restaurant is directly across from the post office. $ Entrees €7-14. ⏰ Open M-F 10am-2:30pm and 5:30-11pm, Su 10:30am-3pm.

ESSENTIALS

Practicalities

- **TOURIST OFFICES:** The Tourist Info Office staff offers numerous brochures and pamphlets, a train schedule, restaurant listings, as well as an extremely helpful free town map. They will also book rooms in town for a €2 fee. *(➡ Minoritenpl. 2 ☎2272 675 66, 💻www.tulln.at ⏰ Open Oct-Apr M-F 8am-3pm; May-Sept M-F 9am-7pm, Sa-Su 10am-7pm.)*
- **BANKS: Erste Bank** has a **24hr. ATM** on the back side. *(Rathauspl. 8. ☎05 0100-20111. ⏰ Open M-Th 8am-noon and 1-3:30pm, F 8am-noon and 1-4:30pm.)* There are also branches of Volksbank, Bank Austria and Oberbank in the Hauptpl., also with 24hr ATMs.
- **PHARMACIES: Bipa pharmacy.** *(⏰ Open M-F 8am-7pm, Sa 8am-6pm.)*
- **POST OFFICE:** The post office also has a **Western Union.** *(Weiner Str. 7-9. ☎0577 677 34 30 💻www.3430.post.at ⏰ Open M-F 8am-6pm.)*
- **POLICE STATION:** *(Nibelungenpl., ➡ behind the Tourist Office and next to the Town Hall.)*

Getting There

Trains to Tulln leave about every half hour from Vienna's most northern train station, **Franz-Joseph Bahnhof** in the 9th district. The trip takes 30-35min. and costs €5.40. When you buy your ticket, check to see which station in Tulln the train will stop at, Tulln an der Donau or Tulln Stadt. **Tulln Stadt** drops you closest to the **city center,** accessed via a short walk up Bahnhofstr. If you get iff at Tulln an der Donau, you can easily take a bus (€1.80) to the city center or, if you already have a map, walk 15-20min.

krems and stein ☎2732

As the gateway to the Wachau region, Krems and its neighboring town Stein are undoubtedly the most picturesque cities from which to begin exploring the Austrian countryside. Located west along the Danube 64km from Vienna, the narrow cobbled streets of Krems seamlessly blend the old and new—cafes and shops along the commercial thoroughfare hide networks of twisted alleyways, where you will stumble across hidden plazas and doors. Wander from one hallowed church to the next (**Pfarrkirche, Piaristenkriche,** and **Frauenbergkirche** are just a few), and take in the view from the hillside beneath the ancient **Pulverturm.** In addition to its historical foundation, Krems has secured its place in the hearts of art-lovers with the **KunstMiele** (Art Mile) and in the livers of wine-lovers as a premiere wine region.

In the neighboring town of Stein, the main street **Steiner Landstrasse** has the most gorgeous old building facades enlivened with flower boxes and in some cases a refreshing coat of paint. Here in Minoritenpl., the **Minoritenkirche** has been altered into a convertible space for artists to rent and display their work. On a warm summer day, stroll along the Danube back to Krems and then take the boat home, just in time to watch the shadows begin to lengthen over the glistening blue of the Donau.

ORIENTATION

If arriving by train, walk through Bahnhofpl. and down Dinstlstr. to reach the main throroughfare of Krems, **Untere Landstrasse** to the right and **Obere Landstrasse** to the left. At the far end of Obere Landstr., you can pass under the *steintor* (gate) and leave the old city into the town of Und. Here you will find the tourist office, **Krems Tourismus.** Continuing west through Und leads to the picturesque neighboring town of Stein, whose main thoroughfare Steiner Landstr. similarly runs parallel to the Danube.

SIGHTS

🏛 GRAFENEGG CASTLE ⊛⊗⌂ CASTLE, GROUNDS
Schloβ Grafenegg ☎2735 550 05 22 ▣www.grafenegg.com
Enter into your own personal fairy tale à la Cinderella as you explore the grounds and ornate rooms of this gorgeous castle nestled in the Austrian countryside a little ways from Krems. The square tower has four mini turrets with clocks in between, and even though the moat is dry, the luminescent white castle is picture perfect. Inside, explore the library, salons, halls, and dining room—be sure to look up at the hammer-beam ceilings for some of the most elaborate Historist woodwork in all of Austria. Today, the castle also hosts about 30 cultural events per year, either in parts of the castle or at the outdoor stage and auditorium, also located on the Castle grounds.

✈ *The ÖBB (Austrian Rail) runs train services from Vienna; Franz-Josefs, Spittelau and Heiligenstadt stations to the station Wagram-Grafenegg, 2km from Grafenegg Castle. Some taxi companies offer* *a fixed-price transfer from Krems for €30 (up to 4 people). Call ☎2732 858 83 or ☎664 210 33 55. If you have a car, getting to Grafenegg is much easier. Driving time from Vienna takes around 40min. Take A22 in the direction of Stockerau. Take the Krems/Tulln/St. Pölten exit S5 to the Grafenegg exit. $ €5, students €3, family ticket €7.50, groups (20+) €4 per person. ⏰ Castle open Apr-Oct Tu-Su 10am-5pm.*

KARIKATURMUSEUM ♿ MUSEUM

Steiner Landstr. 3a ☎2732 90 80 20 💻www.karikaturmuseum.at

The jagged roof and life-size cartoon statues mark this unique Cartoon Museum on Krems' Art Mile. Unlike many cartoon museums, the Karikaturmuseum focuses not only on comic strips and animations but also on political and humor-based cartoons under the motto "laughter is healthy". Most of the exhibits, with the exception of one permanent exhibit, rotate every six months. 2011 marks the 10-year anniversary of the museum, so big (and secretive) plans are in the works!

On the Kunstmiele (Art Mile). $ €9; children, seniors, and students €8. ⏰ Open daily 10am-6pm.

KUNSTHALLE ♿ ART MUSEUM

Steiner Landstr. 3 ☎2732 90 80 10 💻www.kunsthalle.at

This convertible art space hosts primarily modern art exhibits, that rotate every 3-4 months. One of the recent new exhibits focused on "New Realism" and its artists, including **Marcel Duchamp.** Another consisted of Daniel Spoerri's "object boxes," which innovatively used multiple materials in different dimensions. Another was the mixed-media installation *Twelve-O'Clock in London* by an Austrian-American artist.

On the Kunstmiele (Art Mile). $ €9, students €8, family ticket €18, groups of 10 or more €7 per person. ⏰ Open daily 10am-6pm.

FOOD

SCHWARZE KUCHL VIENNESE [2]

Untere Landstr. 8 ☎02732 831 28 💻www.schwarze-kuchl.at

This country-style *kuchl* ("kitchen") offers up traditional Austrian dishes at a tiled stove right before your eyes. As though in a country home, the walls are lined with pots, cooking utensils, and other countryside paraphernalia, though it reads as quaint, not kitsch, and makes Schwarze Kuchl a cozy locale for a hearty meal during your exploration of Krems and Stein.

On the main street in Krems town. $ Entrees €5.50-14. ⏰ Open M-F 8:30am-7:30pm, Sa 8:30am-5pm.

ESSENTIALS

Practicalities

Krems' commercial thoroughfare is Untere Landstr./Obere Landstr. (Upper and Lower), where you can find all the necessary shops and practicalities.

- **TOURIST OFFICES:** *(Utzstr. 1. ☎02732 700 11 💻www.krems.info ⏰ Open Nov 1-Apr 6 M-F 8:30am-5pm; Apr 7-Oct 19 M-F 8:30am-6:30pm, Sa 10am-noon and 1pm-6pm, Su 10am-noon and 1pm-4pm.)*
- **BANK: Bank Austria at Obere.** *(Landst. 19.* **i** 24hr ATM.*)*
- **POST OFFICE:** *(Brandströmstr. 4-6. ☎02732 826 0642)* and *(Steiner Landstr. 68. ☎057 7677 3504)*
- **PHARMACIES: Apotheke.** *(Corner of Untere Landstr. and Marktgasse.)* **Bipa pharmacy.** *(Landstr. 19. ⏰ Open M-Sa 9am-noon and 1:30-5pm.)*

Getting There

Krems is a common excursion from Vienna and is easily accessed from the city. By train, the trip begins at Franz-Joseph Bahnhof *($ €13.90. ⏰ 1hr., 25 per day).* In the summer *(May-Sept),*the **DDSG Blue Danube** runs on Sundays from Vienna to Durnstein, departing Vienna at 8:30am. It stops in Krems at 2pm, and picks up again at 5pm. *(🖥www.ddsg-blue-danube.at $ Round-trip €29.50)* If you are feeling particularly energetic, it is also possible to bike from Vienna to Krems, following the bicycle path that runs alongside the Danube. If you get tired, you can always return via train or boat; in most cases, they allow you to take on a bike free of charge.

essentials

entrance requirements

- **PASSPORT:** Required for citizens of Australia, Canada, Ireland, New Zealand, the UK, and the US.
- **VISA:** Required for visitors who plan to stay in Austria for more than 90 days.
- **WORK PERMIT:** Required for all foreigners planning to work in Austria.

PLANNING YOUR TRIP

Time Differences

Austria is one hour ahead of Greenwich Mean Time (GMT) and observes Daylight Saving Time. This means that Austria is six hours ahead of New York City, 9 hours ahead of Los Angeles, one hour ahead of the British Isles, 9 hours behind Sydney, and 10 hours behind New Zealand.

MONEY

Tipping And Bargaining

Service staff is paid by the hour, and a service charge is included in an item's unit price. Cheap customers typically just round up to the nearest whole Euro, but it's customary and polite to tip 5-10% if you are satisfied with the service. If the service was poor, you don't have to tip at all. To tip, mention the total to your waiter while paying. If he states that the bill is €20, respond "€22," and he will include the tip. Do not leave the tip on the table; hand it directly to the server. It is standard to tip a taxi driver at least €1, housekeepers €1-2 a day, bellhops €1 per piece of luggage, and public toilet attendants around €.50.

Taxes

Most goods in Austria are subject to a Value-Added Tax—or *mehrwertsteuer* (MwSt)—of 19% (a reduced tax of 7% is applied to books and magazines, foods, and agricultural products). Ask for a MwSt return form at points of purchase to enjoy tax-free shopping. Present it at customs upon leaving the country, along with your receipts and the unused goods. Refunds can be claimed at Tax Free Shopping Offices, found at most airports, road borders, and ferry stations, or by mail (Tax-Free Shopping Processing Center, Trubelgasse 19, 1030 Vienna Austria). For more information, contact the German VAT refund hotline (☎0228 406 2880 🖳www.bzst.de).

SAFETY AND HEALTH

General Advice

In any type of crisis, the most important thing to do is **stay calm.** Your country's embassy abroad is usually your best resource in an emergency; registering with that embassy upon arrival in the country is a good idea.

Local Laws and Police

Certain regulations might seem harsh and unusual (practice some self-control city-slickers, jaywalking is a €5 fine), but abide by all local laws while in Germany or Austria; your respective embassy will not necessarily get you off the hook. Always be sure to carry a valid passport as police have the right to ask for identification.

Drugs and Alcohol

The drinking age in Austria is 16 for beer and wine and 18 for spirits. The maximum blood alcohol content level for drivers is 0.05%. Avoid public drunkenness: it can jeopardize your safety and earn the disdain of locals.

If you use insulin, syringes, or any perscription drugs, carry a copy of the prescriptions and a doctor's note. Needless to say, illegal drugs are best avoided. While possession of marijuana or hashish is illegal, possession of small quantities for personal consumption is decriminalized in Germany and Austria. Each region has interpreted "small quantities" differently (anywhere from 5 to 30 grams). Carrying drugs across an international border—considered to be drug trafficking—is a serious offense that could land you in prison.

Specific Concerns

Natural Disasters

Relatively weak earthquakes occur regularly in Germany and Austria, primarily in the seismically active Rhein Rift Valley or in coal mining areas where blasting can set them off. In the event of an earthquake, drop and take cover if indoors. If outside, move away from buildings and utility wires.

Pre-Departure Health

Matching a prescription to a foreign equivalent is not always easy, safe, or possible, so if you take **prescription drugs,** carry up-to-date prescriptions or a statement from your doctor stating the medications' trade names, manufacturers, chemical names, and dosages. Be sure to keep all medication with you in your carry-on luggage.

Common drugs such as aspirin (*Kopfschmerztablette* or *Aspirin*), acetaminophen or Tylenol (*Paracetamol*), ibuprofen or Advil, antihistamines (*Antihistaminika*), and penicillin (*Penizillin*) are available at German pharmacies. Some drugs—like pseudoephedrine (Sudafed) and diphenhydramine (Benadryl)—are not available in Germany or Austria, or are only available with a perscription, so plan accordingly.

Immunizations and Precautions

Travelers over two years old should make sure that the following vaccines are up to date: MMR (for measles, mumps, and rubella); DTaP or Td (for diphtheria, tetanus, and pertussis); IPV (for polio); Hib (for *Haemophilus influenzae* B); and HepB (for Hepatitis B). For recommendations on immunizations and prophylaxis, check with a doctor and consult the **Centers for Disease Control and Prevention (CDC)** in the US or the equivalent in your home country. (☎+1-800-CDC-INFO/232-4636 🖳www.cdc.gov/travel).

austria 101

CUSTOMS

North American manners are considered acceptable in Austria and most German-speaking countries. If you want to impress the locals, eat with your fork in your left hand and your knife in the right without switching. If your funny bones have been itching for a rest, relieve them—elbows on the table are OK in Austria.

FOOD AND DRINK

Food

Traditional Austrian food is a cardiologist's nightmare, which means it has to taste good. Most meals are hearty and focus on *Schweinefleisch* (pork), *Kalbsfleisch* (veal), *Wurst* (sausage), *Eier* (eggs), *Käse* (cheese), *Brot* (bread), and kartoffeln or *Erdapfeln* (potatoes). Some Austrians favorites, however, are foreign, such as *Knödel* (dumplings) and *Dönerkebabs*. For vegetarians, eat your 'shrooms, in the form of *Steinpilze* or *Eierschwammerl*. If you can't stand fungi, look for *Spätzle* (homemade noodles often served with melted cheese) or anything with the world "Vegi" in it. Breakfast options include yogurt and *Müsli* (soaked granola). For a dessert or treat, try the famous Austrian torte in various fruit flavors, or dessert dumplings or panckaes. air that with one of the famous Austrian coffees, like a *Mélange* (Viennese coffee with frothed cream and cinnamon).

Drink

The most famous Austrian wine is probably *Gumpoldskirchen* from Lower Austria. Another good bet is the *Klosterneuburger*. If beer is your alcoholic beverage of choice, you'll find some fanmtastic Austrian choices, inluding *Ottakringer, Gold Fassl,* and *Zipfer Bier.*

HOLIDAYS

As Austria is predominantly Catholic, most of the public holidays, as defined by Austria's federal labor laws, are Catholic.

major public holidays

- **NEW YEAR'S DAY:** Jan 1.
- **THE EPIPHANY:** Jan 6.
- **EASTER MONDAY:** Apr 25
- **NATIONAL HOLIDAY:** May 1
- **ASSUMPTION OF MARY:** Aug 15
- **NATIONAL DAY:** Oct 26
- **ALL SAINTS DAY:** Nov 1
- **IMMACULATE CONCEPTION:** Dec 8
- **CHRISTMAS EVE AND CHRISTMAS:** Dec 24-25
- **ST. STEPHEN'S DAY:** Dec 26
- **NEW YEAR'S EVE:** Dec 31

austria

BELGIUM

When you were planning your trip to Europe, you probably didn't have Belgium at the top of your list of hoppin' spots. Next to the Netherlands, or the Czech Republic, Belgium doesn't scream party central, but um HELLO—this is the home of the French fry; they're doing something right.

If you have a penchant for public urination, you'll probably enjoy yourself in Brussels (that is, if you enjoy watching public urination, you creeper). Peeing statues aplenty await you, from little boys and girls, to dogs, it's hard to turn the corner without seeing something taking a leak. It's cute when you're made out of bronze, but *Let's Go* doesn't recommend trying it yourself—indecent exposure charges don't make good souvenirs.

While you're avoiding criminal charges, you might want to swing by the EU area and Place Schuman. You'll learn quickly why Brussels is known as the capital of Europe as you party with the ambassador from that country you still can't pronounce (and only barely remember). Brussels is also home to dozens of museums, art galleries, and theaters for the the cultural traveler in you.

When you think of all your guilty pleasures, they're probably all elements of Belgian cuisine. Beer? Check. Fries? Check. Waffles? Check. Chocolate? Check. You really can't go wrong if you're eating here, whether it be at a *friterie* in Brussels or a quaint bistro in Bruges. It's time to get after it—let's go.

greatest hits

- **WAX PHILOSOPHIC.** Grab a glass of strawberry wine and talk philosophy at Goupil le Fol (p. 70).

- **YOU CAN HAZ CHOCOLATE?** Belgian Chocolate is famous for a reason. Head on down to the Chocolate and Cacao Museum (p. 63) in the Grand Place to debunk some of those myths you've heard about your favorite guilty pleasure.

- **TIME TO GET SURREAL.** Feed your inner art enthusiast with the works on display at the Magritte Museum (p. 64).

57

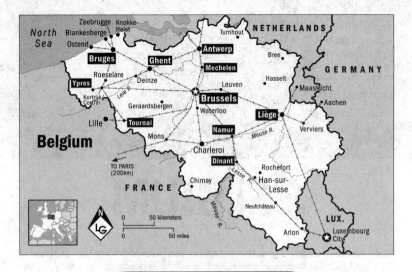

student life

Student life in Brussels is varied and exciting but you'll be happy to know that Let's Go is commited to finding you the best (and cheapest) that Brussels has to offer. What are people doing, you wonder? Get lost in Parc de Bruxelles for the afternoon, but make sure you grab some *frites* before you go. Though you can pick them up on pretty much any corner in the Lower Town, we reccommend going to Friterie Tabora. Fries so good you'll wanna bitch-slap Ronald McDonald for claiming his are better. If you need a beer to wash them down, the Brewer's House offers a great tour and history of beer—with samples!

belgium

brussels ☎02

After cavorting with hash and hookers in Amsterdam, most students see Brussels as a dull hub of Eurocrats, a place to go hole up and detox from Holland just long enough to pass the parents' drug test. That's a mistake. Scratch beneath this city's surface, and you'll uncover an endearingly odd local culture and increasingly relevent sociopolitical scene. Not every city in Europe is collectively enamored with not one, not two, but *three* centrally located statues preoccupied with urinary expulsions (we're obsessed with you too, oh *Manneken Pis*). Not every city in Europe is purportedly home to the world's best beer, chocolate, waffles, *and* fries. And not every city in Europe can be its capital—there can only be one, and it's Brussels. So find a cure for that Holland hangover fast, because this city's a lot more than a parliamentary pit stop.

Brussels is admittedly a small city, and many visitors only spend a few days exploring its cobbled streets and quirky museums. You should certainly visit the "classics," such as the **Manneken Pis** and the **Grand Place,** but we also urge you to head further afield. Get lost in the eclectic **Marolles flea market** or the utterly brilliant **Magritte Museum.** We hope you're not actually coming here to cool down after

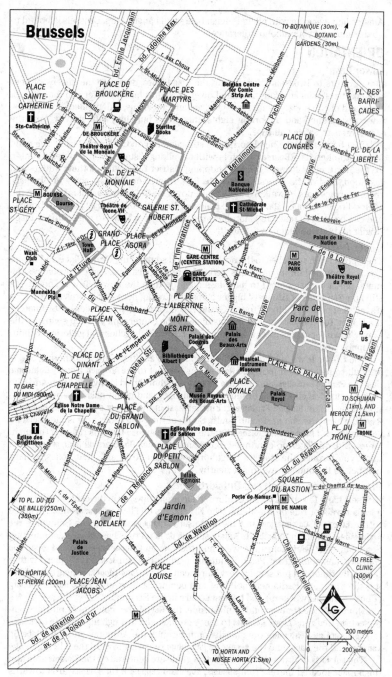

Brussels

brussels

Amsterdam, because with all its Belgian beers and bangin' bars, Brussels is bound to up the ante and your alcohol tolerance.

ORIENTATION

Lower Town

Most visitors to Brussels stick around the **Grand Place**, drawn to the dozens of beer and jazz bars in its environs. But the Lower Town has more to offer you than tourist traps and cheap booze—with local markets and museums, independent bookstores, bars, restaurants, and important sights, this area's bubbling with activity from the side streets to **Sainte-Catherine.**

That being said, the neighborhood's still centered on the Grand Place. The main Metro stop here is Ⓜ**Bourse,** which is within walking distance of the historic center. To the north is **rue Neuve,** a central shopping district filled with clothing outlets and fast food. East of the Bourse is **Place Ste. Géry,** where you will find some of Brussels' trendy terrace bars. A walk from the Place down **rue St-Christophe** will take you to the seafood-heavy area of **Ste.-Catherine. Boulevard Anspach** runs directly past the Bourse, and can be used to reach the Marolles area in the Upper Town to the south, or Place Rogier and Le Botanique to the north.

Upper Town

The Upper Town stretches to the north, east, and south of the Grand Place and Lower Town. Renowned for its musuems, refined shopping districts, and expensive restaurants, this area was bound to have less nightlife than the Lower Town. Though it's still home to some of Brussels' bigger clubs, they're not necessarily Brussels' best, so travelers should stay closer to the Grand Place for a decent bar scene. Fortunately, the Upper Town is within walking distance of the center, and you can swing by the Lower Town for drinks after a visit the Upper Town's churches and galleries without too much trouble.

The Upper Town is quite spread out, splits into additional neighborhoods, and is difficult to navigate on foot. **Rue Royale** runs parallel to **rue Anspach** from Ⓜ**Botanique** past the **Parc de Bruxelles,** and into the historic neighborhood known as **Beaux-Arts.** The neighborhood is chock full of museums, galleries, and grand palaces—not to mention home of the **Belgian Parliament.** Further east is the **Avenue des Arts** and **Boulevard Régent,** which also run north and south. South of the Beaux-Arts area is the **Boulevard de Waterloo** and **Avenue de la Toison d'Or;** the lucrative **Avenue Louise** is right off the main street. Bld. de Waterloo continues round and becomes **Boulevard du Midi,** which then takes you through the **Marolles** neighborhood, a run-down area that poses a sharp contrast to the opulent Av. Louise nearby.

Place Schuman, Heysel, and Outskirts

Brussels has a few areas worth exploring that aren't directly in the center and require a longer walk or ride on the Metro. The EU centers on **Place Schuman,** which is home to the **European Commission** and the **European Parliament.** From Place Schuman, **rue Archimède** runs north to **Ambiorix Square** and **rue de la Loi** runs east to west, connecting Schuman with Ⓜ**Arts-Loi** to the west and the **Parc du Cinquantenaire** to the east. **Rue Froissart** runs south from Place Schuman, leading to **Place Jourdan,** a square with a few restaurants and pubs and a very European crowd. **Parc Léopold** is nearby; behind it is the European Parliament building, and behind Parliament is **Place du Luxembourg** (PLux to the EU workers), the busiest square in the EU area.

Home to the Atomium and Mini-Europe, the **Heysel** area consists of one large intersection that runs from Ⓜ**Heysel** to the Atomium, and through into **Parc de Laeken. Boulevard du Centenaire** runs north-south through the Atomium and into **Place St. Lambert** and the park, and the **Avenue de l'Atomium** runs east toward the A12 highway.

The **outskirts** of Brussels covered in this guide are centered on the **Simonis** area and the **Basilica** located there. From **Simonis, Boulevard Léopold II** runs westwards towards the Basilica, and features a large green park area. If you continue east along the road, you will head back toward Rogier and the center of Brussels.

ACCOMMODATIONS

Accommodations in Brussels fill up quickly, especially during the week. Many thanks to the EU Parliament, expensive and lucrative hotels have sprung up throughout the city, making a cheap hotel even harder to find. Most student-friendly accommodations are slightly north of the **Grand Place;** five of the city's most prominent hostels are within walking distance of the Lower Town. Rooms in the Upper Town get much more expensive, especially if you don't stay in a hostel. Many hotels offer cheap weekend rates, and prices are slashed by nearly 50% when the EU Parliament isn't in session in July and August. Book in advance, especially when Parliament's in session.

Lower Town

SLEEP WELL   ♥♿(ip)♥ HOSTEL ❷

23 rue du Damier   ☎02 218 50 50 ▇www.sleepwell.be

Sleep Well has two options: hostel or hotel. Both are bright, cheerful, and cheap, but the hotel option has a few extra perks, including no lockout and ensuite bathrooms. But you might as well save the money and head to the hostel; the ensuite really isn't worth an extra €20. In keeping with Brussels tradition, the hostel is covered in murals and caters to families, groups, and the lone traveler. The bar downstairs stays busy until closing, so even if you're returning from a night's bar crawl in the center you can continue to sample the local beer until the wee hours.

⚜ ⓂRogier. Follow rue Neuve and take a left onto rue de la Blanchisserie. Rue du Damier is on your right. *i* Breakfast included. Linens provided; towels available for rent. Wi-Fi €1.50 per 15min. ⓈDorms €19-23. Singles €35; doubles €52. ⓏReception 24hr. Lockout 11am-3pm.

2GO4 HOSTEL   ♥(ip) HOSTEL ❷

99 bld. Emile Jacqmain   ☎02 219 30 19 ▇www.2go4.be

2go4 doesn't really look or feel like your typical European hostel. Its strict no-large-groups policy has made it a haven for young solo travelers and students. Shared spaces like the funky common room and the well-trafficked communal kitchen are great places to meet other travelers. Head out with your new friends for a night in Brussels' main town, only a short walk away.

⚜ ⓂRogier. Follow bld. d'Anvers and take a left onto bld. Emile Jacqmain. *i* Linens provided; towels available for rent. Max. 6 people per group. No school groups allowed. Free tea and coffee. Wi-Fi and free internet corner available. ⓈDorms €21-29. Singles €50-55. ⓏReception 7am-1pm and 4-10pm.

GENERATION EUROPE   ♥(ip) HOSTEL ❶

4 rue de l'Eléphant   ☎02 410 38 58 ▇www.aubergesdejeunesse.be

Located in a thriving immigrant neighborhood, Generation Europe is a 10-15min. Metro ride or a 20min. walk outside the Lower Town, but the hostel's stunningly low prices more than make up for the inconvenience. Rooms are big and spacious, and the dorms come with desks, lockers, and shelves. The lounge areas and communal kitchen provide travelers with numerous opportunities to meet other guests. The area isn't especially dangerous at night, but it's probably best not to walk alone.

⚜ ⓂComte de Flandre. Head east, past the police station, and turn left onto rue de l'Ecole. Keep walking along this road and turn right onto rue Chaussée de Grand. Take the first left, which leads onto rue de l'Eléphant. *i* Breakfast included. Linens provided; towels available for rent. Wi-Fi €1.50 per 1hr. ⓈDorms €16-20. Singles €32-34. ⓏReception 24hr. Lockout 11am-2:30pm.

ROYAL HOTEL
HOTEL [3]

8 bld. Jardin Botanique ☎02 218 32 18 www.royal-hotel.be

This small hotel slightly north of the Grand Place offers simple rooms for a lower price than many of the big chains around the Rogier area. The rooms feel a bit worn down and are in need of a new paint job, but the price and location make up for the faded decor. The bathrooms look modern and are a decent size. There are only a few rooms, so be sure to reserve in advance.

[M]Rogier. i Wi-Fi available. $ Singles €45-50; doubles €60. Reception 24hr.

Upper Town

JACQUES BREL
HOSTEL [1]

30 rue de la Sablonnière ☎02 218 01 87 www.laj.be

Surprisingly lively, Jacques Brel provides a modern bar and lounge in its reception area. Although the stairwell is a bit drab, the rooms are comfortable, priced for the student traveler, and not nearly as boring as the exterior suggests. Some of the rooms come with well-furnished ensuites, but be warned that some of the bigger dormitories may not be worth those couple of euros you'll save. Right next to Le Botanique, one of Brussels' most diverse concert spaces, and a 20min. walk from the Grand Place.

[M]Botanique. Head south down rue Royale (away from Botanique) and take the 1st left. i Breakfast and linens included. Free Wi-Fi and computer units in reception. Booking at least 4 weeks in advance is recommended. $ 6- to 14-bed dorms €16.40; 3- to 4-bed dorms €18.50. Singles €32; doubles €45. €2 extra for ages 26 and older. Reception daily 7am-midnight. Lockout noon-3pm. Code access after 1am.

BRUEGEL
HOSTEL [1]

Heilige Geeststraat 2 ☎02 522 04 36 www.youthhostels.be

Bruegel has one of the most important amenities a hostel can have: a **brilliant bar.** This hostel hangout looks like a watering hole you would find in the city center, and stays open until all the guests have gone to bed. Finish out your night with some dancing and karaoke. The rooms here are basic and decent-sized. Only some have ensuite bathrooms, but the communal bathrooms really aren't that bad. Each of the three floors has a lounge or seating area with free Wi-Fi.

[M]Gare Central. Head west along Bld. de l'Empereur. Bruegel is opposite the skate park. i Linens provided. Free Wi-Fi. Some wheelchair-accesible rooms available upon request. $ 3- to 4-bed dorms €18.90. Singles €31; doubles €46. €1.20-4 extra for ages 26 and older. Reception 7-10am and 2pm-1am. Lockout 10am-2pm.

VINCENT VAN GOGH CENTER—CHAB
HOSTEL [1]

8 rue Traversière ☎02 217 01 58 www.chab.be

Between the lack of light, drab exterior, and rickety and uncomfortable beds in the dorms, this hostel feels a little like a prison. Compared to most hostels, though, the communal bathrooms are clean and modern, and you're free to come and go as you please—Van Gogh doesn't feel the need to put a curfew on its residents. The location situates you near some awesome museums and Le Botanique, a brilliant local concert venue, so there is some light at the end of the tunnel. When you really do feel like you're behind bars, go outside and take in the beautiful sights of the Botanic Gardens.

[M]Botanique. Head north along rue Royale, past La Botanique, then turn right onto rue Traversière. i Breakfast and linens provided. Ages 18-35 only. Wi-Fi €2 per hr. $ 8- to 10-bed dorms €18.50; 6-bed €20.50; 4-bed €21.50; 3-bed €27.50. Singles €33.50; doubles €53. Reception 24hr.

SIGHTS

Lower Town

🏛 MANNEKEN PIS   STATUE
Intersection of rue de l'Étuve and rue du Chêne

Prepare to be pretty underwhelmed but pretty amused by the icon of Brussels: a little boy taking a pee into a pond below. This little statue, whose real origins are not known, is one of Brussels' most famous monuments, and he is continually swamped with visitors who stand by his basin in various poses, one of the most popular being to cover his stonely manhood with a hand so that it does not show in the picture. The Manneken likes to celebrate certain national holidays and events, or even just indulge the weird happenings and habits of Brussels; hundreds of Elvis fans once congregated at his feet as he donned his blue suede shoes and classic white jacket. For true insight into the enigma that is the Manneken, start up a conversation with the souvenir vendor directly in front of the sight—he's been there for over 20 years and has some interesting stories to tell. Though, in his own words, the little boy doesn't cause much trouble. Despite his nudity, he is otherwise polite, well-mannered, and pleased to see the whole world coming to visit him.

✈ *Head southwest from the Grand Place along rue de l'Étuve. The Manneken is 3 blocks down.* **i** *Check the vendor's calendar to see what the Manneken Pis will be wearing and when.* ⓢ *Free.*

🏛 MUSÉE DU CACAO ET DU CHOCOLAT   🌐 MUSEUM
9-11 rue de la Tête d'Or   ☎02 514 20 48 🖳www.mucc.be

It is impossible to miss the smell of chocolate that flows out of this small museum just off of the Grand Place. Opened in 1998 by Jo Draps, the daughter of one of the founders of Godiva chocolate company, the Musée du Cacao et du Chocolat is a chocoholic's dream (or worst nightmare if it's Lent). Fresh milk chocolate is churned in the entrance, where you can taste both warm and cold chocolate before proceeding to watch the English-speaking chocolate chef work his magic (and of course taste the results). The museum also aims to promote the role of cacao in the development of chocolate, as so many people do not know about its origin or uses (did you know the Aztecs used cacao as a form of currency?). Although Godiva was sold to the Americans in the 1970s, the museum has been kept in the family and is currently run by Jo Drap's daughter. For those worried about the potential side effects of their chocolate consumption, head up to the third floor to bust some myths about your favorite foodstuff: chocolate does *not* cause acne! Well then, choc's away...

✈ Ⓜ*Bourse. Just south of Grand Place.* ⓢ *€5.50; students, seniors, and ages 12-16 €4.50; under 12 free with parent.* ⏲ *Open Tu-Su 10am-4:30pm.*

GRAND PLACE   SQUARE
Grand Place

The historical center of Brussels is a very grand place known, naturally, as the Grand Place. Standing in the middle of the square, you'll find yourself surrounded by the breathtaking architecture. Soak up the grandeur in one of the square's many cafes, where you can sip coffee and watch the tourists plow on through with their cameras. Don't make the same mistake they often do—look *up* as well as around. The really interesting, intricate architecture is above you, not in front of you. Grand Place really lets down its hair at night, so you should definitely come back and explore once the sun goes down. The famous **Guildhall buildings**, including the **Hotel de Ville** and the **Maison de Roi,** are dramatically illuminated. During mid-August every year, the Grand Place is home to the "Flower Carpet," where green-thumbed Belgian gardeners create a design with colorful native fauna.

✈ Ⓜ*Bourse. Head straight down rue de la Bourse, which leads to the northeast corner of the square.*

SCIENTASTIC ♦ MUSEUM

Bourse Metro Station ☎02 732 13 36 💻www.scientastic.be

Don't be put off by the location of this brilliant museum—although many of Brussels' homeless hang around in the Bourse Metro station, the museum's a load of fun. Head downstairs and follow the large, colorful signs to the Scientastic, which from the outside looks a bit like a fortune teller's tent. The museum's goal is to make science fun, interactive, and accessible for both kids and adults, and the curators have succeeded in making this more than just another science museum. Every visitor can try a "freebie" visit before deciding to pay the entrance or not (!!). Make sure you try out the Manneken Pis recreation to discover how water actually flows, and experiment around with color shadows. The very comical "👍**mirror performance**" demonstrates the magic of reflections, as the tour guide uses various illusions to appear to float, shrink, explode, and even stab himself. Young children and uncoordinated adults should take care not to try the tricks at home.

➜ [M]Bourse. Head toward the Anspach exit and follow the signs for Scientastic. ℹ English-speaking tour guides and English walkthrough guide available. $ €7.70, under 26 and seniors €5.20. ⏰ Open M-Tu 10am-5:30pm, W 2-5:30pm, Th-F 10am-5:30pm, Sa-Su 2-5:30pm.

Upper Town

👍 MAGRITTE MUSEUM ♦ MUSEUM

3 rue de la Régence ☎02 508 32 11 💻www.musee-magritte-museum.be

The Magritte Museum will be one of the most enjoyable, educational and fascinating museum trips you make in Brussels, and maybe in Europe. The museum opened just last year, and until recently tickets had to be booked in advance to ensure you got a spot in line. Now that the crowds aren't as big, swing by and prepare to be amazed. Start your tour at the glass elevator; four Magritte paintings of a man, each at varying stages of completion, are mounted vertically on the opposite wall, and appear to eerily blur together as the elevator rushes by. Each of the museum's three floors conveys a period in the Belgian artist's life through a collection of paintings, drawings, and primary sources (translated into English) that convey the true genius of the man. Make sure you check out the collection of hand-drawn images, compiled by Magritte, Scutenaire, Hamoir and Nougé, in which each of the friends took turns drawing a different limb or cross-section of the human form—without looking at what their colleagues had drawn previously. The results are insightful and brilliant to look at. The audio tour is a very well-compiled and informative guide to this fascinating museum.

➜ [M]Parc. $ €8, students €2, seniors and groups €5, 18 and under free. Audio tour in English €4. Combined ticket with Beaux-Artes €13. ⏰ Open Tu 10am-5pm, W 10am-8pm, Th-Su 10am-5pm.

MUSÉES ROYAUX DES BEAUX-ARTS MUSEUM

3 rue de la Régence ☎02 508 32 11 💻www.fine-arts-museum.be

Brussels' collection of fine art is split into two sections: ancient and modern. A ticket to the Musées Royaux des Beaux-Arts gets you access to both areas. Jan Fobre's massive globe towers over the museum's illustrious lobby; it is crawling with green and blue scarabs, providing a sample of the masterpieces showcased here. The museum's modern arts section displays some of the most mind-boggling works from the 19th-21st centuries, including provocative paintings and sculptures that will either fascinate you or make you wonder why you bought a ticket. The true highlight of the museum is the new 👍**Magritte Museum,** an homage to a modern master if ever there was one, which is housed in the same building complex. Head upstairs for the ancient arts, including a permanent collection called "Art and Finance," which examines historical figures and portraits. Before you head away from the area, make sure you visit the adjacent 👍**Garden of Sculptures,** filled with statues and sculptures watching over you as you eat your lunch.

⇆ Ⓜ Parc. $ €8, students €2, under 18 free. Free first W every month after 1pm. Combined ticket with Magritte Museum €13. ⏰ Open Tu-Su 10am-5pm.

CATHÉDRALE DES SAINTS MICHEL ET GUDULE — CATHEDRAL

15 rue du Bois Sauvage ☎02 217 85 45

Although the Cathedral was only granted status as such in 1962, the building before you has a marvelous history spanning over a millennium and several restorations. The original foundations of Cathédrale des Sts.-Michel et Gudule date back to the 9th century (more recent areas of the foundation can be seen in the crypt for €1). In the 11th century, the building was rebuilt over a 300-year period and heavily influenced by Gothic architecture. Beginning in the mid 1980s and ending in the late '90s, the Cathedral underwent extensive renovations again, restoring the stone work to its original splendor. As you wander through the cathedral, gaze up to the statues of the saints guarding the walls. Each holds an item symbolizing something from the Christian faith: St. Philippe, for example, holds the book of knowledge, while St. Peter posesses a set of golden keys.

⇆ Ⓜ Gare Centrale. $ Free. Crypt €1 Donation. Free choir concerts throughout the year. ⏰ Open M-F 7:30am-6pm, Sa-Su 8:30am-6pm. Mass in French Su 10am, 11:30am, and 12:30pm.

BOTANIQUE — BOTANICAL GARDENS

These beautiful gardens span 6 hectares of land and provide the ideal spot to catch a bit of sun or take a break during the summer. The numerous private enclaves are a welcome break from the touristed city center. Grab a drink at the cafe *(open daily 10am-8pm)* and sit on the terrace overlooking the gardens, or go for a stroll round the fountains and lake. The Botanic Gardens also has a concert venue on its terrace, where up-and-coming European and American artists entertain local students and concertgoers.

⇆ Ⓜ Botanique. $ Free. ⏰ Open daily Oct-Apr 8am-5pm; May-Sept 8am-8pm.

PARC DE BRUXELLES — PARK

Between Belgian Parliament and Royal Palace

Walk the perimeter of what is arguably Brussels' most beautiful park and view the **Palace of the Nation** and other beautiful monuments, or head inward for the trees and foliage. Joggers dominate the dirt tracks at all hours, so take care not to get mowed down. Luckily, there are plenty of places to escape the healthy crowd. The wide green patches, benches, and fountains make the park an ideal place to stop and have a picnic lunch, or just to rest your feet after a busy morning walking around the surrounding museums.

⇆ Ⓜ Parc. ⏰ Open daily 7am-11pm.

Place Schuman

MUSÉES ROYAUX D'ART ET D'HISTOIRE — MUSEUM

10 parc Cinquantenaire ☎02 741 72 11 wwww.mrah.be

This brilliant museum covers a lot of historical ground, so be prepared to cover a lot of ground on foot through the endless exhibits. Immerse yourself in the civilizations of the Aztecs and Egyptians before moving on to the extensive Roman exhibits, which include a wide range of artwork, skeletal remains, and archaeological discoveries. Not all the signs in the museum are written in English, but the collection still lends great insight into the historical periods on display. Make sure to check out the Easter Island section, which showcases one of the island's famous and massive stone heads, before heading over to the medieval and Islamic art sections. The museum could take up a whole morning, and then some. Chances are you won't feel the time pass at all.

⇆ Ⓜ Schuman. In the far southwest corner of Parc Cinquantenaire. $ €5, students and under 18 €4. ⏰ Open Tu-F 9:30am-5pm.

ATOMIUM
◆ HISTORIC BUILDING

Square de l'Atomium ☎02 475 47 77 🖥www.atomium.be

For many, it is the most horrific eyesore of the Brussels' skyline; for others, it is a stroke of architectural genius. Built for the World Expo in 1958, this structure was designed by André Waterkeyn to resemble the atom of an iron crystal—just 165 billion times bigger. The resulting structure is over 100m high, and one of the highlights of visiting the Atomium is a trip to the top in Europe's fastest elevator. As you ascend at 5m per second, you might feel your stomach do a little jump as you take in the panoramic view around you. But the Atomium isn't just a great place for a view of Brussels. Five of the nine spheres of the building are open for you to explore; collectively, they host a restaurant, permanent and temporary exhibits, and a cafe. The permanent collection is a brilliant walk through the history of Expo '58 and the Atomium's construction. Temporary exhibits often focus on science and European culture.

⇆ Take Line 6 to [M]Heysel. $ €11, students and ages 12-18 €8, ages 6-11 €4, under 6 free. Audio tour €2. ⏰ Open daily 10am-6pm.

PARC DU CINQUANTENAIRE
🌳 PARK

This is one of Brussels' beautiful places, with long green lawns and benches for you to lounge on in the sun. The park is home to what you might mistake for the *Arc de Triomphe;* it is in fact Brussels' very own *Arcade Cinquantenaire*, complete with four stone horses drawing a chariot. A walk east along the park will bring you to Autoworld, the Musée Royal de l'Armée et d'Histoire Militaire, and the Musées Royaux d'Art et d'Histoire, which means that, even if it rains, you have some shelter (especially the *free* Military Museum). During the summer, bright green deck chairs are dotted round the park, making for a perfect picnic or sunbathing spot.

⇆ [M]Schuman. At the bottom of rue de la Loi.

STATUE LÉOPOLD
🌳 MONUMENT, STATUE

Parc de Laeken

This monument to the former king of Belgium stands proud on the top of a hill and looks directly down to the residence of the current Belgian royal family. A grand gold statue of Léopold stands in the middle of the castle-like structure. Unfortunately, Léopold's a little camera shy--the area is fenced off from visitors.

⇆ [M]Heysel. In the center of Parc de Laeken.

CHATEAU ROYAL DE LAEKEN
🌳 CHÂTEAU

Av. du Parc Royal

Unfortunately, Prince Philip of Belgium won't be inviting you in for a beer in his grand royal chateau, and if you attempt to get in it's likely that those two stone lions guarding the gate will magically come to life to stop you—well, either them or the police officers surrounding the gates, but *Let's Go* likes to think the odds are 50-50. When King Léopold ascended to the throne in 1831, this chateau was chosen as the royal residence. Although this is the Prince's main residence, however, it is no longer the official royal residence—the Royal Palace in actually located in the Upper Town.

⇆ [M]Heysel. In the southeast corner of Parc du Laeken.

FOOD
🍴

Eating in Brussels can be cheap, which makes the city a student traveler's dream. Locals will even eat out once or twice a week thanks to the inexpensive cost, and Brussels prides itself on quality cuisine. In the Lower Town, avoid the tourist traps on **rue du Bouchers.** Cheap *friteries* and waffle stands can also be found all over the city, and supermarkets are plentiful on **rue Neuve.**

Lower Town

👍 PUBLICO
🥗📶🍸 BELGIAN [3]

32 rue des Chartreux ☎02 503 04 30 💻www.publico.be

The combination of cosmopolitan Brussels with traditional food works brilliantly in this spacious restaurant. The young and courteous owner happily guides travelers through a menu of classic Belgian dishes, including *stoemp* (sausage and mashed potatoes) and various meat stews. There are also some tasty vegetarian options available. The weekday *prix-fixe* menu is a ridiculously good deal: it includes *potage*, an entree choice from the menu, and a coffee, all for €11.50. The contemporary art that lines the walls adds a modern edge to this tasty, traditional dining experience.

➜ ⓂBourse. Just off of rue Orts $ Lunchtime menu €11.50. Entrees €9-16. ⏰ Open daily 11am-midnight. Kitchen open M-F noon-3pm and 6pm-midnight, Sa noon-midnight, Su noon-3pm and 6pm-midnight.

👍 IN'T SPINNEKOPKE
💳🍸 TRADITIONAL, BELGIAN [3]

1 Place du Jardin aux Fleurs ☎02 511 86 95 💻www.spinnekopke.be

Spinnekopke (that's "spider's head" in Flemish) might not sound like an appetizing name for a restaurant. But once you take in this rustic tavern's candlelit tables and crowds of locals, you'll know that you've stumbled across something very exciting. Green-aproned waiters will attend to your table with the utmost attention. For a really tasty meal, try one of the many sauces available for their steak *(steak €15.50, with sauce €3)*, including a brilliant cheese, limbek beer and cream sauce.

➜ ⓂBourse. Head down rue Orts and take a left onto rue des Charteux, which leads to Place du Jardin aux Fleurs. ℹ English menus available. $ Entrees €12-25. ⏰ Open M-F noon-3pm and 6-11pm, Sa 6-11pm.

👍 FIN DE SIÈCLE
🥗🍸 BELGIAN [3]

9 rue des Charteux

With a mishmash of tables outside and no name above the door, this traditional Belgian restaurant may seem a little bizarre at first, and you could easily walk past it. But make sure you backtrack and take a step inside Fin de Siècle's airy interior, its walls lined with modern art by local artists. The antique cash register on the bar and the blue mosaic floor provide cutesy complements to the blackboard menu featuring largely traditional fare. Readers with peanut allergies beware, though—most menu items are cooked in or include a peanut oil, including the salad dressing.

➜ ⓂBourse. Head down rue Orts and then take a left onto rue des Charteux. $ Entrees €9-20. ⏰ Open daily 6pm-1am.

FRITERIE TABORA
🥗 FRITES [1]

4 rue de Tabora

If you're in Brussels, it'd be heresy not to eat *frites*. The famous fried potato is served on every street corner in Brussels, but finding a top-notch *friterie* can prove difficult. Tabora will double fry your *frites* and douse them in a sauce of your choice, from classic ketchup to Samurai sauce. The piping hot fries make for a perfect afternoon snack or, more likely, a brilliant way to end an evening sampling the beers of the local bars.

➜ ⓂBourse. Adjacent to Église St. Michel. $ Small €1.80; large €2.30. Sauce €0.50. ⏰ Open daily 10am-6am.

Upper Town

👍 LES SUPER FILLES DU TRAM
🍴🍸 BURGERS, TARTINES [2]

22 rue Lesbroussart ☎02 648 46 60

With the tram line running outside and the crazy murals painted onto the walls, this little cafe specializing in burgers is far enough off the beaten track to avoid the tourists, but not so much that you get poor quality food. Make sure you look at the walls to get the full effect of the dream-like Brussels skyline being destroyed by monsters and a massive monkey, and look out for the Atomium blasting off from the disaster. All the burgers come stuffed with delicious fillings and a side of *frites* in a little flower pot. If you fancy a burger challenge, try finishing the Big Joe, which overflows with bacon, cheese, pickles, onions, BBQ sauce, and a special house sauce *(€12)*.

 # ⓂLouise. Off of Av. Louise, before you reach Place Flagey. $ Burgers and salads €10-€14. Tartines €9-€12. ⏰ Open M-Sa 10am-11pm, Su 11am-5pm. Kitchen open M-Sa noon-3pm and 6-11pm, Su 11am-5pm.

👍 RESTAURATION NOUVELLE
🍴🍸 TRADITIONAL [3]

2 rue Montagne de la Cour ☎02 502 95 08 💻www.restauration-nouvelle.be

High atop the Museum for Musical Instruments is a modern-looking restaurant with one of the best views in Brussels. Ascend the 10 stories in the glass elevator, reminiscent of something out of *Charlie and the Chocolate Factory*, and be seated by penguin-like waiters. On a sunny day, make sure to request an outdoor seat, but if the weather doesn't permit, try to get a window seat inside very expansive restaurant. The view of Brussels from above is breathtaking; you can see as far as the Atomium, the Grand Place, and the Palaces. The menu, considering the setting, is well-priced and has some traditional Belgian dishes as well as a fish dish of the day.

 # ⓂParc. Enter through museum and head up in the elevator. $ Appetizers €10-19. ⏰ Open M-W 10am-4pm, Th-Sa 10am-4pm and 7-11pm, Su 7-11pm.

LE PERROQUET
🍴🍸 CAFE [2]

31 rue Watteeu ☎02 512 99 22

A stained-glass window of a parrot sets the tone for this Art Deco cafe, popular with the locals and flying under the normal tourist's radar. Locals flock here for one reason: the stuffed pitas. With a menu of over 30 different pita fillings—traditional, vegetarian, adventurous, fruity—your every pita desire will be fulfilled. Why not try the Bangkok *(€7)* with chicken, rice, pineapple, and curry? Served up in small baskets and overflowing with fillings, these piping hot pocket snacks will fill you up for a day of exploring the fashion shops of the Sablon area.

 # ⓂParc. i Credit card min. €12. $ Pitas €6-7. ⏰ Open M noon-11:30pm, Tu noon-midnight, Th-Sa noon-1am, Su noon-11:30pm.

THE MERCEDES HOUSE
🍴🍸 BRASSERIE [3]

22-24 rue Bodenbroek ☎02 400 42 63

Looking for a way to combine your love for cars and Belgian fine dining? Then the Mercedes House Brasserie is the ideal location for a coffee or light lunch. Hot drinks are available for €2-3 and can be enjoyed on the terrace outside with shiny silver cars in the background. At lunchtime, you can sample traditional dishes which won't drive away with your money, but the upmarket setting will put you in the driving seat if you're trying to impress the opposite sex (this can work both ways given the car-heavy setting). If you want to really take a spin, order a bottle of champagne at €50 a pop.

 # ⓂParc. i Coffee still served when kitchen is closed. $ Entrees €14-24. Drinks €2-5. ⏰ Open M-Th 10am-5pm, F 10am-5pm and 7-11pm, Sa 10am-5pm. Kitchen open M-Th noon-3pm, F noon-3pm and 7-11pm, Sa noon-3pm.

Place Schuman

CHEZ MOI
PIZZERIA, BAR ❶

66 rue du Luxembourg — ☎02 280 26 66

The innovative pizza bar has indoor, outdoor, and upstairs seating in which you can enjoy dirt-cheap slices of pizza (without any dirt in it). Avoid the expensive eateries in and around the EU area and just join the other young workers on the grass of Place du Luxembourg as they devour their slices. The daily menu changes regularly, but expect all the standards like mushroom, pepperoni, and vegetarian.

⚑ Ⓜ Maelbeek. *i Takeout and delivery also available.* Ⓢ *Slices €2-3.50.* ⌚ *Open M-W 11am-11pm, Th-F 11am-midnight, Sa-Su 11am-11pm.*

ANTOINE'S
FRITES ❶

1 Place Jourdan

In Place Jourdan at lunch time, two long lines form of children, locals, businessmen, students, and tourists, all hoping to grab a cone of french fries from Brussels' oldest *friterie*. You may have passed out from hunger by the time you reach the counter to place your order, but tasting these *frites* will quickly restore you. Though they may not be Brussels' best *frites*, Antoine's piping hot potatoes are made with the city's oldest recipe and served in some of its biggest portions. Many people head to the grassy banks of Parc Léopold to enjoy their *frites* in the sun, instead of sitting on a dirty bench in Place Jourdan.

⚑ Ⓜ Schuman. *Place Jourdan is just off rue Froissart* Ⓢ *Frites €2-2.20 Sauce €0.50.* ⌚ *Open M-Th 11:30am-1am, F-Sa 11:30am-2am, Su 11:30am-1am.*

CAFÉ PARC AVENUE
CAFE ❸

50 Av. d'Auderghem — ☎02 742 28 10 www.parc-avenue.be

Eating out in the EU area can be expensive. Fortunately, this upscale cafe has a lunchtime option that will suit the budget traveler nicely—a €10 "Business Lunch Menu," which includes the appetizer and entree of the day with tea or coffee. Throw in the free Wi-Fi, the iPads available for patrons to play on, and the selection of international newspapers, and you'll be feeling as ritzy and savvy as the stuffed suits eating around you.

⚑ Ⓜ Schuman. Ⓢ *Breakfast €7-17. Lunch €8-24. Lunch menu €10.* ⌚ *Open M-F 7:30am-3:30pm.*

CAPOLINO'S
ITALIAN ❸

69 Place Jourdan — ☎02 230 37 51 www.capolini.be

Among the expensive restaurants in this "lunching" square, Capolino's plentiful pizza and pasta are some of the best cheaper options. Make sure you grab a seat in the garden out back with wicker chairs and wooden tables. The eating area has a refreshingly earthy feel, but on colder days the indoor seating area also has some character. The welcoming staff will be keen to know where you're from, and will try to make you feel at home—this is one of those places where the pizza is made exactly how you want it, so don't be afraid to ask.

⚑ Ⓜ Schuman. *Place Jourdan is just down rue Froissart. i 8% discount for takeout.* Ⓢ *Pizzas €8.70-14. Pastas €10-16.* ⌚ *Open M-Th noon-2:30pm and 6:30-11pm, F-Sa noon-2:30pm and 6:30-11:30pm, Su 6:30-11pm.*

LA BRACE
PIZZERIA ❸

1 rue Franklin — ☎02 736 57 73

You'd expect to find all types of cuisine in the EU quarter, but there's certainly a lot of Italian places. La Brace is renowned for its authentic Italian pizzas and pastas, and if you walk past the storefront you'll spot the chef through the window, poised over a traditional stone oven; he's there all day and night, so you know that your pizza will be cooked by an expert. The Italian waiters will take your order from either outside on the street or inside the restaurant, which is sometimes complete with guitar music and singing. If you want a real pizza surprise, try the Segreto Pizza—we can't tell you what's on it, because the ingredients are top secret!

✦ Ⓜ*Schuman.* Ⓢ *Pizzas €10-14. Pastas €12-14. Meats €18-24.* ✦ *Open M-Sa noon-3pm and 7-11:30pm.*

RESTO SIMBA
✦✦ AFRICAN ❷

13 Leuvensesteenweg   ☎02 688 43 26 ▨www.lsctraiteur.be

Situated inside Belgium's Musées Royaux d'Art et d'Histoire, Resto Simba offers a few special menu offerings beyond the sandwiches and pastas you might find in the museum's cafeteria. Take a seat among the African art and statues and tuck in to some African cuisune. Dishes include Madagascar chicken, *scampi nin* (a Kenyan curry), and *Croq'Simba* (chicken in palm nut sauce; something tells us that the dish isn't called the "Simba" back in its Motherland). Other sandwiches and baguettes are also available.

✦ *Line 1 to* Ⓜ*Montgomery. Or tram #44 to Tervuren.* Ⓢ *African food €7.80-16.20. Sandwiches €3. Toasted baguettes €5.50-7.50.* ✦ *Open Tu-Su 11:30am-3pm. Kitchen opens at noon.*

NIGHTLIFE

We encourage you to samples as many ▨**good Belgian brews** as humanly possible, but remember: the Metro stops at midnight. Don't forget to plan around it, particularly if you're planning to club your way through the Upper Town area. The cheapest and most popular bars are in Brussels' **Lower Town**, which features a decent mix of tourist traps and well-kept local secrets. **Upper Town** nightlife is less vibrant and more expensive. Bars and lounges for 30-somethings are in abundance, but there aren't that many hubs for students; even the students of Brussels University migrate en masse to the Lower Town for their nightly fix. For a more "European" experience, head to **Place Schuman** or **Place Luxembourg** (that's PLux to the Eurocrats), where young men in suits will undoubtedly ask you what you do and how much you make. Don't be put off by this attitude; they are a friendly bunch in the EU.

Lower Town

▧ GOUPIL LE FOL
✦✦ CABARET

22 rue de la Violette   ☎02 511 13 96

This eclectic *estaminet* (a cafe where the owner is continually present) is the most fantastic, and best hidden, bar you will step into during your time in the Lower Town. From the outside, this pub-like building looks a bit odd, with a few eccentric items in the window—including a stuffed fox—and a sign explaining the bar will not serve coca-cola to its patrons (without alcohol, that is). Step inside and you are thrown into a world of revolution, literature, and art where pictures of the Belgian Royal Family hang from the walls, a library of philosophical thought crowds shelves, and rooms full of artwork are at your disposal. The brilliant owner, Abel, sees his bar as one where people can come in groups or alone to reflect on life, admire the art, and have a slow and quiet drink, while the best of French and Belgian music plays in the background. Goupil le Fol is packed with an intellectual crowd of alternative students and older art lovers, and Abel counts the Prince of Spain and the Prince of Belgium as people who have walked through his doors.

✦ Ⓜ*Bourse. From the Grand Place, head down rue des Chapliers and take a left onto rue de la Violette.* ✦ *Reservations may be required for the weekend.* Ⓢ *Beer €3-6.* ✦ *Open daily 6pm-6am.*

▧ BONNEFOOI
✦✦ BAR

8 rue des Pieriès   ☎048 762 22 31 ▨www.bonnefooi.be

Bonnefooi is one of the most pleasant finds in Brussels, and thanks to its location in an unobtrusive side street off the center, it lacks the tourists who frequent other bars in the area. Even more impressively, the bar is open every night until 8am; the punters at Bonnefooi really know the meaning of an all-night party. Despite the crazy kick-out time, the bar fosters a relaxed atmosphere. The gallery balcony is great for people-watching as locals order from a long list of beers (the Rochefort 8 is a popular and smooth beer). There is a different event going on here every night, from an acoustic session to a DJed dance mix to a jazz performance. Check the board inside the bar for details.

♯ ⓂBourse. Just off of Bld. Anspach. Ⓢ Beer €2-4. Cocktails €7. ⓩ Open daily 6pm-8am.

🎵 MUSIC LOUNGE
✔♀ JAZZ BAR

50 rue des Pierres   ☎02 513 13 45 ✉themusicvillage@skynet.be

One of Brussels' very hip jazz bars, the Music Lounge is popular with all ages and hosts a wide range of jazz throughout the week. The youth jazz section tries to stick to traditional jazz rather than fusion or modern interpretations, so the Music Lounge will suit most jazz purists. The relaxed atmosphere and artsy clientele provide a chill setting to begin a night or end it in style. Check the website or a leaflet for concert details.

♯ ⓂBourse. Just off of Grand Place. ⓘ Cover charge depends on the concert; student discounts available. Ⓢ Drinks €2-7. ⓩ Doors open at 7pm. Concerts start M-Th 8:30pm, F-Sa 9pm, Su 8:30pm.

DELIRIUM
✔♀ BAR

4A Impasse de la Fidélité   ☎02 514 44 34 ▣www.deliriumcafe.be

Situated just opposite the female Manneken Pis, Delirium is the number one stop for anyone visiting Brussels; expect to be drinking among fellow tourists, but this is the bar that anyone will recommend. The bar has over 2000 beers on tap, and you can ask your knowledgeable server to bring you their favorite for a real taste of Belgium (though be warned, you may end up with a very strong 10% beer!). The bar is packed nightly with students, so you'll need to shout to be heard and use hand gestures to order. Don't worry about your rudimentary French or Flemish, as you will most likely be surrounded by English speakers anyway. The interior makes you feel a little like you're inside a brewery, and the giant wooden barrels make for a quirky change from the traditional tables in other bars.

♯ ⓂBourse. Just off rue des Bouchers. Ⓢ Beer €2-6. ⓩ Open M-Sa 10pm-4am, Su 10pm-2am.

Upper Town

🎵 FUSE
✔♀▼ CLUB

208 rue Blaes   ☎02 511 97 89 ▣www.fuse.be

Fuse is one of Brussels' biggest and liveliest clubs, so if you want to escape the calm and casual bar scene in the Lower Town for pounding music and drinks that will make your dancing excusable, this is the place to go. The large dance floor in the main room is a great place to lose your dignity; just make sure that's the only thing you end up losing there. Every month one of the biggest gay events in Europe, La Demance, takes place at Fuse. With male strippers, drag queens, and a lot of semi-naked clubbers, La Demance is infamous in Belgium, and guys travel from just about everywhere to party it up into the early hours.

♯ ⓂPort de Hal. Ⓢ Cover Sa before midnight €5, after midnight €10. Drinks €4-10. ⓩ Open on club nights Th-Sa 11pm-late. Check the website for schedule.

🎵 LA FLEUR EN PAPIER DORÉ
✔♀ PUB

55 rue des Alexiens   ☎02 511 16 59 ▣www.lafleurenpapierdore.be

This brilliant pub just off of the Sablon area counts the artist Magritte and the TinTin cartoonist Hergé among its former clientele. Nowadays, the pub fills its small nooks with locals and artsy types looking for inspiration from the smoke-stained walls (although smoking is now banned inside) and the temporary art exhibits. You can really feel the history in this kooky little pub; La Fleur hosted Magritte's first exhibiton after the war, and the pub is now protected by the Belgian government, presumably for the artsy neurotics of the future.

Ⓜ Gare du Midi. $ Beer €2-7. ⏰ Open Tu-Sa 11am-midnight, Su 11am-7pm.

THE FLAT 🍸 LOUNGE, BAR

12 rue de la Reinette ☎02 502 74 34 💻www.theflat.be

A popular hangout for locals just getting off work and a good place to start your night, The Flat is exactly what it sounds like it is. The layout upstairs resembles an upscale flat that you might find in London or NYC: a spacious living room, a dining area, a grand bathroom, and even a bedroom. Enjoy your mojito from inside the bath, or sip your wine laid out on the bed. Downstairs, a DJ mixes music Thursday through Saturday, and each night three cocktails are selected to have their price fluctuate—as the prices drop dramatically or suddenly shoot up, you'll be reminded of the career on Wall Street that you're never going to have anymore.

Ⓜ Louise. $ Drinks €3-10. ⏰ Open W-Sa 6pm-2am.

KARAOKE SABLON 🍸 KARAOKE BAR

34 rue St. Anne ☎02 512 40 94 💻www.karaokesablon.be

Off a side alley from the Sablon area, this smokey karaoke bar is full of locals until the wee hours of the morn who really feel that they could impress Simon Cowell and co. with their talents. Karaoke Sablon specializes in French music, so expect to hear tone-deaf renditions of Edith Piaf as often as you hear the Beatles. Do not despair—just about any song you can think of is in their encyclopedic playlist, and something you can rock out to is bound to come up. A mixed crowd ranging from children to grandmothers hit the tiny stage, which comes complete with a stool for the slow ballads. This quirky bar will put a smile on your face, even if you just sit and watch the regulars belt it out.

Ⓜ Louise. $ Drinks €3-6. ⏰ Open Tu-Sa 9pm-4am.

Place Schuman

Place Schuman isn't the most lively of places for the student traveler, but it does have a happening club (Soho) and is *the* place to network and exchange business cards. Expect expats, suits, and EU workers, as well as an awful lot of English speakers.

OLD OAK IRISH PUB 🍸 IRISH PUB

26 rue Franklin ☎02 735 75 44

In an area full of English-speaking expats and corporate Eurocrats, this jolly Irish pub caters less to men in suits with BlackBerries and more to a young European crowd. The candlelight and low timbered roof will make you feel like you left Brussels far behind and ended up in Ireland itself. Approaching the bar, the staff will immediately talk to you in English; if you're really in need of it, why not get a team together for the Pub Quiz on Monday nights.

Ⓜ Schuman. $ Drinks €2-5. ⏰ Open daily noon-1am.

THE WILD GEESE 🍸 PUB

2-4 Av. Livingstone ☎02 230 20 07

In an area full of Irish pubs and bars packed with English speakers, The Wild Geese adds a little variety to the European Center's night scene. The bar is large and open with round wooden tables and benches tucked in corners. Enjoy a beer outside on the expansive terrace, or head upstairs for a more reclusive spot. A DJ works the floor Thursday through Saturday nights, and the bar's middle-aged patrons are replaced by a swarm of young Eurocrats who party until the early hours of the morning before deciding to stumble back to their luxury hotels. We're not bitter.

Ⓜ Maelbeek. $ Beer €2.50-4. ⏰ Open M-W noon-1am, Th-Sa noon-3am, Su noon-1am.

SOHO

CLUB

47 Bld. du Triomphe ☎02 649 35 00 🖥www.soho-club.be

Soho is one of Brussels' liveliest clubs, situated just out of the center and near the EU district. If you're bored with the city's laidback bars and fancy a real dance with some loud music, you'd better get yourself here. The 20-something crowd is a perfect match for the student traveler and a welcome break from the older Eurocrats found in the area. Expect a wide variety of music and theme nights, and a dance floor is big enough to get lost in—hopefully people won't be able to notice your not-so-cool dance moves. Taking a taxi home after you leave is advisable, as the distance back to the center is a bit of a walk, and the Metro stops a little after midnight.

[M]Hankar. Take Line 5 toward Hermann-Debroux. $ Cover €10. Drinks €5-10. ⏰ Open Th-Sa 11pm-late.

JORDAN'S

CLUB, LOUNGE

49-50 Place Jourdan ☎02 230 74 66 🖥www.jordans.be

Jordan's is an after-work club, although it doesn't seem to have the pomp associated with such an establishment. The chill atmosphere and chic furniture make it an ideal place to relax and forget about the day (even if you weren't at work). Try one of their special cocktails *(€8)*, including classics or Jordan's specials such as Kiss Kool and Birdie Nam Nam.

[M]Schuman. Place Jourdan is just down rue Froissart. $ Drinks €2-8. ⏰ Open M 11:30am-3pm, Tu-F 11:30am-3pm and 5pm-late, Sa 5pm-late.

ARTS AND CULTURE

Brussels is a hotbed of theater, popular music, and opera, and hosts numerous music and film festivals throughout the year. Make sure you pick up the free weekly culture publication **Agenda** from the Tourist Office, or the free magazine **BruXXL** (available in English), both of which print schedules of all the hot arts and culture events in the city.

Opera

THEATRE ROYALE DE LA MONNAIE

LOWER TOWN

Place de la Monnaie ☎070 23 39 39 🖥www.lamonnaie.be

Brussels' Opera House performed numerous sold-out shows in 2010, including a wildly popular production of *Macbeth*. Perfomances range from classical opera to chamber music performances. Student rush tickets and discounts of up to 50% are available, but performances sell out quickly, especially in June.

[M] De Brouckère. i Box office at 23 rue Léopold. $ Tickets from €20. ⏰ Box office open Tu-Sa 11:30am-5:30pm.

Theater

THEATRE NATIONAL

LOWER TOWN

111-115 Bld. Emile Jacqmain ☎02 203 53 03 🖥www.theatrenational.be

The Theatre National is the official home to a wide range of productions, including well-known plays and experimental theater. The modern building on Bld. Jacqmain sells out fast, and recently announced that the 2011 season will include three original plays.

[M]Rogier. $ Tickets €19, students and under 26 €9. ⏰ Box office open Tu-Sa 11am-6pm.

BEURSSCHOUWBURG

LOWER TOWN

20-28 rue Ortz ☎02 550 03 50 🖥www.beursschouwburg.be

The Beursschouwburg is a haven for up-and-coming artists, and prides itself on supporting newcomers to film, theater, and dance. Contemporary theater is the name of the game here, but you can also catch films, documentaries, dance performances, and temporary exhibits.

[M]Bourse. $ €12, students €10. ⏰ Box office open M-F 10am-6pm.

Concert Venues

LE BOTANIQUE

UPPER TOWN

Bld. du Jardin. 29-31 Botanique ☎02 218 37 32 🖳www.botanique.be

The Botanical Gardens make for a beautiful stroll during the day, but things get a little raunchier at night, when the grand building that towers above the gardens hosts some of the best concerts in the city. Three different stages provide an intimate performance space for artists from the UK, continental Europe, and on occasion the States; in 2010, heavyweight performers included Ellie Goulding, Marina and the Diamonds, and Kate Nash. Brussels' student crowd can't get enough of Le Botanique, and in recent years it's become the city's most popular venue for live music. Make sure you check out a concert there when you head to Brussels.

Ⓜ Botanique. $ Prices vary by show. ⏰ Box office open daily 10am-6pm.

Cinemas

CINEMA ARENBERG

UPPER TOWN

26 Galerie de la Reine ☎02 512 80 63 🖳ww.arenberg.be

Cinema Arenberg is an eclectic little venue that shows European and American films. Catch that movie you missed in the States, or be a little more cultured and head to a Spanish or French documentary. Full schedule and prices can be found online.

Ⓜ Gare Centrale. ℹ Film schedule available online. $ Tickets €8, students €6.60.

Festivals

BRUSSELS FILM FESTIVAL

FILM FESTIVAL

Place St-Croix ☎02 641 10 20 🖳www.fffb.be

European filmmakers flock to the city in late June to screen some of the most promising up-and-coming independent movies of the year. The competition takes place at Flagey, the independent cinema just off of Flagey Square, and tickets for the films are available individually, as well as for the final awards ceremony.

Tram #81 to Ⓜ Louise. $ €7 per film, under 26 €5. 5-film screen pass €25. ⏰ Box office open M 5-10pm, Tu-Sa 11am-10pm, Su 5-10pm.

FÊTE DE LA MUSIQUE

OUTDOOR CONCERT

Considered by some to be a national holiday (it's actually treated as such in France), the Fête de la Musique is an annual jackpot for music lovers that features a variety of musical styles and performers. Stages are set up by the Royal Palace throughout the city, and the musicians perform around the clock. For more information on the 2011 lineup check the website 🖳www.conseildelamusique.be.

$ Free. ⏰ 3rd weekend in June.

SHOPPING

Shopping Malls

CITY2

LOWER TOWN

123 rue Neuve ☎02 22 11 40 60 🖳www.city2.be

Situated just off of rue Neuve, Brussels' central shopping mall dedicates an entire floor to the department store Fnac, and hosts a variety of clothes, electronics, and jewelry shops. A food hall is also located on the first floor. The mall includes an H&M, Sports World, and GB supermarket for your daily needs.

Ⓜ Rogier. ⏰ Open M-Th 10am-7pm, F 10am-7:30pm, Sa-Su 10am-7pm.

GALERIE PORTE LOUISE

✦ UPPER TOWN

235 Galerie de la Porte Louise   ☎02 2 512 97 12 ◻www.galerieportelouise.com
Situated in a more expensive shopping area, this mall is the place to go for independent designers, expensive jewelry, and high-class fashion. Small little boutiques line the walkway, including a pooch pampering shop where the ladies who lunch bring their lap dogs to be spoiled rotten. If you're on a budget you'd better stick to window shopping. The mall can be accessed from the lucrative shopping street of Av. Louise, or off the main road Av. de la Toison d'Or.
✦ Ⓜ Louise. ⏲ Open M-Sa 6:30am-9pm (most shops open from 9am), Su 9am-9pm.

Markets

MAROLLES FLEA MARKET

✦ MAROLLES

Place du Jeu de Balles
The biggest flea market in Brussels. Anything and everything is on sale here, from pocketwatches to plastic pins, taxidermy squirrels to ferret skins. The local vendors will happily bargain with you, but don't try to out-haggle them—they do this job seven days a week, and know all the tricks. The best deals go down early on, so if you want a chance of finding treasure amidst all that junk, get there shortly after the market opens.
✦ Ⓜ Gare du Midi. *i* Most vendors only accept cash. ⏲ Daily market 7am-3pm.

Chocolate Shops

PLANÈTE CHOCOLATE

✦ LOWER TOWN

24 rue du Lombard   ☎02 511 07 55 ◻www.planetechocolat.be
One of the most renowned chocolate shops in Brussels (and that's really saying something), Planète Chocolate displays an infinite array of handmade chocolate creations, inlcuding detailed chocolate bouquets. For €7, you can arrange a trip to their "chocolate salon" and watch the local oompaloompas brew the house specialties, learn a little chocolate history, and then—wait for it—try some of their creations. Call in advance to arrange your visit.
✦ Ⓜ Bourse. Ⓢ Chocolate salon €7. ⏲ Open M-Sa 10am-6:30pm, Su 11am-6:30pm.

LA MAISON DES MAITRES CHOCOLATIERS

✦ LOWER TOWN

4 Grand Place   ☎02 888 66 20 ◻ wwww.mmcb.be
This isn't just any chocolate shop. The 10 chocolate craftsmen employed here work tirelessly to invent scrumptious new tastes and treats, then sculpt their creations into increasingly eccentric shapes—we particularly enjoyed the life-sized chocolate baby in the window. The most innovative chocolatier you'll ever see, with the prices to match—but it's worth checking out, if only to see that for the flowing waterfall of chocolate behind the front desk.
✦ Ⓜ Bourse. ⏲ Open daily 10am-10pm.

Clothes

RUE NEUVE

✦ LOWER TOWN

Rue Neuve is Brussels' main shopping district. Big brand names are tucked between the small cafés and mom-and-pop shops. including H&M, C&A, and Pimkie. On the weekends, the street becomes packed with students and local families looking for a bargain.
✦ Ⓜ Rogier or Ⓜ De Brouckère. Rue Neuve is between the 2. ⏲ Shops usually open M-Sa 10am-6pm. Some shops open Su.

BLENDER01

✦ LOWER TOWN

18 rue des Chartreux   ☎02 503 61 83 ◻www.facebook.com/Blender01
Shop owner Alexis, personally selects designs and gadgets from retailers, and then sells them to the general public. The result is an exceptionally unique collection; currently Blender01 exclusively stocks several designers, including

Grenoble native HixSept L'Oiseau Gris, who makes some rather stylish male clothing. Pieces include a hoodie with a Lego-man printed onto the hood, and a pair of wooden sunglasses (*€130*). Although some items, like the glasses, are expensive, other pieces are more affordable, particularly when it comes to the quirky wallets and bags.

✱ ⓂBourse. ⚇ Open Tu-Sa 11am-7pm, Su 2-6pm.

FOXHOLE
● LOWER TOWN

4 rue des Riches Claires ☎477 20 53 36 ▣info@foxholeshop.com

FoxHole specializes in the 1970s and 1980s vintage gear; this is the place to go if you're looking for a really garish plaid shirt, or just something cool and retro. The prices are student friendly, and many of Brussels' hip arts students buy their clothes here. Expect everything from shoes to bags to shell suits, as well as some really cool hats.

✱ ⓂBourse. ⚇ Open Tu-Sa 12:30-6:30pm.

Books

WATERSTONES
✒ LOWER TOWN

71-75 Bld. Adolphe Max ☎02 219 27 08 ▣www.waterstones.co.uk

One of the UK's biggest bookstores, this renowned English chain is currently staging a hostile takeover of Brussels' book scene. Though *Let's Go* never recommends *coups d'etat*, we approve. You can find just about anything here, from magazines to newspapers to old and new classics. The English-speaking staff will happily advise you on a good read for your trip to Brussels. Check out their "Belgian Classics" section, though you can't go wrong with some Hercule Poirot.

✱ ⓂDe Brouckère. ⚇ Open M-Sa 9am-7pm, Su 10:30am-6pm.

Music

DR. VINYL
✒ LOWER TOWN

1 rue de la Grande Île ☎02 512 73 44

Dr. Vinyl will see you now in this small, hip, and very cool record store. Though most stores in the area specialize in second-hand vinyls and older, retro music, Dr. Vinyl prides himself on selling new and cutting-edge music on vinyl. DJs of tomorrow should come to the Doctor for a check-up and spin some of their own music on the decks that line the edge of the shop. If you're not sure how a record player works and just need some new iPod headphones, the Doctor will also happily point you in the direction of other music shops in the area.

✱ ⓂBourse. ⚇ Open M-Sa noon-8pm.

Jewelry

BETTY DE STEFANO
✒ UPPER TOWN

17 rue Lebeau ☎02 511 46 13 ▣www.collectors-gallery.com

Betty de Stefano is located near the Beaux-Arts area of town, so expect some very *beaux* pieces of jewelry from the 20th century. The small shop also specializes in diamonds, and Betty herself will help advise you on the perfect piece to match your outfit.

✱ ⓂGare Centrale. Just off of Place de la Justice. ⑤ Prices vary. ⚇ Open W-Sa 11am-6pm, Su 11am-3pm.

ESSENTIALS

Practicalities

- **TOURIST OFFICE: Central Office** sells the **Brussels Card,** which includes free public transport, a city map, and free museum access for 24hr., 48hr., or 72hr. (*€24/€34/€40.*)(ⓂBourse, East corner of Grand Place ☎02 513 89 40 ▣www.

brusselsinternational.be ⏰ *Open daily summer 9am-6pm; winter 10am-2pm.)* There is also a second, less central office location *(2-4 rue Royale ☎02 513 89 40 ⏰ Open daily 10am-6pm.)*

- **CONSULATES:** Information available at the **Tourist Office. USA** *(27 Bld. du Régent ☎02 508 21 11);* **UK** *(9/31 Av. des Nerviens ☎02 287 62 48).*
- **CURRENCY EXCHANGE: CBC Automatic Change.** *(7 Grand Place ☎02 547 12 11 ⏰ Open 24hr.)* **Moneytrans** also offers currency exchange *(6 rue Marché-aux-Herbes ☎02 227 18 20).*
- **LAUNDROMATS: Washing 65.** *(65 rue du Midi ⏰ Open daily 7am-9pm.)* **Wash Club.** *(68 rue du Marché au Charbon $ 8kg €4. ⏰ Open daily 7am-10pm.)*
- **INTERNET:** Free Wi-Fi in **McDonald's** and **Quick** on rue de Neuve. **CyberCafés.** *(66 rue du Midi and 86 Bld. Emile Jacqmain $ €1.50 per 30min. ⏰ Open daily 9am-10pm.)*
- **POST OFFICE: Central Office.** *(1 Bld. Anspach ☎022 012345 ⏰ Open M-F 8:30am-6pm, Sa 10am-4pm.)*
- **POSTAL CODE:** 1000
- **POLICE:** ☎101
- **PHARMACIES: Pharmacie Fripiers** is closest to the Grand Place. *(24b rue des Fripiers ☎02 218 04 91 ⏰ Open M-Sa 9am-7pm.)* **Stanby Pharmacies** can be reached at all hours by phone only. *(☎0800 20 600 ⏰ Open 24hr.)*
- **HOSPITAL:** ☎100

Getting There

By Air

The **Brussels airport** *(☎090 07 00 00 💻www.brusselsairport.be)* is 14km from the city center. **Shuttles** run between the airport and **Midi Train Station.** *(💻www.voyages-lelan.be $ One-way €13, round-trip €22. ⏰ Every 30min. 4am-11:45pm.)*

By Train

Brussels has three main train stations: **Gare du Midi, Gare Centrale,** and **Gare du Nord** *(☎02 555 25 55 💻www.scnb.be).* All international trains stop at Gare du Midi, and most stop at Gare Centrale and Gare du Nord as well. Gare Centrale is the stop which will bring you closest to the center and most accommodations. Brussels can be reached from **Antwerp** *($ €6. ⏰ 45min.)*; **Bruges** *($ €12. ⏰ 45 min.);* **Liège** *($ €19. ⏰ 1hr.);* **Amsterdam, the Netherlands** *($ €43. ⏰ 3hr.);* **Paris, France.** *($ €55-€86. ⏰ 1hr.)* **Eurostar** *(💻www.eurostar.com)* runs to **London, UK.** *($ €60-€240. ⏰ 2hr.)*

Getting Around

By Foot

Getting around Brussels is **cheap and simple** because you can do (almost) the whole city by foot and won't need to step onto the Metro unless you head to the Atomium or further on the outskirts.

By Bike

Remember, cars rule the roads in Brussels and bikes are only advisable for the truly brave. If you want to bike around the city there are **villo** (bike rental) points situated at key locations in Brussels; the first half an hour is free and then you pay incrementally for each half an hour afterward *(💻www.villo.be).* **Signposts** are strategically placed in the center to direct you to sights, museums and points of interest in Brussels.

By Metro

The Metro system rings the city, with a tram running vertically through the middle and a further two Metro lines running east to west. The bus system also connects the various quarters of the city such as Ixelles and the European Area. All public transport in Brussels is run by **the Société des Transports Intercommunaux Bruxellois (STIB).** *(☎070 23 2000* 🖳 *www.stib.be* Ⓢ *€0.30 per min.* 🕐 *M-Th 5:30am-12:30am, F-Sa 5:30am-3am, Su 5:30am-12:30am.)* Hence, all tickets are valid for the Metro, the tram and the bus. A **Ten-Voyage ticket** *(€12.30)* is probably the best deal.

By Taxi

If you want to take a taxi after the Metro stops running, you can call **Taxi Bleus** *(☎02 268 00 00)* or **Taxis Oranges** *(☎02 349 43 43.)* Taxi prices are calculated by the fixed price per kilometer *(€1.35-€2.70)* and a fixed base charge *(€2.40-4.40 at night).*

essentials

PLANNING YOUR TRIP

Time Differences

Belgium is 1hr. ahead of Greenwich Mean Time (GMT) and observes Daylight Saving Time. This means that it's 6hr. ahead of New York City, 9hr. ahead of Los Angeles, and 1hr. ahead of the British Isles. In Northern Hemisphere summer they are 8hr. behind Sydney and 10hr. behind New Zealand, while in Northern Hemisphere winter it's 10hr. behind Sydney and 12hr. behind New Zealand. Don't get confused and call your parents when it's actually 4am their time! Note that Belgium changes to Daylight Savings Time on different dates from some other countries, so sometimes the difference will be one hour different from what is stated here.

MONEY

Tipping

In Belgium, service charges are included in the bill at restaurants. Waiters do not depend on tips for their livelihood, so there is no need to feel guilty about not leaving a tip. Still, leaving 5-10% extra will certainly be appreciated. Higher than that is just showing off. Tips in bars are very unusual. Cab drivers are normally tipped about 10%.

Taxes

The quoted price of goods in Belgium includes **value added tax (TVA).** This tax on goods is generally levied at 21% in Belgium, although some goods are subject to lower rates.

SAFETY AND HEALTH

In any type of crisis, the most important thing to do is **stay calm.** Your country's embassy abroad is usually your best resource in an emergency; registering with that embassy upon arrival in the country is a good idea.

Drugs and Alcohol

Though Belgium has fairly liberal attitudes regarding alcohol, with legal drinking ages of 16 and booze widely available, public drunkenness is frowned upon and is a sure way to mark yourself as a tourist.

When it comes to drugs other than alcohol, as is so often the case, things get a little more interesting. Hard drugs are completely illegal in Belgium, and possession or consumption of substances like heroin and cocaine will be harshly punished if caught. Belgium's attitude toward even soft drugs is traditional and conservative.

belgium

Marijuana is both illegal and not tolerated. Coffeeshops in Belgium are just that; the strongest substance you'll be able to buy is a simple *café noir*.

Pre-Departure Health

Matching a prescription to a foreign equivalent is not always easy, safe, or possible, so if you take **prescription drugs,** carry up-to-date prescriptions or a statement from your doctor stating the medications' trade names, manufacturers, chemical names, and dosages. Be sure to keep all medication with you in your carry-on luggage.

Immunizations and Precautions

Travelers over two years old should make sure that the following vaccines are up to date: MMR (for measles, mumps, and rubella); DTaP or Td (for diphtheria, tetanus, and pertussis); IPV (for polio); Hib (for *Haemophilus influenzae* B); and HepB (for Hepatitis B). For recommendations on immunizations and prophylaxis, check with a doctor and consult the **Centers for Disease Control and Prevention (CDC)** in the US or the equivalent in your home country. (☎+1-800-CDC-INFO/232-4636 🖳www.cdc.gov/travel)

belgium 101

facts and figures

- **POPULATION OF BRUSSELS:** 144,784
- **POPULATION OF THE CAPITAL REGION:** 1,089,790
- **AREA:** 62.2. sq. mi.
- **EU BUREAUCRATS:** 24,099
- **FOREIGN JOURNALISTS:** 800
- **GUILDHALLS ON THE GRAND PLACE:** 16
- **GUILDHALLS WITH ANIMAL NAMES:** 4
- **AGE OF BRUSSELS' "OLDEST CITIZEN" (MANNEKEN PIS):** 391

CUSTOMS AND ETIQUETTE

Two Nations, Indivisible...

The Kingdom of Belgium is made up of two fiercely independent regions: French-speaking **Wallonia** (Wallonie, *en français*) to the south, and **Flanders** (Vlaanderen) to the north, which speaks Flemish, a form of Dutch. Brussels is located in the heart of Flanders, but is part of the "French Community"—one of the three official institutions that govern cultural affairs for the speakers of the country's languages. This capital city snub has caused Flemish blood to boil more than a few times. As recently as 2006, television stations were filled with images of Flemish revolution—albeit a fake revolt designed to spur discussion of the language issue. Independence parties routinely receive voter support.

Lost in Translation

Apologies to the Flemish: *francais* is the language of the day here. While there are two official languages, about 90% of people speak French. When giving or receiving directions, it helps to be picky about which language to use. On signs, all streets are listed as one long name made up of two languages, beginning with French and words such as "rue," and ending with the Dutch "straat." When looking for a street, Brussels residents will use only their preferred tongue. Of course, since Brussels is an international city filled with diplomats from across Europe, many people speak English as well.

FOOD AND DRINK

Street Cart/Calorie Chart?

What would the American diner be like without the influence of Belgium? A visit to Brussels reveals that Americana may not be so, well, American after all. Throughout Belgium, vendors with small carts sell **frites**—despite their American name, the Belgians invented the French fry first. Unlike the hometown drive-thru, these fries are always crispy and piping hot, because Belgians cook them twice, including right before they are served.

Chocolat, Chocolat, Chocolat

There are no Oompa-Loompas, but Brussels is likely home to more than a few slightly mad chocolatiers. It certainly has a number of chocolate factories and quaint sweet shops. In his Brussels kitchen in 1912, Jean Neuhaus invented the **praline,** the quintessential Belgian chocolate, when he filled chocolate shells with cream and nut pastes.

Beer!

Need we say more? It's the de facto national drink of Belgium—8700 different varieties are produced in the country. Nowhere will you find more brews than in the bars and cafes of the cosmopolitan Belgian capital. Ordering wine at a Brussels brasserie is basically like ordering beer in Napa Valley. Brussels bars serve beer in all colors (a Flemish red, anyone?) and flavors (do raspberry and peach beer sound appealing?). Brussels even has beer museums, like the Brussels Gueuze Museum, that double as operating breweries and feature remnants of beer making from the middle ages.

FESTIVALS AND FOLKLORE

Is there anyone who doesn't love a good parade? The people of Brussels have certainly loved them for quite a while—since 1549, at least. That's the year when Emperor Charles V and his entourage entered the city in a spectacle not matched since—even though the citizens try every year, in a festival known as **Ommegang.**

GREAT BRITAIN

There once was a country made up of great islands
with peat bogs and moors, great rivers and highlands,
Its people built castles and churches with spires
and started a powerful global empire.
Meanwhile, the hills, filled with white sheep and crofters,
inspired great artists, bold monarchs, and authors.
Today, on a belly of bangers and mash,
the British continue their long, storied past
with Wimbledon, cricket, golf tourneys, and football,
festivals, dubstep, and cold pints on pub crawls.
It's time to discover and leave what you know—
boot up in your wellies, grab your pack, and let's go!

greatest hits

- **MAGICAL MYSTERY TOUR.** Spend a day in the life of John, Paul, George and Ringo by visiting their hometown of Liverpool. Get a ticket to ride through The Beatles Story (p. 172), an entire museum devoted to the legendary band.

- **CHALLENGE THE STATUS QUO.** Or at least hear others with more gumption do so at the Speakers' Corner in London's Hyde Park (p. 94).

- **GET ICED, BRO!** London's hottest drinking spot is inside a block of ice. Throw on some designer thermal wear and head to Absolut Icebar (p. 115).

- **GO ASK ALICE.** Visit Christ Church College (p. 130) in Oxford to see where Lewis Carroll first met the real Alice, before she headed off to Wonderland.

- **GOOD WILL PUNTING.** Need a study break from Cambridge University? Rent a punt from Scudamore's (p. 145) and cruise down the River Cam.

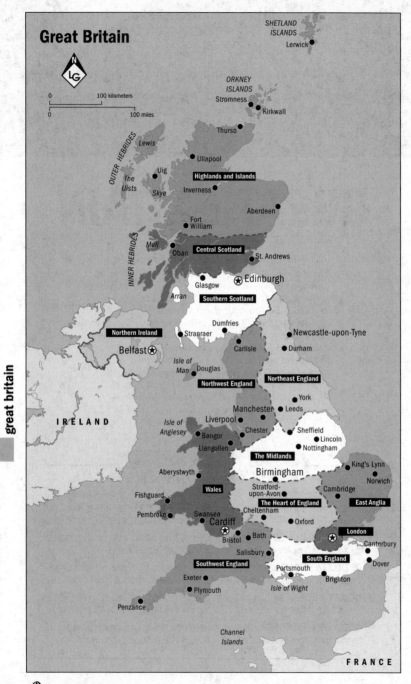

Great Britain

great britain

With Oxford, Cambridge and LSE, Great Britain is home to some of the world's most prestigious universities, attracting local Brits and students from abroad. Nonetheless, Edinburgh, the capital of Scotland, is also Great Britain's capital for student life. **The University of Edinburgh** is home to over 24,000 students who live, study, and drink just south of the **Royal Mile.** The forward-thinking city also has some of Britain's most talented artists, so it's no wonder Edinburgh hosts the world's largest arts festival. Every August, mobs of students from around the globe arrive for **The Fringe,** where you too can hear great music, watch great theater and make some new best friends. Why settle for a pub?

london ☎020

Most people have a well-defined idea of "London": staid tradition, afternoon tea, stuffy Englishmen with cultured accents, heavy ales, and winding lanes—all of it decorated in styles that were popular back when high foreheads were also fashionable. People with this notion of London can easily complete their vacation in 3min. But in London, there's always an underground scene to be found, and a modern pulse beats behind every beautiful old surface. Now, finish your 🍺pint and *Let's Go.*

ORIENTATION

Bayswater

Formerly a watering hole for livestock, Bayswater was built up from a small hamlet in the late 18th and early 19th centuries. In the late 19th century, the neighborhood took on a wealthier set of inhabitants before increased immigration to London spiced up its character and cuisine a bit. It's nestled close to Notting Hill but has much cheaper housing. Get off the Tube at the ⊖**Bayswater** stop for the west of the neighborhood, and at ⊖**Paddington** or ⊖**Lancaster Gate** for the east. Bayswater is east of Notting Hill and west of Marylebone.

Bloomsbury

Once famous for the manor houses, hospitals, universities, and museums that made the area a cultural landmark, Bloomsbury is now a haven for student travelers seeking cheap accommodations in a central location. Providing easy access to the British Museum and the rest of London, Bloomsbury is a perfect location from which to see the city. The borough features a wide range of ethnic restaurants, providing a welcome respite from British specialties like the inimitable "bubble and squeak" (fried leftovers). Especially pleasant are the many beautiful gardens and parks sprinkled throughout the neighborhood. Where once you might have seen **Virginia Woolf** and **John Maynard Keynes,** members of the bohemian Bloomsbury Group, you may now see Ricky Gervais. To reach Bloomsbury, west of **Clerkenwell,** take the Tube to ⊖**Tottenham Court Rd.** or ⊖**Russell Square.**

Chelsea

Chelsea once gained a reputation as a punk hangout, but there is nothing punk about the neighborhood today. Overrun by rich "Sloanes" (preps, in British parlance), Chelsea now has sky-high prices, expensive clubs, and absurd cars. Just about the only thing that's still edgy about the neighborhood is the **Saatchi Gallery.** Current home of **Mick Jagger** and former home of **Oscar Wilde,** most of the action can be found in **Sloane Square, King's Road,** and **Royal Hospital Road.** Visit for the restaurants and the sights, but find your home and nightlife elsewhere. Chelsea is between **Westminster** and **Hammersmith** and beneath **Kensington.** Take to the Tube to ⊖**Sloane Square** to access it.

london • orientation

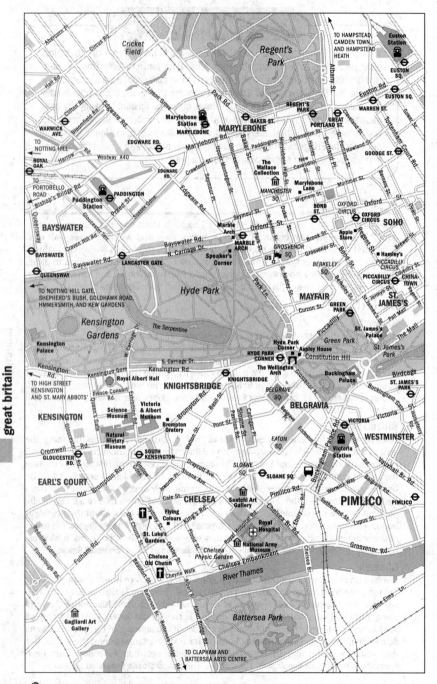

great britain

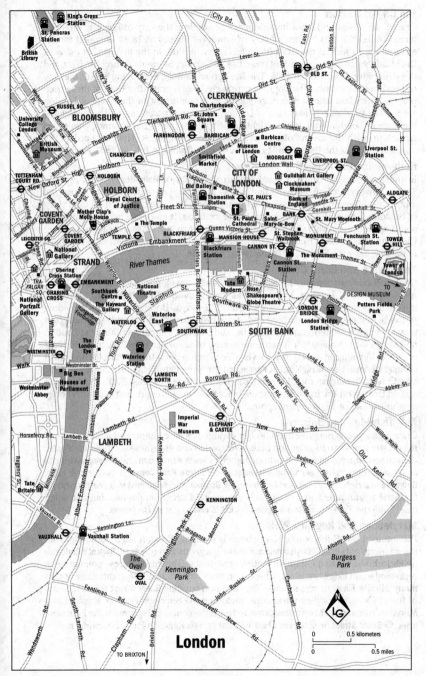

london · orientation

The City of London

One of the oldest and most historic parts of London, the City of London, often referred to as "the City," houses many of London's finest and most crowded tourist attractions, as well as the city's financial center. Written in the histories of many of the buildings are the devastating tragedies of German bombing during the Blitz and the Great Fire of London in 1666. The fire spread rapidly, destroying 80% of the City of London in five days. Much of the current city was rebuilt after both of these tragedies, and its fantastic architecture stands as a monument to the resilient London spirit. "The City" also holds many of London's Roman artifacts, as well as vestiges of the ancient London Wall. It is a neighborhood where the spires of famous churches stretch up with the towers of powerful insurance companies. The City borders the northern bank of the **Thames** and is east of **Holborn.** Take the Tube to ♥**St. Paul's.**

Holborn and Clerkenwell

In the 18th century, Holborn was home to **Mother Clap's Molly House,** a gay brothel. Today, however, it houses many banks, law firms, and upscale pubs, so things are a little bit different. Clerkenwell is a former monastic center, defined by the Priory of St. John, before Henry VIII began the reformation. It has since become a popular spot for excellent meals and hardy night life. Holborn is west of the City of London; Clerkenwell is north of Holborn, with Charterhouse St. serving as part of its southern boundary. Take the Tube to ♥**Farringdon** or ♥**Temple.**

Kensington and Earl's Court

Once a Saxon settlement, Kensington has since developed into one of the most pleasant parts of London. Known as **The Royal Borough of Kensington and Chelsea,** it is sometimes pretentiously referred to as "The Royal Borough." Filled with some of the best museums, nicest bars and swankiest residences in London, Kensington may have more Lamborghinis, Maseratis, and Ferraris per capita than most London neighborhoods. Notable for its museums, ease of access to **Hyde Park,** and laid-back nightlife, Kensington is well worth a visit. Kensington is south of **Notting Hill** and north of **Knightsbridge.** Use ♥**High Street Kensington** for Kensington High St. and Hyde Park, and ♥**South Kensington** for Old Brompton Rd. and the museums. Earl's Court is just up Old Brompton Rd. from Kensington, but it feels worlds apart, and is a much better neighborhood for a quiet evening out.

Knightsbridge and Belgravia

Once a dangerous neighborhood, Knightsbridge has since improved its rep. Appealing mostly thanks to its selection of undercrowded and enjoyable sights and fantastic department stores, this neighborhood between **South Kensington** and **Kensington** merits at least a short visit. Use ♥**Knightsbridge** and ♥**Hyde Park Corner** if you travel here. **Belgravia** is a rich neighborhood bordered by **Chelsea** and **Westminster.** It features many fantastic restaurants and a reasonable selection of accommodations, but not much else. Take the Tube to ♥**Sloane Square** or ♥**Victoria** to get to Belgravia.

Marylebone and Regent's Park

Pronounced (MAR-leh-bone), Marylebone is a classic London neighborhood. From the winding, pub-lined **Marylebone Lane** to the gorgeous and romantic **Regent's Park,** the neighborhood offers a complete British experience. The city's diverse population is represented on Edgware Road, where a predominantly Lebanese community boasts many Middle Eastern restaurants. The area surrounding **Baker Street** features some of the city's more touristy attractions, including the Sherlock Holmes Museum and Madame Tussaud's. Take ♥**Bond Street** to reach the south, ♥**Edgware** for the Lebanese area. ♥**Baker Street** or ♥**Regent's Park** will get you to Regent's Park. Shocking, no?

Notting Hill

Notting Hill is a beautiful neighborhood and, while touristy, it's worth a visit—even if you don't bump into Hugh Grant in a local bookstore. Many shopping options are geared towards an older crowd, but Portobello Market (**Portobello Rd.**, Saturdays from about 6am-6pm) is a blast; you can buy anything from antiques to fresh fruits and vegetables. Aside from the market, the neighborhood's charm lies in its pastel residences, high-end fashion boutiques, and fancy restaurants. These upscale offerings and fantastic houses are what have convinced celebrities like Claudia Schiffer to move to the area. In other celebrity lore, the Clash are rumored to have gotten their start on Portobello Road. Rock on. Notting Hill is just north of **Kensington,** and organizes itself mainly around Portobello Rd. Take the Tube to ⊖**Notting Hill Gate.**

The South Bank

Populated with the renovated factories of yore, the South Bank has undergone a renaissance, reinforcing its status as a hub of London entertainment. This status does, of course, have some history to it: both the **Rose** and **Shakespeare's Globe Theatre** resided on the bank. Now, the **Southbank Centre** hosts exciting classical music concerts. Great theaters abound, as do some of the best museums and galleries in London, including the famous **Tate Modern. "Millennium Mile"** stretches from the London Eye in the west and runs eastward along the **Thames,** making for a beautiful walk, especially around sunset. Head to ⊖**Waterloo** for inland attractions and to ⊖**Southwark** for Bankside. The neighborhood is located in the south of Central London on —you guessed it— the south bank of the Thames.

The West End

The West End is one of the largest, most exciting parts of London. Comprised of **Soho, Covent Garden, Mayfair and Saint James's,** and **Trafalgar Square,** the West End has some of the most affordable shopping in London, as well as arguably the city's best (free!) public museums, such as the **National Gallery,** and the **National Portrait Gallery,** among others. Known by many as the Broadway of London, the West End offers a host of excellent theater options close to Trafalgar Square, accessible by ⊖**Charing Cross.**

Soho, most easily accessed via ⊖**Tottenham Court Road** is one of the hipper and seedier parts of London. Home to one of the most prominent gay communities in London, Soho is teeming with nightlife for the GLBT and straight clubgoers alike. During the day, however, Soho is known for its excellent restaurants. **Chinatown** in particular offers many popular options. It's located off Gerrard St. and is easily accessed from Leicester Square or Piccadilly Circus. The ⊖**Oxford Circus** Tube stop exits onto Regent St. which is one of the more famous and beautiful streets in London, and is home to many chains and famous shops. Most notable here are the gorgeous Apple store and the famous **Hamley's** toy store, which will help anyone rediscover their inner child.

Covent Garden (accessible via ⊖**Covent Garden**—go figure!) is famous for its shops and the Covent Garden Piazza, recognizable from Hitchcock's *Frenzy* and the opening scene of *My Fair Lady.* Though no longer a Cockney flower market or a place where merchants burst spontaneously into song, Covent Garden is known for its rich history of street performers. One could spend a fulfilling trip in the West End only. It should be noted, however, that as the West End is a prime tourist location as well as a nightlife location, it can be quite dangerous. When going out, people should try to travel in groups and stick to the crowded, well-lit streets. If you get tired of walking on foot, you can also travel by rickshaw. Also note that false store fronts with paper signs inside advertising "model" or "girl" are poorly-concealed brothels. If taken in the right spirit, however, and with proper precautions, The West End's relative sketchiness only adds to its color. We prefer to think of it as Dickensian rather than depressing.

london · orientation

Westminster

After the City of London, Westminster lays claim to London's most famous sites. Between the Houses of **Parliament, Buckingham Palace,** and **Westminster Abbey** (as well as many of the modern centers of government), Westminster feels like the seat of the royal empire. Be warned that, outside of the sites, however, there isn't a lot to do. South of Victoria lies Pimlico, a residential neighborhood with several accommodation options, many of them on Belgrave Rd. The ⊖**Westminster** Tube stop is near most sights, but exit at the ⊖**Victoria** or ⊖**Pimlico** stops if you're looking for hostels. Westminster is north of the **Thames** and West of **Belgravia** and **Pimlico.**

North London

North London is a sprawling expanse north of central London. **Hampstead** and **Camden Town** are the two most popular draws. Hampstead provides pleasant dining and a properly British small-town feel. It also offers the glorious and meandering ▧**Heath,** a must for all nature-lovers. Camden was once punk central, but is now more upscale. Still worth a visit, it contains some underground culture and many upscale restaurants and boutiques. Hampstead is accessible via ⊖**Hampstead** and ⊖**Golders Green** on the northern line, and ⊖**Hampstead Heath** via the **National Rail. Camden Town** is accessible on the **Northern Line.** Hampstead is just north of Camden.

South London

South London has been maligned historically as one of London's dodgier neighborhoods. While the area has enjoyed something of a renaissance in recent years, it's still not as safe as many of the areas in London proper; **Clapham** is one of the best neighborhoods to find young professionals who patronize its pub and restaurant scene. Now a cultural center as well, Clapham houses the **Battersea Arts Centre,** renowned for its revolutionary productions. **Brixton** is less quaint than nearby Clapham. Bible-thumpers preach the Apocalypse from convenience store pulpits, and purveyors of all goods at the nearby Afro-Caribbean market make sales despite the overpowering smell of fish. Brixton is also a good place to be if you've been missing fast food. **Stockwell** and **Vauxhall** are less accessible and interesting than the other two neighborhoods in South London, but Vauxhall does claim the **City Farm** in the town park. The local underground stations in many of the southern neighborhoods play classical music, thought by many to be a tactic for keeping young people from accumulating in the Underground, *Clockwork Orange*-style. Access Clapham via ⊖**Clapham North,** ⊖**Clapham Common** or ⊖**Clapham South** or take the **National Rail** services to Clapham Junction. Brixton is accessible via ⊖**Brixton** on the **Victoria Line,** and Stockwell can be easily reached via ⊖**Stockwell.** Those looking to visit Dulwich can take the P4 bus from ⊖**Brixton Station.** Vauxhall is southwest of the **City of London,** Clapham is south of Vauxhall, Brixton is east of Clapham and south of Stockwell.

East London

East London, and especially the **East End,** is known for its cutting-edge galleries and its deliciously affordable markets and restaurants. The neighborhood has all of the spark and edge that **Chelsea** used to, and its massive immigrant community rounds out the culinary landscape nicely. **Brick Lane,** named after the brick kilns brought by Flemish immigrants and defined by the waves of Huguenot, French, Russian, Bengali, and Muslim immigrants who came after, is packed to the gills with fantastic and cheap ethnic cuisine as well as some of the most exciting and youthful nightlife in London. Further east, Greenwich features some of London's more famous sites. Use the **Docklands Light Railway (DLR)** to get to Greenwich, Old St., and Liverpool St. for the East End, ⊖**Aldgate East** for Brick Lane.

West London

West London is one of the more shape-shifting areas of London. **Shepherd's Bush** is a crush of ethnic life, which is evident in the varied restaurants lining **Goldhawk Road,** culminating in the veritable World's Fair that is **Shepherd's Bush Market.** Also unique to Shepherd's Bush is Westfield's, the 43-acre monument to shopping that makes American strip malls look like rinky-dink corner stores. It's essentially a shopping city, and one of those structures where a wavy ceiling constitutes a viable design aesthetic and makes a bold architectural statement. The name Shepherd's Bush is derived from a thorn tree that is deformed by shepherds lying in it while watching their flock. **Hammersmith** is removed from the bustle, feeling more like a seaside resort than a corner of London. The **Thames** provides many water views that would be impossible in the city proper. A good place for a good meal and a quiet day, **Kew** feels like rural London. It is, however, a bit touristy because of the gorgeous **Kew Gardens,** which is the world's largest collection of living plants. (*[i] Wheelchair-accessible. $ £13.50, concessions £11.50, under 17 free. ⏰ Open M-F 9:30am-6:30pm, Sa-Su 9:30am-7:30pm.)* Hammersmith is accessible via the **⊖Hammersmith and City Line** (last stop), and Shepherd's Bush is accessible via the **⊖Central Line.** Kew is on the **Richmond** branch of the **⊖District Line** and is the penultimate stop.

ACCOMMODATIONS

London is an infamously expensive city, and accommodations are no exception to this rule. The cheapest options are the city's hostels, and there are quite a few, especially in **Bloomsbury, Kensington,** and **Earl's Court** and **Bayswater** (extra emphasis on Bloomsbury). Travelers looking for long-term accommodations should look into

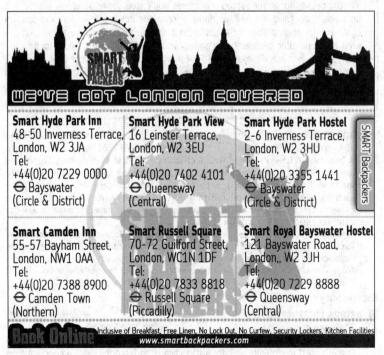

rooms at the colleges. Those unwilling to stay in a hostel can stay in bed and breakfasts as they can offer the privacy and comfort of a hotel at close-to-hostel prices.

Bayswater

👍 THE PAVILION

💳🚭 THEMED HOTEL ❺

34-36 Sussex Gardens ☎020 7262 0905 💻www.pavilionhoteluk.com

All you really need to know about the Pavilion is that the most popular room is named "Honky Tonk Afro." Maybe you need to know more. No, the Pavilion is not a blaxploitation film, but rather a themed hotel with rooms ranging from '70s decor to a Casablanca theme. Many famous and half-naked celebrities have posed here and the hotel is often used by modeling companies.

🧭 ⊖Paddington. Left onto Praed St., right onto London St., left onto Sussex Gardens. ℹ Continental breakfast delivered to your room. $ Small singles £60; large singles £85; doubles £100; triples £120; family (4 people) £130. 4% extra charge when you pay with a credit card.

internet cafe

Many restaurants and cafes offer Wi-Fi, but there are a few surefire ways to get Internet in London. Travelling with a laptop has its challenges and its unexpected joys. No matter how heavy the computer, or how total the hard drive crash after your hostelmate spills beer and vodka, which he, for some reason, thought would "taste really good together, bro," few things compare to the thrill of finding cheap Internet somewhere other than the Internet cafe. Some sure bets include chains like Starbucks, but a true laptop adventurer won't stop there. Sure, you can hit up a Starbucks (and, if it has two floors like the one in Victoria Station, you can camp on the second floor for hours without anyone realizing you're there), but what happens after it closes? That's when you find the cheesiest, most touristy pub you can, and ask if they have Wi-Fi. If they do, you've got internet until 11pm or midnight, plus a killer soundtrack. If, however, that's just not your thing, 💻www.easyinternetcafe.com allows users to search for nearby Internet cafes. Search London for a list of most internet cafes, and to add ratings.

ASTOR QUEST

💳🚭📶 HOSTEL ❷

45 Queensborough Terr. ☎020 7229 7782 💻www.astorhostels.com

A homey and friendly hostel with a chummy staff that lives on-site. The rooms are par for the course in hostel-land, but everything is cleaned and beds are made with fresh sheets daily. Breakfast included and served in a room by the kitchen, which is freely available for use. Hostel-weary travelers have the unique experience of dining under Sid Vicious's drugged-out gaze. Be sure to ask the 24hr. receptionist for deals on clubs.

🧭 ⊖Bayswater. Take right onto Queensway, left onto Bayswater Rd., and left onto Queensborough Terr. ℹ Ages 18-35. 4-bed dorms and twin rooms have shared bathroom. Free luggage storage. Padlocks £2. 1 female-only room available; 6 beds; £19. Laundry wash £2.50, dry £1. Check-out 10am. Check-in any time after 2pm. Hostel renovations should be completed in Jan 2011. $ 4-bed dorm £20; 8-bed £17.00; 6-bed with ensuite bath £19; 4-bed with ensuite £21.

Bloomsbury

👍 ASTORS MUSEUM HOSTEL

💳🚭📶 HOSTEL ❶

27 Montague St. ☎020 7580 5360 💻www.astorhostels.com

This is a true backpackers' hostel, quiet but centrally located. The incredibly friendly staff live on-site and are always ready with a pub-crawl, a good song on the reception speakers, a discount on local sights, and themed parties once a week. Astors is welcoming, comfortable, and exciting all at once. The rooms are spacious and clean, the kitchen is open for guest use, and everything is cleaned at least once a day.

⚲ ⊖*Russell Sq. Go down Guilford toward Russell Sq., turn left onto the square and follow it around until you reach Montague St. Turn left onto Montague St.* **i** *Continental breakfast included. Bring a padlock for the locker under the bed or borrow one with a £3 deposit and a £2 rental fee. Luggage storage free. Laundry £2.50 to wash, £0.50 dry. Wi-Fi throughout building, 40min. free upon arrival, £5 per day, £8 per week. Recommend that you book 2 weeks in advance and 3 weeks in advance for weekends. No ensuite rooms.* ⑤ *4-bed, 6-bed, 8-bed, 10-bed, and 12-bed dorms range £15-25, but prices vary. Doubles £70, but price subject to change.*

GENERATOR HOSTEL
⚲♿(ᵗᵖ)❅ PARTY HOSTEL ❶

37 Tavistock Pl. ☎020 7388 7666 🖳www.generatorhostels.com

Upon waking up in the Generator Hostel after a night of revelry, you may wonder if you forgot to leave the club. The likely answer is that you never went to a club but stayed in to partake in one of the hostel's nightly parties which occasionally feature DJs. Equipped with a bar open late and a 24hr. reception that plays 24hr. of music, the Generator is generating some very good times. The cafeteria-like common spaces and the fact that the staff doesn't live on-site prevents it from feeling homey, but the neon blue lights and steel panels make it look like a hell of a party. Plus, the money you save here will make your evenings just better.

⚲ ⊖*Russell Sq. Go down Colonnade away from Russell Sq. and turn left onto Grenville St.; follow it onto Hunter St. and turn left onto Tavistock Pl.* **i** *Bring your own padlock. Laundry £2 wash, £0.50 per 10min. in dryers. Free Wi-Fi. No private baths.* ⑤ *4-6 bed dorms £20-25; 8-12 bed dorms £17.50-22.50. Singles £55-60; doubles £25-30; triples £17.50-25.00; quads £17.50-20. Call ahead as prices change.* ⌚ *Bar open 6pm-2am. Happy hour 6-9pm.*

CLINK 261
⚲⑤⊗(ᵗᵖ) HOSTEL ❶

265 Gray's Inn Rd. ☎020 7833 9400 🖳www.ashleehouse.co.uk

If you dream of a hostel where every night is movie night (and the film is picked by majority vote and watched from comfortable pleather chairs), where cube chairs fill the entry, and where sleek, retro plastic coverings blanket every surface, then you have dreamed of quirky Clink 261. Centrally located in Bloomsbury, Clink 261 has style, relative grace, and clean and simple rooms that are well-suited to hostelgoers unwilling to commit to grungier options.

⚲ ⊖*King's Cross/St. Pancras. Turn left onto Euston Rd. and follow it as it curves right into Gray's Inn Rd.* **i** *Continental breakfast included. Lockers free, but bring your own padlock. Luggage storage and linens included. The hostel is cleaned and fresh sheets are distributed daily. Laundry £2 wash, 50p per 20min. in the dryer. Wi-Fi £1 per 30min., £2 per hr., £5 per day. Rooms available in 18-bed, 10-bed, 8-bed, 6-bed, 4-bed and private. Shared bath.* ⑤ *Dorms £18-25; private rooms £50-60. Call ahead for current prices.* ⌚ *Breakfast M-F 7:30-9:30am, Sa-Su 8-10am. Free walking tour daily 10:10am.*

Chelsea

No longer a punk-rock haven, Chelsea is now overrun with Ferraris, Benzes, and Porsches, and the hotels have adjusted accordingly. Budget accommodations here are short-stay apartment rentals.

🏙 IES RESIDENCE HALLS
⚲♿❊ STUDENT RESIDENCE HALLS ❶

Manresa Rd. ☎020 7808 9200 🖳www.iesreshall.com

Simple but highly affordable and value-packed (as Chelsea accommodations go), IES Residence Halls fill a large void in the Chelsea housing market, which is dominated by four- and five-star hotels. Three rooms share one spacious kitchen that has chairs, a table, a couch, and a fridge. The style is modern, the concept is simple, and the rates are low. Common rooms on each floor house a TV and the six RAs organize occasional events.

🚶 ⊖Sloane Sq. *Exit the Tube and go straight down Sloane Sq. The street slanting gently left is King's Rd. If you don't want to walk the road (it's manageable but long), the following buses service the area: #11, 19, 22, 211, 319, right on Manresa Rd.* ℹ *Laundry £2 for washer and £1.20 for soap, £1 dryer. No Wi-Fi, but ethernet in every room. Bathrooms cleaned once a week, kitchens cleaned twice a week. Bathrooms ensuite.* $ *1-16 weeks, weekly rates: singles £331-397; twin shared £207. Rates for 16-36 weeks and 36-50 weeks also available. Daily rates: single: £52.86, twin £58.75.* ⏰ *Security 24hr.*

CHELSEA CLOISTERS 💳🚭📶❄ SHORT STAY APARTMENTS ❸

Sloane Ave. ☎020 7584 1002 💻www.chelseacloisters.co.uk

Though a bit old and worn, Chelsea Cloisters offers a viable alternative to the high-cost hotels that might otherwise prohibit a stay in Chelsea. The rooms are clean and efficient, each with its own kitchen and bathroom. It's not the swankiest or brightest building, but the apartments are clean and serviceable. Check carefully what you're paying before you book, as there are a few compulsory charges (cleaning and deposit) not included in the rates. Because of the deposits, it might be wise to book only for very long stays or for stays under a week, in which case no deposit is needed.

🚶 ⊖Sloane Sq. *Exit the tube and go straight down Sloane Sq. The street slanting gently left is King's Rd., go onto it and turn right onto Sloane Ave.* ℹ *Luggage room. BT Openzone vouchers (for Wi-Fi) sold at the desk; £40 per month, £27 per 5 days, £10 per 24hr. Book at least a week in advance.* $ *Compulsory 5-day maid service and linen change £58.75 for a studio, £70.50 for 1 bed, £82.25 for 2 beds. 1-week prices: standard studio apartment £53; large studio apartment £590; 1-bedroom apartment £785. 2-bedroom apartments: double and single £1,025; double and twin £1,075. Deposit: studio £600; 1-bedroom £600; 2-bedroom £800.*

Kensington and Earl's Court

ASTOR HYDE PARK 💳🚭📶❄ HOSTEL ❶

191 Queen's Gate ☎020 7581 0103 💻www.astorhostels.co.uk

Built in the 1800s as a grand Victorian House, the Astor Hyde Park was also a hotel once upon a time. The flagship among Astor Hostels, the Hyde Park location is all high ceilings, aged grandeur, and comfort. The hostel is very close to beautiful Hyde Park. The six-floor hostel has no maximum stay, but it's not meant for long-term stays. Everything is cleaned twice a day, and the kitchen is cleaned three times daily. Careful, though—backpackers subject to delusions of grandeur could easily mistake the other residents for servants in their personal mansion. The hostel keeps some of that old grandeur in the teas with live music and the spacious common room.

🚶 ⊖High Street Kensington. *Turn right onto Kensington High St., then turn right onto Queen's Gate.* ℹ *Free linens; beds are made fresh daily. Laundry: washing machine £2.50, washing powder £1, dryer £1 per 40min. Lockers £1.50 per day, £7 per week. Free Wi-Fi. Coin-operated computers for those without laptops. Every room is ensuite, except 3- to 4-bed rooms, which still have private bathrooms.* $ *Winter prices around £15-20. Summer weekday dorm prices £20-£26; doubles £80 per night; twin £70. Weekend rates go up by £5 per dorm bed and £10 per double and twin.* ⏰ *Reception 24hr.*

YHA EARL'S COURT LONDON 💳🚭📶 HOSTEL ❷

38 Bolton Gdns. ☎020 7373 7083 💻www.yha.org.uk

In one of the pleasant in-between spaces of London which are central yet oddly removed, YHA Earl's Court London is a fairly spacious hostel which, despite its shared bathrooms, grants everyone their own space. Some of the rooms even have their own areas for storage. Frequented by families as well as backpackers, the hostel is welcoming and affordable.

🚶 ⊖West Brompton. *Turn right on Old Brompton Rd., left onto Earl's Ct. Rd., right onto Bolton Gardens.* ℹ *Continental breakfast £2.95. Linens are included; beds are made daily. Shared bathrooms.* $ *Laundry: washer, dryer, and detergent £4.50. Lockers in room, padlocks £3. Internet*

£5 per 24hr., £9 per week. Check ahead, but generally beds in single sex 4-, 6-, and 10-bed dorms £20-24.50.

Knightsbridge and Belgravia

MORGAN GUEST HOUSE
💳🚭📶❄ GUEST HOUSE ❷

120 Ebury St. ☎020 7730 2384 💻www.morganhouse.co.uk

This cozy guest house feels just like a home. Most rooms have a fireplace and all are clean and well decorated, occasionally decked out with chandeliers, huge mirrors, and fresh flowers. In the back, guests can enjoy a patio that's like the Secret Garden. For a pleasant budget stay in Belgravia, you could do worse than the Morgan Guest House.

⇄ ⊖Victoria. Turn left onto Buckingham Palace Rd. With your back to Buckingham Palace Rd., turn right onto Elizabeth, then left onto Ebury St. $ Singles £58; doubles £78, with bath £98; triples £98/138; quads with bath £148. ⏰ Breakfast M-F 7:30-9am, Sa-Su 8-10am.

West End

✎ FIELDING HOTEL
💳🚭📶 HOTEL ❸

4 Broad Court ☎020 7836 8305 💻www.thefieldinghotel.co.uk

Named after the novelist Henry Fielding, who worked next door at Bow St. Magistrate's Court where Oscar Wilde was later tried, the Fielding Hotel is located in pleasant Broad Court. A short walk from the Royal Opera House, the hotel is in one of the most exciting parts of town, but the Fielding doesn't use that as an excuse for poor rooms or exorbitant prices. Book a room at this comfortable, classy, well-located, and reasonably-priced hotel.

⇄ ⊖Covent Garden. Right onto Long Acre. Right onto Drury Ln. Right onto Broad Court. ℹ Book around a month in advance. $ Singles £90; doubles £115.00; superior twins/doubles £140.00, with sitting room £160; suite (sleeps 3) £200. Rates do not include VAT. Call ahead because rates change.

YHA OXFORD ST.
💳🚭📶🍸 HOSTEL ❶

14 Noel St. ☎020 7734 1618 💻oxford@yhalondon.org.uk

The big appeal of YHA Oxford St. is the location, with prime placement in the West End. There are prettier and friendlier accommodations in this city, but you can't complain about the price. Two washer-dryers service 76 beds, and the rooms begin on the third floor, with a battered lift as an alternative to the stairs; don't buy too much of the alcohol served behind reception, as you might not make it up.

⇄ ⊖Oxford Circus. Turn left down Regent St., left onto Noel St.. N13, N15, N18, N136, N159 available from the Oxford Circus Station Bus Stop. ℹ 7-night max. stay. Wi-Fi: £1 per 20min., £5 per 24hr., £9 per 7 days, available in the lounge and some of the rooms. £1.60 for washing, £.50 for a 15-20min. drying cycle. $ 3- to 4-bed dorms £23-32; doubles £56-76; triples £84-117. Alcohol served behind reception: Bottles of beer £2.10-2.75, Irish apple cider £3, Smirnoff Ice £2.85. ⏰ Alcohol served 10am-11:30pm.

Westminster

✎ ASTOR'S VICTORIA
💳🚭 HOSTEL ❸

71 Belgrave Rd. ☎020 7834 3077 💻www.hostelworld.com

A franchise in a chain, Astor's Victoria is especially popular with students. Rooms feel small and run-down but great to live in. Bathrooms are cleaned twice daily, and linens are changed daily. The walls are covered with friendly tips for travelers and low-cost (and specially discounted) outing opportunities. The staff hosts movie nights and pub crawls, and the hostel's excellent location only makes going out easier.

⇄ ⊖Victoria. Left onto Buckingham Palace Rd. Left on Belgrave Rd. ℹ Breakfast included. Storage available. Personal safes £1.50. Wi-Fi £1 for 40min., £5 for 24hr. Common room open until

1am. Check-in after 2pm and before 8am. Check-out by 10am. $ Prices for rooms range wildly; call well in advance. ⏰ Breakfast 8am-10am.

VICTOR HOTEL HOTEL [3]

51 Belgrave Rd. ☎020 7592 9853 🖥www.victorhotel.co.uk

A basic, clean, and—depending on the day—cheap hotel, the Victor is one of the many townhouse establishments lining Belgrave Rd. Boasting a convenient location near the heart of Westminster, the Victor provides well-kept rooms that, while not large, are not nearly as cramped as those of some of the hotels on the same street.

➜ ⊖Victoria. Left onto Buckingham Palace Rd. Left onto Belgrave Rd. i All rooms have an ensuite bathroom. All room prices subject to change based on dates, season, and local events, so check online. $ Doubles M-F £75-85, Sa-Su up to £95. ⏰ Reception 24hrs.

Notting Hill

Notting Hill isn't an ideal place to find budget accommodations—although there are many beautiful residences, travelers short on funds aren't welcome to stay in many of them. Prices hover around £80-120 for doubles. Nearby Bayswater is a much better bet for the penny-pinching traveler.

BOWDEN COURT HOSTEL [2]

24 Ladbroke Rd. ☎020 7727 5665 🖥www.lhalondon.com

This four-floor hostel is just about the only budget-friendly option for people looking to stay in Notting Hill, but luckily, it's close to all the action. In the basement lies a clean and spacious dining room. The food is decent but not terribly healthy. Also in the basement are a laundry room, study room with computers, and TV room. Bathrooms are communal.

➜ ⊖Notting Hill Gate. Exit north, take a right onto Pembridge Rd., and turn left onto Ladbroke Rd. i Lockers £1 per day, £3.50 per week, £10 per month. Washers £3; dryers £1. $ 2-bed dorms £25; 3-bed £23.50. Singles £28-29; doubles £52.00. Weekly 2-bed dorms £114; 3-beds £94.50. Weekly singles £159.50-179.50; doubles £250. ⏰ Breakfast M-F 7am-8:15am; Sa-Su and bank holidays 9:30-10:30am. Dinner M-F 6:30-8pm. Lunch Sa-Su and bank holidays 12:30-1:30pm.

SIGHTS

From the hints of the city's Roman past at the London Wall to the memories of WWII or the unforgettable Great Fire of London, London's long past has not only been documented in stone but also in its art scene, from the masterworks in the West End's National Gallery and the Tate Modern to the cutting edge galleries of Chelsea and the South Bank. And not to worry—this artistic splendor is totally accessible to travelers on a budget, especially those who carry their student IDs. When trying to see a church, look for service times, as you can frequently get in free during masses, Evensong, etc. If you can't afford to visit all of the sights individually, buy a ticket up to the top of St. Paul's—the view from the Golden Gallery is magnificent and the cathedral itself is worth every pence.

Bayswater

SPEAKERS' CORNER HISTORICAL SITE, PERFORMANCE SPACE

Hyde Park, Park Lane. London. W1K 1QB

This innocuous corner of Hyde Park is the stage for political, religious, and social debates. Speakers present ideas, challenge each other, and take questions from the audience. There are no set hours, and anyone is welcome to speak. Come watch free speech in action!

➜ ⊖Lancaster Gate. Take left onto Bayswater Rd. Go in through Victoria Gate and continue left down Hyde Park. Stay close to Bayswater Rd. $ Free. ⏰ Hours vary, but can be 9am-10pm in summer.

Bloomsbury

THE BRITISH MUSEUM

Great Russell Street. ☎020 7323 8299 ▣www.british-museum.org

🚌& MUSEUM

The funny thing about the British Museum is that there's almost nothing British in it. Founded in 1753 as the personal collection of Sir Hans Sloane, the museum juxtaposes Victorian Anglocentricism with more modern, multicultural acceptance. The building itself, in all its Neoclassical splendor, is magnificent; a leisurely stroll through the less crowded galleries is well worth an afternoon visit. The many visitors who don't make it past the main floor miss out—the galleries above and below are some of the museum's best, if not most famous.

The **Great Court** is the largest covered square in Europe, and has been used as the **British Library** stacks for the past 150 years. The blue chairs and desks of the **Reading Room,** set inside a towering dome of books, have shouldered the weight of research by Marx, Lenin, and Trotsky, as well as almost every major British writer and intellectual—and minor ones as well! From the main entrance, the large double doors to the left of the Reading Room lead to the Museum's most popular wing, the **West Galleries.** The **Rosetta Stone** takes center stage in the **Egyptian sculpture** rooms, while the less iconic but enduringly huge monumental friezes and reliefs of the Assyrian, Hittite, and other Ancient Near East civilizations are worth more than a glance. Most famous (and controversial) of the massive array of Greek sculptures on display are the **Elgin Marbles** from the Parthenon, statues carved under the direction of Athens's greatest sculptor, Phidias (Room 18). The Greek government technically bought the Marbles (albeit for a measly price). Other Hellenic highlights include remnants of two of the seven Wonders of the Ancient World: the **Temple of Artemis** at Ephesus and the **Mausoleum of Halikarnassos** (Rooms 21-22).

Upstairs, the **Portland Vase** presides over Roman ceramics and house wares (Room 70). When discovered in 1582, the vase had already been broken and reconstructed, and in 1845, it was shattered again by a drunk museum-goer. When it was put back together, 37 small chips were left over; two reconstructions have reincorporated more and more leftover chips, though some are still missing from the vase. Egyptian sarcophagi and mummies await in the **North Galleries** (rooms 61-66). The newer **African Galleries** display a fabulous collection accompanied by soft chanting, video displays, and abundant documentation (Room 25, lower floor). In Rooms 51-59, musical instruments and board games from the world's first city, Ur, show that leisure time is a historical constant, while Mexico dominates the **Americas** collection with extraordinary Aztec artifacts (Rooms 26-27). **Islamic** art resides in Room 34, and above it, the largest room in the museum holds **Chinese, South Asian,** and **Southeast Asian** artifacts alongside some particularly impressive Hindu sculpture (Room 33). The highlight of the Korean display, in Room 67, is a *sarangbang* house built on-site, while a tea house is the centerpiece of the **Japanese** galleries (Rooms 92-94).

In the **South and East Galleries,** the **King's Library** gallery holds artifacts gathered from throughout the world by English explorers during the **Enlightenment.** While the labeling is poor (and in some places nonexistent), the collection itself is spectacular. The upper level of the museum's southeast corner is dedicated to ancient and medieval Europe, and includes most of the museum's British artifacts. A highlight of the collection is the treasure excavated from the **Sutton Hoo Burial Ship;** the magnificent inlaid helmet is the most famous example of Anglo-Saxon craftsmanship. Along with the ship is the **Mildenhall Treasure,** a trove of brilliantly preserved Roman artifacts (Room 41). Next door are the enigmatic and beautiful **Lewis Chessmen,** an 800-year-old Scandinavian chess set mysteriously abandoned on Scotland's Outer Hebrides (Room 42). Collectors and enthusiasts will also enjoy the comprehensive **Clocks and Watches Gallery** (Rooms 38-39) and **Money Gallery** (Room 68).

🚇 Tottenham Court Rd., Russell Square, or Holborn. ℹ Tours by request. $ Free. Small suggested donation. Prices for events and exhibitions vary. ⏰ Museum open daily 10am-5:30pm. Select exhibitions and displays open Th and F until 8:30pm. Paul Hamlyn Library open M-W 10am-5:30pm, Th 10am-8:30pm, F noon-8:30pm, Sa 10am-7:30pm.

THE BRITISH LIBRARY ♿ LIBRARY

96 Euston Rd. ☎020 7412 7676 💻www.bl.uk

Castigated during its long construction by traditionalists for being too modern and by moderns for being too traditional, the new British Library building (opened in 1998) now impresses all nay-sayers with its stunning interior. The 65,000 volumes of the King's Library, collected by George III and bequeathed to the nation in 1823 by his less bookish son, George IV, are displayed in a glass cube toward the rear. The sunken plaza out front features an enormous and somewhat strange statue of Newton, and also hosts a series of free concerts and events. The heart of the library is underground, with 12 million books on 200 miles of shelving; the above-ground brick building is home to cavernous reading rooms and an engrossing museum. In the **Literature Corner** of the museum, find **Shakespeare's** first folio, **Lewis Carroll's** handwritten manuscript of *Alice in Wonderland* (donated by Alice herself), and **Virginia Woolf's** handwritten notes to *Mrs. Dalloway* (then called *The Hours*). Music-lovers visiting the museum will appreciate **Handel's** handwritten *Messiah*, **Mozart's** marriage contract, **Beethoven's** tuning fork, and a whole display dedicated to the **Beatles,** including the original handwritten lyrics to "A Hard Day's Night"—scrawled on the back of Lennon's son Julian's first birthday card. In the museum, the original copy of the **Magna Carta** has its own room with accompanying Papal Bull that Pope Innocent III wrote in response. **Leonardo da Vinci's** notebooks are in the **Science** section, while one of 50 known **Gutenberg Bibles** is in the **Printing** section.

🚇 Euston Sq. or King's Cross St. Pancras. ℹ Free Wi-Fi. To register for use of reading room, bring 2 forms of ID–1 with a signature and 1 with a home address. ⏰ Open M 9:30am-6pm, Tu 9:30am-8pm, W-F 9:30am-6pm, Sa 9:30am-5pm, Su 11am-5pm. Group tours (up to 15 people) Tu and Th at 10:30am and 2:30pm, £85 per group; call ☎ 020 7412 7639 to book. Individual tours M, W, and F 11am, free; booking recommended; call ☎ 019 3754 6546 to book.

great britain

Chelsea

✓ SAATCHI ART GALLERY ♿ ART GALLERY

Duke of York Sq. ☎020 7811 3085 💻www.saatchigallery.co.uk

It's rare to find a free gallery of this caliber. The rooms are cavernous and bright, providing ample space for each installation. The gallery focuses on contemporary art, all taken from Charles Saatchi's collection. If you see something you really like, be sure to check out the shop where many of the works are condensed into pocket-sized forms. There are 3-4 shows a year, and the pieces run the gamut from paintings, to sculptures, to really frightening installations of plaster people hunched in corners. If you really want to experience the Saatchi Gallery, stand next to one of the wax/plaster humanoid sculptures and argue with it. Sure, it's weird, but is it art?

🚇 Sloane Sq. Go straight once out of the tube and continue onto King's Rd. $ Free as the wind. ⏰ Open M-F 10am-5:50pm, Su-Sa 10am-5:45pm.

CHELSEA PHYSIC GARDENS 🍴♿ BOTANICAL GARDENS

66 Royal Hospital Rd. ☎020 7352 5646 💻www.chelseaphysicgarden.co.uk

The physic gardens are some of the oldest botanic gardens in Europe. Established in 1673 by a society of apothecaries, the gardens contain pharmaceutical and perfumery plant beds, tropical plant greenhouses, Europe's oldest rock garden, and a total of 5000 different plants. The garden was also important to the establishment of the tea industry in India, but apart from that, they're simply beautiful, peaceful, and well worth a visit.

⊖Sloane Sq. Left onto Lower Sloane St.; right onto Royal Hospital Rd. [i] Call ahead to arrange wheelchair-accessible visits. Free guided tours, depending on availability of guides. [$] £8; children, students, and the unemployed £5; under 5 free. ⏰ Open Apr 1-Oct 31 W-F noon-5pm, Su noon-6pm.

Holborn and Clerkenwell

THE TEMPLE

♿ SIGHT

Between Essex St. and Temple Ave. ☎020 7427 4820 🖳www.templechurch.com, 🖳www.middletemple.org.uk

The Temple was a complex of buildings established by the Knights Templar, catapulted into stardom by *The Da Vinci Code*. Established as the English seat for the order in 1185, the buildings were leased to lawyers after the order ended in 1307, and the site is now devoted to legal and parliamentary offices. The medieval church, gardens, and Middle Temple Hall are open to the public. The 1681 Fountain Court is a place for peaceful reflection and was featured in Dickens's *Martin Chizzlewit*. Also beautiful is Elm Court, the small garden enclosed by stone structures. Originally used as a stable for the Knights Templar, Middle Temple Hall became a bit more distinguished later when Shakespeare acted in the premiere of *Twelfth Night* there.

⊖Temple. Go to the Victoria Embankment, turn left and turn left at Temple Ln. [i] 1hr. tours Tu-F at 11am (but not in Aug and Sept when the church is closed); book tours ahead of time. You can book to stay for lunch if you are appropriately dressed. [$] Church and tours free. ⏰ Middle Temple Hall open M-F 10am-noon and 3-4pm, except when in use. Su service 11:15am. Hours for church vary, but are posted oustide. Organ recitals W 1:15-1:45pm. No services in Aug and Sept.

ROYAL COURTS OF JUSTICE

♿ HISTORICAL SITE

Where Strand becomes Fleet St. ☎020 7947 7684

This stunning Neo-Gothic structure was designed by G.E. Street and was opened by Queen Victoria on December 4, 1882. It is home to more than 1000 rooms, and 3.5 mi. of corridor. Justice had better be pretty swift with all the walking it takes to get anywhere in this building. Supposedly, a tributary of the Fleet River, the namesake of Fleet St., runs beneath the building. It is also famous for its large and beautiful mosaic. Guests can sit in the back two rows of the court rooms and listen to the proceedings if court is in session. Order!

⊖Temple. Right onto Temple Pl., left onto Arundel st., right onto Strand. [i] There is a sign with wheelchair accessibility and routes in the entrance to the main building off the Strand. [$] Tours (usually on 1st and 3rd Tu of every month) £10; should be booked in advance. ⏰ Open M-F 9am-4:30pm.

Kensington and Earl's Court

VICTORIA AND ALBERT MUSEUM

♿ GALLERY MUSEUM

Cromwell Rd. ☎020 7942 2000 🖳www.vam.ac.uk

The V and A is one of the most bizarre and all-encompassing museums out there. Originally founded because the director, Henry Cole, wanted to promote different design ideas to the British public, the V and A has examples of styles from all around the world and is as much about the making of things as it is about the artifacts themselves. The many galleries include **Asia, Europe, The British Galleries, Modern,** and **The Fashion Gallery.** With such specific topics, who could possibly be interested in the collections? The **Asia** gallery features everything from ornate, gold Buddhist shrines to traditional suits of armor. Especially popular is the beautiful Iranian Ardabil Carpet, which is lit for 10min. every hour. The **Europe** gallery features the gorgeous Hereford Screen, which is 11m long and 10.5m

london · sights

high, and depicts Christ's Ascension. The British Galleries showcase the ever-popular Great Bed of Ware, which, for a bed, was a remarkably big deal back in 1596 when the first mention of it was made.

South Kensington. Take a right onto Thurloe Pl. and turn left on Exhibition Rd. The museum is to your right across Cromwell Rd. i Wheelchair-accessible guides available at the Grand Entrance Information Desk. Exhibit on "Diaghileu and the Golden Age of the Ballets Russes 1909-1929" from Sept 25 to Jan 9. $ Free, with the exception of the special exhibitions, which are generally £6-£10. Open M-Th 10am-5:45pm, F 10am-10pm, Sa-Su 10am-5:45pm. National Art Library Tu-Th 10am-5:30pm, F 10am-6:30pm, Sa 10am-5:30pm. Free daily tours available; look at screens in entrances for times.

SCIENCE MUSEUM

♿ MUSEUM

Exhibition Rd., South Kensington ☎087 0870 4868 www.sciencemuseum.org.uk

The Science Museum is an exciting look at the history and cutting edge of the discipline. Featuring tons of cool, interactive displays (granted, many of these are directed at children), the Science Museum has myriad valuable and historic artifacts from all areas of science; including many that you won't even realize you wanted to see until you've seen them. A Newcomen-type atmospheric engine dwarfs its surroundings in the Energy Gallery, and the space galleries remind visitors of all ages of the excitement of space travel through their history of rockets and artifacts like a V2 Engine from 1944, and things like wrist watches used on the Apollo missions. Learn about Charles Babbage English, the man responsible for mechanical calculators and shoes for walking on water (conspiracy theorists will be disappointed once reminded that he lived long after Jesus). And if you were wondering what an inventor's brain looks like (we hope this isn't on your mind), they have one in a **jar!**

South Kensington. Take a right onto Thurloe Pl. and turn left onto Exhibition Rd. The museum is to your left just past the Natural History Museum. i A climate change exhibit will open in Nov. The museum also features a popular IMAX cinema. $ Tickets to IMAX 3D shows £8, children £6.25. Concession £6.25. Open daily 10:00am-6:0pm. Last admission at 5:30pm, but it starts closing at 5:40pm.

SAINT MARY ABBOTS

♿ CHURCH

High St. Kensington ☎020 7937 5136 www.stmaryabbotschurch.org

This gorgeous and silent church sits on a site where Christians have worshipped for 1000 years. Designed in 1873 by a famous Victorian architect, Sir George Gilbert, the church is known for its beautiful and simple stained glass by Clayton and Bell and the scorch marks of the 1944 bombing that are visible in the pews. Fridays from 1-2pm musicians from the Royal Academy of Music perform for free.

High St. Kensington. Right onto Kensington High St., left onto Kensington Church St. M 8:30am-6pm, Tu 8:30am-6pm, W-F 7:10am-6pm, Sa 9:40am-6pm, Su 8am-6pm.

Knightsbridge and Belgravia

APSLEY HOUSE

HISTORICAL SITE, MUSEUM GALLERY

Hyde Park Corner ☎020 7499 5676 www.english-heritage.org.uk

Named for Baron Apsley, the house later known as "No.1, London" was bought in 1817 by the Duke of Wellington, whose heirs still occupy a modest suite on the top floor. The house is a stunning architectural triumph, from the gilded mirrors to the gilded oval spiral staircase. Perhaps the most fantastic of all the valuable collections in the house is Wellington's art collection, much of which he received from monarchs around Europe after the Battle of Waterloo. One of the most sought after pieces is Velazquez's beautiful *The Water-Seller of Seville*, which he painted in 1600. Throughout the house you can find various trinkets, such as a silver-gilt dessert plate bearing Napoleon's arms, the key to the city of Pamplona (granted after the Duke captured the city), the death masks of Wellington and Napoleon, and a stunning 6.7m Egyptian service set, given by Napoleon to Josephine as a divorce present. Scholars maintain that the dessert service was meant as a mean joke about Josephine's weight. It's huge.

*➜ ⊖Hyde Park Corner. **i** Arch is wheelchair-accessible; house is not. Complimentary audio tours. June 18th is Wellington Day, so check for special events. $ £6, joint ticket with Wellington Arch £7.40; concessions £5.10, concession joint with Wellington Arch £6.30; children £3, joint £3.70; family joint £18.50. ⏰ Open W-Su Apr-Oct 11am-5pm; Nov-Mar 11am-4pm. Last entry 30min. before closing.*

👍 SERPENTINE BOATING LAKE — 🎟♿ LAKE BOATING

Hyde Park — ☎020 7262 1330 💻www.theboathouselondon.co.uk

Created in memory of Queen Caroline between 1727 and 1731, the Serpentine Boating Lake is one of the most beautiful parts of Hyde Park. Rented boats drift lazily across the placid waters as fat waterfowl battle it out on the shore for pieces of bread. Boats can be rented and taken out for any amount of time. Be sure to check out the nearby Rose Garden.

➜ ⊖Hyde Park Corner. Hyde Park. $ Pedal boats and row boats £7 per person per 30min., £9 per person per hr. ⏰ Open daily 10am-6pm (earlier in low season). Stays open later depending on weather. Boats don't go out if it's raining. Closed in Dec.

Marylebone and Regent's Park

👍 THE REGENT'S PARK — 🎟⛅ PARK

Regent's Park — ☎020 7486 7905 💻www.royalparks.org.uk

In 1811, the Prince Regent commissioned the parks as private gardens, and hired **John Nash** to design them. However, in 1841, the parks were opened to the public, and the city lives all the better for it. Locals, pigeons, thirty couples of herons, and tourists alike frolic among the 10,000 wild flowers and 50 acres of pitches and courts. **Queen Mary's Garden** houses the national collection of delphiniums as well as a gorgeous collection of 30,000 roses. It is also home to an interesting strain of pink flower known as 👍**Sexy Rexy.** The park's popular open-air theater is the setting for all kinds of shows, the screams from the more dramatic performances intermingling with those of children deprived too long of 🍦**ice cream.**

*➜ ⊖Regent's Park. **i** Call ☎020 7486 8117 for information on the deck chairs. Book plays through 💻www.openairtheatre.com. $ Deck chair £1.50 per hr., £4 per 3hr., £7 per 1 day. Boats £6.50 per 1hr., £4.85 per 1½hr. ⏰ Park open daily 5am-dusk. Boating lake open Mar-Oct 10:30am-7pm.*

👍 THE WALLACE COLLECTION — ♿ GALLERY

Manchester Sq. — ☎030 7563 9552 💻www.wallacecollection.org

Housed in the palatial **Hereford House,** the Wallace Collection features an array of paintings, porcelain, and armor collected by over five generations of the Wallace family and bequeathed to the nation by **Sir Richard Wallace** in 1897. The mansion's stunning collection is rendered even more dazzling by its grand gilded setting.

*➜ ⊖Marble Arch. Left onto Oxford St., left on Duke St., right onto Manchester Sq. **i** Private tours W, Sa, Su 11:30am and 3pm; call for details. $ Gallery free. Suggested donation £5. Audio tours £4. ⏰ Open daily 10am-5pm.*

The City of London

Most stereotypical "London" sights are located here and can't be missed—even if having a camera slung around your neck is practically required for entrance.

👍 SAINT PAUL'S CATHEDRAL — 🎟♿ CHURCH

St. Paul's Churchyard — ☎020 7246 8350 💻www.stpauls.co.uk

Entering Saint Paul's Cathedral and not taking the Lord's name in vain is a challenge. Like many churches in the area, Saint Paul's was destroyed in the Great Fire of London. Christopher Wren's masterpiece is the fourth cathedral on the site, with the first building dating to 604 CE. From the start, Wren wanted to include the fantastic dome that is now visible throughout London, but the Church of England was hesitant to include a piece of architecture that was characteristically Roman Catholic. Ultimately, Wren won.

INTERIOR. The first thing you see upon entering the Cathedral is the nave. The baptismal font stands next to an elaborately designed wax candle in the south part of the nave. If you can pull your eyes away from the dome, which was painted by Sir James Thornhill, look out for the terrifyingly huge memorial to the **Duke of Wellington** (on your left in the north aisle as you walk through the nave) and William Holman Hunt's *The Light of the World* which can be found in the Middlesex Chapel, a chapel set aside for private prayer dedicated to the members of the Middlesex regimen of the British army.

SCALING THE HEIGHTS. We know what you're thinking—yes, you are allowed to climb to the top of the dome. After 257 short, dizzyingly tight wooden steps, guests find the Whispering Gallery, a seating area around the inner ring of the dome where, under the right conditions, you can whisper and be heard on the other side. Many people try this at the same time, which makes standing at the rim of Wren's magnificent dome feel a bit like one of the scarier whisper segments in *Lost*, but it's worth giving this acoustic novelty a try. The experience of climbing to the top is greatly enhanced if you make the journey while a choir sings in the nave; the acoustics in the Whispering Gallery are incredible. After 376 steps, visitors can climb out onto the Stone Gallery which is open-air, low-stress, and thoroughly enjoyable. Then it's another 152 steps to the Golden Gallery, an open-air, super high look out onto the city. The army used this gallery in the second World War to spot enemy planes coming from up to 10 miles away. The only drawback is that you can't see the grandeur of St. Paul's itself.

PLUMBING THE DEPTHS. A veritable who's who of famous Britons reside in the loins of St. Paul's. Descend beneath the cathedral to find the tombs and memorials of **Captain John Cooke, Horatio Nelson, Florence Nightingale, the Duke of Wellington** (whose massive tomb is footed by sleeping stone lions), **William Blake, Henry Moore,** and finally **Christopher Wren.** Wren's inconspicuous tomb (to the right of the OBE Chapel) is inscribed *"Lector, si monumentum requiris circumspice"* which translates to "Reader, if you seek his monument, look around." Saint Paul's Cathedral is jaw-droppingly magnificent; there could be no better monument to its visionary architect than the simple words etched on his tomb.

*🚉 ⊖St. Paul's. There are signs outside the station that will lead you to the Cathedral. **i** Guided tours are 1½hr., and they occur at 10:45am, 11:15am, 1:30pm, and 2pm. £3, children £1. A free multimedia tour will be provided starting mid-July to early Sept 2010. Audio tours available in 8 languages including English (adults £4). $ Adults £12.50, students £9.50, seniors £11, children £4.50; family (2 adults, 2 kids) £29.50; group rates (10+) adults £11.50, students £8.50, seniors £10.50, children £4. 🕐 M-Sa 8:30am-4pm (last ticket sold). Least crowded early in the day. Get in for free (though you'll have limited access) at one of the church services; 7:30am is Mattins, 8am is the Holy Communion, 12:30pm is the Holy Communion, 5pm is Evensong. Free Organ Recitals every Su from 4:45-5:15pm.*

👍 MUSEUM OF LONDON ♿ MUSEUM

By the London Wall (London EC27 5HN) ☎020 7001 9844 💻www.museumoflondon.org.uk

The Museum of London is an exhaustive celebration of the city, tracing its history from the pre-Roman days, through the fall of that empire (too bad the city's no longer known as Londinium), up to the present through a series of timelines, walk-in exhibits, and artifacts. Among the fascinating pieces of history on display are a walk-in replica of a London Saxon house from the mid-1000s, a beautiful model of the original St. Paul's cathedral, a taxi from 1908, and Beatlemania paraphernalia. Relatively compact for its sheer scope, the Museum of London yields tremendous bang for your buck, especially because it's free!

➜ ⊖St. Pauls. Go up St. Martins and Aldersgate. ℹ 45min. tours at 11am, noon, 3pm, and 4pm. $ Free. ⏰ Open M-F 10am-6pm.

👍 POTTERS FIELDS PARK ♿ PARK

Tooley St. towards Tower Bridge ☎020 7407 4702 💻pottersfields.co.uk

Providing wide patches of grass for denizens of the park to stretch out on, as well as breathtaking views of Tower Bridge and the Thames, Potters Fields Park is an oasis in such a busy city. It's at the heart of London, but far removed from its bustle. City Hall sits within the park and is just as architecturally magnificent as Tower Bridge. After seeing the park, you may want to check out more of the waterfront and do some shopping in **Hay's Galleria**. Also, be sure to notice the **HMS Belfast,** which is just down the river from the park; a ticket is required to board the vessel.

➜ ⊖London Bridge. Walk down Tooley St. towards Tower Bridge. Go through Hay's Galleria and walk along the river towards Tower Bridge. $ Free.

TOWER BRIDGE 💳♿ BRIDGE

Tower Bridge ☎020 7403 3761 💻www.towerbridge.org.uk

If Fergie had gone to the Tower Bridge exhibition, she would have known that bascule bridges come down more often than London Bridge. Built between 1886 and 1894, Tower Bridge was created because London Bridge had become too crowded. It is a bascule bridge, meaning that, if you're lucky, you'll get to see it rise (and then come down). The exhibition is enjoyable, though if you're afraid of heights, it might not be for you. Hear fun facts about the bridge as well as enchanting anecdotes such as the story of a 1952 double-decker bus that accidentally jumped the bridge while it was rising—clearly the driver never heard the phrase "Mind the gap."

➜ ⊖Tower Hill. Follow signs to Tower Bridge. $ £7, ages 5-15 £3, under 5 free; concessions £5; 1 adult and 2 children £11; 2 adults and 1 child £14; 2 adults and 2 children £16; 2 adults and 3-4 children £18. ⏰ April 1-Sept 30 open 10am-5:30pm daily; Oct 1-Mar 31 open 9:30am-5pm daily.

TOWER OF LONDON HISTORICAL SITE

Between Tower Hill and the Thames ☎084 4482 7777 💻www.hrp.org.uk/toweroflondon

In its 1,000-year history, the Tower of London has been a fortress, a royal palace, a prison, a zoo, a mint, the house of the first royal observatory, and a tourist trap. If tourists were an invading army back in the day of William the Conqueror, he would have surrendered instantly. The Tower has tours led by "Beefeaters," the men and women who guard and live within the tower.

➜ ⊖Tower Hill. ℹ Buy tickets at the metro stop or at the Welcome Center, as these places tend to be less crowded. $ £17; student, senior, and disabled £14.50; under 5 free; family (1-2 adults and up to 6 kids) £47. Audio tours available in 9 different languages; £4, students £3. An individual Membership gives you unlimited, year round access to all the Royal Palaces for £41, with a family membership available for £80. Portions of the site wheelchair-accessible. ⏰ Mar-Oct: M 10am-5:30pm, Tu-Su 9am-5:30pm, last ticket sold at 5pm. Nov-Feb: M-Tu and Su 10am-4:30pm, W-Sa 9am-5:30pm, last entry sold at 4pm. Cafe: Tu-Sa 9:30am-5pm, Su-M 10:30am-5pm. Ceremony of the Keys 9:30pm.

THE MONUMENT 🚫💳🚫♿ HISTORICAL SITE

Monument ☎020 7626 2717 💻www.themonument.info

Built between 1671 and 1677, the Monument stands in memory of the Great Fire of London that burned most of the city in 1666. At 202ft. tall, with an inner shaft containing 311 stairs that must be climbed in order to reach the breathtaking open-air top floor, the Monument is what your Stairmaster would look like in the pre-mechanical age. If you were to lay the tower on its side pointing in a certain direction, it would land on the spot where the fire started. It would also

cause mass hysteria. It is the only non-ecclesiastical Christopher Wren building, though some scholars maintain that it was built to worship 👍**rock hard thighs.**
➔ ⊖Monument. Get off the Tube and it will be directly in front of you as you exit the station. $ £3, children £1; concessions £2. Combined tickets are available with the Tower Bridge exhibition. Combined prices: £8, children £3.50; concessions £5.50. 🕒 Open 7 days a week, 9:30am-5pm. Closed on Christmas and Boxing Day.

The South Bank

👍 IMPERIAL WAR MUSEUM ♿ MUSEUM
Lambeth Rd. ☎020 7416 5000 🖥www.iwm.org.uk

Housed in what used to be the infamous Bedlam insane asylum, the Imperial War Museum is mad for history. The exhibits start out right with two massive naval guns guarding the entrance to the imposing building. The first room is cluttered with enough devices of war to make any general salivate. Highlights include a **Polaris A3 Missile,** the first submarine-launched missile, a full-size **German V2 Rocket,** and the shell (not the inner mechanisms, luckily) of a **"Little Boy,"** the type of bomb detonated above Hiroshima. The bomb is non-functional, but it gets unnerving when kids whack the casing. The third floor houses the expansive **Holocaust Exhibition.** This haunting exhibit traces the catastrophic injustice of WWII Nazi atrocities with cartographic precision and deep feeling, with miles of film exploring everything from the rhetoric of the Nazi party to a history of anti-Semitism. Of course, many visitors may feel like a visit to a museum would be unbalanced with only such light subject matter, and they'll take solace in the **Crimes Against Humanity** exhibition one floor down.
➔ ⊖Elephant and Castle. Turn right onto Elephant and Castle (roundabout), right onto St. George's Rd., and then left onto Lambeth Rd. $ Free. Special exhibits £5, students £4. Multimedia guides available in English £3.50. 🕒 Open daily 10am-6pm. The Blitz Experience daily schedule is downstairs. It lasts around 10min.

👍 TATE MODERN 💳♿ GALLERY
53 Bankside ☎020 7887 8008 🖥www.tate.org.uk

Located in George Gilbert Scott's Brutalist old Bankside Power Station, Tate Modern defies traditional organizational methods, opting out of the chronological in favor of thematic organization. The permanent collection rotates through two floors. Those desperate to see one work in particular should check out the computers on the fifth floor, which enable users to scan through the entire collection.

Level 3 houses the **Material Gestures** gallery, which focuses mainly on postwar European and American art and showcases works by Monet, Francis Bacon and **Anish Kapoor.** Sculptures by Giacometti can also be found here. **Poetry and Dream,** an area centering on Surrealism and its associated themes, displays the work of **Dali** and **Picasso** among others.

On Level 5, **Energy and Process** looks at Arte Povera, the movement from the 1970s that used everyday materials and natural laws to create art. **States of Flux** focuses on cubism and futurism among other important modern movements, displaying the works of **Roy Lichtenstein, Robert Frank, Warhol,** and **Duchamp,** among others.
➔ ⊖Southwark. Left onto Blackfriars Rd. Right onto Southwark St., left onto Sumner, left onto Holland St. $ Free. Multimedia guide available in English, £3.50, concessions £3. 🕒 Open M-Th 10am-6pm, F-Sa 10am-10pm, Su 10am-6pm. Free 10min. talks are given around the various galleries. Check schedule signs for details.

THE LONDON EYE 💳♿ ATTRACTION
Minister Court ☎087 0990 8881 🖥www.londoneye.com

Also known as the **Millennium Wheel,** the 📷**London Eye** is one of the most popular tourist attractions in London. The massive Ferris wheel takes visitors on a 30min. ride, giving them unparalleled arial views of London. An exciting 4D movie experience opens the entire trip which, while gimmicky, is worth it.

🚏 ⊖Westminster. Cross the bridge heading toward the Eye. $ £17.95, ages 4-15 £9.50, under 4 free, seniors and disabled £14.30. Savings of 10% if you book online. ⏰ Hours vary. Call or check the website. In general, Oct-Mar 10am-8pm; Apr 10am-9pm; May-July M-Th 10am-9pm; F-Sa 10am-9:30pm; Su 10am-9pm; July-Aug 10am-9:30pm; Sept 10am-9pm.

The West End

THE NATIONAL GALLERY — 🎧♿ GALLERY

Trafalgar Sq. ☎020 7747 2885 💻www.nationalgallery.org.uk

The National Gallery presides over **Trafalgar Square** and is nearly as impressive as the Square itself. Founded in 1824 and moved to its current location in 1838, the gallery encompasses all the major traditions of Western European art. The more recent **Sainsbury Wing** was opened in 1991, and it encompasses the 13th through 15th centuries. Often, visitors are in such a hurry to see the master works, that they traverse the main steps without looking at the floor. They are ignoring one of the most impressive artworks in the gallery, Boris Anrep's mosaics. The first landing depicts the awakening of the muses, the top landing depicts the modern virtues such as compassion, humor, open-mindedness, pursuit, wonder, and curiosity, all of which will be evoked in a thorough viewing of the gallery. The **West Vestibule** ponders art, astronomy, commerce, music and sacred love among others, for a start, while the **East** celebrates the pleasures of life (Christmas pudding, conversation, cricket, mud pie, profane love, speed). Ask for the pamphlet on the mosaics at the front desk for more details!

🚏 ⊖Charing Cross. $ Free. Audio tours in English £3.50, students £2.50. Maps £1 and are well worth the purchase as the gallery is huge. Special exhibits cost around £10 on average. ⏰ Open M-Th 10am-6pm, F 10am-9pm, Sa-Su 10am-6pm.

TRAFALGAR SQUARE — ♿ HISTORICAL SITE

Trafalgar Square

People flock to Trafalgar Square like pigeons in Hyde Park to bread, and if you're homesick for your native tongue, you'll likely hear it here (yes, American English counts). Designed by Sir Charles Barry, who also designed the Houses of Parliament, Trafalgar Square commemorates Admiral **Horatio Viscount Nelson's** heroic naval victory at the Battle of Trafalgar. The Square serves as a gathering point and has hosted national celebrations and rallies of all sorts. The square is bordered by institutions from many different countries such as the New Zealand House, Uganda House, Canada House, and South Africa House.

✈ ⊖ *Charing Cross.*

NATIONAL PORTRAIT GALLERY
St. Martin's Pl.

☚👣 GALLERY
☎020 7306 0055 🖳www.npg.org.uk

In London, it's easy to get lost in history. You have to remember names of monarchs, gossip stars, the insanely wealthy, the star-crossed lovers—and we haven't even talked about those outside of the royal family. The National Portrait Gallery is less about the art of the portraits themselves than it is about the people behind the portraits and what they meant for England. In fact, the gallery presents excellent short histories of the subjects and organizes them by room in such a way as to trace British history through its greatest asset—its people.

✈ ⊖ *Charing Cross. Walk down Strand to Trafalgar Square and turn right along the square.* ⓢ *Tickets for small special exhibits £5, tickets for large exhibitions £10. Audio tour in English £3.* ⏰ *Open M-W 10am-6pm, Th-F 10am-9pm, Sa-Su 10am-6pm. Guided tours Tu at 3pm, Th at 1:15pm, Sa-Su at 3pm (departing from main room). Certain scheduled nights open until 10pm.*

Westminster

🔖 WESTMINSTER ABBEY
Off Parliament Sq.

☚👣 ABBEY, HISTORICAL SITE
☎020 7222 5152 🖳www.westminster-abbey.org

Founded in 960CE, Westminster Abbey became the royals' church after the crowning of William the Conqueror in 1066. Nearly every monarch since William has been crowned here. Henry III built the modern abbey, but Edward the Confessor built the first church on the site. Inside the abbey, you can see the high altar where kings and queens are crowned and where coffins are displayed during funerals. Especially impressive is the statue of Lord and Lady Norris in the north chapel. Sunlight floods the Lady Chapel during the day, and it's a sight worth seeing. In the Poets' Corner rests the tomb of Chaucer as well as monuments to W.H. Auden, George Eliot, Dylan Thomas, D. H. Lawrence, Lord Byron, Alfred Lord Tennyson, Lewis Carroll, Jane Austen, Charles Dickens, William Shakespeare, and Laurence Olivier.

✈ ⊖ *Westminster. Walk down Westminster Bridge away from the water on the side of the Westminster tube stop. Parliament Square and the abbey will be on your left.* 𝒊 *Audio tours in 11 languages, including English. Definitely take advantage of this free tour (narrated by Jeremy Irons in true Troy Mclure fashion), as there aren't many signs around the abbey.* ⓢ *£15, students and seniors £12, ages 11-18 £6, under 11 (accompanied by adult) free, family ticket (2 adults and 1 child) £30 plus £6 for each additional child.* ⏰ *Open M-Tu 9:30am-3:30pm, W 9:30am-6:00pm, Th-Sa 9:30am-3:30pm. Abbey Museum open daily 10:30am-4pm.*

🔖 CHURCHILL MUSEUM, CABINET WAR ROOMS
Clive Steps, King Charles St.

☚👣 MUSEUM, HISTORICAL SITE
☎020 7930 6961 🖳www.iwm.org.uk/cabinet

The War Rooms opened in 1938, a week before WWII broke out. They were used as a shelter for important government officers, and Winston Churchill spent almost

mind the doors

In many other countries, the train doors for Underground equivalents are pushovers. If you're having a bad hair day and your sleeve is caught in the sensor, the train won't go anywhere. However, things are different in England, and the Brits' gentility is not shared by their train doors. If you try and get on a packed train as the doors are closing, you may wind up leaving your bag and half a limb behind you.

great britain

every day of the war in the windowless, airless subterranean rooms, recreated here and opened for public access. The rooms are tense with wartime anxiety, and the map room, with lights that were not turned off for six years during the war, still burns bright. Connected to the Cabinet War Rooms is the Churchill museum. Visitors can step on the sensors to hear excerpts from some of his most famous speeches and watch videos detailing the highs and lows of his career. Also on display are his alcohol habits, which included drinks with breakfast, lunch, and dinner daily, and his patented "romper," better known as a onesie.

*⇆ ⊖Westminster or St. James's Park. From Westminster, take a right down Parliament St. and a left onto King Charles St. **i** Free sound guide available in English, French, German, Italian, Spanish, Hebrew, Dutch and Mandarin. $ £14.95, students and seniors £12, disabled £9, under 16 free. Special rates available for groups, so call ahead. ⏰ Open daily 9:30am-6pm. Last entry 1hr. before close. Call about scheduling a 2hr. tour.*

Buckingham Palace

George III bought Buckingham House—which wasn't originally built for the royals—in 1761 for his wife, Queen Charlotte. Charlotte proceeded to give birth to 14 out of her 15 children at Buckingham Palace. The house was expanded by George IV, who commissioned John Nash to transform the existing building into a palace. In 1837, Queen Victoria moved into Buckingham Palace, and it has remained a royal residence since then.

Every day at 11:30am from April to late July, and every other day the rest of the year, the **Changing of the Guard** takes place. The "Changing of the Guard" is the exchange of guard duty between different regiments. Forget the dumb American movies where an obnoxious tourist tries in every immature way possible to make the unflinching guards at Buckingham Palace move; the guards are far enough away so that tourists can do no more than whistle every time they move 3 ft. and salute. The entire spectacle lasts 40min. To see it, you should show up well before 11:30am and stand in front of the palace in view of the morning guards. The middle of the week is the least crowded time to watch.

THE STATE ROOMS — PALACE

At the end of the Mall ☎020 7766 7300 🖥www.royalcollection.org.uk

The Palace opens to visitors every August and September while the royals are off sunning themselves. Visitors are granted limited access and are only allowed in the State Rooms, which are used for formal occasions. As a result, these rooms are sumptuous and as royal as you could hope them to be. As you tour them, look for the secret door concealed in one of the White Drawing Room's mirrors, through which royals entered the state apartments. Also not to be missed are the Throne Room and the glittering Music Room. The Galleries display master works from the royal collections, and the gardens display birds that are marginally prettier than the birds you'd see outside.

*⇆ ⊖Victoria. Turn right onto Buckingham Palace Rd. and follow it onto Buckingham Gate. **i** Audio guide provided. Wheelchair users should book by calling ☎020 7766 7324. $ £17, students and seniors £15.50, under 17 £9.75, under 5 free, family (2 adults and 3 children under 17) £45. ⏰ Open daily late July-Oct, 9:45am-4pm (last admission 45min. before close) daily.*

QUEEN'S GALLERY — GALLERY

At the end of the Mall ☎020 7766 7300 🖥www.royalcollection.org.uk

The Queen's Gallery is dedicated to temporary exhibitions of jaw-droppingly valuable items from the Royal Collection. Five rooms, designed to look like the interior of the palace are filled with glorious artifacts that applaud the sovereign. Once purchased, passes can be registered online for 12 months of unlimited access.

*⇆ ⊖Victoria. Turn right onto Buckingham Palace Rd. and follow it onto Buckingham Gate. Entrance to the Mews and Gallery will be on your left. **i** Wheelchair-accessible. ⏰ Open daily*

10am-5:30pm (last admission 1hr. before close), July 27-Oct 1 9:30am-5:30pm (last admission 1hr. before close). Closed Nov 1-Apr 14, 2011.

North London

★ HAMPSTEAD HEATH

♿ PARK

Hampstead ☎020 7332 3030

Hampstead Heath was initially much smaller than its present 800 acres. After Sir Thomas Maryon Wilson tried to develop and sell off the Heath in the early 19th century, the public began to fight for the Heath, culminating in an Act of Parliament in 1872 that declared the Heath open to the public forever. Now it sprawls gloriously in the heart of Hampstead. The **Hill Gardens** are in the southwest corner of the Heath just off North End Avenue. The Hill House was owned by Lord Leverhulme (of Lever Soap), and he modified the surrounding landscapes to create the beautiful, tamer Hill Gardens. A pergola presides over the gardens, its lattice work is entwined with roses, and painters often station themselves around the gardens and pergola. The view through its Georgian columns is best enjoyed around sunset. **Parliament Hill** is one of the higher points in London, offering those willing to climb its deceptively steep sides a glorious reminder that they aren't in the middle of rural England, but are, in fact, only four miles from London proper.

🚶 *Bus #210 will drop you at the north of the Heath, from which you can access Kenwood House and work your way southeast towards Parliament Hill. Alternatively, you can get off at ⊖Hampstead and turn right onto Heath St., up North End Way, left onto Inverforth Close and left onto a path will take you to the hill gardens. Bus #214 allows easy access to Parliament Hill.* 🕐 *Heath open 24hr. Hill Garden open daily May 24-Aug 1 8:30am-8:30pm; Aug 2-May 23 8:30am-1hr. before sunset.*

East London

★ WHITECHAPEL GALLERY

♿ CONTEMPORARY ART

77-82 Whitechapel High St. ☎020 7522 7888 💻www.whitechapelgallery.org

This edgy gallery has been showing important contemporary art since it opened in 1901. Originally an effort of hoity-toity uppity-ups to bring art to the culturally decrepit inhabitants of the East End, the gallery's mission has changed, though its commitment to excellence hasn't. Gallery 7 is dedicated to collections that change four times a year. Gallery 2 features year-long commissioned works, and the rest of the gallery deals with contemporary art and occasional mid-career retrospectives. Art films can be seen running on loop in the cinema space.

🚶 *⊖Aldgate East. Left on Whitechapel High St.* $ *Free. Special exhibits normally under £10, with £2 off for students.* 🕐 *Open Tu-Su 11am-6pm, 1st Th of every month 11am-9pm.*

FOOD

British food doesn't have a great reputation. Yes, it is bad for you and no, it doesn't have complex flavors, but it is so intrinsically a part of British life that to forego it would be a grave error for any visitor to England. **Fish and chips, bangers and mash, tikka masala** (a British invention), and, of course, **warm ale** are all different names for the same thing: comfort food. Neighborhoods like Bloomsbury and Shoreditch serve up wide varieties of ethnic food (read: Indian), but "pub grub" and British food are inescapable. There's a reason that old war propaganda line, "Keep Calm and Carry On," is plastered all over the place; there's a reason the Queen still rolls down the Mall every June 12th; there's a reason the Brits always think England will win the Cup; and there's a reason fair Albion still has the pound; and for that same reason, British food is what it is. Now eat your mushy peas—the cod's getting cold.

Bayswater

Shocking though it may be, most travelers like to take a break from bubble and squeak and bangers and mash. When you get itchin' for a little something from an ethnic kitchen, give Bayswater a shot. A wide range of affordable Middle Eastern and

Indian restaurants abound in this neighborhood.

LA BOTTEGA DEL GELATO — GELATO [3]

127 Bayswater Rd. ☎020 7243 2443

Simply put, this gelato, made in-store, is divine. La Bottega Del Gelato fills the hole in the London ice cream scene with a variety of delicious flavors. Enjoy it outside on Bayswater Rd. in their seating area; even in the heart of the city, this gelato will make you feel like you're on a quiet street in Roma. The Ferrero Rocher is especially good.

⊖Bayswater. Right onto Queensway, follow it until you hit Bayswater Rd. $ 1 scoop £2, 2 scoops £3.50, 3 scoops £4.50; milkshakes £3.50. ⏰ Hours change depending on weather, but the store opens daily 10:30am.

APHRODITE TAVERNA — GREEK [2]

15 Hereford Rd. ☎020 7229 2206 www.aphroditerestaurant.co.uk

Decorated with statues of Aphrodite and a few inexplicable pineapples, Aphrodite Taverna serves up fantastic Greek food at prices that even recession-era Greece can't beat! Too soon? Let's hope not. Come and enjoy a meal of chicken kofta with rice *(£5.90)* or homemade pita *(£4.50)*, and relax as power pop pipes through the store speakers.

⊖Bayswater. Left onto Queensway, left onto Moscow Rd., right onto Hereford toward Westbourne Grove. $ Entrees £5.50-6.80. ⏰ M-Su 8am-5pm.

Bloomsbury

Riddled with cheap student eats, Bloomsbury is an exciting and accessible culinary neighborhood. Here are some of the true gems.

NEWMAN ARMS — BRITISH PIES [3]

23 Rathbone St. ☎020 7636 1127 www.newmanarms.co.uk

Established in 1730, the Newman Arms has been serving succulent British pies about as long as the Queen's relatives have been on the throne. The menu reads like an ode to comfort food, with pies like beef and Guinness, steak and kidney, and lamb and rosemary. The warm upstairs dining room fills up fast, so be sure to reserve a table one day in advance during the summer and much further in advance during the winter (sometimes even months).

⊖Goodge St. Turn left onto Tottenham Court Rd., left onto Tottenham St., left onto Charlotte St., and right onto Rathbone St. i Enter through the corridor next to the entrance to the pub. $ Pies £10. Puddings £11. ⏰ Open M-F noon-2:30pm and 6-9:30pm.

NAVARRO'S TAPAS BAR — TAPAS [3]

67 Charlotte St. ☎020 7637 7713 www.navarros.co.uk

It would make sense if, upon entering this restaurant, you began patting yourself for your passport and looking for the customs agent who won't take "I've nothing to declare" as a personal challenge. Bathed in candlelight and strains of Flamenco music, Navarro's boasts an excellent selection of regional wines that will convince you you're on your way to Spain. Don't forget your castanets.

⊖Goodge St. Turn left onto Tottenham Court Rd., turn left onto Tottenham St. and left onto Charlotte St. i Nicer dress is preferable, as is booking in advance. $ Mainly vegetarian dishes £4.85-4.95, fish and shellfish £5.75-6.10. ⏰ Open M-F noon-3pm and 6-10pm, Sa 6-10pm.

Chelsea

BUONA SERA — ITALIAN [3]

289a King's Rd ☎020 7352 8827

People haven't eaten like this since our ancestors moved out of the trees and onto the ground. The small restaurant manages to fit 14 tables into its tight space by stacking the booths one atop the other. It's sort of like a game of Tetris, except involving delicious and affordable Italian food. Plants on the upper level make the experience feel like it's taking place in the canopy of a tree, but the food will remind you of the pleasures of civilization.

⇞ ⊖Sloane Sq. Exit the Tube and go straight down Sloane Sq. The street slanting gently left is King's Rd. If you don't want to walk the road (it's manageable but long), the following buses service the area: #11, 19, 22, 211, 319 Ⓢ Salads £4.50-5.70, lunch entrees £7.90-8.50. Pasta and risotto £8.60-9.80. Meat and fish entrees £14.50-14.80. Pizza £3.80, plus £1.50 per topping set (tuna and onions, ham and mushrooms, etc.). ⏰ Open M 6pm-midnight, Tu-F noon-3pm, 6pm-midnight, Sa-Su noon-midnight.

The City of London

Many of the culinary offerings in the City of London are geared toward businessmen (expensive) and tourists (expensive, but not very good). Fortunately, there are a few promising options for the budget traveler.

👍 SPIANATA — 🎫⊗ ITALIAN, SANDWICHES, PIZZA ❶

73a Watling St. ☎020 7236 3666 💻www.spianata.com

Enjoy the delicious taste of Italy in every sandwich served on Spianata's freshly baked bread. The businessmen in the city know that some of the best sandwiches and pizzas in the city are served at this authentically Italian shop, so arrive before the peak lunch hour.

⇞ ⊖St. Paul's. Go down Cheapside away from St. Paul's Cathedral; turn right at Bread St. and left at Watling St. Ⓢ Sandwiches £3.25-4; pizza £1.60 cold, £1.90 hot. ⏰ M-F 7:30am-3:30pm.

YE OLDE CHESHIRE CHEESE — 🎫⊗🍸 PUB ❸

145 Fleet St., down Wine Office Court

The current Cheese was built in 1667, but a pub has been in its current location since 1538. **Charles Dickens** and **Samuel Johnson,** author of the first dictionary (a copy is upstairs), frequented the pub. Despite its history, Ye Olde Cheshire Cheese remains a personable, old-timey watering hole, serving traditional English "fayre" alongside their phenomenally cheap and excellent Samuel Smith brews from Yorkshire. If you explore the downstairs dining room, be wary of the sign that says "mind your head." They mean it.

⇞ ⊖St. Paul's. Take a right on New Change, a right onto Cannon St. which becomes St. Paul's Churchyard, Ludgate Hill and then Fleet St. Ⓢ Entrees £9.95-11.95; bangers and mash £3.50. Shots £1.89-2.20; 1/2 pint of lager £1.14, pint of lager £2.27; 1/2 pint of ale £1; pint of ale 1.99. ⏰ M-Sa 11am-11pm, Su 11am-6pm.

great britain

Holborn and Clerkenwell

Holborn offers standard fare plus a few high-class restaurants and bistros mixed in with typical take-away sandwich joints. Clerkenwell has a lot more in the vein of hip, light, and interesting restaurants.

👍 THE CLERKENWELL KITCHEN — 🎫♿☘ HEALTHY, BRITISH, SEASONAL ❸

31 Clerkenwell Close ☎020 7101 9959 💻www.theclerkenwellkitchen.co.uk

Normally when a restaurant advertises "soft drinks," they mean cola and root beer. At the Clerkenwell Kitchen, a "soft drink" means a taste-bud-exploding concoction like their elderflower cordial *(£2)*. Cooking with locally grown ingredients and organic, free-range meat, the Clerkenwell Kitchen welcomes guests to the lighter side of British fare.

⇞ ⊖Farringdon. Right onto Cowcross St., right onto Farringdon, right onto Pear Tree Ct., right onto Clerkenwell Close. Walk straight as if still on Pear Tree Ct. If you see the church, backtrack. Ⓢ Entrees £9-10. Teas and coffees £1.50-1.85. ⏰ Open M-F 8am-5pm and noon-3pm.

Marylebone and Regent's Park

👍 THE GOLDEN HIND — 🎫⊗ FISH AND CHIPS ❷

73 Marylebone Ln. ☎020 7486 3644

The Golden Hind might just have the best fish and chips in London. With a wide selection of fish and a selection of classic sides, the menu will challenge you in ways you never thought fish and chips could.

✦ ⊖*Bond St. Left onto Davies St., right onto Oxford St., left onto Marylebone Ln.* ⑤ *Fish (fried or steamed) £4.70-5.70. Chips £1.50. Peas £1.* ⬚ *Open M-F noon-3pm and 6-10pm, Sa 6-10pm.*

PATOGH
✦⑧ PERSIAN ❷

8 Crawford Pl
☎020 7262 4015

Patogh is the definition of hole-in-the-wall. Small and crowded but nicely decorated and exquisitely scented, Patogh provides traditional Persian food like minced lamb and huge servings of sesame flatbread in a highly atmospheric setting.

✦ ⊖*Edgward Rd. Right onto Chapel St., left onto Edgware Rd., left onto Crawford Pl.* ⑤ *Entrees £8-9.* ⬚ *Open daily noon-11pm.*

The West End

MÔ CAFÉ
✦⑤ ⑼ CAFE, TEA, NORTH AFRICAN ❷

23-25 Heddon St.
☎020 7434 4040 📧www.momoresto.com

When juxtaposed with the absurd decadence of nearby Absolut Icebar (yes, that is a bar...made of ice), the Mo Cafe's own absurd conceit feels a little less ridiculous. With waiters wearing bright red shirts and black pants, chandeliers that are draped in tassels and strings and bronze table tops surrounded by low chairs, the Mo Cafe looks like it's trying too hard. However, try the hummus or the mint tea (made with tea imported from Morocco, obviously), and you'll feel your skull tingle where your fez once was.

✦ ⊖*Piccadilly Circus. Turn left onto Regent St. and left onto Heddon St.* ⑤ *Cold mezze £4.50-4.75. Hot mezze £5.50-5.80.* ⬚ *M-Sa noon-1am, Su noon-11pm.*

KOYA
✦⑧ JAPANESE ❸

49 Frith St.
☎020 7434 4463 📧www.koya.co.uk

Unlike many Japanese restaurants, where Chinese or British cooks pretend to make authentic Japanese dishes, Koya is the real deal. Through the cloth that guards the front door lies a dining room where only the most authentic and delicious *hiya-atsu* and *atsu-atsu* (cold and hot udon) is served. This place is good, and Soho knows it, so try and come sometime other than 6:30pm, as they don't take reservations.

✦ ⊖*Tottenham Court Rd. Turn down Oxford St. with your back to Tottenham Court Rd and then left onto Soho St. Go around Soho Sq to the left and turn left onto Frith.* ⑤ *Udon is around £8.50-9.* ⬚ *Open M-Sa noon-3pm and 5:30pm-10:30pm.*

North London

🔳 LA CRÊPERIE DE HAMPSTEAD
⑧⑤ CRÊPES, STREET STAND ❶

Around 77 Hampstead High St.
📧www.hampsteadcreperie.com

Walking down Hampstead High St. from the underground station, a traveler may notice several people lining the bus stop benches, ravenously eating crêpes out of small conical cups. Walk a bit further down, and you'll see La Crêperie de Hampstead. Serving the community since 1929, the crêperie is not the average street vendor's booth. The crêpes are expertly crafted—a perfect balance of light and doughy—and the ingredients, sweet or savory, are well-blended to create crêpes that burst with flavor.

✦ ⊖*Hampstead. Left onto Hampstead Heath St.* 𝒊 *No seating available, but check the nearby benches.* ⑤ *Savories £4.30-4.65. Sweets £3.40-3.90.* ⬚ *Open M-Th 11:45am-11pm, F-Su 11:45am-11:30pm.*

MANGO ROOM
✦⑧ CARIBBEAN ❸

10-12 Kentish Town Rd.
☎020 7482 5065 📧www.mangoroom.co.uk

Located near bustling Camden Town, the Mango Room is the perfect place to escape the excitement. The cool room decorated with bright paintings that nicely complement the food is perfect for anyone who regrets choosing rainy London over the sunny Caribbean for a vacation. Serving Caribbean dishes like ackee and saltfish with scallions and sweet peppers *(£11)*, the Mango Room is about as escapist and pleasant as the name suggests.

✣ ⊖Camden High St. Left onto Camden High St., left onto Camden Rd., Left onto Kentish Town Rd. ℹ *Minimum £10.* $ *Dinner entrees £10.50-11. Lunch entrees £7-8.50. Mixed drinks £4 during happy hour.* ⏰ *Open daily noon-11pm. Bar open F-Sa until 1am. Happy hour 6-8pm.*

East London

Most of East London's culinary offerings are packed into the unbeatable **Brick Lane.** If you're looking for curry, you'd have to be blind and smell-challenged not to find it. However, if you want to partake in the Shoreditch scene but can't handle the pressure of choosing just one curry restaurant, here are a few good alternatives.

☑ NUDE ESPRESSO

💳🚭📶 CAFE [3]

26 Hanbury St. ☎078 0422 3590 💻www.nudeespresso.com

Most good cafes pride themselves on buying exotic coffee beans, but Nude Espresso takes their gimmick a step further, actually roasting the coffee beans themselves. Serving up some of the best coffee in London, the hip Nude Espresso is a welcome break from the myriad curry restaurants hawking their wares on Brick Ln. With its aluminum cups and stylish interior, Nude Espresso gets the aesthetic right while never forgetting what its clients came for: damn good coffee.

✣ ⊖Aldgate East. Left onto Whitechapel Rd., left onto Osborn St., continue onto Brick Ln.; left onto Hanbury. ℹ *Min. £6 purchase with credit card. Wi-Fi available, but they don't allow plugins.* $ *Breakfast and lunch entrees £6-£7.50. Espresso £2-£2.50. Specialty coffee drinks around £3.60.* ⏰ *Open M-F 7:30am-6pm, Sa-Su 10am-6pm.*

☑ CAFE 1001

💳🚭📶 CAFE [2]

91 Brick Ln. ☎020 7247 9679 💻www.cafe1001.co.uk

Under the overhang connecting Cafe 1001 to the Truman Ale factory, hip East Enders bask in the British sun's occasional appearances and share in the good coffee served from the cafe's year-round outdoor cart. Inside the cafe, numerous patrons listen to music from the likes of Caetano Veloso and kick back in the warehouse-like space. At night, the salad bar turns into a real bar, and the back room becomes a venue for up-and-coming bands and DJs, and sometimes it even serves as a classroom for aspiring swing dancers. Basically, this cafe is as close as a cafe comes to being a cultural center.

✣ ⊖Aldgate East. Left onto Whitechapel Rd., left onto Osborn St., continue onto Brick Ln. ℹ *Credit card min. £4 purchase. F, Sa, Su are club nights from 7pm-midnight, with DJs playing in the back room. Live bands every Tu (rock) and W (folk and jazz). Swing dancing classes Th 11am-5pm.* $ *Coffee £1.20-1.70 for a small, £.40-£2 for a large. Cover charge £3-5 after midnight. Free Wi-Fi.* ⏰ *Open daily 7am-midnight, sometimes no closing F-Su (as in, it stays open continuously).*

Other Neighborhoods

☑ POILÂNE

💳♿ BAKERY [3]

46 Elizabeth St. ☎020 7808 4910 💻www.poilane.com

Poilâne is one of the most famous bakeries from Paris, which means that, by London standards, it's ungodly good. The commitment to excellence at Poilâne is unparalleled. Many of the bakers live above the shop, baking the bread all through the night to ensure that it's fresh for the morning crowd. They use only the oldest, most time-honored traditions and techniques when creating their sourdough masterpieces, and the *pain au chocolat* is to die for. Also worth noting is the fact that they bake in wood-fired ovens of the type that started the Great Fire of London—but don't worry, Poilâne is both safe *and* delicious.

✣ ⊖Victoria. Left onto Buckingham Palace Rd., right onto Elizabeth St. $ *Custard tart £16.*

Walnut bread £4. Pain au chocolat £1.20. Sourdough bread £4.40. 🕐 Open M-F 7:30am-7pm. Sa 7:30am-6pm.

👍 DA SCALZO — 💳♿ ITALIAN [3]

2 Eccleston Pl. — ☎020 7730 5498 💻www.dascalzo.com

You should really be wary of Italian restaurants, especially ones in close proximity to train and bus stations, like da Scalzo, but da Scalzo defies all odds. The food is well-priced and fantastically portioned, making for a real Italian feast to be savored. The waiters and waitresses pal around with each other, putting on informal shows with pizza dough, and they have the incredible ability to make you feel that, though you may have just gotten off the plane, you've been dining at da Scalzo for your whole life.

➡ ⊖Victoria. Left onto Buckingham Palace Rd., right onto Elizabeth St. $ Pasta and risotto £6-7. Stone baked pizza £8.50-9. Meat £12.50-14. Fish £12.50. 🕐 Open M-Sa 8am-11pm, Su 8am-8pm.

👍 BAKER AND SPICE — 💳 NEW EUROPEAN PASTRIES [3]

54-56 Elizabeth St. — ☎020 7730 3033 💻www.bakerandspice.uk.com

Baker and Spice is the *part deux* of the one-two pastry punch on Elizabeth St. The street boasts Poîlane, and, less than a block away, the equally good Baker and Spice. Serving freshly made pastries, strong, delicious coffee, and a wide variety of ready-made meals and salads, Baker and Spice is gourmet on the go. Ideal for takeaway, but delicious enough to be savored slowly in the al fresco dining areas, Baker and Space does it all with ample style and grace.

➡ ⊖ Victoria. Left onto Buckingham Palace Rd., right onto Elizabeth St. 🕐 Open M-Sa 7am-7pm, Su 8am-5pm.

THE GATE — 💳[⊗] VEGETARIAN, VEGAN, GLUTEN FREE [4]

51 Queen Caroline St., 2nd floor. — ☎020 8748 6932 💻www.thegate.tv

Tucked away down Queen Caroline St. in the lofty, sunlit studio of a former puppet-maker, the Gate has been serving a menu composed almost entirely of vegetarian, vegan, or gluten-free dishes for the last twenty years. Everything is made from seasonal ingredients, and the massive window that illuminates the dining room is bordered by sunflowers. If you like what you eat, you can buy their own cookbook, too.

➡ ⊖Hammersmith. Take the south exit from the Hammersmith shopping center toward the London Apollo and follow Queen Caroline St. ℹ Reservations recommended 3 days in advance. $ Entrees £12.50-13.50. 🕐 Open M-F noon-2:30pm and 6-10pm, Sa 6-11pm.

NIGHTLIFE

If you seek the club scene of say, Barcelona, go to Barcelona. The elitist impulse often rears its head in British club life—this is especially evident in Kensington and Chelsea where many clubs are "members only," meaning they'll make you ask to have your name put on a guest list. That doesn't mean that there's no nightlife. Visitors can find evening kicks in bars that serve some exciting drinks (check out Soho for lessons in **mixology**). Music venues like the **Troubadour** in Kensington provide killer atmospheres and young crowds late at night.

Still, pubs are the fabric of British life. Most are open daily 11am-11pm with some variation in regards to the weekend. Pubs are where Brits come to eat and drink too much. At lunchtime, the pubs in Westminster and the City of London fill with men in matching suits. The best are the ones that claim residence in the oldest drinking locations in London, meaning that people have been drunk there since the dawn of time. Be wary of the "George Orwell drank here" or the "Dylan Thomas drank here" line—you will see those names everywhere, because not only were they fantastic drunks, they were also prolific walkers. Parliament even passed the **Defense of the Realm Act** during WWI to limit pub hours in order to keep the munitions workers sober. This law was in effect until 1988, and many pubs still retain the early hours. Always bring cab fare or plan your **night bus** route home as the ⊖**Tube** closes early.

Bloomsbury

👍 VATS WINE BAR
👉♿🍸 WINE BAR

51 Lambs' Conduit St. ☎020 7242 8963 💻www.vatswinebar.com

The epitome of a warm, British restaurant, Vats imports much of its wine while keeping the feel of the place properly British. With a menu boasting around 160 vintages from all over, Vats is an upscale and pleasant evening experience. Upscale pub food like venison sausages with creamed mash, broccoli florets, belotte beans, bacon sauce, and a garnish of cranberries are par for the course. The food is hearty and delicious, and the wine flows freely.

🚏 ⊖Russell Square. Left onto Colonnade, right onto Grenville St., left onto Guilford St. and right onto Lambs' Conduit St. $ Sides £3.75. Entrees £13-15. ⏰ Open M-F noon-2:30pm and 6-9:30pm.

THE FITZROY TAVERN
👉♿🍸 FAMOUS TAVERN

16A Charlotte St. ☎020 7580 3714

Many pubs try to ensnare tourists by claiming they are the oldest pub in England or telling bizarre perversions of famous stories ("and that penny that **Dickens** gave to the little boy was spent on whiskey in our pub...") that lend a historical grandeur to what is actually just a decrepit pub with bad ales. The Fitzroy Tavern actually has a published book about its history, and artifacts from that history coat the walls. Famous for the charitable program instated by the tavern to send kids on outings to the country and for the authors who frequented the pub, most notably **Dylan Thomas** and **George Orwell,** The Fitzroy Tavern is the real deal. Pints are cheap, the history's free, and there's a comedy night too.

*🚏 ⊖Goodge St. left on Tottenham Ct. Rd., left on Tottenham St., left on to Charlotte St. **i** With credit cards, £10 min. and 1.5% surcharge. $ Most pints under £3.15; £2.50 is the average. ⏰ Open M-Sa noon-11pm, Su noon-10:30pm. Comedy night W 8:30pm.*

THE COURT
👉♿🍸 PUB

108a Tottenham Court Rd. ☎020 7387 0183

A true-blue student pub for a student neighborhood, The Court boasts loud music, cheap beers, juke boxes, and a hip crowd. In the upstairs area, there's a pool table, but most of the pubgoers sit outside or inside the brightly-lit pub area, under hanging strings of lights. The burgers are cheap and tantalizing.

🚏 ⊖Warren St. Left on Warren St., right on Tottenham Court Rd. $ Pints £3. Burgers £4.95-5.95. With student discount (you qualify if you buy the yellow student discount card at the pub), the pints are around £2.50. ⏰ Open M-W 11am-midnight, Th-Sa 11am-1am. Food served until 9pm.

PRINCESS LOUISE
👉♿🍸 PUB

208 High Holborn ☎020 7405 8816

A student-packed local hang, the Princess Louise has a classic interior filled with elaborately-designed fogged glass, worn leather seats, and various other pieces of ornate decor. Perhaps the most beautiful things in the pub are the (figurative) price tags on the beers, which are much cheaper than what you'll find in most pubs in the area. A fun atmosphere with a young crowd, the Princess Louise is a neighborhood favorite.

🚏 ⊖Holborn. Left onto High Holborn. $ Pint of bitters £1.99. Pint of lager £2.27. ⏰ Open M-F 11:30am-11pm, Sa-Su noon-11pm.

Chelsea

Chelsea is now one of the more exclusive and pretentious places to find nightlife in London. Many clubs advertise as members-only private establishments, but for many, you only have to call to get on the guest list. There are a few excellent pubs and many clubs, but if you're looking for an easily accessible, young scene, look elsewhere.

THE CHELSEA RAM — PUB

32 Burnaby St. ☎020 7351 4008

A classy neighborhood pub that's more of a quiet hang than it is a rowdy party, the Chelsea Ram specializes in cultivating a pleasant atmosphere. With loads of regulars congregating under the pub's high, bright ceilings, the pub provides friendly staff, good books, fun board games, and interesting art that's for sale (if you tend to buy art when drunk, beware).

Sloane Square. Exit the tube and go straight down Sloane Sq. The street slanting gently left is King's Rd. If you don't want to walk the road (it's manageable but long), the following buses and night buses service the area: #11, 19, 22, 211, 319, N11, N19, N22. Left on Lots Rd., left Burnaby St. $ Pints £4. Entrees £11.50-12.95. Open M-Sa noon-11pm. Su noon-7pm. Lunch served M-Sa noon-3pm and 6-10pm.

HENRY J. BEAN'S BAR AND GRILL — PUB

195-197 King's Rd. ☎020 7352 9255 www.henryjbeans.co.uk/chelsea

Henry J. Bean's attitude toward nightlife is very much embodied in its license-plate map of the states: really cool but a little mixed-up (why is Delaware in the Midwest?) Henry J. Bean's is jam-packed with a super loud young crowd grooving to a wide range of blaring music. Booths provide seating for food, TVs show sporting events, and taps pour beer. The good times await.

Sloane Square. Exit the tube and go straight down Sloane Sq. The street slanting gently left is King's Rd. If you don't want to walk the road (it's manageable but long), the following buses and night buses service the area: 11, 19, 22, 211, 319, N11, N19, N22. $ Pints £3.80. Open M-W 11am-11pm, Th-Su 11am-midnight.

THE ANTELOPE — PUB

22-24 Eaton Terr. ☎020 7824 8512

Established in 1827, The Antelope enjoyed a brief stint as a celebrity pub in the '60s, hosting such rising stars as Roman Polanski. More recently, Prince William came in to drink, but these days The Antelope is otherwise a quiet, small, and cozy neighborhood bar with a Scrabble set and a worn couch that sits by a lamp and under a bookshelf.

*Sloane Sq. Take a right onto Sloane Sq. and another right onto Eaton Gate. Take a left onto Eaton Terr. **i** Free Wi-Fi. Credit card for purchases over £10. $ Pints £3.50. Open M-Sa noon-11pm.*

QUEEN'S HEAD PUB — GLBT PUB

25-27 Tryon St. ☎020 7589 0262 www.the1440.co.uk

Over 100 years old, The Queen's Head (make of that what you will) is one of the oldest gay pubs in London. A friendly and convivial watering hole with an older clientele of both gay and straight patrons. Bingo once a month, karaoke every other week, and quiz night weekly.

Sloane Square. Exit the Tube and go straight down Sloane Sq. The street slanting gently left is King's Rd. If you don't want to walk the road (it's manageable but long), the following buses and night buses service the area: #11, 19, 22, 211, 319, N11, N19, N22. Turn right onto Tryon St. $ Pint of lager £3-4.50. Bitters from £3.15. Pub grub £6.95-7.25, all-day breakfast £6.95. Open M-Th noon-11pm, F-Sa noon-midnight, Su noon-10:30pm.

Holborn and Clerkenwell

Holborn is a pub town, and Clerkenwell is on the up-and-up. Look out for a mix of pleasant, old pubs and hip clubs, most of which can be found on Charterhouse St.

THE THREE KINGS — PUB

7 Clerkenwell Close ☎020 7253 0483

On warm evenings, patrons of The Three Kings line the curbs outside and drink their pints *(£3.30-3.50)* of Timothy Taylor, Staropramer, and Beck's. Inside, customers sit in the arm chairs under the watchful gazes of luminaries like Woody

Allen, Hunter S. Thompson, Smokey Robinson, and that fake rhino the pub has on the wall.

🚶 ⊖Farringdon. Right onto Cowcross St., right onto Farringdon, right onto Pear Tree Ct., right onto Clerkenwell Close. ⏰ Open M-F noon-11pm, Sa. 5pm-11pm.

THE 3 TUNS 💳♿🍸 STUDENT PUB

Houghton St. ☎020 7955 7156

While this place is not rich in the atmosphere department, the 3 Tuns customers are rich in the money department, thanks to this pub's dirt-cheap pints. This London School of Economics pub is frequented by (you guessed it) LSE students and is a good place to come if you want to meet university-aged people or play a game of pool in a sparsely furnished room where people drink beer from plastic cups.

🚶 ⊖Temple. Right onto Temple Pl., left onto Surrey St., cross the Strand. Continue onto Melbourne Pl., left onto Aldwych, right on Houghton St. $ Pints £2.10. ⏰ Term-time hours: M, T and Th 10am-11pm, W 10am-midnight, F 10am-2am, Sa 9pm-3am. During school holidays, call for hours.

Kensington and Earl's Court

👍 JANET'S BAR 💳🚭🍸 BAR

30 Old Brompton Rd. ☎020 7581 3160 💻janetsbar@yahoo.com

Janet's Bar is all about spirits, in both senses of the word. Run by Janet herself, who knows most of the people in the bar and has organized something of a lively ex-pat community around the place, Janet's Bar is a well-formed but instantly welcoming community. All-encompassing memorabilia, photos of club regulars, and the Red Sox and Yankees pennants that are closer than most fans would like. If the atmosphere doesn't make you feel welcome, Beatles sing-alongs will.

🚶 ⊖South Kensington. As you exit, Old Brompton Rd. will be across from you. i Though not wheelchair-accessible, a ramp can be arranged if you call in advance. £3 min. on credit cards. $Bottle of beer around £4.50. Pints £5.95. Shots around £5. Mixed drinks £6.50-8.50. Bottle of wine from £18.50. ⏰ M-W 11:45am-1:00am, Th 11:45am-1:30am, F 11:45pm-2:30am, Sa noon-2:30am, Su 2pm-1am. Live music Tu-Su after 9:30pm.

👍 PIANO 💳🚭🍸 PIANO BAR

106 Kensington High Street ☎020 7938 4664 💻www.pianokensington.com

If you ever dreamed of lying atop a piano in a dimly lit room while someone played sultry jazz, blues, rock and sing-along music, Piano will do you one better: you can eat on the piano, and there's a different pianist every night of the week. Piano is a classy joint loaded with pictures of 🎬**Old Blue Eyes** (Frank Sinatra).

🚶 ⊖High Street Kensington. Turn right on Kensington High Street. i £5 min. on credit cards. $ Most entrees £6.50-7. Bottle of beer £4.50. Glass of house red or white £4.50. ⏰ Tu-Sa 11am-midnight, Su 4:30pm-11:30. Music starts at 6pm Tu-F, 8pm on Sa and the jazz trio goes on Su 8pm.

👍 THE DRAYTON ARMS 💳♿🍸 PUB

153 Old Brompton Rd. ☎020 7835 2301 💻www.thedraytonarmssw5.co.uk

The Drayton Arms is a comfortable, well-kept pub with high ceilings and white string lights that amble up the tree trunk and soft red lights that border the ceiling. Enjoy affordable beers around the fire place, and then go see a film or play in the black box theater on the second floor. Check the site for theater, sporting and film events in the upstairs theater.

🚶 ⊖Gloucester Rd. Turn right onto Gloucester Rd., turn right onto Old Brompton Rd. $ Average pint £3.20. Burgers £7-8.25. Sandwiches £4.25. Entrees £7.50-8.25. ⏰ Open M-F 11am-midnight, Sa-Su 10m-midnight.

Marylebone and Regent's Park

👍 THE GOLDEN EAGLE 💳♿🍸 PUB, MUSIC

59 Marylebone Ln. ☎020 7935 3228

The Golden Eagle is one of the most special pubs in London. Though aesthetically basic, it has some of the kindest patrons and staff that can be found around town. Between the alcohol-induced golden haze, the music, and the unbelievably friendly company, the Pub is a living Capra film, and in no way is that a bad thing.

⇄ ⊖Bond St. Right onto Oxford St., left onto Marylebone Ln. $ Average pint £3.50. ⏰ Open M-Th 11am-11pm, F-Sa 11am-midnight, Su noon-7pm. Music Tu, Th, F 8:30pm.

👍 THE SOCIAL — 💳⊗🍸 CLUB, BAR

5 Little Portland St. ☎020 7636 4992 💻www.thesocial.com

Though the upstairs looks like a typical hip bar with its exposed light bulbs and bare wood floor (though there are DJs on the first floor most nights), the downstairs space at The Social is where the action is. Here is where the ragingly popular hip-hop karaoke night happens every other Th as well as other events like club nights and live performances. Many nights have no cover charge.

⇄ ⊖Oxford Circus. Right onto Regent St., right on Little Portland St. ℹ Credit card min. £10. $ Pints around £3.70. Mixed drinks around £7. Cover £5-7 on club night. Student cards will get you discounts on most covered nights. ⏰ Open M 5pm-midnight, Tu-W noon-midnight, Th-F noon-1am, Sa 7pm-1am.

Notting Hill

Notting Hill is not an ideal neighborhood for nightlife. The pubs thrive on daytime tourists, and many of the locals are young professionals who tend to frequent other spots.

👍 PORTOBELLO STAR — 💳♿🍸 BAR

171 Portobello Rd. ☎020 7229 8016 💻www.portobellostarbar.co.uk

If cafes could have superhero alter egos, the Portobello Star would be Superman. By day, it's a pleasant cafe with internet access; by night, it's a bustling bar... with internet access. It's popular but not too crazy, sophisticated but with fun drinks *("Rock the Kasbah," Grey Goose vodka with lemon juice, mint tea syrup, orange flower water, and egg white, £10)*. You'll hear your favorite classic rock, soft rock, R and B, soul, and hip-hop from the bar or the leather couches in the calmer chill-out room on the second floor of the building. The crowd is in their early 20s to early 30s, and the place is hopping.

⇄ ⊖Notting Hill Gate. Take right onto Pembridge Rd. and then left onto Portobello Rd. $ Mixed drinks £7.50-8. ⏰ Su-Th 10am-midnight, F-Sa 10am-1am.

The West End

👍 ABSOLUT ICEBAR — 💳♿🍸 BAR

31-33 Heddon St. ☎020 7478 8910 💻www.absoluticebarlondon.com

This bar is absurd in the best way possible—the way where everything is made out of ice imported from the Torne River in Sweden. Located in the former wine vault for the monarchy, Absolut Icebar is the perfect place to escape all that British...er, cold. Before entering the hip, "cool" bar, visitors are given designer thermal wear. Each stay is 40 minutes, during which time you drink as much as possible so you don't feel your face as it slowly freezes off. All drinks are served in glasses made of ice. Chipping ice off the wall and into your drink is frowned upon. Highly.

⇄ ⊖Piccadilly Circus. Turn left onto Regent St. and left onto Heddon St. ℹ Tickets include 1st vodka cocktail. Refills £6. Reserve for weekends around 2 weeks in advance. Reservations are taken up to 28 days in advance. $ M-W cover £13.50 (£12.50 if booked in advance), Th until 6:30pm £13.50 (£12.50 if booked in advance), Th night-Sa £15, Th-Sa all day £16 without reservation, Su £13.50 (£12.50 if booked in advance). ⏰ M 3:30pm-11:00pm, T 3:30pm-11pm, W 3:30pm-11pm, Th 3:30pm-11:45pm, F noon-1:15am, Sa 12:30pm-1:15am, Su 3:30pm-11pm, last entry is 45min. before closing. DJs on F and Sa start around 8pm.

👍 GORDON'S WINE BAR — 💳⊗🍸 WINE BAR

47 Villiers St. ☎020 7930 1408 💻www.gordonswinebar.com

Once down the narrow staircase visitors come upon what looks like a cave.

Bottles draped in melted wax and rough, irregularly sloping walls lit by flickering candles fill the space between people sharing bottles of wine from around the world. Out on Watergate Walk, winos sip the fine wines of London's oldest wine bar if the weather permits.

➜ 🚇Charing Cross. Upon exiting, turn 180° and go down Villiers. $ Wine £16-17 per bottle, around £4.50 per glass. Hot meals £9-11, items from the grill are around £6.65. ⏰ Open M-Sa 10am-11pm, Su noon-10pm.

FREUD
💳🚭🍸 BAR

198 Shaftesbury ☎020 7240 9933 💻www.freudliving.com

You wouldn't find Freud unless you were looking for it. With original art decorating the otherwise spare space, Freud is a study in successful understatement. The young and hip come to Freud and get a seat wherever they can, enjoying the reasonably priced drinks.

➜ 🚇Piccadilly Circus. Exit with Haymarket on your right and Regent to your left. turn right around the triangular intersection and right at Shaftesbury. ℹ Credit card min. £10. $ Beer £3.15-3.65. Mixed drinks £5.55-6.50 on average. ⏰ Open M-Sa 11am-11pm, Su noon-10:30pm.

CAFE PACIFICA
💳🚭🍸 MEXICAN BAR TEQUILA

5 Langley St. ☎020 7379 7728 💻www.cafepacifico-laperla.com

Though at first glance Cafe Pacifica may seem a typical Mexican restaurant, its 130 varieties of tequila beg to differ. Though you have to order food to drink, the atmosphere is pleasant, with light Latin music piping through the speakers and classic Mexican entrees like enchiladas. If you're feeling like a real taste in exorbitant spending, pick up a shot of the Cuervo Collecion *(£125)*. If you buy it, you'll get your name on a board in the restaurant, and also possibly on the IRS's auditing list.

➜ 🚇Covent Garden. Left on Long Acre, right on Langley. $ Shots of tequila £3-15. Enchiladas around £9.50. ⏰ Open M-Sa noon-11:45pm, Su noon-10:45pm.

THE EDGE
💳🚭🍸▼ GLBT, MIXED

11 Soho Sq. ☎020 7439 1313 💻www.edgesoho.co.uk

With four floors, The Edge is a full clubbing experience. Disco balls and a crazy light-changing chandelier that looks like an exploding atom decorate the space. The first floor has a lounge bar which is quieter filled with couches. The second floor is the al fresco lounge, serving up massages every night where the recipient pays however much he or she feels it's worth. The third floor has fake trees with climbing blue lights and a dance floor with tiles that change color.

➜ 🚇Tottenham Court Rd. Turn left onto Oxford St., turn left onto Soho St., Edge is on your right. $ Pints £3. ⏰ Open M-Sa noon-1am, Su noon-10:30pm. Dance floor open F-Sa 8pm.

PROFILE
💳♿🍸▼ GLBT BAR

84-86 Wardour St. ☎020 7734 3444 💻www.profilesoho.com

With one of the brightest yellow interiors in Soho, Profile practically screams good time. Serving up American diner food and providing events like Bingo at 6pm on Sundays and psychic Sundays on off-bingo weeks (get your fortune read!), Profile is a great GLBT bar. Downstairs is the cleverly-titled Low Profile, the bar's corresponding nightclub.

➜ 🚇Tottenham Court Rd. Turn down Oxford St. with your back to Tottenham Court Road, turn left onto Wardour St. $ Mixed drinks £6-7. Beer £3.50. ⏰ Profile M-Sa 11am-11pm, Su 11am-10:30pm. Low Profile open Th 10:30pm-2am, F-Sa 10:30pm-4am (drinking stops at 3am). DJs upstairs F 7pm, Sa 8pm. Happy hour at Profile daily 5-7pm.

BAR RUMBA
💳🚭🍸 CLUB

36 Shaftesbury Ave. ☎020 7287 6933 💻www.barrumbadisco.co.uk

Boasting a very young crowd, Bar Rumba is one of the more popular clubs in the area. In a spare space with low ceilings, booths and tables, the dance floor is where all the action takes place among the flashing lights and young crowd.

➦ ⊖Piccadilly Circus. *Turn left onto Great Windmill St. and follow it to Shaftesbury Ave.* ℹ *Credit card £10 min.* $ *Up until 10:30pm guys pay £5, girls get in free. 10:30pm-11:30pm, guys pay £10, girls pay £5. After 11:30pm, everyone pays £10. Cash only for cover.* ⏰ *M-Su 8:30pm-3am.*

MADAME JOJO'S 💳⊗🍸 LIVE ENTERTAINMENT VENUE

8-10 Brewer St. ☎020 7734 3040 💻www.madamejojos.com

Built on the cabaret and live entertainment traditions of yore, Madame Jojo's is not your average club. Every night begins with some form of entertainment before the cabaret tables disappear and the dance floor gets hopping. Dress is smart casual, music is smoking and, when the curtain goes down, the dancing begins.

➦ ⊖*Piccadilly Circus. Go down Shaftesbury and turn left on Wardour St., turn left on Brewer St.* ℹ *Sometimes cover is cash only. Tu is indie night (which is also pretty much a student night). Show finishes around 9:30pm, and then club night begins with DJs. F is northern soul and funk. Sa is 1950s rockabilly and drive. Su is Latin, house, and bebop. W is Trannyshack night, aimed at the transgender community.* $ *Tickets £10-52.50 depending on event, so check website. Single measure spirits and mixer, bottles of beer and glasses of the house red or white £4.50.* ⏰ *Open daily 7pm-3am. 7-9pm is live music, burlesque, comedy, magic, or variety show.*

Westminster

Westminster isn't an ideal location for nightlife, pubs, or clubs. Enjoy it during the day, and then take the party elsewhere, old sport.

THE BUCKINGHAM ARMS 💳♿🍸 PUB

62 Petty France ☎020 7222 3386 💻www.buckinghamarms.com

When the lawmen and -women who keep order in this country need to unwind, they can come here: it is right down the street from the Ministry of Justice. Partially lit by a cool skylight, the pub has comfy armchairs and large windows, so homey charm abounds. It is also worth noting that the Ministry of Justice is on a street named "Petty France." Coincidence? We think not.

➦ ⊖*Victoria. Right onto Grosvenor Pl. Continue onto Victoria St., left onto Buckingham Gate, right on Petty France.* $ *Pint of Youngs £3.* ⏰ *Open M-F 11am-11pm, Sa-Su noon-6pm.*

ARTS AND CULTURE 🎵

You might wonder if the city that brought the world Shakespeare and Harold Pinter has lost its theatrical edge. Not to fear, however—the London theater scene is as vital as ever. From the perennial hard-hitters at the Royal Court to daring musical fare like *Enron: The Musical*, the London stage remains packed with the dramatic flare that put it on the map in the first place.

For those weary of Coldplay, who fear that the country that brought you the Rolling Stones, The Sex Pistols and The Clash hit a roadblock, turn your ears from the arenas and put them to the ground—underground, in fact—to city hotspots where young bands committed to their fans are not interested in seeing their names in gaudy lights.

Cinema

London is teeming with traditional cinemas, the most dominant of which are **Cineworld** and **Odeon,** but the best way to enjoy a film is in one of the hip repertory or luxury cinemas. *Time Out* publishes show times, as does 💻**www.viewlondon.co.uk.** Americans will find the cinema in London to be particularly illuminating, as most films are about a certain kind of American—namely, the stupid, stereotypical kind that would make Europeans hate Americans.

🎬 **BFI SOUTHBANK** 💳♿ THE SOUTH BANK

Belvedere Rd. ☎020 7928 3232 💻www.bfi.org.uk

Hidden under Waterloo Bridge, the BFI Southbank is one of the most exciting repertory cinemas in London. Showcasing everything from art to foreign, British to classic, the BFI provides a range of styles to keep all cinema lovers happy. It runs in seasons, with a different theme each month featuring different elements of film. (For example, a season could be on a director or cinematographer or actor.) The 📺**Mediatech** is free for anyone and allows people to privately view films from the archives.

✈ ⊖*Waterloo.* *i* *Call ☎020 7815 1329 for details on Mediatech hours.* Ⓢ *Evenings M-F £9, concessions £6.65, under 16 and Tu £5.* ⏰ *Mediatech open T-Su noon-8pm.*

Comedy

The English are famous for their occasionally dry, sophisticated wit and often ridiculous ("We are the knights who say Ni!") sense of humor. This humor continues to thrive in the standup and sketch comedy clubs throughout the city. Check *Time Out* for listings, but be warned that the city virtually empties of comedians come August when it's festival time in Edinburgh.

📷 COMEDY STORE ⬥ THE WEST END
1a Oxendon St.   ☎0844 847 1728 🖥www.thecomedystore.co.uk

This comedy venue offers everything from stand-up to the Cutting Edge, a show every Tuesday that does up-to-date topical humor.

✈ ⊖*Piccadilly Circus. Turn left onto Coventry, then right onto Oxendon.* Ⓢ *Tickets £14-20.* ⏰ *Box office open M-Th 6:30-9:30pm, F-Sa 6:30pm-1:15am, Su 6:30-9:30pm. Doors open daily 6:30pm. Bar and diner open daily 6:30pm.*

Dance

As with everything else artistic in London, the dance scene here is diverse, innovative, and first-rate. Come for the famous ballets at older venues like the Royal Opera House or stop by one of the smaller companies for some contemporary dance.

SADLER'S WELLS ⬥♿ CLERKENWELL
Rosebery Ave.   ☎0844 412 4300 🖥www.sadlerswells.com

Encapsulating all forms of dance, Sadler's Wells puts its belief in the power of dance to good use in wide-ranging and always exciting presentations. The site holds 300 years of dance history.

✈ ⊖*Angel. Left onto Upper St., then right onto Rosebery Ave.* *i* *Some shows offer student discounts.* Ⓢ *Tickets £10-£55.* ⏰ *Open M-Sa 9am-8:30pm. By phone M-Sa 9am-8:30pm.*

Music

Clubs are expensive, and pubs close at 11pm. Especially during the current recession, fewer young people are willing to shell out the £10-15 it takes to get into a club, especially since beers cost £4-5 on top of that. Much of the London nightlife scene thus lies beyond pub-and club-hopping in the darkened basements of bars everywhere and the glaringly bright, seismically loud music clubs. With a musical history including **The Beatles, Radiohead,** and **The Clash,** all of the bands from the infamous "British Invasion," and most of the best bands from '90s anthemic pop, the London music scene is very much intact, and makes for both a great night out and an excellent way to forge lasting travel friendships.

Classical

There are several large organizations that supply the city with some of the most renowned classical performances in the world. For free chamber and classical music, check out some of London's churches, where students from famous music schools often give free, professional-quality recitals.

📷 ROYAL OPERA HOUSE ⬥♿ THE WEST END
Bow St.   ☎020 7304 4000 🖥www.roh.org.uk

Though the glorious glass facade of the Royal Opera House makes it look more like a train station than a theater, patrons of the opera enjoy all of the great works of opera and some of the more contemporary pieces too. Though no discounts are offered, students can try and get standby tickets by going online and selecting "student standby" from the website. Top price seats are available for £10 if you get lucky. Booking opens around two months before each performance, so try to book early. The ROH also sponsors free outdoor film screenings, so look out for those on their website.

Covent Garden. Right onto Long Acre, then right onto Bow St. $ Tickets £5-150. Booking office open M-Sa 10am-8pm.

ROYAL ALBERT HALL KENSINGTON

Kensington Gore ☎0845 401 5045 www.royalalberthall.com

Deep in the heart of South Kensington, the Royal Albert Hall was commissioned by Prince Albert in order to promote the arts, and has been in continuous operation since 1871. Offering some of the biggest concerts in London, the famous **BBC Proms** classical festival, and a range of other phenomenal musical events, the hall is an experience in history and culture that's not to be missed.

Knightsbridge. Turn left onto Knightsbridge and continue onto Kensington Rd. $ From £10. Open daily 9am-9pm.

Jazz

RONNIE SCOTT'S SOHO

47 Frith St. ☎020 7439 0747 www.ronniescotts.co.uk

Ronnie Scott's has been defining "hip" in Soho for the last 51 years. It's hosted everyone from **Tony Bennett** to **Van Morrison,** and **Chick Corea** to the **Funk Brothers.** The venue is all flickering candlelight and dulcet reds and blues. Pictures of jazz greats line the walls in black and white, and a diverse crowd imbibes such creations as Jazz Medicine: Jagermeister, sloe gin, Dubonnet, fresh black berries, angostia bitters *(£8)*. The venue's cool, but the jazz is hot.

Tottenham Court Rd. Turn down Oxford St. with your back to Tottenham Court Rd. and turn left on Soho St. turn right onto the square and then right onto Frith St. $ Cover £10, more for big acts. Champagne £8-10. White wine £4.80-5.30. Red wine bottles £22-26. Mixed drinks £8.50-9. Open M-Th 7:15pm-late, F-Sa 6pm-1:30am, Su noon-4pm and 6-10:30pm. Box office open M-F 10am-6pm, Sa noon-5pm.

THE 606 CLUB KNIGHTSBRIDGE

90 Lots Rd. ☎020 7352 5953 www.606club.co.uk

On quiet Lots Rd., opposite what appears to be a rather foreboding abandoned factory, the 606 Club has been quietly hosting the best of the UK music scene since 1969. Properly underground (it's in a basement), the club itself is candlelit and dim.

Sloane Square. Exit the tube and go straight down Sloane Sq. i Non-members have to eat in order to drink. Check website for special Su afternoon lunch and show. $ Cover M £10, Tu-W £8, Th £10, F-Sa £12, Su £10. Entrees £9-18. Bottled beers from £3.45. Open M 7:30pm-midnight, Tu-Th 7pm-midnight, F-Sa 8pm-1:30am, Su 7-11pm.

Pop and Rock

THE TROUBADOUR CAFE KENSINGTON

263-267 Old Brompton Rd. ☎020 7370 1434 www.troubadour.co.uk

Many famous acts have graced the Troubadour's small stage since its founding in 1954. Its hanging string lights and stage lights illuminated **Bob Dylan, Jimi Hendrix,** and **Joni Mitchell,** and pictures of some of these artists are plastered into the tops of the tables. To this day, The Troubadour is a community of aspiring and acclaimed artists bound by great music, good drinks and the intoxicating atmosphere of artistic promise. Come here to see some of the city's most exciting acts before they break.

Gloucester Rd. Turn right onto Gloucester Rd., then turn right onto Old Brompton Rd. i Most nights feature several bands. Every other M poetry night. Cover is cash only. Open M-W 8pm-midnight, Th-Sa 8pm-2am, Su 8pm-midnight. Happy hour Tu-Su 8-9pm.

⬚ KOKO

1a Camden High St. ☎087 0432 5527 ▣www.koko.uk.com

Koko's lodgings are not typical of a rock n' roll venue. Originally a theater, then a cinema, then one of the first BBC radio broadcasting locations, and then the famous Camden Palace Nightclub, Koko holds all its 110 years of history within its beautiful red walls and its gilded, curved wrought-iron fences guarding the balconies from which music-lovers can look down to the stage.

⚡ ⊖*Mornington Crescent. Right onto Hampstead Rd. It's to your right.* *i* *Cash only for in-person purchases. Tickets sold through various outlets online. Indie night (indie music and dancing) F 9:30pm-4am. Credit card at £10 min.* Ⓢ *Concert tickets £10-30. Beer £3.50-4. Mixed drinks £4. For indie night, the first 100 people get in free. Cover for non-students and students after midnight £7, students before midnight £5.* ☒ *Box office open noon-5pm on gig days.*

⬚ BORDERLINE

SOHO

Orange Yd. 16 Manette St. ☎084 4847 2465 ▣www.venues.meanfiddler.com/borderline

A simple venue that, despite its lack of the outlandish Art Deco, theatrical trappings of other similar London concert halls, oozes the spirit of rock and roll from every beer-soaked wall and ear-blowing speaker. Often, big name artists will play the Borderline when starting solo careers. Townes Van Zandt played his last show at the Borderline; Eddie Vedder, Jeff Buckley, and Rilo Kiley have played there; and ⬚**Spinal Tap** played the Borderline right after the movie came out. The amps go to eleven, the music's piping hot, and the location is prime.

⚡ ⊖*Tottenham Court Rd. Right on Charing Cross.* *i* *Club nights W-Sa 11pm-3am.* Ⓢ *Tickets £6-20. Pints £3.40.* ☒ *Doors open for shows daily 7pm. Tickets available at the Jazz Cafe box office M-Sa 10:30am-5:30pm.*

02 ACADEMY BRIXTON

SOUTH LONDON

211 Stockwell Rd. ☎020 7771 3000

Home to Europe's largest fixed stage, the 02 Academy Brixton's set list is rife with the big names of our generation. Past acts include MGMT, Echo and the Bunnymen, Plan B, Pavement, LCD Soundsystem, and the Gaslight Anthem. They also occasionally have club nights (which aren't on a fixed schedule, so check the website).

⚡ ⊖*Brixton. Right onto Brixton Rd., then left onto Stockwell Rd. The area can be a bit rough, so you may want to take a cab.* *i* *Bars are cash only. Call in advance for wheelchair accessibility.* Ⓢ *Ticket prices vary, most £20-35. Pints £4.* ☒ *Venue box office opens 2hr. before doors on gig nights.*

02 EMPIRE

WEST LONDON

Shepherd's Bush Green ☎020 8354 3300 ▣www.02shepherdsbushempire.co.uk

A popular space hosting large rock acts, the 02 Empire is one of the big names on the London music scene. With a classic feel greatly augmented by the bold stonework and old-fashioned hand-placed letters on the awning out front, the Empire hearkens to the heyday of rock and roll.

⚡ ⊖*Shepherd's Bush. Right onto Uxbridge Rd. then left at the end of Shepherd's Bush Green.* *i* *Call ☎084 4477 2000 for tickets.* ☒ *Box office open 4-6pm and 6:30-9:30pm on show days.*

Theater

Ah, "theatre" in London. While in London, many people choose to see a show because the city is renowned for its cheap theater. Tickets for big musicals on the **West End** go for as cheap as £25 the day of, which is pittance compared to the $100 tickets sold on Broadway, the American equivalent. On the West End, the main theater district, you'll find the bigger musicals that are produced in only one theater. For instance, *Phantom of the Opera* is entering its 25th year at Her Majesty's Theatre. Other theaters in the area and throughout London put on more cutting-edge or intellectual plays. Many pubs have live performance spaces in the back where theater groups rehearse and perform for an audience that, thanks to

great britain

a few pints, always finds the second act more confusing than the first. Always check discount prices against the theater itself. Only buy discounted tickets from booths with a circle and check mark symbol that says **STAR** on it. This stands for the Society of Tickets Agents and Retailers, and it vouches for the legitimacy of a discount booth.

▩ ROYAL COURT THEATRE ✈♿ KNIGHTSBRIDGE

Sloane Sq. ☎020 7565 5000 🖳www.royalcourttheatre.com

Famous for pushing the theater envelope, the Royal Court is the antidote to all the orchestral swoons and faux-opera sweeping through the West End. The Royal Court's 1956 production of John Osborne's *Look Back in Anger* (not to be confused with the Oasis song of a similar title) was largely credited with launching Modern British drama. Royal is known as a writers' theater, purveying high-minded works of great drama for audiences that will appreciate them.

‡ ⊖*Sloane Square.* Ⓢ *Tickets M £10, Tu-Sa £12.18-£25. Student discounts available on day of performance, preview and Sa matinees.* 🕐 *Open M-F 10am-6pm or until the doors open, Sa 10am-curtain up on performance days.*

▩ THE NATIONAL THEATRE ✈♿ THE SOUTH BANK

Belvedere Rd. ☎020 7452 3400 🖳www.nationaltheatre.org.uk

Opened in 1976 by appointment of the monarchy, the National Theatre shows great new and classic British drama on its three stages, of which the Olivier is largest. It also revives lost classics from around the world. Special Travelex shows mean half the seats are available for only £10.

‡ ⊖*Waterloo. Right onto York Rd. then left onto Waterloo Rd.* Ⓢ *Tickets £10-44.* 🕐 *Box office open M-Sa 9:30am-8pm, Su noon-6pm.*

▩ THE OLD VIC ✈♿ SOUTH LONDON

The Cut ☎084 4871 7628 🖳www.oldvictheatre.com

This famous theater was built in 1818 and has hosted the likes of **Laurence Olivier.** Though dealing in a huge range of styles, the Old Vic is predominantly a traditional theater showing the classics. Fans of Kevin Spacey will want to visit now, since he is the theater's current artistic director.

‡ ⊖*Southwark. Right onto The Cut.* Ⓢ *Tickets £10-47.* 🕐 *Open M-Sa 10am-7pm on non-show days, 10am-6pm on show days.*

THE YOUNG VIC ✈♿ SOUTH LONDON

66 The Cut ☎020 7922 2922 🖳www.youngvic.org

Formerly the studio space for the Old Vic, the Young Vic puts on a variety of shows, most of which are edgier, more exciting, and newer than the more traditional Old Vic down the road. They frequently do reinterpretations of classic works as well as newer stuff. The three spaces in the theater allow for great versatility, with one main house and two studio spaces.

‡ ⊖*Southwark. Right onto the Cut.* Ⓢ *Tickets £10-22.* 🕐 *Open M-Sa 10am-6pm.*

SHAKESPEARE'S GLOBE ✈ SOUTH LONDON

21 New Globe Walk ☎020 7401 9919 🖳www.shakespeares-globe.org

Though the original Globe theater burnt down in 1613 during a performance of *Henry VIII*, this accurate reconstruction was opened in 1997. Much like the original Globe, it has an open roof and standing area for the "groundlings." Steeped in historical and artistic tradition, the theater stages Shakespeare as well as two new plays a year.

‡ ⊖*Southwark. Left onto Blackfriars Rd., right onto Southwark St., left onto Great Guildford, right onto Park St., left onto Emerson St.* Ⓢ *Standing £5, seats £35.* 🕐 *Box office open M-Sa 10am-8pm, Su 10am-7pm. Telephone line open M-Sa 10am-6pm, Su 10am-5pm.*

london . arts and culture

Festivals

BBC PROMS 🎫♿ KNIGHTSBRIDGE
Kensington Gore ☎0845 401 5045 🖥www.bbc.co.uk/proms

BBC Proms is a world famous classical music festival put on by the BBC in the Royal Albert Hall. What in the world is a "Prom," you ask? "Prom" stands for "Promenade Concert"—a performance at which some of the audience stands on a promenade in the arena. During the proms, there is at least one daily performance in London's Royal Albert Hall, in addition 70-odd events and discussions. Note that performances are broadcast for free.

🧭 ⊖Knightsbridge. Turn left onto Knightsbridge, continue onto Kensington Rd. ***i*** *Check website for specific wheelchair-accessibility information. [S]From £10. ⏰ July-Sept.*

GLASTONBURY FESTIVAL SOMERSET
Pilton, England ☎01458 834 596 🖥www.glastonburyfestivals.co.uk

One of the most famous rock festivals in the world, the Glastonbury Festival explodes onto the scene every June. Possibly as close as you will ever get to going to Woodstock, it's essentially a bunch of festivals jam-packed into one, distributed through the Dance Village, Green Field, Circus and Theatre fields and the Park.

🧭Festival office: 28 Northload St., Glastonbury, Somerset BA6 9JJ. ***i*** *National Express has routes to Glastonbury. Bristol and Glastonbury town shuttles provide transportation to the festival. Disabled patrons must register in order to use the festival's accessible facilities; to get a registration form, request a disabled access packet, which includes information on the site's accessible facilities. [S] Standard ticket £185 + £5 booking fee per ticket + £5 P and P per booking. ⏰ June. Performance dates and times vary.*

SHOPPING

London is known as one of the shopping capitals of the world. With its famous department stores keeping the old flame of shopping as spectacle alive over in Knightsbridge, London has kept some of its old shopping class and the prices that come with it. Vintage stores and hip, independent record stores fill Soho, and the East End has lots of fun boutiques. Notting Hill is famous for **Portobello Market,** but even in off-market days, the road has a host of cute boutique shopping options. Chelsea is for those with a bit more money and a serious commitment to shopping. For you literary junkies, **John Sandoe Books** is our favorite bookstore in the city. Shopping is a significant part of tourism in London, so if you aren't broke and have some extra room in your backpack, window shop the day away.

Westminster

Westminster is filled with chains. The area is worth seeing for the sights, but die-hard shoppers might be best served by looking elsewhere.

HOTEL CHOCOLAT 🎫♿ CHOCOLATE
133 Victoria St. ☎020 7821 0473 🖥www.hotelchocolat.co.uk

One of a chain, Hotel Chocolat is one of the more exciting chains in Westminster. The inside is sleek, like a more efficient version of Willy Wonka's Chocolate Factory. Seventy percent of the chocolate here is made in Britain, and it's packaged into ridiculous items like framed chocolate portraits and chocolate dipping sets, all for sale. For anyone who's ever felt that a chocolate "slab" is preferable to a chocolate bar, you have found your store.

🧭 Victoria. Take right onto Grosvenor Pl and follow it onto Victoria St. ⏰ Open M-F 8:30am-7pm, Sa 9:30am-6pm, Su 11am-5pm.

Bayswater

Bayswater is full of quirky little shops, though it's not a major shopping center like Notting Hill.

BAYSWATER MARKET

        ♿ MARKET

Bayswater Rd.

Every Sunday, local artists of all media and skill levels decorate the Hyde Park Fence with their wares, making it look like an art gallery with commitment issues. It's open all afternoon, so join the crowds as they move from touristy London pictures to more original works from rising stars in the London art scene. Art is for sale at all prices, so come with an open mind and be ready to dig a sizeable hole in your wallet.

   ⌖ ϴ*Lancaster Gate.* ☒ *Open Su late morning through the afternoon.*

Chelsea

Shopping in Chelsea runs the gamut, with stores from the neighborhoods punk-rock salad days to a stifling amount of kitchen and home shops. Still, if you want to trick out your hostel room, we've seen some lovely linoleum.

▪ JOHN SANDOE BOOKS

  ♨♿ BOOKSTORE

10 Blacklands Terr.   ☏020 7589 9473 ■www.johnsandoe.com

While taking the stairs to the fiction section on the second floor, one remembers the joy of independent bookstores. There's barely space for peoples' feet as half of each stair is taken up by a pile of carefully selected books. On the crammed second floor, a cracked leather chair presides over shelves so packed with masterworks and little-known gems that they are layered with moving shelves. There are books everywhere in this store, and the knowledgeable staff is personable and ready to hand with excellent suggestions. Book lovers beware: it would be easy to spend the day in this shop.

   ⌖ ϴ*Sloane Sq. Exit the Tube and go straight down Sloane Sq. The street slanting gently left is King's Rd. Go straight onto it and turn right at Blacklands Terr.* ☒ *Open M-Sa 9:30am-5:30pm, Su noon-6pm.*

Knightsbridge and Belgravia

Mostly posh shops and chains, Knightsbridge isn't the most friendly place for shopping, price-wise. However, the spectacle of its famous department stores make browsing enjoyable.

▪ HARRODS

  ♨♿ DEPARTMENT STORE

87-135 Brompton Rd.   ☏020 7730 1234 ■www.harrods.com

An ode to the shopping experience, Harrods is probably the most famous department store on the planet. Packed with faux-hieroglyphs, a room named "Room of Luxury" or its sequel, "Room of Luxury II," Harrods is just as much a sight to see as it is a place to shop. Especially entertaining are the prices and the people who pay them. Be sure to check out the toy section—it's hard not to rediscover your inner child. Also worth seeing is the candy section of the food court, which is where they sell chocolate shoes (*£84 for a pair*). On the bottom floor, they sell "Personalised Classics" which enable you to insert names in place of the ones already in a given book. Who needs "Romeo and Juliet" when you could have "Fred and Agnes?" "Fred, Fred, wherefore art thou Fred?" The answer: In shopping heaven.

   ⌖ ϴ*Knightsbride. Take the Harrods Exit.* ☒ *Open M-Sa 10am-8pm, Su 11:30am-6pm.*

HARVEY NICHOLS

  ♨♿ DEPARTMENT STORE

109-125 Knightsbridge   ☏020 7235 5000 ■www.harveynichols.com

Whoever was looking for the Fountain of Youth clearly never checked out the ground floor of Harvey Nichols. The entire level is packed with women arming themselves for the battle against age. In fact, four floors of the great department store are taken up by fashion, cosmetics, beauty, and accessories. After that, there's menswear and food and hospitality. Most high-end designers are sold here. Foreigners can shop tax-free if they go to the fourth-floor customer services and fill out a form. The store is upscale, densely populated with women, and a little less of a scene than nearby Harrods.

Knightsbridge. Open M-Sa 10am-9pm, Su 11:30am-6pm (browsing only 11:30am-noon).

Notting Hill

Like we said, Portobello Rd. is truly where it's at. Otherwise, shopping options in Notting Hill consist mainly of antique stores, souvenir sellers and high-end clothing shops.

MUSIC AND VIDEO EXCHANGE — MUSIC

42 Notting Hill Gate — www.mveshops.co.uk

Though part of a chain, this Music and Video Exchange will entertain any audiophile endlessly. The staff engage in Hornby-esque conversations oozing with musical knowledge, while customers browse through the vinyls, CDs, and cassettes in the bargain area. Upstairs in the rarities section, you can find anything from a £12 original vinyl of the Rolling Stones' *Get Yer Ya-Ya's Out!* to the original German sleeve for the Beatles' final record, *Let it Be*. Customers can trade in their own stuff in exchange for cash or—in a move betraying MVE's cold-hearted understanding of a music lover's brain—twice the cash amount in store vouchers.

Notting Hill Gate. Walk out the south entrance and go down Notting Hill Gate. Daily 10am-8pm.

concessions

The British word "concession" is the equivalent of the American "discount." It usually applies to fees for students, seniors, the unemployed with proof of unemployment and, sometimes, the disabled.

The West End

Shopping in the West End is more student-oriented than most areas in London. Filled with cool independent stores, most of them selling books, CDs, vinyls and more vintage clothes than the Motown stars ever wore, the West End is a fun shopping district that tends to emphasize the cheap. Break out the chucks, Ray-Bans, and tight black jeans—your wallet must lighten.

SISTER RAY — INDEPENDENT RECORDS AND CDS

34-35 Berwick St. — ☎020 7734 3297 www.sisterray.co.uk

An old school record shop of the best kind, Sister Ray has every sort of genre, from constant chart-toppers to one-hit wonders. The stellar staff is adept at creating musical matches-made-in-Heaven, directing listeners to artists. Hip, cheap books about music line the check-out counter, and listening stations are throughout the store.

Tottenham Court Rd., left on Oxford St. left on Wardour St., left on Berwick St. **i** *Wheelchair access at the top of the store, ramp available on request. Open M-Sa 10am-8pm, Su noon-6pm. M-W, Sa 11am-7pm, Th-F 11am-8pm, Su noon-6pm.*

ESSENTIALS

Practicalities

- **TOURS: Big Bus Company** *(48 Buckingham Palace Rd. Victoria. ☎020 7233 9533 www.bigbustours.com Buses leave every 15min. 8:30am-6pm.)* offers a **Red Tour** (history) which stops at the Green Park Underground, Hyde Park Corner, Trafalgar Square, Whitehall, Westminster Bridge, London Eye, Tower of London, Buckingham Palace and Victoria. **Original London Walks** *(☎020 7624 9255 $ £8, 65+ and students £6)* has themed walks like "Jack the Ripper Walk" and "Alfred Hitchcock's London." Check the website for schedules. **Britain Visitor Centres** *(1 Regent St. ⊖Piccadilly Circus.* ◼*www.visitbritain.com* ✆ *Open M 9:30am-6:30pm, Tu-F 9am-6pm, Sa 9am-5pm, Su and bank holidays 10am-4pm.)* **London Information Centre** *(Leicester Sq. ⊖Leicester Sq.* ☎*020 7292 2333* ✆ *Open daily 8am-midnight.)*

- **US EMBASSY:** *(24 Grosvenor Sq. ⊖Bond St.* ☎*020 7499 9000* ◼*www.usembassy.org.uk.).*

- **CREDIT CARD SERVICES: American Express** (◼*www.amextravelresources.com)* locations at *(78 Brompton Rd. ⊖Knightsbridge.* ☎*084 4406 0046* ✆ *Open M-T 9am-5:30pm, W 9:30am-5:30pm, Th-F 9am-5:30pm, Sa 9am-4:00pm)* and *(30-31 Haymarket. ⊖Piccadilly Circus.* ☎*084 4406 0044* ✆ *Open M-F 9:00am-5:30pm.).*

- **GLBT RESOURCES: Boyz** (◼*www.boyz.co.uk)* lists gay events in London as well as an online version of its magazine. **Gingerbeer** (◼*www.gingerbeer.co.uk)* is a guide for lesbian and bisexual women with events listings.

- **POST OFFICE: Trafalgar Square Post Office.** *(24-28 William IV St., Westminster. ⊖Charing Cross.* ☎*0207 484 9305* ✆ *Open M 8:30am-6:30pm, Tu 9:15am-6:30pm, W-F 8:30am-6:30pm, Sa 9am-5:30pm.)*

Emergency!

- **POLICE:** Call **City of London Police** (☎*020 7601 2000)* or **Metropolitan Police** (☎*030 0123 1212).*

- **HOSPITAL: St. Thomas' Hospital.** *(Westminster Bridge Rd. ⊖Westminster.* ☎*020 7188 7188.)* **Royal Free Hospital.** *(Pond St. ⊖Hampstead Heath.* ☎*020 7794 0500.)* **Charing Cross Hospital.** *(Fulham Palace Rd. ⊖Hammersmith.* ☎*020 3311 1234.)* **University College Hospital.** *(235 Euston Rd. ⊖Warren Street.* ☎*0845 155 5000.)*

- **PHARMACY: Boots** (◼*www.boots.com)* and **Superdrug** (◼*www.superdrug.com),* the most popular drugstores in London, are scattered throughout the city. **Zafash Pharmacy.** *(233-235 Old Brompton Rd. ⊖Earl's Court.* ☎*020 7373 2798* ◼*www.zafash.com.)* **Bliss Pharmacy.** *(107-109 Gloucester Rd. ⊖Gloucester Rd.* ☎*020 7373 4445.)*

Getting There

By Plane

The main airport in London is **Heathrow** (☎*084 4335 1801* ◼*www.heathrowairport.com).* There are five terminals at Heathrow, which is commonly regarded as one of the busiest international airports in the world. Terminal 2 is closed, and there are exceptions to the rules concerning the location of airlines. The best way to find your terminal is through the **"Which terminal?"** function on the Heathrow website. This tool enables you to search via airline and destination as well as specific flight number.

The cheapest way to get from London Heathrow to Central London is on the Tube. The two Tube stations servicing the four terminals of Heathrow form a distressing looking loop at the end of the ⊖**Piccadilly** line which runs between Central London and the Heathrow terminals *(*✆ *1hr. every 5min. M-Sa 5am-11:54pm, Su 5:46am-10:37pm.)*

Heathrow Express (☎*084 5600 1515* ◼*www.heathrowexpress.com)* runs between Heathrow and Paddington four times an hour. The trip is significantly shorter than many of the alternatives, clocking in at around 15-20min. *(*✆ *M-Sa 1st train from terminals 1, 2 and 3 5:12am; Su 5:08am. M-Su first train from Terminal 5 5:07am),* but the £16.50 *(when purchased online; £18 from station; £23 on board)* makes it a little less enticing. The **Heathrow Connect** also runs to Paddington but is both cheaper and longer because it stops at five places on the way to and from Heathrow. There are two trains per hour, and the trip takes about 25min.

london • essentials

The **National Express** bus runs between Victoria Coach Station and Heathrow three times an hour. Though cheap and often simpler than convoluted Underground trips, the buses are subject to that great parasite of the Queen's country: traffic. There are naysayers roaming the halls of Heathrow moaning terrifying tales about people spending vacations on buses, but if you're looking for a cheap thrill and you're from anywhere with normal driving laws, you can look forward to that first time when they pull onto the highway and your travel-addled mind instructs you to wrench the steering wheel from the driver's mad hands. *(☎08717 818 178 💻www.nationalexpress.com).* Posing a similar traffic threat, **taxis** from the airport to Victoria cost around £60 and take around 45min. In short, they aren't worth it.

Getting to **Gatwick Airport** *(☎084 4335 1802 💻www.gatwickairport.com)* takes around 30min., making it less convenient than Heathrow but less hectic too. The swift and affordable train services that connect Gatwick to the city make the trip a little easier. The **Gatwick Express** train *(☎084 5850 1530 💻www.gatwickexpress.com $ 1-way £15.20; roundtrip £25.80 and valid for a month)* runs non-stop service to Victoria station *(⏰35min., every 15min., 5:50am-12:35am).* Buy tickets in terminals, at the station, or on the train itself.

National Express runs services from the North and South terminals of Gatwick to London. The National Express bus *(☎08717 818 178 💻www.nationalexpress.com)* takes approximately 85min., and buses depart for London Victoria hourly. Taxis take about 1hr. to reach central London. **easyBus** *(☎084 4800 4411 💻www.easybus.co.uk)* runs every 15min. from North and South terminals to Earls Court and West Brompton. *($ Tickets from £20. ⏰ 65min., every 15min.)*

The Europeans are far ahead of Americans in terms of train travel, and London offers several ways to easily reach other European destinations. **Eurolines** *(☎08717 818 181 💻www.eurolines.co.uk ⏰ Open 8am-8pm)* is Europe's largest coach network, providing service to 500 destinations throughout Europe. Many buses leave from **Victoria Coach Station,** which is at the mouth of Elizabeth St. just off of Buckingham Palace Road. Many coach companies, including **National Express, Eurolines,** and **Megabus** operate from Victoria Coach. National Express *(☎087 1781 8178 💻www.nationalexpress.com)* is the only scheduled coach network in Britain and can be used for most intercity travel and for travel to and from various airports. It can also be used to reach Scotland and Wales. **Greenline** *(☎087 1200 2233 💻www.greenline.co.uk)* provides services throughout London. One of its stops is by **Eccleston Bridge,** right next to Victoria, but it also reaches such convenient areas as **Hyde Park Corner** and **Baker Street.**

Getting Around

Though there are daily interruptions to service in the Tube (that's right, not the metro, not the subway, but the Tube, or Underground), the controlling network, **Transport of London** does a good job of keeping travelers aware of these disruptions to service. Each station will have posters listing interruptions to service, and you can check service online at 💻**www.tfl.gov.uk** or the 24hr. travel information service at ☎0843 222 1234. Most stations also have ticket booths and informed TFL employees who can help you and guide you to the proper pamphlets.

Though many people in the city stay out past midnight, the Tube doesn't have the same sort of stamina. When it closes around midnight, night owls have two choices: a cab or **nightbuses.** Most nightbus lines are prefixed with an **N** (N13, for instance) and some stops even have 24hr. buses.

Travel Passes

Travel Passes are almost guaranteed to save you money. The passes are priced based on the number of zones they serve (the more zones, the more expensive), but zone 1 encompasses central London and you will not likely need to get past zone 2. If someone offers you a secondhand ticket, don't take it. There's no real way to verify whether it's valid—plus, it's illegal. Those under 16 get free travel on buses and trams. Children under 5 rule the public transportation system, getting free travel on the Tube, trams, **Docklands Lights Railway (DLR)**, overground, and **National Rail** services (though they must be accompanied by someone with a valid pass). Passengers ages 11-15 enjoy reduced fares on the Tube with an Oyster photocard. Students eighteen and older must study full-time *(at least 15hr. per week over 14 weeks)* in London to qualify for the Student Photocard, which enables users to save 30% on adult travel cards and bus and tram passes. You can apply for one online but you need a passport-sized digital photo and an enrollment ID from your school. It's worth it if you're staying for an extended period of time. (Study abroad kids, we're looking at you...)

Oyster Cards store everything you need and enable you to pay in a variety of ways. Fares come in peak *(M-F 4:30am-9:29am)* and off-peak *(any other time)* varieties and are, again, distinguished by zone. In addition to letting you add Travelcards, Oysters enable users to "pay as you go," meaning that you can store credit on an as-needed basis. The cards have price capping that will allow you to travel as much as you want, while ensuring that you don't pay above the cost of the day Travelcard you would otherwise have purchased. Register your card, especially if you put a lot of money on it. That way, you can ⬛**recover everything if it's lost.**

Weekly, monthly, and annual Travelcards can be purchased at any time from Tube stations. They yield unlimited *(within zone)* use for their duration *(⑤ Weekly rates for zones 1-2 £25.80. Monthly £99.10. Day off-peak £5.60, day anytime is £7.20).*

By Underground

Most stations have **Tube maps** on the walls as well as free pocket maps. Please note that the Tube map barely reflects an above-ground scale, and should not be used for even the roughest of walking directions. Platforms are organized by line, and will have the **colors** of the lines serviced and their names on the wall. The colors of the poles inside the trains correspond with the line, and trains will often have their end destination displayed on the front. This is an essential service when your line splits. Many platforms will have a digital panel indicating ETAs for the trains and sometimes type and final destination. When transferring in stations, just follow the clearly marked routes. Yellow **"WAY OUT"** signs point toward exits.

The Tube runs Monday to Saturday from approximately **5:30am** (though it depends on which station and line) to around **midnight.** If you're taking a train within 30min. of these times (before or after), you'll want to check the signs in the ticket hall for times of the first and last train. The Tube runs less frequently on Sunday, with many lines starting service after 6am. Around 6pm on weekdays, many of the trains running out of central London become packed with the after-work crowd. It's best to avoid the service at this time.

You can buy **tickets** from ticket counters (though these often have lines at bigger stations) or at machines in the stations. You need a ticket to swipe in at the beginning of the journey, and also to exit the Tube. If your train is randomly selected, you will need to present a valid ticket to avoid the £50 penalty fee, which is reduced to £25 if you pay in under 21 days.

By Bus

While slower than the Tube for long journeys (traffic and more frequent stops), **buses** can be useful for traveling short distances covered by a few stops (and several transfers) on the Tube. For one-stop distances, your best bet may be walking.

Bus stops frequently have lists of buses servicing the stop as well as route maps and maps of the area indicating nearby stops. Buses display route numbers.

Every route and stop is different, but buses generally run every 5-15min. beginning around **5:30am** and ending around **midnight.** After day bus routes have closed, **Night Buses** take over. These routes are typically prefixed with an N and operate similar routes to their daytime equivalents. Some buses run 24-hour services. If you're staying out past the Tube closing time, you should plan your nightbus route or bring cab fare.

Singles for adults and students cost £2; fare is only £1.20 with Oyster pay-as-you-go. Sixteen and up Oyster Photocard users get £.60 rates on pay-as-you-go. Eleven- to fifteen-year-olds ride free with Oyster Photocards. Under 11s ride free regardless of Oyster photocard.

oxford ☎01865

Oxford has prestige written all over it. The renowned university has educated some of the most influential players in Western civilization, serving as a home to intellectual royalty, royal royalty, and at least a dozen saints. Students from all around Britain and the world aspire to join the ranks of **Adam Smith, Oscar Wilde,** and **Bill Clinton**...but if you can't join 'em, visit 'em. Swarms of tourists descend on Oxford throughout the year, so don't expect everybody you see to be a local (or a genius). Make room in your budget for some extra-credit **college knowledge.**

ORIENTATION

Cowley Road

If you're looking for an interesting change of pace from blue-blood, tourist-crammed Oxford, take an excursion across **Magdalen Bridge,** then follow the roundabout to Cowley Road. It's Oxford's shopping hub that provides a glimpse into the rich diversity thriving outside the touristy High St. and Cornmarket shops. Cowley Rd. leads through inner-city East Oxford, and into the suburb of Cowley, which **William Morris,** the automobile tycoon, transformed into one of Britain's most significant mass production plants à la Henry Ford. This industry brought a steady flow of immigrants from Wales from the early 1900s.

Today, Cowley Rd. reveals its diversity through its food: in just a quick stroll down the street, you'll see everything from halal groceries to Chinese woks, from Italian dishes to Polish specialties, from tapas to shishas.

Jericho

Jericho is Oxford's bohemian student neighborhood. Home to the **Oxford Canal** with its walking paths, the **Oxford University Press,** and a young, vibrant nightlife (mostly pubs and bars), this part of town is up-and-coming. Bikes and bike shops are everywhere and have become the favorite mode of transport for many Jericho residents. But never fear—Jericho is easy walking distance from Oxford's city center. Walk north up **Saint Giles** (Cornmarket St. becomes Magdalen St., which leads into St. Giles) and make a left onto **Little Clarendon.** The main Jericho drag, **Walton Street,** runs off of Little Clarendon.

Carfax

Carfax is the pulsing heart of the city of Oxford, with both ancient and modern ties. The name comes from the French word *carrefour,* meaning "crossroads." Today, Carfax is at the crossroads of Oxford's main shopping district: **High Street, Saint Aldate's, Cornmarket Street,** and **Queen Street** are the busiest thoroughfares of this tourist-mobbed district. (Cornmarket is pedestrian only, but that doesn't mean its not equally packed.) **Carfax Tower** and **Saxon Tower,** two ancient structures in the city center, serve as convenient orientation points. Meanwhile, the magnificent looming spires of the most centrally-located colleges hover over Carfax, dominating the skyline.

ACCOMMODATIONS

Cowley Road

HEATHER HOUSE   ✦※Ⓧ(ɕ)   BED AND BREAKFAST ❹
192 Iffley Rd.   ☎01865 249 757 ◘www.heatherhouse.plus.com

This cozy home is a good value in otherwise pricey Oxford, with clean, comfortable rooms and a welcoming guest living room, with a homey couch and books about Britain and Oxford, plus the free advice of a local host. Heather House is located on

great britain

a residential main street about a 10min. walk from the colleges. Tea lovers will be pleased that there's a wide selection of herbal teas included with breakfast.

➤ 10-15min. walk from the Magdalen College, but a good 30min. from the train station. Walking: cross the Magdalen Bridge and bear right at the roundabout onto Iffley Rd. From train station, take bus # 4 (A, B, or C) from New Rd. bus stop. Get off opposite the Greyfriars Church bus stop. ℹ Full English breakfast included. Free internet use on a communal computer. Longer stays are cheaper per night. $ Single with private bath £38-£48; ensuite twins £68-80; doubles £70-80. ⏰ Open 24hr.

Carfax

CENTRAL BACKPACKERS 💳🚭📶🍸🍳 HOSTEL ❷

13 Park End St. ☎01865 24 22 88 💻www.centralbackpackers.co.uk

The relaxed rooftop garden with couches and a big screen is the perfect place to kick back and watch a game while throwin' back a pint. The only drawback to a prime downtown location are the sounds of Beyoncé from nearby clubs at 10pm every night. Think of it as motivation, though—shouldn't you be out enjoying Oxford? For those who don't agree, the hostel handily provides free earplugs.

➤ Short walk from Train station; Botley Rd. becomes Park End St. ℹ Continental breakfast included. Free luggage storage. Free lockers. Self-catering kitchen. Laundry £3.50. Beers on the terrace £1. $ 4-bed dorms £21, 8-bed £19, 6-bed female £20, 12-bed £18. £1 per debit/credit transaction. ⏰ Reception open 8am-11pm.

YHA OXFORD 💳♿📶🍸 HOSTEL ❷

2A Botley Rd. ☎01865 727 275 💻www.yha.org

Don't let the less-than-stylish exterior deceive you: YHA Oxford is recently renovated, with modern facilities and spotlessly clean rooms. Special amenities include an intimate library perfect for cozying up to a good book, a "Boathouse" restaurant, an outdoor seating area, and snacks for sale at reception. Like at many YHAs, however, the guest list is made up of significant numbers of schoolkids and other large groups, so you might not find people kicking back and relaxing. If you're lonely, try debating philosophy with the famous Oxfordians in picture frames on the walls. Still and lifeless as they are, they'll give you a run for your money.

➤ Next to train station. ℹ Breakfast not included, full English breakfast £5. Self-catering kitchen. Internet £1 per 15min. Wi-Fi £5 per day. Library and TV lounge. All rooms have ensuite baths, plus extra bathrooms in hallyways. $ Dorms £16-22; singles £28; doubles/twins £45-55. £3 surcharge for non-YHA members. ⏰ Reception 24hr.

University Accommodations

The University of Oxford's conferencing website, 💻**www.conference-oxford.com** lists some individual email contacts for B and B accommodations at the colleges. The process can be a hassle, but worth it if you'd like to stay in the medieval digs of one of Oxford's prestigious colleges.

LINCOLN HALL BED AND BREAKFAST 💳🚭📶 DORMS, BED AND BREAKFAST ❸

Museum Rd. 💻beckie@internal.linc.ox.ac.uk

Lincoln College offers up to 60 single ensuite rooms with shared kitchens in historic, brightly-colored Victorian townhouses. Centrally located to university sights like the **Bodleian Library** and **Pitt Rivers Museum.**

➤ Near the University science area. ℹ Continental breakfast included. Must pay in full before stay. £10 key deposit. Internet access via ethernet port. $ Singles £40. ⏰ Open July-Aug. Reception 24hr.

SIGHTS 👁

Carfax

The **Tourist Information Centre** on **Broad Street** sells the *Oxford What to See and Do Guide* for £.60, which lists all of the colleges' visiting hours and prices and has a handy map. Hours can also be accessed online at 💻**www.ox.ac.uk.** Note that hours and the list of sights open to tourists can be changed at any given time without explanation or notice. Some colleges charge admission, while others are accessible only through the official blue badge tours, booked at the TIC, and a few are generally off-limits. Take this as warning that it's not worth trying to sneak into Christ Church outside open hours. College bouncers in bowler hats, affectionately known as "bulldogs," will squint their eyes and promptly kick you out.

One of the best ways to get into the colleges for free (and also to witness a beautiful, historic ritual) is to check out one of the church services in the college chapels during term-time, for Evensong in particular. Usually, this takes place at around 6pm. Show up 15min. before it starts and tell the people at the gate that you'd like to attend the service; they generally let you in for free.

Christ Church

CHRIST CHURCH ♿ COLLEGE

St. Aldates ☎01865 276 492 🖥www.chch.ox.ac.uk/college

Oxford's most famous college has the university's grandest quad and some of its most distinguished alumni, including 13 saints and past prime ministers. During the English Civil War, "The House" was also the home to **Charles I** and the royal family, who used the Royalist-friendly university as a retreat during Cromwell's advance, and escaped Oxford dressed as servants when the city came under threat. The college is also notable as the place where Lewis Carroll first met **Alice,** the young daughter of the college dean, before she headed to Wonderland. In other cultural references, the dining hall and central quad serve as shooting locations for many *Harry Potter* films (tourists mob to see the site of Hogwarts' dining hall).

Down St. Aldates from Carfax. $ £6.30, concessions £4.80, family ticket £12. 🕐 Open M-Sa 9am-5:30pm, Su 1-5:30pm.

CHRIST CHURCH CHAPEL ♿ CHAPEL

St Aldates ☎01865 276 492 🖥www.chch.ox.ac.uk/cathedral

Christ Church Chapel is the only church in all of England to serve as both a cathedral (for the archdiocese of Oxford) and college chapel. The church was founded in CE 730 by Oxford's patron saint, **Saint Fridesweide,** who built a nunnery here in honor of two miracles: the blinding of her persistent suitor and his subsequent recovery. A stained-glass window, c. 1320, depicts **Thomas à Becket** kneeling moments before his death in Canterbury Cathedral.

Down St. Aldates from Carfax. $ £6.30, concessions £4.80, family ticket £12. 🕐 Hall and cathedral open M-F 10:15am-11:45am, 2:15pm-4:30pm, Sa-Su 2:30-4:30pm only. Last admission 4:30pm. Chapel services M-F 6pm; Su 8am, 10am, 11:15am, and 6pm.

Other Colleges

Oxford's extensive **college system** (distributing its 20,000 students among 38 official colleges and 6 permanent private halls of the university—each with its own structure and rules—means that there are plenty of beautiful grounds to stroll year-round. We've picked out a few of the most frequented to save you the purchase of a guide—well, *another* guide. Full books, however, are published on just single colleges. For information on others, pick up one of the many guides found at the Tourist Information Center or the paperback books found in souvenir shops all over town.

ALL SOULS COLLEGE COLLEGE

Corner of High and Catte St. ☎01865 279 379 🖥www.all-souls.ox.ac.uk.

All Souls College (founded in 1438) is so exclusive that admission is solely offered on an invitation-only basis: the graduate fellows who live here are engaged in intense academic research, and are rumored to rarely leave their rooms because of it.

i The next processions will happen on January 14th, 2011. $ Free. 🕐 Open Sept-July M-F 2-4pm.

BALLIOL COLLEGE
COLLEGE

Broad St.   ☎01865 277 777 ■www.balliol.ox.ac.uk

Along with Merton and University, **Balliol** has a legitimate claim to being the oldest college in Oxford, founded in approximately 1263. Matthew Arnold, Gerard Manley Hopkins, Aldous Huxley, Adam Smith, three British prime ministers, and **six members of the Obama administration** were products of Balliol's mismatched spires.

Ⓢ *£2, students £1, under 18 free.* Ⓩ *Open daily 10am-5pm or dusk.*

MAGDALEN COLLEGE
COLLEGE

High St.   ☎01865 276 000 ■www.magd.ox.ac.uk

Many consider Magdalen (MAUD-lin), with its winding riverbanks, flower-filled quads, and 100 acres of grounds, to be Oxford's best-looking college. Magdalen boys have also been traditionally quite a catch: they've produced seven Nobel Prizes, Dudley Moore, and **Oscar Wilde.** The college has a **deer park,** where deer have grazed aimlessly for centuries.

Ⓢ *£4.50, concessions £3.50.* Ⓩ *Open daily Oct-June 1-6pm or dusk; July-Sept noon-6pm.*

MERTON COLLEGE
COLLEGE

Merton St.   ☎01865 276 310 ■www.merton.ox.ac.uk

Though Balliol and University were endowed before it, **Merton** has the earliest formal college statutes (1274), so it can boast of being the oldest college in its own right. Merton's library houses the first printed Welsh Bible. **JRR Tolkien** was the Merton Professor of English, inventing the **Elven** language and writing some minor trilogy in his spare time. The college's 14th-century **Mob Quad** is Oxford's oldest and one of its least impressive—the "little" quadrangle was where the junior members of the college were housed after the grander Fellows' Quadrangle was built in 1610—but nearby St. Alban's Quad has some of the university's best gargoyles.

Ⓢ *Grounds free. Library tours £2.* Ⓩ *Open M-F 2-4pm, Sa-Su 10am-4pm.*

Museums

🖾 ASHMOLEAN MUSEUM
👆🏻 MUSEUM

Beaumont St.   ☎01865 278 000 ■www.ashmolean.org

Oxford University's Museum of Art and Archeology is newly reopened after a multi-million-dollar renovation that added 39 new galleries and doubled its display space. The Ashmolean collection (named for 17th-century English antiquary, politician, and wealthy collector Elias Ashmole) is the oldest public museum in Europe, with seriously world-class exhibits from every region of the world. In addition to beautiful exhibits that shed light on how world cultures developed through contact with one another, Oxford's only rooftop restaurant lies upstairs. Though the restaurant is pricey, it has excellent views of the city.

⚓ *Opposite the Randolph Hotel.* 𝒊 *Free lunchtime gallery talks for first 12 interested Tu-F 1:15-2pm. Pick up tokens from the information desk.* Ⓢ *Free.* Ⓩ *Open Tu-Su 10am-6pm.*

🖾 BODLEIAN LIBRARY
👆🏻 LIBRARY

Broad St.   ☎01865 277 178 ■www.bodleian.ox.ac.uk

As you enter through the Great Gate into the Old Schools Quadrangle, you'll be in good company—in spirit, anyway. Five kings, 40 Nobel Prize winners, 28 British prime ministers, and writers like Oscar Wilde, CS Lewis, and JRR Tolkien also entered this gate at some point.

⚓ *Entrances on Broad St., Cattle St. and Radcliffe St.* 𝒊 *Extended tour includes visit to underground mechanical book conveyor, tunnel, and the Radcliffe Camera.* Ⓢ *Entrance to the courtyard free. 30min. tour of Library and Divinity Hall £4.50, standard 1hr. tour £6.50, extended tour £13.50. Audio tour £2.50. Entrance to Divinity Hall £1.* Ⓩ *Open M-F 9am-5pm, Sa 9am-4:30pm, Su 11am-5pm.*

Other Sights

OXFORD CASTLE ✎♿ CASTLE

44-46 Oxford Castle ☎01865 260 666 💻www.oxfordcastleunlocked.co.uk

As you wander around the serious students and mobs of tourists, it's easy to forget that Oxford had a history that involved people and things a little more scandalous than philosophers, books, and elegant churches. Oxford Castle reminds one of Oxford's darker past: stories of escapes, betrayal, and romance are told within the walls of the city's 11th-century castle and prison. Tours include a climb up Saxon St. George's tower and a trip down to a 900-year-old underground crypt.

🚏 Off New Rd. $ £7.75, concessions £6.50. ⏰ Tours daily 10am-4:20pm.

CARFAX TOWER ✎♿ TOWER

Junction of St. Aldates/Cornmarket St. and High St./Queen St. ☎01865 792 633

This was the site of the former City Church of Oxford (St. Martin's Church). However, in 1896, university leaders decided that the church needed to be demolished to widen the roads and make room for more traffic in the downtown area. Still, the tower was left untouched. Look for the church clock on the east side of the facade: it is adorned by two "quarter boys," who hit the bells every 15min.

$ Admission £2.20, under 16 £1.10. ⏰ Open daily Apr-Sept 10am-5:30pm; Oct 10am-4:30pm; Nov-Mar 10am-3:30pm.

UNIVERSITY OF OXFORD BOTANIC GARDEN ✎♿ GARDEN

Rose Ln. ☎01865 286 690 💻www.botanic-garden.ox.ac.uk

Back in the day (meaning, of course, the 1600s), this garden, though created to enhance the glory of God and the learning of man, actually had a practical purpose as well: they sold fruit grown in the garden to pay for its upkeep. Today, the garden has another useful purpose: a peaceful haven to resort to if you get overwhelmed by the mobs of tourists on High St. The oldest botanic garden in the UK, it lies outside of the city walls, and it happens to be on top of an ancient Jewish cemetery.

🚏 Off High St. $ £3.50, concessions £3. Year-long season ticket £12, students £10. ⏰ Open Nov-Feb 9am-4:30pm; Sept-Oct and Mar-Apr 9am-5pm; May-Aug 9am-6pm. Glasshouses open at 10am.

OXFORD MUSEUM OF NATURAL HISTORY ♿ MUSEUM

Parks Rd. ☎01865 272 950 💻www.oum.ox.ac.uk

Animal-bone lovers will rejoice at this 150-year-old museum: the collections of zoological, entomological, and geological specimens include dinosaur bones found in the Oxford area, **Charles Darwin's** crustaceans, and the most complete remains of a **dodo** found in the world. A famous debate on evolution that took place inside the building in 1860 between Thomas Huxley and Bishop Sam Wilberforce. Attached is the **Pitt-Rivers Museum** (Archeology and Anthropology), also worth a visit for its collection of lifestyle objects from across the globe—and for its shrunken heads *(☎01865 270 927 💻www.prm.ox.ac.uk).*

🚏 Off Broad St. $ Free. ⏰ Open daily 10am-5pm. Pitt-Rivers Museum open M noon-4:30pm, Tu-Su 10am-4:30pm.

FOOD 🍴

Here's one major perk of living in a student town: **kebab trucks** line High St., Queen St., and Broad St. (we recommend **Hassan's,** on Broad St.) and stay open until 3am during the week and 4 or 4:30am on weekends to fulfill late-night cravings. People think kids here have better things to do, like study? Please.

Cowley

KAZBAR
●ᵕⵣⴾ⵿ TAPAS ❷

25-27 Cowley Rd. ☎01865 202 920 ▦www.kazbar.co.uk

They say this is where southern Spain meets Northern Africa. Granted, Cowley Rd. is very ethnically diverse...but we think their geography might be a little off. Still, the authentic atmosphere almost makes us forget it. Meat, fish, cheese, and vegetable tapas are enjoyed on Moorish-style cushioned benches, with burning incense, colorful tiles, patterned rugs, and an open ceiling. On nice summer days, hip people sip glasses of wine (*£3.25-4.50*) outside in the sun.

☘ *Across from Magdalen Bridge.* *i* *½-price tapas M-F 4-7pm, Sa-Su noon-4pm.* Ⓢ *Tapas £3.10-4.60.* ☒ *Open M-Th 4pm-midnight, F 4pm-12:30am, Sa noon-12:30am, Su noon-midnight.*

ATOMIC BURGER
●ᵕⴾ⵿ BURGERS ❷

96 Cowley Rd. ☎01865 790 855 ▦www.atomicburger.co.uk

A "far-out" selection of homemade beef, chicken, and veggie burgers (*£6.50-8.75*), including a "burger of the week," in a funky outer-space-themed restaurant. If the hanging figurines and comic-book-covered walls don't get you in a cosmic mood, maybe a milkshake with "spacedust" sprinkled on it will do the trick (*£3.50*).

i *All burgers come with free side order. 10% discount on takeaway. Weekend breakfast options, including waffles, muffins, pancakes, and huevos rancheros. Gluten-free options.* Ⓢ *Entrees £4.50-10.50. Double your burger and choose 2 side orders for £5 more.* ☒ *Open M-F noon-2:30pm and 5-10:30pm, Sa-Su 9:30am-10:30pm.*

Jericho

G&D'S
●ᵕⵣ⵿ CAFE ❷

55 Little Clarendon St. ☎01865 516 652 ▦www.gdcafe.com

G&D's is a favorite Oxford haunt, with a Ben-and-Jerry's-caliber obsession with cows. Known for their bagel combinations and their natural, homemade ice cream. Bagels and ice cream—what better combination is there?

☘ *3 locations.* *i* *Lunchtime meal deal M-F noon-2pm: Bagels £3.50. Greek/Caesar salad, regular filter coffee, tea, and pack of chips or piece of fruit. Cow night Tu 7pm-midnight; get 20% off with anything cow-related.* Ⓢ *Bagels £2-5. Ice cream from £2.* ☒ *Open daily 8am-midnight.*

THE STANDARD TANDOORI
●ᵕ⁽ᵖ⁾ INDIAN ❷

117 Walton St. ☎01865 553 557

The decor might look a little dated, but the Indian food is fresh, and the service is friendly. Students say they make one of the best curries in all of Oxford. Many items are £2 cheaper to take out than to eat in, so if you're looking to save a few quid, you might want to call in, stroll over, and pick up.

☘ *Next to Radcliffe Infirmary.* *i* *Vegetarian options. Takeaway available.* Ⓢ *Entrees £3.65-12.* ☒ *Open daily noon-2:30pm and 6-11:30pm.*

Carfax

▨ THE VAULTS AND GARDEN
●⁽ᵖ⁾⵿ CAFE ❷

St. Mary's Church, Radcliffe Sq. ☎01865 279112 ▦www.vaultsandgarden.com

In the summertime, this is possibly the best setting in Oxford for lunch. Based out of the University Church of St. Mary the Virgin, the large garden eating area offers picturesque views of the Bodleian Library, Radcliffe Camera, and nearby colleges. There are even picnic blankets on the grass to stretch out and sunbathe with your coffee, meal, and book. The menu changes daily, with buffet-style serving and fresh salads, sandwiches, and soups, along with coffees, yogurt, and pastries. All vegetables come from nearby organic garden.

☘ *Turn up St. Mary's Passage off Queens St. or High St.* *i* *Menu changes daily for breakfast and lunch. 10% student discount.* Ⓢ *Lunch entrees £4.50-9.* ☒ *Open daily 8:30am-6:30pm.*

oxford • food

BEN'S COOKIES COOKIES ❶

108-109 Covered Market ☎ 01865 247 407 www.benscookies.com

Yes, you might have seen a few of these quaint little cookie stands in London, but this was the original, around for over 25 years in Oxford's 18th-century covered market. This tiny little stall sells what are most definitely the best cookies in town. They come in 10 delicious flavors, like white chocolate chip and triple chocolate chunk, and are served basically fresh out of the oven, nice and gooey.

By High St. $ Cookies £1 and up. Sold by weight. Tins of 3 £5.50, tins of 8 £11.50. Open M-Sa 9:15am-5:30pm, Su 11am-4pm.

THE NOSEBAG ORGANIC CAFE ❸

6-8 St. Michaels St., 2nd fl. ☎01865 721 033 www.nosebagoxford.co.uk

Piping-hot home-cooked dishes in a cozy and relaxed, but informal, setting (don't expect elegance, but rather economical service). The second-floor location in a 15th-century building means nice views of the quaint street below. Healthy organic options, along with vegetarian alternatives. Pastries and wine top off the casseroles, pies, salads, and fish. Menu changes daily.

i Vegetarian options available. $ Entrees £8-£10. Open M-Th 9:30am-10pm, F-Sa 9:30am-10:30pm, Su 9:30am-9pm. Last orders taken 30min. before close.

NIGHTLIFE

The main clubbing area in Oxford is near the train station, on **Park End Street** and **Hythe Bridge Street.** Maybe they figured that there was enough noise already with the trains going by, so a little bit of blasting music couldn't hurt. Both of these streets split off from **Botley Road** (the train station's home). From the center of town, George St. turns into Hythe Bridge St. as you head eastward, and New Rd. likewise becomes Park End.

Carfax

THE BRIDGE CLUB

6-9 Hythe Bridge St. ☎01865 242 526 www.bridgeoxford.co.uk

This mainstream club is very popular with Oxford's crowds of students, English or foreign, especially for their frequent student nights *(Student nights on M and Th; international student night W)*. Come prepared for R and B and the biggest pop hits of the month.

Down the road from the bus station. i No shorts, no hats, no ripped jeans, no white sneakers. $ Cover £3-8. Open M 10pm-2am, W 10pm-2am, Th-Sa 10pm-3am.

THIRST BAR, CLUB

7-8 Park End St. ☎01865 242 044 www.thirstbar.com

This lounge bar is hopping all nights of the week because of its blasting DJs, free cover on weeknights, and spacious outdoor garden, where those who are so inclined can share a hookah (better known as shisha here) to complement their cocktails. Not classy, but not trashy either.

Down the road from the bus station. $ Cover Th-Su £3. Open M-W 7:30pm-2am, Th-Sa 7:30pm-3am, Su 7:30pm-2am.

LAVA AND IGNITE CLUB

Cantay House, Park End St. ☎01865 250 181 www.lavaignite.com/oxford

Perhaps the most popular club in Oxford, the space is newly refurbished and packed with partying packs of patrons. There are three separate and distinct dance floors, plus a separate "chill-out" space for sitting, drinking and talking (three plus one equals four bars), so if you get tired of the scenery, feel free to rotate. Call ahead to be put on the guest list and skip the lines on weekends.

Across the street from Thirst and Central Backpackers. i Student nights M and W. $ Covers £3-8. Open W 9:30pm-2am, Th-Sa 10pm-3am.

great britain

Jericho

◼ THE EAGLE AND CHILD
49 St. Giles
⬤ ⟨♿⟩ ⟨(•)⟩ ☱ PUB
☎01865 302 925

This brick-and-wood pub might be a stop on Oxford's literary trail, but that doesn't mean it shouldn't be on your pub crawl as well. Around as a public house since 1650, this was a former playhouse for Royalist soldiers during the English Civil War and then, four centuries later, a favorite watering hole of **JRR Tolkien, CS Lewis** and the group of writers who dubbed themselves the "Inklings." Have a drink in what used to be the back room (before the garden area was incorporated into the pub), the **Rabbit Room,** where the group had what Lewis referred to as "golden sessions" with drinks in hand and philosophy and literary genius spilling from mouths.

♯ *Down St. Giles, north of the Ashmolean Museum.* ⓢ *Entrees £6.45-10.* ⧖ *Open M-Th 11am-11pm, F-Sa 11am-11:30pm, Su midnight-10:30pm.*

JERICHO TAVERN
56 Walton St.
⬤ ⟨(•)⟩ ☱ ⛲ TAVERN
☎01865 311 775 ◼www.thejerichooxford.co.uk

Radiohead first made its debut here back in 1984; since then, it has been sold and bought, remodeled, rebranded, but thankfully the Jericho Tavern remains a good place to find live music in Oxford. The heated outdoor beer garden is also a plus—especially if you get a Fruli Strawberry Beer *(£3.50)* to enjoy out there—the spacious inside is good for big groups of friends, and there are board games for your entertainment on nights without music. Live acoustic on Sunday nights from 8pm. Check out the music listings on the tavern's website.

♯ *Near the Phoenix cinema.* ⓢ *Entrees £6.50-11.* ⧖ *Open daily noon-midnight. Kitchen open noon-10pm.*

ARTS AND CULTURE

Theater

NEW THEATRE
George St.
⬤♿ CARFAX
☎01865 320 760, 0844 847 1588 for booking ◼www.newtheatreoxford.org.uk

It's showtime. Formerly known as the **Apollo Theater,** this is the main commercial theater in Oxford. The Art Deco building is home to many visiting concerts, musicals, and dramas.

♯ *From the bus station, follow Hythe Bridge St. to Worcester St. Make a right and follow down George St.* ⓢ *Tickets £17.50-42.50. Concessions sometimes for weekday showings. Occasionally £11 student standbys on day of performance. Inquire at box office.* ⧖ *Box office open M-W 10am-5pm; Th 10am-5:30pm; F non-performance days 10am-6pm; performance days 10am-3min. before curtain; Sa 10am-5pm.*

OXFORD PLAYHOUSE
11-12 Beaumont St.
⬤♿ CARFAX
☎01865 305 305 ◼www.oxfordplayhouse.com

Oxford's independent theater, better known to locals as simply "The Playhouse," puts on British and international drama, family shows, contemporary dance and music, student and amateur shows, comedy, lectures, and poetry.

♯ *Down Beaumont St. from the Ashmolean Musem.* ⓢ *Advance concessions £2 off ticket prices. Student standbys available day of show at box office for £9.50.* ⧖ *Box office open M-Sa 10am-6pm or until 30min. before curtain. Su performance days 2hr. before curtain. Cafe open 10am-11pm or until 5:30pm on non-performance nights.*

Music

One of the most popular outlets for music lovers visiting Oxford are the university colleges' **choirs.** These choirs are professional quality—many of them go on international tours, (hopefully) a clear marker of success, and also have CDs that are available for purchase. Many tourists take full advantage of the opportunity to hear them in their natural environment at **Evensong.** Better yet, Evensong is always free. Generally during term time at Oxford *(Oct-Dec, Jan-Mar, and Apr-June),* the college choirs are present at daily evening services, usually held at 6pm *(show up about 15min. beforehand and tell the porter or security that you've come for Evensong).* However, confirm the choir performance information on the college website or with the porters' lodge during the day before showing up for the service.

Shopping

Cornmarket St. is Oxford's chain-happy heaven, turning into Magdalen St. You will find many of the department stores in this area. Jericho has more alternative shopping, while High St. and St. Aldates, with their historic-looking decor, are generally aimed at tourist shopping (i.e. souvenir-hunting). High St. begins directly off Magdalen Bridge, passing colleges and meeting up with Cornmarket St. and St. Aldates to the East before becoming Queen St.

Books

THE ALBION BEATNIK — ♿ JERICHO

34 Walton St. ☎01865 511 345 🖳www.albionbeatnik.co.uk

In this independent bookstore, almost half of the space is dedicated to an impressive collection of Beat poets and music books and general things related to the "Beat" lifestyle. Open up the coolly decorated cupboard in the back corner: inside you'll find hundreds of jazz CDs. There's also a cafe of sorts inside, so you can enjoy a cup of tea *(£1.50)* in an armchair with your book while Dylan and Coltrane play on in the background.

North on St. Giles Rd.; left into Little Clarendon St. At the end turn right. $ New and second-hand books from £1. ⏰ Open M-W noon-7pm, Th-Sa 1-11pm, Su 3-5:30pm.

ESSENTIALS

Practicalities

- **TOURIST OFFICE:** The Tourist Information Centre is crowded with mobs of tourists during the summer. Ask for a free *In Oxford What's On* guide and free restaurant and accommodation guides. Also sells discounted tickets to local attractions. Books rooms for free with a 10% deposit. *(15-16 Broad St. ☎01852 252 200 🖳www.visitoxford.org ⏰ Open M-Sa 9:30am-5pm, Su 10am-4pm.)*
- **STUDENT TRAVEL: STA Travel.** *(Threeways House, 36 George St. ☎0871 702 9839 🖳 www.statravel.co.uk ⏰ Open M-Th 10am-7pm, F-Sa 10am-6pm, Su 11am-5pm.)*
- **TOURS:** The 2hr. official **Oxford University Walking Tour** leaves from the TIC and provides access to some colleges otherwise closed to visitors. The 2hr. tours allow only up to 19 people and are booked on a first come, first served basis, so get tickets early in the day at the TIC, by phone, or online 48hr. in advance. *(☎726 871,☎252 200 to book tickets. 🖳visitoxford.org ⏰ In summer daily 10:45 and 11am, 1 and 2pm; in winter daily 10:45am and 2pm. $ £7, children £3.75.)* Themed tours, like the CS Lewis and JRR Tolkien Tour and Garden run on a varied schedule. *($ £7.50, children £4.)* Check with the TIC or pick up an Official Guided Walking Tours Brochure.
- **CURRENCY EXCHANGE:** Banks line **Cornmarket Street. Marks and Spencer** has a bureau de change with no commission. *(13-18 Queen St. ☎01852 248 075 ⏰ Open M-W 8:30am-6:30pm, Th 8:30am-7:30pm, F 8:30am-6:30pm, Sa 8:30am-6:30pm, Su 11am-4:30pm.)* There is also a bureau of change attached to (but not affiliated with) the TIC, with no commission.
- **INTERNET:** Free at **Oxford Central Library**; however there is often a wait during

prime hours; some stations are open to pre-booking if you know exactly when you'd like to use it. *(Westgate. 🕐 Open M-Th 9am-7pm, F-Sa 9am-5:30pm.)* **C-Work Cyber Cafe.** *(1st fl. of Nash Bailey's House, New Inn Hall St. ☎722 044 $ £1 for 50min. 🕐 Open M-Sa 9am-9pm, Su 9am-7pm.)*

- **POST OFFICE:** *(102-104 St. Aldates. ☎08457 223 344 Bureau de change inside. 🕐 Open M 9am-5:30pm, Tu 9:30am-5:30pm, W-Sa 9am-5:30pm.)*
- **POSTAL CODE:** OX1 1ZZ.

Emergency!

- **POLICE:** *(St. Aldates and Speedwell St. ☎505 505.)*
- **HOSPITAL: John Radcliffe Hospital.** (Headley Way. ➜ *Take bus #13 or 14. ☎741 166.)*

Getting There

By Train

Botley Road Station *(Botley Rd., down Park End. ☎01865 484 950 🕐 Ticket office open M-F 5:45am-8pm, Sa 7:30am-8pm, Su 7:15am-8pm.)* offers trains to **Birmingham** *($ £27. 🕐 1hr. 10min., every 30min.),* **Glasgow** *($ £98.50. 🕐 5-7hr., every hr.),* **London Paddington** *($ £20. 🕐 1hr., 2-4 per hr.),* and **Manchester** *($ £61. 🕐 3hr., 2 per hr.)*

By Bus

Gloucester Green Station has **Stagecoach** buses *(☎01865 772 250 💻www.stagecoachbus.com)* running to **London Buckingham Road** *($ £14, students £11. 🕐 1¼hr., 5 per hr.)* and **Cambridge.** *($ £10.90. 🕐 3hr., 2 per hr.)* Buy tickets on the bus and enjoy free Wi-Fi.

The Oxford Bus Company *(☎01865 785 400 💻www.oxfordbus.co.uk)* runs the **Oxford Express** *(i Free Wi-Fi. $ £13, students £10. 🕐 100min., every 15-30min.)* and the **X70 Airline** services to **Heathrow.** *(i Free Wi-Fi. $ £20. 🕐 1½hr., every 30min.)* Also runs the **X80** service to **Gatwick's** north and south terminals. *(i Free Wi-Fi. $ £25. 🕐 2½hr., every hr.)* All leave from **Gloucester Green.** Tickets can be bought on the bus or at the **National Express** office *(£1 booking fee)*. However, the only way to secure a spot in advance on a particular bus is on the website.

National Express Bus 737 *(☎08717 818 178 💻www.nationalexpress.com 🕐 Ticket office open M-Sa 8:30am-6pm, Su 8:30am-5:30pm)* goes to **London Stansted,** *($ £19.30. 🕐 3½hr., 8 per day.),* **Birmingham** *($ £13.40. 🕐 2½hr., 1 per day.),* and **Bath** *($ £9.50. 🕐 2hr., 1 per day.).*

Getting Around

By Public Transportion

Oxford Bus Company *(☎01865 785 400 💻www.oxfordbus.co.uk)* provides many services within the city. Fares vary depending on distance traveled. *($ DayPass £3.70, weekly pass £13.)* Week passes can be purchased at the Oxford Bus Company office. *(➜ 3rd fl. of Debenham's department store on corner of George and Magdalen St. 🕐 Open M-W and F 9:30am-6pm, Th 9:30-8pm, Sa 9am-6pm.)* **Stagecoach** *(☎01865 772 250 💻www.stagecoachbus.com)* also runs buses in the city and to some surrounding villages. One-way-tickets within the city usually cost £1.80. Be careful when buying DayPasses because they don't apply to both companies (if you buy an Oxford Bus DayPass, it only works on Oxford Bus Company buses). For real-time information on buses in Oxford, use 💻www.oxontime.com, which can also text to your cell phone.

By Taxi

Call **Radio Taxis** *(☎01865 242 424)* or **ABC** *(☎01865 770 077)* for taxis. There are taxi ranks at **Oxford Station, Saint Giles, Gloucester Green,** and **Carfax** in the evening. Taxis (like London black cabs) can be hailed in the street.

By Bike

Bike Rental: Cycloanalysts *(150 Cowley Rd. ☎01865 424 444 🖥www.cycloanalysts.com $ 1 day £17, 2 days £25, 1 week £50. Includes locks. ⏰ Open M-Sa 9am-6pm, Su 10am-4pm.)*

cambridge ☎01223

Cambridge is packed with pubs, clubs, and intimate cafes. Winding lanes twist and turn between the age-old colleges of the university, each one a path through the town's fascinating history. It was here that **Watson** and **Crick** discovered the double helix, **Newton** discovered gravity, **Byron** and **Milton** wrote their famous poetry and **Winnie the Pooh** was born. If you're looking for a simplified Cambridge experience, the "P and P" formula is perhaps best: Punting and Pimm's (in other words, boating and boozing, although the two together could be a disaster waiting to happen).

ORIENTATION

Cambridge has two central avenues: the main shopping street starts at **Magdalene Bridge** north of the River Cam and becomes Bridge St., Sidney St., Saint Andrew's St., Regent St., and Hills Rd. The other main thoroughfare begins as **Saint John's St.** (just off Bridge St.), becoming Trinity St., King's Parade, and Trumpington St. To get into town from the Drummer St. bus station, take **Emmanuel Rd.** This leads to **St. Andrew's St.**, and a bank-heavy block with loads of cash machines. To get to the center of town from the train station, follow **Station Road** and turn right onto **Hills Road.** Then follow it straight until it becomes St. Andrew's St. and turn left on Downing St. and follow to Pembroke St. and turn right onto King's Parade, which will take you past King's College and onto Trinity St. by Trinity College.

ACCOMMODATIONS

The Cambridge lodging scene is notoriously bad. There are few affordable rooms anywhere near the town center, and an excess of overpriced, occasionally sketchy bed and breakfasts fill the north and south of town. Bed and breakfasts cluster on **Arbury Road** and **Chesterton Road** to the north. Several can be found closer to town on **Tenison Road.**

WARKWORTH HOUSE — BED AND BREAKFAST [4]

Warkworth Terr. ☎01223 363 682 🖥www.warkworthhouse.co.uk

Warkworth House is truly a cozy bed and breakfast. It's been owned by the same people for 33 years, and the beautiful rooms are all well furnished. Breakfast is not included....psych! Of course it is.

 # Walk down Parkside away from town center and turn left onto Warkworth Terrace. ℹ Breakfast included. $ Singles from £60; doubles from £80; family room from £100.

TENISON TOWERS — BED AND BREAKFAST [3]

148 Tenison Rd. ☎01223 363 924 🖥www.cambridgecitytenisontowers.com

With more affordable prices than most bed and breakfasts, Tenison Towers offers small, bright, and clean rooms as well as delicious homemade muffins and jams with the complimentary hot breakfast.

 # From the station, go down Station Rd. and turn right onto Tenison Rd. ℹ Breakfast included. $ Singles £40; doubles £64.

YHA CAMBRIDGE — HOSTEL [1]

97 Tenison Rd. ☎0845 371 9728

Though rather worn, the YHA Cambridge is unbeatable for the prices it offers. It's one of the few truly budget accommodations in Cambridge.

 # From the station, head down Station Rd. and turn right onto Tenison Rd. ℹ Internet £1 per 20min., £5 per 24hr., £12 per 3 days, £15 per week. Reservations taken daily 7am-11pm. $ Dorms £14-20. ⏰ Reception 24hr.

A & B GUESTHOUSE BED AND BREAKFAST [3]

124 Tenison Rd. ☎01223 315 702 🖥www.aandbguesthouse.co.uk

A pleasant, relatively centrally located B and B with clean and bright rooms. A & B has a full English breakfast, but can also satisfy vegetarian and gluten-intolerant customers upon request.

From the station, walk down Station Rd. and turn right onto Tenison Rd. i Breakfast included. $ Singles £50; doubles £70; family rooms £90. ⏰ Reception 7am-noon and 6pm-midnight; self check-in after midnight.

SIGHTS

TRINITY COLLEGE — COLLEGE

Trinity Ln. ☎01223 338 400

Trinity is perhaps the most popular of the colleges, drawing phenomenal numbers of tourists. **Henry VIII** intended for Trinity College to be the largest and richest in Cambridge, and with the modern-day college holding its own as third largest landowner in Britain (after the Queen and the Church of England), his wish has clearly been fulfilled. Trinity is famous for its illustrious alumni, including literati Dryden, Byron, Tennyson, and Nabokov; atom-splitter Ernest Rutherford; philosopher Ludwig Wittgenstein; and Indian statesman Jawaharlal Nehru. Perhaps most famously, **Sir Isaac Newton** lived there for 30 years. **The Great Court** in the center of the college is the world's largest enclosed courtyard. Visitors enter the courtyard through the Great Gate, which is guarded by a statue of Henry VIII clutching a wooden chair leg—a substitute for the oft-stolen original scepter. The apple tree near the gate is supposedly a descendant of the tree that inspired Newton's theory of gravity; in the north cloister of Neville's court, Newton calculated the speed of sound by stamping his foot and timing the echo. Lord Byron used to bathe **nude** in the college's fountain. Byron also kept a **pet bear** because college rules forbade cats and dogs. **The Wren Library** is home to alumnus AA Milne's handwritten copies of **Winnie the Pooh** and Newton's personal copy of his **Principia.**

Turn left onto Trinity Ln. off of Trinity St. $ £3, children £1.50. ⏰ Courtyard open daily 9:30am-4:30pm. Wren Library open M-F noon-2pm. Hall open 3-5pm.

KING'S COLLEGE — COLLEGE

King's Parade ☎01223 331 100 🖥www.kings.cam.ac.uk

Founded by **Henry VI** in 1441, King's College was originally a partner school to **Eton** until it slackened its admission policy in 1873 to accept students from other public schools. These days, King's reputation is significantly changed, and it is one of the more socially liberal of the Cambridge colleges, drawing more of its students from state schools than any other. Many visitors come for the Gothic **King's College Chapel,** where the spidering arches and stunning stained glass will stun even the most church-weary tourist. Inside the chapel, the period when Henry's mason left off and the Tudors began building is marked by a change in color of the stone. Note the roses, **dragons,** and unicorns repeated throughout the church's interior, even on its ceiling. These were the symbols of the **Tudors,** and it's a good thing for the church's decor that their coats of arms weren't all skulls, cross-bones, and vampire bats. King's alumni include: **John Maynard Keynes, EM Forster,** and **Salman Rushdie.**

Trumpington becomes King's Parade. $ £5, concessions and children 12-18 £3.50, under 12 free. ⏰ During term time open M-F 9:30am-3:30pm, Sa 9:30am-3:15pm. Outside of term time open M-Sa 9:30am-4:30pm, Su 10am-5pm. Chapel during term-time M-Sa 5:30pm evensong (enter through the front gate at 5:15pm). Su Eucharist 10:30am, Evensong 3:30pm.

THE POLAR MUSEUM — MUSEUM

Lensfield Rd. ☎01223 336 540 🖥www.spri.cam.ac.uk/museum

Founded in 1920 to memorialize **Captain Robert Falcon Scott** and his crew after they died on a return trip from the South Pole in 1912, The Polar Museum has reopened in a sleek, modern renovation packed with memorabilia from various polar expeditions, such as the barrel organ from an 1819 winter trip to the Arctic (it has 40 tunes spread across a five-barrel system) and John Ross's memoirs and narratives which are written in absurdly fine print. Especially of note is the fantastic gallery of Inuit art at the back.

Head down Regent St. away from the city center and turn right onto Lensfield Rd. $ Free. Open Tu-Sa 10am-4pm.

THE FITZWILLIAM MUSEUM — ♿ GALLERY

Trumpington St. ☎01223 332 900 www.fitzmuseum.cam.ac.uk

Named after Richard Fitzwilliam, this beautiful museum was opened in 1848. Through the Corinthian landings of the main hall, visitors will find a variety of paintings, antiquities and applied arts. Among the numerous highlights are paintings by Monet, Pissaro and Renoir, and sculptures by Rodin. There is also a beautiful **John Constable** painting of the Heath upstairs. The museum features Impressionist artwork, Turkish pottery, and objects from everyday Egyptian life on the ground floor.

Trumpington is one of the main roads. Off Pembroke if coming from the east and Silver St. if from the West. $ Free. Audio guides £3, students £2. Guided tours £4. Open Tu-Sa 10am-5pm, Su noon-5pm. Guided tours depart Sa at 2:30pm from the courtyard entrance.

CLARE COLLEGE — ♿ COLLEGE

Trinity Ln. ☎01223 333 200 www.clare.cam.ac.uk

Though initially founded by the **Chancellor of England,** it was refounded by **Lady Elizabeth de Clare** when the chancellor ran out of money. The thrice-widowed, 29-year-old Elizabeth's pain is bluntly referenced in the Clare coat of arms which features golden teardrops ringing a black border. The college has lush gardens of dangling ivy and weeping willows, and you can regularly hear the sound of punts hitting the riverbed. The elegant **Clare Bridge** dates from 1638 and is the oldest surviving college bridge. In wandering through Christopher Wren's Old Court, one can see the **University Library,** where **150 miles** of shelving house **eight million volumes.**

Turn left onto Senate House Passage off of Trinity St. (a continuation of King's Parade). $ £2.50, under 12 free. Open daily 10:45am-4:30pm.

MAGDALENE COLLEGE — ♿ COLLEGE

Magdalene St. ☎01223 332 100

Magdalene (pronounced MAUD-lin) College is housed in a fifteenth-century hostel for Benedictine monks that was, in all probability, nicer than most of the hostels you've been staying in. It's famous for the **Pepys Library,** which holds several diaries by **CS Lewis,** who, despite his status as an Oxford man, lived in Magdalene occasionally.

Bridge St. becomes Magdalene St. [i] Wheelchair access in courtyard but not library. Open daily until 6pm. Library open daily Oct 6-Dec 5 2:30pm-3:30pm; Jan 12-Mar 13 2:30pm-3:30pm; Apr 20-Aug 31 11:30am-12:30pm and 2:30pm-3:30pm.

CHRIST'S COLLEGE — ♿ COLLEGE

St. Andrews St. ☎01223 334 900 www.christs.cam.ac.uk

When it was in its original location, **Christ's College** was known as "God's-house," but it moved in 1448 to the current site where it was known as "Jesus College." Either way, it's holy. The Hall pays homage to two of the most famous residents of the college—**John Milton** and **Charles Darwin**—in the form of a bust and portrait respectively. New Court is a modern concrete building constructed in 1970.

St. Andrew's St. is a continuation of Regent St. [i] Wheelchair access in the church but not tower. $ Free. Open daily 9:30am-noon.

JESUS COLLEGE ♿ COLLEGE

Jesus Ln. ☎01223 339 339 💻www.jesus.cam.ac.uk

Visitors walk down a pathway known as "The Chimney" to get to the college. The arms of Bishop Alcock, the man who founded the College on the grounds of an abandoned Benedictine nunnery, are of a cock standing on an orb, a rather regal-looking visual pun. Stroll through the gardens and courts thronged by roses and enjoy the 25-acre grounds.

‡ Go north on Sidney St. and turn right onto Jesus Ln. ℹ Wheelchair access in the church but not the tower. ⏰ Open daily 8am-dusk.

WHIPPLE MUSEUM OF THE HISTORY OF SCIENCE ♿ MUSEUM

Free School Ln. ☎01223 330 906 💻www.hps.cam.ac.uk/whipple

This university museum is named after Robert Whipple, who donated a collection of roughly 1000 scientific devices to the university, many of which are on display here, such as the *Gömböc* (a strangely shaped object that, despite its homogeneous consistency, will return to the same resting position no matter where you place it), and **Fred,** a 19th-century anatomical model whose parts have been mercilessly scattered across the museum. Several intriguing planetariums, microscopes, telescopes and a wealth of pocket calculators round out the fantastic collection.

‡ Turn left off of St. Andrew's St. onto Downing St., follow it until it becomes Pembroke and make a right onto Free School Ln. ℹ Call ahead for wheelchair access. $ Free. ⏰ Open M-F 12:30-4:30pm.

MUSEUM OF ZOOLOGY ♿ MUSEUM

Downing St. ☎01223 336 650 💻www.museum.zoo.cam.ac.uk

This museum is packed to the gills with fantastic animals (dead, of course). Come for the giant spider crab, and stay for the birds. Some of these guys are enough to make you believe in creationism. Consider the Gorgeted Bird of Paradise: was the Don King hair style necessary for flight? How did the Raggi's Bird of Paradise fly with wings that look like he got in a fight with a Hoover? These are important questions to ask, best followed by a visit downstairs where there's a little history of the fateful 1831 voyage of the HMS Beagle.

‡ Turn left off of St. Andrew's St. onto Downing St. $ Free. ⏰ Open M-F 10am-4:45pm, Sa 11am-4pm.

FOOD 🍴

Though a student town, Cambridge has a lot of upscale dining. The cafes are nestled in its nooks and crannies and often provide delicious, cheap food and excellent coffee. Cambridge is also something of an ice cream town, so look out for the homemade ice cream and gelato that abound. Late-night food is available in the **Market Square** area.

✔ INDIGO COFFEE HOUSE 🌐🚭 CAFE [2]

8 St. Edward's Passage ☎01223 295 688

A student favorite, the Indigo Coffee House has two tiny floors that are sociable out of necessity. With its popular, inexpensive coffee and sandwiches, the cafe is host to a thousand eager, undergraduate debates.

‡ Head toward Trinity on King's Parade and turn right onto St. Edward's Passage. $ Bagels with toppings £1.75-4. Small coffees £1.40-1.85. large £2.65. Sandwiches on ciabatta £4.80 to eat in, £3 to take away. ⏰ Open M-F 10am-6pm, Sa 9am-6pm, Su 10am-5pm.

✔ CB1 🌐🚭🍸🌳 CAFE [1]

32 Mill Rd. ☎01223 576 306

Claiming to be the "oldest internet cafe in UK," CB1 has modern convenience with pre-inflation charm and prices. The sandwiches are delicious and unbelievably cheap, and the creaky wooden bookshelves are bursting with classic novels. Alcohol served with food.

✈ *Go southeast on Parkside until it becomes Mill Rd.* Ⓢ *Sandwiches £2.80. Toasted ciabattas £3.50. Milkshakes £2.60-2.70.* 🕘 *Open M-Th 8:30am-8pm, F 8:30am-9pm, Sa 9:30am-8pm, Su 10:30am-8pm.*

CLOWNS CAFÉ
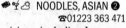 ITALIAN CAFE ❷

54 King St. ☎01223 355 711

This cafe feels like a scene out of an old Italian movie. The effervescent staff playfully jeer at familiar customers and tell regulars they can swing by later to pay the rest of their cash-only bill, while tons of students sit around sipping coffee and tucking into Mediterranean food. There's outdoor seating on the small but pleasant roof terrace.

✈ *Turn right off Sidney St. onto Jesus Ln.; turn right onto Malcolm St. and you'll hit King St.* Ⓢ *Entrees £4-6.50. Full English breakfast £6. W 5-10pm penne carbonara with wine £8.50.* 🕘 *Open daily 8am-11pm.*

BENET'S
ICE CREAM ❸

20 King's Parade ☎01223 329 068

With the soul music blaring, the students chatting, and the homemade ice cream slowly melting in the summer heat, Benet's is a Cambridge summer staple. Their milkshakes are especially delicious.

✈ *King's Parade.* ⓘ *Credit card min. £5.* Ⓢ *1 scoop £2.20, 2 scoops £3.50, 3 scoops £4.40. milkshakes £3.50.* 🕘 *Open daily 8am-9pm.*

MICHAEL HOUSE CAFÉ
CAFE ❸

Trinity St. ☎01223 309 147 🖳www.michaelhousecafe.co.uk

Meals in the Michael House Café are truly transcendent experiences. Between the light that streams through the stained glass and the hearty mains like slow-roasted lamb shoulder with Merguez spices served with oil olive bread, the only thing keeping you from floating with happiness will be the essentially unchanged weight of your wallet.

✈ *Go up King's Parade until it becomes Trinity St.* Ⓢ *Bread £7-9.* 🕘 *Open M-Sa 8am-5pm.*

DOJO'S NOODLE BAR
NOODLES, ASIAN ❷

1-2 Millers Yd. (off Mill Ln.) ☎01223 363 471

Dojo's boasts noodle dishes from all sorts of Asian cuisines, including Japanese, Chinese, Thai, and Malaysian. The quick service, large portions, and low prices make this a popular student haunt.

✈ *Turn left onto Mill Ln. off of Trumpington St. and then left onto Millers Yard.* Ⓢ *Fried entrees £6.45-6.50. Rice dishes £7.15-7.20. Soup entrees £7.20-7.50.* 🕘 *Open M-F noon-2:30pm and 5:30-11pm, Sa-Su noon-11pm.*

RAINBOW CAFÉ
VEGETARIAN, VEGAN, GLUTEN-FREE ❸

9A Kings Parade ☎01223 321 551 🖳www.rainbowcafe.co.uk

Down a small, white-walled alley and under the rainbow arch, vegetarians find their pot of gold: an affordable, exciting, and fast restaurant. Forego the veggie burgers in favor of Libyan Couscous with spinach, chick-peas, zucchini, onion, garlic, green beans, and carrot (£9) or explore a wealth of vegan and gluten-free dishes. Rainbow Café is a true blessing for any vegetarian roaming the meaty wilderness of British cuisine.

✈ *King's Parade.* Ⓢ *Entrees £9-16.* 🕘 *Open M 10am-4pm, Tu-Sa 10am-10pm, Su 10am-4pm.*

CAMBRIDGE CRÊPES
CRÊPES ❶

Corner of Sidney and Market St. 🖳www.cambridgecrepes.co.uk

This popular crêpe stand is packed throughout the day during the summer. With delicious classic sweet crêpes and more inventive fare throughout the menu, Cambridge Crêpes is a solid dining option. Note the finesse with which they make a nutella crêpe: they don't just lather on the stuff, but fling it on until it looks like a Jackson Pollock and tastes 5000 times better. Trust us.

➜ Sidney St. $ Sweet crêpes £2.50; savory crêpes £3.50-3.80. ⏰ Open Tu-Su 11am-5pm.

MASSARO'S 💳🚭 ITALIAN GELATO, SMOOTHIES [3]

85 Regent St. ☎01223 314 236

Massaro's specializes in delicious sandwiches that almost live up to the impossible hype created by their exotic ingredients lists. Between the great sandwiches, the homemade gelato, and the delicious iced drinks (iced coffee with vanilla gelato shaken, not blended), we're sold.

➜ Regent St. $ Sandwiches: £7-7.50 in-store, £5-5.50 takeaway. Iced coffee £1.20-1.50. ⏰ Open M-F 8am-6pm, Sa-Su 10am-6pm.

AUNTIE'S TEA SHOP 💳 BRITISH TEA [2]

1 St. Mary's Passage ☎01223 870 144 💻www.auntiesteashop.co.uk

If you're searching for an authentic British tea, look no further than the calming quietude and lace table cloths of Auntie's Tea Shop.

➜ Go up King's Parade toward Trinity St. and turn right onto St. Mary's Passage. $ Full tea £7.65. Sandwiches £4-4.50. Panini £5.50. ⏰ Open M-F 9:30am-6pm, Sa 9:30am-6:30pm, Su 10:30am-5:30pm.

COPPER KETTLE 💳🚭☀ BRITISH [2]

4 King's Parade ☎01223 365 068

A cozy breakfast place with traditionally English fare. Enjoy a full English breakfast (veggie option available) while basking in the beautiful architecture of King's College.

➜ King's Parade. $ Lunch £7.50-8. Full English breakfast £5.

LA MARGHERITA 💳 GELATO [2]

15 Magdalene St. ☎01223 315 232

Though also an Italian restaurant, La Margherita excels at serving the largest section of delectable gelato in Cambridge. The amaretto is especially fantastic.

➜ Go up Bridge St. $ Small £1.70, medium £2.50, large £3.80. ⏰ Open M-F 10am-4pm and 6-10:30pm, Sa 10am-11pm, Su 10:30am-8pm.

CHOCOLAT CHOCOLAT 💳♿ GELATO, CHOCOLATE [4]

21 St. Andrew's St. ☎01223 778 982

Chocolat Chocolat serves, surprisingly, a wealth of delicious, hand-crafted, French chocolate. They also have fantastic gelato. It's *delicieux delicieux!*

➜ Go up Regent St. until it becomes St. Andrew's St. ℹ Cash only for ice cream. $ 1 scoop £2, 2 £3, 3 for £4. ⏰ Open M-Tu 9am-6pm, W 9am-8pm, Th-F 9am-6pm, Sa 9am-7pm, Su 10:30am-6pm

THE COW 💳📶🍸☀ PIZZA [3]

Corn Exchange St. ☎01223 308 871 💻www.barroombar.com

Housed in an alternative bar, The Cow provides cheap, delicious pizzas in the heart of the city. If Cambridge weather behaves itself, you can enjoy your slices in the outdoor seating.

➜ Go down Downing St. and turn right on Corn Exchange. $ 12 in. pizzas £8-8.25. Wraps £5-5.25. Burgers £8-8.25. ⏰ Open M-Tu noon-11pm, W-Sa noon-1am, Su noon-11pm.

CHARLIE CHAN CHINESE RESTAURANT 💳♿ CHINESE [3]

14 Regent St. ☎01223 359 336

This calm, simple Chinese restaurant is a delicious place for a highly customizable and enjoyable meal. Select from a list of rice and noodles and choose an accompanying meat or seafood dish.

➜ Regent St. $ Chicken, pork, and beef dishes £5.80-7.50. Seafood £7.80. Rice and noodles £1.80-6. Fried rice £3. Boiled rice £1.80. ⏰ Open daily noon-11pm.

NIGHTLIFE

▥ THE FREE PRESS
⚲♈☕ PUB

Prospect Row   ☎01223 368 337 ▥www.freepresspub.com

This small pub is bursting at the seams with character. Cell phones and music are banned, making space for idiosyncratic, pubby conversation that's missing at many modern establishments. Deriving its name from its former life as a newspaper printing shop, the Free Press is a classic watering hole that's well worth the visit for any pub culture fanatic. Get some sun (or clouds) in the beer garden.

⚑ *Left off Parkside (when heading away from town center) onto Warkworth Terrace. Left onto Warkworth St., right onto Prospect Row.* ⑤ *Pints £3.* ⏲ *Open M-F noon-2:30pm and 6-11pm, Sa noon-11pm, Su noon-3pm and 7-10:30pm.*

▥ THE EAGLE
⚲♿♈☕ PUB

8 Benet St.   ☎01223 505 020

On a cool February 28th in 1953, **Francis Crick** and **James Watson** burst into the Eagle and announced to the scientists who were slowly killing their Nobel-prize-winning brain cells that they had discovered the "secret to life," the ▥**double helix.** The history of this charming bar doesn't stop there. Toward the back, messages and squad numbers remain scorched on the ceiling where RAF men burnt them with lighters on the evenings before missions during the war. For your purposes, the bar has history, charm, and affordable alcohol.

⚑ *Head toward Trumpington on King's Parade and turn left onto Benet St.* ⓘ *Credit card min. £5.* ⑤ *Pints £3.* ⏲ *Open M-Sa 10am-11pm, Su 11am-10:30pm.*

▥ CHAMPION OF THE THAMES
⊕♿♈ PUB

68 King St.   ☎01223 352 043

The Champion of the Thames is the sort of pub with comfortably low ceilings and lamps that seem to shed only the warmest, most orange light. Decorated in oars and leather chairs and boasting two rotating guest pints which trend towards excellence, the Champion of the Thames is a great place to grab a brew.

⚑ *Turn right off Sidney St. onto Jesus Ln., then turn right onto Malcolm St. and you'll hit King St.* ⑤ *Carlsberg and IPA pints £2.45.* ⏲ *Open M-Th noon-11pm, F-Sa 11am-11pm.*

▥ THE ANCHOR
⚲♿♈ PUB

Silver St.   ☎01223 353 554

Situated near the river, The Anchor has beautiful bay windows that look onto the water. Get a beer and watch self-punters slowly crash into each other and occasionally sink. The stained glass in the pub is also nice.

⚑ *Off Trumpington.* ⑤ *Pints £3-4.* ⏲ *Open M-Th 10am-11pm, F-Sa 10am-midnight, Su 10am-11pm.*

▥ THE SALISBURY ARMS
⚲♿♈ PUB

76 Tenison Rd.   ☎01223 576 363 ▥www.thesalisburyarms.com

The Salisbury Arms is packed with eight exciting different lagers as well as unique bottled beers (banana bread beer, anyone?). High on local charm, the bar also has one of the more popular pub dogs in the area, Max, an adorable pooch with hair completely covering his eyes.

⚑ *Go down Mill Rd. away from town center and turn right onto Tenison Rd.* ⓘ *Min. credit card £10.* ⑤ *Pints £3.* ⏲ *Open M-Th noon-2:30pm and 5-11pm, F noon-2:30pm and 5pm-midnight, Su noon-2:30pm and 7-10:30pm.*

▥ MILL
⚲⊗♈ PUB

14 Mill Ln.   ☎01223 357 026

Mill is a great old-fashioned pub with excellent river views. They're known for their specialty sausages, all delicious local concoctions like lamb and rosemary.

Choose your own sausage and then your own mash (£6.50).

☞ Go up Trumpington St. toward King's Parade and turn left onto Mill Ln. ⑤ Pints £3.50. ☑ Open daily noon-11pm. Kitchen open M-Sa noon-5pm.

SOUL TREE
♥�♈ CLUB

1-6 Corn Exchange St.　　　　　　　☎01223 303 755 ▇www.soultree.co.uk

Soul Tree is the biggest club in Cambridge, with an impressive three floors of stylishly-graffitied walls. Come enjoy the loud music and dancing in the hip environment.

☞ Go down Downing St. and turn right onto Corn Exchange. *i* Cover cash-only. Credit card over £10. M international student night: cover £3-4, tequila shots £1, bottled beer £1.80. ⑤ F before 11pm cover £4, after £6. Sa before 11pm £6, after £8. Mixed drinks £6. Bottled beer £3.50. ☑ Open M 10am-4pm, F 10am-4pm, Sa 10pm-4am.

FEZ CLUB CAMBRIDGE
♥☈♈ CLUB

15 Market Passage　　　　　　　☎01223 519 224 ▇www.cambridgefez.com

The Fez Club hosts the largest student night in Cambridge. With a striped cloth ceiling and faux-cave walls, it's exotically decorated and hopping with activity.

☞ Left onto Market St. off of Sidney St., right onto Market Passage. *i* Cover cash-only. Inquire about a free membership card from inside and ask about student discounts. ⑤ Cover M students before 11pm £3, after £4; adults before 11pm £4, after £5. Tu before 11pm £3; 11pm-midnight £4, after midnight £5. W £3 before 11pm, after £4; international students before 11pm £1, after £3. Th £6-8. F before midnight £5, after £7. ☑ Open M-Sa 10pm-3am, Su term-time 10pm-3am.

HIDDEN ROOMS
♥⊗♈ BAR, CLUB

7a Jesus Ln.　　　　　　　☎01223 514 777 ▇www.hiddenthing.com

Tucked away under Pizza Express, the Hidden Rooms, while not as secretive as the name would suggest, is a hotspot for nightlife, especially for the more soul-oriented clubbers.

☞ Head north on Sidney St. and turn right onto Jesus Ln. *i* Credit card min. £10. Th is jazz night, F is soul night, Sa is house music. ⑤ Cover for jazz before 10pm £2, after £5. ☑ Open M-Sa 3pm-12:30am. Club open Th-Sa.

THE GRANTA
♥⊗♈⬭ PUB

14 Newnham Terr.　　　　　　　☎01223 505 016

The Granta has gorgeous river views, riverside outdoor seating, and, perhaps most beautiful of all, occasional deals on burgers and pints. Punting available from the dock just next to the pub.

☞ Left onto Silver St. off of Trumpington, left onto Queen's Rd. *i* Credit card min. £5. ⑤ Pints £3. Burger and pint £7. ☑ Open M-Th 11am-11pm, F-Sa 11am-midnight, Su 11am-11pm. Kitchen open M-Sa noon-10pm, Su noon-8pm.

ARTS AND CULTURE

⬓ SCUDAMORE'S
♥ RIVER CAM

Quayside　　　　　　　☎01223 359 750 ▇www.punting.co.uk

Punting is one of those classic Cambridge activities that can't be skipped—not unlike getting soused on Pimm's and falling in the Cam. These vaguely rectangular boats (punts) can be rented for chauffeured tours up and down the river Cam. More adventurous (or possibly idiotic) boaters can try their hand at punting. Simply stand at the back of the boat and thrust the pole into the bottom of the river. As you remove the pole, twist it to ensure it doesn't get stuck and drag you into the water as your boat moves on without you.

☞ Right off Bridge St. underneath Magdalene Bridge. ⑤ Self-hire £18 per hr. plus a £90 deposit taken in the form of an imprint of your credit or debit card. Student ID £14 and a £90 deposit. Guided tours £15, concessions £13.50, under 12 £7.50. ☑ Open daily May-Aug 9am-10pm, Sept-Nov 9am-8pm, Nov-Easter 9:30am-5pm, Easter-mid-May 9am-6pm.

ARTS PICTUREHOUSE

CENTRAL CAMBRIDGE

38-39 St. Andrew's St. ☎0871 902 5720 🖳www.picturehouses.co.uk

Just above one of the raging bars of Cambridge, the Arts Picturehouse screens art flicks, independent films, classics, and more popular movies while its downstairs partner serves alcohol.

*A continuation of Regent St. **i** Off-peak M-F until 5pm; peak is all day Sa and Su and every other day after 5pm. Ⓢ M £7; Tu-F before 5pm £7, after £8; Sa-Su £8. Students £1 off. ⓍBox office opens 30min. before first show, closes 15min. after the start of the last. Phone line open daily 9:30am-8:30pm.*

ADC THEATRE

CHESTERTON

Park St. ☎01223 300 085 🖳www.adctheatre.com

Short for "Arts Dramatic Club," the ADC was a student-run theater for a long time, specializing in new writing and university productions, including frequent performances by the Cambridge Footlights, the comedy group that launched **Hugh Laurie, Steven Fry,** and 🖳**John Cleese.**

Left off Jesus Ln. when you're heading away from town center. Ⓢ M-F £8, concessions £6; Sa-Su £10/£8. Prices subject to change. ⓍBox office open Tu 12:30pm-showtime, W 3pm-showtime, Th 12:30pm-showtime, F-Sa 3pm-showtime.

CAMBRIDGE ARTS THEATRE

CHESTERTON

Peas Hill ☎01223 503 333 🖳www.cambridgeartstheatre.com

This popular Cambridge theater puts on a mix of music, straight plays, comedies, operas, ballet, contemporary dance, and occasional shows from the Cambridge Footlights. Basically, everything.

Head towards Trumpington St. on King's Parade, turn left onto Benet St. and left onto Peas Hill. Ⓢ Tickets £10-35. ⓍOpen M-Sa summer noon-6pm, winter noon-8pm.

CAMBRIDGE CORN EXCHANGE

CHESTERTON

Wheeler St. ☎01223 357 851 🖳www.cornex.co.uk

Probably the largest music venue in Cambridge, the Cambridge Corn Exchange presents many big name musical acts coming through Cambridge.

Head toward Trumpington St. on King's Parade, turn left onto Benet St., and go straight until Benet becomes Wheeler St. Ⓢ Prices vary. Occasional student discounts, depending on the show. ⓍOpen M-Sa 10am-6pm.

SHOPPING

BOOKS FOR AMNESTY

BOOKS

46 Mill Rd. ☎01223 362 496 🖳www.amnesty.org.uk/bookshops

This second-hand charity bookshop is cluttered with an eclectic selection of donated books. The prices are low, making this an excellent place to stock up on road reads. The shelf near the counter houses rare or unique books and is worth a look.

Mill Rd. ⓍOpen M-F 11:30am-6pm, Sa 9:30am-6pm.

BRIAN JORDAN MUSIC BOOKS FACSIMILES

SHEET MUSIC, BOOKS ON MUSIC

10 Green St. ☎01223 322 368 🖳www.brianjordanmusic.co.uk

An old music store, Brian Jordan specializes in elegant editions of classical sheet music as well as a fantastic selection of musical literature.

Go up King's Parade until it becomes Trinity St. and follow it until it becomes St. John's St.; turn right onto Green St. ⓍOpen M-Sa 9:30am-6pm.

HAUNTED BOOKSHOP

BOOKS, ANTIQUITIES

9 St. Edward's Passage ☎01223 312 913 🖳www.sarahkeybooks.co.uk

Legend has it that a woman in white smelling of violets paces the stairway of the Haunted Bookshop. Fact has it that the bookshop contains a massive collection of age-old, elegant editions of a wide variety of literature and children's books. Well worth a look for any bibliophile.

➧ *Go up King's Parade toward Trinity St. and turn right onto St. Edward's Passage.* ⏰ *Open M-Sa 10am-5pm.*

ESSENTIALS

Practicalities

- **TOURIST OFFICE: Tourist Information Centre** at Peas Hill sells National Express tickets, discounted punting tickets, sightseeing bus tickets, and accommodations bookings. Disabled visitors to Cambridge can get an access guide for the city from the TIC. *(☎0871 226 8006 🖳www.visitcambridge.org ⏰ Open M-Sa 10am-5pm, Su 11am-3pm.)*
- **TOURS:** Several walking tours leave from the Tourist Information Centre. The Guided Tour features King's College and Queens' College. *($ £11, concessions £9.50, children £6. ⏰ Leaves M-Sa 11am and 1pm, Su and bank holidays 1pm.)*
- **BUDGET TRAVEL OFFICE: STA Travel.** *(38 Sidney St. ☎0871 702 9809 🖳www.statravel.co.uk ⏰ Open M-Th 10am-7pm, F-Sa 10am-6pm, Su 11am-5pm.)*
- **BANKS: Banks** and **ATMs** line St. Andrew's St.
- **BIKE RENTAL: City Cycle Hire.** *(61 Newnham Road. ☎01223 365 629 🖳www.citycyclehire.com $ £6 per 4 hr., £9 per 8hr., £10 per 24hr., £15 per 2-3 days, £20 per 4-7 days, £30 per 2 weeks, £65 per 9 weeks. ⏰ Open Easter-Oct M-F 9am-5:30pm, Sa 9am-5pm; winter M-F 9am-5:30pm.)*
- **INTERNET ACCESS: Jaffa Net Cafe.** *(22 Mill Rd. ☎01223 308 380 $* £1 per hr. *⏰ Open daily noon-midnight.)*
- **POST OFFICE: Bureau de Change.** *(9-11 St. Andrew's St. ⏰ Open M 9am-5:30pm, T 9:30am-5:30pm, W-Sa 9am-5:30pm.)*
- **POST CODE:** CB2 3AA.

Emergency!

- **POLICE:** Parkside Police Station on Parkside *(☎0345 456 4564).*
- **HOSPITAL: Addenbrookes Hospital.** *(Hills Rd. by the intersection of Hills Rd. and Long Rd. ☎01223 245 151.)*

Getting There

By Train

Trains depart from **Station Road.** *(National Rail Enquiries ☎0845 7484 950 ⏰ Ticket office open M-Sa 5:10am-11pm, Su 7am-10:55pm.)* Nonstop trains to **London King's Cross** *($ £19.10. ⏰ 48min., 2 per hr.)* and to **Ely.** *($ £3.70. ⏰ 20min., 4 per hr.)*

By Bus

The **bus station** is on Drummer St. *(⏰ Ticket office open M-Sa 9am-5:30pm.)* Airport Shuttles run from Parkside. Trains to **London Victoria** *($ £14.40. ⏰ 2hr., every hr.);* **Gatwick** *($ £32. ⏰ 4hr., every 2hr.);* **Heathrow** *($ £29.70. ⏰ 3hr., every hr.);* **Stansted** *($ £13. ⏰ 50min., every hr.);* to **Oxford.** *(Stagecoach Express $ £11. ⏰ 3hr., every 30min.)*

Getting Around

By Bus

Buses run from **Stagecoach** *(☎01223 423 578).* **CitiBus** runs from stops throughout town, including some on **St. Andrew's Street, Emmanuel Street,** and the train station. **Dayrider Tickets** *(Unlimited travel for 1 day. $ £3.40)* can be purchased on the bus, but for longer stays, you can buy a **Megarider** ticket. *(Unlimited travel for 7 days. $ £11.50.)*

By Taxi

For a taxi, call **Cabco.** *(☎01223 525 555 ⏰ Open daily 24hr.)*

edinburgh ☎131

It's a city that moves. Visitors are constantly streaming through Scotland's capital, and the population of the city swells by roughly one million during the month of August. Festival season, or **"Fest"** as it's known to locals, is a time of both great joy and chagrin, as free entertainment reigns supreme but walking down the street takes nearly half an hour. Even when Edinburgh isn't party central, its residents aren't afriad to sing its praises over a **"pint and a blether"** (Scottish-speak for drink and a chat). A majestic city, it's one of those places where you watch the sun go down from the top of a hill and wonder just how you managed to wander into such a spectacular place. However you did it, keep going: Edinburgh was made for it.

ORIENTATION

Edinburgh's most famous neighborhoods **(Old Town, New Town)** are easily divisible, as they are separated by a large gully which houses **Waverly Station** and **Princes's Street Gardens.** This ravine is bisected by three bridges: **Waverly Bridge, North Bridge,** and **The Mound.** Stockbridge is to the north of **New Town** (walk as if you were heading to Leith and the sea) and **Haymarket** and **Dalry** are in the area west of New Town. **The Meadows, Tolcross,** and the **West End** are all over the hill from Old Town, off toward the south end of town.

Old Town

It's heralded by the giant castle that sits atop the rocky crags that divide Old Town from New Town. It's winding streets are surrounded by four-and-five-story Georgian buildings that house everything from storytelling centers to party-driven hostels. Old Town is where it's at. It's where you'll take the most pictures, it's where you'll drink, sleep, shop, and eat. You'll be hard pressed to find another neighborhood some days—there's just so much to do. However, everyone else knows this too, so make sure to hit up Old Town when you're feeling particularly ready for a tourist onslaught.

New Town

New Town isn't actually that new. It would have been new when it was designed by James Craig in the 1760s, but by this point it's down pat. Following a simple, grid-like pattern, it's bordered by **Queen Street** to the north and **Prince Street** to the south. **George Street,** a central thoroughfare, runs through the middle. The various intersecting thoroughfare have branches of their own, usually smaller streets with housing or shops. **Rose Street,** which houses the majority of the pubs in New Town, is one of these.

Stockbridge

Put on your best polo, becase we're heading to the Edinburgh Country Club—Stockbridge. Full of the top tier of upper crust of society, it's a bit like a separate city, with its own restauants, drinking, and way of life. Forgot your monocle? No worries: find one among the posh leftovers sold in the Stockbridge charity shops. As we always say, if you can't beat 'em, join 'em; if you can't join 'em, wear their cast-offs. When you're not scrounging through the thrift stores, you can meander through the streets, pop into a cafe, stop off at a nice restaurant. or just wander on down through the **Water of Leith.**

Haymarket and Dalry

Haymarket and Dalry are not that pretty, at least compared to the rest of Edinburgh. This may be why it is home to some of the city's cheaper housing. A few good food stops are to be found, and those looking for a night out in this area will find cheap drinks. Be warned, there are some Old Guard pubs here that aren't the friendliest.

Tollcross and West End

Owned and dominated by the huge expanse of green that is the meadows, the West End is nevertheless right in the middle of the city, but you'll be seeing far fewer tourists out this way, except during festival time, when it's impossible to open your eyes without seeing a tourist. **Lothian Road** is home to several great pubs, and continuing up to **Home Street** will take you to the local cinema, **The Cameo.** The **University of Edinburgh** is isolated enough from the city that none of the pubs or bars in the area are student-dominated, but you'll find several full of a distinctly younger crowd. If you fancy it, take a putter and a chipping iron and head out to the **Bruntsfield Links,** where you can play on a 30+ chipping course. Get out to Tolcross and the West End. You'll feel better with less tourists around, and the locals will be more kindly disposed to you for the very same reason.

ACCOMMODATIONS

Possibly more so than any other city in the UK, Edinburgh's accommodations options are defined by its neighborhoods. In New Town, you're looking at guesthouses and lodges on the upper end of the price range. Stockbridge has virtually no accommodations to speak of. Old Town is home to the majority of the hostels in town, all of which are right in the center of the action and, for those who wish to keep their distance from the Grassmarket, hostels and hotels fill Haymarket and Dalry, and Tolcross and the West End.

Old Town

👍 ART ROCH HOSTEL 💳♿📶 HOSTEL ❶

2 Westport, Grassmarket ☎0131 228 9981 💻www.artrochhostel.com

The new kid on the block, the Art Roch is already showing everybody else how it's done. With cool, airy dorms featuring sturdy wooden bunks (instead of squeaking metal), this will be a comfortable palce to hit the sack. However, you'll be *really* comfortable when you're hanging out, as the lounge-and-kitchen area is the size of a small airport and fits a kitchen, ping-pong table, TV, chairs and couches, and even a teepee, all with plenty of room to spare.

ℹ Wi-Fi available. $ Dorms high-season £12, £80 per week; low-season £9. Singles £20. ⏰ Reception 24hr.

BUDGET BACKPACKERS 💳⊗📶 HOSTEL ❷

37-39 Cowgate St. ☎0131 226 6351 💻www.budgetbackpackers.com

A surf-green hostel just a few drunken steps from the pub-filled Grassmarket, Budget Backpackers is a vibrant place that's bound to be packed during the summer with young travelers searching for the next party. If you are staying in (we're not going to say you'll be the only one, but...) there's a DVD and movie rental at the lobby.

ℹ Breakfast £2. Wi-Fi £1 per week. Internet £1 per 30min. Book well ahead of July-Aug for summer reservations. $ Dorms high-season £20-40; low-season £10-20. ⏰ Reception 24hr.

EDINBURGH BACKPACKERS 💳⊗📶 HOSTEL ❶

65 Cockburn St. ☎0131 220 1717 💻www.hoppo.com

You'll get those quads in shape hiking up and down the many **stairs** of this tower. Dorms in EB are basic, but with new people coming in all the time, you're certainly not going to be lacking excursion partners. The hostel's kitchen has cupboards with dry erase markers so you can write down which foods are yours (threat level depends on how hungry the bro in the other room is). The lounge shows *Braveheart* (a *lot*) and stag parties have been known to frequent the place, so be ready for a fun, if raucous, time.

🧭 Cockburn St. winds off of High St. ℹ Free Wi-Fi. Internet £1 per 30min. $ Dorms M-F £10, Sa-Su £13-16; Singles £25. ⏰ Reception 24hr.

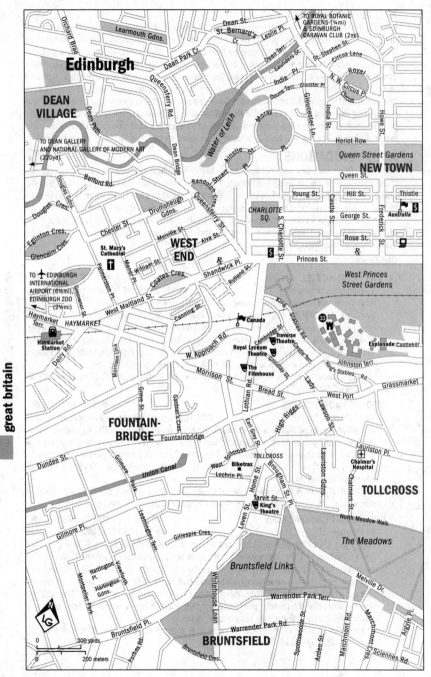

great britain

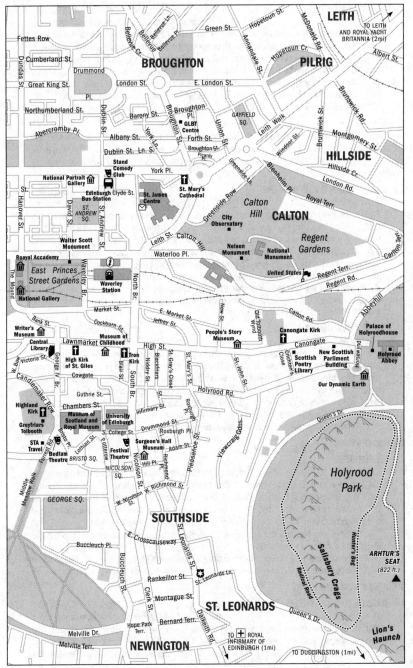

edinburgh · accommodations

COWGATE HOSTEL 💳♿📶 HOSTEL [2]

96 Cowgate ☎0131 226 2153 💻www.cowgatehostel.com

Apartment-style hosteling—now *this* is different. In this series of individual little flats, you'll be bunking with a smaller group of people than at a normal hostel. You'll share the same kitchen, bath, and lounge area as a group. For those traveling solo, this will either be a chance to make some good friends or a really quick way of finding out that the people you're staying with are jerks. Regardless, the place is nice. Head to the blue and orange lobby for internet and tourist information.

i Wi-Fi free. Coffee and tea free. $ Dorms Aug £22, Sept-July £10. ⏰ Reception 8am-11pm.

New Town

Accomodations in New Town, with the exception of Caledonian Backpackers, are usually far out of the budget traveler's pocket. However, should you have a little extra cash to spend, there are some fantastic guest houses in the area. No matter where you stay, you'll be near all the action.

👍 **CALEDONIAN BACKPACKERS** 💳🚭📶 HOSTEL [1]

3 Queensferry St. ☎0131 226 2939 💻www.caledonianbackpackers.com

By far the best budget option in New Town, and not just because it's the only one, this 250-bed monster is comfortable and crazy all at the same time. With free Wi-Fi, internet, and kitchen use, as well as a fully stocked bar, it's not cheap fun, it's cheap *and* fun. Check out the beanbag-filled theater, where you can watch free movies anytime on a projector screen. The murals on the walls depict everything from rock stars to penguins, and the hostel has about as wide a range of people stop in.

➜ West End of the City Center, across from the Caledonian Hotel. i Breakfast 6am-noon. Laundry: washer £1, dryer £1. 18+ only. Female-only dorms available. Wi-Fi, Internet, and kitchen free. $ Dorms £13-20. ⏰ Reception 24hr.

ELDER YORK GUESTHOUSE 💳🚭📶 GUESTHOUSE [3]

38 Elder St. ☎0131 556 1926 💻www.elderyork.co.uk

Providing relatively constant prices throughout the year, the Elder York Guesthouse benefits from three distinct things: a prime location a few yards away from the bus station, a beautiful and shining breakfast area, and large, airy rooms. And then there's the wonderful hospitality of new owners Harry and his wife, who are doing a fine job of running the place.

➜ Right off of York Pl. and St. James Pl. i Cancellations in July-Aug should give 1 week notice. $ Aug £60 per person, Sept-Jul £40 per person.

Haymarket and Dalry

👍 **THE HOSTEL** 💳🚭📶 HOSTEL [2]

3 Clifton Terr. ☎0131 313 1031 💻www.edinburghcitycentrehostels.co.uk

Haymarket and Dalry's hostel, "The Hostel" (this is going to get confusing, isn't it?) is spotlessly clean. Having just undergone a massive renovation and refurbishment, its carefully color-coordinated lounge space has pool tables and a large flatscreen TV as well as free tea and coffee. Bear in mind, though, that The Hostel is intent on maintaining its stellar appearance, as evidenced by the long list of rules on the wall.

➜ Right in Haymarket. i Continental breakfast £1. Towel rental £1, £5 deposit. $ 16-bed dorms £7-12; 5-bed dorms £12-14; 3-bed dorms £14-20. ⏰ Reception 24hr. Lounge open 8am-11pm.

Tollcross and West End

👍 **ARGYLE BACKPACKERS** 💳♿📶 HOSTEL [2]

14 Argyle Pl. ☎0131 667 9991 💻www.argyle-backpackers.co.uk

Argyle is a great place for those who like to keep the party time outside and the cool, lounging-around time in the hostel. A beautiful red kitchen connects to a covered skylight area that in turn links to an outdoor seating area. The lounge space has two computers for guest use as well as a big-screen TV and wood-burning fireplace.

i In Aug, prices generally increase £5 with min. stay 3 days. $ M-F 10-bed dorm £13.50; 6-bed dorm £15; 4-bed dorm £16.50; double £48. Weekend 10-bed dorm £15.50; 6-bed dorm £17; 4-bed dorm £18.50; double £52. ⏰ Reception 9am-10pm; call ahead to arrange a late check-in.

KINGSVIEW GUESTHOUSE GUESTHOUSE [3]

28 Gilmore Pl. ☎0131 229 8004 🖥www.kingsviewguesthouse.com

You can look for hummingbirds buzzing about the entryway garden as you eat breakfast in the front room of this quaint little Victorian guesthouse. The rooms are quaint but comfortable, with tiny desktop flatscreens.

i Dog-friendly. $ Low-season £27.50; high-season £40.

SIGHTS

Old Town

THE SCOTCH WHISKY EXPERIENCE TOUR

354 Castlehill, the Royal Mile ☎0131 220 0441 🖥www.scotchwhiskyexperience.co.uk

Beginning with a carnival ride in giant barrels (it's a good thing that this happens before the drinking), you'll be explained the process of distilling single-malt whisky by a ghostly apparition with a serious penchant for the elixir. Then after a short look at the barrel-making process, you'll be ushered into the tasting room, where an informed guide will offer you smells representative of each whisky-making region in Scotland. At the end of that segment of the tour, you'll select the whisky you want to taste and head to the display room, which houses the Diageo Claive Vidiz Collection of whiskys, almost 3500 of them. There you'll learn how to properly enjoy your whisky and have the opportunity to purchase a bottle from the store, should you find one that you really enjoy. Good luck walking home!

By the bottom of West Princes St. Gardens. $ Silver tour (basic) £11.50, students and seniors £10, children £6, family £27. Gold tour (advanced) £20, students and seniors £17.45. The Collection Tour £20. ⏰ Open daily 10am-6:30pm. Last tour daily 5pm.

NATIONAL LIBRARY OF SCOTLAND LIBRARY

57 George IV Bridge ☎0131 623 3700 🖥www.nls.uk

Yes, it's a working research library and you can get a borrower's card (free with valid ID), but who wants to do that on holiday? Instead, make a stop to check out the exhibit space in the library's large entryway. Each focusing on a different author or theme, the different displays are put up in a large, attractive space that makes it a bit like a museum instead of a library.

i There's a cafe open in the library as well. ⏰ Open M-F 9:30am-8:30pm, Sa 9:30am-1pm, Su (cafe only) 2-5pm.

BRASS RUBBING CENTRE ARTS CENTER

Trinity Apse, Chalmers Close, 42 High St. ☎0131 556 4364

Located in what seems like a one-room cathedral complete with sky-high echoey ceilings and stone gargoyles, is this oddball activity. Pick out a brass plates of Pictish designs *(prices vary according to size)* and the center will supply you with all the materials you need to do a rubbing and create your own take-home artwork. Work on anything from a plate as big as your hand *(£1)*. to a life-size Pictish knight *(£20)*.

⏰ Open M-Sa 10am-noon and 1-5pm. During festival open Su noon-5pm. Last rubbings at 4:15pm.

ST. GILES CATHEDRAL CATHEDRAL

St. Giles Cathedral, High St. ☎0131 225 9442

The stonework on the outside is finer than your granny's lace doily, and the inside's just as beautiful. With glowing stained-glass windows that cast enormous rainbows onto the walls in the late morning and a massive wooden organ near the center of the building, St. Giles is so photo-worthy that you'll find yourself looking like the ultimate tourist and trying to get a shot of everything. However, you won't be the only one, and the constant flow of tourist traffic means that St. Giles is hard-pressed for that calming atmosphere associated with cathedrals. Still, get someone to take your picture in front of a jewel-like window and you'll be more colorful than Captain Planet at Chuck E. Cheese's.

i Tours available, inquire inside. $ Free. ⏰ Open May-Sept M-F 9am-7pm, Sa 9am-5pm, Su 1-5pm; Oct-Apr M-Sa 9am-5pm, Su 1-5pm and for services.

SCOTTISH STORYTELLING CENTRE 🎫♿ CULTURAL EXPERIENCE

43-45 High St. ☎0131 556 9579 💻www.scottishstorytellingcentre.co.uk

Possibly one of a kind, the Scottish Storytelling Centre is just that: a place where people tell tall tales. Featuring Scotsmen and women from all over as well as professional storytellers from Canada, Japan, Africa and beyond, the center also runs storytelling workshops in case you'd like to make sure you have something to say about your trip other than, "Yeah, Scotland. It was cool."

$ £4-10. ⏰ Open July-Aug M-Sa 10am-6pm, Su noon-6pm; Sept-June M, Sa 10am-6pm. Open later when events are on.

THE WRITER'S MUSEUM 🎫🚫 MUSEUM

Ladystairs House, Ladystairs Close, The Royal Mile ☎0131 529 4901

Housed in the majestic Ladystairs mansion is a sanctuary of the works and personal belongings of three of Scotland's greatest authors: **Sir Walter Scott, Robert Burns,** and **Robert Louis Stevenson.** From mannequined displays to locks of hair and writing desks, it's great for a quiet wander whether you've read the collected works of all three or are simply interested in discovering why *Treasure Island* was so damn good.

📍 Half-hidden in one of the small, tunnelled "close" passages off of the Royal Mile. $ Free. ⏰ Open M-Sa 10am-5pm. During the festival, also Su noon-5pm.

THE NATIONAL WAR MUSEUM (NWM) 🎫♿ MUSEUM

Hospital Square, Castle Hill ☎0131 247 0413 💻www.edinburghcastle.gov.uk

Located inside the Castle grounds, the NWM is "free," but only after you've shelled out the cash for a ticket to the castle. Still, it's definitely worth a stop, whether your tastes run to old decorative swords or old decorative admiral's pistols. It turns out that the evolution of the Scottish soldier and his weaponry is a smorgasbord of the instruments of death.

$ Free. ⏰ Open daily in summer 9:45am-5:45pm, in winter 9:45am-4:45pm.

THE NATIONAL MUSEUM OF SCOTLAND 🎫♿ MUSEUM

NMOS, Chambers St. ☎0131 247 4422 💻www.nms.ac.uk

Housed in an enormous modern "castle" complete with winding staircases and enormous open spaces, this museum features nine floors to check out. Here's the crazy part: that's with half of it closed for a massive, £46m renovation that is going to take it "into the 21st century." The exhibits here are as wide ranging as you would expect, from "The Kingdom of the Scots," featuring powder horns and ancient Pictish stonework, to "Scotland: A Changing Nation," showing Scotland in places you'd never expect–inventors, innovators, and even Ewan MacGregors. (Seriously, who knew he was Scottish?) As a final stop, hit up the rooftop terrace for some awesome castle photo ops. But beware: you'll be fair game for the Camera Obscura tours up there. They're watching.

i 3 daily tours at 11:30am, 1:30, and 3:30pm. $ Free. ⏰ Open daily 10am-5pm.

EDINBURGH CASTLE 🎫♿ CASTLE

Castle Hill ☎0131 225 9846 💻www.edinburghcastle.gov.uk

It's the first thing you see on the skyline in Edinburgh and one of the most ar-

resting structures on the planet: the Edinburgh Castle just can't be beat. From the top you'll get all sorts of brilliant photo ops, and there are several different places where you can snap that perfect pic. However, everyone else in town has the exact same idea, so don't be surprised if you find yourself jockeying for frame space. The **"Honours of the Kingdom"** (or the Scottish Royal Jewels) exhibit funnels you along a winding display of murals and mannequins before finally reaching the jewels. If the place is busy, this can take up to 40min., so be warned. Stop by at the top of the hour to see the changing of the guard at the front entrance.
➡ Within West Princes Street Gardens. ℹ Disabled patrons should phone in advance to set up a tour. $ £14, seniors £11.20, children £7.50. ⏰ Open in in summer 9:30am-6pm, winter 9:30am-5pm; last entry 45min. before close.

New Town

👍 NATIONAL GALLERY OF SCOTLAND — 💳♿ MUSEUM

The Mound, just across Princes St. ☎0131 624 6200 🖥www.nationalgalleries.org

At the National Gallery, even the rooms in which the artwork is hung seem designed to make you take your time. The place is octagonally designed and painted a royal red. You'll not want to rush your way through this collection of pre-1900 works, including some fantastic pieces by Raphael and El Greco.
ℹ Free. Special exhibits £5-10. ⏰ Open M-W 10am-5pm, Th 10am-7pm, F-Su 10am-5pm.

NATIONAL TRUST SCOTLAND — 💳🚫 NATIONAL TRUST, GALLERY

28 Charlotte Sw. ☎0844 493 2100 🖥www.nts.org.uk

The group in charge of conserving cultural sites, artifacts, and buildings in Scotland, National Trust Scotland keeps its head office here, where it also maintains a small gallery full of works by 20th-century Scottish artists, a bookshop, a restaurant, and a cafe.
⏰ Gallery open M-F 9am-4:30pm. Cafe, bookshop, and restaurant open M-Sa 9:30am-5pm.

Stockbridge

👍 GLENOGLE SWIM CENTRE — 💳♿ SWIMMING

Glenogle Rd. ☎0131 343 6376 🖥www.edinburghleisure.co.uk

Having just undergone an £18 million renovation, the Glenogle Swim Centre is totally state of the art, with a 25m pool, a sauna, and a steamroom. The best part? It's all available for public use. The best best part? It's all available for public use, for cheap. They also have a gym and fitness classes. Makes you re-consider your wild idea to go down and swim in the freezing Atlantic, doesn't it?
$ Swim costs £4. Sauna and steamroom £.60. ⏰ Open M-F 7am-10pm, Sa-Su 8am-6pm.

STOCKBRIDGE MARKET — MARKET ARCHWAY

At the junction of St. Stephens Pl. and St. Stephens St.

Before you go grab your all-hemp, recycled grocery bag and head off to get your fix of farmers' market veggies, it's worth knowing that the Stockbridge *Market* no longer exists—it's been replaced by houses. However, the **old archway,** with its engraved lettering and protruding lamp is still there, and it makes for quite a picturesque scene. Grab the camera, snap a few quick shots and stroll down through the pathway, now covered by trees. Or just head off to the art gallery next to the entrance.

WATER OF LEITH — NATURE WALK

A beautiful way to spend an afternoon or a date is to take a walk along the paved paths that line this small river, flowing through New Town and Stockbridge. Green trees and foliage hang over the path, providing some shade for when you want to sit down on one of the many benches that line the water. If you follow it long enough, you'll come up underneath the massive, arched underbelly of the Dean Bridge.

THE ROYAL BOTANIC GARDENS 💳♿ BOTANIC GARDENS

20a Inverleith Row ☎0131 552 7171 🖥www.rbge.org.uk

A center for plant research and conservation, this place is nuts (seeds, and spores too) for plants. The entrance and visitors center is beautifully impressive, with a glass facade and white, spinning windmill in front. Entrance to the gardens themselves is free, but to get in to the Glasshouses for the real, misty green experience, you'll have to pay.

$ £4, concessions £3, children £1, family £8. ⏰ Open daily Apr-Sept 10am-6pm, Mar-Oct 10am-5pm.

Tollcross and West End

👍 **THE MEADOWS** PUBLIC PARK

Located on the southwestern end of town, the Meadows are a beautiful, welcome respite from the honking cars and blabbing people inside the city. With wide-open, grass-covered fields intersected by paths covered by the shade of trees, it's no wonder that during the festival the Meadows become a hotspot for people to gather and throw frisbees, barbecue, and generally just have a great time. There are also 16 tennis courts and a playground on one end.

ℹ If you want to make sure of your spot on a tennis court during the summer months, call ahead to reserve at ☎0131 444 1969. ⏰ Courts open Apr-June M-F 4-9pm, Sa-Su 10am-6pm; July-Aug MoF 9am-9pm, Sa-Su 10am-7:30pm; Sept M-F 4-9pm, Sa-Su 10am-6pm.

FOOD 🍎

Edinburgh, like any heavily touristed city, has just about any kind of cuisine you might be hankering for. So if you haven't quite gotten up the gumption to try haggis yet, try some fantastical veggie creations over at **David Bann's** or a huge plate of beef curry over at the **Mosque Kitchen.** You can do a wine and cheese night at the hostel if you stock up at **I. J. Mellis** in Stockbridge. In short, the possibilities are endless.

Old Town

👍 **DAVID BANN** 💳♿ VEGETARIAN [3]

56-58 St. Mary's St. ☎0131 556 5888 🖥www.davidbann.com

At this all-vegetarian restaurant, you're not going be suffering through your salad. How's a watercress, beetroot, and goat cheese salad sound? Good? We thought so. Enjoy your meal and maybe one of the excellently spicy **Bloody Marys** in the attractive, modern interior.

$ Entrees £15-20. ⏰ Open M-Th 11am-10pm, F 11am-10:30pm, Sa 10am-10:30pm, Su 10am-10pm.

LE CAFÉ ROYALE 💳♿ CAFE [2]

274 Cannongate St. ☎0131 652 3534

A people watcher's paradise, the entire front of this café swings open in good weather, leaving you with a covered fresh-air view of the street outside. A few quaint round tables, local artwork on the walls and a central support beam that looks like it was ripped out of the *Titanic* complete the ensemble. Grab a coffee—it's strong and fresh. Let the watch begin.

$ All coffee under £2. ⏰ Open daily 8am-around 8pm.

ELEPHANT CAFÉ 💳♿🍸 CAFE, BAR [3]

21 George IV Bridge ☎0131 220 5355 🖥www.elephanthouse.biz

Harry Potter and company were birthed here on scribbled napkins. The cafe serves both coffee and booze, making you wonder which one **JK Rowling** was drinking when she had her "inspiration." Choose yours. They also have a selection of pastries and pies.

$ £5 minimum. Coffee £1.50-2.75. Beer £3 per bottle. ⏰ Open M-F 8am-11pm, Sa-Su 9am-11pm.

RISTORANTE GENNARO ITALIAN [3]

64 Grassmarket St. ☎0131 226 3706

The best way to pick out an Italian restaurant is obvious—look for the one that's full. The second method requires a quick peek at the menu—is it in Italian? **Ristorante Gennaro** fulfills both of these requirements, seeing its tables fill every night and a menu that has English translations. Dim lighting and a deep red color scheme accentuate the fancy feel, but students as well as a pre-theater crowd are known to turn up.

$ *Appetizers £1.50-9. Pizza £8-12. Fish entrees £12-14, meat entrees £14-19.50.* ⏰ *Open daily noon-11pm.*

New Town

THE UNDERGROUND CAFÉ (TUC) CAFE [1]

34 Eden St. ☎0131 624 7161

A surprisingly great local dive—you'll literally be going down some steep stairs to get to it—located just a few steps away from the Edinburgh bus station, TUC has a charming interior and delicious food. Check out the local artwork on the walls or browse through the festival information resting conveniently on top of an old piano in the entrance.

$ *Soup with bread £1.75-2.75.* ⏰ *Open M-F 7:30am-4pm, Sa 8:30am-4pm.*

WOLFITS RESTAURANT, DELI [1]

200 Rose St. ☎0131 225 5096

We have no idea why this restaurant is called "Wolfits." What we do know is that this small establishment sells good food cheap. Soups and buttered baguettes go for under £3. There's not *really* an atmosphere, but you can watch music videos on the television while you wolf it down.

⏰ *Open daily 7:30am-4pm.*

INDIAN THALI RESTAURANT RESTAURANT [3]

1-3 York Pl. ☎0131 557 9899

With a deep, royal red interior filled with flower vases, this isn't your typical stop-off for a quick bite. The Bollywood music's playing, but if that doesn't drag you in, you can grab some takeaway—it comes with free rice.

$ *Entrees £8-11. Breakfast sandwiches £1-3.* ⏰ *Open Tu-Sa for noon-2:30pm. Open daily 5:30-11pm.*

THE CONAN DOYLE PUB GRUB [2]

71-73 York Pl. ☎0131 557 9539

In the neighborhood where **Sir Arthur Conan Doyle** himself used to live, there's memorabilia—Sherlock Holmes and otherwise—galore in this resto pub. A good value for a full cooked breakfast (veggie or not). Come by on the weekends when it's more of a pub and receive the same kind of value on drinks. Also, enjoy the comfy armchairs.

$ *Breakfast from £5.* ⏰ *Open M-Th 9am-11:45pm, F-Sa 9am-1am, Su 12:30pm-midnight.*

BROWN SUGAR CAFE [1]

39 Queen St. ☎0131 623 7770

There aren't really any attention-grabbing words like "arresting" or "insane" to describe Brown Sugar. And that's what makes it great. Located on a corner just across the street from the park-like Queen's gardens, it's a spot where you can grab a nice coffee, sit back, munch on some homemade **banana bread** and watch the world go by. How's that for arresting?

$ *Americano £1.90. Cadbury's hot chocolate £1.60.* ⏰ *Open M-F 7am-3:30pm, Sa 10am-4pm.*

MIRÓ CANTINA MEXICANA 💳♿☀ MEXICAN ❸

184 Rose St. ☎0131 225 4376

It's a *fiesta* in here! Or at least, that's what the paint job would have you believe. Bright yellows and wild patterns cover the inside (and outside) of this eatery. A little more "Mexican" than "Taco Bell," this place offers a big plate of nachos with beans, jalapeños, melted cheese, salsa, sour cream, and guacamole *(£5)*. Even the outdoor seating has a festive paint job.

$ Selection of Mexican beers £3.10-3.25. ⏰ Open daily in summer noon-10:30pm. Open in winter noon-2:30pm and 5:30-10pm.

Stockbridge

👍 BELLS DINER 💳♿🍸 DINER ❸

7 St. Stephens St. ☎0131 225 4673

We at *Let's Go* are not picky about burgers. For us, as long as it's hot, has a bun, and isn't from a franchise with a "drive-thru," we're pretty happy. However, there are occasions in one's life where one is exposed to burger greatness, and Bells Diner is one of those experiences. The burgers cost a bit more than you'd usually pay *(£8-10)* but are well worth the expenditure. Also, they come with a full plate of chips (fries) and a selection of six different dipping sauces..

i Reservations for weekend evenings recommended. ⏰ Open M-F 6-10pm, Sa noon-10pm, Su 6-10pm.

👍 MADELEINE 🥗♿ CAFE ❷

27b Raeburn Pl. ☎0131 332 8455

An intensely modern, intensely chic cafe with the most futuristic bathrooms you've ever seen (seriously, it's like NASA designed the loo...), Madeleine earns the thumbpick for the macaroons. These light wafery cookied sandwiches are sweet but tart, in flavors like vanilla, chocolate, raspberry, and mango *(£.80 each)*. You can't stop eating them. Seriously, we tried. You can't (mumble crunch yum!) stop...

$ Cakes and coffees £1.40-5. ⏰ Open Tu-Sa 10am-5:30pm, Su 11am-5:30pm.

great britain

GREEN GROCER'S 🥗♿ GROCERY ❶

11 Deanhaugh St. ☎0131 332 7384

Get your fresh apples, nectarines, carrots and any other type of fresh munchable you may be interested in here. Head inside the store for the more sinful foodstuffs, such as chocolates and soft drinks.

⏰ Open daily 6:30am-9pm.

I. J. MELLIS 💳♿ DELI ❸

6 Bakers Pl. ☎0131 225 6566 💻www.mellischeese.co.uk

Yeah, you may be paying the same for some cheese and cured meat as you would for a big plate of fish and chips, but where else are you going to find *Pyrenees Chevre* goat cheese? Not at the chippie's you aren't.

⏰ Open M-F 9am-6:30pm, Sa 9am-6pm, Su 10am-5pm.

Haymarket and Dalry

👍 GOOD SEED BISTRO 💳♿📶☀ BISTRO ❸

100-102 Dalry Rd. ☎0131 337 3803 💻www.goodseedbistro.com

The new kid on the block, the Good Seed Bistro is doing everything right: classy interior, a relaxed vibe. They serve weekday lunch specials *(2 courses, £7.95)*. Interested in coming during the mornings? Coffee and cakes go for just £4.50.

i Wi-Fi available. ⏰ Open M-Th noon-10pm, F-Sa noon-11pm, Su noon-4pm.

CLIFTON FISH BAR 🥗🚭 FISH AND CHIPS ❶

10 Clifton Terr. ☎0131 346 8723 💻www.clifton-fish-bar.justeat.co.uk

A tiny fish and chips joint with two slap-happy fry cooks who are more than ready to play on the job, the Clifton Fish Bar sells cheap pizzas, calzones, and chips. Order the "munchy box," with chicken pakora, vegetable pakora, donner meat, chips, and a can of soda *(just £8.99)*.

Ⓢ *10 in. calzone £4-5.50. 7 in. pizza £3.* Ⓠ *Open M-Th 4:30pm-1am, F-Sa 4:30pm-2am, Su 4:30pm-1am.*

XIANGBALA HOTPOT
63 Dalry Rd.

⊛♿ RESTAURANT ❸
☎0131 313 4408

A slightly different take on restaurant culture, the Xiangbala Hotpot is £15 per person all you can eat for 2hr. With a silver boiling pot in the middle of the smooth black tables, meats, seafood, and veggies are introduced into boiling broths and then eaten.

Ⓠ *Open daily 3-11pm.*

Tollcross and West End

🔲 THE MOSQUE KITCHEN
19a West Nicholson St.

⊛♿ CURRY ❶

The guys at the Mosque Kitchen don't mess around. There's not any "atmosphere" to speak of—just some covered outdoor cafeteria seating—but you don't need it, as you'll be too busy staring at your giant plate of delicious rice and curry to care.

Ⓢ *Veggie curry plate £3.50, meat £4.50, chicken £3.* Ⓠ *Open daily noon-8pm; closed F 1-1:45pm for prayers.*

🔲 VICTOR HUGO CONTINENTAL DELICATESSEN
26-27 Melville Terr.

🍽♿☕ DELI ❷
☎0131 667 1827 🖳victorhugodeli.com

A true combination of deli and cafe, Victor Hugo's has little booths along the walls perfect for snuggling up with a coffee. The inside is a great place to wonder when the pissing rain is going to stop. Or if you've got a slightly more benevolent attitude towards the weather, you can sit outside and enjoy the rain—from underneath the awnings of course. With locals who've been coming back since 1940 as well as students who come for the belly-filling mac and cheese, it's everybody's favorite. Try the award-winning Ramsay of Carluke bacon roll *(£2.85)*.

Ⓢ *Teas £1.60.* Ⓠ *Open M-F 8am-10pm, Sa-Su 8am-8pm. During the festival, open daily 8am-11pm.*

BRAZILIAN SENSATION
117-119 Buccleuch St.

⊛♿ BRAZILIAN ❶
☎0131 667 0400 🖳www.braziliansensation.co.uk

Brazilian Sensation is a smallish but elaborately decorated restaurant that can't get enough of its South American namesake. Even the mannequin in the window is decked out in Brazilian gear. Serving rolls and sandwiches as well as a large variety of tropical fruit smoothies *(£3.50)*.

Ⓢ *Baguettes £2.75.* Ⓠ *Open M-Sa noon-4pm, open Su during the festival.*

PETER'S YARD
27 Simpson Ln.

🍽♿ CAFE ❸
☎0131 229 5876 🖳www.petersyard.com

Peter's Yard, a Swedish-style cafe housed right in the heart of the University of Edinburgh, serves hot cinnammon buns as well as *Kladdkaka* (a Swedish chocolate cake). The cafe is housed in a clear glass box, so those sitting outside on the balcony may 🔲spy on those sitting inside and vice versa. Unfortunately, it seems that most of the people coming to Peter's Yard aren't interesting enough to spy on.

Ⓢ *Kladdkaka £2.70. Coffee £1.75-2.95.* Ⓠ *Open M-F 7am-6pm, Sa-Su 9am-6pm.*

NIGHTLIFE

Edinburgh, despite being the "prettier little sister" to Glasgow, has nowhere near the same club scene. This town full of 🔲**pubs and bars**, however, buzzes happily on the weekends and skyrockets in intensity during the festivals in August. Each specific neighborhood will have its own variations on the classic pub, from the tourist-heavy areas along the Royal Mile, to the strange collection of odd and local watering holes on **Rose Street** in New Town, to the posh, hip new bars in Stockbridge.

Drinking in Scotland, and in Edinburgh especially, isn't about "going on the piss" (though that is a part of it), but about finding the right place for yourself, your group, your night, and your state of mind—no matter how much that last one may be altered throughout the night.

Old Town

BANNERMAN'S — BAR, MUSIC VENUE

212 Cowgate ☎0131 556 3254 www.myspace.com/bannermanslive

With a subterranean, half-barrel auditorium for the live acts, the soundproofing in Bannerman's is so good, if you want to sit in the bar and have a friendly chat, you can...while a rock show goes on next door. A wide selection of beers and cask ales are available, but if you want to try the house special, go for the **"Jager U-boat."** What is a Jager U-boat, you ask? Just place your fingers in your ears, grab a small bottle of Jager with your teeth, tilt your head back and—*Whoosh!* hear the bubbles of the ocean as you decend...into a drunken stupor. Nah, you'll be fine, and Bannerman's is a kick-ass place to hang out.

i Live shows £4-8. $ Jager U-boat £2. Pints £3.40-3.65. ⏰ Open daily Sept-July noon-1am. Aug noon-3am.

WHITE HART INN — PUB

34 Grassmarket ☎0131 226 2806

The Grassmarket's oldest pub (est. 1516), the White Hart Inn retains its olden feel, with faded photographs on the walls, beer steins hanging from the ceilings, and one slightly creepy bust of William Burke by the door. Famous patrons of the pub include Scotland's favorite poet, **Robert Burns.** Grab a pint and see if your poetical stylings are loosed.

$ Pints £2.85-4. Spirits £2.95-12.49. ⏰ Open M-Th 11am-midnight, F-Sa 11am-1am, Su 11am-midnight.

GREYFRIARS BOBBY'S BAR — PUB

30-34 Candlemaker Row ☎0131 225 8328

Named after one of Edinburgh's local legends—Greyfriars Bobby, a terrier so faithful that slept at his owner's grave for the next 14 years until his own death. The citizens here buried him next to his beloved owner and the loyal pooch entered annals of local legend. There's a statue of Bobby outside this pub, and it's a popular photo spot for tourists of all nationalities. The pub itself is a pretty standard alehouse, but if you want to contemplate Bobby's loyalty from across the street you can sit outside and have a beer.

$ Ales £2.80-3. Spirits £3. ⏰ Open M-Sa 11am-midnight, Su 11:30am-midnight.

BLACK BULL — PUB

12 Grassmarket St. ☎0131 225 6636

The floors, the walls, and the ceiling, the place look like the inside of an oak tree. A really big oak tree. The Black Bull is enormous, with ample room for you and a party of any size to find seats in one of the warmly lit booths or on a plush leather sofa. Serving real cask ales, it's more a hang-out than a dance bar, but there are DJs on the weekends.

i Folk session M. Live bands play most Th. $ Spirits £2-2.60. Pints £2.60-3.45. ⏰ Open M-F 11am-1am, Sa-Su 10am-1am.

THE BANSHEE LABYRINTH — CLUB

29-35 Niddry St. ☎0131 558 8209 www.thebansheelabyrinth.com

Built into the side of a hill and just above Edinburgh's famous "haunted vaults" (the Auld Reekie tours actually end here), the Banshee Labyrinth is a maze of stairs and tunnels, low-ceilinged cave-like rooms and Addams Family inspired bars. There are three bars and seven rooms, a pool hall and a cinema, plus a pole-dancing area. Note the sign that absolves the bar from any injuries you may sustain from your "sexy dancing."

Spirits with mixer £2.50. Pints £2.70-3.40. ⏰ *Open daily 12:30pm-3am.*

SIN
⊛♿♀▼ CLUB

207 Cowgate   ☎0131 220 6176 ▪www.club-sin.com

A recently-remade club and one of the Cowgate's newest nightlife options, Sin lives up to its name, getting crazy during the week, on the weekends, whenever. With more fog and spinning lights than that alien spaceship in *Men In Black* and a massive downstairs dance floor, you can head up to the mezzanine level if you—ahem—have just one sip too many and need to find your friends again.

✈ *Cowgate.* Ⓢ *Bottles £2. Pints £2.49.* ⏰ *Open daily 10pm-3am. During fesitval open daily 1pm-5am.*

WHISTLE BINKIES
♥⊗♀ BAR, LIVE MUSIC

46 Southbridge   ☎0131 557 5114 ▪www.whistlebinkies.com

A popular place to see smaller live acts, Whistle Binkies has a sort of "pre-ripped jeans" feel—there are lots of old barrels and comfortable ratty stools, but the holes in the wall with brick underneath are definitely stylized. Framed photos of famous musicians are carefully hung and illuminated, though notably not behind the stage, where things might get messy.

i Live music every night except Sa, when DJs come on. Ⓢ *Pints £3.40-3.60. Spirits £1.60-3.30.* ⏰ *Open M-Th 5pm-3am, F-Su 1pm-3am.*

New Town

▨ CITIZEN SMITH
♥⊗♀♿ BAR

168 Rose St.   ☎0131 225 5979

The only independently owned and run bar on Rose Street, Citizen Smith is a haven for all things folk, blues, rock, alt rock, and indie. There's live music every night on the somewhat improvised stage, but try to show up in August for their own, private "Woodstock," where 50 bands play over the span of three days. Come in, sit down, and admire the giant cardboard arachnid on the ceiling.

Ⓢ *Pints £3.30.* ⏰ *Open daily in summer 4pm-1am, in winter 2pm-1am. During festival, open daily 1pm-3am.*

ROSE AND CROWN
♥♿♀♿ PUB

170 Rose St.   ☎0131 225 4039

In this decent bar with molded ceilings live music is on three nights a week. Other than that and the occasional DJ, however, it's a pretty chill place, simply a nice place to get a cider and sit out in the sun.

Ⓢ *Pints £3-3.30. Spirits £3.15-4.* ⏰ *Open daily 11am-1am.*

JEYKLL AND HYDE BAR
♥⊗♀♿ BAR

112 Hanover St.   ☎0131 224 2002 ▪www.eeriepubs.co.uk

A dark and foreboding—who are we kidding, this place is meant to look creepy on purpose. It's called the Jeykll and Hyde Bar! Still, with iron chandeliers and high-backed "creeeeepy" chairs, they do an okay job. Dracula could have lived here, but he would have been drunk on Bloody Marys the whole time.

i Bring your passportp; the license isn't going to work here. Ⓢ *Pints £1.50-3. Mixed drinks £5, 2 £6.* ⏰ *Open M-Sa noon-1am, Su 12:30pm-10pm.*

QUEEN'S ARMS
♥⊗♀♿ PUB

49 Frederick St.   ☎0131 225 1045

Having recently undergone a massive refurbishment, the Queen's Arms is classier than ever. It's still got that traditional feel, with a padded bar, bookshelf full of classics and wiry chandeliers, but it's all got that new-pub smell. Take it all in over one of their hand-pulled ales. Can we say anymore about its classy classic-ness?

i The Queen's Arms is the 1st pub in Scotland to have Blue Moon on draft. Ⓢ *Pints £3-3.50. Spirits £2.75 and up.* ⏰ *Open M-Sa 11am-1am, Su 12:30pm-1am.*

BLACK ROSE TAVERN BAR

49 Rose St. ☎0131 220 0414 💻www.blackrosetavern.com

If you've ever grown a beard to impress the guys in Pantera or ever bought a guitar with more sharp ends than your Swiss Army knife, you'll enjoy the Black Rose. With "rock karaoke" on Wednesdays and a major skeleton obsession and various tattoos among the staff, the Black Rose is great for rockers of all types. **Jagermeister** is the self-proclaimed house wine. What more do you want?

i Open mic night on T. Quiz on W just before the karaoke. $ Pints £2.80-3.65. Spirits from £1.20-1.60. ⏰ Open M-Sa 11am-1am, Su 12:30pm-1am.

EL BARRIO BAR, CLUB

47 Hanover St. ☎0131 220 6818 💻www.elbarrio.co.uk

New Town's only club is rowdy enough on its own. Open until 3am everyday, this basement of brightly colored walls and Latin music becomes packed with people on the weekends, as the photos on the walls will attest. Laugh at the most intoxicated people you see on the walls and then come back next week to make sure you haven't joined their ranks.

$ Spirits and mixer £3-3.80. Pints £3.50. ⏰ Open daily noon-3am.

ROSE STREET BREWERY PUB

55-57 Rose St. ☎0131 220 1227

A local's pub, the Rose Street Brewery did actually used to be a brewery, but has since been promoted to a place where you can drink it rather than make it. The restaurant upstairs is a popular spot for tourists and serves a mean steak. A plain but comfortable interior, a wooden entry space will take you down a pair of step onto a strangely kilt-like carpet.

i 4 ales available, 2 constant, 2 rotating. $ Pints £2.70-3.40. Spirits £2.55. ⏰ Bar open M-Th 11am-11pm, F-Sa 11am-1am, Su 11am-11pm. Restaurant open daily noon-10pm.

LORD BODO'S BAR BAR

3 Dublin St. ☎0131 477 2563

You could walk by Lord Bodo's bar and say to yourself, "Why, that doesn't look like much of a bar." The exterior's not much to look at, it's true, but the inside is seriously classy, with brown suede chairs and stained wood all around. Grab a martini and get out the tux Bond fans.

$ Pints £2.70-3. Mixed drinks £3.50-4. ⏰ Open M-Th 11am-11:30pm, F-Sa 11am-1:30am, Su 11am-11:30pm.

DIRTY DICK'S PUB

159 Rose St. ☎0131 260 9920 💻dirtydicksedinburgh@gmail.com

I spy, among the bric-a-brac housed in Dirty Dick's: a sea of upside-down golf clubs, a picture of **Alfred Hitchcock,** somewhat creepy teddy bears, a full pint of beer stuck upside down on the ceiling, and an accordion.

$ Pints £3.30. Spirits £2.60. ⏰ Open M-Sa 11am-1am, Su noon-1am.

Stockbridge

THE ANTIQUARIAN PUB

68-72 St. Stephens St. ☎0131 225 2858 💻www.theantiquarybar.co.uk

Its entrance may be hidden at the bottom of a small stairwell in Stockbridge, but this bar let's its people and atmosphere do the talking. A great local crowd with a jovial attitude hang out here, and if you come by on Tuesday night around 8pm you can get in on one hell of a poker game. You probably won't win (some of these guys are legit), but you will have a lot of fun at this bar.

$ Spirits £2.10-3.50. Pints £3-3.55. ⏰ Open M noon-11pm, Tu-W noon-midnight, Th-Sa noon-1am, Su noon-12:30am.

AVOCA BAR

⚆Ⓢ♀ BAR

4-6 Dean St. ☎0131 315 3311 ■www.avocabarandgrill.co.uk

A regulars' watering hole, Avoca is your typical food and booze stop. The building is quite nice, with more of those Victorian moldings we've seen so much of, but the bar itself is fairly spare on decoration. A nice place to come in and have a private chat.

ⓒ *Pints £3-4.15. Spirits £2.70.* Ⓣ *Open M-Th 11am-midnight, F-Sa 11am-1am, Su 11am-midnight.*

HAMILTON'S

⚆♿♀ BAR

16-18 Hamilton Pl. ☎0131 225 8513 ■www.hamiltonsedinburgh.co.uk

With lots of posh, leather couches and very "in" 60s pop art on the back wall, it's no surprise to see that everyone in Hamilton's is well-dressed, mild-mannered and sipping on glasses of wine. Should you like to go and join them, you'd be wise, though it's certainly not necessary, to spiff yourself up a bit. Look at you, you need to wash behind those ears before you go out drinking!

ⓒ *Pints £3.30-4.50. Spirits £3.10.* Ⓣ *Open daily 9am-1am. In Aug and Dec open daily 9am-3am.*

ST. VINCENT BAR

⚆Ⓢ♀♻ BAR

11 St. Vincent St. ☎0131 225 7447 ■www.stvincentbar.com

From the outside the St. Vincent Bar looks like a normal pub...and actually, it looks pretty normal from the inside as well. However, it's a *Let's Go* favorite in terms of pub quirks: St. Vincent's allows you to purchase two pints of your favorite ale "to go." That's right. Tell 'em you feel like drinking at home, and they'll give you a lovely carton of beer. Now that's brilliant.

ⓒ *Pints £3.04-3.85.* Ⓣ *Open M-Sa 11am-1am, Su 12:30pm-1am. During festival open until 3am.*

HECTOR'S

⚆♿♀ BAR

47-49 Deanhaugh St. ☎0131 343 1735 ■www.hectorsstockbridge.co.uk

A hip, trendy bar in the heart of Stockbridge, Hector's burns the candles all night long, until the wax falls on the tables. It's got a classy yet laid-back feel, thanks to wraparound couches complete with funky pillows and a dark purple interior that enhance the aura. A heavily local patronage keeps things from getting too fancy-schmancy. Hector's stocks a wide selection of wines, ales, and beers as well as an organic cider.

ⓒ *Pints £3-3.50. Organic cider £3.10.* Ⓣ *Open M-W noon-midnight, Th-F noon-1am, Sa 11am-1am, Su 11am-midnight.*

THE STOCKBRIDGE TAP

⚆♿♀ PUB

2-6 Raeburn Pl. ☎0131 343 3000

A great local place right next to Hector's, the Stockbridge Tap sees everyone from old men to young girls come in to enjoy the hefty ale selection. If you've got the time and the liver for it, try to drink the spectrum.

ⓒ *Spirits £2.40. Pints £3-3.30.* Ⓣ *Open M-Th noon-midnight, F-Sa noon-1am, Su 12:30pm-midnight.*

Haymarket and Dalry

▪ CARTER'S

⚆♿♀♻ BAR

185 Morrison St. ☎0131 228 9149

Unlike the concept pubs of Haymarket and Dalry, Carter's has an artsy feel accentuated by the candle wax dripping down the stairs and the mismatched couches and chairs in the loft. A place for live music, they set up small shows in the downstairs space. Come on Wednesday for Bluegrass. As the sign painted on the wall says, "Are you gonna piss about all day?—Or are you coming in?" Do the latter.

i Music begins 9-9:30pm. ⓒ *Spirits £2.30-3.30. Pints £2.90-3.20.* Ⓣ *Open M-Sa noon-1am, Su 12:30pm-1am.*

THE MERCAT BAR 🏷♿🍸 PUB

28 West Maitland St. ☎0131 225 8716 🖥www.mercatbar.com

A pub that's renowned locally for it's grub, the Mercat Bar has owners that'll swear it's a bar before a restaurant. Still, with classy tables illuminated under an orange glow and only the lights from the taps to signal out the bar, that'll be up to you to decide.

i Be on the lookout for daily specials. $ *Spirits from £2.20. Pints £3.20-3.70. Entrees £9-12.* ⏰ *Open daily 9am-1am, during the festival 7:30am-1am.*

DIANE'S POOL HALL 💰♿🍸☁ PUB, POOL HALL

242 Morrison St. ☎0131 228 1156

"Diane's" is a bit of a strange name for this pub, considering it's mostly men that frequent it. However, Haymarket could just be lacking in female pool sharks. With nine tables all for £.20 a game, it's a good place to get snookered.

$ *Pints £2.10-2.60. Spirits around £1.55. Cash only.* ⏰ *Open daily 8am-midnight.*

Tollcross and West End

👍 THE LINKS BAR 🏷♿🍸☁ SPORTS BAR

2-4 Alvanley Terr. ☎0131 229 3854

A sports bar with all the typical trimmings—pool tables *(£1 per game)*, pictures of sports greats, cases full of old sporting memorabilia such as ancient golf clubs and stinky old shoes (thank God they're in a case), and a name like The Links Bar (what more do you need?). For those who really don't care what Jack Nicklaus's handicap was during the 1982 British Open, the other half of the bar is an ultra-modern, wooden tube with blue lighting.

$ *Pints £2.95-3.75. Spirits £2-2.50.* ⏰ *Open daily 9am-1am.*

HENDRICKS 🏷♿☁ BAR

1a Barclay Pl. ☎0131 229 2442

A classy young-professionals bar with a decor that could be put up in an interior design catalogue. Thistle wallpaper and little black lamps above the bar illuminate the LBDs that show up on the weekends. No live music or quiz over here though guys. This place is fancy.

$ *Pints £3.15-4.50. Mixed drinks 2-for-1 M-Th £5.49.* ⏰ *Open M-Th 11am-11pm, F-Sa 11am-1am, Su 11am-11pm.*

CUCKOO'S NEST 💰♿ BAR

69 Home St. ☎0131 228 1078

A smaller, student bar with a tiki feel, the booths are lined by a row of bamboo pieces and the mirrors on the walls are framed by what looks to be a bird's nest gatherings. Unless you're really going nuts here though, it looks like the only thing making the name pertinent is the empty bird cage at the back of the bar. There's quiz on Mondays, musical bingo on Thursday and an open mic night the second Wednesday of every month.

$ *Pints £2.50-3.50. Mixed drinks from £3.50.* ⏰ *Open daily noon-midnight or 1am.*

ARTS AND CULTURE 🎵

Edinburgh becomes the world capital for arts and culture every August during the city's **Fringe Festival.** The Fringe publishes its own program of activities, available in hard copy from the Fringe office and online. A world-famous orgy of the performing arts, the Fringe Festival encompasses shows in theater, dance, comedy, opera, and more. The festival was begun in 1947 when eight rebellious theater groups not invited to perform at the International Festival decided that "the show must go on." The organization was formalized, and thus the world's largest arts festival was born. *(180 High Street. ☎131 226 0026 🖥www.edfringe.com.)* For all listings and local events during the rest of the year, check out *The List (£2.25. 🖥www.list.co.uk)* available at newsstands.

Museums and Galleries

👍 SURGEON'S HALL MUSEUM
💳♿ OLD TOWN

Surgeon's Hall, Nicholson St. ☎0131 527 1649 💻www.rcact.ac.uk

Full of some of the nastiest body parts perfectly preserved in formaldhyde and the wickedest-looking tools you've ever seen, this museum showcases every little bit of the history of surgery, and some stuff that must just be there to shock. The exhibit detailing the greusome story of **Burke** and **Hare,** who murdered innocent citizens in order to receive the cash for supplying early doctors with bodies, actually has a pocketbook made from Burke's very **human skin.** Before we had photography we had painting, and there are several *technically* beautiful oils of festering wounds. What can we say? It's great. Just don't come on a full stomach.

ℹ Disabled visitors will want to call in advance to arrange a visit. $ £5, concession £3, family (2 adults, 3 children) £15. ⏰ Open M-F noon-4pm. Aug open M-F 10am-4pm, Sa-Su noon-4pm.

HENDERSON GALLERY
⊗ NEW TOWN

4 Thistle St. Ln. ☎0131 225 7464 💻www.hendersongallery.com

With around nine full rotating exhibitions a year, this isn't just some gallery set up by a sandwich shop, come check out the attractive loft space where paintings from all sorts of artists, from graffitti to fine art.

✤ Out the back door of Henderson's. Ask a member of the staff. ⏰ Open Sept-July M-Sa 11am-6pm, Aug Tu-Sa 11am-6pm.

ALPHA ART
💳♿ NEW TOWN

52 Hamilton Pl. ☎0131 226 3066 💻www.alpha-art.co.uk

With a collection of original and limited-edition prints from artists that are local, UK-based and international, Alpha Art has a huge range of stuff. Great oils, silk-screens, and sculptures abound.

⏰ Open T-F 10am-6pm, Sa 10am-5pm, Su noon-5pm.

Music

👍 HMV PICTURE HOUSE
💳♿🍸 WEST END

31 Lothian Road ☎0131 221 2280 💻www.edinburgh-picturehouse.co.uk

A beautiful place to watch things get messy, the HMV Picture House sees the likes of Imogen Heap and Less Than Jake, plus other big names, on the reg. On Thursday nights they do the intense, "Octopussy Club night," popular with students because of its £1 drinks. Who would have guessed?

⏰ Box office open M-F 12pm-2pm, Sa-Su 12pm-4pm.

THE BONGO CLUB
💳♿🍸 CANONGATE

37 Holyrood Road ☎0131 558 8844 💻www.thebongoclub.co.uk

Half club, half live music venue, half arts space...wait, how many halves is that? Bongo does it all, throwing raging parties on the weekends in their jungle-esque main room, with a stage for bands and live DJ set-up. Head upstairs during the day to check out the revolving art exhibitions in the café.

$ Prices vary. Cover entrance F-Sa £3-12 depending on the act. ⏰ Cafe open 1pm-7pm. Club open 11pm-3am. Open 7pm-10pm when music gigs are on.

THE JAZZ BAR
💳⊗📶🍸 OLD TOWN

1A Chambers St. ☎0131 220 4298 💻www.thejazzbar.co.uk

This is a perfect venue to hear blues, hip-hop, funk, and all that jazz. The Jazz Bar hosts not one, but three shows most nights: "Tea Time" *(Tu-Sa 6-8:30pm)* is acoustic, "The Early Gig" *(daily 8:30-11:30pm)* is jazzy and "Late 'N Live" *(daily 11:30pm-3am)* is funky and electric.

✤ Off of South Bridge St. ℹ Cover cash only. $ Cover after Tea Time £1-5. No cover during Tea Time. ⏰ Open M-F 5pm-3am, Sa 2:30pm-3am, Su 7:30pm-3am. Open until 5am during Fringe Festival in Aug.

Theater

👍 THE BEDLAM THEATRE ⊗♿🍸 OLD TOWN

116 Bristol Pl. ☎0131 225 9893 💻www.bedlamtheatre.co.uk

The oldest student-run theatre in Great Britain, the Bedlam (named after a nearby mental institution) is full of fun and crazy performances, several by the **Edinburgh University Theatre Company (EUTC).** The "Improverts," the university improv group, who play every Friday at 10:30pm and every night at 12:30am during the festival, shouldn't be missed.

ℹ Those requiring disabled access should provide advance notice. $ Tickets £3.50-5, students usually receive a £1 discount. ⏰ Closed June-July. Aug-May, just knock and someone will be there to greet you.

EDINBURGH PLAYHOUSE 💳♿ OLD TOWN

18-22 Greenside Pl. ☎0844 847 1660 💻www.edinburghplayhouse.org.uk

Originally built to be a cinema, which it remained for 40 years, the Edinburgh Playhouse underwent a massive renovation in 1993 and now revels in its status as one of the most popular theaters in the city.

$ Ticket prices vary. ⏰ Box office open M-Sa noon-6pm, show days noon-8pm.

Film

👍 THE CAMEO 💳♿🍸 WEST END

38 Home St. ☎0871 902 5723 💻www.picturehouses.co.uk

Scotland's second oldest cinema and one of the last to show independent, foreign, and cult flicks, the Cameo is a great place to see something other than the next steaming pile of whatever James Cameron has whipped up. Check the calender to see when the monthly showing of the "so-bad-it's-good" cult classic, "The Room" is playing, then head off to the bar after the movie gets out.

$ £6.80, matinee £5.80, student concession £4.50-5.20. ⏰ Open M-Th 11am-midnight, F-Sa 11am-1am, Su 11am-midnight.

SHOPPING 🛍

Clothing

👍 W.M. ARMSTONG AND SONS VINTAGE EMPORIUM 💳♿ OLD TOWN

83 Grassmarket ☎0131 220 5557 💻www.armstrongsvintage.co.uk

The largest vintage store in Britain has three physical shops and an online store. Still, if you're shopping online, you're likely to miss the giant paper-mâché trapeze artist dangling upside down in one of the Grassmarket location's crowded display rooms. You'll probably also miss out on the £1 box, full of all sorts of fun odds and ends. And you miss out on the sunglasses, boots, dresses—hell, just go to the store already.

ℹ Student discounts available. ⏰ Open M-Th 10am-5:30pm, F-Sa 10am-6pm, Su noon-6pm.

W.M. ARMSTONG& SONS VINTAGE EMPORIUM 💳♿ STOCKBRIDGE

64-66 Clark St. ☎0131 667 3056 💻www.armstrongsvintage.co.uk

Hey! You guys already did this one! Guess again: Armstong's is so good they've got multiple stores, and their Clark street location is just as excellent as their Grassmarket spot. This one's got WWI military helmets next to tiny pairs of leiderhosen, elevator shoes and pimpwear—you know the drill. Awesome.

$ Prices vary. ⏰ Open M-W 10am-5:30pm, Th 10am-7pm, F-Su 10am-6pm.

ELAIN'E VINTAGE CLOTHING 💳♿ STOCKBRIDGE

55 St. Stephens St. ☎0131 225 5783

A well-known and fun establishment down in Stockbridge, Elaine's got herself a collection of vintage stuff ranging from the 1920s onward. A great selection of dresses and high-heels (we're not saying they're always there, but **Prada** shoes have been known to frequent this establishment) and a nice collection of men's shirts and jackets.

ⓢ *Prices vary.* ☼ *Open T-Sa 1pm-6pm.*

Books

▨ THE OLD TOWN BOOKSHOP
◆ᕕ OLD TOWN

8 Victoria St. ☎0131 225 9237 ▣www.oldtownbookshop.com

Walking into the Old Town Bookshop, a wonderful little bookstore in the middle of Victoria St., is like walking into an well-tended study. A small space with books rising up to the ceiling, this shop carries an impressive collection of rare and vintage books as well as old paperback books you always wanted to read but never did *(£1).* Antique prints and maps are also available.

ⓢ *Prices vary.* ☼ *Open M-Sa 10:30am-5:45pm.*

BLACKWELL BOOKS
◆ᕕ OLD TOWN

53-62 South Bridge ☎0131 622 8222 ▣www.blackwell.co.uk

A retail chain selling lots of titles at retail prices, there's not a lot of character but you're likely to find that book you couldn't locate in the smaller local shops. Small sale section available.

ⓢ *Prices vary.* ☼ *Open M-F 9am-8pm, Sa 9am-6pm, Su noon-6pm.*

ST. JOHN CHARITY BOOKS PLUS
◆⊗ STOCKBRIDGE

20 Deanhaugh St. ☎0131 332 4911 ▣www.stjohnbookshop.co.uk

A secondhand bookshop with the best of both worlds, St. John's has a collection of old penguin paperbacks *(£1-2)* or a large collection of antiquarian books for those looking to pick up the rare first edition of that ▨**Henry James** book that you never actually finished.

☼ *Open M-Sa 10am-5pm, Su noon-4pm.*

Electronics

LAPTOP REPAIR CENTRE
◉ᕕ OLD TOWN

6 Greyfriars Pl.

A brand-new option for those seeking salvation for their slow or non-functioning computer, PC or Mac. they'll add ram, clean out junk space, or reset your hard drive if necessary. If you're in the market, they also usually have a few second-hand laptops for sale.

ⓢ *All repairs under £69.* ☼ *Open M-Sa 9am-6pm.*

Furniture

▨ HABITAT
◆ᕕ OLD TOWN

32 Shandwick Pl. ☎0844 499 1114 ▣habitat.co.uk

A classy but reasonably priced option, Habitat has everything from couches and chairs to wall decorations and ▨**kitsch.** Think of it as IKEA, but not.

☼ *Open M-W 10am-6pm, Th 10am-7pm, F 10am-6pm, Sa 9:30am-6pm, Su 11am-6pm.*

INHOUSE LIMITED
◆ᕕ NEW TOWN

28 Howe St. ☎0131 225 2888 ▣www.inhouse-uk.com

With a selection of the most Modern of the Modern in furniture pieces, you could make your flat look like a ▨**Samuel Beckett** play—minimalist. It'll cost you though.

ⓢ *Prices vary, but lean towards the high end.* ☼ *Open T-Sa 9am-5:30pm.*

OMNI FURNISHING
◆ᕕ NEW TOWN

6-10 Earl Grey St. ☎0131 221 1200 ▣www.omnifurnishings.co.uk

Specializing in wooden pieces (and, from the lovely smell of fresh-cut wood inside the display rooms, newly-made pieces at that), OMNI has a wide selection of tables, chairs, and other furnishings.

ⓢ *Prices vary.* ☼ *Open M-F 10am-6pm, Sa 9:30am-5pm, Su noon-5pm.*

ESSENTIALS

Practicalities

- **TOURIST OFFICE: Visit Scotland Information Centre** is the largest tourist information centre in Scotland. The friendly representatives from this Edinburgh branch will help you book accommodations, city tours, and coach and bus tours. The office also houses a souvenir shop and Internet center. *(3 Princes Street. ✚ Across from Waverley Station.* ☎*08452 255 121.* ▤*www.visitscotland.com.* Ⓢ *Credit cards accepted.* Ⓧ *Open Sept-June M-Sa 9am-5pm, Su 10am-5pm; July-Aug M-Sa 9am-7pm, Su 10am-7pm.)*

- **INTERNET CAFE: E-Corner Internet.** *(54 Blackfriars St.* ☎*0131 558 7858.* ▤*info@e-corner.co.uk* Ⓢ *Internet £.50 per 10min., £1.80 per 1 hr. Printing £.29 per page. International calls £.10 per min. to landlines.* Ⓧ *Open M-F 9am-10pm, Sa-Su 10am-9pm.)* **PC Emergency Internet.** *(13 Frederick St.* ☎*0754 363 3242.* ▤*info@e-corner.co.uk.* Ⓢ *Internet £2 per hr. Day pass 9am-9pm £6. Printing £.50 per page for first 5 pages, £.25 per page after that.* Ⓧ *Open M-F 9am-10pm, Sa-Su 10am-9pm.)*

- **PHARMACY: Boots Pharmacy.** *(32 West Maitlin St.* ☎*0131 225 7436.* Ⓢ *Credit cards accepted.* Ⓧ *Open M-F 8am-6pm, Sa 9am-6pm.)* **Royal Mile Pharmacy** *(67 High St.* ☎*0131 556 1971.* ▤*royalmilepharmacy@hotmail.com.* Ⓢ *Credit cards accepted.* Ⓧ *Open M-F 9am-6pm, Sa 9am-5pm.)*

- **BANK: Barclays.** *(1 St. Andrews Sq.* ☎*0845 755 5555.* ▤*www.barclays.co.uk.* Ⓧ *Open M-F 9am-5pm, Sa 10am-2pm.)*

- **ATM: Barclays** has 24hr. ATM out front *(72 George St.* ☎*0131 470 6000.* ▤*www.barclays.co.uk.* Ⓧ *Open M-F 9am-5pm, Sa 10am-2pm.)*

- **POST OFFICE: Newington Branch.** *(41 S. Clark St.* ☎*0131 667 1154.* Ⓧ *Open M-Sa 9am-5:30pm, Su 9am-12:30pm.)* **Forest Row Post Office** *(32 Forest Row.* ☎*0131 225 3957.* Ⓧ *Open M-F 8:30am-6pm, Sa 8:30am-5pm.)* **St. Mary's Street Post Office** *(46 St. Mary's St.* ☎*0131 556 6351.* Ⓧ *Open M-F 9am-5:30pm, Sa 9am-12:30pm.)* **Frederick St. Post Office.** *(40 Frederick St.* ☎*08457 740 740.* Ⓧ *Open M 9am-5:30pm, Tu 9:30am-5:30pm, W-F 9am-5:30pm, Sa 9am-12:30pm.*

Getting There

By Train

Waverley Train Station *(between Princes St., Market St. and Waverley Bridge.* ☎*08457 484 950.* ▤*www.networkrail.co.uk.* Ⓧ *Open M-Sa 12:45am-4am, Su 12:45am-6am.)* has trains to **Aberdeen** *(*Ⓢ*£33.20.*Ⓧ *2½hr. M-Sa every hr., Su 8 per day.);* **Glasgow** *(*Ⓢ *£9.70.* Ⓧ *1hr., 4 per hr.);* **Inverness** *(*Ⓢ *£32.* Ⓧ *3½hr., every 2hr.);* **London King's Cross** *(*Ⓢ *£103.* Ⓧ *4¾hr., every hr.);* **Stirling.** *(*Ⓢ *£6.10* Ⓧ *50min., 2 per hr.)* **Haymarket Train Station** is smaller, but has service to destinations throughout Scotland. *(Haymarket Terrace.* ▤*www.scotrail.com.* Ⓧ *Open M-Sa 5:10am-12:30am, Su 7:45am-12:45am. Ticket office open 7:45am-9:30pm.)*

Getting Around

By Bus

Getting around in Edinburgh is always easiest on ▨**foot,** so unless you've just completed your trip through the Himalayas, you shouldn't find you're too sore at the end of the day. However, for those who really dislike hoofin' it, **Lothian Buses** have routes zig-zagging all over the city.

LOTHIAN BUSES

Lothian Buses Plc., Annandale Street, ☎0131 555 6363 ▤www.lothianbuses.com
The first thing you should note about the bus system in Edinburgh is that most

bus stops will have both an electronic screen alerting you to which lines are in service and the ETA of their arrival at the stop. The second is that there is a ticket machine at the stop, so buying your ticket in advance will save the bus driver a lot of chagrin (and perhaps save you from a telling off). Major lines for Lothian buses include the **#24, 29 and 42 buses**, running from Stockbridge, through city center all the way to Newington St. on the South End. The #24 Line heads off toward Mixto St. and Arthur's Seat, the #42 bends west to end at Portobello by Dynamic Earth, and the #29 ends at the Royal Infirmary. The **#12, 26 and 31 buses** all come in from the Northwest and the Haymarket/Dalry area, the #12 bending off to the Northeast after passing through city center, the #26 heading south toward Newington and Mixto St. and the #31 pulling the same route but diverging to head Southwest into Liberton and Gracemount.

[$] Daytime single £1.20, child £.70; day pass £3, child £2.40; city singles (detachable day passes) 20 for £24. All-night ticket for night buses £3.

By Taxi

Call **Central Taxis** to get a cab in Edinburgh.

CENTRAL TAXIS

8 St Peter's Buildings, Gilmore Pl. ☎0131 229 2468 💻www.taxis-edinburgh.co.uk

With over 400 cabs and a 24/7 booking policy, Central cabs are by far the best taxi company to call when you need a lift. Book online if you're lacking in the phone department, and they'll arrive within 5-10min.

liverpool ☎0151

People hear Liverpool and they think Penny Lane, ports, and impossible-to-discern accents, but there's a whole lot more to this young and thriving city. Named the **European Capital of Culture** in 2008, Liverpool in its prime and beginning to reap the full benefits of its ambitious reinvigoration projects of the '80s and '90s that began the redevelopment trend in Great Britain's old industrial cities. With world-class museums, a legendary music scene, two major universities, and a fierce football rivalry, Liverpool challenges long-time cultural competitor Manchester in friendly opposition. A small tidal inlet with a big history, Liverpool oozes with an unwaveringly creative spirit. It is, after all, the hometown of **John Lennon, Paul McCartney,** and **George Harrison.** Today, outsiders flock to Liverpool en masse to soak up its creative juices and see who will be the next great to leave a mark on the city.

ORIENTATION

Liverpool's central district is pedestrian-friendly. There are two main clusters of museums: one on **William Brown Street,** near **Lime Street Station** and the urban oasis of **Saint John's Garden,** and the other at **Albert Dock,** right on the pier. These flank the central shopping district, which is enclosed within **Bold, Church,** and **Lord Streets,** and largely consists of walkways and plazas. The area of shops, cafes, and nightclubs between Bold St. and Duke St. is called the **Ropewalks.** The most tourist part of town, **Cavern Quarter,** located on famous **Mathew Street,** houses the major Beatles sites and gift shops. **Liverpool One** is a sparkling new shopping area, containing **Peter Lane** and **Paradise Street** (pedestrian shopping), **South John Street,** a road with over 160 shops, and a brand-new bus station. To the south of the city, over **Nelson Street,** a glittering arch—recently imported from Shanghai as a gift from the People's Republic—marks the entrance to the **oldest Chinatown in Europe.**

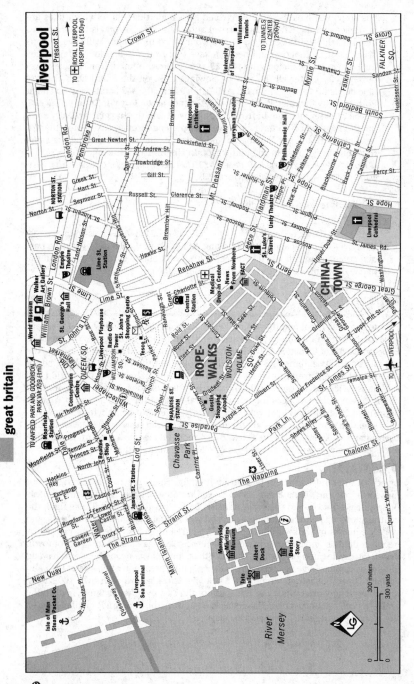

Liverpool

ACCOMMODATIONS 🏠

A wide selection of affordable hostels makes shackin' up in Liverpool is easy to do. **Beatles Week** is especially popular, so if you're stopping in when it takes place at the end of August, make sure to book in advance. The hostels in town often fill up on weekends and therefore charge higher rates on these nights. Additionally, nights before major football matches (Liverpool FC and Everton FC) See hordes of eager fans flood Liverpool hostels in groups larger than the teams themselves. If you forgot to book and are feeling panicked, the TIC's Accommodation hotline *(☎0844 870 0123)* can help you find a bed just in the nick of time.

👍 EMBASSIE BACKPACKERS 💳🚫📶❄ HOSTEL ❷

1 Falkner Sq. ☎0151 708 7193 💻www.embassie.com

All you need is love, and this cozy hostel has lots of it to give. Located in the digs of the former Venezuelan Embassy (hence the name), this beautiful old Georgian house becomes a home away from home for its multinational guests. Embassie Backpackers combines warm, friendly service with excellent facilities—a large room area, an outdoor area for communal barbecues, a downstairs social area, and a self-catering kitchen fully equipped with all kinds of dishes, tea, coffee, and bread 24hr. daily.

➡ Take the 80A, 86A, or 86N bus from Lime St. Station. Ask the driver to drop you off at the corner of Catharine St. and Canning St. If walking, exit station toward The Crown Pub. Turn left onto Lime St. and follow through Renshaw St. At St. Luke's Church, turn right onto Berry St. and at the Chinatown arch, take a left onto Upper Duke St. Keep straight past the Liverpool Cathedral, crossing over Catharine St., continuing onto Canning St. until you reach Falkner Sq. The hostel is on your left, facing the park. ℹ Laundry facilities. Free towels, linens. Lockers available in rooms for £5 deposit. Free coffee, tea, and toast with jam, peanut butter, and marmalade, daily 24hr. Self-catering kitchen. Satellite TV. Free Wi-Fi and free internet use. Scenic backyard with BBQ. Single-sex dorms available. $ Dorms M-Th £15, F £17.50, Sa £20, Su £15. ⏰ Reception 24hr.

👍 INTERNATIONAL INN 💳♿⛅ HOSTEL ❷

4 S. Hunter St. ☎0151 709 8135 💻www.internationalinn.co.uk

This converted warehouse provides a friendly aura, 24hr. service, and guests from all of the world (your first hint are the 20+ flags hanging around reception). It's also conveniently located near the cheap eats of Hardman St. and the city center. Rooms are bright, cheery, and very clean, with ensuite bathrooms. The attached storefront internet cafe (Sam Joe's Cafe) offers breakfast *(from £2.75)*, internet *(£1.50 per ½hr.)*, and live music on some nights.

➡ Off of Hardman St. (Cultural Quarter). ℹ Free Wi-Fi. Free tea, coffee, and toast 24hr. Game room with pool table and free movies. Laundry. $ Dorms M-Th £15, F-Sa £20, Su £15. $ Reception 24hr.

COCOON @ INTERNATIONAL INN 💳♿📶 HOSTEL ❸

4 S. Hunter St. ☎0151 709 8135 💻www.cocoonliverpool.co.uk

In the basement of the International Inn lies the new Budget Pod Hotel. For reasonable prices, couples (or 2 friends) can obtain private hotel-like rooms with HDTVs, blow-dryers, fresh towels, and king beds. However, remember that basement means no windows.

➡ Off of Hardman St. (Cultural Quarter). ℹ Tea & coffee making machines in rooms. Safety deposit boxes in all rooms. Games room with pool table. Only doubles available. Free Wi-Fi. $ Doubles M-Th from £43, F-Sa from £53, Su from £43.

YHA LIVERPOOL 💳♿📶🍸 HOSTEL ❷

25 Tabley St. ☎0845 371 9527 💻www.yha.org/uk

Otherwise standard and non-descript, this YHA tries to lend itself some character by staying in touch with its local roots, as the hallways and lounge areas play off of Beatles themes (rock 'n roll statues, paintings of the Fab Four) a hallway named after "Penny Lane." It is located close to main attractions (museums at Albert Dock), but removed from the hustle-and-bustle of the student nightlife areas (about a 15min. walk to the city center). Almost all the dorms have ensuite bathrooms.

➡ Close to Albert Dock. From the Dock, follow Wapping. Tabley St. is off of Wapping, past Baltic Fleet Pub, to the left. You'll see big signs for YHA. ℹ Breakfast in on-site restaurant for £5; restaurant available for breakfast and dinner. Laundry facilities. Free luggage storage. Internet £1 per 15 min. Wi-Fi £8 for 1 day, £15 for 3-day pass. $ Dorms £16-23; doubles from £41; triples from £52. £3 charge for non-YHA members. ⏰ Reception 7am-11pm.

HATTERS HOSTEL 💳♿📶 HOSTEL ❷

56-60 Mt. Pleasant ☎0151 709 5570 💻www.hattershostel.com/liverpool

With an organic vegetable garden, historic Gothic building, barbecue area, big movie screen, and helpful staff, this member of the super-popular Hatters hostel chain tries to add some character and intimacy to a huge residence of about 200 beds. Otherwise nondescript dorm rooms have modern and very clean ensuite bathrooms. Situated close major nightlife, Hatters is only a 5min. walk from the train station. Book in advance for weekends, or for a Cathedral view.

➡ From train station, head south on Lime St., then make a slight left at Brownlow Hill. Right on Mt. Pleasant. Hostel on right. ℹ Light breakfast included. Laundry facilities. Internet access in lobby £1 per 15min. Lobby Wi-Fi £5 for day pass. 7-day WiFi access (in lobby and rooms) £15. Free luggage storage. Bike storage. Self-catering. Group bookings (6 or more people) require 15% deposit and should be made 2 weeks in advance. $ Dorms M-Th £16.50-17.50, F-Sa £17.50-£18.50, Su £16.50-17.50; singles £40-60; doubles £27.50-35; triples £25. ⏰ Reception 24hr.

EPSTEIN HOUSE ♿💳📶☕ GUESTHOUSE ❸

27 Anfield ☎07810 100 900 💻www.brianepsteinguesthouse.com

Epstein House is the beautiful family home of fames Beatles manager Brian Epstein. Plus, Paul McCartney's father lives on the same road! The house has been converted into a splendid guesthouse. Beatles decor is scattered throughout, and the downstairs lounge area carefully documents Brian Epstein's life story.

➡ From train station, follow signs to Paradise St. bus station. Take the #26 or 27 bus from Paradise St. bus station to Anfield. ℹ Continental breakfast £3, full English breakfast £5. Towels, hairdryers, tea- and coffee-makers ensuite. Parking available. Free Wi-Fi. $ Private rooms from £20 per person. M-F £34 for ensuite room for 2-3 people.

STRAWBERRY HOUSE 🚭💳📶☕ HOSTEL ❶

86 Anfield Rd. ☎07810 100 900

These spacious dorm rooms are good deals. Enclosed within a small row house, the hostel is intimately small with six rooms, a common kitchen, nice patio area, and large common room. Each room has a combination of bunk beds and double beds for three to six people, TVs, and a basin sink.

➡ Anfield. Reception is in the Epstein House, 27 Anfield Rd. (see above). Head there first to pay and pick up keys. Look out for number 86; there are no outer markings for the hostel. ℹ Self-catering kitchen with tea- and coffee-makers. Free Wi-Fi. Common area with TV. $ Dorms £10-12.

SIGHTS

THE BEATLES STORY ♿💳 MUSEUM

Britannia Vaults, Albert Dock ☎0151 709 1963 💻www.beatlesstory.com

Even the most hardcore Beatles fanatic will learn something new about the biggest band that ever was (or, in the words of Lennon, the band that was "bigger than Jesus"). From the group's post-war beginnings to the shag haircuts to the solo careers, the audio guide (included in admission price) will escort you through the quartet's history. You'll hear the voices of Paul McCartney, Alan William, Cynthia Lennon, and others, giving the experience an authentic feel. Learn about the initial meeting of McCartney and Lennon and Sir George's near rejection of the Beatles (that would have been a kicker!). Recreations are all the rage here: wander through the streets of Hamburg, where the Beatles had their first overseas tour, discover the Cavern Club of the 1960s. And maybe you won't be as tripped out as groupies were in the '60s, but exhibits on Sgt. Pepper's Lonely Hearts Club Band will still make for a pretty psychadelic experience.

☭ *Albert Dock (Follow signs from city center).* ⓘ *Headsets available in multiple languages.* Ⓢ *£12.50, concessions £8.50. Includes audio tour and admission to 2 sights.* ⓩ *Open daily 9am-7pm. Last entry 2hr. before close.*

LIVERPOOL ANGLICAN CATHEDRAL
&ᷤ🕊((ᵠ)) CHURCH

St. James Mount ☎0151 709 6271 🖳www.liverpoolcathedral.org.uk

The UK's largest cathedral is surprisingly the product of 20th-century handiwork. Completed in 1978, Liverpool Cathedral has the world's highest and widest Gothic arches, and highest and heaviest peal of bells (you can see them on the tower tour). On Thursday nights in the summer, take a tower tour *(£5)* at dusk and get spectacular views of the Liverpool cityscape.

☭ *From the city center, take Mt. Pleasant St., then right onto Rodney St.* ⓘ *Late-night tours of the tower are available Th nights Mar-Oct until 8pm, or until 10pm in July and Aug. Cafe with free Wi-Fi.* Ⓢ *Free. 2-day attraction pass, tower climb, and a film and audio tour £5, concessions £3.50.* ⓩ *Open daily 8am-6pm.*

WALKER ART GALLERY
&ᷤ🕊 MUSEUM

William Brown St. ☎0151 478 4199 🖳www.liverpoolmuseums.org.uk

A display of over six centuries of fine and decorative art means that items like Napoleon's toothbrush holder and a post-modern espresso coffee maker sit in the same building as pieces by **Monet** and **Degas**. Gallery also features a collection of British art from the last several decades, much culled from Liverpool's own biennial painting competition.

☭ *Close to Lime St. Station, off Victoria Rd.* ⓘ *Special events and exhibitions offered; check website for details.* Ⓢ *Free.* ⓩ *Open daily 10am-5pm.*

MERSEYSIDE MARITIME MUSEUM
&ᷤ🕊((ᵠ)) MUSEUM

Albert Dock ☎0151 478 4499 🖳www.liverpoolmuseums.org.uk

Once upon a time, Liverpool was a small fishing village. Before long, though, it had rapidly developed into one of the most important cities in the British Empire, thanks to its position as a major port and center for exports. Liverpool's role in the shipping industry had major social effects on the city that often get overlooked. Fortunately, this museum explores not only the history of Liverpool at sea but also the characters who drive forward its evolution as a major sea power. From the recreation of a Liverpool ship's journey to a Welsh colony in Patagonia (who knew such a thing existed?) to the stories of the Titanic, Lusitania, and Empress of Ireland disasters, to Liverpool as a site in the bombing raids of WWII, the Museum thoughtfully untangles the role of the sea in Liverpool's story. Meanwhile, the downstairs area offers a unique exhibit on the British Agency of Border and Customs that shows the relevance of Liverpool in the present. Test out your instincts and judge who is a smuggler and who is a legit traveler.

☭ *Albert Dock.* ⓘ *Free Wi-Fi. Lockers on ground floor.* Ⓢ *Free.* ⓩ *Open daily 10am-5pm.*

INTERNATIONAL SLAVERY MUSEUM
&ᷤ🕊 MUSEUM

Albert Dock ☎0151 478 4499 🖳www.liverpoolmuseums.org.uk

Props to Liverpool: rather than deny its strong ties to the slave institutions of the past, the city owns up to them, mourns the evils of its past, and then seeks to move forward in this unique museum. The exhibits here celebrate black heroes and their achievements. Examining the impact of the slave trade on the world and more specifically, the slave-trade capital of Liverpool. (Many of Liverpool's famed streets were named after residents who were somehow tied to the slave trade—even Penny Lane.)

3rd floor of the Merseyside Maritime Museum. i Free. Open daily 10am-5pm.

FACT — ART, FILM

88 Wood St. ☎0151 707 4464 www.fact.co.uk

Housed in a shimmering metallic building, this state-of-the-art facility features film showings, galleries, and exhibitions of new media arts. There is also a cafe, bar, and lounge area.

Chinatown. $ Galleries free. Films £7.40, concessions £5.90. Center open M-Sa 10am-11pm, Su 11am-10:30pm. Galleries open M-Tu 10am-6pm, W 10:30am-6pm. Th-F 10am-6pm, Sa-Su 11am-6pm. Ticket office open M-F 5pm until 15min. after start of last screening, Sa 10:45am until 15min after start of last screening.

TATE LIVERPOOL — MUSEUM

Albert Dock ☎0151 702 7400 www.tate.org.uk/liverpool

This staple of the Albert Docks is part of the legendary Tate institution and features special exhibitions as well as some of the finest modern art in the world. In 2010, for example, a much-heralded Picasso exhibition arrived in town. Permanent galleries feature works from the year 1500 to the present day, including works of **Warhol** and **Pollock.** For some years, this was the largest gallery of modern and contemporary art in the UK outside of London.

Follow signs to Albert Dock. $ Free; some exhibtions have charges. Open Sept-May Tu-Su 10am-5:50pm, June-Aug daily 10am-5:50pm.

VICTORIA GALLERY AND MUSEUM — MUSEUM

Ashton St. ☎0151 794 2348 www.live.ac.uk/vgm

This beautiful museum is hosted in the Gothic, picturesque old library of the **University of Liverpool.** The collection ranges from fine art, sculpture, and ceramics to early X-rays, including a fully re-created dentist's surgery room from the 1930s, dinosaur footprints discovered in this region, hippo skulls, and python skeletons.

From Lime St., continue onto St. Geoge's Pl. and make a left onto Brownlow Hill. Museum is reddish building with clock tower on the corner with Ashton St. i Free guided tours every Tu and Th at 12:30pm. $ Free. Open Tu-Sa 10am-5pm.

FOOD

As a university town, Liverpool is blessed with a healthy endowment of cheap eats. Cheap and classy are hardly synonyms, however, and fast-food dumps are practically as common as Beatles posters. **Hardman Street** (veering off from St. Luke's Church, leading into downtown) is full of low-priced pizza, kebab, and burger joints that live off business from the large student population living in the area.

EVERYMAN BISTRO — BISTRO [2]

5 Hope St. ☎0151 708 9545 www.everyman.co.uk

Everyman serves up gourmet, tip-top quality food in a great setting, and is still mighty cheap. The food is all fresh, made from healthy, local ingredients. Customers head up to the front to order and choose from the twice-daily changing menu of scrumptious treats that's adjusted for the season to take advantage of local produce. The restaurant is always filled with a diverse collection of students, professors, tourists, and locals who come to relish the great quiche and lively atmosphere. Don't skip out on the delicious desserts, like lemon cheesecake or scones *(£1.20-£3.90)*. Gluten-free and vegetarian options available.

Underneath Everyman Theatre, next to Metropolitan Cathedral. $ Entrees £7.50-£9. 3 courses £15. Open M-Th noon-midnight, F noon-2am, Sa 11am-2am.

EGG CAFE 🥦🚭🍸 VEGETARIAN ❶

16-18 Newington ☎0151 707 2755

Hidden off of Bold St., this local vegetarian restaurant offers healthy and homemade dishes for reasonable prices. The funky atmosphere (large wooden communal tables, local artwork for sale on display in boxes, and purple walls with vines painted on them) is indicative of its quirky clientele. Main meal menu changes daily but includes tasty dishes like quiche, hummus, and pita. Vegan options available.

✈ Up 2 flights of stairs, Newington is a side street off of Renshaw St. ℹ Breakfast served M-Sa until noon, Su until 5pm. $ Entrees £4.95. ⏰ Open M-F 9am-10:30pm, Sa-Su 10am-10:30pm.

THE SHIPPING FORECAST 💳🍸 PUB GRUB ❷

15 Slater St. ☎0151 706 8045 💻www.theshippingforecastliverpool.com

This self-proclaimed "Alehouse and Eatery" offers good old comfort food in the form of "Pots of Goodness"—like mac and cheese and vegetable goulash *(£4.60)*, traditional pie and mash with creamy mash, peas, and gravy, and homemade burgers *(from £4.50)*. Live music plays most Thursday, Friday, Saturday, and Sunday nights in the downstairs basement music venue area. Charming in a "pub meets club" kind of way.

ℹ Advance tickets available on 💻ticketweb.co.uk. $ Cover free-£10 when music plays. ⏰ Open M-Th 11am-midnight, F-Sa 11am-3am, Su 11am-midnight.

THE QUARTER 💳♿🍸☀ ITALIAN, CAFE, BAR ❷

7 Falkner St. ☎0151 707 1965 💻www.thequarteruk.com

This classy cobblestone, street-side cafe offers tasty pasta and stone-baked pizzas for moderate prices. Always abuzz with young professionals, tourists, and students (and even **Yoko Ono**), the setting is perfect for a sunny meal outside with a glass of wine, plate of ravioli, and good friends. Sandwiches and salads also available.

✈ Near John Moores University; corner of Hope St. ℹ Special menus of the day available. Cakes £2-2.85. $ Pasta £6-8.75. Pizza £5-7. ⏰ Open M-F 8am-11pm, Sa 10am-11pm, Su 10am-10:30pm.

BAGELS LTD 🥦 DELI ❶

40 Brunswick St. ☎0151 236 5996 💻www.bagelsltd.co.uk

Start spreading the news. They call themselves "New York style" bagels, and this may be the closest you're gonna get in the motherland. Cheap deals: bacon or sausage on a bagel *(£2)* or tea and a toasted bagel *(£1)*. Notice all the photos of the Statue of Liberty and you'll feel like you're state-side.

✈ Ground fl. of India building. ⏰ Open M-F 7:30am-2:30pm.

CAFE TABAC 💳🍸 CAFE, BAR ❶

126 Bold St. ☎0151 709 9502 💻www.cafetabac.co.uk

During the day, Tabac serves a popular breakfast menu, and customers lounge back against their red cushioned chairs, admiring its lighting, funky wallpaper, and stools, all a striking shade of red. At night, the lights go down and the venue transforms into a comfortable, relaxed bar with live performers and weekly film clubs. Check the website for listings.

✈ Edge of Bold St., across from St. Luke's. ℹ Breakfast served 9am-5pm, Lunch and dinner noon-10pm. Free Wi-Fi. $ Breakfast £3.25-5.50. Sandwiches £4-5. Salads £5.50-6.50. Shots £1-2. Beer £1.80-5. ⏰ Open M-W 9am-11pm, Th-Sa 9am-11pm, Su 9am-11pm.

SOUL CAFE 💳♿🍸☀ CAFE, BAR ❶

114 Bold St. ☎0151 708 9470

Soul music plus soul food equals a full stomach and an excellent mood. This cheap Bold St. joint offers all-day breakfast (with yummy American-style pancakes), milkshakes, and homemade soups along with other "soul-warming favorites" and light bites. For the occasionally-needed break from Beatlemania, check out the photos and record covers of soul legends like Otis Redding and hum along to the R and B classics playing in the background on Soul FM, the radio station of choice.

➜ Bold St., corner of Colquist St. $ Breakfast £3-4.50. Sandwiches from £2.50. ⏰ Open M-W 11am-6pm, Th 11am-9pm, F-Su 11am-6pm.

MAHARAJA 💳🍸 INDIAN [2]

34-36 London Rd. ☎0151 709 2006 💻www.maharajaliverpool.co.uk

The first southern Indian restuarant in the northwest of England sticks true to its Keralan roots, mixing delicious spices like cinnamon, ginger, and cloves with curry leaves, black pepper, and garlic to create an appealing taste and distinct flavor. The owners claim that Christopher Columbus sought India in avid pursuit of the spices from Kerala—we don't doubt it.

➜ 2min. walk from Lime Street station. ℹ Business lunch noon-2pm. Vegetarian options available. $ Business lunch £7 (2 or 3 curries, vegetable side dish, rice, and dessert). Entrees £7-14.50.

TOKYOU NOODLE BAR ♿💳 PAN-ASIAN [2]

7 Berry St. ☎0151 445 1023

Simple but reliably tasty, this small Berry St. locale dishes out a wide variety of pan-Asian dishes at reasonable prices. Most of the cuisine is Cantonese, but the menu includes a mix of Japanese and Malaysian. Get your meal with either chopsticks or a fork at one of their communal wooden tables. We won't judge.

$ Entrees £3.80-6.20. ⏰ Open daily 12:30pm-11:30pm.

DELIFONSECA 🚭💳🍸 DELI RESTAURANT [2]

12 Stanley St. ☎0151 255 0808 💻www.delifonseca.co.u

A bustling local favorite situated atop a deli, Delifonseca features local specialites of cheeses, hummus, spices, meats, and plenty of vegetarian options, displayed on a blackboard. No matter what's in season, you're going to get an excellent sandwich.

➜ Down the street from Met and Cavern Quarters, between Victoria St. and Dale St. Granite building, bright green sign. $ Entrees £12 and under. Soups £5. ⏰ Deli open M-Sa 8am-9pm, Dining area open M-Sa noon-late.

THE BEER HOUSE ♿💳🍸 ETHNIC PUB GRUB [3]

41-51 Greenland St. ☎0151 708 3575 💻www.contemporaryurbancentre.org

This huge pub has a lively atmosphere, large tables for groups, a good selection of beers, and specialty curry nights. Traditional English options are supplemeted by all-day breakfasts, pastas, and main-course salads. Quaint wooden tables and chairs lend the place a Victorian feel, and SkySports blasts in the background, displaying your sporting event of choice.

➜ Contemporary Urban Centre. Entry off Jamaica St. ℹ Open mic night on Su. Kitchen closes 9pm. $ Entrees under £10. ⏰ Open daily 11am-11pm.

CAFE LATINO 🚭🚭 CAFE, ITALIAN [2]

28a Bold St. ☎0151 709 4217

Looking out on the frenzy of shoppers and artists of busy Bold St., this upstairs cafe presents simple but affordable meals. The Italian owners offer 10 kinds of pasta and nine types of pizza *(£4)*.

➜ Look for the sign hanging from the 2nd story. Up 3 flights stairs. $ Pizzas and pastas £4-5. ⏰ Open Tu-Sa 9am-5pm.

NIGHTLIFE

Liverpool nightlife has changed dramatically since the days when Lennon and McCartney roamed these streets. With ever-increasing influxes of students (the student population of Liverpool currently stands at about 70,000), the post-dinner party scene has expanded drastically. Luckily for travelers, the pubs and bars here try to tailor their music and prices with the sking student budget in mind. Less felicitously, the newer arrivals lack a distinctive Liverpudlian feel. Chain clubs, Australian bars, and joints with Beyoncé blasting just don't have that Fab Four charm.

Still, the students bring with them many perks. Keep an eye out for special mid-week promotion nights, when clubs offer cheap drinks and no covers. Also, unlike London, Liverpool has many bars and pubs that remain open until 4am to cater to their very young night-owl patrons.

👍 THE PHILHARMONIC — 💳🍸♿ PUB

36 Hope St. ☎0151 707 2837

With the Philharmonic's beautiful woodwork, exquisite mosaic floors, ornate tiling, copper panels, and an excellent bar that serves quality local cask ale, it's no wonder that John Lennon once complained that one of the worst things about being famous was "not being able to go to the Phil for a pint." What is surprising, however, is that this clasically elegant bar has still remained a student haunt at heart, frequented by young people, older locals, and tourists alike. Make sure you check out the unique tiling of the mens' washrooms. (If you're of the female persuasion, ask at the bar for permission to avoid interrupting some poor guy.) Sadly, the women's bathrooms aren't up to the same standards because, when this place opened its doors at the turn of the 20th century, Liverpudlian women didn't probe the pub scene the way they do now.

🪧 Across from Philharmonic Concert Hall. $ Draughts from £2. ⏰ Open daily 10am-midnight.

👍 THE PEACOCK — 💳♿🍸 BAR

49-51 Seel St. ☎0151 709 2146

Classier and with more character than many of the generic Ropewalks haunts. This bar has brick walls, chandeliers, outside patio areas, and a roof terrace. Drinks are reasonably priced and a good rock music selection blasts downstairs, while the upstairs tends to dance music and frenzied partiers.

🪧 Ropewalks. St. Peter's Sq. and Seel St. ⏰ Open M-F noon-2am, Sa noon-3am, Su noon-2am.

HANNAH'S BAR — 💳📶🍸🌳 BAR, RESTAURANT, VENUE

2 Leece St. ☎0151 708 5959 💻www.barhannah.co.uk

While this bar's recent renovation has given it a more posh vibe, it's a student place in essence. Many local musicians of the present-day Liverpool music scene played their first gigs here. Perks include two stories of seating, cozy couches off to the side, a neat skylight roof, and an upstairs outdoor area where you can sit with your drink and enjoy nighttime views of the old church.

🪧 Right next to St. Luke's Church. ⏰ Open M-F 11am-2am, Sa 10am-2am, Su 10am-12:30am.

BAR CA VA — 🎵📶🍸 BAR

4a Wood St. ☎0151 709 9300

This trendy bar tempts the Liverpool youth with its cheap drinks, funky decor, and excellent alternative DJs. Liquor lovers will be smitten: tequila is only £1 a shot and comes in loads of crazy flavors. If the conversation begins to tire, let your eyes wander to the old movie posters, magazine articles, concert fliers, and record covers that plaster the walls from ceiling to floor.

ℹ Free Wi-Fi. ⏰ Open daily 1pm-late (1-2am depending on the crowd and the bouncer's discretion).

MODO — 💳♿🍸🌳 BAR, CLUB

1 Concert Sq. ☎0151 709 8832 💻www.modoliverpool.co.uk

Busy, young, well-established, and trendy, with a huge outdoor beer-garden area Modo is super-popular in the summer and sometimes even gets full mid-week. Beware large crowds and slow service on warm weekend days. If you decide to brave it, bring friends and try a 4-pint cocktail pitcher *(£10).*

🪧 Concert Sq. is between Wood St. and Fleet St. $ Lots of drink deals: 2-4-1 house cocktails £3

(except F and Sa after 8pm), £4.95 cocktails, £8 for pitcher of cocktails or lager pitchers or bottle of wine (except F and Sa after 8pm), £1 chasers, £2.50 double vodka and NRG (except F and Sa after 8pm). ⏰ *Open M-Th noon-2am, F-Sa noon-3am, Su noon-2am.*

THE ZANZIBAR CLUB CLUB

43 Seel St. ☎0151 707 0633 💻www.thezanzibarclub.com

Students flock to hear live music at Zanzibar Club, which features eclectic acts, club nights, and good drink offers. An exotic feel keeps the venue in touch with its chosen name.

Corner of Slater St. and Seel St. ⏰ *Open W-Sa 7:30pm-1am.*

JUPITERS BAR

10 Hackins Hey ☎0151 227 5265

Karaoke is the specialty of this GLBT bar at the edge of Liverpool's gay district. Jupiters boasts reasonably priced drinks, large TVs for sporting events, and pool tables. Popular nights are "Thursgays" and "Sungays."

i Serves food. Free Wi-Fi. ⏰ *Open M-Th noon-11:30pm.*

G BAR CLUB

1-3 Eberle St. ☎0151 236 4416 💻www.g-bar.com

Well-liked by both students and drag queens, this gay-friendly spot is a popular late-night post-clubbing venue. The commercial dance music keeps pumping all night long, and the three floors include a cozy "Love lounge" for canoodling upstairs.

Off of Dale St., by Moorfields Rail. $ *Cover £2-7. Cocktails £3-5.* ⏰ *Open Th 10pm-4am, F 10pm-5am, Sa 10pm-8am, Su 10pm-3am.*

ARTS AND CULTURE

Liverpool was the European Capital of Culture in 2008, and it doesn't let anyone forget it. The city prides itself on its art and music offerings, ranging from Beatles reincarnations to a thriving indie scene to world-class orchestras and theaters.

PHILHARMONIC HALL CLASSICAL MUSIC

Hope St. ☎0151 709 3789 💻www.liverpoolphil.com

This famed Art Deco concert hall stands in the place of the building that burned down in a fire in 1933. While mostly associated with Classical music, this building also has put on contemporary concerts, film screenings, and comedy shows and has hosted Frank Sinatra and the Beatles. There's a plaque dating from the 1912 commemorating the famed Orchestra who perished on the RMS Titanic, because they were contracted for the voyage by music agents from Liverpool.

Between Myrtle St. and Caledonia St. (and between the 2 cathedrals). *i 3hr. tours available.* $ *Tours 15.* ⏰ *Box office open M-Sa 10am-5:30pm.*

EVERYMAN THEATRE THEATRE

5-9 Hope St. ☎0151 709 4776 💻www.everymanplayhouse.com

The Everyman has basically been Everything, from a chapel to a cinema to a boxing arena to a theater space. It was here, for example, that sculptor Arthur Dooley, an ex-boxer, was rumored to engage in a fight with art lecturer Arthur Ballard, also a former boxer. Today, though, the theater puts on its own productions and promotes native Liverpool playwrights, as well as welcoming outside shows from Britain and the world.

Corner of Hope St. and Oxford St./Mt.Pleasant, across from Metropolitan Cathedral. *i Student discounts available.* $ *Tickets £5-50. Standbys (day of) for under 26: £5.* ⏰ *Ticket office open M-F 10am-6pm (11:15am-7:30pm on performance nights). Closed Sa unless there's a performance.*

LIVERPOOL PLAYHOUSE THEATRE

Williamson Sq. ☎0151 709 4776 💻www.everymanplayhouse.com

The counterpart to the Everyman, the Playhouse focuses on traditional theater.

Three times a year it produces its own shows. The building itself dates back to 1866 and is the only Victorian theater still in active use in Merseyside. $ *Tickets £5-£40, concessions £4 off. Standbys (day of) for under 26: £5.* ⏰ *Ticket office open M-Sa 10am-6pm, theater nights until 7:30pm.*

ESSENTIALS

Practicalities

- **TOURIST OFFICES:** *(Whitechapel and Anchor Courtyard, and at Albert Dock. ☎0151 233 2008 🖳www.visitliverpool.com* ℹ Pick up a free copy of **Liverpool Events Guide,** or **Days Out.** Internet use £1 for 15min. Books accommdations for free via accommodation hotline *(☎0844 870 0123)* or in person. ⏰ *Open M-Sa 10am-5pm, Su 11am-4pm.)*
- **TOURS: Mendips and 20 Forthlin Road.** Mendips was the childhood home of Lennon, Forthlin Rd. was the family home of Paul McCartney right through early Beatles Years. Book in advance. *(☎0151 427 7231. 🖳www.nationaltrust.org.uk/beatles. $ £16.80).* **Lime St. Station** *(☎0151 203 3920 🖳www.city-sightseeing.com $ £8, concessions £6)* hop-on, hop-off. Starting from Canada Blvd., Pier Head. **Magical Mystery Tours** offers 2hr. tour of Beatles sites like Strawberry Field and Penny Lane *(☎0151 236 9091 $ £14.95).* If you'd rather explore the sights yourself, pick up a free "How to get to the Beatles Attractions in Merseyside" brochure from the TIC. For the price of a Saveaway day-ticket *(£3.30)* you can take the bus around town to all of the major Beatles sights.
- **BEYOND TOURISM: JobCentre Plus.** *(20 Williamson Sq. ☎0151 801 5700 🖳www.jobcentreplus.gov.uk.* ⏰ *Open M-F 9am-5pm.)* **The Volunteer Centre** *(151 Dale Street. ☎0151 237 3975. 🖳www.volunteercentreliverpool.org.uk.* ⏰ *Open M-F 9am-5pm.)*
- **BANKS:** Located throughout the shopping district. **HSBC.** *(99-100 Cord. St.* ⏰ *Open M 9am-5pm, Tu 9:30am-5pm, W 9am-5pm, Th 9am-7pm, F-Sa 9am-5pm.)*
- **INTERNET ACCESS: Central Library.** *(William Brown St. ☎0151 233 5845.* ⏰ *Open M-Th 9am-7:30pm, Su noon-5pm.)* Free Wi-Fi with food or drink purchase at many cafes around town, including Tabac and the Piazza at Metropolitan Cathedral. Liverpool City Council has placed kiosks around downtown that allow you to send free emails (with 5min. time limit) and look at electronic maps.
- **POST OFFICE:** *(35-37 Leece St. ☎08457 223 344.* ⏰ *Open M-F 8:45am-5:30pm, Sa 8:45am-12:30pm)* and **Liverpool One** *(inside of WHSmith, 1-3 S. John St.* ⏰ *Open M-Sa 9am-5:30pm.)*

Emergency!

- **HOSPITAL: Royal University Liverpool Hospital** *(Prescot St. ☎0151 706 2000.).* For non-emergencies: **NHS Walk-In Centre.** *(Great Charlotte St. ☎0845 46 47* ⏰ *Open M-F 7am-10pm, Sa-Su 9am-10pm.)*

Getting There

By Plane

Liverpool John Lennon Airport, just 7mi. from the city center, has flights from across Europe including Barcelona, Madrid, Paris, and Dublin. #86 or 86A bus will drop you right near Lime St. station. The #500 and 80A also run to the city center *(🖳www.liverpoolairport.com).*

By Train

Liverpool Lime St. Station is located in the heart of the city center, and offers trains (☎08457 48 49 50 ◾www.nationalrail.co.uk) to **Manchester Piccadilly** (Ⓢ £9.80 ⚅ 45 min., 3 per hr.) and **Birmingham** (Ⓢ £24.60 ⚅ 1¾hr., 2 per hr.). **Virgin Trains** (☎08719 774 222 ◾www.virgintrains.co.uk) runs express service to **London Euston** (Ⓢ £65.20 ⚅ 2hr., every hr.).

By Bus

Norton Street Station operates **National Express** buses (☎0845 600 7245) to **Birmingham** (Ⓢ £13 ⚅ 3hr., 4 per day), **London** (Ⓢ£28 ⚅ 5.5hr., 4-5 per day), and **Manchester** (Ⓢ £7 ⚅ 1hr., every hr.).

By Ferry

Ferries arrive at and depart from Pier Head, north of Albert Dock. **The Isle of Man Steam Packet Company** (◾www.steam-packet.com) runs ferries from **St. Nicholas Place, Princes Parade** (⚅ 2½hr.) to the **Isle of Man,** during the summer. **P &O Irish Ferries** (☎0871 66 44 777 ◾www.poirishsea.com) runs ferries from **Dublin** to Liverpool (⚅ 8hr.) from Liverpool Freeport Bootle. **Norfolk Line** (☎0844 499 0007 ◾www.norfolkline.com) has trips to and from Liverpool to **Belfast** and **Dublin,** Tuesday through Saturday, starting from £20 and leaving from 12 Quays Terminal, Tower Rd., Birkenhead.

Getting Around

By Train

Merseyrail Trains (☎0151 227 5181 ◾www.merseytravel.gov.uk) run from three major stops in the city (Moorfields, James St., and Central) on three outbound lines to the surrounding town and out to Southport, to Preston, and to the coast.

By Bus

Local buses (☎0870 608 2608), operated by **Arriva** and **Stagecoach** are based out of Queen's Square Bus Station, Pardise St. Station, and Liverpool One. Each company sells DayRiders for unlimited day travel for £3. Merseyside Saveaways (☎0151 236 6056 ◾www.merseytravel.gov.uk) are good for one-day travel on buses, trains, and ferries in the area after 9:30am weekdays and all day Saturday and Sunday. Available for purchase at Central Train Station for (Ⓢ £3.30 for the main city area, and £4.50 for the surrounding Merseyside areas).

By Taxi

For a **taxi,** call **Mersey Cabs** (☎0151 207 2222) or **Liver Cabs** (☎0151 708 7080). Like London, Liverpool's cabs are black.

glasgow ☎0141

There's a running joke among residents of Glasgow and Edinburgh, that the only good thing about the other is the sign on the highway announcing your departure. A heavy rivalry exists between the two, and Glaswegians often face heavy criticism from their fashionable and trendy neighbor. Glasgow isn't the prettiest city in the world, though it is certainly no longer the predictable industrial giant it used to be. The city teems with students and a fantastic party scene as well as enough different restaurants to make your taste buds sore from overuse. The West End by the University is almost its own city, feeling much more communal and local than the Gothic city center.

ORIENTATION

Glasgow can essentially be divided into two distinct areas: the **city center,** with the shopping center, **Queen Street, Central Station,** and **George Square** all located within walking distance of one another; and the **West End,** home to the **University of Glasgow, Kelvingrove**

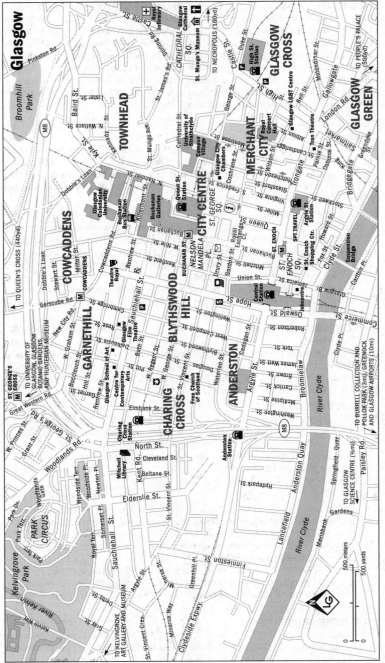

Glasgow

glasgow • orientation

Park and Gallery, and the majority of Glasgow's hostels. The main pedestrian and shopping thoroughfares include the east end of **Sauchiehall Street,** which takes a right turn to become **Buchanan Street,** passing in front of **Nelson Mandela Place.** To get from the city center to the West End, walk from Buchanan onto **Sauchihall Street** and continue until the pedestrian access ends. From there, walk up the hill to **Renfrew St.** (which will take you past a large group of guesthouses and hotels as well as the Glasgow School of Art) and continue onward. At the end of Renfrew St., you will be led over a busy merging of streets by a footbridge. After crossing over you should walk right to get to **Woodlands Road,** which will take you to **Great Western Road** and the West End.

ACCOMMODATIONS

Backpackers who like to hop off the train and directly into a hostel will be disappointed—the majority of Glasgow's budget options require a hike to the West End. The walk from the station is only about 20min., but with that pack on—well, a cab's only around £5. For those looking for something a little higher up the hostel-hotel food chain, Renfrew St. above Sauchiehall St. has a long row of guesthouses and hotels. Expect seasonal rate fluctuations.

👍 WEST END BACKPACKERS — HOSTEL [1]

3 Bank St. ☎0141 337 7000 💻www.glasgowwestendbackpackers.co.uk

West End Backpackers is a laid-back, chill hostel with clean dorms (the sheets smell so lovely) and a great lounge area. Guests receive free computer and kitchen use *and* breakfast. Choose between the larger, sunnier rooms upstairs or the more private basement dorms.

*➔ Just off Great Western Rd. 4 blocks from University of Glasgow campus. **i** Linens and towels provided. $ 10-bed dorms £14, 6-bed £15, 4-bed £16. ⏰ Reception closes at midnight. Breakfast 8-10am.*

👍 THE WILLOW GUESTHOUSE — GUESTHOUSE [3]

228 Renfrew St. ☎0141 332 2332

This is probably the best deal among the guesthouses in terms of quality for money. The rooms in the Willow are tastefully decorated and spacious. Come down in the morning for breakfast, which has been jovially described as "a scorcher."

***i** Large TVs in the rooms. $ Singles £35; doubles £50.*

MCLAY'S GUESTHOUSE — GUESTHOUSE [3]

264-276 Renfrew St. ☎0141 332 4796 💻www.mclays.com

A good, closer-to-budget guesthouse, McLays has a full Scottish breakfast included in the price of the room. There are several standard rooms which, though lacking private baths, do have sinks and mirrors. Relax out on the patio under the umbrellas in rain or shine.

$ Singles £28; doubles £48; family £70. ⏰ Reception 24hr.

SYHA — HOSTEL [2]

7-8 Park Terr. ☎0141 332 3004 💻www.syha.org.uk

Like any hostel that is part of a chain, this hostel is full on beds (around 140) and short on character. It's good if you need to book something at the last minute. They do have their own cafe downstairs where you can get coffee or beer and use the internet or book exchange.

*➔ From St. George's Rd., turn onto Woodlands Rd. and then left onto Duff St. Follow on Lynedoch St. and turn left and then right onto Woodlands Terr. until it becomes Park Terr. Follow around the circle. **i** Kitchen and lounge use available. Non-members will pay approx. £2 more. $ 6-8 bed dorms £20-25.*

THE HERITAGE HOTEL — HOTEL [4]

4 Alfred Terr. ☎0141 339 6955 💻www.theheritagehotel.net

Heritage has a "Best Western" feel and rooms with all the accoutrements—table, chairs, TV, tea and biscuits, soap and shampoos, the whole nine yards—so you can already anticipate the somewhat higher prices.

Off Great Western Rd. *[i] Full Scottish breakfast included.* *Ⓢ Singles £40; doubles/twins £60.*

THE BOTANIC HOTEL HOTEL [3]

1 Alfred Terr. ☎0141 337 7007 www.botanichotel.co.uk

A comfortable and well-decorated (framed photos of palm trees, anyone?) hotel just off Great Western road, the Botanic features large suits, all with windows and TVs.

Off Great Western Rd. *Ⓢ Singles £30-35; doubles £55; family £75.*

ALBA LODGE GUESTHOUSE [2]

232 Renfrew St. ☎0141 332 2588 www.albalodge.co.uk

If you enjoy long, hot showers, take a room at the Alba lodge. Ensuite rooms have enormous bathrooms. A family-run place, this guesthouse benefits from a helpful and friendly staff. Look for the flowers on the front stoop.

[i] Discounts for extended stays. *Ⓢ Singles £35; doubles- £45-60.*

HAMPTON COURT GUESTHOUSE GUESTHOUSE [2]

230 Renfrew St. ☎0141 332 6623 www.haptoncourtguesthouse.co.uk

All the rooms are pink. Pink. Still, this guesthouse with a funky red-patterned carpet and winding staircase has nicely-sized and comfortable rooms. Tourist information is available downstairs.

Ⓢ Singles £28, with bath £33; doubles £52.

VICTORIAN HOUSE HOTEL HOTEL [3]

212 Renfrew St. ☎0141 332 0129 www.thevictorian.co.uk

With 59 clean but somewhat bland rooms, the Victorian hotel has ensuite baths, Wi-Fi, 24hr. reception and plenty of closet space.

Renfrew St. *[i] Breakfast included.* *Ⓢ Singles £32, with bath £35; doubles £55-60.* *Reception 24hr.*

THE RENNIE MACKINTOSH HOTEL HOTEL [2]

218-220 Renfrew St. ☎0141 333 9992 www.rmghotels.com

The lobby of this hotel has been modeled after the interior design of Charles Rennie Mackintosh. The rooms are small but carefully furnished, with glossy furniture and desks in the rooms. Wi-Fi available in the lobby.

[i] 10% discount for stays of 3 nights or more. *Ⓢ July-Aug singles £35; doubles £55. Sept-May singles £30; doubles £48.*

BUNKUM BACKPACKERS HOSTEL [1]

26 Hillhead St. ☎0141 581 4481 bunkumglasgow@hotmail.com

The hostel is located next to a nursery. But that's okay, because you'll be out during the day, right? The dorms in this high-ceiling establishment win the prize for largest rooms and fewest beds, which means you can really spread out and get comfy.

Traveling west on Great Western Rd., turn onto Hillhead St. and walk down 2 blocks. *Ⓢ July-Aug dorms £14, doubles £36; Sept-Jun dorms £12, doubles £16 per person.*

SIGHTS

KELVINGROVE ART GALLERY AND MUSEUM MUSEUM

Argyle St. ☎0141 276 9599 www.glasgowmuseums.com

Built to be a museum and opened in 1901, the gallery is a beautiful red brick structure that looks more like a cathedral than a museum. In fact, if you come around at 1pm, you can hear the giant organ above the main space being played. Oh, and the stuff inside the building is cool too—works by Cézanne, Monet, Gauguin, Van Gogh, and *Christ of St. John of the Cross* by Salvador Dalí.

5min. walk from Kelvinhall subway station and 10min. walk from Kelvinbridge subway station.

i Dalí's Christ of St. John of the Cross on loan until Feb. 2011. $ £1 suggested donation. ⏰ Open M-Th 10am-5pm, F 11am-5pm, Sa 10am-5pm, Su 11am-5pm.

HUNTERIAN MUSEUM — MUSEUM

Gilbert Scott Building ☎0141 330 4221 🖥www.hunterian.gla.ac.uk

Founded in 1807 to display the collections of William Hunter, prominent physician and Scotland's foremost collector of weird crap, the museum exhibits everything from human organs in formaldehyde, the death mask of Sir Isaac Newton, and the side-by-side comparison of the penis bones of a walrus and weasel. (Gents, one of these will boost confidence; the other will not.)

🚏 Glasgow University. i The main display room for the Hunterian Museum will be closed for roof construction until approx. Apr 2011. $ Free. ⏰ Open M-F 9:30am-5pm.

GLASGOW CATHEDRAL AND NECROPOLIS — CEMETERY

Castle St. ☎0141 552 6891 🖥www.historic-scotland.gob.uk

A Glasgow must-see, the cathedral is just as stony, gothic and impressive as the castles from your adventure books growing up. Head into its bowels to view the tomb of the city's patron saint, St. Mungo. The Necropolis, across the bridge from the Cathedral, is even better and spookier. A climb to the peak of the cemetery will give you some of the best views in Glasgow.

🚏 From High St. Rail, follow High St. north until it becomes Castle St. i Volunteer guides give tours of the cathedral during opening hours in the summer. ⏰ Cathedral open Apr-Sept 9:30am-5pm, Su 1-5pm; Oct-Mar M-Sa 9:30am-4pm, Su 1-4pm.

SAINT MUNGO'S MUSEUM — MUSEUM

2 Castle St. ☎0141 276 1625 🖥www.glasgowmuseums.com

St. Mungo's offers a small exhibit of religious artifacts from all over the world, including Catholic stained glass, Greek pottery, statues of Buddha, and religious artifacts from Scotland. Note that the top floor is also the kids "discovery centre," so you may be stepping over construction paper scraps up there.

$ Souvenir shop downstairs accepts credit cards. ⏰ Open M-Th 10am-5pm, F 11am-5pm, Sa 10am-5pm, Su 11am-5pm.

GLASGOW GALLERY OF MODERN ART — ♿ MUSEUM

Royal Exchange Sq. ☎0141 287 3050 🖥www.glasgowmuseums.com

The GOMA, four stories of rotating exhibitions of the most modern (and often the most confusing) works from both Glaswegian and international artists, is so funky inside they've even got the windows painted with a swirling blue. Keep an eye out for the room with the flashing sign that shouts out fun facts like, "the soldier eats your stomach." We can't tell if they're kidding.

🚏 From Glasgow Central Low Level Rail Station, walk east on Gordon St. Turn right onto Buchanan St. and then make a left onto Exchange Pl. $ Free. ⏰ Open M-W 10am-5pm, Th 10am-8pm, F-Sa 10am-5pm, Su 11am-5pm.

SAINT GEORGE'S SQUARE — PLAZA

City Center

An enormous, red-paved, statue-filled plaza in the center of town, St. George's square is lined with wooden benches where you can sit and enjoy the sunshine. Carefully consider your plan to feed the pigeons, as those birds have become drunk with power and think nothing of flying just inches past your head. Those statues of Scotland's greats didn't get their white hair from getting older.

🚏 Take subway to Ⓜ St. George's Cross.

GLASGOW CITY CHAMBERS — CITY HALL

82 George Sq. ☎0141 287 4018 🖥www.glasgow.co.uk

Opened in 1888, the Glasgow City Chambers beats out St. Peter's in Vatican City for largest marble staircase by one flight. Other than that, it's got a giant banquet hall with three different murals depicting different aspects of Scotland's culture.

In the portraits hall, look for the depiction of Lord Provost Pat Lally who, judging from the portrait, must have been Glasgow's first resident supervillain.

🪧 From Glasgow Queen St. Rail Station, walk west on George St. Ⓢ Free. ⏰ Tours 30min., M-F 10:30am and 2:30pm.

GLASGOW BOTANIC GARDENS PUBLIC PARK

West End 💻www.glasgow.gov.uk/en/residents/parks_outdoors

With lots of lawn space for laying out, if and when it's ever sunny, and public greenhouses where you can examine all sort of flora, the Glasgow Botanic ardens is a relaxing place to spend an afternoon. Keep an eye out for an ice cream truck at the entrance, which scoops out delicious cones *(£1)*.

🪧 At the intersection of Byers and Great Western Rd. ⏰ Botanic Gardens visitor's center open daily 11am-4pm.

UNIVERSITY OF GLASGOW 💳 UNIVERSITY

Glasgow University, University Ave., Gilbert Scott building ☎0141 330 5511 💻www.gla.ac.uk

You'll see the heavily Gothic hollowed spire from a distance, but head to University Drive and the visitor's center to pick up a brochure for a self-guided tour. Voted by *Times Higher Education* as having the best campus in Scotland, the U of G is full of cathedral archways and great photo opportunites.

🪧 Located in the West End of Glasgow, 3 mi. from the city center. Ⓢ Self-guided tour pamphlet £3. ⏰ Visitor's center open M-Sa 9:30am-5pm.

FOOD 🍴

Glasgow may look like a big, gritty city (who are we kidding, it *is* a big gritty city), but you will eat like royalty here. The dining options are endless, and cover about as wide a range of tastes as you can imagine. From chippies to bistros and everything in between, you'll be able to take your significant other out for a fancy dinner and then satisfy your drunken 3am craving all on the same block.

👍 **MANCINI'S** 💳🍸❄⛅ ITALIAN [3]

315-321 Great Western Rd. ☎0141 339 5544 💻www.mancini-restaurant.co.uk

Two round chandeliers sit above high wooden tables at this Italian *ristorante*. With generous portions of pasta *(£3.50-7.50)* and soup and sandwich options for just a fiver, you're not going to have to bust your bank to get great food here. However, if you're not hungry, you can simply stop in to grab a glass of champagne or a cocktail.

🪧 Between St. Mary's Cathedral and Napiershall St. ℹ All wines sold by the glass. ⏰ Open M-Th 8am-1am, F-Sa 10am-1am, Su 8am-1am. Restaurant open until 10:30pm.

👍 **NAKED SOUP** 🌿♿⛅ SOUP [1]

6 Kersland St. ☎0141 334 8999

Offering a big cup of great soup, a huge chunk of fresh buttered bread, and your choice of fruit *(£3)*, this place is delicious *and* cheap. It's so good you'll want to keep a Naked Soup menu along with your dirty magazines.

🪧 Just off Great Western Rd. Ⓢ Open M-Th 9am-8pm, F 9am-6pm, Sa 10am-6pm, Su 11am-5pm.

👍 **BIBLOCAFÉ** 💳📶 CAFE [2]

262 Woodlands Rd. ☎0141 339 7645 💻www.biblocafe.co.uk

To put it bluntly, this place is the bomb. A cozy, sit-down coffeeshop and secondhand bookstore, Biblocafé is made really special by the people who frequent it. Lou Munday and her crew of coffee "minions" are some of the most instantly likeable people on the planet. If you enjoy sarcastic humor and witty banter, step in and get hooked.

🪧 ⓂKelvinbridge. Take S. Woodlands Rd. toward St. George's Rd. Ⓢ Coffee from £2. Flavored mochas and lattés from £3. ⏰ Open M-F 8:30am-8:30pm, Sa-Su 9:30am-8:30pm, holidays 10am-6pm.

BEANSCENE 💳 CAFE ❷

40-42 Woodlands Rd. ☎0141 352 9800 🖥www.beanscene.co.uk

Nobody coming to Beanscene plans to take their coffee on the go—the plentiful couches and welcoming creaky wood floor make it hard to tear yourself away. You'll see people studying, chatting or even sleeping (didn't get to the coffee quick enough) at this cafe. Smoothies are also available.

➤ ⓂKelvinbridge. Take S. Woodlands Rd. toward St. George's Rd. ℹ Live music once a month, but inquire within. $ Coffee £1.50-3. ⏰ Open M-Sa 8am-10:30pm, Su 9am-10:30pm.

O'NEILL'S 💳♿🍸 IRISH ❸

453 Sauchiehall St. ☎0141 353 4371 🖥www.oneills.co.uk

O'Neill's is a self-proclaimed Irish restaurant in Scotland, and the schtick feels a bit forced (those Guinness signs are just too clean!). Still, the food is hot and hearty and you can score some Guinness-battered fish and chips *(£6).*

➤ ⓂCowcaddens. ℹ Vegetarian options available. ⏰ Open M-W noon-midnight, Th noon-2am, F-Sa noon-3am, Su noon-2am.

WILLOW TEA ROOMS 💳🚭🍸 CAFE ❸

97 Buchanan St. ☎0141 204 5242 🖥www.willowtearooms.co.uk

With the high-backed chairs based on the original, influential designs of Charles Rennie Macintosh, the Willow Tea Rooms create a dainty, scone-filled paradise for the passing wanderer. Sit by the windows upstairs and enjoy one classy tea experience.

➤ ⓂBuchanan. $ Cakes £12.25. ⏰ Open M-Sa 9am-5pm, Su 11am-5pm. Last orders 30min. before close.

BRADFORD'S BAKERY AND CAFÉ 💳♿🍸 CAFE ❷

245 Sauchiehall St. ☎0141 332 1008 🖥www.hrbradfords.co.uk

The downstairs of this cafe has two rows of pastry shelves in a rainbow of colors. The upstairs, with tables and window views of Sauchiehall St. below, offers full meals as well as coffee and sweets.

➤ ⓂCowcaddens. ℹ Wheelchair accessibility limited to downstairs pastry shop. $ Entrees £5-10. Desserts up to £4. ⏰ Open M-Sa 8am-5pm.

THE LEFT BANK 💳♿🍸 ETHNIC ❸

33-35 Gibson St. ☎0141 339 5659 🖥www.theleftbank.co.uk

One of Glasgow's most varied eateries, you can get everything from chips and salsa to cayenne-dusted squid with homemade lime mayo here. Come during the week for the *prix-fixe* menu if you want to save a little dough.

➤ ⓂKelvinbridge. Walk south to Gibson St. ℹ Vegetarian and vegan options available. $ 2 courses £11, 3 courses £13. ⏰ Open M-F 10am-midnight, Sa-Su 10am-midnight.

BIER HALL REPUBLIC AND PIZZA BAR 🍸☀ PIZZA ❷

9 Gordon St. ☎0141 204 0706

Bier Hall offers a two-for-one pizza deal every day noon-10pm, when you can score two big pizzas for £7-11. They do have an extensive international beer selection, though, so you'll be paying back all the money you just saved, on the £3-4 bottles.

➤ 1 block from Glasgow Central Low Level Station. ℹ Vegetarian and vegan options available. $ Pizza £8-11. ⏰ Kitchen open M-Sa noon–10pm, Su 12:30–10pm. Bar open M–Sa noon–midnight, Su 12:30pm–midnight.

PARADISE RESTAURANT 💳♿ PERSIAN ❷

411-413 Great Western Rd. ☎0141 339 2170 🖥www.persianparadise.co.uk

In Paradise, water streams down the windows into pools with goldfish below and ornamental decorations are everywhere. Now if only the food were as exciting as the decor. Student lunch deal provides a decent two-course meal *(£6).*

ℹ Vegetarian options available. ⏰ Open daily noon-10:30pm.

STRAVAIGIN 🍴 ♿ 🍸 GLOBAL ❹

28 Gibson St. ☎0141 334 2665 💻www.stravaigin.com

Signs that a restaurant must be expensive: they have a cheese section on their menu. Signs that a restaurant must be great: it's packed with people. Stravaigin exhibits both, and is so distinctive that they offer their own recipe of haggis. They even manage to do a vegetarian haggis, though no one's quite sure how.

From Great Western Rd., turn onto Bank St. for 3 blocks, then turn left onto Gibson St. and follow 2 blocks. $ Appetizers £3.65-12. Entrees up to £23. ⏰ Open daily 11am-midnight.

NANAKUSA 🍴 ♿ 🍸 JAPANESE ❸

441 Sauchiehall St. ☎0741 331 6303 💻www.nanakusa.co.uk

Nanakusa offers sushi and Japanese grill options in an atmosphere that leaves modern completely behind in favor of the weirdly futuristic. The long, low tables in front of color-changing window panes make you feel like you're in an extremely relaxed disco while you eat. Staff is courteous and prompt.

[M]Cowcaddens. Take Rose St. south and turn right onto Sauchiehall St. $ Saki singles for £4. Dishes £3-7. ⏰ Open M-Th noon-2:30pm and 5-11pm, F-Sa noon-2am, Su 5-11pm.

NIGHTLIFE

Glasgow plus nightlife equals great parties. That's almost 'nuff said, but we'll go on. Whether you want to sit down and belt out some karaoke or get dolled up to find some classy clubs, Glasgow's got a great scene. There are several good clubs on Bath St. in the city center as well as in the West End. Friday and Saturday nights draw the biggest and sloppiest crowds, but **Sauchiehall Street** has it going on every night of the week.

STEREO 🍴 ♿ 🍸 BAR, RESTAURANT, LIVE MUSIC

20-28 Renfield Ln. ☎0141 222 2254

Much like a vegan, the upstairs restaurant area is thin and green (kidding, kidding). Serving organic ales *(£4.05)* as well as normal brews, the music space downstairs is a concrete box, where a great sound system helps make up for the not-so-great acoustics. Tapas are available until midnight in case you get peckish after all that unadulterated ale.

1 block north of Glasgow Central Low Level Rail Station. $ Entrees £7-7.50. ⏰ Open M-Tu noon-midnight, W-Su noon-3am.

BUFF CLUB 🍴 ♿ 🍸 CLUB

142 Bath Ln. ☎0141 221 7711 💻www.buffclub.com

One of the most popular clubs in Glasgow, the Buff Club is like a '20s speakeasy, with a gold and red interior reminiscent of a classy hotel lobby and a two-floored dance area upstairs reminiscent of awesome. Funk and soul can be heard all night long.

Turn left off of Bath St. at Blytheswood St. and then turn left again. i Electronica night on Tu. Look for weekly vodka+mixer promos. ATM available. $ Pints £3. ⏰ Open daily 11pm-3am.

UISGE BEATHA 🍴 ♿ 🍸 PUB

232-246 Woodlands Rd. ☎0141 332 1622

All right, before you go into the Uisge Beatha, repeat after us: "Ish-kah Vay-ha." Get it right or risk looking like a helpless newbie. With a bar staff guaranteed to know everyone by name (including you, if you give them 5min.) and a wide range of whiskeys and beers, the "Ish" is a must. Stop by on Sundays for a trad band that occasionally swells to two dozen musicians.

[M]Kelvinbridge. Follow Woodlands Rd. i Quiz night on W. $ Pints £2.70-3.45. Spirits £2.80-3. ⏰ Open M-Sa noon-midnight, Su 12:30pm-midnight.

LAKOTA 🍴 ♿ 🍸 BAR

110-114 West George St. ☎0141 332 9724 💻www.lakotabars.co.uk

Lakota is a cocktail bar with plaid-shirted bartenders and deer heads above the bar. This place has a lot of room to roam, with chill booths on one end and a disco ball on the other. Upstairs you'll find the '80s bar Reflex.

✦ Ⓜ*Buchanan St.* ⓩ *Lakota open M-Sa 9am-midnight, Su 10am-midnight. Reflex open F-Sa 8pm-midnight.*

THE HORSESHOE BAR ✦ BAR
17-19 Drury St. ☎0141 248 6368 ▣www.facebook.com/thehorseshoebar

A huge, wraparound bar lined with standing old men greets you in the downstairs segment of this double-sided pub. Yes, the bottom floor is a bit quiet, but head upstairs to the karaoke bar to see tables full of people making conversation over the sweet sounds of the next "star" of the stage. Come in noon-3pm and get a 3-course lunch any day *(£4).*

✦ *1 block west of Glasgow Central Low Level Rail Station.* *i* *Wheelchair accessibility limited to downstairs.* Ⓢ *Pints £2.25-2.70. Wine from £6.* ⓩ *Open M-Sa 10am-midnight, Su 12:30pm-midnight.*

DRUM AND MONKEY ✦♿ PUB
93 Vincent St. ☎0141 221 6636

An ex-bank that now stores whiskey instead of cash, the Drum and Monkey is an old man's bar for sure, but it's also a good drinks bar, with friendly bartenders and a snazzy atmosphere.

✦ Ⓜ*Buchanan St.* ⓩ *Open M-Th 11am-11pm, F-Sa 11am-midnight, Su 11am-10pm.*

HILLHEAD BOOKCLUB ✦♈☕ BAR
17 Vinicombe St. ☎0141 576 1700 ▣www.hillheadbookclub.co.uk

One of the new bars on the block, the Bookclub is in an old cinema, so you're not going to be jockeying for space unless things get really busy. Two floors of booths line an open floor area in this hipster-esque bar. Try their special "Hillhead Strawberry Mojito," which is way more taste and booze than you'd normally be getting for £3. If you see Andrew the barman, tell him we say hi.

✦ Ⓜ*Hillhead. Follow Byers Rd. north to Vinicombe St.* ⓩ *Open daily 11am-midnight.*

THE BOX ✦♈ CLUB
431 Sauchiehall St. ▣www.box-glasgow.co.uk

In comparison to the Nice 'n Sleazy a few doors down, the Box trades beards and flannel for leather bracelets and hard rock. Live music plays 9pm-midnight, and then DJs take over from midnight-3am...every night. The party certainly never stops here, but what's with all the weird bondage images on the walls? Ignore the posters, please, and listen to the music.

✦ Ⓜ*Buchanan. Walk down Rose St. to Sauchiehall St.* Ⓢ *Pints £2-4.* ⓩ *Open M-Th 5pm-3am, F-Su 4pm-3am.*

PIVO PIVO ✦⊛♈ BAR, LIVE MUSIC
15 Waterloo St. ☎0141 564 8100 ▣www.myspace.com/pivopivo

Pivo Pivo is the best place to hear all of the unsigned and unknown Glaswegian music acts. There's a band on every night at this bunker-like former Czech hall. With good acoustics and a nice stage area. You could be feet away from the next Franz Ferdinand or Belle and Sebastian. Jazz happens on Saturday afternoons.

✦ *1 block west of Glasgow Central Low Level Rail.* *i* *Large variety of beers.* Ⓢ *Beer £3-4. Mixed drinks £3. Covers for bands £3-5.* ⓩ *Open M-Sa noon-midnight.*

THE BELLE ⊛♿♈ PUB
617 Great Western Rd. ☎0141 339 9229

With a stone hearth and wood-burning fireplace. The Belle is busiest during the winter months when it may just be the warmest place in the West End...that serves alcohol. With large international selection of bottled beers *(£2-4)* and one weird stag's head with red antlers, this place is definitely worth a closer look.

✦ Ⓜ*Kelvinbridge. Walk west on Great Western Rd.* *i* *The red-antlered stag rejects the term "Demon deer."* Ⓢ *Cash only.* ⓩ *Open daily noon-midnight.*

THE GARAGE 🍸 CLUB

490 Sauchiehall St. ☎0141 332 1120 💻www.garageglasgow.co.uk

The giant truck coming out of the wall above the door says it all—this place is either going to be a traffic jam or an accident. Screaming students dance and drink to the music in one of several bars to be found at the end of the club's many staircases. Wise locals says it's good to go in large groups—heed their advice.

🪧 Ⓜ Cowcaddens. Walk down Rose St. to Sauchihall St. $ Cover M-Th £5, students £3; F-Sa £7/5; Su £5/3. No cover before 11pm. Cash only. ⏰ Open daily 11pm-3am.

HUMMINGBIRD 🍸▼ CLUB

186 Bath St. ☎0845 166 6039

An enormous, four-floor, heavily stylized establishment, the Hummingbird features three private karaoke rooms (each seating 10-15 crooners) as well as a mezzanine bar and a downstairs club space. You may see people wandering around with cocktails larger than their heads—those are the "fishbowls," a house specialty. A late 20s crowd slowly stop acting their age as the night wears on.

🪧 Ⓜ Cowcaddens. Walk down Rose St. and turn right onto Bath St. ⏰ Open M-F 5pm-1am, Sa-Su noon-3am.

NICE 'N SLEAZY 🍸 BAR, LIVE MUSIC

421 Sauchiehall St. ☎0141 333 0900 💻www.nicensleazy.com

A musician's bar, this is the place where you'll see the bartender and the customer in a heated argument—about which Jeff Beck album was the greatest, *Blow by Blow* or *Live with the Jan Hammer Group* (the answer is the latter). With paintings of snakes chasing flowers and hipster mustaches, Nice 'n Sleazy's is a great bar where you can come in and immediately start talking music with the barstaff.

🪧 Ⓜ Cowcaddens. Walk down Rose St. to Sauchihall St. ℹ "Nice 'n Sleazy" T-shirts £20. $ Black and White Russians £2. Pints £2.70-3.30. ⏰ Open M-Sa noon-3am, Su 1:30pm-3am.

KING TUT'S 🍸 BAR, LIVE MUSIC

272 St. Vincent St. ☎0141 221 5279 💻www.kingtuts.co.uk

The names of bands that have played here, and then gone to hit it big, like The Verve, Radiohead, and Florence and the Machine, have been printed on the stairs leading from the bar to the stage area. They're so big that they've even got their own lager, King Tut's, which sells for £3 per pint. Got a band? Drop off your demo in the mailbox inside and hope to be heard.

🪧 Ⓜ Buchanan St. ℹ 10min. concerts daily. $ Lager £3. ⏰ Open M-Sa noon-1am, Su 6pm-midnight.

ARTS AND CULTURE

GLASGOW ROYAL CONCERT HALL (GRCH) CITY CENTER

2 Sauchiehall St. ☎0141 353 8000 💻www.glasgowconcerthalls.com

A music performance space with a capacity of 2000, the GRCH regularly hosts acts of the Elvis Costello/Robert Cray caliber. Shows at this venue offer any sweet sounds you could be yearning for—from jazz to classical to Celtic.

🪧 Ⓜ Buchanan. On the corner of Sauchiehall and Buchanan St. ⏰ Open M-Sa 10am-6pm.

ESSENTIALS

Practicalities

- **TOURIST OFFICE: Visit Scotland,** the tourist information office, books hotels and B and B's (though, strangely, not hostels), in addition to providing free maps, information, and visitors' guides. Of course, there's also a souvenir shop. *(⏰ Open July-Aug M-W 9am-8pm, Th 9:30am-8pm, F-Sa 9am-8pm, Su 10am-6pm. The rest of the year the shop closes at around 5pm or 6pm.)*

- **CURRENCY EXCHANGE: Bank of Scotland.** *(54 Sauchiehall St. ☎0845 780 1801 💻 www.bankofscotland.co.uk ⏰ Open M-Tu 9am-5pm, W 9:30am-5pm, Th-Sa 9am-5pm.)*
- **POST OFFICES: Sauchiehall St.** has a *bureau de change* in addition to regular postal services. *(177 Sauchiehall St. ☎0845 774 0740 💻 www.postoffice.co.uk ⏰ Open M-Sa 9am-5:30pm.)* **Glasgow General Post Office** is the big daddy of post offices in Glasgow and also has a *bureau de change. (47 St. Vincent St. ☎0141 204 4400 💻 www.postoffice.co.uk ⏰ Open M-Sa 9am-5:30pm.)*

Emergency!

- **LATE-NIGHT PHARMACIES: Park Road Pharmacy.** *(405 Great Western Rd. ☎0141 339 5979 💻 www.postoffice.co.uk ℹ Credit cards accepted. ⏰ Open M-F 9am-6pm, Sa 9am-5pm.)* **Boots Pharmacy.** *(200 Sauchiehall St. ℹ Credit cards accepted. ⏰ Open M-W 8am-6pm, Th 8am-8pm, F 8am-6pm, Sa 8am-6pm, Su 10am-6pm.)*

Getting There

Edinburgh Bus Station is the main hub for Edinburgh. Buses come in from Scotland, England, and beyond. *(#9 Elder St. ☎0131 652 5920 💻www.citylink.co.uk $ Luggage storage £2.50-3.50 per 3hr. £5-7 per 24 hr. Lost token £6. Toilets £.30; exact change necessary. ⏰ Ticket office open daily 9am-8pm.)* Several different bus companies run routes to and from Edinburgh, including **National Express** *(☎08705 80 80 80 💻www.nationalexpress.com)* linking England and Scotland, **Scottish Citlink** *(☎08705 50 50 50 💻www.citylink.co.uk)* which connects towns within Scotland, and **Stagecoach** *(☎0870 608 2 608 💻www.stagecoachbus.com).*

Getting Around

The **subway** or **Underground** in Glasgow (called **"Clockwork Orange"**) is operated by the Strathclyde Partnership for Transport. There are 15 subway stops in Glasgow that lie on one circle. The Glasgow subway operates every 4-8 min. Mondays to Saturdays between 6:30am and 11:30pm. On Sundays service is restricted to 11am-6pm, with trains every 8min. Trains take approximately 24min. for an entire circle. *($ Single journey £1.20. 10 trips £10. "Discovery Ticket" for 1 day unlimited travel after 9:30am or all day Su £3.50.)*

belfast ☎028

Finally able to breathe after years of conflict, Belfast is coming into its own as a burgeoning metropolis. Its various shopping centers sell everything from strawberries to luxury watchwear. The city's people are kind and friendly, even though you don't have to go far to find someone who not only remembers "the Troubles," but can also recall a time when a policeman frisked you before you entered the city center. But far from having resentment and a "hush-hush" attitude, the people of Belfast enagage with their history; black cab tours of West Belfast, the area of hottest conflict, have become a popular tourist attraction. Think of Belfast as Dublin's badass older brother who plays in a band: he's cool, gritty, and gets tons of groupies. Head to Belfast to become one yourself.

ORIENTATION

What's with all the Donegalls? Okay, get this: **Donegall Square** surrounds the city hall, **Donegall Road** runs from the west, crossing through town at **Shaftesbury Square** and becoming **Donegall Pass,** and finally, there's **Donegall Street** that runs right through the heart of the cathedral district. Lesson to be learned? If someone gives you directions via a "Donegall" anything, make sure you get a second opinion. Belfast is a slim city, running mostly north to south, with the previously conflicted **Fall** and **Shankill Roads** in

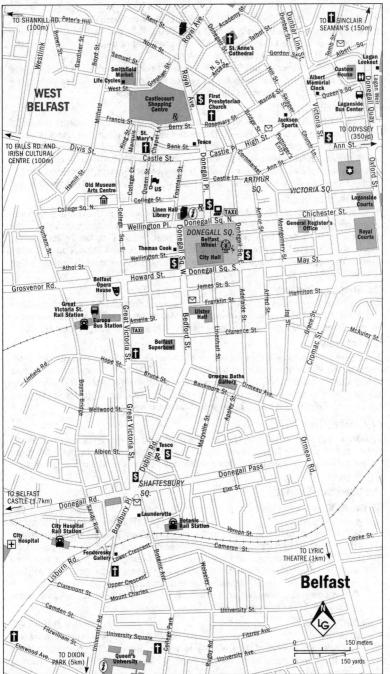

West Belfast usually just being visited by tourists in a cab. **Queen's University** lies south of the city center along **University Road** (follow Bedford St. and Dublin Rd. from City Hall) and houses most of the student life and nearly all of the budget accommodations in Belfast. What was called the "Golden Mile" in past years—the triangle of Dublin Rd., Great Victoria, and Bruce St.—is now pretty much dead. A few fast-food joints and the odd pub can be found there, but the new hotspot for nightlife is the **Cathedral Quarter,** the area above City Hall near the **River Lagan.**

The University District

The University District centers on Queen's University but extends into the residental neighborhoods to the west and south. The **Student Union, The Botanic,** and **Eglantine Inn** are all popular student bars, and there are several hostels and bed and breakfasts on **Eglantine** and **Fitzwilliam Streets. Lisburn Road** provides the other, far-side north-south channel, and also has several good restaurants and cafes. If you ever get disoriented, ask for either Lisburn or University Rd. and you'll be able to point yourself back toward the city center.

The Cathedral Quarter

Boasting the hottest nightclubs and several bars, the Cathedral Quarter is experiencing an upsurge in both popularity and establishments—this is where you'll find the new pub on the block. **High Street** provides a neat "bottom" to the neighborhood, which extends up to the **University of Ulster** and east over to **North Street.** Full of smaller streets, Waring street has some good bars and luxury hotels, and then there's that Donegall street again.

The Shopping District

Right next to the Entries and City Hall, the shopping district houses the more high-end shopping of Belfast as well as the massive **Victoria Square** and **Castlecourt** shopping centers. Shoppers will be happy to note that Belfast is much cheaper than Dublin.

The Entries

A series of cobblestone and brick walking streets, the entries provide all the shopping that the Victoria and Castlecourt centers can't. The term "entry" actually refers to tiny alleyways that have "covered" entrances in between shops on the wider open streets. Chances are you'll see them as you walk around, but if you need help, just ask someone and they'll be happy to point you to the nearest one.

ACCOMMODATIONS

Belfast has a great hostel scene, with several promising options lying close to Queen's University. Most of the B and Bs are down along that area as well. In fact, aside from luxury hotels and the odd hostel down in the city center area, the university district is the place to be.

The University District

👍 VAGABONDS ♿❄🛁🍸 HOSTEL [2]

#9 University Rd. ☎028 9543 8772 💻www.vagabondsbelfast.com

A brand-new, "for backpackers by backpackers" hostel, Vagabonds does everything right. Clean dorms, great common spaces, and a fantastic staff are all the norm here. The manager and his motley crew of employees are guaranteed to show you a good time. So good you might have to stay home for a night and just relax. That's OK, though—Monday movie night means free popcorn. Enjoy.

*➡ From Donegall Sq., follow Bedford St. onto Dublin Rd. and University Rd. **i** Tourist information available. $ Rates vary. Dorms £13-16.*

PADDY'S PALACE 🍴📶🛁 HOSTEL [2]

68 Lisburn Rd. ☎028 9033 3367 💻www.paddyspalace.com

The rules list is sort of long when you walk in the door (no disruption, food and drink only in the kitchen—but Paddy's Palace is pretty nice. The carpets are a different color in every room just to change it up. You can score a free continental breakfast 7:30-9:30am.

⇄ Across the street from Arnie's, on the corner of Fitzwilliam and Lisburn. ℹ Continental breakfast included. $ 12-bed dorm M-F £9.50, Sa-Su £10; 8-bed M-F £13, Sa-Su £14; 6-bed M-F £14, Sa-Su £15; 4-bed M-F £16, Sa-Su £17; doubles £40-45. ⏰ Breakfast 7:30-9:30am.

THE GEORGE B AND B
BED AND BREAKFAST ❸

9 Eglantine Ave. ☎028 9043 9619 💻the-george@hotmail.co.uk

With the help of their fantastic staff, the George provides a budget option for those willing to pay a little bit more for privacy. Relax in the wonderfully decorated sitting room or outside on the front bench in the (occasional) Belfast sun.

⇄ Across the street from Marine House. ℹ Full Irish breakfast included. $ Singles £30; doubles £50. ⏰ Breakfast 7-9am.

LAGAN'S HOSTEL
HOSTEL ❷

121 Fitzroy Ave. ☎0754 041 8246 💻www.laganbackpackers.com

Lagan's is another hostel that has built its reputation entirely on its service. The dorms are plain but clean and you'll enjoy the benefit of free Wi-Fi throughout the hostel, as well as a free full breakfast. Check out the comments in the sign-in book to see just how high the bar has been set.

ℹ Kitchen use available. $ 8-bed dorms M-F £12, Sa-Su £13; 6-bed M-F £13, Sa-Su £14; 4-bed M-F £14 Sa-Su £15; 3-bed M-F £15, Sa-Su £16. Singles M-F £25, Sa-Su £28, doubles M-F £18, Sa-Su £20. ⏰ Reception 24hr.

ARNIE'S BACKPACKERS
HOSTEL ❶

63 Fitzwilliam St. ☎028 9024 2867 💻www.arniesbackpackers.co.uk

Yet another excellent hostel in Belfast, Arnie's has the local vibe going on. Play with Arnie's two dogs in the backyard seating area or sit down in the lounge; the tiny 13 in. TV will help you keep your focus on meeting new friends.

⇄ On Fitzwilliam St., on the Lisburn Rd. side. ℹ The #1 bunk in the 4-bed dorm is lofted and offers more privacy than the rest. Computer £1 per 30min.; proceeds donated to charity. Kitchen available. $ 8-bed dorms £10; 4-beds £12.

MARINE HOUSE
GUESTHOUSE ❸

30 Eglantine Ave. ☎028 9066 2828 💻www.marinehouse3star.com

The amazing rooms in an enormous, classic Victorian home make beautiful Marine House the best B and B on the block. However, the real gem of the establishment is the owner Nat, who is incredibly kind to all of his guests, helping them find attractions and offering advice.

⇄ On Eglantine Ave. near Lisburn Rd. ℹ Full Irish breakfast included. $ Singles £45; doubles £60.

The Shopping District

BELFAST INTERNATIONAL HOSTEL
HOSTEL ❷

22-32 Donegall Rd. ☎028 9031 5435 💻info@hini.org.uk

BIH is like a McDonald's—you only get it really late at night and you don't really want it. Housed in a corporate office space, it has over 200 rooms and less than a pint's worth of character. Still, if you can't find a room in Belfast, head here and you're guaranteed a clean place to stay for the night.

⇄ Just off Shaftesbury Sq. ℹ Presentation of passport or other valid ID necessary for check-in. $ Dorms M-F £11, Sa-Su £12; standard singles M-F £21, Sa-Su £22.

SIGHTS

From the **Saint Anne's Cathedral** with its elegant and pointy architecture, to the **W5 Children Activities Center** (think giant Tinkertoys), Belfast has a multitude of things to see. To recommend just a few, the **city hall** tour is worth either a history lesson or a laugh, depending on how you choose to experience it; **Queen's University** is elegant or overpriced depending on how you choose to look at it; and the **Crown Bar** is either memorable or not, depending on how much you choose to drink.

The University District

👍 ULSTER MUSEUM ♿ MUSEUM

Botanic Ave. ☎028 9042 8428 💻www.nmni.com

Operating on five floors, and covering art, history, and natural history, this museum has a hell of a lot of exhibits. Even better, all of them are very good. See everything from famous Italian art pieces to 📷**T-rex** heads. By the time you finish, you'll have gotten your tourist fix for the entire month.

➜ *Just inside the Botanic Gardens South of Queen's University, on the right.* 💲 *Free.* ⏰ *Open Tu-Sa 10am-5pm.*

THE BOTANICAL GARDENS PARK

Belfast Gardens Park

Not to be confused with "The Botanic Inn" sports bar across the street (serving relaxation of a different genre), the botanical gardens are an excellent spot to check out some scenery, watch people walk their dogs, or examine one of the old-fashioned greenhouses. Bets are still off as to why there's a pine tree in a cage in the middle of the park though.

➜ *Just south of Queen's University on University Rd.* 💲 *Free.*

QUEEN'S UNIVERSITY 🎓♿ UNIVERSITY

Queen's University Belfast, University Rd. ☎028 9097 5252 💻www.qub.ac.uk

Looking more like the cathedrals of Rome than the inside of your third grade classroom, this school should definitely be passed through and admired. If you pick up the "Walkabout Queen's" pamphlet, you'll take a similar route to the guided tours, with no need to tip the brochure when you're done! (Unless, of course, you thought the brochure was cute, and then you could maybe ask it to dinner and then, well...). The nine stops will take you at least an hour to get through.

➜ *To get to the visitor's center, just walk through the main entrance. Call ahead to arrange a guided tour.* 💲 *Free.* ⏰ *Visitors' center open M-Sa 9:30am-4:30pm, Su 10am-1am.*

The Golden Mile

👍 SAINT ANNE'S CATHEDRAL CATHEDRAL

Donegall St.

Possibly the only time that Gothic and modern architecture have been mixed to positive results, the cavernous interior of the gaudy St. Anne's Cathedral is broken up by the "Spire of Hope," a giant space needle (we're not kidding) jutting through the center of the ceiling and extending into the sky above. Dedicated in 2007, this addition proclaims hope to a city that had none for such a long time.

➜ *On the corner of Donegall and Talbot St. 1 block south of the University of Ulster.* 💲 *Free. Donations encouraged.* ⏰ *Open M-F 10am-4pm.*

The Shopping District

👍 BELFAST CITY HALL AND TOUR ♿ CITY TOUR

City Hall ☎028 9027 0456

The free, approximately 1hr. tour of Belfast City Hall offers you the opportunity to do several things: admire giant silver scepters and funny old robes, sit in the seats of all the big-wig politicos that are using that funny clothing, and touch furniture that was supposed to go on the Titanic but never made it inside. It's also informative and historical—we almost forgot that those are important too.

➜ *Donegall Sq. Sign up in the foyer of the building, through the front entrance.* 💲 *Free.* ⏰ *Tours M-F 11am, 2pm, and 3pm. Sa 2pm and 3pm.*

ORMEAU BATHS GALLERY ♿ GALLERY

18a Oremeau Ave. ☎028 9032 1402 💻www.ormeaubaths.co.uk

Housed in an old Victorian bathhouse—you'll see a few hopefully-empty tubs as you walk in the door—the Ormeau Baths gallery rotates between eight and ten exhibits of all sorts throughout the year. It's a perfect space for a gallery. Quiet, spacious and full of strange echoes, you can almost hear splashing Victorians commenting on the paintings.

➥ 3 blocks south of Donegall Sq. on Linenhall St. ℹ Occasionally offers workshops for kids. $ Free. ⏰ Open Tu-Sa 10am-5:30pm.

The Entries

CUSTOM HOUSE HISTORICAL SITE

Custom House Sq.

The Custom House isn't the most interactive of things to visit. In fact, all you can really do here is walk around and admire Charles Lanyon's architectural work. The Custom House was completed in 1857 to help with Belfast's emerging status as a commercial trading giant. Fun factoid: novelist **Anthony Trollope** worked in the Post Office here for several years.

➥ With your back to city hall, walk right on Chichester St., turn left on Victoria St. and it'll be on your left. ⏰ Viewing Gallery open M 10am-6pm, Tu-F 10am-9pm, Sa 10am-6pm, Su 1-6pm.

FOOD

Thank goodness for a city whose food options are drunk-friendly. The number of kebab, burger, chip, and Chinese places open late at night here is astounding. They're everywhere, but especially near **Shaftesbury Square** and the university. When you've woken up and had enough water to feel normal again, however, there are also some places that have especially tasty treats. We've listed some of the best below.

The University District

👍 **MOLLY'S YARD RESTAURANT** 💳♿☀ RESTAURANT [2]

1 College Green Mews, Botanic Ave. ☎028 9032 2600 💻www.mollysyard.co.uk

Come into the weird, garage-like "yard" of Molly's Yard and take a seat at one of the wooden tables outside or one of the candle-graced tables inside. It's your choice—either way you're going to get great eats. Best of all, it's cheap *(dinner £6.95-9.50)*. For this caliber of food, that's amazing. Try the Asian marinated beef skewer with mooli and mango salad with toasted almonds and soy dipping sauce *(£9)*.

➥ 1 block south of University St., above the school campus. $ Dinner entrees £7-9.50. ⏰ Open M-Th noon-9pm, F-Sa noon-6pm. ⏰ Evening menu available M-Th 6-9pm, F-Sa 6-9:30pm.

KOOKY'S CAFÉ 💳📶☀ CAFE [2]

112 Lisburn Rd. ☎029 068 7338

Kooky's Café isn't so much "kooky" as it is a good place to get your morning coffee fix. There are some pieces of modern art on the walls, and yes, those mirrors are wavy instead of square, but the overall feel is much chiller than its name suggests. Grab a "Veggie Works" breakfast with a free-range egg and pull down the morning's paper from the rack.

➥ South of city center. From Donegall Sq., follow Bedford St. straight onto Dublin Rd. and finally Lisburn Rd. $ Lunch sandwiches £3.25-4. ⏰ Open M-F 9am-4pm, Sa-Su 10am-3pm.

THE BARKING DOG 💳♿🍸☀ RESTAURANT [3]

31-32 Malone Rd. ☎028 9066 1885 💻thebarkingdogoffice@gmail.com

Try the homemade linguini with crab meat, chilli and lemon and herb butter *(small £6.50, large £11.50)* at this modern chic restaurant with doggie prints on the fence. The candles on your table are real, and they illuminate the older couples that will be dining all around you.

➥ Next to the Botanic Inn on Malone Rd. $ Entrees £10-20. ⏰ Open M-Th noon-3:30pm and 5:30-10pm; F-Sa noon-3pm and 5:30-11pm; Su 1-9pm.

The Golden Mile

👍 NICK'S WAREHOUSE — 💳♿🍸 BISTRO ❸

35-39 Hill St. ☎028 9043 9690 💻www.nickswarehouse.co.uk

Expressionist paintings sit next to home photos at this bistro-esque restaurant. With an enormous wine selection *(£3-5 per glass)* and a comfortable brick interior, Nick's Warehouse gives you all the frills of a high-end restaurant with none of the pretense.

🚶 5min. walk Northwest of Donegall Sq. Ⓢ Wine £3-5. ⏰ Open Tu-Th noon-3pm and 6-9:30pm, F-Sa noon-3pm and 6-10pm.

THE CHIPPIE — 🥡♿ FAST FOOD ❶

29 Lower North St. ☎028 9043 9619

Absolutely the cheapest option around, everything at the Chippie goes for under £3.30. Several chip variations (that's "fries" to you Amur'can folk) including "gravy chip," "garlic chip," and "curry chip," are here to tempt. If that doesn't whet your palate then go for a ¼lb. Hawaiian burger *(£2.85)*.

🚶 3min. walk north of Donegall Sq. Ⓢ Fish £3.30. Everything else £3. ⏰ Open M-W 10:30am-6pm, Th 10:30am-9pm, F-Sa-6pm.

PRINTER'S CAFÉ — 💳♿🍸☀ RESTAURANT, CAFE ❷

33 Lower Donegall St. ☎028 9031 3406

Down the street from the Duke of York is this BBQ paradise. Get chargrilled Thai beef patties with Asian salad, warm pita bread, satay sauce and sweet chilli sauce *(£8.25)*. Or, if you're just into getting some food in you before heading off to drink at the DOY, grab a sandwich from their takeaway counter at the front of the building.

i Vegetarian options available. Ⓢ Lunch £4-10. ⏰ Open M-Sa lunch 11:30am-3pm. Dinner F-Sa 5:30-9:30pm.

2TAPS — 💳♿🍸☀ TAPAS BAR ❸

42 Waring St. ☎028 9031 1414 💻www.2tapswinebar.com

Why they didn't just call it "2Tapas" is a mystery to us as well. This Spanish-influenced tapas bar serves a "Creme Catalan" (orange-infused brulee) and sangria by the jug *(£12)*. The interior is full of wood paneling and wraparound booths. If you want to head outside, however, the samba music will follow.

🚶 5min. walk northwest of Donegall Sq. Ⓢ Lunch plates £7. Tapas £3.50-5. Entrees £12-15. ⏰ Open in summer daily noon-8pm. Open fall-spring Tu-Sa noon-8pm.

The Shopping District

👍 MADE IN BELFAST — 💳♿🍸 IRISH ❸

Units 1 and 2, Wellington St. ☎028 9024 6712 💻www.madeinbelfastni.com

The welcome mat inside the door declares "Shake your arse for a hip Belfast!" and you best obey, or you're not going to fit in, with the smatterings of wallpaper scraps, mirrors, and spraypaint on the walls set up leopard couches and furry pillows. Even if you're afraid of having a color-induced seizure, you should still come in and eat. The food is all fresh and wholesome and comes in large quantities.

🚶 1 block west of Donegall Sq. i Wine and cocktail menu available. Ⓢ Meals £5-10. ⏰ Open M-W noon-3pm and 5:30-10pm, Th-Sa noon-3pm and 5:30-11pm. Su 12:30-4pm and 6-9pm.

AM:PM — ♿❄☀ RESTAURANT ❸

42 Upper Arthur St. ☎028 9024 9009

Wow, the candelabras here actually get some use. Atmosphere's the thing here, with flowers, mirrors and tiny lamps that hold candles on your table. It's up to you to decide if the quality matches the jump in price.

🚶 1 block east of Donegall Sq. Ⓢ Lunch dishes £5-10. Pints £3.40. ⏰ Open M-Th 10am-midnight, F-Sa 10am-1am, Su noon-midnight.

FOUNTAIN COFFEE

♥ ❖ ⌂ CAFE ❷

27-29 Fountain St.

☎028 9024 6655

These homemade pastries go the extra mile, thanks to the expert chef. Take one out onto the large terrace area in front of the big bay windows. Student discount 10% with ID.

⚘ *North of Donegall Sq.* **i** *Vegetarian options available.* Ⓢ *Sandwiches £5-7. Entrees £6.50-7. Coffee £1.30-2.25.* ⏰ *Open M-W 7am-6pm, Th 7am-8pm, F-Sa 7am-6pm, Su 11am-5pm.*

THE LITTLE CUPCAKE CAFÉ

☻ CUPCAKES ❶

8 Bedford St.

☎028 9024 1751 ▇www.thelittlecupcake.co.uk

Hiding just a minute's walk away from Belfast City Hall, in the middle of the business district, is a tiny little cafe that looks like your grandmother's house. Flowered wallpaper and plaid-embroidered couches don't mean your Grannie can bake like this, though—unless your Grannie actually does make ultra decadent cupcakes of all kinds *(£1.70 each).* Raspberry white chocolate? Latté? Cookies and cream? Yes, yes, yes, please.

⚘ *Directly off Donegall Sq. S.* Ⓢ *Milkshakes £2.20. Coffee £1-2.* ⏰ *Open M-F 8am-6pm, Sa 10:30am-6pm, Su 1-6pm.*

The Entries

▧ SARNIE'S

☻⌂⌂ DELI ❶

35 Rosemary St.

This is a real-deal deli. Squeeze yourself into the tiny interior, wait your turn, order your food (make sure you know what you want beforehand), and wham! Take your foot-long sub outside though, or you'll be trying to get your sandwich to your mouth around somebody else's elbow.

⚘ *North of Donegall Sq.* **i** *Outdoor seating area available.* Ⓢ *Sandwiches £3.50. Soups £2.* ⏰ *Open M-F 6am-3pm.*

CLEMENT'S COFFEE

♥⌂⌂ CAFE ❷

37-39 Rosemary St.

☎028 9032 2293

Clement's motto is "we're religious about coffee." You'd think that, in a city with Belfast's history, such a remark might spark some ire. Well, everybody's too busy enjoying the coffee to care. Possibly the best latte in town can be found here *(£2).* Sandwiches and panini available as well. Sit outside or crash in the leather couches by the big bay windows.

⚘ *North of Donnegal Sq., next to Sarnie's.* **i** *Vegetarian options available.* Ⓢ *Coffee £2-3. Sandwiches and wraps £2-3. Panini £5.* ⏰ *Open M-F 8am-5:30pm, Sa 9am-5:30pm, Su noon-5pm.*

DOORSTEPS

☻⌂❖⌂ RESTAURANT ❶

64 Ann St.

☎028 9024 5544 ▇www.doorsteps.com

A good place to head for hearty sandwiches quick on the spot. Grab and go with any of the cold cuts and either sit outside or take it away. The decor of the restaurant won't intrigue your appetite nearly as much as the food.

⚘ *2 blocks west of Queen's Bridge.* **i** *Vegetarian options available.* Ⓢ *Coffee £1.20-1.65. Sandwiches £3-3.50.* ⏰ *Open daily 7am-5:30pm.*

NIGHTLIFE

Belfast's nightlife thrives in the university district and the Cathedral Quarter. On the weekends it'll seem like everyone in town is out, and toward one or two in the morning, you'll find it harder to get into clubs—and even harder to move once you get in. Drinks abound, and Belfast at 3am sees a lot of singing, staggering, and general merriment. Taxi drivers seem to get a little bit picky in the early hours as well, so try to sober up (or at least look it) when attempting to hail a cab.

The University District

✪ LAVERY'S
🎟♿🍸👍 PUB, CLUB

12-16 Bradbury Pl. ☎028 9087 1106 💻www.laverysbelfast.com

Everybody's heard of it, and if they haven't been there themselves it's only because they haven't gotten off the binky yet. Lavery's is huge, with three floors (a bar, music venue, and club), all of which feel spacious...until the weekends, when the crowd spills out the door. Happy hours Monday-Thursday means all drinks are £2.85. During the week, the third floor is an awesome pool hall.

⇞ At the bottom of Shaftsbury Sq. i Outdoor seating available. $ Pints £3.20. ⏰ Open M-Sa 11:30am-1am, Su 12:30pm-midnight.

KATY DALY'S, THE SPRING AND AIRBRAKE, LIMELIGHT
🎟♿🍸👍▼ CLUB

17 Ormeau Ave. ☎028 9032 7007 💻www.cdleisure.co.uk

Three spots in one! (Well, you still have to pay for each of them, but they're all right together.) Bar-hop without ever leaving the block: start at Katy Daly's bar and check out how many piercings the person next to you has, then move over to the S and A for some live music, and end at Limelight, where all drinks are £2 on Fridays.

⇞ 4 blocks south of Donegall Sq. ⏰ Katy Daly's open M-Sa noon-1am, Su 6pm-midnight. Spring and Airbrake open Tu 9pm-2am; other nights vary. Limelight open Tu 9pm-2am, Th 9pm-2am, F-Sa 10pm-2am.

THE BOTANIC INN
🎟♿🍸👍 BAR, CLUB

23-27 Malone Rd. ☎028 9058 9740 💻www.botanicinnlimited.com

Belfast's sports bar, "the Bot" gets packed on the weekends and during sporting events. Check out signed rugby jerseys, boxing gloves and a trophy case. Show up on Sunday for the carvery menu *(£6)*, and wash it down with some local Belfast Ale. Framed photos of burly men in short-shorts abound.

⇞ Follow University St. to the south until it becomes Malone Rd. i Nightclub upstairs open on the weekends from 10pm. $ Pints £3.10-3.60. ⏰ Open M-Sa 11:30am-1am, Su noon-midnight.

THE STIFF KITTEN
🎟♿🍸👍▼ CLUB

1 Bankmore Sq. ☎028 9023 8700 💻www.thestiffkitten.com

That is some LOUD techno music. The Stiff Kitten on a Saturday compares with Berlin or Amsterdam in terms of pulse-pounding tracks and streaming lights. When you get tired of dancing, head over to the Blue Bar where you can sit down, or head next door to the SK bar, where all age groups mingle in a much more relaxed environment. Who needs perfect hearing anyway?

⇞ Walk south from Donegall Sq. on Bedford St. $ Come on Th and F, for £1.50 and £2 drinks respectively. ⏰ Open M noon-1am, Tu noon-2am, W noon-1am, Th-F noon-2:30am, Sa noon-3am.

The Golden Mile

✪ THE SPANIARD
🎟⊗🍸 BAR

3 Skipper St. ☎028 9023 2448 💻www.thespaniardbar.com

If you can get in over the steep 25+ age requirement, this is the place to be. A hugely popular bar, it's filled with pictures of Salvador Dalí (you get the feeling all of the bartenders wish they had his mustache) and old vinyl. Try the "Extraordinary," with Havana Cuba rum, squeezed lime, and ginger beer.

⇞ Walk west on Donegall Sq. N., down Chichester St. 3 blocks. Make a left onto Victoria St. and follow until you make a left onto High St. Walk 1 block and turn right onto Skipper St. i 25+. $ Pints £3.30. ⏰ Open M-Sa noon-1am, Su noon-midnight.

✪ RAIN
🎟♿🍸👍▼ CLUB

10-14 Tomb St. ☎028 078 1051 8625 💻www.inforainclub.co.uk

The most excellent late-night club spot for Belfastians, Rain is a two-story club powerhouse complete with sunken dance floors, a packed beer garden, and a line out the door that gets longer throughout the night. Arrive early if you want to pay a smaller cover.

⚐ *Near the river Lagan in the Cathedral quarter.* ⑤ *M-Th and Su £2 drinks all night. Sa drinks full price.* ⌚ *Open daily 9pm-3am.*

THE FRONT PAGE ⦿ ⓨ PUB, CLUB
11 Donegall St. ☎028 9024 6369 ▣www.thefrontpagebar.co.uk

Downstairs, you'll find quiet beer drinkers watching their horses at the track. At the club upstairs, a younger crowd grooves everynight at 7pm, with live music and DJs in the place of track condition discussions.

⚐ *Near the intersection of Donegall and Academy St.* ⓘ *Wheelchair accessibility limited to downstairs.* ⑤ *Pints £3.* ⌚ *Open M-Sa 11:30am-1am, Su 11:30am-11:30pm.*

RONNIE DREW'S ⦿ ⓗ ⓨ ⌂ PUB, BAR
78-83 May St. ☎028 9024 2046 ▣www.ronniedrews.com

Right next door to St. George's market, RD's is a bit out of the way, but the booths are comfy, and, more importantly, the drinks are cheap. Come on Thursday or Friday nights to listen to some trad before heading out to the more expensive spots.

⚐ *From Donegall Sq. S., walk down May St. for 3½ blocks.* ⓘ *Dinner deal includes any entree and 2 drinks.* ⑤ *Pints £2.75. Lunch meals £6. Dinner deal £10.* ⌚ *Open M-Th 9am-11pm, F-Sa 9am-1am, Su 9am-midnight.*

The Shopping District

▨ FILTHY MCNASTY'S ⦿ ⓨ ❄ PUB
45 Dublin Rd.

Mannequins in body suits and tutus guard the entrance to this trendy club. FM's is scheduled to open up a big, open-air venue to handle their live-music schedule, so look for that. An alternative crowd hangs out here, and if you wanna get really McNasty, shots are just £3.

ⓘ *Weekly specials on the board.* ⑤ *Pints £3.30.* ⌚ *Open daily noon-1am.*

THE APARTMENT ⦿ ⓗ ⓨ ❄ ⌂ ▼ BAR
2-4 Donegall Sq. W. ☎028 9050 9777 ▣www.apartmentbelfast.com

On the top floor of The Apartment all that separates you from the night air below are big glass panes. And while the exterior of City Hall below is Victorian, the interior of this bar could have come straight out of 1972. Long, flat furniture and funky '70s soul make it a hotspot for an older, slightly more cash-heavy crowd.

ⓘ *Su £0.50 off all cocktails.* ⌚ *Open M-F 7:30am-1am, Sa 9am-1am, Su 10am-midnight.*

CROWN BAR ⦿ ⓗ BAR
46 Great Victoria St. ☎028 9024 3187 ▣www.crownbar.com

One of the most famous bars in Belfast, there are ornaments on the Crown's ornaments. A Victorian era bar with 10 famous "snugs," or enclosed wooden booths, you'll want to call ahead if you're with a group or want to get a snug at peak hours. Take pictures next to the impressive wood and tile work or simply get your snuggie on.

⑤ *Lunch menu £3-9. Pints £3.50-4.* ⌚ *Open M-Sa noon-3pm. Bar open M-Sa noon-10:30pm, Su 12:30-9pm.*

The Entries

▨ THE DUKE OF YORK ⦿ ⓨ ⌂ PUB
2-10 Commercial Ct. ☎028 9024 1062

There's so many bar mirrors inside, you'll think you had "Jameson" tattooed on your forehead—the Duke of York takes bric-a-brac to a whole new level. See live music on Friday and Saturday, and maybe you'll catch the next Snow Patrol (they got their start here).

⚐ *Just off of Donegall St.* ⑤ *Pints £3.10.* ⌚ *Open M-Sa 11:30am-1am, Su 2pm-midnight.*

THE MORNING STAR PUB

17 Pottinger's Entry ☎028 9023 5986 🖳www.morningstar.com

While the party here's not exactly a bumptastic grindfest, Morning Star's an excellent place to have a few afternoon beers or, alternatively, get a massive plate from the ample buffet *(£5)*. If you're feeling like you could eat a horse, go for cow instead and order the 24 oz. rumpsteak. The old men betting on the **horses** will be pissed were you to eat their entertainment.

Walk up Donegall Pl. and turn right onto Castle St. Follow to the intersection of High St. and Pottingers Entry. $ Pints £2.50-3.10. ⏰ Open M-Th 10:30am-11pm, F-Su 10:30am-1am (but you have until 1:30am to finish your drinks).

ESSENTIALS

Practicalities

- **TOURIST OFFICES: Belfast Welcome Centre** is one of the only tourism offices (and by far the biggest) in Belfast and is also the only place to go for luggage storage *($ £3 for up to 4 hrs., £4.50 for over 4hrs).* Aside from taking in your bags and bothering to be open every day except Christmas, the BWC provides all the tourism info you could ever want, assistance booking tours, a gift shop, currency exchange and internet cafe. They must be listening to a lot of Vanilla Ice over there, because their mantra seems to be, "You got a problem? Yo, I'll solve it." *(47 Donegall Pl. Just up the main road extending away from city hall on the left. ☎028 9024 6609 🖳www.gotobelfast.com i Touchscreen information kiosk available. 2 24hr. ATMs located outside Belfast Welcome Centre. ⏰ Open Oct-May M-Sa 9am-5:30pm, Su 11am-4pm and June-Sept M-Sa 9am-7pm, Su 11am-4pm.)*
- **TOURS:** Operating since 1992, **McComb's Tours** has the longest running Giant's causeway tour, and their guides are friendly and knowledgable. However, just because they've been around since 1992 doesn't mean they're behind the times, all of their buses are less than two years old. Take the causeway tour *(£20 full day, £18 express)* or the City Tour *(£12)*. 20% discount available for patrons of the International Youth Hostel, in which McComb's has their office. *(22-32 Donegall Rd. ☎028 9031 5333 🖳www.mccombstravel.com; info@mccombstravel.com ⏰ Open daily 8am-10pm.)*
- **BANKS: Bank of Ireland.** *(28 University Rd. i 2 24hr. ATMs. ⏰ Open M-Tu 9:30am-4:30pm, W 10am-4:30pm, Th-F 9:30am-4:30pm.)* **First Trust Bank.** *(Across the street from the front of city hall. i 2 24hr. ATMs. ⏰ Open M-Tu 9:30am-4:30pm, W 10am-4:30pm, Th-F 9:30am-4:30pm.)* **Belfast GPO** has currency exchange. *(12-16 Bridge St. ☎028 9032 0337 🖳postoffice.co.uk ⏰ Open M-Sa 9am-5:30pm.)*
- **INTERNET ACCESS: Revelations** gives a discount to students and hostelers, if your hostel doesn't have internet already. *(27 Shaftesbury Sq. ☎028 9032 0337 🖳www.revelations.co.uk; admin@revelations.co.uk $ £1.10 per 15min., per 20min. for students and hostelers. ⏰ Open M-F 8am-10pm, Sa 10am-6pm, Su 11am-7pm.)*
- **POST OFFICES: Belfast GPO** can tend to all of your postal service needs. *(12-16 Bridge St. ☎028 9032 0337 🖳postoffice.co.uk ⏰ Open M-Sa 9am-5:30pm.)* You can also head to the **Bedford Street** branch of the post office. *(16-22 Bedford St. ☎028 9032 2293 ⏰ Open M-F 9am-5:30pm.)*

Emergency!

- **POLICE STATION:** *(Ann St. ☎0845 600 8000 for switchboard, ☎999 for emergencies. 🖳www.psni.co.uk ⏰ 24hr. assistance.)*

- **PHARMACIES:** At **Boots,** wade through an enormous make-up section and head upstairs to get to the pharmacy. *(✈ 35-47 Donegall St. ☎028 9024 2332 💻www.belfasttrust.hscni.net ⏰ Open M-F 8am-9pm, Sa 8am-7pm, Su 1-6pm.)*
- **HOSPITALS: Belfast City Hospital** *(Lisburn Rd. ☎028 9032 9241 for switchboard, ☎999 for emergencies. 💻www.belfasttrust.hscni.net ⏰ Open 24hr.)*

Getting There

By Plane

Belfast International Airport *(Belfast BT29 4AB ☎028 9448 4848 💻www.belfastairport.com; info.desk@bfs.aero* **i** *Passengers who require additional mobility assistance should call +44 (0) 28 9448 4957.)* has flights all over Europe, the US, and beyond, and features the following airlines: **Air Lingus** (*☎0871 7185 000 💻www.aerlingus.com*) with flights to and from Barcelona, Faro, Lanzarote (Arrecife), London Heathrow, Malaga, Munich, Rome Leonardo Da Vinci, Tenerife; **Continental** (*☎0845 607 6760 (UK) or 1 890 925 252 (ROI) 💻www.continental.com/uk*) with flights to and from New York; **easyJet** (*☎0905 821 0905 💻www.easyJet.com*), with flights to and from Alicante, Amsterdam, Barcelona, Bristol, Edinburgh, Faro, Geneva, Glasgow, Ibiza, Krakow, Liverpool, London Gatwick, London Stansted, Malaga, Newcastle, Nice, Palma Majorca, Paris Charles de Gaulle; **Jet2.com** (*☎0871 226 1 737 💻www.jet2.com*), with flights to Blackpool, Chambery, Dubrovnik, Ibiza, Jersey, Leeds Bradford, Mahon, Murcia, Newquay, Palma Majorca, Pisa, Toulouse, Tenerife; **Manx2.com** *(☎0871 200 0440 💻www.manx2.com)* with flights to and from the Isle of Man, Galway, Cork; **Thomas Cook** *(☎0871 895 0055 💻www.thomascook.com)*, with flights to and from Lanzarote, Alicante, Antalya, Bodrum, Corfu, Cancun, Dalaman, Faro, Fuerteventura, Heraklion, Ibiza, Larnaca, Las Palmas, Mahon, Monastir, Palma, Puerto Plata, Reus, Rhodes, Sanford Orlando, Sharm el Sheikh, Tenerife, Toulouse, Veronal; **Thompson Airways** *(☎0871 895 0055 💻www.thomson.co.uk)*, with flights to and from Lanzarote, Malaga, Bodrum, Bourgas, Dalaman, Grenoble, Lapland, Las Palmas, Naples, Palma, Reus, Tenerife.

By Train

Belfast Central Train Station runs all over Northern Ireland and down to the Republic as well. Major destinations include Dublin *(2hr.)*, Londonderry *(2¼hr.)* and Neary *(50min.)*. Check the website for times and prices, as both are subject to frequent change. (*Central Station, E. Bridge St. ☎209 066 6630 💻www.translink.co.uk ⏰ Open M-Sa 6:20am-8:10pm, Su 10am-7:30pm.)*

Getting Around

Transportation cards and tickets are available at the **pink kiosks** in Donegall Sq. W. (*⏰ Open M-F 8am-6pm, Sa 9am-5:20pm)* and around the city.

By Bus

Belfast has two bus services. Many local bus routes connect through **Laganside Bus Station, Queens Square Metro** bus service *(☎9066 6630 💻www.translink.co.uk)* operates from Donegall Sq. Twelve main routes cover Belfast. **Ulsterbus** "blue buses" cover the suburbs. *($ Day passes £3. Travel within the city center £1, under 16 £.50, beyond city center £2.30.* **Nightlink** buses travel from Donegall Sq. W. to towns outside Belfast *($ £3.50. 💻 Sa 1 and 2am.)*

By Taxi

Metered taxis run through the city 24hr. Look for the following companies: **Value Cabs** *(☎9080 9080);* **City Cab** *(☎9024 2000);* **Fon a Cab** *(☎9033 3333).*

By Bicycle

For bike rental, head to **McConvey Cycles.** *(183 Ormeau Rd. ☎9033 0322 💻www.mcconvey.com* **i** *Locks included. $ M and F-Su £20; otherwise £10 per day, £40 per week. £50 deposit. ⏰ Open M-W 9am-6pm, Th 9am-8pm, F-Sa 9am-6pm.)*

essentials

entrance requirements

- **PASSPORT:** Required for citizens of Australia, Canada, New Zealand, and the US.
- **VISA:** Required for citizens of Australia, Canada, New Zealand and the US only for stays of longer than 90 days.
- **WORK PERMIT:** Required for all foreigners planning to work in the UK.

PLANNING YOUR TRIP

Time Differences

Great Britain and Ireland are on Greenwich Mean Time (GMT) and observes Daylight Saving Time. This means that they are 5hr. ahead of New York City, 8hr. ahead of Los Angeles, 10hr. behind Sydney, and 11hr. behind New Zealand (note that Australia observes Daylight Savings Time from October to March, the opposite of the Northern Hemispheres—therefore, it is 9 hours ahead of Britain from March to October and 11 hours ahead from October to March, for an average of 10 hours).

MONEY

Tipping and Bargaining

Tips in restaurants are often included in the bill (sometimes as a "service charge"). If gratuity is not included, you should tip your server about 12.5%. Taxi drivers should receive a 10% tip, and bellhops and chambermaids usually expect £1-3. To the great relief of many budget travelers, tipping is not expected at pubs and bars in Britain and Ireland. Bargaining is generally unheard of in UK shops.

Taxes

The UK has a 17.5% value added tax (VAT), a sales tax applied to everything but food, books, medicine, and children's clothing. The tax is included in the amount indicated on the price tag. The prices stated in Let's Go include VAT. Upon exiting Britain, non-EU citizens can reclaim VAT (minus an administrative fee) through the Retail Export Scheme, although the complex procedure is probably only worthwhile for large purchases. You can obtain refunds only for goods you take out of the country (not for accommodations or meals). Participating shops display a "Tax-Free Shopping" sign and may have a minimum purchase of £50-100 before they offer refunds. To clam a refund, fill out the form you are given in the shop and present it with the goods and receipts at customs upon departure (look for the Tax-Free Refund desk at the airport). At peak times, this process can take up to an hour. You must leave the country within three months of your purchase in order to claim a refund, and you must apply before leaving the UK.

SAFETY AND HEALTH

General Advice

In any type of crisis, the most important thing to do is **stay calm.** Your country's embassy abroad is usually your best resource in an emergency; registering with that embassy upon arrival in the country is a good idea.

great britain

Local Laws and Police

Police presence in cities is prevalent, and most small towns have police stations. There are three types of police officers in Britain: regular officers with full police powers, and police community support officers (PCSO) who have limited police power and focus on community maintenance and safety. The national emergency numbers are ☎999 and ☎112. Numbers for local police stations are listed under each individual city or town.

Drugs and Alcohol

Remember that you are subject to the laws of the country in which you travel. If you carry insulin, syringes, or prescription drugs while you travel, it is vital to have a copy of the prescriptions and a note from your doctor. The Brits love to drink while the Irish live to drink, so the presence of alcohol is unavoidable. In trying to keep up with the locals, remember that the Imperial pint is 20 oz., as opposed to the 16oz. US pint. The drinking age in the UK is 18 (14 to enter, 16 for beer and wine with food). Smoking is banned in enclosed public spaces in Britain and Ireland, including pubs and restaurants.

Specific Concerns

Northern Ireland

Border checkpoints in the UK have been removed, and armed soldiers and vehicles are less visible in Belfast and Derry. Do not take photographs of soldiers, military installations, or vehicles; the film will be confiscated and you may be detained for questioning. Taking pictures of political murals is not a crime, although many people feel uncomfortable doing so in residential neighborhoods.

Terrorism

The bombings of July 7, 2005 in the London Underground revealed the vulnerability of large European cities to terrorist attacks and resulted in the enforcement of stringent safety measures at airports and major tourist sights throughout British cities. Allow extra time for airport security and do not pack sharp objects in your carry-on luggage—they will be confiscated. Unattended luggage is always considered suspicious and is also liable to confiscation. Check your home country's foreign affairs office for travel information and advisories, and be sure to follow the local news while in the UK.

Pre-Departure Health

Matching a prescription to a foreign equivalent is not always easy, safe, or possible, so if you take **prescription drugs,** carry up-to-date prescriptions or a statement from your doctor stating the medications' trade names, manufacturers, chemical names, and dosages. Be sure to keep all medication with you in your carry-on luggage.

Immunizations and Precautions

Travelers over two years old should make sure that the following vaccines are up to date: MMR (for measles, mumps, and rubella); DTaP or Td (for diphtheria, tetanus, and pertussis); IPV (for polio); Hib (for *Haemophilus influenzae* B); and HepB (for Hepatitis B). For recommendations on immunizations and prophylaxis, check with a doctor and consult the **Centers for Disease Control and Prevention (CDC)** in the US or the equivalent in your home country. (☎1 800 CDC INFO/232 4636 ▪www.cdc.gov/travel)

Staying Healthy

Diseases and Environmental Hazards

Common sense is the simplest prescription for good health while you travel. Drink lots of fluids to prevent dehydration and constipation, and wear sturdy, broken-in shoes and clean socks. The British Isles are in the gulf stream, so temperatures are mild: around 40°F in winter and 65°F in summer. In the Scottish highlands and mountains temperatures reach greater extremes. When in areas of high altitude, be sure to dress in layers that can be peeled off as needed. Allow your body a couple of days to adjust to decreased oxygen levels before exerting yourself. Note that alcohol is more potent and UV rays are stronger at high elevations.

Many diseases are transmitted by insects—mainly mosquitoes, fleas, ticks, and lice. Be aware of insects in wet or forested areas, especially while hiking and camping. Wear long pants and long sleeves, tuck your pants into your socks, and use a mosquito net. Use insect repellents such as DEET and soak or spray your gear with permethrin (licensed in the US only for use on clothing). Mosquitoes—responsible for malaria, dengue fever, and yellow fever—can be particularly abundant in wet, swampy, or wooded areas. Ticks—which can carry Lyme and other diseases—can be particularly dangerous in rural and forested regions of Britain.

great britain 101

facts and figures

- **TIME WILLIAM THE CONQUEROR ORDERED ALL HIS CITIZENS TO GO TO BED:** 8pm
- **PERSON HER MAJESTY THE QUEEN MUST GAIN PERMISSION FROM BEFORE ENTERING THE CITY OF LONDON:** The Lord Mayor
- **CUPS OF TEA CONSUMED IN BRITAIN ANNUALLY:** 60.2 billion
- **NUMBER OF JOHN SMITHS IN LONDON:** 30,000
- **NUMBER OF MINUTES BIG BEN WAS SLOWED DOWN WHEN A FLOCK OF BIRDS LANDED ON THE MINUTE HAND IN 1945:** 5

PEOPLE AND CUSTOMS

Mother Tongues

"Native" Brits come in four basic flavors–English, Irish, Scottish, and Welsh, and the corresponding languages are all still spoken, although English is the dominant tongue in all four countries. Wales has preserved their native tongue the best, with Welsh translations on every sign and official document and a reasonable percentage of fluent speakers. Irish Gaelic is being aggressively preserved by the Irish government, with classes taught in primary schools. Scottish Gaelic is not as widely taught, and lingers mainly in the outer islands.

Just Ducking Around

When it comes to slang, you might think the British just make it up on the spot. Poultry inspires affectionate names for girls, which include "bird" and "duck." Derogatory language is particularly entertaining. Let's be honest: if you're called a "big girl's blouse" or "namby pamby" (translation for both: wimp) will you be able to keep a straight face?

FOOD AND DRINK

Let's Go Pubbin'

Bars constitute a huge part of culture all over Great Britain, especially tourist-filled London. Pub-goers won't have to tip, but that's only because there's no table service, so sidle up to the bartender for some shots. Ordering at the bar usually proves an exciting way to meet a fellow Carlsberg connoisseur. England predominantly brews ales, a variety of which can be found in any pub with a feisty crowd looking to down some premium bitter pale ale.

Know Your Meats

Fish and chips (to be eaten with malt vinegar rather than ketchup) continue as the go-to "experience" of eating in England. Order "bangers and mash" if you're craving some sausage slathered in onion gravy and mashed potatoes. For the pork lovers, a pork pie cooked from lard pastry with chopped pork bits topped off with pork jelly should satisfy your porker. The more carniverous traveler may also enjoy shepherd's pie, a lamb casserole dish covered with a layer of mashed potatoes.

Are They Pudding Us On?

Bread and butter, sticky toffee, spotted dick suet—just a few of the pudding varieties on the menu in Brtain. The Brits hold pudding in a special place (and it's not their hearts). Mind you, English pudding is not swimply sweet and jiggly. In Britain, the term refers to any rich, dairy-based dessert. Other non-sweet savory dishes also take the name, like Yorkshire pudding, black pudding, and blood pudding.

Tea for Two

Avoid stuffing yourself too much during lunch time when in London in order to make room for afternoon tea, the light English meal eaten a few hours before dinner. Originating in the 17th century when Catherine of Braganza brought the custom over from Portugal, it is now make it an essential part of the day. Loose tea served with milk and sugar accompanies cucumber and cress sandwiches, scones, and other jam pastries. Some Brits prefer High Tea to replace afternoon tea and dinner. This informal meal usually consists of cold meats, sandwiches, and small desserts; don't think it's an elaborate, high-class tea party. It originated when the family was too lazy to cook anything substantial. Oops.

Gastronomic Multiculturalism

London's Chinatown, located just beyond Leicester Square, houses various super-markets, as well as cheap restaurants for a meal with a little bit of (Kung) Pao. Indian food is readily accessible on Brick Lane in East London. Lined with cafés and shops, the area's potent smell of spices and curry is impossible to avoid. Middle Eastern fare is represented by many eateries.

HOLIDAYS AND FESTIVALS

Boxing Day

December 26th is now just a practical post-Christmas day off to be spent lazing in pajamas or traveling home from holiday trips. Originally it was celebrated by the servant classes that were required to work on Christmas Day; the "boxing" part of the name refers to the practice of rich families boxing up their unwanted clothes or gifts and sending them home with the servants. The origin of regifting!

The Queen's Birthday

Her Majesty's day of birth is celebrated on varying Saturdays in June. The current Queen's actual date of birth is April 21st, but the holiday is celebrated in the sum-mertime in the hopes that the weather will cooperate with the agenda of parades, picnics, and announcement of the Birthday Honours or "who's getting knighted."

Bank Holidays

These are public holidays declared each year by the Queen. Bank Holidays occur each year in May and August, as well as several other statutory days, depending on region. St Patrick's Day, for example, is a Bank Holiday in Northern Ireland, but not in England, Scotland, or Wales.

Guy Fakwes' Day

"Remember, remember the fifth of November, the gunpowder, treason and plot." This day commemorates Guy Fawkes' failed attempts to blow up the houses of Parliament. Lots of bonfires, lots of fireworks, lots of burning in effigy.

Cambridge Folk Festival

Held in Cherry Hinton Hall in one of Cambridge's suburban villages, the annual music gathering brings together a widespread variety of folk musicians. Broadcast live on BBC Radio, the festival's two main stages serve as host to burgeoning figures in the British music industry. With previous performers including Paul Simon and Joan Baez, the venue acts as somewhat of a career launcher. Folk lovers usually grab umbrellas and lounge chairs to shelter themselves from weather and relax during the long three-day weekend in late July. Since gaining popularity from its inception in 1964, tickets have sold out immediately in most recent years.

Lord Mayor's Show

When King John granted a charter for the citizens of London to elect their own Lord Mayor in 1215, he may not have imagined the pageantry that would follow Londoners into the modern era, where flamboyant floats and garish costumes decorate the streets each year on the second Saturday in November. Historically, the proceedings took place via horseback or barges on the River Thames—the parade term "floats" was actually derived from the Lord Mayor's traditional romp through the city by boat. In 1710, a drunken flower girl uprooted then-Lord Mayer Sir Gilbert Heathcote from his horse, initiating a change to a state coach procession known for its six-horse coach (only to be outdone by the Queen, who has eight steeds during formal public outings). At 11pm, the parade takes off after swinging by the Mansion House, the Lord Mayor's official residence, to pick the old chap up, stopping by St. Paul's Cathedral to receive the Dean's blessing. The showy ordeal, including the Twelve Great Livery Companies (Merchant Taylors, Haberdashers, Ironmongers and more), usually ends more than three hours later after the procession winds down along the river, followed by an evening spectacle of fireworks.

CZECH REPUBLIC

Throughout the Czech Republic, the vestiges of Bohemian glory and communist rule can be found on the same block. More recently, the '90s sparked the transformation of this country into an alternative, electrifying country. Döner kebabs, *bockwurst*, and Czech cheeses are peddled side by side. Freewheeling youth and a relentless drive toward the modern means endless streets of hip hangouts and vehemently chill attitude, making the cities here, especially Prague, some of the best student urban destinations in Europe. And even though the locals might be too cool for school they do appreciate a tenacity to learn, evident from all the Czechs who cheer your blatantly wrong attempts at their language. Whether they're dishing out heapings of local cuisine on your plate, sharing beers at a lowkey Prague pub, or inviting you to a local party, the citizens will open their arms to you.

greatest hits

- **UNDERGROUND AND UNDER THE INFLUENCE.** Get lost in the subterranean labyrinth of U Sudu bar and club (p. 247).
- **SNACK HOURS.** Support a family business by pigging out on baked goods at Café Šlagr (p. 244).
- **FAST FOOD.** Walk your hot dog through Wenceslas Square before heading to the National Museum (see p. 222).
- **SAMPLE (S)ALE.** Muster up some liquid courage with an 8-beer sampler at Pivovarský Dům (p. 236).

student life

Chock full of amazing hostels, **Nové Město** is the perfect place for penny pinchers to meet frugal friends. But there's more to life than Wi-Fi and luggage lockers, so plan some sightseeing for a steal and venture out into Prague's other neighborhoods. Get your culture on in **Malá Strana** with some state-sanctioned public art, or admire the graffiti in the bohemian paradise of **Žižkov.** Drop some Banksy knowledge on the students walking to lectures at the University of Economics, and convince them to cut class for a cold one at **Vinohrady's** amazing biergartens. Did your pregame turn into a game? Work off your beer belly by busting a move with some dancing queens in the nearby gay district.

prague ☎224

Since the Commies got the boot 20 years ago, Prague has worked overtime to shape up its act. And shape up it has: this former crumbling communist puppet has become a prime tourist Metropolis that showcases the history of a former center of the Western world. And we're talking grade-A top choice history here. Take **Jan Hus**—who kind of invented Protestantism. Jan got into some hot water here back in 1413; it only got hotter on the stake.

Holy Roman Emperor Charles IV ruled one of Europe's largest kingdoms from Prague and built a city of medieval wonders in the process: towers, castles, statues of himself, bridges with his name on it, universities named "Charles," more Charles statues. Real charmer, that Charles.

And let's not forget Prague's defenestration, that classy tradition of tossing politicians from windows, which happened thrice from Prague's various towers. Thanks to the renovations, these towers now shimmer like new, as if calling you to enact a defenstration of your own—maybe of that irritating chatterbox couple in your hostel. Either way, the city will be sparkling clean and a pleasure for the eye.

However, beautification has come at the price of a general Disney-fication of

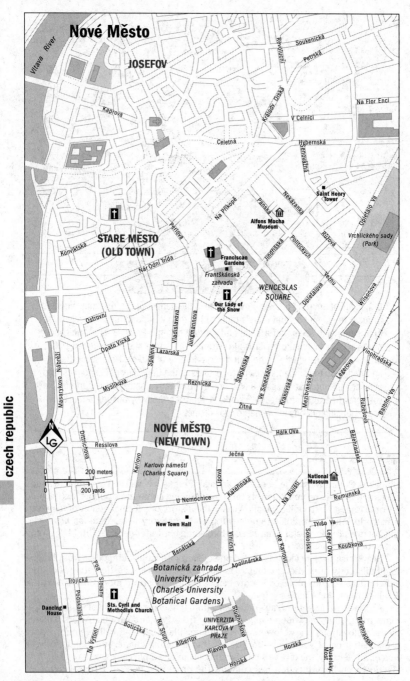

Nové Město

JOSEFOV

Vltava River

Soukenická

Revoluční

Petrská

Kaprova

Kaňov. Dická

Na Flor Encl

V Celnici

Celetná

Hybernská

Senovážná

Na Příkopě

Na Flor Encl

Nekázanka

Saint Henry Tower

Panská

Alfons Mucha Museum

Opletalo Va

Perlová

STARE MĚSTO (OLD TOWN)

Konviktská

Nár Odní Třída

Franciscan Gardens

Frantškánská zahrada

Jindřišská

Politických

Růžová

Vrchlického sady (Park)

Wilsonova

Vežnu

Our Lady of the Snow

WENCESLAS SQUARE

Opletalova

Vinohradská

Ostrovní

Odato Vlčká

Vladislavova

Jungmannova

Spálená

Lazarská

Štěpánská

Ve Smečkách

Krakovská

Mezibranská

Legerova

Rubešova

Babhlno Va

Masarykovo Nábřeží

Myslíkova

Řeznická

Žitná

Bělehradská

Dittrichova

Resslova

NOVÉ MĚSTO (NEW TOWN)

Hálk OVa

czech republic

N

LG

0   200 meters

0   200 yards

Karlovo

Karlovo náměstí (Charles Square)

Ječná

Lipová

Kateřinská

Na Bojišti

National Museum

Rumunská

U Nemochce

Tyršo Va

Leger OVa

Sokolská

Koubkova

New Town Hall

Viničná

Ke Karlovu

Benátská

Apolinárská

Wenzigova

Botanická zahrada University Karlovy (Charles University Botanical Gardens)

Pod Slovany

Trojická

Podskalská

Na Výtoni

Sts. Cyril and Methodius Church

Boticská

Na Slupi

Studničkova

UNIVERZITA KARLOVA V PRAZE

Dancing House

Albertov

Hlavova

Horská

Horská

Nuselský Most

Bělehradská

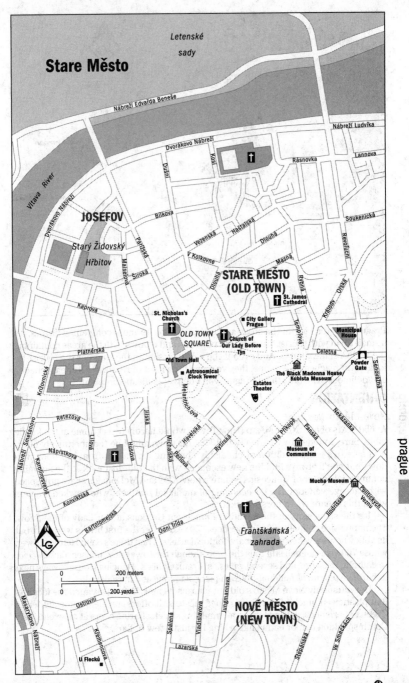

Letenské sady

Stare Město

Nábřeží Edvarda Beneše

Nábřeží Ludvíka

Dvořákovo Nábřeží

Kostí

Rásnovka

Lannova

Vltava River

Dušní

Dvořákovo Nábřeží

JOSEFOV

Bílkova

Vezeňská

Haštalská

Dlouhá

Soukenická

Revoluční

Starý Židovský
Hřbitov

Maiselova

Široká

V Kolkovne

Dlouhá

Masná

Pařížská

Kaprova

Rybná

Krakov Olská

STARE MĚSTO
(OLD TOWN)

Templová

St. Nicholas's
Church ✝

■ City Gallery
Prague

St. James
✝ Cathedral

Platnérská

OLD TOWN
SQUARE

✝ Church of
Our Lady Before
Tyn

Municipal
House

Old Town Hall

Celetná

Powder
Gate

Senovážná

Křižovnická

■ Astronomical
Clock Tower

🏛 The Black Madonna House/
Kublsta Museum

Melantrichova

Estates
Theater

Retězová

Jilská

Michalská

Haveiská

Rytířská

Na Příkopě

Panská

Nekázanka

Náplavní Smetanovo

Liliová

Husova

Perlová

🏛 Museum of
Communism

Náprstkova

✝

Karolínyské

Konviktská

Mucha Museum 🏛

Politických
Veznú

Jindřišká

Bartolomejská

✝

Nár. Odní Třída

Frantškánská
zahrada

Na

N
LG

200 meters

200 yards

Ostrovní

NOVÉ MĚSTO
(NEW TOWN)

Jungmannova

Vladislavova

Masarykovo Nábřeží

Křemencova

Spálená

Lazarská

Štěpánská

Ve Smečkách

■ U Flecků

prague

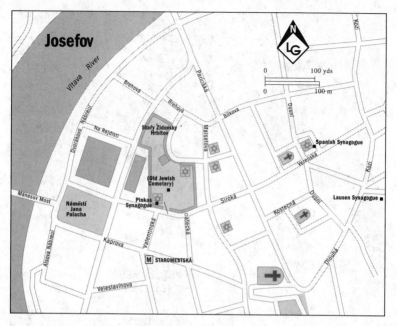

Prague. But don't let this be an excuse to miss out on its more compelling flavors; it's a small town with tourist districts that rub buns and elbows with the areas containing the real Czech Kahunas. And even if the reality is that in the summer the tourist-to-local ratio reaches nine to one, they've come for a a set of reasons: it's cheap, cheery, and delicious. The only thing Prague won't deliver is disappointment.

ORIENTATION

Nové Město *New Town*

At 650 years of age, Nové Město (New Town) would hardly feel at home at the kiddie table. Sure, founded by Charles IV in 1348, this town might be "comparatively new." And sure, it's got a tradition of childishly chucking its leaders from top floor windows but you'll always find the new esconced with the old. Just look at the booming commercial center of Wenceslas Square where KFC and McDonalds share grill space with sausage vendors, the descendants of medieval butchers who hawked weiners when this square was a horse market.

It's the same story at the beautiful Franciscan Gardens at Our Lady of the Snow. The impressive chapel still holds services 650 years after the first bricks were laid, but its abbey now serves as gallery space for local artists. Then there's Saint Henry's Tower, whose 700-year-old bell still tolls the time, though the tower now houses a *whiskeria*, restaurant, museum, and several galleries. Frank Gehry's "Dancing House" sways next to baroque tenement buildings like a hipster skanking at a masquerade.

But ultimately Nové Město's old out-charms its new. Having escaped the facelifts that plasticized much of Old Town, Nové Město still offers travelers some authentic Czech experiences: getting lost on a crumbling street, sharing beers at an exclusively Czech-speaking bar, or eating like a king for just a few dollars.

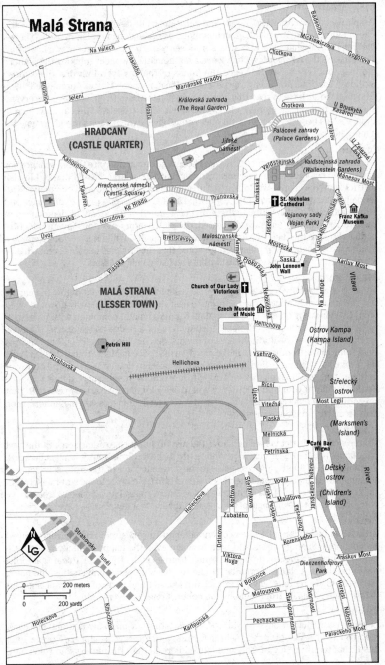

Malá Strana

Na Valech · U Prašného
U Brusnice
Jelení
Mariánské Hradby
Baderího
Mickiewiczova · Gogolova
Chotkova

Královská zahrada
(The Royal Garden)

Mostu

**HRADČANY
(CASTLE QUARTER)**

Jiřské
náměstí

Chotkova
U Brusských
Kasáren

Palácové zahrady
(Palace Gardens)

Klárov
U Železné
Lávky

Kanovnická

Hradčanské náměstí
(Castle Square)

U Kasáren

Valdštejnská

Valdštejnská zahrada
(Wallenstein Gardens)
Mánesův Most

Loretánská · Nerudova
Ke Hradu

Thunovská

Tomašská

Cihelná

St. Nicholas
Cathedral

Úvoz

Bretislavova

Malostranské
náměstí

Vojanovy sady
(Vojan Park)

Mostecká

Franz Kafka
Museum

Vlašská

Prokopská

Saská
**John Lennon
Wall**

Karlův Most

Vltava

**MALÁ STRANA
(LESSER TOWN)**

Church of Our Lady
Victorious

Nebovidská

Na Kampě

Strahovská

Czech Museum
of Music

Hellichova

Ostrov Kampa
(Kampa Island)

■ Petřín Hill

Hellichova

Všehrdova

Říční

Střelecký
ostrov

Viteźná

Most Legií

Plaská

*(Marksmen's
Island)*

Melnická

Petřínská

Holeckova

Vodní

Štefánkova

Elišky Peškové

Janáčkovo Nábřeží

■Café Bar
Wigwa

Dětský
ostrov
*(Children's
Island)*

River

Malátová

Koŕkovská

Zubatého

Drtinova

Korenského

Viktora
Huga

Jiráskův Most

Dienzenhofероvy
Park

Horejsi
Nabrezi

V Botanice

Matoušova

Staropramenná

Svornosti

Lisnicka

Holeckova

Pechackova

Palackého Most

Kartouzská

Kmochova

0 ——— 200 meters
0 ——— 200 yards

Strahovský Tunel

prague · orientation

Stare Město

Despite being overrun with tourists and dog dung while distinctly lacking in authentic Czech culture, Old Town still enchants like a princess doped on charm pills. There's **Old Town Hall,** or what's left of it after sore-loser Nazis bombed it on the war's last day. Then there's the **Astronomical Clock Tower,** a mathematical wonder tracking the planet's motions. **Our Lady Before Tyn** keeps the bones of the guy who first described those motions. Last but not least, there's **Estates Theater** where Mozart "premiered" Don Giovanni. You'll have to read this history between the lines (well, between the crystal shops and marionette stores), but even though wiser travelers will eat and sleep in Prague's less besieged quarters, no one—not even he who passes through Prague for a mere hour—should miss the Old Town.

Josefov

Josefov is the Jewish district of Prague whose main attractions are the six synagogues and the old cemetery. It may seem surprising that such a large, clearly marked Jewish district survives in post-World War II Europe; in fact, during the Nazi occupation Hitler demarcated the area as a future glorified museum of a soon-to-be extinct race and stored pillaged Jewish artifacts there. Because much of the area was demolished in the late 19th century and never restored, the 20th century Art Nouveau architecture is tinged by the district's lingering medieval quality. While it is certainly worth a visit to the synagogues, it must also be noted that the area has become somewhat of a tourist trap, with over-priced restaurants and souvenir peddlers.

Malá Strana

Malá Strana, literally "Lesser Town," is so-called for its placement below the castle, but geographically Malá Strana continues past the Castle, all the way down to what would be **Vinohrady** on the East side. Malá Strana's length, combined with its assortment of yuppie artistic types, make it something of a hodge-podge district. Crowds storm the castle in the northern area of the district, but the sparser southern regions host some of the trendiest digs in the city. The other ace in Malá Strana's hole is **Petřín Hill,** Prague's "Olympus." Petřín has the highest point in Prague and is so full of flower gardens that you'll think you've tripped into one of your sister's dumb romance books. Finally, if your doctor ordered you to see a lot of public art, you can "fill" that prescription in Malá Strana. If he ordered you to avoid unnecessary metaphors, then don't read the previous sentence.

Hradčany

Prague's castle district is located above the rest of the city, providing some of the best panoramas and the biggest crowds. While a trip to the top is obligatory, it might be worth keeping an open mind and a resistance to the magnetic force of the crowds, as some of the quaintest architecture and most serene streets in the city are found several meters in the opposite direction of the cathedral on **Novy Svet.** A grassy knoll hidden by trees above Novy Svet also offers an angle of the gothic cathedral that few tourists have witnessed.

Žižkov

Žižkov is a bohemian paradise with enough graffiti (or "street art") murals sprayed on abandoned garage doors and bars to make even the happy-go-lucky feel a little emo. Perhaps the biggest draw for average tourists is the freaky TV tower that looks like a needle in a stack of crumbs. Home to one of Prague's universities, the quiet, hilly streets are reminiscent of Paris's Latin Quarter and parts of San Francisco, but Žižkov's are set apart from them by the cobblestones on every path.

Vinohrady

Legend has it that in days of yore, Princess Libuse, a probably-fictional-princess, stood on a hill at Vinohrady's Vyšehrad fortress and foresaw the glory of Prague. Fact has it that the first King of Bohemia landed here in the 11th century and ruled here

Hradčany

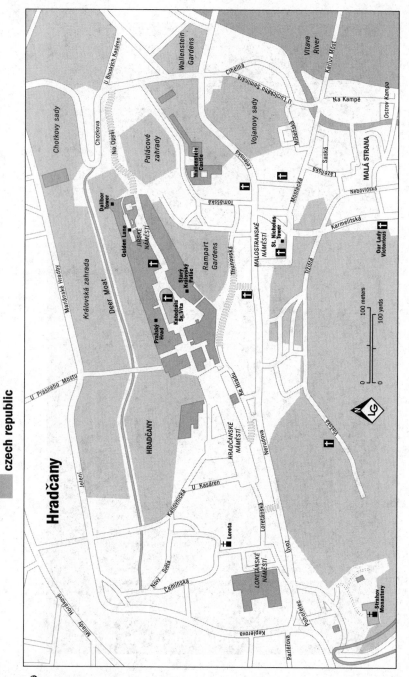

until Charles IV moved across the river. Let's Go has it that Vinhorady is a relaxed neighborhood with the best green spaces and *biergartens* in the city, a lively gay district, and some of the best and cheapest eats. The Vyšehrad cultural monument should really not be missed since it contains the **Church of Saint Peter and Saint Paul**, visible from nearly any point in Prague, and the **Vyšehrad cemetery**, which houses Dvorak's bones and the oldest Roman chapel in the city. Additionally the neighborhood is a great setting for a beautiful afternoon walk with a great view of the river and a better view of Czech kiddies swapping tongues along the fortress wall. For the best sweets in the entire city—maybe the entire world—try out Vinohrady's **Café Šlagr**.

Holešovice

Without question, the most underappreciated neighborhood in all of Prague is Holešovice, which has some of the coolest sites that aren't just enjoyable because a guidebook tells you they're important. From **Cross Club,** which might be the best club in Europe, to **Křižík's Fountain,** an incredible water and light show accompanied by ballet, to Prague's biggest open air market, these sites are alive, fresh and full of Czech youth.

Dejvice

Dejvice is mostly for the old and tired or the middle-aged and child-bearing. It's no surprise that one can barely find a tourist on the streets of Dejvice, because unlike the undiscovered parts behind Prague Castle, this district simply has little to offer the foreigner. Apart from a few good restaurants, most of which are light-years beyond a backpacker's budget, a cool fountain, and a gigantic flowery roundabout, the neighborhood is best left for those to come: the area is under construction, so who knows what the future will hold for Dejvice.

Smichov

Smichov is a area of Prague's fifth district that boasts a giant shopping complex, several quality restaurants that are far less expensive than anything found in central Prague, the Staropramen brewery, and lush greenery that provide visitors with a welcome and off-the-beaten path respite from the main attractions and noise of the Old Town streets.

ACCOMMODATIONS

Accommodations in Prague differ greatly. Thanks to the openning of some new "chic" hostels throughout the city (Mosaic House, Sir Toby's, Miss Sophie's, Czech Inn), travelers willing to pay a bit extra (or sometimes, even not) can find digs with full bedding, in-house restaurants and top quality Wi-Fi. Those who want that hostel-specific thrill of wondering if your roomate's going to kill you won't be disappointed, as there are many "earthy" options throughout the city. In general, Stare Město costs more and offers less, while Nové Město costs less and offers more. Several large hostels in Holešovice start resembling hotels (or fantastic, cushy communes) but require a Metro ride to visit sites, and might be a bit out of the way for most travellers, especially lazy ones. Finally, a note on prices. The prices included are simply approximates. Most Prague hostels price with an algorithm that takes into account the time of year, the fullness of the hostel and the current rate of demand for rooms. This system rewards those who book in advance.

Nové Město *New Town*

▩ MOSAIC HOUSE
Odborů 4

♥♿ HOSTEL, HOTEL ❷
☎725 84 67 73 ■www.mosaichouse.com

Mosaic House, Prague's newest and most luxurious hostel, understands what makes hostels great: a restaurant/bar/stage-venue with live music, a carpeted lounge space with bean bags, and Wi-Fi that's fast and omnipresent. But what makes Mosaic the (pre-hooker) Tiger Woods of Prague hostels is how it improves the tiny annoyances of hostels. Bunks in large dorms have privacy curtains, lighting is indirect instead of overpowering, and the rooms have soft beds and bountiful power outlets. Even

Mosaic's few faults come in pursuit of noble goals, like lights over-eagerly shut off to save power. Still, you gotta respect that this hostel has the only greywater heat recycling system in the Czech Republic. Hotel rooms are 4-star, which bodes well for hostel rooms, which are basically the same with bunks.

*# B: Karlovo namesti. From the station, head north along the west edge of the park. At the northwest corner of the park, take a left at Odborů. **i** Netbooks 40-50Kč per hr. Women-only room available. Non-smoking. 4 computers available 1Kč per minute. Breakfast 150Kč. Towel 100Kč deposit, free for hotel guests. Lockers included. Safe box at desk. $ Dorms 250-550Kč. Doubles (hotel room) 1700-1900/room. ⏰ Reception 24hr. Check-in 3pm. Check-out 11am.*

MISS SOPHIE'S

⊗📶❄ HOSTEL [1]

Meloundvá 3 ☎293 303 0530 💻www.miss-sophies.com

A bit out of the way and a bit more expensive than the cheapest hostel, Miss Sophie's is nevertheless the best bang for your buck in Nové Město. Genuinely cool modern designs including mural-sized original artwork line the newly-painted walls. Steel and glass showers are classier than what you'll find in most hotels. With polished wood floors, comfortable leather couches, flatscreen TV, and DVD library, it's easy to forget this is an accomodation for budget travelers.

*# C: IP Pavlova. Take 1st left from platform, then follow Katerinska to 1st right, onto Melounová. **i** Wi-Fi included and 2 computers with Internet available. Kitchens in some rooms. Most staff members are students. $ Dorms 410Kč; singles 1150Kč. Apartment 1390Kč. Towels 30Kč. 5% discount with ISIC student card if booked online. 4% additional charge if you pay with a credit card. ⏰ Reception 24hr. No curfew. Check-in 3pm. Check-out 11am.*

prague didn't get the memo

You know, the one for buildings that goes something like "brown, black, white or tan, please!" All over this cramped and faded city, the story—the more colorful story—is the same.

Prague just didn't feel the need to bow down to the social norms that dictate which colors a legitimate office building can be painted. Maybe it was a reaction to the communist-era repression of expression, or maybe it's just the Czech effort to offset the Slavic gloom. Whatever the reason, a randomly chosen Prague street wears mostly pinks, yellows, greens and purples, leaving earth tones to its less-daring Metropolitan colleagues.

The real shame is that the city hasn't had a decent paint job since the 1960s, and back then, photographs were taken in black and white.

However, the future may be bright! Tourist boom profits have already done wonders for Prague's impeccably refurbished cobblestone streets, and if tourist swarms continue to descend, we might soon see Prague returned to its former Easter Egg glory.

CHILI HOSTEL

⊗📶🍸 HOSTEL [1]

Pštrossova 7, 110 00 Praha 1 ☎60 311 9113 💻www.chili.dj

Chili Hostel can't be beat when it comes to price and community. Large, comfortable common rooms, kitchens, and dining areas play host to nightly multi-national pregames, supported by the front desk's ample beverage service. Rooms are bunk-heavy and lack adornment besides the occasional chair, but bathrooms are kept very clean and well-stocked.

*# B: Národní trida. From the station, walk south on Spálená, make a right on Myslíkova, and then another right on Pštrossova. **i** Non-smoking. Wi-Fi included and is reliable on most floors. Very large breakfast 89Kč. Linens, towels, and lockers included; laundry available for stays of 5 days or*

more. $ *Dorms from 200Kč; singles 400Kč. Key deposit 200Kč.* ⏰ *Reception 24hr. Quiet time starts at 2:30am. Check-in 2pm. Check-out 10am.*

AZ HOSTEL
🚫⊗📶 HOSTEL ❶

Jindřišské 5, 110 Praha 1 ☎22 424 1664 🖥www.hostel-az.cz

With large rooms at reasonable prices, AZ Hostel is especially ideal for travelers looking to keep to themselves. Full linens come with every room, and no rooms have bunk beds. All the rooms have wood floors and free lockers. No private showers available. Passably comfortable common room has a small TV and free coffee and tea.

🚇 *A or B: Mustek. From the station, walk up the square toward the National Museum, then make a left on Jindřišské; the hostel will be on your left.* ℹ *Laundry service 190Kč per load. Computer use 20Kč per 10min. Wi-Fi and lockers included. Power adapters available upon request.* $ *Dorms 320Kč; singles 950Kč.* ⏰ *Reception 24hr. Check-in noon. Check-out 10:30am.*

THE WELCOME PRAGUECENTER HOSTEL
💳⊗❄ HOSTEL ❶

Žitna 17, 11000 Prague 1 ☎22 432 0202 🖥www.bed.cz

Possibly the worst-named hostel in the city, Welcome Praguecenter provides some impressively luxurious private rooms for, in some cases, dormitory prices. Located on the second floor of an apartment building, its rooms resemble apartments with glass tables and king-sized beds. Refrigerators and safe boxes are available in each room. Small bathrooms, and the lack of common spaces and a kitchen are the only downfalls of this hostel...except for the name, of course.

🚇 *B: Karlovo náměstí. From the station, head away from the river down Žitna.* ℹ *Reservations 1-2 weeks in advance recommended. Sheets and towels included. No breakfast.* $ *All private rooms. 400Kč for bed with shared facilites. 500Kč for bed with private facilties.* ⏰ *Check-in 9am-9pm (call ahead if you'll be later). Check-out by 11:30am. No parties after 10pm.*

Stare Město

OLD PRAGUE HOSTEL
🚫♿🍸 HOSTEL ❷

Benedikstská 2 ☎224 829 058 🖥www.oldpraguehostel.com

Run by the same guys as Prague Square hostel, Old Prague just has a homier, more welcoming feeling to it. Perhaps because an old-school, exposed elevator services the hostel's five stories, but either way, Old Prague does a few things better than its sister hostel. Perhaps most importantly, its desk sells beer in addition to soft drinks. Common areas also have flatscreen TVs and comfortable couches. Rooms are nice and roomy. Beds sit a little close to the ground, and some of the rooms have mental-asylum padded doors, but the brightly colored artwork keeps the experience interesting.

🚇 *B: Náměstí Republiky. From the station, walk north on Revoluční. Take a left on Dlouhá and another quick left onto Benedikstská.* ℹ *Non-smoking. Breakfast, towels, linens, lockers, adapters, irons, and hair dryers included. Wi-Fi available on the mezzanine and in the common area. Key deposit 100Kč.* $ *8-bed dorms 295-430Kč; 4-bed dorms 431-539Kč; doubles 539-700Kč.* ⏰ *Reception 24hr. Check-in 2pm. Check-out 10am.*

PRAGUE SQUARE HOSTEL
🚫♿ HOSTEL ❷

Melantrichova 10 ☎224 240 859 🖥www.praguesquarehostel.com

A well-kept joint in a well-frequented part of town, Prague Square Hostel is uncommonly generous with travel amenities. Unfortunately, it also suffers from some typical Old Town maladies. No laundry service and a sparsely stocked desk store mean travelers are on their own. The rooms are clean, if at times a bit small and the sheets are strangely, but cheerfully, colorful.

🚇 *A or B: Můstek. From the station, head north on na Můstku and continue on it as it turns into Melantrichova. The hostel will be on your right.* ℹ *Non-smoking. Hair dryers, irons, adapters, towels, linens, lockers, and breakfast (8am-10am) included. Free computer access and Wi-Fi in common spaces.* $ *8-bed dorms 300-450Kč; 4-bed 300-530Kč. Singles 645-750Kč; doubles 950-1250Kč.* ⏰ *Reception 24hr. Check-in 2pm. Check-out 10am.*

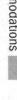

Hradčany

👍 ROMANTIK HOTEL U RAKA
💳♿📶🍸❄🚭 HOTEL [5]

Černínská 10 ☎220 511 100 💻www.romantikhotel-uraka.cz

Housed in the only timbered building in Prague, this romantic little hotel is nestled in a quiet corner of Hradčany. This is a giant splurge for a backpacker, but perfect for a couple in search of a magical stay, providing the best of both worlds: a forest escape from all that is the tourist influx of Prague, while being just a skip down the cobblestone street from it. The hotel is run by a family of genial artists who are only too excited to make your visit to Prague better than the movies.

⇟ Tram #22: Brusnice. From the tram, walk across the street and onto the path that leads towards the trees. Walk down the giant staircase and the hotel will be on the left directly at the base of the stairs. ***i*** *Breakfast included.* [S] *Singles 2280Kč; doubles from 3674Kč.* ⏰ *Reception 8am-10pm. Check-in 2pm. Check-out 11am.*

Žižkov

👍 HOSTEL ELF
💳♿📶🍸🚭 HOSTEL [2]

Husitská 11 ☎222 540 963 💻www.hostelelf.com

The perfect place to stay for those who wouldn't mind crashing on a couch in a friend's apartment that's covered (intentionally) in graffiti. The common room is the center of hostel life, with seven enormous, thoroughly lived-in couches and a communal kitchen nearby. Clean and simply furnished dorms with shared hall baths.

⇟ Trams #5, 9, or 26: Husinecká Tram #stop. From the Tram #stop, follow Husinecká until you reach the square and then make a left at Orebitská, which will run into Husinecká right in front of the hostel. ***i*** *Bike storage available. Breakfast included.* [S] *6-to-9 bed dorms 370Kč; 11-bed dorm 340Kč; singles with bath 1230Kč. Prices go down in low season. 5% discounts in dorms for students.* ⏰ *Reception 24hr. Check-in 2pm. Check-out 10am.*

Vinohrady

CZECH INN
💳♿📶🍸 HOSTEL [1]

Francouská 76 ☎267 26 76 00 💻www.czech-inn.com

Justifiably billing itself as a "designer hostel," Czech Inn takes pains to distinguish itself from the rest of the humdrum hostel world. The lobby and bar areas serve double duty as an art gallery, and every six weeks the hostel changes the art and throws a "gallery opening," complete with wine and snacks. That appreciation for detail extends into the rooms, which have sleek single-sheet glass showers with polished concrete floors.

⇟ A: Náměstí Míru. From the station, walk southeast along Francouská. The hostel will be on your right. ***i*** *Wi-Fi and lockers included. 8 computers available; 1Kč per min. Towels 30Kč with a 100Kč deposit. Breakfast 120Kč at check-in, 140Kč the morning of. Dinner 120-180Kč. Beer 33-55Kč. The entire hostel is smoke-free.* [S] *Dorms 295-472Kč. Singles 1540-2282Kč; doubles 1320-1694Kč. Apartments 1650-2544Kč.* ⏰ *Reception 24hr.*

Holešovice

👍 SIR TOBY'S HOSTEL
💳📶🍸 HOSTEL [1]

Dělnická 24 ☎246 032 610 💻www.sirtobys.com

A quirky, comfortable, feels-like-your-mom-was-involved-in-preparing-your-room kind of hostel where details matter, Sir Toby's combines the efficiency and cleanliness of a large hostel with the intimacy and community of a small one. To start, Sir Toby's room's are identified by respective theme rather than numbers, and they're decorated accordingly. The quirks continue into the grill-equipped back garden where the tables are all old sewing machines. The pub downstiars *(Beer 20-35Kč)* hosts subtitled Czech movie screenings, live concerts, and DJs on a regular basis. There's a hot, all-you-can-shove-down-your-pie-hole breakfast *(100Kč)* from 8:30-11:30am, while Afghani or Czech homemade dinner plates are available nightly *(100-120Kč)*. Guests can also use the modern communal kitchen. Brochures, signs, and homemade guidebooks in the lobby will keep you informed, since you, like Steve Tyler during the filming of Armageddon, "Don't Want To Miss a Thing." But best of all, Sir Toby's is that rarest of things: a hostel without any of the classic hostel musk.

C: Vltavská. From the station, take any Tram #that departs to the left. Ride it 2 stops to Dělnická. Walk to the traffic lights and turn left onto Dělnická. ℹ *Lockers included. Towels 15Kč with a 200Kč deposit. Laundry service costs 200Kč, self-serve 100Kč. Wi-Fi is free, and 5 computers are available at 1 Kč per min.* $ *Dorm 220-400Kč, women's dorm 400-560Kč. Singles 950Kč; doubles 1200Kč.* ⏰ *Reception 24hr. Buzz to enter.*

PRAGUE PLUS HOSTEL ❶

Prívozní 1, 170 00 Praha 7 ☎22 051 0046 🖥www.plusprague.com

A large and tightly-run establishment, Prague Plus feels a bit like foreign summer camp for students. Excitement revolves around the "restaurant," which is secret talk for "enormous effing dining hall" that includes a nightly DJ, a full service bar *(beer 40Kč, mixed drinks 80-120Kč)*, a full service grill *(85-150Kč)*, 5 flatscreen TVs, two tricked out with Nintendo Wiis, a pool and foosball tables, and plenty of horizontal surfaces for getting friendly (wink!). Back at the hotel, a swimming pool and nightly movie screenings let the quiet folk interact quietly. Women-only rooms include hairdryers and vanity sets. The breakfast buffet *(100Kč)* consists of meats, beans, eggs, and cheeses. Prague Plus is one of the best handicap-accessible accommodations in Prague. Before you leave the lobby, say hello to Boris the turtle, who is not dead, but "just sleeping."

C: Nadraží Holešovice. From the station, go 1 stop on any Tram #heading north, or just walk down Ortenovo Namesti in the direciton of the Hotel Plaza Alta. ℹ *Laundry 170 Kč. Breakfast 100 Kč. Linens and lockers included. Free Wi-Fi in lobby and restaurant plus a few free-to-use computers in the lobby and restaurant. Non-smoking.* $ *Sept-June mixed dorms 260-380Kč, women only 300-420Kč; singles 1000Kč; doubles 500Kč. July-Aug 1400Kč/700Kč/380-570Kč/400-590Kč.* ⏰ *Reception 24hr. Check in 3pm. Check out 10am.*

Smichov

ARPACAY HOSTEL HOSTEL ❷

Radlická 76 ☎251 552 297 🖥www.arpacayhostel.com

This hostel—a little ways from central Prague, but a pleasant escape from the throngs of tourist shops—will provide you with a quiet evening for well-rested repose. The hostel has two buildings across from each other and boasts giant breakfast rooms, as well as guest kitchens on each floor. The red building has a terrace on the roof where you can take in the view of Prague and beyond.

Trams #12, 14, 20: Plzeňka. From the tram, walk toward the park and up the stairs, across the train tracks. At the intersection, keep walking straight up the hill on Radlická and look for the Arpacay sign on the right. ℹ *Breakfast, linens, and towels included. Computers available. Smoking deck that overlooks much of the city.* $ *3- to 5-bed dorms from 300Kč.* ⏰ *Reception open 7am-midnight. Check-in flexible. Check-out 10am.*

HOSTEL 5 HOSTEL ❶

Plzeňská 540/23 ☎257 324 908 🖥http://hostel5.pl

A low-key, simple, clean hostel where the selling point is no bunks. Other than that, the place is cheap and has a tiny "terrace" with basically one plastic table and a few chairs. A good option for groups because it offers highly discounted deals, as well as breakfast, for over 15 people.

C: Andel. Walk up Plzeňská about 300m. ℹ *Terrace, kitchen, and linens included.* $ *2- to 5-bed dorms 290-320Kč; singles 250-535Kč.* ⏰ *Reception open 10am-noon and 1pm-11pm.*

SIGHTS

Nové Město

🔲 SAINT HENRY TOWER
                                                                       ♿ BELFRY

Jindřišské ulice, Praha 1 ☎22 223 2429 🖥www.jindrisskavez.cz

Originally built from wood in 1475, then again from stone in 1599, the 67.7m tower was designed as a belfry for the nearby Saint Henry's Church. At one time 10 bells rang out from the tower, but neglect and damage over the years has left just one. The remaining 723kg, 101cm diameter bell rings on the hour and half hour. In recent years, the middle portions of the tower have been ingeniously returned to public use as a restaurant, museum, whiskey bar, and several galleries. Admission gets you into the museum and galleries, but it's worth taking the stairs to peek at the tiny restaurant's tables, which are built around the tower's scaffolding system.

  🚇 A or B: Můstek: follow Jindřišské to the end of the street. *i* Elevator access to all but the last 14 steps. Ⓢ Adult 80Kč. Student 55Kč. 🕐 Open M-F 9am-7pm, Sa-Su 10am-7pm.

🔲 NEW TOWN HALL
                                                                   🖐🚫 TOWN HALL

Karlovo náměstí 1/23, 120 00 Praha 2 ☎22 494 8225 🖥www.nrpraha.cz

A building whose history far outsexes its architecture, the New Town Hall served as the administrative headquarters of New Town for nearly 400 years. The Hall's foundations were laid by Charles IV, the granddaddy of Czech modernity. In 1419, a bunch of angry Hussites threw the town counselors out the top story windows in the first Defenestration. While the hall has a few furnished parlors open for viewing, the building's real thrill comes in climbing the seemingly endless series of wooden platforms leading to the lookout tower. Besides the amazing views of of Prague, the top platforms hold a giant bell, which was described as being "currently broken." It was later discovered that this meant it had been broken for the past 200 years.

  🚇 B: Karlovo náměstí. Exit the station and find the giant tower at the north end of the park. Ⓢ Admission 30Kč. Cash only. 🕐 Open Tu-Su 10am-6pm.

WENCESLAS SQUARE
                                                          🖐♿🛜🍴 CITY SQUARE

Originally built by its namesake as a horse market, Václavské náměstí (Wenceslas Square) now sells everything but. American-style commercial department stores and historic hotels compete for attention with the true stars of the walk—the hot dog and sauerkraut vendors selling up to six different types of sausage. In the olden days, butchers would come selling their wares, and that tradition of sausage excellence has held to the present. Up at the top of the boulevard, check out the 🔲**National Museum**, which in addition to being one of the more beautiful buildings in Prague—especially at night—also contains some impressive zoological and paleological exhibits, mostly in Czech. Also noteworthy are the displayed medals of former president Václav Havel.

  🚇 A or B: Můstek or Můsem. Ⓢ Students 100-150Kč.

ALFONS MUCHA MUSEUM
                                                                  🖐♿ MUSEUM

Panská 7, 110 00 Praha ☎22 421 6415 🖥www.mucha.cz

This medium-sized exhibit focuses on Mucha's works, and is a good introduction for those unfamiliar with the Art Nouveau pioneer and all-around Czech hero. The exhibit pays particular attention to Mucha's time in Paris (1887-1904) during which he painted the famous portraits of Sarah Bernhardt that Americans will likely recognize. For the student price, anyone even remotely interested should check it out. Without the student discount, pre-existing appreciation for Mucha is recommended. Don't miss the hilariously over-the-top video about Mucha's construction of the "Slav Epic."

czech republic

🚇 A or B: Můstek. Walk up Václavské náměstí toward the St. Wenceslas statue. Go left on Jindřišské and left again on Panská. $ Admission 160Kč. Students and seniors 80Kč. Guide sheet 30Kč. ⏰ Open daily 10am-6pm.

OUR LADY OF THE SNOW ♿ CHURCH

Jungmannovo náměstí 18, 110 00 Praha 1

Kostel Panny Marie Sněžně (Our Lady of the Snow) remains one of the most oddly-shaped churches in Central Europe. When commissioned by Charles IV in 1347, the church was intended to be the largest in Prague, with three naves and 30m tall ceilings. When the Franciscans arrived to repair the building in 1603, damage from the Hussite Wars prevented them from carrying out the original plan, and only one nave remained along with the impressively large ceilings. Check the chapel door for a schedule of services in order to listen in on incredible organ music against the sweet the voices of the regular parishioners. While you listen to the music, let yourself wonder how they painted such intricate stars on the ceiling. Don't go without checking the miniature chapel on the church's right side, and the exhibits from local artists displayed in the abbey.

🚇 A or B: Můstek. From the station, walk up Wenceslas Sq. and then turn left on Jungmannovo náměstí; the entrance to the church is behind the statue. ⏰ Open daily 6am-7:30pm. Su services at 9am, 10:15am, 11:30am and 6:30pm.

U FLECKŮ ♿🍸 MUSEUM AND BREWERY

Křemencova 11, 110 00 Praha 1 ☎ 22 49 340 1920 🖥 www.efleku.eu

Skip the tacky, overpriced restaurant if you can help it, and take a guided walk of the museum or an hour-long tour of the brewery. Both are obnoxiously designed to convince guests how important the U Fleků Brewery actually is, but the over-aggrandized tales and obsession over uninteresting U Fleků details more persuasively argue the opposite. Still, it's worth visiting if you want to see old brewing techniques without trecking out to to the brewery at Pilsen.

🚇 B: Národní trida. From the station, walk south on Spálená, make a right on Myslíkova, and then another right on Opatovická. Follow it as it cuves around. When it hits Křemencova, take the second left. $ Museum tour 100Kč. Brewery tour 160 Kč. Groups of 10 or more get a 30% discount. Credit cards discouraged, and no discounts will apply if used. ⏰ Tours available by reservation only M-F 10am-4pm. Sa and Su tours must be accompanied by a meal at the restaurant. Restaurant open daily 9am-11pm.

FRANCISCAN GARDENS ♿ GARDEN

A beautiful couple of acres of land, this little oasis between Our Lady of the Snow and the bustling St. Wenceslas square offers a serene escape from the howl of the city. Massive strange light-bulb-like street lamps line the walk, but unfortunately the park closes before we can ever see them in their full glory. Street performers grab spaces in the shade. The picturesque cottage in the middle of the roses is actually a secondhand clothing store, but don't let that stop you from appreciating its tranquility.

🚇 A or B: Můstek. Enter through the arch to the left of Jungmannova and Národní, behind the statue. ⏰ Open daily dawn-dusk.

DANCING HOUSE MONUMENT

Rasinovo Nabrezi 80 120 00 Praha 2

Now approaching its 15th birthday, the Tančící dům (Dancing House) has comfortably become a national icon after being the source of fierce controversy during its inception and construction. Designed by Vlado Milunic and Frank Gehry (of Guggenheim-Bilbao fame), the eight-story office building allegedly resembles an image of Fred Astaire and Ginger Rogers, earning it the early moniker "Fred and Ginger." The building was known as "Drunken House" for years by Czech traditionalists who felt that it had no place amid the neo-Baroque and Art

Noveau architecture of the neighborhood. Through the help of supporters like Václav Havel, however, the building has become one of Prague's most recognizable landmarks. While the top floor is occupied by Céleste, one of Prague's top French restaurants *(entrées 450-900Kč)*, budget travelers can visit the upstairs patio M-Sa 4-6pm for the price of a drink *(150-200Kč)*.

♯ B: Karlovo náměstí. *From the station, walk down Resslova toward the river. The building is on your left.*

EMAUZY

MONASTERY

Vyšehradská 49/320, Prague 2 ☎221 979 211 ■www.emauzy.cz/en/index.php

Walking through the poorly-maintained cloister of Emauzy is a haunting experience. This cloister, which once served as abode to Jan Hus, the theological martyr and revolutionary, and Johannes Kepler, that dude who explained planetary motion, now sits silent. A train museum for children now occupies part of the old abbey, and the frighteningly empty chapel can be toured for the price of a train admission.

♯ B: Karlovo náměstí. *From the park, follow the brown signs to the monastery down Vyšehradská.* ⑤ 50kč. ⌚ *Mass daily 10am. Open M-F 11am-3pm.*

CHURCH OF SAINT IGNATIUS

CHURCH

Ječná 2, 120 00 Praha 2 ☎221 990 200 ■www.jesuit.cz

This Jesuit church is one of the oldest Baroque buildings in Prague and is the third largest Jesuit complex in all of Europe. Built in the second half of the 17th century, this amazing chapel stands out for its brilliant slabs of green, red and yellow marble. The sculpture work on the altar was done by Matěj Václav Jäckel, who is best known for his work on the statues on the Charles Bridge. The figure of St. Ignatius on the church peak was considered semi-heretical in its day, as clerical rules stated that a full-body halo could only be administered to Christ himself.

♯ B: Karlovo náměstí. *From the station, head away from the river toward Ječná. The church will be on the corner.* ⌚ *Open daily 6:15am-5:30pm. Daily mass 5:30pm.*

Stare Město

🖾 CHURCH OF OUR LADY BEFORE TÝN

⊗ CHURCH

Staroměstské náměstí ■tynska.farnost.cz

Our Lady Before Týn dominates the skyline of Old Town Square with two enormous spires sticking out among the surrounding Baroque buildings. Dating back to the 14th century, the church has seen some bizzare happenings and accumulated some colorful residents in its time. For instance, the church contains the remains of the astronomer **Tycho Brahe,** whose notable achievements include helping to describe planetary motion and peeing himself to death or, more accurately, "unpeeing" himself to death. In 1601, Brahe was at Emperor Rudolf's for dinner, and since it was taboo to leave the table before the Emperor did, Tycho just held it until his bladder burst. But on the bright side, he kept decorum. The church's towers reach a staggering 80m into the air; in traditional Gothic style, one of the spires is just a bit smaller than the other. The church's exterior construction is expected to be finished in 2011.

♯ A: Staroměstská. *Just walk towards the giant twin towers.* ⑤ *Free.* ⌚ *Open Tu-Sa 10am-1pm, 3pm-5pm. Su Mass 9:30am and 9pm.*

🖾 CHARLES BRIDGE

BRIDGE

Probably the most famous site in all of Prague, the Charles Bridge is also the bridge Mr. Phelps falls from in the brilliant movie with mediocre sequels, *Mission Impossible.* Charles IV commissioned the bridge to cross the Vltava River in 1357—if you haven't figured it out already, Charles IV is responsible for everything cool in Prague—but the actual design and construction of the crossing was done by the famous architect Peter Parléř. Although the bridge was originally decorated only by a crucifix, the church commissioned 32 statutes for the bridge between 1600 and 1800, featuring shady characters like St. Augustine, St. Anne, and Lamenting Christ. Weather damage forced the city to remove the original statues, which are now on display at the National Gallery. The bridge also features the Old Town Bridge Tower *(Staroměstská mostecká věž)*, which offers an Ethan Hunt's eye view of the city below. Cross the bridge after sundown for an especially titillating experience.

🚇 A: Malonstranská or Staroměstká. $ Tower 70 Kč, students 50 Kč. 🕐 Open daily Nov-Feb 10am-8pm, Mar-Oct 10am-10pm.

ASTRONOMICAL CLOCK TOWER AND OLD TOWN HALL ♿👁 BELFRY

Old Town Square 1/3 ☎724 911 556

🖥www.prazskeveze.cz/staromestska-radnice-a-vez.html

Here's a free lesson: if you build an amazing clock that tells the position of the sun, the moon, and the planets, people will never stop fabricating legends about it. It's said that after the city council hired the famous clockmaker Mikulas of Kadan to build the clock, they gouged out his eyes so he could never repeat his work (talk about worker's comp issues). In reality, the clock was a collaboration between Kadan and Jan Ondrejuv, a professor of mathematics and astronomy, and Kadan built several clocks after this one. The clock also features another clock that moves once a day and has 365 names on it; Czech tradition "requires" parents to name their children one of said names. The day on which the clock points to your name is your "name day," a kind of bastardized birthday. On the hour, the 12 apostles poke their heads out to the crowd, and a rooster crows. Climb or take the elevator to the top of the tower for amazing views of the city. Also available is a not-that-worth-it tour of the Old Town's halls, highlights of which include the back view of the "apostle clock mechanism" and a walk through the the original romanesque basement. This basement served as the original ground floor before the king raised the level of Old Town by 6m or so.

🚇 A: Staroměstká or A or B: Mustek. $ Halls 100 Kč, students 80 Kč. Tower 100 Kč, students 50 Kč. 🕐 Halls open M 11am-6pm, Tu-Su 9-6pm (last tour starts at 5). Towers open M 11am-10pm, Tu-Su 9am-10pm.

ST. NICHOLAS'S CHURCH CHURCH

Parízská Str ☎224 190 994

St. Nicholas might not be one of the "cool cathedrals" that gets slapped on the cover of every guide book, but the chandelier hanging in its center might be the coolest in the city. Given as a gift to Prague in 1787 by Tsar Nicholas II, this crown is an enormous replica of the royal hat that Russian czars wore. The church contains a succinct but impressive exhibit on the history of the church and of Czech Christianity in general. The church was under the control of Benedictine monks for most of its existence, and a plaque on the former Benedectine monastery attached to the building marks the site where Franz Kafka was born.

🚇 A: Staroměstká. A or B: Mustek. Directly behind the Astronomical Clock Tower. $ Free. 🕐 Open M noon-4pm, Tu-Sa 10am-4pm. Su Mass 10:30am, noon, and 3pm.

MUNICIPAL HOUSE 🎫♿🍸 GOVERNMENT BUILDING, CONCERT HALL

Naměstí Republiky 5 ☎222 002 101 🖥www.obecnidum.cz

It might feel a little uncomfortable to get really excited about a state house and a concert hall, but if you visit the Municipal House, this is what will happen to you. Just go with it. Designed in 1911 by Antonin Balšánek and Osvald Polívka in classic Art Nouveau style, this publicly-commissioned state house features specifically-comissionend works from over 20 of the country's top artists. Every detail, from the shape of the door handles to the doors themselves to the patterns on the banisters, are the careful work of some art Noveau master. Daily guided tours take visitors through Smetana Hall, where the Czech Philharmonic plays, and the Mayor's Hall, decorated by the Czech painter, Alfons Mucha. For a trip to the past, stop by Kavárna Obecní Dům located on the ground floor. This incredible Art Noveau cafe features an oh-so-classic fountain by Josef Pekárek and eight enormous chandeliers hanging overhead.

🚇 B: Naměstí Republiky. Walk across the square; Municipal House is the gigantic building on your left. ℹ Tours in Czech and English. Tickets must be purchased on the day of your visit in the ticket office located in the basement of the Municipal House. $ 270Kč, students 220Kč. ⏰ Open daily 10am-7pm. Tour times vary by week and month; check the calendar for details.

THE BLACK MADONNA HOUSE/KUBISTA MUSEUM ✏⊗❄ MUSEUM

Ovocný trh 19 ☎222 321 459 🖥www.ngprague.cz

The Black Madonna House is the best living example of Cubist architecture—a uniquely Bohemian trend that tried to extract the rules of Cubism into the third dimension. Designed by Gočar, one of 3D Cubism's godfathers, the building now contains a gallery and permanent exhibit analyzing this Bohemian movement. While the exhibit's paintings deliver the whacked-out perspective we expect from cubist masters, what's more bizarre is the Cubist furniture. Chairs, cabinets, and armoires out of an M.C. Escher painting will make you lament that this genuinely awesome movement never became mainstream. Finally, check out the fully-restored "Cubist Cafe" located on the second floor of the building, and if you've got a rich uncle, check out the Kubista Museum store downstairs to pick up some replicas of Cubist jewelry and furniture.

🚇 B: Naměstí Republiky. Walk south through Naměstí Republiky and through Powder Gate, then continue west down Celetná, the museum is right at the fork in the road. $ 100Kč, after 4pm 50Kč. Students 50Kč/30Kč. 1st W of every month free. ⏰ Tu-Su 10am-6pm.

POWDER GATE ⊛⊗ MONUMENT

Na Příkopě 🖥www.prazskeveze.cz/prasna-brana.html

Six hundred years ago, *Horská brán*, or "Mountain Tower," which once stood on this site, actually served a purpose: it protected the city from bad guys and marked the starting point of royal corronation ceremonies. When New Town become a part of the city proper, the tower lost its function and they tore it down to built Powder Gate, an essentially cosmetic and purely symbolic monument. While the tower served as a gundpowder storage center for awhile, now it just kind of chills and lets cars tickle its belly as they drive under it. Climb up to the top for a view of the city and a small rotating exhibition.

🚇 B: Naměstí Republicky. From the Metro, walk south down naměstí Republicky. It's the giant tower in front of you. $ 70Kč, students 15Kč. ⏰ Open daily Mar and Oct 10am-8pm, Nov-Feb 10am-6pm, Apr-Sept 10am-10pm.

ESTATES THEATER ✏⊗🍸 THEATER

Ovocný trh 1, Praha 1, 110 00 ☎224 228 503 🖥www.estatestheatre.cz

The Estates Theater, the legendary stage were Mozart "premiered" *Don Giovonni* in 1787, now has a haunting statue out front commemorating the event. Just one problem: the opera premiered—and bombed—in Vienna. Prague was the back-up premiere. To make a long story short, Prague loved it and it's one of the greatest operas ever written. The film *Amadeus* features a scene with Mozart directing inside the Estates Theater. Popular ballets, dramas, and operas, including *Don Giovonni*, still play nightly in the Estates, and since the theater offers no public tours, the moderate ticket price is definitely worth the experience.

🚇 A or B: Můstek. From the station, head towards Old Town down Na Můstku and take the second right at Rytíšká. The theater and box office will be ahead on your right. $ Tickets 100-1200 Kč. ⏰ Performances at 7pm unless otherwise listed.

ST. JAMES CATHEDRAL ⊗ CHURCH

Malá Štupartsá 6, Old Town

According to legend, a thief once tried to steal a necklace from a Virgin Mary statue in Saint James. Well, as you can imagine, the statue came to life, grabbed the thief's arm, and refused to let go. Anyway, he had to cut his arm off and to this day, a mummified arm still hangs in the church. But this church doesn't need legends to be exciting, because you know what else is exciting? Eleven murals painted on the church ceiling, which are seriously cool. In fact, the entirety of the church is intricately decorated. No kidding, it's beautiful. And finally, here's a true story. When Count Vratislav died, he was placed in one of the most beautiful tombs in all of Prague. But for days after he was buried, terrible noises kept coming from the tomb. Finally the noises stopped when the priests sprinkled holy water on the tomb. Years later, the tomb was opened and scratch marks were found on the inside; this is why you always check that someone's dead before burying him. This church is not to be missed.

➜ From starostka naměstí, take Týnska east, continuing straight through the courtyards as it turns into Týn. The courtyard lets out at Malá Štupartsá where you should take a left. $ Free. ⏰ Open M-Th and Sa-Su 9:30am-noon and 2-4pm; F 9:30am-noon and 2pm-3:30pm. Su Mass 8:30am and 10:30am.

Josefov

The sights of Josefov, mostly syngagogues, are all located within close proximity. *(➜ A: Staroměstská. $ Admission to all synagogues except Staronová 300Kč, students 200Kč. Staronová 200/140Kč. Combined tickets 480/320Kč. ⏰ Synagogues open Apr-Oct M-F and Su 9am-6pm; Nov-Mar M-F and Su 9am-4:30pm. Closed Jewish holidays.)* While ambling through the Jewish district, take note of the beautiful early 20th-century Art Nouveau architecture. While walking down Široká street—"Wide Street" in Czech—take a moment to realize the sheer gravity of the ghetto.

👍 OLD JEWISH CEMETERY (STARÝ ŽIDOVSKÝ HŘBITOV) ♿ CEMETERY

U starého hřbitova 243/3a ☎222 317 191

The Old Jewish Cemetery stretches between the Pinkas Synagogue and the Ceremonial Hall. A winding path snakes through the uneven mounds covered with eroded and broken tombstones jutting out of the ground at unexpected angles. Between the 14th and 18th centuries, the graves were dug in layers, and over time the earth settled so that the stones from the lower layers were pushed to the surface, forcing many of the newer stones out of position and creating an indistinguishable mass of graves. Rabbi Loew is buried by the wall opposite the entrance.

➜ To the right of Pinkasova Synagogue. $ Camera fee 40Kč.

👍 SPANISH SYNAGOGUE (ŠPANĚLSKÁ SYNAGOGA) ♿ SYNAGOGUE

Vězeňská 141/1 ☎221 711 511

The Spanish Synagogue is the most richly decorated of the Josefov synagogues. Built in the Moorish-Byzantine style, the synagogue is covered from floor to ceiling with elaborate geometric patterns in beautiful reds, greens, and golds, and a cupola to top it all. The interior of the synagogue overshadows the exhibit within, which details the history of the Czech Jews from the Jewish Enlightenment to the decades after WWII, and contains an impressive set of silver Torah pointers. The synagogue also hosts classical concerts throughout the year.

➜ On the corner of Široká and Dušní. $ Concerts about 700Kč.

PINKAS SYNAGOGUE (PINKASOVA SYNAGOGA) ♿ SYNAGOGUE

Široká 23/3 ☎221 711 511

At the time of the Nazi takeover, 118,310 Jews lived in the Prague ghetto, many of them refugees from the conquered territories. While a few managed to flee before the terror began, more than 92,000 remained in Prague. Of these remaining Jews, about 80,000 were deported to their deaths at Terezín or other concentration camps. The names of these victims are recorded on the otherwise bare walls of the nearly 500-year-old Pinkas Synagogue. The names were originally added in the 1950s, but under the Communist regime they were whitewashed as part of ongoing efforts to reframe the victims of the Holocaust as anti-fascists. When

Václav Havel was elected president in 1989, his first act was to have the names reinscribed onto the synagogue walls. The second floor contains the haunting drawings of children from their time in Terezín.

⚑ *Between Žatecká and 17. Listopadu* Ⓢ *Yarmulkes 5Kč.*

KLAUSEN SYNAGOGUE (KLAUSOVÁ SYNAGOGA)

♿ SYNAGOGUE

U starého hřbitova 243/3a   ☎222 317 191

The Klausen Synagogue was originally built in 1573, burned down a while later, rebuilt in 1604, and then reconstructed in the 1880s. The inside is dedicated to the role of the synagogue in Jewish life and exhibit various artifacts. Next door, the Ceremonial Hall, maintained by the Prague Burial Society, showcases an exhibit on disease and death in Judaism.

⚑ *Adjacent to the Cemetery.*

MAISEL SYNAGOGUE (MAISELOVA SYNAGOGA)

♿ SYNAGOGUE

Maiselova 63/10   ☎221 711 511

Like most old things in Prague, the Maisel Synagogue has been partially destroyed and subsequently rebuilt several times. While originally built in the Renaissance style, the synagogue is now a hodgepodge of Baroque and Gothic elements. It contains artifacts from the history of Jews in Bohemia and Moravia up until the Jewish enlightenment. Some of the more interesting artifacts include the oldest tombstone from the Old Jewish Cemetery, as well as the robes of a 16th-century Jewish martyr who was burned at the stake by the Inquisition.

⚑ *Between Široká and Jáchymova.*

OLD-NEW SYNAGOGUE (STARONOVÁ SYNAGOGA)

♿ SYNAGOGUE

Červená

The oldest operating synagogue in Europe and one of the earliest Gothic structures in Prague, the relatively small Old-New Synagogue is still the center of Prague's Jewish community. The usual explanation for its oxymoronic name is that it was called the "New" synagogue when it was built in 1270 and took its present name when newer synagogues were built in the 16th century. However, a rumor persists that the synagogue was built with stones from the Temple in Jerusalem and that the name "Old-New" (*Alt-Neu*) is a mistranslation of the Hebrew "Al-Tnai," meaning "on condition"; the stones would be returned when the Temple in Jerusalem was rebuilt. Inside are the remains of a flag flown by the congregation in 1357, when Charles IV first allowed the Jews to fly their own city flag.

⚑ *At the corner of Široká and Žatecká.* 𝒊 *Men must cover their heads. Yarmulkes free.* ☒ *Open May-Aug M-F and Su 9:30am-6pm. Services F and Sa at 8pm reserved for practicing members of the Jewish community.*

STATUE OF FRANZ KAFKA

STATUE

Dušní

The statue of Franz Kafka stands astride an enormous figure that appears to be nothing more than a suit of clothes, as depicted in his story, "Description of a Struggle." At about 12 ft. tall, the statue is nowhere near the height of many of the city's other notable statues (perhaps fittingly so for this short-story writer), but has earned the attention of tourists and locals alike.

⚑ *At the corner of Žatecká, between the Spanish Synagogue and the Catholic church.*

Malá Strana

◪ CHURCH OF SAINT NICHOLAS

● CHURCH

Malostranské náměstí 272/1   ☎257 534 215

If you've spent any time in Europe by now, you've likely seen a church or two, or 50. But this ain't no ordinary house of the Lord. Boldly colored celestial scenes play out on an enormous fresco that spans the entire length of the towering ceilings, and floating above it all, like a magical cherry on a holy sundae (see what we did there?), sits the behemoth, effortless dome. Built by a father-son team in the 17th century, St. Nicholas is considered to be the most beautiful example of high Baroque architecture in central Europe, and was influential in defining the style throughout the continent. Music fans can stay after hours for a concert on an organ that Mozart played.

A: Malostranská. Follow Letenská to Malostranské náměstí. ℹ *Concerts held daily at 6pm.* $ *70Kč, students 30Kč.* ⏰ *Open daily Apr-Oct 9am-4:45pm, Nov-Mar 9am-3:45pm.*

PETŘÍNSKÁ ROZHLEDNA — LOOKOUT TOWER

Petřín hill

If the Petřín lookout tower seems like a shameless knockoff of the Eiffel Tower, it's because it is. The Eiffel Tower debuted at the 1889 World's Fair, and this shorter, fatter cousin popped up two years later at the Czech Jubilee Exposition. So what if it's only 60m tall; it's built at the peak of **Petřín hill,** and from the lookout 299 steps up, you can see a 360-degree panorama of the entire Czech countryside. If you're a lazier breed, take the lift *(50Kč)*, big enough for one fat man or five uncomfortable skinny men. The basement has an impressively blasé exhibit on the tower's history.

It's the giant tower on the hill visible from anywhere in the city. Just walk towards it. $ *100Kč, students 50Kč.* ⏰ *Open daily 10am-10pm.*

THE TOP OF PETŘÍN — 🍸 GARDEN, OBSERVATORY, MAZE

Petřín Hill

The hilltop has a number of sites worth briefly checking out, like the medieval **Hunger Wall,** Charles IV's purposeless welfare project to provide jobs to Prague's starving citizens. For a somewhat more purposeful, or at least aethestic, sight, go see the gardens with hundreds of varieties of roses; Czech lovers like to take up residence on benches there and remind the world how much they love each other. If canoodling Czechs don't do it for you, retreat to the observatory, where guides will help you view sunspots on a clear day, and creep on tourists on the ground when it's shady. There's also an underwhelming mirror labyrinth from the 1891 Jubile Exposition. The maze boasts a mural of the 30 Years' War in the middle of a mirror labyrinth. Go ahead, check it out, since you've already walked all the way up the mountain. When you get back down, see the **Memorial to the Victims of Communism,** a haunting monument near the funicular station that will give you the heebie jeebies at night.

A: Malostranská. Walk southwest towards the hill. If you don't want to take the semi-strenuous 30min. mini-hike to the top of Petřín hill, take the funicular, which leaves from a station in the middle of Malá Strana at Újezd and U tanové drahá. The alpine Tram #runs daily from 9am-11:30pm, accepts normal 26 Metro tickets, and takes 10min. of your time. $ *Observatory 55Kč, students 40Kč. Mirror labriynth 70/50Kč.* ⏰ *Observatory open Nov-Feb Tu-F 6-8pm, Sa-Su 11am-8pm; Apr-Aug Tu-F 2-7pm abd 9-11pm, Sa-Su 11am-7pm and 9pm-11pm; Mar and Oct Tu-F 9-11pm, Sa-Su 11am-6pm and 8pm-10pm. Mirror labyrinth open daily 10am-9:30pm.*

STRAHOV MONESTARY — 🍸 MONASTERY

Strahovské nádvoří 1 ☎233 107 711 🖥www.strahovskyklaster.cz

This 17th-century monastic compound confuses as much as it entertains; just enjoy the beauty and question the craziness later. The compound's principal attraction, the monastic libraries, have some of the most beautiful interiors in Prague: gilded bookshelves flow endlessly under a fresco depicting the story of human progress, while the floor brims with relics like globes that lack Australia or models of an Earth-centered universe. The library's "Hall of Wonders" has everything from a dried whale penis to an eighth century Bible to a set of 68 "tree box/books," bound in a species' bark and filled with its leaves, fruits or cones. Oh, yeah—and a narwal horn, a 12th century spear, and buckets of very ordinary sea shells. Additional non-essentials here include the cloister and attached gallery of 14th-19th century pieces, the church (open only during services), and the cloister's microbrewery (☎233 353 155 🖥www.klasterni-pivovar.cz).

🚶 From Petřín Hill, take the paved asphalt road that leads away from the funicular station. Follow it along the left side of the Hunger Wall for about 10min. ℹ A free guided tour can be arranged by calling ahead (☎233 107 749). $ Monastery admission free. Library 80Kč, students 50Kč. Cloister 30/15Kč. Gallery 30/15Kč. ⏰ Monastery open 10am-9:30pm. Library open daily 9am-noon and 1-5pm. Cloister and gallery open daily 9am-noon and 12:30pm-5pm. Microbrewery open daily 10am-10pm.

OUR LADY VICTORIOUS — 🚫♿ CHURCH

Karmelitská 382/14 — ☎257 537 345

This place might be small potatoes next to St. Nicholas down the street, but for the faithful, it's a must-see. The church houses a wax Christ figurine that's supposed to have protected the city during the 30 Years' War and now posseses healing powers. A museum in the back shows off the more than 80 outfits of this figurine. The church also deserves some attention in its own right, as the oldest Baroque church in Prague, dating back to 1613.

🚶 Follow Letecká through Malostranské náměstí and continue onto Karmelitská. $ Free. ⏰ Open daily 8:30am-7pm. Su Mass (in English) noon.

WALLENSTEIN CASTLE AND GARDENS — 🚫♿ CASTLE

Valdštejnské náměstí 17/4 — ☎257 075 707 🖥www.senat.cz

Originally built from 1623-1626 as a castle for nobleman Albrecht Wallenstein, this immaculate and detail-rich compound now serves as the seat of the Czech Senate. Keep your eyes peeled for live peacocks wandering between the hedge rows and reflecting pools. And don't worry, that albino peacock isn't possessed by Satan, he was just born that way. Some sad-looking owls fill out the aviary next to the "stalagtite wall" with a disorienting concrete array affecting the interior of a cavern. If the statues of Hercules killing all manner of mythical beasts don't impress you, come back on the weekends, when tourists can snoop around the castle's interior.

🚶 A: Malostranská. $ Free. ⏰ Gardens open daily June-Sept 10am-6pm, Oct-May 10am-4:30pm. Interiors open Sa and Su 10am-4:30pm.

FRANZ KAFKA MUSEUM — 🚫♿ MUSEUM

Cihelná 2b — ☎257 535 507 🖥www.kafkamuseum.cz

In an attempt to be as "disillusioning" as Kafka's writing, this museum goes a bit overboard with the shadowy video projections and dramatic lighting effects. Walking through this exhibit feels like riding through Slugworth's evil tunnel from *Willy Wonka and the Chocolate Factory*. Histrionics aside, the facsimiles of Kafka's letters and the images from Kafka's life warrant at least the student admission price. Best thing: Kafka's cartoon drawings of depression and madness, but you could technically also just see these in an anthology in the gift shop.

🚶 A: Malostranská. Go down Klárov toward the river, turn right on U. Luzické Semináré and left on Cilhená. $160Kč, students 80Kč. ⏰ Open daily 10am-6pm.

JOHN LENNON WALL — ♿ MURAL

Velkopřevorské náměstí

After John Lennon got shot, someone painted his face here and then everyone went crazy on it. A lot of mumbo jumbo graffiti decorates it now. Don't get your hopes up, it's just a wall. But it's in a garden, and worth a five-minute walk-by.

🚶 From Charles Bridge, take a left on Lázeňská soon after the bridge ends. Stay on it as it curves around into Velkopřevorské náměstí. $ Free. ⏰ Open as long as walls are open.

Hradčany

Around Prague Castle

👍 PRAŽSKÝ HRAD (PRAGUE CASTLE)

☎224 373 368 🖥www.hrad.cz

One of the largest castles in the world, Prague Castle has been the seat of the

Bohemian government since its construction over a millennium ago. After WWI, Czechoslovakia's first president, Tomáš Masaryk, invited Slovenian architect Josip Plečnik to rebuild his new residence after centuries of Hapsburg neglect. Plečnik not only restored the castle to its former majesty, but also added his own fountains and columns. During WWII, Reinhard Heydrich, the Nazi-appointed governor and notorious "Hangman of Prague," used the castle as his headquarters. An inspiration for *Raiders of the Lost Ark*, Heydrich wore the crown jewels that only rightful Bohemian kings were meant to wear. Though Heydrich's face didn't melt off, he was assassinated less than a year later, as per the film's legend. Arrive on the hour to catch the changing of the guard, complete with fanfare, and stay afterward to take a picture with one of them or try to get them to break their iron stares.

➜ Tram #22 or 23: Pražský hrad. From the stop, go down U Prašného Mostu past the Royal Gardens and into the Second Courtyard. Alternatively, hike up Nerudova. ℹ Ticket office and info located opposite St. Vitus's Cathedral, inside the castle walls. Long tour covers everything, short tour covers the main rooms. Tickets valid for 2 consecutive days. $ Long tour 350Kč, students 175Kč. Short Tour 250/125Kč. ⏰ Open daily Apr-Oct 9am-5pm; Nov-Mar 9am-4pm. Castle grounds open daily Apr-Oct 5am-midnight; Nov-Mar daily 9am-midnight. Changing of the guard daily on the hr. 5am-midnight.

👍 KATEDRÁLA SV. VÍTA (SAINT VITUS'S CATHEDRAL) 📷♿ CHURCH

The centerpiece of the castle complex St. Vitus's Cathedral is an architectural masterpiece, complete with three magnificent towers and more flying buttresses than it knows what to do with (no wonder it took 600 years to complete). The cathedral, not surprisingly, is also the most popular attraction at Prague Castle. During tourist season, expect waits of 20-30min. just to get inside. Once you make it in, though, there's plenty to see. In the main church, precious stones and paintings telling the saint's story line the walls of Saint Wenceslas Chapel (*Svatováclavská kaple*). Don't miss the gorgeous Mucha Window, perhaps the cathedral's most beautiful. For a great view and a healthy hike, climb the 287 steps of the Great South Tower. Many of Prague's most important religious and political figures are buried here. To the right of the altar stands the silver tomb of Saint Jan Nepomuck, of Charles Bridge fame. The Bohemian crown jewels are kept in a room with seven locks, the keys to which are kept in the hands of seven different Czech leaders, both secular and religious.

STARÝ KRÁLOVSKÝ PALÁC (OLD ROYAL PALACE) ♿ PALACE

The Old Royal Palace, to the right of the cathedral, is one of the few Czech castles where visitors can wander largely unattended—probably because its mostly empty. The lengthy Vladislav Hall is the largest Gothic hall in the Czech Republic; it once hosted coronations and indoor jousting competitions. Upstairs in the Chancellery of Bohemia, a Protestant assembly found two Catholic governors guilty of religious persecution and threw them out the window in the 1618 Second Defenestration of Prague, though without paying for an audio tour you would have no way of knowing this; what little information available is kindly written in Czech.

ROYAL SUMMER PALACE AND ROYAL GARDENS ♿ PALACE, GARDENS

The Italian-designed Royal Summer Palace was built in the 16th century to provide entertainment for royals until it fell into the hands of Austrian army, whose stay necessitated extensive rebuilding. Near the entrance, the Singing Fountain uses a vibrating bronze plate to create its rhythmic, enchanting sound, though you have to squat down awkwardly to actually hear it. The surrounding Royal Gardens contain dozens of species of trees and shrubbery, and make for a relaxing stroll at any time of day. The garden is also home to an assortment of birds of prey that a falconer displays daily noon-5pm.

GOLDEN LANE AND DALIBOR TOWER ⊗ TOWER

The small dwellings that line crowded Golden Lane once housed the castle's alchemists. At other times it's been home to the castle's artillerymen and artisans. Franz Kafka worked for a time at a workspace at #22, a small blue house marked with a plaque. At the end of the street you'll come to the base of Dalibor Tower, a cannon tower converted into a prison after a fire. Its most famous resident was the knight Dalibor, the subject of the old Czech adage "Necessity taught Dalibor how to play the fiddle" even though the actual fiddle was a torture—not musical—instrument designed to make the knight change his tune. The tower exhibits a variety of torture and execution implements, including cages, racks, stocks, "Spanish boots," and a headsman's axe.

➜ *To the right of the Basilica, follow Jiřská halfway down and take a right on Zlatá ulička, or "Golden Lane."*

Other Sights

STRAHOVSKÝ KLÁŠTER (STRAHOV MONASTERY) ⊛♿ MONASTERY

Strahovské nádvoří 1 ☎233 107 711 💻www.strahovskyklaster.cz

Part pilgrimage site, part library, and part gallery, the Strahov Monastery has had a rough history; it was built in 1120, burned down in 1258, rebuilt, and then plundered in turn by the Hussites, Swedes, and French. Since the fall of communism, things have quieted down. The renowned library contains thousands of volumes of philosophical, astronomical, mathematical, and historical knowledge, though your admission only entitles you to look from behind a barrier. In the anterior chamber, an 18th-century cabinet of curiosities contains the remains of dozens of crustacean species and other sea fauna, including a crocodile, octopus, and hammerhead shark, as well as various shells, ceramics, and Hussite weaponry. Its most-prized artifact, however, is what is left of a 👍**dodo bird.** If you want a great view that you don't have to pay for, walk down the dirt path at the foot of the monastery to a sign that reads "Grand Panorama." The view from the top of the hill gives you a postcard panorama of Prague.

➜ *Tram #22: Pohořelec. From the tram, walk south and make a right on Dlabačov, then take a sharp left onto Strahovské nádvoří.* $ *Library 80Kč, students 50Kč. Gallery 60/30Kč. Audio tour 90/75Kč.* 🕒 *Open Tu-Su 9am-noon and 1-5pm. Last entry 15min. before closing.*

LORETA ⊛♿ CHAPEL

Loretánské námesti 7 ☎220 516 740 💻www.loreta.cz

Loreta knows the magic of twos. The Loreta complex consists of two chapels and a two-story, arcaded courtyard. The central Santa Casa contains a statue of the Lady of Loreta, holding what is purported to be a piece of Mary's house at Bethlehem. The site is considered the holiest place in the Czech Republic and is the traditional starting point of pilgrimages from the area. On the second floor, a small treasury contains several jewel-encrusted religious texts and an impressive collection of chalices.

➜ *Tram #22: Pohořelec Tram #stop. From the Tram #stop, walk south, turn left on Pohořelec, then left on Loretánské námesti.* $ *110Kč, students 90Kč.* 🕒 *Open Tu-Su 9am-12:15pm and 1-4:30pm.*

Žižkov

CHURCH OF SAINT PROCOPIUS ♿ CHURCH

Čajkovského 36 ☎775 609 952

In 1881, Žižkov became a city independent of Prague. Amidst jubilations over their newfound autonomy, the residents of Žižkov realized that they did not have a Catholic place of worship big enough to accommodate the population within the new city's limits. Eight years after Žižkov's independence, Archbishop Cardinal Frantisek Schonborn ceremonially laid the foundation stone, and the neo-Gothic style church was completed five years later. Of note inside is the side altar adorned by a statue of Madonna with Jesus, an artifact protected during the 30 Years' War in a house in Nové Město.

Trams #5, 9, or 26: Lipanská. Head west 2 blocks on Seifertova. Confession M-W 8:30-11:30am, Th 8:30-11:30am and 1:30-4:30pm.

ŽIŽKOV TELEVISION TOWER — TOWER

Mahlerovy sady 1 ☎242 418 778 www.tower.cz

From a distance, the Žižkov TV Tower looks like a Soviet launch missile that never left Earth. Like the Dancing House and other strikingly modern structures in Prague, the tower was initially met with great hostility during its construction in the mid-1980s, in part because some feared that the tower would hurt infants living around the area with its radio transmissions. After more than 20 years, however, people have grown to at least accept, if not totally embrace, its unusual architecture. In 2000, controversial Czech artist David Černý cast nine figures of babies—perhaps in reference to that earlier paranoia—and attached them to the tower, where they have been suspended ever since. The tower hosts an overpriced restaurant and three observation decks, allowing for impressive views of the city minus the hassle of walking up hundreds of stairs.

A: Jiřího z Poděbrad. From the Metro, cross diagonally through the park and then take Milešovská toward the enormous tower (duh). i Relative level of physical fitness required to reach observation deck. $ 150Kč, students 120Kč. Observation deck open daily 10am-11:30pm.

JAN ŽIŽKA STATUE AND VITKOV HILL — STATUE, HILL

In June 1420, Hussite general Jan Žižka repulsed an attack from King Sigismund of Germany and Hungary on Vítkov Hill, breaking the siege of Prague. The grateful citizens named the area after their savior, and in 1950, an enormous statue by Bohumil Kafka was erected on the hill to commemorate his great leadership. At more than 30 ft. high, the statue remains the largest equestrian statue in the world. Though you can't get very close, the statue is still impressive and worth making the trip uphill. Once there, you can join dogwalkers and picnickers in the surrounding park.

Tram #5, 9, or 26: Husinecká. From the Tram #stop, follow Husinecká, then turn left on Jeronýmova and walk up the hill.

Vinohrady

Vinohrady may not contain the most amazing assortment of historical treasures, but its collection of small parks and beautiful grassy squares is unrivaled. **Riegrovy sady** on the northside of Vinohrady is a set of amazing grassy hills with views of the river—the perfect place for an impromptu picnic. And remember, no open-container laws means your picnic can get as fun as it wants to. For a more romantic setting, try the vine-covered **Havlíčkovy sady** on Prague 2's southern end and enjoy a glass from over 100 varieties of wine *(33-550Kč)* at **Vinični Altán,** the wine bar at the top of the park *(Open dawn to dusk.).*

VYŠEHRAD NATIONAL CULTURAL MONUMENT — MONUMENT

V Pevnosti 5B ☎241 41 03 48 www.praha-vysehrad.cz

Overlooking the beautiful Vltava River, the Vyšehrad monument plays host to scores of Czech couples getting busy on park benches, though **Princess Libuše** spent her time foreseeing the future glory of Prague. See, back then when you claimed to see crazy things, it made you famous instead of, well, crazy. An English guidebook can be purchased from any of the exhibitions *(35Kč),* a worthy investment to understand the signifcance of an afternoon spent here. Historical highlights include the **Church of Saint Peter and Saint Paul** built by Charles IV in the 14th century and the adjoining graveyard featuring some of the wildest and most provocative headstones you'll ever come across, as well as the remains of **Antonin Dvořak** and **Alfons Mucha.** Check out the Gothic Cellar for an archaeological look at the prehistoric inhabitants of the garrison.

🚇 C: Vyšehrad. $ Park admission free. Vyšehrad Gallery 20Kč. The Brick Gate 20Kč. Casemate including guide 50Kč. Church of St. Peter and St. Paul 30Kč, students 10Kč. ⏰ Exhibitions open daily Nov-Mar 9:30am-5pm; Apr-Oct 9:30am-6pm. St Peter and St. Paul open Tu-Th 9am-noon and 1-5pm, F 9am-noon.

Holešovice

LEVETSKÉ SADY ♿ 📶 🍸 PARK

A stroll through this enormous, luscious park with unconquerable views of the Vltava river can brighten your entire day. Meander along its densely forested trails, spectate at its organically-constructed Tony Hawk Skater Pro-style impromptu skate park (unless you're wicked cool and actually join in on the ollies and kick-flips), question the validity of art as you czech out the strange pieces of its sculpture garden, or just get kind of wasted at one of several beer gardens *(shots 30Kč)*. In 1955 the Communists built the largest statue of Stalin ever constructed at the top of the park, but it was torn down in 1962. Now a giant Metronome stands in its place because what says reform like a maintained rhythm? The park also has an array of tennis courts and children's playgrounds, as well as a sometimes-functioning carousel, the oldest in Europe. For a snack you'll never forget, stop at the pricey-but-worth-it **Restaurant Hanavský Pavilon** *(Letensky Sady 173, 170 00 Praha 7 ☎23 332 3641 💻www.anavskypavilon.cz)*. Over 100 years ago, this Art Nouveau Jubile Exposition pavilion was moved to its current perfect location overlooking the city below. It boasts the best dining atmosphere of the city.

🚇 B: Hradčankský. From the station, walk to the other side of the building, and head anywhere in the general south eastern direction—Levetské sady is the enormous park you'll run into. ⏰ Open daily dawn-dusk.

PRAGUE EXHIBITION GROUND PARK

Built on the easternmost section of Stromovka for the 1891 Jubilee Exhibition, this park offers some unique wonders of modern Prague. Coolest among them is the **Křižík's Fountain** *(U Výstaviště 1/20, 170 05 ☎723 665 6941 💻www.krizikovafontana.cz/en)*, a Bellagio-style fountain and lights show that during the summer months is accompanied by live ballet, singers, and musicians *(200Kč)*. Great for a date; if you're single, the fountain will take your mind off of that—sorry, btw. Other stops include the still-used-but-now-ghostly **Industrial Palace,** whose Art Nouveau exterior provides a phantom glimpse at the industrial "newness" of the past. There are also several beer gardens, skate rental shops, an enormous pyramid-shaped performance hall, and the **Lapidary of the National Museum,** which holds major statue structures in their collection—including the original statues on the Charles Bridge. Finally, check out **Marold's Panorama,** an impressive circular mural depicting the Czech Battle of Lipany.

🚇 C: Nádraží Holešovice. From the station, don't cross the street; instead, take Tram #5, 12, or 15 to the next stop, Výstaviště.

PRAGUE MARKET MARKET

Bubenské nábřeží, 170 00 Praha 7 ☎22 080 0592 💻www.holesovickatrznice.cz

A hundred or more street vendors, food peddlers, furniture salesman, and general bargain-gents call Pražská Tržnice (Prague Market), the city's largest market, their home. Sprawled out over an enormous campus of once-abandoned warehouses on the banks of the Vlatava river, flea market junkies, or heck, regular junkies can find hot deals on a variety of mainly manufactured goods. Deals won't walk into your lap, though: bargain hunters need haggling skills in English, Chinese, or Czech. Here's some advice for haggling: decide the honest price at which you value an item before approaching a vendor; then, stick to it. Don't be unreasonable, but don't let yourself get pushed around. Insist on your price, and if you don't get it, no loss. You can still enjoy the haggle-free bargains like ice cream and pastries *(10 Kč)*. Typical merchandise includes clothes, bags, and toys. Check out the smokeless cigarettes, full-sized swords, and the cheapest porno DVDs you'll ever find *(40Kč)*. If you object to pornography, these stands will be the perfect place to try out your jeering skills.

➡ C: Vltavská. From the station, walk to the left along the river. Be careful crossing large lanes of traffic. The market is on your left. ⏰ Open M-Sa 7am-8pm (prime time 9am-2pm).

Dejvice

BRONZE HORSE FOUNTAIN

Between Kafkova and Wuchterlova Streets

Three bronze horses, created by Czech sculptor Michal Gabriel, wade in the waters of the fountain. It's a sight (and bath) for sore eyes on a boiling summer day, and the 24 trees surrounding the fountain will gladly offer shade.

➡ A: Dejvická. Keep right after the round about and turn right at Kafkova.

Smichov

STAROPRAMEN BREWERY — ⊛♿🍸 BREWERY

Nadrazni 84 — ☎257 191 402

Staropramen is the second largest beer producer in the Czech Republic and this venue alone pumps out half a million bottles per day. The tour guides you through a few of the giant copper vats that process malt and provides information on the brewing process, closing with a tasting of the liquid you've drooled over for the past hour. While it might be worth a trek if you've exhausted your options in Prague, the tour itself is quite small for the price.

➡ B: Andel. ℹ Tour takes 1hr. $ Tour and tasting 120Kč. ⏰ Open Tu-Su 11am-5pm.

VYŠEHRAD CASTLE — ⊛⊗ CASTLE

V Pevnosti 159/5b — ☎241 410 348

A 10th-century castle overlooking the Vltava river and adorned by beautiful black Gothic spires, at Vyšehrad one can find the Basilica of Saint Peter and Paul and a cemetery containing the remains of several Czech notables. The castle was once a royal home, as well as a training center for the Austrian army after the 30 Years' War. The castle itself is quite beautiful and goes under the radar of most tourists, giving it a serenely untouched feel. Its location high above the city provides a prime angle to capture Prague Castle in the distance.

➡ C: Vysehrad. Or Tram #7, 8, or 24: Albertov. $ Grounds free. Gallery 20Kč. ⏰ Open daily 9:30am-6pm.

FOOD

If Czech food speaks to you, it will sing to you. Simple, hearty, rich and pork-filled, Czech meals carry weight. Must tries are the fried cheese (both hermelin or eidam), the pork knees, the goulash with dumplings and the schnitzel (think chicken fried steak). Consistent deliciousness, however, comes at the price of variety. Of the thousand or so restaurants in Prague, 800 of them easily share the exact same or nearly the exact same menu, so don't feel bad if you're tempted by the city's mostly-delicious Thai food or it's mostly awful but nevertheless omnipresent Chinese food.

The best thing about Prague, however, is the sausages. Whether you're digging a stand at Wenceslas Square or relaxing at a pub along the river, sausages are served slightly charred in chewy rolls with hearty portions of mustard and a mug of beer. Which brings us to beer, achem, water, achem, the only liquid substance most Czech drink. It comes with every meal (even breakfast), it comes in vending machines (seriously) and it usually costs between 15-40Kč. Beer gets more treatment in Nightlife, but it's also key for food matters since half the Czech cuisine only exists for beer. Pickled sausages, pickled cheese, head cheese (brains), deep-fried bread (which is amazing), pickled onions, pickled cabbage and toasts of cheese and ketchup all serve to supplement drinking and usually won't cost more than 30-40Kč.

In fact, most Czech food is disproportionally cheap. Many restaurants will have a daily lunch menu which offers a lunch with soup (usually a simple garlic, noodle and beef soup) and some entree for 80-110Kč, but be warned, the menus are usually Czech only, and you'll have to ask to see them. The Czech eat small breakfasts, usually just some cheese and hearty bread, but the abundance of tourists has made English and American breakfasts a standard option. Dinner with a mug of beer should come in at below 200Kč, though some items, steaks, pork knees, though available at these prices in some locations, will generally cost you more.

A note about cafes. Hundreds of locations across Prague describe themselves as Cafe Bars. These small-to-large establishments serve both extensive coffee options (including a favorite, Czech rum with coffee) as well as a full bar and usually a small, food menu of beer pairings.

Finally, a note about service and customs. When you enter a Czech restaurant, you are expected to seat yourself, and can even do so at a table already containing other guests. Although Czech service has a bad reputation, things have improved greatly as of late. Bread, pretzels or peanuts at the table are not free, and if you don't want them, don't touch them. Tipping is standard at 10%.

Nové Město *New Town*

🍴 PIVOVARSKÝ DŮM ♿🚭🍸 CZECH [2]

Ječná 15, 120 00 Praha 2 ☎29 621 6666 💻www.gastroinfo.cz/pivodum

Packed with Czech locals and a few wandering randos, this stellar microbrewery does Prague's beer proud. Start off with an 8-beer sampler that includes flavors like coffee, sour cherry, nettle, and banana *(130Kč)*. But make sure you finish it—you'll need the liquid courage to tackle the football-sized roast pork knuckle with mustard and horseradish *(205Kč)*, or the Brewmaster's Pocket *(205Kč)*—deep fried pork stuffed with cheese and more pork. If beer isn't your thing, you should probably leave Prague, but for now, try settling for some red or white wine served hot *(50Kc)*. If pork isn't your thing, fear not: vegetarian choices abound.

🚇 B: Karlovo náměstí. From the station, take Ječná east away from the river; it's on your right at the corner of Ječná and Štěpánská. $ Entrees 140-300Kč. Beer 25-80Kč. ⏰ Open daily 11am-11pm.

🍴 GLOBE BOOKSTORE ♿🚭📶☀ AMERICAN [1]

Pštrossova 1925/6, 110 00 Praha 1-Nové Město ☎22 252 0236 💻www.globebookstore.cz

Americans craving the type of culture that doesn't involve the Czech obsession with pasteurization will find a friend in the Globe. Great American fare like chicken wings *(5Kč)* during happy hour *(M-W 5-7pm)* and one of the best burgers you'll have this side of the pond *(180Kč)* both go well with excellent refillable drip coffee *(40Kč)*, a rarity in Prague. Don't miss brunch *(Sa-Su 9:30am-3pm)* with brilliantly Western dishes like scrambled chorizo *(180Kč)*. The cafe and attached bookstore host ex-pat book readings, movie screenings, or some kind of event most nights of the week. The bookstore itself has the largest collection of English books in the city.

🚇 B: Karlovo náměstí. From the station, take Resslova toward the river and then turn right on Na Zderaze, which becomes Pštrossova; the cafe is on your right. ℹ Make reservations if you have a big party. Three computers have Internet access for 1Kč per min. $ Entrees 100-250Kč. Beer 20-35Kč. Coffee 25-50Kč. ⏰ Open M-Th 9:30am-midnight, F-Sa 9:30am-1am (or later). Attached bookstore keeps the same hours.

🍴 PIZZERIA KMOTRA ♿🚭🍸 AMERICAN [1]

V Jirchářích 12, Praha 1 ☎224 930 100 💻www.kmotra.cz

Tucked downstairs in a little Czech basement, Kmotra's puts most American pizzerias to shame at a quarter of the price. Just one of their 36 pizzas *(110-170Kc)* will fill up two people, but main dishes like gnocchi *(125-145Kč)* or entree salalds *(125-145 Kč)* will appease the pizza skeptic. Try the popular Don Corleone—it's literally soaking in pork fat—or get wild with the Spenatora II, which is cooked with spinach, bacon, and a cracked egg that fries as the pizza bakes. This is serious pizza.

⇆ B: Národní třída. From the Metro, head down Ostrovni towards the river. After 2 blocks, take a left at Vorsilska. $ Entrees 100-200Kč. ⏰ Open daily 11am-midnight.

RESTAURACE U ZALUDO ⊗⊗🍸 CZECH 1

Na Zbořenci 261/5, Praha 2, ☎77 632 7118

Don't look for this place in other guidebooks or at the top of any "Best of Prague" lists. Instead, U Zaludo is the tiniest, salt-of-the-earthiest, most authentic Prague pub experience the city has to offer. This recommendation however comes with a warning: some customers have reported that no one would speak English to them or even present them with a menu. Fear not: simply learn the Czech for a few common food items: fried cheese, *smažený sýr (40Kč),* smoked pork, *uzená krkovice (55 Kč),* beer cheese, *pivní sýr (40Kč),* and grilled sausage, *opečená klobása (40 Kč).* This will be the cheapest meal you have in Prague, or *Let's Go* will eat its hat. And if no one stops to serve you, at least watch old Praguers come in at noon, down five beers and a shot, then return to work. Worth the experience, even if you chicken out.

⇆ B: Karlovo náměstí. From the station, head towards the Resslova. Take the first right, then another immediate right at Na Zbořenci. i Cash only. $ Beer 10-30Kč. Food 40-80Kč. ⏰ Open M-F 10:30am-11pm, Sa-Su 11am-11pm.

LEMON LEAF ♿📶🍸❄ THAI 2

Myslíkově 14 Praha 2 ☎22 491 9656 🖥www.lemon.cz

Besides having great Thai food at reasonable prices *(lunch specials 99-129Kč),* Lemon Leaf has one of the best happy hours in the city with discounts of 25% on meals *(M-F 3:30-6pm).* Plenty of tastes reward the daring eater, like cream of artichoke heart soup with saffron and edible flowers *(49Kč),* but traditional Thai staples are also well executed. Lemon Leaf is at its strongest when Czech and Thai forces work together, as in the milked corn soup with fresh horseradish *(49Kč).*The weekend lunch buffet is suprisingly elaborate *(240Kč),* as are the Thai murals and sculptures around the dining room.

⇆ B: Karlovo náměstí. From Karlovo, take Rasslova toward the river and then make a right on Na Zderaze. Although the address says Myslíkově, the entrance is on Na Zderaze. $ Curry 149-169Kč. Noodle dishes 150-200Kč. Wine 240-800Kč. ⏰ M-Th 11am-11pm, F-Sa 11am-12:30am, Su 12:30pm-11pm.

CAFÉ AND RESTAURANT SLAVIA 📶🍸 CAFE 2

Smetanovo nábřeží 2, Prague 1 ☎22 421 8493 🖥www.cafeslavia.cz

Café Slavia's food, which is deserving of its reputation, is only one reason to visit this historic Czech cafe. During communist rule, this bustling cafe was home base for political dissidents like Václav Havel, and, thanks to a recent renovation, you can now experience it as they did in its full 1930s Art Deco glory. The menu, though somewhat pricey, sets Czech standards like beef fillet with cream sauce *(189Kč)* against more revolutionary fare, like the asparagus-only menu *(70-190Kč).* Or, skip the meal entirely and join well-dressed pre-theater Praguers for a pre-show "ice cup" *(109Kč).* The Hot Love cup features vanilla ice cream, warm raspberries and mint.

⇆ B: Národní třída. From the station, walk north on Spálená and then turn left on Národní. The restaurant is at the end of the street, across from the National Theater. $ Entrees 89-300Kč. ⏰ M-F 8am-midnight, Sa-Su 9am-midnight.

ZVONICE

✦ ♿ ❄ ROMANTIC ❺

Jindřišská věž 110 00 Praha 1   ☎22 422 0009 ▣www.restaurantzvonice.cz

Visitors to this intimate dining spot located on the seventh and eighth floors of the historic Saint Henry's Tower will literally have to compete with tower scaffolding for dining space, but the experience is truly one of a kind. Feel the building shake as the bells in the belfry chime every half hour. Definitely a splurge; a coke will cost you what an entire meal might elsewhere *(99Kč)*, but remember that it's paired with an unbeatable setting. Fancy, exotic main dishes like grilled deer medallions with sour cherry sauce *(730Kč)* or wild boar with coriander and potatoes *(790Kč)* ensure you won't soon forget your meal. There's technically no dress code, but you'll feel rather out of place without a tie, or at least a sweet hat!

🍴 *From Wenceslas Square, walk down Jindřišská. It's the giant tower at the end of the street.* **i** *Reservations recommended.* Ⓢ *Expect to pay 1000 Kč for the full dinner experience.* ⏰ *Open 11:30am-midnight.*

U MATĚJÍČKŮ

♿ ❣ ❄ ♨ CZECH ❷

Náplavni 5, 120 00 Praha 2   ☎22 491 7136

U Matějíčků does solid Czech favorites very right. Start off with the comically enormous "Big Board full of Goodies" *(229Kč)*, which is an all-star sampling of Czech beer pairings: spicy sausage, smoked pork neck, Hermelin and Edam cheeses, *Olomoucke Tvaruzky*, hot peppers and pickled onions. Enjoy main dishes *(90-229Kč)*, like old bohemian roast duck or Czech cheese wrapped in English bacon and fried in beer dough, in the dining room decorated to look like the Czech countryside. For the truly brave, try their homemade "Devils' sauce" *(20Kč)* and wash it down with some dirt cheap wine *(18Kč)*.

🍴 *B: Karlovo náměstí. From the station, head towards the Resslova. Take 2nd right (Dittrichova) and the restaurant will be on your left at the fork.* Ⓢ *Entrees 90-229Kč. Beer 34-40Kč.* ⏰ *Open daily 11am-10pm.*

CAFÉ CÉLESTE

✦♿❄♨ CAFE ❺

Rasinovo Nabrezi 80, Prague 2   ☎22 198 4160 ▣www.celesterestaurant.cz

Great food and a better view if you've got the green for it. Lunch comes in two or three courses M-F *(450/550 Kč)* and dinner means exotic dishes prepared exotically. If you don't believe us, try the Moravian suckling pig with black pudding and jus with rasberries *(555Kč)*, fresh crab meat in a seaweed jelly lagoon *(405Kč)*, or rhubarb *clafouti* with jelly and dark beer milkshake *(205Kč)*. If you just want a peek from the terrace without busting your bank, visit M-F 4-6pm when Céleste opens its roof to mere mortals who order a cocktail *(100-150Kč)*.

🍴 *B: Karlovo náměstí. From the station, walk down Resslova toward the river. The building is on your left.* **i** *Lounge is on street level. Restaurant is through the elevator in the lounge.* Ⓢ *500-1000 Kč* ⏰ *Bar open M-Sa 9am-midnight. Kitchen open noon-2:30pm and 6:30-10:30pm.*

Stare Město

🏛 GRAND CAFE ORIENT

♿ ⦿ ❣ FRENCH, CAFE ❷

Ocovný trh 19   ☎224 224 240 ▣www.grandcafeorient.cz

In 1912, the Czech architect Gočar built the only ever "Cubist cafe" on the second story of the Lady of Black Madonna, the most famous "Cubist building" ever constructed. But at that time, Cubism was a fleeting trend and the cafe closed after just eight short years. After more than 80 years, the cafe was recently reopened with all of the original "Cubist" fixtures. A series of jarring angular lamp posts line the ceiling, and the little terrace out in the front is one of the cutest in the world. One doesn't expect great food out of a place like this, but that's where this little maverick surprises. The food, especially the *galettes*, savory crepes, are incredible. The spinach, ham, bacon, and cheese *galette* is the best experience you'll ever have with spinach—that's a promise.

*B: Náměstí Republiky. From the station, head south to U Prašná Brány and follow it as it becomes Celetná. The cafe is on the left at the fork. *i* The cafe is on the 2nd fl., through the museum entrance. Ⓢ *Galletes 95-135Kč. Coffee 40-60Kč, Desserts 25-60Kč.* 🕑 *Open M-F 9am-10pm, Sa-Su 10am-10pm.*

🏷 APETIT ⊕👤♿♻ CAFETERIA ❶

Dlouhá 23 ☎222 329 853 🖥www.apetitpraha.cz

Slum it like a real Praguer at this local cafeteria chain that might serve up the cheapest grub in Stare Město. Grab a tray, some silverware and select from one of several daily Czech entrees ranging from schnitzel to fried cheese to goulash *(67-78Kč)*. Individual entrees become a dinner with a choice of potatoes, dumplings, or vegetables, and a drink for just a few cents more *(89-92Kč)*. These cafeteria workers are no different from those you remember from grade school—very strict; they've even been known to shush policemen!

C: Republicky Náměstí. From the station, head north up Revoluční and turn left on Dlouhá. Ⓢ *Entrees 89-92Kč.* 🕑 *Open M-F 9am-8pm. Sa-Su 10am-8pm.*

KAVÁRNA OBECNÍ DŮM ♿♻ CAFE ❷

Republicky Náměstí 5 ☎222 002 763

The price of a coffee and dessert *(30-90Kč)* or a light sandwich *(120Kč)* is worth 40 minutes resting under the eight hulking chandeliers in this Art Nouveau masterwork. Each detail, from the design of the chairs, to the Alfons Mucha decorated menus, has been specifically chosen to fit the era, and the fountain at the side of the dining room was built specifically for the cafe by the Czech master Josef Pekárek. So sit back, relax, have an oddly affordable breakfast *(90Kč)*.

*C: Republicky Náměstí. *i* Separate from restaurant across the hall.* Ⓢ *Breakfasts 90-200Kč. Coffee 58-79Kč. Entrees 120-470Kč.* 🕑 *Open daily 7:30am-11pm.*

LEHKÁ HLAVA ⊗♻ VEGETARIAN ❸

Boršov 2 ☎222 220 665 🖥www.lehkahlava.cz

This cozy vegetarian joint whose name means "Clear Mind" hides on a small, quiet street. But that's the genius of the place—its entire experience rests on relaxing its patrons, from the lightly glowing tables to the fish tank to the earthy, "paper bag" menus. And unlike most vegetarian joints whose portions are sized more for hipster toddlers than for hungry human beings, Clear Mind delivers actual quantities of food. The eggplant quesadilla *(145Kč)*, though blasphemous by Mexican standards, has sharp, crisp flavors and loads up on the cheese. The polenta gnocchi in sheep's milk *(175Kč)* takes you outside your comfort zone while comfortably filling you up. For dessert, the millet-based carrot cake is a slice of healthy heaven dipped in chocolate *(70Kč)*. At your meal's end, if you need a little "pep," try Brazilian Guaron juice, with triple the caffeine of coffee *(45-75Kč)*. Also, if you're a monk, ordained clergyman, or "enlightened person," you're in luck; you're saved for time and all eternity, *and* you eat free of charge.

*A: Staroměstského. From the station, head towards the river then south on Křižovnické. Continue as it becomes Smetanovo nábřeží, then make a quick left fork onto Karoliny Světlé. Continue down, them make a left onto Boršov (it's a tiny street). *i* Reservations recommended.* Ⓢ *Entrees 90-185Kč.* 🕑 *Open M-F 11:30am-11:30pm, Sa-Su noon-11:30pm. Between 3:30-5pm, only drinks, cold starters, and desserts available. Brunch served 1st Su of the month 10:30am-2pm.*

BOHEMIA BAGEL ⊕((•))♻ CAFE ❶

Masná 2 ☎224 812 560 🖥www.bohemiabagel.cz

Though it's become something of an institution, Bohemia Bagel still delivers solid breakfast and lunch options at bargain prices. If you've got a youngster, unleash him or her in the playpen while you enjoy bottomless filter coffee *(49Kč)* or a bagel sandwich *(60-90Kč)*. If a plump burger *(125-150Kč)* or American-style sandwich *(95-135Kč)* can't convince you, then maybe you'll be pleased with the

prague · food

ice-cream chipwich *(80Kč)*. Incredible breakfast special of any egg sandwich served with bottomless soft drink, tea or coffee *(89Kč)* offered M-F before noon.

🚇 A: Staroměstského. From the station, take Kaprova away from the river and through Old Town Square. Stick to the left as you cross the square, and take Dlouhá on the opposite side. At the roundabout, take a right on Masná 2. $ Internet 1Kč per min. Bagels 30-50 Kč. ⏰ Open daily 8am-11pm.

KLUB ARCHITEKTŮ 🍴🚭🍸 CZECH, ROMANTIC ❷

Betlémské náměstí 169/5A ☎224 248 878 💻www.klubarchitektu.com

Surprisingly sophisticated and reasonably cheap for Old Town, this little place makes good grounds for a classy evening. Low-vaulted ceilings and the lowest hanging lamps you've ever seen (ask and they'll raise them up for you) will make you feel out of place in shorts or flip flops, but nobody will tell you you can't be there. Don't stop by if you're in a hurry; the fractured and separated serving areas means you can go 10 minutes at a time without seeing heads or tails of a waiter. Food is Czech chic, but if you're not here mostly for the ambience, you'll be disappointed.

🚇 B: Národní třída. From the station, head north on Spálená continuing as it turns into Na Perštýně. When it forks, take the left fork. Restaurant is down a somewhat unmarked staircase through a courtyard on your left. $ Entrees 130-280Kč. Desserts 80-105Kč. ⏰ Open daily 11:30am-midnight.

LA CASA BLU 🍴🍸🚭 MEXICAN ❷

Kozi 15 ☎221 818 270 💻www.lacasablu.cz

A favorite among locals, La Casa Blu provides a meeting place for Latin culture in this city so often lacking thereof; the walls serve as gallery space and Latin musical artists regularly perform. Though it's hidden down a sketchball alley, the scene inside this casa is bright and happening as locals sip *cervezas* in this smoke-free environment. Suprisingly big for the small cafe vibe it maintains, the food here is not to be underestimated, with dishes like Prague's only non-embarrassing selection of nachos *(100-200Kč)* and loaded quesadillas *(128-148Kč)*. La Casa Blu also stays hip late with tequila *(69-139Kč)*.

🚇 C: Republicky Náměstí. From the station, head north up Revoluční and turn left on Dlouhá. At the roundabout, take a right on Kozí. $ Entrees 150-290Kč. ⏰ M-F 10am-late, Sa 11am-late, Su 2pm-late.

U RUDOLFINA 🍴🚭🍸 CZECH ❶

Křížovnická 10 ☎222 328 758

You might have a bit of a struggle ordering here, but you've gotta give up something to eat at the cheapest, most authentic pun in Old Town. This locals-only favorite seems small on the first floor, but opens up downstairs to an impressively large restaurant, with antique photos and street lamps selling the 1930s effect. The staff speaks a wee bit of English, which should be enough to land you a *polévky (soup; 22Kč)* or a plate of *guláš (goulash; 98Kč)*. Even more elaborate dishes like *uzené koleno (smoked pork neck; 149Kč)* or *pečené koleno (sliced roast pork knee; 199Kč)* are incredible deals.

🚇 A: Staroměstského. From the station, head towards the river then south on Křižovnické. $ Entrees 65-199Kč. Beer 18-35Kč. ⏰ Open daily 10:30am-11pm.

CHOCO CAFE 🍴♿📶🍸☕ CHOCOLATE BAR ❸

Liliová 4/250 ☎222 222 519 💻www.choco-cafe.cz

Let's Go highly reccommends a series of fantastic desserts in Choco Cafe's case. The tiramisu *(80Kč)* comes in loaf form and will make your stomach smile. The various hot chocolates might be a little overpriced *(59-95Kč)*, but the espresso *(35Kč)* is actually more of a bargain than you'll find elsewhere in Old Town, especially coming from Choco's ravishing waitresses.

🚇 A: Staroměstského. From the station, head towards the river then south on Křižovnické. At the

bridge, head away from the river down Karlovo and take a left at Liliová. The cafe will be on your left. $ *Toasts 85-93Kč. Desserts 50-100Kč.* ⏰ *Open M-F 9am-8pm Sa-Su 10am-8pm.*

Josefov

LA VERANDA
INTERNATIONAL [3]

Elišky Krásnohorské 2/10 ☎224 814 733 💻laveranda.cz

While its pastel, flowery decor might make La Veranda appear a place for old, lunching ladies, the ingredients used are just as applicable to any man. The tagliolini with tiger prawns and sun-dried tomatoes will surprise both your tongue and your wallet *(295Kč).*

Tram #17: Právnická fakulta. $ *Soup 145Kč. Pasta 225-295Kč. Entrees 430-495Kč.* ⏰ *Open M-Sa noon-11:30pm.*

LA BODEGUITA DEL MEDIO
CUBAN [2]

Kaprova 19/5 ☎224 813 922

It's always a party at this Cuban restaurant where Latin music flows almost as freely as the mojitos. While there are a few vegetarian options *(gorgonzola cheese and raspberry salad 180Kč),* this is the place to go for beef with beef. Don't leave without trying the Mojo—grilled beef fillet served with Cuban baked potatoes *(485Kč).* While most of the meatier entrees are a little pricey, it's certainly possible to keep within budget with an equally hearty appetizer paired with a delicious soup *(85Kč).*

A: Staroměstská. About 25m east on Kaprova from the Metro. ℹ *Latin music and dancing most nights.* $ *Salads 155-190Kč. Entrees 98-485Kč.* ⏰ *Open daily 9am-2am.*

Malá Strana

BAR BAR
PUB [2]

Všehrdova 17 ☎257 312 246 💻www.bar-bar.cz

Discovering Bar Bar anywhere would be an accomplishment, with its saturation of local flavor, infusion of exotic influences, and balance of excitement and hominess. However, this gem hides just off the main street in touristy Malá Strana. The pub's dishes resemble Mom's home cooking. If the thought of Mom's home cooking is too traumatizing, you can cook your own food on a stone grill *(490Kč).* Be warned: this vegetarian-friendly cellar restaurant is becoming more popular; come on the early side, because they don't accept reservations.

A: Malostranská. From the station, take the Tram #to Újezd, walk north on Újezd, then turn right

spread 'em

Spread your cheeses.

Czech-side, the story is sweeter and softer, unlike what we're used to: cheese that rhymes with macho made from 1 part milk and 3 parts industrial plastic. For starters, Praguers spread soft cheese on rolls or toasted bread, not just corn tortilla chips; what's more, soft cheese can comprise a meal in its own right, or be a featured component of a successful larger meal.

Soft, spreadable cheese usually comes as a wheel or as individually-wrapped wedges. If you're thinking, "I've SEEN cheese like this," it's because fortunately, one brand of spreadable cheese has found its way to the colonies. Copyright disputes prevent me from naming the brand, but the image of a "chuckling bovine" may come to mind.

But any Czech would laugh at the idea that this brand could cover the spectrum of soft cheese. Czechs spread the love by adding flavors to the basic creamy base. *Se žampiony* adds mushrooms to the mix, *se šunko* ups the stakes with ham, and other styles add herbs, spices and just about anything else your heart can dream up.

on Všehrdova. $ *Entrees 139-325Kč. Tapas 175Kč. Beer 23-49Kč. Mixed drinks 90-160Kč.* ⏰ *Open Su-Th noon-midnight, F-Sa noon-2am.*

👍 RESTAURANT SOVOVY MLÝNY — 💳♿🍸🌳 CAFE ❹

U Sovových Mlýnů 503/2 ☎257 220 121 💻www.restauracemlyny.cz

If you make it here by 4pm, you're in for an unforgettable treat—a classy, riverside feast for the price of a non-feast thanks to Sovovy Mlýny's ultra cheap "daily menu." Specials like beef over mushrooms and potato gnocchi *(124Kč)* change daily, but are always delicious and filling. To keep things even cheaper, come for the daily dessert menu *(20-85Kč)* for traditional Czech sweets like cottage cake *(75Kč)* or apple strudel *(60Kč)*. But be warned, after 4pm this place comes to its senses and starts charging what it ought to. Sculptures from the attached modern art museum, like the enormous row of plastic yellow penguins, are great conversation pieces.

➜ *A: Malostranská. From the station, head south past the Charles Bridge, sticking to the side of the river. When you reach the park, the restaurant will be in the middle, right long the water, behind the freaky baby statues and the art museum.* $ *Daily menu 100-150Kč. Entrees 255-455Kč.* ⏰ *Open daily 10am-11pm.*

👍 DOBŘÁ TRAFIKA — 🚭⊗🍸🌳 CAFE, WINE BAR ❶

Újezd 37/400 ☎257 320 188 💻www.dobratrafika.cz

An excellent little cafe and wine bar popular with artists, musicians, and other tea-drinking types. Speaking of tea, this place has a four-page menu dedicated to it, and—the rarest sight in all of Prague—a *selection* of different coffees. Food pickings might be a little meager, but who can complain when there are seven different types of mead *(20Kč)*.

➜*A: Malostranská. From the station, take the Tram #to Újezd, walk north on Újezd. Cafe is through the specialty store in front.* $ *Pitas 13-50Kč. Coffee 30-50Kč.* ⏰ *Open M-F 7:30am-11pm, Sa-Su 9am-11pm.*

👍 RESTAURACE TLUSTÁ MYŠ — 🚭⊗🍸 CZECH ❷

Všehrdova 19, 118 00 Praha 1 ☎605 282 506 💻www.tlustamys.cz

Tulstá Myš, "Fat Mouse" directly next door to its neighbor, Bar Bar, has a similar vibe, similarly awesome food, and similarly great prices. Adorable "fat mice" dance around the menu. Grilled sausages *(55Kč)* are cheaper than a street vendor's, and the daily menu has terrific international samplings, like Mexican beans with beef *(99Kč)*. The cozy pub is also a great place to spend an evening sipping "Fire Water," Czech liquors like *Bechorovka*, plum vodka and *Fernet* *(20-40Kč)*.

➜ *A: Malostranská. From the station, take the Tram #to Újezd, walk north on Újezd, and then turn right on Všehrdova.* $ *Entrees 99-150Kč. Soup 24Kč. Beer 20-34Kč. Wine 32Kč.* ⏰ *Open M-F 11:30am-midnight, Sa noon-midnight, Su noon-10pm.*

czech republic

POD PETŘÍNEM — 🚭⊗🍸 CZECH ❶

Hellichova 5 ☎257 224 408 💻www.pivnicepodpetrinem.cz

This friendly, ultra-traditional Czech pub has just a few menu items: goulash *(99Kč)*, schnitzel *(129Kč)*, and pork knee *(139Kč)* among them at medievally cheap prices. The older Czech crowd won't be speaking English, and won't even have an English menu for you, but the few staff members who speak English will happily translate.

➜ *A: Malostranská. From the station, take the Tram #to Hellichova and walk south to Hellichova on your left.* $ *Entrees 99-140Kč. Beer 18-26Kč. Mixed drinks 40-95Kč.* ⏰ *Open 11am-12:30am.*

KAVÁRNA ČAS — 🚭♿📶🍸🌳 SNACKS ❶

Míšenská 92/2 ☎721 959 903

A delicious and cheap stop for a light lunch or dinner comprised entirely of snack food, the delights of this joint are all small, but magical. The snacks are made with recognizable ingredients, but are combined in a 100% foreign way. Toasted cheese sandwiches *(45Kč)* come with ketchup, and strudel pastries *(40-65Kč)* are filled with bologna, sausage, or cabbage. These magical bites won't fill you up, but they won't empty your wallet either.

A: Malostranská. Go down Klárov toward the river, turn right on U. Luzické Semináré. Take a right when you get to Míšenská. $ Toasts 45Kč. Beer 23-30Kč. Espresso 25Kč. Open daily 10am-8pm.

CAFE KAFÍČKE CAFE [2]

Míšenská 10 ☎724 151 795

A quiet stop for expats and other locals smack in the middle of tourist town, Cafe Kafíčke also has the distinction of being the first "non-smoking" cafe in all of Prague, when the American couple running this establishment had a child. You never know who'll be stopping by, from famous Czech film directors, to musicians to actresses. This small cafe's customers include some big names; maybe that's why they also accept euro.

A: Malostranská. Go down Klárov toward the river, turn right on U. Luzické Semináré. Take a right when you get to Míšenská. $ Espresso 38Kč. Sweets 12-52Kč. Open daily 10am-10pm.

Hradčany

U ZLATÉ HRUŠKY SAVE INTERNATIONAL, CZECH [3]

Nový Svět 3 ☎220 514 778 www.restaurantuzlatehrusky.cz

Try the innovative goat cheese in a puff pastry, with arugula and bacon chips *(290Kč)* —and sail away to a far-off galaxy. The place has a terrace for every season, so even if you come in winter you can enjoy the crisp air and snowy landscape while noshing on beef carpaccio *(290Kč)*. Not for the faint of wallet.

Tram #22 or 23: Brusnice. From the stop, walk across the street to the leafy pathway, down the stairs, turn left at the 1st street after the hotel and walk until you see the restaurant terrace on your right. $ Soup 190Kč. Entrees 290-690Kč. Dessert 190Kč. Open daily 11am-1am.

RESTAURACE NAD ÚVOZEM CZECH [3]

Loretánská 15 ☎220 511 532

Tricky to find but worth the search—the view of Petřín Hill and the surrounding area is one of the best you can get. The atmosphere is friendly and casual, and you might even spot a real Czech person eating here on occasion. The menu majors in traditional Czech, with an emphasis in skewers *(169Kč)*.

Tram #22 or 91: Brusnice. From the tram, take U Brusnice south and then turn left on Loretánská. Turn and go down the stairs toward Úvoz; the entrance will be on your left. $ Entrees 159-279Kč. Daily menu 179Kč. Open daily 11am-11pm.

U CÍSAŘŮ CZECH [5]

Loretánská 5 ☎220 518 484 www.ucisaru.cz

This 13th-century cellar, complete with crossed swords and a boar's head, has served the likes of George H.W. Bush, Margaret Thatcher, and Lech Wałęsa. Finally, a *goulash* worth splurging on *(340Kč)*. Other specialties include roast duck in honey and ginger *(420Kč)* and pork sirloin stuffed with carrots and celery *(440Kč)*.

Tram #22 or 91: Brusnice. From the tram, take U Brusnice south and then turn left on Loretánská. $ Appetizers 210-230Kč. Entrees 340-550Kč. i No dress code per se, but you'd probably feel awkward in jeans and a T-shirt. Reservations recommended. Open daily 9am-1am.

Žižkov

ZELENÁ KUCHYNĚ VEGETARIAN [2]

Milíčova 5 ☎222 220 114 www.zelenakuchyne.cz

Clean, fresh, wholesome ingredients combine to make any vegetarian orgasm. Check out the grilled tomatoes with goat cheese and blackberry dressing...do you want to get a room? Top off the pleasurable experience with a little dessert; savor the cinnamon pancakes made from oatmeal and apples and topped with ice cream and blueberry sauce.

Trams #5, 9, 26: Lipanská. From the stop, walk west on and turn right at Seifertova Milíčova. The restaurant is on your left. *$ Menus from 90Kč. Entrees 110-290Kč. 🕐 Open M-F 11am-8pm.*

SPICE INDIA ♿ INDIAN ❷

Husitská 73/37 ☎776 293 320 💻www.spiceindia.cz

No fuss, no muss at this little Indian fast-food joint off the main street. Deliciously spicy cuisine is served up on metal plates by a genial counter staff. Don't forget to order water to wash down the burn.

🚌 Bus #133, 175, or 509: Tachovské náměstí. Keep walking in the direction the bus is going until you find the place on your right. $ Entrees 65-180Kč. 🕐 Open M-F 11am-11pm, Sa Noon-11pm, Su 5pm-11pm.

Vinohrady

★ CAFÉ ŠLAGR ♿🍸 CAFE ❶

Francouzská 72/563 ☎607 27 76 88 💻www.kavarnaslagr.cz

"Mind-blowing" is an appropriate word to describe Café Šlagr's baked goods. If they have it in stock, the *Pářvžký rohlíček (29Kč)* will be one of your finest culinary experiences, while the *krernrole (17Kč)* will help you understand what the Italians were aiming for with cannoli. Be sure to get it with some coffee and milk—the milk comes from a little cow vessel who happily regurgitates into your espresso *(36Kč)*. The family behind this genius operation dressed their little cafe like 1930s Paris and plays cute little swing tunes to sell the effect.

🚌 A: Náměstí Míru. From the station, walk southeast along Francouská. The cafe will be on your right. $ Baked goods 17-40Kč. Breakfast 49-69Kč. 🕐 Open M-F 8am-10pm, Sa-Su 10am-10pm. Breakfast served 8-11am.

LAS ADELITAS 📶🍸 MEXICAN ❷

Americká 8 ☎776 80 53 17 💻www.lasadelitas.cz

Described by some locals as "the only real Mexican restaurant in Prague," this hole-in-the-wall taqueria serves up oddly authentic south-of-the-border fare. Enchiladas, burritos, and tacos all come with legit Mexican *queso*, pickled onions, and hearty refried black beans. Both come with pork and chicken, but pork is the specialty—and boy is it special. Vegetarians will enjoy any major dish served up with sauteed mushrooms, while parched *amigos* can sooth themselves with a cool glass of *horchata (25-69Kč)* or with one of 13 tequilas *(69-150Kč)*. Try the *Sopa Azteca (49Kč)* for a surprisingly filling soup packed with cheese, chicken, and onions.

🚌 A: Náměstí Míru. From the station, walk down Americká. The restaurant is past the square with the dinosaur fountain on your left. $ Entrees 99-179Kč. Margaritas 89-99Kč. 🕐 Open M-F 11am-11pm, Sa-Su 2-11pm. Kitchen open until 10pm.

CAFE ZANZIBAR 📶🍸 CAFE ❷

Americká 15 ☎222 52 03 15 💻www.kavarnazanzibar.cz

This relaxing French cafe has a strange power to improve your mood. Set breakfast menus with combinations of cheese, eggs, pastries, coffee, and baguettes come at great prices *(79-149Kč)*—and yes, some of them come with beer instead of coffee. Lunch includes 20 salad options *(59-149Kč)* and a mess of French and international favorites, like *croques monsieur (ham and cheese super-sandwiches; 65-95Kč)* and Mexican tube sandwiches *(burritos; 129-139Kč)*. Stick around and try a few "beer cocktails"—beers sloshed with things like lemon syrup, Coke, and Sprite *(46-59Kč)*. If you drink enough, you'll get to check out the strangely nautical bathrooms, where a net above the urinals threatens to trap the slow pisser!

🚌 A: Náměstí Míru. From the station, walk down Americká. The cafe is on your right at the square with the dinosaur fountain. ℹ Only the porch is wheelchair-accessible. $ Coffee 36-42Kč. Breakfast 79-149Kč. 🕐 Open M-F 8am-11pm, Sa-Su 10am-11pm. Kitchen open 8am-10pm.

U PALEČKA 🍸 CZECH ❸

Nitranská 1625/22 ☎224 25 06 26 💻www.vinarnaupalecka.cz

U Palečka's simple, rustic interior does not do justice to its gastromically rich menu. One can enjoy its food best from the intimate outdoor porch-boxes in front of the restaurant. On a dry summer day, take in a strange starter like smoked tongue *(60Kč)* or even a well-priced dish of caviar *(110Kč)*. Beef dishes will cost you the most, maybe because of the thick whipped cream they're garnished with *(260Kč)*, but chicken dishes, including mind-blowers like the chicken pocket stuffed with ham and cheese *(155Kč)*, or the turkey stuffed with blue cheese and broccoli *(150Kč)* are more than reasonable.

🚇 A: Jiřího z Poděbrad. From the station, head south on Nitranská, the restaurant will be on your right $ Entrees 90-260Kč. ⏰ Open daily 11am-midnight.

U BULÍNŮ 💳🚭🍸 CZECH ❷

Budečská 803/2 ☎224 25 46 76 💻www.ubulinu.cz

Before you order from this amazing traditional Czech restaurant, read its legend printed in English on the first two pages of the menu. When you're done laughing at the most comprehensive piece of incomprehensible private history you've ever encountered, order anything you want from the large and exciting menu. In keeping with the "devilish" theme of the restaurant (according to legend, the original owners grew horns, a condition called bulinia), chicken dishes *(139-179Kč)* are served with Lucifer skewers and hellish hot sauce. Even vegetarians can get their kicks by ordering any of the several pastas *(89-159Kč)* without chicken, or getting some "traditional Mexican" fare like tortilla with red kidney beans, corn tomatoes, and sour cream.

🚇 A: Náměstí Míru. From the station, walk southeast down Francouzská. The restaurant will be on the corner 3 blocks down. $ Entrees 119-200Kč. ⏰ Open daily 11am-11pm.

Holešovice

👍 LA CRĚPERIE 🥗🚭📶🍸 FRENCH ❶

Janovskéno 4, Praha 7 ☎22 087 8040 💻www.lacreperie.cz

La Crěperie's jive is as hip and French as anyone could hope for. Decor details like a gold-star-striped walls, old photos, even those red bathroom doors Frenchies require for their bowels to work, win this place before we even get to the food. But the food's great too. Sharp "zappy" espresso *(32Kč)* comes *avec* biscuits, the crepes *(35-89Kč)* are perfectly drizzled with honey, and the tunes are hand-selected French grunge rocks and froggie ballads. Someone should film a movie here called, *Amélie II: Czech Out My Quirks!* French *galettes*—buckwheat crepes with savory innards like ham and cheese—are the VIPs of this menu...crunchy and flaky, they're the original Hot Pockets *(72-110Kč)*. Get them with a cup of traditional Brittany cider mixed with black-currant cream.

🚇 C: Vltavská. From the station, head right down Bubenské nábřeží then loop around and cross in front of the giant church; the restaurant is on your left. $ Crepes 35-89Kč. ⏰ Daily 9am-11pm. Kitchen closes at 10pm.

KORBEL 💳🚭🍸 CZECH ❶

Komunardů 1001/30, 170 00 Praha 7 ☎22 298 6095 💻www.restauracekorbel.cz

The building that held Holešovice's oldest restaurant now houses its youngest and hippest one. But don't let the fancy, vaguely-Cubist chairs or the free-form paintings of "sexy Pilsner bottles" give you the wrong idea; the prices and the fare are still solid and traditional. Czech specialties dominate the menu, with options of pork, duck, rabbit, beef, and chicken in a variety of goulashes, stews, and steaks. Vegetarians will also find a selection of vegetables and cheese dinners *(89-95Kč)*. Currently the menu is only available in Czech, but an English menu is in the works, and the staff is friendly and glad to translate.

🚇 C: Vltavská. From the station, take any Tram #that departs to the left. Ride it 2 stops to Dělnická. $ Main dishes 89-175Kč. Beer 24-40Kč. ⏰ M-Sa 11am-2am, Su noon-midnight.

Dejvice

👍 VEGETKA 🚫♿🌤 VEGETARIAN [1]

Kafkova 16 ☎776 343 462 💻www.volny.cz/vegetka

A Buddhist vegetarian restaurant that serves up the freshest of dishes with an Asian twist. It'll be hard not to like tofu after you've eaten here. The "special soup" is especially noteworthy and stocked with noodles, mushrooms, and coriander (among other secret ingredients).

🚇 A: Dejvická. Keep right around the round about, and make a right on Kafkova from Dejvická. $ Entrees 25-120Kč. ⏰ Open M-Sa 10:30am-9pm.

PIVNICE BRUSKA 🚫♿📶🍸❄ INTERNATIONAL [3]

Dejvická 20 ☎224 322 946 💻www.restaurace-bruska.com

Something of a neighborhood landmark that locals have largely managed to keep to themselves. The wooden furniture and ceiling beams and brick floor all signal a typical Czech pub, but the menu contains several surprises for those who can decipher it. Highlights include kangaroo with cranberry sauce and vegetables *(143Kč)* for those who hate adorable animals, and pork stuffed with bacon *(189Kč)* for those who hate themselves.

🚇 A: Hradčanská. From the Metro, walk north on Bubenečská and then turn left on Dejvická. $ Salads 70-125Kč. Entrees 120-190Kč. ⏰ Open M-Sa 11am-11:30pm, Su 11:30am-10pm.

Smichov

ARSLAN KEBAP 🚫♿🌤 KEBAB [1]

Bozděchova 2246/3 ☎257 212 869

Hands-down some of the best kebab and gyros found in the city. The bread used to create the gyros sandwich is a fluffy, airy piece of heaven resembling something akin to ciabatta rather than the soggy pita that most places offer. Way cheaper than anything you'll find around the center and also gives you a giant bang for your tiny little buck.

🚇 B: Anděl. Head away from the mall on Nadrazini and make a right on Bozděchova. $ Gyros from 59Kč. ⏰ Open M-Th 10:30am-10pm, F-Sa 10:30am-11pm.

CUKRÁRNA EVELÍNA 🚫♿ PASTRY SHOP, CAFE [1]

Bozděchova 5 ☎602 891 724

This adorable little pastry shop looks like some place you'd take your dolls out for tea and chocolate cake. Don't spend too long ogling the tiers behind the glass case—a long line waits behind you. Enjoy your find at a little white table and be amused by the drooling passersby.

🚇 B: Anděl. Head away from the mall on Nadrazini and make a right on Bozděchova. $ Cake slices from 18Kč. ⏰ Open daily 9am-7pm.

NIGHTLIFE

Although Prague has one of the greatest clubs in the world (Cross Club) and a few genuinely amazing bars (Chapeau Rouge), most of the nighlife centers on the pub scene. On a typical night, Praguers head out for dinner at a pub (sometimes called Bar Cafe) and just stay there the entire night, drinking beer, smoking cigarettes (indoors, it never gets old) and munching on cold snacks like pickled sausage and fried cheese. Pubs stay open late (midnight Mondays-Wednesdays, 2-4am Thursdays-Saturdays, midnight Sundays) and clubs stay open to 4am or later most night of the week.

Booze across the Czech Republic comes at prices comparable to what you pay for air, but especially cheap and especially delicious are Prague's fire waters: Fernet tastes like a less-syrupy Jagermeister; Becherovka tastes like Christmas in your mouth, and Plum Vodka, tastes--well, the point isn't the taste with the plum vodka.

Nights out in Prague are especially incredible, given that some nights, you can come home completely wasted having spent seven or eight euro. But drink responsibly. Drunk Americans especially become the targets of pickpockets and puking tourists will piss off the tourist police. And then you'll have to sit in the van.

Nové Město

ZACHRAŇTE 02 BAR — CHILLOUT BAR

Karlovo náměstí ☎60 814 4344 www.o2bar.cz

This tiny cabana in the middle of Charles Square Park fits just four cocktail tables. Space is so tight the nightly DJs set their decks on a foosball table in the corner. But it still packs such a huge punch that crowds spill out into the park onto the roof terrace. There's no drink service on the roof, so you'll just have to chill with the punks rolling their own cigarettes and enjoy the surreal view of the New Town Hall lookout tower. Somehow they also fit a kitchen in this place serving cowards a hot dog or some nuts *(15-35Kč)*, while the brave undertake the Delicate Stuffed Cheese with True Story *(55Kč)*. Tell your friends to check the bar's website to see you rocking out on a live web cam.

B: Karlovo náměstí. Exit the station on the side closest to New Town Hall and walk 1 block to the north side of the park. $ Beer 25-40Kč. Mixed drinks 35-80Kč. Open daily 10am-whenever the party stops.

U SUDU — BAR, CLUB

Vodičkova 677/10 ☎222 23 22 07 www.usudu.cz

From the street, U Sudu seems to be a low key five-table pub with a single bar. But if you take the strangely inviting stairway at the back of the club, you'll encounter a large underground pub space. And if you take the enormous brick tunnel leading out of there, you'll find yet another space. And it kind of keeps going like this—snaking below the street in labyrynthine tunnels. It would be easy to spend a night here and not visit all of the different rooms, each of which has a slightly different vibe. Just hope there isn't a fire. In addition to regular drinks, U Sudu has Master 18 proof *(38Kč)* on tap.

B: Karlovo náměstí. From the station, head north towards New Town Tower along the eastern side of the park. Continue past New Town Hall along Vodičkova. The bar will be on your right. $ Snacks 10-55Kč. Beer 23-55Kč. Open M-Th 9am-4am, F 9am-5am, Sa 10am-5am, Su 10am-3am.

CLUB PRDEL — DANCE CLUB

Žitná 4, 120 00 Praha 2 ☎22 223 0890 www.prdelclub.cz

Like the milk bar of Kubrick's "A Clockwork Orange," this sweaty young dance club serves wild nectars amid rather accurate busts of women's rumps, hips and etc. Older (lamer) patrons can chill upstairs sucking on the bitter "Cum of Cucumber" *(185Kč)* or the vanilla vodka-based "Orgasmus" *(120Kč)*, while others can head downtairs for a smoky, steamy romp in the juices of youth. Dress for the occasion: 'cause it's close quarters downstairs and when the second DJ gets spinning, this energetic young crowd makes the temp go up. When 6am rolls around, take five in the "special room" behind the curtains. What you do there is your choice--but there are no chairs, only pillows and bean bags.

B: Karlovo náměstí. From the station, head away from the river down Zitna. The club is on your right. i No dress code, but you'll feel out of place in shorts. $ Beer 40-80Kč. Mixed drinks 120-185Kč. M-Sa 5pm-7am, Su 5pm-5am.

WHISKERIA V — WHISKEY BAR

Jindřišské Věž ☎22 424 8645 www.whiskeria.cz

Travelers who hate dancing, or who don't have legs, will love this brand new whiskey bar where a night can be spent sampling the fruits of rye's labor. Whiskeria offers over 450 varieties of the liquor at prices that are both student-friendly *(100Kč)* and billionaire-friendly *(10,000Kč)*. If malts are all Greek to you, fret not. The bartenders have graduated from booze university and are eager to share their knowledge. You can check their website for classes and tastings. If whiskey's not your thing, they also have other drinks. Non-smoking seathing is available.

A or B: Můstek. From the station, head away from the river down Jindřišské. It's in the giant tower at the end of the street. i Whiskey tastings F. $ Drinks 100-10000Kč. Open daily 10am-midnight or later.

CLUB STŘELEC CLUB

Žitná 51, Praha 2 ☎60 694 7673

This low-key GLBT hangout is so happy with the small set of locals it serves, it almost refused to be listed. A night at this ace hole-in-the-wall where students mix with septuagenarians could end over beers and traded stories or on top of the tables with an impromptu elderly strip tease. Ask the one bartender who speaks English for authentic Czech drinks like the Bloody Back, a combo of cherry liqueur and vodka drunk simultaneously from two separate shot glasses. But be warned, this pub does cater to seniors as well as students, so don't go looking for too wild a time.

C: I.P. Pavlova. From the station, head north on Legerova and make a left on Žitná. The club is on your right. $ Beer 17-31Kč. Mixed drinks 25-50Kč. Happy hour daily 5-8pm.

ROCKY O'REILLYS PUB

Štěpánská 32/620 Praha 1 ☎22 223 1060

Included more as a warning than as a recomendation, this "Irish" pub pegs itself as, and often ends up being, an obligatory stop for British and American tourists. It need not be so. While Rocky's does blast Prague's half liters for actual English "pints," the charm comes with a hefty price tag. Food, like nachos *(145Kč)* or ribs *(295Kč)* is solid enough, and the beer *(30-65Kč)* tastes like beer, but the best things about Rocky's happen on its walls. Sports events get projected onto a big screen, and a hanging poster, "Rockey's 10 Commandments of Travelers," delivers some very wise Prague-specific advice for staying safe and financially responsible while in the city.

A and C: Muzeum. From the station, walk down Václavské náměstí and take a left on Štěpánská. The pub will be on your left. $ Entrees 155-300Kč. Bar open daily 10am-1am. Kitchen open 10am-11pm. Happy hour M-F 5pm-8pm.

Stare Město

CHAPEAU ROUGE BAR, CLUB

Jakubská 2 ☎222 316 328 www.chapeaurouge.cz

Chapeau Rouge is smarter—and hipper—than your average bar. Maybe it's the sprawling Optimus Prime flying over the bar's front room, or the smattering of penis drawings and condom machines around place, but Chapeau Rouge seems to be that quintessential club we all imagine exists in Europe. Downstairs, where the dancing happens, feels like an entirely different club: smokier and darker. Club has a DJ or a band every night of the week. On Friday and Saturday nights, it's hard to imagine a better bar.

C: Republicky Náměstí. From the station, head directly west until you dead end at Rybná. Take Rybná head north up and take a left on Jakubská. $ Beer 25-40Kč. Mixed drinks 60-100Kč. Open M-Th noon-4am, F noon-6am, Sa 4pm-6am, Su 4pm-3am. Dance club open daily from 9pm.

KARLOVY LÁZNĚ CLUB

Smetanovo nábřeží 198 ☎222 220 502 www.karlovylazne.cz

A colossal five-story club with some genuinely impressive lighting and dance floor effects, Karlovy Lázně also manages to be less trashy than you'd imagine from the outside. Each floor plays a particular decade's music, with the exception of one floor that proclaims it plays "black music." The variety of music means that one of the scenes will probably appease you. Drink selection is limited, but the point of this club is mostly to get as drunk as possible and makeout with people: most pub crawls end here. Other highlights include the psychedelic checkerboard dance floor, the Elvis and Marilyn Monroe statues, and the strange laser shooting torso. Huge crowds turn out on weekends, making this place buzz.

A: Staroměstského. From the station, head towards the river then south on Křižovnické. Club is directly past the Charles Bridge through the tunnel of tourist shops. i No dress code. $ Cover until 10pm 70Kč. After 10pm 120Kč. Drinks 40-160Kč. Open daily 9pm-5am.

Malá Strana

JAZZ DOCK — MUSIC CLUB

Janáčkovo nábřeží 2 ☎774 058 838 www.jazzdock.cz

For a little over a year now, this newbie jazz club has been setting trends and making waves, and not just because it's by the water. Impressive when it's empty with laser neon stools, full wall windows, and a black angular interior, Jazz Dock swings hard when it's full of live jazz every night of the week. The gig here is serious; five days of the week include double shows, with programs for children on Saturday and a Dixieland program on Sunday. Due to its genius design, live music can play until 4am without soliciting noise complaints, though on most nights a DJ takes over at 1am or 2am. The ambitious list of progressive cocktails *(135Kč)* is supplemented by a food menu with catches like Tunafish Snails *(85Kč)*—"a rolled surprise"—and the Jazz Hot Dock *(75Kč)*— a hot dog buried in onions and mustard.

B: Anděl. From the station, head north on Nádražní and take a right on Lidická. At the river, take a left on Janáčkovo nábřeží. i Guests who visit the club 3 times receive a card entitling them to a 20% discount on all future club transactions. $ Cover 190Kč. Under 26 or over 65 90Kč. Beer 29-35Kč. Mixed drinks 135Kč. Open M-F 3pm-4am, Sa-Su 11am-4am. Th, F, and Sa shows at 7pm and 10pm. Food served until 4am.

KLUB ÚJEZD — BAR

Újezd 18 ☎251 510 873 www.klubujezd.cz

Klub Újezd attracts guests as wild as its decorations: bathroom doors show monsters taking dumps, a 20 ft. long leviathan snaps above the bar, and corpse faces melt out of the walls. The clientele isn't exactly like that, but three floors do cater to three very different scenes. Upstairs is secluded and smoky, the basement is cold and dungeon-like with a DJ spinning on a mini-stage for the 20 people who can fit there, and the main bar is filled with artists—or posers.

A: Malostranská. From the station, take the Tram #to the Újezd stop. $ Beer 25-60Kč. Mixed drinks 65-100Kč. Open daily 2pm-4am.

Žižkov

PALÁC AKROPOLIS — CAFE, CLUB

Kubelíková 27 ☎296 330 912 www.palacakropolis.cz

Situated in a pre-WWII theater, this entertainment complex has become a landmark in the Žižkov area. The bar and cafe upstairs serve a mix of expats, local artists, and intellectuals, while the multi-level club downstairs has two bars, each with its own nightly DJ and a clientele that changes according to the music. Reggae night on Sunday is always well attended. The space also hosts concerts and regularly collaborates with a group of performance artists.

A: Jiřího z Poděbrad. From the Metro, cross diagonally through the park and then take Milešovská; Kubelíkova is on the other side of the Žižkov tower park. i Cover F and Sa 30Kč. Some concerts cost money; check online before you go. $ Beer 25Kč. Open daily 11am-1am.

Vinohrady

RADOST FX — CLUB

Bělehradská 2334/120 ☎60 319 37 11 www.radostfx.cz

Open as a lounge and cafe every night of the week, Radost takes weekends to unleash its inner world-famous dance club on the city. Glowing rooms and zebra-print couches sell the disco effect, especially when coupled with the eight or so LCD screens flashing crazy images. One of the more advanced light rigs in Prague sexes up the dance floor. If you get tired downtairs, go up for the great but pricey quesadillas and other drunk food *(from 195Kč)* at the cafe. Vegetarians will particularly enjoy getting wasted on veggie and lentil burgers *(185Kc)*. You must try one of the following drinks: Cosmic Granny *(145Kč)*, Lesbian Joy *(110Kč)*, or Sex with an Alien *(145Kč)*.

⚑ C: I.P. Pavlova. From the station, head east on Jugoslávská for a little more than 1 block. when you reach Bělehradská, the club will be on your left. *i* R and B on Th; house, 80s, and 90s on F; funky on Sa. Lounge is wheelchair-accessible; club is not. ⑤ Cover Th 100Kč, F 100-200Kč, Sa 100Kč. ⚉ Cafe open M-Th 11am-midnight, F-Sa 11am-1am, Su 10:30am-midnight. Club open Th-Sa 10pm-5am.

VINÁRNA VINEČKO
⬥ ♿ ♚ (ᵗᵖ) WINE BAR

Lodynská 135/29
☏222 51 10 35 ▣ www.vineckopraha.cz

An upscale wine bar that errs on the side of adult, Vinárna Vinečko is the perfect place to spend a relaxed evening discussing how delightfully you boogie in a non-ironic way. On warm summer nights, the patio lets you decompress even further. Or, if you're lucky enough to be spending the evening with yourself, bring your laptop, use the free Wi-Fi, and treat yourself to a nice glass of *vino*— no buts—you deserve this.

⚑ A: Náměstí Míru. From the station, head west down Rumunská, then take a left down Lodynská. The bar is actually to the right on Bruselská where it meets Lodynská. ⑤ Snacks 68-105Kč. Wine 52-72Kč. Beer 23-60Kč. ⚉ Open M-F noon-midnight, Sa-Su 2pm-midnight.

Holešovice

🏵 CROSS CLUB
Ⓧ (ᵗᵖ) ♚ CLUB

Plynární 1096/23
▣ www.crossclub.cz

Possibly the coolest club you will ever attend, Cross Club exists over five or six stories, including a five-level patio. The club works like this: half of the club is "pay to enter" and the other half, the cafe and restaurant, is free. But here's the rub—none of these places are connected. In other words, you get a stamp and then you wander between the rooms, all decorated with the most amazing assortment of industrial steel. The crowds err on the side of Czech, but internationals can be found about. The real treats are the various "themed rooms" that you discover making your way through the multi-level club. One room is only tall enough to sit in, and you have to crawl to your seat; another is lit only by narrow lamps made from car engines. The club also features several incredibly cheap food options, like hamburgers *(39Kč)* and fried cheese *(39Kč)*, at different stations. As if this wasn't enough, the upstairs has two speciality shops, one featuring a load of original, hip T-shirts, the other selling vinyl records.

⚑ C: Nádraží Holešovice. From the station, head south through the bus station to Na zátorách. Head east on Na zátorách until it becomes Plynámí; the club is on your left. ⑤ Cover 40-100Kč. Beer 25-40Kč. Mixed drinks 40-105Kč. ⚉ Cafe open daily 2pm-2am. Club open Su-Th 6pm-4am, F-Sa 6pm-6am.

Smichov

FUTURUM MUSIC BAR
⬥ Ⓧ (ᵗᵖ) ♚ BAR, CLUB

Zborovská 82/7
☏257 328 571 ▣ www.futurum.musicbar.cz

Perhaps the most stylish bar you will find in Prague, Futurum boasts high ceilings with gorgeous mosaic formations on the floor and ceilings. Set in red low lighting and expansive with its many nooks, the place is perfect for both an intimate evening or a melodic, high-spun night on the town. Order your drink at the long, winding bar that looks like the brim of a tastefully tiled swimming pool and enjoy the live music happening almost every night.

⚑ Trams #4, 7, 10, or 14: Zborovská. Head towards the river ½ block, turn left on Zborovská *i* Check online for event listings. ⑤ Beer from 30Kč. ⚉ Open daily 9am-3am. Concerts begin at 9pm.

ARTS AND CULTURE

Travelers itching for some authentic artistic and cultural experiences are about to get scratched. By Prague. But anyone interested in seeing a show of any kind should be warned: while Prague has incredible art, music, and showmania, there also exist God-awful tourist shows that cost inexcusable sums. The best opera Prague has to offer is available to students for the cost of a sausage from a street vendor. The best music Prague has to offer comes at the cost of *two* said sausages. In other words, any show that costs more than 190Kč for a student ticket is probably going to suck. Prague has three symphonies, each of which is world-class: the **Czech Philharmonic,** the **Czech Radio Symphony Orchestra,** and the **Czech National Sympohny Orchestra.** Opera can be seen at the **State Opera House,** the **Estates Theater,** or the **National Theater.** Additionally, there are private galleries all about the city, even in portions of Old Town where many artists personally show their work. As with all crafts, more legitimate respected artists will sell their wares away from Old Town. The popular music scene can be good at various clubs, but for some awful reason, someone decided it would be a good thing for piano players to play the same five songs at cafes around the city and for cover artists to sing the same five whiney guitar songs ("Wonderwall" included).

While Prague does have a few theaters that consistently show English productions, these shows are mostly tourist traps and in no way reflect the incredible wealth of English theater that actually goes on here. Prague does, however, have a number of companies that more or less consistently put on shows in various venues. Travelers interested in seeing legitimate theater should check 🖥www.expats.cz and 🖥www.prague.tv for extensive theater listings. In recent years, **Prague Playhouse** *(🖥www.prague-playhouse.com)* has produced the highest number of English language shows, while **Blood, Love, and Rhetoric** *(🖥www.bloodloverhetoric.com)* is a great up-and-coming company. The **Prague Shakespeare Festival** *(🖥www.pragueshakespeare.cz)* even produces a few English performances of Shakespeare plays each year. While most Czech theater plays are repertory, or one or two nights over a six-month period, most English language shows play in short runs or in five to six runs scattered over two weeks or so.

Theater

NATIONAL THEATER 🎟♿🍸 NOVÉ MĚSTO

Národní třída ☎224 90 14 87 🖥www.narodni-divadlo.cz

Producing a program of dance, opera, and Czech-language drama, the National Theater is considered one of the most important cultural institutions in the Czech Republic. The theater itself dates back to 1881, though various fires and other setbacks have caused alterations since then. In addition to its regular schedule, during the summertime, smaller, open-air productions consistently grace the surrounding square.

🚇 B: Národní třída. From the station, walk north to Národní and turn left toward the river. $ Tickets 300-1200Kč. 🕘 Open M-F 10am-5:30pm, Sa-Su 10am-12:30pm and 1-5:30pm. Evening box office opens 1hr. before curtain.

STATI OPERA PRAHA 🎟♿🍸 NOVÉ MĚSTO

Wilsonova 4 ☎224 22 72 66 🖥www.opera.cz

Thanks to the State Opera House's student-rush program, travelers can see a fully staged opera for less than the price of a sausage at nearby Wenceslas Sq. Presenting a dozen or so plays at a time, the State Opera sticks with favorites but paints with a bigger brush than the tourist-friendly Estates. Wagner, Mozart, Verdi, and Puccini operas are most frequently produced, with new productions interspersed more occasionally.

🚇 A or C: Muzeum. From the station, head past the National Museum to the left. $ Tickets 100-1500Kč. Students 50-750Kč. 🕘 Open M-F 10am-5:30pm, Sa-Su 10am-12:30pm, 1pm-5:30pm. Evening box office opens 1hr. before curtain.

ESTATES THEATER

STARE MĚSTO

Ovocný trh ☎224 90 14 48 www.estatestheatre.cz

If it's not enough for you to walk by the famous theater where Mozart conducted *Don Giovanni* or the legendary theater where movie Mozart conducted *The Magic Flute* in the movie *Amadeus*, then it'd better be enough for you to see a show here, because otherwise you're out of options. These days, the Estates plays mostly opera hits like *Carmen*, *The Marriage of Figaro*, and you guessed it, *Don Giovanni*.

A or B: Můstek. From the station, head northwest up Na Můstku and turn right on Rytířská. $ Tickets 300-1200Kč. Open M-F 10am-5:30pm, Sa-Su 10am-12:30pm and 1-5:30pm. Evening box office opens 1hr. before curtain.

Festivals

PRAGUE SPRING MUSIC FESTIVAL

MALÁ STRANA

Hellichova 18 ☎257 31 25 47 www.prague-spring.net

An enormous, month-long festival featuring over 70 performances by the world's best soloists, small ensembles, symphony orchestras, and conductors. In addition to public exhibitions ranging in admission price from free to exorbitant, the festival also plays host to an extensive soloist competition. Founded in 1945, the fest survived the pressures of an oppressive communist regime and continues to bring music to the world in a truly unique way.

$ Tickets 100-10,000Kč. Early May-early June. Check website for specific dates.

PRAGUE WRITERS FESTIVAL

STARE MĚSTO

Platýz, Národní 37/416 ☎224 24 13 12 www.pwf.cz

An exciting five-day celebration of writers of all tongues, the Prague Writers Festival prides itself on bringing in the best of the craft. In 2010, the Festival honored Nobel Prize winner Gao Xingjian, among other top writers in the field. Events of the festival include readings, signings, galas, and question-and-answer sessions.

$ Tickets 100-500Kč. During the 1st 2 weeks of June. Check website for specific dates.

SHOPPING

It'd be a bit of a stretch to call Prague a prime shopping destination. While rare items and great deals can be found, they are few and far between. Most of tourist Prague is overrun by Bohemian crystal dealers and marionette shops, but any traveler on a budget would do well to avoid these. Antique and secondhand stores offer the best shots for rare communist artifacts or snazzy, underappreciated clothing.

Clothing

PARAZIT

STARE MĚSTO

Karlova 25 ☎603 56 17 76 www.parazit.cz

An amazing find in any city, Parazit has more unique fashion finds, outrageous wardrobe choices, and other pieces out of some Tim Burton nightmare. Dresses seem like passion projects from *Project Runway;* match one with a bag that looks like a human head. There are definitely more options for women, but men can find a few fiercely original T-shirts. Every item is handmade by Czech designers and Czech design students.

A: Staroméstka. From the station, head down Křižovnická directly along the river. At the Charles Bridge, turn left at Karlova towards Old Town Sq. Keep following Karlova as it snakes around. The shop will be in a courtyard to the left. $ Shirts 200-500Kč. Dresses from 1200Kč. Bags from 300Kč. Open M-Sa 11am-8pm.

Books and Music

GLOBE BOOKSTORE

NOVÉ MĚSTO

Pštrossova 1925/6 ☎222 52 02 36 www.globebookstore.cz

Attached to a cafe with the same name, the Globe caters specifically to American and British expats looking for literary enlightenment in Czech-speaking Prague.

Featuring an impressive collection of literature, travel guides, and general-interest books, the Globe should definitely be a first stop for book-seeking travelers, and we're not just saying this because it sells **Let's Go.**

B: Karlovo náměstí. From the station, take Resslova toward the river and then turn right on Na Zderaze, which becomes Pštrossova; the cafe is on your right. i Attached cafe keeps the same hours. Open M-Th 9:30am-midnight, F-Sa 9:30am-1am (or later).

Specialty Stores

VETEŠNICTVÍ — MALÁ STRANA

Vitězná 16 ☎257 31 06 11

Thrift-store shopping hasn't quite become as posh Prague-side as it has in the States, but one-of-a-kind treasures can still be found here—although at prices that are far from thrifty. Still, if you're looking to pick up a communist-era backpack or a secondhand bed pan, you'll find plenty here. Even if you know you intend to buy nothing, take a few minutes and appreciate the mildly pornographic glassware or the hundreds of strangely personal old photographs.

A: Malostranská. From the Metro, take the Tram #to Újezd then walk towards the river on Vitězná. $ Antiques 10-10,000Kč. Open M-F 10am-5pm, Sa 10am-noon.

GOLD PRALINES — NOVÉ MĚSTO

Rybná 668 ☎222 31 62 27 www.goldpralines.cz

This specialty store offers everything from truffles to miniature chocolate statues to intricately cut chocolate diamonds. With over 40 different types of truffles, each with a unique shape and flavor, Gold Pralines will please even the pickiest of travelers. Non-chocolate treats like marzipan figurines are also available.

C: Republicka námestí. From the Metro, head west. $ Chocolate 30-300Kč. Open daily 9am-8pm.

ESSENTIALS

Practicalities

- **TOURIST OFFICES: Prague Information Services.** *(Arbesovo nám. 4, on the ground floor of Old Town Hall to the left of the Astronomical Clock. ☎221 714 133 www.pis.cz i Other branches at Na příkopě 20, Hlavní nádraží, and in the tower on the Malá Strana side of the Charles Bridge. Look for the green "i" signs throughout the city. Open daily Apr-Oct 9am-7pm; Nov-Mar 9am-6pm.)*
- **LUGGAGE STORAGE:** Lockers in train and bus stations take 25Kč coins. For storage over 24hr., use the luggage offices in the basement of Hlavní nádraží. *($ 40Kč per day; bags over 15kg 60Kč. Open daily 6-11am, 1:30am-5:30pm, and 6pm-5:30am.)*
- **POST OFFICE:** *(Jindřišská 14. ☎221 13 11 11 A or B: Můstek. Open M-F 8am-6pm.)*
- **INTERNET CAFES:** Free Wi-Fi is available at countless cafes and restaurants across the city. Internet cafes are less frequent, but still extremely abundant.

Emergency!

- **EMERGENCY NUMBERS: Medical Emergency** ☎155. **Unified European Emergency Call (operator speaks Czech, English, German)** ☎112. **Fire Department** ☎150.
- **POLICE:** ☎158. **City Police** ☎156.
- **PHARMACY:** *(Paleckeho 5. ☎224 946 982)*
- **MEDICAL SERVICES: Na Homolce (Hospital for Foreigners).** *(Roentgenova 2. www.homolka.cz/en/ Open M 8am-6pm, Tu 8am-8pm, W 8am-6pm, Th 8am-8pm, F 8am-6pm.)* **Doctor Prague Health Centre.** *(Vodickova 28. ☎603 433 833 www.doctor-prague.cz Open 24hr.)*

Getting There

By Plane
Ruzyně Airport is 20km northwest of the city. *(Take bus #119 to A: Dejvická.* ☎*220 111 111* Ⓢ*12Kč, luggage 6Kč per bag. Buy tickets from kiosks or machines.)* Airport buses run by **Cedaz** *(*☎*220 114 296* 🕘*20-45 min., 2 per hr.)* collect travelers from náměstí Republiky *(*Ⓢ *120Kč);* try to settle on a price before departing.

By Train
International trains *(*☎*972 226 150)* run to: **Berlin, DEU** *(*Ⓢ *1400Kč.* 🕘 *5hr., 6 per day.)* **Bratislava, SLK** *(*Ⓢ *650Kč.* 🕘 *5hr., 6 per day.)* **Budapest, HUN** *(*Ⓢ *1450Kč.* 🕘 *7-9hr., 5 per day.)* **Kraków, POL** *(*Ⓢ *950Kč.* 🕘 *7-8hr., 3 per day.)* **Moscow, RUS** *(*Ⓢ *3000Kč.* 🕘 *31hr., 1 per day.)* **Munich, DEU** *(*Ⓢ *1400Kč.* 🕘*7hr., 3 per day.)* **Vienna, AUT** *(*Ⓢ *1000Kč.* 🕘 *4-5hr., 7 per day.)* **Warsaw, POL** *(*Ⓢ *1300Kč.* 🕘 *9hr., 2 per day.).*

By Bus
Eurolines and airport shuttle tickets are sold at the terminal. *(*☎*224 218 680* 🖥*www. eurolines.cz* 🕘*Open M-F 7am-7pm, Sa 8am-7pm, Su 9am-7pm.)*

Getting Around

By Public Transportation
Prague's Metro system alone could sufficiently serve this fun-size city, but Prague also has a Tram #service (light rail), a bus service, a horde of angry taxis and something called a funicular.

An 18Kč public transportation ticket (there's just one type, regardless of the type of transportation) buys a 20min. non-transferable Tram #or bus ride or a five-station non-transferable Metro ride. A 26Kč ticket lasts 1¼hr. with unlimited transfers, and buys a ride on the funicular cable car that runs to the top of **Petřín Hill.** Tickets, which are available at stations and all convenience stores, must be validated at the start of each trip; unstamped tickets are invalid. Although ticket inspections are rare, a hefty fine awaits freeloaders, so pay up. One-, three-, and five-day passes cost 100Kč, 330Kč, and 500Kč, respectively; a monthly pass costs 550Kč. Metro trains run every 2-10min. on line A (green), B (yellow), and C (red) daily 5am-midnight. The dozens of Tram #lines keep different hours, and lines and routes change for late-night service.

Travelers should be mindful of pickpockets and remember that Praguers are big on respect. Persons under 30 should offer seats to seniors or prepare to be shunned like lepers.

karlštejn

Karlštejn Castle was built by Charles IV in 1348 to guard the crown jewels, and unlike its counterpart in Prague, this sucker's actually a full-on castle. We're talking a big-ass wall perched on a mountain top and pawning the cutest little support town you've ever seen, now mostly desperate souvenir shops. The schlep there and back can be done in half a day, and the images of the Czech countryside, run-ins with priceless locals, and the self esteem boost you'll get from imagining you own it all will be some of the most memorable parts of your trip. If you're even thinking of going, make a reservation **now** for the second, extended tour *(available May-Oct),* which takes guests into the heart of the castle including the **Chapel of the Sacred Heart** and some incredible medieval ruins. Those lucky enough to get a reservation can sleep easy knowing they've seen one of the top three sights in the entire Czech Republic. Travelers in less of a hurry can stay over for lunch or take a hike through the woods, which are jurassically overgrown and green in the summer.

SIGHTS

Karlštejn Castle

CASTLE TOUR I

Státní hrad Karlštejn ☎274008154 🖥www.hradkarlstejn.cz

The hour-long tour of Karlštejn Castle takes you through Charles's bedroom and throne chambers as well as the nuns' quarters and the lower rooms of the medium-sized Marian tower. While none of the sights are stunning, it's pretty cool to check out Charles's collection of holy relics, the best of which is the head of a **dragon** St. George killed. Turns out it's a crocodile—imagine that. While the real crown jewels no longer hang in Karlštejn, guests can take a look at some impressive copies. At the height of its power, Karlštejn would hold hundreds of knights at a time, and a few of their original "armor closets" are still on display. Unfortunately, this tour doesn't let visitors into the enormous large tower.

➜ From Karlštejn, walk up the path to the castle. $ 250Kč, students 150Kč. ⏰ Nov-Mar Tu-Su 9am-3pm; Apr, Oct 9am-4pm; May-June, Sept 9am-5pm; Jul-Aug 9am-6pm. Schedule subject to change; check website to confirm times.

CASTLE TOUR II

Státní hrad Karlštejn ☎274008154 🖥www.hradkarlstejn.cz

This tour takes you into the best parts of Karlštejn castle, including the Great Tower, which was never conquered even when the Hussites took the fortification and, as well as the Chapel of the Holy Cross, which was used to store the crown jewels. Best of all, the tour is limited to 15 guests, so you can tap the knowledegable tour guides. Ask questions. They have stories they won't tell you unprompted. For instance, while most castles used wells for water (in case of a siege), Karlštejn couldn't tap its well and had to dig a secret water main from the nearby brook. If anyone found that out, they could poison the brook and take the castle. So, problem solver that he was, Charles IV killed all the workers who built the duct so they wouldn't tell anyone. What makes the tour is the Church of Our Lady, which has an original medieval apocalypse scene violently splayed on its walls. Though some has been destroyed in various sieges, there are still enough nine-headed **dragons,** ghouls made of fire, and skeletons on horses to let you glimpse the horror of the medieval imagination and to haunt your dreams for years to come. The Chapel of the Holy Cross, the final stop on the trek, contains 129 portraits of Bohemian Kings and saints and is covered with the country's largest collection of semi-precious stones. The ceiling, though, is what rocks. It's covered in thousands of glass plates that try (and mostly succeed) to look like a starry sky.

*➜ From Karlštejn, walk up the path to the castle. **i** All reservations must be made in advance. Reservations for Jul and Aug should be made up to 6 months in advance. $ 300Kč, students 200Kč. ⏰ Open Tu-Su Jun 1-Oct 31.*

FOOD

A dozen or so food shops fill this little village, and all of them are more or less fine. But the only one that offers a different, better experience is listed below.

RESTAURACE POD DRACI SKÁLOU CZECH

267 18 Karlštejn 130 ☎311 681 177 🖥www.poddraciskalou.eu

A 5min. walk through the forest from the door to the castle, or a 15min. walk from town, this little forest cafe serves up great authentic food in the middle of what feels like a medieval clearing. None of the items are in English, but a small little picture at the bottom of each section lets you know which animal you're about to eat. If you can find someone to translate, try one of the wild treats like shark steak *(111Kč)* or wild boar *(237Kč).*

➜ From the castle, turn right immediately after you leave the gate (there'll be a sign directing off

into the woods). Follow the path through the woods down the hill. From the town/train station, proceed towards the castle and take the only left that diverts from the main path through the town about 10min. before the castle entrance. Take the road about 10min. through the woods. The restaurant will be on your right. Look for the statue of a ◼dragon. ⑤ Entrees 75-200Kč. Beer 15-35Kč. ◯ Open M-Sa 11am-11pm. Su 11am-8pm.

ESSENTIALS

Getting There

To get to Karlštejn, take the **Beroun train** *(92Kč)* from Prague's Hlavní Nádraží which leaves every hour *(last train leaves at 7pm)*. The train station can be extremely difficult to navigate and the signs poorly marked, so a traveler's best bet is to find any of the information windows and explain your dilemma. The ride takes about 40min. and spends a long time along a river and snaking through the mountains—it's gorgeous. Once you arrive, the castle is a wee bit of a walk *(2km)*, but again, except to the very lazy, this walk will be enjoyable. Just head to your right down the road and across the bridge, then up the hill following the signs that read "hrad." If you're thinking of staying until the evening, make sure to check at the train station when the last train for Prague leaves.

terezín

Although Terezín's most infamous era was WWII when it served as a prison camp for enemies of the Reich (mainly Jews), it was originally built at the end of the 18th century as a strategic stronghold against invaders from the east. It quickly became apparent however, that Terezín was ineffective as a defensive structure, and it was adapted to serve mainly as a prison. The assassins of Archduke Ferdinand—the man whose death started WWI—were jailed and eventually died in Terezin. During WWII, the camp was first used as a prison for political prisoners of the SS, but was slowly converted into a concentration and transit camp for Jews, Romas, Communists, and homosexuals. Terezín was unique, however, in its designation as a prison for high profile prisoners. The abundance of artists, writers, and intellectuals kept in Terezín would produce some of the war's most striking and stark images of life in a Nazi concentration camp. All in all, 200,000 men, women, and children would pass through Terezín's transit centers; 40,000 died at the camp, while 120,000 moved on to death camps in the east. Only 8,000 of the prisoners to pass through Terezín would survive the war.

SIGHTS

The essential sights of Terezín are all administered by a centralized organization, **Terezín Memorial.** A universal ticket can be purchased at any of the sites *(200Kč, students 150Kč)*, or tickets can be purchased separately for each *(160Kč, students 130Kč)*. If you have time, start with the **Ghetto Museum.** For travelers short on time, just see the **Small Fortress.** That being said, Terezín is best experienced as an entire morning and afternoon trip, and given the hour-long bus ride a visit to Terezín requires, it makes sense to spend some time there.

SMALL FORTRESS
Principova alej 304

⊛⑤ MEMORIAL

☎416 782 225 ▣www.pamatnik-terezin.cz

Although the information center provides explanatory maps of the small fortress grounds, definitely try to get a guided tour, which groups of 10 or more can call ahead and book for free (and upon which keen *Let's Go* travelers can usually piggy-back). The Nazis built Terezín as a show prison to demonstrate their humane treatment of prisoners to Red Crosss workers. Only a guide can explain, for instance, that the sinks in the main cell block didn't actually work, or that the swallows building mud nests on the light fixtures had built the same nests during the war; they were a symbol of hope for the winter-frozen prisoners. During the 90min. tour, a knowledgeable and able historian shows you the large holding cells, the solitary confinement cells, the showers and delousing stations, and the various execution grounds. After the tour, travelers can visit exhibits on the WWI and WWII history of the fortress or view documentaries and propaganda films that are shown in an extant Nazi cinema. A relaxed tour of the small fortress can easily take 2hr.

➡ From the bus stop, head east out of the town, over the bridge the bus passed coming in. At the cemetery memorial, take the left fork. $ Combined 200Kč, single 160Kč. Students 150Kč/130. ⏰ Open Nov-Mar daily 8am-4:30pm, Apr-Oct daily 8am-6pm.

GHETTO MUSEUM ⊛♿🍸 MUSEUM

Komenského ulice ☎416 782 225 💻www.pamatnik-terezin.cz

The Ghetto Museum contains a permanent exhibit on the Jewish "Final Solution," specifically with regard to its implementation in Czechoslovakia. Not only does the museum put this tragedy in context, but it contains the most moving exhibit of the entire monument: hundreds of drawings by children who were briefly allowed to attend school during the occupation of the ghetto. The museum also screens a documentary about the memorial and the various events and souls that contributed to the tragedy.

➡ From the bus stop, walk east around the corner from the information center. ℹ A well-stocked cafe in the basement sells lunch and snack fare. Open daily 11am-4pm. $ Combined 200Kč, single 160Kč. Students 150Kč/130. ⏰ Open daily Nov-Mar 9am-5:30pm, Apr-Oct 9am-6pm.

CREMATORIUM ⊛♿ CEMETERY

Principova alej 304 ☎416 782 225 💻www.pamatnik-terezin.cz

The crematorium, where the remains of prisoners were burned, suffered heavy damage in the flooding of 2004. While the facilities have been restored, they have been uncomfortably "over-restored" so that the crematorium now appears to be almost functional. But that's just the inside. From the oustide, the unassuming crematorium could be a small synagogue in the middle of a Jewish graveyard, where a giant stone menorah and various other urns and monuments commemorate the murdered Jews of the Final Solution.

➡ From the bus stop, head across the square to the southwest corner of the Terezín. Continue walking 3-5min. out of town, following the signs that say "Krematorium." ℹ Men should cover their heads before they enter the grounds. Yarmulkes can be purchased inside the crematorium for 20Kč. $ Combined 200Kč, single 160Kč. Students 150Kč/130. ⏰ Open Nov-Mar daily 10am-4pm, Apr-Oct daily 10am-5pm.

MADGEBURG BARRACKS ⊛⊗ MUSEUM

Komenského ulice ☎416 782 225 💻www.pamatnik-terezin.cz

The Madgeburg Barracks house a collection of paintings, drawings, manuscripts, and artisan works produced by Terezín's unusually high proportion of artists, performers, and writers who made these works in the Ghetto—the camps and the Nazi administration buildings where artists were employed to illustrate various announcements. While these secretly produced images were intended to alert the outside world of the atrocities being commited at Terezín, attempts to transmit the pictures were discovered and brutally punished, and most of these images were not uncovered until after the war. The barracks additionally hold the various manuscripts, set pieces, and costumes from the show performances that the Jews were forced to put on for the Red Cross workers.

➡ From the bus station head across the square along Komenského. The barracks is to the left at the end of the street. $ Combined 200Kč, single160Kč. Student 150Kč/130. ⏰ Open daily 9am-5pm.

FOOD

RESTAURACE NA HRADBÁCH ⊛⊗🍸☀ CZECH ❶

Bohušovická brána 335 ☎0723 287 738

A little tiny place where the owners are more than likely to sit down and have a beer with you, Na Hradbách should give you a delicious taste of what it's like to be from the Czech countryside—and it will hardly cost you a dime. Although everything on the menu is great (and virtually free), one surprisingly delicious dish is the fried bread and mustard *(10Kč)*, which could be a meal in itself.

Head to the southwest corner of the garrison. The restaurant is just after you leave the town proper on your way to the Crematorium. $ Entrees 50-95Kč. ⏰ Open M-F noon-10pm Sa-Su noon-8pm.

ESSENTIALS

Getting There

Buses leave regularly from **Nádraží Holešovice** off the metro's C line. The bus station can be difficult to navigate for first-timers. Your best best is to find an information booth, tell them you're trying to get to Terezín, then let them point you in the direction of the proper platform. Tickets are purchased on the bus and cost 80Kč one way. The bus ride takes about 1hr. and drops you directly in front of the Terezín tourist office, 25m from the entrance to the Ghetto Museum. Check the tourist office for the time of return buses. Be warned: the last bus leaves Terezín for Prague around 6pm on most days.

kutnà hora

Kutnà Hora might be the perfect day trip, with cheap grub, untamed countryside, and a set of sights that range from the bone art of 40,000 dead humans to a jaunt 100ft. below the surface of the earth make afternoons here unforgettable. Plus there's one of the most beautiful Gothic cathedrals in central Europe. Even though Kutnà Hora was once a popping city wealthy from its silver mines, the community is now small, quiet, and peaceful, unlike anything you can find in Prague.

ORIENTATION

If you took the bus here, and you should have, the city center (*Palackého náměstí*) sits to the southwest, just up the hill. From there, the tourist center can point you to the nearby Silver Mine Museum and Santa Barbara Cathedral farther up the hill. On your way you can check out St. James Cathedral and the Jesuit College, which are both worth walking by. Visiting the **Cathedral of Our Lady of Assumption** and the **Bone Church** requires a 15min. local bus ride from the bus station.

SIGHTS

ST. BARBARA'S CATHEDRAL — CHURCH

Barborská ☎327 512 115 www.chramsvatebarbory.cz

From the outside, St. Barbara's looks like an ecclesiastical horn toad with spikes and spires jutting willy-nilly. Examined closely, these horns become gargoyles shaped like men or ghouls or rabbits. Inside the church has its own non-traditional charms, like the crests of moneyed families conspicuously floating on the ceiling or the comic book Bible scenes hodgepodged in the gaps between the arches. Then there's the golden organ with its angel band stroking harps and blasting bugles. The Church of St. Barbara (the patron saint of mining) was founded in 1388, and is still worth it today.

From Palackého náměstí, head west on Husova, then take a left on Mincířská another quick right onto Komenského náměstí and another quick left onto Barborská. Follow it as it snakes up the hill and ends at the Cathedral. $ 50Kč, students 30Kč. ⏰ Open daily Nov-Mar 10am-4pm; Apr-Oct 9am-6pm.

THE BONE CHURCH/OSSUARY/ALL SAINTS CHURCH — CHURCH

Zámecká 127 ☎327 561 143 www.kostnice.cz

In the 15th century the Black Death caused the death of a significant portion of the European population. Rumor spread that some traveling monk brought soil to All Saints church from the Holy Land and suddenly, All Saints was *the* place to die and be dead. There were so many people wanting to rest in peace at the church that they decided to expand it. This meant digging up nearly 40,000 bodies. And as everyone knows, when you've got 40,000 exhumed bodies, the only thing to do is give them to a half-blind monk so he can arrange them into crazy designs. The ossuary has skull chandeliers, femur mobiles, streamers of human heads. Try to remember as you're enjoying these decorations that each once had a mother who loved it. Ask to see the hand-pumped organ on the top floor of the church—it's mildly entertaining.

➡ From the bus station, take local bus #1 Bus M-F, #7 Bus Sa-Su to Sedlec. $ 40Kč, students 30Kč. ⏰ Open daily Nov-Feb 9am-4pm; Mar 9am-5pm; Apr-Sept 8am-6pm; Oct 9am-5pm.

CZECH MUSEUM OF SILVER - HRÁDEK — MINE

Barborská 28 — ☎327 512 159 💻www.cms-kh.cz

Rivaling the Bone Church in coolness, this tour of an abandoned silver mine shaft wraps you in miner gear and sends you 35m below the surface of the Earth. The experience is gritty and dirty: ground water streams freely from the rocks around you and in some parts of the tour, vistors must duck and squeeze through the rock. The 1½hr. tour also covers the history of mining in the city and a lot of other stuff that seems weak-sauce compared to the tour of the mine.

*➡ From Palackého náměstí, head west on Husova, then take a left on Mincířská another quick right onto Komenského náměstí and another quick left onto Barborská. **i** Not reccomended for people with even mild claustrophobia or people who have trouble with stairs. $ 120Kč, students 80Kč. ⏰ Open daily Tu-Su Apr, Oct 9am-5pm; May-Jun, Sept 9am-6pm; July-August 10am-6pm. Nov Sa-Su 10am-4pm, M-F through prior booking.*

CATHEDRAL OF THE ASSUMPTION OF OUR LADY — CHURCH

Zámecká, 284 03 — ☎327 561 143 💻www.sedlec.info

A relatively large and empty church, the Cathedral of the Assumption of our Lady definitely won't be the thing you remember from Kutnà Hora, but it's worth a stop in, especially with the combined ticket described below. A group of happy Hussites burned the cathedral down during the war, but it was rebuilt in the Baroque style in the 18th century.

➡ From the bus station, take local bus #1 M-F, #7 Sa-Su to Selecs. $ 30Kč, students 20Kč. Joint ticket to the ossuary and the cathedral 70/40Kč. ⏰ Open Apr-Oct M-Sa 9am-5pm, Su 12pm-5am; Nov-Mar by appointment only.

FOOD

Authentic. Almost free. Delicious.

MCK FAST FOOD — CAFE ❶

Kollárova 590, 284 01 — ☎327 512 127

Despite the idiotic name, McK will be an amazing gastronomical experience for you, if only because the food is basically free. Baguettes of good sizes *(20-30Kč)* and toast *(12-16Kč)* go for a pittance. Entire hamburger meals with fries and a drink are what they could have cost at McDonalds in 1994, and if you just want the hamburger, expect to pay as much as you would for bubble gum *(55Kč)*. Also, the food is good. Vegetarians can dig the big salads *(40Kč)*.

➡ From Palackého náměstí, head down Kollárova. $ Meals 20-50Kč. ⏰ Open M-F 7:30am-5:30pm, Sa 9am-2pm.

ESSENTIALS

Practicalities

- **TOURIST OFFICES:** *(Palackého náměstí 377/5 💻http://kutnahora.cz **i** Contains maps and information, and has an incredibly eager staff. ⏰ Open Mar-Sept M-Su 9am-6pm, Oct-Feb M-F 9am-5pm, Sa-Su 10am-4pm.)*

Getting There

It seems weird, but Kutnà Hora is best reached by bus and best left by train. Buses leave less-than-frequently from Prague's **Florenc** bus station (Metro: B, C) and cost 83Kč each way. For a full day in Kutnà Hora, it's best to be to the train station by 10am. It's 90min. to the Kutnà Hora bus station, and from there it's just a short walk up the hill to the information center and most of Kutnà Hora's sites. Reaching the Ossuary (All Saints Church) from the center of town requires a 20min. bus ride to **Selecs** *(weekdays: # 1, weekends: # 7 $ 10Kč).* From there, it's a 10min. walk to the train station, where trains leave to Prague *(each way 127Kč).* The train ride takes about 1hr. The last train leaves at 9pm. A trip to Kutnà Hora can be properly done in 5hr., not including travel, but most of the city shuts down at 5pm, so a trip to Kutnà Hora should begin with an early morning.

Kutnà Hora, with a decidedly smaller English-speaking population, can be a bit more difficult to navigate than Prague. The best advice is to look for signs, and remember that everything important is in the same basic area.

essentials

entrance requirements

- **PASSPORT:** Required for citizens of Australia, Canada, Ireland, New Zealand, the UK, and the US.
- **VISA:** Required for visitors who plan to stay in the Schengen area for more than 90 days.
- **WORK PERMIT:** Required for all foreigners planning to work in the Czech Republic.

PLANNING YOUR TRIP

Time Differences

The Czech Republic is one hour ahead of Greenwich Mean Time (GMT) and observes Daylight Saving Time.This means that it is six hours ahead of New York City, nine hours ahead of Los Angeles, one hour ahead of the British Isles, nine hours behind Sydney, and 10 hours behind New Zealand.

MONEY

Tipping

Tipping in the Czech Republic is not mandatory, and service staff will not chase after tips. However, it is polite to tip around 5-10% if you're satisfied with your service. Touristy restaurants in the center of town will expect a 15-20% tip, but you have *Let's Go* to help you avoid those places.

Taxes

Most goods in the Schengen area are subject to a Value-Added Tax of 19% (a reduced tax of 7% is applied to books and magazines, foods, and agricultural products). Ask for a VAT return form at points of purchase to enjoy tax-free shopping. Present it at customs upon leaving the country, along with your receipts and the unused goods. Refunds can be claimed at Tax Free Shopping Offices, found at most airports, road borders, and ferry stations, or by mail (Tax-Free Shopping Processing Center, Trubelgasse 19, 1030 Vienna Austria).

SAFETY AND HEALTH

Local Laws and Police

You should not hestitate to contact the police if you are the victim of a crime. Be sure to carry a valid passport, as police have the right to ask for identification. Police in the Czech Republic can sometimes be unhelpful if you are the victim of a currency exchange scam; in that case, you might be better off seeking advice from your embassy or consulate.

Drugs and Alcohol

If you carry insulin, syringes, or any prescription drugs in these cities, you must carry a copy of the prescriptions and a doctor's note. Avoid public drunkenness as it will jeopardize your safety. In the Czech Repubic, drinking is permitted at age 18. The possession of small quantities of marijuana is decriminalized in the Czech Republic. Carrying drugs across an international border—considered to be drug trafficking—is a serious offense that could land you in prison.

Smoking is incredibly popular in the Czech Republic. If you are sensitive to cigarette smoke, ask for a non-smoking room in a hotel or hostel, or to be seated in the non-smoking area of a restaurant.

Natural Disasters

In the event of an earthquake, drop and take cover if indoors. If outside, move away from buildings and utility wires. Flooding occurs fairly frequently in the Czech Republic, but city officials are quick to warn residents, and relief efforts are swift and effective.

Pre-Departure Health

Matching a prescription to a foreign equivalent is not always easy, safe, or possible, so if you take **prescription drugs,** carry up-to-date prescriptions or a statement from your doctor stating the medications' trade names, manufacturers, chemical names, and dosages. Be sure to keep all medication with you in your carry-on luggage. Some drugs—like pseudoephedrine (Sudafed) and diphenhydramine (Benadryl)—are not available in the Czech Republic, or are only available with a perscription, so plan accordingly. Drugs such as aspirin, acetaminophen or Tylenol, ibuprofen or Advil, antihistamines (*antihistaminika*), and penicillin can be found at any local Hungarian pharmacy (*lékárna*).

czech republic 101

FOOD AND DRINK

Food

All the traditional central European staples make an appearance in Czech cuisine, including goulash, brats, and things ending in "kraut" and "schnitzel." Many dishes are served with a side of **knedlik**, i.e. gravy-laden flour dumplings. For vegetarians, **fried cheese** (*smazeny syr*), omelettes, and potato pancakes (*Bramborak*), are local favorites. Other distinctly Czech specialties include *Beefsteak na Kyselo*, which is beef with a tartar sauce-like gravy, and *Kapr Peceny s Kyselou Omackou*, which is carp (the national fish). Soups such as *Cesnekovy Polevka* (garlic soup), *Drstkova Polevka* (tripe soup), and onion soup are also popular. Steer clear from these on date nights, though—unless you're packing industrial strength breath mints.

Drink

With the world's highest per capita beer consumption, it's easy to guess the king of Prague's beverage world. It's actually tough to find a meal for which **beer** isn't an appropriate accompaniment—some Czechs even have it with soup for breakfast. Beer is also a lunch favorite, happy hour standard, and dinner is almost incomplete without this "liquid bread." It doesn't hurt that beer is cheaper than the average can of soda. For authentic local flavor, try brews like **Pilsner Urquell, Budvar, Staropramen** and **Branik.**

HOLIDAYS AND FESTIVALS

Globalization or not, Prague continues to celebrate itself in distinctly Czech ways. Christmas carp, anyone?

festivals

- **MIKULAS (ST. NICHOLAS' DAY-DECEMBER 5TH).** It's reverse trick-or-treating: An elaborately costumed St. Nicholas roams around Prague's Old Town Square, asking children whether they've been good or bad, and doling out treats or coal accordingly. What gives this tradition its Czech flair is St. Nick's entourage: an angel and devil. Don't leave the neighborhood without checking out the Christmas markets loaded with handicrafts and goodies. Get your holiday treats while you can—the traditional Christmas dinner is carp.

- **EASTER.** Prague's Easter markets take over the Old Town Square, selling traditional handcrafts of all kinds. The stars of this show are the hand-decorated Easter eggs. A less commercial (and PC) Easter tradition entails men making bundles of willow twigs called *pomlaskás*, and going to see their favorite girls, who can either decorate the *pomlaská* or throw cold water on their suitors. Seems cute today, but some remember when Easter was still "let's beat women with *pomlaskás*" day.

- **LOVER'S DAY (MAY 1ST).** In Prague, the traditional thing to do is take your honey to the top of Petřín Hill, deposit flowers on the grave of romantic poet Karel Hynek Mácha, and smooch away—nothing like taking in the view and being a spectacle simultaneously. Of course, most participants are too busy to notice others' PDA.

- **ST. VÁCLAV DAY (WEEKEND OF SEPT. 28).** Czechs put the fun in fungi the weekend of this feast day, when thousands travel to the forests around Prague in search of the elusive Václavky mushroom. If Czechs have a national sport, it might just be mushroom hunting—they get pretty competitive about it, so don't even think of honing in on someone else's fungi.

- **WITCHES' NIGHT (APRIL 30).** Another Petřín Hill extravaganza, this tradition involves taking the effigy of a witch up to the top of the hill and burning it. Because it would be a shame if witch burning went out of style entirely.

czech republic

FRANCE

Think of a famous idea. Any famous idea. Or for that matter any brushstroke, article of clothing, architectural style, camera technique, great thinker that should have been medicated, or hip reason to brew a Molotov cocktail. If that idea is Western, then it is probably French (or at least hotly contested and contributed to a French intellectual movement). Your first walk around Paris will be defined by a paralyzing level of excitement. Your first party in Monaco might result in a *Hangover*-esque situation. It's no secret that young Americans "backpack" through France to lose their virginity and construct their identity at a safe distance from their parents. The successes of James Baldwin, Gertrude Stein, and Ernest Hemingway suggest that we couldn't have chosen a better spot; there is a pervading sense in France that *everything* is here.

Students might go to France to be fashionably disaffected artists in boho-chic corner cafes, but this isn't the land of berets and baguettes anymore: it's the land of sustainable energy and the 35-hour work week. As France wrestles with the economic and cultural ramifications of a globalized world, this is also, increasingly, the country of *parkour* and veil bans, sprawling Chinatowns and the Marie Leonie case of 2004. Nowhere is the cognitive dissonance of these cultural collisions more evident than in Marseille, whose burgeoning Little Algeria encroaches upon the city's Old World streets. In the midst if these transitions, the most sacred of French traditions remain gloriously preserved—you might eat a lot of kebabs while you're here, but you can still riot against The Man in the morning and commit adultery by noon.

greatest hits

- **"METAL ASPARAGUS" INDEED.** Lord knows the **Eiffel Tower** wasn't popular at first, but these days the number of people that visits the landmark annually is greater than the entire population of Montana (p. 290).

- **VATICAN-APPROVED T AND A.** France might bill itself as a proudly secular country, but when it comes to church-condoned feathers, falsies, and masquerade balls, Nice conveniently becomes a Catholic stronghold again (p. 383).

- **BEND THAT GENDER.** Soak up the vibrant gay nightlife in Cannes (p. 416).

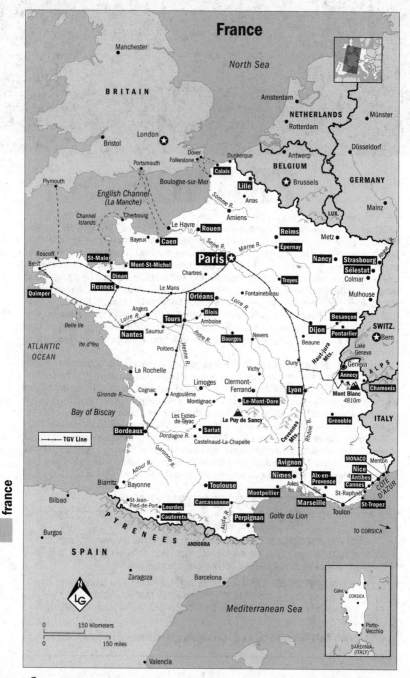

France

france

The trick to a good trip to France is avoiding cliche, so time for some real talk about how you're going to enjoy Paris. Your art history professor told you to go to **the Louvre**, and you should, but there's so much more to see in Paris than the Mona Lisa—and a lot of it is free. Not nearly as morbid as you might think, ▨**Cimitière du Père Lachaise** is hauntingly beautiful, and the final resting place of Jim Morrison of The Doors. If you're staying in the "flavorful" Marais, try staying in ▨**Maubuisson,** a convent-turned-hostel with 3 buildings and breakfast included. Penny-pinching? Try staying somewhere in Canal St-Martin, where prices tend to be a little lower (though you don't want to be traveling alone at night). We'll leave it to you to figure out how to ask for your snails on the side, but the best eats in Paris are most definitely in the 8ème.

Though you could probably spend several satisfied lifetimes in Paris, we encourage you to backpack your way through the rest of the country. Tired of living like a dirty, smelly, backpacker and ready to start living like a king? Well, we can't promise that you'll be able to do that in the Loire Valley, but you can certainly see the chateaux the kings lived in. **Orléans** and **Tours** are major cities of the region, but if you can only hit one make it Tours. If you're hoping to embrace your inner wino (he's probably not hiding too far under the surface away), swing by **Bordeaux** and the surrounding wine country, the viticultural center of the world. Of course, one of the best places in the world to booze and flooze is the **Riviera.** Don't blow your savings in **Monaco** (that is unless you gamble); try to find smaller hot spots in **Cannes** or **Juan-les-Pins** instead.

paris

From students who obsess over Derrida's *Of Grammatology* to tourists who wonder why the French don't pronounce half the consonants in each word, everyone enjoys the city where, by decree of law, buildings don't exceed six stories, *pour que tout le monde ait du soleil* (so that all have sunshine). Though Parisians may English you (speak in English when you speak in French), this city pulls through for those who let themselves indulge in the sensory snapshots around every corner—the aroma of a *boulangerie*, the gleam of bronze balconies, the buzz of a good €2 bottle of red, the jolt of the new fave Metro line 14. For all its hyped-up snobbery (and yes, the waiters are judging you), Paris is open to those willing to wander. The truth is, this city will charm and bitchslap you with equal gusto, but don't get too le tired—by your third or fourth sincere attempt at *s'il vous plaît*, even the waiters soften up. Stick around long enough, and you'll be able to tell the *foux* from the *foux de fa fa*, the Lavazza from the Illy, and the meta hipster bars from the wanna-be meta hipster bars. *Et puis*, we'll see who's judging whom.

ORIENTATION

The Seine river ("SEN") flows from east to west and slices through the middle of Paris, dividing the city into two main sections: the Rive Gauche (Left Bank) to the north, and the Rive Droite (Right Bank) to the south. The two islands in the center of the Seine, the Ile de la Cité and Ile St-Louis, are both the geographical and historical heart of the city. The rest of Paris proper is divided into 20 arrondissements (districts), which spiral clockwise outward from the center of the city, like a snail shell.

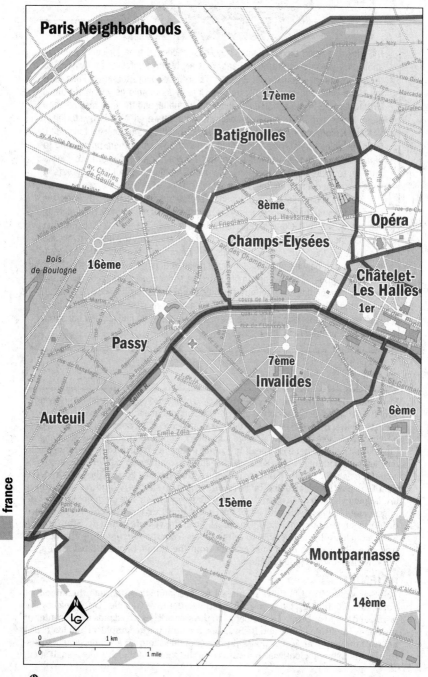

Paris Neighborhoods

17ème

Batignolles

8ème

Opéra

Champs-Élysées

Bois de Boulogne

16ème

Châtelet-Les Halles

1er

Passy

7ème

Invalides

6ème

Auteuil

15ème

Montparnasse

14ème

france

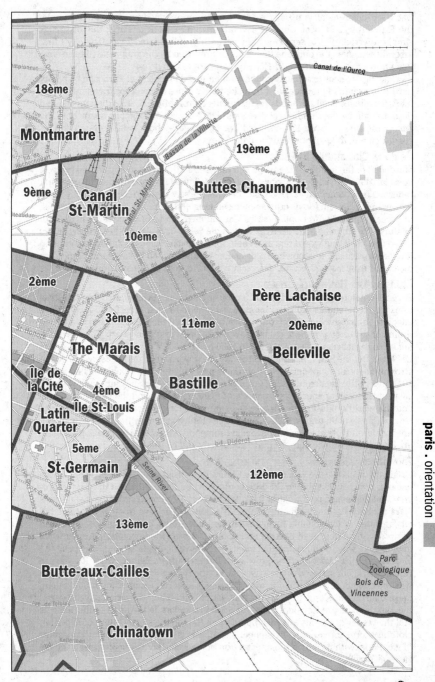

Each arrondissement is usually referred to by an assigned number. For example, the Eiffel Tower is located in the seventh arrondissement of Paris; this district is simply referred to as *le septième* ("the seventh"), abbreviated 7ème. The city's first arrondissement is the only one that is not abbreviated by the grammatical form *ème*; it is known as the *premier* ("PREM-yay") and abbreviated 1er.

The city's organization may sound eminently reasonable, but Paris can be plenty hard to navigate in practice. Just to make things more difficult for travelers, Paris's most prominent neighborhoods regularly bleed into different arrondissements, and do not abide by their numerical divisions. The Marais, for example, spans both the 3ème and the 4ème. We have divided our coverage by both neighborhood and arrondissement, to keep our readers in the know.

Île de la Cité and Île St-Louis

Marooned in the middle of the Seine and tethered to the mainland by arched bridges, **Île de la Cité** is situated at the physical center of Paris. The island hosted Paris's first ramshackle settlement in 300 BCE, and became the seat of the French monarchy in the 6th century CE when Clovis crowned himself king of the Franks; it remained a hotbed of French political power until Charles V abandoned it in favor of the **Louvre** in the 14th century. The stunning **Notre Dame**, as well as the **Sainte-Chapelle** and the **Conciergerie,** ensured that the island would remain a center of Parisian religious, political, and cultural life; unsurprisingly, it is now a major center of tourism. All distances in France are measured from *kilomètre zéro*, a circular sundial in front of Notre Dame.

Châtelet-Les Halles *(1er, 2ème)*

Paris's Châtelet-Les Halles is famous for turning Paris's pet vices into beloved institutions. Its most famous sight, the **Louvre,** was home to French kings for four centuries; absolute monarchy has since gone out of fashion, and the bedchambers and dining rooms of the *ancien régime* palace now house the world's finest art. The surrounding **Jardin des Tuileries** was redesigned in 1660 by Louis XIV's favorite architect, André Le Nôtre, but the Sun King's prized grounds are now a public park, host to crowds of strolling plebeians like ourselves that Louis probably wouldn't have touched with a 10 ft. pole. Still, the arrondissement's legacy of excess is certainly alive and well; we suspect that toilet paper rolls are made of €1000 notes around the **Bourse de Valeurs**, and the world's oldest profession reigns supreme along the curbs of **rue Saint-Denis.** One of Paris's main tourist hubs, Châtelet-Les Halles is heavily frequented by travelers, locals, and lots of scam artists. Seeing somebody run after a pickpocket is not an uncommon occurence here, so move cautiously and confidently.

The Marais *(3ème, 4ème)*

Originally all bog—the name "Marais" literally translates to "swamp"—the Marais became remotely liveable in the 13th century, when monks drained the land to provide building space for the **Right Bank.** With Henry IV's construction of the glorious **Place des Vosges** at the beginning of the 17th century, the area ironically became the city's center of fashionable living; **hôtels particuliers** built by leading architects and sculptors abounded, as did luxury and scandal. During the Revolution, former royal haunts gave way to slums and tenements. The Jewish population, a presence in the Marais since the 12th century, grew with influxes of immigrants from Russia and North Africa, but suffered tragic losses during the Holocaust. In the 1960s, the Marais was once again revived when it was declared a historic neighborhood. Since then, more than 30 years of gentrification, renovation, and fabulous-ization have restored the Marais to its pre-Revolutionary glory. **Rue des Rosiers,** in the heart of the 4ème, is still the center of the city's Jewish population, though the steady influx of hyper-hip clothing stores threatens its existence. The Marais is also unquestionably the center of gay Paris, with its hub at the intersection of **rue Sainte-Croix de la Brettonerie** and **rue Vieille du Temple.**

france

Latin Quarter and St-Germain (5ème, 6ème)

The Latin Quarter and St-Germain tend to be two of Paris's primary tourist neighborhoods. From the hustle and bustle of the predatory cafes around **St-Michel** to the residential areas around **Cardinal Lemoine** and **Jussieu**, the schmoozy galleries of **Odéon** to the best museums Paris has to offer **(Musée de Cluny, Musée Delacroix)**, the fifth and sixth arrondissements truly have it all. They're also eminently walkable. Don't head underground during the day; you'll only encounter pickpockets, scammers, crowds, and—in the summertime—sweaty Metro rides.

Invalides (7ème)

With tourist attractions and museums at every corner, the 7ème bustles with activity, but could use some personality. French military prowess (stop laughing, that's not nice) is celebrated at **Invalides, Ecole Militaire,** and **Champ de Mars,** while the nation's artistic legacy is shown full force at the **Musée d'Orsay** and the **Quai Voltaire.** Formerly one of Paris's most elegant residential districts, the neighborhood is now home to many of the city's embassies. The **Tour Eiffel** appropriately towers over it all, securing the area as one of the most popular destinations.

Champs-Élysées (8ème)

If the Champs-Élysées were a supermodel, it would have been forced to retire for being well past its prime. The arrondissement was synonymous with fashion throughout the 19th century, and the boulevards here are still lined with the vast mansions, expensive shops, and grandiose monuments that keep the tourists coming. But the sense of sophistication and progress has since been dampened by charmless boutiques, office buildings, and car dealerships; these areas are comatose after dark. Only the **Champs** itself throbs late into the night, thanks to its unparalleled nightclubs and droves of tourists. A stroll along **Avenue Montaigne, rue du Faubourg St-Honoré,** or around the **Madeleine** will give a taste of what life in Paris is like for the excessively rich. While low prices usually mean low quality here—particularly for accommodations—there are a few good restaurants and many great museums. The northern part of the neighborhood, near the **Parc Monceau,** is a lovely and less-touristed area for walking.

Opéra (9ème)

The 9th arrondissement is (surprise, surprise) best known for the **Opéra National Garnier,** a magnificent structure steeped in history that is difficult to top in terms of architectural triumph and OCD attention to detail. While the Opéra National is the 9ème's crown jewel, the area is more aptly characterized by a juxtaposition of opposing worlds: this area is home to both one of Paris's chic shopping districts on the Grands Boulevards and the anything-but-classy **Pigalle,** encompassing the red light district and a sickening amount of shops catering to tourists. A residential neighborhood is just a stone's throw away, with the St. Georges Metro at its center, as is the beautiful **Moreau Museum,** housed in the famous painter's former home. A couple of days in the Opéra will probably leave you thinking that it's among the most bizarre city neighborhoods in the world. One comes to learn that the comfortable coexistence of opposing worlds is *très* French.

Canal St-Martin and Surrounds (10ème)

The Canal St-Martin, i.e., the 10th arrondissement, is undeniably one of the sketchier neighborhoods in Paris. During the day as well as at night, you have to constantly watch your back for pickpockets, muggers, and swaying drunks. That being said, the neighborhood boasts some fantastic restaurants around the **Canal St.-Martin,** and some great hotel deals around **Gare du Nord.** The Canal is kind of like a mini-Seine; it's smaller, less touristed, and has just as much trash in it. It becomes a more peaceful area on Sundays, when cars are barred from the streets that run alongside the water.

paris · orientation

Bastille (11ème, 12ème)

As its name attests, the Bastille *(bah-steel)* area is most famous for hosting the Revolution's kick-off at its prison on July 14, 1789. Hundreds of years later, the French still storm this neighborhood nightly in search of the latest cocktail, culinary innovation, and up-and-coming artist. Five Metro lines converge at **République** and three at Bastille, making the Bastille district a transport hub and mammoth center of action—the hangout of the young and fun (and frequently drunk). The 1989 opening of the glassy **Opéra Bastille** on the bicentennial of the Revolution was supposed to breathe new cultural life into the area, but the party atmosphere has yet to give way to galleries and string quartets. Today, with numerous bars along **rue de Lappe,** manifold dining options on **rue de la Roquette** and **rue JP Timbaud,** and young designer boutiques, the Bastille is a great area for unwinding after a day at the museums.

Butte-aux-Cailles and Chinatown (13ème)

The 13*ème* may have served as the setting of Victor Hugo's *Les Miserables*, but these days you're more likely to see a postmodern performance of *Les Miz* than any fashionably starving children. Though Butte-aux-Cailles was once one of Paris's poorest arrondissements, the arrival of the high-speed Metro line and the ZAC Paris Rive Gauche redevelopment project have since transformed the neighborhood into a dynamic community and colorful hub of food and culture. Butte-aux-Cailles attracts a young, artsy crowd that lovingly tags the walls with graffiti. Across the way, Chinatown stretches across multiple Metro stops, and is defined by a unique cultural hybridization rarely seen among immigrant enclaves, in both Paris and beyond.

Montparnasse (14ème, 15ème)

The Montparnasse area is home to two of Paris's most celebrated institutions, the **Catacombs** and the **Cité Universitaire,** and one of its most profitable tourist areas, **Montparnasse Bienvenue.** One of Paris's more dynamic neighborhoods, the 14*ème* provides all the things any self-respecting arrondissement has to offer: a fairly diverse population, fantastic local restaurants, neighborhood specialty shops, leafy parks, mischievous children, and drunks. We recommend staying on the Metro's line 4 past Montparnasse and hopping off at Denfert, or, better yet, Mouton Duvernet. Check out the open-air markets on rue Daguerre, or stroll down **Avenue René Coty,** and go strike up a conversation on the *grande pelouse* at the Cité Universitaire.

Passy and Auteuil (16ème)

Perhaps one of the swankiest neighborhoods in Paris, the 16*ème* is home to the ladies who lunch, their beautiful children, and their overworked husbands. Its elegant, boutique-lined streets are calmer than surrounding areas and offer a glimpse into the lives of Parisian elites. Backlit by fabulous views of the Eiffel Tower, the neighborhood is home to a number of museums and attractions, and elderly local pedestrians are often swamped by mobs of eager sightseers. **Trocadero** witnesses the heaviest tourist traffic, with breakdancing street performers, sprawling gardens, and the best "I've been to Paris" photo ops.

Batignolles (17ème)

Far away from Paris's most touristed destinations, the 17*ème* offers a pleasant respite from the mobs of fellow tourists, and provides the chance to rub elbows (or other appendages, if you so choose) with the locals. A diverse group of Parisians are in residence here; varying widely block to block, bourgeois promenades with flowered trees are abruptly juxtaposed with working-class areas and immigrant neighborhoods. The eastern and southern parts of the arrondissement share the bordering 8*ème* and 16*ème's* aristocratic feel, while the quartier's western edge resembles the shoddier 18*ème* and **Pigatelle.** In the lively **Village Batignolles,** parents and their overly-earnest teenagers take leisurely strolls or sit in the many cafes.

Montmartre *(18ème)*

Montmartre might just be the most eccentric of Paris's neighborhoods. From the scenic vistas at the **Basilique de Sacre-Coeur**, to the historic **cabarets** and **Butte vineyard**, to the (ahem) colorful establishments in the **Red Light District** on bld. de Clichy, you'll see it all in the 18*ème*. Tourism in this part of town can be very difficult. While there aren't too many great options for staying in Montmartre, there are some fantastic sights, decent food, and fun local bars. Keep in mind that while wandering through this neighborhood, you might have to occasionally hike the 130m hill, or Butte, **Montmartre**.

Buttes Chaumont *(19ème)*

In the mid-19th century, Baron Haussman's architectural reforms paved the way for a new working class neighborhood to be settled in the 19th arrondissement, on the northeastern outskirts of Paris. A quiet family neighborhood with a surprisingly lovely **Parc des Buttes Chaumont**, the 19*ème* is now making its best effort at a bohemian revival. The area is rapidly becoming the trendy new hotspot for young professionals and students, and now boasts a growing Asian and North African community. The modern macro-social engineering feat that is the **Parc de la Villette** is also well worth a visit.

Belleville and Père Lachaise *(20ème)*

Belleville is one of Paris's most legendary working-class neighborhoods. Although far from the city center, it is home to one of Paris's most visited tourist sights, the Cimitière Père Lachaise (i.e. that cemetery where Jim Morrison's buried). During the late Second Republic, the 20*ème* became a "red" arrondissement, and was characterized as proletarian and 🔲radical. A legacy of class solidarity and progressivism still characterizes the neighborhood today.

ACCOMMODATIONS

Île de la Cité and Île St-Louis

One of the romantic centers of Paris, the isles attracts honeymooners, swooners, and the like; the hoteliers more than make good on it. Rooms are generally anything but budget and more in the "I need to seduce her" price range.

🔲 HÔTEL HENRI IV ✒ HOTEL ❸
25 pl. Dauphine ☎01 43 54 44 53 🔲www.henri4hotel.fr

It may not have modern-day "necessities" like TVs and hair dryers, but it does have some of the best-located and least-expensive rooms in Paris. Henry IV's printing presses once occupied this 400-year-old and off-beat building; the hotel's porthole doors and a winding staircase make it looks like an ancient ship. Spacious rooms have large windows and charming views.

✚ Ⓜ*Pont Neuf.* ⓘ *Breakfast included.* Ⓢ *Singles €42-59; doubles €49-78; twins €76-81.*

Châtelet-Les Halles

While affordable hotels in this trendy neighborhood tend to be pretty hard to come by, there are a few high-quality budget addresses that are worth checking out. Be sure to make your reservations far in advance—cheap spots in such a central location fill up rapidly at any time of year. Also, be sure to watch yourself around Châtelet. Other tourists will not stick up for you (or even tell you) when a pickpocket or mugger is about to pounce.

🔲 HOTEL DE ROUEN ✒⊗⒴ HOTEL ❷
42 rue Croix des Petits Champs ☎01 42 61 38 21 🔲www.hotelderouen.net

This cozy two-star hotel boasts the lowest prices you'll find in the 1*er* for hotel accommodations. The friendly owner speaks English and is more than happy to tell you about the virtues of all the different rooms. Some of the rooms are decorated with liberated Metro signs and maps, so you won't even have to take advantage of the free Wi-Fi to plan your itinerary. While most rooms come equipped with showers, beware of getting the room without the shower on the first floor; you'll have to walk up five floors (the hotel doesn't have an elevator) to the hallway shower.

✠ Ⓜ*Palais Royal Musée du Louvre, Les Halles.* *i* *Free Wi-Fi. Breakfast €6.* Ⓢ *Singles €40-60; doubles €45-75.* ☒ *Reception 24hr.*

▨ HOTEL TIQUETONNE
⚓♿ HOTEL ❸
6 rue Tiquetonne   ☎01 42 36 94 58

Located a stone's throw from Marché Montorgueil and rue St-Denis' sex shops, Hotel Tiquetonne is surrounded by so many hip shopping spots it could send its hipster clientele into bankruptcy. Simple rooms are generously sized and boast unusually high ceilings (by Parisian standards). Amenities can be hit or miss; the hotel has an elevator, but some rooms don't have showers. Unbeatable prices for this location.

✠ Ⓜ*Etienne-Marcel.* *i* *Breakfast €6. Hall showers €6.* Ⓢ *Singles €35, with shower €45; doubles with shower €55.* ☒ *Reception 24hr.*

▨ CENTRE INTERNATIONALE DE PARIS (BVJ): PARIS LOUVRE
⊕(((•))) HOSTEL ❶
20 rue Jean-Jacques Rousseau   ☎01 53 00 90 90

In an unbeatable location right down the street from the Louvre, this massive hostel has taken over three buildings in total. All guests must be younger than 35, ensuring a young and international crowd. The decor in the lobby, dining hall, and rooms is utilitarian and vaguely influenced by the '60s. Spacious single-sex dorms are available with two to eight beds. A new location is coming to the Opéra district, so stay tuned.

✠ Ⓜ*Louvre.* *i* *Breakfast included. Reservations can be made no more than 15 days in advance by phone or internet, except July-Aug, when they can be made 2 months in advance. Wi-Fi in dining hall €2 per hr., €3 per 2hr. 3-night max. stay; extensions can be arranged on arrival.* Ⓢ *Dorms €29. Extra bed €35.* ☒ *Reception 24hr.*

The Marais

As would be expected, the Marais and its surroundings provide budget accommodations with a bit of flare. Many basic rooms are wallet-friendly, done up in style, and situated in the center of Parisian action. The trendy yet down-to-earth *4ème* is also home to some of the best deals and worthwhile splurges in the city. There's a lot of good stuff to make (and take) home.

▨ MAUBUISSON
⚓ HOSTEL ❸
12 rue des Barres   ☎01 42 74 23 45 www.mije.com

Recognized as a 17th-century historical monument, Maubuisson is a former convent on a quiet street by the St.-Gervais monastery. In keeping with the pious theme, the hostel only accommodates individual travelers, rather than groups. A member of the MIJE hostel group, Maubuisson can arrange airport transportation as well as reservations for area attractions; call for details.

✠ Ⓜ*Hôtel de Ville or* Ⓜ*Pont Marie. From Pont Marie, walk opposite traffic on rue de l'Hôtel-de-Ville and turn right on rue des Barres.* *i* *Breakfast, ensuite shower, and linens included (no towels). No smoking. English spoken. Public phones and free lockers (with a €1 deposit). Internet access €0.10 per min. with €0.50 initial connection fee. Arrive before noon the first day of reservation (call in advance if you'll be late).Individuals can reserve months ahead online and 2-3 weeks ahead by phone. 7-night max. stay.* Ⓢ *MIJE membership required (€2.50). 4-to-9-bed dorms €30; singles €49; doubles €72; triples €96.* ☒ *Reception 7am-1am. Lockout noon-3pm. Curfew 1am; notify in advance if coming back after this time. Quiet hours after 10pm.*

▨ LE FOURCY
⚓(((•))) HOSTEL ❸
6 rue de Fourcy   ☎01 42 74 23 45 www.mjie.com

Le Fourcy surrounds a large, charming, mansion-worthy courtyard ideal for

france

meeting travelers or for open-air picnicking. The adjoining restaurant is located in an authentic vaulted cellar, and offers a main course with drink (lunch only) and 3-course "hosteler special" (€10.50).

✈ Ⓜ St-Paul or Ⓜ Pont Marie. From St-Paul, walk opposite the traffic for a few meters down rue St-Antoine and turn left on rue de Fourcy. *i* Breakfast, in-room shower, and linens are included (no towels). No smoking. English spoken. Public phones and free lockers (with a €1 deposit). Internet access €0.10 per min. with €0.50 initial connection fee. 7 night max. stay. Groups of 10 or more may reserve a year in advance. Individuals can reserve months ahead online and 2-3 weeks ahead by phone. Ⓢ MIJE membership required (€2.50). 4- to 9-bed dorms €30; singles €49; doubles €72; triples €96. Ⓩ Reception 7am-1am. Lockout noon-3pm. Curfew 1am; notify in advance. Quiet hours after 10pm. Arrive before noon the first day of reservation (call in advance if you'll be late).

🏨 HOTEL PICARD ✤📶 HOTEL ❹
26 rue de Picardie   ☎01 48 87 53 82 🖥 www.hotelpicardparis.com

A welcoming, family-owned hotel that's run more like a home with an open door policy. *Let's Go* readers will definitely feel like a member of the family; a 5% discount is given if you flash your copy. The bright and adorable rooms vary in size, but all of them are comfy. Many of them have private bathrooms, most of which have been recently renovated. All rooms come with TVs, safes, and showers.

✈ Ⓜ République. Follow bld. du Temple and turn right onto rue Charlot. Take the first right on rue de Franche Comte, which becomes rue de Picardie. *i* Breakfast €5. Reserve 1 week ahead in summer and 2 weeks ahead the rest of the year. Ⓢ Singles with sink €53-68, with bath €74-93; doubles €59-74/89-112; triples €124-155. Shower €3.

🏨 HÔTEL JEANNE D'ARC ✤📶 HOTEL ❹
3 rue de Jarente   ☎01 48 87 62 11 🖥 www.hoteljeannedarc.com

Joan of Arc may have been one, but you certainly won't be a martyr for staying in this quaint hotel. Charming rooms decorated in mismatched patterns all come with bath or shower, toilet, cable TV, safe and hair dryer. Despite its modern amenities, the place feels more like a homestyle inn than a 2-star hotel; the dining area boasts an absurdly funky mosaic mirror and serves a country-style breakfast.

✈ Ⓜ St.-Paul. From St-Paul, walk against traffic onto rue de Rivoli; turn left on rue de Sévigné then right on rue de Jarente. *i* Breakfast €7. Free Wi-Fi. English spoken. Reserve 2-3 months in advance (longer for stays in Sept-Oct) by emailing or calling with credit card. Ⓢ Singles €62-90; doubles €90-116; triples €146; quads €160.

Latin Quarter and St-Germain

While hotels are generally a bit overpriced in these neighborhoods, it's to be expected given their central location in Paris. Nonetheless, the area boasts some truly luxurious accommodations at very reasonable prices. If you want to be well located while living the (somewhat) high life, *Let's Go* has a few good recommendations for you.

🏨 HÔTEL DE NESLE ✤ HOTEL ❸
7 rue du Nesle   ☎01 43 54 62 41 🖥 www.hoteldenesleparis.com

An absolutely phenomenal place to stay. Every room is unique and represents a particular time period or locale. The Molière room is ideal for the comically minded, and an Oriental room is available for undying proponents of the colonial lifestyle (don't let that be you). The lobby's ceiling is adorned with bouquets of dried flowers, and the peaceful garden has terraced seating and a duck pond. Reserve a good deal in advance, because this unforgettable accommodation fills up quickly, especially during the summertime.

✈ Ⓜ Odéon. *i* Laundry facilities on-site. Ⓢ Singles €55-65; doubles €75-100. Extra bed €12.

Invalides

Budget travel isn't exactly synonymous with the elegant *7ème*. Still, the centrally located arrondissement hosts a number of modern and decently affordable hotels with a friendly staff committed to good service. Many rooms also come with a view of the gilded dome of Invalides.

HOTEL MONTEBELLO — ⊗ HOTEL [2]

18 rue Pierre Leroux ☎01 47 34 41 18 ✉hmontebello@aol.com

From the worn leather couch in the lobby to the faded old photographs lining the walls, Hotel Montebello feels more like a haven for long-lost French grandchildren than an actual hotel. Provides clean and colorful rooms with purple curtains, at some of the best prices in the *7ème*. It's a bit far from most of the neighborhood sights, but the elderly proprietor lends a genuine taste of old Paris. Be warned that credit cards are still considered a bit too new-fangled for this place; you will have to pay by check.

➜ [M]Vaneau. ℹ All rooms with bath. [$] Singles €49; doubles €59; triples €79.

Champs-Élysées

Catering to the Louis Vuitton clientele, accommodations in the posh *8ème* come with a lot of stars and a hell of a nightly rate. Budget travelers might want to look elsewhere. For those absolutely set on location, there are a few quality options.

HÔTEL ALEXANDRINE OPÉRA — HOTEL [2]

10 rue de Moscou ☎01 43 87 62 21 ✉alexandrineopera@gmail.com

Nothing about this hotel could provoke anger (quite the contrary) but you'll still see red (decorators went a little crazy with the color scheme). Apart from that, rooms are well-sized, pleasant and come with a minibar (an unthinkable luxury at this price), hair dryer, TV, phone and shower.

➜ [M]Liège. ℹ Breakfast €9. [$] Singles €65-80, doubles €75-100.

Opéra

👍 PERFECT HOTEL — ⊗ HOTEL [1]

39 rue Rodier ☎01 42 81 18 86

Possibly the best deal in Paris, the Perfect Hotel is, well, practically perfect. For super cheap, visitors have access to a kitchen available for their use whenever they need it. Some of the rooms have balconies, which may be available on request. The cordial owners owners are enthusiastic when it comes to new visitors; they're so concerned about their guests that they installed a surveillance system of the entire hotel to ensure privacy and safety. Or maybe just to watch you. No Wi-Fi, unfortunately, but it's coming soon with upcoming renovations (new painting, wallpaper, and showers).

➜ [M]Anvers. ℹ Reserve 2 months ahead; there are only 10 rooms, and given the cheap prices this hotel fills up weeks in advance during summer. Free breakfast. Credit cards accepted only for weeklong stays or longer. [$] Doubles €25-35 per person; triples €26-28 per person.

Canal St-Martin and Surrounds

Canal St-Martin boasts a wealth of dirt-cheap options around **Gare du Nord.** The following accommodation is among the best that the arrondissement has to offer, but if it's full, ask the proprieters to recommend one of their many competing neighbors. People running hotels around here tend to be pretty no-nonsense, so they'll give you the inside skinny.

👍 HOTEL PALACE — HOTEL [1]

9 rue Bouchardon ☎01 40 40 09 45

Rock-bottom prices and a safe (by *10ème* standards), if not central, location are combined with a very warm and comfortable welcome. Prices are stupifyingly low, with singles going for €20; the greater tourist community is beginning to catch on to this bargain, so be sure to make reservations at least two weeks in advance.

➡ [M]Strasbourg-St-Denis. ℹ Breakfast €4. [S] Singles €20-35; doubles €28-45; triples €60; quads €70.

Bastille

The 11*ème* is littered with hotels (amongst other things), and offers a little bit of something for everybody. Accommodations range from the very cheap to the very not-cheap, but good quality budget hotels are in abundance. The neighboring 12*ème* offers relatively inexpensive and simple accommodations, which work hard to make up for being somewhat on the outskirts. The best options cluster around the **Gare de Lyon.**

AUBERGE DE JEUNESSE "JULES FERRY" (HI) — 💳📶 HOSTEL [2]

8 bld. Jules Ferry — ☎01 43 57 55 60 💻paris.julesferry@fuaj.org

A noble attempt to brighten up the hostel experience, and we mean that quite literally—the brown bunks have recently been painted neon green. A mural of sharks greets you on your walk up the stairs. Colorful rooms with sinks, mirrors, and tiled floors match the carefree atmosphere (though the sharks don't quite scream "Welcome Home!").

➡ [M]République. ℹ Kitchen available. Wi-Fi €5 per 2hr. Breakfast included. [S] Dorms €23. ⏰ Reception and dining room 24hr. Lockout 10:30am-2pm.

Butte-aux-Cailles and Chinatown

Though perhaps not at the center of it all, the 13*ème* is home to several inexpensive accommodations in an ethnically diverse and residential area, providing travelers with an opportunity to escape the steep prices and occasional phoniness of Parisian chic.

👍 OOPS! — ⊗♿📶❄ HOSTEL [1]

50 av. des Gobelins — ☎01 47 07 47 00 💻www.oops-paris.com

The first boutique hostel in Paris, Oops! has the fashion sense of a teen with an attitude problem. Animal print wallpaper, bold colors and a kaleidescope of patterns generate a fun, young feel. The rooms themselves are less remarkable than the decor, but are average in size and include a bathroom and shower, though no lockers are available. Guests are free to use the rainbow-colored lounge and its free Wi-Fi.

➡ [M]Les Gobelins. ℹ Breakfast included. Email to make a reservation. No deposit required if booking made through website. Cancel within 24hr. [S] Dorms €23-€30; private rooms €60-70.

Montparnasse

HOTEL DE BLOIS — 💳♿📶 HOTEL [2]

5 rue des Plantes — ☎01 45 40 99 48 💻www.hoteldeblois.com

Conveniently located a 5min. walk from Denfert-Rochereau and within walking distances of several tasty restaurants, Hotel de Blois is situated in a largely residential area of the 14*ème* on the popular rue des Plantes. Rooms are well-kept and relatively spacious, with full-sized bathrooms and showers. Don't fret about security—the exceptional hostess is extra vigilant about letting in strangers, given the hotel's central location. Her visitors show their gratitude in a proudly displayed collection of thank-you notes. There are five floors and no elevator, so the hotel is far from wheelchair-accessible.

➡ [M]Mouton Duvernet, Alésia. ℹ Breakfast €12. Wi-Fi available. Reserve at least 1 month ahead. [S] Singles €55-95; doubles €60-98; twin suite 65-80. Extra bed €3-5. ⏰ Reception 7am-10:30pm.

Passy and Auteuil

Home to many the posh resident, things get expensive in the 16*ème*, amd accommodations are no exception. Budget hotels and hostels are hard to find and the few options available are a trek from the city's center. On the upside, the neighborhood's more reasonable hotels can offer a welcome respite from the sticky dorms of grungy hostels for those who can afford it.

◼ HOTELHOME PARIS 16 HOTEL ❹

36 rue George Sand ☎010 45 20 61 38 ▥www.hotelhome.fr

As its name would suggest, HotelHome offers a home away from home to the weary traveler. Each of the pre-outfitted apartments comes with a kitchen, dishwasher, bathroom, living room, and delicious potopurri aroma. Thick plush carpets, rich colors, and dark wood make for the kind of luxurious atmostphere one wouldn't dream of when traveling on a budget. Varying apartment styles can accommodate a range of people.

⚑ Ⓜ*Jasmin.* *i* *Breakfast included.* Ⓢ *Junior suite (1-3 people) €123-260; twin suite €180-345; double suite (1-4 people) €207-385; family suite (1-6 people) €288-580. Discounts for early bookings.*

Batignolles

If you're going to stay this far out from the center of town, there better be something good to keeping you here. The 17*ème* hosts a number of more luxurious budget accommodations that will give you a soft bed to come home to after a long day of sightseeing, but it'll be a long Metro ride.

◼ HOTEL CHAMPERRET HELIOPOLIS ⚐♿(ꞯ) HOTEL ❹

13 rue d'Héliopolis ☎01 47 64 92 56 ▥www.champerret-heliopolis-paris-hotel.com

Bright blue, white, and gold rooms with plush, comfy beds and flatscreen TVs. The hotel combines an intimate bed and breakfast vibe with the the amenities of a modern hotel. Book in advance.

⚑ Ⓜ*Porte de Champarret.* Ⓢ *Singles €77; doubles €90, with bath €96; twin €96; triples with bath €120.*

Montmartre

Montmartre's accommodations tend to be a bit pricier, given its position near the top of the list of Paris's most heavily touristed neighborhoods. That being said, we've picked out a few affordable options if you wish to be in the thick of things. Always remember to evaluate the noise level in the neighborhood of your accommodation; while none of these are located in noisy neighborhoods, most locations in the 18*ème* tend to be a bit rowdy at night.

◼ HOTEL CAULAINCOURT ⚐(ꞯ) HOTEL ❷

2 sq. Caulaincourt ☎ 01 46 06 46 06 ▥ www.caulaincourt.com

A friendly, cheap hotel that caters to a slightly younger crowd. Reception will do everything possible to make your stay enjoyable and happy. There's a TV in the lobby, and free internet access up to 30min. Rooms are generally clean, with the exception of a few grimy spots in the bathrooms. Keep in mind that there's a 2am curfew, and 11am-4pm is lockout time; this is not the place to be if you want to party really hard and then sleep in ("*faire la grasse matinée*" in French; doesn't that sound better?). The hotel is located at the top of a long staircase, so its rooms afford some fantastic views.

⚑ Ⓜ*Lamarck-Caulaincourt.* Ⓢ *Singles €50-60; doubles €63-76; triples €89.* ⌖ *Curfew 2am. Lockout 11am-4pm.*

HOTEL ANDRÉ GILL ⚐(ꞯ) HOTEL ❷

4 rue André Gill ☎01 42 62 48 48

A cozy family-run budget hotel, André Gill is located on a side street off rue des

Martyrs, in the thick of the touristy section of Montmartre. The hotel's well-loved cat adds a homey touch, but if you're allergic you should think about heading somewhere else. The rooms here are clean and the reception is friendly. The location is a bit busy; if you're a city slicker, you should be able to sleep like a baby, but country bumpkins should search for something a bit farther out if you want to catch some z's.

☞ ⓂPigalle, ⓂAbesses. *i* Computer use €1.50 per 30min. Breakfast €4. ⑤ Doubles only. Room with sink €60, with bath €89. ⏰ Reception 24hr.

Buttes Chaumont

Buttes Chaumont isn't known for its accommodations for a reason. Largely residential and far away from tourist destinations, it's got hotels that are generally a bit expensive, and impractical for a stay in Paris. La Perdrix Rouge is the great exception.

▨ LA PERDRIX ROUGE   ✎⟨ᵠ⟩ HOTEL ❷
5 rue Lassus   ☎01 42 06 09 53 ▨ www.hotel-perdrixrouge-paris.com

Facing a gorgeous church and just steps from the Metro, La Perdrix Rouge offers a slightly pricey, peaceful home base away from the clamor of central Paris. Surrounded by a bank, grocery store, several bakeries, and restaurants, patrons will find the neighborhood tourist-free and generous in terms of the necessities (fresh bread, pharmacies, crêpes, etc.). Thirty clean, red-carpeted rooms come with bath or shower, hair dryer, toilet, telephone, and TV.

☞ Ⓜ Jourdain. *i* Breakfast €7.50. Minibar deposit €20. ⑤ Singles €79; doubles €85-92; twins €98. Extra bed €12.

Belleville and Père Lachaise

Belleville is pretty far out from most tourist destinations in Paris. Nonetheless, there are some pretty cheap accommodations here. The **Auberge de Jeunesse** has a fantastic sense of community; if you want to meet people at your hostel, but not be able to afford a taxi home after hitting the bars, the 20*ème* is the spot for you.

▨ AUBERGE DE JEUNESSE "LE D'ARTAGNAN"   ✎⟨ᵠ⟩ HOSTEL ❶
80 rue Vitruve   ☎01 40 32 34 56 ▨ www.fuaj.org

A healthy walk from the Metro and a stone's throw from the Lachaise Cemetery, this Auberge boasts an unbecoming design, a friendly reception, and a huge community of transient students. Claiming to be France's largest Youth Hostel, this 440-bed backpacker's republic fosters a fun and irreverent atmosphere with flashing neon lights, a free in-house cinema, and a game room complete with those car-driving games you used to stuff with quarters as a kid. Rooms are clean and have all the basics down pat. The jovial elevator/social facilitator man will make otherwise ordinary elevator rides fun and social.

☞ ⓂPorte de Bagnolet. ⑤ Breakfast included. Internet and Wi-Fi €2 per hr. Linens included. Towels €2.50. Lockers €2-4 per day. Laundry €3 per wash, €1 per dry. Reserve online. ⑤ 9-bed dorms €21; 3- to 5-bed dorrns €23.50. Doubles €28. Discounts for International Youth Hostels Association members. ⏰ Lockout noon-3pm. 4-night max. stay.

SIGHTS   ◉

Île de la Cité and Île St-Louis

The ground zero of Paris, these islands have a lot of big hitters. If you're looking for grand architecture, hundreds of years of history, and mobs of tourists, Île de la Cité is a wonderful place to start. **Notre Dame Cathedral** is it the center of it all, rising above the lesser-known (i.e., not in a Disney movie) but equally impressive locations like **Ste-Chapelle**. Even without all the grandeur, the Île's sheer level of historical significance makes it worth a visit: the birthplace of Paris, the island's narrow streets offer a glimpse of the city's humble beginnings. Just across the way, the rue St-Louis-En-L'Île was historically home to some of the most famous Parisians in history. The

main thoroughfare—the narrow, cobblestone **rue St-Louis-en-l'Île**—strings together a collection of clothing boutiques, gourmet food stores, galleries, and ice cream shops, including the famous **Berthillon glacerie.**

🖼 NOTRE DAME

Île de la Cité

◆ CATHEDRAL
☎01 53 10 07 00

Centuries before it witnessed Quasimodo's attempted rescue of Esmeralda, Notre Dame was the site of a Roman temple to Jupiter and three different churches. Parisian bishop **Maurice de Sully** initiated the construction of the cathedral in 1163. De Sully took care to avoid the poor interior design that characterized Notre Dame's dark and cramped predecessor, and worked to create a more airy structure that would fill with God's light; in the process, he helped engineer a new architectural style that would later be dubbed **Gothic.** De Sully died before his ambitious plan was completed, but the cathedral was reworked over several centuries into the composite masterpiece that stands today.

Like the Île de la Cité itself, Notre Dame has hosted a series of pivotal events in Western history. French royalty used the Cathedral for their marital unions, most notably the marriages of François II to **Mary Queen of Scots** in 1558, and of **Henri of Navarre** to Marguerite de Valois in 1572. The cathedral was also the setting for **Joan of Arc's** trial for heresy in 1455. In a fit of logic, secularists renamed the cathedral The Temple of Reason during the Revolution, and cleverly encased its Gothic arches in Neoclassical plaster moldings. The church was reconsecrated after the Revolution and was the site of **Napoleon's** famed coronation in 1804. However, the building soon fell into disrepair, and for two decades it was used to shelter livestock. Donkeys and pigs were cleared away when **Victor Hugo**, proving that books can change public opinion, wrote his famed novel *Notre-Dame de Paris* (*The Hunchback of Notre Dame*) in 1831, reviving the cathedral's popularity and inspiring **Napoleon III** and **Haussmann** to devote financial attention to its restoration. In 1870 and again in 1940, thousands of Parisians attended masses in the church to pray for deliverance from the invading Germans; God had a thing and couldn't make it, apparently. On August 26, 1944, **Charles de Gaulle** braved Nazi fire to visit Notre Dame and give thanks for the imminent liberation

france

of Paris. His funeral mass was held there many years later, as was the mass of his successor, **Mitterand.** The Cathedral continues to keep up its political prominence, and its place in the public consciousness is demonstrated through its pop culture cameos in movies such as *Amélie*, *Before Sunset*, and *Charade*, as well as the animated films *The Hunchback of Notre Dame* and *Ratatouille*.

Exterior: The oldest part of the cathedral is above the **Porte de Ste-Anne** (on the right), and dates from 1165-1175. The **Porte de la Vierge** (on the left), which portrays the life of the Virgin Mary, dates from the 13th century. The central **Porte du Jugement** was almost entirely redone in the 19th century; the **figure of Christ** dates from 1885. Irreverent revolutionaries wreaked havoc on the facade during the frenzied rioting of the 1790s; not content with decapitating Louis XVI, Parisians attacked the stone statues of the **Kings of Judah** above the doors, under the mistaken impression that they represented the monarch's ancestors. The heads were found in the basement of the **Banque Française du Commerce** in 1977 and were installed in the **Musée de Cluny.**

Towers: Home to the cathedral's fictional resident, Quasimodo the Hunchback, the two towers are the cathedral's most prominent features. Streaked with black soot, they cast an imposing shadow on the Paris skyline for years, but after several years of sandblasting, the blackened exterior has been brightened, once again revealing rose windows and rows of holy saints and hideous gargoyles. It's a long way to heaven: there's always a considerable line to make the 422-step climb to the top of the towers, but the view of Paris is worth it *(20 visitors let in every 10min.).* The narrow staircase leads to a spectacular perch crowded by rows of gargoyles that overlooks the Left Bank's **Latin Quarter** and the Right Bank's **Marais.** In the **South Tower,** a tiny door opens onto the 13-ton bell that even Quasimodo couldn't ring: it requires eight people or one Sumo wrestler to move.

Interior: Notre Dame can seat over 10,000 churchgoers. The arched ceiling is achieved by the spidery **flying buttresses** that support the vaults of the ceiling from outside, allowing light to fill the cathedral through delicate stained-glass windows. Down the **nave** is the **transept** and a view of the **rose windows.** The 21m **north window** (to the left when your back is to the entrance) is still composed almost entirely of 13th-century glass. The Virgin is situated at its center, and depicted as the descendant of the Old Testament kings and judges who surround her. While the north window is spectacularly well preserved, the **south and west windows** have had to undergo modern renovations. The base of the south window shows Matthew, Mark, Luke, and John on the shoulders of Old Testament prophets, while the central window depicts Christ surrounded by his 12 apostles. The cathedral's **treasury,** south of the choir, contains an assortment of glittering robes, sacramental chalices, and other gilded artifacts from the cathedral's past. The **Crown of Thorns,** believed to have been worn by Christ himself, is reverentially presented only on the first Friday of every month at 3pm.

🕆 ⓜCité. Ⓢ *Cathedral €8, ages 18-25 €6, under 18 free. Towers free. Treasury €3, ages 12-25 €2, ages 5-11 €1. Audio tours €5; includes visit of treasury.* ⓐ *Cathedral open daily 7:45am-7pm. Towers open Jan-Mar and Oct-Dec daily 10am-5:30pm; Apr-May and Sept daily 10am-6:30pm; June-Aug M-F 10am-6:30pm, Sa-Su 10am-11pm. Last entry 45min. before close. Tours begin at the booth to the right as you enter. In French M-F 2 and 3pm; call ☎01 44 54 19 30 for English tours. Mass M-F 8, 9am (except July-Aug), noon, 6:15pm; Sa 6:30pm; Su 8:30am, 10am Mass with Gregorian chant, 11:30am international mass with music, 12:45, and 6:30pm. Free recital by a cathedral organists at 4:30pm. Vespers sung Sa-Su 5:45pm. Treasury open M-F 9:30am-6pm, Sa 9:30am-5pm, and Su 1-1:30pm and 6-6:30pm. Last entry 15min. before close.*

🏛 **SAINTE-CHAPELLE**　　　　　　　　　　　　　　　　　　◆✦ CHURCH
6 bld. du Palais　　　　　　☎01 53 40 60 97 ▣www.monuments-nationaux.fr
Everybody needs the occasional diversion to get through a service. For French

royalty in the 13th century, it was the color of the church's walls. When light pours through the floor-to-ceiling stained-glass windows in the **Upper Chapel** of Sainte-Chapelle, illuminating bright dreamscapes of biblical scenes, the church becomes one of the most stunning and mesmerizing sights in Paris. The 15 panes date from 1136, and depict 1113 religious scenes. They narrate the Bible from Genesis to the Apocalypse, and are designed to be read from bottom to top, left to right; the bottom-to-top organization of the stories is meant to represent and enable the elevation of the soul through knowledge. Sainte-Chapelle is the foremost example of flamboyant Gothic architecture, and a tribute to the craft of medieval stained-glass—at 618 square meters, there's more of it than stone. The chapel was constructed in 1241 to house King Louis IX's most precious possession: the Crown of Thorns from Christ's Passion. Bought along with a section of the Cross by the Emperor of Constantinople in 1239 for the ungodly sum of £135,000 (adjust that puppy for about 800 years of inflation), the crown required an equally grand home, though its cost far exceeded that of the chapel. Although the crown itself—minus a few thorns that St-Louis gave away in exchange for political favors—has been moved to Notre Dame, Sainte-Chapelle is still a sight to behold. Down on the bottom floor, the **Lower Chapel** has a blue vaulted ceiling dotted with golden *fleurs-de-lis*, and contains a few "treasures"—platter-sized portraits of saints. This was where mortals served God, while royalty got to get a little closer in the Upper Chapel upstairs.

⇆ Ⓜ Cité. Within Palais de la Cité. $ €8, ages 18-25 €5, EU citizens 18-25 and under 18 free. Twin ticket with Conciergerie €11, ages 18-25 €7.50, under 18 and EU citizens 18-25 free. 🕐 Open daily Nov-Feb 9am-5pm. Mar-Oct 9:30am-6pm. Last entry 30min. before close. Chapel closed M-F 1-2:15pm. Guided tours in French 11am, 3pm, and 4:40pm; in English 3:30pm.

MEMORIAL DE LA DÉPORTATION — ♿ HOLOCAUST MEMORIAL

Paris's Holocaust memorial is a claustrophobic and deeply moving experience. Narrow staircases, spiked gates, and high concrete walls are meant to evoke the atmosphere of the concentration camps; only a few visitors are allowed to enter the exhibition at a time, and the solitude that the museum imposes upon its viewers only increases the pervasive sense of sadness. The focal point of the insitution is a tunnel lined with 200,000 lit quartz pebbles, one for each of the French citizens who were deported. The pebbles are an homage to the Jewish custom of placing stones on the graves of the deceased. Empty cells and walls bear the names of the most infamous camps, as well as a series of humanitarian statements by famous writers like Jean-Paul Sartre and Antoine de St-Exupéry. Near the exit is the simplest and most arresting of these quotes, "Pardonne. N'Oublie Pas." (Forgive. Do Not Forget.)

⇆ Ⓜ Cité. At the western tip of the island in square de l'Île de France, on quai de l'Archevêche. A 5min. walk from the back of Notre Dame cathedral, and down a narrow flight of steps. $ Free. 🕐 Open Tu-Su Apr-Sept 10am-noon and 2-7pm; Oct-Mar 10am-noon and 2-5pm. Last morning entry 11:45am; evening 30min. before close.

CONCIERGERIE — PALACE, PRISON

2 bld. du Palais ☎01 53 40 60 97 💻www.monuments-nationaux.fr

Back in the day, the Conciergerie served as both palace and prison, where kings feasted and criminals rotted. Built by Philip the Fair in the 14th century, the building is a good example of secular medieval architecture—heavy, hard and, somber. The name "Conciergerie" refers to the administrative officer of the Crown who acted as the king's steward, the Concierge (Keeper). When Charles V moved the seat of royal power from Île de la Cité to the Louvre after the assasination of his father's advisors, he endowed the Concierge with the power to run the Parliament, Chancery, and Audit Office. Later, this edifice became a royal prison and was taken over by the Revolutionary Tribunal after 1793. Now blackened by auto exhaust, the northern facade casts an appropriate gloom over the building: 2780 people were sentenced to death here between 1792 and 1794. A full list of the bourgeosie who had their heads chopped up is hung inside. Among its most famous prisoners were Marie-Antoinette, who was kept for 5 weeks, Robespierre, and 21 Girondins.

At the farthest corner on the right, a stepped parapet marks the oldest tower, the **Tour Bonbec,**which once housed the in-house torture chambers. The modern entrance lies between the **Tour d'Argent,** the stronghold of the royal treasury, and the **Tour de César,** used by the Revolutionary Tribunal. Past the entrance hall, stairs lead to rows of cells complete with somewhat blank-faced replicas of prisoners and prison conditions. Plaques explain how, in a bit of opportunism on the part of the Revolutionary leaders, the rich and famous could buy themselves private cells with cots and tables for writing while the poor slept on straw and with each other in pestilential cells. A model of Marie-Antoinette's rather comfortable-looking room suggests the extent to which class distinction remained preserved during the Revolution. If you follow the corridor named for "Monsieur de Paris," the executioner during the Revolution, you'll be tracing the final footsteps of Marie-Antoinette as she awaited decapitation on October 16, 1793. In 1914, the Conciergerie ceased to be used as a prison. Occasional concerts and wine tastings in the **Salle des Gens d'Armes** have, happily, replaced torture and beheadings.

⇟ [M]Cité. $ €7; students €4.50; handicapped and caretaker, EU citizens 18-25 and under 18 free. Includes tour in French. 🕓 Open daily Mar-Oct 9:30am-6pm, Nov-Feb 9am-5pm. Last entry 30min. before close. Tours daily 11am, 3pm.

HÔTEL DE DIEU BUILDING, HOSPITAL

1 pl. du Paris ☎01 42 34 82 34

Upon realizing that it might be helpful to save actual people in addition to their Christian souls (this was the Dark Ages: the idea was new at the time), Bishop St. Landry built this hospital in 651 CE. Today, it is the oldest hospital in Paris. In the Middle Ages, Hôtel de Dieu confined the sick rather than cured them; guards were posted at the doors to keep the patients from escaping and infecting the rest of the city. Over a millennia later, world-renowned chemist and biologist Louis Pasteur utilized the hospital's resources to conduct much of his pioneering research. In 1871, the hospital's proximity to Notre Dame saved the Cathedral from the fires of hell, so to speak—Communards were dissuaded from burning the monument for fear that the flames would engulf their hospitalized comrades nearby. The hospital has seen quieter days for some time now. The serene and well-groomed gardens in the inner courtyard feature sculpture exhibits.

⇟ [M]Cité. $ Free. 🕓 Open daily 7am-8pm.

PALAIS DE JUSTICE COURTHOUSE

4 bld. du Palais ☎01 44 32 51 51

This is *the* place to get a prison sentence. The Palais has borne witness to the German spy Mata Hari's death sentence; Sarah Bernhardt's divorce from the Comédie Française; Emile Zola's trial following the Dreyfus Affair; Dreyfus's declaration of his innocence; and the trial of Maréchal Pétain after WWII. The institution's architecture is organized around the theme of—unsurprisingly enough— "justice," and features symbolic representations of its basic concepts. The portrayals of Zeus and Medusa symbolize royal justice and punishment; the swords and sunlight recall the general concepts of justice and the law. A wide set of stone steps at the main entrance of the Palais de Justice leads to three doorways, each marked with *Liberté*, *Egalité*, or *Fraternité*—words that once signified revolution and now serve as the bedrock of the French legal tradition, not to mention many a photo. All trials are open to the public, and even if your French is not up to legalese, the theatrical sobriety of the interior is worth a quick glance. Plus you don't have to pay to see justice served!

⇞ Ⓜ Cité, within Palais de la Cité, use Ste-Chapelle entrance at 6 bld. du Palais. Enter through the Ste-Chapelle entrance, go down the hallway after the security check and turn right onto a double-level courtroom area. To go in the main entrance, turn right into the courtyard after the security check. $ Free. ⏰ Courtrooms open M-F 9am-noon and from 1:30pm-end of last trial.

five ways to make the louvre cool

As one of the most famous (and bunion-inducing) museums in the world, the Louvre hosts an exceptional crowd of obnoxious international tourists trampling toward the *Venus de Milo,* rowdy French schoolchildren giggling at every naked statue, and security guards that take personal space too seriously. We offer some advice to make that inevitable visit to IM Pei's pyramids a bit more pleasant, albeit less mature:

- **CHECK OUT MONA LISA'S EYEBROWS...** or lack thereof. One painting the size of a mini-magazine. A million American tourists fighting to snap a picture but just getting a shot of each others' cameras. Not enough security guards to fend off the crowd. At some point, should you finding yourself doubting whether you should've just Googled *La Jaconde*, entertain yourself by making a note of her missing eyebrows. The facial aesthetics of the lady in question reflects the style of Florence during an era when it was considered fashionable for women to shave off the only follicular decoration on their face. If only Whoopi Goldberg had been born in the 16th century.
- **MAKE YOUR OWN MUSEUM SOUNDTRACK.** Pick a room on the Richelieu wing on the first floor. Put your iPod on shuffle. Then, for each painting, press next song. As an alternative to stodgy museum cassette tours, your own personalized walk around the museum should make the 400th *Passion of the Christ* triptych more refreshing, especially backed by Nirvana's "Smells Like Teen Spirit."
- **PLAY HIDE AND SEEK IN THE CAROUSEL GARDEN.** Fanning out from the Arc de Triomphe, the outdoor portion of the museum makes botanists everywhere salivate with its various shrubs, trees, flower species, not to mention the naked statues. Find your inner Alice in the Louvre's very own Wonderland. Just don't start painting the roses red or security might ask you to leave—s'il vous plait probably included.
- **ORDER A BEER AT MCDONALD'S.** When the Supersized fast food joint opened up in the Louvre's shopping mall in 2009, the French threw a hissy fit when they realized Americans were trying to make even art connoisseurs fat. But the Mickey D's stayed, and now visitors still have the option of enjoying the European version of the Dollar Menu, as well as the irony of taking a break with a German beverage at an American fast food joint in a French museum.
- **PULL A DUCHAMP.** On your way out, pay a visit to the gift shop in the Allée de Grande Louvre to purchase a postcard of the Mona Lisa. Feel free to add a moustache or a mole here and there, use Duchamp's famous "L.H.O.O.Q"/*"Elle a chaud au cou"* ("She has a hot ass") pun, or come up with your own version. Either way, you'll have a souvenir that's considerably more cool than an Eiffel Tower keychain.

Musée du Louvre

MUSEUM

☎01 40 20 53 17 www.louvre.fr

The cultural importance of the Louvre cannot be overstated. The museum's miles (yes, miles) of galleries stretch seemingly without end, and the depth, breadth, and beauty of their collection spans thousands of years, six continents, countless artistic styles, and a vast range of media.

Successful trips to the Louvre require two things: a good sense of direction and a great plan of attack. *Let's Go* provides general information about the museum, followed by descriptions of its major collections. Those in search of a more detailed itinerary can choose from a selection of curator-designated "Thematic Trails," described on the Louvre's website. We wish you luck.

OVERVIEW

The Louvre is comprised of three connected wings: **Sully, Richelieu,** and **Denon.** These three buildings are centered on the **Cour Napoleon,** the museum's main entrance, which is accessible through I.M. Pei's large, glass **pyramid** (the Cour Napoleon is also accessible directly from the **Palais-Royal/Musée de Louvre Metro station,** by way of the **Carrousel du Louvre,** an underground gallery with high-end shops and a reasonably priced food court.) The Cour sports two ticket counters, a number of automated ticket machines, and a large information desk. Once you've secured your ticket, proceed up the escalators to Sully, Richelieu, or Denon to enter the museum itself on the basement level. Within the museum, each wing is divided into sections according to period, national origin, and medium. Each room within these thematic sections is assigned a number and color that correspond to the Louvre's free map.

*[M]Palais-Royal-Musée du Louvre. **i** Audio tour €6, under 18 €2, disabled visitors and unemployed €4, ages 18-25 rent one audio tour get one free. Visitors with disabilities don't have to wait in line. All entrances except the Passage Richelieu have elevators. At the main desk, you can exchange a piece of identification for a temporary wheelchair. Concerts and films are held in the auditorium in the Cour Napoléon. Concerts €3-30; films, lectures, and colloquia €2-10. Check the website for scheduling and more information. There is a small theater in the hall with free 1hr. films in French relating to the museum (films every hr. 10am-6pm). 1½hr. tours in English, French, or Spanish daily 11am, 2pm, 3:45pm; sign up at the info desk $ Admission €9, after 6pm on W and F €6, unemployed free after 6pm, under 26 free after 6pm. Free admission first Su of every month. Prices include both permanent and temporary collections, except for those in the Cour Napoléon. Tickets also allow same-day access to the Musée Delacroix. ⏰ Open M 9am-6pm, W 9am-10pm, Th 9am-6pm, F 9am-10pm, and Sa 9am-6pm. Last entry 45min. before close; rooms begin to close 30min. before close.*

NEAR EASTERN ANTIQUITIES

The cradle of civilization, the fertile crescent, and the land of epithets, Mesopotamia (also known as the Near East) was also the birthplace of Western Art. The Louvre's collection is one of the largest agglomerations of Egyptian and Mesopotamian artifacts in the world, and includes works that are over ten thousand years old. This area of the museum is generally one of the calmer ones, so you can spend some time marveling at its ancient offerings without feeling overwhelmed by the frenetic crowds. The encyclopaedic exhibits include a few terrific *stelas* (no, not the beer you get ripped off for at the cafes around the Louvre; we're talking slabs of wood or stone inscribed with painting, inscription, etc.) The *Victory Stela of Naram Sim (Room 2)* is a highlight of the collection, depicting the Akkadian King ascending to the heavens, trampling his enemies along the way and sporting the crown of a god. One of the Louvre's most historically significant pieces is the *Law Code of Hammurabi,* or the King of Babylon, currently holding things down in Room 3 of the museum's Near East section.

Richelieu. Ground fl.

GREEK, ETRUSCAN, AND ROMAN ANTIQUITIES

The extensive collection boasts works dating from the Neolithic age, about fourth millennium BCE, up until the sixth century. Many of the works featured here can be traced back to the rich royal collections seized by the rebel government of the French Revolution—which is also, in large part, to thank for transforming the Louvre into a museum. Purchases of various other royal and private collections over the next century solidified the bulk of the modern-day exhibit. The armless *Venus de Milo* is, obviously, the main attraction. As you approach Room 74 on the first floor, you can hear the din of the crowd (not quite Mona Lisa level, but still a din), heartily oohing, ahhing, and snapping pictures of the lady. The *Winged Victory of Samothrace* proves that a head is not a prerequisite for Greek masterpieces; beware of large crowds.

⚓ *Denon and Sully. 1st fl., ground fl., and lower ground fl.*

THE ITALIANS

Leonardo da Vinci's *Mona Lisa*, purchased by Francois I in 1518 *(Room 6)* is the most famous painting in the world. While the lady's mysterious smile and plump figure are still charming, there is nothing charming about fighting for a good view of the painting; if you feel comfortable doing so, now's the time to throw some elbows. The crowds are fierce, the painting is hidden in a glass box that constantly reflects hundreds of camera flashes, and you won't be allowed within 15 ft. of it. In the adjacent hall, an astonishing group of Renaissance master-pieces awaits—everything from Leonardo's *Virgin on the Rocks* to Raphael's *Grand Saint Michael* to Fra Angelico's *Cavalry*. The rest of the exhibit contains Renaissance masterpieces by Caravaggio, Leonardo, and others—an impressive bunch whose work documents the rise of Humanist art in the West. This wing is best visited as soon as the museum opens, as the entire thing turns into a zoo within 15-30min; while crowds are smaller on Wednesday and Friday evening visit times, this part of the museum is always pretty busy.

⚓ *Denon. 1st fl.*

FLANDERS, THE NETHERLANDS

A more relaxed Louvre experience awaits you on the second floor. Vermeer's majestic *Astronomer* and *Lacemaker* occupy Room 38. While Vermeer left behind no sketches or clues related to his preparatory methods, some scholars believe that he used a camera obscura in composing his works; one can make out subtle effects of light that could not have appeared to Vermeer's naked eye without a little assistance, unless he was superhuman (granted, that's a distinct possibility). Also not to be missed is Rubens' *Galerie Médicis*; comprised of 24 huge canvases; the room's paintings are dedicated to episodes from the self-obsessed queen's life. The equally giant tableaux are worth a few minutes of your time. This section of the museum is also filled with works by Rembrandt, Van Eyck, and Van der Weyden.

⚓ *Richelieu. 2nd fl.*

AND NOW FOR THE FRENCH

French paintings? In the Louvre? You would never have guessed it. Extravagant works from the 17th, 18th, and 19th centuries dominate the second floor of the Sully wing. A room dedicated to La Tour, once one of the world's leading Caravaggesque painters, showcases his fascination with hidden sources of light, responsible for the haunting works that occupy Room 28. Once you've had your fill of modernity, peace, and quiet, head back to the first floor of Denon, where the French heavyweights neighbor the *Mona Lisa*. The second most famous painting in these galleries is Delacroix's chaotic *Liberty Leading the People*, in which Liberty is symbolized by a highly liberated (read: partially nude) woman.

france

The rich use of color in the painting is considered seminal in its effect on the Impressionist school of art. Social science types should get a kick out of Ingres' body-twisting *Grande Odalisque* and Delacroix's *Death of Sardanapalus.* The combined chaos and richness of the tableaux are truly fascinating. Both paintings are good examples of Orientalism, a product of France's imperial adventures in North Africa.

⚘ *Sully, 2nd fl. Denon, 1st fl.*

Châtelet-Les Halles

Châtelet-Les Halles is perhaps Paris's most densely touristed area. And that's saying something. From the commercial indulgence of the Place Vendome, to the mind-numbing grandeur and beauty of the Louvre, to the bizarre trends on display at Les Arts Decoratifs, the 1st and 2nd arrondissements have it all.

📷 JARDIN DES TUILERIES   ♿ GARDEN

Place de la Concorde, rue de Rivoli   ☎01 40 20 90 43

Covering the distance from the Louvre to the place de la Concorde (and the Jeu de Paume and L'Orangerie), the Jardin des Tuileries is a favorite hangout for Parisians and tourists alike. The garden was originally built for Catherine de Medici in 1559 when she moved to the Louvre after the death of her husband, Henri II. The original designer was Italian Bernard de Carnesse, who modeled his masterpiece on the gardens of Catherine's native Florence, and the garden was used mostly for royal occasions. About a hundred years later, Louis XIV's superintendent, Jean-Baptiste Colbert, assigned the task of recreating the Tuileries garden to Le Notre (of Vaux-le-Vicomte and Versailles fame), the grandson of one Catherine's gardeners. Straight lines and sculpted trees became the decorative preference for this majestic plot of land, and several generations of kings employed the new and improved Tuileries for massive parties. You don't want to miss the beautiful views of Paris from the elevated terrace by the Seine. There are extremely expensive cafes scattered throughout the grounds. During the summer, confiserie stands, merry-go-rounds and a huge ferris wheel are installed near the rue de Rivoli entrance for the park's younger visitors.

⚘ Ⓜ*Tuileries.* ***i*** *English tours from the Arc de Triomphe du Carrousel.* Ⓢ *Free.* 🕐 *Open daily Apr-May 7am-9pm; June-Aug 7am-11pm; Sept 7am-9pm; Oct-Mar 7:30am-7:30pm. English tours from the Arc de Triomphe du Carrousel. Amusement park open July to mid-Aug.*

📷 ÉGLISE SAINT-EUSTACHE   CHURCH

2 rue du Jour   ☎01 42 36 31 05 🖳www.saint-eustache.org

There's a reason why Richelieu, Molière, Louis XIV, and Mme. de Pompadour achieved greatness in their lives: they were all baptized and/or received communion in the truly awe-inspiring Église de St-Eustache. Construction of the Gothic structure began in 1532 and dragged on for over a century due to lack of funding. The situation was so dire that its head priest sent a letter to the Les Halles community (which was at that point almost entirely Catholic) soliciting money for the project. Construction was essentially completed in 1633, and the church opened in 1637. In 1754, the unfinished Gothic facade was demolished and replaced with the fantastic Romanesque one that stands here today; in this sense, the Church's dysfunctional building process ended up working in its favor. The chapels contain paintings by Rubens as well as by the British artist Raymond Mason's seemingly misplaced relief, "Departure of the Fruits and Vegetables from the Heart of Paris," commemorating the closing of the market at Les Halles in February 1969. Today, St-Eustache stands up to almost any other church in terms of its physical beauty. Not to mention that it collects some serious points because it isn't as heavily touristed as the Basilique Sacre-Coeur, or, obviously, Notre Dame.

⚘ Ⓜ*Les Halles.* Ⓢ *Audio tours are available in English; the suggested donation is €3. A piece of identification is required to use one of the guides.* 🕒 *Open M-F 9:30am-7pm, Sa 10am-7pm, Su 9am-7pm. Mass Sa 6pm; Su 9:30, 11am, 6pm*

COMÉDIE FRANÇAISE, SALLE RICHELIEU ◆ THEATER

pl. Colette, southwest corner of Palais-Royal ☎08 25 10 16 80 🖥www.comedie-francaise.fr

In 1680 Louis XIV ordered that Paris's two most prominent acting troupes, that of the Hôtel Guénégaud and that of the Hôtel de Bourgogne, merge into the Comédie Française. They were lodged originally at the former acting troupe's original location. After the Revolution, in 1799, the government provided for the troupe to move into its legendary location in Palais-Royal's Salle Richelieu. Molière, the company's founder, collapsed on stage here while performing in "Le Malade Imaginaire," and died several hours later. The chair onto which he collapsed is still on display, along with several busts of famous actors crafted by equally famous sculptors. Visconti's Fontaine de Molière is only a few steps from where Molière died at no. 40. Today, the Comédie Française also has locations at the Théâtre du Vieux-Colombier and the Studio-Théâtre.

✈ Ⓜ*Palais Royal-Musée du Louvre.* **i** *Visits not available; you have to get tickets to one of the shows to see the Salle Richelieu.* $ *Spectacles €6-47. Cheapest tickets are available minutes before the show, so try going on a weeknight.* 🕒 *Spectacle start times vary.*

The Marais

There's more to see in the Marais than strutting fashionistas and strolling rabbis. A unique mix of historic and new, the area boasts an impressive list of quirky and worthwhile sights. The eastern section of the arrondissement harbors a labyrinth of old, quaint streets, a smattering churches, and some of Paris's most beautiful *hôtels particuliers*, or mansions (particularly around the **place des Vosges**). The **Centre Pompidou,** the undisputed main attraction of the Marais, breaks up the beige monotony in the western part of the arrondissement. Though the Pompidou, quite like a spoiled child, tends to attract the most attention, there are a number of other museums that are less touristy and just as entertaining. The underrated **Musée Carnavalet** visually portrays the history of Paris, while the **Musée de la Chasse** tells the story of the animals that died here. Even if you aren't the museum-going type, **Vieille du Temple** and **rue des Rosiers** are great streets to explore.

CENTRE POMPIDOU ◆ MUSEUM

pl. Georges-Pompidou, rue Beaubourg ☎01 44 78 12 33 🖥www.centrepompidou.fr

Erected in Beaubourg, a former slum *quartier* whose high rate of tuberculosis earned it classification as an *îlot insalubre* (unhealthy block) in the 1930s, the Pompidou was and still is considered alternately an architectural breakthrough and a montrosity. Pioneered in the '70s by architects Richard Rogers, Gianfranco Franchini, and Renzo Piano at the commission of President Pompidou, the design features a network of yellow electrical tubes, green water pipes, and blue ventilation ducts along the exterior of the building. The range of functions that the Centre serves are as varied as its colors—a sort of cultural theme park of an ultra-modern exhibition, performance, and research space, it most famously hosts the **Musée National d'Art Moderne.** The **Salle Garance** houses an adventurous film series, and the **Bibliothèque Publique d'Information** (entrance on rue de Renard) is a free, non-circulating library with wireless, which is almost always packed with students. Located in a separate building is the **Institut de la Recherche et de la Coordination Acoustique/Musique** (IRCAM), an institute and laboratory for the development of new technologies. The spectacular view from the top of the escalators, which can be reached only by purchasing a museum ticket or by dining at the rooftop restaurant, **Georges,** is well worth the lengthy ascent. From there, look out across at the Parisian skyline and observe the cobblestone square out front, filled with artists, musicians, punks, and passersby.

The **Musée National d'Art Moderne** is the Centre Pompidou's main attraction. While its collection spans the 20th century, the art from the last 50 years is particularly brilliant. It features everything from Philip Guston's uncomfortably adorable hooded figures to Eva Hesse's uncomfortably anthropomorphic sculptures. A large part of its contemporary display is now devoted to work by women artists in a much-needed exhbition called elles@centrepompidou. On the museum's second level, early 20th-century heavyweights like Duchamp and Picasso hold court. Most of the works were contributed by the artists themselves or by their estates; Joan Miró and Wassily Kandinsky's wife are among the museum's founders.

✦ Ⓜ*Rambuteau or Hôtel de Ville. RER Châtelet-Les Halles.* Ⓢ *Library and Forum free. Permanent collection and exhibits €12, under 26 €9, under 18 and EU citizens under 25 free. First Su of month free for all visitors. Visitors' guides available in bookshop.* ☒ *Centre open M 11am-10pm, W-Su 11am-10pm. Museum open M 11am-9pm, W 11am-9pm, Th 11am-11pm, F-Su 11am-9pm. Last ticket sales 1hr. before close. Library open M noon-10pm,W-F noon-10pm, Sa-Su 11am-10pm.*

IGOR STRAVINSKY FOUNTAIN   FOUNTAIN
pl. Igor Stravinsky

This novel installation features irreverent and multichromatic mobile sculptures by Niki de St-Phalle and Jean Tinguely. The whimsical elephants, lips, mermaids, and bowler hats are inspired by Stravinsky's works, and have been known to squirt water at unsuspecting bystanders. While the fountain's colorful quirkiness is in keeping with the Centre Pompidou, it stands in contrast to the nearby historic rue Brisemiche and Église de St-Merri.

✦ Ⓜ*Hôtel de Ville. Adjacent to the Centre Pompidou on rue de Renard.*

HÔTEL DE VILLE   ♿ GOVERNMENT BUILDING
Information office, 29 rue de Rivoli   ☎01 42 76 43 43; 01 42 76 50 49

As the constant stream of tourists and their flashing cameras will attest, the Hôtel de Ville is the most extravagant and picture-worthy non-palace edifice in Paris. The present structure is the second incarnation of the original edifice, which was built in medieval times and, during the 14th-15th centuries, served as a meeting hall for merchants who controlled traffic on the Seine. In 1533, King François I appointed Domenica da Cortona, known as Boccador, to expand and renovate the structure into a city hall worthy of the metropolis; the result was an elaborate mansion built in the Renaissance style of the Loire Valley châteaux. On May 24, 1871, the Communards, per usual, doused the building with gasoline and set it on fire. The blaze lasted a full eight days and spared nothing but the building's frame. Undaunted, the Third Republic built a virtually identical structure on the ruins, with a few significant changes. For one, the Republicans integrated statues of their own heroes into the facade: historian Jules Michelet graces the right side of the building, while author Eugène Sue surveys the rue de Rivoli. They also installed crystal chandeliers, gilded every interior surface, and created a Hall of Mirrors that rivals the original at Versailles. When Manet, Monet, Renoir, and Cézanne offered their services, they were all turned down in favor of the didactic artists whose work decorates the Salon des Lettres, the Salon des Arts, the Salon des Sciences, and the Salon Laurens. Originally called pl. de Grève, pl. Hôtel de Ville is additionally famous for its vital contribution to the French language. Poised on a marshy embankment (or *grève*) of the Seine, the medieval square served as a meeting ground for angry workers, giving France the useful and ever necessary phrase *en grève* (on strike). In 1610, Henri IV's assassin was quartered alive here by four horses bolting in opposite directions.

Today, pl. de Hôtel de Ville almost never sleeps: strikers continue to gather here, and the square occasionally hosts concerts, special TV broadcasts, and light shows. Every major French sporting event—Rolland Garros, the Tour de

France, and any game the Bleus ever play—is projected onto a jumbo screen in the *place*. The information office holds exhibits on Paris in the lobby off the rue de Lobau.

➔ ⓂHôtel de Ville. ℹ Special exhibit entry on rue de Lobau. 🕐 Open M-Sa 9am-7pm when there is an exhibit, 9am-6pm otherwise. Group tours available with advance reservations; call for available dates.

Latin Quarter and St-Germain

Sights, sights, sights, and more sights. There's more to see in the fifth and sixth than there is time to see it in. With that being said, there are a few things that you can't miss. The **Museums of the Middle Ages** (Musée de Cluny) and the **National Delacroix Museum** are two of the finest selections in Paris. The **Jardin de Luxembourg** is magnificent, and, alongside the Tuileries, one of the finest chill spots Paris has to offer. If you're the artsy type, you can't miss the slew of galleries in the **Odéon/Mabillon** area.

📷 PANTHÉON ◆ HISTORICAL MONUMENT, CRYPT

pl. du Panthéon ☎01 44 32 18 04 💻pantheon.monuments-nationaux.fr

Among Paris's most majestic and grandiose structures, the multi-faceted Panthéon is the former stomping ground and final resting place of many great Frenchmen and women of days past. In the 1760s, Louis XV recovered from a serious illness, and, having vowed to transform the basilica of Ste-Geneviève to something bigger if he survived, followed up on his promise. Though the building was originally designed to be the enlarged version of the Abbey of Ste-Geneviève, it was decided during the early stages of the French Revolution to use the massive structure as a secular mausoleum. Some of France's greatest citizens are buried in the Panthéon's crypt, including Marie and Pierre Curie, politician Jean Jaurès, Braille inventor Louis Braille, Voltaire, Jean-Jacques Rousseau, Émile Zola, and Victor Hugo. Now that's a list. There's something here for everybody; if you ever took a high school French class, you'll enjoy paying homage to Antoine de St-Exupéry, writer of "Le Petit Prince." Alexandre Dumas became the crypt's most recent addition, following his November 2002 interment. Compte de Mirabeau, a great Revolutionary orator, received the first nomination for a chunk of real estate at the Panthéon. Although interred there, the government expelled his ashes one year later when the public discovered his counter-revolutionary correspondence with Louis XVI. Beyond the "Ooh, look who's buried here," appeal of the crypt, the Panthéon's other main attraction is a famous science experiment any respectable nerd will have heard of: Foucault's Pendulum. The pendulum's plane of oscillation stays fixed as the Earth rotates around it, confirming the Earth's rotation. While you might be struck by the pendulum's oscillation, don't step in its path. The Earth's not gonna stop for you.

➔ ⓂCardinal Lemoine. ℹ Dome visits Apr-Oct; available in English. $ €7.50, ages 18-25 €4.80, under 18 and 1st Su of every month free. 🕐 Open daily Apr-Sept 10am-6:30pm; Oct-Mar 10am-6pm. Last entry 45min. before close.

📷 LE JARDIN DU LUXEMBOURG GARDEN

Main entrance on bld. St-Michel

"There is nothing more charming, which invites one more enticingly to idleness, reverie, and young love, than a soft spring morning or a beautiful summer dusk at the Jardin du Luxembourg," wrote Léon Daudet in a fit of sentimentality in 1928. The gardens were once a residential area in Roman Paris, the site of a medieval monastery, and later the home of 17th-century French royalty, when Marie de Médici hired architect Jean-François-Thérèse for the task of landscaping the garden's roughly 55 acres of prime Latin Quarter real estate in 1612. Revolutionaries liberated the gardens in the late 18th century and transformed them into a lush public park.

Today, Latin Quarter Parisians flock to Le Jardin de Luxembourg to sunbathe, stroll, flirt, drink, inhale cigarettes, and read by the rose gardens and central pool. The acres are patchworked by lawns of Wimbledon-esque precision, symmetrical pathways, and sculptures; taking in the garden can be a daunting task. Visitors saunter through the park's sandy paths, passing sculptures of France's queens, poets, and heroes. Nerds and chess phenoms challenge the local band of aged chessmasters to a game under shady chestnut trees. Undoubtedly the best, and most sought-after, spot in the garden is the **Fontaine des Médicis,** just east of the Palais, a vine-covered grotto complete with a murky fish pond and Baroque fountain sculptures. You might have to wait a few minutes, or hours, to get one of the coveted chairs bordering the Fontaine. The **Palais du Luxembourg,** located within the park and built in 1615 for Marie de Medicis, is now home to the **French Senate** and thus closed to the public. During WWII, the palace was used by the Nazis as headquarters for the Luftwaffe.

⇄ Ⓜ Odéon or RER: Luxembourg. ⏰ Guided tours in French Apr-Oct 1st W of each month 9:30am. Tours start at pl. André Honorat, behind the observatory. ⏰ Open daily.

👍 MUSÉE NATIONAL DU MOYEN AGE — MUSEUM

6 pl. Paul Painlevé ☎01 53 73 78 00 💻www.musee-moyenage.fr

Located on a site originally occupied by first-to-third-century Gallo-Roman baths and the 15th-century Hotel of the Abbots of Cluny, the Musée National du Moyen Age sits on one of the few prime pieces of historical real estate in Paris. In 1843, the state converted the *hôtel* that stands here today into a medieval museum; post-WWII excavations unearthed the baths. The museum showcases an unusually wide variety of art in its collection and attracts lots of Italian and Japanese tourist groups. While the baths host some Medieval and Roman sculpture, the *hôtel* features a magnificent tapestry exhibit, an expansive ivory collection (the second biggest in Paris, next to the Louvre's), and a number of examples of Gothic sculpture. Plenty of artwork is devoted to everyday life in medieval times.

The museum's collection includes art from Paris's most important medieval religious structures: Ste-Chapelle, Notre Dame, and St-Denis. Panels of brilliant stained glass from Ste-Chapelle are found on the ground floor. The **Galerie des Rois** contains sculptures from Notre Dame—including a series of marble heads of the kings of Judah, severed during the Revolution. The museum's medieval jewelry collection carries daggers; it looks like jewelry has only acquired a recreational purpose in recent times. A series of allegorical tapestries, titled **"La Dame à la Licorne"** (The Lady at the Unicorn), are among the most remarkable and most famous pieces in the museum. Claiming a room all their own, the woven masterpieces depict the five senses. If they look familiar to you, it may because you've seen them before—they deck the halls of the Gryffindor common room in the *Harry Potter* films. The complete cycle comprises the centerpiece of the museum's collection of 15th- and 16th-century Belgian weaving.

The grounds are divided into several sections, including the **Forest of the Unicorn,** which contains uncultivated wild plants, **Le Jardin Céleste** (The Heavenly Garden) dedicated to the Virgin Mary, **Le Jardin d'Amour** (The Garden of Love) which features plants used for medicinal and aromatic purposes, and **Le Tapis de Mille Fleurs** (Carpet of a Thousand Flowers) inspired by the *mille fleurs* tapestries. The museum also sponsors chamber music concerts during the summer.

⇄ Ⓜ Cluny-La Sorbonne. ℹ Audio tour included. $ €8.50, ages 18-25 €6.50, 1st Su of the month free (audio tour €1). ⏰ Open M 9:15am-5:45pm, and W-Su 9:15am-5:45pm. Last entry 30min before close.

👍 MUSÉE DELACROIX — 🎟 MUSEUM

6 rue de Furstemberg ☎ 01 44 41 86 50 💻www.musee-delacroix.fr

The Musée Delacroix combines the personal and scholarly perspectives of 18th-century Romanticist painter Eugène Delacroix, the artistic master behind the famous *Liberty Leading the People* (1830). The museum is situated in the modest, refurbished, three-room apartment and atelier where Delacroix lived and worked for much of his life. Watercolors, engravings, letters to Théophile Gautier and George Sand, sketches for his work in the Église St-Sulpice, and souvenirs from his journey to Morocco constitute the permanent holdings. Temporary exhibits broadcast new developments in Delacroix scholarship. There is a tranquil enclosed garden near the atelier equipped with Delacroix's original palettes and studies.

✣ ⓂSt-Germain-des-Prés or ⓂMabillon. *i* Free same-day entry with a Louvre ticket. Ⓢ €5, under 18 and students free. ⏰ Open June-Aug M 9:30am-5pm, W-F 9:30am-5:30pm; Sept-May M 9:30am-5pm, W-Su 9:30am-5pm. Last entry 30min. before close.

Invalides

Visit this arrondissement more than once if you can. Unsurprisingly, the **Tour Eiffel** towers over all of the 7*ème* attractions, but the posh neighborhood also hosts the French national government, a number of embassies, and an astonishing concentration of famous museums. Be sure to stop by the **Musée de Rodin** and **Musée d'Orsay.**

🏛 EIFFEL TOWER ✈⛄ TOWER

It doesn't need one. You can see it from everywhere. ☎01 44 11 23 23 🖥www.tour-eiffel.fr.

In 1937, Gustave Eiffel remarked on his construction, "I ought to be jealous of that tower; she is more famous than I am." The city of Paris as a whole could share the same lament. A true French synecdoche, the Eiffel Tower has come to stand for Paris itself. Gustave Eiffel designed it to be the tallest structure in the world, intended to surpass the ancient Egyptian pyramids in size and notoriety. Parisians, per usual, were not impressed; the same city-dwellers who cringed at the thought of skyscrapers mumbled disapprovingly before construction had even begun. Critics called it, perhaps not unfairly, the "metal asparagus," and a Parisian Tower of Babel. Writer Guy de Maupassant thought it was so hideous that he ate lunch every day at its ground-floor restaurant—the only place in Paris where you can't actually see the Eiffel Tower. When the tower was inaugurated in March 1889 as the centerpiece of the World's Fair, Parisians forgot their earlier displeasure. Nearly two million people ascended the engineering miracle during the event. Since the expo, over 150 million Parisians and tourists have made it the most visited paid monument in the world.

The cheapest way to ascend the tower is by walking up the first two floors; the third floor is only accessible by elevator. Waiting until nightfall to make your ascent cuts down the line and ups the glamour. At the top, captioned aerial photographs help you locate other famous landmarks. On a clear day it is possible to see Chartres, 88km away. From dusk until 2am (1am Sept-May), the tower sparkles with light for 10min. on the hour.

✣ ⓂBir-Hakeim or Trocadéro. Ⓢ Elevator to 2nd fl. €8.10, ages 12-24 €6.40, 4-11 and handicapped €4, under 3 free; elevator to summit €13.10/€11.50/€9/free; stair entrance to 2nd floor €4.50/3.50/3/free. ⏰ Elevator open daily from Jan to mid-June and Sept-Dec 9:30am-11:45pm, last entry 11pm; from mid-June to Aug 9am-12:45am, last entry 11pm. Stairs open daily from Jan to mid-June and Sept-Dec 9:30am-6:30pm, last entry 6pm; from mid-June to Aug 9am-12:45am, last entry midnight.

🏛 CHAMPS DE MARS ⛄ FIELD, WALK

Lined with more lovers than trees, the expansive lawn that stretches from the École Militaire to the Eiffel Tower is called Champs de Mars (Field of Mars). Close to the neighborhood's military monuments and museums, it has historically lived up to the Roman god of war for whom it is named. In the days of Napoleon's empire, the field was used as a drill ground for the adjacent École Militiare, and in 1780 Charles Montgolfier launched the first hydrogen balloon from its grassy fields. During the Revolution, the park was the site of civilian massacres and political demonstrations. In 2000, a glass monument to international peace was erected at the end of the Champs in quiet defiance of the École Militaire across the way. Named the Mur pou la Paix (Wall for Peace), the structure consists of two large glass walls covered from top to bottom with the word "peace" written in 32 languages. Viewed through the monument's walls, École Militaire appears to have the word "peace" scrawled all over it.

✈ Ⓜ*La Motte Picquet-Grenelle or École Militaire.*

▨ MUSÉE D'ORSAY
62 rue de Lille

☎01 40 49 48 14 🖳www.musee-orsay.com

✦⛐ MUSEUM

Aesthetic taste is fickle. When a handful of artists were rejected from the Louvre salon in the 19th-century, they opened an exhibition across the way, prompting both the scorn of stick-up-their-arses Académiciens and the rise of Impressionism. Today, people line up at the Musée d'Orsay to see this collection of groundbreaking rejects, which were considered so scandalous at the time. Established in 1982 in a dramatically lit former railway station, the collection includes paintings, sculpture, decorative arts, and photography dating from 1848 to WWI. The museum's glorious building is former reject itself. Built for the 1900 World's Fair, the Gare d'Orsay's industrial function was carefully masked by architect Victor Laloux behind glass, stucco, and a 370-room luxury hotel, so as not to offend the eye of the 7*ème*'s sophisticated residents. For several decades, it was the main departure point for southwest-bound trains, but newer trains were too long for its platforms, and it closed in 1939. Decades later, Musée d'Orsay opened in the station as one of Mitterrand's *Grands Projets*, gathering works from the **Louvre, Jeu de Paume, Palais de Tokyo, Musée de Luxembourg**, provincial museums, and private collections to add to the original collection the Louvre had refused.

The museum is organized chronologically from the ground floor up. The ground floor is dedicated to Pre-Impressionist paintings and sculpture, and contains the two scandalous works that started it all, both by Manet. Olympia, rumored to be a common whore whose confrontational gaze and nudity caused a stir, and Déjeuner sur l'Herbe, which shockingly portrayed a naked woman accompanied by fully clothed men. Back in the 19th century, scenes like that never happened. Or at least not publicly. The detailed section study of the Opéra Garnier is situated in the back of the room, and is definitely worth a visit as well. The top floor includes all the big names in Impressionist and Post-Impressionist art: Monet, Manet, Seurat, Van Gogh, and Degas. Degas' famed dancers and prostitutes are a particular highlight. In addition, the balconies offer supreme views of the Seine and the jungle of sculptures in the garden below. Beyond the permanent collection, seven temporary exhibition spaces, called *dossiers*, are scattered throughout the building. One of the most popular museums in Paris with the crowds to match, we recommend that you visit on Sunday mornings or Thursday evenings to avoid the masses.

✈ Ⓜ*Solférino. Access to visitors at entrance A off the square at 1 rue de la Légion d'Honneur.* ⓘ *Baby carriages not allowed. Tickets available online.* Ⓢ *€8, ages 18-25 €5.50, under 18 and EU citizens 18-26 free (free tickets directly at museum entrance).* ⏰ *Open Tu-W and F-Su 9:30am-6pm, Th 9:30am-9:45pm, visitors asked to leave starting 30min. before close. Boutique open daily 9:30am-6:30pm. Restaurant on level 2 open M-W 11:45am-5:30pm, Th 11:45am-5:30pm and 7-9:30pm, F-Su 11:45am-5:30pm.*

ÉCOLE MILITAIRE
1 pl. Joffre

⛐ GOVERNMENT INSTITUTION

Demonstrating the link between sex, war, and power once again, Louis XV founded the École Militaire in 1751 at the urging of his mistress, Mme. de Pompadour, who hoped to make officers of "poor gentlemen." In 1784, 15-year-old Napoleon Bonaparte enrolled. A few weeks later, he presented administrators with a comprehensive plan for the school's reorganization, and by the time he graduated three years later, he was a lieutenant in the artillery. Teachers foretold he would "go far in favorable circumstances." Little did they know. Louis XVI turned the building into a barracks for the Swiss Guard, but it was converted back into a military school in 1848. Today, the extensive structure serves as the living quarters of the Chief of the National Army, and additionally houses the Ministry of Defense and a variety of schools for advanced military studies, such as the Institute for Higher Studies of National Defense, the Center for Higher Studies of the Military, the Inter-Army College of Defense, and the School of Reserve Specialist Officers of State.

✦ ⓂÉcole Militaire.

INVALIDES
✦ HISTORIC BUILDING

Situated at the center of the 7ème, the gold-leaf dome of the Hôtel des Invalides glimmers conspicuously rain or shine, adding a touch of bling to the Parisian skyline. Most visitors assume that the building's history is just as scintillating, but Invalides has always led a life of seriousness and importance. Originally founded by Louis XVI in 1671 as a home for disabled soldiers, it is now the headquarters of the military governor of Paris and continues to serve, on a small scale, as a military hospital. Stretching from the building to the Pont Alexandre III is the tree-lined **Esplanade des Invalides** (not to be confused with the Champs de Mars). The Musée de l'Armée, Musée des Plans-Reliefs, Musée des Deux Guerres Mondiales, and Musée de l'Ordre de la Libération are housed within the Invalides museum complex, as is **Napoleon's tomb,** which lies in the adjoining Église St-Louis. To the left of the Tourville entrance, the Jardin de l'Intendant is strewn with benches and impeccably groomed trees and bushes, a topiary testament to the army's detail-oriented (read: anal) mentality. A ditch lined with captured foreign cannons runs around the Invalides area where a moat used to be, making it impossible to leave by any means beyond the two official entrances. Be aware that certain areas are blocked to tourists, out of respect for the privacy of the war veterans who still live in the hospital.

✦ ⓂInvalides. ⑤ €9; under 18, EU citizens 18-25, and all after 5pm free.

Champs-Élysées

There's a reason that the 8ème remains Paris's most-touristed arrondissement, long after the Champs-Élysées has ceased to be posh. The area harbors more architectural beauty, historical significance, and shopping opportunities than almost any other area in the city, and remains an exhilarating—if hectic—place to spend a day. Champs-Élysées also hosts a variety of art museums in its northern corners; they are often located in *hôtels particuliers*, where they were once part of the private collections.

ARC DE TRIOMPHE
✦ⓗ HISTORIC MONUMENT

pl. de l'Étoile ⬛arc-de-triomphe.monuments-nationaux.fr

The highest point between the **Louvre** and the **Grande Arche de la Defense,** the Arc de Triomphe offers a stunning view down the Champs-Élysées to the **Tuileries** and Louvre. Plans for the monument were first conceived by the architect Charles Francois Ribar in 1758, who envisioned an unparalleled tribute to France's military prowess—in the form of a giant, bejeweled elephant. Fortunately for France, the construction of the monument was not undertaken until 1806, when Napoleon conceived a less bizarre landmark modeled after the triumphal arches of victorious Roman emperors like Constantine and Titus. Napoleon was exiled before the arch was completed, and Louis XVIII took over its construction in 1823. He dedicated the arch to the French military's recent intervention in Spain and its commander, the Duc d'Angouleme, and placed its design in the hands of Jean-Francois-Therese Chalgrin. The Arc de Triomphe was consecrated in 1836;

walk, walk fashion baby

As the home of major luxury fashion flagships such as Chanel and Yves Saint-Laurent, Paris takes its couture to the extreme. With the **Fédération française de la couture** (French Fashion Federation) running biannual fashion weeks at the Carrousel du Louvre, the fashion industry in Paris mostly centers on the rue du Faubourg Saint-Honoré, where anyone wearing a T-shirt and jeans may be heckled and stoned. But France's sartorial history provides some even stranger insight into the country's fashion evolution.

- **NOT SO AMERICAN.** The actual origin of supposedly all-American denim is Nîmes, located in the south of France. Levi Strauss actually imported the unique fabric from the city, which also explains blue jeans' other name—"de Nîmes."

- **THE BANE OF A MILLION WOMEN.** In the 1940s, two Frenchmen became rivals in their quest to claim the bikini as their invention. Jacques Heim first introduced his skimpy two-piece swimsuit design in public, calling it l'Atome. But when Louis Reard hired a skywriter to scrawl his term "Bikini" over the skies of the French Riviera, Heim got shafted, and generations of body image issues began.

- **PRETTY PROPAGANDA.** When Louis XIV reigned over the French court, he became so obsessed with the idea of France as the revolutionary fashion arbiter that he would send life-sized dolls dressed in the most up-to-date gowns to other European courts. It remains unclear whether they were as effective as today's Bratz dolls.

- **FASHION DICTATORSHIP.** The tradition of French rulers manipulating the country's fashion industry runs deep. When Napoleon came into power in the early 19th century, he barred textile imports from England and single-handedly rejuvenated the Valenciennes lace industry, reintroducing *tulle* and *batiste* into popular trends, particularly women's dress. But in typical totalitarian style, Napoleon took it a step further and forbade women in his court to wear the same dress twice for public appearances, in an ongoing effort to stimulate the fashion industry.

in honor of the emperor that conceived of its design, the names of Napoleon's generals and battles are engraved inside. The arch has been a magnet for various triumphant armies ever since. After the Prussians marched through the Arc in 1871, the mortified Parisians purified the ground beneath it with fire. On July 14, 1919, the Arc provided the backdrop for an Allied victory parade headed by Ferdinand Foch. After years under Germany's brutal occupation during WWII, a sympathetic Allied army ensured that a French general would be the first to drive under the Arc in the liberation of Paris.

Today, the arch is dedicated to all French army soldiers and veterans. The **Tomb of the Unknown Soldier,** illuminated by an eternal flame, is situated under the arch, and was added to the structure on November 11, 1920. The memorial honors the 1.5 million Frenchmen who died during WWI. Visitors can climb up to the terrace observation deck for a brilliant view of the **Historic Axis** from the Arc de Triomphe du Carrousel and the **Louvre Pyramid** at one end to the **Grande Arche de la Défense** at the other. There is also a permanent exhibit, "Between Wars and Peace," which reads like the Arc's autobiography.

꛰ ⓂCharles de Gaulle-l'Étoile. *i* Expect daily throngs, although you can escape the crowds if you go before noon. You will kill yourself (and face a hefty fine) trying to dodge the 10-lane merry-go-

paris · sights

round of cars around the arch, so use the pedestrian underpass on the right side of the Champs-Élysées facing the arch. Tickets sold in the pedestrian underpass before going up to the ground level. [$] €9, ages 18-25 €5.50, under 18 and EU citizens 18-25 free. ⏰ Open daily Apr-Sept 10am-11pm; Oct-Mar 10am-10:30pm. Last entry 30min. before close.

AVENUE DES CHAMPS-ÉLYSÉES — SHOPPING DISTRICT

From pl. Charles de Gaulle-Étoile southeast to pl. de la Concorde

Radiating from the huge rotary surrounding the Arc de Triomphe, the Champs-Élysées seems to be a magnificent celebration of pomp and the elite's fortuitous circumstance. Constructed in 1616 when Marie de Medici ploughed the Cours-la-Reine through the fields and marshland west of the Louvre, the Avenue remained an unkempt thoroughfare until the early 19th century, when the city finally invested in sidewalks and installed gas lighting. It quickly became the center of Parisian opulence, and maintained a high density of flashy mansions and exclusive cafes well into the early 20th century. More recently, the Champs has undergone a bizarre kind of democratization, as commercialization is diluting its former glamor. Shops along the avenue now range from designer fashion boutiques to car dealerships to low-budget tchotchke shops: the colossal **Louis Vuitton** flagship emporium stands across from an even larger Monoprix, a low-budget all-purpose store.

Despite its slip in sophistication, the Champs continues to be known as the most beautiful street in the world. In 1860, Louis Vuitton spearheaded a committee to maintain the avenue's luxury, and it still strives to do so today, installing wider sidewalks and trying to prevent certain shops from moving in—H&M was refused a bid in 2007, but eventually won out. With rents as high as €1.25 million a year for 1000 sq. m. of space, the Champs is the second-richest street in the world (New York's 5th Avenue is number one, if you really want to know). The Avenue also continues to play host to most major French events: on **Bastille Day,** the largest parade in Europe takes place on this street, as does the final stretch of the **Tour de France.** And while the Champs itself may be deteriorating into something increasingly (gasp!) bourgeois, many of its side streets, like **Avenue Montaigne,** have picked up the slack and ooze class in their own right.

[M] Charles de Gaulle.

PLACE DE LA CONCORDE — HISTORIC MONUMENT

pl. de la Concorde

In the center of Paris's largest and most infamous public square, the 3300-year-old Obélisque de Luxor stands at a monumental 72 ft. The spot was originally occupied by a statue of Louis XV (after whom the square was originally named) that an angry mob destroyed in 1748. King Louis-Philippe, anxious to avoid revolutionary rancor, opted for a less contentious symbol: the 220-ton red granite, hieroglyphic-covered obelisk presented to Charles X from the Viceroy of Egypt in 1829. The obelisk, which dates back to the 13th century BCE and recalls the royal accomplishments of Ramses II, wasn't erected until 1836. Gilded images on the sides of the obelisk recount its 2-year trip to Paris in a custom-built boat. Today, it forms the axis of what many refer to as the "royal perspective"—a spectacular view of Paris from the **the Louvre** in which the Pl. de la Concorde, the **Arc de Triomphe**, and the **Grande Arche de la Défense** appear to form a straight line through the center of the city. The view serves as a physical timeline of Paris's history, from the reign of Louis XIV to the Revolution to Napoleon's reign, and finally, all the way to the celebration of commerce.

Constructed by Louis XV in honor of, well, himself, the Pl. de la Concorde quickly became ground zero for all public grievances against the monarchy. During the Reign of Terror, the complex of buildings was renamed place de la Révolution, and 1343 aristocrats were guillotined there in less than a year. Louis XVI met his end near the statue that symbolizes the French town of Brest, and the obelisk marks the spot where Marie-Antoinette, Charlotte Corday (Marat's assassin), Lavoisier, Danton, and Robespierre lost their heads. Flanking either side of Concorde's intersection with the wide **Champs-Élysées** are reproductions of Guillaume Coustou's **Cheveaux de Marly.** Also known as Africans Mastering the Numidian Horses, the original sculptures are now in the Louvre to protect them from pollution. The *place* is ringed by eight large **statues** representing France's major cities: Brest, Bordeaux Lille, Lyon, Marseille, Nantes, Rouen, and Strasbourg. At night, the Concorde's dynamic ambience begins to soften, and the obelisk, fountains, and lamps are dramatically illuminated. On **Bastille Day,** a military parade led by the President of the Republic marches through Concorde (usually around 10am) and down the Champs-Élysées to the Arc de Triomphe, and an impressive fireworks display lights up the sky over the *place* at night. At the end of July, the **Tour de France** finalists pull through Concorde and into the home stretch on the Champs-Élysées. Tourists be warned: between the Concorde's monumental scale, lack of crosswalks and heavy traffic, crossing the street here is impossible at best, fatal at worst.

[M]Concorde.

Opéra

OPÉRA NATIONAL DE PARIS/OPÉRA GARNIER — THEATER

pl. de l'Opéra ☎08 92 89 90 90 www.operadeparis.fr

Formerly known as the Opéra National de Paris before the creation of the Opéra Bastille in 1989, this splendid historic structure is now better known as Opéra Garnier. Architect Garnier was extensively inspired by his studies in Greece, Turkey, and Rome, and it definitely shows; the Opéra's wondrous frescoes and dazzling stone and marble designs regularly leave visitors speechless. That being said, visiting the Opéra is a roll of the dice. The building is periodically closed due to performances or set construction, and these interruptions are rarely listed on the website. We also advise that you take one of the guided tours, as the guides are all extremely knowledgeable. You might get a tour guide with a nearly incomprehensible French accent, so try to schedule this visit later in your stay when you're well accustomed to English à la frog.

[M]Opéra. $ €9, under 25 €5. Guided visit €12, over 60 €10, students €9, ages 12 and under €6, big families €30. Open daily 10am-4:30pm; may be closed on performance days, so check the website.

NOTRE DAME DE LORETTE — CHURCH

18bis rue de Châteaudun ☎01 48 78 92 72 www.notredamedelorette.org

Constructed between 1823 and 1836 by architect Hippolyte Le Bas, Notre Dame de Lorette is a remarkably ornate Neoclassical church in an otherwise average residential neighborhood. At the time of its construction, it pushed the limits of socially acceptable extravagance, and even compelled a cadre of church officials, journalists, and other *Parisiens* to disapprove of its borderline-vulgar extravagance. The four massive and intricately carved pillars that support the church's blackening entrance will remind you of the Parthenon; splendid frescoes adorn the ceilings of each of the four chapels, and portray the Virgin Mary and the four principal sacraments (baptism, eucharist, wedding, and anointing of the sick, for those not in the know) in detail. Though a must-see for lovers of art and architecture, Notre Dame de Lorette remains an active neighborhood church, so try to avoid Mass times unless, of course, you want to go for Mass. Given some serious disrepair, the future of the church's renovation or closing is perpetually up in the air. Catch it while it's still here.

[M]Notre-Dame-de-Lorette. Reception M-F 2:30-6:30pm, Sa 5-6:30pm. Open for visitors daily 9am-6pm.

Canal St-Martin and Surrounds

It seems that the number of sketchballs and number of cool sights in a given neighborhood are inversely related. While the 10*ème* doesn't offer much in the way of landmarks or museums, there are a few quick sights that you might want to check out; **Le Marché Saint-Quentin** could take a bit longer.

LE MARCHÉ SAINT-QUENTIN ♿ HISTORIC SIGHT, MONUMENT

Corner rue de Chabrol and bld. Magenta

The largest covered market in Paris, Le Marché Saint-Quentin was constructed in 1865 and renovated in 1982. A series of huge windows allow the sun to pour in, and keep the complex warm even in winter. Come here for the finest cheeses, fish, and meats, or just experience the delicious mix of aromas and mingle with veteran foodies who spend their days browsing for the finest permutation of camembert. There's a bistro in the middle of the market for those who can't wait until they get home to chow down on their produce.

➡ [M]Gard de l'Est. 🕐 Open M-Sa 8:30am-1pm and 4-7:30pm.

Bastille

In the 11*ème*, the term "Sights" is a bit of a misnomer—there are few monumental ones that still exist in this neighborhood, aside from the **place de la Bastille.** Still, the symbolic historical value of the arrondissement remains, and the lively neighborhood provides many of its own contemporary diversions. The 12*ème* boasts giant monoliths of modern architecture, like the **Opéra Bastille** and the **Palais Omnisports.** Most of the construction is commercial, fitting the working-class background of the area, but a bit of old-fashioned charm can be seen in the funky **Viaduc des Arts** near the Bastille. There are generally more hospitals than museums in the neighborhood, but in October 2007 the arrondissement welcomed a new museum, the **Cité Nationale de l'Histoire de l'Immigration,** which is a must-see if only for its present relevance. It is housed in the **Palais de la Porte Dorée** along with the aquarium; if you make it there, hop on over to the nearby **Bois de Vincennes** for the impressive château and grounds.

★ MALHIA KENT WORKSHOP

19 av. Daumesnil ☎01 53 44 76 76 💻www.malhia.com

Fulfilling every Project Runway fantasy, this workshop gives an up-close, behind-the-scenes look at fashion. Artisans weave gorgeously intricate fabrics that become *haute couture* for houses like Dior and Chanel. Also gives you a chance to buy clothing—mostly jackets and blazers—before a label is attached and the price skyrockets.

➡ [M]Gare de Lyon. $ Clothing usually €75-300. 🕐 Open M-F 9am-7pm.

BASTILLE PRISON HISTORIC LANDMARK

Visitors to the prison subsist on symbolic value alone–it's one of the most popular sights in Paris that doesn't actually exist. On July 14, 1789, an angry Parisian mob stormed this bastion of royal tyranny, sparking the French Revolution. They only liberated a dozen or so prisoners, but who's counting? Two days later, the Assemblée Nationale ordered the prison demolished. Today, all that remains is the ground plan of the fortress, still visible as a line of paving-stones in the **place de la Bastille.**

The proletariat masses couldn't have chosen a better symbol to destroy. The prison was originally commissioned by Charles V to safeguard the eastern entrance to Paris; strapped for cash, Charles "recruited" a press-gang of passing civilians to lay the stones for the fortress. Construction was completed by the end of the 14th century, and the Bastille's formidable towers rose 100 ft. above the city. After serving as the royal treasury under Henry IV, the building was turned into a state prison by Louis XIII. Internment there, generally reserved for heretics and political dissidents, was the king's business, and as a result it was often arbitrary. But it was hardly the hell-hole that the Revolutionaries who tore it down imagined it to be. Bastille's titled inmates were allowed to furnish their suites, use fresh linens, bring their own servants, and receive guests; the Cardinal de Rohan famously held a dinner party for 20 in his cell. Notable prisoners included the **☙Mysterious Man in the Iron Mask** (made famous by writer Alexandre Dumas), the Comte de Mirabeau, Voltaire (twice), and the Marquis de Sade, who wrote his notorious novel *Justine* here.

On the day of the "storm," the Revolutionary militants, having ransacked the Invalides for weapons, turned to the Bastille for munitions. Surrounded by an armed rabble, too short on food to entertain the luxury of a siege, and unsure of the loyalty of the Swiss mercenaries who defended the prison, the Bastille's governor surrendered. His head was severed with a pocket knife and paraded through the streets on a pike. Despite the gruesome details, the storming of the Bastille has come to symbolize the triumph of liberty over tyranny. Its first anniversary was cause for great celebration in revolutionary Paris. Since the late 19th century, July 14 has been the official state holiday of the French Republic. It is a time of glorious firework displays and copious amounts of alcohol, with festivities concentrated in the pl. de la Bastille.

✤ ⓂBastille.

JULY COLUMN TOWER

Towering above the the always-busy pl. de la Bastille, this light-catching column commemorates a group of French freedom fighters—though, somewhat illogically, not those who stormed the Bastille. Topped by the conspicuous gold cupid with the shiny bum, the pillar was erected by King Louis-Philippe in 1831 to pay homage to Republicans who had died in the **Trois Glorieuses**, three days of street fighting that engulfed Paris in July of 1830. Victims of the Revolution of 1848 were subsequently buried here, along with two mummified Egyptian pharaohs (we're not sure what their involvement was). The column is closed to the public.

✤ ⓂBastille. In the center of pl. de la Bastille.

Butte-aux-Cailles and Chinatown

There are no monuments in the 13*ème* to speak of, and that's to its credit. Diverse, residential, and pleasantly odd, the neighborhoods here retain the daily rhythm of Parisian life, and remain uninterrupted by the troops of pear-shaped tourists in matching fanny packs that plague the more pristine arrondissements. Though short on medieval cathedrals, hidden gems from Paris's more recent legacy of perturbed Bo(hemian)-Bo(urgeosie)s and globalization are scattered throughout the area. Adventurous wanderers will enjoy getting lost in the quirky and sprawling Chinatown, the and working class Butte-aux-Cailles harbors a thriving street-art culture.

▩ QUARTIER DE LA BUTTE-AUX-CAILLES   NEIGHBORHOOD
Intersection of rue de la Butte-aux-Cailles and rue 5 diamants

Once a working class neighborhood, the Quartier de la Butte-aux-Cailles was home to the *soixantes-huitards*, the activists who nearly paralyzed the city during the 1968 riots. Permutations of the district's original counter-culture remain alive and well: dreadlocks are the hairstyle of choice, and the fashionably disaffected tag walls with subversive graffiti and are armed with guitars at all times. Funky restaurants like **Chez Gladines** and the co-operative **Le Temps des Cerises** line the cobbled streets, and attract a boisterous, artsy crowd. **L'Église de Ste-Anne**, which stands on the corner of rue Bobillot and rue de Tolbiac, boasts a gorgeous stained-glass collection that refracts the afternoon sun into red, blue, and purple light.

✤ ⓂCorvisart. Exit onto bld. Blanqui and then turn onto rue 5 diamants, which will intersect with rue de la Butte-aux-Cailles.

QUARTIER CHINOIS   NEIGHBORHOOD

Just south of rue de Tolbiac

Spread out over four Metro stops just south of rue de Tolbiac, Paris's Chinatown is home to a significant population of Cambodian, Chinese, Thai, and Vietnamese immigrants. Signs change from French to Asian languages, and restaurants advertise steamed dumplings in lieu of *magret de canard*. Non-residents roam the streets looking for the best Asian cuisine Paris has to offer.

Ⓜ Porte d'Ivry, Porte de Choisy, Tolbiac and Maison Blanche are near Chinatown.

BIBLIOTHEQUE NATIONALE DE FRANCE: SITE FRANCOIS MITTERRAND ✦ LIBRARY

11 quai Francois Mauriac   ☎01 53 79 59 59 ▣www.bnf.fr

With its wide windows and and towering steel frame, the library is an imposing piece of architecture worthy of the 13 million volumes it houses. Highlights of the collection include **Gutenberg Bibles** and first editions from the Middle Ages, and are displayed in rotation the Galerie des Donateurs. The exhibit can be accessed for free. Scholars hunker down beneath the vaulted ceiling of the library's imposing reading room, or lounge on the extensive deck, surveying the Seine with cigarettes in hand.

Ⓜ Quai de la Gare. Ⓢ Day pass to reading rooms €3.30; 15-day pass €20; annual membership €35, students €18. Tours €3. ☼ Open M 2-7pm, Tu-Sa 10am-7pm, Su 1pm-7pm. Tours Tu-F 2pm, Sa-Su 3pm.

Montparnasse

CIMITIÈRE MONTPARNASSE   CEMETERY

3 bld. Edgar Quinet   ☎01 44 10 86 50

Opened in 1824, Cimitière Montparnasse is the prestigious final resting place of countless famed Frenchman, and an escape from the touristy hustle and bustle of Montparnasse. Be sure to stop at the security station at the **Boulevard Quinet** entrance for a map marking the resting places of the cemetery's celebrities. The map reads like a *Who's Who?* of French greatness: Charles Baudelaire, Alfred Dreyfuss, Guy de Maupassant, Samuel Beckett, Jean-Paul Sartre and Simone de Beauvoir (the two are buried together), among many others, hold real estate here. The presence of these great minds is surely enough to make humanities buffs shed a tear, and the graves continue to be lovingly adorned with cigarette butts, beer bottles, Metro tickets, and personal statements of gratitude in several languages. The rest of the cemetery, however, leaves a bit to be desired. The broken windows, bright green trash receptacles, and candy-cane-striped "Do Not Enter" signs detract from the solemn beauty of the cemetery. Local residents have co-opted the grounds for their own purposes; kids play tag, older kids from the "banlieues" bum cigarettes off tourists, and locals drink excessively. Nonetheless, the cemetery showcases some delightful architecture, an impressive list of tenants, and relatively few tourists.

Ⓜ Edgar Quinet, opposite the Square Delambre. Ⓢ Free. ☼ Open 24hr.

CATACOMBS   ✦ HISTORIC LANDMARK

1 av. du Colonel Henri Roi-Tanguy   ☎01 43 22 47 63 ▣www.catacombes-de-paris.fr

The Catacombs were originally the site of some of Paris's stone mines, but were converted into an ossuary (i.e., place to keep bones) in 1785 due to the stench arising from overcrowded cemeteries in Paris. A journey into these tunnels is not for the handicapped or the light of heart—it's a 45min. excursion, and there are no bathrooms, so we recommend that all middle-aged men double down on their Maxiflow the night before, and handle business before you descend into the abyss. The visitor enters down a winding spiral staircase, and soon thereafter, is greeted by a welcoming sign: "Stop, here is the Empire of Death." The visuals are quite unlike anything you've ever seen before. Morbid-themed graffiti lines the walls, and the view of hundreds of thousands of bones makes you feel, well, quite insignificant in the grander scheme of things. Try to arrive before the opening at 10am; nestled twice as deep below ground as the Metro, the Catacombs offer a refreshing respite from the midday heat in the summer, and hordes of tourists form extremely long lines to get out of the beating sun. The visitor's passage is well-signed, so don't worry about getting lost. Try trailing behind the group a little for the ultimate creepy experience; you won't be disappointed.

✦ ⓂDenfert Rochereau. Cross av. Roi-Tanguy with lion on your left. Ⓢ €7, over 60 €5.50, 14-26 €3.50, under 14 free. Ⓩ Open Tu-Su 10am-4pm.

Passy and Auteuil

With streets named after Theopold Gautier, Benjamin Franklin, George Sand, and other illustrious figues, the 16ème echoes with previous eras of high culture. Remnants of these periods are now housed in the Quarter's many museums. Fans of *Last Tango in Paris* can wander onto the Bir-Hakeim bridge where scenes were shot, and Honoré de Balzac's devotees can lovingly touch the desk where he wrote. Though packed with tourists, Trocadero and its surroundings feature wonderful views of the Eiffel Tower, and boast a bustling center of street art, not to mention the graves of some of Paris's most notable residents.

◼ CIMITIÈRE DE PASSY   CEMETERY
2 rue du Commandant-Schloesing   ☎01 53 70 40 80

Opened in 1820, this cemetery is home to some of Paris's most notable deceased, including the Givenchy family, Claude Debussy, Berthe Morisot, and Édouard Manet. The idiosyncrasies and enduring rivalries of these figures continue even in death; the graves here look more like little mansions than tombstones. The tomb of Russian artist Marie Bashkirtseff is a recreation of her studio, and stands at an impressive 40 ft. Morisot and Manet are buried in a more modest tomb together. We suspect that Morisot's husband would not have approved. Well-groomed and quiet, the graveyard is more of a shadowy garden, with a wonderful view of the Eiffel Tower.

✦ ⓂTrocadero. Veer right onto av. Paul Doumer. Ⓢ Free. Ⓩ Open Mar 16-Nov 5 M-F 8am-6pm, Sa 8:30am-6pm, Su 9am-6pm; Nov 6-Mar 15 M-F 8am-5:30pm, Sa 8:30am-5:30pm, Su 9am-5:30pm. Last entry 30min. before close. Conservation office open M-F 8:30am-12:30pm and 2-5pm.

PLACE DU TROCADERO   SQUARE

One of the most bustling hubs in the 16th, Pl. du Trocadero offers one of the best views of the Eiffel Tower. Street artists dance to a melange of hip-hop and pop, vendors push their wares on foot, and angsty youth mill about with skateboards. The nearby cafe **Carette** has some of the best hot chocolate in Paris (€7).

✦ ⓂTrocadero.

Batignolles

There's a reason the 17ème isn't a go-to tourist destination. Sights in the traditional sense are few and far between here, but the mostly residential neighborhood and its juxaposition of bourgeois and working class Paris is still worth exploring. The lively **Village Batignolles** is a highlight; stretching from **boulevard de Batignolles** to **place du Dr. Félix Lobligeois**, the area is lined with hip cafes and populated by locals who believe in afternoon drinking. During warmer months, **rue de Levis** turns into an open-air market, and the local groceries and boutiques park their carts of bananas and hang their canopies of frilly skirts outside to tempt passerby.

SQUARE DES BATIGNOLLES   SQUARE

Formerly a hamlet for workers, and then a storage sight for illicit ammunition, Square des Batignolles is now an English-style park where the trees grow wild, unfettered by neutoric French trimmings and metal bars. Monet once sat here to paint the Gare St-Lazare train tracks, before heading over to a favorite cafe at 11 rue de Batignolles. Today, less illustrious but just as ambitious artists line its winding paths, watching the local joggers go by. The gently flowing river and pooling lake make the park an idyllic respite from the bustle of the city.

➡ [M]Brochant. Walk down rue Brochant. Cross pl. du Charles Fillion $ Free. ⏰ Open M-F 8am-9:30pm, Sa-Su and holidays 9am-9:30pm.

Montmartre

One of Paris's most storied neighborhoods, Montmartre was once home to lots of famous artists. Today, the **Place du Tertre,** a former artist hangout, is dominated by drunk portraitists instead. From the hills of Montmartre to the seedy underworld of Pigalle, there's plenty to see here, and plenty of English spoken.

👍 HALLE ST. PIERRE — MUSEUM

2 rue Ronsard ☎ 01 42 51 10 49 💻www.hallesaintpierre.org

Halle St. Pierre is a one-of-a-kind, abstract art museum located right down the street from the Basilica. Exhibits are constantly rotating, so the museum is naturally hard to pin down. The art on display tends to be a bit far out. One of Halle St. Pierre's more recent exhibits was on "Art Brut Japonais," or Japanese Outsider Art; during our visit, a standout among the many mind-bending works was a series of dirty pairs of underwear, or as the French call them, slips. Luckily they didn't smell. Halle St. Pierre also houses rentable workshops, a top-notch bookstore, and a constantly crowded cafe. The museum section is not closed off, so the soft din of cafe chatter accompanies any museum visit.

➡ [M]Anvers or Abesses. $ €7.50, students €6. ⏰ Open Sept-July daily 10am-6pm; Aug M-F noon-6pm.

👍 CIMITIÈRE MONTMARTRE — CEMETERY

20 av. Rachel ☎01 53 42 36 30

A particularly vast cemetery, Montmartre was built below ground on the site of a former quarry, and stretches across a significant portion of the 18th arrondissement. It is now the resting place of multiple famous people: painter Edgar Degas, artist Gustave Moreau, writer Emile Zola, saxophone inventor Adolphe Sax, and ballet dancer Marie Taglioni are among the long-term residents. Fans leave ballet shoes on Taglioni's grave, and coins, notes, etc. at some of the other famous gravestones. The Cemetery itself is in disrepair; several graves have broken windows, and could use some maintenance and cleaning. The mischievous crowd of the Red Light District is surely to thank for this.

➡ [M]Place de Clichy. $ Free. ⏰ Open Nov. 6-May 15 M-F 8am-5:30pm, Sa 8:30am-5:30pm, Su 9am-5:30pm; Mar 16-Nov 5, 8am-6pm, Sa 8:30am-6pm, Su 9am-6pm.

BASILIQUE DU SACRÉ-COEUR — ♿ CHURCH

35 rue du Chevalier-de-la-Barre ☎01 53 41 89 00 💻 www.sacre-coeur-montmartre.fr

Situated 129m above sea-level, the steps of the Basilique offer what is possibly the best view in the whole city. This splendid basilica first underwent construction in 1870. Its purpose? To serve as a spiritual bulwark for France and the Catholic religion, under the weight of a pending military loss and German occupation. The basilica was initially meant to be an assertion of conservative, Catholic power, commissioned by the National Assembly. Today, the Basilica sees over 10 million visitors per year, and is accompanied by an attendant list of tourist traps; outside the Basilica, beware of men trying to "give you" a bracelet or other tourist trinkets, because they'll start to yell emphatically that you have to pay them once you don't. The Cathedral itself is home to two souvenir shops. The Museum has some interesting artistic and architectural features: its slightly muted Roman-Byzantine architecture was a reaction against the perceived excess at the recently constructed Opéra Garnier.

➡ [M]Lamarck-Caulaincourt. $ Free. ⏰ Open daily 6am-11pm. Mass M-Sa 11:15am, 6:30pm, 10pm; Su 11am, 6pm, 10pm.

Buttes Chaumont

Sights in Buttes are pretty much limited to the **Parc des Buttes** and the unique **Parc de la Villette,** a former meat-packing district that provided Paris with much of its beef before the advent of the refridgerated truck. In 1979, the slaughterhouses were replaced with an artistic park, and voilà. Architect Bernard Tschumi's three-part vision took 461 teams from 41 different countries to complete.

▧ PARC DES BUTTES-CHAUMONT   & PARK

This awe-inspiring neighborhood park shrewdly uses impressive, man-made topography to make visitors feel like they're in Atlantis—or some kind of movie. Napoleon III commissioned the park in 1862 to quell his homesickness for London's Hyde Park, where he spent a good deal of time in exile. Construction of the park was directed by designer Adolphe Alphand, whose main triumph was the park's central hill, with its breathtaking exposed crags. The park's area has been a well-trafficked part of Paris since the 13th century, but before Napoleon III it was famous for very different reasons. Once the site of a gibbet (an iron cage filled with the rotting corpses of criminals), a dumping ground for dead horses, a haven for worms, and a gypsum quarry (the source of "plaster of Paris"), the modern-day Parc des Buttes-Chaumont has come a long way. Today's visitors walk the winding paths surrounded by lush greenery and hills, and enjoy a great view of the 19ème, 20ème, and the rest of Paris from the Roman temple at the top of the cliffs. The lower rungs of the Parc provide a lovely and shaded respite on a warm summer's afternoon. Families, rebellious teens, and runners constitute the park's main demographics.

✚ ⓜButtes-Chaumont. ⑤ Free. ⚑ Open daily May-Sept 7am-10:15pm; Oct-Apr 7am-8:15pm.

▧ CITÉ DES SCIENCES ET DE L'INDUSTRIE   ✦& MUSEUM

30 av. Corentin Cariou   ☎01 40 05 12 12 ▧www.cite-sciences.fr

If any structure in Paris has ADHD, it's the Cité des Sciences et de l'Industrie; to call it a multi-purpose complex would be an understatement. The Cité houses the fabulous **Explora Science Museum,** one of the top destinations for the children of Paris. Highlights include a magnificent planetarium, a movie theater, a library, a massive cyber cafe, and an aquarium. The whole structure is an architectural tour de force. Outside of the Cité is the enormous **Géode,** a mirrored sphere that essentially looks like a gigantic disco ball, but somehow doubles as the Cité complex's second movie theater; the 1000 sq. m. surface provides ample screen space. To the right of the Géode, the **Argonaute** details the history of (you guessed it) submarines, from the days of Jules Verne to present-day nuclear-powered subs. If the Argonaute looks like a real naval submarine, that's because it is. The exhibit is fantastic, but will cost you a little extra. At Level -1 in the Cité, you'll find consultation areas for jobs and health; while not exactly a fun outing with the kids, this stuff can be useful if you're looking for a job or wondering how to stay healthy during your time in Paris.

✚ ⓜPorte de la Villette. *i* English or French audio tours included. ⑤ Formule summer (access to all aspects of the Cité) €21, reduced €19. Explora+Planetarium €11, under 25 €8. Argonaute €3. Cinaxe admission €4.80. Explora+Geode €17.50, reduced €14, under 7 €9. ⚑ Open M-Sa 9:30am-6pm, Su 9:30am-7pm. Argonaute open Tu-Sa 10am-5:30pm, Su 10am-6:30pm. Cinaxe open Tu-Su 11am-1pm and 2-5pm; showings every 15min.

Belleville and Père Lachaise

▧ CIMITIÈRE DU PÈRE LACHAISE   CEMETERY

16 rue du Repos   ☎01 55 25 82 10

One of the most prestigious cemeteries in Paris, the Cimitière du Père Lachaise is the biproduct of innovative public health codes and 19th-century publicity stunts. Cemeteries were banned inside of Paris in 1786 after the closure of the

paris · sights

Saints Innocents Cemetery (Cimitière des Innocents); the cemetery was located on the fringe of Les Halles food market, and local officials came to realize that this (shockingly) presented a health hazard. Père Lachaise, in the east of the city, was the biggest of the new cemeteries outside of the city's center, the others being Montmartre and Montparnasse. As any tourist who has visited the 20th arrondissement knows all too well, the 20ème is far removed from the heart of Paris, and the cemetery didn't attract many burials immediately after its creation. In a savvy marketing move, administrators made a grand spectacle of moving the remains of two renowned Frenchmen, Molière and La Fontaine, to Père Lachaise. The strategy worked. Thousands of burials occurred at Lachaise over the next few years, and the cemetery now holds over 300,000 bodies, and many more cremated remains. Today the well-manicured lawns and winding paths of the Cimitière du Père Lachaise have become the final resting place for many French and foreign legends. The cemetery's over-occupied graves house the likes of Balzac, Delacroix, La Fontaine, Haussmann, Molière, and Proust. Expat honorees include Modigliani, Stein, Wilde, and—most visited of all the graves at Père Lachaise—Jim Morrison.

You'll notice that many of the tombs in this landscaped grove strive to remind visitors of the dead's worldly accomplishments. The tomb of French Romantic painter **Théodore Géricault** bears a reproduction of his Raft of the Medusa, with the original painting now housed in the Louvre. On **Frédéric Chopin's** tomb sits his muse Calliope, sculpted beautifully in white marble. Although **Oscar Wilde** died destitute and unable to afford such an extravagant design, an American admirer added bejewelled Egyptian figurines to his grave in 1912. Despite an interdiction on kissing the tomb, dozens of lipstick marks from adoring fans cover Wilde's grave today. Upon entering the cemetery, you might feel a distinctly bohemian "vibe." Well, that's because The Doors' former lead singer, **Jim Morrison,** holds permanent real estate here at Lachaise. Apparently the crooner remains popular even in death. Honored with the most visited, though rather modest, grave in the cemetery, Morrison's final resting place is annually mobbed by hundreds of thousands of visitors. Admirers bearing beer, flowers, joints, poetry, Doors' T-shirts, bandanas, jackets and more surround the resting place of their idol daily.

The monuments marking collective deaths remain the most emotionally moving sites in Père Lachaise. The **Mur des Fédérés** (Wall of the Federals) has become a pilgrimage site for left-wingers. In May 1871, a group of Communards, sensing their reign's imminent end, murdered the Archbishop of Paris, who had been their hostage since the beginning of the Commune. They dragged his corpse to their stronghold in Père Lachaise and tossed it in a ditch. Four days later, the victorious Versaillais found the body. In retaliation, they lined up 147 Fédérés against the cemetery's eastern wall before shooting and burying them on the spot. Since 1871, the Mur des Fédérés has been a rallying point for the French Left, which recalls the massacre's anniversary every Pentecost. Near the wall, other monuments remember **WWII Resistance fighters** and **Nazi concentration camp victims.** The cemetery's northeast corner provokes greater solemnity than the well-manicured central plots' grand sarcophagi, so take playful activities elsewhere.

⚑ Ⓜ Père Lachaise, Ⓜ Gambetta. *i* Free maps at the Bureau de Conservation near Porte du Repos; ask for directions at guard booths near the main entrances. From Apr to mid-Nov free 2½hr. guided tour Sa 2:30pm. For more info on "theme" tours, call ☎01 49 57 94 37. Ⓢ Open from mid-Mar. to early Nov. M-F 8am-6pm, Sa 8:30am-6pm, Su and holidays 9am-6pm; from Nov. to mid-Mar. M-F 8am-5:30pm, Sa 8:30am-5:30pm, Su and holidays 9am-5:30pm. Last entry 15min. before close.

france

FOOD

Île de la Cité and Île St-Louis

The islands are dotted with traditional dimly-lit French restaurants, ideal for the couples who walk hand in hand down the *quais*. But the old heart of Paris is now the tourist center of Paris, and a romantic meal here comes at a price. Expect to pay more than you would for an equivalent meal on the mainland—or just settle for some ice cream. Île St-Louis is perhaps the best place in Paris to stop for a crêpe or a cool treat while strolling along the Seine. And until you're rolling in dough, or dating someone who is, a snack will have to do.

⬛ BERTHILLON   ICE CREAM ❶
31 rue St-Louis-en-l'Île   ☎01 43 54 31 61

You just can't leave Paris without having a bit of this ice cream. The family-run institution has been doing brilliant marketing work since 1954, but it's not all false advertising; Berthillon delivers with dozens of flavors that cater to your every craving. If you can't stand the epic lines, you can get pints of the same stuff at nearby stores.

✦ ⓂPont Neuf. Ⓢ *1 scoop €2.20, 2 scoops €3.40, 3 scoops €4.80.* ⌚ *Open Sept to mid-July W-Su 10am-8pm. Closed 2 weeks in Feb and Apr.*

⬛ CAFE MED   ✦ᵞ RESTAURANT, CRÊPERIE ❷
77 rue St-Louis-en-l'Île   ☎01 43 29 73 17

There may not be doctors in attendance, but they'll fill that hole in your stomach and won't charge you an arm and a leg for your visit. One of the cheapest and most charming options on the isle. The 3-course menu is an astonishing deal.

✦ ⓂPont Marie. Ⓢ *3-course menus at €10, €10,50, €13.90, €19.90. Weekend special tea €6.* ⌚ *Open M-F 11am-3:30pm and 7-10:30pm, Sa-Su 11am-10:30pm.*

Châtelet-Les Halles

Food in the Châtelet area is unabashedly overpriced and often touristy. Nonetheless, there are a few classics that you simply must visit—Angelina comes to mind—and a couple neighborhood options with unique dining experiences that are not to be missed.

⬛ LE PÈRE FOUETTARD   ✦ᵞ☕ TRADITIONAL ❸
9 rue Pierre Lescot   ☎01 42 33 74 17

Boasting a cozy interior dining room and a heated terrace that stays open year-round, Fouettard serves tasty traditional French cuisine at slightly elevated prices. If you can bear to pass up the ambience of a cafe meal, it's better to sit inside; you'll be closer to the bar. Rich wood walls, ceilings and floors are decorated with wine bottles basically wherever they fit. Meals on the terrace are by candlelight at night; how romantic! The location is fantastic, in the midst of the Châtelet-Les Halles neighborhood.

✦ ⓂÉtienne Marcel. Ⓢ *Formules €14.90-19.90. Salads €13.90-14.50. Plats €12.50-23.50.* ⌚ *Open daily 7:30pm-2am.*

ANGELINA   ✦ TEA HOUSE ❸
226 rue de Rivoli   ☎01 42 60 82 00

A hot chocolate at Angelina will make you feel like Eloise at the Plaza. Located right across from the Jardin des Tuileries, this tea house has been around since 1903; bright frescoes, mirrored walls, and white tablecloths have immortalized Angelina as a Paris classic. There's always a long line outside; expect to wait 20-30 minutes to get a table. The wait can obviously get out of hand at peak times (weekends during the summer). The hot chocolate (€7.50) is to die for, even in the heat of the summer. In order to cut down on the line, all food items are available for take-out, but there's often a line for that as well.

ASSIETTE AVEYRONNAISE

✦☺ TRADITIONAL ❷

14 rue Coquillière

☎01 42 36 51 60

A neighborhood favorite: Parisians come from all corners of the city for the delicious traditional saucisse aligot (a sausage engulfed by a mix of mashed potatoes and cheeses), and they won't hesitate to initiate newcomers to the house's best dishes. A half-plate of the house specialty will leave most guests incapable of continuing onto the Millefeuille, the house's dessert specialty. The restaurant's dining room is no-frills and brightly lit, while the terrace (heated when necessary) unspectacularly looks out on the entrance to a parking garage. The service is extremely friendly despite being insanely busy with the droves of regulars.

✦ Ⓜ Les Halles. Ⓢ Entrées €7.20. Plats €13.80. Formules €18.50, €23.80, €28.30. ⏰ Open Tu-Su noon-2:30pm and 7:30-midnight.

AU CHIEN QUI FUME

✦ SEAFOOD, TRADITIONAL ❹

33 rue du Pont Neuf

☎01 42 92 00 24 ▣www.auchienquifume.com

Au Chien Qui Fume has been a staple of the Parisian dining scene since 1740. Chefs arrange mouth-watering seafood platters at the oyster bar (tantalizingly visible from the street). The seafood is fresh from the market the same day. A traditionally decorated dining room and terrace portray the unmistakable class of this establishment, which is arguably Paris's number one for oysters and seafood. The crowd here tends to be pretty old or touristy; the former just trying to revisit the "good old days" and escape the dreadfully multicultural modern Paris, the latter falling into a particularly delicious tourist trap.

✦ Ⓜ Les Halles. Ⓢ Menus €25, €33, €38. Plats €17.50-29.60. ⏰ Open daily noon-2am.

about those snails...

If you're traveling to France, you're sure to get plenty of opinions on eating *escargot,* or snails. Lord knows why, but the snails have been eaten in this area since Ancient Roman times; today, the French are the leading consumers of snails in the world, and devour **40,000 tons** of them per year. A newly-developed (and slightly disturbing) industry, snail-breeding, became necessary when experts discovered that the diet of snails is not always agreeable to the human stomach. Since they eat mainly **decayed matter** and **wild leaves,** snails' stomach contents can occasionally be **toxic.** That's right; eating slimy creepy crawlers can be bad for you. The risks that come with consuming snails can be counterbalanced by removing their stomachs, keeping the snails in isolation for 2 weeks before consumption, feeding them only human-safe materials, or simply buying the snails from a trusted breeder. If you're thinking about a little **snail snack,** look for escargot prepared "*à la Bourguignone,*" with garlic, butter, and spices, or perhaps a *Feuilleté aux escargots*—snails in flaky pastry!

The Marais

Though at times it can feel like eating in the *4ème* is less about food and more about how you look eating it, there are a number of quality restaurants here, specializing in everything from regional French cuisine to new-age fusion. This is not the cheapest place to lunch, but if you're ready for a bit of a splurge your appetite will be more than sated here, even if your bank account is not. Satisfy them both with the unbeatable lunchtime menus, or by grabbing a sandwich from **Le Gay Choc** or a falafel on rue

france

des Rosiers for €5. If you decide on dinner, make sure you make a reservation at the hotter venues. Dozens of charming bistros line rue St-Martin, and kosher food stands and restaurants are located around rue du Vertbois and rue Volta.

👍 CHEZ JANOU — 🍴🍸☀ BISTRO ❷

2 rue Roger Verlomme ☎ 01 42 72 28 41 🖳www.chezjanou.com

The food is so good here it inspires desert-island hypotheticals: if you were stranded on a desert island, would you bring an endless supply of Chez Janou's *magret de canard* or the best lover you've ever had? It's a tough one. Tucked into a quiet corner of the *3ème*, this Provençale bistro serves affordable ambrosia to a mixed crowd of enthusiasts. The chocolate mousse *(€6.60)* is brought in an enormous self-serve bowl, though Parisians count on self-control. Over 80 kinds of pastis.

✈ Ⓜ Chemin-Vert. ℹ Reservations always recommended, as this local favorite is packed every night of the week. $ Entrées start at €8.50. Plats from €14. ⏰ Open daily noon-midnight. Kitchen open M-F noon-3pm and 7:45pm-midnight, Sa-Su noon-4pm and 7:45pm-midnight.

👍 ROBERT AND LOUISE — 🍴 TRADITIONAL ❷

64 rue Vieille du Temple ☎01 42 78 55 89 🖳www.robertetlouise.com

Defined by a firm belief that chicken is for pansies (let's not even talk about vegetarians), Robert and Louise offers a menu that's wholeheartedly carnivorous—we're talking veal kidneys, steak, prime rib, lamb chops. The only concession to white meat is their *confit de canard.* Juicy slabs are grilled in the open wood-fire oven and then served up on cutting boards. There's a definite homey vibe here; you'll feel like you've been given shelter by a generous French family who found you abandoned and shivering when they were coming back from a hunt.

✈ Ⓜ St-Paul or Files du Calvaire. ℹ Reservations recommended. $ Entrées €5-16. Plats €8-18. Desserts €5-6. ⏰ Open Tu-Su noon-2:30pm and 7-11pm.

👍 MARCHÉ DES ENFANTS ROUGES — 🍴 MARKET ❷

39 rue de Bretagne

The oldest covered market in Paris, the Marché des Enfants Rouges originally earned its seemingly politically incorrect name ("market of the red children"?) by providing shelter for orphans. The market is now a famous foodie paradise of hidden restaurants and chaotic stands. Comb through an eclectic selection of produce, cheese, bread, and wine, not to mention Japanese, Middle Eastern, Afro-Caribbean, and every other variety of ethnic cuisine. Parisians often duck in for lunch at one of the wooden tables, which are heated in the winter. The wine bar in the upper right-hand corner, *L'Estaminet*, is airy, relaxed, and offers some cheap glasses *(€3-3.50)* and bottles *(€5-25).*

✈ Ⓜ Filles du Calvaire or Arts et Métiers. ⏰ Open Tu-Th 9am-2pm and 4-8pm, F-Sa 9am-8pm, Su 9am-2pm.

Latin Quarter and St-Germain

The rule with food in these neighborhoods is not to eat on **rue de la Huchette** or at a cafe with English menus on one of the main boulevards. You'll leave with higher cholesterol and a lighter wallet. Venture inland a bit to find a host of terrific selections. The Comptoir Méditerranée is a great cheap lunch option and Le Foyer Vietnam provides a nice change from heavy traditional French cuisine.

LE FOYER DE VIETNAM — ❀ VIETNAMESE ❶

80 rue Monge ☎01 45 35 32 54

It's easy to miss this restaurant, whose meager decor foreshadows this local favorite's meager prices. We suggest that you look for the crowds—Le Foyer de Vietnam is always packed, though it manages to keep hungry patrons waiting for only a few minutes tops. Portions are large but not unmanageable; try one of this hole in the wall's delicious meat- and spice-laced soups, followed by the duck with bananas *(€8.50).* Wash it all down with the delicious and ambiguously titled

Saigon Beer (€2.60). Unconventional desserts prevail; ever heard of lychees in syrup (€2.50)...for dessert? The restaurant appeals to everybody except tourists, offering student discounts on certain menu choices.

✚ ⓂMonge. Ⓢ Menus €9.20, students €7.50. Entrees €3.80-7.50. Plats €6.50-9.20 Ⓩ Open M-Sa noon-2pm and 7-10pm.

CAFE DELMAS
📍 CRÊPERIE, CAFE ❸

2-4 pl. de la Contre Escarpe ☎01 43 26 51 26

Two venues in one, Delmas is the place to while away the hours (stylishly) in a happening part of town. A modern crêperie and cafe on the stylish pl. Contre Escarpe, Delmas's menu boasts a wide variety of choices, from swanky cocktails to traditional cuisines to crêpes. Don't sit inside; the painted library in the back corner is a rather tragic decorative decision.

✚ ⓂCardinal Lemoine. Ⓢ Sweet crêpes €3.50-8.50. Salads €13.50-18. Plats €16-24.50. Ⓩ Open M-Th 7:30am-2am, F-Sa 7:30am-5am, Su 7:30am-2am. Happy hour 7-9pm.

GUEN-MAÏ
📍 VEGAN, EPICERIE ❶

6 rue Cardinale ☎01 43 26 03 24

This healthy-living oasis might have more appeal for vegetarians and vegans than for carnivores (though they do have fish); anyone who craves seitan and soy will find a little slice of macrobiotic heaven here. Also a lunch restaurant, this is a great alternative to yet another heavy traditional French meal; flush out the butter, oil, and richness with one of Guen's homemade vegetarian options. The all-natural food products are made completely in-house. The lunch counter quadruples as a *salon de thé*, food market, bookstore, and vitamin boutique.

✚ ⓂMabillon. Ⓢ Lunch menu entrees €3-5. Plats €7-12.50. Desserts €5. Ⓩ Open M-Sa 9:30am-8:30pm.

Invalides

The chic 7*ème* is low on budget options, but there are a number of quality restaurants that are worth shelling out the extra euros. **Rue Saint-Dominique, rue Cler,** and **rue de Grenelle** feature some of the best gourmet bakeries in Paris, and the steaming baguettes and pastries make for an ideal picnic by the nearby Eiffel Tower.

🏅 LE SAC À DOS
📍🍴 TRADITIONAL ❸

47 rue de Bourgogne ☎01 45 55 15 35 www.le-sac-a-dos.fr

A neighborhood favorite, this intimate restaurant does French dining right—excellent food, good wine and fresh bread cut to order. The standing red lamps and old books on mahogany shelves make Le Sac à Dos feel more like a living room than a restaurant, and the chummy proprieter's hearty jokes and attentive service really makes the experience; don't be surprised if he (jokingly) asks for some of your wine. The *midi* and *soir formule* (€16) will give you most bang for your buck.

✚ ⓂVarenne. Ⓢ Gamas grille €25. Burger and frites €14. Desserts €5. Ⓩ Open M-Sa noon-2:30pm and 7-10:30pm.

🏅 LES COCOTTES
📍 TRADITIONAL ❷

135 rue St.-Dominique ☎01 45 50 10 31

Christian Constant, a famed Parisian chef, realized that not everyone wants to pay their left arm and right leg for a good meal. Thus he opened Les Cocottes. The fourth of his restaurants on the street, the food is just as delicious and half the price. Unsurprisingly, the house speciality is the *cocottes* (€12-17), cast-iron skillets filled with pig's feet and pigeon or fresh vegetables. The decor is a sophisticated take on an American diner, with high upholstered stools at the tall tables, where you can get in and out pretty fast. The best quickie you'll ever have.

✚ ⓂÉcole Militaire or La Tour-Maubourg. Ⓢ Mousseline d'artichaut €16. Salads €10-12. Mousse au chocolat €7. Ⓩ Open M-Sa noon-4pm and 7-11pm, Su with reservation only.

🔲 LA GRANDE ÉPICERIE DE PARIS 🥢 SUPERMARKET, SPECIALITY SHOP ❹
38 rue de Sèvres

If a skinny, chic, Chanel-toting Frenchwoman took on supermarket form, she would become La Grande Épicerie. In addition to its near-obscene bottled water and wine display (€30—*for water? Seriously?*), this celebrated gourmet food store features all things dried, canned, smoked, and freshly baked in itsy-bitsy packets. The butcher actually has a thin twirled mustache. We thought only cartoon French people looked like that. Most items here are overpriced, so it's better to treat La Grande Épicerie de Paris as a fascinating anthropological sample than a supermarket. You might want to avoid the American food section, which showcases such treasured "traditional" cuisine as marshmallows, brownie mix, and Hershey's syrup. The market's refined local patrons cluck their tongues disapprovingly as they walk down the aisle; it's kind of embarrassing.

🚇 Ⓜ*Vaneau.* 𝒊 *No pets allowed.* 💲 *This place is way too expensive for you.* 🕐 *Open M-Sa 8:30am-9pm.*

Champs-Élysées

Once the center of Paris's most glamorous dining and world-class cuisine, the 8*ème's* culinary importance is on the decline, but its prices are not. The best affordable restaurants are on side streets around **rue la Boétie, rue des Colisées,** and **place de Dublin.**

🔲 TY YANN 🥢 CRÊPERIE ❶
10 rue de Constantinople ☎ 01 40 08 00 17

The ever-smiling Breton chef and owner, M. Yann, cheerfully prepares outstanding and relatively inexpensive *galettes* (€7.50-10.50) and crêpes in a tiny, unassuming restaurant; the walls are decorated with his mother's pastoral paintings. Creative concoctions include La Vannetaise *(sausage sauteed in cognac, Emmental cheese, and onions; €10).* Create your own crêpe (€6.40-7.20) for lunch.

🚇 Ⓜ*Europe.* 𝒊 *Credit card min. €12.* 💲 *Crêpes €7.50-10.50.* 🕐 *Open M-F noon-2:30pm and 7:30-10:30pm, Sa 7:30-10:30pm.*

🔲 LADURÉE 🥢 TEA HOUSE ❷
16 rue Royale ☎ 01 42 60 21 79 🖥 www.laduree.com

Opened in 1862, Ladurée started off as a modest bakery; it has since become so famous that a Gossip Girl employee was flown over to buy macaroons here so that Chuck could offer his heart to Blair properly. On a more typical day though, the Rococo decor of this tea salon attracts a jarring mix of well-groomed shoppers and tourists in sneakers. One of the first Parisian *salons de thé*, Ladurée shows its age but remains a must-see (and -taste). Along with the infamous mini macaroons arranged in high pyramids in the window *(16 different varieties; €1.50),* this spot offers little that hasn't been soaked in vanilla or caramel. Dine in the salon or queue up an orgasm to go.

🚇 Ⓜ*Concorde.* 𝒊 *Also at 75 av. des Champs-Elysées,* ☎ *01 40 75 08 75.* 💲 *Macaroons €1.50 each.* 🕐 *Open M-Th 8:30am-7:30pm, F-Sa 8:30am-8pm, Su 10am-7pm.*

FAFOUQUET'S 🥢🍴 CAFE ❺
99 av. des Champs-Élysées ☎01 47 23 50 00

Restaurants can only dream of this kind of fame. The sumptous, red velvet-covered cafe once welcomed the likes of Chaplin, Churchill, Roosevelt, and Jackie Onassis. But as its gilded interior suggests, all that glitters is not gold. Today, Fouquet's owned by a hotel and dining conglomerate, and the only celebrity spottings you'll see are the framed pictures on the wall. Still, it's an experience of quintessential old-time Parisian glamour, easy on the eyes and devastating for the bank account *(appetizers run upwards of €30).* Best to buy a coffee (€8) and see and be seen.

🚇 Ⓜ*George V.* 💲 *Plates €20-55.* 🕐 *Open daily 8-2am. Restaurant open daily 7:30-10am, noon-3pm, and 7pm-midnight.*

paris • food

Opéra

The Opéra district has a few classic food spots, but the area definitely suffered from the loss of one-of-a-kind restaurant Chez Haynes in 2009. Most of the high-quality, affordable options in the district are located in the St-Georges area.

▧ SAVEURS ET COINCIDENCES
⊛ FINE DINING ❸

6 rue de Trévise ☎ 01 42 46 62 23 ▣ www.saveursetcoincidences.com

Saveurs et Coincidences maintains a small, charming dining room; in the summertime, a few tables are set up outdoors and the front windows are flung open, letting the air waft in. Recently purchased by expert chef Jean-Pierre Coroyer—a former semi-finalist in a national gastronomical competition—the new Saveurs et Coincidences combines traditional French cuisine with Japanese, Italian, and other global favors for a succulent and entirely unique collection of entrees. Ingredients are ridiculously fresh. According to the chef, the restaurant doesn't even have a fridge; ingredients are ordered and received from suppliers in the mornings, then sliced, diced and stewed the same day. This process costs Coroyer a good deal of returns, but he proudly declares that he isn't interested in ripping off his customers. It certainly shows in his prices which are incredibly lower than those at most cafes. The lunch formules are such a deal, it should be illegal.

❖ ⓜGrands Boulevards. ⓢ Entrées €8.60. Plats €14.20. Desserts €7.50. Formules midi €10.40, €12.50, €17.

▧ CHARTRIER
⊛❦ TRADITIONAL ❷

7 rue du Faubourg Montmartre ☎ 47 70 86 29 ▣ www.restaurant-chartrier.com

Chartrier has served French traditional cuisine, since 1896, and remains a unique experience that is not to be missed. Think Cheesecake Factory meets Friendly's family vibe, without the obscene portions (portions are a good size here, just not disgustingly huge). We recommend the *tête de veau* (that's sheep's head; €11.80), and then some classic *profiteroles au chocolat chaud* for dessert (€4). If you go alone, you'll be seated with somebody you don't know, which can either be a fantastic experience or a boring, very awkward one. Waiters provide rapid service and are patient with Americans, but only to a point; know what you want to order, because they've got their hands full. If you want to be guaranteed a table, we recommend getting here early—the line stretches about 200m around the block by 7:30pm.

❖ ⓜGrands Boulevards. ⓢ Entrées €2-10.30. Plats €8.50-12.20. Desserts €2.20-4.50. Wine €6.50-34. ⌚ Open daily 11:30am-10pm.

KASTOORI
❧ INDIAN ❷

4 pl. Gustave Toudouze ☎47 70 86 29

Kastoori offers tasty, hearty Indian fare at a collection of tables on the lovely pl. Toudouze; the indoor seating area is cozier, with plush chairs and couches in a small dining room that doubles as the kitchen. Pricewise, the place is a steal during the lunch hour, with a *thali du jour* tasting plate for just €10. There are also plenty of veggie plates for the granola types among you. Waiters are quick to put their cigarettes down to replenish your carafe. Unfortunately, no alcohol is served here; we consider this to be a human right's violation.

❖ ⓜSaint-Georges. ⓢ At lunch (entrée, plat, naan) €10. Menu (entrée, plat, naan, cafe) €17. Desserts €5. Plats €7-13. ⌚ Open Tu-Sa 11am-2:30pm and 7-11pm

Canal St-Martin and Surrounds

The 10ème has a few all-star food spots, and both just happen to be located on the Canal St-Martin. Stay away from the brasseries on the main boulevards, and make the trip down to the Canal (specifically its side streets); great deals on great grub.

france

LE CAMBODGE

CAMBODIAN ❶

10 av. Richerand   ☎ 01 44 84 37 70 ▇ www.lecambodge.fr

Le Cambodge doesn't take reservations, and Parisians of all shapes and sizes regularly wait up to 2hrs for a table. You'd think Lady Gaga was in town; by the time the restaurant opens, the line at the door is already 20 ft. long. We recommend that you arrive 30min. or so before opening time, so as to secure a table on the terrace or in the more secluded dining room—and avoid wandering around the 10ème at night. Incredibly, Le Cambodge is not overrated. This is some of the best Asian food in Paris, and the plentiful main courses will only run you €9.50-13.

✦ ⓂRépublique. Ⓢ Entrées €3-10.50. Plats €9.50-13. Vegetarian plates €8.50-11.50. Desserts €4.50-5.50. ☼ Hours can vary day to day, giving locals a leg-up on early opening notices. Generally, however, M-Sa noon-2pm and 8-11:30pm.

Bastille

With as many kebab stands as people, Bastille swells with fast-food joints. But the diverse neighborhood also boasts a number of classy restaurants with an ethnic touch, many of which are cheaper than those in the more central arrondissements. The most popular haunts line the bustling **rues de Charonne, Keller, de Lappe,** and **Oberkampf.** In terms of food, the 12ème is a generally affordable arrondissement, where casual establishments serve a variety of cuisines, from North African to Middle Eastern to traditional French. Most of the better places are on side streets, scattered throughout the neighborhood. On **rue du Faubourg St-Antoine** there's a slew of nice but overpriced restaurants competing with cheap fast-food spots; the **Viaduc des Arts** hosts a couple of classy terrace cafes where designers take up residence.

CAFE DE L'INDUSTRIE

CAFE ❷

15-17 rue St-Sabin   ☎01 47 00 13 53

There's a reason that podunk cafes specialize in coffee, but the menu at this one will make you forget it. Funky 20-somethings retreat in this always bustling, kind of dark spot, enjoying the extensive, fairly priced menu. The 3-course formule is a steal (€10.50); the chocolate cake is nothing short of divine (€3).

✦ ⓂBreguet-Sabin. Ⓢ Plats €8-14. Desserts €2.50-6. ☼ Open daily 10am-2am.

LE BAR À SOUPES

SOUP BAR ❶

33 rue de Charonne   ☎01 43 57 53 79 ▇www.lebarasoupes.com

It may not have the most personality in the world, but it does have some of the best soups in Paris. Making them fresh daily, the chef commits to creatively combining flavors like leeks and curry or zucchini and ginger. The salad and dessert selection is less spectacular.

✦ ⓂLedru-Rollin or Bastille. *i* Takeout available. Ⓢ Soups €4.90-5.90. Formule midi includes soup, bread roll, salad, dessert or cheese plate, wine, iced tea or coffee. ☼ Open M-Sa noon-3pm and 6:30-11pm.

MORRY'S BAGELS AND TOASTS

BAGELS ❶

1 rue de Charonne   ☎01 48 07 03 03

Trust the French to make bagels fancy; bold statements like the *magret de canard* (bagel with guacamole, cream cheese, and sundried tomatoes (€5.80) and the *foie gras* (self-explanatory; €6) are daring but delicious.

✦ ⓂBastille. Ⓢ Bagels with coleslaw €3-6. Desserts €1.50-3.35. ☼ Open M-Sa 8:30am-7:30pm.

Butte-aux-Cailles and Chinatown

Unbeknownst to many a tourist, the 13ème is a haven for funky, fun and affordable restaurants. Bump elbows with locals over papier-mached tables in the crowded Butte-aux-Cailles, or enjoy the unfathomable delights of Chinatown's many Asian restaurants. Eating on a budget never tasted better, especially in Paris.

MUSSUWAM
✈ AFRICAN ❷

33 bld. Arago   ☎01 45 35 93 67 ▣mussuwam.fr

The new kid on the block, Mussuwam offers Senegalese cuisine in an area dominated by Southern French restaurants. Creole music, chocolate brown walls, and a colorful decor creates an ethnic feel. Fresh juices (€5) are a highlight of the tropical menu.

✦ ⓂLes Gobelins. Ⓢ Plat du jour €15. ⌂ Open M-Sa noon-3pm and 7-11:30pm, Su 11am-3pm.

Montparnasse

LE TROQUET
✦♈ SPANISH, FUSION ❸

21 rue François Bonvin   ☎01 45 66 89 00

This place is worth budgeting for; if you have to eat at sweaty kebab takeout spots for a week, or even two weeks, to afford this, just do it. The food is simply sublime, and the prices are extremely reasonable given the quality. Original recipes developed under the supervision of master chef Christian Ethebest have their origins in traditional Basque cuisine, specifically from the Béarn region. Unlike some other super-gourmet restaurants you may have indulged in, the portions here are hearty. We recommend the *caviar d'aubergine* or the Basque *charcuterie* platter, which are both to die for. For main courses, go with the *joue de cochon* in red-wine sauce. The desserts are beyond tasty too. Menus change every three weeks, but the aforementioned items tend to make frequent comebacks. The service here is super professional and friendly. Could be tough for handicapped travelers, since the dining room is very small and tightly packed. Expect long waits.

✦ ⓂSevres Lecourbe, off of Boulevard Garibaldi. Ⓢ Dinner formule €32. Tasting plate €40.50. Wine €23-77.50 per bottle. Midi entrée, plat, or plat-dessert combo €26. ⌂ Open Tu-Sa 12:30-2pm and 7:30-11pm.

LE DIX VINS
✦♿♈ TRADITIONAL

57 rue Falguiere   ☎01 43 20 91 77

Located on a side street uphill on bld. Pasteur from the Metro stop, Le Dix Vins serves terrific traditional French cuisine at a reasonable price. This is undoubtedly a fine dining experience. In 2010, the restaurant won a prize from the prestigious *Confrerie Gastronomique de la Marmite d'Or* for its cuisine. Located on a quiet street, the restaurant's front windows open up on warm days, and air wafts through the two tightly packed dining rooms. The food is divine, but when we visited the chef told us to write down a few recommendations. For starters, try the artichoke hearts with *foie de veau*, then order the *filets de rougets à la Normande* for your first course. For dessert, the chef proposes the *tartin de poires* with a scoop of vanilla ice cream. The menu switches up periodically, but don't hesitate to ask the gregarious waiter for more suggestions. Technically wheelchair accessible, but it could be a bit tricky space-wise.

✦ ⓂPasteur.

Passy and Auteuil

Like everything in the 16ème, most dining options are on the pricier side, but the food is of the highest quality. If you're willing to spend a little more, the splurge is definitely worth it. Budget-friendly ethnic restaurants are clustered on **rue Lauriston**.

LES FILAOS
AFRICAN ❸

5 rue Guy de Maupassant   ☎01 45 04 94 53 ▣www.lesfilaos.com

The first joint in Paris to specialize in Mauritian cuisine, Les Filaos provides an ethnic touch to the 16th restaurant scene. Delicious punches (€5) are made fresh behind the straw hut bar. Curries (€15-16) can be made as spicy as you like and are topped off with fresh fruit for dessert. Octopus is an island specialty. Saturday night features live Mauritian dancers.

☘ ⓂRue de la Pompe. *i* Prix-fixe lunch €19.50, dinner €30. ⏰ Open Tu-Su noon-2:30pm and 7-10:30pm.

🏠 LE SCHEFFER

22 rue Scheffer

BISTRO ❷

☎01 47 27 81 11

With red-checkered tablecloths, walls papered with posters, and an almost entirely local clientele, Le Scheffer is as authentic as French bistros get. Slightly tipsy diners chat loudly over the din of clattering plates and shouting waiters. Plats include *fois de veau* with honey vinegar (€15) and beef haddock (€15).

☘ ⓂTrocadero. Ⓢ Entrees €15-20. ⏰ Open M-Sa noon-2:30pm and 7:30-10:30pm.

Batignolles

If residents had to make a pilgrimage into central Paris every time they wanted a good meal, no one would live in the 17*ème*. Thankfully, good restaurants are a dime a dozen here, and the diverse population that lives here make for a wide array of choices, from ethnic to French to vegetarian.

🏠 LE MANOIR

7 rue des Moines

CAFE ❷

☎01 46 27 54 51

A true neighborhood favorite, Le Manoir is popular with the kind of cool, fun Parisians you'd want to hang out with. Local parents meet their children in front of the cafe's red awning to pick them up after school. The waiters here are so friendly you'd think there was a catch. When a certain intrepid *Let's Go* researcher left her computer in her nearby apartment, the young waitress offered to watch her drink for her while she ran home to get it—even though the researcher hadn't paid yet. The menu is comprized of local standards, and is particularly well-known for its salads (€11).

☘Brochant. *i* Free Wi-Fi. Ⓢ Plats €13. 2-course menu midi €12. Salmon tartare €13.20. ⏰ Open daily 7:30am-2am.

LA FOURNÉE D'AUGUSTINE

31 rue des Batignolles

TRADITIONAL ❶

☎01 43 87 88 41

It's no mystery why La Fournée d'Augustine won Paris's *medaille d'or* in 2004. Luring in customers with the delicious aroma of freshly baked pastries, this *boulangerie* is everything you thought Paris would smell like: butter, chocolate, and heaven in general. The wide selection of desserts is reasonably priced (cakes €4; *pain au chocolat* €0.80). Fresh sandwiches (€3-4) and other lunch options are also available. The storefront can be hard to spot, so look for the white, wooden tiles painted with lilacs, and follow the smell.

☘ ⓂRome. Ⓢ Donuts €0.60. Loaf of brioche €4.60. ⏰ M-Sa 7:30am-8pm.

Buttes Chaumont

🏠 L'ATLANTIDE

7 av. Laumière

🍴 NORTH AFRICAN ❷

☎01 42 45 09 81 ✉www.latlantide.fr

A relatively hard-to-find type of restaurant in Paris, L'Atlantide practices true North African gastronomy, using meats and spices coming directly from the mountains of North Africa. If you can stand a lot of Oriental-rug patterning (rugs, tablecloths, and waiters' aprons are all coordinated), you'll get a nice hearty plate of couscous you won't forget.

☘ ⓂLaumière. Ⓢ Entrees €5.50-10. Couscous €11-19.50. Plats €13-19.50. Wine €12.50-22.50. ⏰ Open daily 7-10:30pm, Sa-Su 12-2:30pm.

Belleville and Père Lachaise

Belleville doesn't compare to the 19*ème* in terms of food quality. It would behoove you to to hop on the Metro for lunch after your Cemetery visit.

LA BOLÉE BELGRAND

CRÊPERIE, CAFE ❶

19 rue Belgrand   ☎01 43 64 04 03

Across the street from the Gambetta Metro exit, La Bolée Belgrand is a modest crêperie boasting American portions. A local crowd people watches through lace curtains and from outdoor tables while enjoying heaping crêpes and *galettes*. The La Totale, with cheese, eggs, tomatoes, onions, mushrooms, ham, bacon and salad, is a particular favorite.

✦ Ⓜ*Gambetta.* ⓘ *10% off takeout.* Ⓢ *Galettes €7.50-9.50. Crêpes €5-7. Glaces €5.50-7.50.* Ⓩ *Open Tu-Sa noon-2:30pm and 7-10:30pm.*

NIGHTLIFE

Île de la Cité and Île St-Louis

Far from a party spot, the islands are a bit of a nightlife wasteland. Still, there are a few overpriced brasseries that are worth a stop. The bars are a lot more fun and a lot less expensive on either side of the bank, in the neighboring 4*ème* and 5*ème* respectively.

LE LOUIS IX

CAFE, BRASSERIE

25 rue des Deux-Ponts   ☎01 43 54 23 89

The place where the isle's men go to drink, probably because it has the cheapest beer around. As unpretentious as it gets in this neck of the woods.

✦ Ⓜ*Pont Marie.* Ⓢ *Wine €3.50-4.60. Beer €3.80-5.* Ⓩ *Open daily 7:30am-8:30pm.*

Châtelet-Les Halles

BANANA CAFE

BAR, GLBT

13 rue de la Ferronerie   ☎01 42 33 35 31 🖳www.bananacafeparis.com

Situated in the heart of one of Paris's liveliest areas for nightlife, Banana Cafe is the self-declared most popular GLBT bar in the 1*er*—and rightly so. The club suits a wide range of clientele, ranging from the somewhat reticent and straight patrons who occupy the outdoor terrace, to the pole dancers stationed outside on nice days. During the summertime, there's always some kind of hot deal on beer or drinks, and the party regularly spills out onto the rue de la Ferronerie. Head downstairs for a piano bar and more dancing space. There are weekly theme nights; "Go-Go Boys" takes place every Thursday through Saturday from midnight to dawn.

✦ Ⓜ*Châtelet.* Ⓢ *Cover F-Sa €10; includes 1 drink. Beer €5.50. Cocktails €8. Happy hour pints €3, cocktails €4.* Ⓩ *Open daily 5:30pm-6am. Happy hour 6-11pm.*

LE REX CLUB

CLUB

5 bld. Poissonnière   ☎01 42 36 10 96 🖳www.rexclub.com

Definitely the place to be if you're looking to get down on the floor or rock out to a phenomenal DJ set. The club hosts top-notch DJs spanning pretty much any type of music that young people would have the slightest desire to dance to. The crowd is full of students, but due to the high quality of the DJs, there aren't too many Euro-trashy teenagers here. The large sweaty dance floor is surrounded by colorful booths.

✦ Ⓜ*Bonne Nouvelle.* Ⓢ *Cover €10-15. Cocktails €9-11.* Ⓩ *Open W-Th 11:30pm-6am, F-Sa midnight-6am.*

The Marais

There are as many bars and clubs in the Marais as people. It's indisputably the center of Paris's GLBT nightlife scene, and fun and fashionable men's and women's bars and clubs crowd **rue Sainte-Croix de la Bretonnerie.** Hotspots with outdoor seating are piled on top of one another on **rue Vieille du Temple,** from **rue des Francs-Bourgeois** to **rue de Rivoli.** The places on **rue des Lombards** have a rougher and more convivial—though often touristy—atmosphere. The scene in the 3*ème* is a little more laid-back—for

france

the most part, women (and men, too) can leave their stiletto heels at home. There are a number of GLBT bars in the area on and around **rue aux Ours, rue Saint-Martin,** and **rue Michel Le Comte,** but mostly casual bars do live music, especially around the Pompidou.

ANDY WAHLOO — BAR

69 rue des Gravilliers ☎ 01 42 74 57 81 www.andywahloo-bar.com

Everything here is a twist on something else. Andy Wahloo, which means, "I have nothing" in a certain Moroccan dialect, serves delicious and ambitious cocktails *(€10-14)* to a fashionable Parisian clientele in an open courtyard and dark bar. The stop sign tables and paint-can chairs are pushed aside for dancing later in the night. The incredibly attractive clientele will probably catch you staring.

[M]Arts et Métiers. **i** *A good place to wait for a table at 404.* $ *Cocktails €10-14. Open Tu-Sa 5pm-2am.*

RAIDD BAR — GAY BAR, CLUB

23 rue du Temple ☎ 01 42 77 04 88

If you want a penis or just want to see one, come here. Sparkling disco globes light up the intimate space, as do the muscular, topless torsos of the sexy bartenders. After 11pm, performers strip down in glass shower cubicles built into the wall (yes, they take it all off every hour on the hour starting at 11:30pm). Notoriously strict door policy—women are not allowed unless they are outnumbered by a greater ratio of (gorgeous) men.

[M]Hôtel de Ville. $ *Beer €4. Cocktails €10. Open M-Th 5pm-4am, F-Sa 5pm-5am, Su 5pm-4am. Happy hour 5-9pm for all drinks, 5-11pm for beer.*

STOLLY'S — BAR

16 rue Cloche-Perce ☎01 42 76 06 76 www.cheapblonde.com

This small Anglophone hangout takes the sketchy out of the dive-bar and leaves behind the cool. The €13.50 pitchers of cheap blonde beer ensure that the bar lives up to its motto: "hangovers installed and serviced here." Come inside, have a pint, and shout at the TV with the decidedly non-trendy, tattoo-covered crowd. Occasional live music.

[M]St.Paul. On a dead-end street off rue du Roi de Sicile. $ *Cocktails €6.50-8. Happy hour cocktails and pints €5, pitchers €12. Open M-F 4:30pm-2am, Sa-Su 3pm-2am. Terrace closes at midnight. Happy hour 5-8pm.*

Latin Quarter and St-Germain

Nightlife is a bit stronger in the fifth arrondissement; plenty of pricey bars and jazz clubs line the main streets and boulevards around St-Michel. What better way to walk off a few beers than a stroll down the promenade along the Seine? The 6*ème* is more of a bar and student-centered nightlife scene.

LE CAVEAU DE LA HUCHETTE — JAZZ BAR

5 rue de la Huchette ☎01 43 26 65 05 www.caveaudelahuchette.fr

In the past, the Caveau was a meeting place for secret societies and directors of the Revolution; downstairs, you can still see the prison cells and execution chambers occupied by the victims of Danton and Robespierre. WWII brought American soldiers, bebop, and New Orleans jazz to the establishment. Now an eclectic crowd of students, tourists, and locals comes prepared to listen, watch, and participate in an old-school jazz show in this affordable, popular club.

[M]St-Michel. **i** *Live music 10pm-2am.* $ *Cover M-Th €12, F-Sa €14, Su €12, students €10. Beer €6. Cocktails €8. Open M-W 9:30pm-2:30am, Th-Sa 9:30pm-dawn, Su 9pm-2:30am.*

LE WHO'S BAR — BAR

13 rue Petit Pont ☎01 43 54 80 71

This bar stays open super late right in the swing of things—a stone's throw from the Seine and in the heart of the Latin Quarter's bar scene. Live pop and rock music every night at 10:30pm is not exactly original, but it certainly gets the job done. Old and young alike get down on the often sweaty dance floor; the old folks take the cake in terms of funkiness (smell and dancing abilities included).

➜ ⓂSt-Michel. ℹ Disco in the basement W-Su 10:30pm-midnight. $ Beer €5.50-12. Cocktails €10-12. ⏰ Open M-Th 5pm-5am, F-Sa 6pm-6am, Su 5pm-5am.

Invalides

If you want to party into the wee hours of the morn, stumble home to your affordable hotel room, and pass out after consuming another €1 bottle of wine, then you probably shouldn't stay in the *7ème*. Filled with sights but devoid of personality, the neighborhood gets quiet early. The corner-cafe bars at **École Militaire** are packed almost exclusively with tourists, and the **rue Saint-Dominique** has some brassieres frequented by locals. The following venues are a solid bet.

👍 CHAMPS DE MARS — ROMANTIC

Droves of French youngsters march over to the Champs de Mars with the setting sun, schlepping bottles of wine, cases of beer and packs of cigarettes with them. You'll be thankful it's legal to drink outside in Paris as you approach this grassy stretch in front of the the Eiffel Tower. Why? Because you'll find it overflowing with revellers playing guitar and Bocce, exploring the subtleties of each other's faces (read: PDA), and generally being merry. The Eiffel Tower lights up on the hour and makes for a spectacular backdrop to the start of a good night.

➜ ⓂÉcole Militaire or La Motte Picquet-Grenelle.

CLUB DES POÈTES — 💳♿🍸 CLUB, POETRY

30 rue de Bourgogne — ☎01 47 05 06 03 💻www.poesie.net

If you want to drink and feel cultured, this restaurant by day and poetry club by night brings together an intimate community of literati for supper and sonnets. The hip patrons all seem to know each other and may seem intimidating at first, but you'll soon become fast friends as you cram in next to each other the L-shaped long table.

➜ ⓂVarenne. ℹ Poetry readings Tu, F, Sa at 10pm. Come a little before then, or wait for applause to enter. $ Prix-fixe (entrée-plat or plat-dessert) €16. Lunch menu €16. Wine €4-8. ⏰ Open M-F noon-2:30pm and 8pm-1am. Kitchen closes at 10pm.

Champs-Élysées

Glam is the name of the game at the trendy, expensive bars and clubs of the *8ème*. Whether you're going for a mystical evening at **buddha-bar** or a surprisingly accessible evening at **Le Queen,** make sure to bring your wallet, dashing good looks, and if possible, a super-important and/or famous friend.

👍 LE QUEEN — 💳🍸▼ CLUB

102 av. des Champs-Élysées — ☎01 53 89 08 90 💻www.queen.fr

A renowned Parisian institution where drag queens, superstars, tourists, and go-go boys get down and dirty to the mainstream rhythms of a 10,000-gigawatt sound system. Her Majesty is one of the most accessible GLBT clubs in town, and has kept its spot on the Champs for a reason. Women have better luck with the bouncer if accompanied by at least one good-looking male.

➜ ⓂGeorges V. ℹ Disco M, Ladies Night W, '80s Su. $ Cover €20; includes 1 drink. All drinks €10 after that. ⏰ Open daily midnight-6am.

BUDDHA-BAR — 💳🍸 BAR, RESTAURANT

8 rue Boissy d'Anglas — ☎01 53 05 90 00 💻www.buddha-bar.com

Apparently too cool for overdone trends like capital letters, buddha-bar is billed as the most glamorous drinking hole in the city—Madonna tends to drop by when she's in town. If you're sufficiently attractive, wealthy, or well-connected, you'll quickly be led to one of the two floors of candlelit rooms, where your internal organs will gently vibrate to hypnotic "global" rhythms. A two-story

Buddha watches over the chic ground-floor restaurant, while the luxurious upstairs lounge caters to those looking to unwind in style with one of the creative mixed drinks *(€16-21)*. A solid contingent of "atheist drinkers" think buddha is over-rated.

 # Ⓜ Madeleine or Concorde. $ Cocktails €16-21. ⏰ Open daily noon-2am.

Opéra

CAFE LE BARON — BAR, RESTAURANT

11 rue de Châteaudun ☎01 48 78 13 68

A quintessential Parisian cafe, come here if you're really in the mood to receive some disdainful stares from behind sunglasses (if you're obviously American, that is), and cough up the fog of someone else's cigarette smoke. In a good way. Cafe Le Baron's sunny outdoors terrace is right in the thick of things near the Opéra district; the scene here is simply classic, and beautiful. Each cocktail looks like a work of art (*€2.20-7*), and drinks are accompanied by a complimentary tasting plate of olives, veggies, and cheese. Tasteful modern decor graces the interior, with whitewashed walls lined with red wine bottles and an assortment of maroon sofas. The food here is also quite delectable, but expensive; just about everything on the menu is delicious, so you probably won't regret it.

*# Ⓜ Notre Dame de Lorette, Cadette. **i** Happy hour cocktails and pints €5. $ Beer €2.60-7. Wines €2.60-5.50 per glass. Shots €5-18. Appetizers €14-19. Plats €17-26. Desserts €9-10. ⏰ Open daily 11am-1am. Happy hour 5:30-8pm.*

Bastille

Nightlife in the 11*ème* has long consisted of Anglophones who drink too much and the Frenchies who hide from them. With a few exceptions, **rue de Lappe** and its neighbors offer a big, raucous night on the town dominated by expats and tourist-types, while **rue Oberkampf, rue Amelot,** and **rue Thaillandiers** are more eclectic, low-key, and local. Both streets are definitely worth your time, even if you have only one night in the area. **Rue du Faubourg Saint-Antoine** is a world of its own, dominated by enormous nightclubs who only let in the well-dressed. Rue du Faubourg St-Antoine is the dividing line between the lively 11*ème* and the tamer 12*ème*. The hotspots overflow into the streets, and you can hop from one club-lounge to another all night—but it won't be cheap.

FAVELA CHIC — BAR, CLUB

18 rue du Faubourg du Temple ☎01 40 21 38 14 🖳www.favelachic.com

A self-proclaimed Franco-Brazilian joint, this place is light on the Franco and heavy on the brassy Brazilian. Wildly popular with the locals, this restaurant-bar-club has an eclectic decor and equally colorful clients. Dinner in the restaurant segues into unbridled and energetic table-dancing to Latin beats. Exceedingly crowded with sweaty (in a hot way) gyrating bodies during the weekend and a long line snaking out the door. Regulars report that groups high on estrogen and ethnic diversity will get you in more easily.

 # Ⓜ République. Walk down rue du Faubourg du Temple, turn right into the arch at no. 18; the club is to your left. $ F-Sa cover €10; includes 1 drink. Cocktails €9. ⏰ Open Tu-Th 8pm-2am, F-Sa 8pm-4am.

ZERO ZERO — BAR

89 rue Amelot ☎06 68 84 28 57

A tiny, tiny bar covered from head to toe in stickers and graffiti, jammed with the artistic and the unpretentious. DJs spin hip-hop in the lowly-lit corner. The signature drink "Zero Zero," whose size you should not let deceive you, is a dangerously potent mix of dark rum, ginger, and lime (€3).

 # Ⓜ Saint Sebastien Froissart. $ Beer €2.80-4. Cocktails €6.50-8.50. ⏰ Open daily 6pm-2am. Happy hour 6:30-8:30pm.

LE POP-IN
🍺 BAR, ROCK CLUB

105 rue Amelot ☎01 48 05 56 11 💻www.popin.fr

Leaning more towards "popping" than "pop-in," this two-level bar/rock club/90s time warp boasts a basement that's a favorite all-night hangout for Paris's hipster crowd. Pop, rock, folk, and indie fold concerts almost nightly.

‡ [M]St-Sebastien Froissart. i Check website for concerts. Happy hour 6:30-9pm. $ Beer €2.80-5.50. ⏰ Open daily 6:30pm-1:30am.

Butte-aux-Cailles and Chinatown

Blessed with a young and unassuming crowd, the 13*ème's* local haunts are cluttered with vintage instruments, overflow onto maritime concert venues floating along the Seine, and maintain a chill atmosphere you never knew that a city as conscientiously chic as Paris could keep up. Walk down to the Porte de la Gare, grab a bottle of wine with some friends, and watch the Seine go by.

LE MERLE MOQUER
BAR

11 rue de la Butte-aux-Cailles ☎01 45 65 12 43

Capturing the spirit of the neighborhood with its eclectic mix of African art, uneven stools and spray-painted doors, this bar is a little funky, not at all fussy, and the best place on the street to dance. Homemade, flavored rum punches are well worth the €6. Ginger-apple-pear-cinammon is the bartender's choice.

‡ [M]Place d'Italie. $ Drinks €4-6. ⏰ open daily 5pm-2am.

LA DAME CANTON
BAR, CONCERT VENUE

Porte de la Gare ☎01 45 84 41 71 💻www.dame-decanton.com

A quirky alternative to all those passé land-locked watering holes, this floating bar is deliberately odd in the extreme, even by Butte-aux-Cailles standards. A seizure-inducing collection of fishing nets, musical instruments, books on Australia, postmodern takes on the Mona Lisa and small Chinese lamps decorate the walls and ceiling. The floor slopes, the patrons rock dreds, and the owner's been known to wear jean suits. The burly bartenders will serve you Pirate Punch *(€3)* and cocktails *(€7.50)* in plastic cups or out of cans. The lolling waters of the Seine make La Dame Canton a little less than stable, so we advise that you avoid getting plastered on board. But the view of the Seine is spectacular, and the mix of soul funk, hip hop and reggae demonstrate excellent taste. Live concerts every night, starting at about 8:30pm.

‡ [M]Quai de la Gare. $ Cocktails €7.50. Cover Tu-Th €8, students €6; F-Sa €10. ⏰ Open Tu-Th 7pm-2am, F-Sa 7pm-5am.

Passy and Auteuil

The 16*ème* isn't the hottest spot in town, but it does feature a few stylish bars with reasonably priced drinks. You'll be hanging out with the chic and the too-cool-for-school, so leave those frayed sneakers at home.

SIR WINSTON
🍸 BAR, CLUB

5 rue de Presbourg ☎01 40 67 17 37

This cafe/salon/bar/club is a sophisticated hotspot of the young Parisian Bobos (that's bohemian bourgeoisie, for those not in the know). Lean back into a leather chair and sip on a glass of wine *(€5)* or smoke attractively alongside a pensive Buddha. After all, Buddha would have totally done the same. There's a dance space downstairs, though the music is mainly jazz and lounge tunes.

‡ [M]Kleber. i French fries €5. Caesar salad €5. ⏰ Open daily from 9am-4am.

Batignolles

If you're thinking of a wild night on the town in the 17*ème*, forget it. If the people who live here drink here, they do it by themselves; the craziest it'll get is a few drinks with old friends, and maybe a couple of new ones. Sometimes, though, that's all you need.

LE BLOC

21 rue Brochant ☎01 53 11 02 37

Like a good mistress, Le Bloc is always open, accommodating, and kind of cool. This former clinic turned industrial cafe/bar caters to the neighborhood's turtleneck-wearring types from morning till dawn, and will be whatever you want it to be. The food is decent enough *(penne au pisto; €8.80)*, and drinks range from whatever to shocking. Look for the little nook under the stairs with the brown couch, pink walls, and fake skeleton.

✸ ⓜBrochant. *i* Free Wi-Fi. Ⓢ Salads €9-10.20. Most cocktails €6.50. Ⓩ Open daily 8:30am-2am.

Montmartre

Nightlife in Montmartre comes, of course, with the burden of not getting too drunk and staying away from the shady cabarets/strip clubs. The best way to stay safe is to keep your wits about you.

▨ LE RENDEZ-VOUS DES AMIS

☞☿ BAR

23 rue Gabrielle ☎01 46 06 01 60 ✉ www.rdvdesamis.com

You know that you're in for a night of bebauchery when the bar's owners and bartenders drink harder than their customers, pounding shots and beer at random. A true Montmartre institution, Le RVDA has been around for 17 years, and it's not hard to see why. Convivial and untouristed, this bar has a live-free-or-die ethos. Patrons rock out to house music and experimental hip-hop, and occasionally live music. The cocktails are a rip-off, so stick to the beer, though that can also get pricy. Welcome to Montmartre. Cigarettes are sold out front on an informal basis, but don't bring your drink outside—the burly but friendly bouncer will have words for you. Small appetizers are available to help you stomach the beer.

✸ ⓜAbbesses. Ⓢ Beer €2.30-7, pitchers €7. Ⓩ Open daily 8:30am-2am.

▨ L'ESCALE

☞☿ BAR

32bis rue des Trois Freres ☎01 46 06 12 38

A very popular spot among the students of Montmartre, this restaurant serves famously strong cocktails for just €4.50. Young folks huddle around cozy, small tables, and the owner proudly proclaims on the website that L'Escale and its strong drinks are the #1 enemy of the police. There's generally a guest DJ playing house music, or whatever else is super hip at the moment, on Sunday nights.

✸ ⓜAbbesses. Ⓢ Beer €3.50-8. Cocktails €4.50. Ⓩ Open daily 2pm-2am. Happy hour 4-10pm.

THE HARP

☞☿ SPORTS BAR

118 bld. de Clichy ☎01 43 87 64 99

Feel like starting the day off wrong with a beer or two? The Harp's got your back. Open untl 9am on weekends, this sports bar revolves around rugby, soccer, and booze, and hosts plenty of late-night partiers. Boasting a great selection of beer on tap, a pint costs only €6, a hell of a deal for the Red Light District. If the Harp had an anthem, it'd be James Brown and Betty Newsome's "It's a Man's World"; expect lots of bros and the women who love them. Several big-screen TVs make this the ideal spot to watch the game.

✸ ⓜBlanche. Ⓢ Beer €4-6. Ⓩ Open Th-Sa, 5pm-9am. Su-W, 5pm-4am.

Buttes Chaumont

Butte Chaumont doesn't have the most popping nightlife scene, and this is definitely not the safest neighborhood in Paris. That being said, drinks are generally cheap, and the company can get rowdy at the more student-ish bars. If you can only hit up one place, it has to be the Ourcq. The beer goes for only €2.50 and keeps the locals coming.

paris · nightlife

OURCQ

BAR, TEA HOUSE

68 quai de la Loire ☎01 42 40 12 26

Where the students, hipsters, hippies, and other budget-conscious folks go to get down. There's always a party going on, whether it's a Tuesday or a Saturday night. During the day, this classic brasserie doubles as a tea salon and provides its customers with a wide selection of board games and books to go along with their hot beverage of choice *(€2-3)*.

*[M]Laumière. [$] Wine by the glass €2-3. Beer €2.50-4. Cocktails €5. ⏰ Open W-Th 3pm-midnight, F-Sa 3pm-2am, Su 3-10pm.*

ARTS AND CULTURE

Theater

ODÉON THÉÂTRE DE L'EUROPE

LATIN QUARTER, ST-GERMAIN

2 rue Corneille ☎ 01 44 85 40 40 💻 www.theatre-Odéon.fr

The big fish in a theater-themed neighborhood. Even the streets leading towards the Odéon Theatre are named after some of France's most famous playwrights, including Corneille and Racine. The Odéon itself is a classically beautiful theater; gold lines the mezzanine, and muted red upholstery covers the chairs. Considering that this is the Mecca of Parisian theater, the prices are stunningly reasonable. Works range from the classical to the avant-garde.

*[M]Odéon. [$] Shows €5-32. Limited number of extremely cheap rush tickets available right before the show. ⏰ Performances generally M-Sa 8pm, Su 3pm.*

THÉÂTRE DE LA VILLE

CHÂTELET-LES HALLES

2 pl. du Châtelet ☎01 42 74 22 77 💻 www.theatredelavilleparis.com

Built in 1862, the Théâtre de la Ville underwent a rapid number of name changes (and identity crises) in the 1870s. It has since come of age and is now one of the most renowned theaters in Paris—in the '80s it became a major outlet for avant-garde contemporary dance and, therefore, its attendant younger artists. A soiree here should fit into most travel budgets. Bravo!

*[M]Châtelet. [$] Tickets €17-23, students €15. ⏰ Box office open M 11am-7pm, Tu-Sa 11am-8pm.*

Cabaret

LE LAPIN AGILE

MONTMARTRE

22 rue des Saules ☎01 46 06 85 87 💻 www.au-lapin-agile.com

Halfway up a steep, cobblestoned hill that American tourists describe to be "just like San Francisco," Le Lapin Agile has been around since the late 19th century, providing savvy and physically fit (that hill was something!) Parisians and tourists with a venue for music, dance, and theater. The tiny pink, green-shuttered theater was a hotspot of the 20th-century bohemian art scene in Paris—Picasso and Max Jacob are on the list of people who cabareted (is that a word?) there.

*[M]Lamarck-Coulaincourt. [i] Ticket price includes 1st drink. [$] €24, students under 26 €17. ⏰ Open Tu-Su 9pm-2am.*

BAL DU MOULIN ROUGE

MONTMARTRE

82 bld. de Clichy ☎ 01 53 09 82 82 💻 www.moulin-rouge.com

Ever since Christina and Co.'s music video, the only thing people associate with "Moulin Rouge" is that universal question: "*Voulez-vous couchez avec moi?*" But the world-famous cabaret and setting for the song and film isn't just about sex; it's also about glam and glitz. Since its opening in 1889, the Moulin Rouge has hosted international superstars like Ella Fitzgerald and Johnny Rey, and now welcomes a fair crowd of tourists for an evening of sequins, tassels, and skin. The shows remain risqué, but the price of admission is prohibitively expensive. The late show is cheaper, but be prepared to stand if it's a busy night.

✥ ⓂBlanche. *i* Elegant attire required; no shorts, sneakers, or sportswear permitted. Ⓢ Ticket for 9pm show €102, 11pm €92; includes half-bottle of champagne. 7pm dinner and 9pm show €150-180. Occasional lunch shows €100-130; call for more info. ⌚ Dinner at 7pm. Shows nightly 9, 11pm.

Cinema

▨ L'ARLEQUIN ✈ LATIN QUARTER, ST-GERMAIN

76 rue de Rennes ☎01 45 44 28 80

A proud revival theater, L'Arlequin goes heavy on the Hitchcock, mixing in other classic European films and some more modern French selections. The same three films are featured each week, undoubtedly decreasing the prevalence of adolescent movie-hopping. Some films are in English, but beware of certain dubbed selections.

✥ ⓂSaint-Sulpice. Ⓢ €9.50; from M to F afternoon, students and big families €6.50; under 18 €6.50.

Music

▨ ELYSÉE MONTMARTRE ✈ MONTMARTRE

72 bld. Rochechouart ☎01 44 92 45 36 ▨ www.elyseemontmartre.com

Any hip-hop nerd will remember this historic music hall in the Roots' hit song, "You Got Me": "She said she loved my show in Paris at Elysée Montmartre/and that I stepped off the stage and took a piece of her heart." Catch various hip-hop, soul, reggae, rock, indie, and underground acts here.

✥ ⓂAnvers. Ⓢ Prices vary, but generally €13.80-45. ⌚ Hall opens at 11:30pm for all shows.

POINT EPHÉMÈRE ✈ CANAL ST-MARTIN

200 quai de Valmy ☎01 40 34 02 48 ▨www.pointephemere.org

A continuously changing, grungy bar/restaurant/concert hall/dance studio/artist residence, where non-conformity and cigarettes reign supreme. Music acts are usually lesser known. On a concert night, the 300-seat space is packed with guys who collect tattoos and girls who tote helmets instead of purses.

✥ ⓂJaures. *i* Don't walk back late alone. Ⓢ Tickets prices vary per show. ⌚ Open M-Sa noon-2am, Su 1-9pm.

Opera

OPÉRA DE LA BASTILLE ✈♿ BASTILLE

pl. de la Bastille ☎08 92 89 90 90 ▨www.operadeparis.fr

The Opéra Garnier's "ugly" other half, the Opéra de la Bastille tends to do pieces with a more modern spin. Though the building's decor is somewhat questionable, the operas and ballets tend to be breathtaking enough to compensate. There may not be gilded columns, but you'll still feel like you're at the opera. The 2010-2011 season will include the operas *Siegfried* and *Akhmatova*, and the ballets *Romeo and Juliet* and *Swan Lake*.

✥ ⓂBastille. *i* For wheelchair-access, call 2 weeks ahead 01 40 01 18 50. Ⓢ Tickets can be purchased by Internet, mail, phone, or in person. Rush tickets 15min. before show for students under 25 and seniors. Tickets €5-200. ⌚ Box office open M-Sa 10:30am-6:30pm.

OPÉRA GARNIER ✈♿ OPÉRA

pl. de l'Opéra ☎08 92 89 90 90 ▨www.operadeparis.fr

Imagine The Opéra (capital T, capital O) in Paris; now go to the Opéra Garnier. Hosts mostly ballet, chamber music, and symphonies.

✥ ⓂOpéra. *i* Tickets usually available 2 weeks before the show. For wheelchair access call 2 weeks ahead. Ⓢ Ticket prices vary; operas €7-160, ballets €6-80. ⌚ Box office open M-Sa 10:30am-6:30pm. Last-minute discount tickets go on sale 1hr. before show.

paris · arts and culture

SHOPPING

Depending on who you're talking to, Shopping and Paris are almost synonymous. It can be hard to keep yourself from going crazy, but you probably should (nobody likes credit card debt).

look, but no touchy

Below you'll find a list of the big names that you automatically associate with the Paris shopping scene. Unless you found a Parisian ☒sugar daddy (and props to you if you did) you probably won't be leaving with much, but who doesn't like looking at pretty things? Salespeople won't be jumping to help you, but they'll gladly answer your questions if you ask nicely.

- **CARTIER** (*23 pl. Vendôme* ☎*01 44 55 32 20* ▣*www.cartier.com* Ⓜ*Tuileries.*)

- **CHANEL** (*42 av. Montaigne* ☎*01 47 23 74 12* ▣*www.chanel.com* Ⓜ*Franklin D. Roosevelt.*)

- **CHRISTIAN LOUBOUTIN** (*19 rue Jean-Jacques Rousseau* ☎*01 42 36 05 31* ▣*www.christianlouboutin.com* Ⓜ*Les Halles or Louvre Rivoli.*)

- **DIOR** (*8 pl. Vendôme* ☎*01 42 96 30 84* ▣*www.dior.com* Ⓜ*Tuileries.*)

- **GIVENCHY** (*56 rue François 1er* ☎*01 43 59 71 25* ▣*www.givenchy.fr* Ⓜ*George V.*)

- **GUCCI** (*60 av. Montaigne* ☎*01 56 69 80 80* ▣*www.gucci.com* Ⓜ*Franklin D. Roosevelt.*)

- **HERMÈS** (*24 rue du Faubourg St-Honoré* ☎*01 40 17 47 17* ▣*www.hermes.com* Ⓜ*Madeleine.*)

- **JEAN-PAUL GAULTIER** (*44 av. George V* ☎*01 44 43 00 44* ▣*www.jeanpaulgaultier.com* Ⓜ*Charles de Gaulle-Étoile.*)

- **LOUIS-VUITTON** (*101 av. des Champs-Elysées* ☎*01 53 57 52 00* ▣*www.louisvuitton.com* Ⓜ*Charles de Gaulle-Étoile.*)

- **VALENTINO** (*27 rue Faubourg St-Honoré* ☎*01 42 66 95 94* ▣*www.valentino.com* Ⓜ*Madeleine.*)

- **VERSACE** (*45 av. Montaigne* ☎*01 47 42 88 02* ▣*www.versace.com* Ⓜ*Franklin D. Roosevelt.*)

- **YVES SAINT-LAURENT** (*32 rue du Faubourg St-Honoré* ☎*01 53 05 80 80* ▣*www.ysl.com* Ⓜ*Madeleine.*)

Books

☒ **SHAKESPEARE AND CO.**   ✒ LATIN QUARTER, ST-GERMAIN

37 rue de la Bûcherie   ☎01 43 25 40 93 ▣www.shakespeareco.org

Shakespeare and Co. is an absolutely lovable English-language bookshop and miniature socialist utopia. Scenes from the film *Before Sunset* were shot here. Allegedly, the owners allow passing "tumbleweeds" to sleep for free, provided they volunteer in the shop and read a book a day. An adjacent storefront holds an impressive collection of first editions, with empahsis on the Beat Generation.

✚ Ⓜ *St-Michel.* *i* *Bargain bins outside include French classics translated into English.* ⌚ *Open M-F 10am-11pm, Sa-Su 11am-11pm.*

ABBEY BOOKSHOP

LATIN QUARTER, ST-GERMAIN

29 rue de la Parcheminerie ☎01 46 33 16 24 ■www.abbeybookshop.net

Clear your afternoon; if you're going to to Abbey Bookshop, you'll need the time. Set in a back alley, you'll need a few minutes to get used to the sheer number of books surrounding you. With a collection that includes everything from *Why Sex is Fun*, to *Bin Laden: Behind the Mask of a Terrorist*, this Canadian-owned shop probably has what you're looking for, and if not they'll order it for you. Plus they carry *Let's Go*—they've obviously got the right idea.

♯ Ⓜ*St-Michel or Cluny.* ⓘ *Books in English and other langauges available.* 🕐 *Open M-Sa 10am-7pm.*

Clothes and Accessories

LA SAMARITAINE

CHÂTELET-LES HALLES

67 rue de Rivoli ☎08 00 01 00 15 ■www.lasamaritaine.com

Spanning three blocks of the city's prime real estate, La Samaritaine is one of the oldest and most obnoxiously large department stores in Paris, 48,000 square meters of shopping space. The department store was founded in 1869 when Ernest Cognacq, a street salesman who had tired of selling his gentlemens' ties on the often rainy and windy Pont Neuf, decided to bring his operation indoors. La Samaritaine helped usher in the age of conspicuous consumption with an unforgettable slogan: "one finds everything at La Samaritaine." The roof cafe, accessible by a quick elevator ride, has a fantastic, free view of the city. Although the building was renovated in 1928, it closed indefinitely in 2006 for security renovations; murmurs of a reopening in late 2011 have been heard, but those are about as reliable as any other construction timeline in France (read: very unreliable). Check online for progress.

♯ Ⓜ*Châtelet/Pont Neuf.* ⓘ *Closed for renovation.* 🕐 *Information available M-F 10am-6pm.*

FORUM LES HALLES

CHÂTELET-LES HALLES

Les Halles ☎08 25 02 00 20 ■www.forumdeshalles.com

Like most of Paris's monuments, Les Halles history is closely tied to the whims of French royalty and, later on, its politicians. The mall began as a small food market in 1135; Philippe Auguste and, later, Louis-Philippe and François I all considered Les Halles a sort of pet project, and its expansion soon surpassed their expectations. The forum and gardens above ground attract a large crowd. Descend into the pits of one of Paris's storied historical sites to discover its bastard American child; a 200-boutique shopping mall (plus three move theaters), with selections ranging from the Gap, to H&M, to Franck Provost.

♯ Ⓜ *Les Halles.* 🕐 *open M-Sa 10am-8pm.*

Vintage

FREE 'P' STAR

MARAIS

8 rue Ste-Croix de la Bretonnerie ☎01 42 76 03 72 ■ www.freepstar.com

Enter as Plain Jane and leave a star—from the '80s or '90s, that is. Wide selection of vintage dresses (€20), velvet blazers (€40), boots (€30), and military-style jackets (€5) that all seem like a good idea when surrounded by other antiquated pieces, but require some balls to be worn out in the open. There's no way to go wrong with the €10 jean pile and €3 bin.

♯ Ⓜ*Hôtel de Ville.* ⓘ *Credit card min. €20. 2nd location at 61 rue de la Verrerie (☎ 01 42 78 0 76).* 🕐 *Open M-Sa noon-11pm, Su 2-11pm.*

ADOM

BASTILLE

35 and 56 rue de la Roquette ☎01 48 07 15 94 or 01 43 57 54 92

Think of every canonical high school film you've ever seen: *Fast Times at Ridgemont High, The Breakfast Club, Napoleon Dynamite*. The selection at Adom seems to be made up of the wardrobe department from all of them. Cowboy

paris · shopping

boots, acid wash jeans, and letterman jackets are in ample supply here. It's like totally awesome, duh.

✄ ⓂBastille. Ⓢ Boots from €35. Cut-offs €15. ☑ Open M-Sa 11am-8pm, Su 3-8pm.

Specialty

🔲 PYLÔNES
✦ MARAIS

57 rue St-Louis-en-l'Île ☎01 46 34 05 02 🖳 www.pylones.com

An adult version of a toy store with the kind of spunky things you'll impulsively buy, never need, but always marvel at. Like graters topped with doll heads (€18). More useful, but just as fun items include cigarette cases (€12)—you're in Paris now, tobacco's a part of growing up—and espresso cups (€6). The playful, artful objects are fun to look at even if you don't get any.

✄ ⓂPont Marie. 𝒊 5 other locations around the city. Ⓢ Cups €6. Wallets €24. ☑ Open daily 10:30am-7:30pm.

🔲 LA GRANDE ÉPICERIE DE PARIS
✦ INVALIDES

38 rue de Sèvres

The butcher actually has a thin twirled mustache. We thought only cartoon French people looked like that.

✄ ⓂVaneau. 𝒊 No pets allowed. Ⓢ Water €30. This place is way too expensive for you. ☑ Open M-Sa 8:30am-9pm.

ESSENTIALS
🛈

Practicalities

- **TOURS: Bateaux-Mouches** (Port de la Conférence, Pont de l'Alma, Rive droite ☎01 76 99 73 🖳www.bateaux-mouches.fr. ✄ Pont de l'Alma. 𝒊 Free parking throughout the duration of the cruise. Tours in English. Ⓢ €10, children under 12 €5. ☑ Apr-Sept 10:15am-7pm, every 20min. 7-11pm; Oct-Mar 11am-9pm, weekends 10:15am-9pm.) **City Segway Tours.** (24 rue Edgar Faure ☎01 56 58 10 54 🖳www. citysegwaytours.com/paris. 𝒊 All tours leave from beneath the Eiffel Tower and last 4-5hr. Ⓢ €80. ☑ Daily 9:30am, Mar-Dec daily 9:30am and 2pm.) **Canauxrama** (13 Quai de la Loire ☎01 42 39 15 00 🖳www.canauxrama.com ✄ ⓂBastille (Marina Arsenal) or Jaurés (Bassin de la Villette). 𝒊 Reservations recommended. Ticket desk open 40min. before departure or buy online. Departures either from Marina Arsenal or Bassin de la Villette. Ⓢ €16, students €11, children under 12 €8.50, under 4 free. ☑ Both locations with tours 9am-11pm.) **Fat Tire Bike Tours** (24 rue Edgar Faure ☎01 56 58 10 54 🖳www.fattirebiketours.com 𝒊 Tours last 4hr. Ⓢ €28, students €26 ☑ Day tour daily Oct-Mar 11am; Apr-Nov 11am, 3pm. Night tour Mar-Apr daily 6pm; Apr-Nov daily 7pm; Nov Tu, Th, Sa, Su 6pm.)

- **DISABILITY RESOURCES: L'Association des Paralysées de France, Délégation de Paris.** In addition to promoting disabled individual's fundamental rights to state compensation, public transportation, and handicapped-conscious jobs, the association also organizes international and provencial vacations. (17-19 bld. Auguste Blanqui ☎01 40 78 00 00)

- **TICKET SERVICES: FNAC.** (74 av. des Champs-Élysées ☎01 53 53 64 64 🖳www. fnac.fr ✄ ⓂFranklin D. Roosevelt. 𝒊 Also at 77-81, bld. St-Germain; 109 Porte Berger; 30 av. d'Italie, 13ème; 136 rue de Rennes, 6ème; 109 rue St-Lazare, 9ème; 26-30 av. de Ternes, 17ème. ☑ Open M-Sa 10am-11:45pm, Su noon-11:45pm.) **Virgin Megastore.** (52 av. des Champs-Élysées, 8ème ☎01 49 53 50 00 🖳www. virginmegastore.fr ✄ ⓂFranklin D. Roosevelt. ☑ Open M-Sa 9am-6pm.)

- **INTERNET: The American Library** provides free internet access for all members and those with day and week passes. Wireless internet available throughout library. Ask circulation desk for assistance. (10 rue de Général Camou, 7ème ☎01 53 59 12 60

france

www.americanlibraryinparis.org ⚓ ⓜÉcole Militaire. ⌖ Open Tu-Sa 10am-7pm, Su 1-7pm. Reduced summer hours July-Aug. Reference desk closed Su.)

Emergency!

- **EMERGENCY NUMBERS: Police:** ☎17 (for emergencies only). **Ambulance (SAMU):** ☎15. **Fire:** ☎18. **Poison:** ☎01 40 05 48 48 (In French, but some English assistance available). **Rape:** ☎08 00 05 95 95. (⌖ Open M-F 10am-7pm.) **SOS Help!** (☎17) is an emergency hotline for english speakers in crisis.

- **CRISIS HOTLINES: AIDES** is the first French association against HIV/AIDs and viral hepatitis. (☎0800 84 08 00 ■www.aides.org ⌖ Open 24hr.) **Alcoholics Anonymous.** (☎01 46 34 59 65 ■www.aaparis.org) **Red Cross France** provides HIV testing. (43 rue de Valois, 1er ☎01 42 61 30 04 ■www.croix-rouge.fr ⚓ Palais-Royal or Bourse.) **International Counseling Service.** (☎01 45 50 26 49 ■www. icsparis.com.)

- **HOSPITAL/MEDICAL SERVICES: American Hospital of Paris.** (63 bld. Hugo, Neuilly ☎01 46 41 25 25 www.american-hospital.org ⚓ ⓜPort Maillot, then bus #82.) **Hôpital Bichat.** (46 rue Henri Buchard, 18ème ☎01 40 25 80 80 ⚓ ⓜPort St-Ouen.)

Getting There

Paris has three main airports: Roissy-Charles de Gaulle, Orly, and Beauvais.

ROISSY-CHARLES DE GAULLE (ROISSY-CDG)   AIRPORT

23km northeast of Paris   ☎01 40 28 09 39 ■www.adp.fr

Most transatlantic flights land at Aéroport Roissy-CDG. The two cheapest and fastest ways to get into the city from there are by RER and by bus. The **RER train** from Roissy-CDG to Paris leaves from the Roissy train station, which is in Terminal 2. To get to the station from Terminal 1, take the Red Line of the Navette, a free shuttle bus that leaves every 6-10min. From there, the **RER B** (one of the Parisian commuter rail lines) will transport you to central Paris. To transfer to the metro, get off at **Gare du Nord, Châtelet-Les-Halles,** or **Saint-Michel,** all of which are RER and metro stops. The trip should take 35min. in either direction.

Taking a **shuttle bus** the whole distance from the airport to Paris is simple, and it takes about the same amount of time as taking the RER. The ⊠**Roissybus** (☎01 49 25 61 87) leaves from rue Scribe at **Place de l'Opéra** every 15min. during the day and every 20min. at night. You can catch the Roissybus from Terminals 1, 2, and 3 of the airport from 6am to 11pm. Roissybus is not wheelchair accessible. ⌖ Open 24hrs.

ORLY   AIRPORT

18km south of Paris   ☎01 49 75 15 15

Aéroport d'Orly is used by charters and many continental flights. From Orly Sud gate G or gate I, platform 1, or Orly Ouest level G, gate F, take the **Orly-Rail** shuttle bus to the **Pont de Rungis/Aéroport d'Orly** train stop, where you can board the RER C2 for a number of destinations in Paris. Another option is the RATP ⊠**Orlybus** (☎08 36 68 77 14), which runs between Metro and RER stop **Denfert-Rochereau** (lines 4 and 6) in the 14ème and Orly's south terminal. You can also board the Orlybus at **Dareau-St-Jacques, Glacière-Tolbiac,** and **Porte de Gentilly.**

RATP also runs **Orlyval** (☎01 69 93 53 00)—a combination of Metro, RER, and VAL rail shuttle—which is probably your fastest option. The VAL shuttle goes from **Antony** (RER line B) to Orly Ouest and Sud. You can either get a ticket just for the VAL, or combination VAL-RER tickets. Buy tickets at any

RATP booth in the city, or from the Orlyval agencies at Orly Ouest, Orly Sud, and Antony. To Orly: Be careful; it splits into two lines right before the Antony stop. Get on the train that says **"St-Rémy-Les-Chevreuse"** or just look for the track that has a lit-up sign saying **"Antony-Orly."** From Orly: Trains arrive at Orly Ouest 2min. after reaching Orly Sud.

🕐 *Open 24hrs.*

BEAUVAIS
AIRPORT

9 rue des Décharges ☎03 44 11 46 86 🖥www.aeroportbeauvais.com

Aéroport de Paris Beauvais. Buses run between the airport and bld. Pershing in the 17ème, near the hotel Concorde Lafayette (Ⓜ**Porte Maillot**). Tickets are €13 and can be purchased in the arrivals lounge of the airport, at the kiosk just oustide the bus stop, or online. Call for bus schedules.

🕐 *Open 24hrs.*

By Train

Gare du Nord is a central arrival and departure point for trains to northern France, Britain, Belgium, the Netherlands, Scandinavia, Eastern Europe, and northern Germany (Cologne, Hamburg). To **Amsterdam** (🕐 *4-5hr.*), **Brussels** *(🕐 1hr.), and* **London** (*i by the Eurostar Chunnel;* 🕐 *3hr.).*

Gare de l'Est is a central arrival and departure point for trains to eastern France (Champagne, Alsace, Lorraine, Strasbourg), Luxembourg, parts of Switzerland (Basel, Zürich, Lucerne), southern Germany (Frankfurt, Munich), Austria, Hungary, and Prague. To: **Luxembourg** (🕐 *4-5hr.);* **Munich** (🕐 *9hr.);* **Prague** (🕐 *15hr.);* **Strasbourg** (🕐 *1hr.);* **Vienna** (🕐 *15hr.);* **Zürich** (🕐 *7hr.).*

Gare de Lyon is a central arrival and departure point to southern and southeastern France (Lyon, Provence, Riviera), parts of Switzerland (Geneva, Lausanne, Berne), Italy, and Greece. To: **Florence** (🕐 *13hr.);* **Geneva** (🕐 *4hr.);* **Lyon** (🕐 *2hr.);* **Marseille** (🕐 *3-4hr.);* **Nice** (🕐 *6hr.);* **Rome** (🕐 *15hr.).*

Gare d'Austerlitz runs trains to the Loire Valley, southwestern France (Bordeaux, Pyrénées), Spain, and Portugal. (TGV to southwestern France leaves from Gare Montparnasse.) To **Barcelona** (🕐 *12hr.)* and **Madrid** (🕐 *12-13hr.).*

Gare St-Lazare runs trains to Normandy. To **Caen** (🕐 *2hr.)* and **Rouen** (🕐 *1-2hr.).*

Gare Montparnasse runs trains to Brittany and southwestern France on the TGV. To **Rennes** (🕐 *2hr.)* and **Nantes** (🕐 *2hr.).*

Getting Around

By Metro

In general, the Metro system is easy to navigate (pick up a colorful map at any station), and trains run swiftly and frequently. Metro stations, in themselves a distinctive part of the Paris landscape, are marked with an "M" or with the *"Métropolitain"* lettering designed by Art Nouveau legend Hector Guimard. The earliest trains of the day start running around 5:30am, and the last ones leave the end-of-the-line stations (the *portes de Paris*) for the center of the city at about 12:15am during the week, and at 2:15am on Friday and Saturday. Connections to other lines are indicated by orange *correspondance* signs, exits indicated by blue *sortie* signs. Transfers are free if made within a station, but it is not always possible to reverse direction on the same line without exiting the station. **Hold onto your ticket until you exit the Metro,** and pass the point marked *Limite de Validité des Billets;* a uniformed RATP *contrôleur* (inspector) may request to see it on any train. If caught without one, you must pay a hefty fine.

Don't count on buying a Metro ticket late at night. Some ticket windows close as early as 10pm, and many close before the last train arrives. Also, not all stations have automatic booths. It's a good idea to carry one more ticket than you need, although large stations have ticket machines that accept coins. Avoid the most dangerous stations **(Barbès-Rochechouart, Pigalle, Anvers, Châtelet-Les-Halles, Gare du Nord, Gare de l'Est)** after dark. When in doubt, take a bus or taxi.

By RER

The RER *(Réseau Express Régional)* is the RATP's suburban train system, which passes through central Paris. The RER travels much faster than the Metro. There are five RER lines, marked A-E, with different branches designated by a number: for example, the C5 line services Versailles-Rive Gauche. The newest line, the E, is called the Eole *(Est-Ouest Liaison Express)* and links Gare Magenta to Gare St-Lazare. Within Paris, the RER works exactly the same as the Metro, requiring the same ticket. The principal stops within the city, which link the RER to the Metro system, are Gare du Nord, Nation, Charles de Gaulle-Etoile, Gare de Lyon, and Châtelet-Les-Halles on the Right Bank and St-Michel and Denfert-Rochereau on the Left Bank. The electric signboards next to each track list all the possible stops for trains running on that track. Be sure that the little square next to your destination is lit up. Trips to the suburbs require special tickets. You'll need your ticket to exit RER stations. Insert your ticket just as you did to enter, and pass through. Like the Metro, the RER runs 5:30am-12:30am and until 2:30am on weekends.

By Bus

Although slower and often costlier than the Metro, a bus ride can be a cheap sightseeing tour and a helpful introductions to the city's layout. Bus tickets are the same as those used in the Metro, and they can be purchased either in Metro stations or from the bus driver. Enter the bus through the front door and punch your ticket by pushing it into the machine by the driver's seat. If you have a *Navigo* or other transport pass, flash it at the driver. Inspectors may ask to see your ticket, so hold onto it until you get off. Should you wish to leave the paradise that is the RATP autobus, just press the red button so the *arrêt demandé* (stop requested) sign lights up.

Most buses run daily 7am-8:30pm, although those marked **Autobus du nuit** continue until 1:30am. Still others, named **Noctilien,** run all night. Night buses run from Châtelet to the *portes* of the city every hour on the half hour from 12:30-5:30am (1-6am from the *portes* into the city). Look for bus stops marked with a bug-eyed moon sign. Check out **www.noctilien.fr** or ask a major metro station or at Gare de l'Est for more information on Noctilien buses.

versailles

If you descend the great steps of the Versailles garden slowly enough, you might just feel like royalty. A whopping 580m long, this crib won't fit in your camera frame. To be fair, the palace did house all 6000 members of the royal court and serve as the seat of goverment, after **Louis XIV** (1643-1715) decided in 1661 that his father's old brick and stone château needed an upgrade. No less than four men were needed to get it done. Louis XIV, or the Sun King, or the self-aggrandizing narcissist, commissioned two architects, Lous Le Vau and Jules Hardouin-Mansart, painter Charles Le Brun, and landscape designer André Le Nôtre to create an unquestionable symbol of the awesome power of the French monarchy. Later, with the 1789 Revolution, Louis XVI and Marie-Antoinette would learn just how contestable that power was when set under a guillotine blade. In 1837, King Louis-Phillipe initiated a clever piece of PR, opening up parts of the palace to the public and dedicating it to "all the glories of France," emphasis on all, emphasis on France. Since then, the château has remained largely unaltered, though a €370 million renovation and restoration campaign was launched in 2003, and visitors now are hardly ever of royal blood.

ORIENTATION

As the Sun King demanded, a visit to the 800 hectares property must begin at the **terrace.** To its left, the **Parterre Sud** opens up to the **Orangery,** which onces boasted 2000 orange trees. The fresh-squeezed orange juice stands scattered throughout the sight today recall the orangery's historical production. The **Parterre d'Eau,** the first of many ponds and lakes on the premises, stands in the middle of the terrace. Past the **Bassin de Latone** and to the left is the **Jardin du Roi,** a fragant, flower-lined sanctuary only accessible from the easternmost side facing the **Bassin du Miroir.** Near the the grove's southern gate lies the **Bassin de Bacchus,** one of four seasonal fountains, which portrays the Roman god of wine, crowned in vine branches, reclining on a bunch of grapes. Some traveler's report having taken swigs of wine there in honor of the great god. Behind it, the **Bosquet de la Salle de Ball** is a semicircle of cascading waterfalls and torch holders, where royals once late-night bachanalias of their own.

Moving north to the center of the garden leads to the **Bosquet de la Colonnade,** an impressive arrangement of 32 violet and blue mable columns, sculptures, and white marble basins, created by Hardouin-Mansart in 1864. The northern gate to the Colonnade opens onto the 330m long **Tapis Vert,** the main walkway leading to the garden's most ostentatious fountain, the **Bassin d'Apollo,** in which the god himself charges out of the water on bronze horses. On the garden's northern side, you'll find the **Bosquet de l'Encelade.** When the fountain is on, a 25m high jet bursts from Titan's enormous mouth, which is plated, as all mouths should be, with shimmering gold and half buried under rocks.

The **Bassin de Flore** and the **Bassin de Cérès** show ladies, busts out, reclining in their natural habitats—a bed of flowers and wheat sheaves, respectively. The **Parterre Nord** overlooks some of the garden's most spectacular fountains. The **Allée d'Eau,** a fountain-lined walkway, provides the best view of the **Bassin des Nymphes de Diane.** The path slopes toward the sculpted **Bassin du Bragon,** where a beast slain by Apollo spurts water 27m into the air. Next to it, 99 jets of water issue from sea horns encircling Neptune in the **Bassin de Neptuune,** the gardens' largest fountain; make your way here at 5:20pm for a truly spectacular fountain finale.

If you get tired of the grandeur of the main gardens and groves, head up to Marie-Antoinette's Estate, where the quiet, flower-filled paths are much less of an ego display.

SIGHTS

CHÂTEAU

Though the Sun King's palace boasts a whopping 51,200 square meters of floor space, the public is granted access to only a small percentage of it. With over ten million visitors per year, the Versailles staff is practiced in the art of shuttling tourists through. After a walk through the **Musée de L'Histoire de France,** which briefly recounts French history in chronological order, visitors are shepherded down the halls in a single direction. The museum's 21 rooms feature stunning portraits of the royal family, including a smaller copy of Rigaud's famous **depiction of Louis XIV** with red-heeled shoes. Up the main staircase to the right is the two-level chapel where the King heard Mass, built in 1710. Here God competed with the Sun King for attention while the court gathered to watch him pray.

Through the hallway, where the ceiling is covered with marvelous frescoes (don't forget to look up!), are the luxurious **State Apartments,** which include both the king's bedroom, the **Room of Abundance,** the **Apollo Salon,** and the famed **Hall of Mirrors.** Note how tiny the bed is; like Napoleon, Sarkozy, and other French leaders that followed him, Louis XIV was a man of less than average height with an ensuing inferiority complex, and was known to wear shoes with 5" heels. The Apollo Salon houses the Sun King's throne; 3m tall, the throne enabled the

King to tower over his subjects, and enjoy the view of the beautiful fresco of himself on the ceiling, which compares him to Apollo and portrays him as the bearer of Enlightenment. When they weren't trying to figure out how to kill him, French citizens showed great deference to the king and ritualistically bowed or curtsied when they passed the throne, even when great Louis wasn't there. As if the Apollo Salon wasn't elaborate (or pathological) enough, the sumptuous Hall of Mirrors exemplifies the King's opulent taste. Lined with the largest mirrors 17th-century technology could produce and windows that overlook to the grand gardens outside, the room served as a reception for great ambassadors. Today it can be rented out for a hefty sum.

The **Queen's Bedchamber,** where royal births were public events in order to prove the legitimacy of heirs, is much less ornate than the king's, but almost exactly as the queen last left it on October 6, 1789. A rendition of *Le Sacre de Napoleon* by French neo-classicist David depicts Napoleon's self-coronation, and dominates the **Salle du Sacré,** also known as the **Coronation Room.** David painted Napoleon's mother, Letizia, into the scene even though she refused to be there. The more honest painting of **Battle of Aboukir** is positioned on the wall next to it, and portrays the gore of war—and perhaps the price of all the royal splendor that surrounds it.

GARDENS

Gardening *à la française* is nothing short of neurotic. The park of Versailles, with its parterres, groves, statues, fountains, pools, and trees boxed in metal frames, is no exception. Meticulously designed by André Le Nôtre in 1661 and completed by **Jules Hardouin-Mansart,** the château gardens are an impressive 800 hectares. During **Les Grand Eaux Musicales,** almost all the fountains are turned on at the same time, and chamber music booms from among the groves. Wandering through the gardens many walks, you will find a number of marble statues and bursting fountains.

i *Grandes Eaux Musicales Apr-Sept.* Ⓢ *M-F free, Sa-Su and holidays €8, students and under 18 €6, under 6 free.* Ⓔ *Gardens open daily Apr-Oct 8am-8:30pm; Nov-Mar 8am-6pm.*

TRIANONS AND MARIE ANTOINETTE'S HAMEAU

☎01 30 83 78 89 🖳www.châteauversailles.fr.
Contrary to what officials will tell you, the walk up to **Trianons** and **Marie Antoinette's Hameau** does not take 25min. Less ambitious sightseers are overwhelmed by the prospect of leaving the main area, which makes for a quieter and infinitely more pleasant Versailles experience. The garden surrounding Petit Trianon and Marie Antoinette's hameau is one of the most beautiful and tranquil areas of the park. Inspired by Jean-Jacques Rousseau's theories on the goodness of nature, the Queen wanted a simple life, and so commissioned Richard Mique to construct a 12-building compound comprised of a dairy farm, gardener's house, and mill around a pristine and swan-filled lake. Complete with lilac beds, flower pots, and thatched roofs, Marie Antoinette played the peasant and held intimate parties in her **Temple of Love.** We doubt the irony of this idealized pastoralism escaped the Parisian masses of the time. **Petit Trianon** was built between 1762 and 1768 for Louix XV and his mistress Mme. de Pompadour. Some ways away from the palace, the more homey château was intended to serve as a love den. Unfortunately, Pompadour died before it was completed. The **Grand Trianon** was intended to be a château-away-from-château for Louix XIV, who reached the mini château by boat from the Grand Canal. Both the Petit and Grand Trianon provide a less ostentatious view of royal life and allow one to imagine the life of a man rather than the life of a king.

Ⓢ *Admission to palace and audio tour €15, reduced €13. The "passport" one-day pass allows entry to the palace, Trianon palace, and Marie Antoinette's estate €18. Day of Les Grands Eaux*

Musicales €25. Trianon palace and Marie Antionette's Estate €10, reduced €6. 🕐 Château open Tu-Su Apr-Oct 9am-6:30pm; Nov-Mar 9am-5:30pm. Last entry 30 min. before close.

ESSENTIALS

Getting There

RER trains beginning with "V" run from Invaled or any stop on RER Line C5 to the **Versailles Rive Gauche station.** *(🕐 30-40 min, every 15min. $ Round trip €5.80. ℹ Advisable as ticket lines are long at Versailles station.)* Buy your RER ticket before going through the turnstile to the platform; when purchasing from a machine, look for the **Île-de-France ticket option.** While a Metro ticket will get you through these turnstiles, it won't get you through RER turnstiles at the other end and could ultimately result in a significant fine. From RER: Versailles, turn right down **avenue du General de Gaulles,** walk 200m, and turn left at the big intersection onto av. de Paris. You'll know it when you see it.

Getting Around

The **tourist office** is on the left before the château courtyard. Info on local accommodations, vents, restaurants, and sightseeing buses. Also sells tickets for historical guided tours of the town. Not to be confused with office that sells guided tours of the château. *(2bis av. de Paris ☎01 39 24 88 88. 💻www.versailles-tourisme.com. 🕐 Open M 11am-5pm, Tu-Sa 9am-6pm, Su 11am-5pm.)*

orléans ☎0238

Joan of Arc, aptly known as the "Maid of Orléans," marched armies down these crooked cobbled streets when she liberated the city from a brutal seven-month English siege in 1429, a victory which rejuvenated French forces and contributed to their victory in the Hundred Years' War. The historic *petit vieille ville* and its tremendous Cathedral lie at the heart of Orléans, complete with the *patisseries* and *boulangeries* of any traditional French town. Though Orléans should definitely make an appearance on your Loire Valley itinerary, don't anticipate spending more than a few days (or even a day) here— unless, of course, you are a Joan of Arc fanatic and just can't get enough of her. The city devolves into a bustling but run-of-the-mill commercial area further out of the center, with shops and suburban streets which do not compare to the visual beauties on offer closer to the downtown.

ORIENTATION

The train station is a 2min. walk north of the center on **boulevard Alexandre Martin.** From this main road it is possible to reach the *vielle ville* by following the shopping street **rue de la République** (through the *centre commercial* and down the steps) which leads to **place du Martroi**. At pl. du Matroi, continue southwards where rue de la République becomes **rue Royale** and follow this directly southwards to reach the banks of the Loire. Rue Royale intersects with **rue Jean D'Arc**, which will take you to the Cathedral and Tourist Information Office at **place St Croix**, and a little further down rue Royale connects with **rue de Bourgogne** where you will find the best of Orléans's bars and restaurants. A tram service runs between the train station and the river *(€1.40)* which makes transporting luggage nice and simple.

ACCOMMODATIONS

Orléans isn't exactly thriving with budget hotels and funky hostels, but this does not mean that finding a bargain abode around town is impossible. Websites specializing in cheap hotel rooms often provide last-minute offers that are cheaper than advertised rates, so keep your chin up and keep Googling for that deal. Booking in advance for most places is advisable.

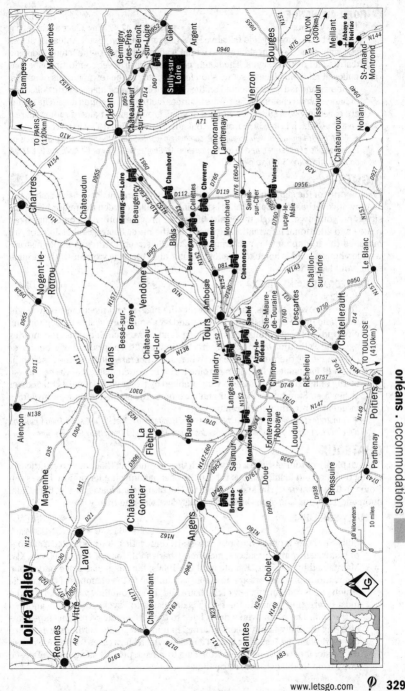

Loire Valley

orléans . accommodations

HOTEL ARCHANGE

HOTEL [4]

1 bld. de Verdun ☎02 32 54 42 42 🖥www.hotelarchange.com

Owned by an outgoing and talkative local man and his son, Hotel Archange places you right near the train station and within walking distance of the major shopping district and historic sights. The hotel cultivates a bizarre yet comforting vibe that makes it an ideal place to set up shop for your stay in the town; murals of angels, rainbows and fairies are painted on the corridor walls, and an eccentric collection of hand-shaped chairs and Star Wars figurines clutter the reception area. The rooms are especially well suited for families or small groups, since pairs of rooms share a vestibule which is lockable from the outside. Free Wi-Fi and TVs in all rooms.

From the train station, walk through the commercial center, down the steps and the hotel is on the other side of the street, next to the McDonalds. $ Singles with shower €43, with bath €47-57; doubles with bath €56-70; triples €70.

SIGHTS

The majority of the sights in Orléans are situated in and around **Place Saint-Croix** in the shadow its overbearring **Cathedral.** It is possible to walk between the major historical sights on your own, though the **Tourist Office** can provide you with some suggested routes and additional information. It was down the **rue de Bourgogne** that Joan of Arc marched the triumphant French army in 1429. The street features multiple historic wooden houses, and is home to most of Orléans' nightlife. One wonders if the virginal saint would approve.

CATHÉDRALE SAINT CROIX

CATHEDRAL

pl. St Croix

Towering over Orléans, the Cathedral is the biggest and most impressive sight to behold in the city. Its Gothic towers and 88m spires are visible throughout the city, and it is easy to imagine the young Joan of Arc marching past it centuries ago. The Cathedral was originally erected in the 13th century, and was built over the course of the next 200 years. When Joan liberated it from the English, it was still unfinished. The city's heroine is not forgotten inside the Cathedral— a statue of her stands in its north wing, flanked by two golden leopards that cower at her feet. Stand near the altar and gaze up to the stained-glass windows for a moment of breathtaking serenity.

From train station take Tram A in the direction of Hôpital and exit at Pl. De Gaulle. Follow rue Jean d'Arc to Pl. St Croix. i Tourist office provides tours. $ Free. ⏰ Open daily 9:15am-6pm.

CHÂTEAUX

Though plenty of tourists hire a car to reach the surrounding Châteaux from Orléans, taking the good old fashioned bus is both the cheaper and simpler option. Buses run from the **Gare Routière** (2 rue Marcel Proust). The **Gien Express** leaves M-F at 6am, 7am, noon and 12:30pm, and stops at **Germingy, Sully-Sur-Loire,** and finally Gien.

SULLY-SUR-LOIRE

CHÂTEAU

☎02 38 36 23 70 🖥www.sully-sur-loire.fr

Sully-Sur-Loire is one of the Loire's most striking castles, and has hosted a number of historically famous visitors, including Charles VII, Joan of Arc, and Louis XIV. Maintained by the Sully Family until the 1960s, the castle has since undergone renovations, and visitors are now able to climb up to the chamber of the guards, which yields a stunning view of the Loire and the surrounding valleys. One of the most interesting rooms in the house is dedicated to Psyche, the Greek goddess of the soul. The room, which dates back to the 17th century, contains tapestries bearing the Sully family's coat of arms. In mid-June, Sully-Sur-Loire is home to the world-famous **Festival de Sully et du Loiret,** which showcases worldwide classical music. **The Forest,** open daily from 8am to sunset, provides a moment of peace away from the busy tourist attraction.

Take the bus from Orléans to Gien, get off at Sully-Sur-Loire. $ €7, groups €5. Open Apr-Sept 10am-6pm; Oct-Dec M 10am-6pm, Tu-Su 10am-noon; Feb-Apr M 10am-6pm, Tu-Su 10am-noon.

GERMINGY-DES-PRÉS (GERMINGY)

CHÂTEAU

☎02 38 58 27 97 www.tourisme-loire-foret.com

The Carolingian church of Germingy-des-Prés is about 30km southeast of Orléans, and dates back to 806 AD, making it one of the three oldest churches in France. The original pillar headings can still be observed in the re-plastered interior. One of the most fascinating displays in the church is a ninth-century "golden" mosaic. The mosaic was actually rediscovered by a group of schoolchildren in 1830 who happened to be playing underneath it. That was almost 200 years ago— see if you can discover anything new in the grand corridors and grounds of this medieval wonder.

Take the bus from Orléans to Gien and get off at Germingy. $ Free. Open daily Apr-Oct 9am-7pm.; Nov-Mar 10am-5pm.

FOOD

Restaurants in Orléans serve classic French cuisine and tastes from around the globe. If you're on a budget, check out the **Carrefour** supermarket, which can be found above of the train station at pl. D'Arc *(Open M-Sa 8:30am-9pm)*. A traditional French market can be found inside **Les Halles Châtelet,** where locals pick up essentials like bread, milk, fish and meats. *(pl. du Châtelet. Open Tu-F 7:30am-7:30pm, Sa 7am-7:30pm, Su 8am-1pm.)* **La rue de Bourgogne** is the busiest street in Orléans, lined with Indian, Thai, British, Lebanese, and traditional French cuisine. In the evening, most places don't open before 7pm, so an early dinner is rarely on the menu.

LA MANGEOIRE

RESTAURANT 3

28 rue du Poirier ☎02 38 68 15 38

This *petit* restaurant is an absolute must with filling French cuisine that won't empty the wallet. Specializing in *les tartines*, or bread topped with meats, cheeses, potatoes, and other ingredients, La Mangeoire provides some of the best portions and price-tags in town. Choose from numerous toppings, including vegetarian options, to create a gigantic rustic meal that could sustain a burly Gaul farmer for several days. For the truly hungry, try the Parisienne, which includes *bris*, beef, mushrooms, and potatoes. The manager, Florent, worked as a chef in NYC for five years and is fluent in English. He'll happily translate the menu for you or offer a few words of advice for making the most of the town. Families and big groups welcome. If you're coming in a big group, call in advance and special arrangements can be made, ranging from flexible opening hours to a set menu.

Rue fu Poirier runs adjacent with rue de Bourgogne. $ Tartines €12, meat and fish €12-16. Open M-Sa noon-2pm and 7-10:30pm.

AU BON MARCHÉ

♿ RESTAURANT 3

12 pl. du Châtelet ☎02 38 53 04 35 www.aubonmarche-orleans.com

Although not as "cheap" as the name suggests, this restaurant offers some high-class French dining for not-so-high-class prices. The restaurant bends around a bar and extends through to a seating area covered in red leather seats, with some high tables that create a modern vibe in an old building. The specialty beef dish *(€15)* comes served on a skewer which could be mistaken for a kebab, until you tuck into the tender meat. The plasma TV screen showing wildlife programmes adds a certain bizarre vibe to the whole setup.

In the Châtelet Square which is a short walk from the Châtelet shopping complex. $ Lunch set menu €7, dinner set menu €18. Open M-F noon-2:30 and 7-10:30pm, Sa noon-2:30 and 7-11pm, Su noon-2:30 and 7-10:30pm.

ESSENTIALS

[i]

Practicalities

- **TOURIST OFFICE:** 2 pl. de l'Étape *(☎02 38 24 05 05. 💻www.tourisme-orleans.com. 🕰 Open daily Apr-June 9:15am-6:15pm; July-Aug 9:15am-6:45pm; Sept. 9:15am-6:15pm; Oct 9:45am-5:30pm; Nov-Mar 9:45am-5pm.)*
- **BANKS:** ATMs along rue de la République.
- **LAUNDROMAT: Laverie Bourgogne.** (176 rue de Bourgogne. *$ Wash €7 per 10kg, dry €1 per 10min. 🕰 Open daily 7am-9pm.)*
- **HOSPITAL: Centre Hospatilier Régional.** 1 rue Porte Madeleine. *(☎02 38 51 44 44).*
- **POST OFFICE:** Pl. du Général de Gaulle. *(☎02 38 77 35 14. 🕰Open M-F 8:30am-7pm, Sa 8:30am-12:15pm.)*

Emergency!

- **PHARMACY:** ☎15. *(🕰Line open daily 7am-9pm.)*
- **POLICE:** 63 rue du Faubourg St-Jean *(☎02 38 24 30 00).*

Getting There

The main train station, **Gare d'Orléans** connects to the other train station **Gare Les Aubrais** by a shuttle which runs roughly every half hour *(€1.20).* You can reach Gare Les Aubrais from **Paris Charles de Gaulle** by a high-speed train *($€30. 🕰1hr-1hr. 30min.)* or take a train from **Paris Austerlitz** from the Gare d'Orléans *($€20. 🕰1hr).* There are frequent trains connecting Orléans with the rest of the Loire Valley, including **Blois** *($€10. 🕰40min.)* and **Tours.** *($€18. 🕰1hr. 30min.)* The Info Desk at Gare d'Orléans is open M-Sa 6am-8pm, Su 8:30am-8pm.

Getting Around

The **tram** system runs in two directions: Jules Verne to the North and L'Hopital de la Source in the South. Tickets for one way on the tram costs €1.30 and must be bought at the stop before getting on. The tram stops at most main points of interest in Orléans, including **Rue de la République** and **De Gualle.**

For a **taxi,** call Radio d'Orléans *(☎02 38 53 11 11).* Taxis run from underneath the train station and cost around €5 to reach the center of town *(€2.10-1.40 per km).*

Buses run around the Centre, but aren't really required for exploring the sights of Orléans, as they are all within walking distance from the vielle ville.

It is possible to hire a **bike** from newly installed **Velo+** bike station outside the Tourist Information Office. The first half an hour is free, and it costs €1 for the next hour, and €2 for the hour after that. There are 33 stops in and around Orléaans which are indicated on the map.

blois ☎02 54

The opposite of blah, Blois (blwah; pop. 51,000) is the hidden gem of the Loire Valley, and the perfect excuse for a few days of exploration and medieval meddling. Indulge your inner Disney princess with a waltz through the incredible Château that overlooks the Loire River, then hit the local bars for a night you'll never forget. The culinary offerings span a variety of palates, with an emphasis on traditional (and even medieval) French food. Though you shouldn't expect to find any banging clubs with massive crowds here, French 20-somethings kick back and bask in the sun outside the numerous bars and cafes in the town's main squares. So if you're looking for a knight in shining armor, rather than a night on the town, Blois also serves as your Camelot crash pad and château launch pad—it's close to Chambord and Cheverny.

ORIENTATION

Remember: what goes up must come down. In Blois, the **train station** rests at the top of a hill, and the main town (and the river) lies at its bottom. Luckily, this makes getting lost nearly impossible, since almost every path or road leading uphill heads toward the station, and every road heading down converges at the river. When in doubt, head down. It is also impossible to miss the **Château** and the **Cathedral**, the towering structures which dominate the town's skyline. There are relatively few museums and sights here, so head for a leisurely stroll along the river if you have extra time.

ACCOMMODATIONS

HOTEL DE FRANCE ET DE GUISE — HOTEL ❹

3 rue de Gallois ☎02 54 78 00 53 www.franceetguise.com

You may feel as if you have just followed Alice down the rabbit hole as you find yourself winding through the twisting corridors of this hotel. We suppose that the creaking staircases and grand mirrors add to the charm of the place. Located a short walk away from all of Blois' attractions, the hotel is ideal for anyone wishing to explore the town.

 # Just north of the rue de Commerce, the hotel is on a corner opposite the Jardins Augustin-Thierry. i Breakfast €7. $ Singles €49-55; doubles €55-65; triples €70-85.

CHÂTEAUX

From Blois as well as the renowned Château de Blois, the Tourist Office runs trips to two of the most magnificent châteaux in the Loire: **Chambord** and **Cheverny**. A bus runs three times a day, departing from the train station at 9am, 11:10am, or 1:40pm, then stopping at Chambord and continuing on to Cheverny at three possible times. The last bus back leaves Cheverny at 6pm. The bus costs €6 for the whole day, and can be used for a reduced entrance into the three châteaux *(€1.50 discount at Blois, €1.50 at Chambord, €1 at Cheverny).*

CHÂTEAU DE BLOIS — CHÂTEAU

pl. du Château ☎02 54 90 33 33 www.châteaudeblois.fr

The highlight of a visit to Blois is by far a trip to its stunning Château. Renowned for its elaborate architectural design—which incorporates Gothic, Renaissance, late 16th-century, and Classical styles—the building will leave you in awe of the minds of those who conceived it. Seven kings and 10 queens of France once used Blois Château as their Royal Palace back in the day, and the rooms were recently renovated and restored to their former glory. Survey the royal study for the secret compartments hidden in the walls, where Alexandre Dumas made Catherine de Medici hide her poisons. Make sure you visit the **Musées de Beaux-Arts** while you're here; it occupies what was formerly the Royal Apartments. The museum houses paintings from the 16th to 19th centuries, including portraits of the royal families and a very explicit painting of John the Baptist's head on a platter. **The Musée Lapidaire** provides insight into recovered rock pieces of other 16th- and 17th-century châteaux located nearby. For a particularly magical tour of Blois, a horse-drawn carriage ride departs from inside the Château every half hour in the afternoon. A light show is produced on the grounds every evening between Apr.-Sept.

 # Follow the rue de Gambetta from the train station. The Château will be directly in front of you, with stairs leading to the courtyard on your right. i Guides available in English, but ring in advance to ensure someone will be there to lead it. $ Tickets can be combined with the Light Show and the Maison de la Magie. All 3 together cost €18, students €13, ages 6-17 €10. The Château alone €8, students €6.50, ages 6-17 €4. 🕘 Open daily Apr- June 9am-6:30pm; July-Aug 9am-7pm; Sept 9am-6:30pm; Oct 9am-6pm; Nov-Dec 9am-12:30pm and 1:30-5:30pm; Jan-Mar 9am-12:30pm and 1:30-5:30pm. Last entry 30min. before close.

all's fair in love and châteaux

If you thought that you had a complicated love life, check out the tale that accompanies the **Château Chenonceau** and **Diane de Poitier**s, the mistress of **Henry II**.

After her husband died, Diane became the most eligible bachelorette in Francis I's court, with her eyes set on the heir to the throne, Henry II. Despite his arranged marriage to **Catherine de Medici**, in 1533, Diane still pursued Henry and became his mistress shortly before the wedding. Rethink your normal ideas of gender roles and age differences in French affairs; Diane was 30, Henry was 14. Henry couldn't be bothered to sleep with his 18-year-old wife, what with puberty and all, and ended up spending all of his time with Diane.

Diane was ever the pragmatist though, and was not keen on being the reason France was without an heir to the throne. She agreed to give Catherine some pointers in the sack in exchange for the freedom to continue to be with Henry. On any given night, Henry would lie with Diane, leave to be with his wife, and then return to Diane. Whatever the cool trick Diane taught Catherine, it worked. Henry fathered several other children, including the future Francis II, Henry III, and Charles IX.

Henry still very much loved Diane and, unbeknownst to Catherine, gave Diane the **Château Chenonceau** in the Loire Valley. Pedophilia clearly has perks, and Catherine resided at Chenonceau until Henry's death. After Henry died in a jousting tournament however, Diane found herself the enemy of the mother of the king. Suddenly without a bargaining chip, Diane was strong-armed into trading Châteaux and downgrading to the lesser Château Anet, where Diane died 7 years after Henry's death (still not a bad deal).

CHAMBORD — CHÂTEAU

Chambord ☎02 54 50 40 00 🖥www.chambord.org

A truly royal experience awaits you as you grace the huge hallways and grand rooms of the former home of Louis XIV. The castle claims to be a "Place aux Rêves"; although Disney may soon want their slogan back, it's hard to deny that the Sun King's crib could take Cinderella's castle in the Magic Kingdom any day. The stunning Renaissance design includes a cool double-helix open staircase on which those who go up never actually cross paths with those going down. The stairs lead up to the chimney rooftops, which boast an exceptional view of the canal and the wildlife reserve below. To bring the château to life and keep the kids entertained, there is a 3D movie room which introduces the history and architecture of Chambord through computer animation. Summer activities on offer include a **Sound and Light show** and an **outdoor market** selling traditional products.

40min. from Blois by bus, departs from the Gare at 9am, 11:10am and 1:40pm. $ High-season €9.50, ages 18-25 €8; low-season €8.50/7. ⏰ Open daily from Apr to mid-July 9am-5:15pm; from mid-July to mid-Aug 9am-7:30pm; from mid-Aug to Sept 9am-6:15pm; Oct-Mar 9am-5:15pm. Sound and light shows from the end of June to mid-Sept.

CHEVERNY — CHÂTEAU

Cheverny ☎02 54 79 96 29 🖥www.château-cheverny.com

Cheverny was opened to the public in 1922, but those who are fans of TinTin may already know plenty about it— the Loire château heavily influenced

france

Moulinsort's creation of the series. Since Cheverny has such a strong connection with the Belgian character, a life-size Tintin exhibition is open for you to enjoy, which includes models, life-sized drawings, and a retelling of the story set in this mysterious château. For those less interested in the activities of a cartoon explorer, the château has extensive grounds which can be explored by boat and electric car, both of which are ideal for experiencing the wildlife living in the flora. Inside the château, the furnished rooms make Cheverny look more like a homey castle than a museum of architecture.

55min. from Blois by bus; departs from the Gare at 9am, 11:10am, and 1:40pm. $ €7.50. Open daily Apr-June 9:15am-6:15pm; July-Aug 9:15am-6:45pm; Sept 9:15am-6:15pm; Oct 9:45am-5:30pm; Nov-Mar 9:45-5pm.

AMBOISE CHÂTEAU

Amboise ☎02 47 57 00 98 www.château-amboise.com

This late 15th-century building was once considered France's most beautiful château, and it housed up to 4000 people during the 16th century. During the reign of Napoleon, most of the château was destroyed or sold off, and what you see now is the result of painstaking rebuilding renovations. Amboise château has a number of exhibits which change throughout the year; during the summer, it is also possible to embark on a guided tour of the underground tunnels, and enjoy the views of the castle by night on a guided "stroll under the stars." Unlike the royal history at most of the other Loire castles, the most interesting and historically fascinating past resident of Amboise was **Leonard da Vinci.** Leonardo's grave is in the **Chapelle Saint-Hubert,** just next the the château; pay your respects to this genius, and reflect on all the salacious revisions Dan Brown has added to his legacy. The rooms are decorated with Gothic and Renaissance furniture that demonstrates the castle's royal history. A deserving resting place for one of the world's greatest artist and academics.

The small town of Amboise is an hour's journey from Orléans by train (€14 every hr). The castle is in the centre-ville between rue Victor Hugo and rue de la Concorde. For free parking follow signs for "parking du château." $ €9.70, students €8.30, ages 7-14 €6.30, under 7 free. Open daily Mar 9am-5:30pm; Apr-June 9am-6:30pm; July-Aug 9am-7pm; Sept-Oct 9am-6pm; early Nov 9am-5:30pm; late Nov to Jan 9am-12:30pm and 2-4:45pm; Feb 9am-12:30pm and 1:30-5pm.

FOOD

Lots of little traditional restaurants can be found in and around the streets of **rue Saint-Lubin** and **place Poids de Rois.** Italian, Chinese, Indian and Greek cuisine can be found in the **place de la Resistance,** which faces the Loire river. You can pick up groceries from the **8 à Huit** at **11 rue de Commerce** *(Open M-Sa 8am-8pm, Su 8am-noon)* or the **Proxi Marché** at 6 Rue Henri Drussy. *(Open M 2:30-8pm, Tu-F 8:30am-1pm and 2:30-8am, Sa 9am-8pm, Su 9am-1pm).*

LE CASTELET 🍴 MEDIEVAL ❸

40 rue St-Lubin ☎02 54 74 66 09 castelet-restaurant@club-internet.fr

Set in a rustic old house, this restaurant offers medieval-themed dishes *(cider marinated chicken with seasonal vegetables; €13)* that will get you in the mood to see the local sights. The friendly owner will be happy to explain the origins and preparation of the dishes he serves. Vegetarian options available.

Situated on the corner of rue St-Lubin. From the bottom of the stairs to the Château, take a right. $ Set lunch menu €16, dinner €21. Open M-Tu noon-2pm and 7-10pm, Th-Sa noon-2pm and 7-10pm.

ESSENTIALS

Practicalities

- **TOURIST OFFICE:** 23 Pl. du Château *(☎02 54 90 41 41. 💻www.bloispaysde-chambord.com. ⏰Open daily June-Aug M-Sa 9am-7pm; Sept 9am-6pm; Oct-Mar 10am-5pm; Apr-May 9am-6pm.)*
- **BANKS:** ATMs available along rue du Commerce and along rue Denis Papin.
- **LAUNDROMAT:** 1 rue Jeanne d'Arc. *($Wash 8kg €5, dry €1 per 10min. ⏰ Open daily 7am-9pm.)*
- **PHARMACY: Pharmacie des 3 Clefs.** 30 rue Denis Papin. *(☎02 54 74 01 35. ⏰Open Tu-F 9am-7pm, Sa 8:30am-7pm.)*

Emergency!

- **POLICE:** 42 quai St-Jean *(☎02 54 90 09 00.)*
- **HOSPITAL: Centre Hospitalier de Blois.** Maile Pierre Charlot *(☎02 54 55 66 33. 💻www.ch-blois.fr.)*

Getting There

The train station is connected to the main Loire Valley stations as well as Paris. **Amboise** is a 20min train journey *(€6)* and **Tours** is a bit further along, taking about 40min. *(€10).* To reach Blois from **Angers,** which is further West, it takes around 1hr. 20min. *(€23)* and **Orléans** is a 30min. train journey east of Blois *(€7.50).* There are also connections to **Paris** which take under 2 hours *(€26).* The ticket office is open M-F 5:30am-8pm, Sa 8:30am-7pm, Su 7:30am-8pm.

Getting Around

Blois train station is within walking distance of the main city center and all the main sights can be reached on foot. Be prepared to walk up many sloping streets and sets of stairs to access different parts of Blois.

Buses are run by TUB *(☎02 54 78 15 66. 💻www.tub-blois.fr)* which depart from the station, going along the river in the direction of the Youth Hostel roughly every half an hour *(Line 4, €1.10)* and 24hr. **Taxis Radio** are stationed at the pl. de la Gare for longer journeys or for heading to the castles *(☎02 54 78 07 65)*. **Bike rental** is provided by Bike in Blois *(☎02 54 56 07 73)* and is located at the pl. de la Gare *($€9 per ½day, €14 per day, €30 per 3 days.)* There are dropoff points all along the Loire, including Orléans, Amboise, Villandry, Saumur, Angers, and Nantes. A leaflet with all dropoff points and contact details are available from the Tourist Office or the Bike Shop.

tours ☎0247

Tours (TOOR; pop. 142,000) is the liveliest of all the Loire cities; it may not have a grand château, but it can certainly be proud of its bustling nightlife. Historically, Tours lacks a local accent and is ultimately home to the "well spoken" of French society. Because of this, students from across the globe flock to Tours to polish their French-speaking skills, and a fellow student is never too far away. The grand Cathedral St-Gatien is one of the architectural highlights of the city, especially given that the Château de Tours has not withstood the test of time. Also home to some diverse museums and modern shopping complexes, Tours has a lot to offer in terms of history, sights, and entertainment for even the most jaded of travelers.

ORIENTATION

A lot of Tours was destroyed during WWII or has since been left to decay; only the *vielle-ville* really represents the true former glory of the town. Luckily, most of the activity in Tours centers on this area, which is very popular with students and younger crowds. **Place Jean Jaurès,** recognizable by its two grand fountains, marks the center of the city, with the Hotel de Ville positioned directly at its center; **bld. Heurteloup** runs east toward the train station, and **boulevard Bérlanger** runs west away from the center. Running north toward the banks of the Loire is the main shopping street **rue Nationale,** which used to be part of the main road and trade route between Paris and Spain; **avenue de Grammont** reaches south toward the Cher river. The majority of Tours's nightlife and restaurants are situated at **place Plumereau** in the northwest *vielle-ville*, which is a 10min. walk from pl. Jean Jaurès. Most of the sights and shopping complexes are closer to, or more east of, the center.

ACCOMMODATIONS

Tours is full of students, so finding a decently priced youth hostel is not difficult at all. For those looking for a bit more luxury, it is possible to bag some dirt-cheap hotel rooms (without actually getting the dirt). Booking in advance is a good idea, especially in the summer.

AUBERGE DE JEUNESSE "VIEUX TOURS" (HI) YOUTH HOSTEL [1]

5 rue Bretonneau ☎02 47 37 81 58 💻www.ajtours.org

A hop, skip, and jump from Tours's best bars and nightlife (so perhaps more of a hop, a trip, and a drunken stumble), this former university housing block is the best deal in the city and is always full of students. Many long-term residents stay here to learn French at the renowned university, and as a result this HI feels more like you're back in the college dorms than your usual youth hostel. All rooms come with a sink and some with a balcony.

A 15min. walk from the train station. Head west along bld. Heurteluop, through pl. Jean Jaurès, and onto bld. Bérlanger. From there, turn right onto rue Chanoineau, which turns into rue Bretonneau. The hostel will be at the far end of the road, on your left. ℹ *Breakfast included. Bedding provided, but bring your own towel. TV and common room/lounge area on 1st, 3rd, and 4th floors. All rooms with shared bath.* Ⓢ *Dorms €19. Required HI membership €7.* ⏰ *Reception 8am-noon and 5-8pm.*

SIGHTS 👁

Museum-hungry tourists should pick up the 👍**Carte Multi-Visite** at any museum for just €8. This little beauty gets you free entry into five of Tours's museums and a guided tour of the city. Just make sure to present the card to them at the museum.

👍 MUSÉE DE COMPAGNONNAGE — MUSEUM

8 rue Nationale ☎02 47 21 62 20 🖥www.ville-tours.fr

Imagine yourself as a child taking a few Lego bricks and building a small little house. Or building a gingerbread house with excessive amounts of frosting. Now, imagine if these designs you had in your head as a child were made in reality. And voila—welcome to the Musée de Compagnonnage, one of the most mind-blowing architectural wonders that you will ever experience. The building houses a semi-secret society of craftsmen from around the world who excel in all kinds of old-school artisanship; legend has it the society stems all the way back to King Solomon's construction of the Temple of Jerusalem. For any budding craftsman (and woman, of course), there is tough competition to ascend to the ranks of the Campagnons, as this museum demonstrates. Highlights include a medieval castle made entirely out of sugar cubes, a bird cage molded to look like a château, model versions of grand stairways, massive wooden clogs the size of a man, and a very impressive sculpture of the human hand. The museum is also connected to a **Museum of Wine,** which documents the history of wine-making in France.

➡ *From pl. Jean Jaurès, head straight down rue Nationale until you meet the Loire. The museum is on your right.* Ⓢ *€5, students and under 25 €3.30, under 12 free.* ⏰ *Open daily June 4-Sept M 9am-12:30pm and 2-6pm, W-Su 9am-12:30pm and 2-6pm.*

👍 CATHÉDRALE SAINT-GATIEN — MUSEUM

pl. de la Cathédrale ☎02 47 70 21 00

After getting the French government on its side, this renovated 14th-century building once again rules the skyline of Tours. The highlight of this Gothic cathedral is undoubtedly its intricate stained-glass windows, which pattern the the floor of the cathedral with fragments of rainbow-colored light. Even more beautiful than the windows, however, is the choir which sings during Sunday morning mass *(11am).* The cathedral is the final resting place for the children of Charles VII, and a very interesting 16th-century sculpture marks their tomb. A visit to the *Psalette* cloister is also a definite must for this sight; not only does it highlight the mix of styles present in the building, but there is also a Gothic library and early Renaissance records office.

➡ *From the train station, head east along bld. Heurteloup and take a left onto rue Jules Simon. The cathedral is just past the Musée des Beaux Arts on the right.* Ⓢ *Free.* ⏰ *Cathedral open daily June-Sept 9:30am-12:30pm and 2-6pm; Oct-Mar 9:30am-12:30pm and 2-5pm; Apr-May 10am-12:30pm and 2-5:30pm. Cloister open daily May-Aug 9:30am-12:30pm and 2-5:30pm; Sept-Mar M 2-5:30pm, T-Sa 9:30am-12:30pm and 2-5:30pm, Su 2-5:30pm; Apr daily 10am-12:30pm and 2-5:30pm.*

CHÂTEAUX

Getting to and from the châteaux of the Loire can prove difficult, as they are not well served by public transportation. The cheapest option, which offers some freedom, is to hire a bike and ride to the châteaux. **Détours de Loire** *(☎02 47 61 22 23 🖥www.locationdevelos.com)* can provide you with a bike and a map, all for just €14 per day.

But getting to and from more than two châteaux in a day by bike will prove difficult. The most freedom and ease is gained from hiring a car at a place like **Avis** *(in the train station ☎02 47 20 53 27)*, but the prices are often prohibitive for the student traveler (upwards of €120 per day). Fortunately, many companies provide plush minibuses which offer half-day and whole-day trips to the châteaux, departing from the tourist office at 9am or 1pm. Some possible choices are **Touraine Evasion** *(☎06 07 39 13 31* ▣*www.tourevasion.com.* Ⓢ *½ day €19-33, full day €44-51.),* **Quart de Tours** *(☎06 30 65 52 01* ▣*www. quartdetours.com* Ⓢ *½ day €21-34, full day €45-50.),*

CHENONCEAU

⊛& CHÂTEAU

Château de Chenonceau　　　　　☎02 47 23 90 07 ▣www.chenonceau.com

The best known of the Loire châteaux, Chenonceau is an incredibly beautiful sight, with Renaissance-era arches that stretch over the Cher River and gardens that expand around the moat. Chenonceau, more so than any of the other châteaux in the area, is a "lady's castle," due to the influence of women on its architectural innovations, restoration, and further development. The original owner, Thomas Bohier, handed over the design of the château to his wife, Katherine, while he was away during the Italian Wars (1513-21). Due to official court rules, Henri II's mistress, Diane de Poitier, was given control of the building in 1547, to which she added luxurious gardens and a bridge that remain to this day. After the death of Henri II, his wife, Catherine de Medici, forced Diane out and designed her own gardens to assert her superiority above her dead husband's mistress.

For a more rural look at the château, follow the pedestrian route that takes you past a donkey field, a flower garden, and a 16th-century farm. The Master Gallery inside Chenonceau houses some stunning portraits, including works by Rubens and Tinoretto; the adjoining wax museum honors exceptional women throughout history. For a beautiful, and potentially wet, view of the river, you can hire a boat during the summer and make a splash on the current of the Cher. The truly magical ▣**Night Walk** in the summer, set to the music of Arcangelo Corelli, allows you to view the château in full illumination.

✈ *Trains run to Chenonceau from Tours every 1½hr.; the trip lasts 30min. The station is by the entrance to the château.* ℹ *Night Walks June F-Su 9:30-11pm; July-Aug nightly 9:30-11pm.* Ⓢ *€10.50, students and under 18 €8.* ☼ *Open daily Apr-May 9am-7pm; June 9am-7:30pm; July-Aug 9am-8pm; Sept 9am-7:30pm; Oct 9am-6:30pm; Nov-Jan 9:30am-5pm; Feb to mid-Mar 9:30am-6pm; late Mar 9:30am-7pm.*

VILLANDRY

⊛& CHÂTEAU

Château de Villandry　　　　　　☎02 47 50 02 09 ▣www.châteauvillandry.com

Built in 1536, Villandry was the last Renaissance château to be built in the Loire but rests on the foundations of a former medieval castle. The only remains of the medieval influence nowadays are the moat that surrounds the château and the gardens. Although the château is an impressive Renaissance building, the real beauty of Villandry comes from its Italian gardens, which are composed of over 125,000 flowers and 85,000 vegetables. For those on a romantic tour of the Loire châteaux, the Ornamental Garden is a must, with its floral representation of the four types of love: Tender Love, Passionate Love, Fickle Love, and Tragic Love. The maze in the Sun Garden is designed to offer a journey of self-discovery and spiritual fulfillment, although unlike the Greek labyrinths it was modeled after, this maze has no dead-ends.

Inside the château, the most impressive sight is the ceiling of the Oriental drawing room, which actually comes from the Maquedaducal Palace in Toledo, Spain. The room is surrounded by artwork and statues which the 20th-century owners of the château, the Carvallo family, built up over the century. Make sure you ascend to the ▣**keep,** which provides a phenomenal bird's-eye view of the gardens below you. The Cher and the Loire are visible through the valleys and forest that surround the château.

Follow the D7 west of Tours. Villandry is approx. 15km from Tours. $ Château and gardens €9, students and under 18 €5, under 8 free. Gardens only €6, students and under 18 €3.50, under 8 free. Open Mar 9am-5:30pm; June 9am-6pm, July-Aug 9am-6:30pm; Sept-Oct 9am-6pm; first half of Nov 9am-5pm; mid-Dec to early Jan 9:30am-4:30pm.

FOOD

For students on a budget, Tours is a dream come true. Almost every restaurant in town will try to entice you with a decently priced set lunch menu *(usually €11-20)*. The restaurants along **rue Colbert** and **pl. Plumereau** are by far the least expensive and most popular, although it's possible to find some good bargains elsewhere. The indoor food market at **places des Halles** *(Open M-Sa 7am-7:30pm.)* can fix you up with fresh produce to make your own meals, and during the summer the market extends outside Wednesday and Saturday mornings *(7am-noon)*. The square in front of the tourist office has a weekly **marché traditionnel** *(Tu 8am-noon)*, where you can pick up typical traditional cheeses, meats, and vegetables. For daily groceries and everyday food, try the **ATAC** by the train station *(5 pl. du Maréchal Leclerc. Open M-Sa 7:30am-8pm)* or the **Monoprix** supermarket. *(63 rue Nationale Open M-Sa 9am-8:30pm.)*

MAMIE BIGOUDE — CRÊPERIE 2

22 rue Châteauneuf ☎02 47 64 53 85

It looks like a house Grandma would build. But grandmas are always a little bit crazy, and Mamie Bigoude is no different; we're just grateful she left out the cats. Enter into her *maison*, which is complete with a kitchen, living room, lounge, garden, bedroom, and even a bathroom for you to eat in (don't worry, there are other bathrooms for when you need *pipi;* they are tastefully decorated with 1960s French advertisements). The restaurant serves crêpes, galletes, and salads named after famous figures. Fancy a bite of Harry Potter? Or a nibble on TinTin, perhaps? And let's not even get into the Chuck Berry salad. For the children, there is even a supervised play area, and for the adults there is enough humor hidden around the house to keep you entertained.

From pl. Plumereau, take rue de Change southward, which leads to rue Châteauneuf. $ Plates €5-15. Open daily noon-2:30pm and 7-11pm.

NIGHTLIFE

The busiest and most popular location for students is around **pl. Plumereau,** where bars, restaurants, and a few clubs fill up with students both inside and outside during the summer months. The streets leading off the *place* are full of pubs and bars, especially the **rue du Commerce,** where finding an Irish pub is almost as easy as if you were in Dublin.

AU TEMPS DU ROIS — BAR

3 pl. de Plumereau ☎02 47 05 04 51

Au Temps du Rois opens up before most people in Tours are awake and stays open long after most people have gone to bed. Owned by two best friends for over 20 years, the bar is decorated with fascinating tidbits, including a pair of golden boots, old theater posters, mosaic tables, and a collection of Petit Robert from across the years. With clocks telling you the time for Tours, Paris, London, New York City, and Japan, this bar manages to combine a traditional French feel with that of the modern world, making it a favorite with Tours's international and French student scene. They've had some very renowned customers in the past, including Mick Jagger, who signed the bar's guestbook. Perhaps second behind Mick was "Miss Mexico 2000," who before conquering the Mexican beauty world used to pull pints here on a Sunday evening when she lived in Tours.

Northeast corner of p. Plumereau. $ All drinks €2.50-7. Open daily 8:30am-2am.

LA GUINGUETTE BAR, RESTAURANT

This very bohemian hangout has neither a fixed address nor a telephone number, but that's because it's on the banks of the Loire river. Situated just by Pont Wilson, this outdoor bar and restaurant was founded around 5 years ago to combat the problem of the homeless not having anywhere to go. Now, the students of Tours populate the banks of the Loire in the summer and drink down beer, wines, and cocktails at La Guinguette while chilling to live music and sitting in chairs susupended from a tree or at the helm of a wooden boat. On summer weekends the riverside hangout is packed with an extremely diverse clientele, and everyone is made to feel welcome; just be careful when returning to the city at the end of the night. Walking home in groups is advisable.

Down the steps by Pont Wilson, at the bottom of rue Nationale. $ Drinks €3-8. Open M-Th 11am-midnight, F-Sa 11am-2am, Su 11am-midnight.

ESSENTIALS

Practicalities

- **TOURIST OFFICE:** 78-82 rue Bernard Palissy *(☎02 47 70 37 37 www.ligeris.com Open daily mid Apr-mid Oct M-Sa 8:30am-7pm, Su 10am-12:30pm and 2:30-5pm; mid Oct-mid Apr M-Sa 9am-12:30pm and 1:30-6pm, Su 10am-1pm.)* If you're looking for a comprehensive **tour** of Tours, the tourist office can suggest a route for you, and provides a **train** for guided tours of the city. *($ €6, under 18 €3.)*
- **BANKS:** ATM machines along rue Nationale. **BNP Paribas** *(86 rue Nationale ☎08 92 70 57 05 Open M 2-6pm, Tu-F 9am-6pm, Sa 9am-12:30pm.)*
- **INTERNET ACCESS: Bureau d'Information Jeunesse (BIJ)** *(78-80 rue Michelet ☎02 47 64 69 13 $ 1hr. free internet access. Open M-Tu 1-6pm, W 10am-noon, Th-F 1-6pm.)* **Tourist Office.** *($ €0.50 per 15min.).* **Top Communications,** 68-70 rue du Grand Marché *(☎02 47 76 19 53 $ €0.50 per 15min., €2 per hr. Open daily 10am-midnight.)*
- **POST OFFICE:** Pl. bd Béranger *(☎02 47 60 34 05 Open M-F 8:30am-6:30pm, Sa 9am-5pm.)* Branch office at 92 rue Colbert.

Emergency!

- **POLICE:** 70-72 rue de Marceau *(☎02 47 33 80 69).*
- **HOSPITAL: Centre Hospatilier Régional.** 2 bld. Tonnellé *(☎02 47 47 47 47).*

Getting There

The **train station** at Tours is one of the busiest in the Loire Valley. There are connections to most of the towns and cities of the Loire; you can reach Tours from **Orléans** in 1hr., and trains run frequently roughly every 30min. *(€17).* **Blois** can be reached on the same train in just over 30min. *(€10).* Tours is connected to **Paris Est** *($ €46. 1½hr.)* by a high speed train. **Bordeaux** connects directly with Tours in under 3hrs *(€50).*

Getting Around

Tours can be easily traveled on foot. Be warned though: what you think is a pedestrian-only zone may very quickly become a road. To reach places farther south, east, or west of Tours, the bus company **Filbleau** *(9 rue Michelet. ☎02 47 66 70 70 Open M-F 7:30am-7pm, Sa 10am-5pm.)* runs daily services. Bus tickets are bought on the bus, and cost €1.25 for a 1hr. ticket or €3.20 for a daypass. For those wishing to explore the Loire Valley by bike, the very helpful **Détours de Loire** can sort you out for €14 per day *(35 rue Charles Giles ☎02 47 61 22 23 www.locationdevelos.com).*

Finally, for travel once public transportation stops running (around 11pm), **Taxis Radio** run 24hr. from outside the train station at €1.40 per km during the day and €2.30 at night *(☎02 47 20 30 40).*

lyon   ☎04

Ultramodern, ultra-friendly, and undeniably gourmet, Lyon (lee-ohn; pop. 453,000) is more relaxed than Paris and claims a few more centuries of history. Its location at the confluence of the Rhône and Saône Rivers and along the Roman road between Italy and the Atlantic made Lyon an easy choice for the capital of Roman Gaul. Today, Lyon has shed its long-standing reputation as a gritty industrial city, emphasizing its beautiful parks, a modern financial sector, and a well-preserved Renaissance quarter. The city is best known as the stomping ground of world-renowned chefs Paul Bocuse and Georges Blanc and as an incubator of contemporary culinary genius.

ORIENTATION

Like Paris, Lyon is split into neighborhoods that have then been numbered, and are often referred to by their number (1èr, 2ème, etc.) For the purposes of this guide, we've split Lyon into four main areas: Presqu'ile, Vieux Lyon, Croix-Rousse and Terreaux. All these areas are west of the Rhône river. To the east of the Rhône, the only landmark of note is the main train station, **Gare Part-Dieu.** The Rhône and the Saône split Lyon into three sections, with the Vieux Lyon on the far west, Croix Rousse to the far north of the center section, Terreaux to the center, and Presqu'ile to the South of the center.

Vieux Lyon

Vieux Lyon is the most beautiful and oldest part of city, with its cobbled streets, religious buildings, and large parks. The Metro stop ⓂVieux Lyon is in the center of the old town, near the Cathedral Saint Jean. The River Saône is to the east; the busy pedestrian streets of **rue du Boeuf, rue Saint Jean,** and **Place du Change** run north to south, and are lined with traditional restaurants. The Funicular at the Metro stop takes you to the top of the Fourvière, where the **Basilica Nôtre Dame de Fourvière** is located with the HI hostel at Saint-Jean.

Croix-Rousse

Croix-Rousse is at the north of the city and perched on top of a very large hill. Head here for some wonderful views of Lyon, and to explore the older buildings of the city, the **Traboulles** and the **La Maison des Canuts.** From the Metro Stop (ⓂCroix-Rousse), **Grand Rue de la Croix Rousse** runs northwards, passing many small shops, boutiques, and La Maison des Canuts. Head eastwards to **rue d'Austerlitz** for some amazing views of the river below and the expansive parks to the northeast; this area is also a hotbed of some brasseries and cafes, so stop and grab a drink before climbing down the hundreds of stairs.

Terreaux

Place des Terreaux (ⓂHôtel de Ville) is to the north of the city center, and mainly in the 1èr. The area is one of the most diverse in Lyon, and hosts the breathtaking buildings of the Hôtel de Ville and the Musée Beaux Arts. From Place Terreaux three streets run southwards; **rue Chenavard** and **rue Herriot** which both lead to **Place des Jacobins,** while **rue de la République** runs to **Place de la République.** North of the square, up the hilly roads, is the Croix Rousse area.

Presqu'ile

The center of Lyon is focussed around **Place Bellecour,** where you will find the tourist office and lots of restaurants around the square. **Rue Herriot** and **rue de la République** both run from the northeast corner of Place Bellecour, which has a lot of shops and cafes along them. **Rue Victor Hugo** runs southwards from the square towards **Place Ampère,** around which you will find a lot of budget hotels close to train station Gare de Perrache. **Place de la République** and **Place des Jacobins,** both north of Place Bellecour, have fountains, restaurants, and shops around them and are useful for orientating yourself.

ACCOMMODATIONS

Most student travelers heading to Lyon check into the only hostel available in Vieux Lyon; consequentially, it can book up pretty fast. If you can't get into the hostel, or if you're in search of more comfortable accommodations, you can find some very quaint and charming places in the city's center, where a single room averages at €40-60.

Vieux Lyon and Presqu'ile

AJ DU VIEUX LYON
🏨 ◆(ᴨ) HOSTEL ❶

41-45, montée du Chemin Neuf   ☎04 78 15 05 50 💻www.fuaj.org

After conquering the massive hill in Vieux Lyon you may be ready to collapse (remember, there *is* a cable car), but the views you get from the HI Hostel in Vieux Lyon are worth the massive climb any day. Sitting on the terrace of the hostel you see the whole city expanding below you, cut by the two rivers, and during the summer you can lounge out and top up your tan. As this is the only hostel in the area, it's full of fellow students. If you can, try and request a room with a view of the city.

☀ ⓜVieux Lyon. Walk up the hill or, take the Funicular to Pl. Saint-Jean. *i* Breakfast and sheets included. Bring your own towel. ⑤ 6-bed dorms €18. ☒ Reception 7am-1pm, 2-8pm, and 9pm-1am.

HÔTEL DE THÉÂTRE
◆ ❖(ᴨ) HOTEL ❸

10 rue de Savoie   ☎04 78 42 33 32 💻www.hotel-du-theatre.fr

The owners of this very homey hotel open up their radiant rooms for rent. The reception area has a petite dining area, complete with wooden floors and a very authentic-looking leather sofa, while the standard rooms are a good size and feel very homey. For those with a few extra euro, the superior rooms are bigger, more spacious, and very plush, promising a peaceful night's sleep in the center of Lyon.

☀ ⓜBellecour *i* Breakfast €6. ⑤ Singles €59-64; doubles €64-70. ☒ Reception open 7am-11pm.

Terreaux

HOTEL LE BOULEVARDIER
◆ ❖(ᴨ) HOTEL ❸

5 rue Fromagerie   ☎04 78 28 48 72 💻www.leboulevardier.fr

This quirky hotel is definitely worth checking out if you want a more interesting stay in Lyon. Compared to the standard offerings in the city center, Hotel le Boulevardier is one of the more eclectic (and good value) places to stay, from the colorful clocks covering the bar wall downstairs, to the old tennis rackets and golf clubs lining the hallways, to the modern art guiding you up the steep staircase to the rooms. The beds themselves are even covered with zany but tasteful covers like pink and green stripes or green polka dots.

☀ ⓜCordeliers. *i* Breakfast €6. ⑤ Singles €41-51; doubles €47-53; triples €62; quads €74. ☒ Reception open from 7am.

HÔTEL IRIS
◆ HOTEL ❸

36 rue d l'Arbre Sec   ☎04 78 39 93 80 💻www.hoteliris.fr

The owner of this hotel personally ensures that the rooms are cleaned to the utmost in this hotel, which used to be a convent. The history of the building shines through, as the high vaulted ceilings make rooms feel much larger than they actually are. Potted plants contribute to an earthy and rather Mediterranean atmosphere for the place.

☀ ⓜHôtel de Ville *i* Breakfast €6. ⑤ Singles €55; doubles €60. ☒ Reception 7am-8pm.

lyon • accommodations

SIGHTS

Vieux Lyon

Vieux Lyon is by far the most beautiful part of the city, with its cobbled streets, the Fourvière Hill, and mazes of streets and spiral staircases. For a more structured tour the Tourist Office provides a guide upon request.

⚑ BASILIQUE NOTRE DAME DE FOURVIÈRE   ⬤ BASILICA

8 pl. Fourvière   ☎04 78 25 86 19 🖵www.lyon-fourviere.com

Despite being built just over 100 years ago and gaining its status as a Basilica in 1897, the Basilica (known in English as *Our Lady of Forvière*) is the crown of the skyline of Lyon. Locals call it *un éléphant renversé*, because the white marble facade makes it look like Dumbo has fallen over at the top of the hill. The beauty of the building is clear as you approach from below, but the closer you get, the more the real spectacles begin to emerge. Inside, there is a fantastic painting dedicated to the Virgin Mary, for whom the Basilica was named as thanks for her protection during the Franco-Prussian Wars. The **Tour de l'Observatoire** is open from July-Sept and offers a fantastic panaromic view of the city below. For a free view, head to the back of the basilica and gaze at Lyons sprawling below. Make sure you descend via the Chemin du Rosaire for a peaceful walk through a sloping park.

⚑ Ⓜ️*Vieux Lyon. Climb the hill until you reach the top, or take the Funicular from Vieux Lyon to Fourvière.* **i** *Two tours of Tour de l'Observatoire are offered. The 45min. short tour takes you up 188 steps of the tower. The 1½hr. long tour takes you up the full 466 steps of the tower.* ⓢ *Basilica free. Short tour €3, under 12 €1.50. Long tour €5, under 12 €3.* 🕐 *Chapel open daily 7am-7pm. Basilica open daily 8am-7pm. Tours July-Sept daily 2:30pm, 4pm.*

lyon: 2000 years and counting

Over the course of two millennia, Lyon has managed to preserve sites from Roman times all the way through the Renaissance. It's your one-stop history tour of Europe in France:

43 BCE to 395 CE: Get a taste of Europe under the iron fist of the Romans by visiting the **Fourvière District**. The original site of the first Roman settlement Lugdunum, you can still visit the amphitheater and basillica, which has been converted to a Catholic Church now featuring a giant golden statue of the Virgin Mary.

12th-16th Centuries: The Middle Ages still very much exist in this district, with narrow streets and open market squares that offered a haven for painters and booksellers on the **Rue Mercière** in the 15th and 16th centuries. Visit the Museum of Printing, and you'll find that no one could read back then.

Renaissance: In Vieux-Lyon, the 5th arrondissement is separated into three sections, all bearring the name of a Saint. St. Paul section is home to expensive hotels, given the original inhabitants were bankers; St. George has corridors and secret passageways that confound unsuspecting tourists and St. Jean is, appropriately, the focus of political power in Lyon.

Late Renaissance 17th–18th Centuries: The "Slopes of **Croix Rousse**" are home to the original European artisan: the silk spinner. In the **Place Tolozan**, you can find the still standing silk industry building, built in the 17th century, and old silk storage buildings that are connected by a series of passageways built by secretive silk workers.

MUSÉE GALLO-ROMAINS AND ARCHEOLOGICAL SITE   RUINS
17 rue Cléberg   ☎04 72 38 49 30 ▨www.musées-gallo-romains.com

Lyon, or "Lugunum," as it was known to the Romans 2000 years ago, was one of the most important cities in the Empire back in the day. The top of this hill was the cultural hub for the city, with amphitheaters and other meeting points for the locals. These beautifully preserved ruins can now be explored and exploited for the great view of the city below. Even more exciting is the fact that the Théatre Romain is used for concerts; Vampire Weekend, Iggy Pop, and REM have all performed here. To learn more about the history of the archaeological site and discover more remains from Lugunum, head to the museum at the top of the site.

⚑ ⓂVieux Lyon. Climb the hill and take a right at the Archéologique. Ⓢ Archaeological site free. Museum €4, students €2.50, under 18 free. 🕐 Ruins open daily Apr 15th-Sept 15th 7am-9pm; Sept 16th-April 14th 7am-7pm. Museum open Tu-Su 10am-6pm.

CATHÉDRALE SAINT-JEAN   CATHEDRAL
Place Saint Jean

Lyon's Cathedral isn't as stunning as the other religious buildings that dominate French cities, but the interesting quirks of this place are worth checking out. The stained-glass window at the east side of the building depicts Lucifer's rejection from Heaven, with Lucifer displayed as a ▧dragon. Not all the windows in the cathedral are religious. During the Nazi's retreat in 1944 some of the windows were destroyed, and have since been replaced with non-religious abstract designs. The 14th-century ▧Astrological Clock chimes several times a day, and features popping automatons that reenact the Annunciation.

⚑ ⓂVieux Lyon Ⓢ Free. 🕐 Open daily M-F 8am-noon and 2-7:30pm, Sa-Su 2-5pm.

Croix-Rousse

LA MAISON DES CANUTS
🎨 MUSEUM

10-12 rue d'Ivry   🖥www.maisondescanuts.com

At the top of the Croix Rousse area (up a very steep set of stairs; you may want to take the Metro) is the location of Lyon's silk haydays. Lyon dominated silk production in Europe for centuries, and in La Maison des Canuts you can have a guided look at how to make silk the old-fashioned way. There's also a free exhibit with information on the history of the city's silk industry; the adjoining shop sells handmade silk scarves, ties, and handkerchiefs, which are expensive but impressive *(handkerchiefs €8.50).*

🚇 Ⓜ*Croix Rousse. Take the Metro from pl. Terreaux.* Ⓢ *Shop and exhibition free. Tours €6, students and under 25€3, under 12 free.* 🕐 *Guided tours daily 11am and 1:30pm; groups can call to arrange a tour.*

Terreaux

MUSEÉ DES BEAUX ARTS
🎨 MUSEUM

20 Place des Terreaux   ☎04 72 10 17 40 🖥www.mba-lyon.fr

Located in the ornate Palais St Pierre, the museum's exhibits range from Egyptian mummies and hieroglyphics to the Ancient Roman bronze models of deities to 14th- and 15th-century Italian artwork. The first floor features an Islamic art collection with some beautiful pieces. Ascend the grand marble staircase to explore artwork from the 20th century, including some zany Picasso pieces. Classical pieces by Monet and Boucher are in the 15th- to 19th-century section, with a big collection of religious artwork further along the floor. Make sure you check out the gardens of Palais St Pierre, which have sculptures by Rodin and Bourdelle.

🚇 Ⓜ*Hôtel de Ville.* Ⓢ *€7, students and under 26 free. Audio tour €3, under 26 and students free.* 🕐 *Open M 10am-6pm, W-Th 10am-6pm, F 10:30am-6pm, Sa-Su 10am-6pm.*

PLACE DES TERREAUX
♿ SQUARE

Heads might roll when you see this square; it was used as a place of guillotine beheadings during the French Revolution. Of course, with the Musée des Beaux Arts on one side and the Hôtel de Ville on the other, no one would suspect that morbid history today. On the far north side is a grand fountain built by Frédéric-Auguste Bartholdi; it used to belong in Bordeaux, but the mayor was unable to afford its upkeep, so in 1890 the mayor of Lyon bought it and transported it to his own city center. The four horses bursting out of the water represent the four tributaries of the Saône river that runs through Lyon.

🚇 Ⓜ*Hôtel de Ville.*

Presqu'ile

MUSÉE DES TISSUS
🎨 MUSEUM

34 rue de la Charité   ☎04 78 38 42 00 🖥www.musee-des-tissus.com

This museum is more for those who like their fashion, but it's not all Gaga and Chanel here. From 4000 year old Egyptian Tunics and fashions from the Ottoman Empire to French fashion from a few years ago, this museum provides a long history of what we wear and why we wear it. At the entrance, check out the family tree that maps a fierce history of fashion. Who knew that your jeggings have ancient Chinese and Italian roots.

🚇 Ⓜ*Ampère Victor Hugo.* Ⓢ *€5.50, students and under 26 €3.* 🕐 *Open Tu-Su 10am-5:30pm.*

FOOD

Lyon is the home of high quality and top notch French cuisine and many will say that this is the city where you will find traditional food alongside modern fusions. Walking through the cobbled streets, you will see areas lined with traditional *bouchons*—little

france

restaurants that serve dishes such as *andouillette* (sausage in a variety of sauces), duck, snails, and frog legs. Most restaurants are accessible on a budget, and every restaurant offers daily set menus; you can expect to pay anything from €12 for set menus, and the more expensive (but oh-so-worth-it) set menus are often worth the splurge. Fast-food options can be found around many squares in the center and just off of Pl. des Terreaux, along with many kebab joints along **rue d'Algérie.** Daily food markets appear along the banks of the Saône from 8am-1pm hawking wares from fruits and vegetables to cheeses and other locally sourced produce.

Vieux Lyon

Vieux Lyon's cobbled streets are lined with *bouchons* and little alcoves housing all types of restaurants. Strolling along **rue Saint Jean** and the little streets off here will throw up many delightful places to sample the local cuisine.

LE PETIT GLOUTON

CRÊPERIE, LYONNAISE ❷

56 rue Saint Jean ☎04 78 37 30 10

This cheery little restaurant feels very homey, with its checkered tablecloths and attentive waiters. If you're in a hurry and don't want to sit down, don't fret— you can grab a cheap crêpe to go *(€3-€5.55)*, and watch as the man makes it in front of you. For a more indulgent meal, we recommend the salmon *(€12)*, or a special pork cooked in a mustrad sauce *(€14.20)*. Their three-course set menu is cheaper than those at other restaurants in the area, but may be slightly less plentiful than other offerings *(€14.25)*.

✚ ⓂVieux Lyon. *rue St Jean runs north from the Metro station* Ⓢ *Meals €10-15. Crêpes €3-5.55.* Ⓩ *Open daily 11:30am-11:30pm.*

LES PAVES DE SAINT JEAN

BOUCHON ❸

23 rue Saint Jean ☎04 78 42 25 13

This traditional *bouchon* offers cheaper set menus than the other restaurants in the area but without sacrificing the standard of the food. The restaurant boasts dishes such as cold pork meats, *andouillette*, and duck in pepper sauce. The high-ceilinged dining area makes it feel like the family are serving you dinner in their own kitchen, and the food is served quickly but still feels as if it's been freshly prepared.

✚ ⓂVieux Lyon. Ⓢ *Set menus €12.50-21. Meats €10-15. Fish €10-16.* Ⓩ *Open daily noon-2pm and 6:30-10:30pm.*

LIBRAIRIE CULTURE CAFÉ

CAFE ❶

16 quai de Bondy ☎04 78 25 56 19 🖳www.book-livre.com

The old owner of this little bookshop has doubled it up as a "culture café," providing a great place to grab a drink, read a book, and watch the locals go by. With a view of the river, this cafe is a great little place to rest your feet, but make sure you explore the crypt of books under the first floor. The menu boasts a great range of 25 teas *(€3 each)*.

✚Ⓜ Vieux Lyon. Ⓢ *Drinks €1.60-3.* Ⓩ *Open daily 10:30am-7:30pm.*

TERRE ADÉLICE

ICE CREAM ❶

1 Place de la Baleine ☎04 78 03 51 84 🖳www.terre-adelice.fr

Terre Adélice is a glacier with a difference—they specialize in bio-ice cream and sorbets. This ice cream is locally made in the Lyon area, and comes in 200 different flavors (though not all of them are served at the same time), including pear sorbet, clementine sorbet, and caramel ice cream.

✚ ⓂVieux Lyon. *On the corner along rue Saint Jean.* Ⓢ *1 scoop €2.30.* Ⓩ *Open daily noon-midnight.*

lyon · food

Croix-Rousse and Terreaux

Rue Austerlitz is lined with brasseries, which are usually open from 10am until late; entrees generally start at €10. **Place Croix Rousse** features lots of boulangeries and supermarkets for the real cheapskates among you. Head down the hill into the Terreaux area for a great selection of traditional and modern cuisine.

L'ESPRESS'O'
39 rue Paul Chenavard

✈((ᵗ))✠ PIZZA, PASTA ❷

☎04 78 91 86 64

Despite a plethora of expensive set menus that rarely dip below €15, L'Espress'o' offers slightly cheaper options in heaping portions. During the week, you can get a steak and chips *(€8)*, and for an extra €2 you can add a drink and a coffee. The traditional pizza and pasta offerings will fill you up nicely if you'd rather not eat steak, and the outside terrace opposite the restaurant is perfect for getting some sun.

✦ Ⓜ*Cordeliers*. ⑤ *Pizza and pasta €9-12. Set menu €13.50.* ⏲ *Open daily 8am-10pm.*

LE NORD
18 rue Neuve

✦✠ LYONNAIS ❸

☎04 72 10 69 69

Although the food is slightly more expensive, heading north will give you some of the best Lyonnais cuisine available, from snails to *quenelle*. Although splurging on a meal here may break your budget, the three-course set menu *(€23)* gives you a rather lavish selection of Lyonnais cuisine. Grab a seat on their covered terrace, complete with faux stained-glass windows.

✦ Ⓜ*Hôtel de Ville*. ⑤ *Meat entrees €15-26, 2-course set menu €20, 3-course set menu €23.* ⏲ *Open daily noon-2:30pm and 7:30-11pm.*

Presqu'ile

The center of Lyon is great for cheap eats and traditional Lyonnais cuisine. Restaurants line **rue Mercière** and **rue des Marronniers** all boast set menus *(€14-25)*, where you will find typical dishes from the south of France. Splurging is not necessarily a bad thing here, as you get what you pay for—spending a few extra euro on dinner will give you a very tasty dining experience.

LA CLÉANOA
33 rue Mercière

✦✠ TRADITIONAL ❸

☎04 78 37 78 37

Although their set menus are slightly more expensive than some of the others in the area, this ultra modern restaurant serves some mouthwatering dishes. This is one of those places where dishing out a little extra pays off. The duck dressed in lavender sauce and pork with peppercorn sauce may cost you a bit more, but you won't care about the damage to your wallet when the immaculate dishes are sizzling in front of you.

✦ Ⓜ*Cordeliers*. *i English menu translations.* ⑤ *Set menus €20-26. Lunch menu €12. Meats €14-20.* ⏲*Open daily noon-2pm and 7-11pm.*

LA MARONNIER
5 rue des Marronniers

✦✠ LYONNAIS ❸

☎04 78 37 30 09

This homey *bouchon* serves Lyonnais cuisine of all varieties. The helpful staff makes you feel like you're eating in someone's house rather than a restaurant. A brilliant three-course menu *(€14)* allows you to choose from several pork dishes, including a sausage in a red wine that which comes complete with potatoes. If you're after a more indulgent cuisine, there is a more expensive set menu giving you a choice of snails, mullet, and duck liver *foie gras*.

✦ Ⓜ*Bellecour*. ⑤ *Set menus €14-23. Meat €8.50-18.* ⏲ *Open M 6-11pm, W-Su 6-11pm.*

CHEZ MARIE-DANIELLE
29 rue des Remparts d'Ainay

✦✠ BOUCHON ❸

☎04 78 37 65 60

Pictures of the Queen of England and Prince Charles indicate which toilet is for the *femmes* and which is for the *hommes* in the quirky Chez Marie. The small restaurant gives off a relaxed vibe, and you don't need to own your own island to pay for your meal. Everyone is made welcome by the staff, even the traveler in shorts and flip-flops. A lot of the dishes are served the "Marie-Danielle way," with a traditional flare to the cooking. Their beef steaks, covered in creamy and sauces, are popular and tasty (€15-€18).

✚ ⓂAmère Victor Hugo. Ⓢ Lunch menu €16. Meat entrees €14-22. ⓩ Open M-F noon-2pm and 7:30-10pm.

NIGHTLIFE

With Irish, English and Scottish pubs in the Vieux Lyon area, busy and noisy boat bars and clubs along the river, cocktail bars and classy establishments near the center, and rum bars specializing in rum cocktails, Lyon's nightlife scene has something for everyone and a bit of everything. A more relaxed scene can be found by sipping wine after your dinner, outside on one of the brasseries' terraces until the early hours.

LE PERROQUET BOURRÉ ●✦ᵞ RUM BAR

18 rue Ste Catherine   ☎06 68 68 03 12 ▣www.perroquetbourre.com

After having a few of the bar's famous cocktails ("Sex'n'Fresh," anyone?), you'll be stumbling on to the next bar like a *perroquet bourré* (drunken parrot). The dancing barmen chuck, throw, toss, and mix the cocktails in time with the music; if they like the looks of you you might even get in on their special handshake. If you're lucky, you might get a glowstick and some candy sweets in your cocktail.

✚ ⓂHôtel de Ville. Ⓢ Rum shots €2-5, cocktails €5-7. ⓩ Open daily 6pm-1am.

THE SHAMROCK ✦ᵞ IRISH PUB

15 rue Ste Catherine

Although this is an Irish pub, complete with the Guiness signs outside, a step inside the ▣Shamrock will quickly remind you that you're in Lyon. Inside the small room with skateboards and buckets hanging from the ceiling, locals show off their musical talents in jam sessions on Wednesdays and jazz nights on Mondays. The back room offers a more chill atmosphere, with old leather sofas where students gather to drink a large bowl of cocktails (€20), or work through a meter of shots (€16). The place can get pretty crowded, though, so be prepared to tussle to get to the bar.

✚ ⓂHôtel de Ville. Ⓢ Beer €2-6. Cocktails €6.50. ⓩ Open daily 7:50pm-late.

SIRIUS ●ᵞ BAR

4 Quai Augagneur

With treasure chests hanging from the top of the boat, a quirky collection of nets and diving suits, and even barrels for bar tables, this boat bar really gets in touch with its pirate side. Order a mojito complete with a glowstick (€8), or try the special "secret" punch that comes in bottles (€10). As the boat gets busier, the heat turns up, so expect to get sweaty on the dance floor in the early hours on the boat.

✚ ⓂCordeliers. Over pont Lafayette and along the waterfront. Ⓢ Drinks €3-10. ⓩ Open daily 9pm-3am.

AYERS ROCK CAFÉ ●ᵞ ROCK BAR

2 rue Désirée   ☎08 20 32 02 03 ▣www.ayersrockcafe.com

No, not *that* Ayers. With music so loud that the bartenders can only just hear your order, Ayers really isn't the place to come for a chat, but it's definitely the place if you're in the mood for a busy and wicked night of loud music, excited barmen, and Australian fun. Bouncers (and a fake kangaroo) guard the door on weekends when it gets busy, so you may have to dress to impress if you want to get in. Watch in awe as the barmen juggle bottles, balance glasses on their arms, and serve you a cocktail or beer with a few other party tricks they've learned along the way. They occasionally bang on the lights that hang above them, so mind your head!

✠ Ⓜ*Hôtel de Ville.* Ⓢ *Beer €3-6. Cocktails €6.50.* ☾ *Open daily 8pm-3am.*

THE SMOKING DOG
16 rue Lainerie

●‡ PUB
☎04 78 28 38 27

With pictures of dogs in smoking jackets and English music playing over the system, The Smoking Dog is a wonderful, if slightly out-of-place, watering hole. There is an old bookshelf full of French and English books in the back seating area, as well as empty boxes of whiskey. For a test of your brain power, visit on Tu night at 9pm for the weekly quiz, including the "Hamster Question" round and the "Yank or Manc" section. Even though the bar is English, the locals lap up the atmosphere, and you will find French people amongst the Anglophones.

✠ Ⓜ*Vieux Lyon.* Ⓢ *Beer €2-6.* ☾ *Open daily 5pm-1am.*

ARTS AND CULTURE
Festivals

LES NUITS DE FOURVIÈRE
1 rue Cléberg

MUSIC, DANCE, THEATER
☎04 72 57 15 40 ◾www.nuitsdesfourviere.fr

Every summer, this massive arts festival takes place in Lyon with everything from public showings of black and white horror classics such as *Dracula* to another kind of vampire, Vampire Weekend. In 2010 Iggy and the Stooges even graced the Théâtre Romain as well as performances of The Tempest, "Let it Be," opera, and classical music performances. Every year Lyon trumps with its selection of arts and performances. Tickets can be bought by calling or visiting the Théâtre Romain or the FNAC store on rue de la République.

Ⓢ *Tickets from €10. Some performances are free.* ☾ *June-July.*

ESSENTIALS
Practicalities

- **TOURIST OFFICE:** In the Tourist Office Pavillion at place Bellecour, 2ème. (☎04 72 77 69 69 ◾www.lyon-france.com. ☾*Open daily 9am-6pm.*) Offers free accommodation bookings, a free public transport map and the ◾**Lyon City Card** (Ⓢ1 day €20. 2 days €30. 3 days €40.). It gets you free entry into Lyon's 21 museums, free public transport for the period, a city tour, a boat tour (*Apr-Oct*) and reductions at certain places, including the National Opera and bicycle rentals. Student reductions on the price of the card are available upon request.

- **TOURS:** Audio tours are offered in English and organized by the Tourist Office. To book one, either call or go into their office (Ⓢ*€9, students €5*). **Le Grand Tour** is also offered. English guides are available (Ⓢ *€17, students €15, ages 4-11 €8* ☾ *1hr. 15mins.*)

- **CONSULATES:** USA (*1 quai Jules Courmant, 2ème* ☎04 78 38 36 88). **Canada** (*17 rue Bourgelat, 2ème* ☎04 72 77 64 07). UK (*24 rue Childebert, 2ème* ☎04 72 77 81 70).

- **CURRENCY EXCHANGE: Goldfinger SARL.**No commission (*81 rue de la République* ☎04 26 68 00 12 ☾ *Open M-Sa 9:30am-6pm*).

- **ATMS:** 24hr. ATMs line the Bellecour Square in the Hôtel de Ville area. An **HSBC** Bank is located at 18 Pl. Bellecour (☎04 78 92 31 00 ☾*Open M-F 8:45am-12:15pm and 2-5pm*).

- **LAUNDROMAT:** 19 rue St-Hélène, 2ème. (Ⓢ *€4 per 7kg* ☾ *Open daily 7:30am-8:30pm*).

france

Another branch at 51 rue de la Charité, 2ème (🕐 Open daily 6am-9pm).

- **INTERNET ACCESS:** Free Wi-Fi at the **Bellecour McDonald's. Raconte Moi la Terre** has Wi-Fi and internet access (14 rue du Plat☎04 78 92 60 22 💲€3 per hr. 🕐Open M noon-7:30pm and Tu-Sa 10am-7:30pm.)

- **POST OFFICE:** Pl. Antoine Poncert, 2ème, next to pl. Bellecour. (☎72 40 65 22 🕐Open M-W 9am-7pm, Th 9am-8pm, F 9am-7pm, Sa 9am-noon).

- **POSTAL CODES:** 69001-69009; last digit corresponds to arrondissement.

Emergency!

- **POLICE:** 47 rue de la Charité (☎04 78 42 26 56).

- **HOSPITAL: Hôpital Hôtel-Dieu** (1 pl. de l'Hôpital, 2ème☎08 20 08 20 69; central city hospital line).

- **EMERGENCY SERVICES:** ☎17.

Getting There

By Plane

Lyon's main airport is **Aéroport Lyon-Saint-Exupéry.** You can reach the city proper from the airport by train run by **Rhônexpress** (🖥www.rhonexpress.fr 💲€13, roundtrip €23; ages 11-25 €11, roundtrip €19. 🕐30min., daily 5am-midnight). You can pick the train up at**Lyon Part-Dieu** station or **Vaulx-en-Velin La Soie**station. Tickets can be bought online in advance to save time. For information on flights, **Air France** has an office on 10 quai Jules Courmont, 2ème (☎08 20 32 08 20) and runs 10 daily flights to Paris's Orly and Charles de Gaulle aiports (💲from €125. 🕐Open M-Sa 9am-6pm.)

By Train

Lyon is served by two main train stations. The main station is **Gare de la Part-Dieu,** where all national and international trains depart from(5 pl. Béraudier ✈ Ⓜ Part-Dieu. 🕐 Info desk open daily 5am-12:45am. Ticket window open M-Th 8am-8pm, F 7am-10pm, Sa 8am-8pm, Su 7am-10pm.) **Gare de Perrache** is where most trains that end their route in Lyon finish. (Pl. Carnot ✈ Ⓜ Perrache 🕐 Ticket office open M 5am-9:45pm, Tu-Sa 5:30am-9:45pm, Su 7am-9:45pm.) Trains leave both stations to **Dijon** (💲€27. 🕐 2hr, every hr.), **Grenoble** (💲 €20. 🕐 1½hr, every hr.), **Marseille** (💲 €44. 🕐 2hr., every hr.), **Nice** (💲 €70. 🕐 6hr., 3 per day.), **Paris** (💲 €80. 🕐 2hr., 17 per day.), **Strasbourg** (💲 €53. 🕐 5hr, 6 per day.), and **Geneva, CHE** (💲 €28. 🕐 2-4hr., 6 per day.). The trains are run by **SNCF.** Their office is located at 2 pl. Bellecour, near the tourist office (🕐 Open M-F 9am-6:45pm and Sa 10am-6:30pm).

Getting Around

Bordeaux can easily be tackled by foot. For longer journeys, the following options are available.

By Bus, Tram, and Metro

All public transport in Lyon is run by **TCL** (☎08 20 42 70 00 🖥www.tcl.fr). There are TCL information offices at the bus and train stations **Part-Dieu** and **Perrache,** and also at major metro stations. A very useful plan of the bus routes and map of the city is available from the Tourist Office or the info centers. All **tickets** are valid for the metro, bus, and tram, and last either one hour (€1.60), or are valid for 10 separate journeys (€13.70; connections and changes included). Public transport runs daily from 5am-12:20am. Th-Sa there is an additional night bus service that runs from Pl. Terreaux to the University areas (every hr., Th-Sa, 1am-4am). The **T1 Metro** line connects the two **train stations,** Part-Dieu and Perrache directly. For reaching the top of **Fourvière** in Vieux Lyon, there are **funiculars** (cable cars) which run between Ⓜ Vieux Lyon, Pl. St-Jean hostle, and St-Just/Fourvière Basilica, until midnight (€2.20).

By Bike

Vélo'v (✉*www.velov.grandlyon.com)* has bike rental spots all around the city center, which makes grabbing a bike cheap, simple and easy. A day card costs €1, which allows you to take a bike from the docking station and use it at your leisure. The first half an hour of travel is free, and the second half hour is €1. Every half hour after that costs €2. You can pick up a map with the points from the internet, the bike points, or the tourist office.

bordeaux ☎05

In addition to its well-deserved reputation as the wine capital of the world, Bordeaux's grand 18th-century architecture makes this city by the river a photographic marvel. In some of France's most elegant streets, hipsters hang out at Pl. de la Victoire in the student quarter, children splash in the waters of the *miroir d'eau,* and tourists with purple-stained mouths taste the best wines on the planet from the legendary vineyards of St-Émilion, Médoc, Sauternes and Graves. Come to Bordeaux first and foremost for the viticulture, but stay for the panoramic views, the sophisticated culture, and the vibrant nightlife.

ORIENTATION

For a mental map of the city of Bordeaux, picture the Garonne River flowing north to south, then add Bordeaux on its west bank. Now let's fill in the details. At the southern end of the city is the **Gare St-Jean** train station, which is a hike from *centre-ville.* To get to town, walk past the sex shops on **Cours de la Marne** until you reach **Pl. de la Victoire,** the student nightlife quarter. From here, turn right under the arch onto the pedestrian street **Rue Ste-Catherine.** *Centre-ville* in a straight shot ahead. You can also take tram C or bus #16 from the train station and get off at Pl. de la Bourse or the Esplanade de Quinconces, but that's jumping the gun.

At the heart of *centre-ville* is **Pl. de la Comédie.** If you're walking along Rue Ste-Catharine from the train station, this is where you'll end up. The square is immediately recognizable by its opulent Grand Théâtre. Ahead on **Cours 30 Juillet** (the continuation of rue Ste-Catherine) you'll find the **Tourist Office,** right before the **Esplanade des Quinconces,** a large plaza and an important public transportation hub. Back at Pl. de la Comédie, you can get to **Pl. Gambetta,** another one of Bordeaux's centers of activity, by walking west for a short distance along **Cours de l'Inentendance.** Most budget hotels are located north of Pl. Gambetta, while the best cheap eateries are south of the Grand Théâtre in the streets coming off rue Ste-Catherine. Head west one one of them, **Rue St-Rémi,** to hit the **Pl. de la Bourse.** This square by the Garonne River is across the street from Bordeaux's iconic public art installation, the 🖼**miroir d'eau.**

ACCOMMODATIONS 🛏

Although Bordeaux's youth hostel is conveniently situated near the train station, the area is home to many a sex shop, and the 5-10min. walk from the nearest tram stop can be freaky at night. Great deals, especially for groups of travelers, can be found farther from the station in the *centre-ville,* on the streets around **Pl. Gambetta.** Reserve one to two weeks ahead in the summertime.

🖼 **HOTEL STUDIO**   ✈((ŋ)) BUDGET BOUTIQUE ❷
26 rue Huguerie   ☎05 56 48 00 14 ✉www.hotel-studio-bordeaux.fr

A long-time Let's Go favorite, Hotel Studio's got a mixture of old and newly renovated rooms that might not be spacious, but have everything you need. From extra-comfy double beds, to cable TV, to futuristic tin showers in the full baths, you'll be hard pressed to find better value in Bordeaux's *centre-ville,* especially given the caring staff who makes this hotel feel like home. Ask for a spiffier renovated room and reserve ahead of time in July and August.

From Pl. Gambetta, walk along Rue Georges Clémenceau until a left turn onto Rue Huguerie just before the statue and traffic circle of Pl. de Tourny. $ Singles €28, renovated €33; doubles €30/38; triples €49; quads €65; quints €70. ⏰ Reception daily 7:30am-8:30pm.

HOTEL CHIC DE LYON

BUDGET HOTEL [2]

31 rue des Remparts ☎05 56 81 34 38

It seems like everything in this lovely hotel sparkles, from the crisp sheets to the white walls. Combined with the fresh smell, the high windows that let in ample air and light, and the occasional garden of potted plants, you're in for a refreshing treat in a superb location. Every room has a full bath, and the staff is warm and welcoming.

Rue des Remparts is the street running past the Hôtel de Ville from Pl. Pey-Berland (where the St-André cathedral is) to Pl. Gambetta. $ Singles €35-37; doubles €49-53; triples €69. ⏰ Reception 24hr., although there is an access code for guests to enter late at night.

a drunkard's guide to france

- **WINE:** Surprise! There's wine in France. There is also cheese and French people. Sarcasm aside, you can find it anywhere, but to go to the source, venture to **Bordeaux,** where Merlot grapes alone cover 50% of the region. Make sure to pick a wine that says *Mis en Bouteille au Château* on the label, which indicates that a wine was bottled at the château where the grapes were grown. If you go for Champagne, French law garentees that your bubbly white wine will have come from the area of the same name 100 miles east of **Paris**. André was barely champagne before, but it's definitely sparkling wine now.
- **PASTIS:** It's way too hot to eat much in **Côte d'Azur**, so sit back in your beach chair and sip Pastis. It's a yellow, licorice flavored alcoholic beverage similar to absinthe, and the French drink 130 million liters of the stuff a year. In Marseille be sure to call it *Pastaga*, and don't use the water served on the side as a chaser, it's supposed to be mixed in with the liquor (like ouzo). Hemingway coined the combo of champagne and Pastis as "Death in the Afternoon," warning us of the misery of a 5pm hangover.
- **KRONENBOURG BEER:** Not one to be outdone by beer chugging Germans, this beer brewed in **Alsace** hasn't changed much since the first pint was fermented in 1664. Its hopsy flavor and alcohol content will make the Alps, and your date, much prettier.
- **LIQUORS:** You can be sure that all those sweet fruits in the **Loire Valley**, in some form or another, have been fermented. If you like oranges, you should be familiar with Anger's Cointreau, but you might not know the cherry version Guignolet, which is also popular. There isn't a restaurant that doesn't have at least one of these liquors mentioned in their dessert menus. Soufflé AU COINTREAU, anyone?
- **ABSINTHE:** The poison of choice of **Parisian** artists of the 19th century, the newly legal spirit was central to Bohemian culture. Known in French as "The Green Fairy" for its, ahem, inspiring effects, absinthe was originally given to French troops as an anti-malarial. Whether you're feeling a bout a malaria coming on or if you're simply seeking hedonistic fun, the Green Fairy surely will not disappoint (unless you're expecting a hallucination).

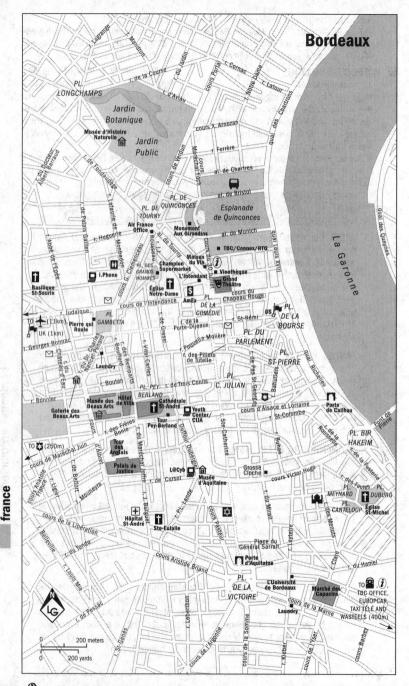

Bordeaux

HOTEL BALZAC — HOTEL ❸

14 rue Lafaurie de Monbadon ☎05 56 81 85 12

Full of character, Hotel Balzac's creaky staircase climbs to irregularly shaped and spacious rooms with rather sensual art on the walls. Between the dim reception, the hotel's namesake, and its *passé* feel, you might just write the next great novel here. If you're not a tortured artist with a rolled cigarette in hand, then at least you have a cheap place to stay and shower in central Bordeaux.

From Pl. Gambetta walk 1 block up Rue Georges Clémenceau and turn left at a 70 degree angle onto Rue Lafaurie de Monbadon. $ Singles €33; doubles €46.

AUBERGE DE JEUNESSE — HOSTEL ❷

22 cours Barbey ☎05 56 33 00 70 www.auberge-jeunesse-bordeaux.eu

Shiny metal, bright colors, and lots of glass characterize the impressive modern architecture of Bordeaux's municipally owned Auberge de Jeunesse. Nevertheless, given the water damage in need of repair and the location near Bordeaux's red-light district, travelers will find better value in *centre-ville.* Dorms for 2, 4, or 6 sleep a total of 108 people in 30 rooms with bunk beds; most rooms come with interior showers, and some with toilets, in addition to cabinets for personal affairs. Relax in the lounge with a flatscreen and a foosball table.

3 large blocks along Cours de la Marne from Gare St. Jean. Follow well-marked signs. i Breakfast, sheets, and internet included. $ Dorms €22. Breakfast 7:30-9:30am. Lockout 10am-2pm. Check-out by 10am. Doors close at 2am.

SIGHTS

Bordeaux isn't short of fun, educational, or quirky ways to pass the time between glasses of wine. Admission to all of Bordeaux's museums is free the first Sunday of every month.

TOUR PEY-BERLAND — TOWER

pl. Pey-Berland ☎05 56 81 26 25

For the best views of Bordeaux, climb 231 steps through an ever-narrowing spiral staircase to the top of the 50m-high Pey-Berland bell tower, named after one of the great archbishops of Bordeaux. Built in 1440 at a distance from the *Cathédrale St-André* in order to protect it from the bell's vibrations, the tower ironically had no bells until 1853.

$ €5. Open daily June-Sept daily 10am-1:15pm and 2-6pm; Oct-May daily 10am-12:30pm and 2-5:30pm.

MIROIR D'EAU — PUBLIC ART

Accessible from the grand buildings of Pl. de la Bourse and beside the banks of the Garonne River, Miroir d'Eau is a spectacular public art installment, and an icon of modern Bordeaux: a mirror made of water. Designed by the architect Michel Corajoud and installed in October of 2006, 2cm of water transform 130m by 42m of black granite into a reflective surface that captures a stunning panoramic view of the city. In additon to releasing billows of fog in computer-controlled cycles, the *miroir d'eau* is a particular favorite of little and not-so-little kids, who love to splash and play in its waters. Bring your camera, sketchpad, and people-watching glasses, especially at sunset.

$ Free. Open 24hr.

CATHÉDRALE ST-ANDRÉ — CATHEDRAL

pl. Pey-Berland ☎05 56 52 68 10

Sculpted angels and apostles adorn the cathedral's facade, while Gothic windows allow natural light to illuminate an interior that has been home to many important royal weddings (a.k.a. alliances)—Eleanor of Aquitaine and Louis VII got hitched here in 1137. Louis XIII and Princess Anne of Austria also tied the knot here in 1615, whereupon Louis walked through the "royal portal" on the north side of the church, an entrance that has allegedly not been used since. Today, the cathedral is a UNESCO World Heritage Site, and one of the stops for pilgrims walking the Camino de Santiago de Compostella.

🔓 *Open daily 10am-12:30pm and 2:30-7:30pm. Guided visits June-Sept Tu-Su 3-5pm.*

MAISON DU VIN   ⬥ WINERY
3 cours du 30 Juillet   ☎05 56 00 43 47

If you're desperate to become a sophisticated oenophile (wine-lover) and you don't have time to venture into the nearby wine country, then head to the *Maison du Vin*, an immense building directly across from the Tourist Office. The *Maison* houses industry offices, an extensive *Bar à Vin* (wine bar) staffed by professionals who guide tastings and an *École du Vin* (wine school) that offers a 2hr. "Introduction to Bordeaux Wines" in English and French with a comparative tasting of two reds and two whites. Those appropriately impressed can purchase the goods at two nearby wine shops. **L'Intendant,** a more intimate wine shop across the street, has an impressive selection of regional wines and a knowledgeable staff. (*2 Allée de Tourny* ☎*05 56 48 01 29* 🔓 *Open daily 10am-7:30pm*). Conoisseurs can then venture across the square to buy high-end bottles, crystal pitchers, and obscure gadgets at the classy **Vinothèque,** a store specializing in all things *vin*. (*8 Cours du 30 Juillet* ☎*05 56 52 32 05* 🖳*www.la-vinotheque.com* 🔓 *Open M-Sa 10am-7:30pm*).

⚑ *Directly across from the tourist office.* ℹ *Tickets for the course can be purchased at the Maison du Vin or at the tourist office.* 💲 *Wine-tasting course €25. Bar à Vin €2-8 per glass of wine.* 🔓 *Courses offered M-Sa 10am in English and 3pm in French. Bar à Vin open M-Sa 11am-10pm.*

FOOD   🛈

Bordeaux boasts a range of local specialties, including oysters straight from the Atlantic, *foie gras* from Les Landes, and beef braised in St-Émilion wine. Restaurants cluster around **Rue St-Rémi** and **Pl. St-Pierre,** while small and budget-friendly options line the narrow streets between **Pl. du Parlement** to the east of **Rue Ste-Catherine.** *Bordelais* don't usually eat before 9pm in the summer and restaurants typically serve meals until 11pm or midnight. Sample local fish and produce at the **Marché des Capucins** (🔓 *Open Tu-Su 6am-1pm*) off **Cours de la Marne,** or head to the conveniently located **Centre Commercial des Grands Hommes** for all your grocery needs. The *Centre* is in the middle of the triangle made by **Pl. Gambetta, Pl. de la Comédie,** and **Pl. de Tourny.** Inside there's a huge **Carréfour** grocery store with super-cheap prepared roasted chicken meals for €3.50. (🔓 *Open M-Sa 9am-9pm.*)

🍽 LA PAPAYA   ⬥ AFRICAN ❷
14 rue Ferdinant Philippart   ☎05 56 44 76 88 🖳www.lapapaya.populus.org

A wonderful Malagasy and Réunionese restaurant (that's the cuisine of Madagascar and the subtropical French island of Réunion due east) that serves up spicy, fruity, and all-round tasty stews on beds of white rice. Try the mutton cooked in *massalé*, a traditional Réunionese composite of cardamum, black pepper, coriander, cumin, and five other spices. Turns out that island food still goes down beautifully with a Bordeaux.

⚑ *From Pl. de la Bourse, with your back to the 3 Graces Fountain and the Garonne River, take the left fork ahead of you. The restaurant is on your left.* 💲 *Appetizers €4.10-8. Plates €9.50-11.80.* 🔓 *Open M-Sa 7:30-10:30pm.*

O'MIRROIR D'O CAFE   ⬥🍴 TRADITIONAL, SEAFRONT ❷
2 quai Louis XVIII   ☎05 56 44 59 59

As close to the banks of the Garonne as you can eat, this friendly cafe serves French dishes like *steak frites* and *confit de canard* that are simply delicious, especially when accompannied by Bordeaux's world-famous wines. Skip dessert—it pales in comparison to the main courses. Afterwards, stroll down the river to the café's namesake, the 👍**miroir d'eau,** which looks best at sunset on a full stomach.

➜ Quai Lousi XVIII is the avenue that follows the Garonne River. The restaurant is in between Pl. de la Bourse and Esplanade des Quinconces. $ Menu (appetizer + plate or plate + dessert) €14. Appetizers €5-7. Plates €9.50-13. Salads €9-11. Pizzas €9-11. Desserts €4-6. ⏰ Open daily 8am-midnight.

TWIN TEA WINE — 🍸 SMALL PLATES ❶

16 rue des Argentiers — ☎05 56 44 63 71 💻www.twinteawine.com

Looking for a truly gourmet experience? Come to this trendy small plates restaurant that doubles as a tea house and wine bar. Using seasonal and fresh produce, the owners have never cooked the same dish twice, but you can expect the likes of lamb and eggplant tajine or organic zucchini sautéed in fennel. If you're not famished, one small plate (€4) and a basket of bread is enough, although 2 plates and a glass of sangria (€10) will ensure your satisfaction. Multi-talented, the owners also prepare homemade cakes and pastries, in addition to entertaining every evening during "happy time" with discounts on wine-tastings.

➜ From Pl. de la Comédie and the Grande Théâtre, walk down rue Ste-Catherine until a left turn onto rue de la Devise. When the street opens into a small square, rue des Argentiers is at the far end beside the church. $ Small plates €4. 2 plates and a drink €10. 4 plates and a drink for brunch €12. Desserts €3,50. Dégustation of 2 wines with a plate €7. Glasses of wine €3. Sangria €2. ⏰ Open Tu-W 11am-11pm, Th-Su 11am-2am. "Happy time" 7:30-9:30pm.

L'OMBRIÈRE — 🍸 TRADITIONAL ❸

14 pl. du Parliament — ☎05 56 48 58 83 💻www.restaurantlombriere.com

Perfectly prepared French cuisine tastes better when it's enjoyed beside a bubbling fountain amidst this chic restaurant's ever-present crowds. Fixed menus include fusion choices like Yakitori-style Scallop and King Prawn Skewers *(€15-25),* but there are plenty of French staples available, including a meal-size salad with baked goat cheese and *foie gras.*

➜ From Pl. de la Comédie and the Grande Théâtre walk down Rue Sainte Catherine until a left turn onto rue St-Rémi. Your next left will be on rue des Lauriers which leads to the open square of Pl. du Parliament. $ Menus €15-25. Appetizers €5.50. Plates €12-16. Desserts €4.50. Wines €3-5.50. ⏰ Open daily July-Aug 10am-2am; Sept-June 10am-3pm and 6pm-midnight.

NIGHTLIFE

Given its student population of 70,000, Bordeaux is full of bars. **Pl. de la Victoire** is *the* student party quarter, and the streets around **Pl. de la Comédie**—especially those south of the Place off of **Rue Ste-Catherine**—are well-stocked with nightlife opportunities. For Bordeaux's large nightclubs, clustered south of the city by mayoral decree, head to **Quai du Paludate** behind the **Gare St-Jean** train station. Travelers should exercise caution when walking in this area at night.

👍 LA CALLE OCHO — 🍸 CLUB

24 rue des Piliers de Tutelle — ☎05 56 48 08 68

This never-ending bar is covered floor-to-ceiling with a love for all things Cuban, not to mention filled wall-to-wall with insane crowds of the young, beautiful, and partying from around the world. Move your hips to rockin' Latin music until you can't resist the allure of a *mojito* any longer.

➜ From Pl. de la Comédie walk along Cours de l'Intendance with the Grand Théâtre to your left. Rue des Piliers de Tutelle is the second right turn. $ Beer €4. Mixed drinks €6. ⏰ Open daily 5pm-2am.

👍 EL BODEGON — 🍸 BAR

14 pl. de la Victoire — ☎ 05 56 96 74 02

This place dominates nightlife in la Victoire, the most popular student party quarter. DJ plays the latest club hits, and bartenders light booze on fire, while the exuberant crowd dances and drinks the night away. Come for karaoke on Wednesdays or weekly theme nights—"Foam Night" and "Vodka Redbull Night" are particularly popular. In addition to the huge drink menu, the bar also serves food daily *(11am-3pm).*

➡ A straight shot down rue Ste-Catharine to Pl. de la Victoire. ℹ W karaoke or theme nights. $ Beer on tap €2.80-4.50. ⏰ Open daily 6am-2am. Kitchen open 11am-3pm. Happy hour 6-8pm.

LE TROU DUCK 🏷🍸▼ BAR

33 rue des Piliers-de-Tutelle ☎05 56 52 36 87

An intimate gay bar that's really more of an excuse to gyrate to '90s music, modern French hits and everyone's favorite: Rihanna. When you're not ordering a drink at the zebra-striped bar or watching wall-size music videos on the projector, take your pick from the young and cute guys.

➡ From Pl. de la Comédie walk along Cours de l'Intendance with the Grand Théâtre to your left. Rue des Piliers de Tutelle is the second right turn. The bar is at the very end of the street. $ Beer €3.50. Mixed drinks €6. ⏰ Open daily 10am-2am.

LE NAMASTHÉ 🏷🍸 TEA HOUSE

16 rue de la Devise ☎06 67 52 69 68

You and the multiple Buddha statues can mellow out together on the leafy brews all night long on the satiny red cushions. This awesome alternative to any ordinary bar has dozens of teas from the Far East in addition to alcoholic beverages, so long as they're not from France. Who knew tea could be so sexy?

➡ From Pl. de la Comédie walk town Rue Ste-Catharine until a left turn on Rue de la Devise. ℹ Credit card min. €10. $ Tea pot €3.80-6. Beer €5. Foreign wine €5. ⏰ Open M-Sa 7pm-1:30am.

ARTS AND CULTURE 🎵

To indulge in other kinds of *Bordelais* culture besides wine, pick up **Clubs and Concerts** at the Tourist Office, which lists every musical happening of all genres in the city. This town is a treasure trove for the indie music scene. Also inquire about a list of weekly free concerts on some of Bordeaux's 40 organs; you're guaranteed a visit to a beautiful church and a dose of good ol' Baroque fun. Of course, for the big daddy of them all, visit the Grand Théâtre, whose ballets, operas, plays, and concerts run from Sept-Jun. When the theater isn't in season, you can still take a guided tour of its magnificent interior.

👍 GRAND THÉÂTRE 🏷 OPERA HOUSE

pl. de la Comédie ☎05 56 00 85 95 💻www.opera-bordeaux.com.

The austere facade of this 18th-century opera house conceals a breathtakingly intricate Neoclassical interior, with a blue dome you will never foget. To see it, attend an opera, concert, ballet, or play—or give your wallet a bit of a break by taking a daytime tour in English or French.

$ Tickets €8-80. Special student discount offers 3 shows for €24. Tours €3. ⏰ The Opera House is closed for performances July-Aug, but open for tours. Ticket office open Sept-Jun Tu-Sa 1-6:30pm.

ESSENTIALS [i]

Practicalities

- **TOURIST OFFICES:** The main tourist office distributes an 80-page *Welcome to Bordeaux* guide and provides maps, brochures, and help with same-day hotel reservations. There's an entire desk dedicated to arranging visits to the *vignobles* (wineries). *(12 Cours du 30 Juillet. ☎05 56 00 66 00 💻www.bordeaux-tourisme.com ➡ Tram line B or C, Pl. de Quinconces. ⏰ Open July-Aug M-Sa 9:30am-1pm and 2-7pm, Su 10am-1pm and 2-6pm; Sept-Oct M-Sa 9:30am-1pm and 2-6pm, Su 10am-1pm and 2-6pm; Nov-Apr M-Sa 10am-1pm and 2-6pm, Su 2-6pm; May-June M-Sa 9:30am-1pm and 2-6pm.)* **Tourist Office Gare St-Jean** helps with transportation and hotel reservations. *(☎05 56 91 64 70 ⏰ Open May-Oct M-Sa 9am-noon and 1-6pm, Su 10am-12pm and 1-3pm; Nov-Apr M-F 9:30am-noon and 2-5:30pm.)*

- **TOURS:** The tourist office offers organized tours in English and French. **Walking tours** take place July 15-Sept 15 daily at 10am and 3pm; Sept 16-July 14 daily at 10am. *(☎05 56 00 66 24 $ €8, students €7. ⏰ 2hr.)* There are also tours with the same duration and price on roller skates, bikes, boat, taxi and *cabriolet.* Woah. More importanty, there are affordable *(€27)* and excellent bus tours to the wine regions of **St-Émilion, Graves,** and **Médoc.** Of course, there are also fancier day-excursions for €90.
- **CURRENCY EXCHANGE:** You have to ring multiple doorbells and climb one flight of stairs to reach the security-heavy **Bureau de Change Kanoo.** *(11 Cours de l'Intendance ☎05 56 00 63 33 $ €8 fixed commission on all cash exchanges. 2.5% commission on traveler's checks. ⏰ Open M-F 9:30am-5:30pm.)*
- **YOUTH CENTER: CIJA** helps with employment and long-term accommodations. Free internet access and SNCF train ticket purchase inside. Also distributes *LINDIC,* a student guide to Bordeaux. *(125 Cours d'Alsace Lorraine. ☎05 56 56 00 56 ⏰ Open July-Aug M 1-6pm, Tu-F 9am-6pm; Sept-June M 1-5pm, Tu-F 9am-5pm. Closed for 1 week in Aug, usually around the 2nd week.)* A branch office is around the corner on 5 Rue Duffour Dubergier. *(⏰ Open M-Th 9:30am-6pm, F 9:30am-5pm.)*
- **INTERNET ACCESS: I.Phone.** *(24 Rue Duplais Gallien ☎05 57 85 82 62 $ €0.50 per 15min. ⏰ Open M-Sa 10am-10pm, Su noon-10pm.)* **L@ Cyb.** *(23 Cours Pasteur ☎05 56 01 15 15 $ €0.75 per 15min. ⏰ Open M-Sa 10am-2am, Su 2pm-midnight.)*
- **POST OFFICE:** The post office has Western Union and **Poste Restante** with Postal Code 33065. *(32 Pl. Gambetta ☎ 05 57 14 24 60 $ €0.58 per letter received. ⏰ Open M-F 9am-6pm, Sa 9am-4pm.)*

Emergency!

- **EMERGENCY NUMBERS: Police** ☎17. **Ambulance** ☎15.
- **POLICE: L'Hôtel de Police.** *(23 Rue Francois Sourdis ☎05 57 85 77 ⏰ Open 24hr.)*
- **HOSPITAL: Hôpital St-André.** *(1 Rue Jean Burguet ☎05 56 79 56 79)*

Getting There

By Plane

There's an airport in **Mérignac** 11 km. west of Bordeaux. *(☎05 56 34 50 50 🖳www.bordeaux.aeroport.fr)* A *navette* run by **Jet'bus** goes from *centre ville* to the airport. *($ €7, under 26 €6; round-trip €12/10. ⏰ 45min., every 45min. 7:45am-10:45pm.)* There are stops at **Gare St-Jean,** the **Tourist Office,** and **Pl. Gambetta. Air France** has an office at 37 Allée de Tourny. *(☎36 54 ⏰ Open M-F 9:30am-6:30pm, Sa 9:30am-1:15pm).*

By Train

Gare St-Jean *(Rue Charles Domercq ☎36 35 ⏰ Ticket office open M-Th 5am-9:40pm, F 5am-10:35pm, Sa 5:40am-9:40pm, Su 6am-10:30pm.)* sends trains to **Lyon** *($ €67.40. ⏰ 8-10hr., 1 per day.);* **Marseille** *($ €75.40. ⏰ 6-7hr., 5 per day.);* **Nantes** *($ €45.70. ⏰ 4hr., 3 per day.);* **Nice** *($ €93.40. ⏰ 9-12hr., 2 per day.);* **Paris** *($ €69.80. ⏰ 3hr., 20 per day.);* **Poitiers** *($ €36.70. ⏰ 2-3hr., 16 per day.)* **Renne** *($€58.50. ⏰ 6hr., 3 per day either through Nantes or Paris.);* **Toulouse** *($ €36.30. ⏰ 2-3hr., 17 per day.)*

By Bus

Réseau TransGironde *(☎05 56 43 68 43 🖥www.citram.com)* buses travel to many small towns surroudning Bordeaux including **St-Émilion** (301 and 302) and **Pauillac** (705), both important viticulture destinations. Ask at the tourist office for schedules and prices. Be aware that buses are decentralized and leave from Esplanade de Quinconces, Gare St-Jean, and several other centers throughout the city.

Getting Around

By Public Transportation

TBC runs a bus and tram system. *(☎05 57 57 88 88 🖥www.infotbc.com, www.reseautbc.com $ 1 ticket €1.40; carnet of 10 or a 7-day-pass €10.60, under 28 €8; 1-day pass €4.10; night pass valid from 7pm-5am €2.30. ⏰ Trams A, B, and C run daily 5am-1am.)* Ticket and information offices at 9 Pl. Gambetta *(⏰ Open M-F 8am-7:30pm, Sa 9:45am-12:25pm and 2-6pm.)*, Esplanade des Quinconces *(⏰ Open M-F 7am-7:30pm, Sa 9:45am-12:25pm and 2-6pm.)* and at the Gare St-Jean train station *(⏰ Open M-F 7am-7:30pm, Sa 8:30am-3pm).*

By Bike

Pierre Qui Roule. *(32 Pl. Gambetta ☎05 57 85 80 82 🖥www.pierrequiroule.fr $ €10 per day, €20 per weekend, €45 per week. In-line skates and pads €6 per half-day, €9 per day. ⏰ Open M 2-7pm, Tu-Sa 10am-7pm.)*

By Taxi

Taxi Télé. *(☎05 56 96 00 34 $ €1.46 per km during the day, €2.19 per km after 7pm. €30-45 to the airport.)*

saint-émilion ☎05

Located 35km northeast of Bordeaux, the famed viticulturists of St-Émilion have been refining their technique since Roman times—and it shows. Local winemakers nourish over 5400 acres, gently crushing the grapes to produce two and a half million liters of wine each year. The medieval village's antiquated stone buildings, twisting narrow streets, and religious monuments ensure a charming visit.

ORIENTATION

St-Émilion is a tiny village, surrounded by miles of vineyards. Indeed, it's small enough that you can walk from one end of town to the other in less than ten minutes. If you arrive at the **train station,** turn right onto the main road and walk 2km north into town on **Rue Porte Bouqueyre** (or take a cab). Once you arrive, there are well-marked signs for the **tourist office,** which is located on **Rue du Clocher,** just opposite the belltower of the *Église Monolithe* church, the tallest structure in the village and your principal landmark. South of the Tourist Office is **Rue Guadet,** where you'll find several wineries and **Montagne D122,** a highway that leaves town. The highway leaves town at the traffic circle, **Pl. Bourgoise,** where **bus #302** from Bordeaux drops you off. Less than one block north on highway D122, where you'll find St-Émilion's grocery store. Continue straight for another 3km to reach the campsites.

ACCOMMODATIONS

It's difficult to plan more than a daytrip to the lovely village of St-Émilion, since you'll be hard pressed to find budget accommodations. St-Émilion's least expensive bed and breakfasts are many miles outside of town, and hotels in the village proper start at €70 per room. Your best option is the campsite, which is 3km north of town on highway D122.

DOMAINE DE LA BARBANNE CAMPSITE ❷

Route de Montagne D122 ☎05 57 24 75 80 🖥www.camping-saint-emilion.com

St-Émilion's closest campsite and most affordable accommodation is 3km out-

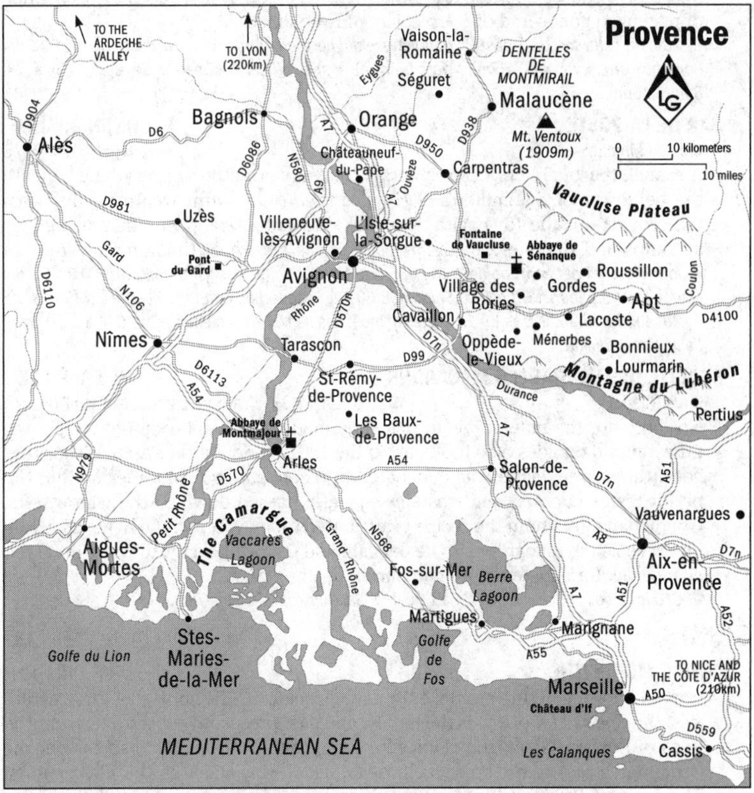

side in the heart of the wine country. With leafy tent sites, an emerald lake for paddleboating, a sparkling pool, and amenities like on-site kitchens, a grocery store, and a restaurant *(plates €9-13)*, the campground is better value than any budget hotel. And, since you won't find budget hotels in St-Émilion, it's your only choice. The downside is the distance from town, so it's best to rent a bike, although take extreme care on the highway.

From Pl. Bourgeoise, walk north on Route Montagne or highway D122 through 3km of vineyards. You'll be turning right at the sign for "Camping." The walk takes 30-45min. but BE CAREFUL since you are walking on a highway. ***i*** *Reserve in advance. Bike rental available.* $ *Apr-June and Sept-Oct tent sites €18, with electricity €22; €6.50 per additional camper. July 2-8 tent sites €26.50/30.50; €8 per additional camper; July 9-Aug tent sites €30/35; €9 per additional camper.* ⏰ *Reception M-Th 8:30am-9pm, F-Su 8:30am-10pm.*

FOOD

St-Émilion's only grocery store is perfect for a picnic among the vines. If you plan to sit down at one of the town's restaurants, expect to pay €10-20 for a plate and search **Pl. du Marché** for typically French fare.

L'ÉPICERIE

GROCERY ❶

pl. Bourgeoise ☎05 57 24 70 08

This cute grocery store is the optimal way to eat for budget travelers. There is an impressive cheese counter, four kinds of fresh bread, fruits, vegetables, all kinds of packaged goods and of course, jars of Nutella.

⊕ 20m on highway D122 past Pl. Bourgeoise, the northern border of town where bus #302 from Bordeaux drops you off. A 2min. walk from the tourist office. ⏰ Open M-Sa 8am-7:15pm, Su 8am-6:15pm.

BAR DE LA POSTE — CONTINENTAL [2]

6 pl. du Marché ☎05 57 24 70 76

A casual, reasonably priced restaurant that serves a little of everything beneath the belltower of St-Émilion's *Église Monolithe.* In warm weather, you'll join the crowds outside for healthy portions of salad, pizza, pasta, fish, or meat—accompanied, of course, by the *pièce de la resistance,* St-Émilion red wine.

⊕ In the square beneath the belltower of Église Monolithe. It's easiest to follow the signs for the church from the Tourist Office. $ Salads €8.50-12. Sandwiches €4.80-6. Galettes €6.50-13.50. Pastas €9.50-16.30. Pizzas €9-13. Plates of meat and fish €12-18. Menu du jour €14.50. ⏰ Open daily 9am-midnight.

RECETTE DES VÉRITABLES MACARONS — BAKERY [2]

9 rue Guadet ☎05 57 24 72 33 💻www.macarons-saint-emilion.com

Not only are the macaroons in this shop made with a 400-year-old recipe, the little almond cookies also took part in the 1867 World Fair in Paris. As the story goes, the secret recipe was concocted in a convent in 1620 under Mother Superior Sister Lacroix, and was subsequently passed down to the widow, Mrs. Goudichaud, to whom the recipe is attributed today. After all the hype, an actual bite reveals the macaroons to be delicate and flavorful. Sadly, they are none too cheap. Ask for a taste before you purchase a box of 36.

$ €10 for a box of 36 macaroons. ⏰ Open M-Sa 8am-7pm, Su 9am-7pm.

SIGHTS

ÉGLISE MONOLITHE — CHURCH

Carved by Benedictine monks out of solid rock over the course of three centuries, the *Église Monolithe* is the largest and best preserved subterranean church in all of Europe. Giant iron clamps keep the columns from collapsing under the combined stress of the heavy bell tower, which was added in the 17th century. The damp underground catacombs, a burial place for infants and wealthy monks, and the adjacent cave of the hermit Émilion, represent only a small portion of the 70 acres of underground galleries that have yet to be excavated. To visit, you must take one of the 45min. guided tours, which depart from the tourist office.

$ €6.70, students €4.20. ⏰ Tours in French at 10:30am, 11:30am, and 2pm-6pm every hr. Tours in English at 2:30pm and 4:30pm.

VINEYARDS

The easiest way to experience the vineyards is to register at the tourist office for guided visits (starting at €18 for a 3hr. tour). Free spirits can pick up a map from the tourist office, rent a bike, and travel to the collection of châteaux several miles outside of town. Plan ahead, since many of them require reservations several days in advance. Luckily, it's not hard to experience St-Émilion wine in the village itself, with a handful of châteaux, associations, and shops offering tours, *dégustation* or wine-tastings and a generally thorough education in some of the world's most renowned red wine.

CHÂTEAU VILLEMAURINE CARDINAL — WINERY

☎05 57 24 64 40

The only château within 2min. of the village promises to teach you all the basics in under an hour. A tour in English or French of this family-run winery comes with a fabulous explanation of the production process, from its hand-picked beginnings to the final corking. Thousands of bottles and barrels in the dark and clammy caves are a sight to behold, and the *dégustation* at the tour's end covers all five steps of wine-tasting. Pay €5 to become an oenophiliac. It sounds dirty, but it means you're beginning a lifelong love affair with wine.

From Pl. Bourgeoise, walk briefly on Saint-Cristophe des Bardes which is highway D243 East and at the fork, veer right. Continue 10m straight ahead, passing the similarly named Château Villemaurine and Château Villemaurine Cardinal will be on your left across from the field of grape vines. $ Visit and dégustation €5. Bottles from €15 and up. Open M-F 9:30am-12:30pm and 1:30-5:30pm. Open by appointment on the weekends.

CLOTS DES MENUTS — CAVES, WINERY

pl. du Chaptire ☎ 05 57 74 45 77

Explore the cool and creepy caves with thousands of bottles from eight regional châteaux, just waiting for you to tase their contents at the *dégustation* table upstairs. Although the wine-tasting is free, it's polite to pay a token amount if you don't plan on purchasing a bottle.

On rue Guadet 2min. from the tourist office $ Bottles from €6. Open daily in summer 10am-7pm; in winter 10am-6pm.

MAISON DU VIN — GALLERY, WINE SHOP

Pl. Pierre Meyrat ☎ 05 57 55 50 55 www.vins-saint-emilion.com

Over 400 wines at wholesale prices, wine-tasting classes run by oenologists, daily visits from St-Émilion châteaux offering free *dégustation* and best of all, an *oflactif* (nasal) guessing game with aromas from raspberry to thyme.

Around the corner from the tourist office next to the church. $ 1½hr. wine-tasting class €21. Open daily Aug 9:30am-7pm; Sept-Oct 9:30am-12:30pm and 2-6:30pm; Nov-Mar 10am-12:30pm and 2-6pm; Apr-July 9:30am-12:30pm and 2-6:30pm. Wine-tasting classes July-Sept daily 11am.

ESSENTIALS

Practicalities

- **TOURIST OFFICE:** To get to the office from the train station, take a right on the main road and walk 20min. up rue de la Porte Bouqueyre toward the clock tower. From the bus stop, just follow the signs. The office distributes *Le Guide St-Émilion*, which details the town's history, provides maps and itineraries, and lists vineyards, accommodations, and restaurants. Note that many of the *châteaux* require reservations to visit. The office organizes daily tours in English and French to the surrounding vineyards: €18 for a 3hr. bus tour of the wine-country with *dégustation* included. *(Pl. des Créneaux ☎05 57 55 28 28 www.saint-emilion-tourisme.com $ Bike rental €12 per half-day, €15 per full day. Open daily June-Sept 9:30am-8pm; Sept-Oct 9:30am-12:30pm and 1:30-6:30pm; Nov-Mar open 10am-12:30pm and 2-5pm; Apr-June 9:30am-12:30pm and 1:30-6:30pm. Tours M-Sa 2:30pm.)*

Getting There

Trains go from **Bordeaux** to the **St-Émilion** train station, 2km outside of town, several times a day; it's a 40min. trip. *($ €7.70. M-F 5:56, 7:06am, 1:33, 4:03, 4:51, 7:19pm; Sa 7:06, 10:42, 10:51am, 1:04, 2:28, 4:03, 7:19pm; Su and holidays 8:33, 10:42, 10:51am, 4:03, 7:19pm.)* **Bus** #32 leaves from the tourist office and takes 1hr. to get to St-Émilion. The benefit is that it drops you off right in the village, whereas the train station is 2km away. Buses leave at 9:20am and 12:25pm.

marseille   ☎0491

We could call Marseille a "true immigrant city" with a "vibrant local culture," but we prefer to think of it as the Tijuana of France. A Tower of Babel, produced by the train-with-cut-brakes that is globalization, this (in)famous port town is the stomping ground of sailors, backpackers, mobs of immigrants, and (we suspect) unsavory characters involved in the import-export business. Expect color, chaos, and a lingering smell of trash. The city is most famous for its dense North African population, and parts of the city are more akin to Algiers or Fez than southern France. People from throughout the Mediterranean converge here to barter and argue loudly with each other in the downtown. Tourists generally observe them from behind the plastic windows of the dinky tour buses. Located in the center of Provence, Marseille is an ideal home base for visits to the calanques along the coasts, or to the Provencal cities of Avignon, Arles, or Cassis. This is not the prettiest town on the French Riviera, but it hosts the closest train station to the prettiest towns on the Riviera. Avoid certain neighborhoods, and schlep it to the sweet smell of lavender only an hour away.

ORIENTATION

Marseille is organized into three main districts. The area bounded by **rue Canebière** and the **calanques** to the East is **Vieux Port; Notre Dame de la Garde** is situated on its central hilltop. Up a few blocks and to the west is **Belsunce,** Marseille's immigrant quarter. Explore "Little" Algeria, Morocco, or Tunisia and people-watch from carpet shops and tea lounges. Just don't walk around there at night. The old quarter to the furthest West is **Le Panier,** where you'll find Marseille's oldest buildings and cramped 6ft.-wide alleys. The **quai du Port** is lined with expensive hotels, boutiques, and upscale seaside cafes.

Vieux Port

Bordered by Cours Julien to the east and the tourism office to the west, Vieux Port is where the bars, restaurants, shopping, and other vibrant parts of the city contain themselves. Crowned by **Notre Dame de la Garde** which overlooks its center, the neighborhood boasts the oldest *boulangerie* in Marseille, not to mention its most happening nightclubs. The port is hemmed by bars and cafes that turn into hotspots at night; upscale restaurants are situated further inland around **Place aux Huiles.** Frustrated single men beware: at night in the Vieux Port, it can be particularly difficult to differentiate between clubs, bars, and strip clubs. The entrepreneurial young women beckoning you to come in at the door are a pretty good hint.

Le Panier

When the Greeks landed in Marseille 2,600 years ago, this is where they landed. Today, le Panier is the oldest and most cramped part of the city, though the area around La Vieille Charité might give it a run for its money. Mostly devoid of bars and clubs at night, this area is best to visit during the day, where the stores and the kooky cafes add charm to the winding narrow streets. At night, the same alleyways are shadowy and somewhat intimidating, since you might be the only one on them.

Belsunce

Little North Africa is bounded by **ave. Belsunce** and the **Canebière**, and teems with little kebab stands and carpet stores; this is an ideal place to shop cheap, and perhaps stop in and enjoy a pastis with a group of old Algerian men. Once dark, the stores close, and the few bars in the area become packed with the city's local flair. Unless you're large, male, and handy in a knife fight, however, take the long way to the port and skip Belsunce at night.

ACCOMMODATIONS

Accommodations in Marseille range from the affordable to the absurd. Stick to Belsunce or on the city's outskirts for the cheapest hotels and hostels, or spend a little more at Vieux Port's quiet B and Bs and nicer, centrally located hotels. If you have money to burn, stroll over to Le Panier and quai du Port for some hotels that are as close to the marina as they are expensive. Unless you're splitting the cost of a terrace room, avoid the area if you're on a budget.

Vieux Port

BALAENA HOTEL ❷

83 av de la Pointe Rouge ☎06 68 42 21 22 www.hebergement-marseille.fr

Conveniently located next to the beach and attached to a wetsuit/dive shop, this spotless hostel remains happily unlisted on English sites because Celine, the owner, speaks no English. A must for those focused on outdoor activites such hiking the Calanques or diving/windsurfing/kiteboarding.

Ⓜ Metro line #2 to Castellene then take Bus #19 (dir. Madrogue de Montredon) to Tibulon. At the end of the alleyway. i Wi-Fi, breakfast, and linens included. Ⓢ Shared rooms €22.50 per person; triples €81.

AUBERGE DE JEUNESSE HOSTEL ❶

Impasse du Docteur Bonfils ☎04 91 17 63 30 www.fuaj.com

Far away from the city, but close to the beach. All the way out in the 8th arrondissment (something most FUAJ hostels have in common) the brightly colored, spacious reception welcomes you with a pool table and bar right as you walk in. Clean, but bare rooms. Organizes wind surfing (*€14 per person for a half day*) and kayaking half days on Saturday (€25) and full days on Su (€44).

Ⓜ Castellene. From there, take bus #44 to Clot Bey Leau. Walk in direction of bus to traffic circle and take a right onto av. Joseph Vidal. Pass the bike rental store and turn left onto Impsse du Docteur Bonfils. Its at the end of the street. Look for Orange circle around blue triangle. i FUAJ Card required. Bar, restaurant, Wi-Fi, kitchen, breakfast included. Ⓢ €19/night. Three nights maximum in summer.

MONTGRAND HOTEL ❺

50 rue Montgrand ☎04 91 00 35 20 www.hotel-montgrand-marseille.com

Clean and well-lit rooms with wide windows that let in lots of sunshine. Triples and quads availiable.

Ⓜ Estrangin, walk along rue Montgrand. Ⓢ Singles €59-65; doubles €75; triples €85; quads €95.

Le Panier

The hotels in this area are freakishly expensive. A few of the better finds on the water sport exceptional views and will only cost you your right arm (unless you're left handed, in which case they will ask for that). For any of the other ones, come back when you've made it in life.

HOTEL HERMES HOTEL ❹

2 rue Bonneterie ☎04 96 11 63 63 www.hotelmarseille.com/hermes

Location, location, location. Hotel Hermes is right on the quai du Port, and next to an innocuous hotel that charges €180 per night. In light of these factors, the prices aren't that bad at this Greek-themed hotel with terrace rooms. While the rooms are reminiscent of a porno shot in a Motel 6 back in 1970s Miami (think pink sheets, loudly patterned carpets, and lingering smell of smoke in the halls), the proximity to cafes and the port more than make up for it.

Ⓜ Vieux Port. i TV, A/C, newly renovated. Breakfast €8. Ⓢ Singles €50; triples with terrace €90. We reccommend springing for the terrace.

They may look peaceful to you, but these oceanside promenades and narrow streets are the stomping grounds of spies, pirates, drug lords, international intrigue, and plain old-fashioned revenge (well, at least on the silver screen).

- **THE COUNT OF MONTE CRISTO.** Edmond Dantès escaped Château d'If, the island prison off the coast of Marseilles, by dressing himself in his dead friend's burial shroud. (Ew.) Over 3500 Huguenots and scores of real-life political detainees found this feared fort-turned-prison escape-proof, but not so with our friend the Count. The prison is open today and frequented by tourists.

- **THE FRENCH CONNECTION.** Sit in a seaside cafe and await your shipment of smuggled heroin from Turkey. (*Let's Go* does not recommend smuggling drugs, because Doyle *will* find you. And he will shoot.) What most people don't know is that the ring leader, Paul Corbone, also smuggled Parmigiano-Reggiano cheese between Italy and France. But whether you're carrying illegal drugs or just illegal dairy products, you'll need to take a break and take in the harbor.

- **THE BOURNE IDENTITY.** If you manage not to fall off the ferry to Corsica, you will officially be more coordinated than Jason Bourne. No, seriously. He takes a spill off the ferry in the opening scene of the movie (two gunshot wounds may have had something to do with the fall, but *Let's Go* doesn't believe in excuses).

Belsunce

LE VERTIGO
♠ ♿ (((•))) ❤ ⌂ HOSTEL ❷

42 rue des Petites Maries ☎04 91 91 07 11 🖳 www.hotelvertigo.com

Right next to the train station. Funky flea market finds decorate the walls and comprise the furniture at this dedicated, youthful hostel. The outside patio explodes with reds and blues and yellows, mimicking the festive streets of Marseille. Clean, cozy shared kitchen is a welcoming haven in this English-speakng, laid-back establishment.

⚑ *From the train station, walk down the Grand Staircase onto bl. d'Athèns. Take the first right. rue des Petites Maries will be on the left, hostel is 20 yards down on the left.* *i Wi-Fi, shared kitchen, 24hr reception, bar open til midnight.* ⓢ *2-6 person dorms €23.90; doubles €55-65.*

SIGHTS
🔘

Most of the must-see sights here are located in the Vieux Port of the city, which hosts **Notre Dame de la Garde** and the **Abbaye St.Vincent**. The museums are decent, and will hypnotize afficionados of 20th-century Cubism, Fauvism or any of those other "-isms" you studied in art school. If you are less than intellectually inclined (you are on vacation, after all), we recommend that you spend most of your time getting out of the city to see **Ile d'If** or the **calanques**. **Le Panier** has the one of the oldest orphanages in France, which also served as a baroque church and now is a museum for Marseille's ancient history. To experience 1,000 years of North African culture in the Med, explore **Belsunce**, which is a sight and smell of its own.

Vieux Port

🖼 NOTRE DAME DE LA GARDE
BASILICA

Top of the hill ☎04 91 13 40 80

You simply won't get a better view of the city than this. As awesome as it is

france

windy, this is where shipwreck survivors went to thank God, and it's where you will too, provided you survive the walk up (take the #60 bus instead). Towering over the Basilica is an 11.2m-tall golden Madonna and Child, which weighs just shy of 10,000 kilos. Services are still held in the crypt of the church, a tradition that's probably a holdover from the days when the Nazis were shooting at the basilica; you can still see the bullet holes in the east wall.

⚑ Take bus #60 from Vieux Port all the way to the end. ⓈFree. ◷ Open daily 7am-7:30pm.

▣ MUSÉE CANTINI
MUSEUM

19 rue Grignan ☎04 91 54 77 75 ▥www.marseille.fr

Housed in a chic warehouse, this museum hosts a permanent collection of Picasso, Cezanne, and Dubuffet paintings. Focuses on Surrealist, Fauvist, and Cubist movements of the last century. The museum is currently undergoing renovations and is expected to be completed in 2013. The new and improved museum is expected to house French artists from all over the country as well as Europe (France is scheduled to be the EU's culture capital in that year).

⚑ ⓂPrefecture. Ⓢ €2.50 entrance fee. Under 10 free. ◷ Open daily 10am-5pm. Jul-Oct open til 7pm.

▣ CHÂTEAU D'IF
CHÂTEAU

quai des Belges ☎04 91 59 02 30

The legendary home to the ▤Man in the Iron Mask and Count of Monte Christo, this island fortress turned prison is less exciting than Alcatraz, but more exciting than just any rock in the middle of the harbor. Forget about the cool, fictitious noble prisoners, though since you were more likely to find Huguenot leaders jailed here during the religious purges of the 1600s. While it's an equally horrific story, somehow it just doesn't have the same ring to it.

⚑ ⓂVieux Port. Quai des Belges. Ⓢ Boat tickets €15, students €10. Château entrance €5. Students free. ◷ Open 9:30am-6:15pm, as a function of the last operating boats to the island.

ABBAYE ST-VICTOR
ABBEY

3 rue de l'Abbaye ☎04 96 11 22 60

An early Christian burial site for saints, the history of the Abbaye St-Victor is (naturally) characterized by power struggles, mob violence, and other things Jesus would totally do. The abbey was originally fortified against pagan invaders, and successfully repelled the barbarian hordes until part of it was destroyed and looted by ▤disgruntled plebeians during the French Revolution. Though Napoleon attempted to restore the Abbey upon taking leadership, many of its treasures had been mysteriously misplaced. In their infinite respect for the dead that are buried here, the Christian faithful have more recently dug up the deceased saints and put their bones on display for tourists in the museum. Hallelujah. The Church also hosts a crypt that is way cooler than Notre Dame de la Garde, though you do have to pay for added awesomeness.

⚑ At the end of rue Sainte. 𝒊 Serves F-Su. Ⓢ Free. Crypt entrance is €2. ◷ Open daily fro 7am-7pm. Will be closed until February 2011.

Le Panier

▣ VIEILLE CHARITÉ
♿ CHURCH

2 rue de la Charité ☎04 91 14 58 80 ▥www.vieille-charite-marseille.org

The Vieille Charité was originally intended to be a tolerant place of worship for the homeless, but they tended to crowd the entrances and make church awkward for the other parishioners. The men and women of the cloth delicately transformed the church into an orphanage, perhaps in an effort to service more lovable charity cases. A wooden plank was strategically placed in front of certain windows so that the nuns couldn't see the local Mother or Father of The Year dropping their kid off in front of the Church. Today, the building hosts the

marseille · sights

Baroque Chapel and the **Musée des Arts Africains, Océaniens, et Amérindiens,** as well as the **Musée dArchéologie Méditerranée,** where you can peruse local ancient history from before and after Roman times.

$ Permanent exhibits €3, students €1.50. French university students (even exchange students) and children under 12 free. Temporary exhibits €4, students €2.50 for students. ⏰ Tu-Sa noon-7pm.

Belsunce

MUSEE DE LA MODE — MUSEUM

11 La Canebière ☎04 96 17 06 00 www.espacemodemediterranee.com

The ultrimate window shopper's dream, this museum houses a history of clothing from the 1940s to the present, and boasts 6000 garments. Lady Gaga's Kermit the Frog dress is sadly omitted. Closed until further notice in preparation for 2013.

[M]Vieux Port, walk up three block, on your left. $ €2 entrance, students free. ⏰ Oct-May 10am-5pm, Jun-Sep 11am-6pm.

LA CANEBIÈRE — MARKET

La Canebière

If you were expecting an open market with the local medicinal hash, we hate to disappoint: "la canabière" is a false cognate. Deriving its name from the Provençal for "hemp," this bustling shopping street is named after Marseille's historic ropemakers and sailors. Look for the really long street that separates Vieux Port from Belsunce.

[M]Vieux Port. Turn around and walk up.

THE GREAT OUTDOORS

Beaches

LA PLAGE POINTE ROUGE

Popular with local windsurfers and kite-boarders, and an oasis for SCUBA divers. Small but awesome windbreak, protected by a jetti.

#19 bus to Toulon.

PRADO PARC

When residents complained about not having easy access to local beaches, this park was created to provide both a community hangout and a buffer between more relaxed tanning beaches and the main road. Packed with both tourists and locals in summer, the park is pretty big, and is conveniently broken up into 4 smaller beaches: Benneveine, Borely, Roucas Blanc, and Vieille Chapele.

Either the #19 bus of #83 to La Plage bus stop.

Hiking

SORMIOU CALANQUE

One of the easiest and most breathtaking of the calanques, this trail leads down to a small cove where it's just too pretty to not swim, even if it means donning your underwater or birthday suit to enjoy it.

Take the #23 bus to the end of the line, and follow the signs for Sormiou down a hike that is all downhill, and takes 25 min.

LUMINY CALANQUE

The calanque to the East of Sormiou, and equally pretty. Windy trail for 30min downhill to the water's edge where cliff jumpers are seen jumping from the high ledges into the lagoon.

End of bus #23, follow signs for Luminy.

FOOD

Vieux Port

⬛ LE SUD DE HAUT   ✦♿♀♨ AFRICAN, HAITIAN ❸

80 cours Julien   ☎04 91 33 75 33

This hippie African/Haitian restaurant specializes in French attitude and American cinema, and is more than willing to provide a little kitsch whenever needed. Few other places offer sit down service with dessert for €10. The walls are painted in bright African colors and papered with American movie and music posters. Oddly enough, the Declaration of Independence too; we've just become more of a fan. The dessert is especially awesome—check out the chocolate covered fried banana.

✤ Ⓜ️Notre Dame -Cour Julien. Ⓢ €10.50 lunch menu with plat du jour and dessert du jour. Make it a three course for €16. Plats €11-16. Cocktails €7. 🕐 Open T-Sa noon-2:30pm, 7-10:30pm.

⬛ AU FALAFEL   ✦♿((•))♨ FALAFEL, SHAWARMA ❶

5 rue Lulli   ☎04 91 54 08 55

Kickass Israeli falafel and shawarma joint. The hummus is homemade, and the falafels are assembled in-house and served hot. The framed pictures of local graffiti art that line the walls are a particular treat, but we nonetheless recommend that you sit outside; the fryer is situated right by the entrance, and the place can get pretty hot. Take-out availible.

✤ Ⓜ️Vieux Port. Ⓢ €4.50 Falafel, Chicken curry and dishes €6. 🕐 Open M-Th noon-midnight, F noon-4pm, Su noon-midnight.

FOUR DES NAVETTES   ♿ BOULANGERIE ❶

136 rue Sainte   ☎04 91 33 65 69 ▧www.fourdesnavettes.com

Founded in 1781, the oldest *boulangerie* in Marseille is famous for its secret recipe of a lemony, hard biscuit that every February 2, the abbey of St-Victor blesses as they first come out of the oven at 6am. Almond cakes and other biscuits fill the air with aromas of marzipan and glazed sugar.

✤ Down the street from the Abbaye St-Victor. Ⓢ 1 Navette €0.75, for a dozen €8. 🕐 Open M-Sa 7am-8pm, Su 9am-1pm and 3-7:30pm. Aug daily 9am-1pm and 3-7:30pm.

CAFE LULLI   ✦♿♨ CAFE ❷

26 rue Lulli   ☎04 91 54 11 17 ▧http://lecafelulli.over-blog.com

The tea jars stacked high behind the register demonstrate the number of available options at this tea cafe. As far as food goes, try the quiche and salade lunch combo (€7.50) or splurge on the dessert maison (€2-6).

✤ Ⓜ️Vieux Port, near the Opera. Ⓢ Open Lunch menu from €7.50-11.

Le Panier

⬛ CHEZ MANON   ✦♨ TRADITIONAL ❷

2 rue Rodillat   ☎06 21 42 30 91

This small cafe may only have 3 tables, but the light blue walls with yellow stripes are oddly soothing, and the proprietess Nacira is a sweetheart who goes out of her way to take care of you. Whether looking for a sandwich (€3.50-4.50) or a more substantial penne dish with salmon, or a combo of three French cheeses (€9-12), this is the perfect escape from the busy *quai du port*.

Ⓢ Tucked away in plain sight 100m from the Vieille Charité. 🕐 Open daily 10:30am-6pm.

LE SOUK   ✦♿♀♨ NORTH AFRICAN ❸

100 quai du Port   ☎04 91 91 29 29 ▧www.restaurantlesouk.com

Tall people watch out in this low-ceiling-ed (we're talking 6' here) restaurant, which serves Maghreb style tea, tahini, and couscous. Tables are accompanied by small cushions in lieu of seats, and dishes served in traditional pottery from across the Med. Choose from wines from Morocco, Algeria, or France to accompany your menu du jour (*€13.50*).

$ Plates from €8-25. Menu du jour offers plat du jour and dessert du jour or entree du jour and plat du jour. ⏰ Open Tu-Su noon-2:30 and 7:30-10:30pm.

CHEZ MADIE LES GALENETTES 💳♿🍸🌳 PROVENÇAL [3]

138 quai du Port ☎04 91 90 40 87

A Provençal cafe specializing in traditional Marseillaise cuisine, located in Marseille? Blasphemy! Not only that, but the beach theme trend applies here as well. Located right on the harbor, the fish tastes fresher and the tourists are louder. Splurge here for dinner when it's not as crowded on the boardwalk.

$ Three course menu featuring local fish and lamb chops €25. Desserts €6. ⏰ Open M-Sa noon-2pm, 8-11pm.

LE WICH 🚫♿ CRÊPERIE [1]

Passage Pentécontore, in between quai du Port and rue de la Loge.

A one window panini and crêpes shop identifiable by the light pink and green storefront and the long line that winds to the other end of the alley. The fare here is sweet and wicked cheap, and features sweet paninis that are rare in a world of grilled ham and cheese (*nutella and banana panini; €4*).

$ Paninis and sandwiches from €3-5. ⏰ Open daily 10am-5:30pm.

MIRAMAR 💳♿🍸🌳 PROVENÇAL [5]

12 quai du Port ☎04 91 91 10 40 💻www.bouillabaisse.com

If food is more important to you than housing, splurge here for over-the-top fish and lobster dishes and more over-the-top service. Named one of France's gourmet restaurants of the year in 2009, Miramar has sure taken pains to keep up its reputation; the outside seating is covered and enclosed, to keep out noise and riff-raff like yourself. Right on the water, reserve a table well in advance, preferably with someone else paying for you. This may well be the best meal you'll have in Southern France.

$ Dishes between €25-44. Daily fish specials. ⏰ Open T-Sa noon-2pm, 7-10pm.

Belsunce

👍 **MARCHÉ PROVENÇAL** 🚫♿ MARKET [1]

7 rue Vacon ☎04 91 54 44 87

Belsunce may well host a largely North African population, but we've noticed that there's plenty of cross-over between French and North African culture—and that most of these commonalities have to do with food. This open air fruit and vegetable market is the heart of Belsunce, and specializes in seasonal fruits from both sides of the Med. Incredibly, given the its size, the market is run by a single local Algerian family.

$ Market prices. ⏰ Open daily 8am-8pm.

👍 **ARABESQUE** ♿ NORTH AFRICAN [1]

20A rue d'Aix ☎04 91 91 96 75

Algerian bakery and tea salon on a main, well-populated street in Belsunce. The neighborhood favorite boasts an array of finely decorated sweets covered in various amounts of carmelized sugar *(€1-3)*. A lunch menu comprised of your standard couscous and kebabs is also available *(€7)*. Try it with the mint tea, which is brewed with real mint leaves.

$ Bakery items €1-3. Lunch kebab or couscous €6.70. ⏰ Open daily 6am-8pm, lunch from 12-3pm. Tea salon open after 3pm.

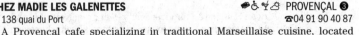

NIGHTLIFE

Most of the bars and clubs here are located in Vieux Port. The more artsy (read: kooky) watering holes are in the area around Cours Julien, while the more hopping, and more expensive hotspots can be easily spotted along the port. Le Panier is devoid of bars, since it's devoid of people at night anyway. Belsunce is where you go when you want to get lost at night and quickly regret doing so.

Vieux Port

PETIT NICE   ♥♥♿ BAR
28 pl. Jean Jaurès

The giant covered patio seating dominates this local fixture of the Cours Julian neighborhood, and is almost three times the size of the bar itself. The inside is decorated with a seemingly random assortment of ropes, hats, Nice posters, and life rings that adhere to the restaurant's general Nice theme (we guess).

⚲ Ⓜ Cours Julien. Ⓢ Half pints €2. Pints €4. Rum and mixed drinks €3.50. ⚘ Open Tu-Th 11am-2am, F-Sa 8am-2am.

SHAMROCK   ♥♿♥♿ IRISH PUB
17 quai de Rive Neuve

A tried and true Irish bar where the city's students and youth hostel workers can always depend on to be open. In true 🍀shamrock fashion, the Shamrock encourages patrons to drink above and beyond the legal limit—on Mondays, all pints are half-off all night. Soccer and rugby scarves cover the walls.

𝒊 Happy hour Tu-Su 6-8pm. Ⓢ Pints €5.50-6. ⚘ Open daily 4pm-2am.

DAN RACING   ♿♥ BAR
17 rue Andre Poggioli   ☎06 09 17 04 07 ▣www.dan-racing.tk

This Harley-themed bar is about as loose and fast as its owner, who never listens to a band before letting them play on stage. More often than not, this tolerant system of letting anyone play only adds to Dan Racing's fly-by-the-seat-of-your-pants vibe, but it occasionally results in the hiring of slasher head-banging groups who sound like some cross between Jacques Cousteau and Iron Maiden.

⚲ Ⓜ Cours Julien. Ⓢ Free entry. Beer €2.50. ⚘ Open F-Sa 6:30pm-2am.

TROLLEYBUS   ♥♿♥▼ CLUB
24 quai de Rive-Neuve   ☎06 72 36 91 10 ▣www.letrolley.com

One of the few clubs in Vieux Port that's not a strip club, this Trolleybus features different kinds of rock, electonica, and world beat in each of their three rooms. Whoever's in charge of the lights here should definitely get a pay raise: when this research-writer visited, a rock concert was projected onto the wall in the first room, fast-paced strobelight pulsed in another, and some moodier, groovier lighting was dappling the third.

Ⓢ €10, free drink with entry. ⚘ Open Jul-Aug W-Sa 11pm-6am, Sep-Jun Th-Sa 11pm-6am.

Le Panier

📓 BAR 13 COINS   ♥♿ BAR
pl. 13 Coins

Identifiable by its dark red exterior and the loud portraits of people painted in bright African yellows, greens, and reds along the walls, this chill bar is ideal for an early start in the afternoon or the first drink of the night. Posters advertising African and Maghreb music concerts paper the doors and windows. While the beer here is not the cheapest, the groovy vibe makes the place more than worth it.

Ⓢ Beer €3-4.50. Mixed drinks €5. ⚘ Open daily 8am-midnight (or later depending on the scene).

marseille · nightlife

ARTS AND CULTURE

Festivals

FESTIVAL DE MARSEILLE

Going strong since 1996, this ginormous music, dance, and movie festival features everything from ballet performances to special screenings to rock concerts. The festival is technically a celebration of Marseille's illustrious history, but appears to be more of an excuse for a two-month party. The festivities start in Le Panier and gradually move east across the city.

$ Prices vary accoring to event. ⏰ June and July. Check out 6 Place Sadi Carnot, or www.festival-demarseille.com for specific information on times.

ESSENTIALS

Marseille is essentially an immigrant town, so if the local resources seem to be overwhelmingly intended for a North African/Arab population, that's because they are. Never fear! There is help for tourists here!

Practicalities

- **TOURIST OFFICE:** Free maps and accommodations bookings. Marseille City Pass includes RTM day pass, access to 14 museums, a walking tour, ferry to Île d'If and varying discounts for city music festivals and events *(4 La Canebière ☎04 91 13 89 00 🖳www.marseille-tourisme.com [M]Vieux Port $ City Pass 1 day, €22; 2 day €29 ⏰ Open M-Sa 9am-7pm, Su 10am-5pm.)* Annex *(At train station ☎04 91 50 59 18 ⏰ Open M-F 10am-12:30pm, 1-5pm)*
- **TOURS:** Tourist office offers walking tours of the city in French daily (*One tour in English per week; ask for schedule*). **Petit Train:** Almost always full of families and tourist groups, this Disneyland-esque trolley takes tourists around the the major sites of the city (*☎04 91 25 24 69* ***i*** Departs on 3 different tracks: Notre-Dame de la Garde basilica, Old Marseille, and Frioul archipelago. *⏰ From quai Belges every 30min.; from Port Frioul to the Saint Estève for the archipelago.The first two routes run Apr-Nov 10am-12:20pm and 2-6pm; the one to the archipelago runs Jul-Aug 10am-12:20pm and 2-6pm. €7/4 for children, €6/3 for children and the one to the archipelago runs Jul-Aug (€3.5/2.5 for children.)*
- **CONSULATES:** UK *(24 av. du Prado ☎04 93 15 72 10 ⏰ Open M-F 9:30am-noon and 2-4:30pm by appointment only).* US (12 pl. Varian Fry *☎04 91 54 92 00 ⏰ Open M-F 9:30am-noon and 2-4:30pm by appointment only).*
- **LOST PROPERTY:** Although it's probably already been resold or put on a ship to Algeria. Good luck. *(41 bd de Briançon ☎ 04 91 14 68 97.)*
- **YOUTH CENTER:** Centre Régional Information Jeunesse (CRIJ) Information on long term housing, short term employment, vacation planning (once you get that job) and services for the disabled. *(96 Canebière ☎04 91 24 33 50 🖳www.crij.com [M]Noailles ⏰Open M 10am-5pm, Tu 1-5pm, W-F 10am-5pm. Limited hours July and Aug.)*
- **GLBT RESOURCES:** *(🖳www.gay-sejour.com)*
- **LAUNDROMATS:** Most hostels have laundry services, even if it's not listed; just ask. *(8 rue Rudolf Pollack. ⏰Open daily 9am-7pm.)*
- **INTERNET ACCESS:** Free internet at the CRIJ. There are also many internet cafes scattered around Belsunce and the Vieux Port. Look for the North African flags in the windows– they advertise that international calls can be made from that cafe.
- **POST OFFICE:** *(1 pl. Hôtel des Postes. Take La Canebière toward the sea and turn right on rue Reine Elisabeth as it becomes Hôtel des Postes. ☎ 04 91 15 47 00*

i *Currency exchange availible.* ✆ *Open M-W 8am-6:45pm, Th 9am-6:45pm, F 8am-6:45pm, Sa 8am-12:15pm. Branch at St-Charles as well scattered libeally around the city.)*

- **POSTAL CODE:** 13001

Emergency!

- **SOS VOYAGEURS:** *(Gare St. Charles* ✆*04 91 62 12 80.)*
- **POLICE:** *(2 rue du Antoine Becker Branch at train station next to Platform A.* ✆*04 91 39 80 00).*
- **PHARMACY:** *(7 rue de la République* ✆*04 91 90 32 27* *i* *English and French spoken.* ✆ *Open daily 8:30am-7pm.)*
- **HOSPITAL: Hôpital Timone.** (264 rue St-Pierre Ⓜ Timone. ✆*04 91 38 00 00).*

Getting There

By Plane

Aéroport Marseille-Provence (✆*04 42 14 14 14* 🖳*www.mrsairport.com).* It's a popular destination, so many carriers offer service to Marseille (*airport code MRS).* Air France offers flights from Paris. Ryan Air also has service to London Airports and to various offshoots of main airports throughout Europe. Shuttles (✆ *08 91 02 40 25* Ⓢ *€.30 per min)* run every 20 minutes between the airport and Gare St-Charles (Ⓢ *€8* ✆ *25min.).*

By Train

Gare St-Charles is the hub of the city, with frequent trains within France. International trains go through Paris (stations differing by ultimate destination). Trains to **Lyon** (✆ *1 hr. 20 per day* Ⓢ *€58),* **Nice** (✆ *2 hr. 20 per day* Ⓢ *€32)* and **Paris** (✆ *3 hr., 15 per day* Ⓢ *€105).* For up-to-date, accurate fare information go to www.sncf.com. For those of you under 25, you can get a TER pass for €15, valid one year, and get a 50% discount on regional travel in Provence-Alps-Côte d'Azur (PACA), or anywhere else for that matter. Trust us, you don't want the TER from Marseille to Paris—its a long haul.

By Bus

Pl. Victor Hugo, behind train station (✆*08 91 02 40 25.* ✆ *Gare St-Charles. Ticket counters open M-F 6:15am-7:30pm, Sa 6:30am-6:30pm, Su 7:45am-noon, 12:45-6pm.)* Depending on location, you can buy tickets on board the bus (i.e. the closer the destination, the more likely) but we reccomend buying tickets at the window and follow ticket-window-guy's advice. To **Aix-en-Provence** (✆ *every 10-15 min 6:30am-8:30pm, two per hour 9-11:30pm* Ⓢ *€5.50),* **Nice** (✆ *2hr, 1 per day* Ⓢ *€28, students €19),* and **Cannes** (✆ *2-3 hr. 1 per day* Ⓢ *€25, students €19).*

By Ferry

SNCM (*61 bl. des Dames* ✆*08 25 88 80 88* ✆ *Open M-Sa 8:30am-8pm. Office open M-F 8am-6pm, Sa 8:30am-noon and 2-5:30pm)* **Corsica Ferries** *(7 rue Beauvau* ✆ *08 25 09 50 95* 🖳*www.corsi-caferries.com* ✆ *Open daily 8am-8pm. To Corsica: €32-65; Algeria €105-315; Sardinia €60-85)*

By Taxi

Expensive, but if you must... **Marseille Taxi** (✆*04 91 02 20 20).* **Taxi Blanc Bleu** (✆*04 94 51 50 00).* 24 hr stands surroung the Gare St-Charles and Vieux Port. To Vieux Port from Gare St-Charles €20-30. To airport €40-55.

Getting Around

Public transport is easily navigable here, with only two metro lines, and two trams covering Belsunce and Vieux Port. Le Panier is only accessible by foot (which adds to the charm, we guess) but buses run along its perimeter. Bus passes can be bought for one journey *(€1.50),* three days *(€10.50)* or 7 days *(€16).* Solo passes can be bought on the buses, and are good for MetroTram or the bus for one hour after they are first validated. All public transport runs frequently Su-W 6am-11:30, Th-Sa 6am-1am.

There are Le Vélo bike stands, but they only work with European bank cards, and require a €150 deposit on your credit card. If you do have a European bank card, though it's a screaming deal at €1 an hour (under 30min free, like in Paris). Buses that you'll care about leave from Gare St-Charles and from Castellene, as well as from Vieux Port. Around the Marina though, walking is your fastest and easiest option.

avignon ☎0490

Avignon is most famous (and rightfully so) as the historical home base for seven rebellious Popes who left Rome during the Babylonian Captivity. Those 39 years made Avignon a center for religion and politics in France, and its famous bridge provided one of the few passes of the river Rhône. A popular camping destination for French campers and historical buffs alike, the medieval alleys and architecture have still held up, making Avignon a city trapped in the 13th century. Its a totally doable daytrip to see everything and not leave feeling disappointed that you didn't see more, while still wondering what was over that little bridge or around that stone turret. Come here and you'll expect to hear tamborines and pipes in the background while you walk around, but it will actually just be the city's vibant bars and cafes with the occasional annoyance of a tourist tram or school group.

ORIENTATION

The town of Avignon is surrounded by a giant wall, so there are only so many ways you can get lost in it. **rue de la Republique,** the main road from the train station, leads straight to the **Palais des Papes,** and divides the town into halves. Most of the cafes and restaurants are on the west side of the street, while the east side is generally comprised of hotels and private housing. Most of the shopping areas are clustered further down the main drag, or at **Halles,** the large shopping center in the middle of town. The **Rhône river** runs right by the city, and sports a very large island, the **Ile de la Barthelasse.** There is camping here for those on a budget, as well as a hostel. The entire town is very walkable, and it would almost be more of a hassle to figure out the public transport; Avignon is comprised of a tangle of one-way streets and alleyways that date back to the 1200s. While you may get lost easily, it's always easy to look up and see the Palais des Papes and re-orient yourself.

ACCOMMODATIONS

HOTEL MIGNON 💳♿📶🍸 HOTEL [3]

12 rue Joseph Vernet ☎ 04 90 82 17 30 💻www.hotel-mignon.com

Small and neat, Hotel Mignon lives up to its name. The centrally-located hotel's wood floors and pristine carpeting make it look like a model home in a Home Depot advertisement. The closet-sized bathrooms appear to be barely able to fit a person, but amazingly pack in a personal sink, toilet and shower. Book well ahead of time in July.

➡ From the main square, go down rue St. Agricole towards the pharmacy. Make your second right onto Joseph Vernet. Hotel on the left. ℹ Breakfast included. $ Singles €45-55; doubles €64-80; triples and quads €81-110.

CAMPING AUBERGE BAGATELLE 💳♿📶🍸⛺ CAMPGROUND, HOSTEL [1]

25 all Antoine Pinay- Ile de la Barthelasse ☎04 90 27 16 23 💻www.campingbagatelle.com

Over the river and through the woods, you can find cheap camping and hostelling less than 5min. from the town center. Auberge features an attached convenience store, as well as a free breakfast for basic double, quad or sextuple rooms. Both camping or hostel options have access to the establishment's facilities, which include a soccer field, basketball court, and pool.

➡ From the Pont d'Avignon, cross the Daladier bridge, and go down staircase on the right on other

side. Turn left towards signs and walk into the campground. Reception is hidden kind of next to the convenience store. *ℹ Camping and Auberge. Wi-Fi, breakfast, and linens included (unless camping). $ Camping €6 per night; 2 people, car, camp is €10 per night in winter, €15 per night in summer; €16 for a bed in a dorm.*

SIGHTS 👁

PALAIS DES PAPES — PALACE

☎04 90 27 50 00 🖥www.avignon-tourisme.com

This giant Gothic palace was built at the height of the Catholic Church's power, when Pope Clement V decided the Vatican was too cramped. The next 6 popes that followed him remained in Avignon during a period known as the Babylonian Captivity (for the record, it wasn't in Babylon, and the popes weren't held captive). Their Palais des Papes is a maze of small passageways that lead abruptly into huge painted chambers. Painted tiles and giant murals ornately decorate select areas, most notably the papal throne room.

ℹ Free audio tour with entrance. $ Nov-Feb €8.50; Mar-Sep €10.50. Includes entrance to Bridge. ⏰ Open Nov-Feb 9:30am-5:45, Mar 1-14 9am-7pm, Mar 15-Jun 9am-7pm, Jul 9am-8pm, Aug 9am-9pm, Sep 1-15 9am-8pm, Sep 16- Nov 1 9am-7pm.

PONT D'AVIGNON — BRIDGE, HISTORIC SIGHT

Port du Rhône ☎04 90 27 51 16

Step aside Palin; the Pont d'Avignon is literally a bridge to nowhere. Stopping half-way across the river Rhône, this bridge is the brainchild of St. Benezet, a shephard who one day heard angels tell him to build a bridge to Avignon. When the townspeople laughed at him, he miraculously threw a large stone into the river, laying foundation for the first arch. No one laughed at him ever again. The bridge eventually collapsed due to flooding and poor construction, and was closed until the 20th century, when they decided to open it again as a museum.

ℹ Free audio tour with entrance. $ Open Nov-Feb €4, Mar-Sep €4.50. Palais and Pont ticket, €11 Nov-Feb, €13 Mar-Sep. ⏰Nov-Feb 9:30am-5:45, Mar 1-14 9am-7pm, Mar 15-Jun 9am-7pm, Jul 9am-8pm, Aug 9am-9pm, Sep 1-15 9am-8pm, Sep 16- Nov 1 9am-7pm.

MUSÉE DU PETIT PALAIS — MUSEUM

pl. du Palais des Papes ☎04 90 86 44 58 🖥www.petitpalais.com

The Musée du Petit Palais starts out slow, with your run of the mill exhibits of 13th-century paintings of saints on wooden boards. We recommend spending more time in the exhibits toward the back, which feature the works of Giotto and other quattrocento Italian artists, 14th century attempts at perspective, and the trials and tribulations of a burgeoning Renaissance. Also of note is the gory 14th-century equivalent of the Passion of the Christ, "The Calvary," depicting a gold, sad, and bleeding Jesus that would make even Mel Gibson cringe.

➜ Behind Palais des Papes at then end of the square. ℹ Info brochures on what you're looking at scattered around the museum. $ €6, students €3. ⏰ Open M 10am-1pm and 2-6pm, W-Su 10am-1pm and 2-6pm..

FOOD 🍴

RESTAURANT NANI — 🌿♿🍸 ITALIAN ❶

rue de la République ☎04 90 82 60 90

Two story Avignonais restaurant specializes in *assiettes*, a pseudo calzone stuffed with meat, olives and tomatoes. Designed to resemble a small farmhouse, you'll definitely rub elbows with the locals in this popular (read: packed like sardines) restaurant.

➜ Corner of rue Théodore Aubanel and rue du Provôt. $ Express lunch with salade, coffee and grande assiette €9.60. Lunch menu for €14 gets you a choice of assiette, chocolate fondue and coffee. Dinner plates €7-15. ⏰ Lunch M-Sa 11:30am-2:30pm, Dinner F-Sa 7-11pm.

FRANÇOISE 💳♿📶 TRADITIONAL [1]

6 rue du Général Léclerc ☎04 32 76 24 77

A weird but trendy combo of cafeteria seating, baked goods and to-go sandwiches. Jams and jellies lure students and *gouteurs* (that's snackers to you) in to chill out for an hour or more over a hot cup of coffee.

i Free Wi-Fi. Credit card min. €10. $ Baked goods and sandwiches €1-5. Salads €4-9. Cafe €1.50 ⏰ Open M-Sa 8:30am-7pm.

NIGHTLIFE

WALL STREET 💳♿🍸👥 BAR

32 rue du Chapeau Rouge ☎06 61 07 11 62

Unlike Wall St., this youthful bar is justly popular with just about everyone. Students and *jouers* alike come on Friday for the stockmarket theme night, where the prices at the bar increase or decrease as randomly as the market itself every 100 seconds. Twice a night the market will "crash" and all prices are slashed by 50%. Prices are posted on their projector screen. Thursday is student night and Saturday is theme night, which changes weekly. Don't let the threat of an economic bubble scare you away—the prices never rise more than €4.50 for pints and shots, and can drop as low as €2. And you thought i-banking was boring.

$ €2.50 shooters and €2.50 half pints, €4.50 pints. Does not include market night. ⏰ Open M-Sa 6pm-1:30am.

LEVEL ONE ♿🍸 BAR

pl. Pie

For the dyed hair and grunge types, this dive bar is both the cheapest and most rough around the edges. Enjoy the 1970s American soundtrack featuring the likes of Janis Joplin and Hendrix while you shoot pool or play fooseball. The orange pleather booths are pretty groovy, unless someone more peirced than you are is sitting in it already.

i Happy hours 5-8pm, half priced pints. $ €2 shooters. €4 pints. Group drinking with €18 giraffes and 10 vodka shooters for €18. ⏰ Open daily 10am-1:30am.

ESSENTIALS

Practicalities

- **TOURIST OFFICE:** Offers maps, guidance, and a free pass that discounts Avignon sights by 20-50%. *(41 cours Jean Juarès. Walk straight down the main drag from the train station. Its on your right after 200 m ☎04 32 74 32 74 💻www.avignon-tourisme.com ⏰ Open Apr-Oct M-Sa 9am-6pm, Su 9am-5pm. Nov-Mar M-F 9am-5pm, Sa 9am-5pm, Su 10am-noon. Closed Dec 12-Jan 1)*
- **PETIT TRAIN:** Lets be real, Avignon is a small city that's easily walkable in a day, so the Petit Trains are mostly packed with, um, let's just say those who are most susceptible to the annual flu. Takes you to all the major sights in Avignon. (*Leaves from Palais des Papes every 20min ⏰ Open daily 10am-8pm. $ €7, children €4*)
- **GLBT RESOURCES:** Le CIDcafe. Loud and proud cafe with brochures to the popular GLBT clubs and bars, such as Le Cage and L'esclave, and a schedule of GLBT theme nights in Avignon *(Pl. St Pierre ☎04 90 82 30 38 💻www.lecidcafe.com).*
- **LAUNDROMAT:** La Blanchisseuse (*24 rue Lanterne ⏰ Open daily 7am-9pm.)*
- **INTERNET:** You can find free internet almost anywhere in Avignon; look out for the green sticker on the entrance to cafes, laundry mats, and stores. Both Françoise or the Laundry mat occasionally have free (but patchy) internet.
- **POST OFFICE:** *(Cours President Kennedy ☎04 90 27 54 10 ⏰ Open M-F 8:30am-6pm, Sa 9am-4pm.)*

Emergency!

- **POLICE:** Caserne de Salle. (*Bld. St. Roch* ☎*04 90 16 81 00*).
- **PHARMACY:** *(11 rue St. Agricole* ☎*04 90 82 14 20 Open daily 9am-7:15pm.)*
- **HOSPITAL: Hôpital Timone.** (264 rue St-Pierre Ⓜ️Timone. ☎*04 91 38 00 00).*

aix-en-provence   ☎0442

In Aix-en-Provence—the city of Paul Cézanne, Victor Vasarely, and Émile Zola—nearly every golden facade or cafe has had a brush with creative genius. In keeping with such a high-art history, Aix continues to boast a flourishing cultural scene with a world-renowned music festival held every July and over 40,000 students who provide the fuel during the year. When it comes to the *vieille ville* (old city), it may very well feel as if there are more restaurants and shops per capita than anywhere else in France. In the summertime, tourists come in droves to take advantage. There's always the escape to nearby Mont Ste-Victoire, but no matter the crowds, Aix's loveliness remains unspoiled.

ORIENTATION

You're in Aix-en-Provence. So far so good. Now you need to find **pl. de la Rotonde,** a large, spritzing fountain and traffic circle that marks the entrance to the *vieille-ville.* This is your homebase and the hub for Aix's public transportation. Thankfully, the **tourist office** is right next door, so you'll probably pick up a map and render this orientation useless. But just in case, here's the lowdown.

From pl. de la Rotonde, **av. des Belges** stretches downhill away from the old city and toward another traffic circle where it meets **av. de L'Europe.** The **Gare Routière** (bus station) is at this intersection, and the **Auberge de Jeunesse** is a 30min. walk straight along av. de l'Europe (or a 5min. bus ride on #4). Back at the fountain and your home-base (keep your eye on the ball), **Cours Mirabeau** is a tree-lined boulevard with numerous cafes. This is your promenading ground for essential services, food, and partying at all hours. Any left turn on Cours Mirabeau leads into the alleys of the old city with shops and restaurants galore. The best way to reach the heart of the old city, **pl. de l'Hotel de Ville,** is by using a map from the tourist office (sorry bud... those medieval streets are confusing.) Other awesome squares in the old city are **pl. des Cardeurs** to one side of pl. de l'Hotel de Ville and **pl. Richelme** just below it.

The remaining main street to know is **av. Bonaparte,** which exits from pl. de la Rotonde in the opposite direction of Cours Mirabeau. The next main street av. Bonaparte hits is the perpendicular **Cours Sextius,** which has nightlife hotspots. It forms one border of the old city. Moving in a circle around the old city from Cours Sextius, **bld. Jean Jaurès/bld. Aristide Briand** (same street, but the name changes), **Cours Saint Louis/bld. Carnot** and **bld. du Roi René** form the other borders. Now that you're oriented, go eat a *trianon* cake at **Patissier Riederer.**

ACCOMMODATIONS

At Aix's most affordable accommodations—the friendly youth hostel and leafy campgrounds—you'll have to accept being at a slight remove from *centre ville.* Thankfully, the bus service is so excellent that you won't feel the difference. The price jumps €20 or more as you approach the middle of town, but the hotels tend to be well situated on the periphery of the old city, and most offer amenities and Provençal charm. Staying in town might be pricey, but you'll get to appreciate Aix from the heart.

▨ AUBERGE DE JEUNESSE   ✈(ʳ)⚲ YOUTH HOSTEL ❶

3 av. Marcel Pagnol   ☎04 42 20 15 99 ▣www.auberge-jeunesse-aix.fr

Aix's most affordable accommodation is a veritable institution that sleeps 140 people in long hallways of four-person dormitories. The uniform bunk beds are comfortable, and although the baths vary in quality—with the occasional absence of a mirror or toilet seat—the porcelain is spotless. Without a doubt, the hostel's best feature is the casual restaurant and lounge, which gets going at 7:30pm. You can eat beautifully *(€5)*, or grab a beer and listen to the music.

➔ From pl. de la Rotonde or the Gare Routière, take bus #4 (dir: La Mayanelle) to the Vasarely stop, and the hostel gates are right there. Alternatively, walk away from the city center down av. de l'Europe. Pass through three traffic circles and follow well-marked signs. ℹ Breakfast included. Dinner €5. $ 4-bed dorms €19 with a HI card (€11). ⏰ Open daily 7am-2:30pm and 4:30pm-1am. Breakfast 7-9am. Vacate rooms by 10am for cleaning.

HOTEL PAUL 🏨 HOTEL [2]

10 av. Pasteur ☎04 42 23 23 90 💻hotel.paul@wanadoo.fr

A charming farmhouse converted into a no-frills hotel with simple rooms. In keeping with the homage to Cézanne in the lobby, there are dozens of flowers in the gorgeous garden. The rooms may not have A/C, and some lack showers, but they are equipped with fans, double beds, and miniature pastoral landscapes. Overall, the feel is lovely and the hotel is perfectly situated with respect to the *centre ville.* Reserve in advance and expect reception to be accommodating but strict about hotel rules.

➔ From pl. de l'Hotel de Ville, walk straight uphill on rue Gastan de Saporta until it exits the old city and becomes av. Pasteur. Continue straight, and the hotel is on your right. 10min. by foot. ℹ Breakfast €5. $ Singles €46-56; doubles €47-57; triples €69. ⏰ Reception opens at 7:15am.

CAMPING ARC-EN-CIEL ⛺📶 CAMPGROUND [1]

50 av. Malacrida ☎04 42 26 14 28 💻www.campingarcenciel.com

The old legend is true: there is a pot of gold at the end of the rainbow, and it's Camping Arc-en-Ciel. A gorgeous campground run by the the Carlier-Berger family since 1950, the 50 campsites are usually filled up with happy campers in vans and tents. Each site has electricity, running water, and free Wi-Fi in addition to shared goods like the public pool, ping-pong table, and TV lounge. The bridge over the green river flowing through the campground is straight out of Monet.

➔ From the city center, take bus #3 down Cours Gambetta until the Les 3 Sautets stop. Walk along av. Malacrida, and the campground is on your right. Signs point the way. $ 1 person €12.55. 2 people €19.20; €6.40 per person thereafter. ⏰ Open Apr-Sept. Gates open daily 8am-8pm. Otherwise, personal keys given upon request with a €10 deposit. Quiet hour 11pm.

SIGHTS 👁

👍 FONDATION VASARELY 🏛 MUSEUM

1 av. Marcel Pagnol ☎04 42 20 01 09 💻www.fondationvasarely.org

It's like nothing you've ever seen before; after all, the very act of seeing changes the dizzying shapes before your eyes. The father of optical-illusion art, the Hungarian-born French artist Vasarely wanted to bring about the "polychromatic city of happiness" with his massive creations of funky geometric forms in vibrant block colors, and the crazy shapes in this gallery can't help but make you happy in any of the museum's eight alcoves, each of which is its own colorful universe. *Gestalt Blue #164* in the "homage to the hexagon" room is an especially cool take on the möbius strip. In addition to the permanent collection, the gallery also holds exhibits of the most avant-garde art around.

➔ Take bus #4 from pl. de la Rotonde to Vasarely. The museum is the very modern building next to the youth hostel, where you're most likely staying. $ €9, students €6. ⏰ Open T-Su 10am-1pm and 2-6pm.

CHEMIN DE CÉZANNE/ L'ATELIER DE CÉZANNE 🏛 MUSEUM

9 av. Paul Cézanne ☎04 42 21 06 53 💻www.atelier-cezanne.com

Golden markers trace the footsteps of the artist on a 2hr. walking tour of the old

city. Lounge at Le Cafe Des Deux Garçons *(53 Cours Mirabeau, #3 on the route)*or marvel at the stained glass of the Cathédrale St-Saveur *(#31)*. In fact, the tour is a good way to get to know Aix's old city in general, since there are few streets Cézanne didn't grace with his presence. Unfortunately, most sights along the tour are only the facades of private bulidings, so the real gem is the last stop: **L'Atelier de Cézanne,** the Impressionist's recreated studio. World-famous wrinkled fruit, a green jug, and a rum bottle sit where Cézanne painted them, and his beret still hangs in the far corner. Staff in the studio are there to answer all questions in fluent English, and the wild garden around the studio transforms in the summer into a performance space for hip music and theater.

Pick up a walking tour from the tourist office to trace Cézanne's footsteps in Aix. For the Atelier, take rue Gaston de Saporta uphill from pl. L'Hotel de Ville until it leaves the old city and turns into av. Pasteur. Keep walking straight and take the right street when the road forks. Walk 10min. uphill on Av. Paul Cézanne and the studio is on your left. The path is well signed. $ €5.50, students €2. ⏰ Open July-Aug daily 10am-6pm; Oct-Mar daily 10am-noon and 2-5pm; Apr-June daily 10am-noon and 2-6pm.

LA CITÉ DU LIVRE — HISTORIC MONUMENT

8-10 rue des Allumettes ☎04 42 91 98 88 🖥www.citedulivre-aix.com

The heart of Aix's literary life can be found in an industrial factory that once produced matches and now invites the likes of Salman Rushdie and Nobel Laureate V. S. Naipaul to give public readings and lectures. The building is also home to the *Méjanes* Library, named for the *Marquis de Méjanes*, a passionate bibliophile who bequeathed his collection to the public in 1790. Since then, the library's stock has only grown and now impressively includes a 40m tall copy of *Le Petit Prince* at the main entrance. In addition to the wonderful books, CDs, and DVDs on loan, the library has the official archives of Albert Camus, a permanent exhibit on Émile Zola, bimonthly festivals, and creative special events. Free internet and tons of study spaces mean the desks are full around exam time. Check the website to see if the festivals coincide with your visit.

From pl. de la Rotonde, walk downhill on av. des Belges until the traffic circle. Turn right onto av. L'Europe and at the next traffic circle turn right again. La Cité du Livre is immediately on the left. ⏰ Open Tu noon-6pm, W 10am-6pm, Th-F noon-6pm, Sa 10am-6pm. Additional hours for festivals and readings. Centre Albert Camus open Tu-Sa 2-6pm.

MUSÉE GRANET — MUSEUM

pl. St-Jean de Malte ☎04 52 52 88 32 🖥www.museegranet-aixenprovence.fr

The large and excellent permanent collection includes nearly 600 works of art, with an emphasis on the French school from the 17th to the 19th centuries. There are rooms with titanic oil paintings of Roman gods and the picturesque pastoral landscapes that typically come to mind when you imagine French art. The room of oil paintings by Aix's favorite native son, Paul Cézanne, is exciting, but you'll beg for more; nine paintings really isn't enough. Temporary exhibits fill the other half of the museum, change annually, and are guaranteed to display someone important.

From pl. de la Rotonde, walk up Cours Mirabeau until the end. Turn right onto rue d'Italie and follow the signs for the the museum 2 blocks ahead and to the right. i Exhibits change year to year, but permanent exhibits are grouped thematically. $ €6, students, handicapped, and under 25 €4. Audio tour €3, students €1. ⏰ Open Tu-W 10am-7pm, Th noon-10pm, F-Su 10am-7pm.

CATHÉDRALE SAINT-SAVEUR — CHURCH

pl. de l'Université

Because construction happened over the course of an entire millenium, there are multiple stylistic elements fused into this mega-church. Begun in the fifth century, the cathedral received its clock in 1430, its Gothic facade in the 1500s, and the Baroque chapel in the 16th century. Through the wooden doors, you'll find

a dark, cavernous, and awe-inspiring interior with a famous triptych painted by Nicholas Fromant called *Brusson Ardent*. There's a room of Roman sculptures by the door as well as the oldest baptistry that still functions in all of France.
➜ On rue Gaston de Saporta, uphill from pl. de l'Hotel de Ville. 🕐 Open daily 8am-noon and 2-6pm. Mass M-Sa 8am, Su 10:30am and 7pm.

FOOD

Aix's *centre ville* is practically all restaurants, which means the city boasts an intensely comprehensive selection of international and Provençal cuisines. The food may be good, but the desserts are even better. The city's staple *bonbon* is the *calisson d'Aix*, an iced almond-and-candied-melon treat. Other specialties include *merveilles de Provence*, which are pralines with kirsch and chocolate available only at Christmastime, and any number of magnificent pastries, notably the decadent *trianon*, at the 200-year-old **Pâtissier Riederer** *(67 Cours Mirabeau ☎04 42 66 90 91 $ €3.80.)* At dinnertime, tables crowd **pl. Ramus** and **pl. des Cardeurs.** For a place to see and be seen, nothing is better than one of the cafes or restaurants on **Cours Mirabeau. Fruit and vegetable markets** are at **pl. de l'Hôtel de Ville, pl. Richelme** *(🕐 Open daily 7am-1pm)* and **pl. de la Mairie** *(🕐 Open Tu 7am-1pm, Th 7am-1pm, Sa 7am-1pm.)* Three **Petit Casinos** serve all your supermarket needs: 5 rue Gaston de Saporta *(🕐 Open M-Sa 8am-8pm)*, 16 rue d'Italia *(🕐 Open Tu-Su 8am-9pm)* and 3 Cours d'Orbitelle. *(🕐 Open M-F 8am-1pm and 4-8pm, Sa 8am-1pm and 4-:7:30pm.)*

BRUNCH — PROVENÇAL [2]

4 rue Portalis ☎06 98 36 00 76

Five tables, a glass counter of fresh food, and two women. That's all it takes to produce beautiful Provençal cuisine in this tiny lunch place. The salads are a meal in themselves, with tuna, chicken, goat cheese, or avocado resting on top of a deep bowl of grated carrots, cabbage, onion, lettuce, and potato. For a heartier meal, order a *quiche* or the perfectly priced *plat du jour*, which is usually a meat dish. And if you only have €2.50 to spend for the day, skip right to dessert, since the strawberries in *crème anglaise* are too good to eat in public. The nursery-rhyme paintings contribute to the joyful ambience, but most of the joy radiates from the grandmotherly woman bustling about to serve your food.
➜ Follow rue d'Italie all the way to pl. des Pecheurs. Turn right onto rue Portalis and look for the grandmotherly figure bustling in the window. $ Lunch €4-7.50. Dessert €2.50. 🕐 Open M-F 10am-7:30pm, Sa 10am-5pm.

PASTA COSY — PASTA [3]

5 rue D'Entrecasteaux ☎04 42 38 02 28

Pasta, pasta everywhere, and all of it to eat. This chic restaurant makes good on its promise of *toutes les pâtes du monde*. Homemade pastas like *fiochetti* (purses) are cooked in woks with eclectic ingredients borrowed from kitchens of the world, but the hunk of reggiano grated freshly onto your noodles still says old-fashioned Italian. A tapas menu also offers tasting portions of dill *crème brulée*, risotto, samosas, and other fusion dishes.
➜ From pl. de la Rotone, walk up rue des Espariat until a left turn onto rue des Tanneurs. Walk straight and take your 3rd left onto what looks like a mostly residential street. The restaurant is on your left. $ Pastas €14-19. 🕐 Open daily 7pm-midnight.

AUX DÉLICES DU LEBAN — LEBANESE [3]

33 rue Lieutaud ☎04 42 26 79 91

This little restaurant serves delicious and well-priced Lebanese basics, including hummus, *baba ganoush*, and plates of meaty *brochettes*. Much of the food is cooked on a decades-old baker's oven in the back of the kitchen. In the warm weather, head straight to the terrace seating area.
➜ At the very bottom of pl. des Cardeurs once it hits rue Lieutaud. $ Mezzes appetizers €6-6.50.

Plates 12-13.50. ⏰ Open daily noon-2pm and 7-11pm.

JACQUOU LE CROQUANT 🍴 PROVENÇAL [3]

2 rue de L'Aumone Vielle ☎04 42 27 37 19

If the French take their dining very seriously, then family-run Jacquou Le Croquant tries to out-French them all with an introduction to their menu that waxes philosophical on *le plaisir de manger* (the pleasure of eating) and *le plaisir de diner* (the pleasure of dining.) The restaurateurs insist on both pleasures, with an abundance of tender game meats like duck and goose in creamy sauces that are served at casual tables in the backyard of an apartment building. The *plat du jour* has the best price tag, but ordering a la carte guarantees a dinner right out of the oven.

🧭 Left turn into pl. Ramus of rue Bédarride. Follow the road right, then left. Le Croquant is past the group of restaurants on the right. $ Salads €9-14. Plates €14-17. Plat du jour €10. ⏰ Open daily noon-3pm and 7-11pm.

NIGHTLIFE

Crowds of students during the year and festival-goers in the summer make partying a year-round pastime in Aix. The nightlife picks up on Tuesday and rocks on until Saturday. Locals and visitors can be found in cafes and bars until closing time at 2am, when the party moves to Aix's clubs. On any given summer weekend, it feels like every seat is taken in the cafes and bars in **pl. de la Richelme, pl. des Cardeurs,** and, of course, along the central **Cours Mirabeau.** As the bars close, student clubs open their doors. Unfortunately, the only option for gay travelers in Aix is **Mediterranean Boy** *(5 rue de la Paix. Turn left on rue Vanloo at the top of Cours Sextius and make your next left onto rue de la Paix ☎04 42 27 21 47 ⏰ Open 10pm-late.)* Since most gay travelers head to Marseille for nightlife, the bar doesn't see too much action.

LE MISTRAL 🍴 CLUB

3 rue Frédéric Mistral ☎04 42 38 16 49 💻www.mistraclub.fr

Your nightly literary and geography lessons: Frédéric Mistral was a Nobel-Prize winning poet whose last name refers to a characteristic west wind that has blown through Provence for millennia. What does that have to do with Aix's most popular nightclub? Not much. Other than the fact that you'll beg for a breeze when the dancing hot bodies around you get too hot. Plus, this super chic club has hosted DJs like Bob Sinclair and and Carl Cox, modern-day poets on the club circuit. Everyday DJs Nikko and Moussa spin house, R and B, and hip hop for the crowds. Themes like '80s and '90s, electro, and ladies' night. Dress to impress.

*🧭 Immediately off Cours Mirabeau on rue Frédéric Mistral. **i** Ladies' Night Tu. Check website for other theme nights. $ Cover for guys €20; girls usually get in free. Gender equality hasn't reached Le Mistral just yet. Drinks €10. Bottles €125. ⏰ Open nightly midnight-6am.*

LE SEXTIUS BAR 🍴 BAR, CAFE

61 cours Sextius

A modern-day Batman in bar format, Le Sextius is an unassuming cafe by day and a life-saving student bar by night. The bartenders might not be superheroes, but the combo of frothy beer and live musicians on weekends will rescue your night from the grip of evil Dr. Banality. Regrettably, the Roman philosopher Sextius, a Stoic and the bar's namesake, would probably disapprove of the frolicking crowds that spread up and down the street in summer time.

🧭 From pl. de la Rotonde, walk along av. Bonaparte and turn right onto Cours Sextius. The bar is ahead on your right. $ Beer €2.20-5. Cocktails €7. ⏰ Open daily 9pm-2am.

LE CUBA LIBRE 🍴 CLUB

4 bld. Carnot ☎04 42 63 05 21 💻www.cuba-libre-aix.com

Le Cuba Libre used to be a taste of island life with cigars and tropical beverages.

Used to be, that is, until the manager gave the place a full makeover, turning former communist fun into a sleek and silvery bar that's meant for casual dancing to the live DJ and blue lights. Castro hasn't left the building just yet, since Monday, Tuesday, and Wednesday are salsa nights *(9pm.)* Tell the gregarious bartender, Yass, that he's the best in Aix and you'll make his night. Maybe he'll return the favor with a free drink?

#From pl. de la Rotonde take av. Victor Hugo until a left turn on bld. du Roi René. Le Cuba Libre is a 10min walk straight ahead. i Salsa night M-W 9pm. $ Beer €4.50. Cocktails €9. Liquor €2.50-7.50. Bottles €72-90. ⏰ Open M-F 5pm-2am, Sa-Su 1pm-2am.

ESSENTIALS

Practicalities

- **TOURIST OFFICE:** Offers a huge number of services, including maps, walking tours, pamphlets on art and culture, a **city guide** for university students, apartment listings, and an entire desk dedicated to helping with accommodations searching. *(2 pl. du Général de Gaulle ☎04 42 16 11 61 🖥www.aixenprovencetourism.com)* **Daily tours** are organized to Marseille *(€49)*, the lavender fields of Luberon *(€59)*, and Van Gogh heritage sights in Arles *(€69)*. The **Aix Pass** gets discounts at museums, concerts, and sights *(€2.)* **Public bus passes** are sold here as well *(☎04 42 26 37 28 🖥www.aixenbus.com ⏰ Open M-Sa 8:30am-7pm, Su 10am-1pm and 2-6pm.)* The office also houses **Ticket Sales** for Aix's concerts *(☎04 42 161 170 ⏰ Open M-Sa 9am-noon and 2-6pm.)*
- **CURRENCY EXCHANGE: Change de l'Agence.** Accepts traveler's checks. *(15 cours Mirabeau ☎04 42 26 84 77 ⏰ Open M-F 9am-noon and 2-6:30pm, Sa 9am-noon and 2-5pm.)*
- **LOST PROPERTY: SOS Voyageurs.** *(☎04 91 62 12 80)*
- **INTERNET ACCESS: Point Com** *(6 rue Gaston de Saporta $€6 per hr. ⏰ Open M-F 10am-1pm and 2-6:30pm, Sa 10am-1pm.)*
- **POST OFFICE: Place Hotel de Ville.** Poste restante and Western Union inside. *(⏰ Open M 8:30am-4pm, Tu 8:30am-12:15pm and 1:30-6pm, W-F 8:30am-4pm, Sa 8:30am-12:30pm.)* The Principal Post Office is at the corner of rue Lapierre and av. des Belges one block south of pl. de la Rotonde.

Emergency!

- **POLICE: Police Municipale.** *(2 cours des Minimes ☎04 42 91 91 11, or the general number ☎17.)*
- **HOSPITAL: Centre Hospitalier Du Pays D'Aix.** *(av. des Tamaris. A 10min. walk north of the old city center on av. Pasteur. Emergency line ☎04 42 33 90 28.)*
- **AMBULANCE:** ☎15. **SOS Medecins.** *(☎04 42 26 24 00.)* Doctors on-call for home visits.
- **PHARMACY:** There are pharmacies every 2 blocks along cours Mirabeau and a collection of 3 at pl. des chapeliers. Among them is **Pharmacie du Cours Mirabeau** *(17 cours Mirabeau ☎04 42 93 63 60 ⏰ Open M-F 8:30am-7:30pm.)* For night service, call the **Commissariat** *(☎04 42 93 97 00)* and they will contact the *pharmacie de garde* (24hr. pharmacy) for that night. For weekend service, check the list of rotating *pharmacies de garde (open 9am-2pm)* posted outside all pharmacies in Aix. Otherwise, call the *Commissariat*.

Getting There

By Train

The **Gare SNCF** train station is located at at Pl. Gustave des Places, and services regional trains *(☎36 35. ⏰Automatic ticketing window open daily 7am-7pm. Reservation and info offices open M-Sa 9am-6pm.)* To: **Marseille** *(💲 €5.30-7. ⏰ 40min., 27 per day);* **Cannes** *(💲 €31. ⏰ 3½hr., 25 per day.);* **Nice.** *(💲€34.40. ⏰ 3-4 hr., 25 per day.)* Note that train numbers decrease substantially on weekends. The **Gare d'Aix-en-Provence TGV** is located 20min. outside of the city, and connects travelers to major cities throughout France via the TGB. To **Paris Charles de Gaulle** *(💲 €80-110.⏰ 3-5 hr. depending on whether you go direct, 18 per day).* The Gare TGV can be reached by **shuttles** from the bus stations *(💲 €5.⏰ 20min., every 10min.)*

By Bus

Gare Routière *(av. de l'Europe.☎08 91 02 40 25.⏰Info desk open M-F 7:30am-7:30-m, Sa 7:30am-12:30pm and 1:30-6pm.)* To: **Marseille** *(🖥www.navetteaixmarseille.com.💲 €5. ⏰ 30 min., theNavette Rapideruns from 6:10am-8:10pm roughly every 10min. Less frequent early morning service from 5:45am and night service until 11:30pm.);* **Nice** *(💲 €30.⏰ 2½hr., 9am, 10:55am, 1:20pm, 2:30pm and 6pm);* **Avignon** *(💲 €14.70.⏰ 1¼hr., run daily 8:30am, M-F 7am, 8:30am, 11:30am, 1pm, 5pm, and 6:45pm.);* **Arles** *(⏰ 1hr.; runs daily 10am, 2pm, and 6:15pm, M-F 6am, 6:50am, 7:55am, 4:35pm, 5:20pm.)* A Youth Card for €15 per month permits a 50% reduction in fares.

Getting Around

Aix-en-Bus is *the* way to get around Aix, with fantastically frequent service *(☎04 42 26 37 28.💲 Tickets €1. 3-day pass 5€. 10 rides €7.)* Complete table of bus schedules and routes, bus passes and maps available at the Tourist Office. The **Association Des Taxis Radio Aixois** is also available *(☎04 42 27 71 11).*

nice ☎04

Nice has been on the backpacker must-see list since the youth of the world discovered its beaches and cheap wine. Combining a wealthy reputation with an affordable underbelly, Nice neatly condenses everything amazing about the Côte d'Azur into one sizzling metropolis. While those of you who'd like to escape the tourists will groan when you see the busloads of cruise-shipping retirees and loudmouthed anglophones in the Vieille Ville, you'll cheer when you see the rock-bottom happy hour prices at the local bars, and grin when you interact with the well-established youth culture that goes out of its way to make travelers feel welcome (a rarity in France). Daytime activities revolve around the rocky beaches and immense seaside promenade; extensive shopping opportunities and an unparalleled array of museums are available for those of you who can't just lie around all day. The city just about explodes at night, with live music in almost every bar and club and non-stop parties that make it hard to keep from dropping dead with exhaustion.

ORIENTATION

Vieux Nice

Vieux Nice is bounded by **bld. Jean Juares** to the north, the **château** to the east, and the **Jardin Albert I** to the west. Its winding steets are sometimes confusing for the tourists that invade the area around lunchtime and after sunset. The **cours Saleya** hosts local markets during the day that give way to cafes at night. Some of the largest crowds gather around the **Église St. Jeaques** and the **Palais du Justice** for street preformers. This is also where you'll find most of Nice's nightlife, backpackers, and cruise ship tourists. Small shops selling liqueurs, oils, and soaps are interspersed amongst the small boutique restaurants and hookah lounges.

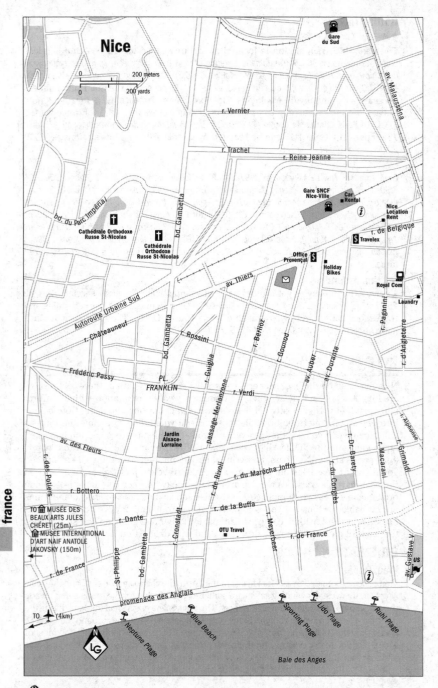

Nice

0 — 200 meters
0 — 200 yards

r. Vernier

r. Trachel

r. Reine Jeanne

Gare du Sud

av. Malaussèna

bd. du Parc Impérial

Cathédrale Orthodoxe Russe St-Nicolas

Cathédrale Orthodoxe Russe St-Nicolas

bd. Gambetta

Gare SNCF Nice-Ville

Car Rental

Nice Location Rent

r. de Belgique

Travelex

Office Provençal

Holiday Bikes

Royal Com

Laundry

Autoroute Urbaine Sud

av. Thiers

r. Châteauneuf

bd. Gambetta

r. Rossini

r. Berlioz

r. Gounod

av. Auber

av. Durante

r. Paganini

r. d'Angleterre

r. Frédéric Passy

PL. FRANKLIN

r. Guiglia

r. Verdi

Passage Merlanzone

Jardin Alsace-Lorraine

r. Alphonse

r. Grimaldi

r. Macarani

av. des Fleurs

r. Dr. Barety

r. des Potiers

r. Bottero

r. de Rivoli

r. du Marécha Joffre

r. du Congrès

r. Dante

r. de la Buffa

r. Meyerbeer

TO 🏛 MUSÉE DES BEAUX ARTS JULES CHÉRET (25m), 🏛 MUSÉE INTERNATIONAL D'ART NAIF ANATOLE JAKOVSKY (150m)

OTU Travel

r. de France

r. de France

r. St-Philippe

bd. Gambetta

r. Cronstadt

promenade des Anglais

US

TO ✈ (4km)

N L G

Neptune Plage

Blue Beach

Sporting Plage

Lido Plage

Ruhl Plage

Baie des Anges

france

👍 VILLA SAINT EXUPERY 💳♿📶🍸❄ HOSTEL [2]

22 av. Gravier ☎08 00 30 74 09 💻www.vsaint.com

One of Europe's coolest hostels, Villa Saint Exupery boasts one of the most extensive lists of organized activities we've ever seen, including sailing trips to St. Tropez and "Anything But Clothes" parties in its newly renovated monastery-turned-social-space. The place used to be one of the farthest hostels from the Vieille Ville, but all that changed in 2010 with the opening of its sister hostel in the pl. Massena. Family-run with English-speaking staff.

➡ From the Comte de Falicon tram stop, walk toward the post office and walk up ave. du Ray. Continue straight as the road turns into ave. Gravier. Walk 2 blocks and make a sharp left turn up the steep hill to the hostel on your left. $ Prices change frequently depending on occupancy. Dorms €16-30; doubles €54-90. ⏰ Reception open 8am-noon and 6pm-2am.

👍 HOTEL BELLE MEUNIERE 💳♿❄ HOSTEL [1]

21 av. Durant ☎04 93 88 66 15 💻www.bellemeuniere.com

This manor-turned-hostel is a backpacker's dream. Forget about the kitsch and the coin-operated soap dispensers; this place is unapologetically simple in its design and home-makeover feel. The rooms are all different and packed with loud social youth, who are attracted by the hostel's ideal location and "Backpacker special." New apartments with kitchenettes are also available for weekly rent not far from hostel.

*➡ From the train station, walk across the street and down the stairs to ave. Durant. Walk half a block and hostel is on your right. **i** Backpacker Special: Breakfast, linen, and shower €18. $ Doubles €49-52; triples €45-60; quads €80. ⏰ Reception until midnight.*

👍 PETIT LOUVRE 💳♿📶❄ HOTEL [3]

10 rue Emma et Phillip Tiranty ☎04 93 80 15 54

Hidden on a side street off the main drag, this hotel is centrally located and one of the best budget options for a long-term stay. The small but clean rooms offer baths, beds, and kitchenettes equipped with pots, pans, and silverware. While it may look like an Ikea catalogue, the prices are much more budget friendly.

*➡ From the tram stop Thiers, walk away from the train station down ave. Jean Medecibout 4 blocks past the Notre Dame cathedral. Turn left onto rue Emma et Phillip Tiranty. Hotel is on your left. **i** Kitchenettes available. $ Singles €45-51, weekly €288; doubles €57/369; triples €68.50/440.*

HOTEL INTERLAKEN 💳♿📶🍸❄ HOTEL [3]

26 rue Durant ☎04 93 88 30 15 💻www.hotelinterlaken.fr

Once upon a time, Picasso and Andy Warhol had a love child. That love child was then asked to decorate a hostel in Nice. This is that hostel. Seemingly random stripes, colors, mismatched kitschy chandeliers, and shiny objects are scattered among the brightly colored and spacious rooms. Just to make everything groovier, the hotel comes with a bar.

➡ Opposite the train station. $ Singles €44-55; doubles €49-62; triples €69-81; quads €84-104.

Sea Front

Not to burst your bubble, but the hotels along the Sea Front are, well, expensive. Who would have thought that such a pristine location right next to the beaches in southern France would be expensive? Surely not us.

HOTEL CRONSTADT 💳♿📶❄ HOTEL [5]

3 rue Cronstadt ☎04 93 02 00 30 💻www.hotelcronstadt.com

One of the most down-to-earth hotels on the seafront, this establishment is run by an old lady who apparently still decorates like it's 1873. Old pictures, chandeliers, quilted bedspreads, and eerie silence add to the feel that this place might be haunted. The only question is if you see Casper, who ya gonna call?

➡ Bus #8, 11, 52, 60, 62 to Gambetta/Promenade. From the bus stop, along the Promenade

*des Anglais, walk towards the Hotel Negresco and turn left onto rue de Cronstadt. Hotel is on your left. **i** Wi-Fi available. Ⓢ Singles €70-75; doubles 90-95; triples €110.*

HOTEL CANADA
💨♿(♥)🛏 HOTEL ❹

8 rue Halevy
☎04 93 87 98 94

A welcomed two-star hotel in this expensive neighborhood. Decorated with replicas of Fernand Leger paintings, this colorful and laid-back hotel has clean rooms and a calm breakfast terrace. If you can stand the heat without A/C, you can live the Niçois lifestyle here.

🚌 Bus #8, 11, 52, 59, 60, 62 to Gustave V. Facing direction of bus, walk across and down the street to the left of Le Meridien. Continue 1 block; hotel is on your right. Ⓢ Singles €52-60; doubles €65-85; triples €89-100.

SIGHTS
👁

Vieux Nice

🖼 MUSÉE D'ART MODERNE ET D'ART COMTEMPORAIN
⦿ MUSEUM

Promenade des Arts
☎04 93 62 61 62 💻www.mamac-nice.org

Located just blocks from the Vieux Nice, Nice's massive Museum of Modern and Contemporary Art offers minimalist galleries that pay homage to the French new Realists, as well as American pop artists like Warhol. Rotating contemporary exhibits showcase artists from around the world. Don't miss the collection of statues by Niki St-Phalle, which routinely frighten even the most hardcore hallucinogen users.

🚌 Promenade des Arts. Take the tram to Catedrale - Vieille Ville. Ⓢ Free. Tours €3, students €1.50. ✪ Open Tu-Su 10am-6pm.

🖼 CHÂTEAU CASTLE HILL
FORTRESS

☎04 93 85 62 33

The remains of an 11th-century fort located on the hill overlooking Vieux Nice, this château is the oldest spot in the city. Celto-Ligurians claimed the sight until the Romans decided it would make a good spot for a fort in 154 CE. Centuries later, Provençal nobles built a castle and cathedral on the hill as a symbol of their authority. During King Louis XIV's great centralization of France, the fortress was destroyed. Today, all that remains is the large park and waterfall that were made from the ruins. The climb may be tiresome, but the view is well worth it, and offers 360 degree views of Nice and the Med.

Ⓢ Free. ✪ Open June-Aug daily 9am-8pm; Sept 10am-7pm; Oct-Mar 8am-6pm; Apr-May 8am-7pm. Info booth open July-Aug Tu-F 9:30am-12:30pm and 1:30-6pm.

COURS SALEYA
SQUARE, MARKET

cours Saleya

Built on the ramparts in the 18th century, the cours Saleya is now a bustling hub of activity ideally situated between Nice Vieille Ville and the beach. Nice's open-air market is located here by day, and a collection of hip cafes set out tables at night. The square is also home to the famous *Marche des Fleurs,* where you can buy opulent bouquets of local flora. A perfect spot to wander through Nice's winding alleyways.

✪ Market daily 7:30am-1pm.

WAR MEMORIAL
MEMORIAL

Place Guynemer

At the foot of the castle hill, this enormous WWI memorial stands in honor of the 4000 Niçois who died in the line of duty between 1914 and 1919. Over 50m tall, this monument was erected in 1924, and cut directly into the old quarries. Some of the most spectacular views of the Mediterranean are along this promenade, which links the port to the Vieille Ville. Although there are signs that warn against

it, don't be surprised to see local kids skateboarding on the memorial steps.
Ⓢ *Free.*

CATEDRALE ST. RÉPARATE

CATHEDRAL

pl. Rossetti

Nice's largest and most opulent cathedral was inspired by early Baroque architectural models from Rome. It is not an accident that the design is a miniature version of the larger and more famous St. Peter's in Rome, complete with a triple nave and a transept.

🕐 *Open daily 7am-6pm. Closed for visits during services.*

ADAM AND EVE HOUSE

HISTORIC SIGHT

rue de la Poissonerie

You'll walk right by this one if you're not careful. The Adam and Eve house, as it's called locally, is one of the last examples in Vieux Nice of the detailed facades that historically decorated the homes here. The house's bas-relief dates back to 1584, and depicts Adam and Eve, naked in the Garden of Eden, threatening each other with clubs. Apparently this WWE version of the Bible never made into the mainstream in English-language trasnlation.

PLACE GARIBALDI

SQUARE

pl. Garibaldi

On the eastern end of the Vieille Ville, the large open space of *place* Garibaldi is lined by elegant, red buildings with green shutters and vaulted porticos. You can see the perfectly integrated Chappelle St-Sepulcre nestled amongst the buildings surrounding the statue and fountain of Garibaldi.

Massena

▨ MUSÉE MATISSE

♿ MUSEUM

164 rue des Arenes   ☎04 93 81 08 08 ▨www.musée-matisse-nice.org

This expertly renovated Genoese villa displays decades of art by one of France's most elusive artists. The permanent collection includes Matisse's early sketches, as well as gouache 3D cardboard cut-outs... er... sorry... "*tableaux.*" If you can't make it up to Vence to see Matisse's whimsical *Chapelle du Rosaire de Vence* for yourself, check out the museum's model of the chapel, and the exhibit that examines his creative process, including the artist's initial attempts to depict the stations of the cross in black and white finger paint. Temporary exhibits generally display more oblique aspects of Matisse's life and work, such as his decades-long artistic obsession for a Russian girl (he drew her and only her for 10 years) named Lydia.

⚑ *Take bus #15, 17, 20, 22 or 25 to Arenes. Free shuttle between Chagall and Matisse museums.* 𝒊 *Tours in English by reservation.* Ⓢ *Free.* 🕐 *Open M 10am-6pm, W-Su 10am-6pm.*

MUSÉE NATIONAL MESAGE BIBLIQUE MARC CHAGALL

⚐ MUSEUM

av. Dr. Menard   ☎04 93 53 87 20 ▨www.musée-chagall.fr

The museum showcases Chagall's interpretation of the Hebrew Bible, comprised of 12 massive canvases that the artist chose to arrange by color rather than chronologically. The adjacent rooms display his "creative" blending of the Bible and the Russian Revolution (because when you say Lenin, we think Crucifixion). The museum also includes an auditorium that hosts concerts and other events, with stained-glass panels by the artist depicting the story of creation.

⚑ *Walk 15min. northeast from the train station or take bus #22 (dir. Rimez to Musée Chagall).* Ⓢ €9.50 *under 26. Art students and EU citizens free.* 🕐 *Open May-Oct M 10am-6pm, W-Su 10am-6pm; Nov-Mar M 10am-5pm, W-Su 10am-5pm. Last entry 30min. before close.*

MONESTERE CIMIEZ

♿ MONASTERY, MUSEUM

av. du Monestere

The monastery was a Franciscan hideout before it was confiscated by the

Revolution. When the Revolution collapse, Monestere Cimiez was returned to the church, and the monks expanded its gardens; they now overlook the port, and stretch to the cemetery where Matisse is buried. Inside the church is a nearly 6m tall marble cross, accompanied by small statues that portray figures from St. Francis' visions.

Take bus #15, 17, 20, 22 or 25 to Arenes. Walk across the park to the Monastery. [$] Free. ⏰ Open M-Tu 10am-5pm, Th-Sa 10am-5pm. Closed on Su during service.

frenchism

If you hear a few familiar words while in Paris, even though you don't speak French, don't be alarmed; the adoption of English words here is both a common and **controversial phenomenon.** *Le hamburger, le jogging,* and *le weekend* are all words that French-speakers use regularly. As the digital age introduced words like *podcast, email,* and *Wi-Fi,* French has struggled to keep up with English in the creation of new terminology. Most French people find it easiest to simply say "podcast" or "Wi-Fi" (pronounced **wee-fee**), but French cultural purists feel that this is an outrage. Enlisting French linguists at the **Academie Francaise**, nationalists associated with the Ministry of Culture have started a movement to invent new French words for the influx of new ideas. Podcast becomes *diffusion pour baladeur* and Wi-Fi, *acces sans fil a l'internet.* It's a valiant crusade, but Wi-Fi is just so much easier to say!

SAINTE JEANNE D'ARC CHURCH ♿ CHURCH

11 rue Grammont

A modern wonder in its day, this church was built in the 1930s entirely out of concrete, then painted white to resemble some blend of sci-fi and Middle Eastern architecture. The domed Byzantine ceiling is laden with symbolism: pat yourself on the back if you can figure out the numerical significance of the seven mini domes supporting the church's three larger domes. Alright, well it has to do with a certain number of virtues supporting a trinity. The church is named after the small chapel to the side, which is dedicated to France's favorite 17-year-old saint (or witch, if you ask the English).

Take the T37 or bus 22 to Église Jean d'Arc. ⏰ Open 8am-4:30pm.

MONT ALBAN FORT ♿ FORT

av. du Mont-Alban

Once a 16th-century fort, this massive and now defunct hilltop bastion boasts a stunning view of Nice, the nearby Cap d'Ail, and even Antibes. The brochure says that on a clear day you can see Corsica, but we sadly didn't. If you're yearning for a long uphill hike in hot weather, this fort's for you. Nice plans to convert the fort into a contemporary art museum in the near future, but for now you'll have to settle for a stroll around the battlements, as visitors are not allowed inside.

Take bus #14 to Chemin du Fort and walk downhill to the fort. Also a footpath exists near the bus stop Escalliers de Verre (bus #81 and 100)

PLACE MASSENA ♿ SQUARE

Place Massena

One of the main centers of the city, this large town square is patterned like a checkerboard, and unlike many areas of Nice, remained relatively untouched during both world wars. The most recent renovations incorporated the tramway into the area, in addition to seven meditating statues perched atop a collection of large poles, designed by Spanish artist Juame Plensa (they supposedly represent each of the seven continents). These figures are joined by breakdancers and street performers during the day and a grittier crowd at night. (Read: take the tram at night.)

Sea Front

The sights that line the Sea Front are largely architectural, with the exception of the villas and estates that have been converted into pretty impressive museums.

MASSENA MUSEUM ♿ MUSEUM

65 rue de France and 35 promenade des Anglais ☎04 93 91 19 10

Once home to (you guessed it!) the prominent Massena family, this giant seaside estate was donated to the city at the turn of the century by Andre Massena, much to the chagrin of the eldest son who had hoped to inherit it. Exhibits include paintings and photographs of Nice's old carnival pier and other neighborhoods, as well as a collection of elaborate dresses that would make Barbie blush. The ornate estate proves that France retained a nobility long after the Revolution.

🕘 *Open M 10am-6pm, W-Su 10am-6pm.* $ *Free.*

MUSÉE BEAUX ARTS ♿ MUSEUM

33 av. des Baumettes ☎04 92 15 28 28 💻www.musée-beaux-arts-nice.org

When you first see its inconvenient location in the far corner of the city, you'll be tempted to blow it off (we almost did). For art lovers, that would be a terrible mistake. This villa turned museum holds works by both Picasso and Rodin. One of the most maccabre collections is a gallery by Niçois artist Gustav-Adolf Mossa, whose work includes the most nightmarish, surrealist paintings imaginable, including clowns with bloody knives and harpies on the piles of dead bodies.

🕘 *Open M 10am-6pm, W-Su 10am-6pm.* $ *Free.*

PROMENADE DES ANGLAIS ♿ PROMENADE

promenade des Anglais

Once a six-feet-wide dirt path, this main artery of Nice was expanded in 1820 by a wealthy Englishman, then inaugurated in 1931 by the Duke of Connaught, one of Queen Victoria's sons. Today it runs along the beach and connects the Sea Front to the Vieille Ville, and provides an easy footpath between private beaches.

BEACHES ♿ BEACH

promenade des Anglais

The public and private **beaches** alternate along the Baie des Anges from Vieux Nice as far as the Sea Front goes. Expect to pay for the umbrellas and chairs at the private beaches, bring multiple towels for padding, or buy a cheap beach mat—the beaches here are pretty rugged, and you don't want to end up sunbathing on jagged rocks. We recommend that you give up the search for sand and just go swimming.

HOTEL NEGRESCO ♿ HOTEL, HISTORIC BUILDING

37 promenade des Anglais

There's a reason we didn't list Hotel Negresco under the accommodations—this place is over €400 a night. The classic Niçois architecture is pretty spectacular, though. The hotel has been clasified as a historical building since 2003, ensuring that its bright white walls and pink dome will be in postcards well in the future.

FOOD

Vieux Nice

Food is plentiful and cheap in this part of town. You'll be able to find the expensive restaurants easily enough, but the charm of Vieux Nice lies in its small snack shacks, markets, and hole-in-the-wall *socca* joints. While heavy on the tourists, Vieux Nice still offers thriving local markets in the Marche des Fleurs and the Cours Saleya *(daily*

7am-1pm), where flowers are sold at slashed prices alongside candied fruits, fresh produce, olives, and Italian cannolis. There are two large **Monoprix** supermarkets located in on ave. Jean Medecin *(⏰ open M-Sa 8:30am-8pm)* and in pl. Garibaldi *(⏰open M-Sa 8:30am-8pm).*

LA FERME SALEYA — TRADITIONAL ❸
8 rue Jules Gilly ☎06 71 84 07 32
This traditional French restaurant will make you think that you're in the rural countryside of Bretagne or Angers. Cute pottery farm animals hint at the largely carnivorous meal that you're about to eat. Call ahead for a group, and the chef will prepare a personalized menu at prices that are comparable to the house *formule.*
$ Formule €15-22. ⏰ Open Tu-Su 12-2:30pm and 7-10pm.

FENOCCHIO — ICE CREAM ❶
2 pl. Rossetti ☎04 93 80 72 52
Serving the best ice cream in France, Fenocchio offers 96 flavors of Italian gelatto, including more eccentric flavors such as beer, avocado, and rose. Traditional flavors like vanilla and pistachio are delicious here too. *Let's Go* recommends one of their decadent sundaes for €10-20.
$ 1 scoop €2, 2 scoops €3.50. ⏰ Open daily 10am-midnight.

RENE SOCCA — SOCCA ❶
2 rue Miralheti ☎04 93 92 05 73
Forget the tourist-frequented *socca* joints—this is the only authentic one you'll find. The lines around the block indicate that this place serves some of the best quality fried Niçois dishes in whole city. Terrace seating with one drink minimum under signs that strongly advise against the use of silverware.
$ Socca €2.50. Plats €5-10. ⏰ Open daily noon-9pm.

FLORIAN — CANDY SHOP ❷
14 quai Papacino ☎04 93 55 43 50 www.confiserieflorian.com
Every sweet tooth's dream come true, this confectionery offers tours of its factory, where you learn how to make candied fruit, crystalized flowers, and candied orange peels. While the tour might make your mouth water, remain in control of you wallet, since you'll want to splurge (understandably so) in the pricey yet delicious boutique after being teased with samples.
In the New Port. i Tours of factory on demand with video in English or French. $ Candied flowers €6. Candied fruit assortment €36. ⏰ Open M-Sa 11am-8pm.

LA MERANDA — PROVENÇAL ❷
4 rue de la Terrasse ☎08 92 68 06 89
A small 12-table gem on the edge of Vieux Nice, Le Meranda's chef Dominique le Stanc produces an outstanding menu that changes daily based on the local market fare. Ratatouille and pizza are regularly served here, in addition to traditional Provençal dishes.
$ Plats €9-13. i Reserve in person for lunch and dinner. ⏰ Open M-F noon-1:30pm and 7-9pm.

Massena

Massena might not offer the backpacker staples of *socca* and cheap fast food, but if you have a little extra to spend on one night out, this is where you want to go. Classy, local, and cheap(er than Vieille Ville), Massena is not as infested with tourists as the rest of the city, and has the traditional cuisine you came to France for.

MANGEZ-MOI — FRENCH ❸
9 rue Blacas ☎04 93 87 54 71 www.restaurantmangezmoi.com
Adorable French/seafood blend restaurant that has all the kitschy decorations

octogenarians go crazy for. Cozy garden seating on ivy-covered terrace. Come for the taster menu of changing daily specials.

$ €15 menu. €25 3-course. ⏰ Open Tu-Th 9am-8:30pm, F-Sa 8:30-10pm.

👍 SPEAKEASY
🚫♿🍸 VEGAN ❷

7 rue Lamartine ☎04 93 85 59 50

A throwback to the Haight-Ashbury circa 1967, this vegan restaurant is run by a friendly American expat hippie. Strangers share the small tables when it gets crowded. The menu changes frequently; cross your fingers and hope that Jane whips up her vegan pie.

$ €14 2-course menu. Specials €9-11. i Open M-F noon-2:15pm and 7-9:15pm, Sa noon-2:15pm.

LE NOLITA
💳♿🍸🌤 CRÊPERIE ❷

8 av. Durant ☎06 23 74 66 67

The small, New York-themed crêpe cafe serves lunch and breakfast specials on the small outdoor patio. Pasta specials accompany dessert *du jour* such as *Mousse au Chocolat* and sweet crêpes.

$ Midi menu €11. Crêpes €7-8. ⏰ Open daily 8am-8pm.

GRAND CAFE DE LYON
💳♿🍸🌤 BRASSERIE ❷

33 av. Jean Medecin ☎04 93 88 13 17 💻www.cafedelyon.fr

One of the oldest brasseries in Nice, this centrally located giant of a bar dominates the shopping area, and is a must for those craving the most elaborate sundae or people-watching combos. Crowds escape the heat by lounging in wicker chairs under rotating fans.

$ Ice cream €5-11. Cocktails €5.30-7.70. ⏰ Open daily 7am-11pm.

Sea Front

Most of the restaurants in this neighborhood are small cafes or more upscale brasseries. While eating out here along the promenade might be out of your reach, any of the small alleys that run perpendicular to the beach have cheap gyro stands and pizza places that sell by the slice. If you do happen to sit down at one of the pricey bistros, go for any of the fruit/ice cream cocktails that are frequently served up.

👍 CAFE DE LA PROMENADE
💳♿🍸🌤 BRASSERIE ❶

3 promenade des Anglais ☎04 93 82 54 55

If you're aching for a real American or English breakfast (as real as France can provide, anyway), come to this cabana-esque diner, which features the plush vinyl booths of your local Denny's and the calorie intake to match.

$ Sandwiches and salads €7-12. Sundaes €7.70-9.70. American breakfast €13.50. ⏰ Open daily 7:30am-2am.

NISS'TANBUL
🚫♿🍸🌤 GREEK ❶

4 bld. Gambetta ☎06 23 12 66 32

A budget traveler's dream. Renowned for its cheap gyros and Turkish fast food, Niss'tanbul whips up hot kebabs and baklava and pours out cheap Greek and Turkish wine.

$ Gyro €5. Plats €9-10. ⏰ Open daily 11am-midnight.

POMODORISSIMO
🚫♿🌤 PIZZA ❶

2 rue Gambetta ☎04 93 02 43 67

Enabling the beach bums of the world one slice at a time, this hole-in-the-wall fast-food joint is ideally located for sunbathers. There's also a small seating area, if you aren't in a hurry to get back to the sand.

$ Pizza slice €2.50. ⏰ Open daily 11am-8:30pm.

NIGHTLIFE

Vieux Nice

◪ BULLDOG PUB POMPEII
●⊗♥♬☎ BAR, LIVE MUSIC

14, 16 rue de l'Abbaye ☎04 93 85 04 06 ▣www.bulldogpub.com

One of Nice's best-kept secrets for locals and intrepid backpackers, this '60s and '70s rock-themed pub hosts live music every night. The house is regularly packed with young people, who resort to barstools and tabletops for standing room.

i Live music, smoking lounge upstairs. Ⓢ Beer €6. Cocktails €8. 6 shots €18. ⓩ Open daily 8am-4am. Live music starts at 10pm.

WAYNE'S BAR
●♿♥♬☎ PUB

15 rue de la Prefecture ☎04 93 13 46 99

Wayne's is a late-night institution in Nice, with an English-speaking staff that caters to rowdy, spitting crowds of unwashed backpackers. Huge crowds at night gather for pop-rock music and drunk, travel story swapping (sounds like a *Let's Go* office party).

i Tourist bookings for bungee jumping, sailing, day trips to towns. Happy hour pints €3.90. Ⓢ Beer €6.20. Cocktails €7.50. ⓩ Open daily noon-2am. Kitchen open noon-11pm. Happy hour 5-8pm.

MA NOLANS
●♿♥♬☎ PUB

2 rue François ☎04 93 81 46 90

Upscale and fun Irish pub that offers karaoke and trivia (with prizes for the winners). House speciality here is pear cider, if you happeneed to be debating a splurge on a pint or whiskey cocktail.

i Trivia night on M 8pm. Karaoke F 10pm-close. Ⓢ Beer €3.90. Cocktails €7.50. ⓩ Open M-Sa noon-2am. Happy hour 5-8pm.

LE SIX
●♿♥♬▼ GAY BAR

6 rue Raoul Bosio ☎04 93 62 66 64

One of the most opulent and creative gay bars in the Riviera. The large space dates back to the Belle Époque, with a room displaying the shower for its nightly shower show. Telephones scattered throughout bar randomly connect to each other for secret chatting with anonymous patrons.

Ⓢ Beer €7. Cocktails €10. ⓩ Open daily 10pm-5am.

3 DIABLES
●♿♥♬ BAR

2 cours Saleya ☎04 93 62 47 00 ▣www.les3diables.com

This bar has become a hopping youth hangout thanks to its Thursday night student prices; just flash your student ID for a dramatic reduction in prices. The two-story bar regularly serves both locals and backpackers. After midnight, DJs turn the bar upstairs into more of a club.

i Karaoke W night. Student night Th, pints €4.. Ⓢ Liquor €3.50. Pints €6.80. Cocktails €8. ⓩ Open daily 5pm-3am. Happy hour 5-9pm.

NOCY-BÈ
●⊗ HOOKAH

4,6 rue Jules Gilly ☎04 93 16 93 20

Traditional Maghreb hookah bar with low lighting, low couches, and no alcohol consumption. Bright cushions, Moroccan lamps, and arched doorways allow you to take a trip across the Mediterranean without the 24hr boat ride.

i No alcohol served. 1-drink min. (as in soda or tea). Ⓢ Hookah €10. Tea €4. ⓩ Open M-Sa 3:30pm-12:30am.

PUB OXFORD
●♿((•))♥ PUB

4 rue Mascoïnat ☎04 93 92 24 54

The cheapest booze in town is served at this new English pub in the center of the old city. Walk through the red telephone booth in the doorway and enjoy the delightfully tacky atmosphere and good company.

i Happy hour shooters €1.50; cocktails €4; pints €3. $ Liquor €6.40. Beer €6.50. ⏰ Open daily 7pm-5am. Happy hour 7-11pm.

THE PLEASURE 💳♿🍸 BAR, SEX SHOP

27 rue Benoît Bunico ☎06 83 81 61 63

For the truly adventurous or hedonistic, this sex shop/bar should take you well past your limits, with its pink feathery decor and extensive drink list of suggestive cocktails such as "Sensual" and "Desire." Friendly owner has experience calming down visibly uncomfortable customers, and regularly reassures patrons that this is a "normal bar."

$ Cocktails €6-10. ⏰ Open Tu-Su 6pm-12:30am.

LES DISTILLERIES 💳♿🍸☀ BAR

24 rue de la Prefecture ☎04 93 62 10 66

Classy bar reminiscent of a turn-of-the-century *brasserie*. Belt-driven fans and antiquated radios complement the veteran adjoining brewery, reminding us that the Niçois have always drank like sailors, even in the classy Belle Époche.

$ Shots €3. Beer €7. Cocktails €7.50. ⏰ Open M-Sa noon-2am. Happy hour 6-8pm.

Massena

Massena might not be the backpacker's first choice for nightlife, but it might tickle your fancy if you're in town for longer than a week and in need of some serious cultural immersion. Few internationals venture beyond the realms of the Vieille Ville and the comfort of Wayne's after all.

LA BODEGUITA DEL HAVANA 💳🚭🍸 BAR

14 rue Chauvain ☎04 93 92 67 24

Papered with Che pics and with rum barrels as tables, this Cuban salsa bar and disco has the feel of a run-down bar in Havana. Serves up Cuban dishes and an extensive list of mojitos *(€10.50)*.

i Salsa dancing W-Th 7:30pm. $ Beer €3. Cocktails €10.50. ⏰ Open Tu-Su 8pm-2am.

LE TONO 💳♿🍸☀ TAPAS, WINE BAR

18 rue Clemenceau ☎04 93 87 84 17

This laid-back wine bar was repeatedly recommended by locals, and serves tapas at an impressively reasonable €6. The menu is mostly vegetarian, but carnivores can find something to eat here too. The outdoor seating and relaxed jazzy vibe lure customers in for late lunches and drinks long after the sun sets.

$ Wine glasses €3-4. Beer €5. Vegetarian tapas €6. ⏰ Open Tu-Su 3pm-midnight.

ARTS AND CULTURE ♫

Festivals and Carnivals

Nice is known for its summer music festivals, particularly the Fête de la Music that occurs on the summer solstice. The bacchanalian Carnival takes place in February or March.

👍 **FÊTE DE LA MUSIQUE** ♿☀ CITYWIDE

This citywide festival is as unofficial as it is awesome. A treasured Niçois tradition since the mid-'80s, this celebration gets every bar, disco, and restaurant in the city puts on free live music in the streets, cafes and alleyways of the city on the summer solstice. Nice comes alive with everything from pop rock to DJ party music. The crowds get particularly rowdy in the *vieille ville*, so make sure to watch out for pickpockets and those who wish to ruin the fun, drunken times. Apart from that minor setback, this is Nice at its best; many of the bars open early and stay open well after 3 or 4am, and the fast food joints take advantage of the partiers and offer *socca* and pizza in the early morning as well. Head to the area around Wayne's and the cours Saleya for the best and most international bands.

⏰ *Summer Solstice (June).*

CARNIVAL — SEA FRONT

💻www.nicecarnaval.com

France might take pride in its secular society, but this annual excuse to get really drunk and dance around owes its existence to the Catholic culture of Nice. The Promenade des Anglais and the quai des Etats-Unis host two weeks of parades, fireworks, and concerts, while confetti falls like rain in Seattle. Flower processions, masked balls, and endless partying make this the liveliest time in Nice's winter.

$ *Tickets €10-30.*

NICE JAZZ FESTIVAL — CIMIEZ

Arenes et Jardins de Cimiez ☎08 20 80 04 00 💻www.nicejazzfestival.fr

Every July, the quiet area of Cimiez and gardens outside of the Matisse Museum swell with over 55,000 spectators, who flock to the city for the eight-day festival, featuring 75 concerts and over 500 individual musicians.

i Free shuttle from the pl. Massena during concerts. $ €29-49 per night, students €22-36; 3-day passes €96-105; 8-day €185. ⏰ Concerts 7pm-midnight.

Cinema, Opera, and Theater

CINEMATHEQUE DE NICE — MASSENA

3 espalande de Kennedy ☎04 92 04 06 66 💻 www.cinematheque-nice.com

The historic theater screens old black-and-white films, documentaries, and art-house staples. The prices here are an absolute steal, but don't expect box office hits or convenient show times. Schedule changes weekly, and is available at the tourism office and local museums.

$ *Tickets €2.* ⏰ *Showings between 11am-8:15pm.*

OPÉRA DE NICE — SEA FRONT

4-6 rue St-François de Paule ☎04 92 17 40 79

Produces stage performances September-May, and hosts visiting orchestras and individual soloists year round. Ballet and Opéra schedule changes and is available at the tourist office.

$ *€7-40.* ⏰ *Box office open M-F 8:30am-4:30pm.*

ESSENTIALS

Practicalities

- **TOURIST OFFICE: Branch on ave. Thiers** has hotel reservations, restaurant and sights guides as well as a city map and practical guide (*Next to the train station. ☎08 92 70 74 07 💻www.nicetourisme.com ⏰ Open Jun-Sept M-Sa 8am-8pm, Su 9am-7pm; Oct-May M-Sa 8am-7pm, Su 10am-5pm.)* **Branches at 5 promenade des Anglais.** (*☎08 92 70 74 07 ⏰ Open Jun-Sept M-Sa 8am-8pm, Su 9am-6pm; Oct-May M-Sa 9am-6pm.)* **Airport Location.** (*Terminal 1 ☎08 92 70 74 07 ⏰ Open Jun-Sept daily 8am-9pm; Oct-May M-Sa 8am-9pm.)*
- **CONSULATES: Canada.** *(10 rue Lamartine ☎04 93 92 93 22 ⏰ Open M-F 9am-noon.)* **UK.** *(Embassy in Monaco, 33 bld. Princesse Charlotte ☎377 93 50 99 54)* **US.** *(7 ave. Gustave V ☎04 93 88 89 55 ⏰ Open M-F 9-11:30am and 1:30-4:30pm.)*
- **YOUTH CENTER: Centre Regional d'Information Jeaunesse (CRIJ)** Posts summer jobs for students and provides info on long term housing, sudy, and recreation. *(19 rue Gioffredo, near the Museum of Contemproary Art. ☎04 93 80 93 93 💻www.crijca.fr i Free internet with Student ID. ⏰ Open M-F 10am-6pm.)*

- **LAUNDROMATS:** These are plentiful in Nice, so check to make sure you're not around the corner from one already before going to. *(7 rue d'Italie* ☎*04 93 85 88 14* Ⓢ *Wash €3.50, dry €1 per 18min.) (11 rue de Pont Vieux* ☎*04 93 85 88 14* Ⓢ *Wash €2.50-6.50. dry €.50 per 8 min.* Ⓩ *Open daily 7am-9pm.)*

- **INTERNET ACCESS:** Internet access is available on almost every street corner in Nice, usually marked by neon signs in Arabic. Free internet at the CRIJ and Wi-Fi at selected Cafes and bars. Closest Internet from the train station is on rue Theirs across from the Thiers tram stop.

- **POST OFFICE:** *(23 ave. Thiers* ☎*04 93 82 65 22* 💻*www.lapost.fr* Ⓩ *Open M-F 8am-7pm. Sa 8am-noon.)* Additional branches everywhere in the city.

- **POSTAL CODE:** 06033.

Emergency!

- **POLICE:** *(1 ave. amrechal Foch* ☎*04 92 17 22 22)*

- **LATE-NIGHT PHARMACY:** Check Nice Matin for rotating Pharmacie de Garde (24 hour pharmacy). Late-night service available by phone.*(7 rue Massena* ☎*04 93 87 78 94).*

- **HOSPITAL:** *(5 rue Pierre Devoluy* ☎*04 92 03 33 75).*

Getting There

By Plane

Aeroport Nice-Côte d'Azur (*NCE;* ☎*08 20 42 33 33*). Municipal Ligne d'Azur Buses leave ever 30 min for the airport from the train station (#98 direct bus; 8am-9pm, €4). Before 8am, bus #23 (*every 15-25min. €1*) Makes several stops, including train station. EasyJet flies to London, Vueling to Barcelona and Air France to Paris and other domestic and international destinations.

By Train

There are two train stations in Nice, although the SNCF is far more useful and centrally located.

Gare SNCF Nice-Ville: ave. Thiers (☎*04 93 14 82 12* 💻*www.sncf.com*) Cannes (*40min., every 20min. 5:15am-12am, €6*); Marseille (*2.5hr., 15 per day, €29-70*); Monaco (*15min., every 20min. €3.30*); Paris (*5hr. 6 per day, €94*).

Gare de Nice CP. (☎*04 97 03 80 80* 💻*www.trainprovence.com*), is located at 4bis rue Alfred Binet, 800 m from Nice-Ville. Chemins de Fer de Provence runs to Digne-les-Bains (*3.5hr., 5 per day, 6:25am-6:15pm, €18*) and Plan du Var (*40min., 10 per day, 6:07am-6:15pm. €3.40*).

By Bus

Gare Routiere: 5 bld. Jean Juares. (☎*04 92 00 42 93*). Buses to national and international destinations. Info booth open M-F 8:30am-5:30pm, Sa 9am-4pm. Bus #100 runs between Nice and Menton via Monaco. Leaves to Monaco every 10-30min. 6am-8pm, Su every 20min. 1hr., puchrchase tickets onbaord for €1. Leaves for Cannes (*40min., every 20min. €1*).

By Ferry

Corsica Ferries (☎*04 92 00 42 93* 💻*www.corsicaferries.com*) and **SNCM** (☎*04 93 13 66 66*) send high-speed ferries from the new port. Reduced rates for those under 25 and over 60. Take bus #1 or 2 to the port. To Corsica (*5-6hr., €15-45; bikes €10; small cars €45-75.*) The two terminals are on opposite sides of the port, so check schedule ahead of time.

nice • essentials

Getting Around

By Bus and Tram

Ligne d'Azur, 3 pl. Massena (☎04 93 13 53 13 🖳 *www.ligneazur.com*), is the public bus company in Nice. Office open M-F 7:45am-6:30pm. Sa 8:30am-6pm. Buses operate daily 6am-9pm. Tourist office gives out bus schedule and posted times are on bus stops. (💲 *Individual passes €1, day pass €4, week-long pass €15.* 🕗 *Night bus runs 9:10pm-1:10am. Tram line runs through Jean Medecin and pl. Massena. Stops every 5 min, 6am-2am along its 9 km route.*)

By Taxi

Central Taxi Riviera (☎04 93 13 78 78) company runs throughout the city (💲 *€20-40 from the airport to the centre-ville*) Be sure to ask for the price before boarding and make sure the meter is turned on. Night fares charged from 7pm-7am.

By Bike

Velo Blue (🖳 *www.velobleu.org*) is Nice's bike rental company. They require that you call or have a French credit card to rent the bike from bike stands. Stands are located all around the city. (💲 *30min. free, €1 per hr.*)

Not every country's synonymous with flashy cars, yachts, gambling, and income taxes; Monaco's a pretty special place. Evading taxes turned out to be such a popular idea that the mega-rich flocked here for centuries, hoping to partake in material excess without being pestered by the IRS. While Monaco's fiscal policies have changed recently, the allure of this tiny principality still revolves around its unparalleled and shameless sense of wealth. Every year, the world stops spinning for the Monaco Grand Prix, where automotive companies and drivers compete to win the world's most difficult course, then party it up in the glamorous clubs near the first place finish. One step off of the train, and you'll realize why Grace Kelly was so quick to ditch US citizenship for a life of luxury in this oasis of old world royalty, jammed in the middle of a modern and jetsetting life.

ORIENTATION

Monaco-Ville

Monaco-Ville sits atop the **rocher de Monaco**, which François Grimaldi climbed and conquered while dressed as a monk (or *monaco*, in Italian) in 1297. Today, it overlooks the **Port of Hercules,** and houses the **Royal Palace** and everything else royal within the city limits. The principality's royal aquarium, palace, car collection, and church are all located atop this neighborhood, which is barely larger than 5x9 blocks. There's a reason that this is the area of Monaco that's most densely packed with tourists. Take some pics, see the sights, then hurry back down the mountain before you feel the need to push past that old lady with a walker who's keeping that extremely slow cruise ship group from moving on.

Monte Carlo

OK, we've all heard of this place. Centered around the **Carre d'Or** and the **Monte Carlo casino,** Monte Carlo boasts the fanciest cars, fastest women, and opulent clubs in Monaco. It might cost you a fortune just to step foot in this part of town, but if you don't mind being Monte Carlo's token pleibian you should put on your best and go people watch. Who knows—you might even find a rich sugar daddy. Keep going past the casino and you'll reach the only **beach** in the principality, as well as the **Forum** and **Sporting Complex.**

La Condamine

This neighborhood boasts the cheapest shops, bars, and general cost of living in Monaco. It's also refreshingly clear of tourists during the day, who are off on excursions to the rocher; at night, it hosts a series of laid-back bars that are seriously lacking in the other parts of Monaco. Located below Monaco-Ville, La Condamine is also where the port's affordable hotels are, but keep in mind that "affordable" in Monaco requires a slight price adjustment, even from the already expensive Riviera.

Fontvieille

This neighborhood is the quiet western side of Monaco. Home to private apartments and yacht clubs, the parties here happen behind close doors, and there isn't much left for the common folk, unless you're looking for a job in the industrial sector. The area is also home to a large **shopping complex** and Monaco's **soccer stadium,** in case you were planning to see the home team.

ACCOMMODATIONS

Oddly enough, the cheapest place to stay in Monaco is in France; the best deals in the area are located in **Beausoleil,** a small town that overlooks Monte Carlo. If you're a purist and want to stay within the principality, **La Condamine** is your best bet for hotels under €100.

Monaco-Ville

There aren't any. Sorry. The Royal Palace and the private apartments of the uber-rich are located here, and they don't want anyone renting a room with a sniper rifle and getting a shot at the prince (thats *Let's Go's* guess, anyway).

Monte Carlo

Actually, these hotels aren't even in Monaco. They're in France, but don't worry about it—Monaco's literally right across the street.

HOTEL VILLA BOERI
♥⊗⒫🛏 BUDGET HOTEL ❹

29 bld. Leclerc   ☎04 93 78 38 10 🖥www.www.hotelboeri.com

It may look sketchy and overgrown from the outside, and the decorative mirrors may date back to the '70s, but this hotel is clean, simple, and cheap for the area. Small rooms with large beds and bath.

⚑ *Take either the #4 or #1 bus to Église St. Charles. With the church on your left, walk along rue bl. des Moulins until coming to a stairwell on your left. Walk up the stairwell and turn right. Walk another 60m. Hotel is on your left.* ℹ *Free Wi-Fi and computer.* ⑤ *Singles and doubles €58-81; 3rd person €8; 4th person €12.*

HOTEL DIANA
♥⚐⒫🍴 HOTEL ❹

17 bld. Leclerc   ☎04 93 78 47 58 🖥www.monte-carlo.mc/hotel-diana-beausoleil

Large comfortable rooms in a classy hotel overlooking the Église St. Charles.

⚑ *Take either the #4 or #1 bus to Église St. Charles. With the church on your left, walk along rue bl. des Moulins until coming to a stairwell on your left. Walk up the stairwell and turn left. Hotel is on your right.* ℹ *Parking and free Wi-Fi.* ⑤ *Singles €45-60, doubles €45-72. Prices vary with inside/port view.*

La Condamine

NI HOTEL
♥⚐🍴⒫ HOTEL ❺

1 rue Grimaldi   ☎97 97 51 51 🖥www.nihotel.com

This zany hotel is a cross between a fun house and a madhouse. Crooked bright orange walls and oddly placed mirrors make Ni Hotel a challenge for the epileptic or criminally insane. Suites and apartments available.

⚑ *From the train station, exit to La Condamine, making a right as you exit the tunnel rue Grimaldi. Continue while the road curves to the left. Hotel on your right.* *Singles €90-140; doubles from €170.*

SIGHTS
🔘

Monaco-Ville

THE PRINCE'S PALACE
⚐⊗ PALACE

Monaco-Ville   ☎93 25 18 31 🖥www.palais.mc

The lavish palace is open to tourists when the flag is lowered and the prince is away, which, it turns out, is quite often. The free audio tour is offered in 11 languages, and will walk you past the silk tapestries, Royal Courtyard, and chambers that combine the opulence of Versailles with the shock of knowing that a monarch still lives here. Judging by the crowds, you could easily mistake the official portrait of Princess Grace as nothing short of the Madonna, herself.

ℹ *Handicapped access not available.* ⑤ *€8, students €3.50.* ☒ *Open Apr 2-Oct 31 daily 10am-6:15pm.*

MUSÉE OCÉANGRAPHIQUE
⚐ AQUARIUM

av. St. Martin, Monaco-Ville   ☎93 15 36 00 🖥www.oceano.mc

Originally a hobby of Prince Albert I, the monarchy's extensive collection of exotic Mediterranean fish is publicly displayed in a palatial, five-story aquarium. The aquarium's main attraction is the shark lagoon and naturalized marine mammals, both alive and stuffed as models. The permanent exhibit on the poles

france

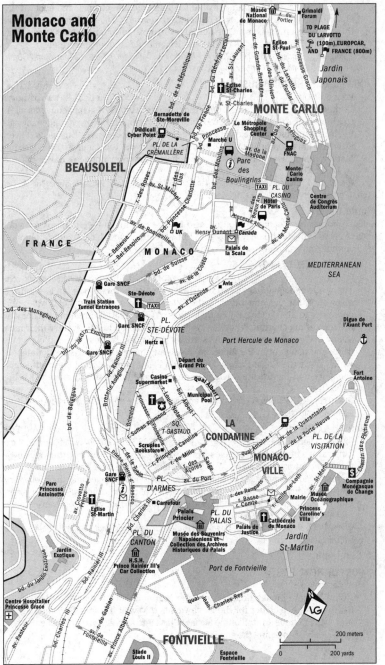

Monaco and Monte Carlo

Musée National de Monaco
r. du Portier
Grimaldi Forum

Église St-Paul

TO PLAGE DU LARVOTTO
(100m), EUROPCAR, AND FRANCE (800m)

Jardin Japonais

Église St-Charles

v. St-Charles

MONTE CARLO

Bernadette de Ste-Moreville

D@dicall Cyber Point

PL. DE LA CRÉMAILLÈRE

Le Métropole Shopping Center

Marché U

FNAC

BEAUSOLEIL

Parc des Boulingrins

Monte-Carlo Casino

TAXI PL. DU CASINO

Centre de Congrès Auditorium

av. de Roqueville

Hôtel de Paris

D UK

av. Henry Dunant

Canada

MONACO

Palais de la Scala

FRANCE

bd. de Suisse

av. de la Costa

Avis

MEDITERRANEAN SEA

Gare SNCF

Ste-Dévote

Train Station Tunnel Entrances

TAXI

Gare SNCF

PL. STE-DÉVOTE

Hertz

Digue de l'Avant Port

Gare SNCF

Port Hercule de Monaco

Départ du Grand Prix

Casino Supermarket

Quai Albert I

Municipal Pool

Fort Antoine

SQ. T-GASTAUD

LA CONDAMINE

av. de la Quarantaine

av. de la Porte Neuve

PL. DE LA VISITATION

Scruples Bookstore

MONACO-VILLE

Gare SNCF

Compagnie Monégasque de Change

Parc Princesse Antoinette

Église St-Martin

PL. D'ARMES

Musée Océanographique

Mairie

Princess Caroline's Villa

Carrefour

Palais Princier

PL. DU PALAIS

Cathédrale de Monaco

Jardin Exotique

Palais de Justice

Jardin St-Martin

PL. DU CANTON

Musée des Souvenirs Napoléoniens et Collection des Archives Historiques du Palais

H.S.H. Prince Rainier III's Car Collection

Port de Fontvieille

Centre Hospitaller Princesse Grace

FONTVIEILLE

Stade Louis II

Espace Fontvieille

0   200 meters
0   200 yards

monaco · sights

has an impressive section dedicated to global climate change, and each of the aquarium's 90 tanks manages to recycle 100% of the 250,000 gallons of water that the institution funnels from the marina every day; considering the 80ft. cliff that houses the museum and its restaurant, it's quite a feat of engineering.

$ Adults €13, students €6.50. ⏰ Open Apr-Jun daily 9:30am-7pm, July-Aug daily 9:30am-7:30pm, Sept daily 9:30am-7pm, Oct-Mar daily 10am-6pm.

NAPOLEONIC HISTORY MUSEUM — ⊗ MUSEUM

Place du Palais ☎93 25 18 31 🖥 www.palais.mc

Containing over 1,000 items from France's First Empire, this museum was a gift to Albert II from his grandfather. Exhibits display letters of correspondence written by the megalomaniacal general concerning his conquest of Europe and even after his imprisonment on St. Helena. Not straying too far from Monegasque history, the museum also contains the charter granting Monaco's independence by Louis XII.

$ Adults €4, students €2. ⏰ Open Jan-Apr 1 (no joke) daily 10:30am-5pm, Apr 2- Oct 10am-6:15pm, Dec daily 10:30am-5pm.

Monte Carlo

Let's be honest: you came to Monte Carlo for the casino, and we don't blame you. Let's Go won't advise you on how to play, but we can tell you that citizens of Monaco are banned from gambling—why take money from the rich?

CASINO MONTE CARLO — ♿🍸 CASINO

☎92 16 20 00 🖥 www.casinomontecarlo.com

The renowned gambling house was infamous well before it was Ian Flemming's inspiration for the first book in the 🎬**James Bond** series, Casino Royale, and continues to this day to conjure up images of Charles Wells breaking the bank at the turn of the century. While the well-dressed and optimistic can try their luck at any of the casino's table games or slot machines, the less intrepid can get a drink and hang out in the **Atrium du Casino** and marvel at the casino's opulence, which rivals the Royal Palace. Dress code is not in effect until 8pm, but jeans, sneakers, and T-shirts are frowned upon. 18+ gambling is strictly enforced. bring photo ID.

$ €10 cover. ⏰ Slots open July-Aug daily from noon, Sept-Jun from 2pm, Sa-Su from noon. Roulette daily from noon.

JARDIN EXOTIQUE — ⊗ GARDEN

62 bld. du Jardin Exotique ☎93 15 29 80 🖥 www.jardin-exotique.mc

This garden of rare plant species from around the world has been growing since the 16th century, when New World explorers brought over cacti and rainforest plants. Accompanying the garden are the Observatory Caves and the prehistory museum, which takes visitors through a series of underground passageways and grottos through the local limerich cave system. Forget which ones are stalagmites and stalagtites? So do we.

$ Adults €7, students €3.70. ⏰ Open May 15-Sep 15 9am-7pm, Sept 16-May 14 9am-6pm (or until nightfall).

La Condamine

PORT OF HERCULES — ♿ PORT

La Condamine

Home to more money floating on water than a Kevin Costner flop, this port is the main service center for the mega yachts that visit the area. Surrounding the port is the famous stretch of the **Monaco Grand Prix,** as well as a series of cafes and bars ideal for escaping the sun.

breaking the bank

If you feel the need to throw your hard-earned euro at one of the richest institutions in the world, do yourself a favor and go for the Roulette wheel. Several resourceful (read: cheating) men have made out quite successfully, including **Joseph Jagger** (distant cousin to Mick) in 1873.

Joseph discovered a slight advantage—one particular wheel landed on 7, 8, 9, 17, 18, 19, 22, 28 and 29 more often than on the other numbers. After placing 7 bets, he quickly made over $1 million on the first day. The casino figured out the flaw and quickly moved tables to throw Jagger off. He was able to find the wheel again in the sea of tables by identifying a chip in the wheel, continued winning, and left with over two million francs, or $5 million in 2005 USD.

Con man **Charles Wells** worked a similar steal, again on the Roulette wheel, in 1891. Wells **broke the bank** (winning more than the chips on the table) 12 times, winning $2.5 million in 11 hours. In one particularly absurd run, he bet the number 5 for five consecutive turns, and won each time. Despite hiring private detectives to investigate, the casino never found out his system. Wells chalked it up to **"luck."**

Fontvieille

HSH PRINCE RAINIER III'S CAR COLLECTION ♿ MUSEUM

Terrasses de Fontvieille ☎92 05 28 56 🖥www.palais.mc

If you thought that the cars parked in front of the casino were impressive, think again—Prince Rainier III's antique car collection puts them all to shame. Highlights include the Cintroen Torpedo that crossed Asia for the Yellow Expedition race in the 1930s, and the sexy '56 Rolls Royce Silver Cloud that carried the prince and Grace Kelly on their wedding day. Don't miss the oldest specimen, the 1903 De Dion Bouton, one of the first widely manufactured steam engine cars.

$Adults €6, students €3. ⏰Open daily 10am-6pm.

LOUIS II STADIUM ♿🍸 SPORTS FACILITY

3 av. des Castelans ☎92 05 40 11

One of the best-funded sports facilities in the world, the stadium is the home feild of AS Monaco, as well as an Olympic swimming pool and multisports hall surrounded by a world class althetic track.

$Adults €4, students €2. ⏰ Tours M, Tu, Th, and F 10:30am,11:30am, 2:30pm, and 4pm. W 10:30am and 11:30am.

MONACO ZOO ♿ ZOO

Terrasse de Fontvieille ☎93 50 40 30 🖥www.palais.mc

Home to 250 animals and 50 different species, this zoo was once the private animal collection of Prince Rainier III before he opened up the grounds to the public in 1954.

$ Adults €4, students €2.. ⏰Open Oct-Feb 10am-noon, 2-5pm, Mar-May 10am-noon, 2-6pm, Jun-Sep 9am-noon, 2-7pm.

BEACHES

PLAGE DU LARVOTTO ♿ BEACH

av. Princess Grace

Well, it's the best and worst beach in Monaco, since it's also the only one. Comprised of two man-made lagoons separated by a divider, this convenient sandy beach does not require a long hike or a daring leap over jagged rocks or cliffs to get to. Larvotto is also one of Monaco's few great equalizers, since everyone in the country who wishes to sunbathe must either come here or, you know, stick to their private yachts' sunbeds.

i Lifgaurd, toilets and handicapped access.

FOOD

Monaco-Ville

CHOCOLATERIE DE MONACO
pl. de la Visitation

✦👤🛏 CHOCOLATIER ❶
☎97 97 88 88

Chocolatier specializing in Monaco-themed chocolates and a Viennese chocolate drink that is richer than the Prince himself.

⑤ Average of €1/10g of chocolate. €4.10 chocolate drinks. ☒ Open daily 9am-6:30pm.

U'CAVAGNATU
12 Comte Felix Gastaldi

✦👤💺🛏 MONEGASQUE ❸
☎97 89 20 40

Traditional *monegasque* cuisine that blends both French and Italian influences into a fusion of Mediterranean styles. Obscure foods include fried zuccini, and olive and onion omelets.

⑤ Lunch plates €12.50-15, €25.50 fixed menu. ☒ Open daily 12-5pm, 7-1pm.

COSTA MONACO
8-10 rue Basse

✦👤💺 CAFE, CRÊPERIE ❷
☎93 50 60 85

Small and relaxed cafe with low, blue couches in a low ceilinged room. Serves tarts, crêpes and drinks.

⑤ Crêpes €3-3.60, Pizza €5.40, Sandwiches €2-5.70. ☒ Open daily 6am-8pm.

Monte Carlo

SAKURA
1 av. Henri Dunant

✦⊗💺 SUSHI ❸
☎93 50 87 33

Sushi restaurant and bar in the Carre d'Or or Monte Carlo. All white interior serves a specialty of fatty tuna and a variety of California rolls. You'll want to dress up to go anywhere near the Carre d'Or, and this chic sushi bar is no exception. Dress to impress.

⑤ €13 rolls, €5 pieces of sashimi. ☒ Open daily 12-2pm, 7-10:30pm.

IL TERRAZZINO
2 rue d'Iris

✦⊗💺 ITALIAN ❸
☎93 50 24 27

Highly praised restaurant known for its festive interior, which is designed to look like an outdoor market. Enjoy fine Italian cuisine while taking in a great view of the casino.

⑤ €45 prix-fixe, €12 plat du jour. ☒Open M-Sa 12-2:30pm, 7:30-11pm.

La Condamine

LA PROVENCE
22 rue Grimaldi

✦👤💺🛏 PROVENÇAL ❸
☎97 98 37 81

Upscale Provençal restaurant in the Condamine. Enjoy specialties like beef tartare in a classy atmosphere. You'll dine at wrought iron tables that give La Provence a mix of traditional flair and modern architecture. Don't worry about getting too dressed up, but make sure you look "nice."

⑤ Lunch menu €16, plates from €9-18. ☒ Open daily 12-3pm, 7-10pm.

NIGHTLIFE

Monaco-Ville

Do you really want to be the backpacker that woke up the royal family? Didn't think so. Monaco-Ville is the sleepy side of town, with no bars or clubs to note.

france

Monte Carlo

This neighborhood hosts some of the glitziest parties and expensive bars and clubs in all of Monaco, not to mention the world. If you're not dressed like a count, be prepared to be turned away at the door (especially if you are a guy or group of guys). While the glam of the **casino** seems to rub off on the surrounding clubs and bars, there are some holdout low-key establishments here that still accept jeans and T-shirts; if it's a **pub,** you're probably in the clear. The **beach** is lined with lounges, and the **Princesse Grace** boasts some of Monaco's mot expensive bars. The more laidback pubs and wine bars run along **rue Portier.**

MCCARTHY'S — IRISH PUB

7 rue du Portier ☎93 50 88 10 www.mcpam.com

The last bastion of normalcy in the ritziest area of Monaco. This laidback Irish pub serves Irish cocktails (read: whiskey and Baileys inspired) and some staple Kilkenny and Guiness in a welcoming atmosphere filled. Whiskey barrels are used for tables, and the walls are covered with Irish road signs.

[$] *€6 beer, €9-12 cocktails. Happy hour prices up to 30% off.* *Open daily 5pm-5am. Happy hour M-F 5-8pm.*

COSMOPOLITAN — WINE BAR

5 rue Portier ☎93 25 78 60 www.cosmopolitan.com

Upscale wine bar where elite patrons blow the bank on €600 bottles of Bordeaux, and backpackers like us sit around and look classy with a €4 glass. Quiet outdoor seating provides an ideal space for a casual conversation and a laidback start to a wild night.

[$] *€10-14 cocktails, €4-5 glass of wine.* *Open daily 12:30-2pm, 6-11pm.*

LA NOTE BLEUE — PIANO, JAZZ BAR

Plage du Larvotto ☎93 50 05 02 www.lanotebleue.mc

For those who as a general rule don't leave the beach if you can help it, this classy jazz and piano bar is spitting distance from the water. The whitewashed walls and low couches make for a comfy place to sip your "Pure Happiness" (vodka, peach) or "Pure Pleasure" (vodka, strawberry, champgane) cocktails.

[$] *€12 cocktails, €7 beer.* *Open daily 6:30pm-3am. Wed-Sat concerts from 6:30pm-12am.*

KARE(MENT) — CLUB

10 av. Princess Grace ☎99 99 20 20 www.karement.com

Located in the Grimaldy Forum, this enormous homage to debauchery is comprised of 3 bars and a dance floor, and hovers 100ft over the water. The views of the ocean from the third bar are particularly dramatic, and the nightly live DJs keep the party hopping. Thursdays are "Salsa Ladies Night"—and features heavily discounted drinks—until 11pm, when the theme changes abruptly to "80's Night." Think those two themes fit well? Neither do we.

[$] *Prices.* *Open summer daily 8am-5am, Winter M-F 8:30am-5am, Sa 6pm-5am.*

THE LIVING ROOM — PIANO BAR, CLUB

7 rue Speluges ☎93 50 80 31

Old school piano bar and throwback to the 1920s and '30s, with a particularly casual patio deck. DJ music gradually incorporates modern music into the bar's repetoire as the night goes on, and expertly syncs modern mixes with the jazz piano.

[$] *€10 beer, €15 cocktails.* *Open M-Sa 11pm-5am.*

La Condamine

The slacker hub of Monaco, La Condamine doesn't require you to dress up completely, though a collared shirt or heels would be nice. Most of the ex-pat bars are located in this area, as well as some of the best Happy hour deals.

⬛ SLAMMERS

♦ ♿ ☕ 🍸 🏠   BRITISH PUB

6 rue Saffren   ☎97 70 36 56

The name says it all. British-run and Morrocan-designed pub with an open mike jam session every Sunday. Low couches on outdoor patio are packed with disaffected youth. Owner encourages ordering takeout for delivery to the bar from neighboring restaurants.

💲€4 beer, €10.50 alcohols. Happy hours almost half price. 🕒 Open M-F 5pm-1am, Sa-Su 1pm-1am. Happy hours 5-8pm.

⬛ STARS AND BARS

♦ ♿ ((♪)) 🍸 🏠   BAR

6 quai Antoine 1er   ☎97 97 95 95 🖥www.starsnbars.com

The ideal guy hangout, Stars and Bars boasts an awesome collection of auto sports memorabilia, a collection of fooseball tables, and crowds that regularly overflow onto the port. The bar serves killer beer cocktails—we recomment the "Exotic," a combo of light beer, pineapple and Malibu rum that will knock you on your ass.

💲€8 beer cocktails, €5 beer. Half priced happy hour. 🕒 Open daily 5:30pm-3 am. Happu Hour from opening to 7:30pm.

RASCASSE

♦ ♿ 🍸 🏠 ▼   BAR, CLUB

Antoine 1er   ☎93 25 56 90 🖥www.larascasse.mc

One of the most upscale bars and clubs in this neighborhood, the Rascasse is well known for its 5hr *Happy hour* and nightly DJs. The bar is located on the famous turn of the Grand Prix, and remains a sure bet for those who want some class in their evening without feeling intimidated or ripped-off.

💲€6 beer, €10 cocktails. Half prices for happy hour. 🕒 Open daily noon-5am, Happy hour 6-11pm M-F. Music F-Sa (Th Jul-Aug)11:30pm til close.

BRASSERIE DE MONACO

♦ 🍸 🏠 ▼   BAR

36 route de la piscine   ☎93 30 09 09

Young, fun hangout for travellers and locals. Right on the port, this bar and pseudo-club has all the traits of a strip club, from the dancing girls to the flatscreen TVs playing looped taps of models' photoshoots. Don't worry; it isn't. The fun crowd gathers around long cafeteria style tables for easy conversation and making friends.

💲€6 beer, €15 cocktails. 🕒 Open daily 11am-3am.

Fotvieille

The only popular bar here is in the **Columbus Hotel,** but it's for stiffs and rich people, and probably not your idea of a good time. As multiple Bond movies suggest, the Columbus serves wicket martinis, but you need to dress up for it and be prepared to leave and catch a bus back to the fun side of town.

ESSENTIALS

🔢

Practicalities

- **TOURIST OFFICE:** 2A bl. des Moulins (☎92 16 61 16), uphill from the casino. English speaking staff provides city maps, extensive pocket guides for restuarants, hotels, nightlife, and attractions, rendering *Let's Go* almost obsolete. Open M-Sa 9am-7pm, Su 11am-1pm. Annexes in the train station at the ave. Prince Pierre exit, in the chemin des Pecheurs parking garage, in the port and outside the Jardin Exotique (open mid-Jun to Aug).

- **EMBASSIES AND CONSULATES: Canada.** (1 av. Henry Durant ☎97 70 62 42); **France.** (1 chemin du Tenao ☎92 16 54 60); **UK.** (33 bl Princess Charlotte ☎93 50 99 54). Nearest **US** embassy is in Nice (☎04 93 88 89 55).

- **CURRENCY EXCHANGE:** Bureau de Change, in Compagnie Monegasque de Change, in the chemins des Pecheurs parking garage. *(Ave. de la Quarantine ☎93 25 02 50 $ Cash advances €50 min. ⏰ Open M-Sa 9:30am-5:30pm.)*

- **INTERNET ACCESS: FNAC,** 17 ave. des Speluges *(☎93 10 81 81)* in Le Metropole Shopping Center. *(ℹ Frequent lines. $ 20min. free. ⏰ Open M-Sa 10am-5:30pm.)* **D@dicall Cyber Point,** 1 impasse General Leclerc (Beausoleil), has Wi-Fi. *(☎04 93 57 42 14 $ Internet €4 per hr. ⏰ Open daily 10:30am-8pm.)*
- **POST OFFICE:** 23 ave. Albert II *(☎98 98 41 41 ⏰ Open M-F 9am-7pm, Sa 8am-noon.)* All mail posted in the principality must bear Monegasque stamps. Annex at av. Prince Pierre train station exit. 4 additional branches.
- **POSTAL CODE:** MC 98000 Monaco.

Emergency!

- **EMERGENCY NUMBERS: Ambulance:** ☎93 25 33 25.
- **POLICE:** *(3 rue Louis Notari ☎93 15 30 15).* 5 other stations in Monaco.
- **HOSPITAL: Centre Hospitalier Princesse Grace,** Ave. Pasteur *(☎97 98 99 00).* Accessible by bus #5 (dir. Hospital).

Getting There

By Train

Gare SNCF has 4 main access points: galerie Prince Pierre, pl. St-Devote, bl. de Belgique, and bld. Princesse Charlotte. *(⏰ Open daily 4am-1am. Info desk and ticket window open M-F 5:50am-8:30pm, Sa-Su 5:50am-8:10pm.)* Trains run to: **Antibes** (1 hr., every 30 min, €6.30); **Nice** (25 min, every 30 min., €2.70); **Cannes** (1 hr. 10 min., every 30 min., €7.50); **Menton** (11min., every 30 min., €1.70).

By Bus

Buses leave from the bl. des Moulins and ave. Princesse Grace, near the tourist office. **TAM** and **RCA** (☎93 85 64 44). To Nice (45 min) and Menton (25 min). Cap d'Ail, St-Jean-Cap-Ferrat and the -sur Mer's via route to Nice. There is also a direct line from the Nice Airport (RCA) via the A8 motorway (45 min., every hour between 9am-9:15pm, €16.10, under 26 €11.50, return €26).

By Helicopter

Hey, you never know. It is Monaco, after all. **Heli Air Monaco** lands in Fontvielle at the Monaco Heliport. *($ €7 min. €120 per 30min.)*

Getting Around

The **bus** system in Monaco is a godsend from its hilly terrain built onto the side of a steep shoreline. The six lines run pretty much to wherever from wherever. *($ Individual ticket €1, 🎫24hr. pass €3. ⏰ M-F every 10min., Sa-Su every 20-30min.)* Buy tickets on board. **Taxis** *(☎93 15 01 01 $ €10 min.)* run 24hr. and wait at 11 taxi stands throughout the city, including the casino, pl. des Moulins, and the train station. If you like control of your own wheels, you can also rent a **scooter** from Auto-Moto Garage, 7 rue de Milo. *(☎93 50 10 80 ℹ Credit cards accepted. $ 50cc scooter €40 per day, €45 per 24hr., €260 per week. €1000 credit security charge. ⏰ Open M-F 8am-noon and 2-7pm, Sa 8am-noon.)*

antibes ☎04 93

Antibes has the largest port on the Mediterranean, attracting sailors and scallywags of all varieties from around the world. A strange island of English-speaking visitors and residents, Antibes has its fair share of rugged British and Irish pubs, with very little of the hopping club scene found in Juan-les-Pins or Cannes. People are either here to drift or to look for work, so the crowd can range from drunk and entertaining to sketchy and intimidating. Antibes has the free beaches that you've been searching for, as well as some good SCUBA diving spots and snorkeling off of the Cap d'Antibes. While the museums, with the exception of the Picasso Museum, might be a tad on the dull side, the real attraction is the laid-back people and easygoing atmosphere, only 10min. from one of the craziest party cities on the Riviera.

ORIENTATION

Antibes is easy to navigate between the **port** and the **Vieux Ville,** even though the streets can be poorly labeled and the helpful tourist arrows can sometimes lead you into a wall. The easiest way to orient yourself is along the town's main streets: **rue de la Republique** and **Bld. d'Aguillon.** Both lead you right into the *Vieux Ville*, while offering totally different attractions along the way. Rue de la Republique is where you'll find upscale restaurants and shopping, while the sleezy port crowd will hang out at the laid-back pubs that line bl. d'Aguillon. Unfortunately the **Cap,**where you'll find secluded beaches and nicer hotels, is either a 20min. walk or a bus ride away. The **#2 bus** goes along the coast. Within the *Vieux Ville*, no matter where you turn you'll almost always end up back at the **Marche Provençale,** a central sqaure that sells fruits and vegetables during the day and turns into a flea market at night.

ACCOMMODATIONS

These are the cheapest ones in town. To find any hotels that are actually budget, you'll have to go to Juan-les-Pins or take a hike up the highway. These places get above €100 in the high season, and its over €200 for rooms of three to four. We don't want to subject our readers to such financial pain and suffering. Please go to Juan-les-Pins. If you're a trust fund baby, don't mind credit card debt, or absolutely must stay in Antibes for some reason, these are the best deals in town:

THE CREW HOUSE — HOSTEL ❷

1 av. St. Roch ☎04 92 90 49 39

Not the most luxurious place to stay, even by hostel standards, but definitely a fun experience for those willing to take a leap outside of their comfort zone and bunk with the rugged sailors and drifters who frequent this predominantly Anglophone hostel. For those used to the cramped living conditions and limited personal space of boats (or for those looking to give it a try).

 # From the train station, walk straight on down ave. de la Libération, take 2nd right on the round about, hostel on your right. $ Apr-Oct dorms €25; Nov-Mar €20. ⏰ No lockout.

RELAIS INTERNATIONAL DE LA JEUNESSE — HOSTEL ❶

272 bld. de la Garoupe ☎04 93 61 34 40 💻www.clajsud.fr

Closer to Juan-les-Pins than Antibes, Relais International provides guests with clean rooms and an escape from the busy city center. Located next to the beach on the Cap, this English-speaking hostel also provides free breakfast and a youthful atmosphere.

 # Take bus #4 to the Telais de Jeunesse stop or the #2 to the Garoupe stop. Facing the water, walk to your right for 10min. i Breakfast included. Free bar and outdoor seating. $ Dorms €18. ⏰ Open Apr-Sep.

france

HOTEL LE PONTEIL — HOTEL ❹

11 impasse Jean Mensier ☎04 93 34 67 92 💻www.leponteil.con

Tucked away at the end of a cul-de-sac under the trees, this quiet hotel will have you itching to leave for the nearby beach, where there is more life and color than in this *hebergement*. The prices really make the establishment's bland character worth it.

 # From the train station, turn left onto Robert Soleau and walk 200m until you get to Place du Général de Gaulle. Walk across the place onto bl. Albert 1er until one block before the beach (6 blocks). Turn right onto ave. du Général Maizière (keeping to the left at the intersection) and walk 200m. Turn left onto Impasse Jean Mensier. Hotel is at the end. i Parking. $ Singles €58-87; doubles €58-105.

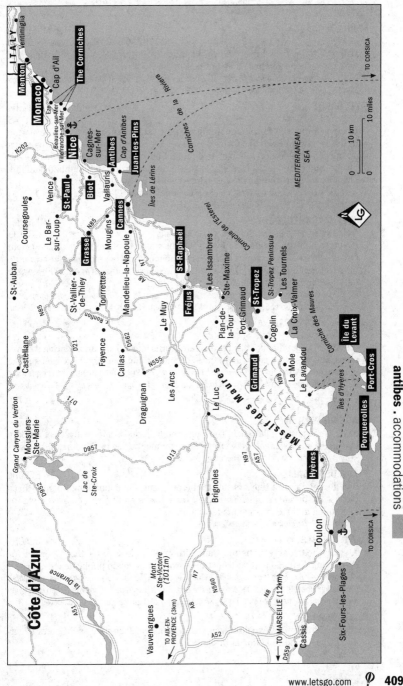

Côte d'Azur

antibes · accommodations

SIGHTS

MUSÉE PICASSO
● MUSEUM

pl. Mariejol   ☎04 92 90 54 20 ▣www.musée-picasso.fr

Displays the artist's lesser-known paintings from the 1940s and video clips of him at work on sketches and paintings.

Ⓢ €8.50, students €6, under 18 free. ☒ Open June 15- Sep15 M 10am-6pm, W-Su 10am-6pm; Sep 15- June 14 M 10am-noon and 2-6pm, W-Su 10am-noon and 2-6pm.

FORT CARRÉ
● HISTORIC SIGHT

Sentier du Fort Carré   ☎06 14 89 17 45

Once an important fortress guarding the port Vauban, the largest private marina in the Mediterranean, this fortress now serves as a showcase for swords and a statue of Napoleon on a horse. Yeah, it still doesn't compensate for his height. Maybe one of those 2400 yachts in the harbor, appropriately dubbed "Millionaire's Row," that would have eased his—well—Napoleon complex.

i Only by guided English or French tour. Ⓢ €3, under 18 free. ☒ Open June 15-Sept 15 Tu-Su 10am-6pm; Sept 15-June 14 Tu-Su 10am-4:30pm.

MUSÉE D'ARCHÉOLOGIE
MUSEUM

On the waterfront in Bastion St-Andre-sur-les-Ramparts   ☎04 95 34 00 39

If you thought the pottery museum in Biot was a hoot, you'll love the ancient Greek and Roman ceramics in this one. The temporary exhibits might be a little more interesting. Past exhibits included present-day objects aged 2000 years to look like archaeological finds from the future.

Ⓢ Students €3. Under 18 free. ☒ Open June 15- Sept 15 M 10am-noon and 2-6pm, W-Su 10am-noon and 2-6pm; Sept 15- June 14 M 10am-1pm and 2-5pm, W-Su 10am-1pm and 2-5pm.

MARCHÉ PROVENÇALE
●⊗ MARKET

rue Aubernon

A market during the day, this covered area turns into a flea market during the evenings, and at seemingly random times during the summer months. Cafes line the market, so the area at the very least makes for good peoplewatching in the shade.

☒ Open June-Aug Tu-Sa mornings, afternoon and evenings in Jun-Aug; Sept-May Tu-Sa mornings.

BEACHES

PLAGE DU PONTEIL
& ⚖ BEACH

Antibes's largest public beach. The long stretch of sand is lined with street vendors and snack stands. It gets very crowded in summer during peak hours of the day.

❉ Turn right from the vieux ville; walk along coast.

PLAGE DE LA SALIS
& ⚖ BEACH

Small public beach that's closer to the port, and the sunbathing hotspot that's closest to the *vieux ville*. The breakwater forms an almost enclosed cove for swimming in the calm, manmade lagoon.

❉ Towards Port Vauban, right from vieux ville.

CAP D'ANTIBES
⚖ BEACH

A rocky beach surrounds the Cap, with crystal clear water that's perfect for snorkeling. Isolated and far from the crowds on the main public beaches.

❉ Take the #2 bus from the bus station to Tour Gandolphe (M-Sa, every 40 min 6:50am-7:30pm). Follow ave. Monseigneurs-Lt. Beaumont to the end. Turn left onto pedestrian road, then right when a small door appears in the surrounding walls; take dirt path to the isolated beach cove.

PLAGE GAROUPE
⚖ BEACH

On the Cap. Sandy beach that was frequented by celebs such as F. Scott Fitzgerald, Picasso, and Cole Porter in the 1920s.

❉ Cap d'Antibes.

FOOD

KEY WEST
♨&♥♨ COMFORT FOOD ❷

30 bld. d'Aguillon ☎04 93 34 58 20 ☒www.lecapdantibes.com

This laid-back restaurant is your go-to place for comfort food like waffles and anything that you could possibly have a craving for. Sailing theme reminiscent of the Florida Keys, with whales and Hemingway featuring prominently on the lime green walls.

Ⓢ *Breakfast food €1.80-6.50. Waffles €2.90-4.90. Cheesecake, salads, sanwiches €3-9.* 🕐 *Open Mar-Dec daily 7:30am-7:30pm (until 2am Jul-Aug).*

BRULOT
♨&♥♨ WOOD FIRED ❸

3 rue Federic Isnard ☎04 93 34 17 76

Wood-fired cuisine in this tavern-like restaurant. Farm implements hang from the ceiling, reminding you where your meat and fish dishes (€12) came from. Three-course *prix-fixe* (€19) features shrimp au pastis and creme brulee to top it off.

Ⓢ *Plats €12-17. Lunch €14. Dinner €19.* 🕐 *Open daily 7pm-12am.*

LE CRÊME BRÛLÉE
♨&♥♨ PROVENCAL, FAMILY ❷

21 rue Thuret ☎04 93 34 56 58

Farm-themed Provençal restaurant serves up crêpes, sandwiches, and *plats*, as well as its dessert namesake. Inside walls are painted to look as though cows are looking in on you while you eat. If that doesn't confuse/frighten you enough, check out the pots hanging from the ceiling that serve as lights.

Ⓢ *Sandwiches €5.50. Crêpes €4-8. Plats €12-15.* 🕐 *Open daily 9am-11pm.*

LE VILLAGE
♨♥ PROVENÇAL ❸

31 rue James Close ☎04 93 34 19 66

This classy joint serves up local mussels, roast duck, and escargots in a traditionally decorated Provençal establishment. Though the decor isn't remarkable, with whitewash plaster walls, the food is quite good. On a tight budget? Go for lunch to get the gourmet taste for almost half the price of the dinner menu.

Ⓢ *Lunch €15. Dinner €28. Kids menu €11.50.* 🕐 *Open M-Tu noon-2pm and 7-10pm, Th-Su noon-2pm and 7-10pm.*

NIGHTLIFE

LA BALADE
&♥ ABSINTHE BAR

25B cours Massena ☎04 93 34 93 00

One of the world's few absinthe bars, La Balade is a famed subterranean hotspot that exclusively serves that one special drink. Don't look naive and ask if you haullucinate. You don't. Thanks to its 140+ proof, you'll be lucky if you see anything at all. Posters and bowler hats cover the walls in tribute to the 19th-centruy avant-garde, who guzzled the drink with a side of laudanum.

🕐 *Open daily 9am-midnight.*

THE HOP STORE
♨&♥♨ BAR

38 bld. d'Aguillon ☎04 93 34 04 06

Antibes's largest pub. With a giant patio that's almost always packed with a young crowd, this two-room bar hosts local rock bands and other live music performances every Wednesday, Friday, and Saturday. Although technically classified as an Irish pub, The Hop Store is the most international spot in all of Antibes.

Ⓢ *Beer €2.50. Cocktails €7.* 🕐 *Open in summer 9am-12:30am, in winter 3pm-12:30am.*

THE BLUE LADY
♨&⟮⟯♥♨ PUB

Galerie du Port ☎04 93 34 41 00

Laid-back pub done up to look like the interior of a steamship in the American

South. The wood and brass bar is decorated with entertaining signs referring to gamblers and loose women. Outdoor seating and live bands every other Friday. Don't miss out on their homemade pub grub, like hand-rolled sausage (€3.50).
$ Beer €3.40-5.50. Cocktails €6.80-9.20. ⏰ Open 7:30am-midnight. Kitchen open until 3:30pm.

ESSENTIALS

Practicalities

- **TOURIST OFFICE:** Free maps, info on hotels, restaurants, and festivals. Help with hotel reservations *(11 pl. de Gaulle ☎04 97 23 11 11 🖥www.antibesjuanlespins.com. ⏰ Open July-Aug daily 9am-7pm; Sept-Jun M-F 9am-noon and 1:30-6pm, Sa 9am-noon and 2-6pm, Su 10am-noon and 2:30-5pm.)*
- **TOURS:** The **Petit Train** covers both Antibes and Juan-les-Pins sights. *(Departure from pl. de la Poste ☎06 15 77 67 47. $ €7. ⏰ July-Aug 10am-10pm; Mar-Oct 10am-6pm.)*
- **INTERNET ACCESS: Xtreme Cyber.** *(8 bld. d'Aguillon in Galerie du Port ☎04 89 89 93 88 $ €5 per hr. ⏰ Open M-F 10am-8pm, Sa 10am-4pm.)*
- **POST OFFICE:** pl. des Martyrs de la Resistance *(☎04 92 90 61 00 ⏰ Open M-F 8am-7pm, Sa 8am-noon.)*
- **POSTAL CODE:** 06600.

Emergency!

- **POLICE:** ☎04 97 21 75 60.
- **PHARMACY:** 1 av. de l'Admiral Courbet. *(☎04 93 61 12 96. ⏰ Open daily 8am-12:30pm and 2-6:30pm.)*

Getting There

By Train

Gare SNCF *(pl. Pierre Semard. ⏰ Ticket desk open daily 5:45am-10:45pm. Info desk open daily 9am-8pm. Station open 5:25am-12:10am.)* runs trains to **Cannes***($ €2.20.⏰ 15min, every 30min.)*; **Nice** *($ €3.40. ⏰ 15min, every 30min.)*, **Monaco** *($ €6. ⏰ 1hr., 5 per day.)*; **Marseille.** *($ €24. ⏰ 2hr., every hr.)*

By Bus

RCA *(☎04 93 39 11 39)* buses run from pl. de Gaulle to **Cannes** *($ €1. ⏰ 20min., every 20-40min.)*, **Nice** *($ €1. ⏰ 1hr., every 20-40min.)*, and **Nice Airport** *($ €1.⏰ 30min., every 20-40min.)*

Getting Around

Walking is the easiest way to get around in the *vieux ville*. From the **train station,**turn left and walk for 5min., and you'll eventually hit the main drag of **rue de la République**, which takes you all the way to the port. To get anywhere farther away, such as the Cap, **buses** *(#2 to the Cap)* leave from the **pl. Guynemer** *(☎04 93 34 37 60 $ €1, day pass €4, week pass €10. ⏰ M-Sa every 40min. 6:50am-7:30pm)*. The **free mini bus** connects the city to the beaches, train station and bus station. **Taxis** are also available from the train station *(☎04 93 67 67 67 $ €18 to Juan-les-Pins. ⏰ 24hr.)*

juan-les-pins   ☎04

Whenever Cannes outprices the Riviera's Spring Break crowd (think Film Festival), Juan-les-Pins subs in as the life of the party. In July and August, the clubs stay open until breakfast—or lunch—and the warm beach welcomes the excessively tan and hungover back into the relaxed rhythm of town life. Situated on the east side of the Cape of Antibes, Juan-les-Pins differs from its historic sister city in that there is little to do other than party, soak in the sun, and play in the water. You'll find actual young people on the beach here, and a very vibrant nightlife that isn't choked by glitz and exploit (cough, Cannes, cough). Be sure to still dress up when you go out—despite the sun and fun, the people here dress to impress, especially during the summer months.

ORIENTATION

Juan-les-Pins is pretty easy to get around; any street from the **train station** leads directly to the beach. A walk down **av. Docteur Favre** takes you right into the middle of the *bar du nuits* and clubs, with the casino conveniently nearby. Walking straight out of the train station down **av. Marechal Joffre** leads you to the main beach and **tourist office**, while **av. l'Esterel** takes you to the budget hotels and cheaper restaurants before hitting the beach on the other side of the train tracks.

ACCOMMODATIONS

HOTEL DE LA PINÈDE   ●❀⊗(ฅ)Ɏ⌂ HOTEL ❸
7 av. Georges Gallice   ☎0648 29 52 74 ◼www.hotel-pinede.com

This classy but funky boutique hotel is a stone's throw from Juan-les-Pins's party district. Don't worry about shut-eye; the windows are soundproof. We're not sure what to make of the paintings of the New York skyline or the Buddha statues, but with a breakfast terrace that's this prime for sunbathing, we don't mind the non sequiturs.

❧ *From the train station, walk down on ave. du Doctueur Fabre. When you reach bl. de la Pinede, make a right. When you reach a 5-point intersection, make a slight right onto ave. George Gallice. Hotel is on your immediate right.* ⓘ *Breakfast €5.50. Soundproof windows.* Ⓢ *Singles €45-50; doubles €60-90; triples €90-120. Prices are higher in summer season.*

HOTEL CECIL   ●❀⊗(ฅ)Ɏ HOTEL ❹
rue Jonnard BP 51   ☎04 93 61 05 12 ◼www.hotelcecil-France.com

Tucked away on the opposite side of town, this quiet Belle Époque hotel will have you thinking about putting some pink furniture in your own house.

❧ *From the train station, turn right and walk down ave. de Esterel 3 blocks. Turn right onto rue Jonnard. Hotel is halfway down the street on your left.* ⓘ *Breakfast €6.50. Prices increase in summer months.* Ⓢ *Singles €55-76; doubles €58-89; triples €105.*

BEACHES

The beaches are ordered from east to west.

PLAGE D'ANTIBES-LES-PINS
bld. du Littoral.

The furthest from the city center (it's almost closer to St-Raphaël), Plage d'Antibes-les-Pins is less crowded than its sister beaches. This is particularly noticeable during the summer months, when it's usually impossible to see any sand in Juan-les-Pins because the umbrellas are so packed together.

PLAGE DU PONT DULYS
bld. Charles Guillaurmont.

One of the most youth-centric beaches in town. It's far enough from the city's center to keep out the elderly and children, but not quite out of the reach for lazy teenagers.

PLAGE LA GALLICE

bld. Boudoin

The closest beach to the town, La Gallice is right next to the port, so you can watch the boats sailing in and out of the harbor. You can also get some good people watching in, since this beach is also the most crowded.

PLAGE EPI HOLLYWOOD

bld. Boudoin

Just out of reach of the city, this beach is where you'll most likely find skinny dippers around 5am who've just been kicked out of the nearby clubs. During the day it's pretty quiet and provides some escape from town.

FOOD

LE SWEET CAFFE

💳♿🍸☀ DINER ❷

16 bld. Baudoiinâ ☎04 93 67 82 12

This relaxing cafe and diner lies on the edge of Juan-les-Pins's party district. Come here after leaving the party early to munch on everything any other restaurant in Juan les Pins has to offer, but at lower prices. The outside patio is lively at night.

$ Pizzas €8.40-11. Crêpes €3.30-9. Salads €7-13. Cocktails €8. Ice cream cocktails €8. ⏰ Open May-Sept 8am-2am or later; Nov-Apr 8am-7pm.

LE RUBAN BLEU

💳♿🍸☀ BRASSERIE ❸

promenade du Soleilâ ☎04 93 61 31 02 🖥plage.rubanbleu@wanadoo.fr

Beachfront brasserie and restaurant that is ideal for watching the young and the fabulous strut their stuff down the boardwalk. You'll pay for the awesome view, unfortunately; the prices here get pretty high. An outdoor seating area opens up on the beach as the night wears on.

$ Plates €19-25. Crêpes €3.50-5. ⏰ Open M-Sa noon-3pm, Su noon-4pm. Beach restaurant open F-Sa 7:30-10:30pm.

LA BAMBA

♿🍸☀ PIZZERIA ❸

18/20 rue Docteur Datheville ☎04 93 61 32 64

Upscale pizzeria and restaurant a block away from the shopping and party center of Juan-les-Pins. Open air restaurant where you can still feel the heat from the woodfired stoves in the back.

$ Dishes €13-15. Pizza €7.80-14. 3-course prix-fixe menu €17.50. ⏰ Open daily noon-10:30pm.

NIGHTLIFE

PAM PAM

♿🍸☀ BAR

137 bld. Wilson ☎04 93 61 11 05 🖥www.pampam.fr

Brazilian bar that serves drinks out of tiki statues. Bright-colored and life-sized tiki gods take the stage with festively dressed dancers at 10pm. Outdoor seating allows some escape from the bongo drums.

$ Apértifs €5. Cocktails €8-12. ⏰ Open daily 3pm-3am.

L'IDEM

🚭🍸▼ BAR, LOUNGE

6 bld. de la Pinede ☎06 09 53 02 49 🖥www.lidem06.unblog.fr

There's 24/7 salsa dancing at this lounge and bar, a block away from the crazy clubs and parties. Skills range from beginner to the pros, who are all too happy to take a greenhorn onto the floor. Lessons are available, and include a night with your instructor or partner on the floor every Thursday night *(€12-22).*

$ Beer €6. Liqueur €5-10. Cocktails €9. ⏰ Open M-Th 7pm-1am (or later), F-Sa 7pm-4am (or later), Su 7pm-1am (or later).

LE CRISTAL BAR

av. Georges Galliceâ ☎04 93 61 62 51

A chill crowd gathers on the terrace to watch local clubbers strut by, or they surround the bar to watch the barmen (literally) juggle bottles as they mix their special ice cream cocktails *(€10).*

[$] Ice cream cocktails €10. ⏰ Open daily 8:30am-2:30am.

ZAPATA BAR

av. du Docteur Dautheville 💻www.juanbynight.com

Think you'll only see someone order 10 shots for himself in Mexico? Think again. We saw it at this Mexican bar, which specializes in shots of "fuego" (gin, run, vodka, spices and lime.) Walls covered in old pre-Revolution photos of Zapata and Hidalgo.

[$] Tequila shots €6. Beer €7. ⏰ Open daily 7pm-3am.

LE VILLAGE DISCOTHÈQUE

1 bld. de la Pinede ☎04 92 93 90 00

Crowds line up early and stretch across the street for this Cuban-themed discothèque and *bar du nuit.* Anticipation for nightly DJ mixes and live performances throughout July and August keeps the city buzzing all year.

[$] Cover €13. Drinks €9. ⏰ Open July-Aug daily midnight-5am; Sept-June F-Sa midnight-5am.

ESSENTIALS

Practicalities

- **TOURIST OFFICE:** 51 bl. de Charles Guillaumont. From the train station, walk down ave. Maréchal Joffre and turn right when you hit the beach. Tourist office is 2min. away on the right, at the intersection of ave. de l'Admiral Courbet and ave. Charles Guillaumont. *(☎04 97 23 11 10 💻www.antibes-juanlespins.com. ⏰ Open M-Sa 9am-noon and 2-6pm, Su 10am-5pm.)*
- **LAUNDROMAT:** On the corner of ave. de l'Esterel and ave. du Docteur Fabre. *(☎04 93 61 52 04 [$] Wash €3.90, dry €.050 per 15min. ⏰Open daily 7am-10:30pm.)*
- **INTERNET: Mediterr@net,** 3 ave. du Docteur Fabre. *(☎04 93 61 04 03[$] €3 per hr. ⏰ Open M-Sa 9am-10pm, Su 10am-9pm.)*
- **POST OFFICE:** Ave. de Maréchal Joffre. *(☎04 92 93 75 50 ⏰ Open M-F 8am-noon and 2-5:45pm, Sa 8:30am-noon.)* ATM available on opposite side (ave. Doctuer Fabre).
- **POSTAL CODE:** 06160.

Getting There

To get to Juan-les-Pins by **train,** go to the Gare SNCF station *(ave. de l'Esterel.⏰Open daily 6:30am-8:55pm. Ticket window open 8:50am-noon and 1:30-5pm.)* To **Antibes** *([$]€1.25.⏰5min., 25 per day.),* **Cannes** *([$]€1.75. ⏰10min., 25 per day.);* **Monaco** *([$]€6.80.⏰1hr., 10 per day.);* **Nice** *([$]€4.10.⏰30min., 25 per day.).* You can also get to Juan-les-Pins by **bus** *(☎04 93 34 37 60.)* **Bus #1** *([$]€1.⏰10min., every 20min. 7am-8pm)* runs from Sillages to pl. Guynemer in Antibes, where you can transfer to the Gare Routiere (regional buses). Night bus #1 between pl. de Gaulle in Antibes and Juan-les-Pins in summer only *(⏰Jul-Aug 8pm-12:30am).* **Taxis** *(☎04 92 93 07 07 or 08 25 56 07 07.)* At the Jardin de la Pinede and outside the train station. The bus from Juan-les-Pins to Antibes is €14-16.

Getting Around

Most of Juan-les-Pins is very walkable; the only problem that we suspect will arise is deciding which beach you should settle on before you start breaking a sweat. If you are completely averse to exercise, the **tourist train** is more than happy to shuttle you around to see the surrounding sights, in case you don't want to walk there yourself. *(☎06 15 77 67 47 ℹ Runs from bld. Boudoin to Antibes, then the vieille ville, and back again to Juan-les-Pins. ⏰ 30min.; Mar-Oct Mo-Su every hr. 10:30am-6:30pm, Jul-Aug runs every hr. 7:30-11:30pm).*

cannes ☎0493

This star-studded, glitzy city on the water definitely has its pricey side, especially during the film festival. If you plan your trip carefully, though, Cannes is probably one of the cheapest places for backpackers to go on the French Riviera. Defined by a distinctly laid back atmosphere for 10 months out of the year (July and August see massive swells in millionaires and their paparazzi, of course), Cannes harbors some of the best that Côte d'Azur has to offer in shopping and beaches, not to mention the fresh shellfish at any of its open air markets. The club scene can be a little intimidating at first, but dressing up just a little bit will go a long way when it comes to getting past the bouncers. In fact, dressing up in general is a good idea here, if only to fit in. Between the hours of 7 and 8pm, locals and tourists magically go from topless and nude (always in vogue here) to full makeup or sports jackets. Don't get caught on the wrong side of this unspoken dress code.

Everyone knows about the Cannes Film Festival, and the city's residents benefit from it; local movie theaters here are able to show Palm d'Or winners before anywhere else in the world. The Palais des Festivals hosts additional expos and concerts throughout the year, which puts Cannes in the party mood almost all the time. You might have to splurge on accommodations—a centrally located place in the city and near the beach is worth the price. Hostels have yet to find their way to the pricey coast of southern France.

ORIENTATION

Cannes is a very easy city to get around; it's a lot smaller than you imagined it was in that last dream of yours where you won Palme d'Or and exchanged room keys with **Matt Damon.** The town can be easily divided into two areas—the expensive part of town and the normal part, where the actual residents live. To the **East of the Palais des Festivals,** the hotels, prices, and breast augmentations get bigger. With names like Dior and Chanel scattered around the private beaches, it's easy to get overwhelmed. If the bling is too much for you, head back towards **the Castre**—the large castle on hill to the West—back to the **Suquet,** where the restaurants are intimate, the prices are lower and people in general are a little more mellow. The nightlife thrives around **rue Doctuer Gerard Monod,** but residents generally stick to the cafes and brasseries that line **rue Felix Fauvre.** The best (and free) bacchanalias are further West past the **Vieux Port,** where you'll find the local population of the young and the restless partying it up almost year round.

ACCOMMODATIONS

HOTEL ALNEA

HOTEL [4]

20 rue Jean de Riouffe ☎04 93 68 72 77 www.hotel-alnea.com

Upscale hotel with walls covered in paintings reminiscent of Gauguin's Tahiti phase. Bright colors make this place come alive, and the beach theme will soon have you dying to go to work on your tanline. Large, clean rooms are each themed according to a famous tropical island or locale.

From the train station, turn right and walk to the MonoPrix. At the intersection, keep going straight one block to rue. Jean de Riouffe. Turn left. Hotel is on your immediate left. ℹ Breakfast €7.50. $ Singles €60; doubles €70; twin €80. ⏰ Check-In 2pm, Checkout 11am. Reception 8am-8pm.

HOTEL 7

🛜♿📶 HOTEL ❹

23 rue Maréchal Joffre ☎04 93 68 66 66

This star-studded hotel opened in January 2010 and still has that new car smell. Pictures of old movies and movie stars are framed on the silver, chic walls. The minimalist decor in the rooms make them feel less small. Handicapped room on ground floor is opened up into a TV lounge when not occupied.

From the train station, turn right and walk until the highway entrance. Walk up the sidewalk to the highway and make a left onto Maréchal Joffre. Hotel will have movie posters on the side facing the train station. ℹ *Breakfast €6. Handicapped room on ground floor.* $ *Singles €60; doubles €70-80. Family room (4 person) €90.*

HOTEL PLM

🛜♿📶 HOTEL ❹

3 rue Hoche ☎04 93 38 31 19 💻www.hotel-plm.com

Boutique hotel with deals if you stay for a while. Clean, nice smelling rooms with purple bathtubs make this simple hotel worth the extra euros, if only to avoid the local dumps.

From the train station, walk right down Juan Juares. Turn left at rue de 24 Aout. Walk for one block until at rue Hoche. Turn right and walk one block. Hotel on right. ℹ *3rd night 25% off. 6th night is 50% off. Breakfast €8.* $ *Singles €46-71; doubles €54-79; superior doubles €59-85.*

HOTEL MIMONT

🛜🚭📶 HOTEL ❷

39 rue Mimont ☎04 93 39 51 64 💻www.canneshotelmimont.com

Still the best budget option in town. Large, clean rooms for relatively cheap, and special *petit chambres* with bed, sink, shared toilet, and shower upon request. On the other side of the train tracks, but still 5min from town. Theincredibly hospitable hosts speak English and are very welcoming to *Let's Go* readers and Americans, who seem to be the majority of their clients.

From the train station, turn left and take the underpass next to the tourist office to rue Mimont. Turn right, and walk fof 3 blocks past the post office. Hotel is on your left. ℹ *Breakfast €6.20.* $ *Petit chambre €30; singles €37-43; doubles €42; triples €58.*

SIGHTS

L'ÉGLISE DE LA CASTRE

CHURCH

Towering over the old city and Vieux Port, this church provides crystal clear views of Cannes all the way to Palm Beach on a clear day. The local landmark nearly bankrupted the city, which had to constantly fundraise for 80 years to complete the stucture and commission its glass and crystal chandeliers, not to mention the neo-Gothic organ that puts Notre Dame's to shame.

$ *Free.* ⏰ *Open daily June-Aug 9am-noon and 3:15-7pm; Sept-May 9am-noon and 2:15-6pm.*

MUSÉE DE LA CASTRE

MUSEUM

☎04 93 38 55 26

Formerly the private castle of the monks of Lérins, this museum houses a permanent collection of ancient relics from the Americas, as well as a display of musical instruments from around the world. The only thing relevant to Cannes is its Provencal art collection from the late 19th and early 20th centuries, which feature depictions of day-to-day life in the city.

$ *€3, students €2.* ⏰ *Open Tu-Su July-Aug 10am-7pm; Sept and Apr-June 10am-1pm and 2-6pm; Oct-Mar 10am-1pm and 2-5pm.*

CASINO CRIOSETTE

CASINO

1 espace Lucien Barrière ☎04 92 98 78 00

The most accessible casino in the area, Criosette features slot machines, blackjack, craps and roulette, as well as a series of fake statues of Greek gods. Kinda like Vegas, only less sleezy. Wait, nevermind: a bunch of guys with slicked hair and their shirts unbuttoned to their belly button just walked in.

i No dress code for slots. No jeans, sneakers, or T-shirts for table games ☼ Slots open at 10am, tables open 8pm-4am.

PLAGE DE LA CROISETTE   BEACH
Between Vieux Port and the Port Canto

A series of private beaches where you will have to shell out €20 for a beach umbrella or beach chair. Pure heresy, in our opinion. The beaches are lined with even pricier restaurants, so you don't need to wander far from your towel to give away even more money.

PLAGES DU MIDI   BEACH
East of the Croisette.

Beautiful sandy beach that's free to the public. Packed in the summertime, this is where you go to meet locals and brush up on some volleyball skills, assuming you know how to say "serve" in French.

FOOD

◆ BELLIARD   ◆♿ BAKERY ❷
1 rue Chabaud   ☎04 93 39 42 72

The 75-year-old *boulangerie* has maintained its humility in one of the priciest areas of Cannes. The neighborhood institution sells an array of charming and affordable *assiettes* (€9.50) as well as tarts, cakes, and a rum raisin ice cream that will put hair on your chest.

Ⓢ Assiette du Jour €9.50. Tarts and cakes €2-3.50. ☼ Open daily 7am-8pm.

AKWABAMO EXOTICK   ◆♿ AFRICAN ❷
36 rue Mimont   ☎04 93 99 89 10

This awesome Côte d'Ivoire restaurant specializes in West African cuisine of chicken and beef *brochettes* (€10). Pick from 6 unpronounceable sauces or endulge in the fish dish with rice (€13). Down it with homemade pineapple and coconut rum. Baskets and crafts cover the walls of this simple establishment.

Ⓢ Dishes €9-18. ☼ Open Tu-F 11am-10pm, Sa-Su 11am-midnight.

LE FREATE   ◆♿△ ITALIAN ❸
26 rue Jean Hibert.   ☎04 93 39 45 39

In business since '47, this Cannes staple sates its clients with grilled meats and pizza, and provides its patrons with that perfect opportunity to escape the hussle in the glitzy part of Cannes for some laidback cafe action near the beach.

Ⓢ Plates €7.50-15. ☼ Open Jun-Sep 6:30am-2am, Oct-May 6:30am-1pm.

LES MAREYEURS DU SUB-EST   ⊛⊗ MARKET ❶
rue Docteur Pierre   ☎04 96 39 39 23

Just cause you're on a budget doesn't mean you can't get lobster. You'll just have to cook it yourself, since this market specializes in live blue lobsters from the daily catch. Make sure you get a fighter, they have the most meat.

Ⓢ €15 per kg. ☼ Open daily 8am-noon.

LA CRÊPERIE   ◆♿△ CRÊPERIE ❷
66 rue Maynadier

A small crêpe place in the heart of the cheap stores on rue Maynadier, its outdoor seating provides the opportunity for judging passerby based on which fake brands they bought.

Ⓢ Crêpes €2.80-8.70. ☼ Open Tu-Su 1pm-8pm.

LAETITIA PASTA   ◆⊗△ ITALIAN ❷
18 av. Maréchal Joffre   ☎04 93 39 52 79

Incredibly cheap pasta and salads for students and budget travelers alike, as the student menu gets you a pasta and drink for ridiculously reasonable prices (€6.50). The simple interior decor matches the simplicity of its menu, while the

france

small stand outside proudly boasts its main dish of the day.

Ⓢ *Students menu €6.50, Normal menu €8 for pasta and drink. Salads €5.90, pastas €5.50-7.10.* ◲ *Open M-Sa 8:30am-7:30pm.*

NIGHTLIFE

▨ THE STATION TAVERN
◆♦♿ Ɏ♨ BAR

18 rue Juan Juares ☎04 93 38 34 91

A godsend for young budget travelers, since cheap beer and karaoke is all you need to fill a small lounge with every under-25 in Cannes. The karaoke nights *(Th-Sa at 9pm)* are completely unpretentious, and totally awesome in its cheesiness.

i Karaoke Th-Sa 9pm. Ⓢ *Beer €3.50, 10 beer for €16, 10 shots for €16.* ◲ *Open M-Sa 6pm-2am.*

BROWN SUGAR
◆♦Ɏ♨▼ BAR, RESTAURANT

17 rue des Frères Pradignac ☎04 93 39 70 10

Kooky Holland-themed bar goes all out with bicycle wheels, accordions, skis, pots and sleds hanging from ceiling. Noticeable family clientele that tapers off as the night goes on. Come before 9:30pm and you get a free tapa with the purchase of a drink. How come you taste so good?

Ⓢ *Beer €4-7, shooters €5, cocktails €8.* ◲ *Open daily 6pm-2:30am.*

SPARKLING AND 4U
◆♦♿Ɏ♨▼ NIGHTCLUB

6/8 rue des Frères Pradignac ☎04 93 39 71 21

And sparkle it does. This joint bar and club is what a club looks like in everyone's wildest dream. Multiple rooms, colors, and textures are enough to keep even the most ADD child interested and focused on this club for the night. A large circular bar (4U bar) sits in the center of the main room, and additional bars are scattered throughout the establishment. Thursday is theme-night. First Thursday of the month is GLBT night.

Ⓢ *Shooters €4, cocktails €12.* ◲ *Open M-Sa 6pm-5am.*

ZANZIBAR
◆♦Ɏ♨▼ BAR

85 rue Felix Fauvre ☎04 93 39 30 75 🖳www.lezanzibar.com

Europe's oldest official gay bar, Zanzibar showcases a classic sailor theme. A small, barrel-like room is covered in images depicting jolly young men drinking and singing on the waterfront. The bar attracts a somewhat older crowd early on in the night, but beckons Americans and youth after midnight.

i GLBT info at www.hexagonegay.com. Ⓢ *Beer €4.50, cocktails €9-10.* ◲ *Open daily 7pm-5am (or later).*

LE 7
◆♦Ɏ▼ CABARET, NIGHTCLUB

7 rue Rouguière ☎04 93 39 10 36 🖳www.discotheque-le7.com

Get prepared for a raunchy all-nighter: this local legend's outrageous drag shows start at 2am, and the drinks and fabulously dressed preformers continue until 5am. Cannes' most famous caberet club, Le 7 caters to all genders and sexual orientations.

Ⓢ *Cover Fri-Sa €12, includes one free drink. Drinks €9.50, shooters €7.* ◲ *Open Th-Su 11:30pm-5am.*

VOGUE
Ɏ♨▼ BAR

20 rue du Suquet ☎04 93 39 99 18

Prepare to be (wo)man-handled. This Hollywood/*fabulous* GLBT bar in the heart of the Suquet compensates for its small size with sparkling mirrors, images of red carpet divas, and a soundtrack fit to accompany your strut down the runway. Come here to play guess-what-gender, then be told very proudly that gender is a construct.

Ⓢ *Cocktails €8.* ◲ *Open daily 8:30pm-2:30am.*

LE MUST

14 rue du Batéguier ☎06 68 14 27 40

Like a scene out of a 1970s porn flick, this *bar du nuit* has chic, glittery plastic barstools, private alcoves in dimly lit areas, and a giant picture of Marilyn Monroe. Outside seating has low couches and a hookah water pipe when you reach sparkley overload. Theme nights include a Russia Night where vodka is discounted.

Ⓢ *Shooters €5, beer €6-8, cocktails €10.* 🕘 *Open Mar-Oct daily 7pm-2:30am, Nov-Feb F-Sa 7pm-2:30am.*

ESSENTIALS

Practicalities

- **TOURIST OFFICE:** In the Palais des Festivals. Booking tickets for events and provides free maps of the city.*(1 bl. de la Croisette* ☎ *04 92 99 84 22* ▇*www.cannes. fr.* 🕘 *Open Jul-Aug 9am-8pm, Sep-Jun 9am-7pm).* Also a branch next to the train station (*☎04 93 99 19 77* 🕘 *Open M-Sa 9am-7pm.*)

- **CURRENCY EXCHANGE: Trevelex.** €80 min cash advance. (*8 rue d'Antibes* ☎*04 93 37 41 45* 🕘 *Open M-Tu 9am-6pm, W 9:45am-6pm, Th-F 8:50am-6pm, Sa 9:45am-6pm.*)

- **AMBULANCE:** (*☎04 92 97 90 21.*)

- **YOUTH CENTER: Cannes Information Jeuenesse.** Info on jobs and housing. (*5 quai St-Pierre* ☎*04 97 06 46 25* ▇*lekiosque@ville-cannes.fr.* 🕘 *Open M-Th 8:30am-12:30pm and 1:30-6pm, F 8:30am-12:30pm and 1:30-5pm.*)

- **INTERNET: Cyber Atlas** (*Corner of Juan Juares and Helene Vagliano* ☎*04 93 69 42 86.* Ⓢ *€3 per hr.* 🕘 *Open Jul-Aug 10am-11pm, Sep-Jun 10am-10pm).*

- **POST OFFICE:** 22 rue de Bivouac Napoleon (*☎04 93 06 26 50* 🕘 *Open M-F 9am-7pm, Sa 9am-noon).* Branch at 34 rue Mimont (*☎04 93 06 27 00* 🕘 *Open M-F 8:30am-noon, 1:30-5pm, Sa 8:30am-noon).*

- **POSTAL CODE:** 06400.

Emergency!

- **PHARMACY: Pharmacie des Allees.** Staff speaks Russian, Italian, German, English and French. (*2 ave. Felix Fauvre* ☎*04 93 39 00 18* 🕘*Open Sept-June M-Sa 9:30am-7:30pm, Jul-Aug 9:30am-9pm.*)

- **POLICE:** 1 ave. de Grasse (*☎04 93 06 22 22*) and 2 quai St-Pierre (*☎08 00 11 71 18*).

- **HOSPITAL: Hopital des Broussailles** (*13 ave. des Broussailles* ☎*04 93 69 70 00*).

Getting There

Trains leave from 1 rue Juan Juares. Automatic ticket booths if you have a European card. (🕘*Station open 5:20am-1:10am. Ticket office open daily 5:30am-10:30pm. Info desk open M-Sa 8:30am-5:30pm.)* To **Antibes** (🕘 *15min.* Ⓢ *€2.75.)*; **Grasse** (🕘 *25min.* Ⓢ *€3.30.)*; **Marseille** (🕘 *2hr.* Ⓢ *€27.40.)*; **Monaco** (🕘*1hr.* Ⓢ *€11)*; **Nice** (🕘 *45min.* Ⓢ *€6.20)*; **St-Rafael** (🕘 *25min.* Ⓢ *€6.30)*; **TGV to Paris via Marseille** (🕘 *5hr.* Ⓢ *€80-100).*

The principal bus company is **Rapide Côte d'Azur,** (*pl. Hotel de Ville* ☎*04 93 48 70 30).* To **Nice** (🕘 *1hr., every 20min.* Ⓢ *€6.)* and **Nice Airport** (🕘 *1hr., every 30min.* Runs M-Sa 7am-7pm, Su 8:30am-7pm Ⓢ *€15.).* Buses to **Grasse** (🕘 *50min., every 45min.* Ⓢ *€1.50.)* leave from the train station.The closest airport is **Nice-Côte d'Azur** (*NCE* ☎*08 20 42 33 33).*

france

Getting Around

Walking is the easiest option in Cannes, since you'll find that its a much smaller city than in your Hollywood dreams and is incredibly manageable by foot. If you have to make it further than local campgrounds, take the **bus** *(€1)* in front of the train station. The Gare Routiere is in front of the Hotel de Ville, and is valid for one hour. The local **train station** leads to any city within reach. There are no subways or tram lines.

saint-tropez ☎0494

St-Tropez is the excess capital of the world. You'd be stunned at the prices, if you weren't distracted by the beautiful yachts and beautiful people. Independent wealth thrives here, as evidenced by the numerous boats flying the flags of blacklisted tax havens. In a town where the tip to the dockmaster can run you as much as €5000, it can be hard to find deals. Apparently rich people just like spending money as a way to keep out the petty-folk. The real attraction here are the party beaches, which light up at night and continue until day break. Unfortunately, these parties are exclusive and hard to access without a yacht or some serious nighttime espionage. Beyond the money, St-Tropez is an incredibly beautiful town, and unlike any other on the Riviera in terms of architecture and layout of the town. Villas and small alleys make up the heart of the town, and it vaguely resembles a seaside village in Spain or Italy with its terra-cotta rooftops and colored tiles. It's easy to see why Hollywood and the mega wealthy fell in love with it, but that means making a serious dent in your wallet to enjoy it yourself.

saint-tropez

ORIENTATION

Its wealth per square kilometer might outdo the Vatican, but St-Tropez is a very tiny town. Walking is the easiest way to get around here between the **old and new ports.** Unfortunately, the **beaches** are far away from the town center, requiring **shuttles** or a 👍**scooter rental** (a good option for those who want freedom from tedious timetables) to get there. The most affordable restaurants, hotels, and shops are on the outskirts of town. The closer you are to the port or the quais, the higher the prices. From the **bus station** or **new port,** turn left and walk right into town. The **pl. des Lices** is the main square that is the most normal, local part of Saint Tropez, with small stands for food, and banks and the market surrounding it. Most of the main roads lead to pl. des Lices. To get to the beaches, either walk around the **citadel** past the cemetery on **Chemin des Graniers,** or take the main road at the entrance of the town **(Route des Plages)** where turning left at any intersection will take you to the beaches.

ACCOMMODATIONS

There are lots of places to stay in St-Tropez, so long as you have lots of money. The cheaper places are located in St. Maxime, the next town over, or just on the outskirts of St.Tropez. The hotels we listed are in the actual town, easy to get to, and under €100.

👍 LE COLOMBIER — 🚭📶🍸☀ HOTEL [5]

impasse des Conquettes — ☎04 94 97 05 31

Beautiful, small hotel just on the edge of the old city. Small rooms, but a private breakfast available in the garden. Cheapest place in St-Tropez, but miraculously still very chic.

➜ From the pl. des Lices (center of town), walk away from the citadel. Take the most left street (bl. Louis Blanc) from the sq. J. Moulin. Walk 1-2 blocks, turn left onto ave. Paul Roussel. Turn left again onto Impsse des Conquettes. Hotel is at the end of street. ***i*** *Cheapest rooms have no A/C and shared bath.* $ *Singles and doubles €63-110.*

LES PALMIERS — 🚭📶🍸☀ HOTEL [5]

24 Lavoir Vasserot — ☎04 94 97 01 61

Small, boutique hotel in the style of a Tropezienne villa. The orange walls and low, plastered ceilings make this affordable hotel even more attractive. Clean rooms and old-fashioned bar. The entry garden is overgrown, so it's an adventure just to find the reception. The villas overlook the garden.

➜ From the pl. les Lices, walk away from the hill and rue joseph Quaranta on your slight right. Hotel is on your left. ***i*** *Breakfast €11.* $ *Singles and doubles €89-189.*

FOOD

Food in St-Tropez is—surprise!—very expensive, especially for sit-down meals. There are some cheaper prix-fixe menus in the old city up near the Citadel, as well as closer to the new port (sailors gotta eat too). All over the pl. des Lices, you'll find cheap food options in the form of stands, and there is a local **Monoprix** *(⏰ Open daily 9am-6pm)* right as you walk into town from the new port.

CRÊPERIE BRETONNE — ♿🍸☀ CRÊPERIE [2]

quai Frederic Mistral — ☎04 94 97 48 53

Authentic Breton crêperie that serves its own cider. Not your typical crêpes, though—these babies are crispy, folded halfway and left partially open, like they do it up north. Right on the port so you can feel like you're rich while you're dining on the patio. Old sailing paraphernalia cover the walls.

$ *Crêpes €3.50-8. Cider €5.* ⏰ *Open daily noon-8pm.*

L'OLIVE — 🚭🍸☀ TRADITIONAL [3]

9 rue Aire du Chemin — ☎04 94 97 09 21

Finally, a three-course meal in St-Tropez that doesn't cost a fortune. Serves

Provençal dishes near the citadel on a patio under a canopy of jasmine.
Ⓢ *Prix fixe 3 course meals €18.* Ⓓ *Open M-Sa 7-10pm.*

LA TANNELLE
Ⓧ⛱🍴 PIZZERIA ❸

Passage Gambetta
☎04 94 54 82 02

Rooftop pizzeria that has a view of the old port. The pizza is cheap, and the ivy growth on the patio provides ample shade. A warning though: the sign out front explicitly states that they don't accept €500 bills. Sorry, Richie Rich.
Ⓢ *Pizza €11.50-13. Order for takeout €10.* Ⓓ *Open daily noon-9pm.*

MIJO CRÊPES
♿🍴 CRÊPERIE ❶

Marché Couvert, pl. des Lices

In the pl. des Lices, there's a covered market with permanent stands of cheap crêpes, which serve the cheapest and the sweetest in town.
Ⓢ *Crêpes €2.50-5.* Ⓓ *Open daily July-Aug 9am-10:30pm; Sept-June 10am-7pm.*

NIGHTLIFE
📷

✍ LE QUAI
🍷🍴▽ BAR

22 quai Jean Juares
☎04 94 97 04 07

Less pretentious lounge and bar that turns into a madhouse of packed bodies and pumping music. When the patrons start to climb onto the furniture, you're not sure if they are drunk or just trying to get out of the mosh pit. Expect absolutely debacherous behavior.
Ⓢ *Beer €5. Cocktails €13.* Ⓓ *Open Mar-Oct noon-4am.*

✍ CABANITO
♿🍷🍴 BAR

16 quai de l'Epi
☎05 14 12 28 60

Pound back shots underneath Che posters to the sounds of Cuban music and reggaeton. The super chill crowd gathers for latin salsa, killer mojitos, and €4 beer. Soirees on Tuesday nights.
Ⓢ *Beer €4. Cocktails €8.* Ⓓ *Open daily 5pm-3am.*

PAPAGAYO
🍴🍷🍴▽ CLUB

Résidence du Port
☎04 94 97 95 95

One of St-Tropez's most famous clubs, where bottles of booze cost more than your starting salary. If you can dress up and get past the bouncer, get ready for a packed house that vibrates with the bass, and keep your eyes out for what color a €500 bill is (hint: it matches the walls). Lounge seating by reservation only. If you forget, the large bouncer will remind you.
Ⓢ *Cocktails €19.* Ⓓ *Open May-June F-Sa 12:30am-6am; July-Aug daily 12:30am-6am; Sept F-Sa 12:30am-6am.*

MICASA SUSHI
🍴🍷🍴 SUSHI, BAR

1 pl. Alphonse Celli
☎04 94 97 04 32

All-white interior sushi bar where everyone sits outside to enjoy the live rock music on the weekends. The older crowd jams and young crowd cases the lines at the exclusive clubs.
Ⓢ *Beer €4. Cocktails €13.* Ⓓ *Open daily 6pm-2am (or later).*

CHEZ MAGGIE
🍴♿🍷▽ BAR

7 rue Sibille
☎04 94 97 16 12

Clubby atmosphere without the stress of not getting in.'70s decor and disco hits make this a popular location for soirees and a slightly older crowd.
Ⓢ *Cocktails €12.* Ⓓ *Open daily 8:30pm-3am.*

TSAR
🍴🍷🍴▽ BAR

1 quai de l'Epi
☎06 11 95 76 43

Gay bar that is frequented by all genders and sexualities for the use of its hookahs. Pink, sparkly, and "fabulously" laid-back (think Claire's, only gay-er), this is the best place for a middle ground thats less than a club and more than a bar.

$ Beer €8. Cocktails €15. Hookah €20. ⏰ Open daily 6pm-3am.

CHEZ LES GARÇONS — 🚭🍸☀▼ GAY BAR

11-13 rue de Crepoun ☎04 94 43 68 70 💻www.chezlesgarcons.com

If the name didn't give it away, the small bar packed with older men will—this is one of the most popular gay bars in St-Tropez, and unlike the Tsar caters almost exclusively to gay men. Outside seating doubles the bar's size. Inside is a DJ and pink and blue arched ceiling.

$ Cocktails €12. ⏰ Open Jun-Aug daily 7pm-3am, Sept-Dec Th-Su 7pm-3am; Feb-May Th-Su 7pm-3am.

ARTS AND CULTURE

PALAIS DES FESTIVALS ET DES CONGRÈS — LA CROISETTE

bld. de la Croisette ☎04 93 39 01 01 💻www.palaisdesfestivals.com

Large venue that hosts every festival or expo that comes through Cannes. Everything from dance, to arts, to concerts to the film festival in May.

$ Prices vary, call director. ⏰ Open M-Sa 9am-noon and 2-6pm.

FESTIVAL DE PLAISSANCE — CENTRE-VILLE

Vieux Port ☎01 46 04 08 62 💻www.salonnautiquecannes.com

In case you wanted to feel worse about yourself for not having giggles of money, check out this aptly named boat show where the entire Vieux Port is filled with multimillion dollar yachts and megayachts during this week long festival in September.

$ €15 entrance for the whole week.

ESSENTIALS

Practicalities

- **TOURIST OFFICE:** On the corner of quai Jean Jaures and rue Victor Laugier. English spoken, free maps, and events guide. *(☎04 94 97 45 21💻www.saint-tropez.st$ €1 bus schedules. ⏰Open daily from late June to early Sept 9:30am-8pm; from mid-Sept to early Oct and from late Mar to mid-June 9:30am-12:30pm and 2-7pm; from mid-Oct to mid-Mar 9:30am-12:30pm and 2-6pm.)*
- **CURRENCY EXCHANGE: Societe Generale,** pl. des Lices. *(☎04 94 12 81 40⏰ Open M-F 8:15am-12:15pm and 2-5:30pm, Sa 8:15am-12:25pm.)*
- **INTERNET: Kreatik Cafe.** *(19 ave. Gen. Leclerc☎04 94 97 40 61 💻www.kreatik.com $ €2 per 10min., €4 per 30min., €7 per hr. ⏰ Open M-Sa 9:30am-noon, Su 2-10pm.)*
- **POST OFFICE:** pl. Alphonse Celli, between old and new ports. *(☎04 94 55 96 50 ⏰ Open M-F 8:30am-noon and 2-5pm, Sa 8:30am-noon.)*
- **POSTAL CODE:** 83990.

Emergency

- **POLICE MUNICIPAL:** Ave. Leclerc *(☎04 94 54 86 65).*
- **AMBULANCE:** ☎04 94 56 60 64.
- **PHARMACY: Pharmacie du Port.** *(9 quai Suffren ☎04 94 97 00 06⏰ Open M-Sa 8:30am-8:30pm.)*

Getting There

St-Tropez is far from any train line, but there is a regular **ferry service** from **Les Bateaux de Saint-Raphaël** (*☎04 94 95 17 46 *▪️*www.tmr-saintraphael.com* Ⓢ *One-way €13, round-trip €23.* 🕐 *1hr.; twice daily at 9:30am and 2:30pm, return at 10:30am and 5:15pm.)* There is also a **bus ride** from the **Saint Raphaël SNCF Gare** (*bus line #7601.* Ⓢ *€2.* 🕐 *1½hr., Sept-June arrivals every hr. 6am-8:15pm, return trips every hr. 6am-8:20pm; July-Aug arrivals every hr. 6am-8:15pm, return trips every hr. 6am-9pm.)*

Getting Around

This is a very easy city to walk. To get to the beaches, take the **shuttle service,** whose schedule you can pick up at the tourist office. You can also take a **taxi** (*☎04 94 97 05 27),* or rent a **scooter** (*Espcae 83, across the street from Cafe Kreatik* *☎04 94 55 80 00* 🕐 *Open M-Sa 9am-noon and 2-6pm.)*

essentials

entrance requirements

- **PASSPORT:** Required for citizens of all countries.
- **VISA:** Required for citizens of any country for stays longer than 90 days.
- **WORK PERMIT:** Required for all non-EU citizens planning to work in France.

You don't have to be a rocket scientist to plan a good trip. (It might help, but it's not required.) You do, however, need to be well prepared, and that's what we can do for you. Essentials is the chapter that gives you all the nitty-gritty you need to know for your trip: the hard information gleaned from 50 years of collective wisdom (and that phone call to France the other day that put us on hold for an hour). Planning your trip? Check. Staying safe and healthy? Check. Plus, for overall trip-planning advice from what to pack (money and as little underwear as possible) to how to take a good passport photo (it's physically impossible; consider airbrushing), you can also check out the Essentials section of ▪️www.letsgo.com.

We're not going to lie—this section is tough for us to write, and you might not find it as fun of a read as 101 or Discover. But please, for the love of all that is good, read it! It's super helpful, and, most importantly, it means we didn't compile all this technical info and put it in one place for you (yes YOU) for nothing.

PLANNING YOUR TRIP

Time Differences

France is 1hr. ahead of Greenwich Mean Time (GMT) and observes Daylight Saving Time. This means that it is 6hr. ahead of New York City, 9hr. ahead of Los Angeles, 1hr. ahead of the British Isles, 8hr. behind Sydney, and 10hr. behind New Zealand.

MONEY

Tipping and Bargaining

By law in France, service is added to bills in bars and restaurants, called *"service compris."* Most people do, however, leave some change (up to €2) for drinks and food, and in nicer restaurants, it is not uncommon to leave 5% of the bill. For other services, like taxis and haircuts, 10-15% tip is acceptable.

Taxes

As a member of the EU, France requires a value added tax (VAT) of 19.6%, which is applied to a variety of goods and services (e.g. food, accommodations), though it is less for food (5.5%). Non-European Economic Community visitors to France who are taking these goods home may be refunded this tax for purchases totaling over €175 per store. When making purchases, request a VAT form, and present them at the *détaxe* booth at the airport. These goods must be carried at all times while traveling, and refunds must be claimed within 6 months.

SAFETY AND HEALTH

General Advice

In any type of crisis, the most important thing to do is **stay calm.** Your country's embassy abroad is usually your best resource in an emergency; registering with that embassy upon arrival in the country is a good idea.

Local Laws and Police

La Police Nationale is the branch of French law enforcement that is most often seen in urban areas. To reach the French police, call ☎17.

Drugs and Alcohol

There is no drinking age in France, but to purchase alcohol one must be at least 18 years old. The legal blood-alcohol level for driving in France is .05%, which is less than it is in countries like the US, UK, New Zealand, and Ireland, so exercise appropriate caution when driving in France.

Specific Concerns

The French Revolution may have been in 1789, but the spirit of the revolution certainly hasn't died. Protests and strikes are frequent in France, but violence does not often occur. You may find yourself in Grenoble on the day of a transit strike (as one LG researcher did) but who hasn't always wanted to see France by Vespa?

france 101

facts and figures

- **NUMBER OF FRENCH NOBEL LAUREATES:** 49.
- **LITERS OF WINE CONSUMED PER PERSON ANNUALLY:** 47.
- **LIKELIHOOD THE PREVIOUS TWO FACTS ARE RELATED:** 93.7%.
- **NUMBER OF MISTRESSES KEPT SIMULTANEOUSLY BY SARTRE:** 9.
- **NUMBER OF PEOPLE LIBERATED FROM THE BASTILLE IN 1789:** 7.
- **NUMBER OF YOUTH ARRESTED ON NOVEMBER 14TH DURING RIOTS OF 2005:** 71.

Let's Go is sure you've heard tell of that infamous French snobbiness—how they think Americans are ignorant, English speakers are inferior, and foreigners in general are pretty sub-par. But they're really not as scary as all that. They've just grown up in the land of Monet and Molière, of Bonaparte and the Bastille, a country that's produced 49 Nobel Prize winners and 31 UNESCO World Heritage Sites, been the seat of three empires and the source of countless artistic movements. It's no wonder they're so proud to be French—and it's also no wonder that they don't think it's cute when you can't tell a Gaul from de Gaulle. So if you don't really like being that kid (who does?), dive into this chapter and read up on the history, art, literature, and customs of France. We'll take you from the first hundred years of the Roman Empire to the Hundred Years' War, from religious repression to artistic expression, and, most importantly, from an oh-you-silly-American Stone Age to an educated Enlightenment. We promise this will be more entertaining and informative than the in-flight movie.

CUSTOMS AND ETIQUETTE

First Impressions

The first time you meet in France, shaking hands is expected, although friends will greet one another with a kiss on the cheek. Women are expected to kiss twice. If you're planning on eating in a restaurant or heading out clubbing, dress it up— the easiest way to stand out as a tourist is to wear shorts and a T-shirt out to dinner. Don't expect to be let into the club wearring sneakers. At restaurants, the tip is included in the bill, but feel free to leave a 5-10% tip for exceptional service.

What Not to Say

In French culture, never discuss money in private or public company. Doing so is seen as tasteless. In restaurants, arguing over who had what when the bill comes up is even more shameless. The host usually is expected to pay; among friends it is more common to split the bill by the number in your party. In addition to money, talking about business is also considered boring.

Demain

If you're invited to dinner at someone's house, you'll find them unprepared if you show up "on time." Try aiming to be 15 to 30 min. late. The attitude of "do it later/tomorrow" is one that France, and Southern Europe generally, embraces. While a German meeting might work differently, a cafe rendezvous typically never starts punctually.

We're Closed

In France, restaurants, cafes, and other serves that usually stay open on Sundays are closed on Mondays instead. If you're planning a hot date on a Monday, make sure to reschedule for later in the week. Besides, who goes on dates on Monday night?

Use Your Crappy French

When entering any sort of establishment, remember that it is the patron's (your) job to initiate conversation. Using French is crucial; it's a sign that you're trying to adapt to the culture and that you're willing to embarrass yourself to do so. French appreciate the struggle and, as most know a few words of English themselves, will often bail you out and start talking in English.

FOOD AND DRINK

A French **breakfast** typically consists of lighter fare— a quick stop for coffee and a *croissant* at the nearest cafe, or a few *tartines* (slices) of bread with jelly. Stop at a *boulangerie* to pick up a pastry or a baguette that was made mere minutes before the shop opened. **Lunch** is a longer affair, but it is becoming less leisurely as even Parisians adjust to the busybody workday of a globalized world. Simple yet savory lunch chow found in cafes and brasseries includes salads, quiche, and tasty croque monsieur (grilled ham and cheese). Eating out for lunch can be more intimidating for non-French speakers, but it's just a matter of having some cojones and testing out your throaty *s'il vous plaît*, no matter how big the waiter's scowl is.

The same goes for **dinner,** where tourists subject themselves to confusion and anxiety as an intimidating *maître'd* recites the menu in rapid-fire French. Stay strong; the food's worth it. A traditional French meal consists of five courses: hors d'oeuvres, soup, a main course, salad, cheese, and dessert, each paired with a wine. Except for the most extravagant five-star establishments, however, a restaurant meal is typically two or three courses depending on your appetite and budget. Some economical travelers may opt to skip the food and just indulge in the ◪wine, but we suggest you do both. Most restaurants open around 7:30pm or 8pm and take orders until 11pm; keep a look out for classic French dishes such as *cassoulet*, a meat stew, or *coq au vin*, wine-cooked chicken. It is law for restaurants to have a *prix-fixe* menu, so if they aren't showing you one but you're interested in the potentially cheaper option, do not hesitate to inquire.

North

Nord Pas-de-Calais, Brittany and Normandy rely heavily on the crustations and bass at the North Sea. Brittany is especially famous for its crêpes, as well as *galettes*, which are made from the buckwheat that grows in the region. Many of the dishes are also paired with cider from northern apple trees, for those who are alcoholically inclined.

South

You'll never get tired of citrus and fruits— unless you go the South of France. This area is one of Europe's main suppliers of herbs (no, not in a Humboldt County sense). Honey is a staple and prized ingredient in this region, as well as goat cheese, sausages, and lamb. Making use of the sea as well, there are also many dishes that include garlic anchovies. Try drinking **pastis**, a yellow anise flavored alcoholic drink. Hemmingway coined the colorful phrase "Death in the Afternoon" to refer to a mix of pastis and Champagne, reminding all of us how much a hangover sucks at 5pm.

West

The Basque cuisine has definitely made its way into this region's food. Even though Bordeaux is known for its wine, it's also famous for its dried meats, including lamb. The region is also France's largest producers of *foie gras*, or fattened goose liver. The food is also heavily influenced by tomatoes, red pepper, wheat products and Arbequina olive oils.

West and Central

The Loire Valley is rich in fruits, as well as the more famous liqueurs that come from those fruits. Most of the meat in this region isd wild game, Charolais cattle, and guinea fowl, while the region is especially famous for its goat cheeses. Go a little to the west and run into Champagne country, which is also famous for its German influenced cakes and beer.

france

GERMANY

Anything that ever made it big is bound to attract some stereotypes, and Germany is no different. Beer, crazy deaf composers, robotic efficiency, sausage, Inglourious Basterds—just to name a few. Germany has some of the best collections of art in the world, incredible architecture, and a history that makes it clear no one bosses Germany around. Whether giving the ancient Romans a run for their money or giving birth to Protestantism, Germany has always been a rebel. Even behind its success as a developed country, it hasn't given that up.

The damage from World War II still lingers in city skyscapes, and the country is keenly embarrassed of its Nazi and communist pasts. Even though its concrete wall has been demolished, Berlin, the country's capital, still retains a marked difference between east and west after decades of strife, tempering the picturesque castles and churches of earlier golden ages.

Plenty of discounts, cheap eats, and a large young population make Germany an exciting place to visit and study. It's also incredibly accessible for Anglophone visitors, as many Germans have no qualms about slipping from their native tongue into English. The nightlife and culture of Berlin or Munich will grab you and never let you go, while thriving smaller university towns will charm you into wanting to stay another semester.

greatest hits

- **COLD WAR KIDS.** Admire the Berlin Wall murals painted by artists from around the world at the East Side Gallery (p. 458).

- **BUTTERFLY KISSES.** Emerge from Cocoon Club (p. 512) as a drunken butterfly after spending the night wrapped in some German hottie's arms.

- **BEAMER, BENZ, OR BENTLEY.** Sport the classiest threads you own, and head to the BMW Welt (p. 525) to test drive a new whip.

- **DOWN IN ONE.** Pace yourself on the Maß and avoid using the vomitorium at Munich's most famous beer hall, Hofbräuhaus (p. 530).

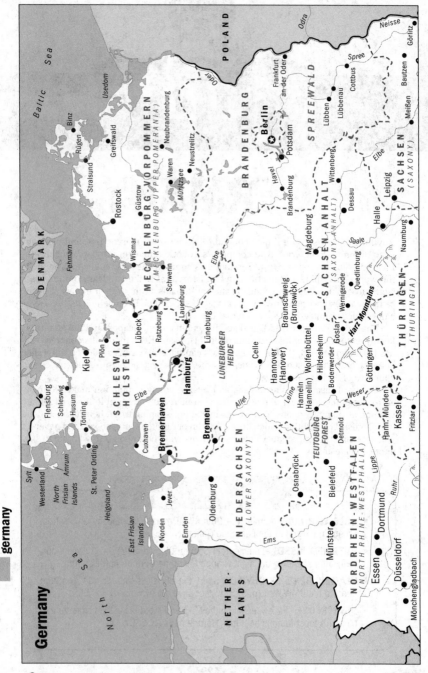

germany

Germany

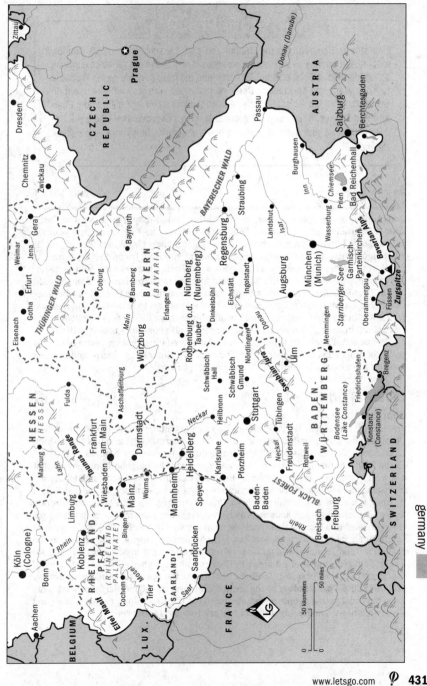

germany

First stop is Berlin, hit up the Bahnof Zoo and the schloß in Berlin's Charlottenburg, but bounce as soon as the sun goes down. Shake the geriatrics, sip wine alongside PYTs at **Solsi e Morsi,** and befriend the legendary bar owner. Continue to Köln, where the spectacular **Dom** will make you with your hangover spin. In Frankfurt, try all the regional specialties and then finish off your night at the **Piper and Red Lounge.** Keep the party going at Munich's **Hofbräuhaus,** where you can even claim that your night of chugging down beers with Germans was a cultural experience.

berlin ☎030

Congratulations on your decision to visit Berlin. Your wussy friends went to Paris. Your snob friends left for London. Your tacky friends chose Florence. And your fat friends stayed home. But you chose Berlin, which makes two things true of you: 1. You're smarter than your friends. 2. You're bad at choosing friends. Everything that rocks in the other European capitals does so in Berlin, but here the beat is faster, the groove is harder, and all of it is covered in more mustard than Mr. French could dream. The Prussians ruled from Berlin's canal-lined boulevards, built the Berliner Dom, pimped out opera houses, and collected enough art to make the Louvre green with envy. In WWII, then there whole "wall" thing where the Soviets literally cut the city in half. In short, "change" more than anything else continues to define Berlin. As a city was simultaneously abandoned and dominated by authority, Berlin became a haven of punks and anarchists in the '70s and '80s. Embracing change and pushing forward has also made Berlin the "cool" capital of Europe.

Your friends are morons.

ORIENTATION

Charlottenburg

Should you forget that Berlin is an old European capital, venture into West Berlin's Charlottenburg. Originally a separate town founded around the grounds of Friedrich I's palace, it was an affluent cultural center during the Weimar years as well as the Berlin Wall era thanks to Anglo-American support. The neighborhood retains that old-world opulence, from its upscale Beaux-Arts apartments to the shamefully extravagant **Kurfürstendamm,** Berlin's main shopping strip. **Ku'damm,** as the locals call it, runs east to west through southern Charlottenburg. It's also home to Europe's largest department store, **KaDeWe,** which comprises five massive floors that keep patrons dressed to a tee and their pantries similarly so with truffle oil. Close to central Charlottenburg is the large **Bahnof Zoo,** a Berlin family favorite, which may join the Ku'damm (and its never-ending flow of teenagers darting in and out of H and M) as the youngest and liveliest areas in Charlottenburg. Other sights include part of the Tiergarten, the sprawling Zoologischer Garten, the Spree River in the northwest, and the **Schloß Charlottenburg** to the west. Otherwise, the higher neighborhood rents keep out most young people and students, so the Charlottenburg crowd is quiet and somewhat older, and the nightlife options are few and far between.

germany

Schöneberg and Wilmersdorf

South of Ku'damm, Schöneberg and Wilmersdorf are primarily middle class, residential neighborhoods, remarkable for their world class mellow cafe culture, bistro tables, relaxed diners, and coffee shops spilling onto virtually every cobblestone street. Nowhere else in Berlin, and perhaps in all of Germany, is the gay community quite as contentedly outrageous as in the area immediately surrounding **Nollendorfplatz.** The gay nightlife scene, ranging from dark and smoky bars to chic and sleek clubs, is diverse in decor and music, but also laid-back and welcoming. To the west lies one of Berlin's most convenient outdoor getaways: **Grunewald,** popular with city-dwellers trading in their daily commute for peaceful strolls with the family dog along pine-lined dirt trails, is reachable by bus and tram in just about 20 minutes.

Mitte

Mitte is without a doubt the most important district in Berlin. It has the **Brandenburg Gate,** the **Reichstag,** the **Jewish Memorial,** the **Column of Victory,** and the **Berliner Dom.** It has the best cultural institutions; **Museum Island** stacks the world's best musuems practically on top of each other. And somehow Mitte manages to multitask as a center for Berlin hipsterdom as well, with sick clubs, indie movie theaters, excellent food, and more walking plaid than that nightmare where the tablecloths came alive. Then, of course, there's the forest-like **Tiergarten** at the center of Mitte, which shelters sunbathers, barbecuers, and grasping lovers. The main street, **Strasse des 17 Juni,** serves as a

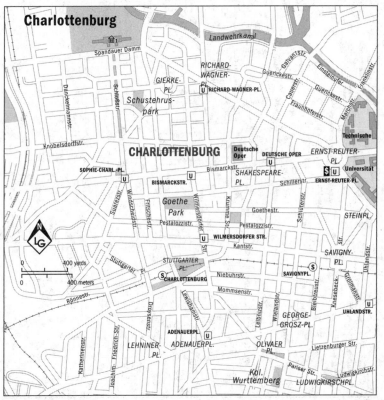

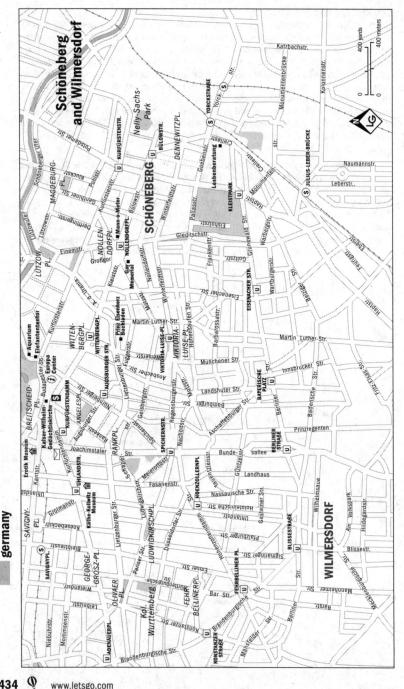

germany

Schöneberg and Wilmersdorf

SCHÖNEBERG

WILMERSDORF

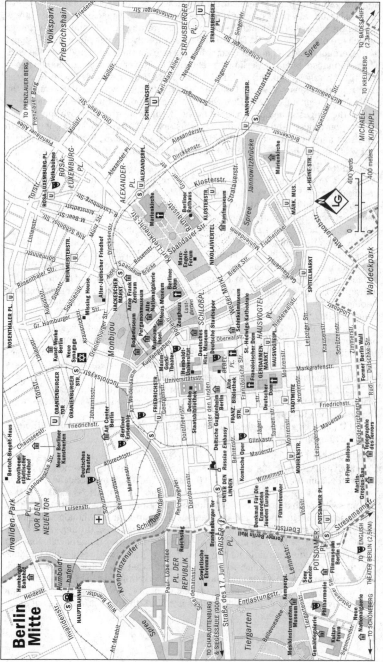

Berlin Mitte

berlin · orientation

populist gathering place where carnivals, markets, protests, and public viewings of the World Cup take precedent over traffic. However, what's most fun about Mitte is tracing the history of Berlin down its streets and through its old and new buildings (which are often combined). The **Berlin Wall** ran directly through Mitte, and East and West Germany made a habit of comparing the sizes of their manhood over the wall. The communists built the Berlin Fernsehturm (TV Tower) as a sign of dominance—it's still the tallest building in Europe. The Americans responded with Congress Hall, now the House of World Cultures, an architectural wonder that's earned the nickname "pregnant oyster." Elsewhere, at the "Topography of Terror" museum, one of the longest standing stretches of the Berlin Wall streaks above the ruins of Hitler's war offices. And even with all this history to fall back on, Mitte continues to construct and reconstruct icons. The **Berlin Schloβ**, the Hohenzollern Imperial Palace that was destroyed in the 1950s, is scheduled to re-open in 2018.

Prenzlauer Berg

What was once Berlin's overlooked Beirke, replete with crumbling cement and graffiti-covered Soviet-era buildings, is rapidly transforming into perhaps the trendiest area in the city. Attracted by low rents, students and artists stormed the neighborhood after reunification, giving the area a bohemian vibe with a unique DDR spin. Today, the streets are owned by well-dressed schoolchildren and their young, effortlessly hip parents, and the city blocks are interrupted by countless small parks, playgrounds, and costly secondhand stores. In Prenzlauer Berg, everything used to be something else. Delicious brunches are served every summer in what were once butcher shops, students party in a horse stable turned nightclub, and cheap cocktails are served from a bar countertop in a former linoleum showroom. For this neighborhood, what's cool is ironic, and what's ironic is the bare-bones, stuck in the '70s, USSR cement siding, burnt-orange shag carpeting past. Cafe-bar owners know what's hip, so even as relics of Prenzlauer Berg's are rapidly disappearing, mismatched sofas and floral wallpaper remain the shabby-chic decorating standard. The bar scene is to Prenzlauer Berg as club culture is to Friedrichshain. After dark, Prenzlauer Berg turns into a not-to-be-missed extravaganza of hole-in-the-wall basement concerts, laid-back wine tastings, and trendy, vegan cafes.

Geographically, Prenzlauer Berg is east of the city center, overlapping in some places with Mitte to the west. Cheaper bars cluster around the **Kastanienallee,** while the area around Lettestr. is ideal for checking out the '70s decorating revival. Only two U-Bahn lines and a single S-Bahn line cut through the area, so plan on trams or walking to explore the berg.

Friedrichshain

Friedrichshain's low rents and DDR edge draw a crowd of punk-rock types ever eastward. From the longest remnant of the Berlin Wall that runs along the river to the oppressive, towering architecture of the neighborhood's central axis, **Frankfurter Allee,** the presence of the former Soviet Union is still strong. Nowhere is that hard edge felt as sharply as in Friedrichshain's famous hardcore nightlife monopolizing every rundown train station and abandoned factory along the Spree, turning graffitied cement sheds into wild raves and electro hangouts. However, some locals complain that gentrification has found its way even here, as traditional residential buildings pop up and chic 20-somethings set up shop on the cafe-ridden **Simon-Dach-Strasse** and **Boxhagenerplatz.** But however legitimate those observations may be, Friedrichshain is still wonderfully inexpensive and fantastically out of the ordinary. Travelers should keep an eye out at night, as Friedrichshain is still a little rough around the edges and even desolate in some spots.

Kreuzberg

If Mitte is Manhattan, Kreuzberg is Brooklyn. Gritty graffiti covers everything here, and the younger population skulks around chowing down street food good enough for the Last Supper. The parties start later, go later, and sometimes never stop. Kreuzberg once ruled as the center of punkdom and counterculture in Berlin. It was occupied by *hausbesetzer* (squatters) in the 1920s and '70s, until a conservative city government forcibly evicted them in the early '80s. Riots ensued, and during Reagan's 1985 visit to the city, authorities so feared protests in Kreuzberg that they locked down the entire district. While these days find it a bit tamer, the alternative heart of Kreuzberg remains. Underground clubs turn on when the lights go down in abandoned basements, burned-out apartment buildings, and shaky rooftop terraces; the clubs that party the hardest in Berlin all find shelter in Kreuzberg. Kreuzberg is also notably home to Berlin's enormous Turkish population. Döner kebabs, those shawarma sandwich-like miracles, go for €2-3 all across this district, and the Turkish Market along the southern bank of the Landwehrkanal is one of the most exciting, raucous, cheap, and authentic markets in Western Europe. If you want to learn things about Berlin, go to Mitte. If you want to not remember your entire trip, come to Kreuzberg.

ACCOMMODATIONS

Charlottenburg

✓ BEROLINA BACKPACKER — 💳📶 HOSTEL ❷

Stuttgarter P. 17 ☎030 32 70 90 72 🖥www.berolinabackpacker.de

This quiet hostel keeps things elegant with pastel walls and bunk-free dorms. Backpackers enjoy the high ceilings and big windows; some rooms even have balconies and intricate molding. Surrounding cafes and close proximity to the S-Bahn make up for its distance from the rush of the city. Communal and private kitchens *(communal €1 per day, private €9.50)* available for use. Relax and enjoy a breakfast buffet *(€7)*, or the "backpackers' breakfast" *(a roll with sausage, cheese and coffee; €3)* in the popular and newly decorated pale blue dining area.

➤ S3, S5, S9, or S75: Charlottenburg. ℹ Internet €0.50 per 15min. Wi-Fi included. $ 5 bed dorms €10-13.50; singles €29.50-35.50; doubles €37-47; triples €39-64; quads €46-60. ⏰ Reception 24hr. Check-out 11am.

A AND O HOSTEL — ⊗ HOSTEL ❶

Joachimstaler Str. 1-3 ☎030 809 47 53 00 🖥www.aohostels.com

On a busy, commercial street, A and O may not have an ideal location unless you plan on frequenting the Erotik Museum 40m away, but it has reliable rooms and close proximity to the Bahnhof Zoo transit hub. The lobby and bar are packed nightly, as is the roof patio despite its resembalence to a dilapidated mini-golf course. Rooms have metal bunks, big windows, personal lockers, and ensuite baths.

➤ 30m from Bahnhof Zoo. ℹ Wi-Fi €5 per day. Breakfast buffet €6. Linens €6. $ 8-10 bed dorms from €10; smaller dorms from €15. Doubles from €25; singles from €39. Prices may change significantly in busy months. ⏰ Reception 24hr.

FRAUENHOTEL ARTEMISIA — 💳⊗📶 HOTEL ❹

Brandenburgische Str. ☎030 873 89 05 🖥www.frauenhotel-berlin.de

This elegant hotel for women only was the first of its kind in Germany. A quiet rooftop terrace with sweeping views of Berlin is adjacent to a sunny breakfast room. Rooms are spacious, with large windows and molding around the ceiling. Named after Italian painter Artemisia Gentileschi, the hotel hosts rotating art exhibitions.

➤ U7: Konstanzer Str. ℹ Breakfast buffet €8. Wi-Fi included. $ Singles €49-54, with bath €64-79; doubles €78/78-108. Additional beds for €20. ⏰ Reception daily 7am-10pm.

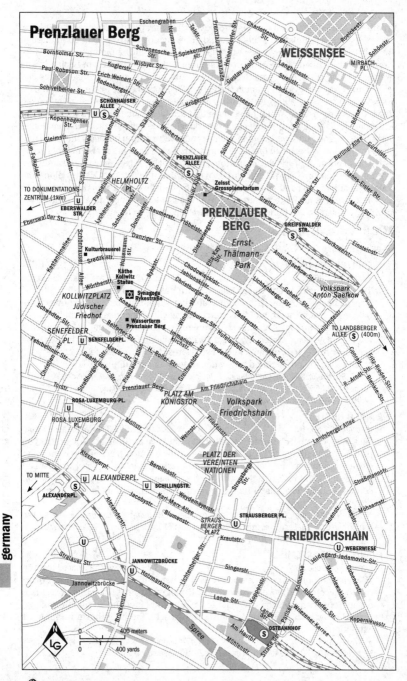

Prenzlauer Berg

germany

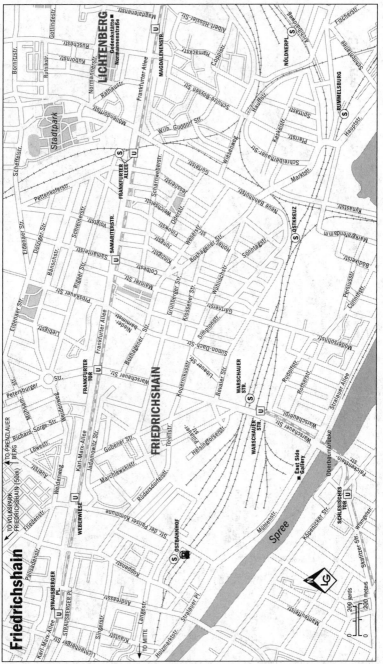

Friedrichshain

berlin · accommodations

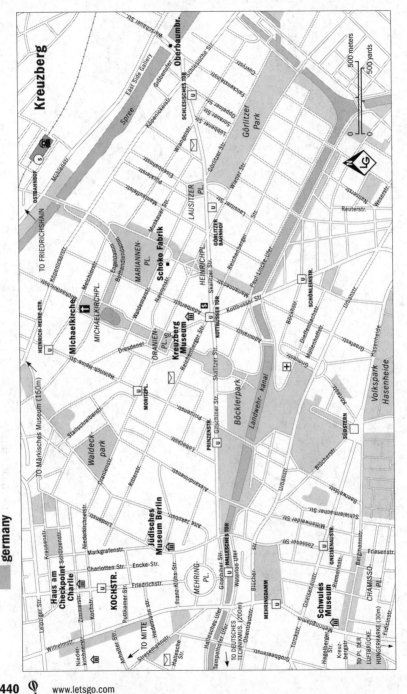

Kreuzberg

germany

How are you doing Germany?

A) Like a berlin party animal

B) Like a HIPPIE ... in Berlin

C) likx a capital city SPACE COWBOY

D) ROCKIN' ALL OVER in BERLIN

E) flying into Frankfurt Airport

F) slxxp xasy in Munich

close to home

Pensions are family-owned guest houses. They are cheaper than hotels, but more expensive than hostels. Many offer long-term rates.

Schöneberg and Wilmersdorf

JUGENDHOTEL BERLINCITY 💳♿📶 HOSTEL [3]

Crellerstr. 22 ☎030 78 70 21 30 🖥www.jugendhotel-berlin.de

Located on a quiet street and bordered by trees, this Jugendhotel Berlincity has first-class rooms, but no dorms. This hostel is a splurge for solo travelers and small groups (think arching-brick-ceilings-and-dark-wood-floors kind of splurge), and usually larger groups get more reasonable rates. The hostel has a strict no smoking and no alcohol policy.

🚇 U7: Kleistpark. i Wi-Fi €1 per 30min., €5 per day. Sheets and breakfast included. $ Singles €38, with bath €52; doubles from €60/79; triples €87/102; quads €112/126; quints €124/150; 6-person rooms €146/168. ⏰ Reception 24hr.

JETPAK 💳🚭 HOSTEL [1]

Pücklerstr. 54 ☎030 83 25 🖥www.jetpak.de

JetPAK is way out in the boonies; if you're even remotely concerned about having a somewhat central location, think hard before booking here. That said, there's a lot that sets this hostel apart, and might make it worth the walk, bus, or train. Converted from an old German army camp, the hostel has been warmed up with colorful walls and comfortable beds and sofas, and is now more convincing as a summer camp. With showers heated by the hostel's own solar panels, this JetPAK is also one of Berlin's most environmentally conscious places to kick back and reap the benefits of nature.

🚇 U3: Fehrbelliner Pl. or U9: Güntzselstr., then bus #115 (dir. Neurippiner Str.): Pücklerstr. Follow the signs to Grunewald, and turn left on Pücklerstr. Turn left again when the JetPAK sign directs you, just before the road turns to dirt. i Breakfast, linens, and Internet included. $ 8-bed dorms €14; doubles €23.

ART-HOTEL CONNECTION 💳🚭▼ HOTEL [4]

Fuggerstr. 33 ☎030 210 21 88 00 🖥www.arthotel-connection.de

Recently redecorated with deep purple walls, crystal chandeliers, and dark wood floors, this hotel is (almost) nothing but class. A gay hotel that describes itself as "hetero-friendly," Art-Hotel boasts some of the most sophisticated style in Schöneberg. But lest we get too serious, this hotel also offers "playrooms," with slings and other sex toys.

🚇 U1, U2 or U15: Wittenbergpl. $ Mar-Oct singles €48; doubles €64; "playrooms" €99. Nov.-Feb. €43/59/89. ⏰ Reception 8am-10pm.

JETPAK CITY HOSTEL 💳🚭 HOSTEL [2]

Pariserstr. 58 ☎030 784 43 60 🖥www.jetpak.de

There's nothing like large rooms with pine bunks, large windows, and brightly colored walls to lessen the institutional hostel feel. Owned by the same people who started the JetPAK in Grunewald, this hostel is much more central and practical for the city traveler, if not quite so one-of-a-kind. But after all, real estate hints at the importance of "location, location, location." The bathrooms are newly tiled, and the common room has couches and a foosball table. Most JetPAK travelers book ahead of time online.

🚇 U3 or U9: Spichernstr. i Linens included. Most breakfast items, including croissants,

€1. $ 8-bed dorms from €18; 6 bed dorms from €19; 4 bed dorms from €20. ⏰ Reception 8am-midnight.

Mitte

Travelers with a limited number of nights should especially think about paying the few extra bucks a night for a place in Mitte. Most of the hostels are nice, and a few of them are literally minutes away from major sights.

CIRCUS HOSTEL — ♿📶🍸 HOSTEL ②

Weinbergswet 1A ☎030 20 00 39 39 (Skype: circus-berlin) 💻www.circus-berlin.de

A cushy place with luxurious beds in the hippest part of Mitte, Circus has a chill cafe, a great bar with nightly specials, DJs, and a pimping karaoke night. Wi-Fi only works well in rooms, and the lack of a "chill-out area" leaves more net-addicted guests wanting, but forgive us for nitpicking. Breakfast is generous and all you can eat, and the mattresses are like clouds. Rooms come with a load of "extras"; the podcast audio tours, jogging route maps, quality food recommendations, and outstandingly helpful staff really do make a difference.

🚇 U8: Rosenthaler Pl. ℹ Linens included. Segways €35 per day. Bikes €12 per day. Breakfast €5. Towels €1. Luggage lockers €10 deposit. $ 8- to 10-bed dorms €19; 4-bed dorms €23. Singles €43; doubles €28. ⏰ Reception 24hr.

HELTER SKELTER — 💻🚬📶🍸 HOSTEL ①

Kalkscheunenstr. 4-5 ☎030 28 04 49 97 💻www.helterskelterhostel.de

The receptionist's warning: "The bar's open all day, but if you're too drunk at breakfast, we cut you off." A bit dirty, a bit worn, but that's just because every night here is wild. If hostel-wide drinking games and late nights are your thing, then take a chance on this place, and years from now you'll remember it as a Berlin highlight.

🚇 U6: Oranienburger Tor. From the station, head south on Friedrichstr. and take a left on Johannisstr. The hostel is on the 3rd fl. through a courtyard. Follow the signs. ℹ Linens, towel, coffee, tea, and Wi-Fi included. Breakfast €3 (free for guests staying longer than 3 days). Smoking allowed in common area. Kitchen available. First 10min. on computer free, €1 per 30min. after. Key deposit €5. $ Megadorm €10-14. Singles €34; doubles €22-27. ⏰ Reception 24hr. Check-in 2pm. Check-out noon.

BAXPAX DOWNTOWN HOTEL/HOSTEL — 💻♿📶🍸 HOSTEL, HOTEL ②

Ziegelstr. 28 ☎30 27 87 48 80 💻www.baxpax.de

Baxpax Downtown has a bag full of fun hostel tricks. Two aboveground pools are revealed in the summer (one on the lower patio, the other on the roof, where, by the way, there's a sweet minibar). Downstairs has its own bar, where a giant stuffed moose head keeps court. The hangout room has a pinball machine, and the patio has a bizzare 6m long bed in case you want to get weird with your friends.

🚇 U6: Oranienburger Tor. From the station, head south on Friedrichstr., then turn left on Ziegelstr. ℹ Key deposit €5. Linens €2.50. Towel €1, free in doubles and singles. Breakfast €5.50. Laundry self-service €5, full-service €8. Non-smoking. $ 20-bed dorms €10-31; 5-bed dorms with private shower €16-36. Singles €29-92; doubles €54-132. ⏰ Reception 24hr. Check-in 3pm. Check-out 11am.

WOMBAT'S CITY HOSTEL — 💻♿📶🍸🏠 HOSTEL ②

Alte Schönhauser Str. 2 ☎030 84 71 08 20 💻www.wombats-hostels.com

Mod, spotless, comfortable, with a rooftop bar and terrace—if Wombats is wrong, we don't want to be right. Hotel-like amenities exclude the possibility of clutch deals, but relax on the beanbags in the lobby and consider that you get what you pay for—that is, except for your first drink at the bar, which is free. The apartments with mini kitchens are nice enough to live in long-term.

🚇 U2: Rosa-Luxemburg-Pl. ℹ Linens, lockers, luggage storage, and Wi-Fi included. Towel €2, free

in doubles and apartments. 8 Internet stations; €.50 per 20min. Breakfast €3.70. Laundry €4.50. Guest kitchen. Non-smoking. Ⓢ *4- to 6-bed dorms €20-24; doubles €58-70; apartments €40-50 per person.* ⏰ *Reception 24hr. Check-in 2pm. Check-out 10am.*

CITYSTAY
💳♿📶⛅ HOSTEL ❷

Rosenstr. 16 ☎030 23 62 40 31 💻www.citystay.de

Besides being the most centrally located hostel in Berlin, a beautiful, well-kept courtyard and an expansive cafe lounge separate this hostel from the pack. Rooms are nice enough with huge windows and adequate beds. But you know what's really nice? A 2min. walk to Museum Island and Unter den Linden.

🚇 *U5, U8, S5, S7, S9, S75: Alexander Pl.* ℹ *Laundry €5. 5 computers in lobby; €3 per hr. Lockers €10 deposit. Sheets €2.50, free with ISIC. Towel €5 deposit. 2 women-only dorms.* Ⓢ *8-bed dorms €17; 4-bed dorms €21; doubles €50, with private shower €65.* ⏰ *Reception 24hr. Check-in 2pm. Check-out 10am.*

ST. CHRISTOPHER'S
💳♿📶🍸⛅ HOSTEL ❷

Rosa Luxembourg Str. 41 ☎030 81 45 39 60 💻www.st-christophers.co.uk

It's rare you find a hostel bar with drinks as cheap as €1 Jager shots, but St. Christopher's delivers this and, subsequently, many a wild night. The Wi-Fi-equipped bar, lobby, and loft spaces blow most hostels out of the water. Rooms are spacious and clean and smell nice, though the same can't always be said of your roommates.

🚇 *U2: Rosa-Luxemburg-Pl.* ℹ *Breakfast, luggage storage, lockers, and linens included. Towels €1. Internet €2 per hr. Non-smoking.* Ⓢ *Prices change in real time based upon availability. Dorms €12-20; doubles €35-50; quads €60-96.* ⏰ *Reception 24hr. Check-in 2pm. Check-out 10am. Bar open daily until 3am.*

Prenzlauer Berg

✍ PFEFFERBETT
🚫💳♿📶🍸 HOSTEL ❷

Christinenstr. 18-19 ☎030 93 93 58 58 💻www.pfefferbett.de

This old, 19th-century brick building is tasteful with a modern edge. The lobby's towering ceilings are supported by brick arches, and the garden out back has a patio popular for socializing. Bathrooms are newly tiled, and spacious rooms have a fun style, with thick stripes running around the walls. Lounge room has a pool, foosball table, and fireplace.

🚇 *U2: Senefelderpl.* ℹ *Breakfast items from €1. Linens €2.50.* Ⓢ *Mar-Oct 8-bed dorms €16; 6-bed €20; 4-bed dorms with bath €25; singles with bath €58; doubles with bath €78. Nov-Feb 8-bed dorms €12; 6-bed €15; 4-bed dorms with bath €20; singles with bath Nov-Feb €47; doubles with €64.* ⏰ *Reception 24hr.*

✍ EAST SEVEN HOSTEL
💳♿📶🍸 HOSTEL ❷

Schwedter Str. 7 ☎030 93 62 22 40 💻www.eastseven.de

Orange and olive walls make this retro hostel a cool, bunk-free place to stay. The indoor lounge area with comfortable sofas and the back patio with a grill are well-used hangouts for backpackers who appreciate cold beer specials *(€1)*. Rooms are spacious, with hardwood floors, old windows, and subtle-hued stripes that would make Martha Stewart proud.

🚇 *U2: Senefelderpl.* ℹ *Free Wi-Fi; Internet terminals €0.50 per 20min. Linens included. Bike rental €10 per day.* Ⓢ *Mar-Oct 8-bed dorms €18; 4-bed dorms with bath €22; singles €38; doubles €26; triples €22. Nov-Feb 8-bed dorms €14; 4-bed dorms with bath €19; singles €31; doubles €22; triples €19.* ⏰ *Reception 7am-midnight.*

ALCATRAZ
🚫💳🚭📶 HOSTEL ❷

Schönehauser Allee 133A ☎030 48 49 68 15 💻www.alcatraz-backpacker.de

Alcatraz is hardly an inescapable prison, but you probably wouldn't mind spending a life sentence here. This hostel's graffiti-chic, spray-painted exterior is as lively as the sociable "chill out room," fully stocked with a foosball table and television. Alcatraz has 80 beds in carefully decorated rooms that contrast the

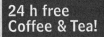

chaos of the common areas. All rooms have ensuite baths, big windows, light yellow walls, and pine bunks.

🚇 U2: Eberswalder Str. ℹ Wi-Fi included. Fully equipped kitchen. Linens €2. Bike rental €10 per day. $ Mar-Oct 8-bed dorms €16; 4-bed €18; singles €40; doubles €50; triples €69. Nov-Feb 8-bed dorms €13; 4-bed dorms €15; singles €35; doubles €44; triples €57. ⏰ Reception 24hr.

LETTE'M SLEEP HOSTEL 💳♿📶 HOSTEL [2]

Lettestr. 7 ☎030 44 73 36 23 💻www.backpackers.de

Located opposite a small park and between the popular bars of the lively Helmholtzpl., this brightly painted hostel is situated perfectly in the middle of Prenzlauer Berg's afternoon and early evening cafe scene. The big kitchen, complete with comfy red couches, a television, and a selection of DVDs, is home base for the hostel's young backpackers. Rooms are spacious and well-lit, with personal lockers and sinks in every room.

🚇 U2: Eberswalder Str. ℹ Linens and Wi-Fi included. $ Apr-Oct 4- to 7-bed dorms €17-23; doubles with sheets and a small kitchenette €55; triples €60. Nov-Mar 4- to 7-bed dorms €11-20; doubles with sheets and a small kitchenette €40; triples €60. ⏰ Reception 24hr.

MEININGER 💳♿📶 HOTEL [3]

Schönehauser Allee 19 💻www.meininger-hotels.com

Meninger is having an identity crisis; the establishment self-identifies as a hotel but charges by the person to fill up its dorms. Decorated in red and white, this neat and clean ho(s)tel is all reliability. Boasting bright white walls, spotless rooms, lots of windows, and just-outside proximity to the U-Bahn station, you really can't lose. Special deals for families.

🚇 U2: Senefelderpl. ℹ Free Wi-Fi, or €1 per 20min. at terminals. Breakfast €5.50. Sheets included. All bathrooms ensuite. $ 3- to 6-bed dorms €28; women-only or small dorms €19; singles €52; doubles €70. Children 6-12 pay 50% of per person fee. ⏰ Reception 24hr. Check-out 1pm.

Friedrichshain

Friedrichshain has built a reputation for itself as Berlin's neighborhood for inexpensive student-friendly housing. Luckily, travelers will enjoy the same wide range of youthful, cheap options for accommodations.

👍 **ALL IN HOSTEL** 💳♿📶 HOSTEL [1]

Grünberger Str. 54 ☎030 288 76 83 💻www.all-in-hostel.com

A bright, open lounge with a welcoming staff make you feel right at home. Rooms have crowded bunks but compensate with high ceilings and big windows. The location is unbeatable—right in the thick of Friedrichshain's popular cafes and bars on a quiet, arboreal street. The crowded lounge area, with big, comfortable couches, is great for socializing.

🚇 U5: Franfurter Tor. ℹ Wi-Fi €1 per hr., hostel terminal €1 per 20min. Breakfast €5. Sheets €3 for 1st night only. $ 10-bed dorms €10; 6-bed dorms with bath €18. Singles with bath €39; doubles with bath €44. ⏰ Reception 24hr.

GLOBETROTTER HOSTEL ODYSSEE 💳📶 HOSTEL [1]

Grünberger Str. 23 ☎030 29 00 00 81 💻www.globetrotterhostel

Right in the middle of Friedrichshain's bars and restaurants, Globetrotter Odyssee is decorated with quirky medieval statues and vaulted ceilings. Muraled walls and rock music in the lounge (furnished with a pool table) give the hostel an East Berlin edge.

🚇 U5: Franfurter Tor. ℹ Free Wi-Fi, hostel terminals €0.50 per 20min. Breakfast €8. Sheets €3 deposit. Credit card min. €25. $ Mar-Oct 8-bed dorms €13.50; 6-bed €15.50; 4-bed €17.50; 3-bed €19.50; singles €36; doubles €47. Nov-Feb 8-bed dorms €10; 6-bed €12; 4-bed €14; 3-bed €16; singles €29, doubles €39. ⏰ Reception 24hr.

U INN BERLIN HOSTEL 💳🚭📶 HOSTEL [2]

Finowstr. 36 ☎030 33 02 44 10 💻info@uinnberlinhostel.com

This small hostel has only 40 beds and is set off a quiet street in Friedrichshain.

Rooms are spacious, with pine bunks and brightly colored walls. U Inn Berlin doesn't consider itself a party hostel; there's a no-alcohol policy, and quiet hours start at 10pm. This hostel's speciality is creating a community for its small number of guests, with events like free German cooking lessons every Friday at 7pm.

🚇 U5: Franfurter Tor. ℹ Linens €2. Breakfast €2. Hostel terminals €1 per 20min. €0.50 daily supplement to pay for "greening" the cleaning supplies and buying fair-trade, organic coffee. $ Apr-Oct 8-bed dorms €15; 5-bed €18; 4-bed €19; 3-bed €23; singles €29; doubles €50. Nov-Mar 8-bed dorms €13; 5-bed €16; 4-bed €17; 3-bed €21; singles €25; doubles €46. ⏰ Reception 7am-1am.

PEGASUS HOSTEL BERLIN

🚫⊗📶 HOSTEL ❶

Str. der Pariser Kommune 35 ☎030 297 73 60 💻www.pegasushostel.de

Set around a courtyard with picnic tables, this hostel has a laid-back atmosphere, but is full of young energy. Towering orange and yellow walls are decorated with canvases of student artwork. There are private lockers in all the rooms. The top floor rooms include loft beds, set right underneath large skylights.

🚇 U5: Weberwiese. ℹ Linens included. Breakfast €6. $ 8- to 10-bed dorms €13; 6-bed €15; quads from €68; triples from €57. Prices vary significantly; call or email ahead to confirm. ⏰ Reception 24hr.

A AND O HOSTEL

💳♿📶 HOSTEL ❶

Boxhagener Str. 73 ☎030 80 94 7 54 00 💻www.aohostels.com

With over 450 beds, this A and O feels like more like a self-sufficient youth community than a hostel. A bright, airy lounge and bar have their own, separate building with foosball and pool tables. Travelers sleep in towering buildings that surround a courtyard. The backyard has a tar volleyball court and single basketball hoop for pick-up games. This A and O might still have some of that chain-hostel look with pre-fab beds and minimal decoration on the walls, but a few quirky touches, like student-made statues in the living area, give it more character.

🚇 U5: Frankfurter Allee. Alternatively, S3, S5, S7, S9 or S75: Ostdreuz. ℹ Breakfast €4. Sheets €3 1st night. Wi-Fi €1 per hr., €8 per week. $ 4- to 8-bed dorms from €10; singles from €19. Prices vary significantly; in the high season, dorms cost as much as €20 per person. Additional €2 for ensuite bath. ⏰ Reception 24hr.

Kreuzberg

Accommodations in Kreuzberg tend to a bit grungier than other parts of the city, but the hostels also have a much better sense of community. Staying in Kreuzberg lets travelers live in a rich community while still being close to the city's major sights.

👍 METROPOL HOSTEL

💳♿🍸 HOSTEL ❷

Mehringdamm 32 💻www.Metropolhostel-berlin.com

The newest addition to the Kreuzberg hostel scene wasn't entirely finished when *Let's Go* stopped by, but the results thus far are pretty promising. The hallways feel a bit like a hospital, but the rooms themselves sometimes verge on near-hotel accommodations. Superb mattresses, clean floors, newly painted walls, and spotless bathrooms all work to this end. Oh, and those century-old-looking doors are actually 100 years old. The building is a historical site and the doors cannot be replaced.

🚇 U6 or U7: Mehringdamm. ℹ Shower and toilet in every room. Breakfast, linens, lockers, luggage storage, safe box, and towels included. $ 6-to 10-bed dorms €9-14; singles €39-49; doubles €49-50. ⏰ Reception 24hr. Check-in 2pm. Check-out 10am.

HOSTEL X BERGER

🚫⊗📶🍸 HOSTEL ❶

Schlesischestr. 22 ☎030 69 53 18 63 💻www.hostelxberger.com

For the quickest jump to the coolest clubs in Berlin, no one outdoes Hostel X

Berger, located right along the canal. While the accommodations are far from new, the rooms somehow feel relaxed, like you've already lived there. A foggy downstairs smoke room with a pool table works like an underground club, while a quiet study upstairs makes good space to work. Rooms are also designed to let you play hard, with a late check-out time and free coffee for the after-party blues.

🏳 *U1: Schlesisches Tor. From the U-Bahn, head south on Schlesischestr.* *i* *Luggage storage and Wi-Fi included. 2 computers with free Internet. Linens €2. Towel €1. Laundry €4. Lock rental €1. Key deposit €6. Guest kitchen open until 9:30pm.* Ⓢ *4-bed dorms €17-18; 16-bed dorms €11-12. Singles €32-36; doubles €40-46.* Ⓠ *Reception 24hr. Check-in 4pm. Check-out 2pm.*

BAXPAX KREUZBERG

⊛ ♿ (ɯ) ୰ ⊠ HOSTEL ❷

Skalitzer Str. 104 ☎030 69 51 83 22 ▥www.baxpax.de

This old-school backpacker hostel offers far from the royal treatment, but a weary traveler will find a bed, lively drunk guests, and staff accustomed to drunk guests. Rooms are themed around countries—someone literally sleeps in a VW bug in the German room. A rooftop terrace connected to the guest kitchen is brilliant in the daytime but unfortunately closes at 10pm. Shoddy Wi-Fi is a major turn-off, but the signal is enough to check mail. Staff wakes you up if you sleep past check-out...not that we would know.

🏳 *U1: Görlitzer Bahnhof.* *i* *Breakfast options €1-2.50. Linens and towel €2.50. Internet €2 per hr. Laundry €7. Lockers, luggage storage, and safebox included. Guests can smoke in the common room after 6pm.* Ⓢ *32-bed dorms €9-14; 8-bed €10-17; 4-bed €14-20. Singles €26-37; doubles with bath €24-30.* Ⓠ *Reception 24hr. Check-in 3pm. Check-out 11am.*

HOSTEL 36 ROOMS

⊛⊛⊗(ɯ)୰ HOSTEL ❶

Spreewaldpl. 8 ☎030 53 08 63 98 ▥www.36rooms.com

Nice large rooms and a beautiful outdoor patio are somewhat robbed of fun by the hostel's no-outside-alcohol policy. Guests can beer it at the hostel bar or wait until Thursday, Friday and Saturday, when one of Kreuzberg's hippest underground clubs rocks in the hostel's basement. Hot travelers can dip in the wave pool across the street at the hostel's discounted price *(€2 per hr.)*. Old World rooms have chandeliers and great views of the nearby park. Unfortunately some also have an Old World smell.

🏳 *U1: Görlitzer Bahnhof.* *i* *Locker rental €2. Linens and towel €2.50. Bike rental €10 per day. Key deposit €10.* Ⓢ *8-bed dorms €14-17; 4-bed €18-21. Singles €35-39; doubles €50-58.* Ⓠ *Reception 24hr. Check-in 1pm. Check-out 11am. Patio and kitchen open until 10pm.*

COMEBACK PACKERS HOSTEL

⊛⊛⊗(ɯ)୰ HOSTEL ❶

Alabertstr. 97 ☎030 60 05 75 27 ▥www.comebackpackers.com

As you climb the fish-smelling stairs, you'd never guess that this relaxed hostel waited at the top, just chilling there. The large common room feels more like your mother's kitchen and stays open all night. Guests can jump out the windows... onto the roof for a smoke or some sun at the picnic tables. The showers are pretty exposed—as in, people will definitely see you naked, and you definitely should not pee because everyone will know, and it will be embarrassing. Anyway—beds are adequate and tend to not be bunked. Rooms are large, wood-floored, and climb-on-the-roof-able, but otherwise unremarkable. The only remarkable thing is the goose lamp in the goose room. It's a goose. But it's also a lamp. Staff has a very German sense of humor.

🏳 *U1 or U8: Kotbusser Tor.* *i* *Coffee, linens, and Wi-Fi included. Key deposit €10. Full-service laundry €5. Towel €2. Continental breakfast (€3) must be requested.* Ⓢ *Dorms €14-20.* Ⓠ *Reception 24hr. Check-in 3pm. Check-out 1pm.*

SIGHTS

Charlottenburg

Most of Berlin's sights are located outside of residential Charlottenburg, closer to the center of the city. That said, Charlottenburg has certain sights that recommend themselves to the traveler with more than a day or two to spend in Berlin. Unique museums, grand palaces, and one of the world's most historic stadiums are spread out all over the neighborhood.

KÄTHE-KOLLWITZ-MUSEUM — MUSEUM

Fasanenstr. 24 ☎030 32 69 06 00 www.kaethe-kollwitz.de

Through both World Wars, Käthe Kollwitz, a member of the Berlin Sezession (Secession) movement and one of Germany's most prominent 20th century artists, protested war and the situation of the working class with haunting sketches, etchings, sculpture and charcoal drawings of death, poverty, and starvation. The series of works entitled, "A Weaver's Revolt," on the 2nd floor are the drawings that skyrocketed Kollwitz to fame. The death of the artist's own son, who was killed in Russia during WWII, provides a wrenching emotional authenticity to her depictions of death, pregnancy, and starvation, and her own revealing self-portraits.

U1: "Uhlandstr." $ Admission €6, students €3. Open daily 11am-6pm.

SCHLOß CHARLOTTENBURG — PALACE

Spandauer Damm 10-22 ☎030 320 9275

This expansive Baroque palace, commissioned by Friedrich I in the 1600s as a gift for his wife, Sophia-Charlotte, stands impressively at the end of a long treelined walkway on the outer north end of Charlottenburg. The Schloß is made up of several parts. **Altes Schloß,** the oldest section (marked by a blue dome in the middle of the courtyard), has rooms chock full of historic furnishings (much of it reconstructed due to war damage) and elaborate gold guilding. **Neuer Flügel** (New Wing), includes the marble receiving rooms and the more somber royal chambers. **Neuer Pavillion** houses a museum dedicated to Prussian architect Karl Friedrich Schinkel. Other sections include the **Belvedere,** a small building housing the royal family's porcelain collection, and the **Mausoleum,** the final resting place for most of the family. Behind the palace extends the exquisitely manicured Schloßgarten, full of small lakes, footbridges and fountains.

Bus #M45 from Bahnhof Zoo to Luisenpl./Schloß Charlottenburg or U2: Sophie-Charlotte Pl. $ Altes Schloß €10, students €7; Neuer Flügel €6/5; Belvedere €2/1.50; Mausoleum free. Audio tours available in English included. Altes Schloß open Apr-Oct Tu-Su 10am-6pm; Nov-Mar Tu-Su 10am-5pm. Neuer Flügel open year-round M and W-Su 10am-5pm. Belvedere and Mausoleum open Apr-Oct daily 10am-6pm, Nov-Mar daily noon-5pm.

MUSEUM BERGGRUEN — MUSEUM

Schloßstr. 1 ☎030 326 95 80

Think Picasso is a jerk whose art didn't deserve the hype it got? This intimate three-floor museum will put away your anti-Picasso sentiments. The first and second floor are Picasso-packed, with added bonuses of French Impressionist Matisse's art and African masks. The third floor showcases paintings by Bauhaus teacher Paul Klee and Alberto Giacometti's super-skinny sculptures of human forms.

Bus #M45 from Bahnhof Zoo to Luisenpl./Schloß Charlottenburg or U2: Sophie-Charlotte Pl. $ €12, €6 students, children free. Audio guide included. Open Tu-Su 10am-6pm.

BRÖHANMUSEUM — MUSEUM

Schloßstr. 1A ☎030 32 69 06 00 www.broehanmuseum.de

If you're wondering where all the stuff you couldn't sell at your great-aunt's estate sale went, here it is. The Bröhanmuseum showcases epic brös ißing bròs... Just kidding, we mean Art Nouveau and Art Deco paintings, housewares, and furniture. Along with figurines and lampshades that resemble knicknacks you sneered at (and now regret not buying) at neighborhood garage sales, the ground floor also pairs several groupings of period furniture with paintings from the same era (1889-1939). The first floor is a small gallery dedicated to the Modernist Berlin *Sezession* painters, though occasionally upstaged by oddly chosen shocking green walls, and the top floor houses special exhibitions.

Bus #M45 from Bahnhof Zoo to Luisenpl./Schloß Charlottenburg or U2: Sophie-Charlotte Pl. The museum is next to the Bergguen, across from the Schloß. [$] Admission €6, students €4. ⏰ Open Tu-Su 10am-6pm.

OLYMPIASTADION STADIUM

Olympischer Pl. 3 (Visitor Center) ☎030 25 00 23 22 💻www.olypiastadion-berlin.de

This massive Nazi-built stadium comes in a close second to Tempelhof Airport in the list of monumental Third Reich buildings in Berlin. It was erected for the infamous 1936 Olympic Games, in which African-American track and field athlete Jesse Owens won four gold medals. Hitler refused to congratulate Owens, who has since been honored with a Berlin street, Jesse-Ownes-Allee and his name has been engraved into the side of the stadium with the other 1936 gold medal winners. The six stone pillars flanking the stadium were originally intended to signify the unity of the six "tribes" of ethnicities that Hitler believed fed into true German heritage. Recent uses have included the 2006 World Cup final. The independently operated **Glockenturm** (bell tower) provides a great lookout point and houses an exhibit on the history of German athletics.

S5, S7, or U2: Olympia-Stadion. For Glockenturm, S5 or S7: Pichelsburg. [$] €4, students €3. Tour with guide €8, students €7, children under 6 free. ⏰ Open daily Mar 20-May 9am-7pm, June-Sept 15 9am-8pm, Sept 16-Oct 31 9am-7pm, Nov-Mar 19 9am-4pm.

ZOOLOGISCHER GARTEN ZOO

8 Hardenberg Pl. ☎030 25 40 10 💻www.zoo-berlin.de

Germany's oldest zoo houses around 14,000 animals of 1500 species, most in open-air habitats connected by winding pathways under dense cover of trees and brush. While you're there, pay your respects to the world-famous polar bear **Knut,** or he may go nuts. Originally deemed the cutest polar bear alive, Knut has been diagnosed by animal specialists as a psychopath addicted to human attention. Luckily, he's still pretty cute.

U2 or U9: Zoological Garten, or S5, S7 or S75: Bahnhof Zoo. Main entrance is across from the Europa Center. [$] €12, students €9, children €6. Combination to zoo and aquarium €18/14/9. ⏰ Open daily from 9am-7pm (last entry 6pm). Animal houses open 9am-6pm.

AQUARIUM AQUARIUM

Budapester Str. 32 ☎030 25 40 10 💻www.aquarium-berlin.de.

Within the walls of the zoo, but independently accessible, is an aquarium with three floors of fish, reptiles, amphibians and insects. Highlights include the pychadelic jellyfish and the slimey carp petting zoo.

U2 or U9: Zoological Garten, or S5, S7 or S75: Bahnhof Zoo. [$] €12, students €9, children €6. See above for aquarium-zoo combination tickets. ⏰ Open daily 9am-6pm.

Schöneberg and Wilmersdorf

Schöneberg sights are a mix of gorgeous parks and whatever cultural bits and pieces ended up in this largely residential neighborhood. Travelers with limited time in Berlin should note that attractions here are few and far between, and aren't easily and efficiently visited.

GRUNEWALD AND THE JAGDSCHLOß PARK

Am Grunewaldsee 29 (Access from Pücklerstr.) ☎030 813 35 97 💻www.spsg.de

This 3 sq. km park, with winding paths through wild underbrush, gridded pines, and a peaceful lake, is popular dog-walking turf and a great change from the rest of the bustling Berlin. About a 1km walk into the woods is the **Jadgschloß,** a restored royal hunting lodge that houses a gallery of portaits and paintings by German artists like Graff and Cranach. The house is the picture of understated elegance, surrounded by even more blooming botany. The one-room hunting lodge is worth skipping, unless you find pottery shards particularly gripping. Instead, walk around the grounds, or take a hike north in the forest to **Teufelsberg** ("Devil's Mountain"), the highest point in Berlin, made of rubble from World War II piled over a Nazi military school.

U3 or U7: Fehrbelliner Pl., or S45 or S46: Hohenzollerndamm then bus #115 (dir. Neuruppiner Str. of Spanische Alle/Potsdamer): Pücklerstr. Turn left on Pücklerstr. following the signs and continue straight into the forest to reach the lodge. ℹ Check the Jadgschloß visitor's center for a map. $ Admission to the hunting lodge €4, €3 students. Tours in German offered on the weekends €1. ⏰ Open Tu-Su 10am-6pm.

BRÜCKE MUSEUM — MUSEUM

Bussardsteig 9 ☎030 831 20 29 💻www.brueckemusuem.de

This museum displays an uncommon collection of Brücke art, German impressionism inspired by its French contemporaries. The brief *Die Brücke* ("The Bridge") stylistic period was characterized by bright, fierce colors. The Brücke Museum building, inside the Grunewald forest, is a work of contemporary art itself. The staff loves the collection (which says something), and often rotates special exhibitions displaying pieces related to the Brücke period, including the obvious French Impressionist works, but also world art, such as African craft works.

U3 or U7: Fehberlliner Pl., then bus #115 (dir. Neuruppiner Str. to Spanische Allee/Potsdammer): Pücklerstr. $ €4, €3 students. For a ticket including special exhibits, €5/4. ⏰ Open M and W-Su 11am-5pm.

GAY MEMORIAL — MEMORIAL

Just outside the Nollendorf U-Bahn station

Blink and you might miss it. This unassuming, unmarked memorial is shaped like a Crayola crayon, and striped with as many colors as a box of the art supply. The small monument commemorates the homosexuals killed in World War II.

U1, U3, U4, or U9: Nollendorfpl.

ST. NORBERT KIRCHE CEMETERY — CEMETERY

Access from Belzinger Str., between Martin-Luther-Str. and Eisenacher Str.

Sunken in a few feet from street level and walled off by unlocked gates, this enchanting cemetery brings R.I.P. to the living. With a mix between manicured shrubs and a patch of wild, over-grown ivy in front of every tomb, a quick stop here on a busy day is beautiful. An adjoining children's playground outside the gates brightens things up. We wouldn't say this is worth a trip itself, but the cemetery is good for a stroll after stepping out of one of Schöneberg's popular cafes.

U7: Eisenacherstr. ⏰ Gate usually locked by 6pm.

Mitte

Like any KFC, Mitte contains 95% good stuff and 5% crap. Stick with the recommendations, and you'll be fine. You're on your own with KFC.

PERGAMON MUSEUM — ♿ MUSEUM

Am Kupfergraben 5 ☎0302 090 55 77 💻www.smb.museum

If it kept its two main exhibits, the Pergamon temple and the Ishtar Gate, the rest of this museum could show off cotton balls and it'd still be worth it. The museum reconstructs the Pergamon temple nearly to its full size, and the battle mural on the wall displays jagged toothed snakes ripping off heroes' arms while titans rip lions' mouths apart. The Mesopotamian Ishtar Gate, reconstructed tile-by-original-tile, rises 30m into the air, then stretches 100m down a hallway. You'll hardly believe it.

U2, U5, U8: Alexanderpl. $ €10, students €5. Free Th after 6pm. Open M-W 10am-6pm, Th 10am-10pm, F-Su 10am-6pm.

TOPOGRAPHY OF TERROR — MUSEUM

Niederkirchner Str. 8 ☎0302 545 09 50 www.topographie.de

This exhibit opened May 2010 and looks at the origins, development, and deployment of Nazi terror from 1930 to 1946. This detailed, personalized, fair, and informative exhibition provides one of the best insights into Nazi strategies and the extent of the horror. No detail (or image) is deemed off-limits, and travelers with weak stomachs are warned. That said, the conclusions of this exhibit are so incredibly important and so poorly understood that a trip here should really be considered a must. A bookshop, cafe, and library take up the bottom floor, while a segment of the Berlin Wall and the excavated foundations of Hitler's old terror headquarters fill out an enormous, otherwise empty, courtyard.

U2: Potsdamer Pl. From the Metro, head east on Leipziegerstr. and take a right on Wilhelm-Leipziegerstr. The exhibit is directly across from the Hi-Flyer. $ Free. Open daily 10am-8pm.

MEMORIAL TO THE MURDERED JEWS OF EUROPE — MEMORIAL

Cora-Berliner-Str. 1 ☎0302 639 43 11 www.stiftung-denkmal.de

Imposing concrete blocks equidistant from each other commemorate the Jews who were killed by the National Socialists. If you're looking for reflection or somberness, you won't find it aboveground, where kids play hide and seek, tourists nap on blocks, and policemen from the nearby American embassy work in a paranoid frenzy to keep cars from stopping. See the memorial quickly, then head below ground for a moving, informative exhibit on the Jewish history of WWII. Especially devastating is the "family" room, which presents pre-war Jewish family portraits and then investigates the individual fates of the family members. The last room continuously plays one of thousands of compiled mini-biographies of individuals killed in the Holocaust. To read the bios of every murdered Jew would take over six years.

U2: Potsdamer Pl. From the Metro, walk north on Ebertstr. $ Free. Open daily Apr-Sept 10am-8pm; Oct-Mar 10am-7pm.

HOMOSEXUAL MEMORIAL — MEMORIAL

On Ebertstr. www.stiftung-denkmal.de/en/homosexualmemorial

While Berlin now accepts homosexuality like few places do in the world, it wasn't so until 1969, before which homosexuality was illegal under a law passed by the Nazis. As a result, homosexuals were not included in many memorials against Nazi violence. This memorial, which opened in 2008, consists of a giant block with a screen that plays a video of two men kissing on loop—though part of the memorial, this video is set to change every two years.

U2: Potsdamer Pl. From the Metro, walk north on Ebertstr. The memorial will be on your left, in the garden. Open 24hr.

HOUSE OF WORLD CULTURES — EXHIBIT HALL

John-Foster-Dulles-Allee 10 ☎3039 78 70 www.hkw.de

Originally built by the Americans to show off to the nearby East Berliners, the House of World Cultures now hosts festivals, movie screenings, lectures, and an incredible anarchist bookstore in a bizarre structure that's been affectionately called "The Pregnant Clam." The formless statue in the pool out front becomes a butterfly when you view its reflection.

U55: Bundestag. From the Metro, head southwest down Paul Löbe Allee. $ Free. Event prices vary. Open daily 10am-7pm. Exhibitions open M 11am-7pm, W-Su 11am-7pm.

NEUES MUSEUM ♿ MUSEUM

Bodestr. 1 🖥www.neues-museum.de

One of the top museums in the city, this collection of Egyptian and Greek antiquities goes beyond what you'd expect. Mummies abound, sarcophogi run rampant, and somewhere in it all, that famous bust of Nefertiti—yeah, that one—sits glowing in her own room. The building was heavily damaged in the war, and this new New Museum does a brilliant job of incorporating the old structure into a fantastically modern creation. To avoid the lines, reserve a ticket online.

🚏 U6: Friedrichstr. S5,S7,S75,or S9: Hackescher Markt. ℹ Tickets correspond to a time, and after they've been purchased visitors must return at the time printed on their ticket. No line Th 6-8pm. $ €10, students €5. Free Th after 6pm. ⏰ Open M-W 10am-6pm, Th-Sa 10am-8pm, Su 10am-6pm.

SOVIET MEMORIAL ♿⛅ MEMORIAL

Str. des 17 Juni

WWII tanks and anti-aircraft guns flank this memorial built by the Soviets in 1945. It is estimated that between eight to 10 million Soviets died fighting in the war, including 80,000 who died in the Battle of Berlin. The memorial is expected to be finished by late 2010.

🚏 Bus #100: Pl. der Republik. Head south through Tiergarten to Str. des 17 Juni and take a right. $ Free. ⏰ Open 24hr.

BRANDENBERG GATE ♿ GATE

Pariser Pl. ☎0302 263 30 17

During the day, tourists swarm this famous 18th-century gate; the wise traveler will return at night to see it lit in a blaze of gold. Friederich Wilhelm II built the gate as a symbol of military victory, but Germans these days prefer to shy away from that designation, you know, because of WWI and, uh, WWII. A system of gates once surrounded it, but today only this most famous gate remains.

🚏 U55: Brandenburg Tor. $ Free. ⏰ Open 24hr.

HUMBOLDT UNIVERSITY ♿ UNIVERSITY

Unter den Linden 6

Home to some of the greatest thinkers of the modern age, including Freud and Einstein, this university is closed to the public and doesn't make much of a sight touring-wise, but it's neat to stop by and feel like you're somehow being involved in something. During the day, vendors sell used books out in front. Maybe you'll find Einstein's old unread copy of *The Mayor of Casterbridge*.

🚏U2: Hausvogteipl. From the Metro, walk north along Oberwalstraße.

VICTORY COLUMN 🎫🚭🍸 MONUMENT

Großer Stern 1 ☎030 391 29 61 🖥www.monument-tales.de

This 27m tall monument celebrates Prussia's victory over France in 1880. The statue of Victoria at the top is made of melted-down French cannons, and during WWII, Hitler had the statue moved to its present location to increase its visibility. The column is under renovation; an exhibition that examines the significance of various "monuments" built throughout the world is expected to be finished in 2011.

🚏 U9:Hansapl. ℹ Present your ticket at the cafe to get a €0.50 discount on all drinks. $ €2.20, students €1.50. ⏰ Open Apr-Oct M-F 9:30am-6:30pm, Sa-Su 9:30am-7pm; Nov-Mar M-F 10am-5pm, Sa-Su 10am-5:30pm.

NEUE WACHE ♿ MEMORIAL

Unter den Linden 4 ☎030 25 00 25

This building was built as a guard house for the nearby city palace (hence, "New Watch"). The building has been used as a number of memorials since then, and in 1969 the remains of an unknown soldier and an unknown concentration camp victim were laid to rest here. Since 1993 the Neue Wache has served as the central memorial of the Federal Republic of Germany for the Victims of War and Tyranny. A statue of a mother holding her dead son stands alone in the center of an enormous empty room.

🚇 U2: Hausvogteipl. From the Metro, walk north along Oberwalstr. $ Free. ⏰ Open daily 10am-6pm. The interior of the monument is still visible when the building's gate is closed.

SCHLOßPLATZ ♿ SQUARE

Schloßpl.

Schloßplatz manages to be a sight where castles themselves are feuding. The Berliner Schloß, the Hohenzollern imperial palace stood on this spot until the communists tore it down in 1950 to build the Palast der Republick. After reunification, the Palast der Republick was torn down, this time to make way for a replica of the Berliner Schloß. The new building will house the collections of Humboldt University among other exhibitions. Construction is set to start in 2013 and finish in 2019. Currently, the field sits open in some parts, while others are under excavation. A nearby visitors center has German-only information on the forthcoming building.

🚇 U2: Hausvogteipl. From the Metro, walk north along Oberwalstr. and take a right on Französische Str. Continue it across the canal bridge. ⏰ Visitors center open daily 10am-6pm.

FERNSHEHTURM 🚫💳🚫♿🍸 TOWER

Panoramastr. 1A ☎030 242 3333 💻www.tv-turm.de

At 368m, the Fernshehturm, literally "TV Tower," trumps all other sky-ticklers in the EU. It's shaped like a lame 1950s space probe on purpose; commies wanted folk to think of Sputnik when they saw it. In the DDR's defense, it wasn't its biggest miscalculation. This supposed "triumph of Soviet technology" was actually completed by Swedish engineers when construction faltered. Elevators now shoot more than a million people each year to a height of 200m where they can dig a 360° panorama, grab a drink at the bar, or stomach an incredibly pricey meal. The height plays especially well in Berlin, which has few tall buildings.

🚇 U2, U5, U8: Alexanderpl. $ €10.50, under 16 €6.50. ⏰ Open daily Mar-Oct 9am-midnight; Nov-Feb 10am-midnight.

ROTES RATHAUS CITY HALL

Rathausstr. 15 ☎0309 02 60

This imposing red brick structure looks like the world's most intense East Coast private high school, but it used to be the East Berlin City Hall and now houses the Berlin Senate. Senate? In Berlin? But Berlin's a city! Well, actually, traveler, Berlin is one of the 16 states that make up the Federal Republic of Germany. Each district of Berlin has a mayor, and individual state senators who conduct business at the Rotes Rathaus.

🚇U2: Klosterstr. From the Metro, head north.

MARIENKIRCHE 🚫♿ CHURCH

Karl-Liebknecht-Str. 8 ☎0302 500 25 💻www.marienkirche-berlin.de

The oldest still-standing medieval church in Berlin (est. 1270) has one of the most frightening murals you'll ever see: a line of saints and kings perform the dance of death alongside a line of skeletons who look more like space creatures from *The X-Files.* There's a Dan Brown novel here waiting to be written.

🚇 U2, U5, U8: Alexanderpl. $ Free. ⏰ Open daily in summer 10am-9pm; in winter 10am-6pm.

REICHSTAG 💳♿🍸 PARLIAMENT

Pl. der Republik 1 ☎0302 273 21 52 💻www.bundestag.de

Visitors to the German parliament building can climb the roof's 1200-ton glass dome that looks down into the main chamber as a symbol of the "openness" of German democracy. It also serves to focus sunlight into the government chambers via an aggressive spire of mirrored fragments that juts down toward the floor. A free, automated audio tour tracks your movements up and down the nearly 300m ramp. Stop off at the very top for a swell view of the Berlin skyline and to marvel at the fact that this dome—and therefore the Reichstag—has no roof. Rain, snow, and sleet all fall into the building and land in a giant "cone" located on the dome's floor. Visitors can trek around the roof terrace to avoid the solar panels that make the Reichstag the world's only zero-emission congress. Across the way stand a series of futuristic government offices that have been affectionately termed "the Washing Machine." If viewing democracy makes you hungry, stop at the restaurant located on the roof.

Bus #100: Pl. der Republik. $ Free. Open daily 8am-10pm.

SCHLOß BELLEVUE PALACE

Spreeweg 1 ☎0302 00 00

This palace, home of the German president, was the first Neoclassical building in Germany. What? That doesn't excite you? Then try this: when there's a gala, watch from the street as the privileged drink cocktails.

U9: Hansapl. From the Metro, head east past the Victory Column. Never open to you.

BERLINER DOM ♿ CHURCH

Am Lustgarten ☎0302 026 91 19 www.berlinerdom.de

You'll probably spend the whole time thinking how big a bowl of cereal the inverted dome would make; in other words, it's a fantastically enormous dome and a ridiculously beautiful church. "Dom" means cathedral in German; since this 1905 church belongs to the Protestants, it's technically not a cathedral, but in terms of grandeur it blows away most cathedrals you've seen. A museum upstairs shows various failed incarnations of the church, and if you climb some sketchy-feeling backstairs, you can actually get to a roof terrace lookout. Don't forget the basement with the most luxurious crypt you've ever seen, housing the ghosts of lightweights like the Hohenzollern kings.

U2, U5, U8: Alexanderpl. $ €5, students €3. Open Apr-Sept M-Sa 9am-8pm, Su noon-8pm; Oct-Mar Ma-Sa 9am-7pm, Su noon-7pm.

ALTES MUSEUM ♿ MUSEUM

Am Lustgarten www.smb.museum

A newly organized collection of Roman and Estruscan antiquities now takes up the entire first floor of this incredible musuem. Though this museum's cool in another context, those who've seen its flashier cousins, the Pergamon and the Neues, might be a bit disappointed. Check it if you've got the time; skip it if you don't.

U2, U5, U8: Alexanderpl. $ €8, students €4. Free Th after 6pm. Open M-W 10am-6pm, Th 10am-10pm, F-Su 10am-6pm.

TIERGARTEN ♿🍸 PARK

Tiergarten

Stretching from the Brandenburg Gate in the east to the Bahnhof Zoo in the west, this Balrog-sized park is at the heart of Berlin and contains some of its most famous iconic monuments including the Column of Victory and the Soviet War Memorial. Str. des 17 Juni bisects the park from east to west, and frequently hosts parades or celebrations. During the 2010 World Cup, the city blocked off the entire street from June to July and presented the World Cup on 10 enormous screens to daily hordes of thousands of fans. It was drunk and it was loud. The park also contains some beautiful paths and gardens that can offer solace from the hipster invasion.

Bus #100 or #200: Brandenburg Tor.

TACHELES GALLERY

Oranienburger Str. 53

An unforgettable experience day or night, this bombed-out department store has become a living, breathing street-art Metropolis. Bars, galleries, a movie theater, faux beach exterior, and sculpture garden/workshop all exist where every available space is covered in graffiti art, human piss, or both. *But it's worth it.* Seating options in the outside bars range from lifeguard towers to forklifts.

U6: Oranienburger Tor. $ Free to enter; most galleries cost €1-5. Open 8am-late.

CENTRUM JUDAICUM: NEW SYNAGOGUE SYNAGOGUE

Oranienburger Str. 28-30 ☎030 88028 316 centrumjudaicum.de

The New Synagogue, built in 1866, was once one of the most awesome Jewish temples in Europe, with 3200 seats and a 50m dome. Almost completely destroyed, first by Nazi violence, then by American bombs, after 1989 the building's exterior and dome were restored, and the building became the museum, cultural center, and miniature synagogue that it remains today. The exhibit on the original synagogue is small and only justified by a pre-existing interest in the building's history. The dome, too, disappoints somewhat, and most visitors will be satisfied with a strut past the front.

U6: Oranienburger Tor. i Information in English. $ Permanent exhibition €3, reduced €2. Dome €1.50, reduced €1. Open Apr-Sept M 10am-8pm, Tu-Th 10am-6pm, F 10am-5pm, Su 10am-8pm; Oct and Mar M 10am-8pm, Tu-Th 10am-6pm, F 10am-2pm, Su 10am-8pm; Nov-Feb M-Th 10am-6pm, F 10am-2pm, Su 10am-6pm.

NEUE NATIONAL GALLERIE MUSEUM

Potsdamer Str. 50 ☎0302 66 42 45 10 www.smb.museum

The be-all end-all of early 20th-century painting in Berlin, this museum's building is almost as famous as its collection. Strange temporary exhibits live upstairs in the so-called "Temple of Light and Glass" designed by Mies van der Rohe, while the basement holds a treasure trove of primarily German paintings and sculptures. Works by Edward Munch, Franz Marc, and Max Ernst are just a few of the highlights. Sadly, in the 1930s, key works were labeled "degenerate" by the Nazis and have since disappeared from the collection. Missing works appear as black-and-white photocopies and are still hung throughout the gallery.

U2: Potsdamer Pl. i Audio tour included in the price of admission. $ €10, students €5. Free Th after 6pm. Open M-W 10am-6pm, Th 10am-10pm, F-Sa 10am-6pm.

MUSEUM FOR FILM AND TELEVISION MUSEUM

Potsdamer Str. 2 ☎030 300 903 0 www.deutsche-kinemathek.de

A fun little exhibit on the history of German cinema, with a special emphasis on the work of Fritz Lang and Marlene Dietrich. Not a must-see, but the production photos and set drawings of *The Cabinet of Dr. Caligari* and *Metropolis* are worth the admission price alone. Film buffs will be rewarded, and film gruffs will still find a few things to tickle them. A TV library lets visitors watch old German TV. If you thought their *wars* were crazy...

U2: Potsdamer Pl. $ €5, students €3. Audio tour €4/3. Open Tu-W 10am-6pm, Th 10am-8pm, F-Su 10am-6pm.

BERTOLD BRECHT HAUS MUSEUM

Chausseestr. 125 ☎030 200 57 1844 www.adk.de

Bertold Brecht revolutionized theater with such masterworks as the *Threepenny Opera*, and this tour lets you glimpse into his personal life. While Brecht only lived (and died) here from 1953 to 1956, the same is true of his other addresses—Brecht "changed countries as often as shoes," so don't feel like you're getting a raw deal. Preserved by his wife, the Brechtian actress Helen Weigel, Brecht's apartment (two studies and the bedroom where he croaked) contains his library and other small artifacts of note. Come with an English-speaking crew so they do the tour in English; otherwise you'll be stuck reading along and wondering if the Germans are mocking you each time they laugh.

🚆 U6: Oranienburger Tor. From the U-Bahn, head north on Chausseestr. The house will be on your left. There isn't a good sign or anything, so look for the address. ℹ All tours are guided. $ €4, students €2.50. ⏰ Tours every 30min. Tu 10-11:30am, 2-3:30pm. W 10-11:30am. Th 10-11:30am, 5-6:30pm. F 10am, 10:30am, and 11:30am. Sa 10-noon, 1-3:30pm. Su 11am, noon, 1, 2, 3, 4, 5, and 6pm.

Prenzlauer Berg

BERLINER MAUER DOKUMENTATIONZENTRUM — MUSEUM, MONUMENT

Bernauer Str. 111 ☎030 464 1030 🖥www.berliner-mauer-dokumentationzentrum.de

A remembrance complex, museum, chapel, and entire city block of the preserved Berlin Wall, two concrete barriers separated by the open *Todesstreife*, or death strip, come together in a memorial to "victims of the communist tyranny." The church is made of an inner oval of poured cement walls, lit from above by a large skylight, with gaps that look out over a field of tall grasses and poppies. The museum has assembled a comprehensive collection of all things Wall. Exhibits include photos, film clips, and sound bites. Climb up a staircase to see the wall from above.

🚆 U8: Bernauer Str. $ Free. ⏰ Open Tu-Su Apr-Oct 9:30am-7pm; Nov-Mar 9:30am-6pm.

JÜDISCHER FRIEDHOF — CEMETERY

On Schönehauser Allee; enter by the Lapidarium

Prenzlauer Berg was one of the major centers of Jewish Berlin during the 19th and early 20th centuries. The ivy-covered Jewish cemetery contains the graves of Giacomo Meyerbeer and Max Liebermann and is studded by impressively high, dark tombs under towering old trees. Nearby, **Synagogue Rykstrasse** *(Rykestr. 53)* is one of Berlin's loveliest synagogues. It was spared on *Kristallnacht* thanks to its inconspicuous location. Unfortunately, visitors are not allowed in, as the synagogue still operates as a school.

🚆 U2: Senefelderpl. $ Free. ⏰ Open M-Th 8am-4pm, F 8am-1pm.

ZEISS-GROSSPLANETARIUM — PLANETARIUM

Prenzlauer Allee 80 ☎030 421 84 50 🖥www.astw.de

In 1987 this planetarium opened as the most modern facility of its kind in the DDR. Compared to its peers in the West, it seems about as technologically advanced as a tricycle, but it can still show you the stars. No exhibits here, only shows; check the website or call in advance for times.

🚆 S8, S41, S42, or tram M2: Prenzlauer Allee. From the stop, the planetarium is across the bridge. $ €5, students €4. ⏰ Open Tu 9am-noon, W 9am-noon and 1:30-3pm, Th 9am-noon, F 7-9pm, Sa 2:30-9pm, Su 1:30-5pm.

Friedrichshain

✓ VOLKSPARK — PARK

Volkspark is the second-largest park in Berlin and its oldest. This 52-hectare park is too big to feel crowded, even with masses of dog-walkers and suntanners filling the paths and grassy lawns. Since opening in 1840, monuments and memorials have been added here and there around the green spaces. In 1913 the **Fairy Fountain** was added, representing 10 characters from the book *The Brothers Grimm.* The rubble from two bunkers that were bombed and destroyed in World War II was piled into a war monument in 1950, now called **Mont Klemont,** and is sometimes used as a platform for open-air concerts and movie screenings in the summer. Statues that commemorate the Polish soldiers and German antifascists were built in 1972.

🚆 S8 or S10: Landsberger Allee. Alternatively, U5: Strausbgr. Pl. Bounded by Am Friedrichshain to the north, Danziger Str. to the east, Landsberger Allee to the south, and Friedenstr. Str. to the south.

👍 EAST SIDE GALLERY — MONUMENT

Along Mühlenstr. 💻www.eastsidegallery.com

The longest remaining portion of the Berlin Wall, this 1.3km stretch of cement slabs has been converted into the world's largest open-air art gallery. The Cold War graffiti wasn't preserved; instead, the current murals were painted by an international group of artists who gathered in 1989 to celebrate the end of the city's division. One of the most famous contributors is artist Dmitri Wrubel, who depicted a wet kiss between Leonid Brezhnev and East German leader Eric Honecker. The stretch of street remains unsupervised and, on the Warschauer Str. side, open at all hours, but vandalism is surprisingly rare.

🚇 U1, U15, S3, S5, S6, S7, S9, or S75: Warschauer Str. Alternatively, S5, S7, S9, or S75: Ostbahnhof. From the stops, walk back toward the river. $ Free.

Kreuzberg

While sights don't quite compare to the grand historical scope of Mitte, there is still a fair amount to see in this more real section of town. The greenery in itself is an amazing sight.

👍 DEUTSCHES TECHNIKMUSEUM BERLIN — 💳♿🍸 MUSEUM

Trebbiner Str. 9 ☎03090 25 40 💻www.sdtb.de

Don't tell the National Air and Space Museum about this place. With 30 full-sized airplanes, 20 boats—including a full-sized Viking relic—and a train from every decade since 1880, this museum could be a city in itself. Most impressive are the large mechanical demonstrations conducted throughout the day. The museum also has a garden with two windmills and a brewery.

🚇 U1 or U2: Gleisdreieck. ℹ Many exhibits in English. $ €4.50, students €2.50. ⏰ Open Tu-F 9am-5:30pm, Sa-Su 10am-6pm.

CHECKPOINT CHARLIE — ♿ HISTORIC SIGHT

Zimmerstr. and Friedrichstr.

This tourist trap once had significance as the entrance point into the American sector from East Berlin. For reasons unknown to Let's Go, it has recently become a prime tourist destination, where buses of photo-snapping lemmings buy into this scheme. Germans in American uniforms stand in the middle of the street and charge you €3 to take a picture of them; this is the most lucrative business since prostitution. A set of placards along Kochstr. provide a somewhat interesting history on the checkpoint and the various escapes it saw. Skip the musuem.

🚇 U6: Kochstraße $ Free. ⏰ Open 24hr.

JEWISH MUSEUM — 💳♿🍸🍴 MUSEUM

Lindenstr. 9-14 ☎0302 599 33 00 💻www.jmberlin.de

Modern, interactive exhibits treat subjects ranging from explanations of the Torah to the philosophies of Moses Mendelssohn to the anatomy of Jewish discrimination under Charles V. Architect Daniel Libeskind designed the museum's building to reflect the discomfort, pain, and inherent voids in Jewish history. While most attempts at "conceptual buildings" suck grandly, this one amazingly succeeds and the effect is moving, disorienting, and thought-provoking. No two surfaces are parallel to each other; the floor is uneven, and the doors and windows seem like portals from a nightmare.

🚇 U1 or U6: Hallesches Tor. From the station, head east on Gitschinerstr. and take a left at Lindenstr. $ €5, students €2.50. Audio tours €2. ⏰ Open M 10am-10pm, Tu-Su 10am-8pm. Last entry 1hr. before close.

SCHWULES MUSEUM (GAY MUSEUM) — 🍸 MUSEUM

Mehringdamm 61 ☎0306 959 90 50 💻www.schwulesmuseum.de

This little indie-feeling museum is actually state-supported, making it the world's only state-funded exhibit on homosexual persecution. Temporary exhibits take up over half of the museum, and displays are far from extensive, but the museum does offer a history rarely presented. The permanent exhibit focuses on German homosexual history from 1800 to the present.

U6 or U7: Mehringdamm. From the station, head south on Merhringdamm. The museum will be through a courtyard on your left. i English exhibit guide available. ⑤ €5, students €3. ⓧ Open Tu-F 2-6pm, Sa 2-7pm.

FOOD

rule of thumb

While ordering beer (or anything else), be careful which finger you use to indicate "one." As you may have seen in *Inglourious Basterds,* Germans use the ▧**thumb** to ask for one, while adding the pointer finger means two. Simply holding up the second finger may earn you some confused looks from the occasional bartender.

Charlottenburg

Charlottenburg's history of wealth and opulence is still visible to the visitor in the upscale Ku'damm or in its elegant hotels. It's not surprising that inexpensive meals are difficult to come by. In north Charlottenburg, the neighborhood called Moabit (right next to Mitte) is home to strong Middle Eastern and Asian ethnic communities. For cheap, authentic Turkish or Vietnamese food, it may be worth the trip of 20min. from the Zoo.

▧ SCHWARZES CAFE

⟶☺ ⚲⚐ BAR, RESTAURANT ❸

Kantstr. 148   ☎030 313 80 38

Pharmacies, grocery stores, and even whole neighborhoods might close down at night, but Schwarzes Cafe will still be open. Drink absinthe after dark inside the frescoed walls of the area's most popular boho cafe. The artistically peeling paint on the floors will increasingly bewilder as the absinthe gets to your head. Chase it down with breakfast when the sun comes up, or at a mere bohemian hour: all meals are served around the clock.

S3, S5, S7, S9, or S75: Savignypl. ⑤ Weekly specials €7-13 served 11:30am-8pm. Breakfast €5-8.50. Cash only. ⓧ Open M 24hr., Tu 4am-10am, W-Su 24hr.

ABBAS

⟶☺ MIDDLE EASTERN ❶

Huttenstr. 71   ☎030 34 34 77 70

Abbas and the restaurants around it belong to Arabic and Asian immigrants attracted by the area's low rent. This sprawling sweet and nut shop sells a wide range of authentic Middle Eastern desserts on the cheap, from chocolate-covered lentils to pistachio-cashew pastries. Try its specialty baklava *(€1.30 for 2 pieces).*

Bus M27: Turmstr./Beusseistr. ⑤ Cash only. ⓧ Open M-Th 10am-5pm, F and Sa noon-8pm.

Schöneberg and Wilmersdorf

Schöneberg's relaxed cafe culture is best experienced around the intersection of **Maaßenstrasse** and **Winterfeldstrasse.** More popular cafes and inexpensive restaurants crowd the **Akazienstrasse,** from the U-Bahn station at Eisenacherstr., to Hauptstr.

▧ CAFE BILDERBUCH

⟶☺(•) CAFE ❷

Akazienstr. 28   ☎030 78 70 60 57 ▨www.cafe-bilderbruch.de

Even if you couldn't eat here, Cafe Bilderbuch's antique cabinets, fringed lamps, deep-cushioned sofas, and adjoining library would still make this a place to visit. Fortunately, their unbeatable Sunday brunch buffets *(€8)* have us shoving

berlin · food

grandmothers out of the way to get in the door. The dinner specials *(€5-8.50)* are always affordable and never stuffy.

🚇 U7: Eisenacher Str. ℹ Free Wi-Fi. $ Soup from €3.70. Salads from €6. Entrees €8. Coffee €1.50. ⏰ Open M-Th 9am-1am, F-Sa 9am-2am, Su 10am-1am. Kitchen closes Su-F 11pm, Sa midnight.

👍 BAHARAT FALAFEL

🚫⛅ TURKISH ❶

Winterfeldtstr. 37 ☎030 216 83 01

This isn't your average *döner* stand. First, because it doesn't serve *döner*. Second, because this vegetarian Turkish restaurant makes all its falafel fried to order, in fluffy pita with lots of tomatoes, lettuce, and mango or chili sauce *(€3-4)*. Wash Baharat's plates, with hummus, tabouleh, and salad, all down with fresh-squeezed *Gute Laune Saft (good-mood juice, €1-2)*. Indoor seating with bright walls and flowers on the table, or an outdoor bench under a striped awning.

🚇 U1, U3, U4 or U9: Nollendorfpl. $ Entrees €6-8. ⏰ Open M-Sa 11am-2am, Su noon-2am.

👍 HIMALI

💳🍸⛅ TIBETAN, NEPALESE ❷

Crellerstr. 45 ☎030 78 71 61 75 💻www.himali-restaurant.de

Nepali and Tibetan classics are cooked up and served piping hot from a tandoori oven. Food is never short on spices, either in quantity or variety, which are grown and ground by hand. This restaurant offers a huge range of vegetarian dishes, curried or grilled, with tofu, vegetables and *naan* with your choice of seasonings. The Nepali tea *(€2.50)* is to die for.

🚇 U7: Kleistpark. $ Entrees €6.50-10. ⏰ Open daily noon-midinight.

Mitte

BERLINER MARCUS BRÄU

💳♿🍸 GERMAN ❷

1-3 Münzstr. ☎0302 47 69 85 💻www.marcus-brau.de

This corner shack's been brewing its own beer and liqueurs since before its country tried to conquer the world. The liqueurs, especially the coffee liqueur, taste as good as your mom smells, assuming she smells great. The food isn't exactly free, and the decor isn't exactly Ritz Carlton, but it's authentic, hearty, and German. Try the beer *(from €3 for 5L)*; it's among the best in the city.

🚇 U2, U5, U8, S5, S7, S9, or S75: Alexanderpl. $ Entrees €7.50-9. Drinks €1-7. ⏰ Open daily noon-late.

GOOD MORNING VIETNAM

💳♿🍸⛅ VIETNAMESE ❷

Alte Schonhauser 60 ☎030 30 88 29 73 💻www.good-morning-vietnam.de

The name is great. Explanation for the name is even better: "A yesterday's movie title, a salutation that reminds us of the past, a past full of starvation and war..." Brimming with such great food, this restaurant is hardly about starvation. Entrees *(€7)*, are cheaper than much-hyped Monsieur Vuong's down the street, and include crispy duck, mango chicken skewers, and tofu platters.

🚇 U2: Rosa-Luxemburg-Pl. $ Entrees €7-7.50. ⏰ Open daily noon-midnight.

DOLORES BURRITOS

🚫⛅ MEXICAN FUSION ❶

Rosa-Luxemburg-Str. 7 ☎030 28 09 95 97

Modeled after the Mexican fusion of Baja Fresh or Chipotle, this "California Burrito" shop sells hulking tubes under €5. While we won't go as far as calling these suckers "Californian," the place does a good job of supplying a real spread of chipotle chicken *(€1)*, spiced *carnitas (€1.30)*, and vegetables *(€0.80)* and lets you combine them in burrito *(€4)*, bowl *(€4)*, or quesadilla *(€3.70)* form. The staff could be nicer, but with the rush of students they're dealing with, you hardly blame them.

🚇 U2, U5, U8, S5, S7, S9, or S75: Alexanderpl. $ Burritos around €5; prices vary depending on your ingredients. ⏰ Open M-Sa 11:30am-10pm, Su 1-10pm.

Prenzlauer Berg

W-IMBISS
VEGETARIAN ❶

Katanienallee 49   ☎030 48 49 26 57

Maybe it's Indian food, or maybe it's Mexican. We can't really tell, but one thing we do know: this food is good. W-Imbiss specializes in fusing ethnic food types to make something interestingly novel, and damn good. Their specialty is the *naan* pizza—freshly baked bread in a tandoori oven spread with anything from pesto to avocado to chipotle sauce and served piled high with arugula and feta or mozzarella. W-Imbiss also sells cold wraps and quesadillas to an international crowd.

U8: Voltastr. ⑤ Pizza €2-5.50. Wraps €4-5. ☺ Open May-Aug daily noon-midnight; Sept-Apr daily 12:30-11:30pm.

HANS WURST
VEGAN ❷

Dunckerstr. 2A   ☎030 41 71 78 22

This small cafe serves only organic, vegan foods with no flavor enhancers. Readings, DJs, and acoustic concerts spice up the evenings in this minimally decorated, laid-back venue. The menu changes daily, with seasonal and innovative offerings. Try the tofu burger on toast with original, spicy sauces.

U2: Eberswalder Str. Or M10: Husemannstr. ⑤ Entrees €3.70-8. Tofu burger €4. ☺ Open M-Th noon-midnight, F-Sa noon-late.

DAS FILM CAFE
BURGERS, THEATER ❷

Schliemannstr. 15   ☎030 810 11 90 50 ▧www.dasfilmcafe.de

Das Film Cafe serves up homemade burgers to fans hungry for a good meal and even better movies. This cafe has two screenings a night in a small, high-resolution theater downstairs, usually around 8pm and 10pm, and prides itself on selecting films with an international, independent flair. Films are never dubbed over and are usually shown in English.

U2: Eberswalder Str. ⑤ Tickets €4.50, students €4. Burgers €7. Hummus plates €5.50. Cappuccino €2. ☺ Open M-F 2:30pm-late, Sa-Su 11:30am-late.

Friedrichshain

Friedrichshain is famous for its inexpensive, student-centered living, and its restaurants, bars and cafes don't disappoint. In the area bounded by Frankfurter-Allee to the north, Jennerstr. to the east, Simon-Dach-Str. to the west, and Wühlschischerstr. to the south, streets overflow with bistro tables, outdoor umbrellas, and cheap food.

FRITTIERSALON
GERMAN ❶

Boxhagener Str. 104   ☎030 25 93 39 06

Yes, we know, ever since you set foot in Berlin, you've been drowning in bratwurst, currywurst, and fried potatoes. But for anyone in Friedrichshain, this all-organic "frying salon" is unique enough to merit a visit. In addition to a traditional prize-winning Berliner currywurst, this restaurant serves a number of German classics with a twist: try the wheat-based vegetarian currywurst or bratwurst or a hamburger or veggie burger with strawberries and avocado. All sauces and french fries are homemade, and all dishes are cooked to order.

U5: Frankfurter Tor. ⑤ Bratwurst and currywurst €2.20. Burgers €6. ☺ Open M 6pm-late, Tu-F noon-late, Sa-Su 1pm-late.

CARAMELLO EIS
ICE CREAM ❶

Wühlischerstr. 31   ☎030 50 34 31 05 ▧www.caramello-eis.de

Caramello Eis scoops some of the best ice cream in town all night long to a following of devoted students. All of Caramello's ice cream is handmade, organic, and vegan. Don't leave Friedrichshain without trying the dark chocolate *eis* with

berlin . food

chili powder; the staff says it's the best chocolate ice cream in all of Berlin, and we're not about to argue.

⇞ U5: Frankfurter Tor. Ⓢ Cones €1. ⏰ Open daily 11am-late.

Kreuzberg

Good food lives and dies all over Kreuzberg, but the best food is stacked up in the area near **Oranienestrasse.**

👍 CAFE MORGANLAND ⊛🚭🍸⛅ CAFE ❶

Skalitzer Str. 35 ☎03061 132 91 💻www.cafemorgenland.eu

Its Parisian breakfast—a fresh butter croissant, a large dish of perfect vanilla custard with fresh fruit, and the best milk coffee you've ever had—breaks the laws of economics. The all-you-can-eat brunch buffet *(€9.50)* on the weekends will literally make your jaw drop: eight types of meat, five types of bread, 15 spreads, sausages, eggs, curries, potatoes, fish, vegetables, fruits—it's paradise. Solid international fare fills out the rest of the menu.

⇞ U1: Görlitzer Bahnhof. Ⓢ Entrees €5-15. ⏰ Open daily 10am-1am.

👍 RESTAURANT RISSANI ⊛🚭🍸 MIDDLE EASTERN ❶

Spreewaldpl. 4 ☎3061 62 94 33

A lot of döner kebab places around town call themselves authentic. Well, Rissani doesn't serve döners—they call them chicken shawarma sandwiches—but they're twice as delicious and half as expensive *(€2)*. Dinner plates, with shawarma, falafel, tabbouleh, hummus, and salad will make you forget your bad day.

⇞ U1: Görlitzer Bahnhof. From the station, head east down Skalitzer str. and take a right at Spreewaldpl. Ⓢ Entrees €2-5. ⏰ Open M-Th 11am-3am, F-Sa 11am-5am, Su 11am-3am.

👍 MUSTAFAS ⊛♿🍸 MIDDLE EASTERN ❶

Mehringdamm 32 💻www.mustafas.de

Some say that this place serves up the best döner kebabs in the city—that's debatable, but what's not is that Mustafas has the best *durum (shawarma burrito with sauce; €4)* in the city. It tastes like the best thing in the world stuffed with the second-best thing in the world. Vegetarians who usually scrounge through various falafel options will rejoice over the delicious grilled vegetables in the veggie *durum (€3.10)*. If you want to check it out yourself, their website has a live webcam.

⇞ U6 or U7: Mehringdamm. Ⓢ Entrees €2.50-5. ⏰ Open 24hr.

👍 HENNE ALT-BERLINER WIRTSHAUS GASTSTÄTTEN ⊛🚭🍸⛅ GERMAN ❷

Leuschnerdamm 25 ☎3061 477 30 💻www.henne-berlin.de

Henne provides the most German experience imaginable. An antler-lined parlor crammed with plaid tablecloths, sturdy German damsels hauling mugs of beer, and a menu that consists of a single dinner: a piece of bread, creamy potato salad, and enormous, perfectly crispy, internationally renowned chicken that will forever redefine "fried food." The chicken skin whispers as you crunch it, "I'm better than the girls you'll miss out on by eating me and gaining weight." She only speaks the truth.

*⇞ U1 or U8: Kottbusser Tor. From the station, head northwest on Oranienstr. Take a right at Oranienpl. **i** Reservations needed for outdoor seating. Ⓢ Entrees from €8. ⏰ Open Tu-Sa 7pm-late, Su 5pm-late.*

NIGHTLIFE ♪

Charlottenburg

Charlottenburg's quiet cafes and music venues cater to the 30-something set. Great for a mellow evening, or a chance to hear the city's best jazz, but the real parties are eastward. The Ku'damm is best avoided after sunset, unless you enjoy fraternizing with drunk businessmen.

👍 A TRANE ◉🍸 BAR AND CLUB

Bleibtreustr. 1 ☎030 313 25 50 💻www.a-trane.de

Small in size, big on talent. Hanging black and white photographs of jazz greats, some who even performed at A Trane (like legends Herbie Hancock and Wynton Marsalis), look down on crowded tables filled with jazz enthusiasts. First-class musicians still entertain guests on a quiet street corner.

🚇 S3, S5, S7, S9, or S75: Savignypl. $ Cover €7-15, students €5-13. Sa from 12:30am no cover. 🕐 Open M-Th and Su 9pm-2am, F-Sa 9pm-late.

CASCADE ◉⊗🍸 CLUB

Fasanenstr. 81 ☎030 31 80 09 40 💻www.cascade-club.de

The walk down to the large basement club is bookended by steps flooded by flowing water, hence the name Cascade. With a high cover, this club might be a bit of a splurge, but in return travelers get a dance floor of underlit blocks (à la 👍**John Travolta**), a wall-to-wall bar, and a young crowd–there might even actually be dancing! There are ways to get around the high admission price; stop by on a Friday and pick up a voucher for free entry, good the next evening, or next weekend.

🚇 U1: Uhlandstr. $ Cover €10. Beer €3.50, shots €4. 🕐 Open F-Sa 11am-late.

Schöneberg and Wilmersdorf

Schöneberg is still Berlin's unofficial gay district, full of GLBT nightlife. We've picked some of our favorites, but the neighborhood is full of outrageously popular bars and clubs that serve a vibrant gay community. From what we can tell, there aren't happier partiers in all of Berlin.

👍 HAFEN ◉🍸▼ GAY BAR

Motzstr. 19 ☎030 211 41 18 💻www.hafen-berlin.de

Nearly 20 years old, this bar has become a landmark for Berlin's gay community. The sign outside may only specifically invite "drop dead gorgeous looking tourists," but you'll find plenty of locals all along the spectrum of attractiveness. The mostly male crowd spills out onto the streets during the summer. The weekly pub quiz, Monday at 8pm, is wildly popular (first Monday of the month in English), and every Wednesday features a new DJ. On April 30th, Hafen hosts their largest party of the year, in honor of the Queen of the Netherlands. They promise us that the "Queen" makes an appearance.

🚇 U1, U3, U4 or U9: Nollendorfpl. $ No cover. 🕐 Open daily 8am-4am.

👍 PRINZKNECHT ◉🍸▼ GAY BAR

Fuggerstr. 33 ☎030 23 62 74 44 💻www.prinzknecht.de

Prinzknecht serves a mostly male clientele from a huge central wooden bar. Even with so many bar stools and couches, the bar fills up way past capacity on event nights, and people begin to resemble waves on the street. Check the website for upcoming events, including an incredibly popular 👍**ABBA** night.

🚇 U1 or U2: Wittenbergpl." $ No cover. 🕐 Open M-F 2pm-3am, Sa and Su 3pm-3am.

BEGINE 🍸▼ LESBIAN BAR

Potsdamer Str. 139 ☎030 215 14 14 💻www.begine.de

In a neighborhood dominated by male gay clubs, Begine is a welcome retreat for women. Named after a now-defunct Lesbian WC, Berlin's biggest lesbian community center has a popular, low-key cafe/bar with comfortable sofas, live music, and readings at night.

🚇 U2: Bülowstr. $ No cover. 🕐 Open M-F 5pm-late, Sa 3pm-late, Su 7pm-late.

Mitte

👍 BANG BANG CLUB ◉🍸 CLUB

Neue Promenade 10 ☎030 604 053 10 💻www.bangbangclub.net

Hiding beneath the S-Bahn tracks in groovy, smoky caverns of arched brick, the Bang Bang club plays it cool without being snooty. Weave through the tight hallways and dance the night away with Berliners.

🚇 *S5, S7, S9, S75: Hackescher Markt. U.* ⓢ *Admission free–€20.* 🕐 *Usually open F-Sa 10pm-late. Check website for details.*

🏛 COOKIES
🍴🍸 CLUB

Friedrichstr. 158 ☎030 274 929 40 🖥www.cookies-berlin.de

Hot, sweaty, sexy, and packed, Cookies jams in a former Stasi bunker that operates as a restaurant during the day. Locals claim that this party originally started in some guy's basement before moving to hip venues. The party don't start till 1am, so save your tears if you show up alone at midnight. Entrance can be a little exclusive—don't dress up, dress down—so it helps if you know the name of the DJ playing that night.

🚇 *U6: Französische Str. From the U-Bahn, head north.* ⓢ *Admission €5-15.* 🕐 *Club open Tu 10:30pm-6am, Th 10:30pm-6am.*

Prenzlauer Berg

Far less techno and far more laid-back than other parts of Berlin, Prenzlauer Berg's trendy cafes and late-night restaurants each have a devoted local following. Opt for bars over clubs in this part of town.

🏛 THE WEINEREI: FORUM
🍷🍸🍺 BAR

Veteranenstr. 14 ☎030 440 6983

This unmarked wine bar has gone from a local secret to a local legend, catapulted by its comfortable elegance and unique paying system. Pay €2 for a glass, sample all the wines, and then sample again, and again, and before leaving, pay what you think you owe. Enjoy your vintage at an outdoor table, on an indoor sofa, or in the downstairs wine cellar (by request).

🚇 *U2: Senefelderpl.* ⓢ *Depends on how drunk you get.* 🕐 *Open M-Sa 10am-late, Su 11am-late.*

🏛 SOLSI E MORSI
🍷🍸🍺 BAR

Marienburger Str. 10

It's not often that an owner becomes as loved as his bar, but Johnny Petrongolo is that rare exception. Buzzing about tables, opening wine bottles, and handing out plates of free parma ham, cheese, bread and olives, Johnny and his familial staff have won over the hearts of their young regulars, and ours as well. If you're not sure where to start, let the Petrongolos help you pick your wine.

🚇 *U2: Senefelderpl.* ⓢ *Wine from €3 a glass.* 🕐 *Open daily 6pm-late.*

🏛 KLUB DER REPUBLIC (KDR)
🍷🍸🍺 CLUB

Pappelallee 81

There are few museums that have as many authentic Soviet artifacts as KDR has hanging on its walls. Once the showroom of the DDR carpet and linoleum supplier, KDR kept the old formica bar and leaded glass, and added lamps from the original Palast Republik, collected as the building was being torn down. The furniture is from the DDR landmark Cafe Moscow. DJs play every night to a mixed crowd attracted by the club's no cover policy.

🚇 *U2: Eberswalder Str. Turn into what looks like a deserted parking lot and climb the metal stairs.* ⓢ *Drinks €5, beer €4.* 🕐 *Open from "dark to light." In more definite terms, that's around 9pm in the summer, in the winter 8pm-late.*

INTERSOUP
🍷🍸🍺 BAR

Schliemannstr. 31 ☎030 23 27 30 45 🖥www.intersoup.de

With worn '70s furniture, retro floral wallpaper, and soup specials, this is your East-Berlin Soviet-era grandmother's living room turned ironic. Named after the DDR-era general store Intershop, Intersoup has been keeping things quintessentially Prenzlauer Berg-esque and getting quite the local following doing it. The upper level always has a DJ, but the real highlight is the downstairs **undersoup**, where international bands perform every night at 10pm, in genres from folk to rock, to an audience seated in comfortable mix-matched chairs covered in lurid orange and olive patterns. There's almost never a cover.

U2: Eberswalder Str. $ Soup €4.50-5. Open M-Sa 6pm-3am, Su.

Friedrichshain

When people think of Berlin techno clubs, they're picturing Friedrichshain. You won't find more legendary converted factory or warehouse clubs in any other neighborhood in Germany, and maybe even all of Europe. Most of these raging dance venues are spread out along the river and railroad tracks, between the car dealerships and empty lots on **Mühlenstrasse.** More low-key, but equally popular bars are clustered around **Simon-Dach-Strasse.** In fact, even as we've recommended our favorite laid-back and hoppin' bars below, you really can't go wrong with any place along **Simon-Dach.**

ASTRO-BAR — BAR

Simon-Dach-Str. 40 — www.astro-bar.de

This popular bar gets back to the basics with cheap prices and generously poured alcohol. A DJ plays vinyl records every night starting at 10pm, featuring classics like the Stones and the Beatles, along with some newer indie tracks. Run by a bunch of guys who like their music, love their whiskey *(€4),* and decorate the back of their bar with Transformers nailed to the wall.

U5: Frankfurter Tor. $ Beer from €2.50. Mixed drinks from €5. Open 6pm-late.

ABGEDREHT — BAR

Karl-Marx-Allee 150 — ☎030 29 38 19 11 www.abgedreht.net

This no-frills bar is located right next to Frankfurter Tor, so you can soak up Soviet ambiance while you practically sit on the laps of locals. Sheet music papers the walls, and leather couches are clumped around antique sewing tables. This bar caters to the 30+ crowd, and is a little removed from most of the action on Simon-Dach, but if you're looking to drink a beer with a view of the DDR main street, this is the place to go.

U5: Frankfurter Tor. $ 0.5L beer €3-4. Open daily 5pm-late. Happy hour 7-9pm, cocktails from €5.

Kreuzberg

CLUB DER VISIONAERE — CLUB

Am Flutgraben 1 — ☎030 695 189 44 www.clubdervisionaere.com

Though this river-front cabana/bar/club/boat is packed, the experience is worth the sweaty armpits. A mini-indoor club has a DJ spinning, but the fun is outside with rum-based drinks, feet dipped in the river, and large pizzas *(€8).* This club is like a mix of the Bayou, New York, and Cancun. One of the best experiences you will have anywhere. So relaxing, so engaging, so Berlin.

U1: Schlesisches Tor. From the U-Bahn head southeast on Schleissichestr. $ Admission €4-15. Open daily 10pm-late.

WATERGATE — CLUB

Falckensteinstr. 49 — ☎030 61 28 03 96 www.water-gate.de

This ultra-exclusive club lights up the river with an eye-popping display of lights, but from the street, not even a sign marks its entrance. You'll have to rely on the enormous line of partiers who've come for a club that lives up to its reputation. Tired guests can "chill out" on the floating dock, while raging rhinos can tear up one of two dance floors. The place won't get packed until 2am—but then it roars until the sun shushes it down. Groups of more than two should pretend like they're separate, and couples should pretend like they're single—seriously.

U1: Schlesisches Tor. Head toward the bridge. It's the unmarked door at the top of those stairs immediately before the river. $ Cover €8-20. Mixed drinks €6.50. Open W 11-late. F and Sa midnight-late.

ARTS AND CULTURE

Music and Opera

BERLINER PHILHARMONIKER — MITTE

Herbert-von-Karajan-Str. 1 ☎030 25 48 89 99 💻www.berlin-philharmonic.com

It may look strange from the outside, but acoustically, this yellow building is pitch-perfect; all audience members hear the music exactly as it's intended to reach their ears. The Berliner Philharmoniker, led by the eminent Sir Simon Rattle, is one of the world's finest orchestras. It's tough to get a seat; check 1hr. before concert time or e-mail at least 8 weeks in advance.

🚇 S1, S2, or S25 or U2: Potsdamer Pl. $ Tickets from €7 for standing room, from €13 for seats. ⏰ Open July-early Sept. Box office open M-F 3-6pm, Sa-Su 11am-2pm.

DEUTSCHE STAATSOPER — MITTE

Unter den Linden 7 ☎030 203 545 55 💻www.staatsoper-berlin.de

The Deutsche Staatsoper is East Berlin's leading opera theater. Though it suffered during the years of separation, this opera house is rebuilding its reputation and its repertoire of classical Baroque opera and contemporary pieces.

🚇 U6: Französische Str. Or bus #100, 157, or 348: Deutsche Staatsoper. $ Tickets €50-160; students €12, if purchased 30min. before shows and ½-price on cheaper seats for certain performances. ⏰ Open Aug to mid-July. Box office open daily noon-7pm, and 1hr. before performances.

DEUTSCHE OPER BERLIN — MITTE

Bismarckstr. 35 ☎030 34 38 43 43 💻www.deutscheoperberlin.de

The Deutsche Oper is Berlin's newest opera house. If you have the chance, don't pass on a cheap ticket to go see one of Berlin's best performances.

🚇 U2: Deutsche Oper. $ Tickets €12-118. 25% student discounts. ⏰ Open Sept-June. Box office open M-Sa 11am until beginning of the performance, or 11am-7pm on days without performances; Su 10am-2pm. Evening tickets available 1hr. before performances.

Film

Finding English films in Berlin is anything but difficult. On any night, choose from over 150 different films, marked **O.F.** or **O.V.** for the original version (meaning not dubbed in German), **O.m.U** for original version with German subtitles, or **O.m.u.E.** for original film with English subtitles.

KINO BABYLON — 🚭 🍸 MITTE

Rosa-Luxemburg-Str. 30 ☎030 242 59 69 💻www.babylonberlin.de

A spunky little independent film house with a commitment to quality films, Kino Americans and Berliners alike who flock here for pure film culture. Occasional summer screenings happen outdoors on the beautiful Rosa-Luxemburg-and an epic screening of Rocky Horror Picture Show goes down regularly here.

🚇 U2: Rosa-Luxemburg-Pl. $ Tickets €4-8. ⏰ Schedules change daily. Check website for details.

ARSENAL — KREUZBERG

In the Filmhaus at Potsdamer Pl. ☎030 26 95 51 00 💻www.fdk-berlin.de

Run by the founders of Berlinale, Arsenal showcases indie films and some classics *(€6.50)*. Frequent appearances by guest directors make the theater a popular meeting place for Berlin's filmmakers.

🚇 U2, S1, S2, or S25: Potsdamer Pl.

Theater

ENGLISH THEATER BERLIN — ♿ 🍸 KREUZBERG

Fidicinstr. 40 ☎030 693 56 92 💻www.etberlin.de

For over 20 years Berlin's only all English-language theater has been defying German-language totalitarianism with everything from 10-minute short festivals to full length productions. Leave your *umlauts* at home.

U6: Pl. der Luftbrücke. $ €14, students €8. Box office opens 1hr. before show time. Shows are at 8pm unless otherwise noted.

DEUTSCHES THEATER MITTE

Schumann Straße 13a ☎030 28 44 10 www.deutschestheater.de

Built in 1850, this world-famous theater that legendary director Max Reinhardt once controlled is still a cultural heavy hitter in Berlin. Performances tend to be in German, and they tend to change frequently, so check the website for details.

U6: Oranienburger Tor. From the U-Bahn, head south on Friederichstraße, take a right on Reinhartße and another right on Albrecthstr. $ €5-30. Box office open M-Sa 11am-6:30pm, Su 3-6:30pm. Shows are at 8pm unless otherwise noted.

SHOPPING

Flea Markets

ARKONAPLATZ PRENZLAUER BERG

Arkonapl. ☎786 9764

Craftsmen sell jewelry. Farmers juice oranges. That guy down the street hawks his CDs from a towel. Arkonaplatz brings out the weird, the old, the desperate, and everyone who wants their stuff. The market's enormous size makes the junk spread incredible: DDR relics, massive rolls of fabric, pictures of vendors' babies, antique space hats? Stick around in the afternoons when the unnamed Irish man comes by with a karaoke machine on his bike. He's been doing it for years now.

U8: Bernaurstr. Open Su 9am-6pm.

TURKISH MARKET KREUZBERG

Along the south bank of the Landwehrkanal

Fruit vendors shout to passersby about their fruit, bakers shout about their baking, clothing dealers shout about their clothing. The Turkish Market is not just an amazing place to find great deals on fruit and clothing, it's one of the best experiences of the entire city. The fruit stands have fruits you've never seen, and they only cost €1. The clothing stands have deals like three pairs of socks for the price of one. On top of this, musicians play at the ends of the market. Not exactly a "flea" market, but an incredible market, and one you won't forget.

U1: Kottbusser Tor. From the U-Bahn, head south toward the canal. Open Tu and F noon-6pm.

MAUERPARK FLEA MARKET PRENZLAUER BERG

On Eberswalderstr.

The Mauerpark Flea Market is the biggest and best-known in all of Berlin. A labyrinth of booths and stalls sells everything from hand-ground spices to used clothing to enamel jewelry to potted plants. Hoards of bargain hunters, hipsters, and gawking tourists crowd the park, drinking fresh-squeezed orange juice and listening to the street musicians who swarm the market. Like all secondhand stores in Prenzlauer Berg, Mauerpark is rarely dirt-cheap. You can still find good values, but expect slightly higher prices.

U2: Eberswalderstr.

Books

ST. GEORGE'S BOOKSTORE PRENZLAUER BERG

Wörtherstr. 27 ☎0308 179 83 33

You'll be hard-pressed to find a better English-language bookstore on the continent. St. George's owner makes frequent trips to the UK and US to buy up loads of titles so that his customers can find any book they're looking for, and then some. Over half of the books are used and extremely well-priced *(paperbacks*

€4-6), with a number of books for just €1. This shop also carries new books and can order absolutely any title they don't already carry. If you're looking for travel reading material, there's absolutely no better place to go in Berlin. Pay in euros, British pounds, or American dollars (oh my!).
🚇 U2: Senefelderpl. 🕐 Open M-F 11am-7pm, Sa 10am-4pm.

Music

SPACE HALL KREUZBERG
Zossenerstr. 33, 35 ☎306947664 🖥www.spacehall.de
They don't make them like this in the States no more. The CD store is two doors down from the vinyl store. The vinyl store just keeps going, with a "bunker" vibe and a courtyard where DJs sometimes spin and sample turntables. They also have an inspiring collection of rubber duckies.
🚇 U7: Gneisenaustr. 🕐 Open M-W 11am-8pm, Th-F 11am-10pm, Sa 11-8pm.

ESSENTIALS

Practicalities

- **TOURIST OFFICES:** Now privately owned, tourist offices provide far fewer free services than they once did. 🖥www.berlin.de has quality information on all aspects of the city. **EurAide** sells rail tickets, maps, phone cards, and walking-tour tickets. *(☎1781 828 2488 🚇 In the Hauptbahnhof, across from the McDonald's.)* **Tourist Info Centers.** *(Berlin Tourismus Marketing GmbH, Am Karlsbad 11, 10785. Office located on the ground floor of the Hauptbahnhof. The entrance is on Europl. ☎030 25 00 25 🖥www.berlin-tourist-information.de i Service in English. Siegessäule, Sergej, and Gay-Yellowpages have gay and lesbian event and club listings. $ Reserve rooms for a €3-6 fee. Transit maps free; city maps €1. The monthly Berlin Programm lists museums, sights, restaurants, and hotels, as well as opera, theater, and classical music performances, €1.75. Full listings of film, theater, concerts, and clubs in German Tip, €2.70, or Zitty, €2.70. English-language movie and theater reviews are in Ex-Berliner €2. 🕐 Open daily 8am-10pm.).* **Alternate location.** *(Brandenburger Tor 🚇 S1, S2, or S25 or bus #100: Unter dne Linden. On your left as you face the pillars from the Unter den Linden side. 🕐 Open daily 10am-6pm.)*
- **STUDENT TRAVEL OFFICES: STA** books flights and hotels and sells ISICs. *(Dorotheenstr. 30 ☎030 20 16 50 63 🚇 S3, S5, S7, S9, S75, or U6 to Friedrichstr. 🕐 Open M-F 10am-7pm, Sa 11am-3pm.)* **Second location.** *(Sleimstr. 28 🚇 S4, S8, S85, or U2: Schönhauser Allee. 🕐 Open M-F 10am-7pm, Sa 11am-4pm.)* **Third location.** *(Hardenbergerstr. 9 🚇 U2: Ernst-Reuter-Pl. 🕐 Open M-F 10am-7pm, Sa 11am-3pm.)* **Fourth location.** *(Takustr. 47 🕐 Open M-F 10am-7pm, Sa 10am-2pm.)*
- **CURRENCY EXCHANGE AND MONEY WIRES:** The best rates are usually found at exchange offices with *Wechselstrube* signs outside, at most major trainstations, and in large squares. For money wires through Western Union, use **ReiseBank.** *(Hauptbahnhof ☎030 20 45 37 61 🕐 M-Sa 8am-10pm)* **Second location.** *(Bahnhof Zoo ☎030 881 7117)* **Third location.** *(Ostbahnhof ☎030 296 4393.)*
- **LUGGAGE STORAGE:** *(🚇 In the Hauptbahnhof, in"DB Gepack Center," 1st fl., East side. $ €4 per day.)* Lockers also in Bahnhof Zoo, Ostbahnhof, and Alexanderpl.
- **INTERNET ACCESS:** Free Internet with admission to the **Staatsbibliothek.** During their renovation, Staatsbibliothek requires a €10 week-long pass to their library. *(Potsdamer Str. 33 ☎030 26 60 🕐 Open M-F 9am-9pm, Sa 9am-7pm.)* **Netlounge** *(Auguststr. 89 ☎030 24 34 25 97 🖥www.netlounge-berlin.de 🚇 U-Bahn: Oranienburger Str. $ €2.50 per hr. 🕐 Open daily noon-midnight.)* **Easy Internet** has several locations throughout Berlin *(Unter den Linden 24, Rosenstraße 16, Frankfurter Allee*

32, Rykestraße 29, and Kurfürstendamm 18). Many cafes throughout Berlin offer free Wi-Fi.

- **POST OFFICES: Main branch** *(Joachimstaler Str. 7 ☎030 88 70 86 11 🚇 Down Joachimstaler Str. from Bahnhof Zoo and near Kantstr. ⏰ Open M-Sa 9am-8pm.)* **Tegel Airport** *(⏰ Open M-F 8am-6pm, Sa 8am-noon.)* **Ostbahnhof** *(⏰ Open M-F 8am-8pm, Sa-Su 10am-6pm.)*
- **POSTAL CODE:** 10706.

Emergency!

- **POLICE:** *(Pl. der Luftbrücke 6. 🚇 U6: Pl. der Luftbrüche.)*
- **EMERGENCY NUMBERS:** ☎110. **Ambulance and Fire** ☎112. **Non-emergency advice hotline:** ☎030 46 64 46 64.
- **MEDICAL SERVICES:** The American and British embassies list English-speaking doctors. The **emergency doctor** *(☎030 31 00 31 or ☎01804 2255 2362)* service helps travelers find English-speaking doctors. **Emergency dentist.** *(☎030 89 00 43 33)*
- **CRISIS LINES:** English spoken at most crisis lines. **American Hotline** has crisis and referral services. *(☎0177 814 15 10)* **Poison Control.** *(☎030 192 40)* **Berliner Behindertenverband** has advice for the handicapped. *(Jägerstr. 63d ☎030 204 38 48 💻www.bbv-ev.de ⏰ Open W noon-5pm and by appointment.)* **Deutsche AIDS-Hilfe.** *(Wilhelmstr. 138 ☎030 690 0870 💻www.aidshilfe.de)* **Drug Crisis.** *(☎030 192 37 ⏰ 24hr.)* **Women's Resources.** Frauendrisentelefon Women's crisis line. *(☎030 615 4243 💻www.frauenkrisentelefon.de ⏰ Open M and Th 10am-noon, Tu-W, F 7pm-9pm, Sa-Su 5pm-7pm)* **Lesbenberatung** offers lesbian counseling. *(Kulmer Str. 20 ☎030 215 2000 💻www.lesbenberatung-berlin.de)* **Schwulenberatung** offers gay men's counseling. *(Mommenstr. 45 ☎030 194 46 💻www.schwulenberatungberlin.de)* **Maneo.** Legal help for gay violence victims. *(☎030 216 3336 💻www.maneo.de ⏰ Open daily 5pm-7pm)* **LARA.** Sexual assault help. *(Fuggerstr. 19 ☎030 216 88 88 💻www.lara-berlin.de ⏰ Open M-F 9am-6pm.)* **Children's emergency helpline.** *(☎030 610 061)*

Getting There

By Plane

Capital Airport Berlin Brandenburg International (BBI) will open in the southeast Berlin in 2012. Until then, **Tegel Airport** will continue to serve travelers. *(Take express bus #X9 or #109 from Jakob-Kaiser Pl. on U7, bus #128 from Kurt-Schumacher-Pl. on U6, or bus TXL from Beusselstr on S42 and S41. Follow signs in the airport for ground transportation. ☎49 30 6091 2055 💻www.berlin-airport.de)*

By Train

International trains *(☎972 226 150)* pass through Berlin's **Hauptbahnhof** and run to: **Amsterdam, NTH** *($ €130. ⏰6½hr., 16 per day.)*; **Brussels, BEL** *($ €165 ⏰ 7hr., 14 per day.)*; **Budapest, HUN** *($ €165 ⏰ 13hr., 4 per day.)*; **Copenhagen, DNK** *($ €155 ⏰ 7hr., 7 per day.)*; **Paris, FRA** *($ €200 ⏰ 9hr., 9 per day.)*; **Prague, CZR**; *($ €80 ⏰ 5hr., 12 per day.)* **Vienna, AUT.** *($ €155 ⏰ 10hr., 12 per day.)*

By Bus

ZOB is the central bus station. *(Masurenallee 4. 🚇 U2: Kaiserdamm. Alternatively, S4, S45, or S46: Messe Nord/ICC. ☎030 301 30 80 ⏰ Open M-F 6am-9pm, Sa-Su and holidays 6am-8pm.)*

Getting Around

By Bike

The best way to see Berlin is by bike. Unless your hostel's out in the boonies, few trips will be out of cycling reach, and given that U-Bahn tickets verge on €3 and that the average long-term bike rental costs €8 per day, pedaling your way is just a better deal.

FAT TIRE BIKE RENTAL MITTE

Alexanderpl. ☎030 24 04 79 91 www.berlinfahrradverleih.com

Rents bikes for half- and full-days.

East location U2: Alexanderpl. Directly under the TV Tower. West location U2 or U9: Zoological Garten. $ €7 per ½-day (up to 4hr.), €12 per day. Open May-Oct 15 daily 9:30am-8pm; Oct 16-Nov and Mar-Apr daily 9:30am-6pm.

The BVG

The heart of Berlin's public transportation system is the U-Bahn and S-Bahn Metro trains, which cover the city in a spidery and circular patterns, respectively. Trams *(Straßenbahn)* and buses (both part of the U-Bahn system) scuttle around the remaining city corners. *(BVG's 24hr. hotline ☎030 194 49 www.bvg.de)* Berlin is divided into three transit zones. Zone A has central Berlin, including Tempelhof Airport. The rest of Berlin is in Zone B; Zone C consists of outlying areas, including Potsdam and Oranienburg. An AB ticket is the best deal, since you can later buy extension tickets for the outlying areas. A one-way ticket is good for 2hr. after validation. *($ Zones AB €2.10, BC €2.50, ABC €2.80, under 14 reduced fare, under 6 free.)* Within the validation period, the ticket may be used on any S-Bahn, U-Bahn, bus, or tram.

Most train lines don't run Monday through Friday 1-4am. S-Bahn and U-Bahn lines do run Friday and Saturday nights, but less frequently. When trains stop, 70 night buses take over, running every 20-30min. and tending to follow major transit lines; pick up the free Nachtliniennetz map of bus routes at a **Fahrscheine und Mehr** office. The letter "N" precedes night bus numbers. Trams also continue to run at night.

Buy tickets, including monthly passes, from machines or ticket windows in Metro stations or from bus drivers. **Be warned:** machines don't give more than €10 change, and many machines don't take bills, though some accept credit cards. Validate your ticket by inserting it into the stamp machines before boarding. Failure to validate becomes a big deal when plainclothes policemen bust you and charge you €40 for freeloading. If you bring a bike on the U-Bahn or S-Bahn, you must buy it a child's ticket. Bikes are forbidden on buses and trams.

Single-ride tickets are a waste of money. A **Day Ticket** *($ AB €6.10, ABC €6.50)* is good from the time it's stamped until 3am the next day. The BVG also sells **7-day tickets** *($ AB €26.20, ABC €32.30)* and **month-long tickets** *($ AB €72, ABC €88.50).* Another option are the popular tourist cards: the **WelcomeCard** (sold at tourist offices) buys unlimited travel. *($ AB 48hr. €17, ABC €19; 72hr. €23/26)* and includes discounts on 130 city sights. The **CityTourCard** is good within zones AB *($ 48hr. €16, 72hr. €22)* and offers discounts at over 50 attractions.

By Taxi

Taxis: Call 15min. in advance. Women can request female drivers. Trips within the city cost up to €30. *(☎030 26 10 26, ☎0800 263 0000 toll-free)*

köln *cologne* ☎0221

The Roman city of Colonia made headlines many times in history before becoming a staple of Germany travel guides. Housing valuable relics of the Three Kings, Köln first made its name as a hubbub of pilgrimage activity. Later, its port along the Rhein made it a commercial entrepeneur's dream city. In the 18th century, Farina's invention of the fragrant Eau de Cologne made Köln's citizens, and then the rest of the world, smell nice. Finally, in 1880, the City's Dom was completed.

Today, pilgrims take the form of chatty tourists who leave with suitcases full of perfume and dozens of photos of the Dom (in their defense, it's pretty incredible). Yet the city still clings to its roots, and the many archaeological excavation sites around the Altstadt attest to Köln's obsession with historical preservation. True to form, many Kölners also converse with each other in the city's own dialect, called *Kölsch—*

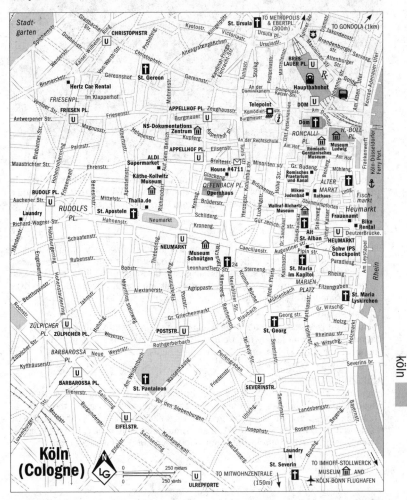

which, coincidentally, is also the name of the city's own beer, made exclusively in breweries whose windows have a clear view of the Dom. With all that *Kölsch* and a robust nightlife scene fueled by students from Germany's largest university, you're bound to have a good time.

ORIENTATION

The Rhein River runs north-south through the middle of the city, though most of the river runs to the west. There, a long semi-circular street comprised of **Hansaring, Hohenzollernring, Hohenstaufenring, Sachsenring,** and **Ubierring,** divides the city's **Altstadt** inside the ring along the river and the **Neustadt** outside. On the other side of the river is **Deutz,** home to Köln's trade fairs.

Altstadt-Nord

The beloved Dom takes center stage the heart of the Altstadt-Nord, next door to the Hauptbahnhof. Bounded by the Deutzer Brücke to the south, this part of town is one-third historical sights, one-third shopping malls, and one-third overpriced German brewhouses.

Altstadt-Sud

Admittedly, there's not much in this part of town—yet. While the **Schockoladen Museum** remains this quarter's greatest asset, recent construction along the banks of the Rhein have transformed the formerly defunct **Rheinhaufen** harbor into a posh new residential area. The three inverted L-shaped apartment buildings, called the **Kranhaus (Crane House),** have brought the city some modern architectural street cred.

Neustadt

The western end of this part of town is the university. You'll find plenty of cheap eats and student-friendly nightlife in the area around **Zülpicher Platz**. Along the northwestern end, the **Belgisches Viertel** neighborhood is populated by chic boutiques and designer furniture stores, along with a few of the city's more upscale bars.

ACCOMMODATIONS

Köln's hotels raise rates from March to October, when trade winds blow conventioners into town. The hotel haven is **Brandenburger Strasse,** on the less busy side of the Hauptbahnhof. Looking for last-minute deals during **Karneval** is foolish—book up to a year ahead and expect to pay a premium.

Altstadt-Nord

🏨 STATION HOSTEL FOR BACKPACKERS ♦⊛(ᵗᵖ) HOSTEL ❷
Marzellenstr. 44-56 ☎0221 912 53 01 🖳www.hostel-cologne.de

The most conveniently located hostel in Köln also boasts the best atmosphere, with chalkboards telling you about all the goings-ons around the city and knowledgeable staff quick to help you with whatever you need. The dorms are often not bunked, meaning you don't have to fumble around ladders in the middle of the night.

🍴 *From the Hauptbahnhof, take the Dompropst-Ketzer-Str. exit with the Dom to the left and the Rolex building to the right, and turn right behind the Rolex building onto Marzellenstr.* *i* *Linens and Wi-Fi included.* ⑨ *6-bed dorms €17; singles €32-39; doubles €44-55; triples €66-75; quads €80-88; quints €90.* 🕐 *Reception 24hr. Check-in 3pm. Check-out noon.*

Altstadt-Sud

🏨 HOSTEL KÖLN ♦🚽(ᵗᵖ)❄🔲 HOTEL ❸
Marsilstein 29 ☎0221 998 77 60 🖳www.hostel.ag

Sleek rooms, friendly reception, and a great location by Neumarkt make this hostel (though more like a hotel) a great deal for travelers. Although it's called a hostel because of the multiple-bed rooms, the place actually functions like a hotel: if you book a dorm you have to book the entire room. So come with friends, and enjoy your free breakfast on the rooftop balcony with some great views.

🍴 *U1, U3, U4, U7, U9, U16, or U18: Neumarkt, then head west and turn left onto Im Lach and right onto Marsilstein to hostel on right.* *i* *Breakfast, linens, and towels included. Free Wi-Fi and computers for guest use.* ⑨ *3- to 8-bed dorms from €24; singles from €45; doubles from €60.* 🕐 *Reception 24hr. Check-in 3pm. Check-out 11am.*

Neustadt

MEININGER CITY HOSTEL ♦⊛(ᵗᵖ)🍽 HOTEL ❷
Engelbertstr. 33-35 ☎0221 355 33 20 14 🖳www.meininger-hostels.com

This trendy hostel boasts a game room, lounge, cinema, and bar, along with a breakfast room decorated with chandeliers and velvet wallpaper. Rooms are quiet and clean, if not small, and all come with private bathrooms.

🍴 *U1, U7, U12, or U15: Rudolfpl., then exit station, turn left (south) onto Habsburgstr., right on Lindenstr., and left on Engelbertstr.* *i* *Breakfast €4.50. Linens included. Towels available with deposit. Free Wi-Fi in lobby; €5 per day in room.* ⑨ *8-bed dorms from €19; 3- to 6-bed dorms from €25; women-only 6-bed dorms €22; singles from €49; doubles from €68.* 🕐 *Reception 24hr. Check-in 3pm. Check-out 10am.*

SIGHTS 🔵

Altstadt-Nord

🏛 DOM ♦🚽❄ CATHEDRAL
Domkloster 3 🖳www.koelner-dom.de

This towering structure, which took over 600 years to build, has defined Köln

köln · sights

with its colossal spires since its completion in 1880. A canopied ceiling towering 44m above the floor, and 1350 sq. m of exquisite stained glass casting a harlequin display of colored light, the cathedral is the perfect realization of High Gothic style. Despite the endless construction that guarantees constant scaffolding along the ornate exterior, thousands of visitors flock to this landmark daily.

Begin your tour at the plaza out front where a conglomeration of street performers and camera-touting tourists interact. Directly opposite the front door, a scale replica of the cathedral's crowning pinnacles lets you marvel at their size. Enter the church and head to the choir, keeping to the right-hand side. The stained-glass window in the South Transept might look a little different than the others; called the **"pixel window"** by some, this piece of modern art was created in 2007 to replace the original destroyed in World War II, using a computer program to position squares of 72 different colors for a mystical effect. As you walk further toward the back of the cathedral, a small chapel houses a **15th-century triptych** painted by Stephen Lochner to represent the city's five patron saints: St. Ursula and her bevy of female attendants (a whopping 10,000 virgins, according to legend) dominate the left wing; St. Gereon is on the right; in the center, the Three Kings pay tribute to a newborn Christ. Continue along the back of the church to take a peek at the **Shrine of the Three Kings** inside the iron gates. On the left side of the choir is the **Chapel of the Cross,** which holds the 10th-century **Gero Crucifix,** the oldest intact sculpture of *Christus patiens* (a crucified and deceased Christ with eyes shut). Nearby, a doorway leads outside and a right turn will get you into the cavernous **Schatzkammer** (treasury), which holds clerical relics: thorn, cross, and nail bits, as well as liturgical vestments and pieces of 18 saints.

To ascend the tower, go back outside and turn left to head down the stairs. 15min. and 509 steps (100m) are all it takes to scale the **Südturmb** (south tower) and catch an impresive view of the city and river below, as well as a birdseye view of the inside of the cathedral itself. Catch your breath at the **Glockenstube** (about ¾ of the way up), a chamber for the tower's nine bells. Four of the bells date from the Middle Ages, but the 19th-century upstart known affectionately as **Der Große Peter** (at 24 tons, the world's heaviest swinging bell) is loudest.

*➜ By the Hauptbahnhof. **i** The Dom Forum (located across the street, ☎0221 92584720 💻www.domforum.de) organizes guided tours in English M-Sa 10:30am and 2:30pm, Su 2:30pm, €6, students €4. A 20min. film shown inside the Dom Forum building also gives an introduction to the cathedral, in German M-Sa noon, 1:30pm, 3pm, 4:30pm, Su 3pm and 4:30pm; in English M-Sa 11:30am and 3:30pm, Su 3:30pm; €2, students €1. $ Entry free. Schatzkammer €4, students €2; tower €2.50/1; combined €5/2.50. 🕐 Church open daily May-Oct 6am-9pm, Nov-Apr 6am-7:30pm. Schatzkammer open daily 10am-6pm. Tower open daily May-Sept 9am-6pm, Oct and Mar-Apr 9am-5pm, Nov-Feb 9am-4pm.*

✎ MUSEUM LUDWIG ✎♿❄ MUSEUM

Heinrich-Böll-Pl. ☎0221 22 12 61 65 💻www.museum-ludwig.de

This attractive museum features works by virtually every big-name artist of the 20th century, with displays of pop art, photography, and one of the world's largest Picasso collections. The museum also houses sculptures by artists more known for their paintings, including Picasso, Lichtenstein, and Warhol.

*➜ Behind the Dom to the right and the Römisch-Germanisches Museum. **i** Audio tour €3, or download the entire thing online before you go. $ €10, students €7. First Th of the month ½-price after 5pm. 🕐 Open Tu-Su 10am-6pm, first Th of the month 10am-10pm.*

✎ KOLUMBA ✎♿☁ MUSEUM

Kolumbastr. 4 ☎0221 933 19 30 💻www.kolumba.de

This enormous concrete building, constructed over the ruins of the Gothic cathedral St. Kolumba, is the art museum of the archbishop of Köln. On the ground floor, a cavernous room reveals the cathedral's excavation, where a bridge guides you along the rubble. Elsewhere in the museum, ancient relics and church artifacts are juxtaposed with modern secular works, all of them dramatically presented. Art aside, a gorgeous reading room with high-backed and comfortable leather chairs on the top floor invites you to sit and contemplate the art, or to peruse through their collection of art books and German literature.

🍴 *U3, U4: Appellhofpl., then walk through the Opern Passage and turn left onto Glockengasse and go a block past 4711.* ℹ *Free guidebooks available in English.* Ⓢ *€5, students €3, under 18 free.* ⏰ *Open M-Th 9am-noon and 2-6pm, F 9am-noon.*

EL-DE HAUS (NS-DOKUMENTATIONSZENTRUM) ✦⚬❀ MUSEUM
Appellhofpl. 23-25   ☎0221 2212 6332 🖳www.museenkoeln.de/ns-dok

The city's former Gestapo headquarters now educates visitors on the city's history under Nazi rule. Prison cells in the basement, once overcrowded with political wrong-doers and wrongly accused bystanders, have been meticulously preserved, and impart harrowing first-hand accounts of torture that prisoners inscribed into the walls. The inscriptions also include poems of protest, simple calendars, love letters, and self-portraits. The top floors exhibit stories and artifacts from Köln under the Third Reich.

🍴 *U3, U4, U16, or U18: Appellhofpl., then follow the signs.* ℹ *English explanations in the downstairs jail, but not in the upstairs exhibits. Audio tour €2.* Ⓢ *€3.60, students €1.50.* ⏰ *Open Tu-Su 11am-5pm.*

Altstadt-Sud

🏛 SCHOKOLADEN MUSEUM ✦⚬❀ MUSEUM
Am Schokoladenmuseum 1a   ☎0221 931 88 80 🖳www.schokoladenmuseum.de

Yes, it's every child's dream: a full-blown chocolate museum and factory! Yet beyond the demonstrations of how to make hollow chocolate balls and the mesmerizing packaging machine, the museum is surprisingly thorough and some sections even downright academic. The anthropologists will appreciate the numerous profiles of cocoa farmers, the activists the explanations of fair trade, and the economists the charts and figures of global chocolate price-setting. Much more than just a fun excuse to immerse yourself in chocolate, the museum is a great opportunity to learn just about everything (and then some) about your favorite food. Be sure to stop at the gold fountain, which spurts a stream of free samples.

🍴 *Bus #106 to Schokoladen Mueum, or walk south along the Rhein past the Deute Brucke and turn left onto the small footbridge.* ℹ *All explanations in English.* Ⓢ *€7.50, students €5.* ⏰ *Open Tu-F 10am-6pm, Sa-Su 11am-7pm. Last entry 1hr. before close.*

DEUTSCHES SPORT AND OLYMPIA MUSEUM ◉⚬ MUSEUM
Im Zollhafen 1   ☎0221 33 60 90 🖳www.sportsmuseum.info

Race through the history of German sportsmanship and the Olympic games in this interactive museum. Hands-on exhibits include a pommel horse, bicycle wind tunnel, boxing ring, and tiny turf soccer field on the roof. Extended exhibits also highlight the design and events of Germany's own Olympic games, 1936 in Berlin and 1972 in Munich. There's plenty of German memorabilia (think old sneakers and tennis racquets) displayed as well. No air conditioning means that it gets quite stuffy.

🍴 *Bus #106 to Schokoladen Mueum, or walk south along the Rhein past the Deute Brucke and turn left onto the small footbridge. The museum is behind the Schokoladen.* ℹ *Captions in English.* Ⓢ *€6, students €3.* ⏰ *Open Tu-F 10am-6pm, Sa-Su 11am-7pm.*

MUSEUM SCHNÜTGEN ✦⚬❀ MUSEUM
Cäcilienstr. 29-33   ☎0221 22 12 36 20 🖳www.museenkoeln.de/museum-schnuetgen

This museum opened in a brand new space in October 2010, showcasing one of the world's largest collections of medieval art from the early Middle Ages to

the end of the Baroque period. With over 5000 Romanesque and Gothic stone sculptures and 2000 works in silver, gold, ivory, and bronze, this museum is a bastion of ecclesiastical art from its very beginnings. Also included is an extensive collection of stained glass windows, tapestries, and priestly fashions.
➡ U1, U3, U4, U7, U9, U16, or U18: Neumarkt, then head east a tiny bit on Cäcilienstr. $ €5, students €3. ⏰ Open Tu-W 10am-6pm, Th 10am-8pm, Su 10am-6pm.

Neustadt

The Romanesque period saw the construction of 12 churches in a semi-circle around the Altstadt, each containing the holy bones of saints to protect the city. Though dwarfed by the splendor of the Dom, these churches attest to the glory and immense wealth of what was once the most important city north of the Alps. The most memorable, owing to its glorious imprints on the city skyline, is the **Groß St. Martin.** Near the Rathaus and the Altstadt, the church was re-opened in 1985 after near destruction in WWII. The interior is tiled with mosaics from the Middle Ages, and crypts downstairs house an esoteric collection of stones and diagrams *(An Groß St. Martin 9 ☎0221 257 79 24 $ Church free. Crypt €0.50. ⏰ Open Tu-F 10am-noon and 3-5pm, Sa 10am-12:30pm and 1:30-5pm, Su 2-4pm).* In addition, **St. Ursula,** north of the Dom, commemorates Ursula's attempts to maintain celibacy despite her betrothal. This was easier after she was struck by an arrow in 383 AD during an untimely attack in the midst of a Hunnish siege. Relics and more than 700 skulls line the walls of the Goldene Kammer *(Ursulapl. 24☎ 0221 13 34 00 $ Church free. Kammer €1, children €0.50. ⏰ Open M-Sa 10am-noon and 3-5pm, Su 3-4:30pm).* The other Romanesque churches include **St. Gereon** *(Gereonsdriesch 2-4),* **St. Cäcilien** *(Cäcilienstr. 29),***St. Maria im Kapitol** *(Marienpl. 19),* **Alt St. Alban** *(Martinstr. 39),* **St. Maria** *(An Lyskirchen 10),* **St. Georg** *(Georgspl. 17),* **St. Pantaleon** *(An Pantaleonsberg 2),* **St. Severin** *(Im Ferkulum 29),* **St. Kunibert** *(Kunibertsklosterg. 2),* and **St. Aposteln** *(Neumarkt 30).*

FOOD

Köln's local cuisine centers on sausage and *rievkooche*, slabs of fried potato to dunk in *apfelmus* (apple sauce). Don't pass through without sampling the city's smooth Kölsch beer, a local favorite whose shield adorns most bars. Local brews include Sion, Küppers, Früh, Gaffel, and Dom. They usually come in small 0.2L glasses for freshness, but don't worry—waiters are quick to refill. Cheap restaurants and cafes packed with students line the trendy **Zülpicher Str.** *(U9, U12, U15: Zülpicher Platz)* Mid-priced ethnic restaurants are concentrated around the perimeter of the Altstadt, particularly from **Hohenzollernring** to **Hohenstaufenring.** For groceries, head to **Rewe City** *(Hohenstaufenring 30, by Zülpicher Pl. ⏰ Open M-Sa 7am-midnight.)* or **Aldi Süd** *(Richmodstr. 31, by Neumarkt. ⏰ Open M-Sa 8am-8pm.)*

Altstadt-Nord

FRÜH AM DOM GERMAN [3]
Am Hof 18 ☎0221 2613-211 🖥www.frueh.de
It's enormous, it's right across the street from the Dom, and it's always filled with tourists, but even native Kölners will take their out-of-town guests to this massive beer hall for the epitome of the Köln experience. The excellent food is reasonably priced, and the terrace outside offers spectacular views of the Dom.
➡ By the south plaza of the Dom to its right. $ Entrees €4.10-23. Kölsch €1.60. ⏰ Open daily 8am-midnight.

Altstadt-Sud

TOSCANINI ITALIAN [2]
Jakobstr. 22 ☎0221 310 9990
Transport yourself to an Italian country villa with this restaurant, where your food comes out piping fresh from the stone oven. While stone oven pizzas are

all the rage in Germany, there are few that do them as well as Toscanini's; try the Rustica *(€8.90)*, a delicious combination of cheeses, serrano ham, and arugula. The subdued ambience means it's nice enough for a date, yet casual enough for jeans.

U3 or U4: Severinstr. Head south down Severinstr. and turn right onto Jakobstr. $ Entrees €5-20. ⏰ Open M-F noon-3pm and 6-11pm, Sa 6-11pm., Su noon-3pm and 6-11pm.

Neustadt

HABIBI FALAFEL — CAFE ❶

Zülpicherstr. 26 ☎0221 271 71 41 💻www.habibi-koeln.de

Cheap and hearty falafel *(€1.50)* and shawarma *(€3)* make this a popular student joint, especially on late nights after a few rounds of drinks. The falafel is always perfectly moist and the meat is perfectly juicy, and all entrees come with a free cup of tea.

U9, U12, or U15: Zülpicher Pl., then head down Zülpicherstr. to restaurant on right. $ Entrees €1.50-7.70. ⏰ Open M-Th 11am-1am, F-Sa 11am-3am, Su 11am-1am.

BEI OMA KLEINMANN — CAFE ❷

Zülpicherstr. 9 ☎0221 23 23 46 💻www.beiomakleinmann.de

Though the dear Oma Kleinmann who founded this popular schnitzel joint passed away in 2009, her spirit lives on. The framed prints of photos and other memorabilia from the '50s attest to the restaurant's vintage character; a plaque of sorts to the left of the bar with names of students who have eaten the most schnitzel attests to the place's popularity. A convivial atmosphere permeates the restaurant, so come by for dinner and a few obligatory glasses of Kölsch.

U9, U12, or U15: Zülpicher Pl., then head down Zülpicherstr. to restaurant on left. $ Schnitzel €9.90-12.80. Kölsch €1.40. ⏰ Open Tu-Su 5pm-1am. Kitchen open 5-11pm.

CAFE ORLANDO — CAFE ❷

Engelbertstr. 9 ☎0221 42 34 84 03 💻www.cafeorlando.de

This small cafe, decorated with a red-and-gold vintage French theme, is filled in the mornings with locals enjoying a lazy breakfast and the morning paper. Slow service make this a poor choice for frenzied see-it-all travelers, but a stop here for some coffee or a superbly fresh fruit bowl will not disappoint.

*U9, U12, or U15: Zülpicher Pl., then head down Zülpicher Pl. and turn right onto Engelbertstr. **i** Free Wi-Fi. $ Breakfast €3.30-7.50. Omelettes €5.50-5.80. Pasta entrees €5.50-6.80 ⏰ Open daily 9am-midnight.*

NIGHTLIFE

For a good time, head over to the Neustadt for your nightlife adventures; the closer to the Rhein or Dom you venture, the quicker your wallet will empty and the more tourists you're likely to encouter. After dark in Hohenzollernring, crowds of people move from theaters to clubs and finally to cafes in the early hours of the morning. Students congregate in the **Bermuda-Dreleck** (Bermuda Triangle), bounded by **Zülpicherplatz, Roonstr.,** and **Luxemburgstr.** The center of gay nightlife runs up **Matthiasstr.** to **Mülhenbach, Hohe Pforte, Marienplatz,** and up to the **Heumarkt** area by **Deutzer Brücke.** Radiating westward from Friesenpl., the **Belgisches Viertel** (Belgian Quarter) is dotted with more expensive bars and cafes.

Kölners will often visit four or five establishments in one night, and true to their wanderlust nature, a favorite pasttime includes grabbing bottles of beer at the numerous small **kiosks** that dot the streets, walking and drinking, then refilling at another kiosk. On summer nights, the **Brüsslerplatz** area in the shadow of the St. Michael Church is always packed with students on the prowl, with rowdiness that the city has imposed heavy fines against (look for the PSCHT! sign).

Altstadt-Nord

GLORIA

♠ ♿ ❤ ❀ ☎ ▼ BAR, CLUB, CAFE, THEATER

Apostelnstr. 11 ☎0221 66 06 30 ▣www.gloria-theater.com

A former movie theater, this popular local cafe, comedy theater, and occasional club is at the nexus of Köln's trendy gay and lesbian scene. Call or visit the website for a schedule of themed parties, which alternate between gay and mixed.

☞ *U1, U3, U4, U7, U9, U16, or U18: Neumarkt, then walk west towards the St. Apostein cathedral and follow Apostelnstr. as it curves to the right.* ⓢ *Cover €7-30, may include show ticket. Beer €1.60-4.70. Cocktails €6.50.* ☼ *Open M-Sa 10am-11pm, until 5am on party nights. General ticket office open M-F noon-6pm.*

Neustadt

DAS DING

☺❀⊗❤ CLUB

Hohenstaufenring 30-32 ☎0221 24 63 48 ▣www.dingzone.de

This smoky, eclectic student bar and disco has dirt-cheap specials *(often under €1, F-Sa 10-11pm)* and themed parties parties. The required student ID at the door keeps the age down and the party hopping.

☞ *U9, U12, or U15: Zülpicher Pl.* ⓢ *Cover €3-5. Almost all drinks under €3.* ☼ *Open Tu 9pm-3am, W 9pm-2am, Th 10pm-3am, F-Sa 10pm-4am.*

DIE WOHNGEMEINSCHAFT

♠⊗❤❀ CLUB

Richard-Wagner-Strasse 39 ☎0221 39 75 77 18 ▣www.die-wohngemeinschaft.net

Meet your newest housemates, and sit in the rooms of Annabel, Mai Li, Easy, and JoJo at this novelty club, meant to give 20-somethings the nostalgia of dorms and shared apartments. Annabel's cutesy white bed with floral sheets is the perfect setting for a girl-talk, while Mai Li's room has a ping pong table where you can practice her favorite hobby, and the backseat of JoJo's vintage mini-bus is the perfect place for a bit of privacy (ahem).

☞ *U1, U7, U12, or U15: Rudolfpl., then walk south 1 block to Richard-Wagner-Str. and head west.* ⓢ *Beer €1.60. Mixed drinks €5-6.* ☼ *Open daily 3pm-2am.*

ARTS AND CULTURE

🎵

Köln explodes with festivity during **Karneval** *(late Jan-early Feb)*, a week-long pre-Lenten "farewell to flesh." Celebrated in the hedonistic spirit of the city's Roman past, Karneval is made up of 50 neighborhood processions in the weeks before Ash Wednesday. The festivities kick off with **Weiberfastnacht** *(Mar 1, 2011; Feb 28, 2012)*, where the mayor mounts the platform at Alter Markt and abdicates city leadership to the city's *Weiber* (a regional, untranslatable, and unabashedly politically incorrect term for women). In a demonstration of power, women then traditionally find their husbands at work and chop off their ties. In the afternoon, the first of the big parades begins at **Severinstor.** The weekend builds up to the out-of-control parade on **Rosenmontag,** the last Monday before **Lent** *(Mar. 7, 2011; Mar. 5, 2012)*. Everyone dresses in costume and gives and gets a couple dozen *Bützchen* (*Kölsche* dialect for a kiss on the cheek). While most revelers nurse their hangovers on **Shrove Tuesday,** pubs and restaurants set fire to straw scarecrows hanging out of their windows.

For shows, get your tickets from **KölnTicket** *(*☎*0221 2801▣www.koelnticket.de)*, which has multiple locations throughout the city, most notably in the basement of the **Tourist Office** in the same building as the **Römisch-Germanisches Museum.**

OPER DER STADT KÖLN & KÖLNER SCHAUSPIELHAUS

♠♿❀ OPERA, THEATER

Offenbachpl. ☎0221 22 12 84 00 ▣www.buehnenkoeln.de

These two venues, part of the same complex, form Köln's cultural center and are home to the city's opera and theater companies. Both are under plans for

germany

major renovation to begin sometime in the next few years, but don't worry—the companies will just move to alternate venues.

🚏 U3 or U4: Appellhofpl. $ Open €10-70, students €10 or 50% off. Schauspielhaus €9-33, students €6. ⏰ Box office open M-F 10:30am-7pm, Sa 11am-4pm.

KÖLN PHILHARMONIE ♿ ❄ ORCHESTRA

Bischofsgartenstr. 1 ☎0221 221 20 40 80 🖳www.koelner-philharmonie.de

This amphitheater is home to the Köln's very own symphony orchestra. During the normal season, come by on Thursdays at 12:30pm for PhilharmonieLunch, a free 30min. concert. When the orchestra goes on break over the summer, the Kölner Sommerfestival takes over, staging opera and popular musicals on tour.

🚏 Behind the Römisch-Germanisches Museum and Museum Ludwig. $ Prices vary for each concert; students get a 25% discount. Tickets includes local public transportation 4hr. before and 4hr. after the concert.

ESSENTIALS

Practicalities

- **TOURIST OFFICE: KölnTourismus.** *(Kardinal-Höffner-Platz 1, right across from the Dom. ☎0221 221 🖳www.cologne-tourism.de **i** The basement contains a souvenir shop and a Ticket Office. Several companies have hop-on hop-off bus tours for about €15; inquire in the tourist office. $ City maps (€0.20) and guides (€0.50) and books rooms for a €3 fee. Do-it-yourself 1.5hr.* ***iGuide*** *€8 per 4hr. English-language walking tour €9, students €7. ⏰ Open M-Sa 9am-8pm, Su 10am-5pm, to 6pm in summer. 1.5hr. English-language walking tour every Sa at 1pm.)*
- **BUDGET TRAVEL: STA Travel.** *(Zülpicher Str. 178 ☎0221 44 20 11 🚏 U9: Universität. **i** Sells ISICs and books flights. ⏰ Open M-F 10am-7pm, Sa 11am-3pm.)*
- **CURRENCY EXCHANGE: Reisebank.** *(In the Hauptbahnhof. ⏰ Open daily 7am-10pm.)* Inside the tourist office is also **Exchange.** *(⏰ Open M-F 9am-6pm, Sa 9am-4pm.)*
- **WOMEN'S RESOURCES: Frauenamt.** *(Markmannsgasse 7 ☎0221 26482 ⏰ Open M-F 8am-4pm, Tu 8am-6pm, F 8am-midnight.)*
- **ROOM SHARE: Zeitwohnen** arranges furnished apartments for 1 month to 3 years. *(Konrad-Adenauer-Str. 4 ☎0221 8002340 🖳www.zeitwohnen.de ⏰ Office open M-F 9am-6pm.)*
- **LAUNDROMAT: Eco-Express Waschsalon.** *(At the corner of Richard-Wagner-Str. and Händelstr. $ Wash 6-10am €1.90, 10am-11pm €2.50. Soap €0.50. Dry €0.50 per 10min. ⏰ Open M-Sa 6am-11pm.)*
- **GAY AND LESBIAN RESOURCES: SchwIPS Checkpoint.** *(Pininstr. 7, just around the corner from Hotel Timp. ☎0221 92 57 68 11 🖳www.checkpoint-koeln.de **i*** **Emergency helpline.** *☎0221 19228. ⏰ Open W-Th 5-9pm, F-Sa 2-7pm, Su and holidays 2-6pm.*
- **INTERNET ACCESS:** Most cafes have free wireless, including the **Starbucks** in the Hauptbahnhof. **Gigabyte.** *(Across the street from the Hauptbahnhof. $ 24hr. internet terminals €2.79 per hr. Wireless €0.50 per hr.)*
- **POST OFFICE:** *(Trankgasse 11, right by the Hauptbahnhof. ⏰ Open M-Sa 7am-10pm, Su 8am-10pm.)*
- **POSTAL CODE:** 50667.

Emergency!

- **POLICE:** ☎110.
- **FIRE AND AMBULANCE:** ☎112.
- **PHARMACY: Dom Apotheke.** *(In the courtyard between the Dom and the Hauptbahnhof. ⏰ Open M-F 8am-8pm, Sa 9am-8pm.)*

Getting There

By Plane

Köln-Bonn Flughafen. *(Halfway between Köln and Bonn. The S13 runs between the Köln Hauptbahnhof and the airport every 20-30min. 🖥www.koeln-bonn-airport.de ℹ Flight information ☎02203 4040 0102.)*

By Train

The Köln **Hauptbahnhof** is centrally located right by the Dom in the Altstadt-Nord. Trains to: **Berlin** *($ €60-115. ⏰ 5-8hr., 1-2 per hr.)*; **Frankfurt** *($ €30-90. ⏰1-3hr., 2 per hr.)*; **Bonn** *($ €7-12. ⏰ 0.25-1hr., 4-5 per hr.)*; **Munich** *($ €70-150. ⏰ 5hr., 2 per hr.)*; **Amsterdam, NED** *($€30-55. ⏰ 3-4hr., 2 per hr.)*; **Brussels, BEL** *($ €40-80. ⏰ 2-4hr., 13 per day)*; **London, GBR** *($ €70-130. ⏰ 5hr., 7 per day)*; **Basel, CHE** *($ €60-140. ⏰ 4-6hr., 1 per hr.)*; **Vienna, AUT** *($ €60-180. ⏰ 8-12hr., 1 per hr.)*.

Getting Around

By Public Transportation

Köln's buses, trams, and subways are served by the KVB, or Kölner Verkehrs-Betriebe *(🖥www.kvb-koeln.de)*. A short ride (less than 4 stops) is €1.60, kids 6-14 €0.90. A ride anywhere in the city is €2.40, kids €1.20, and the prices increase with farther distance. You can also get 4 tickets at a time for a cheaper price *(€8.60, kids €4.50)*, or get a day ticket *(€7.10, €10.40 for up to 5 people)*. Validate your tickets at the start of your trip by getting them stamped in the rectangular box. If you're caught without a ticket, you face an immediate €40 fine.

By Ferry

Köln-Düsseldorfer. *(☎0221 2088318 🖥www.k-d.com ℹ Boats leave from the dock in the Altstadt halfway between the Deutzer and Hohenzollern bridges. Offers trips up and down the Rhein. $ A trip all the way to the end at Mainz is €52.50, with return €58.50. Trips to Bonn €12.80/€14.90. Students ½-price with ID. 1hr. panoramic cruises up and down the Rhein along the Köln area €7.80 per person. 2hr. afternoon cruises €11.10. ⏰ 1hr. panoramic cruises daily Apr-Oct at 10:30am, noon, 2, and 6pm. 2hr. afternoon cruises leave at 3:30pm.)*

By Gondola

Kölner Seilbahn sells gondolas trips on the Rhein from the Zoo to the Theinpark across the river. *(Rhiehlerstr. 180, U18: Zoo/Flora. ☎0221 547 4184 🖥www.koelner-seilbahn.de $ €4, children ages 4-12 €2.40; round trip €6/3.50. ⏰ Open Apr-Oct daily 10am-6pm.)*

By Bike

Kölner Fahrradverleih rents bikes. *(Makmannsgasse, in the Altstadt. ☎0171 629 87 96 🖥www.koelnerfahrradverleih.de $ €2 per hr., €10 per day, €40 per week. ⏰ Open daily 10am-6pm.)*

By Car

Ride Share: CityNetz Mitfahrzentrale. *(Maximinenstr. 2. ☎0221 19444 ⏰ Open M-F 9am-6pm, Sa-Su 10am-2pm.)🚇 U70, U74, U75, U76, U77, U78, U79, Tram 706, 713, or 715: Heinrich-Heine-Allee. $ Novels from €1.50. h Open Tu-Su 10am-8pm.)*

Hamburg is a city of paradoxes. One of the most historic port cities in northern Europe, Hamburg is over 100km from the North Sea. A city of old money, beautiful churches, and an extravagantly ornate **Rathaus** are mere miles away from camps of the homeless and unemployed set up under stone bridges. Some of Germany's renowned orchestras and symphonies share a 3km radius with the unapologetically trashy strip joints and erotic shops on the infamous **Reeperbahn.** The only constant is the Elbe, tying Hamburg to the world. Massive commercial ships and a crane-studded industrial district just across the Elbe from Hamburg bring global products and people. Portugese and Turkish immigrants coalesce in the west, in Altona and Schanzeenviertel, and tapas bars and falafel stands stand side-by-side with Irish pubs and German breweries. Hamburg's notable **Altstadt,** recognizable by its mammoth churches and towering spires, is split by canals, streams, and bridges at every bend. A total of 2,479 bridges connect Hamburg, out-bridging Venice.

Any visitor will note the tragedies left by the Great Fire of 1842 and the devastating Allied WWII bombing. In a single night in July of 1943, air raids simultaneously leveled the city and killed over 50,000 tenants in the crowded buildings lining the waterfront. As a result, many of the architectural masterpieces that once filled the city are lost. Fortunately, a massive 1960s reconstruction effort restored many of Hamburg's beloved buildings, including the **Große Michaeliskirche,** an aqua-blue and gold-gilded oceanic masterpiece of a church. In shocking contrast to this opulence are the coal-black ruins of St. Nikolai, whose dark Gothic spire is a reminder of the cost of war. Despite it's cautioning remembrances, Hamburg has seen changes like the St. Georg district, which today is home to a flourishing gay community. And, of course, Hamburg is incomplete without the 🎵**Beatles.** The music legends performed here pre-fame, and so the city has become a magnet for independent musical artists.

ORIENTATION

Hamburg lies on the northern bank of the **Elbe** river, 100km south of the North Sea. The city's **Altstadt,** full of old buildings and mazes of canals, lies north of the Elbe and south of the **Alster lakes.** Of the two Alster lakes, **Binnenalster,** the much smaller of the two, is located in the heart of the Altstadt, bordered by Jungfernstieg to the south and Ballindamm to the West. The much larger **Außenalster,** popular for sailing in the summer and skating in the winter, is slightly further north, just separated from the Binnenalster by the **Kennedybrücke.** Five beautiful churches, whose spires spear the Hamburg skyline, outline Hamburg's Altstadt. Anchoring the center of the Altstadt is the palacial **Rathaus,** the ornate town hall, and **Rathaus market,** home to political protests and farmers' markets alike. **Alsterfleet canal** bisects the downtown area and separates Altstadt on the eastern bank from the Neustadt on the west. The city's best museums, galleries, and theaters are located within these two districts.

The **Hauptbahnhof** lies at the eastern edge of the city center, along Steintorwall. Starting from the Kirchenallee exit of the Hauptbahnhof, Hamburg's unofficial gay district, **St. Georg,** follows the **Lange Reihe** eastward, where quiet cafes populate the streets. Outside the Hauptbahnhof's main exit on Sheintorwall is the **Kunstmelle** (Art Mile), a row of museums extending southward from the Alster lakes to the banks of the Elbe. Perpendicular to Seintorwall, **Mönickebergstraße,** Hamburg's most famous shopping street, runs westward to the **Rathause,** which connects the city center to the train station. The Neustadt's **Hanseviertel,** between Rathausmarkt and Gänsemarkt, is full of shops, galleries, and auction houses. Hanseviertel is striped with canals, giving the area a Venetian glamour.

Just south of the Rathaus, **St. Pauli** houses large stretches of walkways along the

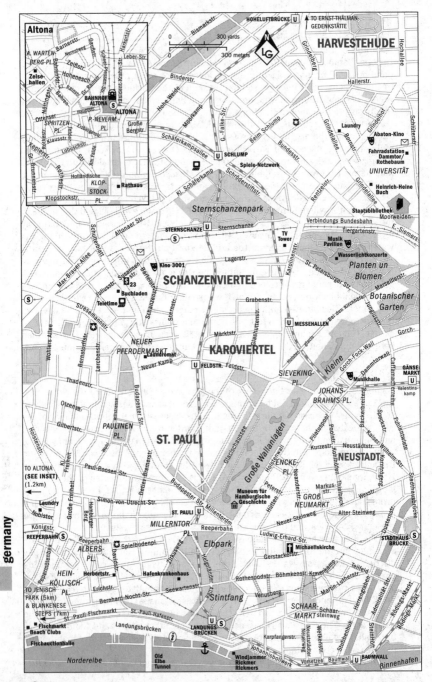

Altona

0 | 300 yards
0 | 300 meters

A. WARTEN-BERG-PL.

Zeise-hallen

SPRITZEN-PL.

KLOP-STOCK-PL.

Rathaus

Klopstockstr.

BAHNHOF ALTONA

ALTONA

P.-NEVERM.-PL.

HOHELUFTBRÜCKE

TO ERNST-THÄLMAN-GEDENKSTÄTTE

HARVESTEHUDE

Bismarckstr.

Binderstr.

Hohe Weide

Moorkamp

G.-Falke-Str.

Beim Schlump

Bundesstr.

SCHLUMP

Spiele-Netzwerk

Laundry

Abaton-Kino

Fahrradstation Dammtor/Rothebaum

UNIVERSITÄT

Heinrich-Heine Buch

Staatsbibliothek

Sternschanzenpark

Schäferkampsallee

Kl. Schäferkamp

Schröderstiftstr.

STERNSCHANZE

Sternschanze

TV Tower

Lagerstr.

Musik Pavillon

Wasserlichtkonzerte

Planten un Blomen

Botanischer Garten

Kine 3001

SCHANZENVIERTEL

Buchladen

Teletime

23

Grabenstr.

MESSEHALLEN

NEUER PFERDERMARKT

Laundromat

Neuer Kamp

FELDSTR. Feldstr.

KAROVIERTEL

Marktstr.

Kleine

Gorch-Fock-Wall

SIEVEKING-PL.

Musikhalle

GÄNSE-MARKT

JOHANS BRAHMS-PL.

PAULINEN PL.

ST. PAULI

Große Wallanlagen

NEUSTADT

TO ALTONA (SEE INSET) (1.2km)

Laundry

Nobistor

Königstr.

REEPERBAHN

ALBERS-PL.

Paul-Roosen-Str.

Simon-von-Utrecht-Str.

ST. PAULI

MILLERNTOR PL.

Reeperbahn

Spielbudenpl.

HEIN-KÖLLISCH-PL.

Herbertstr.

Hafenkrankenhaus

TO JENISCH PARK (5km) & BLANKENESE STEPS (7km)

Fischmarkt Beach Clubs

Fischauctionhalle

St.-Pauli-Fischmarkt

Norderelbe

Old Elbe Tunnel

LANDUNGS BRÜCKEN

Windjammer Rickmer Rickmers

Elbpark

Stintfang

Museum für Hamburgische Geschichte

GROSS NEUMARKT

Michaeliskirche

SCHAAR-MARKT

BAUMWALL

Binnenhafen

germany

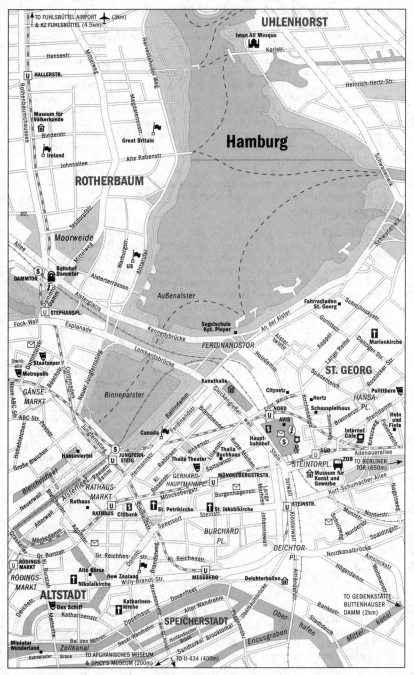

TO FUHLSBÜTTEL AIRPORT (3km)
& KZ FUHLSBÜTTEL (4.5km)

UHLENHORST

Iman Ali Mosque

Karlstr.

Hansastr.

Mittelweg

Harvestehuder Weg

Heinrich-Hertz-Str.

HALLERSTR.

Rothenbaumchaussee

Magdalenenstr.

Museum für
Völkerkunde

Binderstr.

Great Britain

Hamburg

Ireland

Johnsallee

Alte Rabenstr.

Schwanenwik

ROTHERBAUM

Str.

Tesdorfstr.

Moorweide

Allee

Mittelweg

Warburgstr.

Alsterufer

US

Schwanenwik

Bahnhof
Dammtor

Alsterterrassen

DAMMTOR

Außenalster

Fahrradladen
St. Georg

Schmilinskystr.

STEPHANSPL.

Alsterglacis

Fock-Wall

Esplanade

Kennedybrücke

Segelschule
Kpt. Pieper

An der Alster

Gurlittstr.

Koppel

Danziger Str.

Marienkirche

Lombardsbrücke

FERDINANDSTOR

Alster-
twiete

Lange Reihe

Rostocker Str.

Drehb-
ahn

Staatsoper

Metropolis

Neue ABC-Str.

**GÄNSE-
MARKT**

ABC-Str.

Colonnaden

Neuer Jungfernstieg

Binnenalster

Holzdamm

Kunsthalle

Ballindamm

Ferdinandstr.

Brandstwiete

Glockengießer-
wall

Citynetz

Spadenteich

Ernst-Merck-Str.

NORD

AVIS

Haupt-
bahnhof

Hertz

Schauspielhaus

Kirchenallee

Brennerstr.

Steindamm

**HANSA-
PL.**

Politthburo

Internet
Cafe

Hein
und
Fiete

ST. GEORG

SÜD

Adenauerallee

Hansaviertel

Große Bleichen

Hohe Bleichen

Jungfernstieg

**JUNGFERN-
STIEG**

Canada

Hermannstr.

Kl. Rosenstr.

Gr. Rosenstr.

Rosenstr.

Thalia
Buchhaus

Thalia Theater

Spitalerstr.

Kurze Mühren

Steintorwall

STEINTORPL.

ZOB

TO BERLINER
TOR (650m)

Bleichenfleet

Alsterfleet

Ressen-
damm

**RATHAUS-
MARKT**

*GERHARD-
HAUPTMANNPL.*

MÖNCKEBERGSTRSTR.

Mönckebergstr.

Burgenhagenstr.

Museum für
Kunst und
Gewerbe

Kurt-Schumacher-Allee

Neuerwall

Altstwall

Rathaus

RATHAUS

Citibank

St. Petrikirche

St. Jakobikirche

Steinstr.

Lange Mühren

Klosterwall

STEINSTR.

Nagelsweg

Mönkedamm

Gr. Burstah

Agrafstr.

Speersort

*BURCHARD
PL.*

Johanniswall

Münzstr.

Norderstr.

Spaldingstr.

Graskeller

Kl. Burstah

Gr. Reichenstr.

Donstr.

Brandstwiete

Kl. Reichenstr.

*DEICHTOR-
PL.*

Nordkanalbrücke

Högerdamm

Amsinckstr.

Spaliwstr.

Wollinerstr.

**RÖDINGS-
MARKT**

RÖDINGS
MARKT

Alte Börse

New Zealand

Willy-Brandt-Str.

MESSBERG

Deichtorhallen

Altlandstr.

TO GEDENKSTÄTTE
BUTTENHAUSER
DAMM (2km)

ALTSTADT

Nikolaikirche

Deichstr.

Das Schiff

Katharinen-
kirche

Dovenfleet

Alter Wandrahm

Stadtdeich

Bankstr.

Katharinenstr.

Deichtorstr.

Zippelhaus

SPEICHERSTADT

Hollandischer
Brook

*Ober-
hafen*

Ericusgraben

Miniatur
Wunderland

Zollkanal

Kehrwieder

Brook

Bei den Mühren

Neuer Wandrahm

Sandtorkai

Brooktorkai

Pickhuben

Oberbaumbrücke

Holzbrücke

Kleiner
Grasbrook

Mittel-
kanal

TO AFGHANISCHES MUSEUM
& SPICY'S MUSEUM (200m)

TO U-434 (400m)

hamburg · orientation

industrial Elbe, the **Landungsbrücke,** and the weekly Hamburg **fischmarkt.** Also in St. Pauli is the infamous **Reeperbahn,** running parallel to the river, packed with strip joints and erotic shops. To the north of St. Pauli, students and academics inhabit the **Dammtor** district, home to Hamburg's university and the Planten un Blomen botanical gardens. The city's wealthiest neighborhoods, including **Winterhunde** and **Harvesthude,** are just opposite Dammtor on the shores of the lake. Farther west, **Schanzenviertel** is a more liberal community of students, artists, and sizable immigrant populations. Here, rows of street-art-covered restaurants and a busy late-night bar scene impart the area's new-found edge. On the westernmost side of Hamburg, **Altona** celebrates with a nightlife and restaurant scene similar to Schanzenviertel. The area was an independent city ruled by Denmark in the 17th century before eventually being absorbed by Hamburg. Altona's pedestrian zone, the **Ottenser Hauptstrasse,** runs west from the Altona station. To the far east of Hamburg lies one of the city's most important, if distant sights. The former concentration camp, **KZ Neuengamme,** is now a memorial to victims of forced labor in World War II. On the extreme opposite side of the city past Altona, **Klein-Flottbek** has two of Hamburg's most beautiful museums, set in the scenic **Jenisch Park** along the Elbe.

ACCOMMODATIONS

INSTANT SLEEP — HOSTEL ❶

Max-Brauer-Allee 27 ☎040 43 18 23 10 www.instantsleep.de

Bright, spotless dorms, colorful murals, and personal lockers in every room for safety ensure what the name promises. The real highlight, which causes more staying up than the opposite, is the common room complete with foosball table, hammocks, benches, and a comfortable loft for lounging. A young backpacking crowd gathers here every morning and evening for socializing.

U3, S11, S21, or S31: Sternschanze. [i] Sheets included. Free Wi-Fi and Internet at guest terminals. $ Dorms €16.50; singles €31; doubles €45; triples €62. ⏰ Reception W-Sa 8am-2am, Su-Tu 8am-11pm. Check-in 3-8pm; call ahead if you're arriving outside these hours. Check-out 11am.

SCHANZENSTERN ÜBERNACHTUNGS-UND GASTHAUS — HOSTEL ❷

Bartelsstr. 12 ☎040 439 84 41 www.schanzenstern.de

In the middle of the upbeat Schanzenviertel, this guesthouse has bright, hotel-like rooms on the upper floors of a converted pen factory. Big windows look out over the red-tiled rooftops of Hamburg, and the hostel shares a block with an independent film theater. The hostel owns a laid-back adjoining cafe with a shady courtyard and porch swings. All showers ensuite.

U3, S11, S21, or S31: Sternschanze. [i] Breakfast €4.50-6.50. Laundry €5. Sheets included. Free Internet terminals for guests, Wi-Fi €2 per hr. $ Dorms €19; singles €38.50; doubles €54; triples €64; quads €78; quints €95. ⏰ Reception 6:30am-2am. Check-out 11am.

SCHANZENSTERN ALTONA — HOSTEL ❷

Kleiner Rainstr. 24-26 ☎040 39 91 91 91 www.schanzenstern-altona.dess

On a quiet residential street, this bright hostel is filled with light from the common area's full wall of windows looking over the adjacent courtyard. Spacious rooms with pine beds and ensuite baths.

S1, S2, S3, S11 or S31: Altona. [i] Wi-Fi €2 per hr., Internet on guest terminals free. Sheets included. Breakfast €6.50. $ Dorms €19; singles €44; doubles €59-69; triples €74; quads €84; apartments €79-100. ⏰ Reception 7am-11pm. Check-out 11am.

SIGHTS

PLANTEN UN BLOMEN — BOTANICAL GARDEN

Next to the Hamburg Messe. ☎040 428 23 21 25 www.plantenunblomen.hamburg.de

This perfect mix of manicured gardens, tranquil lily-pad laden ponds, and wide expanses of grassy lawns is enjoyed by newspaper readers, picnickers and sun worshippers alike. Wander for miles through scenic paths overgrown with lavender bushes, or sit on white wooden chairs under the shade of towering chestnut trees. Planten un Blomen also contains the largest **Japanese Garden** in Europe, a rose garden with over 300 varieties of blooms, and a botanical garden with an exotic variety of plants. Children or the young at heart can play on three playgrounds,a water slide, trampoline, minigolf, or water-jet soccer. For the more serious Harry Potter enthusiast, a giant, though inanimate chess set is the arena of many a blood-thirsty competition. Daily performances by groups ranging from Irish step dancers to Hamburg's police choir fill the outdoor Musikpavillion at 3pm from May to September. The nightly **Wasserlichtkonzerte** draws crowds to the lake with choreographed fountains and underwater lights.

S21 or S31: Dammtor. ⏰ Open May-Sept 7am-11pm, Oct-Apr 7am-8pm. Japanese Garden open Mar-Oct M-F 9am-4:45pm, Sa-Su 10am-5:45pm; Nov-Feb M-F 9am-3:45pm, Sa-Su 10am-3:45pm. Wasserlichtkonzerte May-Aug. nightly 10pm, Sept. 9pm.

MUSEUM FÜR KUNST UND GEWERBE — MUSEUM

Steintorpl. 1 ☎040 42 81 34 🖥www.mkg-hamburg.de

This museum of applied arts sets the tone for it's collection with a hammock hanging between two fake palms in a plexiglass bubble suspended above the entrance. Quirky Art Nouveau pieces will have you asking, "Is this art?," but enjoying the absurdity of foam cactuses all the same. More conventional and equally impressive are the extensive photography exhibits on the first floor, featuring post-war German photographers. Another hall contains over 430 historical keyboard instruments including harpsichords, clavichords, and hammer-klaviers all the way up to the modern piano, and another exhibit traces the history of porcelain through region, which an expansive array of Asian pottery.

Walk 1 block south from the Hauptbahnhof. $ €8, students €5, children under 18 free. ⏰ Open Tu-Su 11am-6pm, Th from 11am-9pm.

HAMBURGER KUNSTHALLE (HALL OF ART) — ART MUSEUM

Glockengießerwall ☎040 428 13 12 09 🖥www.hamburger-kunsthalle.de

It would take days to fully appreciate all the world-class art displayed in the expansive Kunsthalle, one of the best art museums in Germany. The collection is organized chronologically. Old Masters and 19th century work is on the upper levels, prints and drawings downstairs, and a contemporary art collection is in the adjacent Galerie der Gegenwart. An impressive French Impressionist and German Realist collection is a can't-miss, especially the gigantic Renoir canvases. The revolving exhibitions in the Galerie der Gegenwart are one of the museum's biggest highlights.

Turn right from the "Sitalerstr./City" exit of the Hauptbahnhof and cross the street. The Kunsthalle is identifiable by its domed ceiling. $ €10, €5 students, under 18 free. ⏰ Open Tu-W 10am-6pm, Th 10am-9pm, F-Su 10am-6pm.

RATHAUS — TOWN HALL

Accessible from Bergerstr. ☎040 428 31 24 70

With more rooms than Buckingham Palace, the 1897 Hamburg Rathaus, which replaced the one that was burned down in the Great Fire of 1842, is an ornate stone-carved monument to Hamburg's long history as a wealthy port city. Its lavish chambers, accessible only through a worthwhile guided tour, are furnished with expansive murals and mind-blowingly designed chandeliers. The building still serves as the seat of both city and state government, while the Rathausmarkt out front hosts a slew of festivities, from political demonstrations to medieval fairs.

U3: Rathaus. $ Tours €3. ⏰ Only accessible on a tour. English tours run M-F at 11:15am, 1:15pm and 3:15pm, Sa 11:15 and 1:15, and Su 11:15am, 1:15pm, 3:15pm, and 5:15pm. Tours don't run on days that the state government convenes, so call ahead.

DEICHTORHALLEN HAMBURG — ART MUSEUM

Deichtorstr. 1-2 ☎040 32 10 30 💻www.deichtorhallen.de

Hamburg's contemporary art scene thrives in these two former fruit markets, which house rotating photography, painting, sculpture and film installations. The south hall features photography, while the north hall divides its attention among several creative mediums. Both halls are worth the trip, but check ahead to find what exhibit you'll be visiting—some are more "experimental" than others.

🚉 *U1: Steinstr. Follow signs from the U-Bahn station.* $ *Each building €7, students €5, families €9.50. Combination ticket to both halls €12/8/16.50, or €4.50 Tu after 4pm. Under 18 free.* ⏰ *Open Tu-Su 11am-6pm.*

FISCHMARKT — FISH MARKET

Große Elbstraße 137 ☎040 38 01 21 💻www.fischmarkt-hamburg.de

A Hamburg tradition since 1703, the Su morning Fishmarkt is an anarchic mix of vocal vendors hawking fish, produce, flowers, and clothing. Early risers mix with Reeperbahn partyers fresh from a long night out at clubs and bars. Make yourself the least conventional breakfast you'll ever have: fish and beer just as the sun's coming up. Everything's delicious and cheap. Bands of all genres entertain shoppers with loud rock music from the stages of the beautiful three-story brick and stained-glass fish auction hall, but the real action is outside.

🚉 *S1, S3 or U3: Landugsbrücken.* ⏰ *Open Apr-Oct Su 5-9:30am, Nov-Mar Su 7-9:30am.*

OUTSIDE CENTRAL HAMBURG

Hamburg's sights are fascinating and varied, but many of the most unique attractions are located away from the city center; making it to one of these can carve out a good chunk of your day.

KZ-GEDENKSTÄTTE NEUENGAMME — CONCENTRATION CAMP

Jean-Dolidier-Weg 75 ☎040 428 13 15 00 💻www.kz-gedenkstaette-neuengamme.de

Between 1938 and 1945, this camp held 110,000 people as forced laborers. Close to half the occupants died from overwork or execution. Walk around the camp buildings, from the cafeteria to the dorms to the work-camps, and the thoughtful, well-presented and heart-wrenching exhibits of Neuengamme's former prisoners. Several paths lead from the meticulously labeled multilingual main exhibition, which features recorded stories from survivors, and a series of red photo albums, each detailing the life of one of Neuengamme's victims. Outside, follow a path through to the brick-making factory, labor barracks, and war memorials.

🚉 *S21: Bergedorf (about 20min.), then bus #227 or #327: KZ-Gedenkstätte, Aussellung (about 35min.). Buses leave the train station and the camp every 30min., Su every 2hr.* $ *Free.* ⏰ *Museum and memorial open Apr-Sept M-F 9:30am-4pm, Sa-Su noon-7pm; Oct-Mar M-F 9:30am-4pm, Sa-Su noon-5pm. Paths open 24hr. Tours in German Su noon and 2:30pm.*

FOOD

LA SEPIA — SEAFOOD ❶

Schulterblatt 36 ☎040 432 24 84 💻www.la-sepia.de

This Spanish and Portuguese restaurant serves some of the most affordable and generously served seafood in town. See your meal prepared in front of you fresh from the harbor. The lunch special *(€4-6)* is a steal; try the grilled salmon, served with potato soup and a heaping side of (more!) potatoes and vegetables.

🚉 *U3, S11, S21, or S31: Sternschanze.* $ *Entrees €7.50-22.* ⏰ *Open daily noon-3am.*

HATARI PFÄLZER CANTINA — GERMAN ❷

Schanzenstr. 2 ☎040 43 20 88 66

This eclectic restaurant is decorated with Chinese **dragons** and hunting trophies. A young student crowd flocks here for hamburgers *(€7.30-7.90)* and

people watching on this busy street corner. Hatari also serves German specialties, including the misleadingly-named French pizza, a Bavarian dish of thin
cooked dough spread with cream and piled with toppings.

⚑ *U3 or S11, S21, or S31 to "Sternschanze."* Ⓢ *Entrees from €7.* Ⓣ *Open noon-late.*

HIN & VEG
⊛Ⓨ⌂ VEGETARIAN ❶

Schulterblatt 16
☎040 594 534 02

If you've been holding back on trying the meat-heavy German classics, this
is your chance to fill up on some Deutschland staples served up by an Indian
owner. Hin & Veg is a completely meat-free restaurant that serves up vegetarian
versions of *currywurst (€3)* and *döner (€4),* all with vegan sauces.

⚑ *U3, S11, S21, or S31: Sternschanze.* Ⓢ *South Asian specialties €5.50-8.50.* Ⓣ *Open M-Th
11:30am-11:30pm, F-Sa 11:30am-midnight, Su 12:30pm-10pm.*

OMAS APOTHEK
⊛Ⓨ⌂ FUSION ❷

Schanzenstr. 87
☎040 43 66 20

Omas serves up large meals at low prices in a retro-themed bar, outfitted with
floral wallpaper and the apothecary drawers that give the restaurant its name.
The food is as eclectic as the decor; a mix of German, Italian and American cuisine, and some of the friendliest bar staff on Schanzenstraße, draws in a relaxed
crowd of all ages. A popular pick is the breakfast platters, served M-F 9am-noon,
and Sa-Su 9-3pm *(€7.30, students €6.30).*

⚑ *U3, S11, S21, or S31: Sternschanze.* Ⓢ *Schnitzel platter €7.50. Hamburger and fries €6.60.* Ⓣ
Open daily 9am-1am, F-Sa until 2am or later.

HOFFSKI MÜSLI BAR
⊛Ⓨ CEREAL ❶

Bartelsstr. 8
☎040 79 69 68 78

A wholesome change from the German diet, this cereal bar let's you design your
own perfect bowl of nuts, grains, cornflakes, chocolate chips, and even the
fierce German gummy 🐻bears. Also enjoy the *bircher müesli,* a Swiss morning
specialty of cereals soaked over-night in yogurt. Antique white chairs and dark
wood floors with gilded accents give this cafe an elegant touch, while keeping
the vibe relaxed and low-key.

⚑ *U3, S11, S21, or S31: Sternschanze.* Ⓢ *€1.80 for 100 grams, about €3 for a large bowl.* Ⓣ
Open M-F 8:30am-7pm, Sa 10am-5pm, Su 11am-4pm.

NIGHTLIFE
◾

Reeperbahn and St. Pauli

ROSI'S BAR
⊛⌂ BAR

Hamburger Berg 7

On a strip of almost-identical bars running along the Hamburger Berg, Rosi's
stands out with a playlist of mostly soul music, and a 60-year history of serving
up drinks to thirsty Hamburgers and Hamburgerins. Rosi, the one-time wife of
Tony Sheridan who began managing the bar at 18, still runs it with her son. Wood
paneled walls are dressed up with a single disco ball. DJs almost every night
starting at 11pm.

⚑ *S1, S2, or S3 to "Reeperbahn."* Ⓢ *Beer €2.50, cocktails €5.* Ⓣ *Open Su-Th 9pm-4am, F-Sa
9pm-6pm.*

BARBARABAR
⊛Ⓨ BAR

Hamburger Berg 11
☎016 090 36 15 19 ▣www.barbarabar.de

Hamburger Berg is full of laid-back retro bars. Think every-night DJs, cheap(ish)
drinks, and sagging sofas. Barbarabar stays true to this form. Its foosball table is
a big hit with a crowd of young students, where matches can get almost as heated
as the deep red wallpaper. Music is mostly pop, with a tad of electro on the side.

⚑ *S1, S2, or S3: Reeperbahn.* Ⓢ *Beer €2.40, mixed drinks about €5.* Ⓣ *Open daily 8pm-late.*

St. Georg

👍 CAFE GNOSA ⊛🍸⛅▼ CAFE, GAY BAR

Lange Reihe 93 ☎040 24 30 34 🖥www.gnosa.de

A Hamburg institution, if an unconventional nightlife pick. More cafe than bar, Cafe Gnosa has been serving up drinks and city-famous cakes in a well-lit, quiet restaurant since WWII. Hamburg's first gay bar has a laid-back, yet sophisticated atmosphere, with damask walls and revolving art exhibitions in the back room. Free gay publications like *hinnerk* and *Hamburg's Gay Map* available.

⇄ *Follow Ernst-Mecke-Str. from the north entrance of the Hauptbahnhof as it turns into Lange Reihe.* $ *Beer €2.50, mixed drinks €5.5-7.50. Cakes €3-5.* ⏰ *Open daily 10am-1am.*

KYTI VOO ⊛⛅▼ GAY BAR

Lange Reihe 82 ☎040 28 05 55 65 🖥www.kytivoo.de

This large and relaxed gay bar keeps things upbeat with quiet electro beats and strategic red lights and disco balls. A huge outdoor seating area under a large awning is a popular place to drink for a young, mellow crowd.

⇄ *Follow Ernst-Mecke-Str. from the north entrance of the Hauptbahnhof as it turns into Lange Reihe.* $ *Espresso €1.60. Beer €2.90. Cocktails €5.50-8.* ⏰ *Open M-F 9am-open end, Sa-Su 10am-late.*

Schanzenviertel

SHAMROCK IRISH BAR 🍸⛅ BAR

Feldstr. 40 ☎040 43 27 72 75

This is about at Irish as it gets outside of Dublin. Three smoky, dark wood rooms are filled to capacity with a young, often English-speaking crowd. Irish football banners hang from the ceiling, and some of the funniest bartenders this side of the Channel fill up huge steins while Celtic tunes, big band music, and classic rock keep the atmosphere upbeat.

⇄ *U3: Feldstr.* $ *Beer €3.50. Guiness €3.80.* ⏰ *Open M-Th 6pm-late, F 5pm-late, Sa-Su noon-late.*

YOKO MONO ⊛🍸 BAR

Marktstr. 41 ☎040 43 18 29 91 🖥www.yokomono.de

Plywood tops the counter of this smoke-filled, no-frills bar. Busy with a young, alternative crowd, Yoko Mono boasts a popular pool table and DJs most nights. Let vinyl booths and rock music throw you back to a different decade.

⇄ *U3: Feldstr.* $ *Beer €2.80, wine €2.50.* ⏰ *Open daily noon-2am or later.*

Altona

FABRIK 🍸⛅ CLUB

Barnerstr. 36 ☎040 39 10 70 🖥www.fabrik.de

This former weapons factory now only kills on the dance floor. For years, crowds have packed the two level club, complete with a rusted crane on the roof, to hear big-name rock acts and an eclectic mix of other bands, with styles ranging from Latin to punk. Check the website ahead of time for a schedule of events; the club also hosts a "Gay Factory" night each month.

⇄ *S1, S3, or S31: Altona.* $ *Cover €7-8.* ⏰ *Music nearly every night, starting at 9pm. Live DJ most Sa nights at 10pm.*

AUREL ⊛🍸⛅ BAR

Bahrenfelder Str. 157 ☎040 390 27 27

This laid-back bar draws the ultimate "mixed crowd." Students rub shoulders with architects who sit side-by-side with artists and travelers. But the real appeal is the international vibe; bartenders are from France, US, and England, and their guests are from all around the world. Aurel gets its fair share of locals as well, who come for the mojito happy hour *(daily from 9pm)* and the relaxed feel.

🚇 *S1, S3, or S31: Altona.* $ *Beer €2.90. Mixed drinks €6-8.* ⏰ *Open daily from 10am-3am.*

ARTS AND CULTURE

STATSOPER — OPERA

Große Theaterstr. 36 ☎040 35 68 68 💻www.hamburgische-staatsoper.de

The Statsoper was opened in 1678 as the first theater in Hamburg for aristocrats and nobles. Today, it houses one of the best opera companies in Germany as well as the national dance powerhouse, the John Neumeier Ballet company. And with low prices, we lowly peasants can still get a seat.

🚇 *U2: Gänsemarkt* $ *Tickets starting from €8.* ⏰ *Box office open M-Sa 10am-6:30pm and 90min. before performacnces.*

DEUTSCHES SCHAUSPIELHAUS — THEATER

Kirchenallee 39. ☎040 24 87 13 💻www.schauspielhaus.de

This theater produces contemporary international works mixed with Shakespeare and Sophocles. Its quirky off-beat plays, and the tried-and-true classics, are usually performed in German.

🚇 *Located diagonally across from the Hauptbahnhof.* $ *Student prices from €7.50.* ⏰ *Box office open M-Sa 10am-7pm, or during showtimes.*

HAMBURG SYMPHONIKER — ORCHESTRA

Rothenbaumchaussee 77. ☎040 44 02 98 💻www.hamburgersymphonkier.de

The Hamburg Symphoniker performs at the Hamburg Musikhalle *(Johannes-Brahms-Pl. 20, ☎040 34 69 30 💻www.musikhalle-hamburg.de)*, which is is home to many of Hamburg's great orchestras, including the Philharmonie *(💻www.elbphilharmonie.de)* and the Norddeutscher Rundfunk Symphony *(💻www4.ndr.de)*.

🚇 *U2: Gänsemarkt.* $ *Tickets from €8.* ⏰ *Box office open M-F 10am-6pm.*

ESSENTIALS

Practicalities

- **TOURIST OFFICES:** Hamburg's main tourist offices supply free English-language maps and pamplets. All sell the **Hamburg Card.** The **Hauptbahnhof** office books rooms for a €4 fee. *(In the Wandelhalle, the station's main shopping plaza, near the Kirchenallee exit. ☎040 30 05 12 01. 💻www.hamburg-tourism.de ⏰ Open M-Sa 9am-7pm, Su 10am-6pm.)* The **Sankt Pauli Landungsbrücken** office is often less crowded than the Hauptbahn office. *(Between piers 4 and 5. ☎040 30 05 12 03. ⏰ Open Oct-May daily 10am-5:30pm; Apr-Sept M, W, Su 8am-6pm, Tu and Th-Sa 8am-7pm.)*
- **TOURS: Top-Tour Hamburg** offers double-decker bus tours. If a sight requires a little further exploration, you can hop off anytime for a look and jump back on the next bus. (Tours depart from the Kirchenallee exit of the Hauptbahnhof for landlubbers (Top-Tour) and the St. Pauli Landungsbrücken for the nautically inclined (Maritim-Tour); combine the two in an all-encompassing Gala Tour. *(☎040 641 37 31. 💻www.top-tour-hamburg.de* ℹ *English-language tours available upon request.* $ *€15, students €13, children free.* ⏰ *Buses leave every 30min. daily Apr-Oct 9:30am-5pm; fall and winter tours every 1hr. 10am-3pm.)* **Strattreisen Hamburg** offers offbeat 1-2hr. themed walks, with titles like "Reeperbahn by Night," "Merchants and Catastrophes Downtown," and "Neon-Lights, Seedy Bars, and Catholics in St. Pauli." *(Kuhberg 2. ☎040 430 3481. 💻www.stattreisen-hamburg.de* ℹ *Most tours are offered in German; however, English language tours are also given on a less frequent basis.* $ *€7-46.* ⏰ *Call ahead for times.)* See Hamburg with a water-bird's eye view on a 50min. boat rides around the lakes with **Alster-Touristik** *(On Jungfernstieg by the Außenalster. ☎040 357 4240. 💻www.alstertouristik.de* $ *€10, under 16 €5. Group discounts available.* 🚇 *U1, U2, S1, or S3: Jungfernstieg; follow the swan*

signs. ☺ *Tours leave daily late Mar-Oct every 30min. 10am-6pm.)*

- **CONSULATES: Canada** *(Ballindamm 35, between Alestertor and Bergstr.* ☎*040 460 02 70.* ✇ *U1, S1, S2, or S3: Jungfernstieg.* ☺ *Open M-F 9:30am-12:30pm.)* **Ireland** *(Feldbrunnerstr. 43.* ☎*040 44 18 61 13.* ☺ *Open M-F 9am-1pm.)* **New Zealand** *(Domstr. 19, on the 2nd fl. of block C of Zürich-Haus.* ☎*040 442 55 50.* ✇ *U1: Messberg.* ☺ *Open M-Th 9am-1pm and 2-4:30pm.)* **UK** *(Harvesthuder Weg 8a.* ☎*040 448 03 20.* ✇ *U1: Hallerstr.* ☺ *Open M-Th 9am-4pm, F 9am-3pm.)* **US** *(Alsterufer 27/28.* ☎*040 41 17 11 00.* ✇ *S11, S21 or S31: Dammtor.* ☺ *Open M-F 9am-noon.)*

- **CURRENCY EXCHANGE: ReiseBank** arranges money transfers for Western Union, cashes traveler's checks. *(2nd fl. of the Hauptbahnhof near the Kirchenallee exit.* ☎*040 32 34 83.* ✦ *ReiseBank also has branches in the Altona and Dammtor train stations as well as in the Flughafen.* Ⓢ *1.5% commission, charges €6.50 to cash 1-9 checks, €10 for 10 checks, and €25 for 25 checks, and exchanges currency for a fixed charge of €3-5.* ☺ *Open daily 7:30am-10pm.)* **Citibank** cashes traveler's checks, including AmEx. *(Rathausstr. 2* ☎*040 30 29 62 02.* ✇ *U3: Rathaus.* ☺ *Open M-F 9am-1pm and 2-6pm.)*

- **BOOKSTORES: Thalia-Buchhandlungen** is one of the city's largest bookstores. *(Spitalerstr. 8.* ☎*040 48 50 11 22.* ▣*www.thalia.de* ✇ *U2: Mönckebergstr.)* **Europa Passage** offers the city's biggest English language selection.*(Ballindamm 40.* ☎*309 549 80.* ✇ *U1, U2, S1 or S3: Jungferstieg.)* **Heinrich-Heine Buchhandlung** has an excellent travel section and a decent selection of English-language novels. *(Grindelallee 26-28.* ☎*040 441 13 30.* ▣*www.heinebuch.de* ☺ *Open M-F 9:30am-7pm, Sa 10am-4pm.)*

Emergency!

- **POLICE:** *(✇ From the Kirchenallee exit of the Hauptbahnhof, turn left and follow signs for "BGS/Bahnpolizei/Bundespolizei."* ☎*110.* ✦ *Another branch is located on the Reeperbahn at the corner of Davidstr. and Spielbudenpl. and in the courtyard of the Rathaus.)*

- **FIRE AND AMBULANCE:** ☎112.

- **PHARMACY: Senator-Apotheke.** *(Hachmannpl. 14.* ☎*040 32 75 27* ✦ *English-speaking staff.* ☺ *Open M-F 8am-6:30pm, Sa 9am-1pm.)* **Hauptbahnhof-Apotheke Wandelhalle.** *(In the station's upper shopping gallery.* ☎*040 32 52 73 83.* ☺ *Open M-F 7am-8pm, Th-F 7am-10pm, and Sa-Su 8am-9pm.)*

- **INTERNET ACCESS: Internet Cafe** offers one of the best deals in town. *(Adenauerallee 10, directly across from the ZOB.* ☎*040 28 00 38 98.* Ⓢ *€0.75 per 30min.* ☺ *Open daily 10am-11:55pm.)* **Teletime** doubles as a hookah bar at night. *(Schulterblatt 39.* ☎*040 41 30 47 30.* Ⓢ *€0.50 per 15min.* ☺ *Open M-F 10am-10pm, Sa-Su 10am-7pm.)* Free Wi-Fi is available in **Wildwechsel** *(Beim Grünen Jäger 25.* ☺ *Open daily from 4pm.)*and at **Altan Hotel** *(Beim Grünen Jäger 23.* ☺ *Open 24hr.)* **Staats- und Universitätsbibliothek** Computers on the 2nd fl., but internet access is limited to library cardholders; some temporary internet access for non-cardholders may be arranged. *(Von Melle-Park 3.* ☎*040 428 38 22 33.* ▣*www.sub.uni-hamburg.de* Ⓢ *Library card €5 per month or €15 for 6 months.* ☺ *Open to the public M-F; hours vary by department, but generally 10am-6pm.)*

- **POST OFFICE:** At the Kirchenallee exit of the Hauptbahnhof. *(☺ Open M-F 8am-6pm, Sa 8:30am-12:30pm.)*

- **POSTAL CODE:** 20099.

germany

- **HOME SHARE: Mitwohnzentrale Homecompany.** *(Schulterblatt 112. ☎040 194 45. 💻www.hamburg.homecompany.de ⏰ Apartments available for 1 month or more. Passport and deposit of 1-2 months' rent required. 🚇 U3, S21 or S31: Sternschanze. Then follow the Schulterblatt under the bridge. ⏰ Open M-F 9am-1pm and 2-6pm, Sa 9am-1pm.)*
- **LAUNDROMAT: Schnell und Sauber** *(Neuer Pferdemarkt 27. $ Wash €3.50 for 6kg or €7 for 12kg. Dry €0.50 per 10min. 🚇 U3: Feldstr. ⏰ Open daily 7am-10:30pm.)* Or enjoy a beer while laundering at **Loundromatte.**
- **GLBT RESOURCES:** St. Georg is the center of the gay community. **Cafe Gnosa** offers delicious refreshments and several free publications concerning Germany's gay community.*(Lange Reihe 93.)* **Hein unt Fiete,** a self-described switchboard, gives advice on doctors, disease prevention, and tips on the gay scene. *(Pulverteich 21. ☎040 24 03 33. 🚇 Walk down Steindamm away from the Hauptbahnhof, turn right on Pulverteich and look for a rainbow-striped flag on the left. ⏰ Open M-F 4-9pm, Sa 4-7pm.)* **Magnus-Hirschfeld-Centrum** offers daily film screenings, counseling sessions, and a gay-friendly evening cafe. *(Borgweg 8 . ☎040 27 87 78 00. 🚇 U3: Borgweg.)* **Dementy** operates hotlines for gays and lesbians *(☎040 27 87 78 01.* ℹ Gay hotline *(☎040 279 0069 ⏰ Open M and Th-F 2-6pm, Tu-W 2-6pm and 7-10pm.)* Lesbian hotline *(☎040 279 0049, W 7-9pm. ⏰ Open M-Th 5pm-11pm, F 5pm-late, Su 3-10pm.)*

Getting There

By Plane

Air France *(☎01805 83 08 30)* and **Lufthansa** *(☎01803 80 38 03)*,among other airlines, service Hamburg's **Fuhlsbüttel Airport** *(☎040 507 50).* **Jasper Airport Express** buses *(☎040 22 71 06 10 💻www.jasper.de)* run from the Kirchenallee exit of the Hauptbahnhof directly to the airport *($ €5, under 12 €2. ⏰ 25min., every 10-15min. 4:45am-7pm, every 20min. 7-9:20pm.)* Alternatively, you can take U1,S1, or S11 to Ohlsdorf, and then an **express bus** to the airport *($ €2.60, children 6-14 €0.90. ⏰ Every 10min. 4:30am-11pm, every 30min. from 11pm-1am.).* The same modes of transporation are available from the airport to the center of the city.

By Train

The **Hauptbahnhof,** Hamburg's central station, has connections to: **Berlin** *($ €56. ⏰ 2hr.);* **Copenhagen, Denmark** *($ €80.⏰ 4.5hr.),* **Frankfurt** *($ €150. ⏰ 5hr.);* **Hanover** *($ €55.⏰ 1.5hr.);* **Munich** *($ €185. ⏰ 7hr.).*Be advised that prices may vary on day of travel, time of year, and proximity of purchase date to travel date. The efficient staff at the **DB Reisezentrum** sells tickets *(⏰ Open M-F 5:30am-10pm, Sa-Su 7am-10pm),* which are also available at the ticket machines located throughout the Hauptbahnhof and online at 💻**www.db.de. Dammtor** station is near the university, to the west of Außenalster; **Harburgdorf** is to the southeast. Most trains to and from Schleswig-Holstein stop only at **Altona,** while most trains toward Lübeck stop only in the Hauptbahnhof. Frequent locals trains and the S-Bahn connect the stations.

By Bus

The **ZOB** terminal is across the Steintorpl. from the Hauptbahnhof *(⏰ Open M-Th 5am-10pm, F-Sa 5am-midnight, Su 5am-10pm.).*

Ride Share

Mitfahrzentrale Citynetz, Ernst-Merke-Str. 12-14. *(☎040 194 44 💻www.citynetz-mitfahrzentrale.de $Prices vary by driver.⏰ Open M-F 9:30am-6:30pm, Sa 10am-2pm.)*

Public Transportation

HVV operates the efficient U-Bahn, S-Bahn, and bus network. Short rides within downtown cost €1.65, one-way in greater Hamburg €2.60; 1-day pass €5.60, 3-day pass €15.90. Passes are available for longer, though anything over a week requires a photo. Frequent riders can bring a photo or take one in the nearby ID booths for €5. The **Hamburg Card** provides unlimited access to public transportation, reduced admission to museums, and discounts on souvenirs, restaurants, theater, and bus and boat tours for groups of 1 adult and up to 3 children under 15. *(Available at tourist offices and in some hostels and hotels.* Ⓢ *€8 per day, €18 for 3 days, €33 for 5 days.)* The Group Card provides the same benefits for up to 5 people of any age *(*Ⓢ *1-day €11.80, 3-day €29.80, 5-day 51).*

By Ferry

HADAG Seetouristik und Fährdienst AG, St. Pauli Landungsbrücken *(☎040 311 7070).* Most locals suggest taking the HVV-affiliated ferries in lieu of the expensive tour boats for an equally impressive view of the river Elbe. Departing every 15min. from the docks at St. Pauli to 21 stops along the river. Full circuit lasts 75min. Price included in HVV train and bus passes; €2.60 for a new ticket.

By Taxi

All Hamburg taxis charge the same rates. **Taxi Hamburg,** *(☎040 666 666).* **Das Taxi,** *(☎040 22 11 22).* **Autoruf,** *(☎040 44 10 11).*Normally about €2.40 to start, then €1.75 or less per additional km.

Car Rental

Avis *(⚥ In the Hauptbahnhof near track #12 on the Spitalerstraße side.☎040 32 87 38 00, international ☎018 05 55 77 55 🖥 www.avis.de i Lower prices online.* Ⓢ *Cars from €242 per week, with insurance and 24hr. emergency assistance.* ☼ *Open M-F 7:30am-9pm, Sa 8am-6pm, Su 10am-6pm.)* Lower prices online at **Hertz,** *(Kirchenallee 34-36⚥ Across the Kirchenallee from Ernst-Merck-Str. ☎040 280 1202, international ☎01805 33 35 35 🖥 www.hertz.de i Lower prices online.* Ⓢ *Cars from €243 per week, including insurance.* ☼ *Open M-F 7am-7:30pm, Sa 8am-4pm, Su 10am-4pm.)* **Europecar,** *(Holstenstr. 156⚥ U3: Feldstr. ☎040 306 8260 🖥 www. europecar.de i Lower prices online.* Ⓢ *Cars from €245 per week.* ☼ *Open daily 24hr.)*

Boat Rental

Die Segelschule Pieper, *(An der Alster/Atlantickstieg ⚥ Directly across form the Hotel Atlantic at the intersection of Holtzdamm and the An der Alster on the Außenalster. ☎040 24 75 78 🖥www. segelschule-pieper.de) i Must be 14+ to rent.* Ⓢ *Pedalboats and rowboats for €12-13 per hr., and sailboats for up to 6 people for €16-19 per hr.* ☼ *Open May-Sept daily 10am-9pm.)*

Bike Rental

Hamburg is very bike-friendly, with wide bike lanes built into most sidewalks. **Fhrrandstation Dammtor/Rotherbaum** *(Schlüterstr. 11. ☎040 41 46 82 77),* Ⓢ *€3 per day.* ☼ *Open M-F 9am-6pm).* **Fahrandladen St. Georg** *(Schmilinskystr. 6. ⚥ Off the Lange Reihe near the Außenalster. ☎040 24 39 08* Ⓢ *€8 per day, €56 per week with a €50 deposit.* ☼ *Open M-F 10am-7pm, Sa 10am-1pm.)*

dresden ☎0351

In 1945, a two-night-long Allied air raid completely destroyed Dresden, killing between 25,000 and 50,000 Germans. Until the reunification of Germany in 1989, many of the historic buildings burned in the bombing were left untouched as a monument to the war. As striking as these ruins must have been, we're thrilled the city of Dresden ultimately decided to reconstruct its stunning riverside view (with substantial help from the German and British national governments.) The ongoing, incredibly successful restoration has resurrected the "Florence on the Elbe" to its old Baroque beauty, and given rise to a vibrant youth culture. With world-class museums, operas, and palaces to fill your day, and nightclubs and bars busy late into the night, we suggest you come for the *Kirches* and stay for the *Klubs* (or vice versa.).

ORIENTATION

Dresden is located about 60km northwest of the Czech border and 200km south of Berlin, with its population of 500,000 heavily concentrated around the banks of the **Elbe.** The river bisects the city, with **Neustadt** to the north, and **Altstadt** to the south. **Hauptbahnhof,** which is located in Alstadt, is linked to the **Altmarkt** (with its beautiful historic buildings) by **Prager Strasse,** a pedestrian zone lined with shops and fountains. **Altmarkt** is connected to Neustadt by **Austusbrucke,** the Elbe's central walking bridge, which links Alstadt to Neustadt's pedestrian walkway, **Haupstrasse.** Most of Dresden's historic sights are located along the Elbe, with the majority found in Altstadt. Neustadt is the younger, more alternative side of Dresden, full of hostels, inexpensive restaurants, and unbeatable nightlife.

ACCOMMODATIONS

With the Hauptbahnhof and river sights located in Altstadt, it may be tempting to book your stay on the south side of the river. However, far more hostels, with lower prices and a more youthful clientele, are in the Neustadt. Public transportation makes everything easily accessible from either side of the river, so don't let proximity keep you from finding your bunk to the north of the Elbe.

Altstadt

JUGENDGÄSTEHAUS
HOSTEL ❷

Masternistraße 22   ☎0351 49 26 20 ✉www.dresden.jugendherberg.de

Jugendgästehaus, a member of Hosteling International, is one of few hostels located in Dresden's Altstadt, and, at just a 7min. walk away, is the closest to Dresden's historic river sights. The hostel's interior is admittedly asylum-esque, with stark white walls, fluorescent lighting and hospital waiting room furniture. Rooms have either two or four beds, and are mostly popular with families.

⚐ *From the (H) at Post Platz, follow Feiberger to Maternistrasse.* ⓘ *In-room full bath is available for an extra €4.50.* Ⓢ *May-Oct with breakfast from €21.25, with either lunch or dinner €26.75, with lunch and dinner €32.25. Nov-Apr from €20.25.* ⏲ *Reception 24hr.*

CITY HERBERGE
▰(ᵗʸ) HOSTEL, HOTEL ❸

Lingnerallee 3   ☎0351 485 99 00 ✉www.cityherberge.de

If you are set on staying in the Altstadt, this is the place to do it. From the outside the building looks a bit like an insane asylum, and it's located across from a happening skate park, but the rooms themselves are cozy, comfortable, and can be personalized based on your budget. The hostel rooms share toilets on the floor while the hotel-style rooms come with a bathroom and amped-up decor (like paintings and fluffier pillows). Suitable for all age groups; the great lobby area is stocked with board games.

⚐ *Tram 7 or 12: Pirnaischer Platz. From the stop, walk down St. Petersburger Strasse towards the Rathaus (City Hall with the big tower).* ⓘ *Breakfast and internet access included.* Ⓢ *Basic rooms €16-35; standard €21-42; comfort €30-56.* ⏲ *Reception 24hr.*

Neustadt

▦ LOUISE 20
▰⊗ HOSTEL, PENSION ❶

Louisenstr. 20   ☎0351 889 48 94 ✉www.louise20.de

The golden hardwood floors and dainty glass canisters with cereal conjure feelings of comfort, with impeccable cleanliness and in-room sinks to match. You may feel so at home that you don't want to leave, except to find nourishment in

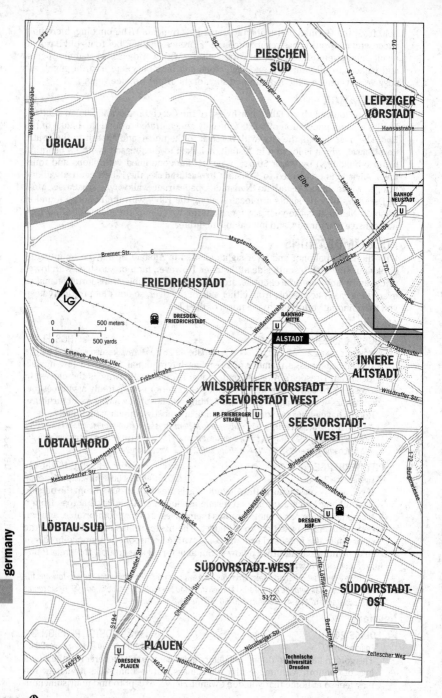

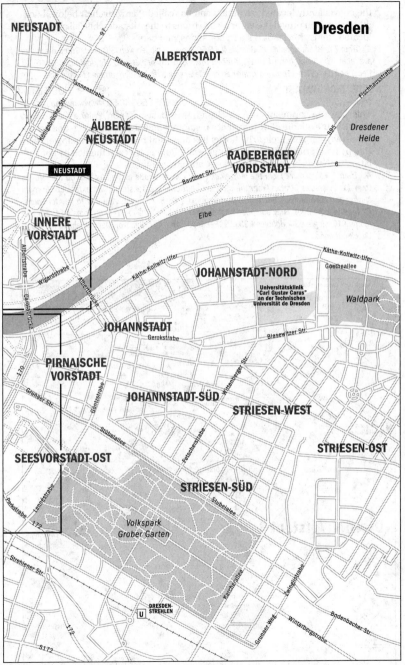

Dresden

NEUSTADT

ALBERTSTADT

Stauffenbergallee

Tannenstraße

97

Königsbrücker Str.

ÄUßERE
NEUSTADT

RADEBERGER
VORSTADT

Bautzner Str.

Fischhausstraße

S95

Dresdener
Heide

6

NEUSTADT

INNERE
VORSTADT

Albertstraße

Wigardstraße

Albertbrücke

Carolabrücke

6

Elbe

Käthe-Kollwitz-Ufer

JOHANNSTADT-NORD

Käthe-Kollwitz-Ufer

Goetheallee

Universitätsklinik
"Carl Gustav Carus"
an der Technischen
Universität de Dresden

Waldpark

JOHANNSTADT

Gerokstraße

Blasewitzer Str.

PIRNAISCHE
VORSTADT

170

Grunaer Str.

Güntzstraße

JOHANNSTADT-SÜD

Stübelallee

Fetscherstraße

Wittenberger Str.

STRIESEN-WEST

STRIESEN-OST

SEESVORSTADT-OST

Parkstraße

Lennéstraße

172

STRIESEN-SÜD

Stübelallee

Volkspark
Großer Garten

Strehlener Str.

172

S172

DRESDEN-
STREHLEN
U

Karcherallee

Gruaner Weg

Zwinglistraße

Winterbergstraße

Bodenbacher Str.

dresden . accommodations

the conveniently located restaurant and bar called Planwirtschaft below. Luckily, the location provides easy access to trams to the Altstadt while also centrally located amidst Neustadt restaurants, shops, and bars.

*➔ Tram 7 or 8: Louisenstr. **i** Breakfast €5.50. Linens included with ISIC card. Group discounts available. $ 5-bed dorm €14-17; 3-4 bed room €16-18; singles €29-35; doubles €38-46. ⏰ Reception daily 7am-11pm. If arriving earlier or later with a reservation, arrange in advance.*

HOSTEL MONDPALAST
📶🍸 HOSTEL [1]

Louisenstr. 77 ☎0351 563 40 50 💻www.mondpalast.de

This place is seriously cosmic. Hostel Mondpalast (Moon Palace) is nestled smack in the middle of of Neustadt's restaurant and nightlife district, and serves a mostly young clientele. The hostel has a bar and restaurant on its lower level (happy hour prices all day long for guests!). Rooms are each themed by constellation with pine beds, private lockers, and stellar murals.

*➔ Tram 7: Louisenstr.. From the stop, walk along Louisenstraße to Mondpalast, on the left. Or, tram 11: Pulsnitzer Straße. From the stop, turn left onto Louisenstr. **i** Breakfast €6. In-room shower and bathroom available, usually for an extra €6-8. All guests required to pay for linens, €2 (one time charge). Fully equipped kitchen. Wi-Fi included. $ 8-10 bed rooms €14; 5-6 bed rooms €16; single €34; doubles €39. ⏰ Reception Apr-Oct 24hr.; Nov-Mar call ahead for hours. Check-out noon.*

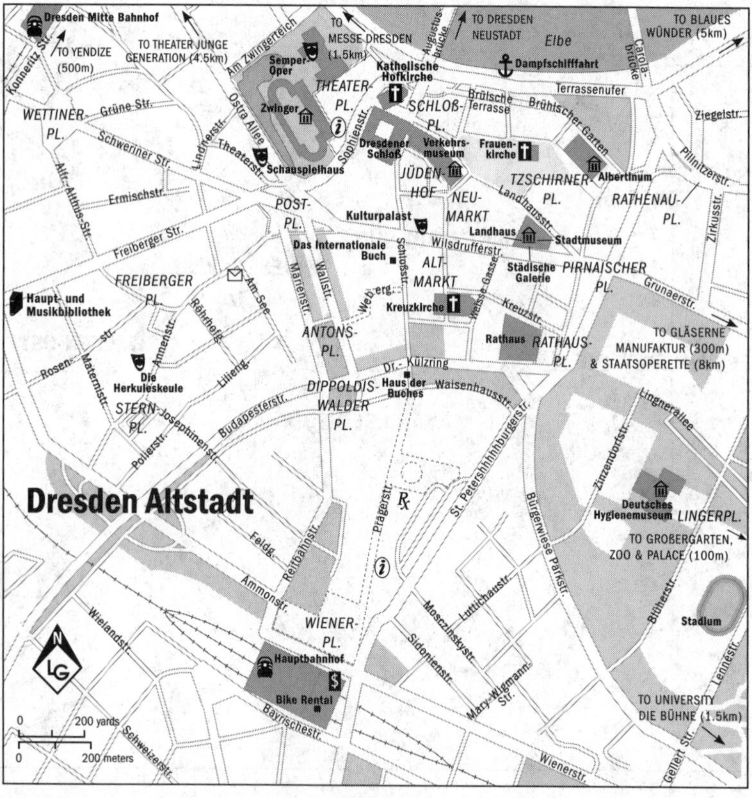

Dresden Altstadt
Dresden Mitte Bahnhof
TO YENDIZE (500m)
TO THEATER JUNGE GENERATION (4.5km)
TO MESSE DRESDEN (1.5km)
TO DRESDEN NEUSTADT
Elbe
TO BLAUES WÜNDER (5km)
Semper-Oper
Katholische Hofkirche
Dampfschifffahrt
Terrassenufer
Zwinger
THEATER-PL.
SCHLOß-PL.
Brülsche Terrasse
Brühlscher Garten
WETTINER-PL.
Dresdener Schloß
Verkehrs-museum
Frauen-kirche
Albertinum
Schauspielhaus
JÜDEN-HOF
NEU-MARKT
TZSCHIRNER-PL.
RATHENAU-PL.
POST-PL.
Kulturpalast
Landhaus
Stadtmuseum
Das Internationale Buch
ALT-MARKT
Städische Galerie
PIRNAISCHER PL.
FREIBERGER PL.
Haupt- und Musikbibliothek
Kreuzkirche
ANTONS-PL.
Rathaus
RATHAUS-PL.
TO GLÄSERNE MANUFAKTUR (300m) & STAATSOPERETTE (8km)
Die Herkuleskeule
DIPPOLDIS-WALDER PL.
Haus der Buches
STERN-PL.
Deutsches Hygienemuseum
LINGERPL.
TO GROßERGARTEN, ZOO & PALACE (100m)
Stadium
WIENER-PL.
Hauptbahnhof
Bike Rental
TO UNIVERSITY DIE BÜHNE (1.5km)
0 200 yards
0 200 meters
Konneritz Str.
Grüne Str.
Schweriner Str.
Ermischstr.
Freiberger Str.
Ostra Allee
Theaterstr.
Sophienstr.
Wilsdrufferstr.
Marienstr.
Wallstr.
Schloßstr.
Kreuzstr.
Grunaerstr.
Pillnitzerstr.
Ziegelstr.
Zirkusstr.
Landhausstr.
Waisenhausstr.
Dr.-Külzring
Budapesterstr.
Josephinenstr.
Rosen-str.
Ammonstr.
Feldg.
Reitbahnstr.
Pragerstr.
St. Petersburgerstr.
Bürgerwiese Parkstr.
Lingnerallee
Zinzendorfstr.
Lüttichaustr.
Mosczinskystr.
Sidonienstr.
Mary-Wigmann-Str.
Blüherstr.
Lennéstr.
Wienerstr.
Bayrischestr.
Schweizerstr.
Wielandstr.
Gellert Str.
Carolabrücke
Augustusbrücke
Am Zwingerteich
Am See
Alt-Althus-Str.
Lindnerstr.

SIGHTS

We'd tell you that there's too much for a traveler to see in just a few days, but fortunately for you and your weary feet, many of Dresden's major sights are clumped close together on the beautiful scenic banks of the Elbe. With the **Royal Cathedral** right next to the **Royal Palace** right next to the **City Opera House,** the original city-plan was either drawn up by the incurably lazy for their own convenience, or the admirably considerate for ours. Most of the places to see are in the Altstadt, but there's plenty to keep you busy in the Neustadt as well.

Altstadt

FRAUENKIRCHE

Neumarkt

CHURCH

☎0351 656 06 💻www.fauenkirche-dresden.de

Frauenkirche (Church of Our Lady) was first bombed and destroyed in 1945. Originally, left in ruins as a monument to the terrors of war, it was decided after the German reunification that the church would be rebuilt, incorporating the black, burned stones from the old church into the new, lighter stones. Because the British financed a substantial portion of the reconstruction, Dresden now regards the church as a symbol of reconciliation. Unfortunately, the light blue, green, and pink painted interior seems to be visually more symbolic of an Easter egg or a Miami condo than the mended relations between previously warring states. Visitors can see Altstadt from the top of the dome.

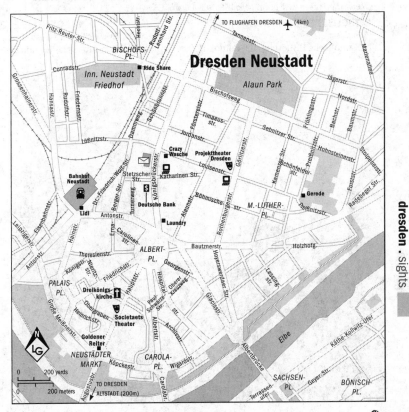

dresden • sights

🚋 Tram 1, 2, 4, or 12: Altmarkt. Tram 3, 6, 7 or bus 75: Pirnaischer Platz. $ €8. ⏰ Open Mar-Oct M-Sa 10am-6pm, Su 12:30-6pm. Nov-Feb M-Sa 10am-4pm, Su 12:30-4pm. Weekend times restricted due to rehearsals.

DRESDENER RESIDENZ SCHLOSS ROYAL PALACE

Taschenberg 2 ☎0351 49 14 20 00 💻www.skdmuseum.de

Originally built as a residential palace for Saxony's Wettin dynasty of electors (you can see their portraits in the palace's Gallery of Electors, if you're curious), it was ruined in the 1945 Allied bombing. Currently, the palace is being restored as a museum, with four different exhibits open at different times and for different admission prices. High on the list of those to see are both the New and Historic Green Vaults, which have recently found a home back in the palace. The **Historic Green Vault,** a collection of Augustus the Strong's jewelry, ivory carvings, and intricate work by goldsmiths, might be worth the admission fee. The **New Green Vault,** is a smaller exhibit, but less of a hassle to visit, and features a separate part of Augustus's treasure collection. Visitors can also visit the **Rüstdammer** (Armory), **Münzkabinett** (Coin Cabinet), and **Kupferstich-Kabinett** (Cabinet of Prints and Drawings).

🚋 Tram 4, 8 or 9: Theaterpl. ℹ Historic Green Vault ticket reservation at least one day prior to visit. Reservations can be made online at www.dresden.de.). No reservations necessary for the New Green Vault. $ Historic Green Vault €10, including audio tour. Children under 7 free. New Green Vault €6, students €3.50. ⏰ Historic Green Vault open M and W-Su 10am-7pm, last entry 6pm. New Green Vault open M and W-Su 10am-6pm.

KATHOLISCHE HOFKIRCHE CATHEDRAL

Schlossplatz ☎0351 484 48 12 💻www.kathedrale-dresden.de

Katholische Hofkirche (the Catholic Court Cathedral) adjoins the palace. Though

destroyed in 1945, it was quickly restored to near perfect condition, with a striking bright white marble interior. The cathedral still displays its original organ on the second floor, which, having miraculously survived the bombing, represents the last surviving work of world-famous organ-builder Gottfried Silbermann. Because the church is still very much used by worshippers, remember to behave respectfully (confessionals aren't photobooths, folks).

🚋 Tram 7, 8 or 9: Theatpl. ℹ Guided tours M-Th 2pm, F-Su 1pm, Sa 1pm. $ Free. ⏰ Open M-Tu 9am-6pm, W-Th 9am-5pm, F 1-5pm, Sa 10am-5pm, Su noon-4pm.

SEMPERBAU MIT ZWINGGER — MUSEUM

Theaterpl. 1 ☎0351 491 46 22 💻www.skd-dresden.de

Contains collections including the **Gemäldegalerie Alte Meister** (Old Masters Picture Gallery). The Old Masters Gallery has large, tightly packed canvases reaching from the ground to the high ceilings, often organized by artist. Walk past **Canaletto's** paintings of Venice, or Carriera's room of portraits on the third floor. Don't miss Canaletto's 18th century iconic paintings of the Dresden waterfront to see how successful the reconstruction of Altstadt has been. Other works by **Raphael, Botticelli, Titian, Rembrandt,** and **Correggio** also make this worth the visit. Part of the **Rüstkammer** (armory) collection is also housed here, in addition to the **Porzellansammlung** (porcelain collection), the largest ceramics collection in the world, with over 20,000 works. Collected by Augustus the Strong, a porcelain aficionado, the display traces pottery specimens from the Ming Dynasty to Japanese Imari wares from the early 17th and 18th centuries.

🚋 Tram 7, 8 or 9: Theaterpl. The Zwingger is right across from the Hofkirche. $ Gemäldegalerie Alte Meister €3, students €2, entire collection €10/7.50. Under 16 free. ⏰ Open Tu-Su 10am-6pm.

DIE GLÄSERNE MANUFAKTUR (THE TRANSPARENT FACTORY) 💳♿❄ — FACTORY

Lennestr. 1 ☎01805 89 62 68 💻www.glaesernemanufaktur.de

Join a guided tour through this glass extravaganza that houses the Volkswagen's Phaeton, and watch men in white moon-suits piece the luxury cars together by hand. Each Phaeton on the assembly line is unique, and will eventually be delivered to its owner through an elaborate display in which the car ascends into the room on a platform. If cars aren't your thing, the almost transparent building is still a spectacle. At the end of the tour, there is a parked Phaeton to play with (no test driving allowed). Be sure to sit in the driver's seat and turn on the back massager.

🚋 Tram 12 or 13: Strassburger Platz. ℹ The factory is occasionally open for independent exploration, but the areas for independent visit are restricted. $ €4, students, seniors, disabled €2. Family card €10 (two adults, up to 5 children). Group discounts available. ⏰ English tours daily at noon and 3pm, but hours and tours subject to change; call in advance to confirm and reserve.

Neustadt

DREIKÖNIGSKIRCHE (CHURCH OF THE MAGI) — CHURCH

Hauptstr. 23 ☎0351 812 41 00

Only the original clock and bell tower, designed in 1730, survived the 1945 Dresden bombing, but a new structure has been built around it to allow church services to continue. Climb to the top of the bell tower, up a dizzying series of spiral staircases, to see panoramic views of all of Dresden.

🚋 Tram 8: Neustädter Markt. $ Admission to the tower €1.50, children €1. Church service free. ⏰ Tower open Mar-Oct Tu 11:30am-4pm, W-Sa 11am-5pm, Su 11:30am-5pm. Nov-Feb W noon-4pm, Th-F 1pm-4pm, Su 11:30am-4:30pm.

GOLDEN REITER (GILDED HORSEMAN) — STATUE

This gold-plated August the Strong faces the Augustusbrücke on Neustädter Markt. Some locals find the statue of a "fat man on a fat horse" unappealing and gaudy, but there's something to be said for large gold equine statues...probably.

Augustus' commendatory suffix has two suggested derivations. First, it alters his physical strength, supposedly displayed by his indented thumbprint on the **Brühlsche Terrasse.** Since the thumprint was made after his death, this would indeed be quite a show of strength. Second, it speaks to his his virility—legend has it that he fathered 365 children, though the official tally is 15.

 # Tram 8: Neustädter Markt. $ Free.

ALAUNPARK — PARK

On sunny days, families have picnics, children eat ice cream, students study on the grass, and everyone else runs around playing soccer and frisbee. This expansive park occasionally hosts a local produce market during the summer, and is always a perfect place to bring a meal and take a stroll.

 # Bordered by Bischofsweg, Alaunstraße, Kamenzer Str. and Tannenstr. $ Free.

The Great Outdoors

PURO BEACH — ♿🍸☀ POOL, BAR

Leipziger Str. 15 ☎0351 215 27 71 🖥www.puro.de

Where the wanna-be beach babes of Dresden come to see and be seen; wear your sparkly bikini, flex your abs, and lay out stylishly on the large cushions under sweeping white umbrellas. The small pool even has a waterfall.

 # Tram 11: Antonstr. From the stop, walk towards the bridge, down the stairs, and follow the path along the Elbe. $ Mixed drinks €2-7. ⏰ Open daily 11am-late; the party continues at the neighboring club, Pier 15.

CITY BEACH DRESDEN — ♿🍸☀ BEACH, BAR

Leipziger Str. 31 ☎0152 24 39 43 04 🖥www.citybeachdresden.de

The down-to-earth brother of Puro Beach, City Beach Dresden is the summertime hang-out for locals with an expanse of sand, beach beds, and picnic tables. Get a group together and reserve a beach volleyball court—once play begins it almost feels as though you are on the beaches of California.

 # A little past Puro Beach, also on the path along the Elbe. $ Mixed drinks €2-5. Beach volleyball court €10-15 ⏰ Open daily 10am-dusk.

FOOD

Dresden is full of inexpensive and great tasting food. Affordable restaurants in Altstadt are difficult to come by; travelers will have to sacrifice their budgets and eat alongside masses of tourists to enjoy a meal with great views of reconstructed Baroque buildings. Luckily, markets are open relatively frequently in the summer months in **Altmarkt,** where good food is available for a lot less. Neustadt, however, has a wide range of eateries with plenty of low-budget options. Make sure you pick up a free *Dresden by Locals* map in any hostel or tourist office to see a long listing of places Dresdeners go to be fed and watered.

Altstadt

Restaurants around the Altstadt market let visitors in on the incredible views of the Frauenkirche and the Elbe. Unfortunately, these places are expensive and overrun by hoards of tourists. If you're looking to stay on a budget, your cheapest options are the *bratwurst* stands scattered around the **Markts,** which sell their fare for €2-3. It's usually safe to bet that at least one vendor will be on **Münzgasse,** which runs from the river to the Frauenkirche. Restaurants in the area, which have similar prices and serve similar crowds, apparently attempt to differentiate themselves by emulating different countries, which makes them look slightly ridiculous in such a quintessentially German *platz.*

CAFE AHA — 🥬♿☀ CAFE, VEGETARIAN ❷

Kreuzstr. 7 ☎0351 496 0673 🖥www.ladencafe.de

If your German meat-heavy diet is starting to take a toll on your arteries, you will breathe "aha" with relief at the veggies here. The meals are mostly vegetarian, the products are organic, and the outdoor seating beneath the Kreuzkirche is the table to grab. The Saxon potato soup *(€4)* is a local specialty, while the classic Spinach lasagna is another favorite *(€9)*.

🚋 *Tram 1, 2, or 4: Altmarkt, next to Kreuzkirche.* Ⓢ *Soups and salads €4-10. Entrees €5-11. Desserts €2-4.* ⏰ *Open daily 10am-midnight.*

AUGUSTINER AN DER FRAUENKIRCHE — 💳🍸⛅ GERMAN ❷

An der Frauenkirche 16/17 — ☎0351 48 28 97 🖥www.augustiner-dresden.de

If you feel like splurging on one of the Altmarkt restaraunts, consider eating at Augustiner an der Frauenkirche. With outdoor seating only about 50 yards from the Frauenkirche, and an extensive beer and liquor menu, it might be worth the extra cost. Entrees include pan-seared mushrooms with bread dumplings *(€10.80)*, beer stew (bet you didn't see that one coming) with carrots and dumplings *(8.80)*, and schnitzel with salad and fried potatoes *(€15)*.

🚋 *Tram 1, 4, 8, 9,11 or 12: Postpl.* Ⓢ *Beer €3.20-€6.40. Entrees €8-15.* ⏰ *Open daily 10am-1pm.*

RAUSCHENBACH DELI — 💳♿🍸⛅ CAFE, BAR ❷

Weissegasse 2 — ☎0351 821 27 60 🖥www.rauschenbach-deli.de

Breakfast, lunch, dinner, drinks—Rauschenbach Deli is a classic of the Weissegasse cafe row at any time of day, and doesn't seem quite as touristy as the surrounding restaurants. The ample outdoor seating, also in the shadow of Kreuzkriche, is the perfect place to people-watch as you sip a beer *(€2.20)* and snack on mozzarella sticks *(€3.50)*.

🚋 *Tram 1, 2, or 4: Altmarkt, next to Kreuzkirche.* Ⓢ *Breakfast €4-7. Salads and pasta €7-11. Entrees €13-15. Ice cream €4-7.* ⏰ *Open M-W 9am-midnight, Th 9am-1am, F-Sa 9am-2am, Su 9am-midnight.*

Neustadt

👍 HOT SPOON — 🚫♿ CAFE ❶

Konigsbrucker Str. 74 — ☎0351 89 96 08 75 🖥www.hotspoon.de

A large yellow spoon with a smiley face will lead you to this soup-happy haven. Inside, the lime green walls, hanging lanterns, and black and white checked floor look like something from *Alice in Wonderland*. The soup is served in brightly colored bowls from a large pot-shaped counter. The Italian tomato soup *(small €2.60, medium €3.70, large €4.20)* has basil, fresh hunks of mozzarella, and bow-tie pasta. Vegans can delight in Russian borscht *(€2.60/3.70/4.20)* with mushrooms, tomatoes, potatoes, and sauerkraut. Menu changes frequently.

🚋 *Tram 7 or 8: Bischofsweg.* ℹ *Another branch located at Kunsthandwerkerpassage 9 is open 11:30am-4pm.* Ⓢ *Small soups €2.30-2.70, medium €3.60-3.80, large €4.10-4.30.* ⏰ *Open M-F 11:30am-11pm, Sa-Su noon-11pm.*

BAGEL'S DRESDEN — 🚫🍸⛅ BAGELS, SANDWICHES ❶

Louisenstr.77 — ☎0152 06 84 65 84 🖥www.bagels-dresden.de

Bagel's Dresden offers huge bagels for very little. Try the Italian bagel, with salami, fresh balsamic cheese, and olive spread, or the Torro, with pesto, pastrami, and camembert. *Bier und bagel*, you ask? Just add an extra €1.80-2.

🚋 *Tram 7: Louisenstr. From the stoop, walk along Louisenstr. to Mondpalast, on the left. Or, tram 11: Pulsnitzer Str. Turn left onto Louisenstr.* Ⓢ *Bagel sandwiches from €3.80.* ⏰ *Open daily noon-1am.*

CAFÉ KOMISCH — 🚫⛅ CAFE ❶

Bischofsweg 50

Café Komisch is both a cafe and ice cream (*eis*) parlor. The cafe has indoor seating and inexpensive drinks, but the outdoor ice cream window is the local hotspot, with lines sometimes stretching around the block. Get the soft ice cream in orange or banana, and happily lick away as you make your way across the street to Alaunpark.

Tram 7: Bischofsweg. From the stop, follow Bischofsweg for about 3 minutes to the café. $ Small ice cream €1.30, large €2. Cappuccino €1.80. Espresso €1. ⏰ Coffee shop open M-F 3-6:30pm, Sa-Su 2-6:30pm. Ice cream window open daily 10am-10pm. Winter hours subject to change.

NIGHTLIFE

Dresden's nightlife scene is one of the best in Germany. Bars and small live music venues overflow with students and locals in the Neustadt every Friday and Saturday, and often on other days of the week as well. Further up, about 15 minutes by tram *(Tram 7 or 8: Industriegeländ)*, a crowded block of industrial buildings turned nightclubs stand their ground, with more dance floors and bars than we care to count, and the occassional, unbeatable, rave concert.

Altstadt

BIERSTUBE — BAR

Bergstrasse 1 ☎0351 47 16 09 www.klubneuemensa.de

Bierstube roughly translates to "beer living room," which pretty much sums up this student hangout. The beer is oh-so-cheap *(0.5L for €1.90)* and the heaping meals fill the stomachs of procrastinating students who drink, smoke, and play cards, before reluctantly returning to the library. Or not.

Tram 8 or 66: Nurnberger Str. At the intersection, walk down Bergstrasse away from the city. It will be on the left amidst the other campus buildings. $ Entrees €2-5. Beer from €2. ⏰ Open M-F 9am-1am, Sa noon-1am, Su 5pm-1am.

CLUB AQUARIUM — BAR, MUSIC VENUE

St. Petersburger Str. ☎0351 497 66 70 www.club-aquarium.de

Once located on the rooftop of the student dorm at the same address, this student bar had to move to the basement because of noise complaints, just in time for the flood of 2002. During the flood, the bar was filled with water (and fish), and thus Aquarium was born. Now the venue is a student hotspot during the week for strong, cheap drinks like a classic gin and tonic *(€2.80)*. There is often live music and game nights.

Tram 3, 7, 8, 9, or 11: Walpurgistr. $ Beer and mixed drinks €2-8. ⏰ Open M-F 1pm-1am.

Neustadt

WASHROOM — CLUB, LOUNGE, MUSIC VENUE

Hermann-Mende-Str. 1 ☎0351 80 44 41 57 08 www.washroom.de

Part of the Industriegelände community, the Washroom is part lounge, part dance club, and part concert venue (on certain nights). If you can, try to catch a hip-hop, techno, or rap concert at the Washroom—the price is well worth the experience. When the performers take a break, jump around to the electro music under blue, red, and black lights.

Tram 7 or 8: Industriegeläende. Follow the flashing lights and blaring bass. $ Concert tickets from €8, but the cost varies depending on the performer. Cover €5-10 without show. Beer and mixed drinks from €2.50. Keep an eye out for €1 drink nights. ⏰ Hoursvary; generally open F-Sa 10pm-4am.

STRASSE E — CLUB

Werner-Hartmann-Str. 2 ☎0351 213 85 30 www.strasse-e.de

Strasse E, another Industriegalaende club, is a three-story, six-dance-floor club (including one outdoors). The club gets packed even before midnight with both young people and middle-aged auto-designers by day/dance divas by night types. Come to watch (and join) Germans get their groove on (some better than others), to electro and rock music.

Take the 7 or 8: Industriegelaende. $ Cover around €8. ⏰ Open F-Sa 10pm-5am.

ARTS AND CULTURE

Entertainment

SÄCHSISCHE STAATSOPER (SEMPER OPER)

☛OPERA HOUSE

Theaterpl. 2   ☎0351 491 10 ▣www.semperoper.de

The ornate Baroque Semper Oper offers visitors one of the best cultural experiences in Dresden. For as little as €8, you can see operas, ballets, and concerts, including performances by the Staatskapelle Dresden, the city's premier orchestra in the beautiful city theater.

> ⚐ Tram 4, 8 or 9: Theaterpl. The box office is located across from the Semper Oper. ⓘ Order tickets online at www.semperoper-erleben.de. Guided tours of the opera house are the only way to see the interior without attending a performance. Ⓢ Tours €8, students €4. ⓐ Tours M-F 1:30-3:30pm, Sa-Su 8:30am and 1:30pm-3:30pm; schedule varies greatly, so call ahead to confirm. Box office open M-F 10am-6pm, Sa-Su 10am-1pm, and 1hr. before the show starts.

STAATSOPERETTE DRESDEN

☛OPERETTAS, MUSICALS

Staatsoperette Dresden   ☎0351 20 79 90 ▣www.staatsoperette-dresden.de

This small performance venue is about a 35-minute tram ride away from central Dresden, but if you're looking for a change of scenery or a certain musical (or operetta, as it were), it could be worth the trek. Be sure to take a look at the Himmelfahrtskirche, just across the street, to make your trip complete.

> ⚐ Tram 6: Altleuben. Ⓢ Tickets vary in price. Students generally €8-24. ⓐ Box office open M 10am-4pm, Tu-F 10am-7pm, Sa 4-7pm, Su 1hr. before curtain.

STAATSSCHAUSPIEL

☛THEATER

Theaterstr. 2   ☎0351 491 35 55 ▣www.staatsschauspiel-dresden.de

With four different venues at two locations in the city, this theater offers contemporary comedies, as well as works by Shakespeare and Chekhov. The main location at Theaterstr. 2 is more expensive; the second venue Kleines Haus has cheaper shows.

> ⚐ Tram 8, 11, 12: Postplatz. From the station, walk down Ostra-Allee, left on Theaterstr. Ⓢ Tickets €9-20. ⓐ Box office open M-F 10am- 6:30pm, Sa 10am-2pm.

ESSENTIALS

Practicalities

- **TOURIST OFFICES:** The tourist office staff books rooms (from €25) for free and sells the Dresden City Card and the Dresden Regio Card (see below). *(General information ☎0351 49 19 21 00. Room reservations ☎0351 49 19 22 22. Group tours ☎0351 49 19 21 00. Advance ticket purchases ☎0351 49 19 22 33. ▣www.dresden-tourist.de Ⓢ English language city guides €.50. Audio-walking tour in English €7.50 for 4hr. ⓐ Open M-F 10am-6pm, Sa-Su 10am-4pm.)*

- **TOURS: Stadtrundfahrt** double-decker bus tours include 30min. walking tours of the Zwinger Palace and Fauenkirche. Stay onboard for the 90min tour, or go freestyle and jump on and off as you please at any of the 22 stops. *(Depart from Theaterpl. ☎0351 899 56 50 ▣www.stadtrundfahrt.de Ⓢ Day pass €20, children €1. ⓐ Tours Apr-Oct 9:30am-5pm every 15-30min., Nov-Mar 9:30am-3pm every 30-60min.)*

- **CURRENCY EXCHANGE:** Western Union money transfer service is available at **ReiseBank.** *(Located in the Hauptbahnhof. ☎0351 471 21 77 Ⓢ min. €2 max. €10 fee for any exchange, plus 2.5% charge on the amount exchanged. ⓐ Open M-F 8am-8pm, Sa 9am-6pm, Su 10am-6pm.)* **Deutsche Bank.** *(Located on the corner of Königsbrücker Str. and Katharinenstr. in the Neustadt. ☎0351 482 40 ▣www.db.com ⓐ Open M-Tu 9am-1pm and 2-6pm, W 9am-1pm, Th 9am-1pm and 2-7pm, and F 9am-1pm and 2-4pm.)*

- **LUGGAGE STORAGE:** Lockers are located in all train stations. Follow suitcase symbol. (Ⓢ €3-4 per 24hr.)

- **HOME SHARE: Mitwohnzentrale** offers flats available in outer districts from €150 per month. (Dr.-Friedrich-Wolf-Str. 2, on Schlesischer Pl. ☎0351 194 30 🖳www. dresden-mitwohnzentrale.de 🕐 Open M-F 10am-8pm, Sa-Su 10am-2pm.)

- **GAY AND LESBIAN RESOURCES: Grenede.** (Prießnitzstr. 18. ☎3051 802 22 51. Counseling ☎0351 804 44 80 🖳www.gerede-dresden.de 🕐Open M-F 8am-5pm.)

- **WOMENS RESOURCES: Frauenzentrum "sowieso" (Frauen für Frauen)** specializes in addressing sexual harassment and assault, eating disorders, and employment. (Angelikastr. 1. ☎0351 804 14 70 🖳www.frauenzentrumsowieso.de ⚡ Tram 11: Angelikastr., or walk 30min. up Bautzner Str. from Alpertpl. 🕐 Open M, W, and F 9am-3pm, Th 9am-6pm. Advice in person or by phone M, W, F 9-11am, Th 3-6pm. Psychologist by appointment M-F or walk-in Th 3-6pm.)

- **LAUNDROMATS: Eco-Express.** (2 Königsbrücker Str., on Albertpl. Ⓢ Wash €1.90 before 11am, €2.40 after 11am. 14kg machine €5. Dry €0.50 per 10min. Soap €0.30. 🕐 Open daily 6am-11pm.) Staff books rooms (from €25) for free and hands out city map.

- **INTERNET ACCESS: Mondial.** (Rothenburgerstr. 43. Enter on Louisenstr. ☎0351 896 14 70 𝒊 Wi-Fi available. Ⓢ €2 per hour. 🕐 Open M-F 10am-1am, Sa-Su 11am-1am.) **Haupt- und Musikbibliothek.** (Freiberger Str. 35, in World Trade Center. ☎0351 864 82 33 𝒊 Some English books. Free internet 30min. at a time. Music scores, CDs and DVDs. Bring a passport to check out items. 🕐Open M-F 11am-7pm, Sa 10am-2pm.)

- **POST OFFICE:** (Königsbrücker Str. 21-29. ☎0180 304 05 00r 𝒊 Western Union available. Wheelchair accessible. 🕐Open M-F 9am-7pm, Sa 10am-1pm.) An alternate branch is located in the Altstadt. (Wilsdruffer Str. 22 🕐Open M-Sa 10am-7pm.)

- **POSTAL CODE:** 01099.

Emergency!

- **POLICE:** (☎110.)

- **AMBULANCE AND FIRE:** (☎112.)

- **PHARMACY:** Saxonia Apotheke Internationale. (Prager Str. 8a. ☎0351 490 49 49 🖳www.saxoniaapotheke.de 𝒊 Carries international medicines. The Notdienst sign outside lists rotating 24hr. pharmacies. 🕐 Open M-F 9am-8pm, Sa 9:30am-5pm.)

Getting There

By Plane

The **Dresden Airport** information desk (☎0351 881 33 60 🖳www.dresden-airport.de) is reachable by public transit on the S-Bahn, line S2, which leaves every half hour, 4am-11:30pm. The shuttle (tickets €1.90) will pick up or drop off at Dresden-Neustadt and most Dresden hotels (15min.), or the Dresden Hauptbahnhof (20min.).

By Train

Dresden has two main stations: the **Hauptbahnhof** (south of Altstadt), and **Bahnhof-Dresden-Neustadt,** across the Elbe on the western edge of the Neustadt. A third station, **Dresden Mitte,** lies between the two but is rarely used because of its location. Trains to: **Bautzen** (Ⓢ €10.50. 🕐 1 hr., every hour.); **Berlin** (Ⓢ €37. 🕐 3hr., 1 per hr.); **Budapest, Hungary**(Ⓢ €103. 🕐 11hrs., 3 per day.); **Frankfurt am Main** (Ⓢ €87. 🕐 4hr., every hr.); **Görlitz**

germany

(☎ €19. 🕐 1hr., every hr.); **Leipzig** *(☎ €21. 🕐 1hr., 1-2 per hr.);* **Munich** *(☎ €101. 🕐 7hr., 1-2 per hr.);* **Prague** *(☎ €31. 🕐 2hr., 7 per day.).*

Getting Around

By Tram

Dresden is largely a walking city, and there aren't many places you'll need to go that you can't get to on foot. For trips across the city, use the tram system *(Single ticket €1.90; 4-trip card €4; one-day ticket €5; one-week travel pass €14.50).* Tickets are available from **Fahrkarten** dispensers at major stops, and on trams. Validate your tickets in the red boxes onboard the tram. For information and maps, visit ◼www.vvo-online.de, or try the **Service Punkt** stands in front of the Hauptbahnhof or at Postpl., Albertpl., and Pirnaischer Pl. Most major lines run every 10min. or so during the day, and every 30min. after midnight—look for the moon sign marked "Gute-Nacht-Linie."

By Metro

The **S-Bahn,** or suburban train, travels along the Elbe from **Meisßen** to the **Czech border.** Buy tickets from the Automaten and validate them in your red machines at the bottom of the stairwells to each track.

By Taxi

☎0351 211 211 or ☎888 88 88.

By Car

Sixt-Budget *(☎1805 25 25 25)* is located at Hamburger Str. 11, is open M-F 6am-10pm. Sa-Su 8am-noon.

By Bike

Bike rental is available at all train stations. **German Bahn** at Neustadt station and Hauptbahnhof offers bikes for €8 per day. *(☎1805 15 14 15. 🕐 Open M-Sa 6am-8pm, Su 8am-8pm.)*

By Ferry

Sächsische Dampfschiffart *(☎0351 86 60 90 ◼www.sächsische-dampfschiffart.de)* offers daily cruises on steamers along the Elbe, usually departing from the terrace bank in Dresden, to destinations including **Pillnitz** and **Bad Schandau.** *(Office and info desk open M-Th and Su 8am-6pm, F-Sa 8am-7:30pm.)*

Ride Share

Mitfahrzentrale *(Dr.-Friedrich-Wolf-Str. 2, on Schlesischer Pl., across from Bahnhof Neustadt. (☎0351 194 40 ◼www. mitfahrzentrale.de 🕐 Open M-F 9am-8pm, Sa-Su 10am-4pm.)*

frankfurt   ☎069

Forget the cobblestone roads and half-timbered houses of German back in the day: this city on the banks of the Main River is one big financial center, with enough skyscrapers to earn it the nicknames "Mainhattan" and "Bankfurt." Legend has it that the city was auspiciously founded when Charlemagne and his Franks were fleeing the Saxons; they saw a deer crossing the Main River in a shallow *Furt* (ford) and followed it to safety on the opposite bank, and that very spot is where they founded Frankfurt. In 1356, Frankfurt rose to prominence when the Golden Bull of imperial law made it the site of emperors' elections and coronations until the Holy Roman Empire dissolved. Trade fairs—mass conglomerations of merchants all bartering with each other—regularly took place in the city.

Fast forward to the 21st century; Frankfurt now houses the EU's bank, marked by an enormous statue of the euro symbol. Skyscrapers loom over crowded streets and dark-suited stock traders busily jaywalk across avenues. Though Frankfurt has a reputation for being the most Americanized city in Europe, the government works to preserve the city's rich history, and the medieval charisma of **Marburg** and the towns along the **Bergstrasse Wine Road** remain blessedly secluded. By rail, the line running between Frankfurt and Heidelberg also hits all the major towns.

ORIENTATION

The Main River runs east to west through Frankfurt, conveniently splitting it into two parts, though most of the city is located in the north.

North of the Main

The city center is called the **Innenstadt,** the site of the Römerberg and the spired Dom. Its northern end is the city's commercial district, with high-class shops and restaurants stretching along the **Zeil** between the subway stops **Hauptwache** and **Konstablerwache.** Immediately west of that, around **Taunusanlage,** is the city's financial district. To the west lies the **Hauptbahnhof,** surrounded by cheap restaurants and the city's red light district. In the northwest corner is Bockenheim, home to students and the wallet-friendly eateries that join them. Some of the city's most upscale and exclusive nightlife can be found along **Hanauer Landstrasse** in the east side of the city, amid automobile dealerships.

South of the Main

Immediately south of the Main is the **Museumsufer,** a network of museums stretching along Schaumankai running along the river. Collectively, the neighborhood to the south is known as **Sachsenhausen.** In the middle around **Schweizer Platz,** you'll find a collection of age-old Apfelwein eateries, while to the east by **Frankensteiner Platz** is a hopping nightlife district, with bars and throngs of young people.

ACCOMMODATIONS

As the financial center of Europe, Frankfurt doesn't really offer deals, and hotels are often full of bankers and businessmen. The **West End/Bockenheim** area has affordable options in a quiet setting, though nightlife is more accessible from accommodations in **Sachsenhausen** and near the **Hauptbahnhof.**

North of the Main

FRANKFURT HOSTEL — HOSTEL, HOTEL ❷

Kaiserstr. 74 ☎069 247 51 30 www.frankfurt-hostel.de

A convenient location and great prices attract young internationals to this bustling hostel, where new friends hang out in the sunny pastel-colored rooms or the homey lobby. Nab a seat on the balcony and people-watch on the Kaiserstr. below. For a cheap meal, take advantage of the free pasta for guests on Saturday evenings, and free tastings of Frankfurt's signature green sauce on Thursdays.

From the Hauptbahnhof, head along Kaiserstr. to the hostel on the left. ℹ *Breakfast and Wi-Fi included.* $ *Singles and doubles €59; 3-10 bed dorms €19-22.* ⏰ *Reception 24hr. Check-in 2pm. Check-out 11am.*

FIVE ELEMENTS — HOSTEL ❷

Moselstr. 40 ☎069 24 00 58 85 www.5elementshostel.de

This posh hostel right by the Hauptbahnhof offers a bunch of student-friendly amenities, including a 24hr. bar with stylish leather cube seats and a bike rental. Rooms are also stylishly decked in stainless steel bunks with personal reading lamps and under-bed lockers. All this makes it worth overlooking the fact that this hostel is smack-dab in the middle of Frankfurt's red light district—just don't speak to those strangers outside late at night.

From the Hauptbahnhof, walk down Kaiserstr. and then turn left onto Moselstr. ℹ *Towels and Wi-Fi included. Linens €1.50. Breakfast €4. Laptops available to borrow with deposit.* $ *5-7 bed dorms from €18; singles €40; doubles from €50; quads from €88.* ⏰ *Reception 24hr. Check-in 4pm. Check-out noon.*

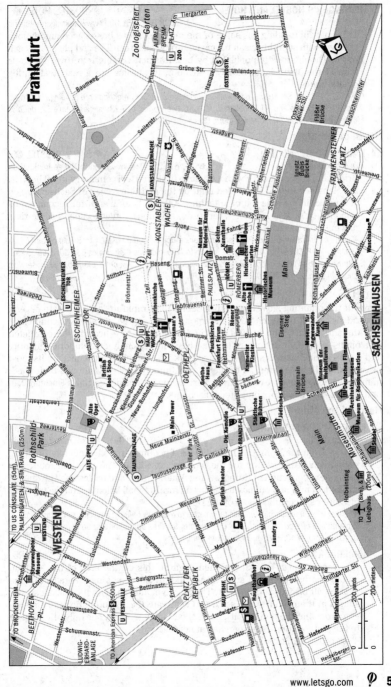

Frankfurt

frankfurt . accommodations

MEININGER'S HOSTEL AND HOTEL

●⊗⁽⁽ᵖ⁾⁾Ⴤ❄❉ HOSTEL, HOTEL ❷

Europaallee. 64 ☎030 66 63 61 00 ■www.meininger-hotels.de

This colorful building has some of the most luxurious hostel accommodations in town, with superbly clean rooms featuring flatscreen TVs and phones in each room. Though mostly populated by businessmen coming into town for trade fairs at the Messe immediately next door, the rooms are a real steal during quieter times.

➹ *S3, S4, S5, or S6: Messe, then walk south towards a blocky multi-colored building.* *i* *Break-fast €7.50. Linens and Wi-Fi included.* Ⓢ *3-6 bed dorms €19-28; singles from €52; doubles €70.* Ⓒ *Reception 24hr. Check-in 3pm. Check-out 10am.*

South of the Main

▨ HAUS DER JUGEND (HI)

●Ⴤ⁽⁽ᵖ⁾⁾Ⴤ HOSTEL ❷

Deutschherrnufer 12 ☎069 610 01 50 ■www.jugendherberge-frankfurt.de

Bright and cheery, though with a slight institutional feel common with HI hostels, the Haus der Jugend is situated right by the nightlife frenzy of Sachsenhausen and packs in a whole ton of amenities. Ask the helpful staff for recommendations if you're at a loss for what to do, and don't forget to spend some time playing with the giant chess set!

➹ *Bus #46: Frankensteiner Pl., then backtrack a tiny bit to the hostel.* *i* *Breakfast and linens included. Wi-Fi €5 per day. Laundry €2.* Ⓢ *8- to 10-bed dorms €18; singles €36.50; doubles €53-63; triples €63-76.50; quads €84-102.* Ⓒ *Reception 24hr. Lock-out 2-6:30am; call for service. Check-in 1pm. Check-out 10am.*

SIGHTS

Ⓖ

Beneath the daunting skyscrapers that define the Frankfurt landscape are several historic sights, all of which have undergone some degree of reconstruction since the Altstadt's destruction in 1944. Old and new come to a head in the conflicted metropolis—some attractions reflect the city's increasingly contemporary identity and others remain as relics of a bygone Frankfurt. The city's museums are its most prized cultural possessions, all of them exceptionally well-done though their sheer number is enough to leave any tourist overwhelmed. Consider getting a **Frankfurt Card** or a **Museumsufer Ticket** for some steep discounts.

North of the Main

▨ MUSEUM FÜR MODERNE KUNST

●ჄჄ MUSEUM

Domstr. 10 ☎069 21 23 04 47 ■www.mmk-frankfurt.de

Blocks from the Dom, this highly stylized postmodern "slice of cake" building provides a fitting setting for the modern art within. The museum rotates its permanent collection of European and American art, and prides itself on special exhibits of new and unknown artists and forms. Small balconies on the top floor also offer spectacular views of the Dom.

➹ *U4 or U5: Römer/Dom. From the station, walk to the curvy building 1 block north of the Dom.* *i* *Explanations offered in English.* Ⓢ *€8, students €4. Free admission last Sa of month.* Ⓒ *Open Tu 10am-6pm, W 10am-8pm, Th-Su 10am-6pm.*

RÖMERBERG

SQUARE

A voyage through Frankfurt should begin in this central area of the Altstadt, among the half-timbered architecture and medieval-looking fountains that appear on all postcards of the city. The Statue of Justice, with its delicate scales, stands in the center of the square to celebrate the 13 coronations of German emperors once held in the city. Once spouting wine, today she only offers shade to the plethora of pigeons perched at her feet.

➹ *U4 or U5: Dom/Römer.*

germany

RÖMER

⏺ CITY HALL

Römerberg 25

At the west end of the Römerberg, the gables of Römer have marked the site of Frankfurt's city hall since 1405. It was also the original stop on the Main for the merchants who began the city's long trade tradition. Today, the building's upper floors are open to the public. Visit the **Kaisersaal**, a former imperial banquet hall adorned with portraits of 52 German emperors, from Charlemagne to Franz II. Be forewarned, however, that private events held in the Römer close the building to the public entirely.

⚟ *U4 or U5: Dom/Römer.* Ⓢ *€2.* ⧗ *Open daily 10am-1pm and 2-5pm.*

ARCHÄOLOGISCHER GARTEN

ARCHAEOLOGICAL SITE

Between the Dom and the rest of the Römerberg are the Schirn Kunsthalle and a plantless "garden" of crumbled building foundations dating back to the 2000-year-old Roman settlement. Three sets of ruins, from the first century BC and the ninth and 15th centuries AD, were uncovered during excavations in 1953. Today, they are preserved in a well-maintained urban garden landscape. Over the summer, theater performances often take place on scaffolding straddling the garden.

⚟ *U4 or U5: Dom/Römer. From the stop, head towards the Dom.*

DOM

⏺&⟡ CHURCH

Dompl. 14 ☎069 13 37 61 84 🖳www.dom-frankfurt.de

East of the Archäologischer Garten stands the only major historical building in the city center that escaped complete destruction in WWII. The seven electors of the Holy Roman Empire chose emperors here, and the Dom served as the site of coronation ceremonies from 1562 to 1792. The **Dom Museum** inside the main entrance has architectural studies of the Dom, intricate chalices, and the ceremonial robes of imperial electors. The **Haus am Dom**, across the courtyard from the church itself, also houses a branch of the museum.

⚟ *U4 or U5: Dom/Römer.* Ⓢ *Cathedral free. Dom Museum €3, students €2. Tours €3, students €2.* ⧗ *Cathedral open M-Th 9am-noon and 2:30pm-8pm, F 2:30-8pm, except during services. Tours in German Tu-Su 3pm. Museum open Tu-F 10am-5pm, Sa-Su 11am-5pm. Haus am Dom open M-F 9am-5pm, Sa-Su 11am-5pm.*

GOETHEHAUS

⏺⏺ HOUSE

Großer Hirschgraben 23-25 ☎069 13 88 00 🖳www.goethehaus-frankfurt.de

The house in which the father of Faust was born was meticulously reconstructed after its WWII destruction and has since been preserved as a shrine to the author, with all of his family's fine furnishings on display. Wind your way up the four stories of sitting rooms, bedrooms, and writing chambers and learn more than you ever thought possible about the childhood home of Germany's most beloved literary giant. The memorable writing chamber, puppet-show room, and personal library should not be missed. If you still want more, the neighboring **Goethe Museum** promises to offer obsessed fans a more in-depth look at the author's life when it reopens after an extensive renovation in early 2011.

⚟ *U1, U2, U3, U4, or U5: Willy-Brandt-Pl. From the stop, follow the signs.* 𝒊 *English placards available.* Ⓢ *€5, students €2.50. Interactive audio tour €3.* ⧗ *Open M-Sa 10am-6pm, Su 10am-5:30pm.*

MAIN TOWER OBSERVATION DECK

⏺& OBSERVATION DECK

Neue Mainzer Str. 52-58. ☎069 36 50 47 40 🖳www.maintower.de

Vistors will agree that a trip to the top of Frankfurt's only observation deck is a must. Take the elevator to the 54th floor and walk three floors up to the outdoor observation deck, where your 250m height will let you see for miles (kilometers) on end. You can also sip a cocktail *(from €4)* at the bar just one floor below.

frankfurt • sights

🚇 *S-bahn: Taunusanlage. From the stop, walk along Junghofstr. and then turn right onto Neue Mainzer Str.* $ *€5, students €3.50.* ⏰ *Ground floor exhibit open M-F 8am-8pm, Sa-Su 10am-5pm. Platform open in summer M-Th 10am-9pm, F-Sa 10am-11pm, Su 10am-9pm; in winter M-Th 10am-7pm, F-Sa 10am-9pm, Su 10am-7pm. Restaurant and bar open Tu-Th 5:30pm-1am, F-Sa 5:30pm-2am.*

South of the Main

Museumsufer

The Museumsufer (that's Museums-ufer, not Museum-sufer, and most definitely and most unfortunately not Museum-surfer) is a strip along the southern bank of the Main that hosts an eclectic range of museums mostly housed in opulent 19th-century mansions. The sheer diversity of topics covered in the museums means that there's something for everyone, from film to anthropology to impressionist art. The Museumsufer is also home to Frankfurt's **Museumsuferfest,** a huge cultural celebration held every August with art showings, music, and general revelry among the Main. To get there, take the U1, U2, or U3 to Schweitzer Pl. and then walk north towards the river. Alternatively, take bus #46 from the Hauptbahnhof, which runs along the Museumsufer.

👍 MUSEUM FUR ANGEWANDTE KUNST (MUSEUM FOR APPLIED ART) 🎟♿🍸

Schaumankai 17 ☎069 21 23 40 37 💻www.angewandtekunst-frankfurt.de

With an impressive display of art spanning over 5000 years, the modern wing of the museum is perhaps the most fun, with plenty of quirky chairs and lamps and other simple household items that highlight the evolution of industrial design. The futuristic new building is also connected to the original villa via a bridge on the second floor, inside of which furnished rooms represent unique styles and time periods.

🚇 *On the eastern end of the Museumsufer, by the Eierner Steg footbridge.* $ *€8, students €4.* ⏰ *Open Tu 10am-5pm, W 10am-9pm, and Th-Su 10am-5pm.*

👍 STÄDEL 🎟♿🍸 MUSEUM

Holbeinstr. 1 ☎069 696 05 09 80 💻www.staedelmuseum.de

The crown jewel of the Museumsufer presents seven centuries of art, from Old Masters like Botticelli, Rembrant, and Vermeer, to the fathers of modern art including Monet, Renoir, and Picasso. The permanent collection will be closed until summer 2011 for a top-down renovation, which will result in more space to house the museum's expanded modern art collection. In the meantime, rotating temporary exhibits are on display.

🚇 *By the Holbeinsteg, the colorful suspended footbridge.* **i** *All captions in English. All prices and hours are set to change once the permanent collection reopens.* $ *€12, students €10, under 12 free. Audio tours €4, students €3.* ⏰ *Open Tu 10am-8pm, W-Th 10am-10pm, and F-Su 10am-8pm.*

LIEBIEGHAUS 🎟♿🍸 MUSEUM

Schaumankai 71 ☎069 650 04 90 💻www.liebieghaus.de

The impressive building and gardens contain classical, medieval, Renaissance, Baroque, and Rococo statues, friezes, and other sculptures. A climb up the tower also leads you to several rooms still furnished in the house's original style, full of cozy nooks and outstanding views of the Main.

🚇 *Next door to and west of the Städel.* $ *€9, students 7, under 12 free. Audio tours €4, students €3.* ⏰ *Open Tu 10am-6pm, W-Th until 10am-9pm, F-Su 10am-6pm.*

DEUTSCHES FILMMUSEUM 🎞♿🍸 MUSEUM

Schaumankai 41 ☎069 961 22 00 💻www.deutschesfilmmuseum.de

Observe the progression of film from a 19th-century obsession with optical illusions to the first pictures by the Lumière Brothers. Under renovation until spring 2011, the new museum promises more space and a larger soundproof theater.

🚇 *By the Untermainbrücke.* **i** *Hours and prices will be set when the museum reopens.*

FOOD

Frankfurters love sausages and beer, but they have their own regional specialties as well. Feast on *Handkäse mit Musik*, a gel-like translucent yellow cheese with a strong flavor, served with vinegar and topped with onions. *Grüne Sosse*, or green sauce, is actually a white sauce made green with borrage, sorrel, chives, and other assorted green herbs and served with peeled potatoes and boiled eggs. Wash both of these specialties down with *Apfelwein* (also called *Ebbelwoi*), apple wine, poured from a blue and white porcelain *Bembel* into small 0.3L *Geripptes* glasses. Portions of apple wine should never exceed €2 and are regularly enjoyed in **Sachsenhausen,** the old district on the southern side of the Main.

The most reasonably-priced meals can be found around the Hauptbahnhof, with a large variety of ethnic (mostly Asian) eateries, and in the university district of Bockenheim (take U4, U6 or U7: Bockenheimer Warte). A number of inexpensive food carts and stands populate the Zeil as well as the large shopping district around Hauptwache. For cheap do-it-yourself meals, keep your eyes peeled for **Penny Markt** *(Hanauer Landstr. 1-5, right off the Zeil. ⏰ Open M-Sa 7am-10pm)* or **Aldi Süd** *(Darmstädter Landstr. 10, in Sachsenhausen. ⏰ Open M-Sa 8am-8pm).* At Hauptwache, the **Galeria Kaufhof** *(Zeil 116-126. ⏰ Open M-W 9:30am-8pm, Th-Sa 9:30am-9pm)* also has a grocery store in the basement.

North of the Main

👍 DAS LEBEN IST SCHÖN — 💳⊗🍸❄☀ ITALIAN ❷

Hanauer Landstr. 128 — ☎069 43 05 78 70 💻www.daslebenistschoen.de

This restaurant proclaims "life is beautiful," and looking upon the portraits on the walls, one can't help but agree. A bite of the piping hot pastas or freshly baked pizzas will confirm the sentiment. A summer patio is decorated with nautical themes.

🚏 Tram 11: Schwedlerstr, then keep heading west for a ½-block. Ⓢ Entrees €6.80-16.80. ⏰ Open M-Th 11:30am-midnight, F 11:30am-1am, Sa noon-1am, Su 6pm-midnight.

👍 KLEINMARKTHALLE — ⊛♿🍸 MARKET ❶

Hasengasse 5 — ☎069 21 23 36 96 💻www.kleinmarkthalle.de

Make your own lunch in this three-story warehouse of bakeries, butchers, and produce stands. Cutthroat competition among the many vendors keeps prices low. Find enough meat to feed a small nation, though most of it is raw.

🚏 U4 or U5: Römer/Dom, then head toward the Dom and continue north about a ½ block past the Museum für Moderne Kunst. ⏰ Open M-F 8am-6pm, Sa 8am-4pm.

IMA MULTIBAR — 💳⊗🍸☀ WRAPS ❷

Kleine Bockenheimer Str. 14 — ☎069 90 02 56 65 💻www.ima-multibar.de

One of the only affordable eateries by the opulent Goethestr., IMA Multibar serves up delicious and hearty wraps and salads to throngs of shoppers and young professionals. The fast-paced (pay up at the front) and hip (check out the bathroom sinks) combo makes for a popular spot both for lunch and for nighttime drinks.

🚏 U6 or U7: Alte Oper, then head west on Kalbacher Gasse, turn right onto Goethestr., then turn left into the small back alley. Ⓢ Wraps €7.50-9. Salads €4.50-12. ⏰ Open M-W 11am-10:30pm, Th-Sa 11am-1:30am. Kitchen open M-W 11am-9:30pm, Th-Sa 11am-midnight.

CAFE LAUMER — 💳♿🍸☀ CAFE ❷

Bockenheimer Landstr. 67 — ☎069 72 79 12 💻www.cafe-laumer.de

Dine like a local on the outdoor patio or backyard garden of this celebrated cafe in the West End, only a few blocks from the university. Young businessmen on their lunch break enjoy the hearty special of the day *(€6.40-9.80)* while neighborhood residents read the newspaper, drink a cup of coffee *(€2.20)* and eat generous slices of cake *(€2.40-3.20).*

🚇 U6 or U7: Westend, then head east on Bockenheimer Landstr. to restaurant on right. $ Entrees €4.60-9.80. ⏰ Open M-F 9am-8pm, Sa 8:30am-7pm, Su 9:30am-7pm.

JADE-MAGIC WOK ♿🍸 CHINESE [2]

Moselstr. 25 ☎069 27 13 59 88

This cozy little Chinese restaurant not far from the Hauptbahnhof serves up cheap and tasty meals. Try the entrees with *Sa-Cha Soße,* a flavorful difficult-to-describe Chinese sauce. The recommended specials have plenty of entrees for only €5.

🚇 From the Hauptbahnhof, walk straight down Kaiserstr. and turn right onto Moselstr. ℹ If you speak Chinese with the owners, they're likely to give you free dessert. $ Entrees €4.10-12.50. ⏰ Open daily 11:30am-11pm.

South of the Main

ADOLF WAGNER ♿🍸 GERMAN [3]

Schweizer Str. 71 ☎069 61 25 65 🖥www.apfelwein-wagner.de

Saucy German dishes and some of the region's most renowned *Apfelwein* keep patrons of this famous corner of old Sachsenhausen jolly. Sit with storied regulars and try some of the *Grüne Sosse* that you keep hearing about. Head inside for classic German decor, or stay outside for prime people-watching.

🚇 U1, U2, or U3: Schweizer Platz, then head south on Schweizerstr. to restaurant on left. ℹ English menu available. $ Entrees €7.30-13. 0.3L Apfelwine €1.60. ⏰ Open daily 11am-midnight.

NIGHTLIFE

If you're just looking for a low-key night with a few drinks, head to Sachsenhausen on the southern side of the city. Head between **Bruckenstrasse** and **Dreieichstrasse** for an authentic German experience, with rowdy pubs and taverns specializing in local *Apfelwein* (also known as *Ebbelwoi*). The complex of cobblestone streets centering on **Grosse** and **Kleine Rittergasse** teems with cafes, bars, restaurants, and Irish pubs. While nightlife can be fickle, Frankfurt has thriving clubs and prominent DJs, mostly between **Zeil** and **Bleichstrasse** and the nearby **Hanauer Landstrasse.** In general, things don't heat up until after midnight. Wear something dressier than jeans and sneakers if you want to get past the picky bouncers.

North of the Main

COCOON CLUB 🍸 CLUB

Carl-Benz-Str. 21 ☎069 90 02 00 🖥www.cocoonclub.net

Oozing with ultra-hip coolness, this popular club epitomizes trend-setting design with intergalactic decor, curvy walls, fluorescent pods, and "membranous" separators. Dress well to get past the bouncers.

🚇 U11, U12: Dieselstr., then walk down Carl-Benz-Str. until you get to the club. $ Cover €15. ⏰ Open F-Sa 9pm-6am.

PULSE AND PIPER RED LOUNGE 🍸 BAR, CLUB

Bleichstr. 38A ☎069 13 88 68 02 🖥www.pulse-frankfurt.de

An all-in-one with two dance halls, two lounges, a restaurant, and a summer beer garden, Pulse is swanky and chic. Despite its size, the club manages to maintain a cozy feel as bartenders warmly greet regulars on their way in. A smoking section, Piper, comprised of a separate bar and lots of lounge space is one of the largest public smoking areas in Frankfurt. Although officially a gay club, Pulse enjoys a mixed clientele, especially at their restaurant.

🚇 U1, U2, or U3: Escehenheimer Tor, then move 1 block north and 2 blocks west on Bleichstr. ℹ Martini M, all martinis €5. Happy hour Th, all cocktails €6.50. $ Restaurant entrees change monthly, generally €6-22. Beer €2.80-4. Cocktails €8-10. ⏰ Pulse open M-Th 11am-1am,

F 11am-4am, Sa noon-4am, Su noon-1am. Piper Lounge (entry within Pulse) open daily at 6pm and closes with Pulse. Kitchen open until 11pm.

JAZZKELLER JAZZ CLUB

Kleine Bockenheimer Str. 18a ☎069 28 85 37 www.jazzkeller.com

Founded in 1952, Jazzkeller is the oldest jazz club in Germany and has hosted a large number of jazz masters, including **Louis Armstrong** and **Dizzy Gillespie.** Wednesday nights are reserved for jam sessions by local groups, while Friday nights are the DJ-ed "Swingin'-Latin-Funky" dance nights. Live performances take place the other nights of the week.

U6 or U7: Alte Oper, then head west on Kalbacher Gasse, turn right onto Goethestr., then turn left into the small back alley. $ *Cover W and F €5, €12-20 on other nights.* ⏰ *Open W-Th 9pm-late, F 10pm-3am, Sa 10pm-late, Su 8pm-late. Opening time subject to change.*

SWITCHBOARD CAFE

Alte Gasse 36 ☎069 29 59 59 www.ad36.de

More a community center than an actual club, Switchboard is Frankfurt's go-to for the gay and lesbian community. An information center in the basement has walls filled with free pamphlets, and the bartenders (all volunteers) are also extremely knowledgable about the city's sexual health resources. Although much of the clientele is older, many students also go for the homey atmosphere.

U1, U2, or U3: Eschenheimer Tor, then move with traffic down Bleichstr. for 3 blocks and you'll see it on the right. **i** *2nd floor has counseling offices, schedule appointments in advance by phone. Anonymous AIDS testing M 5-7:30pm, €15.* $ *Beer €2.30-3.20. Shots €1.80. Long drinks €5.80.* ⏰ *Open M-Th 7pm-midnight, F-Sa 7pm-1am, Sa-Su 7pm-11pm.*

South of the Main

SAM'S SPORTSBAR BAR

Kleine Rittergasse 28-30 ☎069 66 36 90 20 www.samssportsbar.de

The American theme of this bar might make it a turn-off, low drink prices excuse any kitsch. With €4 cocktails all day and €1 shots after midnight, Sam's is the cheapest bar in the popular Sachsenhausen district, and you'll always find it brimming with young people. Its signature burgers were voted the best in Frankfurt, though in Germany, that statement doesn't go quite as far as it would in America.

Bus #46 (from the Hauptbahnhof) or Tram 14: Frankensteiner Pl., then head down Frankensteinerstr. which turns into Kleine Rittergasse. $ *Beer €2.50-4.10. Mixed drinks €7-8. Entrees €6-29.* ⏰ *Open M-W 4:30pm-1am, Th 4:30pm-2am, F 4:30pm-4am, Sa noon-4am, Su noon-1am.*

ARTS AND CULTURE

Frankfurt has a large variety of venues that bring you everything from opera to musical theater, rock bands to symphony orchestras. Tickets can be bought from Frankfurt Ticket *(☎069 1340-400 www.frankfurt-ticket.de ⏰ Open M-F 9am-8pm, Sa 9am-7pm, Su 10am-6pm.)*, or at its office at the B level of the Hauptwache U-Bahn station *(open M-F 10am-6pm, Sa 10am-4pm)*.

Stadtische Buhnen

This modern complex in the financial Willy-Brandt-Platz is home to two main companies: the **Oper Frankfurt** and the **Schauspiel.** Both also hold regular performances in the **Bockenheimer Depot,** a converted train depot *(Carlo-Schmid-Platz 1, take the U4, U6, or U7: Bockenheimer Warte. ☎069 134 0400 www.bockenheimer-depot.de)*.

OPER FRANKFURT OPERA

Untermainanlage 11 ☎069 134 04 00 www.oper-frankfurt.de

The new digs of Frankfurt's renowned opera company are situated by the financial district, and the chunky building suits the modern interpretations performed within. Check out the big cloud sculpture that drapes around the lobby.

✈ *U1, U2, U3, U4, or U5: Willy-Brandt-Platz, then head toward the big euro statue.* ℹ *Tickets include use of local public transit 5hr. before the performance until the transit shutdown.* Ⓢ *Tickets €9-130, students ½-price.* 🕐 *Box office open M-F 10am-6pm, Sa 10am-4pm.*

SCHAUSPIEL
✦&❀ THEATER

Neuer Mainzer Str. 17 ☎069 134 04 00 💻www.schauspielfrankfurt.de

Frankfurt's premier theater company puts on about 25 productions a year, many of them experimental. The complex consists of three venues: the **Schauspielhaus** is the largest theater stage in all of Germany, the **Kammerspiele** is kept completely black to prevent distractions, and the **Box** is an intimate venue with only 66 seats.

✈ *U1, U2, U3, U4, or U5: Willy-Brandt-Pl., then head toward the river on Neuer Mainzer Str.* ℹ *Tickets include use of local public transit 5hr. before the performance until the transit shutdown.* Ⓢ *Tickets €10-44, students €6-10.* 🕐 *Box office open M-F 10am-6pm, Sa 10am-4pm.*

Other Venues

THE ENGLISH THEATRE
✦&❀ THEATER

Gallusanlage 7 ☎089 242 316 20 💻www.english-theatre.org

The largest English-language theater in continental Europe, the English Theatre has 300 seats and puts on between 6-8 shows per season, ranging from dramatic tragedies to light-hearted musicals.

✈ *U1, U2, U3, U4, or U5: Willy-Brandt-Pl., then walk past the Euro statue and turn right onto Gallusanlage.* Ⓢ *Tickets generally €21-34, student tickets (not available for Sa performances) €14-23.* 🕐 *Performances Tu-Sa 7:30pm, Su 6pm. Box office open M noon-6pm, Tu-F 11am-6:30pm, Sa 3pm-6:30pm, Su 3pm-5pm.*

ALTE OPER
✦&❀ CLASSICAL MUSIC

Opernpl. 1 ☎069 134 03 75 💻www.alteoper.de

Once an ornate opera house, performances here now mostly consist of classical music rather than opera. Although Frankfurt does not have their own symphony orchestra, the city is often a tour stop for internationally renowned orchestras, including the New York Philharmonic and the Berlin Philharmonic. The hall is also home to the Sir Georg Solti Conducting Competition, held every other October.

✈ *U6 or U7: Alte Oper.* Ⓢ *Shows vary in price, students under 27 pay ½-price.* 🕐 *Box office open M-F 10am-6:30pm, Sa 10am-2pm.*

DIE KOMÖDIE
✦&❀ THEATER

Neue Mainzer Str. 14-18 ☎069 28 43 30 💻www.diekomoedie.de

This cozy little theater produces lighter theatrical fare, with all productions in German.

✈ *U1, U2, U3, U4, or U5: Willy-Brandt-Pl., then walk toward the river along Neue Mainzer Str.* Ⓢ *Tickets generally €20-30.* 🕐 *Box office open M-F 9am-5pm.*

ESSENTIALS 🔁

Practicalities

- **TOURIST OFFICE:** (☎069 21 23 88 00 💻www.frankfurt-tourismus.de ✈ *In the Hauptbahnhof near the main exit, next door to the car rental.* Ⓢ *Brochures, tours, and maps €0.50-1. Books rooms for a €3 fee, free if you call or email ahead.* 🕐 *Open M-F 9:30am-5:30pm, Sa-Su 9am-6pm.)* **Alternate location.** *(Römerberg 27* ℹ *Books rooms.* 🕐 *Open M-F 9:30am-5:30pm, Sa-Su 10am-4pm.)*

- **TOURS:** (Ⓢ *Afternoon tours €26, students €21, under 12 €10. 25% discount with a Frankfurt-Card. Evening tours €16, students €12, under 12 €5.* 🕐 *Afternoon tours depart daily 10am and 2pm (in winter 2pm) from the Romerberg tourist office, 15min. later from the Hauptbahnhof tourist office. Tours available in 14 different* *languages and last 2½hr. Evening tours (1½hr.) depart from the Hauptbahnhof at 5:45pm.)*

- **BUDGET TRAVEL: STA Travel.** *(Bergerstr. 118 ☎069 904 36 970 💻www.statravel.de 🚏 U4: Höhenstr., then walk with the flow of traffic down Bergerstr. ℹ Books national and international flights and sells ISICs. ⏰ Open M-F 10am-7pm, Sa 10am-4pm.)*
- **CONSULATES: Australia.** *(Neue Mainzer Str. 52-58, 28th fl. ☎069 90 55 80 ⏰ Open M-Th 9am-4:30pm, F 9am-4pm.)* **US.** *(Gießenerstr. 30 ☎069 753 50 ⏰ Open M-F 8am-4pm. Closed holidays and the last Th of the month.)* **Ireland.** *(Gräfstr. 99 ☎069 977883883 ⏰ Open by appointment only.)*
- **CURRENCY EXCHANGE:** At any bank. Banks in the airport and the **ReiseBank** at the Hauptbahnhof *(☎069 24278591 ⏰ Open daily 7:30am-9pm.)* have slightly worse rates but, unlike most banks, stay open during the weekend. **Deutsche Bank.** *(🚏 Right across the street from the Hauptbahnhof.)* **American Express.** *(Theodor-Heuss-Allee 112 ☎069 9797 1000 ⏰ Open M-F 9:30am-6pm, Sa 10am-2pm.)* Germany's only remaining American Express branch exchanges currency, handles travelers' checks, and arranges hotel and rental car reservations.
- **INTERNET ACCESS:** Plenty of Internet-Telefon stores can be found on Kaiserstr., directly across from the Hauptbahnhof. **CyberRyder** *(Töngegasse 31 $ Internet €1.30 per 15 min. Drinks €1.50-3. ⏰ Open M-F 9:30am-10pm, Sa 10am-10pm, Su noon-9pm.)* Boasts itself as Frankfurt's 1st internet cafe, CyberRyder has computers and Wi-Fi in a cozy cafe setting.
- **POST OFFICE:** *(inside the Hauptbahnhof, opposite track 16. ⏰ Open M-F 7am-7pm, Sa 9am-4pm.)*
- **POSTAL CODE:** 60313.

Local Services

- **GAY AND LESBIAN RESOURCES:** The **Switchboard** contains a gay information center. *(Alte Gasse 36 ☎069 29 59 59 💻www.ag36.de 🚏 Take the U- or S-Bahn to Konstablerwache.)* It also has the **Cafe der AIDS-Hilfe Frankfurt,** a popular bar/cafe run by the local AIDS foundation. *(ℹ Anonymous AIDS testing M 5-7:30pm, €15. ⏰ Open Sept-June M-Th 7pm-midnight, F-Sa 7pm-1am, Su 2-11pm; Jul-Aug M-Th 7pm-midnight, F-Sa 7pm-1am, Su 7-11pm.)* Another solid resource is the **AIDS Anoyme Beratungsstelle.** *(AIDS Anonymous Information Center ☎069 21243270 💻www.gesundheitsamt.stadt-frankfurt.de.)*
- **LAUNDROMATS:** *(SB Waschsalon, Wallstr. 8 🚏 Near Haus der Jugend in Sachsenhausen. $ Wash €3.50, dry €0.50 per 10min. ⏰ Open daily 6am-11pm.)*

Emergency!

- **EMERGENCY:** ☎110.
- **FIRE AND AMBULANCE:** ☎112.
- **PHARMACY: Apotheke im Hauptbahnhof.** *(train station's Einkaufspassage ☎069 23 30 47 🚏 Take the escalators heading down towards the S- or U-Bahn trains, then turn left. ⏰ Open M-F 6:30am-8pm, Sa 8am-9pm, Su 9am-8pm.)*

Getting There

By Plane

The largest and busiest airport in Germany, Frankfurt's **Flughafen Rhein-Main** *(☎0180 537 24636)* is the gateway to Germany for thousands of travelers from all over the world. From the airport, S-Bahn trains S8 and S9 travel to the Frankfurt Hauptbahnhof every

15min. *($ Tickets €3.80. Buy from the green Fahrkarten machines before boarding.)* Most public transportation and trains to major cities depart from **Airport Terminal 1.** Take the free bus *(every 15min.)* or walk through the skyway to reach the terminal from the main airport. Taxis to the city center *(around €20)* can be found outside every terminal.

By Train

The Hauptbahnhof is located in the west side of the city, close to the river: 0180 519 4195; www.bahn.de for reservations and information. Trains leaving from Frankfurt include those to **Berlin** *($ €90-150. ⏰4 hr., 2 per hr.)*; **Köln** *($ €30-90. ⏰1-2hr., 3 per hr.)*; **Munich** *($ €40-90.⏰ 3-4hr., 2-3 per hr.)*; **Heidelberg** *($ €16-26.⏰ 1-1.5hr., 2-3 per hr.)*; **Dresden** *($ €60-110.⏰ 5-8hr., every hr.)*; **Amsterdam, NED** *($ €49-140.⏰ 4-5hr., every 2 hr.)*; **Paris, FRA** *($ €59-140.⏰ 4-5hr., 6 per day)*; **Basel, CHE.** *($ €60-100.⏰ 3hr., 1 per hr.)*

By Ride Share

Mitfahrenzentrale, *(Stuttgarterstr. 12. Take a right on Baselerstr. at the side exit of the Hauptbahnhof (track 1) and walk 2 blocks toward the river. ☎069 19440 💻www.mfz.de ⏰ Open M-F 9:30am-5:30pm, Sa 10am-2pm.)* Arranges rides to Berlin *(€20)*, Munich *(€15)*, Köln *(€11)*, Amsterdam *(€20)*, Vienna *(€24)*, and other cities.

Getting Around

By Public Transportation

Buy your tickets from the green-blue Fahrkarten machines immediately before boarding; tickets are automatically validated upon purchase and are valid for 1hr. Check first if your destination qualifies for a "short ticket" by looking through the stops at the top of the machine, and then punch in the appropriate number before selecting the type of ticket you want. For rides within Frankfurt, use the code "50" *($ €2.30. ⏰ Open M-F 6-9am and 4-6:30pm and Sa-Su all day €2.40, children €1.40. Short rides €1.50, children €1. Day tickets €6, children €3.60, group of up to 5 adults €9.50.)* Failure to buy a ticket results in an immediate €40 fine, and Frankfurt is notorious for checking, especially during rush hour.

By Taxi

☎069 23 00 01, ☎069 23 00 33, or ☎069 79 20 20.

By Car Rental

At the Hauptbahnhof by the Reisezentrum, you'll find the offices of **Avis** *(☎0180 55577 ⏰ Open M-F 7am-9pm, Sa and holidays 8am-5pm, Su 10am-4pm)*, **Europcar** *(☎0180 58000 ⏰ Open M-F 7am-8pm, Sa 8am-7pm, Su 8am-7:30pm)*, **Hertz** *(☎01805 333535 ⏰ open M-F 7am-9pm, Sa-Su and holidays 8am-5pm)*, and **Sixt.** *(☎0180 5252525 ⏰ Open M-F 6:30am-9pm, Sa 8am-5pm, Su and holidays 8am-7pm.)*

By Boat

Several companies offer Main tours, departing from the Mainkai on the northern bank near the Romerberg. **KD.** *(☎069 285728 💻www.k-d.com $ €7.80 per person. ⏰ 1hr. round trips aboard the MS Palladium daily between Apr and Oct at 10:30am, noon, 2, 3:30, 5, and 6:30pm.)* **Primus-Linie** *(☎069 1338370 💻www.primus-linie.de)* cruises to a variety of towns along the Main, making for great day trips.

By Bike

Deutsche Bahn (DB) runs the citywide bike rental, **Call a Bike.** Look for the bright red bikes with the DB logo on street corners throughout the city. Retrieve unlocking code by phone or online *(☎0700 05225522 💻www.callabike.de)*, bikes are €0.10 per min., €15 per day. Another similar company is **NextBike,** but you must return bikes to specific locations throughout the city *(💻www.nextbike.de $ Bikes are €1 per hr., €8 per day.)*

If you ask the average traveler about this Bavarian capital, you'll hear beer, beer, and more beer. The birthplace of **Oktoberfest,** Munich (pop. 1,350,000) prides itself on making some of the world's finest brews, providing beer gardens and halls with the source of merriment and pleasure. Yet those who look past the city as a bastion of alcohol will find that it has much more to offer. As the third largest city in Germany, Munich is also a thriving center of European commerce, and some residents even call the city "Toytown" for its relative wealth and ease of living. World-class museums, parks, architecture, and a rowdy art scene mix the archaic with the modern in a city that is, contrary to some misconceptions, not drowning in booze. Most of the time. Many Muncheners (not Munchkins) also head to Salzburg for a day (only 1½hr. away by train).

ORIENTATION

City Center

The city center is the hub of all tourist activity in Munich. Most of Munich's historical sights and name-brand stores are jam-packed into the few blocks between **Marienplatz** and **Odeonsplatz.** Struggle through the throngs of ubiquitous international camera-flashers and get yourself the stereotypical Bavarian experience, complete with a night at the infamous **Hofbräuhaus** and a stroll through the **Residenzmuseum** and the adjoining **Hofgarten.** South of Marienplatz is the neighborhood **Isarvorstadt,** once home to the city's underground nightlife scene. Today it's more a bustling, yuppie neighborhood, but the bars have retained their original bohemian splendor. This neighborhood also houses Munich's GLBT district. To its west is **Isarvorstadt-Ludwigvorstadt, Theresienwiesen,** otherwise known as the Oktoberfest field, or what we call the stuff of legend. Immediately north of that is the **Hauptbahnhof,** Munich's central train station, where numerous hostels provide an excellent atmosphere for meeting fellow travelers.

University Area

Hear "university area," think culture and retail. Many of the city's impressive art museums dot **Maxvorstadt,** home of the **Königsplatz,** as well as fancy-pants restaurants, quaint coffee houses, and secondhand shops. **Schwabing,** to the north, is a student's dream district; Ludwig-Maximilian Universität erudites keep the area trendy and cozy yet upscale bars and eateries running with their patronage. To the west of Schwabing everything goes greener with the charming **Englischer Gartens** and Munich's beloved beer gardens by the **Chinesischer Turm** (Chinese pagoda).

Olympic Area

The 1972 Olympics was Germany's chance to prove itself in the international spotlight after the racist diasters that had riled 1936 Berlin Olympics under the Nazi regime. However, its success was largely shadowed by the killing of 11 Israeli athletes by Palestinian terrorists. Now known as the **Munich Massacre,** it was immortalized through Steven Spielberg's 2005 film *Munich.* Today, you can visit the **Olympiapark** and marvel at the site of the Games. The imposing **Olympiaturm** (Olympic Tower) is the highest point in all of Munich at 291 meters, and the iconic **Olympiastadion's** (Olympic Stadium) curtains of acrylic glass drape over lime green seats. Also on-site is all things **BMW,** with a museum, factory, and showroom, and the enormous shopping mall, **Olympia-Einkaufzentrum,** for all your food and fashion needs.

munich . orientation

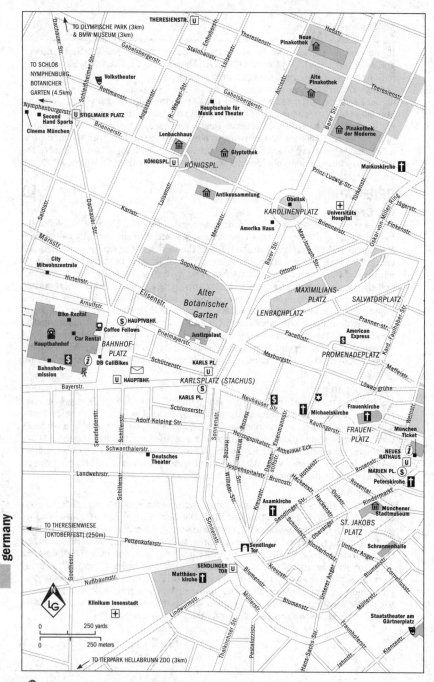

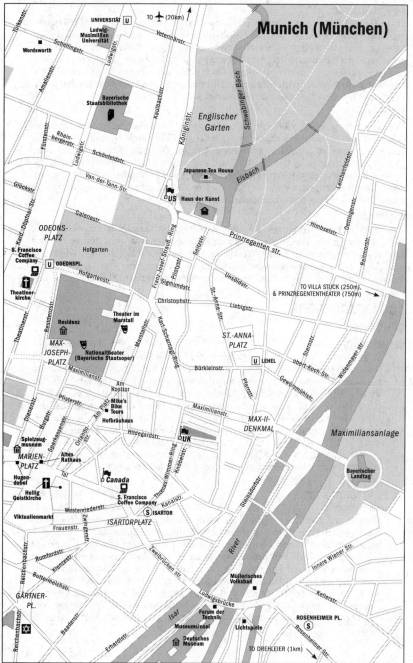

Munich (München)

munich . orientation

Au-Haidhausen

These two neighborhoods across the Isar used to house laborers before WWII bombing nearly demolished Au, though Haidhausen was left surprisingly intact. Today, these regions play a large role in Munich's cultural scene. **Gasteig** cultural complex contains Munich Philharmonic, a conservatory, the main branch of the public library, and an experimental theater all in one. On the flip side, staples of Munich nighlife line **Westbahnhof** station, with enormous clubs dedicated to all things glitter and party. Talk about being on the right side of the tracks.

Neuhausen

Neuhausen remains one of Munich's hidden gems, relatively undiscovered by tourists, so it still actually has character. Take Tram 17 towards Amalienburgstr. and you'll find some of Munich's prettiest landscapes, from the world's largest beer garden at **Hirschgarten** to the beautiful and extravagant **Schloss Nymphenburg** to the tranquil **Botanischer Garten**. For a more urban feel, head to **Rotzkreuzplatz** and meander down Nymphenburgstr. for the city's best cafes and ice cream, then end your night with a rousing chorus at the **Lowenbräukeller** beer hall.

Thalkirchen

This quiet and relatively unexplored neighborhood is actually the Circle of Life. Well, not really, but Thalkirchen's **Tierpark Hellaburn** is the world's first zoo to put animals in their "native habitats." Today, the zoo remains a delight for children and wildlife photographer wannabes, while others take in the beauty of the **Isar River** with extended rafting trips on floating beer gardens and kayaking or rafting along a few legendary whitewater patches.

ACCOMMODATIONS

City Center

WOMBATS — HOSTEL [2]

Senefelderstr. 1 ☎089 59 98 91 80 🖥www.wombats-hostels.com/munich

With its bright fluorescent colors and curvy lobby furniture, Wombats caters to hip hostel-hoppers. Redeem the free drink voucher you got at check-in at the bar while you play a few games of pool with some new friends, and relax on a hammock in the sunny winter garden. Many rooms facing the winter garden have poor ventilation, though the noisy fans (provided) offer a little respite. All rooms have private bathrooms, high-tech key-card lockers, and clothing hangers.

➡ S1, S2, S3, S4, S5, S6, S8, U1, U2, U4, or U5: Hauptbahnhof. Across the street from the Hauptbahnhof (south side). ℹ Linens included, but you'll have to make and strip your own bed. Wi-Fi in the lobby (spotty connection in rooms) included. $ 4- to 10-bed dorm rooms from €12-27; doubles €35-38. ⏰ Reception 24hr.

EURO YOUTH HOTEL — HOSTEL [2]

Senefelderstr. 5 ☎089 59 90 88 11 🖥www.euro-youth-hotel.de

Cozy rooms, good company, and knowledgable staff define this centrally-located hostel, which also offers complimentary tea and coffee for its guests. The 12-person dorms are a bit cramped, but doors to the outdoor terrace provide excellent (and much-needed) ventilation. An outlet at each bed lets you charge your electronics overnight with ease. With its 360-degree wrap-around bar, the lounge here is a popular hangout and final stop for many beer tours through Munich.

➡ S1, S2, S3, S4, S5, S6, S8, U1, U2, U4, or U5: Hauptbahnhof. Across the street from the Hauptbahnhof. ℹ Shared and private bathrooms available. Free Wi-Fi. $ 12-bed mixed dorms €18.80-22.00; singles €50-52. Doubles, triples, quads, and quints also available. ⏰ Reception 24hr.

University Area

PENSION AM KAISERPLATZ
🚫⊘📶❄ PENSION [3]

Kaiserpl. 12 ☎089 34 91 90

Each elegantly decorated room in this 10-room pension has its own unique period style, from Victorian to Baroque, with every detail down to the patterend bedsheets from Italy selected meticulously by the owner herself. The quiet neighborhood is slightly removed from the touristy hubbub of the city center, but only a stone's throw from the student-infested Schwabing.

🚉 *U3 or U6: Münchener Freiheit. Walk past Vanilla Lounge down Herzogstr., then turn left onto Viktoriastr.; the pension is on the right at the end of the street.* ℹ *Breakfast (served in-room) included. Rooms fill up quickly, so book in advance.* $ *Singles from €31, with shower €47; doubles €49; triples €72; quads €92; quints €110; 6-bed rooms €138.* ⏰ *Reception 8am-8pm.*

PENSION ISABELLA
🚫⊘📶❄ PENSION [4]

Isabellastr. 35 ☎089 271 35 03 🖥www.pensionisabella.de

Each room offers plenty of space and seating areas, with unique decor and in-room sink. Bathrooms are shared, but they're large and clean.

🚉 *U2: Hohenzollernpl. Walk west on Hohenzollernpl. and turn left onto Isabellastr.; it's on the right.* ℹ *English-speaking owner. Wi-Fi included.* $ *Singles €38-53; doubles €60-80; triples €78-108; quads €88-128.* ⏰ *Reception 8am-8pm.*

Olympic Area

HAUS INTERNATIONALE
💳⊘📶🍸❄ HOSTEL [2]

Elizabethstr. 87 ☎089 12 00 60 🖥www.haus-internationale.de

Clean rooms, an expansive cafeteria, and serene courtyard make this quiet and out-of-the-way hostel a good bet if you're in the area. A discotheque downstairs, open until 1am, pretty much makes up the local scene since the only thing nearby is a gas station across the street. Haus Internationale has 573 beds, so you're sure to meet other travelers, though most of them are with large groups.

🚉 *U2: Hohenzollernpl., then Bus #53 (dir.: Aidenbachstr.) or Tram #12 (dir.: Romanzplatz): Barbarastr.* ℹ *Breakfast, linens, towels, and Wi-Fi included. Single beds in dorms not available, you must book the entire room.* $ *Singles €33-49; doubles €58-78; triples to 7-bed rooms €30-26 per person. Packages with lunch and dinner (half and full board) also available.* ⏰ *Reception 24hr.; after 11:30pm show room key to security guard for entry.*

Au-Haidhausen

MOTELONE
💳♿📶🍸 HOTEL [3]

Orleansstr. 87 ☎089 59 97 64 90 🖥www.motel-one.de

Turquoise is no longer only Tiffany's. Indeed, MotelOne has taken over the brand's signature shade for their interior decor for their mostly business traveler clientele. Despite translucent tables in the lounge or dramatic black-and-white floor-to-ceiling photos of Munich's greatest sights, the building does not even remotely resemble the famous shop. Cozy rooms are decked out in—you guessed it—turquoise blankets and upholstery.

🚉 *S1, S2, S3, S4, S5, S6, S7, or S8: Ostbahnhof. Turn right onto Orleansstr.* ℹ *Free Wi-Fi in lobby, or €5 per room. No phones in rooms.* $ *Singles from €59; doubles from €74.* ⏰ *Reception 24hr.*

Neuhausen

JUGENDLAGER KAPUZINERHOLZL (THE TENT)
🚫⊘📶🍸 CAMPGROUND [1]

In den Kirschen 30 ☎089 141 43 00 🖥www.the-tent.com

When Munich prepared to host the 1972 summer Olympics, the government kicked out all the hippies camping out at the English Gardens, who then skipped out to the northeast corner of town to set up a permanent camp. There the Tent

munich . accommodations

was born. Sing songs with other campers around the large bonfire before heading to bed in the giant 160-person tent, or get a floor mat (provided) and set yourself up in the unfurnished tent next door. Bathroom facilities are much cleaner and well-maintained than your summer camp ever was, and, true to hippie culture, the cafeteria serves almost exclusively organic foods. A communal kitchen also makes cooking for yourself a breeze.

*# Tram 17: Botanischer Garten, take a right onto Franz-Schrankstr. and a left at the end of the street. **i** Wi-Fi included. Free street parking available (first-come first-served). $ Floor €7.50 (including blankets and floor pad), bed €10.50. Camping €5.50 per person with additional charge from €5.50 per tent. Credit card required for advanced reservation, but only cash payments accepted. ⏰ Reception 24hr except between 10:30-11:30am and 5:30-6:30pm. Quiet hours begin at 1am.*

Thalkirchen

JUGENDHERBERGE MÜNCHEN PARK (HI) HOSTEL [3]

Miesingstr. 4 ☎089 78 57 67 70 🖥www.muenchen-park.jugendherberge.de

This recently renovated hostel is the Hilton of hostels, with brightly-colored, well-designed rooms, each named after a prominent German scientist). Ample shelving and storage make unpacking a real possibility, and glass-enclosed hangout spaces with smart orange sofas encourage relaxation. No bar, but there is a giftshop full of gimmicky jewelry and all sorts of HI memorabilia. A "family room" on the first floor includes a ball pit and slide for youngsters, as well as a spotless kitchen.

*# U3: Thalkirchen, take the Fraunbergstr. exit and then follow the signs. **i** Breakfast and linens included. Wi-Fi €5 per 24hr. In-room lockers require a €2 deposit. $ Singles €38-41; doubles €69-74; 4- to 6-bed dorms €24-30. Age 26+ additional €4 per night. ⏰ Reception 24hr.*

SIGHTS

City Center

MARIENPLATZ SQUARE

Marienpl. 1

Towering spires surround this social nexus, major S- and U-Bahn junction, and pedestrian zone of Munich. The **Mariensäule,** an ornate 17th-century monument of the Virgin Mary, sits at the center of this large square as a tribute to the city's near-miraculous survival of both the Swedish invasion and the plaugue. To the north sits the equally ornate **Neues Rathaus,** the new city hall, built in the early 20th century in a neo-gothic style. Camera-touting tourists can always be found staring at its central tower during the thrice-daily **Glockenspiel** mechanical chimes display, considered to be one of the most overrated attractions in all of Europe *(daily 11am and 12pm, in summers also at 5pm).* To the right of the Neues Rathaus is the **Altes Rathaus,** the old city hall, which now houses a toy and teddy bear museum, **Spielzeugmuseum,** *(open daily 10am-5:30pm, €3, under 15 €1, family €6).* A busy open space, Marienplatz is also often used for political demonstrations.

 # S1, S2, S3, S4, S5, S6, S7, S8, U3 or U6: Marienplatz. $ Free. ⏰ Square open daily.

ALTER PETER CHURCH

Rindermarkt 1 ☎089 260 48 28

An enormous Gothic-inspired church sitting right in the city center, Alter Peter was severely damaged during WWII. It was meticulously rebuilt with true German precision, down to original cannonballs lodged in the church wall (walk around the outside of the church to the back, take the steps leading up to Cafe Rischart, and look around the top right corner of the window frame). Nowadays a 306-step climb to the top of the 92m tower offers the best birds-eye view of Munich: on clear days, you can see over 70 miles.

S1, S2, S3, S4, S5, S6, S7, S8, U3 or U6: Marienplatz. $ Church entry free. Climb to the top €1.50, students and children €1. Tower open M-F 9am-6:30pm, Sa-Su 10am-6:30pm.

RESIDENZ AND HOFGARTEN MUSEUM

Residenzstr. 1 89 26 06 71 www.residenz-muenchen.de

Once the quarters of the Wittelsbach dynasty, the Residenz is now a museum aptly called the Residenzmuseum displaying all its lavish treasures. Get ready for blinding gold leaf gilded rooms decked out in the Baroque, Rococo, and Neoclassical styles. Highlights include the Rococo **Ahnenglerie,** hung with over 100 family portraits tracing the royal lineage, the spectacular **Renaissance Antiquarium,** the oldest room in the palace, replete with stunning frescoes, and large and in charge Chinese and Japanese porcelain. On the same property is the **Treasury,** which houses royal crowns and jewels, and the **Cuvilliés Theatre,** the stunning royal theater that saw the premiere of several Mozart operas. Treasury and theater require a separate ticket for entry. Directly behind the museum is the **Hofgarten**, popular for post-dinner strolls and ballroom dancing under the central pavilion on weekend evenings.

U3, U4, U5, or U6: Odeonsplatz. i Free audio tours available in German, English, French, Italian, and Spanish. Many of the rooms, including those in the Königsbau (King's Tract), will be under renovation for another few years. $ Residenz and Treasury each €6, seniors €5, free for students and children; Residenz and treasury ticket €9/€8/free; Theater €3/€2/free. combination of all three €11/€9/free. Residenz and treasury open daily Apr-mid-Oct 9am-6pm, mid-Oct to Mar 10am-5pm. Theater hours vary based on season schedule; check the website for details. Last entry 1hr. before close.

University Area

The Kunstareal *(www.pinakothek.de)* is a museum district near the edge of Maxvorstadt that comprises the overwhelming majority of Munich's art museums, making it home to a veritable buffet of art. Like all buffets, you can get too much of a good thing and be left feeling nauseated, so try to take in a few each day to truly appreciate the offerings. Most of these museums are free *(all state-run Pinakotheks and the Museum Brandhorst €1)* or reduced price on Sundays (though you will also have to pay for the audio tour, which is usually free every other day), while on other days combination tickets can gain you entry for a discount. A ticket *(€12)* will get you into the three Pinakotheks, the Museum Brandhorst, and the Sammlung Schack for a day, while €29 will get you into them for 5 days, allowing you to time digest between courses.

KÖNIGSPLATZ SQUARE

Literally "The King's Square," Konigsplatz was comissioned by King Ludwig I to be Munich's cultural center. What resulted is a field with three enormous Greek buildings: the **Propyläen,** an ornate gateway, the **Glyptothek,** houses the king's collection of Greek and Roman statues, and the **Antikensammlung,** housing royal antiques. While World War II transformed this "German Acropolis" into a center for Nazi rallies and offices, the entire area was restored back to its original splendor in 1988, and you can now visit both the Glyptothek *(☎089 28 61 00)* and the Staatliche Antikensammlung *(☎089 59 98 88 30 www.antike-am-koenigsplatz.mwn.de)* for their incredible works of ancient art.

U2 or Bus #100: Königsplatz. $ Each museum (Glyptothek and Antikensammlung) €3.50, students €2.50. Museums open Tu-W and F-Su 10am-5pm, Th 10am-8pm.

ENGLISCHER GARTEN GARDEN

Stretching majestically along the city's eastern border, the Englischer Garten (English Garden) is one of the largest metropolitan public parks in the world, dwarfing both New York's Central Park and London's Hyde Park. The possibilities of activities here are numerous, from nude sunbathing (areas are designated FKK, Frei Körper Kultur, or Free Body Culture, on signs and maps) and bustling beer gardens to pick-up soccer games and shaded bike paths. On sunny days, all of Munich turns out to fly kites, ride horses, and walk their beloved dogs. The main park ends with the **Kleinhesseloher See,** a large aritifical lake, but the park extends much further and becomes ever more wild, although the fiercest thing you might get is a roaming flock of sheep. Several beer gardens on the grounds as well as a Japanese tea house offer respite, while the Chinese pagoda and Greek temple make the park an international cultural festival. Need some American spirit? Don't miss the surfers illegally riding the white-water waves of the Eisbach, the artificial river that flows through the park (near the Haus der Kunst, on the southwest corner of the park).

✈ *U3: Universität, Giselastr., or Münchner Freiheit, and head east.*

Olympic Area

OLYMPIAPARK

⬦ SPORTS COMPLEX

☎089 30 67 27 07 ▪www.olympiapark.de

Built for the 1972 Olympic Games, the lush Olympiapark offsets the curved steel and transparent spires of the impressive **Olympia-Zentrum** and the 290m tall **Olympiaturm,** Munich's tallest building. A 1-3hr. self-guided audiowalk gives highlights of the entire park. Otherwise, three English-language tours are available. The 90min. **Adventure Tour** gives an introduction to the history and construction of the entire park with a walk through the Swimming Hall, site of Mark Spitz's then-record 7 gold medal win, the Olympic Hall, and the Olympic Stadium. The 1hr. **Stadium Tour** details the large stadium. The **Roof Climb,** a daring two-hour exploration of the stadium with a rope and hook, is for adrenaline junkies only. Tourists can also marvel at the view from the top of the tower and stroll around the **Rock (and Roll) Museum** at the top.

germany

🚇 U3: Olympiazentrum. ℹ Other tours available in English upon reservation; see website for details. $ Adventure Tour €8, students 5.50. Stadium Tour €6/4. Roof climb €39/29. Tower and Rock Museum €4.50, under 16 €2.80. Discounts with receipt from admission to Sea Life, BMW Welt/Museum. ⏰ All tours offered daily Apr-Nov. Adventure Tour: 2pm, Stadium Tour 11am, Roof Climb 2:30pm (weather permitting). Tower and Rock'n'Roll Museum open daily 9am-midnight. Audiowalk hours vary on season, generally 9am-4:30pm (winter) to 8:30am-8pm (mid-summer); check the website for details.

SEA LIFE — 🎟♿ AQUARIUM

Willi-Daume-Platz 1 ☎018 05 66 69 01 01 💻www.sealifeeurope.com

Seahorses and stingrays and sharks, oh my! This extensive aquarium showcases organisms from many different environments, including Nemo's cousins and fat, ugly groupers. Discovery stations along the way allow you to feel the textures of different aquatic creatures for yourself, and the grand finale—a 10m shark tunnel—will leave you humming Jaws for the rest of the day.

🚇 U3: Olympiazentrum, head towards the tower and then follow the signs. $ €15.50, students €14.50, age 3-14 €9.95; €5 discount if you book online. ⏰ Open Apr-Sept daily 10am-7pm; Oct. M-F 10am-6pm, Sa-Su 10am-7pm; Nov-Mar M-F 10am-5pm, Sa-Su 10am-7pm. Last entry 1hr. before closing.

BMW WELT AND MUSEUM — 🎟♿ MUSEUM

Petuelring 130. ☎018 02 11 88 22 💻www.bmw-welt.com

A marvel of architectural daring, the enormous steel and glass spiral of the BMW museum houses state-of-the-art interactive exhibits detailing the history, development, and design of Bavaria's second-favorite export. Illuminated frosted glass walls and touch-sensitive projections lead visitors past engines, chassis, and concept vehicles with exhibits in both English and German. The award-winning kinetic sculpture features 714 suspended metal balls in a variety of shapes, many of them of historic and current BMW vehicles. Visitors can also tour the adjacent **production factory** with a tunnel that runs through the entire production line, or enjoy the video games and customizable test cars in the **BMW Welt** building.

🚇 U3: Olympiazentrum. BMW Welt will be the large steel structure on your left; a ramp accessible from inside the building will lead you across the street to the museum. ℹ Factory and museum tours available by appointment only. $ Museum €12, students €6. BMW Welt free. Special discounts with Olympiapark ticket or the City Tour Card. ⏰ Museum open Tu-Su 10am-6pm; BMW Welt open daily 9am-6pm.

Au-Haidhausen

VILLA STUCK — 👁♿ MUSEUM

Prinzregentenstr. 60 ☎089 45 55 51 25 💻www.villastuck.de

This elegant villa, designed by Munich artist Franz von Stuck, provides a sophisticated backdrop for the art of the early 20th-century German Jugendstil, a movement that celebrated nature and the smooth lines of the body. Gold mosaic arches, marble fireplaces, and recessed black ceilings offset the colorful landscapes and still lifes. For contrast, rotating exhibits in the basement highlight contemporary artists.

🚇 Bus #100 or Tram #18: Friedensengel. $ €6, students €3. ⏰ Open Tu-Su 11am-6pm.

Neuhausen

★ SCHLOß NYMPHENBURG — 🎟♿❄ CASTLE

Schloss Nymphenburg ☎089 17 90 80 💻www.schloss-nymphenburg.de

The breathtaking Schloß Nymphenburg, a favorite summer residence for Bavarian royalty modeled after Versailles, was built in 1662. Now open to the public, the palace opens with the lavish two-story **Stone Hall,** bursting with extravagant Rococo decor and Neoclassical themes. Make your way through electors' apartments, including the bedroom in which King Ludwig II was born, and feast your eyes on the portraits in the Gallery of Beauties, featuring 36 of whom King Ludwig I considered to be the most beautiful women (nymphs?) in all of Bavaria. Situated in the expansive landscaped gardens are four other equally ornate pavilions: the **Amalienburg, Badenburg,** the grottoed **Magdalenenkrause,** and the oriental **Pagodenburg.** Summertime brings plenty of classical concerts to the park grounds; check kiosks for details. German-speaking science enthusiasts will not want to miss the **Museum Mensch und Natur** *(Museum of Man and Nature, to the right of the palace, www.musmn.de),* a two-story tribute to natural history with superb interactive exhibits.

🚏 Tram 17: Schloss Nymphenburg. ℹ The gardens are free, so you'll often see morning joggers or bikers traversing the grounds. $ Palace €5, students €4; porcelain museums €4/3; pavilions each €2/1; combination ticket for palace and porcelain museums €10/8, €4/3 for all pavilions. Audio tours (English available) €3.50. Museum Mensch und Natur €3/2, Sundays €1. Everything free for under 18. 🕐 Entire complex open daily Apr-Oct 15 9am-6pm, Oct 16-Mar 10am-4pm. Badenburg, Pagodenburg, and Magdalenkrause closed in winter. Museum Mensch und Natur open Tu-W 9am-5pm, Th 9am-8pm, Fr 9am-5pm, Sa-Su 10am-6pm.

HIRSCHGARTEN 🎫♿🍸❄ PARK, BEER GARDEN

Hirschgarten 1 💻www.hirschgarten.com

This seemingly modest park filled with playful children and zen sunbathers is also home to Europe's largest Biergarten, seating a whopping 8000 jolly clinkers. Grab a *Maß* and take a seat in the boisterously delightful atmosphere, and have your heart melted by to all the cute little kids running around the premises. During the summer, the carousel is a constant source of joy. To think, if only you had grown up in a beer garden.

🚏 Tram 17: Romanplatz, then walk south to the end of Guntherstr. ℹ Credit cards accepted in restaurant but not in the a la carte. $ Entrees €7-14. Maß €7.20. 🕐 Kitchen open 11am-10pm.

Thalkirchen

In the summertime, Thalkirchen plays host to flurries of visitors floating (in every sense of the word) down the Isar River. The *Flosslände,* a natural wave along the river (from U3 Thalkirchen, take Bus #135 towards Campingplatz), sees its share of surfers and kayakers. In warm weather, look for kayak rentals along the river. Serenity-seeking visitors instead take a *Flossfahrt,* a day-long trip down calmer waters on an enormous rafts, complete with food, drink and music for a beer garden on the water. Most of these actually begin south of Munich and float to the *Flosslände* as the final stop, see 💻www.isarflossfahrten.biz for more information.

TIERPARK HELLABURN 🐾 ZOO

Tierparkstr. 30 ☎089 625 08 34 💻www.tierpark-hellabrunn.de

Munich's zoo was created in 1911 as the world's first "Geo-zoo," meaning that animals are separated by their original geographic locations and kept in environments as close possible to their original habitats. Dodge the screaming four-year-olds and wander around the four continents represented. Flock with flamingos, elephants, and elks, and make sure to stop in Villa Dracula for the bat house. Vending machines distributing portions of food *(€0.50)* let you get up close and personal with your favorite creatures.

🚏 U3: Thalkirchen, or Bus #52 from Marienpl.: Tierpark. ℹ All explanations in German only. For a more interactive experience, check the feeding schedule at the front gate. $ €9, under 14 €4.50, students €6. 🕐 Open daily Apr-Sept 8am-6pm, Oct-Mar 9am-5pm. Animal houses close 30min. before zoo.

Outside Munich

👍 NEUSCHWANSTEIN CASTLE 🎫♿ CASTLE

Neuschwansteinstr. 20, Schwangau ☎083 62 93 08 30 💻www.neuschwanstein.de

No visit to this castle is complete without a walk across **Marienbrücke**, a slightly rickety wooden-bottomed bridge built by Maximillian, Ludwig's father, for his wife Mary. The bridge sits over a slim and elegant waterfall and gives a stunning side view of Neuschwanstein. Also on-site at Neuschwanstein is the yellow **Hohenschwangau,** King Ludwig II's favorite summer retreat in his youth. Here you can see Ludwig's bedroom, with inlaid crystals on the ceiling to represent stars in the night sky, and the piano and bed that Richard Wagner used during his visits..

*DB: Füssen (about 2 hrs.); once there, walk right across the street to take either the 73 or 78 bus (10 min., 2 per hr., €1.90 per way or free with the Bayern ticket): Königsschlößer (Royal Castles). To get to the castle, you can either walk up the hill (many routes available; 20-50min.), take a bus (up €1.80, down €1, and round-trip €2.60; 10 min.; drop-off behind Neuschwanstein between the castle and Marienbrücke), or take a horse-drawn carriage (up €6, down €3; 15min.). **i** Purchase tickets for tours at the main ticket office located a 3-minute walk uphill. Tours available in 14 different languages, last 35min., and are required for entry into the castle. The summer months bring loads of fairy-tale-seeking tourists, so get there early to reserve your spot. Make sure to save time for some hiking to the Marienbrücke (15min. from Neuschwanstein) and other mountaintop-top destinations. Special wheelchair-accessible tours available with advance registration on Wednesdays. $ Guided tours of castle €9, students €8, under 18 free with an adult. Tickets can also be reserved in advance via phone for an extra €1.80 per ticket. The two castles share a ticket office, though the Hohenschwangau office is open 30min. after Neuschwanstein's closes; combination tickets for the two castles are available (€17/15). ⏰ Castle open Apr-Sept 9am-4pm, Oct-Mar 10am-4pm; ticket office open an hour before opening and closing.*

DACHAU CONCENTRATION CAMP MEMORIAL SITE ♿ MEMORIAL SITE

Alte Römerstr. 75, Dachau ☎081 31 66 99 70 🖥www.kz-gedenkstaette-dachau.de

The first thing prisoners saw as they entered Dachau was the inscription *Arbeit Macht Frei*, "work will set you free" on the iron gate to the camp. Dachau was the Third Reich's first concentration camp, opened in 1933 to house political prisoners on the former grounds of a WWI munitions facotry. After Hitler visited the work camp in 1937, it became a model for over 30 other camps through Nazi-occupied Europe and a training ground for the SS officers who would work at them. Those who volunteered for medical experiments in hopes of release were frozen to death in hypothermia experiments or infected with malaria, all in the name of "science." The barracks, designed for 5,000 prisoners, once held 30,000 men at a time - two have been reconstructed for visitors, and gravel-filled outlines of the other barracks stand as haunting reminders. The camp's crematorium and gas chambers have also been restored. On the site are also Jewish, Catholic, Lutheran, and Russian Orthodox prayer spaces, each designed to offer guidance and solace to visitors. The museum at the Dachau Memorial Site, in the former maintenance building, examines pre-1930s anti-Semitism, the rise of Nazism, the establishment of the concentration camp system, and the lives of prisoners through photographs, documents, videos, interactive exhibits, and artifacts. An additional display in the bunker chronicles the lives and experiences of the camp's most prominent prisoners, including Georg Elser, the SS officer who attempted to assassinate Hitler in 1939.

*S2 (dir.: Petershausen): Dachau (4 stripes on the Streifenkarte, or get a €7 Munich XXL ticket to cover all transportation for the entire day), and then bus 726 (dir.: Saubachsiedlung): KZ-Gedenkstätte (1 stripe, €1.20, or free with Munich XXL ticket). **i** Due to graphic content, museum not recommend for children under 12. All displays have English translations. There is a small cafeteria at the welcome center, but the grounds are extensive, so bring a snack $ Audio guides in English, French, German, Italian, and Hebrew €3.50, students €2.50. Tours €3 per person. Museum and memorial grounds free. ⏰ Open Tu-Su 9am-5pm. Tours (2.5hr.) in English daily at 11am and 1pm, in German at noon. 22min. documentary shown in German at 11am and 3pm, English at 11:30am, 2pm, and 3:30pm.*

FOOD

City Center

👍 AUGUSTINER BEERHALL AND RESTAURANT
💳♿🍸☁ GERMAN [3]

Neuhauserstr. 27 ☎089 23 18 32 57 🖥www.augustiner-restaurant.com

Get your hearty authentic German standards here; try two *weisswurst (white sausages; €4.50)* with a bowl of fresh asparagus soup *(€3)*, or go for gravy-laden roasted pork with a giant potato dumpling and sauerkraut *(€10.50)*. Watch out: the pretzels at your table will actually set you back a little *(€0.90)*. Enjoy the subdued beer-hall ambience in either the main hall or the picturesque courtyard with a .5L Augustiner Edelstoff *(€3.60)*. Though this place may seem like a tourist haven with its multilingual staff and menus, rest assured that most patrons are actually faithful locals.

🚇 SB or UB: Karlsplatz (Stachus), walk past the fountain and under the arches to Neuhauser Str.; restaurant will be on right. ℹ Multilingual menu. $ Entrees €4-24.80. ⏰ Open daily 9am-midnight.

WEISSES BRAUHAUS
💳🚭🍸☁ GERMAN [3]

Tal 7 ☎089 290 13 80 🖥www.weisses-brauhaus.de

Weisses Brauhaus has been serving up excellent renditions of traditional fare since 1540. Try the pork, braised in Aventinus beer, with a selection of house Tegernseer Hell beer *(0.5L €3.50)*. Minimizing on meat? The Weisses Brauhaus salad *(€8.90)* offers a refreshing balance between leafy greens and crispy meat.

🚇 S1, S2, S3, S4, S5, S6, S7, S8, U3, or U6: Marienplatz; walk past the arches or Altes Rathaus to restaurant on the left. ℹ Multilingual menus available. $ Entrees €6.30-13.50. ⏰ Open daily 8am-1am; kitchen open until 11pm.

CAFE RISCHART
🚫💳♿🍸❄☁ CAFE [1]

Marienpl. 18 ☎231 70 03 10 🖥www.rischart.de

Locals complain endlessly about the hordes of tourists that crowd their beloved Cafe Rischart, known for its baked goods and gelato. Thankfully for them, Cafe Rischart has several other locations around the city, but its Marienplatz location is undoubtedly the most iconic. Grab an enormous melt-in-your-mouth slice of butter cake as you people-watch from the patio. In addition, delicious sandwiches *(€3-4)* and pretzels *(€1)* make a great lunch. Definitely do not leave without a scoop of gelato *(€1)*! The sit-down menu is considerably more expensive than take-away, so make a picnic out of it.

🚇 S1, S2, S3, S4, S5, S6, S7, S8, U3, or U6: Marienplatz; located in the SE corner of the square. $ Entrees €4-9. ⏰ Open M-Sa 7am-8pm, Su 9am-7pm.

University Area

👍 BAR TAPAS
🚫💳🚭🍸☁ TAPAS [2]

Amalienstr. 97 ☎089 39 09 19 🖥www.bar-tapas.com

Dark red walls and candlelit tables set the tone at this romantic Iberian outpost. Grab a pen and a slip of paper from the bar to make your selections from the displays of tapas. Especially recommended are the spicy chorizo and the tortilla pie with cheese, potatoes, and onions. The place fills up on the weekends, so get there early.

🚇 U3or U6: Universität. Turn west (left) onto Adalbertstr. ℹ 2-4 tapas recommended per person. Cocktails €5 daily after 10:30pm. $ Each tapas dish €4.20. ⏰ Open daily 4pm-1am.

CAFE IGNAZ
🚫💳🚭☁ VEGETARIAN [3]

Georgenstr. 67 ☎089 271 60 93 🖥www.ignaz-cafe.de

Newton's third law states that for every reaction there is an equal and opposite reaction. In the land of meat and potatoes, that equal and opposite reaction comes in the form of this quaint vegetarian and vegan cafe, its carrot logo the antithesis of Bavarian cuisine. The pastries are delicious with the savory gnocchi and crepes guaranteed winners.

U2: Josephsplatz. Take Georgenstr. west for two blocks. *i* *English-language menu.* *[$] Entrees €7-12. Breakfast buffet M and W-F 8am-11:30am €7 including warm drink. Lunch buffet M-F noon-2:30pm, €6.90. Happy hour M-F 3pm-6pm, one entree for €6. Brunch buffet Sa-Su 9am-2pm, €9.* *⏰ Open M, W-F 8am-11pm, Sa-Su 9am-11pm.*

Au-Haidhausen

WRITSHAUS IN DER AU

GERMAN ❹

Lillienstr. 51 ☎089 448 14 00 🖳www.wirtshausinderau.de

Writshaus in der Au claims to serve the largest dumplings in all of Munich, both in size and variety. Try the Original Münchner Knödel, an enormous hash of pretzel dough, roast pork, and—of course—beer *(€10.50)*. Other favorites include the *Hofente*, Bavarian-style duck fresh from the oven *(€13.80 per portion, €17.90 per half duck)*, and the chocolate dumplings served with a berry compote *(€6.90)*.

Tram 18: Deutsches Museum, then cross the bridge and head past Museum Lichtspiele to turn right onto Lillienstr. *i* *English menu available.* *[$] Entrees €7.70-18.80* *⏰ Open M-F 5pm-1am, Sa-Su 10pm-1am.*

CAFE VOILA

CAFE ❸

Wörthstr. 5 ☎089 489 16 54 🖳www.cafe-voila.de

Locals flock here, maybe because they can sit in the sunny atrium and wonder at the color-changing sign behind the bar over breakfast. Or, more likely, it's the over 100 cocktail choices.

Tram 19: Wörthstr., or S1-8 or U5: Ostbahnhof, head straight out through the entrance onto Wörthstr. one block past the small park between the roads. *i* *Happy hour M-Th and Su 5pm-1am: all cocktails €5.* *[$] Breakfast €4-10.50. Entrees €5.50-21.50.* *⏰ Open daily 8am-1am.*

Neuhausen

RUFFINI

CAFE ❷

Orffstr. 22-24 ☎089 16 11 60 🖳www.ruffini.de

This whimsical cafe on a quiet residential street buzzes with locals catching up with each other or the morning paper. Expert baristas churn out perfect cups of frothy cappucino; order yours with a flaky croissant *(€5.70)* and take it to the sunny rooftop terrace. Downstairs, sample some wines at the bar from an extensive menu *(.25L €4.60-7.40)*, or practice your German reading comprehension with the provided magazines.

Tram 12: Neuhausen, then turn perpendicular to tram route such that park is immediately to the left. Cafe is two blocks down Ruffinistr. *i* *Rooftop terrace is self-service, so order downstairs before you sit down. Small bakery attached, entrance on Ruffinistr.* *[$]Breakfast entrees €5.70-8.30* *⏰ Open Tu-Fr 8:30am-6pm, Sa 8:30am-5pm, Su 10am-5pm.*

AUGUSTINERKELLER

GERMAN ❸

Arnulftr. 52 ☎089 59 43 93 🖳www.augustineerkeller.de

Augustiner is widely viewed as the most prized of ☐Bavarian brews since its birth in 1824, and its beer garden is no less precious. Clinking beer glasses resound as early as 11am at this favorite, where residents enjoy enormous pretzels and dim lighting beneath century-old chestnut trees. The restaurant serves up authentic Bavarian dishes, though the real attraction is the namesake beer.

S1, S2, S3, S4, S5, S6, S7, and S8: Hackerbrucke; turn right onto Anulfstr. *[$] Maß €7.20. Restaurant entrees €9-23. Beer garden is cash only.* *⏰ Beer garden open daily 11:30am-midnight, restaurant open 10am-1am.*

Thalkirchen

ALTER WIRT IN THALKIRCHEN 💳🚭🍸☀ GERMAN ❷

Fraunbergstr. 8 ☎089 74 21 99 77

This traditional Bavarian kitchen also cooks up various international classic cheap eats like burgers and quesadillas. But you didn't come to Germany for that, and honestly you're better off sticking to the traditional stuff. Cheap and hearty food with large portions make this a local favorite.

🚇 U3: Thalkirchen, then head down Fraunbergstr. ℹ Specials include Schnitzel Thursdays (enormous plate of schnitzel with fries, €5.10 with the purchase of a drink). $ Entrees €7-16. ⏰ Open Su-Th 9am-1am, F-Sa 9am-3am. Kitchen closes at midnight.

MANGOSTIN RESTAURANTS 💳🚭🍸☀ ASIAN ❹

Maria-Einsiedel-Str. 2 ☎089 723 20 31 💻www.mangostin.de

Half kitschy, half classy, this orientally-inspired Mangostin cooks up pricey Germanized "Asianese" food in a Japanese garden setting. The other restaurants on the same premises also feature artful decor. You're definitely paying for the miraculous cultural fusion, not the food.

🚇 U3: Thalkirchen, take the Tierpark exit and you'll see it on the corner. $ Entrees €12-25. ⏰ Open 11:30am-midnight, though each restaurant's hours may vary.

NIGHTLIFE

City Center

👍 **HOFBRÄUHAUS** 💳♿🍸 BEER HALL

Platzl 9 ☎089 29 01 36 0 💻www.hofbraeuhaus.de

No trip to Munich is complete without a trip to its most famous beer hall. Steeped in history, Hofbrauhaus remained royalty-only until the King Ludwig I opened it to the public in 1828. Seat yourself at one of the crowded benches and make some new friends. Beer here only comes in liters *(€6.90)*; if you ask for anything less, they'll chortle and bring you a *Maß* anyway. By the end of the night, you'll be singing at the top of your lungs with complete strangers, and if you're not feeling so well, ask to visit the celebrated vomitorium, an ergonomic device built for those occasions.

🚇 S1, S2, S3, S4, S5, S6, S7, S8, U3 or U6: Marienplatz.; take a left right before the Altes Rathaus onto Burgstr., walk past the Alter Hof courtyard and take a right onto Pfisterstr. Restaurant will be on your right. ℹ Get here early to guarantee a spot, especially for large groups. $ Entrees €7-14. ⏰ Open daily 9am-11:30pm.

👍 **CAFE AM HOCHHAUS** 💳🚭🍸☀▼ CLUB

Blumenstr. 9 ☎089 290 13 60 💻www.cafeamhochhaus.de

One of the first clubs in the area, Cafe am Hochhaus defines itself by its musicality, with DJs spinning anything but mainstream, either from jazz to funk. This draws an assorted clientele, and on any given night you might run into some of Germany's most famous models or the 50-year-olds who practically live there. Dance under the vodka-bottle-shaped disco ball, and pause to contemplate the quirky wallpaper. Sunday nights are gay-friendly, though straights are always welcome.

🚇 U1, U2, U3 or U6: Sendlinger Tor; walk towards the tram stop such that the brick arches of Sendlinger Tor are behind you, and turn left onto Sonnenstr. The road will turn into Blumenstr. and curve multiple times before you reach the cafe on your right. ℹ No food. $ Shots €3-5. Cocktails €7-8. ⏰ Open daily 8pm-3am, later on the weekends. The party usually doesn't get started until 10pm.

University Area

👍 **ALTER SIMPL** 💳🚭🍸❄☀ BAR

Türkenstr. 57 ☎089 272 30 83 💻www.eggerlokale.de

Once a second home to Munich's bohemian artists and intellectuals, Alter Simpl today contains all the cozy fixings of a neighborhood bar, with a rich history to boot. Founded in 1903, the bar takes its name from an old satiritical magazine called "Simplicissmus," with the magazine's iconic logo of a dog breaking the chains of censorship reworked into a dog breaking open a champagne bottle. Coupled with great Bavarian food and a lively student scene, what's not to love?

🚇 *U3 or U6: Universität, then turn right on Schellingstr. and right onto Türkenstr.* $ *Beer 3 per .5L. Snacks and entrees €5.50-14. Daily lunch specials €7.77.* ⏰ *Open M-Th and Su 11am-3am, F-Sa 11am-4am. Kitchen closes 1hr. before.*

👍 SCHELLING SALON

●⊘🍸❄ BAR

Schellingstr. 54 ☎089 272 07 88 💻www.schelling-salon.de

A Munich institution since 1872, rack up at the tables where Lenin, Rilke, and Hitler once played *(€9 per hour)*. The walls, filled with newspaper articles and other memorabilia, attest to the salon's cred. Unwind with a cheap beer and friends after a hectic week of real drinking.

🚇 *U3 or U6: Universität, then head away from the Siegestor and take a right onto Schellingstr.* ℹ *Foosball and ping pong also available.* $ *Breakfast €3-6, German entrees €5-12, beer 0.5L €2.90.* ⏰ *Open M and Th-Su 10am-1am. Kitchen open until midnight.*

Au-Haidhausen

👍 MUFFATWERK

●♿ LIVE MUSIC

Zellstr. 4 ☎089 45 87 50 10 💻www.muffatwerk.de

This former power plant hosts techno, hip-hop, spoken word, jazz, and dance performances. The massive performance hall features international DJs and artists, while the attached beer garden and cafe provide a more relaxed venue for enjoying the afternoon or evening.

🚇 *Tram 18: Deutsches Museum, then cross the bridge and turn left (follow the signs).* $ *Cover generally €5-9, though many events are free; concert tickets vary in price. Check website for events.* ⏰ *Shows generally begin between 9-10pm with entry one hour earlier. Beer garden open M-Th 5pm-1am, F-Su noon-1am. Clubbing nights generally begin between 10-11pm.*

OPTIMOLWERKE AND KULTFABRIK

●⊘ CLUB COMPLEXES

Friedenstr. 6 and Grafingerstr. 6 ☎089 450 69 20, 089 45 02 88 99

💻www.optimolwerke.de and www.kultfabrik.de

In adjacent lots lie **Kultfabrik** and **Optimolwerke**, two powerhouses of adolescent fury, each with enormous candy-store assortments of smaller venues. Many locals complain that the enormity of these complexes lends an impersonal feel, and their location in abandoned factories by the train tracks is just gritty, but here's where you'll find Munich's youth into the wee hours. Hours, covers, and themes vary between each of the invididual venues, which range from the fun-in-the-sun **Bamboo Beach** (Kultfabrik), complete with imported sand, to the darker **Drei Turme** (Optimolwerke) with its castle-like interior. Also within Kultfabrik is **Kalinka**, where you can fill up on vodka and party it up against a giant 7ft. bust of Lenin *(open F-Sa)*. Kultfabrik also offers a monthly publication with schedules that you can find in many hostels and other places where young people congregate.

🚇 *S1, S2, S3, S4, S5, S6, S7, or S8: Ostbahnhof, then walk through the underground tunnels past all the tracks to the back of the station and follow the crowds.* $ *Prices vary, but covers are generally around €5 and cheaper if you go earlier in the night.* ⏰ *Hours vary, but most parties begin between 10-11pm; check online for directories for each club.*

Neuhausen

👍 LÖWENBRÄUKELLER

💳♿🍸❄⛅ BEER HALL AND GARDEN

Nymphenburgerstr. 2 ☎ 089 54 72 66 90 💻www.loewenbraeukeller.com

Marienplatz has Hofbräuhaus, and Neuhausen has Löwenbräukeller. Across the street from the Löwenbräu distillery, Löwenbräukeller is easily identifiable by its elaborate tower of green and the characteristic Lowenbrau lion sitting on the terrace. Renovated in 2008, Löwenbräukeller offers the best of all worlds—an ornate indoor beer hall, a relaxed rooftop terrace, and a 1000-seat beer garden. Dine on traditional Bavarian fare while downing Löwenbräu lager under the stars, and you sing your way back home in the company of new friends.

 # U1: Stiglmaierpl. i English menu available. $ Maß €7.80. Entrees €8-20 ⏰ Open daily 10am-midnight.

BACKSTAGE BAR

Wilhelm-Hale Str. 38 ☎089 126 61 00 🖳www.backstage.eu

Housed in a converted gas station, Backstage features music, often live, from the indie underground scene. Local crowd varies depending on the evening's act, but during the summer you can always expect a crowded *Biergarten* with one of the best beer deals in town *(Maß €4.80)*.Sports games and movies make for raucous parties.

 # SB: Hirschgarten, or Tram 16 or 17: Steubenpl. i Check the website for details. $ No cover for most events. ⏰ Summer Biergarten open M-Th 6pm-2am (or later), F-Sa 6pm-4am, Su 6pm-2am (or later). Check website for specific events; nightly dance parties usually start between 10-11pm.

ARTS AND CULTURE

Though the culture here seemingly centers around beer, you're never at a loss for world-class music and theater. For comprehensive listings of performances, check out *Munich Found (🖳www.munichfound.de $€3 at newsstands)*. Tickets for most events can be purchased at *München Ticket*, a counter at either of the tourist offices *(☎018 054 81 81 81 🖳www.muenchenticket.de)*.

Theater, Opera, and Classical Music

As a Wagnerian capital, Munich has a thriving classical music and opera scene, especially in the summertime, as many historic attractions host their own concert series. Get a taste for King Ludwig II's Wagner obsession by attending an opera yourself; the opera festival *(🖳www.muenchener-opern-festspiele.de)* in July features performances in the Pavilion 21 Mini Opera Space, a contemporary expanse of angular steel set up at the square behind the National Theater, as well as Oper für Alle (Opera for All), free open-air concerts and Jumbotron-broadcasted operas under the summer stars.

NATIONAL THEATER ♿ OPERA

Max-Joseph-Pl. 2 ☎089 21 85 19 20 🖳www.bayerische-staatsoper.de

Built by Max Joseph to bring opera to the people, this magnificent theater is now home to the Bayerische Staatsoper and has soaring white balustrades, an enormous chandelier, and rich velvet seating. Student tickets *(from €9)* sold 1hr. before shows at the entrance on Maximilianstrand or two weeks in advance from the box office at Marstallpl. 5 behind the theater. Tickets can also be purchased online.

 # U3 or U6: Odeonspl. or Tram 19: Nationaltheater. i Subtitles in German. ISICs not accepted for student tickets; bring alternate forms of IDs. $ Guided tours €5, students €4. ⏰ Box office open M-Sa 10am-7pm and 1 hr. before shows. Guided tours of the theater almost daily in the summer in German; English-language tours offered four times a year in July. All tours start at 2pm and last 1hr. See website for details.

STAATSTHEATER AM GÄRTNERPLATZ ♿ THEATER

Gärtnerpl. 3 ☎089 20 23 86 84 🖳www.gaertnerplatztheater.de

This theater in the nightlife hub of Gartnerplatz shows a mix of comic operas, musical theater, and, true to the cultured bohemian atmosphere of the area, artsy-fartsy works from the early 20th century. The steps outside are also a popular hangout spot, perfect for people watching over a meal on the go.

 # Tram 17 or 18: Reichenbachpl. $ Tickets generally €4-60; students always get half price, or certain shows have "KiJu" €8 student tickets. ⏰ Box office open M-F 10am-6pm, Sa 10am-1pm.

PRINZREGENTENTHEATER 🎟♿ THEATER

Prinzregentenpl. 12 ☎089 21 85 02 🖳www.prinzregententheater.de

A magnificent theater built as a festival hall for the performance of Wagner's operas, the Prinzregententheater now houses the Bayerische Theaterakademie and shows a number of productions ranging from theater, classical music, opera, to ballet.

🚇 U4: Prinzregentenplatz. $ €8 student tickets available for most shows at the door. ⏰ Box office open M-F 10am-1pm, 2-6pm; Sa 10am-1pm.

Film

English films are usually dubbed in German - look for "OV" (original language) and "OmU" (subtitled) on posters or listings. Pick up some facts on the world's most obscure (and some not-so-obscure) topics at Munich's Internationales Dokumentarfilmfestival *(🖳www.dockfest-muenchen.de)*, a weeklong international documentary competition held every May. For the more mainstream, the broader Filmfest München *(🖳www.filmfest-muenchen.de)* takes place in mid-summer and is spread out in theaters all throughout the city. Listings for these festivals, as well as some of the larger cinemas in Munich, can be found in *in München*.

CINEMA 🎬♿ MOVIE THEATER

Nymphenburgerstr. 31 ☎089 55 52 55 🖳www.cinema-muenchen.com

This theater plays almost exclusively English-language films, along with live satellite broadcasts of operas and concerts from all around the world. Sip a *bier* during the movie to remember you're in Munich, or grab some Ben and Jerry's and pretend you're back home.

🚇 U1: Stiglmaierpl., then 2 blocks west on Nymphenburgerstr. ℹ Reserve tickets online, as movies often sell out. $ €7.50-8.50, students €6.50-7.50. Matinees M-F before 5:30pm €4.50/€3.50.

MUSEUM LICHTSPIELE 🎬♿ MOVIE THEATER

Lilienstr. 2 ☎089 482403 🖳wwwmuseum-lichtspiele.de

This cute, quirky little theater is perhaps best known for their weekly showing of Rocky Horror *(F-Sa 11:30pm)*, a tradition that has continued for 34 years. Films are all shown in their original versions, with most of them in English.

🚇 Tram 18: Deutsches Museum, cross the bridge, and head to the right. $ Tickets vary by day and time, ranging from €5.50-7.50. Student tickets generally €1 less.

Other Music

Big-name pop stars usually perform at the Olympiahalle and the Olympiastadion. These being outdoor venues, though, you can always sit on the grass at the Olympiapark and enjoy the music for free. Smaller venues for less mainstream artists can be found at Muffatwerke and Backstage.

✔ **TOLLWOOD FESTIVAL** FESTIVAL

Olympiapark South ☎0700-38 38 50 24 🖳www.tollwood.de

Munich's annual culture festival attracts a young and active German audience for hundreds of concerts, theatrical productions, and circus shows from the world's leading performers. These spectacular presentations compete for attention amid Oktoberfest-style tents serving delicacies, including Munich's own sweet nectar, beer. Tollwood Magazine, available from the tourist office, lists performances, many of which are free.

🚇 U3: Olympiazentrum, or take the special MVV bus (Tollwood 99) that runs from Westfriedhof (U1) and Schiedplatz (U2 and U3). ⏰ Held mid-June-mid-July and late Nov-Dec. Festival grounds open M-F 2pm-1am, Sa-Su 11am-1am.

GLOCKENBACH WERKSTATT BÜRGERHAUS 🎬 COMMUNITY CENTER

Blumenstr. 7 ☎089 26 88 38 🖳www.glockenbachwerkstatt.de

By day, this community center hosts a kindergarten and other kid-friendly courses, including dance, soccer, and African drumming. By night, the place transforms into a hub that showcases local talent, with open mic nights, jam sessions, live concerts, and DJ dance parties. A summer courtyard cafe is a choice snack spot for many local.

🚇 S1, S2, S3, S4, S5, S6, S7, S8, U3 of U6: Marienpl., then wrap around Viktualienmarkt, turn right onto Reichenbachstr., right onto Frauenstr., which turns into Blumenstr. when the road curves. ℹ Events vary widely from day to day, so check the schedule online. $ Cover charges free-€8. ⏰ Open daily; nighttime events start between 5 and 10pm.

ESSENTIALS

Practicalities

- **TRAVEL OFFICES: EurAide** is Deutsche Bahn's English-speaking office. Staff books train tickets for all European destinations for free. Tickets for public transit and discounted tickets for English-language walking, bus, and bike tours also available. Pick up a free copy of the helpful brochure*Inside Track. (Inside Hauptbahnhof. ☎59 38 89. 💻www.euraide.com ⏰ Open daily May-Sept M-Sa 8am-noon and 2pm-6pm, Su 8am-noon, Oct-Apr M-Sa 8am-noon and 1pm-4pm, Su 8am-noon.)*
- **TOURIST OFFICES:** English-speaking staff books rooms for free with a 10% deposit. Also on-site at each tourist office is Muenchen-Ticket, a booking agency for concerts, theater, and other events. *(Bahnhofsplatz 2, Marienplatz 2. ☎23 39 65 00. 💻 www.muenchen-tourist.de $ English city guides€2, and maps €0.40. 🚇 Take a right out of the main Hauptbahnhof entrance (Bahnhofsplatz), or find it at the base of the Neues Rathaus (Marienplatz). ⏰ Gahnhofsplatz loc. open M-Sa 9am-8:30pm, Su 10am-6pm. Marienpl. loc. open M-Sa 10am-8pm, Su 10am-4pm.)*
- **BIKE RENTAL AND TOURS:** Pedal, laugh, and down a few beers as you pick up some creative history on one of 👍**Mike's Bike Tours.** *(Bräuhausstr. 10. ☎089 25 54 39 88. 💻www.mikesbiketours.com $ English city guides €2, maps €0.40. Hefty backpackers' discount with receipt from stay at certain hostels (see website for details). 🚇 S1, S2, S3, S4, S5, S6, S7, S8, U3, or U6: Marienplatz. Tours start at by the tower of the Altes Rathaus. ⏰ Tours daily from mid-Apr to Aug 11:30am and 4pm, Sept-mid-Nov and Mar-mid-Apr 12:30pm. Office open mid-Apr-Oct 7 10am-8pm; Mar-mid-Apr and Oct 8-Nov 18 10:30am-1pm and 4:30-5:30pm when not raining.)* **Radius Tours** offers historical walking tours of the city in English, including a 2hr. tour of the Altstadt. Bike tours also available. *(Opposite track 32 of the Hauptbahnhof. ☎089 55 02 93 74. 💻www.radiusmunich.com $ Bike tours €18. 🚇 S1, S2, S3, S4, S5, S6, S7, S8, U3, or U6: Marienplatz. Look for the guides in blue and white checkered shirts. ⏰ Office open Apr-Nov M-F 9am-6pm, Sa-Su 9am-8pm. Tours offered Apr-Oct daily 10:45 and 11:45am. Bike tours May-Oct, every Tu, Th, and Su at 10:30am.)*
- **CONSULATES: Canada** *(Tal 29. ☎089 219 95 70. 💻www.canadainternational.gc.ca 🚇 S1, S2, S3,S4, S5, S6, S7 or S8: Isartor; look for the gold door to the righ of Conrad. ⏰ Open M-Th 9am-noon.)* **Ireland** *(Dennigerstr. 15. ☎089 20 80 59 90. 💻www.dfa.ie 🚇 U4: Richard-Strauss Str. ⏰ Open M-F 9am-noon.)* **UK** *(Möhlstr. 5. ☎089 21 10 90. 💻ukingermany.fco.gov.uk 🚇 Tram 18: Effnerpl. ⏰ Open M-Th 8:30am-noon and 1pm-5pm, F 8:30am-noon and 1pm-3:30pm.)* **US** *(Koniginstr. 5. ☎089 288 80. 💻www.munich.usconsulate.gov 🚇 U3, U3, U4, U5, or U6: Odeonspl. ⏰Open by appointment only.)*
- **CURRENCY EXCHANGE: ReiseBank** has decent rates and Western Union money-wiring office. *(at the front of the Hauptbahnhof. ☎089 55 10 80. www.reisebank.de ⏰ Open daily 7am-10pm.)* **Exchange AG** will cash travelers' checks with a hefty commission. *(Peterspl. 10. ☎089 235 09 20. ⏰ Open M-F 10am-6pm.)*
- **LUGGAGE STORAGE:** Available at the airport. *(☎089 97 52 13 75. 📶www.munich-airport.de).* Also available at the Hauptbahnhof. *(☎089 97 52 13 75.)*

- **LOCKERS:** Accessible in the main hall of Hauptbahnhof. ($ €3-5 per 24hr. for up to 3 days. ⏰ Open from 4am-12:30am. A staffed storage room in the main hall is open M-F 7am-8pm, Sa-Su 8am-6pm.)
- **LOST PROPERTY:** Anything lost in the Hauptbahnhof or on DB or S-Bahn trains will find its way to the **DB Lost Property Office** *(In the Hauptbahnhof by track 26. ☎089 13 08 66 64. 💻www.fundservice.bahn.de ⏰ Open M-F 7am-8pm, Sa-Su 8am-6pm.).* Those searching for lost property on the U-Bahn subway lines will be taken to the **Infopoint Office of the MVV** *(In the Hauptbahnhof. ☎089 21 91 32 40. ⏰ Open M-F 8am-noon and 12:30pm-4pm, Sa-Su 9am-12:30pm and 1pm-5pm.).* **Official Lost Property Office** *(Ötztalerstr. 17. ☎089 23 39 60 45. 💻fundbuero.kvr@muenchen.de ⏰ Open M 8am-noon, Tu 8:30am-noon and 2-5:30pm, W-F 8am-noon.).*
- **HOME SHARE: Mitwohnzentrale Wolfgang Sigg GmbH/An der Uni** offers apartments available by the month and a helpful multi-lingual website. *(Fendstr. 6 ☎089 330 37 40. 💻www.mrliving.de 🚇 U3 or U6: Munchener Freiheit. Walk south on Leopoldstr., turn left onto Fendstr. At #6, ring buzzer, and go through the corridor to the 2nd building. ⏰ Open M-F 9am-noon, other hours by appointment.)* **City Mitwohnzentrale** rents apartments for a stay of over 4 days. *(Lämmerstr. 6 ☎089 592 51 01. 💻www.mitwohn.org $ Sublets usually for €300-400 per month. 🚇 By the Arnulfstr. exit of the Hauptbahnhof.)* **Studentenwerk** offers inexpensive housing options for students, though you usually need a university affiliation. *(Leopoldstr. 15 ☎089 38 19 62 83. 💻www.studentenwerk.mhn.de 🚇 U3 or U6: Giselastr.)* **Apartment-Börse Studentenstadt Freimann** offers temporary dormitory housing. *(☎089 324 32 88. 💻aboerse@gmx.de 🚇 U6: Studentenstadt. ⏰ Open M-F 6-8pm.)*
- **VISITOR PUBLICATIONS: New in the City** is an annual publication in German and English covering everything from apartment registration to popular nightlife. Available at local newsstands. *(💻www.newinthecity.de)*
- **GLBT RESOURCES: Publications:** All available at gay and lesbian nightlife spots. **Leo,** the queer magazine of Bavaria, is published monthly and includes gay-interest articles as well as an events listing. **Blu** is geared towards a younger crowd and reads like a fashion magazine, also with events listings in the back *(💻www.blu.fm)* **Rosa Muenchen** is a quarterly directory of all things gay, covering everything from shops to pharmacies to escorts to gay sports teams. **Gay Services Information** *(☎089 260 30 56. ⏰Open daily 1pm-midnight.).* **Lesbian Resources: Lesbenberatungsstelle LeTra** *(Angertorstr. 3. ☎089 725 42 72. 💻www.letra.de ⏰ Hotline open M 2:30-5pm, Tu 11:30am-1pm, W 2:30-5pm, Th 7-9pm.).* **Other Resources: Schwules Kommunikations und Kulturzentrum,** also called the **"sub,"** has a wealth of resources, counselors, and also staffs a small cafe and library for gay men. English spoken. *(Müllerstr. 43. Information Hotline ☎089 260 33 20. Violence Hotline ☎089 192 28. ⏰ Center open M-Th 7-11pm, F-Sa 7pm-midnight, Su 7-11pm. Their information hotline is staffed daily 7-11pm and their violence hotline is staffed daily from 10am-7pm.)*
- **WOMEN'S RESOURCES: Kofra Kommunkationszentrum für Frauen** offers job advice, knowledge on lesbian politics, books, magazines, and a small cafe. *(Baaderstr. 30. ☎089 201 0450. 💻www.kofra.de $ Internet €1 per hr. ⏰ Open M-Th 4-10pm, F 2-6pm.)* **Frauentreffpunkt Neuperlach** offers venues and services for women, including an international coffeehouse and English conversation nights. Check website or call for dates and times. *(Oskar-Maria-Graf-Ring 20-22. ☎089 670 64 63. 💻www. frauentreffpunkt-neuperlach.de)* **Lillemor's Frauenbuchlader** is a women's bookstore. *(Barerstr. 70. ☎089 272 12 05. ⏰ Open M-F 10am-7pm, Sa 10am-2pm.)*

- **DISABLED RESOURCES: Info Center für Behinderte** *(Schellingstr. 31. ☎089 211 70. 🖳www.vdk.de/bayern ⏰ Open M-Sa 9am-8pm, Su 10am-6pm.)*
- **TICKET AGENCIES:** Advance tickets are available at **München Ticket**'s retail locations within the tourist offices in the Rathaus in Marienpl. and at the Hauptbahnhof. *(☎018 054 81 81. 🖳www.muenchen-ticket.de $ Phone €0.14 per min. ⏰ Rathaus location open M-Sa 10am-8pm, Marienplatz location open M-F 10am-8pm, Sa 10am-4pm.)*
- **LAUNDROMATS: Waschomat** is a bright and cheery laundromat with English-language instructions. *(Parkstr. 8. $ Wash €3.90 (soap €0.40), dry €0.60 per 5min. high-spin or €0.80 per 15min. Happy hour daily 6am-9am wash €3.30. ⇄ Tram 18 from Hauptbahnhof (dir.: Gondrellpl.) or 19 (dir.: Pasing): Holzapfelstr. Turn onto Holapfelstr., take the second right onto Schwanthalerstr., and then turn left onto Parkstr. ⏰ Open daily 6am-midnight.)*
- **INTERNET: San Francisco Coffee Company** *(Im Tal 15, with other locations throughout the city. $ Free Wi-Fi with the purchase of a coffee.)* **Coffee Fellows Cafe** has an internet cafe on the second floor. *(Schuetzenstr. 14. $ Free Wi-Fi for an hour with any €5 purchase. Wireless or PC use €1.30 per 30min or €2.50 per hour. Black-and-white printing €0.30 per sheet. Faxing €0.50 per sheet within the country, €1.00 outside the country.)*
- **POST OFFICE:** *(☎018 03 00 30 08. ⇄ The yellow bulding opposite the Hauptbahnhof. ⏰ Open M-F 8am-8pm, Sa 9am-4pm.)*
- **POSTAL CODE: 80335.**

Emergency!

- **POLICE:** ☎110.
- **AMBULANCE AND FIRE:** ☎112
- **EMERGENCY MEDICAL SERVICE:** ☎089 19 222
- **EMERGENCY ROAD SERVICE:** ☎089 018 02 22 22 22
- **RAPE CRISIS SUPPORT: Frauennotruf München** *(Gullstr. 3. ☎089 76 37 37. 🖳www.frauennotrufmuenchen.de ⏰ Available daily 6pm-midnight.)*
- **AIDS HOTLINE: IN GERMAN.** *(☎089 194 11 OR ☎089 23 32 33 33 ⏰ M-F 7-9pm.)*
- **PHARMACIES:** *(Bahnhofpl. 2. ☎089 59 98 90 40. ⇄ On the corner of the Hauptbahnhof; take a right upon exiting. ⏰ Open M-F 7am-8pm, Sa 8am-8pm.)*
- **MEDICAL SERVICES: Klinikum Rechts der Isar** *(Across the river on Ismanigerstr. ⏰ Open 24hr. for emergencies.)* **Münchner Aids-Hilfe e.V.** offers free risk analysis and advice for AIDS and other STDs. *(Lindwurmstr. 71. ☎089 54 33 30. 🖳www.muenchner-aidshilfe.de $ Most tests require a small fee. ⏰ Open M, W, and Th 5-8pm.)*

Getting There

Transportation to Munich is never a problem, with direct flights arriving daily from many international locations. In addition, many European cities are accessed with the **Deutsche Bahn,** the German railway system, with trains arriving at the Hauptbahnhof (central station).

By Plane

Munich's international airport, Flughafen München *(Nordalee 25 ☎089 975 00 🖳www.munich-airport.de)* is a 45-minute train ride from the city center. Take S1 or S8 to Flughafen *(runs every 10 min.)*

By Train

Munich's central train station, **München Hauptbahnhof,** *(Hauptbahnhof 1☎089 130 81 05 55 ◼www.hauptbahnhof-muenchen.de)* has arrivals and departures to a host of European cities. All major trains arrive at the HBF. Take S1, S2, S3, S4, S5, S6, S7, S8, U1, U2, U3, U4, or U5 to Hauptbahnhof. Connected cities include **Berlin** *(Ⓢ €79. ☒ 6hr., 2 per hr.);* **Frankfurt** *(Ⓢ from €50. ☒ 3hr., 2 per hr.);* **Köln** *(Ⓢ from €120. ☒5hr., 2 per hr.);* **Füssen** *(Ⓢ from €20. ☒ 2hr., every 2hr.);* **Hamburg** *(Ⓢ from €60. ☒ 4hr., every hr.);* **Hanover** *(Ⓢ from €50. ☒ 5hr., every 1hr.);* **Dusseldorf** *(Ⓢfrom €40. ☒3hr., 2 per hr.);* **Dresden** *(Ⓢ from €80. ☒ 6hr., 2 per hr.);* **Bonn** *(Ⓢ from €70. ☒ 6hr., 4 per hr.);* **Leipzig** *(Ⓢ from €60. ☒ 4.5hr., 1 per hr.);* **Innsbruck, AUT** *(Ⓢ from €30.☒ 2hr., ever 2hr.);* **Salzburg, AUT** *(Ⓢ from €20.☒ 2hr., every hr.);* **Zurich, CHE** *(Ⓢfrom €50. ☒5hr., 4-5 per day);* **Prague, CZR** *(Ⓢ from €60. ☒ 6hr., 4 per day);* **Paris, FRA** *(Ⓢ from €129. ☒ 6-10hr., 6 per day);* **Amsterdam, NHE.** *(Ⓢ from €50. ☒ 8-12hr., ever 1hr.)* The station also serves as a hub for the city's own public transportation system (the **MVV**).

Getting Around

Munich's pubilc transportation system consists of four integrated components: the **S-Bahn,** a surburban train; the **U-Bahn,** an underground municipal train; **trams,** and **buses.**

Deutsche Bahn

The S-Bahn is under the operation of the Deutsche Bahn network, so Eurail, InterRail, and German railpasses are vaild. S-Bahn to the airport starts running at 3:30am

Ticket Validation: Before you begin your journey, validate your ticket by getting it stamped in the blue boxes. Plainclothes officers often check for tickets, and those without properly validated tickets are charged a hefty €40 fine. Don't get caught!

MVV Network

The U-Bahn, trams, and buses are all part of the city's MVV network *(☎089 41 42 43 44◼www.mvv-muenchen.de)* and require separate ticket purchases. Pick up maps at the tourist office or at the MVV Infopoint office in the Hauptbahnhof. The MVV network runs M-Th and Su 5am-12:30am, F-Sa 5am-2am. Separate NachtTrams (night trams) run every 20 minutes and go to just about everywhere in the city. Tickets come in multiple forms based on how far you're traveling and how long the pass is valid. The simplest form is the single Einzelfahrkarte ticket *(€2.40),* which is good for two hours for a trip in one direction. All other trips depend on the distance, for which the Munich area is split into 16 different zones of concentric circles around the city center. For short trips (within the same zone), get a Kurzstrecke *(€1.20).* For multiple rides, buy a stripe ticket (Streifenkarte) which usually comes with 10 stripes *(€11.50).* Cancel two stripes per zone or one stripe if traveling within the same zone. The zones are further grouped into four different groups for which you can get one-day or three-day passes and single or partner tickets (covering up to 5 adults or children and a dog, with 2 children = 1 adult). There are several cards available.

- **ISARCARDS:** An IsarCard is a week- or month-long pass only available for single travelers that costs only a little more than the 3-day passes. IsarCards, however, only run during the week or month proper (e.g. weekly passes work from Sunday to Sunday, and monthly passes are bought for each specific month), so plan accordingly.

- **CITY TOUR CARD:** This card gets you transportation along with some discounts to Munich attractions. That said, most of these attractions are actually not the more popular ones, and the discounts are tiny. Unless you are planning on going to most of these attractions with a partner ticket, it's probably not worth it.

- **BAYERN TICKET:** The Bayern Ticket gets you access to any public transportation within Bavaria for an entire day *(M-F 9am-3am, Sa-Su midnight-3am)*. The ticket also covers bordering cities including Ulm and Salzburg, making the ticket perfect for day trips to Salzburg and Neuschwanstein. A single ticket costs €20, which is already a considerable savings, but get a group of 5 friends together and pay only €28, which comes to only €5.60 per person.

By Taxi

Taxi-München-Zentrale *(☎089 216 10 or 194 10 🖳www.taxizentrale-muenchen.de)*. Large oasis of waiting taxis immediately outside the Hauptbahnhof, or call them directly from one of the 130+ taxi stands located throughout the city (tram and subway maps will usually indicate which stops have taxi stands). Call ahead to make special requests for pet-friendly or large-capacity cars.

By Car

Upstairs at the Hauptbahnhof (opposite track 24) are **Budget** *([i] Online reservations only. ⏰ Open M-F 7am-9pm, Sa-Su 8am-5pm)*, **Avis** *(☎01805 55 77 55 ⏰ Open M-F 7am-9pm, Sa-Su 8am-5pm)*, **Europcar** *(☎01805 8000 ⏰ Open M-F 7am-9pm, Sa-Su 8am-7pm)*, **Hertz** *(☎1805 33 35 35 or ☎089 550 2256 ext. 2. ⏰ Open M-F 7am-9pm, Sa-Su 9am-5pm)*, and **Sixt** *(☎1805 26 02 50⏰ Open daily 6am-9pm)*.

By Bike

RADIUS BIKES — BIKE RENTAL

☎089 55 02 93 74 🖳www.radiusmunich.com

Bike rentals available for an hour or longer.

 # Opposite track 32 of the Hauptbahnhof. [i] Helmet included. Deposit €50. $ Bike rental €3-7 per hour, €14.50-18 per day. ⏰ Open Apr-Nov M-F 9am-6pm, Sa-Su 9am-8pm.

MIKE'S BIKE TOURS — BIKE RENTAL

Bräuhausstr. 10 ☎089 25 54 39 87 🖳www.mikesbiketours.com

Bike rentals available for one day or longer.

 # Behind the Hofbräuhaus. From Marienpl., go past Altes Rathaus onto Tal, then turn left onto Hochbrückenstr. [i] Helmet, map, lock, and other accessories included. $ Rental €12 per first day and €9 per day afterward. ⏰ open mid-Apr-Oct 7 10am-8pm; from Mar-mid-Apr and Oct 8-Nov 18 10:30am-1pm and 4:30-5:30pm when not raining.

DB CALL A BIKE — BIKE RENTAL

☎0700 05 22 55 22 🖳www.callabike.de

DB Call a Bike is a Deutsche Bahn service available by phone after registering online.

[i] €5 deposit. $ Rental €0.08 per min. €15 max.

SECOND HAND SPORTS — BIKE SALE

Nymphenburgerstr. 29 ☎089 59 70 74 🖳www.secondhand-sport.de

This shop sells used bikes from €50 with buyback options. Good selection of outdoor adventure gear, snowboards, skis, and helmets. English-speaking staff also services bikes with a speedy turnaround.

#U1 to Stiglmaierpl. $ Rental €0.08 per min. €15 max. ⏰ Open M noon-7pm, Tu-F 10:30am-7pm, Sa 10:30am-4pm.

essentials

entrance requirements

- **PASSPORT:** Required for citizens of Australia, Canada, Ireland, New Zealand, the UK, and the US.
- **VISA:** Required for visitors who plan to stay in Germany for more than 90 days.
- **WORK PERMIT:** Required for all foreigners planning to work in Germany.

PLANNING YOUR TRIP

Documents and Formalities

You've got your visa, your invitation, and your work permit, just like *Let's Go* told you to, and then you realize you've forgotten the most important thing: your passport. Well, we're not going to let that happen. **Don't forget your passport!** Citizens of Australia, Canada, Ireland, New Zealand, the UK, the US need valid passports for entrance into Germany.

Visas

EU citizens do not need a visa to globetrot through Germany. Citizens of Australia, Canada, New Zealand, and the US do not need a visa for stays of up to 90 days, but this three-month period begins upon entry into any of the countries that belong to the EU's **freedom of movement** zone. Those staying longer than 90 days may purchase a visa at the German mission that covers your residence. A visa costs €60 and allows the holder to spend 90 days in Germany.

Double-check entrance requirements at the nearest embassy or consulate of Germany for up-to-date information before departure. US citizens can also consult ◼http://travel.state.gov.

Entering Germany to study requires a student visa. For more information, see the **Beyond Tourism** chapter.

Work Permits

Admittance to a country as a traveler does not include the right to work, which is authorized only by a work permit. For more information, see the **Beyond Tourism** chapter.

Time Differences

Germany is one hour ahead of Greenwich Mean Time (GMT) and observe Daylight Saving Time. This means that they are is six hours ahead of New York City, 9 hours ahead of Los Angeles, one hour ahead of the British Isles, 9 hours behind Sydney, and 10 hours behind New Zealand.

MONEY

Getting Money from Home

Stuff happens. When stuff happens, you might need some money. When you need some money, the easiest and cheapest solution is to have someone back home make a deposit to your bank account. Otherwise, consider one of the following options.

Wiring Money

Arranging a **bank money transfer** means asking a bank back home to wire money to a bank in Germany. This is the cheapest way to transfer cash, but it's also the slowest and most agonizing, usually taking several days or more. Note that some banks may only release your funds in local currency, potentially sticking you with a poor exchange rate; inquire about this in advance. Money transfer services like **Western Union** are faster and more convenient than bank transfers—but also much pricier. Western Union has many locations worldwide. To find one, visit ☐www.westernunion.com or call the appropriate number: in Australia ☎1800 173 833, in Canada and the US 800-325-6000, in the UK 0800 735 1815, in Germany ☎0800 180 7732 or in Austria ☎0800 29 6544. To wire money using a credit card in Canada and the US, call ☎800-CALL-CASH; in the UK, 0800 833 833. Money transfer services are also available to **American Express** cardholders and at selected **Thomas Cook** offices.

US State Department (US Citizens only)

In serious emergencies only, the US State Department will forward money within hours to the nearest consular office, which will then disburse it according to instructions for a US$30 fee. If you wish to use this service, you must contact the Overseas Citizens Services division of the US State Department. (*☎+1-202-501-4444, from US 888-407-4747*)

TIPPING AND BARGAINING

Service staff is paid by the hour, and a service charge is included in an item's unit price. Cheap customers typically just round up to the nearest whole Euro, but it's customary and polite to tip 5-10% if you are satisfied with the service. If the service was poor, you don't have to tip at all. To tip, mention the total to your waiter while paying. If he states that the bill is €20, respond "€22," and he will include the tip. Do not leave the tip on the table; hand it directly to the server. It is standard to tip a taxi driver at least €1, housekeepers €1-2 a day, bellhops €1 per piece of luggage, and public toilet attendants around €.50. Germans rarely barter, except at flea markets.

Taxes

Most goods in Germany are subject to a Value-Added Tax—or *mehrwertsteuer* (MwSt)—of 19% (a reduced tax of 7% is applied to books and magazines, foods, and agricultural products). Ask for a MwSt return form at points of purchase to enjoy tax-free shopping. Present it at customs upon leaving the country, along with your receipts and the unused goods. Refunds can be claimed at Tax Free Shopping Offices, found at most airports, road borders, and ferry stations, or by mail (Tax-Free Shopping Processing Center, Trubelgasse 19, 1030 Vienna Austria). For more information, contact the German VAT refund hotline (*☎0228 406 2880; www.bzst.de*).

SAFETY AND HEALTH

General Advice

In any type of crisis, the most important thing to do is **stay calm.** Your country's embassy abroad is usually your best resource in an emergency; registering with that embassy upon arrival in the country is a good idea.

Local Laws and Police

Certain regulations might seem harsh and unusual (practice some self-control city-slickers, jaywalking is a €5 fine), but abide by all local laws while in Germany; your respective embassy will not necessarily get you off the hook. Always be sure to carry a valid passport as police have the right to ask for identification.

germany

Drugs and Alcohol

The drinking age in Germany is 16 for beer and wine and 18 for spirits. The maximum blood alcohol content level for drivers is 0.05%. Avoid public drunkenness: it can jeopardize your safety and earn the disdain of locals.

If you use insulin, syringes, or any perscription drugs, carry a copy of the prescriptions and a doctor's note. Needless to say, illegal drugs are best avoided. While possession of marijuana or hashish is illegal, possession of small quantities for personal consumption is decriminalized in Germany. Each region has interpreted "small quantities" differently (anywhere from 5 to 30 grams). Carrying drugs across an international border—considered to be drug trafficking—is a serious offense that could land you in prison.

Specific Concerns

Natural Disasters

Relatively weak earthquakes occur regularly in Germany, primarily in the seismically active Rhein Rift Valley or in coal mining areas where blasting can set them off. In the event of an earthquake, drop and take cover if indoors. If outside, move away from buildings and utility wires.

Pre-Departure Health

Matching a prescription to a foreign equivalent is not always easy, safe, or possible, so if you take **prescription drugs,** carry up-to-date prescriptions or a statement from your doctor stating the medications' trade names, manufacturers, chemical names, and dosages. Be sure to keep all medication with you in your carry-on luggage.

Common drugs such as aspirin (*Kopfschmerztablette* or *Aspirin*), acetaminophen or Tylenol (*Paracetamol*), ibuprofen or Advil, antihistamines (*Antihistaminika*), and penicillin (*Penizillin*) are available at German pharmacies. Some drugs—like pseudoephedrine (Sudafed) and diphenhydramine (Benadryl)—are not available in Germany, or are only available with a perscription, so plan accordingly.

Immunizations and Precautions

Travelers over two years old should make sure that the following vaccines are up to date: MMR (for measles, mumps, and rubella); DTaP or Td (for diphtheria, tetanus, and pertussis); IPV (for polio); Hib (for *Haemophilus influenzae* B); and HepB (for Hepatitis B). For recommendations on immunizations and prophylaxis, check with a doctor and consult the **Centers for Disease Control and Prevention (CDC)** in the US or the equivalent in your home country. (☎+1-800-CDC-INFO/232-4636 ▣*www.cdc.gov/travel).*

germany 101

ETIQUETTE AND CUSTOMS

Dining

Traditionally, German restaurants allow self-seating if no host is present. Water with your meal is on request and you must specify if you want tap water. Otherwise, the restaurant will rack up your bill by bringing you expensive bottled water. Also, before you satiate a ravenous appetite with a fluffy roll, consider the unfortunate extra charge for rolls or bread.

Gratuity

At the end of the meal, the bill includes gratuity. However, it is appropriate to add a 5% tip for good service, and a 10% tip for exceptional service.

germany 101 . etiquette and customs

Meet and Greet

Unlike workaholics in the United States, Germans look down upon working after hours as evidence of poor planning. Germans face tasks at work and in their personal life with an approach of careful scheduling and organization.

When entering a room, shake hands with everyone in the room individually, including children. Until you are told otherwise, address a person with their official title and surname. When entering a store, always greet with a "Guten Tag." Upon leaving the store, even if you did not buy anything, it is polite to say goodbye, or, "auf Wiedersehen."

So You Want to Meet the Parents...

If you are invited to a German home, it is best to bring chocolates or flowers as a gift. Since many flowers carry particular stigmas, it is safest to bring yellow roses or tea roses. After all, you don't want to give funeral flowers to your kind host.

Germans eat meals with forks in the left hand and the knives in the right hand. German etiquette requires keeping elbows off the table, although hands should always be visible on the table. Sorry, no under the table deals. When you are finished (try to finish everything on your plate), lay your knife and fork parallel to each other on the right side of the plate. Finally, for all salad lovers out there, always fold your lettuce with your knife, instead of cutting it.

HOLIDAYS AND FESTIVALS

DATE	NAME	DESCRIPTION
January 6	Three Kings Day	Children dress up as kings and participate in parades
42 days before Easter	Fasching	A Carnival similar to Mardi Gras, celebrated the week of Lent.
Friday before Easter	Good Friday	Shops closed all day
late March/early April	Easter	Shops closed all day
late September/early October	Oktoberfest	Beer festival with tasting tents and events
October 3	Unity Day	Celebration of the reunification of East and West Germany
December 5	St. Nicolas Day	On the eve of December 6th, children leave their shoes outside for Saint Nick to fill with treats
December 21	St. Thomas Day	People late to work have to wear a cardboard donkey all day. Don't be a slow ass on this day!
December 24	Christmas Eve	Shops close early today
December 25	Christmas Day	Shops closed all day

germany

Karneval

Colorful costumes, blaring pop music, and uninhibited dancing take over Germany during Carnival, also called **Karneval, Fastnacht,** or **Fasching**. The Carnival officially starts on November 11th at 11:11 am, but the festivities don't commence until February, coinciding with the start of Lent. A myriad of masquerades and costume parties cumulate with grand parades on the 42nd day before Easter, **Rosenmontag** (known as Rose Monday in the U.S.). In some cities, such as Munich, the wild celebrations hit on Tuesday, when dance parties overflow blocked off streets. The best festivities are found in Munich, Muenster, Aachen, Köln, and Mainz.

Oktoberfest

Where can you drink a one-liter beer at 9 am and with a million people doing the exact same thing? Only at **Oktoberfest**. Every year, from late September to early October, you can be drunk in Munich for 16 straight days, surviving on enormous pretzels and even larger mugs of beer. Oktoberfest starts with the official tapping of the first barrel of beer at the Schottenhamel tent. For the following two weeks, over six million people attend the festival to pay patronage to beer tents. Beer tents are exactly what they sound like: Massive tents filled with tables, where attendees can settle down and get down to the business of beer. The tents open at 10 am on weekdays and 9 am on the weekends, and close at 11:30 pm. Tents only serve beer until 10:30 pm, although you may be passed out on the tent floor by then. If you remain conscious, just remember to bring cash only. Always tip the waitresses (usually a euro per beer), otherwise you might not get seconds. Or thirds. Most importantly, it is difficult to get into a tent without a reservation. One must make reservations directly through the landlord of each tent. Often, a reservation requires a minimum group of 6 to 8 people. If you do not have a reservation, arrive at the tents by 12 pm on weekdays or by 10 am on the weekends. For landlords' contact information, go to ◼www.oktoberfest.eu.

FOOD AND DRINK

Prepare for the Wurst

Carnivores look no further. Germany beckons your presence with a cornucopia of processed pork and meat, placed under the umbrella term *wurst*. Know how to deal with the wurst when venturing through restaurants and street vendors.

An Apple a Day

The other main food groups in Germany include bread, cheese, and alcohol. If you crave produce to balance your meals, head to the weekly **Wochenmarkt**. The Wochenmarkt opens one to two times a week in most towns and suburbs. Although slightly pricier than the grocery store, the market is always abundant with ripe, local harvest. When shopping at the grocery store, bring your own bag or money to buy them at checkout. Don't look for a bagger either, since you must bag your own groceries.

We Love Our Bread, We Love Our Butter

Breakfast, or **Fruhstuck,** is typically consists of buttered bread with a topping of cheese, jam, or some variety of pork. Don't look for hot pancakes or crispy hashbrowns here; cooked breakfasts are rare in Germany.

Lunch, or **Mittagessen,** is the main meal, typically served between 12 and 2 pm. This one to three course meal starts with everyone proclaiming, "Guten Appetit."

From 3 to 5 pm is afternoon teatime. Indulge in desserts like Black Forest cake, marble cake, firm pudding molds, or the infamous Berliners.

Dinner, or **Abendessen,** is from 6 to 8 pm. Dinner is ordinarily another carb loaded meal, featuring buttered bread topped with deli meat. At this point, it may be time to consider the Atkins diet.

Shots, Shots, Shots, Everybody

Yes, it is true that Germany is second in the world for beer consumption. But, you will not be zealously chugging from **Das Boot** every time yo enter a bar. Normally, **Kleines Bier** is a quarter-liter of beer while **Grosses Bier** is a half-liter. In Bavaria, many places serve a **mass** of beer, which equals one liter.

Germans might be famous for their over 1200 breweries, but there are also plenty of other spirits available. Many Germans enjoy a shot of Schnapps, called **Korn**, with their beer. If you are looking to cut back on sugar, steer clear of liqueurs, which (by law) must contain 100 grams of sugar per liter.

GREECE

In any history or philosophy class, chances are Athens came up more than a few times. Democracy, theater, and the foundations of Western thought all began in this beautiful *polis*. Socrates, Plato, and Herodotus called this city home, and architectural wonders like the Parthenon, Dionysus's Theater, and the Ancient Agora still stand after thousands of years. By all accounts, Athens is a city for the ages. However, even today life goes on in this capital. Athens' modern age has its own angsty populace, financial burdens, nightlife, and transit system. Though much of what is worth seeing in Athens is from thousands of years ago, getting to the ancient ruins requires navigating through a city of winding streets and tons of people living daily life—drink some *ouzo* and munch on *souvlaki* while you take it all in. The Cyclades in the Greek isles are storied sites of ancient marauders, Greek gods, and modern fishing enclaves that have embraced tourism wholeheartedly.

greatest hits

- **ACROPOLIS MUSEUM:** You'll probably be disappointed by some of the ruins in Athens (understandable, since they've been around for almost 3000 years), but this museum has the best of the best—don't miss it (p. 555).
- **BUST OUT YOUR HIKING BOOTS:** Hike up the hill on the uninhabited island of Delos to see all of the excavated sites of this UNESCO World Heritage Site (p. 575).
- **GOLDEN BEACH:** Head to this classy beach on Batsi with hordes of other sunbathers (p. 578).

Don't go to the Ancient Agora to make any new friends—you're about 2600 years too late. Instead, head to **Exharia** after dark, the student hub of Athens. It's always packed with young people and is the least touristy part of Athens you're likely to find. Better yet, there are foosball tables in the square for public use. So find two Spaniards and two Dutchmen, pit them against each other, and see if they have the same outcome as the 2010 World Cup final.

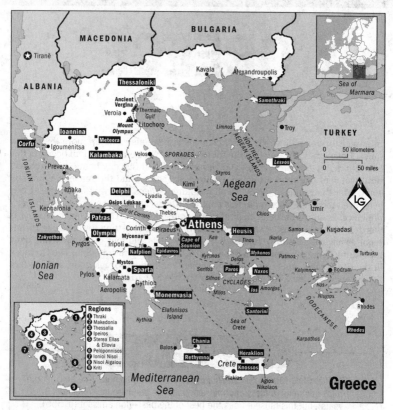

athens ☎210

ORIENTATION

Syntagma

Syntagma Square is the center of Athens' transportation hub. The stately, Neoclassical **Parliament building** and the **Tomb of the Unknown Soldier** mark the foot of the nature lovers' haven, the **National Gardens.** Looking in the opposite direction, the long stretch of **Ermou** teems with high-fashion shops and trend-seeking teenagers on skateboards. The bustling square has gum spots blackening the white tile floor and is surrounded by roads crammed with public transport. Airport-bound buses leave from the right edge of the square, and the main metro entrance is across from the Parliament on **Amalias.** The trolley lets out on the top right corner of the square, and cabs are everywhere. **Georgiou, Filelinon,** and **Othonos** border the other three sides of the square. Step out of the main square and Syntagma quiets significantly. Streets wind along, cafe tables sit in wait, and shop owners attempt to lure in customers. **Mitropoleos, Ermou,** and **Karageorgi Servias** (which turns into Perikleous, then Athinados) start here and extend far into Monastiraki and Psiri. The occasional public concert, the changing of the guard at the Parliament Building, and the abundance of unlicensed vendors around the square add to Syntagma's status as an energetic center of human activity.

Plaka

Situated in the middle of the triangle formed by **Syntagma Square, Monastiraki Square,** and the **Acropolis,** Plaka is a plush, touristy section of Athens that's surprisingly the best place for low-budget travelers to live while in the city. Many of the streets are pedestrian thoroughfares with only a few wayward motorbikes, and vendors take full advantage of this extra sidewalk space. While **Kydatheneon** and **Adrianou** have scores of tourist-oriented *tavernas* and souvenir shops, the smaller and quieter streets have retained an antique charm.

Monastiraki

Behind the metro station, which borders on Hadrian's Library, and across Ermou, is a maze of streets speckled with bead shops, artisan's stores, scrumptious restaurants, and interesting nooks. Nowhere in Athens are pedestrians as stylish nor ice cream shops so picturesque. Sticking to the main straightaway of **Athinas,** perpendicular to Ermou at the square, is far more touristy but after a few blocks leads to the **Meat Market,** which is certainly worth a visit for those with strong stomachs.

Exarhia

In 1973, students in Exarhia participated in a powerful demonstration against the right-wing dictatorship that was then in control of the Athenian government. Today, this section of Athens is still a hotspot for youth culture and is filled with graffiti, coffeeshops, and shisha (think hookah, you westerners). Be wary of getting lost on the way to a destination in this sometimes desolate neighborhood, but don't let the difficulty stop you from seeing this anarchist-enclave-turned-bohemian-mecca in the flesh—especially for a hip dinner.

ACCOMMODATIONS

Syntagma

"JOHN'S PLACE" GUEST HOUSE

Patrou 5

◉❋ HOTEL ❷
☎210 32 29 719

For a trip back to another era, stay in this parquet-floored, steep-staired yet somehow homey hotel. "John" seems to have forgotten all modern amenities when founding this hotel that lacks internet, television, elevator, and credit card capabilities. However, A/C is available in each fresh-linened room, and the white embroidered drapes let in a pleasing amount of afternoon sunlight. High ceilings and Tiffany blue walls add charm to each floor's common space. Make sure to lock valuables in the room's safe; it has been said that the woman at the front desk seems to be fond of her afternoon naps.

✈ *From Syntagma square, walk down Mitropoleos 4 blocks; Patrou is on the left.* ⑤ *Singles €35, doubles €50, triples €60.*

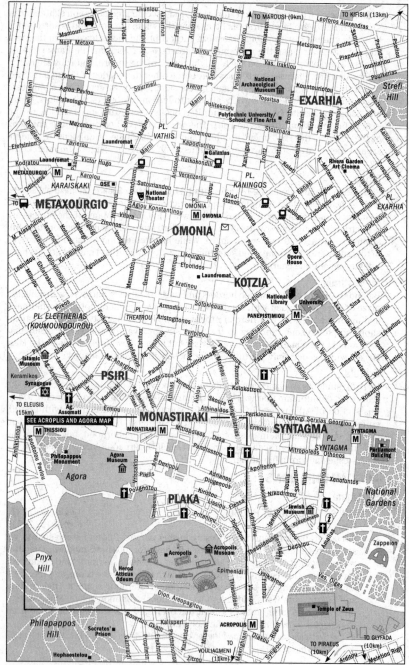

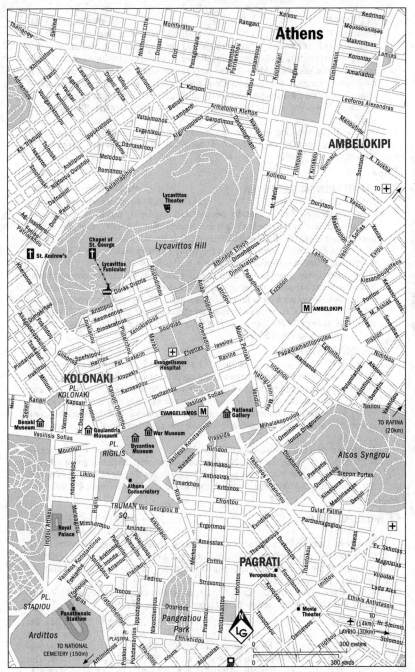

HOTEL KIMON

◆●(((•)))❄ HOTEL ❹

Apollonos 27 ☎210 331 4658 🖳www.kimonhotelathens.com

Long and quiet hallways, a fire extinguisher on every landing, and an attentive man behind the desk make this is a well-tended hotel. Cantaloupe-colored walls and prismatic glass windows on the stairway landings add some pizzazz to the otherwise cramped space—including some rooms with balconies just large enough to cram two people—expertly magnified by full-length mirrors at the entrance. Not the cheapest hotel, Kimon might be saved by the diligence of its staff.

✣ *From Syntagma square, walk down Mitropoleos 3 blocks.* *i* *Request a room with a safe. Breakfast of eggs and juice can be added for €5 per person.* ⌚ *Late June-Sept doubles €60-€70; Oct-June doubles €50-€60.*

Plaka

🏨 STUDENT AND TRAVELLER'S INN

◆⊗(((•)))💺❄⛱ HOSTEL ❶

16 Kydathineon ☎210 32 44 808 🖳www.studenttravellersinn.com

Centrally located, full of friendly people, and constantly pulsing with a Top-40 playlist, Student and Traveller's Inn is a backpacker's dream come true. Every need is met in this no-frills establishment. This hostel is located right at the top of a street lined with restaurants in the heart of every sight worth seeing, so if there's room and you don't mind bunk beds, this is the place to go.

✣ ⓂSyntagma. *Walk along Filelinon in the same direction as traffic. Turn right onto Kydatineon. Walk a few blocks and pass a church on your right.* *i* *Same-day laundry €8 for 2kg wash, dry, and fold. Daily happy hour 6:30pm. Breakfast options around €5.* Ⓢ *June-Sept: 8-bed dorms €20; 4-bed €23, with bath €25. Singles €45, with bath €55; doubles €65, with bath €73; triples €81, with bath €90. From Oct-Mar prices drop by roughly €10.* ⌚ *Reception 24hr. Quiet hours from 10:30pm. Happy hour daily 6:30pm.*

HOTEL ACROPOLIS HOUSE

●(((•)))❄ HOTEL ❺

6-8 Kondrou ☎210 32 22 344, 210 32 26 241 🖳www.acropolishouse.gr

Located within an old mansion near Syntagma Square, this hotel offers a charming stay for travelers looking to find a taste of home in Greece. The cozy rooms, though not large, have all the amenities one could want, and the family staff is warm. From the third floor hallway there is a fabulous view of the Acropolis, and a few rooms have balconies that overlook the neighborhood. Potted greenery abounds.

✣ *At intersection of Iperidou and Kondrou just a few blocks from Syntagma.* *i* *TV and phone in all rooms. Wi-Fi included but works only on ground floor for most computers. Breakfast included.* Ⓢ *May-Oct singles €68; doubles for 1-2 nights €91, for over 2 nights €83; triples €119/108. Nov-Apr singles for 1-2 nights €56, for over 2 nights €51; doubles €70/64; triples €91/83.*

Monastiraki

🏨 HOTEL PELLA INN

●⊗(((•)))💺❄⛱ HOTEL ❹

104 Ermou ☎210 32 50 598 🖳www.pella-inn.gr

This hostel reminiscent of a ski lodge is run by a maternal woman who cares for the hostel like it is her own offspring. Though the decor is a bit dated, everything is clean. Bring a drink or snack up to the roof—the view of Athens and the Acropolis is phenomenal.

✣ *From* Ⓜ*Monastiraki, walk down Ermou and take a right onto Karaiskaki; the hotel will be on the left.* *i* *Breakfast included. Laundry €6.* Ⓢ *Doubles €50-60; triples €120.*

CECIL HOTEL

◆♿(((•)))💺❄ HOTEL ❺

Athinas 39 ☎210 32 17 079 🖳www.cecil,gr

Located in the heart of Monastiraki and graced with a metal grate elevator perfect for travelers schlepping huge bags around, this hotel is larger than most. The charming dining room has upholstered chairs that seat a well-dressed clientele.

greece

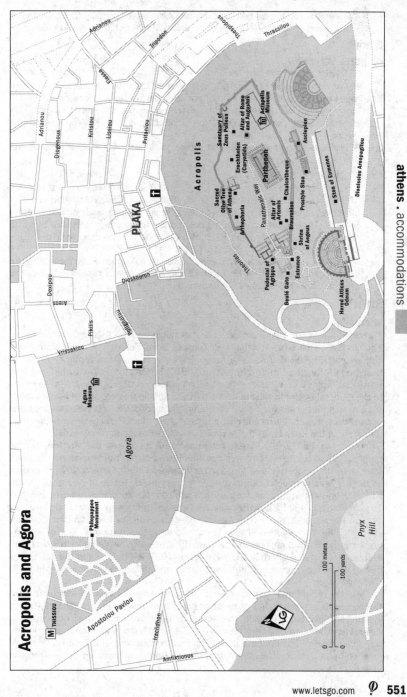

Acropolis and Agora

M THISSIOU

Philopappos Monument

Agora

Agora Museum

PLAKA

Acropolis

Sacred Olive Tree of Athena
Arrhephoria
Panathenaic Way
Altar of Artemis
Brauronion
Shrine of Aegeus
Entrance
Beulé Gate
Pedestal of Agrippa

Erechtheion (Caryatids)
Parthenon
Chalcotheque
Prostyle Stoa
Asclepion

Sanctuary of Zeus Poileus
Altar of Rome and Augustus
Acropolis Museum

Stoa of Eumenes

Herod Atticus Odeum

Dionisiou Areopagitou

Pnyx Hill

100 meters
100 yards

Apostolou Pavlou
Iraclidhon
Amfiktionos

Adrianou
Tripodon
Thrassilou
Adrianou
Kiristou
Lissiou
Pritaniou
Diogenous
Erissa
Dexipou
Areos
Dioskouron
Pikilis
Vrissakiou
Polignotou

☝ From Ⓜ Monastiraki, cross Ermou and walk down Athinas a few blocks; Cecil Hotel will be on the left. *i* Breakfast included. Ⓢ Singles €60; doubles €70; triples €120; family suits €160.

Exarhia

🏨 HOTEL EXARCHION
55 Themistokleous

📞210 38 00 731

 🌊 ♿ (((•))) ♈ ❄ HOTEL ❸

Right in the middle of Exharia's hipster-zone, Exarchion is a convenient spot to get a taste of Athens' youth culture. This part of town is lively at night and close to plenty of coffeshops and *tavernas* that are popular with the locals. Very clean and wheelchair-accessible, Hotel Exarchion is the best sleeping option in the area.

☝ Half a block down from the base of Pl. Exharia. *i* Breakfast €5. Ⓢ Singles €50; doubles €50; triples €70; family suite €90.

HOTEL ORION AND DRYADES
105 Em. Benaki and 4 Dryadon

📞210 33 02 387 ✉www.orion-dryades.com

 🌊 ♿ ♈ ❄ HOTEL ❷

This hotel is an amalgamation of 2 hotels that used to exist side-by-side, and it's a bit scattered as a result. Located at the extremity of Exharia, Orion and Dryades is off the beaten track and houses dated decor and a creaky elevator. But with great prices and clean rooms, think of walking back to the hotel from the sights as a free daily workout.

☝ From Pl. Syntagma, take bus #230 to Kalidromiou. Or, walking from Pl. Syntagma, follow Panipistimiou and take a right onto Em. Benaki. *i* Breakast €6. Laundry €3 per load. Wi-Fi €10 per week. Ⓢ Singles €25; doubles €35, with bath €60.

SIGHTS

Acropolis

Throughout its 2,500 year existence, the Acropolis has seen its fair share of action. Though somewhat worn for the wear (oh hey, Lord Elgin), it is a fascinating and quintessentially Athenian site. The Acropolis began as a political center in the Mycenean period from the 15th to 12th centuries BC. The king lived atop the hill that now provides tourists a breathtaking view of the entirety of Athens, from the Aegean Sea to the mountains. But in the 8th century BCE a temple was erected to honor **Athena,** the patron goddess of Athens, and ever since the story of the Acropolis has been one of construction, demolition and changing religious orders. Perhaps no site other than the Dome of the Rock rivals the Acropolis' multi-denominational appeal.

The first temple, called the **Hekatompmedos** for its measly 100 foot length, was made of wood and probably was not much to look at. So, just under 50 years later, the Athenians decided to construct a more elaborate temple, now known as the **Old Temple.** In celebration of their victory in the battle of Marathon in 490 BCE, the ancient Athenians decided that a third renovation was in order. But just 10 years later in 480 BCE, **Xerxes** and his Persian army swept Sparta and in order to fight the intruder at sea (the Athenians' strong suit) rather than land (Xerxes' strength), the Athenians fled the city, abandoning the Acropolis. Xerxes and his crew vandalized the newest temple, smashing statues' heads and wreaking general havoc. Not until Pericles' heyday from 450 BCE-429 BCE did the Athenians decide to face the ruins and build yet again, and this reconstruction resulted in the Parthenon.

After its tumultuous, extended, and awkward growth spurt, the Acropolis went through an angsty, religiously unsound period. From the 4th century AD until Greece claimed independence in 1833, the Acropolis went from its original dedication to Athena to a Christian Orthodox church to a Catholic church under the Byzantine Empire to a center of Muslim faith under Ottoman occupation—if this doesn't confuse you, well done. During this phase, **Lord Elgin,** a British ambassador to the Ottoman

Empire, carried some of the Parthenon's remains with him back to Britain, where they now remain in the British Museum—much to the dismay of many Greeks.

Now, centuries after its founding, the Acropolis is a tourist site and is currently undergoing another renovation started in 1983. Even through the throngs of tourists, looking down on Athens from a vantage point that must be like that of Mount Olympus, it is possible to imagine why the Acropolis and its turf have been fought over for so long.

i Admission gets you into the archeological site of the Acropolis, the archeological site and museum of the Ancient Agora, the north and south slopes of the Acropolis, the Theatre of Dionysis, the Roman Agora, Kerameikos, the Temple of Olympian Zeus, and Hadrian's Library. $ €12, students and EU seniors €6, EU students and internationals under 19 free on Su. ⏰ Open daily 8am-7:30pm.)

Parthenon

The Parthenon is the pinnacle of the Acropolis—historically, geographically, and artistically. Designed at the height of Periclean democracy by Iktinos, the structure, though now only the remnants of what once stood, is commonly seen as a symbol of Western culture. It took only nine years to build the Parthenon, but many layers of design went into its construction. The temple, which consists of over 16,500 pieces of white marble, is Doric but has Ionic features, and eight columns line each of its narrow sides. Now only white, the Parthenon was formerly painted inside with friezes and a deep blue hue. There were three key design features to the Parthenon. First, the **metopes,** or relief slabs, depicted scenes from Greek mythology like the war between the gods and the giants and the fight the centaurs had over women. Second, the Parthenon had Ionic **friezes.** The last, and perhaps the most notable design feature is that of the **pediments,** which were mounted between 438 and 432 BCE along the top of the columns. The East pediment, laid out in great detail on the third floor of the Acropolis museum, tells the story of the moment of Athena's birth when she sprung from Zeus' head. The West pediment shows the contest between Athena and Poseidon for Athens, when her olives won out over his salt water.

Erechtheum

Set to the left of the Parthenon, the Erechtheum is divided into two parts—the East portion to **Athena,** the West portion to her losing foe in the bid for Athens, **Poseidon.** The monument was built during the Peloponessian War between 421 BCE and 409 BCE. Work was paused while Athens went to war with Sicily and resumed at the completion of that battle, which did not go well for Athens. The Erechtheum is notable for the six **Caryatid** statues—women standing in a horseshoe shape supporting the roof—and is named after a hero Poseidon supposedly smote in his losing bid for Athens.

Propylaea

The Propylaea is the gateway to the Acropolis. Once a majestic entryway through which all walked, it is now a somewhat haggard collection of columns. First constructed in 437 BCE under Pericles' instruction, the Propylaea was never fully completed because of a series of wars that interrupted its construction. The same blast that damaged the Temple of Athena Nike in 1686 also damaged the structure, ambitious in its many tiers and mixed Doric and Ionic styles. A renovation project began in 1984 was recently completed, so enjoy the Propylaea in all its dilapidated splendor.

Theater of Dionysus

Down a path to the right of the main entrance to the Acropolis sits a giant, steep-stepped ancient theater that must strike fear in anyone who stands on its stage. Originally constructed in honor of **Dionysus,** the ancient Greek god of making merry through the aid of dance and wine, the theater became a place of celebration and artistic ecstasy. One ceremony led to another, and in 500 BCE a contest for playwrights that had been in Athens' outskirts was moved to the city. It was in this theatre that Aeschylus', Sophocles', Euripides', and Aristophanes' plays were first performed in honor of the gods. Recently, the theatre was renovated, and it now serves as a fully functional performance space.

Temple of Athena Nike

As you and hundreds of other travelers ascend the steep, slippery steps toward the Parthenon and walk through the Proplyaea, glance to your right: you will see the Temple of Athena Nike. Designed in the Ionic style by the famed architect **Kallikrates** during the Peace of Nikias from 421-415 BCE, the temple is now in its third iteration. Like the Parthenon, this temple has been ransacked many times throughout its history, primarily during the Turkish-Venetian War (1686-1687 AD). The temple initially had a frieze that was more than 25m long and depicted scenes of Athenian military success, but four parts of the initial 14 are now in the British Museum, and other portions have been destroyed. Make sure to check out some of the sections that are inside the Acropolis Museum on the second floor.

Agora

If the Acropolis was the showpiece of the ancient capital, the Agora was its heart and soul. It served as the city's marketplace, administrative center, and focus of daily life from the sixth century BCE through the sixth century CE. Socrates, Demosthenes, Aristotle, and St. Paul all debated democracy in its hallowed stalls. The 500-person **Boule**, or senate of ancient times, met in the **Bouleuterion** to make decisions for this city, and the **Monument of the Eponymous Heroes** functioned as an ancient tabloid, where the government posted honors and lawsuits. Following its heyday, the Agora, like the Acropolis, passed through the hands of various conquerors. The ancient market emerged again in the 19th century, when a residential area built above it was razed for excavations. Today, the Agora is a peaceful respite from the bustling Athens around it.

TEMPLE OF HEPHAESTUS

The impressive temple atop Kolonos Agraraiso Hill is dedicated to Hephaestus, the Greek god of metal working. The temple is made mostly of Pentelic marble in the Doric style and has **friezes** that depict the battle between Athenian hero **Theseus** and the Pallantids along its ceiling. Built from 460-415 BCE, the temple was in use through 1834 but is now the best-preserved Classical temple in all of Greece.

SKIAS

Civic offices that held the polis' official **weights and measures** were managed in 35-day segments by each of Athens' different factions in the round building now known as the Tholos—Greek for "circle"—on the left side of the Agora beneath the Temple of Hephaestus. Next to the **altars to the gods** and across from the **gymnasium,** the Skias' location is a prime example of what the Agora was in its heyday—a mix of everything Athenian.

ODEION OF AGRIPPA

Designed for performances, this structure originally had a thatched roof, orchestra pit, and seating for nearly 1000 people—no small feat for a building in 15 BCE. Like many other structures in the Agora, the original was destroyed by the Herulian invasion of 267 CE.

ROMAN AGORA

When the Ancient Agora filled with administrative buildings and crowded out vendors, the shop owners picked up their commerce and moved to the Roman Agora. The structure was built from 19-11 BCE and had two **propyla,** or Doric vestibules at the entrance, one of which was given by Julius Caesar himself. Today, all that remains beyond the five imposing columns at the entrance is an open, grassy expanse ringed by white marble pieces. In the far end of the Agora stands the **Tower of the Winds,** built by Andronikos, an astronomer from Macedonia. Also, the far side of the Agora is the foundation of the Vespasianae, or public latrines, that showcase Greece's advanced sewage system.

Enter the Agora either off Pl. Thission, off Adrianou, or as you descend from the Acropolis. ***i*** *For holiday schedule, call ☎210 32 16 690. Map kiosks are plentiful throughout the park, but it might be helpful to bring your own maps.* [$] *€2, students and EU seniors €1. EU students and under 19 free.* 🕐 *Open daily 8am-8pm. Last entrance 7:30pm.*

Syntagma

ACROPOLIS MUSEUM — MUSEUM

Dionyssiou Areopagitou 15 ☎210 32 10 185 www.theacropolismuseum.gr

A must-see—preferably before heading up the hill to the Acropolis—this modern museum has an astounding collection of ancient artifacts within its somewhat controversial modern design. Opened in 2007, it holds statues, terracotta wine vases, coins, and dioramas designated with placards that give great historical context in both Greek and English. Five of the original 6 Caryatids from 420-415 BCE are inside on the second floor; copies now stand in their stead on the Erechtheumn. Make sure to watch the video about the Parthenon on the 3rd floor for a great dose of information, and ask the archaeologists wandering the exhibits in black pants, white shirts, and nametags any pertinent questions.

[M]Acropolis. Located 300m from the Acropolis itself. ***i*** *The entrance to the museum has glass flooring, allowing visitors to see ruins beneath where they walk. Very cool and very reflective: make sure not to wear a skirt. Cafe on 3rd floor.* [$] *€5, students €3.* 🕐 *Open Tu-Su 8am-8pm, last entry 7:30pm.*

NATIONAL GARDEN — GARDEN

The land between Amalias, Vas. Olgas, Vas. Sofias, and Irodou Atikou

Step through the gates of the National Garden and the honks, heat, and general havoc of Athens fades into the shade, soft paths, and bird sounds within the park. This lush, expansive patch of peace has been public since 1923 and boasts, along with benches, marigolds, and winding pathways, a Botanical Garden, turtle pond, and cafe. In antiquity, the sacred grove of Cyceum stood in the same place.

From Syntagma facing the Parliament building, turn right. The many entrances to the park are behind the stalls and bus stops. ***i*** *Don't go alone at night.* [$] *Free.* 🕐 *Open 24hr.*

PARLIAMENT BUILDING — PUBLIC BUILDING

Stadiou 13 ☎210 32 37 315 www.nhmuseum.gr

Every hour on the hour, a small crowd of tourists assembles in front of the Parliament building to witness the changing of the guard, an absurd ritual that involves five men in tan colored shirts holding guns walking in a way that must resemble a loon mating dance. As part of the procedure for switching the soldiers need to touch their shoes' humongo pompoms. Between the hourly embarrassments, times two lucky men get to stand in the garb and get stared at by crowds without responding (a la Buckingham Palace). On Sunday at 11am there is an even more elaborate proceeding. All in all, the process takes about 5min.

Yellow building at the head of Syntagma, along Amalias. ***i*** *Changing of the guard every hour on the hour all day and night.*

PANATHENAIC STADIUM — STADIUM

Renovated for the Athens Olympics in 2004, the stadium is a massive construction of marble with no hot dog vendors of the standard American stadium. Sadly, this stadium might be better appreciated through pictures—the angle that visitors are allowed does not provide much of a vantage point, and honking from the road 50m away undermines the structure's glory.

On Vas. Konstantinou. From Sydagma, walk down Amalias 10 min. to Vas. Olgas and follow it to the left. Or take trolley #2, 4, or 11 from Syntagma. $ Free. Open 24hr.

NATIONAL ARCHAEOLOGICAL MUSEUM — MUSEUM

Patision Street 144 ☎210 90 00 901

At home if you dig in the dirt, you find worms. In Athens, it seems, one finds ancient artifacts. And worms. The quantity of vases and statues in this museum, founded in 1892, is astounding, and to look at every exhibit would take days. Room after room is full of perfectly chiseled, nude forms, and the second floor is entirely pottery. Decide ahead of time how long you want to spend at the museum, but don't expect to breeze through. The placards are like textbooks, so read them like you do a textbook: skim.

Walk 20 min. from Pl. Syntagma down Stadiou to Aiolou. Turn right onto Patission; or take trolley #2, 4, 5, 9, 11, 15, or 18 from the uphill side of Syntagma or trolley #3 or 13 from the north side of Vas. Sofias From Victoria, walk straight to the 1st street, 28 Oktuvriou; turn right and walk 5 blocks. Museum will be on the left i Photos without flash permitted. $ €7; students and EU citizens over 65 €3; EU students, under 19, and disabled persons free. Open Apr-Oct M 1:30pm-8pm, Tu-Su 8am-8pm. Nov-Mar 1:30pm-3:00pm, Tu-Su 8:30am-3pm.

Plaka

HADRIAN'S LIBRARY — RUINS

☎210 32 49 350

Built in 132 CE in the architectural style of the Roman Forum, this library was once the scene of a pool, a garden, and as the name suggests...a library. The books made of papyrus are long gone, but some columns still stand.

[M]Monastiraki. Walk up the hill. i Included in the €12 Acropolis ticket. $ Students and over 65 €2. EU students and under 19 free. Open daily 8am-8pm.

ARCHAEOLOGICAL SITE OF KERAMEIKOS — RUINS

End of Ermou ☎210 346 3552

Come to this burial ground to walk on over 1000 years of ancient, rotting nobility. No markers indicate who lies where, but blooming flowers, huge funerary statues, and remains of the ancient walls of Athens dot the landscape, making this former cemetery a beautiful archaeological excavation site. Look for the Dipylon gate, once the city's main entrance, where Pericles gave a memorable speech honoring those who perished during the first year of the Peloponnesian War. Supposedly, the hill to the immediate right of the museum is where the most famous remains rest.

[M]Monastiraki. Walk down Ermou. i Included in the €12 Acropolis ticket. $ €2, with student ID €1. Open daily 8:30am-3pm.

NUMISMATIC MUSEUM — MUSEUM

12 Panepistimiou ☎210 36 52 057 www.nma.gr

It takes money to see money. More **coins** than you could ever imagine are displayed in glass cases in this formal house of a German benefactor. As you walk through the displays, take note of the overzealous guards that watch your every move, almost assuming that you are going after one of these old pieces of change. With a huge variety of ancient currencies, this museum is worth your money—especially because it offers a complimentary hour-long audio tour of the first floor.

[M]Syntagma. Go left down Panepistimiou, and the museum will be on the right. i Complimentary hour-long audio tour of the 1st floor. $ €3, students and over 65 €2, EU students and under 19 free. Open Tu-Su 8:30am-3pm.

Monastiraki

👍 MUSEUM OF CYCLADIC ART
⊗♿❄ MUSEUM

4 Neophytou Douka ☎210 72 28 321 💻www.cycladic.gr

This museum's informative and well-labeled contents highlight a style of Greek art different from the other museums of its caliber. The first floor holds prime examples of Cycladic art, which is defined by its violin-shaped figures that capture human form in extreme simplicity. The fourth floor also holds dioramas about life in seventh-century Athens.

➹ Ⓜ Syntagma. Walk to Pl. Konolaki; the museum is 2 blocks past the square. ℹ Pictures without flash permitted. $ €7, over 65 €3.50, students €2.50, under 18 free. ⏰ Open M 10am-5pm, W 10am-5pm, Th 10am-8pm, F-Sa 10am-5pm, Su 11am-5pm.

BENAKI MUSEUM
⊗♿❄ MUSEUM

1 Koumbari and Vas. Sofias ☎210 36 71 000 💻www.benaki.gr

Founded in 1930 from a collection accumulated by Antony Benaki in his family's mansion, this museum—the central one of the Benaki museum network—houses an extensive collection of art from Greek history to the present. Pottery, busts, paintings, and a gold crown are shown behind glass in the museum that reopened in 2000.

➹ Ⓜ Syntagma. Walk along Vas. Sofias; the museum is at the intersection of Vas. Sofias and Koumbari. $ €6, students and over 65 €3, EU students and under 19 free. ⏰ Open M 9am-5pm, W 9am-5pm, Th 9am-midnight, F-Sa 9am-5pm.

NATIONAL GALLERY
⊗♿❄ MUSEUM

Vas. Konstantinou 50 ☎210 72 35 937 💻www.nationalgallery.gr

Greece is not renowned for its modern art, yet it seems the National Gallery showcases work mostly from the last few hundred years. The main collection holds a large number of Greek portraits, whose prominent moles have been immortalized forever, but lacks any artwork that really stands out.

➹ Located on the intersection of Vas. Konstantinou and Vas. Sofias by the Hilton Hotel. ℹ Photos without flash permitted. $ €6.50; students, children, and over 65 €3. ⏰ Open M-Sa 9am-3pm, Su 10am-2pm.

Exarhia

HOLY TRINITY
⊗ CHURCH

Fillelinon 21A ☎210 32 31 090

Gilt-laden, the Holy Trinity is the largest of the Byzantine churches in Athens and easily accessible from Syntagma. With 1000 years of history, this church is still young relative to other sights of Athens. After being amazed by the giant chandelier in the church's center, don't miss a nook on the right that displays a fresco painted 850 years ago. Other than this piece, most of the paintings on the walls are from the 19th century.

➹ Ⓜ Syntagma. Follow Fillelinon at the base of the square. The church will be a few blocks down on the left. $ Free. ⏰ Open daily 8am-noon.

FOOD

Syntagma

👍 PARADOSIAKO
🍴🍸☀ GREEK ❷

Voulis 44 ☎210 321 4121

While many lunch places sit idle with empty chairs, this stop does not lack customers—and for good reason. The Greek salad *(€6)*, though ubiquitous in Athens (and oddly enough listed on menus as "Greek salad" rather than just... salad), is particularly scrumptious. Mop up the extra olive oil with the hearty, solid bread that comes with your meal. Sitting either inside or outside on a quiet side street, meet the wonderful owners—a husband and wife team that has worked here since the restaurant's opening.

✈ Ⓜ*Syntagma. Walk along Filellinon, take a right down Nikodimou. Voulis is 3 blocks down. Para-dosiako is on your right.* Ⓢ *Meals €5-15.* ⏲ *Open daily noon-midnight.*

CAFE VOULIS
Voulis 17

⊛ ☕ ❄ CAFE ❶
☎210 32 34 333

Chat over a prosciutto and mozzarella sandwich *(€3.70)* along with some coffee *(€1.50-€3.20)* at this reasonably-priced coffee shop where customers smoke from their metal bar stools and relax for hours on end. Fairly crowded and just a few blocks from Syntagma, Cafe Voulis is not gourmet but is very convenient.

✈ *Behind hordes of motorcycles, set back on a corner just off Ermou.* *i Delivery available.* Ⓢ *Entrees €6.* ⏲ *Open M-F 7:30am-9pm, Sa 8am-5pm.*

PETROS GRILL HOUSE
Kidathineon 28

✒☕ GRILL HOUSE ❶
☎201 32 46 229

Petros is a great place to grab a chicken or pork gyro *(€2)* for the road. While this restaurant does double as a locals' evening hangout, stick to their lunch menu and ask for the waiter from New York who moved to Greece to turn his life around after losing his job at Lehman Brothers.

✈ *Head 3 blocks down Kidathineon; it's on the right.* Ⓢ *Entrees €12.* ⏲ *Open daily 9am-2am.*

Plaka

🔖 YIASEMI
23 Mnisikleous

⊛Ⓧ☕❄⌁ CAFE ❶
☎213 04 17 937 🖳www.yiasemi.gr

This cafe belongs by the sea rather than in the heart of Athens. With its adorable daisy-painted tables and stone staircases, it's a shame there's no view to go with this relaxed beach town vibe. The portions are small, but this cafe is better for sitting with a friend and catching up over coffee or tea *(€3.50)*. If hungry, try the lemon pie *(€5)* or meatballs *(€5)* that offer a hearty portion for their price.

✈ *Up the hill past the Roman Agora. To the right down the street with the red track paint and lanes drawn on the ground.* Ⓢ *Coffee €3.50. Entrees €5-10.* ⏲ *Open daily 10am-2am.*

🔖 BENETH
Adrianou 97

⊛Ⓧ☕❄ BAKERY ❶
☎210 32 38 822

If it's your birthday, if you want to pretend it's your birthday, or even if you just want to eat something delicious, go to Beneth. Pastries made on location and baklava that leaves you craving more even after eating your own body weight in these treats are well worth their price tags *(€2)*. Packaged yogurt and beverages are sold in a cooler on the left of the shop. Though Beneth offers no seating, try standing at the high metal tables out front.

✈ *Striaght down Adrianou.* Ⓢ *Pastries and fresh-baked bread €1-3. Cappuccino €1.50.* ⏲ *Open daily 7am-10pm.*

SCHOLARHIO OUZERI KOUKLIS
Tripodon 14

✒☕❄⌁ TAVERNA ❷
☎210 32 42 603 🖳www.scholarhio.gr

This self-proclaimed traditional family restaurant is in actuality the neighborhood's restaurant best adapted to tourism. Waiters sneakily bring out bottled water before you can think to ask for tap and fill your table with platters of small plates whose prices add up quicker than you can eat. Keeping track of the tab aside, the food is pretty good, and green peppers in the Greek salad *(€4)* are a nice touch.

✈ *Up the hill past the Roman Agora. Down the street on the right with the red track paint and lanes drawn on the ground.* Ⓢ *Individual dishes €3. Meal of 2 side plates, bread, beverage, and dessert €14.* ⏲ *Open daily 11am-2am.*

EAT AT MILTON'S
91 Adrianou

◆⊗♀※🛆 FANCY ❺

☎210 32 49 129 ▣www.eatmiltons.gr

Perfect for the fanciest date of your life, this white-tiled restaurant serves fish so fresh that there's not even a freezer on-site. For those attempting to win over a heart—and willing to have a heart attack when the bill comes—there is a lobster special *(€50 per person)* that will impress the most gourmet of companions. If you're not trying to impress anybody, order one of the few modest options on the menu to save your wallet from extinction. Organic food fans will be pleased to learn that they serve a "BIO" Greek salad *(€12)* made with fresh local ingredients.

☃ *Up the hill past the Roman Agora. Take the street with red track paint and lanes drawn on the ground to the end, and then turn left at the next road. Milton's will be on the opposite corner at the end of the block.* ⑤ *Salads and soups €9-12. Entrees €25-30. Lobster special €50.* ☼ *Open daily noon-5pm and 7:30pm-midnight.*

Monastiraki

🏴 MANDRAS
Ag. Anarguron 8 and Taki

◆⊗♀※🛆 GREEK ❸

☎210 32 13 765

Delicious food defines this classy establishment near a large square in the depths of Monastiraki. *Tzatziki* dip comes with olive oil drizzled on top and one regal olive perched in the center of the serving. Those craving a healthy serving of meat should try the lamb *(€16)* or grilled chicken *(€9.50)*.

☃ Ⓜ*Monastiraki.* ⓘ *Live music nightly after 8pm.* ⑤ *Appetizers €5; entrees €8-25.* ☼ *Open daily 2pm-2am.*

SAVVAS
Mitropoleos 86

◆⊗♀🛆 TAVERNA ❶

☎210 32 45 048

These gyros are cheap and delicious, and you'll almost feel like Pavlov's dog after eating your first. The cost of a gyro skyrockets to €8.50 if you eat at the restaurant, so grab a few to go and eat them in Pl. Monastiraki.

☃*Opposite* Ⓜ*Monastiraki.* ⑤ *Gyros from €1.80.* ☼ *Open daily 9am-2am.*

IRIDANOS
Adrianou 9

◆⊗♀※ TAVERNA ❷

☎210 32 79 678

A standard taverna at the base of the Agora, Iridanos serves Greek classics like lamb and potatoes *(€8)* to clients resting in wicker chairs with blue cushions. Steer clear of the fancy beverages—they may cost more than your meal.

☃ *Down Adrianou.* ⑤ *Entrees €6-12. Mixed drinks from €5.* ☼ *Open daily 9am-2am.*

Exarhia

🏴 BARBA YIANIS
94 Em. Benaki

⊛⊗♀※ TAVERNA ❶

☎210 38 24 138

This *taverna* has been around for 90 years, and it hasn't lost any of its charm. Pale yellow walls, high ceilings, and a cafeteria-style food selection make this a cozy place to sit and enjoy some classic Greek "homefood," in the words of the manager. Try the beef in small pieces *(€8)*, roast pork in lemon sauce *(€8)*, and the green beans *(€5)*.

☃ *Straignt up Em. Benaki from Panepistimiou by Pl. Syntagma.* ⑤ *Entrees €5-€12.* ☼ *Open M-Sa noon-1am, Su noon-7pm.*

BOE
Araxobis 56

⊛⊗(ᵗ)♀※🛆 CAFE ❶

☎210 38 35 811

A hipster coffee shop in a hipster area. In a giant corner venue with umbrellas and chairs out front, this cafe stays busy until closing every night. Settle in with a book or laptop and pass the afternoon away in the cool, marble-floored environment, then head outside with friends at night for some cappuccino and

athens • food

conversation. On a budget? Take your beverages to go—Boe, like many restaurants in Athens, has cheaper prices for takeout.

➜ Opposite Club Creperie Xarchia in Pl. Exarhia. $ Cappuccino freddo €3.80. Fresh orange juice €5, €3 if taken to go. ⏰ Open daily 9am-midnight.

KAVOURAS 🍴🍸❄ SOUVLAKI [1]

64 Themistokleous ☎210 38 38 010

Cheap *souvlaki* and beer in a great location make Kavouras a great spot for a quick lunch or dinner. Add a vegetarian *souvlaki* to any meal for just €0.90. Though variety isn't this place's forte—the menu consists entirely of *souvlaki*—it does this Greek fast food staple well.

➜ Half a block from the base of Pl. Exharia. $ Souvlaki with meat €1.70; vegetarian €0.90. Beer €1.50-2.50. ⏰ Open daily 11am-3am.

CLUB CREPE XARCHIA 🍴♿🍸❄☁ FAST FOOD [1]

Corner of Ikonomou and M. Themistokleous on Pl. Exarhia ☎210 38 40 773

Delicious crepes right on Pl. Exarhia. Huge salads *(€5)* come with tons of ingredients, but the food is made to order and not as quick as the self-proclaimed "fast food" moniker would suggest. Fidgety people and late-night eaters beware: seating is on a bit of a slant and you may topple over on accident.

➜ At the tip of Pl. Exarhia. ℹ Food made to order. $ Salads €5. Crepes €3. ⏰ Open daily noon-4am.

BARBARA'S FOOD COMPANY 🍴🚭🍸❄☁ INTERNATIONAL [3]

Em. Benaki 63 ☎210 38 03 004 💻www.bfoodcompany.gr

Wide, white-painted boards and metallic countertops give this spacious eatery an airy feel. Greek yuppies sit at tables and try the rigatoni with mozzarella *(€6)*, the salmon with ginger and orange *(€8.50)*, and fettuccini with swordfish and tomatoes *(€7.50)*.

➜ At the tip of Pl. Exarhia. $ Entrees around €8. ⏰ Open M-Sa 12:30pm-12:30am, Su 1-11:30pm.

Pagrati

CUCINA POVERA 💳♿🍸❄ RESTAURANT [5]

Eforionos 13 ☎210 75 66 088 💻www.cucinapovera.gr

Though this restaurant's name translates to "poor man's kitchen," Cucina Povera is anything but cheap. Its menu is written daily based on market specials, and its sage green walls and pine wood tables create an atmosphere that is both earthy and classy. Some of the dishes are vegetable-based, like the green salad with beet root and warm goat cheese *(€9)*, and others might turn a sensitive stomach, like the assortment of cooked intestines on the menu. Regardless of preference, Cucina Povera is sure to satisfy; be forewarned that these rich panhandlers will take all your spare change and then some.

➜ Walk east from the Panathenaic Stadium (away from the Acropolis) on Vas. Konstandinou, then turn right on Eratosthenous and left onto Eforionos. ℹ Wine selection tops 350 choices. $ Meals €25, excluding wine. ⏰ Open in summer M-Sa 8pm-midnight; in winter, Tu-Sa 1-5pm.

POSTO CAFE 🍴♿📶🍸❄☁ CAFE [1]

Pl. Plastira 2 ☎210 75 62 379

With red plastic chairs and lots of green plants around the patio area, this super-cheap cafe has a slight Gilligan's Island feel to it. Though they claim to be open 24/7, the cafe is closed for the brief window of 7-9am on Monday mornings. Otherwise, though, this is a great spot to sit with a cheap *frappe*, crepe, or beer and take advantage of the free Wi-Fi.

➜ In Pl. Plastira. Look for it behind the green potted plants. ℹ Free Wi-Fi. $ Soda €1. Coffee €2. Orange juice €3. Small draft beer €2, large €3; bottle of beer €2.50. Crepes €2.50. ⏰ Open M midnight-7am and 9am-midnight, Tu-Su 24hr.

NIGHTLIFE

Plaka

CHANDELIER PLAKA BAR

4 Benizelou ☎210 331 6330 www.chandelier.gr

This quirky, ultra-modern bar is a hotspot Thursday through Saturday but quieter during the week. It serves up a variety of alcoholic concoctions, from standard beverages like strawberry daiquiris *(€9)* and mojitos *(€4.50)* to specialty drinks like the "Green Boy" that mixes cucumbers, lemon, and mustard with alcohol *(€4.50)* and the "Honey Love" that combines banana, lemon, honey, orange, and pineapple with a mixed drink to form a fruity frenzy *(€4.50)*. If alcohol isn't your thing, a plethora of booze-free drinks fill up two whole pages of the establishment's menu.

[M]Syntagma. Walk down Mitropoleos, take a left onto Evangelistrias after 7 blocks. Chandelier Plaka is 2 blocks down. $ €4-10. Open daily 7pm-2am.

BRETTOS BAR

Kolonaki 41 ☎210 33 17 793

In the mood to stomp on some 40-year-old's toes when fighting for a seat? Maybe brush up on someone else's fanny pack or jean shorts? Try Brettos, a bar in the heart of Tourist Land, Athens. With brightly colored bottles illuminating the high ceilings and functional barrels of beer lining the right wall, Brettos looks like fun, but its size and crowds make it almost too jam-packed to enjoy. With no room for dancing, conversation flows as freely as the wine or the *ouzo (bottles from €19)*.

[M]Syntagma. Walk down Filelinon to Kidathineon. 4 blocks down on the left. $ Red wine by the glass from €2. Ouzo from €2.50. Open M-F 10am-2am, Sa-Su 10am-3am.

CINE PARIS ROOF GARDEN CINEMA OUTDOOR CINEMA

Kyd ☎210 32 22 071 www.cineparis.gr

Want to get drunk and see a movie at the same time? Don't try to sneak that six pack of Natty into the nearby theater. Instead, head to Cine Paris Roof Garden Cinema to booze while you watch films in an ivy-laced rooftop garden in the middle of Plaka. Opened in the '20s by a Greek hairdresser who had lived in Paris, this cinema showcases thrillers like the "King of Mykonos" and recent blockbusters like *Knight and Day*.

[M]Syntagma. Walk down Filelinon to Kidathineon. 3 blocks down on the right. i All movies in English subtitled in Greek. $ €8, students €6. Drinks at the rooftop bar €2-6. Movies begin daily at 8:45pm.

Monastiraki and Psiri

OINOPNEUMATA BAR

Miaouli 21 ☎210 32 39 370

Located on a street that is almost exclusively bars, Oinopneumata is the most crowded. Filled with teenagers unabashedly making out and others actively disputing the rules of soccer, this is a great place to come for some beers *(from €4)* in an unadorned, raucous environment.

From [M]Monastiraki, cross Ermou street and walk down Miaouli 2 blocks. $ Rakomelo €8 for 8 shots. Shisha €10. Open daily 6pm-2am.

PSIRA BAR

Miaouli 19 ☎210 32 44 046

Order some *rakomelo*, Greece's local alcohol sweetened with honey, for €8 at this bar serviced by a friendly staff. Enjoy a slight breeze and good company in the outdoor seating, or head inside for a lively conversation.

[M]Monastiraki. Cross Ermou street and walk down Miaouli 2 blocks. $ Beer €4. Ouzo €7. Rakomelo €8. Open M-Th noon-2am, F-Sa noon-4am, Su noon-3am.

KAZOZA ♿🍸❄☁ BAR

Miaouli 13 ☎210 32 16 469

The actual countertop to this bar is around the corner from Miaouli street in a hole in the wall, and customers only set foot inside to search for the bathroom. Most just sit down at a table outside along Miaouli proper and wait for the waiter to come take their order. With just plain chairs and tables and no real decoration, enjoy the free peanuts—what else do you need with your beer?

➡ From [M]Monastiraki, cross Ermou street and walk down Miaouli 2 blocks. [$]Beer €4-5. Wine €6. Ouzo €7. Honey and wine €12 per ½L. Shisha €10. ⏰ Open daily 7:30pm-4am.

Exarhia

TRAIN CAFE 🍸❄ CAFE, BAR

Em. Benaki 72 ☎210 38 44 355

A train carved into a slab of wood and painted with red and blue paint gives this well-lit wood bar its name. Though customers are sparse in the summer, crowds come in the wintertime to try the *psimeni raki (€4),* a cocktail made of raki, honey, sugar, and herbs.

➡ [M]Syntagma. Follow Panepistimiou to Em. Benaki. [$] Beer €3. ⏰ Open daily 10am-3am.

UNDERGROUND ♿🍸❄☁ BAR

Metaxa 21 ☎210 38 22 019

If this bar could make a noise, it would be a gruff and sustained "grrr!" Black decor and bartenders wearing headbands and piercings give this bar a slight punk feel, and alternative music gives this place a truly underground vibe.

➡ [M]Syntagma. Follow Panepistimiou to Em. Benaki. Take a left onto Andrea Metaxa. Underground is half a block down on the left side of the street. Look for the glass panel with the doorknob. [$] Draft beer €4. Special cocktails €7. ⏰ Open M-Th 10am-2am, F-Sa 10am-4am, Su 10am-2am.

Kolonaki

SHOWROOM ♿🍸❄ BAR

12 Milioni and 4 Iraklitou ☎210 36 46 460 www.showroomcafe.gr

Settle into a comfortable white leather barstool at this local hangout not yet discovered by tourists. Although it's not cheap, Showroom is worth the splurge. As evidenced by the pineapple and bananas in the silver bowl prominently on display at the bar, its drinks are all made with fresh fruit. Soft, bongo-like background music gives the bar a relaxed feel, so order a drink and stay for a while.

➡ [M]Syntagma. Follow Vas. Sofias past the Parliament Building to Sekeri. Take a left onto Sekeri and then a right onto Konstantinou Kanari. Milioni is 1 block down on the left side of the street. [$] Beer €7. Mixed drinks €12. ⏰ Open daily 8am-2am.

TRIBECA ♿🍸❄☁ BAR

Skoufa 46 ☎210 36 23 541

Hunter green walls and dark wood line this bar geared toward an older crowd. Few under 30 can be seen at Tribeca, where most of the customers are graying. Dancing isn't the MO for this mature crew, but settle in at a standard outdoor table for a ginger mango daiquiri *(€9.50)* for a palette-confusing experience.

➡ [M]Syntagma. Follow Panepistimiou to Omirou. Turn left on Skoufa. [$] Cocktails €9.50. ⏰ Open M-Sa 9:30am-3am, Su 10am-2am.

ARTS AND CULTURE

Festivals

ATHENS FESTIVAL ☁

Panepistimiou 39 ☎210 32 72 000 www.greekfestival.gr

Also known as the Hellenic Festival, this outpouring of the arts takes place from early June to July in a number of venues throughout Athens. Ranging from classical music concerts and dance recitals to plays and concerts by modern artists like Rufus Wainwright (of *Shrek* "Hallelujah" fame), performances are not so much insights into Athenian culture or tradition as a promise of a fun summer night in a beautiful city.

⇄ To get to the box office from [M]Syntagma, follow Filelinon in the direction of traffic for 2 blocks to Nikodimou, which turns into Flessa. Make a slight right onto Kiristou; take Kiristou to Mnissikleous, and follow Mnissikleous to the end. ℹ See website for annual list of performances. $ Tickets from €15-50. ⏰ Open daily 9am-2pm and 6-9pm.

VIRGIN MARY DAY

Virgin Mary Day is actually a three-day-long festival beginning on August 15, the day Greeks celebrate the birth of Mary. With free foods, orchestra concerts, dancing, partying and other things the Virgin Mary probably didn't partake in too much during her time, the Greeks enjoy themselves during this 72hr. holiday.

SHOPPING

Athens' shopping can be divided into three categories: the touristy, the everyday necessities, and the posh. Shopping for tourist memorabilia is best done in the **Athens Flea Market,** located directly to the right of **[M]Monastiraki,** or in **Plaka** along Kydathineon. Amongst the *tavernas* there are a shocking number of shops selling exactly the same cotton dresses, keychains, magnets, packaged soaps, and T-shirts that will make great gifts for Aunt Darlene and Uncle Jim. For the everyday non-Greece specific shopping, head to **Ermou.** Follow it from **Pl. Syntagma** down to **Pl. Monastiraki** and pass staples like H and M and Sephora, in addition to their Greek equivalents. This area is where most Athenian teenagers buy their wardrobes, and it's the place to look for that last-minute pair of shorts or bathing suit. The **posh shopping** is in **Kolonaki,** along **Tsakalof** or any street branching off of Panepistimiou up toward Pl. Kolonaki. Foreign designers from Theory to Lacoste to Longchamp have their stores here.

Outdoor Markets

FISH AND MEAT MARKET 🚭♿🍸⛅ SYNTAGMA

On Athinas between Armoudiou and Aristogeitonos

Squeamish beware: this place is not for the soft-hearted or for people who coo over pictures of kittens. Carcasses swing from behind glass encasements, and the thwack of butchers chopping their meat echoes through the concrete enclosure. Men in bloody aprons parade around as whole lambs stare with vacant eyes. The fish market smells horrendous but is a bit tamer.

⇄ From [M]Syntagma, walk down Ermou street and turn left on Athinas. ⏰ Open daily 4am-6pm.

VARNAKIOS 🚭♿⛅ SYNTAGMA

On Athinas between Armoudiou and Aristogeitonos

Like a supermarket with one aisle and a rougher crowd of check-out people, Varnakios has everything needed to stock an Athenian kitchen or cook a fresh meal. In fact, make it your one-stop shop for finding the makings of a fresh Greek meal. On the right side of this side-street-turned-grocery-store are tables invisible beneath cartons of tomatoes, cucumbers, peaches, cherries, and other varieties of fresh produce. On the left side of the "aisle" are shops with prepackaged edibles and soaps as well as eggs and dairy.

⇄ [M]Syntagma. Walk down Ermou and turn left onto Athinas. ℹ Produce €1-3; shop prices vary. ⏰ Open M-Th 6am-7pm, F-Sa 5am-8pm.

ESSENTIALS

Practicalities

- **TOURIST OFFICES:** The **Information Office** travel brochures are helpful and their **Athens map** indispensable. Ask for the lists of museums, embassies, and banks. Most up-to-date bus, train, and ferry schedules and prices also available. (*Amalias 26* ☎210 33 10 392 ■*www.visitgreece.gr* ☼ *Open M-F 9am-7pm, Sa-Su 10am-4pm.)*

- **BUDGET TRAVEL OFFICES:** **Academy Travel** specializes in custom island-hopping routes. *(Iperidou 3* ☎210 32 45 071 ■*www.academytravelgreece.com* ☼ *Open daily 9am-10pm.)* **STA Travel.** *(Voulis 43* ☎210 32 11 88 ■*www.e-travelshop. gr* ☼ *Open M-F 9am-5pm, Sa 10am-2pm.)* **Adrianos Travel, Ltd.** *(Pandrossou 28* ☎210 32 20 702 ■*www.ticketgreece.gr* ☼ *Open daily 9am-6pm.)* **Meliton Travel** *(23b Apolonos* ☎210 32 47235 ■*www.melitontravel.gr* ☼ *Open in summer M-F 9am-6pm, Sa 10am-2pm; winter M-F 9am-5pm.)*

- **CURRENCY EXCHANGE:** **National Bank**, Karageorgi Servias 2, in Pl. Syntagma. *(*☎21033 40 500 ☼ *Open M-Th 8am-2:30pm, F 8am-2pm.)* **Citibank,** the post office, some hotels, and other banks offer currency exchange. Commission is usually around 5%.

- **LUGGAGE STORAGE:** **Pacific Ltd.** is in El. Venizelos Airport's arrivals terminal, across from the large cafe. *(*☎210 35 30 160 ■*www.pacifictravel.gr* Ⓢ *€2 per day. €30 per month.* ☼ *Open 24hr.)* Main branch at 26 Nikis in Syntagma. *(*☎210 32 41 007 Ⓢ *€2 per day, €30 per month.* ☼ *Open M-F 9am-6pm.)* Many **hotels** have free or inexpensive luggage storage. Lockers are also available at Ⓜ Monastiraki, Ⓜ Piraeus, and Ⓜ Omonia.

- **LAUNDROMATS:** Most *plintirias* (launderers) have signs reading "Laundry." **National.** *(Apolonos 17 in Syntagma* ☎210 32 32 226 ■*www.nationaldrycleaners. gr* Ⓢ *Wash, dry, and fold €4.50 per kg., min. 2 kg. Dry cleaning: men's shirt €3, dress pants €5.* ☼ *Open M 8am-5pm, Tu 8am-8pm, W 8am-5pm, Th-F 8am-8pm.)* **Zenith** *(Apolonos 12 and Pendelis 1* ☎210 32 38 533 Ⓢ *Wash, dry, and fold €4 per kg.* ☼ *Open M 8am-4pm, Tu 8am-8pm, W 8am-4pm, Th-F 8am-8pm.)*

- **INTERNET ACCESS:** Free Wi-Fi is now available through the athenswifi network in **Pl. Syntagma, Pl. Kotzia,** and **Thissio.** Athens also teems with Internet cafes. Expect to pay €3-6 per hr. **Bits and Bytes,** Kapnikareas 19 in Plaka *(*☎210 32 53 142 *)* and Akadamias 78 in Exharia *(*☎210 52 27 717*)*, is the mother of new-age internet cafes with fast connections, and 2 floors with A/C and internet 24hr. (■*www.bnb.gr* *i* *Cash only.* Ⓢ *€2.50 per hr. min. charge €2 for 30min. ISIC cardholders €1.80 per hr. Black-and-white printing €0.30 per page; color €0.50 per page.* ☼ *Open 24hr.)* **Lobby Internet Cafe** is mainly a cafe with a few computers and a printer. *(Imittou 113 by Pl. Pangratiou, in Pagrati.* ☎210 70 14 607 Ⓢ *Internet €4 per hr. Printing €0.25 per page.* ☼ *Open daily 9am-1am.)*

- **POST OFFICES:** For customer service inquiries call the **Greek National Post Office (ELTA)** *(*☎210 32 43 311*)*. For shipping abroad, try parcel post at the Syntagma ELTA branch at Mitropoleos 60 *(*☎210 32 42 489 Ⓢ *Stamps for postcards and letters up to 20g. €0.72, plus €3.22 for registered mail and €2.90 for express.* ☼ *Open M-F 7:30am-8pm.)* **Acropolis/Plaka** branch exchanges currency and accepts Poste Restante. Sends packages up to 2kg abroad. *(*☎210 92 18 076 ☼ *Open M-F 7:30am-6pm.)* **Exharia** branch, at the corner of Zaimi and K. Deligiani, exchanges currency and accepts Poste Restante. *(*☼ *Open M-F 7:30am-2pm.)* **Omonia** distributes stamps 24hr. and accepts Poste Restante and parcels up to 2kg to ship abroad. *(Aiolou 100* ☎210 32 53 586 *i* *Credit card required.*

Open M-F 7:30am-8pm, Sa 7:30am-2pm.) **Syntagma** branch is on the corner of Mitropoleos. Sells stamps, exchanges currency, and accepts Poste Restante *(☎210 33 19 500).*

- **POSTAL CODES: Acropolis and Plaka:** 11702. **Exharia:** 10022. **Omonia and Syntagma:** 10300.

Emergency!

- **EMERGENCY:** ☎112. **Ambulance:** ☎106. **SOS Doctors:** ☎1016. **Poison Control:** ☎210 77 93 777. **AIDS Help Line:** ☎210 72 22 222. For medical information in Greek and English *(☎210 89 83 146).*

- **TOURIST POLICE: Airport Police** *(☎210 35 36 899).* **Athens Tourist Police** Station at 43-45 Veikou Str, Koukaki *(☎210 92 00 724).* **Athens Police Headquarters** 173, Alexandras Avenue *(☎100 on local phones, 210 64 76 000).*

- **LATE-NIGHT PHARMACIES:** Marked by a green cross. About 1 every 4 blocks is open 24hr.; they rotate. Once a pharmacy closes, it will list on its door the nearest ones that are open 24hr.

- **HOSPITALS:** Emergency hospitals or clinics on duty can be reached at ☎106. **KAT** *(Nikis 2 ☎210 62 80 000)* is located between Marousi and Kifisia. **Geniko Kratiko Nosokomio** is a public State Hospital at Mesogion 154 *(☎210 77 78 901).* State hospital **Aeginitio** *(Vas. Sofias 72 ☎210 72 20 811)* and *(Vas. Sofias 80 ☎210 77 70 501)* is closer to Athens' center. Near Kolonaki is the public hospital **Evangelismos** *(Ypsilantou 45-47 ☎210 20 41 000.)*

Getting There

By Air

Greece's international airport, **Eleftherios Venizelos (ATH)** *(☎210 35 30 000 ◨www.aia.gr),* has 1 massive but navigable terminal. Arrivals are on the ground floor. **Metro Line 3** (blue) connects the airport to Ⓜ️Syntagma in the Athens city center *(Ⓢ €6).* **Suburban Rail,** which serves the airport and runs along the Attiki Odos highway, connects with **Line 1** (green) at Ⓜ️Neratziotissa and with the blue line at Ⓜ️Doukissis Plakentias—the most central stations in Omonia and Syntagma, respectively *(🕐 About 30min.)* To get from **Plateia Syntagma** in the city center to the airport, take the X95 bus *(Ⓢ €3.20. 🕐 45min.-1hr. depending on traffic, every 10-15min.),* which runs 24hr. Pick it up on Othonos near the top right corner of Pl. Syntagma. From Ⓜ️**Ethniki Amyna**, take the X94 *(Ⓢ €6, students €3. 🕐 Every 15min. 7:20am-8:40pm.)* or the X95, and from Ⓜ️**Dafni** take the X97 *(Ⓢ €6, students €3. 🕐 Every 30-60min).* From **Piraeus,** take the X96. *(Ⓢ €6, students €3. 🕐 Every 20-25min.)* Catch the bus in Pl. Karaiskaki on the waterfront, on Akti Tzelepi, across from Philippis Tours. From **Kifisia,** catch the X92 from Pl. Platanos. *(Ⓢ €6, students €3. 🕐 Every 45min.-1hr.)* If your travels have taken you to **Kifisos Intercity Bus Station,** take the X93. *(Ⓢ €6, students €3. 🕐 Every 20-45min.)* **KTEL** regional bus lines serve the airport as well. From **Rafinam,** a bus *(Ⓢ €3)* leaves every 30min. from the stop midway up the ramp from the waterfront, and stops at **Loutsa** (Artemis) along the way. Buses drop off at the 1 or the 4 departure entrances and wait outside the 5 arrival exits. You can catch the bus from Lavrio at Keratea, Kalivia Thorikou, and Markopoulo as well.

There are a number of ways to get from the **airport** to the center of town, like taking the **X95 bus.** *(Ⓢ €3. 🕐 40-70 min., every 15min.)* Bus tickets can be bought right outside the exit near baggage claim. The blue Metro line, **line 3,** is fast, clean, and also runs from the airport to Pl. Syntagma. *(Ⓢ €6.)* Signs for the metro are clearly marked by baggage claim. When in doubt, ask the **information booth** how to get to Syntagma and they will point you on the right path. Make sure to exchange a bit of currency to buy your bus or metro ticket to Syntagma. **Cabs** are also available, but they cost upwards of €40 and come with a €3.40 airport surcharge and additional baggage fees *($ €0.35 per bag)*. If sticking to a budget, the bus or the metro is the way to go.

By Train

Hellenic Railways (OSE) *(Sina 6 ☎210 52 97 777 🖳www. ose.gr)*. Contact the railway offices to confirm schedules before your trip. **Larisis Station** has trains that go to Northern Greece *(☎210 52 98 829)*. Take trolley #1 from El. Venizelou (Panepistimou) in Pl. Syntagma *(⏰ Every 10min. 5am-midnight)* or take the metro to Sepolia. Trains depart for **Thessaloniki.** *($ €14. ⏰ 7hr., 5 per day.)* To get to **Bratislava, Bucharest, Budapest, Istanbul, Prague, Sofia,** and other international destinations, take a train from Larisis Station to Thessaloniki and change there. **Peloponnese Train Station** has trains to **Albania, Bulgaria,** and **Turkey.** Ticket office open daily 5:45am-9pm. From Diligani, easiest entry is through Larisis Station; exit to your right and go over the footbridge. From El. Venizelou (Panepistimiou) in Syntagma, take blue bus #057. *($ €0.45. ⏰ Every 15min., 5am-11:30pm.)* To **Nafplion** *($ €5. ⏰ 3hr., 2 per day.)* and **Patra** *($ €5.30. ⏰ 4hr., 3 per day.)*

By Bus

Athens has four bus terminals, two of which serve the regional bus line and two of which serve the suburban bus lines. Check regional schedules *(☎210 51 14 505)* or suburban schedules *(🖳www.ktelattikis.gr)*.

Terminal A is located at Kifissou 100 *(☎210 51 24 910)*. Take blue bus #051 *($ €1. ⏰ Every 15min. 5am-midnight.)* from the corner of Zinonos and Menandrou near Pl. Omonia. Don't mistake the private travel agency at Terminal A for an information booth. Buses from here run to various regional destinations; ask at information booth for schedule.

Terminal B is at Liossion 260 *(☎210 83 17 153)*. Take blue bus #024 from Pl. Syntagma on the National Garden side of Amalias, or from Panepistimiou. *($ €1. ⏰ 45min., every 20min. 5:10am-11:40pm.)* Buses to **Delphi** leave from here.

Mavromateon 29 is in Exharia *(☎210 82 10 872)*. Walk up Patission from the National Archeological Museum and turn right onto Enianos 9 Alexandras Av.; it's on the corner of Areos Park. Take trolley #2, 5, 9, 11, or 18. Buses from this stop go to the Rafina ferry stop, the Sounion Peninsula via Coast Road or Lavvio. Tickets are sold at two stands 50m apart.

Plateia Eleftherias has probably the fewest buses that will be of use to tourists. To get here from Pl. Syntagma, go west on Ermou, turn right onto Athinas, turn left onto Evripidou, and walk to the end of the street. From here, buses A16 or B16 will take you to Daphni Monastery and Eleusis. *($ €1. ⏰ 10-20min., 5am-11pm.)*

By Ferry

Check schedules at the tourist office, in the Athens News, with the Port Authority of Piraeus *(☎210 42 26 000; 210 41 47 800)*, over the phone *(☎185 from within Athens only)*, or at any travel agency. Most ferries dock at Piraeus; others stop at nearby Rafina. Ferry schedules are not regular and are formed at the beginning of each week, so checking ahead is very important.

Piraeus

Take the M1 (green) south to its terminus, or take bus #040 from Filellinon and Mitropoleos right off Pl. Syntagma. *(⏰ Every 15min.)* Ferries from Piraeus run to Tinos, Mykonos, Pyros, Naxos, Ios, Santorini, and Milos.

Rafina

From Athens, buses leave for Rafina from Mavromateon 29, two blocks up along Areos Park or a 15min. walk from Pl. Syntagma. *($ €2. ⏰ 1hr., every 30min. 5:40am-10:30pm.)* Ferries from here head to Andros, Mykonos, Naxos, Pyros, and Tinos. Flying Dolphoins sail to Andros, Mykonos, Naxos, Pyros, and Tinos.

Getting Around

Buy **yellow tickets** at most **street kiosks** and validate them yourself at the purple machine on buses, trolleys, trams, and metros. (**$** *€1.* 🕒 *1½hr. of use.)* Those who plan to use public transportation frequently should opt for a 24hr. ticket (**$** *€3),* which grants unlimited travel on city bus, trolley, tram, and metro after its validation. A weekly card (**$** *€10)* is also available. Hold on to your ticket: if you drop it or don't validate it, you can be **fined** up to €72 on the spot by police. Getting caught might not seem likely, but it's not worth the risk. As a general note, be wary of **public transit strikes.** If there is a general strike, chances are that **taxis** are still running, so even though the price will be far higher, you can get where you need to go.

By Metro

Most of the Athens **metro** (🕒 *M-Th 5:30am-midnight, F-Sa 5:30am-2am, Su 5:30am-midnight.)* was rebuilt for the 2004 Olympics. It consists of three lines. **Metro Line 1** is green and runs from northern **Kifisia** to the port of **Piraeus,** connecting to **Suburban Rail** at **Neratziotissa. Metro Line 2** is red and currently runs from **Agios Antonios** to **Agios Dimitrios,** eventually continuing to **Anthoupoli** and **Helliniko** toward the **Saronic Gulf. Metro Line 3** is blue and now runs from **Egaleo,** west of the city center, to **Doukissis Plakentias,** where it intersects the Suburban Rail and the **airport.** After renovations it will continue northwest to **Haidari,** and ultimately may be extended to **Port Zea** in Piraeus. A new metro line is planned to run from **Alsos Veikou** to **Maroussi,** looping across both the red and blue lines.

By Foot

Aside from the heat, Athens is also a pedestrian-friendly city. Base your directions from central **Syntagma Square** and you'll be able to navigate almost anywhere in the city from this central location.

By Bus

Yellow **KTEL** buses leave from **Terminals A and B, Mvromateon 29,** and **Pl. Eleftherias,** and travel all over the Attic peninsula. Check schedules at Terminal A (☎*210 51 24 910* 🕒 *M-Sa 5am-11:30pm, Su 5:30am-11:30pm.)* or B. (☎*210 83 17 153* 🕒 *M-Sa 5am-11:30pm, Su 5:30am-11:30pm.)* Certain buses like the **X95** from **Syntagma** to **El. Venizelou airport,** the **X96** from **Piraeus** to **El. Venizelou airport,** and **#40** from **Piraeus** to **Syntagma** run 24hr. Buy KTEL bus tickets on board or in the terminal. The other buses frequently visible around Athens and its suburbs are blue, designated by three-digit numbers. Both are good for travel throughout the city and ideal for daytrips to **Daphni** and **Kesariani,** the northern suburbs, **Glyfada** and the coast, and other destinations in the greater Athens area. The metro stations' and tourist offices' maps of Athens label all of the most frequented routes.

By Trolley

Yellow trolleys (**$** *€1.* 🕒 *M-Sa 5am-midnight, Su 5:30am-midnight.)* can be differentiated from buses by their electrical antennae. Service is frequent and convenient for short hops within town. See the detailed metro and tourist office map for routes and stops.

By Taxi

Meter rates start at €1.10, with an additional €0.60 per km within city limits and €1.10 outside city limits; min. fare €2.80. From midnight-5am everything beyond the start price is €1.10 per km. There's a €3.40 surcharge for trips from the airport, and a €0.95 surcharge for trips from port, bus, and railway terminals. Max 20min. waiting time would cost €9.60. Add €0.35 extra for each piece of luggage over 10kg. Pay what the meter shows, rounding it up to the next €0.20 for a tip. Hail your taxi by shouting the destination, not the street address (e.g. "Pangrati"). The driver will pick you up if he feels like heading that way. Get in the cab and tell the driver the exact address or site. Many drivers don't speak English, so write your destination down (in Greek

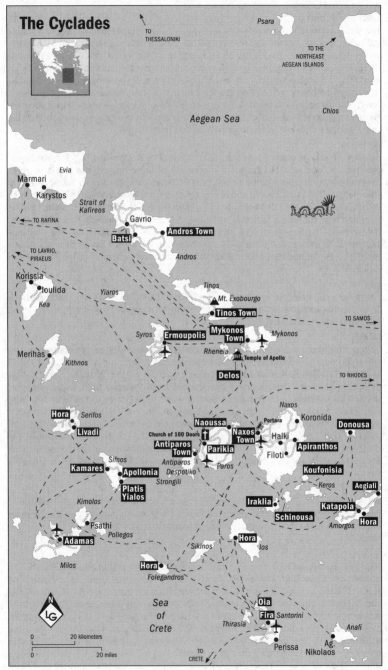

The Cyclades

TO
THESSALONIKI

Psara

TO THE
NORTHEAST
AEGEAN ISLANDS

Aegean Sea

Chios

Evia

Marmari

Karystos

Strait of
Kafireos

TO RAFINA

Gavrio

Batsi

Andros Town

Andros

TO LAVRIO,
PIRAEUS

Korissia

Ioulida

Kea

Yiaros

Tinos

Mt. Exobourgo

Tinos Town

TO SAMOS

Merihas

Kithnos

Syros

Ermoupolis

Mykonos Town

Mykonos

Rheneia

Temple of Apollo

Delos

TO RHODES

Naxos

Hora

Serifos

Livadi

Church of 100 Doors

Naoussa

Portara

Koronida

Donousa

Antiparos Town

Parikia

Naxos Town

Halki

Apiranthos

Antiparos

Paros

Filoti

Kamares

Simos

Apollonia

Despotiko

Strongili

Koufonisia

Keros

Aegiali

Platis Yialos

Kimolos

Iraklia

Schinousa

Katapola

Amorgos

Hora

Psathi

Poliegos

Adamas

Sikinos

Hora

Ios

Milos

Hora

Folegandros

Sea
of
Crete

Oia

Fira

Santorini

Thirasia

Anafi

Perissa

Ag.
Nikolaos

TO
CRETE

N

0   20 kilometers

0   20 miles

greece

if possible) and be prepared to try to type the address into the GPS system yourself. Include the area of the city, since streets in different parts of the city may share the same name. It's common to ride with other passengers going in the same direction. Schedule a pickup with Radio Taxi. (*$ €3-5 additional charge;* **Acropolis** *☎210 86 95 000 or 210 86 68 692;* **Ikaros** *☎210 51 52 800;* **Ermis** *☎210 41 15 200;* **Kosmost** *☎210 52 18 300).*

mykonos ☎22890

Mykonos is renowned as an island of hedonism where the sea glistens next to the equally sparkling, sweaty bodies of the naked old men beside it. Here, brown netting passes as a shirt, beaches are clothing optional, and happy hours come three times a day. Island-revelers sleep from 7am-2pm and then head to the beach to bring the day in with a piña colada and a discussion of their alcohol intake the night before. Tourists less inclined to relax on the scantily-clad beaches or rage at the local club scene can wind through the intertwined streets of Mykonos Town. In the middle of the island between Mykonos Town and Paradise Beach, houses are as white as Crest models' teeth and jut out from the parched earth, disturbed only by the lizards scuttling amongst long forgotten (or never remembered) Red Bull cans. Mykonos' gay scene far surpasses that of other Greek islands, and here men or women walking holding hands or kissing does not elicit so much as a second glance.

ORIENTATION

Mykonos Town is located on the western side of the 41mi. island. On the south side of the island, **Paradise Beach** neighbors **Paraga Beach.** If you're staying at one of the island's campgrounds, the day will likely involve passing from one side of the island to the other by way of winding pathways that count as roads: it's a miracle that bus drivers don't ram into every stone wall along their routes. Along these roads, goats, cows, and the occasional donkey can be seen behind pens, a dramatic shift in scenery from both the classy development of Mykonos Town and the seedy developments of Paradise Beach.

ACCOMMODATIONS

ZORZIS HOTEL — HOTEL ❹

30 Nik. Kalogera ☎228 90 22 167 www.zorzishotel.com

Elaborate wooden beds, mismatched cushions by the breakfast tables, and a community fridge are just a few of the special touches that make Zorzis Hotel feel homey. Located down a quiet street in Mykonos Town, this hotel has all the amenities that can be desired, including an eager-to-please staff. Highly visible security cameras will keep a watchful eye over your things while you are out at the beach or a nearby bar.

Down the street from Hotel Philippi. ***i*** *Breakfast included. Laundry service, safety deposit box, and currency exchange available. Community fridge. Fans in every room.* $ *Singles €85; doubles €113.* *Reception 24hr.*

PARADISE HOSTEL — HOSTEL ❷

Behind Paradise Beach www.paradiseclub-mykonos.com

Only 100m from the water and the site of some of the island's most advertised parties, Paradise Hostel is for those who want to pay as little as possible to be near the action. Cabins are cheap, tiny, and stripped of all but the basics, though the mattresses are plush. When filled to capacity in the summer months, nearly 800 beach-goers stay here, making this an agoraphobic's nightmare and a social butterfly's paradise.

⇞ *Right behind Paradise Beach.* ℹ *Breakfast included. Electrical outlet in each cabin. Luggage storage available.* $ *Singles €25-60; doubles €34-80. Motorbike rental €14 per day.* ⏰ *Reception 8am-11pm.*

HOTEL APOLLON
HOTEL [5]

On the waterfront ☎228 90 22 223

With incredible views of Mykonos' waterfront from its porch, Hotel Apollon has the best real estate in town. Rooms are spacious and well-kept, but the entrance has accumulated knick-knacks and paintings through the years and is running low on usable wall space. Without many additional offerings beside bed and bath, Hotel Apollon is a convenient hotel—just don't expect to be able to check your email from the premises.

⇞ *On the waterfront a few blocks to the left (when looking at the water) of Taxi Sq. Entrance is behind Yialos outside seating.* ℹ *Refrigerator in every room.* $ *Doubles Sept-June €60, with bath €80; Jul-Aug €65/90.* ⏰ *Reception 8am-11pm.*

SIGHTS

LENA'S HOUSE
MUSEUM

On Matoyanni's extension ☎228 90 28 764

Originally an upper-middle-class home in 18th-century Mykonos, this house was donated as a museum by sibling-less resident Lena in 1970. The house stands as it did when she lived there and is notable for the amount of imported wood it contains, as no timber trees grow on Mykonos. As a result, only those with wealth could afford wooden tables, beds, and homes. Lena's father was a timber trader in the Black Sea, and he filled his house with this status symbol. The house provides an interesting glimpse into the island before it was a tourist destination.

⇞ *From Fabrika, walk down the main street, take the 1st right, and turn right at Jimmy's souvlaki shop. Continue down the street as it winds and Lena's House will be on your left.* ℹ *Walk only on the carpets.* $ *€2, students free.* ⏰ *Open daily 7-9pm.*

FOLKLORE MUSEUM
MUSEUM

The House of Kastro ☎228 90 22 591

Built in 1958, the Folklore Museum is the type of place that would never be built today: there are no ropes, placards explaining the rooms' contents, or plexiglass cases separating viewers from the displays. The disorganized explosion of plates, model ships, earrings, and votive offerings from the Mediteranean ports of the 18th and 19th centuries is a fun, quick walk through that feels like stepping into a really old treasure chest. Beware of the doll in the bedroom and the mannequin sitting at the table in the first room as their eyes creepily follow you as you explore the oldest house on the island.

⇞ *From Taxi Sq., walk along the waterfront to the left. Right before passing the port, take a left onto the street that has a visible upward slant; the Folklore Museum will be on the right before you reach the church.* $ *€2, students free.* ⏰ *Open M-Sa 5:30-8:30pm, Su 6:30-8:30pm.*

THE GREAT OUTDOORS

Scuba

MYKONOS DIVING CENTER
DIVE SHOP

Behind Tropicana Bar at Paradise Beach ☎228 90 24 808 www.dive.gr

Though your typical Mykonos tourist is known more for valuing what's on the surface than for looking beneath, the pale blue seas hold reefs and even a cement boat that sunk 30m that entertain divers of all abilities. At this official PADI dive center, beginners willing to dedicate three days to the activity can earn scuba certification, and those who already have a beginner license can take classes to become advanced. Those who want to try wearing the mask but don't want to sacrifice three days of tanning time to wear a wetsuit can try the "Discover Scuba Diving" course and dive to a depth of 12m.

☩ *Set back behind Tropicana Bar on Paradise Beach.* ***i*** *PADI dive center. All equipment included in prices. Minors need guardian signature. Make reservations 48hr. in advance and cancel more than 24hr. in advance; cancellation fee €60.* Ⓢ *Snorkeling €40. "Discover Scuba Diving" course €70. Full-day diving for certified divers €100. Night diver training €150.* ☒ *Open daily 9am-7pm.*

Beaches

Mykonos is surrounded by beaches that give many a visitor a sun-kissed glow (or in the more dramatic cases, the appearance of having been submerged in a vat of tanning oil and then fried). Beaches fall into two categories—the pulsing music sort and the quieter, more family-friendly variety. The two main "pulsing music" beaches are **Paradise Beach** and **Paraga Beach,** which neighbor each other on the southern end of the island. Both have small rocks rather than sand and are harpooned with reed-covered umbrellas. Throughout the day both play top-40 dance tunes with added bass tracks, and at 5pm both beaches push the limits of the speakers' capacity and turn the volume way up. Many gaudy bathing suits make their debut here, and nudity is welcome though not so common among the younger set: those most willing to disrobe are the older men.

Past these two beaches are **Super Paradise, B. Agrari,** and **B. Elia.** Super Paradise is a small but busy pebbly beach that lacks the pulsing soundtracks of its beach brethren. Most beachgoers here are in their mid-30s and still fit, though not buff enough to swim in the nude. **B. Agrari** is a quiet couples beach, and you probably need to ask the water taxi to stop here if it is your destination of choice. There are many open chairs and a floating wooden platform a bit out into the water for snuggling couples to lay on during sunsets. **Elia** (*☎228 90 27 000),* the last beach that water taxis hit on their usual route, is renowned as the gay beach, and a rainbow flag waves proudly above the sandy shore.

On the other side of Paraga and Paradise Beach are **Psarou** and **Ornos.** Ornos, the launching pad for many water taxis, is a family-friendly beach where an open space has been left open in the center of the beach for those who do not want to purchase chairs. Virtually no one opts out of swim trunks on this stretch of pebbly sand, where colorful straws mix with the stones. Psarou is also fairly quiet and family friendly. Off the water taxi route are two treasures of beaches, **B. Panormos** and **Ag. Sositis.** Both of these quiet beaches are on the northern side of the island and an ideal destination for those who do not want to be disturbed.

FOOD

▨ SUISSE CAFE
End of Matoyani

CAFE, CREPERIE ❶
☎228 90 27 462

Build your own salad of succulent tomatoes and cheeses topped with the cafe's special dressing or indulge in a powdered crepe in this Alice-in-Wonderland-esque cafe and dessert place. With pinks, blues, and greens accenting the white tablecloths, the fantasy decor makes every female feel like a princess. Well-priced and a welcome break from the ubiquitous *tavernas* and in-your-face Greekness of many other eateries in the same price bracket, Suisse Cafe is a treasure.

☩ *From the Fabrika bus station, take the 1st right and follow that road down to the left. Turn right when you reach the intersection with the gyro place with bright blue window shutters, and then make a left.* Ⓢ *Ice cream from €2.50. Crepes €3.50-6. Banana split €9. Fresh-squeezed orange juice €3.50. Cocktails €6. Sandwiches from €5.* ☒ *Open daily 9:15am-midnight.*

▨ PASTA FRESCA
Kouzi Georgouli 15

ITALIAN ❸
☎228 90 22 563

For some good ol' Italian pasta come to...Mykonos? Down one of the main streets, a man in a white apron can be seen handmaking tortellini on a wooden table, with multicolored noodles spread out in front of him. Directly behind him, the products of his labor are served atop white tablecloths in the glow of candlelight and the sparkle of wine glasses. A variety of sauces are offered with these fresh pastas, and a wide selection of wines complement the course. This elaborate table is an ideal stage for romantic hand-holding.

On the main street from the bus station. $ Salads €11. Pasta dishes from €9. ⏰ Open daily 3pm-3am.

PICCOLO SANDWICH SHOP [1]

18 Drakopoulou ☎228 90 22 208 www.piccolo-mykonos.com

An adorable sandwich place just a few blocks from the waterfront, Piccolo offers up scrumptious bite-size concoctions with prices a bit out of proportion with the size but worth the splurge. Fresh ingredients like tomatoes, olives, and eggplant brighten the deli counter, and fresh oranges for juice adds a colorful splash. Order from the extensive menu right inside the door, or make your own sandwich combination from the displayed ingredients. Top off the meal with a pastry on display in the glass case at the end of the deli counter.

From the waterfront, walk straight up Drakopoulou for 2 blocks. $ Sandwiches from €4.90 ⏰ Open daily 9am-12:30am.

NIGHTLIFE

Many travelers arrive at Mykonos with two goals: get drunk and stay drunk. Both of those goals are readily achievable on an island that has built a reputation for itself as party-until-dawn-and-maybe-a-bit-after central. All varieties of spandex and skimpy shirts and dresses make their appearance every night of the week, because on Mykonos, the weekend knows no bounds. From the beach clubs to the bars in Mykonos Town, everyone has a place to go to mix with other sweaty bodies. DJs from around the world come to the island to spin at the clubs, and events are well-advertised. Just don't make the mistake of going out too early: bars and clubs in town don't heat up until around 1am, and the beach clubs don't hit their full groove until 3am.

SKANDINAVIAN BAR AND DISCO BAR, DANCE CLUB

Agios Ioauis, Barkia ☎22190 22 669 www.skandinavianbar.com

If you go to one club in Mykonos, this should be it. While the beach clubs advertise heavily, their giant venues leave partygoers with too much room around them for the appropriate sweaty club feel. The Skandinavian is just the right size for clubgoers to feel packed in and still have room to shimmy. Rather than spin over-played Top-40s, classics to the tune of "I Will Survive" set the tone for the night (though Drake has his turn), and bartenders are incredibly friendly and willing to add some extra booze to a drink upon request. If you are going to run into that tantalizing guy or girl you saw on the beach earlier, it will be on top of the heart-tiled Skandinavian Bar dance floor.

From the waterfront, walk up 2 blocks by the Hotel Apollon. $ Wine and beer €5. Vodka €7. Cocktails €8. ⏰ Open daily 10pm-sunrise.

PIERRO'S GLBT

Ag. Kiriaki ☎228 90 22 177 www.pierrosbar.gr

At around 1am, the street outside Pierro's is filled with a throng of men—some in loafers, some in sneakers...and some in heels. This bar founded over 30 years ago has taken on the motto of "gay bar, straight friendly," according to the owner's wife, and every night the chocolate-colored decor is the backdrop for the heart of Mykonos' gay scene. Most of the socializing takes place outside in a night breeze that ruffles the feathers of drag-queen headdresses rather than in the extensive space indoors. Though the crowd tends toward 30-year-olds, and women are few and far between, all are welcome.

⚓ *Next to Taxi Sq.* *i* *Drag show nightly 1am.* Ⓢ *Beer €5. Whisky €8. Cocktails €10.* Ⓩ *Open daily 10:30pm-4am.*

BAR DOWN UNDER
Ag. Ioanninou

●⅁⅌❀ BAR
☎687 46 82 554

This appropriately named bar is a magnet for the many Australians who for one reason or another find themselves in Mykonos. The clientele tends to be quite attractive, but under the flashing bright blue and red lights, even these attractive bar-hoppers seem to bob awkwardly in place like buoys in the ocean. In an attempt to reel people into the bar's dance space, a promoter stands by the door distributing cards worth a free shot. Take a card, take a free shot, and then move on for the rest of your night.

⚓ *From the waterfront, walk up one block.* Ⓢ *Cocktails until midnight €5. Orgasm specialty drink €8. Mojitos €10. Buckets of each cocktail €25.* Ⓩ *Open daily 9pm-2am or later.*

ESSENTIALS

Practicalities

- **TOURIST OFFICE: Sea and Sky Travel Agency.** (*Above Remezzo bus station.* ☎228 90 28 240).

- **BUDGET TRAVEL OFFICES: Windmills Travel.** (*Next to South Station.* ☎228 90 26 555 ▤*www.windmillstravel.com*).

- **CURRENCY EXCHANGE: Alpha Bank** (*Matogianni 41* ☎228 90 23 180 Ⓩ *Open M-Th 8am-2:30pm, F 8am-2pm.*) offers **currency exchange,** as does **Eurochange** in Taxi Sq.

- **LAUNDROMAT: Quick Clean** offers laundry services. (*☎228 90 27 323* Ⓢ *Wash and dry €10.*)

- **INTERNET ACCESS:** Several cafes on the waterfront and by Fabrika station offer Wi-Fi with a food or beverage purchase. **Fast Internet** (*☎228 90 28 842* ▤*www.fastinternetgreece.com* Ⓩ *Open daily 10am-12:30am.* Ⓢ *€2.40 per hr.*) is immediately on the right by Fabrika and next to Quick Clean.

- **POST OFFICE:** The post office (*☎228 90 22 238* Ⓩ *Open M-F 7:30am-2pm.*) is located across the street from Space Club.

- **POSTAL CODE:** 84600.

Emergency!

- **EMERGENCY NUMBER:** ☎108.

- **POLICE: Local police.** (*☎228 90 22 716* Ⓩ *Open 24hr.*) **Tourist police.** (*☎228 90 22 482* Ⓩ *Open daily 8am-9pm.*) Both are located by the airport.

- **HOSPITAL/MEDICAL SERVICES:** (*On the road leading from Fabrika station* ☎228 90 23 994 Ⓩ *Emergency care 24hr.*)

Getting There

Mykonos is accessible from **Athens** by ferry *(4hr.)* and by plane *(20min.)*.

By Plane

Olympic Airways, (*☎228 90 22 490*), **Aegean Airlines** (*☎228 90 28 720*), and **Athens Airways** all fly to Mykonos Airport (JMK).

By Ferry
Most boats dock at the New Port near Ag. Stefanos beach, 3km away from Mykonos Town, but some sea jets still dock at the Old Port. For information about which boats arrive where, call the **port authority** *(☎228 90 22 218)*. Buy tickets at **Sea and Sky Travel Agency** *(☎228 90 28 240)*, on the road above the Remezzo bus station and on the waterfront at Matogianni, where the latest ferry schedules are posted on its front porch. Ferries arrive from **Andros, Naxos, Paros, Rafina, Piraeus, Syros,** and **Tinos.**

Getting Around

Mykonos Town's main entrance is the **Fabrika bus station.** Streets are rarely labeled, and if they are labeled, buildings are not numbered. If looking for somewhere specific, know its name and ask for directions from shop owners along the way. The windy roads date back to when pirates claimed Mykonos' land and wanted to make their treasure chests as inaccessible as possible—and they succeeded. Be prepared to walk some as you find your destination. Though the town covers only a small geographic area, the paths loop around and you might get disoriented.

By Bus
Crossing from Mykonos Town to **Paradise Beach** or vice versa can be done by bus. *($ €1.40 each way, €1.70 after midnight.)* **KTEL** *(☎228 90 23 360 $ €1.40-1.70)* has two stations on Mykonos. Tickets can be purchased on the bus from the driver, in the KTEL ticket station by the bus stop, or in many of the bodegas surrounding the bus stops. Bus stations are more like glorified parking lots than actual stations.

By Bike
Bikes are available for rent beside the **Fabrika bus station** in numerous and well-labeled shops and at Paradise Beach and Paraga Beach Camping. Bikes on Mykonos are full-throttle, and only some places require previous experience with the fast-moving two-wheelers in order to rent one for 24hr. But roads are hilly and windy, and it is often impossible to see oncoming traffic because of curvatures in the roads, so be careful. *Let's Go* does not condone drinking and driving—no matter what the vehicle.

By Taxi
Taxis *(☎228 90 22 400 $ €5-12, depending on destination)* are an easy way to get around the island at any hour of the day. Wait for a cab at Taxi Sq., by the waterfront, or by the Fabrika bus station. Allow plenty of time, as there aren't usually enough taxis to meet demand.

By Water Taxi
Water Taxis run in a loop from **Ornas Beach** and scallop around the beaches on the southern side of the island, including **Super Paradise, Agrari, Ellia, Paranga,** and **Platy Gialos.** At Ornas, tickets can be purchased from the shack on the back of the sand in the middle of the beach or on the boat. Make sure to specify to the person steering where you would like to get off, and ask about the return schedule. Signs are unclear and faded, and the boats do not always run on whatever schedule does exist, so don't use water taxis if you are pressed for time.

By ATV or Motorbike
ATV *($ €15 per 24hr.)* and **motorbikes** *($ €10 per 24hr.)* can be rented near the bus stops or at some hotels.

delos ☎22890

Delos's history is rich—literally. On virtually every cultural and historical level, this island has been the stage for a notable occurrence. Let's start at the beginning, with the island's name. Delos translates to "visible." According to Greek mythology, this dollop of land just 40min. from Mykonos by ferry was brought to the surface from Poseidon's underwater kingdom. The god took pity on Leto, Zeus' most recent mortal crush, when she was ready to give birth to Zeus' godly children but could not find land on which to bear them. Supposedly Hera, the archetypal jealous wife, had forbidden all lands from hosting the roaming pregnant woman. So who else but Zeus' brother to come to Leto's rescue? Bros before hos. Thus, the island, "seen," is the mythical birthplace of Apollo and Artemis, the God of the Sun and Goddess of the Moon, respectively. From 900 BCE to 100 CE the island was the site for cult worship of the two gods, as well as Dionysus.

In commerce, the island was also central. The Delian League—founded in 478 BCE and membered by 173 Greek city-states (Sparta not among them)—was based here, meaning that for about 400 years Delos was the closest thing to NATO or the World Bank until, well, NATO and the World Bank. Politically, the Delian League also had an agenda. Its member states paid a tribute to the league, funds which they could reclaim at any point in time, so long as the money was dedicated to defeating the Persians. Artistically, the island was home to marvelous, painstakingly thorough mosaics, frescoes, and architectural feats that, though now mostly washed away, can be glimpsed in the few remaining patches that have made it through the millenia. In terms of human rights, Delos' record is less stellar; the island was a former port city and had a busy slave trade. Delos had residents of Greek, Egypt, and other civilizations living side by side, and in that sense it was among the first cosmopolitan cities.

SIGHTS 👁

The ruins on Delos are so phenomenal that the island is now a World Heritage Site and has been for over two decades. Only one-fifth of the island is excavated, but that small fraction has unearthed an archaeological gold mine. Old mansions, a unique street design, and many temples devoted to the Greek gods still remain in some form on the multicultural island. Walk around; there will be no shortage of ancient marble on which to focus your camera.

📷 HIKE UP THE HILL
⊗ HIKE

Once you reach the top of this winding, heavy-breath-inducing path, you will never want to go down—not just because it's too steep, but because the view from the top is magical. Nearby islands are hazy in the distance, and the whole of excavated Delos is at your feet. When you are splayed on the smooth rocks at the peak of the hike, the sun god Apollo kissing you with abundant affection, the crowds and cacophonous Top-40 noise of Mykonos Town feel a lot more than a ferry ride away.

⚑ Facing the museum, go right and follow the path. Roughly 15min. to the top. i The terrain is steep in parts and the stones are not cemented together and sometimes wiggle underfoot. Be wary of where you step. Stable shoes advised. Bring water.

📷 THE THEATER QUARTER
⊗ RUIN

Built in the 3rd century BCE with a seating capacity of over 5000 people, this theater is where the magnitude of ancient Delos is most tangible. The giant arch of seats bears down on the stage, which initially was home to only one actor but soon grew to a cast of three. In annual free performances funded by wealthy sponsors, ancient Delians would watch three tragedies, two comedies, and one satire in one rousing weekend of theater.

➔ #95 on the free map by the ticket booth. Wind your way through the ancient homes inland from the agora.

TEMPLE OF ISIS 🚫 RUIN

Reaching this Egyptian temple involves embarking on a beautiful 10min. hike on a path that leads to the highest point on Delos. The temple itself is fairly intact; a Doric-style marble structure with still-standing columns of impressive but not daunting height or breadth. It was erected in the beginning of the Roman period in honor of Isis, the Egyptian goddess of maternity.

➔ Facing the museum, go right and follow the path. The temple will be on the left side and is marked Temple D'Isis.

DELOS MUSEUM MUSEUM

Holding the real Lions of the Naxians in a room to the back right, a number of pots and engravings, and a mosaic from the floor of a mansion from the town, this museum is absolutely worth a few minutes of your time. The labels are short and generally provide nothing more than a name and date, but the contents are self-evident.

➔ On the right side of the island, inland from where the boat docks, behind the agora. ℹ Photos permitted. $ Included in €5 admission fee to island. ⏰ Open Tu-Su from when the 1st ferry arrives to 2:40pm.

TEMPLE OF APOLLO ♿ RUIN

Constructed in the 4th century BCE, the temple is now a giant 33-ton hunk of marble on the ground. The statues of Apollo and a giant building once stood on the slab, but now the base is empty. Although the current remains of the temple are not much to see, the fact that the Greeks could move so much marble to one place is impressive in itself.

➔ Close to the waterfront behind the agora.

HOUSE OF DIONYSUS 🚫 RUIN

Step into this semi-restored mansion from ancient times and get a sense of the splendor that has dissolved into rock and weeds. The old plumbing aqueduct is still visible, as is the mosaic on the floor of the courtyard next to the giant columns. The house was initially for more than one family—think along the lines of a modern co-op—but no sign explains how many. On the right of the entrance are the beginnings of a flight of stairs that once led to upper levels of the house but now lead to the sky.

➔ In the back of the winding paths through the houses, on the left side of that part of the island.

ESSENTIALS

Practicalities

Delos is a World Heritage Site, so everything has been done to preserve the island as it stands. Therefore, the island allows no hotels, only one shop behind the ticket booth, and one restaurant. If you're a picky eater or really looking to scrimp on funds, bag a lunch. While food in the restaurant beside the museum is not exorbitantly priced, it's also not the cheapest. Make sure to wear shoes that can provide stability on a rocky terrain, and bring any medications necessary for your trip as there is no pharmacy.

Getting There

Delos is accessible by ferry from **Mykonos.** Ferries dock at a port located on the far left side of the waterfront, and tickets can be purchased from the booth at the base of the dock or from a travel agency. Ferries *($ €15 round trip. ⏰ 40min.)* depart for the island at 9am, 10am, and 11am, and ferries return to Mykonos from Delos at 12:15pm, 1:30pm, and 3pm. No one is permitted to stay on the island past the last ferry.

Getting Around

Delos is geographically small, but there is much to take in from that small patch of land. All moving about the island is done on foot. There are no roads on the island. It is best to grab a map from the booth you pass by when entering the island and where you pay the €5 entrance fee. In a stack to the right of the plexiglass window are maps that suggest different paths through the island's sights, each based on how much time the visitor will be on the island. Pressed for time? The blue arrows lead to a shorter path than the red arrows.

batsi ☎22820

Batsi is a small town where tourists are welcomed with a smile. A former fisherman's base snuggled into a cove at the base of Andros Island's mountainous terrain, Batsi is peaceful and tiny enough that sometimes the old men sitting in the shop doorways nod kalimera, which means hello. Chances are the person whose *domatia* you stay in will be cousins with the shop owner who sold you a T-shirt yesterday or with your waiter from dinner the night before. Local kids run around the harbor's sand beach nude, burying things in the slightly silt-spoiled ground. Local businesses close for an afternoon siesta and any of the *tavernas* lining the harbor is great for an extended cup of coffee. The most central beach in Batsi is in the middle of the harbor. While this sandy area might not resemble the lavish beaches of other islands, it is still a great place to lounge and pick up some rays.

ORIENTATION

Batsi is set along a harbor, and everything fans out from the crescent of the waterfront. The harbor has two arcs and is shaped like a W when seen from the land looking toward the water. The left concave of the W is the **warf side.** Boats dock here, and the bank and tourist agency are along the main road near the water. The right concave of the W is a string of shops and buildings. The middle of the W is a row of *tavernas* and coffee shops, all fairly priced. Other roads lead away from the town up the hill. When facing the waterfront, the main road, if followed to the right, leads to **Gavria** and **Golden Beach.** From the same perspective, the main road, if followed to the left, leads to **Chora,** also known as **Andros Town.**

The entirety of Batsi is not ideal for handicapped visitors. While it can be explored via car, most of the town is set up along a series of step risers to compensate for the enormous grade in the land that slopes down to the waterfront, making getting around in a wheelchair difficult. The main waterfront level would be passable but the next level of shops might be difficult to access.

ACCOMMODATIONS

Batsi is bursting at the seams with *domatia*, or rooms to let. Even if you show up to the town without sleeping arrangements, chances are you will be able to find somewhere to sleep with little difficulty. Though there are no cheap hostels to soften the blow to your budget, most *domatia* are worth the few extra euro. For a listing of *domatia* in the town, call **Andros Information** (☎228 20 41 575).

◪ VORONOFF'S

⊛⊛⁽ᵠ⁾ 𝄇 ⌂ DOMATIA ❷

Main Street — ☎228 20 41 650

A powerful fan compensates for Voronoff's lack of A/C, and Voronoff himself only adds to the rest of this *domatia's* appeal with his genuine kindness. Spacious rooms, good lighting with switches right above the clean-linened bed, a stone patio outside the rooms, and speedy Wi-Fi all over are just a few of the amenities that make Voronoff's go from a good place to stay to a great one.

🎯 Follow the main street uphill 5min. *i* Free Wi-Fi. Voronoff's also acts as Batsi's post office. Ⓢ Singles and doubles €25. Ⓧ Reception 9am-3pm.

HOTEL SKOUNA
Nik. Damianos

☺⊗Ÿ❄♨ HOTEL ❷
☎237 50 71 183

For a hotel that smells like your grandmother's attic, head to Hotel Skouna. Flower-patterned bathroom tiles and upholstered chairs straight from the '50s decorate a hotel that has scents from the same era. There are no computers or Wi-Fi, but the rooms are spacious and clean.

🎯 On the right side of the waterfront. *i* Prices can be negotiated. Breakfast €6 Ⓢ Singles €35; doubles €45. Ⓧ Reception 24hr.

SIGHTS

Batsi itself may not be the most historic of destinations, but within 45min. of the town by car or motorbike lie two old stone remains, and if possible, both are worth the trip. Beaches, of course, abound.

CASTLE OF THE OLD WOMAN
⊗ RUINS

If the difficulty of finding the parking lot didn't make it clear, it will be evident once you arrive at this castle that you are in the wilds of Andros Island. This gorgeous remoteness is the charm of the Castle of the Old Woman, now only rubble and a few scattered stone arches left over from its construction in medieval times when the island was occupied by the Venetians. No picture can accurately capture the full panorama of seeing mountain and sea in every direction. While the ruins of this castle are historically significant, the real gem here is the view.

🎯 Roughly 1½hr. from Batsi. Follow the road to Bay of Korthi. On the roundabout at the Bay of Korthi, take the road that runs perpendicular to the water out of town for about 8km. Turn right at the sign for Kohilu. From that road, there is a shoddily paved windy road on the left side. Follow the road to the end, and climb the stairs and follow the path to the top. *i* Wear comfortable shoes. No signs. Ⓢ Free. Ⓧ Open 24hr.

TOWER OF AGIOS PETROS
♨ RUINS

Off the main road to Gavrio

In the crook of the mountain, this stone tower looks exactly like where Rapunzel let her hair down. Round and composed of grey stone, it's a relic of the Hellenistic period and was built to function as a lookout tower. The tower is amazingly well-preserved and located about 5min. past Golden Beach by car. Though it is impossible to climb the tower now, it once stood over five stories high.

🎯 About 15min. from Batsi on motorbike. Ⓢ Free. Ⓧ Open 24hr.

GOLDEN BEACH
☺♿♨ BEACH

Along the road to Gavrio

Golden Beach, its name apt both for the color of the sand and the color it will turn your skin after a few hours on the sand, is Batsi's most developed beach. Although a few other sandy patches speckle the coastline, this is the first one with an accompanying beach bar and advertisements. But even with this added attention, the beach stays clean and classy.

🎯 Along the road to Gavrio about 15min. by car or motorbike; 45min. by foot. Ⓢ 2 chairs and an umbrella €12.

FOOD

Unlike on some of the other islands, Batsi's food is decently priced. Eat at one of the many tavernas along the waterfront, sip coffee from cushioned benches, or grab some fresh fruit from the centrally located fruit market. Don't expect to be amazed by the variety of food here, but chow down on the classic Greek cuisine.

TAVERNA STAMATIS
Wharf side of the harbor

♨⊗💲❄☺ TAVERNA ❶

☎228 20 41 975

For lack of a better word, Taverna Stamatis, open since 1965, is perfect. The lamb falls off the bone, the beetroot salad (€5) has just enough olive oil, and the waitstaff comes over three times a meal to ask about the food. Climb the steps to this taverna, claim a navy chair, and enjoy the sunset over the Batsi harbor with some fresh calamari. This is why life is worth living.

🍴 *Opposite the wharf along the left side of the waterfront, up the flight of stairs.* 💲 *Tzatziki €4, fried zucchini €3.50. Meatballs €5. Beetroot salad €5. Greek salad €6. Stuffed tomatoes €5.50. Fish €8-60.* 🕐 *Open daily noon-midnight.*

TOUNTA'S
To the right of Taverna Stamatis

👄⊗💲 BAKERY ❶

☎228 20 41 411

Loaves of freshly baked bread line the walls of Tounta's, while dishes of sugar-coated cookies and glimmering baklava sit along the shelf space. It is nearly impossible to leave the shop without a few calories in a bag or already in your belly. The offerings are simple—all things that are delicious and bad for you—and the woman behind the counter is generous. Even if you are not in the market for some *kourampies* (almond cookies with a powdered sugar coating), chances are she will give you a free taste.

🍴 *On the 2nd tier of shops on the left side of the waterfront, facing the water. Past the tavernas along the steps from Taverna Stmatis.* 💲 *One big piece of baklava €1.50. Cookies 20 for €9. Fresh bread €1.80 per kg.* 🕐 *Open daily 7am-11pm.*

NIGHTLIFE

When it comes to nightlife, Batsi is no Mykonos. During the day the clubs moonlight as coffee shops, but at night the dance floors open up to willing patrons. Enjoy a leisurely drink looking out over the harbor early in the night, as dancing does not get started until around 2am.

NAMELESS
In the corner on the wharf side of the waterfront

⊛⊗⟨ᵗᵖ⟩💲❄☺ BAR, DANCE CLUB

☎228 20 41 488

The last stop of the night for locals and tourists alike, Nameless has earned itself a reputation as the best place to go in Batsi. In the midst of renovations, the inside combines an ultra-modern atmosphere—think white tea-cup barstools and black-tiled bathrooms—with chandeliers and brick walls that look like they are straight out of a dungeon. Try a late-night Juliet, a mojito with gin (€8), at the bar with the cheapest cocktails in Batsi.

🍴 *In the corner on the left side of the waterfront, before the road rounds to Taverna Stamatis.* ⓘ *Newly designed garden behind the main entrance serves coffee during the day and cocktails at night. Free Wi-Fi with purchase.* 💲 *Cocktails €8. Coffee €2.50-3.50.* 🕐 *Open 24hr.*

CAPRICCIO
Along the wharf side of the waterfront

♨💲☺ BAR

Taglined "The Island Bar," Capriccio can be recognized by its white outdoor tables and the '90s music that plays from its speakers throughout the day. Inside the chairs are low to the ground, and playful marbles decorate the windowsills. Views of the harbor from the outdoor seating are beautiful, so feel free to make a night of this place with a post-dinner coffee and then a late-night cocktail.

🍴 *On the left side of the waterfront before you reach Taverna Stamatis.* 💲 *Coffee from €2.50. Beer €5-8. Cocktails €11.* 🕐 *Open daily 9am-3am.*

ESSENTIALS

Practicalities

- **TOURIST OFFICE:** Batsi has no tourist office, but **Andros Information** has pamphlets and contact numbers for *domatia.* (☎*228 20 41 575.*)

- **BUDGET TRAVEL OFFICES: Greek Sun Holidays** *(☎228 20 41 771)* is the only travel agency in the town.
- **CURRENCY EXCHANGE: National Bank** has a **24hr. ATM** and offers currency exchange. *(☎228 20 41 400 ⏰ Open Tu-W 9am-1pm, F 9am-1pm.)*
- **INTERNET ACCESS: Nameless** offers Wi-Fi. *(☎228 20 41 488 ⇄ In the corner on the left side of the waterfront, before the road rounds to Taverna Stamatis. ⏰ Open 24hr.)*
- **POST OFFICE:** Mail letters and postcards at **Voronoff's** at the top of the hill above the harbor. *(☎228 20 41 650 ⏰ Open M-F 9:30am-1:45pm.)* For packages, go to **Gavrio** *(☎228 20 71 254)* or **Andros Town** *(☎228 20 22 260).*

Emergency!

- **POLICE:** Batsi's police station was closed, so **Gavrio's police station** *(☎228 20 71 220)* is the nearest one. You can also contact the Port Police. *(☎228 20 71 213.)*
- **LATE-NIGHT PHARMACIES:** The one **pharmacy** on the island is behind Dino's bike rental shop, around the block on the street that leads to Hotel Kaparesy. *(☎228 20 41 451 ⏰ Open M-Sa 9am-1:30pm and 6:30-8:30pm.)*
- **HOSPITALS/MEDICAL SERVICES:** For medical emergencies, contact the **Medical Center.** *(☎228 20 22 222; 228 20 22 333.)* In Andros Town, to the left of the beach, behind a playground is a small **medical office.** *(☎228 20 41 326 ⏰ Doctor available daily 9am-1pm.)*

Getting There

Batsi can be accessed by **ferries** from **Mykonos** *(⏰ 2hr., 3 per day.),* **Rafina** *(⏰ 2hr., 3-4 per day.),* and **Tinos** *(⏰ 2½hrs., 3 per day.),* all of which dock in **Gavrio.** To reach Batsi from Gavrio, board one of the **minibuses** that waits at the port for each incoming ferry and runs from Gavrio to Andros Town, stopping in Batsi on the way. You can also take the **bus** which runs from Gavrio to Andros Town and stops in Batsi on the way, or take a **taxi** *($ €20).*

Getting Around

Navigating Batsi is tricky. Walking up and down the slope of the town is not a small feat for the less athletically-inclined. Though it is possible to spend time in the town and never leave the main waterfront, the excursions to sights and distant beaches are worthwhile. To make such treks, it is hugely advantageous to rent a motorbike or car. If these aren't options, see if the bus or minibus will stop where you want to go; if not, there are always taxis, and some drivers will be willing to negotiate the meter price.

You can rent **bikes** at Dino's Bikes *(☎228 20 41 003 $ €16 per day.),* on the right side of the waterfront.

naxos ☎22850

Step off the ferry in Naxos and immediately look left to see what remains of the temple to Apollo, a beautiful marble archway that serves as a reminder of the island's past. Next, look right and you will see what the island has become: land cultivated for maximum tourist appeal. Luckily, even what has become of Naxos is wonderful in its own way. The beaches still rinse away the troubles, the food—particularly in the nearby town Halki—makes you want to stuff your face, and the nightlife is vivacious without the grimy feel of Mykonos. For a travel experience with all the resources at your disposal, head to Naxos.

ORIENTATION

Naxos centers on the **waterfront.** When facing inland, the port is on the left side of the waterfront. The **bus station** is directly in front of the port, and the **Temple of Apollo** is beyond the port all the way to the left. To the right is what is best referred to as *taverna* row. Interspersed with the *tavernas* are bars, cafes, and some tourist shops. Nightlife stretches all the way to the right on the waterfront and one street back from taverna row. **Kastro** is the area deeper into town, which can be accessed by turning left at the top of the street behind **OTE,** the telephone office.

ACCOMMODATIONS

Naxos is a great place to sleep on budget. More expensive housing can be found along the waterfront, but the campgrounds are the best place to stay when on a budget.

MARAGAS CAMPING — CAMPGROUND [1]

At Agia Anna beach — ☎228 50 42 552 💻www.maragascamping.gr

If you came to Naxos to go to the beach, Maragas Camping is the place to stay. The road between the campground and the beach across the street sees so much foot traffic from the water to the campground and back that sand has been dragged across the pavement. Kids walk around the site barefoot, and four-wheelers sit under their cover ready for rental. The place is not fancy—the towels in the bathroom come frayed—but all is clean and family-friendly.

🧭 From the port, take the bus headed to Agios Prokopios and get off at Maragas Camping 12km away. ℹ 30min. bus ride from town. Bus comes every 30min. Free Wi-Fi in the taverna. Motorbike and 4-wheeler rental. Safe box if requested. On-site supermarket. $ Doubles €20-45; studios and apartments €30-90. ⏰ Reception 8am-10pm.

GLARONISSI 1 — HOTEL [4]

Past Maragas Camping along Agia Anna beach — ☎228 50 41 201 💻www.glaronissi1.com

Somehow those who run Glaronissi 1 have coerced grass into growing from sand in front of their small establishment, which holds a few clean rooms decorated with shimmery blue bedspreads and metallic bunk-bed ladders. Located next door to Maragas Camping, Glaronissi 1 is just steps away from the mellow waves of the beach.

🧭 From the port, take the bus headed to Agios Prokopios and get off at Maragas Camping, which is about 12km from town. Glaronissi 1 is just past Maragas; look for the grass on the ground out front. ℹ Refrigerator, coffee stovetop, and silverware in every room. $ High-season doubles €75; quads €90. Low-season doubles €30; quads €40.

NAXOS CAMPING — CAMPGROUND [1]

Middle of Agios Georgios beach — ☎228 50 23 500 💻www.naxos-camping.gr

Naxos Camping's biggest appeal is its proximity to town. Though still 2km from the port, the public bus runs by the campground's entrance every 20min., and it's easy to walk from town to the site by following Ag. Giorgios all the way to where the windsurfers gather in the wide cove. Unfortunately, the premises lack all creature comforts. The shower faucet is so high that bathing is like shampooing in the rain, some mattresses have cigarette holes, beds come without sheets, and, when we visited, the bathrooms did not stock toilet paper.

🧭 From the port, take the bus to Agios Prokopios and get off at Naxos Camping. By foot, walk along the main taverna row street by the waterfront, which leads to Agios Georgios beach. Walk along the beach past the main stretch of sand and around to the cove where windsurfers gather. At the back of that cove the highway is visible; cross the street and into the campground. It is 1.5km from town to the campground. ℹ Mini-mart, self-serve restaurant, pool, and refrigerators for communal use. $ €7 per person. Huts €2 extra.

SIGHTS

Kastro is the area of town set back behind the first streets you see when stepping off the ferry. The area has winding, twisting, and confusing streets that date back to when the Venetians settled Naxos. The area used to house around 400 people in giant mansions. Now, some of the structures remain, but the luster of the place—which throughout the century has enticed guests like the Kennedys and Rockefellers—has somewhat diminished.

👍 PORTARA — RUINS

This archway, visible from basically anywhere along the waterfront, is a gem of a sight. Dedicated to Apollo, the remains now lay scattered around the archway from their original construction in the fifth century BCE. On the far right of the waterfront when looking out on the water, the Portara is at the end of the island and looks out at an incredible view of ocean, mountains, and sky.

➜ On the far right of the waterfront when looking at the water. Up the steps. $ Free.

👍 VENETIAN MUSEUM — MUSEUM

☎228 50 22 387

When as a boy the owner of the museum saw his neighborhood, the Kastro area, becoming commercialized and the old mansions being turned into shops and *domatia*, he decided he wanted to preserve his home in its original state. He opened his doors to the public, and now all can wander through the rooms where he grew up to see the French couches where he sat with his parents and entertained movie stars and politicians decades ago. Make sure to find the piano which Leonard Bernstein once played.

➜ Pass the Byzantine Museum and walk under the archway. The Venetian Museum is under the arch. i Nighttime concerts during the summer. $ €5, students and over 65 €3. ⏰ Open daily in summer 10am-3pm and 7-10pm.

CATHOLIC CHURCH — ♿ CHURCH

At the top of the hill ☎228 50 22 725

A flood in 1915 destroyed the decorative tombstones of the ancient families of the Kastro area, but the tall white dome is still impressive inside. Behind the altar is supposedly one of the oldest examples of the Virgin Mary standing alone, without Jesus in her arms. Unless Catholic churches are your passion, this is just as well enjoyed in passing from outside as when stepping into the silent dome.

➜ At the top of the hill by the Archaeology Museum in Kastro. To get there, turn from the main waterfront road aroud the corner of OTE; walk uphill along the street until it branches 3 ways at the top of the hill. A pharmacy will be on the corner. Turn onto the left most street and follow it until you reach another fork; bear left and follow the street as it winds. Pass Taverna Kastro on your right and continue following the main street as it winds up. i Modest dress required. $ Free. ⏰ Open daily 10am-7pm.

THE GREAT OUTDOORS

Beaches

Naxos is chock-full of beaches: if there are two things the island is not short on, it's sand and sun. For the beach nearest to town, walk along the waterfront past OTE and the post-office playground to the far right of the port (when facing inland) to reach **Agios Giorgios,** where people play actively with paddle balls, toddlers splash in the shallow water, and European men rock swimsuits close to Speedos. Expect crowds and convenience. For a little more space on the sand, head to **Agios Prokopios, Agioa Anna,** and the nude beach **Plaka** just north of Maragas Camping. On this stretch of sand you will find gentle waves and a crew with fewer kids. All can be accessed by bus from Naxos Town. Check a map for more secluded beaches farther from town. Cabs are ready to take beachgoers nearly anywhere. For waterskiing, windsurfing, tubing, wakeboarding, and basically any watersport you can think of, head to Plaka beach for **Plaka Watersports** *(☎694 46 33 194 🖥www.plaka-watersports.com ℹ Cash only. $ €15-40. ⏰ Open daily 10am-7pm.),* located right across the highway from the beach a few minutes walk from Maragas Camping.

FOOD

Beware of bland, touristy tavernas here; there are plenty of them. A key to identifying a more touristy establishment from a less touristy one is how prevalent English is in the menu. If dishes are listed in English second and the translation seems to have been made from a menu originally written in Greek, the restaurant is a go. If the menu is only or predominantly in English, steer clear.

BOSSA — BAR, CAFE ❶

On the waterfront

The light fixtures here hang like giant, white dandelions about to blow away with a puff of wind from the sea. Many tables and chairs fill the extensive outdoor seating area, and even more chairs fill the modern, inside space as well. Popular with a crew of younger, more stylish foreigners, Bossa has both great views and great people-watching.

Follow the waterfront street to the end and turn right when you reach OTE. Walk toward the water past the cluster of cafes, and Bossa will be there on the left. Look for the light fixtures. ℹ At night it becomes a happening bar. $ Coffee €3.50. Beer €4. Cocktails €7. ⏰ Open daily 9am-2am.

TAVERNA KASTRO — TAVERNA ❷

In Kastro ☎228 50 22 005

A traditional eatery with dishes like rabbit stew *(€9.50)* and *choriatiko*, veal baked in a clay pot with cheese and vegetables *(€12)*, this taverna is the place to go to experience the culinary culture of Kastro. The stone patio seating area awards diners here with views of the sea from the heights of the old, Venetian part of the city.

Turn from the main waterfront road aroud the corner of OTE; walk uphill along the street until it branches 3 ways at the top of the hill. Turn onto the leftmost street and follow it until you reach another fork; bear left and follow the street as it winds. The taverna will be on your right. $ Salads €3.50-5. Entrees €7-15. Coffee €1.50-2.50. Beer €2.50. ⏰ Open daily 6:30pm-1am.

MANOLIS' GARDEN TAVERNA — TAVERNA ❸

End of Market St. ☎228 50 25 168

This taverna is about as far from the main tourist stretch as you can get within Naxos, and its food is equally far from the competition. Try the fresh fish served with lemon to remember the best thing about being on an island.

Old street can be accessed from a sidestreet on the left in the main taverna row along the waterfront by turning left where you see the sign for the secondhand bookstore. Follow this street to the end, then follow sign to Manolis' Garden and walk through the archway. $ Salads €3.50-6. Seafood €6.50-17. ⏰ Open daily 6pm-midnight.

NIGHTLIFE

Naxos's nightlife centers on the outer edges of the waterfront. The dancing doesn't get started in earnest until around 1:30am, but beers and cocktails are consumed by the dozens earlier in the evening. Nightlife here ranges from the casual guitar-jamming bar to the full-on club with a bouncer, so nearly any sort of fun can be had. If you don't want to wait until 1:30am to start dancing, bring an iPod to the beach and have a silent rager. Who cares what the others think? You're in Naxos!

JAM BAR — BAR

The street behind taverna row ☎698 85 08 024

The enterprising singer, guitarist, or drummer can find an audience here, where bands set in the corner play for the lively crowd. A British flag with the Rolling

Stones' mouth emblazoned in the center flies high above the wood tables and bartop, and Red Hot Chilli Peppers and soul music croon from the speakers. Beer is the most popular drink of the somewhat older clientele, but cocktails are served up as well at this music-lovers' bar.

Take the 1st left after Krik Cafe when walking along taverna row away from the port. It is on the right opposite Waffle House. $ Beer €3-5. Cocktails €7. Open Apr-Oct daily 8pm-3am.

MOJO BAR

On the waterfront ☎228 50 26766

The bartender here works magic, so watch him splash liquor and fruit juices into glasses. Just as there's no doubt that Yo-Yo Ma was born to play the cello, this man was born to make cocktails. Perhaps this art is less valued, but show your appreciation by paying the steep price of a pomegranate martini, a Hollywood-lipstick-red concoction that he creates with real pomegranate juice and serves with fresh pomegranate seeds in a martini glass. You will not regret it, even if the price means you forego lunch tomorrow.

Follow the waterfront street to the end and turn right when you reach OTE. Walk toward the water past the cluster of cafes and turn left. Pass Bossa and you will see the sign for Mojo on the left. [i] The outdoor seating is in high demand, so get there on the early side or ask to reserve a table. $ Beer €5. Cocktails from €7. Open in summer daily 7pm-5am.

ESSENTIALS

Practicalities

- **BUDGET TRAVEL: Zas Travel** provides ferry and airplane booking services and can answer questions about the island. Find the location two doors down from the tourist center and another 50m away from the port, both on the waterfront. *(☎228 50 23 330 www.zastravel.com Open daily 8:30am-noon.)*
- **TELEPHONE: OTE** offers phones and calling cards as well as help with broken phones. *(☎228 50 23 333 Open M-F 8am-2pm.)*
- **INTERNET ACCESS: Citron Cafe and Cocktail Bar** provides free Wi-Fi and great beverages in a super hip, clean environment. *(☎228 50 27 055 Open daily 8am-2am.)*
- **POST OFFICE:** *(☎228 50 22 211 Open M-F 7:30am-2pm.)*
- **POSTAL CODE:** 84300.

Emergency!

- **POLICE: Police** station is located on Amortou, the main road heading toward Ag. Giorgios beach from Pl. Prodikiou, 1km out of town. *(☎228 50 22 100, 228 5023 039 Open 24hr.)*
- **PORT POLICE:** ☎*228 50 22 300*
- **PHARMACY:** It's located right before the OTE on the far right of the waterfront street when looking inland. *(☎228 50 24 946 Open M-Tu 8:30am-2:30pm and 6-10pm, W 8:30am-2:30pm, Th-F 8:30am-2:30pm and 6-10pm, Sa 8:30am-2:30pm.)*
- **MEDICAL SERVICES:** For health care questions, turn inland at the fork in the road past the OTE, at the right end of the waterfront when looking inland. It is 500m farther on the left. *(☎228 50 23 333, 228 53 60 500 [i] Helicopter to Athens available in emergencies. Open 24hr.)*

Getting There

Getting to Naxos can be done by ferry or by plane. If planning to fly from Athens, book tickets far in advance. Ferry tickets are easier to come by last-minute.

By Plane

Flights leave from **Naxos Airport (JNX). Olympic Airways** *(☎228 50 23 292)* has a desk in **Naxos Tours** *(☎228 50 22 095 🖳www.naxostours.gr)*, on the left end of the waterfront. Air tickets also sold at **Zas Travel** *(☎228 50 24 330 🖳www.zastravel.com)*. Flights go to **Athens** *($ €80)* and come in from Athens *($ €95)*. Book tickets months in advance; planes seat only 40 people and fill quickly.

By Ferry

All ferries from Naxos leave from Naxos Town. Two docks are at the left end of town, one for large ferries and the other for smaller ferries and daily cruises. For updated schedules and prices, consult travel agencies. To: **Amorgos** *($ €14. ⏰ 2-6hr., depending on stops; 2-5 per day.)*; **Astypalea** *($ €23. ⏰ 3hr., 1 per week.)*; **Donousa** *($ €8.50. ⏰ 1-4hr., 4 per week.)*; **Ios** *($ €9.30. ⏰ 1½hr., 6 per week F-Su.)*; **Koufonisia** *($ €7.50. ⏰ 3hr., 1-2 per day.)*; **Paros** *($ €7.50. ⏰ 1hr., 4 per day.)*; **Santorini.** *($ €15.50. ⏰ 2-6hr., 1-3 per day.)*

By Boat

High-speed boats go to: **Ios** *($ €20.50. ⏰ 45min., 1 per week.)*; **Mykonos** *($ €18.50. ⏰ 45min., 1 per day.)*; and **Santorini.** *($ €27.50. ⏰ 30min., 1-2 per day.)*

Getting Around

Getting around Naxos Town is best done on foot, and most of the streets other than the main waterfront one on the outside of the *tavernas* are pedestrian-only. Naxos's streets are particularly windy and mostly unnamed, so working your way through town can be complicated. Don't be shy about asking for directions from people in shops and on the street, particularly in Kastro. To reach distant beaches, buses or cabs are best. Buses head to Maragas Camping until 2:30am, so even those out late don't need to spend the extra money on cabs unless it's a really late night.

By Bus

Tickets for all buses *(☎228 50 22 291 $ €1.40-5.50.)* must be purchased before boarding the bus. Sometimes drivers will let you board and then purchase tickets at the next open station, but be prepared just in case. Current schedules are available at the station, located across from the largest dock and at tourist offices. Buses to **Apollon** *(⏰ 2 per day 9:30am-1:30pm.)* and **Filoti-Chalki-Sagri** *(⏰ 6 per day 9:30am-3pm.)* are often packed. Buses also run to: **Ampram** *(⏰ Tu and Th 2:30pm.)*; **Apiranthos** *(⏰ 5 per day 7:15am-3pm.)*; **Apollon** *(⏰ Tu and Th 2:30pm.)* via the coast; **Engares** *(⏰ Tu and Th 2:30pm.)*; **Glynado-Tripodes** *(⏰ 4 per day 7:30am-3pm.)*; **Kastraki** *(⏰ 3 per day 7:30am-3pm.)*; **Korono-Skado** *(⏰ 2 per day 9:30am-1:30pm.)*; **Melanes-Miloi** *(⏰ 2 per day 12pm-3pm.)*; **Mikri Vigla** *(⏰ 3 per day 7:30am-3pm.)*; **Pyrgaki Beach.** *(⏰ 3 per day 7:30am-3pm.)*

By Taxi

Taxis are located on the waterfront next to the bus depot. *(☎228 50 22 444)*

IOS ☎22860

If you aren't drunk when you arrive, you will be when you leave—sobriety is the antithesis of Ios' ethos. The most bodacious, juiced-up, accented, and horny travelers find their way here, where boxed wine is passed around on the public bus and phone calls home include gems like: "We're staying in a really beautiful place, but I don't know how long we're going to be there because we've vomited on everything." And, "Anus? No it's Ios." The most intrepid game-spitters find themselves at Mylopotas beach by day and the town clubs by night. The literati can escape the broey bacchanalia by driving about 30min. to Homer's burial site on the far side of the island, bearing down on the sea and mountains which he immortalized in his epics. Beaches galore dot the coastline and range from the silent cove-type to the girls-seeking-ass-while-drunk type, so know where you are headed before you board the bus.

ORIENTATION

Ios is a sizable island with beaches spread along its coast, but the two main hubs of activity are the town and Mylopotas Beach. The main road from the port passes through town on its way to Mylopotas. Ios Town and Mylopotas Beach are under 10min. apart by bus and about 25min. apart by foot. To get to Mylopotas Beach from town, follow the main road to the right when looking at the big blue-roofed church in town. Town itself is set up like a piece of terraced land; streets run parallel to each other along its slope. The main nightlife stretch—most easily found by following the music and crowds at 1:30am—is three terraces in the depths of town. To get to the first terrace, walk toward the church through the big parking lot in front, and bear right.

ACCOMMODATIONS

FRANCESCO'S — HOTEL [2]

In town ☎228 60 91 223 🖥www.francescos.net

This complex of buildings, a pool, cafe, and bar is a student traveler's ultimate destination. The complex forms a social world unto itself in the sparkling white buildings, and at night the crew rallies together when they hit **Blue Note.** The rooms are quite clean, though sparsely decorated. Breakfast is served for the extended morning of 8am-2:30pm on a patio that overlooks the ocean, and the fully-stocked bar opens at 6pm for those who need only a few hours awake before beginning the party circuit again.

In the village. With your back to the bank in the main plateia, take the steps up from the left corner of the platei, then take the 1st left. ℹ *Safety deposit boxes and luggage storage. Free*

greece

pick-up at port. Free Wi-Fi. Computers €1 per 15min. $ Singles €28-55; doubles €33-70; triples €48-75; quads €60-80. ⏰ Reception open 9am-2pm and 6-10pm.

FAR OUT BEACH CLUB CAMPGROUND ❶

End of Mylopotas Beach ☎228 60 91 468 💻www.faroutclub.com

Far Out is the epicenter of Ios' daytime revelry. If you want to wake up in the early afternoon and head to the beach to be hit on by foreigners already on their third piña colada, this is the place to stay. Accommodations range from the bring-your-own-tent area to the "bed tent" (which looks like a giant dog house and holds two small, sheetless cots) to the bungalow (which comes with electricity, beds with sheets, and a fan). All the sleeping quarters are set up along a very steep hill, so be prepared to lug your backpack up. Bathrooms dot the ascent and are clean, though it's best to check for toilet paper in the stall before sitting down.

*➜ At the end of Mylopotas beach. Take the public bus to Mylopotas beach. **i** Laundry service available. Movies nightly 9pm. Computer station with internet €1 per 15min. Self-serve restaurant. Mini-mart. Connected to the Far Out Village, which has rooms from €12-55 per person. $ €5-11. Tents €6-15 per person. Bungalows €8-22 per person. ⏰ Reception 24hr. Mini-mart open daily 8am-11pm. Restaurant open daily 8am-10pm. Pool open daily 11am-8pm.*

SIGHTS

HOMER'S TOMB TOMB

Plakatos

For those who like mountains or heroes or honor or beauty or harrowing death, those forced to read *The Odyssey* in high school and secretly loved it, or those just amazed by the idea that a blind man 2000 years ago was able to dictate two epic tales that are still around today, this grave will feel like holy ground. At the end of a dirt path, the tomb is a stone platform with a stunning view that looks down on a tiny island that is reminiscent of the Sirens' island.

*➜ On the northern tip of the island. **i** Wear comfortable shoes. $ Free.*

SKARKOS RUIN

Main Road

A ruin from the Early Bronze Age, the middle of Ios' height as a Cycladic civilization, the site was first excavated in 1986 and is where most of the contents of the Ios Archeology Museum were found.

➜ About 5min. outside town toward's Homer's Tomb. $ Free. ⏰ Open Tu-Su 8:30am-3pm.

BEACHES

Ios is a beach and party island (if you didn't already get the gist); there's little to do here but eat, sleep, sunbathe, and copulate. Appropriately, there's no shortage of sand. **Mylopotas Beach** is a 25min. walk from town and can also be reached by public bus, which leaves from the town center every 20min. Here, the music's as loud as it can be and the bikinis are as small as they come. **Saint Theodotis Beach,** on the northeast side of the island, is the quietest of the beaches and remains impeccably clean. Lounge by the pool at the debaucherous **Far Out Beach Club** at the end of the stretch of sand to start your daydrinking early. This is the place to go if seeking scantily clad, young Aussies. **Koumbara,** just under 2km down the road that follows Gialos beach, draws a much smaller crowd to its large cove, which is a popular place for windsurfing. For those who want quiet and natural beauty, check out **Manganari,** accessible by bus. Locals head to **Kolitsani,** a crystal pool of water at the little bay. Those who want to forgo all pretense of bathing suits should head to **Psathi,** the nude beach on the eastern coast. The port beach Gialos, Mylopotas, and Manganari all offer **watersports** ranging from paddleboats to windsurfing and tubing.

FOOD

👍 POMODORO

💳🚭🍸❄☁ RESTAURANT [2]

South of the main plateia ☎228 609 1387

Walk up the marble stairs into Pomodoro—which means pomegranate in Greek—and you're face-to-face with the restaurant's Italian pizza chef. The food is out-of-this-world delicious, made with fresh ingredients and cooked by a diligent and smiling staff. The Halloumi salad *(appetizer €5; entree €9)* is made with a cheese from Crete that has been grilled, placed on a bed of lettuce, oranges, and hazelnuts, and topped with a honey-based dressing. Once you eat it, there's no way you will be able to resist coming back the next night for another. The decor is equally irresistible, a classy concoction of stone archways, sparkling glasses, and a scenic rooftop garden.

➡ From the main plateia, when facing the bank, walk down the street to the right and look for the Pomodoro sign above a side street. The entrance is about 20m up on the left side. ℹ Head upstairs to enjoy views of Ios's town from the rooftop garden. $ Salads €5-9. Pizzas €12. Gnocchi €12. Brownies €7. ⏰ Open May-Oct daily 6pm-1am.

ALI BABA'S

💳♿🍸❄ ASIAN FOOD, COMFORT FOOD [2]

On the north side of town ☎228 60 91 558

Want to get 12L of cocktails served in two goldfish bowls with neon-colored straws for €35? Really craving that pad thai even though you're in Greece? If so, Ali Baba's is the place for you. The owner takes meticulous care of his restaurant, which started as an Asian food place but has recently expanded to include basic comfort food like meat and potato pie. Despite its location, make sure to try the Thai fare prepared by the chef straight from Thailand. And a brief warning: don't do anything particularly embarrassing while you eat. When it gets late and the restaurant fills up, the waitstaff takes covert pictures and then flashes them up on the restaurant's big screen.

➡ From the bus stop, walk alongside the church into the archway by the Ios Gym. Take a right, and Ali Baba's will be 2 blocks up on your left. From other parts of town, look at the maps posted around; Ali Baba's has a star on the map. $ Most entrees from €9.50. ⏰ Open daily May-Oct 6pm-2am.

NIGHTLIFE

At night, Ios Town erupts into a giant, cacophonous party. Any street is likely to have at least two full bars by 1am. Because everything is so close, there's bound to be a bar just for you nearby.

👍 BLUE NOTE

🎵🚭🍸❄ CLUB

Off the main plateia ☎228 60 92 271

Because Francesco, of Francesco's, owns this club, it fills up every night with people from his hotel at around midnight. Dark with unexciting decor, this bar collects the liveliest group of partiers around. The doormen are chatty and announce entrances with seemingly genuine excitement. Smoke hangs in the air above the crowd, punctured only by fist-pumping dance moves.

➡ Past the main plateia walking away from Disco 69, past the fast food joints. ℹ Scandinavian music after 2am. $ Shots €3. Cocktails €5. Long Island Iced Tea special 2 for €5. ⏰ Open daily 11pm-3am.

👍 JÄGER BAR

🎵🚭🍸❄ BAR

Off the main plateia ☎693 77 94 324

Jägerbombs—Jäger Bar—Jäger Bar. Hop on the Blue Note bandwagon when that bar's early night crew swings around to Jäger Bar at around 1am. When they come the disco ball spins, the pine wood decor reflects light, and bodies pack in so tightly that you can't help but find your arms wrapped around that beautiful girl or guy to your right. It's not the best place to get your most elaborate dance moves on, but the bar is exciting and perfect for some sweaty dancing.

❦ *Walk through the main plateia away from Disco 69 and continue down the street to the right past Rock Bar; it'll be on the left.* **i** *Busiest from 1-3am.* Ⓢ *Jägerbombs €5, 4 for €10. Cocktails 2 for €5.* ⓓ *Open daily 11pm-4:30am.*

DISCO 69   ●●⊗Ⴡ❀ CLUB
Main plateia   ☎228 60 91 064 ▉www.disco69club.com

With the ever-subtle name of Disco 69, this place draws hordes of girls to its bartop and dance floor. While girls get in free all night long, guys need to pay a €6 cover charge, the result being that until late the girl-to-guy ratio is very favorable for the heterosexual males willing to pay the entrance price. The bartenders promote their "sex on the beach" cocktails with a two for €5 special during the extended happy hour.

❦ *In the main plateia.* Ⓢ *Cover €6 for men; includes 2 shots and 2 drinks. Shots €3. Cocktails €5.* ⓓ *Open daily 11pm-6am. Happy hour 11pm-2am.*

ARTS AND CULTURE   🎵

OPEN THEATER FESTIVAL PROGRAM   ●と♨ CULTURAL EVENTS
Theater of Odysseus Elytis

Every summer, a series of events take place at the Theater of Odysseus Elytis, a modern venue designed to look like an ancient theater. Events range from concerts to plays, and informational pamphlets with the schedule are available at the Ios Archeological Museum and tourism offices.

❦ *By Scorpios Bar on the right on the way to Mylopotas.* Ⓢ *Some events free. Price varies.*

ESSENTIALS   ⓘ

Practicalities

- **BUDGET TRAVEL OFFICE: Acteon Travel** provides ferry and flight booking. *(☎228 60 91 343 by the port; 228 60 91 004 in town; 228 60 91 005 by the supermarket.* ▉*www.acteon.gr* **i** *Also has a branch by the port and across the street from the bus stop.* ⓓ *Main port office open daily 8am-11pm. Town office open daily 9am-11:30pm. Supermarket office open daily 9:30am-10pm.)*

- **CURRENCY EXCHANGE AND ATM: National Bank** provides **currency exchange** and a **24hr. ATM** in the main plateia. *(☎228 60 91 565* **i** *Bring a passport for currency exchange.* ⓓ *Open M-Th 8am-2:30pm, F 8am-2pm.)*

- **LAUNDROMAT: Sweet Irish Dream Laundry** provides wash and dry by the club with the same name on the main road from the port. *(☎228 60 91 584* **i** *Cash only.* ⓓ *Open daily 10am-9pm.)*

- **INTERNET: Acteon Travel, Francesco's, and Far Out Beach Club** provide Wi-Fi and computers with internet access in the port, at the end of Mylopotas, and in the town, respectively. *(☎228 60 91 343 in the port; 228 60 91 468 at the end of Mylopotas; 228 60 91 223 in the town.* Ⓢ *All charge €1 per 15min. of computer use. Cash only.)*

- **POST OFFICE: Post Office** provides mail service and stamps on the main road coming from the port. *(☎228 91 235* ⓓ *Open M-F 7:30am-2pm.)*

- **POSTAL CODE:** 84001.

Emergency!

- **POLICE:** The **police station** is on the road to Kolitsani beach. *(☎228 60 91 222* ⓓ *Open 24hr.)*

- **HOSPITAL/MEDICAL SERVICES:** The **Medical Center** provides routine health care and emergency services, located about 200m from the dock. *(☎228 60 28 611* *i Specializes in drunken mishaps. ⏰ Open M-F 8:30am-2:30pm and 6-8pm for emergencies only.)* The local doctor provides emergency and routine medical help on the main road next to Fun Pub opposite the bus stop. *(☎228 60 91 137; 693 24 20 200 i If the door is closed, bang loudly in an emergency; Yiannis sleeps inside. ⏰ Open 24hr.)*

Getting There

By Ferry

Ios is accessible by **ferry.** The price and time ranges vary according to ferry line and type of boat. Inquire at travel agencies throughout the port and town for specific timetables and prices. To: **Mykonos** *($ €35. ⏰ 2hr., 1 per day.);* **Naxos** *($ €12-22. ⏰ 1-1½hr., 1-4 per day.);* and **Santorini** *($ €7-16. ⏰ 1½hr., 2-4 per day.)*

Getting Around

While in Ios Town, the best and only way to navigate the twisty streets, often narrow and fraught with steps, is by foot. To get from Mylopotas beach to the town, or to reach some of the more distant beaches, board the bus at Mylopotas beach, the port, or the parking lot in town. Tickets are purchased once on board. To get to Homer's tomb and a few of the farther beaches, rent a car or four-wheeler, or shell out the cash for a cab. To get back to Far Out Camping late at night, wait opposite the bus stop in town by the 24hr. food shops and hail a cab.

By Bus

Frequent buses shuttle between port, village, and beach. *(⏰ Every 10-20 min. 8am-midnight $ €1.40.)* There are clearly marked stops in all three locations: near the square of the port, along the main road in town, and all along the beach road in Mylopotas. Bus schedules are posted outside the bus stand in town along the main road in front of the church.

By Taxi

Taxis can take you where you need to go at any time during your stay on Ios. *(☎697 87 34 491; ☎697 70 31 708; or ☎697 77 60 570 $ Cash only.)*

santorini ☎22860

Santorini has had its share of catastrophes—it acquired its present shape in one of the biggest volcanic eruptions in recorded history, and an earthquake in 1956 razed many of the island's buildings. Since then, tourism has allowed for Santorini to rebuild itself; in fact, most of the island's annual income is still earned during its high season. Many establishments close for the winter, and people have to live off money earned in August—partially explaining why Santorini is one of the most expensive islands in Greece.

Today, Santorini is close on the heels of Mykonos and Ios in its popularity with partiers, who come to revel nights away on the steep cliffs of the caldera in Fira. The island is also popular with honeymooners who come to gaze at sunsets in Oia and window-shop in the town's jewelry stores and art galleries. The island's black sand beaches are perfect places to tan the day away, while hiking trails up to the ruins of Ancient Thira and boat tours to active volcanoes elevate any adventure seeker's heart rate. Due to this versatility, armies of tourists pour into Santorini from across the world. Because of the popularity and cost of importing its water and produce from the mainland, however, the prices of the island are about as steep as the cliffs of the caldera.

ORIENTATION

Fira is Santorini's principal town, set against a steep caldera, or volcanic cliff. Its center is **Plateia Theotokopoulou,** a small square with plenty of travel agencies, banks, and cafes. To get here from the bus station, walk uphill through the taxi park and then turn right. **25 Martiou** is the main road, running through the *plateia* and toward the town of Oia. Above the *plateia* is a web of small streets that connect to the **Golden Street,** which is parallel to the cliff and is home to many pay-us-for-the-magnificent-view restaurants and hotels. **Ethnikis Stavrou** (or simply the "bar street") can be found above the *plateia* and is home to some of Fira's liveliest restaurants and bars. A **cable car** further up the *caldera* connects the town with its port.

Oia is a town in the very north of the island. The central *plateia* is just above the town's beautiful main church. To get here from the **bus station,** turn away from the sea and zigzag your way uphill to the right. The **main street** runs both ways from the *plateia* along the cliffs—westward toward the **Ammoudi Beach** and eastward toward the small village of **Finikia.**

ACCOMMODATIONS

LETA HOTEL

PENSION [3]

Fira ☎228 602 2540 www.leta-santorini.gr

An alluring swimming pool is in the center of this colorful pension. The rooms are big and clean, and while they may get rather pricey during the high season, they are a safe bet for a comfortable stay. Enjoy the view of the Aegean from some of the balconies, or head down to the *plateia* to join the crowds.

To get here from the plateia, walk along the main road in the direction of Oia, past Pelican Tours and the food court; the pension will be to your right. ℹ *Breakfast included. Swimming pool. Shuttle service to and from the port and airport.* $ *High-season doubles €70. Low-season singles €35-45.* ⏰ *Reception 24hr.*

PENSION PETROS

PENSION [3]

Fira ☎228 602 2573 www.villapetros-santorini.gr

With its convenient location and glittery-clean interiors, Pension Petros is one of the best accommodation options in Fira. Try to stay here outside of the month-long high season, when the price doubles. The pension's small swimming pool isn't the liveliest spot on the island, but you probably didn't come all the way to Greece to spend time in a pension's pool.

From Pelican Tours in the plateia head downhill. When you reach the end, make a left and then an immediate right; Petros is further down the hill on the left. ℹ *Breakfast included. Swimming pool. Shuttle service to and from the port.* $ *High-season doubles €60; low-season €30-45.* ⏰ *Reception 24hr.*

SANTORINI CAMPING

CAMPING, HOSTEL [1]

Fira ☎228 602 2944 www.santorinicamping.gr

One of the most affordable accommodations in Fira is the no-frills Santorini Camping. It's a bit of a walk away from the center, but its popular pool and loud party music make it pretty lively. You can find better private rooms elsewhere, so come here if you want to camp, stay in a dorm, or stay in one of their tents equipped with a bed. The most hardcore of budget travelers can simply bring a sleeping bag and crash on their campgrounds *(€6-10).*

The camping is about 400m from the plateia. From Pelican Tours, walk downhill until the end of the road, turn left ,and then take the 1st right; continue down the hill until you reach the camping. ℹ *Swimming pool. Free shuttles to and from the port. Locks €2. Internet €3 per hr. Double rooms have free A/C, Wi-Fi.* $ *Bed tents €8-20; dorms €10-20. Doubles with bath €30-70.* ⏰ *Reception 24hr.*

SIGHTS

MUSEUM OF PREHISTORIC THYRA

MUSEUM

Fira ☎228 602 3217

"A masterpiece by an avant-garde painter" which combines "restraint in color and drawing with freedom of composition, intense movement, varied poses, and a registering of the momentary." No, that's not a description of a modern painting—it's the Bronze Age wall painting of monkeys that was recovered from the ruins of Akrotiri. This Minoan village was completely blanketed by lava after a volcano eruption in the 17th century BCE and wasn't excavated until 1967. The museum exhibits many objects that were found during the excavations, offering an insight into the lives of people living here during the Minoan civilization (apparently, they had a "consumer society" back then). Among the most interesting exhibits here are a gold ibex figurine which was discovered hidden inside of a wooden box in 1999 and the miniature 3-D model of what the city looked like before the eruption. There are a few samples of Minoan jewelry as well—it is thought that since so little of it was found, people must have anticipated the eruption and collected their valuables before leaving the city.

From the plateia, walk toward the bus station; the museum's entrance will be to your right. $ *€3, students free.* ⏰ *Open in summer M 1:30-8pm, Tu-Su 8am-8pm; in winter M 1:30-3pm, Tu-Su 8am-3pm.*

PYRGOS AND ANCIENT THIRA — HIKING

Pyrgos, Kamari, Perissa

If you're a mountain goat in your heart of hearts, we know just the hike for you (and maybe the psychiatrist as well). Start in **Pyrgos,** a beautiful little town that used to be the capital of the island and is the site of a Venetian fortress. Wander through its labyrinthine, sloping streets and discover tiny blue-domed churches (there are over 30 of these). If you continue up past Franco's Cafe and the large church, you'll discover a small set of steps that leads to a rooftop offering a panoramic view of the island. From Pyrgos, it's a 45min. walk up to **Profitis Ilias Monastery** *(☎31812).* The monastery was built in 1711, and for some reason, it now shares its site with a military radar station. The old monastery is open only for formal liturgies *(usually between 6:00-6:30am, modest clothes required),* but there's a smaller, newer church which is easier to visit. The unmarked entrance can be found by walking to the left of the final path, and you might be greeted by a friendly, multilingual monk who will answer your questions *(10am-1pm, free).* From here, it's a 1hr. hike over slippery gravel and craggy rocks which demand good footwear to the ruins of **Ancient Thira** *(⏰ Open Tu-Su, 8:30am-2:30pm $ €3, students free).* Be on a lookout for stacks of rocks, red spots, and views of the path ahead to navigate the poorly marked first part of the trail. At Ancient Thira, you'll see the ruins of an ancient theater, a church, various baths, and even a forum, most of which date back to the Hellenic period. Look out for carved dolphins and ruined columns, and don't forget to take in the magnificent view.

To get to Pyrgos, take a local bus going to Perissa or any bus that goes to Vlichada. If you want to reach the ruins of Ancient Thira directly, you can hike from Kamari or Perissa—the former has a paved road leading up the hill, while the latter has only a footpath. Hikes from both places should take about 1hr.

VOLCANO, THIRASIA, AND HOT SPRINGS — ISLANDS

Santorini, Caldera Rim

If you feel a burning desire to experience the volcano and other parts of Santorini's *caldera* rim first-hand, you should take one of the many tours. Excursions typically go to the volcano first, where guides lead hikes up the black rocks to the active crater. After a 30min. up-close look at lava, the tours move on to the waters around Palea Kameni or Nea Kameni, where you can jump off the boat and swim to the (rather lukewarm) sulfur hot springs. Some excursions continue on to the small island of Thirasia, where tourists get a few hours to wander up to explore the towns above the port. The sleepy villages of Manolas and Potamos offer some decent views of Santorini's western coast and have quite an authentic feel. The most complete tour packages also include a sunset dinner at Oia.

$ *Tours start at around €13 (just the volcano) and go up to €35 and higher. Ask around at multiple agencies to find the right tour.*

AKROTIRI RUINS RUINS

Akrotiri

The famous fate of Pompeii is just an imitation of an earlier disaster—in the 17th century BCE, a volcanic eruption destroyed Santorini and covered the maritime Minoan city of Akrotiri with lava. As a result, Akrotiri was preserved in time better than almost any other Minoan site. Only around three to five percent of the entire city has been excavated so far, but what's been found has been enough to show the sophistication of this Bronze Age culture. Akrotiri had multi-story houses and extensive sanitation, drainage, and sewage systems. Each house had at least one room decorated with wall paintings (which are now exhibited in Athens and Fira). No skeletons were found in the ruins, one more piece of evidence suggesting that the inhabitants escaped before the eruption. The site has been closed for a while now due to reconstruction and "technical reasons" involving a lawsuit, but ask around whether it's open when you come to Santorini. A (non-) visit to the ruins can be conveniently combined with a visit to the **Red Beach,** which is a 15min. walk away.

Take a bus from Fira to Akrotiri. The ruins are a 15min. walk from the village of Akrotiri, down the main road that continues toward the Red Beach. ⏰ Temporarily closed.

BEACHES

The best-known beach on Santorini is **Red Beach,** a small strip of pebbles and black sand under towering red-brick cliffs. You'll have to climb a small ridge to get here, but the beach, overflowing with umbrellas and beach chairs, is worth the 15min. walk from the Akrotiri ruins bus stop or the 30min. walk from Akrotiri village.

The island's most popular beach is **Kamari,** a large expanse of fine black sand with hordes of sunbathers, but locals love the festive beach towns of **Perissa** and **Perivolos,** which lie on a 9km stretch of black sand just south from the Ancient Thira mountain. In fact, beaches in Kamari and Perissa were awarded a Blue Flag for their beauty. While beach chair and umbrella rentals can be expensive *(from €7),* some restaurants in Perissa will let you stay on their beach beds without charge if you buy a drink.

To get away from the crowds, try **Vlihada,** a pleasant, medium-sized beach near some impressive white cliffs. There are only a few buses per day to Vlihada from Fira, so either come with your own transport, or carefully check the bus schedule before your trip. When you're in Oia, don't miss the **Ammoudi Beach,** a small, rocky affair that's more of a dock than anything else. The cheap, infrequent boats for Thirasia leave from here as well. The closest beach to Fira is **Monolithos,** with thin, yellow sand and shallow water. All of these harder-to-find beaches can be reached by bus from Fira *(€1.40-2),* but some of the best and most peaceful beaches on the island are only accessible by car.

FOOD

CAFE NRG CREPES ❶

Ethnikis Stavrou, Fira ☎24997

NRG (read: energy) has got some of the biggest and best crepes around. The menu items are more like suggestions than anything binding, so feel free to build your own monster crepe from the listed ingredients. Our suggestion: go for the simple but unbeatable combination of Nutella, chopped bananas, and Chantilly cream *(€4.50).* NRG has long opening hours, so it's a good place for late-night takeout.

Located on the bar street, right next to the Koo Club. From Pelican Tours on the plateia's corner, walk uphill, take the 1st right, and walk until you see it on your left. $ Crepes €3.20-6.60. ⏰ Open daily 9:30am-4am.

👍 POLSKI LOKAL 🚫💳 📶 🍸 ⛅ POLISH, GREEK [2]

Oia ☎228 607 2083

This is the go-to place in Oia if you're a budget-conscious traveler (assuming that a budget-conscious traveler goes to Oia at all). Run by good-natured Polish immigrants and seasonal migrants, it offers some traditional Polish dishes (goulash, pirogi, bigos) paired with a *Zywiec* beer. If you're not feeling like Polish food, go for their gyros, which harbor a delectable special sauce.

➜ *From the plateia, walk down the main street in the direction of Ammoudi until you reach public toilets. Turn left, walk under the archway, and head downhill. Pass the parking lot and continue until you see the restaurant to your left.* ℹ *Free Wi-Fi.* $ *Pitas €2.50-2.70. Greek dishes €7.50-9.50. Polish dishes €6.50-9. Beer €2.80-4.50.* ⏰ *Open M-Sa 1-11pm, Su 5-11pm.*

DOLPHINS FISH TAVERN 💳 🍸 ⛅ FISH [3]

Akrotiri ☎228 608 1151

Customers can sit on one of the two piers that extend onto the sea and eat amongst dolphins—hence the name. If you're feeling audacious, try the fresh swordfish—just remember that each fish is sold by the kilogram and can get outrageously expensive if you aren't paying attention. What you don't finish should be thrown to Paki, the restaurant's small but fierce-looking dog.

➜ *The restaurant is a 10min. walk from the Akrotiri ruins bus stop in the direction of the Red Beach.* $ *Seafood €6.50-13. Fish dishes with salad and potatoes €20-22 per person.* ⏰ *Open daily 11am-midnight.*

NIGHTLIFE

There's a reason Ethnikis Stavrou in Fira is also known as simply the "bar street." You're not likely to find nightlife anywhere else.

👍 KOO CLUB 💳 🍸 CLUB

Ethnikis Stavrou, Fira ☎228 602 2025 💻www.kooclub.gr

There's both an indoor bar and a luxurious, open-air garden, which together provide plenty of space for both talking and dancing. Head to the crowded dance floor for some loud music and flashing lights, just make sure to keep your sandals in your room—the bouncers are quite serious about the dress code.

➜ *On the bar street next to NRG Cafe.* ℹ *No beachwear.* $ *Cover €10; includes 1 drink. Beer from €6. Cocktails €10.* ⏰ *Open daily 11pm-6am.*

MURPHY'S 💳 🍸 IRISH BAR

Ethnikis Stavrou, Fira ☎228 602 2248 💻www.murphys-bar.eu

Supposedly the first Irish bar in Greece, Murphy's is a reliable spot to do some social mingling. The traditional bar decoration is rather invisible in the nighttime hours, but you won't care much. There are a few very similar competitors on and around bar street like Highlander and 2 Brothers, so pick based on your aesthetic preferences.

➜ *It's on the bar street next to Enigma.* $ *Cover charge F-Sa €10; includes 1 drink and 1 shot. Beer from €5. Cocktails €9.* ⏰ *Open daily noon-6am. Happy hour 9:30-10:30pm.*

ESSENTIALS

Practicalities

- **TOURIST OFFICE: Tourist Information Booth** provides maps and general information. *(Fira, in the plateia* ☎*228 602 5940* ⏰ *Open 8am-10pm.)*
- **TOURS: Pelican Tours** sells ferry tickets and organizes boat trips to the volcano, hot springs, and Thirasia. Assists with airline tickets, helicopter or plane chartering, and currency exchange. *(Fira, in the plateia.* ☎*228 602 2220* 💻*www.pelican.gr* ⏰ *Open daily 8am-11pm.)* In Oia, similar services are provided by **Ecorama Holidays.** *(At the bus station* ☎*2286071508* ℹ *Free internet for customers.* ⏰ *Open 8am-10pm.)*

- **CURRENCY EXCHANGE: National Bank** exchanges currency, traveler cheques, and has a **24hr. ATM** *(Fira, near the plateia.* ☎228 602 3318 ◼*www.nbg.gr.* 🕗 *Open M-Th 8am-2:30pm, F 8am-2pm.)* In Oia, there's a **24hr. ATM** on the main road, near the *plateia.*

- **LAUNDROMAT: AD Laundry Station** in Fira does washing, drying, and folding. *(Below the plateia.* ☎228 602 3533 *i* €10 per basket. 🕗 Open M-Sa 9am-2pm and 5-8pm.)*

- **INTERNET ACCESS: PC World.** *(Fira, in the plateia.* ☎228 60 5551 *i* Internet €2.50 per hr., Wi-Fi €4 per hr. 🕗 Open M-Sa 10am-10pm, Su 11am-7pm.)*

- **POST OFFICE: Post Office** *(Fira, main road* ☎228 602 2238 🕗 *Open M-F 7:30am-2pm.)*

- **POSTAL CODE:** 84700.

Emergency!

- **EMERGENCY NUMBERS: Medical Emergency:** ☎166. **Local Medical Emergency:** ☎228 636 0300. **Police:** ☎100. **Local Police:** ☎228 602 2649. **Port Police:** ☎228 602 2239.

- **POLICE:** The local **police station** is in the nearby village of Karterados. It can be reached at ☎228 602 2659 or ☎228 602 2649.

- **LATE-NIGHT PHARMACIES:** *(Fira, plateia* ☎228 602 3444 🕗 Open 8am-11pm.)*

- **MEDICAL SERVICES: Santorini Hospital** in Fira provides 24hr. emergency care. *(*☎228 632 2863 *i* Note that the phone code for the hospital is "22863" and not "22860" like the rest of the island. 🕗 Open 24hr.)*

Getting There

By Air

Flights *(* 💲 From €80. 🕗 1hr., 8 per day.)* between **Athens** and Santorini National Airport **(JTR)** *(*☎228 602 8405)* are operated by Olympic Airways *(*☎228 602 8400), Aegean Airlines *(*☎228 602 8500), and Athens Airways *(*☎228 603 2020). There are also flights from **Thessaloniki.** *(* 💲 From €120. 🕗 1hr., 1-2 per day.)* From the airport there are public buses to Fira *(* 💲 €1.40.), but hotels and pensions often provide free transport.

By Ferry

Ferries *(* 💲 €8-34)* and **Flying Dolphins** *(* 💲 €16-56.)* connect Santorini with Piraeus and other islands—the latter are much faster and about twice as expensive. Note that ferry schedules often list Santorini as **Thira.** Ferries travel to: **Ios** *(*🕗 30min.-1½hr., 3-5 per day.); **Mykonos** *(*🕗 3hr., 2 per day.); **Milos** *(*🕗 1½-3hr., 1-3 per day.); **Naxos.** *(*🕗 1½-2½hr., 3-4 per day.)* To check current schedules, ask at Pelican Tours or any other travel agency. If you're arriving by ferry, you'll be dropped off at one of the three ports (Fira, Oia, Athinios), but most likely at **Athinios** (even if your ticket says Thira). There are public buses from here to Fira *(* 💲 €2. 🕗 20min.)* meeting the ferries, but hotels often provide free transport from here as well. To get to and from Fira's port, either walk down the 588-step footpath, take the **cable car** *(*☎228 602 2977 💲 €4, children and luggage €2. 🕗 Every 20min. 6:30am-10:40pm), or hire a donkey *(* 💲 €5)* at the red donkey station.

Getting Around

By Bus

Local buses *(*☎25404 ◼*www.ktel-santorini.gr)* connect most towns on Santorini. From the Fira bus station, buses head to: **Akrotiri** *(*🕗 30min., 10 per day. 💲 €1.70.); **Athinios** *(* 💲 €2. 🕗 25min., 4 per day.); **Kamari** *(* 💲 €1.40. 🕗 20min., every 30min. 7:30am-12am.); **Monolithos** *(* 💲 €1.40. 🕗 30min., 8 per day.); **Oia** *(* 💲 €1.40. 🕗 30min., every 30min. 6:50am-11pm.)* via the airport; **Perissa** *(* 💲 €2. 🕗 30min., every 30min. 7:10am-12am.); **Vlihada** *(*🕗 5 per day €1.40.).

Transferring in small towns isn't very convenient, as the waiting times can be quite long. You can get a **taxi** at Fira's taxi park *(☎228 602 2555 🕒 24hr.)*, just above the bus station.

By Moped and ATV

Many **moped and ATV rental** agencies can be found in the streets around Fira's *plateia*. In mid-season, expect to pay around €10-20 per day for a moped and €15-25 for an ATV, with higher prices in August. Most car rental companies are open between 8am and 8pm, and you'll need a driver's license. Ask around for the best price, and make sure they give you a helmet.

milos ☎22870

greece

Milos is pretty much the opposite of a party island—it's slow-paced and not excessively popular with foreign tourists. Instead, explore volcanic beaches amidst colorful cliffs to sea caves and strange rock formations. You can go lie down on the moon-like beach of Sarakiniko, or take a boat cruise to the pirate hideouts of Kleftiko. Even if you abandon the dramatic shoreline and head inland, you can find the remnants of early Christian catacombs, a smattering of tiny museums, and a ton of Orthodox churches. The island's hilltop capital, **Plaka,** offers some great views of the island's entirety, while the port of **Adamos** is where you'll find some semblance of nightlife (there were around five bars last time we counted). There are no hostels on the island, but there are plenty of *domatia* and some reasonably cheap hotels to accommodate the budget traveler. Even though the island isn't exactly a whirlwind of activity, the tourist infrastructure is very developed—Milos maintains several websites that give a good overview of the main attractions and direct you to many interesting places.

ORIENTATION

The best place to stay in Milos is probably **Adamos,** the port city with a lot of tourist-oriented infrastructure. Most activity is concentrated along the **waterfront,** where you'll find many restaurants and tourist agencies. The **bus stop** is opposite the ATE Bank, where the Plaka-bound **main road** adjoins the waterfront. Plenty of cheap *domatias* can be found in the labyrinthine streets directly behind the waterfront. The island's capital is **Plaka,** a hilltop city some 6km north of Adamos. Its upper part is a maze of narrow streets with many cafes that offers many unexpected scenic views, while down the hill you'll find the Archeological Museum, the hospital, and the road that will lead you to Trypiti's **catacombs.** While you're in Plaka, don't forget to climb the hill to **Panagia Thalassitra Monastery,** where you can see the entire island.

ACCOMMODATIONS

HOTEL SEMIRAMIS — 📶❄ HOTEL [2]

Adamas ☎228 702 2117 💻www.semiramishotel-milos.com

This place may be one of the cheapest hotels on the island, but you wouldn't be able to guess that from the cozy, clean, and spacious rooms. The genuine owner will be happy to give you local advice on what to see on the island, while the leafy backyard is an excellent place to wait through the midday sun. For the most frugal of travelers, there are two rooms that share a bathroom and go for an even lower price.

➜ From ATE Bank, walk down the main road for 30m; on the left you'll see a sign pointing you to the hotel. ℹ Airport transportation available. $ High-season doubles €55-65; low-season €28. Triples 20% extra. 🕒 Reception 9am-4pm and 7:30-9pm.

ELENI HOTEL — 📶❄ HOTEL [3]

Adamas ☎228 702 1972 💻www.hoteleleni.com

A bit of a walk away from the hustle and bustle of the waterfront, this 15-room hotel is among the cheaper options, offering competent rooms with A/C and balconies and a very personable owner.

✈ From the dock, continue down the waterfront away from the restaurants and tourist agencies. After you reach the Lagada beach, walk 50m inland, take a left turn, and walk until you see the hotel to your right. $ Doubles €30-70. ⏰ Reception 8am-midnight.

SANTORINI CAMPING — 🏕 CAMPGROUND ❶

Achivadolimni ☎228 703 1410 💻www.miloscamping.gr

If you don't have your own transportation, staying here can be a bit inconvenient (it's some 6km away from Adamas, and buses run infrequently), but there are many advantages. The campground is just a few minutes away from Hivadolimni, the island's most popular beach, and there's a swimming pool and open-air cafeteria, both on a steep cliff overlooking the beach. You'll also be able to use the communal kitchen, mini-mart, and cheap laundry service *(€5)*.

✈ Take the bus from Adamas. i Free airport and port transportation. $ 2-person bungalows €30-98; 3-person bungalows €60-116; 4-person bungalows €70-131. ⏰ Reception 8am-12am.

SIGHTS

✓ CATACOMBS AND ROMAN THEATER — 🏕 RUINS

Trypiti ☎228 702 1625

Among the first Christian places of worship in the world, the **catacombs** at Milos were used for secret religious ceremonies and burying the dead in the days when Christians had to worship in secrecy to avoid persecution. A Christian community was on the island as early as the first century, and it grew considerably in the following centuries. Carved in soft volcanic rock, the catacombs were pillaged in the 19th century, and not much remains to see today. Still, the place remains strangely fascinating. Vaults in the sides contain graves which accommodated anywhere from one to seven bodies, and it's estimated that thousands of people were buried here. Only one of the three galleries can be accessed today, and that only on a guided tour. The guides don't speak much English, so don't expect thorough explanations. Notice the primitive inscriptions on the walls—no, these weren't made by early Christians; it's vandalism from a few years back when the catacombs didn't have a night guard. The **ancient Roman theater** is a few minutes on foot away from the catacombs. It is quite well preserved and used to host musical performances. If you continue further up the hill, you'll come across the site where **Venus de Milo** was found, and further up is a small hill topped by a tiny chapel—the view from here is worth the climb.

✈ Trypiti is 1km away from the lower bus stop in Plaka. To get to the catacombs, follow the downhill road that adjoins the square above the lower bus stop. Pass the Ancient Theater sign but stay on the road, and the catacombs will be further down at the end of the winding road. To get to the theater, backtrack from the catacombs and turn left (just before the flight of steps) onto a path that will lead you there. i Guided tours of catacombs every 20min. $ Catacombs €2, reduced ticket €1, EU students free. ⏰ Open Tu-Sa 8:30am-6:30pm, Su 8:30am-3pm.

✓ KIMOLOS — ISLAND

Kimolos Island, north of Milos

Kimolos is an island stuck in time—some say the precise date is 1955, but decide for yourself. When you arrive by ferry at the port of **Psathi,** you might be awaited by the island's single bus *(☎6973 700 033 $ €1.50)*, and bus driver, who's allegedly the only person on Kimolos who speaks some English. The bus will take you to **Chorio,** the island's capital, where you can find a number of small museums—the **Folk and Maritime Museum** *(☎228 705 1118, €1)* run by a friendly doctor, the **Archaeological Museum** where you can walk on a glass floor over tombs from the Archaic period, and a volunteer office dedicated to the **monk seal** (*Monachus monachus*), which is one of the most endangered mammals in the world and which lives on this island. Don't forget to wander around Chorio's **kastro,** the town's castle center. The opening times of these sights vary, but if you come outside of the visiting hours, you can always try banging on the door to win a personalized visit. If you have your own transport, you can go see **Skiadi,** an enormous mushroom-like rock structure in the northwest of the island—it can be reached by driving down a road from Chorio and then walking for some additional 30min. on an arrow-marked path. If you don't have a car, you can call the island's sole **taxi** *(☎228 705 1552).* Finally, south of Kimolos is the uninhabited island of **Polyaigos** (fittingly, the name means "many goats") which has some interesting volcanic caves. **Delphini Sea Taxi** *(☎228 705 1437)* organizes boat trips to this island from Psathi (these generally leave at 9am and cost €25). Since Kimolos is a small, untouristy island, things do not always run on fixed schedules—before going there, always get advice from local sources.

⇟ To get to Kimolos, drive or take a bus from Adamas to Pollonia, and then take one of the ferries to Kimolos (there are 2 per day in winter, 4 per day in fall and spring, 5-6 per day in July and August. Check the current schedules at a travel agency. The ferry can carry road vehicles as well. Tickets cost €2). There are ferries from Adamas as well, but these are more expensive and run only about once a week.

KLEFTIKO AND GLARONISSIA ROCK FORMATIONS

Milos shores

Some of the best-known structures on Milos can't be accessed without a boat. One of these is Kleftiko, an impressive rock formation on the southwest shore of the island. It is said that the Ottoman pirate Barbarossa used to hide his boats in the marine caves of Kleftiko to avoid his pursuers. If you're lucky, you might glimpse an old cannon still lying on the seafloor. Glaronissia islands are home to 20m basalt blocks protruding out of the water. Composed of small crystals, they are shaped like hexagons and are often compared to organ pipes. To get to either of these rock formations, you'll have to join in on one of the many cruises organized around the Milos shoreline *(€20-60),* take part in a kayaking excursion, or do some rather audacious long-distance swimming.

THE GREAT OUTDOORS

MILOS KAYAKING KAYAKING

Triovasalos ☎228 702 3597 🖳www.seakayakgreece.com

If you feel like having a firsthand experience of the caves, arches, and cliffs that line the uneven shoreline of Milos, you'll be interested in some of the five different beginner-friendly **kayak** routes offered by Milos Kayaking. Among the major draws are the daytrips to Kleftiko and Glaronisia, but Klima, Gerakas, and the sulfur mines are interesting as well. The price includes a picnic lunch, snorkeling equipment, and transport to and from the paddle site.

⇟ For information about trips and bookings, go to a travel agency in Adamas or contact the company directly. [i] Availability of trips depends on weather. $ €65 per person. ⏰ Trips are usually 10am-5pm and involve 3hr. (7½-10 mi.) of paddling.

MILOS DIVING CENTER DIVING

Pollonia ☎228 702 8077 🖳www.milosdiving.gr

For fans of sea anemones and shipwrecks from WWII, the Pollonia-based Milos Diving Center organizes diving trips and awards diving certificates (CMAS, PADI, IAHD). Southwest Aegean Milos Sea Club *(☎6977 288 847)* based in Adamas offers diving trips as well.

[i] For information about trips and bookings, go to a travel agency in Adamas or contact the companies directly. $ Self-equipped dive €35; dive with equipment provided €50; 10 dives €400.

FOOD

ARTEMIS
BAKERY ❶

Adamas ☎228 702 2998

Artemis has an unbelievable selection of freshly baked croissants, cookies, breads, and pies, all very suitable for a fast breakfast or a picnic at a secluded beach. Try the big slice of watermelon pie *(€2)*, or supply yourself with the traditional Milos dessert, *koufeto*, made of pumpkin, honey, and almonds *(€3-8)*. Pizza, cheese buns, and other savory baked goods are also available.

The bakery is on the fork opposite ATE Bank and the bus stop. $ Bread €1 per kg. Croissants €2. Cookies €9 per kg. ⏰ Open daily 5am-midnight.

FORAS
TAVERNA ❷

Plaka ☎228 702 3954

This traditional taverna in Plaka serves cheap, fresh food in generous portions. In fact, if you ask the boss Nikolas about which menu items are good, he'll pat his well-nourished belly and tell you that everything is good. Try their tasty rabbit with bread and onions *(€8)* or the swordfish *(€8)*—the more exotic meals come at good prices. Foras also serves white wine produced in Milos, so order half a carafe *(€2.50)* and get your drink on.

From the upper bus stop in Plaka, head downhill on the main road; it will be on your right. $ Salads €2.50-5.50. Entrees €4.50-8. Beer €2.20-2.50. ⏰ Open daily 8am-1am.

PITSOUNAKIA
GRILL ❶

Adamas ☎228 702 1739

Less expensive than most restaurants down on the waterfront, Pitsounakia is especially good for a quick gyro or *souvlaki*. Coming later in the day seems to be more common than coming here for lunch. If you want a proper meal, go linger in the asphalt garden in the back of the restaurant. The gyros line gets quite long sometimes, so if you're running for a ferry or something, you may have to hit up somewhere with a higher price but shorter line.

Pitsounakia is some 20m from ATE bank down the main road, on the left. $ Souvlaki €1.80. Entrees €5.50-7. Beer €2.50. ⏰ Open daily 1pm-1am.

NIGHTLIFE

AKRI
BAR

Adamas ☎228 702 2604

Akri ("edge") has a more laid-back feel and a nicer view than its neighbors down the hill. The sprawling terraces have many tables and stools from which you can observe the green-lit waters of Adamos harbor. The two levels of slick interiors are suitable for dancing, but Akri is also a good place to come for an evening coffee. This is not a place for you if you hoped to listen to Greek music, but they play just about everything else.

Continue up the hill beyond Vipera Lebetina and Aragosta cafe, Akri will be to your left. $ Coffee €2-3.5. Small beer €5-6. Cocktails €8-9. ⏰ Open daily 8pm-4am.

ARAGOSTA
BAR

Adamas ☎22292 www.aragosta.gr

One of the few nightlife establishments in Adamas, Aragosta gets very lively at night. The laid-back, white-and-red terrace overlooks the pedestrian zone of the waterfront, so this is the place to go if you want to be seen partying it up. A few meters up the hill, Aragosta has a small open-air cafe that has an excellent view of the harbor that serves as a refuge from the loud music inside the bar.

Climb up the stairs near Milos Travel, it's the bar on the right. $ Small beer €5-5.50. Cocktails €10. Desserts €5-7. ⏰ Open daily 7pm-5:30am. Cafe open daily 9am-2pm and 7pm-3am.

VIPERA LEBETINA 🍸 BAR

Adamas

This bar is named after the island's famous venomous snake, but let's hope none of that stuff made its way into their drinks. With a dock-facing terrace outside and a small dance floor inside, Vipera is one of the more compact bars here, but that doesn't make its charisma any smaller at night when rock music is playing at full volume.

➡ *Find it a few meters above Aragosta.* 💲 *Shots €3. Beer €5-6. Cocktails €9.* ⏰ *Open daily 9pm-5:30am*

BEACHES

Beaches in Milos are a cut above any other beach—they are natural works of art. After years of volcanic eruptions, mineral deposits, and aquatic erosion, the shoreline of Milos is a wonderland of multicolored sand, steep cliffs, and fascinating caves and arches. One of the most remarkable beaches is 👍**Sarakiniko,** a shallow pool of water in the middle of white volcanic moonscape. **Papafragas,** close to the ruins of Fylakopi, is a long, water-filled canyon ending in a small sandy beach. **Hivadolimni** is the longest beach on the island, named after the small saltwater lake behind it, while 👍**Paliochori** is known for its colorful cliffs and turquoise water. Out of the 60-something beaches on Milos, around 30 are accessible only by car, while the best-known ones have infrequent bus connections running from Adamas. Boats will take you to beaches that are hard to access by road, including the sea cavern of **Sykia.** For more information about individual beaches, ask for a brochure at the tourist office.

ESSENTIALS

Practicalities

- **TOURIST OFFICES: Tourist Information** provides maps, brochures, ferry and bus timetables, and has a complete list of the island's hotels. *(Adamas, waterfront* ☎*228 702 2445* 💻*www.milos.gr* ⏰ *Open M 8:30am-midnight, Tu-Sa 8:30am-11pm.)*
- **TOURIST AGENCIES: Brau Kat Travel** has very helpful staff and sells ferry tickets, rents cars, and arranges tours. *(Adamas, waterfront* ☎*228 702 3000* 💻*www.milosisland.gr* ⏰ *Open daily 8:30am-1am.)* **Sophia Travels** provides similar services. *(Adamas, waterfront* ☎*228 702 1994* 💻*www.milosferries.gr* ⏰ *Open daily 8:30am-1am.)*
- **CURRENCY EXCHANGE: National Bank** provides currency exchange. *(Adamas, waterfront* ☎*228 702 2332* ⏰ *Open M-Th 8:30am-2pm, F 8:30am-1:30pm.)*
- **ATM: ATE Bank** *(*☎*228 702 2330, near the bus stop)*
- **LAUNDROMAT: Smart and Fast Clean** *(Adamas, main road* ☎*228 702 3271* 💲 *€8 for 5-6kg of laundry.* ⏰ *Open M-Sa 8am-10pm, Su 11am-10pm.)*
- **INTERNET:** The municipality of Adamas has a **free Wi-Fi hotspot** on the waterfront. **Internet Info.** *(Adamas, main road* 💲 *€3 per hr., €0.50 per 5min.* ⏰ *Open daily 9am-3pm and 4pm-12:30am.)*
- **POST OFFICE: Hellenic Post** provides Poste Restante and express mail services. *(Adamas, waterfront* ☎*228 702 2345* ⏰ *Open M-F 9am-1pm.)*
- **POSTAL CODE:** 84800.

Emergency!

- **EMERGENCY NUMBERS:** ☎166. **Local Emergency:** ☎*228 702 2700.* **Police:** ☎100. **Local Port Police:** ☎*228 702 3360.* **Local Tourist Police:** ☎*228 702 1378.*
- **POLICE: Police Station.** *(Plaka, main road* ☎*228 702 1378* ⏰ *Open 24hr.)*

- **LATE-NIGHT PHARMACIES: Pharmacy** *(Adamas, main road ☎228 702 2178 ⏰ Open daily 8:30am-3pm and 6pm-midnight.)*
- **MEDICAL SERVICES: Health Center** in Plaka provides 24hr. emergency care. *(Plaka, lower square ☎228 702 2700 ⏰ Open 24hr.)*

Getting There

By Plane

About twice a day there are government-subsidized **flights** between Athens and Milos Airport **(MLO)** (☎*228 702 2381*) operated by Olympic Airways *(Adamas, waterfront ☎228 702 2380)*. Flights are cheap *($ €45-50)* and get sold out easily, so book in advance. There is no public transportation from the airport, so you'll have to take a taxi or arrange it with your hotel.

By Ferry

Ferry and **fast ferry** schedules change very often (three or four times just in June), but at the time of writing, the following connections were available: **Piraeus** *(4-7 per day, 2½-7hr.)*, **Amorgos, Anafi, Folegandros, Heraklion, Ios, Karpathos, Kimolos, Kithnos, Koufonisi, Mykonos, Naxos, Rhodos, Santorini, Serifos, Sifnos, Sikinos, Sitia,** and **Syros.** Check the current schedules at any travel agency. Ferries travel to and from Adamas.

Getting Around

By Bus

Local transportation is provided by **buses** *($ €1.50-1.70)* which run from Adamas to different parts of the island. Among the destinations are **Plaka** *(via Triovassalos and Tripiti ⏰ Every hr. 7:30am-12:30am.)*, **Pollonia** *(via Pahena and Filakopi ⏰ 9 per day 6:45am-10:15pm.)*, **Paleochori** *(via Zefiria ⏰ 7 per day 10:30am-7:15pm.)*, **Achivadolimni** and **Provata** *(⏰ 8 per day 10:15am-6:20pm.)*, **Milos Camping** *(⏰ 11 per day 8am-11:15pm.)*, and **Sarakiniko.** *(⏰ 11am, 1pm, 3pm.)*

By Taxi

Taxis line up by the waterfront in Adamas *(☎228 702 2219 for Adamas; ☎228 702 1306 for Triovassalos)*. Check the taxi price list at the tourist office. The best way to explore the island is with your own transport, since many beaches aren't accessible by bus.

essentials

entrance requirements

- **PASSPORT:** Required for citizens of all countries. Must be valid for 90 days after the period of intended stay.
- **VISA:** Not required for citizens of Australia, Canada, Ireland, New Zealand, the UK, and the US.
- **WORK PERMIT:** Required for all foreigners planning to work in Greece.

PLANNING YOUR TRIP

Time Differences

Greece is 2hr. ahead of Greenwich Mean Time (GMT) observes Daylight Saving Time. This means that it is 7hr. ahead of New York City, 10hr. ahead Los Angeles, 2hr. ahead of the British Isles, 7hr. behind Sydney, and 9hr. behind New Zealand.

MONEY

Tipping and Bargaining

In Greece, law requires that restaurant and cafe prices include a 13% gratuity. Additional tipping is unnecessary, unless you are particularly pleased with the service, in which case leave 5%.

Bargaining in a street market or bazaar is a life skill, but trying to get a cheaper price in an established shop can be considered disrespectful. The price tends to be more flexible in informal venues. If it's unclear whether bargaining is appropriate in a situation, hang back and watch someone else buy first. Be warned, merchants with any pride in their wares will refuse to sell to someone who has offended them in the negotiations, so don't lowball too much.

Taxes

Currently, Greece's value-added tax (VAT) is 21%; however, in return for the EU bailing them out of their tar pit of debt, the VAT will increase to 23%. Also, Greece will introduce a 10% excise tax on tobacco, fuel, and alcohol. Theoretically, Greece's VAT that you pay on your trip can be reclaimed at most points of departure, but this requires much persistence and hassle.

SAFETY AND HEALTH

General Advice

In any type of crisis, the most important thing to do is **stay calm.** Your country's embassy abroad is usually your best resource in an emergency; registering with that embassy upon arrival in the country is a good idea.

Local Laws and Police

Greek police are used to having foreigners around, but that does not mean they allow them to break the law. Photographs and notes cannot be taken near military establishments (including docks). The purchase of pirated goods (including CDs and DVDs) is illegal; keep your receipts for proof of purchase. Taking objects or rocks from ancient sites is forbidden and can lead to fines or prison sentences. Drunk driving and indecent behavior also can result in heavy fines, arrest, and imprisonment. Although legal in Greece since 1951, homosexuality is still frowned upon socially. GLBT individuals are not legally protected from discrimination. That said, destinations like Athens, Thessaloniki, Lesvos, Rhodes, Ios, and especially Mykonos offer gay and lesbian hotels, bars, and clubs.

Drugs and Alcohol

Visitors of all ages generally have very little difficulty obtaining alcohol in Greece. In contrast, drug laws are very strict. Conviction for possession, use, or trafficking of drugs, including marijuana, will result in imprisonment and fines. If you use prescription drugs, have a copy of the prescriptions and a note from the doctor, if possible. Authorities are particularly vigilant at the Turkish and Albanian borders.

SPECIFIC CONCERNS

Natural Disasters

Located in one of the world's most seismically active areas, Greece experiences frequent and occasionally large **earthquakes.** The most recent serious quake in 1999 wreaked an estimated US$3 billion worth of damage and caused nearly 1,800 casualties in Athens and 45,000 casualties in Turkey. Earthquakes are unpredictable and can occur at any time of day. If a strong earthquake does occur, it will probably only last one or two minutes. Protect yourself by moving a sturdy doorway, table, or desk, and open a doorway to provide an escape route. In mountainous regions, landslides may follow quakes.

Demonstrations and Political Gatherings

Strikes and demonstrations occur frequently in Greece, especially now during the current economic crisis. Although generally orderly and lawful, they can spiral out of control: most recently, in December 2008, riots and violent demonstrations involving destructive vandalism and forceful clashes between civilians and the police rocked Athens and other major cities across the country. Disruption of public services, such as public transportation and air traffic control, can occur unexpectedly due to union strikes. Common areas for protest include the Polytechnic University area, Exharia, Omonia, Syntagma Square, and Mavii Square in Athens.

Terrorism

Terrorism is a serious concern for travelers to Greece. Terrorist activity has been on the rise because of domestic terrorist groups with marxist-anarchist leanings and anti-globalization agendas. **Revolutionary Struggle,** an extreme leftist paramilitary organization, launched a rocket at the US Embassy in Athens in early 2007. Its successor organization, **Revolutionary Nuclei,** has claimed responsibility for numerous attacks since, involving the use of Molotov cocktails, small-scale arms, and homemade explosives. The best thing you can do to be safe is to be aware of your surroundings, especially in crowded areas and tourist sites.

Pre-Departure Health

Matching a prescription to a foreign equivalent is not always easy, safe, or possible, so if you take **prescription drugs,** carry up-to-date prescriptions or a statement from your doctor stating the medications' trade names, manufacturers, chemical names, and dosages. Be sure to keep all medication with you in your carry-on luggage.

Pharmacists often speak English reasonably well and can help you find common over-the-counter drugs like aspirin in the pharmacy.

Immunizations and Precautions

You should consult with your doctor before traveling to Greece and she or he may recommend getting Hepatitis A, typhoid, and rabies vaccinations, especially if you are traveling to rural areas.

Travelers over two years old should make sure that the following vaccines are up to date: MMR (for measles, mumps, and rubella); DTaP or Td (for diphtheria, tetanus, and pertussis); IPV (for polio); Hib (for *Haemophilus influenzae* B); and HepB (for Hepatitis B). For recommendations on immunizations and prophylaxis, check with a doctor and consult the **Centers for Disease Control and Prevention (CDC)** in the US or the equivalent in your home country. (☎+1-800-CDC-INFO/232-4636 www.cdc.gov/travel)

Staying Healthy

In Greece, water is safe to drink, except in certain isolated areas. Wear plenty of sunscreen and always have a bottle of water to avoid dehydration.

greece 101

CUSTOMS AND ETIQUETTE

Invitation Explanation

Don't know anyone in Greece? Don't worry. Greek culture puts a high value on warmth and hospitality. Don't be surprised if you wind up with multiple invitations to chat over lunch at a local cafe or join a family for a home-cooked meal. If you're invited out for dinner or a drink, keep in mind that the host usually pays the bill. If you are lucky enough to land an invitation to a Greek home, be prepared for VIP treatment! Arriving 30min. late is considered punctual, and it is customary to bring a small gift, like flowers or chocolate. Perplexed by an invitation to a "nameday" party? Greeks tend not to celebrate birthdays, but rather "namedays," the birth date of their namesake saint. Take note: gifts are expected—and don't forget a funny nameday card!

Godly Garments

Sightseers are welcome to visit Greek Orthodox churches, but conservative dress is expected, so leave your beachwear behind. For both men and women, this means covering up from shoulders to knees. Respect worshippers by refraining from photography and other disruptive behaviors.

Don't Ruin the Ruins

Inanimate objects deserve respect too: observe posted signs and avoid touching monuments so that visitors can appreciate the sights for another few thousand years. Found a broken shard of marble that bears a striking resemblance to Socrates? Leave him in his homeland for other visitors to enjoy—taking anything from historical or archaeological sights is not only disrespectful, it is grounds for arrest.

FOOD AND DRINK

Eat Up!

After traveling through centuries of magnificent art and architecture and across miles of dazzling beaches, pause to give your hungry stomach some relief. If you're in the mood for a little bite to eat, stop for *meze*, small dishes that make an ideal snack. Vegetarians can choose from *meze* including *melitzanosalata*, eggplant salad, and *dolmades*, leaves stuffed with pine nuts, currants, and rice. For the carnivorous at heart, *bekrí-mezé*, diced pork stew, and savory meatballs like *keftédes* and *soutzoukákia smyrnéika* are sure to hit the spot. No trip to Athens is complete without sampling local olives, fresh feta, and authentic gyros made with rotisserie-coooked meat and *tzatziki* (garlic, yogurt, and cucumber sauce) served in pitas. Try specialties like *aïdakia*, seasoned lamb chops, or *chtapodi sti skhara*, grilled octopus.

For a budget-friendly option, stop for *souvlaki*, tender skewers of meat (choose from pork, chicken, beef, or lamb) grilled to perfection. Enjoy *souvlaki* fresh off the skewer or in a pita sandwich with garnishes and sauces. *Phyllo* pastry is another Greek favorite, used in dishes ranging from *spanakopita*—made from spinach, feta cheese, onions, and egg wrapped in delicate sheets of pastry—to *baklava*, a desert consisting of thin pastry layers filled with nuts and drenched in sweet syrup. Don't worry–they aren't too Greece-y!

Buy You a Drink?

Wet your whistle after climbing the Acropolis at local coffee shops serving sweet, strong Greek coffee, or trya frappe, foamy iced instant coffee. If you're in the mood for wine, you've come the right place–Greece has a 6500-year history of wine production. Even small *tavernas* often serve a wide variety of local wines. If you're in the mood for something stronger, take a sip of Greece's favorite alcoholic drink, *ouzo*. *Ouzo's* intense black-licorice flavor and powerful kick are not for everyone. *Ouzo* often accompanies *meze*, and is sometimes drunk diluted with water or ice, which causes the drink to turn an opaque white color.

HUNGARY

Throughout Hungary, the vestiges of Ottoman and communist rules can be found on the same block. Castles stand staunchly and thermal baths pool beside concrete Soviet monuments, overlooking the graves of 20th-century writers and medieval poets.

Döner kebabs, *bockwurst*, and cheeses are peddled side by side, while Budapest locals frequent Turkish bathhouses. Freewheeling youth and a relentless drive toward the modern means endless streets of hip hangouts and vehemently chill attitude, making the cities some of the best student urban destinations in Europe. And even though the locals might be too cool for school, they do appreciate a tenacity to learn about their culture. That includes the medieval gems of Szentendre and Ersztergom.

greatest hits

- **RUBBER DUCKIE, YOU'RE THE ONE.** Make out in the bathtub upstairs at Szimpla Kert (p. 631), Budapest's original ruin pub.

- **GET ICED.** In the winter, an area of Hősök tere (Heroes' Square, p. 618) functions as an ice rink.

- **FRESH TO DEATH.** Learn proper hummus-and-pita-eating techniques at Hummus Bár (p. 626).

- **NOTHING IS GIVEN SO FREELY AS ADVICE.** The staff at Aventura Boutique Hostel (p. 613) gladly doles out suggestions on the where and what.

hungary

budapest ☎01

Perhaps the single most underrated city in Europe, Budapest is a city for lovers and dreamers, a place where the grocery store clerk will chat you up even if he can't understand a word you say, a land where ruins become hang-outs, where hipsters drink beer and watch experimental films, where people flock to museums until three in the morning, where every building has its own character, its own name and color. Nowhere else can you play chess with half-naked men three generations older than you in the warm waters of a Turkish bath. You might be hard-pressed to find a picture comparable to one taken at sunset from Fisherman's Bastion on the top of Buda Castle. Enjoy a stroll down Andrássy boulevard, with its tree-lined walkway where purple and yellow flowers bloom to tickle your feet as you pass. In the past few years since Hungary entered the European Union and Union money began to flow into the once severely impoverished nation, Budapest has become a city under constant repair and reconstruction; the result is a city of juxtaposition. Newly erected buildings stand hand-in-hand with ancient 18th-century ones whose crumbling facades become endearing rather than appalling. Bridges seem to crumble into the waters below and then suddenly reemerge polished. Perhaps what makes the city most remarkable is that rather than discarding its scars from a bloody history, it scrambles to preserve them. It's not that it seeks to distance itself from the brutality of what was, but instead to learn from and at times even embrace the past toward the nurture of a future through acts of filial affection.

ORIENTATION

The Belváros, District V

You can't say you've conquered Budapest until the Belváros, Budapest's downtown, has been checked off your list. Keep in mind, though, that this is the most heavily touristed area of the city; restaurants will gladly strip you of all you've got and stores will sell you the cheapest, well, garbage at high prices. That being said, this neighborhood's hostels will give you a lot of bang for your buck in an unbeatable location. **Grand Market Hall** at the foot of the green **Szabadság Bridge** is a place for the faint of wallet; rows of freshly baked bread and spicy strung salami create a visceral experience—free of charge. Perhaps the greatest asset this part of town has to offer the penny-pinching backpacker is the walk along the **Danube,** one street over from Váci utca. Benches line the boardwalk, folk musicians play their accordions in the summmertime, kids run after balls and puppies, and you can experience one of the most beautiful views of Buda and **Castle Hill** this side of the city.

Lipótváros, District V and XIII

Lipótváros includes parts of District V and XIII, beginning after Arany János utca, adjacent to the Belváros, and continuing along the river past Margit Island. This neighborhood boasts the majestic **Parliament Building** with its Gothic spires, as well as St. Stephen's mummified hand carefully preserved in the Basilica. Lipótváros also extends into Budapest's former factory district. Now home to a few dozen giant apartment buildings, the area is one of the few places yet to be refurbished in the city. While not much attracts the average tourist past Margit bridge, the more adventurous will find a few hidden treasures nestled between the towering residential complexes.

Erzsébetváros, District VII

Named for the beloved wife of **Emperor Franz Joseph,** Erzsébetváros has been the center of Jewish life in Budapest for over 150 years. Almost entirely destroyed during WWII, the area has been in a state of reconstruction since the late '80s. "Elizabeth Town" now boasts some of the city's most beautiful architecture and inviting streets, not to mention to her Great Synagogue and many kosher delis. While the Jewish label remains, unfortunately, many of the area's once flourishing kosher, family-style restaurants have closed due to economic hardship. Although the mealtime establishments have dwindled, Erzsébetváros still plays host to the city's greatest number of ruin pubs, keeping it a bustling and exciting climate during the late night and early morning hours.

Terézváros, District VI

Perhaps the busiest district of Budapest, **Terézváros** hosts an international train station, corporate offices, giant supermarkets, import stores, and the most globally diverse selection of dining opportunities you'll find in the city. The district line begins at **Nyugati station** and extends eastward to **Erzsébet körút** and runs north-to-south along Andrássy út from **Heroes Square** to the **State Opera House.** The area to the south on and near Hajós utca boasts some of the city's coolest new ruin pubs, while **Liszt Ferenc tér,** a few blocks from the **Oktogon,** offers outstanding budget eateries from Hungarian canteen-style joints to fancier sit-down ordeals. As in most cases, a busier environment means more commotion, and while there's no reason to fret on an average day, heed the area around the train station for pickpockets, peddlers, and obnoxious drunks—especially at dawn.

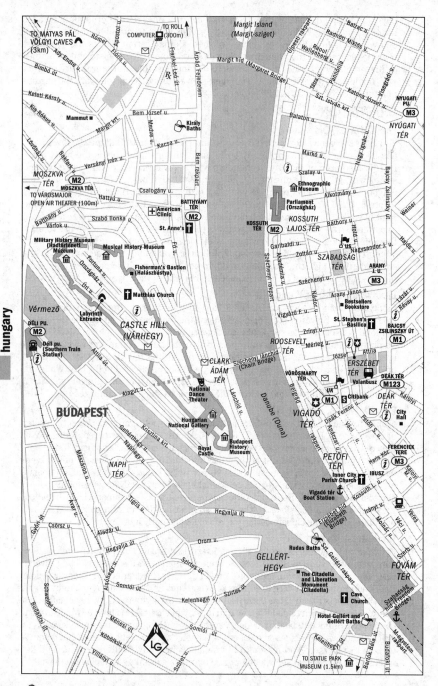

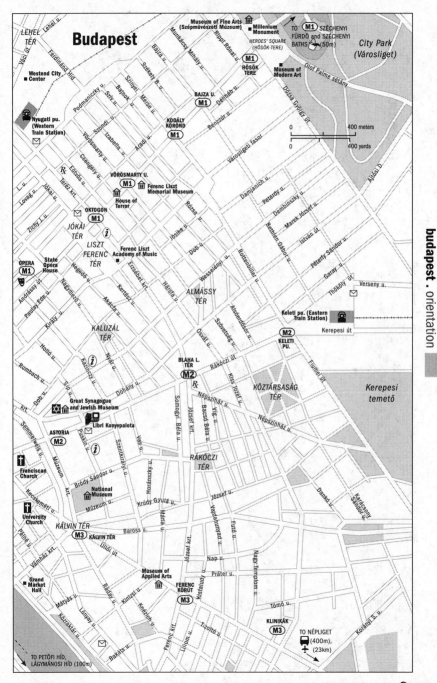

Budapest

LEHEL TÉR

Museum of Fine Arts
(Szépművészeti Múzeum)
Millenium Monument
HEROES' SQUARE
(HŐSÖK-TERE)

TO **M1** SZÉCHENYI
FÜRDŐ and SZÉCHENYI
BATHS (50m)

City Park
(Városliget)

M1
HŐSÖK
TERE

Museum of
Modern Art

Westend City
Center

Nyugati pu.
(Western
Train Station)

BAJZA U.
M1

KODÁLY
KÖRÖND
M1

0   400 meters
0   400 yards

VÖRÖSMARTY U.
M1   Ferenc Liszt
Memorial Museum

House of
Terror

OKTOGON
M1
JÓKAI
TÉR   (i)

LISZT
FERENC
TÉR   Ferenc Liszt
Academy of Music

OPERA
M1   State
Opera
House

KALUZÁL
TÉR

ALMÁSSY
TÉR

Keleti pu. (Eastern
Train Station)

Kerepesi út

M2
KELETI
PU.

Verseny u.

BLAHA L.
TÉR
M2

KÖZTÁRSASÁG
TÉR

Kerepesi
temető

Great Synagogue
and Jewish Museum

Libri Konyvpalota

ASTORIA
M2   (i)

Franciscan
Church

RÁKÓCZI
TÉR

National
Museum

University
Church

KÁLVIN TÉR
M3   KÁLVIN TÉR

Grand
Market
Hall

Museum of
Applied Arts

FERENC
KÖRÚT
M3

KLINIKÁK
M3

TO NÉPLIGET
(400m),
(23km)

TO PETŐFI HÍD,
LÁGYMÁNOSI HÍD (100m)

budapest . orientation

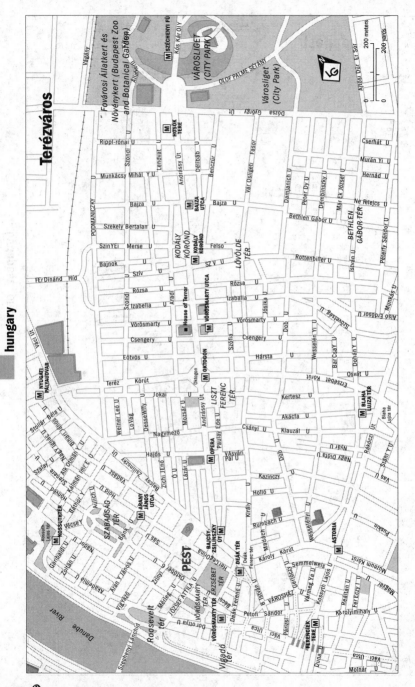

Terézváros

hungary

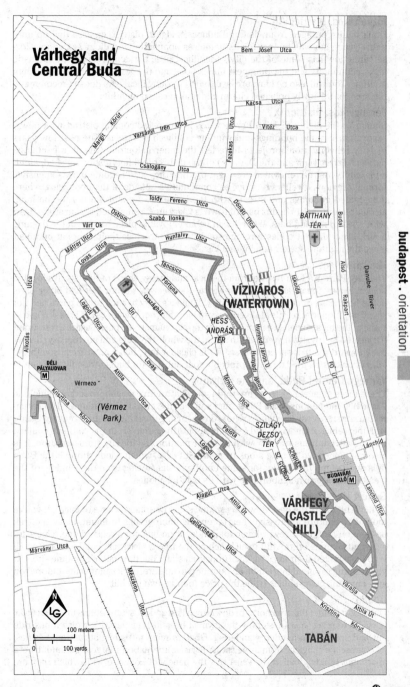

Várhegy and Central Buda

Bem Jósef Utca

Kácsa Utca

Varsányi Irén Utca

Margit Körút

Vitéz Utca

Fazekas Utca

Csalogány Utca

Toldy Ferenc Utca

Donáti Utca

Ostrom

Szabó Ilonka

Várf Ok

BÁTTHANY TÉR

Budai

Mátray Utca

Hunfalvy Utca

Lovas Utca

Iskola

Alsó Rakpart

Táncsics

VÍZIVÁROS (WATERTOWN)

Utca

Logodi Utca

Fortuna

Danube River

Úri

Országház

HESS ANDRÁS TÉR

Hunyadi János Ú

Alkotás

Hunyadi János U

Ponty

Fő Út

DÉLI PÁLYAUDVAR Ⓜ

Attila

Lovas

Táncsics Utca

Krisztina Körút

Vérmezo

Utca

(Vérmez Park)

SZILÁGY DEZSO TÉR

Logodi U

Palota

Lánchíd

Aladár Utca

Attila Út

BUDAVÁRI SIKLÓ Ⓜ

SZ GYORGY

SZINHAZU

Lánchíd Utca

Gellérthegy Utca

Márvány Utca

VÁRHEGY (CASTLE HILL)

Mészáros

Utca

Váralja

Krisztina Körút

Attila Út

N
LG

0   100 meters
0   100 yards

TABÁN

Józsefváros, District VIII

Don't be discouraged from visiting Budapest's eighth district, an area that up until a few years ago was known for its homeless population and dicey sex shops. Józsefváros now has some of the city's friendliest little parks and squares, a fantastic artist community and the Budapest film school, and the gorgeous National Museum building. You will also be hard-pressed to find a young local who doesn't recommend the area for its newly polished charm and underground nightlife.

Ferencváros, District IX

Similar to the eighth district, Ferencváros is an up-and-coming district with newly renovated Baroque buildings and winding cobblestone streets. The past few years of "city rehabilitation" projects have left the inner half-circle (the area contained between **Ferenc körút** and the Danube) of the district looking freshly polished, albeit a bit empty. As the renovated areas get prettier, they also become more expensive, forcing previous dwellers to move to communities outside of the boulevard, where delapidated buildings and streets with the homeless are still the norm. The main attraction for tourists in this part of town is **Ráday utca,** a small pedestrian street lined with restaurants and bars. While it can be an enjoyable place to dine in the evening hours, strict district codes forcing establishments to close their doors at midnight leave the nightlife seeker at a bit of a loss.

The Városliget *City Park*

The City Park is a lush respite from the heat and messy chaos of the city. It's located behind **Heroes' Square** and is the gateway to the freeway roward **Eger** and other parts in the northeastern corner of the country. While it's easy to stick to the parks and not spend any money here, it is also very easy to blow all your savings as the area is home to some of the most expensive restaurants in the city, namely the posh **Gundel,** a restaurant frequented by royalty. If you want to spend the whole day here and are too lazy to walk back toward the **Oktogon** on **Andrássy út** for cheaper fare, make great friends with the *lángos* makers, as fried dough is probably your only bet for budget-friendly gnawing.

Várhegy, Central Buda, and the Vizivaros

These three adjacent districts are Buda's most attractive neighborhoods and include **Castle Hill,** the famous **Chain Bridge,** and some of the city's most authentic Hungarian restaurants. It's easy to spend a whole day perusing the cobblestone streets of Castle Hill, marveling at the view and learning about Hungarian art in the National Gallery. For the adventurous traveler with a day or month pass for city transportation, it is also recommended to take a bus from **Margit Bridge,** which winds through the Buda hills and behind the castle, for some unofficial sightseeing from the window of the wealthy **Rózsadomb** neighborhood with its palatial abodes.

Gellért Hegy *Gellért Hill*

Gellért Hill offers the best view of **Pest** (and some peripheral views of **Buda**). If you're looking to capture impressive, heart-stopping photographs to flaunt, make the trek up here on foot, for a rewarding experience, or on bus, for a relaxed one. There are a few attractions on the hill itself, such as the **Liberty Monument** commemorating all who have risked their lives for the Hungarian state, but they fail to steal the show. If you're going to spend more than an hour or two up here, pack sandwiches before you go—anything being sold is triple the price found down the hill.

Óbuda

Óbuda is a residential area north of downtown **Pest** and most attractions in **Central Buda.** If you're looking to witness how the layman lives in Budapest, it's worth a bus ride out and some open-minded wandering. Óbuda's most intriguing attraction, besides, of course, the magical Roman **Aquincum Ruins,** is the nation's largest communist-era apartment building called the **Panel** (for the panels of concrete with which they are assembled) at **Flórián tér.** A recent restoration project of this panel to make them a little more humane has left Flórián tér a giant block of apartments painted neon green.

Margit-Sziget *Margaret Island*

Margaret Island—an oasis of lush greens, expansive parks and a 5km running loop that wraps around the perimeter—is hands-down the most relaxing place in the city. Mostly a summer haunt for locals and tourists seeking respite from the blazing sun and dirty streets, this place offers something akin to Central Park in New York City, but even better as the river rushes past and building views are almost non-existent. It feels as if you've stumbled into a rain forest big enough to find your own secret nook.

ACCOMMODATIONS

The Belváros

☑ ALL CENTRAL HOSTEL ✈♿📶 HOSTEL [2]

Bécsi u. 2 ☎01 328 0955 💻www.allcentral.hu

A no-frills hostel with friendly staff, sleek metal bunks, pristine bathrooms and unbeatable location and prices. An elevator whisks weary pack-toting travelers up to one of the four floors for a night of urban-style repose. While the place functions as a hostel during the summer months, foreign students might find this the cheapest deal in the city for term-time housing. A couple blocks away from the Parliament building, Danube River, Basilica and Váci utca, this place is a steal.

➜ M1, M2, or M3: Deák Ferenc Tér. Head down Bárczy István utca towards river and turn right on Bécsi utca. ℹ Wi-Fi included. Laundry 800Ft. Kitchen. Luggage and safe included. Lockers available. $ Dorms 3000-5000Ft; doubles 14,000Ft. ⏰ Reception 24hr. Check-out 10am.

☑ THE LOFT HOSTEL ✈♿📶 HOSTEL [2]

Veres Pálné u. 19 ☎01 328 0916 💻www.lofthostel.hu

Gorgeous wood paneling, modern decor, tons of leisure activities to keep you occupied (if you choose to stay inside), and carefully-scrubbed bathrooms make this an oasis from tourism. The giant common room can keep the introverted busy and an energetic clientele will gladly team up for a night out. The helpful staff can point you in the right direction for excursions in and just outside of the city.

➜ M3: Ferenciek Tere. Walk toward river, turn left on Veres Pálné. It's the 3rd street up, parallel to the river. ℹ Wi-Fi included. Kitchen. Printing, DVDs, and games available. $ Dorms 3400-4400Ft. ⏰ Reception 24hr.

Lipótváros

☑ AVENTURA BOUTIQUE HOSTEL ✈⊗📶 HOSTEL [2]

XIII, Visegrádi utca 12. ☎01 239 0782 💻www.aventurahostel.com

The lofted floors of this hostel feel like your neighborhood playground jungle gym. All the beds have locked storage compartments, and a super-friendly staff gladly doles out suggestions on the where- and what-to's. An amply-stocked kitchen offers free snacks, while a laid-back clientele keeps the ruckus at a low frequency.

➜ M3: Nyugati. From the Metro head down Szent István körút toward the river and turn right onto Visegrádi. ℹ Wi-Fi, food, spices, and cooking supplies included. Walking audio guide rental of the entire city 3000-5000Ft. $ Dorms from 3500Ft; doubles 11,000Ft. ⏰ Reception 24hr. Flexible check-out.

☑ THE GROOVE HOSTEL ✈⊗📶 HOSTEL [2]

XIII, Szent István krt 16. ☎01 786 8038 💻www.groovehostel.hu

This hostel has inviting hardwood floors, a cheery interior, plush cubes and beanbags scattered around, and views of downtown Budapest that leave other hostels in the dust. Check out the TV loft above the reception desk or head next door to the famous Comedy Theater for a night of laughs.

➜ M3: Nyugati. From the Metro head down Szent István krt towards the river; the hostel will be on your right. ℹ Wi-Fi, lockers, and linens included. $ Dorms from 2700Ft. ⏰ Reception 24hr.

Erzsébetváros

👍 10 BEDS — HOSTEL ❷

Erzsébet krt 15. ☎01 3620 933 59 65

Feels like you've stumbled into a long-lost cousin's apartment. A happy and friendly hostel where long-term guests sometimes become quasi-staff members and welcome you to the city with a trip to a bath or a pub crawl. Eat your breakfast at the stylish new bar or take a bath in the relaxing tub.

*➡ M2: Blaha Lujza tér. Head north on Erzsébet krt from the Metro for a block and a half; the hostel is on your right. **i** Laundry, lockers, linens, and Wi-Fi included. $ Dorms from 3000Ft. ⏰ Reception 24hr.*

THUMBS UP HOSTEL — HOSTEL ❷

Kertész utca 18. ☎01 3630 318 44 43 🖥www.thumbsuphostel.com

A great deal in the center of town. Two giant common rooms give you something to do for a night and comfy beds at a low price will make you sleep like a baby. A giant flatscreen and loads of DVDs will make you feel right at home. Head to the kitchen to chat with the laid-back clientele.

*➡ M2: Blaha Lujza tér. Head north on Erzsébet krt and veer left at the first intersection; the hostel is near the corner of Kertész and Wesselényi. **i** Breakfast, Wi-Fi, lockers, and linens included. Towels 300Ft. Laundry 2000Ft. Quiet after 10pm. $ Dorms from 2500Ft; doubles from 4500Ft. ⏰ Reception 24hr. Check-out 11am.*

Terézváros

👍 HOME-MADE HOSTEL — HOSTEL ❷

Teréz Körút 22 ☎01 302 21 03 🖥www.homemadehostel.com

A happy, earthy, and surprisingly quiet little hostel in an apartment building on the main boulevard a block from the Oktogon. Extremely friendly staff cooks delicious food a few times per week to ease you into Hungarian living. Antique TVs, radios, rugs, and no bunks give a unique experience for the traveler looking for a safe and sound stay.

*➡ M1: Oktogon. From the Metro, take Teréz krt east from Oktogon; the hostel is on your left. **i** Scooter rental. Towels, linens, and Wi-Fi included. Locker deposit 1000Ft. $ Dorms from 3600Ft; doubles from 12,000Ft. ⏰ Reception 24hr.*

👍 BROADWAY HOSTEL — HOSTEL ❷

Ó street 24-26 ☎01 688 16 62 🖥www.broadwayhostel.hu

Your name won't be in lights on Broadway, but you'll find a hammock in the courtyard to hang in and wonderfully comfortable beds upon which to sleep away your traveling hardships. Smaller rooms make the experience more personal and each bed has its own giant cupboard that locks. The location is perhaps one of the most happening streets in town and you can't miss the building covered in murals and colorful—intentional—graffiti.

➡ M1: Opera. From the Metro head north on Hajós utca and take the 1st right; hostel is on the left and adorned by graffiti. $ 10- to 16-bed dorms from 3300Ft. ⏰ Reception 24hr.

Józsefváros

👍 MANDRAGORA BOUTIQUE HOSTEL — HOSTEL ❷

Krúdy Gyula utca 12. ☎01 789 95 15 🖥www.mandragorahostel.com

This phenomenal budget option doesn't offer dorm rooms, but there is no place in the city, especially with such a great location, that offers private singles and doubles for less. Its gorgeous interior decor looks like something out of a magazine and most of the rooms come with a bathtub. A kitchen and common dining room give the communality of a hostel, but the retreat into a private space gives you the comfort of home.

*➡ M2: Blaha Lujza tér. Across from the Metro. **i** Wi-Fi included. TV and DVDs available in the common area. $ Singles from 5500Ft; doubles from 8000Ft. ⏰ Reception 24hr. Check-out 11am.*

hungary

Ferencváros

MAXIM HOSTEL — HOSTEL [2]

Ráday utca 34 ☎01 2360 404 02 22 💻www.maximhostel.com

Maxim is a new hostel located on the main street of Ferencváros, Ráday. Amazing wooden beds will help you rest easy under crazy wall murals. A spacious bathtub will wash the city grime off your skin and help you relax from the energy of the street. Cool movie theater seats in the common area provide a fun repose and the staff is always on hand to give advice about the city. Occasional free Hungarian meals cooked by staff members cap off an unbeatable deal.

➡ M3: Ferenc körút. From the station, head west on Üllői and make a left at Kinizsi utca. The hostel is on the corner of Knizsi and Ráday. ℹ Wi-Fi, linens, towels, and breakfast included. $ Dorms from 2250Ft; doubles from 7000Ft. 🕐 Reception 24hr.

Gellért Hegy

BUDA BASE — HOSTEL [2]

Döbrentei utca 16 ☎01 3620 543 74 81

Probably the coolest location to stay in this city. At the foot of Gellért Hill you can see the **Liberty Statue, Parliament, Chain Bridge,** and the beautiful buildings lining Pest's shore from your window. Two- and eight-bed dorms usually cost the same and depend on availability. A spacious living room that opens to the kitchen and dining room decorated with the owner's personal furniture give the place an inviting feel. Don't let the Buda location deter you: Pest's buzzing streets are only a 10min. walk away.

➡ Tram 18 or 19: Döbrentei tér. From the tram stop, head south toward the square. ℹ Lockers and linens included. Free Internet and Wi-Fi extends into the garden so you can surf the net in the cool breeze. $ 2- to 8-bed dorms 2000-3300Ft; doubles 8200-10,950Ft. 🕐 Reception 24hr.

SIGHTS

The Belváros

GRAND MARKET HALL (NAGYCSARNOK) — MARKET

Váci utca and Vámház körút

While it looks more like the Nyugati train station, this hall was built in 1894 to emulate the trend of indoor markets in major Western European cities. If you are looking for legit local fruits and veggies, though, don't be fooled by this tourist trap, and head instead to the Buda side markets for a better value. Grand Market Hall *is* worth a trip to witness the infamous Hungarian assertiveness and to gawk at the arched windows, colorfully tiled roof, and Hungarian folk costume peddlers. If you do end up doling out some cash, be sure to haggle like crazy. Head downstairs for some fish and pickled delicacies like pearl onion, stuffed paprika, and cabbage.

➡ M3: Kálvin Tér. From the Metro take Vámház toward the river. 🕐 Open M 6am-5pm, Tu-F 6am-6pm, Sa 6am-2pm.

UNIVERSITY CHURCH — CHURCH

Papnövelde utca 7

Once the site of a Turkish mosque, University Square is accented by the glowing orange Baroque architecture of University Church, built in 1725. Pauline monks spent 17 years building and then perfecting every nook and cranny of the church, while hiding valuable goblets and costumes in the cupboards lining the interior. This easy-to-miss chapel is between rows of tall buildings and several streets up from the main downtown tourist area, but is worth a gander if you like secret spots. Take it easy under one of the trees in front of the church, or head inside and marvel at its unsung glory.

➡ M3: Ferenciek tere. From the Metro head east on Kecskeméti utca and turn right on Papnövelde. 🕐 Services M-F 7am and 6pm, Su 8am, 9am, 11am, 12:30pm, 5pm, 7:30pm.

ERZSÉBET TÉR ♿🌳 CITY PARK

The largest green space in the downtown Pest area, this unassuming chunk of nature has undergone a series of name changes. Initially Queen Elizabeth Square, it became New Square, and then changed to simply Market Place. After WWII it became Stalin Square, then Engels Square from 1953, until its final christening as Elizabeth Square in 1990. An overeager administration planned to construct the new National Theatre Concert Hall at the site just over a decade ago—much to the dismay of the city—and even broke ground just before they were ousted from office. The beginnings of the dig were abandoned and residents began referring to the gaping hole in the middle of the downtown as "*gödör*" (pothole). Fortunately, an ambitious urban renewal project has turned the area into the city's most beloved park, equipped with rolling picnicking greens and a twinkling pool-fountain. The multi-function **Gödör Klub** hosts art shows and live music in what was once intended as a theater. Sit and enjoy the hum of melodies, the smell of *kolbász* grilling, and the grind of skate punks ripping past, with a cold brew and amiable company.

M1-3: Deák Tér.

Lipótváros

ORSZÁGHAZ (PARLIAMENT) GOVERNMENT BUILDING

Plaza Kossuth ☎01 441 4000 www.parlament.hu

"The motherland does not have a house," lamented Hungarian poet Mihály Vörösmarty in 1846. In response to the growing sense of Hungarian nationalism during the period, the palatial Gothic building looks more like a cathedral than a seat of government. The building is the largest in Hungary and towers at 96m, a number symbolizing the date of Hungary's millenial anniversary. The building once required more electricity than the rest of the city combined to supply power to its 692 rooms. The gold and marble interior shines proudly on the original Holy Crown of Hungary.

M2: Kossuth Tér. Head towards the river. ℹ *Tours start at Gate XII. Tours last about 50min.* $ *Entrance and tour 2850Ft, students 1410Ft, free with EU passport. Ask a guard for permission to buy a ticket at Gate X.* ⏰ *English-language tours daily 10am, noon, 2pm; buy tickets early, especially in summer. Ticket office opens at 8am.*

SAINT STEPHEN'S BASILICA (SZT. ISTVÁN BAZILIKA) CHURCH

Hercegprímás utca 7

Completed in 1905 after 50 years of construction, this towering monument and its majestic cupola smile on Budapest's Wall Street. Built in the Neo-Renaissance style, the edifice was damaged during the siege of Budapest in WWII and has undergone a series of renovations. The red-green marble and gilded interior attracts both local worshippers and gaping tourists who come to see the Panorama Tower and the highest 360° view of the city. The Basilica's most prized treasure is St. Stephen's mummified right hand, removed from his body by a priest and hidden in the countryside until it was stolen during WWII and subsequently returned. A 100ft donation dropped in the box will illuminate the hand for 2min.!

Metro to Deák Tér. Follow the signs. $ *Church free. Tower 500Ft, students 400Ft.* ⏰ *Church open daily 7am-7pm. Chapel May-Oct M-Sa 9am-5pm, Su 1-5pm; Nov-Apr M-Sa 10am-4pm. Mass M-Sa 8am and 6pm, Su 8, 9, 10am, noon, 6, 7:30pm. Tower open daily Apr-Oct M-Sa 10am-6pm.*

LIBERTY SQUARE ♿🌳 SQUARE

Szabadság Tér 8-9 ☎01 428 2752 www.english.mnb.hu

Built on the site of a former prison facility meant to tame rebellious Hungarians, the square is now a green space with benches and a cafe. It also contains the only remaining Soviet monument in Budapest proper, a massive obelisk commemorating the Russian soldiers who liberated the city from the Germans in WWII. Nearby, the

Hungarian National Bank's elegant facade and the American Embassy ironically (or symbolically) stand face-to-face with the red star-topped obelisk.

✣ *M3: Arany János. Directly diagonal from the Metro toward the river.*

Erzsébetváros

GOZSDU UDVAR
WALKWAY

Between Király utca 13. and Dob utca 16   ▣www.culture.hu

A 200m stretch of six connected courtyards under six apartment and office buildings, the walkway feels like a secret little market with restaurants, cafes, shops and a stage for concerts, comedy, and promo events in almost every courtyard. Perfect for a cool respite from the summer heat or a warm, friendly place in the winter to amble in the energy of Budapest's coolest locals.

✣ *M1: Oktogon. Head east on Erzsébet krt and turn right on Király utca.* ⓘ *Summer months bring open-air concerts and events.*

SYNAGOGUE AND JEWISH MUSEUM
☺& MUSEUM, SYNAGOGUE

Corner of Dohány utca and Wesselényi utca.   ☎3670 533 5696 ▣www.greatsynagogue.hu

The largest synagogue in Europe and the second-largest in the world, Pest's Great Synagogue (Zsinagóga) was built in 1859 and heavily damaged during WWII when the Nazis used it as a radio base during the Siege of Budapest. The 20-year effort to restore the towering onion domes and Moorish Revival-style building is only now coming to a head. The enormous metal weeping willow called the Tree of Life stands in the courtyard as a beautiful Holocaust memorial. Next door, the Jewish Museum (Zsidó Múzeum), built at the birthplace of Zionist Theodor Herzel, displays Budapest's most prominent Jewish artifacts.

✣ *M2: Astoria.* ⓘ *Covered shoulders required. Men must cover their heads inside; yarmulkes available at the entrance. Admission to museum included with entrance to the synagogue.* ⓢ *1400Ft, students 750Ft. Tours 1900Ft/1600Ft.* ⓩ *Open May-Oct M-Th 10am-5pm, F 10am-2pm, Su 10am-2pm; Nov-Apr M-Th 10am-3pm, F 10am-1pm, Su 10am-1pm. Services F 6pm. First entry 10:30am. Tours M-Th 10:30am-3:30pm every 30min.; F and Su 10:30, 11:30am, 12:30pm.*

Terézváros

ANDRÁSSY ÚT
BOULEVARD

Hungary's grandest boulevard, **Andrássy út** extends from **Erzsébet tér** northeast to **Heroes' Square** (*Hősök tér*). Its elegant gardens and balconies, laid out in 1872 and renovated after the fall of the Iron Curtain in 1989, recall the grandeur of Budapest's Golden Age. While the Metro runs directly under the boulevard, it would be a shame to miss the walk, which takes you past rows of UNESCO-preserved buildings. At the intersection with **Felsőerdősor utca, Kodály körönd** is surrounded by beautifully painted buildings and statues of three of Hungary's greatest Ottoman-killers as well as a poet who celebrated the anti-Ottoman exploits of the other three when he wasn't celebrating more erotic exploits.

NYUGATI PÁLYAUDVAR
GRASSY KNOLL

A brand-spanking new nook next to the train station, transformed from a parking lot to a grassy knoll for reading and lounging, along with a terrace for nightlife activities. Revel in the beautiful architecture of Nyugati as a backdrop for this secret little respite off the main boulevard. The venue boasts two cafes and bars and is an up-and-coming host to live concerts, plays, and broadcasts.

✣ *M 1-3: Nyugati pályaudvar. At the intersection of Teréz körút, Szent István körút, Váci út, and Bajcsy-Zsilinszky út.*

EIFFEL TÉR
➹&(ⁿ)♈☺ RAILWAY STATION
▣www.eiffelter.hu

This railway station is smaller than its eastern cousin, though it has the advantage of being in a neighborhood you'll actually want to visit. The building was designed and built by the Eiffel Co., though it's notably less phallic than the company's Parisian masterpiece. The station itself is a beautiful Baroque construction connected to the most lavish McDonald's you'll ever see.

➡ *M 1-3: Nyugati pályaudvar. To the right of the station if you're looking at the big clock.*

The Városliget

👍 HŐSÖK TERE (HEROES' SQUARE) ♿ MONUMENT

At the Heroes' Square end of Andrássy út, the **Millennium Monument** commemorates Hungary's heroes. Built for the city's millennial celebration, the sweeping structure dominates the square. The pillar in the center is topped by the Archangel Gabriel, presenting the Hungarian crown to St. Stephen. At its base are equestrian statues of the seven chieftains said to be the leaders of the Magyar tribes that settled the Carpathian Basin. The pillar and the surrounding structures contain statues of other national heroes: it's a veritable hit parade of awesome hats through the ages from St. Stephen to King Matthias Corvinus. During the summer, concerts and other events are often held in the square and in the winter an area of the square functions as an ice rink. The square is flanked by the Museum of Fine Arts on the left and the Palace of Art on the right.

➡ *M1:Hősök tere. You can't miss it!*

👍 SZÉCHENYI-GYÓGYFÜRDŐ (SZÉCHENYI BATHS) 🎟♿🍸⛅ BATH, MONUMENT

Állatkerti körút 11 ☎01 363 32 10 💻www.szechenyibath.com

Statues and a fountain adorn the Neo-Baroque exterior of the biggest and one of the most luxurious bath complexes in Europe. A popular destination for locals and tourists alike, you could spend an entire day just relaxing in the swimming pool. Those looking to exercise their minds while their bodies unwind can challenge older intellectuals to a game of chess. Be warned that the games are often intense; don't be surprised if you find yourself surrounded by eager spectators. After your embarrassing defeat, swim away in shame and treat yourself to a consolation massage. The complex's 12 pools and three thermal baths mean you can probably avoid everyone who saw you lose.

➡ *M1: Széchenyi Fürdő.* ℹ *Bring your own bathing suit and towel.* $ *Swimming pool 2500Ft per 2hr., 2800Ft per day. Thermal tub tickets 1500Ft per day. Massages from 2000Ft.* ⏰ *Open daily 6am-10pm.*

SZÉPMŰVÉSZETI MÚZEUM (MUSEUM OF FINE ARTS) 🎟♿ MUSEUM

Hősök tere ☎01 469 71 00 www.szepmuveszeti.hu

Built to look like a worn temple from antiquity, this building's exterior is as much a work of art as the collections it houses. The museum's main focus is a large collection of Italian and Renaissance pieces. Many of Europe's artistic luminaries can be found here, from **Giotto** and **Bruegel** to **Monet** and **Rodin.** An excellent collection of Dutch work appears on the top floor. The basement juxtaposes the modern art collection with an awe-inspiring Egyptian collection focusing on all things mummified. Some of the striking pieces include mummified hawks, cats, and alligators. One of the museum's prized pieces, a magic wand that looks something like a boomerang, was once used to protect children and expectant mothers from harm.

➡ *M1: Hősök tere.* $ *1400Ft, students 700Ft.* ⏰ *Open Tu-Su 10am-6pm. Ticket booth open Tu-Su 10am-5pm.*

Várhegy, Central Buda, and the Vizivaros

👍 ROYAL PALACE 🚫🎟🚫♿ MUSEUM

Szent György tér 2

Towering above the Danube on Várhegy, the Castle District has had something of a rough history. Built between the 12th and 14th centuries, the original castle was occupied by the Ottoman invaders, who turned it into barracks and then left it to decay. During the campaign to retake Buda by the allied Christian forces, much of the palace was destroyed by heavy artillery bombardment. It wasn't until the middle of the 18th century that the palace was completely rebuilt, only to be destroyed again less than a century later, when the Hungarian revolutionary army laid siege to it during the 1848 revolution. In the last decades of the 19th century, the palace became one of the most lavish royal residences in the world. For the Hungarians, it was an emblem of national pride. For the Axis forces at the end of WWII, it was the best place to stage a last-ditch defense of the city against the advancing Red Army. Once again, heavy artillery reduced the palace to smoldering wreckage. The communists saw the ruined Royal Palace as a symbol of the old regime and completely gutted its interior. Today Buda Castle version 4.0 closely resembles its Hapsburg incarnation, with flowery courtyards, statues, and panoramic views of the rest of the city. The interior of the palace now houses the **National Széchényi Library** as well as some of the city's finest museums.

M1, M2, or M3: Deák tér. From the Metro, take bus #16 across the Danube. Or, from M2: Moszkva tér, walk up to the hill on Várfok u. "Becsi kapu" marks the castle entrance.

FISHERMAN'S BASTION (HALÁSZBÁSTYA) — MONUMENT

Szentháromság tér

Named for the fisherman's guild that was charged with defending this stretch of Castle Hill during the Middle Ages, Fisherman's Bastion is, despite its parapets and towers, a purely decorative structure. Frigyes Schulek, the same architect who restored Matthias Church, designed the bastion with a melange of Neo-Gothic and Neo-Romanesque elements that harmonize with the surrounding structures. The seven towers represent the seven Magyar chiefs who first settled Hungary in 896. The view of Parliament, St. Stephen, and downtown Pest is breathtaking, especially at sunset and at night.

In front of Matthias Church, walk toward the river. $ Daytime 300Ft, nighttime free.

MATTHIAS CHURCH (MÁTYÁS TEMPLOM) — CHURCH

Szentháromság tér 2 — www.matyas-templom.hu

The colorful roof of Matthias Church on Castle Hill is one of Budapest's most photographed sights. The church was converted to a mosque in 1541, but 145 years later, the Hapsburgs defeated the Turks, sacked the city, and then reconverted the building, in that order. The church's decorations reflect its mixed heritage. Inside, intricate geometric patterns line the walls alongside murals by famed painter Károly Lotz, who also decorated the ceiling of the State Opera House. Facing the altar, turn left and you will find the tombs of **King Béla III** and his first wife, the only tombs in the church to survive the Ottoman occupation; in 1967, archeologists stripped the bodies of their royal jewelery to be included in the National Museum. Ascend the spiral steps to view the exhibits of the **Museum of Ecclesiastical Art,** where you'll find plenty of gold and a replica of the Hungarian crown, complete with a slanted cross.

*Bus #16, 16a and 116: Szentháromság tér. Or Morada: Estação acessível. Both take you right to the church. **i** Because of extensive renovations that may extend into 2011, the church's normal hours of operation change daily. Check online prior to visit to confirm. $ Church and museum 750Ft, students 500Ft. ⏰ Open M-F 9am-5pm, Sa 9am-2:30pm, Su 1-5pm. High Mass M-Sa 7, 8:30am, 6pm; Su 7, 8:30, 10am, noon, 6pm.*

SZÉCHENYI CHAIN BRIDGE (SZÉCHENYI LÁNCHÍD) — BRIDGE

Built in 1849, the Széchenyi Chain Bridge was the first permanent bridge across the Danube in Budapest and one of the longest bridges in the world. At the time of its construction, it was a sensation in Budapest, its imperious structure symbolizing Hungary's national awakening. During WWII, the Chain Bridge (along with every other bridge in the city) was destroyed by the retreating Axis forces, and was later rebuilt with a pair of noble-looking lions flanks at either end of the abutments. A popular myth states that the sculptor forgot to give the lions tongues and that the public's merciless mocking caused him to throw himself into the Danube. In reality, the tongues are just hard to see from below. At the Buda end of the bridge you can see the Zero Kilometer Stone that marks the place from which all Hungarian highways are measured.

MAGYAR NEMZETI GALÉRIA (HUNGARIAN NATIONAL GALLERY) ♿ MUSEUM

Buda Palace, wings A, B, C, and D ☎01 356 0049 🖳www.mng.hu

The halls of Buda Castle now house the world's largest collection of Hungarian fine arts. Spread across three floors and divided by historical period, the permanent collection traces the development of Hungarian painting and sculpture from the Gothic period to the second half of the 20th century. The collections of painters like Gyárfás Jenő and Károly Lotz are some of the museum's best, though it's the sculptures that stop hearts and open minds. In the 20th century galleries, look for pieces by Impressionist **Béla Czóbel.** The basement of the museum contains the crypt of the Hapsburg palantines, though admission can only be obtained through prior arrangement with a guide.

Hike up or take the tram to Buda Castle. The museum is housed in the giant building that you couldn't possibly miss. $ Museum 900Ft. Hapsburg crypt 600Ft. ⏰ Open Tu-Su 10am-6pm. Last entry 30min. before close.

wet and wild

I took a bath for the first time since I've been in Budapest today. Today marks my one-month-and-one-week in this city. Now before you start scrunching up your pretty little noses in your primly scrubbed apartments, fully-equipped with hot showers and clean toilets, I'd like to clarify that this was a special type of bath—yes, I have showered and kept myself tidy since I've been here, thank you very much. What I am talking about here are the magnificent, magical, surreal, entrancing, phenomenally orgasmic Turkish baths where you can float around for hours in warm mineral water and rub elbows with sexy septuagenarians.

The bath I went to, **Széchenyi,** is housed in a beautiful building in the center of the City Park and is the only bath where you can witness said 70-year-old men playing chess on floating chess boards. I'm not sure if you've ever seen a cat play an accordion, but it's kind of like that. Anyway, I seriously recommend bathing when in Budapest. It will make you feel even more refreshed than half an hour of Bikram yoga and provide you with a tale you could never tell your grandchildren. It will be that wild.

-Vanda Gyuris

KIRÁLY BATHS (KIRÁLY FÜRDŐ) ♿ BATH

Fő utca 82-84 ☎01 202 3688 🖳www.spasbudapest.com

Tiny holes in the top of the giant cupola draw in delicately crafted lines of light, producing the sensation that you're bathing inside Heaven's gates. Construction began on the monumental Király Baths by order of the Pasha of Buda in 1565. Unlike most of the area baths, the Király Baths are not connected directly to the thermal springs, taking water from another nearby bath instead. The Pasha ordered them built far from the springs so that bathing could continue even during an inevitable siege by Christian forces. Renovated and rebuilt after damage from WWII, the Király baths, perhaps more than any other in the city, evoke the spirit of the Turkish tradition with their crescent-topped domes and octagonal bath surrounded by pillars.

Trams #4, 6. From the tram stop, take south Frankel Leó utca; it will become Fő utca. i Bathing-suit rental available. $ 2100Ft. Open daily M 8am-7pm (women only), Tu 9am-8pm (men only), W 8am-7pm (women only), Th-Sa 9am-8pm (men only), Su 9am-8pm.

CASTLE LABYRINTHS (BUDAVÁRI LABIRINTUS) — LABYRINTH

Úri utca 9 or Lovas út 4/a. ☎01 212 0207 www.labirintus.com

Formed naturally by thermal springs that extend 1200m underground, the Castle Labyrinths were once home to Neanderthals. For a time, the caves served as personal wine cellars for the residents of Castle Hill. In the 1930s, the tunnels were connected and expanded to create a bomb shelter that housed up to 10,000 people. Nowadays, the caves have been converted into a series of chambers that toe the line between museum and haunted house. The caves are divided into several themed sections filled with decorations of dubious authenticity, including cave paintings and statues. Most memorable, perhaps, is a fountain of red wine that the wise are advised not to drink and the foolish are likely to splatter on their clothes. The final stretch of labyrinth, named the **Labyrinth of Another World,** is a bizarre mix of social and self-reflexive critique centered on "artifacts" like enormous stone Coke bottles from a species of man called "Homo Consumes."

M1, M2, or M3: Deák tér. The labyrinths are toward the opposite end of Castle Hill from the Royal Palace. i Not the best place for those claustrophobic types. The best time to visit the labyrinths is between 6 and 7:30pm, when they turn out the lights and hand out woefully and comically ineffective oil lamps. Children under 14 and people with heart conditions are advised not to take part in the spooky festivities. $ 2000Ft, students 1500Ft. Open daily 9:30am-7:30pm.

Gellért Hegy

LIBERTY MONUMENT (SZABADSÁG SZOBOR) — MONUMENT

Gellért Hill

Visible from all over the city, Budapest's Liberty Monument has a complicated history. One story goes that the figure was originally designed to hold a propeller by the order of Regent Horthy, Hungary's right-wing leader during the interwar period. Before anyone got around to building the statue, however, the Soviets had "liberated" a then-grateful Budapest, which replaced the propeller with a palm leaf and dedicated the statue to their Soviet heroes. After half a century of communist rule, the citizens of Budapest no longer felt quite so liberated, and, in 1989, the statue of a Soviet soldier was relocated from the base of the monument to Memento Park. The monument was rededicated to everyone who has ever fought for Hungary's freedom and success. The steep hike up the mountain is worth the trek for an unparalleled panorama of the city and surrounding neighborhoods.

The monument is at the top of the hill, near the Citadella. i Only wheelchair-accessible if you take bus #27 from Moricz Zsigmond.

HOTEL GELLÉRT AND GELLÉRT BATHS — BATH

Szent Gellért tér 1 ☎01 466 61 66 www.spasbudapest.com

At the foot of Gellért Hill and directly facing the green Szabadság Bridge, the world-famous hotel was built in the Vienna Secession style and incorporates gorgeous elements of the then-emerging Art Nouveau. While the hotel itself is probably beyond most student budgets, the equally famous adjoining baths are certainly not. Probably the most popular of the Buda baths for tourists, the Gellért Baths feature a richly tiled interior with statues and columns surrounding the main bath. Outside, an enormous sitting bath is popular with visitors of all ages.

Tram #49: Szent Gellért tér. i Bathing-suit and towel rental available. Check www.danubiushotels.com for hotel details. $ Admission with locker 3500Ft. Open M-F 6am-7pm, Sa 6am-10pm, Su 6am-8pm. Last entry 1hr. before close.

THE CITADELLA

VIEW

Citadella Sétány 1 ☎01 279 19 63 www.citadella.hu

This structure was originally built by the gloating Hapsburgs after the failed 1848 revolution to remind Hungarians who was in charge. The angled walls occupy most of the hill's plateau and must have provided the imperial soldiers garrisoned there with great views of the city that resented them. During WWII, the interior was converted into a massive, three-level air-raid shelter, which served as one of the strong points for the German and Hungarian forces during the bloody Siege of Budapest. Today, the Citadella is home to a luxury hotel and expensive restaurant. The former air-raid shelter contains an overpriced museum filled with wax figures depicting scenes from the war, ranging from not very to quite interesting. During the summer, the surrounding area is swamped with food vendors and souvenir stands. If you can, go at night to take in the view in relative peace.

The citadella is at the top of the hill, near the Liberty Monument. $ 1200Ft. Museum open daily May-Sept 9am-8pm, Oct-Apr 9am-5pm.

Óbuda

PÁL-VÖLGYI AND MÁTYÁS CAVES

CAVES

☎01 325 95 05 www.caving.hu

Budapest is famous for its thermal baths, but few people know that the heated water that eats up entire afternoons has also spent hundreds of thousands of years eating through the limestone hills beneath the city. The result: over 100km of caves directly below many of Budapest's residential areas. The second longest of Hungary's cave systems, the Pál-völgyi and Mátyás Caves offer the unskilled numerous spelunking opportunities. The no-climbing walking tours are informative and interesting without asking you to do anything more stressful than climb a short ladder. These walks descend 30m below the surface, where you'll see many dripstones and even the occasional 40-million-year-old fossil. Many people bring a sweater, though during the hot summer nothing feels better than descending into the caves, which keep cool at 50°F all year long. Those looking for something a little more challenging should consider taking on The Sandwich of Death.

Bus #86: Kolosy tér. From the stop, backtrack up the street and take the 1st right to reach the bus station. From there, catch bus #65 to get to the caves. i Bring warm clothing. English tours available; call ahead for times. $ 1050Ft, students 785Ft. Open Tu-Sa 10am-4pm. Tours every hr.

AQUINCUM RUINS

RUINS

Szentendrei út 135 ☎01 250 16 50 www.aquincum.hu

Long before the mighty Magyars settled the Carpathian basin, the Roman Empire had a thriving settlement of 40,000 inhabitants on this spot. The ruins of this ancient settlement can be seen all over northern Buda. The Military Amphitheater at the corner of Lajos utca and Pacsirtamező utca in Óbuda is especially awesome. The largest collection of ruins can be found at the **Aquincumi Múzeum,** just north of Budapest proper. The museum includes thousands of artifacts from the town like pottery, bricks, and jewelry. Upstairs, an exhibit recreates parts of the proconsul's palace as well as the famed Aquincum organ. Outside, you can explore more than an acre of ruins, including the workshops of various craft guilds. When in the former Roman Empire, do as the former Romans did and spend an afternoon hanging around the former thermal baths.

From Batthyány tér, take the HÉV 7 stops to Aquincum, then get off and backtrack about 0.5km; the ruins and museum are on your left. $ 1300Ft, students 500Ft. Museum open Apr 16-30 Tu-Sa 10am-5pm, May-Sept daily 10am-6pm, Oct Tu-Sa 10am-5pm. Park open Apr 16-Oct 9am-dusk.

Outer Buda

✓ MEMENTO PARK (SZOBORPARK)

♿ MONUMENT

On the corner of Balatoni út and Szabadkai utca. 🖳www.mementopark.hu

While in the rest of the former Soviet republics people were happily dismantling and demolishing the symbols of their hated regimes, the monument-loving people of Budapest decided it might be worthwhile to keep theirs around, even if they didn't want them anywhere near the city itself. Forty of these statues now reside a bus ride away in Memento Park *(25min.)* as a testament to a bygone political and artistic period. At the gates to the park you can see an authentic replica of the infamous Stalin statue that was torn down so thoroughly during the 1956 revolution that only the dictator's boots remained; the remains of the statue became a symbol of the revolution. Other notable statues include a striking metallic mass of bayonet-wielding soldiers charging past a podium as well as the deranged-looking Soviet soldier that used to stand at the base of the Liberty Monument, clutching his Soviet flag and machine gun. An indoor exhibition shows unnerving clips from old secret police training videos. If you pay attention, you may even learn a thing or two about how to hide secret messages in crushed soda cans.

⇟ Express bus #7: Etele tér. From the stop, take the yellow Volán bus from terminal #7 bound for Diosd-Érd and get off at Memento Park. You'll need to buy a separate ticket from the Volánbusz ticket office. There is also a white direct bus from Deák tér (1, 2, or 3) Jan-June and Sept-Dec daily 11am, July-Aug daily 11am, 3pm for 3950Ft, students 2450Ft; includes price of admission and return ticket. $ 1500Ft, students 1000Ft. ⏰ Open daily 10am-dusk.

Margit-Sziget

RUINS

♿ RUINS

Margit Sziget

Though it may be hard to imagine now, there was once a time when the island was used for something besides outdoor drinking and sunbathing. For several centuries, Margaret Island was the place to be cloistered in Budapest. The Franciscans were the first on the scene, building their priory in the 13th century only to have it destroyed under the Ottomans in the 16th century. King Béla IV built a convent during the height of the Mongol invasion in the 13th century. At that time, he vowed to send his daughter, Margaret, to the convent if he ever had the chance to rebuild the country after the Mongol assault, though nobody seemed to have consulted Margaret on this arrangement. When the Mongols were finally beaten back, the king made good on his vow and sent his 11-year-old daughter to become a nun. While taking orders may not have done much for Margaret's social life, at least it guaranteed her a kind of immortality when the island was renamed after her death. Today, you can still see the ruins of both structures. Princess Margaret is buried at the site of the old nave.

⇟ Take the main road from the Margit Bridge entrance. You'll pass the Franciscan priory 1st, on your left, between the Hajós Alfréd Swimming Pool and the Palatinus Baths. The convent is farther along, on your right near the water tower.

ZENÉLŐ SZÖKŐKÚT (MUSIC FOUNTAIN)

♿ FOUNTAIN

Margit Sziget

Built in 1936, the Musical Fountain consists of multiple waterjets choreographed to music from nearby speakers. Even if you can't make out the music, the sight of the jets pulsing and changing is mesmerizing. A favorite of local parkgoers, the Musical Fountain attracts visitors who love to set up picnics and hookahs in the shaded area nearby. At night, colorful lights add a whole new dimension to the show. While the sight of the enormous central jet is certainly impressive, perhaps someone should tell UNESCO that the island's beloved musical fountain is actually just a copy of an older fountain built by a Transylvanian handyman.

⇟ From the Margit Bridge entrance, take the main road north; the fountain is just past the statue.

Outside Budapest

VISEGRÁD

Visegrád is a tiny town in Pest County home to the summer palace of King Matthias Corvinus of Hungary. Its main attraction is the two-part 13th century castle nearby. The center of the lower castle area is adorned by the giant Solomon Tower that was once a royal residence and now houses the **King Matthias Museum of Visegrád.** A trip to Visegrád would not be complete without a visit to the Royal Palace that was originally built in the early 14th century and later completely reconstructed by King Matthias Corvinus in the 15th century. Considering it was a vacation spot of one of the most powerful leaders in Hungary's history, the building is quite unassuming and looks more like a Mediterranean villa than a royal palace. Only limited rooms in the building's interior are open to the public, but they're worth the visit to marvel at the king's jewels. Without a doubt the most fun to be had in the area is the summer bob-sledding course on **Mogyoró Hill.** Check the tourist office for information.

✠ *Buses depart from Árpád híd bus station in Budapest every 30min. No trains go to Visegrád. The bus to the castle departs from the ferry boat pier (Nagymaros) at 9:26am, 12:26, and 3:26pm. The last bus from the castle back to the pier is at 4pm.* ℹ *Check with Budapest Tour Inform before you leave for maps and information, as there is no tourist office in Visegrád.*

VÁC

The Vác cathedral is the main attraction of this tiny town. Built in the late 18th century and modeled after St. Peter's Basilica in Rome, the gorgeously restored columns invite visitors to meditate in holy peace. The **Stone Gate** built in 1764 for Empress Maria Theresa's visit to the town looks like Paris' Arc de Triomphe. Perhaps most intriguing, and also most overlooked, are the **Statue of the Holy Trinity** columns.

✠ *Buses depart from Árpád híd station in Budapest every half-hour. The train departs from Nyugati toward Szob via Vác every 30min. The train station is at the northern end of Széchényi utca adjacent to the bus station. Follow Széchényi utca toward the river for 0.5km which will lead you toward the main square at Március 15 tér.* Ⓢ *Prices vary depending on time of year.*

FOOD

The Belváros

▨ **CENTRAL KÁVÉHÁZ**   ✦⊗♈⚲ CAFE ❸

V, Károlyi Mihály utca 9.   ☎01 266 2110 ▥www.centralkavehaz.hu

Doors and windows bust open to reveal local clientele, from cramming students to old men sucking on cigars to women gabbing about the latest he-said she-said at this larger-than-life coffee and sandwich shop. Don't let the marble tables and leather couches fool you; if you linger for long enough the laid-back waiters will find you and you'll begin to groove with the chill atmosphere.

M2: Ferenciek Tere. From the Metro take Károly Mihály east. $ Nosh 1800-2650Ft. Entrees 2300-3900Ft. Mixed drinks 500-1100Ft. ⏰ Open daily 7am-midnight.

CAFE ALIBI — CAFE ❷

V, Egyetem Tér 4 — ☎01 317 4209 💻cafealibi.hu

An old-fashioned cash register and your grandmother's fine china will greet you at this little coffee shop in the center of student-city. Don't let the white tablecloths scare you--while the price is up there, you're unlikely to find a more tasteful cafe in this neighborhood away from all those foreign loudmouths.

M3: Kálvin Tér. From the Metro take Kecskeméti utca west and turn left on Egyetem tér. $ Salads 900-1600Ft. Coffee from 320Ft. ⏰ Open M-F 8am-2am, Sa 9am-1am.

KICSIMAMA KONYHÁJA — HUNGARIAN, FAST FOOD ❶

Lónyay u. 7. — ☎01 216 4178

A get-in-get-out kind of place perfect for backpackers on the run. Delectable Hungarian quick-eats for a tight budget. Not your grandma's kitchen, nor is it a five-star *resto*, but you get the idea. Try anything breaded or soaked in sauce.

M3: Kálvin Tér. Head towards the river and make a left on Lónyay.ß. $ Breaded cauliflower 580ft. Spinach ricotta pasta 280ft. Specials from 780ft. ⏰ Open M-F 10am-6pm, Sa 10am-3pm.

KÁRPÁTIA — HUNGARIAN ❺

V, Ferenciek Tere 7-8 — ☎01 317 3596 💻www.karpatia.hu

The up-and-coming executive chef doles out revamped Hungarian cuisine, mixing ancient spices and recipes with Mediterranean, Asian, and Latin flavors. An immaculate Baroque interior with red, gold, and green patterns cover a vaulted ceiling at one of the city's oldest restaurants. Dishes like venison filet with balsamic strawberries and maize polenta with black truffles *(7050Ft)* will blow your taste buds away. Your wallet will be crushed by debris from the explosion, so save it for a last-night-in-town-splurge.

M3: Ferenciek Tere. i Reservations recommended. $ Appetizers 1900-3100Ft. Entrees 3300-7500Ft. ⏰ Open daily 11am-11pm.

1000 TEA — TEA HOUSE ❸

Váci utca 65 — ☎01 337 8217 💻www.1000tea.hu

Take your shoes off and sip tea in one of the many arched alcoves of this Japanese-style tea house, located in a tranquil courtyard away from the buzz of Váci. With an impressive menu and worldly staff, you might receive a bit of knowledge along with your tea condiments. Couples can relish the tea samplers *(from 1400ft)*. Get your Zen on, you're in tea land now.

M3: Kálvin Tér. From the Metro take Vámház toward the river and turn right on Váci utca. $ Teas 420-1100Ft. ⏰ Open M-Sa noon-11pm, Su 1-11pm.

Lipótváros

SZERÁJ — TURKISH, FAST FOOD ❶

V, Szent István krt.

Turkish fast food with a Hungarian touch. Perfect for a quick, delicious meal without the fuss of waiters and tips. If you've got more time on your hands, sit outside in the summer on the patio overlooking bustling Szent István krt or at one of the tables inside illuminated by massive windows. You can even smoke inside in the upstairs balconies. Try the Hungarian twists on Mediterranean classics, like the kebab sandwich with red cabbage *(650Ft)*.

M3: Nyugati. Head down Szent István towards the river, the restaurant is on your left. $ Entrees from 400Ft. Desserts from 300Ft.

TRÓFEA GRILL ÉTTEREM — GOURMET, BUFFET [3]

XIII, Visegrádi utca 50A ☎01 270 0366 www.trofeagrill.com

Gourmet meal and all-you-can-eat buffet don't usually hold hands on the playground, but somehow this place pulls it off. The large wooden dining area is lined with the skulls of the various species you'll be enjoying. An over 100-dish menu will leave you either unsurpassably satiated or slobbering indecisively. Stand-up and occasional folk dancing during the summer make for a somewhat bizarre (but entertaining) dining experience.

M3: Nyugati. From the Metro take Szent István krt toward the river and turn right on Visegrádi. i Wi-Fi included. $ Buffet M-F lunch 3400Ft; M-Th dinner 3800Ft; F dinner and all day Sa-Su 4600Ft. Open M-F noon-midnight, Sa 11:30am-midnight, Su 11:20am-8:30pm.

Erzsébetváros

CASTRO BISZTRÓ — BISTRO [1]

1075 Madách tér 3. ☎01 215 01 84 www.castrobistro.hu

An easy cafe where you can sit alone and read or chat with friends over an espresso. An eclectic decor boasts Buena Vista Social Club posters and a handsome bar serves a sizzling Illy roast and a selection of beer and wine. Windows bring in ample light and the summertime opens a whole new world and vibe with the outdoor terrace. Clientele ranges from artsy cafe regulars to the occasional tourist.

M1, M2, or M3: Deák Ferenc tér. From the Metro head north on Király utca, right on Rumbach Sebestyén utca and right on Madách. $ Espresso 200Ft. Sandwiches from 700Ft. Open M-Th 10am-midnight, F 10am-1am, Sa noon-1am, Su 2pm-midnight.

HUMMUS BÁR — ISRAELI [1]

Kertész utca 39 ☎01 321 74 77 www.hummusbar.hu

An explosion of olive oil, lemon zest, and chickpeas makes you feel like you're trotting the ancient limestone streets of Jerusalem. A young and modern decor (that's clientele included) rendez-vous with old recipes to birth some of the city's most delectable Jewish fare. Check out the "hummusology" posters for proper hummus-and-pita-eating technique. Don't leave without trying the *Laffa*, a giant flat bread stuffed with meat (or veggies), spices, and hummus.

M1: Oktogon. Head east on Erzsébet krt, right on Király and left on Kertész. $ Falafel from 800Ft. Entrees 400-1800Ft. Open daily noon-11pm.

Terézváros

MENZA — HUNGARIAN [3]

Liszt Ferenc tér 2 ☎01 413 14 82 www.menza.co.hu

Makes you feel like you're one of the locals eating the cuisine of champions. Don't be deterred by the large crowds—this *menza* (canteen) is packed for a reason. Large portions of real Hungarian lunch food in an atmosphere that can't be any more mundane (in the best sense). Go for the daily menu *(890Ft)* and you'll get a real bang for your buck, with meals like fried turkey breast and a rice-and-peas side.

M2: Oktogon. From the Metro, take Andrássy út west and then turn left onto Liszt Ferenc tér; the restaurant is at the corner with Paulay Ede utca. $ Salads 1390-1690Ft. Pasta 1290-1990Ft. Entrees 1890-3990Ft. Open daily 10am-1am.

FŐZELÉK FALO — HUNGARIAN [1]

Nagymező utca 18

You can't go to Hungary and not try *főzelék*—a truly Hungarian everyman dish composed of vegetables and spices cooked into a thick soup. This tiny place boasts every kind of *főzelék* and makes you feel like you've dropped in at grandma's. Be sure to try the squash *(380Ft)*; those looking to bypass the nostalgia for something a little more hearty should try the *weiner schnitzel (350Ft)*.

M1: Oktogon. Head south from the Metro on Andrássy and right on Nagymező. $ Főzelék 380Ft. Entrees 390-690Ft. M-F 10am-9:30pm. Sa noon-8pm.

KAJA.HU 🚭♿📶🌳 HUNGARIAN [2]

Nagymező utca 41 ☎01 374 04 68 🖥www.kaja.hu

One of the cheapest deals in the city. A simple canteen-style eatery serving traditional and delicious Hungarian fast food in huge portions to a local student and working crowd. Order the fried camembert with blueberry sauce *(950ft)* and you'll fit right in. A great place for lunch, but also for a quick starter drink and meal before a night out.

🚏 M1: Oktogon. Head south from the Metro on Andrássy and right on Nagymező. ℹ Delivery available. $ Menus 640Ft. Salads 890Ft. Entrees from 990Ft. ⏰ Open daily 10am-midnight.

ZSÁKBAMACSKA 💳♿🍸 HUNGARIAN [3]

Lovag utca 3 ☎01 354 18 10 🖥zsakbamacska.hu

Finally some decent Hungarian sit-down food without the inauthentic gypsy music drilling in the background. A simple cellar setting invites guests almost as warmly as the staff does. Hit some Hungarian fish soup *(1250Ft)* for a spicy time and couple it with crispy duck topped with sour cherry sauce *(2750Ft)*. The prices are just as spicy as the food, but you can save by getting a hearty soup or a small meat dish with a salad.

🚏 M3: Arany János utca. From the Metro, take Bajcsy-Zsilinszky út north, then make a sharp right onto Nagymező utca, and then turn left onto Lovag utca. $ Appetizers 1350-2350Ft. Soups 750-1150Ft. Salads 550-950Ft. Entrees 1950-4550Ft. Vegetarian entrees 1550-2150Ft. ⏰ Open M-F 5pm-midnight, Sa-Su noon-midnight.

CSIRKE CSIBÉSZ 💳♿🍸 FAST FOOD [1]

Nagymező utca 35 ☎01 269 39 62

The haunt for locals after a night of drinking. Open until the wee hours, this place serves up sizzling whole chickens for you to devour (with your hands, if you wish). Stand at the counters or sit in a high stool and be amazed at how great the fare tastes—even during the day in a sober state of being.

🚏 M1: Oktogon. Head south from the Metro on Andrássy and right on Nagymező. $ Sandwiches and entrees from 290Ft. ⏰ M-F 7am-6pm and W-Sa 7:30pm-5am.

CACTUS JUICE 💳🚭🍸❄ HUNGARIAN, AMERICAN [3]

Jókai Tér 5 ☎01 302 21 16 🖥www.cactusjuice.hu

As you pull up to this little joint you might be thinking, why in the great heavens did you send me to some Western pub in the middle of Budapest!? Don't you worry! Just head on downstairs and join the hoards of chilled-out local 20-to-30-somethings enjoying cheap beer and feasting on a Hungarian-American fare that's truly unlike any other restaurant in the city. If you're scrimping, go for the goulash *(860ft)*. If you're in the mood to dole out a little more loot, take a stab at the tenderloin steak and *lecsó*, Hungarian tomato and pepper sauté *(2990Ft)*.

🚏 M1: Oktogon. Head south on Andrássy and turn right on Jókai. ℹ Often hosts DJs. Check online for listings. $ Salads from 1490Ft. Entrees from 1590Ft. ⏰ Open M-Th noon-2am, F-Sa Noon-4am, Su 4pm-2am.

Józsefváros

✓ SIRIUS KLUB 🚭🚭 TEA HOUSE [1]

Bródy Sándor utca 13. ☎01 266 17 08

A giant selection of teas served through a small window connected to the main seating area, Tibetan prayer flags, and floor cushions invite you to kick off your walking shoes and mellow out. If you're starved you might head to a restaurant, but for a quick nosh try their chocolate cookies.

🚏 M3: Kálin tér. From the station, head north on Múzeum krt and turn right on Bródy Sándor. $ Tea from 540Ft. Cookies 250Ft. ⏰ Open daily noon-10pm.

✓ DARSHAN UDVAR 💳♿🍸🌳 INTERNATIONAL [2]

Krúdy Gyula utca 7. ☎01 266 5541 🖥www.darshan.hu

Housed in a mosaic-tiled building with a magnificent inner courtyard, this restaurant boasts a menu as eclectic as its decor. From Buddha statues to Hungarian-style tablecloths, this place combines world cuisine with Hungarian spice. Relax in the courtyard over a meal, or stay for a beer and live music in the later hours. *🧭 M3: Ferenc körút. From the station, head north on József krt and turn left on Krúdy Gyula. $ Soups from 690Ft. Entrees 990-2350Ft. Dessert 590-720Ft. ⏰ Open daily 11am-midnight.*

Ferencváros

PINK CADILLAC PIZZERIA 🚫♿⛅ ITALIAN ❷

Ráday utca 22 ☎01 216 14 12 💻www.pinkcadillac.hu

Pink Cadillac is a stylish pizza joint that offers some of the best pies in the city. Its specialties include the *Pirata*, *Dolce Vita*, and the massive signature Pink Caddy *(mushroom, ham, salami, olives; 2860Ft)* after which you may need a forklift to exit the building. The decor includes some vintage advertisements as well as the front of the eponymous pink Cadillac, sticking out of the wall with headlights on. *🧭 M3: Kálvin tér. From the station, take Kálvin tér toward the river and turn left on Ráday. $ Pizza 750-2860Ft. Pasta 1140-1900Ft. ⏰ Open daily 11am-1am.*

PASTA NEGRA 🚫♿🍸❄⛅ TAPAS ❸

Kálvin tér 8 ☎01 215 56 16 💻www.patanegra.hu

This wonderful tapas joint in the middle of Kálvin tér will make you happy you chose Budapest over Madrid for a summer vacation. Tapas range from the banal Catalan bread *(350Ft)* to the exotic crispy fried baby squid *(950Ft)*. Don't let the big scary bull standing outside frighten you—the patio is where it's at if you want a true fusion of Spanish slow-cooking in the bustle and noise of Hungary's capital. *🧭 M3: Kálvin tér. From the station, walk across the street. $ White wine from 690Ft. Red wine from 750Ft. Entrees 840-1300Ft. Tapas 350-1950Ft. ⏰ Open M-W 11am-midnight, Th-F 11am-1am, Sa noon-1am, Su noon-midnight.*

hungary

The Városliget

👍 ROBINSON RESTAURANT 💳♿🍸⛅ HUNGARIAN ❸

Városligeti tó ☎01 663 68 71

Certainly commands one of the more interesting locations in Budapest atop an artificial pond in the middle of City Park. Serves a mix of Hungarian and international dishes. Grilled goose liver *(2790Ft)* is the house specialty. *🧭 M1: Hősök tere. From the station, walk through Heroes' Sq. and then turn left; the restaurant is in the park across from the zoo. $ Soups 1200-1400Ft. Entrees 1900-5890Ft. ⏰ Open daily noon-4pm, 6pm-midnight.*

GUNDEL ÉTTEREM 💳♿🍸❄⛅ CLASSY ❹

Állatkerti út 2 ☎01 603 24 80 💻www.gundel.hu

If you dare to enter, remember your best posh accent and pretentious gaze—this is the only area restaurant classy enough for both the Queen of England and Pope John Paul II to have graced it with their presence. Most of the menu is well outside a backpacker's budget, and the style probably diverges as well. The best deal is the three course lunch menu *(3800Ft)*, which comes with a glass of house wine. *🧭 M1: Hősök tere. From the station, walk through Heroes' Square and then turn left; the restaurant is right next to the zoo. ℹ Men must be in blazers or sport jackets. Reservations not required, but recommended. $ Sandwiches 1990-2190Ft. Salads 3190-3790Ft. Entrees 3980-6200Ft. ⏰ Open daily noon-4pm and 6:30-midnight.*

BARAKA 💳♿🍸❄ INTERNATIONAL ❸

Andrássy út 111 ☎01 483 13 55

Located on the ground floor of a former historic hotel, Baraka is one of Budapest's most celebrated restaurants. The exterior overlooks the beautiful boulevard and Heroes' Square, while the interior has the feel of a sleek New York lounge. Start off with the Thai-marinated salmon *tataki* in coconut crust

(1800Ft). The five-spice duck breast *(4900Ft)* is one of the chef's specialties.

✈ *M1: Bajza utca. Walk toward Heroes' Sq.; the restaurant is on the right.* ℹ *Reservations recommended.* Ⓢ *Appetizers 1500-1900Ft. Entrees 2400-6200Ft.* ☎ *Open M-Sa noon-3pm and 6-11pm, Su noon-3pm.*

Várhegy, Central Buda, and the Vizivaros

▨ DAUBNER CUKRÁSZDA
●ᕗ⌂ CAFE ❷

Szépvölgyi út 50 ☎01 335 22 53 ▩www.daubnercukraszda.hu

While locals rave about the cakes and ice cream, the place is all too easy for tourists to miss due to its off-the-beaten-path location. A sweet place to get something to go and eat in the privacy of your hostel bed; or stay a while and couple a chocolate cake *(380Ft)* with some nutty coffee *(300Ft).* While the glass cases are stocked with more things than you could ever work off at the gym, don't stand and slobber too long—the line of people out the door will slip into a premature sugar coma.

✈ *Tram 17: Kolosy tér. From the tram stop, walk a few blocks up Szépvölgyi út; the cafe will be on your left.* Ⓢ *Sweets from 300Ft. Coffee from 300Ft.* ☎ *Open daily 9am-7pm.*

ARANYSZARVAS BISZTRÓ
🍴ᕗ❄☼⌂ HUNGARIAN ❹

Szarvas tér 1 ☎01 375 64 51 ▩www.aranyszarvas.hu

An enormous gilt deer head greets guests at this fancy coffeehouse where many of the 18th century's most renowned literary luminaries gathered to reinvigorate the Hungarian language and invent modern Serbian. For decades, this revered Buda landmark was the only restaurant in Budapest that served game. Nearly 40 years later, venison, boar, and pheasant are still the only game in town. Don't be petrified after a cursory glance at the menu—it is possible to keep the price down if you go for a fairly filling starter like smoked pork joint salad with horseradish *(1450Ft)* or a schmancy after-dinner dessert like baked yogurt with raspberry ice cream *(990Ft).*

✈ *Trams 18 or 19: Döbrentei tér. From the tram stop, take Döbrentei tér away from the river, turn right onto Attila út, and then veer left; the restaurant is on the corner.* ℹ *Reservations recommended.* Ⓢ *Appetizers 1200-1800Ft. Entrees 1600-2900Ft. Desserts 990-1400Ft.* ☎ *Open daily noon-11pm.*

NAGYI PALACSINTÁZÓJA
●ᕗ⌂ FRENCH ❷

Hattyú utca 16 ☎01 212 48 66

Literally "your grandmama's creperie," this tiny joint fries up thin pancakes Hungarian-style, stuffing them with delicious fatteners like sweet cocoa powder, rice pudding, and sour-cherry sauce. It's a perfect early-morning place to soak up all that booze from a raunchy night and watch the sun rise over Parliament.

✈ *M2: Moszkva tér. From the station, walk toward the river; at the big intersection, veer right on Hattyú utca.* ℹ *Another location is at Batthyány tér 5.* Ⓢ *Sweet crepes 130-640Ft. Savory crepes 240-620Ft.* ☎ *Open 24hr.*

Óbuda

▨ EMIL CUKRÁSZDA
●ᕗ⌂ CAFE ❶

Bécsi út 314 ☎01 240 75 35 ▩www.emilcukraszda.hu

While it may seem like a random shop thrown in between some other odd shops on a main road leading out of the city, beware this type of dismissive thinking! Don't miss out on one of the best confectionaries in the land, stocked with finger- (and if it drops on the ground, ground-) licking good treats. Limited seating area (i.e., a bench next to the entrance) means it's an in-and-out sort of ordeal, but the courageous traveler will not be disappointed once he's taken his first bite of triple chocolate cake with raspberry filling and buttercream accents.

✈ *Bus #260: ATI. Keep walking a bit in the direction of the bus and cross the road.* Ⓢ *Sweets from 250Ft. Coffee from 210Ft.* ☎ *Open daily 10am-6pm.*

CSÜLÖK CSÁRDA 🚫♿🍸🌤 HUNGARIAN [3]

Szentendrei út 89 - 95 ☎01 240 02 54 💻www.emilcukraszda.hu

Csülök Csárda is for the real meat lover. A sea of wooden tables greets ravenous guests ready to mangle their prey, and traditional Hungarian cuisine served in an interesting decor makes you wonder where these Hungarians get their decorators. The food is delicious, despite its surroundings' lack of aesthetic beauty, and the giant portions come at an unbeatable price.

➡ HÉV: Köles Street. From the stop, backtrack on Szentendrei út 1 block. $ Soups 500-620Ft. Entrees 1100-2500Ft. ⏰ Open M-F 10am-10pm, Sa-Su 11am-11pm.

Margit-Sziget

HOLDUDVAR 💳♿🍸🌤 HUNGARIAN, MEDITERRANEAN [2]

Margit Sziget ☎01 236 0155 💻www.holdudvar.net

Orange lanterns and hipster-type furniture welcome the hungry traveler. If it's not enough that this place turns into one of the coolest open-air venues come nightfall with film screenings, live music, and dancing 'til dawn, it also serves up some of the most delicious fare in the middle of the river. The food is Hungarian with a Mediterranean tinge. Try the Mediterranean tomato soup with mozzarella *(850Ft)* and you'll leave happy and satisfied. Turns into a fun bar come nightfall.

➡ From the Margit Bridge entrance, take the main road; the garden will be on your right, across from the Hajós Alfréd Swimming Pool. ℹ Film screenings in the open-air cinema Su 9pm. $ Appetizers 1700-2500Ft. Pasta 1700-2900Ft. Entrees 1500-4500Ft. ⏰ Open daily in summer 11am-5am.

CHAMPS SPORTS PUB 💳♿🍸🌤 PUB [2]

Margit Sziget ☎01 413 1655 💻www.champs.hu

An expansive wooden deck invites guests to sip beer or relax and chat with friends on beanbags. More than 30 plasma TVs broadcast the latest game and the kitchen serves up wholesome portions of pizza, Mexican food, and other delicious odds and ends.

➡ Tram #1: Jászai Mari tér, walk across the bridge to the island. The pub is across the way from Holdudvar. $ Pizza 900-1500Ft. Quesadillas 1000Ft. ⏰ Open in summer daily 11am-2am.

NIGHTLIFE

The Belváros

KATAPULT 💳🚭🍸 PUB

V, Dohány u. 1 ☎01 266 7226

Local 20-somethings squeeze into this tiny but lively pub that functions as a cafe by day. Red walls and trippy lamps bring a range of evenings, from political debates to head-banging and grinding; the space leaves it up to the clientele to decide its vibe for the night. Try to eat beforehand as the kitchen closes in the afternoon.

➡ M2: Astoria. Walk west up Károly krt from the Metro and backtrack to the right onto Dohány. $ Beer from 500Ft. ⏰ Open daily 9am-2am.

GÖDÖR KLUB 💳🚭🍸🌤 CLUB

V, Erzsébet Tér ☎01 201 3868 💻www.godorklub.hu

The conspicuously bare concrete walls of the club, situated in the former foundation of what was supposed to be the new National Concert Hall, might seem unfinished, but on weekends you can hardly move in the crowded concert arena where rock, jazz, world, techno, and folk deafen patrons. If you arrive early enough you might snag a table on the long staircase or a seat on one of the benches along the retaining walls. For a more relaxing time head there during the week for Pilates.

➡ M1-3: Deák Tér. $ Beer from 350Ft. Shots 200-1000Ft. ⏰ Open M-Th 10am-2am, F-Sa 10am-4am, Su 10am-2am.

CAPELLA CAFE 💳🚭🍸▼ GAY CLUB

V, Belgrád rakpart 23 ☎70 328 6775 💻www.capellacafe.hu

Budapest's first gay discotheque draws a crowd of all orientations to its three levels even during the week. Themed dance rooms, a variety of music and occasional drag nights promise an evening unlike any other in the city. Upstairs you'll find a laid-back bar with a balcony surrounding the dance floors for those wallflower types.

✦ *Trams #2 and 2a: Március 15 tér. Follow the river towards the castle.* ⓘ *Cover W-Sa usually 1000ft.* Ⓢ *Beer and wine 600Ft. Shots from 800Ft.* ☺ *Open daily M-Sa 10am-5am.*

scrub pub

Ruin pubs—the number one trend in nightlife in Budapest these days—are installed in the courtyards and gardens of empty, crumbling old communist-era residential buildings. You won't see anything from the outside (except people drifting in and out with their plastic beer glasses, or perhaps a beefy guard controlling the noise levels of these residential party pads), but the inner courtyard is decorated with a hodgepodge of hipster-eque furniture: bathtubs for sofas, a table with eight different chairs, etc. Concerts, DJs, films, and alternative exhibits provide the entertainment at these hot hangouts.

Lipótváros

BECKETT'S IRISH PUB ●●⊗💲 PUB

V, Bajcsy-Zsilinszky út 72 ☎01 311 1035 🖳www.becketts.hu

The only Irish pub in Budapest that is owned and operated by an actual Irishman, it's mostly expats with hearty laughs and iron livers here. Get a kick out of Irish culture juxtaposed with Hungarian locals debating politics or soccer. Fall and winter months bring live concerts in the form of Oasis cover bands.

✦ *M3: Nyugati. From the Metro walk south. The pub is on the right.* Ⓢ *Sandwiches 950-1950Ft. Beer from 600Ft. Shots from 445Ft. 10% discount with student ID.* ☺ *Open M-Th noon-midnight, F-Sa noon-2am, Su noon-midnight. Kitchen open until midnight.*

Erzsébetváros

🏮 SZIMPLA KERT ●●♿💲🍸 RUIN PUB

Kazinczy utca ☎01 352 41 98 🖳www.szimpla.hu

Graffiti designs adorn the crumbling walls, a hodgepodge of furniture ranging from your grandmother's Victorian love-seat to the old beach lounger you threw in the garage, colorful lighting, a movie screen, and concert stage make for a chilled out night in hipster glory at Budapest's original ruin pub. Smoke in the courtyard, eat crepes by the bar, or make out upstairs in the bathtub. Mind-blowing films screened almost every night nicely compliment the dream-like atmosphere.

✦ *M2: Astoria. Head east on Rákóczi út and turn left on Kazinczy.* ⓘ *Check the website for event listings.* Ⓢ *Beer from 350Ft. Shots from 600Ft. Mixed drinks 1400-2500Ft.* ☺ *Open daily noon-3am.*

🏮 MUMUS ●●⊗💲 RUIN PUB

Dob utca 18

If you can figure out how to keep mellow at this laid-back bar where the booze runs cheaper than penny candy, shoot us an email. Local students and artists along with the occasional with-it backpacker haunt the place with an off-the-grid atmosphere: non-sloppy, all-night boozing. A classy ruin pub with a simple decor that invites an intelligent clientele to sip, chat, and listen to floaty music.

✦ *M2: Astoria. Head north on Károly krt and turn right on Dob utca.* Ⓢ *Beer from 240Ft. Shots 250-500Ft. Wine from 200Ft.* ☺ *Open M-Sa 3pm-3am, Su 4pm-midnight.*

🏮 MOST ●●⊗💲🍸 RUIN PUB

Zichy Jenő utca 17 🖳www.szilvuple.hu

A new take on the ruin pub, Most offers a diverse array of styles; classic grunge furniture to sleeker decor on the terrace means a good night for everyone. Three venues, each with its own personality, guarantee to serve a clientele base just as unique. Head upstairs to the balcony for a romantic drink, chill indoors on the first floor amidst the books and odds-and-ends to get your hipster on, or never leave the unassuming garden where you entered—a plot of land transformed into a quiet oasis of happy conversation and cheap drinking.

M1: Opera. East on Andrássy, left on Nagymező and left on Zichy Jenő. $ Beer 550Ft. Wine 450Ft. ⏰ Open daily 11am-3am.

Józsefváros

CORVINTETŐ CLUB

Blaha Lujza tér 1-2 ☎01 772 29 84 💻www.corvinteto.hu

As you're walking up in anticipation of what's to come, don't be fooled by the graffiti-stained stairs and concrete monstrosity in front of you: this dance-and-drink party place on top of a former state-owned department store is a stylish club offering one of the most breathtaking views in Budapest. Regular DJs and live acts are a popular draw in the red-lit lounge area, but head outside in the summer to the three bars and non-stop grooving.

M2: Blaha Lujza tér. From the station, walk towards the Corvin building; the entrance is along Somogy Béla út, up the stairs. $ Beer from 320Ft. Shots 600-950Ft. ⏰ Open daily 6pm-5am.

Ferencváros

RUMBA CAFÉ BAR

Lónyay utca 27 ☎3670 503 69 69 💻www.rumbacafe.hu

A super-relaxed bar that makes you feel like you're in your best friend's den. Worn sofas, an eclectic mix of posters, '70s-esque armchairs, and wooden tables offer a nice flashback as you sip island drinks—the house specialty is Sex on the Rumba *(rum, pineapple juice and apricot brandy; 950Ft).*

M3: Ferenc körút. From the station, head west on Üllői and left on Kinizsi and right on Lonyay utca. $ Shots from 660Ft. ⏰ Open Tu-Sa 6pm-midnight.

Várhegy, Central Buda, and the Vizivaros

ZÖLD PARDON ENTERTAINMENT COMPLEX

Goldmann György tér ☎01 279 1880 💻www.zp.hu

"Green" Pardon has gained a bit of a bad name over the past few years for catering primarily to 16-year-olds yearning to escape their parents and have a night of unrestricted smoking and paying their elders to buy them drinks. Contrary to stereotype, however, the rising number of savvy Budapestians who know what's up would wholeheartedly recommend this expansive open-air venue to anyone young, old, short, or tall looking for a good time. The summer months bring countless DJs, rappers, hip-hop stars, and dancers, while the constantly changing drink specials at the multiple bars will have you seeing green elephants well into the morning hours.

Trams 4 or 6: Petőfi híd, budai hídfő. i Check website and Facebook for event listings. $ Cover 300Ft. Beer from 350Ft. Mixed drinks from 1000Ft. ⏰ Open Apr-Oct daily 11am-5am.

Margit-Sziget

HOLDUDVAR OUTDOOR BAR

Margit Sziget ☎01 236 01 55 💻www.holdudvar.net

Built on 13th century ruins, this giant garden venue doles out the best tunes, tastiest fare, and wildest nights on the island. Hit up the place during the day and gorge on such tasty things as "paprika chicken breast with curded ewe cheese dumplings" *(1900Ft)* and come back by the midnight hours to watch a film outdoors, dance like there's no tomorrow, and, most importantly, drink the cheapest beverages on the island until you forget what tomorrow means.

From the Margit Bridge entrance, take the main road; the garden will be on your right, across *from the Hajós Alfréd Swimming Pool. i Film screenings on the open-air cinema Su 9pm. $ Beer from 300Ft. Shots 790-1400Ft. Appetizers 1700-2500Ft. Pasta 1700-2900Ft. Entrees 1500-4500Ft. ⏰ Open in summer daily 11am-5am.*

ARTS AND CULTURE

Music and Opera

ACADEMY OF MUSIC — TERÉZVÁROS

Liszt Ferenc tér 8 ☎01 342 0179 🖥www.zeneakademia.hu

Find the nation's young musical prodigies all in one room at the prestigious Academy of Music. Pray to the music gods to make you lucky enough to catch a concert in the majestic Art Nouveau building that houses the school in Franz Liszt's honor.

M1: Oktogon. From the station, head east on Teréz krt and turn right on Király utca; the academy will be on your right 1 block down. i Check the website or call for concert listings. Schedules vary and there are rarely concerts in summer. $ Prices vary. ⏰ Box office open daily 2-8pm.

MAGYAR ÁLLAMI OPERAHÁZ (STATE OPERA HOUSE) — TERÉZVÁROS

Andrássy út 22 ☎01 353 0170 🖥www.opera.hu

Housed in a magnificent Neo-Rennaissance building that took nine years to construct, the Hungarian State Opera hosts some of the continent's finest operas, ballets, and classical performances. While some tickets sell out a year in advance, rush tickets are sometimes available at a fraction of the normal price 1hr. before the performance.

M1: Opera. i Call for show schedules, or check the poster at the gate. $ Tickets 1000-9000Ft. ⏰ Box office open M-Sa 11am-7pm, Su 4-7pm. Closes at 5pm on non-performance days.

Theater

MADÁCH SZÍNHÁZ — ERZSÉBETVÁROS

Erzsébet körút 29 ☎01 478 2041 🖥www.madachszinhaz.hu

A local favorite, Madách Színház is one of the few theaters in the city that suits all tastes. From *Cats* to *Monty Python* to *Anna Karenina*, you can get your fill of culture in all its many shades.

Tram 4 or 6: Wesselényi utca. From the station, walk across the street. i Check online for listings and prices. $ Prices vary; approximately 800-5200Ft. ⏰ Box office open daily 1pm-6:30pm.

Dance

NEMZETÍ TÁNCSZÍNHÁZ (NATIONAL DANCE THEATRE) — THE BELVÁROS

Színház utca 1-3 ☎01 201 4407 🖥www.dancetheatre.hu

The only 18th-century theater building in Hungary that's still a theater has been home to many key events in Hungarian cultural history. The first Hungarian-language play was performed here in 1790, and many of classical music's luminaries, including Beethoven, played here. Today the theater is home to Budapest's dance performances, which encompass ballet, modern dance, and folk.

Castle Hill, just north of the royal palace. Facing the castle, the theater is to the right, up the stairs. $ Tickets 2500Ft. ⏰ Box office open M-Th 10am-6pm, F 10am-5pm.

SHOPPING

Music

FERENC LISZT MUSIC SHOP — TERÉZVÁROS

Andrássy út 45 ☎01 322 4091

Named after Hungary's most famous composer, the store mostly carries classical music as well as musical necessities like sheet music and instructional how-to tapes.

M1: Oktogon. From the station, walk south toward the Opera. ⏰ Open M-F 10am-6pm, Sa 10am-1pm.

WAVE MUSIC

◆& TERÉZVÁROS

Révay köz 1 ☎01 269 0754 ■www.wave.hu

A carefully selected collection of CDs, LPs, and DVDs to satisfy tastes that range from alternative punk to jazz.

✦ *M1: Bajcsy-Zsilinszky út. From the station, head north on Bajcsy-Zsilinszky and turn right on Révay köz.* ℹ *Check out the online library coming soon.* ☒ *Open M-Sa 10am-8pm.*

Books

PENDRAGON

◆& TERÉZVÁROS

Pozsonyi út 21-23 ☎01 340 4426

A diverse selection of English novels and travel guides, neatly stacked by a helpful and friendly staff.

✦ *Tram 4 or 6: Jászai Mari tér. From the station, walk up Pozsonyi út.* ☒ *Open M-F 10am-6pm, Sa 10am-2pm.*

Clothes

JAJCICA

◆& ERZSÉBETVÁROS

Dohány utca 94 ☎01 321 2081 ■www.jajcica.hu

Hip, alternative clothing and an awesome selection of retro shoes and leather boots.

✦ *M2: Blaha Lujza tér. From the Metro walk north on Erzsébet körút, turn right on Dohány utca, the store will be on your left.* ☒ *Open M-F 10am-7pm, Sa 10am-2pm.*

G-STAR RAW

◆& THE BELVÁROS

Andrássy út 2 ☎01 484 6484 ■www.g-star.com

Stylish denim that's quite pricey, but the store itself is worth a gander. Gives new meaning to the word Metro-polis.

✦ *M1: Bajcsy-Zsilinszky. From the station, walk across the street.* ☒ *Open daily 10am-6pm.*

Food

LEHEL PIAC

◉&⚸ DISTRICT XIII

Lehel tér

The best open-air market to buy fruit and veggies for pennies or less. All local growers and the lack of a middle man makes it an authentic price.

☒ *Open M-F 6am-6pm, Sa 6am-2pm, Su 6am-1pm.*

Specialty

LEKVÁRIUM

◉& ERZSÉBETVÁROS

Dohány utca 39 ☎01 321 6543

This place sells homemade jam almost as good as your grandmother makes. Try the strawberry jam—the older, the tastier.

✦ *M2: Blaha Lujza tér.* ☒ *Open M-F 10am-6pm.*

ESSENTIALS

Practicalities

- **TOURIST OFFICES: Tourinform** arranges tours and accommodations. *(V, Sütő u. 2.* ☎*01 429 97 51.* ■*incoming@vista.hu* Ⓢ **Budapest Card** (Budapest Kártya) provides discounts, unlimited public transportation, and admission to most museums *(2-day card 6300Ft, 3-day 7500Ft.* ☒ *Open M-F 9am-6:30pm, Sa 9am-2:30pm.)*

- **DOMESTIC OPERATOR:** ☎*190*

- **INFORMATION:** ☎*199*

- **GLBT RESOURCES: GayGuide.net Budapest** posts an online guide and runs a hotline with info and a reservation service for GLBT-friendly lodgings. *(*☎*01 06 30 932 33 34.* ■*www.budapest.gayguide.net* ☒ *Hotline open daily 4-8pm.)* **Na Végre!** publishes an up-to-date guide to gay nightlife, available at any gay bar. *(*■*www. navegre.hu).*

hungary

- **POST OFFICE:** *(V, Városház utca 18 ☎01 318 4811. ℹ Poste Restante, Postán Mar, is in office around the right side of the building. ⏰ Open M-F 8am-8pm, Sa 8am-2pm.)* Alternative branches at Nyugati station, VI, Teréz körút; 105/107 Keleti Station, VIII, Baross tér 11/c; and elsewhere. Open M-F 7am-8pm, Sa 8am-2pm.
- **POSTAL CODE:** *Depends on the district—postal codes are 1XX2, where XX is the district number.*

Emergency!

- **TOURIST POLICE:** *(V, Sütő utca 2, inside the Tourinform office. ☎01 438 80 80. 🚇 M1, M2, or M3: Deák tér. ℹ Beware of imposters demanding to see your passport. ⏰ Open 24hr.)*
- **PHARMACIES:** *(II, Frankel Leó út 22 ☎01 314 36 95. ℹ Generally, look for green signs labeled Apotheke, Gyógyszertár, or Pharmacie. ⏰ Open M-F 7:30am-9pm, Sa 7:30am-2pm. Minimal after-hours service fees apply.)*
- **MEDICAL SERVICES: Falck (SOS) KFT.** *(II, Kapy út 49/b. ☎01 224 90 90. ℹ The US embassy maintains a list of English-speaking doctors.)*

Getting There

By Plane

Ferihegy Airport *(BUD; ☎01 235 38 88).* From the airport to the center, take bus #93 *($ 270Ft. ⏰ 20min., every 15min. 4:55am-11:20pm),* then #3 to Kőbánya-Kispest (15min. to Deák tér, in downtown Budapest). **Airport Minibus** *(☎01 296 85 55)* goes to hostels *($ 2990Ft).*

By Train

The major stations, **Keleti Pályaudvar, Nyugati Pályaudvar,** and **Déli Pályaudvar,** are also Metro stops *(☎3640 49 49 49).* Most international trains arrive at **Keleti Station,** but some from Prague go to **Nyugati Station.** For schedules, check 💻www.mav.hu, part of which is in English. Prices change often and sometimes depend on time of day and time of year. To: **Berlin** *($ 15,800Ft. ⏰ 12-13hr., 4 per day);* **Bucharest, ROM** *($ 23,600Ft. ⏰ 14hr., 5 per day);* **Prague, CZR** *($ 16,300Ft. ⏰ 7-8hr., 5 per day);* **Vienna, AUT** *($ 3600Ft. ⏰ 3hr., 17 per day);* **Warsaw, POL** *($ 18,500Ft. ⏰ 11hr., 2 per day).* The daily **Orient Express** stops on its way from Paris, FRA to Istanbul, TUR. Trains run to most major destinations in Hungary. Purchase tickets at an **International Ticket Office** *(⏰ Keleti Station open daily 8am-7pm; Nyugati Station open M-Sa 5am-9pm; info desk 24hr.).* Or try **MÁV Hungarian Railways,** VI, Andrássy út 35. *(☎461 55 00. Branches at all stations. Open Apr-Sept M-F 9am-6pm, Oct-Mar M-F 9am-5pm.)* The **HÉV Commuter Railway Station** is at Batthyány tér, opposite Parliament. Trains head to Szentendre *($ 460Ft. ⏰ 45min., every 15min. 5am-9pm).* Purchase tickets at the station for transport beyond the city limits.

By Bus

Buses to international and some domestic destinations leave from the **Népliget Station,** X, Üllői út 131. *(🚇 M3: Népliget. ☎01 329 14 50. ⏰ Cashier open 6am-8pm.)* Check 💻www.volanbusz.hu for schedules.

Getting Around

By Train

The **HÉV Commuter Rail Station** is across the river from Parliament, one Metro stop past the Danube in Buda at Batthyány tér. On the list of stops, those within the city limits are displayed in a different color. For these stops, a regular Metro ticket will suffice. Purchase tickets at the counter to travel beyond the city limits. Békásmegye is the final stop within the city limits.

By Budapest Public Transit

The **subways** and **trams** run every few minutes. **Buses** are generally on time and some run 24hr.; schedules are posted at stops. **Budapest Public Transport** (BKV; ☎3680 40 66 86 🖥www.bkv.hu) has information in Hungarian and an English website. Single-fare tickets for public transport (one-way on 1 line Ⓢ 320Ft) are sold in Metro stations, Trafik shops, and by sidewalk vendors at tram stops. Punch them in the orange boxes at the gate of the Metro or on buses and trams; punch a new ticket when you change lines, or face a fine of 6000Ft from the undercover ticket inspectors. (Ⓢ Day pass 1550Ft, 3-day 3850Ft, 1-week 4600Ft, 2-week 6200Ft, 1-month 9400Ft.)

The Metro has three lines: **M1 (yellow), M2 (red),** and **M3 (blue).** M1 runs west to east from downtown Pest past City Park along Andrássy út. M2 runs west to east and connects **Deli Train Station** in Buda with **Keleti Train Station** in Pest along Rákóczi út. M3 runs north to south through Pest and provides a transfer bus to the airport from the southern terminus (Kőbánya-Kispest). A fourth Metro line is currently under construction that will connect southern Buda to northeastern Pest, though it is not expected to open until 2012. The Metro runs 4:30am-11:30pm.

Most buses and trams stop running at 11pm. After you've missed the last tram, transportation is available in the form of **night (É) buses** which run midnight-5am along major routes: #7É and 78É follow the 2 route; #6É follows the #4/6 tram line; #14É and 50É follow the #3 route.

szentendre ☎06

This tiny town of 20,000 is home to many Budapest businessmen and their families seeking refuge from the commotion of the big city. Its cobblestone streets and tiny little nooks under lush greenery give it something of a romantic character. A small trek up to the top of Church Hill will give you the perfect pictures to send home, and the tiny art galleries and museums are great for any troubled genius.

ORIENTATION

Boats (☎484 40 00) leave from the pier below **Vigadó tér** (Ⓢ 2000Ft. ⏱ 1½hr., 2 per day.). The train and bus stations are 10min. from Fő tér; descend the stairs past the HÉV tracks and through the underpass up Kossuth utca. At the fork, bear right on Dumtsa Jenő utca. From the ferry station, turn left on Czóbel sétány and left on Dunakorzó utca.

SIGHTS

🏛 CHURCH HILL (TEMPLOMDOMB) ⊛ VIEW

The best place to capture panorama photos of old houses, tons of church spires and a majestic Danube below.

✦ Walk up the hill from the Town Hall.

🏛 HUNGARIAN OPEN AIR MUSEUM ⊛&♿ MUSEUM

Sztaravodai út ☎0626 502 500

This museum is a 3km preservation of traditional Hungarian country towns and villages from the end of the 18th century to the beginning of the 20th. Traditional feasts, everyday tasks, and craft-making are also represented to teach foreigners about Hungarian pastoral life.

$ 600Ft, students 400Ft, family 1600Ft. ⏰ Open daily 9am-4pm.

SZAMOS MARZIPAN MUSEUM AND CONFECTIONERY
♿ MUSEUM

Dumtsa Jenő utca 12 ☎0626 412 626 💻www.szamosmarcipan.hu

Have you ever seen a life-sized replica of the Hungarian crown jewels, scenes from the *Wizard of Oz*, and a 160cm long replica of the Hungarian parliament—all made from marzipan? If that won't get you to make the trip, maybe the 80kg white-chocolate statue of Michael Jackson will be a draw—a thriller even. On your way out, it's hard to resist getting at least a little something from the confectionery or the adjoining cafe.

➡ 2 blocks down the street from Tour Inform. $ 400Ft. ⏰ Open daily May-Oct 10am-7pm, Nov-Apr 10am-6pm.

CZÓBEL MUSEUM
♿ MUSEUM

Templom tér 1 ☎06 26 310 244

The Czóbel Museum exhibits work by noted artist Béla Czóbel, including his bikini-clad "Venus of Szentendre." Admission includes access to the adjoining exhibit of works by the Szentendre Artists' Colony, which are either hit-or-miss.

➡ Head west from Fő tér. i English captions. $ 500Ft, students 300Ft. ⏰ Open W-Su 10am-6pm.

PARISH CHURCH OF SAINT JOHN
♿ CHURCH

Church Hill

One of the few surviving medieval churches in Hungary that was rebuilt after Ottoman occupation in the 18th century. The holy ghosts have put a curse on all those hoping to snap a photo from inside the church, which costs 100Ft to evade.

➡ On Church Hill. $ Free. 100Ft to take pictures. ⏰ Open Tu-Su 10am-4pm. Services Su 7am.

NEMZETI BORMÚZEUM (NATIONAL WINE MUSEUM)
♿ 🍷 MUSEUM

Bogdányi utca 10 💻www.bor-kor.hu

The grandiose National Wine Museum consists of little more than a cellar with some displays set up to elaborate on Hungary's various wine regions. The museum tour is available with a wine-tasting course, which features eight Hungarian wines as well as Hungarian appetizers. During the hot, sticky summer, the mercifully cool wine cellar is worth the trip alone, even if you wine connoisseurs might be less than impressed.

$ Exhibit 200Ft. Tasting and English-language tour 2200Ft. ⏰ Open daily 10am-10pm.

FOOD

CAFE CHRISTINE
♿ 🍷 ☀ HUNGARIAN 3

Görög utca 6 ☎0626 369 7008 💻www.cafechristine.hu

Enjoy reasonably priced tourist food right by the Danube. In the summer, the small cafe opens up onto the sidewalk with plenty of seating and shade with a mix of umbrellas and trees. Those with little regard for their arteries will spring for the traditional Hungarian beef stew with ewe cheese gnocchi *(2100Ft).*

➡ From Fő tér walk towards the river; the restaurant is on your right. $ Entrees 900-4100Ft. ⏰ Open daily 8am-11:30pm.

LÁNGOS
♿ FRIED DOUGH 1

Dumsta Jenő utca

For some delicious fried dough, stop at this little lunch counter on your way to the tourist office.

➡ Next to Tourinform. $ Lángos 165-250Ft. ⏰ Open daily 10am-8pm.

ART CAFÉ
♿ 🍷 ☀ CAFE 2

Fő tér 11 ☎0626 311 285

The best pastries in town, as well as gigantic, out-of-this-world ice cream sundaes. Much less assuming than the other places in the main square.

⇡ *On the right as your heading to the main square.* $ *Sundaes from 800Ft. Sandwiches from 650Ft.* 🕐 *Open daily 10am-10pm.*

ESSENTIALS

Practicalities

- **POST OFFICE:** on Fő tér. *(☎06 26 310 011 🕐 Open M-F 8am-5pm, Sa 8am-noon.)*
- **POLICE:** *(2000 Szentendre Dunakorzó ☎06 26 310 233).* In the neighboring city of **Dunakeszi** *(Tábor utca 2 ☎06 27 341 055).*
- **HOSPITAL:** *(Kanonok utca 1 ☎06 26 501 440).*
- **TOURIST OFFICES: Tourinform** is between the center and the stations. Open from mid-Mar to Oct daily 9:30am-1pm and 1:30-4:30pm; from Nov to mid-Mar M-F 9:30am-1pm and 1:30-4:30pm.*(Dumtsa Jenő út. 22, ☎06 02 631 79 65)*

Getting There

HÉV **trains** go to **Szentendre** *($ 480Ft. 🕐 45min. 3 per hr.)* depart from Budapest's Batthyány tér station. **Buses** run from Szentendre to Budapest's **Árpád híd** Metro station *($ 280Ft. 🕐 30min., 1-3 per hr.),* **Esztergom** *($ 660Ft. 🕐 1hr., 1 per hr.),* and **Visegrád** *($ 375Ft. 🕐 45min., 1 per hr.).* **Boats** *(☎484 4000)* leave from the pier below Vigadó tér *($ 2000Ft. 🕐 1½hr., 2 per day.).*

esztergom ☎033

Atop the **Esztergom Basilica,** as the breeze of a thousand years cools your face, looking out at the hills in the distance and the domed bridge that whisks travelers effortlessly across the border into Slovakia, you might feel a bit light-headed. The city of Esztergom produces a kind of ethereal haze, giving it a glow that extends far beyond its historical significance as the birthplace of King St. Stephen. It's the perfect "city upon a hill," nestled in the Danube Bend, where the awe-struck traveler will be surprised when he or she runs into locals who live day-to-day in the magical land; many will scramble to share their town and the stories of their great past.

ORIENTATION

Just down the street from the train station is St. Anne Church (Szent Anna Templom), a domed yellow church with a lovely green-lined walkway. On the way from the station to the Basilica you can take a detour to the left at **Árok utca** and check out the **Prímás island** for a view of the river. Just a little ways down from Árok you'll find **Lőrinc utca,** which will take you to **Párkányi híd,** the bridge that crosses the border to **Slovakia.** If you continue down **Kiss János altábornagy út** from the station, past **Hősök Tere,** you should keep left towards **Bajcsy-Zsilinszky Endre utca** to hike up to the fortress and Basilica.

SIGHTS

BASILICA OF ESZTERGOM

BASILICA

☎033 40 23 54 🖥www.bazilika-esztergom.hu

The nave lacks much of the ornamentation of other cathedrals, which gives it a sense of quiet stoicism. The organ, adorned with angelic statues, is one of the largest in Hungary. To one side you can find the millennia-old skull of Saint Stephen, founder of the Kingdom of Hungary. The beautiful Bakócz Chapel, to the left of the nave, is the only surviving chapel from the Middle Ages. The builders disassembled the chapel into 1600 pieces and reincorporated it into the new church while preserving its original form. The church crypt, also a worthy sight, contains the remains of Hungary's archbishops. Perhaps the greatest attraction is the hike up to the cupola. Four hundred stairs whisk travelers up a tightly wound spiral staircase (not for the claustrophobic) to a magnificent view of the city and neighboring area. On clear days you can see the beautiful pine-covered peaks of the Slovak Low Tatras.

Ⓢ *Chapel free. Cupola 400ft. Crypt 200ft.* Ⓩ *Open Mar-Oct Tu-Su 9am-4:30pm; Nov-Dec Tu-F 9am-4:30pm, Sa-Su 10am-3:30pm.*

CASTLE RUINS

RUINS, MUSEUM

☎033 41 59 86

Around the Basilica you can see the ruins of the castle where St. Stephen was born, which once dominated the same hilltop. A museum now occupies the former ruins and showcases many artifacts from the medieval and Renaissance periods. Some areas allow you to look through the ▨**glass floor** into the excavation site below.

Ⓢ *800Ft.* Ⓩ *Open Tu-Su 10am-4:45pm.*

FOOD

CSÜLÖK CSÁRDA

●♨♈❀ HUNGARIAN ❷

Batthyány Lajos utca 9

☎33 41 24 20 ▨www.csulokcsarda.hu

Traditional, but somewhat over-played, here you'll find Hungarian cuisine in a picnic-esque atmoshphere. Dishes range from the ancient recipe of smoky ox tongue *(1390Ft)* to aquatic treasures like the Hungarian classic, mixed fish soup *(1890Ft).* Don't be turned off by the restaurant's logo—the ghost from *Ghostbusters*—the restaurant is usually packed with hungry tourists and locals alike, especially during the summer.

Ⓢ *Appetizers 790-1395Ft. Entrees 1690-3990Ft.* Ⓩ *Open July-Aug M-F 8am-5pm, Sa 9am-noon; Sept-June M-F 8am-4pm.*

ESSENTIALS

Getting There

Trains run from Budapest's **Nyugati station** *(*Ⓢ *750Ft.* Ⓩ *1½hr, 22 per day).* The train station is about a 15min. walk from town. Facing away from the station, go left on the main street. Follow the street around the bend to the left and turn right at **Kiss János Vezérezredes út.** Buses run from **Szentendre** *(*Ⓢ *500Ft.* Ⓩ *1½hr, 1 per hr.)* and **Visegrád** *(*Ⓢ *350Ft.* Ⓩ *45min., 1 per hr.).* From the bus station, walk by **Simor János út** toward the market. The most spectacular way to get there is by ▨**MAHART ferry** *(*☎*484 40 13* ▨*www.mahartpassnave.hu),* which leaves the pier at Gőzhajó utca on **Prímás Sziget** for Budapest *(*Ⓢ *2985Ft.* Ⓩ *5hr., 6 per day).*

essentials

PLANNING YOUR TRIP

Time Differences

Hungary is one hour ahead of Greenwich Mean Time (GMT) and observes Daylight Saving Time. This means that it is six hours ahead of New York City, nine hours ahead of Los Angeles, one hour ahead of the British Isles, nine hours behind Sydney, and 10 hours behind New Zealand.

MONEY

Tipping and Bargaining

Tipping is customary in all situations where the customers and service workers—waiters, taxi drivers, and hotel porters—come face to face. Depending upon how satisfied you are with the service, plan to tip 10-15%.

- **PASSPORT:** Required for citizens of Australia, Canada, Ireland, New Zealand, the UK, and the US.

- **VISA:** Required for visitors who plan to stay in the Schengen area for more than 90 days.

- **WORK PERMIT:** Required for all foreigners planning to work in Hungary.

Taxes

Most goods in the Schengen area are subject to a Value-Added Tax of 19% (a reduced tax of 7% is applied to books and magazines, foods, and agricultural products). Ask for a VAT return form at points of purchase to enjoy tax-free shopping. Present it at customs upon leaving the country, along with your receipts and the unused goods. Refunds can be claimed at Tax Free Shopping Offices, found at most airports, road borders, and ferry stations, or by mail (Tax-Free Shopping Processing Center, Trubelgasse 19, 1030 Vienna Austria).

SAFETY AND HEALTH

General Advice

In any type of crisis, the most important thing to do is **stay calm.** Your country's embassy abroad is usually your best resource in an emergency; registering with that embassy upon arrival in the country is a good idea.

Local Laws and Police

You should not hestitate to contact the police in Budapest (☎107) if you are the victim of a crime. Be sure to carry a valid passport, as police have the right to ask for identification. Police can sometimes be unhelpful if you are the victim of a currency exchange scam; in that case, you might be better off seeking advice from your embassy or consulate.

Drugs and Alcohol

If you carry insulin, syringes, or any prescription drugs in these cities, you must carry a copy of the prescriptions and a doctor's note. Avoid public drunkenness as it will jeopardize your safety. In Hungary, drinking is permitted at age 18. Marijuana is entirely illegal in Hungary. Carrying drugs across an international border—considered to be drug trafficking—is a serious offense that could land you in prison.

Smoking is incredibly popular in Hungary. If you are sensitive to cigarette smoke, ask for a non-smoking room in a hotel or hostel, or to be seated in the non-smoking area of a restaurant.

Specific Concerns

Pre-Departure Health

Matching a prescription to a foreign equivalent is not always easy, safe, or possible, so if you take **prescription drugs,** carry up-to-date prescriptions or a statement from your doctor stating the medications' trade names, manufacturers, chemical names, and dosages. Be sure to keep all medication with you in your carry-on luggage. Some drugs—like pseudoephedrine (Sudafed) and diphenhydramine (Benadryl)—are not available in Hungary, or are only available with a perscription, so plan accordingly. Drugs such as aspirin (*aszpirin*), acetaminophen or Tylenol (*paracetamol*), ibuprofen or Advil, antihistamines (*antihisztaminok*), and penicillin can be found at any local Hungarian pharmacy.

hungary 101

facts and figures

- **ELEVATION OF BUDAPEST:** 185m/607ft.

- **NUMBER OF CITIES IN BUDAPEST:** 2. Separated by the Danube, Buda and Pest still have autonomy though their compound name came into use more than a century ago. Just like Minneapolisstpaul.

- **NUMBER OF THEATRES IN BUDAPEST:** 86

- **SEATS IN BUDAPEST'S DOHÁNY STREET SYNAGOGUE:** 3000.

- **AGE OF THE MILLENNIUM UNDERGROUND:** 114 years old in 2010.

- **"TIME WHEEL" TURNOVER TIME:** Exactly one year. The sand in this 8m-tall hourglass takes a full year to sift down. How they flip it over is another story.

FOOD AND DRINK

Food

Hungarians don't take food lightly. Accordingly, traditional Hungarian fare is as heavy as it comes, usually starring meat, potatoes and **paprika** (the Hungarian kind, which is HOT). No city does savory stews and meaty pancakes better than Budapest, but for those adverse to eating things that once had hooves, there are definitely options. Fortunate constants among most Budapest eateries are generous portions and reasonable prices, no matter what the cuisine. Some local specialties:

- **FŐZELÉK.** A hearty vegetable stew. Vegetarians, rejoice! It can be flavored with bacon or sausage, though; so ask first, then rejoice.

- **HORTOBÁGY PANCAKES.** *(Hortobágyi Palacsinta)* An ooey-gooey amalgam of fried pancakes, veal chunks, sour cream and paprika.

- **GOULASH.** The ubiquitous meat, potatoes and paprika stew. Hard to mess up, but beware if you're sensitive to heat.

- **KOLBÁSZ.** Hungarian sausage.

- **FATÁNYÉROS.** A barbeque dish of mixed meat, including mutton, beef, veal, and/or pork.

- **HALÁSZLÉ.** This "fisherman's soup" is a spicy showcase of river fish, heated up with (yep) a good dose of paprika.

Drinks

Hungary has become an active **wine** producer in recent years (especially since the fall of the Soviet Union), a point of pride among modern Budapestians—so much so that a national wine festival is celebrated in the city each September. To impress the locals or expand your palate, try ordering a *Budai Zöld, Furmint, Juhfark, Hárslevelu, Kadarka, Kéknyelu,* or *Királyleányka* (and if you successfully get one, make sure to toast your pronunciation skills). Budapest also boasts numerous *czardas* (old-fashioned taverns), *pinces* (beer/wine cellars) and *sorozos* (pubs) that serve as good a selection of local and international beers as anywhere on the continent. Just be careful to order what you want by name—order just *sor* (beer), and restaurants will often automatically bring you their expensive imported beer, instead of a cheaper Hungarian brand.

HOLIDAYS AND FESTIVALS

There's nothing Hungarians take more seriously than celebrating, especially when their city is the star of the party. Consequently, Hungary's calendar is filled with festivals featuring everything from wine tasting to gladiator fights.

festivals

- **INTERNATIONAL BOOK FESTIVAL (APRIL 14-17).** The name says it all.

- **FLORALIA FESTIVAL (MAY 22-23).** Party like it's 50CE! Held at the **Aquincum Museum in Óbuda** (Old Buda, district 3), this event revives an ancient Roman tradition, including theater, flower exhibitions, and even gladiator fights (the family-friendly kind).

- **NATIONAL GALLOP (JUNE 2-6).** Heroes' Square, Andrássy Ut. If you don't mind being inundated with Hungarian national pride, this exhibition of traditional equestrian skills is worth the trek.

- **SUMMER ON THE CHAIN BRIDGE (JULY 3-AUGUST 15).** This Budapest institution takes over the famous Chain Bridge with various performances and programs against the cerulean backdrop of the Danube.

- **SZIGET ROCK MUSIC FESTIVAL (AUGUST 11-16).** College students and motorcycle dudes descend on the city for this four-day rock-out, which has attracted crowds of over 300,000.

- **FESTIVAL OF FOLK ARTS (AUGUST 20-22).** Explore Buda's castle district to hear traditional Hungarian folklore and see handicraft demonstrations. The festival kicks off with celebrations for St. Stephen's Day on August 20 that include an artisans' parade and the "blessing of the bread" in front of St. Matthias' church.

- **JEWISH SUMMER FESTIVAL (AUGUST 26-SEPTEMBER 6).** Part celebration and part education, this festival is a full introduction to Hungarian Jewish culture, centered on (where else?) the Dohány Street Synagogue.

- **WINE FESTIVAL (FIRST WEEK IN SEPTEMBER).** Beginning with the harvest parade, this week-long toast to Hungarian vinters includes traditional costumes, dance, handicrafts, and of course lots of refreshments. Every year's a good year.

hungary

IRELAND

There's a neat little still at the foot of the hill
Where the smoke curls up to the sky
By a whiff of the smell you can plainly tell
That there's poitín boys close by.
For it fills the air with a perfume rare
And betwixt both me and you
As home we roll, we can drink a bowl
Or a bucketful of mountain dew.

Now learned men as use the pen
Have writ' the praises high
Of the sweet poitín from Ireland green
That's made from wheat and rye
Away with your pills, it'll cure all ills
Be ye pagan, Christian, or Jew
So take off your coat and grease your throat
With a bucket of the mountain dew.

greatest hits

- **SICK FLICKS.** Hit up the DVD collection at the Irish Film Institute (p. 652), then catch a movie or two.

- **REJOYCE.** At the James Joyce Centre (p. 655), you can pay homage to one of the forefathers of literary Modernism.

- **SHAMROCK AND ROLL.** Whelan's bar (p. 662) features predominantly alternative music, with not one but *two* stages.

- **CLUBLIN.** Head to Tripod (p. 662) on Harcourt St. in Dublin for top-shelf live music.

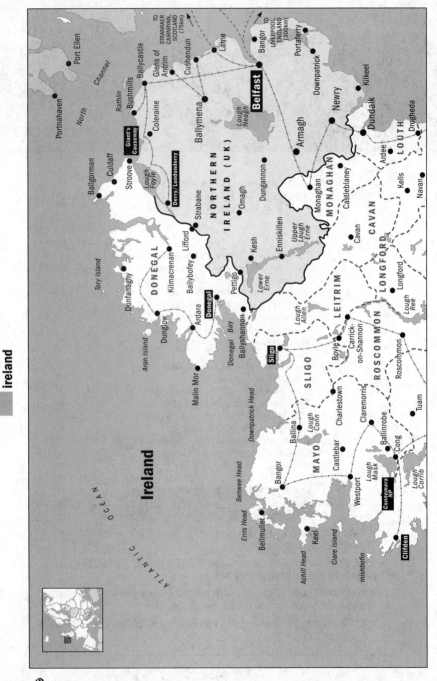

Ireland

Port Ellen

Portnahaven

North Channel

TO STRANRAER CAIRNRYAN, SCOTLAND

TO LIVERPOOL (300km) ENGLAND

Bangor

Portaferry

Larne

Belfast

Ballycastle

Cushendun

Glens of Antrim

Rathlin

Bushmills

Downpatrick

Kilkeel

Giant's Causeway

Coleraine

Ballymena

Newry

Dundalk

Armagh

Ballygorman

Culdaff

Lough Neagh

LOUTH

Drogheda

Stroove

Derry/Londonderry

NORTHERN IRELAND (UK)

Monaghan

Ardee

Lough Foyle

Dungannon

MONAGHAN

Kells

Navan

Dunfanaghy

Strabane

Omagh

Castleblaney

CAVAN

Tory Island

DONEGAL

Lifford

Kesh

Enniskillen

Cavan

LONGFORD

Kilmacrenan

Ballybofey

Upper Lough Erne

Pettigo

Longford

Donegal

Lough Ree

Dunglow

Ardara

Lower Erne

Lough Allen

LEITRIM

Carrick-on-Shannon

ROSCOMMON

Aran Island

Donegal Bay

Ballyshannon

Sligo

Boyle

Malin Mor

Sligo

SLIGO

Roscommon

Downpatrick Head

Tuam

Benwee Head

Ballina

Lough Conn

Charlestown

Claremorris

ATLANTIC OCEAN

Erris Head

MAYO

Castlebar

Ballinrobe

Bellmullet

Bangor

Cong

Lough Corrib

Keel

Westport

Lough Mask

Connemara NP

Achill Head

Clare Island

Clifden

Inishbofin

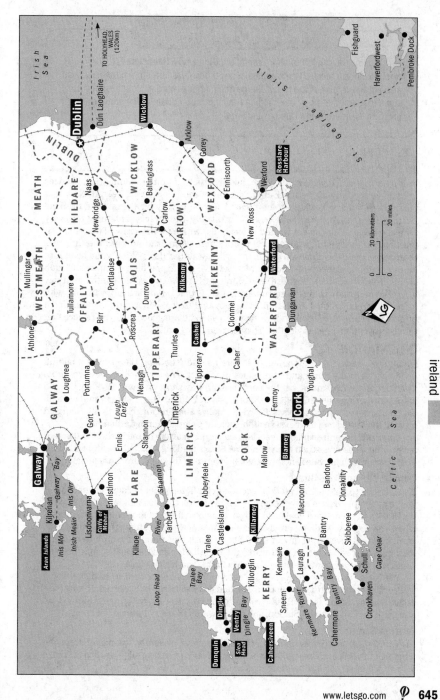

For students traveling to Dublin, a trip to the **Guinness Storehouse** is a no-brainer. Not only do you receive free samples during a how-to-drink-a-pint tutorial, but you also get a free pint at the top of the building. After ascending countless flights of stairs to reach the top of the building (which is, appropriately, pint-shaped), you'll probably be ready throw one back anyway.

dublin ☎01

Pull up a pint of ▨**Guinness,** sit down, and listen up. If you're reading this, chances are you've recently arrived in Dublin, capital of the Republic of Ireland. Now that you're here, however, what's to be done? You can('t) very well sit around drinking Guinness the *whole* time you're there. Fortunately, Dublin has something for every type of traveler. You can get wasted in **Temple Bar** with a motley crew of tourists, visit museums of everything from natural history to modern art, tour both the Guinness Storehouse *and* the Jameson Distillery, wile away the day poking your head into luxury clothing stores on Grafton Street, see live music and hit the impressive club scene around Camden, Wexford, and Harcourt Streets...we could continue all day long. The important thing to remember, though, is that Dublin is a fantastic city, with incredibly friendly inhabitants and a vibrancy that never seems to dim. See as much of it as you can—don't constrain yourself to specific areas because you're sure that things just couldn't get any better. They can, and they will.

ORIENTATION

Dublin's an easy city to get around, despite its size. The **River Liffey** draws a natural divide between the north and south sides of the city. The south side is known for its swankier, more ritzy areas, but the north is in no way short on gems. Dividing the two halves further are the different neighborhoods of Dublin. They range from the small-ish, touristy area known as **Temple Bar** to the **Grafton Street** region to the South Georgian area, to the Viking and medieval section, including Christchurch Cathedral.

Large north-south dividing streets include the major artery on the north side, **O'Connell Street** (which has pedestrian **Henry** and **Talbot Streets** flanking it on either side) and **Parliament Street,** which provides another street-bridge-street thoroughfare farther inland.

Temple Bar and the Quays

It's a bit silly to put an "Orientation" section in for Temple Bar because chances are if you're in Temple Bar on a weekend, you'll be so drunk that just making it to the end of the block will seem like a challenge. However, maybe the next morning (or afternoon), when you feel like walking around, take the main east-west street (**Temple Bar Street,** go figure) and diverge on any of the multiple lanes that run north-south from there. Heading north will take you up towards the River Liffey and the Quays while heading south will take you towards **Dame St., Dublin Castle,** and **Trinity College.**

The Quays (pronounced "Keys") are even more straightforward to navigate. You'll walk either on the north side (**Ormond Quay** and **Bachelors Walk**) or on the south side (**Wellington** and **Merchant's Quay**). Head west to go inland towards the Guinness Storehouse and the Irish Rail Heuston Station, and east towards the ferry terminal and port.

Grafton Street

Ah Grafton Street, pedestrian highway of purchase pleasure. Taking off from the meeting of **Suffolk** and **Nassau Streets,** Grafton Street climbs on a slight incline (*Let's Go* listings will refer to Grafton directions as being either "up" or "down") up from **Trinity**

ireland

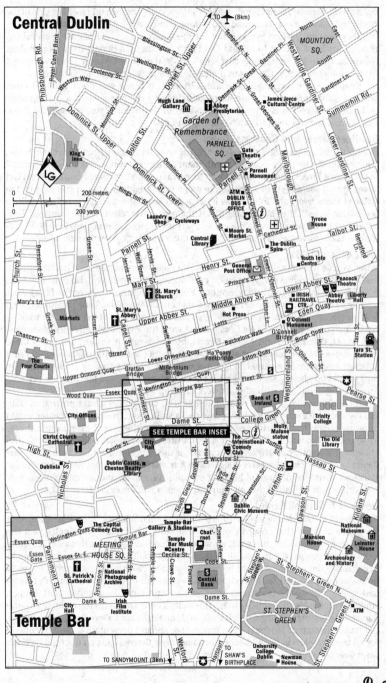

Central Dublin

Blessington St.
Temple St. N.
TO ✈ (8km)

North
West Middle Gardiner St.
East

MOUNTJOY
SQ.

South
Gardiner Ln.

Wellington St. Upper
Denmark St. Great
Hill St.
N. Great Georges St.
Summerhill Rd.
Lower Gardiner St.

Fontenoy St.
Dorset St. Upper
Great Denmark St.
Gardiner Pl.

Western Way
Phibsborough Rd.
Royal Canal Bank
Mountjoy St.
Bolton St.
Dominick Pl.

Dominick St. Upper

Hugh Lane
Gallery 🏛
Abbey 🕇
Presbyterian

James Joyce
Cultural Centre

Garden of
Remembrance

Dominick St. Lower

King's
Inns
N
LG

PARNELL
SQ.

Gate
Theatre

Marlborough St.

0   200 meters
0   200 yards

Kings Inn St.

Parnell St.

Parnell
Monument

Thomas Ln.

Tyrone
House

Talbot St.
Beresford Ln.

Laundry
Shop
Cycleways

Moore St.
Market

ATM ■
DUBLIN
BUS ■
OFFICE
ⓘ

Upper O'Connell St.

Cathedral St.
The Dublin 🕇
Spire

Bernard St.
Green St.
Wolfe Tone St.
Jervis St.

Central
Library

Henry St.
General
Post Office ✉

Youth Info
Centre

Church St.
Parnell St.
Mary's Ln.

St. Mary's 🕇
Church

Liffey St.
Prince's St. N.

Lower Abbey St.
Peacock
Theatre

Greek St.
St. Mary's 🕇
Abbey

Upper Abbey St.
Middle Abbey St.
Hot Press

IRISH
RAILTRAVEL
CTR. ■

Abbey
Theatre
Liberty
Hall

Markets

Capel St.
Smithfield Row

Great Strand St.
Great
Lotts

O'Connell
Monument ■

Eden Quay

Chancery St.
Strand St.

Lower Ormond Quay
Bachelors Walk

O'Connell
Bridge

Burgh Quay
D'Olier St.
Hawkins St.

Tara St.
Station

The
Four Courts

Grattan
Bridge

Millennium
Bridge

Ha'Penny
Footbridge
Aston Quay

Westmoreland St.

Upper Ormond Quay
Wood Quay
Essex Quay

Wellington

Temple Bar

Quay
Fleet St.

💲

Pearse St.

City Offices

Parliament St.

Dame St.

SEE TEMPLE BAR INSET

Anglesea St.

Bank of
Ireland 💲

College Green

Molly
Malone
statue

Trinity
College

Christ Church
Cathedral 🕇

Castle St.
City
Hall

✉
The ⓘ
International
Comedy
Club

Suffolk St.

The Old
Library

High St.
Nicholas St.

Dublinia ■

Dublin Castle ■
Chester Beatty
Library

Dame Ct.
Dame St.

Wicklow St.

Fade St.

Drury St.
South William St.
Clarendon St.

Nassau St.

Grafton St.

Dawson St.

Kildare St.

National
Museums 🏛

Dublin
Civic Museum 🏛

Mansion
House

Leinster
House 🏛

Archaeology
and History 🏛

Temple Bar

Essex Quay
The Capital 🛡
Comedy Club

Wellington Quay

Temple Bar
Gallery & Studios 🛡

Temple Bar

Chat'
rnet

Crown Alley

Essex
Gate

Parliament St.
Exchange St.

Essex St. E.
Essex Gate

MEETING
HOUSE SQ.

Sycamore St.

Eustace St.

Temple Ln. S.

Temple
Bar Music ■
Centre
Cecilia St.

Cope St.

St. Patrick's 🛡
Cathedral

National ■
Photographic
Archive

Crowe St.
Fownes St.

💲
Central
Bank

City
Hall

Dame St.

Irish ■
Film
Institute

Dame St.

St. Stephen's Green N.

Wexford St.

TO SANDYMOUNT (3km)

Harcourt St.

✠

TO
SHAW'S
BIRTHPLACE

ST. STEPHEN'S
GREEN

St. Stephen's Green W.
St. Stephen's Green E.

ATM ■

University
College
Dublin ■

Newman ■
House

College to **St. Stephen's Green.** Small, pedestrian walkways branch off on either side of the street and lead to more shops and, more importantly, several excellent pubs.

Shopping on Grafton Street is not for the faint of heart—or of cash. Several top tier brands have outlets here, and Dublin's not exactly a pennypincher's paradise. However, there are some gems that won't rob you of all the money you saved to get from Dublin to Prague. Check out the clothing listings for more detail there.

Even if you're not buying, Grafton Street is a place you don't want to miss. Window shopping here is made more enjoyable by the presence of a hodge-podge collection of street performers, who busk from dawn until (yes, we said it), dusk. Visit during the weekend to catch some great acts.

Gardiner Street and Customs House

Dublin City Council might as well just get it over with and rename Gardiner Street "Hostel Row." The place is littered with them. The street runs north to south parallel to O'Connell Street, and the easiest way to get there is to take the pedestrian **North Earl Street** from **O'Connell** (you'll know you're going in the right direction if you pass by the **statue of James Joyce**) and follow it as it turns into **Talbot Street,** which is only partially a pedestrian street. After **Marlborough Street,** the next cross street will be Gardiner. Turn left or right, you won't escape the endless stream of signs offering you free Wi-Fi, full Irish breakfasts, and clean sheets. That last one's a priority, so make sure to ask.

West of Temple Bar

When you've had enough of Temple Bar's late night shenanigans and Grafton street's lost it's charm (read: when your credit card maxes out), head west. Like the cowboys of old, strike out for gold and adventure. Follow the northern side of the Liffey west and along the quays until you reach **Bow Street** on the **Arran Quay.** Turn right and walk a few blocks up—Eureka! Gold! Liquid gold Jameson whiskey at the distillery tour! Now that you're rich, take **Lord Edward Street** west through nearly all of its changes— **High Street, Cornmarket,** and **Thomas Streets,** but it's worth it to turn left on to **Crane Street,** enter the **Guinness Storehouse,** scale the stairs (or take the elevator if you find yourself exceptionally parched) to the **Gravity Bar,** where you may survey the long, dusty trail you blazed. Accept your pint of Guinness gladly, and feel the rich rewards that accompany the neighborhoods west of Temple Bar.

All banter aside, the area west of Temple Bar constitutes a huge portion of Dublin. Phoenix park sits on its inland edge, and a walk there from the city center would take up a significant portion of your day. However, there are several great things to see along the way. On the south side, **Christchurch Cathedral, Dublinia,** and the **Irish Museum of Modern Art;** on the left, in contrast, is the impressive architecture of the **Four Courts** and the **National Museum of Decorative Arts and Military History,** housed at Collins Barracks. Don't be afeared o' heading out into the sunset and making a day out of enjoying a part of Dublin that all your lazy friends will never get to.

North of O'Connell Street

Past the **O'Connell Monument,** with it's bullet-riddled Victory, past the spire, that unequivocal proof that absurdly phallic sculpture is not dead, and finally, past the **Parnell Monument,** which, uh, well...so we can't think of a joke for that one. It's there anyway and you're past it. Past all of these things you'll find a neighborhood caught in a strange limbo—somewhere between being too close to the city center to really be residential, but not far enough away to escape all of downtown Dublin's hustle-and-bustle. The result is an area with smaller and more local shops, and a much smaller percentage of tourists on the sidewalk. There are things to see up here—the **Gardens of Remembrance** are worth a look, and the **Hugh Lane Gallery** might just beat out the Irish Museum of Modern Art in terms of scale and presentation. And of course, for all the Joyceans in the audience, the **James Joyce Centre** is just up the road on **North Great George's Street.**

Dorset Street and Drumcondra

Okay, things to know about Dorset Street. It's dodgy. Like, not a place you want to take Fluffy for a walk after dark. Located far past the **Parnell Monument** and running east to west, it has a few hostels and restaurants, but there's really nothing to see. If you're thinking about trying to find a place away from the city proper, a much better place is **Upper Drumcondra Road.** The top of this street, near **Griffith Avenue,** is a very safe residential area, and the B and Bs in that part of town bring none of the hassle of the city center and have the added benefit of a real neighborhood feel.

ACCOMMODATIONS 🏠

Dublin is expensive, no two ways about it. Expect to pay at least €15 per night for a hostel dorm room, and often times more. Banking on the heavy party traffic, hostels, guesthouses and hotels in Dublin have all adopted a "week" and "weekend" rate, with the latter usually being around a one-quarter increase from the weekday price, so bear that in mind if you're planning a weekend trip.

Temple Bar and the Quays

Temple Bar accommodations are usually filled with younger travelers—backpackers especially—who are interested in going out and having a good time. Note that any hostel in the Temple Bar area is bound to be noisy at night, and that you might have to deal with people coming into the dorm room at late hours.

👍 BARNACLES TEMPLE BAR HOUSE — 💳📶 HOSTEL ❶

19 Temple Ln. ☎01 671 6277 💻barnacles.ie

Have a great time and meet fellow travelers at this Temple Bar funhouse. The exterior looks small but hides several different dorms and private rooms, a large common room, and a kitchen, the latter of which serves a free light breakfast. The modern decorating will appeal to hipsters traveling through Dublin, while the friendly staff is always happy to help GLBT guests find gay-friendly nightlife in the area.

⇆ Down towards the Liffey from Dame St. ℹ Laundry €7 per bag. Towel and lock rental €1.50 plus €5 returnable deposit. $ Dorms €10-33; private rooms €30-44. ⏰ No curfew; present hostel-issued security pass after 11pm.

👍 FOUR COURTS HOSTEL — 💳♿📶⛅ HOSTEL ❷

15-17 Merchants Quay ☎01 672 5839 💻www.fourcourtshostel.com

Unless you're *really* lazy and don't want to walk the two blocks down to Temple Bar from the Quay, this might just be the best hostel in Dublin. "Staff Drink fund: We need beer!" reads the tip jar, and the staff are determined to keep things lighthearted. Tons of complimentary services (DVD, Wii or guitar rental) are all available with a presentation of ID. The dorms themselves are comfortable with lofty ceilings that serve as stuffiness reducer or snore amplifiers, depending on your perspective.

⇆ Riverside, Merchant's Quay. ℹ Credit card min. €15, 24hr. cancellation policy. $ Dorms €15 per week, €19 per weekend. ⏰ No curfew; present hostel-issued security pass.

LITTON LANE HOSTEL — 💳♿📶 HOSTEL ❷

Litton Ln. ☎01 872 8389 💻www.irish-hostel.com

If you ever looked at Freddie Mercury's sweaty pantsuit in a Hard Rock Café and didn't gag, you'll love this hostel. Housed in what used to be a recording studio for the likes of U2, Van Morrison, and The Cranberries, it's now been completely remodeled. The rock vibe remains, however, as painted murals of artists and lyrics follow you down the hallways of each floor.

⇆ On Bachelor's Walk, north side of the Liffey. ℹ Bathrooms shared. Group discounts available. $ 10 bed dorm weekday €12, weekend €14; 8 bed dorm €13/15; 6 bed dorm €14/16; private twins €45; doubles €50; 3-bed apartment €75 per night. ⏰ No curfew; present hostel-issued security pass.

RIVERHOUSE HOTEL 💳 HOTEL ❹

23-24 Eustace St. ☎01 670 7655 💻www.riverhousehotel.com

For those who are able to spend a bit more but still want to stay in the Temple Bar area, the Riverhouse Hotel is the place to go. A local feel carries throughout, despite its heavily touristed neighborhood.

*➜ Temple Bar; look for a deep-red front with gilded lettering. **i** Discounts for extended stays. $ High season €50-110; low season €45-90.*

Grafton Street

👍 **AVALON HOUSE** 💳♿📶 HOSTEL ❷

25 Aungier St. ☎01 475 0001 💻www.avalonhouse.ie

A hugely popular hostel on the south end of town, Avalon house boasts free Wi-Fi, computers for guest use, a movie projector and DVD rental, ping-pong, pool table, and book exchange. And those are just the perks. Also available are laundry machines and an ISA 10% student discount for the first night. Chill out downstairs with a good flick, or head upstairs to the cafe to chat up your fellow travelers.

➜ Follow South Great George's St. until it turns in Aungier St. $ Rates change daily, so check website for more information. ⏰ Reception 24hr.

CENTRAL HOTEL 💳♿📶 HOTEL ❺

1-5 Exchequer St. ☎01 679 7302 💻www.centralhotel.com

Plush green carpets, huge framed mirrors, Victorian paintings of stockings and petticoats, and that's just in the lobby! This posh hotel's rates change daily, so check the website for booking info. However, expect to pay double on the weekends. Continental *(€5)* and full Irish *(€10)* breakfasts available.

***i** Tourist kiosk available in lobby. ⏰ Reception 24hr.*

KELLY'S HOTEL 💳🚭📶 HOTEL ❸

36 South Great George's St. ☎01 648 0010 💻www.kellysdublin.com

If you're into white walls and minimalist furniture you'll be quite at home in this ultra-chic, ultra-modern hotel. The rooms are comfortable, with big beds and modern bathrooms. The doubles are a little on the small side, however. Free breakfast available at Le Gueulenton next door. Both Kelly's hotel and Grafton Guesthouse get noisy at night from the bars below, so make sure to request a quiet room.

➜ Turn right off of Grafton St. and continue until you reach South Great George's St. $ Rates change daily. Check website for more information. ⏰ Reception 24hr.

GRAFTON GUESTHOUSE 💳🚭📶 HOTEL ❸

26-27 South Great George's St. ☎01 648 0010 💻www.kellysdublin.com

A more traditional version of what is to be found over at Kelly's Hotel, the Grafton Guesthouse offers comfortable, not-white ensuite rooms. The creaking wooden stairs and high ceilings of the hotel will only serve to remind you that you're residing in one of the oldest parts of Dublin.

*➜ Just down the street from Kelly's Hotel. **i** Reception in Kelly's Hotel. $ Prices change daily, so check the website for more information. ⏰ Reception in Kelly's hotel, 24hr.*

ALBANY HOUSE 💳🚭📶 BED AND BREAKFAST ❹

84 Harcourt St. ☎01 475 1092 💻www.albanyhousedublin.com

Okay, this one's a bit on the steep-side, pricewise, but it's worth it. The Albany House is located in a wonderful Georgian home, with more elaborate molding than month-old bread. Rooms are large with very modern bathrooms. All rooms ensuite.

*➜ From the top of Grafton St. continue straight the length of St. Stephen's Green and continue on to Harcourt St. It will be on the left. **i** Continental breakfast included. Wi-Fi available in lobby. $ Check website for rates.*

Gardiner Street and Customs House

Gardiner Street might as well be called Hostel Row. There are tons of hostels, hotels, guesthouses, lodges, and B and Bs all the way down the street. If it's a place where people stay, chances are it's located here. It's a quick walk down to the city center and Temple Bar, though if you're coming back late from a night out you'll want to be careful. A taxi might be the best bet.

👍 **HOLYHEAD B AND B** 💳📶 BED AND BREAKFAST ❷

42 Lower Gardiner St. ☎01 873 5889

A bed and breakfast with a real, classic feel to it, Holyhead has winding stairways take you up to beautitul window landings where you can sit and enjoy the morning sun. The rooms themselves are nice (although some of them sport a paint job that is radically different than the classic decor of the interior).

i *Breakfast and Wi-Fi available.* [$] *Rooms range from €30-60 during the week, with an increase on the weekends.*

👍 **GLOBETROTTERS HOSTEL** 🚭📶❄ HOSTEL ❸

47-48 Lower Gardiner St. ☎01 873 5893 💻www.globetrottersdublin.com

There's a reason "Hostelworld" has ranked Globetrotters as one of the best more than once—it lives up to its self-styled high standards. With comfortable dorms and incredibly swanky singles and doubles, all the rooms here are ensuite and come with a full Irish breakfast. Hidden perk: if you're staying in single or double rooms, dial 0 on your phone to order a drink from the bar to be delivered up to your room.

i *Kitchen and Wi-Fi available.* [$] *Dorms M-F €18, Sa-Su €20. Singles ensuite €60-70; doubles €40-45 per person.*

ABBOTT LODGE 💳🚭📶 HOTEL ❸

87-88 Lower Gardiner St. ☎01 836 5548 💻www.abbottlodge.com

A beautiful lodge, where, if you book at the right time, you can get a room at a decent price. Book in advance to secure the best rates. Breakfast is included—full Irish from 8:30-10am, with continental available before that.

i *Breakfast included.* [$] *Singles from around €30; doubles €50.*

ABRAHAM HOUSE 💳🚭📶 HOSTEL ❶

82-83 Lower Gardiner St. ☎01 855 0600 💻www.abraham-house.ie

One of the good bargain options on Lower Gardiner St. There are no lockers—just a luggage storage room, so bring along your own lock or pay for one. The dorm rooms are small but clean. Meet other travelers over breakfast.

i *Breakfast included. Sheets included. Safety deposit boxes are €1 per night+€10 deposit. Free Wi-Fi in the lobby, as well as a TV and DVD rental in the sitting room. All rooms ensuite.* [$] *Beds from €9. Expect a raise in prices for weekend and holiday stays.* ⏰ *Reception 24hr.*

HAZEL BROOK GUEST HOUSE 💳🚭📶 BED AND BREAKFAST ❷

85-86 Lower Gardiner St. ☎01 836 5003 💻www.hazelbrookhouse.ie

A well-furnished and comfortable Gardiner St. option, Hazel Brook offers free Wi-Fi in all rooms, as well as a full Irish or contitnental breakfast from 8-10am. Another high-ceilinged Georgian option, this one differs from the others in that you won't have bunk beds or lockers in the rooms.

i *Breakfast and Wi-Fi available. Coffee and TV available in all rooms.* [$] *€40-100+ depending on the day, so check the website for rates.*

Dorset Street and Drumcondra

Dorset Street and Drumcondra both lie on the outskirts of Dublin city center, so you're looking at a long walk or bus ride into town. That being said, it can be a nice escape. However, you should always be careful about how you find your way home late at night. Walking is not a good idea, and the buses stop running at 11:30pm, so if you plan on staying out later than that, make sure to set aside some of your cash for a taxi.

ASHLING HOUSE/AZALEA LODGE
BED AND BREAKFAST ❹

168 Upper Drumcondra Rd./67 Upper Drumcondra Rd. ☎01 837 5432/01 837 0300

Owned by the same couple, these two B and Bs might just be the greatest thing since sliced bread. Or, perhaps, scones, which you'll receive upon entering the door of the Azalea Lodge. Breakfast at the Ashling is continental, and the prices slightly cheaper because of it. But if you're willing to splurge, everything in the full Irish at Azalea is fresh and cooked to order. Amazing.

i All rooms ensuite. $ Rooms €70-80 per night.

THE DUBLIN CENTRAL HOSTEL
HOSTEL ❶

5 Blessington St., Dublin 7 ☎01 086 385 3832

Having just been recently renovated, this hostel is spotless but unfortunately lacks flavor. Hopefully things pick up with time, but meanwhile you can enjoy kitchen use, a pool table, and free TV inside its freshly painted walls.

From the top of Parnell Sq., cross Dorset St. and on to Blesington. i Lockers free for those staying under 1 week. All rooms ensuite. Credit cards will be accepted soon. $ 4-bed dorm M-F €12, Sa-Su €16; 8-bed €10/14; private room €40/50.

TINODE HOUSE
GUESTHOUSE ❷

170 Upper Drumcondra Rd. ☎01 837 2277 tinodehouse.com; info@tinodehouse.com

A spotless, cozy option up drumcondra, this B and B features a glass covered sitting area (complete with board games!) as well as a outside patio. The dining room will make you feel like you're back at home.

i All rooms with cable TV. $ €40-45 per person.

SIGHTS

Temple Bar and the Quays

The good thing about sightseeing in Temple Bar is that everything's so close together. And the Quays? Hit the river and run in either direction.

JAMESON DISTILLERY TOUR
WHISKEY DISTILLERY TOUR

Bow St., Smithfield Dublin 7 ☎01 807 2355 www.jamesonwhiskey.com

Hooray! Another tour that rewards you by offering free drinks! It's common knowledge now, but if you volunteer at the end of a short video that introduces the tour, you'll get to participate in a whiskey tasting at the end of the walk through Jameson Distillery. If your hand isn't called upon, you'll still get that complimentary whiskey at the end, but those who are chosen will receive a certificate denoting them as Jameson "official whiskey tasters." Whatever that means. The tour lasts around 1hr. 15min. and showcases the process of whiskey distillation from start to finish. Restaurant and gift shop in the lobby.

Walk on the north side of the Liffey down to Arran quay, turn right and follow the signs to the Jameson distillery. $ Tour: €13.50, student €11, senior €10, child €8, family (2-4) €30. Open M-Sa 9am-5:15pm, Su 10am-5:15pm (last tour 5:15pm).

IRISH FILM INSTITUTE
CINEMA

#6 Eustace St. ☎01 679 5744 www.irishfilm.ie

Walking down a long hallway paved in movie reels and plastered with classic movie posters, this refurbished Quaker building is a movie junkie's dream-come-true. Skylights let the natural light filter in as you can enjoy a drink in the bars, a bite to eat from the restaurant, or check out the in-house DVD store. Then hit up the cinema, checking out indie and Irish flicks. Look for the monthly director's retrospectives; if the director's Irish, you might just get to attend a Q and A session.

$ Movie tickets €7.75 until 6pm, afterwards €9.20. Film institute open M-F 10am-6pm; cinema open M-F 10am-9:30pm.

NATIONAL WAX MUSEUM PLUS

MUSEUM

Foster Pl., Dublin 2 ☎01 671 8873 www.waxmuseumplus.ie

This is how wax museums should be: get your educational quota done early (you start with the "Writers' Room" and "History Vaults") and then move on into the fun stuff (Hannibal horror rooms and waxen celebrities). Get closer to Pierce Brosnan's ruggedly strong chin than you ever thought possible.

Across from the Trinity College entrance near Grafton street. i Parental advisory for 16 and under for Horror room. $ €10, students and seniors €9, children €7, family €30. Open daily 10am-7pm.

DUBLIN GRAPHIC STUDIO GALLERY

ART GALLERY

"Through the arch" off Cope St. ☎01 679 8021 gallery@graphicstudiodublin.com

An artist-owned gallery where 99% percent of the works on display are up for sale, any purchase you make will help fund artist workshops and give awards to local art students. But even if you're not buying, the gallery is a great stop.

$ Prices vary. Open M-F 10am-5:30pm, Sa 11am-5pm.

GALLERY OF PHOTOGRAPHY

PHOTOGRAPHY GALLERY

Meeting House Sq., Temple bar ☎01 671 4654 www.galleryofphotography.ie

A photo gallery that showcases both graduate student and professional work two stories of winding exhibit space makes for a wonderful—and free, free is always good—wander. Check out their large selection of photography books and pick up a postcard in the lobby.

At the back of the square. $ Free. Open Tu-Sa 11am-6pm, Su 1-6pm.

Grafton Street

TRINITY COLLEGE

UNIVERSITY TOUR

Trinity College, College Green www.tcd.ie

Tours given by Trinity students describe a history of the college that is full of fun and quirky historical facts. Ghosts, deadly student feuds and more await you, stories told with all the college sarcasm money can buy. The climax of the tour is at the **Old Library,** where participants are led into the room that showcases the famous **Book of Kells.** The book itself is housed in a dark and crowded room, so you have to squint and jostle to get a good look. More easily enjoyed is the **Long Room,** a wonderful, wood-paneled room that stretches the length of the building and houses (in shelves upon shelves) some of the university's oldest and rarest books. A rotating themed exhibition of some of them is available for perusal in the glass display cases that run the length of the room.

Crossing O'Connell Brige onto Westmoreland St., walk 5min. It will be on your left. $ Tour plus admission to the Old Library and Book of Kells €10, tour without admission to library €5. Admission to library without tour €9. Tours M-Sa 10:15, 10:40, 11:05am, 11:35am, 12:10, 12:45, 2:15, 3, 3:40pm.

NATIONAL LIBRARY OF IRELAND

LIBRARY

7 Kildare street ☎01 603 0200 www.nli.ie

The main show, so to speak, is the exhibition detailing the life and works of **William Butler Yeats.** A circular space with a bench allows you to listen to recordings of Yeats's poetry accompanied by associative images projected on the screens. Several items from Yeats's life are on display as well, including his ring, collections of his poetry, and even a lock of his hair.

Follow Nassau St. along Trinity College, and turn right on Kildare. $ Free. Open M-W 9:30am-9pm, Th-F 9:30am-5pm, Sa 9:30am-1pm. Guided tours led through the exhibit daily at 3:30pm.

NATURAL HISTORY MUSEUM

MUSEUM

Merrion St., Dublin 2 ☎01 677 7444 www.museum.ie

The ground floor of this museum houses fauna from all over the island, including skeletons of the Ancient Irish Elk (it's like Bambi from hell), as well as tons of other birds and bugs and fish. When you've finished with that, head upstairs to the world exhibit, where you can get your fix for rhinos, hippos and giraffes.

⚓ *Follow Nassau St. (it turns into Clare St.) and then turn Merrion Sq. west.* Ⓢ *Free.* ⓣ *Open T-Sa 10am-5pm, Su 2pm-5pm.*

DUBLIN CASTLE ⊛& CASTLE/GOVERNMENT BUILDING
Dublin Castle, State Apartments, Dame St. ☎01 677 7129 🖳www.dublincastle.ie

Built by the English in the 13th century, the original "Dublin Castle" burned down in an accidental fire. Whoops. The castle was rebuilt in the 18th century, and was the headquarters of British rule in Ireland until the Irish revolution in 1920. Now it's a series of governmental buildings. The tour will take you through several impressive state rooms, including the blue carpeted "ballroom," where the President of Ireland is now inaugurated. The tour ends in the bowels of one of the castle's original towers. You can see the darkly colored waters that once formed a pool in the castle gardens, giving the city its name—the Irish *"Dubh"* (black), and *"Linn"* (pool).

⚓ *Walk over the O'Connell Bridge past Temple Bar and turn right onto Dame St. Follow Dame St. for 10min. and Dublin Castle will be on the left.* Ⓢ *€4.50, seniors and students €3.50, under 12 €2.* ⓣ *Open M-F 10am-4:45pm, Sa-Su and public holidays 2pm-4:45pm.*

West of Temple Bar

Okay, so some of the places out here require a bit of a hike, but you're up for it, right? No? Don't feel like walking for 45min. during your vacation? Not a problem. Take the Dublin sightseeing bus tours—part of their circuit involves stops at all of the places listed below.

🗋 GUINNESS STOREHOUSE ⊛&ⵝ BEER TOUR
St. James' Gate ☎01 471 4668 🖳www.guinness_storehouse.com

The Guinness storehouse is a 5-story exhibit centered entirely around...just kidding. How's this? It's a tour of an old beer factory. At the Guinness storehouse you get to spend time examining old Guinness ads, learning how to properly drink a pint (free samples!), and, at the top of the building, have a free pint of Guinness at the Gravity Bar, a circular glass bar that looks out over all of Dublin. Here's what you need to know: great tour, great views, free beer. Sound good? You bet.

⚓ *Follow Dame street as it turns into: High, Cornmarket, and Thomas St., and then turn left on Crane St. The Dublin hop-on, hop-off tour buses are also a good way to go. i Tour brochures available in mulitple languages. Huge selection of Guinness merchandise for sale.* Ⓢ *€15, seniors and students €11, students under 18 €9, children 6-12 €5.* ⓣ *Open daily Sept-June 9:30am-5pm; July-Aug 9:30am-7pm.*

NATIONAL MUSEUM OF DECORATIVE ARTS AND HISTORY &🏛 MUSEUM
Collins Barracks, Benburb St. ☎01 677 7444

Fitting: that an old military barracks should now house a military history museum. Not so fitting: that the same barracks should house a decorative arts museum. Admittedly, it's a weird combination—exhibits of Ireland's tumultuous history side by side with cabinets housing oriental plates, but it's something you shouldn't miss. Check out the interactive features of the "barracks life" exhibit in particular.

⚓ *Walk inland on the north side of the Liffey for approx. 30min. i No photos of the exhibits allowed.* Ⓢ *Free.* ⓣ *Open T-Sa 10am-5pm, Su 2pm-5pm.*

IRELAND MUSEUM OF MODERN ART (IMMA) & MUSEUM
Royal Hospital, Military road, Kilmainham ☎01 612 9900 🖳www.imma.ie

Located in an old military hospital, the rooms here are so white and blank you'll have trouble figuring out whether they're part of the exhibition or not. Usually housing three or four separate exhibits, the long halls and quiet atmosphere of the

IMMA are perfect for contemplating whether the artist you're seeing was actually influenced by Jackson Pollock, or just spilled some extra paint on the canvas.

ℹ Guided tours are given for free every W, F, and Su at 2:30pm. $ Free. ⏰ Open T 10am-5:30pm, W 10:30am-5:30pm, Th-Sa 10am-5:30pm, Su 12pm-5:30pm.

North of O'Connell Street

For the Hugh Lane Gallery and the Gardens of Remembrance, you'll want to head behind the Parnell monument and to the top of Parnell Sq. Leaving the Hugh Lane Gallery, turn left to get to the Writers Museum, and the James Joyce Centre is just a few blocks down in the same direction.

👍 DUBLIN WRITERS MUSEUM 🎫🚭❄⛅ MUSEUM

18 Parnell Sq. ☎01 872 2077 💻www.writersmuseum.com

James Joyce may have his own digs just up the road, but Ireland's other greats are also being remembered in style. The DWM showcases old manuscripts, first editions, and tons of memorabilia (read: old pipes and typewriters up the ying yang). Head upstairs to see the one thing the James Joyce Centre doesn't have—his piano—and then come back down and admire both the artistry on the wall and the beautiful home itself. If you really like the house, thank the father of Irish whiskey, John Jameson, who lived in it from 1891 to 1914 and is responsible for much of the renovation.

🚶 Continue walking along Parnell St. north with the Hugh Lane Gallery on your left; the museum is at the end of the block. ℹ Cafe and gift shop. $ €7.50, seniors and students €6.30, children €4.70, family (2+2) €18.70. ⏰ Open M-Sa 10am-5pm, Su 11am-5pm. Last entry 45min. before close.

THE HUGH LANE GALLERY ♿⛅ ART GALLERY

166 Parnell Sq. ☎01 222 5564 💻www.hughlane.ie

A modern art gallery that's so modern, it doesn't even have to show you just art: the works of the famous painter Francis Bacon are here, but so is his studio. Literally. An exact replica of one of his studios has been brought in and assembled right in the gallery, so now you can see just how much disorder it takes to create art. Upstairs and downstairs collections are interesting and slightly less messy, at least the art there is restricted to the canvas.

🚶 At the top of Parnell Sq., across the street from the Gardens of Remembrance. ℹ Cafe and bookstore downstairs. $ Free. Suggested donation €2. ⏰ Open Tu-Th 10am-6pm, F-Sa 10am-5pm, Su 11am-5pm.

JAMES JOYCE CENTRE 🎫🚭⛅ MUSEUM

35 North Great George's St. ☎01 878 8547 💻www.jamesjoyce.ie

A Georgian house on North Great George's St. now houses the James Joyce Centre. Part museum, part headquarters for Joyce fanatics of Dublin, it's also a mecca for Joyce fanatics from the rest of the world. And trust us, there are plenty. Pieces of note include a copy of Joyce's deathmask, a table at which part of "Ulysses" was written, and the door to 7 Eccles St., the fictional residence of Leopold Bloom.

🚶 Walk up O'Connell St. to the Parnell Statue, turn right onto Parnell St. and then left onto North Great George's St. ℹ Group discounts available. $ €5, students and seniors €4. ⏰ Open Tu-Sa 10am-5pm, Su noon-5pm.

Dorset Street and Drumcondra

Croke Park is a little bit, okay, a lotta bit, out of the way. However, it's also roughly the size of an aircraft carrier, so it's hard to miss. Take a taxi, or walk your way up along Drumcondra.

👍 CROKE PARK 🎫♿❄ SPORTS STADIUM

Croke Park, Jones Rd. ☎01 819 2323 💻www.crokepark.ie

Taking you for a run-around the magnificent Croke Park Stadium, home of Gaelic football and hurling, this tour covers the stadium from top to bottom, literally.

You'll hit the locker room, players lounge, and corporate top boxes. Holding 82,300 occupants when full, Croke Park is the 4th largest stadium in Europe—pretty impressive when you consider that all Gaelic sports are amateur sports. Those burly players? Yeah, they all have day jobs. The museum is informative for those interested in picking up the history, but for those who've really been wondering what it's like to play Gaelic sports can try them out on the second floor, where you can try your luck with a hurling bat or test your foot accuracy kicking a Gaelic football. Of course, the truest way to experience Croke Park is to see a game, so ask about tickets while you're there.

🚌 *Buses that pass by Croke Park are the 3, 11, 11a, 16, 16a, 46a and 123.* 🄢 *Tour and museum €11, museum only €6; students and seniors €8.50/4.50; under 12 €7.50/4; under 5 free/free; family €30/16.* 🕗 *Open Sept-June M-F 9:30am-5pm, Su noon-5pm; July-Aug M-F 9:30am-6pm, Su noon-6pm. Last tour at 3pm.*

GARDENS OF REMEMBRANCE ⛲ PUBLIC PARK
Up past the Parnell Monument, just below Dorset St.

A nice place to escape and rest your legs or get out of the hustle-and-bustle of the city around you, the Gardens of Remembrance are defined by a giant, cross-shaped pool at the bottom, and a large statue of falling men and women and rising geese at the end. Mind you don't sit on the grass, though—they've got signs there to tell you it's a no-no.

🄢 *Free to the public.*

FOOD

Dublin's food is, contrary to popular belief, very good. Sure, there are a lot of boiled and fried foods liberally doused in salt, but time and practice have honed those dishes down to their delicious cores. More exotic flavors have come to Dublin thanks to the **Celtic Tiger,** and a huge variety of ethnic restaurants can be found all over the city. Unfortunately, there are also a slew of bad fast food chains. Here's the traveler's rule of thumb: if it smells the same back home as it does in Dublin, shy away.

Temple Bar and the Quays

If there's a place to escape Ireland's infamy as a country with "bad" or "dull" food options (though these are words that are thrown around by other people, and *Let's Go* has always held Irish cuisine in high regard), that place is Temple Bar. It's got traditional Irish fare, rest assured, but it's also become quite the cosmopolitan neighborhood. You also won't have far to go to find several international options.

PANEM ♿ CAFE ❶
21 Lower Ormond Quay, Dub 1 ☎01 872 8510

Run by a Sicilian man and his Irish wife, Panem has got your coffee and pastry fix covered. With imported Italian coffee (€2.50-3) and the mind-meltingly delicious Sicilian almond biscuits for just (€1) each, Panem will become your morning, or afternoon, or evening, ritual.

🚌 *Over the Millenium Bridge from Temple Bar.* 🄢 *€.90-6.50. Cash only.* 🕗 *Open M-Sa 9am-5pm.*

TANTE ZOE'S CREOLE ❹
1 Crow St., Temple Bar ☎01 679 4407 🖳www.tantezoes.com

The food's all Creole, all the time (jambalayas and gumbos are the *plat du jour*, *toujours*), but the ambience is divided. Sit upstairs for the feel of a French bistro or head downstairs for a close-quartered jazz club. Come Saturday nights to hear the singing waitress.

🚌 *1 block west of Central Bank Plaza, head north on Crow St.* 🄢 *€7-30.* 🕗 *Open M-Th noon-10pm, F-Sa noon-11pm, Su noon-10pm.*

BOTTICELLI'S 🚫♿ ICE CREAM ❶

No. 3 Temple Bar St. ☎01 672 7289 🖥www.botticelli.ie

Providing Temple Bar's ice cream fix, Botticelli's serves Italian gelato in cups or cones from €2.50-5. Flavors include banana, tiramisu, and Italian *cioccolato.* Coffee is served as well.

🚏 Temple Bar St., across from The Temple Bar. Ⓢ Cash only. ⏰ Open 11am-midnight everyday.

GERTRUDE'S CAFE AND RESTAURANT 💳♿🍸⛅ CAFE ❷

3-4 Bedford Row, Temple Bar ☎01 677 9043

A comfortable cafe both in view of the Quays and Temple Bar street, Gertrude's is a good place to grab your morning coffee and watch the passers-by. Gertrude's offers coffee varieties *(€2.50-3.25)* as well as sandwiches *(€7-9)* and pizzas *(€9-14).* Servers are affable, but you can push the doorbell outside on the terrace if you don't see anyone.

🚏 Just north of Gogarty's, Temple Bar. Ⓢ €2.50-14. ⏰ Open daily 8am-6pm.

ISKANDERS 🚫♿ LATE NIGHT ❶

30 Dame St. ☎01 670 4013

After a long night of drinking, you'll swear it's the greatest thing you've ever eaten. Oh, and it's good sober, too. Iskander's is a Dublin institution and its massive shawarma with fries and a coke *(€10)* should not be missed.

Ⓢ Cash only. ⏰ Open daily 11am-5am.

STAGE DOOR CAFÉ 🚫♿🍸⛅ CAFE ❶

10b-11 East Essex St., Temple Bar ☎01 677 6297

Though the sign from its old namesake, the "Lemon Jelly Café" is still on, this cafe has undergone a serious renovation to make the atmosphere as fun and eclectic as the food and drink are tasty. A full Irish breakfast is available all day, or you can select from fresh pastries, cakes, and quiches. There's also a "create your own" sandwich or wrap option available *(€6.95.)* Take your meal out on the terrace to allow the sun's rays curative powers to work on your hangover.

ℹ Wi-Fi coming soon. Ⓢ Coffee €2-6. Food €3-9. ⏰ Open M-F 8am-9 or 10pm, Sa-Su 9am-10:30pm.

GALLAGHER'S BOXTY HOUSE 💳♿🍸 IRISH ❸

20-21 Temple Bar st., Temple Bar ☎01 677 2762 🖥www.boxtyhouse.ie

Nearly all of the pubs in the Temple Bar area serve some kind of Irish food, but Gallagher's takes it a step further with an interior most reminiscent of a 19th-century Irish household. It features "Boxty," a dish of potato pancakes with meat and veggie fillings, that'll fill you up, even if it doesn't exactly shock your taste buds. You might find it hard to choose a drink at this joint's full bar.

🚏 On Temple Bar St., just off Anglesea St. Ⓢ Appetizers €4-11. Entrees €19-23. ⏰ Open M-Th 10am-11pm, F-Sa 10am-11:30pm, Su 10am-11pm.

MILANO 💳♿❄ ITALIAN ❷

19 East Essex St., Temple Bar ☎01 670 3384 🖥www.milano.ie

Serves fresh, made-in-front-of-you pizzas in either a "classic" or "romana" style, a thinner, crispier crust. The modern interior, with sweeping lines and tiny table lamps, ensures a nice evening out, even in the screaming Temple Bar.

Ⓢ €7-15. ⏰ Open M-Sa noon-10:30pm, Su noon-10pm.

Grafton Street

👍 **CORNUCOPIA** 💳⊗🍸 VEGETARIAN ❷

19-20 Wicklow St. ☎01 677 7583 🖥www.cornucopia.ie

Prepare to get your health on. Cornucopia serves meals that are vegan, gluten-free, wheat-free, yeast-free, dairy-free, egg-free, and (of course) low-fat. Despite their alarming lack of harmful ingredients, the food is delicious and comes served up hearty buffet style. You can even try some organic wine *(€5.35 per glass, €21.50 per bottle)*.

➤ *Just down Wicklow St. from the tourist information office.* ℹ *Upcoming bands post flyers for shows in the entrance.* ⏰ *Open M-W noon-9pm, Th-Sa noon-10:30pm, Su noon-8:30pm.*

BUTLER'S CHOCOLATE CAFÉ 💳♿☀ CAFE ❷

Wicklow St. ☎01 671 0591 🖥www.butlerschocolates.com

The Butler's advertising is very, very good. First, you walk in and delicious looking chocolate is shown being made on the TV. "No," you tell yourself, and you approach the counter but...gasp! They have all of their delicious truffles on display under a glass counter at the register!

➤ *Wicklow St. across the street from Munchies Cafe.* $ *Coffee €2-3.50. Boxes of take-away chocolate €2-50.* ⏰ *Open M-F 7:45am-7pm, Sa 9am-7pm, Su 10:30am-7pm.*

CAPTAIN AMERICA'S 💳🚭🍸 STEAKHOUSE ❹

44 Grafton St. ☎01 671 5266 🖥www.captainamericas.com

Believe it or not, Captain America's is an Ireland-themed rock memorabilia restaurant that's heavy on the U2. Plates here are pricey, but if you're willing to swing it, head down towards the seats by the window. That way, you'll have a window to distract you from Sinead O'Connor's portrait.

➤ *At the top of Grafton street on the left.* $ *Plates run from €10-17, steaks more.* ⏰ *Open M-W noon-10:30pm, Th-Su noon-9 or 10pm-ish.*

HANLEY'S CORNISH PASTIES 💳♿☀ PASTIES ❶

Dawson St., across from the Mayor's residence 🖥www.hanleyspasties.com

Serving up hot and fresh Cornish pasties, croissants filled with cheese, meats and veggies, grab one of these for just a few euro and continue moving—they just beg to be eaten on the go.

ℹ *Coffee available as well.* $ *Pastries generally under €5. Veggie and cheese €3.95, cheese, leek and bacon €4.95.*

CEDAR TREE LEBANESE RESTAURANT 💳♿🍸 LEBANESE ❷

11 St. Andrew's St. ☎01 677 2121

Offering cheap but delicious lunchtime options such as *kafta harra*, *kibbe say-neih* and falafel, this is a good lunchtime spot, with excellent mosaic work on the tables and walls. Complement your meal with Almaza, the Lebanese beer.

➤ *Turn off of Suffolk street onto St. Andrews street.* $ *Wraps €5.50. Entrees €7.75.* ⏰ *Open M-Sa 11:30am-11pm, Su 2pm-10:30pm.*

BEWLEY'S ORIENTAL CAFÉ 💳♿🍸☀ CAFE ❸

78-79 Grafton St. ☎01 672 7720 🖥www.bewleys.com

A Grafton Street institution, Bewley's is something to see in itself. Beautiful stained glass windows by Dublin artist Harry Clark line the downstairs walls, making the place look more cathedral than cafe. If you're looking for a "cafe's cafe" then head upstairs, where you can sit out on the tiny balcony overlooking the street. Oh, and did we forget to mention the amazing coffee and extensive dessert section of the menu?

➤ *About midway up Grafton St. on the right hand side.* $ *Coffee €2-4.50. Lunch €6-16.* ⏰ *Open M-Th 7:30am-10pm, F-Sa 7:30am-11pm, Su 7:30am-10pm.*

North of O'Connell Street

TESCO 💳 SUPERMARKET ❷

Moland House, Talbot St. ☎01 887 0980

Don't feel like going out to eat? Pick up some goods to go at Tesco. There's also a 24hr. ATM outside that accepts just about any credit card.

➤ *Across from the Irish Life shopping mall.* ⏰ *Open M-Sa 7am-11pm, Su 8am-10pm.*

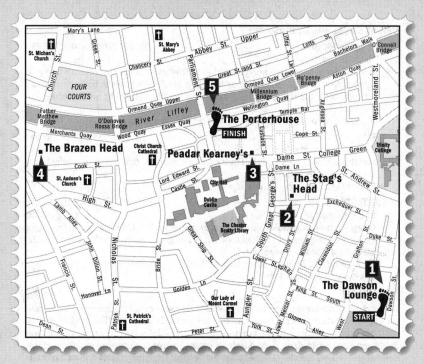

publin walking tour

The capital of Ireland is known for a few things: James Joyce, brogues, and, of course, brew. For those steadfast enough to tackle a true pub crawl, we've consoliated some of the city's best pubs below. Pace yourself, though.

1. THE DAWSON LOUNGE. Start your pub tour at the Dawson Lounge at 25 Dawson St. This pleasantly traditional pub is the smallest pub in Ireland. What it lacks in size, it makes up for with its robust brews.

2. THE STAG'S HEAD. Next on the itinerary, head to the Stag's Head at 1 Dame Ct. To get here from Dawson Lounge, head northeast all the way down Grafton St.; take a left onto Wicklow St. and a left onto Exchequer St; take a right onto Dame Ct., and you're there. Everything's very Victorian here; and, of course, there's taxidermy on the wall.

3. PEADAR KEARNEY'S. Once you've re-hydrated, soldier onto Peadar Kearney's, just a couple of blocks from the Stag's Head. This joint is named for the composer of the Irish National Anthem, and before the night is over, you, too, will be belting that tune.

4. THE BRAZEN HEAD. When you walk out of Peadar's, take a left and continue west for a few blocks; you'll stumble upon the Brazen Head at 20 Lower Bridge St., Merchant's Quay. This establishment, my friends, is Dublin's oldest bar.

5. THE PORTERHOUSE. It'll be a bit of a trek, but once you've sufficiently shot the breeze (and the shots) with the old chaps at the Brazen Head, head on over to The Porterhouse at 16-18 Parliment St. This place boasts three stouts, three ales, and three lagers. Try some, but not all of them. By this point in the evening, we're not sure how you'll be holiding up.

WALKING TOUR
Let's Go
www.letsgo.com

Dorset Street and Drumcondra

👍 THE LOVIN' SPOON — ❀☕ RESTAURANT/CAFE ❶

13 N. Frederick St.

A small, local place that serves good food fresh, the Lovin' Spoon isn't into putting up pretense. Go in, grab your food and keep rolling seems to be the overall attitude here. Sandwiches come in several varieties *(€3.60-6)*, while coffee and juice are also available *(€2.20)*.

➡ Between Parnell Sq. and Dorset St. ⏰ Open M-F 7am-6pm, Sa 9am-4pm.

TESCO — ❄💳 GROCERY ❷

22 Upper Drumcondra Rd. ☎01 837 7632

For those staying way out in Drumcondra's boonies, this Tesco is available for your grocery shopping.

⏰ Open M-Sa 8am-10pm, Su 10am-10pm.

THE TASTY HUT — 💳♿❄ RESTAURANT ❷

61 Upper Dorset St. ☎01 8733756

Okay, so the place looks like a dump. Don't be fooled. Offering cheap late-night grub (both burgers and Indian food), it tastes great. So great you might actually stay to eat it in the restaurant.

$ Burgers €3.50-5. Indian plates up to €13.50. ⏰ Open daily noon-4am. Delivery Tu-Su 5pm-midnight, F-Sa 5pm-1am.

NIGHTLIFE

Holy crap. Dublin knows how to party. Temple Bar sees crazy parties every night, and on the weekends the locals come out and things really get goin'. The best cluster of real, honest-to-goodness house-pumpin', beat layin' clubs can be found on **Harcourt Street** and **Harcourt Road,** up by **St. Stephen's Green.** An area with several excellent clubs, **Camden** and **Wexford Streets** (referred to as the **"Village"**) is nearby. **South William Street** has some great bars and pub options as well.

Temple Bar and the Quays

There's one neighborhood in Dublin where you're nearly guaranteed all of the following: public drunkenness, public vomiting, public nudity, a stag party, a hen party, women in high heels and halter tops, men in high heels and halter tops, beer, beer, and more beer. If you're staying at a hostel here, chances are you're not planning on making the most of their foosball table. On any given night, Temple Bar's streets fill with tourists walking about in various stages of inebriation. It might not be the thing you want to do every night, but it's certainly something you can't miss.

👍 PANTI BAR — ♿🍸❄▼ BAR, CLUB

7-8 Capel St. ☎01 874 0710 💻www.pantibar.com

Panti Bar gives the Dragon a run for its money at its across-the-river location that fills up quickly on the weekends. Go early to grab a table or show up whenever to mingle. There's a dance floor downstairs. Just follow the breasted Absolut bottle running down the "Absolut Panti" sign.

➡ From Parliament St. and Temple Bar, take the Grattan bridge over the Liffey to Capel St. The bar will be on your right. $ Drinks half price on Sunday.

👍 PEADAR KEARNEY'S — ❀♿🍸 PUB

64 Dame St. ☎01 707 9701

Named for the composer of the Irish National Anthem who grew up upstairs, it's only fitting that this pub has great live music, seven nights a week. Come in early and score a cheap drink *(€3.50)*, or wait until the band starts up at 9pm. Brian Brody is a one-man musical powerhouse on Saturday nights. Don't miss it.

⚓ On Dame St. on the south side of Temple Bar. ***i*** *No cover.* **ⓢ** *When daily specials end, look for drinks to be approx. €5. Cash only.* **✆** *Open noon-1am everyday. Happy hour M-F noon-7pm, Sa-Su noon-5pm.*

🏴 ALCHEMY   ⊗Ψ❄ CLUB

Fleet St., Temple Bar   ☎01 612 9390 📧www.alchemydublin.ie

While the design of the building may be poor (two flights of stairs to get down to the club?), especially poor for drunks, the interior of the club could have been taken straight from NYC. Top 40 hits blare all night long, and upturned liquor bottles behind the bar get constant use. Students should come on Wednesday, when there are discounted drinks or on Sunday when admission is free.

ⓢ *Cover F-Sa €9. Guinness and lager €5.* **✆** *Open W-Su 10:30pm-3am.*

GOGARTY'S   ♥♿Ψ🛋 BAR

58 Fleet St.   ☎01 671 1822 📧www.gogartys.ie

Okay, it's basically a tourist trap, and you'll be hard-pressed to find a local here, but it's a pretty cool tourist trap, with three floors, two bars, a beer garden and a very posh a la carte restaurant on the top. Live music from 1:30pm, moving upstairs at 8pm, and continuing all night long.

⚓ On the easter edge of Temple Bar. **ⓢ** *Bar food approx. €5-15, upstairs expect a price jump. AE/ MC/V.* **✆** *Open M-Sa 10:30am-2:30am, Su 12pm-1am.*

TEMPLE BAR   ♥♿Ψ🛋 BAR

47-48 Temple Bar St.   ☎01 672 5287 📧www.templebarpubdublin.com

With possibly the best "beer garden" in the area, *the* Temple Bar (not the neighborhood, we're trying to be specific here) is a pun-merited hotspot on a sunny day. Expect to pay the TB standard €5 for a pint and slightly more for a mixed drink. Music starts with Traditional Irish songs at 2pm and moves onto U2 at night.

⚓ On Temple Bar street, in Temple Bar. If you can't find it there's nothing we can do for you.) ***i*** *No cover.* **ⓢ** *Guinness €4.95, lager €5.50.* **✆** *Open M-W 10:30am-12:30am, Th 10:30am-2am, F-Sa 10:30am-2:30am and Su noon-1am.*

FITZSIMON'S BAR AND CLUB   ♥♿Ψ🛋 BAR, CLUB

21-22 Wellington Quay   ☎01 677 9315 📧www.fitzsimonshotel.com

A tourist-heavy bar, but with good reason. Located in the heart of Temple Bar, Fitzsimon's has five different floors, including a nightclub, cocktail bar and open-air rooftop terrace. Hugely popular on the weekends, this emporium of nightlife entertainment is open until 2:30am daily. Be forewarned, there's no AC in the club downstairs, so it can turn into a sweatbox.

⚓ On the corner of Eustace and East Essex St. ***i*** *Fitzsimon's also has a hotel and restaurant. A €6 vodka and coke and a €5.50 gin and tonic are both available until 11pm.* **ⓢ** *Stout €4.85, lager €5.35.* **✆** *Open daily noon-2:30am.*

THE BRAZEN HEAD   ♥♿Ψ🛋 PUB

20 Lower Bridge St., Merchant's Quay   ☎01 679 5186

The oldest pub in Ireland, The Brazen Head was opened in 1198. That's 561 years before the invention of Guinness and 737 years before the founding of AA. This place knows what being a pub is all about. In fact, it still looks pretty Medieval: walls are covered with pictures of an Irish past, benches are well-worn, and the outdoor courtyard is reminiscent of something you'd find in the Middle Ages. In celebration of the 250th anniversary of Guinness, and its founder, Arthur Guinness, in 2009, Tom Jones came to sing at the Pub. How cool is that?

⚓ A few blocks west down the Quay from Temple Bar, turn south on Lower Bridge St. ***i*** *No cover.* **ⓢ** *Pints around €5, food €5-20.* **✆** *Open M-Th 10:30am-midnight, F-Sa 10:30am-12:30am, Su 10:30am-midnight.*

THE PORTERHOUSE

🍴♿🍸 BAR, PUB

16-18 Parliment St. ☎01 679 8847 💻www.porterhousebrewco.com

Imagine it: a three story bar, with live music every night, the wall lined with beers of amber and gold. Sounds like heaven, right? Well, it exists. The Porterhouse is the largest independent Irish brewing company, putting out nine of their own beers year-round and several seasonals. Try the "daily beer promotion," which allows you to pick up a different brew from around the world every day *(€4)*. Musical acts perform on a stage in between floors, so you can look up from the groundfloor, or down from the third floor balcony.

⇟ 1 block up Parliment from the Quay. ℹ Food available until 9:30pm. $ Pints run around €4.30-5. ⏰ Open M-W 11:30am-midnight, Th 11:30am-1:30am, F-Sa 11:30am-2:30am, Su 12:30pm-11pm.

THE MEZZ

🍴♿🍸▼ BAR, CLUB

23-24 Eustace St., Temple Bar ☎01 670 7655 💻www.mezz.ie

Your hard rock option in Temple Bar, the Mezz is actually two different venues: the upstairs bar, where the decor is a magazine and poster collage straight out of your "angsty" phase and the downstairs, which is even louder and more raucous with walls painted by a professional graffiti artist. Don't be fooled if you can't hear the music from the outside. The Mezz spent loads of money in the 2009 to completely soundproof the place. Just hop inside and get your jam on.

⇟ Head south from the Milennium Bridge up Eustace street and the Mezz will be on your left. ℹ No cover $ Pints around €5. ⏰ Open daily 5pm-2:30am.

Grafton Street

✓ TRIPOD

🍸❄☁ CLUB

37 Harcourt St. ☎01 475 9750 💻www.pod.ie/venue_tripod.php

Some stone towers hide dragons, this one hides great live music and dance venue. The main hall houses international DJs and other forms of dance music. Early in the morning on a Friday or Saturday night, this place is packed with sweaty dancers. Heading over the Pod around the base of the tower will put you in—well, a pod—that's running a different beat, with house music and a lightshow to make drugged-out hippies jealous.

$ Beamish €4. Mixed drinks €5. Mid-week deals for students. ⏰ Open T-Sa 4:30pm-3am.

✓ COPPER FACE JACKS

♿🍸❄☁ CLUB

29-30 Harcourt St. ☎01 475 8777 💻www.jackson-court.ie

Rumor has it that the longstanding Copper Face Jacks is a good place for those looking for love. Without saying anything about whether it's true or not (gentlemen never kiss and tell), Copper's, as it's affectionately called, makes for a great time. With two floors, two dance floors, and two big bars, you'll have a great time. Say hello to an intoxicated Cupid for us.

ℹ 20+ only. $ Guinness €4.50. Lager €4.80. Cover €5+. Ages 20+ only. ⏰ Open daily 4pm-3am.

✓ WHELAN'S

🍴♿🍸☁ BAR, MUSIC VENUE

25 Wexford St. ☎01 478 0766 💻www.whelanslive.com

The place for Dublin's alternative music, Whelan's boasts a large interior, with several bars, a excellent balcony area, and two stages. The main stage hosts the biggest names in up-and-coming music, while the smaller stage upstairs handles local and acoustic acts. Whelan's is a must. (Note that the view from the main stage balcony may be better, but the sound will not be. Choose carefully.)

⇟ Follow South Great George's street 15min. away from the river. Whelan's is on the right. $ Guinness €4.40. Lagers €4.90. €5-10 cover for the club after 10:30pm on weekends. ⏰ Open M-F 2:30pm-2:30am, Sa 5pm-2:30am, Su 5pm-1:30am.

THE DAWSON LOUNGE 💳🚭🍸 PUB

25 Dawson street ☎01 671 0311 💻www.dawsonslounge.ie

Protect yourself from nuclear fallout by climbing down the stairs into "the smallest pub on earth" (or at least, Dublin). A bit of a novelty, it's a fun place to stop by during the afternoons when you can benefit from its dimly lit, cool ambience. Let it get crowded, however, and you'll uncomfortably realize that it's really just a walk-in closet with a Guinness tap.

✣ From the top of Grafton St., walk 1 block left. Turn left again, the pub will be on your left. ***i*** *Tiny packages of peanuts also available for purchase. ⏰ Open M-Th 12:30pm-11:30pm, F-Sa 12:30pm-12:30am, Su 3pm-11pm.*

GRAFTON LOUNGE 💳♿🍸❄ CLUB

Unit 2, Royal Hibernian Way, Dawson St. ☎01 679 6260 💻www.thegraftonlounge.ie

With weird, funky furniture, a pool table downstairs, and so many people wearing white you might actually need to put on your sunglasses at night: the Grafton Lounge is a place for beautiful people to be seen. Don't think of showing up looking scruffy. DJs pump out the tunes from Th-Su.

$ Guinness €5. Mixed drinks from €10. ⏰ Open M-W 11am-11:30pm, Th-Sa 11am-2:30am, Su 4:30pm-1:30am.

DAVY BRYNE'S 💳♿🍸⛅ PUB

21 Duke St. ☎01 677 5217 💻www.davybrynes.com

Getting a famous mention in James Joyce's "Ulysses," this literary pub fills up on Bloomsday with patrons looking for gorgonzola sandwiches and glasses of "burgundy" (the same meal consumed by the novel's main character). On days that *don't* celebrate major Irish writers, the pub is also a pretty great place to get a pint and hang out.

✣ Heading on Grafton St. towards St. Stephen's Green. Turn left on Duke St. $ Food runs between €5-17. Extensive wine selection €5-7.50 per glass. ⏰ Open M-Th 11am-11:30pm, F-Sa 11am-12:30am, Su 11am-11pm.

D TWO ♿🍸❄⛅ CLUB

60 Harcourt St. ☎01 476 4600 💻www.dtwonightclub.com

This is where George of the Dublin jungle comes to get his pint. A popular club, its enormous jungle themed beer gardens is packed on the weekends, especially during the summer. Come in before 8pm and all drinks are €3.50.

$ Lagers €5. Guinness €4.90 after 11pm.

CAPITOL LOUNGE ♿🍸❄▼ CLUB, COCKTAIL LOUNGE

1-2 Aungier St. ☎01 475 7166 💻www.capitol.ie

Cocktails are the thing at the Capitol lounge—€5, all day, everyday. With over 100 different variations on the menu, you're going to have watch yourself to make sure you don't get sloppy. Head upstairs where the music's slightly softer to chat with friends or wade through the crowd downstairs as the DJs put out that house music pulse.

i *21+ only. $ No cover. ⏰ Open daily 3pm-3am.*

PYGMALION 💳🚭⛅▼ BAR, CLUB

Powerscourt Centre, South William St. ☎01 633 4479 💻pygmaliondublin@gmail.com

An attractive bar with attractive people, the biggest pull for Pygmalion is their half-price drinks on Sundays. Look for it to really fill up then. Drinks at their normal prices are reasonable, and there's an extensive cocktail menu from €8.50-10. Guinness after church, anyone?

i *Outside seating available. $ Guinness €4.70. Lagers €4.90.*

DICEY'S GARDEN 💳🍸❄⛅ CLUB

21-25 Harcourt St. ☎01 478 4066 💻www.russellcourthotel.ie

Another club that looks like somebody threw some lights in the hotel lobby—

and then you hit the beer garden, or two levels of wrap-around balconies and a dance floor below.

i 21+ only. Ⓢ Cover: T €2, W €3.50, Th €3, F €4, Sa €5. ◷ Open daily noon-2:30am.

THE "NO NAME BAR" ✦♨▼ BAR
#3 Fade St. (Next to Hogan's Bar on South Great George's St.)

Looking like a sweet Manhattan flat from the early 1960s, this place could have been a sweet beat hangout. The brick walls and sparse furniture in this bar gives the 20-something crowd a chance to mingle. And mingle they do, over much-craved mojitos and homemade Bloody Marys. Get your groove on weeknights as the DJs take over from 8pm til close.

⚑ Follow South Great George's St. until you see Hogan's Bar; turn left. Ⓢ Guinness €4.50. Lager €5. Barfood on weekdays €10 or less. ◷ Open M-W 1pm-11:30pm, Th 1pm-1am, F-Sa 1pm-2:30am, Su 1pm-1am.

THE DRAGON ✦♿♨▼ BAR, CLUB
64-65 South Great George's St.   ☎01 478 1590 ✉thedragon@capitalbars.com

A heady combination of Paris chic, neon Vegas, and the Addams family, the Dragon is a gay bar popular with a younger crowd than the Georges, and it really gets hopping around midnight. Check out the extremely entertaining drag/dance shows on Monday, Saturday or Thursday and join in under the light of the spinning disco ball.

⚑ From Dame St., follow South Great George's St. up a few blocks. *i* Mezzanine and second dance floor upstairs. Ⓢ Pints €3-6. ◷ Open M 8pm-3am, Tu 8-11:30pm, W-Sa 8pm-3am, Su 8-11:30pm.

THE CAMDEN PALACE ✦♈❄♨ CLUB
84-87 Lower Camden St.   ☎01 478 0808 ▣www.camden-deluxe.com

Dear. God. Somebody let out the crazy. The Camden Palace takes everything over-the-top and then throws it overboard. In a huge ampitheater of a club, people get freaky on the light-up go-go platforms (and with each other). Can't seem to find it? Look for the guys swinging fire-tipped chains outside the entrance on a weekend night.

⚑ Follow Great St. George's street as it turns into Aungier, and then into Camden. The club will be on your right. *i* IDs are a must. Ⓢ Guinness €4.70. Lagers €5. Mixed drinks €8. Cover €10 on weekends. ◷ Pool hall and bar open daily noon-3am. Nightclub only open Th-Sa.

THE STAG'S HEAD ✦♿❄ PUB
1 Dame Ct.   ☎01 679 3687 ✉thestagshead@fitzgeraldgroup.ie

Established in 1895, the Stag's Head is the everyman pub of Dublin. Everybody drinks here. Businessmen drinking next to soccer hooligans drinking next to punk rockers. Oh yeah, and there actually is a giant stag's head in there.

⚑ Dame Court has a small entrance on Dame St. Ask around. Ⓢ Guinness €4.55. Lager €4.90.

ARTS AND CULTURE
Theater

▨ THE GAIETY THEATRE ✦♈ THEATRE
South King St.   ☎01 677 1717 ▣www.gaietytheatre.ie

A beautiful old house theater with three levels of red velvet seating. Student discounts are offered up to 15%, but another good money saving tip (regular prices run anywhere from €25-55) is to go for the "restricted view" seats. Rumor has it that the large drop in price is only coupled with a small loss of stage visibility. Check the website for a complete show schedule. Riverdance comes for two months every summer—Riverdance!

⚑ Walk to the top of Grafton St. and turn right. *i* No exchanges or refunds. Doors close promptly when the show begins. Concessions available. Ⓢ Tickets prices vary. ◷ Box office open M-Sa 10am-7pm.

ireland

BEWLEY'S CAFÉ THEATRE 🎫 THEATRE

78-79 Grafton St. ☎01 086 878 4001 🖥www.bewleys.com

A good place for lunchtime entertainment as well as jazz or cabaret in the evenings.

⇟ About halfway up Grafton St. on the right. i Call or email the office for booking about. $ Tickets range €10-20.

PROJECT ARTS CENTRE ❄ THEATRE

39 East Essex St. ☎01 881 9613 🖥www.projectartscentre.ie

A big, hard-to-miss blue building sitting in the middle of Temple Bar, the Project Arts Centre has upstairs and downstairs theaters, as well as a gallery space. Stop in to check out upcoming shows and take advantage of some free coffee and W-Fi. Check the website for show schedules.

$ Tickets €20-25. ⏰ Box office open M-Sa 11am-7pm. Gallery open M-Sa 11am-8pm.

ABBEY THEATRE ♿❄ THEATRE

26-27 Lower Abbey St. ☎01 878 7222 🖥www.abbeytheatre.ie

First opened in 1904 through the efforts of a certain Mr. William Butler Yeats, the Abbey Theatre has burned down, been moved away, moved back, and rebuilt on its original location, and is supposed to move again in 2012. Apparently the physical space is doing its best to mimic the creative atmosphere, which has been promoting an ever-changing landscape of new Irish writers.

⇟ From O'Connell St., turn right.

Dance

These two shows make up for their touristy atmospheres with all the dancin' and jiggin' you could ever want.

ARLINGTON HOTEL TEMPLE BAR 🎫♿❄ IRISH DANCE

16-18 Lord Edward St. ☎01 670 8777 🖥www.arlingtonhotel.ie

With a raised stage in contrast to the Blarney Inn, where the dancing is done right on the pub floor, the Arlington hotel knows they've got quite a show. Spring for the three course dinner plus a show *(€30)*, and you'll get set up at a table front and center. If you don't feel like eating, however, you're still welcome to enjoy the performance. Just make sure you grab a drink from the bar.

i "Pour your own pint" tables available as well. ⏰ Shows daily 8:30-11pm.

BLARNEY INN PUB 🚭 IRISH DANCE

1-2 Nassau St. ☎01 679 4388 🖥www.blarneyinn.com

Irish dancing from Thursday to Saturday. The show begins at 8pm, but the dancers don't usually come on until 9pm. Performers are either co-ed or all-female, depending on the day.

⇟ From Trinity college, follow Nassau St. with the College on your left. The Blarney Inn Pub will be on your right on the corner of Kildare St. $ Entrees €15. ⏰ Open M-F 10:30am-11pm or midnight, Sa-Su 9am-11pm or midnight.

Festivals

STREET PERFORMANCE WORLD CHAMPIONSHIPS ☀ FESTIVAL

Merrion Sq. 🖥www.spwc.ie

The best street performers in the world come to compete for honor, glory, and that €2-coin you've got rolling around in your pocket (but admission is free). A must-see.

⇟ From Trinity College follow Nassau St. east, along Clare Street to Merrion Sq. $ Free. Donations encouraged. ⏰ June.

TRINITY COLLEGE DUBLIN SHAKESPEARE FESTIVAL FESTIVAL

Trinity College, College Green Dublin 2 ☎01 896 2242 🖥www.dublinshakespeare.com

Running during the first or second week of June, this festival is put on by Trinity College's drama club, the Dublin University Players, and offers main event shows on campus, as well as free shows in parks across Dublin throughout the week. You can buy tickets inside Trinity College, or just ask the nearest person you see strumming a lute.

🪧 From O'Connell Bridge, follow Westmoreland St. to Trinity College on the left. $ €18, seniors and children €12.50, students €10.

SHOPPING 🛍

Clothing

👍 THE HARLEQUIN 💳♿ TEMPLE BAR AND THE QUAYS

13 Castle Market ☎01 671 0202 💻susannaharlequin@hotmail.com

The Harlequin is a great little vintage shop where you'll have trouble finding something that *doesn't* totally match your new retro ensemble. With three floors, costume jewelry, and the sexiest collection of men's velvet jackets this side of the Channel, it's a must-hit for any clothing shopper.

ℹ Upstairs and downstairs not wheelchair-accessible. ⏰ M-W 10am-6pm, Th 10am-8pm, F 10am-6pm, Th 10am-8pm, Sa 9:30am-6pm, Su 12:30-5:30pm.

GENIUS ⊘❄ WEST OF TEMPLE BAR

Powerscourt Centre, Clarendon St. ☎01 679 7851 💻www.genius.ie

A store whose merchandise seems designed to make you feel stupid in whatever *you're* wearing, Genius offers a classy assortment of name brand jackets and men's accessories, as well as a large selection of stylish leather boots. It's up to you to decide if throwing down €100+ for boots is a smart move or not.

ℹ Annual sales in June and Jan. ⏰ Open M-W 10am-6pm, Th 10am-8pm, F-Su 10am-6pm.

AVOCA 💳♿❄ TEMPLE BAR AND THE QUAYS

11-13 Suffolk St. ☎01 677 4215 💻www.avoca.ie

This home of Irish-made items has it all. Women's clothing, throws and scarves, a cafe upstairs, and a pantry full of their own homemade scones, jams and other sweet things.

🪧 Down the street from Dublin Tourism on Suffolk St. ⏰ Open M-W 10am-6pm, Th 10am-7pm, F-Sa 10am-6pm, Su 11am-6pm.

INDIGO AND CLOTH 💳⊘ WEST OF TEMPLE BAR

Basement 27, South William St. ☎01 670 6403 💻www.indigoandcloth.com

Down in a little basement shop on South Williams St. lies God's own collection of trendy clothing. Carrying alternating top tier brands, this little shop makes sure you get your bang for your buck. Unfortunately, a lot of bang means a lot of buck, and simple tops or T-shirts here can run up to €60, and jackets or dresses up to €350. If you can spring, you'll be one impeccably dressed individual walking the streets of Dublin.

⏰ Open M-W noon-6pm, Th noon-7pm, F noon-6pm, Sa 10am-6pm, Su 1pm-5pm.

FLIP 💳⊘ TEMPLE BAR AND THE QUAYS

4 Fownes St. Upper ☎01 671 4299 💻www.flipclothing.com

Open since the mid-'80s when Temple Bar had none of its present day veneer, Flip clothing is a combination of vintage and not, with leather and military jackets, funky Hawaiian prints, and a liberal price negotiation policy. You're getting a great deal might just depend on how willing you are to beg.

$ T-shirts from €15. Jeans from €20. ⏰ Open M-W 10am-6pm, Th 11am-7pm, F-Sa 10am-6pm, Su 1-6pm.

GREAT OUTDOORS 💳♿ GRAFTON ST.

Chatham St. ☎01 679 4293 💻www.greatoutdoors.ie

If you need bugspray, tents, sleeping bags, or a waterproof anything, head to Great Outdoors to find it. A wide range of outdoor equipment, it'll help you survive your trek through the mountains...or just stay dry under Ireland's never ending rain.

🪧 Turn right on Chatham St. just before you get to the top of Grafton street. ℹ Some outdoor clubs' discounts honored. ⏰ Open M-W 10am-6pm, Th 10am-8pm, F 10am-6pm, Sa 9:30am-6pm, Su 12:30-5:30pm.

THE EAGER BEAVER 💳♿ TEMPLE BAR AND THE QUAYS

17 Crown Alley ☎01 677 3342

The longest operating vintage shop in Temple Bar lives up to its name, you won't be able to wait before getting in here to check out their selection of new and vintage wear. An extensive collection brought in from Germany, UK, and Holland. Check out the downstairs collection of tweeds or ask the owner Robert for a good place to get a beer. He'll pint you in the right direction. Ha.

$ Levis from €20-30. Tweed jackets from €35-40. ⏰ Open M-Sa 10am-7pm, Su noon-6pm.

FAT FACE 💳♿ TEMPLE BAR AND THE QUAYS

31 Exchequer St. ☎01 677 2415 💻www.fatface.com

Okay, so the name doesn't exactly scream style, but that's all advertising...we think. An England-based company begun when a couple of "ski bums" (again, their words, not ours), Fat Face offers surfer chic reminiscent of Quiksilver, but with a much funnier name.

PATAGONIA 💳♿ TEMPLE BAR AND THE QUAYS

24-26 Exchequer St. ☎01 670 5748 💻www.patagonia.com

A European outlet store, this Patagonia sells discontinued stock at reduced prices. If you're looking for durable but attractive travel wear, this is a good bet.

⏰ Open M-Th 10am-6pm, W 10am-8pm, F 10am-6pm, Sa 9:30am-6pm, Su 1pm-5pm.

Books

BARGAIN BOOKS 🚫💳♿ GRAFTON ST.

37 Grafton St.

Damn. You've just finished that new Dan Brown novel and the hostel's book exchange is looking a little weak. Head over to Bargain Books, where factory outlet prices are the thing. Copies of *Ulysses* run just €3. Do you dare?

➜ Almost to the top of Grafton St. on your left. $ Cash only. ⏰ M-Tu 9am-7pm, W 9am-8pm, Th-F 9am-8:30pm, Sa-Su 9am-7pm.

TEMPLE BAR BOOK MARKET TEMPLE BAR AND THE QUAYS

Temple Bar Sq. 💻www.templebar.ie

Every Saturday and Sunday local booksellers set up tents and deal new, used, and antique books here at good prices.

➜ Just through Merchant's Arch on Temple Bar St. $ Books from €3. ⏰ Sa-Su 11am-6pm.

DUBRAY'S BOOKS 💳♿ GRAFTON ST.

36 Grafton St. ☎01 677 5568 💻www.dubraybooks.ie

A multi-level bookstore offering new titles. Check out either the sale section or the staff recommends, available in a handy pamphlet available at the counter.

➜ Almost to the top of Grafton street on the left. ⏰ Open M-F 9am-9pm, Sa 9am-7pm, Su 9am-6pm.

CENTRAL LIBRARY ♿ EAST OF O'CONNELL ST.

Ilac Shopping Centre, 12 Earl St. N. ☎01 873 4333 💻centrallibrary@dublincity.ie

In Dublin for a while and low on cash? Looking to read something other than the *Let's Go* in your hands? Take out a free library card at this convienent location. Just bring along an ID and proof of address.

➜ From O'Connell St., turn left onto Henry street. The iLac Centre is on your right. $ Free. ⏰ Open M-Th 10am-8pm, F-Sa 10am-5pm.

BOOKWORMS ♿❄ WEST OF O'CONNELL ST.

75 Middle Abbey St. ☎01 873 5772 💻booba@eircom.net

A long-standing discount and secondhand bookstore, the emphasis here is on prices. Cheap prices. Very few of the titles here are sold retail. With books upon shelves, boxes and other strange forms of display, it's a chaotic yet organized book-lovers paradise.

➜ From O'Connell St., turn left on to Middle Abbey St. i Children and young readers sections. ⏰ Open M-F 9:30am-7:30pm, Sa 9:30am-7pm, Su 1-6pm.

THE SECRET BOOK AND RECORD STORE
♿ ❄ WEST OF GRAFTON ST.

15a Wicklow St. ☎01 679 7272

It's hard to find, but worth finding. The SBARS has extensive used and new sections, including a classics section *(€3 each)*. Combine that with a charming staff and mellow mood music from Freebird records and you've got one hell of a music/literary combo.

➶ Look for a little door with a small sign, and follow the hallway. ⏰ Open daily M-W 11am-6:30pm, Th 11am-7:30pm, F-Su 11am-6:30pm.

BOOKS UPSTAIRS
💳 ⊗ TEMPLE BAR AND THE QUAYS

36 College Green ☎01 679 6687 💻info@booksirish.com

A fun bookstore divided into many different subjects, including fiction, philosophy, religion, gay, and many others. Articles and book reviews tacked to the bulletin board alert you to what's hot off the press.

➶ Across the street from Trinity College at the bottom of Grafton St. ⏰ Open M-F 10am-7pm, Sa 10am-6pm, Su 2-6pm.

THE WINDING STAIR BOOKSTORE
💳 ♿ TEMPLE BAR AND THE QUAYS

40 Lower Ormond Quay ☎01 872 6576 💻bookshop@winding-stair.com

A fun, local bookstore that gives a 10% discount to students. Come in to find a hefty selection of new and used titles.

➶ Across the Milennium Bridge from Temple Bar. ⏰ Open M-W 10am-7pm, Th-Sa 10am-8pm, Su noon-7pm.

Outdoor Markets

SOUTH CITY MARKET OR ST. GEORGE'S ARCADE
⊛ ♿ NORTH OF O'CONNELL ST.

South Great George's St.

This open-air market is a good place to find vintage wear, old LPs, used CDs and DVDs, weird Asian goods ("Hello Kitty" bra, anyone?), coffee, flowers, jewelry, used books and more.

➶ Walking up Grafton St., turn right onto Johnson's St. and follow it to the South City Market. ⏰ Open M-F 10:30am-6:30pm, Sa 10:30am-6:30pm, Su noon-6pm.

Liquor Stores

Ah, the fine art of boozin'. The establishments below have been chosen for their selection and for the personable, welcoming nature of their staff. If you're interested in become a professional whiskey drinker, or at least maintaining the claim when you're sober, head to either of these bottle shops. If you're just interested in finding a cheap bottle of wine to take to the party, there are liquor stores located all over Dublin, handily marked with the vaguely black-market sounding "off license." Cheers.

✓ CELTIC WHISKEY SHOP
💳 ♿ SOUTH OF GRAFTON ST.

24 Dawson St. ☎01 675 9744 💻www.celticwhiskeyshop.com

Whether you're looking to get a bunch of those tiny bottles that you find in hotel minibars, or paying €3000 for a single bottle, you can find what you're looking for here. Wine, whiskey, and microbrews available. Daily whiskey tastings make even the shopping experience smooth.

➶ Walk to the top of Grafton St. and turn left, and then left again on Dawson St. $ Prices vary.

JAMES FOX
💳 ♿ GRAFTON ST.

119 Grafton St. ☎01 677 0533 💻www.jamesfox.ie

Besides having an extensive selection of Irish and Scotch whiskeys from all prices ranges, James Fox specializes in cigars. If you've been thinking about grabbing that Cohiba, now's the time to do it.

➶ At the bottom of Grafton street. ℹ Cigar accessories available as well. ⏰ Open M-Sa 9:30am-6pm, Su 12:30-5:30pm.

Electronics

👍 COMPUB AND MAC EXCHANGE ♿❄ GRAFTON ST.

11 Grafton St. ☎01 507 9107 💻www.compub.com

Apple users, you didn't think we were going to leave you out in the cold, did you? Compub offers a wide selection of Mac products, including iPods and Macbooks. They also have a tech support group, and, if you've got a warranty they'll gladly accept it. If not, however, it's €75 for a diagnostic test plus the cost of your repair.

⇆ Just Down Grafton St. from the Molly Malone statue. ⏰ Open M-W 9am-7pm, Th 9am-9pm, F-Sa 9am-7pm, Su 11am-6pm.

PHILLIPS ♿❄ TEMPLE BAR AND THE QUAYS

19-22 Dame St. ☎01 474 0788 💻www.phillipsshop.ie

Phillips on Dame St. has adapters for your gear, though bear in mind they don't have converters. No cameras either. They do have a large selection of headphones (including the noise-cancelling ones) though.

⏰ Open M-W 10am-6pm, Th 10am-7pm, F-Sa 10am-6pm, Su 1-5pm.

SONY CENTRE ♿❄ LOWER O'CONNELL ST.

17 Lower O'Connell St. ☎01 873 1512 💻www.sonycentres.co.uk

This store offers cameras and memory cards, as well as laptop cases and other travel accessories. The boys at Sony Centre will help you with troubleshooting problems, but they don't have a certified tech center.

⇆ When heading up O'Connell St., it will be on the right. ⏰ Open M-W 10am-6pm, Th 10am-7pm, F-Sa 10am-6pm, Su 1-5pm.

Furniture

👍 NOONE FURNITURE 💳♿❄ NORTH OF THE QUAYS

36 Talbot St. ☎01 855 6731 💻www.noonefurniture@eircom.net

Offers a large selection of all types of furniture, but if you don't see what you're looking for, just inform the staff and they'll order it for you from the catalogue. Free assembly and delivery with purchase. It doesn't get much better than that.

⇆ On Talbot St., down near Connolly Station. $ Prices vary, but single beds from €300. ⏰ Open M-Sa 9:30am-5pm.

BEDROOM ELEGANCE 💳⊘❄ UPPER DORSET ST.

55-56 Upper Dorset St. ☎01 872 8210 💻bedroomelegance.ie

Offering made-to-measure furniture, this stuff is custom, so go in with an idea of what you want. That wrap-around couch with the 10 cupholders can be done, they just need to know about it.

⏰ Open M-F 9:20am-5:30pm, Sa 9:30am-4pm.

Antiques

👍 COURTVILLE ANTIQUES 💳♿❄ WEST OF TEMPLE BAR

Powerscourt Townhouse, South William St. ☎01 679 4042 💻www.courtvilleantiques.com

Sick of people telling you that their 1999, oversized Aerosmith concert T-shirt is an "antique?" Come to Courtville Antiques, where almost all of the items are certified as being *at least* 100 years old. A fine selection of women's jewelry, old paintings, and some beautiful glassware from County Cork.

⏰ Open T-F 11am-5:30pm, Sa 10am-5:30pm.

THE CARBOOT SHOP 🚫♿ THE QUAYS

Eden Quay 💻www.thecarbootshop.com

Right on the river, the Carboot hop is your best bet for antiques north of the Liffey. Bric-a-brac and curio are in abundance. If things look busy, stay away: you may be charged a €1 entrance fee. However, if the shop is empty, enter with the hope of getting a great deal.

➡ Across the brige to the north side, turn right and walk a few blocks. $ Prices vary. 🕐 Open M-Sa 11am-6pm.

JOHNSON'S COURT VINTAGE EMPORIUM ⊛⊗ SOUTHWEST OF GRAFTON ST.

12A Johnson's Ct. ☎01 670 6825

A store full of so many knick-knacks and interesting pieces you'll wonder how you're ever going to leave. The owner has a large selection of items from Ireland as well as a significant collection brought in from the rest of Europe.

➡ From Grafton St., follow Johnson St. 🕐 Open M-Sa 10:30am-5:30pm.

Department Stores

☑ **PENNYS DEPARTMENT STORE** 💳♿❄ O'CONNELL ST.

O'Connell St. ☎01 656 6666 💻www.pennys.ie

Imagine if Wal-mart were Irish. Now imagine that it's good, and even cheaper. Now you've got Pennys. This department store chain is beloved in Ireland, and with T-shirts or sneakers from €5, the love is well-deserved. Traveling long? Get yourself some new undies stat *(€2-3)*.

➡ On O'Connell St., just below the GPO. $ Cheap. 🕐 Open M-W 8:30am-8pm, Th-F 8:30am-9pm, Sa 8:30am-7pm, Su 11am-7pm.

☑ **POWERSCOURT CENTRE** 💳♿❄ WEST OF GRAFTON ST.

59 South William St. 💻www.powerscourtcentre.com

The "artsy" shopping center, the Powerscourt is the place to go for antiques (there's a whole wing dedicated to them), as well as painting and photography galleries. Sit down in the café on the ground floor and enjoy the sunshine filtering down through the massive skylight installed over the courtyard.

➡ Take Johnson's St. right from Grafton and walk 1 block. 🕐 Open M-F 10am-6pm, Th 10am-8pm, Sa 9am-6pm, Su noon-6pm.

ST. STEPHEN'S GREEN SHOPPING CENTRE 💳♿❄ GRAFTON ST.

At the top of Grafton St. ☎01 478 0888 💻www.stephensgreen.com

A mall offering your usual collection of retail chains (Quiksilver, GameStop, etc.), there's no real reason to go in here if you're not shopping, except maybe to observe the incredibly large clock that hangs from the ceiling.

*➡ At the top of Grafton St., across from St. Stephen's Green. **i** Toilet use €.20. 🕐 Open M-W 9am-7pm, Th 9am-9pm, F-Sa 9am-7pm, Su 11am-6pm.*

CLERYS DEPARTMENT STORE 💳♿❄ O'CONNELL ST.

18-27 O'Connell St. ☎01 878 6000 💻www.clerys.com

Much more your Mom's store, Clerys doesn't really hold much appeal for the student traveler. Still, if you're looking for an easy way to browse for a few hours it has 4 floors of shopping, including a restaurant on the top floor.

*➡ Across the street from Pennys. **i** Customer service desk located on the 2nd floor. 🕐 Open M-W 10am-6:30pm, Th 10am-9pm, F 10am-6:30pm, Sa 9am-7pm.*

ESSENTIALS

Practicalities

- **TOURIST OFFICES: College Green Tourism Office,** Dublin's only independent tourist agency, will help you get a jump on any tour you have in mind. From booking tickets to the Guinness storehouse to reserving your stay for the night, they do it all. However, it's worth stating that they are a booking service, and while they can answer most of your questions, if you're looking for information in general you should head over to Dublin Tourism on Suffolk street. *(37 College Green, Dublin 2. ☎01 410 0700 💻info@daytours.ie 🕐 Open daily 8:30am-9pm.)* To get to **Dublin Tourism (O'Connell St. branch),** from the river, walk up O'Connell street. It's on the right. An off-shoot of the Dublin Tourism head offices in the converted St. Andrew's cathedral, this office

ireland

offers many of the same services (tour bookings, room reservations and general tourist information), just in slightly more boring building. Tourist gift shop available. *(14 O'Connell St. ☎01 874 6064 💻visitdublin.com ⏰* Open M-Sa 9am-5pm.) To get to the **Northern Ireland Tourist Board,** from college green, walk up Suffolk St. Dublin Tourism will be on your right. The Dublin place to go for information on Belfast and Northern Ireland, they're also a booking service, and will make you any reservations you require, free of charge. *(Inside Dublin Tourism. ☎ 01 605 7732 💻www.discovernorthernireland.com ⏰ Open Sept-June M-Sa 9am-5:30pm, Su 10:30am-3pm; July-Aug M-Sa 9am-7pm.)* Finally, to get to **Dublin Tourism,** from the college green, walk up Suffolk St. Dublin Tourism will be on your right. Located in a converted church with beautiful arched ceilings and stained glass windows, this may be the only tourist office that's a sight in itself. The staff are knowledgeable and friendly. Head to the general information desk with broad questions, or head over to one of the many tour companies that have desks in the office. *(The former St. Andrew's church, Suffolk St. ☎01 605 7700 💻www.visitdublin.com ⏰ Open M-Sa 9:30am-5pm, Su 10:30am-3pm.)*

- **LUGGAGE STORAGE:** To get to **Global Internet Café** head over the bridge and on to O'Connell St.; it will be on the right. A nice internet café (and they actually do serve coffee), possibly the best thing about this place is their luggage storage rates. A lot of hassle averted for a little money. *(8 Lower O'Connell St. ☎01 873 9100 💻www.globalhq.ie $ Internet: first 20min. €1.45, student €1.30; 20-40min €2.25/2; 40-60min. €2.95/2.65). Luggage storage: 1st day €3.95, each additional day €1.95. ⏰ Open M-F 8am-10pm, Sa 9am-9pm, Su 10am-9pm.)*
- **ATMS:** A 24hr. ATM can be found at the bottom of Grafton Street, across Nassau Street from the Molly Malone statue. There are two 24hr. ATMs at the **Ulster Bank** on Dame street across from the Wax Museum Plus.
- **CURRENCY EXCHANGE:** Does paper exchanges as well as card withdrawls. €6000 limit. *(1 Westmoreland St. ☎01 670 6724 ⏰ Open M-Th 9am-6pm, F-Sa 9am-8pm, Su 10am-6pm.)*
- **POST OFFICES:** To get to **Dublin General Post Office,** walk up O'Connell St. from the river for 5min., the post office is on the left hand side. At the time of this book's printing, a museum detailing the 1916 Easter uprising (which took place in front of the Post Office) was scheduled to be opened. Oh, and they send mail too. *(O'Connell St., Dublin 1 ☎01 705 7000 💻www.anpost.ie ⏰ Open M-Sa 8:30am-6pm.)*
- **POSTAL CODE:** Dublin 1 (General Post Office). Even-numbered codes are for areas south of the Liffey, while odd-numbered codes are for the north.

Emergency!

- **PHARMACIES: Hickey's Pharmacy** is up Grafton St. on the left. *(21 Grafton St. ☎ 679 0467 ⏰ Open M-Th 8:30am- 8:30pm, F 8:30am-8pm, Sa-Su 10:30am-6pm.)* Another branch is on O'Connell St., right after the bridge. It's the same company as the Grafton St. branch—this one's just open a little later. *(55 Lower O'Connell St. ☎01 873 0427 💻www.hickeyspharmacy.ie $ Prices vary. ⏰ Open M-F 7:30am-10pm, Sa 8am-10pm, Su 10am-10pm.)* **Temple Bar Pharmacy** *(21 Essex St. ☎670 9751 ⏰ Open M-W 9:30am-7pm, Th-Sa 9:30am-8pm, Su 1pm-5pm.)*
- **WOMEN'S ASSISTANCE: Dublin Rape Crisis Center** provides a 24 hr. hotline, free counseling, advocacy and legal advice for victims of recent rape or sexual abuse. *(70 Lower Leeson St. ☎24hr. toll-free national hotline 1800 77 8888; office number 661 4911 💻www.drcc.ie $ Services are offered free of charge. ⏰ Open M-F 8am-7pm, Sa 9am-4pm.)*

Getting There

By Air

Flights go through **Dublin International Airport** (◼www.dublinairport.com; information.queries@ daa.ie). The DIA houses desks for several different flight companies, some of which do flight bookings at the desk.

- **RYANAIR:** Available for last minute changes to your tix, no phone or booking done here. Do that on ◼www.ryanair.com.

- **LUFTHANSA:** German based airline has both a reservations number and the weirdest hours ever. (☎01 855 4455 ◻ Open daily 5am-7am, 8:15am-12:30pm, 3:30pm-5:30pm.)

- **AERARANN:** For domestic flights in Ireland. Book online or reserve at the desk. (☎0818210210 ◼www.aerarann.com ◻ Open daily 5:30am-10pm.)

- **AERLINGUS:** Book flights, change flights, collect excess baggage (*i* There's a 20kilo weight limit). Rebooking. (◼www.aerlingus.com.)

- **U.S. AIRWAYS:** Rebookings, delayed flights and customer service. (☎8090925065 ◼www.usairways.com ◻ Open daily 7:30am-noon.)

- **CONTINENTAL AIRLINES:** (☎189 092 5252 ◼www.continental.com).

- **AIRFRANCE:** (☎ 01 605 0383 ◼www.airfrance.ie ◻Open M-F 4am-7:50pm, Sa 4am-5:45pm, Su 4am-7:50pm.)

- **DELTA:** (☎1850 088 2031 ◼www.delta.com ◻ Open 6am-1pm. May change according to day's flight schedule.)

By Car

- **BUDGET:** (☎01 844 5150 ◼www.budget.ie ◻ Open daily 5am-1am.)

- **HERTZ:** (☎01 844 5466 ◼www.hertz.ie ◻ Open daily 5am-1am.)

- **EUROPCAR:** (☎01 844 4199 ◼www.europcar.com ◻ Open daily 6am-11pm.)

- **SIXT RENT-A-CAR:** (☎01 018 1204 ◼www.sixt.ie ◻ Open daily 6am-midnight.)

- **AVIS:** (☎01 605 7563 ◼www.avis.ie ◻ Open M-F 5am-11:30pm, Sa 5am-11pm, Su 5am-11:30pm.)

Getting Around

By Bus

The price of your bus fare in Dublin depends on how far you're traveling (listed in stages) and run 1-3 €1.15, 4-7 €1.60, 8-13 €1.80 and over 13 stages €2.20. The "Rambler Pass" allows you to travel on any bus for a set amount of time, is pretty steep, so only buy it if you're sure to be moving around quite a bit (1 day pass €6, 3 day €13.30, 5 day €20). The buses themselves run all over Dublin. Times vary, but buses can usually be caught every 8-20min. from 6am-8am and every 30min. from 8pm-midnight. (59 O'Connell St. ☎01 973 4222 ◼www.dublinbus.ie.)

By Taxi

Taxis in Dublin are, much like everything else, expensive. Expect to pay anywhere from €7-10 to get from one destination to another, and more if you're heading across town. Obey the general rules of foreign taxi travel—ask ahead to find the shortest route to your destination, and then make sure the cabbie follows it. Blue Cabs is the predominant taxi company in Dublin. They offer wheelchair-accessible cabs. Call ahead of time to book. (66/67 Butterly Business Park, Kilmore Rd., Dublin 5 ☎01 802 2222 ◼www.bluecabs.ie.)

There are groups of taxi cabs (called "ranks") in four neighborhoods in Dublin. In

Temple Bar, the ranks can be found on the Aston Quay and on the college green in front of the Wax Museum and Bank of Ireland. In the **Grafton Street area,** find taxis near the intersection of Dawson and Duke St. (on Harry St., off the top of Grafton St. and to the right). Next, in the **Viking/Medieval area** of town, pick up taxis on Christchurch Pl. across the street from the Christchurch Cathedral. Finally, a rank can be found **north of O'Connell Street** on Eden Quay just to the right of the O'Connell Monument, in the median of O'Connell St. just south of the Parnell Monument, and on Sackville Pl., (walk ¼ of the way up O'Connell St. and turn right).

essentials

entrance requirements

- **PASSPORT:** Required for citizens of Australia, Canada, New Zealand and the US.
- **VISA:** Required for citizens of Australia, Canada, New Zealand, and the US only for stays of longer than 90 days.
- **WORK PERMIT:** Required for all foreigners planning to work in Ireland.

PLANNING YOUR TRIP

Time Differences

Ireland is on Greenwich Mean Time (GMT) and observes Daylight Saving Time. This means that it is 5hr. ahead of New York City, 8hr. ahead of Los Angeles, 10hr. behind Sydney, and 11hr. behind New Zealand (note that Australia observes Daylight Savings Time from October to March, the opposite of the Northern Hemispheres—therefore, it is 9hr. ahead of Britain from March to October and 11hr. ahead from October to March, for an average of 10hr.).

MONEY

Tipping and Bargaining

Tips in restaurants are often included in the bill (sometimes as a "service charge"). If gratuity is not included, you should tip your server about 12.5%. Taxi drivers should receive a 10% tip, and bellhops and chambermaids usually expect £1-3. To the great relief of many budget travelers, tipping is not expected at pubs and bars in Ireland. Bargaining is generally unheard of in shops.

Taxes

Ireland has a 21% value added tax (VAT), a sales tax applied to everything but food, books, medicine, and children's clothing. The tax is included in the amount indicated on the price tag. The prices stated in *Let's Go* include VAT. Upon exiting Ireland, non-EU citizens can reclaim VAT (minus an administrative fee) through the Retail Export Scheme, although the complex procedure is probably only worthwhile for large purchases. You can obtain refunds only for goods you take out of the country (not for accommodations or meals). Participating shops display a "Tax-Free Shopping" sign and may have a minimum purchase of £50-100 before they offer refunds. To claim a refund, fill out the form you are given in the shop, and present it with the goods and receipts at customs upon departure (look for the Tax-Free Refund desk at the airport). At peak times, this process can take up to an hour. You must leave the country within three months of your purchase in order to claim a refund, and you must apply before leaving Ireland.

SAFETY AND HEALTH

General Advice

In any type of crisis, the most important thing to do is **stay calm.** Your country's embassy abroad is usually your best resource in an emergency; registering with that embassy upon arrival in the country is a good idea.

Specific Concerns

Pre-Departure Health

Matching a prescription to a foreign equivalent is not always easy, safe, or possible, so if you take **prescription drugs,** carry up-to-date prescriptions or a statement from your doctor stating the medications' trade names, manufacturers, chemical names, and dosages. Be sure to keep all medication with you in your carry-on luggage.

Immunizations and Precautions

Travelers over two years old should make sure that the following vaccines are up to date: MMR (for measles, mumps, and rubella); DTaP or Td (for diphtheria, tetanus, and pertussis); IPV (for polio); Hib (for *Haemophilus influenzae* B); and HepB (for Hepatitis B). For recommendations on immunizations and prophylaxis, check with a doctor and consult the **Centers for Disease Control and Prevention (CDC)** in the US or the equivalent in your home country. (☎1 800 CDC INFO/232 4636 ▣www.cdc.gov/travel)

Staying Healthy

Diseases and Environmental Hazards

Common sense is the simplest prescription for good health while you travel. Drink lots of fluids to prevent dehydration and constipation, and wear sturdy, broken-in shoes and clean socks. When in areas of high altitude, be sure to dress in layers that can be peeled off as needed. Allow your body a couple of days to adjust to decreased oxygen levels before exerting yourself. Note that alcohol is more potent and UV rays are stronger at high elevations.

Many diseases are transmitted by insects—mainly mosquitoes, fleas, ticks, and lice. Be aware of insects in wet or forested areas, especially while hiking and camping. Wear long pants and long sleeves, tuck your pants into your socks, and use a mosquito net. Use insect repellents such as DEET and soak or spray your gear with permethrin (licensed in the US only for use on clothing). Mosquitoes—responsible for malaria, dengue fever, and yellow fever—can be particularly abundant in wet, swampy, or wooded areas. Ticks—which can carry Lyme and other diseases—can be particularly dangerous in rural and forested regions of Britain.

ireland 101

FOOD AND DRINK

Grublin

Irish food can be fairly expensive, especially in cities and in restaurants. The basics—and that's what you'll get—are simple and filling. Quick and greasy staples are **chippers** (fish n' chip shops) and **takeaways** (takeout joints). At chippers, "fish" is a whitefish, usually cod, and chips are served with salt and vinegar; ketchup sometimes costs extra. Fried food delicacies include chips with gravy, potato cakes (pancakes made of potato flakes), or the spiceburger (fried patty of spiced breadcrumbs). Most pubs serve food and pub grub is a good option for a cheap but substantial meal. Typical **pub grub** includes Irish stew (meat, potatoes, carrots, and onions), burgers, soup, sandwiches.

Most Irish meals are based on a simple formula: meat, potatoes, and greens.

Preparation usually involves frying or boiling. *Colcannon* (a potato, onion, and cabbage dish), "ploughman's lunch," and Irish stew are Irish specialties. Loud and long will Irish bards sing the praises of the Clonakilty man who first concocted **black pudding.** As one local butcher put it, this dish consists of, "some pork, a good deal of blood, some grains and things—all wrapped up in a tube." **Irish breakfasts,** often served all day and given at any B and B, include eggs, sausage, porridge, rashers (a more thickly sliced version of American bacon), a fried tomato, brown bread, and toast.

A true culinary merit of the Irish is their bread. Most famous is **soda bread:** heavy, white, sweetened by raisins, and especially yummy when fried. Most common are **brown bread** and **batch loaves.** The brown stuff is thick and grainy, while batch loaves are square-shaped, white, and ideal for sandwiches.

Publin

In Ireland, **beer** is always on tap. Cocktails are an oddity found mainly in American-style bars and discos, and most pubs stock only a few bottles of wine. Beer comes in two basic varieties, **lagers** (blond, bizzy brews served cold, a bit weaker than ales or stouts) and **ales** (slightly darker, more bitter, and sometimes served warmer than lagers). **Stout,** a type of ale, is thick, dark-ruby colored, and made from roasted barley to impart an almost meaty flavor. **Guinness** stour inspires a reverence otherwise reserved for the Holy Trinity.

Irish whiskey, which Queen Elizabeth once claimed was her only true Irish friend, is sweeter than its Scotch counterpart, spelled "whisky." In Ireland, whiskey is served in larger measures than you might be used to. Jameson is popular everywhere. Dubliners are partial to **Powers and Sons. Irish coffee** is sweetened with brown sugar and whipped cream and laced with whiskey.

ireland 101 . food and drink

holidays and festivals

- **JAMESON DUBLIN FILM FESTIVAL:** Featuring more than 120 films from all over the world, this 11-day festival strikes Ireland's capital every February.

- **BLOOMSDAY:** The official Bloomsday, named for Leopold Bloom, the protagonist of *Ulysses*, takes place on June 16th and commemorates Irish Modernist writer James Joyce. In true Irish fashion, festivities occur scattershot a few days before and after the 16th.

- **DUBLIN LGBTQ PRIDE FESTIVAL:** "Created by the LGBTQ community, for the LGBTQ community," the Dublin Pride Festival takes place every year from mid- to late-June. All types of festivities—from film screenings to art exhibitions to proms—lead up to the epic parade toward the end of the month.

- **DUBLIN FRINGE FESTIVAL:** Every year from mid- to late-September the Dublin Fringe Festival fosters up-and-coming artists in all different performance media, whether dance, theater, visual art, or music.

- **ST. STEPHEN'S DAY/BOXING DAY:** One of nine public holidays in Ireland, Boxing Day or the Feast of St. Stephen is celebrated on December 26th—yup, more fun just after Christmas. On that day in Dublin celebration ensues on Sandymount Green.

ITALY

For the home of the papacy, Italy sure knows how to do sensual pleasures right: stylish Vespas, intoxicating *vino*, vibrant *piazze*, and crispy pizzas covered in garden-fresh produce populate this country where *la dolce far niente* (literally, the sweetness of doing nothing) is a national pastime. While some travelers let Italy's quirks (supermarkets closed on Sunday and spotty A/C) impede their pursuit of *la dolce vita*, as a student traveler, you are uniquely situated to experience "the boot" in all its ridiculousness and sublimity. Striking out on your own, likely on a budget, you'll open yourself up to what someone who stays at the swankiest hotels and eats at all the five-star restaurants misses: making connections with the people and way of life of this chaotic wonderland. *Let's Go* researchers have reported being given co-pious amounts of free food, receiving unsolicited assistance, and sharing drinks with natives who were more than ready to help them navigate the caprices of a country where things we take for granted ("the customer is always right," street signs, etc.) are conspicuously absent. It's not like our researchers wear neon orange *Let's Go* T-shirts while they're traveling the country—they were treated this way because in their quests for the most divine scoop of gelato or the best-deal happy hour buffet, they reached out to the locals who know how much of the country's untainted energy can be found in its most affordable pleasures. You too can learn to see the beauty of Italy's sometimes befuddling customs, as getting acquainted with its people becomes as much a priority as taking in all its Renaissance art, Roman grandeur, and religious relics. Who knows? Maybe by the time you're ready to leave, some of those Italian oddities will be looking practically divine.

greatest hits

- **ANCIENT ANTIQUES.** The relics of Ancient Rome pop up all over the place. Rome is obviously the place to start (p. 680), but even places like Verona (p. 803) and Milan (p. 734) share this fascinating history.

- **WHERE REBIRTH WAS BORN.** Thanks to the Renaissance, there is a lot of art in Italy. The Uffizi in Florence is the king of Italian museums (p. 828).

- **MONDO MANGIA.** Italian restaurants are all over the world, so you might as well sample where they began, right? For where pizza was invented, head to Naples (p. 862). For the birthplace of lasagna, try Bologna (p. 807).

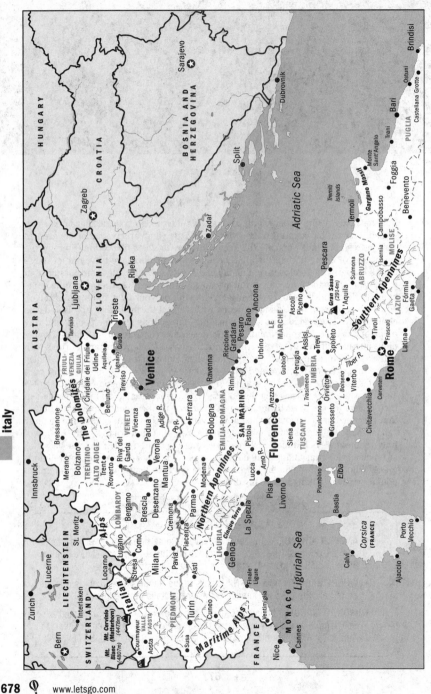

italy

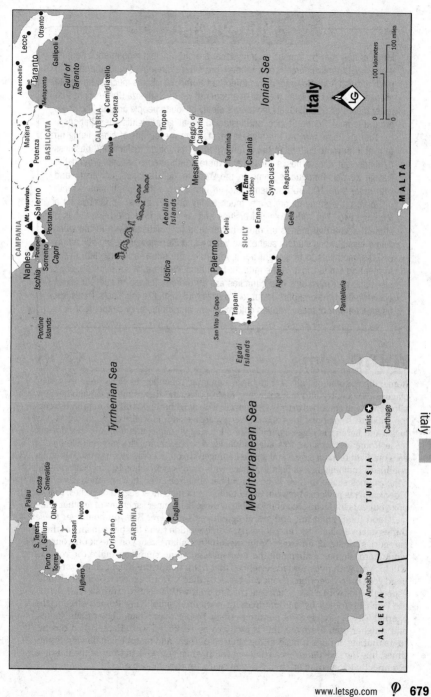

Italy

Much of Italy may be famous for things that are old (ancient monuments, Renaissance art, Catholic churches everywhere), but a huge amount of youth manages to push through it all. Nowhere is this truer than **Rome**, which has much of Italy's old attractions and yet also an incredible amount of youth. Sapienza University has no fewer than 147,000 students, so there's plenty of young people around. The areas around Termini, Centro Storico, and Testaccio are all great nightlife destinations.

Though Rome may be the biggest beast, there are dozens of cities lining up to rival it for youth culture. **Milan** is renowned for its uptight fashion and business dealings, but it also has a looser and more youth-oriented scene around the Navigli district. **Bologna** is home to the Western World's oldest university, and with more than 100,000 students packed into a city with a population a tenth of Rome's, the students are pretty much taking over. **Pisa** may be famous for a leaning tower, but with three universities and an awful lot more bars, it has a student scene that stands up much better than its buildings. Even in the cities with a less obvious student scene, like **Venice** and **Florence,** there are still plenty of 20-somethings to be sought out if you make the effort—try Dorsoduro in the former and Santa Croce in the latter to find them. Wherever you are in Italy, don't just think that museums and churches are all there is for you to see. Hit up an *aperitivo* bar or take a pitcher out to a *piazza* and drink like the locals. That's just as much a part of today's Italian culture as any amphitheater or chapel roof.

rome *roma* ☎06

Rome: the epitome of Italy, and its biggest enigma. It condenses every stereotype that plagues the country into one sprawling metropolis...and then rambles on another few kilometers and centuries to reverse them all. With neighborhoods off the map and streets too small to *be* mapped, this is a city as expansive as it is walkable, as global as it is local. And here's the biggest paradox of all: it's as young as it is old. And that doesn't mean Rome averages out to some middle-aged soccer mom. This city will blow your ears out with teenage gusto and shake its finger at you in codgerly reproval. Within its confines, crumbling bricks fight for space with candy-colored hotels, and centuries-old cobblestones shake to their bones as rubber tires roll over their weathered surface. Video cameras peek out between the columns of Rome's most sacred churches, as if to box your ears for feeling too comfortable in these dank inner sanctums of another era.

Good food, great art, and grand people—it's all here. But you could get these things in any Italian city (and honestly, Rome wouldn't win the prize in any of these categories). Instead, for every "quintessentially Italian" item you check off your list while here, Rome, challenging the tourists who come simply to make the rounds, will hit you with five more experiences that *truly* define the Italian character—and bend your preconceptions about what exactly that is. Don't expect to conquer Rome, especially not with a list. (Carthage tried to do it with an entire army and failed.)

Don't be fooled by the hundreds of postcards simplifying Rome's streets: the Eternal City is anything but picture perfect. Dirtier than Milan, bigger than Naples, and rougher than Florence, this is a city to be reckoned with. Rather than bowing to its tourists, it nods it head in recognition of them and marches on its way. Sometimes, like the speeding Vespas that only stop when you walk in front of them, Rome requires that you stand up to it. Are you ready for the challenge?

ORIENTATION

Ancient City

With one of the highest camera-to-square-inch-of-sidewalk ratios in Rome, the Ancient City doesn't exactly feel "ancient" anymore. This vast stretch of tourist heaven, whose sights are the single reason many people come to Italy, is a stunning mix of old and new. For every ruin you'll see (and there are plenty), there's a plastic replica to match; for every nude statue, an overpriced sweatshirt to cover you up. With so many sights worth seeing, it is all right for once to abandon your pride and surrender yourself to tourism in its full glory—photos with costumed gladiators, lines that only seem short compared to the 190m frieze on Trajan's column, and enough overpriced gelato to make even Augustus's purse feel a little empty. Unlike most neighborhoods, which actually have an epicenter, the Ancient City is as scattered as some of its ruins. But don't worry; by the time you reach your destination—be it ruin or restaurant—you'll have forgotten the crowds and costs you endured to get there. Perhaps it's that feeling of traveling through time as you survey the remains of a civilization extinct for more than a millennium, or maybe it's the mouth-watering aroma of fresh-baked pizza dough that does it, but, whatever the cause, tourist travails pale in comparison to the pleasures of the Ancient City.

Centro Storico

To the traveler who has paid one too many euro after waiting in one too many 4hr. lines, the Centro Storico offers a reprieve: nearly all of the churches, monuments, and *piazze* in this part of town are free of charge, and the only lines you'll be waiting in are the ones for overpriced gelato or food. With most of the main attractions compactly clustered on either side of **Corso Vittorio Emanuele,** this tangled web of streets is manageable in size, though not as easily navigable as a more grid-like pattern might be. Expect to get lost as *vias* suddenly split into numerous *vicolos*, so use the Corso as a departure point and the vibrant urban living rooms of **Campo dei Fiori** and **Piazza Navona** on either side as your major landmarks.

Piazza Di Spagna

Rome has a 5th Avenue too, and this is it. Bordered by the overbearing **Via del Corso,** the grid-like streets surrounding the Spanish Steps are full of people shopping and goggling in front of windows at Rome's highest end stores. It's hard to find a well-priced meal or a respite from the congestion unless you make a return to nature along the Tiber River or in the Villa Borghese park, both of which cushion the tourist enclave. Also redeeming the area are some of the best sights in the city. As in the **Centro Storico,** many landmarks are outside and free to the public, so the only obstacle to an enjoyable experience will be the crowds.

Jewish Ghetto

You could pass through the Jewish Ghetto and notice nothing more than a surprisingly quiet Friday evening and Saturday morning and slightly more ethnic cuisine than Rome's majority. Now occupying little more than a few streets near the Tiber River, this compact neighborhood was actually home to the first real community of Jews in Western Europe. Originally a true ghetto blocked off from the city proper with sturdy walls and plagued by an unfortunate tendency to flood, today it is a pleasant stretch of residential houses and excellent restaurants that dish up some of the best artichoke around. A low-key and less-touristed area to meander through on the way to the nearby Centro Storico, the Jewish Ghetto may be small, but it is rich in history and flavor.

Vatican City

The people-to-square-foot ratio is significantly cockeyed in this tiny state: an expected madhouse of crowds in the Vatican contrasts sharply with the mostly empty boulevards in the surrounding region of **Prati,** making any attempt to measure population density a joke. That's actually a good thing though—after forging through the

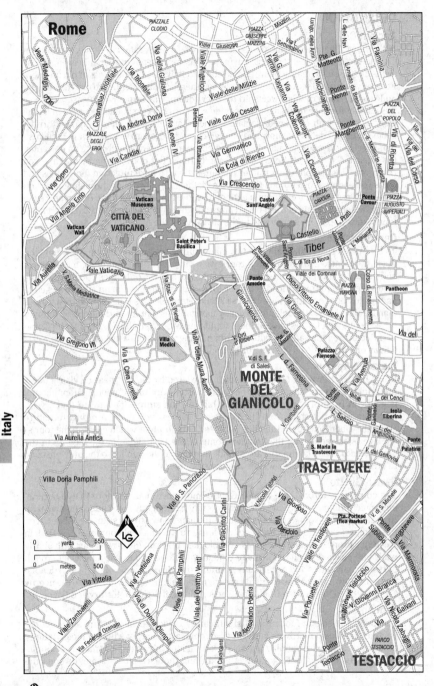

Rome

italy

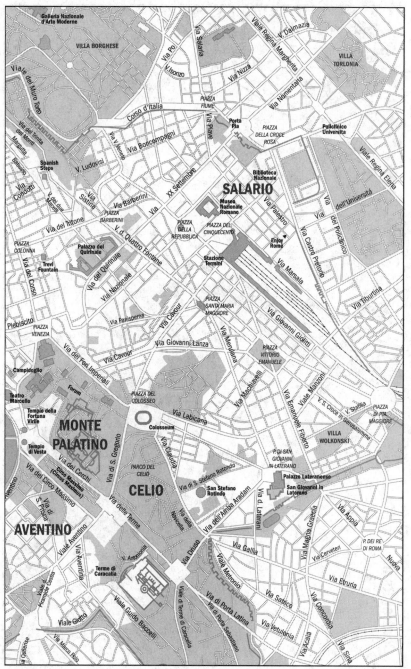

rome • orientation

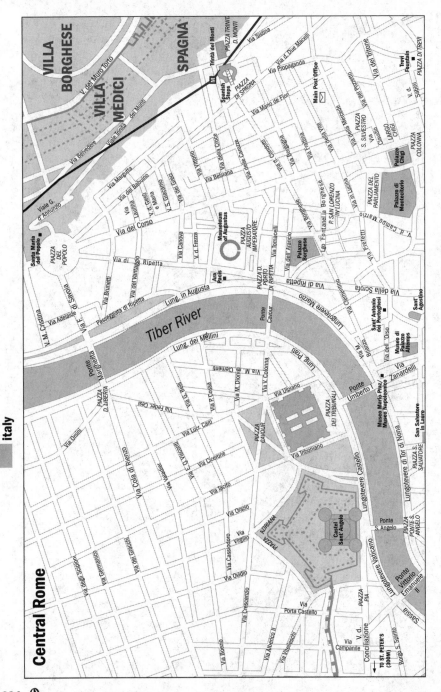

Central Rome

italy

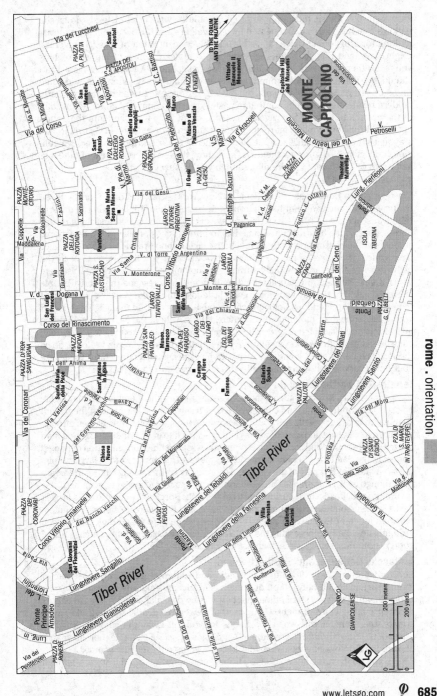

crowds to pay a visit to the pope, you'll be able to wander effortlessly down the region's tree-lined streets, frequented by dog-walkers and the occasional lost tourist looking for a big dome (a.k.a. **St. Peter's**). If the concentration of plastic souvenirs, bright flags, and English menus isn't enough to indicate which of the two regions you're in, then the brick wall which physically separates Vatican City from Prati should give you a clue. Walk around outside its boundary on the Prati side, and you'll find surprisingly affordable hotels and casual trattorias scattered throughout fairly modern residential buildings colored in pastel greens and pinks. And for all this talk of the crowds in Vatican City, even when you make your way back into the pope's digs, the throng of people is more manageable than what you'll find in Central Rome. Maybe it's the gargantuan size of St. Peter's and its *piazza*, or perhaps peoples' religious consciences that check them, but somehow the tourist crush west of the Tiber and north of Trastevere is more diluted than you'd expect.

Trastevere

Trastevere is to Rome what Brooklyn is to New York—overlooked by tourists, loved by locals, and removed from the metropolitan center while still being in the thick of things. Just across the Tiber River, this enclave of cobblestone streets and small *piazze* boasts some of the best nightlife Rome has to offer; it's as popular with international students at the nearby university as it is with neighborhood residents whose families have called Trastevere home for generations. Although you likely won't spend the night here, as there are few budget-friendly accommodations, dinner in Trastevere won't break the bank. Restaurants that have managed to escape the tourist bubble abound—just throw away your map, get a little lost, and make your way into one of the tasty and unpretentious homegrown establishments that fill the neighborhood. If you've had enough of monuments and ruins, take a walk in the lush gardens leading into Monteverde (which has "green" in its name for a reason). You knew you weren't going to get through this book without reading that old saying, "When in Rome, do as the Romans do." Well, if living like a true Roman means making friendly Trastevere your home as well, following that well-worn adage can't do you wrong.

Termini And Northeast Rome

Ask people if they saw the Vatican, the Colosseum, or any other number of famed sights on their last trip to Rome, and chances are they'll say no to at least one of them: with so much to take in, something's got to give. Ironic, then, that everyone passes through Termini, as mundane and unromantic as it is. It seems like everyone sticks around here as well—the area around the station is home to an astonishing concentration of budget hotels. In the San Lorenzo neighborhood is Sapienza University, Rome's largest, helping to ensure that this part of the city has a thoroughly vibrant young culture. Be aware that, though lively, this area is hardly charming, and many pickpockets work here.

For charm, head a little further north to the Villa Borghese, one of Rome's largest parks. The surrounding neighborhoods of Parioli and Flaminio are also more chilled-out than much of Rome (especially Termini), so come here for a break. In between Termini and Villa Borghese runs the Via Nomentana, the area around which is full of good restaurants, serene streets, and a more residential feel.

Testaccio, Ostiense, and Southern Rome

Located south of the Colosseum, Testaccio and Ostiense are left off most tourist itineraries and are literally left off of Rome's central map. Take advantage of this relative anonymity and get lost in their quiet streets by day, making sure to save energy for their pulsing clubs at night. Comprised of newer, residential housing and paved streets, these uncongested neighborhoods let you put away the guidebook for an afternoon (though studies have shown that copies of *Let's Go* double their lifespan if exposed to ample sunlight, so consider keeping yours out) and just wander a bit.

As you go even further south, you'll find more quiet residential streets, enough churches to convert you to Catholicism, and, yes, more ruins of sorts. Though it takes a while to reach the more serene stretch of the Appian Way, once you do, you'll feel miles away from bustling Rome.

ACCOMMODATIONS

Finding lodging in Rome is not as daunting as it may seem, even though the tourist offices do not provide as extensive listings as those in other cities. Options range from cheap hostels to four-star hotels and a slew of places in between. Expect the most standard and comprehensive services at hotels, with a price to match. Better hostels have kitchens, no curfew, and services geared to students such as maps, internet access, tours, and even bars. Smaller *pensione,* bed and breakfasts, and *alberghi* (the Italian word for hotels) are often located within a larger building of apartments and thus may be harder to find without advance knowledge. Such establishments often offer fewer rooms and services but more availability during high season, even at the last minute. Disregard the rule for hotels and hostels at these lodging houses and make reservations in person. These are often more convenient for the proprieters and may get you a lower rate. Discounts are often given for longer stays and for payments made in cash.

Termini is the best place to find last-minute and conveniently-located accommodations, especially for travelers arriving by train. If you have not booked in advance, however, be wary of hotel scouts who will jump at the opportunity to advertise overpriced rooms late in the evening. Before booking, be sure to ask about services offered: some places charge for breakfast, A/C, internet, or, even worse, all three.

Ancient City

Home to some of the biggest monuments in Rome, the Ancient City is not the cheapest place to plant yourself during a visit to Italy's capital, though if you're willing to shell out at least €100 a night, you'll have more than enough four-star options to choose from. Never fear, however; plenty of bed and breakfasts and *pensioni* offer decent services at a much lower cost.

CASA SANTA PUDENZIANA
⊛⊘(ᵖ)⌂ CONVENT ❷
V. Urbana 158 ☎06 48 80 56

If you're of the female persuasion and don't mind a 10:30pm curfew (12:30am on Sa), the quiet and spatious grounds of Casa Santa Pudenziana might just provide a welcome relief from the more crowded (and somewhat pricier) hostels nearby. This convent's six-bed dorm, double, and single make for a small community of guests—and that's if there are no vacancies. Guests here often run into each other at breakfast, dinner, or throughout the day in the peaceful central garden. Library and chapel upstairs as well as clean common spaces with television, refrigerator, and microwave. Wi-Fi from nearby hotels floats through some parts of the convent, but *Let's Go* does not recommend relying on stolen Wi-Fi. No lockers or keys, so get ready to greet the friendly staff every time you buzz to get in.

✦ Ⓜ A: Cavour. From V. Cavour, turn onto V. Urbana. *i* Women only. Breakfast included 7-9am; dinner 8pm, €10. Ⓢ Dorms €22; singles €40; doubles €52. Inquire about discounts for longer stays. ☒ Strict curfew M-F 10:30pm, Sa 12:30am, Su 10:30pm.

STUDENT HOUSE
⊛⊘(ᵖ) HOSTEL ❶
V. Merulana 117 ▣www.hostelworld.com

This small hostel does indeed feel like a house—the central reception area is more like a living room complete with bookshelves, photos, TV, and colorful furniture than a place to check in and out. Student House's rooms consist of two six-bed co-ed dorms, so don't plan on making it your private getaway. The living spaces are sunny and equipped with bunks and mirrors. The hall bathrooms might not be convenient, but the small communal kitchen and free Wi-Fi are. Brush up on your Italian before you get here—the owner speaks no English.

✦ Ⓜ A: Manzoni. From V. Emanuele Filberto, walk straight on V. Manzoni and make a right onto V.

Merulana. **i** *Reserve your space at hostelworld.com. Set up check-in time in advance to avoid arriving when the owner is out. Towels €1.* $ *Dorms €20.*

HOTEL SAN DANIELE BUNDÌ 💳⊗📶❄ HOTEL [4]

V. Cavour 295 ☎06 48 75 295 💻www.hotelsandanielebundi.it

Neighboring establishments recommend Hotel Bundì for its simple rooms and accommodating staff. Although the hotel is small, its central location, competitive prices, and surprising tranquillity make it a good bet. Rooms have Wi-Fi, air-conditioning, private bathrooms, and TVs. Complimentary breakfast is an added perk.

➔ *[M]A: Colosseum. From V. dei Fori Imperiali, make a right onto V. Cavour. Buzz at the doors and take Scale B to the 3rd fl.* $ *Singles €65; doubles €85.* ⏰ *Reception closes at 8pm.*

PENSIONE ROSETTA 💳⊗📶❄ PENSIONE [4]

V. Cavour 295 ☎06 47 82 3069 💻www.rosettahotel.com

A friendly staff and clean, though spartan, rooms make Pensione Rosetta a convenient option for those who hope to roll out of bed and check out the Colosseum in their pajamas. Each of Rosetta's 20 rooms have a private bathroom, a telephone, a TV, and air-conditioning; free Wi-Fi is available in public areas. The central courtyard provides a welcome respite from the busy V. Cavour.

➔ *[M]A: Colosseum. From V. dei Fori Imperiali, make a right onto V. Cavour. Buzz at the doors and take Scala B to the 1st fl.* $ *Singles €65; doubles €90; triples €105; quads €120.*

CESARE BALBO INN 💳⊗📶❄ HOTEL [4]

V. Cesare Balbo 43 ☎06 98 38 60 81

Conveniently located entirely on the first floor, Cesare Balbo Inn is the perfect choice for those too lazy to climb a flight of stairs or walk more than a mile to Rome's ancient sights. Rooms here are big, colorful, and sunny. The staff is friendly, but they might get a little confused if you ask questions about topics as complicated as how much a room costs. Free internet, private bathrooms, in-room breakfast, and air-conditioning round out this small establishment.

➔ *[M]A: Cavour: From V. Cavour, make a right on V. Panisperna; walk 2 blocks and make a right on V. Cesare Balbo.* $ *Doubles €90; triples €100; quads €110.* ⏰ *Reception 24hr.*

SANDY HOSTEL 🌐⊗📶 HOSTEL [1]

V. Cavour 136 ☎06 48 84 585 💻www.sandyhostel.com

If all of Termini's more popular hostels are full, this spot offers a very cheap, if barely passable, alternative. While the sound of music (not the von Trapp family kind) coming from neighbors in the building can make for a less-than-peaceful experience, and the strong cigarette smell permeating the rooms may gross you out, the sunny rooms will help appease at least one of your five senses. The staff hardly strives to deliver great service, but that's to be expected at this no-frills establishment.

➔ *[M]A: Cavour. Walk up Cavour. Buzz and walk to the 5th fl.* **i** *Computer with ethernet provided. Reserve online.* $ *Co-ed 4- to 6-bed dorms €20-30.* ⏰ *Reception 7am-midnight. 2-week max. stay.*

italy

Centro Storico

The Centro Storico is not the cheapest place to stay, but hotels here often have a lot more character and offer better services than those found elsewhere. Reserve rooms well in advance and don't expect them to be cheap.

ALBERGO DEL SOLE 🌐⊗📶❄ HOTEL [5]

V. del Biscione 76 ☎06 68 80 68 73 💻www.solealbiscione.it

Especially well-furnished rooms with antique furniture, paintings, and curtains make this place feel more like a home than a hotel. Great common spaces, including a garden terrace and sitting rooms on each floor, give Alberge del Sole a lived-in quality. Knowledgable staff are welcoming and straight-forward.

➔ *Exit P. di Fiori onto V. del Biscione.* **i** *Most rooms with A/C, otherwise with fan. Wi-Fi €1.50 per hr.* $ *Singles €70, with bath €110-125; doubles €100-105/€120-160.* ⏰ *Reception 24hr.*

HOTEL SMERALDO
💳⊗📶❄ HOTEL [5]

Vicolo dei Chiodaroli 9 ☎06 68 75 929 💻www.hotelsmeraldoroma.com

Somewhat tight rooms are clean and bright, sporting well-coordinated decor. The gracious reception staff inspires confidence in guests by happily giving advice to travelers. There are no surprises here—rooms are well-equipped and neatly kept.

➜ From Campo dei Fiori, walk down V. dei Giubbonari, turn left onto V. dei Chiavari and right onto Vicolo dei Chiodaroli. i Breakfast included. All rooms have private bath. Wi-Fi €5 per hr. in common areas; public computer available. [$] Singles €70-110; doubles €90-145. ⏰ Reception 24hr.

ALBERGO POMEZIO
💳♿📶❄ HOTEL [5]

V. dei Chiavari 13 ☎06 68 61 371

This hotel's fast-paced and assertive owner offers large and nicely decorated rooms with curtains and matching trimmings. Good services, including free Wi-Fi, for the location and price. The large breakfast room is one of the few common spaces for guests.

➜ From Campo dei Fiori, walk down V. dei Giubbonari and turn left onto V. dei Chiavari. i All rooms have private bath. Free Wi-Fi. [$] Singles €70-100; doubles €100-140. Weekends tend to be more expensive.

Piazza Di Spagna

Staying in the Piazza di Spagna area is a pricey affair, and though you might be getting newer accommodations and slightly better services, you'll be surrounded by more crowds than are present in the Ancient City or Centro Storico. Boasting little nightlife to boot, this neighborhood is a better bet for older folks who want reliable services than for youth seeking value and fun.

👍 HOTEL PANDA
💳⊗📶❄ HOTEL [4]

V. della Croce 35 ☎06 67 80 179 💻www.hotelpanda.it

Luckily (or not), there are no panda bears around, but you'll feel as warm and fuzzy as one of these bamboo-chomping cuties while staying at this small, family-run hotel. Simply decorated rooms come with A/C, Wi-Fi, and TV at a better price than the spiffier hotels down the street. Opt for a bigger room if you can, as the small ones really are small. Though there isn't much common space (read: narrow hallways and no breakfast room), the rooms are enough of a retreat for this shortfall to be inconsequential.

➜ ⓂA: Spagna. From the Spanish Steps, take V. Condotti, turn right onto V. Belsiana and right onto V. della Croce. Hotel is on the 2nd fl. i Breakfast €5 at downstairs bar. A/C €6. Free Wi-Fi. [$] Singles €55-68, with bath €65-80; doubles €68-78/€85-108; triples €120-140. ⏰ Reception 24hr.

DEPENDANCE ANAHI
💳⊗📶❄ HOTEL [5]

V. della Penna 22 ☎06 36 10 841 💻www.hotellocarno.com

Dependance Anahi boasts a prime location and stellar services, if less history and pomp than its sister across the street. Mostly double rooms and two singles all have TV, A/C, private bath, minibar, and free Wi-Fi, and Art Nouveau detailing gives the place more flavor than your standard rooming house. Head across the street to enjoy a buffet breakfast in the quiet, vine-covered patio or relax in the palatial lounge rooms.

➜ ⓂA: Flaminio. From P. del Popolo, exit near V. di Ripetta and immediately turn right onto V. Penna d'Oca. Across the street from Hotel Locarno; reception at V. della Penna 22. i Breakfast included. Bath, minibar, and safe ensuite. Free bike rental. Free Wi-Fi. [$] Singles €90-120; doubles €110-190. ⏰ Reception 24hr.

HOTEL DE PRETIS
💳⊗📶❄ HOTEL [5]

V. Rasella 142 ☎06 48 19 626 💻www.hoteldepetris.com

Not only are rooms equipped with all the basics—TV, A/C, free Wi-Fi, and minibar—but they're especially elegant. Superior rooms have hardwood floors and modern furniture, while the standards are less luxe, though bigger than average. Expect no surprises from the reliable rooms and staff.

✚ ⓂA: *Barberini. From P. Barberini, take V. del Tritone, turn left onto V. Boccaccio and left onto V. Rasella.* **i** *Breakfast included. All rooms have ensuite bath. Free Wi-Fi.* ⓢ *Singles €94-136; doubles €113-171. Extra bed €46.* ⓩ *Reception 24hr.*

DOMUS JULIA
✦⊗⟨ᵖ⟩❄ HOTEL ❹

V. Rasella 32 ☎06 47 45 765 ◫www.domusjulia.it

The friendly dog at Domus Julia makes up for the reception staff who can be a bit short of temper at times. The hotel's 18th-century building retains its historic look but brings itself up to the 21st century with all the expected comforts, including free internet. If you've gotten a bit bored of seeing Roman ruins, rent one of their bikes for free or even earn an extra euro by walking the dog. The breakfast room is a nice hang-out even in the evening.

✚ ⓂA: *Barberini. From P. Barberini, take V. del Tritone, turn left onto V. Boccaccio and left onto V. Rasella.* **i** *Breakfast included. All rooms have minibar and ensuite bath. Free Wi-Fi.* ⓢ *Singles €60-100; doubles €78-180; triples €89-210.* ⓩ *Reception 24hr.*

Vatican City

When it comes to hotels, the area immediately around the Vatican is as overpriced as the pizza and souvenirs. However, the quieter streets nearer the river and Prati offer many affordable options, mostly small hotels within residential buildings. A nice area in which to stay due to its proximity to the sights and distance from the *centro*'s chaos, it may only be lacking in nightlife, which is (expectedly) quiet.

🏨 COLORS
✦⊗⟨ᵖ⟩❄ HOTEL, HOSTEL ❶

V. Boezio 31 ☎06 68 74 030 ◫www.colorshotel.com

The rooms smell fresh like wood and look bright, as colors should. The boldly pigmented adornments of their 23 rooms help keep guests' stays comfortable, while the free Wi-Fi is simply convenient (and rare for this neighborhood). If the rainbow inside has you wanting some straight-up green, head to the rooftop terrace. One dormitory with five beds gives this hotel a hostel spirit. The room has A/C though, putting it miles beyond most hostels.

✚ ⓂA: *Ottaviano. Walk down V. Ottaviano; turn left onto V. Cola di Rienzo and right onto V. Terenzio; at the intersection with V. Boezio.* **i** *Breakfast included at hotel; €7 in dorm. Common terrace, TV room, and mini-kitchen. Free Wi-Fi.* ⓢ *Dorms €15-30; singles €30, with bath €50-80; doubles €70-100.* ⓩ *Reception 24hr.*

HOTEL AL SAN PIETRO
✦⊗⟨ᵖ⟩❄ HOTEL ❸

V. Giovanni Bettolo 43 ☎06 37 00 132 ◫www.sanpietrino.it

Small green frogs (don't worry, they're ceramic) and the smell of flowers greet guests at this small hotel, located only 5min. from the Vatican museums. Though the rooms aren't particularly large, free Wi-Fi and staff that matches the upbeat decor make it a better deal than hotels advertised nearby. No breakfast, but there's an organic grocery store down the street.

✚ ⓂA: *Ottaviano. Exit onto V. Barletta and turn left onto V. Bettolo.* **i** *Singles with shared bath. Free Wi-Fi.* ⓢ *Singles €40-50; doubles €70-89; triples €115.* ⓩ *Reception 24hr.*

HOTEL GIUGGIOLI
✦⊗⟨ᵖ⟩❄ HOTEL ❺

V. Germanico 198, 2nd fl. ☎06 36 00 53 89 ◫www.hotelgiuggioli.it

The silver accents and geometric furniture give this top-notch hotel a distinctly modern feel. Carpeted rooms are very clean and generously sized, though a bit dimly lit. If long lines at the Vatican aren't your thing, bike rental gives you another reason to travel elsewhere in the city. The lovely bar and kitchen area *(open 1-9pm)* feels more like an upscale restaurant then a hotel add-on.

✚ ⓂA: *Lepanto. Walk down V. Ezio and turn right onto V. Germanico.* **i** *Breakfast included. All*

italy

rooms have private bath and minibar ensuite. Wi-Fi €1 per hr. $ Singles €70-110; doubles €80-130. Bike rental €12 per hr. 🕐 Reception 24hr.

HOTEL LADY
💳⊗📶 PENSIONE ❹

V. Germanico 198, 4th fl. ☎06 32 42 112 🖥www.hotelladyroma.it

Aesthetics trump amenities here: the old-fashioned charm of this former monastery is unfortunately accompanied by a lack of A/C and Wi-Fi. Still, the original wood-beamed ceilings and amber stained-glass windows create a comforting feel that most modern hotels can't replicate. Fans and antique wooden furniture that looks like it's been here for a century add to Hotel Lady's appeal. Rooms without bathrooms may be less convenient but are significantly bigger.

➡ Ⓜ A: Lepanto. Walk down V. Ezio and turn right onto V. Germanico. ℹ Singles and triples with shared bath only. Internet room available. $ Singles €60; doubles €75, with bath €90; triples €120. 🕐 Reception 24hr., but call about arrival time.

A ROMA SAN PIETRO B AND B
💳⊗📶❄ B AND B ❸

V. Crescenzio 85 ☎06 68 78 205 🖥www.ftraldi.it

Though it may not be quirkier than a hotel, this small bed and breakfast offers brightly colored (though somewhat blandly furnished) rooms with excellent perks: A/C, free Wi-Fi, and complimentary breakfast make it better than some hotels. Reserve in advance and schedule arrival time, as there are only five rooms and the owner might be out. Watch out for the dripping water in the courtyard.

➡ Ⓜ A: Ottaviano. Walk down V. Ottaviano and turn left onto V. Crescenzio. ℹ Breakfast included. Free Wi-Fi. $ Singles €40-50; doubles €60-110; triples €70-140. Extra bed €10-25. 🕐 Call to schedule arrival time.

Termini and Northeast Rome

Termini abounds with hotels, hostels, bed and breakfasts, and *pensioni*. There's a roughly one-to-one ratio of extremely cheap to extremely overpriced options, so do research beforehand and try to book at least one week in advance, especially for summer stays. Although the proximity to Termini station makes living here convenient, the area is not the safest place at night. Be wary of pickpockets and, if possible, avoid walking about in the late hours.

👍 M AND J PLACE HOSTEL
⊛⊗📶❄ HOSTEL ❷

V. Solferino 9 ☎06 44 62 802 🖥www.mejplacehostel.com

A prime location, helpful staff, and clean rooms grace this wonderful hostel. M and J Place boasts great common spaces (kitchen, balcony, and TV lounge) as well as a calm feel enhanced by rooms that are neat and not too crowded. Private rooms are more reminiscent of a hotel with A/C, computers, TV, and towels ensuite. The reception desk posts weekly events in the city, provides laptop rentals, lends books, offers printing and photocopying services, and has public computers in case you need to get organized. If you'd rather relax, the downstairs restaurant, bar, and club provide food all day, an *aperitivo* hour at 6pm, and a chance to dance at 11pm.

➡ Ⓜ Termini. Walk down V. Marsala away from the station, and turn right onto V. Solferino. ℹ Breakfast included in some reservations; book online and choose (€3 otherwise). Lockers outside room. Free luggage storage until 9pm. Towels €2. 1hr. free internet with booking; €2 per hr. or €5 per 4hr. thereafter. All-female dorms available. $ 10-bed dorms €25; 8-bed €26; 6-bed €32-35; 4-bed €35-37.50. Singles €75; doubles €80-120; triples €150; quads €180. 🕐 Reception 24hr. Restaurant/bar open daily 7am-late. Kitchen open 3-10pm.

👍 ALESSANDRO DOWNTOWN
💳⊗📶 HOSTEL ❶

V. C. Cattaneo, 23 ☎06 44 34 0147 🖥www.hostelsalessandro.com

This conveniently located hostel is a bit less party-hardy than its sister, the **Palace,** but offers great services to backpackers and students. Large common spaces, communal kitchen, and dorms make it less cramped than nearby hostels, although bunk beds can take down the comfort level of the largest dorms. Other than the midday cleaning which prevents you from resting in your room until after 3pm, Alessandro Downtown is ready to take care of you after a long day in the city.

✚ ⓜTermini. Take V. Giovanni Giolitti and turn left onto V. C. Cattaneo. *i* Breakfast included. Free pasta dinners M-F 7pm. Lockers ensuite; free luggage storage before 2pm. Towel rental. Book online 1 week in advance Apr-Aug. 30 min. free Wi-Fi daily; €2 per hr. thereafter. ⓢ 8-bed dorms €14-29; 6-bed €15-30; 4-bed (co-ed) with bath €19-40; doubles €50-53, with bath €55-110. ⓞ Reception 24hr. Rooms must be evacuated 10am-3pm for cleaning.

prego

Prego. The word is like pizza: Italians have somehow found a way to top or dress it with anything; to have it in any context, at any time of day; and to make it hot, cold, or even lukewarm to match the occasion. Whatever the situation, it all flies:

- **"PREGO?"** The first thing you'll hear as you walk into a *pasticceria.* Translation: "How can I help you?" or "What do you want?" And they expect you to know, immediately. (Standing around asking prices doesn't fly too well.)

- **"PREGO!"** A favorite of the Sistine Chapel guards. Amid the clamor of docents shushing people and telling them not to take pictures, you hear the word muttered sternly, more like a reprimand than anything else. Translation: "Geez...thanks for being quiet after the 15th time I've told you to turn off your camera and shut your trap!"

- **"PREGO."** The sweetest version of them all, when it's just a simple statement, often following *"grazie."* After you buy a gelato or compliment someone, the recipient of your cash or flattery will often acknowledge his or her thanks by calmly uttering the word. Translation: "You're welcome" or "I'm honored."

- **"PREGO" (WITH OPTIONAL "!")** Actually used in its dictionary sense, this *prego* can mean "I pray." Now, Italians pray for all kinds of things—in religious contexts, in which case the exclamation mark probably isn't necessary, but also in more mundane or demanding contexts. It's often a favorite of cleaning ladies. Walking into a room full of strewn backpack contents, you might catch a despairing *"Pre-e-g-o-ooooo."*

ALESSANDRO PALACE
V. Vicenza 42   ☎06 44 61 958   www.hostelsalessando.com   HOSTEL ❶

A historically decorated bar (check out the "frescoed" ceiling) turned modern (check out the speakers and TV!) makes this one of the most social hostels around. While the nightly pizza giveaway *(8:30pm)* goes fast, great happy hours and drink specials keep guests around all evening. A/C keeps the rooms bearable in the mid-July Roman heat, though big dorm size can make restful sleep difficult. Still, this is as close as a hostel gets to being a palace.

✚ ⓜTermini. Walk up V. Marsala away from the station and turn right onto V. Vicenza. *i* Breakfast included; free pizza daily Apr-July 8:30pm. Lockers ensuite. Fridges in some doubles. Reserve online at least 1 week in advance during high season. 30min. free Wi-Fi daily. all dorms have private bathroom. ⓢ 8-bed dorms €15-30; 6-bed €16-36; 4-bed €18-38, with bath €21-42. Doubles €55-115, with bath €65-130; triples €75-135/€81-147. ⓞ Reception 24hr. Free luggage storage before 3pm. Bar open daily 6pm-2am.

THE YELLOW
V. Palestro 44   ☎06 49 38 2682   www.the-yellow.com   HOSTEL ❶

This hostel isn't called "yellow" because it's scared, but because it's so darn happy. The perfect place for social butterflies, this establishment boasts a full bar (customers will likely spend more time here than in their somewhat small rooms) and over five floors of dorms as well as colored lights and funky posters in the hallways. Skype headsets, locks, and even laptops are conveniently available to rent or purchase at the reception desk. Come here for fun times . . . not to wake up at 6am for a hike to the Vatican.

✣ ⓜTermini. Take V. Milazzo away from the station and turn left onto V. Palestro. *i* Breakfast €2-10 at the bar next door. Lockers ensuite; free luggage storage before 1:30pm. €10 towel deposit. 30min. free internet per day on public computers. No Wi-Fi. Ⓢ 12-bed dorms €18-24; 7-bed €20-26; 6-bed €22-34; 4-bed €24-35. Ⓩ Reception 24hr.

LEGENDS HOSTEL
➡Ⓧ⬥(ᵀ) HOSTEL ❷

V. Curtatone 12 ☎06 44 70 32 17 🖳www.legendshostel.com

This cramped but well-equipped hostel close to Termini brings in a mixed crowd of backpackers and older folk. There's little common space, and rooms are fairly distant from one other (some in a separate building). However, the small kitchen gives the place a sense of community, especially during delicious breakfasts and pasta dinners. The friendly and low-key staff is ready to assist you during your stay in Rome. Shared bathrooms can be a bit messy, but at least they come with soap.

✣ ⓜTermini. Walk up V. Marsala away from the station; turn right onto V. Gaeta and right onto V. Curtatone. Buzz and walk to 1st fl. *i* Breakfast included; free pasta offered M-F 7pm. Lockers ensuite. 5hr. free Wi-Fi; €1 per hr. thereafter. Public computers at reception desk. Fans in rooms. Ⓢ 8-bed dorms €23-33; 6-bed €25-37; 5-bed €28-41; 4-bed €30-44. Triples €48-51; doubles €41-71. Ⓩ Reception 24hr.

FREEDOM TRAVELLER
➡Ⓧ(ᵀ)❄ HOSTEL ❶

V. Gaeta 23 ☎06 48 91 29 10 🖳www.freedom-traveller.it

Freedom Traveller is a friendly and slightly less crowded hostel with the same great perks as nearby spots. Its sunny reception area and common spaces (TV room, backyard, and kitchen) immediately make you feel welcome. The first-floor location and proximity to Termini make it especially convenient for weary travelers. Free Wi-Fi is luxurious compared to most hostels that charge by the hour.

✣ ⓜTermini. Take V. Marsala away from the station and turn right onto V. Gaeta. *i* Free pizza and beer party Tu evenings. Free luggage storage until 2.30pm. All-female dorms available. Free Wi-Fi in common spaces and some rooms. Ⓢ 6- and 4-bed dorms €17-32; doubles €60-110; triples €75-135; quads €80-160. Ⓩ Reception 24hr. Lockout 10:30am-2pm (except for private rooms). Quiet hours 11pm-8am. Communal kitchen open until 10:30pm.

MOSAIC HOSTEL
➡Ⓧ(ᵀ)🛏 HOSTEL ❷

V. Carlo Cattaneo ☎06 44 70 4592 🖳www.hostelmosaic.com

Right below the busier **Alessandro,** this similar hostel's reception boasts a comfy leather couch, warmly painted walls, and a helpful staff that immediately fosters a sense of home. Rooms that feel less utilitarian than those of your typical hostel (despite the requisite bunks) provide everything you need for a comfortable stay in Rome.

✣ ⓜTermini. Take V. Giovanni Giolitti and turn left onto V. C. Cattaneo. On the 2nd fl. *i* Breakfast included; free pasta dinner M-F. Lockers ensuite; free luggage storage upon arrival. Towels €2. Kitchen access M-F. Female-only dorms available. Reserve online at least a week in advance. 30min. free Wi-Fi daily; €1 per hr. thereafter. Ⓢ 8-bed dorms €22; 6-bed €24; 5-bed €25; 4-bed €27. Ⓩ Reception 24hr.

CASA OLMATA
➡Ⓧ(ᵀ) HOSTEL ❶

V. dell'Olmata 36 ☎06 48 30 19 🖳www.casaolmata.com

This quiet, well-kept, and cheerfully-run hostel finds itself in a nicer region than most. Mixed 6-bed dorms, triples, doubles, and singles are a bit cramped, but wooden bunks and homey decorations (check out the old clocks and lace curtains in some rooms) provide a comfy, lived-in feel. Many rooms come with fully-equipped ensuite kitchens, TV, fans, and private bath; others have access to a communal kitchen down the hall with microwave and fridge. Definitely not a party hostel (quiet hours after midnight), but all the better for it.

✈ ⓂTermini. Walk toward P. Santa Maggiore and down V. Paolina. Turn left onto W. Quattro Cantoni and left onto V. Olmata. *i* Breakfast included. Lockers in hallway and ensuite. 15min. free internet per day at public computer. Roof terrace. Free Wi-Fi. Ⓢ Dorms €18-20; singles €38; doubles €56-58. Inquire about discounts for longer stays. Ⓩ Reception 8am-2pm and 4pm-midnight.

HOTEL PAPA GERMANO
♥⊗(ɕ)❄ HOTEL ❷

V. Calatafimi 14/A ☎06 48 69 19 🖳www.hotelpapagermano.com

Hopefully, Hotel Papa Germano's tacky decor will make you smile rather than judge, for if you write this place off too swiftly, you'll be missing out on its many great services. If the wallpaper doesn't make you grin, maybe the especially friendly reception or free Wi-Fi will. The modest rooms' TVs, A/C, and telephones make them good deals. If you're not looking for a private room, the dormitory is an economical alternative that remains slightly nicer than hostel options.

✈ ⓂTermini. Take V. Marsala away from the train station, proceed straight as it becomes V. Volturno, and turn right onto the small V. Calatafimi. *i* Breakfast included. 3 public computers available. Ⓢ Dorms €15-30; singles €30-60; doubles €40-95, with bath €50-120; triples €50-100/€60-140; quads €70-130/€80-150. Ⓩ Reception 7am-midnight.

BED AND BREAKFAST A CASA DI ZIA SERAFINA
●⊗(ɕ)❄ B AND B ❹

V. Filippo Turati 107 ☎06 44 66 458 🖳www.casaserafina.it

A gracious host welcomes you to her four furnished and immaculately kept rooms off the bright central hallway of her apartment at this intimate bed and breakfast. A great deal amid most of Termini's less-than-charming accommodations, Signora Serafina's rooms are equipped with Wi-Fi, TVs, A/C, and cheerful decor. Chambers without bathrooms have access to a sparkling clean one in the hallway. Homemade breakfast cooked each morning by the signora herself.

✈ ⓂTermini. Walk down V. Ratazzi and turn left onto V. Filippo Turati. Buzz and proceed to 3rd fl. Call in advance to set up arrival time; key given to enter building and room. Ⓢ Doubles €70, with bath €80; triples €110.

AFFITTACAMERE ARIES
♥⊗(ɕ)❄ HOTEL ❹

V. XX Settembre 58/A ☎06 42 02 71 61 🖳www.affittacamerearies.com

The lovely owner might be reason enough to stay here—she'll be happy to offer you coffee upon arrival. A bit removed from the Termini cluster, this charming hotel decorated with flowers and frescoes offers six simple but spacious rooms. The stone floors and metal-framed beds might not be the warmest and fuzziest things around, but the accommodating service, friendly dog (which sometimes follows the owner around), and great amenities make up for it.

✈ ⓂTermini. Veer left toward P. della Repubblica, proceed onto V.V.E. Orlando, and turn right onto V. XX Settembre. Buzz and take Scala B to the 2nd fl. *i* Breakfast included. Free Wi-Fi. Ⓢ Singles €50; doubles €80; triples €105. Ask about a discount for longer stays. Ⓩ Guests are given a key to enter, but reception essentially 24hr.

SIGHTS
◉

Do the sights of Rome even require an introduction? Like the extrovert who will shake your hand before you take your coat off, Rome's famous destinations have no trouble themselves known: interrupting, side-tracking, and dragging out your itinerary before you even get started, they seem to beckon from every street corner and *piazza*. Don't worry—that's a good thing. If they were anything less than spectacular, the gargantuan number of must-sees in Rome would feel burdensome. Luckily, they *are* spectacular and, luckily again, fairly concentrated within the city. You'll run into about half of them by default. On your way to get gelato, for example, you'll come across a fountain that looks, to put it mildly, vaguely familiar. The sights you won't stumble upon while hunting for a good pizzeria can be tackled with a good pair of walking shoes, a whole lot of ambition, and an espresso to keep you going. Our suggestion: take at least one day without the guidebook or map and simply see where you end up. Chances are you'll hit a lot of those "must-sees" without even trying.

Ancient City

▣ COLOSSEUM ⊛⊗ ANCIENT ROME
Bordered by V. di San Gregorio, V. Cello Vibenna, and V. N. Salvi ☎06 39 96 77 00
🔲www.pierreci.it

A walk through the Colosseum provides an interesting mix of old and new—crumbling bricks and empty "cells" evoking the unfortunate ancients who once occupied them are juxtaposed against the vision of dozens of modern-day tourists who eagerly peer into the Colosseum's arena, a formerly sandy pit in which bloody (and sometimes not so bloody) combat took place. For the ⑤**best view** of the arena, climb to the upper tiers, where you can see the structure in its entirety—a massive 188m by 156m oval. Looking down, you'll get a feel for what it was like to witness the combats that took place in this amphitheater. This is famously the place where **gladiators**, men who were often slaves or prisoners but whose number once included an emperor, met for battle in the frenzy of the Roman games. Trained from the age of 17 and given rankings based on the number of fights they won, these combatants were seldom actually killed as they usually begged for mercy when defeat seemed imminent. It wasn't until the Middle Ages that massacre became the norm. Check out the detailed costume and weaponry exhibits in display cases on the upper level. If you want to see the gladiator armor on something other than a stuffed mannequin, consider getting your picture taken with one of the costumed dudes accosting middle-aged women around the concession stands out front *(usually €5)*. While the arena takes center stage for most visitors, peer around the back side for a great view of the Arch of Constantine, the tree-lined V. San Gregorio, and the Roman Forum just across the way.

✠ Ⓜ B:Colosseo or Ⓜ Termini, then bus #75. ⑤ Tickets are purchased for entrance to the Colosseum, Palatine Hill, and the Roman Forum, 1 entrance per sight, used over the course of 2 days. €12, EU students ages 18-24 €7.50, EU citizens under 18 and over 65 free. Guided tour €4; audio tour €4.50; video guide €5.50. All available in English. ⌚ Open daily 8:30am until 1hr. before sunset.

▣ ARCO DI CONSTANTINE ♿ ANCIENT ROME, MONUMENT
V. San Gregorio, South of the Colosseum near the Palatine Hill entrance.

Although most people only pass the Arch of Constantine on the way to the Colosseum or the Roman Forum across the street, its size and beauty are reason enough to seek it out. Towering an impressive 70 ft. over the V. San Gregorio, the arch stands in commemoration of Constantine's victory over Maxentius at the Battle of the Milvian Bridge in 312 CE. Despite the metal gates that prevent visitors from walking through the arch, those interested can take a closer look at the beautiful engravings and inscriptions depicting Constantine's battles and victories that etch the structure. The Romans, who seem awfully good at "borrowing" things (check out the torn-away marble sections of the Colosseum), continued the tradition here, decorating the side of the arch with medallions stolen from other monuments nearby. Guess there's something to be said for kleptomania after all.

✠ Ⓜ B: Colosseo or Ⓜ Termini, then bus #75. Walk down V. San Gregorio from the Colosseum. ⑤ Free.

ROMAN FORUM ⊛⊗ ANCIENT ROME
A walk through the Roman Forum provides a pleasant (though somewhat bumpy) one-hour respite from the busy city just outside its gates, even if you don't know a bit of its history or read a single plaque. Chances are, though, you didn't pay €12 for a walk in the park. For that, try the **Domus Aurea.** To justify spending cash on ruins instead of gelato, consider picking up an audio tour that will at least

clue you in to the history of a few of the sections you'll pass. There isn't much information posted along the way, so unless you're enough of a Latin scholar to understand the original inscriptions, your map (provided at the ticket office) and audio tour are the only things helping you tell your *templi* from your basilicas.

The individual attractions are numerous, and you'll pass them if you spend an hour or two walking around. **Via Sacra,** the oldest street in Rome, runs through the center of the Forum and will deliver you to most of the places you could want to go. To the right, you'll find the remains of the **Basilica Fulvia-Aemilia,** originally built in 179 BCE by two Marcuses—Fulvius and Aemilius—but then renovated by the Aemilia family, perhaps as a mode of self-promotion. If you're having trouble finding the basilica, that's because it no longer exists—just the skeleton of a floor plan and some remains housed under a roof are still here. Step inside the **Curia,** originally the meeting place of the Senate, for a museum-like display of coins, columns, and recovered friezes that once decorated the basilica, including ⊠**The Rape of the Sabine Women.** Outside again, you'll find the **Temple of Saturn** and the **Basilica Julia** flanking the sides of the central area. Duck into the tiny hut dedicated to Caesar, where flowers and photos add a bit of color to the dirt-covered area. Past a couple of temples, you'll come to the **Arch of Titus,** built in 81 CE by Emperor Domitian to commemorate the victory over Jerusalem by his brother Titus. Although smaller than Constantine's, Titus' arch boasts a coffered archway and beautiful interior frieze depicting a hoard of horses, a menorah, and crowds of people after the victory that make it especially stunning. Further on, walk down the dirt paths of the **Severan Horrea** which are bordered by brick cell enclosures and excavation areas.

☘ Ⓜ*B: Colosseo or* Ⓜ*Termini, then bus #75. Enter at V. San Gregorio (near the Arch of Constantine), V. dei Fori Imperiali (halfway between Trajan's column and the Colosseum), or directly opposite the Colosseum. Entrance to the Forum is joint with that to the Palatine Hill, a neighboring site.* ℹ *Tickets are purchased for entrance to the Colosseum, Palatine Hill, and the Roman Forum, 1 entrance per sight, used over the course of 2 days. €12, EU students ages 18-24 €7.50, EU citizens under 18 and over 65 free. Audio tour to the Forum €4, combined with the Palatine €6; available in English.* 🕐 *Open daily 8:30am until 1hr. before sunset.*

tip!

Tickets to the Colosseum can be purchased at the Palatine Hill/Roman Forum entrance on V. San Gregorio. Head there midday, after the early morning frenzy, to avoid waiting in a 2hr. line at the Colosseum.

PALATINE HILL
☻☻ⓩ ANCIENT ROME

The Palatine Hill, occupying the stretch of elevated land between V. dei Cerchi, V. di San Gregorio, and V. di San Teodoro, was once *the* place to live (even Cicero and Mark Antony had their homes here). Today, it consists mostly of grassy patches and ruined temples, though it still provides some of the best views of the city and the adjacent Roman Forum. At the very least, bring a camera, some water, and maybe a sandwich for a pleasant stroll through its grounds.

Entering at V. San Gregorio, you can either head right (which will lead you into the Roman Forum) or left (which will lead you to the Palatine Hill). The ascent up the hill is a bit steep and winding, but some convenient steps make getting to the top much easier and faster. On the left, you'll find the **Stadium and Severan Complex** whose huge territory was once used as a riding school. Immediately onward is the **Domus Augustana.** (Its lower floor is on the left, the upper on the right.) Cushioned between the domus' remnants is the **Palatine Museum,** which houses a small collection of statues, tiles, busts, and other archaeological items from wealthy Roman households. *(Open daily 8am-4pm, 30 people per fl., 20min. at a time. Free.)* Next along your walk is the start of the **Domus Flavia,** a huge region which includes reception rooms, a peristyle, and the Nymphaeum, a space which houses an octagonal fountain that once covered the entire area and symbolized power but today is dried up. The **Casa di Livia,** sectioned between, was property of the Roman aristocracy during the first century BCE and today provides a welcome escape from the sun. Play a little "Theseus and the Minotaur" (a classic game for children circa 200 BCE), and walk through the surrounding labyrinth of dank tunnels containing placards that describe the area. The **Casa di Augustus** and the **Casa di Romolo** are immediately on the left, surrounded by tiny Romulean Huts. Most scenic of all are the 👍**Farnese Gardens,** which offer an unparalleled vista of the Roman Forum, the Colosseum, and Capitoline Hill. They're also a good place to stop for a picnic (which some travelers supplement with oranges from one of the nearby trees). Descend the stairs to check out the **Nymphaeum of the Rain,** a small cave with running water.

➜ [M]B: Colosseo or [M]Termini, then bus #75. Enter at V. San Gregorio (near the Arch of Constantine), V. dei Fori Imperiali (halfway between Trajan's column and the Colosseum), or directly opposite the Colosseum. Next to the Roman Forum. ℹ Tickets are purchased for entrance to the Colosseum, Palatine Hill, and the Roman Forum, 1 entrance per sight, used over the course of 2 days. €12, EU students ages 18-24 €7.50, EU citizens under 18 and over 65 free. Audio tour to the Palatine Hill €4, combined with the Forum €6, available in English. ⏰ Open daily 8:30am until 1hr. before sunset.

FORI IMPERIALI

♿ ANCIENT ROME

V. dei Fori Imperiali ☎06 67 97 702

Walking down V. dei Fori Imperiali, it's impossible to miss—you guessed it—the Imperial Fora. Built in the 150 years after Caesar's reign, the four fora located here marked a new period of Roman dominance that ushered in a return to Hellenistic architecture. The open area enclosed by a colonnade to sequester the center from the surrounding, urban activity was the place where the business of the forum took place. This central region used for government affairs was topped off by a small temple decorated with friezes and paintings commissioned by the day's ruler to display his financial and political power. The first two fora were constructed by Caesar and Augustus, the next (christened the "Forum of Peace" to mark a calmer period in the empire's history) by Vespasian, and the last (called the Forum of Nerva) by Domitian. Down the way, you'll find the biggest forum of all, the **Forum of Trajan,** built between 107 and 113 CE.

In 1924, some of the land that once held the fora was paved over to make way for V. dei Fori's modern-day, less-than-regal central thoroughfare. Although the grounds themselves have been closed to the public for years, you can still admire them from the sidewalk, pick up a map of them at the tourist office and give yourself a tour, or explore them on a guided tour.

➜ From the Colosseum, walk down V. dei Fori Imperiali. Ruins are on the right. ℹ Call the tourist office above for more information. $ Free. ⏰ Exhibition and info center open daily 9:30am-6:30pm.

DOMUS AUREA

♿ ANCIENT ROME, PARK

Vle. della Domus Auerea 1 (Colle Oppio Gardens) ☎06 39 96 7700

The expansive grounds of Domus Aurea sit between the Colosseum and busy V. Merulana. Shallow hills, patches of grass, and small children's playgrounds make a walk through this park a refreshing change of pace from the tourist crowds just next door. In the morning and early evening, the park is especially populated with dog walkers and joggers. Although you probably aren't here to see any monuments (by now, you might be eager to escape them), make sure to check out the **Trajan Baths,** which lie near the V. delle Terme di Traiano.

➜ From the Colosseum, walk down V. Terme di Tito. Park is on the right and continues until V. Merulana $ Free. ⏰ Open daily 7am-9pm.

CHIESA DI SAN PIETRO IN VINCOLI [®] CHURCH

P. di San Pietro in Vincoli, 4/a ☎06 97 84 49 50

Sitting atop a small hill just off V. Cavour, this fourth-century church houses Michelangelo's famous statue of Moses. After gazing at the bigger-than-life sculpture, take some time to admire the brightly-colored fresco ceilings and meander through the clean, white colonnade.

‡ From V. Cavour turn onto V. S. Francis di Pacia and walk down V. Eudossiana. The church is on the left. i Fully covered legs and shoulders required. $ Free. ⏰ Open daily 8am-12:30pm, 3-6pm.

CIRCUS MAXIMUS ♿ ANCIENT ROME

It's only logical to pay a visit to the Circus Maximus after a long tour of the Colosseum and the Palatine Hill. While only a shadow of what it used to be, the Circus Maximus rounds out the key sights of your tour through Ancient Rome. At the end of V. di San Gregorio (near the P. di Porta Capena), this grassy plot of land was once Rome's largest stadium, home to more than 300,000 screaming Romans who came to watch the chariot races. Now, the fields only reach similar volumes during summer concerts and city celebrations, scheduled on a monthly basis.

‡ [M]B: Circo Massimo or bus #118. $ Free.

CAPITOLINE HILL [®] PIAZZA, MUSEUM

Rome's small but magnificent capital sits nestled between the **Monumento a Vittorio Emanuele II** (a massive white building resembling a tiered wedding cake) and the Roman Forum. From both these sights, views of the little Capitoline Hill are hard to miss. Coming up V. Arco di Settimio at the backside of the hill, you'll arrive at the **Piazza di Campidoglio,** designed by Michelangelo in 1536. At the center of the piazza sits an equestrian statue of **Marcus Aurelius.** It's actually a replica of the original, which you can view in a weatherproof chamber located in the Palazzo Nuovo. Still, this oft-photographed bronze statue is an impressive monument to one of Rome's more philosophically-inclined emperors. Piazza di Campidoglio is ringed by the **Capitoline Museums,** which hold a treasure trove of Roman and Greek sculpture as well as the oldest public collection of ancient art in the world. If you instead arrive at the piazza from V. del Teatro Marcello, you will be forced to climb a somewhat awkwardly slanted staircase. But get ready to be greeted by two symmetrical (and seductive) stone statues of Castor and Pollux on their horses.

‡ From V. dei Fori Imperiali, veer left towards the Monumento a Vittorio Emanuele II. Turn onto V. Teatro Marcello and head uphill $ Capitoline Museums €6.50, EU students 18-25 €4.50, EU citizens under 18 and over 65 free. Audio tour €5. Available in English. ⏰ Capitoline Museums open Tu-Su 9am-8pm. Ticket office closes 1hr. before museums close.

Centro Storico

The Centro Storico abounds with sights that are as quintessentially Roman as pasta is Italian. Luckily, you won't have to pay or wait in line to see many of them, and their close proximity to one another makes it possible to visit all these sights in one rewarding afternoon.

PANTHEON ♿ ANCIENT ROME

P. della Rotunda ☎06 68 30 02 30

Even without looking at your map, you're bound to stumble upon the Pantheon as you wander through the Centro Storico: signs pointing the way and crowds hovering outside will indicate that something great is coming. Corinthian columns and the large pediment atop give the edifice, which is currently under construction, the look of a Greek temple. An impressive 20 tons each, the bronze doors (originally plated in gold) leading into the Pantheon are enough to make visitors feel miniscule. Inside, the circular building is full of people craning their necks to admire the perfect hemispherical dome (142 ft. in diameter and height) which, until Brunelleschi's Duomo in Florence, was the largest in the world. If you ever thought concrete was a poor man's material, think again. A mix of pumice, ash, sand, water, and chemical solidifiers, this material made the dome's casting possible by providing a viable alternative to the heavier stone blocks typically used. The coffered ceiling looks almost modern in form—a true geometrical abstraction—especially in contrast to the more traditional frescoes around it. Consider that the Pantheon's only source of light is the 27 ft. oculus at its center: over the course of the day, the beam of sun shining through it slowly moves along the temple's beautiful marble floor. (The best time to come, nevertheless, is on a rainy day, when water droplets flow directly through the central ring.) Notable for the architectural accomplishment of its design alone, the Pantheon is also a significant reflection of religious tolerance, dedicated to every god (of Ancient Rome, that is).

➡ *From P. Navona, follow signs for the Pantheon toward V. della Dogana Vecchia.* $ *Free.* ⏰ *Open M-Sa 8:30am-7:30pm, Su 9am-6pm.*

👍 CAMPO DEI FIORI ♿⛅ PIAZZA

Between P. Farnese and C. Vittorio Emmanuele

Cushioned between stately Palazzo Farnese one block away and the busy C. Vittorio Emanuele, Campo dei Fiori is an enclosed world of its own where students, merchants, nighttime revelers, and performers make it their home. At its center, the somewhat ominous statue of a cloaked Giordano Bruno towers above the crowds. Aside from his imposing figure, street mimes clad in ridiculous garb are the only other even remotely statuesque shapes around. During the day, check out the market where merchants sell everything from **👍fish** to fresh produce to **👍alcohol** to clothes (⏰ *Open M-Sa 7am-2:30pm*). At night, the Campo is literally abuzz with the chatter of diners, while the clink of wine glasses and the thumping of a few disco-like clubs add to the jocular clatter of this happening center for city life.

➡ *From P. Navona, head towards C. Vittorio Emanuele and cut straight across to Campo dei Fiori.* ℹ *Watch your valuables at night.* $ *Free.*

PIAZZA NAVONA ♿⛅ PIAZZA

Surrounded by V. di Santa Maria dell'Anima and C. del Rinascimento.

One of Rome's most picturesque *piazze*, Navona is right up there with the Colosseum and the Vatican in tourist popularity. Luckily for visitors, there's neither a 4hr. line nor a hefty admission price. Rather, the oval arena, originally a stadium built by Domitian in 86 CE, is full of tourists snapping pretty pictures, mimes performing at either end, artists selling trite watercolors, and musicians playing what sounds like the soundtrack of a Frank Sinatra film. This scene makes everything you heard about "classic Italy" seem true. Weave your way through the crowds—even grab a seat if you can—to take a closer look at Bernini's magnificent **Fontana dei Quattro Fiumi,** a massive stone sculpture that depicts four river gods, each representing a continent. Flanking it, the less spectular **Fontana di Nettuno** and **Fontana del Moro** draw significantly smaller crowds but provide good spots to take a seat and view the scene from afar.

➡ *Entrances into P. Navona at Palazzo Braschi, V. Agonale, V. di Sant'Agnese di Agone, and Corsia Agonale.*

CHIESA DI SAN LUIGI DEI FRANCESI ⊗ CHURCH

P. San Luigi dei Francesi 5 ☎06 68 82 71

From the exterior, this 16th-century church could easily be overlooked by pedestrians: its French facade is pretty unimpressive by Roman standards. Consequently, the surprise inside is even sweeter than it might have been. Three of Caravaggio's most impressive works, **👍The Calling of St. Matthew, St. Matthew and the Angel,** and **The Crucifixion,** grace the Contarelli Chapels in back. (If you're having difficulty finding them, it might be because they are not illuminated. Deposit €1 to light them up, or wait for someone else to step up.) Because they occupy the inner wall, it is

slightly hard to get enough distance to view the paintings properly. However, these three works rival the private collection of Caravaggio's work held by the Galleria Borghese, so make sure to take them in as best you can. Their intense chiaroscuro, characterized by high contrast between light and dark, is characteristic of the religious and emotional meaning Caravaggio is famed for bringing out in his subjects.
➜ From P. Navona, exit onto Corsia Agonale, turn left onto C. del Rinascimento and right onto V. Santa Giovanna d'Arco. $ Free. 🕘 Open M-W 10am-12:30pm and 4-7pm, Th 10am-12:30pm, F-Su 10am-12:30pm and 4-7pm.

VITTORIO EMANUELE II MONUMENT 🚫♿ MONUMENT, MUSEUM

In P. Venezia ☎06 67 80 664; museum ☎06 67 93 526 💻www.risorgimento.it

The stunning Vittorio Emanuele II Monument towers—grandiose, theatrical, and triumphant—above P. Venezia. In fact, this flamboyant building remains a captivating presence. Even in far-away P. del Popolo, it towers in the distance down V. del Corso. The monument is affectionately (and a bit mockingly) referred to as "The Wedding Cake"—and justly so: its multiple tiers and pristine white facade look good enough to eat and garish enough to flaunt. Out front, huge Italian flags wave majestically as gladiators—or rather plump men in metal garb—pose alongside confused tourists. Designed in 1884 and finally finished in 1927 by Mussolini, the huge building is as close as you can get to a giant megaphone that constantly yells out, "We are Italy! We are great!" The monument is best seen from P. Venezia or even from a few blocks away, but if you venture up its mighty steps, you'll find the **Museo del Risorgimento,** a slightly dull (and extremely dark) collection of artifacts tracing the course of Italian unification, inside. Though the museum is free, the view from outside is lighter, brighter, and more worth your time.
➜ In P. Venezia. $ Free. 🕘 Monument open M-Th 9:30am-6:30pm, F-Su 9:30am-7:30pm. Museum open daily 9:30am-6:30pm.

PALAZZO VENEZIA ♿ PALAZZO

V. del Plebiscito 118 ☎06 69 99 41; info and booking ☎06 32 810 💻www.galleriaborghese.it

In the northwest corner of P. Venezia, the Palazzo stands out as a result of its simple, brick facade rather than any particularly beautiful or ornate characteristic. As one of Rome's first Renaissance buildings, it certainly reflects an air of stateliness and grace, though it seems like a shy, quiet wallflower in comparison to the Vittorio Emmanuele Monumento across the way. Though today it is not a site of governmental power, Mussolini once used it as his headquarters. The museum inside the Palazzo holds an impressive collection of documents, tapestries, paintings from the early Renaissance, and sculptures.
➜ Across the way from Monumento a Vittorio Emanuele II, in P. Venezia. $ €4, EU citizens 18-25 €2, EU citizens under 18 and over 65 free. 🕘 Open Tu-Su 8:30am-7:30pm. Ticket office closes at 6:30pm.

PIAZZA DELLA ROTUNDA ♿ PIAZZA

P. della Rotunda, right outside the Pantheon

The P. della Rotunda is either the *antipasto* or the *dolce* to your exploratory entree (which is the 🏛**Pantheon,** in case you haven't guessed). Before or after strolling under the beautiful dome of Rome's stately temple, crowds throng around the Egyptian obelisk crowning the center of this *piazza*. An 18th-century monument was created out of this obelisk when Clement XI "de-paganized" it by sticking a cross on top. The somewhat whimsical fountain in the square sports serpents and sharp-toothed heads that spew water out of their mouths. The *piazze* surrounding this central spot are noticeably less crowded but contain some monuments of their own worth checking out. **Piazza della Minerva** features yet another obelisk sitting atop Bernini's elephant statues, whose figures supposedly represent the powerful "mind" needed to support the obelisks' wisdom. **P. di Sant'Eustachio** is full of small cafes and bars, including the famous **Sant'Eustachio Il Caffè** coffee den.
➜ Outside the Pantheon. $ Free.

Piazza Di Spagna

▨ PIAZZA DEL POPOLO ⓖ PIAZZA

At the end of V. del Corso

From the center of P. del Popolo, you can see the magnificent **Vittorio Emanuele Monument** glowing (yes, it's so white, it glows) in the distance. Likewise, from the monument, a straight shot up V. del Corso has you gazing at this gigantic *piazza*, the "people's square," no ▨**Communist connotation** intended. Despite the Corso's noise and crowds, this street is probably the best way to arrive at and appreciate the openness of the *piazza* which, for being so famous, is surprisingly uncongested. Perhaps it merely appears so thanks to its size and an oblong shape which makes its edges feel wider. At the center, the **Obelisk of Pharaoh Ramses II** stands triumphantly, attracting a few tourists to sit at its base. The ▨**Santa Maria del Popolo** church is worth a visit, as it contains two Caravaggio masterpieces in the Capella Cerasi: *The Conversion of St. Paul* and *Crucifixion of St. Peter*, both of which are stunning examples of the artist's attention to chiaroscuro and the religious import this stylistic technique carried.

⚐ Ⓜ*A: Flaminio.* Ⓢ *Church is free.* ⓩ *Church open M-Sa 7am-noon and 4-7pm, Su 8am-1:30pm and 4:30-7:30pm.*

▨ MUSEO DELL'ARA PACIS ⓖ MUSEUM

At intersection of Lungotevere in Augusta and P. Porto di Ripetta ☎06 06 08 🖳www.arapacis.it

This truly serene museum is a befitting space for its central monument, the **Ara Pacis.** The bare white walls and huge windows of the space reflect the peace of the monument, a frieze-covered enclosure constructed in 13 BCE to commemorate Augustus' victories throughout Spain and Gaul. Visitors can walk inside the structure to get a closer look at the 40m string of acanthus plant carved in the marble to represent renewal and unity under Augustus' Golden Age. On the outside, a mostly intact frieze of the ruler and his family reflects the tranquility of the period—the figures seem at ease, carved with an eye towards realism. Ironically, Augustus' body is chipped off in the procession and only his head remains. In the front of the museum, a row of busts including the head of Ottavia lie across from a reconstructed family tree. Check out the small model and accompanying map which shows the monument's original location in the context of Rome's current street layout.

⚐ Ⓜ*A: Spagna. Take V. del Carrozze towards V. del Corso and proceed into P. Augusto Imperiale.* ⓘ *Audio tour available in English €3.50.* Ⓢ *€6.50, EU students 18-25 €4.50, EU citizens under 18 and over 65 free.* ⓩ *Open Tu-Su 9am-7pm. Last entry 1hr. before close.*

FONTANA DI TREVI ⓖ FOUNTAIN

Right beyond P. Acc. S. Luca

The best time to see the fountain is at 4:30 in the morning, because it's probably the only hour where you'll be able to sit on one of the stone ledges without hearing the sounds of vendors selling overpriced trinkets and tourists snapping picture-perfect shots in the background. That's certainly the hour that Anita Ekberg, actress of Fellini's *La Dolce Vita*, came by when she took a dip in the fountain's gushing waters. (While you can make a late-night visit, don't follow her lead or you risk a steep fine.) Even if you don't make it during this empty hour, Nicolo Salvi's mix of masterfully cut rock and stone in the raw is phenomenal. Neptune, surrounded by the goddesses of abundance and good health as well as two brawny horsemen, is carved with exacting detail, while the environment in which he sits is realistic merely because it has been left untouched. As good as gelato might be, save your coins for the fountain: one will ensure a prompt return to Rome, two will bring you love in the Eternal City, and three will bring about your wedding.

⚐ Ⓜ*A: Barberini. Proceed down V. del Tritone and turn left onto V. Stamperia.*

PIAZZA DI SPAGNA AND THE SPANISH STEPS
⊗ MONUMENT, PIAZZA

P. di Spagna

In every sense, the P. di Spagna is a conglomeration of international roots—not only does it draw a global tourist crowd to its sandy-colored steps, but its history encompasses the Italians (who designed it), the British (who occupied it), the French (who financed it), and, oh yeah, the Spaniards (you've got this one). Built in 1723 as a way to connect the Piazza with the new **Trinità dei Monti** church above it, the magnificent steps now seem to be more of a hangout spot for tired shoppers, gelato eaters, and youth looking to avoid the expensive bar scene of this commercial neighborhood. The best view of the steps and Piazza is actually from the church's steps directly above—from there, you can get a better sense of their size while avoiding the cluster of people below. When you do make your way down, check out the **Fontana della Barcaccia** built by Bernini the Elder before the steps were even constructed. The absurdly pink house and its two palm trees might remind you of leisurely beach life, but they actually commemorate the death of John Keats, who died there in 1821.

✝ Ⓜ*A: Spagna.*

Jewish Ghetto

The Jewish Ghetto consists of a few blocks just off Isola Tiberina. Come here for great food and a look back at one of the first Jewish communities in Western Europe.

▨ THE GREAT SYNAGOGUE
Ġ SYNAGOGUE

Corner of Lungotevere dei Cenci and V. Catalana ☎06 68 40 06 61 ▧www.museoebraico.roma.it

From afar, the Synagogue occupies a place in the Roman skyline right up there with many of the city's other, more famous cupolas. The Synagogue's beautiful, palm-tree-surrounded roof is distinct from the architecture and ruins which surround it, so stroll by to glimpse a different element of Rome's urban design. Construction of the Synagogue began in 1904 as part of an effort to revitalize and rebuild the Jewish Ghetto, which had for many decades suffered from flooding and unsanitary conditions. By 1904, the Synagogue, designed with a curious mix of Persian and Babylonian influences, had been completed. Its unique design was intended to make it stand apart from the city's many Catholic churches. Inside, highlights include a stunning mix of painted floral patterns by Annibale Brugnoli and Domenico Bruschi and an upper section of stained glass. Look up top for the small portion of clear glass commemorating a child who was killed in a 1982 plane crash.

✝ *At the corner of Lungotevere dei Cenci and V. Catalana.* ⅈ *Open for services.* Ⓢ *Free.*

PIAZZA MATTEI
Ġ PIAZZA

Between V. dei Falegnami and V. dei Funari

The tiny P. Mattei is the center of the Jewish Ghetto, though today most of the neighborhood's culinary and social activity occurs on V. del Ottavio. Visit this *piazza* for a look at the **Fontana delle Tartarughe,** a 16th-century monument by Taddeo Landini that depicts four figures bearing tortoises and a strange basin atop their heads. The rest of the Piazza is comprised of merchants and residential houses, save the **Chiesa di Sant'Angelo** in Pescheria, an unimposing eighth-century church named for its proximity to the fish market that once operated near Porta Ottavia. Though technically the center of the ghetto, this square feels more like a quiet respite from the busier streets nearby.

✝ *From the Area Sacra, walk down V. Arenula and turn left onto V. dei Falegnami; P. Mattei is on the right.* ⅈ *The church cannot be entered due to repairs.*

Vatican City

More so than any other region of Rome, Vatican City fuses Roman history, artistic mastery, and Catholic ideology. As the administrative and spiritual headquarters of the Catholic Church, it has historically remained relatively independent from the rest of Rome, minting its own currency (the Italian *lire*), using colorfully-clad Swiss guards at its entrance, and running its own postal system. Expect some of the longest lines in the city but the greatest art to match, contained most notably in **St. Peter's Basilica** *(Basilica di San Pietro)* and the **Vatican Museums.**

ST. PETER'S BASILICA ♿ CHURCH

At the end of V. della Concilizione ☎06 69 81 662 🖳www.saintpetersbasilica.org

If the Vatican's special post boxes aren't enough to remind you that you've entered another jurisdiction, then perhaps the airport-like security required before entering the Basilica will be. Though lines here don't get nearly as long as those for the **Vatican Museums** (see below), people are required to pass through scanned security before entering the church during visiting hours. Once you've cleared the metal detectors, head through any one of the colossal doors. You won't be able to use the **Porta Sancta** (last door on the right of the entrance porch) though: it's only opened during Holy Years.

Depending on the time of day, the church's interior appears in incredibly varied degrees of illumination—the ceilings are so high that on dark days the small windows near the Basilica's top do little to illuminate the nave. Immediately to the right, find Michelangelo's **Pietà,** one of the most moving renderings of Mary and Jesus ever created. Since 1972, when a vandal attacked it with an axe, breaking Jesus's nose and Mary's hand, it has sat behind the bulletproof glass that slightly obscures the view even while it protects the precious piece of art. As you proceed onward, notice the strip of gold mosaics studded with Latin letters lining the perimeter of the nave and adding to the incredibly dogmatic and somewhat overbearing feel of the church.

Though it's hard to pinpoint the church's crowning element, Michelangelo's dome at least wins in size—at a spectacular 138m in height and 42m in width, it remains the largest in the world. Directly below it, the somewhat ridiculous *baldacchino* (note the sculpted bumblebees buzzing around its twisting columns) marks the altarplace used by the pope. The supposed tomb of St. Peter sits immediately below the altar.

Despite the hordes of people who frequent the Basilica each day, its size is enough to dwarf even the biggest crowds (60,000 and counting). Though most people come to the church as tourists, and the flash of cameras is nearly constant, consider participating in Mass, which is conducted before Bernini's bronze **Cathedra Petri** and lit from behind by glowing alabaster windows. If you're feeling really ambitious, it's even possible to hold your wedding in the Basilica, though the wait and price for the most famous church in the world could leave you eternally single. Only Catholics need apply.

ℹ Free guided tours in English leave from the Pilgrim Tourist Information Center. No shorts, miniskirts or tank tops. For information on weddings visit 🖳www.saintpetersbasilica.org $ Free. 🕐 Open daily Apr-Sept 7am-7pm; Oct-Mar 7am-6:30pm. Tours in English Tu at 9:45am, Th-F at 9:45am. Mass M-F 8:30am, 10am, 11am, noon, and 5pm; Su and holidays 9am, 10:30am, 11:30am, 12:15pm, 1pm, 4pm, and 5:45pm. Vespers daily 5pm.

VATICAN MUSEUMS ♿ MUSEUM

Entrance at Vle. Vaticano ☎06 69 88 38 60 🖳www.museivaticani.va

After waiting in a 4hr. line, we hope you spend at least half as much time in the galleries themselves. Unfortunately, the lure of the Sistine Chapel (and frequent arrows pointing the way) pull people onward, creating a human stream with a very strong current. But you're not a **fish!** Jump out and admire some of the more obscure treasures which are not only on display but comprise the building itself. If this is your first time through these museums, forget the itinerary and just wander a bit, stopping at whatever piques your fancy. If you try to read and see everything in a guidebook, you will tire before getting halfway through.

After entering the complex, most people start in the **Museo Pio-Clemetino,** which contains the world's greatest collection of antique sculptures, including the famous **Laocoon** in an octagonal courtyard. Before heading upstairs, make sure to circumnavigate the 👍**Sala Rotonda,** a small room with unbelievable mosaics on the floor and a domed roof recalling the **Pantheon's** coffered ceiling and oculus.

Head directly upstairs to find the **Etruscan Museum,** which contains a daunting 18 rooms' worth of Etruscan artifacts, sarcophagi, and vases that offer a glimpse into Italy's earliest civilization. The **Candelabra Gallery** and dimly lit **Tapestry Gallery** are often treated as thoroughfares, but the **Map Gallery** is worth a stop. Huge frescoed maps of Italy line the walls and provide an eye into the country's diverse geographical regions. You can carry on via a shortcut to the Sistine Chapel from here, but if you can wait, meander through the **Stanze di Rafaele.** These four rooms, originally Julius II's apartments, were decorated by the great Raphael, and include the 👍**School of Athens** fresco on one large wall.

In no other collection would all the aforementioned works possibly be considered a *precursor* to the main show. But you're in the Vatican Museum, and it's time for the main course. The 👍**Sistine Chapel** is undoubtedly the most sought out, crowded, and monumental part of the museum. Every few minutes, the guards shush the mass of people, reminding them not to take photos and ushering them onward. Expect an unpleasant experience in the way of people but a remarkable one in the way of art. If craning your neck to see the ceiling hurts after a few minutes, imagine Michelangelo actually making the work—he painted the frescoes on a platform while bending backward and never recovered from the strain. Even those not versed in art history will recognize the famous **Creation of Adam,** one of nine panels depicting scenes from the story of Genesis. Occupying the entirety of the altar wall, the **Last Judgment** can be viewed with much less physical contortion. This huge fresco is, in a way, free of composition—it is a massive conglomeration of muscular figures, clouds, and land masses—but this adds to its uncontainable and inconceivable force. Though it can be difficult to focus on one area, look for the flayed human skin that hangs between heaven and hell, a self-portrait included by Michelangelo.

*➔ ⓂA: Ottaviano. Head down V. Ottaviano, turn right onto V. dei Bastioni di Michelangelo, and follow the wall until you see the end of the line to the museums. Entrance is on Vle. Vaticano. **i** A wheelchair-accessible itinerary is available as well as wheelchairs for rent. Call ☎06 69 88 15 89 for info. [$] €15, EU citizens aged 18-26 and ages 6-18 €8; under 6 free. Last Su of every month all enter free. Entrance with guided and audio tours €31/€25. 🕐 Galleries open M-Sa and last Su of each month 9am-6pm.*

italy

👍 PIAZZA DI SAN PIETRO ♿ PIAZZA

At the end of V. della Concializione ☎06 69 81 662 🖳www.vaticanstate.va

There is no way to escape the arms of St. Peter—from the start of V. della Conciliazione they beckon pedestrians into the *piazza*, and once you've made your way inside, their embrace is enough to silence even the chattiest tourist in your group. If Bernini had seen this effect more than 400 years after the square's construction, he would have smiled. He intended the colonnade enclosing the *piazza*'s ovular area to symbolize the welcoming arms of the Catholic Church and greet tired pilgrims after a circuitous trek through the city.

*➔ Bus #23, 34, 40, 271, or 982 to P. Pia or bus #62 down V. della Conciliazione. **i** The Pilgrim Tourist Office, to the left of the Basilica, has a multilingual staff, a gift shop, free bathrooms, a first-aid station, brochures, maps, currency exchange, and Vatican post boxes inside or nearby. Call the number or visit the website above for more info. [$] Free. 🕐 Piazza open 24hr. Tourist Office open M-Sa 8:30am-6:15pm.*

MUSEO NAZIONALE DI CASTEL SANT'ANGELO ❀♿ CASTLE, MUSEUM

Lungotevere Castello 50 ☎06 68 19 111 🖳www.castelsantangelo.com

If you thought all of Rome was basilicas and ruins, think again: that circular, brick structure on the river is a castle, complete with moat (OK, it's dried up) and torches (fine, they're electric). Castel Sant'Angelo dates from the first century CE—when it was built as a mausoleum for Hadrian and his family—and is notable for its whimsical frescoes, winding staircases, and a rooftop offering magnificent views of Rome and the nearby Vatican City.

➔ Bus #23, 34, 40, 271 or 982 to P. Pia. At the end of V. della Conciliazione and at the intersection with Ponte S. Angelo. $ €8.50, EU students ages 18-25 €6, EU citizens under 18 and over 65 free. Audio tour €4. ⏰ Open Tu-Su 9am-7:30pm. Ticket office closes 6:30pm.

Trastevere

Ahhh, Trastevere. With old cobblestone streets, hidden-away trattorias, and bustling nightlife, this oft-forgotten gem of a neighborhood is not one to miss. Even if you're only in Rome a few days, ditch some of those churches you had planned to visit and head across the Tiber to enjoy more intimate *piazze* (Santa Maria in Trastevere is our favorite), basilicas that rival their more-famous brethren on the other side of the river, and a tight-knit community proud of their unpretentious neighborhood.

👍 ISOLA TIBERINA ♿ OPEN SPACE

With most of Rome's major sights located further "inland," tourists tend to forget about Rome's river, the Fiume Tevere, and the land out yonder. On your way to Trastevere, take the tiny **Ponte Fabriccio (aka the Ponte dei Quattro Capi),** which, in case you couldn't tell by its name, bears four stone heads, allegedly those of the architects who originally restored the bridge. You'll find yourself standing on **Isola Tiberina**, a small plot of land that, according to legend, is actually composed of the silt-covered bodily remains of Tarquin, an Etruscan ruler who was thrown in the river for raping the beautiful Lucretia. The island is only home to a few establishments, so most people only stay to check out the hard-to-pronounce **Fatebenefratelli Hospital**, which looks more like a church than a healing facility. If you want to stick around, head down the slope to the open expanse directly on the river. A few people might be fishing, but more will be 👍**lying in the sun** on what is the closest thing Rome has to a beach.

➔ From V. del Teatro Marcello, walk towards the water and onto Lungomare dei Pierleoni. Turn left and cross Ponte Fabricio. $ Free.

GIANICOLO HILL ♿ OPEN SPACE

While people-produced monuments (or at least their remains) take center stage in Central Rome, those in Trastevere are rivaled by the neighborhood's natural wonders. The highest peak in this part of Rome, Gianicolo Hill, is a large expanse of land highlighted by the **Fonte Acqua Paola**, a fountain which marks the end of an aqueduct honoring Pope Paul V. While the crystal-blue pool of water and elaborate white facade above it are marvels of human design, the 👍**surrounding landscape** really steals the show.

➔ From Fonte Aqua Paola, continue uphill, onto V. Aldo Fabrizi and enter the park. You will pass Monumento a Garibaldi on the pleasant walk. $ Free.

CHIESA DI SANTA MARIA IN TRASTEVERE ♿ CHURCH

P. Santa Maria in Trastevere ☎06 58 14 802

Located in the heart of Trastevere, this church is a tourist favorite, and for good reason: beautiful mosaics decorating the facade are matched by an equally stunning gold interior where more mosaics depicting Jesus, Mary, and a slew of other Biblical figures grace the apse. This *chiesa* was the first in Rome built exclusively for the Virgin Mary. The **piazza** out front is a lovely place from which to admire this Byzantine structure.

➔ From Vle. Trastevere, turn right onto V. San Francesco a Ripa and walk 5min. until you get to the piazza. $ Free. ⏰ Open M-F 9am-5:30pm.

Termini and Northeast Rome

This large area is unsurprsingly full of a great deal of fascinating sights. The area north of Termini around **Via Nomentana** and **Via XX Settembre** is a lovely place to walk. The former is lined with beautiful houses and the latter offers a beautiful vantage point at V. delle Quattro Fontane, where you can see the monuments of Via dei Quirinal, the Spanish Steps, and Santa Maria Maggiore.

★ VILLA BORGHESE ♿ (( )) GARDENS

Bordered by Vle. Trinita dei Monti and V. Porta Pinciana. ☎06 32 16 564

The Villa Borghese sits north of Termini and provides a needed respite from the city's bustle. Mostly flat pathways cut through gardens, lawns, and various museums, including the **Galleria Borghese,** the **Museo Nazionale Etrusco di Villa Giulia,** and the **Galleria Nazionale d'Arte Moderna,** which actually sits right outside the park. Though most visitors choose to stroll or picnic in the park, there is also a bike rental stand just beyond the entrance of the Galleria Borghese.

⇄ [M]A: Spagna or Flaminio. $ Free. ⏰ Open daily Apr-Aug 7am-9pm; Sept 7am-8pm; Oct-Dec 7am-6pm; Jan-Feb 7am-6pm; Mar 7am-8pm.

★ BASILICA DI SANTA MARIA MAGGIORE ♿ CHURCH

In P. Esquilino ☎06 69 88 68 02

It's a good thing this basilica is so close to Termini, or the slew of cheap eats and hostels might be the only first impression visitors received of Rome. Just a 5min. walk from the station, this fifth-century church is a stunning combination of Baroque and classic Roman design. With its white marble artifice and huge flight of stairs, the back of the church (close to V. Cavour) might be even more stunning than the front. Although the frescoes that line the side chapels are impressive, it's the gold-coffered ceiling and wide apse that really impress. Adjoining the basilica is a small museum containing artifacts and artwork relating to the church's history, even though the basilica itself offers enough to see.

*⇄ [M]Termini. Turn right onto V. Giolitti and walk down V. Cavour. **i** Modest dress required. $ Basilica free. Museum €4, EU students and over 65 €2. Loggia €5, reduced €3. Audio tour (available in English) €4. ⏰ Basilica open daily 7am-7pm. Museum open daily 9am-6pm.*

GALLERIA BORGHESE 🍂♿ MUSEUM

Piazzale del Museo Borghese 5 ☎06 84 16 542 💻www.galleriaborghese.it

While the beautiful gardens in which it sits are reason enough to make the trek up to this fabulous museum, the Galleria Borghese is a must-see while in Rome. Inside the villa, Cardinal Scipione's collection includes such standouts as Bernini's *David* and the dynamic *Apollo and Daphne*, Caravaggio's gruesome *David with the Head of Goliath*, and other masterpieces by Correggio, Titian, Raphael, Veronese, and Rubens. Note that reservations are required in advance of your visit to the galleria. They are easy to make over the phone or online, but you won't be able to wander in on a whim. On par with the Vatican Museums and less crowded because of the required reservation, the Galleria Borghese is a true Roman gem.

*⇄ Enter on V. Pinciana, near V. Isonzo. Proceed up Vle. dell'Uccelleria for about 5min. **i** Reservations required; call ☎06 855 5952 or visit 💻www.ticketeria.it. $ €10.50, EU students ages 18-25 €7.25, EU citizens under 18 and over 65 €4. Tours €6, ages 9 and under free. 90min. audio tour (available in English) €5. ⏰ Open Tu-Su 9am-7pm. Reservation phone line open M-F 9am-6pm, Sa 9am-1pm. Guided tours available in English at 9:10am and 11:10am.*

PORTA PIA ♿ MONUMENT

Piazzale Porta Pia

The magnificent Porta Pia marks the end of **Via XX Settembre** and the start of **Via Nomentana,** the tree-lined street that leads out of the city center. Michelangelo was commissioned by Pope Pius IV to construct this gate to replace the Porta

Nomentana, which was not accessible at the time. There is much debate about the degree to which Michelangelo's plan was altered, especially because he died shortly before the gate's completion. Today, Porta Pia marks the end of Termini and the beginning of the more residential zones beyond. At the center, a statue of La Patria di Bersaglieri presides over an ideal spot in which one can admire the *piazza* or grab a lunch break.

[M]A: Repubblica. Turn right onto V. XX Settembre and proceed straight until you reach the Porta Pia; after that, the street becomes V. Nomentana. $ Free.

GALLERIA D'ARTE MODERNA — MUSEUM

Vle. delle Belle Arti 131 ☎06 32 29 81 www.gnam.beniculturali.it

The Galleria d'Arte Moderna is not only a beautiful building but one that contains a superb collection of art dating from the past 200 years—certainly a relief to visitors who've spent days touring the sights of Ancient Rome. The museum's light-filled central room for greeting visitors offers an impressive display of works by Klimt, Mondrian, Giacometti, Balla, and Klee. Proceeding immediately ahead, you will reach the most contemporary of the rooms, which is crowned with a hanging sculpture by Calder and adorned with a number of white and black sculptural paintings by Castellani. The rest of the museum is well-organized by century and period, starting with works by Courbet, Van Gogh, Cezanne, Manet, and Degas and heading into the 20th century with a huge collection of De Chirico, Boccioni, Balla, Morandi, Miro, and Modigliani. Make sure to pass through famed modernist Marcel Duchamp's collection of ready-mades, including the famous Urinal.

From Vle. del Giardino in the Villa Borghese, veer right and exit the park onto Vle. delle Belle Arti. Museum is on the right. $ €8, EU students 18-25 €4, ages under 18 and over 65 free.

CHIESA DI SANTA MARIA DEGLI ANGELI — ♿ CHURCH

P. della Repubblica ☎06 48 80 812 www.santamariadegliangeliroma.it

At the crest of the expansive P. della Repubblica, this 16th-century church (Michelangelo's last, at age 86) is monumental, starting with its front doors: the façade is actually taken from the remains of Diocletian's hot baths (see below), on which Pope Pius IV commissioned the church to be built. Inside, a small rotunda leads into an especially open interior whose design underwent many revisions before it was finally completed. The scarcity of seats makes it less crowded than most churches.

[M]Termini. Walk into the P. del Cinquecento and veer left toward V. Viminale. ⏰ Open M-F 7am-6:30pm, Sa-Su 7am-7:30pm.

BATHS OF DIOCLETIAN — MUSEUM, ANCIENT ROME

V. Enrico de Nicola 79 ☎06 39 96 77 00

In the heart of busy Termini, the Baths of Diocletian have weathered the city grime. Begun in 298 CE by Maximianus, brother of Diocletian, the baths took nearly 10 years—and more than 40,000 Christian slaves—to build. Upon completion, they were able to accommodate 3000 people in what ended up being much more than a mere "bath"—the Diocletian complex contained libraries, gardens, gallery spaces, gyms, and even brothels. Though the baths may no longer exist in the same state of glory, a visit to them is surely worth it.

[M]Termini. Walk into P. dei Cinquecento; enter on V. Volturno. i Part of the Museo Nazionale Romano group; buy 1 ticket for entrance to all 4 sights over 3 days. $ €7, EU students €3.50, EU citizens under 18 and over 65 free. ⏰ Open Tu-Su 9am-7:45pm.

Testaccio, Ostiense, and Southern Rome

THE APPIAN WAY — ♿ ANCIENT ROME

V. Appia Antica ☎06 51 35 316 www.parcoappiaantica.it

When you've had your way with Rome's busy *corsi*, it might be time to try the

Appian on for size. Stretching 16km from Porta San Sebastiano to Frattocchie, it tends to be a little big for most people: walking itineraries generally end around the **Tomb of Cecilia Metella,** though the road extends another 5-6 mi. Don't expect that first stretch to be all dirt roads surrounded by fields and crumbling aqueducts. Since being paved over, the Appian Way has become, somewhat unfortunately, a modern-day reincarnation of its ancient self: a very busy road. That means you'll see your fair share of whizzing cars and walking tourists as you follow the street.

In the third century, V. Appia Antica—the main branch of the trail—extended about a mile from Porta Capena to Porta S. Sebastiano. Today that stretch has become V. delle Terme di Caracalla and V. di Porta San Sebastiano, and the true "Way" officially begins after you exit the **Aurelian walls.** At the time of its use, the ancient road served as the burial ground of the highest Romans and early Christians, since they were forbidden to keep their tombs within the city walls. That means that there are a number of catacombs filled with paintings, sarcophagi, and of course bodies, along the way. **Catacombo San Callisto** (V. Appia Antica 110 ☎06 51 30 15 80 🖳www.sdb.org) is 20km long and 20m deep. Fifty-six martyrs and 18 saints, many of whom were popes, are down there. The other famous catacomb is **Catacombo di San Sebastiano** (V. Appia Antica 136 ☎06 78 50 350 🖳www.catacombe. org), the resting place of Saints Peter and Paul, and 160,000 other people. If all the dead bodies are too gross an idea for you, **Basilica di San Sebastiano** offers a more holy respite, and features Bernini's masterpiece, **Jesus Christ the Redeemer,** which was finished when the Baroque master had reached the ripe old age of 81.

As you get further along the Appian Way it becomes more and more rewarding. After **Cecilia Metella,** you can walk on the road's original paving stones and gaze at miles of unsullied land. If that sounds more appealing to you but you don't want to wander that far south, consider walking down V. della Caffarella (to the left of V. Appia Antica) and the pedestrian trails surrounding it instead of hitting the catacombs.

✦ ⓜB: Circo Massimo or Piramide, then bus #118, which runs along V. Appia Antica to the S. Sebastiano Catacombs. If you want to walk, head down V. delle Terme di Caracalla from the Circo Massimo. At Piazzale Numa Pompilio, veer right onto V. di Porta S. Sebastiano, through the city wall and onto V. Appia Antica. ⓘ Info office is located at V. Appia Antica 42, right before Domine Quo Vadis. It offers bike rental, free maps, historical pamphlets, a self-service bus ticket machine, and opportunities for activities along the way. Ⓢ Road and park free. Catacombo San Callisto and Catacombo di San Sebastiano €8, ages 6-15 €5. Basilica di San Sebastiano free. Ⓩ Road is closed to cars on Su, making it the best day to walk the trail. Catacombo San Callisto open Mar-Jan M-Tu 9am-noon and 2-5pm, Th-Su 9am-noon and 2-5pm. Catacombo di San Sebastiano open M-W 9am-noon and 2-5pm, F-Su 9am-noon and 2-5pm. Basilica di San Sebastiano open daily 8am-6pm.

🖾 BASILICA DI SAN PAOLO FUORI LE MURA   ♿ CHURCH

Piazzale San Paolo 1   ☎06 69 88 08 00 🖳www.basilicasanpaolo.org

This is the light at the end of the tunnel, but unlike the kind you might see during a near-death experience, you should definitely make your way toward this light. After a 30min. walk down the empty-ish V. Ostiense, this magnificent basilica and its gold mosaics are the shining reward you've been waiting for. The second-largest church in Rome, the often overlooked Basilica di San Paolo Fuori le Mura shares extraterritorial status with the **Vatican, Santa Maria Maggiore,** and **San Giovanni in Laterano.** Though this sounds cool, it pretty much means that if you buy a stamp from the church's gift shop, you can only mail the letter in a post box on the premises. Historically, the basilica might be most famous for housing the body of St. Paul after his beheading, but for the aesthetically inclined, the gold mosaics both inside and out steal the show.

✦ ⓜB: Basilica San Paolo, or bus #23 to Ostiense/LGT S. Paolo stop. Ⓢ Basilica free. Cloister €4. Ⓩ Basilica open daily 7am-6:30pm.

▨ BASILICA DI SAN GIOVANNI IN LATERANO

⊗ CHURCH

P. San Giovanni in Laterano 4
☎06 69 88 64 33

Practically off the radar in central Rome, San Giovanni in Laterano is hardly something to be overlooked. Before St. Peter's became such a hot spot, this massive basilica was the home of the papacy. Big windows and a white mosaic floor make the nave feel lighter than that of St. Peter's (though the lack of huge crowds also helps). The dynamic statues of apostles glaring down from their elevated position make you feel just as small and inconsequential, however.

✦ ⓜA: San Giovanni or bus #16 from Termini. ⑤ Basilica free. Cloister €2, students €1. Museo della Basilica €1. ⌚ Basilica open daily 7am-6:30pm. Cloister open daily 9am-6pm. Museo della Basilica open M-F 9:30am-6:15pm, Sa 9:30am-6pm.

CENTRALE MONTEMARTINI

●⊗ MUSEUM

V. Ostiense 106
☎06 42 88 88 88 ▣www.centralmontemartini.org

You might have believed that central Rome is *the* place for seeing old ruins juxtaposed against modern constructions, but the Eternal City is nothing compared to this museum. A relatively new addition to the **Musei Capitolini** family, this building—the first public electricity plant in the city—now houses an impressive collection of Roman statues, busts, and mosaics excavated during the early 1800s.

✦ ⓜB: Ostiense. A 10min. walk down the V. Ostiense. ⑤ €4.50, EU students 18-25 €2.50, EU citizens under 18 and over 65 free. Combined ticket with Musei Capitolini €8.50/6.50. ⌚ Open Tu-Su 9am-7pm.

DOMINE QUO VADIS?

⊗ CHURCH

At the intersection of V. Appia Antica and V. Ardeatina. ☎06 51 20 441 ▣www.catacombe.org

Even its questioning name reflects the speculation that surrounds this tiny church on the Appian Way. Supposedly, Christ's ▣**footprints** are set in stone up the middle aisle, though San Sebastiano down the way claims the same novelty. The church's name ("Lord, where are you going?") derives from the question St. Peter asked Christ when he feared the Lord was fleeing Rome. Though speculation surrounds the footprints, the tourist office's brochures indicate that this church is winning the debate.

✦ Bus #218. ⑤ Free. ⌚ Open in summer M-Sa 8am-7:30pm, Su 8:15am-7:40pm; in winter M-Sa 8am-6:30pm, Su 8:15am-6:45pm.

FOOD

If Italy is the king of fine food, then Rome is its crown jewel. The sheer number of trattorias, cafes, *alimentari* (local grocery stores), *osterie, tavole calde* (cafeterias), pizzerias, and *gelaterie* is enough reason to be overwhelmed without even picking up your fork. With so many options, it's tempting to simply settle for the most convenient—but don't. Always head away from the blocks immediately surrounding major sights: food here is overpriced and usually not well made. Avoid "tourist menus" with bright photos illustrating the plates and English translations. Restaurants with nonstop hours (no midday closing) are often those that cater to tourists rather than locals.

Ancient City

It's a shame that eating's necessary. Well, not really, but since everyone has to do it—and nearly everyone in Rome comes to the Ancient City—restaurants in this region are often overcrowded and overpriced. For the best deals, avoid places closest to the sights and meander down some of the quieter streets.

▨ PIZZERIA DA MILVIO

●⊗ PIZZERIA ❶

V. dei Serpenti 7
☎06 48 93 01 45

A sign that reads, "40 Types of Pizze e Pane," hangs above this pizzeria's bright red walls, a little reminder to passersby that this is the spot for variety, convenience, and flavor. Architecture students crowd the casual stools in back for

simple *primi* like *pomodoro con riso (€5)* and *secondi (€6)* served from hot trays. Up front, the friendly servers cut dozens of thin-crust pizzas into slices sold by the ounce. Be ready to eat on the go; lunch is the busiest hour.
➡ *From V. Cavour, turn onto V. dei Serpenti and walk 2min.* $ *Primi €5; secondi €6. Pizza €0.80-1.40 per etto.* ⏰ *Open daily 7am-midnight.*

👍 LA CUCCUMA 💳♿☀ RISTORANTE [1]
V. Merulana 221 ☎06 77 20 13 61
Even if you're not sitting at their outdoor tables, La Cuccuma's warmly colored walls, arched ceilings, and airy interior will make you feel like you're in the warm Roman sun. The €9 fixed meal *(primi, secondi, contorni, and bread)* is hard-to-beat with huge portions. Still, this restaurant threatens to outdo itself, selling thin-crust pizza by the kilo to hungry students looking for a meal on the go. Generous slices loaded with toppings will set you back less than €4.
➡ Ⓜ*A: Vittorio Emanuele. Walk down V. d Statuto, and turn right onto V. Merulana.* $ *Pizza €8-12.90 per kg.* ⏰ *Open daily 11am-midnight.*

ANTICA BIRRERIA PERONI 💳♿🍸 RISTORANTE, DELI [2]
V. San Marcello 19 ☎06 67 95 310 💻www.anticabirreriaperoni.net
Pizza and panini may abound in Rome, but far harder to come by are the German-Italian plates Antica Birreria Peroni has been making for over 100 years. This popular establishment's tiny interior feels a bit like an old-fashioned candy shop—albeit, a candy shop filled with adults instead of children and beer instead of sweets. It is constantly teeming with customers ordering takeout plates like grilled pork sausage *(€4)* or the smoked pork with sauerkraut *(€10)*. Four types of beer on tap go for as little as €3 to wash down the wurstel *(€6.50-13)*. Be ready to stand or scramble for one of the few stools at the bar.
➡ *From the Vittorio Emanuele monument, turn right on V. Cesare Battisti, left into P. dei Santissimi Apostoli, and walk 2 blocks down.* $ *Primi €5-7; secondi €4-19. Buffet €3.50-6.50.* ⏰ *Open M-Sa noon-midnight.*

LA TAVERNA DA TONINO E LUCIA 🚭♿🍸 RISTORANTE [3]
V. Madonna dei Monti 79 ☎06 47 45 325
You'll feel like you're in some Italian *madre*'s home as soon as you walk into this local favorite: mouthwatering aromas, a view into the kitchen, and a cork-lined wall full of pictures and lights give La Taverna da Tonino e Lucia its cozy feel. Tight quarters may just have you becoming *amico* with your neighbors at the next table by meal's end, but that's par for the course here where the regulars already know each other. The small menu's limited selection is actually a blessing in disguise—the plates are so good that a bigger selection might make choosing impossible. Try the veal rolls with tomato sauce or the specially recommended *paglia ai funghi*.
➡ Ⓜ*B: Cavour. Walk down V. Cavour towards the Fori Imperiali, turn right onto V. dei Serpenti and left onto V. Madonna dei Monti.* $ *Primi €8; secondi €9-13.* ⏰ *Open M-Sa noon-2:30pm, 7-10:30pm.*

LA CARBONARA 💳🚭🍸 RISTORANTE [3]
V. Panisperna 214 ☎06 48 25 176 💻www.lacarbonara.it
The wall of handwritten comments and the massive collection of wine corks beside it should give you an idea of how long this standby has been around (try over 100 years). Despite its history and fame, La Carbonara has remained well priced and down to earth—just read some of the comments made by customers and family members as you gobble down classics like *carciofio alla giulia* (fried artichoke) and *cacio e pepe* (cheese and peppers). If you like what you get (and you surely will), don't hesitate to scribble your own sweet nothings on the wall. Just try to compose something a bit more poetic than the graffiti on your hostel bunk bed.
➡ *From S. Maria Maggiore, walk 5min. down V. Panisperna.* $ *Primi €6-9; secondi €9-15.* ⏰ *Open M-Sa 12:30pm-2:30pm and 7pm-11pm.*

IL GELATONE GELATERIA ❶

V. dei Serpenti 28 ☎06 48 20 187

Il Gelatone deserves every bit of its name: the suffix "*one*," which means big, translates to plentiful scoops and an expansive selection of flavors. Twenty-eight types of sorbet, more than 30 creamier gelati, and four flavors of yogurt make ordering hard—it's a good thing even small cones *(€2)* come with a choice of three flavors. To make matters better (or worse, if you have a hard time making up your mind), you can top off your frosty delight with anything from meringue to pistachio to fresh fruit, whipped cream, and chocolate.

From the Fori Imperiali, walk up V. Cavour and make a left onto V. dei Serpenti. $ Cones or cups €2-4. Open daily 10am-10pm.

HOSTARIA I BUONI AMICI RISTORANTE ❷

V. Aleardo Aleardi ☎06 70 49 19 93

Hand-decorated plates, countless bottles of wine, and quirky paintings line the walls of this tightly-packed, locally loved spot where *buoni amici* do indeed come to dine and drink. The plaid-covered tables are small, but the servings are large; pasta plates like *bucatini* with bacon, cheese, and chili are hot in more ways than one *(€7)*.

[M]B: Colosseo. From the Colosseum, take V. Labicana; then take a right on V. Merulana and a left on V. Aleardo Aleardi. $ Primi €7-8; secondi €7-12. Open M-Sa 12:30-4pm and 7:15pm-midnight.

Centro Storico

Catering to hungry tourists, food in the Centro Storico tends to be overpriced. Your best bet for a quick meal is to head to a *panificio*, *pasticerria*, or pizzeria and eat your grub in a nearby *piazza*. For a sit-down meal, try to wander down narrow and out-of-the way streets rather than stay in more central regions.

DAR FILETTARO A SANTA BARBARA FISH ❶

Largo dei Librari 88 ☎06 68 64 018

We're glad that some places never change. Despite its fame and hordes of customers—families and fancily clad couples alike—Dar Filettaro a Santa Barbara has remained reliably excellent. The *piazza* fills with the sound of chatter from those who dine and those in line. It won't be hard to make an order: the one-sheet menu features only salad, *antipasti*, and the classic fried cod fillet. Plus, nearly everything is €5, so feel free to leave your calculator at home.

From Campo dei Fiori, walk down V. dei Giubbonari and turn left onto the tiny Largo dei Librari. $ Salads, antipasti, and fried fish €5. Desserts €0.50-3.50. Beer €2.50-4.50. Open M-Sa 5:30-11:30pm.

FORNO MARCO ROSCIOLI BAKERY ❷

V. dei Chiavari ☎06 68 64 045 www.anticofornoroscioli.com

If you can find a stool at this bakery, grocery, and fresh food "deli," grab it or else you'll be forced to eat standing at one of the beer barrel tables outside (which frankly, isn't too bad of an option). Most people grab a slice of something to go—a strip of thin-crust pizza or *kranz*, a flaky, twisted roll with almonds and raisins. But the best deals are Forno's fresh plates of *primi*, like its cold rice salad and hot tomato gnocchi, which customers order at the counter according to portion size as they stealthily nab one of the coveted stools. At only €5-7 a plate, this Forno's prices beat those of any restaurant around.

From Campo di Fiori, walk down V. dei Giubbonari and turn left onto V. dei Chiavari. $ Primi €5-7. Pizza €9.50-18 per kg. Strudel €1.80 per etto. Open M-Sa 7am-8pm.

GELATERIA DEL TEATRO GELATERIA ❶

V. di San Simone 70 ☎06 45 47 880

Ever wondered what makes Italian gelato so darn good? Well, much like Willy Wonka, the friendly owners here offer customers a peek into the magic makings of their product—and it really is a *teatro*-tastic experience watching fruit and milk get churned into creamy perfection. The result of Gelateria Del Teatro's alchemy? Over 40 flavors of truly unique gelato, and the owners pride themselves on individually developing each one.

⌘ *From P. Navona, turn left onto V. dei Coronari and look for the tiny V. di San Simone on the left.* *i* *Free tours offered for groups; call (or unwrap a golden ticket) to reserve a spot. Credit cards €20 min. purchase.* Ⓢ *Cones and cups €2-8.* Ⓞ *Open daily noon-midnight.*

PIZZERIA DA BAFFETTO

◉❖ᵹ♈⌂ PIZZERIA ❷

V. del Governo Vecchio 114   ☎06 68 61 617

At Pizzeria da Baffetto, the doors stay sealed and the menu stays hidden until the server lets you in. When the doors do open, a cloud of warm, pizza-infused air slips out to tempt the many eager patrons waiting in line. The service here may be brusque, but that's because they need a Soup-Nazi demeanor to control the crowds waiting for a table. This pizzeria cooks up some of the best pizza in the city, served in a no-frills, packed dining room.

⌘ *From P. Navona, exit onto P. Pasquina and continue as it becomes V. del Governo Vecchio.* *i* *Long waits and no reservations; arrive early if you want a table.* Ⓢ *Pizza €5-9.* Ⓞ *Open M-W 6:30pm-12:30am, Th-Su 6:30pm-12:30am.*

CUL DE SAC

❖ᵹ♈⌂ RISTORANTE ❸

P. Pasquino 73   ☎06 68 80 10 94

When it's so close to Rome's most famous *piazza* (P. Navona, if you weren't sure), it's surprising that Cul de Sac's fresh mix of international flavors is the only touristy thing about the place. Though Roman classics abound, the "international thing" seems to be catching: try the *escargots alla bourguignonne (€6.60),* an order of *babaghanuush (€6.20),* or a cup of hot chocolate made with cocoa from Ghana, Ecuador, Venezuela, and Trinidad. The cool marble bar up front is surrounded by hundreds of wine bottles to pair with the dishes on the diverse menu (written in four languages). Wooden benches and the vine-decorated walls and floors create a laid-back, picnic feel.

⌘ *From P. Navona, walk onto P. Pasquino.* Ⓢ *Primi €7.10-8.90; secondi €6.70-9.80. Desserts €4.30.* Ⓞ *Open daily noon-4pm and 6pm-12:30am.*

Piazza Di Spagna

Between Prada, the Spanish Steps, and the teems of tourists frequenting both, it might be hard to find a tasty and economical bite midday. For lunch, try heading to *panifici* (bakeries) or pizzerias and eating on the *piazze*. For dinner, veer onto smaller streets for better quality and service, even if it will cost you a bit more.

◪ GUSTO

❖ᵹ♈⌂ RISTORANTE, BAR ❸

V. della Frezza 23 and P. Augusto Imperatore 9   ☎06 32 26 273 ▣www.gusto.it

The difference between good taste and bad is as clear as black and white—and by taste we mean flavor *and* style. Black-clad waiters whisk around Gusto's white, brick interior that's divided between a wine lounge and a sit-down restaurant opening onto P. Augusto Imperatore. Tall mirrors make the place feel even bigger than it is, but petite tables near the bar bring it back to life-size for you and your date. On the *piazza* side of things, your best bet is one of the stellar pizzas cranked out of their open brick oven. The real action (and the best deal), however, is to be found at the bar during nightly happy hours: Gusto's buffet of gourmet treats like vegetable couscous and curious black-bread *tramezzini* is better than a sit-down meal. If it weren't for the accompanying cocktails, you'd swear your mom was feeding you right out of her kitchen.

⌘ *Directly across from Mausoleo Augusto on the piazza or, from P. del Popolo, exit onto V. di*

Ripetta and turn left onto V. della Frezza. ***i*** *Happy hour buffet with drink €10.* Ⓢ *Primi €10; secondi €10-18.50. Pizza €6-9.50. Beer €3-5.50. Wine €4.50-12. Cocktails €9.* ⏰ *Open daily 10am-2am. Happy hour daily 6-9pm.*

FRASCHETTERIA BRUNETTI RISTORANTE ❷

V. Angelo Brunetti 25b ☎06 32 14 103 www.fraschetteriabrunetti.it

Save your messiness for a melting gelato after dinner—there'll be no greasy pizza fingers or spaghetti mishaps here. Instead, Fraschetteria Brunetti focuses primarily on baked pasta dishes, including 11 types of lasagna in varieties that you won't find anywhere else: try the rich gorgonzola and walnut. Covered in handwritten notes from loyal patrons, this place is legit, managing to avoid jacked-up prices and watered-down cuisine despite its proximity to the sights.

*[M]A: Flaminio. From P. del Popolo, exit onto V. di Ripetta and turn right onto V. Angelo Brunetti.* ***i*** *Fixed lunch of entree, coffee, and drink €7.50.* Ⓢ *Primi €8. Panini €3.50. Cocktails €4.* ⏰ *Open M-Sa 11am-midnight, but may close earlier or later depending on the crowd.*

CAMBI PIZZERIA, BAKERY ❶

V. del Leoncino 30 ☎06 68 78 081

Better than a cheapo pizzeria and cheaper than a sit-down restaurant. The mix of salty and sweet scents perfuming the area has most folks starting with a loaded slice of pizza and following it up with a €1 fruit torte. But don't overlook their real specialties: unleavened bread (hard bread lightly doused in oil) and *crostata* (cookies filled with chocolate or fruit). When you see tourists paying three times the price down the street, your meal will taste even better.

*From Ara Pacis/Mausoleo Augusto, walk down V. Tomacelli and turn right onto V. Leoncino.* ***i*** *No seating. Only vegetable oil used. Also sells basic groceries.* Ⓢ *Cookies €0.80, €33 per kg. Panini €3.50. Pizza €7.50-15 per kg. Crostatine €11.* ⏰ *Open M-Sa 8am-8pm.*

BAR SAN MARCELLO CAFE ❶

V. D. San Marcello 37-8 ☎06 69 92 33 15

Don't let the curt service turn you off from this small *tavola calda*, a lunchtime favorite among local workers. The ratio of Italians to tourists means you won't hear much English as you munch on fresh pasta salads, grilled fish, or panini. Take advantage of the linguistic discrepancy: with the **Trevi Fountain** right around the corner, you can easily get your full share of English chatter for the day just a short walk away.

*From Palazzo Venezia, take V. del Corso; turn right onto V. S.S. Apostoli and left onto V. D. San Marcello.* ***i*** *Takeout available. Limited seating in back.* Ⓢ *Panini €3.50-4. Primi €4-5.* ⏰ *Open daily 6am-5:30pm.*

FIASCHETTERIA BELTRAMME RISTORANTE ❸

V. della Croce 39

When a restaurant has managed to limit its menu to one page and survive for over 100 years without a phone, you know it's doing something right. Don't expect creative culinary concoctions but classic dishes made with family love. Their *cacio e pepe* might be some of the best in the neighborhood, and locals will let you know it when you end up sitting next to them in the restaurant's close quarters. We're glad that despite the modern fashion flash surrounding it, this traditional standby hasn't changed.

*[M]A: Spagna. From the Spanish Steps, take V. Condotti; turn right onto V. Belsiana and right onto V. delle Croce.* Ⓢ *Primi €10; secondi €15-18; verdure and contorni €6-10.* ⏰ *Open M-Sa noon-2:30pm and 7-10:30pm.*

NATURIST CLUB RISTORANTE, VEGETARIAN ❸

V. della Vita 14, 4th fl. ☎06 67 92 509

Like its street name, this restaurant is all about *"la vita"*—that is, saving a few *vite* by serving up an entirely macrobiotic menu. Climb up four well worn flights of stairs (which might be part of the health kick) to enjoy totally atypical Roman fare like ravioli stuffed with creamy tofu and pesto *(€8)* or seitan escalope with grilled vegetables *(€9)*. Despite their exotic twists, dishes here taste like they might have been made at any one of the trattorias down the street. Those skeptical of macrobiotic food might find that this place changes their mind.

➜ Directly off V. del Corso around P. San Lorenzo in Lucina; turn right onto V. della Vita from V. del Corso and look for #14. Buzz and walk to 4th fl. ℹ 90% organic and totally macrobiotic; fish is the only non-vegetarian option. $ Primi €8-9; secondi €9-11. Fixed vegetarian meal €14; lunch/dinner combo €8-10/€20-25. Organic wine €12-16 per bottle. 🕐 Open M-F 12:30-3pm and 7-10:30pm.

Jewish Ghetto

Though the Jewish Ghetto is one of the smaller neighborhoods in Rome, it is rich in fine cuisine and character. Most restaurants are on V. del Portico d'Ottavia, and while not exactly cheap, they are a great alternative to classic Italian fare if that's all you've been eating. Most are kosher and closed early Friday through Saturday.

ANTICO FORNO DEL GHETTO — BAKERY, GROCERY ❶

P. Costaguti 31 ☎06 68 80 30 12

You don't have to resort to a slice of pizza in order to avoid the overpriced plates of a sit-down restaurant: grab a loaf of to-die-for bread, a few slices of smoked meat, and a hunk of cheese at this family-run neighborhood staple instead. Locals flock to the small store to buy anything from fresh pasta to cookies and milk to a hot slice of flatbread or focaccia topped with veggies.

➜ From Ponte Garibaldi, walk down V. Arenula, turn right onto V. S. Maria d. Pianto and into P. Costaguti. ℹ Only pizza and bread guaranteed kosher. Cheese, bread, cookies, and meat sold by lb. $ Pizza and focaccia €1.20-2 per piece, €7.70-9.70 per kg. 🕐 Open M-F 7:45am-2:30pm and 5-8pm, Sa-Su 7:45am-1pm.

LA TAVERNA DEL GHETTO — KOSHER ❹

V. del Portico d'Ottavia 7/b-8 ☎06 68 80 97 71 💻www.latavernadelghetto.com

The small dining area out front might have you thinking that this is an intimate cafe with Middle Eastern music and delicious food to match. But head around the block, and you'll see that this popular spot opens up into an expansive dining space that can play host to bigger parties and more festive dining. The first kosher restaurant in Rome, La Taverna del Ghetto is an expert in the classics: *bacala* (fried catfish), *fiori di zucca*, and any variation of artichoke. Soy-based desserts are dairy-free and pleasantly mild after an otherwise heavy meal.

➜ From Teatro Marcello, walk down V. del Piscaro and veer right as it becomes V. del Portico d'Ottavia. ℹ Strictly kosher. $ Primi €11.50; secondi €15.90-19.50. 🕐 Open M-Th noon-11pm, F noon-4pm, Sa 9-11pm, Su noon-11pm.

PASTICCERIA BOCCIONE LIMENTANI — BAKERY ❷

V. Portico D'Ottavio 1 ☎06 68 78 637

This tiny, unadorned *pasticceria* doesn't need the cuteness factor to promote itself: its small assortment of baked goods is strong enough to bring customers running, no advertisements needed. Only about four products are made here—freshly baked tortes and a range of *biscottini* with nuts and fruits—so all you have to do is know what you want, order, and enjoy.

➜ Right on the corner of V. Portico D'Ottavio; look for numbers, as it's practically unmarked. $ Cookies around €18 per kg. Tortes €18-22 each. 🕐 Open M-Th 7:30am-7:30pm, F 7:30am-3:30pm, Su 7:30am-7:30pm.

KOHSER BISTROT CAFE — CAFE, KOSHER ❸

V. Santa Maria del Pianto 68/69 ☎06 68 64 398

This cheerful and brightly lit cafe doubles as an early evening spot for cocktails and an anytime spot for delicious kosher food. Picnic-like wooden tables on the street are often full of locals munching on finger food with their wine or enjoying fuller plates like curry chicken with artichokes. The modern interior has a full bar and a few shelves with packaged food items for sale.

From Ponte Garibaldi, walk up V. Arenula and turn right onto V. Santa Maria del Pianto. $ Primi €9-11; secondi €8-9. Beer and wine €6-7. Cocktails €7-8. 🕒 Open M-Th 9am-9pm, F 9am-sundown, Su 9am-9pm. Aperitivo happy hour 5-9pm.

Vatican City

The longest line in Rome eventually becomes a hungry crowd. The selection of neighborhood trattorias and small stores that lines the quieter streets outside the Vatican walls won't disappoint, but the bright English menus and beckoning waiters closer to the museums will.

CACIO E PEPE — RISTORANTE ❸

V. Avezzana 11 ☎06 32 17 268 www.cacioepeperistorante.com

If you're in the area (and by that, we mean as far as 1 mi. away), it will be well worth your time to trek to this true trattoria. Welcoming owner Gianni will personally seat you and make sure your *cacio e pepe* (fresh egg pasta topped with oil, grated cheese, and black pepper) is everything it should be: big, flavorful, and perfectly *al dente.* Its popularity with locals instead of tourists has kept the vibe casual and the service as good as the food...and that's saying a lot.

[M]A: Lepanto. From Metro, walk up V. Lepanto (away from the Vatican), turn right on Vle. delle Milizie and left onto V. Avezzana, a 5min. walk. $ Primi €8; secondi €9-10. 🕒 Open M-F 12:30-3pm and 7:30-11:30pm, Sa 12:30-3pm.

OLD BRIDGE GELATERIA — GELATERIA ❶

V. Bastioni di Michelangelo 3/5 ☎06 38 72 30 26 www.gelateriaoldbridge.com

Gelato so sinfully good you might need to visit the Vatican just to confess it. Despite being practically on the doorstep of the most touristed sight in the city, this hole-in-the wall *gelateria* has thankfully remained just that. It's tiny and unadorned yet amazingly good. Beware: lines may rival those of the Vatican, but the size of your order (huge) will make the wait worthwhile.

Off P. Risorgimento and across the street from the line to the Vatican Museums. $ Cones €1.50-3; cups €3-4. 🕒 Open M 3pm-2am, Tu-Su 9am-2am.

FA BIO — CAFE, ORGANIC ❶

V. Germanico 43 ☎06 64 52 58 10 www.fa-bio.com

If you're going to pay €4 for a panini, it might as well be organic, right? And if all that pizza and gelato have you craving something green, then Fa Bio will be your Eden. Just walking in, you'll be refreshed by the smell of blended smoothies and fresh salads alone. Organic pie *(€1.50),* hearty tofu salads *(€4.50),* and bread that is, for once, not white are enough to sustain you for a heavy afternoon of sightseeing. If you still need a pick-me-up after the 4hr. waits, re-energize with *"L'energizzante,"* a potent shake of milk, pear, ginger, and cacao.

[M]A: Ottaviano. Walk down V. Ottaviano and turn left onto V. Germanico. i All food organic. $ Panini €4. Salads €4.50. Cookies €0.50-1. Fruit juices and smoothies €3.50. 🕒 Open in summer M-Sa 9am-8pm; in winter M-Sa 9am-5pm.

FABBRICA MARRONS GLACES GIULIANI — CIOCCOLATERIA ❷

V. Paolo Emilio 67 ☎06 32 43 548 www.marronglaces.it

This is the kind of place you visit first for yourself, second to do some gift-shopping for friends back home, and third...for yourself again. The shop's old school '40s feel adds to the delight of ordering your sweet confections from the family owners. Their specialties—*marron glacés* (candied chestnuts) and chocolate—are the perfect match of sweet and rich. Though they might not make a boxed trip home to your folks, the candied fruits are stellar—shiny and big as crown jewels.

[M]A: Lepanto. Take Vle. Giulio Cesare toward the Vatican and turn left onto V. Paolo Emilio.

Ⓢ Marron Glacés €3.50 per etto (100g). Candied fruit €4.50 per etto. Chocolates €4.50 per etto. 🕐
Open in summer M-Sa 8:30am-1pm and 3:30pm-7:30pm; in winter M-Sa 8:30am-8pm, Su 9am-1pm.

WINE BAR DE' PENITENZIERI

🍴⊗☕ CAFE, BAR ❸

V. dei Penitenzieri 16/A ☎06 68 75 350

Before hitting the inescapable nest of pizzerias surrounding the Vatican, grab a bite at this small but hugely popular lunch spot. The stand-up bar makes it easy to munch on a panino (€4-5) and sip your cappuccino (€0.90-2.50) without having to pay for table service. A rotating list of classics—mostly pastas and salads—is reserved for those who nab a seat in the adjoining room. If you don't want real sustenance, have a cocktail instead. Hey, you're not in St. Peter's yet.

⚑ From St. Peter's, take V. della Conciliazione toward the river, turn right onto V. dei Cavalieri del San Sepolcro, and keep straight as it becomes V. Penitenzieri. Ⓢ Primi and meat-and-cheese plates €10. Panini €4-5. Beer €3-4.50. Wine €3.50-4. Cocktails €6. 🕐 Open M-Sa 6am-8:30pm.

L'ARCHETTO

🍴⊗🍽 PIZZERIA ❷

V. Germanico 105 ☎06 32 31 163

Tired of the same old pizza toppings and overpriced slices? Order one in the round from a menu that trumps the regular list. Try L'Archetto's namesake speciality with cooked mozzarella, arugula, sausage, and peppers or, for a smaller bite, an order of bruschetta (€1.50-2.80). Though the setting might not be anything special, their lunch special—€8 *primo* with a choice of soup—makes the pizzeria popular with the economically minded and hungry midday crowd.

⚑ Ⓜ A: Ottaviano. Walk V. Ottaviano toward the Vatican and turn left onto V. Germanico. *i* Primi served only at lunch. Ⓢ Bruschettas €1.50-2.80. Pizza €3.50-8. Primi with soup €8. 🕐 Open daily 12:30-3pm and 7pm-midnight.

Trastevere

There are plenty of dining options in Trastevere, whether you want a luxurious sit-down meal, a bite on the go, or something in between. While the *piazze* are full of great choices, explore smaller side streets for some of the harder-to-find gems.

🏛 LA RENELLA

🍴♿ PIZZERIA, BAKERY ❶

V. del Politeama 27 ☎06 58 17 265

La Renella is as close to a true neighborhood eatery as you're likely to find, with locals coming here at all hours of the day for everything from their morning bread to lunchtime pizza to after-dinner cookies. The handwritten menu looks like it hasn't changed for years, but with Roman classics like the *fiori di zucchini* (huge orange petals topped with anchovies and cheese), why should it?

⚑ From P. Trilussa, walk down V. della Renella; the front entrance is here, but there's also a back entrance on V. del Politeama. Ⓢ Pizza €5-12 per kg, sweet tortes and crostate €10-18 per kg, biscotti €10-16 per kg. 🕐 Open daily 7am-10pm (closing time can vary).

SIVEN

🍴♿ PIZZERIA, DELI ❶

V. San Francesco a Ripa 137 ☎06 58 97 110

There's hardly a moment of the day when someone isn't entering or exiting this tiny spot, where cheap pizza and hot pasta *primi* are sold by weight. Lasagna, gnocchi, eggplant parmigiano, and calzones would make meals on their own, but most people come away with a few slices of thin-crust pizza, loaded with all the standards—think zucchini, potatoes, mushrooms, or steak. There's nowhere to sit and the service is fast, so be ready to eat on the go. And make sure you know what you want, or you'll just get in the way of the regulars behind you.

⚑ From Vle. Trastevere, turn right onto V. San Francesco a Ripa. Ⓢ Pasta €0.75-0.80 per etto. Calzones €2.50. Pizza €1-1.30 per etto. 🕐 Open M-Sa 9am-10pm.

LE FATE

🍴♿((•))☕❀ RISTORANTE ❸

Vle. Trastevere 130 ☎06 58 00 971 🖥www.lefaterestaurant.it

Inspired by the fable of Aurora, this festive restaurant has taken on the themes of love and solidarity in both its ambience and the quality of its food. The warmly lit dining area has the feel of a woodland cottage, with a bookshelf of cookbooks in the corner, twinkling star lights, and a string of vines covering the wall. All ingredients come from Lazio, so you can expect especially fresh plates; the homemade gnocchi with steak, cream, spinach, and ricotta is as rich in flavor as Princess Aurora was in gold. Students who aren't blessed with riches like the fairytale heroine should take advantage of the €10 meal, complete with bruschetta, pasta, dessert, and a glass of wine. Just say the magic word (or show your student ID).

 # About 15min. down Vle. Trastevere from P. G. Belli. i Free Wi-Fi. Inquire about cooking classes and apartment rentals for students. $ Primi €10-13; secondi €12-25. ⏰ Open daily 6-11pm.

PIZZERIA DA SIMONE ♿ PIZZERIA, DELI ❶

V. Giacinto Carini 50 ☎06 58 14 980

After a long trek up to Ponte Acqua Paola and the surrounding gardens, there's no better way to replenish yourself than with a hot slice of Da Simone's pizza. Pies topped with anything from shrimp to the more classic sundried tomatos and *mozzarella di bufala* go for about €1.50-4 per slice. Down the counter, you'll find freshly-made pasta dishes, steamed vegetables *(€12-16.90 per kg)*,and huge legs of chicken *(€3)* that are filling enough to be a complete dinner. If you're hoping to grab dinner here, be ready to take your food and make a picnic of it in the park, as there's no seating.

 # From the Porta San Pancrazio on Giancolo Hill, walk downhill on V. Giancinto Carini for about 7min. $ Pizza €6.96-16.90 per kg. ⏰ Open M-Sa 7am-8pm.

CASETTA DI TRASTEVERE ♿🍸 RISTORANTE ❷

P. de Renzi, 31/32 ☎06 58 00 158

Inside is like outside at this budget-friendly restaurant. A hanging clothesline, painted Italian facade, and terra-cotta rooftop transform the spatious interior of Casetta di Trastevere into just what its name implies—a *casetta*, or little house. Upstairs, a banquet-sized table serves especially large groups, but downstairs, smaller clusters of students consistently fill the tables. With the cheapest pizza in town *(marinara pie €3)*, this little house is a very, very, very fine house, allowing you to save your euros for Trastevere's teeming nightlife just down the street.

 # From S. Maria in Trastevere, walk down V. di Piede until you hit V. della Pelliccia. P. de Renzi is just beyond. $ Pizza €3-6. Primi €5-8; secondi €5-16; dessert €3-5. ⏰ Open daily noon-11:30pm.

BISCOTTIFICIO ARTIGIANO ♿ BAKERY ❶

V. della Luce 21 ☎06 58 03 926

With piles on piles of freshly baked cookies, this place seems more like a factory than a humble bakery. With no seats or decorations to speak of, Biscottificio Artigiano's success rests solely on its scrumptious cookies and ever-growing reputation. (Note the wall of newspaper clippings.) Try the paper-thin *stracetti*—a slightly sweet cookie made from nuts and eggs. Family-run for over a century, this bakery cooks with recipes that are like no one else's in Rome.

 # From P. Sonnino, take V. Giulio Cesare Santini and turn left on V. della Luce. $ Most cookies €7.5-16 per kg. Rustic and fruit tortes €15. ⏰ Open M-Sa 8am-8pm, Su 9:30am-2pm.

Termini and Northeast Rome

The area around Termini is dominated by restaurants representing both extremes of the price range: cheap eats and over-priced tourist menus catering to hungry travelers. Avoid restaurants immediately surrounding the station and head into some side streets for higher quality options. If you head too far from the station, though, things will get much pricier around the Villa Borghese.

ANTICA PIZZERIA DE ROMA ♿❄ PIZZERIA ❶

V. XX Settembre 41 ☎06 48 74 624 💻www.mcmab.net

Businessmen may take home a big paycheck, but that doesn't mean they don't like bargains when they see them: midday, this tiny pizzeria is full of men in suits, munching some of the best-priced and freshest pizza in the neighborhood. Though this pizzeria offers the same standard fare that infiltrates all of Rome (thin crust pizza sold by weight), watching the workers cut, weigh, and serve up fresh pies like a science (or whip out an individual one in less than 10min.) is a real pleasure—and you haven't even taken your first bite. Once you do, you'll be ready to join the businessmen every day.

➡ From P. della Repubblica, walk down V. V. E. Orlando and turn right onto V. XX Settembre. Proceed 7min. $ Individual pizzas €2.20-5.50, €0.70-2 per etto. ⏰ Open daily 8am-9:30pm.

PASTICCERIA STRABBIONI ROMA — ⊛ ♿ 🍸 🥡 CAFE, BAKERY [2]

V. Servio Tullio 2a-2b — ☎06 48 73 965

Not much has changed at Strabbioni since it opened in 1888: not the hand-painted flowers gracing the ceiling or the old-fashioned lamps, and definitely not the good service and food. (While *Let's Go* might not have been around in 1888, we're pretty sure this place would have merited a listing in *Let's Go Grand Tour 1889.*) The second-oldest bar of its type still in Rome, this is the place where locals come for a cheap lunch (*primi* classics are written daily on a chalkboard outside), a freshly baked pastry, or even an afternoon mixed drink. At only €3.50-4 a drink, how can you resist?

➡ From Porta Pia, walk down V. XX Settembre and make a right onto V. Servio Tullio. $ Primi €6-7; secondi €8. Pastries €0.80-3. ⏰ Open M-Sa 7am-8pm.

STAROCIA LUNCH BAR — ⊛ ♿ 🍸 🥡 FOOD BAR [1]

V. Sicilia 121 — ☎06 48 84 986

Pop into this bustling, modern cafe after a stroll in the Villa Borghese. Chic white decor and a small patio out front distinguish it from other bars offering the same, standard fare. Fresh (and huge) panini, pasta, cocktails, and coffee are surprisingly well priced given Starocia's hip vibe. Especially popular with the lunch crowd, though its evening happy hour buffet for only €4 *(with wine €6)* means you'll probably make it your dinner spot.

➡ Walking south on V. Po (away from the Villa Borghese), make a right onto V. Sicilia. $ Pasta and secondi €4-7. Tramezzini and panini €1.80-3. Coffee €0.80-1.80. Cocktails €4.50-5.50. ⏰ Open M-Sa 5:15am-9:30pm. Happy hour M-Sa 6pm.

FASSINO — ⊛ ♿ 🍸 CAFE, GELATERIA [2]

V. Bergamo 24 — ☎06 85 49 117

The folks at Fassino will have you know gelato isn't just a summer thing. Their famous *Brivido Caldo* reinvents the favorite frozen treat, sticking a cookie in its middle and turning it into a hot delight topped off with whipped cream. After the sugar rush (or before, if you're one of those people who's been brainwashed into the dessert-after-dinner rule), settle down for a savory crepe, which the Sicilian owner makes with no butter fat—only extra virgin olive oil—for a lighter taste. Though their fixed lunch meal *(a crepe, drink, dessert, and coffee; €8.50)* is a steal, consider coming in the evening when a classical pianist plays until the customers leave.

➡ From the end of V. XX Settembre, turn left onto V. Piave and walk until you hit P. Fiume. Turn right onto V. Bergamo. $ Gelato €1.50-3. Brivido Caldo €3 (winter only). Cocktails €4.50-5. ⏰ Open M-F 9:30am-1am, Sa 3:30pm-1am, Su 9:30am-1:30pm and 3:30pm-1am.

RISTORANTE DA GIOVANNI — 💳 ⊗ 🍸 RISTORANTE [2]

V. A Salandra 1 — ☎06 48 59 50

A hand-written menu, shelf of old typewriters, and even a hanging carcass greet customers at this subterranean trattoria. Don't worry: the meat is dangling in the kitchen, ensuring that your entree will be that much fresher. With only a few windows near the ceiling and a wood-lined interior, this family-run Roman restaurant oozes with dark warmth that matches its classic dishes. You've seen it written dozens of times at numerous establishments, but you'll never get tired of Da Giovanni's *cacio e pepe*, which they've been making for over 50 years.

From P. della Repubblica, walk up V. V. E. Orlando and turn right onto V. XX Settembre. Walk 5min. and turn left onto V. M Pagano; veer left onto V. A. Salandra. $ Primi €5.50-6.50; secondi €4.50-12. Open M-Sa noon-3pm and 7-10:30pm.

RISTORANTE AFRICA — AFRICAN ❷

V. Gaeta 26-28 — ☎06 49 41 077

The area around Termini abounds with cheap, international dives, but this African restaurant distinguishes itself with better quality food and a more welcoming decor. The staff will be happy to recommend a dish to the customer ignorant of African cuisine, but English translations provide ample assistance. Vegetarians can finally feast on something other than pasta: the *aliccia* is a healthy dish of puréed vegetables simmered in onion and herb sauce and served with traditional African bread *(€9).*

[M]Termini. Walk in the direction of P. del Cinquecento and turn right onto V. Gaeta. $ Appetizers €3-4; entrees €9-12. Open M-Sa 8am-midnight.

BUBI'S — RISTORANTE ❸

V. G.V. Gravina 7-9 — ☎06 32 60 0510 www.bubis.it

The small menu and serene pistachio walls of this elegant restaurant cater to diners with refined taste. Terrace seating behind a wall of leaves is great for a more intimate meal and makes you feel far removed from the busy V. Flaminia. Though specializing in classic Roman cuisine, the restaurant serves entrees like *straccetti di pollo* with curry and Canadian rice as well as a range of gourmet hamburgers that add a little bit of international flare.

[M]A: Flaminio or tram #19 to Belle Arti. Walk up V. Flaminio from the Metro for about 5min. and turn left onto V. G.V. Gravina. $ Primi €9-12; secondi €12-18. Panini €12-14. Open M-Sa 12:30-3pm and 8-11pm.

Testaccio, Ostiense, and Southern Rome

Testaccio is known among Roman residents as one of the best spots for high-quality, well-priced food. Its location farther from the sights means it evades the tourist crowds of the city center. Whether you want an upscale restaurant or a cheaper trattoria, you won't have any trouble finding it here. If you're out exploring the Appian Way, it's best to bring food with you, since there aren't many options around there and those that are there are seriously overpriced.

IL NOVECENTO — RISTORANTE ❸

V. dei Conciatori 10 — ☎06 57 25 04 45 www.9cento.com

Fresh. Homemade. Family-run. You've heard these adjectives used all too often to describe Italian cuisine, but here, they actually come to life. Watch the owner's son roll out pasta dough, cut it into *tagliatelle*, and dump it into boiling water before it ends up on your plate topped with their own pesto *(€9).* If pasta isn't your thing, then how about pizza or roasted meat—again, you can see both sliced and diced minutes before you eat them. Though the wood-lined rooms up front are especially cozy, try to grab a table in the huge dining room in back so you can take in all the kitchen action.

[M]B: Piramide. Walk down V. Ostiense and make a right onto V. dei Conciatori. $ Primi €8-10; secondi €12-18. Pizzas €5-9 (only at dinner). Open M-F 12:30-2:30pm and 7:30-11pm, Sa-Su 7:30-11pm.

FARINANDO — PIZZERIA, PANIFICIO ❷

V. Lucca della Robbia 30 — ☎06 57 50 674

At Farinando, you can get top-notch pizza by the kilo or pie, huge calzones, and anything from cookies to fruit tarts without having to pay for expensive table service or retreat to a park bench. Stock up before hitting the long V. Ostiense for some sightseeing.

❖ ⓂB: *Piramide. Walk up V. Marmorata; turn left onto V. Galvani and right onto V. Lucca della Robbia.* ⓢ *Calzones €3. Whole pizza €4-7, €7-18 per kg.* ⓩ *Open M-Th 7:30am-2pm and 4:30-8:30pm, F 7:30am-9pm, Sa 5-9pm.*

LA MAISON DE L'ENTRECÔTE

🌐♿Ⴤ♨ RISTORANTE, ENOTECA ❸

P. Gazometro 1 ☎06 57 43 091 🖂www.lamaisondelentrecote.it

You don't need a plane ride or a time machine if you want to return to bohemian Paris: just retreat to Le Maison's dim downstairs, where stained-glass lamps and slow music put you at ease. The small menu lets you pair classic French dishes like cheesy onion soup (€7) with Italian staples. Try their *crema* gelato topped with Grand Marnier. Check out the antique mirror and the 10% discounted menu scribbled atop it, then check yourself to see if your cheeks are pink like Moulin Rouge from the wine you've hopefully been sipping.

❖ ⓂB: *Ostiense. Walk down V. Marmorata away from Piramide for 5min. and turn right onto P. Gazometro.* ⓢ *Primi €7-10. Salads €5-7. Meats €9-14. Beer €4. Cocktails €6. Wine by the bottle €12-16.* ⓩ *Open Tu-Th 1-3pm and 8pm-midnight, F-Sa 8pm-midnight.*

OSTERIA DEGLI AMICI

✒♿Ⴤ❄❋ RISTORANTE ❸

V. Nicola Zabaglia 25 ☎06 57 81 466 🖂www.osteriadegliamici.info

Besides the excellent cheese-topped pasta dishes, there's nothing cheesy about this place. Enjoy hot saffron risotto sprinkled with smoked Scamorza cheese and drizzled in balsamic vinegar while downing a glass of their stellar wine (whose cork might get added to the gigantic collection up front). If the relaxed setting makes you want to linger, split a spicy chocolate souffle—almost as hot as the entrees—with your *amico*, who's hopefully bringing the heat as well.

❖ ⓂB: *Piramide. Walk up V. Marmorata; turn right onto V. Luigi Vanvitelli and left onto V. Nicola Zabaglia.* ⓢ *Primi €7-9; secondi €12-16.* ⓩ *Open W-Su 12:30-3pm and 7:30pm-midnight.*

L'OASI DI BIRRA

✒♿Ⴤ RISTORANTE ❷

P. Testaccio 40 ☎06 57 46 122

Most liquor menus round off their selection at a few pages, but this two-floor mecca of food and alcohol has six pages devoted to Belgian beer *alone*. It requires a book to catalogue the rest of their international collection, which also includes wine, grappa, rum, and whiskey. The floor-to-ceiling bottles (both upstairs and down) probably make up less than 10% of their actual collection. The best way to tackle the menu is to order a bottle for the table (some upwards of €200) and match it up with a few six- or eight-variety plates of *salumi*, cheese, or bruschetta which come in nearly as many combinations as the alcohol. If you're bad at making decisions, drop in during happy hour when you can endlessly sample the goods for only €10 at the *aperitivo* buffet.

❖ ⓂB: *Piramide. Walk up V. Marmorata and turn left onto P. Testaccio.* ⓘ *Also carries a small selection of bottled food products.* ⓢ *Bruschettas €8. Salumi and formaggi plates of 6-8 types €16-19. Draft beer €4-10. Wine €12-200+ per bottle.* ⓩ *Open M-Sa 4:30pm-12:30am, Su 7:30pm-12:30am. Happy hour nightly 5-8:30pm.*

NIGHTLIFE

Don't spend all your euros and energy at the museums—Rome's nightlife is varied and vast, giving you a whole other itinerary to attack after the guards go home and the cats come out to prowl the ruins. Generally, you'll be able to find whatever nightlife you're into, though each neighborhood has its own flavor and characteristic selection. The only areas where your nights might end a bit early are, unsurprisingly, Vatican City and the region near Villa Borghese.

Ancient City

Nightlife in the Ancient City is confined mostly to Irish pubs, upscale wine bars, and small cafes open until the late hours. While there's nothing like walking down a cobblestone street after a few glasses of wine, if you're looking for young, pumping clubs, head elsewhere.

👍 ICE CLUB

💳⊗🍸❄ CLUB, BAR

V. Madonna dei Monti 18/19 ☎06 97 84 5581 💻www.iceclubroma.it

Gelato isn't the only way to cool off from the hot Roman sun: enter Ice Club, the only bar in Italy made entirely of ice. For €15, you get a silver cloak, a pair of gloves, and one free drink at what may be Rome's (literally) coolest spot, an ice tube of colored lights, pulsing music, and stellar drinks. Vodka goes down smooth as, you guessed it, ice and not only because it's served in an ice cup: with over 40 flavors ranging from strawberries and cream to chocolate, you'll never know you're drinking your liquor straight. Clearly, this is how the place keeps its clientele, since after a few shots, it's hard to tell that the temperature is below freezing.

➜ From the Fori Imperiali, turn right onto V. Madonna dei Monti. ℹ Su-M and W-F drop by between 6-9pm and get in free after 11pm. Open bar Tu €15. Buy 1 shot, get 4 free Th. Credit cards accepted for cover. Cash only at the bar (because credit cards would just be impractical in that weather). $ Cover €15; includes 1 drink. Shots €2.50. Straight vodka €7. Cocktails €8. Ice luge €10. ⏰ Open daily 6pm-2am.

SCHOLAR'S LOUNGE

💳♿🍸 IRISH PUB

V. del Plebiscito 101/B ☎06 69 20 2208 💻www.scholarsloungerome.com

There'll be no scholars reading here: with nine TVs (including two that are over 5 ft. wide) and over 250 kinds of whiskey (the biggest collection in Italy), they're probably dancing on the table. Don't bother bringing your Italian phrasebook, because the Irish bartenders, huge Irish flag hanging over the bar, and steady stream of Irish dishes *(beef in Guinness stew, €9.50)* make this a of Dublin on the Tiber. Although you can keep it cheap at only €3.50 for a pint of beer, those looking for a splurge should check out the whiskey list: a shot of Jameson Rarest Vintage Reserve goes for a whopping €133.50. Ask to see their private collection, which might as well be at a museum.

➜ From P. Venezia, follow V. del Plebiscito to just where it intersects V. del Corso. ℹ Live music Th-F. Karaoke on Tu and Su. $ Pints €3.50-5.50. Cocktails €7.50-9.50, €5 during the day. Student specials: long drinks €4.50, shots €1. ⏰ Open daily 11am-3:30am. Happy hour until 8pm.

LIBRERIA CAFÉ

💳⊗🍸 CAFE

V. degli Zingari 36 ☎06 33 97 22 4622

Libreria's "business card" is a bookmark, just in case you want to remember the address—or perhaps the page number—where you left off. You'll find yourself in relaxed company at this bohemian cafe, accoutered with draped cloths, antique couches, votive candles, lamps that might as well have come from a Lewis Carroll novel, and, of course, walls of books by Karl Marx, Victor Hugo, Freud, and any number of Italian authors. Smooth jazz playing in the background will feel even smoother after a glass of one of the 47 varieties of wine *(€5)* offered. If you do, in fact, want to read, try a cup of tea instead, hailing from Russia, Japan, or even South Africa *(€5)*.

➜ [M]B: Cavour. From V. Cavour, turn right onto P. degli Zingari and left onto V. degli Zingari. $ Beer €3-5. Wine €5. Cocktails €5-6. Appetizers €6-10. ⏰ Open M 6pm-2am and W-Su 6pm-2am. Aperitivo buffet 7-9pm, €8.

Centro Storico

The Centro Storico might be old, but it packs in a young crowd at night. One of the best places to find bars and clubs, both in terms of location and quality, this area remains fairly safe after sunset due to its bustle at most hours. If you don't feel like heading inside, check out the Campo dei Fiori, where many spend the evening enjoying the outdoor scenery.

DRUNKEN SHIP

BAR, CLUB

Campo dei Fiori 20/21 ☎06 68 30 05 35 www.drunkenship.com

Wait, is this the campo or the campus? Walking into Drunken Ship, you might very well think you're back at college, as it comes complete with nightly beer pong, TVs airing sports games, a DJ spinning Top 40 tunes, and a raucous crowd of students ready to enjoy it all. Great weekly specials, including Wednesday night power hours and Pitcher Night Thursdays *(€10)*, make this one of the most popular spots for young internationals aching for some university-style fun.

 # In Campo dei Fiori. i M-Th half-price drinks for women until 11pm, Tu buy-1-get-1 free until 11pm; check online for more specials. Student discounts nightly. Happy hour pint of wine with free buffet €4. [$] Shots €3-6. Long drinks €6. Cocktails €7. ⏰ Open M-Th 3pm-2am, F-Sa 10am-2am, Su 3pm-2am. Happy hour M-F 4-8pm.

d-squared

Drinking and dining are two of Italy's most famous attractions. For all the great cuisine on offer, however, sit-down meals in Italy can equal time and money. If you're looking to save on both those fronts while indulging your stomach and liver (livers *want* alcohol, right?), the Italians are have something to help you out: the *aperitivo* happy hour. This works as follows. Anytime after 5:30pm, most places put out a buffet spread containing anything from finger food to *primi*, into which customers are free to dive after purchasing a drink. Though you don't get the service of a sit-down meal, the food is often extremely fresh and well-made, the vibe is casual, and the value unbeatable: as much food as you want and well-priced cocktails for under €10. The only thing to prevent you from loading up your plate with refill after refill is pride. After your fifth trip back to the food table in the course of two hours, you'll probably realize you don't have too much of that.

SOCIETE LUTECE

BAR

P. di Montevecchio 17 ☎06 68 30 14 72

The total opposite of an American-college-student-ridden bar, Societe Lutece attracts an artsy late 20s to early 40s crowd. Homemade bags made from recycled material hang from the ceiling, and the menu is a fabric-covered panel of wood into which prices are etched. To complete the natural feel, all food and drinks are organic or locally produced. If you're hunting for high-quality and low-stress nightlife, how could you look any further than this place's nut colada *(€8)*?

 # From P. Navona, exit and turn left onto V. Coronari; continue and make a sharp left onto V. Montevecchio. i Happy hour drinks with free buffet €8. [$] Beer €5. Wine €6. Cocktails €8. ⏰ Open Tu-Su 6pm-2am. Aperitivo 6:30-10pm.

MOOD

CLUB

C. Vittorio Emanuele 205 ☎06 32 90 64 22 40

It may be painted entirely silver, but it meets the golden standard as far as Roman discos go. Room after room in Mood's cavernous downstairs lets guests choose between lounging or dancing. But with the stereo blaring Top 40 early on and drinks flowing generously (student specials abound), most people will be up on the floor by the time 1am rolls around. Because it's downstairs, the Centro Storico's 2am norm for closing may as well not exist.

 # Near Campo dei Fiori. i Americans get in free. 2 drinks for €10 or open bar €15 until 1am. €2 shots for ladies. Student specials; show ID. [$] Cocktails €10. ⏰ Open daily 11pm-4am.

FLUID
♥⊛🌿❄ BAR, CLUB

V. del Governo Vecchio 46
☎06 68 32 361 ■www.fluideventi.com

Fluid seems to be working a "natural" theme—though the fake tree branches, caged rocks, and faux ice cube stools don't exactly scream "crunchy granola." With a lounge early in the evening and an upbeat DJ set later in the night, this is the place to come for post-dinner drinks and company. The drink menu, which is essentially a book of cocktails, features unorthodox mixes, like the cinnamon red: a smoothie of *cannella rossa* liqueur, yogurt, *crema di limone*, and whipped cream (€7.50).

✵ *From P. Navona, exit onto P. Pasquina and continue as it becomes V. del Governo Vecchio.* ⓘ *DJ nightly. Aperitivo buffet €7.50.* Ⓢ *Beer €5-6. Cocktails €7.50.* Ⓩ *Open daily 6pm-2am. Aperitivo 6-10pm.*

ARISTOCAMPO
♥占🌿⚄ BAR, RESTAURANT

P. Campo dei Fiori

On the doorstep of Campo dei Fiori, this fast-paced bar gets crowded early thanks to its better-than-average *aperitivo* buffet. Pumping music pulses from the small bar inside, but most of the action is on the patio where nearly every stool is occupied. Great panini—good for carni-, herbi-, and omnivores—satisfies those late night cravings wrought by yet another cocktail.

✵ *In Campo dei Fiori.* ⓘ *Aperitivo €5.* Ⓢ *Beer €5-6. Cocktails €7. Panini €4-5. Salads €8.* Ⓩ *Open daily noon-2am. Aperitivo 6-8pm.*

ANIMA
♥⊛🌿❄ CLUB, BAR

V. di Santa Maria dell'Anima 57

Anima's copper entrance leads into a dim lounge, complete with black lights, low couches, and two bars. Lounge music plays in the early evening as a mixed crowd of students and 20-somethings wander in. Starting around midnight, the dance floor heats up with house and commercial tunes spinning until the wee hours. Head up the tiny spiral staircase if you want to step off the floor and people-watch from above.

✵ *From P. Navona, turn left onto V. di Santa Maria della'Anima.* ⓘ *Ladies' night 2-for-1 drinks on M. Open bar Th and Su. Happy hour beer €2.50, cocktails €4.50.* Ⓢ *Beer €4-5. Cocktails €6, €10 after midnight.* Ⓩ *Open daily 7pm-4am. Happy hour 7-10pm.*

Piazza Di Spagna

There's a reason the Spanish Steps are so popular at night, and it's not their beauty (though that's a definite perk). Young travelers seeking nightlife in this neighborhood would rather lounge on the steps than pay €15 for drinks and light music at a lounge nearby. There's no reason to stay in this neighborhood for a night out, unless you like walking down empty streets of closed boutiques or rubbing shoulders with business-men and the residents of five-star hotels.

ANTICA ENOTECA DI V. DELLA CROCE
♥占🌿⚄ RESTAURANT, ENOTECA

V. della Croce 76b
☎06 67 90 896

Escape the pretentiousness of the surrounding snazzy bars and head to this old-fashioned *enoteca* for a drink and a meal. The airy feel set by tall ceilings and rustic arches is refreshing compared to nearby places. A plate of homemade pasta with duck sauce and a glass of wine will cost you less than €15 and can be enjoyed in comfort at the long bar or a small side table. Unfortunately, there's no happy hour, but that just means you can enjoy €5 draft pints at 3pm.

✵ Ⓜ*A: Spagna. From the Spanish Steps, walk down V. della Croce.* Ⓢ *Wine €4-10 per glass (also available by the bottle). Beer €5. Cocktails €8. Primi €8-9; secondi €12-16.* Ⓩ *Open daily 11am-1am.*

GILDA 🍷⊗🍸❄ CLUB

V. Mario dè Fiori 97 ☎06 67 84 838 🖥www.gildabar.it

We don't think the gold walls and chichi leather couches are a coincidence—dress sharply and prepare to schmooze with Rome's elite (or those with aspirations). One of the city's most famous discos, this upscale spot caters to an exclusive crowd wanting only the best cocktails and music. Pay for a table or rent a private room while you sip that martini and wait for the dance floor to fill up with stylishly-clad clubbers. Colored lights, multiple stereos, and ceilings rivaling St. Peter's in height don't disappoint. Our advice: if you make it here, just forget that "budget" thing and resign yourself to weeping in the morning.

 # [M]A: Spagna. From the Spanish Steps, walk down V. Condotti and turn left onto V. Mario de Fiori. ℹ *Disco open Sept-mid-June; moves to the beach at Ostia during the summer. Happy hour buffet with drink €8.* $ *€20-30 for a table, includes 1 drink. Cocktails €15.* ⏰ *Disco open Sept-June Th-Su midnight-4am. Restaurant open daily from noon. Happy hour 5-9pm.*

Trastevere

Trastevere is home to some of the best nightlife in the city—student and otherwise. Whether you want a small bar, a classy lounge, or somewhere where you can move around a bit, make the trek over the river and get ready for a late night.

FRENI E FRIZIONI 🍷♿🍸☀ LOUNGE, BAR

V. del Politeama 4-6 ☎06 45 49 74 99 🖥www.freniefrizioni.com

To find this place, don't look for a street number: turn your head skyward until you spy a jam-packed bar. Located just up the stairs off Via del Politeama, Freni e Frizioni has essentially created its own *piazza*. (And you thought only high Roman authorities could do that.) The white interior, decorated with art work and bookshelves, feels more like a living room than a lounge. The extensive bar is only a precursor to the *aperitivo* room in back—a dining table to rival that of the Last Supper's, constantly replenished with fresh entrees served directly from the pots they were cooked in, awaits you.

 # From P. Trilussa, head down the tiny V. del Politeama and look for the steps on the left. $ *Wine €6. Cocktails €7-8. Aperitivo buffet €6-10.* ⏰ *Open daily 6:30pm-2am. Aperitivo 6:30-10:30pm.*

CAFE FRIENDS 🍷♿📶🍸☀ CAFE, BAR, CLUB

P. Trilussa 34 ☎06 58 16 111 🖥www.cafefriends.it

Like good friends (well, even mere acquaintances) should, the servers here know your name. Locals and international students alike crowd this hip cafe-lounge at all hours of the day. Fully decked out with a swanky silver bar, stylish cartooned walls, and spatious indoor and patio seating, Cafe Friends caters to more American tastes: a full breakfast is served daily 8:30am-12:30pm. But abandon those early-morning ways for the more typically Italian *aperitivo* mixed-drink buffet, served nightly 7-10pm *(€6-8)*, which draws the biggest crowd. The special Friends drinks, like the "Zombie" *(rum, Jamaicano, cherry brandy, orange juice, and lime; €6.50)* will keep you going to music that blasts all the way into the early evening.

 # From Ponte Sisto, head into P. Trilussa. $ *Beer €3.50-5. Martinis €7. Cocktails €8. 15% discount for international students with ID.* ⏰ *Open M-Sa 7am-2am, Su 6:30pm-2am.*

PEPATO 🍷♿🍸☀ BAR, LOUNGE

V. del Politeama 8 ☎06 58 33 52 54

Follow the illuminated red Pepato sign into this dim haven of drinks and music, where predominantly black decor sets a sophisticated vibe. Sleek black stools line the silver bar where young staff serve Pepato specials like the "Royal," a powerful mix of Absolut Peppar, peach vodka, and champagne *(€7)*. Although there are plenty of couches and tucked-away corners for sitting, rock and house tunes blaring on the stereo will probably have you moving before the night is out. The wooden patio outside offers some reprieve from the pulsing interior, reminding you that you are on a historic, cobblestone street in a good ol' Catholic city.

✦ *From Ponte Sisto, turn left onto Lungotevere Raffaello Sanzio; head down the stairs in the piazza on the right, and make a left.* Ⓢ *Shots €3. Beer €4-7. Wine €5-7. Cocktails €6. Aperitivo buffet €10.* Ⓞ *Open Tu-Su 6:30pm-1am. Aperitivo 6:30-10pm.*

GOOD CAFFE

✦♿ (♥) ♀ ☕ CAFE, BAR

V. di San Dorotea 8/9 ☎06 97 27 79 79 ▣ www.goodcaffe.it

Alcohol really finds a home here—a refrigerator full of white wine, a bookshelf full of red, and an armoire of liquor make the place especially homey. Of course, the twinkling lights, colorful chandeliers, and festive red walls don't take away from the comfy feel. Most customers come for casual conversation over drinks, but live jazz and blues M and Th and a DJ F-Sa make Good Caffe a better-than-good place to check out any night.

✦ *From P. San G. de Matha, take V. di San Dorotea as it veers left.* *i* *Free Wi-Fi.* Ⓢ *Beer on tap €4.50-7. Cocktails €8. Aperitivo buffet with wine €5, with cocktail €8.* Ⓞ *Open daily 8am-2am. Aperitivo 7-9pm.*

BEIGE

✦♿ ♀ ❄ BAR, LOUNGE

V. Politeama 13-14 ☎06 58 33 06 86 ▣ www.beigeroma.com

Somehow swanky black and white decor equals... Beige? Distinguishing itself from some of the more low-key establishments nearby with its plush stools, modern black arches, and dark green lounge, Beige caters to a sophisticated crowd all evening long. Its 12 page menu, organized solely into pre- and post-dinner beverages, gives a drink to match nearly every hour until 2am. Mellow music and plenty of seats.

✦ *From Ponte Sisto, turn left onto Lungotevere Raffaello Sanzio, head down the stairs in the piazza on the right, and make a left.* Ⓢ *Cocktails €8.* Ⓞ *Open Tu-Su 7:30pm-2am. Aperitivo 7:30-10:30pm.*

Termini and Northeast Rome

There are plenty of bars surrounding Termini, most of them close to hostels and thus especially popular with students. If staying out late, travel with a group and watch your purse. Stay away from the station as much as possible. If you want to venture slightly further north, **Via Nomentana** and its surrounding streets are also home to plenty of good bars.

▨ BOEME

✦⊗ ♀ ❄ CLUB

V. Velletri 13 ☎06 84 12 212 ▣ www.boeme.it

An expansive downstairs disco lined entirely in black and white stripes and funky flowered wallpaper brings in a happening crowd on the weekends. Multiple platforms for dancing, flashing lights, a sound system blaring house and Top 40 hits, a huge bar, and neon accents create a psychedelic experience for partiers willing to drop a few euros.

✦ *From P. Fiume, walk up V. Nizza and turn left onto V. Velletri.* Ⓢ *Cover €15-20; includes 1st drink. Drinks €10.* Ⓞ *Open F-Sa 11pm-5am.*

AI TRE SCALINI

✦⊗(♥) ♀ CAFE, ENOTECA

V. Panisperna 251 ☎06 48 90 74 95

Look down V. Panisperna and you'll see two things: a hanging curtain of vines and a crowd of people. The *sorridenti* customers at this socially-conscious *enoteca* and cafe often spill out onto the street, wine glass in hand. Inside, the giant blackboard menu features only locally grown and seasonally harvested products hailing from Lazio. The beverage selection is just as sustainable, including organic and hand-cultivated wines (the Sangiovese was made by prison inmates); the restaurant also refuses to sell bottled mineral water. Blues in the background, frescoed walls, tiny tables, and dim lights make this the perfect spot for casual conversation, a game of chess (check out their antique set), or some Roman history catch-up (their mini bookshelf should help).

rome · nightlife

From the intersection of V. XIV Maggio and V. Nazionale (near Trajan's column), walk up V. Panisperna. *i* Free Wi-Fi. 10% discount at lunch hours. Ⓢ Beer on tap €3-5. Wine €3.50-6 per glass, €11-70/bottle. Sfizi (bite-sized appetizers) €2.50-3; primi €3-8. Ⓩ Open M-F noon-1am, Sa-Su 6pm-1am. Aperitivo 6-9pm.

YELLOW BAR
◆♣&♥⚏ CAFE, BAR

V. Palestro 40 ☎06 49 38 26 82 🖳www.the-yellow.com

Feeling a bit homesick for college, or perhaps just your home country? Whatever locale you have a hankering for, the international folks at Yellow Bar are sure to cure your case of the blues. Next door to its hopping hostel, this bar caters to a mixed crowd of travelers and students who come for cheap drinks, relaxed music, and good company. Order one of their special cocktails like the 🚫**Chuck Norris Roundhouse Kick to the Face Crazy Shot** (don't ask what's in it...just drink up) before heading downstairs to the beer pong room, fully equipped with two regulation-size tables and an official list of house rules.

✦ Ⓜ*Termini. From V. Marsala, near track 1, walk down V. Marghera and then turn left onto V. Palestro.* *i* *Pub quiz on W €5. Open bar on F €15.* Ⓢ *Cocktails €8. Beer pong pitchers €14.50. Happy hour spirits €2.50; wine €1.50.* Ⓩ *Open daily 7:30am-2am. Kitchen open 7:30am-noon. Happy hour 3-9pm.*

TWINS
◆⊗✗♥❉ BAR, CLUB

V. Giolitti 67 ☎06 48 24 932 🖳www.twinbar.com

Flashing lights, loud music, and red walls set a lively stage for the international crowd that packs Twins every night. Located just outside of Termini's station, this club is as busy as the street outside. The front bars cater to those seeking more of a lounge, while the back room and its private outdoor courtyard pack it in with loud beats and dancing. Though it's easy to get carried away here, keep your wits about you and your wallet close to your body—Termini's station is known for pickpockets.

✦ Ⓜ*Termini. Right outside the station.* Ⓢ *Beer €3.50-5. Cocktails €8. Primi €7-13; secondi €12-23.* Ⓩ *Open daily 6am-2am. Happy hour 5-7pm.*

DRUID'S DEN
◆♣&♥⚏ IRISH PUB

V. San Martino ai Monti 28 ☎06 48 90 4781 🖳www.druidspubrome.com

Wait, we're in Italy? You'd never know it in this green-lit Irish pub, the second oldest in the country. The brick walls are lined with memorabilia from the owner's frequent trips back home, an assortment ranging from flags to wooden place-name placards. Popular mostly with Italians and expats in the neighborhood, this is the place to come for quality drinks against a backdrop of national soccer games or traditional live Irish music, depending on the night.

✦ Ⓜ*B: Cavour. Walk down V. Giovanni and veer left onto V. San Martino ai Monti.* *i* *Live music F-Sa around 10pm.* Ⓢ *Special whiskeys €4-5. Cocktails €4.50. Drafts €5.50.* Ⓩ *Open daily 5pm-2am. Happy hour 5-8:30pm.*

L'ISOLA CHE NON C'È
◆♣(((•)))♥⚏ LIBRERIA

V. San Martino ai Monti 7/A ☎06 48 82 134

Lavender walls and a sleek wooden catwalk lined with books and bottles make up the little *isola* that, according to its name, "is not here." (Maybe that's because it's a paradise?) Books are only a starting point for discussion, an excuse for intellectual folk to gather over good wine and food. Occasional lectures on environmental concerns and live music on select nights provide other reasons to pop by this place and see what's going on. While classically Italian in its low-key style, Isola's tiny menu is a bit spunkier, with specials like smoked swordfish and pineapple or vegetarian delights like tabbouleh with zucchini.

✦ Ⓜ*B: Cavour. Walk down V. Giovanni and veer left onto V. San Martino ai Monti.* *i* *Free Wi-Fi. Live music most Th and Sa. Free buffet with purchase of a drink.* Ⓢ *Wine and beer €3-5. Cocktails €4-8. Primi €7-11.* Ⓩ *Open M-Th 11am-midnight, F-Sa 11am-2am.*

Testaccio, Ostiense, and Southern Rome

Off Rome's central map, Testaccio and Ostiense cater to in-the-know partygoers: locals who've sought out the best clubs and the savvy tourists or students who've sought out the locals. The strip of clubs, restaurants, and lounges surrounding **Via di Monte Testaccio** begs to be explored, though as the evening rolls on longer lines make it harder to gain admission. The streets closer to the train station tend to have smaller, low-key establishments that stay open late, an option if you don't feel like heavy-duty clubbing. Too far south gets quiet, though.

👍 CONTE STACCIO — 💳🚭🍸❄⛱ BAR, CONCERT VENUE

V. di Monte Testaccio 65/b ☎06 57 28 97 12 💻www.myspace.com/contestaccio

If bumping and grinding to DJ'd music isn't your thing, then you'll probably love Conte Staccio. Live music ranging from indie rock to electro-funk draws a mixed crowd of internationals and not-so-mainstream students and locals. Two rooms—one with a stage, the other with tables for late-night nibbles—give you the option to enjoy the music from afar or rock out up close, though the smallish quarters mean that the huge stereos might blow your ears out before long, regardless of room. Head to the outdoor steps if you need a break from the music, but chances are the crowd outside will be just as packed.

✢ ⓂB: Piramide. Walk up V. Marmorata towards the river, turn left onto V. Galvani ,and veer left onto V. di Monte Testaccio. $ Beer €2.50-5. Wine €3-5. Cocktails €6-7. Primi €8; secondi €10. ⏰ Open daily 8pm-5am. Restaurant 8pm-3am. Music 11pm-5am.

👍 AKAB — 💳♿🍸❄⛱ CLUB

V. di Monte Testaccio 69 ☎06 57 25 05 85 💻www.akabcave.com

It's hard to tell what's inside and what's out at Akab, where the switch is so subtle that you don't know if your feeling is a cool summer breeze or some powerful A/C. During the summer most of the action starts in the central room, as live bands warm up the crowd and customers load up at the blue-lit bar staffed by buff bartenders. When the DJ starts, head back to room after room of dimly lit lounges and dance halls that, with ramps and flashing lights galore, feel somewhat like a psychedelic amusement park for adults. During the winter, the neon-colored upstairs lounge opens to accommodate the crowds. Though the cover and drinks cost a pretty penny, you'll be paying for one of Testaccio's hottest clubs and crowds.

✢ ⓂB: Piramide. Walk up V. Marmorata towards the river, turn left onto V. Galvani, and veer left onto V. di Monte Testaccio. ℹ Beer €5 on Tu. Electronic on Tu. House on Th. Rock on F. Commercial and house on Sa. $ Cover €10-20 on F-Sa includes 1 drink, free some other nights. Cocktails and beer €10. ⏰ Open Tu 11:30pm-4:30am, Th-Sa 11:30pm-4:30am.

COYOTE — 💳🚭🍸⛱ BAR, CLUB

V. di Monte Testaccio 48/B ☎340 24 45 874 💻www.coyotebar.it

Cowboys might ride off into the sinking western sun; but night visitors at Coyote will wander home as the sun rises in the east. Get here early to avoid Colosseum-sized lines and an entrance fee to match. Once inside, ascend the curving ramp to a huge outdoor patio where beer flows generously under green and red lights. Once the clock strikes midnight, what started out as a casual cocktail bar becomes a full-fledged disco spinning house, Latin, and Top 40 tunes. The wooden floors give the place an extra bounce as the stereo cranks up and the crowds begin to move. If you're sober enough before leaving, check out the trail of American license plates lining the wall—last time we checked, the eastern seaboard was heavily outweighed by the wild west and the sultry south. New Yorkers, donate a plate, please?

✢ ⓂB: Piramide. Walk up V. Marmorata toward the river, turn left onto V. Galvani, and veer left onto V. di Monte Testaccio. ℹ No food—hit **Top 5** *(see below) downstairs if you get hungry. $ Cover €10 F-Sa after midnight. Beer and wine €5. Cocktails €8. ⏰ Open daily 9pm-5am. Bar 9pm-midnight. Disco midnight-5am.*

ON THE ROX 🚬♿🍸 BAR

V. Galvani 54 ☎06 45 49 29 75

The lively crowd that frequents this huge lounge still "rox" out big time, even if the place isn't technically a club. Rustic arches offset by twinkling chandeliers give the place a spunky vibe that matches its nightly mix of students and locals. Pop music plays in the background, but the real buzz comes from conversation and the cheers of customers watching sports on the flatscreen TVs. With great nightly specials, even Tu becomes an ideal day for a night out.

➡ [M]B: Piramide. Walk up V. Marmorata toward the river and turn left onto V. Galvani. ℹ Pitcher night on M, €10. Buy 1 get 1 free on W. Ladies' night 2-for-1 cocktails on Th. Live music 4 nights per week in the winter. Student special long drinks €5. Happy hour buffet €7. $ Shots €2.50. Beer €4. Cocktails €6. Food €6-8. ⏰ Open M-W 6pm-4am, Th-Su 6pm-5am. Happy hour daily 6-10pm.

LA CASA DELLA PACE 🚭🚫🍸🎵 CULTURAL CENTER, CONCERT VENUE

V. di Monte Testaccio 22 ☎329 54 66 296 💻www.myspace.com/bigbang

More than a nightlife haven for artsy and intellectual folks, this "House of Peace" holds multicultural events, art exhibitions, and live music performances throughout the year. In the evening, join a truly mixed crowd on any of the floors as live music ranging from reggae to electro-funk plays on the stripped-wood dance floor. Multiple adjoining rooms, including the upstairs gallery space, slowly fill up with beer sippers, conversationalists, performers, and artists. Drop by F or Sa for La Casa's "Big Bang" nights or check online for a schedule of upcoming events. Be sure to try out the ✪**mosaic-tiled bathroom,** which rivals some of Rome's greatest—bathrooms, that is.

➡ [M]B: Piramide. Walk up V. Marmorata towards the river, turn left onto V. Galvani, and veer left onto V. di Monte Testaccio. ℹ €7 membership card required to enter; buy at the desk and reuse for all events. $ Shots €2.50. Beer €2.50-4. Cocktails €6. ⏰ Open M-Th 3-10pm, F-Sa 10pm-5am, Su 3-10pm.

CARUSO 🚬🚫🍸❄ CLUB, LATIN

V. di Monte Testaccio 36 ☎06 57 45 019 💻www.carusocafe.com

Move your hips to merengue rather than the same old pop mix. The distinctive orange glow in this club's cluster of dance rooms will warm you up for dancing; cool (though slightly pricey) drinks and strong A/C will cool you down when things get too hot. Plenty of tables and padded chairs sit beside rather random Buddha sculptures, so take this opportunity to lounge next to the big enlightened guy. Live bands take the small stage when the DJ steps down.

➡ [M]B: Piramide. Walk up V. Marmorata toward the river, turn left onto V. Galvani, and veer left onto V. di Monte Testaccio. ℹ Live and DJ'd Latin music. $ Cover Su-Th €8, F-Sa €10; includes 1st drink. Beer €6. Cocktails €6-11. ⏰ Open M-Th 11pm-2am, F-Sa 11pm-4am, Su 11pm-2am.

ARTS AND CULTURE

"Arts and culture?" you ask. "Isn't that Rome, *itself?*" Psshh. Well, yes, Renaissance paintings, archaeological ruins, and Catholic churches do count. But aside from these antiquated lures, Rome offers an entertainment scene that makes it much more than a city of yore. Soccer games might not quite compare to man-fights-lion spectacles, but with hundreds of screaming Italians around, it comes close. If you need more ideas, check Rome's city website (*💻www.060608.it*) for a schedule of upcoming events ranging from live music to festivals. Other good resources are *Roma C'è* (*💻www.romace.it*) and 💻www.aguestinrome.com. Or just wander the streets scouting out advertisements and flyers, which are nearly as common as ruins. In Rome, it's definitely possible to experience "arts and culture" in places where an alarm won't go off when you get too close.

Jazz

Unfortunately, most jazz places close during the summer months, either re-opening in September or heading outdoors. For a current schedule of other jazz events check out █www.romace.it, █www.romajazz.com, or █www.casajazz.it.

█ FONCLEA ✎⊗🍸 VATICAN CITY

V. Crescenzio 82A ☎06 68 96 302 █www.fonclea.it

Crowds linger on the street and trickle down the steps into this den of live jazz and food. Amid hanging skis and teapots, nightly performers pay homage to anything from swing to The Beatles. Munch on chips and guacamole during the *aperitivo* hour while trumpeters and saxophonists warm up their lips. Drinks and food are a bit overpriced, but with music this good, who's thinking of eating?

✦ ⓂA: Ottaviano. From P. Risorgimento, head away from the Vatican on V. Cresenzio. Ⓢ Cover F-Sa €6. Beer €7. Cocktails €10. ⏰ Open from mid-Sept to mid-June M-Th 7pm-2am, F-Sa 7pm-3am, Su 7pm-2am. Music at 9:30pm. Aperitivo hour 7-8:30pm.

BIG MAMA ✦👌🍸 TRASTEVERE

Vicolo San Francesco a Ripa 18 ☎06 58 12 551 █www.bigmama.it

She's not just a "Mama"—when it comes to the blues, she's a *big* mama. Nightly concerts by jazz and blues performers.

✦ Bus #75 or 170 or tram #8. From P. Garibaldi, walk down Vle. Trastevere, turn left onto V. San Francesco a Ripa, and veer right onto the tiny vicolo. Ⓢ Year-long membership card (€14) or monthly card (€8) grants free admission to most shows. A few big shows require an additional ticket fee. ⏰ Open daily from late Sept to late May 9pm-1:30am. Music at 10:30pm.

Classical Music and Opera

TEATRO DELL'OPERA ✦👌 TERMINI

P. Beniamino Gigli 7 ☎06 48 16 02 55 █www.operaroma.it

Once you've caught a glimpse of the 6m chandelier and frescoes by **Annibale Brugnoli** gracing this four-tier theater, you'll be happy you shelled out the extra euro even if opera and ballet aren't your thing. From July to early fall, additional performances are held outdoors at the **Baths of Caracalla** (*Terme di Caracalla*).

✦ ⓂA: Repubblica. Walk down V. Nazionale, then turn left onto V. Firenze and left onto V. del Viminale. Ⓢ Opera €17-130, ballet €11-65; students and over 65 receive 25% discount. Check website for last-minute tickets with 25% discount. ⏰ Regular box office open Tu-Sa 9am-5pm, Su 9am-1:30pm, and 1hr. before performance until 15min. after its start. Box office for Baths of Caracalla open Tu-Sa 10am-4pm, Su 9am-1:30pm.

ACCADEMIA NAZIONALE DI SANTA CECILIA ✦ NORTHEAST ROME

Vle. Pietro de Coubertin 30 ☎06 808 2058; ☎06 89 29 82 for tickets █www.santacecilia.it

Founded in 1585 as a conservatory, the Accademia is now both a place of training for aspiring and renowned musicians and a professional symphonic orchestra. Past conductors have included **Debussy, Strauss, Stravinsky,** and **Toscanini.**.

✦ ⓂA: Flaminio and then tram #2 to P. Euclide. Or take the special line "M" from Termini (every 15min. starting at 5pm) to Auditorium. Last bus after last performance. ⓘ Box office at Largo Luciano Berio 3. Ⓢ Tickets €18-47. ⏰ Box office open daily 11am-8pm.

Spectator Sports

STADIO OLIMPICO 👌 OUTSKIRTS

V. del Foro Italico 1 █www.asroma.it, www.sslazio.it

Soccer matches—the favorite game of the Romans since their gladiator days—are held here. The stadium serves as the battleground for **A.S. Roma** and **S.S. Lazio.** The easiest way to tell them apart is by color (red and sky blue, respectively). Tickets aren't easy to come by: check the spots below or ask around.

✦ ⓂA: Ottaviano. Then take bus #32 to Piazzale della Farnesina. ⓘ Tickets can be purchased at the stadium, online at sites like █www.listicket.it, or at various ticketing spots around the city such

as Lazio Point (V. Farini 34/36 ☎06 48 26 688). ⓢ Tickets €20-80. ◵ Most matches Sept-May
Su afternoons. Lazio Point box office open daily 9pm-1am and 2:30-6pm.

SHOPPING

When it comes to shopping, it would be significantly easier to make a list of what
Rome *doesn't* have than what it does. Fashionista, artista, or "intelligista," you won't
leave Rome unsatisfied, though your pocketbook might be significantly lighter.
European chains like United Colors of Benetton, Tezenis, Motivi, and even H and
M speckle the city. Those with a taste for high fashion should head to the **Piazza di
Spagna** region, Rome's equivalent of Fifth Ave., which is home to the regular gamut
of designer stores. Smaller (though no less costly) boutiques dominate the Centro
Storico. Major thoroughfares like **Via del Corso, Via Cavour, Via Nazionale,** and **Via Cola di
Rienzo** abound with cheap clothing stores touting a similar collection of tight, teeny-
bopper glitz and fare that comes unattached to a brand name. The regions around
Termini, Vle. Trastevere, and the **Vatican** contain a fair number of street vendors selling
shoes, lingerie, dresses, and sunglasses, usually for under €15, though established
open-air markets will have a bigger selection.

Outdoor Markets

One of the few things that tourists and locals appreciate with equal enthusiasm are
Rome's outdoor markets. You can find real bargains if you're willing to rifle through the
crowds and stacks. With early hours on both their opening and closing ends, make sure
you set that alarm. It's best to stick to official markets rather than take on merchants
who set up shop individually. The fine for buying fake designer products rests on the
buyer, not the seller, and can reach into the hundreds of thousands of euro.

spagna stores

It's not Milan. It's not Paris. It's Rome—and that's no small thing. The area around
Piazza di Spagna has all the glitz you might want—ice-cold stores with ice-cold staff
hovering about making sure you don't paw through their precious items. You'd think
you were in another museum or something. Here's where to find the priciest and
snobbiest of stores:

- **DOLCE AND GABBANA.** *(P. di Spagna 94 ☎06 69 38 08 70 ▇www.
  dolcegabbana.it ◵ Open M-Sa 10:30am-7:30pm, Su 10:30am-2:30pm
  and 3:30-7:30pm.)*

- **EMPORIO ARMANI.** *(V. del Babuino 140 ☎06 32 21 581 ▇www.
  giorgioarmani.com ◵ Open M-Sa 10am-7pm.)*

- **GUCCI.** *(V. Condotti 8 ☎06 679 0405 ▇www.gucci.com ◵ Open M-Sa
  10am-7:30pm, Su 10am-7pm.)*

- **PRADA.** *(V. Condotti 92/95 ☎06 679 0897 ▇www.prada.com ◵ Open
  M-F 10am-7:30pm, Sa 10am-8pm, Su 10am-7:30pm.)*

- **VALENTINO.** *(V. del Babuino 61 and V. dei Condotti 15 ☎06 36 00 19 06
  and ☎06 67 39 420 ▇www.valentino.com ◵ Open daily 10am-7pm.)*

- **VERSACE.** *(V. Bocca di Leone 26/27 ☎06 67 80 521 ▇www.versace.com
  ◵ Open M-Sa 10am-7pm, Su 2pm-7pm.)*

italy

PORTA PORTESE

⊕& TRASTEVERE

From P. di Porta Portese to P. Ippolito Nievo
🖳www.portaportesemarket.it

The legs of this U-shaped market seem to extend forever and are of markedly different qualities. The longer V. Portuense is occupied by clones—vendors selling the same selection of cheap garments, toiletries, furniture, plastic jewelry, and shoes. We're talking 2m stacks of €2 clothes. If you're not exhausted by the madhouse (reminiscent of the hustling crowds of the Vatican Museums), make it to the antiques section where cooler treasures reside: old comic books, records, jewelry, and furniture.

🚌 Bus #40 to Largo Argentina and tram #8. 🕘 Open Su 7am-2:30pm.

VAN SANNIO MARKET

⊕& SOUTHERN ROME

V. Sannio
☎06 06 08

Cheap doesn't have to mean mass-produced and homogenous. Head here early to be the first of many to dig through mostly used clothes and items. A refreshing change from the ubiquitous street merchants spattering Rome, this large market is the outdoor equivalent of a New York thrift store. Hipsters rejoice.

🚌 ⓂA: San Giovanni. 🕘 Open M-Sa 9am-1:30pm.

CAMPO DEI FIORI

⊕& CENTRO STORICO

Campo dei Fiori

Thank God there's a place to buy fresh fruit and vegetables in the middle of overpriced trattorias: the lively Campo makes a great lunch spot if you don't mind the crowds. Giving as much flavor to the *piazza* during the day as bars give it at night, the market's open stalls vend cheap clothing, produce, fish, and even alcohol—no need to head to San Marino to pick up some absinthe.

🚌 Bus #116 or tram #8. 🕘 Open M-Sa 7am-2:30pm.

MERCATO DELLE STAMPE

⊕& PIAZZA DI SPAGNA

Largo della Fontanella di Borghese

The small *piazza* and academic assortment of goods keep this market more manageable than most others in Rome—after all, how rowdy can a crowd get around a stack of books? Older crowds weave through the stalls, where you can find a curious selection of used books, old prints, and other dusty articles.

🚌 Bus #224 or 913 to P. Imperatore or bus #492, 116, or 81. 🕘 Open M-Sa 9:30am-6pm.

ESSENTIALS

Practicalities

- **TOURIST OFFICES: Comune di Roma** is Rome's official source for tourist information. Green **P.I.T. Info booths** are located throughout the city around most major sights. English-speaking staff provide limited information on hotel accommodations and events around the city, though plenty of free brochures and a city map are available. The booths also sell bus and Metro maps and the **Roma Pass** *(PIT booth locations include V. Giovanni Giolitti 34 in Termini, P. Sidney Sonnino in Trastevere, and V. dei Fori Imperiali ☎06 06 08 for main info center; check online for individual booth numbers 🖳www.turismoroma.it, 🖳www.060608.com 🕘 Most locations open daily 9:30am-7pm; Termini location open 8am-8:30pm.)*

- **CURRENCY EXCHANGE: Money exchange** services are especially abundant near Termini and major sights but tend to have high rates. **Western Unions** are also readily available. *(🕘 Most banks open M-F 8:30am-1:30pm and 2:30-5pm.)*

- **LUGGAGE STORAGE: Termini Luggage Deposit.** *(☎06 47 44 777 🖳www.grandistazioni.it 🚌 In Termini, below Track 24 in the Ala Termini wing. 𝒊 Takes bags of up to 20kg each for 5 days max. Cash only. 💲 €4 for 1st 5hr., €0.60 per hr. for 6th-12th hr., €0.20 per hr. thereafter. 🕘 Open daily 6am-11:50pm.)*

- **LOST PROPERTY: La Polizia Municipale** holds property a few days after it is lost; check the closest branch to where you lost your item. After that point, all lost property is sent to **Oggetti Smarriti,** run by the Comune di Roma. To retrieve an item, you must present a valid form of ID, a statement describing the lost item, and a cash payment of €2.97. *(Circonvallazione Ostiense 191 ☎06 67 69 3214 ▪www.060608. it or email oggettismarriti@comune.roma.it with questions ✚ Ⓜ️B: Piramide or Ⓜ️B: Garbatella. ☼ Open M 8:30am-1pm, Tu 8:30am-1pm and 3-5pm, W 8:30am-1pm, Th 8:30am-5pm, F 8:30am-1pm.)*

- **GLBT RESOURCES:** The Comune di Roma publishes a free guide to gay life in Rome, *AZ Gay,* with listings for gay-friendly restaurants, hotels, clubs, and bars. Pick one up at any P.I.T. Point. **ARCI-GAY** is a resource for homosexuality awareness, offering free courses, medical, legal, and psychological counseling, and advice on gay-friendly establishments in the city. *(V. Zabaglia 14 ☎06 64 50 11 02; ☎800 71 37 13 for helpline ▪www.arcigayroma.it ✚ Ⓜ️B: Piramide. Walk up V. Marmorata and turn right onto V. Alessandro Volta; it's at the intersection with V. Zabaglia. i ARCI-GAY cards allow access to all events and services run by the program throughout Italy; €15 (valid 1 year). ☼ Open M-Sa 4-8pm. Helpline open M 4-8pm, W-Th 4-8pm, Sa 4-8pm. Welcome Groups Th 6:15-9pm, Young People Groups F 6:30-9pm.)*

Emergency!

- **POLICE: Police Headquarters.** *(V. San Vitale 15 ☎06 46 86 ✚ Ⓜ️A: Repubblica.)* **Carabinieri** have offices at V. Mentana 6 *(☎06 58 59 62 00 ✚ Near Termini.)* and P. Venezia *(☎06 67 58 28 00).* **City Police** *(P. del Collegio Romano 3 ☎06 69 01 21).*

- **CRISIS LINES: Rape Crisis Line: Centro Anti-Violenza** provides legal, psychological, and medical counseling for women of all nationalities. *(V. di Torre Spaccata 157, V. di Villa Pamphili 100 ☎06 23 26 90 49; ☎06 58 10 926 ▪www.differenzadonna. it ☎ Phone lines open 24hr.)* **Samaritans** provides psychological counseling on the phone in many languages; call for in-person guidance. *(☎800 86 00 22 ▪www. samaritansonlus.org ☼ Line operating daily 1-10pm.)*

- **LATE-NIGHT PHARMACIES: Farmacia della Stazione** is by Termini Station. *(P. dei Cinquecento 49/51 ☎06 48 80 019 ☼ Open 24hr.)* **Farmacia Internazionale** is toward the Centro Storico. *(P. Barberini 49 ☎06 48 25 456 ✚ Ⓜ️A: Barberini. ☼ Open 24hr.)* **Farmacia Doricchi** is toward the Villa Borghese. *(V. XX Settembre 47 ☎06 48 73 880 ☼ Open 24hr.)* **Brienza** is near the Vatican City. *(P. del Risorgimento 44 ☎06 39 73 81 86 ☼ Open 24hr.)*

- **HOSPITALS/MEDICAL SERVICES: Policlinico Umberto I** is Rome's largest public hospital. *(Vle. del Policlinico 155 ☎06 44 62 341 ▪www.policlinicoumberto1.it ✚ Ⓜ️B: Policlinico or bus #649 to Policlinico. Ⓢ Emergency treatment free. Non-emergencies €25-50. ☼ Open 24hr.)*

Getting There

By Plane

DA VINCI INTERNATIONAL AIRPORT (FIUMICINO; FCO)

30km southwest of the city   ☎06 65 951

Commonly known as Fiumicino, Da Vinci International Airport oversees most international flights. If you're arriving in Rome from a different continent, you'll almost certainly land here, as it's serviced by most carriers. To get from the airport—which is located right on the Mediterranean coast—to central Rome, take the **Leonardo Express** train to **Termini Station.** After leaving customs, follow signs to the **Stazione Trenitalia/Railway Station,** where you can buy a train ticket at an automated machine or from the ticket office. *(Ⓢ €14. ☼ 32min., every 30min. 6:47am-11:37pm.)*

ROME CIAMPINO AIRPORT (CIA)

15km southeast of the city ☎06 65 951

Ciampino is the rapidly growing airport serviced by $**budget airlines** like Ryanair and EasyJet. There are no trains connecting the airport to the city center, but various options for getting into Rome from Ciampino exist. The **SIT Bus Shuttle** *(☎06 59 23 507 🖥www.sitbusshuttle.it $ €4. ⏰ 40min., every 45-60min. 7:45am-11:15pm.)* runs from the airport to V. Marsala, outside Termini Station.

By Train

All **Trenitalia** trains run through **Termini Station,** the main transport hub in central Rome. International and overnight trains also run to Termini. City buses #C2, H, M, 36, 38, 40 64, 86, 90, 92, 105, 170, 175, 217, 310, 714, and 910 stop outside in the P. del Cinquecento.

Trains run to and from **Florence** *($ €16.10-44. ⏰ 1½ -4hr., 52 per day, 5:57am-8:15pm.),* **Venice** *($ €42.50-73.50. ⏰ 4-7hr., 17 per day, 6:45am-8pm.),* **Milan** *($ €46-89. ⏰ 3-8hr., 33 per day, 6:45am-11:04pm.),* **Naples** *($ €10.50-44. ⏰ 1-3hr., 50 per day, 4:52am-9:39pm.),* and **Bologna** *($ €36-58. ⏰ 2-4 hr., 42 per day, 6:15am-8:15pm.).*

Getting Around

Rome's public transportation system is run by **ATAC.** *(☎06 57 003 🖥www.atac.roma.it ⏰ Open M-Sa 8am-8pm.)* It consists of the **Metro, buses,** and **trams,** which service the city center and outskirts, as well as various **Ferrovie urbane** and **Ferrovie metropolitane,** which service more distant suburbs including Ostia Lido, Tivoli, Fregene, and Viterbo. Transit tickets are valid for any of these lines and can be bought at *tabacherrie* throughout the city, at some bars, and from self-service machines or ticket windows at major stations including Termini, Ostiense, and Trastevere. A **BIT** *(integrated time ticket; €1)* is valid for 1¼hr. after validation and allows unlimited bus travel plus one Metro ride within that time frame; it is generally the most economical choice. A **BIG** *(integrated daily ticket; €4)* is valid until midnight on the day of validation and allows unlimited bus and Metro use. The **BTI** *(integrated tourist ticket; €11)* grants unrestricted access for three days after validation. The **CIS** *(integrated weekly ticket; €16)* grants unrestricted access for seven days after validation. Tickets **must be validated** at Metro station turnstiles and stamping machines on buses and trams.

By Bus

The best way to get around the city other than by walking is by bus: dozens of routes service the entire city center as well as outskirts. **Bus stops** are marked by yellow poles and display a route map for all lines that pass through the stop.

By Metro

Rome's **Metro** system consists of two lines: ⓂA, which runs from Battistini to Anagnina (hitting P. di Spagna and S. Giovanni), and ⓂB, which runs from Laurentina to Rebibbida (hitting the Colosseum, Ostiense, and southern Rome); they intersect only at **Termini Station.** While the Metro is fast, it does not service many regions of the city and is better used for getting across long distances than between neighborhoods.

By Tram

Electric trams make many stops but are still an efficient means of getting around. A few useful lines include **tram #3** *(Trastevere, Piramide, Aventine, P. San Giovanni, Villa Borghese, P. Thorwaldsen),* **tram #8** *(Trastevere to Largo Argentina),* and **tram #19** *(Ottaviano, Villa Borghese, San Lorenzo, Prenestina, P. dei Gerani).*

By Bike

ATAC runs **Bikesharing** *(☎06 57 03 🖥www.bikesharing.roma.it).* Purchase a card at any ATAC ticket office. *(➡ ⓂA: Anagnina, Spagna, Lepanto, Ottaviano, Cornelia, Battistini or ⓂB: Termini, Laurentina, EUR Fermi, or Ponte Mammolo. ⏰ Open M-Sa 7am-8pm, Su 8am-8pm.)* Bikes can be parked at 19 stations around the city. Cards are rechargeable. *($ €5 initial charge, €0.50 per 30min. thereafter. ⏰ Bikes available for a max. 24hr. at a time.)*

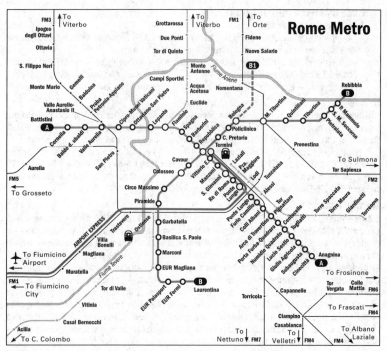

Rome Metro

By Taxi

Given the scope of Rome's bus system, taxis should only be reserved for desperate or time-sensitive affairs. Legally, you may not "hail" a cab on the street—either call **RadioTaxi** (☎06 66 45) or head to a taxi point (near most major sights) where drivers wait for customers.

milan *milano* ☎02

An intersection of fashion and finance, Milan is a city whose residents are ready to proclaim their pride in the sophisticated metropolis they call home. Italy's moral capital is the antithesis of the chaotic south. Citizens speak in a refined dialect, the government officials actually work, and even the scooters stop for red lights. Although the cost of living is high and traffic can be a nightmare, the spires of the city's intricately carved **Duomo**, the echoing notes of the renowned **La Scala** theater, and the gleaming boutiques of the **Fashion District**, where casually parallel parking a cherry-red Ferrari is no big deal, help prove the Milanese's point: this is a truly cultured town. But in addition to its role as a national and global trendsetter, Milan plays an essential part in the Italian economy, home as it is to rubber giant Pirelli and scores of banks, hedge funds, and other GDP-boosting institutions that remain mysterious to the layperson. While the city's dark-suited bankers walk its streets with a clear purpose, meandering tourists can find many artistic treasures that remain less known. Leonardo's *Last Supper*, one of the world's best-known paintings, is here, as are the collections at the **Pinoteca di Brera** and **Pinoteca Ambrosiana,** both filled with priceless Italian art dating from the Renaissance to the 20th century. And of course there's soccer, with the fanatically followed Inter and A.C. Milan. The city

italy

has everything that's to be expected from a world-class metropolis—wealth, culture, sport, and more—all carried off with that cosmopolitan, stylish élan of which the Vespa-driving, street-smart Milanese are so proud.

ORIENTATION

Piazza Del Duomo and Fashion District

Sitting in the heart of downtown *centro*, the Duomo is the geographical and spiritual center of Milan. It is also the city's tourist hub, from which many tours make their start. Consequently, this neighborhood is characterized by overpriced chain restaurants and souvenir stalls. A little to the north, the Fashion District is the home of every designer brand you're ever heard of, and ten more too. Its central location makes it all the more convenient for the Bentley chauffeurs and Ferrari-driving executives who populate the place.

Giardini Pubblici

The neighborhoods near Giardini Pubblici connect the Porta Venezia area and the public gardens themselves to Stazione Centrale. Many hotels can be founds near the station and along the main roads of **Corso Buenos Aires** and **Viale Tunisia.** The area's primary Metro station, ⓜPorta Venezia, is located on C. Buenos Aires at P. S. F. Romano, a maze of traffic and trams that can't be missed.

Castello Sforzesco

This part of Milan contains an eclectic mix of neighborhoods and attractions, ranging from a major tourist center and transportation hub to upscale apartments and the artsy neighborhood of Brera. At the center of it all is the castle, which—like the Duomo—is surrounded by hawkers toting their wares to tourists. To the west, upscale, brand-name stores; high-class residences; and da Vinci's *Last Supper* can be found on C. Magenta.

Navigli and Outskirts

While it seems at first that most of Milan's attractions are packed within the city center, many cultural heavyweights and affordable accommodations can be found farther afield. Because of Milan's extensive Metro and tram system, most outskirts are easily accessible from the *centro*. The Navigli area, in the southwest of the city, is a triangle bounded by two waterways, the Naviglio Grande to the northwest and the Naviglio Pavese to the east, though the area's many bars and restaurants spread a few blocks beyond. Northwards, **Corso Garibaldi** leads to the lively nightlife street of **Corso Como** and the vast **Cimitero Monumentale,** resting place of many Italian luminaries. Northwest of the city is the wealthy **Fiera** neighborhood, home to Milan's business expos as well as less affluent residential areas around ⓜ**Lotto** and ⓜ**QT8.** Soccer fans will swoon when they see the **San Siro** stadium complex, home to Milan's famous soccer teams. Some areas are seedy, especially near Stazione Centrale, where travelers should be careful walking alone late at night.

ACCOMMODATIONS

As you would expect in any large city, Milan's accommodations run the gamut. A few youth hostels can be found scattered around the city, and some are very conveniently located in quiet residential areas just a short Metro ride from the *centro*. A number of quality one-star hotels surround the **Giardini Pubblici** and lie to the southeast of Porta Venezia as well as along **Via Giorgio Washington.** International chains are clustered closer to the city center, where budget accommodations can be hard to come by.

Piazza Del Duomo and Fashion District

Checkbooks out, please, this part of the city might as well be called Five Star City. Trust us: it's not just the handbags that are expensive. We recommend you stay somewhere else and take advantage of Milan's public transit systems. The following are already on the edge of the city center.

milan • accommodations

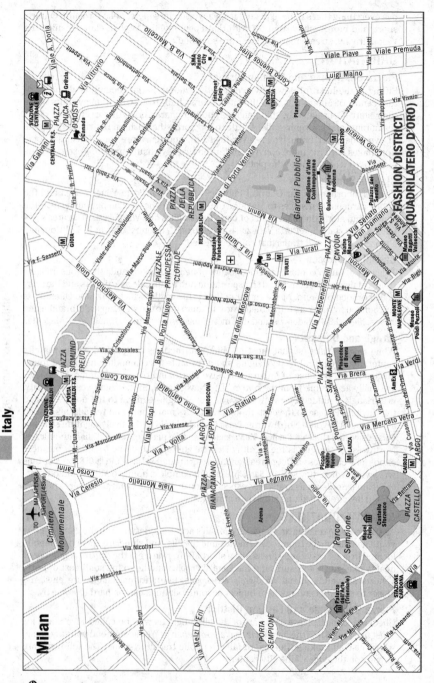

Milan

italy

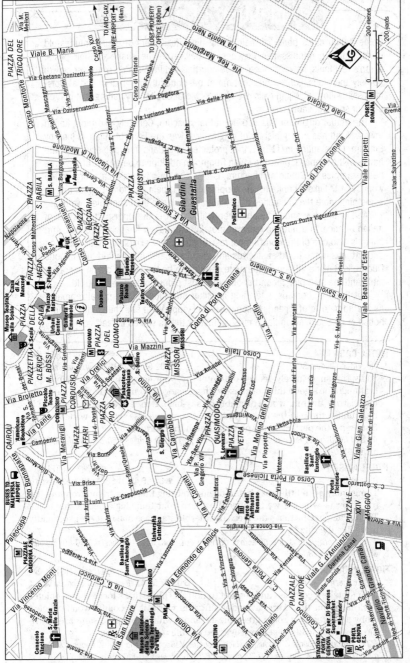

milan · accommodations

a question of morality

Some Italian cities boast of their raging nightlife. Others of their centuries-old ruins, stunning Renaissance frescoes, or hell, even the shape of their pasta. Milan's residents, however, seem to be courting a different kind of tourist crowd: namely, the pious. For reasons that are at best quaintly misguided, and at worst impossibly illogical, Milan calls itself Italy's "Moral Capital." Try getting that printed on your souvenir shot glass.

The actual origins of this title are rather obscure. Certainly, like most Italian towns, Milan has a long history of religiosity. It was the Edict of Milan, signed by Emperor Constantine in 313 CE, that protected Christians from persecution at the hands of the Romans, while the Milan Duomo, in addition to being one of the city's best examples of Gothic architecture, is also the fourth-largest cathedral in the world. But Milan's inhabitants are emphatic that it being a Moral Capital means something more than churches or proclamations. It's in the intangibles, we hear.

And really, why should we be skeptical? Milan is the undisputed center of Italian finance. And nothing reeks of morality like Italian financial dealings. And Milan is also one of the world's most fashionable cities, exhibiting all that is good and virtuous in the world of stilettos and shoulder bags. Just behind that famous Duomo is Galleria Vittorio Emmanuele, reputed to be the world's oldest shopping mall, and the stomping ground of only the most pious holders of Visa Gold.

But there is, perhaps, one thing in Milan absolutely above moral reproach. As the hometown of legendary composer Giuseppe Verdi and the glorious opera house of La Scala, Milan has a musical history that is sacred indeed.

HOTEL CASA MIA HOTEL ❹

Vle. Vittorio Veneto 30 ☎02 65 75 249 🖳www.casamiahotel.it

Sadly, this small, nicely decked-out hotel isn't your home, despite the name. But that might be a good thing because with a location a 10min. walk from the Fashion District, the rent would probably be sky-high. Better to enjoy the views of P. Repubblica through the large windows of someone else's yellow-walled breakfast area—the perfect sunny place to watch the world go by.

➧ [M]3: Repubblica. Hotel is on the corner of the piazza. $ Singles €50-65; doubles €70-90; triples €100-120.

HOTEL ALISEO HOTEL ❸

C. Italia 6 ☎02 86 45 01 56 🖳www.hotelaliseo.it

Things may get a little cozy if you decide to bring that new friend from the bar (or church—who are we to judge?) back to your thin single bed at this hotel. Then again, maybe that's the idea. The marble staircase makes it ever so slightly more like the Ritz.

➧ [M]3: Missori. Hotel is directly across from the exit on C. Italia. $ Singles €40-80; doubles €50-110; triples €80-130.

HOTEL VECCHIA HOTEL ❹

V. Borromei 4 ☎02 87 50 42 🖳www.hotelvecchiamilano.it

It might take a compass and sextant to find this place that's located on a quieter back lane, but the extra navigation effort is worth it. A comfy, wood-paneled lobby and breakfast room greet guests, and a whimsical spiral staircase above the front desk leads to generously sized double rooms upstairs.

➧ [M]1: Codusio. Follow V. Cordusio, which becomes V. Boccheto and then V. Podone. At P. Borromeo, turn right. $ Singles €50-70; doubles €70-90; triples €90-110.

Giardini Pubblici

The area between Stazione Centrale and the Giardini Pubblici is packed with hotels, some of them cheap and seedy, others with a doorman and concierge.

👍 HOTEL EVA AND HOTEL ARNO — 💳🚭📶 HOTEL [2]

V. Lazzaretto 17, 4th fl. ☎02 67 06 093 🖥www.hotelevamilano.com, www.hotelarno.com.

Friendly staff and comfortable rooms make this quirky dual-hotel setup (the two are across the hall, and share a reception) a good choice for budget travelers.

➜ Ⓜ1: Porta Venezia. Follow V. Castati, then turn right onto V. Lazzaretto. Ring bell. Ⓢ Singles €30-45; doubles €50-100; triples €65-90.

HOTEL ITALIA E NAZIONALE — 💳🚭📶🍸 HOTEL [3]

V. Vitruvio 44/46 ☎02 66 93 826 🖥nazionaleeitalia@tiscalinet.it

Despite the slight smell of smoke in some rooms, the prices at this establishment—including breakfast and in-room TV—are hard to beat in central Milan.

➜ Ⓜ2/3: Centrale FS. Ⓢ Singles €35-55; doubles €55-95; triples €110-120.

HOTEL BAGLIORI — 💳♿📶🍸⛰ HOTEL [4]

V. Boscovich 43 ☎02 29 52 68 84 🖥www.hotelbagliori.com

The idyllic front garden might have been plucked straight out of Versailles and the breakfast room stolen from a country club. Conveniently located and excellently appointed.

➜ Ⓜ1: Lima. Follow C. Buenos Aires south. Ⓢ Singles €50-180; doubles €130-250.

HOTEL SAN TOMASO — 💳🚭📶 HOTEL [1]

V. le Tunisia 6, 4th fl. ☎02 29 51 47 47 🖥www.hotelsantomaso.com

The rooms are clean, but plastic vines on white walls provide the only decoration at this thimble-sized hotel. More importantly, hotel staff do not necessarily speak English, making booking a room here somewhat difficult.

➜ Ⓜ1: Porta Venezia. Ⓢ Dorms €20; singles €35-85; doubles €50-95; triples €70-120.

Castello Sforzesco

The neighborhoods around Castello Sforzesco offer very few inexpensive hotels. Milan is a wealthy city, and staying in its center is going to take a bit of change.

HOTEL PANIZZA — 💳🚭📶 HOTEL [2]

V. Panizza 5 ☎02 46 90 604 🖥www.hotelpanizza.it

Don't get discouraged walking down the street: we're not sure why this small, simple, and cheap hotel decides to hide itself with only a small plaque announcing its presence, but it is indeed ready and waiting for your patronage. Inside, stained glass on the guestroom doors recalls Milan's Duomo.

➜ Ⓜ1: Conciliazione. Follow V. Porta Vercellina and turn right onto V. Biffi and again onto V. Panizza at the piazza. Ⓢ Dorms €25-27; singles €30-45; doubles €45-90; triples €65-120.

HOTEL LANCASTER — 💳🚭📶🍸❄ HOTEL [5]

V. Abbondio Sangiorgio 16 ☎02 34 47 05 🖥www.hotellancaster.it

The elegant Hotel Lancaster offers relatively enormous rooms, gigantic beds, and humongous showers.

➜ Ⓜ1/2: Cardona F.N. Take tram #19 towards Ospedale Sacco and get off at P. Giovanni XXIII. Follow V. Savoia to V. Sangiorgio. Ⓢ Singles €65-130; doubles €90-230; triples €130-300.

Navigli and Outskirts

Outside of the *centro*, accommodations vary widely in both price and quality. The area east of Stazione Centrale has some of the cheapest *pensione*, though these are often located on seedy streets.

👍 ZEBRA HOSTEL — 💳🚭📶 HOSTEL [2]

Vle. Regina Margherita 9 ☎02 87 23 66 83 🖥www.zebrahostel.it

Fortunately, the zebra theme is muted, and there are no tacky striped walls to keep you awake at night. But staying up late must be seriously fun in this new, clean hostel's gigantic common room, which features classic arcade games.

➔ Ⓜ3: Crocetta. Take V. A. Lamarmora to V. Margherita, and turn left. Hostel is up the stairs and to the left. $ Dorms €24-26; singles €35; doubles €30-32. €4 linen deposit.

✔ POP HOUSE — 🅟🚭📶☀ HOTEL [3]

V. Menabrea 13 ☎335 80 56 883 💻www.pophouse-milano.com

At Pop House, a cell phone is your doorman, a computer your concierge, and you're the room service. The three fashion industry workers who run this simple, modern spot are often off around the globe, but they're available to open the door from a thousand miles away thanks to high-tech gadgetry. Both the two-room "loft" and three-room "house" are comfortable lounge areas with compact kitchens. Small spiral staircases connect the ground floor to the sleek, stone-walled bathrooms and bright bedrooms—plus a rooftop terrace.

➔ Ⓜ3: Maciachini. Follow V. Menabrea 2 blocks. ℹ No reception; call on arrival. $ Singles €35-50; doubles €50-70; triples €60-75.

✔ OSTELLO LA CORDATA — 💳♿📶 HOSTEL [2]

V. Burigozzo 11 ☎02 58 30 35 98 💻www.ostellolacordata.com

Home to a lively, international backpacking crowd headed for the disco lights of the Navigli district, Ostello La Cordata has a party-hostel reputation.

➔ Ⓜ3: Missori. From P. Missori take tram #15 2 stops to Italia S. Luca; continue in the same direction for 1 block and turn right onto V. Burigozzo. Entrance around the corner on V. Aurispa. $ Dorms €21-25; singles €50-70; doubles €70-100; triples €90-120. ⏰ Lockout 11am-2:30pm.

MISTER BEEM — 🅟🚭📶 HOSTEL [1]

V. Goldoni 84 ☎380 46 72 253

Though the doorknob may be falling off the front door, this hostel is located in a safe and quiet residential area southeast of the city center. If you have an allergy to flowers—tacky paintings of sunflowers, that is—the orange-colored common room might make you want to sneeze.

➔ Ⓜ1: Porta Venezia. Take tram #5 or 33, in direction of Ortica or Limbrate, to P. Savoia. Continue walking in the same direction 4 blocks and turn right onto V. Cicognara. Make a left onto V. Goldoni. $ Dorms €18-23. ⏰ Lockout 11am-1:30pm.

HOTEL BRASIL — 💳🚭 HOTEL [3]

V. G. Modena 20, 4th floor ☎02 70 10 22 76 💻www.hotelbrasilmilano.com

Descisions, decisions, decisions. Hotel Brasil offers a myriad of different room setups at varying prices. All are brightly colored with an abundance of natural light in the high-up floor of an apartment building southeast of C. Venezia. Even though bags of linens are sometimes left in the hallway, guests in every room receive the same basic hospitality from the helpful staff.

➔ Ⓜ1: Palestro. From C. Venezia, turn right onto V. Salvini, which becomes V. Vitali. Make a slight left at V. de Bernardi, which becomes V. Belloti. Walk 5 blocks and turn right onto V. Modena. ℹ Small breakfast buffet €3. $ Singles €35-45; doubles €40-55; triples €50-65; quads €65-80.

RIPA DEL NAVIGLIO — 💳📶❄ B AND B [5]

Ripa de Porta Ticinese 71, 4th fl. ☎02 89 69 33 43 💻www.ripadelnaviglio.it

The red blankets and cozy double beds make this bed and breakfast ripe for romance. Want to impress that cute Italian girl? Take her here—with a flowered balcony overlooking the rooftops and an airy breakfast room in sunburst colors, Ripa del Naviglio is a hidden oasis.

➔ Ⓜ2: Porta Genova. Walk down V. Casale. Cross the footbridge and turn right. ℹ Only 3 rooms. $ Doubles €110, can sometimes be negotiated lower for stays over 3 days.

HOTEL CALAIS — 🅟🚭📶 HOTEL [4]

V. Washington 26 ☎02 46 94 760 💻www.hotelcalaismilano.com

Even given the two world clocks set to Havana and Moscow in the hotel's lobby, we won't pass judgment on the owner's political leanings. What we can say is that he (and his little dog, too!) is helpful and runs a quirky establishment—guestroom walls painted with turquoise waves to mimic the breaking surf of *La Manche* and all.

⚡ Ⓜ1: Wagner. *From the large traffic circle, follow V. Washington to the south.* Ⓢ *Singles €50-65; doubles €65-80; triples €85-100.*

OSTELLO A.I.G. PIERO ROTTA (HI) 〰️Ⓧ🛜🍴 HOSTEL ❶

Vle. Salmoiraghi at V. Calliano ☎02 39 26 70 95 📧ostellomilano.it

Comparing this hostel to an aging supermodel probably gives it a little too much credit—or too much insult to supermodels—but it's certainly ready for some plastic surgery. Built in the 1950s, this large, 400-bed hostel has dark hallways and aging bathrooms, but recently began a major renovation.

⚡ Ⓜ1: QT8. *When facing park after exiting station, follow V. Salmoirghi to the right.* Ⓢ *6-bed dorms €22; private rooms €25. €5 cash key deposit required.* 🕐 *Lockout 10am-2pm.*

SIGHTS 👁️

Is this a city without a history? An *Italian* city without a history, at that? Of course not, though compared to Rome, Venice, and Florence, Milan can sometimes seem rather without roots. With a city center that's grown up around the 14th-century **Duomo**, Milan does indeed have a robust past of politics, art, and culture that is revealed in its sights.

Piazza Del Duomo and Fashion District

🏛️ DUOMO ♿ CHURCH

P. del Duomo ☎02 72 02 33 75 📧www.duomomilano.it

The second-largest Catholic cathedral in the world, the Duomo takes up the largest spot in the hearts of Milan's residents. With a construction spanning from 1386 to the 1900s, the building juxtaposes an Italian Gothic style with Baroque architectural elements added at the order of Archbishop Borromeo, who sought to show solidarity with Rome during the Protestant Revolution. The rooftop, accessible by elevator or stairs, offers one of Milan's best vistas. The nearby **Museo del Duomo** remains closed for renovation but normally houses paintings, tapestries, and artifacts dating back to the cathedral's construction.

⚡ Ⓜ1: Duomo. *i Modest dress code strictly enforced.* Ⓢ *Free. Rooftop elevator €8. Stairs €5.* 🕐 *Open daily 7am-7pm. Roof open daily Feb 16-Nov 14 9am-10pm.*

🏛️ TEATRO ALLA SCALA 〰️Ⓧ❄️ OPERA

P. della Scala ☎02 88 79 24 73 📧www.teatroallascala.org

They say it's not over until the fat lady sings. Similarly, no opera can be complete without having been performed at La Scala, the world's preeminent venue. Opera season runs from December to July and September to November, overlapping the ballet season. The theater also has a museum that lets you trace its history through a series of small, lavishly designed rooms on an upper floor of the building. You can also get a slimpse into the main hall, which even if you don't care for opera can still be absolutely stunning.

⚡ Ⓜ1/3: Duomo. *Pass through the Galleria to P. della Scala. i Dress code: jacket and tie for men, appropriate attire for women.* Ⓢ *Ticket prices vary widely depending on performance. Any remaining tickets sold at a 25% discount 2hr. before the performance; student discounts available. Museum €5.* 🕐 *Box office open daily noon-6pm in* Ⓜ1: Duomo, *and at theater 2hr. before performances. Theater closed Aug. Museum open daily 9am-12:30pm and 1:30-5:30pm.*

🏛️ PINACOTECA AMBROSIANA ♿ MUSEUM

P. Pio XI 2 ☎02 80 69 21 📧www.ambrosiana.it

When a gallery's halls themselves count as art, how much more spectacular does that make the works they house? It's a fair question at this museum just blocks from the Duomo. The palatial rooms of the Ambrosiana feature walls of vibrant colors and molded ceilings in gold leaf. The masterworks on the walls include the first Italian still-life, Caravaggio's *Basket of Fruit*. Raphael's expansive sketch of the ◾**School of Athens** fills an entire wall in a room darkened for preservation.

✦ Ⓜ1: Duomo. Follow V. Spadari off V. Torino, and turn left onto V. Cantu. Ⓢ €8, under 18 or over 65 €5. Ⓩ Open Tu-Su 9am-7pm. Last entry 30min. before close.

MUSEO BAGATTI VALSECCHI
◆⊗ MUSEUM

V. Gesu 5 ☎02 76 00 61 32 🖳www.museobagattivalzecchi.org

This stunningly preserved 19th-century *palazzo* has no business calling itself a museum—it's more like a time machine. Built to appear several centuries older than it actually is, this former home of brothers Fausto and Giuseppe Bagatti Valsecchi is full of Renaissance artwork and artifacts, including paintings by **Giovanni Bellini.**

✦ Ⓜ3: Montenapoleone. Walk down V. Monte Napoleone and turn left onto V. Gesu. Ⓢ €8, students and over 65 €4. €4 for all on W. Ⓩ Open Tu-Sa 1-5:45pm.

MUSEO POLDI PEZZOLI
◆⛪ MUSEUM

V. Manzoni 12 ☎02 78 08 72 🖳www.museopoldipezzoli.it

Enter the home of one of Milan's most storied collectors, Gian Giacomo Poldi Pezzoli. His broad collection includes a number of famous Italian works, including Botticelli's *Madonna* and Pollaiuolo's *Portait of a Young Woman*. Works by some Flemish and Northern European painters, including Brueghel the younger, are on display as well. Jewelry, furniture, and timepieces round out this *palazzo*'s marvelous trove of *objets d'art*.

✦Ⓜ1/3: Duomo. Follow V. Manzoni past La Scala. Ⓢ €8, students and seniors €5.50, under 10 free. Ⓩ Open M 10am-6pm, W-Su 10am-6pm.

GALLERIA VITTORIO EMANUELE II
⛪ ARCHITECTURE

P. del Duomo

Welcome to what may be the world's first shopping mall. But as they say, oft-imitated, never duplicated, and no suburban teen hangout can match the Galleria in intricacy and expense. Light streams in through the 48m glass and iron cupola, making this five-story arcade of offices, restaurants, and overpriced shops a marvelous sight.

✦ Ⓜ1/3: Duomo. To the left when facing the Duomo. Ⓢ Free (entry at least).

Giardini Pubblici

If you feel as if you're running low on oxygen in Milan's treeless concrete jungle, here's your neighborhood.

◾ **GIARDINI PUBBLICI**
⛪ GARDENS

C. Venezia at Bastioni di Porta Vinezia ☎02 67 06 093

More than just a park and namesake to the neighborhood, the Giardini Publicci brings a swath of green to a city in which all streets feel walled-in by buildings and most foliage is confined to private interior courtyards. Milan's main park is a popular spot among the city's residents who come here to walk their dogs, lie in the sun, or simply wander amidst the garden's shady ponds, open lawns, and mossy cliffside trails.

✦ Ⓜ1: Porta Venezia or Palestro. Ⓢ Free. Ⓩ Open June-Aug 6:30am-11:30pm, Sept 6:30am-11pm, Oct 6:30am-9pm, Nov-Dec 6:30am-8pm, Jan-Feb 6:30am-8pm, March-April 6:30am-9pm, May 6:30am-10pm.

◾ **GALLERIA D'ARTE MODERNA**
⛪ MUSEUM

V. Palestro 16 ☎02 88 44 59 47 🖳www.gam-milano.com

Located in the historic Villa Reale—whose ornate ballrooms-turned-galleries are nearly a sight unto themselves—this gallery on the fringe of the Giardini Pubblici features a vast array of modern Italian art focusing on the 18th and 19th centuries. Among the best-known artists represented here are the Post-Impressionist **Paul Gauguin** and the Futurist **Giacomo Balla.**

✦ Ⓜ1: Porta Venezia. Ⓢ Free. Ⓩ Tu-Su 9am-1pm and 2pm-5:30pm.

Castello Sforzesco

Welcome to Milan's tourist district, part two. The Castello is a hub for many visitors, hawkers, and museums, but the surrounding area, with less trodden ground, hides a few extraordinary gems.

CASTELLO SFORZESCO
CASTLE, MUSEUM

P. Castello ☎02 88 46 37 00 🖳www.milanocastello.it

Visiting Castello Sforzesco is just like being in a toy shop: A castle! With a moat! And gates that crash down! And knights in shining armor! And princesses! And museums of ancient art and Egypt and prehistory and decorative arts and musical instruments! (OK, so maybe not all of us had ancient art museums at our local toy store.) Really, Milan's dominant fortress, constructed in 1368 to defend the city, is way better than a toy box. Leonardo's studio could once be found within the castle which today pays tribute to him and many other artists in its **Museum of Ancient Art,** where Leonardo's frescoes cover the ceiling.

⚕ Ⓜ1: Cairoli. Ⓢ Grounds free. All-museum pass €3, students and seniors €1.50. Ⓞ Castle grounds open Apr-Oct daily 7am-7pm; Nov-Mar 7am-6pm. Museums open Tu-Su 9am-5:30pm.

CHIESA DI SANTA MARIA DELLE GRAZIE AND CENACOLO VINCIANO
CHURCH

P. Santa Maria delle Grazie 2 ☎02 89 42 11 46 🖳www.cenacolovinciano.org

Leonardo's **The Last Supper** is one of the world's most famous paintings and—unlike another famous Leo da Vinci masterpiece—it isn't surrounded by hundreds or thousands of gawkers. Due to the fragility of the painting, which was restored and returned to public display in 1999, groups of only 25 are granted 15min. slots in which to view the painting. Still, as any economist will tell you, this limited supply creates a significant shortage of tickets, so book ahead (☎02 92 80 03 60).

⚕ Ⓜ1: Conciliazione or Ⓜ3: Cardona. From P. Conciliazione, take V. Boccacio and then turn right onto V. Ruffini for 2 blocks. ⓘ Many tickets for the Last Supper are bought up by tour companies months in advance, so be sure to reserve early online. Ⓢ Church free. Refectory €6.50, EU residents 18-25 €3.25, EU residents under 18 or over 65 free. Reservation fee €1.50. Ⓞ Church open daily 7am-noon and 3-7pm. Refectory open Tu-Su 8am-7:30pm; last entry 6:45pm.

PINACOTECA DI BRERA
MUSEUM

V. Brera 28 ☎02 72 26 31 🖳www.brera.beniculturali.it

One of the Pinacoteca di Brera's most unique aspects is that, within a glass enclosed cube in Gallery 14, conservators work on paintings, providing a glimpse into how art museums keep their priceless works fresh. Founded for the private study of art students, this museum also includes highlights such as Raphael's *Marriage of the Virgin* and Caravaggio's *Supper at Emmaus* in addition to numerous other works spanning from the 14th to 20th centuries.

⚕ Ⓜ2: Lanza or Ⓜ3: Montenapoleone. Walk down V. Pontaccio and turn right onto V. Brera. ⓘ Visitors with disabilities enter V. Fiori Oscuri 2. Ⓢ €5, EU citizens under 18 or over 65 free. Ⓞ Open Tu-Su 8:30am-7:30pm.

MUSEO NAZIONALE DELLA SCIENZA "DA VINCI"
MUSEUM

21 V. San Vittore ☎02 48 55 51 🖳www.museoscienza.org

No automobiles here, but there *are* planes, trains, ships, and a submarine—some designed by Italy's most famous inventor and the museum's namesake, whose sketches have been reconstructed in 3D so kids can try to make that outrageous whirlybird fly.

⚕ Ⓜ2: Sant'Ambrogio. Ⓢ €8, under 18 and students with ID €6. Ⓞ Open Tu-F 9:30am-5pm, Sa-Su 9:30am-6:30pm.

MUSEO CIVICO ARCHEOLOGICO
MUSEUM, ANCIENT ROME

C. Magenta 15 ☎02 86 45 00 11

Whoa—the ancient Romans had central heating? And Milan was at one point their imperial seat? You bet, as this museum of Milan's ancient history reveals.

With its collection of stonework, knives, and pottery as well as the patrician residence and Roman rampart in its backyard, the Museo Civico Archeologico offers a rare glimpse into the city's ancient history. Don't miss the ruins of Emperor Maximian's residence. *(V. Brisa 16 ➔ Off C. Magenta. $ Free.)*

➔ Ⓜ1/2: Cardona F.N. Follow V. Carducci and turn left onto C. Magenta. $ €2, students and seniors €1. 🕐 Open Tu-Su 9am-1pm and 2-5:30pm.

Navigli and Outskirts

While Milan's monuments are concentrated in the city center, beyond this area a number of museums whose scope stretches past the classical art and history found near the Duomo await. From sports to modern sculpture and poster art, there's much to explore beyond Milan's ring roads.

CIMITERO MONUMENTALE — ♿ CEMETERY

Piazzale Cimitero Monumentale ☎02 88 46 56 00 💻www.monumentale.net

Imagine Arlington Cemetery in Virginia, with its rows of even, identical gravestones. Then imagine the exact opposite. That's Cimitero Monumentale, whose often gaudy mausoleums and sculpted headstones offer an everlasting image of the departed. Famed conductor Toscanini makes this graveyard his final resting place. Try to spot his tomb, which was designed for his son who died at the age of four. It's pockmarked with scars left from the WWII bombs that battered Milan. When the tomb was recently restored, the holes were left as a reminder of Toscanini's staunch resistance to Mussolini's regime.

➔ Ⓜ2: Porta Garibaldi. Walk parallel to the tracks and under the overpass. Cross V. Farini to the cemetery parking lot. $ Free. 🕐 Open Tu-Su 8am-6pm.

STADIO GIUSEPPE MEAZZA, SAN SIRO — 💳♿🍸 OUTSKIRTS

V. dei Piccolomini 5 ☎02 48 70 71 23 💻www.acmilan.com, www.inter.it

There's just one thing that all *Milanese* can be said to take too seriously: soccer. With two world-renowned squads occupying the same city—and stadium—every single citizen has picked a side. Matches in this 85,000-seat complex are raucous affairs, especially when the city's two teams, AC Milan and Inter, go head-to-head twice a year. Tickets can be hard to come by, so buy them early. You also get a tour a visit the museum, which traces the history of both clubs through displays of everything from posters to jerseys to vintage noisemakers.

*➔ Ⓜ1: Lotto. From P. Lotto, a long walk down Vle. Caprili, which becomes Piazzale del Spor. **i** Tickets can be purchased at local banks–AC Milan at Intesa San Paolo and Inter at Banca Populare di Milano, both of which have many locations throughout the city. $ Tickets €7-135. Museum €7, under 18 and over 65 €5. Museum and tour €12.50/€10. 🕐 Most games Sept-June Su afternoon. Museum open daily 10am-5pm. Sometimes varies on gamedays and during special events.*

BASILICA DI SAN LORENZO MAGGIORE AND LORENZO COLUMNS — ♿ CHURCH

C. di Porta Ticinese 39 ☎02 89 40 41 29 💻www.sanlorenzomaggiore.com

Up, up, and away is the feeling as San Lorenzo's soaring dome draws eyes to the heavens. Its gold-plated altar and organ make for another holy feast for the eyes. The columns outside the building are the most significant Roman ruin remaining in Milan and act not only as a historical reminder but as a social gathering spot. The basilica itself also has historic relevance, as its round floorplan became a symbol of the circle's perfection during the Renaissance.

➔ Ⓜ1: San Ambrogio. Follow V. de Amicis. $ Free. 🕐 Open daily 7:30am-12:30pm and 2:30-6:45pm.

TICINESE CITY GATE — ♿ ARCHITECTURE

P. XXIV Maggio

Originally part of a wall built to protect Milan in the 1100s, today this gate is wide open to the onslaught of cars, scooters, and trams that invade the city. As the only gate from the period remaining in the city, Ticinese is an impressive survivor. Today, a countercultural scene can be found making its weekend home under the gate's arches, with impromptu concerts filling the Friday night air, bars sprouting from the back of parked VW buses, and ⚲**communist** rallies bringing out the *carabinieri*.

⚑ Ⓜ2: *Porta Genova.* Ⓢ *Free.*

PIRELLI TOWER
                 ♿ TOWER
P. Duca d'Aosta 3

If the Duomo is the elegant symbol of Milan's heart and soul, the Pirelli tower is the manifestation of its industrial brawn and economic prosperity. Upon orders from Alberto Pirelli, president of the famous tire company, construction began in 1956. Soon the 30-story tower was the tallest building in Italy. It is now one of the city's best known buildings.

⚑ Ⓜ2/3: *Centrale F.S.* *i* *Interior not open to the public.* Ⓢ *Free.*

FOOD

There's much to be had from Milan's culinary scene, from slices of pizza enjoyed while sitting on the sidewalk to fine dining in the city's venerable sit-down, button-up establishments. Starting the night off right is easy with happy hour *aperitivo* buffets offered by many bars, especially near the Navigli—all-you-can-eat spreads of breads, pasta, meats, and cheeses come included with the purchase of one drink. Sadly overlooked most everywhere except inside the city's ring road, Milanese cuisine with its risotto and *cottoletta alla milanese* (breaded veal cutlet) is still served up in a number of quaint trattorias. Often hard to find in Italy, ethnic cuisines from Argentina to Eritrea and beyond take center stage in some neighborhoods, particularly around **Giardini Pubblici.**

Piazza Del Duomo and Fashion District

When it's time to sit down and eat after your sightseeing, identify the touristy spots nearby...then steer clear. A better bet is to venture down a few side streets, where there are a number of great, inexpensive options.

▦ PRINCI
           ◉✲ BAKERY, PIZZERIA ❶
V. Speronari 6
         ☎02 87 47 97 ▧www.princi.it

Restaurant idea lab, circa the foundation of Princi: "Hey, I've got an idea! Let's put an Italian bread shop into an Egyptian tomb!" In such a manner, this dimly lit, sandstone-walled bakery might have been conceived. The hubbub of locals swarming the counter can be intimidating to tourists unfamiliar with the place, but to order a tasty pizza slice *(€3.50-5)* or pastry *(€1-4)*, just be assertive and push through the throngs to reach the counter.

⚑ Ⓜ1/3: *Duomo. Take V. Torino and make first left.* Ⓢ *Primi and secondi €5-10.* ⊘ *Open daily 7am-8pm.*

▦ BREK
           ✦♿✲❄ BUFFET ❶
Piazzetta Giordano 1
       ☎02 76 02 33 79 ▧www.brek.com

Grab and go is not the motto here. This is fast food Fashion District style, so the buttoned-up throngs take their meal on china from the buffet and walk down the wide, grand staircase to eat. Typical Italian entrees like lasagna and pizza accompany sides ranging from meat and cheese plates to chocolate cake and tiramisu.

⚑ Ⓜ1: *San Babila. From P. San Babila, walk through Galleria San Babila arcade to Piazzetta Giordano.* Ⓢ *Salads €3-4. Pizza slices €3-4. Primi €4-6.* ⊘ *Open daily noon-3pm and 6:30-10:30pm.*

PIZZA AND FRIENDS
            ✦♿✲ PIZZERIA ❷
V. F. Baracchini 9
       ☎02 87 23 81 33 ▧www.pizzaandfriends.com

If you believe the names of its dishes, this place should cost a fortune. Luckily, it doesn't. The "St. Tropez" *(tomato, mozzarella, tuna, leek, and basil; €9)* ain't nearly as expensive as the vacation destination it's named after, and the "Rockefeller" *(mozzarella di bufala, truffles, egg yolk, arugula, and parmesan; €12)* doesn't require the bank account of America's famous oil tycoon. The greatest part? These pizza pies taste like a million bucks.

🍴 Ⓜ️3: Missori. From P. Missori, follow V. M. Gonzaga. At P. Diaz, turn right onto V. Baracchini. Ⓢ Pizzas €5.50-12. Sandwiches €5-6.50. 🕐 Open daily 11:30am-1am.

GROM
🍴 ♿ GELATERIA ❶

V. Santa Margherita 16 ☎02 80 58 10 41 🖥www.grom.it

This place's gelato is so good that they have to hide it. While other establishments have mounds of the stuff on display, at Grom, only the privileged few get a chance to see the masterpiece frozen treats that servers keep covered under American-style tin lids.

🍴 Ⓜ️1/3: Duomo. Pass through the Galleria to P. Scala. Follow V. San Margherita to the right. Ⓢ Gelato €2.50-3.50. 🕐 Open M-Th noon-11pm, F-Sa noon-midnight, Su noon-11pm.

CAFE VECCHIA BRERA
🍴⊗🍴 CAFE ❷

V. dell'Orso 20 ☎02 86 46 16 95 🖥www.creperiavecchiabrera.it

Crepes and beer. What's not to love? Even better, this casual establishment claims to offer an entire "world" of different and exotic brews (€3-15), and the bar has the bottles and taps to prove it. No matter which brew you choose, combine that cool golden beverage and a steaming golden crepe (€5-7).

🍴 Ⓜ️1: Cairoli. From Largo Cairoli, follow V. Cusani until it becomes V. dell'Orso just before the cafe. Ⓢ Cover €1. Crepes €5-7. Sandwiches €7-8. 🕐 Open M-Sa 7am-2am, Su 11am-2am.

3CAFE
🍴♿🍴❄ ARGENTINE ❷

C. di Porta Ticinese 1 ☎02 45 49 60 85 🖥www.3cafe.it

In Milan, a place of refined taste and class, it seems practically vulgar to put a picture of a big, juicy, hunking piece of meat in your window. But that's just how 3Cafe adorns itself, and this method seems to work, as the restaurant draws people in for steaks prepared in a way that you just can't get at most *ristoranti*.

🍴 Ⓜ️2: Sant'Ambrogio. Follow V. de Amicis and turn left onto C. di Porta Ticinese. Ⓢ Primi €6; secondi €7.50. 🕐 Open M-Sa noon-3pm and 7:30-11:30pm.

Giardini Pubblici

The streets surrounding Giardini Pubblici offer an (eventually welcome) respite from the Italian fare that dominates the city. Locals—who are adamant about cooking their own homegrown recipes—come to this neighborhood for its selection of cuisines from Asia, Africa, and even the Americas.

▨ CASATI 19
🍴⊗🍴 RISTORANTE ❸

V. F. Casati 19 ☎02 29 40 29 94 🖥www.ristorantepizzeriacasati19.it

This family-run establishment has gotten a reputation as Giardini Pubblici's go-to neighborhood *ristorante*. Its pizzas, including the featured "Casati 19" with artichokes and cured beef (€7.50), are always filling.

🍴 Ⓜ️1: Porta Venezia. Ⓢ Cover €1.50. Primi and secondi €8-16. 🕐 Open Tu-Su noon-3pm and 7-11pm.

RISTORANTE ASMARA
🍴⊗🍴 ERITREAN ❸

V. L. Palazzi 5 ☎02 89 07 37 98 🖥www.ristoranteasmara.it

Prepare your taste buds before entering this African establishment that features spicy food beneath Eritrean flags and portraits of tribesmen. Use your ▨hands to scoop up *zighini* with meat and vegetables into a flatbread (€10).

🍴 Ⓜ️1: Porta Venezia. Ⓢ Cover €1.60. Appetizers €4-5.50; entrees €8-10. 🕐 Open M-Tu 10:30am-3:30pm and 6pm-midnight, W 6pm-midnight, Th-Su 10:30am-3:30pm and 6pm-midnight.

L'OSTERIA DEL TRENO
🍴⊗🍴♿ RISTORANTE ❶

V. San Gregorio 46/48 ☎02 67 00 479 🖥www.osteriadeltreno.it

Step right up to this cozy self-service restaurant, where locals gather at lunchtime to catch up with friends and meet for work dates with colleagues. The menu changes daily, but you can count on a number of pasta and meat options.

✦ Ⓜ2/3: *Centrale F.S.* Ⓢ *Primi €4.50; secondi €6.50.* Ⓩ *Open M-F 10am-7pm and 8:30pm-12:20am, Sa noon-7pm and 8:30pm-12:20am, Su 10am-1pm and 7pm-12:30am.*

RISTORANTE INDIANO NEW DELHI ◈⊗Ⓨ INDIAN ❸

V. Tadino 1 ☎02 29 53 64 48 🖳www.ristorantenewdelhi.it

Italians turn to Ristorante Indiano New Delhi for something they *don't* know how to prepare: the best Indian food in the neighborhood. If you're feeling particularly native, join the crowd and chow down on a fresh-cooked samosa, enjoy one of New Delhi's lunch specials *(vegetarian €8, with meat €9),* or sample from the Indian-style antipasti *(€3.50-6).*

✦ Ⓜ1: *Porta Venezia.* Ⓢ *Tandoori and curry dishes €11-14.* Ⓩ *Open daily 11am-4pm and 6pm-midnight.*

AZZURRA GRILL ◈⊗Ⓨ SEAFOOD ❸

V. San Gregorio 11 ☎02 29 40 61 15

The deep blue sea is pretty far from Milan, but fresh fish still come in daily at this grill. At Azzura, you can sample all of the ocean's bounty in pastas, cooked as main dishes, and on pizzas. Try the thin sliced swordfish *(€13)* or Azurra's signature pizza, which is topped with tomatoes and seafood *(€9).*

✦ Ⓜ1: *Porta Venezia.* Ⓢ *Primi €7-12. Seafood dishes €11-19.* Ⓩ *Open daily 7-11pm.*

Castello Sforzesco

As is the case with the Duomo, restaurants within sight of the Castello Sforzesco are designed to catch tourists who don't know where else to eat. Try **Corso Magenta** and some parts of the Brera district instead.

▩ CHOCOLAT ◈⊗♨ GELATERIA ❶

V. Boccaccio 9 ☎02 48 00 16 35 🖳www.chocolatmilano.it

Six different flavors of gelato, and that's just counting those of the chocolate variety. You'll find that this *gelateria* not only earns its name but goes beyond the call of duty, serving up white chocolate, coffee, nougat, and fruit flavors as well. Locals say that the unique, spicy Chilli Chocolate flavor is a must-have.

✦ Ⓜ1/2: *Cardona F. N.* Ⓢ *Gelato €2.50-3.50.* Ⓩ *Open M-F 7:30am-midnight, Sa 8am-midnight, Su 10am-midnight.*

JAMAICA BAR ◈♿Ⓨ♨ CAFE ❷

32 V. Brera ☎02 87 67 23 🖳www.jamaicabar.it

Don't visit this Brera establishment for a serving of modesty—it's not on the menu at this historic cafe that's played host to a line of important artists, writers, and even Nobel prize winners. What is on sale here is Milan's culinary classic, *cottaletta alla milanese,* a fried veal cutlet served with risotto *(€14.50).*

✦ Ⓜ1: *Lanza. Take V. Tivoli, which becomes V. Pantaccio. Turn right onto V. Brera.* Ⓢ *Panini €5-6. Antipasti €5-7. Pizza €7-9.* Ⓩ *Open daily 9am-2am. Closed Su for 5 weeks in July and Aug.*

PASTICCERIA MARCHESI ◈⊗Ⓨ BAKERY ❶

V. Santa Maria alla Porta 11/A ☎02 87 67 30 🖳www.pasticceriamarchesi.it

Ouch! Our sweet tooth is aching just looking at this place's pastel-colored frosted cakes and chocolate delights laid out to tempt the weak of will.

✦ Ⓜ1: *Cairoli. Follow V. San G. Sul Moro to intersection with C. Magenta.* Ⓢ *Pastries €2-5.* Ⓩ *Open Tu-Sa 8am-8pm, Su 8am-1pm.*

Navigli and Outskirts

The best of the best in Milan's hinterlands aren't necessarily near one another, but the search just adds to the reward. In the Navigli, try to hit up the *aperitivo* buffets of the area's countless bars.

milan ∙ food

BIG PIZZA: DA NOI 2
●&♥♨ PIZZERIA ❶

V. Giosue Borsi 1 ☎02 83 95 677 ▣www.danoi2.com

The name is no lie. These pizzas are big—bigger than the plate, bigger than a New-York-style slice, maybe bigger even than the Big Apple itself. Get your belly ready for these thin-crust puppies.

♯ Ⓜ2: Porta Genova. Ⓢ Cover €1.50. Pizza €6.50-8.50. ⚑ Open M-Sa noon-2:30pm and 7pm-midnight. Sometimes stays open later on weekends, depending on crowds.

CHOCO CULT
●⊗♥❅ GELATERIA, BAKERY ❶

V. Buonarroti 7 ☎02 48 02 73 19 ▣www.chococult.it

Both an early morning coffee stop and a refreshing afternoon ice cream stand, this establishment actually makes most of its revenues from the sale of hard chocolate (€50-200 per kg). Luckily, its chocolate-making skills are also put to good use in all of its other delicacies., including a lot of gelato.

♯ Ⓜ1: Wagner. Ⓢ Gelato €2.50-3.50. Coffee and espresso €1-3. ⚑ Open daily 7am-midnight.

AMERICAN DONUTS
●⊗♥❅ CAFE, AMERICAN ❶

V. Sirtori 4 ☎02 89 05 77 79 ▣www.americandonut.it

Oh beautiful, for sprinkle skies, and amber rings of dough! In fact, such a soundtrack might be the last touch missing from this clever diner that certainly doesn't take itself too seriously—Old Glory graces everything from the coffee mugs to the servers' aprons. For a breakfast on the go, grab a doughnut (€1.80), or take on a more leisurely and fattening American meal and enjoy a burger or fried chicken (€7-10).

♯ Ⓜ1: Porta Venezia. From P. Romana, take V. Melzo and turn right onto V. Malpighi, then a quick left onto V. Sirtori. Ⓢ Cookies and muffins €1.50. Sandwiches €3-4.50. ⚑ Open M-F 7:30am-7:30pm, Sa 8:30am-7:30pm, Su 9am-7pm. Brunch served Sa-Su 10am-4pm.

PICHANAS
●⊗♥❅ BRAZILIAN ❸

Piazzale Lotto 14 ☎02 39 21 44 08 ▣www.pichanas.com

If you're on the one-meal-a-day diet but not really feeling it, here's the place for you. One meal is all you will need after Pichana's gigantic buffet of meat, pastas, and vegetable side dishes. The dinner buffet (€40) is accompanied by live Latin music and features 20 appetizers and 12 different meats, but the real deal is the smaller lunch (€15).

♯ Ⓜ1: Lotto. On the circle in Hotel Oro Blu. Ⓢ Lunch €15; dinner €40. ⚑ Open daily 12:30-3pm and 8pm-2am. Will sometimes stay open later than officially stated.

LA CANTINA DI MANUELA
●⊗♥❅ RISTORANTE ❸

V. Procaccini 41 ☎02 34 52 034 ▣www.lacantinadimanuela.it

Wine bottles for sale hang on the wall at this intimate brasserie, which claims to focus first and foremost on that most sacred art of drinking *vino*. Small-batch Italian vintages and well-known brands are all available from behind the bar. In the kitchen, dishes range from rissotos to fish and beef filets, and many courses feature wine-based sauces.

♯ Ⓜ2: Garibaldi F.S. Walk alongside the tracks on V. Sturzo, then continue in front of the cemetery building to V. Procaccini on the other side of the piazza. Ⓢ Antipasti and primi €8-10; secondi €19-22. ⚑ Open M-Sa 11:30am-3pm and 6:30pm-2am.

GHIRERIA GRECA
●&♥ GREEK ❶

Ripa di Porta Ticinese 13 ☎02 58 10 70 40

Take a quick trip across the Adriatic—or at least the Naviglio Grande—to stop at this quick and scrumptious Greek sandwich shop that provides a satisfying alternative to nighttime bar food.

♯ Ⓜ2: Porta Genova. Ⓢ Entrees €6-13. ⚑ Open M-F noon-2:30pm and 6pm-2pm, Sa noon-3am, Su noon-2pm.

RUGANTO

♥ℤ☺ RISTORANTE ❸

V. Fabbrini 1.

☎02 89 42 14 04

Ah, Italia. Pasta and pizza on the *piazza*, and in the shadow of ancient Roman columns to wit. Here, the cuisine is classic Italian, made as it should be.

✦ Ⓜ2: Sant'Ambrogio. Walk down V. Edmondo de Amicis, turn right onto C. Porta Ticinese. Ⓢ Beer €4-5. Pizza €6-12. Primi and secondi €9-20. ☒ Open daily 12:30-3pm and 7:30pm-midnight.

NIGHTLIFE

In terms of sheer variety, very few places on earth can rival Milan when it comes to nightlife—and there are plenty of locals eager to rave about their city's vibrant after-hours scene. **Corso Como** is home to the city's most exclusive and expensive clubs, where mere mortals can mingle with models and football stars. Dozens of small bars with big (and inexpensive) *aperitivo* buffets line the canals of the **Navigli** area, drawing students and young people to the neighborhood in droves. Beyond these hubs, the nightlife spokes stretch to all edges of the city, throughout which both local bars and international clubs are scattered.

Piazza Del Duomo and Fashion District

Nightlife on P. del Duomo is pretty much the same as the daylife: a lot of tourists gawking at the pile of intricate stonework that is the Duomo and Galleria Vittore Emmanuelle. The Fashion District is a business area, so most things close early.

▣ TASCA

✦⊗⅄ ENOTECA

C. di Porta Ticinese 14

☎02 83 76 915 ▣www.iltasca.it

In vino, veritas, the saying goes. Does that translate to Spanish? After several glasses of wine from this lively spot, there are more than a few people—inhibitions erased—who are willing to tell the whole truth to any passerby who will listen. Inside, the owners focus on Spanish cuisine, fixing up tapas as they take a few sips of Chardonnay themselves.

✦ Ⓜ2: Sant'Ambrogio. Follow V. de Amicis and make a left onto C. di Porta Ticinese. Ⓢ White wine €5-6, red €5-9. Tapas €5-10. ☒ Open M-Sa 12:30pm-1:30am.

CUORE

✦⊗⅄ BAR

V. Gian Giacomo Mora 3

☎02 58 10 51 26 ▣www.cuoremilano.it

Interesting fact: in Italy certain liquor licenses prohibit dancing, as places are supposed to be bars not clubs. Cuore is a bar, but some travelers report getting their illicit dance on here, even though busting out your interpretation of The Robot is technically illegal after 11pm in the small dance floor brought to life by a pumping DJ set.

✦ Ⓜ1/3: Duomo. Follow V. Torino to C. Porta Ticinese, and turn right onto V. G. G. Mora before the columns. Ⓢ Beer €5. Cocktails €7-8. ☒ Open daily 6pm-2am.

Giardini Pubblici

Nightlife is possibly the only category where "crowded" isn't a dirty word. In the summer months at Giardini Pubblici's tiny bars, it's not just the buildings themselves that fill up, but the sidewalks, too, as patrons march to their next cocktail.

▣ ATOMIC BAR

⊛⊗⅄ BAR

V. Casati 24

☎02 89 05 91 69 ▣www.atomicbar.it

Thirsty students recline beneath Pop Art murals as their overstuffed and well-worn space-age chairs burst at the seams. Students don't stay seated for too long, however, as the dance floor heats up to beats spun by a different DJ every night of the week (starting 11pm).

✦ Ⓜ1: Porta Venezia. Ⓢ Cocktails €10, €8 during happy hour. ☒ Open daily 7pm-2am.

L'ELEPHANT

✦⊗⅄❄▼ BAR

V. Melzo 22

☎02 29 51 87 68 ▣www.lelephant.it

Small groups of men and a few women recline on couches and chitchat at

L'Elephant, one of Milan's oldest hangouts for the GLBT community. The buttoned, plastic-feeling faux-leather on the walls makes the whole place seem a little like the couches that sit off to one side, but the palms overhead and pink boas draped about will remind you where you are.

✚ Ⓜ1: Porta Venezia. Ⓢ Cocktails €5-8. Ⓩ Open Tu-Su 6:30pm-2am.

MONO ●⚹♿♀ BAR

V. Lecco 6   ☎33 94 81 02 64 ▣www.myspace.com/monomilano

Hipsters in fedoras mingle outside this über-retro corner bar. Definitely a hipster bar, Mono is full of molded plastic chairs, dim lamps, and an old-school radio and record player.

✚ Ⓜ1: Porta Venezia. Ⓢ Cocktails €8. Ⓩ Open Tu 6:30pm-1am, W-Th 6:30pm-1:30am, F-Sa 6:30pm-2am, Su 6:30pm-1am.

Castello Sforzesco

Home to one of Milan's most student-friendly clubs, the area around Castello Sforzesco is otherwise full of quieter bars and lounges, some of which cater to an older crowd.

▨ OLD FASHION CAFE ●♿♀ CLUB

Vle. Emilio Alemagna 6   ☎02 80 56 231 ▣www.oldfashion.it

If you're under 30, this is the place to see and be seen in Milan—everyone you know will probably be here on Friday, and Tuesdays could bring some familiar faces too. If you're over 30, you'll probably be driven crazy within 100m of the place when your ears first catch the sappy pop songs mixed in with bass beat.

✚ Ⓜ1/2: Cardona F. N. Walk up V. Paleocapa and turn slight right onto Vle. Alemagna. The club is to the left of Palazzo dell'Arte along a cobblestone path. Ⓢ Cover €10. Ⓩ Open M-Tu 10:30pm-4:30am, W 10:30pm-4am, Th-Sa 10:30pm-4:30am, Su 11am-4pm and 7pm-midnight.

Navigli and Outskirts

Areas outside of Milan's *centro* feature some of its best known clubs as well as a few exotic outliers. Students on a budget frequent the Navigli to chow down on the *aperitivo* buffets during happy hour then hit up one of the clubs for DJs and live music. Elsewhere, **Corso Como**, north of the Duomo near Porta Garibaldi, showcases the city's world-renowned nightlife. It also plays host to an informal fashion show as well-dressed out-and-abouts strut the street on weekend nights. East of **Corso Buenos Aires** and **Stazione Centrale** are a number of bars popular with locals. You'll also find much of the city's GLBT scene here. To the south and west are a number of scattered clubs and bars, the more suburban of which can be hard to find.

▨ LE TROTTOIR ●⊗♀♿ CLUB

P. XXIV Maggio 1   ☎02 83 78 166 ▣www.letrottoir.it

This ever-crowded Navigli club attracts all comers with live nightly music (11pm-3am) ranging from rock and pop to reggae and soul. Upstairs, where a DJ spins (Th-Sa 11pm-3am), a rotating art exhibit showcases alternative—and sometimes raunchy—pieces. If the art is too hot and heavy for your taste, park yourself outside in one of the comfy seats on the deck.

✚ Ⓜ2: Porta Genova. Located in P. XXIV Maggio as its own island in a sea of roads. *i* Concert schedule online. Ⓢ Cover €8, with table service €9. Beer €6-7. Cocktails €8. Pizza and sandwiches €6-8. Ⓩ Open daily 11am-3pm.

▨ ONDANOMALA ●♿♀♿ CLUB

V. Lampugnano 109   ☎393 33 60 025 ▣www.ondanolmala.it

Here, in a trendy club tucked behind a housing development, there's sand between the toes and bamboo on the bar, even in the center of northern Italy. On weekends, hundreds of people pack the sandy main room and seven private areas.

✚ Ⓜ1: Uruguay. About a 15min. walk. From V. Croce, turn left onto V. Omodeo. Turn right at V. Montale, which becomes V. Lampugnano. Ⓢ 1st drink €7-15, depending on day of the week; afterward cocktails €7. Ⓩ Open May-Sept Tu-Su 6pm-3am; Oct-Dec Th-Su 6pm-3am; Feb-Apr Th-Su 6pm-3am. Happy hour 6-10pm.

ATMOSPHERE SOUL JAZZ

⊕⊗Ψ✄ BAR, JAZZ CLUB

V. Sidoli 24   ☎335 69 42 059 ■www.atmospheresouljazz.com

There's live music every night—if the employee banging drumsticks on the bartop counts as live music. Otherwise, Friday and Saturday are the evenings to come for live jazz, soul, and "funky" blues.

✦ Ⓜ1: Porta Venezia. Take tram #5 or 33 in direction of Ortica or Limbrate to Piazza Savoia. Continue walking in the same direction 5 blocks. The bar is on the right before Piazzale Susa. Ⓢ Beer €3-4. Cocktails €6. Happy hour €6. ⏰ Open daily 6pm-2am. Happy hour 6-10pm.

TAXI BLUES

●♿Ψ✄ BAR

V. Bocconi 6   ☎02 58 31 52 46 ■www.taximilanoblues.it

Local students enticed by Taxi Blues' €6-7 *aperitivo* (though vegetarians might want to steer clear on Friday when sushi is served) sink into plush, white leather couches in this psychedelic wonderland of a bar.

✦ Ⓜ3: Porta Romana. Follow Vle. Sabotino to Vle. Bligny. Ⓢ Beer €5. Cocktails €7. ⏰ Open daily 7am-2am. Happy hour 6:30-9:30pm.

SPRITZ NAVIGLI

⊕♿Ψ BAR

Ripa di Porta Ticenese 9   ☎02 83 39 01 92 ■www.spritz-navigli.it

A big sliced orange—and crowd of waiting 20-somethings—marks the entrance to this student favorite known for its varied and scrumptious happy hour food.

✦ Ⓜ2: Porta Genova. Ⓢ Happy hour buffet €8. ⏰ Open daily 6pm-2am. Happy hour 6-10pm.

HOLLYWOOD

●⊗Ψ❋ CLUB

C. Como 15   ☎02 65 98 996 ■www.discotecahollywood.com

The spotlight is on at this celeb-filled club, among the most elite in Milan. Man or woman, the dress code here isn't just elegant but "dress to impress" if you want to make it past the ropes into the blue-tinted lobby. Tuesday's Erasmus night is packed with students seeking half-price admission and the attraction of deafening bass in a strobe-lit basement that not any old dorm room can provide.

✦ Ⓜ2: Garibaldi F.S. Exit the station to the right, follow Vle. Sturzo and turn right onto C. Como. *i* Dress code is described as "elegant." Some female travelers report being able to get in for free earlier in the evening. Ⓢ Cover €20-25. Cocktails €10. ⏰ Open Tu-Sa 11pm-5am.

BLANCO

●⊗Ψ✄ BAR

V. Morgagni 2   ☎02 29 40 52 84 ■www.blancomilano.com

Wearing sunglasses inside might be cool all over Milan, but Blanco's blindingly white interior virtually requires it. Fortunately, the majority of patrons at Blanco's well-known happy hour flow into the street, where the pulsating beat can be heard (and felt) over the din of hundreds of voices.

✦ Ⓜ1: Porta Venezia. Head north on C. Buenos Aires, until making a right at V. Stoppani. At the park, Blanco is across and to the left. Ⓢ Cocktails €8. ⏰ Open M-Sa 6:30am-2am.

ESSENTIALS

⏻

Practicalities

- **TOURIST OFFICES: Informazioni Accoglienza Turistica** is Milan's central tourist office. It publishes *Hello Milano*, which offers information in English on events and nightlife, and the monthly *Milanomese*, which has a comprehensive listing of events and exhibitions in Italian and English. (P. Duomo 19A ☎02 77 40 43 43 ■www.visitamilano.it ✦ Next to the pharmacy, on the left when facing the cathedral, and down the stairs or elevator. ⏰ Open M-Sa 8:45am-1pm and 2-6pm, Su 9am-1pm and 2-5pm.) **Stazione Central Branch.** (☎02 77 40 43 18/19 ✦ Directly across from the tracks.)

- **GLBT RESOURCES: ARCI-GAY "Centro D'Iniziativa Gay."** (V. Bezzeca 3 ☎02 54 12 22 25 ■www.arcigaymilano.org ⏰ Open M-F 3-8pm.)

designer stores

If any city can claim its designer fashions are worth their astronomical pricetags, it's Milan. That's because clothes really do make the man (or woman) in this world center of fashion. Particularly after the semiannual shows held here, wealthy disciples of the current season flock to **Via Montenapoleone** and the surrounding environs to buy up the newest style of suit or handbag in one of the street's temples to fashion. Here are the main designer stores you might be seeking out.

- **ARMANI.** *(V. Manzoni 31 ☎02 72 31 86 00 💻www.armani.com ⏰ Open M-W 10:30am-7:30pm, Th-F 10:30am-9pm, Sa 10:30am-7:30pm, Su 2:30-7:30pm.)*
- **GUCCI.** *(V. Monte Napoleone 5-7 ☎02 77 12 71 💻www.gucci.com ⏰ Open M-F 10am-7pm, Sa 10am-7:30pm, Su 10am-1pm and 2pm-7pm.)*
- **PRADA.** *(V. Monte Napoleone 6-8 ☎02 77 71 771 💻www.prada.com ⏰ Open M-Sa 10am-7:30pm, Su 11am-7pm.)*
- **SALVATORE FERRAGAMO.** *(V. Monte Napoleone 3 and V. Monte Napoleone 20/4 ☎02 76 00 00 54 and 02 76 00 66 60 💻www.ferragamo.com ⏰ Open M-Sa 10am-7:30pm, Su 11am-7pm.)*
- **VERSACE.** *(V. Monte Napoleone 11 ☎02 76 01 12 71 💻www.versace.com ⏰ Open M-Sa 10am-7pm, Su 11am-6pm.)*

- **DISABLED SERVICES: AIAS Milano Onlus.** *(V. Paolo Mantegazza 10 ☎02 33 02 021 💻www.aiasmilano.it)*

Emergency!

- **POLICE:** *(In P. Cesare Beccaria, near Duomo ☎02 77 271)*
- **LATE-NIGHT PHARMACIES:** These can be found in **Stazione Centrale** *(☎02 66 90 735)* and **Stazione Porta Garibaldi** *(☎02 29 06 32 62)*. Most other pharmacies post after-hours rotations.
- **HOSPITALS/MEDICAL SERVICES: Ospedale Fatebenefratelli** *(C. Porta Nouva 23 ☎02 63 631)* and **Ospedale Maggiore di Milano.** *(V. Francesco Sforza 35 ☎02 55 031 ⇄ 5min. from Duomo on inner ring road.)* **Ospedale Niguarda Ca'Grande** is in the north of the city *(P. Ospedale Maggiore 3 ☎02 64 441)*.

Getting There

By Plane

Milan is served by three primary airports. **Malpensa (MXP)** is the main airport, 48km northeast of the city. There's a 50min. shuttle to Stazione Centrale *($ €7.50.)* **Linate (LIN)** is just 7km away and receives mainly European flights. It also has a shuttle to Stazione Centrale *($ €5.)* **Bergamo** airport is 58km northeast of Milan, but services a number of budget airlines and is often the cheapest way to reach the city. There is an hour-long shuttle ride to Stazione Centrale *($ €7.90.)*

By Train

Milan's main train station—Italy's second busiest—is **Stazione Centrale.** *(☎89 20 21 ⇄ Northeast of the city center in P. Duca d'Aosta.)* Trains to **Florence** *($ Eurostar €52, regional trains €27.50. ⏰ Eurostar 2hr., departs every hr. 5:45am-8:15pm. Regional train 3hr., departs every 3hr. 6:50am-8:15pm.)*; **Rome** *($ Eurostar €89, regional trains €46. ⏰ Eurostar 3½hr., more than once* an hr. 5:45am-9pm. Regional train 6½hr., every 3hr. 6:50am-11:30pm.); **Turin** (Ⓢ €9.55. ⌚ 2hr., every hr. 5:15am-12:15am.); **Venice** (Ⓢ €30. ⌚ 2hr., every hr., 6:35am-9pm.); and numerous local destinations.

Getting Around

By Public Transportation

Milan's extensive and efficient transit network is the pride of the city. The Ⓜ**Metropolitana Milanese** underground system runs from 6am-midnight and is the quickest and most useful branch of public transit. **Line 1** (red) streches from the suburbs of Sesto northeast of the city (Sesto 1 Maggio F.S.) to the exposition centers of **Rho-Fiera** in the northwest and to **Bisceglie** in the southwest. **Line 2** (green) links Milan's three primary train stations while spanning from **Cologno Nord** and **Gessate** in the east to **Abbiategrasso** in the west. It crosses Ⓜ1 at **Cardona** and **Loreto**. **Line 3** (yellow) runs south from the up-and-coming neighborhoods near **Maciachini** to **San Donato,** crossing Ⓜ2 at **Stazione Centrale** and Ⓜ1 at **Duomo.**

The subway's reach is not all-encompassing, so beyond its range a system of **trams** and **buses** connects Metro stations to the less accessible parts of the city. Trams #29/30 circle the city's outer ring road, while bus #94 circles the inner road. Tickets (€1) are good for Metro, trams, and buses for a period of 1hr. after validation; €3 buys a 24hr. pass, and €5.50 gets 48hr. Evening tickets (€1.80) are valid after 8pm until close on the day validated. For late-night travel, ATM operates a **Radiobus** service (☎02 48 03 48 03), which will pick up passengers holding valid ATM tickets anywhere in the city for a €2 surcharge (€1.50 if purchased in advance from the locations above), from 8pm-2am.

By Taxi

White taxis are omnipresent in the city, and cab stands in major *piazze* usually have cabs day and night. Otherwise, call one of the three major companies: **Autoradio Taxi** (☎02 85 85), **Taxi Blue** (☎02 40 40), or **RadioTaxi** (☎02 69 69).

By Bike

If you want to ride around town, try the new bikesharing program **bikeMi** (☎800 80 81 81 ▦www.bikemi.it), which has installed dozens of pick-up and drop-off locations where locals and visitors can check out bikes and leave them at their destination. These are sprinkled throughout the city and its outskirts. (Ⓢ Daily subscriptions €2.50, weekly €6, plus fees of €0.50 per 30min. after 1st 30min. up to 2hr. maximum. After 2hr., fines of €2 per hr. apply.)

turin *torino* ☎011

The ⚑**2006 Winter Olympics** put "Torino" on the map—literally. The confusion over which name to use, the hard English "Turin" or the smooth, rhythmic Italian has heightened since the city insisted on its native tongue back when it got the games. Regardless of which name it goes by, the often overshadowed northern city is universally admired now that it's had a chance to show off its many wonders. One of the greenest big cities in Italy, with vast public parks, the river Po, the hills beyond, and tree-lined boulevards blazed by Napoleon, Turin can in some ways feel more French than Italian in character. Espresso is *caffé*, the downtown is filled with royal history, and isolated *castelli* dot the hillsides surrounding the city.

ORIENTATION

Geographically, there are really two Turins. On the left bank of the **River Po,** there's a dense Neoclassical city and a street grid with—gasp—right angles at nearly every corner. On the right bank, there's an Alpine village, with roads winding up the mountainside and castle-like homes clinging to the slopes. Key points in the former include **Piazza Castello,** the spiritual home of the city, **Stazione Porta Nuova,** the point of arrival for most travelers, and **Piazza Vittorio Veneto,** a major nightlife destination by the river.

ACCOMMODATIONS

Turin's budget accommodations consist of a wide variety of hostels, hotels, and B and Bs that can suit anyone's tastes, but there's seemingly no rhyme or reason to the geographical layout of these many properties.

👍 OPEN 011
💳♿📶 HOSTEL ❶

C. Venezia 11 ☎011 25 05 35 💻www.openzero11.it

This hostel has amazingly high ceilings and no bunk-beds in its 34 gleaming rooms, each of which has a bathroom inside. There's ample space to spread out and relax.

➡ From Porta Nuova, take bus #52 (67 on Su) to V. Chiesa della Salute. Turn right at the next intersection and then left onto C. Venezia. $ 3- to 4-bed dorms €18; singles €31; doubles €44.

HOTEL CAMPIDOGLIO
💳♿📶❄ HOTEL, HOSTEL ❷

V. Corio 11 ☎011 77 65 808 💻www.hotelcampidoglio.it

Located down an alley "paved" with grass and smoothed stones, this place truly earns the seemingly contradictory title of "luxury hostel." Private rooms have had modern renovations and look damn good as a result, the dorm rooms retain their unfortunate pink floral wallpaper. All are bunk free.

➡ Take tram #9 toward Stampala and get off at the Ospedale Maria Vittoria stop. After exiting, turn around and make the 1st right onto V. Cibrario, then turn left onto V. Corio. $ 3- to 4-bed dorms €22-24; singles €35-40, with bath €50-55; doubles €52-57/€65-70.

HOTEL ALPI RESORT
💳🚭📶❄ HOTEL ❹

V. Alfonso Bonafous 5, 3rd fl. ☎011 81 29 677 💻www.hotelalpiresort.it

This hotel is no more in the Alps than any part of Turin. It's still got a great location, though, one block from the city's bustling nightlife hub. There're also spacious rooms and free internet in this restored apartment building.

➡ Just off P. Vittorio Veneto. $ Singles €50-65; doubles €69-85; triples €89-120.

ALBERGO AZALEA
💳🚭 HOTEL ❸

V. Mercanti 16 ☎011 53 81 15 💻www.hotelazalea.it

Whether you're watching a football game or playing poker, Albergo Azalea's spacious common room that overlooks a bright courtyard provides the perfect venue for enjoying the company of others (and the TV). The hotel has 10 meticulously clean and brightly colored rooms in an apartment building just minutes from the heart of Torino's *centro.*

➡ 100m from P. Castello. Take V. Pietro Micca from the piazza's southwest corner, and turn right onto V. Mercanti. $ Singles €40-55; doubles €55-70; triples €75-80; quads €85-90.

SIGHTS

👍 MOLE ANTONELLIANA
💳♿ TOWER, MUSEUM

V. Montebello 20 ☎011 81 38 560 💻www.museocinema.it

Once the world's tallest structure built from traditional masonry (read: brick) as its construction neared completion in the 1880s (before the builders added some concrete—brilliant), the Mole Antonelliana is at the very least Turin's highest structure. Home to the **Museo Nazionale de Cinema,** the Mole holds the distinction of being the world's tallest museum. Head here for magnificent views and lots of movies and movie paraphernalia.

➡ From P. Castello, walk east on V. Giuseppe Verdi and turn left onto V. Montebello. $ Museum €7, students and over 65 €5. Elevator €5/3.50. ⏰ Museum open Tu-F 9am-8pm, Sa 9am-11pm, Su 9am-8pm. Elevator open Tu-F 10am-8pm, Sa 10am-11pm, Su 10am-8pm.

👍 PALAZZO DELL'ACCADEMIA DELLE SCIENZE 🎫♿ MUSEUM

V. Accademia delle Scienze 6 ☎011 44 06 903 💻www.museoegizio.it

It's not King Tut's tomb, but this *palazzo* is still the final resting place of some well-known Egyptian royalty. The first Egyptian collection outside of Cairo, Turin's **Museo Egizio** consists of many artifacts that were acquired in the Italian Archaeological Mission of 1903-1937, which was responsible for the acquisition of thousands of artifacts currently on display. Upstairs in the same building is the **Galeria Sabuda,** the Savoy Gallery, which houses the art collections that were once kept for the personal enjoyment of the Palazzo Reale and Palazzo Carignano's residents. Renowned for its 14th- to 18th-century Flemish and Dutch paintings, the museum also contains works by Rembrandt and other noted artists.

➜ 2 blocks from P. Castello. [S] Egypt museum €7.50, students 18-25 €3.50. Savoy Gallery €4/2. ⏰ Egypt museum open Tu-Su 8:30am-7:30pm. Savoy Gallery open Tu 8:30am-2pm, W 2-7:30pm, Th 10am-7:30pm, F-Su 8:30am-2pm.

CATTEDRALE DI SAN GIOVANNI ♿ CHURCH

V. Palazzo di Città 4 ☎011 43 61 540

The **👍Holy Shroud of Turin,** one of the most enigmatic relics in all of Christianity, is kept in the Turin cathedral's **Capella della Santa Sindone.** Said to be Jesus's burial cloth and bearing a faint image of his face, the 3 by 14 ft. cloth itself is available for viewing by tourists only a few weeks every 25 years—the most recent exhibit was 2010, so book now for 2035. Its full-size reproduction is in **Chiesa di San Lorenzo,** although this image pretty much resembles one found anywhere in the world with a good search engine.

➜ To Cattedrale di San Giovanni from P. Castello, take V. Palazzo di Citta 1 block and turn left onto V. XX Settembre. San Lorenzo's entrance is on P. Castello, in front of and to the left when facing the Palazzo Reale gates. [S] Free. ⏰ Open M-Sa 7am-noon and 3-7pm, Su 8am-noon and 3-7pm.

PALAZZO REALE 🎫♿ MUSEUM

Piazzetta Reale ☎011 43 61 455 💻www.ambienteto.arti.beniculturali.it

The Princes of Savoy's residence for more than 200 years, since 1865, the Palazzo Reale has been as much a relic representing a time that predates Italy's current republic. It is the most central of the *"Crown of Delitie,"* a ring of Piedmont castles that became a UNESCO World Heritage Site in 1997. See it on a guided tour that is the only way to see the palace's interior.

➜ On P. Castello. ℹ Guided tour in Italian with available English audio tour. [S] €6.50, students €3.50. Gardens free. ⏰ Open Tu-Su 8:30am-6:20pm. Required guided tour lasts 1hr., departs every 30min. Gardens open daily from 9am to 1hr. before sunset.

BASILICA DI SUPERGA 🎫🚫 CHURCH

Superga Hill ☎011 89 97 456 💻www.basilicadisuperga.com

"The most enchanting position in the world." That's how the famous modernist architect Le Corbusier described the site of this basilica perched on a summit 672m above sea level. The view from the summit is spectacular in all directions (when the sky is clear), with Turin and the Alps beyond in clear focus.

➜ Tram #15 to Stazione Sassi, then bus #79 or a cable railway for an 18min. ride uphill. [S] Cable car €4 round-trip, €5.50 on Sa-Su. Basilica free. Royal tombs and royal apartment €4, students €3. Dome €3/2. ⏰ Cable car open M 9am-noon and 2-8pm, W-F 9am-noon and 2-8pm, Sa-Su 9am-8pm. Returns on the ½hr. Basilica open M-Sa 9am-noon and 3-6pm, Su 12:45-6pm. Tombs and Royal Apartment open daily 9:30am-7:30pm; 30min. guided tour in Italian required with translation available. Dome open M-F 10am-6pm, Sa 10am-7pm, Su 12:45-7pm.

THE GREAT OUTDOORS

Turin city proper wasn't the only thing onstage at the **👍2006 Winter Olympic Games;** the majestic white-capped Alps beyond also got their fair share of TV time. While they made an occasional pretty backdrop for the TV cameras in town for the Games, they have always been woven into the fabric of Torinese life. The **Via Lattea** ski area *(☎0122 79 94 11 🖥www.vialattea.it)*, or "Milky Way," hosted Olympic Alpine and cross-country skiing and ski jumping events. The village of **Sestriere,** just 17km from the French border, hosted Alpine skiing at the Games and got most of the press attention. Farther away, outside of the long Olympic reach, is **Alagna** *(☎0163 92 29 22 🖥www.freerideparadise.it)* in the Monte Rosa region. This place is known for its 1200m vertical drop, expert-only trails, and wide open *pistes* that allow skiers to chart their own path down.

The Piedmont Region tourism office *(☎011 43 21 504 🖥www.piemontefeel.it)* in Turin provides abundant information about planning a ski trip in the area.

FOOD

The Savoys first drank *cioccolato* in the 1600s, and since then, it's been all chocolate all the time in the ex-capital city that's home to the famous 👍**Nutella** and **Ferrero Rocher** brands. Beyond chocolate, Piedmont's cuisine has little international stature. Even within the city, food is focused around cafes and bars rather than elaborate sit-down restaurants. Where it's available, Piedmontese food blends northern Italian cooking with French influences.

👍 EATALY — MARKET [2]

V. Nizza 224 ☎011 19 50 68 11 🖥www.eataly.it

Eataly feels like a town of its own, with dozens of house-like stores set up shop under this market's tremendous glass skylights. With outlets serving gelato, pizza, pasta, meat, cheese, and more, plus a full gourmet grocery and wine shop, the 10,000-square-foot facility that is Eataly could practically take a half-day of sightseeing on its own.

→ Take bus #1, 18, or 35 to Lingotto. $ Variable. ⏰ Open daily 10am-10:30pm

👍 AGNOLOTTI AND FRIENDS — RISTORANTE [3]

P. Corpus Domini 18/b ☎011 43 38 792 🖥www.agnolottiandfriends.it

The pedestrian-only *piazza* here allows patrons to sit outside and enjoy the Piedmont region in more ways than one—*agnolottti*, a beef- and-vegetable-stuffed ravioli that is the restaurant's specialty, is a signature Piedmont dish.

→ Take V. Palazzo della Citta 2 blocks from P. Castello. $ Appetizers €7.50. Agnolotti €12. ⏰ Open daily 12:30-3pm and 8pm-midnight.

IL PUNTO VERDE — VEGETARIAN [2]

V. San Massimo 17 ☎011 88 55 43 🖥www.il-punto-verde.it

Where do you go to eat when you don't want meat? Heading toward the university's always a good bet—that whole "liberal bastion" thing—and doing so will lead weary vegetarian travelers right to Il Punto Verde's €5 student lunch menu and vast array of options, including vegan dishes.

→ Off V. Po, near P. Carlo Emanuele II. $ Cover €1.80. Primi and secondi €8. ⏰ Open M-F 12:30-2:30pm and 7-10:30pm, Sa 7-10:30pm.

CAFFÉ CIOCCOLATERIA AL BICERIN — CAFE [1]

P. della Consolata 5 ☎011 43 69 325 🖥www.bicerin.it

Count Chocula is wondering why he didn't think of this. Coffee, cream, and chocolate together in a glass mug that permits the layers of goodness to be revealed in all their glory. This delightful confection—Bicerin *(€5)*—has been served here since 1763.

→ Take C. Regina Margherita through P. della Repubblica, then turn left onto V. del Orfane and right onto the small piazza. $ Bicerin cake €4.50. ⏰ Open M-Tu 8:30am-7:30pm, Th-F 8:30am-7:30pm, Sa-Su 8:30am-1pm and 3:30-7:30pm.

NIGHTLIFE

It's hard to tell when *Torino* sleeps—things are happening every night of the week. From the pounding bass of dance clubs, to quiet wine bars and even calmer cafes, Turin offers something for just about every taste. 👍**I Murazzi,** a long boardwalk between Ponte V. Emanuele I and Ponte Umberto along the west bank of the Po, is unquestionably the epicenter of nighttime revelry.

🔲 OLÉ MADRID
●◎⊗💲⌣⛶ BAR

V. Murazzi del Po 5   ☎338 58 02 884

Spanish theme? Rather unclear where that came from. But this is for sure: strutting in on a Saturday night in a sombrero would be rather inconvenient, as the dance floor is packed with students swaying to the rhythms of the club's DJs.

🍴 *On the banks of the Po. From Porta Nuova, walk or take tram #9 or bus #34, 52, or 67 to C. Massimo d'Azeglio. Walk to the bridge and down the ramps to the left.* 💲 *Shots €2. Beer €4. Cocktails €6.* 🕗 *Open M-Th 9:30pm-3am, F-Sa 9:30pm-5am, Su 9:30pm-3am.*

SIX NATIONS MURPHY'S PUB
●◎⊗💲⌣⛶ BAR

C. Vittorio Emanuele II 28   ☎011 88 72 55 ▣www.sixnations.it

Come for the English, stay for the pints. Even when no football match is on the big screen (and especially if one is), this pub draws British expats and international students looking for a place to speak their mother tongue.

🍴 *On C. Vittorio Emanuele, to right when exiting Porta Nuova.* 💲 *Beer €3-5. Cocktails €5.50* 🕗 *Open daily 6pm-3am.*

FLUIDO
●◎⊗💲⌣⛶ CLUB

Vle. Umberto Cagni 7   ☎011 66 94 557 ▣www.fluido.to

Everything in Fluido flows down from the natural amphitheater, really a large grassy depression, that serves as its late-night seating bowl. Live music fills this happening spot outside the club's front doors with beach ball-bouncing students and hipsters.

🍴 *On the banks of the Po.* 💲 *Shots €3. Cocktails €6.* 🕗 *Open Tu-W 10am-2am, Th 10am-3am, F-Sa 10am-4am, Su 10am-1:30am.*

ESSENTIALS
🔢

Practicalities

- **TOURIST OFFICES: Turismo Torino** has helpful staff who speak English, French, German, and Spanish (oh, and Italian, too). They offer an excellent map of Turin and its transit system as well as info on museums, cafes, and tours. *(P. Castello 161* ☎*011 53 51 81* ▣*www.turismotorino.org* 🍴 *At the intersection of P. Castello and V. Garibaldi.* ℹ *Also has an info booth at Porta Nuova, opposite platform 11.* 🕗 *Open daily 9am-7pm.)*

Emergency!

- **LATE-NIGHT PHARMACIES: Farmacia Porta Nuova.** *(V. Paulo Sacchi 4* ☎*011 51 75 237* 🍴 *Exit Porta Nuova to the left.* ℹ *Pharmacies post after-hours rotation, available at* ▣*www.farmapiemonte.org.* 🕗 *Open daily 8am-7:30pm.)*

- **HOSPITALS/MEDICAL SERVICES: San Giovanni Batista,** commonly known as Molinette *(C. Bramante 88-90* ☎*011 63 31 633* ▣*www.molinette.piemonte.it),* **Maria Adelaide** *(V. Zuretti 29* ☎*011 69 33 111* ▣*www.cto.to.it),* **Mauriziano Umberto I** *(Largo Turati 62* ☎*011 50 81 111).*

Getting There
🔳

By Plane

Caselle Airport *(*▣*www.aeroportoditorino.it),* 20km from the city, serves European destinations. From Porta Nuova, take the blue Sadem buses to "Caselle Airport" via Porta Susa. *(*☎*011 22 72 022* 💲 *€5.50.* 🕗 *30min.)* Buses depart frequently to airport *(5:15am-11:15pm)* and to the city *(6:05am-12:05am).* Buy tickets in bars and newstands right outside the station or onboard *(€0.50 surcharge).* Train to the airport departs from Stazione Dora *(*💲 *€3.40.* 🕗 *20min., every 30min.)* to the airport 5:04am-11:09pm and to Turin 5:05am-9:45pm. The DoraFly bus connects Stazione Dora to Porta Susa and the underground line, or take tram #10 from Porta Susa or buses #46 or 49.

By Train

Stazione Porta Nuova *(☎89 20 21 or ☎011 66 53 098)*, on C.Vittorio Emanuele II, is the main hub. Trains to: **Milan** *($ €9.55. 🕑 2hr., departs every hr. 4:50am-10:50pm.)*; **Rome** *($ From €41. 🕑 6-7hr., 9 per day 6:37am-9:55pm.)*; **Venice.** *($ From €35. 🕑 5hr., departs every hr. 4:50am-10:50pm.)* Turin's **Stazione Porta Susa** is one stop toward Milan and has TGV trains to **Paris** via **Lyon.** *($ Around €95. 🕑 5-6hr.; 8:11am, 9:40am, 5:35pm, 7:05pm, 9:18pm.)*

Getting Around

Buy public transportation tickets at *tabaccherie*, newstands, or bars. Buses run daily 5am-1am; some routes stop at midnight. Friday through Saturday, a few special "Night Buster" routes run until 5am, so if you're paying attention, you'll realize that means 24hr. service. *($ 70min. tickets to city buses and trams €1, 1-day tickets €3.50, weekly passes €9.50.)* The **Metro** is less useful for seeing the city and, because it is still under construction, can be unreliable. Tickets *(€1)* are single-use only, but valid for 70min. on other forms of transport. Get a public transit map that include all bus and tram routes from the tourist office. **Taxis** can be found throughout the city or phoned for service *(☎011 57 37 or ☎011 57 30)*. For **Bike Rental,** try **Tourinbike.** *(V. Fiochetto 39 ☎011 57 93 314 🖥www.tourinbike.com $ €10 per 4hr., €15 per day, discounts for multiple days.)*

tourin' card

Boy, does Turin have a deal for you! The biggest steal in the city is the **Torino+Piemonte Card** *($ 48hr. €20, 7-days €35)*, which provides free entrance to all the museums and monuments in Turin and Piedmont, rides on public transportation (except underground), access to the hop-on, hop-off TurismoBus Torino, the panoramic lift in the Mole, the Sassi-Superga cable car, and the boats for river navigation on the Po, as well as discounts on guided tours and shows. The card is available at any Turismo Torino info point and at most hotels.

venice *venezia* ☎041

On any given day, the number of tourists in Venice—20 million annually—constitutes a larger percentage of the city's population than do locals—all 60,000 of them. This has given the city an unfairly reductive reputation as a tourist hub whose beauty and charm have been eviscerated by camera-toting yokels without an appreciation for anything outside a good photo op. Though you're certain to encounter the neon fanny pack crowd in the major squares, churches, museums, and monuments, if you let yourself escape down any one of Venice's many labyrinthine side streets, you'll discover traces of Venice's glorious past preserved in dilapidated *palazzi*, beautiful syncretic architecture hinting at Eastern influences, and street signs written in the vanishing Venetian dialect. Moreover, you'll find a vibrant and resilient local culture impervious to the tourist onslaught. Characterized by an incredible performance art and music scene, some of Italy's best seafood, bustling docks where local artisans still repair **boats** by hand, and numerous schools dedicated to building upon Venice's artistic legacy in the modern era, this hardy spirit makes modern Venice a joy to explore. This collection of 117 islands in a lagoon of the Adriatic Sea is famously both a difficult city to know and an easy city to love, but if you're not afraid to step off the beaten path, you'll come to appreciate the subtleties of the Venetian character that can't be discovered on a gondola ride or captured in a postcard.

ORIENTATION

Venice's historical center is comprised of six main *sestieri* (neighborhoods). Often divided along vague boundaries, the neighborhoods each consist of several islands. **San Marco** is at the geographic center of the city, across the Grand Canal from **San Polo** and **Santa Croce**. **Cannaregio** lies to San Marco's north and **Castello** to its northeast, while **Dorsoduro** marks the city's southern edge. Outside of the city proper, a set of numerous islands including Giudecca, Lido, Murano, and Burano are not to be forgotten.

San Marco

While walking along the quiet canals of Venice's residential neighborhoods, it's easy to forget that on an average day the city is populated by just as many tourists as full-time residents. Cross over to San Marco, and that fact hits you with full force—dozens of museums, upscale hotels, designer stores, art galleries, and, of course, thousands upon thousands of tourists. The crisis of conscience most travelers undergo when planning their time in Venice is usually this: "How much time should I spend in San Marco?" Because let's be honest—as crowded and expensive as San Marco is—the neighborhood is popular for good reason. The museums and sights here are as impressive as you'll find anywhere in Europe, and the tourist industry has brought world-class shopping, hotels, and cuisine to the area, particularly to the region closest to **Piazza San Marco**. Travelers who want to spend just a couple days in Venice but want to see all of the city's typical postcard attractions should look for a budget hotel on the fringes of the neighborhood. This won't put you more than a 10min. walk from either the Rialto Bridge or P. San Marco. Be forewarned, however, that San Marco is conspicuously less residential than any other neighborhood in Venice—if you're in a section that isn't currently overrun by tourists, it's likely to seem a bit abandoned or even post-apocalyptic.

Cannaregio

Cannaregio is one of Venice's largest neighborhoods, and for travelers willing to step off the beaten path, it offers a great opportunity to see a less touristy side of Venice than is on display in places like San Marco. Most hotels are located on the eastern and western edges of the neighborhood (by the Rialto Bridge and train station, respectively) in areas with a fair amount of tourist traffic, but the beauty of Cannaregio is that you're never more than 10min. away from both the liveliest, most crowded *piazze* and the quiet residential neighborhoods that are more representative of typical Venetian life.

San Polo

San Polo is the smallest of Venice's six *sestiere*, but its location in the heart of the city makes it a prime tourist destination. The **Rialto Bridge** markets and **Frari Church** are among San Polo's highlights. Many tourists also favor the neighborhood for shopping, both for souvenirs and upscale clothing, and dining, as San Polo's concentration of high-quality restaurants sets the city standard. Surprisingly, despite the heavy tourist traffic, there are relatively few hotels. However, those that are available tend to be reasonably priced affairs with good access to the city's points of interest. Despite the neighborhood's small size, it's surprisingly easy to get lost, especially if you think that the signs reading "San Marco" are actually leading you toward the square—in many cases, they're not. Your best bet is use a map and stick to wider streets with more tourists. If you try to take shortcuts, you'll probably end up walking in circles.

Santa Croce

Although a small neighborhood by Venetian standards, Santa Croce is incredibly diverse and easily accessible from western Cannaregio, San Polo, and Dorsoduro. **Piazzale Roma,** the main stop for most buses and taxis coming into Venice, is located in Santa Croce and defines the character of the neighborhood's western side. Restaurants and hotels around this transportation hub tend to be of a generic international style, so visitors to Santa Croce who see only this section of the neighborhood will leave

venice . orientation

unimpressed. The small area near San Polo, however, offers some of the best restaurants and hotels in Venice at exceptionally reasonable prices. From the main street of **Salizada San Pantalon,** the sights of Cannaregio as well as the restaurants and nightlife of Dorsoduro are easily accessible. For travelers willing to trek a bit in order to reach Venice's main sights, Santa Croce can serve as a budget-friendly base camp.

Dorsoduro

As neighborhoods go, Dorsoduro is a *Let's Go* favorite. Unlike some of the other *sestiere*, Dorsoduro possesses the ideal combination of awesome local flavor, proximity to major sights, great nightlife, and exceptional restaurants. Granted, if you want to stay in Dorsoduro, you'll probably pay 25% more than you would for a comparable room in Santa Croce or Cannaregio, but, as in most Italian cities, with a little luck and a little haggling you can still end up with a bargain. Moreover, the intersection of San Polo, Santa Croce, and Dorsoduro is the heart of Venice. From here, or just about anywhere else in Dorsoduro, you shouldn't be more than a few minutes from some of Venice's best museums. You also won't have to struggle too much to make it back to your hotel after a night out. Dorsoduro has its fill of unique side streets but remains an easily navigable neighborhood (at least by Venetian standards), with more incredible restaurants, fabulous art galleries, and cool shops than any other district in Venice. Whether you stay in Dorsoduro or not, do not make the mistake of relegating the neighborhood to the bottom of your itinerary—there is no better way to experience Venice than by wandering through Dorsoduro, *sans* map, in a day spent getting lost in the neighborhood's winding roads and alleyways.

Castello

With proximity to two of Venice's prime tourist destinations, the Rialto Bridge and P. San Marco, Castello is in many ways a less expensive alternative to San Marco. If you know where to look, you can find great hotels and restaurants at much more competitive prices. While Castello tends to get a lot of spillover tourist traffic from San Marco, the farther north and east you go, the more apparent Castello's charming, quaint local character becomes. Since Venice lacks traditional streets, neighborhoods can change from block to block. This is especially evident here, where crowded, loud, and overdeveloped thoroughfares suddenly give way to quiet and scenic side streets. If you have a few days in Venice, it's certainly worth exploring this neighborhood, including its eastern portion; however, there are few notable sights, and it's easy to get lost. Though residents proudly proclaim that eastern Castello represents the true, vanishing Venice, visitors will find the west more to their liking, with excellent restaurants and easy access to the rest of the city.

ACCOMMODATIONS

Though Venice has very few hostels, there are dozens upon dozens of great budget hotels throughout the city that are typically worth the extra cost. Save money by requesting a room with a shared bathroom. Your bedroom will be private (and typically with its own sink), but you will share a shower and toilet with the other people on your floor. Since most small hotels offering Wi-Fi, A/C, or wheelchair-accessibility only have a limited number of rooms with these features, particular requests for room selection should be made ahead by phone or email. Booking in advance can also help you find a lower rate. Nightly rates almost always include breakfast, which can range from some toast and coffee to an extravagant affair. Don't be afraid to negotiate prices; offering to pay in cash sometimes helps travelers finagle a lower rate. If you want to sleep right by Venice's major sights or in a room with views of the Grand Canal, it'll cost you. Most travelers, however, will probably find the minor inconvenience of being a few minutes removed from the hot spots worth the few dozen euro they save nightly by staying at one of Venice's numerous budget accommodations.

San Marco

Unlike most other Venetian neighborhoods, which are home to primarily 1- and 2-star hotels, San Marco is packed with establishments of the 4- and 5-star variety whose luxury is exceeded only by the amount you'll have to drop to book one of their rooms. Still, there are bargains to be had, particularly if you're willing to stay on the western side of the neighborhood, farther from the **Rialto Bridge** and **Piazza San Marco.**

👍 NOVECENTO

💳🚭📶❄ HOTEL [5]

Calle del Dose 2683 ☎041 52 12 145 💻www.novecento.biz

Incorporating South and East Asian design influences, trendy Novecento sets the standard for boutique hotels in Venice. With excellent lounge areas, top-notch rooms (each with its own unique design theme), and access to a nearby fitness club free of charge, Novecento offers amenities and a quality of service unmatched by the vast majority of budget hotels in Venice.

➜ V: Santa Maria del Giglio. Walk north approximately 45sec.; hotel is on the right. ℹ Breakfast included. $ Singles €100-130; doubles €160-260; triples €180-300.

👍 HOTEL CASANOVA

💳♿ HOTEL [5]

Frezzeria 1284 ☎041 52 06 855 💻www.hotelcasanova.it

Approximately 1min. away from P. San Marco, Hotel Casanova is an incredible value for the area. Though you'll have to contend with chaos on the narrow street below from dawn until dusk, you can't get much closer to Venice's main attractions. With Hotel Casanova's exceptional accommodations, the largest and most comfortable you'll find anywhere in Venice in this price range, you get convenience without sacrificing quality.

➜ Exit the southwest corner of P. San Marco, opposite Basilica di San Marco, and take 1st right onto Frezzeria; the hotel is less than 1min. ahead on the right. ℹ Breakfast included. $ Singles €70-120; doubles €90-170; triples €120-200; quads €150-230.

HOTEL SERENISSIMA

💳🚭📶❄ HOTEL [5]

Calle Goldoni 4486 ☎041 52 00 011 💻www.hotelserenissima.it

Close to P. San Marco yet far enough away to evade most tourist traffic, the aptly named Hotel Serenissima sits on a quiet street with great shopping and fine dining nearby. The rooms are full of white decorations, meaning that any smidge of dirt could show up tenfold. Perhaps that's why the management keeps every room strikingly clean. If you've been trudging around the canals all day, make sure to take your boots off so as not to dirty this place's immaculate interior.

➜ From P. San Marco, exit west opposite Basilica di San Marco, turn right, and continue straight for 2-3min. across 1 bridge; the hotel is on the left. ℹ Breakfast included. $ Singles €81-120; doubles €120-180; triples €150-235; quads €190-275.

Cannaregio

Cannaregio has some of the best budget hotels in Venice, particularly on the western islands near the train station. Luckily, the rest of the traveling world hasn't caught on yet, and even if you're arriving in Venice without a reservation during the busy season, Cannaregio has many top-notch accommodations that can be booked at reasonable rates. The neighborhood itself is mostly residential and has a more laidback vibe than other areas of Venice.

👍 HOTEL SILVA ARIEL

💳♿❄ HOTEL [4]

Calle della Masena 1391/A ☎041 72 93 26 💻www.arielsilva.it

If you're able to negotiate a good price with the manager, Hotel Silva Ariel is one of the best values you'll find in all of Venice. A couple blocks removed from the more tourist-laden area around Campo San Geremia, this beautiful and spacious hotel sits relatively close to almost anything you would want to see in Cannaregio.

➜ Left from the train station, then 5min. walk over Guglie Bridge and left onto Calle della Masena. ℹ Breakfast included. $ Singles €55-75; doubles €80-100.

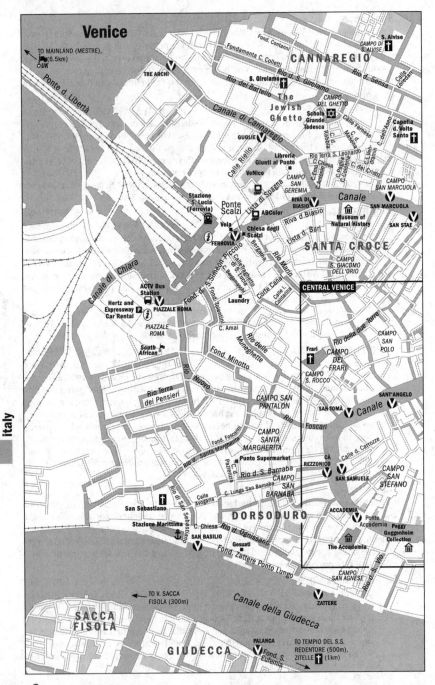

Venice

TO MAINLAND (MESTRE),
(6.5km)
UK

Ponte d. Libertà

TRE ARCHI

Fond. Contanni

Fondamenta C. Colletti

Rio d. S. Girolamo

CANNAREGIO

Rio d. Sensa

Calle Loredan

S. Alvise

CAMPO DI
S. ALVISE

S. Girolamo

Rio del Battello

The
Jewish
Ghetto

CAMPO
DEL GHETTO

Schola
Grande
Tedesca

Calle Farnese

Rabbia

Capella
d. Volto
Santo

Calle dell'Aseo

Canale di Cannaregio

GUGLIE

Calle Riello

Libreria
Giunti al Punto

VeNice

Rio Terra S. Leonardo

C. Chiesa

C. Cantoni

C. Emo

C. Poglia

C. Coletta

C. del Cristo

CAMPO
SAN MARCUOLA

Stazione
S. Lucia
(Ferrovia)

Ponte
Scalzi

Lista di Spagna

CAMPO
SAN
GEREMIA

RIVA DI
BIASIO

ABColor

Riva d.Biasio

Canale

SAN MARCUOLA

Museum of
Natural History

SAN STAE

Vela

FERROVIA

Chiesa degli
Scalzi

Lista d. Bari

SANTA CROCE

Fond. d. S. Simeon Piccolo

Callefragetto
d. S. Lucia

C. Bergamaschi

Rio Marin

Bergama

Rio L.
Contarina

CAMPO
S. GIACOMO
DELL'ORIO

Canale di Chiara

ACTV Bus
Station

Hertz and
Expressway
Car Rental

PIAZZALE ROMA

PIAZZALE
ROMA

C. Fond. Tolentini

Laundry

Corte Canal

Calle L.
Contarina

CENTRAL VENICE

South
African

C. Amai

Rio delle
Muneghette

Fond. Minotto

Rio
della due Torre

Frari

CAMPO
DEI
FRARI

CAMPO
SAN
POLO

Rio Nuovo

Rio Terra
dei Pensieri

Fond. Foscari

CAMPO SAN
PANTALON

CAMPO
S. ROCCO

SAN TOMA

Canale

Foscari

SANT'ANGELO

CAMPO
SANTA
MARGHERITA

RIO D. Santa Margherita

Punto Supermarket

Rio d. S Barnaba

C. d.
Patena

Calle
Avogaria

C. Lunga San Barnaba

CAMPO
SAN
BARNABA

CÀ
REZZONICO

SAN SAMUELE

Calle d. Carrozze

CAMPO
SAN
STEFANO

San Sebastiano

Stazione Marittima

C. Chiesa

Rio d. Ognissanti

DORSODURO

SAN BASILIO

Gesuati

Fond. Zattere Ponto Lungo

ACCADEMIA

Ponte
Accademia

Peggy
Guggenheim
Collection

The Accademia

CAMPO
SAN AGNESE

Rio d. S. Vio

TO V. SACCA
FISOLA (300m)

Canale della Giudecca

ZATTERE

**SACCA
FISOLA**

GIUDECCA

PALANCA

Fond. S.
Eufemia

TO TEMPIO DEL S.S.
REDENTORE (500m),
ZITELLE (1km)

italy

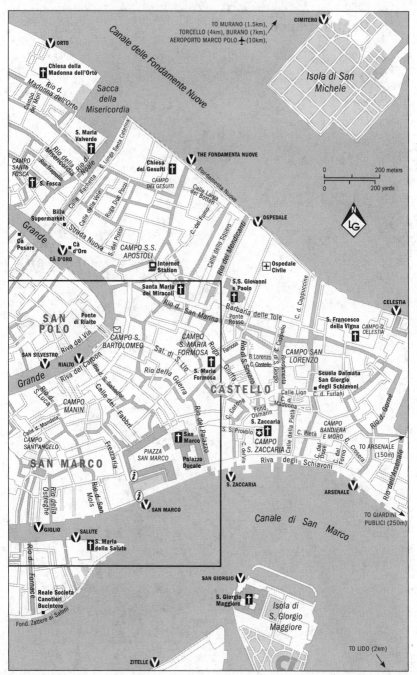

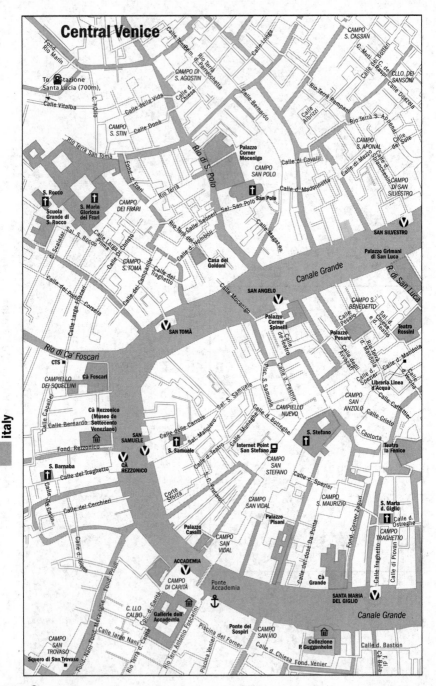

Central Venice

To Stazione Santa Lucia (700m),

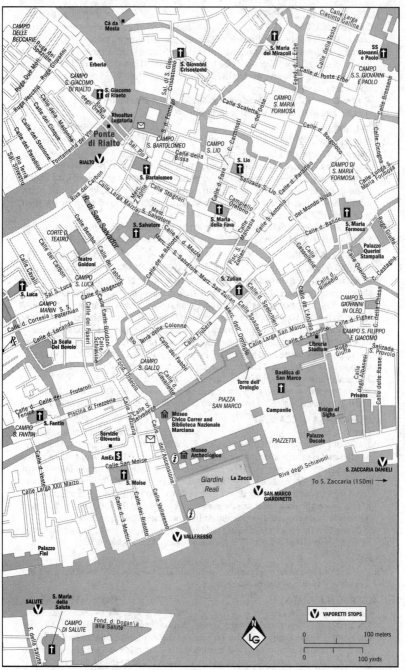

HOTEL BERNARDI SEMENZATO

◆⊗⟨ᵖ⟩❈ HOTEL ❷

Calle dell'Oca 4366 ☎041 52 27 257 ▣www.hotelbernardi.com

Lots of hotels on the eastern side of Cannaregio are overpriced and poorly maintained, but Hotel Bernardi bucks the trend by offering great rooms at ridiculously low prices (well, for Venice at least). The singles without private bathrooms can get uncomfortably warm during the summer, but the free Wi-Fi more than makes up for this minor discomfort.

⚒ *From Campo SS. Apostoli, head north on Salizada Pistor and take the 1st left.* *i Breakfast included. Free Wi-Fi.* Ⓢ *Singles €30-35; doubles €54-78.*

HOTEL ROSSI

◆⊗⟨ᵖ⟩❈ HOTEL ❸

Lista di Spagna 262 ☎041 71 51 64 ▣www.hotelrossi.ve.it

Just a few steps off Lista di Spagna, Hotel Rossi's peaceful setting seems miles (kilometers?) away from Cannaregio's more active center. Next to one of the neighborhood's nicest gardens, this hotel has reasonably large rooms, air conditioning, and understated classic Italian decor—all of which make it popular with middle-aged tourists, but perhaps less so with students scared away by the high Wi-Fi fee *(€14 per 24hr.).*

⚒ *Walk 3min. from the train station, then turn left down a side street immediately before Campo San Geremia.* *i Breakfast included.* Ⓢ *Singles €45-72; doubles €80-95.*

HOTEL STELLA ALPINA

◆♿⟨ᵖ⟩❈ HOTEL ❺

Calle Priuli 99/D ☎041 52 45 274 ▣www.hotel-stellaalpina.com

If you've been on the road for a while and the thought of another night spent in a sleeping sack is making you wish you'd stayed home and taken that summer job at Taco Bell, look no further than Hotel Stella Alpina, which offers budget-friendly luxury to the tired traveler. From the classic, almost formal, furnishings in the lobby to the modern decor in the dining room and bedrooms, this hotel's ambience certainly tops that of your local fast food franchise. But you'll have totally forgotten about your lost opportunity in the food service industry once you've laid yourself down in one of the hotel's air-conditioned rooms on the most comfortable bed you might ever find. Just make sure to get the job next summer to pay for this splurge . . .

⚒ *From train station, turn left at the 1st st. past Calle Carmelitani and walk for about 1.5min.* *i Breakfast included. Discount for booking ahead online.* Ⓢ *Singles €70-90; doubles €75-105.*

ALBERGO CASA BOCCASSINI

◆♿ HOTEL ❺

Calle Volto 5295 ☎041 52 29 892 ▣www.hotelboccassini.com

You could walk right past Albergo Casa Boccassini and never know it was there, nestled as it is in an unassuming residential area removed from Cannaregio's major thoroughfares. However, you'd be missing one of this neighborhood's little-known all-stars. Casa Boccassini's comfortably-sized and thoughtfully-decorated rooms seem well priced (especially if you haggle down the rate), but the true standouts of this inconspicuous hotel are its gorgeous garden and the delightful indoor and outdoor seating you can enjoy while eating your complimentary breakfast.

⚒ *Coming from Fondamenta Nuove along Calle del Fumo, turn right at the 1st st. past Calle Larga dei Boteri.* *i Breakfast included* Ⓢ *High-season singles €70, low-season €50.*

San Polo

Though San Polo is home to relatively few hotels and hostels, the ones that are here offer a central location at double-take rates.

ALBERGO GUERRATO

◆⊗⟨ᵖ⟩ PENSIONE ❹

Calle drio la Scimia 240/a ☎041 52 85 927 ▣www.pensioneguerrato.it

Located in an 800-year-old *palazzo* just steps away from the Rialto Bridge, Albergo Guerrato offers competitive rates on some of the most desirable rooms in Venice. Characterized by simple but neat aesthetics that focus less on excessive decoration and more on comfort, they're perfectly suited to hard-living travelers.

*From the Rialto Bridge, continue west and turn onto the 3rd street on the right; the hotel is shortly ahead on the right. **i** Breakfast included. **$** Doubles €95-140; triples €120-155; quads €185; quints €195.*

A VENICE MUSEUM

Calle del Traghetto 2812

🖢⊗⊗⁽ᵖ⁾❄ HOSTEL ❷

☎340 73 57 468

The owners of A Venice Museum, one of the very few true youth hostels in Venice, are so committed to running a fun, vibrant, engaging, and social establishment that they've banned everyone over 40 (not a joke—check the age requirements). The price is unbelievable, you can do laundry on-site (an indescribably huge perk given the lack of laundromats in Venice), and the hostel hosts dinner every night for only €3. If you're the type who doesn't mind waiting for the shower and loves to party with loud music until late at night, you're sure to have a blast here.

*V: San Tomà. Go straight, make the 1st right, take the next right, and then take the next right. The hostel is not conspicuously advertised; look for a dark green door with several doorbells. Ring the one that says "Museum" for entrance to the hostel. **i** Breakfast included. Linens €5 per night; towels €2. Dinner €3. Under 40 only. **$** Dorms €28-35.*

approximations

Enrico Fermi—physicist, quantum theorist, statistician. Italian.

Fermi had one of the greatest scientific minds of the 20th century, but spending time in Italy is enough to make you question his method of informal approximation. Basically, Fermi argued that one could accurately estimate the answers to complex problems by appropriately analyzing their necessary factors and assumptions. Fermi's theory has clearly been taken to heart by the people of Italy, because everyone here approximates. Everything. All the time. And, sadly, not always as well as Fermi did.

Directions tend to be kind of dicey approximations—we're pretty sure that over 75% of hotels in Venice claim to be within 5min. walking distance of the Rialto Bridge. Wi-Fi availability is also a source of wild estimation. If a hotel advertises wireless internet access, what they really mean is that they have some *approximation* of Wi-Fi—even if it's only in the lobby and working roughly 3hr. per day. Most restaurants and hotels boast of their A/C, which they definitely have...at least in one room. But it might not be working this week.

There are perks to this system of guesstimation as well. In the states, we tend to think of prices as set in stone, but here, they are simply estimates—estimates that can be recalculated based on how charming a shop owner finds you. The approximation of opening and closing times also tends to work out well: in Venice, you'll never have a restaurant door closed on you because you arrived 5min. after business was supposed to end. Also, if you sleep past check-out time, don't sweat it—as long as you exit your room *approximately* on time.

To strung-out, type-"A" Americans, the blurry lines of Venetian approximation can be frustrating to no end. If you, like *Let's Go* researchers, make a habit of hanging around in hotel lobbies, you'll see plenty of arguments between managers and customers over technicalities to which the customer adheres rigidly and the proprietor, well, not so much. Venice is a wonderful city with a lot to be appreciated, but to most enjoy the city, it's best to quickly learn how to chill out and take things as they come. And trust that they will turn out right...more or less.

venice • accommodations

LOCANDO CA' SAN POLO 💳♿📶❄ HOTEL ❹

Calle Saoneri de la Malvasia 2697 ☎041 24 40 331 💻www.casanpolo.it

If you want luxurious accommodations in Venice without spending all your money at once, do you (a) seduce a rich Venetian heiress, (b) sneak into Palazzo Ducale and take up residence in the Doge's Apartments, or (c) stay here? Ca' San Polo is by far the most legal, moral, and plausible of these three options. With study desks, blackout curtains, comfortable king-size beds, and beautiful views of the neighborhood from the third-floor terrace and dining area, this hotel proves that budget and luxury are not mutually exclusive.

🧭 *V: San Tomà. Continue north toward Frari, turn right, continue across the bridge, turn right, and take the 1st left; the hotel is ahead on the right. Signs indicate the direction toward the hotel.* ℹ *Breakfast included.* [$] *Doubles €80-110; triples €100-120; quads €140-180.*

HOTEL ALEX 💳🚭 HOTEL ❸

Frari 2606 ☎041 52 31 341 💻www.hotelalexinvenice.com

A small family hotel just across the bridge from the Frari, Hotel Alex prides itself on offering clean, quiet, and comfortable rooms. Though students may feel out of place in the family atmosphere, quads that go for €20 per person per night make hosteling look like a crummy deal. Consider booking in advance to request a room with a balcony overlooking the street.

🧭 *V: San Tomà. Continue north toward Frari, turn right, continue across the bridge, turn right, and turn left; the hotel is ahead on the left.* ℹ *Breakfast included.* [$] *Singles €35-56; doubles €40-120; triples €60-162; quads €80-200.*

Santa Croce

Although Santa Croce isn't known for its budget accommodations, you can find a room at the right price to make the neighborhood your home-away-from-home. Santa Croce is centrally located, with San Marco and the Rialto Bridge just minutes away and the nightlife in Dorsoduro easily accessible. At the same time, the neighborhood enjoys wide, quiet streets that aren't overrun with tourists. It's best to stay away from its western side, as you're more likely to discover good deals in the eastern section.

👍 **ALBERGO AI TOLENTINI** 💳🚭📶 HOTEL ❹

Santa Croce 197/G ☎041 27 59 140 💻www.albergoaitolentini.com

Albergo ai Tolentini is a small hotel without many different options accommodations-wise, but what it does have is exceptional. Start with what are in all likelihood the largest double rooms you'll find for less than €100 in Venice, decorated in an elaborate Venetian style and featuring private baths. Add on the hotel's convenient location, which is about as central as you can get in Venice, and you've got the makings of one very serviceable little hotel.

🧭 *Follow Piazzale Roma east, cross consecutive bridges, turn left, and continue along canal for 3-4min. before turning right away from Hotel Sofitel. Continue for 2min.; hotel is on the left.* ℹ *Breakfast included.* [$] *Doubles €85-115.*

ALBERGO CASA PERON 💳🚭 HOTEL ❸

Salizzada S. Pantalon 84 ☎041 71 00 21 💻www.casaperon.com

A small, family-owned hotel with tons of personality, Albergo Casa Peron is worth the time to book in advance. A prime location on one of Santa Croce's main streets put this hotel in our good graces from the outset, but Albergo Casa Peron scores extra points with *Let's Go* for its supremely cool owner and the pet parrot who helps oversee the hotel from his shoulder.

🧭 *Follow Piazzale Roma east, cross consecutive bridges, and continue for approximately 2min.* ℹ *Breakfast included.* [$] *Singles €30-90; doubles €50-100; triples €80-130.*

PENSIONE DA IVANO 💳♿ PENSIONE ❸

Santa Croce 373 ☎041 524 66 48 💻www.daivanovenezia.it

Close to Piazzale Roma, Pensione da Ivano possesses a peaceful location, despite being a bit out of the way. The spacious, well-decorated rooms are only brightened by the friendly presence of their dedicated manager, who has owned the *pensione* and nearby Caffé Las Ramblas for the past 37 years. Feel free to chat him up, as he loves to talk with travelers about his city.

✦ *East from Piazzale Roma, turn right at the 1st canal you see and turn right onto Sestiere Santa Croce. Go to Caffé Las Ramblas, where you can be redirected to the pensione (4min. away).* ✦ *Breakfast included.* Ⓢ *Rooms €45-100.*

HOTEL FALIER
✦�(ᵠ)❄ HOTEL ⑤

Salizada S. Pantalon 130 ☎041 71 08 82 ◼www.hotelfalier.com

Most of the hotels in the Santa Croce area are rather pricey, but Hotel Falier bridges the gap between luxury and budget fairly well. The price of a single room is as far from inexpensive as Venice is from Sicily, but the doubles are a good value compared to some of the luxury hotels in the neighborhood, without any compromise in quality. You won't be cheated the extra bucks you're shelling out: the hotel's phenomenal location is accompanied by an excellent dining room, a desk manager fluent in English, a lovely balcony, and other subtle pleasantries.

✦ *Follow Piazzale Roma east, cross consecutive bridges, and continue for approximately 2min.* ✦ *Breakfast included.* Ⓢ *Singles €100-150; doubles €120-170.*

Dorsoduro

Finding a good hotel at the right price can be tricky in Dorsoduro, but if you're patient and willing to put in a little bit of legwork calling places or checking their websites, you should be able to find a solid rate on a great hotel in the heart of Venice's best neighborhood.

🏨 HOTEL MESSNER
✦�(ᵠ)❄ HOTEL ⑤

Fondamenta di Cà Bala 216/217 ☎041 52 27 443 ◼www.hotelmessner.it

Described by its owner as "three hotels in one," Hotel Messner offers one-, two-, and three-star accommodations—great for budget travelers who want to save money but still have the flexibility to choose their room's amenities. Regardless of star ranking, most rooms are brightened by floor-to-ceiling windows that prove a blessing in the humid Venetian summer.

✦ *V: Zattere. Turn right, walk 4-5min., turn left onto Fondamenta di Cà Bala and continue for about a min. Reception is approximately 1min. past the hotel in Ristorante Messner.* ✦ *Breakfast included.* Ⓢ *Singles €70-105; doubles €95-160; triples €135-180; quads €150-200.*

🏨 HOTEL ALLA SALUTE
✦�(ᵠ) HOTEL ③

Fondamenta di Cà Bala 222 ☎041 52 35 404 ◼www.hotelsalute.com

A lot of hotels in Venice overdo the whole Venetian theme, making you feel as if you're trapped in an antique dealer's storage facility. Hotel alla Salute, by contrast, presents a simple, modern take on Venetian aesthetics with some of the least cluttered and most beautiful hotel rooms in the city. Given the hotel's prime location and generous breakfast buffet, staying here is quite a deal.

✦ *V: Zattere. Turn right, walk 4-5min., turn left onto Fondamenta di Cà Bala and continue for about 2min.* ✦ *Breakfast included.* Ⓢ *Doubles €64-95; family rooms (fit 3-5) €75-135.*

HOTEL AMERICAN
✦�(ᵠ)❄ HOTEL ④

San Vio 628 ☎041 52 04 733 ◼www.hotelamerican.com

If you can book Hotel American anywhere at the bottom of their price range, we strongly advise you to do so. In addition to its regal old-world-hotel regal air, the American possesses all the amenities you could possibly want from a budget hotel.

✦ *V: Zattere. Turn right, walk 3-4min., turn left onto San Vio and continue for just over 1min.* ✦ *Breakfast included.* Ⓢ *Singles €60-230; doubles €80-370; suite €150-460. Extra bed €20-70.*

ANTICA LOCANDA MONTIN
✦⊗ B AND B ④

Fondamenta Eremite 1147 ☎041 52 25 151 ◼www.locandamontin.com

Although it is less than 2min. from each of Dorsoduro's two biggest streets,

Antica Locanda Montin feels removed from these heavily trafficked areas. This is a small inn that lacks some of the conveniences available at large hotels, but it makes up for this inadequacy with a quaint small-town ambience and excellent values on exceptionally comfortable rooms.

➡ V: Zattere. Turn right, take the first possible left, cross the bridge, turn left, turn immediately right, and the hotel is shortly ahead on the left. i Breakfast included. $ Singles €50-70; doubles €130-160.

ALBERGO HOTEL ANTICO CAPON 🚭📶❄ HOTEL [2]

Campo San Margherita 3004 ☎041 52 85 292 🖥wwww.anticocapon.altervista.org

Hotel Antico Capon's location is both a blessing and a curse. If you want to party every night, the location right in Campo San Margherita, Dorsoduro's prime nightlife spot, will be perfect. If you want to sleep early, good luck ignoring the din echoing through the square. The rooms here are cheap for a reason: they're tiny.

➡ Opposite the northeast corner of the square. i Breakfast included. $ Doubles €45-95; triples €60-75; quads €120.

Castello

Castello is bursting at the seams with overpriced hotels looking to exploit tourists who mistakenly believe they just have to be within a 5min. walk of the Rialto Bridge and P. San Marco. Hidden among these flashy establishments, however, are a good number of hotels that are accessible to the major sights but manage to maintain the quiet neighborhood ambience that makes Venice so charming.

👍 **LA RESIDENZA** 💳🚭📶 HOTEL [4]

Campo Bandiera e Moro 3608 ☎041 52 85 315 🖥www.venicelaresidenza.com

Every hotel in Venice wants to claim that it is located in a former palace, but at La Residenza, you can tell that they aren't lying. The regal decor, stately reception area, and magnificently decorated guest rooms evoke a sense of Venice's extravagant mercantile history. Although this is far from the typical budget hotel, staying here provides a uniquely Venetian experience.

➡ From P. San Marco, walk towards the water, turn left, and cross 4 bridges; then turn left and continue to Campo Bandiera e Moro. i Breakfast included. Free Wi-Fi. $ Singles €50-110; doubles €60-200. Extra bed €35.

italy

👍 **THE GUESTHOUSE TAVERNA SAN LIO** 💳🚭📶❄ B AND B [4]

Salizada San Lio 5547 ☎041 27 77 06 69 🖥www.tavernasanlio.com

Staying in Venice on a budget means foregoing a lot of luxuries that might be taken for granted in American hotels, but if you book a room at the Guesthouse Taverna San Lio at the right time, you can get an incredible room that feels authentically Venetian yet still includes Wi-Fi, A/C, a private bathoom—creature comforts certainly not enjoyed by the city's Renaissance residents—and, perhaps most importantly, a mouth-watering breakfast.

➡ From Rialto Bridge, go east along Salizada San Lio for 3-4min.; hotel is on the right. i Breakfast included. Free Wi-Fi. $ Doubles €70-150; triples €100-180; quads €130-200.

FORESTERIA VALDESE 💳♿ HOSTEL, HOTEL [2]

Palazzo Cavagnis 5170 ☎041 52 86 797 🖥www.foresteriavenezia.it

One of the few places in Venice to get a shared dormitory room more typical of a hostel, Foresteria Valdese is an oasis of value in a sea of €90-per-person, one-star hotels. The hotel is run by a Protestant church that maintains the house in which the hotel is located. While the reservation system can be tricky, especially for dorms, Foresteria Valdese offers both a unique experience and a great deal in Venice.

➡ From Campo Santa Maria Formosa, take Calle Larga Santa Maria Forma; Foresteria Valdese is immediately across the 1st bridge. i Breakfast included. $ Dorms €23-29; doubles €78-96; triples €90-111; quads €114-144.

ALBERGO DONI
💳🚭 HOTEL [4]

Calle del Vin 4656 ☎041 52 25 267 💻www.albergodoni.it

Rooms at the low end of the price range here are an absolute steal. Although you'll pay for proximity to P. San Marco with heavy tourist traffic and some street noise, the hotel's 17th-century building features spacious rooms, excellent antique furniture, and even some breathtaking ceiling frescoes.

➜ From P. San Marco, walk toward the water, turn left, and cross 2 bridges; take the 1st left and walk 30sec. ℹ Breakfast included. $ Singles €50-65; doubles €60-120.

CASA QUERINI
🛁🚭📶❄ HOTEL [5]

Campo San Giovanni Novo 4388 ☎041 24 11 294 💻www.locandaquerini.com

Situated in a quiet square apart from the madding crowds of P. San Marco, this hotel is an excellent choice for anyone who wants to be near Venice's tourist center but still enjoy a tranquil stay in a hotel with all the amenities. The decor is a bit minimalist and lacks the same Venetian touch of most other hotels in the area, but with private bathrooms, Wi-Fi, and A/C, this hotel's comfort-inducing features present a good trade-off for a lot of exhausted travelers.

➜ From P. San Marco, walk toward the water, turn left, cross Ponte della Paglia, turn left onto C. dei Albanesi, walk 2min., and turn left at Campo S. Giovanni Novo. ℹ Breakfast included. Wi-Fi €6 per hr. $ Doubles €110-150; triples €135-175.

Outskirts

By staying in the outskirts, you can upgrade your digs on the cheap or go even more bargain-basement than is possible in the *centro*. Lido is loaded with hotels that are less expensive than their Venetian counterparts, and ⛺**camping** on the islands or the Italian mainland is a popular alternative for even more saving. While camping might conjure up images of improvised tents and fishing for dinner, Italians campsites offer RV-park luxury, with fully furnished trailers or at least fairly decent permanent tents.

👍 OSTELLO DI VENEZIA (HI)
💳🚭📶❄ HOSTEL [2]

Fondamenta Zitelle 86 ☎041 52 38 211 💻www.hostelvenice.com

Ostello Venezia sets the standard for hostels in Venice. With 260 beds, a restaurant, common room, bar, and state-of-the-art facilities, it's an incredible value. Located in Giudecca, it's not too far from Dorsoduro or San Marco. Groups can often book rooms in advance, but outside of those cases, dorms are strictly divided by gender. For those apprehensive about leaving their belongings unattended in a room with a dozen other people, the hostel provides free private lockers with keys and padlocks. Though having to use the vaporetto system can be a bit of a hassle, the hostel's great facilities and efficient and helpful staff more than make up for any inconvenience caused by its out-of-the-way location.

➜ V: Zitelle, turn right and continue for less than 1min. The hostel is on the left. ℹ Breakfast included. €3 daily surcharge for those without YHA membership. Wi-Fi €2.50 per 12hr., internet terminals €3 per hr. $ Dorms €22. ⏰ Lockout 10am-1:30pm.

CAMPEGGIO SAN NICOLÒ
💳♿ CAMPING [1]

V. dei Sanmichieli 14 ☎041 52 67 415 💻www.campingsannicolo.com

Lido's only major camping site, Campeggio San Nicolò is a great budget option. Though the site is removed from Lido's major vaporetto stops, bike rentals make the island extremely accessible. Tents offer reasonable short-term accommodations, and campers are surprisingly nice given the cost per person. This kind of camping is an interesting and uniquely European experience—something worth trying before you leave Italy (though not cool enough to be attempted when rain is in the forecast).

➜ From dock Lido San Nicolò, turn right, and continue north for about 5min. There will be signs indicating the direction of the campsite. ℹ Laundry €3. Parking €2. Bike rental €7. $ Prices vary depending on what exactly you're looking for, but will probably cost about €18 per person per night.

CAMPING JOLLY
V. Giuseppe de Marchi 7

♠☀♿☼ CAMPING ❶

☎041 92 03 12 🖳www.ecvacanze.it

This is a place to stay if you want to *say* you came to Venice but actually spend your whole trip partying on the Italian mainland. It takes about 45min. to get from Camping Jolly to Venice proper, so don't pop your tent here if you want to be in the city. Instead, come here for the nice pool, awesome bar, tons of backpackers, and a DJ who seems to love Kanye West. Lots of people think that traveling is a lost art in the age of the internet, but dancing to 🔊Thriller with backpackers from Japan, some hair-metal fans from Germany, and a pair of Italian bartenders is a great reminder of what it can be when done right.

⚑ There are several ways to get to Camping Jolly. The best route from Venice is to take bus #6 from the train station toward Marghera, get off at V. Paleocapa, turn onto V. Beccaria, and continue for about 10min. until you reach V. Della Fonte. Turn right onto V. Della Fonte and continue until the street ends. You'll see an outdoor park/sports complex. Follow the walkway along the park until you reach an underpass. Go through the underpass, and you will emerge at Camping Jolly. ⑤ 1- to 3-person tents €12.50; bungalows (up to 3 people) €39-58.50; casa mobile (up to 4 people) €60-79; chalet (up to 5 people) €84-116.

SIGHTS

An incredible number of churches, museums, palaces, and historic sights line Venice's canals—you could easily spend a month in the city and still be stumbling across new places to check out on a daily basis. If you're planning to spend any time sightseeing here, you should seriously consider purchasing the **Rolling Venice Card** (available at any IAT/VAT Tourist office for €4), a tourist pass for visitors to the city between the ages of 14 and 29 which provides unlimited use of ACTV public transit, free admission to the Civic Museums of Venice, free admission to the churches that are a member of the Chorus Pass collective, reduced admission at any number of other sights, and discounts at various hotels and restaurants.

San Marco

It's easy to be overwhelmed by the number of sights in San Marco. In fact, before you even head out into the wider neighborhood, it's easy to be overwhelmed by the number of sights in **Piazza San Marco** alone. In the *piazza*, the two main attractions, **Basilica di San Marco** and **Palazzo Ducale,** are found easily enough, but several other sights of great interest are often overlooked by visitors. In the wider *sestiere* closer to **Rialto Bridge,** for example, attractions like the excellent **Palazzo Grassi** await. Perhaps most importantly, before braving this area be sure to meditate for a couple of minutes, have a glass of Venetian wine, pop a couple of Xanax, or do whatever else is necessary to prepare yourself for the jostling, shoving, elbowing, shouting, and general rudeness that crops up as inevitably in the heart of *La Serenissima* as it does in any overcrowded tourist area. Once you've done that, you'll be ready to experience one of the densest concentrations of spectacular sights in the whole of Europe.

🏛 PALAZZO DUCALE
P. San Marco 1

♠♿ PALAZZO, MUSEUM

☎041 27 15 911 🖳www.museiciviciveneziani.it

This massive palace that served as the residence of Venice's pseudo-monarchical mayor and the seat of his government throughout most of Venetian history is, perhaps, the best showcase of Venetian history, art, and architecture you'll find in a single building. Unfortunately, it has lost much of its character in recent years as it has increasingly sought to traffic as many visitors as possible through its exhibits with the most minimal inconvenience. Unlike the serene **Accademia** or **Guggenheim Museum,** where it's possible to move leisurely through the galleries and follow no particular path, the Palazzo Ducale poses challenges to those who would like to meander through its halls, as numerous guided tours block hallways and crowd some of the museum's most famous attractions. For the best way to

italy

see the Palazzo, rent a handheld audio tour *(€5)* or stop by the the museum shop to purchase a guide before you enter. Then, proceed at your own pace. While there are many bottlenecks in some of the more famous rooms, where guides tend to linger, if you time things well, you should be able to evade clusters of tourists while still managing to see everything. And there is a remarkable amount to see, from Sansovino's statues in the courtyard to Veronese's *Rape of Europa*.

Every room open to the public is worth visiting, and *Let's Go* recommends allowing yourself to wander through the Palazzo, spending more time in the rooms that are of particular interest to you. If you decide to go all-in and read about the history of every room, you could easily spend 4hr. in the place, but in any case, budget at least 90min. for your visit. No visit to the Palazzo Ducale can be complete without seeing Tintoretto's *Paradise*, an impossibly massive oil painting with strongly religious themes that gives the **Great Council Room** an ominous, foreboding air. The numerous exhibitions in the **Doge's Apartments,** including the Doge's private libraries and dining room, should prove fascinating to anyone with an interest in Venetian history or high culture. Surprisingly, one of the least crowded sections of the palace is the area containing the **Bridge of Sighs** and prisons, which constitute an extensive labyrinth throughout the lower eastern side of the palace and provide stark contrast to the opulence and majesty of the floors above.

 # Entrance to the Palazzo Ducale is along the waterfront. $ Apr 1-Oct 31 €13, students ages 18-25, ages 6-14, over 65, and holders of the Rolling Venice card €7.50; Nov 1-Mar 31 €12/6.50. 🕐 Open daily June-Oct 8:30am-6:30pm; Nov-March 9am-6pm; Apr-May 9am-7pm. Ticket office closes 1hr. before museum.

✓ BASILICA DI SAN MARCO ♿ CHURCH

P. San Marco ☎041 27 08 311 🖥www.basilicasanmarco.it

This basilica is maybe the top "can't miss" sight in all of Venice, and not just because admission is free. Lines to the Basilica are often long, but don't be deterred. Visitors rarely spend more than 15min. inside the Basilica, so even if you're behind a few hundred people, it shouldn't take more than a wait of 20min. or so for you to enter what is universally considered the most impressive church in Venice. If you're planning a day in P. San Marco, either go to the Basilica first thing in the morning before it is crowded or mid-afternoon when light streams in through the windows and provides some of the most striking natural illumination you'll find anywhere in the world.

Even before you enter the church, you cannot help but be struck by its size and intricate design. Spend a few minutes admiring the basilica's facade, overlooked by far too many visitors. It is every bit as impressive as the inside's soaring domes, marble inlay, and gorgeous golden mosaics that acquire an eerie life-like quality in the proper lighting. The majesty of the church is a testament to the history of Venice, as the Basilica di San Marco dates back to the origins of the city. Founded in the ninth century by two Venetian merchants who daringly stole St. Mark's remains from the city of Alexandria and smuggled them past Arab officials by hiding them in a case of pork meat, the church was originally a much smaller, more modest wooden building that suffered serious damage during a fire in the 11th century. Venice, emerging as a powerful city state, dedicated substantial time, effort, and funding to the construction of the new Basilica di San Marco, which was further embellished as the Republic of Venice rose in stature. Today, it stands more or less as it was completed in the 17th century. The church's interior is clearly the product of the various cultural influences that have affected the Venetian identity, seamlessly incorporating Byzantine, Roman, and Northern European influences into an interior that is simultaneously ostentatious in its gilded excess and mysterious in the dark, rich detail of its altars and mosaics.

Though admission to the Basilica is free, those interested in further exploration of the remarkable building's history will have to pay extra to see its three affiliated sights: the Pala d'Oro, treasury, and St. Mark's Museum. Anyone intrigued by the Byzantine influences in the Basilica should take a few minutes to appreciate the **Pala d'Oro**, an altar retable that is widely regarded as one of the most spectacular intact examples of Byzantine artwork. A visual history of the life of Saint Mark, the Pala d'Oro was meticulously designed with thousands of precious gemstones adorning what is certainly one of the most breathtaking pieces of religious artwork you'll see anywhere in Italy. The **treasury** houses various precious objects of religious significance, a collection that anyone with an interest in the history of the Basilica will enjoy exploring even if it includes a small fraction of the number of artifacts it featured prior to the Napoleonic invasions. **St. Mark's Museum** helps to contextualize the Basilica and is a great primer in Venetian history for anyone with a short stop in Venice. Nevertheless, visiting the museum isn't essential to appreciating the astounding beauty of the Basilica, which is the main attraction here.

✳ *Entrance on east side of P. San Marco, north of Palazzo Ducale.* ⓘ *Modest dress required—no bare shoulders or revealing skirts or shorts.* ⓢ *Basilica free. St. Mark's Museum €4. Pala d'Oro €2. Treasury €3. All prices reduced 50% for groups of 15 or more.* 🕐 *Basilica open Easter-Nov M-Sa 9:45am-5pm, Su 2-5pm; Nov-Easter M-Sa 9:45am-5pm, Su 2-4pm. Pala d'Oro and treasury open Easter-Nov M-Sa 9:45am-5pm, Su 2-5pm; Nov-Easter M-Sa 9:45am-4pm, Su 2-4pm. Museum open daily 9:45am-4:45pm.*

▨ PALAZZO GRASSI
Campo San Samuele 3231   ☎041 52 31 680 🖥www.palazzograssi.it

♥🔥 MUSEUM

A highbrow museum of contemporary art that's not afraid to laugh at itself, Palazzo Grassi is at once entertaining and refreshing. Sponsored by François Pinault and affiliated with the **Punta della Dogana** museum in Dorsoduro, Palazzo Grassi features artwork in numerous media from prominent contemporary artists such as **Matthew Day Jackson, Cy Twobly,** and **Jeff Koons.** The Palazzo's signature piece is a series of canvases that constitute a visual interpretation of events in Japanese history. Created by Takashi Murakami over the course of six years, the work was initiated at the behest of Pinault for installation specifically in this gallery. Even if you aren't familiar with modern art, there are enough pieces in enough media here that something is bound to interest, challenge, or even just amuse you. Unlike other sights in Venice, Palazzo Grassi doesn't shy away from self-parody. This is exemplified in Rob Pruitt's "101 Artistic Ideas," a work featured in the Mapping the Studio exhibition. Some of Pruitt's ideas have been put into practice throughout the museum. You might think you've seen every imaginable take on the Renaissance fresco after a few days in Venice, but until you've seen Idea #72 ("Put 👁googly eyes on things") put in practice on a priceless 17th-century mural, you really don't know what you're missing. Palazzo Grassi's sense of humor makes its collections more accessible to those with a casual interest in artwork, as do the frequent events that the museum hosts to introduce visitors to prominent artists and the artistic process. Such events seek to contradict, defy, and critique notions about art while maintaining a certain levity that gives the museum its welcoming, cheeky character.

✳ *Follow the signs to Palazzo Grassi/Palazzo Fortuny from anywhere in San Marco. If coming from the Rialto Bridge, continue along the streets running parallel to the Grand Canal, staying near the Canal, until you see signs directing you toward Palazzo Grassi. Palazzo Grassi is also immediately adjacent to vaporetto stops S. Samuele (line 2) and S. Angelo (line 1).* ⓢ *€15, with affiliated Punta della Dogana in Dorsoduro €20.* 🕐 *Open M 10am-7pm, W-Su 10am-7pm. Last entry 1hr. before close.*

PIAZZA SAN MARCO
P. San Marco

🔥 SQUARE

Indisputably the most important square in Venice and home to many of the city's most important historical and cultural attractions, P. San Marco is a study in contrasts. Chaotic despite its spectacular views of Venice's serene lagoon, this dignified, historical home of Venetian government is now overrun by tour groups of texting teenagers and foreigners who chase pigeons for amusement. In this way, P. San Marco encapsulates both the best and worst of Venice. When you stand in the square, you're only moments from the **Basilica di San Marco,** the **Campanile,** the **Palazzo Ducale, Saint Mark's Clock Tower,** and almost half a dozen notable museums. You're also just a few steps away from Venice's most upscale shopping and dining establishments, which draw visitors from all over the world. Though not without its high-end attractions, the *piazza* has mass appeal as well, with occasional street performers, numerous salesmen offering knock-off designer goods, gelato galore, and the infamous pigeons who have given rise to an industry of their own. Shrewd locals sell stale bread to tourists who want to feed the birds. The **bold**est (or dumbest) of these avian-loving visitors cover themselves in bread so as to attract dozens of the flying scourge to roost on them. (Why anyone would want pigeons sitting on their shoulders is a mystery.) It takes a rare disposition to appreciate the *piazza* at its chaotic midsummer peak. It is best to visit early in the morning or late at night, when the Piazza evokes memories of a time before Venice had become one of the world's tourist capitals. In recent years, the Piazza has been known to flood at high tide, so when you are ready to soak up San Marco's old-world glamour, make sure to leave those new Ferragamo pumps you just bought at home.

This is possibly the only place in Venice that isn't hard to find. $ Free.

a chorus of churches

For a small city, Venice sure has a lot of churches—a lot of very memorable ones that are worth your time, too. Most of them charge €3 for entry, though, which might make you ask if they're worth your money. Eliminate this calculation, however, with the Chorus Pass, which can be purchased for €10 and grants unlimited entry to participating churches (there are 18 of them) for a year. Buy it at participating churches and then feel free to wander in and out as much as you wish: it won't cost you another cent (unless the collection plate comes around).

CAMPANILE ♿ TOWER

P. San Marco ☎041 27 08 311 www.basilicasanmarco.it

One of the most prominent buildings in P. San Marco, the Campanile is undeniably the dominant fixture of the Venetian skyline—so much so that in 1997, a group of separatists advocating the political division of Italy decided to storm the tower to proclaim their message from its heights. The incident, which marked the 200-year anniversary of the end of the Venetian Republic, is one of the tower's few claims to legitimate historical significance, since the original (completed in 1514) spontaneously collapsed in 1902. Remarkably, given the size and central location of the tower, no one was killed during the collapse, and the reconstruction of the tower was completed a decade later. The Campanile has a fully functioning elevator capable of taking over two dozen people to the top of the tower, from which you can enjoy fantastic views of the city. Unfortunately, it's a complete tourist trap, since access to the lift costs €8 and usually requires a substantial wait. Most visitors, at least those without a political message to proclaim from the heights of the tower, will likely be content to admire the simple brick structure of the Campanile from ground level.

In P. San Marco. $ Entrance and lift access €8. ⏰ Open daily July-Sept 9am-9pm; Oct 9am-7pm; Nov-Easter 9:30am-3:45pm; Easter-June 9am-7pm.

Cannaregio

To get the most out of Cannaregio, take the locals' advice and treat your stay here as an opportunity to experience the real Venetian lifestyle rather than as a time for sight-seeing. Most of the notable attractions in the neighborhood are churches which hold architectural as well as religious interest, but the two can't-miss destinations in Cannaregio are the Ca' d'Oro and the Jewish Ghetto.

CA' D'ORO

Strada Nova 3932 ☎041 52 00 345 www.cadoro.org

A truly Venetian institution, this palace of a few centuries ago now houses one of the most impressive art collections in the region. Comprised of works dating from the city's earliest days, the museum's assortment of art is surprisingly extensive, easily meriting a visit of 2 or 3hr. The ex-*palazzo*'s architecture rivals the art for splendor, as do the views of Venice (perhaps the best you'll find) from the museum's balconies. All of these aesthetic delights make the somewhat pricey tickets *(€6.50)* well worth the expense, even if you're not that into art. Plus, you'll be able to tell your parents of at least one high-culture experience you had while you were in Italy. Ah, *la dolce vita.*

Going east on Strada Nova, find the Ca' d'Oro on the right immediately before reaching Calle della Testa. Bookshop and Loggias only accessible by staircase. $ €6.50, EU citizens 18-25 €3.25, EU citizens under 18 and over 65 free. Open M 8:15am-2pm, Tu-Su 8:15am-7:15pm. Last entry 30min. before close.

THE JEWISH GHETTO

Sestiere di Cannaregio 1146,Campo di Ghetto Nuovo ☎041 71 50 12 www.moked.it/jewishvenice

Stepping into Venice's Jewish Ghetto, the first neighborhood in the world to bear a title that has now become so ubiquitous that suburban teens questionably use it to describe their two-year-old cell phones, will give you a taste of what this part of the city was like a few centuries ago. Much of the ghetto's original architecture has been preserved, including several synagogues. Although you'll be able to see the buildings of Venice's past, don't expect to witness any Shylock-ian angst—unlike residents who lived here in the 16th century, today's inhabitants of the ghetto are not forced here by government edict. The area remains uniquely Jewish, however, with strong Israeli and Italian-Jewish influences. Many of the signs in this section of Cannaregio are written in Hebrew as well as Italian.

Across the Guglie Bridge going northeast, turn left onto Fondamenta Pescheria, walk 1 block and turn onto Ghetto Vecchio.

CHIESA DEI GESUITI

Campo dei Gesuiti

Duck into Chiesa dei Gesuiti and be rewarded by the impressive art it contains, including an original work by Titian. Gesuiti was built later (by Venetian standards) than many other churches in Cannaregio, so a visit here will give you a sense of what was hip and happenin' back in the 18th century. Cannaregio's streets are dotted with churches, but if you only have time for one holy encounter, make a beeline for Gesuiti.

From Sestiere Cannaregio, going east, turn right onto Campo del Gesuiti. Open M-Sa 10am-noon and 4-6pm.

San Polo

Though a small neighborhood, San Polo has several sights that are well worth visiting. In addition to the **Rialto Bridge** and the area immediately surrounding it, several nearby churches and museums count among Venice's most rewarding destinations.

RIALTO BRIDGE

BRIDGE

Over the Grand Canal

Even before the Rialto Bridge, or *Ponte di Rialto*, was built in 1591, its site at the

italy

intersection of four of Venice's six *sestiere* (San Marco, Canareggio, San Polo, and Castello, to be precise) served as a major point of transfer among Venice's islands. In the 12th century, construction began on a series of bridges to accommodate pedestrian traffic across the **Grand Canal,** but as trade in the Republic of Venice continued to expand, the need for a permanent structure that wouldn't interfere with **boat** traffic became apparent. Though numerous famous Italian artists of the day were considered, ultimately **Antonio da Ponte** directed the project, deciding on the controversial stone construction that has become a Venetian trademark. The bridge today stands in essentially the same form in which da Ponte designed it, with three lanes of pedestrian traffic divided by two narrow lanes of shops, and it continues to be a center of shopping and dining for Venetian locals and tourists. With glass shops, stores stocked with souvenirs, athletic apparel sellers, trendy boutiques, and *haute couture*, the shopping options on the Rialto Bridge offer something for almost anyone. Those who grow tired of browsing should enjoy the vantage point from the bridge's high point, which affords the city's best view of the Grand Canal. Facing north, you'll be able to see some of Venice's best-preserved *palazzi*, while facing south you're sure to be graced with breathtaking visions of the San Marco and San Polo waterfront and gondolas docked along the canal. Those seeking the perfect picture of the bridge should head south on San Marco from the Rialto Bridge, cross two smaller waterfront bridges, and then take a snapshot that captures Rialto's entire span.

From anywhere in the city, follow the bright yellow signs that say Per Rialto and you will eventually make it to the bridge.

FRARI — ♿ CHURCH

Campo dei Frari 3072 ☎041 52 22 637 www.basilicadeifrari.it

From the outside, Basilica di Santa Maria Gloriosa dei Frari might look like it belongs more in the industrial section of **Giudecca** than in the pantheon of Venice's great churches, but if you make it inside this rough, foreboding brick structure you'll be awestruck by one of the city's largest and most spectacular churches. Second only to the **Basilica di San Marco** in size, the Frari houses numerous notable works by famous artists such as **Bellini** and **Titian** as well as remarkably well-preserved wooden seating that once cradled the bottoms of Venetian nobility and several spectacular mausoleums dedicated to the church's early patrons. The church is large enough to have several smaller rooms that function as museums of the church history and house frescoes, stonework, and historical golden artifacts. Unlike most churches in Venice, which can take just a couple of minutes for the typical tourist to enjoy, it can take an hour to fully appreciate the artistic subtleties of the Frari. The numerous altars are all masterpieces in their own rights, while the mausoleums are a spectacular display of Venice's artistic prowess as well as the egotism and incredible wealth that characterized the city's elite throughout most of its history. Though the church is a spectacular sight to visit at any time of day, try to make it near opening or closing, when there are fewer tour groups around. At these times, every footstep that hits the church's stone floor can be heard echoing under its towering arches, and its serene beauty can be best appreciated.

V: Campo San Tomà. Proceed straight until you reach a T intersection, turn right, make the 1st left, and continue to the square; the entrance to the church is immediately ahead. $ *€2.50, with Chorus Pass free. Audio tour €2.* *Open M-Sa 9am-6pm, Su 1-6pm.*

SCUOLA GRANDE DI SAN ROCCO — MUSEUM

Campo di San Rocco 3054 ☎041 52 34 864 www.scuolagrandesanrocco.it

Home to some of Tintoretto's greatest works as well as canvases by **Titian,** Scuola Grande di San Rocco is not as extensive as many other galleries in Venice, but its works are every bit as impressive. Originally designed as a place for laypersons of the Catholic faith to meet and promote various acts of religious piety, the Scuola has been preserved primarily as an art museum, and though the displays are small, the collection is well-organized and quite accessible to visitors. Anyone who has spent hours craning their necks to admire paintings on the ceilings of Venetian museums, *palazzi*, and churches will appreciate the mirrors provided for examining Tintoretto's magnificent religious scenes painted on the second-floor ceiling.

 # From Campo dei Frari, walk to the west end of the church, turn right, and follow the signs north toward San Rocco. The school is on the left. $ €7, students €5, under 18 €3. ⏰ Open daily 9:30am-5:30pm. Last entry 30min. before close.

CAMPO SAN POLO ♿ PIAZZA

Campo San Polo

As Venice's second-largest public square—you may have heard of the largest, **Piazza San Marco**—Campo San Polo is the default winner of the award for largest Venetian square that doesn't spend half its time under a flood of seawater or tourist traffic. It's also home to some of the city's most important events, including outdoor concerts, screenings for the **Venice Film Festival,** and numerous pre-Lenten festivities during **Carnevale**. During major events, the square is transformed from a quiet, open space housing a few street vendors and gelato stands into the Venetian equivalent of an amphitheater, packed with tourists and locals enjoying some of the best partying Venice has to offer. Even if there aren't any major events going on in Campo San Polo while you're visiting Venice, this historic square deserves a visit. Formerly the site of bullfights and religious services, the square is now quiet most days and home to several small restaurants and cafes. It's worth spending some time looking at San Polo's historic buildings, including the **Palazzo Tiepolo Passi,** a 16th-century palace that has been converted into a hotel, and the **Chiesa di San Polo,** which houses several works by **Giovanni Tiepolo.**

 # From the Rialto Bridge, walk through the markets along Ruga dei Oresi, turn left onto Rughetta del Ravano, continue for approximately 4min., and you'll arrive at Campo San Polo.

Santa Croce

MUSEUM OF NATURAL HISTORY ♿ MUSEUM

Santa Croce 1730 ☎041 27 50 206 💻www.museicivicivenezianі.it

Venice's Museum of Natural History is one of those rare museums that can be as much fun for adults as it is for children. Unlike many Venetian museums, which house great collections that are presented devoid of context in empty *palazzi*, the Museum of Natural History almost seems like a museum of modern art when you first enter. Fossils hewn into simulated archaeological sites rather than housed in glass cases successfully draw the visitor more into the museum experience. Rooms detailing the history of earlier life forms build up the ambience with judicious use of theatrical lighting, while the quiet primordial soundtrack is as entertaining on its own as anything the museum houses. A full visit to the museum takes 30-60min. and may take even less time for visitors who aren't able to read Italian, since information about the exhibits is displayed in only the one language.

 # V: San Stae. Continue down Salizada San Stae, make the 1st right that leads to a bridge, continue straight across 2 bridges, then make the 2nd right, and continue until you reach the museum. It will be difficult to find, but if you follow the signs to Fontego dei Turchi, you will get there. $ €4.50, students ages 15-25, ages 6-14, over 65, and holders of the Rolling Venice Card €3, under 6 and holders of the Civic Museums pass free. ⏰ Open W 9am-5pm, Sa-Su 10am-6pm.

CA' PESARO ♿ MUSEUM

Santa Croce 2070 ☎041 72 11 27 💻www.museicivicivenezianі.it

Though in most cities Ca' Pesaro would be deserving of a **thumbpick,** the otherwise spectacular museum is just one of many impressive modern and contemporary art collections in Venice. This museum features an interesting mix of paintings and sculpture—mostly from the late 19th and early 20th centuries—that chronicles the development of modern art as a transnational movement. As one of Venice's more famous art museums, Ca' Pesaro has the added advantage of hosting frequent temporary exhibitions, which generally feature pieces from the mid- to late 19th century and tend to be more lowbrow, general-interest affairs than the more esoteric exhibits in its permanent collection. Even those left unimpressed by the art can still marvel at the *palazzo*'s intact ceilings, which far too many visitors miss completely. Others may explore the second floor's gallery of East Asian artwork. Though this exhibit is not nearly as well-presented as the first floor's modern art gallery, the assemblage of Japanese ornamental weaponry accompanied by informational videos about the extensive decorating process is far different from anything else you'll find in Venice.

V: San Stae. Exit the church square left (facing away from the Grand Canal), cross the 1st bridge possible, continue straight, make the 1st possible left, and you should see the entrance to the museum. There will also be signs indicating the direction toward the museum. $ €6.50, students ages 15-25, ages 6-14, over 65, and holders of the Rolling Venice Card €4, under 6 and holders of the Civic Museums pass free. ⏰ Open Tu-Su Apr-Oct 10am-6pm; Nov-Mar 10am-5pm. Last entry 1hr. before close.

Dorsoduro

THE PEGGY GUGGENHEIM COLLECTION — ♿ MUSEUM

Dorsoduro 704 — ☎041 24 05 411 www.guggenheim.org

When you walk into a museum and the first room features works by Miró, Picasso, Dalí, and Magritte, you know it's exceptional. The Peggy Guggenheim Collection is a great museum to visit, both for art aficionados and for those who think of karate-kicking turtles when they hear the names of Leonardo, Michelangelo, Donatello, and Raphael. The collection is a relatively small one that includes notable works from almost every major movement of the late 19th and early 20th centuries. It is comprised of works that notable traveler Guggenheim collected during her lifetime, and thus contains pieces that hail from all over Europe and the Americas. Her assortment of artwork emphasizes the international character of art produced during this period while retaining a certain Venetian flair: a substantial number of works are by Venetian and Italian artists. Even if you have no interest in artwork, the *palazzo* itself is well worth the price of admission. Its immaculately maintained gardens and house make it one of the most beautiful *palazzi* in all of Venice.

From Santa Maria della Salute, follow the signs west towards the Guggenheim Museum for approximately 4min. $ €12, students €7, seniors €10. ⏰ Open M 10am-6pm, W-Su 10am-6pm. Last entry 5:45pm.

SANTA MARIA DELLA SALUTE — CHURCH

Campo della Salute — ☎041 52 25 558

Don't make the mistake of contenting yourself with views of Santa Maria della Salute across the water from P. San Marco. While the vision of the sun setting behind the church is incredible, the sanctuary itself is just as impressive—and equally free to enjoy. Santa Maria della Salute, built between 1631 and 1687, was intended to be an homage to the Virgin Mary, who many Venetians believed was capable of protecting them from the ravages of the plague. Since 1629 marked the last great outbreak of the plague in Venice, it is unclear whether the church's construction did anything to end the spread of the disease. Regardless, the church stands today as an architectural and aesthetic wonder, with its innovative dome remaining perhaps the most recognizable sight in Venice. Paintings by Tintoretto and Titian highlight the interior of the church, which also features numerous statues, arches, columns, and altars that have led some to call Santa Maria della Salute the most beautiful church in Venice.

From the Ponte dell'Accademia, turn left and continue to the eastern tip of Dorsoduro (approximately 6-8min.). ⏰ Open daily 9am-noon and 3-5:30pm.

PUNTA DELLA DOGANA

♠♿☼ MUSEUM

Fondamenta della Dogana alla Salute 2   ☎041 52 31 680 🖥www.palazzograssi.it

A new museum by the über-chic François Pinault, the Punta della Dogana-Palazzo Grassi complex is an absolute must-see for anyone with an interest in contemporary art. Simultaneously more interactive, more accessible, and more intimidating than any conventional art museum, Punta della Dogana features artwork that is visceral, graphic, and that blurs the distinctions between low and high art—even in a country famed for its Renaissance celebration of the human form, you'd be hard-pressed to find a museum with more phallic representations. A great complement to the collection of earlier works found in the Accademia and the assortment of modernist art featured in the Guggenheim, Punta della Dogana's collection of contemporary art is one of the most impressive in Italy. Due to the combined entry fee, it is especially worth seeing if you also plan to check out the Palazzo Grassi in San Marco.

⌗ *From the Ponte dell'Accademia, turn left and continue to the eastern tip of Dorsoduro for 6-8min.* ⓢ *€15, with affiliated Palazzo Grassi in San Marco €20.* ⓩ *Open M 10am-7pm, W-Su 10am-7pm. Last entry 1hr. before close.*

THE ACCADEMIA

♠♿ MUSEUM

Campo della Carità   ☎041 52 00 345 🖥www.gallerieaccademia.org

Venice's premier museum for pre-19th-century art, the Accademia is currently undergoing extensive renovations that limit the number of vistors it can accommodate daily. These renovations have also changed the museum layout, but the Accademia still remains chock-full of important Italian art. Unlike the **Peggy Guggenheim Collection** or **Punta della Dogana,** which feature relatively few works, the Accademia is home to a substantial collection that will likely leave most casual visitors overwhelmed. Nonetheless, there are several truly awe-inspiring works to be found in its hallways, and there is perhaps no better place than the Accademia to enjoy Venice from an artistic perspective, as many of the works featured represent scenes and sights that will be familiar to travelers who have already spent a few days in the city.

⌗ *Immediately across the Ponte dell'Accademia from San Marco.* ⓢ *€6.50, EU citizens 18-25 €3.25, EU citizens under 18 and over 65 free.* ⓩ *Open M 8:15am-2pm, Tu-Su 8:15am-7:15pm.*

🏖Lido

Once the world's most popular beach resort, Lido is largely forgotten by the 20 million travelers who visit Venice annually. Though the island's beautiful and historic hotels still fill up each summer, it's now a quiet counterpart to the city center rather than the main draw for international travelers. As a result, visitors to the island can enjoy scenic bike rides along the coastline, strolls along gorgeous tree-lined streets, and sun-bathing spots on one of its eastern coast's pristine (if occasionally crowded) beaches—all without too much trouble. Since the vaporetto #1 line regularly makes stops at the island, and frequent ferries run from Piazzale Roma, the seeming wall between Lido and the city center is more of a psychological barrier than anything else. If you're in San Marco or eastern Castello, you can easily make a quick 3hr. trip to Lido and see a lot of the island without difficulty.

GRAND VIALE

♿ PROMENADE

Grand Viale

This famous promenade cuts from eastern Lido—with its majestic hotels and fine restaurants—to the western portion of the island, where you'll find miles of sandy shoreline, gorgeous beach resorts, and the glamorous theaters and hotels that support Lido's annual film festival. A walk along the Grand Viale can take as little as 15min. or as long as several hours, depending on how intent you are on enjoying the sights. Since Lido was largely uninhabited until the 20th century, it lacks the grandly historic character that distinguishes Venice, but you'd never mistake it for a Hawaiian or Caribbean resort community. Walking along the Grand Viale, you'll experience Lido as a resort town worthy of an F. Scott Fitzgerald novel, with beautiful hotels that feature towering columns, breathtaking mosaic facades, and a spectacularly anachronistic sense of Old World aristocracy. If you make it to the eastern side of the island and turn right onto Lungomare Gabriele D'Annuzio, you'll see what may be Lido's most impressive sight, the grandiose and slightly preposterous **Grand Hotel des Bains** (the setting of Thoman Mann's novella *Death in Venice*), which still annually hosts the most impressive gathering of celebrities this side of Cannes during Venice's own film festival.

⚑ *From dock Santa Maria Elizabetta, walk straight ahead. The Grand Viale runs east-west.*

SPIAGGE DI VENEZIA
🏖♿♨ BEACH

Piazzale Ravà ☎041 52 61 249 🖵www.veneziaspiagge.it

With hotels limiting access to a lot of the prime stretches of ⚑**beach** in Lido, just spending a day on the shore can end up costing over €50 per person simply for chairs, umbrellas, and towels. Spiagge di Venezia—which manages two popular stretches of beach in Lido—is the more budget-conscious option if you want to soak up the sun without spending too much cash. You could certainly rack up the charges with food, drinks, a changing room, and umbrella and chair, but none of these are necessary to enjoy Lido's magnificent sandy expanses and pristine waters.

⚑ *From dock Lido San Nicolò, go east on V. Giannantonio Selva for 6-8min. and you'll reach the Spiagge.* ⑤ *Beach free. Umbrella and chair €12. Private changing room €23.* 🕓 *Open daily 9am-7pm.*

Giudecca

Giudecca, technically a part of Dorsoduro but separated from the neighborhood by the Giudecca Canal, is the most easily accessible of the lagoon islands, as the vaporetto #2 line zigzags the Giudecca Canal and makes several stops on the island. A €2 ticket for crossing the Giudecca canal supposedly exists, but the vaporetto operators *Let's Go* spoke with said they didn't care if we hopped on for one stop free of charge. Thanks, guys! In recent years there has been talk of constructing a tunnel between Dorsoduro and Giudecca, but it appears no such plans will be implemented in the foreseeable future. Giudecca seems to have a rather cyclical history. It was first inhabited by wealthy families who claimed a preference for large estates with gardens but were really being pressured to leave the city due to political controversy. The lack of large-scale residential development on the island later made Giudecca the center of the city's early 20th-century industrial boom, and for a time, the island produced the vast majority of commercial ⛴**boats** used in the city. After WWII, Giudecca lacked viable industry and fell into disrepair but is completing the cycle again with the development of upscale housing and hotels. Though Giudecca is coming back into fashion, its industrial history remains an influence: the island's most prominent landmark and one of Venice's most prestigious hotels, **The Molino Stucky Hilton,** is located in a former granary and flourmill which retains a sternly industrial exterior despite its interior's refinement and elegance.

IL REDENTORE
🏛❌ CHURCH

Campo S.S. Redentore 195 ☎041 27 50 462 🖵www.chorusvenezia.org

One of Venice's most celebrated churches, Il Redentore is by far the biggest attraction on Giudecca. The church, which was constructed to give thanks for divine deliverance from the plague (perhaps a bit prematurely) in 1577, is considered one of ⚑**Andrea Palladio's** greatest works, displaying his acute awareness of proportion in architectural design. Inside the church, paintings from some of the city's greatest artists, including **Saraceni, Veronese,** and **Tintoretto** hang, underscoring the prominence of the church in Venetian society. So highly regarded was Palladio's masterpiece that it gave rise to its own festival, the ⚑**Festa del Redentore,** which began as an annual political procession from the **Doge's Palace** to the church and, though now largely devoid of religious sentiment, continues to be celebrated every third weekend in July.

⇟ Take vaporetto line #2 to Redentore; the church is immediately ahead. $ €2.50, with Chorus Pass free. Elevator to campanile €4. 🕐 Open M-Sa 10am-5pm. Last entry 15min. before close.

Murano

Known colloquially as "The Glass Island," Murano is one of the largest lagoon islands and has been the center of Venice's glass industry since the 13th century, when concerns about the possibility of fires in the city center led politicans to ban glass production. Of course, safety concerns never stopped enterprising Venetians from *selling* the glass anywhere, and buyers of the stuff are everywhere. Nevertheless, Murano remains the glass headquarters of Venice. Though the large brick buildings, open kilns, and occasional abandoned workshops give the island a slightly gritty industrial feel, it also features a few beautiful tree-shaded streets with glass shops displaying the work of the island's top artisans. If you spend more than a few minutes exploring Murano, you're almost certain to find a *fornace* in operation where you can see some of the world's most talented artisans practicing their craft. If you're lucky, you might even find a studio that lets visitors try their hand at glass blowing. Travel times to Murano vary, but expect to spend at least 30min. getting there by vaporetto lines #41, 42, or LN, which are generally the most accessible options.

islands of the lagoon

The islands in the lagoon surrounding Venice are often given short shrift by travelers on tight schedules, but they have played a vital role in Venetian history and remain fascinating to this day. If you have a couple of hours of free time and the foresight to plot a good vaporetto route from island to island, you can visit a half-dozen of them with relative ease. The one thing shared by the islands is their ability to retain distinct identities. The major islands remain strikingly different from one another and proud of their independent cultural and historical legacies. Some are strongly provincial and have generally eschewed economic diversification, while others have maintained a strong sense of local community despite being subject to change and turmoil. Many are still virtually uninhabited. Visitors tend to have mixed feeling about the islands of the Venetian Lagoon, some considering them not worth the time or trouble, others maintaining that the islands are the main reason to visit the city. If you want a complete overview of the city of Venice, get on a ⛵**boat** and explore the myriad opportunities the lagoon offers.

MUSEO DEL VETRO 💳♿ MUSEUM

Fondamenta Giustinian 8 ☎041 73 95 86 🖥www.museicivicivenziani.it

Anyone with enough interest in artisan glass to visit Murano shouldn't leave without checking out the Museo del Vetro, which traces the development of Murano's glass industry from its earliest stages to the present day. The museum features several exceptional pieces, both contemporary and historical, that reflect the ways in which glass has been historically used both practically and aesthetically. Though the collection is impressive, the real draw is the wing dedicated to glass production that gives an overview of how different glasses are made and the minerals that are used to give the material its different colors and textures. Don't miss the museum garden and its fascinating artifacts.

⇟ V: Museo (accessible by lines R, 41, 42, N, and DM). Follow the signs to the museum. $ €6.50, students ages 15-25, ages 4-14 and over 65, and Rolling Venice Card holders €4. Admission

included in Civic Museums Pass. ⏰ *Open daily Apr-Oct 10am-6pm; Nov-Mar 10am-5pm. Last entry 30min. before close.*

BASILICA DI SANTA MARIA E SAN DONATO ♿ CHURCH

Calle San Donato 11 ☎041 73 90 56

A unique church, Murano's Basilica contrasts sharply with the Renaissance architecture that you'll find throughout Venice and Italy as a whole. With distinct Byzantine influences in its exterior, elaborate arches, and strong geometric patterns, the Basilica embodies Eastern influences that have profoundly shaped the development of Venetian culture and society. The floors within the church, comprised of thousands upon thousands of jewel-like tiles, are incredibly intricate and some of the city's most breathtaking mosaics. The church also houses a set of bones reputed to be from a **dragon.**

V: Museo (accessible by lines R, 41, 42, N, and DM). Walk past the museum along the canal for about 2min.; the church is ahead on the left. $ *Free.* ⏰ *Open daily 8am-7pm.*

Burano

Burano—about an hour away from Venice by vaporetto lines LN and N—is a relatively small island best known for its handmade lace production and fishing industry. Visitors to Burano almost inevitably stop in Murano first, since that island is on the way from Venice, and are consistently surprised at the contrast between the two. Whereas Murano is populated by brick and stone buildings and is almost as devoid of vegetation as Venice, Burano boasts several large parks, lots of open space, and famously colorful houses. Originally, at least according to legend, the fishermen of the island painted their homes ostentatious shades of blue, pink, red, green, yellow, and orange so that each could readily identify his home from a distance when returning to the island, and the fantastically colorful homes have evolved into a Burano trademark. While this tradition is now somewhat obsolete given technological improvements in nautical navigation, lace production in Burano continues in much the same fashion that it has for centuries. Though you can shop for Burano-style lace in Venice (see **Venetian Artisan Goods**), Burano itself is the best place to find a wide selection of lace goods that are guaranteed to be handmade. Be forewarned, however, that the lace production process is labor-intensive, and that labor will be reflected in the price of pretty much anything you buy. Even if you're not shopping for lace, it's still absolutely worth paying a visit to Burano. An hour or two of wandering will bring you to the beautiful **Church of San Martino** and its infamous leaning campanile; the **Lace Museum** *(P. Galuppi 187 ☎041 73 00 34)*, which is returning in 2011 after an almost year-long sabbatical; and some of the most beautiful and whimsical buildings in all of Venice.

Torcello

Accessible by vaporetto line N and a ferry (T) from Burano, Torcello isn't the easiest island to get to but definitely rewards those who make the effort. Though the island—the first settlement in the lagoon—was once home to over 20,000 people, from the 12th to the 15th centuries it was largely abandoned as the lagoon surrounding it became a swamp. Torcello is now home to only a few dozen people managing a couple of restaurants, a hotel, and the scant attractions that bring tourists to the island. Walking around this bit of land can be a surreal experience; it's hard to comprehend that this largely abandoned and overgrown island once was home to the largest population center of the Venetian Republic. So few relics remain.

CATHEDRAL OF SANTA MARIA ASSUNTA CHURCH

Isola di Torcello ☎041 27 02 464

Founded over 13 centuries ago, the Cathedral of Santa Maria Assunta offers a strong reminder of the thriving community that once existed on Torcello. It's definitely not worth making the trip all the way out to Torcello just for this small church, but as an example of the eclecticism in Venice's early places of worship, its mosaics and incredible rendering of the Last Judgment are engaging. The campanile, once abandoned, is again in operation and affords the best view of the northern lagoon you'll find anywhere. Also affiliated with the cathedral are the smaller churches of **Santa Fosca** and **Museo di Torcello,** both of which are sure to fascinate any visitors intrigued by the strange history of Venice's abandoned island.

From the island's only vaporetto stop, follow the path to the island's only substantial settlement. It's a 7-10min. walk; just look for the tower in the distance. Ⓢ *Church €4. Campanile €4. Both €7.50.* *Open daily Mar-Oct 10:30am-6pm; Nov-Feb 10am-5pm.*

FOOD

As you might expect in a city visited by over 20,000,000 tourists each year, Venice has no shortage of restaurants. Almost all are receptive to international travelers and offer English-language menus and service, particularly those where the tourist industry is centered.

Since visitors to Venice range from international celebrities to student backpackers, most restaurants try to accommodate all tastes and budgets. Even in the most upscale Venetian restaurants, you should typically be able to get a pizza for less than €10. That being said, a few restaurants in prime locations bank on being able to overcharge hungry tourists who don't have the energy to look beyond the first place they see. Avoid suffering a less-than-memorable *and* expensive meal and do a bit of comparison shopping before settling on an eatery. Also take note of whether you should expect a service charge. These should be written on the menu of most establishments that have one. While common, the service charge can come as an unpleasant surprise.

Most restaurants in Venice serve food typical of the Veneto region, which shouldn't offer any particular surprises for travelers familiar with the basics of Italian cuisine. Risotto, beans, and polenta are particularly popular here. Menus tend to be rather seafood-heavy, but pasta, chicken, and steak are also fairly standard offerings. Pizza, of course, is a staple of almost every dining establishment. Since the tradition of eating cat in Northern Italy has been banned, there shouldn't be anything too troubling on the menu for English-speaking tourists, with the possible exceptions of squid-ink pasta *(nero di seppia)* and **horse** meat *(cavallo)*, which aren't too common. For students really looking to save time and money, sandwich shops, snack bars, kebab shops, and small pizzerias often offer decent and reasonably filling meals, including drink, for less than €6.

italy

San Marco

Like most things in San Marco, dining tends to be expensive and upscale. You'll find some of Venice's best restaurants here, but they tend to be some of the priciest as well. Despite this trend, there are a surprising number of restaurants that offer great values, particularly if you're willing to trek a couple blocks away from P. San Marco and the Rialto Bridge.

TRATTORIA PIZZERIA AI FABBRI TRATTORIA, PIZZERIA [3]

Calle dei Fabbri 4717 ☎041 52 08 085

An eclectic pizzeria that cooks up more than just your conventional margherita and *quatro formaggi* varieties, Pizzeria Ai Fabbri is distinguished by a high degree of culinary creativity, evident in their unusual appetizers (including sumptuous duck dumplings) and wide selection of side dishes that wouldn't find their way onto a typical Venetian menu. Though a flatscreen TV by the entrance tuned into news or soccer matches gives the restaurant a bit of a bar-ish feel, those who would prefer a quiet meal in the back dining room can enjoy the same excellent menu in a more serene setting.

Go through the St. Mark's Clock Tower, turn left, continue to Calle dei Fabbri, and continue for 2-3min.; the restaurant is on the right. Ⓢ *Entrees €7.50-23.* *Open daily 11am-midnight.*

👍 BISTROT DE VENISE
💳♿🍸❄⛅ RISTORANTE [4]

Calle dei Fabbri ☎041 52 36 651 💻www.bistrotdevenise.com

With an innovative menu that features historic recipes citing origins in the 16th century (which appears to be when the restaurant won its first award, given the incredible number of honors it has since racked up), Bistrot de Venise specializes in traditional Venetian food prepared to the absolute highest standard. Though the sticker shock might dissuade some budget travelers, if you want a world-class meal in San Marco, you won't find anything nearly this good for anything less.

🪧 Go through the St. Mark's Clock Tower, turn left, continue to Calle dei Fabbri, and continue for about 2min.; the restaurant is on the right. [$] Entrees €18-28. ⏰ Open M-Th noon-3pm and 7pm-midnight, F-Sa noon-3pm and 7pm-1am, Su noon-3pm and 7pm-midnight.

RISTORANTE NOEMI
💳♿🍸❄⛅ RISTORANTE [5]

Calle dei Fabbri 912 ☎041 52 25 238 💻www.ristorantenoemi.com

For those of you craving a steak or some veal after weeks spent subsisting on a carb-heavy Italian diet, Ristorante Noemi should make its way onto your radar, as it is reputed to serve up some of the best grilled food in Venice. Affiliated with the upscale Hotel Noemi but catering to a clientele that goes beyond the hotel's guests, this restaurant offers high-quality traditional Venetian food at respectable prices, especially if you manage to avoid the temptation to order the menu's highest-priced items.

🪧 Go through the St. Mark's Clock Tower, turn left, continue to Calle dei Fabbri, and continue 2min.; the restaurant is on the right. [$] Entrees €8-34. ⏰ Open daily 11:30am-midnight.

ACQUA PAZZA
💳♿🍸❄⛅ SEAFOOD [5]

Campo San Angelo 3808 ☎041 27 70 688 💻www.veniceacquapazza.it

Acqua Pazza, roughly translated as "Crazy Waters," is both the name and the motif of this fine restaurant near San Marco's two modern art museums. Featuring excellent seafood and bizarre, though amusing, acquatically inspired decor—Acqua Pazza is just as sweet as it is salty—its €12 house desserts are some of the best confections Venice has to offer.

🪧 From Teatro La Fenice, continue northwest on Calle de la Verona for less than 2min., take the 1st left after crossing a bridge, take the next right, and take the next left; the restaurant is in Campo San Angelo. ℹ Men are required to wear long pants to dinner. [$] Entrees €18-35. ⏰ Open daily noon-3pm and 7pm-11pm.

BAR MIO
💳♿🍸 SNACK BAR [1]

Frezzeria 1176

If you're feeling bold, try to claim a spot at Venice's most heavily trafficked snack bar. You'll be rewarded with a sandwich crisped to perfection—though never overheated—at a pleasantly low price. You're unlikely to see any other tourists in Bar Mio, but that doesn't mean the place is starving for business. The incredibly efficient employees don't have a moment's rest from opening to close, as locals constantly stream in for first-class coffee and sandwiches.

🪧 Exit the southwest corner of P. San Marco, opposite Basilica di San Marco, and take 1st right onto Frezzeria; the restaurant is less than 1min. ahead on the right. [$] Sandwiches €4.50-7. ⏰ Open daily 6:30am-9pm.

RISTORANTE ANIMA BELLA
💳♿🍸 RISTORANTE [3]

Calle Fiubera 956 ☎041 52 27 486

A quirky and small restaurant that bills itself as a combination *ristorante*, pizzeria, and grill, Anima Bella is more reminiscent of the dining room in a typical Italian villa than a tourist-filled restaurant in San Marco. Since Anima Bella tends to focus on relatively few dishes prepared exceptionally well, you could order anything off the menu without regretting it. However, while everything here is prepared with care, you could eat ravioli for weeks in Venice and find none that match the quality you'll get at Anima Bella.

⇞ Exit P. San Marco beneath St. Mark's Clock Tower, take 1st possible left onto a street with a bridge and cross the bridge; the restaurant is on the right. $ Entrees €8-20. ⏰ Open daily 11am-10pm.

Cannaregio

As many great places as there are to eat in Cannaregio, there are just as many mediocre and touristy options. Stay away from the main streets and menus targeting out-of-towners, and you'll find some of the best cuisine Venice has to offer.

✓ RISTORANTE CASA BONITA

💳♿🍸🌳 RISTORANTE [3]

Fondamento S. Giobbe 492 ☎041 52 46 164

One of the trickiest things about eating in Venice is that almost every restaurant claims to be authentically Venetian and displays a mouth-watering menu—then you walk in and realize that there are more Germans than Italians in the house. Casa Bonita is the rare Venetian restaurant that is both accessible from the main thoroughfares and genuinely Venetian. Often packed throughout the day, this restaurant caters to local tastes with excellent food in generous portions for a reasonable price. The canal-side outdoor seating is excellent, and the bar gives you any number of excuses to stay at your table and people-watch after your meal.

⇞ From the train station, turn left and walk 5min. down Lista de Spagna. Immediately before Guglie Bridge, turn left and continue for 4min. $ Entrees €12-18. ⏰ Open Tu-Su 10am-3pm and 5:30pm-1am.

OSTERIA BOCCADORO VENEZIA

💳♿🍸🌳 RISTORANTE [5]

Campo Widmann 5405/a ☎041 52 11 021 💻www.boccadorovenezia.it

Unlike your typical Venetian restaurant, Osteria Boccadoro Venezia offers an haute-cuisine reinterpretation of the region's traditional foods. Although Osteria Boccadoro's prices may seem excessive, rest assured that its food merits the cost. The restaurant's minimalist, modern aesthetic might not match up to your standard idea of what a fine Venetian restaurant looks like, but in sacrificing a bit of tradition, this osteria has foregone nothing in terms of stomach-pleasing fare, winning over discerning locals and tourists alike with its quality dishes.

⇞ Halfway along Calle Widmann. $ Entrees €20-28. ⏰ Open Tu-Su noon-2:30pm and 7-10:30pm.

TRATTORIA STORICA

💳♿🍸🌳 RISTORANTE [3]

Ponte dei Gesuiti 4858 ☎041 52 85 266 💻www.trattoriastorica.it

Trattoria Storica is an upscale, family-operated Venetian restaurant with exceptionally friendly service and great food. An excellent choice for anyone looking to savor a longer meal in a quieter section of Cannaregio, Storica offers generous portions that make for a very filling dinner, though you might consider splitting one of their dishes for lunch with a fellow traveler. With a helpful English-language menu, the restaurant does a great job welcoming foreigners without compromising its Venetian character.

⇞ Exiting the Gesuiti to Campo dei Gesuiti, turn left and cross the bridge; Storica is on the left. $ Entrees €16-22 . ⏰ Open daily 11am-4pm and 7pm-midnight.

GAM GAM

🥗♿ KOSHER [3]

Canale di Cannaregio 1122 ☎041 71 52 84

Perhaps the premier kosher restaurant for the more-than 1000 Jewish residents of Venice, Gam Gam brings together traditional Italian kosher cooking (and if that phrase sounds like an oxymoron to you, you really should try out Gam Gam), Venetian cuisine, and newer Israeli culinary influences in a menu unlike any other you'll find in Venice. Although almost all of Gam Gam's patrons are Orthodox or Conservative Jews, this restaurant is also a great place for gentiles to experience Venice's small but remarkably vibrant Jewish community.

⇞ From Campo S. Geremia, cross the Guglie Bridge and turn left. $ Entrees €8-15. ⏰Open M-Th noon-10pm, F noon-4pm, Su noon-10pm.

PASTICCERIA MARTINI BAKERY ❶

Rio Terà San Leonardo 1302 ☎041 71 73 75

At first glance, Pasticceria Martini is a lot like other pastry shops in Cannaregio, but once you try one of their croissants, you'll realize why so many residents pass by a half-dozen other pastry shops on their way here.

➔ Just past the Guglie Bridge going North. $ Pastries €1. Coffee €1.50. ⏰ Open daily 6am-9pm.

NAVE DE ORO ♿🍸 ENOTECA ❶

Rio Terà San Leonardo 1370 ☎041 71 96 95

Essential for any traveler seeking lots of alcohol for little money, the Nave De Oro in Cannaregio is one of six locations in Venice where wine is sold by the liter and "BYOB" stands for bring your own (empty) bottle. Provided you have €2 and an empty bottle of any kind (yes, even an old water bottle will do), you can get a liter of one of the surprisingly good regional wines offered by the friendly and knowledgeable staff. Welcome to Venice—you know you're in Europe when the wine is less expensive than the water.

➔ East of the Guglie Bridge along Rio Terà San Leonardo. $ Wine €1.70-2.20 per L. ⏰ Open M-Sa 8am-1pm and 4:30-7:30pm.

San Polo

Along the Grand Canal, San Polo suffers from the same generic tourist cuisine that you'll find near all of Venice's sightseeing destinations, but if you manage to get away from the main drag around the Rialto a little bit, you'll be rewarded with the unique specialities and terrific ambience of Venice's best small restaurants.

👍 **ANTICO FORNO** ♿🍸 PIZZERIA ❷

Ruga Rialto 970/973 ☎041 52 04 110

Let's Go's top recommendation for pizza in Venice, Antico Forno makes standard pies with top-quality ingredients as well as adventurous vegetarian options (olives, a variety of peppers, feta cheese, etc.) and deep-dish pizza that will put anything from Chicago to shame. The price might seem a bit high for single slices, but a large piece of their perfectly crisped and seasoned deep-dish pizza is substantial enough to serve as a meal.

➔ From Rialto Bridge, go straight ahead to Ruga Rialto and turn left onto Ruga Rialto; Antico Forno is ahead on the right. $ Slices €2-3.50. ⏰ Open daily 11am-10pm.

👍 **CIOCCOLATERIA VIZIOVIRTÙ** 💳♿ CIOCCOLATERIA ❶

Calle Balbi 2898 ☎041 27 50 149 💻www.viziovirtu.com

Venice's premiere chocolatier, Cioccolateria VizioVirtù crafts an incredible selection of creative, delicious, and (unfortunately) expensive chocolates in-house daily. While VizioVirtù does an excellent job with staples such as pralines, truffles, and baked goods, its mastery of the fine art of confectionery is best on display in its unconventional chocolates, including ones spiced up with red pepper, and replica Venetian masks that make great, site-specific gifts.

➔ V: San Tomà. Walk straight until you reach a T intersection and turn left; the shop is on the right. $ Various chocolate creations €1-2.50. ⏰ Open daily 10am-7:30pm.

OSTERIA NARANZARIA 💳♿🍸❄ RISTORANTE ❹

Naranzaria 130 ☎041 72 41 035 💻www.naranzaria.it

Osteria Naranzaria is a trendy, international-style restaurant and lounge with a menu as diverse as its clientele. Without completely abandoning its Venetian roots, the restaurant takes risks, dishing up unusual items such as fresh sushi, supposedly the best of its kind available in the city. Naranzaria also tends to serve smaller portions, so it's a great place to have a light lunch by Rialto Bridge or enjoy some sushi and drinks before heading out for the night.

➔ From Rialto Bridge, walk past San Giacomo, turn right, and cross the square; the restaurant is directly ahead. $ Entrees €7-18. Sushi 10 pieces for €15. ⏰ Open Tu-Su noon-2am.

BIRRARIA LA CORTE 💳♿🍸❄⛅ RISTORANTE 3

Campo San Polo 2168 ☎041 27 50 570 🖥www.birrarialacorte.it

The top restaurant in Campo San Polo, Birraria la Corte boasts a pretty adventurous repertoire without abandoning the staples of every Italian menu. Two unconventional entrees it has perfected include buffalo steaks and chicken curry, both of which go great with any number of the imported beers the restaurant has on tap.

🚶 From the Rialto Bridge, walk through the markets along Ruga dei Oresi, turn left onto Rughetta del Ravano, continue for approximately 4min., and cross the square; the restaurant is in the northwest corner. [$] Entrees €6.50-19. ⏰ Open daily noon-2:30pm and 7-10:30pm.

MURO VENEZIA FRARI 💳♿🍸❄⛅ RISTORANTE 4

Rio Terà dei Frari 2604 ☎041 52 45 310 🖥www.murovenezia.com

Muro Venezia eschews the dry, regal ambience typical of most fine Venetian restaurants in favor of a more cutting-edge aesthetic. This preference for the avant-garde is also on display in the restaurant's creative interpretations of classic Venetian recipes, including one of the most incredible vegetable risottos you'll ever have. If you like the feel here, you should check out the bar owned and operated by the same people near the Rialto Bridge, **Muro Venezia Rialto.**

🚶 From Campo dei Frari, cross a bridge to the east, turn right, continue for 30sec. to the end of the street, and turn left. [$] Entrees €7-25. ⏰ Open M-W 11am-1am, F-Su 11am-1am. Kitchen open noon-3pm and 7-10:30pm.

PIZZERIA DUE COLONNE 💳♿🍸 PIZZERIA 3

Calle della Chiesa 2343 ☎041 52 40 685

Pint-sized Pizzeria Due Colonne features a menu with great seafood, pastas, and pretty much every kind of pizza you could imagine. The portions are a whopping size for the low prices, which should save you enough that you don't feel too bad about spending a bit extra on their famous fried calamari.

🚶 From Campo dei Frari, exit the square east, cross a bridge, turn left, cross another bridge, continue right along Calle Dona, and cross another bridge; the restaurant is ahead on the right. [$] Entrees €6.50-15. ⏰ Open daily noon-2:30pm (3pm for pizza) and 7-10:30pm.

Santa Croce

If you're looking to get a meal in Santa Croce, stay toward the east side of the neighborhood. You can walk around the western end for half an hour without finding anything worthwhile, but if you stick to the eastern side, especially immediately southeast of Piazzale Roma, you'll discover a lot of small, personality-filled neighborhood restaurants that offer great values for budget travelers.

RISTORANTE RIBOT 💳♿🍸⛅ RISTORANTE 3

Fondamenta Minotto 158 ☎041 52 42 486

Venice is an incredible culinary city, but Ristorante Ribot manages to stand out, with exceptional food at real-world prices. The restaurant pays tribute to the best of traditional Venice—regional cuisine, excellent Italian wines, and a beautiful patio garden—but keeps it fresh with an innovative kitchen, modern design, and live music three to four times a week. It's tough to find better food anywhere in Venice, let alone at comparable prices.

🚶 Follow Piazzale Roma east, cross consecutive bridges, and continue for approximately 2min. [$] Entrees €8-14. ⏰ Open daily noon-2:30pm and 7-10:30pm.

PANIFICO BAROZZI 🚫♿ BAKERY, GROCERY STORE 1

Salizada S. Pantalon 86/A ☎041 71 02 33

One of the trickiest things about Venetian pastries is that, from a window shopper's perspective, every store's baked goods look practically identical. Sadly, looks can be deceiving, meaning that identical-looking cookies can in fact vary in quality from barely palatable to incredibly delicious. Panifico Barozzi's pastries, however, taste as scrumptious as they appear. With an impressive number

italy

of different delicacies to sample and the added bonus of a small grocery store (surprisingly tough to find in most neighborhoods) stocked with inexpensive and convenient snacks, this is a one-stop shopping experience you can't miss.

⚑ *Follow Piazzale Roma east, cross consecutive bridges, and continue for approximately 3min.* Ⓢ *Pastries €1-2.* Ⓐ *Open daily 6am-7:30pm*

ANTICO GAFARO
◆♿♥☕ RISTORANTE, PIZZERIA ❸

Salizada S. Pantalon 116/A
☎041 52 42 823

A traditional restaurant with excellent pastas (especially lasagna) and serviceable pizzas, Antico Garafo is so perfectly Venetian that it could pass for a movie set. With the gorgeous backdrop of a canal frequented by quiet 🚤**boats** and some of the neighborhood's most beautiful buildings, this restaurant is a great place to relax and enjoy a long meal.

⚑ *Follow Piazzale Roma east, cross consecutive bridges, and continue for approximately 3min.* Ⓢ *Entrees €8-22.* Ⓐ *Open daily 11:30am-11:30pm.*

AGLI AMICI
◆♿♥☕ SNACK BAR, RISTORANTE ❸

Sestiere Santa Croce 189
☎041 52 41 309

With impressive omelettes and a great selection of cheeses, Agli Amici is a welcome anomaly in Venice, where breakfast usually consists of nothing more than tea and toast. Although the seafood options are a bit expensive, everything else here is of solid value, making this restaurant a quick but hearty lunch stop.

⚑ *Follow Piazzale Roma east, cross consecutive bridges, immediately turn left, and continue for 90sec.* Ⓢ *Entrees €6-20.* Ⓐ *Open daily 8am-7:30pm.*

LAS RAMBLAS
◆♿♥☕ CAFE ❸

Santa Croce 373
☎041 52 46 648

Inspired by Barcelona's famous pedestrian street, Las Ramblas does not quite recreate the famous Catalan circus feel: its tranquil atmosphere is a far cry from the street-performing madness of its namesake. Nevertheless, the restaurant serves delicious food at reasonable prices that are, rain or shine, far better than most restaurants you'll find around Piazzale Roma. It's worth waiting for a sunny day, however, to appreciate the restaurant's beautiful patio.

⚑ *Following Piazzale Roma east, turn right at the 1st bridge you see; continue for 30sec.; turn right again and continue for 30sec.* Ⓢ *Entrees €8-20.* Ⓐ *Open daily 9:30am-11pm.*

TRATTORIA ALLE BURCHIELLE
◆♿♥☕ SNACK BAR ❷

Fondamenta delle Burchielle 393
☎041 71 03 42

Close to Piazzale Roma, Trattoria Alle Burchielle offers authentic Venetian food at exceptional prices. The outdoor seating by the canal is wonderful, and given the prices, you can enjoy several courses without breaking the bank.

⚑ *Following Piazzale Roma east, cross the 1st bridge you see and turn right immediately; the restaurant is on the right.* Ⓢ *Entrees €7.50-15.* Ⓐ *Open daily noon-10pm.*

TRATTORIA IN CAMPIEO
◆♿♥☕ RISTORANTE ❸

Campieo Mosca 24
☎41 71 10 61

A step back from Salizada S. Pantalon, Trattoria in Campieo has Campieo Mosca almost entirely to itself and uses this space to full effect, offering a great outdoor setting in which to enjoy a tasty Venetian meal. Although the food is excellent, be forewarned that portions tend to run on the small side. Consider stopping here for a light lunch unless you don't mind lightening your wallet considerably.

⚑ *Follow Piazzale Roma east, cross consecutive bridges, continue for approximately 3min., and turn right into Campieo Mosca.* Ⓢ *Entrees €10-22.* Ⓐ *Open daily noon-3pm and 6-10:30pm.*

ALIBABA KEBAB
◉♿ KEBAB, PIZZERIA ❶

Salizada S. Pantalon
☎041 52 45 272

Anyone staying in Venice for an extended period of time should seriously consider trying some sort of kebab, one of Venice's major ethnic foods. Alibaba

venice ● food

Kebab offers pretty exceptional and authentic kebab at a reasonable price and in one of the nicest kebab restaurants you'll find in the city. Also serves pizzas, but seeing how there's a pizzeria on every corner, you might as well take the opportunity to try something a little different.

➡ Follow Piazzale Roma east, cross consecutive bridges, and continue for approximately 5min. $ Pizza €1.50. Kebab €4. ⏰ Open daily 11am-3pm and 5:30-9:30pm.

Dorsoduro

Most of the nice restaurants in Dorsoduro tend toward the expensive side, but the neighborhood also offers some of the best cafes and pizzerias in the city, which makes the area appealing to travelers on a budget.

👍 RISTORANTE LINEADOMBRA 💳♿🍸⛅ RISTORANTE ❺

Ponte dell'Umiltà ☎041 24 11 881 💻www.ristorantelineadombra.com

Probably not the type of restaurant most budget travelers can afford to eat at more than once a trip, but if you're prepared to spring for an expensive meal, you won't find a restaurant that takes its work more seriously than Ristorante Lineadombra. The food is reputed to be some of Venice's best and is served in a beautiful, modern restaurant aesthetically similar to the nearby **Punta della Dogana** in its minimalist sensibility. Since you're going to pay a premium anywhere you eat along Zattere, you might as well go all-out and enjoy a truly excellent meal.

➡ V: Zattere. Turn right and continue for 6-7min. The restaurant is on the left, with patio seating on the right. $ Entrees €21-35. ⏰ Open daily noon-3pm and 7-10:30pm.

👍 SUZIE CAFE 💳♿🍸 CAFE ❷

Dorsoduro 1527 ☎041 52 27 502 💻www.suziecafevenice.com

With tons of classic-rock memorabilia, highlighted by a sweet guitar boasting half a dozen signatures on its body, Suzie Cafe distinguishes itself from other snack bars and cafes with both great food and high-personality decor. You could spend weeks in Venice without finding a better place to sit down and enjoy an €8 meal.

➡ V: Zattere. Turn left; walk 5-7min. to end of Zattere, turn right, and continue for 2-3min.; the snack bar is in the corner of a square. $ Sandwiches and light meals €4-11. ⏰ Open M-Th 7am-8pm, F 7am-1am.

RISTORANTE AI GONDOLIERI 💳🚫♿🍸 RISTORANTE ❹

San Vio 366 ☎041 52 86 396 💻www.aigondolieri.com

An upscale restaurant that is famous for its catering, having hosted multiple events for the nearby Guggeneheim Museum, Ristorante Ai Gondolieri is a great place to take a date after a day of visiting art galleries. Although Ai Gondolieri can be expensive, especially if you order a bottle off of their extensive wine list, the quality is proportionate to the price.

➡ From Santa Maria della Salute, walk east towards the Guggenheim, past the museum; when you reach the bend in the canal, the restaurant will be immediately across the water. $ Entrees €11.50-32. ⏰ Open M noon-3:30pm and 7-10:30pm, W-Su noon-3:30pm and 7-10:30pm.

IL DOGE 🚫💳♿ GELATERIA ❷

Campo San Margherita 3058 ☎041 52 34 607

Sure, there are gelato places on pretty much every street corner in Venice, but Il Doge is unique. It doesn't use syrups or artifical flavors in its ice cream, opting instead for fresh ingredients that make for a better taste and texture. And, although the quality is high, the prices are among the lowest you'll find in a Venetian *gelateria*. With a few unique flavors that defy description, Il Doge has quickly helped at least one *Let's Go* researcher fatten up.

➡ The southwest corner of Campo San Margherita. $ 1 scoop €1.20, 2 scoops €2, 3 scoops €2.80. ⏰ Open daily noon-11pm.

PIZZA AL TAGLIO 💳♿🍸 PIZZERIA ❷

Sacca de la Toletta 1309 ☎041 52 36 518

The Pizza Academy diploma on the wall doesn't lie—the owner of this shop

italy

knows how to cook up some serious pizzas and sandwiches. Unlike the bland, flat, lukewarm stuff you'll find at many pizzerias, Pizza Al Taglio's pizza and sandwiches are fresh, filling, and delicious. The nutella calzones *(€1.50)* are sure to make your day but ruin your diet.

➜ From the Accademia, go east, turn left at the 1st canal you meet, and turn right at the 1st bridge ahead on the left; continue straight for 2-3min. [$] Slices of pizza €2. Sandwiches €3. Calzones €3. ⏰ Open daily 10:30am-10:30pm.

RISTORANTE CANTINONE STORICO 💳♿🍸⛅ RISTORANTE ❸

Fondamenta di Ca' Bragadin 660/661 ☎041 52 39 577

Situated between the Guggenheim and Accademia, Ristorante Cantinone Storico is the rare Dorsoduro restaurant that offers great Venetian cuisine in a relaxed setting at prices more commonly seen in the backroads of Cannaregio and the eastern reaches of Castello. Stop here for a long lunch break between visits to the neighborhood's museums.

➜ V: Zattere. Turn right, walk 3-4min., and turn left onto Fondamenta Bragadin. Continue for 2-3min.; the restaurant is on the right. [$] Entrees €10-24. ⏰ Open daily 12:30-5:30pm and 7:30-10:30pm.

Castello

Since Castello is so close to P. San Marco, it gets a lot of tourist traffic, and restaurants with well-priced cuisine tend to be few and far between. There are quite a few good restaurants in Castello, but they're typically a bit pricier than comparable restaurants in other neighborhoods. In a lot of cases, you're going to have to compromise either on quality (and opt for a cheap restaurant) or convenience (and trek out to Cannaregio or eastern Castello), or just be prepared to pay a bit more than you otherwise might.

👍 **TAVERNA SAN LIO** 💳♿🍸⛅ RISTORANTE ❹

Salizada San Lio 5547 ☎041 27 70 669 💻www.tavernasanlio.com

One of the best restaurants you'll find in all of Venice, Taverna San Lio serves an incredible Venetian menu with a bit of international flair. Reflecting the owner's eclectic taste, both the decor and the cuisine are strongly Venetian but reflect the city's increasingly cosmopolitan identity. If the quality of the food isn't enough to turn heads, the bright colors of the walls will catch your attention.

➜ From Rialto Bridge, go east along Salizada San Lio for 3-4min.; restaurant is on the right. [$] Entrees €12-26. ⏰ Open M noon-11pm, W-Su noon-11pm.

RISTORANTE AI BARBACANI 💳🚫♿🍸 RISTORANTE ❸

Calle del Paradiso 5746 ☎041 52 10 234 💻www.ristoranteaibarbacani.com

Far and away the most impressive restaurant in the area around Santa Maria Formosa, Ristorante ai Barbacani boasts an excellent Venetian menu, extensive wine list, subtle yet elegant Venetian decor, and gorgeous floor to ceiling windows that open on to a canal trafficked by gondoliers and kayakers. If you're looking to impress a date, consider calling ahead to reserve the table for two closest to the window near the bridge.

➜ From Campo Santa Maria Formosa, immediately across westernmost bridge off the square. [$] Entrees €9-20. ⏰ Open daily noon-2:30pm and 6-10:30pm.

CIP CIAP 🚫💳🚫♿🍸 PIZZERIA ❶

Calle del Mondo Novo 5799/A ☎04 15 23 66 21

You'll be hard pressed to find pizza of this quality for a better price in Venice. The calzones and pizza are made fresh several times daily and then cooked to order. Budget travelers weary of the sensibly-sized portions found in most Venetian restaurants may find themselves suffering a stomachache after gorging themselves on Cip Ciap's cheap pies.

➜ Immediately across bridge to Calle del Mondo Novo from S. Maria Formosa. [$] Calzones €3. Pizza €1.50 per slice. ⏰ Open M 9am-9pm, W-Su 9am-9pm.

RISTORANTE AL COVO
💳♿🍸⛱ RISTORANTE [4]

Campiello della Pescaria 3968 ☎041 52 23 812 💻www.ristorantealcovo.com

From the outside, there isn't anything too striking about Ristorante al Covo, but this modest restaurant offers the most incredible Venetian cuisine in Castello, if not the entire city. Though pricey for budget travelers, a €25 meal here is an absolute steal when compared to other restaurants of comparable quality.

➡ East from P. San Marco, cross 4 bridges and turn left onto the last street before the 5th bridge going east. $ Entrees €16-29. ⏰ Open daily 12:45-3:30pm and 7:30-midnight.

RISTORANTE PIZZERIA SAN PROVOLO
💳♿🍸⛱ RISTORANTE [3]

Campo San Provolo 4713 ☎041 52 85 085

If you're looking to get a meal around San Marco at a good restaurant that caters to tourists, Ristorante Pizzeria San Provolo is a great choice. The staff is very friendly and speaks English well, the menu has many options in various price ranges, and the patio seating is exceptional.

➡ From P. San Marco, walk south toward water, turn left, cross 2 bridges, make the 1st left, and continue through Campo San Provolo; the restaurant is on the left. $ Entrees €9-29. ⏰ Open M-Th 11:30am-10:30pm, Sa-Su 11:30am-10:30pm.

NIGHTLIFE

For all of its fascinating history, awe-inspiring architecture, and delightful cuisine, the one thing that Venice desperately lacks is nightlife. Whereas the ubiquity of historic *palazzi*, excellent seafood, and lovely hotels in Venice means you could find them while blindfolded, if you head out in search of a random bar you'll likely end up heading home an hour later with nothing more than a kebab to show for it. Stick to the major hot spots listed here, and you'll have a lot more success. Additionally, be prepared for a much more laid-back bar scene than that of most major Italian cities. You're not going to find much dancing or serious partying, but there are a couple great places to sit back, enjoy a few drinks, and appreciate Venice at night. **Campo San Margherita** in Dorsoduro is the city's biggest nightlife hub, and that whole neighborhood is the place to be after 9pm. Crime in Venice is less of a concern than it is almost anywhere else in Italy, but use common sense: don't carry too much cash or walk alone at night, and you will probably be fine.

San Marco

After tourists head out for dinner at around 7pm, the bells of the Campanile stop chiming every few minutes, and pigeons and seagulls are left to drift aimlessly in the sky as the tourists who fed them bread during the day disappear. It is at this time of day that P. San Marco is at its finest.

After the beauty of the early evening, things get slower and duller. Dozens of places market themselves as "bars," but that term is more likely to denote a light-fare restaurant that serves alcohol than a nightlife hotspot. There are certainly a couple of places worth visiting, but since San Marco caters to the city's typical tourist, expect to see a lot more middle-aged couples holding hands and a lot fewer students downing body shots.

BACARO LOUNGE BAR
💳♿🍸❄ BAR

Sestiere San Marco 1345 ☎041 29 60 687

An ultra-chic minimalist bar just steps away from P. San Marco, Bacaro Lounge is one of the few establishments in San Marco that caters to the young and fashionable post-dinner crowd. Whereas most bars here are filled with middle-aged tourists rocking fanny packs and visors, Bacaro Lounge recalls the scene at an exclusive club in Manhattan or LA. With an understated playlist, sleek lounge set-up conducive to free conversation and mingling, and an extensive list of wine and cocktails, Bacaro Lounge is clearly the hottest place to be after dark in San Marco.

➡ Exit the southwest corner of P. San Marco, opposite Basilica di San Marco; the bar is shortly ahead on the left. $ Drinks €3.50-13. ⏰ Open daily until 2am.

RISTORANTE GRAN CAFFÉ QUADRI — CAFE

P. San Marco 121 ☎041 52 22 105 💻www.quadrivenice.com

Caffé Quadri isn't a bar or club, and the tone tends more toward refinement than debauchery, with a string quartet dressed in formalwear setting the soundtrack. Sipping one of their excellent drinks (the wine list is unbeatable, and the coffee is reputedly some of Venice's best) to the tune of the strings playing in the background, you'll experience P. San Marco as it ought to be, showcased in the lovely setting provided by this cafe.

In the northwest corner of P. San Marco. $ Drinks €3-8. Dessert €3-7. ⏰ Open daily until 12:30am.

GRAND CANAL RESTAURANT AND BAR — HOTEL BAR

Calle Vallaresso 1332 ☎041 52 00 211 💻www.hotelmonaco.it

A welcoming hotel bar, the Grand Canal Restaurant and Bar in upscale Hotel Monaco manages to avoid pretention and cultivate a clientele that stretches beyond the hotel's guest list. The wine list is exceptionally good, the bar has comfortable seating, and the dock opens into a nice summer breeze and excellent views across the water to **Santa Maria della Salute.**

From P. San Marco, walk towards the water, turn right, and continue for 2min.; Hotel Monaco is at the end of the street. $ Drinks €4-10. ⏰ Open daily until midnight.

Cannaregio

People don't travel to Cannaregio for its nightlife, but anyone can enjoy sitting outside with a good bottle of wine or a couple scoops of gelato while taking in this low-key neighborhood's nighttime scene. The natives here are generally more receptive to out-of-town visitors than are the residents of Venice's more popular destinations, probably because Cannaregio remains free of the floods of gondola-searching tourists that fill places like P. San Marco. Cannaregio's decidedly more intimate Campo San Marco on Lista di Spagna is a particularly pleasant place to while away the night hours, as Venetian locals and tourists socialize in restaurants and on benches well into the evening.

CASINO' MUNICIPALE DI VENEZIA: CA' VENDRAMIN CALERGI — CASINO

Cannaregio 2040 ☎041 52 97 111 💻www.casinovenezia.it

One of the first things you might notice after getting off the plane at VCE is that Venice takes its gambling seriously—even the baggage carousels have a roulette-wheel theme, sponsored by the (in)famous Venetian Municipal Casino. While serious gamblers might want to head straight to Lido where the historic casino's main branch still operates, the Cannaregio location should be fun for anyone who just wants to play (or count) some cards and have a few drinks.

Going east on Strada Nova, take the 1st left past Calle Vendramin. i Male guests should wear formal jackets. $ Entry €5, guests at some hotels get in free. Ask at your reception desk. ⏰ Open M-Th 3pm-2:30am, F-Sa 3pm-3am, Su 3pm-2:30am.

THE IRISH PUB VENEZIA — BAR

Cannaregio 3847 ☎041 528 1439 💻www.theirishpubvenezia.com

A friendly crowd of boisterous locals and rowdy tourists brings The Irish Pub Venezia some of the best nightlife in the neighborhood. The drinks are strong and the bar is crowded, but patrons tend to be jovial and are happy to strike up a conversation on Venice, politics, or just about any other subject at the drop of a hat. Loud music and the pub's proximity to the late-night restaurant Neapolis Kebab keep it hopping long into the evening, even on weekdays.

Just off Strada Nova, on the left going east. $ Drinks €3-6. Snacks €6-12. ⏰ Open daily until 1:30am.

San Polo

Nightlife-wise, San Polo is second only to Dorsoduro. The area around the **Rialto Bridge** in particular is home to some of Venice's best bars, popular with both Venetian locals and tourists.

👍 JAZZ CLUB 900

💳♿🍸☁ JAZZ CLUB

San Polo 900 ☎041 52 26 565 🖥www.jazz900.com

Just down Ruga Rialto from the bars near the Rialto Bridge, Jazz Club 900 is a live-music hot spot. With shows up to several times each week, top-notch pizza, and reasonable prices on bottles, glasses, and pitchers of beer, this venue can be a chill hangout or a lively music bar, depending on what groups the club is hosting.

🚶 From the Rialto Bridge, continue straight, turn left onto Ruga Rialto, continue for 2min., and turn right: it's ahead on the left. Signs lead to the jazz club. $ Drinks €2.50-5. Pizza €6-11. ⏰ Open Tu-Su 11:30am-4pm and 7pm-2am.

MURO VENEZIA RIALTO

💳♿🍸❄☁ BAR

Campo Bella Vienna Rialto 222 ☎041 24 12 339 🖥www.murovenezia.com

With chic metal-and-dark-leather decor reminiscent of trendy bars in downtown Manhattan, Muro Venezia Rialto is one of Venice's most popular drinking spots for travelers and locals in their mid-20s. A bit more upscale than most other bars around the Rialto Bridge, Muro Venezia keeps the music low and emphasizes its lounge ambience.

🚶 From Rialto Bridge, continue straight ahead for less than 2min., and turn right; the bar is on the left. $ Drinks €3-7. ⏰ Open M-Sa 9am-3:30pm and 4pm-1:30am, Su 4pm-1:30am.

ANCÒRA VENEZIA

💳♿🍸❄ BAR

Rialto 120 ☎041 52 07 066 🖥www.ancoravenezia.it

One of Venice's most popular (and crowded) bars, Ancòra complements the subtle Asian and modernist aesthetics of its decor with some of the most universally lauded bartenders in the city. If the bar is overly crowded, grab a drink to enjoy outside in Campo di San Giacometto.

🚶 From the Rialto Bridge, continue straight; Ancòra is the last bar on the right side of the Campo di San Giacometto. $ Drinks €3-6.50. ⏰ Open M-Sa 9:30am-2am.

BAR AI 10 SAVI

💳♿🍸 BAR

Rialto 55 ☎041 52 38 005 🖥www.ai10savi.com

A popular hangout for local teens and groups of tourists alike, Bar Ai 10 Savi lacks the pretense of some other Rialto nightspots and sticks to the basics: ☑**strong drinks** at great prices. The bar is crowded enough that patrons spill out onto the street in chatting groups to enjoy a cold one and the Campo di San Giacometto.

🚶 From Rialto Bridge, continue straight; the bar is on the left side of Campo di San Giacometto. $ Drinks €2.50-5.50. ⏰ Open daily 8:30am-1am.

Santa Croce

In a city not known for its nightlife, Santa Croce is about the last place you'd want to go for an evening out. Unlike some other neighborhoods with at least a few bars and restaurants open late, Santa Croce offers only a couple of places that keep the home-fires burning after midnight.

BAR AL CARCAN

💳♿🍸☁ BAR ❸

Salizada S. Pantalon ☎041 71 32 36

While most of Santa Croce shuts down around 11pm (even on weekends), Bar Al Carcan stays crowded well into the night with tourists and locals alike looking to get a quick nightcap or enjoy a few drinks on the patio. The bar is small and fairly popular, though never overcrowded, and offers cheap drinks and good music.

🚶 Follow Piazzale Roma east, cross consecutive bridges, and continue for approximately 2min. $ Drinks €3-6. ⏰ Open until 1am most days during the summer.

Dorsoduro

Dorsoduro has far and away the best nightlife of any neighborhood in Venice. Though there are dozens of bars and clubs, the vast majority of them are concentrated around **Campo San Margherita,** which is located just minutes away from Santa Croce and San Polo. As there isn't any action to be found on the island's western and southern edges, your best bet is to barhop near this vibrant campo. Nightlife in Dorsoduro begins before sunset during the summer, and the infamous **Club Piccolo Mondo** keeps it going almost until daybreak. So if you're looking for some bacchanalian revelry in the surprisingly sober city of Venice, Dorsoduro is the place to go.

CLUB PICCOLO MONDO — CLUB

Accademia Dorsoduro 1056 ☎041 52 00 371 www.piccolomondo.biz

The definitive epicenter of Venetian nightlife, Club Piccolo Mondo puts most other bars in the city to shame. Small and down a dark side street near the Accademia, it might not impress from the outside, but if its world-class bar, excellent music, chill lounge areas, and awesome dance floor are enough to draw Mick Jagger and Naomi Campbell, they should be able to earn your patronage, even with the steep cover charge *(€10).* The club prides itself on the diversity of its clientele, which ranges from students to middle-aged patrons and includes locals as well as tourists, so anyone should feel welcome here. A lot of visitors opt to start the night at another bar before coming to Club Piccolo Mondo, due to the place's expensive drinks. As a result, things usually don't get too crazy until after midnight.

From Ponte Accademia, facing the Accademia, turn right; continue onto the 1st street directly ahead (running parallel to the Grand Canal); continue for approximately 2min.; club is on the right. $ Cover €10. Drinks €9-12. Open daily 11pm-4am.

VENICE JAZZ CLUB — JAZZ CLUB

Ponte dei Pugni/Fondamenta del Squero 3102 ☎041 52 32 056 www.venicejazzclub.com

The Venice Jazz Club is a great place to begin a night out in Dorsoduro. While most bars are still in restaurant mode, this club is serving drinks to the tune of excellent music. It tends to attract an international crowd of 20-somethings and empty out once concerts end, despite technically remaining open. Given that it's the premier spot for live jazz music in Venice, perhaps this focus on the jams is to be expected.

From Campo San Margherita, walk towards Campo San Barnaba; turn right immediately before the bridge; the club is just ahead on the right. $ Cover €20; includes 1 drink. Drinks €5-10. Appetizers €5-15. Opens daily at 7pm. Concerts start at 9pm and usually last about 2hr.

MADIGAN'S PUB — IRISH PUB

Campo San Margherita 3053/A

Madigan's Pub seeks to replicate the ambience of an Irish pub and does so to great effect, creating the loudest, rowdiest bar in Campo San Margherita and maybe in all of Venice. On weekend nights, the pub is packed, both inside and on the patio, with international patrons drinking beers, taking shots, and shouting to old (and new) friends over the bar's deafening music.

At the southwest end of the Campo San Margherita. $ Drinks €4-8. Open daily until 1:30am.

MARGARET DUCHAMP — BAR

Campo San Margherita 3019 ☎041 52 86 255

One of the biggest bars in Venice and a Dorsoduro institution, Margaret Duchamp is the most prominent watering hole in Campo San Margherita. Though the bar typically plays jazz or pop, the music isn't overwhelmingly loud, making this an excellent place for a few hours of chill time spent enjoying some of the best cocktails in Venice.

At the southwest end of the Campo San Margherita. $ Drinks €3.50-9. Open daily 9am-2am.

ORANGE RESTAURANT AND CHAMPAGNE LOUNGE BAR

Campo Santa Margherita 3054/A ☎041 52 34 740 www.orangebar.it

With an excellent patio, comfortable lounge furniture, and an awesome terrace looking out over Campo San Margherita, Orange Restaurant and Champagne Lounge has a more refined ambience than other Venetian bars. It might not get as crazy as some Dorsoduro hotspots, but make no mistake: with a wine list featuring over 60 Italian vintages and 20 imports, mega-screen TVs, and a top-notch bartender, Orange is a choice place for a night out.

At the southwest end of the Campo San Margherita. $ Drinks €4.50-12. Open daily 10am-2am.

BISTROT AI DO DRAGHI BAR

Campo San Margherita ☎041 52 89 731

More bohemian than most bars in Campo San Margherita, Bistrot Ai Do **Draghi** tends to draw grungier travelers than the other bars in the square. In fact, this place is so full of such when-did-you-last-shower travelers that it's a surprise there isn't a stack of backpacks in the corner. The bar itself has an exceptionally relaxed and social character, with conversation rather than music constituting the dominant background noise.

The northeast corner of Campo San Margherita. $ Drinks €1.50-6. Open M-Tu 7:30am-2am, Th-Su 7:30am-2am.

BLUES CAFE BAR

Crosera San Pantalon ☎348 24 06 444

Like most bars east of Campo San Margherita, Blues Cafe has a calm, sophisticated vibe that draws patrons in their late 20s and early 30s. Unlike a lot of other bars, Blues Cafe keeps the good times rolling well into the evening every night of the week, especially when there is live music. *Let's Go* gives Blues Café bonus points for musical diversity, as it spins jazz, pop, and the best old-school hip hop playlist this side of the South Bronx.

From Campo San Margherita, go west, and cross the 1st bridge you come to; continue across the square; the bar is on the 1st cross street you come to. $ Drinks €4-10. Open M-F 10am-2am, Sa-Su 3pm-2am.

IMAGINA CAFE CAFE, BAR

Campo San Margherita 3126 ☎041 24 10 625 www.imaginacafe.it

Part art gallery, part cafe, and part bar, Imagina Cafe is a favorite hangout of the Venetian *intelligentsia*. With awesome white, leather couches, consistently changing artwork, and sophisticated drinks, Imagina Cafe is a great place for stimulating conversation about the latest exhibit in François Pinault's **Punta della Dogana** contemporary art museum, but probably not the best bar if you want to get crunk or hear Miley Cyrus's latest hit.

The southwest end of the Campo San Margherita, near Ponte dei Pugni. $ Drinks €2-8. Open Tu-Su 8am-2am.

Castello

A great place to sit outside at a cafe and relax well into the night, Castello isn't particularly notable for its nightclub scene. However, its good number of bars and cafes still draw large crowds during the summer. Most nightlife hotspots are along the waterfront that marks the southern boundary of the neighborhood, but there are a couple of places worth checking out further north close to the Rialto Bridge as well as on the eastern side of Castello.

TAVERNA L'OLANDESE VOLANTE BAR

Castello 5658 ☎041 52 89 349

Blasting reggae beats until 2am, Taverna L'Olandese Volante is one of the most popular bars in the neighborhood. It seems to have wide appeal, drawing tourists, locals, students, and middle-aged customers to its great selection of beers on tap, prime location in one of Castello's best squares, and thoroughly impressive (and surprising) reggae playlist. Excellent, mahn.

🚶 From Rialto Bridge, walk east toward Salizada San Lio; continue along Salizada San Lio, then turn left at T-intersection at end of street; the bar is shortly before the 1st canal. $ Drinks €2.50-6. Snacks €5-12. ⏰ Open Sa-Su until 2am in high season.

BAR VERDE 💳♿🍸☁ SNACK BAR

Calle de le Rasse 4525 ☎041 52 37 094

Bar Verde isn't an overwhelmingly unique establishment, but it's a great place to grab a couple of drinks and something quick to eat late at night near P. San Marco in Castello. The bar is frequented mainly by tourists staying at hotels in the area, so your neighbor at the bar may run the gamut from a budget traveler sipping inexpensive beer to a middle-aged couple stepping out for some late-night gelato.

🚶 From P. San Marco, walk south toward water, turn left, cross 1 bridge, turn left onto 2nd street on the left, and continue for about 2min. $ Drinks €3-6. Gelato €1.50-4. Snacks €6-12. ⏰ Open Sa-Su until 2am in high season.

CAFFE INTERNAZIONALE 💳♿🍸☁ CAFE, BAR

Riva degli Schiavoni 4183 ☎041 52 36 047

A great place to grab a coffee or beer and maybe a quick snack right along the water, Caffe Internazionale is distinguished by an excellent patio with incredible views of the canals. This is a convenient stop at which to refuel before catching the vaporetto home after a long night in Castello or San Marco, and the nearby docks serve as an intriguing vantage point for people-watching the party 🌙**boats** and luxurious yachts that constantly drift past.

🚶 From P. San Marco, walk south toward water; turn left and continue for 2-3min., crossing 2 bridges; the bar is on the left. $ Drinks €2-5. Snacks €5-10. ⏰ Open Sa-Su until 1:30am in high season.

ARTS AND CULTURE 🎵

At the height of its power during the Italian Renaissance, the Venetian Republic was one of the centers of artistic and cultural innovation, and the profound legacy of the Renaissance is evident in the architecture, music, painting, and theater that so many tourists flock to Venice to enjoy. Things have been changing quickly, though, and particularly in recent years, Venice has begun to incorporate more contemporary and modern influences in its creative scene. As a result, you'll find an incredible diversity of artistic and cultural experiences here, from the classical to the avant-garde and from the expensive to the remarkably affordable.

Orchestral Music

👍 **INTERPRETI VENEZIANI - CHIESA DI SAN VIDAL** 💳♿ SAN MARCO

Campo San Vidal 2862/B ☎041 27 70 561 💻www.interpretiveneziani.com

Held in the beautiful San Vidal Church in San Marco, Interpreti Veneziani's concert series has garnered the acclaim of the most discerning critics and is regarded by many as the best orchestral music in Venice. While many churches host concerts that are more casual and better suited for those who feel like they should listen to this kind of music but don't really understand it, Interpreti Veneziani caters to serious aficionados, and their concerts are much more akin to a performance at La Fenice than your typical church choir.

🚶 Immediately across the bridge from the Ponte dell'Accademia. $ Tickets are usually €40.

FRARI CONCERT SEASON - BASILICA DEI FRARI 💳♿ SAN POLO

Campo dei Frari 3072 ☎041 52 22 637

Famous for its organ, which serves as the centerpiece of many concerts, Basilica dei Frari keeps things a bit less formal than some of the other orchestral events in the city but no less praiseworthy. Concerts here tend to be less predictable than those at other venues, since the church often welcomes guest choirs (and offers reduced ticket prices for the occasion), but the venue is in high demand, meaning that performances are invariably of the highest quality.

⚜ *V: Campo San Tomà. Proceed straight until you reach a T intersection; turn right, make the 1st left, and continue to the square; the entrance to the church is immediately ahead.* Ⓢ *Tickets €18.*

Theater

⬛ TEATRO LA FENICE ♨♿Ÿ SAN MARCO
Campo San Fantin 1965   ☎041 78 65 11 🖳www.teatrolafenice.it

Venice's most versatile and prestigious venue, Teatro La Fenice is the place to go if you can only see one musical or theatrical performance during your stay. The theater itself is a remarkable building, having earned its name (The Phoenix) after rising from the ashes of three separate fires, and it's worth the price of admission just to experience the space on the night of a show. However, La Fenice is more than just a beautiful building. Its world-class acoustics draw some of the globe's top musical and theatrical talent.

⚜ *Exit the southwest corner of P. San Marco, take the 1st right onto Frezzeria, continue for 3-4min., following the turn left in Frezzeria as the road becomes Calle del Frutariol, and turn left at Calle de la Verona; the theater is shortly ahead on the right.* Ⓢ *Opera €10-180, concerts €10-60, ballet €10-100.* ⌚ *Performances most weekday evenings and weekend afternoons and evenings.*

TEATRO FONDAMENTA NUOVE ♨♿ CANAREGGIO
Fondamenta Nuove 5013   ☎041 52 24 498 🖳www.teatrofondamentanuove.it

A smaller venue that often hosts less conventional and more avant-garde performances than Venice's best-known theaters, Teatro Fondamenta Nuove is the favorite of many locals and quickly endears itself to tourists who see its shows. Visitors who want to see artistically innovative performances with challenging content would be wise to check out Fondamenta Nuove's programming.

⚜ *From Ca' d'Oro, turn left onto Strada Nova, then right onto Corte Longa Santa Caterina; continue for 5-7min., then turn left onto Fondamenta Nuove.* Ⓢ *Prices vary according to seatings and shows; contact box office for up-to-date information.*

Festivals

Venice is home to two of the premier arts festivals in Europe, the Venice Biennale and the Venice Film Festival. Although Venice is a popular tourist destination year-round, the number of visitors spikes during these two events as art and film aficionados flock to the city.

LA BIENNALE DI VENEZIA
Ca' Giustinian, San Marco 1364/A   ☎041 52 18 711 🖳www.labiennale.org

First held as a relatively small art exhibition in 1895, the Venice Biennale has sky-rocketed into one of the world's most celebrated festivals of contemporary artwork. Though war, politics, and changes in the artistic community intervened to dramatically restructure the festival several times during the 20th century, it continues to attract some of the world's most talented and original artists. The festival is organized around 30 national pavilions that display contemporary artwork from the sponsor countries but also incorporates various special exhibitions. Critics laud the national pavilion format of presentation, which encourages expression of each participating nation's unique perspectives on contemporary artwork and makes visiting the Biennale as culturally informative as it is aesthetically challenging. While the Biennale is held only once every two years (that is, after all, what the name boils down to), it has become such a popular event that it has given rise to other festivals including the **International Architecture Exhibition** and **International Festival of Contemporary Music,** which have run for 12 and 54 years, respectively. The Biennale is held in years ending with an odd number (so 2011 is in luck), while the other festivals are typically held during years ending in an even number.

In the Giarddini Pubblici in Castello. Get there via vaporetto line #1, 2, 41, 42, 51, 52, or N. ⏰ June 4-Nov 27 2011. Odd-numbered years only.*

MOSTRA INTERNAZIONALE D'ARTE CINEMATOGRAFICA

Ca' Giustinian, San Marco 1364/A ☎041 52 18 711 💻www.labiennale.org

Venice is home to the world's oldest film festival, which was first held in 1932 and continues to draw thousands of artists, actors, directors, and film critics to the city each fall for film screenings and celebrations of Italian and international cinema. The festival, held on Lido, has endured political turmoil (which saw Mussolini Cups awarded as the festival's top prize) and its home island's gradual decline as a popular tourist destination, yet it hasn't waned in popularity. Famous actors from all over the world, including popular Hollywood stars, continue to come to the festival each year, bringing extra verve to the peaceful beaches of eastern Lido. At this time of the year, members of the film industry, along with the journalists, fans, and paparazzi they attract, fill 1000-seat auditoriums for showings of both popular and smaller-market films.

ℹ Contact information above is for La Biennale di Venezia offices, which operate the administration of the Venice Film Festival. ⏰ Early Sept.

SHOPPING

With innumerable designer stores, clothing boutiques, Murano glass shops, Burano lace vendors, Carnival mask workshops, and other stores operated by local artisans, Venice is a shopper's paradise. Every neighborhood has something to offer, but the best places can be found along the main streets of San Marco, Cannaregio, and San Polo as well as the areas adjacent to the Rialto Bridge. Though there are a fair number of shops with generic, overpriced merchandise who prey on tourists who haven't done sufficient comparison shopping, there are also a lot of great stores with incredible deals, especially for the shrewd negotiator. While the amount of English that shop owners speak is usually inversely proportional to how hard you press for a discount, prices can often be talked down. Failing that, tax refunds are often offered by stores that specialize in high-priced goods. If you're spending more than a few euros, it's worth asking about every possible discount, including those affiliated with *Let's Go* and **Rolling Venice** (if you have the card) as well as those that come from paying in cash. Some owners will deduct as much as 10% if any of these apply.

Venetian Artisan Goods

Of the top three artisan goods made in Venice—glass, masks, and lace—only the masks are typically produced in the city itself. Glass is produced in the northern lagoon island of **Murano,** which has been a world capital for high-quality artisan glass goods since Venice's glass furnaces were banished from the city center in 1291, while lace is generally produced in **Burano,** a quiet island to the north of Murano whose economy is based primarily on fishing and the production of handmade lace. Though the islands offer numerous stores and the most extensive selection of glass and lace, there's no need to make a trip to the northern lagoon just to go shopping, as Venice itself has a solid number of reputable stores.

CA' MACANA ♿ DORSODURO

Dorsoduro 3172 ☎041 27 76 142 💻www.camacana.com

Venice is overrun with mask shops, but Ca' Macana is one of the few places that focuses exclusively on Carnival masks and regards its work as a serious art form. Though the shop has an unmatched selection of masks, it's Ca' Macana's workshops, where you can see masks being made by hand, that truly set it apart.

From Campo San Barnaba go south; the store is ahead on the left. The showroom and mask-making courses are in 2 different storefronts just north of Campo San Barnaba. $ Masks €15-60. ⏰ Open daily 10am-7pm.

MA.RE 🛍♿ SAN MARCO

V. XXII Marco 2088 ☎041 52 31 191 💻www.mareglass.com

MA.RE is stylish and cutting-edge without being jarringly avant-garde and offers pieces that are practical and functional rather than just glass for glass's sake. Unlike other stores specializing in kitsch and easily mass-produced artifacts, MA.RE makes sensible yet innovatively designed products. This is particularly evident in the beautiful wine, cocktail, and drinking glasses that manifest the talent of their Murano artists.

⇟ Exit the southwest corner of P. San Marco, continue west across a bridge, and keep walking for less than 2min.; the store is ahead on the right. $ Prices vary depending on quality of glass and product. ⏰ Open daily 10:30am-7pm.

DUE ZETA 🛍 SAN MARCO

371-368 Calle Larga San Marco ☎041 63 17 79 💻www.duezeta.net

A lot of the glass sellers around San Marco greet tourists with a smile and a 50% markup, but the manager of Due Zeta is much more likely to introduce himself with a sneer and offers of steep discounts. The expansive store—which fills its three storefronts with an incredible selection—offers everything from inexpensive glass jewelry and souvenirs to high-end glass artwork that is worth taking some time to admire, even if you're not in the market for a €2500 chandelier.

⇟ From P. San Marco, 2nd street to the north. $ Earrings and other jewelry as little as €3. Chandeliers up to €2500. ⏰ Open daily 9am-11pm.

P. SCARPA 🛍♿ SAN POLO

Campo Frari 3007 ☎041 52 38 681

One of the few lace shops outside of Burano that sells high-quality handmade products from the island, P. Scarpa captures the atmosphere of Burano perhaps better than any other store in Venice proper.

⇟ Along the southern edge of the square. $ Prices vary. A lot. ⏰ Open daily 10:30am-7pm.

gondolas

Probably the most recognizable (and cliché) symbol of Venice, the gondola once filled the city's canals, serving as the city's main mode of water transportation. They were decorated with brilliant colors and designs that rivaled the extravagance of the famed Venetian Carnevale masks, but the city put the kibosh on the artistic arms race in the 16th century and mandated black as the standard color. In the centuries that followed, the gondola eventually fell out of favor as more efficient means of aquatic transportation became available, but several hundred still remain for the enjoyment of tourists. To prevent unsanctioned price-gouging, legal standard rates *(€80 for 40min. and up to 6 people, €40 for each additional 20min., 25% price increase for night tours)* have been established for gondola rides. Some gondoliers manage to circumvent these by charging for add-ons such as tours, singing, or other amusements. The gondola is certainly a Venetian novelty and many travelers will feel that their trip is incomplete without a ride in one, but budget travelers unwilling to shell out more for a 40min. ride than they're spending on the night's accommodations can hop on the *traghetti* for a much abbreviated, more goal-oriented (getting from one side of the Grand Canal to the other) version of the same experience. It's €0.50, and comes without the funny hats and singing (usually).

Markets

Though Venice has relatively few open spaces and streets, it is the setting for a number of respectable outdoor markets selling fresh fruit, vegetables, and seafood. Though the markets can be a bit intimidating to the timid traveler—you might be surprised by the vendors' brusque manners—if you're assertive, you'll find excellent values on the freshest and most delicious produce in the city. Prices are typically posted, so you don't have to worry about getting overcharged. Do make sure you're paying for produce that isn't blemished or bruised, though, since some vendors try to pass the damaged wares off on tourists who are less likely to complain.

👍 RIALTO MARKET ⊘♿ SAN POLO

San Polo

Once the biggest market in the Mediterranean, the Rialto Market still does business largely the way it has for nearly the past millennium. With wholesalers, retailers, restaurateurs, local shoppers, and tourists, things can get kind of crazy, but the spectacle of the market is part of what makes it great.

➡ On the San Polo side of the Rialto Bridge, walk toward the Grand Canal and continue west. $ Prices are variable but cheap. ⏰ Open M-Sa 8am-noon. Fish available Tu-Sa 8am-noon.

TRADITIONAL ▣ BOAT MARKET ⊘♿ DORSODURO

Campo San Barnaba

A relic from Venice's past without a fixed name or address, the boat market docked near Campo San Barnaba is the best remaining example of Venice's answer to the supermarket. If you want to actually buy things, it's not really worth coming here. But if you want a cool experience, this is a great choice. In theory, it's a market run out of a boat, but it's actually so popular that it also occupies a storefront opposite the boat's moorings.

➡ Exit Campo San Margherita in the southwest corner and continue west until you reach the bridge; the market is on the water. $ Prices are variable but quite cheap. ⏰ Open M-Sa 8am-6pm. Hours may vary, especially during winter.

ESSENTIALS ▪

Practicalities

- **TOURIST OFFICES: APT Tourist Office** provides information, maps, tours, the Rolling Venice Card, and theater and concert tickets. Outposts are located throughout the city. *(Main Office: P. Roma ☎041 24 11 499 🖥www.turismovenezia.it ℹ Additional offices near P. San Marco (San Marco 71) and on Lido (Gran Viale 6/A). ⏰ Open daily 9:30am-1pm and 1:30-4:30pm.)*
- **LUGGAGE STORAGE: Stazione Santa Lucia.** *(⊘ ☎041 785 531 🖥www.grandistazioni.it ➡ At the train station. $ First 5hr. €4, €0.60 per hr. up to 12, €0.20 per hr. thereafter. ⏰ Open daily 6am-midnight.)*
- **DISABILITY SERVICES: Informahandicap** provides information to physically disabled travelers in Venice, which, given the city's crazy design, is potentially a very useful thing. *(San Marco 4136 ☎041 27 48 144 🖥www.comune.venezia.it ➡ Nearest vaporetto stop is Rialto. On Riva del Carbon, 2-3min. southwest of Rialto Bridge. ⏰ Open Th 9am-1pm.)*
- **POST OFFICES: Poste Venezia Centrale.** *(Main office at San Marco 5554, with branches all over the city ☎041 24 04 158 🖥www.poste.it ➡ Nearest vaporetto stop Rialto. The post office is off of Campo San Bartolomeo, directly in front of the Rialto Bridge. ⏰ Open M-Sa 8am-7pm.)*

Emergency!

- **POLICE:** There are police stations all over the city, but the main one is the **Carabinieri** office. *(Campo San Zaccaria, Castello 4693/A ☎041 27 411 ✈ Walk straight and follow the signs from vaporetto San Zaccaria.)*

- **HOSPITALS/MEDICAL SERVICES: Ospedale Civile.** *(Campo Giovanni e Paolo Santissimi, Castello 6777 ☎041 52 94 111 ▣www.ulss12.ve.it ✈ Walk east from vaporetto Fondamenta Nuove and turn right after 1st bridge. i Be forewarned: the hospital has limited hours and is likely to redirect you elsewhere for further treatment.)*

Getting There

By Plane

As many tourists are crestfallen to discover, though **Aeroporto Marco Polo (VCE)** (☎041 26 09 260 ▣www.veniceairport.it) is billed as Venice's airport, once you've made it there, the journey to Venice's historic center has only just begun. You could opt to take a water taxi to reach the *centro*, which would cost about €100, but there are several more economical ways to make it to Venice from the airport. **Alilaguna** (☎041 24 01 701 ▣www.alilaguna.it) offers transport directly from VCE to the city center at €12 per passenger, but the service isn't necessarily the most expedient option. The ultimate budget solution is to take any one of a number of bus lines to **Piazzale Roma,** located near the Calatrava Bridge just minutes away from **Stazione Santa Lucia.** The buses, which offer convenient transportation throughout the region, are operated by **ACTV** (☎041 24 24 ▣www.hellovenezia.it) and cost as little as €2.50. This is comparable to the **ATVO Shuttle** bus, which also stops at Piazzale Roma and costs €3 for a one-way trip. Regardless of how you plan to get from Aeroporto Marco Polo to the city, be sure to get your ticket before leaving the airport—tickets for transportation services are most easily purchased at the windows there.

By Train

Most travelers who are already in Italy will reach Venice by train. Several train lines run through **Stazione Santa Lucia** (☎041 26 09 260 ▣www.veneziasantalucia.it), in the east of the city, bringing people from **Bologna** (Ⓢ €8.90. ⌚ 2hr., 30 per day.), **Florence** (Ⓢ €22.50. ⌚ 2-3hr., 20 per day.), **Milan** (Ⓢ €14.55. ⌚ 2½-3½hr.), **Rome** (Ⓢ €42.50. ⌚ 3½-6hr., 20 per day.), and numerous local destinations.

Getting Around

By Foot

Though Venice is a wonderful city with many great things to offer visitors, convenience of transportation isn't one of them. Within the city's six *sestiere*, there are absolutely no cars, buses, or trains. While poets, musicians, and various members of the literati have waxed nostalgic about the beauty of Venice's romantic, tangled streets, those same winding walkways are likely to provoke less lyrical outbursts from those unfamiliar with the city. Even experienced travelers will likely find themselves frustrated when navigating the city, since maps struggle to provide adequate detailing of the city's smaller thoroughfares. Additionally, streets are often nameless or change names unexpectedly, and street numbers organized by neighborhood give only a general indication of where particular addresses are to be found. Your best bet is to memorize a few major landmarks, know the vaporetto stop nearest your hotel, know at least one *campo* near your hotel or hostel, and keep the cardinal directions in mind.

By Boat

In some cases, particularly when bridges are scarce, travelers will find it more convenient to get to their destination by boat. Before you spend a lot of money on an expensive vaporetto ticket, consider whether a **traghetto** might get you to your destination more quickly. There are several major stops in the city where you can catch these small ferries, essentially gondolas without the kitsch, that will take you across the Grand Canal for only €0.50. Signs toward *traghetti* stops tend to be clearly indicated, and odds are, wherever you are, there will be one nearby. *Traghetti* hours vary and are limited during the winter, but in general, they remain an excellent means of transport around Venice. The vaporetti offer more extensive service throughout the city and operate 24hr. per day but are also more expensive. A single vaporetto ride costs €6.50 and longer-term passes which offer unlimited service are also available *(🕐 12hr. pass €16; 24hr. €18; 3-day €21; 4-day €28; 7-day €50)*, but the best option for students visiting in the short-term may be to purchase a three-day pass *(€22)* that includes unlimited transport via vaporetti and mainland-connecting buses as well as the benefits of the **Rolling Venice Card.**

verona ☎045

Fair Verona, best known to most English-speakers as the site of Shakespeare's *Romeo and Juliet*, has come a long way since the days when the Houses of Montague and Capulet fought in its streets. (OK, maybe the Bard embellished the history a bit, but a real-life Capello family did live here long ago.) Currently home to a thriving population of over 260,000 people, Verona is one of the liveliest and most economically important cities in northern Italy. Its ability to reconcile this modernity with its storied history through the preservation of numerous historic buildings and architecturally significant works from the Middle Ages has earned it a designation as a **UNESCO World Heritage Site.**

ORIENTATION

Verona is a sprawling city with over 700,000 people in its greater metropolitan area, but the good news for visitors is that it's actually fairly manageable. Getting around requires a fair amount of biking or walking, which is the best means of transit since car travel will likely leave out-of-towners frustrated, but pretty much everything of interest is within a 15-20min. walk of the **Arena.** Given the incredible number of well-preserved historic sights and buildings, the journey can be even more interesting than the ultimate destination.

ACCOMMODATIONS

Verona is one of the most difficult places in Italy to find budget accommodations. Often the city's visitors are older opera aficionados, so most hotels cater to a wealthier clientele.

HOTEL SAN LUCA — HOTEL ❺

Vicolo Volto San Luca 8 ☎045 59 13 33 www.sanlucahotel.com

Hotel San Luca might be beyond the price range of many budget travelers, but anyone willing to shell out for a top-quality hotel should seriously consider this one since you get what you pay for and then some.

From the southwest corner of P. Bra, continue south on C. Porta Nuova and turn right onto Volto San Luca. $ Singles €78-181; doubles €116-208; triples €146-258.

B AND B ALLE ERBE — B AND B ❸

Corte Sgarzarie 5 ☎39 29 15 50 00 www.alleerbe.it

By far our favorite bed and breakfast in Verona, B and B Alle Erbe sits in a picturesque courtyard no more than 10min. from any of the city's major sights.

From P. Bra, go northwest on V. Fratta, turn right onto C. Cavour, and continue straight for about 5min. $ Singles €45-60; doubles €60-180.

HOTEL SIENA HOTEL [4]

V. Marconi 41 ☎045 80 03 074 www.hotelsiena-verona.it

Complementing its lovely enclosed garden and excellent-value rooms with unparalleled service, Hotel Siena is small but nonetheless very accommodating of international travelers, although quite far from the *centro*.

From P. Bra, exit west onto V. Roma, turn left onto V. Daniele Manin, and continue straight for 3-5min. $ Singles €50-90; doubles €65-135.

HOTEL ARENA HOTEL [3]

Strada Porta Palio 2 ☎045 80 32 440 www.albergoarena.it

A great value hotel, Hotel Arena has some of the cheapest rooms on offer, particularly for travelers booking singles or doubles. Central location.

From Castelvecchio, continue south along Strada Porta Palio for about 2min.; the hotel is on the right. $ Singles €35-75; doubles €60-115.

SIGHTS

If you invest in a **Verona Card** *(1-day pass €10; 3-day €15)*, you'll get free access to 12 sights, plus four more at a reduced charge. The card is available at most major sights and local *tabaccherie.* If you're tempted by the many Romeo-and-Juliet attractions, do bear in mind that they tend to be overcrowded and of relatively little historic signficance. A more interesting time can be found visiting **Piazza delle Erbe,** the hub of Verona's political and cultural life since Roman times.

ARENA DI VERONA ANCIENT ROME

P. Bra ☎045 80 03 204 www.arena.it

The Verona Arena, one of the best preserved and maintained Roman ampitheaters in the world, is both the city's most prominent Roman edifice and its top venue for theatrical and musical performances. Used in antiquity for less refined (i.e. brutal) spectacles, the arena was lauded in modernity for its remarkable history as well as its excellent acoustics, and the summer operas here are one of the biggest reasons visitors come to Verona.

From Stazione FS, bus #11, 12, 13, or 72 on M-Sa or #90, 92, 93, 96, or 97 on Su. $ Entry €3, free with Verona Card. Opera tickets €23-198. Open M 1:30-7:30pm, Tu-Su 8:30am-7:30pm. Most performances at 9pm.

MUSEO DI CASTELVECCHIO CASTLE, MUSEUM

C. Castelvecchio 2 ☎045 80 62 611 www.comune.verona.it

The castle of Castelvecchio itself is as much of an attraction for many visitors as the museum to which it's home. Built by the **Scaliger dynasty** of Verona in the 14th century on the site of a defunct Roman fortress, the castle is the city's most notable medieval building for both architectural and historical reasons. The interior, however, has been completely renovated to accommodate an extensive collection of medieval and Renaissance artwork from the region.

From Stazione FS, take bus #21, 22, 23, 24, or 41 on M-Sa or #91, 93, 94, or 95 on Su. $ €6, students and over 60 €4.50, ages 8-14 €1, free with Verona Card. Open M 1:30-7:30pm, Tu-Su 8:30am-7:30pm.

COMPLESSO DEL DUOMO CHURCH

P. Duomo ☎045 59 28 13 www.chieseverona.it

An architecturally fascinating cathedral, the Complesso del Duomo was originally consecrated in the fourth century as a small and relatively simple church and was rebuilt several times over the next few centuries due to natural disasters. The cathedral's structure suffered during the 1177 earthquake that sparked Verona's Romanesque movement, a period which profoundly shaped the development of the modern cathedral.

➤ Bus line #72. [$] €2.50, free with Verona Card. ⏰ Open Mar-Oct M-Sa 10am-5:30pm, Su 1:30-5:30pm; Nov-Feb Tu-Sa 10am-4pm, Su 1:30-5pm.

CASA DI GIULIETTA
⊛♿ PALAZZO, MUSEUM

V. Cappello 23 ☎045 80 34 303 💻www.comune.verona.it

This building is purported to be the home of Juliet Capulet—and is a rare exception to the classiness you'll find all over Verona. The house is of dubious historical significance at best, given that it has yet to be proven that the Juliet featured in Shakepeare's work was even a real person, but that doesn't deter hundreds of thousands of visitors from flocking to the house each year.

➤ Bus #72 or 73. [$] €4. ⏰ Open M 1:30-7:30pm, Tu-Su 8:30am-7:30pm.

FOOD ▣

Verona is one of the Veneto's top culinary cities and is famous above all else for its excellent wines. While visitors to Verona expect great *vino*, many are also surprised by the number of fantastic cafes and restaurants.

👍 TIGELLA BELLA
💳♿🍸❄ RISTORANTE [2]

V. Sottoriva 24 ☎045 80 13 098 💻www.tigellabella.it

Tigella Bella is an unconventional restaurant featuring small plates rather than full entrees, but it serves up delicious fried dumplings and *tigella* bread, a unique regional delight.

➤ From the southeast corner of P. Bra, exit onto V. Pallone; take the last left before the bridge onto V. Marcello and continue until the street ends; turn left then immediately right. [$] Entrees €8.90. ⏰ Open Tu-Su noon-2:30pm and 7pm-12:30am.

CANGRANDE OSTERIA AND ENOTECA
💳♿🍸❄☁ RISTORANTE [3]

V. Dietro Listone 19/D ☎045 59 50 22 💻www.enotecacangrande.it

A popular restaurant among locals and visitors, Cangrande has garnered resoundingly positive reviews for its Veronese specialities, which range from exceptional meat and cheese plates to more unique regional delicacies.

➤ From the southwest corner of P. Bra, exit west onto V. Roma and take the 1st right onto V. Listone; the restaurant is shortly ahead on the left. [$] Entrees €7-21. ⏰ Open M-Sa 10am-1pm and 5pm-1am.

LA TAVERNA DI VIA STELLA
💳♿🍸❄ RISTORANTE [3]

V. Stella 5/C ☎045 80 08 008 💻www.trovaristorantiverona.com

La Taverna di Via Stella is a true tavern, featuring a cozy, welcoming ambience and excellent, hearty portions of local specialties. You'll find several innovative preparations of duck, some of the best polenta you'll ever eat, and numerous vegetable side dishes that complement any meal on their well-rounded menu.

➤ From the Arena, exit northeast onto V. Anfiteatro and continue for 3-5min.; the restaurant is shortly ahead after V. Anfiteatro becomes V. Stella. [$] Entrees €7.80-19.50. ⏰ Open daily 12:15-2pm and 7:15-11pm.

CREPERIA CUOVE AND AVANZI
💳♿🍸❄ CREPERIE [1]

V. Marconi 58 ☎32 91 69 98 34

After a long night out, crepes may be one of the few foods that rival kebabs on the list of crave-worthy foods available in Italy. This place takes it to the next level.with an astonishing menu of sweet and savory crepes for next to nothing.

➤ From the southwest corner of P. Bra, exit west onto V. Roma, make the 1st left onto V. Daniele Manin, and continue for 6-8min.; the creperie is on the right. [$] Crepes €2.60-3.60. ⏰ Open Tu-Th noon-2:30pm and 6pm-1am, F noon-2:30pm and 6pm-3am, Sa 5pm-3am, Su 5pm-midnight.

TRATTORIA AL SOLITO POSTO
💳♿🍸❄ RISTORANTE [2]

V. Santa Maria in Chiavica 5 ☎045 80 14 220 💻www.alsolitoposto.verona.it

A restaurant that is among the city's best according to locals, Trattoria al Solito

Posto tends to keep it simple with top-quality Veronese cuisine prepared with fresh, local ingredients.

From the Arena, exit northeast onto V. Anfiteatro, continue for 4-6min., turn left onto V. al Cristo, and make the 3rd right onto V. Santa Maria in Chiavica; the restaurant is shortly ahead $ Entrees €7.50-14. ⏰ Open M noon-2:30pm, W-Th noon-2:30pm, F-Su noon-2:30pm and 7:30-10pm.

NIGHTLIFE

Verona acquits itself surprisingly well for a quiet town mainly famous for an Elizabethan tragedy—several bars and clubs stay packed well into the night, even on weekdays.

PASION ESPAÑOLA — BAR

V. Marconi 4 ☎045 59 60 38

The best late-night bar in the city, Pasion Española is the place to go for drinks, music, and a great Spanish-infused atmosphere after 1am.

From the southwest corner of P. Bra, exit west onto V. Roma and make the 1st left onto V. Daniele Manin. $ Drinks €2-6. ⏰ Open M-Th 10pm-3am, F-Sa 10pm-4am, Su 10pm-3am.

BLOOM CAFE — CAFE

P. Erbe 24 ☎045 20 68 160

Bloom Cafe is distinguished by its excellent patio, attentive service, selection of high-end liquors, and great lounge music.

Northwest corner of P. Erbe. $ Drinks €3.20-6.70. ⏰ Open daily 9:30am-2am.

CASA MAZZANTI CAFFÉ — CAFE

P. Erbe 32 ☎045 80 03 217 www.casamazzanticaffe.it

Casa Mazzanti Caffé might be the most sophisticated bar in the city, but it avoids taking itself too seriously. Sit on the patio to relax and make small talk.

Northwest corner of P. Erbe. $ Drinks €3-8. ⏰ Open daily 8am-2am.

ESSENTIALS

Practicalities

- **TOURIST OFFICES:** The central tourist office is at V. degli Alpini 9. *(☎045 80 68 680 Accessible by bus #13, 51, 61, 62 70, 71, or 73. Walk south from Arena di Verona into P. Brà. ⏰ Open M-Sa 9am-7pm, Su 9am-3pm.)*

Emergency!

- **POLICE:** *(V. Salvo D'Acquisto 6 ☎045 80 561 Bus #72. From city center, continue along C. Porta Nuova and turn right onto V. Antonio Locatelli.)*
- **HOSPITALS/MEDICAL SERVICES: Ospedale Civile Maggiore** provides emergency and non-emergency medical care. *(Piazzale Aristide Stefani 1 ☎045 81 21 111 www.ospedaleuniverona.it Bus #41, 62, 7, or 71.)*

Getting There

By Plane

Verona has a small international airport, **Aeroporto Valerio Catullo (VRN)** *(Valerio Catullo ☎045 80 95 666 www.aeroportoverona.it)*. A shuttle from the airport to the train station runs every 20min.

By Train

Verona Porta Nuova station *(☎045 89 20 21 www.grandistazioni.it)* is where most travelers arrive. It offers service to and from: **Bologna** *($ €7.20. ⏰ 50-90min., 1-2 trains per hr.)*; **Milan** *($ €9. ⏰ 1hr. 20min.-2hr., 2-3 per hr.)*; **Rome** *($ €45-85. ⏰ 3hr., about 1 per hr.)*; **Venice.** *($ €6.15. ⏰ 1-2 hr., 2-4 per hr.)*

bologna ☎051

Bologna la grassa, la dotta, la rossa. It's a common refrain among locals trying to describe their city's greatest attributes. Fat, learned, and red—in these terms, the city sounds kind of like an obese Commie professor, but, really, they sum up the place quite nicely. First, *la grassa.* The people of Bologna love their food, and they're famous for it. Stuffed pastas like tortellini are among the local creations, and *lasagna alla Bolognese* has of course gathered popularity far from Emilia-Romagna's dark, fertile soil. The town's other primary exports are caps and gowns—*la dotta.* Bologna is home to the Western hemisphere's oldest university, the very first "Alma Mater," whose 100,000 students swamp the city while classes are in session and leave it feeling decidedly roomy come summertime. With youthful exuberance (and livers), these students lend the city hopping nightlife and plenty of inexpensive booze. What Bologna hasn't been so successful at spreading around Italy these days are the works of the national 👍**Communist Party,** *la rossa,* which is headquartered in the city and has the sympathies of a number of its citizens.

ORIENTATION

Welcome to Bologna, a pedestrian's town. Almost everything happens inside the *centro* walls, and a walk straight across takes less than 40min., meaning anywhere worth going is easily reached on foot. Most travelers arrive at **Stazione Centrale,** in the north of the city. Just left of the station exit, **Via dell'Indipendenza,** which runs south to the *centro* at **Piazza Nettuno,** begins. The larger **Piazza Maggiore,** Bologna's medieval center, connects to P. Nettuno. From here, streets branch off and lead to the city's many museums. **Via Rizzoli** runs east from P. Nettuno to the **Two Towers of Bologna,** one leaning, and to **Via Zamboni,** hub of the city's university and a major student gathering spot. **Via Ugo Bassi** runs west from the *piazze* to **Via del Pratello's** numerous bars. **Via Archiginnasio** heads south alongside the basilica to Bologna's classiest quarter, where the entrances to designer shops gleam beneath elaborately patterned portico ceilings.

ACCOMMODATIONS

For a place with so many students, Bologna is woefully lacking in hostels—there's just one, and it's several kilometers from the *centro.* Other accommodations can be pricey and fill up quickly, especially at the beginning and end of the school year in September and May. Though no other hotels are too far apart, the most affordable properties can be found near **Via Marconi** and **Via Ugo Bassi.**

👍 ALBERGO ATLANTIC
HOTEL [4]

V. Galleria 46 ☎051 24 84 88 🖥www.albergoatlantic.net

This new, immaculate hotel near Stazione Centrale can, in places, resemble a surrealist maze of stairs, but its rooms and public areas are flooded with light, its wooden decor is classy, and the amenities are plentiful.

‡ From the train station, head straight down V. Galleria. [$] Singles €50-130; doubles €80-190; triples €100-250.

ALBERGO GARISENDA
HOTEL [3]

V. Rizzoli 9/Galleria Leone 1 ☎051 22 43 69 🖥www.albergogarisenda.com

The beds and bathrooms may be modern, but that's about it—and at Albergo Garisenda, that's a good thing. The owners have decorated the halls and guestrooms of this third-floor hotel with an electic collection of antiques ranging from carved armoires and a piano to turn-of-the-century sewing machines.

‡ Take V. Rizzoli and turn right up the steps into Galleria Leone, where the door is on the left. [$] Singles with shared bath €45-55; doubles €60-85, with bath €75-110.

ALBERGO CENTRALE 💳🚭📶❄ HOTEL [4]

V. Della Zecca 2, 3rd fl. ☎051 22 51 14 💻www.albergocentralebologna.it

With two separate sitting rooms in which to relax and sweeping views of Bologna's rooftops (ask for a room on the hotel's upper floor), Albergo Centrale has some features more befitting of a luxury hotel than one with two stars (and one that's located one the third floor of an office building to boot).

➡ Just off V. Ugo Bassi. $ Singles €65-80; doubles €85-120; triples €105-150.

HOTEL DUE TORRI 💳🚭📶🍸❄ HOTEL [4]

V. degli Usberti 4 ☎051 26 98 26 💻www.hotelduetorri.net

Travelers bothered by flowers, pastel colors, or frilly white tablecloths best steer way clear of this one. Those who can handle baby-blue fabric draped above their bed will be pleased with Hotel Due Torri's nicely sized, comfortable rooms.

➡ From P. Maggiore, take V. degli Usberti and turn left onto V. Gessi; then make the 1st left and 1st right. $ Singles €55-130; doubles €60-160; triples €80-200.

ALBERGO PANORAMA 💳🚭❄ HOTEL [3]

V. Livraghi 1, 4th fl. ☎051 22 18 02 💻www.hotelpanoramabologna.it

The flowers welcoming guests outside the elevator, *and* at the front desk, *and* in the hall may be fake, but the benefits of staying in this great location sure aren't. In addition to its proximity to most of Bologna's sights, the very well-appointed singles make this hotel an excellent choice for solo travelers.

➡ Just off V. Ugo Bassi. ℹ Only credit card accepted is Visa. $ Singles €40; doubles €60, with bath €80; triples €80-90; quads €90-100.

OSTELLO DUE TORRE SAN SISTO (HI) 💳♿📶 HOSTEL [1]

V. Viadagola 5 ☎051 50 18 10 💻www.ostellodibologna.com

This quiet spot is 4km outside Bologna's center and surrounded by farmland. Though the large dorm rooms are bunk-bed-free and the comfortable common room is full of student travelers, the hostel's remote location is a major drawback.

➡ Take bus #93 from V. Mille at P. dei Martiri to San Sisto. At night, take bus #21B from the train station. $ Dorms €17; singles €23-25; doubles €38. ⏰ Lockout 10am-2pm.

SIGHTS 👁

Bologna's academic heritage has given it dozens of 👍**free** museums. The **University Museums,** too many to count on one hand (or two hands and two feet, for that matter), cover every imaginable discipline and are clustered at the far end of V. Zamboni while the **Civic Museums** are more spread out. 👍**Piazza Maggiore** and **Piazza del Nuttuno** are the city's main squares featuring Romanesque architecture, countless monuments, and, in the latter, the surprisingly sexual stone and bronze fountain of **Neptune and Attendants.** In P. di Porta Ravegnana you can see **The Two Towers,** one of which is leaning at an angle that would make Pisa proud.

👍 **BASILICA MADONNA DI SAN LUCA** ⛪ CHURCH, PANORAMIC VIEW

34 V. San Luca ☎051 61 42 339 💻www.sanlucabo.org

On a hilltop high above Bologna, this basilica holds a mysterious and prized icon of the Virgin Mary. The current church (not the first on the site) was constructed in 1723. Outside, views over the rolling countryside of Emilia-Romagna testify to the fertility of this region's land, though there are no stunning vistas of the city from here.

➡ Bus #20 to Villa Strada. Then take tourist bus or a 40min. hike to the church. $ Free. ⏰ Open Mar-Oct M-Sa 6:30am-7pm, Su 7am-7pm; Nov-Feb M-F 6:30am-5pm, Su 7am-5pm.

PALAZZO ARCHIGINNASIO ♿ PALAZZO

P. Galvani 1 ☎051 27 68 11 💻www.archiginnasio.it

Built in 1563, the first permanent seat of Bologna's famous university has a lot of grafitti to show for its age, though maybe not the kind you have in mind.

italy

The coats of arms of over 5000 instructors and students cover the walls and ceilings of the palace's courtyard and hallways. Today, the building houses the 800,000-volume **Biblioteca dell'Archginnasio,** arguably Italy's most important public library.

Walk down V. Archiginnasio alongside the basilica from P. Maggiore. $ Free. Open M-F 9am-6:45pm, Sa 9am-1:45pm. Closed 1st 2 weeks of Aug.

PINACOTECA NAZIONALE — MUSEUM

V. delle Belle Arti 56 ☎051 42 09 411 www.pinacotecabologna.it

The focus on religious artwork at this *pinacoteca* (art gallery) can be staid, but the brushwork is astounding. God seems to pop right out of the frame in many of these pieces, especially the more Realist ones, which are the youngest works in this collection spanning from Ancient Rome era to the 18th century. Artists include **Raphael** and Vasari.

From the 2 towers, take V. Zamboni. Turn left at the opera house and then right onto V. delle Belle Arti. $ €4, students and seniors €2. Open Tu-Su 9am-7pm.

PALAZZO COMMUNALE — MUSEUM

P. Maggiore 6 Collezioni Communali ☎051 21 93 526 www.comune.bologna.it/culture
Museo Morandi ☎051 21 93 332 www.museomorandi.it

Two museums for the price of one—and that price is zero! The **Collezioni Communali d'Arte** showcases art of the area around Bologna dating from the 13th through 20th centuries, while the **Museo Morandi** pays tribute to Bologna's own master, Giorgio Morandi. Though acclaimed by critics, Morandi may be less appreciated by artistic neophytes encountering the numerous beige still-lifes covering these walls.

On the west side of P. Maggiore. $ Free. Open Tu-F 9am-6:30pm, Sa-Su 10am-6:30pm.

MUSEO CIVICO MEDIOEVALE — MUSEUM

V. Manzoni 4 ☎051 21 93 930 www.comune.bologna.it/iperbole/museicivici

A medieval city has to store all its history somewhere. For Bologna, that place is here. From images and busts of the city's patron saints to wax seals and weaponry of local nobility, this museum offers an insight into the city's past.

Off V. dell'Indipendenza. $ Free. Audio tour €4. Open M-F 9am-3pm, Sa-Su 10am-6:30pm.

FOOD

Whatever locals list as Bologna's claims to fame (admittedly, quite a lot), this city is known internationally for one thing: its food. Heard of *lasagna alla bolognese?* How about tortellini? Yep, both were invented here. In the *centro,* restaurants galore pack the side streets.

OSTERIA DELL'ORSA — RISTORANTE ❷

V. Mentana 1/F ☎051 23 15 76 www.osteriadellorsa.com

It's a new day, and that means a new pasta at Osteria dell'Orso, which specializes in Bolognese cuisine at tremendously affordable prices. Sit down with friends or strike up a conversation with the next group at the long benches of the several communal tables that constitute three quarters of the restaurant's indoor seating. The pasta menu changes daily, but a wide variety of panini *(€4-5)* and *crostini (€4)* are always available. Though *"Orsa"* means **bear**—as the osteria's logo will show—we're feeling bullish that this place will satisfy any eater.

From P. Nettuno, take V. dell'Indipendenza, then turn right onto V. Marsala and left onto V. Metana. $ Entrees €6-10. Open daily noon-1am.

SPACCA NAPOLI — PIZZERIA ❷

V. San Vitale 45/A ☎051 199 80 262

Diners at this sit-down pizza joint relax surrounded by kitschy fake bricks, but fear not: they're soon living the dream in a separate world of crisp, doughy crust and melty mozzarella (plus whatever toppings they've added on).

Head down V. San Vitale from the 2 towers. $ Pizza €3-7.50. Primi and secondi €7-10. Open M-F noon-2:30pm and 7pm-midnight, Sa-Su 7pm-midnight.

TRATTORIA ANNA MARIA RISTORANTE ❸

V. Belle Arti 17/A ☎051 26 68 94 www.trattoriaannamaria.com

Anna Maria has been instructing her chefs to use the freshest ingredients to make traditional Bolognese dishes for 20 years. No one's complaining about taking her orders, because clearly it's working. The restaurant's walls are covered in letters from satisfied diners as well as articles about the cuisine.

From the 2 towers, take V. Zamboni, turning left onto V. Castagnoli at the opera house. Then make a right onto V. Belle Arti. $ Cover €3. Primi €13-14; secondi €11-14. Open Tu-Su noon-3pm and 7-11:30pm.

PIZZERIA TRATTORIA BELFIORE PIZZERIA ❶

V. Marsala 11/A ☎051 22 66 41

Pizza's bargain basement—at street level, and with outdoor seating! The pizza is great and a great deal at this small, wood-paneled sit-down joint. The menu also features a number of pastas.

Just off V. Indipendenza. $ Cover €2. Pizza €2.60-6. Primi €6.50-7.50; secondi €7-9. Open M 12:30-2:30pm and 7:30pm-12:30am, W-Su 12:30-2:30pm and 7:30pm-12:30am.

AMBASCIATORI RISTORANTE ❷

V. Orefici 19 ☎051 22 01 31 www.liberie.coop.it

Here two of Bologna's favorite things, books and food, can be found in one place. In a quirky juxtaposition, Ambascatori places three restaurants on three floors amid shelves of Italian-language novels and memoirs. Bags of pasta for sale sit next to shelves of books on cooking pasta.

Take V. Rizzoli away from P. Nettuno and turn right onto V. Orefici. $ Panini €3.50-4.50. Primi €8-10; secondi €9-15. Eateries open daily 7am-midnight. Bookstore open daily 9am-midnight.

NIGHTLIFE

One hundred thousand students require a lot of booze. Bologna provides generously, with a vast selection of bars, pubs, and nightclubs. **Via Zamboni** is student central and home to a mass of nightspots, while across town, **Via del Pratello** hosts a slightly older and more subdued crowd at its own multitude of watering holes. In summer, nightclubs close, and the partying moves to a number of outdoor discos, particularly in **Parco Magherita,** south of the city.

COLLEGE BAR BAR

Largo Respighi 6/D ☎051 34 90 03 73 66

Cheap drinks and outdoor seating draw students to this small but packed watering hole. Books above the bar attempt a scholarly air, but it is fair to say that studying is on few people's minds here. Special deals appeal to many—six shots for €5 is sure to get the night off to a fast start. Couples make increasing use of the couches in the dark back room as the night gets older.

Take V. Zamboni and turn left before the opera house. The bar is on the left. $ Beer €3-5. Cocktails €4. Open M-F noon-3am, Sa-Su 6pm-3am.

CLURICAUNE IRISH PUB

V. Zamboni 18/B ☎051 26 34 19

The best Irish pub in Bologna—just ask an Irishman. (And there are only—only!—six of them. Pubs that is, not Irishmen.) Students and groups of expats gather to watch every soccer game and converse over their choice of one of the eight beers *(€4.50; Guinness €5)* on tap.

Take V. Zamboni from the 2 towers. $ Cocktails €5.50. Open June-Aug M-Th noon-2am, F-Sa noon-2:30am; Sept-May daily 4pm-2am.

ALTO TASSO ENOTECA
P. San Franceso 6/D ☎051 40 88 06 79 💻www.altotasso.com

As well as providing for thirsty students—a task this bar carries out well—Alto Tasso puts a lot of effort into showcasing the art on its walls. It's a bright display that rotates among young, local artists every two weeks.

➜ Take V. Ugo Bassi and make a slight left onto V. Pratello, then the first left to V. San Francesco. $ Wine €2-5. Beer €2.50-5. Cocktails €5. ⏰ Open M-Th 4:30pm-2:30am, F-Sa 4:30pm-3am, Su 4:30pm-2:30am.

CASSERO CLUB
V. Don Minzoni 18 ☎051 649 4416 💻www.cassero.it

A cavernous dance floor and thumping beat inside plus a vast, sunken *piazza* for dancing, carousing, and occasional live music outside add up to plenty of space for the locals and students who frequent this popular party spot, Bologna's best-known gay and lesbian club.

➜ Take V. Marconi to P. dei Martiri and turn left onto V. Don Minzoni. $ Cover M-Tu €10, W €3, Th-Su €10. Beer €3. Cocktails €7. €15 ARCI-GAY card required for entrance. ⏰ Open daily in summer 7pm-6am; in fall, winter, and spring 9pm-6am.

ESSENTIALS

Practicalities

- **TOURIST OFFICES: IAT** provides information on sights and the city. Walking and bus tours start here. *(P. Maggiore 1/E ☎051 23 96 60 ➜ In Palazzo di Podesta. ⏰ Open daily 9am-7pm.)* **Bolognaincoming** books hotels, but not hostels. *(P. Maggiore 1/E ☎800 85 60 65 💻www.bolognaincoming.it ➜ Located inside the tourist office. ⏰ Open daily 9am-7pm.)*
- **INTERNET: Sportello Iperbole** provides free Wi-Fi, limited rather generously to 3hr. per day, and internet access limited a little less generously to 2hr. per week on non-personal computers. *(P. Maggiore 6 ☎051 20 31 84 ➜ In Palazzo Comunale. i Reserve ahead for Wi-Fi. ⏰ Open M-F 8:30am-7pm, Sa 8:30am-2pm and 3-7pm.)*

Emergency!

- **POLICE:** *(P. Galileo 7 ☎051 16 40 11 11).*
- **LATE-NIGHT PHARMACY: Farmacia Communali.** *(P. Maggiore 6 ☎051 23 85 09 ➜ In Palazzo Communale. ⏰ Open 24hr.)*
- **HOSPITALS/MEDICAL SERVICES: Policlinco San Orsala Malpighi.** *(V. Pietro Albertoni 15 ☎051 63 61 111 💻www.aosp.bo.it ➜ Follow V. San Vitale to V. Massereti and turn left.)*

Getting There

By Plane

Aeroporto Guglielmo Marconi (BLQ) *(☎051 647 9615 💻www.bologna-airport.it)* is northwest of the city center. ATC operates the **Aerobus** *(☎051 29 02 90)*, which runs from the airport to the train station's track D, with several stops in the *centro* along V. Ugo Bassi. *($ €5. ⏰ Every 15min. 6am-12:15am.)*

By Train

Stazione Centrale, in the north of the *centro*, is the main point of arrival. Trains arrive from **Milan** *($ From €19. ⏰ 2-3hr., 2 per hr. 5:15am-11am.)*, **Florence** *($ €24. ⏰ 90min., 2 per hr. 7:15am-10:30pm.)*, **Rome** *($ From €36. ⏰ 3hr., 2 per hr. 7:15am-10:30pm.)*, and **Venice** *($ €15. ⏰ 2hr., every 30min.-1hr. 5:57am-11:11pm.)*

cinque terre ☎0187

Once an undiscovered paradise, the Cinque Terre now offers a break to backpackers tired of city-hopping through Europe. Frequent train service makes the five charming cliffside villages that dot this stretch of the Italian Riviera easily accessible, yet the region's unique landscape, characterized by terraces built up over thousands of years of grape and citrus farming, prevents this Italian Shangri-La from becoming a tourism-fueled playground-by-the-sea. Yes, out-of-town visitors now account for a large majority of the summertime population, and English at times feels like the area's first language. But visitors willing to trek along the trails that connect the region's five towns find that a number of unrivaled vistas and secluded beaches remain.

It would be a lie and a cliché to say that, in the Cinque Terre, there's not a car in sight. They're here, along with scooters and motorboats too. But in the face of all the beachfront hustle and tourist bustle, it's still possible to slip away into the vineyards, look down on the towns, and witness the beauty and majesty that make the Cinque Terre seem too perfect to be real.

ORIENTATION

Part of the pleasure of exploring the five towns that give Cinque Terre its name comes from getting to know each of the five coastal towns' distinct personalities. Furthest north, **Monterosso** is blessed with a welcoming expanse of sand, making it a perfect modern beach town. **Vernazza** is the quieter but more beautiful sister by the sea. Hilltop **Corniglia** is tiny and withdrawn from the tourist circuit but offers the most stunning vistas of all five towns, but no beach and few practical services. **Manarola** has the best (and wackiest) swim spot. Finally, **Riomaggiore** is larger and beachless, but sees backpackers trying, successfully or not, to find last-minute rooms.

ACCOMMODATIONS

Most hotels can be found in the large towns at either end of the Cinque Terre: Monterosso and Riomaggiore, with a few options dotted in between. Across the five villages you'll easily find *affittacamere*, apartments let out by locals on a short term basis. They often offer cheap and extremely pleasant living quarters.

Monterosso

Monterosso contains most of the Cinque Terre's hotels—probably as many as fill all the other villages combined.

HOTEL SOUVENIR HOTEL ❷

V. Gioberti 24 ☎0187 81 75 95

Though the owners urge their guests to party on the beach, the groups of backpack-lugging students who stay at Souvenir seem content to hang out in the in the hotel's large and comfortable rooms, many with bunk beds to accommodate bigger groups.

Head up V. Roma from the waterfront; turn right onto V. Gioberti, and walk to the end. $ Dorms €25-35; singles €45.

HOTEL AMICI HOTEL ❹

V. Buranco 36 ☎0187 81 75 44 www.hotelamici.it

Far, far away from the touristed world of Monterosso, there is a secret garden of terraces, citrus trees, and bright flowers. That garden just happens to be this hotel's roof. After going up five floors in the elevator, guests can keep going up and up through the foliage if the lounge chairs and patio tables aren't good enough. The hotel also has spacious rooms with large bathrooms to match.

From the waterfront, take V. Emanuele to P. Matteotti, turning left onto V. Buranco. Hotel has a large sign on the right. i Breakfast included. Wi-Fi €2.50 per hr., €3.50 per 2hr. $ Bed in doubles or triples €50-70; singles €60-80. €5 surcharge per night for stays under 3 nights.

Vernazza

With a few exceptions, Vernazza's accommodations are almost all rental rooms owned by private citizens. Look for signs advertising *camere* in front of stores, restaurants, and doorways all over town.

▨ ALBERGO BARBARA
●⊗ HOTEL ❹

P. Marconi 30, top fl. ☎0187 81 23 98 ▣www.albergobarbara.it

Ahoy there! Lifting that giant suitcase up a spiral staircase with only a rope to cling to may not be fun (though it really makes the nautical theme work), but it's worth it to get to the rooms above. Many have sea views and wooden rafters, and even those that look out the back are bright and airy.

⚑ *To the right when coming from V. Roma.* ⓘ *No elevator. Several flights up.* ⓢ *Doubles €50, with bath €60-65, with sea view €100.* ⌚ *Closed Dec-Feb. Check-in until 5pm; later, call ahead.*

Corniglia

Although Corniglia is best as a daytrip because of its small size and inconvenient hilltop location, there are a number of *affittacamere* that tend to be more affordable than those in other towns.

▨ OSTELLO CORNIGLIA
●⊗((ŋ)) HOSTEL ❷

V. alla Stazione 3 ☎0187 81 25 59 ▣www.ostellocorniglia.com

Among a sea of signs advertising rooms, the bright yellow ostello stands out, and for good reason. This two-year-old, 24-bed hostel offers the most affordable accommodations in town, with colorful common spaces to match.

⚑ *In the yellow building to the right before the centro storico.* ⓘ *Breakfast €3.* ⓢ *Single-sex 8-person dorms €24; doubles €55. Extra bed €20.*

Manarola

▨ OSTELLO CINQUE TERRE
●⅋((ŋ)) HOSTEL ❷

V. Riccobaldi 21 ☎0187 92 02 15 ▣www.hostel5terre.com

It may have a summer camp atmosphere, but this is no wood-board bunkhouse. All rooms look out over Manarola and the sea beyond, and an airy restaurant with terrace serves as a gathering spot. What's more, an extensive board game collection and snorkel equipment for rent keep patrons entertained.

⚑ *From the train station tunnel, turn right and walk 300m uphill to the church, where the hostel will be to the left.* ⓘ *Wi-Fi €1 per 15min.* ⓢ *6-bed dorms €23; doubles €65; quads €100.* ⌚ *Reception 7am-1pm and 4pm-1am. Lockout 10am-5pm. Closed Nov-Feb.*

CAPELLINI AFFITICAMERE
●⊗ AFFITTACAMERE ❹

V. Birolli 88 ☎0187 92 04 10

Although she doesn't own a computer, the kind, motherly keeper of these simple but comfortable rooms literally goes out of her way to make guests feel at home, as she has to descend from the fourth floor for every request. The rooms, on Manarola's main street, each have a few pieces of antique furniture like leather armchairs, plus a table, chairs, and fridge: perfect for a quiet night in.

⚑ *Turn left from the tunnel, over the piazza; the property is on the right.* ⓢ *Doubles €60; triples €75.*

Riomaggiore

At the extreme end of Cinque Terre, Riomaggiore has more than its fair share of room rentals and *locande* (inns), meaning that this is the best place to look for last-minute lodging (though that doesn't guarantee anything will be available if you arrive in mid- to late summer). Most hotels and room rentals are on **Via Colombo,** but looking on a few back streets and above the town center can yield rewards.

▨ MAR-MAR
●⊗ AFFITTACAMERE ❷

V. Malborghetto 4 ☎0187 92 09 32 ▣www.5terre-marmar.com

Talk about assorted flavors—from student dorms to vast apartments, this room rental company seems to have it all. Each room includes an ensuite bath, but beyond that, little is shared by the 30 different properties. Some have TV, others balconies, and prices vary accordingly. Those who choose to spend less can still benefit from the community terrace, a space for all renters that overlooks the water.

→ After the tunnel, turn left up V. Colombo. Mar-Mar is ahead on the left. $ Dorms €15-20; doubles and apartments €60-120. ⏰ Office open daily 9am-1pm and 2-5pm.

EDI
💳🚭 AFFITTACAMERE [4]

V. Colombo 111 ☎0187 92 03 25

With many boasting full kitchens and terraces, Edi's apartments are dressed to impress and priced to please. (One-bedroom apartments with living room and bathtub for €60?! It's a real possibility.) The best deals, however, are on the couple of rooms reserved for young people, which include many of the same amenities—minus the sea view, but you can find that at the beach—for even lower rates.

→ From the tunnel, head about halfway up V. Colombo, where Edi is on the right. $ Student rooms for 2-3 people €50-75; doubles €60-100; apartments €60-180.

LOCANDA DALLA COMPAGNIA
💳🚭📶❄ B AND B [4]

V. del Santaurio 32 ☎0187 76 00 50 💻www.dallacompagnia.it

The most popular accessory at this cheery bed and breakfast should probably be a skateboard for guests to zoom down the steep hill of V. Colombo. Though perched at the top of the road, this *locanda* is still only minutes (perhaps seconds for those on wheels) from the water and restaurants in the lower end of the town. It features five brightly colored rooms and an open breakfast area as well as a few "mini-apartments" farther from the main building but with similar amenities.

*→ At the top of V. Colombo, in the small piazza on the right. **i** Breakfast included in most rates. $ Doubles outside the hotel €30-50, in main building €60-100. Small discount for payment in cash. ⏰ Check-in noon-6pm.*

SIGHTS 👁

Beaches and hike routes are the most important sights to be found in the Cinque Terre. You'll also find a few charming spots with great views, and the odd remnant of the area's history as an important trading post.

Monterosso

👍 IL GIGANTE
♿ MONUMENT, BEACH

V. Mollina, near V. Fegina

He's the best-looking lifeguard on the beach. Too bad he's so hard to get into bed. That's because he's a stone giant carved from a cliff, watching over one of Monterosso's 👍**free beaches.** Beyond the giant's gaze, you'll be able to view more of the town's public shores, the most of any of the Cinque Terre towns. The uncontrolled stretches tend to be mixed in with roped-off private areas for hotel guests and paying customers. Look for the *ingresso libero* signs by the stairs or beach access to be sure that no cabana boys will come chasing you down with a bill.

→ Turn right out of the train station onto Lungomare Fegina. $ Free.

Vernazza

👍 CASTELLO DORIA
👁🚭 CASTLE

V. G. Guidoni

The Cinque Terre and its seas were a playground for the powerful families of Vernazza early in the last millennium, and from this castle, they observed and manipulated their domain...with the help of a strategic location and some artillery. (And thank goodness someone was protecting this harbor: at one point in the 13th and 14th centuries it was the primary port exporting the region's wine.) The power may be gone, but the view from the castle, the commanding and description-defying view, remains for all to see.

➡ Turn left onto V. G. Guidoni and walk up many steps, following the signs for "Castello." Ⓢ €1.50. All proceeds benefit local charity. ⏰ Open daily 10am-7pm.

VERNAZZA PORT ♿ BEACH

P. Marconi

Once upon a time, this minuscule inlet was home to much of the wine shipping on the Italian Riviera. Now it sees a lot of toddlers in swim diapers taking their first dip with mom and dad. The small strip of sand located right in the heart of Vernazza has no services or lifeguard, but its small size and protected water mean it remains very family friendly.

➡ At the end of P. Marconi. Ⓢ Free. ⏰ Open daily sunrise-sunset.

Manarola

👍 **ROCKY BEACH** ⊗ BEACH

At the end of V. Birolli

A ▣**boat** putters by, a swimmer uses it to screen the defender, and—he scores! Yes indeed, water polo is one of the primary pastimes—after fishing from small, enthusiastically colored boats, of course—practiced in Manarola's compact cove. The rock face leading down from the town doesn't dissuade swimmers from nearby homes or from two continents away, and neither does the occasional marine traffic. Sunbathers populate the hard surfaces, both slanted and flat, along the boat ramp, while more adventuresome types jump 15 ft. from the central outcropping.

➡ Turn left from the tunnel and head down to the water on V. Birolli. Ⓢ Free.

MUSEO DI SCIACCHETRÀ 🍷⊗ MUSEUM

V. Discovolo 203

This one-room museum showcases the history of the Cinque Terre region, a story very intertwined with wine. The now-famous trail linking the towns was once a trade route through which grapes, lemons, and thyme were brought to the wider world. Also, see the tools used to harvest the tens of kilos of delicate grapes needed to produce just one liter of *sciacchetrà*. A 15min. video on the process *(available in English)* is played on request.

➡ Turn right from the tunnel; the museum is up the hill on the right. Ⓢ Free with Cinque Terre Card, which is required for admisison. ⏰ Open daily 9:30am-1pm and 1:30-7pm.

Riomaggiore

👍 **ARTWORK OF SILVIO BENEDETTO** ♿ PUBLIC ART

In P. Rio Finale, the tunnel, and all over town 💻www.silviobenedetto.it

Buenos Aires native Silvio Benedetto has made it his mission to beautify Riomaggiore through monumental works of art, and all visitors to the town are beneficiaries of his project. Exploring the town, visitors will unexpectedly find Benedetto's murals glorifying the area's history in many places, including in the tunnel from the train station and on Riomaggiore's municipal building.

➡ First admire the mural outside the train station. Then proceed through the tunnel to town, focusing on the mosaic to the right, and don't miss the tile installation outside the tunnel's end. Above town, the municipal building on V. T. Signori also has a mural. Ⓢ Free.

FOOD 🍴

Monterosso

Monterosso's food offerings are as broad and varied as can be found in the Cinque Terre. This means nothing exotic, but a selection of Italian-style restaurants from several pizzerias and Ligurian seafood shops as well as focaccerias and *gelaterie* lining the waterfront streets. To make a picnic, visit **SuperConad Margherita.** *(P. Matteotti 9 🕐 Open June-Sept M-Sa 8am-1pm and 4:30-8pm, Su 8am-1pm.)*

👍 CANTINA DI SCIACCHETRÀ — 💳🚭🍸 WINE SHOP ❶

V. Roma 7 — ☎0187 81 78 28

The one stop on V. Roma required for wine connoisseurs and thirsty students alike, this bottle-filled shop offers regional wines including its namesake, the world-renowned sweet wine, at dirt-cheap prices. Plus, samples are available at the lowest price of all: zero. The enthusiastic and kind English-speaking staff are always eager to pour something but will also help customers navigate the selection of marmalades and sauces *(€5-10)*. For many backpackers, this place's outdoor seating is the beach (just ask the staff to open the bottle before you leave).

➔ On the left before the first underpass over V. Roma. $ Cinque Terre wine €5-20. Sciacchetrà €27. 🕐 Open daily 9am-11pm.

RISTORANTE L'ALTAMAREA — 💳🚭🍸⛱ SEAFOOD ❸

V. Roma 54 — ☎0187 81 71 70

Fresh fish and even fresher homemade pasta are the hallmarks of this well-loved restaurant's traditional Ligurian menu. Most locals already know the chef and his scrumptious creations, but tourists just discovering them for the first time come away equally satisfied. Fish ravioli is among the unique dishes recommended by diners and the staff alike.

➔ On the right after the 1st underpass on V. Roma. $ Primi €10; secondi €14-18. 🕐 Open M-Tu noon-3pm and 6-10pm, Th-Su noon-3pm and 6-10pm.

PIZZERIA LA SMORFIA — 🚫💳🚭🍸⛱ PIZZERIA ❷

V. Vittorio Emanuele 73 — ☎0187 81 83 95

A huge selection of 50 different pizzas (and 16 white pizzas, plus 10 calzones) draws locals, including workers from other nearby restaurants, to this crowded joint. Three employees frantically wait tables, cut pizzas, and make change to keep up with the rush and calls for beer that flow from the groups of young people under the awnings. The large pizzas will feed an army. The calzones shaped like bloated croissants are filled with deliciously melty cheese and sauces.

➔ Take the 1st left on the piazza after the tunnel onto V. Vittorio Emanuelle. The pizzeria is up on the left. $ Pizzas €4.50-7, large €9-14. Calzones €8. 🕐 Open daily 10:30am-3pm and 6-11pm.

Vernazza

👍 BAIA SARACENA — 🚫💳🚭🍸⛱ PIZZERIA ❶

P. Marconi 16 — ☎0187 81 21 13 💻www.baiasaracena.com

The location—in an arcade next to Vernazza's quaint fishing port—is special, and so is the pesto pizza. For just €5 (€4.50 for margherita), patrons can get a large and amazingly filling slice as well as a soda. Even when it's raining, dozens of visitors gather with their slices to eat on the rocky sea wall as waves crash at their back. For table service (when it's sunny), sit on the patio and savor the majestic view from a table.

➔ Far down on the left side of the piazza, right before the seawall. $ Whole pizzas €6.50-8.50. Bruschetta €5-6. Salads €5-8. 🕐 Open M-Th 10:30am-10:30pm, Sa-Su 10:30am-10:30pm.

BLUE MARLIN BAR — 🚫💳🚭🍸⛱ CAFE ❶

V. Roma 43 — ☎0187 82 11 49 💻bluemarlin2@lycos.it

Here's something many travelers haven't seen in a while: eggs and bacon. And what a relief it can be to find those two staples on one's breakfast plate, as is possible here in the heart of Vernazza. And if eggs *(€4)* keep Americans happy, adding sausage or bacon *(€2)* should really put them in hog heaven. Despite a cuisine that seems particularly suited to Uncle Sam, this bar fills with patrons of all nationalities by mid-morning and tends not to empty out until just before closing, when the day's first meal is a distant memory.

➥ Down the hill from the train station; on the right. $ Pastries €1. Bruschetta €3-4. Pizza €5-7. Espresso drinks €1-2. ⏰ Open daily 7am-6:30pm. Hot breakfast served 8:40-11:30am.

Corniglia

As a waypoint for backpackers, Corniglia offers a number of simple but satisfying dining options as well as several sit-down restaurants catering to those staying in town.

LA GATA FLORA — PIZZERIA [1]
V. Fieschi 109 — ☎0187 82 12 18

Once the trail-fatigued backpacker realizes it's not vertigo that's making her see pots and pans hanging from the ceiling—they've been recycled as lights—she must deal with another sight quite uncommon in these parts: a rectangular pizza. Yes, with corners. The thick crust makes a filling meal, while the focaccia, also square, with toppings including tomato and olives can hold you over as a tasty snack.

➥ From centro storico, turn right onto V. Fieschi; the pizzeria will be on the left. $ Whole pizzas €4.50-7, slices €2.50-3.50. Focaccia €1.80-3. ⏰ Open M 10am-3pm and 6-8pm, W-Su 10am-3pm and 6-8pm.

CANTINA DI MANANAN — RISTORANTE [3]
V. Fieschi 117 — ☎0187 82 11 66

Whether it's a desire to create exclusivity or a European dislike of working that keeps this restaurant open for just over 4hr. per day doesn't really matter: make time to visit the small stone-walled restaurant during its operating hours. The front entrance is covered in chalkboards scrawled with the dishes of the day, including the popular stuffed pastas.

➥ From centro storico, turn right onto V. Fieschi; the restaurant will be on the left. $ Cover €1.80. Primi €10-12; secondi €12-18. ⏰ Open M 12:45-2:30pm and 7:45-9:15pm, W-Su 12:45-2:30pm and 7:45-9:15pm.

Manarola

TRATTORIA DAL BILLY — RISTORANTE [2]
V. Rollandi 122 — ☎0187 92 06 28

The long hike up the steep road to reach this place is worth it—locals love the fresh seafood (caught by a fisherman whose gleaming mug adorns the walls) and homemade Ligurian pastas.

➥ Turn right from the tunnel, then follow the road uphill 300m to the church piazza. Then turn right up the steps at the far side of the piazza and follow the small street to the trattoria. $ Cover €2. Primi €6-10; secondi €9-17. ⏰ Open M-F noon-2:30 and 6-10:30pm, Th 6-10:30pm, F-Su noon-2:30pm and 6-10:30pm.

LA CAMBUSA — PIZZERIA [1]
V. Birolli 110 — ☎0187 92 10 29

The display case is always full. Maybe that's because there are so many choices that no customer can bear to pick just one dish. Beneath the hand-painted sign and fake ivy of this seatless establishment (not counting a few benches outside) every bread product and delicacy known to humanity awaits, from cannoli *(€1)* and pastries to focaccia with tons of different toppings.

➥ Turn left from the tunnel and cross the piazza. The pizzeria is on the right. $ Focaccia €1.80-2.50. Panini €3. Pizza slices €2. ⏰ Open daily 8am-8pm.

Riomaggiore

TE LA DO IO LA MERENDA — PIZZERIA, TAKEOUT [1]
V. Colombo 161 — ☎0187 92 01 48

Can the menu at this tiny hole-in-the-wall takeout joint get any bigger? Sure it can: the staff hangs handwritten pages of new dishes and specials all over the outside and from the clotheslines inside. Serving more than typical pizza and pasta, this quick and scrumptious spot draws patrons all day with local specialities including crispy *farinata* and vegetarian Ligurian pastas, even without giving their hungry guests a single place to sit down.

 # At the bend in V. Colombo, on the right. $ Medium pizzas €5-7, slices €2-3. Ligurian dishes to go €5-8. ⏰ Open daily 8am-8pm.

DAU CILA SEAFOOD [3]

V. San Giacomo 65 ☎0187 76 00 32

Some townspeople say that this is not only their favorite restaurant in town, but it is also the only restaurant that serves fresh fish brought into the town's harbor. While that's probably not true, great fresh fish is certainly to be had.

 # From the tunnel, take the steps down toward "Marina." Once outside, Dau Cila is on the left. $ Salads and primi €9-12; secondi €12-18. ⏰ Open daily noon-3pm and 6-11pm.

NIGHTLIFE

Don't expect to find much of anything going on after sundown in the smaller villages of Vernazza and Corniglia. But in the bigger towns there are quite a few bars populated by more than quite a few backpackers.

Monterosso

FAST BAR BAR

V. Roma 13 ☎0187 81 71 64

It's fast times at Cinque Terre in this all-American bar, where it is the rare customer who speaks Italian rather than English. Visiting students chat at tables and mingle by the bar over draft beers and colorful cocktails sipped from long neon straws (apparently they weren't flashy enough already).

 # After exiting the tunnel, pass under the railroad bridge and head left onto V. Roma. The bar will be on the left. $ Shots €3. Beer €4-4.50. Cocktails €5-6. ⏰ Open daily 10am-2am. Aperitivo 6:30-8pm. Closed 2 weeks in Dec and all of Jan.

CA DI SCIENSA BAR

P. Garibaldi 17 ☎0187 81 82 33

Don't worry about missing any of the action of the sporting world at Ca di Sciensa. TVs are everywhere you go and every way they come—outside, upstairs, flatscreen, big-screen, and even vintage versions with knobs. Join your friends in the extensive but frequently full outdoor seating for once-a-week live music.

 # From the tunnel, walk along the opposite side of the railroad bridge to P. Garibaldi. $ Beer €2-4. Cocktails €5. Sandwiches €5. ⏰ Open May-Sept daily 10:30am-2am; Oct-Apr M 10:30am-2am, W-Su 10:30am-2am. Aperitivo 7-8:30pm.

Manarola

The Cinque Terre's undiscovered hotspot is here in Manarola, but it's close to the only game in town.

LA CANTINA DA ZIO BRAMANTE BAR

V. Birolli 110 ☎0187 76 20 61

How much more fun would elementary school music class have been with a few bottles of wine? Ignore the flagrant illegality of that proposal for a moment, then look to this cantina for the answers. The owner and friends jam on the guitar (or didgeridoo) nightly at the front of the room cluttered with microphones, amps, and songbooks.

 # Turn left from the tunnel and cross the piazza; it is on the right. $ Wine €2.50-4.50. Cocktails €5-6. ⏰ Open M-W 9:30am-1am, F-Su 9:30am-1am.

italy

Riomaggiore

Not to be confused with that other Rio (look a few thousand miles west), this Cinque Terre town certainly lacks a hard-partying club scene, but has a couple of nice bars.

BAR CENTRALE 🍸 BAR

V. Colombo 144 ☎0187 92 02 08

The central gathering point for Riomaggiore's visiting international crowd isn't much to see on its own (except for caffeine-junkies itching to see its high-tech espresso machine). When the people start flowing in and the backpacker crowd begins to swap travel tales, however, it becomes easy to see why visitors return night after night.

⇞ Up V. Colombo on the left. $ Beer €3.50-5. Cocktails €5.50-7. ⏰ Open daily 7am-1am.

A PIE DE MA, BAR AND VINI 🍸 BAR

V. dell'Amore ☎0187 92 10 37

Who knows how many lovers have taken a break from smooching on the path above for a cocktail overlooking the sea—a pretty romantic location in itself? The A Pie de Ma drinks can't hurt the relationship either.

⇞ From the train station, take the steps up to V. dell'Amore. Turn right at the sign just before the ticket booth. i Live music most F-Sa at 9pm or 9:30pm. $ Wine €2-6. Beer €2.50-4.50. Cocktails €5-6. ⏰ Open daily 10am-midnight.

HIKING

The trails connecting the five villages were once used to carry grapes and wine from the vineyards that fill the hilltops. Today they offer the chance for a spectacularly beautiful and not especially difficult hike. The tourist office says it should take five hours, experienced hikers say four hours or less.

Monterosso To Vernazza

The hike from Monterosso to Vernazza *(90min.)* is the most challenging of the four town-linking hikes, but without question, the pain is worth the gain: breathtaking vistas of the towns and spectacular panoramas of the sea crown the uphill journey. There are rocky and uneven steps at both ends of the trail, but in between the trail becomes a relatively flat track notable for its wildflowers, butterflies, and gorgeous views over terraced vineyards back to Monterosso.

Vernazza To Corniglia

The trail from Vernazza to Corniglia *(75min.)*, while still difficult due to a significant number of steps throughout, is more open than the previous walk. It begins along a wide trail with continuous views of the ocean over a brush-covered hill. With less shade comes more cacti (in Italy, who knew?). The hike's most impressive point is near **Marker 15**, over 200m up, where the trail overlooks Corniglia—itself a city on a hill—with Manarola's orange and pink hues standing out against the many azure inlets in the distance.

Corniglia To Manarola

Talk about an inauspicious start to this trail *(40min.)*. Even after climbing down 382 steps from Corniglia (a good reason to do the trail in this direction), the scenery scarcely improves, as the entry to this portion of the trail is past the train station, through a bunker-like concrete gully, and past a number of abandoned warehouses. Compared to the first two sections of trail, the scenery here is only decent. The trail is much flatter and paved with gravel in many places, making it easier for hikers of all abilities.

Manarola To Riomaggiore

All's fair in love and walking, as the final stretch of Cinque Terre's famous "Trail #2" (the blue line on the tourist-office map) demonstrates. Known as **Via dell'Amore,** or the "Lover's Trail," this 20min. walk can be completed by anyone, and with elevators at both ends, it is nearly wheelchair accessible except for a few steps in the middle. *(Disabled visitors should call the park in advance at ☎0187 76 00 91 for lift information.)* Smooth and paved, this hike provides more than just a mild introduction to the sea views further along. Its uniqueness comes from the so-called "tunnel of love" graffiti-ed with sappy hearts and Cupid's arrows by countless paramours over the years, though some have painted elaborate murals. A cheesy but nonetheless popular trail tradition is to affix a lock to the park fences with your one and only and throw away the key as a symbol of everlasting affection.

ESSENTIALS

Practicalities

- **TOURIST OFFICES:** You can find **Cinque Terre National Park Offices** in or next to the train stations in Monterosso, Corniglia, and Riommagiore. They provide information on trails and sells **Cinque Terre Cards,** which are necessary for hiking. *(☎0187 81 25 23 for Monterosso 🖳www.parconazionale5terre.it ⏰ All 3 open daily 8am-7pm, somtimes slightly later.)*
- **INTERNET:** As with most services, Monterooso is the best bet. If your accommodation doesn't provide internet, **The Net** has computers and Wi-Fi. *(V. Vittorio Emanuele 55 ☎0187 81 72 88 🖳www.monterossonet.com $ €1.50 1st 10min., €0.10 per min. thereafter, or €10 per 2hr. ⏰ Open daily 9:30am-9pm.)* In Vernazza, try **Phone Home Internet Point,** which has computers and Wi-Fi. *(V. Roma 38 $ €0.15 per min. 1st 30min., €0.10 per min. thereafter. Wi-Fi €3 per 30min. ⏰ Open daily May-Oct 9:30am-10pm; Nov-Apr 9:30am-8pm.)*
- **POST OFFICES:** All five towns have their own post office, in **Monterosso** at V. Roma 73 *(⏰ Open M-F 8am-1:30pm, Sa 8am-12:30pm.)* and in **Riomaggiore** at *V. Pecunia 7 (☎0187 80 31 60 ⏰ Open M-F 8am-1pm, Sa 8am-noon.)*

Emergency!

- **POLICE: Carabinieri** in Monterosso *(☎0187 81 75 24)*. There are also municipal police offices in all the towns except Manarola.
- **LATE-NIGHT PHARMACIES:** The pharmacies at **Via Fegina 44** in Monterosso, **Via Roma 2** in Vernazza, and **Via Colombo 182** in Riomaggiore post after-hours rotations outside.
- **MEDICAL SERVICES:** There is a **doctor's office** in the municipal building in Monterosso *(P. Garibaldi)*.

cinque terre card

Cinque Terre Cards can be bought in the train stations and Cinque Terre National Park offices in each of the five towns. If you have any intention of hiking while in the area, you will need to purchase one, as they are required for access to the paths. They also grant reduced entry fees to various attractions in the towns and access to the bus routes within each town. A one-day pass costs €5, two-day is €8, three-day is €10, and seven-day is €20. You also have the option of buying an obviously-titled "with train" pass that includes unlimited access to the trains connecting the villages. This pass costs €8.50/€14.70/€19.50/€36.50, and is not worth the extra money since a) a train ride costs €1.40, so you'd have to ride it three times in one day to make it worth your money and b) you're buying what is essentially a hiking pass, who needs trains?

Getting There

By Train

All the towns lie on the Geona-La Spezia line. If you're coming from far afield, you will almost certainly have to change trains at least once to get here. All trains from **Genoa** (Ⓢ €5. ⏲ 90min., about every hr., departing Genoa 5am-10:20pm.) and **La Spezia** (Ⓢ €1.40. ⏲ 20min., every 30min. or more, departing 4:30am-12:50am.) stop in Monterosso and Riomaggiore, but many skip the towns inbetween. Some direct trains arrive from Turin, Florence, and Milan, but generally you need to change train to get here from one of those destinations. Local trains run between **Levanto** and **La Spezia**, with stops at each of the five villages (Ⓢ M-F €1.40, Sa-Su €1.50. ⏲ 2-19min., every 30min. or less 4:51am-11:39pm.) Train schedules to the towns are available at tourist offices. Note that for some of the villages (particularly Corniglia) the train station can be as much as a 15min. steep walk from the town itself.

Getting Around

In each of the towns, **walking** is the best way to do it. **National Park Buses,** a.k.a. green vans run through several of the villages to connect their coasts with their uphill attractions, but note that you cannot get between the villages via bus.

florence *firenze* ☎055

With Michelangelos crammed into every corner and Botticellis stacked clear to the sky, Florence isn't quite a real city—it's more like a storage facility for the Renaissance. Race through the Tuscan capital in three to five days, consuming masterpieces like a fresco-eating Pac-Man, and you're bound to remember Florence as a beautiful—if blurry—delight. Look too closely, though, and the seams begin to show. A large portion of the city's seemingly 16th-century buildings and frescoes are actually 19th-century reproductions, sometimes making it feel as if you're in a chase scene out a cheap cartoon where the same handful of background cells have been reused over and over again. Add in the overwhelming tourist crush and the lack of any local industry aside from the manufacture of plaster *Davids*, and it can all start to seem a bit Disney World.

So don't stretch out your stay. With little green space, performance art, or nightlife, Florence is the place for concentrated sightseeing at its best. In the end, you'll find it's better to give the city just a few days of intense museum- and church-going and leave feeling as though you've seen only the tip of a remarkable iceberg than overstay and never want to visit another gloriously frescoed cathedral again. Because really, they truly are glorious.

ORIENTATION

Duomo And Piazza Della Signoria

The center of the city contains Florence's two most famous attractions: the **Duomo** and the **Uffizi.** In a city where the streets were lain with 15th-century logic and everything looks pretty much the same, you'll find the Duomo an invaluable navigational aid. No matter how lost you get, you'll probably be able to find your way back here. A little further to the south, P. della Signoria offers the chance to hang out with the well-heeled, honeymooners, and a replica of the *David*. Given its high number of tourists, this area contains fairly high-priced and busy restaurants, so is notable far more for its sights than for any practical concerns.

The Outer Ring

Surrounding all the tourists at the Duomo and Uffizi are a series of neighborhoods that offer (slightly) less-tourist-filled establishments and a still high number of great museums. In the northwest is **Santa Maria Novella** train station, your likely point of arrival in the city. Heading east from there to the area around **Piazza San Lorenzo** you'll find cheap hotels, 99 cent stores, and huge outdoor markets. Continuing east, you'll go past the **San Marco** area, characterized by an amazing density of museums and bus stops. Furthest east in the city is **Santa Croce,** home of the city's university, and therefore by far its best nightlife.

The Oltrarno

The Oltrarno is the area across the Arno river. The western side is one of the most authentic parts of the city, while still retaining a high density of hostels and museums. As you go further east it becomes more residential, with only the **Piazzale Michelangelo** and the nightlife around **Ponte San Niccolo** to really draw visitors.

ACCOMMODATIONS

Travel in a small group to get your money's worth in Florence, particularly during the low season. Two to four people can score gorgeous rooms in three-star hotels for a lower per-person rate than you'll find at a hostel. Although most hotel rooms are doubles, it is not difficult to find triples, quads, and even family suites. For the solo traveler, options are a little more limited. Florence is home to only a few good hostels, and most otherwise affordable accommodations charge a pretty penny for singles. However, if you're only in town for a few days, there are plenty of acceptable options in central locations. Ikeep in mind that low season is called "low" for a reason: nightly room rates can drop by €10-20 when the city is less flooded with out-of-towners seeking beds. In our listings, we've stuck to high-season rates, so those of you traveling to Florence in February can silently gloat every time you read a price estimate and think about how much lower your rate will be.

Duomo And Piazza Della Signoria

There are a lot of options in the most central part of the city, though none are super cheap. The Academy is your best bet, particularly if you can book in advance. To go up a notch, check out the many nice small hotels, mostly found to the east and north of the Duomo. While Florence *is* tiny, it's still nice to be at its center.

ACADEMY HOSTEL — HOSTEL [2]

V. Ricasoli 9 — ☎055 23 98 665 www.academyhostels.com

This is the poshest hostel in Florence, and if you're planning ahead, it is the place to stay. For a few euros more than Archi Rossi and Plus Florence—the other good hostel options in town—you get free pasta and wine every evening at 6:30pm as well as towels, privacy screens, bedside tables, and no bunk beds. Academy is also far smaller than the other options, sleeping only 30 people at a time. For better or for worse, the price keeps away the hordes of drunk teenagers and the more adventurous backpackers, so the Academy mostly attracts middle-ground types who book in advance. The uncommonly helpful day staff learn names and, like the ritziest of concierges, know the city inside and out. Lockout may seem inconvenient, but it keeps the place spotless.

 # Less than a block north of the Duomo, on the left. i Breakfast and dinner included. Credit card min. €150. Free Wi-Fi. $ Dorms €29-34. ⏰ Reception 24hr. Lockout 11am-2pm.

HOTEL BRETAGNA — HOTEL [4]

Lungarno Corsini 6 — ☎055 28 96 18 www.hotelbretagna.net

Beautiful historic suites with frescoed ceilings merit a pricetag that's twice as high, and even this hotel's standard rooms are lovely. A tiny balcony off the lobby looks out on the Arno—at sunset, it's a fine place for a coffee or smoke. Breakfast is served in a hall lined with antique porcelain adjacent to a banquet hall that would not be out of place in one of the city's major *palazzi*.

 # Facing the river, it's 2 blocks right of Ponte Vecchio. i Breakfast included. $ Doubles €90-110; historic rooms €110-140. Several larger suites available. ⏰ Reception 24hr.

HOSTEL VERONIQUE / ALEKIN HOSTEL

🍴♿(ᵗᵖ) HOSTEL ❷

V. Porta Rossa 6, 2nd and 4th fl.

☎055 260 8332

These are two barebones hostels on two floors of the same building, run by mother and son. Rooms are all private and sleep two to four. The bathroom on the hall is shared. The place could use a better paint job, but otherwise it's clean and serviceable.

⌖ *Just north of Mercato Nuovo.* ⓘ *Free Wi-Fi. Cash preferred.* Ⓢ *Beds around €25.* Ⓒ *Alekin (he of the title) will sleep in the hostel if there are any late arrivals expected.*

HOTEL LOCANDA ORCHIDEA

🍴♿(ᵗᵖ) HOTEL ❸

V. Borgo Degli Albizi   ☎055 24 80 346 💻www.hotelorchideaflorence.it/history.html

A lovely, homey little place, with tile floors, leather couches, and a narrow terrace that's overgrown in a romantic sort of way. It's charmingly cluttered and den-like in most of the common space, but the shared bathrooms are large and clean.

⌖ *V. Borgo Degli Albizi leads from the southeast of the Duomo piazza.* ⓘ *Tea and coffee all day. Good ceiling fans.* Ⓢ *Singles €30-55; doubles €50-75; quads €80-120.* Ⓒ *Reception 8am-10pm.*

The Outer Ring

Unless you're here with your parents or you have a specific reason to stay south of the Arno, this is where you'll probably stay. As in almost any city, there are plenty of budget hotels located right next to the train station. If you roll into town late and are just looking for somewhere to crash, head straight to **Via Fiume,** which is lined with hotels. **Via Nazionale** and **Via Faenza** are a little further east but still have plenty of budget options. Further east from those, though, and you'll reach more residential areas with far fewer options, so it's best to stick to the north and northwest of the city.

🏚 OSTELLO ARCHI ROSSI

🍴♿(ᵗᵖ) HOSTEL ❷

V. Faenza 94r   ☎055 29 08 04 💻www.hostelarchirossi.com

The large garden courtyard might be the only green space you'll see in Florence outside of church cloisters. The quirky garden is charming enough that you will forget you are in a massive 100+ bed hostel, and the walls packed with notes, drawings, and signatures from previous guests will give you something new to look at every time you walk up the stairs. Pay a little extra for an ensuite room, because the communal bathrooms are shared by too many. On the plus side, this hostel has more computers than most American public schools. Despite some trade-offs, this is the best hostel in Florence. Good luck trying to find somewhere to scrawl your own name—look for *Let's Go* across from the water cooler.

⌖ *From the train station, take V. Nazionale and then a left onto V. Faenza.* ⓘ *Beer on sale at desk.* Ⓢ *Dorms €21-27.* Ⓒ *Reception 6:30am-2am.*

🏚 HOSTEL PLUS

🍴♿(ᵗᵖ) HOSTEL ❷

V. Santa Caterina D'Alessandria 15   ☎055 46 28 934 💻www.plushostels.com

It's a chain hostel, sure, but it's the nicest darn chain hostel our *Let's Go* researchers have ever seen. With so many rooms, it can feel a little empty when there aren't nine million tourists around, but that just means more space for you on the spacious terrace bar. Climb up another level to the flat roof, which sports some folding chairs, a guard rail, and, the best panoramic 💻**view** of Florence you'll find outside Giotto's tower. Down in the basement is a restaurant (*€10 for breakfast, pasta dinner, or a bottle of wine*), another full bar, a disco complete with ball, a sauna, a Turkish bath, and a heavily chlorinated swimming pool flooded with colored lights.

⌖ *Follow V. Nazionale way up until it changes names.* ⓘ *Breakfast €10.* Ⓢ *Dorms €20-25.* Ⓒ *Reception 24hr.*

🏚 PENSIONE LA SCALA

🍴⊗❄ PENSIONE ❹

V. della Scala 21

☎055 21 26 29

Don't be scared off by the name of the building in which Pensione La Scala is situated—Residence Bellevue. This place may be a bit mental, but it's no institution. Rather, it's a comfy, personal bed and breakfast with a stuffed crocodile, frescoed ceilings, a nifty vintage radio that sometimes works, and a dining room table full of books and papers. It will be cleared for breakfast only if you're able to get on avuncular proprietor Gabriel's good side. Gabriel lives on premises and describes himself as Santa Claus—especially to those who are quick to flash a smile, show up on an under-booked night, or pay cash.

♯ *Down from the train station, on the left.* **i** *Cash preferred.* ⓢ *Doubles €80-90; triples €120-135; quads €160-180.* ⌚ *Reception 24hr., but Gabriel would rather not be woken up at odd hours.*

▨ SOGGIORNO ANNAMARIA / KATTI HOUSE   ⬤♿ (⌾) B AND B ❸

V. Faenza 21   ☎055 21 34 10 ▣www.kattihouse.com

If you are traveling with a small group and don't mind sharing queen-size beds, stay here. This lovely B and B feels more like a flat that you're borrowing from some posh aunt. Wood-beamed ceilings, grandfather clocks, and comfortable living rooms characterize these suites of rooms. On the second floor, four bedrooms share a big, sunny living room with a built-in bar. Each bedroom sports a TV and a tea kettle (as we said, posh aunt).

♯ *On V. Faenza, look for the doorway with all the Let's Go stickers.* **i** *Breakfast included.* ⓢ *Singles €70; doubles €85; quads €130.*

HOTEL CONSIGLI   ⬤♿ (⌾)❈ HOTEL ❸

Lungarno Amerigo Vespucci 50   ☎055 214 172 ▣www.hotelconsigli.com

If you are traveling in a small group, this gorgeous hotel on the Arno is a no-brainer. The grand staircase of the 16th-century building leads to airy rooms with original frescoes on the ceilings: the family-size suites are an especially

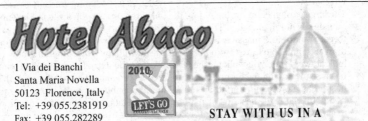

italy

impressive option for a well-behaved group of four. Brave a narrow spiral staircase to have a glass of wine on the enormous terrace overlooking the river. And with the American consulate right next door, you're sure to be first in line for the airlift if Florence is invaded by zombies.

➥ Follow the river west, up past the consulate. ℹ Breakfast included. Remodeling project underway in 2010, prices (and quality) may rise thereafter. $ Doubles €90; triples €120; family suite €130.

HOTEL ESTER 💳♿📶 HOTEL [3]

V. Largo Alinari 15 ☎055 23 02 185 🖥www.roominflorence.com

Down the block from the train station, the two levels of Hotel Ester boast an array of private rooms with flatscreen TVs, mini-fridges, and overhead fans. The longer the hike, the better the view—the third story rooms boast a lovely prospect, while the larger rooms across the street at sister hotel Luna Rossa are a good deal for groups *(quad €120).*

➥ From train station, turn left at the McDonald's; Hotel Ester is about 1 block down on the right. Luna Rossa and Maison de Charme are across the street and adjacent, respectively, but share Hotel Ester's reception. $ Mar-Oct doubles €75, with bath €90; Nov-Feb €55/60.

DAVID INN 🖱🚭📶 HOSTEL [2]

V. Ricasoli 31 ☎055 21 37 07 🖥hostelfirenze.splinder.com

One of the few small hostels in Florence, David Inn sits on the top floor of an otherwise residential building, and is the sort of place that provides you with somewhere to sleep—and not much else. No common space except for a couple squashy couches against an orange wall. The dorms are your basic bunk-bed situation, and the kitchen is tiny. But the small hostel scene in town is fairly dire, so if Academy is full or too posh for your hosteling tastes, then try here.

➥ About a 5min. walk north of the Duomo, on the right. ℹ Luggage storage. $ Dorms €24-26. 🕒 Reception 24hr.

The Oltrarno

This side of the river has a decent concentration of good hostels, but they aren't significantly cheaper than the more centrally located places. You have to really want to be in the Oltrarno to stay here.

✓ OSPITALE DELLE RIFIORENZE 🖱♿📶 HOSTEL [1]

P. Piattellina 1 ☎055 21 67 98 🖥www.firenzeospitale.it

Carved out of an old monastery, this socially aware hostel still feels like a religious escape. Live like a monk in a little pre-fab cell for two or three and hang out in the cavernous common space, featuring an ornate but decaying 15th-century ceiling that looks like something off the Titanic. All kinds of classes are run here including yoga, capoeira, and ceramics. Some of them are free, others are free for your first session. The folks at this nonprofit, co-operative hostel are a special sort—take one of their booklets providing walking tours of the people's Florence, which shift the historical perspective from the Medici to the Medici's handmaids.

➥ From P. Santo Spirito, the "ostello" signs direct you to this one. ℹ Free Wi-Fi. $ 3- to 4-bed dorms €15; doubles €40; triples €45. 🕒 Reception 7am-noon and 3pm-2am. Curfew 2am.

HOSTEL SANTA MONACA 💳🚭📶 HOSTEL [1]

V. Santa Monaca 6 ☎055 26 83 38 🖥www.ostello.it

This former monastery has all the charm of a local community center, despite the occasional cast-iron gate or vaulted ceiling. Rooms are simple, bathrooms are shared, and everything is kept clean during a strict 10am-2pm lockout. A nice large mess hall lined with picnic tables and a digital projector for sporting events are the few perks. A small grocery store is next door, but the"kitchen" is poorly equipped and overcrowded at meal times. You'll reap the benefits of

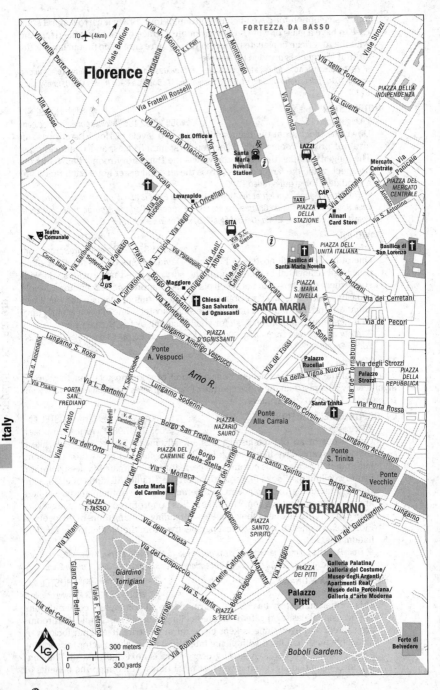

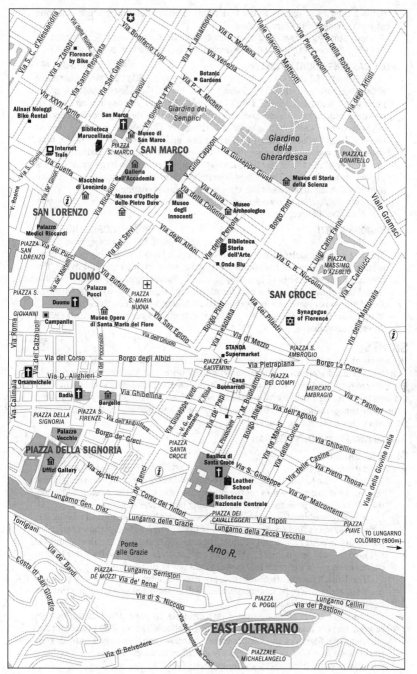

florence · accommodations

Santa Monaca's proximity to the P. di Santo Spirito after-dinner scene—as long as you're back for the 2am curfew.

➡ From P. Santo Spirito, take a right onto V. Sant'Agostino and then a left onto V. Santa Monaca. ℹ Free Wi-Fi. $ Dorms €17.50-20.50. ⏰ Reception 7am-2am. Curfew 2am. Lockout 10am-2pm.

PLUS CAMPING MICHELANGELO — CAMPING ❶

Vle. Michelangelo 80 — ☎055 68 11 977 💻www.camping.it

Camping sure sounds nice, doesn't it? A bit of the **great outdoors,** some greenery, roughing it a little? Don't be fooled. Whether you're packing a tent or renting a bungalow, this campsite has all the appeal of the neighboring Piazzale Michelangelo—which is to say, of a parking lot. The bungalows sleep two or three in bunk beds. You have to share a key, and there's no locker in the tent, so we don't recommend going halvsies on one with a stranger. Bathrooms are in a facility at the top of the hill akin to the locker room at a large gym. Wi-Fi is expensive and limited. The cafe is your only option for food that doesn't require a good walk, though at least the view is nice from its seating area.

➡ To the left of Piazzale Michelangelo, or take the #12 bus to the Camping stop. $ 2-bed tents €29; 3-bed €36. ⏰ Reception 24hr.

SOGGIORNO PITTI — HOSTEL, HOTEL ❷

P. Pitti 8 — ☎329 06 40 765 💻www.soggiornopitti.com

This is a sort of a hotel-hostel combo—the feel is hostel, with a big comfy common space, but most of the rooms are private, with double beds and twins. The bathrooms are clean but not terribly plentiful. That being said, it is a serviceable hostel and benefits from the best location of the three in the western Oltrarno. But if you look elsewhere in Florence you'll find nicer options than this.

➡ Across the street from Palazzo Pitti. $ Dorms €20; doubles with bath €70; quads €92. ⏰ Reception 8am-11pm.

SIGHTS

Hope you like the Renaissance! Seriously, that's the big game in town here. If you search really hard you can find museums or attractions that don't have their roots in the 16th century, but there aren't many. If you do like the Renaissance, this is literally the best place in the world for you. Options abound, so it's best to take your time and appreciate things rather than letting them become a devalued mush of crucifixes and portraits of semi-attractive women.

Duomo And Piazza Della Signoria

UFFIZI GALLERY — MUSEUM

Piazzale degli Uffizi 6 — ☎055 23 88 651 💻www.firenzemusei.it

Welcome to the Uffizi. The first thing you should know about this museum is that the *David* is not here—he's on the other side of town, in the Accademia. Also, the *Mona Lisa* is in France, and de Nile ain't just a river in Egypt.

If you're looking for an art history lesson, don't expect to find one in this listing. You won't find one in the galleries' texts either: although the explanatory panels are in both Italian and English, they are not hugely informative. Your best bet is to take an audio tour *(€5.50)* or to stick with *Let's Go.* We'll do our best to point out some of the main things you might not notice on your own.

The Uffizi's rooms are numbered. Look to the lintel of the doorway to figure out what room you're in. Our instructions will assume that you are going through the galleries sequentially.

Start the Uffizi from the top. Don't crumple up your ticket at the bottom of your bag (or paste it directly into your notebook like we did) because, after climbing two flights of the Uffizi's grand staircase, you'll be asked to flash your ticket once more. At this point, you're standing in an enormous hallway lined with statues and frescoed to within an inch of its life.

The first room you'll actually enter is **Room 2,** which begins the long parade of Jesuses that you'll be visiting today. **Rooms 3-4** are particularly gilded. In Martini's *Annunciation,* Gabriel literally spits some Latin at Mary, who responds with the mother of all icy stares. In **Room 6,** take some time with Beato Angelico's fun *Scenes From the Lives of Hermits.*

The next few rooms are all well and good, but **Rooms 10-14** are the main event. Where there be crowds and benches, there be the postcard works. Not that you need us to tell you this, but Botticelli's *Birth of Venus* is on the left—that's right, behind all those people. Push your way to the front to enjoy all the little details that don't come across in the coffee mug and mousepad reproductions, like the gold trim on the trees, the detail of the fabrics, and Venus's rather poor haircut. It's like she tried to get the Rachel but left on an extra 4ft.

Room 15 features works by a fellow named Leonardo da Vinci. If you're able to tell which are by him without reading the plaques, give yourself a pat on the back for being a good art historian.

If you're getting sick of Catholicism, skedaddle to **Room 20** to view a couple rare portraits of Martin Luther. Ninety-five theses, three chins. **Room 22** has a Mantegna triptych on the right with a curved center panel that makes it seem almost 3D. **Room 25** varies the Jesus-ness with some scenes from Joseph's story in Exodus on the right. There's a seriously ginormous baby in **Room 29's** Parmigianino painting, which is called *Madonna of the Long Neck* for reasons that will be obvious.

A really interestingly composed painting of a woman bathing hangs on the near-right wall of **Room 31.** What do you look at first? Don't be shy, we know you're eyeing her luscious breasts. And then you probably look at her legs and thighs, and perhaps the rest of her. And then, if you haven't yet turned away, maybe you will notice King David in the top left corner. The woman is Bathsheba, and Brusasorci's painting is remarkable for making you, the viewer, mimic the intensity of David's ogling gaze.

On the left in **Room 35** is a *Massacre of the Innocents* by Daniele Ricciarelli. Though feminists might be excited about the painter's vaguely female name, sadly, Daniele was a dude like every other artist in the Uffizi. Despite the pile of dead babies in this painting, *Let's Go* does not condone the making of **dead baby jokes.**

Finally you'll reach the **Room of Niobe,** an impressive palatial space full of statues posed as if frozen while cowering in horror, not unlike the poses of the ash corpses in Pompeii. These statues were discovered in the Villa Medici gardens and are supposed to be the unfortunate children of Niobe about to be slain by the gods as revenge for their mother's pride in her progeny.

The last couple of rooms have some 18th-century stuff. But you don't care about that. You waited in line for 3hr. and then proceeded through an endless line of rooms filled with Renaissance art, so maybe it's time to just go home. **Congratulations** on finishing the Uffizi; now you can go act like a Botticelli expert among all your friends, even if the only thing you remember is Venus's terrible haircut.

It's the long narrow part of P. della Signoria. Enter (or stand in line) on the left, reserve tickets on the right. To avoid the lines without paying for a reservation, try arriving late in the day, when your time in the museum will be limited by closing. ℹ *2-3hr. wait in line is average.* $ *€10, EU citizens ages 18-25 €5, EU citizens under 18 and over 65 and the disabled free. €4 reservation fee. Audio tour €5.50.* 🕐 *Open Tu-Su 8:50am-6:50pm.*

THE BARGELLO — ♿ ❄ MUSEUM

V. del Proconsolo 4 ☎055 23 88 606 🖥www.firenzemusei.it

For a change of pace, the Bargello offers a nice dose of 19th-century eclecticism:

it's a bit like London's Victoria and Albert Museum, with objects organized by function and material. The building was once a brutal prison, but fortunately for visitors, there's no trace of this original purpose left in the architecture. The courtyard, once the site of public executions, is now adorned with terra-cotta coats of arms and family crests. Several statues remain from what must have been an extremely suggestive fountain. Look for the water spigots located in such charming locations as between a lady's legs. There's also an enormous cast cannon bearing the head of St. Paul, a devoted disciple of the prince of peace who probably wouldn't be too happy about having his face emblazoned on heavy artillery. Pass the pair of great stone lions wearing iron crowns—very *Narnia*—to find a hall full of pagan (not so *Narnia*) sculptures such as Adonis, Bacchus, and a 1565 work celebrating Florence's victory over Pisa.

The courtyard stairs bring you to some stone fowl and a series of numbered galleries. Minutely carved ivories, from tiny portraits to hair combs to a giant chess board are in **Room 4.** The variety of objects that people have thought to carve from elephant tusk is astounding.

Room 6 holds a huge collection of Maiolica, an earthenware pottery that is decorated before being glazed. **Room 8** will introduce you to the Ninja Turtle you know least well. This *Salone Di Donatello* was designed for his 500th birthday in 1887, and has remained unchanged since.

Room 9 contains probably the only Arabic script you'll see in Tuscany. This chamber is devoted to Islamic art and has some very interesting ceramics and fabrics.

Room 10 is a true Victorian *wunderkammer* (or wonder-cabinet). There's the case of pipes, the case of bottles, and the collection of keys and locks. There are even table settings, scientific instruments, metalwork, jewelry, and that 17th-century spork you've been missing.

On the third floor, check out the fantastic tiny bronzes in **Room 15. Room 13's** glazed terra cotta in blues, greens, and yellows creates a color scheme that will make you feel as if you've been sucked into a game of old-school Oregon Trail.

 # Behind the Palazzo Vecchio. $ €4, EU citizens ages 18-25 €2, EU citizens under 18 and over 65 free. ⏰ Open daily 8:15am-5pm. Closed 1st, 3rd, and 5th Su each month, and 2nd and 4th M.

DUOMO ♿ CHURCH

P. del Duomo 1 ☎055 23 02 885 🖳www.operaduomo.firenze.it

Honestly, it's better on the outside. The Duomo complex is enormous and distinctive, looming over every other Florentine building. All roads seem to lead to the Duomo and its shockingly colorful facade, capped with that giant red gelato-cone of a dome. It's famous, it's old, and it's free: clearly it must be the greatest tourist attraction known to humanity.

Well, it's all right. There are a lot of really great churches in Florence, and the Duomo just happens to be the biggest. It truly is enormous, but once you've stood in line behind half a dozen cruise-ship excursion groups to file your way inside the mighty cathedral, you might find yourself wondering—"is that all there is?"

Fortunately, it's not. Unfortunately, all the good parts have been divvied up, so you can only sample a bit at a time. All the statues, paintings, and other adornments—including a *pietà* that Michelangelo originally intended for his own tomb and the incredibly creepy 👁**Mary of the Glass Eyes**—have been moved into the **Museo Opera di Santa Maria del Fiore** across the street. The octagonal building by the entrance to the cathedral is the **Baptistery,** where you also have to pay for entrance, although you can admire Ghiberti's splendid golden eastern doors —dubbed the **"Gates of Paradise"** by Michelangelo—for free. The final attractions are the **dome** and the **campanile,** both of which involve 400+ steps of climbing (unless you're training for some kind of stair-climing race, there's really no reason to do both). For free, all you get is a rather empty, cavernous church.

In the church, there are certainly highlights. The inside of **Filippo Brunelleschi's** vast dome is ornately frescoed and extremely impressive, even from ground level. On the opposite side of the nave a 24hr. clock by **Paolo Uccello** oxymoronically runs counter-clockwise. If you take the stairs in the middle of the church's floor down to the basement, you can pay €3 to see the archaeological remnants of the Duomo's previous incarnations, which is cool if you like that sort of thing.

And in a bit of irony, that notable green-white-and-pink marble facade that's so impressive from the outside—well, it's a fake. Or rather, it's not contemporary to the cathedral itself. The Duomo's facade was left unfinished in the 16th century and was eventually removed completely, leaving the great cathedral buck naked. Only in the late 19th century—last Thursday by Florentine standards—did the Duomo receive its famous decoration. Like much of Florence, it's not actually from the Renaissance—it's the Victorian equivalent of a Renaissance Faire.

Still really pretty, though.

⚑ *Come on, you can't miss it.* *i* *Audio tour available in English.* Ⓢ *Duomo free. Dome €8. Campanile €6. Museum €6. Baptistery €4.* 🕐 *Duomo open M-F 10am-5pm, Sa 10am-4:45pm, Su 1:30-3:30pm. 1st Sa each month only open 10am-3:30pm. Dome open M-F 8:30am-7pm, Sa 8:30am-5:40pm. Campanile open daily 8:30am-7:30pm. Museum open M-Sa 9am-7:30pm, Su 9am-1:40pm. Baptistery open in summer M-W 12:15-6:30pm, Th-Sa 12:15-10:30pm, Su 8:30am-1:30pm; in winter M-Sa 12:15-6:30pm, Su 8:30am-1:30pm. In both seasons open 1st Sa of the month 8:30am-1:30pm.*

PIAZZA DELLA SIGNORIA
P. della Signoria

            ♿ PIAZZA

Don't be fooled by the *David* in front of the **Palazzo Vecchio**—the real deal is in the **Accademia.** The reproduction in the *piazza* fills David's original location and stands just as proud as his original did when he (allegedly) was installed facing Pisa to celebrate Florence's dominance over the Tuscan region. To the left of the statue is a giant fountain which Michelangelo despised so much that he called it a waste of perfectly good marble. To the big guy's right you'll find the **Loggia,** a portico full of statues that's as legit as any room in the Uffizi. Hang out amid the art students sketching, listen to the street musicians, and enjoy the free outdoor art. Don't miss Giambologna's spiraling *Rape of the Sabines.*

⚑ *This is the main piazza to the north of the Uffizi.* Ⓢ *Free.*

PONTE VECCHIO
Ponte Vecchio

            ♿ BRIDGE

This is Florence's famous shop-covered bridge. It has been called the "old" bridge for, oh, 400 years or so, ever since the Florentines first built a second bridge over the Arno and had to find a way to distinguish this one from their new *ponte.* When the Nazis evacuated Florence, Ponte Vecchio was the only bridge they didn't destroy. Now it is full of gold and jewelry shops—more like kiosks, in many cases—as well as shadier street vendors and buskers. Come on a weekend afternoon, and you are guaranteed to be in the wedding photos of at least half a dozen bridal parties. Come at night for a romantic view of the river—and of other couples seeking the same.

⚑ *From the Uffizi, walk to the river. It's the one with the shops on it.* Ⓢ *Free.*

PALAZZO VECCHIO
In P. della Signoria

        ◉♿ MUSEUM
        ☎055 27 68 465

The real draw here is that it's the only museum you can visit post-*aperitivo.* In addition, the place has got some pretty impressive architecture and views. The vast and ornate **Room of the 500's** gilded ceiling is divided into panels that frame truly massive paintings. On the second floor, the **Salon of Leo X,** a terrace with an incredible view of the city and the surrounding hills, provides a great photo op. There's a lot of repetition in this *palazzo*, though, and it can all begin to look the same. That's until you reach the **Sala dei Gigli,** which boasts a pretty rocking view of the Duomo as well as a fantastic map room that's worth all the chintz before it.

The huge one in P. della Signoria. $ €6, ages 18-25 and over 65 €4.50. Tours free if requested at time of ticket purchase. ⏰ Open M-W 9am-midnight, Th 9am-2pm, F-Su 9am-midnight. Activities and tours with costumed reenactors, skits, etc. available; call for times.

The Outer Ring

Florence has numerous sights outside of the Uffizi and that big pink gelato cone. The city is so full of museums and churches that we just don't have space to list all of them. These are what we think are the best, if you wonder around the city enough you're bound to find a bunch more.

GALLERIA DELL'ACCADEMIA — MUSEUM

V. Ricasoli 60 ☎055 23 88 612 www.firenzemusei.it/accademia

Sometimes tourist attractions gain their reputation for a reason. The *David* is pretty legit. Do you see those veins on his hand? The guy's a beast.

Four other statues by Michelangelo share *David*'s hall. They're unfinished, with figures that appear to be trapped in the remaining block of marble, like Han Solo encased in carbonite. You may understand on an intellectual level that the master's statues are carved from a single piece of marble, but seeing these unfinished works drives it home. One big damn rock. One man. A bunch of chisels. It's kind of miraculous, really.

Beyond its main event, the Accademia is a small museum, albeit a good one. The musical instruments gallery, to the right when you enter, is surprisingly informational. Past the *David* gallery on the left is a 19th-century workroom overflowing with sculpted heads and busts. Notice the little black dots freckling the pieces? They harken back to the Accademia's days as an actual academy. These are plaster casts were created for teaching, and the black dots are nails that students used as reference points as they made copies for practice. Gorgeous crucifixes and Russian Orthodox stuff make a quick spin through the upstairs worthwhile. At your most contemplative pace, the Accademia won't take more than an hour. Bear that in mind when weighing the choice between paying extra for a reservation or waiting in a line that lasts far longer than you'll spend in the actual museum.

*Line for entrance is on Ricasoli, off of San Marco proper. **i** Make reservations at the Museo Archeologico, the Museo di San Marco, or the Museo del'Oficio. The non-reservation line is shortest at the beginning of the day. Try to avoid the midday cruise ship excursion groups. $ €6.50, EU citizens ages 18-25 €3.25, EU citizens under 18 and over 65, and art students free. €4 reservation fee applies to all. ⏰ Open Tu-Su 8:15am-6:50pm. Last entrance 30min. before close..*

SYNAGOGUE OF FLORENCE — SYNAGOGUE, MUSEUM

V. Luigi Carlo Farini 4 ☎055 21 07 63 www.firenzehebraica.net

It may not be Renaissance vintage, but this is one Florentine house of worship that is well worth a visit. Florence is mum when it comes to the history of its working class, minority, or otherwise non-Medici population, and the synagogue is one of the only sights where average citizens get the spotlight. The story of the Jewish community and Italy's role in WWII is every bit as vital to your understanding of the city of Florence as a stack of Botticellis. Prior to WWII, there were 40,000 Jews in Italy, 2400 living in Florence. The synagogue contains a memorial to the Florentines killed in the camps; although the list is relatively short, the number of shared surnames indicates that a handful of large families were wiped out completely. That this building is still standing is miraculous—when the Nazis evacuated the temple was rigged to explode, but amazingly all but one of the bombs failed to detonate, saving it from total destruction—and a visit to it offers an incredibly moving and different experience from anywhere else in Florence.

↗ From the Basilica di Santa Croce, head north on V. dei Pepi for 7 blocks. Take a right onto Pilastri and an immediate left onto V. Luigi Carlo Farini. ***i*** *Yarmulkes required and provided. Check bags and cameras at lockers before entering. $ €5, students €3. ⏰ Open Apr-Sept M-Th 10am-6pm, F 10am-2pm; Oct-Mar M-Th 10am-3pm, F 10am-2pm. Closed Jewish holidays. The 1st fl. of the museum is open during the 2nd half of every hr.*

👍 MUSEO DI FERRAGAMO — 💵♿ MUSEUM

P. Santa Trinita 5r — ☎055 33 60 456 💻www.museoferragamo.it

That's right, the shoe guy. This small but excellently designed museum celebrates the work of the great cobbler to the stars, whose eloquent and anecdotal memoirs are liberally quoted in the museum's display text. Exhibits rotate every two years; a new installation is arriving in late 2010, focusing on footwear in the second half of the 20th century. We know you may have a skeptical look on your face right now, but you don't have to be Carrie Bradshaw to appreciate a fashion and culture exhibit as thoughtfully assembled as this one. The gift shop is surprisingly tiny, but check out the real Ferragamo store upstairs to ogle shoes you can't possibly afford.

↗ Enter at P. Santa Trinita, the side of the building facing away from the river. ***i*** *Ticket proceeds fund scholarships for young shoe designers. $ €5, under 10 and over 65 free. ⏰ Open M 10am-6pm, W-Su 10am-6pm.*

PALAZZO STROZZI — 💵♿ MUSEUM, PALAZZO

P. degli Strozzi — ☎055 27 76 461 💻www.palazzostrozzi.org

While this may seem like yet another old palace, impressive like all the others, it isn't the seen-one-seen-'em-all Renaissance decor that makes Palazzo Strozzi worth visiting. The Center for Contemporary Culture Strozzina, which produces shows of recent and contemporary art in the palace's exhibit halls, is the main draw here. Recent shows have included an exhibit of De Chirico, Ernst, and Magritte as well as a series of interactive installations tracing the effect of media on modern living. The programming changes regularly, so check the website or stop by if you want to shake a little 21st century into Florence's 15th-century aesthetic.

↗ West of P. della Repubblica. $ Prices and hours vary; check website for details.

BASILICA DI SANTA MARIA NOVELLA — 🚫♿ CHURCH

P. di Santa Maria Novella — ☎055 21 59 18 💻www.chiesasantamarianovella.it

If you're only going to bother with one of the non-Duomo churches, consider making it this one. The cavernous church features some glorious stained glass which, due to the church's north-south orientation, reflects beautifully on to the floors in the morning and late afternoon. The Filippino-Lippi-designed chapel to the right of the altar is almost cartoonish in the drama and action of its panels. Cappella Strozzi on the left has a sadly faded fresco of Purgatory, inspired by Dante. Try to make out the goblins, centaurs, and less familiar mythological figures like the man-dove. The basilica also features an impossibly handsome gift shop in a room dominated by a gold-trimmed reliquary cabinet and a red and blue ceiling so bright it must have been restored yesterday.

↗ Just south of the train station; can't miss it. ***i*** *Audio tour stations in the middle of the sanctuary for €1; some travelers wait around for others to pay up the euro and get bored, then finish their turn. $ €3.50, over 65, the disabled, and priests free. ⏰ Open M-Th 9-5:30pm, F 11am-5:30pm, Sa 9am-5pm, Su 1-5pm.*

PALAZZO MEDICI RICARDI — 💵♿ MUSEUM

V. Camillo Cavour 1 — ☎055 27 60 340 💻www.palazzo-medici.it

After innumerable treks through the detritus of the Medici's public life, you may be wondering what they were like at home. Answer: more of the same. In their tiny chapel, the frescoes are so cluttered with faces of generations of Medici attending the Adoration of the Magi that you'll find just as much to look at as you would in a grander commission. The *palazzo* still plays a key role in provincial government today. The **Quattro Stagioni** hall hosts the provincial council, and the gold-on-white stucco panels of the **Sala Luca Giordana,** flanked by painted mirrors and frolicking cherubim, are incongrously complemented by a projection screen, a conference table, and rows of plexiglass chairs. If nothing else, be happy for the members of the provincial council who get to gaze at fleshy angels when they zone out during dull meetings.

From San Lorenzo you can see the back of the huge brown palace. Enter from the reverse side, on V. Cavour. $ €7, groups of 15 or more and ages 6-12 €4. ⏰ Open M-Tu 9am-7pm, Th-Su 9am-7pm.

a man with a plan

After 100 years of construction, the Duomo still had a gaping hole. The architects found themselves stumped—during construction, they had not realized that the dome the design called for would have to be larger than anything previously built or even considered possible. After several decades of leaving the church open to the elements, the commission for the construction was awarded to an unlikely candidate: **Filippo Brunelleschi,** who had been trained as a goldsmith, not an architect. How did Brunelleschi end up gaining the commission for the largest dome of his age? Legend states that he proposed a competition: whichever architect could make an egg stand up on a slab of marble would take over the dome's construction. When everyone else attempted and failed, Brunelleschi cracked the egg at the bottom and placed the newly flat edge on the marble. Fortunately, he was as talented at architecture as he was at rule-bending, and his ingenuity led to the spectacular dome that is still the most stunning sight on Florence's skyline.

MEDICI CHAPELS

♿ MUSEUM

P. Madonna degli Aldobrandini 6 ☎055 23 88 602 💻www.firenzemusei.it

Ah, the Medici. If you thought they were opulent alive, wait until you see them dead! The **Cappella Principe,** an octagonal chapel that's the final home of a handful of Medici, is the grander of the two on display in this museum, despite being unfinished. Some of the Medici were smart enough to commission their own statues, and they're doing swell. Others went with the popular trend of having sons commission honorary statues after their fathers' death. This, of course, led to lots of empty statue slots. There are other late additions as well—the frescoes may look the part, but they were painted in the 1870s. As some tour guide quipped while we were eavesdropping, while the French were inventing Impressionism, the Florentines were still in the Renaissance.

The roundish building to the right of San Lorenzo. [i] Likely visit length: 30min. tops. $ €6, EU citizens 18-25 €3, EU citizens under 18 and over 65 free. ⏰ Open fairly daily 8:15am-4:50pm. Closed 1st, 3rd, 5th M and 2nd and 4th Su each month.

MUSEO DI SAN MARCO

♿ MUSEUM

P. San Marco 3 ☎055 23 88 608 💻www.firenzemusei.it

The first floor of this museum is divided into small cubbies the size of West Village studios. These are the cells of old monks, and each one has a different painting on the wall. Pop inside and imagine spending four decades copying manuscripts by hand in here. Then imagine what it would be like if an angel arrived to announce that you were about to experience an unplanned pregnancy—twice—by looking at Fra Angelico's two **Annunciation** frescoes. The most famous, which you'll probably recognize from postcards, is at the top of the staircase, while a less popular incarnation is on the wall of one of the cells.

➜ The north side of the piazza. ℹ Approximate visit time: 30min. $ €4, EU citizens age 16-25 €2. ⏰ Open M-F 8:15am-1:50pm, Sa 8:15am-6:50pm, Su 8:15am-7pm.

BASILICA DI SAN LORENZO — 🎟♿ CHURCH

P. San Lorenzo — ☎055 26 45 184 💻www.sanlorenzo.firenze.it

The Basilica di San Lorenzo was consecrated in 393 CE: this is why Europeans scoff at Americans who think of 19th-century churches as old. The austere basilica is grey and white, but the cupola by the altar is a bit more glam. In the old sacristy is a small cupola painted with gold constellations on a midnight blue background that represent the sky over Florence on July 4th, 1442. Cool if you care about that sort of thing, but otherwise, spend your €3.50 on a big gelato and take it to the cloister on the left side of the basilica. The cloister is free and peaceful and has some of those rare Florentine trees. The domes and towers of nearby attractions peek out over the walls of the courtyard, making for a nice panorama.

➜ In P. San Lorenzo, which is just a little north of the Duomo. $ €3.50. ⏰ Open M-Sa 10am-5pm, Su 1:30-5pm.

BASILICA DI SANTA CROCE — 🎟♿ CHURCH

P. Santa Croce — ☎055 24 66 105

This basilica is an enormous complex worthy of costing more than the other big churches in town, though really it's the dead celebrities buried here that jack up the price of admission. Fork over the dough and pay your respects to Florence's greats. Rossini's tomb is subtly decorated with treble clefs and violin bridges. Galileo gets a globe and an etching of the solar system (*his* solar system) to mark his grave. Machiavelli is just sort of chilling. Dante's tomb is probably cool, but it was blocked with scaffolding when we visited. Michelangelo, all things considered, really should have a grander place of burial, but since he didn't design it, we take what we can get. Even Marconi is here—that's right, the guy who invented the radio.

➜ Take Borgo de' Greci east from P. della Signoria. $ €5, ages 11-17 €3, disabled free. Combined with Casa Michelangelo €8. Audio tour €5. ⏰ Open M-F 9:30am-3:30pm, Sa-Su 1-5:30pm.

The Oltrarno

👍 PALAZZO PITTI — 🎟♿ MUSEUM, GARDENS

P. de' Pitti

The major sights of West Oltrarno are all helpfully condensed into the enormous Palazzo Pitti. Built by Lucca Pitti and eventually bought by—who else—the Medici, it is a phenomenal complex of museums and gardens. The museums are batched under two ticket combos: **Ticket One** gets you into Galleria Palatina, Galleria d'Arte Moderna, and Apartamenti Reali. **Ticket Two** is for the Boboli Gardens, Museo degli Argenti, Galleria del Costume, and Museo della Porcellana. Overall, if you're choosing one ticket combo over the other, we recommend 👍**Ticket Two.**

As wonderful as the museums are, it's the 👍**Boboli Gardens** that are the most remarkable attraction here. They're like a cross between Central Park and Versailles, which means they are really wonderful. Imagine you're a 17th-century Medici strolling through your gardens—but don't imagine your way into a corset, ladies, because the gardens are raked at a surprising incline. Ticket Two will also get you into **Galleria del Costume,** essentially a fashion museum that is worth visiting for its interesting curatorial decisions—clothes are arranged thematically rather than chronologically. There's also the **Museo degli Argenti**—a treasure museum—and the **Museo della Porcellana**—which is much less dull than you might expect a porcelain museum to be.

If you ignored out advice and purchased Ticket One, your main attraction will be the **Galleria Palatina,** an enormous gallery that would be more of a draw in a city that didn't also include the Uffizi. In a typically Florentine move, the permanent collection is housed in rooms named not for the art, but for the ceilings. We are still in a *palazzo*, remember, so the organizational logic is still that of a rich royal wanting to clutter his brocaded walls with all the big-ticket masterpieces he could commission. At the back end of the gallery is the **Apartamenti Reali,** which gets it right by doing away with the pesky art and sticking to the rich people's bedrooms. Take a quick stroll through the apartments of the great and pick out tapestries, tassels, and toilettes for your own palace. Finally, there's the **Galleria d'Arte Moderna.** Only in Florence could people define "modern art" as stuff that predates the French Revolution. The gallery is mostly mired in 19th-century Naturalism, so don't let the name fool you into thinking that you'll find anything remotely challenging or aesthetically engaging here. Fortunately, the Palazzo Pitti complex as a whole is large enough that one disappointing museum is not enough to derail what is, even in this city, an extraordinary collection of displays.

Cross the river at Ponte Vecchio and walk straight, bearing right with the street, until you reach the extremely obvious palace. [i] *Official guidebook €8, available at ticket office. Audio guide €5.50, double €8.* $ *Ticket 1 €12, EU citizens age 18-25 €6, EU citizens under 18 and over 65 free. Ticket 2 €10/€5/free.* 🕐 *Ticket 1 attractions open Tu-Su 8:15am-6:50pm. Ticket 2 attractions open daily June-Aug 8:15am-7:30pm; Sept 8:15am-6:30pm; Oct 8:15am-5:30pm; Nov-Feb 8:15am-4:30pm; Mar-May 8:15am-6:30pm. Closed 1st and last M of each month.*

PIAZZALE MICHELANGELO ♿ PANORAMIC VIEWS

Piazzale Michelangelo

It's a parking lot. Still, it's the most scenic damn parking lot you'll ever see. Cross the river and bear east until you reach the base of the steps. It's about a 10min. walk uphill to the *piazzale*—a walk both pleasanter and cheaper than the one up the Campanile, but still requiring decent shoes. You can take the #12 or 13 bus if you're lazy, but the short **hike** is rather pleasant itself. At the summit, you'll be rewarded with a broad cement *piazza* upon which an oxidized reproduction of the *David* and a whole lot of parked cars enjoy a killer view. Ignore everything behind you and watch the sun set over the city.

From pretty much any bridge, walk left along the river until P. Guiseppe Poggi, where you will find the base of the steps. It's up from there. [i] *Wheelchair-accessible only by bus.* $ *Free.* 🕐 *Open 24hr.*

FOOD

While Florence isn't a culinarily distinct city, it remains a great place to find good food. There are trattorias everywhere, and almost every one of them is tasty. The only major variance between them all will be in cover charge and distance from a major *piazza.* If they begin to feel a bit too similar to one another, head to smaller places: the markets, the hole-in-the-walls, the local favorites. Whatever you do, you can't go wrong.

Duomo And Piazza Della Signoria

The places in the city center all seem to have been cast from the same mold. They cost about the same, they offer similar fare, and most of them have a rockin' view. For slightly more variety, venture a couple blocks from the main *piazze.*

GROM ♿ GELATERIA [1]

V. del Campanile ☎055 21 61 58 www.grom.it

Grom is a high-end *gelateria,* which means it has a posh location right off the

Duomo, a branch in New York City, and a slightly higher starting price than the city's other top-notch *gelaterie.* Nevertheless, it's the best of the sweet stuff in the Duomo area. Sure, you'll find it mentioned in every guidebook and, if you catch it at the wrong time of day, you'll be waiting in line for 15min. Just come back later. The gelato will still be delicious.

Just south of the Duomo. $ From €2. Open daily Apr-Sept 10:30am-midnight; Oct-Mar 10:30am-11pm.

DA VINATTIERI SANDWICHES [1]

V. Santa Margherita 4r ☎055 29 47 03

This is a literal hole-in-the-wall that's well worth tracking down. Unlike most of the panini in town, these are actually made to order. As in, the guy picks up the leg of ham and cuts off a slice for your sandwich. You can step into the tiny shop or just order a quick *lampridotto (€3.50)* from the alley through the counter window. Choose from the long menu of sandwich suggestions or invent your own—they all cost the same anyway.

Across the alley from Casa di Dante, so just follow the signs for that attraction. Shares a corner with Lush, which you can smell from 2 blocks away. $ Panini €3-3.50. Open daily 10am-8pm.

FESTIVAL DEL GELATO GELATERIA [1]

V. Del Corso 75r ☎055 29 43 86

We had dismissed this tacky, neon-flooded *gelateria* as a certain tourist trap, but when a local recommended it, we caved and gave the disco gelato a try. At our first bite of *ciociolata fondante,* the garish flourescence melted into warm candlelight and fireflies and a violinist in white tie began to...OK, no, the place still looked ridiculous, but hot damn that be good gelato.

Look for the neon. You seriously can't miss it. $ Gelato from €1.80. Open daily noon-midnight.

OSTERIA DELL PORCELLINO RISTORANTE [3]

V. Val di Lamona 7r ☎055 26 41 48 www.osteriadelporcellino.com

This beautiful osteria has an alleyway to itself which it fills with wrought-iron tables and colored lights. Don't come for lunch, when the adjacent Mercato Nuovo is bustling. Instead, wait until the evenings when the *piazza* clears out and the space is well worth the €2 cover.

Right off Mercato Nuovo. i Vegetarian menu. $ Cover €2. Primi €7-10; secondi €14-22. Open daily noon-3pm and 5-11pm.

CAFFE DUOMO RISTORANTE [2]

P. del Duomo 29-30r ☎055 21 13 48

There are a number of nice trattorias all in a row here, staring up at the Duomo. They're all roughly equivalent and offer specials, so browse them all and decide which you like best. We prefer this one for its lighter lunch specials, particularly the cheese and cold cut platter with a glass of Chianti *(€12 for 2 people).* The young staff have also been known to dance to Justin Bieber when business is slow.

In the shadow of the Duomo. $ Entree and a glass of wine for €9. Open daily noon-11pm.

CORONAS CAFE CAFE [1]

V. Calzaiuoli 72r ☎055 23 96 139

Cheap sandwiches and pastries *(€1-3.50)* as well as an open layout on the corner make this cafe a good spot for eating alone and people-watching. The excellent gelato is available in enormous American-appetite-sized cones if you want to be *that* guy.

Just north of P. della Signoria, on the corner. $ Pastries €1-3.50. Panini €3.50. Open daily 10am-1am.

The Outer Ring

One of the best options outside of the immediate center is to grab food at the great markets to the north of the Duomo, particularly Mercato Centrale. You can also head east to the **Santa Croce** area—where there are students, there's cheap food.

🍴 EBY'S BAR — ⊛♿🍸☼ MEXICAN [1]

V. dell'Oriuolo 5r and Borgo Pinti 2r — ☎055 90 62 116

Heck yes, burrito joint! America has the leg up on Europe in a certain area—Mexican food just ain't a thing on the continent. Imagine our joy, then, when we found a top-notch burrito joint right on the edge of Santa Croce's nightlife scene. Eby's is even good! This is a place that knows its purpose: a boasting sign on the door proudly announces the availability of "LATE NIGHT CHICKEN QUESADILLA." Order your €4 burrito on the corner of Borgo Pinti and Dell Orioulo, then cross to Eby's colorful bar and upstairs dining room. The food is so good that you can even come here sober.

➜ Head away from Santa Croce, west from P. de Salvamini. [$] Nachos €3. Burrito €4. Sangria pitcher €12. ⏰ Open daily 10am-3am.

🍴 GELATERIA DEL NERI — ⊛♿ GELATERIA [1]

V. Dei Neri 20/22r — ☎055 21 00 34

Our job description compels us to have our thrice-daily dose of gelato at a different *gelateria* each time to sample Florence's wide range of offerings. So why can't we stop eating at this one? It might have something to do with the mousse-like semifreddo—try the tiramisu—or the insanely spicy Mexican chocolate, which we found too intense to even finish.

➜ On the right when heading to city center. [$] Cups and cones from €1.50. ⏰ Open daily 9am-midnight.

🍴 TRATTORIA MARIO — ⊛⊗🍸 RISTORANTE [2]

V. Rosina 2r — ☎055 21 85 50 💻www.trattoriamario.com

If you're starting to wonder where all the Italians are hiding, show up late for lunch at Trattoria Mario. Diners are packed into tables with strangers, and regulars will flag the waitress if they want a newcomer to be seated at their table. And then perhaps they will buy you wine. Lots and lots of wine. The food is pretty good too, with the day's offerings written on brown paper by the kitchen.

➜ Just off Mercato Centrale, on the right. [$] Daily specials €6-9. ⏰ Open M-Sa noon-3:30pm.

🍴 NEGRONE — ⊛♿🍸 RISTORANTE [1]

P. del Mercato Centrale — ☎055 21 99 49

Mercato Centrale isn't just for groceries. The edges are lined with cafes, cafeterias, and panini stands that cater to workers and wise visitors. Negrone stands out as both the oldest, dating back to 1872, and the best. Crowd around the counter to order whatever happens to be on offer, take your tray, and squeeze in somewhere at the picnic tables along the wall. The food is fantastic and dirt-cheap, plus the atmosphere is far livelier than any cookie-cutter trattoria. Don't forget to bus your tray when you're done!

➜ Along the wall of the Mercato. [$] Primi and secondi €4-7. Cup of house wine €1. ⏰ Open M-Sa 7am-2pm.

🍴 LA GHIOTTA — ➶♿❄ CAFE [1]

V. Pietrapiana 7r — ☎055 24 12 37

Take a number at this student-y rotisserie with student-y prices—the line is out the door during lunchtime. Pick your meal from platters behind the counter or order one of 20 varieties of pizza *(all €5.50)* and cram into the seats in the back. You'll eat even cheaper if you take it to go—get half a rotisserie chicken for a couple euros, go for a giant slab of eggplant parmigiana, or try whatever else they happen to have when you visit.

⚓ *From Borgo Alegri, take a right.* Ⓢ *Primi €5-6; secondi €5-7. Liter of wine €6.* 🕙 *Open daily noon-5pm and 7-10pm.*

ANTICA GELATERIA FIORENTINA

◉&️ GELATERIA ❶

V. Faenza 2a   ☎388 058 03 99 🖳www.gelateriafiorentina.com

Off-beat flavors like rosewater, cheesecake, and green tea will add some variety to your gelato diet, and although the peanut butter chocolate was probably concocted to please Americans starved of their lunchbox staple, it at least succeeds in its goal. Antica is super cheap too, with cones starting at a single flavor for €1. If you want to go whole-hog American, there's a ginormo cone (€15) in which you can try every flavor on tap. Don't mix the cheesecake and green tea.

⚓ *Toward the far end of V. Faenza, on the left.* Ⓢ *Cones from €1.* 🕙 *Open daily noon-midnight.*

OPERA ET GUSTO

♿&️♈❀ RISTORANTE, CONCERT VENUE ❸

V. Della Scala 17r   ☎055 28 81 90 🖳www.operaetgusto.com

This sleek joint is a little-black-dress sort of place, with black and red decor and limited lighting. The draw is the live performances most nights, which tend towards jazz combos and light world music but sometimes encompass diverse theatrical art forms. Considering the entertainment, the cover (€2) is a steal.

⚓ *Coming from Santa Maria Novella, on the left.* 𝒊 *Show 9-10:30pm.* Ⓢ *Cover €2. Primi €10-12; secondi €11-22.* 🕙 *Open daily 8:30pm-2am.*

GRAN CAFFE SAN MARCO

♿&️(( ))♈❀⌂ CAFE ❶

P. San Marco 11r   ☎055 21 58 33 🖳www.grancaffesanmarco.it

This place just keeps getting bigger. Enter from the main *piazza*, and it's a *gelateria*. Enter from the side street, and it's a pizzeria. Walk further in, and it's a cafeteria, coffee bar, and garden cafe. Make your way to the tented garden for a bit of quiet. It's a bit chintzy but cheap. The enormous gooey bowls of lasagna (€4.50) are reheated, but since when has a bit of reheating hurt lasagna?

⚓ *The south end of the piazza.* Ⓢ *Huge variety of options, but meal-type food will run you from €3 panini to €7 secondi.* 🕙 *Open daily 8am-10pm.*

IL GIOVA

♿⊗⌂ RISTORANTE ❷

Borgo la Croce 73r   ☎055 24 80 639 🖳www.ilgiova.com

Settle down with a giant slice of watermelon on the mismatched chairs of this busy little lunch joint. At night, the outside tables fill the otherwise deserted intersection with couples and young people sipping wine. Menu changes daily.

⚓ *At the corner of V. della Mattonaia.* Ⓢ *Primi €5; secondi €7.* 🕙 *Open M-F noon-5pm and 7:30-11pm, Sa 12:30-4:30pm and 7:30-11pm.*

RUTH'S KOSHER VEGETARIAN FOOD

♿⊗❀ KOSHER ❷

V. L.C. Farini 2/A   ☎055 24 80 888 🖳www.kosheruth.com

There are probably some visitors to Florence who are stuck eating every meal here, and that must get old. For the carnivorous Christian getting sick of all that *bistecca alla fiorentina* or the nostalgic New Yorker who misses the Lower East Side, however, Ruth's provides some nice variety. Have a falafel while surrounded by Israelite kitsch like Hebrew calendars, maps of Israel, and photos of bearded old Jews. If you look Jewish, the locals may stop by your table to say hi.

⚓ *On the right of synagogue.* 𝒊 *Kosher.* Ⓢ *Falafel platter €9. Entrees €9-12.* 🕙 *Open M-Th 12:30-2:30pm and 7:30-10pm, F 12:30-2:30pm, Sa 7:30-10pm, Su 12:30-2:30pm and 7:30-10pm.*

OSTERIA E PIZZERIA CENTROPOVERI

♿&️♈❀ PIZZERIA, RISTORANTE ❷

V. Palazzuolo 31r   ☎055 21 88 46 🖳www.icentopoveri.it

Two adjacent restaurants with the same name but different menus. The long dining rooms with curved ceilings will make you feel like you're eating in a tunnel,

florence • food

but the light at the end is the excellent pizza *(€4-9)* on the pizzeria side, and the Tuscan specialties in the osteria, with a *prix-fixe* menu *(€35)* featuring *bistecca alla fiorentina.*

🍴 *Corner of Porcellana.* Ⓢ *Cover €2 in osteria. Pizza €4-9. Primi €7-10; secondi €9-19.* Ⓩ *Open daily noon-3pm and 7pm-midnight.*

TRATTORIA ZAZA
🍷♿🍸🛏 RISTORANTE ❷

P. del Mercato Centrale 26r ☎055 21 54 11 🖥www.trattoriazaza.it

The tented alfresco seating is typical for a *piazza ristorante*, but the quirky logo on the menu—a naked child being stung on the buttocks by a bee—should give you a clue to the offbeat glamour of the inside dining rooms. Lurid frescoes coat the vaulted ceilings, while staid dead white men watch you devour fresh pasta from gilded portraits. For those not inclined to the bloody *bistecca alla fiorentina*, there are abundant creative salad options—try Zaza's, with chicory lettuce, walnuts, brie, and Roquefort dressing.

🍴 *Behind Mercato Centrale.* Ⓢ *Cover €2.50. Primi €7-11.* Ⓩ *Open daily 11am-11pm.*

The Oltrarno

A lot of the Oltrarno's restaurants are quirkier than their counterparts on the other side of the river. Unfortunately, they're also a little bit more expensive and more likely to have a cover. Still, the locals who frequent these joints must know something we don't.

🏷 DANTE
🍷♿🍸 RISTORANTE ❷

P. Nazario Sauro 12r ☎055 21 92 19 🖥www.trattoria-dante.net

An excellent choice for students—with any meal, students get a free bottle of wine. No joke. The pizza is the same as anywhere, but dude, ⚡**free wine.** Also hosts lots of images of Dante on the wall, as you'd expect. Free wine!

🍴 *A block south of Ponte alla Carraia, on the right.* Ⓢ *Cover €2.50. Pizzas €6-9. Pastas €8-10.* Ⓩ *Open daily noon-11pm.*

OSTERIA SANTO SPIRITO
🍷♿🍸🛏 RISTORANTE ❷

P. Santo Spirito, 16r ☎055 23 82 383

Delightful wooden tables behind bamboo screens line the street in front of this osteria, while inside large round tables are suffused with a flickering red light. Linger after your pasta for the *crème brulée (€6)* and other posh desserts.

🍴 *Far end of the piazza from the church, on the right.* Ⓢ *Pizza €6-9. Primi €7-12. Wine by the bottle from €12.* Ⓩ *Open daily noon-11:30pm.*

NAPO LEONE
🍷♿🍸🛏 RISTORANTE ❸

P. del Carmine, 24 ☎055 28 10 15

The most famous rule of naming your restaurant Napo Leone is to never get involved in a land war in Asia, but only slightly less well-known is this: never have dinner in a parking lot when romance is on the line. Thankfully, Napo Leone is compensating quite well, thank you, creating a romantic atmosphere despite the location, with stained-glass lanterns and curlicue chairs. The menu features inconceivable appetizer platters like the spread of prosciutto, salami, artichokes, baked tomatoes, olives, peccorino cheese with jam, liver pate, *mozzarella di bufala*, and fried dough for €12.

🍴 *Against the wall in the back of the piazza.* Ⓢ *Cover €3. Pastas €8-10. Meat entrees €10-24.* Ⓩ *Open daily 7pm-1am.*

BIBO
🍷♿🍸❄🛏 RISTORANTE ❷

P. di Santa Felicita 6r ☎055 23 98 554

A quiet restaurant right past the Ponte Vecchio, Bibo is kinda on the tacky side of niceness, with electric candles on pink tablecloths, but it works.

🍴 *Bear left after crossing Ponte Vecchio.* Ⓢ *Pastas €9-10.* Ⓩ *Open daily noon-11pm.*

GELATERIA LA CARRAIA
💳♿ GELATERIA [1]

P. Nazario Sauro 25r ☎055 28 06 95 🖥www.lacarraiagroup.eu

An excellent gelato option right across the river, with cones starting at €1. Try the After Eight. Not much ambience in the shop itself, but go stand by the river—it's right outside.

➡ Right over the Ponte alla Carraia. $ Gelato from €1. ⏰ Open daily 11am-11pm.

NIGHTLIFE

People don't come to Florence to party. They come to Florence to stare at pretty things. During peak season, major sporting events, and other cultural happenings, the streets will fill with young people clutching wine bottles. At other times, you will be better off simply hanging out with the people in your hostel. For more hopping after-hours entertainment, head to Santa Croce or deal with one of the bazillion American or Irish pubs that litter the city.

Duomo and Piazza Della Signoria

This isn't exactly a traditional nightlife area. You'll find a couple of bars around, but generally you should head a little further outside the center. There is some DIY nightlife. The **Loggia, Piazza della Repubblica,** and **Ponte Vecchio** are all excellent places to hang out with a 👍**beer,** so get one to go from Old Stove or a watering hole in a pubbier part of town. It should also be noted that the Ponte Vecchio is a fine place for a snog and that *Let's Go* does not condone drunk-riding the P. della Repubblica carousel.

NOIR
💳♿🍸❄ BAR

Lungarno Corsini 12/14r ☎055 21 07 51

This super-classy watering hole spills over to the other side of the street, where patrons balancing cocktails and munchies lean against the wall of the Arno. Inside is dark, trendy, and loud, with low, cushioned benches lining the walls. Fill your plate from the extensive *aperitivo* buffet and go watch the sunset over the river.

➡ Facing Ponte Vecchio, it's on your right. $ Bottled beer €5. Cocktails €6-7. ⏰ Open daily noon-3am.

OLD STOVE
💳♿🍸🍺 IRISH PUB

P. della Signoria 30r ☎055 29 52 32 🖥www.theoldstovepub.com

Hey look, it's another Irish pub! Which, of course, actually means American because Irish people know better than to go to Florence for drinking. The dive-bar inside pales in comparison to the social and open outdoor seating. Wednesdays are Dollar Days—pay in US$ all day long. Other branches by the Duomo and *Il Porcellino.*

➡ Walk to the side of P. della Repubblica that doesn't have the carousel, and look down the street to the left. There it is. ℹ Happy hour pints €4. $ Pints €6. Cocktails €7. ⏰ Open M-Th noon-2am, F-Sa noon-3am, Su noon-2am. Happy hour M-Th 5-9pm.

SHOT CAFE
💳♿📶🍸 BAR

V. dei Pucci 5 ☎055 28 20 93

At least it looks different from the other American bars? This aggressively quirky little bar is covered in inner tubes and stuffed fish because, well, why not? The music is American "oldies," if you define oldies as anything recorded between 1920 and 2005. The TV is usually tuned to MTV—now that's retro.

➡ A block north of the Duomo. ℹ Happy hour 1st drink €3.50, 2nd €3, 3rd €2.50. Free Wi-Fi. $ Shots €2.50. Pitchers €9. ⏰ Open daily 5pm-3am. Happy hour until 9pm.

The Outer Ring

Although there are bars to be found in many areas around here (except around P. San Marco), by far the best nightlife is to the east in the university area. On nice evenings, **Piazza Sant'Ambrogio** and **Piazza Ghiberti** are swarmed with young people carrying drinks from the few area bars.

👍 LAS PALMAS
💳♿🍸☀ BAR

Largo Annigoni ☎347 27 60 033 💻www.laspalmasfirenze.it

Hundreds of locals pack this stretch of blacktop, transforming what may or may not qualify as a *piazza* by day into a rowdy block party by night. There's a lovely neighborhood feel here, with groups of students, families, and older folk crammed into the scores of tables covered by piles of food from the generous *aperitivo* buffet and children entertaining themselves at the foosball and table tennis games off to the side. A big stage bordering the space features performances and movies all summer as well as live screenings of sporting events.

🧭 Off of P. Ghiberti, in front of the La Nazione building. ℹ Check website for full-season performance and screening schedule. Ⓢ Beer €5. Pizza €5-8. Primi €7-10. ⏰ Open daily May-Sept, hours vary.

👍 SANT'AMBROGIO
💳♿🍸☀ BAR

P. Sant'Ambrogio 7r ☎055 24 10 35

This bar seems to single-handedly service the entire P. Sant'Ambrogio scene. And since this *piazza* is responsible for about 40% of Florentine nightlife overall, that's saying something. The plentiful outdoor seating located across the *piazza* from the bar itself spills over onto the steps of the church, creating a pleasant evening bustle. By nightfall, the whole area is full of young people sipping drinks from Sant'Ambrogio.

🧭 The piazza is at the end of V. Pietrapiana. Ⓢ Wine €4-7. Hard liquors €6-7. ⏰ Open M-Sa 8:30am-2am. Aperitivo happy hour 6-9pm.

SPACE CLUB ELECTRONIC
💳♿🍸 CLUB

V. Palazzuolo 37 ☎055 29 30 82 💻www.spaceelectronic.net

Do you wish you could go clubbing in Epcot? Then this utterly ridiculous club is the place for you. Descend into the depths of its space-age neon dance hall for a taste of the European clubbing scene, or as close as you'll get to that in central Florence. If the bouncer waves you in, don't be fooled into thinking you got a free entrance—you pay the steep cover *(€16)* when you leave. And hold tight to your drink ticket when crowding around the aquarium bar, because the fine for losing it is sky high.

🧭 From river, take V. Melegnano to V. Palazzuolo, then turn right. Ⓢ Cover €16 and it only goes up from there. ⏰ Open daily 10pm-4am.

italy

PLAZ
💳♿📶🍸☀ CAFE, BAR

V. Pietrapiana 36r ☎055 24 20 81

Sit under a tent on this busy little *piazza* and do some quality web surfing (courtesy of free Wi-Fi) while attacking an enormous salad *(€8)* or sweet crepe *(€5)*. At night the scene shifts, and you'll begin to see drunk university students stumble past as you sip an aromatic *(€9-10)*.

🧭 On P. die Ciompli. Ⓢ Cover €1.50. Aperitivo buffet from €8. ⏰ Open daily 8am-3am.

JOSHUA TREE
💳♿🍸❄ BAR

V. della Scala 37r 💻www.thejoshuatreepub.com

The dark, bold colors of this Irish-style pub may remind you of the nicer of your college haunts. It is smaller than similar places in town which means it doesn't feel deserted in the early hours of the evening. Good place to start your adventures, or to just hang out on a weeknight.

🧭 At corner of V. Benedetta. Ⓢ Pints €5. ⏰ Open daily 4pm-2am. Happy hour 4-9:30pm.

MOSTODOLCE
💳♿🍸❄ BAR

V. Nazionale 114r ☎055 23 02 928 💻www.mostodolce.it

The one pub around San Lorenzo likely to have one or two Italians present. Large and comfortable, with big crowds for sporting events and artisanal beers brewed in Prato. If you're around for a while (or drink fast) there's a "10th beer free" punch-card.

➜ *On the corner of V. Guelfa.* $ *Pints from €6.* ⏰ *Open daily 5pm-2am.*

KITSCH BAR 💳♿🍸🌤 BAR, CONCERT VENUE

Vle. Gramsci 1r ☎055 23 43 890

If a summer evening's booze-fueled wanderings take you straying to the edge of the historic city center, a small outdoor stage featuring local musicians will probably attract you to Kitsch. On evenings that don't feature live music, you can still find a bar that, bedecked with a giant Buddha, knock-off Klimt, and patio with glowing floors, certainly lives up to the place's name.

➜ *The traffic circle on the far right edge of your map, just above the river.* $ *Aperitivo buffet €8. Happy hour beer and cocktails €5.* ⏰ *Open daily 6:30pm-2am. Aperitivo buffet 6:30-10:30pm. Happy hour 10pm-1am.*

DUBLIN PUB 💳♿🍸🌤 BAR

V. Faenza 27r ☎055 27 41 571 💻www.dublinpub.it

Dartboards, beer ads, drunk Americans—the works. There are a few tables outside, but beware the splash of street-cleaning zambonis after midnight. Across the street is a fine *gelateria* for when you want to wash down the beer with something sweet.

➜ *The far end of V. Faenza.* $ *Pint of cider €4.40. Pint of Guinness €6. Pizza €5.* ⏰ *Open daily 5pm-2am.*

I VISACCI 💳♿🍸 BAR

V. Borgo degli Albizi 80/82r ☎055 26 39 443

Five shots for €5 is a deal offered at a few places in town, but it's good to know which they are. This is an excellent joint for a pre-game—if you ever make it out the door after the €5 cocktails and three beers for €10.

➜ *Coming from Duomo, take a left off Proconsolo.* $ *5 shots for €5. 3 beers for €10. Cocktails €5.* ⏰ *Open daily 10am "till late."*

The Oltrarno

This is the part of the city that the locals go to party. Since they're real people with real jobs, things tend to be much more happening on the weekends. In the west, **Piazza di Santo Spirito** is the most lively, while in the east, investigate **Piazza Poggi**, at the base of Piazzale Michelangelo, and the area just over the **Ponte San Niccolo** to get your game on. In late summer, bars along the southern banks of the Arno enliven the entire scene.

👍 **VOLUME** 💳♿🍸🌤 BAR

P. di Santo Spirito 5r ☎055 23 81 460

There's a great quirky atmosphere in this *"museo libreria caffè."* Cluttered and busy, Volume sports mismatched chairs low to the ground and stacks of books, a juke box *(€0.50 per play)* and a giant old printing press for good measure. The place is just as much about gelato and sweets as it is about cocktails, but the gelato is fancy, starting at €2.50. Don't drunkenly nibble on the cones in the display case—they're coated with something icky to keep the flies away.

➜ *Right of the church, sandwiched between 2 larger establishments.* $ *Cocktails €7. Crepes €4-7.* ⏰ *Open daily 11am-3am.*

JAMES JOYCE PUB 💳♿🍸🌤 BAR

Lungarno b. Cellini 1r ☎055 65 80 856

This enormous, popular bar is lively with students, particularly on nice weekend evenings. You don't even have to step inside to order another round of drinks—a window in the bar opens onto the patio. There's foosball and literary kitsch on the walls, and a generally local, fun vibe.

➜ *On the right, following the perilous traffic circle after the Ponte San Niccolo.* $ *Shots €3-4. Wine from €4.50. Bottled beer €5.* ⏰ *Open daily until 3am.*

NEGRONI

🍸♿🍸☀ BAR

V. de' Renai 17r ☎055 24 36 47 💻www.negronibar.com

This is the principal bar of the lovely P. Poggi, where patrons spill out of the official outdoor seating to populate the small green square and the banks of the Arno. The petite interior is hopping when the DJ's there or the weather's bad.

 # On P. Poggi. $ Grappa €4. Beer €5.50. Aperitivo buffet €7-11. ⏰ Open M-Sa 8am-2am, Su 6:30pm-2am. Aperitivo 7-11pm.

POP CAFE

🍸♿🍸☀ BAR

P. di Santo Spirito 18a ☎055 21 38 52 💻www.popcafe.it

This simple setup on a lively *piazza* is enlivened by a DJ and cheap drinks. Beer, shots, and *prosecco* are all €3 at the bar, €4 at the outside tables. Non-carnivores take heed—the *aperitivo* buffet is vegetarian, as is the weekday lunch menu. Stumble back in the morning, because they proudly offer bagel sandwiches.

 # To the left of the church. $ Beer, shots, and prosecco €3-4. Bagel sandwiches €5. ⏰ Open daily 11:30am-2am.

FLO

🍸🚫🍸☀ BAR

Piazzale Michelangelo 84 ☎055 65 07 91 💻www.flofirenze.com

If the climb to the Piazzale at night leaves you needing a drink to recover, check out Flo. The scene is noisy and crowded, but the view is divine. If you're staying at the camping hostel next door, then the music from Flo is likely to keep you up. Might as well join the party.

 # To the left of the Piazzale, or take the #12 or 13 bus. $ Beer €6. Cocktails €8. ⏰ Open daily 7pm-3am.

glbt nightlife

A number of bars and clubs in the Santa Croce area cater to a **GLBT** clientele—however, they would prefer not to be listed in guidebooks. Many of these establishments are unmarked or tucked down alleys. If you can get yourself in the correct general vicinity, the staff at neighboring bars can usually direct you the rest of the way. For a list of gay-friendly nightlife options, contact Arcigay (💻*www.arcigay.it).*

ARTS AND CULTURE

You may have heard there was this Renaissance thing here once. As you might guess, this is very much a visual arts town. To read about Florence's prodigious collection of art, see **Sights.** If you're hoping to encounter art other than paintings and sculptures, head to Lucca.

Theater and Music

There's not much of a scene for original theater in Florence, but when something comes to town you'll know about it—the city is emblazoned with posters for theatrical events up to a month away.

CHIESA DI SANTA MARIA DE' RICCI

♿ DUOMO

V. del Corso ☎055 21 50 44

An unassuming little church with a loud voice, this *chiesa* boasts a pretty spectacular pipe organ. Fortunately for the music-starved traveler, it likes to show it off. Organ vespers are played every evening at 7pm, followed by a recital of organ music from 8-10 pm.

 # From the Duomo, take V. dei Calzaioli south and turn left onto del V. del Corso. $ Free. ⏰ Daily vespers 7pm, recital 8pm.

TEATRO VERDI
V. Ghibbellina 99r

☛ THE OUTER RING

☎055 21 23 20 ■www.teatroverdionline.it

This grand concert hall lined with box seats is home to orchestra concerts and other live music events.

✴ *From P. Santa Croce, walk up V. Giovanni da Verazzano.* ℹ *Credit card required for phone or online reservations.* ⌚ *Box office open daily 4-7pm during the theater season. Alternative box office at V. Alammani 39 (near the train station) open M-F 9:30am-7pm, Sa 9:30am-2pm.*

Spectator Sports

STADIO ARTEMIO FRANCHI
Vle. Manfredo Fanti 4/6

☛ OUTSKIRTS

☎055 58 78 58 ■www.fiorentina.it

As is true for most Italian cities, Florence has a soccer team, and that soccer team is one of the primary obsessions of the city's residents. Purple-clad Fiorentina waver on the brink of success but never quite seem to achieve it, making them a great team to support if you're more into roller-coaster rides than easy victories. Catch a game here on Sundays throughout most of the year. The stadium is mostly uncovered, though, so pick a day when it's not raining.

✴ *Take bus #7, 17, or 20 or train from Santa Maria Novella to Firenze Campo Marte. The bus takes you directly to the stadium; it's a short walk from the train.* ℹ *Call ahead for wheelchair-accessible seats.* ⌚ *Ticket office open M-F 9:30am-12:30pm and 2:30-6:30pm. Most matches Su afternoons Sept-May.*

SHOPPING

Florentines cook up some of the snazziest window displays you'll ever see—you'll be tempted to stop in nearly every store you pass. If you're going to be in the city for a while, wait for the sales. The best months for shopping are January and July. As retailers prepare for the August slump, when the locals desert the city for the seashore, they chop prices drastically. Mid-July is also the season of scorching temperatures, so you'll have more than one reason to stay inside the air-conditioned stores.

Open-Air Markets

▨ MERCATO CENTRALE
P. Mercato Centrale

☛ THE OUTER RING

It's best to come here to eat, but you can come to sightsee too. Watch real Florentines (and clever tourists) peer at tomatoes and squeeze melons in the vast produce market.

✴ *It's the huge green-and-red building in the middle of all those sidewalk vendors.* ℹ *Some stalls accept credit cards, others don't.* ⓢ *Market rate.* ⌚ *Open M-F 7am-2:30pm, Sa 7am-5pm.*

▨ SAN LORENZO
San Lorenzo

☛ THE OUTER RING

Unless you're very serious about going off the beaten path, this is where you'll come for souvenir and knockoff shopping. You'll find leather bags, jackets, belts, journals, and gloves, as well as stationery, hats, tapestries, pashminas, doodads, and tourist schlock.

✴ *The area around San Lorenzo and Mercato Centrale* ℹ *Some are cash only, some take credit cards.* ⌚ *Open daily 9am-7pm.*

MERCATO NUOVO (MERCATO DEL PORCELLINO)
P. di Mercato Nuovo

☛ PIAZZA DELLA SIGNORIA

A similar selection to the San Lorenzo market can be found here, but the posher location means higher prices in this ancient marketplace. Then again, there are instances of the real deal mixed in with the knock-offs, so this is a good spot if you know enough to judge the quality of what you're looking for. Also check out the bronze boar *(il Porcellino)* and pop a coin in his drooling fountain mouth for good luck.

➔ From Ponte Vecchio, take V. Santa Maria north. ℹ Most, but not all, take credit cards. ⏰ Open daily 9am-7pm.

Clothing

Many department stores dot the area around P. della Signoria and Santa Maria Novella. Here are some good picks for filling out a travel wardrobe with more European styles.

PROMOD 💳♿ THE OUTER RING

V. dei Cerretani 46-48r ☎055 21 78 44 💻www.promod.eu

Akin to H and M or Forever 21, Promod sells bargain-priced, relatively disposable current fashions. Stocks mostly women's clothing.

➔ Take V. Cerretani west from the Duomo. ⏰ Open daily 10am-8pm.

GOLDENPOINT 💳♿ THE OUTER RING

V. dei Cerretani 40r ☎055 28 42 19 💻www.goldenpointonline.com

Goldenpoint deals in women's swimsuits and lingerie. It offers no bargains, but there's a bigger selection of swimsuit sizes and styles than elsewhere. Curvy women take note: Italian swimsuits offer far better support than American styles. Other locations at V. Panzani 33 *(☎055 21 42 96)* and V. dei Calzaioli 6 *(☎055 27 76 224).*

➔ Take V. Cerretani west from the Duomo. ⏰ Open daily 10am-7pm.

ESSENTIALS [7]

Practicalities

- **TOURIST OFFICES:** Tourist Information Offices, or **Uffici Informazione Turistica,** are staffed by qualified, multilingual personnel who can provide general information about visiting Florence and city services in addition to specifics about events, exhibitions, accommodations, and tours. There are numerous locations around the city, but one of the most useful is at **Piazza Stazione 4.** *(☎055 21 22 45 ⏰ Open M-Sa 8:30am-7pm, Su 8:30am-2pm.)*
- **CONSULATES: UK** *(Lungarno Corsini 2 ☎055 28 41 33).* **USA** *(Lungarno Vespucci 38 ☎055 26 69 51).*
- **LUGGAGE STORAGE:** At Stazione di Santa Maria Novella, by platform 16. *(ℹ Cash only. $ 1st 4hr. €4, 6th-12th hr. €0.60 per hr., then €0.20 per hr. thereafter. ⏰ Open 6am-11:50pm.)*
- **INTERNET: Internet Train** can be found all over the city. For a central location, try V. de' Benci 36r. *(☎055 26 38 555 💻www.internettrain.it ➔ From P. Santa Croce, go left onto V. de' Benci. $ Wi-Fi €2.50-3 per hr. Internet €3-4.50 per hr. ⏰ Open daily 10am-10:30pm.)*
- **POST OFFICES:** *(V. Pellicceria 3 ☎055 27 36 481 ➔ South of P. della Repubblica. ⏰ Open M-F 8:15am-7pm, Sa 8:15am-12:30pm.)*
- **POSTAL CODE:** 50100.

Emergency!

- **POLICE: Polizia Municipale** *(☎055 32 85).* 24hr. non-emergency helpline *(☎055 32 83 333).* Help is also available for tourists at the mobile police units parked at V. de' Calzaioli near P. della Signoria and Borgo S. Jacopo in the Oltrarno near the Ponte Vecchio.
- **LATE-NIGHT PHARMACIES: Farmacia Comunale** is in Stazione Santa Maria Novella and is open 24hr. *(☎055 21 67 61).* Other 24hr. pharmacies include **Farmacia**

Molteni *(V. Calzaioli 7r ☎055 21 54 72 ➡ Just north of P. della Signoria.)* and **Farmacia All'Insegna del Moro.** *(P. San Giovanni 20r ☎055 21 13 43 ➡ A little east of the Duomo.)*

- **HOSPITALS/MEDICAL SERVICES: Ospedale Santa Maria Nuova** near the Duomo has a 24hr. emergency room *(P. Santa Maria Nuova 1 ☎055 27 581).* Tourist medical services can be found at V. Lorenzo Il Magnifico 59. *(☎055 47 54 11 ➡ In the north of the city, near P. Liberta.)*

Getting There

By Plane

Aeroporto Amerigo Vespucci. *(V. del Termine 11 ☎055 30 615 main line; 055 30 61 700 for 24hr. automated service 💻www.aeroporto.firenze.it ℹ For lost baggage, call ☎055 30 61 302.)* From the airport, the city can be reached via the **VolainBus shuttle.** Pick up the shuttle from the Departures side—exit the airport and look to the right. Drop off is at Santa Maria Novella station. *($ €5. ⏰ 25min., every 30min. 5:30am-11:30pm.)*

By Train

Stazione Santa Maria Novella will likely be both your entry point to and exit point from the city. The ticket station is open daily 6am-9pm. Self-service kiosks are available 24hr. The Information Ofice is next to track 5. *(⏰ Open daily 7am-9pm.)* Luggage storage is by platform 16. Trains run to and from **Bologna** *($ €42. ⏰ 37min., 2 per hr. 7am-10:35pm.)*, **Milan** *($ €52. ⏰ 1¾hr., 1 per hr. 7am-9pm.)*, **Rome** *($ €44. ⏰ 95min., 2 per hr. 7am-10:45pm.)*, **Siena** *($ €6.20. ⏰ 90min., 6 per hr. 8:10am-8:10pm.)*, **Venice** *($ €42. ⏰ 2hr., 2 per hr. 8:30am-8:30pm.)*, and numerous local destinations.

By Bus

Three major intercity bus companies run out of Florence. **SITA** *(V. Santa Caterina da Siena 17 ☎800 37 37 60 💻www.sita-on-line.it)* runs buses from **Siena, San Gimignano,** and other Tuscan destinations. **LAZZI** *(P. Stazione 4/6r ☎055 215155; for timetable info 055 35 10 61 💻www.lazzi.it)* buses depart from P. Adua, just east of the train station. Routes connect to **Lucca, Pisa,** and many other local towns. **CAP-COPIT** *(Largo Fratelli Alinari 10 ☎055 21 46 37 💻www.capautolinee.it)* runs to local towns. Timetables for all three companies change regularly, so call ahead or check online before traveling.

Getting Around

By Bus

Since buses are the only public transportation in Florence, they are surprisingly clean, reliable, and easy to manage. Not to mention adorably orange and tiny! They are operated by **ATAF** and **LHNEA.** Buy a ticket before boarding from most newsstands and tabacconists, from a ticket vending machine, or from the ATAF kiosk in P. Stazione *(☎800 42 45 00 $ 90min. ticket €1.20, €2 if purchased on board; 24hr. €5; 3-day €12.)* Time-stamp your ticket when you board the bus—there are sporadic ticket checks, and if you forget, are caught without a stamped ticket, or can't successfully play the "confused foreigner" card, it's a €50 fine. You're unlikely to need to use the buses unless you're leaving the city center. The network is extensive, with several night-owl buses taking over for the regular routes in the late evenings, so if you are venturing out of town, pick up a schematic bus map from the ATAF kiosk or use the trip planner at 💻www.ataf.net.

By Taxi

To call a cab, try calling ☎055 4390, 055 4499, 055 4242, or 055 4798. Tell the operator your location and when you want the cab, and the nearest available car will be sent to you. Designated cab stands can be found at P. Stazione, Fortezza da Basso, and P. della Repubblica. Cabs between fares can also often be found at Santa Maria Novella.

By Bike

It takes some confidence to bike in the crowded parts of central Florence, but cycling is a great way to check out a longer stretch of the Arno's banks or to cover a lot of territory in a fast-paced day. **Mille E Una Bici** (☎055 65 05 295) rents out 200 bikes in four locations, and they can be picked up and returned at any of four locations: P. Stazione, P. Santa Croce, P. Ghiberti, and Stazione F.S. Campo Di Marte. **Florence By Bike** (V. San Zanobi 91r and 120-122r ☎055 48 89 92 🖳www.florencebybike.it) is another good resource. Staff will help renters plan routes, whether for an afternoon or for a multi-day trip outside of town.

siena ☎0577

Thanks to the biannual Palio, Siena shares a reputation with Spain's Pamplona for being a city that's completely crazy two days of the year and asleep the other 363. That's really not a fair rep though, because the Sienese provide plenty to see even when they aren't racing bareback around Il Campo. The city's completely befuddling medieval layout is Tuscany taken to its illogical—and seriously charming—extreme. Amid the trapped-in-time Gothic architecture, you'll find that Siena is also a respectable university town with a campus indistinguishable from the city around it—you'll only realize you're at the university when you poke into a church and discover it's actually a Linguistics department. Offering pleasant Campo-centric nightlife, relative freedom from overwhelming Florentine tourist crowds, and a twisty jumble of streets hiding secrets that will take a semester to unlock, Siena is perhaps the best study-abroad city in Tuscany—and one of the best to visit as well.

ORIENTATION

Siena is a tricky maze of dead ends and twisting streets going to who-knows-where. Learn the key locales of the city center (**Il Campo** and the **Duomo**) and orient yourself as best you can from them. Note that the train station is well to the north of the city center, so it may be better to arrive by bus, which will drop you off in **Piazza Matteotti,** in the northwest of the *centro*.

ACCOMMODATIONS

We are sad to report that there are exactly eight dormitory beds in the entirety of Siena. If you have a friend with whom to share a bed-and-breakfast double, however, there are quite a few good options. No matter what you're looking for, you need to plan ahead when trying to visit in early July or early August—at these times, every room in the city is booked (and has been months in advance) for the Palio.

CASA DI ANTONELLA   ✦⊗ B AND B ❸
V. delle Terme 72   ☎339 30 04 883 🖳anto.landi@libero.it

You'll feel like you've scored your own flat at this hands-off B and B where check-in consists of wandering inside to find the room marked by a Post-it with your name on it. Although the owner, Antonella, only comes round to prepare breakfast, you won't be lacking for anything in the six airy, comfortable doubles.

✦ *From P. Matteotti, take V. dei Termini and turn right onto V. delle Terme.* Ⓢ *Doubles €50-60.*

SIENA IN CENTRO   ✦ㅊ⒭ B AND B ❸
V. di Stalloreggi 14-16   ☎0577 43 041 🖳www.bbsienaincentro.com

Three B and B properties are bundled together as Siena in Centro. All boast similar decoration and amenities. Casa del Giglio, with ornate headboards and fancy curtains, is the nicest, but Casa del Conte and B and B dei Rossi are lovely as well.

✦ *For reception, follow signs from the Duomo to the Pinacoteca but bear right onto V. di Stalloreggi.* Ⓢ *Singles €40-80; doubles €60-120; triples €90-150.*

PICCOLO HOTEL ETRUSIA
♠ & ❋ HOTEL ❸

V. delle Donzelle 3   ☎0577 28 80 88 ▣www.hoteletruria.com

Look for an ivy-covered entryway to find this pleasant little hotel with a comfortable sitting area. The hotel keeps a 1am curfew, but a few of the rather straightforward rooms have a separate entrance from the street.

⚑ *North of V. Banchi di Sotto. In the area north of Il Campo, there are signs directing you here.* ⑤ *Singles €40-55; doubles €80-110; triples €90-138. Extra bed €10-28.*

YHA OSTELLO DI SIENA
●& ⑼ HOSTEL ❶

V. Fiorentina 89   ☎0577 52 212 ▣www.ostellosiena.com

Sadly, Siena's one hostel barely counts as a hostel and it's barely in Siena. Offering mostly double rooms and a single eight-bed dormitory, the place is a 15min. bus ride from the *centro*. What it lacks in location it also lacks in character.

⚑ *From train station, take bus #77 or 4. From the centro take #10, 15, or 77. Ask the driver to let you off at the ostello.* ⑤ *Dorms €20; doubles €40.*

TRE DONZELLE
♠⊗⑼ HOTEL ❸

V. delle Donzelle 5   ☎0577 28 03 58 ▣www.tredonzelle.com

Rooms are bare-bones but spacious, and a nice lounge sits off the lobby. Hope you're planning to party with the crowds in Il Campo at night, because you'll be hearing them all evening anyway.

⚑ *North of V. Banchi di Sotto. In the area north of Il Campo; look for the signs.* ⑤ *Singles with shared bath €38; doubles €49, with bath €60; triples €70/€85; quads with bath €105.*

SIGHTS
◉

You'll find a wealth of things to see in Siena, but the biggest attractions are **Il Campo** and the area around the **Duomo.** The six sights of the Duomo complex—Duomo, Baptistery, Crypt, Museo dell'Opera, Santa Maria della Scala, and Museo Diocesano—can be visited with a single cumulative ticket, available at the ticket booth to the right of the cathedral up until 30min. before the sights close. The ticket is valid for 48hr. from first use, so you don't even have to cram all the sights into one day, and with the exception of the Museo Diocesano, they are all helpfully clustered in the same *piazza*. At €12 regular and €5 for students, this is one of the best cumulative ticket deals in the region. The cathedral, crypt, and Santa Maria della Scala are particularly worth visiting. Call ahead for specific accessibility information for the different venues.

▧ IL CAMPO
& PIAZZA

P. del Campo

Originally conceived as a space for large civic events, Il Campo continues to be the heart of the *centro*. During the twice-annual ▧**Palio,** this shell-shaped *piazza* is crammed with as many bodies as can be packed into its boundaries when the famous horse race tears around the square's outer edge. Even without the Palio, the *piazza* hums with the life of the town. By day, Il Campo is a restaurant-lined expanse of gently slanted, sun-warmed brick. In the evenings, Il Campo is transformed into a communal patio, as the students of Siena plop themselves on the brick in small clusters to drink and hang out until the early hours.

⚑ *Follow the ubiquitous signs pointing you to Il Campo.*

▧ DUOMO
♠& CHURCH

P. Duomo 8   ☎0577 28 30 48 ▣www.operaduomo.siena.it

Of the many impressive cathedrals in Tuscany, Siena's Duomo might be the best. The first thing you notice is the floor—or rather, the abundant metal posts cordoning off chunks of the floor to stop distracted tourists from trampling over the large marble cartoons underfoot. The earlier examples from the 14th century use a technique called *graffito*—thin grooves were chiseled out of slabs of white marble and then filled in with black *stucco*, creating an image worthy of a coloring book. The later examples also use marble inlay to create richly

siena ‧ sights

colored designs that almost look as if they had been painted. Overhead, carved busts of centuries of popes look down on visitors. Imagine what *they* talk about at night. Turn around to check out the beautiful stained-glass representation of the Last Supper. Off the left aisle, the small, richly adorned **Piccolomini Library** displays an excellent collection of graduals and illuminated manuscripts. And don't skip the gift shop, which has a rather nice selection of stationery modeled on the library's illuminated manuscript collection. Sadly, no one has yet been clever enough to turn those *graffito* designs into a proper coloring book.

🧭 Follow the ever-present signs. Ticket booth is on the right of the cathedral. 💲 €3. Combined ticket with other Duomo sights €12, students €5. ⏰ Open June-Aug M-Sa 10:30am-8pm, Su 1:30-6pm; Sept-Nov M-Sa 10:30am-7:30pm, Su 1:30-5:30pm; Nov-Feb M-Sa 10:30am-6:30pm, Su 1:30-5:30pm; Mar-May M-Sa 10:30am-7:30pm, Su 1:30-5:30pm.

SANTA MARIA DELLA SCALA — 🎟♿ MUSEUM

P. Duomo 1 — ☎0577 53 45 11 💻www.santamariadellascala.com

Actively tending to pilgrims, the poor, and the orphaned for over a millennium, the Santa Maria della Scala complex is one of the oldest hospitals in Europe. It was also a mighty and wealthy institution, the city's third-biggest site for artistic installations after the Duomo and **Palazzo Pubblico.** Today, the building is no longer in use as a hospital—instead, it is currently under renovation to become the new home of the city's Pinacoteca in 2013. Sadly, you'll find little on display relating to the building's fascinating history. One brilliantly frescoed ward displays a photograph of the same ward in the early part of the century, when a row of cots stood under the same frescoes. For even more reductiveness, check out the second-to-last fresco on the right, which illustrates a scene in this very ward from many centuries before. Another notable section of the complex is the church of **Santissima Annunziata**—an enormous 1730 painting of a scene from the Gospel of John fills the church's entire apse. Unlike much 18th-century work in the region, this one actually looks like it's from 1730. The complex's many other galleries are filled with the permanent collection from the hospital's history as well as rotating exhibits from the Pinacoteca and elsewhere. If you want to learn more about the Palio, check out the small exhibit of contrada flags and other ephemera related to the famous race in the lower level.

🧭 Across from the entrance to the Duomo. ℹ Individual tickets available at the museum, combined tickets at the general Duomo ticket booth. 💲 €5.50, students €3. Combined ticket with other Duomo sights €12, students €5. ⏰ Open daily 10:30am-6:30pm.

CRYPT — 🎟♿ CHURCH

P. Duomo — ☎0577 28 30 48 💻www.operaduomo.siena.it

The crypt is not actually a crypt, but you can see why they thought it was when they discovered the space during a 1999 excavation. Imagine digging along the outer edge of a cathedral to lay some new pipes and suddenly breaking into an underground cavern lined with 13th-century frescoes, still brightly colored thanks to centuries of being sealed off. That's a tale to tell at your next dinner party. Visiting the discovery today, you walk through the crypt on a false floor several feet above the real one, with windows underfoot allowing you to see the brickwork and floor of the cavern as it was found. It's quite a nifty space.

🧭 Just past the ticket booth, on the left. 💲 €6. Combined ticket with other Duomo sights €12, students €5. ⏰ Open daily June-Aug 9am-8pm; Sept-Oct 9:30am-7pm; Nov-Feb 10am-5pm; Mar-May 9:30am-7pm.

MUSEO DELL'OPERA — 🎟♿ MUSEUM

P. Duomo — ☎0577 28 30 48 💻www.operaduomo.siena.it

The Duomo's museum houses Sienese masterpieces that were once displayed in the cathedral, including an excellent collection of statues of prophets by Pisano. On the upper floors, check out a beautiful silver rosebush and a jumble of reliquaries that hold bits of saints. Follow the signs to the **Facciatone,** at the end of the Hall of Vestments. A staircase inside the wall leads to what would have been the top of the facade of the New Cathedral had construction not been halted by the Black Death in 1348. From here, enjoy a splendid view of the city and the surrounding mountains. It's also enjoyable to look down on Il Campo and watch all the little tourists scurrying about.

Opposite the Duomo, on the left. $ €6. Combined ticket with other Duomo sights €12, students €5. Open daily June-Aug 9am-8pm; Sept-Oct 9:30am-7pm; Nov-Feb 10am-5pm; Mar-May 9:30am-7pm.

BAPTISTERY

CHURCH

P. San Giovanni ☎0577 28 30 48 www.operaduomo.siena.it

This building where, for centuries, Sienese children were baptized is small but sumptuously decorated, with a ceiling fresco illustrating the Apostles' Creed and a 15th-century marble, bronze, and enamel baptismal font. The polychrome marble exterior is quite grand and a worthwhile pairing with the Duomo.

From the ticket booth, ahead and downstairs. $ €3. Combined ticket with other Duomo sights €12, students €5. Open daily June-Aug 9am-8pm; Sept-Oct 9:30am-7pm; Nov-Feb 10am-5pm; Mar-May 9:30am-7pm.

PALAZZO PUBBLICO

MUSEUM, PALAZZO

P. Il Campo 1 ☎0577 29 26 14 www.comune.siena.it/main.asp?id=885

This grandiose town hall, begun in 1297, forms the lower wall of Il Campo. Built to show up hotshot Florence, the tower here is slightly taller than that of its rival's. (Proving that size doesn't matter, Siena was decimated by the Black Death shortly after the tower's completion, while Florence went on to become the birthplace of the Renaissance.) The *palazzo* is also home to the **Museo Civico,** which showcases the building's elaborate frescoes and architecture, including a chapel with a fantastic wood-carved choir and a series of paintings illustrating the unification of Italy. Also includes a **tower** with great views over the city.

It's the big thing at the bottom of Il Campo. $ Museum €7.50, students €4. Tower €8. Both €13. Museum open Mar 16-Oct 10am-7pm; Nov-Mar 15 10am-6pm.

FOOD

Thanks to Siena's slightly higher population of homegrown residents than those of similar Tuscan cities, the town has a large number of groceries and delis—great news for cheapskates. Avoid the restaurants that border Il Campo unless you want to pay €9 for a bowl of pasta.

LA PIZZERIA DI NONNO MEDE

PIZZERIA [2]

V. Camporeggio 21 ☎0577 24 79 66

It takes a little bit of effort to find this pizzeria, but that's because it's hiding itself for the locals. There's a bunch of patio seating overlooking the town skyline, and on clear summer evenings, every inch of that seating will be packed.

There are stairs behind Fontebranda that lead uphill and to the right—they'll take you there. $ Cover €1.60. Pizza €5-7.50. Primi €6-7.50. Open daily noon-3:30pm and 7pm-1am.

LA FONTANA DELLA FRUTTA

GROCERY [1]

V. delle Terme 65-67 ☎0577 40 422

For a budget lunch, you can't beat the takeout counter at this corner grocer. The packaged goods and produce are reasonably priced and lovely, but head to the counter for excellent cold pastas, stuffed tomatoes, sauces, and vegetable dishes sold by the kilogram.

At the corner of V. S. Caterina. $ Most pastas around €11 per kg. Open daily 8am-8pm.

SALE E PEPE

RISTORANTE [1]

V. Garibaldi 23 ☎0577 60 00 89 www.ristorantesalepepe.it

This extremely affordable dinner option is making a funny in its name—it's just off Piazza del Sale, you see, and Sale e Pepe means salt and pepper. Not laughing? A better reason to eat here are the dozen pastas that come with 0.5L of water and a coffee (€5.50).

❖ Off P. del Sale. ⑤ Pasta, secondo, water, and coffee €10. ☼ Open daily 11am-11pm.

SAVINI ⑳☧ BAKERY ❶
V. dei Montanini 9 ☎055 91 21 61 💻www.dolcezzesavini.com

Since 1959, this bakery has been producing delicious Sienese specialties like *panforte*, a sort of trail mix from the Crusades now sold by the paper-wrapped block, and *ricciarelli*, sugary almond cookies. Savini now has locations in half a dozen Tuscan cities.

❖ From P. Gramsci take V. Cavallerizzo, then turn right onto Montanini. ⑤ Most pastries €1-2.50. ☼ Open M-Sa 7:30am-7:30pm, Su 8am-1pm.

NIGHTLIFE

There are plenty of nice bars in Siena, but the cheerful efforts of the student population have brought about a true BYOB scene. Pick up a couple of bottles and head to Il Campo for the nightly block party. The tourist-trappy restaurants surrounding the *piazza* become tourist-trappy bars at night, so load up elsewhere to avoid €8 pints.

▨ SAN PAOLO PUB ⑳☒☧ PUB
Vicolo San Paolo 2 ☎0577 22 66 22 💻www.sanpaolopub.com

For reasonably priced drinks and food that's *almost* on Il Campo—if you sit outside and crane your neck a bit, it's like you're there—this alleyway pub is your best bet. It's small enough to seem crowded all day, and the alley allows for spillover when the place is legitimately crowded at night.

❖ In a little covered alley, just off Il Campo—it's 1 of the streets directly opposite the Palazzo. ⑤ Beer €4.20. Cocktails €5. Hot and cold sandwiches €3.50. ☼ Open daily noon-2am.

▨ ENOTECA ITALIANA ☧ ENOTECA
P. Libertà 1 ☎0577 22 88 11 💻www.enoteca-italiana.it

Unique to Italy, the Enoteca Italiana is a public institution founded in 1960 to educate the people about Italian wine and wineries. The collection includes over 1600 different wines—1607 at last count, according to one waiter—which are presented on a rotating tasting menu each week. At €11, they're fairly reasonable, considering you're getting educated and tipsy at the same time.

❖ Inside Fortezza Medicea. ⑤ Tasting menu of 2 glasses of wine €11. ☼ Open M-Sa noon-1am.

CAFFE DEL CORSO ☧ BAR
V. Banchi di Sopra 25 ☎0577 22 66 56 💻www.caffedelcorsosiena.it

If you've been mystified by Italian distinctions between different types of cocktails, then Caffe del Corso is here to help! One wall of this corner pub is covered with the drink list, helpfully divided into categories like *aperitivi* (Bloody Mary, martini, cosmo), after dinners (margarita, Sidecar, whiskey sour), and long drinks (Screwdriver, Gin Fizz, mojito). The drinks may have lots of distinctions, but they have one thing in common—they all cost €5.

❖ 2 blocks up from Il Campo, on the right. ⑤ Cocktails €5. ☼ Open Tu-Su 8:30am-3am.

DUBLIN POST ☧ IRISH PUB
P. Gramsci 20/21 ☎0577 28 90 89 💻www.dublinpost.it

Yet another Irish pub in Italy. You know the drill. This one has a lot of outdoor seating.

❖ Directly across from the end of the bus lines. ⑤ Beer €5. ☼ Open M-Sa noon-1am, Su 3pm-1am.

ESSENTIALS

Practicalities

- **TOURIST OFFICES: APT Siena** provides maps for a small fee. Also has pamphlets, brochures, and a bookstore. *(P. del Campo 56 ☎0577 28 05 51 🖳www.terresiena.it ⇟ Right in Il Campo; look for the"i.")*

Emergency!

- **POLICE:** *(V. del Castoro 1 ⇟ Near the Duomo.)*
- **HOSPITALS/MEDICAL SERVICES: Santa Maria alle Scotte.** *(Vicolo delle Scotte 14 ☎0577 58 51 11 ⇟ Take bus #3 or 77 from P. Gramsci. ⏰ Open 24hr.)*

Getting There

Siena is surprisingly difficult to reach. Coming from Florence is easy, but if you're arriving from elsewhere, you're almost certainly going to have to transfer train or bus at least once.

By Bus

Siena is one of the few Italian towns that possesses a train station but might actually be better reached by bus. From Florence at least. **TRA-IN/SITA** *(☎0577 42 46 🖳www.trainspa.it)* buses drop off in P. Antonio Gramsci, about 5min. north of P. del Campo. (Some also drop off at the train station, see below.) The ticket office is in the underground terminal. *(⏰ Open 7am-7pm.)* From **Florence.** *($ €6.80. ⏰ 90min., at least 1 per hr.)*

By Train

The train station is in **Piazza Rosselli,** 15min. outside town by bus #3, 4, 7, 8, 10, 17, or 77. *(Ticket office open daily 6:30am-1:10pm and 1:40-8:10pm.)* Trains arrive from **Florence** *($ €6.30. ⏰ 90min., every hr. 8am-8pm.)* and Poggibonsi. *($ €2.40. ⏰ 30min., 2 per hr.)*

pisa ☎050

This is what Pisa has to offer: one tower, leaning. One airport, budget airline hub. Three universities.

That may not sound like much, but the tower is actually really cool, the airport is remarkably easy to get to, and the universities, well, you can thank them for the city's many student-friendly bars. If Florentine nightlife left you doubting the Tuscan party scene, come to Pisa, where the density of pubs will leave you leaning at a 3.99° angle too.

Unless you're visiting someone at one of the universities or flying out of the airport, however, there's little reason to stay overnight in Pisa. The tower doesn't take long to see, and the theoretically picturesque alleys along the Arno would be far more charming if they didn't smell like urine. *Let's Go* recommends staying a night or two in nearby **Lucca,** and making Pisa a half-day trip from there.

ORIENTATION

Whether arriving in Pisa by train or by plane, you will enter the *centro* via the **train station.** The city knows why people visit it, so street signs bearing the image of a leaning tower and an arrow are abundant. When you leave the station, you will be south of the Arno—the **Piazza dei Miracoli** is on the other side of the river, in the northwest of the *centro.* Follow either the "Torre" or "Centro" signs to get there. Otherwise, walk straight—leaving the *stazione* you will be on **Corso Italia**—to reach the river.

ACCOMMODATIONS

Those staying overnight in Pisa are likely in transit—therefore, our picks weigh access to the train station and airport over proximity to the tower.

▨ WALKING STREET HOSTEL

@@⊗ HOSTEL ❷

C. Italia 58   ☎393 06 48 737 ▉www.walkingstreethostel.com

This hostel is nice enough to make you wish you had a reason to stay in Pisa longer. The dorm rooms that face C. Italia have an entire wall of 300-year-old stained glass—that's floor-to-ceiling stained glass, in your dorm room—and common space is plentiful and comfortable, with a pool table and dart board in two Chinese-themed red lounges.

⌗ *On C. Italia, equidistant between the train station and the river.* Ⓢ *Dorms €22.*

HOSTEL PISA

@@⊗⑽ HOSTEL ❶

V. Sainati 8   ☎349 68 88 446

If you get the sense that some dude just decided to turn his house into a hostel and called it Hotel Pisa, then you are absolutely correct. Carlo is a backpacker himself, but the sort who cares more about community than security. If you're the same, you'll love it here. Also lends out bikes, which is helpful since this is a bit far from the *centro*.

⌗ *Leave the train station at track 14, take a right onto V. Quarantola, then, after 5min., make a left onto V. Sainati.* Ⓢ *Dorms €20.*

HOTEL HELVETIA

✦♿⑽ HOTEL ❸

V. Don Gaetano Boschi 31   ☎050 55 30 84

Our pick for slanty-building-proximity is this lovely bargain hotel with a beautiful, well-kept garden that proudly features a cactus to rival the city's famous tower. Four floors of private rooms have brick trim, ceiling fans, wood shutters, and iron bedstands.

⌗ *V. Don Gaetano Boschi begins in the southeast corner of P. dei Miracoli.* **i** *Only 1 wheelchair-accessible room, which is a suite.* Ⓢ *Singles €35; doubles €45, with bath €62; quad suite €100.*

ALBERGO ARISTON

✦⊗⑽✳ HOTEL ❸

V. C. Matti 42   ☎050 56 18 34 ▉www.hotelarisonpisa.it

You are paying for extreme proximity to the monuments here—many of the rooms have a view dominated entirely by a certain crooked belltower. (Of course, the prime real estate also comes along with a certain amount of noise and bustle.) Otherwise, the chambers are simple doubles with iron-frame queen beds. In the lobby, a bar and a few leather armchairs surround a TV.

⌗ *Just outside the east gate of P. dei Miracoli.* **i** *Doubles only.* Ⓢ *Doubles €70-90.*

RELAIS UNDER THE TOWER

✦⊗⑽ HOTEL, HOSTEL ❷

V. Santa Maria 165   ☎050 52 00 231 ▉www.hotelpisacentro.it

Twins and bunk beds share rooms in this semi-hostel where rooms are private or dorm depending on demand. Though it can't make up its mind about what kind of rooming house it is, Relais Under The Tower's name is pretty literal—you won't find another hostel-like place closer to the monuments.

⌗ *Just south of the tower.* Ⓢ *Dorms €20-25; doubles €45-50, with bath €65-100.*

SIGHTS

All of Pisa's grime and crass tourism instantly melt away when you walk among the glistening white monuments of **Piazza Duomo**. The writer Gabriele D'Annunzio called this medieval square the *Piazza Dei Miracoli*, or Piazza of Miracles, and the name is both apt and widely used. If you want to expand your visit beyond the big shiny buildings, there are plenty of churches into which you can wander or you could take a bus from P. Vittorio Emanuele to **Marina di Pisa,** the nearest beach.

▨ LEANING TOWER

✦⊗ TOWER

P. Duomo   ☎050 83 50 11 ▉www.opapisa.it

Jaded travelers that we are, we expected Pisa's famous tower to be something of a tourist trap, on par with a leaning Big Block of Cheese. We were very wrong.

italy

Turns out the postcards, placemats, and neckties simply cannot do justice to the ridiculous slant of this seriously tipsy structure. It really is awesome, shocking as that may be. And if you're getting sick of the sense o' wonder inspired by most great European monuments (we told you we were jaded), get stoked for the tower. Your first reaction will be less OMG and more LOL. LMAO, even. It really is hilariously tilted. Oh man, Tower, you crack us up.

➜ Follow the abundant signs to "Tower." ℹ Wheelchair-accessible only by arrangement, call ahead. Make reservations in the Museo del Duomo, online, or next to the tourist info office. $ €15. ⏰ Open daily June-Sept 8am-11pm; Oct 9am-7pm; Nov-Dec 24 10am-5pm; Dec 25-Jan 6 9am-6pm; Jan 7-Feb 10am-5pm; Mar 9am-6pm; Apr-May 8am-8pm. Last entry 30min. before close. Visit lasts 30min. and is guided.

PIAZZA DEI MIRACOLI SIGHTS — 🎟♿ CHURCH, MUSEUM, CEMETERY

P. Duomo

Outside of the famed leaning attraction, P. Duomo contains many other notable attractions in which you could spend an entire day. The impressive **Duomo** itself would not be at all out of place in Florence. Everything from the ceiling to the pews is stylish. The **Battistero** is the great round thing in front of the cathedral, and its acoustics are so spectacular that a choir singing inside can supposedly be heard from 2km away. The **Camposanto** (cemetery) remains impressively peaceful amongst all the tourists. It retains fragments of frescoes that were heavily damaged by Nazi shelling. When preservationists finally began reconstructing the frescoes in 1979, they discovered enormous preparatory drawings underneath. In response, **Museo delle Sinopie** was created so that visitors could see these sketches, with catwalks providing multiple vantage points from which to view the drawings. Finally, **Museo dell'Opera del Duomo** contains yet more information on the construction, reconstruction, and preservation of the cathedral and its surrounding buildings. If you ever happen to travel back in time to Pisa in 1064, you'll be able to tell them exactly how they can keep their buildings from getting all tilty.

➜ In P. Duomo, in the north of the city. ℹ Wheelchair-accessible only by arrangement; call ahead. $ All sights have joint admission: 1 monument €5, 2 monuments €6, all 5 €10. Handicapped persons and 1 guest free. Buy tickets at the biglietteria north of the tower or at the Museo delle Sinopie. ⏰ Open daily Apr-Sept 8am-8pm; Oct 9am-7pm; Nov-Dec 24 10am-5pm; Dec 25-Jan 6 9am-6pm; Jan 7-Feb 10am-5pm; Mar 9am-6pm.

GIARDINO SCOTTO — ♿ PARK

Lungarno Leonardo Fibonacci ☎050 83 50 21

For a small park, Giardino Scotto sure brings the goods. Its main draws are the ruins and Roman walls, upon which you can go clambering around if you'd like. There's also a permanent outdoor movie theater in the park where first- and second-run films are screened every night of the summer.

➜ South of the river, east of the centro.. ⏰ Open daily July-Aug 9am-8:30pm; Sept 9am-8pm; Oct 9am-6pm; Nov-Jan 9:30am-4:30pm; Feb-Mar 9am-6pm; Apr 9am-7pm; May-June 9am-8pm.

FOOD

This port city is blessed with lots of seafood, plus restaurants that double as bars offering lovely *aperitivo* buffets and late hours. Just south of the monuments on **Via Santa Maria,** you will find about a half dozen pizzerias.

ARGINI MARGINI — 🎟♿🍸 SEAFOOD ❷

Lungarno Galilei ☎329 88 81 972 💻www.arginiemargini.com

The Arno smells far sweeter when you're sipping wine on a dock along its sandy shore. In the summer months at the edge of the south shore, head to Argini Margini's small floating dock for fresh seafood and live jazz and classical music.

➜ Look over the edge of the river, and you'll see it. $ Cover €1. Seafood priced at market rate, by the kg. ⏰ Open in summer M-Th 6-11pm, F-Sa 6pm-midnight, Su 6-11pm.

LA BOTTEGA DEL GELATO ♿ GELATERIA [1]

P. Garibaldi 11 ☎050 57 54 67 💻www.labottegadelgelato.it

Big scoops of good-by-all-but-Florentine-standards gelato, right on Pisa's main bridge. Take your cone and stroll along the Arno.

➡ On P. Garibaldi. $ Gelato from €1.50. 🕐 Open daily in summer 11am-1am; in fall, winter, and spring 11am-10pm.

DOLCE PISA ♿🍸 CAFE [1]

V. Santa Maria 83 ☎050 56 31 81

At this pleasant cafe a bit farther down the otherwise busy street off the monuments, entire swaths of the menu are €5, including the lunch menu (lasagna, gnocchi, etc.), a large selection of salads, and a long list of smoothies.

➡ From the monuments, it's about a 5min. walk down V. Santa Maria; it's on the right. $ Pastries €0.90. Most entrees €5. Cappuccino €1.20. 🕐 Open M-Tu 7:30am-11pm, Th-Su 7:30am-11pm.

OSTERIA I SANTI ♿🍸❄ RISTORANTE [2]

V. Santa Maria 71/73 ☎050 28 081 💻www.osteria-isanti.com

With a real canopy, tall green plants, and twinkling Christmas lights, Osteria i Santi offers nicer outdoor seating than most of the options in this area.

➡ From the monuments, walk down V. Santa Maria; it's on the right. $ Cover €1.50. Dishes €6.50-9. 🕐 Open daily noon-3pm and 7-10:30pm.

IL BARONETTO ♿🍸❄ RISTORANTE [1]

V. Domenica Cavalca 62 ☎340 25 91 646 💻www.ilbaronetto.com

Il Baronetto's quiet side street is far less foul-smelling than other Pisan side streets, so it's a good place for a nice lunch. The pizza menu is extremely diverse—pies come in a phenomenal 45 varieties, many of them under €6.

➡ Off V. Curatone. From river, turn right. $ Cover €1.50. Pizza €4-8. Primi €7-10. 🕐 Open M-Sa 8:30am-3:30pm and 5:30-9:30pm.

NIGHTLIFE

You really don't need our help with this one. Pisa is jam-packed with bars and pubs, many of them quite cheap. Basically, if you are paying more than €2.50 for a bottle of beer, then you'd better really like the place. Florentine *piazza*-based nightlife is less popular here, if only because the *piazze* aren't as pretty and the pubs are more plentiful. The main gathering spot, **Piazza delle Vettogaglie,** is a near-hidden square lined with small pubs, picnic tables, and cheap late-night food options.

BAZEEL ♿🍸 BAR

Lungarno Pacinotti 1 ☎340 28 81 113 💻www.bazeel.it

A big corner bar on a major *piazza*, Bazeel dominates the scene around the Ponte di Mezzo, the most central of the *centro* bridges. When it's hot, there are frozen cocktails *(€6.50).*

➡ Just over the north side of the bridge. $ Beer €3-4.50. 🕐 Open daily 2pm-2am.

AMALTEA ♿🍸 BAR

Lungarno Mediceo 49 ☎050 58 11 29

Munch from a generous *aperitivo* buffet while watching the sun set over the river from this other *piazza* dominator with a *gelateria* conveniently located next door.

➡ In P. Cairoli, on the river. $ Beer €3.50-4.50. Cocktails €4.50-6. 🕐 Open daily 5pm-2am.

ESSENTIALS

Practicalities

- **TOURIST OFFICES:** The office at **Piazza Vittorio Emanuele II** provides maps, an events calendar, and other assistance. *(P. Vittorio Emanuele II 13 ☎050 42 291 💻www.pisaunicaterra.it 🕐 Open daily 9:30am-7:30pm.)*

Emergency!

- **POLICE: Polizia Locale** for non-emergencies *(☎050 58 35 11).* **Polizia Municipale** *(V. Cesare Battisti 71/72 ☎050 91 08 11).*
- **LATE-NIGHT PHARMACIES: Lugarno Mediceo 51.** *(☎050 54 40 02 ⇆ North shore of river, in the east. ⏰ Open 24hr.)*
- **HOSPITALS/MEDICAL SERVICES: Santa Chiara** provides emergency assistance. *(V. Bonanno ☎050 99 21 11 ⇆ Near P. del Duomo.)*

Getting There

By Plane

Galileo Galilei Airport *(☎050 84 93 00 💻www.pisa-airport.com)* is so close to the city you could walk, but assuming you don't want to do that, the train shuttle *(€1.10)* is only 5min. The shuttle arrives at platform 14 **Pisa Centrale.**

By Train

Pisa Centrale will be your main port of entry from other Italian destinations. *(P. della Stazione ☎050 41 385 ⇆ South of P. Vittorio Emanuele II.)* Trains run to **Florence** *(Ⓢ €5.70. ⏰ 60-80min., on the 32s and 54s 4:15am-1:12am.),* **Rome** *(Ⓢ €17.85. ⏰ 4hr., approx. every hr., 5:45am-7:56pm.),* and **Lucca.** *(Ⓢ €5.10. ⏰ 27min., approx. 2 per hr., 6:20am-9:50pm.)*

By Bus

Lazzi *(☎058 35 84 876 💻www.lazzi.it)* and **CPT** *(☎050 50 55 11 💻www.cpt.pisa)* run buses that leave from and arrive in P. Sant'Antonio. *(Ticket office open daily 7am-8:15pm.)* To **Florence** *(Ⓢ €6.10. ⏰ 2hr., 1 per hr.)* and **Lucca** *(Ⓢ €2. ⏰ 40min., 1 per hr.)*

lucca ☎0583

Ask a native of Lucca to compare Florence to his beloved hometown, and he is likely to mutter dismissively about canine excrement. The fiercely proud Lucchesi have every reason to be protective of their little fortified Brigadoon, as it is everything Florence is not: musical, uncrowded, green, and slow-paced. You can throw away your map here and just get lost—the walls will keep you safe as you wander amid labyrinthine alleys, distinctive *piazze,* and bicycling Lucchesi balancing cappucinos. The amazingly intact 16th-century walls that hug the city not only provide a gorgeous 4km stroll, but also keep out most cars, generic trattorias, and two-days-per-country Round-the-Worlders. As the birthplace of **Puccini,** Lucca is also an extremely musical city, with at least one concert every day of the year—your first stop might be at one of the ubiquitous poster kiosks to find out which university choir is touring through town that day.

Let's Go recommends staying at least a night or two in Lucca and using it as a base to visit Pisa rather than the other way around. You don't want to miss the walls at sunset.

ORIENTATION

Lucca is not a place for checklist tourism. Whether you are here for an afternoon or a week, the best thing to do is get lost. Put a map in your pocket in case of emergency, resist the temptation to follow the stops of the carefully signposted Tourist Route, and have at it. You'll find that despite the secret passages, hidden *piazze,* and winding alleys, these medieval streets are so distinctive that in a day you'll know your way around.

To spell it out for you, **Piazza Napoleone** is in the south, a little west of the cathedral, and is a main entrance point through the city walls. **Via Fillungo,** lined with posh shops and department stores, runs roughly north-south. **Piazza San Michele** is in the center of the Roman section and left of center of the modern city. The other major gateway to the town is **Piazzale Verdi** in the west. If the streets seem like they are begining to spiral in on themselves, you are probably nearing the elliptical **Piazza dell'Anfiteatro** in the north. East of the canal on **Via Del Fosso** you'll find the city's "new" section—a 16th-century extension that does feel rather different from the original city's grid. It's also a bit more lived-in and every bit as lovely. The walls, of course, are all around you.

ACCOMMODATIONS

There's just one hostel in town, but it's big enough to accommodate everyone. You can also get a room at a great B and B for what you would've spent on a hostel in Florence.

★ LA GEMMA DI ELENA — B AND B [2]

V. Della Zecca 33 ☎0583 49 66 65 💻www.virtualica.it/gemma

Most B and Bs feel like they were decorated by a chintzy aunt. This one feels like it was decorated by that awesome guy from college who lived in Tibet and now edits an antiquing blog. It's spacious yet cluttered in an utterly lived-in way, with colorful sarongs on the wall and a wind chime hanging from the chandelier.

➜ Off of V. Del Fosso. $ Singles €35; doubles €55, with bath €65. In low season €5-10 less.

OSTELLO DELLA GIOVENTU (HI) — HOSTEL [1]

V. della Cavallerizza 12 ☎0583 46 99 57 💻www.ostellionline.org

Goodness knows why someone thought Lucca needed an enormous HI hostel, but that means all the more space for you! This former library has impossibly high ceilings and cavernous common spaces. If only there were more people to fill them.

➜ Just past V. San Frediano. $ Dorms €18-22.

B AND B LA TORRE — B AND B [3]

V. del Carmine 11 ☎0583 95 70 44 💻www.roomslatorre.com

Small but tidy rooms feature brass beds and wicker furniture, but the real deal here is the apartment for two to four people that's rented as part of the hotel. True story: the proprietor met his girlfriend when she stayed at La Torre...on *Let's Go*'s recommendation. (Send *your* Let's Go-enabled love stories to us at 💻feedback@letsgo.com.)

➜ Across from the Mercato. $ Singles €35, with bath €50; doubles €50/80; quads €120.

GUESTHOUSE SAN FREDIANO — B AND B [3]

V. Degli Angeli 19 ☎0583 46 96 30 💻www.sanfrediano.com

There's nothing generic in this very personal B and B decorated with letters from former guests, photos of the owner's family, and a mannequin wearing the military uniform of the guesthouse chef's grandfather. The nine rooms have an Alpine lodge feel, with pointed wood-beam ceilings and the occasional skylight.

➜ Off V. Cesare Battisti. $ Singles €40-50, with bath €60-70; doubles €50-70/70-95.

RELAIS SAN LORENZO — B AND B [4]

V. Cesare Battista 15 ☎0583 19 90 191 💻www.sanlorenzorelais.it

The rooms in this floral-scented B and B are named after Puccini operas, but you won't find Mimi's garret here. If you want to go all out, the suite is stunning.

➜ Off V. San Giorgio. $ Singles €55-80; doubles €75-95; suite €130-140.

SIGHTS

This is not a city for tick-box tourism: the main sight is the town itself. Just go have a wander. We're here if you want to read about the things you see.

★ THE WALLS — ♿ WALLS

All around the city

Some cities have a park. This park has a city. Lucca's walls were built as fortification in the second half of the 16th century, an expansion of previous Roman and medieval walls. Despite all their ramparts, sally ports, and cavaliers, however, they never had to face an enemy worse than an 1812 flood. Metaphorically, the walls continue to be a defense—they protect this Tuscan Atlantis from the outside world, keeping this ancient, tiny city's rhythm from being disrupted by the frantic tick-tock of tourism and modernity. "Once it was a place for military protection," says the city's official guide of the walls, "and now it protects memories."

➡ *Walk away from the town center and you're certain to hit them.*

👍 PIAZZA ANFITEATRO — ♿ PIAZZA

In the north of the city

If Lucca's streets begin to seem like they're curving in on themselves, you are probably nearing P. Anfiteatro. Once the site of a Roman amphitheater—hence the name—this is now simply an elliptical *piazza.* Which, when you think about it for a moment, is probably not something you've seen before. There's nothing here except for a handful of nice trattorias and a Puccini gift shop, but the "square's" artful shape alone makes it entirely worth seeking out.

➡ *Follow V. Fillungo to its northernmost point, to P. degli Scalpellini, there's an entrance there.*

👍 TORRE DELL'ORE — 🚫💳🚫♿ TOWERS

V. Fillungo 24

The city of Lucca began renting Torre Dell'Ore to clock-runners in 1390, and it has told Lucca's time ever since. The steep climb to the top takes you through the innards of a working timepiece, with all its mechanisms and bits on display. At the top, you'll have an incredible view of this teeny walled city and the surrounding Tuscan hills.

➡ *Roughly in the center of the city.* $ *€3, students and over 65 €2.* ⏰ *Open daily June-Sept 9:30am-7:30pm; Oct-May 9:30am-6:30pm.*

PUCCINI OPERA — ♿ MUSEUM

V. Santa Giustina 16 ☎0583 95 58 24 💻www.pucciniopera.it

Whether you're a Puccini diehard or haven't even seen *RENT,* this small and free exhibit should be mandatory viewing during a visit to Lucca. It's only a couple rooms, but the texts go a long way towards explaining why Puccini is important to opera and his hometown.

➡ *Off P. San Salvatore.* $ *Free.* ⏰ *Open M 10am-7pm, W-Su 10am-7pm.*

ORTO BOTANICO — 🚫💳♿ GARDEN

V. del Giardino Botanica 14 ☎0583 44 21 61 💻www.comune.lucca.it

The Tuscans love their botanical gardens, even in cities that are already so green and beautiful that it's almost besides the point. This one is superbly maintained, with a winding path up a little hill and a pond full of extremely vocal frogs. Friday evenings in the summer are the best times to visit thanks to the free performances in the courtyard.

➡ *In the southeast corner of the city.* $ *€3, under 14 and over 65 €2, disabled persons and 1 guest free.* ⏰ *Open daily July-Sept 14 10am-7pm; Sept 15-Oct 10am-5pm; Mar 20-Apr 10am-5pm; May-Jun 10am-6pm. Nov-Feb only available by reservation.*

FOOD 🍴

Many of Lucca's loveliest dining spots are tucked into alleyways and hidden courtyards, but at night they are easy to find. Just follow the candles or paper lanterns lining the sidewalk: they likely lead to a quiet and charming dinner spot.

👍 SAN COLOMBANO — 💳♿🍸⛅ RISTORANTE, CAFETERIA ❷

Baluardo di San Colombano ☎0583 46 46 41 💻www.caffetteriasancolombano.it

San Colombano is carved into the city walls, pretty cool, no? The Lucchese specialties are excellent—try the macaroni with gorgonzola and pear sauce. Bottles of wine will run you anywhere from €12 to €200.

➜ In the walls in the southeast. $ Cover €2. Primi €7-9. ⏰ Open Tu-F 8am-1am, Sa 8am-2am.

LUCCA IN TAVOLA

💳♿🍸⛱ CAFE [1]

V. San Paolino 130/132 ☎347 81 55 631 💻www.luccaintavola.it

Diners are encouraged to draw on the plain brown placemats at this sidewalk cafe, and the walls are adorned with past visitors' drawings of Lucca and love letters to the bruschetta *(€4.50)*. Although the four-language menu and the location right off Piazzale Verdi would imply that Lucca in Tavola caters to tourists, the food is nonetheless excellent and cheap.

➜ Just off Piazzale Verdi. $ Bruschettas €4.50. Pizza €5-6.50. ⏰ Open daily 10am-11pm.

ANTICO SIGILLO

💳♿🍸❄⛱ RISTORANTE [2]

V. degli Angeli 13 ☎0583 91 042 💻www.anticosigillo.it

Candles in white paper bags invite passersby on busy V. Fillungo to peer down a passageway and into a romantic courtyard. The restaurant proper is across the street, but the seating is nestled under the arches of the candle-lit courtyard.

➜ Courtyard entrance off V. Fillungo. $ Cover €1.50. Primi €7-12. Chef's specials €8-15. ⏰ Open daily 2-11pm.

FUORI DI PIAZZA

💳♿🍸❄⛱ PIZZERIA [2]

P. Napoleone 16 ☎0583 49 13 22

With beer available by the liter, this place would be listed under nightlife if only it were open later. No matter. For a €1 cover, you can sit right on P. Napoleone with your own personal tap and a giant pizza.

➜ On P. Napoleone. $ Pizza €4.50-6.50. L of beer or wine €8. ⏰ Open daily 10:30am-9:30pm.

GINO'S BAR

💳🚫♿🍸⛱ RISTORANTE [2]

P. XX Septembre 4 ☎335 70 15 311

The inside of Gino's Bar is nothing much, but sitting on the raised deck while having a simple *primi* or a cocktail and watching everyone else hurrying around on the *piazza* is a thing of beauty.

➜ Just off P. Napoleone. $ Primi €6-8. Cocktails €5. 0.5L wine €6. ⏰ Open Tu-Su 11am-11pm.

NIGHTLIFE

Smatterings of nice bars and *enoteche* dot the old city, but areas of particular concentration include the intersection of V. Vittorio Veneto and C. Garibaldi, **Piazza San Michele,** and **Piazza San Frediano.**

👍 ENTE ENTO

💳♿🍸❄⛱ ENOTECA

V. della Polveriera 8 ☎0583 14 52 21

There are a half dozen bars, pubs, and *enoteche* around the intersection of V. Veneto and C. Garibaldo, but the super-mod Ente Ento is our favorite. This *enoteca* fancies itself an old movie. The chic interior is entirely black and white, with glossy photos of Bogie and James Dean on the wall—a splash of red on Marilyn's lips provides the space's only dash of color.

➜ Across from Baluardo Santa Maria. $ Bottled beer €4. Cocktails €5. ⏰ Open M-Tu 7am-1am, Th-F 7am-1am, Sa 7am-2am, Su 7am-1am.

PULT

💳♿🍸⛱ ENOTECA, RISTORANTE

V. Fillungo ☎0583 49 56 32 💻www.pult.it

You will pass PULT many times—its location in the center of V. Fillungo makes it hard to miss. This is definitely a place to hang out conspicuously. If you know anyone in Lucca, you'll probably see him or her while you're sitting here with a glass of wine, and you'll certainly be seen by whoever walks by.

➜ In the middle of V. Fillungo, more or less. $ Liqueurs €4. Bottled beer €5. Wine bottles €25. Primi €10-18. ⏰ Open Tu-Su noon-3:30pm and 7:30-1am.

GELATERIA VENETA

◆&♨ GELATERIA

V. Vittorio Veneto 74 ☎0583 16 70 37 ◩www.gelateriaveneta.net

While it may seem odd to list a *gelateria* as a nighttime destination, visit adorable Veneta in the evening and you'll understand. The locals have made it an after-dinner hotspot in the manner of a 1950s ice cream parlor full of bobby-soxers and drugstore Romeos.

✚ At intersection with C. Garibaldi. ⑤ Cover €1. Cones from €2. ⌚ Open daily 10:30am-1am.

ARTS AND CULTURE

♫

Lucca is an extremely musical town. The **Puccini Festival** ensures at least one performance every single day of the year, and summertime sees an explosion of concerts and musical events.

⬛ PUCCINI E LA SUA LUCCA

◆& OPERA

Chiesa di San Giovanni ☎340 81 06 042 ◩www.puccinielasualucca.com

Hometown hero **Giacomo Puccini** is celebrated every single night of the year in Lucca with recitals of his arias and art songs often paired with vocal music by Mozart and Verdi. That makes this the only permanent ⬛festival in the world and suggests that these folks don't really understand the concept behind festivals.

✚ Off V. Duomo. ⑤ Nightly concerts €17, students €12. ⌚ Tickets on sale at Chiesa di San Giovanni daily 10am-7:15pm.

ESSENTIALS

❷

Practicalities

- **TOURIST OFFICES: Ufficio Regionale** includes an internet point, currency exchange, booking assistance, and a tourist bus checkpoint. (*P. Santa Maria 35* ☎0583 91 99 31 ◩www.luccaturismo.it ✚ Look for "i" sign, on the right. ⌚ Open in summer 9am-8pm; in fall, winter, and spring 9am-1pm and 3-6pm.)

Emergency!

- **POLICE: Polizia Municipale.** (*Vle. Camillo Benso Conte di Cavour 1* ☎0583 45 51 ✚ Outside the walls to the south.) **Carabinieri.** (*Cortile degli Svizzeri* ☎0583 47 821 ✚ In the southwest of the centro.)

- **LATE-NIGHT PHARMACIES: Farmacia Comunale.** (*P. Curatone* ✚ Outside the city walls, opposite Baluardo San Colombano. ⌚ Open 24hr.)

- **HOSPITALS/MEDICAL SERVICES: Campodi Marte** provides emergency medical attention. (*V. dell'Ospedale* ☎0583 95 57 91 ✚ Outside the city walls, in the northeast corner. ⌚ Open for emergencies 24hr.)

Getting There

✈

By Train

The **train station** is in Piazzale Ricasoli, just south of the city walls. (⌚ Ticket office open daily 6:30am-8:10pm. Station open M-F 4:30am-12:30am, Sa-Su 5:30am-12:30am.) To **Florence** (⑤ €5.10. ⌚ 80min., on 32s and 39s 5:05am-10:32pm.), **Pisa** (⑤ €2.40. ⌚ 30min., on 42s and 12s 7am-9:42pm.), and numerous local destinations.

By Bus

Lazzi (☎0583 58 78 97 ◩www.valibus.it) in Piazzale Verdi. To **Florence** (⑤ €5.10. ⌚ 70min., 1-2 per hr.), and **Pisa.** (⑤ €2.40. ⌚ 50min., 1-2 per hr.)

naples *napoli* ☎081

Naples is a bustling, hectic city—revel in it if you like, revile it if you must, just don't be scared by it. Travelers who know where they're going (or just look like they do) will fare best. Traffic zooms through the streets in lanes half the width of the painted lines. Red lights are mere suggestions. Crossing the street is a battle of wills—one of which has a V8 engine on its side. Yet Neopolitans take it all in stride. Cheerful chaos is a lifestyle they have eagerly adopted, though they now take out the trash, and much of the crime and grime has gone with it. Laughing together in one hearty chuckle, locals seem to spend every waking hour on the town, drinking, smoking, carousing, and eating.

It's a shame tourists often treat this city as a mere stopover while exploring nearby attractions. All they see is the train station—unruly and unclean, the worst of stereotypical Naples, but many areas have the beauty of a resort town. Scrub off the grime and graffitti, and there's much to be found in the city's architecturally masterful *centro*. Don't trust us? Trust UNESCO, which recently deemed Naples' historical center a **World Heritage Site.** For millennia, the city has been an outpost for the world's greatest civilizations, so forgive Naples its untidiness and petty crime: the continent and, really, the world as they stand in the modern era owe a lot to this scrappy city.

ORIENTATION

Stazione Centrale and Centro Storico

Naples's transit hub, Stazione Centrale opens onto the vast, chaotic **Piazza Garibaldi,** full of vendors and traffic that stops for no man or woman. Hotels surround the *piazza* and fill its nearby streets. The neighborhood is seedy, and many streets are, in fact, lined with trash. A little further west, the Centro Storico, also known as Spaccanapoli, is Naples's oldest neighborhood, filled with tiny alleys and beautiful architecture.Though you may stay near the train station, for sightseeing, eating, and nightlife, you should definitely head to more central parts of the city.

Western Naples

The neighborhoods just get nicer as you get further away from the train station. **Piazza del Plebiscito** was once one of the most important locations in Naples, home to the Palazzo Reale and a stunning church. Today, it has declined in vitality but remains central to the city. The **Spanish Quarter** is to the northwest and features a number of small but bustling streets heading up the hill. On a hill high above the city (best ascended by funicular), **Vomero** is classy and serene. Going even further west, **Chiaia** is fashionable while closer to sea level.

ACCOMMODATIONS

The first thing most travelers see upon arriving in Naples is a neon junkyard of hotels in the hectic and unpleasant area near **Stazione Centrale.** Don't trust anyone who approaches you in the station—people working on commission are happy to lead naive tourists to unlicensed and overpriced hotels seedier than those you could find on your own. There are several comfortable and inexpensive options in this area; just be careful when returning at night. **Centro Storico** and **Piazza del Plebiscito** have much better-located options, though at noticeably higher prices. Progressing further west, **Vomero, Chiaia,** and **Mergellina** boast numerous hospitable bed and breakfasts in quiet areas that provide excellent views of the city or the sea.

Stazione Centrale and Centro Storico

Accommodations in Naples's historical heart are more convenient and thus pricier, but they'll put travelers just a dough's throw away from the ancient streets that are the pizza capital of the world.

6 SMALL ROOMS

HOSTEL ❶

V. Diodato Lioy 18 ☎081 79 01 378 www.6smallrooms.com

Modesty may be a virtue, but the Australian owners of this beautiful hostel seem to be taking it a bit far with the name of this place. Most of the "small" rooms are huge, with high ceilings and fun, elaborate murals of the city and ancient Roman gods.

 # [M]1: Dante. Walk down V. Toledo, turn left onto V. Tommaso Senise, and make the 1st right onto V. Diodato Lioy. i Some rooms with A/C. $ Dorms €20; singles €25-45; doubles €50-65; triples €60-75; quads €80-95. 10% Let's Go discount.

NAPLES PIZZA HOSTEL

HOSTEL ❶

V. San Paulo ai Tribunali ☎081 19 32 35 62 www.naplespizzahostel.com

When guests open the door to their room, it's clear this hostel is a step above the rest. Most chambers have loft beds up a set of steps above the other bunks, creating a secret, secluded single within a dorm. One guest apparently enjoyed her stay so much that she painted a mural of—what else?—happy students eating Neopolitan pizza on the orange walls of the common room.

 # Taking V. Tribunali from the station, turn right onto V. San Paulo ai Tribunali. $ 5-bed dorms €15-18; singles €25-40; doubles €35-55; triples €49-70, quads €65-79.

HOTEL GINEVRA

HOTEL ❷

V. Genova 116 ☎081 28 32 10 www.hotelginevra.it

Exiting Naples's train station is always an adventure, but few expect a full-blown safari. Get ready for it as you walk into this hotel and investigate its "ethnic" rooms, which come with elephant carvings on the door, bamboo on the walls, and vines on the ceiling.

 # Take the 1st right out of the station onto C. Novara, then the next right onto V. Genova. $ Singles €25-45; doubles €35-65; triples €45-75. 10% Let's Go discount.

HOSTEL PENSIONE MANCINI

HOSTEL, PENSIONE ❶

V. P.S. Mancini 33 ☎081 55 36 731 www.hostelpensionemancini.com

The helpful owners make this hostel, located in a distinctly average building, stand out. Bedrooms are comfortable, some with balconies. But the overwhelming hospitality of an owner who organizes outings for and shares extensive knowledge of the city with his guests is the real bonus of staying here.

 # Directly across the piazza from the station. $ Dorms €13-16; singles €25-30, with bath €40-45; doubles €35-45/40-50; triples €54-66/60-70; quads €60-68/70-80. 10% Let's Go discount.

HOTEL ZARA

HOTEL ❷

V. Firenze 81 ☎081 28 71 25 www.hotelzara.it

Comfy common areas with deep couches, large TV, and a fish tank make socializing easy, while the simple rooms make for a good night's sleep.

 # Walk down the right side of P. Garibaldi from the station and turn onto V. Milano, then right onto V. Firenze. $ Singles €25-35; doubles €30, with bath €35; triples €50/60.

Western Naples

HOSTEL OF THE SUN

HOSTEL ❶

V. Melisurgo 15, 7th fl. ☎081 42 06 393 www.hostelnapoli.com

This hostel is quite simply the most fun place you can stay in Naples. The exuberant—somehow even that strong word seems too weak—staff begins everyone's stay with an in-depth and amusing introduction to the city and a collection of free maps to stuff in pockets. They keep it going by hosting several outings weekly, occasionally cooking for guests, and relaxing with them in the colorful and comfortable common room which features a flatscreen TV, DVDs, computers, and Nintendo Wii. (The owner has been known to challenge guests; those who beat him get a free stay, though he claims an undefeated record.)

 # Take the R2 bus from C. Umberto I near the station, get off at the 2nd stop on V. Depretis.

i *Breakfast included. Private rooms with ensuite A/C. Free lockers. Free internet and Wi-Fi.* Ⓢ *5- to 7-bed dorms €16-20; doubles €55-60, with bath €60-70; triples €75-80/€70-90; quads €80-90/€85-100. 10% Let's Go discount.* ⏰ *Reception 24hr.*

🏨 CAPPELLA VECCHIA 11 ✈⊗(ⁿ)❄ B AND B ❹

Vicolo Santa Maria a Cappella Vecchia 11, 1st fl. ☎081 24 05 117 🖥www.cappellavecchia11.it
Meeting other travelers has never been easier than at the communal breakfast
table of this well kept B and B. The common room has comfortable couches and
a public computer, while the beds are cozy and the bathrooms large. If cappella
Vecchia is full, head across the hall to **Napoliday,** (☎081 24 81 106 🖥www.napoliday.it)
which is equally nice and only slightly pricier.
🚶 *From V. Santa Caterina just before P. dei Martiri, turn onto the small alleyway of Vicolo Santa
Maria a Cappella Vecchia. Take the stairs to the right.* Ⓢ *Singles €50-70; doubles €80-110.*

🏨 HOTEL AND HOSTEL BELLA CAPRI ✈⅋(ⁿ)❄ HOSTEL ❶

V. Meilsurgo 4, 6th fl. ☎081 55 29 494 🖥www.bellacapri.it
The ground-floor hotel for people over 30 here is kept well-hidden from the
groups of students who occupy the upper floor. Every night is a social occasion,
with guests cooking in the communal kitchen, chatting, and gathering for near-
nightly outings to bars in the *centro*.
🚶 *R2 bus from C. Umberto I near the station to the 2nd stop on V. Depretis. After hours, ring
bell.* Ⓢ *Dorms €15-21; singles €40-50, with bath €50-70; doubles €50-60/€60-80; triples €70-
80/€80-100; quads €80-90/€90-110. 10% Let's Go discount.*

HOTEL TOLEDO ✈⊗(ⁿ)❄ HOTEL ❹

V. Montecalvario 15 ☎081 40 68 00 🖥www.hoteltoledo.com
The peaceful rooftop terrace is just one highlight of this Spanish Quarter property's common areas. They also include a large bar with throne-like dining chairs
and couches that guests sink into while enjoying a nightcap.
🚶 *From P. Dante, walk down V. Toledo and turn right onto V. Montecalvario.* Ⓢ *Singles €50-65;
doubles €70-100; suites €100-120.*

SIGHTS

Been there, done that. So the Greeks, Romans, and Spanish have each said about the
city of Naples, and each of their conquests has left a unique mark on this remarkably historical metropolis. Home to a world-renowned antiquarian museum and an
ancient underground system that remains a remarkable feat of engineering, Naples
has got the really-old thing covered.

Stazione Centrale and Centro Storico

Part wide boulevards with ornate achitecture, part Roman alleys, Naples's Centro
Storico has a history that is palpable.

🏛 NAPOLI SOTTERANEA (UNDERGROUND NAPLES) ⊙⊗ ANCIENT ROME

P. San Gaetano 68 ☎081 29 69 44 🖥www.napolisotterranea.org
Get down and dirty 35m below the city exploring ancient Greek aqueducts,
World War II bomb shelters, and more. Visitors wander through passageways,
grottoes, and catacombs, and while most of the tunnels are cavernous and well
lit, the last part of the tour has patrons shimmying through a tiny tunnel in the
rock with only candles illuminating the way.
🚶 *Take V. Tribunali and the entrance is to the left of San Paolo Maggiore church.* Ⓢ *€9.30, students €8.* ⏰ *90min. tours depart every 2hr. M-F noon-4pm, Sa-Su 10am-6pm.*

🏛 MUSEO ARCHEOLOGICO NAZIONALE ⊙⅋ MUSEUM, ANCIENT ROME

P. Museo Nazionale 19 ☎081 29 28 23 🖥museoarcheologiconazionale.campaniabeniculturali.it
Even if the prospect of more archaeological specimens has no appeal for
you, you've got to be intrigued by the more salacious stuff on display at this
museum. It's home to the ever-popular **Gabinetto Segreto** ("Secret Cabinet"),

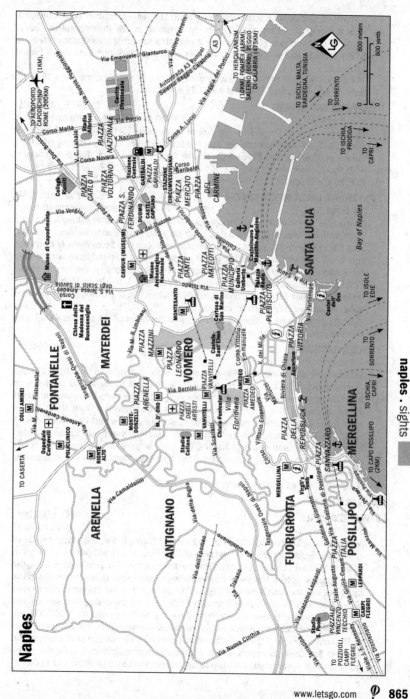

Naples

TO AÉROPORTO
CAPODICHINO (1KM);
ROME (200KM)

Via Don Bosco

TO CASERTA

V.C. Lahalle

Corso Malta

Via Emanuele - Gianturco

Via Nuova Poggioreale

Stadio Albricci

Autostrada A3 Pompei
Salerno Reggio-Calabria

Via Reggia del Portici

A3

(TO HERCULANEUM
(10KM); POMPEII (18KM);
SALERNO (60KM); REGGIO
DI CALABRIA (475KM)

Corso Novara

PIAZZA
NAZIONALE

V.Nazionale

Centro
Direzionale

Via Porzio

PIAZZA
CARLO III

PIAZZA
VOLTURNO

Collegio
Ruoti

Stazione
Centrale

GARIBALDI

Corso A. Lucci

Stazione
CIRCUMVESUVIANA

PIAZZA
GARIBALDI

Corso
Garibaldi

TO SICILY, MALTA,
SARDEGNA, TUNISIA

PIAZZA
FERDINANDO

CASTEL
CAPUANO

Via del Duomo

Via S.

PIAZZA S.

Via Foria

Via Vergini

Museo di Capodimonte

Corso S. Teresa degli Scalzi di Savoia

PIAZZA
MERCATO

DEL
CARMINE

TO SORRENTO

TO ISCHIA,
PROCIDA

CAVOUR

Museo
Archeologico
Nazionale

DUOMO

PIAZZA
DANTE

PIAZZA
MATEOTTI

Castelnuovo o
Maschio Angioino

TO CAPRI

Chiesa della
Madonna del
Buonconsiglio

FONTANELLE

MATERDEI

MONTESANTO

Certosa di
San Martino

PIAZZA
MUNICIPIO

Galleria
Umberto I

Palazzo
Reale

SANTA LUCIA

Bay of Naples

COLLI AMINEI

Via M. Pietravalle

Via Antonio Cardarelli

Tangenziale Ovest di Napoli

PIAZZA
MAZZINI

VOMERO

Castello
di Sant'Elmo

Corso Vittorio
Emanuele

PIAZZA
PLEBISCITO

PIAZZA
VITTORIA

Via N. Sauro

Castel
dell'Ovo

TO ISOLE
EOLIE

Ospedale
Cardarelli

POLICLINICO

Via M.-R.Imbriani

PIAZZA
LEONARDO

PIAZZA
ARENELLA

Via Bernini

VANVITELLI

Villa
Floridiana

V. del Molo

Via Scarlatti

Via Parterope

Aquarium

PIAZZA
AMEDEO

Riviera di Chiaia

TO
SORRENTO

MONTE-
DONZELLI

M.D.'ORO

PIAZZA
DEGLI
ARTISTI

Chiaia Funicolare

AMEDEO

Corso Vittoria Emanuele

TO ISCHIA
CAPRI

RIONE
ALTO

Stadio
Collana

PIAZZA
VANVITELLI

PIAZZA
DELLA
REPUBBLICA

MERGELLINA

Virgil's
Tomb

SANNAZZARO

PIAZZA

TO CAPO POSILLIPO
(2KM)

ARENELLA

ANTIGNANO

Via Camaldolilir

Via della Pigna

Via dell'Epomeo

Tangenziale Ovest

FUORIGROTTA

Galleria di Napoli

Galleria A. Giornate

Via F. Galiani di Posillipo

PIAZZA
ITALIA

LEOPARDI

POSILLIPO

Via Marechiaro

MERGELLINA

Via Nuova Cinthia

Via Giacomo Leopardi

Via Giustiniano

Viale Augusto

Viale Giulio-Cesare

CAMPI
FLEGREI

Stadio
S. Paolo

PIAZZALE
VINCENZO
TECCHIO

PIAZZALE

Via Diocleziano

TO
POZZUOLI,
CAMPI
FLEGREI

Viale J.-F. Kennedy

800 meters

800 yards

Bay of Naples

naples · sights

a trove of sexual artifacts recovered from the ash-entombed archaeological site at Pompeii. Of course, the entire museum is not pornographic—heck, some of it's even good for kids—as it contains the most significant collection of artifacts from the nearby towns that were destroyed by Vesuvius's famed eruption.

‡ Ⓜ Cavour. Turn right from the station and walk 2 blocks. $ €10, EU citizens ages 18-24 €5, under 18 and over 65 free. 🕐 Open M 9am-7:30pm, W-Su 9am-7:30pm.

CAPPELLA SAN SEVERO

◉⊗ CHURCH, MUSEUM

V. de Sanctis 19 ☎081 55 18 470 🖥www.museosansevero.it

Here's one fewer church in a city full of them—this 1590 chapel has been converted to a private museum. Several remarkable 18th-century statues, of which Giuseppe Sanmartino's ✪**Veiled Christ** is by far the best known, fill the corridors.

‡ To the right when walking away from P. San Domenico Maggiore $ €6, ages 10-25 €4, with Artecard €5. 🕐 Open M 10am-5:40pm, W-Sa 10am-5:40pm, Su 10am-1:10pm.

PIO MONTE DELLA MISERICORDIA

◉⊗ MUSEUM

V. Tribunali 253 ☎081 44 69 44 🖥www.piomontedellamisericordia.it

Life on the run was good to Caravaggio, or so it appears. After killing a man in a 1606 duel, the master became a fugitive from justice and fled to Naples, where he was commissioned to paint one of his masterpieces, **The Seven Works of Mercy,** for this small chapel. That painting is the centerpiece of a round nave surrounded by works of art. More hang above, in the former offices of the centuries-old charitable organization that commissioned the chapel. Works by **Mattia Preti** and **Francesco de Mura** fill several rooms, while a balcony in one office offers a superb view of Caravaggio's work from above.

‡ On V. Tribunali, before V. Duomo when coming from the station. $ €5, students €4. 🕐 Open M-Tu 9am-2pm, Th-Su 9am-2pm.

PIAZZA GARIBALDI

♿ PIAZZA

P. Garibaldi

Don't worry about missing this *piazza*—it truly is a sight to behold, if not the prettiest picture to put on a postcard. P. Garibaldi is to Naples as Naples is to Italy: its most incomprehensibly chaotic outpost. Street vendors stake out their sidewalk claims like 1849 California miners, only here the Gold Rush comes from tourists' pockets in exchange for cheap sunglasses and knockoff bags. A spider web of roads and Neopolitan drivers who won't stop add to the disorder. Unlike the streets in much of Naples, the ones here really are lined with trash. At the end of the *piazza* farthest from the trains, **Garibaldi** himself watches over the scene.

‡ Outside Stazione Centrale and at the end of C. Umberto.

Western Naples

✪ PALAZZO REALE

◉⊗ MUSEUM

P. del Plebiscito 1 ☎081 40 05 47

Visitors can play royalty for a day wandering through the magnificent halls of this sprawling structure, once the seat of Bourbon kings and Spanish viceroys in Naples. Wander through artwork-filled rooms and see—but don't dare sit in—the velvet-draped golden throne of former kings, whose exploits are recounted in the aptly but not succinctly named fresco, *The Splendor of the House of Spain and Some Episodes in the Life of Ferrante of Aragon*, on the ceiling in a subsequent room. The palace is also an intellectual mecca, as it contains the 1,500,000 volume **Biblioteca Nazionale,** which holds carbonized scrolls from the Villa dei Papiri in Herculaneum. As if this *palazzo* wasn't packed with enough stuff already, the **Teatro di San Carlo**, Europe's oldest continuously active theater, calls the place home as well. Its acoustics are reputedly better than those of Milan's **La Scala.**

➡ *In P. del Plebiscito.* $ *€4, students €2.* ⏰ *Open M-Tu 9am-8pm, Th-Su 9am-8pm.*

👍 CASTEL SANT'ELMO — ⊗ ♿ CASTLE, MUSEUM

V. Tito Angelini 20 ☎081 22 94 401 💻www.polomusealenapoli.beniculturali.it

Stop, gulp in some air, and step up to the wall and gaze out. You'll need that oxygen, because this view—standing eye level with airplanes—truly takes the breath away. Once a defensive outpost, the ramparts of P. d'Armi atop this castle are one of Naples's loveliest places. They're also now part of a creative art installation by **Giancarlo Neri** which uses lighting to artificially "compete" with the moon in certain parts of the city. **Napoli Novecento,** an extensive modern art museum featuring canvases and sculpture from the last century of Neopolitan modern art, can be found in the old fortress as well.

➡ *In Vomero. From the funicular at P. Fuga, turn right up the steps and follow the signs along V. Morghen to the castle.* $ *€5, EU students ages 18-25 €2.50.* ⏰ *Open M 8:30am-7:30pm, W-Su 8:30am-7:30pm. Guided tours of the museum offered hourly 9am-6pm.*

BASILICA DI SAN FRANCESCO DI PAOLO — ⊗ CHURCH

P. del Plebiscito 10 ☎081 76 45 133

Designed to mimic the Pantheon in Rome, this towering domed church is no copycat. It's interior is soaring—54m high and 34m in diameter—and bright like its Roman counterpart, but the basilica is not exactly like its pagan counterpart, as it features carved statues of saints surrounding the nave (though we could get into an interesting conversation about Catholicism's use of sainthood as a way to appeal to pagan polytheism here if we really wanted to get deep). The building dominates P. del Plebiscito.

➡ *The building with the large dome.* ℹ *Modest dress required.* $ *Free.* ⏰ *Open M-Sa 8am-noon and 3:30-7pm, Su 8:30am-1pm and 4-7pm.*

MUSEO NAZIONALE DI CAPODIMONTE — ⊗ ♿ MUSEUM

V. Miano 2 ☎081 74 99 111 💻www.museo-capodimonte.it

Here is a true rarity among museums, especially in Italy: a collection that features classical works alongside contemporary art. Though it's famous for its **Farnese Collection,** once owned by a family of the same name, the museum has much more going for it than that. Formerly a royal palace, the *museo* boasts many rooms that are precious artifacts in themselves, though unlike 2D paintings, these works of art can hold visitors inside them. In the second floor's Neopolitan collection, works by **Caravaggio** and numerous 19th-century masters from the city are on display.

➡ *In the north of the city.* Ⓜ*Cavour, then bus C63 or R4.* $ *€7.50, EU students ages 18-25 €3.75.* ⏰ *Open M-Tu 8:30am-7:30pm, Th-Su 8:30am-7:30pm.*

CASTEL DELL'OVO (EGG CASTLE) — ♿ CASTLE

Borgo Marinari ☎081 24 00 055

All that fuss over an egg? Yes indeed, throughout the city's history one measly egg has caused a string of panics. According to legend, the enchanted egg in question was placed in this castle's foundation by **Virgil.** If its fragile shell were to break, the city of Naples would crumble. After the yellow-brick castle sustained significant damage when one of its arches collapsed, none other than the queen herself had to reassure the public that the egg was safe. Originally a monastery, the castle was later converted to be used for defensive purposes but is now mostly used for its beautiful views, especially at sunset.

➡ *Walk down V. Santa Lucia from south of P. del Plebiscito.* $ *Free.* ⏰ *Open M-Sa 8:30am-7pm, Su 8:30am-2pm.*

SPAGGIA ROTONDA DIAZ — ⊗ BEACH

V. Francesco Caracciolo

Capri and Ischia, Sorrento and Amalfi—they're all so far away. Spaggia Rotonda is right here in the heart of Naples, and it's a Neopolitan **beach** at its finest. This is the perfect spot for working on the southern Italian tan you see on everyone around you.

🚶 Walk down V. Caracciolo along the waterfront from Mergellina or Chiaia. $ Free. ⏰ Open daily sunrise to sunset.

FOOD

When in Rome, do as the Romans do. When in Naples, eat 👍**pizza**. If you ever doubted that Neopolitans invented the crusty, cheese-covered pie, the city's pizzerias will take that doubt, beat it into a ball, throw it in the air, spin it on their collective finger, punch it down, cover it with sauce and mozzarella, and serve it *alla margherita.* Centro Storico is full of excellent choices, especially along **Via Tribunali,** the pizza corridor of the world.

Stazione Centrale and Centro Storico

👍 ANTICA PIZZA DA MICHELE ♿🚭🍸 PIZZERIA [1]

V. Cesare Sersale 1/3 ☎081 55 39 204 💻www.damichele.net

All the people here must know something. They take numbers from the chef inside, then wait around in the hot midday sun, sometimes for 1hr. What they're waiting for has been called, by some, the best pizza in the world. The options may be limited to margherita and marinara *(€4.50),* with the option of double cheese *(€5.50),* but once a pie is in front of you, you know it's the real deal.

🚶 Walk down C. Umberto I and turn right. ⏰ Open M-Sa 10am-11pm.

👍 GINO SORBILLO 💳🚭🍸❄ PIZZERIA [1]

V. dei Tribunali 35 ☎081 44 66 43 💻www.sorbillo.eu

Making pizza and children since 1935, Gino Sorbillo has created a dynasty: a family of 21 pizza-making children, several of whom own their own shops nearby. His eponymous shop also gave birth to the *ripieno al forno* (literally "fried in the oven"), a.k.a. the calzone.

🚶 Between V. Arti and Vico San Paolo. $ Pizza €3-8. ⏰ Open Sept-July M-Sa noon-3:30pm and 7-11:30pm.

👍 PIZZERIA DI MATTEO 💳🚭🍸❄ PIZZERIA [1]

V. dei Tribunali 94 ☎081 45 52 62 💻www.pizzeriadimatteo.it

This place has its priorities straight: while diners at Pizzeria Di Matteo have to take the stairs, the pizza rides to the dining room in an elevator. The Neopolitans that fill the tables aren't bothered by the unhurried service.

🚶 On V. dei Tribunali near V. Duomo. $ Pizza €2.50-6. ⏰ Open M-Sa 9am-midnight.

ANTICA TRATTORIA DEL CARMINE 💳🚭🍸❄ RISTORANTE, SEAFOOD [3]

V. dei Tibunali 330 ☎081 29 43 83

Recommended by locals as a great date spot or stop for some quality fish or pasta, this trattoria with a multi-level dining room under brick arches retains the rustic, ancient charm of Naples's historic center.

🚶 Directly across from Napoli Sotteranea. $ Primi €4-13; secondi €7-10. Fish €7.50-13. ⏰ Open Tu noon-4pm, W-Su noon-4pm and 7-11pm.

SORRISO INTEGRALE ♿🚭🍸❄☁ VEGETARIAN [2]

Vico S. Pietro a Maiella 6 ☎081 45 50 26 💻www.sorriosointegrale.com

Naples making you feel like you're becoming round and sprouting tomato sauce and mozzarella? At some point, take a break from pizza and pasta to try this small, hidden organic and vegan restaurant with a constantly changing menu.

🚶 Near P. Miraglia, on the small connecting street between Vico S. Pietro a Maiella and P. Bellini. Inside the gate on the right when heading to P. Bellini. $ Cover €2. Primi €4.50; secondi €5.50-7.50. ⏰ Open daily noon-4pm and 7-11pm.

Western Naples

This area has plenty of nice cafes and a little diversity for a break from pizza.

👍 **HOSTERIA TOLEDO** 💳🚭🍸❄ RISTORANTE ❷

Vicolo Giardinetto 78/A ☎081 42 12 57 🖥www.hosteriatoledo.it

Specializing in pasta and seafood, this homey spot has axed pizza from its menu in a dramatic, anti-establishment move largely unheard of in the Neopolitan culinary scene.

➜ Take Vicolo Giardinetto off V. Toledo. $ Primi €6.50-8; secondi €7-14. ⏰ Open M 1-4pm and 7pm-midnight, Tu 1-4pm, Th-Su 1-4pm and 7pm-midnight.

👍 **TRATTORIA NENNELLA** 🚭♿🍸⛅ RISTORANTE ❷

Vicolo Lungo Teatro Nuovo 105 ☎081 41 43 38

From construction workers to bankers, Neopolitans gather here for long and leisurely lunches at unbelieveably low fixed prices from a menu consisting of a *primo*, *secondo*, *contorno*, fruit, and wine.

➜ Walk up Vicolo Teatro Nuovo and look for the signs near Vicolo Lungo Teatro Nuovo $ Prix-fixe menu €10. ⏰ Open M-Sa noon-3pm and 7-10:30pm. Closed in Aug.

👍 **FRIGGITORIA VOMERO** 🚭🚭 BAKERY ❶

V. Domenico Cimarosa 44 ☎081 57 83 130

Super-quick, super-cheap, and about as Neopolitan as a place can be, this no-frills fast-food joint fills its flour-dusted display cases with fried dough creations.

➜ In Vomero. Head away from the funicular at P. Fuga and look across the square. $ Fried foods €0.20-2. Panini €2.50 ⏰ Open M-Sa 9:30am-2:30pm and 5:30-8:30pm.

PIZZERIA GORIZIA 💳🚭🍸❄⛅ PIZZERIA ❷

V. Bernini 29-31 ☎081 57 82 248

From late lunch through late at night, this place is packed with local diners. They're rewarded with a delicious pizza *crudaiola (€8)*, a piping-hot and pie with *mozzarella di bufala*, tomato, prosciutto, oregano, and olive oil.

➜ In Vomero. From the funicular at P. Fuga, take V. Cimarosa to the left and turn right onto V. Bernini. $ Cover €1. Pizza €5-8. Primi €6-13; secondi €8-15. ⏰ Open Tu-Su 12:30-4pm and 6:30pm-midnight.

HAPPY MAX KEBAB 🚭♿ KEBAB ❶

P. Giulio Rodino 35

Try what locals call the best kebab in Naples—just don't look for any seating or superfluities.

➜ In Chiaia. Take V. Chiaia from V. Toledo and turn right onto the small piazza and V. Filangieri before P. dei Martiri. $ Sandwiches €3.50. ⏰ Open daily 11:30am-midnight.

NIGHTLIFE

The discos in Naples may be few and far between—literally—but the city is not without after-hours activity. Its *centro* and fashionable outer neighborhoods bustle with bars and students in *piazze* drinking cheap beer from—where else?—local pizza joints. Just avoid the area around **Stazione Centrale;** it's extremely sketchy at night.

Stazione Centrale and Centro Storico

👍 **TROPICANA** 🚭🚭🍸❄ CLUB, LATIN

V. San Giuseppe dei Ruffi 14 ☎338 23 08 288

Whether they come from Buenos Aires or Bolivia, Brazil or Bogota, they're welcome here. Those who don't speak a Latin language are warmly welcomed too, but their nation's flag won't be on the wall at this salsa and Latin music club, one of Naples's most hopping hidden spots. A packed, small dance floor moves into a frenzy when the DJ starts spinning.

➜ Just off V. Duomo. $ 1st drink €5, €3.50 per drink thereafter. ⏰ Open daily midnight-6am.

LEMME LEMME BY INTERNET BAR 🚭🚭📶🍸❄⛅ BAR

P. Bellini 74 ☎081 29 52 37

Sway to the beat, check your email, grab a drink, or check the score—the free internet at this popular bar is great for everything except your social life. Stay away from the screen and mingle with the locals who gather on this pretty *piazza*. You can friend them all on Facebook later.

➔ ⓂDante. Walk through Porta Alba and turn left onto V. Santa Maria di Constantinopoli; the piazza is immediately to the right. Ⓢ Beer €3-5.50. ⏰ Open M-Sa 9am-3am, Su 5pm-3am.

ARTS CAFE
◆🚭🍸❄ CLUB

V. San Giuseppe dei Nudi 9 ☎081 21 88 467 💻www.artscafe.eu

An older crowd gathers for an old-school spectacle nightly at this club featuring everything from jazz quartets to Vaudeville-esque shows in its simple venue near the Museo Nazionale.

➔ From V. Santa Teresa degli Scalzi (V. Roma) across from the museum, take the zigzagging street upward to the cafe. Ⓢ Drinks €5, with dinner €20. ⏰ Open daily 6pm-1am.

CAFFÉ LETTERARIO INTRA MOENIA
◆🚭📶🍸❄⛅ BAR

P. Bellini 70 ☎081 29 07 20 💻www.intramoenia.it

A more relaxed, literary crowd gathers here in an attempt to escape the nightly beat on the bar-filled *piazza*. This place's interior might appeal to those with an insatiable desire to drink in a library—it's filled with shelves, wood paneling, and an interesting collection of old clocks.

➔ ⓂDante. Walk through Porta Alba and turn left onto V. Santa Maria di Constantinopoli; the piazza is immediately to the right. Ⓢ Beer €4-5. Cocktails €7-8. ⏰ Open daily 10am-1am.

Western Naples

👍 GOODFELLAS
◆🚭🍸❄ BAR

V. Morghen 34 ☎340 92 25 475 💻www.goodfellasclub.com

This is a good old sports bar—except there's hardly any sports on TV. Screens show MTV along with the occasional soccer match, while cover bands take to the stage three nights weekly at 11pm. There are some sports around—the Chicago Bulls jerseys and baseball posters on the wall ensure that.

➔ In Vomero. Up the stairs from the funicular in P. Fuga and to the left. Ⓢ 0.5L wine €3.50. Beer €5. Cocktails €7. ⏰ Open Tu-Su 8pm-2am.

👍 S'MOVE
◆🚭🍸❄⛅ BAR

Vico dei Sospiri 10/A ☎081 76 45 813 💻www.smove-lab.net

This bar is the closest one can come to getting groovy in summertime Naples, as a DJ spins house, funk, or rap most nights to create the feeling of being at a disco, without most of the dancing.

➔ In Chiaia. From P. dei Martiri, take V. Alabardieri, then make the 2nd left. Ⓢ Beer €5. Cocktails €7-8. ⏰ Open daily 7pm-4am. Aperitivo 7-9pm.

LES BELLES CHOSES
●🚭🍸❄⛅ IRISH PUB

V. Cesario Console 15/16 ☎081 24 51 166

Les Belles Choses is a little like a pug: not so beautiful, but oh-so-friendly. The beers are cool and the staff and patrons are warm.

➔ Just south of P. del Plebiscito. Ⓢ Beer €3-4. Cocktails €6.50. ⏰ Open M-Tu 6:30pm-1:30am, W-Sa 6:30pm-4am, Su 6:30pm-1:30am. Sometimes open later depending on crowds.

VINTAGE
◆🚭🍸❄⛅ ENOTECA

V. Bernini 37/A ☎081 22 95 473 💻www.vintageweb.it

Vomero's first wine bar makes quite an impression. On nights when a DJ plays inside, the sound bursts onto the street and draws in a line of young people who would otherwise stay at the tables outdoors. Then the dance floor gets hot and sweaty in an almost anti-*enoteca* way. (This is not your mother's wine bar.)

➔ In Vomero. From the funicular at P. Fuga, take V. Bernini past P. Vanvitelli. Ⓢ Wine €5. Cocktails €7. ⏰ Open M-Th 7pm-1am, F-Sa 7pm-3am. Happy hour 7-9:30pm. Closed 2 weeks in Aug.

Practicalities

- **TOURIST OFFICES: EPT** offers booking services, free maps, and the indispensible guide ▨**Qui Napoli,** which includes abundant hotel and restaurant listings. (*P. dei Martiri 58* ☎*081 41 07 211* ▣*www.eptnapoli.info* 🕐 *Open M-F 9am-2pm.*)

- **INTERNET:** Internet points are clustered around V. Mezzocannone and P. Bellini. **Lemme Lemme by Internet Bar** offers computer terminals and free Wi-Fi. (*P. Bellini 74* ☎*081 29 52 37* 🛢 *Computers €0.05 per min.* 🕐 *Open M-Sa 9am-3am, Su 5pm-3am.*)

Emergency!

- **POLICE: Polizia Municipale** (☎*081 75 13 177*). **Polizia del Stato** can be found at V. Medina, near P. Matteoti, or at P. Garibaldi 22, directly across the *piazza* from the station.

- **HOSPITALS/MEDICAL SERVICES: Incurabili** is more helpful than its name might suggest. (*P. Cavour* ☎*081 25 49 422* ✠ Ⓜ*Cavour (Museo). The emergency ward is directly up V. Maria Longo.*)

Getting There ☒

By Plane

Aeroporto Capodichino (NAP) (*Vle. Ruffo Fulco di Calabria* ☎*081 84 88 87 73 or 081 75 15 471* ▣*www.gesac.it* 🕐 *Open daily 5:30am-11:30pm.*) is located in the northeast of the city and is a great point of access to the whole Bay of Naples area. The red and white **Alibus** shuttle travels from the airport arrivals terminal to the seaport near P. Municio and to P. Garibaldi. (🛢 *€3.10.* 🕐 *15-20min.*)

By Train

Stazione Centrale is in the crazy part of Naples, by P. Garibaldi. Trains come from **Rome.** (🛢 *From €12.* 🕐 *1-3hr., every 30min. 5:40am-10:10pm.*) **Eurostar** trains operated by Trenitalia arrive from **Milan** via **Bologna, Florence,** and **Rome.** (🛢 *€98.* 🕐 *5hr., every hr. 6:30am-5:15pm.*)

Getting Around 📱

The **UnicoNapoliticket** (☎*081 55 13 109* ▣*www.napolipass.it*) is valid for all modes of transportation in the city. Tickets come in three varieties: 90min. (*€1.10*), full-day (*€3.10*), and weekend (*€2.60*) and can be bought at newsstands and *tabaccherie*. All regional buses and trains are included in the **UnicoCampania** system (▣*www.unicocampania.it*).

By Bus

Public bus lines crisscross the city; most accommodations and tourist offices provide maps. Most buses run from 6:30am to just before midnight.

By Taxi

A number of companies operate the city's white taxis (☎*081 88 88; 081 570 70 70; 081 55 60 202; 081 55 15 151*). Only take official, licensed taxis with meters and always ask about prices upfront.

pompeii *pompei*

Sailing around the Bay of Naples, you'll see Mt. Vesuvius from nearly all vistas. It lurks formidably as though to say, "Don't forget about me." Well, given the crowds that stream to Pompeii annually, we hardly think the massive volcano is being forgotten (even if it *has* been dormant more than half a century.) On August 24, 79 CE, it earned its infamy, erupting and blanketing the nearby city of Pompeii in a cloud of ash. Tragic though the eruption was for the residents of this ancient metropolis, the preservation of its streets, artifacts, and even people is unparalleled, making this frozen snippet of life nearly two millennia ago a gold mine for archaeologists and a sort of morbid historical "playground" for tourists.

SIGHTS

For the price of one ticket at Pompeii, you'll have the run of an entire ancient city, but that doesn't mean touring the ruins is a simple undertaking. Pompeii was a true metropolis, complete with basilicas, bars, and brothels, and that kind of scope can be intimidating. Rather than taking any kind of tour, one of the most fun ways to experience Pompeii is to navigate its maze-like streets solo—you'll likely get lost even with a map. Before heading out, pick up a free map and guidebook at the info office by showing your ticket. (*€11, EU citizens age 18-24 €5.50, EU citizens under 18 and over 65 free. Valid 1 day; no re-entry. ☼ Ruins open daily Apr-Oct 8:30am-7:30pm; Nov-Mar 8:30am-5pm.*) Of course, the pleasure of going it alone can be mitigated when the city is packed, and at times it's hard to walk down one of Pompeii's cobbled streets without running into another visitor. Come in the early summer or fall for slightly less crowded circumstances.

Near the Forum

Entering from Porta Marina, you first hit the **Basilica,** the remains of a building originally used for legal purposes and business matters. Now an open space occupied by columns that resemble tree stumps, it's a small taste of the many columned structures to come. To the left is the grassy **Forum,** the first-century city's political, religious, and economic center. Head to the **Granai del Foro** on the left for a startling peek at four body casts created by pouring plaster into air pockets in the ash that were formed by disintegrated bodies. You may not be able to tell that one of them is a dog, but the three human figures, one of whom is a pregnant woman, are contorted in heart-wrenching positions of fear. As this area is closest to the main entrance and the cafeteria, it is predictably the most crowded. Head elsewhere for a quieter walk.

Near the House of the Faun

The wide V. delle Terme and V. della Fortuna surround the area around the stunning **Casa del Fauno,** the biggest and perhaps best preserved residence in the ruins. Your attention will undoubtedly be drawn to the bronze faun statue at the house's center, but don't miss the mosaic-covered surrounding rooms—unfortunately, these mosaics can only partially make up for the absent Alexander mosaic now displayed at the Naples Museo Archeologico Nazionale. At the time of its discovery, that tiled decoration suggested some relation between the house's wealthy owner and Alexander the Great.

Near the Brothel

While all of Pompeii's ruins are full of strolling tourists, none are as packed as the **Lupanare,** the ancient city's brothel. Looks like it's just as popular now as it was centuries ago. If you can squeak past the tourist groups, take notice of the explicit frescoes lining the walls, which show popular bedroom positions as a source of "inspiration" for the men who frequented the place. Nearby, the large **Stabian Baths** feature a body cast and a wall of impressive mosaics.

Near the Amphitheater

That big green block on your map indicates the **amphitheater,** a massive structure that could hold 20,000 spectators and hosted Colosseum-like gladiator battles in its day. Much quieter now, the arena stands as another vivid reminder of what this city used to be. The adjacent **Great Palaestra** provides a nice break from the hard-to-navigate stone blocks scattered about the rest of the city and some shade under its trees. Less serene is the **Garden of the Fugitives,** where you'll find more plaster casts of the bodies of individuals who didn't flee the city in time.

ESSENTIALS

Practicalities

- **TOURIST OFFICES:** Tourist Offices (🖳*www.pompeiturismo.it* 🕐 *Open daily 8:30am-6:30pm.*) are located at the Circumvesuviana station (☎*081 85 07 255*) and at V. Sacra 1 (☎*081 536 32 93*).

Getting There

The best way to get to Pompeii's archaeological site is by the **Circumvesuviana train** from Naples's Stazione Centrale (💲 *€2.40.* 🕐 *20-30min., every 15min.*) or from Sorrento. (💲 *€1.90.* 🕐 *20-30min., every 20min.*) Get off at Pompei Scavi. From the train, the ruins' main entrance, **Porta Marina**, is to the right. If you proceed onward down V. Villa dei Misteri, you can enter at the less crowded entrance at **Piazza Esedra**.

👍herculaneum *ercolano*

Once you've gotten over Herculaneum's hard-to-pronounce name, there's very little to begrudge this delightful ancient Roman town. A smaller archaeological site than the more famous Pompeii, Herculaneum is much easier on the sightseer than its big sib—you can cover its grounds in an afternoon without fatigue or boredom ever setting in. Not only is it better preserved and less crowded than good old Pompy, but it's also situated in a beautiful natural enclave. Sparkling water less than 1 mi. away and lush green trees surrounding the ruins make Herculaneum worth a daytrip even if you're not an archaeological fanatic. Best of all, the modern city that cradles the ancient one has not become a tourist trap, meaning you'll find plenty of residential life, shops, and cheap restaurants if you want to spend the afternoon. Slow down and gear up for this undiscovered lost city.

SIGHTS 🔘

🏛 HERCULANEUM (ERCOLANO SCAVI) ✎⊗ ANCIENT ROME

At the intersection of C. Resina and V. IV Novembre   ☎081 732 4338 🖳www.pompeiisites.org

Herculaneum is a city upon a city. You'll know you've reached the ancient Ercolano when cotton-candy pink houses suddenly cede to dusty, copper-colored ones. Even before buying a ticket to enter the ruins, take a moment to look around. The public walkway leading to the information desk provides one of the best views of the city in its entirety. To the right is the 4.5 hectare region open to the public. (Another 16 or so hectares are not visible.) From this elevation, you get the best sense of how deeply the city was buried by the explosion and of how much was vertically preserved. About 16m of pyroclastic rock covered the region, making its second-story structures even better preserved than those of Pompeii.

Though this city is smaller than Pompeii, you could easily spend hours exploring its nooks and crannies. Make sure not to miss the **Casa del Tramezzo di Legno,** one of the site's largest and most detailed complexes: large frescoes, a marble table at its center, and wooden dividers give the room its name. The **Casa della Cervi** (House of the Deers) is a bit like a museum: still-life frescoes (now covered in Plexiglas) line the walkway, while the central courtyard was once home to life-size statues depicting dogs destroying deers. (No evidence that Herculaneum's citizens were alliteration authorities.) Not only were they artistically inclined, but the people of Herculaneum knew how to live: the **Larga Taberna** contains a series of holes that were used for serving food and wine. They cleaned themselves in style too—the **Terme Suburbane** (Suburban Baths) is a three-room complex whose middle area contains an intricate black-and-white mosaic on its floor.

Appreciate the age of this sight, but allow the modernity that rubs up against old Herculaneum to enrich your experience of the ancient town. Rooftops of modern dwellings peek out beyond the ruins' perimeter, and the sounds of city residents penetrate the otherwise silent streets of the remains. Like a remarkable mini-Rome, where rubble and modern brick live side by side, Herculaneum is maybe not as much a city upon a city, as it is two cities in one.

§ €11, EU citizens ages 18-24 €5.50, EU citizens under 18 or over 65 free. Audio tour €6.50, 2 for €10. ☼ Open daily Apr-Oct 8:30am-7pm; Nov-Mar 8:30am-5pm.

ESSENTIALS

Practicalities

- **TOURIST OFFICES:** (V. IV Novembre 82 ☎081 78 81 243 ▨www.comune.ercolano. na.it ⚑ 3min. down the hill from the train station. ☼ Open M-Sa 8am-6pm.)

Emergency!

- **POLICE:** Carabinieri (V. Nicolo Marcello Venuti 30 ☎081 77 76 022). **Local Police** (☎081 78 81 400). **State Police** (☎081 78 87 111).

Getting There

Take the **Circumvesuviana train** from Naples's Stazione Centrale to Ercolano Scavi (§ €1.80. ☼ 17min., every 15min.) or head to the same destination from Sorrento. (§ €1.90. ☼ 45min.) From the station, head downhill 500m to the main gate.

capri ☎081

Capri certainly qualifies as an oasis. Before even landing at its dock, visitors have their cameras going, snapping postcard shots of the aquamarine water and pastel houses dotting the island's cliffs. Pebble beaches, stunning vistas, and rocky hikes add to this escape's at times unbelievable beauty. Yet walking around the narrow streets of the isle's residential area, you may feel as though you're in a Disneyland for the Bill Gateses of this world.

ORIENTATION

The Isle of Capri consists of two towns: **Capri,** closer to the port, and **Anacapri,** higher up and further west. Capri centers on **Piazza Umberto I.** Radiating from here, the main streets are **Via Roma** (mostly practical stores), **Via Vittorio Emanuele** (designer shops), **Via Botteghe,** and **Via Longano** (mostly restaurants). Take the bus uphill to get to Anacapri, it will drop you off in **Piazza Vittoria,** the town's center. Most of the action is down the long **Via Giuseppe Orlandi,** which is full of restaurants, merchants, and most of the interesting places to visit.

ACCOMMODATIONS

Rooms in both Capri and Anacapri are pricey year-round, thanks to the popularity of the lovely island they call home. The most conveniently located hotels also tend to be the most expensive, making any stay here at least a bit of a splurge.

▨ HOTEL QUATTRO STAGIONI ⊛⊗(ᵒ)✲ HOTEL ❸

V. Marina Piccola 1 ☎081 83 70 041 ▨www.hotel4stagionicapri.com

The humorous and hospitable staff make this one of the sunniest spots on the island, even if its look isn't as refined as other options. Simple furnishings, a removed location, and quiet but sunny rooms make Quattro Stagioni a break from the glitz of the *centro.*

⚑ Bus to V. Marina Piccola. § Singles €40-70; doubles €70-130. 10% Let's Go discount.

VILLA PALOMBA

📧⊗⌖❄ B AND B ❸

V. Mulo 3 ☎081 83 77 322

Possibly the best deal on the island if you can manage the slight trek to get here. A vine-covered patio with great views gives you plenty of relaxing space, while the wicker furniture and flower-decorated sheets' old-fashioned feel matches the motherly attention paid to you by the hostess.

⚑ *From V. Marina Piccola, walk down stairs on the right onto V. Mulo; walk through tunnel and slightly downhill, following signs.* 𝒊 *A/C €10 per day.* Ⓢ *Singles €45-65; doubles €80-130.*

VILLA MIMOSA BED AND BREAKFAST

📧⊗⌖❄ B AND B ❸

V. Nuova del Faro 48/A ☎081 83 71 752 🖥www.mimosacapri.com

Anacapri might already resemble a fairy-tale land, but if you had any doubts, Villa Mimosa's hanging bird cages and antique sculptures adorning the garden will do the trick. Rooms are equipped with private terraces.

⚑ *100m down the hill on the right from the last stop of the Marina Grande-Anacapri bus.* Ⓢ *Doubles €70-100.*

HOTEL IL PORTICO

📧⊗⌖❄ HOTEL ❹

V. Truglio 1/C ☎338 18 28 700 🖥www.ilporticocapri.com

Ideally located between the port and Capri's *centro*, this spot offers the reliability of a hotel and the feel of a bed and breakfast. Sparkling clean rooms (and since they're white, you can tell) smell like flowers and, if you step out onto the balcony, the sea.

⚑ *Off V. Marina Grande on the way to Capri's centro.* Ⓢ *Doubles €80-160; triples €140-190.*

THE GREAT OUTDOORS

Beyond Capri's rampant commercialism lies its stunning natural beauty—and that's the best reason to come. Most ◪hikes are hilly but not terribly rugged, making a pair of sneakers enough for hitting the paths. The **Arco Naturale**, a triumphant stone arch, can be reached by starting in P. Umberto I, heading down V. le Botteghe, and finally veering right onto V. Matermania. Head down a steep staircase, and you'll hit the spot. Turn back around and make your way left, passing the Grotta di Matermania and the **Villa Malaparte**, a rare work of modern architecture. When the road opens out onto V. Pizzolungo, the **Faraglione**, Capri's famous three rocks, is around the way. The walk is about 1½hr. Head to the tourist office for detailed maps of other suggested hikes.

GROTTA AZZURRA

📧⊗ CAVE

On the island's northwest coast, below Anacapri ☎081 83 70 973

Despite being blue, this is Capri's golden star—and when we say blue, we mean swimming-pool aquamarine. The walls of this water-filled cave shimmer almost artificially when sunlight beams through from beneath the water's surface. Roman statues were discovered here and legend has it that spirits reside in the caves—if the authorities don't catch you taking a prohibited swim, maybe the ghosts will.

⚑ *Take the bus from Anacapri to Grotta Azzurra leaving from Vle. de Tommaso (15min., every 10-20min. 6:30am-10:30pm). Once there, catch a Cooperativa Battellieri rowboat to the entrance.* Ⓢ *Cooperativa Battellieri boat €7.50. Entry €4.* ⏱ *Last boat at 5pm.*

MONTE SOLARO

📧⊗ PANORAMIC VIEWS

V. Caposcuro 10 ☎081 83 71 428 🖥www.capriseggiovia.it

It might be nearly as expensive as the ferry to Capri, but the ascent 589m above the island is worth it. For 13min., titillate or tremble as your chairlift climbs up to the summit. From the island's highest point, you can enjoy an unrivaled panorama of land and sea: Ischia, Naples, and the Appenines loom in the distance, though standing there you wouldn't wish yourself anywhere else.

⚑ *The chair lift leaves from V. Caposcuro 10, just off P. Vittoria in Anacapri.* Ⓢ *Round-trip €9.* ⏱ *Ticket office open 9:30am-5pm. Last ride to Monte Solaro at 5pm; last ride back at 5:30pm.*

FOOD

Capri is famous for the **Caprese salad**—rich mozzarella balls tossed with sweet red tomatoes and fresh basil. *Limoncello*, a lemon-flavored yellow liqueur, seems to epitomize the island's sweetness and bright feel. It's hard to find a budget meal here, but cafes often have decently priced panini to tide you over. Anacapri is generally more budget-friendly.

PASTICCERIA GELATERIA SAN NICOLA — BAKERY, GELATERIA [1]

V. San Nicola 7 ☎081 83 72 199

Size *does* matter. What this shop lacks in square footage, it makes up for in the size of its pastries. Unlike more glamorous spots, this closet-sized bakery makes treats that are actually fresh and well-priced.

➡ In Anacapri. Take V. Giuseppe Orlandi away from P. Vittoria and turn right onto V. San Nicola. $ Pastries €0.80-3. Cannoli €1.50. Gelato €2.50-3. 🕐 Open daily 7am-9pm.

TRATTORIA IL SOLITARIO — PIZZERIA [2]

V. Giuseppe Orlandi 96 ☎081 83 71 382 💻www.trattoriailsolitario.it

Tucked away behind a garden and with its *own* garden inside, this pizzeria feels miles away from the commerical flare of Anacapri. It has probably the best prices on the island for a sit-down pizza, yet it isn't lacking in flavor or creativity.

➡ A short walk down V. Giuseppe Orlandi from P. Vittoria. $ Cover €1.50. Pizza €3.50-8. Primi €5.50-15. Caprese salad €6. 🕐 Open in summer daily noon-3pm and 7:30-11:30pm; in fall, winter, and spring M noon-3pm and 7:30-11:30pm, W-Su noon-3pm and 7:30-11:30pm

TINELLO — SEAFOOD [2]

V. L'Abate 3 ☎081 83 76 578

Finally, a restaurant without a photo-supplemented (dear Italy: we know what pasta carbonara is; we don't need a picture), touristic, or pages-long menu: this tiny spot feels like it could be in an old city center rather than ritzy Capri. The only thing reminding you of the water is the exquisite seafood menu.

➡ From Chiesa Santo Stefano, walk up stairs to the covered V. L'Abate. $ Primi €7-15; secondi €10-15; dolci €5-7. 🕐 Open daily noon-2:30pm and 7:30-11pm.

VERGINIELLO — RISTORANTE [3]

V. Lo Palazzo 25 ☎081 83 70 944

The whole package: terrace seating for a view, straw covering for some shade, and great value for some help re-padding that dented wallet. Despite its central location and amazing panorama, this large restaurant retains the feel of a family-run trattoria, with its light-hearted staff generous portions.

➡ Take V. Roma from P. Umberto I and walk down the stairs on the right past the post office. $ Cover €2. Primi €7-14; secondi €12-22. 🕐 Open daily noon-3pm and 7:30pm-midnight.

NIGHTLIFE

With ferry and hotel costs what they are, the Isle of Capri is not the young traveler's party town that other beach locales sometimes are. People who can afford to stay here head to expensive lounges and discos. The economically minded might consider the ridiculously early 5:40am ferry back to Naples, which means you can "stay the night" partying in Capri instead of booking a hotel room. Given the cost of most spots however, sleeping in Naples or living it up in Capri will probably end up costing about the same.

BYE BYE BABY — CLUB

V. Roma 6 ☎081 83 75 065 💻www.byebyebabycapri.com

Funky furniture sits in the lounge areas of this downstairs disco, though you won't be doing much sitting as the night wears on. The hefty price of drinks draws a sophisticated crowd, so don't expect to get in donning beachwear.

➡ Take V. Roma from P. Umberto and descend steps on right. $ Entry M-F with purchase of drink.

F-Sa and special events cover €20; Includes 1 drink. Cocktails €10. ⏰ Open Tu-Su 11pm-5am.

NUMBER 1/NUMBER 2 CLUB

V. Vittorio Emanuele III 53/55 ☎081 83 77 078

Follow the blue lights down to this spectacular double-whammy of a spot—but only if you're prepared to rub shoulders with a pretty crowd and their pretty pennies. The two adjoining rooms let guests drift seamlessly between live vocals and jazz (Number 1) and commercial and house (Number 2).

✈ Take V. Vittorio Emanuele III from P. Umberto I. ℹ Dress to impress. $ M-Th entry with drink; F-Su cover €30+. Cocktails €20, at a table €40. ⏰ Open daily 11pm-3am.

MEDJ PUB PUB

V. Oratorio 9 ☎081 83 75 148

The cheapest spot to get a cocktail or beer, even by non-resort standards. Without the hip decor or nightly DJ of nearby clubs, it attracts a younger crowd looking for good conversation loosened up by a few too many drinks.

✈ From P. Umberto I, take V. P.S. Cimino and turn left onto V. Oratorio. $ Beer €2.50-4. Shots €4. Cocktails €5-6. ⏰ Open in summer daily 8pm-2am; in fall, winter, and spring Tu-Su 8pm-2am.

ESSENTIALS

Practicalities

- **TOURIST OFFICES: Info points** can be found to the right of the dock at **Marina Grande** *(☎081 83 70 634)*, in **Piazza Umberto** in Capri *(☎081 83 70 686)*, and in Anacapri just off P. Vittoria at **Via Giuseppe Orlandi 59** *(☎081 83 71 524 💻www.capritourism.com, www.infocapri.molti ⏰ All branches open M-Sa 8:30am-8:30pm, Su 9am-3pm.)*
- **INTERNET: Capri Graphic** offers internet and office supplies in Capri. *(V. Listrieri 17 ☎081 83 75 212 ✈ From P. Umberto I walk down V. Longano and make a right onto V. Listrieri. $ €2 per 10min., €6 per hr. ⏰ Open M-Sa 9am-1pm and 4-8pm.)* In Anacapri try **Hotel Due Pini.** *(P. Vittoria 3 ☎081 83 71 404 $ €1 per 10min., €5 per hr. ⏰ Open daily 8am-6pm.)*

Emergency!

- **POLICE: Carabinieri** have offices in Capri *(V. Provinciale Marina Grande 42 ☎081 83 70 000 ✈ By the port. ⏰ Open until 8pm.)* and Anacapri *(V. Caprile ☎081 83 71 011).* There is also **City Police** in Capri *(V. Roma 70 ☎081 83 74 211).*
- **HOSPITALS/MEDICAL SERVICES: G. Capilupi** in Capri. *(V. Provinciale 2 ☎081 83 81 205 ✈ At the 3-pronged fork at the end of V. Roma. ⏰ 24hr. service for emergencies.)*

Getting There

Capri's main port is Marina Grande. Various companies run ferries to and from Naples and Sorrento. **Caremar** *(☎89 21 23 💻www.caremar.it)* is the cheapest option but not the most frequent, running both ferries and hydrofoils to and from **Naples** *($ Ferries €10, hydrofoils €14.50. ⏰ 50-80min.; depart Naples every 2-4hr. 5:40am-9:10pm, depart Capri every 2-4hr. 5:45am-10:20pm.)* and hydrofoils to **Sorrento.** *($ €9.80. ⏰ 25min.; depart Sorrento 7:45am, 9:25am, 2:30pm, 7pm; depart Capri 7am, 8:40am, 1:40pm, 6:15pm.)* **SNAV** *(☎081 42 85 555 💻www.snav.it)* runs the most frequent hydrofoils to and from **Naples** *($ €16. ⏰ 45min., every 30-80min. 6:50am-7:10pm.)* and **Sorrento** *($ €13.50. ⏰ Every 20-85min. 7:35am-6:30pm.)* Having arrived, you can either walk 20min. up the winding streets to Capri or take a **funicular.** *($ €1.40. ⏰ Every 15-30min. 5:25am-1:45am.)*

Getting Around

Once in Capri and Anacapri's town centers, navigating the narrow and steep streets is only practical on foot. To get between major points, take **buses** or the **funicular** *(€1.40 per ride).* You can buy a €1 rechargable card and fill it with €2.20 for 1hr. (includes one bus and one funicular ride) or €6.90 for the week. Rechargable cards are rarely worth it for daytrips but are practical if you're here for a while and planning to bus around the island a lot. From Capri *centro*, ATC buses run to **Anacapri.** *(⏰ Every 10min. during the day, 20min. early and late, 6am-2am.)* All buses depart from the start of V. Roma in Capri. From Anacapri *centro*, buses head to other island destinations like Grotta Azzurra and Faro. All buses stop in P. Vittoria in Anacapri. For a **taxi,** head to the hubs at the Marina Grande port, P. Umberto I in Capri *(☎081 83 70 543),* or P. Vittoria in Anacapri *(☎081 83 71 175).*

sorrento ☎081

Sorrento is the practical traveler's paradise. Located on a train, bus, and ferry route that connects it with the Amalfi Coast's other cities, Sorrento makes dazzling, high-cliffed Bay of Naples beauty easily accessible. While many travelers use Sorrento as a springboard for daytrips, its mix of paved streets and urban grit with shopping and beach bumming—the epitome of leisure—make it worth exploring in its own right. Before hopping on that train to more serene destinations, kick back with a glass of *limoncello* (as common as water here) and a *cono* of mint gelato for some daytime relaxation. Don't forget your heels, though—staying out into the wee hours of the morning is as popular with Sorrento's young crowds.

ORIENTATION

With its flat layout and paved sidewalks, Sorrento is very easy to navigate. Circumvesuviana trains and SITA buses pull into **Piazza de Curtis.** From there, head up the steps to **Via degli Aranci,** which has plenty of cheap accommodations and stores along its sidewalks, or down the hill to **Corso Italia,** which leads into the *centro.* A short walk will take you to the palm-tree-filled **Piazza Tasso** and the parallel **Via San Cesareo,** which is cluttered with souvenir and *limoncello* shops. From the *piazza,* steep stairs lead to the waterfront, a small public beach, and the port.

ACCOMMODATIONS

Being a beach town, Sorrento has its fair share of hotels—sometimes it feels as though they make up a third of the buildings here. With so many cheap hostels and one-star hotels only a few minutes from the *centro,* Sorrento is a great base for hopping around the Amalfi coast.

ULISSE DELUXE HOSTEL 💳🚭📶 HOSTEL [1]

V. del Mare 22 ☎081 87 74 753 💻www.ulissedeluxe.com

With its air-conditioned rooms, marble foyer, and discounted access to its private fitness center, Ulisse Deluxe is not easily reconciled with conventional expectations about hostel living. Doubles are more like those of a hotel.

➡ Walk down C. Italia nearly to its end and then head downstairs just before the hospital. Walk 3min. toward the right down V. del Mare. $ Dorms €18-25; doubles €60-80; triples €90-120; quads €120-160.

BED AND BED DIANA CITY 💳🚭📶 HOTEL [3]

C. Italia 5 ☎081 80 74 392 💻www.dianacity.com

You don't have to veer out of central Sorrento or resort to dormitory living to find an affordable room: this newly opened spot is as convenient as it is cheery. Colorful rooms decorated with bright paintings and linens remind you of the beach, and the sand is only 10min. away.

From P. Tasso, head 10min. down C. Italia, away from the train station. $ Doubles €59-79.

OSTELLO LE SIRENE HOSTEL ❶

V. degli Aranci 160 ☎081 80 72 925 www.hostellesirene.com

The bunk beds in the small rooms at this hostel don't allow for much wiggle room, but le Sirene's proximity to the beach and train is convenient. Rooms have ensuite baths, which would be a plus if the floors weren't wet and a bit dirty.

From train station, follow signs down V. degli Aranci and walk 5min. i $ 8-10 bed unisex dorms €16; 6- to 7-bed (co-ed) €18; 4-bed (co-ed) €19-20. Doubles €45-60.

THE GREAT OUTDOORS

Sorrento doesn't offer much in the way of religious and artistic must-sees, but its location on the coast makes it a great starting point for scenic **hikes** and leisurely days on the sand. Most visitors hit the **beach,** head up **Corso Italia** for shopping, or hop on a SITA bus to hit nearby cities on the Amalfi coast. Sorrento's main beach is the **Marina Grande,** easily accessible by walking down V. de Maio and climbing down 100 steps to the winding road. From there, the port is to the right and a sizeable stretch of private beach is to the left. The tiny public area, which will undoubtedly be crowded, is just beyond. For a break from crowded beaches head west on C. Italia and then V. Capo for about 30min. to the Capo di Sorrento, a small protrusion of beach and cliff off the otherwise flat coast. When you reach Calata di Punta del Capo, head right down the steep cobblestone road which eventually becomes soil and winds to the coast. Near the base, you'll pass a small sign marking the **Ruins of Villa di Pollio Felice.** They truly are ruins—without the post, you would barely know they existed. Continue on past the few crumbling arches and make the steep descent to an aquamarine pool of water which will most likely be occupied by swimmers, though far fewer than fill Sorrento's main beaches.

FOOD

Eating good food and staying cool in Sorrento is easy—*gelaterie* and *limoncello* merchants seem to come in pairs. If you've never tasted the sweet yellow drink, pop into **Limonoro** for a free sample and a piece of *limoncello*-filled chocolate. *(V. San Cesareo 49/53 ☎081 807 2782 www.limonoro.it. Open daily 8am-9pm.)* Sit-down restaurants line the touristy C. d'Italia, and while they're not as expensive as those in most beach towns, better spots can definitely be found on peripheral streets.

PRIMAVERA GELATERIA GELATERIA, PASTICCERIA ❶

C. Italia 142 ☎081 80 73 252 www.primaverasorrento.it

When the Pope and bikini-clad supermodels can agree on something, you know it's good: photos of each line the walls of this famed *gelateria*, where proud owner Antonio Cafiero dishes up over 70 flavors of gelato and sweets.

5min. down C. Italia from P. Tasso. $ Pastries €1.50-3. Cones €2.50-12. The €12 cone is unimaginably large. Open daily summer 9am-1am; fall, winter, and spring 9am-midnight.

IL GIARDINIELLO RISTORANTE ❷

V. dell'Accademia 7/9 ☎081 87 84 616 www.giardiniellosorrento.com

Retreat from the sun and crowds to this leaf-covered restaurant while watching Nonna Luisa mix dough for her namesake *torta di nonna.* Classic *Sorrentina* dishes, like gnocchi with tomatoes and basil, are accompanied by a large selection of wine and often served by the owners themselves.

From P. Tasso, head down V. de Maio, turn left onto V. Santa Maria Grazie, and continue as the street becomes V. Accademia. $ Cover €1. Pizza €4.50-7. Primi €4-7. Fish and meat €6-14.50. Open in summer daily 10:30am-midnight; in winter M-W 10:30am-midnight, F-Su 10:30am-midnight.

SALTO PIZZERIA ❶

V. degli Aranci 147 ☎334 31 22 016

Portions and menu sizes are rarely this gigantic, even in Naples. Drop by Salto's miniscule shop before hitting the beach or the train for a pizza, made any way you like it.

➡ *From the train station, head down V. degli Aranci away from the centro. Across the street from hostel.* $ *Pizza €2.50-4, slices €0.80. Panini €3-3.50. Primi €3.50.* ⏰ *Open daily 9am-1am.*

NIGHTLIFE

For such a small town, Sorrento is home to a surprising number of hopping evening spots. Head down **Corso Italia** for a lively array of bars and cafes. Though this town doesn't boast the beach discos of other coastal cities, you can still break it down at spots like **Daniele's Club,** which has a small dance area and caters to a distinctly tourist crowd. *(P. Tasso 10* ☎*081 877 3992* 💻*www.bagattelle.net* ⏰ *Open daily 9pm-4am.)*

👍 ENGLISH INN — 🍸 CLUB, BAR, RISTORANTE

C. Italia 55 — ☎081 807 4357 💻www.englishinn.it

English keeps the crowd hustling every night and well into the morning. The real action happens upstairs in the vine-covered rooftop garden. A nightly DJ, plenty of TVs, and a cheap bar (with bartender's choice happy hours) give rowdy guests their choice between dancing, drinking, or watching it all unfold.

➡ *5min. from P. Tasso.* $ *Shots €2. Beer €3-3.50. Cocktails €5. Pizza, pasta, and panini €5-9.* ⏰ *Open daily 8am-4am. Upstairs garden open 7:30pm onward. Happy hour 10pm.*

INSOLITO — 🍸 BAR, CLUB

C. Italia 38/E — ☎081 87 72 409 💻www.insolitosorrento.it

If you want to disguise your foreign status and slip in with a sleeker Italian crowd, Insolito's glass bar and modern mini-disco will fit the bill. Despite its "prettier-than-thou" look, the place stays down-to-earth thanks to its cheap happy hours. Just don't expect the raucous crowd that can be found at other touristy spots.

➡ *5min. down C. Italia from P. Tasso.* $ *Cocktails €5-8.* ⏰ *Open daily 8am-5am.*

ESSENTIALS

Practicalities

- **TOURIST OFFICES: Info Points** are the most convenient sources of information and are scattered throughout the town. Locations at the **Marina Piccola** *(near the port),* in **Piazza de Curtis** *(outside the train station),* in **Piazza Tasso,** and in **Piazza Andrea Veniero** *(near the end of C. Italia). (*⏰ *All open daily at 10am; some close at 8pm, others at 9pm.)* The main **Tourist Office** is at V. Luigi de Maio 35. *(*☎*081 807 4033* 💻*www.sorrentotourism.com* ⏰ *Open M-Sa 8:30am-4pm.)*
- **INTERNET: Insolito.** *(C. Italia 38/E* ☎*081 877 2409* 💻*www.insolitosorrento.it* $ *Wi-Fi €4 per hr.* ⏰ *Open daily 8am-5am.)*

Emergency!

- **POLICE: Carabinieri** *(Vicolo III Rota* ☎*081 80 73 111).* **Police** *(Vicolo III Rota* ☎*081 80 75 311)* right off C. Italia heading toward St. Agnello.
- **HOSPITALS/MEDICAL SERVICES: Santa Maria della Misericordia** keeps miserable hours. *(C. Italia 129* ☎*081 533 1112* ⏰ *Open to public for appointments M-Sa 1-3pm and 7-8:30pm, Su 1-4pm and 7-8:30pm.)*

Getting There

By Train

Circumvesuviana trains roll into the station in P. de Curtis 6. *(*☎*800 05 39 39* ⏰ *Every 15-30min. 5:01am-11:26pm.)* The train runs to **Naples** *(*$ *€3.40.* ⏰ *1hr.)* and makes stops along the way in **Pompeii** *(*$ *€1.90.* ⏰ *20-30min.)* and **Herculaneum.** *(*$ *€1.90.* ⏰ *45min.)*

By Ferry

Ferries arrive at the port on the Bay. **Linee Marittime Partenopee** (☎*081 80 71 812* 🖥*www. consorziolmp.it*) runs hydrofoils from **Naples** (Ⓢ *€10.* 🕓 *Every 2hr. from Naples 9am-6:25pm, from Sorrento 7:20am-4:25pm.)* and **Capri.** (Ⓢ *€14.* 🕓 *Roughly every hr. from Capri 8am-7pm, from Sorrento 7:20am-6:20pm.)* **Metro del Mare** (☎*199 60 07 00* 🖥*www.metrodelmare.net*) runs ferries from **Amalfi.** (Ⓢ *€11.* 🕓 *1hr.; 4-5 per day from Amalfi 8:35am, noon, 1:50, 5, 5:40pm; from Sorrento 9:30am-1:15pm and 6:05pm.)*

By Bus

SITA buses (☎*089 405 145* 🖥*www.sitabus.it*) stop in P. de Curtis in front of the Circumvesuviana train station and are the best way to travel to Sorrento from the Amalfi Coast. Buy tickets from **Unicocampania** bus drivers or the kiosk in P. de Curtis. For prices and logistics see the box "bay of buses." Buses run to and from **Amalfi.** (🕓 *90min., every 30min. 6:30am-midnight.)*

amalfi ☎089

Amalfi is the cool kid on the block—universally known, the subject of wild rumors, the one everyone else wants to be. Not surprising, as it's the perfect marriage of waterfront and commercial *centro* yet somehow escapes becoming either fully urban or completely beach resort. More than any other coastal spot, Amalfi walks the line between artificial and natural beauty.

ORIENTATION

Amalfi is shaped like an upside-down "T": its base lying on the waterfront and its thin center extending slightly uphill. It's all easily walkable in an hour. **Piazza Flavio Gioia** (the bus and boat hub) leads into **Piazza Duomo,** which funnels into the narrow **Via Lorenzo d'Amalfi** and **Via Pietro Capuano.** 🔳**Corso delle Repubbliche Marinare** runs along the coast and becomes **Via Pantaleone Comite.** Follow this road to get to neighboring **Atrani,** a 10min. walk around the large cliff.

ACCOMMODATIONS

Cheap accommodations in Amalfi are few and far between. For better prices, head to **Atrani.** If you do want to shell out your euros, you'll likely get good services and great views of the water, though you'll still have to pay to step on the sand.

HOTEL LA CONCHIGLIA
●⊗(•) HOTEL ❹

Piazzale dei Protontini ☎089 87 18 56 🖥www.amalfihotelconchiglia.it

The bright aquamarine shutters and decorative tiling of this hotel match Amalfi's beautiful water. This family-run place 10min. from the *centro* is secluded from crowds but still provides guests with beach proximity and plenty of relaxing space on the terraces and garden.

✴ *Facing the water from the bus stop, walk right on the waterfront along Lungomare dei Cavalleri for 10min. Look for hotel sign when you reach Salita S. Caterina.* Ⓢ *Singles €55; doubles €80-90; triples €110-120. Beach access, 2 chairs, and umbrella €18.*

A SCALINATELLA HOSTEL
●⊗(•) HOSTEL ❷

P. Umberto I ☎089 87 14 92 🖥www.hostelscalinatella.com

Helpful staff and cheap prices are the only appealing thing about an otherwise bare-bones hostel. Its location in the more secluded Atrani is a plus, though you won't have anything near hotel-like amenities.

✴ *In P. Umberto in the center of Atrani.* Ⓢ *4-bed dorms €25; 2-4 person private rooms €70-140.*

THE GREAT OUTDOORS

Beaches are the reason most people come to Amalfi. The town's main beach is the **Marina Grande,** which, though unremarkable, is well-loved and easily accessible (translation: crowded). Head around the Torre di Amalfi to neighboring **Atrani,** where a much quieter sandy stretch awaits. You can also try a rigorous **hike** through Amalfi's stunning countryside. One of the most popular hikes connects Amalfi to Ravello through Pontone. The 2hr. uphill climb starts at the **Museo della Carta.** The tourist offices in both Ravello and Amalfi provide detailed hiking maps.

FOOD

Most higher-quality restaurants are located up side steps off the main streets. The local favorite dish is *scialatelli* (a coarsely cut pasta), often topped with excellent seafood.

BAR BIRECTO — CAFE ❶

P. Umberto I ☎089 87 10 17 www.ilbirecto.com

You've had pizza, gelato, and beer before—the first two are practically Italy's middle names—but finding them on the cheap, especially in Amalfi's touristy streets, is another story. So Bar Birecto's happy hour combo *(all the above for €5)* is nothing less than spectacular.

In Atrani. From Amalfi, walk 10min. along V. Pantaleone Comite overlooking the waterfront; after the tunnel, head down the circular ramp on the right into Atrani's centro. $ Gelato €2-3.50. Pizza €4-6. Primi €5-7. Beer €2.50-6. Cocktails €4-5. Open daily 7am-2am. Happy hour 3-7pm.

TRATTORIA E PIZZERIA DA MEMÉ — RISTORANTE ❸

Salita Marino Sebaste 8 ☎089 83 04 549

This family restaurant is set back away from Amalfi's beach going crowds. Locals gather at small tables scattered on stone steps leading to the fresh interior. Though the brick-oven pizza is a real steal, their specialty is homemade pasta topped with fresh seafood.

Walk up V. Lorenzo d'Amalfi from P. Duomo. Look for signs on the left of the street and turn up the stairs. $ Cover €1.50. Primi €6.50-15; secondi €8-15. Open in summer daily noon-3pm and 6:30pm-midnight; in fall, winter, and spring Tu-Su noon-3pm and 6:30pm-midnight.

PIZZA EXPRESS — PIZZERIA ❶

V. Pietro Capuano 46

Pop into this tiny joint for the best prices and quickest service in town. Its hole-in-the-wall status, however, means you'll have to head elsewhere with your goods.

From P. Duomo, walk up V. Lorenzo d'Amalfi and continue as it becomes V. Pietro Capuano. $ Pizza €2.50-5, slices €1-1.50. Calzones €4. Open in summer daily 9am-10pm; in fall, winter, and spring M-Th 9am-10pm, Sa-Su 9am-10pm.

ESSENTIALS

Practicalities

- **TOURIST OFFICES:** The **Azienda Autonoma Soggiorno e Turismo di Amalfi.** *(C. delle Repubbliche Marinare 27, through the courtyard. ☎089 87 11 07 www.amalfitouristoffice.it 5min. from P. Flavio Gioia, in the direction of Atrani. Open M-Sa 9am-1pm and 2-6pm, Su 9am-1pm.)*

Emergency!

- **POLICE: Carabinieri.** *(V. Casamare 19 ☎089 87 10 22 To the left of V. delle Cartiere's start, on the way to the Museo della Carta.)* **Police.** *(In P. Municipio ☎089 87 16 33 Around the corner from Tourist Office.)*
- **HOSPITALS/MEDICAL SERVICES: Guardia Medica** *(V. Casamare before the Carabinieri ☎089 87 14 49).*

To get around Sorrento and the Amafi Coast, buses are your friend. Tickets work on a system where you buy them for a given amount of time, and then are entitled to unlimited rides within that timeframe. Tickets are also valid for EAVBUS service within Sorrento, and the Circumvesuviana trains. A 45min. ticket costs €2.40, 90min. €3.60, 24hr. €7.20, and a 3-day pass €18.

Getting There

By Bus

Amalfi is best reached by blue **SITA** buses which run up and down the coast (☎089 87 35 89 ▣www.sitabus.it). Buses arrive in and depart from P. Flavio Gioia near the port.

By Boat

Ferries and hydrofoils (docks beside the bus stop) are a more expensive option, but provide nice views and service some places buses don't reach. **Metro del Mare** (☎199 60 07 00 ▣www.metrodelmare.net) runs ferries to **Naples** (⑤ €14-15. ☒ 2hr.; 6 per day; from Naples 8:25-9:20am, 3:10pm, and 5:20pm, from Positano 8:35am-5:40pm.), and **Sorrento** (⑤ €11. ☒ 1hr.; 4-5 per day; from Sorrento 9:30am-1:15pm and 6:05pm; from Amalfi 8:35am, noon, 1:50pm, 5pm, 5:40pm.).

ravello ☎089

If the Amalfi Coast is a house, Ravello is the attic a lot of visitors don't see but actually stores much of the coolest stuff. This tiny town sits quite literally above all of Amalfi's coastal cities and offers phenomenal views down on them. It has beautiful gardens, elegant villas, and a classical music festival that makes you think the place might be heaven itself (it certainly has enough altitude to make you wonder). Come here to get away from the bustle—everything from the music to the older crowds begs you to slow down.

ORIENTATION

Ravello is a small hilltop town, easily walkable in an hour. After getting off the bus at **Via G. Boccaccio,** walk through the tunnel into **Piazza Duomo.** From there, a few main streets, including **Via Roma** and **Via della Francesca** (headed for **Villa Cimbrone**), branch off, leading to stunning views and Ravello's outdoor sights.

SIGHTS

Like the aforementioned attic, Ravello packs a lot of cool stuff into a small space. If you don't want to go the more cultural route, consider doing some hiking around the area. Routes are well marked and fairly easy.

▦ VILLA RUFOLO ✦�& GARDENS
P. Duomo ☎089 85 76 21 ▣www.villarufolo.it

These grounds are so stunning that they inspired **Richard Wagner:** it was in his honor that the town initiated its classical music festival. The villa's lands, once the possession of Ravello's wealthiest family, feature a cloister and the **Torre Maggiore** (visible from outside the walls), but the natural beauty is its most obvious and pleasing element. A garden full of diverse and rare flora complements the blue seascape gleaming below.

✦ Right off P. Duomo. ⑤ €5, under 12 and over 65 €3. ☒ Open daily 9am-9pm.

ravello • sights

FOOD

The restaurants in musical Ravello serve up some seriously delicious food that'll have you singing their praises, but you may end up singing the blues when the bill arrives—things here aren't cheap.

CUMPÀ COSIMO

RISTORANTE ❸

V. Roma 44/46 ☎089 85 71 56

After 81 years of business, this family-run trattoria has carved itself a spot in Ravello's cliffs and in the hearts of its residents. Rich crepes with ham and cheese are a family specialty *(€11)*, but for those who can't make up their mind, the testing plate *(€15)* may be the better choice.

Down V. Roma, just past the tourist office. $ Primi €9-15; secondi €9-40. Open Mar-Sept daily noon-3:30pm and 6:30-10:30pm; Oct-Feb Tu-Su noon-3:30pm and 6:30-10:30pm.

RISTORANTE PIZZERIA VITTORIA

RISTORANTE ❷

V. dei Rufolo 3 ☎089 85 79 47 www.ristorantepizzeriavittoria.it

For a twist on the old pie, try the 0.5m pizza "plank," with your choice of three toppings *(€18)*. The inner garden's small tables may barely accommodate the giant-sized entree, but with a friend, you'll have no trouble finishing it off.

From P. Duomo, head out onto V. dei Rufolo for 2min. $ Cover €2. Pizza €5-9. Primi €9-12; secondi €15-18. Open daily 12:15-3pm and 7:15-11pm.

FESTIVALS

RAVELLO FESTIVAL

SUMMER

P. Duomo 7 ☎089 85 84 22 www.ravellofestival.com

As if the view wasn't enough, Ravello goes and gives us one of the world's largest classical music festivals each summer. If classical music's your thing, you'll probably be in heaven. If it's not, you can just look at the view. Inspired by an 1880 visit here by Richard Wagner, the festival now encompasses dance and art shows, as well as remarkable concerts in the Villa Rufolo gardens.

Most performances take place in Villa Rufolo gardens, although the reach of the festival extends over the whole town. $ Concert tickets €20-70. Festival runs July-Sept. Ticket office open daily May-Sept 10am-8pm.

ESSENTIALS

Practicalities

- **TOURIST OFFICES: Azienda Autonoma Soggioro e Turismo di Ravello** provides free maps of the town and surrounding area (including hiking maps), information on the Ravello Festival, and hotel and restaurant listings. *(V. Roma 18 ☎089 85 70 96 www.ravellotime.it A 2min. walk from P. Duomo. Open daily 9:30am-1pm and 2-6pm.)*
- **INTERNET: Bar Calce** provides internet and Wi-Fi. *(V. Boccaccio 11 ☎089 85 71 30 Beside SITA bus stop. i Cash only. $ €1.50 per 15min., €5 per hr. Discounts on internet if you buy food. Open daily 8:30am-1:30pm and 3:30-10pm.)*

Emergency!

- **POLICE: Carabinieri.** *(V. Rogadeo 1 ☎089 85 71 50 At the end of V. Roma, make a right.)* **Polizia Locale.** *(P. Fontana Moresca ☎089 85 74 98 At the end of Vle. Gioacchino D'Anna.)*

Getting There

Ravello is a 25min. ride from **Amalfi** on a blue **SITA bus.** Buses arrive and leave from the end of V. Giovanni Boccaccio regularly. (🕑 *Every 10-30min. 5:45am-12:25am.*) Alternatively, 🚶hike 1hr. up fairly even stairs from **Atrani** (through Castiglione and Scala) or 2hr. from Amalfi (through Pontone).

essentials *i*

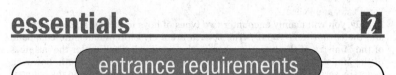

entrance requirements

- **PASSPORT:** Required of any citizens, of anywhere.
- **VISA:** Required of non-EU citizens staying longer than 90 days.
- **WORK PERMIT:** Required of all non-EU citizens planning to work in Italy.

PLANNING YOUR TRIP

Time Differences

Italy is 1hr. ahead of Greenwich Mean Time (GMT) and observes Daylight Saving Time. This means that it is 6hr. ahead of New York City, 9hr. ahead of Los Angeles, 1hr. ahead of the British Isles, 8hr. in Northern Hemisphere summer and 10hr. in Northern Hemisphere winter behind Sydney, and, in the same fashion, 10hr./12hr. behind New Zealand. Don't get confused and call your parents while it's actually 4am their time! Note that Italy changes to Daylight Savings Time on different dates from some other countries, so sometimes, though not often, the difference will be one hour different from what is stated here.

MONEY

Tipping And Bargaining

In Italy, as in the rest of Europe, tips of 5-10% are customary, particularly in restaurants. Italian waiters won't cry if you don't leave a tip—just get ready to ignore the pangs of your conscience later on. Taxi drivers expect the same kind of tip, but lucky for you alcoholics, it is unusual to tip in bars. Bargaining is appropriate in markets and other more informal settings, though in regular shops it is inappropriate. Hotels will often offer lower prices to people who arrive looking for a room that night, so you will often be able to find a bed cheaper than what is officially quoted.

Taxes

The **Value Added Tax** (**VAT;** *imposto sul valore aggiunta*, or IVA) is a sales tax levied in EU countries. Foreigners making any purchase over €155 are entitled to an additional 20% VAT refund. Some stores take off 20% on-site. Others require that you fill out forms at the customs desk upon leaving the EU and send receipts from home within six months. Not all storefront "Tax-Free" stickers imply an immediate, on-site refund, so ask before making a purchase.

SAFETY AND HEALTH
General Advice
In any type of crisis, the most important thing to do is **stay calm.** Your country's embassy abroad is usually your best resource in an emergency; registering with that embassy upon arrival in the country is a good idea.

Local Laws and Police
In Italy, you will mainly encounter two types of boys in blue: the *polizia* (☎113) and the *carabinieri* (☎112). The *polizia* are a civil force under the command of the Ministry of the Interior, whereas the *carabinieri* fall under the auspices of the Ministry of Defense and are considered a military force. Both, however, generally serve the same purpose—to maintain security and order in the country. In the case of attack or robbery, both will respond to inquiries or desperate pleas for help.

Drugs and Alcohol
Needless to say, **illegal drugs** are best avoided altogether, particularly when traveling in a foreign country. In Italy, just like almost everywhere else in the world, drugs including marijuana, cocaine, and heroin are illegal, and possession or other drug-related offenses will be harshly punished.

If you carry **prescription drugs,** bring copies of the prescriptions as well as a note from your doctor, and have them accessible at international borders.

The legal drinking age in Italy is (drumroll please) 16. Remember to drink responsibly and to **never drink and drive.** Doing so is illegal and can result in a prison sentence, not to mention early death. The legal blood alcohol content (BAC) for driving in Italy is under 0.05%, significantly lower than the US limit of 0.08%.

Specific Concerns
Travelers with Disabilities
Those in wheelchairs should be aware that travel in Italy will sometimes be extremely difficult. Many cities predate the wheelchair—and sometimes it seems even the wheel—by several centuries and thus pose unique challenges to disabled travelers. Venice is particularly difficult to navigate in a wheelchair given its narrow streets and numerous bridges (many with steps). Be aware that while an establishment itself may be wheelchair-accessible, getting to the front door in a wheelchair might be virtually impossible. **Accessible Italy** (☎+378 941 111 ▣*www.accessibleitaly.com*) is an organization that offers advice to tourists of limited mobility heading to Italy, with tips offered on subjects ranging from finding accessible accommodations to organizing wheelchair rental.

Natural Disasters
Italy is liable to occasional earthquakes and volcanic eruptions (see **Pompeii** or **Herculaneum**). If Vesuvius decides to become active during your trip (this could actually happen), your best resource will be your country's embassy.

italy 101

CUSTOMS AND ETIQUETTE
Undeniably a friendly bunch, Italians do have their own ways of doing things. Italians place a lot of emphasis on first impressions, so don't get yourself into a *mi scusi* situation. When meeting someone for the first time, a handshake is the way to go—**air kissing** (left side first!) generally comes with a little more familiarity. The Italian people are known to stand pretty close, so get ready to readjust your personal space boundaries. When it comes to clothing, Italians find having

- **AREA:** 116,400 sq. miles
- **POPULATION:** 58 million
- **REGISTERED CATHOLICS:** 51.6 million
- **ACTIVE VOLCANOES:** 3
- **MONEY THROWN INTO TREVI FOUNTAIN DAILY:** €30,000
- **ANNUAL WINE CONSUMPTION PER CAPITA:** 26 gallons
- **ANNUAL BREAD CONSUMPTION PER CAPITA:** 183 pounds
- **FIFA WORLD CUP WINS:** 4
- **TEENAGE MUTANT NINJA TURTLES NAMESAKES:** 4

una bella figura, or a good image, very important and tend to value quality over quantity. They dress more formally, more frequently than Americans. Women should be warned that short skirts and shorts are slightly more risqué in Italy than America—revealing tops are a little less so.

At meals, Italian etiquette is not so very different from the American—at home, courses are served one by one and passed around the table, and at restaurants, the waiter should bring all dishes at once. What you may not be used to are the meal*times:* lunch is usually served anywhere from 1pm to 3pm, and dinner can be as late as 10pm, but hey, at least it's not Spain.

FOOD AND DRINK

If you're headed to Italy, it is not unlikely that one of the highlights of your trip will come in a culinary form: people have been known to visit Italy just for the food. Whether you're enjoying wine (from the number one exporter in the world) or the internationally famous pasta, you're sure to be impressed by the local fare.

The first meal of the day in Italy generally isn't anything too elaborate: *la colazione* may consist simply of coffee and a *cornetto* (croissant). Lunch (*il pranzo*) can go either way: in rural regions you may find it to be a hugely elaborate affair that precedes a nap and separates the two halves of the workday. However, most Italians will just grab a simple panino or salad. The last meal of the day, *la cena,* is generally the most important, and starts at approximately 8pm. It can continue through most of evening, seeing as it may contain any or all of the following courses: an *antipasto* (appetizer), a *primo piatto* (starchy first course like pasta or risotto), a *secondo piatto* (meat or fish), a *contorno* (vegetable side dish), a *dolce* (dessert), a *caffè* (espresso), and often an after-dinner liqueur.

POTENT POTABLES

You can't write about Italian food without acknowledging the drinks that accompany it. Coffee and wine in particular enjoy an unrivaled respect from the Italian people, and therefore come in infinite delicious varieties. Italian-style coffee, or *espresso,* is famous, though the blend of coffee beans used is often from **Brazil.** The beans are roasted medium to medium-dark in the north, getting progressively darker as you move toward the south.

Leading the world in both wine exports and national wine consumption, Italy is a country that values a good *vino.* Every year over one million vineyards

italy 101 · potent potables

cultivate grapes for *rosso* (red wine) and *bianco* (white wine). Try such regional beauties as *Barolo*, a classy (read: expensive) staple of Piedmont made from red grapes that are fermented for over 20 years, or *Frascati*, a cold, clean Roman white.

THE NETHERLANDS

There are few places in the world that can pull off the Netherlands' unique combination of reefer-clouded progressiveness and folksy, earnest charm. Like your straight-edge, ex-hippie high school math teacher, this part of Europe somehow manages to appeal both to tulip-loving, wooden-shoe-lusting grandmas and ganja-crazy, Red-Light-ready students. So, like every other college student, come to Amsterdam to gawk at the coffeeshops and prostitutes, but don't leave thinking that's all there is to this quirky country. Take some time to cultivate an appreciation for the Dutch masters; people will think you're so cool when you declare that the Northern Renaissance was really the site of Western culture's rebirth. Take time to pick the brains of the friendly, largely English-speaking natives. Obviously, most Dutch people aren't pot-heads—they'll tell you that if marijuana was legalized in the states, 700,000 less people would need to be incarcerated annually. Put that in your pipe and smoke it. Consider what it would be like to live in a place where hookers are unionized and public works like windmills, dikes, canals, and bike lanes define the national character, and get ready to go Dutch!

greatest hits

- **LET'S (VAN) GOGH.** The area around Museumplein in Amsterdam features not one, but two of the world's greatest art museums. Savor the Dutch Golden Age at the Rijksmuseum (p. 911) or *Sunflowers* at the Van Gogh Museum (p. 910).

- **CENTRAAL PERK.** It's no cliché to say that the Netherlands' coffeeshops are like no others in the world. No matter what your tastes, a visit to even just one is sure to be an enlightening experience (p. 915).

- **DAM GOOD BARS.** Rotterdam is a nightlife haven, with laidback and musical bars littering the streets (p. 948).

- **RULE THE WORLD.** The Hague isn't only the Netherlands' political capital, it's also home to much of the world's international judicial system. Wannabe world leaders, watch your step: you don't want to end up in the dock at the International Criminal Court (p. 940).

It's hard to think of many countries anywhere in the world that are as friendly to students as the Netherlands. Student scenes and discounts are easy to find, while the wealth of things to do means young people never need constrain themselves to any one place or activity. The Dutch make their cultural institutions extremely accessible, you can purchase a **Museumjaarkaart** for unlimited access to most of the Netherlands' numerous museums—it comes at half price for anyone under 26. Many places actively court student customers. If you're hungry, try 'Skek in **Amsterdam,** where you'll receive a 33% discount by showing a student ID. This might be the first place in the world where people try to borrow IDs from people *under* 21.

Of course, two of the most (in)famous attractions in the Netherlands are its coffeeshops and its nightlife. Fortunately, neither disappoint, and both are key reasons why this is such a great student country. In **Amsterdam,** coffeeshops are everywhere, but pick carefully, as quality varies enormously. Check out our extensive listings to help you decide where to visit. Though the best coffeeshops are very much confined to Amsterdam, great nightlife is common across the country. In Amsterdam, parties rage nightly in Leidseplein and Rembrandtplein, while the central areas like the Red Light District offer a seedier, but uniquely "Amsterdam," experience. Elsewhere, **Rotterdam** and **Utrecht** are both lively destinations featuring plenty of young professionals in the former and students (often of the study abroad kind) in the latter. While **The Hague** may be the quieter counterpart to its neighbors, it is a great place to take your parents if they decide to tag along, and has a solid youth culture of its own as well. Wherever you are in the Netherlands, take advantage of this great student country, an essential experience in any trip through Europe.

amsterdam ☎020

Tell someone you're going to Amsterdam, and you'll be met with a chuckle and a knowing smile. Yes, everyone will think you're after hookers and weed, but the tolerant laws here are shared by many Dutch cities that can't claim Amsterdam's title as the liberal capital of the West. Its characteristic tolerance has defined the city for centuries, long before the advent of drug tourism and prostitutes' unions. A refuge for Protestants and Jews fleeing Belgium in the 16th century, this center of sea trade and capital of a formerly imperialist nation has grown to be a tremendously diverse and progressive place that is more remarkable for letting its residents (and visitors) be whoever they please than for being a pothead's paradise.

As you stroll the streets, appreciate the culture and vitality of this pretty city. You can walk it in under an hour, moving from the peaceful canals of the **Jordaan** to the leering men and gaudy porn stores of the **Red Light District.** Old trading money lives on in graceful canal houses, while a few blocks away, repurposed squats are now clubs and cinemas. The city makes a strong effort to aid its burgeoning arts and culture scene, so Amsterdam is truly getting cooler by the day. And as long as you really like beer, food and drink here are far cheaper than the fare in other European cities.

Whether you're obsessed with Dutch painting, want to dance all night at a GLBT club, or just want to sit in a coffeeshop and get high, you're guaranteed to have a

good time in Amsterdam. If you're the stoner, make sure to mix it up and go to Vondelpark every once in a while. And if you're the art student, we hear that *Sunflowers* looks really cool when you're high.

ORIENTATION

The first step to getting a handle on Amsterdam's geography is to learn about its canals. The **Singel** encloses the heart of the Centrum, made up of the **Oude Zijd, Red Light District,** and **Nieuwe Zijd** from east to west. Barely 1km in diameter, the Centrum overflows with bars, brothels, clubs, and tourists wading through wafts of marijuana smoke. **Centraal Station** sits at the northern end. After that, running in concentric circles you have the **Herengracht, Keizergracht,** and **Prinsengracht,** a somewhat classier area filled with good restaurants and intriguing museums. **Rembrandtplein** and **Leidseplein** are nestled into the central part of the ring. To the east of the canal ring is **Jodenbuurt and Plantage,** the city's historically Jewish district. Continuing around the south of the canal ring to the west, you've got **De Pijp,** an artsy neighborhood filled with immigrants and hipsters, then **Museumplein,** home to some of the city's most important museums and its biggest central park. Moving farther clockwise, you'll find the **Oud-West** and **Westerpark,** two largely residential neighborhoods that are experiencing a boom in popularity and culture. In between Westerpark and the canal ring is the lovely **Jordaan,** north of which (and just west of Centraal Station) lies **Scheepvaartbuurt.**

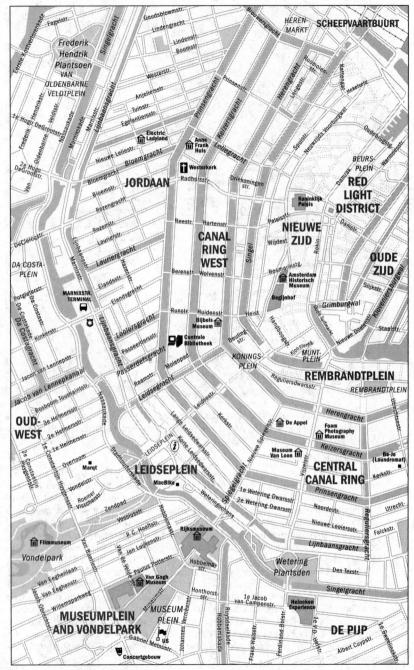

the netherlands

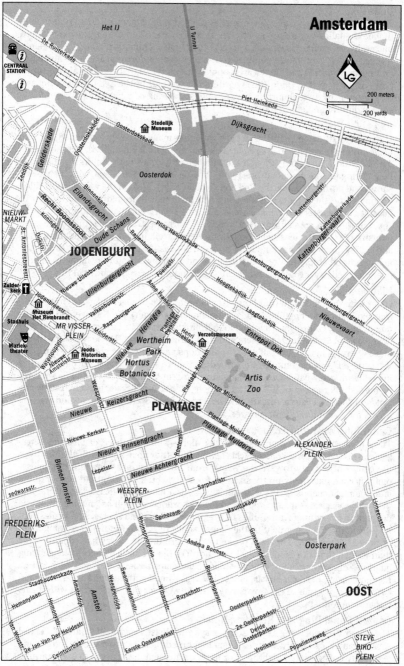

Amsterdam

Oude Zijd

The centrally-located Oude Zijd manages to encapsulate many of Amsterdam's multifaceted qualities in a narrow stretch of real estate. The northern strip, centered on **Zeedijk**, is as close as Amsterdam gets to having a Chinatown. Zeedijk spills into **Nieuwmarkt**, a lovely square dominated by a medieval ex-fortress. The bars and cafes lining Nieuwmarkt's perimeter are popular places for tourists and locals to rub elbows over a beer. The Oude Zijd is bordered on one side by the Red Light District and on the other by Jodenbuurt and represents something of a balance between those starkly different neighborhoods.

Red Light District

Like it or not, the Red Light District is what draws many travelers to Amsterdam. The neighborhood's goings-on are remarkably well regulated and policed, but the area is definitely no Disneyland (though the number of families with children sightseeing here during the day might surprise you). The **Oudezijds Achterburgwal**, with its live sex shows and porn palaces, is the Red Light's main artery. Most of the working-girl-filled windows line the streets perpendicular to this main thoroughfare and stretch to **Oudezijds Voorburgwal** and **Warmoesstraat.** Yes, this is very much a neighborhood about sex, but the high concentration of hotels on Warmoesstraat means that there is an industry here for the less red-blooded traveler as well. In fact, you'll find many bars and coffeeshops that have nothing to do with prostitution. If you want to see the neighborhood at its most hedonistic, come on a Friday or Saturday night; to be less overwhelmed, try strolling through on an afternoon, especially midweek.

Nieuwe Zijd

Older than the Oude Zijd (but home to a church that's younger than the Oude Kerk, thus explaining the neighborhoods' confusing name swap), the Nieuwe Zijd offers a mix of history, culture, and a whole lot of tourists. **Damrak,** its eastern edge, stretches from **Centraal Station** to **Dam Square** and then turns into **Rokin.** These are some of the busiest streets in the city, full of souvenir shops and shawarma stands. As you head west, the streets become less crowded and more hip. **Spuistraat,** in particular, is loaded with artsy cafes and boutique stores. All in all, the Nieuwe Zijd is a not-to-be-missed microcosm of the city as a whole. Either **Dam Square,** lined by the **Nieuwe Kerk** and **Koninklijk Palace,** or cafe- and bookstore-filled **Spuistraat,** make good starting points for an exploration of the area.

Canal Ring West and Scheepvaartbuurt

The Canal Ring West comprises—spoiler alert—a ring of three canals: the **Herengracht, Keizersgracht,** and **Prinsengracht** (helpful hint: they go in alphabetical order from the center of the city toward the west), from Brouwersgracht down to the Leidseplein. It is an extremely pretty stretch of the city, chock-full of grand canal houses and quaint houseboats. Three major sights—the **Anne Frank House, Westerkerk,** and the **Homomonument**—are located in this neighborhood as well as smaller museums devoted to everything from Bibles to eyeglasses. The **Nine Streets,** small lanes running from the Prinsengracht to the Singel, south of Raadhuisstraat, are a highlight of the neighborhood. They are packed with more unique stores and vibrant cafes than we can fit in our guidebook. To the north of the canals is the city's old shipping quarter, Scheepvaartbuurt, which would make quite a round of *Wheel of Fortune.* Its main street, **Haarlemmerplein,** is worth a visit—lined with restaurants, stores, and coffeeshops, it's one of the few parts of the city center that is crowded with locals rather than tourists.

Central Canal Ring and Rembrandtplein

The Central Canal Ring is, in some ways, the least remarkable part of central Amsterdam. Fortunately, it at least has Rembrandtplein to provide some great and extremely concentrated nightlife. For more excitement, head north to the Centrum, for better sights and food, go south to Museumplein or De Pijp. It's certainly not an unpleasant area, however, and the **Golden Bend** boasts some of Amsterdam's most impressive architecture.

West Of Town

To the west of the Canal Ring, **Jordaan** has developed from a working class neighborhood into one of Amsterdam's prettiest and most fashionable. You won't find any of the sights that make Amsterdam famous here, but the restaurants and cafes are not to be missed. Further west is the residential **Westerpark**, with a loyal and vocal—don't expect to hear much English out here—community spirit. South of Westerpark is the **Oud-West,** still dominated by locals but with a few large streets (Kinkerstraat and Overtoom in particular) full of small ethnic cafes and cheap chain stores that keep the area busier.

Museumplein and Leidseplein

Museumplein feels distinctly different from the rest of the city center. With its excellent cultural sites, it draws larger groups of older and more affluent tourists than do the backpacker-filled areas to the north. The square itself is a large, grassy field lined with some of the best museums in the world—it may be the obvious touristy thing to do, but no visit to Amsterdam is complete without a trip to the Van Gogh Museum or Rijksmuseum. To the north is the incredibly different Leidseplein, a massive nightlife hub rivaled only by Rembrandtplein. A busy and touristy region, this part of Amsterdam has a polarizing effect on those who pass through it, inspiring devotion or disapproval but very rarely anything in between.

De Pijp

De Pijp may lack in traditional history or cultural sights, but it more than makes up for that in terms of modern culture. A mix of different immigrant communities, students, and artists enjoy the relatively inexpensive (for the pre-gentrified moment) housing, the excellent ethnic restaurants, and the fun cafes of the area. **Albert Cuypmarkt,** one of the largest markets in the city, is a focal point.

Jodenbuurt and Plantage

Jodenbuurt and Plantage are two of the less-touristy neighborhoods that travelers are still likely to visit. A high concentration of sights and museums is the real draw here, but don't overlook the few excellent restaurants and small bars that dot the area. Jodenbuurt, centered around **Waterlooplein,** takes its name from its history as a 17th-century Jewish immigrant neighborhood. The Holocaust tragically devastated Amsterdam's Jewish population, lowering the population from 55,000 to just over 5000. Today, many moving and informative museums recount the Dutch Jewish community's experience. Stretching around Jodenbuurt to the east is **Plantage,** with its large streets and many lovely parks. Most commercial establishments can be found in the streets near the **Artis Zoo.**

ACCOMMODATIONS

Unless you're going to be shelling out for one of the glitzy, multi-star hotels in Amsterdam, chances are you'll either be staying in a big backpacker hostel or a small hotel in a converted canal house. For the most part, pretty much anything you find in the city center will be at lease decent, but there's a huge variety in value—some rooms are simply small white boxes with a bed, while others are lovingly decorated with modern elegance or a cool theme. To stretch your euro the most, consider staying in one of the neighborhoods outside of the main canal ring. Otherwise, the hostels in the center are well-maintained and home to vibrant social scenes.

Oude Zijd

Most accommodations are concentrated in the Red Light District and Nieuwe Zijd, leaving the Oude Zijd with slim pickings. However, it's here that you can find two of the city's best and most affordable hostels.

▨ SHELTER CITY ✦⊗⁽ᵗ⁾ HOSTEL ❶

Barndesteeg 21 ☎020 62 532 30 ▣www.shelter.nl

Shelter City is a large and friendly Christian hostel (with no religious requirements for guests) in the heart of the Oude Zijd. Dorms range in size from 4 to 16 beds per room. All are single-sex, and most come with shared baths. There are many comfortable common spaces, including a cafe and courtyard garden in this hostel that's extremely popular with young backpackers from all over.

✦ ⓂNieuwmarkt. Just off the southwestern edge of the square. *i* No drugs or alcohol allowed. Ⓢ Dorms €14.50-32.50. Discounts available for longer stays.

▨ STAYOKAY AMSTERDAM STADSDOELEN (HI) ✦⊗⁽ᵗ⁾ HOSTEL ❶

Kloveniersburgwal 97 ☎020 62 468 31 ▣www.stayokay.com/stadsdoelen

Located in a tranquil part of the Oude Zijd, this hostel is near to Jodenbuurt. Rooms are plain and clean, with a slightly older feel than many of the other Stayokays (a Dutch hostel chain) due to its location in an old canal building.

✦ Tram #4, 9, 16, 24, or 25 to Muntplein. Walk down Nieuwe Doelenstraat; Kloveniersburgwal will be on the right over the bridge. Ⓢ 8- to 20-bed dorms €15-27.50; private rooms €39-70.

Red Light District

Lined with popular hotels and hostels, **Warmoesstraat** is great if you're looking for a place with a bustling backpacker atmosphere. While the prices here vary seasonally as they do in most of the city's neighborhoods, rates in the Red Light District also tend to fall drastically during the middle of the week.

▨ THE GREENHOUSE EFFECT HOTEL ✦⊗⊗⁽ᵗ⁾ HOTEL ❸

Warmoesstraat 55 ☎020 62 449 74 ▣www.greenhouse-effect.nl

The Greenhouse Effect has some of the nicest rooms in all of Amsterdam, so they're definitely miles above the Red Light District average. The hotel's location above a welcoming bar and next door to a great coffeeshop is also special, particularly since guests receive discounts at both establishments.

✦ From Centraal Station, go south on Damrak, turn right onto Brugsteeg, and veer left onto Warmoesstraat. Ⓢ Singles €65-75; doubles €95-110; triples €130.

DURTY NELLY'S HOSTEL ✦⊗⁽ᵗ⁾ HOSTEL ❶

Warmoesstraat 115-117 ☎020 63 801 25 ▣www.durtynellys.nl

A deservedly popular hostel, Durty Nelly's boasts co-ed dorms that are, ironically, very clean. They aren't terribly spacious, but the rooms feel more cozy than cramped. Guests receive a discount on food and drink at the pub below, and the staff is happy to help arrange sightseeing around the city.

✦ From Centraal Station, go south on Damrak, turn right onto Brugsteeg, and veer right onto Warmoesstraat. Ⓢ 4- to 10-bed dorms €25-50.

MEETING POINT YOUTH HOSTEL ✦⊗⁽ᵗ⁾ HOSTEL ❶

Warmoesstraat 14 ☎020 62 774 99 ▣www.hostel-meetingpoint.nl

The cheapest prices and most spacious dorms in the Red Light District—you know this place is gonna be popular with young backpackers. The eight- or 18-bed co-ed dorms are plain but large and airy. There's a 24hr. bar downstairs.

✦ From Centraal Station, turn left onto the far side of Prins Hendrikkade, then bear right onto Nieuwebrugsteeg, then a right onto Warmoesstraat. Ⓢ 18-bed dorms €18-25; 8-bed €25-30.

HOTEL INTERNATIONAAL ✦⊗⁽ᵗ⁾ HOTEL ❸

Warmoesstraat 1-3 ☎020 62 455 20 ▣www.hotelinternationaal.com

Similar to many of the other small bar-hotel setups along the street, Hotel Internationaal nevertheless stands out thanks to its extra-amicable staff and extra-pastel-green walls. The rooms are otherwise a bit nondescript—though those on the top floor have cool Tudor-style exposed beams.

🪧 *From Centraal Station, turn left onto Prins Hendrikkade, then go right onto Nieuwebrugsteeg, then right onto Warmoesstraat.* [$] *Doubles €65-85, with bath €85-110; quads €120-140.*

Nieuwe Zijd

The Nieuwe Zijd is packed with accommodations, making it easy to stumble straight from **Centraal Station** into your room. Hotels here tend to be pricey for what you're getting. Luckily, top-notch hostels abound.

☑ FLYING PIG DOWNTOWN

💳🚭📶 HOSTEL [1]

Nieuwendijk 100 ☎020 42 068 22 💻www.flyingpig.nl

A lively bar (it doesn't call itself a "party hostel" for nothing), a comfy smoking lounge, and spacious dorms make this a perennial favorite among backpackers. The young and cheerful staff makes the place feel like home, and frequent events, like live DJs three times a week, enhance the sociable atmosphere.

🪧 *From Centraal Station, walk toward Damrak. Pass the Victoria Hotel and take the 1st alley on your right, which leads to Nieuwendijk.* [$] *4- to 18-bed dorms €20-30.*

☑ AIVENGO YOUTH HOSTEL

💳🚭📶 HOSTEL [1]

Spuistraat 6 ☎020 42 136 70

If you find the white walls and minimal decoration in most hostels a little boring, this is the place for you. Deep colors and gauzy purple curtains give the dorms a decadent, *Arabian Nights* sort of vibe. A mix of bunks and normal beds fills the large and sociable dorms.

🪧 *From Centraal Station, walk down Martelarsgraacht; keep straight onto Hekelveld, which will turn into Spuistraat.* [$] *Dorms €20-35; in winter prices as low as €12. Private rooms €70-110.*

☑ BOB'S YOUTH HOSTEL

🚫💳🚭📶 HOSTEL [1]

Nieuwezijds Voorburgwal 92 ☎020 62 463 58 💻www.bobsyouthhostel.nl

A slightly hippie-er counterpart to the Flying Pig, Bob's Youth Hostel attracts flocks of young travelers who enjoy lounging in the graffiti-filled bar area or outside on the steps (often with acoustic guitars). To leave room for more spontaneous travelers, only a small number of reservations are taken.

🪧 *From Centraal Station, go down Martelaarsgracht and bear left as it becomes Nieuwezijds Voorburgwal.* [$] *4- to 16-bed dorms €22; apartment €90 for 2 people, €120 for 3.*

☑ HOTEL BROUWER

🚫💳🚭 HOTEL [4]

Singel 83 ☎020 62 463 58 💻www.hotelbrouwer.nl

If you want to get a sense of what it would be like to live in an old Dutch canal house, this is your best bet (and value). Of all the rooms (each named after a Dutch artist), the small double Bosch room is the real delight, with a living room space featuring antique furniture and a traditional box bed set into the wall.

🪧 *From Centraal Station, cross the water, go right on Prins Hendrikkade, and left onto Singel.* [$] *Doubles €100; triples €120.*

HOTEL GROENENDAEL

💳🚭📶 HOTEL [1]

Nieuwendijk 15 ☎020 62 448 22 💻www.hotelgroenendael.com

Simple, slightly worn rooms are more than just bed-filled boxes thanks to lovely touches like molding around the wall edges, large windows, and a few small terraces. Breakfast is served in a cozy common area.

🪧 *From Centraal Station, turn right, go left at Martelaarsgracht, and then head right onto Nieuwendijk.* [$] *Singles €35; doubles €60; triples €90.*

Canal Ring West and Scheepvaartbuurt

Raadhuisstraat is a row of hotel after hotel, making it a great place to try and find a room if everywhere else is full. For a quieter and more picturesque location, try one of the places in the **Nine Streets** or along a canal.

🏨 FREDERIC RENT-A-BIKE
Brouwersgracht 78

🔲⊘ HOTEL, APARTMENTS ❷
☎020 62 455 09 💻www.frederic.nl

Three amazing, homey rooms, each named after a different artist, sit at the back of Frederic's bike rental shop. The rooms are surrounded by the cozy shop that's filled with pianos, statues, and other knickknacks (including a small suit of armor). Frederic also rents out a number of houseboats and apartments in the area. You can end up saving quite a bit by staying in these impeccable apartments, which come at a price that's more than competitive given their quality and location. Adding to the experience are the supremely helpful owners, who know the city inside and out and will give you some of the best Amsterdam advice you can find. They also have some great stories to tell; make sure to ask them about their experiences with other luminaries of the travel-writing world.

⚑ *Leaving Centraal Station, make a right, cross the Singel, then walk 2 blocks down Brouwersgracht.* ⑤ *Smaller rooms €40-50 as singles, €60-70 as doubles; Mondrian room €90-100. Apartments and houseboats range from €100 for 2 people to €225 for 6, with 15% reservation fee.*

🏨 HOTEL CLEMENS
Raadhuisstraat 39

🔲⊘((ɬ)) HOTEL ❷
☎020 62 460 89 💻www.clemenshotel.com

Every room in this small hotel is lovingly decorated with French patterned wallpaper and tiered curtains. Enjoy breakfast on the balcony with a view of the Westerkerk. Best of all: it's cheap.

⚑ *Tram #13, 14, or 17 to Westermarkt.* ⑤ *Singles €40-60; doubles €60-120; triples €120-150.*

🏨 NADIA HOTEL
Raadhuisstraat 51

🔫⊘((ɬ)) HOTEL ❸
☎020 62 015 50 💻www.nadia.nl

Nadia Hotel boasts luxurious rooms with elegant bedspreads, large windows, and built-in wooden shelves. The double overlooking the canal will make you feel like you're on a 🔲**boat.**

⚑ *Tram #13, 14, or 17 to Westermarkt.* ⑤ *Singles €50-90; doubles €65-100.*

HOTEL PAX
Raadhuisstraat 37B

🔫⊘ HOTEL ❷
☎020 62 497 35 💻www.hotelpax.nl

The common spaces in Hotel Pax are brightly painted and hung with mirrors and prints, giving it a much nicer feel than other budget hotels nearby. The no-frills rooms are outfitted with plain metal-frame beds but remain spacious and airy.

⚑ *Tram #13, 14, or 17 to Westermarkt.* ⑤ *Singles from €35; doubles €60-90; quads €120-150.*

Central Canal Ring and Rembrandtplein

Despite the neighborhood's slim hotel pickings, the Central Canal Ring is an excellent place to call home. You'll be close to Museumplein, Leidseplein, and the Nieuwe Zijd—pretty much wherever you might want to go in Amsterdam. To top it all off, these relatively quiet hotels come at a better value than those in the city center.

🏨 HEMP HOTEL
Fredericksplein 15

🔫⊘((ɬ)) HOTEL ❸
☎020 62 544 25 💻www.hemp-hotel.com

Each of Hemp Hotel's rooms has a different geographic theme—the Caribbean, Tibet, and India are regions represented—brought to life by hemp fabrics, handmade wood carvings, and vibrant pictures. Book far in advance—the hotel is deservedly popular and fills up quickly. Make sure to try the hemp rolls at breakfast.

⚑ *Tram #4, 7, 10, or 25 to Fredericksplein. Walk diagonally across the square.* ⑤ *Singles €60; doubles €70, with bath €75.*

the netherlands

👍 THE GOLDEN BEAR
💳⊗📶▼ HOTEL [3]

Kerkstraat 37 ☎020 62 447 85 💻www.goldenbear.nl

Since 1948, this has been Amsterdam's premier openly gay hotel (about 75% of the guests are male, though women and straight couples are certainly welcome). Besides its forward-thinking attitude, the hotel is notable for its welcoming staff and elegantly modern rooms at excellent prices. Management is changing in late 2010, so call ahead to find out if policies have changed.

➜ Tram #1, 2, or 5 to Keizersgracht. Continue down Leidsestraat and make a right. [$] Singles with shared bath €63-70; doubles €73-90, with bath €90-130.

👍 CITY HOTEL
💳⊗📶 HOTEL [3]

Utrechtstraat 2 ☎020 62 723 23 💻www.city-hotel.nl

Large, brightly decorated, and perfectly clean rooms with colorful bedspreads and oversized pictures of flowers characterize this beautiful hotel. Some rooms have balconies, and those on the top floor have great views of Rembrandtplein and the rest of the city. Many of the rooms are made for five to eight people (some with bunk beds), but none feel cramped. There are no singles, though.

➜ Tram #9 or 14 to Rembrandtplein; off the southeast corner of the main square. [$] Doubles €135; triples €150; 6-person rooms €270.

HOTEL KAP
💳⊗📶 HOTEL [2]

Den Texstraat 5b ☎020 62 459 08 💻www.kaphotel.nl

In the summer, when you can eat breakfast or simply relax in the leafy garden out back, Hotel Kap is a really lovely option. The rooms have high ceilings and great windows, though the furnishings are rather plain.

➜ Tram #4, 7, 10, 16, 24, or 25 to Weteringcircuit. Walk down Weteringschans, make a right at 2e Weteringplantsoen, and then a left at Den Texstraat. ℹ Breakfast included. Singles with shared bath; doubles available with shared or ensuite bath. Wi-Fi €5 per stay. [$] Singles €40-65; doubles €60-95.

West Of Town

If you want to live like a local but not commute like one, camp out in the Jordaan. Westerpark is extremely residential and has few accommodations, while Oud-West has a few more, particularly in the area close to Leidseplein.

👍 SHELTER JORDAAN
💳⊗📶 HOSTEL [1]

Bloemstraat 179 ☎020 62 447 17 💻www.shelter.nl

Smaller and in a quieter location than its sister hostel in the Oude Zijd, the Shelter Jordaan has the same excellent prices, clean facilities, and comfortable atmosphere. Single-sex rooms are large and bright, with colorful beds and lockers that avoid the institutional feel to which many hostels succumb.

➜ Tram #10 to Bloemstraat or tram #13, 14, or 17 to Westermarkt. Follow Lijnbaansgracht for 50m, then turn right onto Bloemstraat. [$] 4- to 8-bed dorms €16.50-30.50.

👍 HOTEL JUPITER
⊘⊗📶 HOTEL [2]

2nd Helmersstraat 14 ☎020 61 871 32 💻www.jupiterhotel.nl

Charming both inside and out, this hotel's rooms are a welcome break from the usual monochromatic hotel palette, with colorful walls and sleek modern furniture, and they're only a 5min. walk from the Leidseplein.

➜ Tram #3 or 12 to Overtoom. From Overtoom, walk 2 blocks away from Vondelpark on 1e C. Huygensstraat and make a right. [$] High-season singles €54, with bath €64; doubles €74/99. Low-season singles €39/49; doubles €59/79. Triples and quads also available.

HOTEL VAN ONNA
⊘⊗📶 HOTEL [2]

Bloemgracht 104 ☎020 62 658 01 💻www.vanonna.nl

The rooms on the top floor of this hotel are truly remarkable, with slanted ceilings and exposed wood beams, plus a view over the rooftops of the whole Jordaan. Rooms are impeccably clean.

➡ *Tram #10 to Bloemgracht or tram #13, 14, or 17 to Westermarkt. Cross Prinsengracht and make a right; Bloemgracht is 2 blocks away.* $ *Singles €45; doubles €90; triples €135.*

Museumplein and Leidseplein

Hotels around Museumplein are removed from the city's best food and drink but ooze residential luxury. And, of course, they put you a stone's throw from the area's great museums, so you can go back and see *Night Watch* again and again and again. Leidseplein also offers a few great options.

STAYOKAY AMSTERDAM VONDELPARK — 💳♿📶 HOSTEL [1]

Zandpad 5 — ☎020 58 989 96 💻www.stayokay.nl/vondelpark

This is a large, slightly institutional-feeling hostel in between Vondelpark and Leidseplein. The dorms are spacious and incredibly clean, and each room has its own bathroom (the larger rooms have two). Staff are more than willing to help with any questions you may have about the city. Guests tend to be on the younger side of the backpacker set.

➡ *Tram #1, 2, 5, 7, or 10 to Leidseplein. Walk across the canal toward the Marriott, take a left, then make a right onto Zandpad after 1 block.* $ *2- to 20-bed dorms €20-34; singles €50-80.*

FLYING PIG UPTOWN — 💳🚭📶 HOSTEL [1]

Vossiusstraat 46-47 — ☎020 40 041 87 💻www.flyingpig.nl

We find it a little confusing that the Flying Pig Uptown is actually south of Flying Pig Downtown in Nieuwe Zijd, but then again, we can't quite wrap our heads around the fact that the Nile runs south to north—no matter. This is the original Flying Pig, and with a tranquil location across from Vondelpark, this winged swine is a little less rowdy than its younger sibling. Nevertheless, it's still a phenomenally popular and friendly hostel. With proximity to the Leidseplein, guests frequently start off here before going pubbing and clubbing—and then nurse their hangovers the next day.

➡ *Tram #2, 3, 5, or 12 to Van Baerlestraat. Walk down Van Baerlestraat toward Vondelpark and make a right onto Vossiusstraat.* $ *2- to 10-bed dorms €14-40.*

HOTEL BEMA — 💳🚭📶 HOTEL [2]

Concertgebouwplein 19b — ☎020 67 913 96 💻www.bemahotel.com

Just across from the stunning **Concertgebouw** and the grassy expanse of Museumplein, Hotel Bema boasts rooms with incredible romantic elegance boosted by high ceilings, crystal chandeliers, and old-fashioned floral wallpaper. Topping off the luxury, breakfast is brought to your room between 8:30am and 9am. We could get used to living like this, especially at such low prices.

➡ *Tram #3, 5, 12, 16, or 24 to Museumplein. Walk down the left side of the Concertgebouw and cross the street.* $ *Singles with shared bath €35-45; doubles €65-75, with bath €75-85.*

BACKSTAGE HOTEL — 💳🚭📶 HOTEL [2]

Leisegracht 114 — ☎020 62 440 44 💻www.backstagehotel.com

We at *Let's Go* may not be rock stars, but even without Keith Richards' life experience under our belts, we can safely say that there is no way in hell any backstage area is as glorious as the rooms of this hotel. The decor adheres strictly to a concert-venue theme: backboards are made to look like trunks, lamps like spotlights, ceiling lights have drum lampshades, and certain rooms have dressing tables that even Lady Gaga would envy. Some suites are quads and quints big enough to house your whole band. One room has been sponsored by Activision and is Guitar Hero themed, with your very own Xbox and game setup.

➡ *Tram #1, 2, or 5 to Leidseplein.* $ *Singles €35-85; doubles €48-145; quints €150-250.*

FREELAND — 💳🚭📶❄ HOTEL [3]

Marnixstraat 386 — ☎020 62 275 11 💻www.hotelfreeland.com

Freeland is an unbelievably fresh and cheerful hotel, miles away in character from the crowds and grit of the nearby Leidseplein. Rooms are airy and floral, but in a pastel take on modern design that's breezier than the cloying sweetness of your great-aunt Mildred's living room. Book early, as this place's charm isn't exactly a well-kept secret.

Tram #1, 2, 5, 7, or 10 to Leidseplein. $ Singles €58-70; doubles €78-120.

INTERNATIONAL BUDGET HOSTEL HOSTEL ❶

Leidsegracht 76 ☎020 62 427 84 www.internationalbudgethostel.com

On the opposite side of the Leidsegracht from the Leidseplein in a classic, narrow canal house sits this student-friendly hostel. Each dorm has four single beds—no bunk beds, a boon for those prone to either hitting their heads on or rolling off the top bunk. Very welcoming and friendly staff.

Tram #7 or 10 to Raamplein. Continue walking down Marnixstraat and make a left at the canal. $ Dorms €20-32.

De Pijp

Though far from the city's true center, De Pijp has character and easy transport options, making it the perfect place to see what it's like to be the hip, young thing living in an up-and-coming 'hood.

BICYCLE HOTEL HOTEL ❷

Van Ostadestraat 123 ☎020 67 934 52 www.bicyclehotel.com

A certain current of yuppie environmentalism runs through De Pijp, so it's appropriate that this eco-conscious hotel sits within its borders. Not only does the hotel have solar panels and a "green roof" (something about plants growing on it and saving energy—the owners explain it better than we can), but the whole theme of clean freshness permeates the building. Large windows in the rooms overlooking leafy gardens let in light and air. There are even some real balconies to sit on. Plus, the per-day bicycle rental costs almost exactly equal the price of a 24hr. transport ticket, so there's no excuse for you not to go green as well.

Tram #3, 12, or 25 to Ceinturbaan/Ferdinand Bolstraat. Continue 1 block farther and make a left onto Van Ostadestraat. $ Singles €35-70; doubles €40-85, with bath €60-120. Bike rental €7.50 per day.

SARPHATI HOTEL HOTEL ❸

Sarphatipark 58 ☎020 67 340 83

This bright and modern hotel is just across the street from Sarphatipark and a few blocks away from Albert Cuypmarkt. Rooms have bright yellow walls and high ceilings; all are impeccably clean.

Tram #3 or 25 to 2e van der Helstraat. Walk along the park. $ Singles €60-90; doubles €80-140.

Jodenbuurt and Plantage

Slightly removed from the city center (though in pocket-sized Amsterdam you're never really far from anything), these establishments will make for a more tranquil and local-feeling stay.

BRIDGE HOTEL HOTEL ❹

Amstel 107-111 ☎020 62 370 68 www.thebridgehotel.nl

The massive rooms in this family-run hotel are well worth the splurge. Done up in a mod palette of black, red, and white, rooms are large enough for a table and chairs and some have a view of the Amstel outside. The location may feel remote, but you're just across the bridge from Rembrandtplein.

Tram #9 or 14 to Waterlooplein or Mr. Visserplein. Walk down Weesperstraat; make a right onto Nieuwe Prinsengracht, then a left onto Amstel. $ Singles €85-115; doubles €98-140.

HERMITAGE HOTEL HOTEL ❸

Nieuwe Keizersgracht 16 ☎020 62 382 59 www.hotelhermitageamsterdam.nl

A newer addition to the street, Hermitage also has a younger feel than most of the neighboring hotels.Combining two of Amsterdam's predominant hotel aesthetics, modern minimalist and old-fashioned floral, Hermitage covers its walls in stylized silver-and-black flowered wallpaper, and the rooms continue the cozy yet urban look.

❖ *Tram #9 or 14 to Waterlooplein or Mr. Visserplein. Walk down Weesperstraat and make a right onto Nieuwe Keizersgracht.* Ⓢ *Singles €44-90; doubles €55-120.*

SIGHTS 👁

Walking around Amsterdam, you'll come across more than enough sights to fill your visit. Between old churches, quaint houses, and peaceful canals, this is one of the prettiest modern cities around. Behind those picturesque walls, however, there's a whole lot more waiting to be explored. The large, famous galleries on Museumplein are rightly celebrated for their collections of new and old Dutch art; modern photography exhibitions are held in 17th-century canal houses or 14th-century churches; and a whole host of excellent museums and monuments are reflections upon the Netherlands's tribulations during WWII. Most historical museums focus on Dutch or colonial topics, while the newer art exhibitions have an international bent. Of course, there are also a few less highbrow options like the Sex Museum and the Hash, Marijuana, and Hemp Museum. Plus the First Museum of **Fluorescent** Art, which is just too awesome to be sufficiently honored by mere prose.

If you're planning on visiting a number of museums, it's strongly recommended to invest in the **Museumjaarkaart** (💻*www.museumjaarkaart.nl).* For €40, or €20 if you're under 26, you get free entrance to most museums in Amsterdam and the Netherlands for a whole year. Though only a few museums have admission fees of more than €10, the little €5 and €7 tickets do add up. With the Museumjaarkaart, there's nothing to stop you from popping into one of the smaller or weirder museums and then skipping right out if it's not up to snuff. You *cannot* get the card at the tourist office, but instead should go to one of the participating museums, such as the Bijbels Museum, the Rijksmuseum, or the Van Gogh museum. If, on the other hand, you're only in town for a few days, consider getting the **I Amsterdam card** (💻*www.iamsterdam.com)* at the tourist office, which is more expensive and only valid for 24-72hr. but also gives you access to public transport.

Oude Zijd

The Oude Zijd doesn't have many traditional sights or museums, but it is home to a number of interesting architectural landmarks.

👍 NIEUWMARKT ♿🍸 SQUARE

Nieuwmarkt

Dominated by the largest still-standing medieval building in Amsterdam, Nieuwmarkt is a calm square lined with diverse cafes and bars, making it one of the best places in the city for some relaxed people-watching. **De Waag,** the 15th-century castle-like structure in Nieuwmarkt's center, was originally a fortress gate. When the walls surrounding the city were demolished to enable Amsterdam's expansion, the fortress became a weighing house. In later centuries it housed a gallery for surgical dissections (Rembrandt's *The Anatomy Lesson of Dr. Tulp* depicts one such event), the **Jewish Historical Museum,** and, now, a restaurant and cafe. Nieuwmarkt is beloved by tourists and locals alike: in the 1970s, a plan to build a Metro and highway going through the neighborhood triggered the demolition of many surrounding buildings, which in turn prompted heavy rioting here in 1975. The highway idea was scrapped, but the Metro plan persisted, the product of which you can see in the corner of the square. Daily markets selling everything from souvenirs to organic food take place daily here and are at their largest on the weekends.

❖ Ⓜ*Nieuwmarkt or from Centraal Station walk 10min. down Zeedijk.*

FO GUANG SHAN HE HUA TEMPLE ⊘ TEMPLE

Zeedijk 106-118 ☎020 42 023 57 🖳www.ibps.nl

You can't miss this brightly painted, gabled building along Zeedijk. It's Europe's largest palace-style Buddhist temple. Queen Beatrix herself officially opened the temple, associated with the Taiwan-based Fo Guang Shan Buddhist order, in 2000. The goals of the temple include both spiritual development and cultural exchange. Most travelers come to peek inside the temple at the ornate Buddha statues, but the building also hosts lectures on Buddhism and Chinese as well as holiday and festival celebrations.

⇄ [M]Nieuwmarkt. [$] Free. ⏰ Open Tu-Sa noon-5pm, Su 10am-5pm. Services Su 10:30am; open to the public.

Red Light District

No one comes to the Red Light District to go museum-hopping. However, if you decide to take a break from pretending not to look at the window prostitutes, there are a few sights here that you can examine without feeling nearly as embarrassed.

👍 **OUDE KERK** ⊛♿ CHURCH

Oudekerksplein 23 ☎020 62 582 84 🖳www.oudekerk.nl

Since its foundation in 1306, Oude Kerk, the oldest church in Amsterdam, has endured everything from the Protestant Reformation to the growth of the Red Light District which today encroaches naughtily on its very square. Oude Kerk didn't escape all this history unscathed: during the Alteration of the 16th century, the church lost much of its artwork and religious figures. However, it remains a strikingly beautiful structure, with massive vaulted ceilings and gorgeous stained glass that betray the building's Catholic, pre-Calvinist roots. Oude Kerk is now largely used for art and photography exhibitions, including the display of the prestigious **World Press Photo** prizewinners.

⇄ From Centraal Station, walk down Damrak, take a left onto Oudebrugsteeg, and turn right onto Warmoesstraat; the next left leads to the church. [$] €7.50; students, seniors, and under 13 €5.50; with Museumjaarkaart free. ⏰ Open M-Sa 10am-5:30pm, Su 1-5:30pm.

HASH MARIJUANA HEMP MUSEUM ⊛⊘ MUSEUM

Oudezijds Achterburgwal 148 ☎020 62 359 61 🖳www.hashmuseum.com

No matter how much weed you've encountered in Amsterdam, this place probably has something you haven't seen before. More valuable for the kitsch factor than for actual information (if you want that, go a few doors down to **Cannabis College**), this museum explores the history and myriad uses of the cannabis plant. Displays detail ancient mentions of smoking marijuana, the importance of the hemp industry in the 17th and 18th centuries, the science of THC, and the costs of America's war on drugs—among much other ganga-related information. You can see a collection of pipes from around the world and a copy of the Declaration of Independence printed on hemp paper. Scattered somewhat incongruously throughout are Bible verses that could be liberally interpreted as support for the freedom to toke up.

⇄ From Dam Square, walk east on Dam and make a left onto Oudezijds Achterburgwal. [$] €9, groups of 10 or more €7 per person. ⏰ Open daily 10am-11pm.

CANNABIS COLLEGE ⊛⊘ INFORMATION CENTER

Oudezijds Achterburgwal 124 ☎020 42 344 20 🖳www.cannabiscollege.com

Get your druggie "diploma" (a bachelor's in blunts? a master's in marijuana? a doctorate in doobies?) by taking a short quiz on all things cannabis-related. Don't just come to pad your credentials, though: this is a repository of any and all information you could ever want about the funny stuff. Friendly volunteers on staff are happy to answer any questions visitors may have about the history, science, and usage of the drug. They're so knowledgeable that they run training programs for coffeeshop staffers, and they're hoping to expand with even more educational opportunities in the future. Downstairs, a wide variety of plants grow in a lovingly tended organic garden.

From Dam Square, walk east on Dam and make a left onto Oudezijds Achterburgwal. $ Free. Garden €2.50. Open daily 11am-7pm.

Nieuwe Zijd

The Nieuwe Zijd (despite the name) is one of the oldest parts of the city. Both important historical architecture and museums dedicated to the past can be found within its borders. Some of the more recent and gimmicky museums, such as **Madame Tussaud's** and the **Amsterdam Dungeon,** are located here as well.

NIEUWE KERK — CHURCH, MUSEUM

Dam Sq. ☎020 63 869 09 www.nieuwekerk.nl

Built in 1408 when the Oude Kerk became too small for the city's growing population, the Nieuwe Kerk is a commanding Gothic building that manages to hold its own amid the architectural extravaganza that is Dam Sq. Inside, the church is all vaulted ceilings and massive windows. Don't miss the intricate organ case designed by **Jacob van Campen,** Koninklijk Palace's architect. Today, the church is no longer used for religious purposes but is the site of royal inaugurations (the last one being that of **Queen Beatrix** in 1980) and some royal weddings (**Prince Willem-Alexander,** the heir to the Dutch throne, was married here in 2002). Most of the year, however, the space serves as a museum. Each winter, the church holds exhibits on foreign cultures, with a specific focus on world religions, and recent topics have included Islam and Ancient Egypt. Organ concerts are held here every Sunday, while shorter and more informal organ recitals are performed on Thursday afternoons.

Any tram to Dam. Nieuwe Kerk is on the northeastern edge of the square. $ €5, students €4, with Museumjaarkaart free. Organ concerts €8.50, recitals €5. Open daily 10am-5pm. Recitals Th 12:30pm. Concerts Su 8pm.

BEGIJNHOF — COURTYARD, CHURCH

Begijnhof www.begijnhofamsterdam.nl

The **Beguines** were medieval groups of Roman Catholic laywomen who took vows of chastity and chose to serve the Church without retreating from the world and formally joining a convent. After seeing this beautiful 14th-century courtyard (the Beguines lived in the houses surrounding it), you'll agree that they made a good call: this is a pretty sweet crib.

Tram #1, 2, or 5 to Spui/Niuewezijds Voorburgwal. Walk down Gedempte Begijnsloot; the gardens are on the left. $ Free. Open daily 9am-5pm.

AMSTERDAM HISTORICAL MUSEUM — MUSEUM

Nieuwezijds Voorburgwal 357, Kalverstraat 92 ☎020 52 318 22 www.amh.nl

People, schmeople. This place is about Amsterdam, the *city.* Watch the introductory video that shows how this northern powerhouse has grown from a tiny settlement by the Amstel to a familiar horseshoe ring of canals to the recognizable urban destination of the past century. Don't miss the room dedicated to Golden Age art, with some stomach-churningly gruesome paintings of the anatomy lessons that were fashionable during the 17th century. Also fascinating is the corner that shows various city planning designs from the past century, driving home the fact that Amsterdam is an entirely manmade city and that building more housing today entails building more land.

Tram #1, 2, or 5 to Spui/Niuewezijds Voorburgwal. Head up Niuwezijds Voorburgwal; the museum is on the right. $ €10, seniors €7.50, students and ages 6-18 €5, under 6 and with Museumjaarkaart free. Open M-F 10am-5pm, Sa-Su 11am-5pm.

DAM SQUARE

                                                                    ♿ SQUARE

Dam Sq.

Once upon a time, lively Amsterdam was just two small settlements on either side of the Amstel River. Then one day, the settlers decided to connect their encampments with a dam. Three guesses where that dam was built. Since then, Dam Square has been the heart of the city, home to markets, a church, the town hall, and a weigh house (until Napoleon's brother had it torn down because it blocked his view). The obelisk on one end is the **National Monument,** inside of which soil from all twelve Dutch provinces and the Dutch East Indies is stored. The monument was erected in 1956 to honor the Dutch victims of WWII. Across from the monument, next to the Nieuwe Kerk, you'll find the **Koninklijk Palace,** which is currently closed for restoration. Louis Napoleon took it over in 1808, deciding that the building, constructed in the 17th century as Amsterdam's town hall, would make an excellent fixer-upper. Since then, it has been an official royal palace of the Netherlands, though Queen Beatrix only uses it for official functions and actually lives elsewhere. Too bad—she's wasting a unique view of the crowds, street performers, and occasional concert-type events that take place in the square.

⬧ *Tram #1, 2, 4, 5, 9, 13, 14, 16, 17, 24, or 25 to Dam. Yeah, it's pretty easy to get here.*

AMSTERDAM SEX MUSEUM

◉✕ MUSEUM

Damrak 18   ☎020 62 283 76 📩www.sexmuseumamsterdam.nl

Unless you were previously unaware that people have been having sex since the species's origin, there is not much information about sex or sexuality to be had at this museum. (The brief "Sex Through the Ages" presentation is hilariously simplistic, though the elegant British accent narrating it is priceless.) Instead, there's a lot of pornographic paintings, photographs, books, and statues, mainly from the late 19th and early 20th centuries, though most historical periods are represented in some form or another. Scattered throughout are models of various sexual icons: there's Marilyn Monroe with her skirt fluttering over the subway vent, a 1980s pimp, and even a 👨flasher who thrills the audience like clockwork every few seconds. If you really want to see a parade of pictures of people having sex, you could just walk through the Red Light District and get it for free. At least this place charges a low rate for the high kitsch factor.

⬧ *From Centraal Station, walk straight down Damrak.* *i* *Must be 16+ to enter.* Ⓟ *€4.* ⏲ *Open daily 9:30am-11:30pm.*

Canal Ring West and Scheepvaartbuurt

The Canal Ring West has none of the city's large art museums, but it is where you'll find some of Amsterdam's quirkiest spots as well as the notable **Anne Frank House** and nearby **Westerkerk.**

▣ ANNE FRANK HOUSE

✈✕ MUSEUM

Prinsengracht 267   ☎020 55 671 00 📩www.annefrank.nl

From July 6, 1942, until they were betrayed by a still unknown informant and arrested on August 4, 1944, Anne Frank and her family, along with four others, lived in a "secret annex" above the warehouse of her father's company in this building. Since its publication in 1950, the diary Frank kept during her stay in the annex has become one of the world's most-read books; it stands as one of the most moving accounts of war and persecution to date as well as a testament to the strength and depth of the human spirit. This wonderfully presented museum illustrates the story of Frank and her fellow annex inhabitants and accompanies their tale with more information about the fate of Jews in the Netherlands and throughout Europe under Nazi oppression. Many traces of the annex's clandestine residents have been preserved, including the pictures Anne glued to the walls in hopes of cheering up the place and the pencil marks that tracked the growth of the children throughout their years in hiding. The rooms are no longer furnished, but models of their earlier setup (as well as blacked-out windows and the size of the rooms themselves) give some idea of the close quarters Anne struggled with in her diary. An exhibit near the end brings forth one of Otto Frank's main motives for establishing the museum: not just to remember the victims of the Holocaust, but to use that memory to work for a future in which such atrocities remain a thing of the past.

Tram #13, 14, or 17 to Westermarkt. ℹ Lines are shortest before 10am and after 6pm. $ €8.50, ages 10-17 €4, under 10 free. ⏰ Open daily July-Aug 9am-10pm; Sept 1-14 9am-9pm; Sept 15-March 14 9am-7pm; March 15-June 9am-9pm.

WESTERKERK — CHURCH

Prinsengracht 281 ☎020 62 477 66 🖥www.westerkerk.nl

The 85m tower of the Westerkerk stands out starkly amid the relative height uniformity of central Amsterdam's buildings. This church was completed in 1631 according to a design by **Hendrik de Keyser.** On the top of the tower is the symbol of the crown of Maximilian of Austria, a gift he gave to the city in thanks for Amsterdam's support of the Austro-Burgundian princes. Despite the apparent narcissism of the gesture, Maximilian's crown and the tower it caps have become an enduring symbol of the city. On the outside, the church's brick-and-stone exterior is a fine example of Dutch late Renaissance style. Inside, its plain white walls and clear glass windows are an example of the clean Calvinist aesthetic. Nevertheless, the church is by no means restricted to perpetual austerity: Queen Beatrix and Prince Claus were married here in 1966, which must have been quite the event. Rembrandt is buried somewhere within the church, although no one seems to know exactly where. (Yeah, we don't know how they forgot where they put one of the most famous painters of all time either.)

A trip up the **Westerkerkstoren** (part of a 30min. guided tour) is a must, affording phenomenal views of the surrounding city. Also up in the tower's heights is an astounding set of 47 bells, one of which weighs in at an astonishing 7509kg, making it Amsterdam's heaviest. On Tuesdays, the carillon plays from noon to 1pm. Free organ concerts are held every Friday at 1pm, and the church hosts many other concerts throughout the year.

Tram #13, 14, or 17 to Westermarkt. $ Free. Tower tour €5. ⏰ Open Apr-Oct 11am-3pm. Tower tours every 30min.

HOMOMONUMENT — ♿ MONUMENT

Westermarkt 🖥www.homomonument.nl

Designed by Karin Daan and officially opened in 1987, the Homomonument was the culmination of a movement to erect a memorial dedicated to those who were persecuted by the Nazis for their sexuality, but it is also meant to stand for all homosexual men and women who have been and are being oppressed because of their sexual orientation. The monument is constructed of three pink granite triangles (in remembrance of the symbol the Nazis forced homosexuals to wear) that are connected by thin lines of pink granite to form a larger triangle. Built so that it would merge seamlessly with the daily life of the city, the Homomonument can, in fact, be hard to discern under picnicking tourists and whizzing bikes. One triangle is set down into the water of the Keizergracht and points toward the **National War Monument** in Dam square, representing the present. The raised triangle stands for the future and points toward the headquarters of the COC, a Dutch gay rights group that was founded in 1946, and, as such, is the oldest continuously operating gay and lesbian organization in the world. The third triangle points toward the **Anne Frank House,** symbolizing the past; it is engraved with the words *"Naar Vriendschap Zulk een Mateloos Verlangen"* ("such an endless desire for friendship") from the poem *To a Young Fisherman* by Jacob Israel de Haan (1881-1924), a gay Dutch Jewish poet.

Tram #13, 14, or 17 to Westermarkt. The Homomonument is between Westerkerk and the Keizersgracht. $ Free.

Central Canal Ring and Rembrandtplein

The grand buildings in the center of the canal ring, architectural landmarks themselves, house some excellent historical museums as well as galleries highlighting more cutting-edge culture.

FOAM PHOTOGRAPHY MUSEUM — MUSEUM

Keizersgracht 609 ☎020 55 165 00 www.foam.nl

Foam—the **Fo**tografiemuseum **Am**sterdam—showcases photography exhibits on pretty much every topic imaginable, from ultramodern, gritty documentary shots to glossy fashion photos. Both renowned and up-and-coming photographers are shown here in a sparse wood-and-metal space. A place for study as well as exhibition, the cafe reading room has books and magazines for your perusal. No need to feel ashamed for simply grabbing a coffee and feeling like one of the artsy Dutch students who hang out here though.

Tram #4, 16, 24, or 25 to Keizersgracht. FOAM is about 50m east of the stop. $ €8, students and seniors €5.50, under 12 and with Museumjaarkaart free. Open M-W 10am-6pm, Th-F 10am-9pm, Sa-Su 10am-6pm. Cafe open daily 11am-5pm.

MUSEUM VAN LOON — MUSEUM

Keizersgracht 672 ☎020 62 452 55 www.museumvanloon.nl

The Van Loons have been so integral to the city's history, their family tree might as well be drawn on a map of Amsterdam. One of the family's earlier members was a founder of the Dutch East India Company, and since then many have been mayors, political advisors, and the like. However, this house was not originally owned by this powerful lineage. Its first resident, **Ferdinand Bol,** was Rembrandt's most famous student. The house as you see it now, though, is clearly of the Van Loon tenure, with family portraits lining the walls. Indeed, while here, it's easy to feel as if you're creeping around someone's house (which, really, you are). Set up to look like the elegant, upper-class home it was when the Van Loons still lived here, the museum preserves a record of what traditional wealthy Dutch life was like, as per the intentions of the family when they donated their residence to the city. Weird last name or no, you'll wish that you had grown up a Van Loon after seeing this place—everything is stunningly beautiful.

Tram #4, 16, 24, or 25 to Keizersgracht. The museum is about 50m east of the stop. $ €7, students €5, with Museumjaarkaart free. Open M 11am-5pm, W-Su 11am-5pm.

REMBRANDTPLEIN — SQUARE

Rembrandtplein

Once upon a time (a.k.a. the late 17th century), the area now known as Rembrandtplein was home to Amsterdam's butter market (*Botermarkt*). Unless there are things we don't know about the dairy trade, we suspect that the neighborhood was quite a bit tamer then than it is today. Around the end of the 19th century, hotels and cafes began to spring up around the square, which led to more tourists visiting the area, which led to people trying to figure out how to get more money from the tourists, which meant trying to get tourists drunk: thus, the explosion of bars and clubs nearby. Rembrandtplein is now home to Amsterdam's largest club, **Escape,** underneath Europe's largest LCD TV screen. From the middle of the square, **Rembrandt van Rijn** looks benevolently down at the madness.

Tram #9 or 14 to (surprise!) Rembrandtplein.

GOLDEN BEND

 ♿ ARCHITECTURE

Herengracht, between Leidsestraat and Vijzelstraat

If the tiny, teetering canal houses of Amsterdam are beginning to make you feel a bit claustrophobic, head to this scenic stretch of the Canal Ring. In the 17th century, the ring canals were extended all the way to the Amstel. This required a fair bit of cash, so in order to encourage investment, the city decided to loosen restrictions on house width and allow Amsterdam's rich to build homes that were twice as wide as had been previously allowed. Termed the "Golden Bend" for the wealth that subsequently flocked here, this is a grand and beautiful stretch of former residences, all featuring Neoclassical facades and glimpses of sparkling chandeliers through latticed windows. Today, most are inhabited by banks, life insurance agencies, and the occasional philanthropic organization. For a few days in June, it's possible to tour many of the houses' gardens on the **Open Garden Days.** For more information, check out ⛶www.opentuinendagen.nl.

✈ *Tram #1, 2, or 5 to Koningsplein.*

MUSEUM WILLET-HOLTHUYSEN

✍✘ MUSEUM

Herengracht 605   ☎020 52 318 70 ⛶www.willetholthuysen.nl

Not technically on the "Golden Bend" but still an extremely elegant canal house, this building has been preserved by the **Amsterdams Historisch Museum** to demonstrate what wealthy Dutch life was like in the 19th century as seen through the eyes of **Abraham Willet** and **Louisa Willet-Holthuysen,** the house's last inhabitants. Three opulently decorated floors feature many of the pieces acquired by this couple of avid art collectors. Painted by **Jacob de Wit,** the ceiling in the Blue Room was poached from a house on Keizersgracht. Throughout the museum, small paragraphs detail the culture and customs of life in the Willets' time. It makes a striking contrast to some of the other historic house museums such as **het Rembrandt** due to its grandeur and scale. A lovely garden in the back is open to museum visitors.

✈ *Tram #9 or 14 to Rembrandtplein. Walk down Utrechtsestraat and make a left.* Ⓞ *€7, students and ages 6-18 €3.50, under 6 and with Museumjaarkaart free.* Ⓢ *Open M-F 10am-5pm, Sa-Su 11am-5pm.*

West Of Town

▪ ELECTRIC LADYLAND

◑✘ MUSEUM

2e Leliedwarsstraat 5   ☎020 42 037 76 ⛶www.electric-lady-land.com

The "First Museum of Fluorescent Art" and a sight unlike any other, Electric Ladyland deserves a good chunk of your sightseeing time. The endearingly eccentric and passionate owner, Nick Padalino, will happily spend hours explaining the history, science, and culture of fluorescence and fluorescent art to each and every visitor who walks through the door. He's collected a spectacular assortment of rocks and minerals, many exceedingly rare, that hail from New Jersey to the Himalayas and glow all kinds of colors under the different light Padalino expertly shines upon them. Other artifacts tell the history of fluorescence and its popularity in the early part of the century: paintings made from fluorescent paint or ground mineral pigments, some dating to as early as the 1940s, hang on the walls. Most intriguing, though, is the fluorescent cave-like sculpture that Padalino terms "participatory art"—don a pair of foam slippers and poke around the glowing grottoes and stalactites, flick the buttons on and off to see different fluorescent and phosphorescent stones, and look for the tiny, hidden Hindu sculptures. Completing the psychedelic trip is a quiet soundtrack of classic rock from Hendrix to The Beatles. Upstairs, you can buy your own fluorescent art or blacklight kits to take home a part of the experience.

✈ *Tram #13, 14, or 17 to Westermarkt. Cross Prinsengracht and walk 1 block down Rozengracht,*

the netherlands

then make a right and walk a few blocks—the museum is just before you reach Egelantiersgracht. [$] €5. ⏰ Open Tu-Sa 1-6pm.

MUSEUM HET SCHIP ♿ MUSEUM

Spaarndammerplantsoen 140 ☎020 41 828 85 🖥www.hetschip.nl

As Amsterdam expanded at the turn of the 20th century, its workers lived in increasingly cramped and squalid conditions. Socialist movements led to laws regulating housing (requiring, for example, that apartments have windows) and to the construction of affordable, higher-quality living spaces. **Het Schip** ("The Ship") was one such housing project, built in 1919 and designed by Michel de Klerk. Its unusual design makes it a leading example of the Amsterdam School, an expressionist movement in architecture and design. You can get a feel for the characteristics of the Amsterdam School just by walking around the large building: notice the unusual curves inspired by organic shapes, the creative use of different kinds of brick and roof tiles, and the intricate sculptural decorations lurking in various corners. A visit to the museum, however, is worth the extra time, as it provides you with the opportunity to explore inside the remarkable post office nestled in one corner as well as an example of one of the building's original apartments (the rest are still in use).

🚋 Tram #3 to Haarlemmerplein. Walk across the canal toward Westerpark, up Spaarndammerstraat, and left onto Zaanstraat; the building will be a few blocks down the street. [$] €7.50, students €5, with Museumjaarkaart free. ⏰ Open Tu-Su 11am-5pm. Tours every hr. 11am-4pm.

STEDELIJK MUSEUM BUREAU AMSTERDAM ♿ MUSEUM

Rozenstraat 59 ☎020 42 204 71 🖥www.smba.nl

As the Stedelijk Museum's project space, the Stedelijk Museum Bureau Amsterdam (SMBA) seeks to promote cutting-edge contemporary art, primarily from the Netherlands. The bright white room hosts around six exhibitions a year, with everything from sculpture to painting to performance art represented. Lectures and discussions are also organized by the gallery. Check the website to see what's currently running. Given the free admission, there's no reason not to drop by.

🚋 Tram #13, 14, or 17 to Westermarkt. Cross Prinsengracht, make a left, and walk 1 block. [$] Free. ⏰ Open Tu-Su 11am-5pm.

HOFJES ♿ GARDENS, DUTCH HISTORY

Located in the northern third of the Jordaan

One theory regarding the origin of the Jordaan's name speculates that the moniker is derived from the French word *jardin* (garden), as a number of French Huguenots immigrated here in the 17th century. Such a hypothesis may provoke skepticism, however, since Jordaan is one of Amsterdam's few areas that doesn't have a park—it all starts to make sense, though, once you've stepped behind some of the neighborhood's closed doors. Here, you will find a number of *hofjes*, courtyards surrounded by almshouses that were originally designed to provide housing for poor older women. Nowadays, the buildings have been turned into private houses, but many of the gardens are still open to the public. In the northern part of the Jordaan, at Palmgracht 28-38, you can find the **Raepenhofje,** named after the founder (Pieter Raepe) who had it built in 1648 for orphans and widows to enjoy. A few blocks down is the **Karthuizerhof,** at Karthuizersstraat 21-131. This larger *hofje* has two flowering gardens dotted with benches and a pair of old-fashioned water pumps. Finally, head to Egelantiersgracht 107-145 for the **Sint-Andrieshof** *(⏰ Open M-Sa 9am-6pm.)*, another oasis of tranquility. These gardens are surrounded by residences, so be quiet and respectful.

🚋 To start off at the Raepenhofje, take tram #3 to Nieuwe Willemstraat, cross Lijnbaansgracht, make a left, and then a right onto Palmgracht. [$] Free.

WESTERPARK   ♿ PARK

The park that gives the neighborhood west of the Jordaan its name is small but worth a visit on a sunny day. Along the Haarlemmerweg grassy slopes roll down to the water and invite lounging; dirt paths around the park are great for biking, walking, or jogging. In the middle, a duck-filled pond accompanied by some very curious statues, including a headless woman in fancy dress, presides.

Tram #10 to Van Limburg Stirumstraat. Walk up V. L. Stirumstraat, cross the Haarlemmerweg, and enter the park on the right. Main entrance on Spaarndammerstraat, across from the Naussauplein (buses #22 and 348). Ⓢ *Free.*

HOUSEBOAT MUSEUM   ⓈⓈ MUSEUM

Prinsengracht, facing #296   ☏020 42 707 50 ▤www.houseboatmuseum.nl

You can't avoid seeing ■houseboats floating in the canals as you wander through Amsterdam, and this museum is designed to answer the inevitable questions that arise when landlubbers contemplate living on the water. The museum *is* a houseboat, and it appears deceptively large—it's actually the same size as the average Amsterdam apartment. It's cozily set up to look like a real home, too, but it's more than just a model: the informative guide available in dozens of languages, slideshows, and photos tell you all about the history, construction, and maintenance of the boats. If you're inspired to get on the water yourself, you can always rent a houseboat at **Frederic Rent-a-Bike.**

Tram #13, 14, or 17 to Westermarkt; cross Prinsengracht, make a left, and walk to the intersection with Elandsgracht. Ⓢ *€3.50, with Museumjaarkaart €2.75.* □ *Open Mar-Oct Tu-Su 11am-5pm; Nov-Jan 3 F-Su 11am-5pm; Jan 30-Feb F-Su 11am-5pm.*

Museumplein and Leidseplein

Surprise! The Museumplein is filled with museums. Good ones, at that, with two of the city's best and most famous just a few steps away from each other. Besides the listings below, the beautiful **Concertgebouw** at the southern end of Museumplein is a concert hall worth visiting even when the music isn't playing.

■ VAN GOGH MUSEUM   ♨♿ MUSEUM

Paulus Potterstraat 7   ☏020 57 052 00 ▤www.vangoghmuseum.nl

We think this may be the best museum in Amsterdam—unfortunately, so do a lot of other people. The lines can get pretty painful, so to avoid them, reserve tickets on the museum's website or arrive around 10:30am or 4pm. By all means, don't let the fear of crowds deter you: this museum is absolutely worth the wait. Van Gogh was an artist for only about 10 years, yet he left a remarkable legacy of paintings and drawings—most of which are owned by this museum. The exhibit is arranged in chronological order, and wall plaques do an excellent job of describing and analyzing each phase of Van Gogh's life. On the ground floor, you'll find works from the **French Barbizon School** and the **Dutch Hague School,** both of which were influential to Van Gogh's early development. The next floor up contains the bulk of Van Gogh's works. His early phase is exemplified by dark, gloomy works like the *Potato Eaters* and *Skull of a Skeleton with Burning Cigarette.* After moving to Paris and becoming more involved in the modern art movement there, Van Gogh began to experiment with a different, brighter tone. Some clearly show the influence of the late 19th-century Orientalism craze and the period's popular Japanese woodblock prints. Others reflect his friendships with Modernist painters like **Paul Gauguin** (more on him and others later). The eye-catching works in this later period include paintings like *Bedroom at Arles* (undergoing restoration at the time of press) with its bright impasto hues and the delicate *Branches of an Almond Tree in Blossom.* It's particularly poignant to track the theme of Van Gogh's descent into depression and suicide which threads throughout the commentary accompanying the paintings.

The second floor contains works from the **Mesdag Museum,** one of Holland's earliest museums of modern art whose collection is now in the hands of the Van Gogh Museum. More works by the Barbizon and Hague schools are also on display here. While you won't find any blockbuster names, the works are incredibly diverse and provide a helpful overview of Impressionism's precursors. One more flight up, works of Van Gogh's French contemporaries are displayed, with some of Van Gogh's works hanging among them to emphasize their connection. There are lovely works by Toulouse-Lautrec, Gauguin, Renoir, Manet, Seurat, and Pissarro. Following these, works by artists influenced by Van Gogh, such as **Derain** and **Picasso** are featured. Finally, a small exhibition on Symbolism explains what besides Impressionism was going on in the French art world of the 19th century. Temporary traveling exhibitions fill an adjacent space. All in all, the museum presents a remarkable concentration of top-quality art in an accessible dose.

🚋 *Tram #2, 3, 5, or 12 to Van Baerlestraat. Walk 1 block up Paulus Potterstraat.* ⑤ *€14, under 18 and with Museumjaarkaart free.* ⏰ *Open M-Th 10am-6pm, F 10am-10pm, Sa-Su 10am-6pm.*

RIJKSMUSEUM
Jan Luijkenstraat 1

●⚓♿ MUSEUM

☎020 67 470 00 🖥www.rijksmuseum.nl

If something feels familiar when you see the Rijksmuseum for the first time, don't be surprised: the palatial building was designed by **Pierre Cuypers,** the architect responsible for Centraal Station. The museum has been under construction for years and, at the time of writing, plans to fully reopen in 2013. For now, highlights of the collection are on display in the **Philips Wing.** As the national museum of both history and art, the Rijksmuseum holds vast stores of art and artifacts from the Middle Ages through the 19th century, a comprehensive exhibit on Dutch history, a collection of Asian art, and an enormous selection of furniture, Delftware, silver, and decorative objects (including two detailed 🅿**dollhouses** that probably cost more than many student apartments). Some of this stuff is temporarily on loan to other European museums, but a good cross-section remains in the Philips Wing on the ground floor. Here, the museum tells the story of the Netherlands as it grew from Dutch Republic to world power, commanding a fair share of the seas and international trade. However, the real heart of the museum is the art on the floor above, where the outstanding Dutch paintings of the Golden Age are housed. Numerous still lifes (cheese figures prominently, typical Dutch), landscapes, and portraits set the tone for 17th-century Dutch art, reflecting the trends and culture of the history lesson on the first floor. Next up, they pull out the big guns in a room full of deep, beautiful works by **Rembrandt van Rijn** and his pupils, evocative landscapes by **Jacob van Ruisdael,** and four luminous paintings by **Vermeer,** including *The Milkmaid.* A whole room is devoted to the *Night Watch,* probably Rembrandt's most famous painting, which depicts a military company on a gargantuan scale. Finally, a spot for temporary exhibits often connects these early Dutch masters to more modern painters. A recent show displayed the influence 17th-century Dutch painters exerted on the Spanish Modernist **Joan Miró.**

🚋 *Tram #2 or 5 to Hobbemastraat. Or tram #7 or 10 to Spiegelgracht. Museum is directly across the canal.* ⑤ *€12.50, under 18 and with Museumjaarkaart free.* ⏰ *Open daily 9am-6pm.*

VONDELPARK
Vondelpark

♿ PARK

One hundred and twenty acres of rolling streams, leafy trees, and inviting grass—in the summer, at least—make Vondelpark central Amsterdam's largest and most popular open space. Founded in the 1880s to provide a place for walking and riding, the park is now a hangout for skaters, senior citizens, stoners, soccer players, sidewalk acrobats, and more. Head here on the first sunny day of the spring and you'll see the whole city out in full force. The park is named after **Joost van den Vondel,** a 17th-century poet and playwright often called the Dutch Shakespeare. Not only is Vondelpark a great outdoor space, but it also has some excellent cafes, a weekly group roller skate that leaves every Friday at 8pm in front of the Filmmuseum, and an open-air theater (◼*www.openluchttheater.nl)* with free music and theater performances in the summer. If you're looking for a different sort of outdoor entertainment, be happy to know that it was determined in 2008 that ◼**having sex** would be legal in Vondelpark—provided it wasn't taking place near the playground. Local police, however, decided that they wouldn't let this fly. We're not too sure what the law's status is today, so we recommend playing it safe and exhibiting restraint (or letting us know what happens if you try taking advantage of the 2008 measure). Even without a bit of afternoon delight, you can still spend a delightful afternoon here taking a break from the rest of the city.

➹ *Tram #2, 3, 5, or 12 to Van Baerlestraat. Walk down Van Baerlestraat to the bridge over the park and take the stairs down.*

MAX EUWEPLEIN   ♿ SQUARE
Max Euweplein   ◼www.maxeuweplein.net

This small square tucked in the corner of a space dominated by megabar patios remains the heart of the Leidseplein. Somewhat inexplicably, the inscription above the pillars of the main entrance to the square reads *Homo sapiens non urinat in ventum* ("A wise man does not piss into the wind")—perhaps a useful reminder to the barflies of the Leidseplein. The sight to be seen is a large chessboard with oversized pieces (Max Euwe was a famous Dutch chess master), generally presided over by a cluster of grizzled old men as younger chess enthusiasts eagerly watch every move. The square occasionally plays host to live music and dance performances.

➹ *Tram #1, 2, 5, 7, or 10 to Leidseplein. Facing the ABN-Amro bank, make a left along Wetering-schans; the square will be on your right.*

De Pijp
De Pijp's sights are of a decidedly different variety than those in nearby Museum-plein. Rather than staring at paintings you'll never have a chance to own, haggle for wares at **Albert Cuypmarkt,** and instead of contemplating what life would be like in the Dutch Golden Age, find out what it's like being a bottle of beer at the Heineken Experience.

SARPHATIPARK   ♿ PARK
Sarphatipark

In the 1860s, Amsterdam's chief architect was convinced that the center of the city would move south, and that this spot in De Pijp (then just marshlands and a windmill or two) would be the ideal place for Centraal Station. We all know how that one turned out (though one wonders what would have happened to the Red Light District if visitors couldn't stumble straight into it from the station). Not one to be deterred, the architect decided to build a park instead. And not a bad one, either. Sarphatipark is fairly small, but its crisscrossing paths and central monument give it a genteel, 19th-century feel. It's rarely as crowded as Vondelpark, so you can have more grassy sunbathing space to yourself. The monument commemorates the same guy who gave his name to the park, the Jewish philanthropist and doctor **Samuel Sarphati.** Under the Nazi occupation, his statue was removed and the park was renamed for a Hegelian philosopher; one of the first acts after the liberation was to restore the park to its rightful name.

➹ *Tram #3 or 25 to 2e Van der Helstraat.*

HEINEKEN EXPERIENCE — MUSEUM

Stadhouderskade 78 ☎020 52 392 22 💻www.heinekenexperience.com

Beer hasn't been made here since 1988 (if you want an actual brewery tour, check out **Brouwerij 't IJ**), which is why this is an "experience." And what an experience, indeed. Four floors of holograms, multimedia exhibits, and virtual reality machines tell you everything you'll ever want to know about the green-bottled beer. We particularly enjoyed the ride that replicates the experience of actually becoming a Heineken beer. (There's something very Zen-alcoholic about the whole "in order to enjoy the beer you must BE the beer" idea.) And don't worry—it would be inhumane to be surrounded with all of that beer-related information without actually letting you drink, so the ticket includes two oat sodas of your very own. Lines can be long in the afternoon, so the best time to arrive is before 1pm. Yeah, you'll be drinking early, but we won't judge. It *is* Amsterdam, after all.

Tram #16 or 24 to Stadhouderskade, or tram #4, 7, 10, or 25 to Weterincircuit. Cross the canal and you'll see the building. $ €15. ⏰ Open daily 11am-7pm, last entry 5:30pm.

Jodenbuurt and Plantage

Jodenbuurt and Plantage are filled with some of the city's lesser-known but no less interesting museums. Due to its history as the Jewish Quarter, Jodenbuurt has its share of museums focusing on Jewish culture and history. Spacious Plantage offers the open spaces of the **Botanical Gardens** and **Artis Zoo.** The phenomenal **Brouwerij 't IJ** can be found north, by the water.

VERZETSMUSEUM (DUTCH RESISTANCE MUSEUM) — MUSEUM

Plantage Kerklaan 61 ☎020 62 025 35 💻www.verzetsmuseum.org

Nazi Germany occupied the Netherlands for five years during WWII, and this museum is designed to present the various responses of Dutch people during that time to the question "What do we do?" The permanent exhibition begins in the 1930s, painting a picture of what life was like during that time and building a backdrop to the traditions and conflicts within Dutch society. In the early days of the occupation, many struggled with the decision of whether to adapt to their relatively unchanged life under Nazi rule or to openly resist the occupiers. As time went on, the persecution of Jews, gypsies, and gays intensified, and numerous political and social regulations were put into place; as a result, the forces of the resistance grew. This museum does a masterful job of combining the ordinary and the extraordinary by placing visitors in the shoes of average Dutch citizens and also sharing the stories of individuals who risked (and often lost) their lives to publish illegal newspapers, hide Jews, or pass information to Allied troops. A smaller portion of the exhibit details the effects of the war on Dutch colonies in East Asia.

Tram #9 or 14 to Plantage Kerklaan. Across from Artis Zoo. $ €7.50, ages 7-15 €4, under 7 and with Museumjaarkaart free. ⏰ Open M 11am-5pm, Tu-F 10am-5pm, Sa-Su 11am-5pm.

JOODS HISTORISCH MUSEUM (JEWISH HISTORICAL MUSEUM) — MUSEUM

Nieuwe Amstelstraat 1 ☎020 53 103 10 💻www.jhm.nl

Four 17th- and 18th-century Ashkenazi synagogues were incorporated to form this museum dedicated to the history and culture of the Jews of the Netherlands. One part of the museum highlights the religious life of the community using artifacts (including a number of beautifully decorated Torahs), explanations of Jewish traditions, and videos that recount personal anecdotes. Above this section, an exhibit details the history of the community from 1600-1900, from the first settlements in Amsterdam under the city's unusually early religious tolerance to the struggles Jews faced in gaining full civil and political liberties. Paintings and documents detail different aspects of Dutch Jewish life.

Particularly noteworthy is the small display on Spinoza, including an early copy of the *Tractatus Theologico-Politicus*. The next part of the museum chronicles 1900 to the present, showing the growth of the Jewish community up until WWII, the persecution and devastation of the war period, and then the rebuilding efforts after the war's end.

🚊 Trams #9 or 14 or Ⓜ*Waterlooplein*. Ⓢ €9, students and seniors €6, ages 13-17 €4.50, under 13 and with Museumjaarkaart free. 🕙 Open daily 11am-5pm.

TROPENMUSEUM
●� MUSEUM

Linnaeusstraat 2
☎020 56 882 00 ◾www.tropenmuseum.nl

In a palatial building that is part of the Koninklijk Instituut voor de Tropen (Dutch Royal Institute of the Tropics), this museum provides an anthropological look at disparate "tropical" regions from the distant past to today. A running theme throughout the exhibits is the complicated relationship between Europe and these areas during the rise and fall of Western imperialism. From Thai bridal jewelry to African presidential folk cloths, an astounding collection of cultural artifacts is on display. An extensive portion of the first floor is devoted to the Dutch colonial experience in Indonesia (from the perspective of both colonizers and colonized), from which a large part of the museum's collection was initially drawn.

🚊 Tram #9, 10, or 14 to Alexanderplein. Cross the canal and walk left along Mauritskade. Ⓢ €9, students €5, under 18 and with Museumjaarkaart free. 🕙 Open daily 10am-5pm.

BROUWERIJ 'T IJ
●ġ♈ BREWERY

Funenkade 7
☎020 62 283 25 ◾www.brouwerijhetij.nl

What could be more Dutch than drinking beer at the base of a windmill? What's even better is that the beer brewed and served here is much, much tastier than more internationally famous Dutch brands (we won't name any names). Once a bathhouse, this building was taken over as a squat in the 1980s. Today, its brewers craft 10 different beers, some seasonal but all organic, unfiltered, and non-pasteurized. You can try a glass or three of their wares at the massive outdoor terrace of the on-site pub or at a few cafes and bars in the city. Brews range from the *Zatte*, a golden triple beer, to the *Plzen*, their pilsner, to a variety of bocks and a delicious wheat beer. If you're at the bar, make sure to notice the long collection of bottles on the shelves—it's one of Europe's largest.

🚊 Tram #10 to Hoogte Kadijk or #14 to Pontanusstraat. Head toward the windmill. Ⓢ Beer €1.90-2.30. 🕙 Pub open daily 3-8pm. Free tours of the brewery F 4pm, Su 4pm.

MUSEUM HET REMBRANDT
●⊛ MUSEUM

Jodenbreestraat 4
☎020 52 004 00 ◾www.rembrandthuis.nl

Flush with success at the height of his popularity, Rembrandt van Rijn bought this massively expensive house in 1639. Twenty years later, after a decline in sales and failure to pay his mortgage, he sold the house along with his possessions. It probably sucked to be him, but his misfortune turned out to be a great boon for historians—the inventory of Rembrandt's worldly goods taken at the time of sale meant that hundreds of years later curators were able to reconstruct his house almost exactly as it was when he lived there. Now visitors can see where Rembrandt slept, entertained guests, sold paintings, made paintings, and got attacked by his mistress after a fight over alimony (that would be in the kitchen). The most interesting rooms are those on the top floor: Rembrandt's massive studio (with many of his original tools still there) and the room where he stored his *objets d'art*—armor, armadillos, and everything in between. The museum also holds a hundred-fold collection of Rembrandt's etchings, a rotating selection of which are on display. Every 45min. on the third floor, guides reenact Rembrandt's etching and printing techniques. An exhibition space for rotating collections of more contemporary art is attached to the main building.

🚋 *Tram #9 or 14 or [M]Waterlooplein.* $ *€9, ages 6-17 €2.50, under 6 and with Museumjaarkaart free, with ISIC card €6.* ⏰ *Open daily 10am-5pm.*

ARTIS ZOO ♿ ZOO

Plantage Kerklaan 38-40 ☎020 900 278 4796 💻www.artis.nl

If all of Amsterdam's culture is blowing your brain, join the animals at this zoo, one of Europe's oldest. The sprawling complex includes an aquarium, a planetarium, and a geological museum in addition to the critters themselves. Areas are devoted to regions like the South American Pampas and the African Savannah, and all the classics like elephants, lions, leopards, giraffes, and a variety of monkeys can be found among the hundreds of species living here. Some of our favorites include the teeny black-footed penguins, playful sea lions, and **Lemurland,** a special island where visitors can get up close and personal with the fuzzy beasts.

🚋 *Tram #9 or 14 to Plantage Kerklaan.* $ *€18.50, seniors €17, ages 3-9 €15.* ⏰ *Open daily Apr-Oct 9am-6pm; Nov-Mar 9am-5pm. Zookeeper presentations daily 11am-3:30pm.*

PORTUGEES-ISRAELIETISCHE SYNAGOGUE ♿ SYNAGOGUE

Mr. Visserplein 1-3 ☎020 62 453 51 💻www.esnoga.com

This beautiful synagogue has remained largely unchanged since the local community of Sephardic Jews constructed it in 1671. Most of them had fled persecution in the Iberian peninsula—hence the common practice of calling the synagogue an *Esnoga,* the Portuguese word for synagogue. The building's large vaulted interior is dominated by massive stone pillars and hung with brass candelabra. Sand is scattered on the floor in the Dutch tradition to absorb dirt and muffle the noise of footsteps. Information and artifacts from the Dutch Jewish community's past 300 years are on display, but this is still very much a space of worship—services are held on Sabbaths and holidays.

🚋 *Trams #9 or 14 or [M]Waterlooplein.* $ *€6.50; students, seniors, and with Museumjaarkaart €5; ages 13-17 €4.* ⏰ *Open M-F 10am-4pm, Su 10am-4pm. Closed on Jewish holidays.*

COFFEESHOPS AND SMARTSHOPS

The first experience of walking into a store, reading a menu, and ordering a few grams of weed as casually as you would a sandwich may feel surprising to those used to buying their magic **dragon** from a shady guy with an unregistered cell phone number and a 1970s car. Sure, there are plenty of ways to enjoy yourself in Amsterdam without lighting up, and lots of people won't set foot in a coffeeshop over the course of their entire visit. Nevertheless, it's undeniable that liberal drug laws *do* draw people to the city from far and wide.

However, just because you can do things here that you'd get arrested for elsewhere doesn't mean that anything goes. Certified coffeeshops will have a green-and-white **BCD sticker** that denotes their credibility. Shops aren't allowed to advertise the fact that they sell marijuana or hash, and in theory, you're supposed to have to ask for the menu, though in most places they'll have it on the bar as long as it's towards the back of the store. You are only allowed to buy 5g of drugs from an establishment per day. It's recently become illegal to smoke tobacco indoors in most places, though some coffeeshops have special smoking areas where you can indulge in a mixed joint. Don't walk down the street smoking a blunt—just because the Dutch are OK with THC doesn't mean that they smoke all that much of it, and doing so will mark you as an obvious tourist. (And a stoned one, at that—hi, pickpockets!) If you do want a smoke in the open air, find a store with an outdoor patio or hit up one of the city's parks.

The variety at many shops can be overwhelming for those who aren't used to choosing what strain they're smoking. Ask coffeeshop staff for advice if you have any questions, as they are usually used to explaining their wares. In general, the more expensive a brand is, the stronger or better you can expect it to be. If you want to smoke some really good stuff, look for prestigious **Cannabis Cup winners.** When it comes to hash, most places stock blonde (Moroccan), which is lighter than black (Indian). Neither of them is anywhere near as potent as the special varieties of Dutch **ice-o-lator.** It can cost €20-50 per gram, but that's because it's basically purified THC and will, to put it "blunt"-ly, fuck you up. Europeans generally stick to smoking joints, but quite a few stores provide bongs or even vaporizers for tourists. If you want to roll a doobie yourself, most stores will let you take a few papers for free. You can also buy pre-rolled joints with a limited selection of strains. If there's something you really want to try that doesn't come pre-rolled, many shops offer paper cones that allow the truly lazy (or uncoordinated) to simply pop the weed in and be set to light up. Coffeeshops also sell space cakes, muffins, and brownies. As cute as they sound, these should be eaten with caution, as it's impossible to verify how strong they are and the effects often don't kick in for 1hr. or more—and then can last for up to a day.

If you have any questions regarding the effects or legality of drugs options in Amsterdam, hit up **Cannabis College** or the **Jellinek Clinic,** both of which keep extensive, up-to-date information. It is *imperative* to keep in mind that hard drugs (ecstasy, cocaine, heroin, etc.) are not legal in the Netherlands, despite what dealers approaching you on the street at 3am might try to tell you. Seriously, there are stores with DRUG MENUS here. Isn't that enough? Finally, though we may list a wide array of coffeeshops and smartshops in this guidebook, *Let's Go* does not recommend drug use in any form.

Coffeeshops

There are well over 200 coffeeshops in Amsterdam, and honestly the quality doesn't really vary that much. Most tourists visit for the experience, and this is hardly like a restaurant where the majority of patrons really know that much about what they're consuming. Below are our 11 favorite coffeeshops in the city. As totally groovy as they are, *Let's Go* definitely does not recommend trying to hit all of these in one day...

👍 DE TWEEDE KAMER 🚫♿ NIEUWE ZIJD

Heisteeg 6 ☎020 42 222 36

Probably stocks the widest selection of weed in Amsterdam. This coffeeshop is run by the same people as the more famous Dampkring, but here you'll find fewer tourists and a cozier atmosphere. Plus, there's a certain pleasurable irony in smoking in a store named after one of the Dutch chambers of Parliament.

➔ Tram #1, 2, or 5 to Spui/Nieuwezijds Voorburgwal. Walk down to Spui, up Spuistraat, and left onto Heisteeg. $ Weed €4-13 per g; joints €3-9; hash €8-40 per g; space cakes and muffins €6. ⏰ Open daily 10am-1am.

👍 AMNESIA 🚫🚫⛱ CANAL RING WEST

Herengracht 133 ☎020 63 83 03

One of Amsterdam's best-decorated coffeeshops, in all senses of the word. The spacious interior has long couches and tables done up in black and purple; picturesque canalside seating is available outside. The menu, highlighted by nine Cannabis Cup winners, includes both standard fare and specialty brands. It also has a big coffee bar for those who prefer the stimulating effects of caffeine to those of the other drugs on offer. Those whose greatest vice is dessert should try Amnesia's frothy shakes.

➔ Tram #1, 2, 5, 13, 14, or 17 to Dam/Radhuisstraat. Continue along Radhuisstraat and make a right onto Herengracht. $ Weed €8.50-13 per g, specialty brands €13-17 per g; joints €4-6. ⏰ Open daily 10am-1am.

👍 **RUSLAND** ◉⊗ OUDE ZIJD

Rusland 17 ☎020 62 794 68

According to some, this is the oldest coffeeshop in Amsterdam. We won't take a stance on that issue, but we will say that this is definitely one of the city's better shops. Two floors inside are decorated with stenciled images of the Kremlin and other Moscow buildings, and the low ceilings combined with comfy cushion-lined seating will make you feel as cozy as you might while sitting inside on a snowy Russian day. The drug menu isn't terribly extensive, but it is complemented by an astonishing selection of teas, fresh juices, and milkshakes.

‡ Tram #4, 9, 14, 16, 24, or 25 to Muntplein. Walk up Nieuwe Doelenstraat and make a left. $ Weed €4-12 per g; joints €2.50-4.50; hash €3-30 per g; space muffins €5. ⏰ Open daily 10am-midnight.

HILL STREET BLUES ◉⊗ RED LIGHT DISTRICT

Warmoesstraat 52 ☎020 63 879 22 🖳www.hill-street-blues.nl

So named because of its location next to a police station, Hill Street Blues benefits from a great view over the water at the back of its smoking room, reached through a narrow entrance that hides the large two-level shop. Every inch of the walls, floor, and ceiling is covered with graffiti—you can add to it yourself (buy a marker at the counter if you happened to forget your own). The place, like everywhere on Warmoesstraat, is busy but manages to remain relaxed.

‡ From Centraal Station, walk down Damrak; make a left onto Oudebrugsteeg and then a left onto Warmoesstraat. $ Weed €3-14 per g; joints €10, with tobacco €3-5; hash €4-20 per g. ⏰ Open daily 9am-1am.

PARADOX ◉♿ WEST OF TOWN

1e Bloemdwarsstraat 2 ☎020 62 356 39 🖳www.paradoxcoffeeshop.com

Paradox boasts a wonderfully laid-back atmosphere with the staff to match. A smattering of wooden tables and chairs fill the cafe-like space, and the chill feel is continued in a soundtrack that tends toward reggae and other types of world music.

‡ Tram #13, 14, or 17 to Westermarkt. Cross Prinsengracht and continue on Rozengracht, then make a left onto 1e Bloemdwarsstraat. $ Weed €5.50-11 per g; joints €3-4; hash €7-15 per g; space cakes €6. ⏰ Open daily 10am-8pm.

KANDINSKY ◉⊗ NIEUWE ZIJD

Rosmarijnsteeg 9 ☎020 62 470 23

Eschewing the Rasta-psychedelic-jungle themes of many neighboring coffeeshops, Kandinsky has a multilevel interior with sleek leather booths, mod tables, and tastefully colored lighting that make it feel like some sort of hip lounge club. No pretension in the attitude, though: the staff is chatty and cheerful.

‡ Tram #1, 2, or 5 to Spui/Nieuwezijds Voorburgwal. Walk up Nieuwezijds Voorburgwal and make a left onto Rosmarijnsteeg. $ Weed €8.25-13 per g; joints €4.50, with tobacco €3.70; hash €7.50-35 per g. ⏰ Open daily 9:30am-1am.

YO YO ◉⊗ DE PIJP

2e Jan van der Heijdenstraat 79 ☎020 66 471 73

The kind of store where they take their weed seriously, but you'd never tell from the supremely laid-back attitude. Only sells outdoor, organic marijuana and hash. Pastel green walls and large windows letting in lots of light continue the whole earth-happy theme. It's a nice place to come for a slice of pie and a coffee, even if you don't plan on smoking.

‡ Tram #3, 4, or 25 to Ceinturbaan/Van Woutstraat. Walk north on Van Woutstraat, then make a right onto 2e Jan van der Heijdenstraat. $ €5 gets you 0.6-1g of weed or 0.8-1.1g of hash; joints €2.50. ⏰ Open M-Sa noon-7pm.

STIX ❀⊗ CENTRAL CANAL RING

Utrechtsestraat 21 🖥www.stix.nl

If you want to feel like a local, come to this uncrowded shop in the Central Canal Ring where the drugs are cheap and strong. Stix is a simple shop—no big smoking rooms with couches and Ganesh statues here, just picnic-table seating and a bright, airy atmosphere. Staff cheerfully welcomes both newcomers and loyal regulars.

➡ Tram #9 or 14 to Rembrandtplein. Walk down Utrechtsestraat; the store is near Herengracht. $ Weed €6-13 per g; joints €10, with tobacco €3.20-3.80; hash €9-25. ⏰ Open daily 11am-1am.

THE BUSH DOCTOR ❀⊗☃ REMBRANDTPLEIN

Thorbeckeplein 28 ☎020 33 074 75

Rembrandtplein tends to be more about drinking than smoking, but the crazy selection of potent strains here makes it a worthwhile stop. This is one of the best places to try specialty strains of weed and hash: not only do they have a variety of their own potent mixes, various fruity options, and organic wares, but they also carry over half a dozen kinds of the infamous ice-o-lator hash You might want to leave plenty of time between smoking and hitting the clubs, though, or the strobe lights could be a bit overwhelming.

➡ Tram #9 or 14 to Rembrandtplein. Thorbeckeplein is across the square from the giant TV screen. $ Weed €7.50-12.50 per g; joints €4-6.50; hash €10-12 per g, ice-o-lator €22-55 per g; space cakes €7. ⏰ Open daily 9am-1am.

GREY AREA ❀⊗ CANAL RING WEST

Oude Leliestraat 2 ☎020 42 043 01 🖥www.greyarea.nl

One of the only coffeeshops in Amsterdam run by Americans. These guys really know their stuff, as do many of the loyal patrons. Try one of their vaporizers. With many celebrities frequenting the store, there's a chance you'll be able to say that you've used the same one as Willie Nelson.

➡ Tram #1, 2, 5, 13, 14, or 17 to Dam/Radhuisstraat. Continue on Radhuisstraat, make a right onto the far side of the Singel; it will be on your left. $ Marijuana €8.50-13 per g; joints €5. ⏰ Open daily noon-8pm.

DAMPKRING ❀♿ NIEUWE ZIJD

Handboogstraat 29 ☎020 63 807 05 🖥www.dampkring.nl

The same extensive menu as Tweede Kamer but a very different atmosphere. Scenes from *Ocean's Twelve* were filmed in the warmly painted, psychedelic lounge. This newfound celebrity and the quality of options on the menu have catapulted Dampkring to a stardom that brings in the crowds. Has smoking-accessories shop on Prins Hendrikkade and an extensive online store.

➡ Tram #1, 2, or 5 to Koningsplein. Cross the canal and continue onto Heiligeweg, then make a left onto Handboogstraat. $ Weed €4-13 per g; joints €3-9; hash €8-40 per g; space cakes and muffins €6. ⏰ Open M-Sa 10am-1am, Su 11am-1am.

Smartshops

Smartshops do not sell weed and hash, though they usually stock marijuana seeds and smoking accessories. What they do offer in terms of instant psychedelic gratification are truffles (the only type since the banning of hallucinogenic psilocybin mushrooms that are still legal), salvia, and all sorts of herbs and extracts that can promise everything from ecstasy-like effects to heightened sexual arousal.

CONSCIOUS DREAMS KOKOPELLI ⊗ RED LIGHT DISTRICT

Warmoesstraat 12 ☎020 42 170 00 🖥www.consciousdirect.com/shops/kokopelli

A bright emporium for all kinds of consciousness-altering substances and souvenirs, this smartshop sells sex toys, lava lamps, and trinkets. On the drug-related side, they offer a huge array of herbal substances like Philosopher's Stones, salvia, and herbal XTC. They also sell drug-testing kits that can evaluate the composition of the drugs you're going to take or the state of your body after you've already taken them. Ask the well-informed staff any questions you may have regarding psychedelic substances.

From Centraal Station, turn left onto Prins Hendrikkade, bear right onto Nieuwebrugsteeg, and then keep right onto Warmoesstraat. [$] Philosopher's Stones €12.50-20; salvia, herbal XTC, and most other substances around €9-17. ⏰ Open daily 11am-10pm.

AZARIUS CENTRAL CANAL RING

Kerkstraat 119 ☎020 48 979 14 🖳www.azarius.net

The physical manifestation of the largest online smartshop, Azarius sits in the building once inhabited by the city's oldest smartshop (Conscious Dreams—see above). Azarius is a small and friendly store, with a knowledgeable staff ready to answer any questions about their many products. They sell magic truffles, salvia, herbal XTC, and many other herbs and extracts in addition to cannabis seeds and smoking-related accessories. If you can't find what you're looking for in the store, you can always check online.

Tram #1, 2, or 5 to Prinsengracht. Walk 1 block up Leidsestraat and make a right onto Kerkstraat. [$] Truffles €10-14 per dose. ⏰ Open in summer daily noon-9pm; fall, winter, and spring M-Tu noon-9pm, Th-Sa noon-9pm.

dutch desserts

Whether it's from roaming through museums or lazing in coffeeshops, sightseeing in Amsterdam is bound to make you a bit peckish. You can continue the cultural immersion *and* satiate your hunger with these traditional sweets.

- **STROOPWAFELS.** Literally "syrupwaffles," these crunchy-on-the-outside, gooey-on-the-inside Dutch treats are made from two thin waffle-like cookies glued together by a brown sugar and butter syrup. You won't be able to go a block in the Netherlands without finding a store that sells them in some form.
- **HAGELSLAG.** Breakfast in the Netherlands tends to be quite an affair, and one of the things that may stand out most is a box of these chocolate (or fruit-flavored) sprinkles. The common way to eat them is on buttered toast, so the sprinkles don't roll off. The name *hagelslag* is derived from the Dutch word for "hail," surely fueling dreams of chocolate falling from the sky in the minds of many a Dutch child.
- **OLIEBOLLEN.** A somewhat unappealing name—"oil balls"—comes with a fun story. Legend has it that the Germanic goddess Perchta would fly around during midwinter, slicing the belly off anyone she met. Germanic tribes ate *oliebollen* so that the oil in their stomachs would cause her sword to slide off. The science may be dubious, but these balls of dough studded with raisins, deep-fried, and then dusted with powdered sugar are certainly delicious.

MAGIC MUSHROOM GALLERY NIEUWE ZIJD

Spuistraat 249 ☎020 42 757 65 🖳www.magicmushroom.com

Large smartshop with all kinds of herbal extracts, dried herbs, mushroom seeds, and grow kits, plus more knick-knacks than you can shake a stick at. Patient staff will walk you through the book of all their options, or you can peruse it yourself in the small seating area. Another, smaller location is on the Singel, by the Bloemenmarkt.

Tram #1, 2, or 5 to Spui/Nieuwezijds Voorburgwal. Walk down to Spui and then right up Spuistraat. [$] Salvia €12-30; mushroom seeds €22-30. ⏰ Open daily 10am-10pm.

TATANKA LEIDSEPLEIN

Korte Leidsedwarsstraat 151 ☎020 42 121 39

This smartshop sells a variety of mushrooms, marijuana seeds, salvia, and all kinds of smoking accoutrements—pipes, grinders, and anything else you might need. Also sells T-shirts and other souvenirs. Very helpful staff will walk you through the mechanics of any prospective purchase.

Tram #1, 2, 5, 7, or 10 to Leidseplein. $ Mushrooms €12-20; seeds from around €30 to over €100. Open daily 11am-10pm.

MUNCHIES

For some reason, when we think "Northern Europe," we don't think "awesome food." Now, that's a little bit prejudiced, but it's telling that in the vast world of Amsterdam restaurants, very few of them actually serve Dutch cuisine. (Here's a quick run-down of what that looks like: pancakes, cheese, herring, and various meat-and-potato combinations.) Instead, most of the terrific food you'll find comes from the cuisines of all the others who, just like you, have been drawn to Amsterdam by its reputation of awesome. Also, Amsterdam has this thing with sandwiches—they are everywhere, and they tend to be really, really good.

De Pijp, Jordaan, and the Nine Streets in Canal Ring West boast the highest concentration of quality eats. De Pijp is the cheapest of the three. If you really want to conserve your cash though, **Albert Heijn** is the largest and most visible chain of supermarkets in the city *(find your nearest location at www.ah.nl).*

Oude Zijd

Zeedijk is overwhelmingly packed with restaurants of all shapes and sizes, so be careful to compare menus when selecting a place to eat, since some can be touristy rip-offs. Don't cross the neighborhood off your list for fear of that possibility though—there are some really great places.

'SKEK CAFE, GLOBAL ❷

Zeedijk 4-8 ☎020 42 705 51 www.skek.nl

A "cultural eetcafe" where all students with ID get a 33% discount, 'Skek prepares food that is a sort of European fusion, with options like a Greek hamburger with *tzatziki* mayonnaise, grilled vegetable lasagna, or salmon with lentils. This is a place that begs you to stay a while—tables are painted with whimsical fantasy board games, student art lines the walls, and live music is featured many nights. The free Wi-Fi is a draw as well.

At the beginning of Zeedijk, near Centraal Station. $ Appetizers €4.25-5; entrees €12.50-13.50. Did we mention the 33% student discount? Open M-Th noon-1am, F-Sa noon-3am, Su noon-1am.

LATEI CAFE ❶

Zeedijk 143 ☎020 62 574 85 www.latei.net

Colorful and eccentric, Latei is filled with mismatched furniture and interesting knick-knacks—every single one of which is for sale. Save your money for the simple and impeccable food, though: sandwiches are made with artisan bread and the cafe's own olive oil and filled with everything from chorizo to hummus and grilled eggplant. Indian cuisine makes a guest appearance at dinner Thursday to Saturday nights.

[M]Nieuwmarkt. $ Sandwiches €3-5. Open M-W 8am-6pm, Th-F 8am-10pm, Sa 9am-10pm, Su 11am-6pm.

BIRD THAI ❸

Zeedijk 72-74 ☎020 62 014 42 www.thai-bird.nl

Zeedijk might be considered Amsterdam's Chinatown, but the best Asian restaurant is arguably Thai eatery Bird. Seriously, this is the most authentic Thai food you can get outside the Land of Smiles. *Let's Go* really likes their green curry.

[M]Nieuwmarkt. [i] Snack bar cash only. $ Entrees €11-14, at snack bar €9-11. Open daily 5-11pm. Snack bar open daily 2-10pm.

Red Light District

Gluttony is one of the few sins you can't indulge in the Red Light District. There are some good, reasonably-priced cafes, but if you're looking for a quality meal, head next door to the Oude Zijd.

👍 DE BAKKERSWINKEL — 🥦♿ CAFE [1]

Warmoesstraat 69 — ☎020 48 980 00 🖥www.debakkerswinkel.nl

As cute and homey as the surrounding streets are neon and sordid. In the large pastel dining room you can enjoy terrific quiches, breakfast menus, or homemade sourdough bread and cheese. High tea is also available, replete with different combinations of scones, sweets, and sandwiches.

🚏 From Centraal Station, walk down Damrak, make a left onto Oudebrugsteeg, and then a right onto Warmoesstraat. $ Sandwiches €4. Slice of quiche €5.20. Breakfast menus €5.95-12.25. High teas €13.95-40. ⏰ Open Tu-F 8am-6pm, Sa 8am-5pm, Su 10am-5pm.

THEEHUIS HIMALAYA — 🥦♿ CAFE, VEGETARIAN [1]

Warmoesstraat 56 — ☎020 62 608 99 🖥www.himalaya.nl

At the back of a New Age-y bookstore, this surprisingly large cafe with welcoming staff and a tranquil canal view offers an all-vegetarian menu with many vegan options. Choose from a selection of sandwiches, bagels, and desserts or try the special vegan Himalaya burger. This may be the one place where you can find inner peace in the Red Light District (without paying a little extra).

🚏 From Centraal Station, walk down Damrak, make a left onto Oudebrugsteeg, and then a left onto Warmoesstraat. $ Sandwiches and bagels €3-5. Burgers €7.95. ⏰ Open M noon-6pm, Tu-W 10am-6pm, Th 10am-8pm, F-Sa 10am-6pm, Su noon-5:30pm.

Nieuwe Zijd

Eating in the Nieuwe Zijd is less than ideal: it tends to be packed with overpriced, low-quality tourist traps. Try the southern half of **Spuistraat** or head to La Place for a quick lunch.

👍 LA PLACE — 💳♿🍸☀ CAFETERIA [1]

Kalverstraat 203 — ☎020 62 201 71 🖥www.laplace.nl

In most parts of Amsterdam, it's often the cute cafes that have the best informal food. In the Nieuwe Zijd, many of those cafes will try to charge you €10 for a sandwich, so embrace the rampant commercialism in the area and head to this cafeteria inside the giant **Vroom and Dreesmann** department store. You'll be rewarded by a vast buffet of pizzas, pastas, salads, sandwiches, meats, and pastries for incredibly reasonable prices.

🚏 Tram #4, 9, 14, 16, 24, or 25 to Muntplein. You'll see the giant V and D store; enter through the Kalverstraat door; the entrance to the cafeteria is on the left. $ Sandwiches €3-5. Pizzas €7. ⏰ Open M 11am-8pm, Tu-W 10am-8pm, Th 10am-9pm, F-Sa 10am-8pm, Su noon-8pm.

CAFE SCHUIM — 💳♿🍸☀ CAFE [2]

Spuistraat 189 — ☎020 63 893 57

With bright, abstract shapes on the wall and massive padded-leather chairs surrounding small tables, this artsy spot is the antithesis of the McDonald's a few blocks away. Try sandwiches like the club with smoked chicken and avocado at lunch, or their creative pastas, steak, and entrees at dinner.

🚏 Tram #1, 2, 5, or 14 to Dam/Paleisstraat. Walk down Paleisstraat toward Singel and make a left onto Spuistraat. $ Sandwiches €4-7. Pastas €9.50-12.50. Beer from €2.20. ⏰ Open M-Th noon-1am, F-Sa noon-3am, Su 1pm-1am.

RISTORANTE CAPRESE — 💳🚫🍸☀ ITALIAN [3]

Spuistraat 259-261 — ☎020 62 000 59

The service here is leisurely at best, but that just makes it feel more authentically Italian. With the massive wall mural of a Neapolitan bay view, you might even be convinced that you're a few countries to the south (at least in the summer).

🚋 *Tram #1, 2, or 5 to Spui/Nieuwezijds Voorburgwall. Cross over to Spuistraat and make a right.* $ *Pastas €9-14. Meat entrees €18-22. House wine from €4 per glass.* ⏰ *Open daily noon-11pm.*

Canal Ring West and Scheepvaartbuurt

This is one of the best places for high-quality eats in Amsterdam; restaurants in this neighborhood take food and style very seriously. The Nine Streets area is especially packed with hip and delicious cafes. To the north, **Haarlemmerstraat** and **Haarlemmerdijk** are lined with restaurants, from cheap sandwich joints to upscale bistros.

OPEN CAFE-RESTAURANT FRENCH, ITALIAN [3]
Westerdoksplein 20 ☎020 62 010 10 www.open.nl

This restaurant inhabits one of the coolest locations in Amsterdam—a renovated segment of a train bridge perched high above the waters between Westerdok and the IJ. The Mediterranean-style food is elegant, with dishes like lamb ravioli, stewed oxtail, and sea-bass salad. Conveniently, most dishes come in both half and full portions, so you can enjoy the view without breaking the bank.

🚋 *From Haarlemmerstraat, walk from Korte Prinsengracht through the tunnel under the train tracks and then cross the bridge; you can't miss the restaurant on your right.* $ *Sandwiches and salads €7-14. Half-entrees €7-14, full €14-22.* ⏰ *Open daily 10am-10:30pm.*

FOODISM SANDWICHES, ITALIAN [1]
Oude Leliestraat 8 ☎020 42 751 03 www.foodism.nl

This lovely little joint is bursting with color, from the lime green walls to the glossy cherry tables. The food is even brighter: choose from a menu of creative sandwiches like chicken and mango chutney or hummus with alfalfa or go for one of the daily homemade pastas. The baked goods are sinfully delicious.

🚋 *Tram #1, 2, 5, 13, 14, or 17 to Dam/Radhuisstraat. Continue on Radhuisstraat and make a right on the far side of the Singel; it will be on your left.* $ *Sandwiches €5.50. Pastas €10-12.* ⏰ *Open M-Sa noon-10pm, Su 1-6pm.*

HARLEM: DRINKS AND SOUL FOOD AMERICAN [2]
Haarlemmerstraat 77 ☎020 33 014 98

No, they didn't leave out a vowel: this place is the Dutch outpost of good ol' American soul food. Here, you can indulge your culinary homesickness without the shame of being seen in a Burger King. Fill up on a variety of club sandwiches, soups, and salads at lunch or sup on dishes like macaroni and cheese and fried chicken at dinner.

🚋 *Make a right when leaving Centraal Station, cross the Singel, and walk down Haarlemmerstraat a few blocks; Harlem's on the corner with Herenmarkt.* $ *Sandwiches €5-8. Entrees €12-18.* ⏰ *Open M-Th 10am-1am, F-Sa 10am-3am, Su 10am-1am. Kitchen closes 10pm.*

'T KUYLTJE SANDWICHES [1]
Gasthuismolensteeg 9 ☎020 62 010 45 www.kuyltje.nl

A no-frills takeout spot that makes tremendous, filling Belgian *broodjes*. The proprietor used to be a butcher, a fact which is immediately evident from the fresh and flavorful meat products—no prepackaged cold cuts here.

🚋 *Tram #1, 2, 5, 13, 14, or 17 to Dam/Radhuisstraat. Continue down Radhuisstraat and make a left at the Singel.* $ *Sandwiches €3.50.* ⏰ *Open M-F 7am-4pm.*

I QUATTRO GATTI ITALIAN [3]
Hartenstraat 3 ☎020 42 145 85

This tiny restaurant serves up Italian dishes exquisitely made by a native-born chef. Menus change to reflect seasonal ingredients, and everything is homemade. It boasts a great wine selection.

🚋 *Tram #13, 14, or 17 to Westermarkt. Make a right after crossing Keizersgracht and then a left onto Hartenstraat.* **i** *Reservations strongly recommended.* $ *Entrees €12-20.* ⏰ *Open Tu-Sa 6-10pm.*

Central Canal Ring and Rembrandtplein

You'll eat well in the Central Canal Ring, where restaurants are affordable, tourist crowds are low, and you're never too far from Amsterdam's major sights. **Utrechtsestraat** in particular boasts a high concentration of diverse restaurants. Rembrandtplein is mostly filled with enormous international restaurants and oversized cafes,but there are some good spots mixed in.

👍 **RISTORANTE PIZZERIA FIRENZE** 💳♿🍸 ITALIAN ❶
Halvemaansteeg 9-11 ☎020 62 733 60 🖥www.pizzeria-firenze.nl

The wine bottles sitting on every table and the murals of Italian scenery on the walls will make you feel like you're actually in *Italia*. Not the world's most gourmet pizza, but with large pies beginning at €5, no one's complaining. Definitely one of the best values for a restaurant meal around Rembrandtplein.

⇞ Tram #9 or 14 to Rembrandtplein. Halvemaansteeg is the street to the left of the line of buildings with the giant TV screen. $ Pizza and pasta €5-9. ⏰ Open daily 1-11pm.

👍 **VAN DOBBEN** 💳♿📶 SANDWICHES ❶
Korte Reguliersdwarsstraat 5-9 ☎020 62 442 00 🖥www.eetsalonvandobben.nl

An old-school deli and cafeteria that is everything most restaurants in Rembrandtplein are not: cheap, fast, and simple. Choose from a long list of sandwiches or a more limited selection of soups, salads, and omelettes. We're not sure how this place stays in business, seeing as how everywhere else seems to charge five times as much, but we hope they keep the magic going.

⇞ Tram #9 or 14 to Rembrandtplein. It's on a small street, get onto Reguliersdwarsstraat and look for where the street veers off on the right. $ Sandwiches €2.50-4.25. ⏰ Open M-Sa 9am-6pm.

B AND B LUNCHROOM 🚫💳♿ CAFE, SANDWICHES ❶
Leidsestraat 44 ☎020 63 815 42

It's hard to walk by this storefront and not be drawn in by the window heaped high with pastries and muffins. The shop sells filling sandwiches that go beyond the ordinary offerings with combinations like roast beef and "citron mayonnaise" or gorgonzola and asparagus.

⇞ Tram #1, 2, or 5 to Keizersgracht. The cafe is on the southwestern corner. $ Sandwiches €3.50-6. Salads €6.50-7.50. ⏰ Open daily 10am-6pm.

LOS PILONES 💳♿🍸☀ MEXICAN ❸
Kerkstraat 63 ☎020 32 046 51 🖥www.lospilones.com

While popular with tourists, locals, and expats from all over, this restaurant remains steadfastly Mexican—their website is only in Spanish, and you should have seen the crowds here watching Mexico play in the World Cup. The menu is full of tacos, enchiladas, and other entrees like *pollo con mole*.

⇞ From Leidseplein, walk up Leidsestraat and make a right on Kerkstraat. $ Appetizers €3-8; entrees €15-17. Margaritas €7.25. ⏰ Open Tu-Th 4pm-1am, F-Sa 4pm-2am, Su 4pm-1am.

West Of Town

Some of the quirkiest eats, most distinctive spaces, and highest-quality food can be found in these neighborhoods. In this residential area, you're likely to be the only foreigner at the table.

👍 **RAINARAI** 🚫💳🚭 ALGERIAN ❷
Prinsengracht 252 ☎020 62 497 91 🖥www.rainarai.nl

Algerian fare means you can count things like spicy lamb meatballs, grilled asparagus, stuffed artichokes, and curry among your options. No matter what the daily dishes are when you arrive, you won't be disappointed—everything is delicious.

⇞ Tram #13, 14, or 17 to Westermarkt. Cross Prinsengracht and make a left. $ Entrees €10-14.50. ⏰ Open Tu-Su noon-10pm.

TOMATILLO

★✦♿ MEXICAN ❶

261 Overtoom   ☎020 68 330 86 🖳www.tomatillo.nl

Tomatillo bills itself as "Tex-Mex to go," but its crisp, clean interior and fresh ingredients set it apart from the rest of the ethnic fast food eateries along Overtoom. The food steers clear of the greasy, over-cheesiness of many gringo attempts at Mexican cuisine (though we suspect the friendly proprietors would give you extra cheese if you asked—this is the Netherlands, after all).

🍴 *Tram #1 to J. P. Heijestraat. Tomatillo is a block north of Vondelpark.* Ⓢ *Burritos and tostadas €7.50-9.50. Tacos €2.75-3.50.* ⏲ *Open Tu-Su noon-9pm.*

BELLA STORIA

●♿♿♙⚖ ITALIAN ❷

Bentinckstraat 28   ☎020 48 805 99 🖳www.bellastoria.info

For people who miss their Italian granny's home cooking (or missed out on having an Italian granny entirely), this is the place to be. It's truly a family affair, run by a mother and her sons who chatter in Italian as they roll out dough.

🍴 *Tram #10 to Van Limburg Stirumplein. Facing Limburg Stirumstraat, Bentinckstraat is on your right.* Ⓢ *Pastas €10-17.* ⏲ *Open daily 10am-10pm.*

DE VLIEGENDE SCHOTEL

●♿♙ VEGETARIAN ❷

Nieuwe Leliestraat 162-168   ☎020 62 520 41 🖳www.vliegendeschotel.com

It's a little unclear what aliens have to do with vegetarian cuisine (this restaurant's name translates to "The Flying Saucer"), but we'll let the mystery slide because this restaurant is down-to-earth even if its food is out-of-this-world good.

🍴 *Tram #10 to Bloemgracht. Cross Lijnbaansgracht, make a left, and then a right onto Nieuwe Leliestraat.* Ⓢ *Entrees €11-13.* ⏲ *Open daily 4-11:30pm.*

WINKEL

●⊗♙⚖ CAFE ❷

Noordermarkt 43   ☎020 62 302 23 🖳www.winkel43.nl

Winkel serves up a cuisine that's hard to classify: you can get miso soup, a club sandwich, or lamb stew depending on your whim. No matter how you're feeling, you should do as everyone else does and order the apple pie. Winkel occasionally hosts live music and dancing.

🍴 *Tram #3 or 10 to Marnixplein. Cross Lijnbaangracht, walk up Westerstraat, and make a left onto the square.* Ⓢ *Entrees €6-15.* ⏲ *Open M 7am-1am, Tu-Th 8am-1am, F 8am-3am, Sa 7am-3am, Su 10am-1am.*

Museumplein and Leidseplein

This whole area can tend to be a little overpriced—Museumplein because it attracts real grown-ups and Leidseplein because it attracts drunk backpackers who don't know better. For the best values, look for restaurants that have special set menus or daily deals, or grab a sandwich and snack from a grocery store.

CAFE VERTIGO

★⊗♙⚖ CAFE, MEDITERRANEAN ❶

Vondelpark 3   ☎020 61 230 21 🖳www.vertigo.nl

Cafe Vertigo finds itself in a remarkable, ornate building with a seemingly endless patio that makes the place look like it should be a lot more expensive than it is. On a summer day, there's no better place to enjoy a sandwich and a drink (except, perhaps, for the grass of Vondelpark itself). Though the cafe sits on the edge of the park, it faces an expanse of green that will make you feel quite outside the city.

🍴 *Tram #1, 3, or 12 to 1e Constantijn Huygensstraat/Overtoom. Walk down 1e C. Huygensstraat, make a right onto Vondelstraat, and enter the park about 1 block down; the cafe is on your left.* Ⓢ *Soups and sandwiches €3.50-6.75. Entrees €11.75-19.50.* ⏲ *Open daily 10am-1am.*

BAGELS AND BEANS

★⊗⚖ CAFE ❶

Van Baerlestraat 40   ☎020 67 570 50 🖳www.bagelsbeans.nl

This charming chain now has over 40 stores across the Netherlands, but this is where it all began. You can get something as simple as a bagel with cream cheese (though with dozens of bagels and cream cheese options, it's not as simple as it sounds), or go for one of their creative sandwiches like chicken and avocado or goat cheese, honey, and walnuts. Given the dearth of affordable food around here, this place is magical. Check out the absurd opening times.

➔ Tram #2, 3, 5, or 12 to Van Baerlestraat. Ⓢ Bagel with cream cheese €3.35. Sandwiches €3.95-6.50. ⏰ Open May-Sept M-F 7:59am-6:02pm, Sa-Su 9:31am-6:02pm; Oct-Apr M-F 8:28am-6:01pm, Sa-Su 9:31am-5:59pm.

✔ EAT AT JO'S
🚫 ♿ 🍸 AMERICAN [2]

Marnixstraat 409 ☎020 63 833 36 💻www.eatatjos.com

This cafe inside the **Melkweg** complex gives you the opportunity to rub elbows with performers and locals over outstanding, impeccably fresh food. The menu changes daily, accommodating seasonal variation and the chef's multiethnic whims, but always with a vegetarian and vegan option.

➔ Tram #1, 2, 5, 7, or 10 to Leidseplein. Make a right down Marnixstraat. Ⓢ Sandwiches €5. Salads €7. Entrees €13. ⏰ Open W-Su noon-9pm. Dinner service begins at 5:30pm.

SAMA SEBO
💳 ♿ 🍸 ☀ INDONESIAN [3]

P. C. Hooftstraat 27 ☎020 66 281 46 💻www.samasebo.nl

Just next to the temporary entrance to the **Rijksmuseum,** this restaurant exemplifies the Dutch fondness for Indonesian food—authentic *rijsttafels* are served in a place that looks like a quintessential Dutch pub. Not the cheapest meal available, but the lunch deals are a good value for the neighborhood.

➔ Tram #2 or 5 to Hobbemastraat. Walk down the street with the Rijksmuseum on your right; the restaurant is at the intersection with P. C. Hooftstraat. Ⓢ Entrees €2.50-8. Lunch menus €16. Rijsttafel €30 per person. ⏰ Bar open M-Sa 9am-1am. Kitchen open noon-3pm and 5-10pm.

J. J. OOIJEVAAR
🚫 ⊘ 🍸 DELI [1]

Lange Leidsedwarsstraat 47 ☎020 62 355 03

This is the place for the cheapest sandwiches on the Leidseplein—perhaps in all of Amsterdam. Rolls start at €1.30, and all manner of fillings are available to stuff them with: cheeses, meats, vegetables, etc.

➔ Tram #1, 2, 5, 7, or 10 to Leidseplein. Ⓢ Sandwiches €1.30-3.50. ⏰ Open M-F 8:30am-6pm.

De Pijp

If you could somehow work it so that you ate every meal in De Pijp during your time in Amsterdam, you would be a happy **camper.** In a radius of just a few blocks, you'll find a tremendous variety of cuisines dished up at significantly lower prices than in most other parts of the city. **Albert Cuypstraat** and **Ferdinand Bolstraat** are good places to start looking, but don't neglect the side streets that radiate off of them as well.

✔ CAFE DE PIJP
🚫 ⊘ 🍸 ☀ MEDITERRANEAN [1]

Ferdinand Bolstraat 17-19 ☎020 67 041 61 💻www.goodfoodgroup.nl

20-somethings linger over drinks, dinner, or more drinks at Cafe De Pijp, something of a catch-all local hotspot. The menu is filled with tapas-esque offerings, like Merguez sausage with Turkish bread and aioli, or more Italian-inspired dishes along the lines of eggplant parmesan. On weekend nights, DJs spin dance tunes to help you work off your meal.

➔ Tram #16 or 24 to Stadhouderskade. Walk 2 blocks down Ferdinand Bolstraat. Ⓢ Entrees €5.50-8. ⏰ Open M-Th 3:30pm-1am, F 3:30pm-3am, Sa noon-2am, Su noon-1am.

✔ BAZAR
💳 ♿ 🍸 MIDDLE EASTERN [2]

Albert Cuypstraat 182 ☎020 67 505 44 💻www.bazaramsterdam.com

The crush of Albert Cuypmarkt feeling a little overwhelming? Pop into this former church where the vaulted ceilings remain, now decorated with Arabic Coca-Cola signs and old Dutch advertisements. Bazar serves inexpensive and super tasty Middle Eastern food.

➔ Tram #16 or 24 to Albert Cuypstraat. Walk through the market a few blocks. Ⓢ Sandwiches

and lunch entrees €4-10. Dinner entrees €12-16. ⏰ *Open M-Th 11am-midnight, F 11am-1am, Sa 9am-1am, Su 9am-midnight.*

WARUNG SPANG MAKANDRA ⊗♿🍸 INDONESIAN ❶

Gerard Doustraat 39 ☎020 67 050 81 💻www.spangmakandra.nl

Imperialism may have been a pretty terrible thing, but at least it has given us delicious culinary combinations like the Indonesian-Surinamese mix at this neighborhood favorite. Enjoy noodle and rice dishes, satays, and *rotis*—pancakes with different meat or vegetable fillings—for incredibly low prices.

✥ *Tram #16 or 24 to Albert Cuypstraat. Walk 1 block north on Ferdinand Bolstraat and make a left.* $ *Entrees €5.50-9.* ⏰ *Open M-Sa 11am-10pm, Su 1-10pm.*

BURGERMEESTER ⊗♿ BURGERS ❶

Albert Cuypstraat 48 ☎020 67 093 39 💻www.burgermeester.eu

Thankfully, the burgers here are better than the store's punny name (*burgemeester* is "mayor" in Dutch). This is something of a designer-burger bar—you can get a patty made from fancy beef, lamb, salmon, falafel, or Manchego cheese and hazelnuts, then top it with things like Chinese kale, truffle oil, or buffalo mozzarella. Burgers can be ordered normal-sized or miniature, because food is always more fun when it's tiny. They sell salads, too, but who goes to a burger joint for a salad?

✥ *Tram #16 or 24 to Albert Cuypstraat. Walk down the street away from the market.* $ *Burgers €6.50-8.50. Toppings €0.50-1.* ⏰ *Open daily noon-11pm.*

DE TAART VAN M'N TANTE ⊗♿🍸 DESSERT ❶

Ferdinand Bolstraat 10 ☎020 77 646 00 💻www.detaart.com

What started as a customized cake bakery now has its own restaurant where you can try slices of delicious cakes and pies—apple, pecan, and all kinds of more exciting combinations (including ones made "tipsy" with dashes of Amaretto and other liqueurs).

✥ *Tram #16 or 24 to Stadhouderskade/Ferdinand Bolstraat. The store is on the corner.* $ *Tart slices €4.30-5.20.* ⏰ *Open daily 10am-6pm.*

Jodenbuurt and Plantage

👍 **EETKUNST ASMARA** ⊗♿🍸 ERITREAN ❷

Jonas Daniel Meijerplein 8 ☎020 62 710 02

Jodenbuurt started out as a neighborhood of immigrants, and this East African restaurant is a testament to the area's continuing diversity. The menu consists of different types of meat or vegetables cooked in delicately blended spices, all served with *injera*, a traditional spongy, slightly tangy bread.

✥ *Tram #9 or 14 or* Ⓜ*Waterlooplein. Restaurant is just after the Jewish Historical Museum.* $ *Entrees €9.50-11.50. Beer €1.50.* ⏰ *Open daily 6-11pm.*

ROSARIO 💳🚫🍸 ITALIAN ❹

Peperstraat 10 ☎020 62 702 80 💻www.restaurantrosario.nl

If you're in the neighborhood and ready to drop a tidy sum, then this is the place to come. Everything from the bread to the pasta is fresh and homemade. Dishes are classic Italian with a twist, like curry *tagliatelle* with salmon or avocado *panna cotta*.

✥ *Tram #9 or 14 or* Ⓜ*Waterlooplein. Walk along Nieuwe Uilenburgerstraat until it becomes Peperstraat.* $ *Antipasti €11-12.50; primi €13.50-15; secondi €22-24.* ⏰ *Open W-Su 6-10:30pm.*

PLANCIUS 💳♿🍸⛅ CAFE, SANDWICHES, FRENCH ❷

Plantage Kerklaan 61A ☎020 33 094 69 💻www.restaurantplancius.nl

Capturing that elusive stylish yet unpretentious feeling, Plancius is a one-stop-shop for everything from breakfast to after-dinner drinks. The menu rotates seasonally, but trust that lunch will have a selection of creative spins on the traditional sandwich, while dinner tends toward more formal French fare like lamb shank or shrimp croquettes.

Tram #9 or 14 to Plantage Kerklaan. Across from Artis Zoo. $ Sandwiches €2.65-8.50. Dinner appetizers €8; entrees €15-19. ⏰ Open daily 11am-11pm. Cheaper items served until 6pm.

NIGHTLIFE

It goes without saying that experiencing the nightlife in Amsterdam is an integral part of any trip to the city. Certainly, you can go to the Rijksmuseum and see a dozen Rembrandts, but there's nothing like stumbling out of a bar at 5am and seeing the great man staring down at you from a pedestal in the middle of **Rembrandtplein.** That's one of the main after-dusk hotspots, where you can find glitzy clubs lined up next to raucous tourist bars and dance spots where the music invites choruses of drunken revelers to sing along. **Leidseplein** offers a similar mix of quality dance venues with live DJs, cool cocktail spots, and rowdy pubs. A few additional clubs are scattered throughout the city, but mostly what you'll find in the way of nightlife are some hipper lounge bars and a whole lot of *bruin cafes,* cafe-pub combinations populated by old Dutch men and hipster students, depending on what neighborhood you're in. The closer you get to the **Red Light District,** the more the local presence fades away and is taken over by groups of large British men on bachelor party trips wearing matching T-shirts.

▼**GLBT nightlife** is very visible and prominent. Around Rembrandtplein, especially on Reguliersdwarsstraat, you'll find both gay clubs and bars that cater primarily to men, though some women often turn up, too. The northern part of **Zeedijk** also has a couple of gay bars, and on the end of Warmoesstraat, near Dam, you'll find smaller, darker clubs that are strictly men-only and feature a fair bit of rubber and leather.

Oude Zijd

Both **Zeedijk** and **Nieuwmarkt** are lined with bars, so you certainly won't be at a loss for options when you head out to grab a drink in the evening. The watering holes on Zeedijk tend to be more popular with tourists, while Nieuwmarkt's crowd is mixed. If you head east toward Jodenbuurt, you will find more locals. Heading west will bring you to the Red Light District in all its glory. Though some overflow energy from the busier neighborhoods to the west spills into the Oude Zijd, things are generally a bit tamer at night. It's telling that most of the establishments listed here have "cafe" in their name. The northern part of Zeedijk, near Centraal Station, has a smattering of ▼**GLBT** bars, identified by their rainbow flags.

HET ELFDE GEBOD — BAR

Zeedijk 5 ☎020 62 235 77 🖥www.hetelfdegebod.com

Named "The Eleventh Commandment" after a now nonexistent Belgian beer, this bar sets itself apart from the endless row of pubs along the street with its incredible beer selection.

At the beginning of Zeedijk, near Centraal Station. $ Beer from €3. ⏰ Open M 5pm-1am, W-Su 3pm-1am.

CAFE DE JAREN — BAR

Nieuwe Doelenstraat 20-22 ☎020 62 557 71 🖥www.cafedejaren.nl

Incredibly popular with locals and tourists of all ages, Cafe de Jaren has an expansive interior and a two-tiered terrace overlooking the Amstel, making it one of the nicest spots to sit in Amsterdam. Thanks to its size and elegance, it looks a lot more expensive than it is. It also serves a diverse lunch and dinner menu.

Tram #4, 9, 16, 24, or 25 to Muntplein. Cross the Amstel and walk a ½-block. $ Beer from €2.50. Wine from €3. ⏰ Open M-Th 9:30am-1am, F-Sa 9:30am-2am, Su 9:30am-1am.

COTTON CLUB — JAZZ CLUB

Nieuwmarkt 5 ☎020 62 661 92 🖥www.cottonclubmusic.nl

An old and storied jazz club on the edge of Nieuwmarkt. Legendary musicians have played here, and every Saturday 5-8pm, you can hear the talented house musicians play, often with special guests. The rest of the week this is still a tuneful and relaxed place to enjoy a drink.

✠ Ⓜ*Nieuwmarkt*. Ⓢ *Beer from €2.50. Weekly concerts are free.* ⧖ *Open M-Th noon-1am, F-Sa noon-2am, Su noon-1am.*

CAFE NAGEL

⊛ ⅋ ⚥ BAR
☎020 51 684 93

Krom Boomssloot 47

Cafe Nagel is a truly local spot that feels miles away from tourist-filled Nieuwmarkt (though it's just a 2min. walk). It's packed with a regular crowd of locals in their 20s and early 30s on weekend nights. The good selection of beers and spirits (at some of the cheapest prices in town) should be enjoyed at the cafe's simple wooden tables or bustling bar.

✠ Ⓜ*Nieuwmarkt. Walk down Keizersstraat; it's across the canal.* Ⓢ *Beer from €2.50. Spirits from €3.* ⧖ *Open M-Th 11am-1am, F-Sa 11am-3am, Su 11am-1am.*

Red Light District

Ah, the Red Light District at night. Most of the neon glow bathes **Oudezijds Achterburgwal** and the nearby alleyways. Farther over on **Warmoesstraat,** you can still get a tinge of the lascivious luminescence but will find far more non-sex-related establishments. Especially on weekends, the whole area is filled with crowds of predominantly male tourists. Despite getting very busy, the hotel bars on Warmoesstraat and Oudezijds Voorburgwal can be fun places to mingle with fellow backpackers.

▓ CLUB WINSTON

⚥ ⅋ ⚥ CLUB

Warmoesstraat 129   ☎020 62 539 12 ▤www.winston.nl

A surprisingly large spectrum of musical genres fills this club each night with young locals and tourists. Live bands often play earlier in the evening, while DJs take over after 11pm. Once the bands clear out, the stage is free for intrepid dancers. You can hear everything from rock, metal, and drum 'n' bass to electronica, indie pop, or hip hop.

✠ *From Centraal Station, go south on Damrak, turn right onto Brugsteeg, and left onto Warmoesstraat.* Ⓢ *Cover usually around €5. Beer from €2.50.* ⧖ *Open daily, usually 9pm-4am.*

GETTO

⚥ ⊗ ⚥ ▼ BAR
☎020 42 151 51 ▤www.getto.nl

Warmoesstraat 51

A fun, everyone's-welcome-here cocktail bar crossed with a diner, Getto offers a phenomenal cocktail menu as well as their very own homemade infused vodka (flavors range from vanilla to cucumber). Though the bar's considered a GLBT establishment, the crowd is really as diverse as they come.

✠ *From Centraal Station, go south on Damrak, turn right onto Brugsteeg, and veer left onto Warmoesstraat.* Ⓢ *Cocktails from €6.* ⧖ *Open Tu-Th 4pm-1am, F-Sa 4pm-2am, Su 4pm-midnight. Happy hour Tu-Sa 5-7pm.*

CAFE AEN'T WATER

⊛ ⊗ ⚥ ♨ BAR
☎020 65 206 18

Oudezijds Vorburgwaal 2a

Smack in the middle of the two busiest Red Light District drags, you'll be surprised by how relaxed you feel and how much Dutch you hear. The star attraction is the large outdoor patio that hugs a bend in the canal, but if you choose to sit inside, you'll be able to enjoy the soundtrack of quality rock and indie music.

✠ *From Centraal Station, turn left onto Prins Hendrikkade and then bear right onto Nieuwebrugsteeg; continue straight as it becomes Oudezijds Vorburgwaal.* Ⓢ *Beer from €2.* ⧖ *Open M-Th noon-1am, F-Sa noon-3am, Su noon-1am.*

ROCK PLANET

⊛ ⅋ ⚥ ♨ BAR
☎020 42 164 00

Oudezijds Voorburgwal 246

This bar serves as an appropriate reminder that though some in the Red Light District may try, no one does debauchery like a rock star. The staff happily takes any music requests (as long as they're for rock), but you can also select from a vast collection of live concert DVDs and watch the performances while you drink. Reasonably mellow on weekdays (despite the high decibels), Rock Planet really fills up on weekend nights.

🚶 From Dam Sq., walk east on Dam and make a right onto Oudezijds Voorburgwal. $ Beer from €2. ⏰ Open M-Th 9am-1am, F-Sa 9am-3am, Su 9am-1am.

Nieuwe Zijd

Though not very concentrated, nightlife in the Nieuwe Zijd is diverse. **Spuistraat** is the place to go for artsier cafes and bars, while **Dam Square** and **Rokin** are lined with larger, rowdier pubs. The small streets in the southern part of the neighborhood are home to quite a few good beer bars and a couple of energetic clubs as well.

👍 PRIK

💳♿🍸⛅▼ BAR, CLUB

Spuistraat 109 ☎020 32 000 02 💻www.prikamsterdam.nl

Voted both best bar and best gay bar in Amsterdam on multiple occasions, Prik attracts pretty much everyone—locals and tourists, gay and straight people, men and women—though the majority of patrons tend to be men. It's a place that is as light and fun as its name ("bubble"). Serves great inventive cocktails and tasty bar snacks. Come for cocktail specials all day Thursday and Sunday evenings. On weekends, DJs spin pop, house, and disco classics.

🚶 Tram #1, 2, 5, or 14 to Dam/Paleisstraat. Walk down Paleisstraat and right onto Spuistraat. $ Beer from €2. Cocktails from €6. ⏰ Open M-Th 4pm-1am, F-Sa 4pm-3am, Su 4pm-1am. Kitchen open until 11pm.

👍 DANSEN BIJ JANSEN

🚫💳🚫♿🍸 CLUB

Handboogstraat 11-13 ☎020 62 017 79 💻www.dansenbijjansen.nl

A student-only club (must have ID or be accompanied by someone who does), Dansen bij Jansen attracts those from both the nearby University of Amsterdam and local hostels. The music in the crowded main dance floor may feel a bit three-years-ago, with a slightly cheesy mix of Top 40, R and B, and disco, but it certainly gets people dancing.

🚶 Tram #1, 2, or 5 to Koningsplein. Cross a canal, walk up Heiligeweg, and turn left onto Handboogstraat. $ Cover M-W €2; Th-Sa €5. Beer from €2. ⏰ Open M-Th 11pm-4am, F-Sa 11pm-5am.

CLUB NL

💳♿🍸 CLUB

Nieuwezijds Voorburgwal 169 ☎020 62 275 10 💻www.clubnl.nl

This is a swanky lounge club with surprisingly low cover charges. Patrons are slinkily dressed, and you'd be advised to spruce up a bit before trying to get in, especially later on a weekend night. The carefully crafted cocktail menu is just as image-conscious as the club itself, with delicious results.

🚶 Tram #1, 2, 5, or 14 to Dam/Paleisstraat. Just south of the stop on Nieuwezijds Voorburgwal. $ Cover F-Sa €5. Beer from €2.50. Cocktails from €8. ⏰ Open M-Th 10pm-3am, F-Sa 10pm-4am, Su 10pm-3am.

GOLLEM

🚫💳🚫♿🍸 BAR

Raamsteeg 4 ☎020 67 671 17 💻www.cafegollem.nl

This is not a bar for the indecisive. Beer aficionados from all across the city (and the world) flock to Gollem's slightly Gothic interior for the brews: this was one of the first cafes in Amsterdam to serve specialty Belgian beers way back in the '70s, and now the bar sells over 200 different kinds, with eight on tap. They even have the famed **Westvleteren,** made by reclusive monks in incredibly small batches to prevent it from becoming commercialized.

🚶 Tram #1, 2, or 5 to Spui/Nieuwezijds Voorburgwal. Walk up Spui and make a left onto Raamsteeg. $ Beer from €2.50. ⏰ Open M-F 4pm-1am, Sa-Su 2pm-2am.

Canal Ring West and Scheepvaartbuurt

This area doesn't go wild after sunset, although there are plenty of bars in which to grab a cheap beer and make friends with some locals.

👍 DULAC
◆⊗🍸⛱ BAR

Haarlemmerstraat 118 ☎020 62 442 65 💻www.restaurantdulac.nl

This bar is a popular place with local and foreign-exchange students. (There's a 50% student discount on the food served by the restaurant within.) The interior presents a fantastical mix of vintage designs, crazy sculptures, and found objects, including a pair of antlers and an antique saxophone. A garden terrace is in the back, and a pool table is inside.

➔ From Centraal Station, make a right, cross the Singel, and walk down Haarlemmerstraat. $ Beer from €2.50. Entrees €10-18. 🕐 Open M-Tu 4pm-1am, W-Th 1pm-1am, F-Sa 1pm-3am, Su 1pm-1am.

👍 DE PRINS
●⊗🍸⛱ BAR

Prinsengracht 124 ☎020 62 493 82 💻www.deprins.nl

One of the few unassuming bar-and-cafes in town, De Prins serves a variety of beers on tap (five, to be precise). Enjoy your brew in the wooden interior that inexplicably has pictures of the Queen facing portraits of Al Pacino and Humphrey Bogart or at the canalside seating outside. Music ranges from country blues to indie rock at this favorite haunt of young locals.

➔ Tram #13, 14, or 17 to Westermarkt. 2 blocks up Prinsengracht, on the far side. $ Beer €2.10-3.40. Liquor €3.50-5. 🕐 Open M-Th 10am-1am, F-Sa 10am-2am.

THIRSTY DOGG
●⊗🍸⛱ BAR

Oude Leliestraat 9

Small bar in the Nine Streets that shares the neighborhood's urban, alternative charm. Excellent selection of liquor, including a half-dozen types of absinthe. Some travelers consider Thirsty Dogg a marijuana-friendly environment.

➔ Tram #13, 14, or 17 to Westermarkt. Walk down Raadhuisstraat, make a left onto Herengracht, and then a right onto Oude Leliestraat. $ Beer €2.50. Wine €3. Absinthe €4. 🕐 Open M-Th 4pm-1am, F 4pm-3am, Sa noon-3am, Su noon-1am.

Central Canal Ring and Rembrandtplein

Rembrandtplein *is* its nightlife. Yeah, there's a pretty sweet statue of Rembrandt in the middle of this square, but if you were interested in the man himself, then you would be at one of Amsterdam's many fine museums—none of which can be found here. This is home to the art of looking good and getting down, not the art of the Dutch Renaissance. The square itself is lined with massive bars and clubs, while the streets that fan out from it are home to smaller establishments. **Reguliersdwarstraat,** particularly once you cross Vijzelstraat, is well known as **▼"the gayest street in Amsterdam,"** lined with a diverse array of gay bars and clubs, though many more are to be found on other neighboring streets as well. Rembrandtplein is conveniently serviced by night buses #355, 357, 359, 361, and 363; taxis also loiter around the main square at all hours. Outside of that mecca, **Spiegelgracht** and **Utrechtsestraat** house most of the neighborhood's other bars.

👍 ESCAPE
◆⊗🍸 CLUB

Rembrandtplein 11 ☎020 62 211 11 💻www.escape.nl

This is Amsterdam's biggest club, with a capacity for thousands. Although it may no longer be considered the hottest spot in town, it still reliably draws large crowds and excellent DJs. The main dance floor is a glam space with a massive stage (VIP area behind the DJ) and platforms strewn throughout for those brave enough to take the dancing spotlight. A lounge, another dance space, and a balcony from which to observe the bacchanalia below can all be found upstairs. The crowd is a mix of large groups of tourists and chic young Dutch. On weekends lines can grow long after 1am, and some suggest that upping your style will increase your chances of getting in.

➔ Tram #9 or 14 to Rembrandtplein. $ Cover €5-10, students €6 on most Th. Beer from €2.60.

Spirits €3.80-5.80. ⏰ *Open Th 11pm-4am, F-Sa 11pm-5am, Su 11pm-4am.*

◙ STUDIO 80
⊛⊗⅋ CLUB

Rembrandtplein 17 ▥www.studio-80.nl

A grungier alternative to the more polished clubs around Rembrandtplein, Studio 80 is extremely popular with the young student crowd. The emphasis is on dancing and music at this club, where you'll be rocking out on plywood planked floors. Sound varies from minimal electro to deep house to hip hop. Be prepared for a thorough pat down by bouncers at the door.

☂ *Tram #9 or 14 to Rembrandtplein. The entrance is next to Escape (see above), under the large balcony.* ⑤ *Cover depends on the night, usually €6-10. Beer €2.50.* ⏰ *Open W-Th 11pm-4am, F-Sa 11pm-5am, Su 11pm-4am.*

LELLEBEL
⊛⊗⅋⌂▼ BAR

Utrechtstraat 4 ☎020 42 751 39 ▥www.lellebel.nl

A terrifically fun and welcoming bar presided over by outrageous drag queens. With decor that's as campy as the costumes, Lellebel is all the more ready to help you make friends with your fellow drinkers. While it attracts a primarily gay male crowd, absolutely all genders and sexualities will feel comfortable here, as the ladies behind the bar are eager to assert. It plays host to a variety of theme nights—karaoke, Transgender Cafe, and Salsa Night, to name a few—and events such as the frequent Miss Lellebel contests and a Eurovision party.

☂ *Tram #9 or 14 to Rembrandtplein. Just off the southeast corner of the square. Karaoke on Tu. Transgender Cafe on W. Red Hot Salsa Night on Th.* ⑤ *Beer €2.50.* ⏰ *Open M-Th 8pm-3am, F-Sa 8pm-4am, Su 8pm-3am.*

MONTMARTRE
⊛⊗⅋▼ BAR

Halvemaansteeg 17 ☎020 62 076 22 ▥www.cafemontmartre.nl

A sinfully luxurious ◖**Garden of Eden** inspired interior provides the backdrop for this popular spot, regularly voted the best gay bar in Amsterdam. The crowd is dominated by gay men, but all are welcome. As the night wears on, the dancing heats up to Euro and American pop and bouncy disco.

☂ *Tram #9 or 14 to Rembrandtplein. Off of the northwest corner of the square.* ⑤ *Beer from €2.50. Liquor from €3.50.* ⏰ *Open M-Th 5pm-1am, F-Sa 5pm-3am, Su 5pm-1am.*

ARC
♥♿⅋⌂ BAR

Reguliersdwarsstraat 44 ☎020 68 970 70 ▥www.bararc.eu

Dim, red lighting and leather couches complement one of the hipper bars in the area. The crowd is trendy, and the music goes from nouveau disco to R and B, getting you ready for a night spent dancing nearby. Arc's real draw is its exquisite and inventive cocktail menu; Wednesday and Sunday are cocktail nights when selected libations are only €6. Arc also serves a varied menu of tapas and other European dishes.

☂ *Tram #9 or 14 to Rembrandtplein. On the stretch of Reguliersdwarsstraat that is across Vijzelstraat from the main square.* ⑤ *Beer from €2.50. Cocktails €8-10.* ⏰ *Open M-Th 4pm-1am, F-Sa 4pm-3am, Su 4pm-1am. Kitchen closes at 11pm.*

DE DUIVEL
⊛⊗⅋ BAR

Reguliersdwarsstraat 87 ☎020 62 661 84 ▥www.deduivel.nl

Amsterdam's premier hip-hop joint, visited by top names from Cypress Hill to Ghostface. Even without famous guests, De Duivel remains a nighttime favorite, with DJs who spin a terrific mix drawing a diverse crowd of patrons.

☂ *Tram #9 or 14 to Rembrandtplein.* ⑤ *Beer €2.50.* ⏰ *Open M-Th 10pm-3am, F-Sa 10pm-4am, Su 10pm-3am.*

VIVE LA VIE
⊛♿⅋⌂▼ BAR

Amstelstraat 7 ☎020 62 401 14 ▥www.vivelavie.net

This long-established lesbian bar draws a diverse crowd of women and a few

amsterdam • nightlife

of their male friends thanks to its unpretentious atmosphere focused on having a fun time. Excellent drink selection includes the **Clit on Fire** shot *(€4)*, whose ingredients are a closely guarded secret.

🚋 Tram #9 or 14 to Rembrandtplein. $ Beer from €2.50. Spirits from €4. ⏰ Open M-Th 3pm-3am, F-Sa 3pm-4am, Su 3pm-3am.

West Of Town

Nightlife in the Jordaan is much more relaxed than in Leidseplein or the Nieuwe Zijd, but that doesn't mean it's not popular or busy. Establishments tend more toward cafe-bars or local pubs than clubs, though some excellent music can be found in the neighborhood's southern stretches. If you're looking to seriously mingle with the locals, try one of the places along **Lijnbaansgracht** and **Noordermarkt** that really get going on weekends. Further west can get a little dead at times, although it there are some up-and-coming spots to be found.

👍 FESTINA LENTE — ♿ 🍸 BAR

Looiersgracht 40b ☎020 63 814 12 💻www.cafefestinalente.nl

Looking something like what you would get if you stuck a bar in the middle of an elegant vintage living room, this spot is enduringly popular with fun and cultured young Amsterdammers. Bookshelves line the walls, and games of chess and checkers are readily available for use—just try to find a free spot to play.

🚋 Tram #7, 10, or 17 to Elandsgracht. Go straight on Elandsgracht and make a right onto Hazenstraat; the bar is 2 blocks down on the corner. $ Beer from €2. Wine from €3.30 per glass. ⏰ Open M noon-1am, Tu-Th 10:30am-1am, F-Sa 10:30am-3am, Su noon-1am.

👍 'T SMALLE — ♿ 🍸 CAFE

Egelantiersgracht 12 ☎020 62 396 17

One of the most revered and popular *bruin cafes* in the city, 't Smalle was founded in 1780 as a spot to taste the products of a nearby *jenever* distillery. Today, the interior is appropriately old-fashioned and classic, but the real place to be is outside at one of the many tables lining Egelantiersgracht, for our money one of the prettiest canals in Amsterdam. Be warned, though: on nice days, you may have to get here very early or very late to claim a chair. An alternative location—in Nagasaki, Japan (*🚋 Head east about 9200km. The bar is on your right.*)—features a replica of the cafe that stands in the model "Holland Village."

🚋 Tram #13, 14, or 17 to Westermarkt. Cross Prinsengracht, make a right, and walk a few blocks. $ Beer from €2. ⏰ Open M-Th 10am-1am, F-Sa 10am-2am, Su 10am-1am.

👍 OT301 — 🍸 CLUB

Overtoom 301 💻www.ot301.nl

This establishment plays home to everything even remotely entertaining—a temporary handicrafts store, a cinema, live music, yoga and acrobatic classes, a vegan restaurant, and excellent DJ parties on most weekend nights make some strange bedfellows. The building was a squat inhabited by artists in the late '90s who brought in art and music, causing the city to consider it a cultural breeding ground. Check the website for upcoming events; the parties have music that ranges from electro house to soul and funk. The crowds who come to dance are as diverse and laid-back as one would expect from the surroundings.

🚋 Tram #1 to J. Pieter Heijestraat. $ Cover €3-5 most nights. ⏰ Hours vary depending on programming; check website for details.

CAFE CHRIS — ♿ 🍸 BAR

Bloemstraat 42 ☎020 62 459 42 💻www.cafechris.nl

Workers building the tower of the nearby Westerkerk used to stop here to pick up (and then probably spend) their paychecks—the bar first opened its doors in 1624, making it the oldest in the Jordaan. Today, it is just as popular with the local after-work crowd as it was with the construction dudes, and the antique interior of deep wood and stained glass keeps history at the forefront.

✠ *Tram #13, 14, or 17 to Westermarkt. Cross Prinsengracht, make a right, and walk 1 block.* Ⓢ *Beer €3-5.* ⌚ *Open M-Th 3pm-1am, F-Sa 3pm-2am, Su 3-9pm.*

SAAREIN
●●((º)) ⍦ ▼ BAR

Elandsstraat 119   ☎020 62 349 01 ▇www.saarein.info

A *bruin cafe* very much in the tradition of the Jordaan but with a GLBT focus, Saarein attracts mainly older lesbians, though all genders and orientations are heartily welcome. Hosts a variety of events, from a pool competition every Tuesday to discussion groups about issues of gender and sexuality.

✠ *Tram #7, 10, or 17 to Elandsgracht. Make a left onto Lijnbaansgracht and walk 2 blocks.* Ⓢ *Beer from €2.* ⌚ *Open Tu-Th 4pm-1am, F 4pm-2am, Sa noon-2am, Su noon-1am.*

Museumplein and Leidseplein

"Leidseplein" translates to "more diverse nightlife per square foot than anywhere else in the city" (don't listen to anyone who feeds you a story about how it means something to do with a road to the city of Leiden). Some native Amsterdammers scoff at this area, considering it a sea of drunken British and American tourists, but the bars that cater to the liquored-up crowd are primarily confined to the Korte and Lange Leidsedwarsstraats. The rest of the area, a bit to the south, plays host to some very hip and friendly bars as well as a few terrific nightclubs. Scattered within the whole of the neighborhood are several bastions of incredible live music (including the aforementioned nightclubs). Unless you are going to a big-name event at **Paradiso** or **Melkweg**, prices in the neighborhood are extremely reasonable. Many establishments are just as full of locals, young and old, as they are with tourists. And if you want to be one of the revelers that gives the Leidseplein its bad name, check out the Leidseplein Pub Crawl (promoters lurk in the main square all day long). There's little reason to head much further south, though, museums don't stay open after 6pm and neither does much else around Museumplein post-dinner.

PARADISO
●●⍦ CLUB, CONCERT VENUE

Weteringschans 6-8   ☎020 62 645 21 ▇www.paradiso.nl

Paradiso hosts an infinity of live music performances (generally less well-known artists than nearby Melkweg, though it has played host to some big names like Wu-Tang Clan and Lady Gaga) every day and club nights five nights a week—including *Noodlanding!* ("emergency landing"), a party with "alternative dance hits" on Thursdays.

✠ *Tram #1, 2, 5, 6, 7, or 10 to Leidseplein. Take a left onto Weteringschans.* Ⓢ *Prices vary by event; tickets are usually €5-20 plus a €3 monthly membership fee.* ⌚ *Hours vary by event.*

MELKWEG
●●⍦ CLUB, CONCERT VENUE

Lijnbaansgracht 234A   ☎020 53 181 81 ▇www.melkweg.nl

The name translates to "milky way"—a pun on the fact that this cultural center is housed in an old milk factory. One of Amsterdam's legendary night spots and concert venues, Melkweg hosts rock, punk, pop, indie, reggae, electronic...basically, any type of music that exists in the big Milky Way has probably been played in this little one. After the concerts on Friday and Saturday, there are club nights with techno, house, and alternative music.

✠ *Tram #1, 2, 5, 6, 7, or 10 to Leidseplein. Turn down the small street to the left of the Stadsschouwburg theater.* Ⓢ *Tickets generally €10-30 plus €3.50 monthly membership fee.* ⌚ *Concerts usually start around 8 or 9pm, with clubbing getting going around 11pm or midnight.*

SUGAR FACTORY
●●⍦ CLUB

Lijnbaansgracht 238   ☎020 62 650 06 ▇www.sugarfactory.nl

Billing itself as a *nachttheater*, Sugar Factory is, at its core, just a very cool place to dance. Live music and DJs are often accompanied by mind-bending video displays, dancers, and other performers. Music tends toward house, electro, and "club jazz." The sizeable dance floor fills with a mix of young Dutch hipsters,

from the road

Everyone knows that the Dutch have a thing for 🚲**bicycles.** I have seen people do everything while riding their two-wheelers around town–they eat, talk on cell phones, smoke cigarettes, and apply makeup. Bikes really are an excellent way to get around the city, but because Amsterdam is also so easily traversed on foot, I never got around to renting one. Part of me felt, though, that in not pedaling around the city, I was missing out on an important aspect of local culture.

At least, that was the case until I went to research the Leidseplein. This square is renowned for its nightlife, so to make the best use of my time and the biggest dent in my list of establishments, I decided to try and research as many bars and clubs as possible in one night. My last stop was the Sugar Factory. I didn't get there until after 1am, and the music was so good and the people so friendly that I ended up staying until closing. Exiting to the disconcertingly bright morning (it seems that during the Dutch summer it's only really dark from 11pm-3am), my newfound Dutch pals asked me how I planned on getting home. "The tram," I replied. They all looked at me in astonishment. "You don't have a bike?" they asked. Somehow, in my foreign naïveté, I had assumed that people surely didn't bring their bicycles when they went out for a night on the town. What if you get drunk? Or are wearing high heels? Or are just tired from dancing all night?

Such things, while obstacles to an ungainly and inexperienced cyclist like myself, are barely even considerations for a native Amsterdammer. Sure enough, the phalanx of people pouring out from the clubs on the Leidseplein were all headed toward the bicycle racks outside. I think that my new friends must have seen a certain wistfulness in my eyes, and they kindly offered to give me a ride home. So I perched on the back of a bike, and we zipped off along the canals in the 5am sunshine. Only if I had been eating some Gouda at the same time could I have felt more Dutch.

—Beatrice Franklin

older locals, and a smattering of tourists. The cocktail balcony provides the perfect spot to people watch, while the smoking lounge upstairs is the perfect place to...smoke. Check the website for upcoming events; it's a safe assumption that there will be something going on Friday and Saturday nights midnight-5am.

🚋 Tram #1, 2, 5, 6, 7, or 10 to Leidseplein. Turn down the small street to the left of the Stadsschouwburg theater. $ Cover usually €8-12. Beer from €3. Cocktails €6.50. ⏰ Hours vary.

🏆 WEBER — ⊛⊘🍸 BAR

Marnixstraat 397 ☎020 62 299 10

A bar that's tremendously popular with young locals and a few stylish tourists alike, Weber is the place to be. Come early or late (once people have departed for the clubs) if you want to get a seat on a weekend night. Tiny, frilly red lampshades and vintage pornographic art give the place a cheeky bordello feel, which is complemented by jazzy French pop. But don't be fooled: this bar steers clear of the tawdriness that plagues so much Amsterdam nightlife. Small balcony seating raised above the bar area and a large downstairs room are great spots to grab a drink and chat with friends.

🚋 Tram #1, 2, 5, 6, 7, or 10 to Leidseplein. Walk south of the square and make a right onto Marnixstraat. $ Beer €2.50. Spirits from €4. ⏰ Open M-Th 8pm-3am, F-Sa 8pm-4am, Su 8pm-3am.

DE PIEPER

CAFE

Prinsengracht 424 ☎020 62 647 75

One of Amsterdam's oldest cafes, De Pieper calls a building that's been around since the 17th century its home. The interior reflects the building's age, with low ceilings, dark wood paneling, and Delft mugs hanging behind the bar, but De Pieper also makes a quirky nod to modernity, with strings of fairy lights and posters from performances at nearby venues. This is the perfect place to escape from the internationalism of the Leidseplein and just have a good *bier* like a local. It has a jovial and loyal following, especially on weekend nights.

Tram #1, 2, or 5 to Prinsengracht or #7 or 10 to Raamplein. At the corner of Prinsengracht and Leidsegracht. $ Beer from €2.50. ⏰ Open M-Th 11am-1am, F-Sa 11am-3am.

BOURBON STREET

BLUES CLUB

Leidsekruisstraat 6-8 ☎020 62 334 40

This is a jovial and bustling home of nightly live blues, soul, and funk. Walls are packed with memorabilia and photos from past events. At the jam nights on Monday, Tuesday, and Sunday, all are welcome to bring their own instruments and play along. (We assume that this works, because if you're willing to haul your gear to the Leidseplein, then you're hopefully pretty good.) Bourbon attracts large crowds of locals and tourists alike.

Tram #1, 2, 5, 6, 7, or 10 to Leidseplein. Make a right onto Korte Leidsedwarsstraat and Leidsekruisstraat will be on your left. $ Beer from €3. ⏰ Open M-Th 10pm-4am, F-Sa 10pm-5am, Su 10pm-4am.

PIRATES BAR

BAR

Korte Leidsedwarsstraat 129

Belly up to the bar here for some cheap grog; weekly deals have beer going for as little as €1.50. The atmosphere is perhaps a bit more frat boy than salty sea dog (though ship accoutrements abound); if you end up intersecting the Leidseplein Pub Crawl as it makes its way through this watering hole, be prepared for a lot of crowded, sweaty bumping and grinding to the Top 40, hip hop, and dance music. It's a great place to get yourself ready for an evening of debauchery on the town.

Tram #1, 2, 5, 6, 7, or 10 to Leidseplein. $ Cover €2.50 for men, includes 1 drink. Beers around €2.50. Shots €3.50. ⏰ Open M-Th 6pm-3am, F-Sa 6pm-4am, Su 6pm-3am.

De Pijp

What De Pijp does—laid-back hipster bars with good beer, good food, and good company—it does very well.

CHOCOLATE BAR

BAR

1e Van Der Helststraat 62A ☎020 67 576 72 www.chocolate-bar.nl

While most bars in the neighborhood have a cafe-like vibe, this place veers more toward cocktail lounge. It's certainly not a dressy affair, but the long, glossy bar and seating area peppered with small, chic tables up the cool factor. The outdoor patio is a special place, with couches and picnic tables—a prime place to survey the De Pijp scene. On weekends, DJs spin laid-back dance tunes inside.

Tram #16 or 24 to Albert Cuypstraat. Walk 1 block down Albert Cuypstraat and make a right. $ Beer from €2. Cocktails €7. ⏰ Open M-Th 10am-1am, F-Sa 10am-3am, Su 11am-1am.

TROUW AMSTERDAM

CLUB

Wibautstraat 127 ☎020 46 377 88 www.trouwamsterdam.nl

This club's not strictly in De Pijp, but just across the Amstel. Housed in the former office building of the newspaper *Trouw*, this complex includes a restaurant, exhibition space, and club. It's a rather gritty, industrial-feeling space that's extremely popular with local students. The music ranges from dubstep to electronic to house and more; check the website for specific events. It occasionally hosts after-parties that begin at 6am.

➜ Ⓜ Wibautstraat. The stop is right next to the building. Or tram #3 to Wibautstraat. Walk a few blocks south on Wibautstraat. You're looking for a giant white office building that says "Trouw" on the upper corner. $ Cover €10-17. 🕐 Club generally open F-Sa 10:30pm-5am.

KINGFISHER

♿🍸 BAR

Ferdinand Bolstraat 24 ☎020 67 123 95

One of the original bars that set the stage for the rise of cool in De Pijp, Kingfisher hasn't let the popularity go to its head, and it remains a wonderful spot to enjoy one of their international beers and a chat in the spacious wood interior. The place is filled to the gills on weekend nights, but on a sunny afternoon, you should still be able to grab a coveted table outside.

➜ Tram #16 or 24 to Stadhouderskade. Walk 1 block down Ferdinand Bolstraat. $ Beer from €2. 🕐 Open M-Th 11am-1am, F-Sa 11am-3am, Su noon-1am.

Jodenbuurt and Plantage

This is not the neighborhood for rowdy nightlife. If you're looking for a big night out, you'd do better to head to nearby **Rembrandtplein** or **Nieuwmarkt.** However, there are a few excellent laid-back local bars in the neighborhood, befitting its overall character.

👍 DE SLUYSWACHT

♿🍸 BAR

Jodenbreestraat 1 ☎020 62 576 11 💻www.sluyswacht.nl

This tiny, tilting 17th-century building houses the kind of bar you would expect to find on a lone seacoast, not a bustling street. The outdoor patio sits right above the canal, with giant umbrellas ready in case the weather should turn rainy. When it gets really inclement, the plain wooden interior is invitingly snug. A good selection of draft and bottled beers is available.

➜ Tram #9 or 14 or Ⓜ Waterlooplein. $ Beer €2.10-4. 🕐 Open M-Th 11:30am-1am, F-Sa 11:30am-3am, Su 11:30am-7pm.

HET GENOT VAN RAPENBURG

🍸 BAR

Rapenburg 16-18 ☎020 62 231 50 💻www.hetgenotvanrapenburg.nl

A welcoming bar tucked away on an out-of-the-way corner of Plantage, this watering hole is populated mostly by locals from the nearby offices. Music at the bartender's discretion—usually leaning toward relaxed British and American indie rock—add to this unfussy watering hole's charm.

➜ Tram #9 or 14 or Ⓜ Waterlooplein. Walk along Nieuwe Uilenburgerstraat until it becomes Peperstraat; the bar is at the corner. $ Beer €2.20-4 🕐 Open M-Th 5pm-1am, F-Sa 5pm-2am, Su 5pm-1am.

ARTS AND CULTURE ♫

Besides its stunning collection of visual arts, Amsterdam offers a whole host of cultural attractions to travelers and locals alike. The music and film scenes here rival those of any other city in Europe, and many argue that the **Concertgebouw** concert hall has the best acoustics in the world. Comedy shows have been increasing in popularity, and with large summer festivals held each year, you can see some wonderfully innovative theater and dance if you time your visit right.

👍 CONCERTGEBOUW

♿ MUSEUMPLEIN

Concertgebouwplein 2-6 ☎020 57 305 73 💻www.concertgebouw.nl

Even if you don't catch a concert here, it's worth taking a look at this magnificent 1888 building when you're in Museumplein. However, with some of the best acoustics in the world and a highly renowned classical ensemble, the **Royal Concertgebouw Orchestra,** this performance space is more than just a pretty sight. Some 900 concerts, primarily classical but also programs of jazz and world music, are held here each year. Free lunch concerts are held Wednesdays in the small concert hall, while even performances in the main hall have some tickets in the €20 range.

🚋 Tram #3, 5, 12, 16, or 24 to Museumplein. ⓢ Varies by concert; main events generally €20-100. ⌚ Ticket office open M-F 1-7pm, Sa-Su 10am-7pm.

▨ MELKWEG ●⊗♉ LIVE MUSIC
Lijnbaansgracht 234A ☎020 53 181 81 💻www.melkweg.nl

A legendary venue for all kinds of live music as well as clubbing.

🚋 Tram #1, 2, 5, 6, 7, or 10 to Leidseplein. Turn down the small street to the left of the Stadsschouwburg theater. ⓢ Generally €10-30, with €3.50 monthly membership fee. ⌚ Concerts usually start around 8pm or 9pm.

▨ PARADISO ●⊗♉ LIVE MUSIC
Weteringschans 6-8 ☎020 62 645 21 💻www.paradiso.nl

Everything from big-name pop acts to experimental DJs.

🚋 Tram #1, 2, 5, 6, 7, or 10 to Leidseplein. Take a left onto Weteringschans. ⓢ Prices vary by event; tickets usually €5-20 plus a €3 monthly membership fee. ⌚ Hours vary by event.

▨ ALTO ●⊗♉ JAZZ
Korte Leidsedwarsstraat 115 ☎020 62 632 49 💻www.jazz-cafe-alto.nl

Amsterdam's most respected jazz joint, Alto is small, dark, and cozy—as any such place should be. Look for the giant saxophone outside marking the location. With live performances every night by renowned artists, the place fills up quickly, so come early to get a seat.

🚋 Tram #1, 2, 5, 6, 7, or 10 to Leidseplein. ⌚ Open M-Th 9pm-3am, F-Sa 9pm-4am, Su 9pm-3am. Music starts daily at 10pm.

▨ BOOM CHICAGO ●♿♉ COMEDY
Leidseplein 12 ☎020 42 301 01 💻www.boomchicago.nl

Boom Chicago is the place for extremely popular English-language improv comedy shows with plenty of audience participation, every night of the week.

🚋 Tram #1, 2, 5, 7, or 10 to Leidseplein. ⓢ Tickets €20-25. ⌚ Most shows begin 8-9pm.

SHOPPING

With shopping, as with pretty much every other aspect of life in Amsterdam, a wide range of options is at your fingertips. The **Nine Streets** just south of Westerkerk are packed with vintage stores and interesting boutiques. **Haarlemmerstraat,** in Scheepvaartbuurt, is also an up-and-coming neighborhood in terms of clothing design. For more established brands, look to **Kalverstraat,** with its string of international chains and large department stores. If you're looking for something really pricey, **P. C. Hooftstraat,** near Museumplein, is the part of town with the big-name designers. On the other end of the spectrum, markets like **Albert Cuypmarkt** offer dirt-cheap and, at times, flat-out bizarre clothing and other wares.

▨ ALBERT CUYPMARKT ●♿ MARKET
Albert Cuypstraat

Stretching almost half a mile along the length of Albert Cuypstraat in De Pijp, this is the most famous market in Amsterdam. Need a motorcycle helmet, sundress, and cinnamon all in one afternoon? This is the place to go.

🚋 Tram #16 or 24 to Albert Cuypstraat. ⌚ Open M-Sa 9am-6pm.

▨ LAURA DOLS ●⊗ VINTAGE CLOTHING
Wolvenstraat 7 ☎020 62 490 66 💻www.lauradols.nl

An amazing collection of vintage gowns includes taffeta prom dresses, fluffy shepherdess-y numbers, and things you could actually get away with wearing outside of the house. Also sells shoes, bags, and old-school lingerie (including some awesome metallic bras).

➜ *Tram #1, 2, or 5 to Spui/Nieuwezijds Voorburgwal. Walk west to the far side of Herengracht, make a right, and then a left onto Wolvenstraat.* $ *Most dresses €30-60, though some go up into the hundreds.* ⏰ *Open M 1-6pm, Tu-W 11am-6pm, Th 11am-7pm, Sa 11am-6pm, Su 1-6pm.*

THE BOOK EXCHANGE — BOOKS

Kloveniersburgwal 58 ☎020 62 66 266 🖥www.bookexchange.nl

A tremendous selection of hardcover and paperback secondhand English books, ranging from New Age philosophy to poetry and beyond. Largest choice is with paperback fiction. Knowledgeable expat owner is more than happy to chat at length with customers. Store also buys and trades books.

➜ *From Nieuwmarkt, cross to the far side of Kloveniersburgwal and make a left.* ⏰ *Open M-Sa 10am-4pm, Su 11:30am-4pm.*

STUDIO 88 — ♿ CLOTHING

Gerard Douplein 88 ☎020 77 065 84 🖥www.fashionstudio88.nl

The clothes at Studio 88 might not be as cheap as at naerby Albert Cuypmarket, but for an overstock and sample store, it sells some very nice high-end pieces for a fraction of what they would ordinarily cost. It carries mostly women's clothes with a few racks of men's things in the back.

➜ *Tram #16 or 24 to Albert Cuypstraat. Walk 1 block up and make a right onto Gerard Doustraat; the store is up ahead on the right.* $ *Prices vary by brand. Most shirts average around €20. Dresses around €40.* ⏰ *Open M 1-6pm, Tu-F 11am-6pm, Sa 10am-6pm.*

ESSENTIALS

Practicalities

- **TOURIST OFFICES: VVV** provides information on sights and accommodations. They also sell the **I Amsterdam** card, which gives you unlimited transport and free admission to many museums within a certain number of days. *(Stationsplein 10 ☎020 188 00 🖥www.iamsterdam.com ➜ Across from the eastern part of Centraal Station, near tram stops 1-4. ⏰ Open M-W 9am-6pm, Th-F 9am-9pm, Sa-Su 9am-6pm.)* There's another location at **Leidseplein 26.** *(⏰ Open M-Sa 10am-7:30pm, Su noon-7:30pm.)* **GAYtic** is a tourist info office authorized by the VVV that specializes in GLBT tourist info. *(Spuistraat 44 🖥www.gaytic.nl ⏰ Open M-Sa 11am-8pm, Su noon-8pm.)*
- **INTERNET: Openbare Bibliotheek Amsterdam** provides free Wi-Fi and free use of computers that can be reserved through the information desk. *(Oosterdokskade 143 ☎052 309 00 🖥www.oba.nl ➜ From Centraal Station, walk straight east. You'll cross a canal, and the street will become Oosterdokskade. ⏰ Open daily 10am-10pm.)*
- **POST OFFICES: Main branch**. *(Singel 250 ☎020 55 633 11 🖥www.tntpost.nl ➜ Tram #1, 2, 5, or 14 to Dam/Paleisstraat. Walk 1 block north and make a left onto Raadhuisstraat. ⏰ Open M-F 9am-6pm, Sa 10am-1:30pm.)*

Emergency!

- **POLICE: Politie Amsterdam-Amstelland** is the city's police department. The following are the most convenient bureaus to central Amsterdam. All can be reached at ☎020 900 8844, where you will be connected to the nearest station or rape crisis center. **Lijnbaansgracht.** *(Lijnbaansgracht 219 ➜ Tram #7 or 10 to Raamplein. Walk 1 block south and make a left onto Leidsegracht. ⏰ Open 24hr.)* **Nieuwezijds Voorburgwal.** *(Nieuwezijds Voorburgwal 104-108 ➜ Tram #1, 2, 5, 13, or 17 to Nieuwezijds Kolk. Walk 1 block down Nieuwezijds Voorburgwal. ⏰ Open 24hr.)* **Prinsengracht.** *(Prinsengracht 1109 ➜ Tram #3, 4, 7, 10, or 25 to Fredericksplein. Walk diagonally through the square, up Utrechtsestraat, and make a right onto Prinsengracht. ⏰ Open 24hr.)*

- **CRISIS HOTLINES: Amsterdam Tourist Assistance Service** provides help for victimized tourists in Amsterdam, generally those who have been robbed. Can offer assistance with practical matters like money transfers, replacing documents, and finding temporary accommodations. *(Nieuwezijds Voorburgwal 104-08 ☎020 62 532 46 💻www.stichtingatas.nl 🚋 Tram #1, 2, 5, 13, or 17 to Nieuwezijds Kolk. Walk 1 block down Nieuwezijds Voorburgwal. It's inside the police station. ⏰ Open daily 10am-10pm.)*
- **LATE-NIGHT PHARMACIES:** There are no specifically designated 24hr. pharmacies, but **Afdeling Inlichtingen Apotheken hotline** provides information about what pharmacies are open late on a given day. *(☎020 69 487 09 ⏰ Available 24hr.)*
- **HOSPITALS/MEDICAL SERVICES: Academisch Meidsch Centrum** is located southeast of the city. *(Meibergdreef 9 ☎020 56 691 11 💻www.amc.uva.nl 🚋 Bus #45, 47, 120, 126, 153, 155, 158 or night bus #375, 376, 377, 378, and 379 to Paasheuvelweg. Hospital is directly across.)* **Doctors Service Foundation of Amsterdam** will put you in touch with a doctor's clinic open after hours or on weekends. *(☎088 00 30 600 💻www.shda.nl ⏰ Line open daily 5pm-8am.)*

Getting There

By Plane

Schiphol Airport (AMS) *(☎090 001 41 inside the Netherlands; 31 207 940 800 outside 💻www.schiphol.nl)* is the main international airport for both Amsterdam and the Netherlands. It's located 18km outside the city center, and the easiest way to reach it is by **train** *($ €4.20. ⏰ 15 min., 4-10 per hr. 6am-1am, then 1 night train per hr.)* Trains also go to other Dutch cities from here.

By Train

Almost all trains arrive in **Centraal Station** *(Stationsplein 1 ☎0900 9292 💻www.ns.nl)*, Trains from **The Hague** *($ €10.10. ⏰ 1 hr., 3-6 per hr., 4:45am-12:45am.)*, **Rotterdam** *($ €13.30. ⏰ 1hr., 3-8 per hr. 5:30am-12:45am, 1 per hr. 12:45am-5:30am.)*, and **Utrecht.** *($ €6.70. ⏰ 30min., 4 per hr. 6am-midnight, 1 per hr. midnight-6am.)* International trains from Belgium run by **Thalys** *(💻www.thalys.com)*. Trains from **Brussels.** *($ €25-64. ⏰ 2hr., 1 per hr. 7:50am-8:50pm.)*

Getting Around

By Public Transportation

Trams are generally the fastest and easiest modes of transport, going to all major points within the city center (except for the Oude Zijd and Red Light District, which have almost no public transport stops but are easily accessible by the stops on their northern or southern ends). Buses are good if you are going to more residential areas or spots outside of the center, though trams extend to farther distances as well. The Metro is rarely useful, as it only goes down the eastern side of the city and has few stops within the center.

The **OV-chipkaart** has replaced the strippenkaart as the only type of ticket used on Amsterdam public transport. One-hour tickets can be purchased directly on trams and buses for €2.60. One- to seven-day tickets (valid also on night buses) cost €7-29. Otherwise, you can purchase an OV-chipkaart for €5 and add money to it as you need. With the chipkaart, a ride on the bus, tram, or Metro costs €0.78 plus €0.10 per km. A ride pretty much anywhere in the city center will only cost you around €1. An ordinary chipkaart does not work on night buses; you have to buy special tickets, which cost €3.50 per ride or 12 for €25. Make sure to both tap in *and* tap out with your chipkaart to avoid being charged for more than you actually travel.

Bike Rentals

Bikes are a huge part of Amsterdam culture, and if you choose to go without one and then make friends with locals, expect them to mock you for relying on your feet or the trams. **Frederic Rent-a-Bike** (*Brouwersgracht 78* ☎*020 62 455 09* 🖥*www.frederic.nl*) is run by Frederic, a guru of all things Amsterdam, who rents out rooms and also bikes. **Bike City** (*Bloemgracht 68-70* ☎*020 62 637 21* 🖥*www.bikecity.nl*) in Jordaan is another option. In the centrum, try **Damstraat Rent-a-Bike** (*Damstraat 22* ☎*062 550 29* 🖥*www.bikes.nl*).

the hague *den haag* ☎070

The official name of The Hague is *'s Gravenhage*, translating to "The Count's Domain." That's a pretty awesome name for a city, so we're going to be using it for the rest of this introduction. The Count's Domain was birthed when **Floris IV**, Count of Holland, decided around 1230 that the land surrounding the pond that is now the Hofijver would be a good place to go hunting. Later Counts agreed that this was a nice tract of land, so they built more palaces here. Over time, this became an important administrative center for the Counts of Holland. After a bit of messy political history, The Count's Domain officially became the home of the government of the Dutch Republic and the residence of the House of Orange in the 16th century. In order for the national government to control the area, The Count's Domain didn't officially become a city until the Napoleonic period.

Today, in addition to being the capital of the Netherlands, The Count's Domain is extremely important for international matters, serving as the home of all embassies to the Netherlands, the judicial body of the UN, the UN's tribunal on the former Yugoslavia, the International Criminal Court, and EU organizations like EUROPOL.

If all this makes The Count's Domain sound important (as though you weren't tipped off by the regal name), that's because it is. This is a city full of politicians, diplomats, and businesspeople. Unsurprisingly, it feels a bit more sedate than the other large Dutch cities. However, its international character makes it a pleasure for travelers, as you're pretty much guaranteed to find someone from your own country mixed in with all the locals.

ORIENTATION

Coming into The Hague, you'll probably be arriving at **Den Haag Centraal** which marks the eastern border of the city center. The Hague's real heart is the area around the palatial **Binnenhof**, the Dutch Parliament (the surrounding area is called **Buitenhof**). North of here, the city gets increasingly more residential. South and west of Buitenhof are the more commercial areas with the best shops, food, and nightlife. Running south from Buitenhof is **Spui**, which heads toward the **Stayokay**, lined first with theaters, then with some cheap takeout restaurants. West of Buitenhof is the busy shopping area on **Grotemarktstraat** and the surrounding streets. This region gives way to the popular nightlife area around **Grote Markt**. Northwest of Buitenhof a tangle of small streets like **Molenstraat** and **Papestraat** contains more relaxed bars and good restaurants. Fifteen minutes north of the city by tram, you'll find the beach town of **Scheveningen**.

ACCOMMODATIONS

With so many people rolling into The Hague on business, there are few rooms for those seeking a cheap roof over their heads. Budget hotels tend to be either quite plain or located outside the city center. The Stayokay, the one hostel in town, is a good option.

🏠 STAYOKAY DEN HAAG ✦♿(ᵗᵖ) HOSTEL ❶
Scheepmakersstraat 27 ☎070 31 578 88 🖥www.stayokay.nl
The only hostel in The Hague, and a good one at that. About 5min. from Holland

the netherlands

Spoor train station and 15min. from the city center, this Stayokay has the same quality facilities (large, clean rooms, and helpful staff) as the other Stayokays around the Netherlands, though it also shares their slightly bland character.

From Den Haag Centraal, take tram #17 to Rijswijkseplein. $ 4- to 8-bed dorms from €20.

JORPLACE BEACH HOSTEL — HOSTEL 1

Keizerstraat 296 ☎070 33 832 70 www.jorplace.nl

Located in Scheveningen, the beach town 15min. away from The Hague, this is a great option if you want a bit more bustle and fun than the Stayokay. And if you want to go to the beach, of course.

From Den Haag Centraal, take tram #16 to Buitenhof and switch to tram #1. $ 4- to 20-bed dorms €19-30; doubles €35-60.

STATEN HOTEL — HOTEL 2

Frederik Hendriklaan 299 ☎070 35 439 43 www.statenhotel.nl

Located outside the city center but quite close to the excellent **Gemeentemuseum,** Staten Hotel is family-run, and it shows in the kind and helpful service.

Tram #17 to Museon/Gemeentemuseum. Continue walking toward the museums, go left onto Frederik Hendriksplein, then right onto Frederik Hendriklaan. $ Singles €45-70; doubles €77-83.

HOTEL LA VILLE — HOTEL 2

Veenkade 5 ☎070 34 636 57 www.hotellaville.nl

Recent renovations have left this hotel with ultramodern, all-white decor (occasionally broken up by the odd wall print here and there). The rooms can be on the small side, but the location is pretty ideal for the price: you're just around the corner from the heart of the city.

Tram #17 (from either Holland Spoor or Den Haag Centraal) to Noordwal. The hotel is ahead on your left. $ Singles €45; doubles €80; royal suites €125. Apartments €115.

SIGHTS

As the political center of the Netherlands and one of the most important diplomatic cities in the world, The Hague is full of political and historic heavyweights. Also, a few excellent art museums dot the city.

VREDESPALEIS (PEACE PALACE) — GOVERNMENT

Carnegieplein 2 ☎070 30 242 42 www.vredespaleis.nl

It might be difficult to think of **Tsar Nicholas II** as a big supporter of international peace and demilitarization. But he and **Andrew Carnegie** were the two big players behind the construction of this formidable building dedicated to the promotion of cooperation between nation states. The Peace Palace is home to both the **International Court of Justice (ICJ)** (the judicial organ of the United Nations) and the lesser-known **Permanent Court of Arbitration (PCA)** (an older court for settling interstate disputes). There are two ways to get yourself inside: attend a session of the ICJ (the PCA hearings are usually closed to the public) or take a tour around the building. (There is a third way to get inside: being on trial there. But note that *Let's Go really* does not approve of crimes against international justice.)

*Tram #1 or 10 to Vredespaleis. You can't miss the place. **i** To attend a session of the ICJ, check the website's calendar (www.icj-cij.org) or call ☎030 223 23. Unless it's a very high-profile case, you do not need to make reservations to attend. Bring a passport or driver's license for entry. Reservations must be made for the tours, recommended at least a week in advance. $ Tour €5, under 13 €3. Tours May 1-Sept 30 M-F at 10, 11am, 2, 3, 4pm.*

MAURITSHUIS — MUSEUM

Korte Vijverberg 8 ☎070 30 234 56 www.mauritshuis.nl

The outside of this museum, an elegant 17th-century building next to the Binnenhof and the water of the Hofijver, is so pretty that you may not want to actually go inside. But that would be foolish, as this is one of the best collections of Dutch

Golden Age art in the country (and the world). Concentrated in just two floors, you've got works by **Rubens, Van Ruisdael, Holbein, Hals,** and **Steen.** The most famous pieces in the collection are Rembrandt's *The Anatomy Lesson of Dr. Tulp*, and Vermeer's luminescent ***Girl with a Pearl Earring*** and *View of Delft*. Given that only 36 works by Vermeer exist, this is a pretty good showing.

Tram #10 or 17 to Buitenhof. Walk along the water and make a right at the end; the museum is straight ahead of you. $ €12, under 18 free, with Museumjaarkaart €1.50. ⏰ Open Apr-Aug M-Sa 10am-5pm, Su 11am-5pm; Sept-Mar Tu-Sa 10am-5pm, Su 11am-5pm.

GEMEENTEMUSEUM — ♿ MUSEUM

Stadhouderslaan 41 — ☎070 33 811 11 www.gemeentemuseum.nl

A perfect counterpoint to the Mauritshuis (above), this museum is the home of a wide collection of 19th- and 20th-century art, with a special focus on Dutch and other Northern European artists. A great selection of German Expressionist works gives way to a large body of paintings by **Piet Mondrian,** including his last work, *Victory Boogie Woogie*.

Tram #17 to Gemeentemuseum/Museon. The museum is just across the street. $ €10, under 18 or with Museumjaarkaart free. ⏰ Open Tu-Su 10am-5pm.

BINNENHOF AND RIDDERZAAL — ♿ GOVERNMENT

Binnenhof 8a — ☎070 36 461 44 www.binnenhofbezoek.nl

This complex of palace-like buildings next to the waters of the Hofijver is one of the most central and photogenic sights in The Hague. And it's important, too. This is the home of Dutch democracy, where the upper and lower chambers (the *eerste kamer* and *tweede kamer*) of Parliament live. Also in the complex is the **Ridderzaal,** or Hall of Knights, where Queen Beatrix officially opens Parliament each year on the third Tuesday in September (after traveling to the hall in a gilded carriage). Guided tours, which begin with a video on the history of the Binnenhof, can take you through the Ridderzaal and the **First or Second Chambers of Parliament** (except when they are in session). The tours are pretty lengthy and will tell you all you'd ever want to know about the workings of the Dutch political system. If you don't fancy a lecture, you can still wander through the courtyard of the Binnenhof and peek into the windows of the Ridderzaal.

Tram #1 to Centrum, or #10 or 17 to Buitenhof. It's the giant castle-like building by the water. ℹ Reservations recommended for the guided tours. $ Tour of Ridderzaal €4, Ridderzaal and a chamber of Parliament €6. ⏰ Tours M-Sa 10am-4pm.

COFFEESHOPS AND SMARTSHOPS

The Hague doesn't have much of a coffeeshop scene—the few that are here aren't as bare bones as the ones in Rotterdam, but you won't find anything near the concentration or luxury of the Amsterdam shops.

EUPHORIA — ♿ SMARTSHOP

Schoolstraat 11 — ☎070 35 625 51 www.euphoria.nl

It's kind of surprising that a city with so few coffeeshops has such a good smartshop. Euphoria cuts the crap, stocking the same good selection of smoking gear (bongs, water pipes, etc.) as Amsterdam smartshops but eschewing the kitschy souvenirs those outposts hawk.

From the Grote Kerk, walk 1 block down Riviervismarkt toward Buitenhof and make a right onto Schoolstraat. $ Herbal XTC €8-14; philosophers' stones €17 per dose. ⏰ Open Tu-W noon-7pm, Th-Sa noon-9pm, Su noon-6pm.

THE GAME — ♿ COFFEESHOP

Nieuwstraat 4 — ☎070 34 505 74

As far as coffeeshops in The Hague go, this is one of the better ones. A spacious interior, a cool mural behind the bar, and sparkling lights complete the chilled-out look that is enjoyed by locals and tourists alike.

Walk down Buitenhof toward Riviervismarkt and make a left onto Nieuwstraat. $ Weed and hash €4-11 per g. ⏰ Open M-Th 11am-1am, F-Sa 11am-1:30am, Su 2pm-1am.

FOOD

The Hague does have some budget options, but they are largely the kind of places best for 3am pizza or post-clubbing shawarma. You can find them in the streets surrounding the **Grote Kerk** and along **Spui** (which is conveniently on your way home if you're stumbling back to the Stayokay). A higher quality but slightly more expensive meal can be enjoyed at one of the number of good restaurants around **Molenstraat.** **Chinatown,** the area surrounding Wagenstraat, is chock full of Asian restaurants.

HNM CAFE
CAFE, FUSION ❷

Molenstraat 21a ☎070 36 565 53

HNM is somewhat along the lines of a classic *bruin cafe*, but with brighter chairs, larger windows, and more international food. Try the Thai chicken soup or the pasta Bolognese and enjoy the eclectic mix of indie music playing overhead.

From Binnenhof, walk through Plaats square, make a right onto Noordeinde, and a left onto Molenstraat. $ Entrees €11-14. ⏰ Open M-W noon-midnight, Th-Sa noon-1am, Su noon-6pm.

VERY ITALIAN PIZZA
ITALIAN ❷

Kettingstraat 13-15 ☎070 36 545 41 www.veryitalianpizza.nl

Dozens of different oven-baked pizzas and pastas can satisfy just about any craving for a mixture of carbs, cheese, vegetables, and meat.

Walk down to the end of Buitenhof, away from the water toward Riviervismarkt, and make a left onto Kettingstraat. $ Pizzas and pastas €5-10. Schaals €21-36. ⏰ Open daily 11am-1am.

BAKLUST
VEGETARIAN ❶

Veenkade 19 ☎070 75 322 74 www.baklust.nl

This cheery little cafe feels like a homey kitchen, with colorful decor, cool comic posters on the wall, and nice wooden tables. The food is all vegetarian, with many vegan options. Their tarts and other bakery items are particularly mouth-watering.

Tram #17 to Noordwal. The restaurant is at the beginning of the canal. $ Sandwiches €3.50-6. Entrees €4-10 ⏰ Open Tu-Su 10am-6pm.

HARVEST
CHINESE ❷

Sint Jacobstraat 1 ☎070 39 209 60

At the edge of Chinatown, this simple restaurant offers an excellent selection of dim sum. The pork buns are doughy, the dumplings steamy, and the rice flour rolls slippery.

Tram #2 or 6 to Spui. Walk south on Spui and make a right onto Sint Jacobstraat; Harvest is at the corner with Wagenstraat. $ Dim sum €2.50-4. Entrees €8-13. ⏰ Open daily noon-midnight.

LOS ARGENTINOS
ARGENTINE ❸

Kettingstraat 14 ☎070 34 685 23 www.los-argentinos.nl

This rough wood-paneled, bar-like spot boasts the best steaks in town—just ask the locals. If steak isn't your thing, entrees like grilled salmon should fit the bill, but don't come here expecting a good salad.

Walk down to the end of Buitenhof, away from the water toward Riviervismarkt, and make a left onto Kettingstraat. $ Steaks €10-20. ⏰ Open daily 3pm-midnight.

NIGHTLIFE

Given the city's reputation as a center for business and politics, nightlife in The Hague is perhaps livelier than one would expect. You'll only find a handful of clubs, but some of the larger bars turn into dance spots late on weekend nights. The best places to go for boisterous crowds are the bars around **Grote Markt,** which have large terraces from which people spill out into the square. Near **Oude Molstraat,** a number of excellent bars and *bruin cafes* offer the working men and women of The Hague a place at which to drown their geopolitical sorrows.

BOTERWAAG BAR
Grote Markt 28 ☎070 36 238 62 🖳www.boterwaag.nl
The vaulted ceilings in this large bar make it feel like you're drinking in a cathedral, which seems appropriate given that so many of the excellent Belgian beers they serve were brewed by monks.
🚋 Tram #2 or 6 to Grote Markt. Or from Buitenhof, walk straight down the square with your back to the Hofijver, follow signs for Grote Kerk, and then make a left at the church. $ Beer from €2.20. ⏰ Open M-W 10am-1am, Th-Sa 10am-1:30am, Su 10am-1am.

DE PAAP BAR, CONCERT VENUE
Papestraat 32 ☎070 36 520 02 🖳www.depaap.nl
De Paap is simply the best rock cafe in town, attracting a fairly diverse group of rock, punk, funk, and cover bands. After the live acts end, the music keeps going until late, either with a DJ or whatever the bartenders feel like playing.
🚋 Tram #17 to Gravenstraat. Walk up Hoogstraat and left on Papestraat. $ Beer from €2. ⏰ Open Th 7pm-4am, F 5pm-5am, Sa 7pm-5am.

PAARD VAN TROJE (TROJAN HORSE) CLUB, CONCERT VENUE
Prinsengracht 12 ☎070 36 018 38 🖳www.paard.nl
Probably the largest and most diverse nightlife spot in the city, Paard van Troje hosts an assortment of bands and DJs. Things die down a bit in the summer, but at least that means there is usually no cover. Some nights are more concert-y, some more club-y—generally dancing will get going after 1am.
🚋 Tram #2 or 6 to Grote Markt. $ If there is cover, usually €5-12; free entrance with student ID on Th. Beer from €2.20. ⏰ Hours vary, generally open Th-F 11pm-4am, Sa 11pm-5am.

ESSENTIALS

Practicalities

- **TOURIST OFFICES: VVV.** *(Hofweg 1 ☎070 36 188 60 🖳www.denhaag.nl ⏰ Open M-F 9:30am-6pm, Sa 9:30am-5pm, Su 11am-6pm.)*
- **INTERNET: Bibliotheek Den Haag.** *(Spui 68 ☎070 35 344 55 🖳www.bibliotheekdenhaag.nl 🚋 Tram #2 or 6 to Spui. $ Free Wi-Fi. Internet €2.80 per hr. ⏰ Open June-Aug M noon-8pm, Tu-F 10am-8pm, Sa 10am-5pm; Sept-May M noon-8pm, Tu-F 10am-8pm, Sa 10am-5pm, Su noon-5pm.)*

Emergency!

- **POLICE: Politie Haaglanden** is the regional police department for The Hague. *(Jan Hendrikstraat 85. ☎070 900 88 44 🖳www.politie.nl/haaglanden)*
- **LATE-NIGHT PHARMACIES: Dienstapotheeks** are the 24hr. pharmacies. They rotate depending on the day. To find the nearest one in your neighborhood, check at your closest pharmacy or call ☎070 34 510 00.
- **HOSPITALS/MEDICAL SERVICES: Bronovo Hospital.** *(Bronovolaan 5 ☎070 31 241 41 🖳www.bronovo.nl 🚋 Tram #22, 23, or 28 to Bronovo Ziekenhuis.)*

Getting There

Den Haag Centraal is the main **train** station. Trains from **Amsterdam** *($ €10.10. ⏰ 1hr., 1-6 per hr.)*, **Rotterdam** *($ €4.30. ⏰ 30-45min., 1-6 per hr.)*, and **Utrecht** *($ €9.70. ⏰ 35-40min., 1-6 per hr.)*

Getting Around

HTM *(🖳www.htm.net)* is the public transport network for The Hague, Scheveningen, and Delft. If you're staying in a hotel outside the center, want to visit one of the more distant museums, or intend to check out the beach at Scheveningen, the tram network is your best bet. HTM uses the **strippenkaart** system that has gone out of style in Amsterdam; you can purchase the tickets *(€7.60 for 15 strips)* at the train station and then present the tickets to be stamped by the driver or stamp them yourself on the tram. Most rides within The Hague will cost two to three strips. Or, take a **bike,** which you can rent from Rijwielshop Den Haag *(Koningin Julianaplein 10 ☎070 38 532 35 💻www.rijwielshopdenhaag.nl)* or Rent a Bike The Hague *(Noordeinde 59 ☎070 32 657 90 💻www.rentabikethehague.nl).*

rotterdam ☎010

If you've spent a lot of time in other parts of the Netherlands, you may have forgotten what a skyscraper looks like. **Rotterdam** is here to remind you. It's strategic importance as a port city drew Nazi attention during WWII, and in May 1940, a massive bombing campaign razed virtually the entire city center. The reconstruction effort that followed in the postwar period focused on building a modern, revitalized city, and those efforts have left an indelible mark, creating a legacy of fascinating architecture and cutting-edge art that continues to this day. Rebuilding also imbued Rotterdammers with a fierce sense of city pride, most evident when you hear them talk about Amsterdam, their bitter rival in soccer and just about everything else. There's certainly a lot for the port city's residents to be proud of: Rotterdam, in addition to being a center for architecture and culture, boasts terrific festivals, live music, and some of the hippest nightlife you can imagine—all with an extremely laid-back attitude.

ORIENTATION

Rotterdam is the second-largest city in the Netherlands, but pretty much all points of interest lie within a fairly small perimeter. The two main arteries are **Coolsingel/Schiedamsedijk,** which passes the main historical museums as it runs south from **Stadhuis** to the **Erasmus Bridge,** and **Westblaak/Blaak,** which stretches from the Erasmus Medical Center west toward the Cube Houses, passing Museumpark and the principal art museums along the way. These two roads intersect at **Beurs,** a huge commercial center filled with lots of shopping and fast food.

ACCOMMODATIONS

The accommodations in Rotterdam pretty accurately reflect its split between business-focused industrial city and youthful cultural hotspot. Some really excellent hostels can be found here in addition to a few reasonably priced hotels.

ROOM HOSTEL — HOSTEL [1]

Van Vollenhovenstraat 62 ☎010 28 272 77 💻www.roomrotterdam.nl

Ask anyone who has stayed here about the hostel, and the first thing they'll mention is the fun-loving and extremely kind international staff. Everyone who works here loves the hostel and loves Rotterdam and they'll help you to do the same as you chat over a beer in the popular hostel bar. The rooms aren't half bad, either.

Tram #4 or 7 to Westplein. Walk back the way the tram came and then 1 block up Van Vollenhovenstraat. $ 4- to 10-bed dorms €18.50-25.50; doubles €50-55.

STAYOKAY ROTTERDAM (HI) — HOSTEL [1]

Overblaak 85-87 ☎010 43 657 63 💻www.stayokay.com

This hostel embraces the ultramodern aesthetic of its architectually unique setting: the lobby and bar are glossy and bright orange, and the rooms are done up in space-age white and gray. True to the standard of Stayokays everywhere, the rooms are impeccably clean.

[M] Blaak. Exit the station and look up; you'll see the houses. It's easiest to find the hostel if you go under the houses toward the water and follow the signs up the ramp. $ Dorms €20.50-31.

HOTEL BAZAR — HOTEL [3]

Witte de Withstraat 16 ☎010 20 651 51 💻www.bazarrotterdam.nl

Enjoy exquisitely decorated rooms based on the Middle East, Africa, and South

America: the colors of each theme are vibrant and the furnishings lovely. And you're right in the heart of the nighttime action on Witte de Withstraat.

➜ Tram #7 or 20 to Museumpark. Walk away from the water down Witte de Withstraat. $ Singles €70; doubles €80-130.

SKYLINE HOTEL
💳🚭📶 HOTEL [2]

's-Gravendijkwal 70-72 ☎010 43 640 40

Skyline is surprisingly nice for the price, with a location that's conveniently near both Centraal Station and the bustling area by Witte de Withstraat and the Binnenwegs. A brightly tiled bar is downstairs.

➜ Tram #4 to 's-Gravendijkwal then walk north a little. $ Singles €49; doubles €75; triples €95.

SIGHTS 👁

Rotterdam's architecture is one of its most famous attractions, and the post-war explosion of modernity has given the city not just an impressive skyline but also a vibrant contemporary art scene.

👍 MUSEUM BOIJMANS VAN BEUNINGEN
💳♿ MUSEUM

Museumpark 18-20 ☎010 44 194 00 💻www.boijmans.nl

Absolutely one of the foremost art museums in the Netherlands, Boijmans van Beuningen boasts a collection that spans hundreds of works and multiple centuries but nothing in the exhibits feels superfluous. The permanent collection begins with medieval art from Italy and Northern Europe, then has a few rooms with works by Dutch masters like Bruegel, **Bosch,** and Rembrandt. Further along, there are rooms of Impressionism, a terrific group of Surrealist works (Dali and Magritte in particular), and a remarkable set of Expressionist pieces, notably those by **Kandinsky.**

➜ Ⓜ Eendrachtsplein. Walk south on Westersingel and make the 1st right; you'll see the flags of the museum. $ €10, students €5, under 18 or with Museumjaarkaart free. Free entrance on W. ⏰ Open Tu-Su 11am-5pm.

👍 NETHERLANDS ARCHITECTURE INSTITUTE (NAI)
💳♿ MUSEUM

Museumpark 25 ☎010 44 013 58 💻en.nai.nl

It's appropriate that a city with architecture as interesting as Rotterdam's would be home to one of the best institutes for architecture in the world. The glass and steel building, designed by **Jo Coenen,** contains an exhibition space, library, and a huge architecture archive. The museum is scheduled to re-open from construction in January 2011. When it does, it will feature a segment dedicated to the Institute's conception of "architecture as consequence"—the idea that architecture can be promoted as a solution to many of the world's social and environmental problems.

➜ Ⓜ Eendrachtsplein. Walk south on Westersingel and make the 1st right; it's just past the Boijmans Museum. $ €8, students and seniors €5, under 18 or with Museumjaarkaart free. ⏰ Museum and Sonneveld House open Tu-Sa 10am-5pm, Su 11am-5pm. Library open July-Aug M-F 10am-5pm; Sept-June M-Sa 10am-5pm.

KUBUSWONIG (CUBE HOUSES)
🚭♿ ARCHITECTURE

Overblaak 70 ☎010 41 422 85 💻www.kubuswonig.nl

These exceptionally weird additions to Rotterdam's architecture were designed by **Piet Blom** in 1982 as a new sort of housing complex. Bright yellow cubes, rotated and set atop concrete columns, form a "forest," with commercial establishments on the lower promenade and residences inside the cube.

➜ Ⓜ Blaak or tram #21 to Station Blaak. $ €2.50. ⏰ Show Cube open daily 11am-5pm.

ST. LAURENSKERK
♿ CHURCH

Grote Kerkplein 15 ☎010 41 314 94 💻www.laurenskerkrotterdam.nl

This magnificent 17th-century building seems out of place in modern Rotterdam.

It was virtually destroyed in the 1940 bombing, but its remains became a symbol of the wartime city. Since those tragic years, the building has been restored to its original design, a huge, vaulted neo-Gothic structure with amazing space and light.

➡ ⓂBlaak or tram #21 to Station Blaak. Facing the Cube Houses, walk to your left; you'll see the church tower a few blocks up ahead. ⏰ Open Tu-Sa 10am-4pm.

MUSEUM HET SCHIELANDSHUIS (HISTORICAL MUSEUM) 💳♿ MUSEUM
Korte Hoogstraat 31 ☎010 21 767 67 💻www.hmr.rotterdam.nl

This excellent museum on the history of Rotterdam lies in one of the few buildings of the city center that survived the bombing. The permanent collection on the first floor consists of a well-designed exhibit that takes you on a tour of the growth, destruction, and rebuilding of the city.

➡ ⓂBeurs or tram #8, 23, or 25 to Churchillplein. Walk down Blaak and make a left onto Korte Hoogstraat. $ €5, under 17 or with Museumjaarkaart free. ⏰ Open Tu-Su 11am-5pm.

COFFEESHOPS AND SMARTSHOPS

Of the few coffeeshops in Rotterdam, virtually all are merely takeout spots—none of the comfy, pillow-strewn interiors familiar to smokers in Amsterdam here. On the plus side, the weed and hash do tend to be slightly cheaper. Head to **Nieuwe Binnenweg** to find numerous shops.

REEFER 🚫♿📶 COFFEESHOP
Oppert 1 ☎010 41 226 13

This is one of the only coffeeshops in Rotterdam where people—virtually all locals—actually stick around after buying their weed. The large smoking room (tobacco allowed) has couches, pool, foosball, and free computers.

➡ Tram #7 or 8 to Meent. Walk down Meent and make a right onto Oppert. ℹ Extremely strict about ID. $ Weed and hash €4-12 per g; joints €2.50-3.50. ⏰ Open daily 10am-midnight.

FOOD

Eating is a pleasure in Rotterdam, whose international character brings in a plethora of affordable ethnic options. For cheap Chinese and shawarma, check out **Witte de Withstraat,** where the stores are conveniently open as late as most of the bars. Slightly nicer sit-down ethnic places are to the north on **Nieuwe Binnenweg.** The area north of the Cube Houses, behind the Laurenskerk, is full of interesting cafes.

👍 **BAGEL BAKERY** 💳♿🍸⛅ BAGELS, MEDITERRANEAN ❶
Schilderstraat 57a ☎010 41 121 560

Both businesspeople and tourists pop into this fresh and airy restaurant with plenty of outdoor seating to enjoy bagels and a variety of toppings (all kinds of cream cheese, mozzarella and tomato, tuna with olive tapenade, etc.).

➡ ⓂBeurs or tram #8, 23, or 25 to Churchillplein. Walk south on Schiedamsedijk and make a right onto Schilderstraat. $ Bagels €2-8. Entrees from €11. ⏰ Open Tu-W 9am-5:30pm, Th-F 9am-10pm, Sa 10am-10pm, Su 10am-5:30pm.

👍 **FAFI** 🚫♿ CHINESE, INDONESIAN ❶
Witte de Withstraat 93b ☎010 41 400 02

Just what every bar-filled street needs: a Chinese greasy spoon where you can satisfy your drunkies with some pork fried rice. This one ups the ante by adding even more kinds of noodles and curries to its extensive menu.

➡ Tram #7 or 20 to Museumpark. It's right on the corner with Eendrachtsweg. $ Sandwiches €2-3. Entrees €7-12. ⏰ Open M-Th 11:30am-2am, F-Sa 11:30am-4am, Su 2pm-2am.

BAZAR 💳♿🍸⛅ MIDDLE EASTERN ❷
Witte de Withstraat 16 ☎010 20 651 51 💻www.bazarrotterdam.com

Festive Arabian fairytale decor (including some very cool glass and beaded lanterns) makes Bazar's dining room feel quite magical. The food is a mix of Middle

Eastern and Mediterranean fare, with an assortment of dishes that includes falafel salads, Turkish pizzas, fancy kebabs, and baked vegetarian plates.

➔ Tram #7 or 20 to Museumpark. Walk away from the water down Witte de Withstraat. Ⓢ Sandwiches and lunch entrees €4-10. Dinner entrees €12-16. ⏰ Open M-Th 8am-1am, F 8am-2am, Sa 9am-2am, Su 9am-midnight.

LEBKOV AND SONS — ♿ CAFE, SANDWICHES [1]

Stationsplein 50 — ☎010 24 006 17 💻www.lebkov.com

You can find this purveyor of top-notch sandwiches in a random corner next to the train station. The selection of sandwiches on wonderfully plump bread is mouth-watering, though the store also does soups, salads, and desserts.

➔ Facing Rotterdam Centraal, it's on the left of the main square. Ⓢ Sandwiches €2.25-3.50. ⏰ Open M-F 6am-7pm, Sa 9am-5pm.

NIGHTLIFE

Nightlife in Rotterdam is painted as the only Dutch scene to rival Amsterdam's. The **Witte de Withstraat** and **Oude Binnenweg** area offers a fantastic bar scene, with live music or sweet stuff on the stereo at practically any watering hole you hit up. Student nightlife is centered on **Oudehaven,** in the west of the city. For clubs, head to the area near **Kruiskade and Stadhuis** just south of the station. Rotterdam's **GLBT** nightlife isn't as extensive as Amsterdam's, but there are a few good bars and clubs surrounding **Van Oldenbarneveltstraat.**

DE WITTE AAP — ♿ 🍸 BAR

Witte de Withstraat 78 — ☎010 41 495 65 💻www.dewitteaap.nl

De Witte Aap is filled with a sizeable crowd of urban-artsy locals lingering on the street patio or along the curvaceous bar pretty much every night of the week. Besides the friendly bartenders and the overall air of hip-dom, the main attraction here is the well-chosen soundtrack of mashed-up hip hop.

➔ Tram #7 or 20 to Museumpark. Walk straight down Witte de Withstraat. Ⓢ Beer from €2. ⏰ Open M-Th 4pm-4am, F-Sa 4pm-5am, Su 4pm-4am.

DIZZY — 🍸 BAR, JAZZ CLUB

's-Gravendijkwal 127 — ☎010 47 730 14 💻www.dizzy.nl

An established institution in a city renowned for the largest jazz festival in Europe, Dizzy has quite the reputation. With jam sessions on Monday, live jazz Tuesday and Thursday, funk DJs on Friday, and Brazilian jazz on Saturday, there's no shortage of things to hear.

➔ Tram #4 to 's-Gravendijkwal. Ⓢ Beer from €2.20. ⏰ Open M-F noon-2am, Sa 4pm-2am, Su 4-11pm. Music usually starts at 10pm.

DE SCHOUW — ♿ 🍸 BAR

Witte de Withstraat 80 — ☎010 41 242 53

A stubbornly simple and local bar plastered with old concert posters and photographs, De Schouw is full of regulars enjoying a drink and possibly a game of chess. Attached to the exterior is **de Aanschouw Rotterdam,** quite possibly the smallest gallery in the world—it's just a glass box with a single piece of art inside.

➔ Tram #7 or 20 to Museumpark. Walk away from the water down Witte de Withstraat. Ⓢ Beer from €2. ⏰ Open M-Th 11am-1am, F-Sa 11am-3am, Su 11am-1am.

CATWALK — 🍸 CLUB

Weena Zuid 33 — 💻www.catwalkclub.eu

This intimate, welcoming club (wait that sounds really sexual in a way we don't intend) sits in a former pedestrian tunnel near Rotterdam Centraal and is cheaper and less about being seen than some of the area's other clubs. Dancing alongside you, you'll find a stylishly laid-back group of diverse students and locals.

➔ Tram #4, 7, 8, 21, 23, or 25 to Weena. Walk away from the roundabout, left onto Lijnbaan, and

right onto Weena Zuid. $ Cover €5. Beer from €2.20. ⏰ Usually open Th-Sa 11pm-whenever the people go home (they have a 24hr. license). Check website for specific events.

GAY PALACE CLUB

Schiedamsingel 139 ☎010 41 414 86 💻www.gay-palace.nl

No false advertising here—this is, in fact, a palace fit for a queen. The largest gay club in Rotterdam attracts a pretty mixed crowd of partygoers with one thing in common: their fondness for the dance floor. You'll find mostly men but quite a few women as well, all shaking it under the big paper lanterns and neon lights.
Tram #7 or 20 to Museumpark. Walk down Witte de Withstraat, make a right when you get to Bazar, and keep right on that street as it loops around $ F cover varies by event; Sa cover €5 before midnight, €10 after. ⏰ Open some F; check website or flyers. Otherwise open Sa 11pm-5am.

FESTIVALS

NORTH SEA JAZZ FESTIVAL JAZZ

Ahoy Complex, Zuiderpark ☎0900 1010 2020 (€0.45 per min.) 💻www.northseajazz.com

One of the largest jazz festivals in the world, North Sea draws over 70,000 people to three days of top-notch music. Past performers have included Stevie Wonder, Norah Jones, B. B. King, Joss Stone, **Herbie Hancock,** and many more.
[M]Zuidplein. Walk down Metroplein to Zuiderpark. $ Day tickets €88; 3-day pass €204. Some concerts require an extra €15 ticket. ⏰ Usually held the 2nd weekend of July.

ESSENTIALS

Practicalities

- **TOURIST OFFICES: Use-It** is a great one-stop shop for everything you could need in Rotterdam, including free Wi-Fi. *(Schaatsbaan 41-45 ☎010 24 092 58 💻www.use-it.nl ⏰ Open May 15-June Tu-Su 9am-6pm; July-Aug M noon-5pm, Tu-Su 9am-6pm; Sept 1-Sept 15 Tu-Su 9am-6pm; Sept 16-May 14 Tu-Sa 9am-5pm.)* **VVV.** *(Stationsplein 45 ☎0900 403 4065 💻www.vvvrotterdam.nl ⏰ Open M-Sa 9am-5:30pm, Su 10am-5pm.)*

Emergency!

- **POLICE: Politie Rotterdam-Rijnmond** is the local police department. *(Doelwater 5 ☎0900 88 44 💻www.politie-rotterdam-rijnmond.nl Metro or tram #21 or 23 to [M]Stadhuis. It's 1 block south of Hofplein, on the right. ⏰ Open 24hr.)*
- **LATE-NIGHT PHARMACIES: Night Pharmacy**. *(Schiedamsedijk 80 ☎010 43 399 66 ⏰ Open daily 5:30pm-8am.)*
- **HOSPITALS/MEDICAL SERVICES: Erasmus MC.** *('s-Gravendijkwal 320 ☎010 70 401 45 💻www.erasmusmc.nl Tram #8 to Erasmus MC. ⏰ Open 24hr.)*

Getting There

Trains arrive into **Rotterdam Centraal** from **Amsterdam** *($ €13.30. ⏰ 1hr.-1hr. 15min., 1-7 per hr.),* **Brussels** *($ €25.50. ⏰ 1hr. 10min., 1 per hr., 8am-9pm.),* **The Hague** *($ €4.30. ⏰ 30 min., 1-5 per hr.),* and **Utrecht** *($ €9.10. ⏰ 40 min., 1-4 per hr.).* You can also theoretically fly into the small Rotterdam international **airport,** serviced by **budget airlines** like Transavia and City Jet, but it's easy to get there from Amsterdam's Schiphol Airport *($ €10.70. ⏰ 45 min., 1-5 per hr.),* where you'll have many more flight options.

Getting Around

RET is the transport network for Rotterdam. There are numerous **Metro** lines in the city; the D line runs north-south, with Rotterdam Centraal as its northern terminus, and the A, B, and C lines run east-west, intersecting D at Beurs. However, since there are only a few Metro stops within the city center, it is much more convenient for tourists to use the **tram** network, which costs the same as the Metro *(trips €0.78 to* start and then €0.15 per additional km. 1- to 3-day ticket €6-12. Single-use tickets, valid for 1hr. on tram and bus or 2hr. on tram, bus, and Metro €2.50-3.50). As with most Dutch cities, **biking** is the most popular and convenient method of transportation. You can rent bikes at most hostels and hotels or at **Use-It** for €6 per day *(€50 deposit required)*.

utrecht ☎030

First settled under the Romans around the turn of the millennium, Utrecht was, for a long time, the Netherlands's cultural and religious capital. Given its ideal placement in the center of the country, the city is a good staging ground for all kinds of festivals and events and remains at the heart of Dutch life even though it is no longer the country's capital. Remnants of the city's religious past live on in the beautiful medieval churches and the stunning Domkerk. Not being the modern-day capital, however, means that Utrecht is small, easily accessible, and pedestrian friendly. Its rows of old-fashioned houses, church spires, and long walkways lining canals set below street level make it quite the *belle ville*. But we wouldn't have you thinking it's all sweetness and quiet here: with one of the Netherlands's largest universities and a student population pushing 60,000, Utrecht's got great nightlife and a buzzing, youthful feel. This makes it the ideal stop for those who want to experience the Netherlands at its most picturesque without totally leaving the urban jungle behind.

ORIENTATION

Arriving at Utrecht Centraal, you'll enter the city through the gargantuan Hoog Catharijne shopping center. Unless you're tempted to do some shopping, follow the signs toward **Vredenburg** and eventually emerge at a square about a 5min. walk from the city center, or **Museumkwartier.** This part of town, a long strip bordered on the west by **Oudegracht** and on the east by **Nieuwegracht canal,** contains the most points of interest in the city. **Domtoren,** Utrecht's most easily recognizable landmark, is located smackdab in the middle of the two canals (well, in the middle of where Nieuwegracht would be if extended just a little bit farther). The primary east-west street is the many-named **Vredenburg/Lange Viestraat/Potterstraat,** which then becomes **Nobelstraat** after Janskerkhof. While Utrecht is an affluent and peaceful city, the area around Utrecht Centraal is best avoided at night.

ACCOMMODATIONS

Utrecht is a pretty swanky town, and this is immediately apparent when you're trying to find a hotel in the center that's under €200 a night. Fortunately, **Strowis** has great dorms and private rooms, and there are a few really excellent hotels on the city's outskirts.

STROWIS ★⦿◉ HOSTEL ❶
Boothstraat 8 ☏030 23 802 80 ■www.strowis.nl

Run by the same former squatters' organization as the **ACU,** Strowis is a beautiful hostel located right in the city center. It's got high ceilings, brightly-painted walls, and spotless dorms and bathrooms.

⎯ *15min. east of the train station.* ⓒ *4- to 14-bed dorms €15.50-18.50; singles and doubles €60.* ⓒ *Curfew M-Th 2am, F-Sa 3am.*

DE ADMIRAAL ★⦿◉ HOTEL ❸
Admiraal van Gentstraat 11 ☏030 27 585 00 ■www.hoteldeadmiraal.nl

This hotel is about a 20min. walk from the city center, but don't let the distance put you off. It's an incredibly beautiful and well-designed place; ask for a room with a garden-view terrace.

⎯ *Bus #8 to Jan van Galenstraat.* ⓒ *Singles €70, with bath €90; doubles €110.*

HELLO B AND B HOTEL ❷

Herenweg 32 ☎030 22 692 124

It's hard to tell that there is a hotel in the middle of the long line of houses here, and this non-commercial feeling continues inside, where you'll feel like a guest in a welcoming home. The rooms are incredibly cozy, with hearty wood furniture and floral patterns on walls and bedspreads.

‡ 15min. walk along Oudegracht to the north of the city center. $ Singles €45; doubles €65.

SIGHTS

Utrecht is home to a lot of churches and a lot of offbeat museums on topics ranging from Aboriginal art *(Oudegracht 176 ☎023 801 00 🖥www.aamu.nl)* to street organs *(Steenweg 6 ☎023 127 89 🖥www.museumspeelklok.nl).*

DOMKERK CHURCH

Domplein ☎030 23 600 10 (tour reservations) 🖥www.domkerk.nl, www.domtoren.nl

At 369 ft., this intricate Gothic spire belonging to Utrecht's cathedral is the tallest church tower in all of the Netherlands. Besides its unique height, it is distinguished by being the only Dutch church built in the Northern French Gothic style, which can be seen in its characteristic pointed arches and large windows. In the church you can observe its altarpieces bearing the marks of the 16th century's iconoclastic violence, its huge 19th-century organ, and the tomb of sea hero Admiral van Gendt. Make sure to stop by the peaceful cloister next door.

‡ In the city center, it's the tallest thing around—you'll be able to find it. $ Church free. Tour €8, students and seniors €6.50, under 13 €4.50. ⏰ Church open May-Sept M-F 10am-5pm, Sa 10am-3:30pm, Su 2-4pm; Oct-Apr M-F 11am-4pm, Sa 11am-3:30pm, Su 2-4pm.

CENTRAAL MUSEUM MUSEUM

Nicolaaskerkhof ☎030 23 623 62 🖥www.centraalmuseum.nl

This is the Netherlands's oldest municipal museum (dating from 1838). The collection's eclectic mix tells the story of Utrecht's artistic and cultural development. Particularly notable is the selection of 17th-century Caravaggist painters, like **Hendrik ter Brugghen** and **Gerrit van Honthorst.** A modern art wing with works by Surrealist artists and Magic Realists such as **Pyke Koch** also merits mention.

‡ From Domkerk, head south on Korte Nieuwstraat, which becomes Lange Nieuwstraat. Turn right onto Agnietenstraat; it becomes Nicolaaskerkhof. $ €9, students and ages 13-17 €4, seniors €7.50, under 12 and with Museumjaarkaart free. ⏰ Open Tu-Su 11am-5pm.

CATHARIJNECONVENT MUSEUM

Lange Nieuwstraat 38 ☎030 23 138 35 🖥www.catharijneconvent.nl

In honor of Utrecht's history as the Christian center of the Netherlands, this convent has been converted into a museum dedicated to the treasures of Dutch Christianity. Here you'll find beautiful religious paintings by artists like Rembrandt and **Frans Hals,** while in the treasury, ornate chalices and illuminated manuscripts explain the development of Christianity in the Netherlands.

‡ From Domkerk, walk down Korte Nieuwstraat, which then becomes Lange Nieuwstraat. $ €11.50, under 18 €7.25, with Museumjaarkaart €2.50. ⏰ Open Tu-F 10am-5pm, Sa-Su 11am-5pm.

COFFEESHOPS AND SMARTSHOPS

Utrecht is home to a few coffeeshops, though not as many as one might expect in a place this packed with students.

COFFEESHOP ANDERSON COFFEESHOP

Vismarkt 23 ☎030 23 286 65

Coffeeshop Anderson is more touristy than many Utrecht shops, but that's just because of its prime location and its two large and well-decorated smoking rooms, one of which has a window overlooking the canal. Many patrons linger over juice and joints for hours while playing games of backgammon or chess.

➤ *From Domkerk, walk to Oudegracht and make a right.* $ *€10 gets you 1-1.6g weed or hash; joints €3.50-5.* ⏰ *Open M-W 10am-11pm, Th-Sa 10am-midnight, Su noon-11pm.*

BORDEAUX ROOD ⊗♿ COFFEESHOP

Voorstraat 81 ☎030 23 696 86

The name makes Bordeaux Rood sound like an establishment in Amsterdam's Red Light District, but other than some red velvet curtains, there's little resemblance to a bordello here. Small but quality selection of weed.

➤ *From Domkerk, walk behind the church to get to Oudekerkhof and continue onto Drift; make a left onto Voorstraat.* $ *Weed and hash €4-12 per g.* ⏰ *Open M-W 10am-10pm, Th-Sa 10am-11pm, Su noon-10pm.*

FOOD

Eating in Utrecht is a delight for the stomach but certainly not for the bank account. **Museumkwartier** tempts with one elegant bistro after another. None are exorbitantly expensive (€25-30 for a meal, perhaps), but they're not exactly budget-traveler friendly.

BIGOLI ⊗♿🍸 ITALIAN, DELI [1]

Schoutenstraat 7-12 ☎030 23 688 48 🖥www.bigoli.nl

This Italian deli and sandwich shop sets out a mouthwatering display case full of meats, cheeses, and spreads. You can pick up a sandwich to go or stock up on deli items, pastas, oils, and wine.

➤ *Just off Neude square, in the direction of Domkerk.* $ *Sandwiches €3-4.* ⏰ *Open M 11am-6pm, Tu-W 10am-6pm, Th 10am-9pm, F 10am-6pm, Sa 10am-5pm.*

STAMPOT TO GO ⊗♿ DUTCH [1]

Nobelstraat 143 ☎030 22 323 62 🖥www.stampottogo.nl

Disappointed by the dearth of fulfilling Dutch comfort food in a sea of shawarma and pizza joints, the owner of this sleek green and white shop took matters into her own hands and opened a place where you can get classic Dutch food to go.

➤ *From Domkerk, walk down Korte Jansstraat to the Janskerk and make a right onto Nobelstraat.* $ *Stampot €5-6.* ⏰ *Open M-W 4-8:30pm, Th 4-9pm, F 4-8:30pm. Closed most of July.*

RESTAURANT SWEETIE ♿🍸 CHINESE, SURINAMESE [2]

Predikherenstraat 21 ☎030 23 227 24 🖥www.restaurant-sweetie.nl

One of Utrecht's most popular ethnic restaurants, Sweetie has an impressive menu of dishes that are a mix of Chinese and Surinamese cuisine (leaning more toward the latter)—think lots of rice and noodles, satays, and rotis.

➤ *From Domkerk, walk down Schoutenstraat toward Neude, cross the square, and head down Predikherenstraat.* $ *Entrees €9-17. 3-course menu €17.50.* ⏰ *Open Tu-Su 4-10pm.*

ZIZO ⊗♿ CAFE, SANDWICHES [1]

Oudegracht 281-283 ☎030 23 004 63 🖥www.zizo-online.net

This lunch cafe is part of a complex staffed almost entirely by mentally-handicapped men and women and that includes a colorful gift store and a copy service. The menu consists of large sandwiches made fresh to order, salads, soups, and homemade desserts.

➤ *On Oudegracht, near the Catharijneconvent.* $ *Sandwiches, soups, and tarts €2.75-4.75. Salads €9.90.* ⏰ *Open Tu-F 10am-5pm, Sa 10am-4:30pm.*

NIGHTLIFE

For a picturesque medieval town, Utrecht sure does have some bumping nightlife, thanks in large part to the thousands of students that call it home. Thursday is a big night for clubbing, as many establishments grant free entrance with a student ID. Check out the streets of the **Museumkwartier** for bar-cafes and the **Oudegracht** for beautiful terraces along the canal. **Janskerkhof** has something of a monopoly on student bars, with a number of them clustered in a corner just down the road from the student club, **Woolloo Moolo** *(Janskerkhof 14)*, that's run by a local fraternity.

TIVOLI
CLUB, CONCERT VENUE

Oudegracht 245 ☎0900 235 84 86 🖥www.tivoli.nl

Utrecht's premier spot for good music and a good night, Tivoli hosts all kinds of bands, mainly indie rock and some blues, reggae, and hip-hop acts. Three nights a week, local and international DJs spin house, electro, hip hop, and pop to keep the crowd moving. With a capacity of 1000, it can get quite crowded—it's mainly packed with students, especially on Thursdays.

From Domkerk, walk down to Oudegracht and make a left. $ Cover €4-10; students with ID free Th. Beer from €2.30. ⏰ Open Th-Sa 11pm-5am; other times depend on concerts.

KAFE BELGIË
BAR

Oudegracht 196 ☎030 23 126 66

It's a safe bet that any bar referencing Belgium in its name will have a good beer selection. True to form, this bar delivers—within its simple stucco interior you'll find 20 beers on tap and over 200 bottled varieties. Enjoy your pint amid a faithful crowd of locals young and old.

From Domkerk, walk down to Oudegracht and make a left. It's on the near bank of the canal, just past the Aboriginal Art Museum. $ Beer from €2. ⏰ Open daily noon-1am.

'T OUDE POTHUYS
BAR, JAZZ CLUB

Oudegracht 279 ☎030 23 189 70 🖥www.pothuys.nl

A sunken, candlelit bar with live jazz, blues, or funk every night, 't Oude Pothuys is somewhat labyrinthine. It's got a stage-filled bar area, a restaurant, and a canalside terrace from which people have been known to take a drunken dive.

From Domkerk, walk down to Oudegracht and make a left. The bar is the one on the far side of the canal, at the corner with Korte Smeestraat. $ Beer from €2.10. ⏰ Open M-W 3pm-2am, Th-Sa 3pm-3am, Su 3pm-2am. Live music 11pm.

ESSENTIALS

Practicalities

- **TOURIST OFFICES: VVV.** *(Domplein 9 ☎0900 128 87 32 🖥www.utrechtyourway.nl Across from Domkerk. ⏰ Open M noon-6pm, Tu-W 10am-6pm, Th 10am-8pm, F 10am-6pm, Sa 9:30am-5pm, Su noon-5pm.)*
- **INTERNET: Openbare Bibliotheek Utrecht.** *(Oudegracht 167 ☎030 28 618 00 🖥www.bibliotheek-utrecht.nl $ Free Wi-Fi. Internet €3 per hr. ⏰ Open M 1-9pm, Tu-W 11am-6pm, Th 11am-9pm, F 11am-6pm, Sa 10am-5pm.)*

Emergency!

- **POLICE: Politie Utrecht.** *(Kroonstraat 25 ☎030 900 8844 🖥www.politie.nl/utrecht ⏰ Open 24hr.)*
- **HOSPITALS/MEDICAL SERVICES: Universitair Medisch Centrum Utrecht.** *(Heidelberglaan 100 ☎088 75 555 55 🖥www.umcutrecht.nl Take any of the numerous buses that run to Academisch Ziekenhuis. The stop is right at the hospital.)*

Getting There

Trains roll into **Utrecht Centraal,** an easy walk from the city center, from **Amsterdam** *($ €6.70. ⏰ 30min., 1-4 per hr.)*, **Rotterdam** *($ €9.10. ⏰ 40min., 1-4 per hr.)*, and **The Hague.** *($ €9.70. ⏰ 35-40min., 1-6 per hr.)*

essentials

PLANNING YOUR TRIP

Time Differences

The Netherlands are 1hr. ahead of Greenwich Mean Time (GMT) and observe Daylight Saving Time. This means that they are 6hr. ahead of New York City, 9hr. ahead of Los Angeles, and 1hr. ahead of the British Isles. In Northern Hemisphere summer they are 8hr. behind Sydney and 10hr. behind New Zealand, while in Northern Hemisphere winter they are 10hr. behind Sydney and 12hr. behind New Zealand. Don't get confused and call your parents when it's actually 4am their time! Note that, like the rest of the EU, the Dutch change to Daylight Savings Time on different dates from some non-European countries, so sometimes the difference will be one hour different from what is stated here.

MONEY

Tipping

In the Netherlands, service charges are included in the bill at restaurants. Waiters do not depend on tips for their livelihood, so there is no need to feel guilty about not leaving a tip. Still, leaving 5-10% extra will certainly be appreciated. Higher than that is just showing off. Tips in bars are very unusual. Cab drivers are normally tipped about 10%.

Taxes

The quoted price of goods in the Netherlands includes **value added tax (BTW).** This tax on goods is generally levied at 19%, although some goods are subject to lower rates.

SAFETY AND HEALTH

General Advice

In any type of crisis, the most important thing to do is **stay calm.** Your country's embassy abroad is usually your best resource in an emergency; registering with that embassy upon arrival in the country is a good idea.

Drugs and Alcohol

The Netherlands has a fairly liberal attitude regarding alcohol, with legal drinking ages of 16 and booze widely available. Public drunkenness, however, is frowned upon and is a sure way to mark yourself as a tourist.

When it comes to drugs other than alcohol, as is so often the case, things get a little more interesting. Hard drugs are completely illegal in the Netherlands, and possession or consumption of substances like heroin and cocaine will be harshly punished if caught. In the Netherlands, soft drugs like marijuana and mushrooms are tolerated, and you are very unlikely to face prosecution for using them. Consumption is confined to certain legalized zones, namely coffeeshops (for marijuana) and smartshops (for herbal drugs). Both are heavily regulated but very popular: the number of smartshops in particular has exploded in recent years. When visiting a coffeeshop or smartshop for the first time, it may be a

the netherlands

good idea to take a sober friend with you. Even experienced drug users may be surprised at the hotbox effect created in shops where the fumes of several pot-smokers accumulate. Having a friend to guide you home could turn out to be helpful if not absolutely essential.

Prostitution

The "world's oldest profession" has flourished in the Netherlands, particularly in the liberal capital of the world, Amsterdam. Prostitution in Amsterdam has always centered on what is today called the Red Light District, though it is practiced elsewhere in the city as well.

Legal prostitution in Amsterdam comes in two main forms. Window prostitution, which involves scantily clad women tempting passersby from small chambers fronted by a plate-glass window, is by far the most visible. Sex workers of this kind are self-employed and rent the windows themselves. Accordingly, each sets her own price. This form of commercial sex gave the Red Light District its name, as lamps both outside and inside the windows emit a red glow that, at night, bathes the whole area. Whether shopping or "just looking," be sure to show the women basic respect. Looking is fine and even expected, but leering and catcalling are absolutely uncalled for. Keep in mind that prostitution is an entirely legal enterprise, and windows are places of business. Most of the prostitutes whom you see belong to a union called "The Red Thread" and are tested for HIV and STIs, although testing is on a voluntary basis. Do not take photos unless you want to explain yourself to the angriest—and largest—man you'll ever see.

If you're interested in having sex with a window prostitute, go up to the door and wait for someone inside to let you in. Show up clean and sober; prostitutes always reserve the right to refuse their services. Anything goes as long as you clearly and straightforwardly agree to it beforehand. Specifically state what you want to get for the money you're paying—that means which sex acts, in what positions, and, especially, how much time you have in which to do it. Window prostitutes can set their standards; by no means are they required to do anything you want without consenting to it in advance. Negotiation occurs and money changes hands before any sexual acts take place. Always practice safe sex; a prostitute should not and will not touch an un-condomed penis. Don't ask for a refund if you are left unsatisfied: all sales are final. There is no excuse for making trouble; if anyone becomes violent or threatening with a window prostitute, she has access to an emergency button that sets off a loud alarm. Not only does it make an ear-splitting noise but it also summons the police, who invariably side with prostitutes in disputes. If you feel you have a legitimate complaint or have any questions about commercial sex, head to the extremely helpful Prostitution Information Centre (below) and talk it through.

Another option is the recently legalized brothels. The term usually refers to an establishment centered on a bar. There, women—or men—who are avilable for hour-long sessions will make your acquaintance. These brothels, also called sex clubs, can be pricey. They are also controversial, and in the last few years the authorities have sought to close brothels associated with trafficking and criminal gangs.

The best place to go for information about prostitution in Amsterdam is the **Prostitution Information Centre.** *(Enge Kerksteeg 3, in the Red Light District behind the Oude Kerk, ☎020 420 7328 ▇www.pic-amsterdam.com ☒ Open Sa 4-7pm. Available at other times for group bookings, call ahead.)* Founded in 1994 by Mariska Majoor (once a prostitute herself), the center fills a niche, connecting the Red Light District with its eager frequenters. The center's staff can answer any question you might have, no matter how blush-worthy the query.

facts and figures

- **POPULATION:** 16,609,000
- **AGE:** 430 years old in 2011
- **SIZE:** 41,526 sq. km
- **INHABITANTS PER SQ. KM:** 400
- **ETHNIC GROUPS:** 173
- **POT SMOKERS:** 5.2% of *Nederlanders* in any given year (compared with 12.5% of Americans)
- **COFFEESHOPS IN AMSTERDAM IN 1960, THE FIRST TIME LET'S GO WENT TO AMSTERDAM:** 5
- **COFFEESHOPS TODAY:** 241
- **TOURISTS THAT VISIT A COFFEESHOP:** 30%
- **BICYCLE THEFTS IN AMSTERDAM PER YEAR:** 80,000

CUSTOMS AND ETIQUETTE

We know you're expecting some culture shock in the Red Light District of Amsterdam, but there's plenty to be aware of in (ahem) your slightly more "professional" encounters with Amsterdam natives.

Upon being introduced to someone, a firm handshake is customary, though close friends greet each other with three kisses, *comme le style français*. When sharing a meal, it is still common for men to wait for women to be seated. Soft drugs and prostitution may be legal in Amsterdam, but abusers and law-breakers are punished harshly.

HOLIDAYS AND FESTIVALS

HOLIDAY OR FESTIVAL	DESCRIPTION	DATE
Queen's Birthday	A day of national pride. Orange clothing and street parties everywhere. Not the queen's real birthday.	April 30
WWII Remembrance Day	A solemn day to remember the Netherlands' WWII dead. A moment of silence is observed.	May 4
Liberation Day	A day of public *fêtes* to celebrate the country's liberation from Nazi occupation. Controversy often erupts over Dutch appeasement of their conquerors.	May 5
National Windmill Day	Windmills throw open their doors, and many have special (often educational) events.	2nd Saturday in May
Amsterdam Gay Pride	Three days of tolerance and partying, with a parade and street festivals for all sexual orientations.	Early August
Aalsmeer Flower Parade	Flower floats, flower art, and flowery music in the world's flower capital.	Early September
High Times Cannabis Cup	One long tokefest. At the end of the festival, awards are given to the best hash and marijuana.	November
Amsterdam Leather Pride	The premier gathering for "leather men." Features fetish parties and a lot of leather outfits.	late October early November
Sinterklaas Eve	Dutch Santa Claus delivers candy and gifts to nice Dutch children. The naughty ones are kidnapped (hope you're on the nice list).	December 5

the netherlands

PORTUGAL

Portugal draws hordes of backpackers by fusing its timeless inland towns and majestic castles with industrialized cities like Lisbon, whose graffiti-covered walls separate bustling bars from posh *fado* restaurants. The original backpackers, Portuguese patriarchs like Vasco da Gama, pioneered the exploration of Asia, Africa, and South America, and the country continues to foster such discovery within its borders, with wine regions like the Douro Valley, immaculate forests and mountains in its wild northern region, and 2000km of coastline for tourists to traverse and travel.

greatest hits

- **BARRIO ALTO NIGHTLIFE:** Don't fear crowd-induced pit stains in this neighborhood—everyone drinks on the sidewalks (p. 967).
- **FADO:** Because you're where this music was born (p. 969).
- **CLUBBIN' BY THE WATER:** Lisbon has some of the hottest clubs this side of the Pyrenees, located on the riverfront (p. 967).

Portugal

ATLANTIC OCEAN

MINHO

Vila Nova de Cerveira
Valença do Minho
Caminha
Viana do Castelo
Minho
Lima
Cávado
Barcelos
Braga
Guimarães
Amarante
Tâmega
Espinho
Ovar
Aveiro

Parque Nacional da Peneda-Gerês
Serra-Do Gerês
Caldas de Gerês
Parque Natural de Montesinho
Bragança
TRÁS-OS-MONTES
Mirandela
Miranda do Douro
Parque Natural do Alvão
Vila Real
Parque Natural do Douro Internacional
DOURO ALTO
Serra Do Marão
Douro

DOURO LITORAL
Porto

BEIRA ALTA
Viseu
BEIRA LITORAL
Luso
Buçaco
Coimbra
Mondego
Serra Da Estrêla
Guarda
Manteigas
Parque Natural da Serra da Estrêla
Sabugal
Sortelha
Serra Da Gardunha
Monsanto
BEIRA BAIXA
Castelo Branco

Costa Da Prata
Figueira da Foz
Conímbriga
Zêzere
Leiria
Batalha
Fátima
Tomar
Nazaré
São Martinho do Porto
Alcobaça
Ilhas Beriengas
Caldas da Rainha
Cabo Carvoeiro
Óbidos
Peniche
Serra De Aire
Tejo
ESTREMADURA
RIBATEJO
Santarém
Ericeira
Vila Franca de Xira
Mafra
Sintra
Queluz
Cascais
Estoril
Lisbon
Parque Natural de Arrábida
Setúbal
Cabo Espichel
Tróia Peninsula
Sesimbra
Alcácer do Sal
Baía de Setúbal
Costa Azul

Serra De São Mamede
Castelo de Vide
Marvão
Crato
Portalegre
SPAIN
ALTO ALENTEJO
Estremoz
Elvas
Évora Monte
Évora

Santiago do Cacém
Sines
Beja
BAIXO ALENTEJO
Guadiana
Costa Dourada
Mira
Mértola

ALGARVE
Lagos
Silves
Cabo de São Vicente
Sagres
Portimão
Albufeira
Faro
Olhão
Tavira
Vila Real de Santo António
Golfo de Cádiz

0   50 kilometers
0   50 miles

portugal

student life

Northern Portugal's most famous export, port, is named after the city of Porto, and guess what the entire country is named after? It really all centers on this delicious alcoholic beverage made from wine that, by virtue of residual sugar, has become more than four times as alcoholic as regular wine. With half the proof of vodka and more than twice its tastiness, port can be quite the temptress, and before you know it, you're passed out at the tasting. Port is no old-person's drink either—students at Coimbra are just as likely as seniors playing cards to be imbibing the ruby drink.

lisbon ☎21

ORIENTATION

Lisbon's historic center has four main neighborhoods: **Baixa,** where accommodations, shopping, and tourists galore can be found; **Chiado,** the cultural center just uphill west of Baixa; nightlife-rich **Bairro Alto,** still farther west; and ancient **Alfama,** on the east side of Baixa. The narrow, windy streets and stairways of Alfama and Bairro alto can be confusing and difficult to navigate without a good map. The **Lisboa Mapa da Cidade e Guia Turístico** *(€3)* has nearly every street in these neighborhoods labeled, and is a good investment if you're going to be exploring Lisbon for a few days. The maps at the tourist offices are reliable but do not show the names of many streets, particularly in Alfama and Bairro Alto. **Tram 28E** runs east-west, parallel to the river, and connects all these neighborhoods, with its eastern terminus in the inexpensive and off-the-beaten-path neighborhood of **Graça.**

ACCOMMODATIONS

In recent years Lisbon has experienced an explosion of budget tourism, and new, low-priced accommodations have sprung up to cater to this crowd. The large number of hostels in **Baixa** and **Bairro Alto** means there is an impressive level of competition between them (one *Let's Go* researcher was even accused of being a spy for a different hostel), which keeps prices low and forces the owners to constantly attempt to improve to gain an edge.

Camping is fairly popular in Portugal, but campers can be prime targets for thieves. Stay at an enclosed campsite and ask ahead about security. There are 30 campgrounds within a 45mi. radius of the capital. The most popular, **Lisboa Camping,** is inside a 2,200-acre *parque florestal* and has the highest rating given to campsites in Portugal. They also have a hotel for dogs *(€10 per day)*. Seriously. *(Parque Municipal de Campismo de Monsanto, Estrada da Circunvalação ☎217 62 82 00 🖥www.lisboacamping.com ⇄ Bus 714 runs from Pr. do Comércio to Parque de Campismo. $ July-Aug €6.50 per person; €6-7 per tent; €4 per car; May-June and Sept €5.50/5-6/3.50; Oct-Apr €5/4.10-5/3.)*

Baixa

✓ KITSCH HOSTEL — HOSTEL [1]

Pr. dos Restauradoes, 65, 2nd fl. ☎213 47 43 62 🖥www.kitschhostel.com

Eponymous kitsch covers the walls of this hidden hostel (you have to go through a back door in a tobacconist's to get there), which is a little rougher and edgier than its clean-cut counterparts on the other side of Rossio. The dorm rooms are simple and small, the private rooms not much better, but you're not going

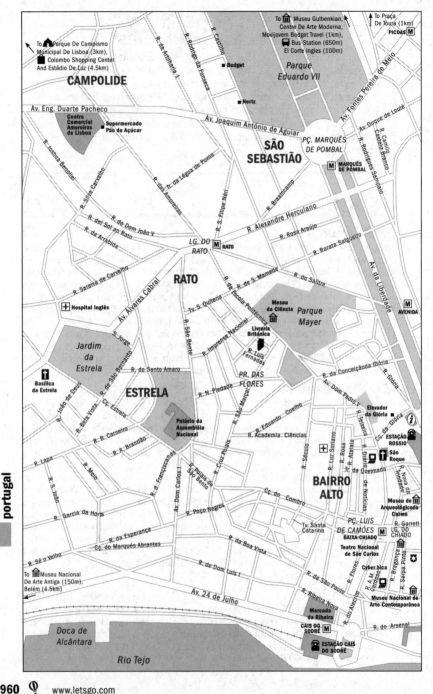

portugal

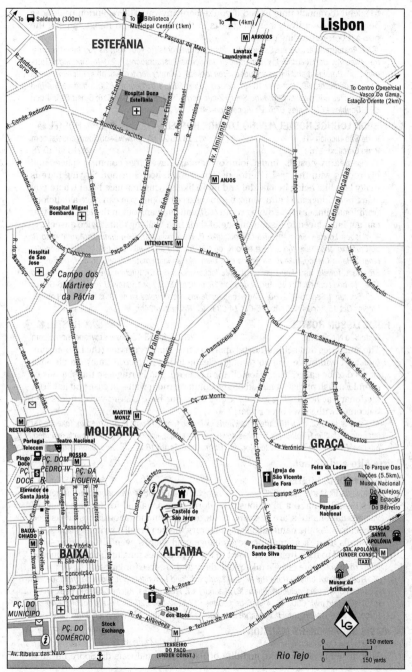

Lisbon

ESTEFÂNIA

lisbon · accommodations

to spend too much time in bed if you're here anyway. The reception desk does double-duty as a lively bar for guests in the evenings who mingle among the pop-art before heading out.

✝ ⓂRestauradores. On east side of Pr. dos Restauradores (to your right as you face the long, tree-lined Av. da Liberdade); enter through Tabacaria Restauradores, next to Santander Totta bank. *i* Breakfast and linens included. Free lockers. Laundry service available. Kitchen. Towels €1. Shared baths. ⓈOct-May 10- to 12-bed dorms €12; 8-bed dorms €14; 6-bed €16; 4-bed €18. Doubles €40; triples €60. June-Sept 12-bed dorms €14; 8- to 10-bed €16; 6-bed €18; 4-bed €20. Doubles €60; triples €75. ⌚ Reception 24hr.

▨ LISBON LOUNGE HOSTEL/LIVING LOUNGE HOSTEL ⬤⊗⒣ HOSTEL ❶
R. de São Nicolau, 41 ☎213 46 20 61 ▧www.lisbonloungehostel.com
R. do Crucifixo, 116 ☎213 46 10 78

These nearby hostels, under joint ownership, have large common spaces and big rooms with the best interior design around, hostel or not. Staying here is really less like being in a hostel and more like staying in a nice hotel where you share bedrooms and bathrooms: if you reserve by 6pm, you can have a delicious traditional dinner in the dining room (€8), you can hang out in the lounge, or you can get introduced to Lisbon on one of their free walking tours twice a week.

✝ Lisbon Lounge: From ⓂBaixa-Chiado, take R. da Vitória exit, then immediate right onto R. do Crucifixo, then take the 1st left onto R. de São Nicolau and walk for 4 blocks. Living Lounge: From ⓂBaixa-Chiado, take R. da Vitória exit, then take an immediate left onto R. do Crucifixo. *i* Breakfast, towels, and linens included. Free lockers. Laundry €7. Kitchen. Free city tours Tu and F. Ⓢ Lisbon Lounge: Oct 15-Apr 14 dorms €18; doubles €50. Apr 15-May 31 and Sept 16-Oct 14 €20/60. Jun 1-Sep 15 €22/60. Living Lounge: dorms and doubles same rates as Lisbon Lounge. Singles Oct 15-Apr 14 €30; Apr 15-Oct 14 €35. ⌚ Reception 24hr.

HOME LISBON HOSTEL ⬤⊗⒣ HOSTEL ❷
R. de São Nicolau, 13 ☎218 88 53 12 ▧www.mylisbonhome.com

The amenities that set this hostel apart are free laundry service (the Lisbon summer heat will make you go through clean clothes in record time), an elevator (it used to be called "Easy Hostel" for a reason), and Portuguese translations of useful English phrases painted on the common room wall—in case you left your dictionary at home. The rooms aren't huge but have classic wood floors and balconies with views over Baixa.

✝ From ⓂBaixa-Chiado, take the R. da Vitória exit, then turn right onto R. do Crucifixo. Take the 1st left onto R. de São Nicolau; it's 5 blocks down. *i* Breakfast, linens, lockers, and towels included. Kitchen. Free laundry service. Elevator. Ⓢ Dorms June-Sept €18-22. ⌚ Reception 24hr.

Bairro Alto and Chiado

▨ LISBON POETS HOSTEL ⬤♿⒣ HOSTEL ❷
R. Nova da Trinidade, 2, 5th fl. ☎213 46 10 58 ▧www.lisbonpoetshostel.com

This hostel is flat-out luxurious. The dorm rooms, named for famous poets of various nationalities, are large and clean, and the common room is best measured in hectares. As the name suggests, a literary theme prevails: writers' quotes line the walls, there's a small book exchange, and there's even a typewriter—but you'll need to fix it first if you want to use it. Activities ranging from city tours to *fado* nights to cafe crawls take place daily and are free for guests.

✝ From ⓂBaixa-Chiado, take the Pr. do Chiado exit, and turn right up R. Nova da Trinidade. *i* Breakfast and linens included. Towels €1. Laundry €7. Free lockers. Kitchen. Shared bath. Elevator. Credit card min. €50. Ⓢ 4- or 6-bed dorms €17-21; 2-bed €20-24. Private doubles €40-60. Discount with 5 nights total if 1 or more is in Oporto Poets Hostel. ⌚ Reception 24hr.

▨ OASIS BACKPACKERS MANSION ⬤♿⒣ HOSTEL ❷
R. de Santa Catarina, 24 ☎213 47 80 44 ▧www.oasislisboa.com

This hostel is close to the nightlife of Bairro Alto and Cais do Sodré but in a quiet neighborhood just down the street from the pleasant Miradouro de Santa Catarina. It has its own nightlife, too, in the private patio bar *(open 6pm-1am)* just off the street, and the rooms are large and comfortable. Large, private doubles are located up the street on a lovely courtyard. This building also has a kitchen and trendily decorated common space.

⚡ Ⓜ*Baixa-Chiado (Chiado exit). From Pr. de Luís de Camões, follow R. do Loreto (at far right side if entering plaza from direction of Metro station) 4 blocks, then left down R. Marechal Saldanha to the Miradouro de Santa Catarina (lookout point), then right; it's the big yellow house at the end of the street.* *i* *Breakfast, linens, and towels included. Kitchen. Free safe. Laundry €7.* Ⓢ *Dorms €18-22; doubles €45-56.* 🕐 *Reception 8am-midnight.*

Alfama

LISBON AMAZING HOSTEL
✎⊗⊗(()) HOSTEL ❷

Beco do Arco Escuro, 17 ☎218 88 00 54

The rooms in this hostel certainly aren't the biggest, and it's more expensive than comparable accommodations in neighborhoods to the west, but stay in this hostel for the true Alfama experience. It's literally right above one of the ancient neighborhood's arches, one block from the cheap restaurants on R. dos Bacalhoeiros and the cathedral. The neighborhood is much quieter at night than Bairro Alto, so you can actually get some sleep, if you want.

⚡ Ⓜ*Terreiro Paço, tram 28E, or bus 737 to Sé. From the north side of Pr. do Comércio (farthest from the river), facing the river, head left along R. da Alfândega 3 blocks, then left, then left on R. dos Bacalhoeiros, then right through the arch and up the steps; follow signs for "LAHostels."* *i* *Breakfast, linens, and towels included.* Ⓢ *June-Sept dorms €30; doubles €55. Oct-May dorms €20-25; doubles €45-55.*

Around Praça do Marquês de Pombal

BLACK AND WHITE HOSTEL
✎⊗⊗(()) HOSTEL ❶

R. de Alexandre Herculano, 39, 1st fl. ☎213 46 22 12 ▣www.costta.com

This hostel is in a slightly more upscale neighborhood (though less than a block from a supermarket), and staying here is like living in an artist's studio. Massive, colorfully bold murals and random pieces of art floating around the dorm rooms make the entire hostel feel like a large piece of performance art. The common spaces are large and comfortable, and the building itself feels charmingly worn.

⚡ Ⓜ*Marquês de Pombal, or buses 1, 74, 202, 706, 709, 713, 720, 727, 738, 758, 773 to Rato. From ⓂMarquês de Pombal metro stop, take the exit toward R. de Alexandre Herculano, then walk down Av. da Liberdade away from the giant statue. Then turn right onto R. de Alexandre Herculano; the hostel is 4 blocks down on the left.* *i* *Breakfast and linens included. Towels €1. Kitchen.* Ⓢ *Dorms €15-20.* 🕐 *Reception 24hr.*

SIGHTS

Lisbon's history can be seen on every street in the city, stretching from the present back 3,000 years. Moorish *azulejos* (painted and glazed tiles) line the ancient facades and interiors of Alfama; the fortress-like 12th-century Sé (cathedral) looms over the city with its imposing Romanesque presence; the 11th-century Castelo de São Jorge sits on a high hill over the center. The whole city is essentially one large sight to experience, from confusing Alfama to rigid and (more) modern Baixa. Those planning on doing a lot of sightseeing in a few days should consider purchasing the tourist office's Lisboa Card for a flat fee. Many museums and sites are closed Mondays and free Sundays and holidays before 2pm.

Baixa

Baixa doesn't have many historical sights—the whole neighborhood was leveled and rebuilt after the earthquake of 1755. The pedestrian streets and *praças*, though, have their own newer brand of beauty and excellent people-watching. **Rossio,** known more formally as **Praça de Dom Pedro IV,** is Lisboa's heart. The city's main square has been used as a cattle market, public execution stage, bullring, and carnival ground—today it is home to tourists and the large central statue of Dom Pedro IV, with circling drivers making the plaza their own Indianapolis Motor Speedway. At the north end of the plaza is the magnificent Teatro Nacional de Dona Maria II, with a statue of Gil Vicente, Portugal's first great dramatist, peering down onto Baixa.

Bairro Alto and Chiado

The culture in Chiado is as high as its altitude, and the area is home to plenty of museums and historic sites. Neighboring Bairro Alto offers great views of the city from its *miradouros.*

MUSEU ARQUEOLÓGICO DO CARMO ⊘⊗ CHURCH, MUSEUM

Lg. do Carmo ☎213 47 86 29

Sick of those big, boring churches that all look the same? This archaeological museum is housed in a 14th-century Gothic church like any other, except it's **missing its roof.** The ruins became ruins in the 1755 earthquake and ensuing fire, and today they stand as an open courtyard under empty arches where the roof once stood. Highlights of the museum, whose collection spans four millennia and the entire globe, include mummies from Peru and Egypt, but the real sight here is the ruined building itself.

➔ ⓂBaixa-Chiado (Chiado exit) or bus #58, 100, or tram 28. From Rossio, walk (steeply) up Cç. do Carmo to Lg. do Carmo. $ €3.50, students and seniors €2, under 14 free. ⏰ Open M-Sa June-Sept 10am-7pm; Oct-May 10am-6pm.

👍 CASTELO DE SÃO JORGE 💳⊗ CASTLE, HISTORIC SITE, VIEWS

Castelo de São Jorge ☎218 80 06 20 💻www.castelosaojorge.egeac.pt

Built by the Moors in the 11th century on the highest point in Lisbon, this hilltop fortress was captured by Dom Afonso Henriques, Portugal's first king, in 1147. Later Portuguese kings made it their residence, and today visitors can walk all around the ramparts to enjoy phenomenal panoramic views of Lisbon. There is a small museum of artifacts found at the site that date back to the sixth century BCE.

➔ Bus #737, or trams 12E and 28E; follow signs to Castelo. $ €7, students and seniors €3.50, under 10 free. ⏰ Open Mar-Oct 9am-9pm; Nov-Feb 9am-6pm. Last entry 30min. before close. Museum has guided tours daily at noon and 4pm.

👍 SÉ CATEDRAL DE LISBOA ⊘⊗ CHURCH, MUSEUM

Largo da Sé ☎218 86 67 52

Lisboa's 12th-century cathedral is massive and intimidating, built to double as a fortress, if needed. Its austere Romanesque style makes the few brightly colored stained-glass windows leap out of the walls, where the same ornamentation is often lost in a busy Gothic or Baroque church. The cloisters, an archaeological site perpetually under scaffolding, contain a collection of tombs with brilliant carvings of various scenes from daily life and the Bible. The treasury houses a small collection or religious objects and manuscripts.

➔ Bus #737, or tram 28E. From Baixa, follow R. da Conceição east (to the left as you face the river) up past the church, then turn right onto R. de Santo António da Sé and follow the tram tracks; it's the large, simple building that looks like a fortress. $ Free. Cloister €2.50. ⏰ Church open M 9am-5pm, Tu-Sa 9am-7pm, Su 9am-5pm. Treasury open M-Sa 10am-5pm. Cloister open May-Sept M 10am-5pm, Tu-Sa 10am-6pm; Oct-Apr M-Sa 10am-5pm. Mass Tu-Sa 6:30pm, Su 11:30am.

Graça

PANTEÃO NACIONAL 💳♿ TOMBS, HISTORIC SITE

Campo de Santa Clara ☎218 85 48 39 💻www.igespar.pt

The Igreja de Santa Engrácia was started in the late 17th century, but once the architect died, the king lost interest in the project and the funding dried up, leaving the church unfinished for some 250 years. Eventually, General Salazar's regime took control of the construction and completed the dome, though the pinnacles the original architect intended for either side were never added. Salazar rededicated the building as the National Pantheon, a burial place for important statesmen, in 1966. However, when democracy was restored in 1975, the new government used the Panteão to house the remains of Salazar's most prominent opponents, while those who had worked with Salazar were prohibited from entering the building. The dome is a distinctive feature of the Lisbon skyline, and the much beloved Amália Rodrigues, queen of *fado*, is among those buried there.

⇟ [M]Santa Apolonia, bus #12, 28, 34, 35, 704, 745, 759, 781, 782, or tram 28E. Get off tram 28E at Voz do Operário stop in front of Igreja e Mosteiro de São Vicente de Fora, then follow Arco Grande de Cima (to the left of church), then take the 1st right, 1st left, and then another right; you can't miss it. $ €3. Students and under 14 free. Seniors €1.50. Su before 2pm free. ⏰ Open Tu-Su 10am-5pm.

Belém

The Belém waterfront, a couple of kilometers west of Lisbon's center, is one of the most majestic tributes to Portugal's Age of Discovery and its legendary seafaring spirit. Almost as famous as the historic sights is **Pasteis de Belém,** a pastry shop with a reputation as rich as its pastries. *(R. de Belém, 84-92 ☎213 63 74 23 $ Pastries €0.90 each ⏰ Open daily 9am-11pm.)*

MOSTEIRO DOS JERÓNIMOS — CHURCH, MUSEUM

Pr. do Império — ☎213 62 00 34 🖥www.mosteirojeronimos.pt

The Hieronymite Monastery was established in 1502 to honor Vasco da Gama's expedition to India. We're guessing the explorer's spirit is pleased with this ornate tribute. The Manueline building has the detail of its Gothic predecessors and the sweeping elegance of the oncoming Renaissance. In the '80s the monastery was granted World Heritage status by UNESCO, and it is in pristine condition inside and out. The church contains tombs (both symbolic and actual) of Portuguese kings and bishops. Symbolic tombs include areas of tribute to Vasco da Gama and Luís de Camões, Portugal's most celebrated poet. Entrance to the cloister is not cheap (€7, but free Su before 2pm), but it's worth it to see one of Lisbon's most beautiful spaces, which somehow retains its charm despite being filled with hordes of tourists.

⇟ Tram 15E, or bus #28, 76, 201, 204, 714, 727, 729, 751 to Mosteiro dos Jerónimos. $ Free. Cloister and museum €7, over 65 €3.50, under 14 free; F-Su before 2pm free for all. Combined ticket with Torre de Belém €10. ⏰ Open May-Sept Tu-Su 10am-6:30pm; Oct-Apr Tu-Su 10am-5:30pm. Last entry 30min. before close.

TORRE DE BELÉM — DEFENSE TOWER, VIEWS

Torre de Belém — ☎213 62 00 34

Portugal's most famous tower has risen out of the water (except at low tide, when it's connected to the shore by a narrow, sandy isthmus) from the banks of the Tejo for nearly 500 years, gracing visitors' memories and souvenir stores' postcards since its completion in 1519. It's a short and lovely walk (if you walk along the river—the other side of the road is less scenic) from the Mosteiro dos Jerónimos. There is a shady park in front of it and a tiny strip of beach next to it. The tower has many levels to maximize artillery efficiency, as well as stunning 360-degree views of the Tejo and the city of Lisbon. Don't miss the detailed carvings shaped like a rhinoceros (there are signs pointing to it), and take a minute to relax in one of the shady turrets with stone window seats and stunning views.

⇟ From Mosteiro dos Jerónimos, take unmarked underground walkway in front of the monastery (from entrance, head toward the river; it's a small stairway) to other side of road and tracks and walk west along the river (to the right as you face the water) about 15min. Alternatively, walk in

the same direction on the monastery's side of the road and take the pedestrian walkway over the road at the tower. $ *€5. Students and under 14 free. Over 65 €2.50. Su before 2pm free for all. Combined ticket with Mosteiro dos Jerónimos €10.* 🕐 *Open May-Sept Tu-Su 10am-6:30pm; Oct-Apr Tu-Su 10am-5:30pm. Last entry 30min. before close.*

FOOD

Some of the best and least expensive meals can be found in the ubiquitous **pastelarias:** don't be fooled by the name (it means pastry shop) or the appearance (the centerpiece is usually the counter with heaps of sweets), because these places can cook, too. That said, don't skip the pastries: **pasteis de nata** are generally less than €1 and are the city's most popular sweet. Local specialties include *caracois* (small snails; look for a restaurant with a sign that says "Há caracois" in the window), **lombo de porco com amêijoas** (pork with clams; much tastier than it sounds at first), and the Portuguese staples *alheira* (smoked chicken sausage), *sardinhas assadas* (grilled sardines), and *bacalhau* (cod) just about any way you can think of. Some of the best deals, in terms of getting a lot for a little, are the *tostas*, large grilled sandwiches that usually cost €2-3. The local traditional drink is **ginjinha** (pronounced "jee-JEE-nyah;" also often called *ginja*), a sour cherry liqueur served ice-cold in a shot glass and meant to be sipped. If it's bad, it tastes like cough syrup, but if it's good it's delicious and refreshing, particularly on hot Lisboa afternoons. It usually costs €1-1.50, and is sometimes served in a glass with chocolate for a little extra.

Baixa

MOMA — RESTAURANT ❷

R. de São Nicolau, 47 — ☎914 41 75 36

A delicious oasis of good food in the desert that is Baixa. Moma's menu is printed new daily and posted in beautiful handwriting on a large slate out front. The dishes tend to be cool, light, and creative for the hot summer months, but heavier meals are there for the taking as well. The interior is simple and clean, but the outdoor seating is the place to enjoy your meal, in the middle of the R. de São Nicolau but separated from the touristic madness by umbrellas and bamboo blinds. Get there on the early side if you're going for lunch, though, as it tends to fill up quickly with local suits in the middle of their workday.

[M]Baixa-Chiado (Baixa exit). Exit Metro station onto R. da Vitória, then right 1 block, and then left onto R. de São Nicolau. $ *Entrees usually €6-8.* 🕐 *Open M-Sa noon-7:30pm.*

BONJARDIM — GRILL ❷

Tv. de Santo Antão, 12 — ☎213 42 74 24

A little bit past Rossio from the main part of Baixa, this restaurant just off the food-filled R. de Santo Antão serves massive portions of various styles of chicken, meat, and fish. Dine outside and enjoy your meal from the "king of chicken" while watching crabs and lobsters duke it out in the aquarium in the window, or the similarly bizarre spectacle of the plethora of lost tourists trying to get back to the main plazas and easily gridded streets to the south.

[M]Restauradores or buses #36, 44, 90, 205, 207, 702, 709, 711, 732, 745, 746, 759. Take Travessa de Santo Antão from the east side of Pr. dos Restauradores. $ *Whole chickens €9. Grilled meats €8-12.* 🕐 *Open Tu 6-11:30pm, W-Su noon-11:30pm.*

Bairro Alto and Chiado

CERVEJARIA TRINDADE — TRADITIONAL ❸

R. Nova da Trindade, 20C — ☎213 42 35 06 www.cervejariatrindade.pt

Cervejaria Trindade is famous all over Lisbon for the *molhos* (sauces) made from beer that were invented here. Eateries throughout the city will often offer a course "à trindade," named for this establishment. Cervejaria Trindade's location was occupied from the end of the 13th century by a convent and became one of Lisbon's first breweries at the start of the 19th century. Sagres, Portugal's second best-selling beer brand, came out with a beer called Bohemia 1835, created especially to celebrate the 170th anniversary of Cervejaria Trindade. The enormous dining rooms are covered with *azulejos* from this period, and the cloister of the convent is used for dining as well.

From [M]Baixa-Chiado, exit onto Lg. do Chiado, then take a sharp right up R. Nova da Trindade (to left of A Brasileira). $ Meat plates à trindade €9-18. Pratos do dia M-F €7.50. ⏰ Open daily noon-1:30am.

NOO BAI CAFE — CAFE, VIEWS 1

Miradouro do Adamastor (Santa Catarina) ☎213 46 50 14 www.noobaicafe.com

The food and drink here are perfectly fine, but few come here on a culinary quest. It's the sweeping view of the Tejo, including the burnt-orange 25 de Abril bridge and the giant statue of Christ signalling an incomplete pass, that really brings the crowds. If you see an open table by the railing, leap for it and don't leave until you feel like it.

[M]Baixa-Chiado (Chiado exit) or tram 28E to Santa Catarina. From Pr. de Luís de Camões, follow R. do Loreto (far right corner of plaza with your back toward Metro station) 4 blocks, then turn left down R. Marechal Saldanha to the miradouro. $ Sandwiches €3-5. Coffee €1-2.50. Beer €2-4. ⏰ Open M-F noon-midnight, Su noon-10pm.

Alfama

FLOR DA SÉ — PASTELARIA 1

Lg. de Santo António da Sé ☎218 87 57 42

This *pastelaria* is known throughout Lisbon for having the best pastries this side of Belém and for its cheap *pratos do dia* (around €5). Its location near the border between Alfama and Baixa makes it a good place to start or to end your tour of Alfama.

Take tram 28E to Sé, then walk back a block along the tracks toward Baixa; it's on the left. $ Pratos do dia €4.50-5.50 ⏰ Open M-F 7am-8pm, Su 7am-8pm.

CHURRASQUEIRA GAÚCHA — GRILL 2

R. dos Bacalhoeiros, 26 ☎218 87 06 09

Great, traditional Portuguese fare in a simple but very large dining room. The meat and fish are displayed in a window on the street, so you can just walk by and pick what looks good.

From Baixa, follow R. do Comércio east (to the left as you face the water) until R. da Madalena, then slight right onto R. dos Bacalhoeiros. $ Main courses €7.50-14. ⏰ Open M-Sa noon-midnight.

ÓH CALDAS — TRADITIONAL 3

R. de São Mamede, 22 ☎218 87 57 11

This traditional restaurant has favorites like *sardinhas assadas* (grilled sardines; €6.50), *alheira* (smoked chicken sausage; €6), and an ever-changing three-course daily menu (€12). Its location on the scenic route between the Sé (cathedral) and the Castelo de São Jorge makes it a convenient Alfama stop.

From Baixa, follow R. da Conceiçao east toward Alfama (to left as you face the river), just past the Igreja da Madalena. Head left up Travessa d'Almada for 3 blocks, then left on R. de São Mamede. $ Daily menu €12. ⏰ Open daily noon-4pm and 8pm-midnight.

NIGHTLIFE

Bairro Alto is one massive street party every night (even Sunday!) until 2am, and is where just about everyone in town starts their evening. Few people actually stay in the plethora of bars that line these narrow streets: you go into one of the places, get your massive beer or cocktail (generally about 9 parts alcohol and 1 part not), and take a seat on the **sidewalk.** Or, head to **Parraxaxá** convenience store and buy ice-cold liters of Super Bock for €2 each.

Bairro Alto

🏛 PORTAS LARGAS   ⊜⊗✆Ƴ   BAR, MUSIC
R. da Atalaia, 105   ☎213 46 63 79

This staple of the Bairro Alto scene has live music every night (sometimes really good, other times unfortunate covers of '80s songs that are so bad they're good) and some of the biggest, strongest *caipirinhas* and mojitos around (€4-6). It gets crowded inside, but you can enjoy the music and drinks just outside. Don't expect to be able to loiter inside and enjoy the music without buying a drink.

   ✦ Ⓜ*Baixa-Chiado (Chiado exit). Bus #1, 202, 758, 590, or tram 28E. Walk up R. da Misericórdia 4 blocks from Pr. de Luís de Camões, then left for 5 blocks.* Ⓢ *Beer €2. Caipirinhas and mojitos €4.* Ⓩ *Open Oct-June M-Th 8pm-2am, F-Sa 8pm-3am, Su 8pm-2am; July-Sept M-Th 7pm-2am, F-Sa 7pm-3am, Su 7pm-2am.*

🏛 BICA ABAIXO   ⊜⊗✆Ƴ   BAR
R. da Bica de Duarte Belo, 62   ☎213 47 70 14

This bar is located on the steep slope of the shiny silver Elevador da Bica funicular, just to the south of the center of Bairro Alto. It's perfect for those making the trek down to the river or for those sick of Bairro Alto's cheaply made drinks: the native Brazilians who own and run this small bar make the native *caipirinhas* (€3) in town, crushed and mashed and mixed together right in front of you.

   ✦ Ⓜ*Baixa-Chiado (Chiado exit) or tram 28E to Calhariz-Bica. From Pr. de Luís de Camões, follow R. do Loreto (far-right corner of plaza, with your back to the Metro station) 3 blocks, then turn left down R. da Bica de Duarte Belo; it's on the left.* Ⓢ *Beer €1.50. Mixed drinks €3-4.* Ⓩ *Open daily 9pm-2am.*

Alfama

🏛 LUX   ✦⊗✆Ƴ   DISCOTECA ❸
Av. do Infante Dom Henrique   ☎218 82 08 🖳www.luxfragil.com

This club is known far and wide as one of the best clubs in Western Europe; Lisboans abroad will tell you that if you visit one *discoteca* in Lisbon, it has to be this one. The enormous riverside complex has three stories of debauchery. Chill on the calm rooftop with amazing views, start to get schwastey at a slightly more intense bar on the floor below that, then descend into the maelstrom on the lowest level to find a raging disco howling and shrieking with techno. The bouncers tend to be very selective, so just act cool and try to get on their good side by being polite and speaking Portuguese (even the most pathetic attempt at the difficult language is greatly appreciated, and it might even decrease your cover charge). Dress well—only wear jeans or sneakers if the jeans are super-skinny and the sneakers are canvas high-tops, since the stylin' hipster look tends to play well.

   ✦ Ⓜ*Santa Apolónia, bus #12, 28, 34, 35, 206, 210, 706, 745, 759, 781, 782, 794. Just east of Santa Apolónia train station, on the side of the tracks closest to the river.* Ⓢ *Cover usually €12.* Ⓩ *Open Tu-Sa 11pm-6am.*

🏛 GINJA D'ALFAMA   ⊜⊗Ƴ⊿   GINJINHA ❶
R. de São Pedro, 12

Hidden in the heart of Alfama, this tiny hole-in-the-ancient-wall bar specializes in *ginjinha*, Lisbon's native wild-cherry liqueur, and serves it up cheap and ice cold (€1). You can take it outside to the small tables around the corner, which are much cooler than the stifling bar itself. It's a great place to start the night, serving sandwiches to carbo-load with before heading back out to hilly and confusing Alfama.

   ✦ *Bus #28, 35, 206, 210, 745, 759, 794. Walk down R. de São João da Praça, to right of Sé Cathedral as you're facing it, and follow the same street (bear left at the fork 1 block past the cathedral) as it becomes R. de São Pedro; it's a small store on the left side.* Ⓢ *Ginjinha €1. Sandwiches*

€1.50-2.50. ⏰ *Open M 9:30am-midnight, W-Su 9:30am-midnight.*

RESTÔ BAR, CIRCUS ❷

Costa do Castelo, 7 ☎218 86 73 34 💻www.chapito.org

This bar has amazing views over Alfama and the Tejo, though those are best enjoyed during the daytime. At night the outside patio comes alive with a carnival feel, and not without reason—it's on the grounds of Chapitô, a government-funded clown school. On most evenings there are circus shows, with tightrope walkers and trapeze artists practicing aerial acrobatics over the party below. Check the schedule online to make sure you're around for a show.

*Bus #737 to Costa do Castelo. From Baixa, it's a long walk uphill: follow R. da Conceiçao east toward Alfama (left as you face the river), past Igreja da Madalena, and up Travessa d'Almada to the left to R. de São Mamede. Go up the steep and windy Travessa da Mata, then left up Çç. do Conde de Penafiel to Costa do Castelo, then right.* $ *Beer €2. Cocktails €4-7.* ⏰ *Open M-F noon-3pm and 7:30pm-1am, Sa-Su noon-1:30am.*

Cais do Sodré, Santos, Alcântara, and Docas de Santo Amaro

Once the bars in Bairro Alto close, the party walks down R. do Alecrim to Cais do Sodré, where there are more than a dozen clubs. The area looks pretty unsavory 7am-2am, but the lines for the clubs stretch around the block for the other five hours. Many party enthusiasts then continue westward toward the **25 de Abril bridge,** where the neighborhoods of Santos, Alcântara, and the newly redeveloped Docas de Santo Amaro have chic and exclusive clubs, like **Op Art**.

FADO

A mandatory experience for visitors, Lisbon's trademark form of entertainment is the traditional *fado*, an art combining music, song, and narrative poetry. Its roots lie in the Alfama neighborhood, where women whose husbands had gone to sea would lament their *fado* (fate). Singers of *fado* traditionally dress in black and sing mournful tunes of lost love, uncertainty, and the famous feelings of *saudade* (to translate *saudade* as "loneliness" would be a gruesome understatement). Almost all *fado* houses are rather touristy, since not all that many Portuguese want to hear *fado* sung by anyone other than the beloved Amália Rodrigues. Expensive *fado* houses with mournfully high minimums include **Cafe Luso** *(Tv. da Queimada, 10 ☎213 42 22 81 💻www.cafeluso.pt $ $25 min.* ⏰ *Open daily 7:30pm-2am.)* and **Adega Machado** *(R. do Norte, 91 ☎213 22 46 40 $ €16 min.* ⏰ *Open Tu-Su 8pm-2am.)* The places listed below are free.

VOSSEMECÊ ALFAMA

R. de Santo António da Sé, 18 ☎218 88 30 56

This *fado* joint, conveniently located near Baixa, is housed in a beautiful, if oddly shaped, stable; arched ceilings and heavy stone columns run farther than the eye can see into the darkness of the ground-level restaurant. The *fadistas* rotate, each singing a couple of songs ranging from lively and funny to mournful. There's no cover charge or drink minimum, but the drinks are reasonably priced *(€3.50-6.50)* and quite good.

*[M]Baixa-Chiado (Baixa exit), or tram 28E. Follow R. da Conceiçao east toward Alfama (to the left as you face the river) past Igreja da Madalena; it's on the corner across the street to the left.* $ *Drinks €3.50-6.50. Main courses €8-15.* ⏰ *Open M-Tu noon-4pm and 8:30pm-midnight, Th-Su noon-4pm and 8:30pm-midnight; fado 9pm-midnight.*

A TASCA DO CHICO BAIRRO ALTO

R. do Diário de Notícias, 39 ☎965 05 96 70

This Bairro Alto *fado* location is popular with locals and has no cover charge or drink minimum. You're going to want a cold drink, however, as it gets crowded and stiflingly hot early on. Many choose to grab a spot at the open window and watch from the cool(er) street outside. Pretty much any amateur *fadista* who wants to take a turn can sing, so on a given night you could hear something you'd rather forget immediately, followed by the next big thing in *fado*.

Ⓜ Baixa-Chiado (Chiado exit). From Pr. de Luís de Camões, head up R. do Norte (to the right near the far side of the plaza if your back is to the Metro station) for 1 block, then take a quick left. Next, turn right up R. do Diário de Notícias. $ Beer €1.50. ⏰ Open M-Sa 8pm-2am. Fado starts around 9:30pm, but arrive much earlier to get a seat.

FESTIVALS

June in Lisbon is essentially one month-long festival, with food, drink, music, and dancing filling the streets from Bairro Alto to Graça and far, far beyond. The night of June 12 is the peak of the festivities, when Lisbon's adopted patron Saint Anthony is celebrated during the **Festa de Santo António.** Confetti falls by the metric ton on the **Avenida da Liberdade** during the parade. The crowded streets of Alfama, particularly around the **Igreja de Santo António da Sé,** erupt with zealous revelry, and everyone consumes *sardinhas assadas* (grilled sardines) and *ginjinha* (wild cherry liqueur). Decorations hang in Alfama for months after the **festas de Lisboa** end, and serve as reminders of the crazy month. For three days during the second week in July, the **Optimus Alive** music festival takes over the Algés waterfront, drawing some of the world's most popular artists and fans from across the globe *(☎213 93 37 70 💻www.optimusalive.com).*

Feiras *Markets*

The *feiras* can be great places to pick up one-of-a-kind souvenirs and other items on the cheap. *Feiras* that take place regularly include the **Feiras das Velharias,** antique fairs held in Lisbon's western suburbs (in **Oeiras** and **São Julião da Barra** on the first Sunday of the month, in **Caxias** on the second Sunday of the month, in **Paço de Arcos** on the third Sunday of the month, and in **Algés** on the fourth Sunday of the month) and the **Feira de Carcavelos,** one of the area's oldest markets that carries cheap clothing, which takes place in Carcavelos every Thursday.

FEIRA DA LADRA GRAÇA

Campo de Santa Clara

The so-called "thief's market" is Lisbon's best known, held in Graça near the edge of Alfama. The stalls at this market, which takes place every Tuesday and Saturday, stretch from the Mosteiro de São Vicente da Fora to the Panteão Nacional, with vendors selling antique books, vintage vinyls, old postcards, and just about anything else you might want. Prices are flexible and bargaining is encouraged, but initially posing too low of an offer can be thought of as an insult. Get there early before the tour groups pick the place clean.

Take tram 28E to Igreja e Mosteiro de São Vicente de Fora, then walk to the left of the big white church. ⏰ Open Tu 7am-2pm, Sa 7am-2pm.

ESSENTIALS

Practicalities

- **TOURIST OFFICE:** The Tourist Office on Pr. dos Restauradores has information for Lisboa and all of Portugal. *(Pr. dos Restauradores, 1250 ☎213 47 56 60 💻www.visitlisboa.com Ⓜ Restauradores, or bus #36, 44, 91, 205, 207, 702, 709, 711, 732, 745, 746, 759. On west side of Pr. dos Restauradores, in Palácio da Foz. ⏰ Open daily 9am-8pm.)* The **Welcome Center** is the city of Lisboa's main tourist office where you can buy tickets for sightseeing buses and the Lisboa Card, which includes transportation and discounted admission to most sights for a flat fee. *(R. do Arsenal, 15 ☎210 31 27 00)* The **Airport branch** is located near the terminal exit. *(☎218 45 06 60 ⏰ Open daily 7am-midnight.)* There are also information kiosks in Santa Apolónia, Belém, and on R. Augusta in Baixa.

- **INTERNET: Biblioteca Municipal Camões** has free internet access. *(Lg. do Calhariz, 17 ☎213 42 21 57 ▇www.blx.cm-lisboa.pt ⚜ Ⓜ️Baixa-Chiado, tram 28E OR bus #58, 100. From Pr. de Luís de Camões, follow R. do Loreto for 4 blocks. ◫ Open Sept 16-July 15 Tu-F 10:30am-6pm; July 16-Sept 15 M-F 11am-6pm.)*

- **POST OFFICE: Correios** main office is on Pr. dos Restauradores, but the Pr. do Comércio branch *(◫ Open M-F)* is less crowded. *(Pr. dos Restauradores, 58 ☎213 23 89 71 ▇www.ctt.pt ⚜ Ⓜ️Restauradores or bus #36, 44, 91, 205, 207, 702, 709, 711, 732, 745, 746, 759. ◫ Open M-F 8am-10pm, Sa-Su 9am-6pm.)*

Emergency!

- **POLICE: Tourism Police Station** provides police service for foreigners. *(Pr. dos Restauradores, 1250 ☎213 42 16 24 ⚜ Ⓜ️Restauradores or bus #36, 44, 91, 205, 207, 702, 709, 711, 732, 745, 746, 759. On west side of Pr. dos Restauradores, in Palácio da Foz next to the tourist office.)*

- **LATE-NIGHT PHARMACIES: Farmácia Azevedo and Filhos** in Rossio posts a schedule of pharmacies open late at night, as do most other pharmacies, or just look for a lighted, green cross. *(Pr. de Dom Pedro IV, 31 ☎213 43 04 82 ⚜ Ⓜ️Rossio or buses #36, 44, 91, 205, 207, 709, 711, 732, 745, 746, 759. In front of metro stop at the side of Rossio closest to river. ◫ Open daily 8:30am-7:30pm.)*

- **HOSPITAL/MEDICAL SERVICES: Hospital de St. Louis** is in Bairro Alto. *(R. de Luz Soriano, 182 ⚜ Ⓜ️Baixa-Chiado. From Pr. de Luís de Camões, follow R. do Loreto 4 blocks, then right up R. de Luz Soriano. ◫ Open daily 9am-8pm.)* Lisboa's main hospital is **Hospital de São José.** *(R. de José António Serrano ☎218 84 10 00 ⚜ Ⓜ️Martim Moniz or bus #8, 799. ◫ Open 24hr.)*

Getting There

By Plane

All flights land at **Aeroporto de Lisboa** *(☎218 41 37 00)*, near the northern edge of the city. The cheapest way into town from the airport is by **bus**: to get to the bus stop, walk out of the terminal, turn right, and cross the street to the bus stop, marked with yellow metal posts with arrival times of incoming buses. Buses #44, 91, and 745 *(Ⓢ €1.45. ◫ 15-20min., every 12-25min. 6am-12:15am.)* run to Pr. dos Restauradores, where they stop in front of the tourist office. The express AeroBus 91 runs to the same locations *(Ⓢ €3.50. ◫ 15min., every 20min. 7am-11pm.)* and is a much faster option during rush hours. A **taxi** downtown costs about €10-15, but fares are billed by time, not distance, so watch out for drivers trying to take a longer route.

By Train

Those traveling in and out of Lisboa by train are regularly confused, since there are multiple major train stations in Lisboa, all serving different destinations. The express, inexpensive **Alfa Pendular** line runs between Braga, Porto, Coimbra, and Lisboa. **Urbanos** trains run from Lisboa to Sintra and to Cascais, with stops along the way, and are very cheap and very reliable; make sure you go to the right station, though. Contact **Comboios de Portugal** for more info *(☎808 20 82 08 ▇www.cp.pt)*. **Estação do Barreiro** is across the Rio Tejo from Lisboa and runs trains to destinations to the south of the city. *(Ⓢ €2.15. ◫ 30min., 2 per hr.)* **Estação Cais do Sodré** runs trains to the west of the city, with the line ending in Cascais. Take trains labeled "Oeiras" or "Cascais Todos" to get to Belém *(Ⓢ €1.25)* and trains labeled "Cascais" or "Cascais Todos" to Estoril *(Ⓢ €1.75)* and Cascais *(Ⓢ €1.75)*. **Estação Rossio** is the gorgeous neo-Manueline building that services the northwestern suburbs, with the line ending in Sintra. *(Ⓢ €1.75. ◫ 40min., every 10-20min.)* **Estação Santa Apolónia** runs trains to the north and east. It is located on the river to the east of Baixa; to get there, take the blue Metro line to the end of the line. Trains between **Santa Apolónia** and **Aveiro**

($ €16.50-25. ⏰ 2½hr., 16 per day 6am-10pm.), **Braga** *($ €31. ⏰ 3½hr., 4 per day 6am-10pm.),* **Coimbra** *($ €20-31. ⏰ 2hr., 20 per day 6am-10pm),* **Porto** *($ €20-28.50. ⏰ 3hr., 16 per day 6am-11pm.),* and **Madrid** *($ €59. ⏰ 10hr., daily at 10:30pm.)* **Estação Oriente** runs southbound trains between Oriente and Faro *($ €18.50-21. ⏰ 3½-4hr., 6 per day 8am-8pm.)* with connections to other destinations in the Algarve.

By Bus

Lisboa's bus station is close to Ⓜ Jardim Zoológico, but it can be hard to find. Once at the Metro stop, follow exit signs to Av. C. Bordalo Pinheiro. Exit the Metro, go around the corner, and walk straight ahead 100m; then cross left in front of Sete Rios station. The stairs to the bus station are on the left. Rede Expressos *(☎707 22 33 44 💻www.rede-expressos.pt)* runs buses between Lisboa and **Braga** *($ €19. ⏰ 4-5hr., 14-16 per day 7-12:15am.),* **Coimbra** *($ €13. ⏰ 2hr., 24-30 per day 7am-12:15am.),* and **Lagos.** *($ €18.50-19. ⏰ 4hr., 14-16 per day 7:30am-1am.)*

Getting Around

By Public Transportation

Carris *(☎213 61 30 00 💻www.carris.pt)* is Lisboa's extensive, efficient, and relatively inexpensive transportation system that is the easiest way to get around the city of Lisboa. The city is covered by an elaborate grid of subways, buses, trams, and *elevadores* (funiculars, useful for getting up the steep hills). Fares purchased on board buses, trams, or *elevadores* cost €1.45; the subway costs €0.85 but you must first purchase a rechargable *viva viagem* card *($ €0.50).* The easiest and most cost- and time-effective option for those who will use a lot of public transportation is the unlimited 24hr. **bilhete combinado** *($ €3.75),* which can be used on any Carris transport and means you don't have to go into a Metro station to recharge your card before getting on a bus or tram.

By Taxi

Taxis in Lisbon can be hailed on the street throughout the center of town. Good places to find cabs include the train stations and main plazas. Bouncers will be happy to call you a cab after dark. Rádio Táxis de Lisboa *(☎217 93 27 56)* and Teletáxis *(☎218 11 11 00)* are the main companies.

essentials

PLANNING YOUR TRIP

Time Differences

Portugal is on Greenwich Mean Time (and is thus one hour behind Spain) and observes Daylight Savings Time. During the summer, from the end of March until the end of October, time is shifted forward one hour (GMT +1).This means that it is 5 hours ahead of New York City, 8 hours ahead of Los Angeles, the same time as the British Isles, 9 hours behind Sydney, and 11 hours behind New Zealand.

MONEY

Tipping and Bargaining

Native Portuguese rarely tip more than their spare change, even at expensive restaurants. However, if you make it clear that you're a tourist — especially an American one — they might expect you to tip more. Don't feel like you have to tip; the servers' pay is almost never based on tips. No one will refuse your money, but you're a poor student so don't play the fool.

Bargaining is common and necessary in open-air and street markets. Especially if you are buying a number of things, like produce, you can probably get a better deal if you haggle. However, do not barter in malls or established shops.

Taxes

Portugal has a 7-8% value added tax (IVA) on all meals and accommodations. The prices listed in Let's Go include IVA unless otherwise mentioned. Retail goods bear a much higher 16% IVA, although the listed prices generally include this tax. Non-EU citizens who have stayed in the EU fewer than 180 days can claim back the tax paid on purchases at the airport. Ask the shop where you have made the purchase to supply you with a tax return form, but stores will only provide them for purchases of more than €50-100. **Taxes,** presently 21%, are included in all prices in Portugal. Request a refund form, an *Insenção de IVA*, and present it to customs upon departure.

SAFETY AND HEALTH

General Advice

In any type of crisis, the most important thing to do is **stay calm.** Your country's embassy abroad is usually your best resource in an emergency; registering with that embassy upon arrival in the country is a good idea.

Local Laws and Police

Travelers are not likely to break major laws unintentionally while visiting Portugal. You can contact your embassy if arrested, although they often cannot do much to assist you beyond finding legal counsel. You should feel comfortable approaching the police, although few officers speak English. In Portugal, the **Policía de Segurança Pública** is the police force in all major cities and towns. The **Guarda Nacional Republicana** polices more rural areas, while the **Brigada de Trânsito** is the traffic police, that sport red armbands. All three branches wear light blue uniforms.

Drugs and Alcohol

Recreational drugs are illegal in Portugal, and police take these laws seriously. The legal minimum drinking age is 16. Portugal has one of the highest road mortality rates in Europe. Do not drive while intoxicated, and be cautious on the road.

SPECIFIC CONCERNS

Natural Disasters

Apart from the occasional mild earthquake evey 200 years, there is little to fear from nature in Portugal. However, it is worth noting that if more than an inch of snow falls, many cities will shut down totally and driving will be incredibly slow, as Portuguese drivers will be freaked from the weather conditions.

PRE-DEPARTURE HEALTH

Matching a prescription to a foreign equivalent is not always easy, safe, or possible, so if you take **prescription drugs,** carry up-to-date prescriptions or a statement from your doctor stating the medications' trade names, manufacturers, chemical names, and dosages. Be sure to keep all medication with you in your carry-on luggage. Pharmacists in Portugal often speak very good English and can help you find common over-the-counter drugs.

portugal 101

facts and figures

- **OFFICIAL NAME:** Portuguese Republic
- **POPULATION:** 10.7 million
- **MOST FAMOUS INVENTION:** The Hot Air Balloon (1709)
- **AGE:** 872 in 2011
- **NUMBER OF CASTLES:** 101

CUSTOMS AND ETIQUETTE

The Portuguese are generally friendly, easygoing, and receptive to foreigners. Any attempt on your part to speak in the native tongue will be appreciated.

Taboos

Though dress in Portugal is more casual in the hot summer months than in the cold of winter, strapless tops on women and collarless t-shirts on men are generally unacceptable; shorts and flip-flops may be seen as disrespectful in some public establishments and rural areas even during a heat wave. Skimpy clothes are always a taboo in churches, as are tourist visits during masses or services. Do not automatically assume that those you meet will understand Spanish; one of the best ways to offend a local is to tacitly suggest that Portugal is part of Spain.

Public Behavior

Politeness is key in Portuguese society. Be sure to address a Portuguese as *senhor* (Mr.), *senhora* (Ms.), *senhora dona* (Mrs.), followed by their first name. To blend in, it's a good idea to be as formal as possible at first impression. Introduce yourself in detail; you'll be welcomed openly if you mention who you are, where you're from, and what you're doing in Portugal. Don't be surprised if you get pecked on both cheeks by younger Portuguese, but handshakes are generally the standard introductory gesture by most of the population.

FOOD AND DRINK

Portugal is a paradise for fresh seafood. Whether you're a seasoned fan of nautical fare or a shellfish skeptic, the Portuguese offer up an enticing selection of marine cuisine. While *bacalhau* (cod) is by far the fish of choice for most in Portugal, *peixe espada* (swordfish) is also a popular option. When it comes to cephalopods, *choco grelhado* (grilled cuttlefish), *polvo* (boiled or grilled octopus), and *lulas grelhadas* (grilled squid) should not be missed. For those less enamored of seafood, don't fear—the Holy Trinity of Portuguese fare remains pork, potatoes, and pastries.

Many Portuguese pastry names have a distinctly religious air, from *barriga de friera* (nun's belly) to *papos de anjo* (angel's chins) to *toucinho do céu* (bacon from heaven). Despite its name, no pigs are harmed in the making of *toucinho do céu;* while the name derives from a time when bacon lard was used in its preparation, today all three of these divine treats are reliant upon egg yolks and sugar for their rich taste, providing a PETA-friendly pastry for the Portuguese.

portugal

SPAIN

Despite being fiercely proud of their individuality, Spain's regions share a common rhythm. From the lull of afternoon siestas to the riotous tapas bars and *discote-cas*, Spain harbors an invigorating lifestyle that galvanizes any traveler. For daring backpackers looking to elevate their adventures, hiking the Camino in the north can provide history lessons laced with continental views. If the flatlands are more your cup of tea, check out the beaches of Sitges in Catalonia or the chic northern city of San Sebastian to soak up rays and see local birthday suits. If the only buff part of your body is your brain, head north to Madrid's Museo del Prado: with almost 10,000 pieces of art, they don't have enough room to display their entire collection.

greatest hits

- **SEE GUERNICA AT THE REINA SOFIA :** This piece of modern art by Picasso immortalized the atrocities of the Franco regime (p. 986).

- **CITY AT YOUR FEET:** Climb up the Columbus Monument (p. 1011) at the end of La Rambla and gaze out over the entirety of Barcelona.

- **RAGE:** Go to Ibiza (p. 1087). Go to Sevilla (p. 1094). Go to Granada (p. 1055.) Seriously, pretty much any town with more than 1000 people will be poppin' at 3am.

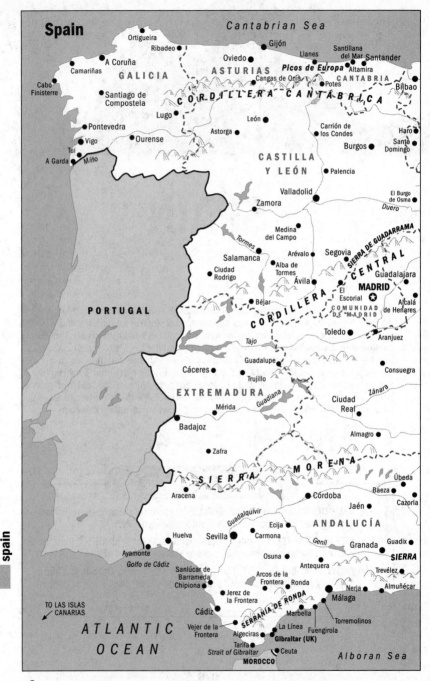

Spain

Cantabrian Sea

Ortigueira
Ribadeo ● Gijón ● Llanes Santillana del Mar Santander ●
A Coruña ● Oviedo ● **Picos de Europa** Altamira **CANTABRIA**
Camariñas ● **GALICIA** **ASTURIAS** Cangas de Onís Potes ● Bilbao ●
Cabo Finisterre ● Santiago de Compostela **CORDILLERA CANTÁBRICA**
Lugo ● León ● Carrión de los Condes ● Haro ●
Pontevedra ● Astorga ● Burgos ● Santo Domingo
Vigo ● Ourense ● **CASTILLA Y LEÓN** Palencia ●
Tui ● A Garda ● Miño
Valladolid ● El Burgo de Osma ●
Zamora ● *Duero*
Tormes Medina del Campo ● **SIERRA DE GUADARRAMA**
Salamanca ● Arévalo ● Segovia ● **CORDILLERA CENTRAL**
Ciudad Rodrigo ● Alba de Tormes ● Ávila ● Guadalajara ●
PORTUGAL Béjar ● El Escorial **MADRID** ☆ Alcalá de Henares ●
COMUNIDAD DE MADRID
CORDILLERA Toledo ● Aranjuez ●
Tajo
Cáceres ● Guadalupe ● Consuegra ●
Trujillo ● *Zánara*
EXTREMADURA *Guadiana*
Mérida ● Ciudad Real ●
Badajoz ●
Zafra ● Almagro ●
SIERRA **MORENA** Úbeda ●
Aracena ● Córdoba ● Báeza ●
Cazorla ●
Jaén ●
Guadalquivir Ecija ● **ANDALUCÍA**
Huelva ● Sevilla ● Carmona ● *Genil* Granada ● Guadix ●
Ayamonte ● Osuna ● Antequera ● **SIERRA**
Golfo de Cádiz Sanlúcar de Barrameda Arcos de la Frontera Ronda ● Trevélez ●
Chipiona ● Jerez de la Frontera Nerja ● Almuñécar ●
SERRANÍA DE RONDA Marbella ● Málaga ● Torremolinos
TO LAS ISLAS CANARIAS Cádiz ● La Línea Fuengirola
Vejer de la Frontera Algeciras ● **Gibraltar (UK)**
ATLANTIC OCEAN Tarifa ● Ceuta ●
Strait of Gibraltar **MOROCCO** *Alboran Sea*

spain

Ever since dictator Franco's death in 1975, the *madrileños* have been going out like it's going out of style. *La movida*, the youth countercultural movement post-1975, broke all those pesky Franco-era taboos by over-indulging in everything from alcohol to fornication. While few places are as countercultural as they were in the '70s, the student nightlife scene is just as jammin'—but maybe with fewer drugs. Start your night off at **Kiyo** in Chueca and sip a kiwi, vodka, and *sake* concoction in the heart of Madrid's gay nightlife. Next, head to **Kapital,** a classic huge disco that will please any clubgoer with four levels of themed dance floors, go-go dancers of both genders, and enough fog to give you asthma. Don't stop grinding until sunrise, and then cap off the evening with *chocolate con churros,* fried dough dipped in thick, molten hot chocolate at **Chocolateria San Ginés.**

madrid ☎91

ORIENTATION

El Centro

Bordered by the beautiful Palacio Real in the west and the relaxing Parque del Retiro in the east, El Centro, the heart of Madrid, encompasses the city's most famous historical sites and modern venues. Ancient churches, plazas, and winding cobblestone streets are set beside hip clubs and lively bars. In the middle is **Puerta del Sol,** the "soul of Madrid," where thousands descend to ring in each New Year. By day it is filled with tourists and locals checking out the restaurants and shopping that fill the eight streets meeting at Sol, and by night clubbers continue the party until 6am or later. Also in El Centro is **Plaza Mayor,** a vibrant square bordered by restaurants and filled with street performers and vendors. Finally, **Plaza Santa Ana** provides a popular meeting place where locals and tourists can escape for lunch and pre-club drinks. If you only have a few days in Madrid, El Centro gives a great taste of Madrid's culture and people. You can get around quickly with the Metro, but the area is also easily walkable, as the main sights are close to one another. When in doubt, stick to the main streets: **Calle de Alcalá, Calle Mayor, Calle de las Huertas,** and **Calle de Atocha** for great restaurants, nightlife, hostels, and cafes.

La Latina and Lavapiés

Known as the multicultural center of Madrid, La Latina and Lavapiés burst at the seams with international restaurants, bars, and cafes. Less frequented than the Sol or Plaza Mayor areas, these districts are where the locals go to drink and eat before heading out to enjoy more popular nightlife in other quarters. If you find yourself in La Latina, be sure to barhop on **Cava Baja,** a narrow street packed with enough cocktail bars, beer stops, restaurants, and tapas bars to suit any taste. With a relatively recent influx of immigrants from North Africa, the Middle East, and India, Lavapiés is a great place to eat if you're looking for an alternative to Spanish tapas. **Calle de Lavapiés** is filled with Indian restaurants, many of which specialize in tasty tandoori dishes.

Huertas

Huertas street's walls are etched with quotes from writers like Cervantes and Calderón de la Barca who lived in this historically literary neighborhood during its Golden Age. Today, the neighborhood centers itself on **Plaza Santa Ana** and **Calle de las Huertas** and is bordered by C. Alcalá (north), Pasea del Prado (east), and C. Atocha (south).

Get rid of your writer's block with Huertas' many tapas bars, lively nightlife, and delicious food along Plaza Santa Ana, C. del Principe, and C. de Echegaray.

Avenida del Arte and Retiro

Once reserved for royalty, the beautiful **Parque del Buen Retiro** is a peaceful gem in the middle of hectic Madrid—much like a Spanish Central Park. Full of wide walkways, gardens, cafes, and entertainers, this is the perfect place to exercise or take a load off and people-watch. Rent a rowboat for 45min. for €5 and paddle around the lovely man-made lake near the northern entrance to the park. Next door to these grounds is the **Paseo del Prado,** home to some of the world's best art museums including the **Museo Nacional del Prado** and the **Reina Sophia** modern art museum. Walk along this tree-lined boulevard to get shade and see some of the best sights that Madrid has to offer.

Gran Vía

Though it celebrated its centennial in 2010, Gran Vía isn't ready for retirement yet. The bustling "Broadway Madrileño" has evolved from a musical mecca to a bustling thoroughfare full of theaters, fast-food restaurants, shopping, and nightlife. Indeed, Gran Vía has just gotten younger with age. It may once have been where grandma came to see the opera, but now it's where the young and the trendy come for international shopping and clubbing.

Chueca and Malasaña

Madrid's famous gay neighborhood **Chueca** is centered on [M]Chueca and encompasses **Hortaleza, Infantas, Barquillo,** and **San Lucas** streets. Packed with modern restaurants, a wide variety of bars, and some of the best nightlife in Madrid, the district is a go-to neighborhood for anyone—regardless of orientation. The **Malasaña** area is named after **Manuela Malasaña,** a seamstress who became an unwilling martyr for Spain in the Peninsula War when she was executed by French forces for holding scissors that were interpreted as a weapon. Today, Malasaña is home to the city's hipster crowd and attracts hard-rock and grunge fans to its many venues. Both neighborhoods are funky and colorful and maintain a paddle-your-own-canoe mentality.

Argüelles and Moncloa

Just north of Plaza España is Argüelles, a series of crisscrossing streets centered on shopping-filled **Calle de la Princesa.** The neighborhood is highly residential and not really geared toward tourists, but the beautiful **Templo de Debod** is worth any traveler's time. The lookout points behind this temple present a scenic view of western Madrid. The **Paseo del Pinto Rosales** on the border of the beautiful **Parque del Oeste** offers excellent cafes and a quiet atmosphere in which to enjoy lunch. To the north of Argüelles is Moncloa, which is right beside the university area. Although not as touristy as the center, **Moncloa** has some worthwhile stops, including the **Arco de La Victoria** and the **Museo de America.**

ACCOMMODATIONS

El Centro

HOSTEL IVOR — HOSTEL [4]

C. Arenal, 24, 2nd fl. ☎91 547 10 54 🖥www.hostal-ivor.com

This beautiful hostel, located between Puerta del Sol and Plaza Mayor, home to many of El Centro's most prominent restaurants, cafes, clubs, and bars, is more like a mid-range hotel in terms of accommodations and service. Bright, clean, and well-decorated, Ivor's 25 rooms are comfortable but pricey. Extremely friendly service sets Hostel Ivor apart from its competition, with free Wi-Fi, ensuite bathrooms, and a cozy room make for a pleasant stay.

‡ From Puerta del Sol, walk down C. del Arenal a little bit past C. de las Hileras. $ Singles €44; doubles €65. ⏰ Reception 24hr.

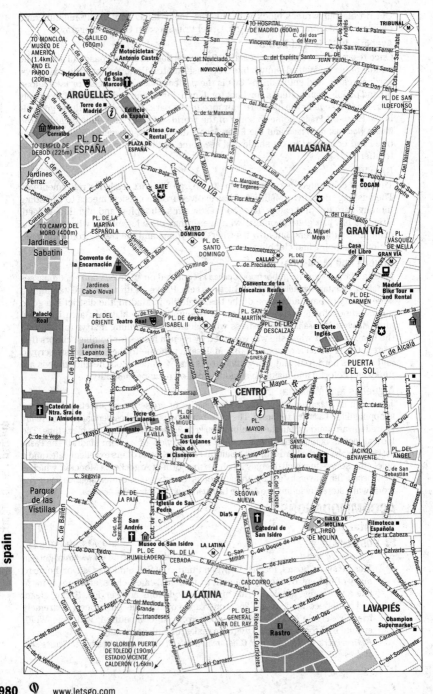

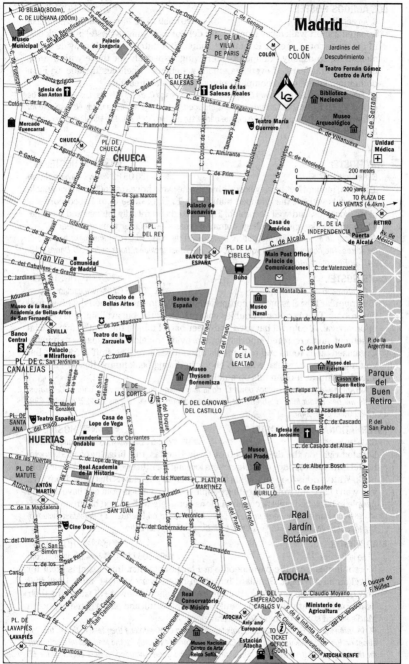

Madrid

LOS AMIGOS HOSTEL

●⊗(ʈ)❈ HOSTEL ❶

C. Arenal, 26, 4th fl.   ☎91 559 24 72 ▇www.losamigoshostel.com

Located a short walk away from Puerta del Sol, Los Amigos Hostel is smack dab
in the center of C. Arenal. Rooms are shared, but unbunked beds provide a nice
alternative to usually cramped hostel living, especially for those with *grande*
neighbors and fears of even the smallest heights. Amenities include Wi-Fi, a
communal kitchen, and complimentary continental breakfast.

✈ *From Puerta del Sol walk down C. del Arenal until you pass C. de las Hilerias; Los Amigos will be
on your right.* **i** *Breakfast included. Linens included. Extra large lockers and towels available for
rent. Free Wi-Fi.* Ⓢ *Dorms €17, with private bath €19; doubles €45-50.* ⚇ *Multilingual reception
8am-midnight.*

Huertas

▧ WAY HOSTEL

●⊗(ʈ)❈ HOSTEL ❷

C. Relatores, 17   ☎91 420 05 83 ▇www.wayhostel.com

This new, modern-but-homey hostel charges the same prices as youth and backpackers' hostels without the cramped bunk beds. Each of these 6- to 10-bed dorms is
clean, spacious, and well decorated. The relaxed and friendly kitchen and the large
TV room feel like upscale college common areas—perfect for your next beer.

✈ ⓜ*Tirso de Molina. From the station, walk toward the museum district and make a left up C.
Relatores. The hostel will be on your right.* **i** *Breakfast included. Book online.* Ⓢ *Dorms €18-
24.* ⚇ *Reception 24hr.*

CAT'S HOSTEL

●⊗(ʈ)❈ HOSTEL ❶

C. Cañizares, 6   ☎91 369 28 07 ▇www.catshostel.com

This popular hostel is mostly comprised of basic dorms (2-14 beds) with shared
bathrooms. There are some doubles with private baths, but availability is decided
upon arrival. A colorful bar area with beer barrel tables, the "Cat's cave" social
basement, and a restored Moorish patio provide travelers with spaces to mingle.
Organized tapas tours and pub crawls often meet here. The staff is friendly, but
you might have to wait a while to check in during peak hours. Reserve a room
ahead of time as it often fills up quickly.

✈ ⓜ*Antón Martín. Walk 1 block down C. de la Magdalena and make a right onto C. Cañizares.
Cat's will be on your left.* **i** *Breakfast included. Laundry €5.* Ⓢ *Dorms €17-22; doubles €38-
42* ⚇ *Reception 24hr.*

INTERNATIONAL YOUTH HOSTEL

●⊗(ʈ)❈ HOSTEL ❶

C. de las Huertas, 21   ☎ 91 429 55 26 ▇www.posadadehuertas.com

Located right on the drinking hub of C. de Huertas, this brightly painted, social
hostel is ideal for groups of backpackers looking for other people to join their wolf-
pack. With various food and sights tours as well as pub crawls that leave from IYH,
you won't have any trouble meeting people—even your bedroom can have up to 10
people in bunk-bed-style accommodations complete with shared bathrooms.

✈ ⓜ*Antón Martín. Walk north up C. de Leon, make a right on Huertas.* **i** *Breakfast included.
Luggage storage. Free Wi-Fi.* Ⓢ *Dorms €16-22.* ⚇ *Reception 24hr.*

MAD HOSTEL

●⊗(ʈ)❈ HOSTAL ❶

C. de la Cabeza, 24   ☎91 506 48 40 ▇www.madhostel.com

Mere minutes from the party people at Plaza Santa Ana, this hostal is great for
travelers on a budget. Standard but clean rooms vary with 4-6 bunk beds that
may or may not be single-sex. Bottom bunkers should beware of smacking their
heads on the relatively low top bunks. Pick up a drink and play a game of pool in
Mad's social space to meet fellow travelers.

✈ ⓜ*Antón Martín. From the station, walk forward down C. Magdalena then take C. Olivar, the 2nd
street on the left. Walk until you see C. Cabeza and turn right. Look for the Mad Hostal signboards
on the left side of the street.* **i** *Breakfast, safe, and linens included. Towels available for €5*

deposit. Laundry machines available. Small 4-piece gym and rooftop terrace. €10 key deposit. Reserve ahead. [$] *Dorms €16-23.* ⏰ *24 hours.*

Gran Vía

👍 LA PLATA — 💳🚭📶❄ HOSTAL [5]

Gran Vía, 15 — ☎91 521 17 25 💻www.hostal-laplata.com

Owned and operated by the Garrido brothers, this hostel exudes quirky charm, from its brightly painted lobby to the unnecessary chandeliers in every room. Thanks to this place's incredibly helpful and friendly staff, *Let's Go* recommends this hostal out of all the options in this building.

➔ [M]Gran Vía. Walk straight east; building will be on your right. [$] *Singles €45; doubles €60.* ⏰ *Reception 24hr.*

👍 HOSTAL FELIPE V — 💳🚭📶❄ HOSTAL [5]

Gran Vía, 15, 4th fl. — ☎91 522 61 43 💻www.hostalfelipev.com

Felipe V runs itself like a hotel with spacious rooms and friendly service. Family owned and operated, this hostal has been recently renovated and offers guests a daily newspaper and concierge-like services in its lobby.

➔ [M]Gran Vía. Walk east; building will be on your right. ℹ *Breakfast €4.50. Offers travel agency service and reservations for airport shuttles* [$] *Singles €46; doubles €64; triples €78.* ⏰ *Reception 24hr.*

HOSTAL A. NEBRIJA — 💳🚭📶❄ HOSTAL [3]

Gran Vía, 67, 8th fl. — ☎91 547 73 19 💻www.hostalanebrija.com

The best part of this hostal is its spectacular views of the Palacio Real, the cathedral, and the nearby gardens. The second-best part is the eclectic collection of religious paintings and porcelain decorations in its lobby. With attractive prices in this neighborhood of expensive hostels, Hostal A. Nebrija is hard to turn down.

➔ [M]Plaza de España. [$] *Singles €28; doubles €36; triples €55.* ⏰ *Reception 24hr.*

Chueca and Malasaña

HOSTAL LOS ALPES — 💳🚭📶❄ HOSTAL [4]

C. de Fuencarral, 17, 3rd and 4th fl. — ☎91 531 70 71 💻www.hostallosalpes.com

Located on one of the best shopping streets in Madrid, Hostal Los Alpes is a great place for you and your wallet to rest after a day of shopping. You'll breathe easy large rooms, spacious bathrooms, and nice common area with leather seating and a community computer. Your wallet will stay pleasantly plump, as the prices here are remarkably reasonable for the service provided.

➔ [M]Chueca. Make a right onto C. de Gravina and a right onto C. de Hortaleza. [$] *Singles €28; doubles €50.* ⏰ *Reception 24hr.*

HOSTAL MARIA LUISA — 💳🚭📶❄ HOSTAL [4]

C. de Hortaleza, 19, 2nd fl. — ☎91 521 16 30 💻www.hostalmarialuisa.com

This well-kept hostal has all the amenities of a small hotel at a much lower price. Nightstands, patterned bed coverings, and wooden wardrobes make the rooms look like they belong in someone's house, and the common area includes living-room-style couches with a TV and pictures on the wall. All it's missing is a mom and some meatloaf.

➔ [M]Chueca. Make a right on C. de Gravina and a right on C. de Hortaleza. [$] *Singles €39; doubles €50; triples €69; quads €85.* ⏰ *Reception 24hr.*

Argüelles and Moncloa

HOSTAL ANGELINES — 💳🚭📶❄ HOSTAL [4]

Hilarion Eslava, 12 — ☎91 543 21 52

This well-kept hostal puts you near Madrid's university district. Although several metro stops away from the city center, it's a better value than closer hostals and will save you some money. Big, sparkling white bathrooms and huge beds make it an excellent place to take refuge after a long day exploring the city.

[M]Moncloa. Walk south down C. de la Princesa and make a left on C. de Romero Robledo. Keep walking until you reach Hilarion Eslava, then make a left. $ Singles €40; doubles €45. ⏰ Reception 24hr.

tooth mouse

Most countries have some tradition involving children's baby teeth. In America, we're used to a tooth fairy replacing them with coins as we sleep. However, in Spain (and other Spanish-speaking countries like Argentina), the agent of tooth-to-coin transformation is actually a mouse! His name, in the legend, is Ratoncito Pérez. Ratoncito translates to "cute little mouse," and Pérez is a generic last name (think Smith). The tooth-mouse story came into being—allegedly—when the royal Prince Alfonso XIII lost one of his first baby teeth. The royal parents, in an effort to reassure him, asked a certain priest to formulate some sort of nice story for the toothless prince. So, as he didn't have much of a choice, the priest wrote a book about a boy, Bubi (the prince's nickname), who loses a tooth but is later rewarded by a mouse. It probably had a bunch of priestly morals thrown in there as well, but what really stuck was the idea of a mouse swapping teeth for presents. You might think it's a bit of a one-sided deal, but rumor has it that Ratoncito Pérez is actually building a modernista mansion out of all the baby teeth.

Outside the City Center

CAMPING ALPHA CAMPING [1]

12.4km down Ctra. de Andalicia in Getafe ☎916 958 069 💻www.campingalpha.com

This clean and welcoming campground features paved roads, pool, tennis courts, showers, laundry, and an internet center. Outside, it might get uncomfortable in the middle of Madrid's infamously hot summers.

Walk down Vada Santa Catalina, cross the bridge, and bear right. Take bus #447, which stops across from the Museo de Jamón. Cross the footbridge and walk 1½km back toward Madrid along the busy highway following the signs. $ Apr-Sept €7 per person; €7.10 per tent. Oct-Mar €5.56 per person; €5.68 per tent. 2- to 5-person bungalows €51-100.

SIGHTS

El Centro

PALACIO REAL MONUMENT

C. de Baillén ☎34 91 454 87 00 💻www.patrimonionacional.es

After the previous Muslim fortress was destroyed in a fire, Philip V began building the almost entirely marble Palacio Real. Its size and opulence are overwhelming, with each displayed room filled with vast collections of priceless furniture, tapestries, paintings, porcelain, and other things you'd expect to find in a house made of marble. Go on the 1hr. tour (in English or Spanish) that takes you through the palace's most richly decorated and renovated rooms and gives you behind-the-scenes stories about palace quirks. One can't-miss room is the Salón del Trono, where the king and queen used to greet visitors (today the palace is only used by the royal family on official state occasions). Still want more after the palace tour? Check out the **Real Armeria** (Armory) with an awesome collection of knights' armor and the **Oficina de Farmacia** (Royal Pharmacy), which features crystal and porcelain medicine receptacles. If you're in town on the first Wednesday of the month between September and May, check out the changing of the guard at noon.

→ *Ⓜ Opera. Walk west down C. de Arrieta. Palacio Real will be at the end of the road.* **i** *Come early to avoid long lines.* $ *€8, with tour €10; students, seniors, and children 5-16 €3.50.* ⏰ *Open Apr-Sept M-Sa 9am-6pm, Su 9am-3pm; Oct-Mar M-Sa 9:30am-5pm, Su 9am-2pm.*

PLAZA MAYOR
⊗🍸☀ PLAZA

Plaza Mayor

Built in the 15th century as a market square and home to important members of the court during the 17th century, the Plaza Mayor is steeped in history and architectural beauty. Today, it keeps the flavor of both its historic uses. By day, its hundreds of restaurants, shops, and street performers function as a modern-day market square. By night, live flamenco and music performances provide entertainment fit for a king's court. During the week-long **Fiesta de San Isidro** that begins on May 15, the plaza comes alive in celebration to honor Madrid's patron saint. The tourist office located in the plaza is quite helpful for free maps and suggestions for activities and other sights.

→ *Ⓜ Sol or Ⓜ Opera. From Puerta del Sol, walk 2min. down C. Mayor toward the Palacio Real. It will be on your left.*

PUERTA DEL SOL
⊗🍸☀ PLAZA

C. de Cedaceros, 10

Located in Puerta Del Sol is Spain's *Kilometre Zero*, the point from which all distances in Spain are measured. The Esquilache mutiny of 1766 began here in 1808, when *madrileños* took up arms against French troops in a historic resistance captured in Goya's *Dos de Mayo* and *Tres de Mayo*. Today, it is the headquarters of Madrid's regional government, hundreds of restaurants and cafes, and some of the best shopping in the city. This common meeting spot for *fútbol* game celebrations, protests, and celebrations is the true "soul" of the city.

→ *Ⓜ Sol.*

CATEDRAL DE LA ALMUDENA
◆⊗❄ CATHEDRAL

C. Bailen ☎91 542 22 00

Located right next to the Palacio Real, this cathedral has an incredible cavernous marble interior. Walk in for free and take in the 66ft. diameter dome and featured statues and artwork. In the 11th century, the image of the Virgin over the entrance was hidden by Mozarabs. When Madrid was reconquered by King Alfonso VI of Castile, the soldiers endeavored to find the statue to no avail. According to legend, after days of prayer, the spot on the wall hiding the icon crumbled to reveal this magnificent statue.

→ *Right next to Palacio Real.* $ *Free.* ⏰ *Open daily 10am-2pm and 5-8pm.*

PLAZA DE ORIENTE
⊗☀ PLAZA

Plaza de Oriente, 2

This beautiful plaza is filled with perfectly manicured hedges, fountains, and statues in honor of former Spanish kings and queens that surround the equestrian statue of Philip IV by Montañes. Lovers, tourists, sunbathers, and sunbathing tourist-lovers all lounge around the plaza.

→ *Across from the Palacio Real.* $ *Free.*

JARDINES DE SABATINI
⊗☀ GARDEN

C. de Baillen, 9 ☎91 588 53 42

Jardines de Sabatini is an outdoor reflection of the wealth and opulence of the royal palace. Immaculately kept trees, hedges, and fountains create a relaxing atmosphere, and tourists with children stroll through this soccer-mom haven during the day. Buy a gelato at one of the many cafes across the street and come here for a mid-afternoon break from reality.

→ *Right next to the Palacio Real.* $ *Free.* ⏰ *Open until dusk.*

La Latina and Lavapiés

BASILICA DE SAN FRANCISCO EL GRANDE

⊗ CATHEDRAL

C. de San Buenaventura, 1 ☎91 365 38 00

This Roman Catholic Church is one of the most distinctive structures in La Latina. The basilica was designed in a Neoclassical style in the second half of the 18th century and comes to life when lit up at night. The cathedral has three chapels, including the Chapel of San Bernardino de Siena, where Goya's magnificent painting of the chapel's namesake rests. Pay close attention to the picture and you will see that the figure on the right not looking up is Goya himself. Don't forget to check out the adjacent gardens outside that hold spectacular views of western Madrid.

✦ From ⓂLa Latina, walk straight west down Carrera S. Francisco. ⑤ Free. Guided tours €3. ⍟ Open Tu-F 11am-12:30pm and 4-6:30pm, Sa 11am-noon.

Huertas

REAL ACADEMIA DE BELLAS ARTES DE SAN FERNANDO

✦⊗❋ MUSEUM

C. de Alcalá, 13 ☎91 524 08 64 ▪rabasf.insde.es

The oldest permanent art institute in Madrid, the Real Academia de Bellas Artes is a short walk away from bustling Puerta del Sol. With a small collection, it can be comfortably visited in a couple of hours. If you need to blast through this museum, don't forget to check out the Goyas in room 20.

✦ From Puerta del Sol, walk east down C. de Alcalá. Real Academia de Bellas Artes de San Fernando will be on your left. ⑤ €5; groups of 15-25 €2.50; students, under 18, and over 65 free. ⍟ Open M 9am-2:30, Tu-F 9am-7pm, Sa-Su 9am-2:30pm.

Avenida del Arte

MUSEO NACIONAL REINA SOFÍA

✦⊗ ART MUSEUM

C. Santa Isabel, 52 ☎91 774 10 00 ▪www.museoreinasofia.es

This public collection of 20th-century art has burgeoned since Juan Carlos I declared the building a national museum in 1988 and named it after his wife. The building is a work of art in itself, with two futuristic-looking glass elevators ferrying visitors up and down the museum as they look north over the skyline. The museum's 10,000-piece collection of paintings, sculptures, installation pieces, and film is amazing by anyone's standards. The second and fourth floors are mazes of permanent exhibits charting the Spanish avant-garde and contemporary movements. If that's not for you, the second-floor galleries dedicated to **Juan Gris, Joan Miro,** and **Salvador Dalí** display Spain's vital contributions to the Surrealist movement. If you're pressed for time, make sure not to miss Pablo Picasso's ▪**Guernica,** the highlight of the Reina Sofía's permanent collection and the centerpiece of its knockout Gallery 206. Make sure to read about this paintings symbolic ties to the Spanish Civil War.

✦ ⓂAtocha. *i* €6, ages 17 and under and over 65 free Sa afternoon and Su. Temporary exhibits €3 ⑤ €6, €3 temporary exhibitions. ⍟ Open M 10am-9pm, W-Sa 10am-9pm, Su 10am-2:30pm.

MUSEO THYSSEN-BORNEMISZA

✦⊗ ART MUSEUM

Paseo del Prado, 8 ☎91 369 01 51 ▪www.museothyssen.org

Unlike the Prado and the Reina Sofía, the Thyssen-Bornemisza covers international art from many periods: exhibits range from 14th-century canvases to 20th-century sculptures, and its collection encompasses periods of art overlooked by the other two. The museum is housed in the 19th-century **Palacio de Villahermosa** and contains the collection of the late Baron Henrich Thyssen-Bornemisza. Today, the museum is the world's most extensive private showcase. Take advantage of the spread by checking out its **Baroque** collection that includes pieces by **Caravaggio, Riber,** and **Claude Lorraine.** Also, don't forget to explore the **Impressionist, Fauvist,** and early **avant-garde** pieces that paved the way to modern art as we know it today. To be honest, there's too many famous artists to namedrop—just come here to be wowed and won over by its gigantic collection.

🍴 *From the Prado, walk straight north up the Paseo Del Prado. Museum is at the corner of Carrera de San Jeronimo and Paseo Del Prado.* 💲 *€7, children under 12 free.* 🕐 *Open Tu-Su 10am-7pm.*

MUSEO NACIONAL DEL PRADO　　　　　　　　　🕊⊗ MUSEUM
C. Ruiz de Alarcón, 23　　　　　　　　☎91 330 28 00 🖳www.museodelprado.es

With its Goyas and El Grecos, Rembrandts, Raphaels, and Rubens, the Prado has enough alliterative artistic awesomeness to make the Louvre look not so special after all. Organized by country, the ground floor houses Spanish (12th to 16th century), French, Dutch, and Italian (17th-19th century) works. While Let's Go recommends that you spend a few hours here, if you're in a rush, be sure to catch the can't-miss works. **Velázquez's** masterpiece ⬛*Las Meninas,* considered one of the finest paintings in the world, captures a studio scene centered on the Infanta Margarita. Velásquez himself stares out from behind his easel in the left side of the painting. It may look like just another picture of wealthy Spaniards in big dresses, but this piece has been praised as the culmination of Velázquez's career—a meditation on reality, art, illusion, and the power of easel painting. That pouting dog in the corner looks a lot more profound now, doesn't it? **Goya's** ⬛*Majas*—two paintings with differing states of clothing side-by-side of a woman believed to be the Duchess of Alba—wows audiences with its intricate brushstrokes. Take a free museum map and get the English audio tour *(€3.50)* for background information on the museum's 1500+ displayed paintings. To get the most masterwork for your moola, try to make it during free entrance.

🍴 *Ⓜ Banco de España and Ⓜ Atocha. From Ⓜ Atocha, walk north up Paseo del Prado; the museum will be on your right just past the gardens.* ⓘ *Free entry Tu-Sa 6-8pm, Su 5-8pm. Consult website for up-to-date schedule.* 💲 *€8, students €4, under 18 and over 65 free.* 🕐 *Open Tu-Su 9am-8pm.*

REAL JARDÍN BOTÁNICO　　　　　　　　　⊗⊗⊗⊘ GARDEN
Plaza de Murillo, 2　　　　　　　　☎91 420 30 17 🖳www.rjb.csic.es/jardinbotanico/jardin

The perfect place to rest after a visit to the Prado, this small garden is full of well-kept flowers and exotic collections. Sit in the shade on one of the many benches of this oasis in the middle of Madrid's museum district as you ruminate on the countless pieces of art you just cranially ingested.

🍴 *Next door to the Prado.* ⓘ *.* 💲 *€2.50, students €1.25, groups €0.50.* 🕐 *Open daily Jan-Feb 10am-6pm; Mar 10am-7pm; Apr 10am-8pm; May-Aug 10am-9pm; Sept 10am-8pm; Oct 10am-7pm; Nov-Dec 10am-6pm.*

Chueca and Malasaña

CONVENTO DE LAS SALESAS REALES　　　　　　⊗ CATHEDRAL
C. Barbara de Braganza　　　　　　　　　　　☎91 319 48 11

This mostly empty church is a calm getaway from the hustle and bustle of Chueca. Next door to some of the district's classiest shopping, its beautiful monastery was designed by Francois Carlier and is worth a pit-stop and a photo. Go inside to see the dome, which features painted biblical scenes and the tombs of Fernando VI and Barbara de Braganza, constructed by Francesco Sabatini and Francisco Gutierrez.

🍴 *Ⓜ Colon. From Pl. Colon, go down Po. de Recoletos and take a right onto C. de Barbara de Braganza.* 💲 *Free.* 🕐 *Open M-F 9:30am-1pm and 5:30-8pm, Sa 9:30am-2pm and 5-9pm, Su 9:30am-2pm and 6-9pm. Closed to tourists during mass.*

MUSEO DE HISTORIA　　　　　　　　　　🕊⊗ MUSEUM
C. Fuencarral, 78　　　　　　　　☎91 588 86 72 🖳www.munimadrid.es/museodehistoria

This renovated 18th-century building built during the reign of Felipe V now holds a collection of sketches, models, paintings, drawings, and documents that showcase the history of Madrid. Saved from destruction in 1919 by the

madrid • sights

Spanish Society of Friends of Art, the museum is now considered one of Madrid's historical-artistic monuments. Come for a cultural break from all the shopping on C. Fuencarral. Closed for renovation until early 2010.

✿ ⓂTribunal. Walk straight north up C. Fuencarral. Ⓢ Free. ☼ Open Tu-Sa 10am-9pm, Su 11am-2:30pm.

Gran Vía

▨ PLAZA DE ESPAÑA   ⊗♿ PLAZA

On a sunny day the Plaza de España is filled with street performers, vendors, sunbathers, and Spanish couples showcasing some serious PDA. In the middle of the plaza, look for the statues of Don Quixote and Sancho Panza, and then head west to scope out the statue of celebrated wordsmith Cervantes.

✿ The western end of Gran Vía. Ⓢ Free.

Argüelles and Moncloa

▨ TEMPLO DE DEBOD   ⊗♿ TEMPLE, PARK

C. de Ferraz, 1   ☎91 366 74 15 ▣www.munimadrid.es/templodebod

On a nice day, this is one of the most beautiful spots in Madrid. In the '60s, when massive flooding threatened to destroy the ancient temple complex at Au Simbel, Egypt, a team of Spanish archaeologists helped to rescue these national treasures. In appreciation, the Egyptian government shipped the Templo de Debod to Madrid's Parque de la Montana, where you can now see the small archaeology exhibit housed inside. Outside of the temple is a series of original archways that are even more impressive at night, lit up and reflected in the adjacent pool. The park surrounding the temple teems with families, runners, tourists, and locals lounging in the afternoon sun. Go to the lookout point behind the temple for one of the most beautiful views of Madrid.

✿ ⓂPl. de Espana. Walk to the far side of Pl. de Espana, cross the street, walk a couple of blocks right, and it will be on the left. Ⓢ Free. ☼ Open Apr-Sept Tu-F 10am-2pm and 6-8pm, Sa-Su 10am-2pm; Oct-Mar Tu-F 9:45am-1:45pm and 4:15-6:15pm, Sa-Su 10am-2pm. Rose garden open daily 10am-8pm.

ARCO DE LA VICTORIA   ✦♿♿ ARCH

Near Parque Del Oeste

If you're getting off at the Moncloa stop, be sure to snap a picture by the Arco de la Victoria, a monument built in 1956 by order of General Franco to commemorate the rebel army's victory in the Spanish Civil War. Of course, judging by the monument, you'd think that Franco and his friends came to power stomping through the country Julius-Caesar-style, but that glorious horse and chariot at the top of the arco is unfortunately just a few centuries too anachronistic. Surrounded by traffic, it looks almost like Madrid's version of the Arc de Triomphe.

✿ ⓂMoncloa.

PARQUE DEL OESTE   ✦⊗♿ PARK

C. de Francisco y Jacinto Alcântara

A nice shaded place to come exercise during hot summer months, the Parque del Oeste is popular with families and tourists looking to take a nice stroll after a day of museum-hopping. Less crowded than the popular Retiro Park, Parque del Oeste is a lush break from the concrete jungle of western Madrid. If you're parched, plenty of tiny cafes line Paseo del Pinto Rosales near the park. However, exercise caution as nighttime approaches, as the park gets a lot less charming and a lot more alarming after sunset.

✿ ⓂMoncloa. 𝒊 Do not walk here after dark. Ⓢ Free. ☼ Open 24hr.

CASA DE CAMPO   ✦⊗♿ PARK

Avenida de Portugal

Madrid's biggest park, the sprawling Casa de Campo is a popular sight for locals and tourists alike. The park offers various exercise options, including long running and biking trails as well as kayak and rowboat rentals in its lake. For another type of heartrate booster, the amusement park **Parque de Atracciones** has roller coasters and more cotton candy than you could ever eat.*(Ⓜ️Batan or bus #33 or 65. From the metro station, turn right and walk up the paved street away from the lake. ☎914 63 29 00 🖥️www.parquedeatracciones.es 🕐 Open M-Sa 9am-7pm.)* To hang out with some new feathered friends, look no further than the park's **zoo and aquarium.** *(☎915 12 37 70 🖥️www.zoomadrid.com. 🕐 Open daily, but check website for hours as schedule changes.)*

❧ Ⓜ️*Lago, Batan, and Casa de Campo are all within the park.* ⓘ *Let's Go does not advise walking here after dark.* Ⓢ *Free.* 🕐 *Open 24hr.*

Outside the City Center

🏛️ EL PRADO
Paseo del Prado

🌿Ⓧ❄️ PALACE
☎91 376 15 00

Originally built in the 15th century as a hunting lodge for Enrique IV, El Prado was also the permanent residence of Franco, who remained there until his death in 1975. On display are Franco's bathroom, private prayer room, and bedroom cabinet where he kept Saint Teresa's silver-encrusted petrified arm, one of his most treasured possessions. The palace also holds a Velázquez painting and Ribera's *Techo de los Hombres Ilustres* (Ceiling of the Illustrious Men).

❧ Ⓜ️*Moncloa. Take bus #601 from the underground bus station adjacent to Moncloa.* Ⓢ*€4, students and over 65 €2.30.* 🕐 *Open Apr.-Sept M-Sa 10:30am-5:45pm, Su 9:30am-1:30pm; Oct-Mar. M-Sa 10:30am-4:45pm, Su 10am-1:30pm. Mandatory 45min. guided tour in Spanish; last tour leaves 45min. before closing.*

FOOD

El Centro

Food in El Centro tends to be on the pricey side, as the area is rampant with tourists. If you're sitting outside on the terrace, just grab a seat and the waiter will come to you. Many places will charge you for table bread, so don't touch it if you don't want to pinch pennies. Most restaurants in El Centro don't provide free water, either, but will instead bring you their most expensive bottled mineral water with a fine vintage year—so stick to the house wine or explicitly ask for beverage prices. If you go down a winding cobblestone street, you're bound to find a hole-in-the-wall restaurant with more reasonable prices. For those on an even tighter food budget, a nice alternative to eating out is to go to a local grocery store such as **Dia** or **Carrefour** or a small shop labeled *alimentaciones* to buy sandwich fixings and fruit for a bargain. You'll find even better bargains at the Plaza de San Miguel marketplace.

🏛️ EL ANCIANO REY DE LOS VINOS
C. de Bailén, 19

🌿Ⓧ🍸❄️ SPANISH ❸
☎91 559 53 32 🖥️www.elancianoreydelosvinos.es

Right across the street from the Catedral de la Almudena, this is the perfect place to relax after a tour of the cathedral or Palacio Real. Sit outside on the terrace and sip an afternoon drink *(€3.50)*. Try the *Tinto de Verano*, a refreshing wine-based drink similar to Sangria. El Anciano offers *canapés (€6.50)*, salads *(€10-15)*, a variety of tapas *(€6-13)*, and sandwiches *(€6)* that all can be topped off with dessert *(€5)*.

❧ *Walk across the C. de Bailén from the Catedral de la Almudena.* Ⓢ *Canapés €6.50. Tapas €6-13. Salads €10-15. Sandwiches €6.* 🕐 *Open daily 10am-midnight.*

CHOCOLATERÍA SAN GINÉS
Plaza de San Ginés, 5

🌿Ⓧ🍸❄️ CHOCOLATERÍA ❶
☎91 366 54 31

An absolute late-night must for clubbers and early risers, this chocolatería is famous for its classic chocolate *con churros (€4)*. After dancing off just as many calories, come here around 5 or 6am to cap your night off with a sweet treat.

madrid • food

🧭 *From Puerta Del Sol, walk down C. Arenal until you get to Joy nightclub. It will be tucked in the tiny Plaza de San Ginés.* $ *Chocolates from €4.* ⏰ *Open 24hr.*

CERVECERÍA LA PLAZA
💳🚭🍸❄ TAPAS [2]

Plaza de San Miguel, 3 ☎91 548 41 11

Locals and tourists come here to get relatively cheap tapas and entrees *(under €10)* to go with their *cerveza.* Hugely popular, Cervecería la Plaza has two locations, one in the Plaza de San Miguel and one in Plaza de Santa Ana. Both with packed outdoor terraces shaded by large umbrellas to protect against intense sun, they offer lively atmospheres with generous portions.

🧭 *From the Palacio Real, walk down C. Mayor toward Puerta del Sol. Plaza de San Miguel will be on your right.* $ *Beers €3. Entrees and tapas under €10.*

La Latina and Lavapiés

✔ MANO A MANO
💳🚭🍸❄ SPANISH [3]

C.Lavapiés, 16 ☎91 468 70 42

This small restaurant in Lavapiés cooks up authentic Spanish favorites in family-style portions. Bringing a family or a few friends who can seriously chow down? Go splitsies on one of their gigantic rice dishes packed with seafood and vegetables, or order solo and try one of their *raciones* like the Iberian ham *(€12).*

🧭 *ⓂLavapiés. Walk straight uphill up C. Lavapiés.* $ *Raciones €7-12. Rice dishes for 4 to 6 people €28.* ⏰ *Open daily 2-5pm and 9pm-1am.*

MARIMBA
💳🚭📶🍸⛱ CAFE, BAR [1]

C. de Lavapiés, 11

Marimba is one of the more modern cafes in the Lavapiés district, offering beverages accompanied by tapas during the day and cocktails at night. You might have to stand with your drink next to Marimba's sparse seating, but super attentive service makes up for the lack of space.

🧭 *ⓂLavapiés. Walk uphill on C. Lavapiés.* $ *Tapas €3.50. Coffee and tea €2. Cocktails €6.* ⏰ *Open daily 11am-2am.*

EL PALADAR
🚭🍸⛱ CAFE [1]

C. Argumosa, 5 ☎91 467 85 35

This tiny place only offers outdoor seating, but it's a local favorite and a nice place to sit and relax in Lavapiés. Get a small snack *(€3.50)* or a larger *racion (€6.50)* of one of their regional specialities. If you've never had it, be sure to try *horchata,* a sweet refreshing summertime milk-like drink made from tigernuts.

🧭 *ⓂLavapiés. Walk east down C. Argumosa.* $ *Tapas €2-5. Raciones €5-10.* ⏰ *Open daily 11am-midnight.*

Huertas

✔ DIBOCCA RESTAURANTE ITALIANO
💳🚭🍸❄ ITALIAN [2]

Paseo de los Olmos, 28 ☎91 517 22 19 💻www.dibocca.com

If you're sick of tapas and craving some Italian in the middle of Espagne, look no further than DiBocca, upscale environment without the pricetag. Try one of their regular or stuffed pastas *(€10),* salads *(€8),* meats and fish *(€11),* or desserts *(€4.65)* to get a taste even Snookie would enjoy.

🧭 *From Puerta del Sol walk straight south down Pasea de los Olmos (tiny street).* ℹ *English menus available.* $ *Entrees €5-12.*

✔ LA NEGRA TOMASA
💳🍸 CUBAN [2]

C. de Cádiz, 9 ☎91 523 58 30 💻www.lanegratomasa.es/

Come to this fun Cuban restaurant for big portions, big drinks, and a raucous good time. Waitresses in Cuban garb serve up traditional Cuban fare in a restaurant with walls lined floor to ceiling with memorabilia. Try one of the main dishes like the *Ropa Vieja Habanera* (€8-12). Order *para picar*, tiny appetizers to share *(€3-7)*, and while you're there be sure to get a cocktails *(€6-7)*.

🧭 From Puerta del Sol, walk south down C. de Espoz y Mlna, restaurant will be on your right. $ Entrees €8-12. ⏰ Day prices for drinks: 1:30-11pm.

TABERNA DE ANTONIO SANCHEZ — TAPAS [2]

Meson de paredes, 13 ☎34 915 397 826

Founded in 1830 by bullfighter Antonio Sanchez, this taberna has had a lot of time to perfect its delicious tapas and entrees. Get a variety of tapas *(€1-3)* to share as two *tapas calientes* are filling enough for dinner. If you can find this restaurant, the inside covered in dark-wooded walls and Spanish paintings feels like a step back in time. Make sure to try the *Mortados Calientes de Chizo* or the *Escalipines à la Madrilena* for a taste of the old world.

🧭 From [M]Tirso De Molina, walk past the Plaza de Tirso de Molina until you get to C. del Meson de Paredes. It will be on your left. $ Entrees €3-15.

CASA ALBERTO — TRADITIONAL [2]

C. de las Huertas, 18 ☎91 429 93 56 🖥www.casaalberto.es

Founded in 1827, Casa Alberto is one of the oldest taverns in Madrid. Come for a taste of some of the best tapas in the city, made from carefully selected ingredients and true to the recipes of past generations. Lancers and *banderilleros* used to come here to imbibe a "cup of courage" before entering the bullring. Feeling adventurous? Enter your own bullring of fear by trying tripe (stomach...yum), or pig's ear. If you'd rather stay in your comfort zone, go with customer favorites such as snails, lamb's knuckles, oxtail, veal meatballs, or Madrid-style Salt Cod.

🧭 From Plaza Del Angel, walk down C. de las Huertas towards the Prado. It will be on your right. $ Entrees €5-20 ⏰ Open daily noon-1:30am

O'PULPO MESON RESTAURANTE — TAPAS [2]

C. de los Cañizares, 8 ☎91 369 02 46 🖥www.opulpo.com

Right next door to Cat's Hostel, O'Pulpo serves up traditional local tapas with a one-big-family attitude. Try the Tortilla Tapa—a mixture of potatoes, eggs, and onion, with the *Tinto de Verrano*, a beverage made with wine and lemon Fanta.

🧭 From Plaza Santa Ana, walk south down C. Olivar and pass C.Magdalena. It will be on your right. $ €5-15. ⏰ Open daily 10am-4:30pm and 8:30pm-midnight.

LA SOBERINA — TAPAS [2]

C. Espoz y Mina ☎91 531 05 76 🖥www.lasoberbia.es/

For a traditional Spanish dish try the *Arroz Abanda* at La Soberina. Originally a way to use up leftovers from the week, *Arroz Abanda* is a gumbo-like seafood rice dish. From 1-5pm get the special: an appetizer and entree *(€9.50)*. *Tapas calientes (€4)* and drinks *(€1.90)* also served.

🧭 From Plaza de Santa Ana head down C. Espoz y Mina towards Puerta Del Sol. $ Entrees €4-12. ⏰ Open daily 8:45am-2am.

Gran Vía

RESTAURANTE LA ALHAMBRA DE SANTO DOMINGO — MEDITERRANEAN [2]

Jacometrezo, 15 ☎91 548 43 31

Come to La Alhambra de Santo Domingo to order cheap and fast Mediterranean food. Their menú of the day includes an appetizer, entree, bread, drink, and dessert *(€8)* and is a great deal for backpackers looking to fill up for cheap. For a smaller meal, explore their kebab plates *(€4)*, pizzas *(€3)*, or desserts *(€3.50)*.

🧭 [M]Callao. Walk east down Jacometrezo, restaurant will be on your left. $ Meals around €10.

[H]ARINA — SANDWICHES, DESSERTS, COFFEE [2]

Plaza de la Independencia, 10 ☎91 522 87 85 🖥www.harinamadrid.com

Go through the sliding glass doors of this chic bakery for a delicious dessert and drink or a small salad before visiting nearby Retiro Park.

➔ *Outside the entrance to Retiro park in the Plaza de la Independencia.* Ⓢ *Food €5-15.* ⏰ *Open M-Su 9am-9pm.*

MERCADO DE LA REINA 💳🚭🍸❄ TAPAS [3]

C. Gran Vía, 12 ☎91 521 31 98 💻www.mercadodelareina.es

The classy Mercado de la Reina is an upscale break from Gran Vía shopping. Business suits flock to this mercado's back tables during their lunch breaks, so plop down into one of the high stools in the front of the restaurant to taste *pinchos* made from organic ingredients that come paired with wine.

➔ *From* Ⓜ*Gran Vía metro stop walk straight east down Gran Vía, restaurant will be on your right.* Ⓢ *Entrees €10-20.* ⏰ *Open M-Th 9am-midnight, Sa-Su 10am-1am.*

Chueca

BAZAAR 💳🚭🍸❄ MEDITERRANEAN [2]

C. de la Libertad, 21 ☎91 523 39 05 💻www.restaurantbazaar.com

With immaculate white tablecloths, plush seats, and romantic candles, you'd expect this restaurant to be forebodingly expensive. Think again. Bazaar boasts cheap dishes *(€8-10)* in a ritzy atmosphere, but some portions are on the smaller side.

➔ Ⓜ*Chueca. Make a left on C. Augusto Figuroa, and a right on C. de la Libertad, 21.* Ⓢ *Entrees €8-10.* ⏰ *Open daily 1:15-4pm and 8:30-11:45pm.*

MAGASAND 💳🚭🍸📶❄ CAFE, SMOOTHIES [1]

Travesía de San Mateo, 16 ☎91 319 68 25 💻www.magasand.com

With an advertising slogan like, "incredible sandwiches, impossible magazines," Magasand is a cafe you need to experience to understand. Have one of their fresh sandwiches, salads, smoothies, or coffees made-to-order by the jovial staff, and then move upstairs to lounge on hip couches and colorful stools as you read one of their many alternative artsy magazines.

➔ Ⓜ*Chueca. Make a right on C. Augusto Figuroa, and another right on C. Hortaleza. Turn right onto Travesía de San Mateo (there's a sign on Hortaleza pointing you in the right direction).* Ⓢ *Sandwiches €5-8. Salads €4-7.* ⏰ *Open daily 9:30am-1:30pm and 4-9pm.*

STOP MADRID 💳🚭🍸❄ TAPAS [1]

C. de Hortaleza, 11 ☎91 521 8887 💻www.stopmadrid.es

Founded in 1929, this traditional Madrid tavern offers Iberian ham, Spanish cheeses, and 70 different kinds of wine. Marble walls, wine bottle decor, and wooden stools make this place feel like you've hot tub-time-machined your way back to the old country.

➔ Ⓜ*Gran Vía. From the Gran Vía stop, walk straight up C. de Hortaleza.* Ⓢ *Entrees €5-10* ⏰ *Open daily noon-2am.*

DIURNO 💳🚭🍸❄ CAFE, VIDEO RENTAL [1]

San Marcos, 37 ☎91 522 0009 💻www.diurno.com

Get your freshly prepared sandwiches, desserts, pastas, and more at this yuppie haven reminiscent of an iPod commercial. With a huge selections of DVDs for you to rent and buy, take your food to-go and catch up on the last season of *Modern Family.*

➔ Ⓜ*Chueca. Make a left onto C. Augusto Figuroa, and a right onto C. de la Libertad, 21. Diurno is across from Bazaar.* Ⓢ *Sandwiches €5-10.* ⏰ *Open daily 10am-midnight.*

EL TIGRE 💳🚭🍸❄☁ TAPAS [1]

C. de las Infantas, 30 ☎91 532 00 72

El Tigre is crowded, hectic, loud, and fun. Buy a round of drinks (try one of their big mojitos) and get free plates full of tapas to go with it. Enough to fill you up, the tapas here are deep fried and delicious, and even hardy eaters can fill up for under €5. Prepare to fight your way through the crowd to grab a ledge to perch your food and drink. Originally a local favorite, El Tigre was recently discovered by travelers who now make up a large part of their clientele.

➔ Ⓜ*Gran Vía. Walk north up C. de Hortaleza and make a right on C. de las Infantas. It will be on your right.* $ *Beer €1.50. Drinks with tapas €3-10.* ⏰ *Open daily 10am-2am.*

Malasaña

★ LA DOMINGA
🍴⊗🍸❄ SPANISH [3]

Espíritu Santa, 15 ☎915 244 809 🖥www.ladominga.com

Come to this upscale restaurant for fancy Spanish food even the pickiest of eaters can enjoy. With wood furnishings, a large bar, and dark red walls, this is the perfect place to try conservative Spanish fare for the first time. On weekdays, go for their *menú* of the day *(€10.90).*

➜ [M]Tribunal. Go west on C. de San Vincente Ferrer, make a left on C. del Barco, and make a right on C. del Espíritu Santo. $ *Entrees €10-15.* ⏰ *Open daily 1pm-4:30pm and 8:30pm-noon.*

CRÊPERIE LA RUE
🍴⊗🍸❄ CRÊPERIE [2]

C. Espíritu Santo, 18

This tiny crêperie calls itself a "un pedacito de Francia en el centro de Madrid," or a little bit of France in the center of Madrid. We agree. French music, paintings of Parisian landmarks, and the delicious smell of savory and sweet crêpes make this place seem like the set from *Amélie* and the perfect stop for a mid-afternoon snack. Order your crêpe to go as there is limited seating.

➜ [M]Tribunal. Go west on C. de San Vincente Ferrer, make a left onto C. del Barco, and make a right onto C. del Espíritu Santo. $ *Crêpes €4-8.* ⏰ *Open daily 11:30am-midnight.*

OLOKUN
🍴⊗🍸❄ CUBAN [3]

C. Fuencarral, 105 ☎914 45 69 16

If you'd like to taste classic Cuban food, look no further than Olokun. Get a tropical drink *(€5-7)* to go along with the beach scenes on the walls. Try Cuban classics like *tostones* *(€6)* or *Ropa Vieja*, *(shredded beef served over rice; €10).* For a little taste of everything, go for the menú *(€11.90).* If you get bored waiting for your meal, you can always go play with the foosball table in the basement.

➜ [M] Tribunal. From the Tribunal metro stop walk straight north up C. Fuencarral. Restaurant will be on your left $ *Entrees €10-15.* ⏰ *Open daily noon-5pm and 9pm-2am.*

Argüelles and Moncloa

★ LA TABERNA DE LIERIA
🍴⊗🍸❄ SPANISH [4]

C. del Duque de Liria, 9 ☎915 414 519 🖥www.latabernadeliria.com

This offbeat restaurant serves up classy Basque food in interesting flavor combinations in an atmosphere that seems like your distant relative's living room. To get a taste of everything, try their preset menu combinations made for two or more people. Wine and cheese tastings as well as lessons in how to cook duck *foie gras* are offered periodically, so consult their website for a schedule of these tasty exhibitions.

➜ [M]Ventura Rodriguez. Walk forward, take the left fork in the road (C. San Bernardino), and walk straight forward. $ *Entrees €15-20.* ⏰ *Open daily 10am-2am.*

EL JARDÍN SECRETO
🍴⊗🍸❄ CAFE [1]

C. de Conde Duque, 2 ☎91 541 80 23

Tucked away in a tiny street close to C. de la Princesa, El Jardín Secreto is Arguelles's best-kept secret. Walk into this eclectic cafe filled with beaded window coverings, wooden ceiling canopies, and crystal-ball table lights to enjoy one of their dozens of coffees, hot chocolates, and snacks. For a real taste of the varied treats Secreto has to offer, try the Chocolate El Jardín served with chocolate Teddy Grahams and dark chocolate at the bottom of your cup *(€6)* or the George Clooney cocktail with *horchata*, crème de cocoa, and cointreau *(€7.25).*

➜ [M]Ventura Rodriguez. Walk straight, take the left fork in the road (C. San Bernardino) and walk forward. $ *Coffee and tea €3-6. Cocktails €7.25. Desserts €4.20.* ⏰ *Open M-Th 6:30pm-1:30am, F-Sa 6:30pm-2:30am, Su 6:30pm-1:30am.*

KURTO AL PLATO 💳🚭🍸❄ SPANISH [5]

Serrano Jover, 1 ☎917 585 946 💻www.kultoalplato.com

Described as Basque haute cuisine in miniature, Kurto al Plato is a great place to try designer tapas in a swanky atmosphere. Located right next to the El Corte Ingles department store, Kurto al Plato is your perfect stop for a post-shopping dinner, but make sure your wallet isn't wiped before you order. High black chairs, funky plates, and a colorful chalk drink menu all add to the upscale but slightly offbeat decor.

➜ [M]Argüelles. Walk straight south down C. de la Princesa. $ Meals €12-20. ⏰ Open M-Th 8:30-11:30pm, F-Sa noon-1am, Su 8:30-11:30pm.

NIGHTLIFE

El Centro and Gran Vía

👍 OHM/BASH LINE 💳🚭🍸❄ CLUB

Plaza de Callao, 4 ☎91 532 01 32 💻www.pacha-madrid.com

Known as Bash Line on weekdays and Sundays and Ohm on Fridays and Saturdays, this lively club has drag queens out front and DJs who keep the beats going until the sun comes up. Organized themed parties are regular features.

➜ [M]Tribunal. $ Cover M-F €10-15; Sa €10-14; Su €10-15. ⏰ Open W-Su midnight-6am.

👍 PALACIO GAVIRIA 🚭🍸❄ CLUB

C. del Arenal, 9 ☎915 266 069 💻www.palaciogaviria.com

Built in 1850 and inspired by the Italian Renaissance, the Palacio Gaviria is a beautiful palace turned nightlife hotspot. Make your royal entrance by heading down the grand marble staircase onto the dance floor powered by techno beats and electric dance moves. Be on the lookout for promoters of Palacio Gaviria in Puerta del Sol, as they will often have vouchers for free entry or drinks.

➜ From Puerta del Sol walk straight down C. del Arenal. $ Cover M-Th €10, F-Sa €15, Su €10. ⏰ Opens at 11pm.

JOY ESLAVA 🍸❄ CLUB

Arenal, 11 ☎91 366 37 33 💻www.joy-eslava.com

An old standby, this converted theater has stayed strong amid Madrid's rapidly changing nightlife scene. Number one among study-abroad students and travelers, this club plays an eclectic mix of music and features scantily clad models (of both sexes) dancing on the theater stage. Balloons and confetti periodically fall from the ceiling New-Year's-Eve-style.

$ Cover M-W €12; Th €15; F-Su €18. ⏰ Open M-Th 11:30pm-5:30am, F-Sa 11:30pm-6am, Su 11:30pm-5:30am.

EL CHAMPANDEZ 💳🚭🍸❄ BAR

C. de Fernando, 77 ☎91 54 29 68 💻www.chapandaz.com

With manmade stalactites hanging from the ceiling, this unique bar is designed to look like a cave (complete with a specialty drink that bartenders drip from the ceiling). Although it's pretty quiet earlier in the evening, it starts getting packed with pre-clubbers fast.

➜ From [M]Moncloa, get to the intersection of C. de Fernando and C. de la Princesa and walk straight east down Fernando. $ Drinks €10. ⏰ Open daily 10pm-3am.

La Latina and Lavapiés

👍 SHOKO 💳🚭🍸 DISCOTECA

C. de Toledo, 86 ☎913 541 691 💻www.shokomadrid.com

With massive "bamboo" shoots that reach to the ceiling, a huge stage featuring internationally acclaimed acts, and a swanky VIP section *Let's Go* wishes it could live in, Shoko is an Oriental-inspired *discoteca* that follows the rules of Feng Shui and breaks any rules against a good time.

➜ [M]La Latina. Head straight south down C. de Toledo. $ Cover €10-15. ⏰ Open daily 11:30pm-late.

CASA LUCAS BAR

Cava Baja, 30 ☎91 365 08 04 www.casalucas.es

The inviting orange walls, paintings, and corked wine bottles create a friendly vibe, and once you've opened that wine bottle, you'll never want to leave this mellow, comfortable *casa.* Casa Lucas is a comfortable place to grab a glass of wine. Calmer than some of La Latina's rowdy options, Casa Lucas also has tapas and *raciones*—just pay attention to the prices, as some expensive *raciones* can turn into a brutal bill.

[M]La Latina. Walk west down Plaza de la Cebada. Make a right onto C. de Humilladero and continue right on Cava Baja. $ Raciones €5-20. Open daily 8:30pm-midnight.

LA PEREJILA TAPAS, BAR

C. Cava Baja, 25 ☎91 364 28 55

This place immediately stands out because of the live parakeets out front. The tropical theme continues inside with green walls, fake shrubbery, and quirky knick-knacks that make this feel like a themed restaurant at an amusement park. Come to see the eclectic decor, stay for a taste of their homemade tapas, and spend the night for *cerveza* and sangria.

[M]La Latina. Walk west down Plaza de la Cebada. Make a right onto C. de Humilladero, and continue right on Cava Baja. $ Cocktails €5-10. Open daily 1-4pm and 8:15pm-12:30am.

Huertas

KAPITAL CLUB

Atocha, 125 ☎91 420 29 06

If you only have one night in Madrid, be sure to make it to Kapital, one of the biggest clubs in Spain (if not the world). With seven different floors of music and a huge variety of drinks to encounter, this sprawling discoteca has something for every party animal—even you, Mom. Don't come too early; the place starts going strong around 2am.

2min. walk up Atocha street from [M]Atocha. $ Cover €15; includes 1 free drink. Drinks €10-15. Open Th-Sun 11:30pm-5:30am.

SWEET CLUB

C. del Doctor Cortezo, 1 ☎918 694 038

Suspended cages, a disco-ball dance floor, and men and women in daring apparel are staples of this hot nightclub. Whips may be confiscated upon entrance.

From [M]Anton Martin, walk uphill on Atocha and make a left on C. del Doctor Cortezo. $ Cover €10-14 cover; includes one drink Open F-Sa 11pm-daybreak.

DUBLINERS BAR

C. Espoz y Mina, 7 ☎34 915 227 509

Come to this Irish bar for a bucket of beers *(€15)*, a huge screen for sporting events, and a good ol' time. Filled with travelers from all over the world, Dubliners has a fun, international vibe and gets packed and crazy during major sports games. Ever seen grown men from around the world attempt their own drunken rendition of "We are the Champions"? You can even go in for the Dubliners' breakfast *(€5.70).*

From Puerta del Sol walk straight south down C. Espoz y Mina. Bar will be on your left. $ Drinks €5-10. Open M-Th 11am-3am, F-Sa until 11am-3:30am, Su 11am-3am.

VINOTECA BARBECHERA BAR, RESTAURANT

C. del Principe, 27 ☎91 420 04 78 www.vinoteca-barbechera.com/

With tables and chairs made out of beer barrels, Vinoteca Barchechera is a fun place to grab a reasonably priced drink while still enjoying the bustle of Plaza Santa Ana. Part of a chain of wine bars, Vinoteca Barbechera also serves a good range of tapas, including rolls stuffed with chorizo, ham or anchovies, smoked tuna and trout, and a range of desserts.

Plaza Santa Ana. $ Drinks €5-15. Open daily 10am-midnight daily.

VIVA MADRID 🍸 BAR

C. de Manuel Fernández y González, 7 ☎91 429 36 40

Students, travelers, artists, and artists who sometimes travel as students come to party in this crowded and noisy bar, decorated in turn-of-the-century decor. It is rumored that during the 1950s, Ava Gardner and the bullfighter Manolete got handsy here—watch out for some perverted Picasso looking to buy you a drink.

➜ *From [M]Sol, walk towards the museum district on Carrera de San Jeronmino; make a right onto C. de Manuel Fernandez y Gonzalez.* $ *Beer €4. Other drinks €6.* ⏰ *Open F noon-1am, Sa noon-2am.*

Chueca

👍 **KIYO** 💳🚭🍸❄ BAR

C. de Barbieri, 15 ☎91 522 01 82

This lime green bar stands out even in the eclectic Chueca district. Come in for their signature kiwi cocktail drink made with fresh crushed kiwi, vodka, and sake *(€7)* served by bartenders passionate about this newly opened spot—just don't be surprised when pop like Lady Gaga is blasting on replay.

➜ *[M]Chueca. Walk straight south down C. Barbieri towards Gran Vía. Discoteca will be on your right* $ *Cocktails €5-9.* ⏰ *Open daily 9pm-3am*

SHORT BUS 💳🚭🍸❄ BAR

C. Pelayo, 45

The motto of this funky bar is "open your mind and everything else," and we're sure they mean just about everything. With questionable cartoons on the walls and bright colors everywhere, this is a haven for the weird and wonderful.

➜ *[M]Chueca. Walk straight north up C. Pelayo; bar will be on your left.* $ *Cocktails €5-10.* ⏰ *Open daily 11am-2pm and 9pm-3am.*

STUDIO 54 💳🚭🍸❄ DISCOTECA

C. Barbieri, 7 ☎34 615 12 68 07 💻www.studio54madrid.com

Steps away from the Chueca metro station, this packed discoteca has enough beautiful people, booze, and beats to do the original Studio 54 proud. Filled with a mostly gay clientele dressed to the nines, this place is fun for anybody with an open mind. Women even get in for free sometimes, depending on the time and night.

➜ *[M]Chueca. Walk straight south down C. Barbieri towards Gran Vía. Discoteca will be on your right.* $ *Cover €10.* ⏰ *Open Th-Sa 11:30pm-3:30am.*

Malasaña

👍 **LA VÍA LÁCTEA** 💳🚭🍸❄ DISCOTECA

Velarde, 18 ☎91 446 75 81

This discoteca dates back to the beginning of the *movida* era and has the bric-a-brac to prove it. It's covered floor to ceiling with pop music memorabilia like album covers, concert posters, photographs, and more. Jams from the'50s through the '80s prove to be a popular mix and continue to delight young, international ravers more than 30 years after the club's inception.

➜ *[M]Tribunal. Walk north up C. Fuencarral and make a left onto Velarde.* $ *Cover €8-12.* ⏰ *Open daily 7:30pm-3:30am.*

CLUB NASTI 💳🚭🍸 DISCOTECA

San Vicente Ferrer, 33 💻www.nasti.es

Come to Club Nasti on Saturday nights for a hipster heaven of synthesized pop, electro beats, and punk jams. For a lighter touch try Friday nights, when house DJs spin indie rock like The Strokes, The Artic Monkeys, and The Ramones. Small dance floor gets packed as the night progresses, and you might end up wanting to shimmy out of your sweaty plaid shirt to dance only in your Ray Bans. Just remember: what happens at Nasti stays at Nasti.

♯ ⓜ*Tribunal. Walk south down C. de Fuencarral and make a right onto San Vicente Ferrer.* Ⓢ
Drinks €8-12. ⌚ *Open Th 2-5am, F 1-6am, Sa 2-6am.*

Argüelles and Moncloa

MI BOHIO
C. Luisa Fernanda, 9

♥⊗⊗♈❀ BAR, CUBAN
☎915 41 58 91

A small bar and Cuban restaurant tucked away near C. de la Princesa, Mi Bohio looks like the place in this neighborhood where everybody knows the locals' names. Since nightlife is slim in this area, head to this watering hole for some drinks and a game on its large TV.

♯ ⓜ*Ventura Rodriguez. Walk north up C. de la Princesa and make a left onto C. Luisa Fernanda.* Ⓢ *Beer €1.50. Cocktails €7.50.* ⌚ *Open daily 11am-1am.*

ARTS AND CULTURE

With some of the best art museums, public festivals, and performing arts groups in the world, Madrid's arts and culture scene is thriving. From street performers in Retiro Park to Broadway musicals, you can find anything you're looking for in this metropolis. Come for traditional entertainment such as **classic flamenco,** or push the envelope at one of Madrid's contemporary art, music, or theater venues.

la corrida de toros

Bullfighting has an ancient pedigree: it stems from the Roman tradition of making things fight other things for fun. Back in the day, there were man versus man fights, tiger versus man fights, tiger versus bull fights, and any number of other permutations. While a tiger versus man fight in this day and age would likely cause a small riot, for some reason bullfights are still quite popular. Bullfighting has had its detractors throughout the ages: Pope Pius X declared bullfighting forbidden, but not for the reason you might think. No, the Pope was worried about the immortal souls of the matadors who were voluntarily risking their lives. Later in Spain's history, Dictator Francisco Franco deemed bullfighting one of the true Spanish sports and greatly fostered its growth. Most people believed that Franco's support would be the death knell of the bullfighting following after the end of his rule: however, for some reason it continued on, bloody as ever. Today, the president of Spain, Jose Luis Rodriguez Zapatero, has banned children younger than 14 from even viewing the bullfights, and banned its broadcasts on public television. Since the bull is traditionally killed within the ring in Spain, this seems a valid opposition.

If you're really squeamish about this kind of thing, you could go to Portugal, where the bulls are never killed in the arena—they're moved off-site first. If you're just kind of squeamish, we would suggest leaving before the matador is awarded his trophy of an ear, a hoof, or perhaps a tail—the skill of the matador is positively correlated with the number of body parts awarded. On a related note, bull tail is a delicacy in Spain, said to be of a consistency resembling gelatin.

madrid • arts and culture

Corridas de Toros *Bullfights*

Whether you see it as animal torture or as national sport, the spectacle of *la corrida*, or bullfighting, is a cherished Spanish tradition. Although it has its origins in earlier Roman and Moorish practices, today it's considered Spain's sport, and some of the top *toreros*, or bullfighters, are true celebrities in Spain. The bullfight has three stages. First, the *picadores*, lancers on horseback, pierce the bull's neck muscles.

Then, assistants thrust decorated darts called *banderillas* into the bull's back to slightly injure and tire it. Finally, the *matador* kills his large opposition with a sword in between the bull's shoulder blades, instantly causing its demise. The best place to see bullfighting in Madrid is at the country's biggest arena, **Plaza de las Ventas,** where you can buy tickets in *sol* or *sombra* (sun or shade) sections. Get your tickets at the arena the Friday and Saturday leading up to the bullfight. (*C. Alcalá 237* ☎*913 56 22 00* ▉*www.las-ventas.com* ✿ ⓂVentas ☒ *Ticket office open 10am-2pm and 5-8pm.*) You'll pay more to sit out of the sun, but either way you'll have a good view of the feverish crowds who cheer on the matador and wave white handkerchiefs called *pañuelos* after a particularly good fight. Bullfights are held on Sundays and holidays throughout most of the year. During the **Fiesta de San Isidro** in May, fights are held almost every day, and the top bullfighters come face to face with the fiercest bulls.

Flamenco

▨ CARDAMOMO ♠⊗♈☀ PUERTA DEL SOL

C. de Echegaray, 15 ☎91 369 07 57 ▉www.cardamomo.es

For classic flamenco in the middle of a nightlife hub, check out Cardamomo. Offering nightly shows at 10:30pm, Cardamomo is a great place to start an evening of barhopping on C. de Echegaray. Check online for show times, performers, and special events. ✿ ⓂSol. Walk east toward Plaza de las Cortes, and make a right on C. de Echegaray. ⓈTickets €10-15. Check with your hostel for discounts. ☒ Nightly shows 10:30pm.

LAS TABLAS ♠⊗♈☀ GRAN VÍA

Plaza de España, 9 ☎91 542 05 20 ▉www.lastablasmadrid.com

Las Tablas offers authentic flamenco at lower prices than some of the other nearby establishments. Located at the corner of C. Bailen and Cuesta San Vicente, it's the perfect place to stop and experience some Spanish culture after a day shopping along Gran Vía. ✿ ⓂPl. de España. Head to the far end of the plaza. Ⓢ Tickets €24; includes 1 drink. ☒ Shows M-Th 10:30pm, F-Sa at 8pm and 10pm, Su 10:30pm.

Fútbol

Fútbol games are a beloved tradition throughout Spain but especially in Madrid. Fans of **Real Madrid** line the streets and pack into bars to watch the match. If the team wins, celebrations continue until early the next morning. For the best fútbol experience, head to Estadio Santiago Bernabeu. Tickets to games in this massive stadium will be steep *(€50-100)* unless you can find discounts. Tickets for **Atlético** and **Getafe,** two other local teams, are a bit cheaper.

▨ ESTADIO SANTIAGO BERNABEU ♠⊗♈⚶ FÚTBOL STADIUM

Av. Cochina Espina, 1 ☎91 464 22 34 ▉www.santiagobernabeu.com, www.realmadrid.com

Site of the 2010 European Final Cup, Estadio Santiago Bernabeu is also home to the Real Madrid fútbol team, named the greatest club of the 20th century by FIFA. Come watch a match and feel the tumultuous energy of the crowd as it cheers on its beloved home team. Come early, as navigating your way through this humongous stadium is almost impossible. During the summer, tours of this massive stadium are available. ✿ ⓂSantiago Bernabeu. Stadium is across the street from the metro station. Ⓢ Tours €15, under 14 €10. ☒ Check online for tour times and dates.

Festivals

FIESTAS DE SAN ISIDRO SALAMANCA

C. de Alcalá, 237 ▉www.esmadrid.com/sanisidro

From mid-May to early June there are bullfights almost every day at **Plaza de las Ventas,** where some of the best bullfighters in Spain come to battle some of the country's fiercest bulls. ☒ May 15-early June.

MADRID CARNIVAL

The week before Lent, Madrid celebrates with a Mardi Gras-esque spectacle of parades, costume parties, and extravagant masks. There is also a tradition called "The Burial of the Sardine," in which participants decked out in black cloaks and hats walk through the streets with a coffin containing an effigy of a dead sardine. Don't understand? Neither do we, but it's seriously awesome.

🗓 *Feb 18-25, 2011.*

FIESTAS DE SAN LORENZO

🖳 www.fiestasdesanlorenzo.com

August is the traditional month for festivals in Madrid. During the Fiestas de San Lorenzo in mid-August, *madrileños* celebrate with dancing in the streets, processions, and outdoor concerts. Check online for specific activities and times.

🗓 *Varies.*

NOCHEVIEJA

PUERTA DEL SOL

To ring in the new year, hundreds of *madrileños* gather at Madrid's version of Times Square, Puerta del Sol, to watch the ball drop from the clock tower. Instead of counting down, the clock chimes 12 times to represent good fortune for the 12 upcoming months of the year. According to tradition, you're supposed to eat a grape at every toll and drink at midnight.

ᛦ Ⓜ*Sol.* 🗓 *Dec 31.*

El Rastro

If you're in town on a Sunday, don't miss El Rastro, the biggest and most frantic flea market in Madrid. Beginning at **Pl. Cascorro** off **C. Toledo** and ending at the bottom of **C. Ribera de Cortidores,** rows of vendors in makeshift stalls set up outside permanent shops to pawn off their goods. From modern art and handmade trinkets to international clothing and knock-off jewelry and fragrance, *Let's Go* imagines you can pretty much buy anything your heart desires at this Spanish bazaar. Locals and tourists swarm this market, so come in the early hours to beat the heat and avoid the crowds from 9am-3pm. Buyers beware: this market is notorious for **pickpockets.** Stay alert, don't bring anything flashy, and guard your valuables. Always keep your hand on your bag while walking. After haggling for that used *paella* recipe book, drift to the **Plaza Mayor** for lunch and more shopping or the **Plaza de Tirso de Molina** for cheerful flower stands and fountains.

ESSENTIALS

Practicalities

- **TOURIST OFFICES:** Start off at the **Madrid Tourism Centre** in Plaza Mayor (☎91 588 16 36 🖳*www.esmadrid.com),* where you can get city and transit maps as well as suggestions for activities, food, and accommodations. English and French are spoken at most tourist offices located throughout the city and can be incredibly helpful in planning your day. Additional tourist offices and stands are all over the city, labeled by large orange stands with exclamation marks.

- **TOURS:** Different themed tours leave regularly from the Madrid Tourism Centre. For dates, times, and more information visit 🖳www.esmadrid.com. Also, many youth hostels host tapas tours, pub crawls, and walking tours for reasonable prices and are great for meeting people and finding awesome food in the process. Check out www.toursnonstop.com for tours (Ⓢ*€10 tapas and pub tours).* Run by historian and writer Stephen Drake-Jones, the **Wellington Society** offers different themed tours of Madrid and day excursions to places like Toledo and Segovia (☎609 143 203 🖳*www.wellsoc.org).* Another option is **Madrid Vision** (☎91 779 18 88 🖳*www. madridvision.es),* which runs the double-decker red buses that you see throughout the city. You can choose between the *historicó* and *moderno* routes, each making 15-20 stops throughout the city (Ⓢ €17; certain discounts available online).

madrid · essentials

- **CURRENCY EXCHANGE:** The easiest place to change your money is the airport. You can also change your money in stations in both Puerta Del Sol and Gran Vía (see booths that say "change"), but try to use these as a last resort, as rates are bad and commission charges are high. Most hostals and hotels will also be able to change your money, with rates varying by location.

- **LUGGAGE STORAGE:** Store your luggage at the **Aeropuerto Internacional de Barajas** (☎91 393 68 05 Ⓢ 1-day €3.70; 2-15 days €4.78 per day. Open 24hr.) or at the **bus station** (Ⓢ €1.40 per bag per day; open M-F 6:30am-10:30pm, Sa 6:30am-3pm).

- **POST OFFICES:** Buy stamps (*sellos*) from a post office or tobacco stand (yellow/brown sign). Madrid's **central post office** is at Plaza de Cibeles (☎91 523 06 94; 902 19 71 97 ☼ Open M-F 8:30am-9:30pm.) Post boxes are usually yellow with one slot for "Madrid" and another for everywhere else.

- **POSTAL CODE:** 28008.

Emergency!

- **EMERGENCY NUMBERS:** In case of a **medical emergency**, dial ☎061 or ☎112. For non-emergency medical concerns, go to **Unidad Medica Angloamericana,** which has English speaking personnel on duty by appointment. (*C. del Conde de Aranda, 1, 1st fl.* ☎914 35 18 23 ☼ Open M-F 9am-8pm, Sa 10am-1pm.)

- **POLICE: Servicio de Atención al Turista Extrarijero** (SATE) are police who deal exclusively with tourists and help with contacting embassies, reporting crimes, and canceling credit cards. (*C. Legantos, 19* ☎915 48 85 27; 902 102 112 ☼ Open daily 9am-midnight.)

Getting There

By Plane

All flights come in through the **Aeropuerto Internacional de Barajas** (☎902 404 704 🖳www.aena.es). The **Barajas** metro stop connects the airport to the rest of Madrid. (Ⓢ €2.) The **Bus-Aeropeurto 200** leaves from the national terminal T2 and runs to the city center through the **Avenida de America** metro station (☎902 50 78 50 ☼ Every 15min. 5:20am-11:30pm.) **Taxis** are readily available outside of the airport, and it takes about 30min. and €35 to get to the city center. For more information on ground transport, check out 🖳**www.metromadrid.es.**

By Train

Trains (☎90 224 02 02 🖳www.refe.es) from northern Europe, France, and **Barcelona** (including the high-speed AVE train) arrive on the north side of the city at Chamartin. Trains to and from the south of Spain and Portugal use **Atocha.** Buy tickets at the station or online. There is a **RENFE** information office located in the main terminal. (☎902 24 02 02 ☼ Open daily 7am-7pm.)

By Bus

AVE trains offer high-speed service to southern Spain, including **Barcelona** and **Sevilla.** (*Estacion Chamartin, C. Agustin de Foxa* ☎913 00 69 69; 91 506 63 29.) Be sure to keep your ticket, or you won't be able to pass the turnstiles. Call **RENFE** for both international destinations and domestic travel. (☎90 224 34 02 for international destinations; 902 24 02 02 for domestic.) Ticket windows open daily 6:30am-9pm; buy tickets at vending machines outside of these hours. Check online for prices, as plane tickets may be cheaper depending on season. If you prefer four wheels, any private bus company runs through Madrid, and most pass through **Estación Sur de Autobuses** (*C. Mendez Alvaro* ☎91 468 42 00 🖳www.estacionautobusesmadrid.com. *i* Info booth open daily 6:30am-1am.) National destinations include **Algeciras, Alicante, Oviedo,** and **Toledo,** among others. Inquire at the station, online, or by phone for specific information on routes and schedules.

spain

Getting Around

By Metro

The Madrid metro system is by far the easiest, cheapest way to get you almost anywhere you need to go in the city. Service begins at 6am (7am on Sunday) and ends around 1:30am. Try to avoid rush hours at 8-10am, 1-2pm, and 4-6pm. The fare is **€1** for a one way trip. If you're making multiple trips, you can save by purchasing a combined **10-in-one metrobus ticket** for €7. Be sure to grab a **free metro map** (available at any ticket booth or tourist office). **Abonos mensuales,** or monthly passes, grant unlimited travel within the city proper for €46, while **abonos turisticos** (tourist passes) come in various lengths (1, 2, 3, 4, or 7 days) and sell for €5-24 at the metro stations or online. For metro information go to 💻**www.metromadrid.es**.

By Bus

Buses cover areas that are inaccessible by metro and are a great way to see the city. Try the nifty handout "Visiting the Downtown on Public Transport" to find routes and stops. *(💲 Free at any tourist office or downloadable at 💻www.madrid.org.)* Tickets for the bus and metro are interchangeable. From midnight-6am, the *Búho* (owl), or night bus, travels from Pl. de Cibeles and other marked routes along the outskirts of the city *(M-Th every 30min. midnight-3am, every 1hr. 3-6am; F-Sa every 20min; Su every 30 min. midnight-3am.)* These buses, marked on the essential **Red de Autobuses Nocturnos** *(available at any tourist office or from 💻* run along 26 lines covering regular daytime routes. For info, call **Empresa Municipal de Transportes** *(☎902 50 78 50 💻www.emtmadrid.es).* **Estacion Sur** *(C. Mendez Alvaro ☎91 468 42 00)* covers mainly southern and southeastern destinations out of Madrid such as **Granada, Sevilla, Málaga,** and **Valencia.** Go to 💻**avanzabus.com** for timetables and routes.

By Moped and Bike

You can hire a bike from **Karacol Sport** for €18 per day *(C. Tortosa 8 ☎91 539 9733 ℹ Cash deposit of €50 and photocopy of your passport required 💻www.karacol.com ⏰ Open M-W 10:30am-3pm and 5-8pm, Th 10:30am-3pm and 5-9:30pm, F-Su 10:30am 3pm and 5-8pm.)* Biking in the city is ill-advised, but Casa de Campo and Dehesa de la Villa both have easily navigable bike trails. **Motocicletas Antonio Castro** rents mopeds from €23-95 per day including unlimited mileage and insurance , but you'll need your own lock and helmet—you just need to be 25 years old and have a driver's license for motorcycles *(C. Clara del Rey, 17 ☎914 1300 47 💻www.blafermotos.com ⏰ Open M-F 8am-6pm, Sa 10am-1:30pm.)*

barcelona ☎93

ORIENTATION

Barri Gòtic and Las Ramblas

If there is one thing to know about Barri Gòtic, it's this: you will get lost. Knowing this, the best way to properly orient yourself to the neighborhood is to spend an entire day learning your way around. **Las Ramblas** provides the western boundary of the neighborhood, stretching from the waterfront north to Plaça Catalonia. **Vía Laietana** cuts through the city nearly parallel to Las Ramblas, running directly in front of the Catedral, through **Plaça de l'Àngel**, and marks the eastern border of the Barri. The primary east-west artery, **Carrer de Ferran**, runs perpendicular to Las Ramblas and Via Laeitana, separating the Barri Gòtic into the **lower** (from C. de Ferran to the water) and **upper portions** (C. de Ferran to Carrer de Fontanella). Street names are located on plaques located on the upper stories of buildings, facing the named street, along with names of the squares. For these areas, the **L3 and L4 lines** of the metro will be most helpful, with Ⓜ**Drassanes**, Ⓜ**Liceu**, and Ⓜ**Catalonia** dropping along Las Ramblas (L4), and Ⓜ**Jaume I** located in the heart of the Barri Gòtic, at the intersection of **C. Ferran** and **Via Laietana**.

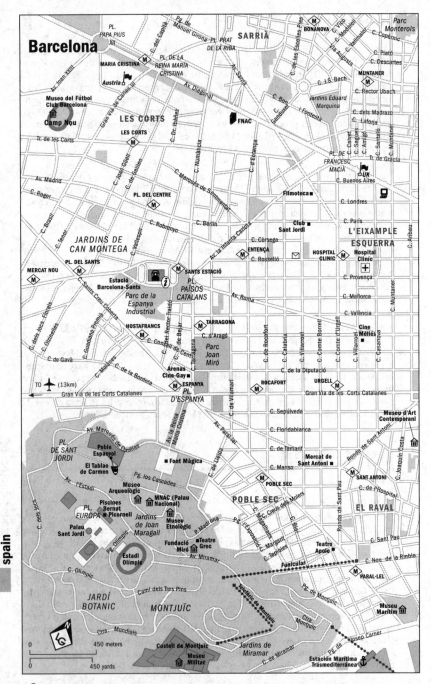

Barcelona

spain

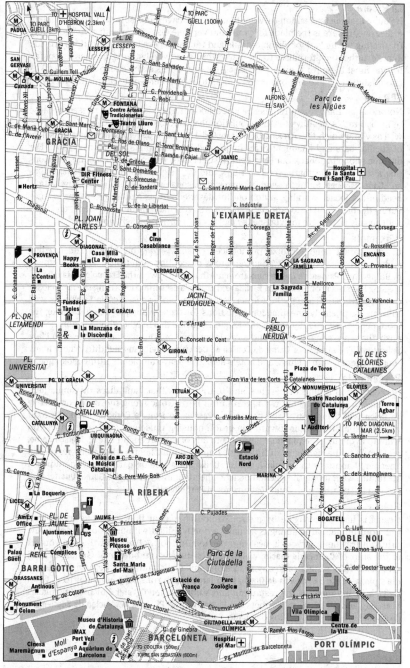

La Ribera

If you're looking for fashion-forward boutiques or cavernous *botegas* housed in medieval stone, Ribera is the place for you. For everyone else, the area may be incredibly frustrating for its lack of cheap options and tourist accessibility, but it does provide a more authentic alternative to the Barri Gòtic's crowded streets. For those looking for the most bang for their buck, **Passeig del Born** offers some cheap eats, as well as enough bars to make any pub crawl a night to remember—or to drunkenly forget.

El Raval

Notorious as Barcelona's rougher neighborhood, Raval shouldn't be missed because of its bad rap. A healthy student population makes for quirky (and cheap) eateries as well as vibrant nightlife. Areas around **Rambla del Raval** and **Carrer Joaquim Costa** boast lots of smaller bars and late-night cafes frequented by Barcelona's alternative crowd. For daytime shopping, check out **Riera Baixa,** a street lined entirely with secondhand shops that also hosts a fleamarket on Saturdays, and the neighborhood around **Carrer Dr. Dou** and **Carrer Elisabets** for higher-end (though still reasonably priced) shops. Be sure to take heed of the locals' warning: watch out for deserted streets and aggressive prostitutes during the night, and be aware that sometimes streets may still be eerily empty and filled with equally aggressive men or sneaky pickpockets during daylight hours.

L'Eixample

In this vibrant neighborhood, pronounced *eh-sham-plah,* big blocks and dazzling architecture means lots of walking and tons of exciting storefronts. The modernista building-lined **Passeig de Gràcia** runs from north to south, with the **Eixample Dreta** encompassing the area around **Sagrada Familia** and **Eixample Esquerra** comprising the area closer to the University. Though the former contains the notorious **Sagrada Familia,** as well as some surprisingly cheap accommodations for those willing to make the hike, the more pedestrian-friendly area is the Esquerra. While this neighborhood is notoriously posh, there are some cheaper and more interesting options as you get closer to **Plaça Universitat.** The stretch of **Carrer de Consell de Cent** boasts vibrant nightlife, where many "hetero-friendly" bars, clubs, and hotels help give "Gay-xample" its fitting nickname.

Barceloneta

Barceloneta is a land of beaches and tourist traps that capitalizes on sunbathers flocking to beaches. A short walk from the Barri Gòtic along the water on **Passeig de Colon** will bring you to Ⓜ**Barceloneta.** **Passieg de Joan de Borbó** is the main road curving along the water toward the **beach,** housing museums and restaurants you want to avoid like the plague. Venture onto any of the streets off of **Psg. Joan de Borbó,** and you'll find a tight grid of little shops and more authentic (though by no means cheaper) haunts, with the plaza around **C. del Baluart** being particularly lucrative. A 10-15min. walk along the packed beaches heading away from the **Gothic Quarter** will get you to the ritzy clubs and restaurants of **Port Olímpic.**

Gràcia

Gràcia is hard to navigate by metro. While this may at first seem like a negative, this poor municipal planning is actually a bonus. Filled with artsy locals and a few drunken travelers, Gràcia is best approached on foot. Ⓜ**Diagonal** will drop you off at the start of **C. Gran de Gràcia,** which creates the eastern border of Gràcia up until Ⓜ**Fontana.** Take a right onto any road along this walk, and you'll be navigating Gràcia's plaza-centric **C. de Ros de Olano/C. de Terol,** which runs perpendicular to C. Gran de Gràcia, intersecting the restaurant and student-laden **C. Verdi.** For bustling plazas both day and night, your best bets are **Pl. del Sol** and **Pl. de la Revolución de Septiembre de 1868,** both off of C. de Ros de Olano.

ACCOMMODATIONS

Barri Gòtic and Las Ramblas

HOSTAL MALDÀ
⊛⊗(ᵞ) HOSTAL ❶

C. Pi, 5   ☎93 3317 30 02 ▤www.hostalmalda.jimdo.com

Hostal Maldà provides a dirt-cheap home away from home, complete with your mother's cat, kitschy clocks, ceramics, and confusing knickknacks. A comfy lounge with books and TV feels more like a living room than a dorm common space. Unlike many hostels, the price does not change with the season, nor will this hostal be booked months beforehand during the summer months—knowing their audience and popularity, the owners only accept sixty percent of capacity through reservations, so try stopping by if you're stranded or weren't quick enough to snag a room beforehand.

⚑ ⓂLiceu. *Begin walking in front of the house with the dragon and take an immediate left onto C. Casañas. Stay on this road as it passes in front of the church and through the Plaça del Pi. Enter the Galerias Maldà (interior shopping mall) and follow the signs to the hostel.* **i** *Sheets included. Luggage storage available. All rooms have shared bath.* ⓢ *Singles €15; doubles €30; triples €45; quads €60.* ⌚ *Reception 24hr.*

YOUTH HOSTEL ALBERGUE
⊛⊗(ᵞ)✳ HOSTEL ❶

C. Palau, 6   ☎93 319 53 25 ▤www.bcnalbergue.com

Clean dormitory-style rooms fitting 4-8 people with pleasant views onto the street and courtyard below. All rooms include cheerily colored ceilings and wooden floors, and some include balconies—perfect for scoping out fellow travelers, restaurants, or even the nearby trinket store. Common space provides a bright, albeit sterile seating area to veg out and watch TV, grab snacks from the vending machine, and even challenge fellow hostelers to a riveting game of chess.

⚑ ⓂLiceu. *Walk down C. Ferran toward Las Ramblas. Take the first left once reaching the Plaça Sant Jaume, onto C. de la Ciudad. Right onto C. d'Arai. Second left, onto C. del Palau.* **i** *Free breakfast 8-9:30am. Lockers included. Sheets €2. Kitchen open 7-10pm.* ⓢ *4- to 8-bed dorms €13-24.50.* ⌚ *Reception 24hr.*

HOSTAL-RESIDÈNCIA REMBRANDT
⊛⊗(ᵞ) HOSTAL ❷

C. de la Portaferissa, 23   ▤www.hostalrembrandt.com

Unlike most hostels, which only offer a practically infinite number of small, dark rooms that look exactly the same, the Hostal-Residència has a variety of large, spacious rooms with pleasant quirks and details. Many rooms include multiple large windows or balconies looking out over the corner of the street or into the courtyard, and one triple even has a loft. For once, it's worth the price to have a bathroom ensuite—even the ones that aren't equipped with jacuzzis are still big enough to spend an entire week in relaxing. The rooms are a real steal in the low season, and the location and charm are still worth it in the high season.

⚑ ⓂLiceu. *Walk down Las Ramblas toward Plaça Catalonia and take a right onto C. Portaferissa; the hostal is by Galerias Maldà.* **i** *Linens and towels included.* ⓢ *Singles €20-30, with bath €20-35.* ⌚ *Reception 9am-11pm.*

HOSTAL-RESIDENCA LAUSANNE
⊛♿(ᵞ) HOSTAL ❸

Avinguda del Portal de l'Àngel, 14   ☎ 933 02 11 39 ▤www.hostallausanne.es

An incredibly classy stairwell (marble stairs, blue- and gold-glazed tile) leads to an equally classy hostel. Each room sports excellent views, but try getting one that faces the patio—the view is better and it will be quieter at night, so long as your hostelmates aren't total hooligans. Enjoy the view from your own room, chat up some fellow travelers in the bohemian common space with free internet, microwave, and TV, or chill out on the back patio and look out over the neighboring rooftops.

⚑ ⓂCatalonia. *Exit the metro and walk along the street toward the Corte Ingles, the rounded building with horizontal bands. Upon reaching the far corner of the square, turn right onto Avinguda del Portal de l'Àngel.* **i** *Towels, sheets, and toiletries included. Fridge and luggage storage available.* [$] *Singles €28-35; doubles €47-54; triples €68-75. Call for most up-to-date prices.* ⏰ *Reception 24hr.*

QUARTIER GOTHIC
💳♿📶 HOSTEL [2]

C. Avinyó, 42 ☎93 318 79 45 💻www.hotelquartiergothic.com

Flags from many countries and the hostel's own propaganda and regalia deck the walls and halls of Quartier Gothic. Rooms overlooking the courtyard have the best views and the least noise from the nightlong babbling of the Gothic Quarter. Though the attached baths are more spacious than in comparable hostels in the area, the shared bath is practically a room of its own (though only intended for one person at a time). With some rooms including TV and DVD players and a relatively impressive breakfast (selection of juices, coffee, tea, bread, and pastries), this hostel shows up many in its price range in terms of ammenities while still being in a central location. Short-term apartment by Casa Milà also available through informal arrangement with one of the employees.

⇄ *[M]Drassanes. Head toward Plaça de Catalonia on Las Ramblas. Turn right onto C. dels Escudellers, then right onto C. Avinyó. .* **i** *Breakfast €3. Safety box in room, lockers available for day after checkout for €2. Linens included. Rooms with private bath also have TV and DVD player.* [$] *Singles €19-27; doubles €32-57; triples €42-75. Discount for booking online.* ⏰ *Reception 24hr.*

PENSIÓN LA CALMA
❀🚭📶 PENSIÓN [2]

C. Lleona, 8-10 ☎93 318 15 21 💻www.pensionlacalma.com

Ask to see the rooms yourself to find the one sporting the most beautiful balcony view in all of the cheap hostels in the Gothic Quarter—hanging laundry, latticed gardens, terraced roofs, and all. A refreshing break from the nondescript, chain-like interiors being adopted by many hostels with private rooms, the Pensión La alma instead promises sheets that look like they came out of the '70s, tile from the '80s, and paintings that would look at home in any secondhand store. If you're looking for a clean and convenient place with character, then this is definitely a place to consider.

⇄ *[M]Liceu. Head toward the sea on Las Ramblas. Turn left onto C. Ferran, then right onto C. Raurich. Take the second left, C. Lleona.* **i** *Towels and linens included. Microwave and fridge available.* [$] *Doubles €42, with bath €50, triples €63/€75.* ⏰ *Reception 24hr.*

HOSTAL LEVANTE
💳❄ HOSTAL [3]

Baixada de San Miquel, 2 ☎933 17 95 65 💻www.hostallevante.com

Considering the rumors that the place used to be a haunt of Picasso when it was previously a whorehouse, Hostal Levante is now almost eerily clean and upstanding, with only a few stained chairs hinting dirtier days. Spacious yet simple private rooms cater to an older (or at least older acting) crowd than most similarly priced places in the area, and the hostel is much calmer as a result. If you don't mind shared facilities, save the €10 for the closet-sized bathroom.

⇄ *[M]Liceu. Walk down Las Ramblas toward the sea. Take a left onto C. Ferran and a right onto C. Avinyó. Baixada de San Miquel is on the left, and Hostal Levante is right at the corner.* **i** *Lock box in room. Towels and linens included.* [$] *Singles €35, bath €45, doubles€55, with bath €65; triples €90.*

KABUL YOUTH HOSTEL
💳♿📶🍸❄ HOSTEL [1]

P. Reial, 17 ☎93 318 51 90 💻www.kabul.es

One of the biggest and most popular hostels in Barcelona, the Kabul Youth Hostel has hosted nearly one million backpackers since its establishment in 1985. The hostel offers bare-bones, dormitory-style accommodations and a rooftop terrace. Lower-capacity rooms are often cramped and more expensive, but if you can get one with a balcony (just ask), then it's worth the added expense. The common space boasts backpacker photo galleries, a pool table, other table games, music, and a never-ending swarm of chatty younger travelers that are genuinely excited about meeting other travelers. Free breakfast and dinner make the price of a room here a steal.

✦ Ⓜ Liceu. *Walk toward the sea along Las Ramblas and turn left onto C. Ferran. Take the first right and enter the Plaça Reial. Kabul Youth Hostel will be on the far left, with well-marked glass doors.* *i* *Complimentary breakfast (8-10am and dinner (8:30pm) first come, first served. Lockers included with €15 key deposit. Luggage storage available. Blanket included; sheets €2. Laundry facilities available. 20min. free internet per day. Guestlist access to local clubs.* Ⓢ *Dorms €15-29.* ⏰ *Reception 24hr.*

HOSTAL NITZES BCN

✦⊗⁽ᵗ⁾ HOSTAL ❹

C. Calella, 1 ☎93 302 11 05 🖳www.hostalnitzbcn.com

Up the stairs from Pensión Coral is a much hipper, much more stylish alternative with a younger clientele—12 newly renovated rooms sporting sleek and funky decor are complemented by chic common areas. Although the comfy common room, basic kitchen, and shared bathrooms may appeal to the backpacking set on paper, expect rooms a step up from your normal youth accommodations—we're talking towels, shelves, ritzy ceiling fans, and even colored accent walls.

✦ Ⓜ Liceu. *With C. de la Boqueria to your left, walk down Rambla and take the first left onto C. de Ferran. Take a right onto C. Avinyó and take your third left, onto C. Calella.* *i* *Towels included. A/C in hallway, fans in rooms. Free Wi-Fi.* Ⓢ *Singles €40-45; doubles €40-90, with bath €55-90; triples €60-90.* ⏰ *Reception 24hr.*

La Ribera

🏠 PENSIÓ 2000

✦⁽ᵗ⁾ PENSIÓN ❷

C. Sant Pere Més Alt, 6 ☎93 310 74 66 🖳www.pensio2000.com

Brightly colored and well-lit rooms provide excellent views of the Palau de la Música Catalana across the street (and, reportedly, some complementary music performances on louder nights). High ceilings and a relaxed, college-living-room-like common space (without the empty beer cans and hookah, of course) make for a friendly home away from home, complete with concerned and super helpful hostel-owners-cum-parents.

✦ Ⓜ Jaume I. *Walk on Via Laietana toward the Cathedral and take a right onto C. Sant Pere Més Alt, 6. Pensió 2000 is located directly across from the Palau.* *i* *Breakfast €5. Internet €1 per day.* Ⓢ *Doubles €55, with private bath €60. Extra bed €20, second extra bed €16.* ⏰ *Reception 24hr.*

🏠 GOTHIC POINT YOUTH HOSTEL

✦⁽ᵗ⁾❄ HOSTEL ❶

C. dels Vigatans, 5 ☎932 68 78 08 🖳www.gothicpoint.com

This youth hostel sports a social life as vibrant as its nearly flourescent lime green walls, with a ping-pong table along the huge terrace for those nights when you just need to duke it out. The chutes-and-ladders-esque bedrooms provide standard youth hostel fare with one significant improvement: most are enclosed in their own wall of curtains for some semblance of privacy.

✦ Ⓜ Jaume I. *Walk down C. Argenteria and take a left onto C. dels Vigatans.* *i* *Kitchen available. Inquire about working to pay for your stay. Sheets €2. Towels €2.* Ⓢ *Dorms €15-23.* ⏰ *Reception 24hr.*

HOTEL TRIUNFO

✦⁽ᵗ⁾❄ HOTEL ❹

Pg. de Picasso, 22 ☎933 10 40 85 🖳www.atriumhotels.com

Chic upscale rooms with curtains that actually match the covers, luxurious bathrooms with slick black tubs, and flatscreen TVs on the wall make this expensive option worth its price tag. A small common room with black leather couches, a contrasting white sculpture, and posters of worldwide art exhibitions provide the perfect place to prep before heading across the street to catch a classical performance in the Parc de la Ciutadella.

✦ Ⓜ Arc de Triumf. *Walk on Passeig de Lluís Companys through the arch and toward the Parc. Follow the curve to the right once it meets the park to walk onto Pg. de Picasso. Hotel Triunfo is on the*

barcelona • accommodations

HOSTAL RIBAGORZA
◆●《(ŋ)※ PENSIÓN ❷

C. de Trafalgar, 39 ☎933 19 19 68 🖥www.hostalribagorza.com

Brown- and blue-tiled floors paired with orange covers make for a funky color palette ensuite, while knick-knack ceramics make you feel as if you're staying with your Spanish grandmother. Let this place spoil you with clean rooms, balconies, and surprisingly large shared bathrooms.

♯ ⓂArc de Triumf. Stand on the far side of the Arc farthest from the Parc with your back to the arch. C. Trafalgar is the first street on your left. Ⓢ Doubles €45, with bath €55-62; triples €60/€75. Ⓩ Reception 24hr.

BARCELONA 4 FUN
◆●Ⓧ《(ŋ) HOSTAL ❷

C. Ample, 24 ☎93 268 41 50 🖥www.barcelona4fun.com

An unmarked door in an unmarked building hides private rooms with the social life (and shared bathrooms) of a hostel (if you can find the place, anyway). Young travelers pack this hostal's 2- and 3-person rooms, though most time is spent either in the kitchen or in the living room with a sunny view to the street, comfy furniture, and computers with free internet. Close to Barceloneta if you can't stay too far from the clubs.

♯ ⓂBarceloneta. While facing the water, walk to your right along Psg. Isabel II/Psg. Colom. Walk for 5min. and turn right onto C. Avinyó. At the 2nd street (C. Ample), take a right. Look for a huge stone doorway on your left and doors leading into black-and-white checkered marble hallway. Go up grand staircase—door is unmarked, but it's door #2 on the 1st floor. *i* Free internet and Wi-Fi. Breakfast included. Towels €1. Ⓢ Doubles €54-60; triples €81-90.

El Raval

🏠 HOTEL PENINSULAR
●●♿《(ŋ)※ HOTEL ❸

C. Sant Pau, 34 ☎93 302 31 38 🖥www.hpeninsular.com

Four stories of rooms wrap around a well-lit courtyard with hanging plants. Comfortable rooms with pale green doors, little desks, and windows overlooking the picturesque surroundings make for a gigglishly quaint place to rest your head.

♯ ⓂLiceu. On Las Ramblas, turn your back to Plaça Catalonia. C. Sant Pau will be on your right. *i* Free Wi-Fi and toiletries. Ⓢ Doubles €60; triples €85; quads €100. Ⓩ Reception 24hr.

IDEAL YOUTH HOSTEL
●●♿《(ŋ)※ HOSTEL ❶

C. la Unió, 12 ☎933 42 61 77 🖥www.idealhostel.com

An industrial-chic common space with foosball and amoeba-like couches hosts to a revolving door of vibrant backpacking youth. The bathroom facilities in this standard youth hostel smell so soapy you know they're clean. Young, helpful staff will point you in the right direction and may even end up going with you to show you the ropes.

♯ ⓂLiceu. Walk toward the water on Las Ramblas and take a right onto C. de la Unió. *i* Breakfast included. Safebox available. Ⓢ Dorms €18. €9.50 deposit. Ⓩ Reception 24hr.

L'Eixample

🏠 SANT JORDI: HOSTEL ARAGO
◆●《(ŋ) HOSTEL ❸

C. Aragó, 268 ☎93 215 67 43 🖥www.santjordihostels.com/hostel-arago

Sit back in their gloriously bright, home-like kitchen and common space, or gather round on one of the couches and listen to hostelmates play covers of Bob Dylan and Andrew Bird on the communal guitar. Any hostel with quotes from Guy Debord, Wittgenstein, and Nietzsche on its board has to be a little different, and this one is in the best way. Modern wooden and steel bunks offer a little more privacy and comfort than most hostels, though with nightly outings and a solid, exciting community, chances are you'll be spending little time in them.

♯ ⓂPasseig de Gràcia. Walk along Psg. de Gràcia away from Plaça Catalonia and the Corte Ingles.

spain

Take a left onto C. d'Aragó. ℹ Lockers and luggage storage included. Sheets and blankets included. Laundry available. Kitchen and computers with internet. $ Dorms €30-35. ⏰ Reception 24hr.

👍 SANT JORDI: APARTMENTS SAGRADA FAMILIA 💳♿📶❄ HOSTEL [2]

C. del Freser, 5 ☎93 446 05 17 💻www.santjordihostels.com/apt-sagrada-familia/

For those sick of dining on takeout, coffee, and beer, Sant Jordi's apartment-style lodging offers the chain's characteristic laid-back style, communal guitar, employee dedicated to arranging nightly parties, and guarantee of social hostelmates as cool as you (or as cool as you want to be). Each apartment includes a private bath (or two), a stylish and comfy living room, free washing machine, and stocked kitchen, with the added benefit of hostel style sociability. With rooms for one, two, or four people, you can pick your privacy without *pension*-style isolation.

➔ [M]Hospital Sant Pau. Walk along C. del Dos de Maig toward C. Corsega. Take a left onto C. Roselló and stay left as the road splits to C. del Freser. ℹ Apartments include living room, TV, washing machine, ensuite bathrooms, and kitchen. Free Wi-Fi. Lockers, sheets, and blankets included. $ 4-bed dorms €16-28; singles €20-38; doubles €36-64. Towels €2. ⏰ Quiet hours after 10pm.

👍 HOSTEL SOMNIO 💳♿📶 HOSTEL, HOSTAL [3]

C. de la Diputació, 251 ☎93 272 308 💻www.somniohostels.com

This ultra-sleek hostel offers the best of both worlds—beautifully decorated private rooms and cost-efficient and dorm-style bunking. Cool wooden floors and modern decor will leave you expecting to pay the price, but you'll be thankfully disappointed. Super helpful and friendly staff will direct you to the best little tapas bar or the only cost-efficient driving tour in Barcelona. Watch for more locations in the near future, as they look to expand throughout Spain.

➔ [M]Passeig de Gràcia. Walk along Gran Vía toward the University and take the first right onto Rambla de Catalonia. Somnio is on the corner of C. Diputacio and the Rambla. ℹ Breakfast €2. Locker, towel, and bedding included. Free Wi-Fi $ Dorms €26; singles €44; doubles €78, with bath €87.

EQUITY POINT CENTRIC 💳♿📶❄ HOSTEL [2]

Psg. de Gràcia, 33 ☎93 215 65 38 💻www.equity-point.com

Equity Point's location can't be beat, especially for its price. Though the expansive number of rooms and the gargantuan, but beautiful, reception area in this modernista building might intimidate you, their website puts it most accurately when it states that this hostel is "like a cuckoo that's muscled into the very plushest of nests." Great views from the bunk-style rooms and a ton of amenities, including a terrace and bar, provide the perfect reprieve if somehow you don't feel like spending the day out front along Passeig de Gràcia.

➔ [M]Passeig de Gràcia. Walk along Psg. de Gràcia away from Plaça Catalonia and the Corte Ingés. Equity Point is on the corner of C. Consell de Cent and Psg. de Gràcia. ℹ Lockers available. Free Wi-Fi; computers with internet free for 20min. Top sheet and blanket €2 each. Towel €2 with €2 deposit. $ Dorms €18.50-30. ⏰ Kitchen open until 10pm.

GRAFFITI HOSTAL 💳🚭📶☀ HOSTEL [1]

C. Aragó, 527 ☎93 288 24 99

True to its name, this hostel has graffiti, ranging from impressive works of art spanning entire walls to incredibly mundane scratchings by drunk hostelmates. An unmarked door hides the cheapest rooms in Barcelona complete with lockers, two outdoor terraces, and a common room. If you've visited before, be sure to stop by again—the hostel is under new management and has a facelift to show for it.

➔ [M]Clot or [M]Encants. From Clot, face the rocket-shaped Agbar Tower and head directly to your right along C. d'Aragó. From Encants, walk along C. del Dos de Mag toward Agbar Tower and take a left onto C. d'Aragó. $ Dorms €10-13. ⏰ Common areas closed midnight-8am.

BARCELONA URBANY HOSTEL 💳♿📶 HOSTEL [2]

Avinguda Meridiana, 97 ☎93 503 60 04 💻www.barcelonaurbany.com

The tons of young people flocking to this hostel guarantee a fun, social experience, and the free gym access and nightly clubbing outings provided by Barcelona Urbany simply greaten the potential. Rooms are supermodern, but don't be surprised if you want to spend most of your night on the terrace bar sipping super cheap beer and sangria (€1) instead.

✚ ⓂClot. Walk along Av. Meridiana toward the rocket-shaped Agbar Tower. Urbany will be on your right, on the corner of Meridiana and C. de la Corunya. *i* Breakfast included. Luggage storage. Laundry available. Ⓢ All-female dorms €23-34; mixed dorms €20-31. Singles and doubles €68-94. ⓏReception 24hr.

HOSTAL EDEN
💨📶 HOSTAL ❷

C. Balmes, 55   ☎93 452 66 20 ◾www.hostaleden.net

Don't expect another white-walled sleeping box—bright, pastel colored walls mimic the vivid blues, greens, yellows, and reds of the covers. The interior bathrooms are just big enough to get around in easily, and each comes with a hair dryer for when the windblown look isn't cutting it. The rooms aren't incredibly spacious, but also aren't closet-sized—just be nimble if you take the far side of the bed.

✚ ⓂPasseig de Gràcia. Walk along Passeig de Gràcia away from Plaça Catalonia and the Corte Ingles. Take a left onto C. d'Aragó just after Casa Battló. Take a left onto C. Balmes. *i* Towels, safety boxes, and fans included. ⓈSingles €25-30, with bath €35-55; doubles €35-45/€50-60.

Gràcia

ALBERGUE-RESIDENCIA LA CIUTAT
💨📶❄ HOSTEL ❶

C. de ca l'Alegre de Dalt, 66   ☎93 213 03 00 ◾www.laciutat.com

Colorful dorm-style rooms for offer a cheerily saturated, modern place to rest your head. Useful facilities dot every floor, including a fully-equipped kitchen, common room with TV, and showers. Single and double rooms are also available, with discounts given to those who stay longer than seven days. The Disney-meets-graffiti murals lining the corridors exemplify the vibrant and young social atmosphere, and the terrace provides a welcome break for a breath of fresh air. Getting there from the city center may be a pain, but the bustling student-friendly (and cheap) nightlife of Gràcia is just a short walk away.

✚ ⓂJoanic. Walk along C de l'Escorial through the plaza and follow for 5-10min. Take a right onto C. de Marti before the Clinic and take the first left onto C. de ca l'Alegre de Dalt. *i* Lockers and towels included. Sheets €1.80. Free internet at public computers. Equipped kitchens and shared bathrooms on each floor. Laundry service available. Ⓢ 4- to 6-bed dorms €17-20; singles €35-50; doubles €26-30. First night deposit required for online booking. ⓏReception 24hr.

HOSTAL LESSEPS
💨⊗📶 PENSIÓN ❸

C. Gran de Gràcia, 239   ☎93 218 44 34 ◾www.hostallesseps.com

Recently renovated, this *pension* boasts 16 larger rooms, all with huge baths and sleek flatscreen TVs. With these amenities, some people decide to not leave their rooms. Even for the area, this hostel is surprisingly quiet.

✚ ⓂLesseps. Walk away from the giant road along C. Gran de Gràcia. Hostal Lesseps is a few blocks down on the right. *i* All rooms with ensuite bath. Free internet at public computers. Ⓢ Singles €40; doubles €65; triples €80.

Camping

Almost all of Barcelona's campsites come equipped with baffling ammenities, and even the more reserved campsites have basic bathing and laundry facilities as well as a super-market and restaurant. If you're not the tenting type, affordable 4- to 6-person bungalows are usually available with kitchens and complete bathrooms. Many have minimum stay requirements, so be prepared to kick back and settle down for a few days.

CÀMPING TRES ESTRELLAS
♿📶 CAMPSITE ❶

Autovía de Castelldefells, km. 186.2, Gavá   ☎93 633 06 37 ◾www.camping3estrellas.com

If you get any closer to the beach, you'd be washed out to sea at high tide. Camping facilities dot the beautiful beach of Gavá, 12km from the city center *(35min. by bus).* Extensive facilities boast not one but two swimming pools (in case you're afraid of sharks), volleyball nets, and a grill area, along with the expected supermarket, bar, and restaurant.

 # Gavá stop on bus L94 or L95 from Plaça Catalonia. Campsite 5min walk from station. ℹ Pools, restaurant, supermarket, and BBQ area available. $ Camping €6-8 per person; €7.50-9 for tent. 2-person cabin €26-38; 4-person cabin €38-60. ⏰ Open Mar 15-Oct 15.

CÀMPING MASNOU ♿ CAMPSITE [1]

Carretera. N-II km 633 Camil Fabra, 33. ☎93 555 15 03 💻www.campingsonline.com

A more rustic and down-to-earth alternative to many of the resort-esque campsites. Camping Masnou is close to the water, recommended for those looking to indulge in the outdoors or just rest their head inside a tent after sightseeing in the city. Cheap bungalows provide a warmer alternative to your frigid tent during the winter months.

 # [M]Masnou or N80 bus from Plaça Catalonia. Campsite 5min. walk from station. ℹ Bike rental, laundry, supermarket, pool, and restaurant available. Pet-friendly. $ Camping €5.20 per person. 4-to 6-person bungalows €60-90. ⏰ Open year-round.

Outskirts

Though a trek from the city center, the following two youth hostels offer astounding views and ammenities for prices that would get you a basic bed with a view to the wall in the touristy areas. You're not stuck out in the boonies unless you want to be, either—with nearby bus and trains stations, the city is just a short and cheap ride away.

MARE DE DÉU DE MONTSERRAT YOUTH HOSTEL ☕♿📶 HOSTEL [1]

Pg. Mare de Déu del Coll, 41-51 ☎93 483 83 63 💻www.xanascat.cat

This renovated *modernista* oasis houses 209 cheap beds within its antique walls. Now owned and operated by the government, the basic rooms offer huge lockers for all of your hiking gear. The real draw is the breathtaking stained glass and Moorish detail in the foyer and common rooms, and with the Parc Güell just a short hike away, there's no reason to stay in the monk-like confines of the dormitories.

 # Bus #28, 92, and N5 stop across the street. Behind Parc Güell. ℹ Breakfast and sheets included. Lockers and safety boxes available. Wi-Fi €.90 per 30min. Laundry €4.50. $ Dorms €15-25. ⏰ Reception 24hr.

IN/OUT YOUTH HOSTEL ☕♿📶 HOSTEL [2]

Major del Rectoret, 2 ☎93 280 09 85 💻www.inoutalberg.com

Situated in the Parc de la Colserolla, In/Out offers a homey place to rest your head (no metal frames or cold tile here). The hostel also has heart, as it is staffed almost entirely by people with mental disabilities. A pool, restaurant, TV, and easy access to the train to Barcelona sweetens the deal, though you may be tempted to spend your days getting lost in the surrounding hills instead.

 # [M]Baixador de Vallvidrera (S1, S2), exit Barri of the Rectoret. Follow road to right, Mare is a few minutes up the mountain. ℹ Breakfast included. All rooms have fridge and lockers. Pool and restaurant. $ Dorms €14-22. Blankets €2. towels €2. Food €7-16.

SIGHTS 👁

Barri Gòtic and Las Ramblas

👍 COLUMBUS MONUMENT TOWER

Portal de la Pau ☎93 302 52 24

Located where Las Ramblas meets the water, the Columbus Monument offers an unbeatable view of the city and a certain heart attack for those afraid of heights for just €3. The 60m statue was constructed from 1882-1888 in time for Barcelona's World's Fair in order to commemorate Barcelona's role when Christopher Columbus met with King Ferdinand and Queen Isabella upon his return from the New World. Though it is said that the 7.2m statue at the top of the tower points west to the Americas, it actually points east, supposedly to his hometown of Genoa. Around the base of the column are reliefs depicting the journey, as well as bronze lions that are guaranteed to be mounted by tourists on any given hour.

⚡ Ⓜ*Drassanes. Entrance located in base facing water.* Ⓢ *€3, seniors and children €2.* ⏲ *Open daily May-Oct 9am-7:30pm, Nov-Apr 9am-6:30pm.*

MUSEU D'HISTORIA DE LA CIUTAT ⚲ HISTORY
Pl. del Rei ☎93 256 21 00 🖳www.museuhistoria.bcn.es

If you thought the winding streets of the Barri Gotíc were old school, check out the Museu d'Historia de la Ciutat nestled 20m underneath Pl. de Reial. Underneath this unassuming plaza lies the excavation site of **archaeological remains** of ancient Barcino, the Roman city from which Barcelona sprouted. One thing has remained the same—the people of this area love their booze, and huge ceramic wine flasks can be seen dotting the site, as well as intricate floor mosaics and strikingly well-preserved ruins ranging from the first to 6th centuries AD. The second part of the museum in the area features the comparatively new **Palacio Reial Major**, a 14th-century palace for Catalan-Aragonese monarchs that was built in part using the fourth-century Roman walls. Inside the palace, the expansive and impressively empty Gothic **Saló de Tinell** (Throne Room) is the seat of legend: here Columbus was received by Fernando and Isabel after his journey to the New World, while the **Capilla de Santa Àgata** avoids the fame of kitschy tales and goes right for the goods, hosting rotating exhibits about modern and contemporary Barcelona.

⚡ Ⓜ*Jaume I.* 𝒊 *Free multilingual audio guides.* Ⓢ *Museum and exhibition €7, students and under 25 €5, under 16 free. Museum €6, students €4. Exhibition €1.80/1.10.* ⏲ *Open Apr-Sept Tu-Sa 10am-8pm, Su 10am-3pm; Oct-Mar Tu-Sa 10am-2pm and 4-7pm, Su 10am-3pm.*

CITY HALL ⚲ GOVERNMENT
P. de Sant Jaume–Ciutat, 2 ☎93 402 70 00 🖳www.bcn.es

The government-appropriate 18th century Neoclassical facade facing the Plaça hides a more interesting 15th century Gothic facade located at the old entrance to the left of the building (which is now also the tourist entrance). Inside City Hall are a myriad of treasures, both fantastical and more somber—the lower level is home to many pieces of sculpture from the Catalan masters (many of these same artists have work in the Museu Nacional d'Art de Catalonia), while the upper level boasts impressively lavish architecture and interiors such as the *Saló de Cent*, where the *Consell de Cent* (Council of One Hundred) ruled the city from 1372-1714. Around certain holidays, the Giants of the Old City may be seen lurking the halls, towering figurines representing past kings and queens, horses, indecipherable monsters, and 🗲dragons.

⚡ Ⓜ*Jaume I. Take a right onto C. de Jaume I after exiting the station. Once in Plaça de Jaume I, City Hall is on your left.* 𝒊 *Tourist info available at entrance. To enter, take alley to the left of City Hall and take a right onto C. Sant Miquel.* Ⓢ *Free.* ⏲ *Tourist info open M-F 9am-8pm, Sa 10am-8pm, Su and holidays 10am-2pm. City Hall open to public Su 10am-2pm.*

LA BOQUERIA (MERCAT DE SANT JOSEP) ⚲ MARKET
La Rambla, 89

If you're looking for the freshest tomatoes, leeks the size of a well-fed child's arm, fruit prickly enough that it could second as a shirukin, sheep's head (eyes included), or maybe just some nuts, the Boqueria has you covered in the most strikingly beautiful way. Though each neighborhood in Barcelona lays claim to its own *mercado*, Mercat de Sant Josep is not only the biggest and impressive in the city, but it also claims the title of largest-open air market in all of Spain. As a consequence, expect to have to fight your way through wildebeest-like hordes of locals and tourists alike to get those cherished lychee for your picnic on the beach. If filling your stomach from the glowing rows of perfectly arranged, perfectly ripe produce doesn't satisfy your famished gut, restaurants surrounding the market offer meals made of fresh produce straight from the nearby vendors.

For the frustrated vegans in the city, the market will be your godsend—just turn a blind eye to the ham legs hanging on the outskirts.

✤ ⓂLiceu. Walk on Las Ramblas toward Plaça Catalonia and take a left onto Plaça de Sant Josep. 🕰 Open M-Sa 8am-8pm, though some individual stands stay open after 9pm.

CATEDRAL DE CANTA CRUZ Y SANTA EULALIA DE BARCELONA   ♿ CATHEDRAL
P. de la Seu   ☎93 315 15 54 ▪www.catedralbcn.org

Behold: the Cathedral of the Holy Cross and Santa Eulalia (La Seu, for short) and its ever-present construction-related accoutrements, Barcelona's only cathedral and a marvel of beauty and perserverance. The impressive scaffolding rig and skeletal spire drawing attention away from the Gothic facade are actually signs of what you'll see advertised with the "Sponsor a Stone" campaign in the interior—costly renovations that began in 2005. The cathedral is no stranger to drawn out projects, however. Although construction on the cathedral began in 1298, the main building wasn't finished until 1460, the front facade until 1889, and the central spire until 1913.

Once you've been funneled through the scaffolding and into the main building's interior, almost all signs of construction disappear. Soaring vaulted ceilings mark the nave, and decadently decorated chapels—28 in all—line the central space. Most important, however, is the *cathedra* (bishop's throne) that designates this building as a cathedral and is found on the altar. Don't miss the crypt of Saint Eulalia, located at the bottom of the stairs in front of the altar.

To the right of the altar (through a door marked "Exit") is the entrance to the cloister, a chapel-laden courtyard enclosing palm trees and thirteen white ducks that are intended to remind visitors of Saint Eulalia's age at the time of her martyrdom. Here you will find the cathedral's museum, which hides various religious paintings and altarpieces in various stages of needing to be cleaned, a very gold monstrance (used during communion), and, in the Sala Capitular, Bartolomé Bermejo's *Pietà*. If you only have €2 to spend, pay to take the lift instead—you'll get up close and personal with one of the church's spirals and find yourself with a breathtaking view of the city.

✤ ⓂJaume I. Left onto Via Laietana and then left onto Av. de la Catedral. Ⓢ Catedral free. Museum €2. Elevator €2.50. Tours €5. 🕰 Free admission M-F 8am-12:45pm and 5:15-7:30pm, Sa 8am-12:45pm and 5:15-8pm, Su 8am-1:45pm and 5:15-8pm. Visitor admission M-Sa 1-4:30pm. Inquire about guided visit to museum, choir, rooftop terraces, and towers.

PALAU DE LA GENERALITAT   GOVERNMENT
☎90 240 00 12 ▪www.gencat.cat/generalitat/eng/guia/palau/index.htm

Facing the Plaça Sant Jaume I and the Ajuntament, the Palau de la Generalitat provides a second reason this plaza is incredibly popular with protestors and petitioners. The Renaissance facade dates from the early 17th century, hiding a Gothic structure that was obtained by the Catalan government in 1400. Although the majority of visitors will be stuck admiring its wonderfully authoritative feel from the exterior, with a bit of magic in the way of good timing it is possible to see the interior. Inside, visitors will find a Gothic gallery, an orange tree courtyard, St. George's Chapel, a bridge to the house of the President, many historic sculptures and paintings, and the **Palau's carillon**, a 4898 kg instrument consisting of 49 bells that is played on holidays and for special events.

✤ ⓂJaume. Take a right onto C. de Jaume I after exiting the station. Once in Plaça de Jaume I, Palau is on your right. Ⓢ Free. 🕰 Open to the public on Apr 23, Sep 11, and Sep 24, and on 2nd and 4th Su of each month from 10am-2pm.

GRAN TEATRE DEL LICEU   ♿❈ THEATER
La Rambla, 51-59   ☎934 85 99 00 ▪www.liceubarcelona.com

Along the sometimes dirty paths, animal cages, and peddlers of Las Ramblas is one of the Europe's grandest stages that specializes in opera and classical performances. The Baroque interior of the auditorium will leave you gawking at the fact that it dates back only to 1999 when the interior was reconstructed after a 1995 fire (though, to be fair, it is an exact reconstruction of the previous auditorium). A 20min. tour provides a glimpse of the ornate *Sala de Espejos* (Room of Mirrors), where Apollo and the Muses look down upon opera-goers during intermission, and the five-layered bedazzled auditorium, where you may catch a director yelling furiously during a rehearsal if you are lucky. For a more in-depth tour that won't leave you spending half of your time looking at stackable chairs in the foyer or being told about the donors list (though it does include Placido Domingo), be sure to either come for the 1hr. tour at 10am, arrange a behind-the-scenes tour with the box office, or attend a performance in person.

⚐ Ⓜ*Liceu.* *i* *Discount tickets available.* Ⓢ *20min. tour €4, 1hr. tour €8.* ☒ *Box office open M-F 10am-2pm and 2-6pm. 20min. tours start every 30min. daily 11:30am-1pm; 1hr. tour daily at 10am.*

P. DE L'ÀNGEL
&♿ HISTORY

Corner of Via Laietana and C. de la Princessa

The square immediately surrounding the Ⓜ Jaume I may now seem like nothing but a place to grab a good pastry, but in the days of Roman Barcino this spot was the main gate into the city. To revel in some of this seemingly absent history, simply walk parallel to **Via Laietana**, the busy street forming one side of the square's border. For a more contemporary piece of history (though sitll dating from the triple digits CE), look no further than the the angel statue facing the street that happens to be pointing to her toe. This sculpture commemorates the event from which the plaza got its name—reportedly when carrying the remains of Saint Eulalia to the cathedral from Santa Maria del Mar, the caravan came to the plaça. Suddenly, the remains became to heavy to carry, and upon setting down the remains, an angel appeared and pointed to her own toe, alerting the carriers that one of the church officials had stolen Santa Eulalia's little digit.

⚐ Ⓜ*Jaume I.* Ⓢ *Free.*

ROMAN WALLS
♿ HISTORY

Scattered throughout the Ciutat Vella, portions of the Roman remains are marked clearly with orange and black info plaques by the city, and it's hard not to run into at least one of them. For those history buffs looking for the most bang for their buck, walk down C. Tapineria (it's to your back as you exit the metro station), a narrow street connecting Plaça de l'Angel and Plaça Ramon Berenguer. This street holds the most concentrated number of fourth-century wall remains, though they may be hard to spot, as they are entirely incorporated into the base of the 14th-century Palau Reial Major. The second area of interest is the **Plaça Seu** in front of the Cathedral, which may be reached by following C. Tapineria and taking a left onto Av. de la Catedral. To the left of the Cathedral is the only remaining octagonal tower, and to the right are a reconstruction of the Roman aqueduct and other smaller remains. For those hankering for more, a map listing all visible Roman remains in the city may be found on the information placards near each site.

⚐ Ⓜ*Jamue I.* Ⓢ *Free.*

Las Ramblas

Beginning along the sea and cutting straight through to Plaça Catalonia, Las Ramblas is Barcelona's world-famous main pedestrian throughfare that attracts flocks of visitors and flocks of people attempting to draw money from said visitors. Lined with trees, cafes, tourist traps, human statues, beautiful buildings, and pickpockets, the five distinct promenades combine seamlessly to create the most lively and exciting pedestrian area in the city. The **Ramblas**, in order from Plaça Catalonia to the Columbus Monument are: **La Rambla de les Canaletes, La Rambla dels Estudis, La Rambla de Sant Josep, La Rambla dels Cataputxins,** and **La Rambla de Santa Monica.**

LA RAMBLA DELS ESTUDIS

                                                ♿ PROMENADE

Las Ramblas

Named for the university that was once located here (*estudis* means "studies" in Catalan), the path is now closer to a lesson in animal taxonomy than scholarly topics. Known as "Las Ramblas dels Ocells" (literally, of the birds), the shops along this stretch of pavement sell everything from rabbits to guinea pigs, iguanas to turtles, ducks to parrots, and much more. Here is your place to pick up a pigeon, and with some good training, you may soon be able to sidestep Spain's postal service. This area justifiably becomes the target of Barcelona's active and outraged animal rights proponents, but there seems to be no indication that Las Ramblas will be any less furry, fluffy, or feathery anytime soon.

✢ Ⓜ*Catalonia. Walk toward the water.*

LA RAMBLA DE SANT JOSEP

                                               ♿ PROMENADE

Las Ramblas

If you're looking for a bouquet for that special someone, or you've just decided that your hostel bathroom could really benefit from a few rose petals, La Rambla de Sant Josep is your place. Flower shops line this stretch of the pedestrian avenue, giving it the nickname "La Rambla de les Flors." Following the theme of living things now dead, the impressive Boqueria is found along this stretch, along with the once-grand and now practically gutted **Betlem Church.** The end of this promenade is marked classily by Joan Miró's mosaic in the pavement at Plaça Boqueria.

✢ Ⓜ*Liceu. Walk toward Plaça Catalonia.*

LA RAMBLA DELS CATAPUTXINS

                                        ♿ PROMENADE

Las Ramblas

La Rambla dels Cataputxins boasts access to Ⓜ Liceu and a straight shot to Plaça Sant Jaume I via C. Ferran, which runs directly through the center of the Gothic Quarter. Cafes and restaurants line this portion of Las Ramblas, and eager business owners will try desperately to pull you into their lair—if "tapas" and specials listed in English don't do it first. Littered with eye candy such as the **Casa Bruno Cuadros** (corner of C. Boqueria and Las Ramblas, the one with the 🐉**dragon** in front), Teatre Liceu, and a mosaic by Joan Miró, this portion of Las Ramblas is often the busiest.

✢ Ⓜ*Liceu. Walk toward the sea.*

LA RAMBLA DE SANTA MÒNICA

                                        ♿ PROMENADE

Las Ramblas

Ending at the feet of Christopher Columbus himself, La Rambla de Santa Monica leads the boulevard to the waterfront. This portion of the path is the widest and, unlike its saintly name would suggest, the most packed with vices and temptation. Though filled with artists peddling their takes on Miró, your face, or dolphins in the shape of letters during the day, at night the area becomes thick with prostitutes agressively looking for confused potential clients. In the same debaucherous spirit, Santa Mònica is also the only place on Las Ramblas home to peep shows.

✢ Ⓜ*Drassanes.*

LA RAMBLA DE LES CANALETES

                                        ♿ PROMENADE

Las Ramblas

The head of Las Ramblas when walking from Plaça Catalonia to the water, this rambla is named after the fountain that marks its start—Font de les Canaletes. Surprisingly unceremonious, the fountain is not a spewing spectacle of lights and water jets but instead a fancy drinking fountain with four spouts, rumored to make those who drink its water fall in love with the city. These days the fountain has amusingly run dry, however, so be sure to fill your Nalgene elsewhere, sans love potion.

✢ Ⓜ*Catalonia.*

barcelona · sights

BETLEM CHURCH

 ♿ CHURCH

La Rambla, 89

Upon its construction in 1680-1729 on the site of an earlier church dating from 1553, the"Our Lady of Bethlehem" Church served as an important nucleus for the Jesuit school in Barcelona until their explusion from Spain in 1767. Today, Betlem Church's fortification-like facade running along Las Ramblas is hard to miss. The church does have a softer side, however—facing the C. Carme is a Baroque facade flanked by sculptures of Jesuit saints Ignacio de Loyola and Francisco de Borja, both completed by Catalan sculptor Andreu Sala. Also stretching over the entrance is a representation of the Nativity by Francesc Santacruz.

With such an intriguing exterior, the interior of the church is bound to disappoint. Once considered one of the most beautiful churches in Spain, the unadorned single nave and sparsely populated surrounding chapels leave knowledgeable visitors wondering just what happened to its former glory. Though the edifice itself has been largely restored, the Church's simple interior remains a victim of the Spanish Civil War, when Leftist fire caused the entire vaulting system to collapse and destroyed the interior. Some chapels have been refurbished using altarpieces from other churches and private collections with some of the more beautiful and elaborate pieces located in the chapels along the left side of the nave. Betlem currently functions as a parish church and offers daily mass in both Spanish and Catalan.

⚛ Ⓜ*Liceu. Walk on Las Ramblas toward Plaça Catalonia. Betlem Church is on the left after the Boqueria.* Ⓢ *Free.* ⏲ *Open daily 8:30am-1:40pm and 6-9pm. Masses in Catalan and Castellano.*

La Ribera

■ DISSENY HUB BARCELONA (DHUB)

✈♿ DESIGN, ART

C. Montcada, 12; Av. Diagonal, 686   ☎93 256 23 00 ▣www.dhub-bcn.cat

Ever dream of making a chair simply with a beam of light? Chances are you haven't, but just in case you have (or you're curious how it's even possible), Disseny Hub Barcelona will show you said chair, let you touch it, and even explain every single step of its magical creation. Split over two buildings nearly a town apart, Disseny Hub Barcelona focuses on showcasing Barcelona's cutting edge contemporary art with a commercial edge through amazing historical displays, video supplements, and a creative laboratory that fosters the budding designer in even the least creative visitor. The **Montcada branch**, located across from the Museu Picasso, houses temporary exhibitions and study galleries that test the limits of the imagination, including everything from heat sensitive wallpaper to an automated dessert printer. Just across town, the Palau de Pedralbes hosts the **Museu de les Arts Decoratives** and the **Museu Tèxtil i d'Indumentària**, both highlighting the evolution of art objects and fashion from the Romanesque to the Industrial Revolution with enough quirky artifacts and period dress to make it worth the trek. Currently, the price of admission provides access to both museums, but look for both to be housed under the same roof in the upcoming year as the primary home of the Disseny Hub Barcelona is finished in Plaça de les Glorièss Catalanes in 2011.

⚛ *Montcada:* Ⓜ*Jaume I. From Metro, walk down C. de la Princesa and turn right onto C. de Montacada. Pedralbes:* Ⓜ*Palau Reial.* ℹ *New combined museum to be opened in 2011 in Plaça de les Glories.* Ⓢ *Admission to both centers €5. Free Su 3-8pm.* ⏲ *Montcada open Tu-Sa 11am-7pm, Su 11am-8pm. Pedralbes open Tu-Su 10am-6pm.*

PICASSO MUSEUM

✈♿ ARCHITECTURE, ART

C. Montcada, 15-23   ☎93 256 30 00 ▣www.museupicasso.bcn.es

Tucked away amongst the *bodegas* and medieval charms of Ribera is the Museu Picasso—five connected mansions dedicated to showcasing what Picasso's work was like before he was cool. His early years' collection is organized chron-

spain

ologically, providing insight into his development into the international star of Cubism. However, the collection is not completely Barça-centric. Paintings from after his time in Paris show the influence of the Impressionists he encountered, while several works from his Blue and Rose periods help to literally paint a picture of his past. The most sweeping gesture of influence is easily the room of the artist's 58 renditions of Velázquez's *Las Meninas*, where the iconic Spanish painter's work is spiked and contorted into a nightmare landscape of Cubist forms. Temporary exhibits highlight the work of Picasso's contemporaries, though the museum would easily attract the same droves of visitors without them. Expect a long wait along the crowded street of Montcada during any day of the week, especially on Sundays when the museum is free. To beat the throngs of people, try hitting up the museum early or waiting until the later hours.

⚐ Ⓜ*Jaume I. From the Metro, walk down C. de la Princesa and turn right onto C. de Montacada.* ⓘ *Free entrance on first Su of each month.* Ⓢ *€8.50 (valid for 2 days, only for permanent exhibits). Annual subscription (permanent and temporary exhibits included) €14.* ⌚ *Open Tu-Sa 10am-7pm, Su 10am-2:30pm.*

PARC DE LA CIUTADELLA
♿(ᵗᵖ) PARK, MUSEUMS

Between Psg. de Picasso, C. Pujades, and C. Wellington

Once the site of the Spanish fortress built by King Felipe V in the 18th century, the park was transformed into its current state after the citadel was destroyed in preparation for the Universal Exhibition of 1888. This sprawling complex designed by Josep Fontserè includes copious green space as well as various *modernista* buildings from the period. Points of architectural interest span from two areas: the antique fort holds the governor's palace, arsenal, and *capilla*, and the Exhibition in 1888 area showcases century-old gems, many of which are still in use today. The steel and glass **Hivernacle**, a greenhouse-turned-civic-space near the Pujades entrance, maintains its original function as well as its newer one as a concert venue. The **Natural History Museum** (☎93 319 69 12) continues educating crowds and completing conservation work between its two locations. The **Museu Martorell** functions as a geology museum, and the ⌂**Castillo de los Tres Dragones**, designed by Lluís Domènech i Montaner (of Palau de Música Catalana and Hospital de Santa Creu fame) comprises the **Zoological Museum** building and the entrance to the **Barcelona Zoo** (☎90 245 75 45 ▣www.zoobarcelona.cat). The extravagant **Cascada Monumental** fountain located in the center of the park, designed in part by Antoni Gaudí, still provides a spectacle for any visitor. Though a newer addition, the ⌂**mastodon** near the entrance of the zoo makes for an excellent photo opportunity.

For those just looking to use the park as, well, a park, bike trails run around the exterior walls, and dirt pedestrian paths break up the lush grass and tree-shaded pockets. Expect to see nearly every corner covered by picnickers during the summer months, and be sure to stop by and join the locals for a bath in the fountain.

⚐ Ⓜ*Arc de Triomf. Walk through the arch and down the boulevard to enter the park.* ⓘ *Free Wi-Fi available at the Geological Museum, Parliament building, and Zoological Museum.* Ⓢ *Park free. Museum €4.10-5.60, Su 3-8pm free. Zoo €16.* ⌚ *Park open daily 10am-dusk. Natural History Museum open Tu-Sa 10am-6:30pm, Su 10am-8pm. Zoo open May 16-Sep 15 10am-7pm; Oct 10am-6pm; Nov-Dec 10am-5pm; Jan-Feb 10am-5pm; Mar-May 15 10am-6pm.*

PALAU DE LA MÚSICA CATALANA
♥♿❋ MUSIC HALL

C. Sant Francesc de Paula, 2 · · · · · · ☎902 47 54 85 ▣www.palaumusic.com

Serving as a home to both Barcelona's Orfeo Choir and the Catalan musical spirit, the Palau is a one-stop shop for every kind of music—from flamenco to blues to classical to pop. Even if you can't find a concert to fit your fancy (or budget), the guided tour of the building (the only other way possible to see the interior) is a must-see. In this 1908 *modernista* masterpiece, Lluís Domènech i Montaner, architect of the **Hospital de Sant Pau,** **Casa Fuster,** and the ⌂**Castell**

dels Tres Dragons, shaped an awe-inspiring building from brick, stone, iron, and glass. The frustrating impossibility of getting a good view of the exterior is due to Montaner assuming a plaza would be constructed in the front; unfortunately, this never happened, and now tourist pictures are taken from the windows of neighboring buildings facing the façade. Luckily, the exquisite interior more than makes up for this visual tease. The breathtaking stained-glass dome and long, tall stained glass windows shed light on the seating-turned-garden, complete with intricate ceramic flowers decorating the ceiling. Above and around the stage, angels representing musical instruments interact with musicians such as Wagner and Beethoven, trees, and stampeding horses. Back in commission after a 30 year hiatus, the Palau's 3000-tube organ stands front and center on the upper portion of the hall. Although they offer reduced admission concerts regularly, if you're dying to hear what it sounds like, just ask your tour guide—chances are they'll play a pre-programmed song just for your group.

✈ ⓂJaume I. Walk on Via Laietana toward the Cathedral. Walk for about 5min. and take a right onto C. Sant Pere Mas Alt. Palau will be on your left. 𝒊 Schedule of events and ticketing info available on website. Ⓢ Guided tours €12, students €10. 🕓 50 min. guided tours daily 10am-3:30pm, with English on the hour and Catalan and Spanish on the half hours. Aug and Easter week tours 10am-6pm. Box office open 9am-9pm.

El Raval

CENTRE DE CULTURA CONTEMPORÀNIA DE BARCELONA (CCCB)   ✦♿ ART
C. de Montalegre, 5   ☎93 306 41 00 🖥www.cccb.org

A literal hub for anything involving the more contemplative ideas of the city, the Centre de Cultural Contemporània de Barcelona boasts everything from art exhibitions to lectures on Gilles Deleuze to theater to literature to help trying to figure out what the hell public and private space really means. Three exhibition galleries, two lecture halls, an auditorium, and a bookstore fill the striking architectural complex, consisting of an early 20th-century theater-turned-supersleek glass-expansion-wing. Paired with the thought-provoking collections of nearby MACBA, the CCCB offers everything you'll need to inspire that next existential crisis.

✈ ⓂUniversitat. Walk down C. Pelai and take the 1st right and then a left onto C. Tallers. Take a right onto C. Valldonzella and a left onto C. Montalegre, which will place you in front of the Museum complex. 𝒊 Guided visits in Spanish Th 6pm, Sa 11:30am. Ⓢ One exhibition €4.50. Two or more exhibitions €6, under 25 €3.40, under 15 free. €3.40 on W; free on 1st W of month, Th from 8-10pm and Su 3-8pm. 🕓 Open Tu-W 11am-8pm, Th 11am-8pm, F-Su 11am-8pm. Last entry 30min. before close.

MUSEU D'ART CONTEMPORANI DE BARCELONA (MACBA)   ✦♿ ART
P. dels Angels, 1   ☎93 412 08 10 🖥www.macba.cat

If the teeny art galleries and student-studded eateries around El Raval have struck your fancy, consider checking out the culture hub that helped to spawn them all. Bursting out of the narrow streets and into its own spacious plaza, the bright white geometries of American architect Richard Meier's 1995 building have made an indelible mark on the land, both architecturally and culturally, by almost single-handedly turning the area into a regional cultural and artistic center. The stark, simple interior plays host to an impressive collection of contemporary art, with particular emphasis on Spanish and Catalan artists, including a world-renowned collection of interwar avant-garde art. Due to its prime location near the Universitat and its undeniable appeal to local youth, MACBA prides itself on hip happenings. During the summer, "Nits de MACBA" keeps the doors open until midnight on Thursday and Friday nights, with free guided tours and reduced admission. Students and art afficionados alike flock to the popular hangout to catch one of the more experimental rotating exhibits, exciting complements to the static permanent collection. As if this weren't enough, the museum completely transforms during Barcelona's Sonar music festival every year, magically converting into the Sonar Complex stage and denying admittance to all those without a festival ticket.

✈ ⓜUniversitat. Walk down C. Pelai and take the 1st right and then a left onto C. Tallers. Take a right onto C. Valldonzella and a left onto C. Montalegre, which will place you in front of the Museum complex. *i* Guided tours in English included in ticket purchase. ⓢ Entrance to all exhibits €7.50, students €6; temporary exhibits €6/4.50. One-year pass €12. ⓣ Open June 24-Sept 24 M 11am-8pm, W 11am-8pm, Th-F 11am-midnight, Sa 10am-8pm, Su 10am-3pm; Sept 25-June 23 M 11am-7:30pm, W-F 11am-7:30pm, Sa 10am-8pm, Su 10am-3pm.

RIERA BAIXA
C. de la Riera Baixa

ⓢ♿☺ FLEA MARKET, SECONDHAND
◪www.facebook.com/pages/Riera-Baixa

A street lined entirely with secondhand shops, Riera Baixa is a mecca for any bargain or vintage shopper. The main attraction happens on Saturdays when clothes, records, trinkets, cameras, and an unfathomable amount of other stuff combine with Raval's largely student population, giving birth to the most exciting flea market in the city.

✈ ⓜLiceu. Walk down C. de l'Hospital and take a slight right onto C. de la Riera Baixa. ⓣ Flea-market Sa 11am-9pm. Shops open daily.

PALAU GÜELL
C. Nou de la Rambla, 3

☺ ARCHITECTURE
☎933 17 39 74 ◪www.palauguell.cat

Commissioned by Eusebi Güell, a wealthy textile industrialist of Parc Güell fame, Güell Palace was designed by renowned architect Antoni Gaudí and completed in 1888. The Palace holds the distinction of being the only building that Gaudí completed, and it hasn't been significantly altered since. The building is currently closed for restoration and renovation, but it will be open for public visits beginning in April 2011.

✈ ⓜLiceu. Walk toward the water on Las Ramblas and take a right onto C. Nou de la Rambla. *i* Closed until April 2011. No tourist information available until reopening.

L'Eixample

◪ FUNDACIÓ ANTONI TAPIES
C. Aragó, 255

✦♿ ARCHITECTURE, ART
☎93 487 03 15 ◪www.fundaciotapies.org

Housed in a building by *modernista* architect Lluis Domenech i Montaner, the Fundació Antoni Tapies is made unmissable by its mess of wire and steel atop a low brick roofline, a sculpture by its namesake Antoni Tapies entitled "Núvol i Cadira," or "Cloud and Chair" (1990) that supposedly shows a chair jutting out of a large cloud. Once inside, the lower two levels are dedicated to temporary exhibitions on incredible modern and contemporary artists and themes, recently holding work by Eva Hesse and Steve McQueen. Ascend to the top floor to find the gallery space dedicated to famous Catalan artists, including Antoni Tapies himself. Paintings and sculpture using found materials shed new light on Catalonia's turbulent past, while summer nights light up with DJ nights, free drinks, and after-hours galleries.

✈ ⓜPasseig de Gràcia. Walk toward the mountain on Psg. de Gràcia and take a left onto C. Aragó. The museum has a funky mess of wire on top. ⓢ €7, reduced €5.60. Free May 18 and Sept. 24. ⓣ Open Tu-Su 10am-8pm.

◪ SAGRADA FAMILIA
C. Mallorca, 401

✦♿ ARCHITECTURE
☎93 208 04 14 ◪www.sagradafamilia.cat

If you know Barcelona, you know Sagrada Familia—its eight completed towers and fanciful forms befitting of its Gaudí nametag have been plastered on tourist magazines, highlighted in movie advertisements, and featured in every panorama of the city ever photographed in the modern era. And with over 120 years of construction, the cranes surrounding the Sagrada Familia complex have become as iconic as the temple itself.

Although still a work in progress, Sagrada Familia's construction began way back in 1882. The super-pious, super-conservative **Spiritual Association for Devotion to St. Joseph (or the Josephines)** commissioned the building as a reaction to the liberal ideas spreading through Europe in the decades prior. It was intended as an Expiatory Temple for Barcelona in commemoration of the Sacred Family—Mary, Jesus, and Joseph. When searching for an architect, the Josephines looked in-house and picked Diocesan architect Francisco de Paula del Villar as their main man, but the relationship quickly turned sour, and one year later the church replaced him with Gaudí after only the Gothic foundations had been laid.

At the time of employment, Gaudí was just 30 years of age, and he would continue to work on the building until his death over forty years later. Modest private donations founded the construction of the church in the beginning, but after the completion of the **crypt** in 1889, the church received an incredibly generous private donation allowing Gaudí to step up his game. This extra cash gave birth to the design that would make the building both the most ambitious and the most impossible to complete in the city. After building the **Nativity Facade,** a drop in private donations slowed construction, and in 1909 temporary schools were built next to the church for workers' children. Gaudí set up shop on-site a few years later, living next to his incomplete masterpiece until his brutal death by tram just outside of the church's walls in 1926. Fittingly, he was buried inside the **Carmen Chapel** of the crypt.

Gaudí's bizarre demise marked the start of a tragic period for the temple. The Civil War brought construction entirely to a hault, and in 1936 arsonists raided Gaudí's tomb, mashed the plaster models of the site, and burned every document in the workshop, effectively destroying all artifacts of the architect's original intention. Since then, plans for the construction have been based off of the remaining reconstructed plaster models, with computers only recently being used to help understand their complex mathematics.

Currently, the building remains under the auspices of the Josephines, and architect Jordi Bonet, whose father worked directly with Gaudí, remains in charge of the overall direction. The Cubist **Passion Facade** (Passion being the crucifixion, death, and resurrection of Christ) faces Pl. de la Sagrada Família, and was completed by Josep Marià Subirachs in 1998. Its angular and abstracted forms are a far cry from Gaudí's original plans for the facade in 1911 and provide a stark contrast to his own more traditional Nativity Facade on the opposite face. The first mass was held inside the gutted church in 2000 for celebration of the milennium, and the church's apse is projected for completion in the upcoming year thanks to a continuous stream of popular donations (read: your ticket price).

If all goes well, the projected completion date is 2026, coincidentally both the 100th anniversary of Gaudí's death and the date that hell is predicted to freeze over. Until then, paintings of the completed building line the adjacent **Casa Museu Gaudí,** and an exhibition dedicated to the mathematical models let you imagine the completed building that you'll probably never get to experience.

⌖ [M]Sagrada Familia. ℹ Guided tours in English May-Oct at 11am, 1pm, 3pm, and 4pm; Nov-Apr at 11am and 1pm. $ €11, students €9, under 10 free. Elevator €2.50. Combined ticket with Casa-Museu Gaudí €13, students €11. 🕐 Open daily Apr-Sept 9am-8pm, Oct-Mar 9am-6pm. Last elevator to the tower 15min. before close.

CASA BATTLÓ ♿ ARCHITECTURE

Pg. de Gràcia, 43 ☎93 216 03 06 🖥www.casabatllo.es

From the spine-like stairwell wrapping around the scaled building's interior to the undulating 📷**dragon-esque** curve of the ceramic rooftop, the Casa Battló will have you wondering what kinds of drugs Gaudí was rectally injecting. This architectural wonderland was once the home of the fantastically rich and is now the most heavily frequented of the three *modernista* marvels in the **Manzana de la Discordia** lining Passeig de Gràcia. A self-guided audio tour lets you navigate the dream-like environs at your own pace, so be sure to spend some time with the curved wood and two-toned stained glass of each of the doors (from both sides—the glass changes color), the soft scale-like pattern of the softly bowed walls, and the charybdis-esque light fixture that pulls the entire ceiling rippling into its center. Gaudí's design spans from the incredibly logical to the seemingly insane, including a blue lightwell that passes from deep navy to sky as you descend in order to distribute light more evenly.

If you're having a problem parting with the cash to get in, just try this logic, heard in line at the box office: if your flight to Barcelona had cost €18 more than you paid, would you still have taken it? Then why miss this gem for the same price? Like the guy who needed convincing, you won't be disappointed.

✦ Ⓜ*Passeig de Gràcia. Walk away from Plaza Catalonia on Passeig de Gràcia. Casa Battló is 2½ blocks down on the left.* ℹ *Tickets available at box office or through TelEntrada. Entrance includes free self-guided audio tour.* Ⓢ *Tours €17.80, students and BCN cardholders €13.* 🕐 *Open daily 9am-8pm.*

CASA MILÀ (LA PEDRERA)

✦♿ ARCHITECTURE

Pg. de Gràcia, 92   ☎93 484 59 00 🖥www.lapedreraeducacio.org

No, this building's facade didn't melt in the Barcelona sun, though it has garnered some equally unflattering comparisons. Its nickname "La Pedrera" literally means "the quarry," and stems from popular jokes, criticism, and caricatures about the house upon its construction 100 years ago. Although wealthy businessman Pere Milà hired Gaudí after being impressed by his Casa Battló a few blocks away, his wife began to loathe her version of Gaudí's signature style as construction progressed, and eventually refused to let the costly venture proceed. Not one to let the difficult couple have the last word, Gaudí sued the rich pair over fees and gave his winnings from the suit to the poor. Not ones to have Gaudí have the last say, the couple then looked elsewhere to complete their home interior, making La Pedrera the only house designed by Gaudí that isn't graced by his furniture.

La Pedrera still functions as a home to the rich, famous, and patient—the wait list for an apartment is over 20 years long—as well as offices of the Caixa Catalonia. Many portions of the building are open to the public, including an apartment decorated with period furniture (and, true to the house, not designed by Gaudí) and the main floor. The attic, a space known as **Espai Gaudí,** boasts a mini-museum to the man himself, including helpful exhibits explaining the science behind his beloved caternary arches and what exactly it means for the architect to be "inspired by natural structures." Up top, a terrace holds the perfect photo opportunity, whether with the desert-like sculptural outcroppings or the view overlooking Barcelona to Gaudí's Sagrada Familia. During the summer the terrace lights up both literally and metaphorically with jazz performances on Friday and Saturday nights in a series known as *La Nit de Pedrera*.

✦ Ⓜ*Diagonal. Walk on C. Rosselló toward Passeig de Gràcia and take a right. La Pedrera is on the left at the corner of C. Provença.* ℹ *Free audio tour with entrance.* Ⓢ *€9.50, students and seniors €5.50. Concerts €12; glass of cava included.* 🕐 *Open daily Mar-Oct 9am-8pm; Nov-Feb 9am-6:30pm. Last entry 30min. before close. Concerts last weekend of June and July F-Sa 9pm-midnight.*

CASA AMATLLER

✦ ARCHITECTURE, CHOCOLATE

Pg. de Gràcia, 41   ☎93 4487 72 17 🖥www.amatller.com

The severe, rational counterpart to Gaudí's neighboring acid trip **Casa Battló,** Casa Amatller was the first of the trio of buildings that has come to be known as the **Manzana de la Discordia.** In 1898, chocolate mogul Antoni Amattler commissioned **Josep Puig i Cadafalch** to spruce up the facade of his prominent home along Passeig de Gràcia, and out popped a mix of Catalan, neo-Gothic, Islamic, and Dutch architecture in a strict geometric plane. A carving of Sant Jordi battling the pesky ◧**dragon** appears over the front door, accompanied by four figures engaged in painting, sculpting, and architecture. Amattler's peddling in the muses is more than just decorative. Inside the building, find the **Amattler Institute of Hispanic Art,** including a library accessible to visiting scholars and students of art history. Although the house is currently undergoing renovations, the main floor is still open to visitors by reservation every Friday at noon, though times will change as the work progresses. If you're in the area and feel like stopping by to take a look at this gem, the lower level gift shop includes a free exhibition of the house and its sculpture and informs you as to exactly how Amattler got so filthy rich, with bars of the company's delicious chocolate for sale on your way out the door.

✢ ⓂＰ*asseig de Gràcia. Walk away from Plaza Catalonia on Passeig de Gràcia. Casa Amatller is two and a half blocks down on the left.* 𝒊 *Reservation by phone or email required for tour.* Ⓢ *Tours €10;include chocolate tasting.* ◱ *Guided tours F at noon.*

HOSPITAL DE LA SANTA CREU I SANT PAU   ♿ ARCHITECTURE

C. Sant Antoni Maria Claret, 167   ☎90 207 66 21 ▣www.santpau.es

Notoriously the most important piece of *modernista* public architecture, this hospital's practice is anything but *nouveau*. Dating back to 1401, the Hospital de la Santa Creu i Sant Pau is the newest embodiment of the medical practice formerly housed in the Antique Hospital de la Santa Creu in Raval. Wealthy benefactor Pau Gil bequested funds for the building upon his death with strict instructions, including the name appendage. Construction then began in 1902 under the design of **Lluís Domènech i Montaner,** who in almost Gaudían fashion (only made more appropriate by Gaudí's anonymous death in the old hospital), died before its completion. His son then saw the work to fruition, giving the hospital 48 large pavilions connected by underground tunnels and bedazzled with luxurious modernist sculptures and paintings. Although the hospital still functions as a world class medical facility today, you won't need to break a leg to appreciate its beauty. Guided tours are offered daily as a part of Barcelona's Ruta de Modernisme.

✢ Ⓜ*Hospital Sant Pau.* ◱ *Guided tours in English daily at 10am, 11am, noon and 1pm. Information desk open daily 9:30am-1:30pm.*

Gràcia

PARC GÜELL   ⊛♿ PARK, ARCHITECTURE

Gràcia

Now a mecca for countless tourists and outdoor-loving locals alike, Parc Güell was originally intended for the eyes of a select few. Catalan industrialist, patron of the arts, and all-around man of disgusting wealth Eusebi Güell called upon his right-hand man **Antoni Gaudí** in 1900 to collaborate on an endeavor completely unlike the previous Güell Palau. The patron envisioned a luxurious community of 60 lavish homes wrapped around an English-inspired, Ebenezer-Howard-esque garden paradise overlooking Barcelona—rich, elite, and pleasantly removed from the mundane realities of the city and its plebian people. Unfortunately for the complex, other members of Barcelona's upper class weren't convinced; they weren't about to abandon the amenities of the city for a cut-off hunk of grass dotted by Gaudí's seemingly deranged buildings, which that at the time lacked even basic living luxuries. Construction came to a halt in 1914, and in 1918 the area became a park when the Barcelona City Council bought the property.

The park was opened to the public in 1923 and has since been declared a UNESCO World Heritage Site. Buses bring flocks of visitors directly to the **Palmetto Gate,** a structure flanked by a guardhouse-turned-museum and giftshop. Hand-drummers stationed outside of the facing alcove often provide a dream-like soundtrack for walking through the gingerbread-esque architecture. Those with sturdy shoes lacking a fear of heights often choose to take the metro and climb the escalators to the nature-clad side entrance. The main attractions of the park (and, consequently, the areas most packed with people) are the brightly-colored mosaics and fountains, like the **salamander fountain** just across from Palmetto Gate. The pillar forest of the **Hall of One Hundred Columns (Teatre Griego),** dotted with sculptural pendants by **Josep Maria Jujol,** musicians, and people peddling fake handbags. The intricate vaults of the hall support **Plaça de la Nautralesa** above, enclosed by the winding **serpentine bench,** decked in colorful ceramics, including 21 distinct shades of white that were castoffs from the **Casa Milà.** If you catch yourself wondering how a ceramic bench can be so comfortable, thank the woman rumored to have sat bare-bottomed in clay for Jujol to provide the form.

Paths to the park's summit provide amazing views, and one in particular showcases what the park has left to offer: walk to the right when facing the salamander fountain from its base. Follow the wide path and veer right toward the shaded benches and continue climbing uphill to come across the **Casa-Museu Gaudí** *(C. d 'Olot, 7 ☎93 284 64 46 🖳www.casamuseugaudí.org.)* As you continue, the third and last original building of the complex, **Juli batllevell 's Casa Trías** lays inconspicuously ahead, still privately owned by the Doménech family. **El Turo de Les Tres Creus** greets visitors at the top of the wide path. This, the park's highest point with appropriately incredible views, was originally intended to be the residents' church and now serves instead to mark the end of the ascent.

Although the main areas of the park are regularly full during the dog days of summer, it's possible to ditch the toddlers and fannypacks by showing up at or before the park's opening—chances are they won't turn you away, and even if you have to wait, at least there's an incredible view.

🚏 [M]Lesseps. Walk uphill on Travessera de Dalt and take a left to ride escalators to safety. Bus #24 from Plaça Catalonia stops directly in front of the park. [$] Free. Museum €5.50, students €4.50. ⏰ Open daily Oct-Mar 10am-6pm; Apr-Sept 10am-8pm.

Montjuïc and Poble Sec

👍 FUNDACIÓ MIRÓ ♿ ARCHITECTURE, ART

Parc de Montjuïc ☎93 443 94 70 🖳www.fundaciomiro-bcn.org

From the outside in, the Fundació serves as both a shrine to and a celebration of the life and work of Joan Miró, one of both Catalonia and Spain's most beloved contemporary artists. The bright white angles and curves of the Lego-esque Rationalist building were desigend by Josep Lluís Sert, a close friend of Joan Miró. Since its first opening, the museum's holdings have expanded beyond Miró's original collection, with many works by those inspired personally by the artist being donated or acquired in the years after his death. A rotating collection of over 14,000 works now fills the open galleries with views to the grassy exterior and adjacent **Sculpture Park.** Highlights of the collection include paintings and gargantuine *sobreteixims* (paintings on tapestry) by Miró, as well as works by Calder, Duchamp, Oldenburg, and Léger. Like much of Barcelona, the foundation refuses to be stuck in its past—although an impressive relic of a previous era, the foundation continues to support the contemporary arts in the present day. Temporary exhibitions have recently included names such as Olafur Eliasson, Pipllotti Rist, and Kiki Smith, while the more experimental **Espai 13** houses exhibitions by emerging artists selected by freelance curators. Overwhelmed? You should be. This is one of the few times we recommend paying for the audio tour *(€4).*

🚏 [M]Parallel and then take the funicular to the museum. [$] €8.50, students €6. Audio tour €4. Sculpture garden free. ⏰ Open July-Sept Tu-Sa 10am-8pm, Su 10am-2:30pm; Oct-June Tu-Sa 10am-7pm.

NATIONAL ART MUSEUM OF CATALONIA

♦♿ ARCHITECTURE, ART

Palau Nacional, Parc de Montjuïc   ☎93 622 03 76 ⬛www.mnac.es

This majestic building perched atop the escalator summit of Montjuïc isn't quite as royal as it would at first appear. Designed by Enric Català and Pedro Cendoya for the 1929 International Exhibition, the Palau Nacional has housed the Museu Nacional d'art de Catalonia (MNAC) since 1934. Though the sculpture-framed view over Barcelona from the museum's front can't be beat, more treasures await inside. Upon entrance you'll be dumped into the gargantuan colonnaded **Oval Hall,** which, although empty, gets your jaw appropriately loose to prepare for its drop in the galleries. The wing to your right houses a collection of Catalan Gothic art, complete with wood-paneled paintings and sculptures Pier 1 would die to duplicate. To your left in the main hall is the wing housing the museum's impressive collection of Catalan Romanesque art and frescoes, removed from their original settings in the '20s and installed in the museum space—a move for the best considering the amount of churches devastated during the Civil War just a decade later. Upstairs are the more modern attractions, with MNAC's collections of modern art to the left, numismatics (coins, for you non-collectors) to the slight right, and drawings, prints, and posters to the far right. For those intoxicated by the quirky architecture of the city, Catalan *modernisme* and *noucentisme* works dot the galleries, from Gaudí's 1907 "Confidant from the Batlló House" chair to Picasso's Cubist "Woman in Fur Hat and Collar." Ranging from 1800-1940, the collection highlights both the shape of Barcelona's avant-garde movements at the time and paints a pictures as to how they got that way. If art isn't your thing, check out the currency collection—though beauty may be in the eye of the beholder, this 140,000-piece brief in the history of Catalan coin will hardly have any detractors.

💠 Ⓜ*Espanya. Walk through the towers and ride the escalators to the top—the museum is the palace-like structure.* ⓘ *Free entrance on first Su of each month.* Ⓢ *Permanent exhibits €8.50 (valid for two days). Annual subscription (permanent and temporary exhibits) €14.* ⌚ *Open Tu-Sa 10am-7pm, Su 10am-2:30pm.*

POBLE ESPANYOL

♦♿❈ ARCHITECTURE, ART

Av. de Francesc Ferrer i Guàrdia, 13   ☎93 508 63 00 ⬛www.poble-espanyol.com

One of the few original relics from the 1929 International Exibition still dotting the mountain, the Poble Espanyol first aimed to present a unified Spanish village from its disparate, disjointed parts. Inspired by *modernista* celebrity Josep Puig i Cadafalch's original idea, the four architects and artists in charge of its design visited over 1600 villages and towns throughout the country to construct its 117 full-scale buildings, streets, and squares. Though intended simply as a temporary arts pavilion, the outdoor architectural museum was so popular that it was kept open as a shrine (or challenge) to the ideal of a united Spain that never was and never will be. Nowadays, the Poble Espanyol is all of this and more, with artists' workshops lining the winding roads peddling goods, spectacles during the day, and Terrazza and other parties raging on during the night.

💠 Ⓜ*Espanya. Walk through the towers and take a right after climbing the escalators to the top.* Ⓢ *€8.90, students €6.60. Night entrance €5.50.* ⌚ *Open M 9am-8pm, Tu-Th 9am-2am, F 9am-4am, Sa 9am-5am, Su 9am-midnight. Shops open daily in summer 10am-8pm; in winter 10am-6pm.*

CASTLE OF MONTJUÏC

⊗ ARCHITECTURE

Ctra. de Montjuïc, 62-68   ☎93 256 44 45 ⬛www.bcn.catl

Built in 1640 during the revolt against Felipe IV, this former fort and castle has seen its fair share of both Catalan and Spanish struggles. The fortress first saw action in 1641 against Castillian forces and continued its function as a military implement until 1960 when it was ceded to the city and refurbished as a military museum by Francisco Franco. Despite being handed to the city, the fort was controlled by the army until 2007, when its direction was finally handed to the Barcelona City Council. Since then, Barcelona has really enjoyed having a castle—maybe a little too much. A current exhibition named "Barcelona té castell!" (Barcelona has a castle!) explores and celebrates the possibilties for the space, while the castle itself remains, you know, a castle. Incredible views of the harbor and city as well as a moat-turned-beautifully-manicured-garden await those that make the hike.

✦ ⓂEspanya. Montjuïc Cablecar on Avenida Miramar. ⑤ Free. 🕐 Apr 1-Sept 30 9am-9pm; Oct 1-Mar 31 9am-7pm.

THE GREAT OUTDOORS

Beaches

Let's talk 🅵platges—that's beaches in Catalan. For basic information on all of the city beaches, contact the **city beach office** (☎932 21 03 48 🖥www.bcn.cat/platges). Tents, motorcycles, soap, loud music, littering, and dogs (though we've only seen dogs and trash) are all prohibited. Showers, bathrooms, police, first aid, and basic info are available at each individual beach June-Sept 10am-7pm. Lifeguards are present at all beaches June-Sept daily 10am-7pm; Mar-June Sa-Su 10am-7pm. Lockers are available at the police station during certain hours. For the gym rats and juice heads, almost all beaches have some sort of outdoor workout facility.

PLATJA SAN SEBASTIÀ
♿ BEACH

Mouth of the Port to C. del Almirall Cervera 🖥www.bcn.cat/platges

The first of Barcelona's public beaches when stumbling out of the Ciutat Vella, Platja San Sebastià, along with Barceloneta, is one of the oldest beaches in the city. Older residents of the Barri Gótic fill the available sand and are joined by a mix of tourists attracted to its convenient location. Like all beaches closer to Las Ramblas and the center of the city, San Sebastià will fill up quickly, especially on weekends. If you're looking for a place a little more private, the end furthest from Barceloneta—near Torre San Sebastià—promises something at least remotely resembling peace and quiet.

✦ ⓂBarceloneta. 𝒊 Bathrooms, swimming area, and showers available. ⑤ Free. 🕐 Wheelchair-accessible bathing services available June and second half of Sept on holidays and weekends. Open daily July-1st week of Sept 11am-6pm.

PLATJA BARCELONETA
BEACH

From C. del almirall Cervera to Port Olimpic 🖥www.bcn.cat/platges

The most popular (read: crowded) beach in Barcelona, Barceloneta attracts a vibrant mix of visitors, tourists, and brave locals regardless of the weather. In short, good luck finding a place to sunbathe even when there's no sun to be seen. With three volleyball courts, an outdoor gym, information center, various restaurants, a boardwalk, skating area, ping pong, and a *biblioplaya* (beach-centric library), Barceloneta offers (nearly) everything but a spot to lay your towel.

✦ ⓂBarceloneta or ⓂCiutadella 𝒊 Info center. Book rental. Showers, public restrooms, volleyball courts, ping pong tables, and gym available. ⑤ Free. 🕐 Open 24hr.

PLATJA MAR BELLA
BEACH

From Mar Bella Pier to Bac de la Roda 🖥www.bcn.cat/platges

Past the Bogatell naval base, rocky outcroppings provide cover for Barcelona's only designated portion of nude beach. Past this short stretch of plentiful skin is a gay beach, marked by a rainbow flag flying at the beachside restaurant. Mostly frequented by younger and local people, the two sections provide a perfect place to shed some inhibitions (among other things).

✦ ⓂSelva del Mar. 𝒊 Showers, public restrooms, ping pong tables, skating area, and basketball available. ⑤ Free. 🕐 Open 24hr.

PLATJA NOVA MAR BELLA

                                              ✦ BEACH

Bac de Roda Pier to Selva de Mar Pier   ▣www.bcn.cat/platges

The furthest of all the beaches and consequently the least crowded, Platja Nova Mar Bella is the stomping ground of local youth, teenagers, and students. Still easily accessible by metro, this beach boasts a more relaxing alternative to the tourist-pushing match of Barceloneta, especially on weekends.

✦ ⓂSelva de Mar and ⓂEl Marisme. *i* Showers and public restrooms available. Ⓢ Free. ♿ Wheelchair-accessible bathing services available on holidays and weekends during June and second half of Sept. Open daily July-1st week of Sept 11am-6pm.

Parks

PARC DE COLLSEROLA

                                             ♨ PARK

Crta. de l'Església, 92   ☎93 280 35 52 ▣www.parccollserola.net

Just twenty minutes outside the center of Barcelona by train lies the largest metropolitan park in the world. At 84.65sq. km, Parc de Collserola makes Paris' Bois de Boulogne look like a playground and New York's Central Park like a grade school shoebox diorama. The park stretches along the **Collserola mountain range** from the **Besos River** to the **Llobregat River**, with **Barcelona** and the **Vallés basin** forming its southern and northern boundaries, respectively. Although the park is easily accessible by public transportation, few people from outside of Barcelona and its environs make the short trek, so expect to find all signs and informational material in Catalan.

Collserola isn't your typical "city park." The city grid is nowhere to be seen, and there are more than pigeons and squirrels here. The park offers a refreshing dose of fresh air and wildlife that the gridded city misses. Due in part to straddling two distinct climates, the coastal **Mediterranean** and the more deciduous **Euro-Siberian,** Collserola shelters a wide range of flora and fauna, including the occasional wild boar. For a greatest hits showcase of the variety that the park has to offer, the trail from **Parc del Laberint** (ⓂMundet) to **Sant Cugat** is highly recommended. Besides a relaxing place to birdwatch and improve your classification skills, the park also offers many opportunities for exercise, with a ton of hiking trails and the **Carrertera de les Aigües** (Water Road), a cycling track that follows the ridge of the mountain range.

For those who do not find never-ending delight in the birds and the bees, the park is littered with places to eat, benches to relax on, and historic pieces of architecture and ruins to mentally digest. History buffs will want to check out the 12th-century **Sant Adjutori** and **Sant Medir**, while modernists should be sure to make a stop at the **Collserola Tower,** a telecommunications tower designed by architect Normal Foster for the 1992 Olympic Games. Although the games have long past, its 10th-floor observation room and unbeatable location on Vilana hill make it an ideal place to look out over all of Barcelona, Montserrat, and, if the day is clear, even the Pyrenees.

✦ ⓂBaixador de Valvidvera for Information Center (S1, S2), ⓂPeu de Funicular (S1, S2), ⓂLes Planes (S1, S2), ⓂLa Floresta (S1, S2, S5, S55), or ⓂMundet (L3). *i* Tourist information center, museum, and restaurant near ⓂBaixador de Valvidvera entrance. Other museums and restaurants scattered throughout; see website for full listing. Ⓢ Free. ♿ Tours daily 10am-2pm. Info center open daily 10am-3pm.

FOOD   ▣

Barri Gòtic and Las Ramblas

LA COLMENA

                                       ✦✦✦ PASTRY SHOP ❶

P. de l'Àngel, 12   ☎933 15 13 56

Directly facing the Plaça l'Angel, *pastelería* and *bombonería* La Colmena sweetly greets visitors as they appear bleary-eyed from the labyrinth of the Barri Gòtic and the Catalonian Sun. La Colmena offers a variety of pastries, chocolates, sweets, and hard drinks (of the dessert variety) to take the buzz off a day of continually getting lost. Mirrored walls and marble inlaid floors covered with confectioneries make you feel as if you've suddenly walked into an old-time mix between the shop in *Charlie and the Chocolate Factory* and the gingerbread house of Hansel and Gretel. Offerings range from the expected—chocolate (€1.30) and truffles (€2)—to those specific to Cataluña, like the *pastellitas de l'Angel* (€1.25), a small and flaky pastry shell with sugary pumpkin filling. If you're overwhelmed (as you should be), just ask the knowledgeable staff.

✦ ⓂJaume I. La Colmena is at your back after exiting the metro. ⓈSweetsNo €1.30-4. ⏰ Open daily 9am-9pm.

ESCRIBÀ
                                                          ⏳❊⏏ DESSERT ❶

La Rambla, 83   ☎93 301 60 27 🖳www.escriba.es

Grab a coffee and ogle the stained-glass peacock or one of the many just as impressive works of art waiting to be devoured in the front display case. With tarts, croissants, cakes, and deceivingly beautiful and life like rings made of caramel, Escribà is waiting to tempt you from every corner of the store. If you're not in the mood for sweets, select one of their savory dishes, such as the croissant with blue cheese, carmelized apple, and walnuts (€4.50) or the "bikini" bread mold with ham and brie (€3.50).

✦ ⓂLiceu. Walk toward Plaça Catalonia. Escribà is almost immediately on the left. Ⓢ Sandwiches €3.50. Salads €3. Menú €5.90. ℹ Open Tu-Su 9am-9pm.

VEGETALIA
                                       ✦ℽ ORGANIC, VEGETARIAN ❷

C. Escudellers, 54   ☎93313 33 31 🖳www.restaurantesvegetalia.com

Vegetalia delivers delicious organic, natural, and environmentally conscious foods at reasonable prices that will please any customer, no matter the need. Relax at the bar and chat with the friendly, laid-back staff about the ironic history of the Plaça de George Orwell, or experience the square for yourself after ordering at their walk-up window. Try one of their pizzas (€9.50) topped off with the carob vegan chocolate cake (€4.50), or gorge yourself on their daily menú (€10). A range of organic foods, teas, and coffees is located in the back of the store.

✦ ⓂLiceu. Walk down Las Ramblas toward the sea. Take a left onto Carrer dels Escudellers and walk for about 5 minutes. Gopal is 3 doors down on the right after entering Plaça George Orwell. ℹ Organic store in rear. Ⓢ Appetizers €4-9.90; entrees €6.20-9. Menú €10. ⏰ Open M 1-4pm and 8-11:30pm, Tu-Sa 8-11:30pm, Su 1-4:30pm, Su 1-4:30pm and 8-11:30pm.

L'ANTIC BOCOI DEL GÒTIC
                                      ✦⏳ℽ CATALAN ❸

Baixada de Viladecols, 3   ☎933 10 50 67 🖳www.bocoi.net

Enter the lair of L'Antic Bocoi del Gòtic, where walls of rustic stone are somehow made impressively classy. The restaurant specializes in Catalan cuisine with fresh, seasonal ingredients and prides itself on bringing new ideas to traditional food. The staff recommends their selection of cheeses and their own take on the *coques de recapte*, a traditional regional dish made of a thin dough with delicious fresh produce and thickly layered meats. This hip joint fills up quickly after opening.

✦ ⓂJaume I. ℹ Reservations recommended. Ⓢ Appetizers €7-10, entrees €9-20. ⏰ Open M-Sa 8:30pm-midnight.

ARC CAFE
                                      ✦❊ FUSION, THAI ❷

C. Carabassa, 19   ☎9330 52 04 🖳www.arccafe.com

Down the narrow Carrer d'en Carabassa, Arc Cafe is easy to miss. For this reason, it's a great place to stop in when you're sick of the fanny packs and sneakers that crowd Las Ramblas—it's virtually guaranteed to be tourist-and bustle-free. The restaurant boasts a vegetarian-friendly menu that rotates every three months as well as popular Thai nights Th-F (regular menu still available). Luckily, their curries are always available—choose between chicken, bean curd, and jasmine rice (€10.50-11.50)—just be sure to order a mojito with Malibu to cool off (€6) if you're brave enough to go for spice. Cheaper midday menu also offered daily (€9.60).

✈ Ⓜ*Drassanes. Walk toward the Sea on Las Ramblas, take a left onto Carrer de Josep Anselm Clavé. Walk 5 min. and stay on this road as it changes names to Carrer Ample. Take a left onto Carabassa. Arc Cafe on right.* **i** *Reservations recommended on weekends.* Ⓢ *Appetizers €4.90-8; entrees €8.50-11.90. Wine €2. Beer €2-3.* ⚄ *Open M-Th noon-1am, F-Sa noon-2am.*

LES QUINZE NITS
✈♿♥♨❄ MEDITERRANEAN ❷

P. Real 6 ☎93317 30 75 ▧www.lesquinzenits.com

Despite the restaurant's white tablecloths, leather chairs, and fabulous view of the Plaça Reial, the line outside of Les Quinzes Nits is enough to make any weary traveler looking for a classier dinner reconsider their priorities. Where else would you woo your most recent roadside romantic acquisition on a backpacker's budget? Try the duck confit with triaxat and pesto sauce *(€10)* or the leek pie with tomato and arugula *(€6.31)*. Expect a 30min. wait upon opening, but reportedly the line diminishes around 9pm.

✈ Ⓜ*Liceu, walk down Las Ramblas toward the Sea and take a right on C. Ferran, then right onto Passeig Madoz. Restaurant on the left as you enter Plaça Reial .* **i** *No reservations.* Ⓢ*Appetizers €3-6; entrees €6-10. Bread €.85.* ⚄ *Open daily 1-3:45pm and 8:30-11:30pm.*

TUCCO
✈⊗♥ PASTA ❶

C. d'Aglà, 6 ☎933 01 51 91

True to its name, Tucco "fresh pasta" offers just that—a selection of fresh pastas topped with your choice of sauce and cheese *(€4)*. The limited seating in the teeny store serves as a revolving door for hip, young locals and internationals wandering far off the beaten paths of the Gothic Quarter. If pasta isn't your thing, a selection of wallet-and veggie-friendly sandwiches, pizzas, desserts, salads, and snacks fill the nutritional void a meal of carbs creates. Don't expect to sit if you come at mealtime; instead, take your plasticware and hit the road.

✈ Ⓜ*Licue. Walk on Las Ramblas toward the water. Take a left onto C. Escudellers. Left onto C. d'Aglà.* Ⓢ *Pasta €3.95. Pizza from €9.* ⚄ *Open M-F 1-11:30pm, Sa 1-6pm.*

ELS QUATRE GATS
✈⊗♥ CATALAN ❹

C. Montsió, 3 ☎93 302 41 40 ▧www.4gats.com

Named after the hostal that served as a vital grounds for the artistic and literary community in Barcelona in the last decade of the 19th century, Els Quatre Gats now attracts the flocks as much for its historic affiliations as for the quality of its offerings. Hand-painted tiles, drawings from the period, and a rustic wooden interior remind patrons of Barcelona's days of yore, even if the whole shtick is somewhat constructed. The sheer beauty of the Casa Figuras in which the restaurant sits is in itself worth a visit, and considering the prices are not too inflated for the food, the experience is well worth the money.

✈ Ⓜ*Catalonia. Face the station from the street and walk to the right corner of the Plaça, by el Corte Ingles. Turn right onto Av. Portal de l'Angel and then take a left onto C. Montsió.* **i** *Live piano daily 1-4pm.* Ⓢ *Entrees €13-25.55.* ⚄ *Open daily 10am-2am.*

CAFE DE L'OPERA
✈♿♥ CAFE ❷

La Rambla, 74 ☎93 317 75 85 ▧www.afeoperabcn.com

Beginning in the 18th century as a boarding tavern and later a chocolate shop, the cafe assumed its current form in 1929, adopting the amusing mix of modernist curves, Grecian women, and pastel paint colors that can be seen today. Don't be fooled by the fancy Parisian facade or the impressive historical pedigree—although famous as a Barcelonan post-opera institution, Cafe l'Opera offers affordable fare and a wide list of beers (including "Cannabis Club"; €3.60, which purportedly tastes like, well, you can guess), wines, drinks, and tapas.

✈ Ⓜ*Liceu. On La Rambla when walking toward the water.* **i** *Credit card only over €20. Other/ miscellaneous hard info.* Ⓢ *Tapas €2-4. Sandwiches €3-6.70. Specials €10.50-13.* ⚄ *Open daily 8:30am-2:30am.*

spain

TRAVEL BAR 💳♿📶🍸❄🌳 BAR [2]

C. de Boqueria, 27 ☎93342 52 52 💻www.travelbar.com

Predictably, this bar unabashedly caters to travelers. Unpredictably, it's a fantastic outside-the-hostel resource for people on the road, whether to meet fellow backpackers, chow down on a cheap meal, watch the game on the big screen, indulge in free internet, or browse their collection of travel books. Empty pockets? Stop in at 8pm for their €1 meals and to peruse their community bulletin board for deals on tours, rentals, and flamenco dance lessons. Older readers take note: complete with an endorsement from MTV, this place seems to cater almost exclusively to the college crowd. Menu is uncreative, overpriced, and downright cruel to vegetarians, but luckily it's near many delicious (and cheap) culinary alternatives.

➡ *[M]Liceu. Exit and walk down C. de Boqueria. Bar on the left. [S] Tapas €2-3. Entrees €6-12.50. Beer €3-5. €1 meals nightly at 8pm. 10% charge to sit on terrace. ⏰ Open daily 12:30pm-11:30pm.*

La Ribera

👍 **EL XAMPANYET** 💳♿🍸 TAPAS [2]

C. de Montcada, 22 ☎933 19 70 03

The cup doeseth overfloweth, with sheepskin wine bags, an overwhelming selection of *cava*, and crunchy old locals spilling out the door and onto the street at all hours. Inside is a museum of casks, blackened bottles, and kitschy bottle openers displayed against a handpainted ceramic tile background. We recommend you try their cask-fresh *cerveza* *(€3.50)* or their house wine *xampanyet* *(€2)*, and pad your stomach with some of their delicious tapas *(€1.10-12.50)*.

➡ *[M]Jaume I. Walk down C. de la Princesa and take a right onto C. de Montcada, towards the Museu Picaso. Xampanyet is on the right before reaching Plaçeta Montcada. [S] Tapas €1.10-12.50. Beer €3.50. Wine and cava from €2. ⏰ Open Tu-Sa noon-4pm and 7-11pm, Su noon-4pm.*

👍 **PETRA** 💳♿🍸❄ RESTAURANT [2]

C. dels Sombrerers, 13 ☎93 319 99 99

With dark wood, stained glass, art nouveau prints, menus decaled onto wine bottles, and chandeliers made of silverware, Petra will have you expecting a high price for its eccentricity. Luckily, the bohemian feel is matched by bohemian prices. Pastas like the delicious gnocchi with blue cheese and asparagus *(€5.15)* and entrees *(€7.85)* are nice on the wallet.

➡ *[M]Jaume I. Walk on C. Princesa and take a right onto C. del Pou de la Cadena. Take an immediate left onto C. de la Barra de Ferro and a right onto C. dels Banys Vells. Petra is located where C. dels Banys Vells terminates at C. dels Sombrerers. [S] Menú €6.50. Appetizers €4.85-7.05; entrees €7.85. ⏰ Open Tu-Sa 1:30-4pm and 9-11:30pm, Su 1:30-4pm.*

👍 **LA BÁSCULA** ♿ VEGETARIAN [2]

C. dels Flassanders, 30 ☎93 319 98 66

A working cooperative that serves cheap vegetarian sandwiches, *empanadas*, and salads. Doors serve as tables and a mixture of art, environmentally-friendly sodas, and protest flyers hanging up around the walls set this restaurant apart from the rest. Though discretely robed in the same antique exterior as more expensive places, Báscula provides a cheaper alternative to the upscale eateries in other stone hideaways surrounding Ribera. Hours and seating availability may change as the restaurant fights for its right to serve in-house, but takeout is available no matter the outcome.

➡ *[M]Jaume I. Walk down C. de la Princesa and take a right onto C. dels Flassanders. [S] Entrees and salads €7-9. Sandwiches €4-4.50. Piadinas €6. ⏰ Open W-Su 1-11pm.*

HOFMANN PASTISSERIA 💳♿❄ PASTRY SHOP [1]

C. dels Flassaders, 44 ☎932 68 82 21 💻www.hofmann-bcn.com

Pastry school meets storefront in this Seussian mindbender in a French countryside setting. Artisans work on delectable goods in clear view on the mindbending spiral staircase above, while glass cases and wooden cabinets filled with adorable gelatos (€3.50), precious marmalade jars (€8), and a selection of not-so-sickeningly-cute-but-utterly-delectable tarts and cakes wait below. For breakfast, try a coffee and one of the fresh croissants.

✚ ⓜJaume I. Walk down C. de la Princesa and take a right onto C. dels Flassanders. Hofmann is located immediately before crossing Passeig del Born. ⓢ Croissants €1-1.50. Gelato €3.50. Marmalades €8. Chocolates €1-5. Coffee €1.20-1.50. ⓩ Open Tu-W 9am-2pm and 3:30-8pm, Th-Sa 9am-2pm and 3:30-8:30pm, Su 9am-2:30pm.

BODEGA LA TINAJA
✚ ⓔⓖ❄ WINERY, RESTAURANT ❸
C. de l'Esparteria, 9 ☎93 310 22 50 🖥www.bodegalastinajas.com
With so much wine lining the walls that you'll feel tipsy just looking in, this dark, earthy den behind a huge Gothic door provides bottle after bottle, ▮jug after jug, and even barrel after barrel for whatever your thirst (or just eyes) may desire. The smell of seasoned meat fills the air with typical Catalan entrees (€10-21).

✚ ⓜBarceloneta. Walk away from the water on Plà del Palau and turn right onto folo Plà del Palau at the end of the plaza. Turn left onto Plaça de les Olles and follow it as it veers into C. de les Dames. Turn right onto C. de l'Esparteria. ⓘ Large selection of wine. Sometimes hosts guitar and flamenco concerts. ⓢ Salads €7.25-8.75. Full entrees €10-21, half €4.25-11. ⓩ Open Tu-Su 8am-midnight.

EL ROVELL
✚ⓔⓖ❄ CATALAN ❸
C. de l'Argenteria, 6 ☎932 69 04 58🖥www.elrovelldelborn.com
Literally "the yolk" and not so literally "the place to meet," El Rovell satisfies both claims with a special egg-centric menu section and a large TV for congregating around the game. Don't be fooled by the screen in the back and the buckets hanging from the tables—this is no spit-your-shells-on-the-floor sports bar. Classy red leather stools and a clean wood interior match equally refined clientele and cuisine, like *huevos rotos* (scrambled eggs) with *foie gras* (€9.25).

✚ ⓜJaume I. Exit to C. de l'Argenteria and walk down C. de l'Argenteria away from Via Laietana. ⓢ Entrees €7.50-24. Salads €6.50-14. Tapas €5.50-11. ⓩ Open daily 1-4pm and 7pm-midnight.

VA DE VI
✚ⓔⓖ❄ CATALAN ❸
C. dels Banys Vells, 16 ☎933 19 29 00
This 15th-century tavern was once home to Christopher Columbus, though nowadays the rustic, earthy interior is caught in a decorating rift between 19th-century cellos and random flourescent lightning bolts ripping through the main room. The menu hearkens back to its historic past with a selection of traditional Catalan dishes, cheeses from France and Spain, and enough wine and *cava* to get you to believe you discovered the ▮New World.

✚ ⓜJaume I. Walk down C. de l'Argenteria and take a left onto C. Rossic. Take a right onto C. dels Banys Vells. ⓢ Meats €4-14.20. Cheeses €4-9. Tapas €1.50-6.50. Wine €2. Cava €2.50. Beer €1.50. ⓩ Open M-Th 6pm-2:30am, F-Sa 6pm-3am, Su 6pm-2:30am.

LA PIZZA DEL BORN
✚ⓔⓖ PIZZERIA ❶
Pg. del Born, 22 ☎933 10 62 46
True to its name, La Pizza del Born serves pizza along the oh-so-fashionable Passeig del Born—something worth noting for the important role it serves for budget travelers drowning in the dollar signs of boutiques and botegas. A slice will cost you just €1.80, and stools and a TV make finding new friends easy during any fútbol match.

✚ ⓜJaume I. Walk down C. de la Princessa and take a right onto C. dels Flassanders. Pizza del Born is in front and to the right upon entering Passeig del Born. ⓢ Slice of pizza €1.80; 2 slices and a drink €3.90. ⓩ Open M-Th noon-1am, F-Sa noon-2am, Su noon-1am.

El Raval

👍 SOHO
💳♿🍸 PITA, HOOKAH [1]

C. Ramelleres, 26

One of the most recent additions to Raval, Soho is also one of the most welcome, serving cheap and simple eats like pitas and pastas with meat and vegetarian options *(€1.95)* without sending you off in a rush. Low-slung seats with smaller, intimate rooms make the perfect setting for test-driving a hookah from the impressive wall of smoking paraphernalia *(€10).*

➡ ⓂUniversitat. Walk down C. Tallers and take a right onto C. de les Ramelleres..Ⓢ Pitas €2. Pasta €3. Hookah €10. ⏰ Open M-Sa 1pm-midnight.

👍 JUICY JONES
💳♿🍸❄ VEGETARIAN [2]

C. Hospital, 74 ☎934 43 90 82 🖥www.juicyjones.com

The big brother of the Juicy Jones in the Barri Gotíc, this version of the vegetarian eatery offers a Raval-inspired twist—daily specials of Indian dahl and curries spice up the normal selection of sandwiches, plates, and an impressive selection of juices. If you have ever wondered what M.C. Escher's art would have looked like in the times of LSD, the interior will satisfy your curiosity.

➡ ⓂLiceu. Walk down C. de l'Hospital. Juicy Jones is on your right on the corner of C. Hospital and C. d'En Roig, before you hit Rambla del Raval. Ⓢ Menú €8.50. Daliy thali plate €6. Tapas €2-3.50. Sandwiches €3.85-4.50. ⏰ Open daily 1-11:30pm.

👍 NARIN
🚫♿🍸 MEDITERRANEAN [1]

C. Tallers, 80 ☎933 01 90 04

Sitting discretely along the shops and cafes of C. Tallers, Narin is hiding the best baklava in Barcelona and equally scrumptious falafel, *shawarma*, and kebabs. If you can't stand the heat, get out of the kitchen—the inside feels like a sauna with wooden walls and sweaty people. Luckily, beers come cold and cheap *(€1.80)* for those looking to brave the bar area, and a tiled dining room provides a reprieve from the buzz of the kebab shaver.

➡ ⓂUniversitat. Walk down C. dels Tallers. Ⓢ Pitas €3-4. Snacks €2.50-4.80. Baklava €1. Beer €1.80. ⏰ Open M-Th 11am-2am, F-Sa 11am-3am, Su 11am-2am.

SHALIMAR
💳♿🍸 PAKISTANI, INDIAN [2]

C. Carme, 71 ☎933 29 34 96

Shalimar serves authentic Pakistani and Indian dishes tandoori style. Generous

the art of *tapear*-ing

You may be under the (very common) impression that tapas are a type of Spanish food. However, it would be better to say that tapas are a Spanish way of eating.

Tapas are said to have been invented out of necessity. According to *The Joy of Cooking,* the original tapas were the slices of bread or meat which sherry drinkers in Andalusian taverns used to cover their glasses between sips, explaining the verb's origin: *tapar*, to cover. The reasoning behind this was protection from the fruit flies that abound during hot Spanish summers, and their penchant for sherry. Eventually, the bartenders realized that by diversifying their food offerings, they would net more customers, and the idea of tapas came into being. Today the tapas themselves may be any type of Spanish food, served in small portions. The verb tapear contains the essence of tapas, as it means, colloquially: to go out to several bars and order a drink and a few tapas at each. It's the quintessential method of Spanish socializing: similar to a pub crawl, but with way more food.

portions and delicious meat-based curries including chicken (€7), lamb (€8.20), and shrimp (€9) punctuate a menu that would make any vegetarian happy. Handpainted tiles and warm lighting perk up the interior as lace curtains block out the busy streets of Raval.

✣ ⓂLiceu. Walk down C. de l'Hospital and take a right onto C. d'En Roig. Left onto C. del Carme. Shalimar is on the left before the fork in the road. Ⓢ Appetizers €2-8. Veggie specials €3.70-4. Shrimp curry €9.30. Chicken €7. Beer €2. ⌚ Open M-Tu 8pm-midnight, W-Su 1-4pm and 8pm-midnight.

MADAME JASMINE ⅙ ⅋ CAFE ❶
Rambla del Raval, 22

Allow yourself to be seduced either by the 19th-century French-brothel-chic interior or the scrumptious *bocadillos*. Orange and red lighting sets the mood, incense fills the nostrils, and a selection of sultry Latin, electro, and lounge music will get you in the mood to partake in the less literal red light activities lining the streets of Raval.

✣ ⓂLiceu. Walk down C. de l'Hospital and take a right onto Rambla del Raval. Madame Jasmine will be on your left nearly two thirds down. Ⓢ Sandwiches and salads €4.75. House vermouth €2.20. Cocktails €5.50. Shots €2. ⌚ Open M-F 5:30pm-2:30am, Sa-Su 1:30pm-2:30am. Kitchen open daily until midnight.

MENDIZABAL ⓔ⅙⚐ FOODSTAND ❶
C. Junta de Comerç, 2

A crowd of young, artsy students out front and vibrant multicolored tiles in the back make this otherwise inconspicuous foodstand hard to miss. Take your cheap eats to go, or grab a seat on the terrace in the neighborhing plaza for an extra 10% (look for the coordinating chairs). Some veggie-friendly options are available—we recommend the tomato, brie, and avocado sandwich (€3.60).

✣ ⓂLiceu. Walk down C. l'Hospital. Mendizabal is at the corner of C. l'Hospital and C. Junta de Comerç. ℹ Terrace seating located in plaça across the street, but will cost 10% extra. Ⓢ Bocadillos €3.60-4.10. Beer €2.50. Postres €1.30-2.80. ⌚ Open daily 8am-12:30am.

L'ANTIC FORN ⓔ⅙⅋ CATALAN ❸
C. Pintor Fortuny, 28 ☎93 412 05 86 🖳www.lanticforn.com

White tablecloths and an unremarkable interior hide high quality Catalan cuisine at a reasonable price. The dining room is bright and airy during the day, with the crowd getting younger and the lighting sultier as the night progresses. Order the cooked artichokes (€6.50) or grilled goat breast (€9) as you get prepared for a rowdier end to your night elsewhere.

✣ ⓂCatalonia. Walk toward the sea on Las Ramblas and take a right onto C. Pintor Fortuny. ℹ Reservations recommended on weekends. Ⓢ Appetizers €4.50-11; entrees €8.70-18. Daily menú €11. ⌚ Open daily 9am-5pm and 8pm-midnight.

ORGANIC ⓔ⅙⚐❈ CAFE, MEDITERRANEAN ❷
C. Junta de Comerç, 11 ☎933 01 09 02 🖳www.antoniaorganickitchen.com

For once, you won't have to worry about space for seating—organic has enough room to fit an entire youth hostel and their luggage. A vegan buffet (€7) surprises and delights with croquettes, pasta, and salad fixings, while all vegetarian Mediterranean dishes will please even the most outspoken carnivores. Be sure to say thanks to Mother Earth as you leave—she'll be looking down on you approvingly, surrounded by peas, earth, and fire, to your left.

✣ ⓂLiceu. Walk down C. l'Hospital and take a left onto C. Junta de Comerç. Ⓢ Vegan salad buffet €7. Pizza €9. Menú €9.50. ⌚ Open daily 12:30pm-midnight.

BAR RESTAURANT ELISABETS ⓔ⅙⅋ BAR, RESTAURANT ❷
C. Elisabets, 2-4 ☎933 17 58 26

Hopping local bar by night, this crypt for decrepit old radios offers a daytime menu of cheap sandwiches and lighter fare (€2.40-3.45), as well as heavier homemade dishes *(€6-12)* and cheese and meat platters *(€9-10)* to satisy midday hunger. Be prepared to get cozy with a younger crowd no matter what time you eat.

➡ Ⓜ*Universitat. Walk down C. Tallers and take a right onto C. Elisabets..* $ *Sandwiches €2.40-3.45. Lunch menú €8.50. Tapas €2-3.55. Appetizers €2.40-3.50; entrees €6-12. Beer €1.40-2.15. Mixed drinks €5-7.* ⏰ *Open M-F 7:30am-2am, Sa 7:30am-11pm.*

CHULO 🌿♿🍸☀ CAFE ❶

Pl. Vincenç Martorell ☎933 02 40 95

Gold indoor couches and painted cherry trees inject a shabby chic upscale twist into the interior of this little cafe, but the real life is outside on the terrace in Plaça Vincenç Martorell, where it helps form the trifecta of cafes lining the side of the courtyard. Cheap breakfasts like the *toasta* with brie and tomato *(€3.50)* and *bocadillos*, like salmon and cream cheese *(€4.90)*, make this cafe the best of the bunch.

➡ Ⓜ*Catalonia. When facing Las Ramblas, take the road to your right (C. de Petal) along the plaza. Turn left onto C. de Jovellanos at the end of the plaza. Follow C. de Jovellanos as it becomes C. de les Ramelleres, and Plaça de Vincenç Martorell is on the left.* $ *Breakfast €2-4.20. Sandwiches €4.50-5.50. Salad €5.75-7.* ⏰ *Open daily 10am-midnight.*

CAFE D'ANNUNZIO 💳♿🍸❄☀ CAFE ❷

Pl. Vincenç Martorell ☎933 02 40 95

Rainbow stickers mark the glass doors of the last of the three cafes that line the arcade of Plaça Vincenç Martorell. Pictures of Venice and sculptures of Roman heads dress up the otherwise generic interior that sells delicious coffee supplied by Cafe del Dog. Sit inside to find an anachronistic, ill-fitting mix of '80s alternative hits playing over the stereo.

➡ Ⓜ*Catalonia. When facing Las Ramblas, take the road to your right (C. de Petal) along the plaza. Turn left onto C. de Jovellanos at the end of the plaza. Follow C. de Jovellanos as it becomes C. de les Ramelleres, and Plaça de Vincenç Martorell is on the left.* $ *Appetizers €1.60-4. Platters €10-15. Beer €2.70-3. Sandwiches €5-8, small €3.25-5.50.* ⏰ *Open daily 9:30am-1am.*

L'Eixample

👍 **OMEÍA** ♿🍸❄ JORDANIAN ❷

C. Aragó, 211 ☎93 452 31 79

When you're (literally) sick of gorging yourself on cheap shwarma from stands, stop in to Omeía for some authentic Middle Eastern fare that will only make you regret not having a bigger stomach. Start off with their roasted red pepper soup *(€6.50)* and fill up with one of their traditional Jordanian dishes *(€9-13)*. A word of advice: be prepared to take a long walk around the long blocks of l'Eixample after you finish to ease digestion.

➡ Ⓜ*Universitat. Walk on C. d'Aribau to the left of the University. Take a right onto C. Aragó.* $ *Starters €6-7. Entrees €6-13. Menú €7.50.* ⏰ *Open daily 10am-4pm and 8pm-midnght.*

👍 **EL JAPONES** 💳♿🍸❄ JAPANESE, SUSHI ❸

Passatge de la Concepció, 2 ☎93 487 25 92 💻www.grupotragaluz.com

This sushi costs more than the price of your hostel for the night, but it's more than worth shortening your trip. Bulk up on noodles or rice and order a mixed sushi platter *(€10.50-21.80)* for a cheaper (though by no means cheap) alternative. A sleek interior and romantic ambience makes for the perfect place to bring a date or make new friends.

➡ Ⓜ*Diagonal. Walk toward Passeig de Gràcia and take a right onto it. Take a right onto Passatge de la Concepció, the first smaller road on the right.* $ *Appetizers €5.70-10.20. Noodles €5.90-6.40. Sushi €5-10. Sushi platters €10.50-21.80.* ⏰ *Open M-W 1:30-4pm and 8:30pm-midnight, Th-Sa 1:30-4pm and 8:30pm-1am, Su 1:30-4pm and 8:30pm-midnight.*

CERVESERIA CATALANA 💳♿🍸❄☀ TAPAS, CATALAN ❸

C. Mallorca, 236 ☎93 216 03 68

Tapas, *flautas*, seafood, burgers, beer, wine, and more—it's easy to see why locals flock to Cerveseria Catalana's warmly lit interior in the dark of night. During the evening hours, the bar and outdoor seats are abuzz with the lively chatter of 20-somethings, while the crowd gets older (though no less lively) as you move back through the proper tables. Plan on waiting to get a seat, or give in and join the barside party.

✣ ⓂDiagonal. *Walk away from Passeig de Gràcia and take a right onto Rambla de Catalana. Take a right onto C. Mallorca.* Ⓢ *Starters €3.85. Salads €3.10-6.10. Tapas €3-12.* ☿ *Open daily 8am-1:30am.*

FRIDA'S MEXICAN RESTAURANT
♥ ♿ ❤ ❄ MEXICAN ❷

C. Bruc, 119 ☎93 457 54 09

Reportedly the most authentic Mexican restaurant in Barcelona, Frida's serves anti-TexMex quesadillas, *tostadas*, and a range of platos, including *cochinita pibil* (*€11.65*) and *michoacan carnitas* (*€11.35*), generally for much less than they're worth. Kick back with a Jamaican-flavored margarita (*€5.70*) at the bar, sit under a fitting picture of Frida Kahlo, or take your food to go and picnic along nearby Passeig de Gràcia.

✣ ⓂGirona. *Walk on C. Girona toward C. Aragó and take a left onto C. de Mallorca. Frida's is on the corner of Mallorca and Bruc.* Ⓢ *5 tacos €9 Th and F. Salads €5.90-6.30. Tostadas and quesadillas €3. Entrees €7.80-11.35. Margaritas €5.70.* ☿ *Open Tu-Sa 1-4pm and 8:15pm-midnight.*

MAURI
♥ ♿ ❤ ❄ PASTRY SHOP, TEA SHOP, DELI ❶

Rambla del Catalonia, 102 and 103 ☎93 215 10 20 🖳www.pasteleriasmauri.com

This tripartite pastry-deli-dessert shop has something to enchant whatever your hunger. Dine in the 102 shop over little sandwiches, croquettes, and croissants, or order something from the deli next door and dine in the wood and plaster salon. Across the street you'll find their *bomboneria* and tearoom, offering adorable giftbaskets in case you're looking to woo a fellow traveler.

✣ ⓂDiagonal. *Walk away from Passeig de Gràcia and take a right onto Rambla de Catalonia. The pastisseria is on the right and the tea shop on the left.* Ⓢ *Pastries and snacks €1.50-2.50. Lunch menú €13.* ☿ *Open M-F 9am-9pm, Sa 9am-9pm, Su 9am-3pm.*

LAIE BOOKSTORE CAFE
♥ (((•))) ❤ ❄ CAFE, CATALAN ❸

C. Pau Claris, 85 ☎93 318 17 39 🖳www.laie.es

Laie's is the perfect place to curl up with a purchased book after impressing your friends with your memorization of one of their literary quotes along the windows. Choose from a sunny yellow backroom with palm trees and burlap shades or chill out in the dark, shaded couches of the front. A veggie-friendly snack bar with gourmet mini sandwiches and pastries provides snacks during the odd hours, while an all-you-can-eat lunch buffet satisfies the hunger knowledge can't fill.

✣ ⓂGràcia. *i Internet €1 per 15min.* Ⓢ *Coffee and snacks €1.35-4.50. Beer €2-2.60. Wine €1.55-3. Lunch menú M-F €14; Sa-Su €17.* ☿ *Open M-F 9am-1am, Sa 10am-1am.*

COLMADO DE SOL
♥ ♿ ❤ ❄ BEER, CAFE ❷

C. Consell de Cent, 383 ☎93 533 19 47 🖳www.colmadodelsol.com

Although this little cafe offers a variety of deli-style items for takeout or enjoyment at one of their few tables, the real attraction is in their almost limitless selection of beer. Over 300 different types line the walls, all chilled and ready for your stomach. Knock back a few before heading to their tapas bar next door, or pick up a couple of classy brews so you're not stuck paying €1 for Estrella from a six-pack later in the night.

✣ ⓂGirona. *Walk along C. Consell de Cent toward C. del Bruc. Colmado de Sol will be right after the intersection.* Ⓢ *Plates of the day €8. Dinner menú €10.* ☿ *Open M-Sa noon-10pm.*

LA FLAUTA
♥ ♿ ❤ ☁ TAPAS, SANDWICHES ❷

C. Aribau, 23 ☎93 323 70 38

La Flauta takes its name from the long, thin crusty Catalan sandwich that puts other *bocadillos* to shame. Bearing no resemblance to the stale bread and two slices of cheese you drunkenly paid €4 for at 3am, these sandwiches are stuffed full of mouth-

spain

watering veggies, meat, and cheese *(half €3.65-6.90; whole €4.75-8.75).* Lots of veggie options, tapas, and other plates fill out the menu in a decor that would never leave you believing that they're known for two pieces of bread and some filling.

⚑ Ⓜ*Universitat. Walk down C. d'Aribau, the road to the left of the University. La Flauta is 1 block down on the left.* Ⓢ *Weekday lunch menú €10.50. Entrees €4.50-7.90. Sandwiches €3.65-7.90.* ⏲ *Open M-Sa 7am-1:30am.*

LA MUSCLERIA
💨♥❦✿♨ SEAFOOD ❷
C. Mallorca, 290
☎93 458 98 44 🖳www.muscleria.com

Would you eat them in a can, would you, could you, in a van? Would you eat them in a boat, could you eat them on a float? Although you probably won't be able to answer these questions, La Muscleria will let you try—they offer up more mussel options than a single mind can muster, though you'll have to order takeout (at a 20% discount) to experiment with eating locales. Ordering in gets you a bucket of mussels and a smaller dish of fries. Other seafoods (calamari and oysters, to name a few) round out the menu.

⚑ Ⓜ*Girona. Walk along C. de Girona toward C. d'Aragó and take a left onto C. Mallorca. La Muscleria is located on the left, in a basement.* ℹ *20% discount for takeout.* Ⓢ *Salads €6.75-7.05. Mussels €9-10.85.* ⏲ *Open M-Sa 1-4pm and 8:30-11:30pm, Su 1-4pm.*

CAN CARGOL
💨♿❦✿ CATALAN ❸
C. València, 324
☎93 458 96 31 🖳www.cancargol.es

A fun selection of snail dishes *(including "grandfather" or "mother-in-law" style; each €9.25)* are complemented with a range of charcoal grilled veggies and meat-centric entrees, ranging from pig's feet *(€5.25)* to *bacalau* with garlic mousseline *(€7.50).* Though obviously nicer than your average kebab stand, the relatively laid-back atmosphere with exposed rafters and blackened wine bottles won't make you feel too out of place when you show up in your shirt and cargo shorts.

⚑ Ⓜ*Girona. Walk along C. de Girona toward C. d'Aragó and take a left onto C. de Valencia.* ℹ *Reservations recommended F-Su.* Ⓢ *Appetizers €3.75-8.75; entrees €5.75-18.25.* ⏲ *Open daily 1:30-4pm and 8:30pm-midnight.*

LA PULPERÍA
💨♿❦✿♨ SEAFOOD ❷
Consell de Cent, 329
☎92 487 53 98 🖳www.restaurantelapulperia.com

In a masochistic turn of events, this restaurant lets you eat fantastic *pulpo,* or octopus, under the watchful eye of an eight-legged friend (admittedly, he's painted and presumably holds no grudges). Just to be sure there are no hard feelings, a selection of Galician tapas are available around the dark wooden bar, and there's always room to escape his gaze on the terrace.

⚑ Ⓜ*Passeig de Gràcia. Walk up Pg. de Gràcia and take a right onto Consell de Cent.* Ⓢ *Tapas €4-5.60. Octopus €8.25-33.* ⏲ *Open M-Th noon-midnight, F-Sa noon-2am.*

LA RITA
💨♿❦✿ CATALAN ❸
C. Aragó, 279
☎93 487 23 76 🖳wwww.laritarestaurant.com

The stomping ground of locals looking for an unbeatably priced midday meal. The cuisine spans a small range of traditional items with a twist, including potatoes and black sausage, duck breast with apples, raspberry *coulis,* and mango chutney. Though the price is near dirt cheap for the quality, the interior is anything but; expect an upscale but relaxed ambience that will make you question wearing that T-shirt—but not quite regret the decision.

⚑ Ⓜ*Girona. Walk toward C. d'Aragó and take a left onto the street. La Rita is a flew blocks down on your right.* Ⓢ *Appetizers €4.75-7; entrees €7-11.* ⏲ *Open daily 1-3:45pm and 8:30-11:30pm.*

TAPAS, 24
💨⊗❦✿☁ TAPAS ❷
C. Diputació, 269
☎93 488 09 77 🖳www.carlesabellan.com

Climb down the stairs and into the den of delicious tapas. Chef Carles Abellan, formerly of El Bulli, serves up food that you can actually afford at this alternative to his acclaimed Comerç 24. Marble countertops and colorful paintings of the menu spruce up this cafeteria-esque alcove. Try a plate of *patatas bravas* (€3.75) with either a glass of *cava* (€3) or their house *sangría* (€3.75).

➧ *[M]Passeig de Gràcia. Walk away from Plaça Catalonia. Tapas, 24 is on the corner of C. Diputació and Pg. de Gràcia.* [$] *Tapas €2.50-8. Raciones €9-12. Wine and cava €3.* ⏰ *Open daily 9am-midnight.*

RODIZIO GRILL 💳♿🍸❄ BRAZILIAN GRILL, CATALAN [3]

C. Consell de Cent, 403 ☎93 265 51 12

Not only is this buffet food delicious, fresh, and of high-quality, but some of the fare, including Brazilian meats, make their way around to each of the tables. The buffet will cost you €18-20, so come hungry enough to eat the entire blue-and-white cow looking down from overhead.

➧ *[M]Girona. Walk along C. de Girona toward C. Consell de Cent and turn right onto the road. Rodizio Grill is to the left.* [$] *M-Th lunch buffet €18.20; nights and F-Sa €20.50. Desserts €3.24-4.30. Cocktails €5.* ⏰ *Open M-Th 1-4:30pm and 9pm-midnight, F-Sa 1-4:30pm and 9pm-1am, Su 1-4:30pm and 9pm-midnight.*

Barceloneta

👍 **BOMBETA** 💵♿🍸 TAPAS [3]

C. Maquinista, 3 ☎93 319 94 45

Take heed of the warning scrawled above the bar, "No hablamos inglés, pero hacemos unas bombas cojonudas"—or, for the non-Spanish speaking set, "We don't speak English, but we make *bombas* that are out of this world." A retro facade with windows plastered with menu listings offers typical Spanish fare like *tostadas*, tortillas, and tapas, but really—just get the *bombas*.

➧ *[M]Walk down Pg. Juan de Borbó (toward the beach) and take a left onto C. Maquinista.* [$] *Appetizers €3-9.50; entrees €5-18.* ⏰ *Open M-Tu 9am-11:45pm, Th-Su 9am-11:45pm.*

SOMORROSTRO 💳♿🍸❄ SEAFOOD [3]

C. Sant Carles, 11 ☎93 225 00 10 🖥www.restaurantesomorrostro.com

This eatery is one of the few restaurants that is a part of Barceloneta's restaurant association, a recently established organization dedicated to making the inflated prices of Barceloneta actually worth the cost while bringing the best of the port to its tables. Somorrostro is also one of the best priced of this group, with reasonable seafood dishes, *paella*, and curries (€13-19) and a nighttime *menú* (€15). The real draw for the restaurant comes midday on weekdays—a seafood buffet lets you pay for fish, prawns, and more fresh from the port and cooked to your liking for unbelievably cheap prices (€13 per kg).

➧ *[M]Barceloneta. Walk on Pla del Palau over Ronda Litoral to follow the harbor. Take the 5th left after crossing Litoral, onto C. Sant Carles.* [$] *Weekday lunch buffet €13 per kg. Dinner menú €15. Appetizers €5.50-10; entrees €13.60-18.50.* ⏰ *Open Tu-Sa 8pm-11:30pm, Su 2-4pm and 8-11:30pm.*

BAR BITACORA 💵♿🍸 TAPAS [3]

C. Balboa, 1 ☎93 319 11 10

During the summer months, the giant neon 📷eyeball of this establishment looks onto a small terrace full of young people flocking from the beach. A sparse interior offers lots of seats for those looking to get out of the sun, with scarves from around the world hanging from the pipes as a reminder of colder weather to come. Beautiful salads offer a refreshing alternative to the fried *bombas* and beer around the beach—try the Salad Bitácora *(mezclun, avocado, apple, and walnuts with a honey vinaigrette, €6.50.)*

➧ *[M]Barceloneta. Walk down Pg. Juan de Borbó (towards the beach) and take the 1st left after Ronda del Litoral onto C. Balboa.* [$] *Tapas €2.50-8. Sangria €3.* ⏰ *Open M-W 10am-midnight, F-Sa 10am-2am, Su noon-5pm.*

CAN MAÑO

👄&🍸 SEAFOOD ❷

C. Baluart, 12

☎93 319 30 82

A no-frills bar-restaurant that has been serving fresh seafood for good prices to a never ending crowd of locals for years. Tile floors, white paint, and a random assortment of old framed newspaper clippings provide a refreshing break from those restaurants that make any attempt at interior decoration. If you had any doubts about just how little pretension this place harbors, just ask 🖾Tommy the Trout to start singing, "Take Me to the River" to you from his wall plaque.

🍴 Ⓜ*Barceloneta. Walk on Pla del Palau over Ronda Litoral to follow the harbor. Take the first left after crossing Litoral, onto C. Balboa. Take the 2nd right onto C. Baluart.* Ⓢ *Meat and fish dishes €3-10. Combination plates €6-8.* 🕐 *Open M-F 8am-5pm and 8-11pm, Sa 8am-5pm.*

Gràcia

🖾 LA NENA

👄❋ CAFE, ORGANIC ❶

C. Ramon i Caja, 36

☎93 285 14 76

An extensive menu of gourmet chocolates, ice creams, crepes, sandwiches, and quiches with ridiculously low prices. Don't try ordering a cold beer to beat the heat, though—the huge banner overhead alerts visitors that they may be the only spot in Barcelona that doesn't serve alcohol. Chill jazz plays over the speakers and kids' games and books line the tall, bright walls. For a filling treat, try one of their *tostadas*, like the goat cheese (goat cheese, tomato, and mushroom on bread), that will have you wishing you too had an extra stomach for more room.

🍴 Ⓜ*Follow C. d'Asturies, the one-way road leading from the metro stop and take a right onto Torrent de l'Olla. Walk a few blocks and take a left onto C. Ramon i Caja.* Ⓢ *Sandwiches €3.50. Quiches €5.50.* 🕐 *Open daily 1pm-1am.*

🖾 GAVINA

👄&🍸❋ PIZZA ❷

C. Ros de Olano, 17

☎93 415 74 50

Although there's not yet a market for pizza places where you can dine under life-sized patron saints, Gavina is just ahead of the curve. Don't misinterpret their slant, though—George Washington and a plethora of other nations' money serve to secularize this sanctuary of informal Italian cooking. The big draw is the gigantic, delicious pizzas. Try their namesake the Gavina (potatoes, ham, onion, and mushrooms), but be sure to bring friends or an otherworldly appetite.

🍴 Ⓜ*Fontana. Walk on Gran de Gràcia away from C. d'Asturies and take a left onto C. Ros de Olano.* Ⓢ *Pizza €6.50-14. Wine €8.50-15.* 🕐 *Open M-Th 1pm-1am, F-Sa 1pm-2am, Su 1pm-1am.*

CHIDO ONE

👄&🍸 MEXICAN ❷

C. Torrijos, 30

☎93 285 03 35 🖳www.chidoone.es

This Mexican restaurant has more *luchador* mettle than Strong Bad, complete with brightly painted walls splattered with murals, crafty animals, and other knick-knacks brought from the homeland. Try one of their handmade tortillas in their delicious quesadillas *(€8.50-10)*, and grab a Mexican beer to wash them down.

🍴 Ⓜ*Joanic. Take a right onto C. de l'Escorial and a left onto C. de Sant Lluis after a block. Left onto C. Torrijos.* Ⓢ *Appetizers €8.50-9.50; entrees €9.50-11.* 🕐 *Open M-Th 1-5pm and 7pm-midnight, F-Su 1pm-2am.*

L'ARMARI

👄&🍸❋ FRENCH ❷

C. Montseny, 13

☎93 368 54 13

Relaxed French cuisine including foie gras, truffles, cheeses, and a range of tartars fill this bistro. Young locals gather under delicate lighting for a midday meal with friends on mismatched chairs (some of which are somehow sporting a classy zebra stripe), while the black-and-white photos and French books on the walls set an appropriately refined scene. But with €4 mixed drinks before 10pm, don't feel as if you need to stay straight-laced.

🍴 Ⓜ*Fontana. Walk on Gran de Gràcia away from C. d'Asturies and take a left onto C. Montseny.*

BARCELONA REYKJAVÍK

📶♿ BAKERY ❶

C. Astúries, 20 ☎93 237 69 18 🖥www.barcelonareykjavik.com

This difficult-to-pronounce bakery is perfect for the discerning backpacker that's tired of white bread and sugary, mass-produced *magdalenas*. This eatery bakes mindblowing breads—if you've been in Spain long enough you'll find their sourdough a godsend—as well as delicious muffins, brioche, and other baked goods. Ingredients and potential flags for each are listed, making people with dietary restrictions' lives a little easier, if only for a short second before they venture back out into the world of meat, cheese, sugar, and gluten. Be prepared to eat on your feet or save it for later—this little storefront has no seating.

✚ Ⓜ*Follow C. d'Asturies, the one-way road leading from the metro stop.* **i** *Each item labeled for gluten, dairy, eggs, sugar.* $ *Items sold by weight. Breads normally €3-5. Baked goods €1-2.* ☼ *Open M-Sa 11am-9:30pm.*

ASKA DINYA

📶❄ MIDDLE EASTERN ❸

C. Verdi, 28 ☎93 368 50 77

Garden views abound in this crumbling rock-walled oasis. Pesky cats look down from overhead as an intoxicating smell of incense fills the nostrils. Afraid of a feline messing with your meal? Well, don't fear—it's all a painted ruse (or at least the cats are), but the serious quality of their food isn't. Loads of Palestinian-inspired options fill the menu, including *babaganoush* (*€6.50*), hummus, falafel, and tons of vegetarian options. In fact, this is one of the few places where you're given the option to *add* meat to your liking instead of trying to keep it out.

✚ Ⓜ*Follow C. d'Asturies, the one-way road leading from the metro stop and take a right onto C. Verdi after crossing Torrent de l'Olla.* $ *Appetizers €6.50-8.50; entrees €9-13.50. Menú €8.* ☼ *Open daily 1pm-1am.*

UGARIT

📶♿❖ SYRIAN ❷

C. Verdi, 11 ☎93 217 86 22 🖥www.ugarit.es

If you're trying to decide among the plethora of food places dotting C. Verdi, all it takes is one step inside Ugarit to make the decision for you. Incredible smells from the Syrian cuisine will have you salivating before you can put down your foot. Named after an ancient city from the area, this restaurant serves seriously fresh cous cous, bread dishes with roasted peppers called *mohamora* (*€5.95*) and Syrian vegetarian offers.

✚ Ⓜ*Follow C. d'Asturies, the one-way road leading from the metro stop, and take a right onto C. Verdi after crossing Torrent de l'Olla. Ugarit is down a few blocks.* $ *Salads €4.90-6.75. Tapas €3.50-4.30. Entrees €6-12. Menú served M-F 1-5pm €10.* ☼ *Open daily 1pm-1am.*

NIGHTLIFE

Barri Gòtic and Las Ramblas

🔲 BARCELONA PIPA CLUB

🌐⊗❖ BAR, CLUB

P. Reial, 3 ☎933 02 47 32 🖥www.bpipaclub.com

With pipes from four continents, smoking accoutrement decorated by Dalí, and even an "ethnological museum dedicated to the smoking acccessory," the only pipe-related article missing from this club—albeit somewhat appropriately—is Reneé Magritte's *"Ceci n'est pas une pipe."* Despite its cryptic lack of signage and an ambience of a secret society, the combination bar, pool room, and music lounge boasts a surprising number of travelers. The dark wood, low lights, and provincial furnishings make for a perfect place to transport yourself from the more collegiate nightlife of the Plaça Reial, even if the only experience you have with smoking is toting a candy cigarette.

♫ ⓜLiceu. Walk on Las Ramblas toward water. Left onto C. Ferran and first right to enter Plaça Reial. Pipa Club is an unmarked door to the right of Glaciar Bar. To enter, ring the bottom bell. *i* Rotating selection of tobacco available for sale. Special smoking events. Tango and salsa lessons M and T 8:30-10:30pm. Jam session Su 8:30pm. ⓢ Beer €4-5. Wine €4-5. Cocktails €7.50-9. ⓩ Open daily 6pm-6am.

HARLEM JAZZ CLUB ●⅋♉ MUSIC CLUB, BAR

C. Comtessa de Sobradiel, 8 ☎933 10 07 55 ✉www.harlemjazzclub.es

With two live music performances each night and a drink included with admission, Harlem Jazz Club promises to beat those empty-wallet blues. A performance schedule online and on their door lets you choose whether you'll drop in to hear lovesick English crooning or a little saucier Latin flavor. With acts ranging from Bossa Nova to gypsy punk, blues to funk, and soul to salsa, the club is a fantastic place for any music lover to spend the evening.

♫ ⓜLiceu. Walk toward the water on Las Ramblas. Left onto C. Ferran. Right onto C. Avinyó. Left onto C. Comtessa de Sobradiel. *i* Live music M-Th 11:30pm and midnight, F-Sa 11:30-m and 1am, Su 11:30pm and midnight. Calendar of events for the month available online or at door. ⓢ Cover M-Th €5, includes 1 drink; F-Sa €8, includes 1 drink; Su €5. Beer €3.80. Cocktails €7.80. ⓩ Open M-Th 9pm-4am, F-Sa 9pm-5am, Su 9pm-4am.

SMOLL BAR ●⊗♉▼ BAR

C. Comtessa de Sobradiel, 9

The chic '60s decor and friendly, burly bartenders combine to please an ever-present hip, gay-friendly, and young crowd. When there's room at the bar, squeeze in tight and try one of over 25 cocktails or a signature shot. The Rasmokov (vodka shot with a lime wedge topped in sugar and espresso powder) will leave you caffeinated, sugar-buzzed, and full of fuzzy, extroverted feelings.

♫ ⓜLiceu. Walk toward the water on Las Ramblas. Left onto C. Ferran. Right onto C. Avinyó. Left onto C. Comtessa de Sobradiel. ⓢ Beer €3.50. Cocktails €5.60. ⓩ Open M-Th 9:30pm-2:30am, F-Sa 9:30pm-3am.

MANCHESTER ●⊗♉ BAR

C. Milans, 5 ☎663 07 17 48 ✉www.manchesterbar.com

The long listing of bands on the exterior—Joy Division, The Cure, Arcade Fire, The Smiths, and many, many more—leaves little to the imagination. After passing the turning record table on the interior, you'll find a dark world of intimate seating, band references, and people who love both chatting and drinking the night away. A 7-10pm happy hour with €1.50 Estrellas gets the night started off right, and a vending machine selling tobacco is open until closing.

♫ ⓜLiceu. Walk toward the water on La Rambla, left onto C. Ferran. Right onto C. d'Avinyó. Left onto C. Milans before hitting C. Ample. Manchester is located where the street curves. *i* Happy hour beer €1.50. ⓢ Beers €2-4. Shots from €2.50. Mixed drinks €6. ⓩ Open M-Th 7pm-2:30am, F-Sa 7pm-3am, Su 7pm-2:30am. Happy hour daily 7-10pm.

TRECE ●⊗♉ BAR

C. Lleona, 13

If you can fight your way through the crowd of international 20-somethings into this pocket-sized hangout, Trece offers some of the best mojitos in Barcelona (€6). Bare walls with exposed brick show off local artwork and an assorted selection of dismembered body parts, including a set of mannequin legs sticking out over the restroom door and a torso functioning as the primary light source. Hits from the'80s abound, and a projector plays a selection of music videos and YouTube clips over the heads of the clientele.

♫ ⓜLiceu. Walk on Las Ramblas toward the sea, left onto C. Ferran. Right onto C. d'Avinyó and left onto C. de la Lleona. ⓢ Beer €3. Cocktails €6-7. ⓩ Open M-Th 7pm-3am, F-Sa 7pm-5:30am, Su 7pm-3am.

barcelona • nightlife

OVISO
CAFE, BAR

C. Arai, 5 www.barnawood.com

Cafe Oviso is where ancient Roman villa meets bohemian dive bar. A myriad of frescos adorn the walls, including images of peacocks, myths, and a curious scene in which a man appears to be putting the moves on a lion. Benches and larger tables invite clients to continue the theme and lounge at their discretion like a drunken Bacchus. A delicious variety of food and juices are served during the day, while at night the bar fills up quickly with a mix of locals from the Plaça Trippy.

[M]Liceu. Walk toward the water on Las Ramblas. Left onto C. Ferran. Right onto C. Avinyó. Left onto C. Arai; Oviso is on the right as you enter the plaça. i Food and juice served during the day. $ Beer €3. Cocktails €7. Open M-Th 10am-2:30am, F-Sa 10am-3am, Su 10am-2:30am.

EL BOSQ DE LES FADES
CAFE, BAR

Pg. de la Banca, 16 ☎933 17 26 49 www.museocerabcn.com

If you have ever wondered what it's like to be a hobbit and drink a whole pitcher of Sangria *(€12)*, Bosq de les Fades provides the perfect opportunity to settle your burning curiosity. A wooded canopy creates an enchanted forest deserving of the bar's name. If you're not the outdoorsy type and prefer something more domestic, you can hang out in a haunted bedroom, so long as you don't mind a woman behind a false mirror dropping in on your conversation. Be prepared for as many gawkers as diners, as the fantastical facade across from the Wax Museum is a popular photograph point.

[M]Drassanes. Walk briefly along Las Ramblas toward the water. Turn left onto Pg. de la Banca. El Bosq de les Fades is at the end of the road, in front of the Museu de Cera. $ Cava glass €3, bottle €16. Sangria €3.50, pitcher €12. Wine €2.30. Cocktails €6.10-7.20. Open M-Th 10:30am-1am, F-Sa 10:30am-1:30am, Su 10:30am-1am.

BOULEVARD CULTURE CLUB
NIGHTCLUB

Las Ramblas, 27 ☎933 01 62 89 www.boulevardcultureclub.com

With three rooms, dizzying lights, and a clientele that borders on barely legal, Boulevard Culture Club plays host to the nightclubbers of the traveler-laden Las Ramblas. Promoters draw in dancers with discount fliers along the street. If you don't like the techno playing in the first room, just move on to the next to hear some Missy Elliott instead.

[M]Liceu. Walk on Las Ramblas toward the water, destination on right. i Reduced admission with flyer distributed along Las Ramblas. Calendar of special events and theme nights on website. $ Cover €15; includes one drink. Open daily midnight-6am. Free for men before 1am and women before 2:30am.

KARMA
NIGHTCLUB, BAR

Pl. Reial, 10 ☎933 02 56 80 www.karmadisco.com

Karma: for those who dream of disco in a partified subway station. A bizarre mix of blues, soul, and '80s music plays for a largely uninterested older set while rainbow lights wrap around two barrel vaults that mark the bar and dancefloor. You may be better off living your actual dream by grabbing a boombox, some streetside beer, and a metro ticket—not that *Let's Go* suggests (illegally) drinking in public.

[M]Liceu. Walk on Las Ramblas toward the water. Left onto C. Ferran, Right to enter Plaça Reial. $Club cover €10; includes 1. Beer €4. Cocktails €6-8. Club open Tu-Th and Su 12am-5am, F-Sa 12am-6am. Bar open daily 6pm-2:30am.

La Ribera

ALMA
BAR

C. de Sant Antoni dels Sombrerers, 7 ☎93 319 76 07

A quieter alternative for those too cool to bother with the packed houses and inflated prices of nearby Passeig del Born. Cheap drinks provide bait for any traveler, while relaxed seating, rotating art exhibitions, and a bartender that stays surprisingly laidback even when drunkenly berated about the lack of mojitos give solid reasons to stay for the night.

⯮ [M]Jaume I. Walk down C. de la Princesa and take a right onto C. Montcada. Upon entering Psg. del Born, take a right onto C. dels Sombrerers and then take a right again onto the 1st street on your right, C. de Sant Antoni dels Sombrerers. $ Cava €1.80. Beer €2. Cocktails €6. ⏰ Open Tu-Th 8:30pm-2:30am, F-Sa 8:30pm-3am.

EL BORN — BAR

Pg. del Born, 26 ☎933 19 53 33

Shed the pretense and shabby themes and stop in to El Born for a straight-up bar—no more, no less. Marble tables and a green palette provide gametime seating and trenches for those brave enough to claim them on weekend nights. With cheap beer *(€2-2.50)* and ambient music, it's no wonder this place is always full.

*⯮ [M]Jaume I. Walk down C. Princesa and take a right onto C. Montcada. Follow until you hit Psg. del Born. **i** Free Wi-Fi. $ Beer €2-2.50. Mixed drinks €6. ⏰ Open Tu-Su 10am-2:30am.*

EL COPETÍN — LATIN BAR

Pg. del Born, 19 ☎607 20 21 76

Shimmy your hips at this dance floor that doesn't stop. Cuban beats blare the entire night from shortly after opening onward, attracting a laid-back, fun-loving crowd that knows how to move. A cafe-like portion up front provides some reprieve for those needing a breather, though the waitstaff may be too busy dancing along to tend to your every beck and call.

⯮ [M]Jaume I. Walk down C. Princesa and take a right onto C. Montcada. Follow to Psg. del Born. $ Mixed drinks €7. ⏰ Open M-Th 6pm-2:30am, F-Sa 6pm-3am, Su 6pm-2:30am.

BERIMBAU — LATIN BAR

Pg. del Born, 17 ☎933 19 53 78

This Brazilian *copas* bar, reportedly the oldest Brazilian bar in Spain, offers a range of drinks you won't easily find this side of the Atlantic. Try the *guarana* with whiskey *(€8)* or an orange and banana juice with vodka *(€9)*. Relaxed, beachy beats fill the air, with wicker chairs to let you live out the summer dream.

⯮ [M]Jaume I. Walk down C. Princesa and take a right onto C. Montcada. Follow to Psg. del Born. $ Cocktails €8-10. ⏰ Open M-Th 6pm-2:30am, F-Sa 6pm-3am, Su 6pm-2:30am.

PRINCESA 23 — BAR

C. Princesa, 23 932 68 86 18

Cheesy quotes line the wall, '80s and '90s hits flood the stereo, and young tourists unashamed of both of these details pack the club to the gills. Shamelessly capitalizing on an inauthentic medieval-esque Spanish theme, the continually stuffed house dishes out cheap mojitos and *caipirinhas* *(€4)* until 11pm and offers up a selection of nachos, tapas, and wraps so you can eat away the embarassment of actually enjoying yourself.

⯮ [M]Jaume I. Walk down C. Princesa. $ Mojito and Caipirinha €4 until 11pm. Cocktails €7. Sandwiches, wraps, and nachos €4.50-10.50. Salads and tapas €4-7.70. ⏰ Open daily noon-3am. Kitchen open noon-midnight.

El Raval

MARSELLA BAR — BAR

C. de Sant Pau, 65 ☎93 442 72 63

Walls lined with antique mirrors, cabinets, old advertisements, and dusty bottles will have you waiting to witness your first saloon brawl. Luckily, the crowd is genial and friendly, even after a few absinthes *(€5)*—not that there's room to fight in this crowded place anyway. Crackling paint and fuzzy chandeliers will have you feeling every month of the bar's 190 years of business.

⯮ [M]Liceu. Walk down C. Hospital and take a left onto C. Junta de la Comerç. Take a right at the end of the street onto C. de Sant Pau. $ Beer €3.50. Absinthe €5. Mixed drinks €5-6. ⏰ Open M-Th 11pm-2am, F-Sa 11pm-3am.

👍 PLASTIC BAR

⊛♿🍸❄ BAR

C. Sant Ramón, 23 💻www.myspace.com/plasticobar

This hip bar is big enough to host as many people as are cool enough to enter. Dark paisley walls with a green lit bar let you squeeze through to the back portion, where the real life awaits. The upper level is for lounging, while the scratchy soundsystem of the lower portion pumps a mix of modern indie and '60s rock to a crowd excited to dance the night away.

➔ Ⓜ Liceu. Walk on Las Ramblas toward the Sea. Take a right onto C. Nou de la Rambla and right onto C. de Sant Ramón. $ Shots €3. Beer €3-3.50. Mixed drinks €6. ⏰ Open M 11pm-2:30am, W 11pm-2:30am, Th 11pm-2:30am, F-Sa 11pm-3am.

👍 BAR BIG BANG

⊛♿🍸❄ BAR, MUSIC CLUB

C. Botella, 7 💻www.bigbangbcn.net

The back room attracts a collegiate crowd to watch free nightly performances like the jazz acts, standup comedy, and vaudeville-esque theater. Out front, customers are serenaded by big band favorites—both local and national—over the stereo and black-and-white projector screen. Creepy eyes look down from every corner, whether from the frames of outsider art or from the jazz star photos lining the dark walls.

➔ Ⓜ Sant Antoni. Walk down C. de Sant Antoni Abad (in the corner of the square where C. del Comte d'Urgell and C. de Manso meet) and take a hard right onto C. Botella. ℹ Schedule of performances and special events on website. Variety show on Tu, DJ on F and Sa at midnight. $ Shots €3. Beer €3-4. Cocktails €6.50. All cheaper before 11pm. ⏰ Open Tu-Sa 9:30pm-2:30am, Su 10:30pm-2:30am.

VALHALLA ROCK CLUB

⊛♿🍸❄ BAR, MUSIC CLUB

C. Tallers, 68 💻www.myspace.com/valhallaclubderock

Be prepared to see burly men air-guitaring Slayer in the place where a normal dance floor should be. At times serving as a concert hall, this dark and industrial-esque nightclub is a haven for those sick of flashing lights and throbbing techno. Free cover on non-show nights means you can use the saved cash to try their entire selection of *chupitos del rock*, specialty shots named after bands from Elvis to Whitesnake *(€1)*.

➔ Ⓜ Universitat. Walk down C. Tallers. ℹ Draught beer €1.50-2.50 daily until 10pm. Check myspace for calendar of concerts and special events. $ Shots €1-2. Sangria €2.50. Beer €2.50-5. Mixed drinks €6-7. ⏰ Open daily 6:30pm-2:30am.

SANT PAU 68

🏷♿🍸❄ BAR

C. Sant Pau, 68 ☎934 41 31 15

An absurdist bar with an identity crisis. The Van Gogh-esque wall of ears is paired with gas tank-inspired lights and a metal chandelier with circuit board cutouts casting geeksheek patterns of light across the stairwell. If you're looking to get away from the crowd, grab a bloody mary *(€6)* and head upstairs to scrawl your regards on the graffiti wall.

➔ Ⓜ Liceu. Walk down C. Hospital and take a left onto C. Junta de la Comerç. Take a right at the end of the street onto C. de Sant Pau. $ Beer €2. Mixed drinks €6. ⏰ Open M-Th 8pm-2:30am, F-Sa 8pm-3:30am, Su 8pm-2:30am.

L'OVELLA NEGRA

⊛♿🍸❄ BAR

C. Sitges, 5 ☎933 17 10 87 💻www.ovellanegra.com

Think Viking beer hall without the possibility of a funeral pyre burning into the night. Cheap beer flows freely, which makes stomaching the kitsch—anyone care to take a picture with the drunken black sheep cutout?—possible. Split-log benches and a selection of foosball, pool tables, and TVs provide all the charm of a frathouse in Valhalla.

➔ Ⓜ Catalonia. Walk toward the sea on Las Ramblas and take a hard right onto C. dels Tallers. then take a hard left onto C. Sitges. $ Tapas €1.50-4. Shots €2.30-3. Beer €1.20-3.60. Pitchers of beer and sangria €10.70-12.50. ⏰ M-Th 9am-2:30am, F 9am-3am, Sa 5pm-3am, Su 5pm-2:30am. Drinks cheaper before 11pm.

L'Eixample

👍 LES GENTS QUE J'AIME

💳🚫♿🍸 BAR

C. Valencia, 286 ☎93 215 68 79

Come down the stairs into this sultry red velvet underworld for antique photographs, jazz covers of "Tainted Love," and vintage chandeliers that set the mood for you to partake in their sinful pleasures. Not sure where to head for the rest of the night? Cozy up next to the palm-reader, or have your tarot cards read to keep from indecision.

⇆ ⓂDiagonal. Turn right onto Passeig de Gràcia and walk for 3 blocks. Take a left onto C. Valencia. Les Gents is downstairs next to Campechano. ℹ Palm reading and tarot cards M-Sa, €30 and €25. $ Wine €3. Beer €3.50. Cocktails €7. ⏰ Open M-Th 7pm-2:30am, F-Sa 7pm-3am, Su 7pm-2:30am.

👍 LA FIRA

🚫💳🚫♿🍸 CLUB

C. Provença, 171 ☎65 085 53 84

Decorated entirely with pieces from the old Apolo Amuseument Park in Barcelona, this club is like a debaucherous family reunion without having to worry about the faux pas of incest. The walls act as a masoleum to innocent years past, sporting dioramas of the fair, fortune tellers, and masks of questionable racial politics. Dance away under the big top, and try not to get too creeped out while downing *Espit Chupitos* under the glare of the knowing sphynx.

⇆ ⓂHospital Clinic. Walk away from the engineering school on C. del Rossello and take a right onto C. de Villarroel when it dead-ends. Take the first left onto Provença; La Fira is a few blocks down. ℹ Often hosts shows or parties, sometimes with entrance fee or 1-drink min. $ Beer €5. Cocktails €8. ⏰ Open Th-Sa 11:30pm-3am.

ZELTAS

💳♿🍸❄▼ BAR

C. Casanova, 75 ☎93 450 84 69 🖥www.zeltas.net

Like a story lifted from a sultry romance novel about an all-male harem with impeccable taste, Zeltas pleases the eyes in more ways than one. An all black interior draped in white, flowing fabric sets the tone, while chic white couches and a bar seemingly dedicated to those looking to dance shirtless sets the mood. Musky cologne floats through the air, and beefy male dancers in tight black spankies make the air somehow thicker.

⇆ ⓂUniversitat. Face the University building and walk left on Gran Vía. Turn right onto C. Casanova. Zeltas is down 2 blocks. ℹ Male dancers nightly. $ Beer €5. Cocktails €7.50. ⏰ Open daily 11pm-6am.

LA CHAPELLE

💳♿🍸❄▼ BAR

C. Muntaner, 67 ☎93 453 30 76

A wall of devotional figurines and paintings with mostly nude men in front allows La Chapelle to show a gayer side of the sacrament. Solemn red lighting mixed with modern bubble lights cut through the veil of testosterone—apparently debaucherous religious imagery is bait for bears. Get a little closer to God while getting a lot closer with some grizzly guys.

⇆ ⓂUniversitat. Face the University building and walk left on Gran Vía. Turn right onto C. Muntaner. La Chapelle is 2 blocks down. $ Beer €2.50. Mixed drinks €5. ⏰ Open daily 4pm-2:30am.

DOW JONES

💳♿🍸❄ BAR

C. Bruc, 97 ☎93 476 38 31 🖥www.bardowjones.es

During the day this English-centric bar has enough television screens to keep every fútbol fan happy, no matter his allegiance. At night, the bar lights up with raucous foreigners trying desperately to order their favorite drink before the price spikes—like the stock market, drinks' prices vary based on their popularity during the day. Wait for the prices to crash if you're counting on a winner, or keep buying low and be glad the staff speaks English fluently for when you're slurring your Spanish.

⇆ ⓂGirona. Walk toward C. Aragó on C. Girona and take a left onto C. Valencia after passing Arago. Walk 1 block and take a left onto C. del Bruc. Dow Jones is close to the corner. $ Food

€2.75-7.50. Beer €2-5.50. Cocktails €4-7. ⌚ *Open M-F 7am-2:30am, Sa-Su noon-3am.*

AIRE
⬥⊗⍦❄▼ CLUB

C. Valencia, 236 ☎93 454 63 94 🖳www.arenadisco.com

If you're looking for a queer-centric party spot that isn't overwhelmingly male (i.e. the rest of l'Eixample), check out Aire for all of the non-guy company the neighborhood seemed to be lacking. This huge club is packed nearly as soon as its doors open and continues to party with a mix of pop hits, R and B, and electronica well into the night. Don't worry about feeling left out—no matter your gender or orientation, unless you show up at one of their Women-only strip shows (*6-10pm one Su each month*)—the owner says the club is, "for girls...and friends."

✦ Ⓜ️*Universitat. Face the university building and walk down the street that runs along its right side, C. Balmes. Turn left onto C. Valencia, 1 street after crossing Arago.* ⓘ *Women-only strip show 6-10pm 1st Su of every month.* Ⓢ *Cover €5-10; includes 1 drink.* ⌚ *Open Th-Su 11:30pm-3am.*

ANTILLA
⬥♿⍦❄ LATIN CLUB

C. Aragó, 141 ☎93 451 45 64 🖳www.antillasalsa.com

Watch yourself upon entering—this saucy Latin bar and dance club is so full of energy that dancers often find themselves dancing right out the door. Little Cuban *maracas*, bongos, and cowbells are littered along the sandy bar, and painted palm trees dot the walls. For those intimidated by joining the frantic shimmying without some practice, salsa lessons are offered before the club opens to the public Tu-Sa 5-11pm so you can shake it like a pro—or at least not like you just crawled out of the womb.

✦ Ⓜ️*Urgell. Walk along Gran Vía to the closest intersection (C. Comte d'Urgell) and take a right onto the street. Walk 3 blocks and take a left onto C. Arago.* ⓘ *No cover W-Th and Su, but 1-drink min.* Ⓢ *Cover F-Sa €10. Beer €6. Cocktails €8.* ⌚ *Open W-Th 11pm-4am, F 11pm-6am, Sa 11pm-5am, Su 7pm-1am.*

ESPIT CHUPITOS (ARIBAU)
⬥♿⍦❄ BAR

C. Aribau, 77 🖳www.espitchupitos.com

If you want shots, they've got 'em—580 different delectable little devils will let you party as if you'd gone to Cancun on vacation instead of the Mediterranean. Be prepared for a little more than just drinking, though. Spectacle shots such as the *Harry Potter* literally light up the night, while others have the bartenders getting down and dirty. If you can't get enough, Espit Chupitos has gotten so popular that it now has two other locations in the city, a sister store in l'Eixample called Gato Negro, and an outpost inside La Fira.

✦ Ⓜ️*Universitat. Walk on C. Aribau to the left of the university building. Espit Chupitos is 4 blocks down.* Ⓢ *Shots €2. Cocktails €8.50.* ⌚ *Open M-Th 8pm-2:30am, F-Sa 8pm-3am, Su 8pm-2:30am.*

LUZ DE GAS
⬥♿⍦❄ CLUB, CONCERT HALL

C. Muntaner, 244-256 ☎93 209 77 11 🖳www.luzdegas.com

The most well-known club in the city, and for good reason. Red velvet walls, gilded mirrors, and sparkling chandeliers will have you wondering how you possibly got past the bouncer. Big name jazz, blues, and soul performers occasionally take the stage during the evening hours, while after 1am it becomes overrun by swanky partygoers. Ritzy young things dance to deafening pop, from Outkast to Nancy Sinatra, pounding through the lower area, while the upstairs lounge provides a much-needed break for both your feet and ears.

✦ Ⓜ️*Diagonal. Take a right onto Rambla de Catalonia, walk 1 block and take a slight left onto Av. Diagonal. Walk 5min. and take a right onto C. de Muntaner.* ⓘ *For show listings and times check the Guía del Ocio or their website.* Ⓢ *Club cover €18. Beer €7. Cocktails €10.* ⌚ *Dance club open daily 11:30pm-5:30am.*

DBOY/LA MADAME/DEMIX
⬥⊗⍦❄▼ CLUB

Ronda Sant Pere, 19-21 ☎93 453 05 82 🖳www.matineegroup.com

Three clubs in one, this single spot hosts a downright confusing variety of nightlife options depending on the night. **DBoy** is no-girls allowed, with a young and lively gay crowd dancing in a laser-lit wonderland. **La Madame** fems it up, offering a hetero-centric alternative geared mosty towards women, and **Demix** supplies just like what it sounds—a mixed crowd. Check the website beforehand to see which way the club swings.

➤ Ⓜ Urquinaona. With your back to Plaça Urquinaona, Ronda Sant Pere runs to the right from the P.. Follow it a few short steps and look for the LED sign. $ Cover varies €10-15. ⏰ DBoy open in summer F-Sa midnight-6am. La Madame open in summers Su midnight-5am. Demix open Jan-July F-Su midnight-6am; Sept-Dec F-Su midnight-6am.

Barceloneta

👍 ABSENTA — 💳♿🍸 BAR

C. Sant Carles, 36

Not for the easily spooked, Absenta is like an episode of the Twilight Zone if you were trapped inside the television looking out. Staticky TV sets with flickering faces dot the walls, and a life-sized angel hovers above while you sinfully sip your absinthe *(€4-7)*. A young crowd brings this *modernisme*-inspired beauty up-to-date in an appropriately artsty manner.

➤ Ⓜ Barceloneta. Walk down Pg. Joan de Borbó toward the beach and take a left onto C. Sant Carles. $ Beer €2.30. Mixed drinks €7. Absinthe €4-7. ⏰ Open Tu-F 11pm-2am, Sa 11am-3am, Su 6pm-2am.

CATWALK — 💳🚭🍸❄⛅ NIGHTCLUB

C. Ramón Trias Fargas, 2-4 ☎69 264 14 29 💻www.clubcatwalk.net

Though you'll only get access to the ritzy elevated walk above if you're a VIP, there's enough glam below to ward off your jealousy, so be sure to leave your T-shirts and sneakers back in your hostel. Beautiful people deck the lounges and dancefloor, while the brave (or possibly drunk) take advantage of the lit dancing boxes to strut their stuff to a mix of pop, electro, and R and B.

➤ Ⓜ Port Olímpic. ℹ No T-shirts, torn jeans, or sneakers permitted. Events listing on website. $ Cover €18. Beer €7. Mixed drinks €12. ⏰ Open Th midnight-5am, F-Sa midnight-6am, Su midnight-5am.

OPIUM MAR — 💳♿🍸⛅ NIGHTCLUB, RESTAURANT

Pg. Marítim de la Barceloneta, 34 ☎90 226 74 86 💻www.opiummar.com

Slick restaurant by day and an even slicker nightclub by night, this lavish indoor and outdoor party spot still knows how to kick it up a notch despite its facade of decorum. Seafood is served until 1am, after which a mix of electronica and American pop pounds from the stereo and lures dancers off of the fashionable white chairs and onto the dance floor.

➤ Ⓜ Port Olímpic. ℹ Events listing on website. DJs every W. $ Cover €20; includes one drink. ⏰ Restaurant open daily 1pm-1am. Club open M-Th midnight-5am, F-Sa 1-6am, Su midnight-5am.

GRAN CASINO — 💳♿🍸❄ CASINO

C. Marina, 19 ☎93 225 78 78 💻www.casino-barcelona.com

The most beautiful casino in Barcelona, nestled within the requisite amount of glitz and glam surrounding Port Olímpic. Slot machines above in the Sala Americana start the night off slowly, while things get more serious (and addictive) below with tables of blackjack, American and French roulette, a theater hosting Vegas-esque shows, and a killer buffet. Admission to the main floor will cost you *(€4.50)* unless you bring a flyer, but that's nothing compared to the money you'll be lured into gambling away the entire night anyway.

➤ Ⓜ Port Olimpic. Under the Fish. ℹ Must be 18 to play. No sneakers or beach clothes allowed; collared shirt recommended for men. Passport required. Live jazz in Sala Principal F-Sa. $ Entrance to Sala Principal €4.50 ⏰ Sala Americana (slot machines and bar) open M-Th 10am-5pm, F-Sa 10am-5:30pm, Su 10am-5pm. Sala Principal (theater, game tables) open daily 3pm-5am.

Montjuïc and Poble Sec

ROUGE CAFE
❤❄ BAR

C. Poeta Cabanyes, 21 ☎93 442 49 85

When you walk into a sultry rouge-lit lounge decked in leather chairs and a cavalcade of vintage decor (including a shoddy copy of the Arnolfini wedding portrait), you know you're doing something right. Luckily, a crowd of hip, friendly locals are there to join you. The prettiest, most stereotypically girly drinks in the city are some of the most delicious, so try the melon Absolut Porno (€6) or the vodka-based Barcelona Rouge (€6.50).

✦ ⓂParallel. With Montjuïc to your left, walk along Av. Parallel. Take a left onto C. Poeta Cabanyes. Rouge Cafe will be on your left before Mambo Tango Youth Hostel. ⏰ Open daily in summer 7pm-3am; in winter 8pm-3am.

TINTA ROJA
❤♿ 🍸❄ BAR

C. Creu dels Molers, 17 ☎93 443 32 43 🖳wwww.tintaroja.net

Named after the 1941 tango "Tinta Roja" by Cátulo Castillo and Sebsatián Piana, this cafe-bar mixes literal Latin flavor with the flair of the theater. Argentine drinks are their specialty, ranging from a little boost of maté (€4.80) to a full range of the country's liquors and beers. Scattered seating under questionably erotic Impressionistic paintings populate the front, while a back stage plays host to popular tango classes on Wednesday nights at 9pm. Don't mind the mannequins looking down over your footwork—chances are they're just admiring your work.

✦ ⓂPoble Sec. With Montjuïc to your right, walk along Av. Parallel. Take the second right onto C. de la Creu dels Molers; Tinta Roja will be on the left. ℹ Tango classes W 9-11:30pm. ⓢ Beer €2.30-4. Wine €2.50-3.70. Maté €4.80. Argentinian liquors €5.50-6. Mixed drinks €7. ⏰ Open Th 8:30pm-2am, F-Sa 8:30pm-3am.

242
❤ CLUB

C. Entença, 37 ☎932 28 90 73 🖳www.myspace.com/club242

Fearing a hangover after that massive night of partying? One of the longest running after-hours clubs in the city of Barcelona, 242 lets you skip right over those painful waking hours and relive the night you already enjoyed. A crowd trickles in after 6am as the other clubs close to enjoy drinks, electronica, air conditioning, and movies. If you find yourself winding down, they even have food for breakfast.

✦ ⓂEspanya. Walk away from Montjuïc on Gran Vía and take a right onto C. de' Entença. 242 is right before the intersection with Sepúlveda. ℹ Special events listed on Myspace. ⓢ Cover €15; includes 1 drink. Beer €5. Mixed drinks €10. ⏰ Open F-Su 6am-whenever the party stops.

SALA APOLO
❤♿ 🍸❄ CLUB

Nou de la Rambla, 113 ☎93 441 40 01🖳www.sala-apolo.com

Looking for a party, but lamenting that it's Monday? Sulk no longer—for the last number of years Sala Apolo has been drawing locals to start the week off right with Nasty Mondays, featuring a mix of rock, pop, indie, garage, and '80s (€11). In fact, the night is so popular that it spawned an equally persuasively named Crappy Tuesdays (indie and electropop; €10-12), which take over after the American one-woman Broadway-esque show "Anti-Karaoke." Stop by later in the week to catch a varied crowd, and check the website for the latest bigger name indie concerts rolling through the venue.

✦ ⓂParal-lel. Walk along Parallel with Montjuïc to your right. Take a hard right onto Nou de la Rambla. Not to be confused with Teatre Apolo, which is on Av. Parallel. ⓢ Anti-karaoke €8. Nasty M €11. Crappy Tu €10-12. W Rumba €6-10. Other tickets €15-23.

LA TERRAZZA
❤♿ 🍸 CLUB

Avda. Marquès de Comillas ☎68 796 98 25 🖳www.laterrrazza.com

One of the most popular clubs in Barcelona, La Terrazza lights up the Poble Espanyol after the artists call it a day. The open-air dance floor gets packed early, with flocks of youth clamoring to get inside to dance to the techno beat. This bizarre mix of giant naked lady murals, Buddha sculptures, and Greek revival arcades nestled in the courtyard of the fake Spanish village is bound to confuse you, but chances are that after the music starts you won't really care.

✠ Ⓜ Espanya. Head through the Venetian towers and climb the escalators. Follow the signs to the Spanish Village. *i* Free bus from Plaza Catalonia (Hard Rock Cafe) to club every 20min. 12:20am-3:20am; free buses from Terazza to Plaza Catalonia non-stop 5:30am-6:45am. Ⓢ Cover €18, with flyer €15. Beer €6. Mixed drinks €8-10. ☾ Open Th 11pm-5am, F-Sa midnight-6am.

Gràcia

▨ EL RAÏM

✦⚕♥ BAR

C. Progrés, 48 ⬚www.raimbcn.com

Though a little farther from Gràcia's roaring plazas, this time capsule with an identity crisis is well worth the short trek. A mix between a Catalan bodega and '50s Cuban bar, this traditional winery has been in business since 1886, when it served as the diner for the old factory across the street. Since then, the owner has transformed the place into a shrine to Cuban music and memorabilia, rum, and incredible mojitos. It consistently attracts a flock of down-to-earth locals looking for one (or all) of the three.

✠ Ⓜ Fontana. Walk down C. Gran de Gràcia and make a left on C. Ros de Olano. Walk for about 4 blocks and take a right onto C. Torrent de l'Olla. Take the 4th left onto Siracusa, and El Raïm is on the corner of its intersection with C. del Progrés. Ⓢ Beer €2-3. Mixed drinks €5.50. ☾ Open daily 8pm-2:30am.

▨ VINIL

❀⚕♥ BAR

C. Matilde, 2 ☎66 917 79 45 ⬚www.vinilus.blogspot.com

Those expecting a fetish club—whether for LPs or something of a kinkier persuasion—may be disappointed. Though this is certainly no shrine to a musical era past (or present), the warm lighting and comfy pillows make the perfect place to kick back and watch their daily screened movie. Feel free to geek out over their giant phonograph or the Velvet Underground song playing over the speakers—chances are the hip clientele will perfectly understand.

✠ Ⓜ Diagonal. Ⓢ Beer €3-3.50. Mixed drinks €5. ☾ Open in summer M-Th 8pm-2am, F-Sa 8pm-3am; in winter M-Th 8pm-2am, F-Sa 8pm-3am, Su 8pm-2am.

LA CERVERSERA ARTESANA

✦⚕♥❀ BAR, BREWERY

C. Sant Agustí, 14 ☎93 237 95 94 ⬚www.lacervesera.net

When you visit the only pub in Barcelona that makes its own beer, you better order their beer no matter what vows you've taken with PBR. With a huge variety of brews—dark, amber, honey, spiced, chocolate, peppermint, fruit-flavored, and more—there's literally something for everyone, along with seasoned bar snacks to encourage your thirst. If beer isn't your thing, at least come to hear the music—you probably won't hear Pink Floyd and Phil Collins played back-to-back anywhere else in the city.

✠ Ⓜ Diagonal. Take a left onto Psg. de Gràcia and a right (exact right, 90 degree angle) onto C. Corsega at the intersection of Psg. de Gràcia and Via Diagonal. C. Sant Agustí is the 3rd street on the left. Ⓢ House brews €4.80-5. ☾ Open M-Th 6pm-2am, F-Sa 6pm-3am, Su 6pm-2am.

VELCRO BAR

✦⚕♥ BAR

C. Vallfogona, 10 ☎61 075 47 42

Though Velcro Bar is a bit farther from Gràcia's popular plazas, its screenings of nightly movies attract a young and hip clientele that ends up paying little attention to the moving pictures. True to its name, this is a bar where bright green and pink velcro waits to hold the bottom of your drink.

✠ Ⓜ Fontana. Follow C. Asturies to C. Torrent de l'Olla and make a right. Follow for three blocks, make a left onto C. Vallfogona. Ⓢ Mixed drinks €5-8. ☾ Open daily 7pm-2:30am.

barcelona . nightlife

OTTO ZUTZ 💳⊗🍸❄ CLUB

C. Lincoln, 15 ☎93 238 07 22 💻www.ottozutz.com

Like a tiered layer cake with an impeccably designed party inside (or maybe a portion of Dante's Inferno, depending on the night), three floors of dancing and drinks await. At least four different DJs pound out a huge variety of music to a chic and shiny crowd, with a reprieve from the throbbing masses only available up top. Watch out—during the summer this heaven gets hellishly hot.

🚶 *Ⓜ Fontana. Walk along Rambla de Prat and take a right as it dead-ends into Via Augusta. Take the first right onto C. Laforja and the first right again to reach C. Lincoln.* $ *Cover €10-15; includes 1 drink. Beer €6. Miixed drinks €6-12.* ⏰ *Open W-Su midnight-6am.*

KGB ⊛⊗🍸 CLUB

C. Alegre de Dalt, 55 ☎93 210 59 06 💻www.salakgb.net

In Soviet Russia, KGB dances you. No, but really—the only indications of the eastern block are the oppressive KGB posters hanging from the walls like propaganda and the sheer utility of the decorations—expect lots of black, lots of metal, and little glitz or bourgeois sparkle. Scrappy youth join the bartenders and live DJ and VJ in a sweaty countdown to get down. Entrance is free with a flyer; otherwise you'll be paying €12-15 to join this Communist party.

🚶 *Ⓜ Joanic. Walk along C. Pi i Maragall and take the 1st left. To get a cab home, come back to Pi i Maragall.* $ *Cover €12 with 1 drink, €15 with 2 drinks until 3am. Free with flyer.* ⏰ *Open Th 1-5am, F-Sa 1-6am.*

Tibidabo

👍 **MIRABLAU** 💳♿🍸⛅ BAR, NIGHTCLUB

P. Dr. Andreu ☎934 18 58 79 💻www.mirablaubcn.com

With easily the best view in Tibidabo and arguably the best view in Barcelona, Mirablau is a favorite with posh internationals and the younger crowd. It also happens to be near the top of Collserola mountain range's highest peak. Reasonable drinks for the area *(cocktails €7-9.50)* and a view that will leave you feeling like you've ascended to heaven—a heaven that plays the Village People—earns this bar a *Let's Go* thumbpick. A relaxed bar and lounge area upstairs changes into a energy-filled dance floor on the lower level, leaving those with two left feet room to spill out onto the terrace.

🚶 *Take the L7 to Ⓜ Avinguda de Tibidabo or the Tramvia Blau to Pl. del Doctor Andreu. From the metro, walk up the mountain on Av. de Tibidabo to Plaça Dr. Andreu. From the tram, it's to your left when facing the city.* ℹ *Credit card minimum Th-Sa €4.70. Drinks discounted M-Sa before 11pm, Su before 6pm.* $ *Beer and wine €1.80-6. Cocktails €7-9.50.* ⏰ *Open M-Th 11am-4:30am, F-Sa 11am-5:45am.*

MERBEYÉ 💳♿🍸⛅ BAR

Plaça Dr. Andreu ☎934 34 00 35

More like a den than the clifflike Mirablau on the opposite side of the road, Merbeyé provides a classy, red-velvet atmosphere for those looking to embrace the romantic side of the picturesque surroundings. With a lounge whose lights are so low that seeing your companion may be a problem, Merbeyé creates the perfect setting to bring a date or possibly find another at the seemingly neverending bar. Smooth jazz serenades throughout, and with just one Mirabeye *(Cava Brut, cherry brandy, and Cointreau; €9-10)* you'll be guaranteed to find yourself at the requisite level of chill.

🚶 *Take the L7 to Ⓜ Avinguda de Tibidabo or the Tramvia Blau to Pl. del Doctor Andreu. From the metro, walk up the mountain on Av. de Tibidabo to Plaça Dr. Andreu. From the tram, it's to your back when facing the city.* $ *Non-alcoholic drinks €8-9. Cocktails €9-10. Food €2-7.60.* ⏰ *Open W 7pm-1am, Th noon-2am, F-Sa noon-4am, Su noon-2am.*

ARTS AND CULTURE

Music and Dance

For comprehensive guides of large events and information on cultural activities in the city, contact the **Institut de Cultura de Barcelona (ICUB)** *(Palau de la Virreina, La Rambla, 99* ☎*93 316 10 00* ✉ *www.bcn.cat/cultura* 🕐 *Open daily 10am-8pm)* or the the **Guía del Ocio** *(*✉ *www.guiadelociobcn.com).*

Although a destination for musicians year-round, Barcelona especially perks up during the warmer months with an influx of touring bands and impressive music festivals. The biggest and arguably baddest of these is the three-day electronic music festival **Sónar** *(*✉*www.sonar.es)* taking place in mid-June, which attracts internationally renowned DJs, electronica fans, and party people from all over the world. The **Grec** summer festival *(*✉*www.bcn.cat/grec)* takes place throughout the summer months, using mutiple venues throughout the city to host international music, theater, and dance. The indie-centric **Primavera Sound** *(*✉*www.primaverasound.com)* at the end of May is also quickly becoming a regional must-see. More information on local festivals is available in the *Mondo Sonoro*, which lists happenings across the world.

Classical and Opera

PALAU DE LA MÚSICA CATALANA
👌♿❄ L'EIXAMPLE

St. Francesc de Paula, 2   ☎90 244 28 82 ✉www.palaumusica.org

Although the Bach- and Verdi-studded stage still hosts primarily classical concerts, this *modernista* structure also hosts a surprising variety of musical acts almost every night. Over 300 performances of choral and orchestral pieces, pop, acoustic, jazz, and flamenco grace its stage every year, including those from its very own **Orfeo Català** (Catalan choir) for which the building was constructed. If you're just looking for an excuse to see the breathtaking Secret Garden-esque interior without a tour (or you really like giant air-driven, tubed instruments), drop by for one of their frequent and cheap organ performances—they need them to keep the organ pipes clean.

✈ Ⓜ*Jaume I. Facing Via Laietana from the Plaça de l'Angel exit, take a left onto the road. Walk for 10min. and take a right onto the plaza-like C. Sant Pere Mas Alt.* ⓘ *Check the Guía del Ocio for listings.* Ⓢ *Concert tickets €8-175.* 🕐 *Box office open M-Sa 10am-9pm, Su from 2hr. before show time. No concerts in Aug.*

GRAN TEATRE DEL LICEU
👌♿☂❄ LAS RAMBLAS

La Rambla, 51-59   ☎93 485 99 13 ✉www.liceubarcelona.com

A Barcelona institution since its founding in 1847, the Gran Teatre del Liceu is actively reclaiming its role as the premier venue for upscale performances after being closed due to fire in 1994. Classical, opera, and ballet grace the stage of its impressively restored auditorium, while a smaller reception room hosts discussions about the pieces and smaller events. If you're afraid of committing to a ticket, drop in for a tour and hope to catch a sneakpeak of the rehearsal for the night's performance.

✈ Ⓜ*Liceu. Face the plaza and the house with umbrellas on its side and walk to your right down La Rambla. Teatre is about a block away.* ⓘ *Tickets available at box office, online, or through ServiCaixa.* 🕐 *Box office open M-F 1:30-8pm.*

Pop and Rock 'n' Roll

RAZZMATAZZ
👌☂❄ LAS RAMBLAS

C. Pamplona, 88 and Almogàvers, 122   ☎93 272 09 10 ✉www.salarazzmatazz.com

This massive, converted warehouse hosts big-name popular acts from reggae to electropop and indie to metal. The big room packs the popular draw (bands like Motorhead, Alice in Chains, and Gossip), while the smaller rooms hide up-and-comers like the Vivian Girls. Wherever there isn't a throng of people for the concerts, you'll find a young crowd pulsing to the beat of one of their nightly

DJs. The labyrinthine nightclub spans across multiple floors in two buildings, connected by industrial stairwells and a rooftop walkway—definitely not intended for the navigationally deficient.

✦ ⓂBogatell. Walk down the diagonal street (C. Pere IV) away from the plaza and take the 1st slight left onto C. Pamplona. Razzmatazz is immediately on the right. 𝒊 Tickets available online through website, TelEntrada, or Ticketmaster. ⓢ Tickets €12-22.

SALA APOLO
✦🚹♿🍸❄ BARCELONETA

Nou de la Rambla, 113 ☎93 441 40 01 🖥www.sala-apolo.com

Host to major indie acts that come through the area (think Crystal Castles and Nouvelle Vague) as well as some touring hip hop and electronica artists. A regular Rumba club on Wednesday nights features a different saucy band every week, and popular Nasty Mondays (midnight, €11) and Nasty Tuesdays (midnight, €8) shake up the atypical party nights of the week.

✦ ⓂParal-lel. Walk along Parallel with Montjuïc to your right. Take a hard right onto Nou de la Rambla. Not to be confused with Teatre Apolo, which is on Av. Parallel. 𝒊 Tickets available on website. ⓢ Rumba tickets €6-10. Other concert tickets €15-23.

Folk and Jazz

JAMBOREE
✦⊗🍸❄ LAS RAMBLAS

Plaça Reial, 17 ☎93 319 17 89 🖥www.masimas.com

The black-and-white portraits of jazz musicians lining the walls tell of the club's long-standing history. Jamboree has been hosting jazz acts for over 50 years, and manages to mix this rich history with a surprising dose of relevant contemporary artists—expect to hear a Billie Holiday tribute one night and the Markus Strickland Quartet the next. If you're looking for something a little less predictable, their WTF Jam Sessions are popular with local musicians and will only cost you €4 to peep.

✦ ⓂLiceu. Facing the house with the 🐉dragon and umbrellas on it, walk down La Rambla to your right and take a left onto C. Ferran. Take the 1st right to enter Plaça Reial. Jamboree is in the far corner to your right. 𝒊 Tickets available through TelEntrada. ⓢ Jazz tickets €10-25 (normally €10-15), Su jam session €4, flamenco €6. 🕙 Jazz performances Tu-Su 9 and 11pm, check site for exact times as some performances start at 8pm. WTF Jam Sessions M 9pm-1:30am. Upstairs Tarantos holds flamenco shows daily 8:30, 9:30, and 10:30pm.

Theater

TEATRE LLIURE
✦🚹♿❄ LA RIBERA

Plaça Margarida Xirgu, 1 ☎93 218 92 51 🖥www.teatrelliure.com

Established in 1976 by the artsy inhabitants of Gràcia, the Teatre Lliure has become known for presenting works in Catalan, including contemporary pieces and classics from around the globe, and many original Catalan pieces birthed from its own theater cooperative. The present location at the foot of Montjuïc has housed the theater since 2001 but still maintains the feel of its bohemian homeland. Most tickets are more than reasonably priced, and many include entrance to a discussion after the show with the crew and theater critics.

✦ ⓂEspanya. Face Montjuïc and go right on Av. Parallel. Take a right onto C. de Lleida and a left through the gate to enter the plaza. 𝒊 Tickets available by box office or ServiCaixa. Some original productions include talk with the artists and critics afterward; check website for info. Language of performance listed on website. Art exhibitions relating to current shows. ⓢ Tickets €15-24. 🕙 Art exhibitions on view on days of performances Tu-F 6-8:30pm, Sa-Su 4-6pm.

TEATRE GREC
♿ LA RIBERA

Passeig de Santa Madrona, 36 ☎93 316 10 00 🖥www.bcn.cat/grec

No, this theater isn't left over from the good ol' days, no matter what its name may imply. This open-air Grecian-style amphitheater instead dates just from 1929, when it was carved out of an old stone quarry for the International Exhibition that gave birth to many of Montjuïc's existing spectacles. These days the theater hosts a range of theater, opera, dance, and music performances during the summer months and is the main venue of the city's annual Festival Grec, which takes place from mid-June to early August. Be sure to bring mosquito repellent—being nestled in the Jardins Amargós comes with a price.

✈ ⓂEspanya. *Head through the 2 bell towers marking the entrance to Montjuïc and follow the escalators to the top. When facing the palace-like art museum, walk along the street to the left and be sure to stay left as it breaks. Teatre Grec is on this road (Passeig de Santa Madrona) just after the Ethnological Museum..* **i** *Tickets available at Tiquet Rambles (Rambla, 99 ☎93 316 11 11) ⓏTiquet Rambles open daily 10am-8:30pm), Telentrada, and ServiCaixa. Most theater performances in Catalan or Spanish.*

TEATRE NACIONAL DE CATALONIA
📧& BARCELONETA

Plaça de les Arts, 1 ☎93 306 57 00 🖳www.tnc.es

This modern structure designed by Ricardo Bofill is a confusing steel and glass nod to the Parthenon. Inaugurated on September 11, 1997, the National Day of Catalonia, it has since been posed as the next cultural center of Barcelona, with an adjacent auditorium with a capacity of 36,000 slated to be completed in the near future. The two performance halls of the main building host contemporary Catalan and foreign plays, classics, and traditional Catalan dances and music from time to time, while the second building of the complex houses all of the workshops that make the stage tick. Take advantage of youth, if you have it— tickets for shows start from €12 if you're under 25.

✈ ⓂGlories. *Face the rocketshaped Torre Agbar and take the 1st road to your right, Av. Meridiana. Teatre Nacional de Catalonia will be on your right.* **i** *Tickets available through TelEntrada, ServiCaixa, Tiquet Rambla, and box office.* ⓢ *Tickets €15-32, under 25 from €12.* Ⓩ *Box office and info open W-F 3-8pm, Sa 3-9:30pm, Su 3-6pm.*

Festals

Barcelona loves to party. Although *Let's Go* fully supports this endeavor to its fullest extent, we still need to include some nitty-gritty things like accommodations and, you know, food, so we can't possibly list all of the annual festivals around Barcelona. For a full list of what's going on during your visit, be sure to stop by the **tourist information office** once you arrive in the city. As a teaser, here are a few of the biggest, most student-relevant shindigs:

FESTA DE SANT JORDI
La Rambla

This provides a more intelligent, civil alternative to Valentine's Day. Celebrating both St. George (the city's patron saint) and the deaths of Shakespeare and Cervantes, Barcelona gathers along Las Ramblas in search of flowers and books to gift to lovers. Ⓩ *April 23.*

LA DIADA
Fossar de les Moreres

This festival is Catalonia's national holiday celebrating the end of the city's siege in 1714 as well as of reclaiming national (whoops, we mean regional) identity after Franco. Celebrations will be had and flags will be waved. Ⓩ *Sept 11.*

FESTA DE SANT JOAN
The beachfront

These days light a special fire in every pyromaniac's heart as fireworks, bonfires, and torches light the city and waterfront in celebration of the coming of summer. Ⓩ *June 23-24.*

FESTA MERCÈ
Placa de Sant Jaume

This multi-week celebration of Barcelona's patron saint Our Lady of Mercy, it is the city's main annual celebration. More than 600 free performances and 2000 entertainers cloak the city in multiple venues, all of which are free. There is a contest in the Placa de Juame every year in which contestants have to build a human tower and have a small child climb up it.

🗓 *Weeks before and after Sept 24.*

BARCELONA PRIDE

Parade ends in Avinguda Maria Cristina

This week is the Mediterannean's biggest GLBT celebration and takes place throughout Catalonia. Multiple venues throughout the city and surrounding region take active part throughout the festival, culminating with a parade and festival on the final weekend.

🗓 *Last week of June.*

Fútbol

Although Barcelona technically has two football teams, **Fútbol Club Barcelona (FCB)** and the **Real Club Deportivo Español de Barcelona (RCD),** you can easily pass a stay in the city without ever hearing about the latter. It is impossible to miss the former, however, and for good reason. Besides being a really incredible athletic team, FCB lives up to its motto as "more than a club."

During the years of Francisco Franco, FCB was forced to change its name and crest in order to banish any nationalistic references to Cataluña, and thereafter became a rallying point for oppressed Catalan separatists. Once the original name and crest were reinstated after Franco's fall in 1974, the team retained its symbolic importance and is still seen as a sign of democracy, identity, and pride for the region.

This passion is not entirely altruistic, however—FCB has been one of the best teams in the world in recent years. In 2009 they were the first team to win six out of six major competitions in a single year. Their world-class training facilities (thanks in part to the 1992 Olympics) supply many World Cuppers each year, leaving many Barcelonans annoyed that they are not permitted to compete as their own nation, similar to Ireland or Wales in the United Kingdom. Much to the chagrin of some hardheaded FCB fans, Spain won the World Cup in 2010.

Because FCB fervor is so pervasive, you will not need to head to Camp Nou to join in the festivites—almost every bar off the tourist track boasts a screen dedicated to their games. Sit down, kick back with a brew, and just don't root for the competition.

ESSENTIALS

Practicalities

- **TOURIST OFFICES: Plaça de Catalonia** is the main office along with Pl. de Sant Jaume. *(Pl. de Catalonia, 17S* ☎*93 285 38 34* 🖥*www.barcelonaturisme.com* ✴ Ⓜ*Catalonia, underground across from El Corte Inglès. Look for the pillars with the letter i on top.* 𝒊 *Free maps; brochures on sights, transportation, tours, and about everything else you could want to find; booking service for last-minute accommodations; gift shop; money exchange; and box office (Caixa de Catalonia).* 🗓 *Open daily 9am-9pm.)* **Plaça de Sant Jaume** *(C. Ciutat, 2*☎*93 270 24 29* ✴ Ⓜ*Jaume I, located in the Ajuntament building in Plaça Sant Jaume.* 🗓 *Open M-F 9am-8pm, Sa 10am-8pm, Su and holidays 10am-2pm. Closed Jan 1 and Dec 25.)* **Oficina de Turisme de Barcelona** *(Palau Robert, Pg. de Gràcia, 107*☎*93 238 80 91,*☎*012 in Catalonia* 🖥*www.gencat.es/probert* ✴ Ⓜ*Diagonal.* 🗓 *Open M-Sa 10am-7pm, Su 10am-2pm. Closed Dec 25 and 26, and Jan 1 and 6.)* **Institut de Cultura de Barcelona (ICUB)** *(Palau de la Virreina, La Rambla, 99* ☎*93 316 10 00* 🖥*www.bcn.cat/cultura* ✴Ⓜ*Liceu.*🗓 *Info office open daily 10am-8pm.* **Estació Barcelona-Sants** *(Pl. Països Catalans*☎*90 224 02 02* ✴ Ⓜ*Sants-Estació* 𝒊 *Info and last-minute accommodation booking.* 🗓 *Open June 24-Sept 24 daily 8am-8pm; Sept 24-June 23 M-F 8am-8pm, Sa-Su 8am-2pm.)*

- **TOURS:** **Self-guided tours** of Gothic, Romanesque, *modernista*, and contemporprary Barcelona available; pick up pamphlets in tourism offices. A wide variety of **paid walking tours**also exist, with information available in the brochures at the tourism office. The **Pl. de Catalonia tourist office** hosts its own walking tours and has information about bike tours. (☎93 285 38 32. €12, ages 4-12 €5). ⚐ Ⓜ*Catalonia, underground across from El Corte Inglès. Look for the pillars with the letter i on top. i 2hr. walking tour of the Barri Gòtic.* ⚐ *Tours daily at 10am (English) and Sa at noon (Catalan and Spanish* **Picasso tours** *(☎93 285 38 32) of Barcelona* ⚐ Ⓜ*Catalonia i Check for English, Spanish, and Catalan tour availability. Tour includes entrance to* **Museu Picasso.** Ⓢ €19, ages 4-12 €7 ⚐ *Tu, Th, Sa 4pm (English) and Sa at 4pm (Spanish or Catalan tours with pre-booking).*

- **LUGGAGE STORAGE:** **Estació Barcelona-Sants** (⚐ Ⓜ*Sants-Estació.* Ⓢ *Lockers €3-4.50 per day.* ⚐ *Open daily 5:30am-11pm.)***Estació Nord** (⚐ Ⓜ*Arc de Trimof.* Ⓢ *Lockers €3.50-5 per day, 90-day limit.)* **El Prat Airport** (Ⓢ *€3.80-4.90 per day.)*

- **GAY AND LESBIAN RESOURCES:** **GLBT tourist guide** includes a section on GLBT bars, clubs, publications, and more *(Pl. de Catalonia tourist office.)* **GAYBARCELONA** (🖳*www.gaybarcelona.net.)* and **Infogal** (🖳*www.colectiugai.org.)* have up-to-date information. **Barcelona Pride** has annual activites during the last week of June *(🖳www.pridebarcelona.org/en.)* **Antinous** specializes in gay and lesbian books and films *(C. Josep Anselm Clavé, 6 ☎93 301 90 70* 🖳*www.antinouslibros.com* ⚐ Ⓜ*Drassanes* ⚐ *Open M-F 10:30am-2pm and 5-8:30pm, Sa noon-2pm and 5-8:30pm.)*

- **INTERNET ACCESS:** **Barcelona City Government** offers free Wi-Fi access at over 500 places including some museums, parks, and sports centers. (🖳*www.bcn.es.)* **Easy Internet Cafe** *(La Rambla, 31 ☎93 301 75 07* ⚐ Ⓜ*Liceu.* Ⓢ *Decent prices and around 300 terminals. €2.10 per hr., min. €2. 1-day unlimited pass €7; 1wk. €15; 1 mo. €30.* ⚐ *Open daily 8am-2:30am.)* **Easy Internet Cafe** *(Ronda Universitat, 35.* Ⓢ *€2 per hour; day pass €3, 1 wk. €7, 1 mo. €15.* ⚐ *Open daily 8am-2:30am.)* **Navegaweb** *(La Rambla, 88-94 ☎93 318 90 26* 🖳*nevegabarcelona@terra.es* ⚐ Ⓜ*Liceu.* Ⓢ *€0.20 per min. to USA. Internet €2 per hour.* ⚐ *Open M-Th 9am-midnight, F 9am-1am, Sa 9am-2am, Su 9am-midnight.)* **BCNet (Internet Gallery Cafe)** *(C. Barra de Ferro, 3 ☎93 268 15 07* 🖳*www.bornet-bcn.com.* ⚐ Ⓜ*Jaume I.* Ⓢ *€1 for 15 min., €3 per hr., 10 hr. ticket €20.* ⚐ *Open M-F 10am-11pm, Sa-Su noon-11pm.)*

- **POST OFFICE:** *(Pl. d'Antoni López* ☎*90 219 71 97* 🖳*www.correos.es* ⚐Ⓜ*Jaume I or* Ⓜ*Barceloneta.* Ⓢ *Open M-F 8:30am-9:30pm, Su noon-10pm.)*

- **POSTAL CODE:** 08001.

Emergency!

- **EMERGENCY NUMBERS:** ☎061.

- **POLICE:** **Local police:** ☎092. **National police:** ☎091. **Tourist police** *(La Rambla, 43*☎*93 256 24 30* ⚐ Ⓜ*Liceu.* ⚐ *Open 24hr.)*

- **LATE-NIGHT PHARMACY:** Rotates. Check any pharmacy window for the nearest on duty, contact the police, or call **Información de Farmacias de Guardia** *(☎93 481 00 60).*

- **HOSPITALS/MEDICAL SERVICES:** **Hospital Clínic i Provincal** *(C. Villarroel, 170* ☎*93 227 54 00* ⚐ Ⓜ*Hospital Clínic. Main entrance at C. Roselló and C. Casanova.)* **Hospital de la Santa Creu i Sant Pau** *(☎93 291 90 00; emergency*☎*91 91 91* ⚐ Ⓜ*Vall d'Hebron.)* **Hospital del Mar** *(Pg. Marítim, 25-29 ☎93 248 30 00* ⚐ Ⓜ*Ciutadella or* Ⓜ*Vila Olímpica.)*

Getting There

By Plane

AEROPORT DEL PRAT DE LLOBREGAT BCN

08820 El Prat de Llobregat ☎93 478 47 04 for Terminal 1, ☎93 478 05 65 for Terminal 2B

To get to Pl. Catalonia, take the **Aerobus** *(☎92 415 60 20)* in front of terminals 1 or 2 *($ €5, round-trip ticket valid for 9 days €8.65. ⏰ 35-40min.; every 6-15min. to Pl. Catalonia daily 6am-1am, to airport 5:30am-12:14am.)* To the airport, the A1 bus takes you to Terminal 1, A2 bus to Terminal 2. For early morning flights, the Nitbus **N17** runs from Pl. Catalonia to all terminals *($ €1.40. ⏰ from Pl. Catalonia every 20min. daily 11am-5am, from airport every hr. 9:50pm-4:50am.)* Cheaper, and usually a bit faster, than the Aerobus is the **RENFE train** *(☎90 224 34 02 $ €1.40 or free with T10 transfer from metro. ⏰ 20-25min. to Estació Sants, 25-30min. to Pg. de Gràcia; every 30min., from airport 6am-11:38pm, from Estació Sants to airport 5:35am-11:09pm.)* To reach the train from Terminal 2, take the pedestrian overpass in front of the airport (it's on the left when your back is to the entrance). For those arriving at Terminal 1, a shuttlebus is available outside the terminal to take you to the train station. *➤ ⓂSants-Estació. ℹ Info and last-minute accommodation bookings, as well as transport connections from the airport to the city center and other locations. ⏰ Open daily 9am-9pm.*

AEROPORT DE GIRONA GRO

☎90 240 4704 💻www.girona-airport.net

Transport to Barcelona is available from the airport by **Barcelona Bus** *($ €12, round-trip €21. ⏰ 1hr. 10min. from Girona to Estacio d'Autobusos Barcelona Nord ℹ Buses from the airport to Estacio d 'Autobusos Barcelona Nord are timed to match flight arrivals. Buses from Estacio d 'Autobuses arrive at Girona Airport approximately 3hr. before flight departures. ⏰ Open 24hr.*

By Train

Depending on the destination, trains can be an economical option. Travelers may find trains at **Estació Barcelona-Sants** in Pl. Països Catalans (ⓂSants Estació) for most domestic and international traffic, while **Estació de Franca** on Av. Marques de l'Argentera (ⓂBarceloneta) serves regional destinations and a limited number of international locations. Note that trains often stop before the main stations; check the schedule. **RENFE** *(reservations and info ☎90 224 02 02, international ☎24 34 02 💻www.renfe.es)* runs to **Bilbao, Madrid, Sevilla,** and **Valencia** in Spain. Trains also travel to **Milan** (via **Turin** and **Figueres**) in Italy and **Montpellier** in France, with connections to Geneva, Paris, and the French Riviera. There's a 20% discount on round-trip tickets. Call or check website for train times and seasonal schedules.

By Bus

Buses are often considerably cheaper than the train and should be considered for those traveling within the region on a budget. The city's main bus terminal is **Barcelona Nord Estació d'Autobuses** *(☎902 26 06 06 💻www.barcelonanord.com ➤ ⓂArc de Triomf or #54 bus),* with buses also departing from the Estació Sants and the airport. **Sarfa** *(Ticket office at Ronda Sant Pere, 21 ☎90 230 20 25 💻www.sarfa.es)* is the primary line, but **Eurolines** *(☎93 265 07 88 💻www.eurolines.es)* also goes to **Paris** via **Lyon** and offers a 10% discount to travelers under 26 or over 60. **ALSA/ENATCAR** *(☎90 242 22 42; www.alsa.es)* goes to **Alicante, Bilbao, Madrid, Sevilla, Valencia,** and **Zaragoza.**

By Ferry

Ferries to the **Baleares Islands, Mallorca,** and **Ibiza** leave daily from the port of Barcelona at **Terminal Drassanes** *(☎93 324 89 80)* and **Terminal Ferry de Barcelona** *(☎93 295 91 82 ➤ ⓂDrassanes).* The most popular ferries are run by **Transmediterránea** *(☎902 45 46 45 💻www.transmediterrana.es)* in Terminal Drassanes.

Getting Around

By Metro

The mode of transportation used most in the city is the Barcelona **Metro** *(☎93 318 70 74 🖳www.tmb.cat)*. Get to know it well—the extensive train and bus system provides cheap, easy access to nearly the entire city. Different lines are identified by L and then their number *(L1, L2, L3, L4, L5, L8, L10, L11)*. **Trains** run Monday through Thursday and Sundays from 5am to midnight, Friday and days prior to holidays 5am to 2am, and Saturday all day. Stops are marked by a red sign with a white capital M.

By Bus

For more remote or hard-to-access places, the bus may be an important complement to the metro during your journey. Barcelona's tourist office also offers a **Tourist Bus** *(🖳bcnshop.barcelonaturisme.com $ 1 day €22)* that frequents sights of particular interest in the city and allows riders to hop on and off for a 24hr. period. Depending on how much you plan to use the route (and how much you loathe hopping off of a red double decker labeled "Tourist Bus" when you're traveling), the bus may be a worthwhile investment upon arriving in the city.

Rentals

Motocicletas (motos for short—scooters, and less frequently motorcycles) are a common sight, and **bicycles** are also becoming more popular. Many institutions rent motos by hour, day, and month, but you need a valid driver's license recognized in Spain in order to rent one for personal use. Many places also offer bike rental. If you will be staying in the city for an extended period, it is possible to buy a bike secondhand or register for **Bicing** *(☎902 31 55 31 🖳www.bicing.cat)*, the municipal red and white bikes.

By Taxi

When all other cheaper and more exciting options fail, Barcelona offers a taxi service to get you back home safely on those nights when revelry lasts after metro hours. The official taxi service is **Radio Taxi** *(☎93 225 00 00)* and is identifiable by the black and yellow cars.

granada ☎858 or 958

So *Let's Go* rents a time machine, and it's the 15th century. You're the queen of Spain (a queen who supposedly wore the same dress for the entire extent of her reign, no less), and you can live anywhere in your kingdom. Where do you choose to reside? If you're **Isabela la Católica,** the Spanish queen who, with the help of her far-less-powerful husband, **Ferdinand,** gobbled up the Iberian peninsula for the sake of the kingdom and the church, then you're picking Granada. In 1492, Granada had spent centuries under Moorish Rule, and **Boabdil,** the last sultan on the Iberian Peninsula, was holding strong to his city while his brethren fell left and right. However, with a little persuasion and a whole lot of gold, Isabela was one persuasive lady. It may look like she's holding a grenade in all the city statues, but the city got taken without a drip of bloodshed, and she's really just gripping a pomegranate. This city symbol was part of Granada's draw—the citrus fruits like figs, oranges, and pomegranates were making bank for Boabdil, so the Spaniards wanted the goods.

Now let's fast-forward a good couple of hundred years. Today, you have a city still glowing with a North African influence, including stunning remnants of Boabdil's crown like the Alhambra. You have a combination of Mediterranean, Moroccan, and Spanish cuisine on every block. Excitement from the urban, commercial city center, all the way into the hippie-inhabited caves of Sacramonte give this city an energy unlike any other. Granada may have a population under 250,000, but you pack that crowd into a small city without anything but mountains for hours, and it can feel like

NYC. So enjoy the high-speed lifestyle in Realejo and by the university, and then get in touch with the nearby nature.

ORIENTATION

Plaza Nueva

The area around Plaza Nueva connects main street **Calle Gran Vía** to the more northern **Albacin** region that holds **La Alhambra.** All the Moroccan restaurants, tea stops, shops, and hookah bars can be found around **Calle Cria Nueva** and **Calderería Vieja,** and there are plenty of falafel options and tapas bars on **Calle Elvira.** Follow **Calle Santa Ana** up towards the Alhambra, and you'll travel along old, picturesque streets. Generally, the streets are small and winding, so make sure to bring a map. One of the main squares of the city is **Plaza San Nicolas;** and the adjacent **Mirador Nicolas** is one of the best places to get a view of the Alhambra. You'll also find a fresh produce market in **Plaza Larga.** Furthest north, the **Sacromonte** region is generally classified as the hippie and gypsy area of Granada.

Catedral and University

South of **Calle Gran Vía,** the streets become much more organized and manageable. This area is right by the university, and the student vibe is strong. School-supply shops, bookstores, and cafes with internet can be found on nearly every corner. **Plaza Trinidad** and **Plaza Bib Rambia** are lined with restaurants and small shops, and they're great places to stop for relaxing meals or some retail therapy. **Calle Pedro Antonio de Alarcon** is a great street for late-night tapas and drinks, especially if you're looking to run into the student crowd. If you're looking to relax with some reading or a picnic, **Parque Fuente Nueva** *(☎ Open daily 8am-10pm.)* is a student favorite, located right around university grounds.

Elsewhere

You'll find Granada's commercial district along **Calle Reyes Catolicos** and **Arcera del Darro**—the shops get bigger, the streets get wider, and the general effort of the city grows with decorations, fountains, and landscaping as you walk closer to the intersection. This area, **Realejo,** is a wonderful spot to explore on a weekend stroll. You'll find families brunching and relaxing on **Carrera del Genil,** some of the city's most traditional tapas along **Calle Navas,** and a major square with lots of food options at **Campo Principe.**

Located around the outskirts of the city clockwise from the Alhambra, you'll find the **Sierra Nevada** mountain range, the major science center **Parque de las Ciencias,** the **Parque Garcia Lorca,** the **Renfe** and **bus stations,** and **La Cartuja.**

ACCOMMODATIONS

Plaza Nueva

▦ OASIS GRANADA

★((•))✿ HOSTEL ❷

Pl. Correo Viejo, 3   ☎958 215 848 ▦www.oasisgranada.com

This hostel chain definitely has hostel living down to a science. Arriving at Oasis Granada, you're guaranteed one of the most luxurious, convenient, and generally pleasant hostel stays around. With top-notch facilities including a massive cafeteria (where your free breakfast is served), full bar (with a free drink upon arrival and nightly happy hour), and a rooftop terrace to soak up some sun, this place really delivers on the promise of its name. If you can get yourself to leave, Oasis will make sure you're acquainted with the city in a variety of ways. Check out the welcome board in front to get the daily list of activities, including themed tours. Socialize at the evening dinner parties or tapas outings, use their friendly staff to get some nightlife tips, and then come home to your multi-room dorm suite with a thick mattress, clean sheets, and a fuzzy blanket to keep you cozy.

The only drawback of living in an oasis is that you won't be alone: this busy accommodation is always overflowing with partiers on the weekends.

 # From the bus station, take bus #3 or 33 to Gran Vía de Colon 1, make a right onto Carcel Baja and a left onto Placeta Correo Viejo. i Breakfast included. Towel rental €1. Free activities and tours. $ Dorms €15-18. ⏰ Reception 24hr. Breakfast 8am-11am.

PENSIÓN BRITZ PENSIÓN [2]

C. Cuesta de Gomerez, 1 ☎958 223 652 🖥www.lisboaweb.com

While high-quality backpackers' hostels can be found all around the area, that type of stay isn't for everyone. For the more selective voyager, Pensión Britz provides a great private alternative. You'll find your quiet room with large armoir, checkered comforter and drapes, and particularly springy mattress to be a great place to relax in peace. The rooms with ensuite bathrooms are definitely a bit more expensive, but they are larger and brighter than the other rooms, which only have a sink in the corner of the room. The spunky Spanish staff will hop out of their seats to help you plan reservations and tours at all the sights and fight to get you special offers around town. If you're planning a longer stay, they may even offer to include breakfast if you ask nicely enough.

 # C. Reyes Católicos becomes Pl. Santa Ana and Cuesta Romerez branches off to the right. i Ventilation in rooms. Washing machine available. $ Singles €17-25, with bath €33-38; doubles €30-36, with bath €40-48; triples €45-48, with bath €51-57; quads €50-55, with bath €60-68. ⏰ Reception 24hr.

Catedral and University

FUNKY BACKPACKERS HOSTEL [2]

C. Conde de las Infantes ☎958 800 058 🖥funky@alternativeacc.com

Funky Backpackers describes itself as the "multicultural" hostel of Granada, and we couldn't agree more. You'll find murals from all over the world all over the walls, nightly dinners of international cuisine *(€4-5)*, and a full cultural activity agenda including salsa dancing, flamenco shows, inter-language discussions, and music jam sessions. Regardless of your cultural background, it's impossible not to be stunned and impressed by the dorm living—each room has a kitchen, sofa, and lockable private closet. The English-speaking staff has the knowledge to answer even the most difficult tourist questions, and there are schedules and travel ideas posted around the lobby. If you've stayed or plan to stay at Picasso's Corner in Málaga or Terrace Backpackers in Córdoba, you'll get a 10% discount off the already shockingly low prices.

 # Conde de las Infantes intersects with Plaza Trinidad. i Credit card min. €50; €1 surcharge for smaller sums. Breakfast included. Female-only dorms available. $ 7-bed dorm €12.75; 6-bed €13.35-€15.75; 4-bed €16.75; female-only €16.75. Doubles €38. ⏰ Reception 24hr.

HOSPEDAJE ALMOHADA HOSTAL [2]

C. Postigo de Zarate, 4 ☎958 207 446 🖥www.laalmojada.com

Admit it—you used to play those simulation computer games with your friends (or more likely by yourself) where you'd build a cute little cyber-house and have little people try to live inside of it. Well, if you could design the cutest, quaintest, just-pinch-its-cheeks home, it might look a bit like Hospedaje Almohada. From the colorful and cushioned living room with packed bookshelves and a TV to the fully stocked kitchen and bright patio dining space, you'll be itching to relax or cook yourself up something warm and yummy. The entire place is even decorated, and you'll find classic Andalucian paintings on all the walls along the hallways and inside the rooms. These private abodes are clean, quiet, and spacious and equipped with sink, bedside tables, and even a small seating area.

 # From Pl. Trinidad, take C. Trinidad to the T intersection and make a right onto Postigo de Zarate. i Towels and linens included. $ Singles €20; doubles €36; triples €51. ⏰ Reception 9:30am-3pm and 4:30-9:30pm.

Elsewhere

ALBERQUE INTURJOVEN GRANADA (HI) HOSTEL ❷

C. Ramon y Cajal, 2 ☎958 002 900 www.inturjoven.com

Run by the Andalucian government, Inturjoven hostels like this gem always feel particularly safe and organized. Even though Alberque Inturjoven Granada is situated in a more industrial area south of the university that has quite the assortment of graffiti, the hostel is a nice escape from the surroundings. Rooms are big and simple, each with large closets and tons of space. Even though it's not centrally located, the nearby Camino Ronda bus stops catch a wide array of city lines. Despite the hostel not having a public kitchen, daily meals are offered and vending machines line every floor.

Take the circular bus lines (#11, 21, or 23) to Camino Ronda 10 and turn right at Ramon y Cajal. i Parking available. Towels €2. Breakfast €2; lunch and dinner €8. $ Ages 25 and under singles €16-19; doubles €16-19; triples €16-19. Ages 26 and over singles €22-25; doubles €22-25; triples €22-25. ⏰ Reception 24hr.

SIGHTS

The sights of Granada are unlike any other you'll visit in Spain. Rather than a simple checklist of museums, churches, and monuments (although Granada does have quite the impressive array of those as well), Granada's history can be explored by just grabbing a map and wandering around the different historic barrios of the city. You'll find a unique vibe in the **Albaicin** and **Sacramonte,** get a taste of the Spanish history around the **Cathedral,** and find yourself in complete awe as you make your way around **the Alhambra.**

Plaza Nueva

CASA-MUSEO FREDERICO GARCIA LORCA MUSEUM, PARK

C. Virgen Blanca s/n ☎958 258 466 www.huertadesanvicente.com

Probably one of Granada's best spots for a picnic or a morning jog (there are signs posted all around recommending stretching and toning exercizes), the entirety of Parque Frederico Garcia Lorca smells of the roses that line its paths. Whether you want to sit at the duck pond or enjoy one of the two restaurants in the park, you cannot leave without stopping at the main event. The Casa-Museo Frederico Garcia Lorca is the original summer house of the famous Spanish poet, playwright, and director who was assassinated after his disappearance during the Spanish Civil War. This emblem of Granadan culture is now honored in the home where he found some of his greatest inspiration. You can tour his kitchen, his grand piano, and his desk of work and even see his high-school diploma, which rats out his barely passing grades.

Take the circular bus to the intersection of C. Recogidas and Camino de Ronda and follow the signs. i Tours available in English and Spanish. $ €3, students €1, W free. ⏰ Open Tu-Su July-Aug 10am-2:30pm; Oct-Mar 10am-12:30pm and 4-6:30pm; Apr-June and Sept 10am-12:30pm and 5-7:30pm.

Alhambra

In 1238, **Sultan Al-Ahmar** of the Nasrid Dynasty took a look around Granada and realized that he had an opportunity to make something of the old **alcazaba** in the Albayzin area, an already centuries-old fortress with foundations constructed by the Romans. Al-Ahmar had a vision of turning this protective city wall into a palace and getaway for Arab royalty and top government officials. However, by 1491, Granada wasn't a princely paradise but a scrappy survivor. It was all that remained of the kingdom of al-Andalus, and *los reyes Católicos* were sieging the city in what would become the final act of the 780-year *Reconquista.* By 1492, Granada belonged to Ferdinand and Isabella, and we're sure that once all-powerful Isabella saw the this city's Alhambra, she decided that the couple was never going to leave this place.

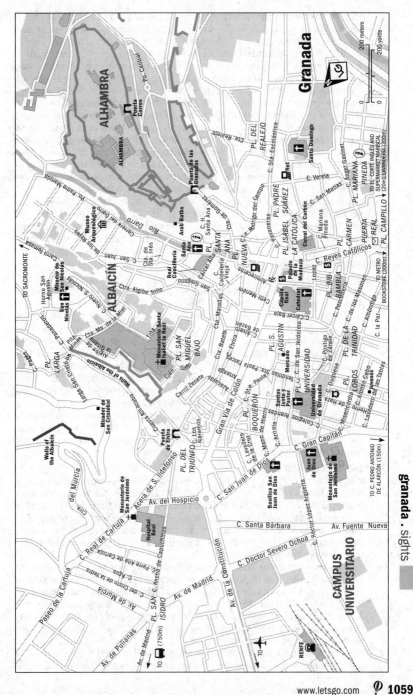

Granada

granada · sights

Today, we definitely need to give a big thank you to good old Al-Ahmar (much more interesting than Weird Al or that creepy Uncle Al) for creating the Alhambra, one of the most historic and symbolic sights in all of Spain. It's the government's biggest moneymaker—Sagrada Familia has a higher income, but it loses tons to renovations—and it will soon be one of your favorite spots on the map. When visiting the Alhambra, be prepared to devote a good 3½-4hr. to your visit, as there is a ton to see. The Alhambra isn't simply a single sight—it's a fortified city full of gardens, museums, towers, and baths, not to mention a UNESCO World Heritage Site.

There are a few ways to get tickets to the Alhambra. *(C. Real s/n* ☎*902 441 221* ▣*www.alhambra-patronato.es* ⓢ *€12.)* To purchase your ticket in advance, inquire at any of the La Caixa dispensers around the city, including one at the **Tienda de la Alhambra** *(C. Reyes Católicos, 40* ☎*902 888 001* ▣*www.alhambra-tickets.es).* Many hostels will also book tickets for you at an additional charge of €2. You can buy tickets on the day of your visit at the entrance, either at the ticket office or the automated machines in the **Access Pavilion.** The ticket office is open from 8am until 1hr. before close.

The general daytime tickets allow access to all sights on the grounds—either in the morning *(🕐 8:30am-2pm.)* or in the afternoon. *(🕐 Mar 15-Oct 14 2-8pm; Oct 15-Mar 14 2-6pm.)* An evening ticket includes access to the gardens or Nasrid palaces, but not both, for €12 as well. *(🕐 Mar 15-May 31 and Sept 1-Oct 14 Th-Sa 10-11:30pm; Oct 16-Nov 14 F-Sa 8-9:30pm.)* These later visits allow you to see the Alhambra when the grounds are lit up against the night sky.

NASRID PALACES

Once on the grounds, the **Nasrid Palaces** are definitely the hot spot of the Alhambra. They're so hot, in fact, that you have to pick a specific time slot upon which to enter when purchasing your ticket to the Alhambra. You're limited to 1hr. of exploration, and there's a ton to see, so be ready for quite the journey through these remarkable grounds. Making your way through the **Sala de la Barca, Salon de Comares,** and **Sala de las Albencerrajes,** you'll be impressed by the detailed original plasterwork curving and winding its way up to the tall pointed ceilings of the rooms. The turquoise, yellow, and green tiles add a splash of lovely color to these once-royal rooms. Remember that the lion is king of the jungle and the **Patio de los Leones** is definitely the ruling architectural spot in the entire Alhambra. A complex system of aqueducts used gravity to power this fountain (and all the plumbing of the Alhambra), and such creativity and technical prowess blew the conquering Catholic royalty "out of the water." (Yeah, we went there.)

PALACIO DE CARLOS V

| Museo de Bellas Artes | ☎958 895 430 ▣www.museosdeandalucia.es |
| Museo del Alhambra | ☎902 441 221 ▣museo.pag@juntadeandalucia.es |

While the Palacio de Carlos V is often referred to as the "unfinished" and thus "forgotten" palace, there are definitely memories to be made here. At this 16th-century Renaissance-style palace, you'll not only get to explore the striking circular courtyard with two stories of marble columns, but you can also enjoy the two museums on the grounds.

The **Museo de Bellas Artes** is Granada's main art museum and actually the oldest public museum in Spain. The exhibitions begin in the historic year of 1492—yes, yes, it's the year when Columbus ▣**sailed the ocean blue,** but it's also the year when Granada shifted from Arab to Catholic control—and make their way into the modern day. There's a lot of local pride going on, from works by Granada natives to works inspired by the city itself. The museum also holds temporary rotating multimedia exhibits.

Also in the palace is the **Museo del Alhambra,** which holds a wide breadth of information and objects from the Alhambra itself. Luckily, since Ferdinand and

Isabella settled into the Alhambra in the 15th century, all of the decorations, building elements, and possessions of the royal couple have been preserved and moved around the palaces. But now it's come time to share the spotlight—the museum, in development since 1940, now houses one of the world's best collections of Spanish-Moorish and Nasrid art.

Ⓢ *Museo de Bellas Artes €1.50, EU students free. Museo del Alhambra free.* Ⓩ *Palacio box office open daily Mar-Oct 8am-7pm; Nov-Feb 8am-5pm. Museo de Bellas Artes open Mar-Oct Tu 2:30-8pm, W-Sa 9am-8pm, Su 9am-2:30pm; Nov-Feb Tu 2:30-6pm, W-Sa 9am-6pm, Su 9am-2:30pm. Museo del Alhambra open July 1-Sept 15 Tu-Su 8:30am-2pm; Sept 16-June 30 Tu-Su 8:30am-2:30pm.*

ALCAZABA

The **Alcazaba** is largely to thank for the survival of the sight you're enjoying today. This fortress was definitely hard to get around (especially when traveling by donkey and wearing cloth slippers), and it protected the Alhambra for hundreds of years. However, today you can go where all those would-be conquerers wanted to be. Climb the Torre del Cubo, Torre de Homenaje, and Torre de la Vela to survey your kingdom: you'll be lost in the panoramic views of all of Granada, snapping pictures of the hundreds of thousands of tiled rooftops extending into the horizon.

GENERALIFE

The **Generalife** was definitely built for a king—or should we say a sultan? Constructed between the 12th and 14th centuries, this maze of gardens, patios, and fountains was intended to be the sultan's place of rest. And it's not all just nature up here. You'll also enter the stunning royal villa, decorated with the beautifully detailed plasterwork, as well as the outdoor theater where the dance portion of the annual **Festival Internacional de Música y Danza** is held. You'll climb the **escalera de agua**, a staircase lined with laurel trees and streams of water running down either handrail, and exit through the **Promenades of Oldeander and Cypress Trees.** And in case your eyes weren't already aesthetically overwhelmed, you can also look down over the entire Alhambra below.

Albaicín *Albayzín*

The history and conceptualization of the Albaicín barrio may seem a little conflicted: some say that the name of this ancient Muslim barrio could translate to "the miserables" in Arabic; others proudly explain that this quarter is actually the oldest, most historic portion of Granada, where the first Muslim court of the city was established in the 11th century. Today, the romantic Albaicín area, dipping into a valley that will send back a booming **echo** if you shout from the right place along **Calle Santa Ana**, still holds strong remnants of its Muslim past. Despite later alterations by Ferdinand and Isabella, this UNESCO World Heritage Site still has a Nasrid-style flair.

OLD MUSLIM BARRIO

C. del Darro, 41 ☎958 225 640

The signs that you've entered this area are subtle at first. Walking the streets, you'll start to notice churches like the **Iglesia de Santa Anat** that have oddly mosque-like entrances. Walking up C. Carmen de Darro, you can enter the **buñuelos,** or Arab baths. (☎*958 027 800* Ⓩ *Open Tu-Sa 10am-2pm.* Ⓢ *Free.)* These are now a public monument. You can freely explore the **carmens,** or classic patio-gardens of the wealthy, at **Casa del Chapiz** on C. Cuesta del Chapiz and discover a whole new way of showing off your wealth (nothing was flashier than a snazzy garden with citrus trees and a few bamboo shoots). Along Carmen de Darro or Cuesta de Acahaba, you can visit the **original city walls** of Granada that once protected last sultan Boabdil's five Granadan castles. In the marketplace of Plaza Larga, you'll encounter the **Puerta de Pesa.** Notice the remaining weights hanging from this entryway—they were once used as a warning and reminder to merchants that consequences awaited if they were to cheat the customers of the marketplace.

While a few remain to sustain the warning (so yes, you really did just buy three kilos of pomegranates), most of the weights have today been moved to the Albaicín's **Archeological Museum**, along with many other pieces of Granada's history

$ *€1.50, EU citizens free.* ⏰ *Open Tu 2:30-8:30pm, W-Sa 9:30am-8:30pm, Su 9:30am-2pm.*

Sacromonte

Let's look at those monthly bills: rent, electricity, plumbing, heat. It all really adds up. But you know what's a cheaper option? Digging yourself a cave in the mountains across from the Alhambra. That must have been the thought process (more or less) of the Indian gypsies who dug into the mountainside when arriving on the Iberian peninsula in the 15th century. While they were living comfortably for centuries along the Río del Darro, the boom came when the lower classes packed their bags for Sacromonte between the late 19th and mid-20th century—by 1950 there were 3682 known cave dwellings along the mountainside.

But a genius for econonomical living wasn't the only talent these gypsies had. Walking the **Camino del Sacromonte,** you'll come across flamenco bar after flamenco bar, all ready to present the gypsy *zambra* style of this famous dance. You can also stop in at the museum honoring *zambra* and one of its top performers, **Cueva Maria la Canastera** *(Camino de Sacromonte, 89 ☎958 121 183 💻cuevacanastera@yahoo.es).*

👍 MUSEO CUEVAS DE SACROMONTE — MUSEUM, CAVES

Barranco de los Negros s/n ☎958 215 120 💻www.sacromontegranada.com

In this museum, you'll get to see many of the original, though restored, cave dwellings—and they look surprisingly cozy. They might be dug-in holes, but you'll see stables, kitchens, bedrooms, and workspaces all comfortably kept up in these small, manmade caves. You'll also learn about the unique ecology of the **Darro River Valley,** which houses La Alhambra on one bank and Sacromonte on the other, and get an awesome view of this unbeatable duo.

$ *€5.* ⏰ *Open daily Apr-Oct 10am-2pm and 5-9pm; Nov-Mar 10am-2pm and 4-7pm.*

HOLY CAVE — CAVE, RELIGIOUS SITE

At the Abadía del Sacromonte

Sacromonte, or "holy mountain," is named such because of years of myth and legend. The holiest of these myths centers on the appropriately named **Holy Cave,** where a pile of ashes, supposedly being those of Granada's patron saint, San Cecilio, were discovered along with some leaden books suggesting the best means of converting Muslims to Catholicism. It was thought that the books were written by the saint. When Ferdinand and Isabella got word of this cave, they invested huge sums to create the *via crucis*, a line of over 1000 crosses along the mountain. Today, even though the legends have been proven false—the leaden books were actually written by a random Moorish scholar and are now stored in the **Abadía del Sacromonte**—the mountain remains a religious emblem and the **Procession to Sacromonte** is held on the first Sunday in February each year to honor San Cecilio.

Catedral Quarter

CATEDRAL DE GRANADA — ®♿ CHURCH

C. Gran Vía de Colon, 5 ☎958 222 959

Queen Isabella grew up in a nunnery, so it only makes sense that she'd put one hell of a church in her favorite city (should we not be saying "hell" in the same sentence as "church"?). The Catedral de Granada, formerly connected to the Capilla Real where Isabella is actually burried, is a massive, circular building lined with 13 golden *capillas*, or chapels, all of which are the Capilla Mayor in the center of the church outshines. This sanctuary, surrounded by multiple organs and thick marble pillars (you'd need at least three people to give them a good hug), was definitely made for presentation's sake. It looks more like a theater than a church—two levels of balconies and stained-glass windows are the backdrop for the enormous red-carpeted altar in front. You'll also get to visit the Sacristía when entering the Catedral, which stores religious artwork and artifacts from centuries of Catholic royalty in Granada.

Entrance on C. Oficios. i Information in Spanish only. $ €3.50. Audio tour €3. Open M-Sa 10:45am-1:30pm and 4-8pm, Su 4-8pm. Ticket office closes 15min. before close.

FOOD

Food in Granada takes on three main types: Spanish-Granadan (think bold cuisine—*tortrilla sacramonte* is scrambled up with marrow, brains, and bull's testicles), North African, and Mediterranean. Everyone will have their favorite falafel spot that they can't name but can loosely direct you toward as well as their idea of the best *teteria*, or Arabic tea shop, packed with people sitting on cushions and sharing puffs of hookah. The tapas of Granada are what will really make you never want to leave—order a drink at any tapas bar and they'll bring it out with a selection of free small plates of food.

Plaza Nueva

BAR KIKI — TAPAS, BAR 3

Pl. de San Nicolas, 9 ☎958 276 715

You're sitting enjoying your view from Pl. de San Nicolas when you notice booming conversation from your peripheral. That's definitely Bar Kiki—unless some hippie vendors are getting extra chatty. The huge tented patio out front is always packed with locals, who come for the creative menu that uses fresh products purchased at the local Mercado Daria. Kiki serves up massive rations intended to be split between two people *(€14-20)*. Their specialty, Solomillo Nacional, celebrates Granada's Moorish influence with a hefty slab of tenderloin topped with almonds, apples, dates, raisins, and a reduction of sweet Pedro Ximenez wine *(€20)*. If the market has fresh tuna that day, you'll be lucky to get a free tapa of Atun de Barbate, fish marinated with olive oil, white wine, onions, and almonds, alongside a big mug of beer *(€2)* or a glass of Spanish wine *(€3)*.

Located right behind the viewpoint at Pl. de San Nicolas. $ Plates for 2 €14-20. Beer €2. Wine €3. Open M-Tu 10am-midnight, Th-Su 10am-midnight.

CASA LOPEZ CORREA — TAPAS 3

C. de los Molinos 5 ☎958 223 775

You might be caught off guard when walking into Casa Lopez Correa. It smells Spanish, but it looks Granadan. It's serving free tapas, but most of the patrons are speaking English. First off: this is not a tourist trap! Casa Lopez Correa just happens to be the stand-in "town bar" for all the Aussies, Brits, Kiwis, and Americans who decided to settle down in Granada. The crowd is likely inspired by the British owners: the wife works behind the stove and the husband works the bar, each preparing the house specialties. The worldly options are homemade and include Italian, English, Moroccan, and Spanish dishes. The *menú* of the day *(2 courses €10; 3 courses €12)* involves massive portions whose fragrances pour out from the open kitchen into the small restaurant. The extensive cocktail selection is especially impressive as there's not a syrup in sight, and all the mojitos, *caipirinhas*, and margaritas are made with fresh fruits and quality liquors *(€6)*. The tapa you get alongside these beverages is a hefty sampling of the *menú's* daily special.

From Pl. Isabel La Catolica, take C. Pavaneras until it curves into C. de los Molinos to the right. $ Appetizers €3.50-7.50; entrees €7.50-9.50. Mid-size rations €5-10. Beer €1.70. Wine €2.10. Open M-F noon-4pm and 8pm-1am, Sa 8pm-1am, Su 1-5pm with reservation only.

Catedral and University

POE — OPEN LATE 1

C. Verónica de la Magdelena 40 www.barpoe.com

Poe may very well be the destination for the most delicious and least expensive meal in Granada. Walk in and snag a spot at the small loungey tables or at the wooden bar stools, then check out the warm yellow walls, woven grass lamps, and eclectic collection of African art. Chat with the British owner if you can catch him between his conversations with all the university regulars who come in and report about their recent exams, the latest soccer game, and even that special someone who's stealing their heart. Order a beer *(€1.50-4)* or glass of wine *(€1.50-2.70)*–both of which are available in non-alcoholic versions *(€1.50)*–and take your pick of free tapas. The chicken with a sweet and spicy Thai sauce is their most popular option, but the Portuguese *bacaloa* and Brazilian black bean and pork stew are both pretty irresistible. If you can't stop eating, just tack on an extra tapa for €1.20, a half-ration for €3.50, or a full ration for €6.

➜ From Plaza Trinidad, take C. Alhondiaga to C. La Paz and turn right. ℹ Vegetarian options available. $ Beer €1.50-4. Wine €1.50-2.70. ⏰ Open Tu-Su 8pm-2am.

LA CAMPERERIA 🍴🍸 BAR [2]

C. Duquesa, 3 ☎958 294 173

Walking down C. Duquesa, it's impossible to miss the sleek, metallic sign denoting La Campereria in all-bold caps—that, and the crowd of loud, young, socializing students overflowing out of its front door. This restaurant-bar has an extensive menu of meat, fish, and salad options but specializes in its *camperos*, or round, pressed sandwiches sliced up pizza-style for sharing. Although they're pressed, it's hard to flatten out these absolutely stuffed savories. The vegetarian *(tomato, corn, pineapple, heart of palm, lettuce, fried onion, and mayo; €7.50)* and the chef special *(tomato, York-style ham, cheese, chicken or beef, egg, herbs, fried onion, lettuce, and mayo; €9)* are two irresistable favorites. Order your drink at the white bar that glows with red lights and is lined with beer taps and bottles of champagne and get a free slice of *campero* matched with a hearty, hot side dish like fresh spinach tortellini.

➜ From Plaza Trinidad, follow C. Duquesa and the restaurant is on the left. $ Camperos €6-9. Meat €10.50-18. Fish €12-14. Menú of the day €9.50. Dessert €2-4. Beer €1.90. Wine €2.50. Mixed drinks €4. ⏰ Open M-Th 8am-1am, F-Sa 8am-2am, Su 8am-1am.

Elsewhere

👍 CASA JUANILLO 🍴🍸☀ TRADITIONAL [2]

Camino del Sacramonte, 81-83 ☎958 223 094

This one is definitely worth the hike up Sacramonte. Casa Juanillo serves some of the most traditional Granadan dishes with one of the best views in the city. While the owner and his children will greet you at the street-level terrace, walk up to the classic Andalucian patio for a real treat. The brick and clay construction borders the dollhouse-esque blue panes and huge windows that give you the perfect view of the Alhambra and Darro River Valley below. And it's not just the design that's classic: whether you go with tapas and share a big jar of sangria *(€9)* with your free small plates (cross your fingers for the top knotch *albondigas*) or taste the *tortilla al monte*, full of the traditional pig's brains and purple peppers *(€9)*, you will leave stuffed and smiling.

➜ Take bus #34 or 35 to Camino del Sacramonte. $ Entrees €7-14. Beer €1.80. Wine €2-3. Free tapa with drink. ⏰ Open Tu-Sa noon-4:30pm and 8pm-midnight, Su noon-4:30pm.

👍 LA CHICOTÁ 🍴🍸☀ TAPAS [2]

C. Naves, 20 ☎958 220 349 💻www.lachicota.es

We know it can be overwhelming to choose a place to eat on C. Navas; the street is lined with restaurants and packed with locals trying to take their pick. Should you draw straws? Spin a wheel? Have your llama sniff it out? While all three of those could work, you may just be better off taking our word for it and sitting down at La Chicotá. The meant-to-be-shared rations and oversized tapas taste as good as they look. Even the waiters are excited about the stunning presentation—some store pictures on their cell phones of the house favorite *cremoso de queso con miel* (€10), a plate of hefty cheese pieces dripping in fresh honey and accompanied by fresh veggies. The stuffed potatoes (€5.50) are cheap, filling, and always ordered. The *patata relleno Chicotá* is overflowing with ham, mushrooms, and the secret spicy sauce. Even if it requires a little squirming or a mid-meal jog, make room for the homemade profiteroles doused in chocolate and hazelnut sauce and freckled with powdered sugar (€5). While you can't make reservations for those busy dinner hours, the speedy waiters won't leave you hanging for more than a few minutes.

#From C. Reyes Catolicos, walk through Plaza Carmen to C. Naves. $ Vegetable plates €7-12. Entrees €7.50-14. Desserts €2-5. Beer €1.70. Wine €2.50-3. ⏰ Open daily noon-midnight.

MEKNES RAHMA

🍴 MOROCCAN [2]

C. Peso de Harina, 1 ☎958 227 430 💻www.restaurantemeknes.com

Meknes Rahma is as traditional as they come. Take one step through the door and the colorful drapes, tiled walls, patterned cushions, and carved ceiling immediately tell your stomach to prepare for some quality Moroccan cuisine. The waiters enthusiastically share their cultural knowledge as they recommend their couscous (€11-12.50), baked casseroles (*tajins*; €7.50-10), and vegetable soup *harira* (€3.50). Feel free to light up a hookah and snack on a massive bowl of hummus (€3.50), a fresh cup of Moroccan tea with peppermint, or the homemade Arabic pastry of the day (€1.50).

#At the corner of Cuesta de Chapiz and where you turn for Camino del Sacramonte. $ Salads €3-4. Entrees €7.50-12.50. Teas €2.50. Hookah €10. ⏰ Open daily noon-midnight.

extra virgin

A little-known fact about Spain is that it is the world's leading producer of olive oil, squeezing out about 44% of the world's oil. Therefore, you'll find a lot of foods are cooked in the stuff: meats, potatoes, toast—whatever we in America might put butter on. In fact, it is estimated that each Spaniard consumes an average of 14 liters of olive oil per year.

NIGHTLIFE

GRANADA 10

🍴🍸 CLUB, THEATER

C. Carcel Baja, 10 ☎610 219 910 💻granada.10@hotmail.com

Granada 10 has got this double-life thing down better than Clark Kent; it's a movie theater and cabaret by day (€4) and a hot dance club at night. Just because it transitions from screening small local films into a party haven, it doesn't lose the underlying theme. When Granada 10 is packed (pretty much every night after 2am), party people fill up the huge theater space that's converted into the dance floor. The decadent marble bar and golden couches line the different areas, and a fancy light show gets the energy up. The only simple thing about this spot is the drink menu: just beer (€3), soda (€2), and cocktails (€6). While you can't expect tons of locals, you'll be hanging with an enthusiastic, reckless, college-age crowd any night of the week. Be ready for salsa Sundays, ladies night Wednesdays, or student special Thursdays.

#From C. Gran Vía, turn onto Carcel Baja; the club is on the right. i Cover varies by night. $ Beer €3. Cocktails €6. Movie ticket €4. ⏰ Open daily noon-6am; movie screenings in early evening.

✔ CLUB AFRODESIA

🎵🍸 CLUB

C. Almona del Boqueron s/n 💻www.afrodesiaclub.com

Time to shake your groove thing! Club Afrodesia, brought to you by the same owners as local favorite **Booga Club** *(C. Santa Barbara 3 🖳www.boogaclub.com),* is one of Granada's top spots to bump and grind without twiddling your thumbs until that 2am opening time. Check out hip-hop Tuesdays, Jamaican Club Wednesdays, or the Thursday through Saturday funk nights that energize the crowds. The party doesn't really get started until 2 or 3am (even later in the summers), but come early and relax on leather couches near swanky wood paneling and a leopard-print DJ booth. Go for a simple beer *(€3)* or take the Afrodesia route and just mix something with a Redbull *(€4.50).*

⇟ Almona del Boqueron branches off Gran Vía at C. Cedran. $ Shots €2.50. Beer €2.50-3. Redbull €3. Mixed drinks €5-5.50. ⏰ Open Tu-Th 11pm-3am, F-Sa 11pm-4am.

PERRA GORDA 🍸 CLUB

C. Almonda del Boqueron s/n

It's time to whip out those ripped jeans and studded leather jackets, because Perra Gorda is Granada's hot spot for rock and roll. This dark, red-and-black-themed club centers on the massive square bar ringed by posters for local concerts. Whether you're enjoying your cheap mojito *(€3),* taking advantage of the three Buds for €5, or making it in time for the happy hour where all mixed drinks are two for €3, your wallet will catch a ton of breaks. Check out Perra Gorda's weekly entertainment—from throwing up your index and pinkie fingers at the Wednesday acoustic concerts, to playing your heart out in the Monday night foosball tourney (winner gets a free bottle of gin or rum in the fall), or dancing along the hallway with the late-night local crowd.

⇟ Almona del Boqueron branches off Gran Vía at C. Cedran. $ Shots €1-2. Beer €1.20-2.50. Mojitos €3. Mixed drinks €4. ⏰ Open M-Th 10pm-3am, F-Sa 10pm-4am, Su 10pm-3am. Happy hour 10pm-midnight.

SALA VOGUE 🍸 CLUB

C. Duquesa, 35 🖳www.salavogue.es

Sala Vogue is a double-trouble student favorite: you've got two dance floors, two DJs, and two absolutely massive bars surrounding each dance floor. With all these options, Vogue can feed your partier soul no matter what mood you're in. *Sala 1* will be spinning indie, pop, rock, and '80s hits, while *Sala 2* can soothe your cravings for electronic and house. While you may have to pay a little extra for the guest DJs (Vogue rakes in some international hot shots), you can enjoy the 3 beers for €5 during the week, or the one-mixed-drink or two-beer deal with your cover on the weekends. You'll bump into your university buddies like Lucy from Psych 101 and Ricky from Rocks for Jocks year-round, and the tourists swarm in during the summer months. However, don't expect a crowd until 3 or 4am at least—they'll be finishing their homework first, right?

⇟ On C. Duquesa between Gran Capitan and Horno de Abad Málaga. $ Cover Th-Sa €6; includes 1 mixed drink or 2 beers. Beer €3. Mixed drink €5. ⏰ Open M-Th midnight-6am, F-Sa midnight-7am, Su midnight-6am.

Elsewhere

Along Camino del Sacromonte in the evenings, you'll find bar upon bar offering cheap drinks (with free tapas, of course) and even cheaper flamenco, jazz, and poetry readings. **Pena las Cuevas de Sacromonte** *(Camino de Sacromonte, 21 ☎920 182 663 🖳www.erasmusgranada.com)* has free shows every night *(11pm)* and special flamenco-poetry combos on Fridays and Saturdays *(10pm).* **Museo Cuevas del Sacromonte** screens open-air independent films Tuesdays and Thursdays *(10pm; €3)* and has flamenco shows on Wednesdays *(10pm; €12)* throughout July and August.

ARTS AND CULTURE
Flamenco and Jazz

VENTA EL GALLO   BAR, RESTAURANT, FLAMENCO
Barranco Los Negros, 5   ☎958 228 476 💻www.ventaelgallo.com

Though pricier than many of the divier flamenco-jazz bars around Granada, Venta el Gallo is known for being one of the highest-quality options for traditional Granadan flamenco. Since it's located in Sacromonte, you know you're getting the authentic thing—you're where the *zambra* dance style started, for goodness's sake! This classic Andalucian house has an arched clay stage decorated with hanging pots and pans that supports a full band and multiple performers.You and over 100 other audience members can enjoy the show with a classy drink or stuff yourself with the multi-course menu of classic Granadan recipes and "El Gallo" specialty preparations. Since they know their location is only convenient for cave dwellers, they offer a pickup and dropoff service (€6) if you don't feel like taking the bus.

🚌 *Take bus #34 or 35 to the base of C. del Sacromonte and follow the signs.* 🛈 *Pickup and dropoff €6.* 💲 *Dinner and show €52. Drink and show €22.* 🕐 *Restaurant open daily 1-4:30pm and 7:30pm-midnight. Dinner with show 8:30pm. Shows 9:30 and 10:30pm.*

Festivals

CORPUS CHRISTI   SPRING

While this citywide party is technically intended to celebrate the presence of Jesus Christ in Holy Communion, Corpus Christi has become more debaucherous than religious over the years. The Catholic monarchs brought the festivities to Granada hoping to use the excitement to win over the large Muslim and Jewish populations. Some say that the royalty even urged the local government to invest huge sums of money in the celebrations and make this party as wild, crazy, and fun as possible— you'll be glad that these "suggestions" were taken seriously. The Thursday of the festival, when the **Corpus Christi Parade** is held and the throne created by Miguel Moreno is carried through the streets, is the most important day of the event and is always 60 days after Easter. In its entirety, the festival lasts from the *Encendio*, or lighting of all the city lights Monday at midnight, until the **fireworks** extravaganza the following Sunday. Over the course of the week, *casetas* and a fun fair are set up on the outskirts of the city, and *Carocas*, or satirical cartoons depicting the events of the past year, are played in **Plaza Bibrambla.** Direct bus lines run to the festival grounds for €1.40. Hostels and hotels tend to fill up, so book in advance.

🕐 *60 days after Easter.*

FESTIVAL INTERNACIONAL DE MÚSICA Y DANZA   SUMMER

The Festival Internacional de Música y Danza is one of Granada's most prized events. Held now for over 50 years, this summertime festivity brings together a wide variety of music and dance forms, including flamenco, piano, zarzuela, orchestral, and vocals. Performances are held all over the city, including such awe-inspiring spots as the outdoor theater of the **Generalife** and the Alhambra's **Palacio de Carlos V.** For tickets and the festival program of events, contact the festival box office at the **Corral del Carbón.** (*C. Mariana Pineda s/n* ☎958 221 844 💻*taquilla@granadafestival.org*) or **Ticketmaster** (☎*902 150 025* 💻*www.ticketmaster.es/granadafestival*).

ESSENTIALS
Practicalities

- **TOURIST OFFICES:** There are over 25 tourist offices in the greater Granada area, including one at the airport (☎*958 245 269* 💻*iturismo.aeropuerto@dipgra.es*), at Plaza del Carmen (☎*958 248 280* 💻*informacion@granadatur.com*), and in the Alhambra (*Avda. Generalife s/n* ☎*958 544 002* 💻*www.andalucia.org*).

- **TOURS:** The tourist bus line for Granada runs year-round English tours (🖳*www.citysightseeing-spain.com/html/es/tour* $ *€10.* ⏰ *1hr. 15min., every 15min.)* that stop at 10 major sights. You can also hop on the free walking tour, officially run out of Oasis Granada, that leaves from the fountain at Plaza Nueva every day at 11am (€3-5 tip recommended).
- **CURRENCY EXCHANGE: Interchange** *(C. Reyes Católicos 31* ☎*958 224 512* ⏰ *Open M-Sa 9am-10pm, Su 11am-3pm and 4-9pm.)* is a money-exchange office that provides services with all major credit cards, including American Express.
- **INTERNET:** The **Biblioteca de Andalucía** *(Profesor Sainz Cantero, 6* ☎*958 026 900* 🖳*www.juntadeandalucia.es/cultura/ba* ⏰ *Open M-F 9am-9pm, Sa 9am-2pm.)* has eight computers that you can use for free for up to an hour. You can also use the facilities at the **university,** including the free Wi-Fi. **Idolos and Fans** is an internet cafe *(Camino de Ronda, 80* ☎*958 265 725* ⏰ *Open daily 10am-midnight.* $ *€1.80 per hr., €9 per 6hr., €12 per 10hr.)* that has facilities for photocopying, fax, scanning, video chat, computer use, Wi-Fi, and even a Playstation 3.
- **POST OFFICE:** The closest post office is at Puerta Real *(intersection of C. Reyes Católicos and Acera del Darro* ☎*958 224 835* ⏰ *Open M-F 8:30am-8:30pm, Sa 9:30am-2pm.)*

Emergency!

- **EMERGENCY NUMBERS: Municipal police:** ☎092. National police: ☎091.
- **LATE-NIGHT PHARMACIES:** You'll find a few 24hr. pharmacies around the intersection of C. Reyes Catolicos and C. Acera del Darro, including **Farmacia Martin Valverde** *(C. Reyes Catolicos, 5* ☎*958 262 664).*
- **HOSPITALS/MEDICAL SERVICES:** Call the **Hospital Universitario Vírgen de las Nieves** *(Av. Fuerza de las Armadas, 2* ☎*958 020 002)* or the **Hospital San Juan de Dios** *(C. San Juan de Dios s/n* ☎*958 022 904).* For an ambulance, contact a local emergency team *(☎958 282 000).*

Getting There

By Air

Airport Federico García Lorca *(☎958 245 200)* is located about 15km outside the city in Chauchina and can be accessed along the A-92 highway. It connects to the **Madrid, Barcelona,** and **Mallorca** airports domestically as well as Britain's **London-Stansted** and **Liverpool** Airports, Germany's **Frankfurt-Hahn Airport,** and Italy's **Bologna** and **Milano Bergamo** Airports. Air Europa, Iberia, SpainAir, RyanAir, and Vueling Airlines all fly through Granada.

By Train

The main **train station** *(Av. de Andaluces s/n* ☎*958 204 000)* runs Renfe trains (🖳*www.renfe.es)* to and from **Barcelona** *($ €60.50.* ⏰ *11½hr.; 8am, 9:30pm.),* **Madrid** *($ €66.80.* ⏰ *4hr. 25min.; 9:05am, 5:05pm.),* **Sevilla** *($ €23.90.* ⏰ *3hr., 4 per day 7am-6pm.),* and **Algeciras** *($ €20.40.* ⏰ *4½hr.; 7am, 12:15, 3:45pm.),* as well as many other smaller cities.

By Bus

The **bus station** *(Caretera Jaén s/n* ☎*958 185 480)* runs Alsa buses (🖳 *www.alsa.es)* around Andalucia *(☎958 185 480 for the regional line),* as well as connecting to **Madrid** *(☎958 185 480)* and the **Valencia-Barcelona** *(☎902 422 242)* lines. You can arrive from **Sevilla** *($ €20.* ⏰ *3hr., 9 per day 8am-11pm.),* **Cadiz** *($ €31.* ⏰ *5hr., 4 per day 9am-9pm.),* **Madrid Estación Sur** *($ €17.* ⏰ *5hr., 15 per day 1am-11:30pm.),* or **Málaga** *($ €10.* ⏰ *1½hr., 15 per day 7am-9:30pm.),* as well as many other destinations. Autocares Bonal *(☎958 46 50 22)* also runs a direct route to and from **Sierra Nevada** ski resorts *(⏰ 25min.; M-F 3 per day, Sa-Su 4 per day.)* during ski season.

Getting Around

Transportes Rober (☎*900 710 900* ✉*www.transportesrober.com*) runs almost 40 bus lines around the city (ⓢ *€1.20, 7 rides €5.*), as well as smaller direct buses to the **Alhambra,** the **Albaicín,** and the **Sacromonte.** These **tourist lines** are #30, 31, 32, and 34, and the **circular lines** (#11, 21, and 23) make full loops around the city. Rober also runs a special Feria line. (ⓢ *€1.40.*) While most lines generally run between 6:30am and 11:30pm every day, the **Buho lines** (*#111 and 121* ⓢ *€1.30.* 🕐 *Midnight-5:15am.*) Lines #3 and 33 from the **bus station** and lines #3, 6, 9, and 11 from the **train station** take you to **Gran Vía de Colon.** Also, there's an airport shuttle from the 2nd stop on Gran Vía. (ⓢ *€3.* 🕐 *45min.; 11-13 per day.*)

pamplona *iruña* ☎948

If people know one thing about Pamplona (pop. 200,000), it's the **Running of the Bulls.** If they know two things about Pamplona, it's the **Running of the Bulls** and the ■**earth-shattering week of partying** that accompanies the former. Hemingway may have made this town famous in *The Sun Also Rises,* but Pamplona has had no trouble keeping itself in the headlines. The week of *los Fermines* fills the city to the gills with revelers, and the high demand leads to skyrocketing prices. Pamplona takes its name from the Roman general Pompey, who is said to have founded the town in the first century BCE, after which it grew and developed under the Romans and later the Visigoths. Despite its Roman history, though, Pamplona has a strong sense of its **Basque heritage:** almost all public signage in Pamplona (*Iruña* in Basque) is in both *castellano* and Basque (*euskera* in Basque). The heavily fortified Pamplona has been a border city since the eighth century, caught between various Iberian kingdoms, France, and Spain. Since the Middle Ages, the *Camino de Santiago* has connected Pamplona with the rest of Europe across the Pyrenees and has kept it economically and culturally prosperous. The *casco antiguo* and nearby areas are largely tourist-oriented, but are still heavily frequented by locals in the low season.

ORIENTATION

Most of the action in Pamplona takes place east of the parks (**la Ciudadela** and Parque de la Taconera) and to the south and west of the río Arga. At the north end of this area is the *casco antiguo,* the old quarter, which has narrow streets lined with shops, bars, and plazas. The **Catedral** is in the *casco's* northeast corner; the massive ■**Pl. del Castillo** is in the center at the south end. The wide, pedestrian *Av. Carlos III* connects the *casco* to the *segundo ensanche,* an urban zone certainly newer than the *casco,* but not without its own charm. The **Av. de la Baja Navarra** is the city's main thoroughfare, and it cuts east-west through the *segundo ensanche,* with the **bus station** at its western end.

ACCOMMODATIONS

Most of the accommodations in Pamplona are in the *casco antiguo.* Cheaper and quieter places can be found in the **segundo ensanche.** The city's just not big enough to worry about being 3 blocks away from all the action.

■ HOSTEL HEMINGWAY ◄⊗(�) HOSTEL ❶

C. Amaya, 26, 1izq. (2nd fl., on the left) ☎948 98 38 84 ✉www.hostelhemingway.com

Traveling alone and looking for a group to go tapas-tasting or barhopping with? This recently opened hostel's communal spaces (like its common area with a giant TV) create instant bonds among the young crowds that stay here, facilitated by the fact that English is Heminway's *lingua franca.* The hostel was opened in 2009 by three young friends traveling through Pamplona who realized there wasn't a hostel in town save those for pilgrims, so they decided to open their own. The shared bedrooms aren't exactly spacious, and it's in the *segundo ensanche,* a short walk from the *casco antiguo*, but the free breakfast and camaraderie among guests and hosts more than make up for it.

🧭 From bus station, take Av. de la Baja Navarra east 8 blocks, then right on C. Amaya for 3 blocks. ***i*** *Breakfast included. Laundry €3 wash, dry €4. Kitchen available. All rooms with shared bath. Computers with internet €0.50 per 15min.; €1.50 per hr.* $ *6-bed dorms €19; 4-bed €20. Singles €21; doubles €22; Su-Th €15 for pilgrims with accreditation. During San Fermín €55/€65/€14. Bike rental €2 per 2hr., €3 per 4hr.* ⏰ *Reception 8am-midnight, but keys are available to guests with a €10 deposit.*

PENSIÓN ARRIETA PENSIÓN [4]

C. Arrieta, 27., 1izq. 2nd fl. on the left ☎948 22 84 59 💻www.pensionarrieta.net

Though it's located a few blocks out of the *casco antiguo* in a more modern part of town, this *pensión* is close to both the wide, pedestrian Av. de Carlos III, and the bus station. The rooms are large and bright, and don't worry about that squawking noise—the house parrot goes to sleep at night, so he won't keep you up.

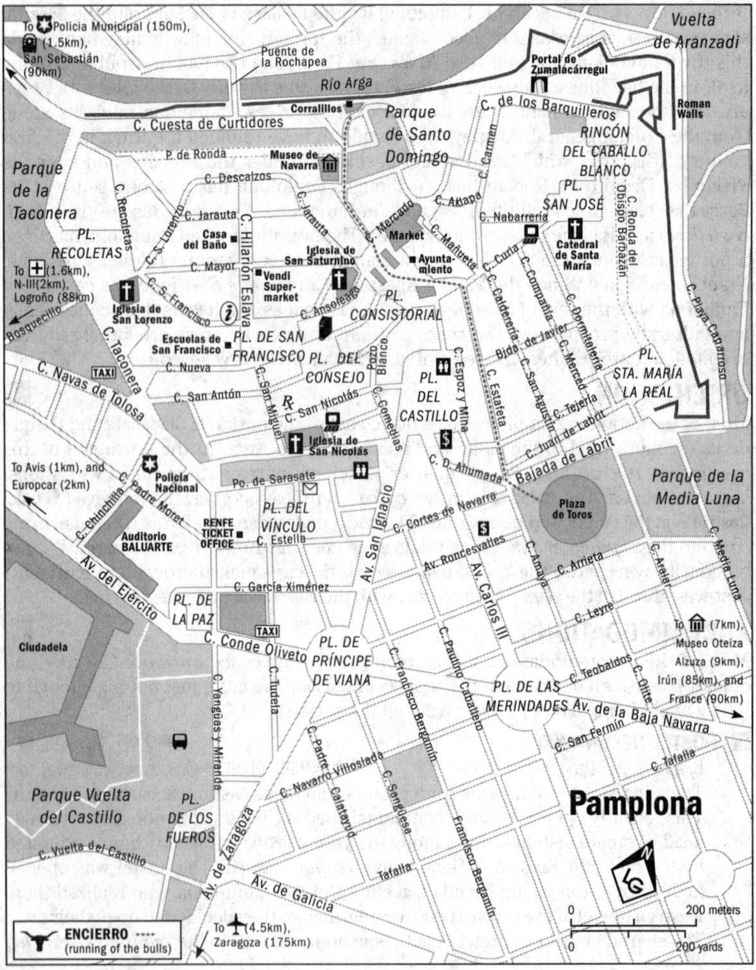

spain

⚡From bus station, take Av. de la Baja Navarra east, then left onto C. Caballero, then right onto C. Arrieta. From casco antiguo, take Av. de Carlos III south, then right onto C. Arrieta. *i* Laundry service. English spoken. Ⓢ July 5-14 doubles €150, with bath €200; triples €200. Jul 15-Sept 15 singles €40; doubles €50; triples €60. Sept 16-July 4 €35/45/55. Ⓩ Reception 9am-8pm.

PENSIÓN ESLAVA
C. Eslava, 13, 2nd fl.

●⊗ PENSIÓN ❶
☎948 22 15 58

A shrewd old woman operates this *pensión* on the second floor of a purple-painted building at the end of C. Eslava. The rooms are bare-bones: beds, closets, and windows. Some rooms come with a sink, while others have balconies looking onto one of the few relatively quiet streets in the *casco antiguo*. The few rooms here fill up quickly in the summer.

⚡ From Pl. San Francisco, take C. Eslava 3 blocks north. *i* Shared baths. Ⓢ Singles €15; doubles €20-25. During San Fermín singles €60-70; doubles €100.

SIGHTS

Ⓞ

Walk around the **old quarter** enough and you're bound to see some historic sight that catches your eye. The northeast corner of the *casco*, by the cathedral, is one of the most beautiful areas of the town. Don't miss the **Pl. Consistorial,** with its unbelievably florid **city hall.**

CATEDRAL DE SANTA MARÍA Y MUSEO DIOCESANO
C. Dormitalería, 3-5   ☎948 21 25 94 ▣www.catedraldepamplona.com

●& CHURCH

This Gothic cathedral was built over the course of the 15th century on and around the ruins of its 12th-century Romanesque predecessor, whose larder still stands. The larder is currently part of the museum, and may contain more silver and jewel-encrusted crosses than the entire rap music industry. The facade was added later, completed in 1799. The cloister is considered one of Europe's most beautiful, though it hides a dark secret: the numbers on the floor tiles correspond to tombs beneath them.

⚡ From Pl. del Castillo, head east on Bajada Javier 3 blocks, then left onto C. Dormitalería. *i* Facade undergoing renovations due to be completed in 2012, but the sides and rear of the cathedral are unaffected and can still be seen in all their Gothic splendor. Free information pamphlets with plenty of pictures available in English. Ⓢ €4, children €2.50, pilgrims €2, groups €3.35 per person. Ⓩ Mar 16-Nov 14 M-Sa 10am-7pm; Nov 15-Mar 15 M-Sa 10am-5pm.

LA CIUDADELA
Av. del Ejército

& PARK, HISTORIC SITE
☎948 22 82 37

What would you do if you had an unused medieval fortress half the size of the *casco antiguo* just sitting around? If you were Pamplona, you'd make it a public park. *La Ciudadela* is a fascinating mix of vegetation and crumbling fortifications. Its a great place to lounge during the *siesta*, or while waiting until your bus leaves from the station next door.

⚡ From Pl. del Castillo, take Paseo de Sarsate to C. Taconera, then left onto C. Chinchilla; the entrance is on the other side of Av. del Ejército. Ⓢ Free. Ⓩ Park open M-Sa 7:30am-9:30pm, Su 9am-9:30pm. Rotating art exhibitions open M-F 6-8:30pm, Sa 11am-2pm and 6-8:30pm, Su 11am-2pm.

FOOD

Ⓒ

MESÓN PIRINEO
C. Estafeta, 41

●& ❣ TAPAS ❶
☎948 20 77 02

This bar serves up great tapas and *pinchos* at some of the lowest prices around. Just look at the counter, find something you like, and order it; all the *tapas* are delicious and under €2. The *pincho* with mushrooms and ham and the *tapa* with *bacalao* (cod) are particularly tasty.

⚡ From the Pl. del Castillo, head east one short block on Bajada Javier, then left onto C. Estafeta. Ⓢ Tapas and pinchos €1.80-5. Ⓩ Open daily 11am-3:30pm and 5:30pm-midnight.

pamplona . food

LA MEJILLONERA
🚭 ♿ 🍸 TAPAS ❶

C. Navarrería, 12 ☎948 22 91 84

This *cervecería* and tapas bar is a favorite among locals who come to enjoy the *mejillones (mussels; €2.50-3)* from which the bar takes its name. The drinks cost about half what you could expect to pay a couple of blocks away at the Pl. del Castillo—€1.20 for a *caña* of beer, €1.50 for a *sangría.* The tapas selection is mostly seafood-based, but still varied. They also claim "the best *patatas bravas* in Pamplona."

⇄ From Pl. del Castillo, head east on Bajada Javier, then left onto C. Caldereria, then right onto C. Navarrería. ℹ Standing room only. $ Tapas and mussels €2-5. ⏰ Open M 6:30-11pm, Tu-Su 12:30-3pm and 6:30-11pm.

ÑAM
🚬 ♿ 🍸 📶 BAR, CAFE ❸

Paseo de Sarasate ☎948 22 05 49 💻www.tmservicios.com/nam

A small, newer bar and restaurant on the Paseo de Sarasate, Ñam has far and away one of the coolest names to pronounce in Pamplona. It also has excellent *bocadillos (€2)* and cheap *pinchos del día (€0.90).* The weekend *menú (€20)* is more expensive than those at some of the other establishments in the area, but the selection is wider and the dishes are of higher quality. A young crowd takes over this restaurant's bar F-Sa after 10pm.

⇄ From Pl. del Castillo, take Paseo del Sarasate from southwest corner. $ €8-18, weekend menú €20 ⏰ Open M-Th 8:30am-11pm, F-Sa 8:30am-1am, Su 8:30am-11pm; during San Fermín open 24hr.

NIGHTLIFE

The claustrophobic streets of the **casco antiguo** are the main arteries of the Pamplona nightlife scene. Most of the bars are more or less the same, and after a couple of minutes of wandering around to find one with the kind of crowd you're looking for (younger, older, loud, mellow—they often change from weekend to weekend and vary by night), head in and order. The main locales for this type of barhopping are C. San Nicolás, C. San Gregorio, C. Caldereria, C. Navarrería, and C. San Agustín, but **following the shouts** echoing down the streets can also help you start your night. Fair warning: things are dead around here on Sunday or Monday nights. But of course, during *los Sanfermines,* the party practically never stops.

DISCOTECA REVERENDOS
🚬 🚭 🍸 CLUB

C. Monasterio Velate, 5 ☎948 26 15 93 💻www.reverendos.com

For those who don't mind a little evening stroll (20-30min. from *casco antiguo*), head to the *barrio de San Juan.* This futuristic *discoteca* tends to draw a big student crowd from the nearby university and pumps house music and hip hop until the early morning.

⇄ Follow Av. de la Baja Navarra west, then follow Av. del Ejército along the northern edge of la Ciudadela, then take a slight left onto Av. de Bayona, then stay right at the fork onto C. Monasterio Velate for 2 blocks; Reverendos is on the left. $ Mixed drinks €6-11. ⏰ Open M-Th 12:30-6am, F-Sa 12:30-6:30am, Su 12:30-6am.

BAR BAVIERA
🚬 ♿ 🍸 ⛅ BAR, CAFE

Pl. del Castillo, 10 ☎948 22 20 48

Find yourself looking to grab a drink late at night early in the week, but you've noticed that every place in the *casco antiguo* closes around midnight? Bar Baviera is open until 2:30am and is a convenient alternative to wandering around an otherwise dead part of town. It's a little pricey (€2 for a *caña*), but that's the Pl. del Castillo for you.

⇄ On the east side of the Pl. del Castillo. $ Mixed drinks €2-8. ⏰ Open daily 11am-2:30am; during San Fermín open 23hr. (must close 1hr to clean).

FIESTA DE SAN FERMÍN

Las Fiestas de San Fermín, also known as **los Sanfermines**, is considered by many the greatest, **wildest week of partying in Europe** (or anywhere, for that matter). The nine-day festival encapsulates two crucial facets of Navarra's culture: millennia-old religious conservatism and a fervent desire to **party like it's going out of style.** The festival celebrates the third-century Saint Fermin *(San Fermín)* of Amiens, Navarra's patron saint and first bishop of Pamplona, whose mentor, Saint Saturninus, was martyred by being dragged to death after having his feet tied to a bull. The religious components of the *fiesta* take place alongside the nonstop debauchery of the red-scarved revelers, and despite the city's relatively small size, the two manage to coexist.

The *Sanfermines* begin the morning of July 6, when the entire city of Pamplona and visitors from around the world gather at the Pl. Consistorial. At noon (though the plaza is too crowded to get into by 10am), the mayor appears amid shouts and traditional *San Fermín* cheers and songs, such as the famous *"Uno de enero, dos de febrero, tres de marzo, cuatro de abril, cinco de mayo, seis de junio, siete de julio, ¡San Fermín! A Pamplona hemos de ir, con una media, con una media, a Pamplona hemos de ir, con una media y un calcetín."* ("January 1, February 2, March 3, April 4, May 5, June 6, July 7, San Fermín! To Pamplona we must go, with a stocking, with a stocking, to Pamplona we must go, with a stocking and a sock!") The mayor then fires a rocket from his balcony and yells in Spanish and Basque, "People of Pamplona! Long live *San Fermín!"* Whatever can be found (food, clothing, trash, small animals) is then thrown up in the air and rained down on the partiers, as the *fiesta* begins and everyone fans out from the Pl. del Consistorial to fill the streets of the *casco antiguo*, which won't empty again for another nine days. The religious side of the festival makes an appearance with the **procession of San Fermín** at 10am on July 7, when church and city officials march the 16th-century statue of *San Fermín* from its home in the **Iglesia de San Lorenzo** through the *casco antiguo*, in the hope that it will protect the runners in return for the extravagant adulation.

THE RUNNING OF THE BULLS

Encierro route

The most famous component of *los Sanfermines* is the *encierro*, the running of the bulls each day July 7-13 at 8am. The *encierro's* roots lie in the Middle Ages, when the bulls would be driven at dawn from the *corralillos* outside the city walls to certain death at the *plaza de toros*. At some point, young men began a tradition of running in front of the bulls during this daily routine, an act of lunacy and courage much like riding on top of subway cars today. Though the authorities tried to stop this dangerous ritual for the first couple of centuries of its establishment, they eventually decided to embrace it. In 1776, the Pamplona City Council passed a law that fences must be put up along the whole route, and thus began the centuries-old tradition. The route used for the *encierro* today has been in place since 1927. At exactly 8am the first *txupinazo* (rocket, pronounced and sometimes spelled *chupinazo*) is set off and the *encierro* begins. The first segment is a steep uphill section that is quite dangerous, as the bulls handle the incline much better than the bipedal humans. Once all the bulls are in the street, the second *txupinazo* is set off. The runners—who have just finished praying for San Fermín's blessing—and bulls then go through the Pl. Consistorial, past the *Ayuntamiento* (town hall), and make a left turn and then a 90° right turn. At this last turn, the Mercaderes bend, and the speeding bulls tend to skid and pile up against the wall; the runners who aren't pinned use this brief distraction to get away. After another few hundred yards, they all enter the bullring (cue *txupinazo* number three), where the bulls are rounded up and put into holding pens (final *txupinazo*) for bullfights later in the day. For those who think about running with the bulls and hear their mother's voice unbidden in the back of their heads shrieking, **"You're going to do WHAT?"** the *encierro* can be watched from a safe distance, in the bullring or behind the fences. Those who wish to watch the spectacle at the *plaza de toros* should arrive no later than 6:30am, as tickets *(€4.50-6)* go on sale at 7am at the bullring box office. There is a free section, but the danger of suffocation and trampling is significantly higher. To watch from behind the fences, arrive as early as you can get up (or as late as you can stay up, as the case may be), around 6am to get a decent spot. If you want to see one of the bullfights *(Jul 7-13, 6:30pm)*, chances are pretty slim that you'll get in, as only a few tickets are on sale each day; the rest belong to season ticket-holders. Some travelers purport that the easiest way to procure tickets is to buy them from scalpers *(usually €50 or higher; lower as the start of the fight approaches)*.

THE PARTY

Plaza del Castillo

Seriously. This is The Party, capital T, capital Plaça 9 days of chaos, shennanigans, fireworks, dancing, singing, music, drinking, and just about anything else you can think of adding to make things crazier. Sleeping often occurs (when it does occur, that is) in streets, parks, or any free square inch that can be found in the packed city. Many of the bars are open 23hr. per day—they are legally obligated to close 1hr. each day to clean up a bit—or at least give the drunken masses a second to breathe between beers. The Pl. del Castillo, in the heart of the *casco antiguo* but close to the *segundo ensanche*, is the center of this orgiastic glory. The plaza becomes one massive 24hr. *discoteca*, with the ever-swelling sea of partiers dressed in white with red *fajas* *(sashes; about €6)* and *pañuelos* *(handkerchiefs; €2-5)*, which can be bought at stands throughout Pamplona. At midnight on July 14, the festival officially ends, as the revelers that remain sing the *Pobre de mí: "Pobre de mí, pobre de mí, que se han acabado las Fiestas de San Fermín."* ("Woe is me, woe is me, *San Fermín* has ended.")

ESSENTIALS [i]

Practicalities

- **TOURIST OFFICE:** The tourist office has excellent maps and information on the city of Pamplona, as well as on the region of Navarra and *camino*-specific sights. It also offers an essential **San Fermin Fiesta Programme** guide, with just about everything you would want to know about the *encierro* and festivals. Ask about guided tours. English, French, and **Basque** spoken. *(C. Eslava, 1, on northwest corner of Pl. San Francisco ☎848 42 04 20 💻www.turismo.navarra.es ⏰ Open Sept 22-June 20 M-Sa 10am-2pm and 4-7pm, Su 10am-2pm; June 21-Sept 21 M-F 9am-6pm, Sa 9am-2pm and 4-6pm, Su 10am-2pm; San Fermín daily 9am-2pm and 3-5pm.)*
- **CURRENCY EXCHANGE:** The **Banco Santander Central Hispano** has a 24hr. **ATM** and will exchange American Express travelers checks commission-free if they are for euros. *(Pl. del Castillo, 21, and Paseo Sarasate, 15 ☎948 20 86 00 ⏰ Open daily Apr-Sep M-F 8:30am-2pm; Oct-Apr M-F 8:30am-2pm, Sa 8:30am-1pm; during San Fermín open M-F 9:30am-noon.)*
- **LUGGAGE STORAGE:** is available at the bus station for €5.10 per day *(⏰ Open M-Sa 6:15am-9:30pm, Su 6:30am-1:30pm and 2-9:30pm; closed for San Fermín, when the* **Escuelas de San Francisco,** *across Pl. San Francisco from the library, is open instead. ℹ Passport or ID required. ⏰ Open 24hr. Jul 4-Jul 16 8am-2pm. $ €3.40 per day.)*
- **LAUDROMAT AND PUBLIC BATHS:** The **Casa del Baño** offers wash-and-dry services as well as showering facilities. *(C. Eslava, 9 ☎948 22 17 38 $ Wash and dry €10.60. Showers €1.10. ⏰ Open M-Sa 8:30am-8pm, Su 9am-2pm. Wash and*

dry not offered during San Fermín.)

- **INTERNET ACCESS:** For **free internet access,** go to the **library** on Pl. San Francisco. (🕐 *Open Sept-May M-F 8:30am-8:45pm, Sa 8:30am-1:45pm; Jun-Aug M-F 8:30am-12:30pm. During San Fermín open M-F 12:15-1:45pm.)*

- **POST OFFICE:** The **post office** is just a couple minutes' walk from the Pl. del Castillo *(Paseo de Sarasate, 9 ☎948 20 68 40* 🕐 *Open M-F 8:30am-8:30pm, Sa 9:30am-2pm. Jul 6 9am-2pm. Closed Jul 7.* ℹ️ *If you're walking the camino, it will send any excess luggage—up to 20kg—to Santiago to await your arrival (up to €13.40.)*

- **POSTAL CODE:** 31001.

Emergency!

- **EMERGENCY NUMBERS: Municipal police** are at C. Monasterio de Irache, 2 *(☎092 or 948 42 06 40).* **National police** are at C. General Chinchilla, 3 *(☎091).*

- **24HR. PHARMACIES: Farmacia Yangüas** is located opposite the bus station. *(C. Yangüas y Miranda, 17 ☎948 24 50 30* 🖥️*www.farmayanguas.com* 🕐 *Open 24hr.)*

- **MEDICAL SERVICES:** The **Hospital de Navarra** is at the corner of C. Irunlarrea and Av. de Pío XII *(C. Irunlarrea, 3 ☎848 42 22 22 or ☎112 for emergencies).* During *San Fermín,* the **Red Cross** sets up stations at the bus station, along the *corrida,* and at various points in the *casco antiguo.*

Getting There

By Bus

The bus station is located along the eastern edge of la Ciudadela *(Av. de Yangüas y Miranda* ☎948 20 35 66 🖥️www.estaciondeautobusesdepamplona.com 🕐 *Open daily 6:30am-11pm).* Buses arrive from: **Barcelona** (💲 €31-37. 🕐 *6hr.; M-Sa 3 per day 7:30am-3:35pm, Su 5 per day 7:30am-11:30pm); Bilbao* (💲 €13. 🕐 *2½-3hr.; M-Sa 6 per day 7am-8:30pm, Su 5 per day 8:30am-8pm.);* **Irún** (💲 €7. 🕐 *2hr.; 1 per day M-Sa 8am, Su 9am.);* **Logroño** (💲 €8. 🕐 *2hr.; M-F 9 per day 6:45am-8pm, Sa 7 per day 7:45am-8pm, Su 5 per day 10am-8pm.);* **Madrid** (💲 €38. 🕐 *5¾hr., M-Th 6 per day 1am-7:30pm, F 7 per day 1am-7:30pm, Sa-Su 6 per day 1am-7:30pm.);* **San Sebastián** (💲 €7. 🕐 *1¼-2hr.; M-Th 13 per day 7am-8:15pm, F 17 per day 7am-9:15pm, Sa 13 per day 7am-8:15pm, Su 15 per day 7am-9:15pm.)*

By Train

The RENFE train station *(☎902 24 02 02* 🕐 *Open M-Sa 6am-11:30pm, Su 8am-11:30pm.)* is a bit far away from the *casco antiguo,* but is serviced by bus #9 *(€1.10),* which goes to the center of town in about 15min. Trains arrive from **Barcelona** (💲 €56, *if booked a week in advance €34.* 🕐 *3¾hr.; M, Tu, Th, Sa 3 per day 7:35am-3:35pm, W, F, Su 4 per day 7:35am-4:35pm.)* and **Madrid.** (💲 €56, *if booked a week in advance €33.* 🕐 *3hr.; M-F 4 per day 7:35am-7:35pm, Sa 3 per day 7:35am-3:05pm, Su 3 per day 10:35am-7:35pm.)*

By Plane

Aeropuerto de Pamplona-Noáin *(☎902 40 47 04* 🖥️www.aena.es), about 4mi. out of town, is serviced by bus #21 *(€1.10).* Planes arrive from destinations throughout Spain; check **Iberia's** website *(*🖥️*www.iberia.es)* or **TAP-Air Portugal's** *(*🖥️*www.flytap.com)* for prices and schedules, as they vary.

Getting Around

The easiest way to get around Pamplona is **by foot.** The *casco antiguo* is tiny, and the *segundo ensanche* is not so big that you can't walk from one end to the other in 10min. There is a **bus** system *(☎901 50 25 03* 🖥️www.mcp.es/tuc/index.asp💲 €1.10, *with tarjeta monedero €0.56; free transfers. Wheelchair-accessible except lines #13, 21, and 23.)* The #4, 10, 12, 13, and 18 buses go to the **bus station;** bus #9 goes to the **RENFE train station,** and bus #21 goes to the **Aeropuerto de Pamplona-Noáin. Taxi** stands near the *casco* *antiguo* and *segundo ensanche* can be found at Hotel 3 Reyes (C. Navas de Tolosa, 25), Pl. del Vínculo (intersection of C. de Estella and C. de Sancho "El Mayor"), Pl. Duque de Ahumada (just south of Pl. del Castillo, on east edge of Av. Carlos III), C. Amaya between Av. de la Baja Navarra and C. Teobaldos, Pl. de la Cruz (Bergamín, 6), inside and outside the bus station, and at Pl. Conde Rodezno; there is also a stand at the RENFE station. Alternatively, call Teletaxi San Fermín (*☎948 23 23 00 or ☎948 35 13 35)*.

logroño ☎941

The Roman town that stood where Logroño is today (if it's a town and it's in southern or western Europe, it's safe to assume the Romans founded it) was destroyed by the Visigoths in the sixth century; the city's current incarnation began around that time. The name Logroño most likely comes from the Latin *illo* ("that") and the Germanic *gronio* ("river's ford"); in a similar multicultural mishmash, the Romance culture in Logroño has grown and flourished out of the ruins left by the Goths. The city owes much of its local prominence to its location along the pilgrimage route known as the **Camino de Santiago,** which has made Logroño a hub of travel and commerce since the Middle Ages. This town was also strategically important in the Middle Ages, as it was located near the border between Castile, Navarre, and Aragón. Today, Logroño is the capital of the **Comunidad Autónoma de La Rioja** and is home to over 150,000 citizens. The region is famous for its █wines, which make up a large portion of the region's economy and draw oenophiles from around the world. Since Logroño tends to be a bit off the typical tourist's path, there is more of a focus on commerce than on tourism, and it is clear that this is a modern, growing city that is open to tourism but not driven by it.

ORIENTATION

Logroño can essentially be divided into two sections: the **casco antiguo** (old quarter) and **everywhere else.** The *casco* is bordered by the Río Ebro to the north and the **Paseo del Espolón** (a large open area, somewhere between a park and a plaza) on the south, and it is cut into quarters by the C. Sagasta (north-south) and the C. Portales (east-west). The **Gran Vía Rey Juan Carlos I,** lined with tall apartment and office buildings, is the main east-west thoroughfare and is generally seen as the old town's southern border. The **Calle del General Vara de Rey** is the major north-south avenue and goes past the **bus station** and **train station**. The train station's entrance is temporarily on the side of the tracks away from the center of town; from the station, head right on C. Marqués de Larios, which bends left and becomes C. Hermanos Hircio; then turn right at C. Poeta Prudencio and right on C. del General Vara de Rey, which goes to the Paseo del Espolón.

ACCOMMODATIONS

Most hotels and *hostals* in Logroño can be found in the **casco antiguo,** but the more modern living areas have better prices and aren't too far away. Besides, living in an apartment building in a residential neighborhood where it seems like only five tourists have been since the city's founding in the 11th century makes you really █**feel like a badass local.**

█ PENSIÓN REY PASTOR ⊛⊗(ᵗ) PENSIÓN ❷

C. Marqués de Murrieta, 35, 1D, 2nd fl. ☎630 50 23 50 █www.pensionreypastor.com

About a 10min. walk from the *casco antiguo*, this *pensión* is in an apartment building in a more modern part of town, across the street from two supermarkets and surrounded by shops and restaurants. The affordably priced rooms with free Wi-Fi and a TV are spacious and cheerfully decorated with orange walls and rainbow-colored comforters.

⚑ *From the casco antiguo, follow C. Portales to Pl. Alférez Provisional, then take C. Marqués de Murrieta, passing through the Gran Vía. From the bus or train stations, take C. del General Vara de*

Rey to the Gran Vía, then make a left; make another left at the C. Marqués de Murrieta. ℹ *Shared baths.* $ *Singles €20; doubles €30; triples €55. F-Sa €25/49/69.* ⏰ *Reception 8am-midnight.*

ASOCIACIÓN RIOJANA DE AMIGOS DEL CAMINO DE SANTIAGO ⊘ ⊘♿ ALBERGUE ❶

Ruavieja, 32 (enter on Travesado Palacio) ☎941 26 02 34 🖥www.asantiago.org

This is probably the cheapest place you'll find to spend a night in Logroño (€3), but it's just for pilgrims walking the Camino de Santiago. If you don't have a stamped pilgrim passport and a backpack, you will be turned away. To stay in one of their 88 beds (you share a room with 21 of your closest new friends), you must come *"andando, a caballo, o en bicicleta"* ("on foot, on horse, or on bicycle"), and beds are given on a first-come, first-served basis.

➡ *Head north on C. Sagasta, then right at C. Ruavieja.* ℹ *Must have pilgrim passport (available at Federación Española Asociaciones de Amigos del Camino de Santiago, C. Ruavieja, 3 bajo, open M-F 8am-3pm) and stamp from Logroño (available at tourism office or cathedral).* $ *€3.* ⏰ *Backpack pickup and showers noon-4pm. Reception open 4-10pm. Lights-out 10pm.*

SIGHTS 👁

👍 MUSEO WÜRTH ♿⛅ MUSEUM

Av. de los Cameros, 86-88 ☎941 01 04 10 🖥www.museowurth.es

Don't let this museum's location (in an industrial park in Agoncillas, 15min. by car from Logroño) drive you away; instead, let the museum drive you to it with its complimentary bus service. Opened in 2007 by industrial manufacturing company Würth Spain, the Museo Würth's architecturally stunning white cement, red steel, and tinted glass building stands in stark contrast to the cheaply made industrial buildings of the surrounding *polígono industrial.* Inside, bright and spacious galleries display works from the Würth collection—mostly 20th-century European art, including works by Picasso and Braque—and exhibitions by contemporary artists based in Spain and around the world.

➡ *Free bus provided by museum (large white coach, not a city bus) on M, W, F at 6pm (returns 8pm); Tu, Th varies, check schedule; Sa at 11:30am and 6pm (returns 2pm and 8pm), Su at 11:30am (returns 2pm). Bus leaves from Logroño's Glorieta del Doctor Zubía bus stop* $ *Free.* ⏰ *Open M-Sa 10am-8pm, Su 10am-3pm. Guided visits M-Sa 6:30pm, Su noon.*

👍 EL CUBO DEL REVELLÍN ♿ MUSEUM, HISTORICAL SITE

C. Once de Junio, 6 ☎941 50 31 16 🖥www.logro-o.org/cubo_revellin/index.htm

El Cubo, the artillery fortification at the northwest corner of Logroño's city walls, was built in the 1520s when Logroño was Castile's main stronghold on the border with Navarre. Today, it houses a museum opened in 2006 after renovations and restoration. The old structure's architecture represents a middle phase between medieval and more modern building techniques, while the recent glass, metal, and faux-old-wood additions highlight the best of modern design.

➡ *Just up C. Once de Junio from the tourism office.* ℹ *Call ahead or email cubodelrevellin@logro-o.org for tours. Free 6min. film every 15min.* $ *Free.* ⏰ *Open W 10am-1pm; Th-F 10am-1pm and 5-8pm, Sa 11am-2pm and 5-8pm; Su 11am-2pm.*

SALA AMÓS SALVADOR ♿ MUSEUM

C. Once de Junio ☎941 25 92 02 🖥www.logro-o.org/culturalrioja/sala_amos.htm

On the northwestern edge of the *casco antiguo* is a building that has been a convent, military hospital, barracks, warehouse, jail, tobacco factory, and, most recently, a space for art exhibitions. It still says "Fábrica de Tabacos" above the entrance, but the building is now 640 sq. ft. of exhibition space where tourists and locals can come for free to browse an exhibition of photography, sculpture, or whatever is on display at the time; there is usually a new exhibition every couple of months.

➡ *Head north on C. Sagasta, then left at C. Portales, then right at C. Once de Junio.* ℹ *Closes occasionally to take down and install exhibitions; check website to make sure it will be open.* $ *Free.* ⏰ *Open Tu-Sa 11am-1pm and 6-9pm, Su noon-2pm and 6-9pm.*

THE GREAT OUTDOORS

If the tree-lined Paseo del Espolón and the thrilling mile or so of Camino that runs through Logroño don't satisfy your thirst for natural beauty and adventure, just keep following the **Camino de Santiago.** You can head northeast, crossing the Ebro via the Puente de Piedra and heading up into the hills. All the pilgrims heading west will think you're quite lost, though, since Santiago de Compostela is in the other direction. To take the Camino westward, you can find a backpacker and follow him, or you can follow the **yellow arrows and signs,** which will lead you along C. Marqués de Murrieta and C. Duques de Nájera, and into the Parque San Miguel. From there, the route goes across the highway and into the countryside, through fields and toward Santiago de Compostela. The next stop on the Camino after Logroño is Navarrete (7½ mi.), then Nájera (another 9½ mi.).

FOOD

👍 JUAN AND JUAN — 💳♿🍸⛅ BAR, RESTAURANT ❶

C. Albornoz, 5 — ☎941 22 99 83

Juan and Juan, owned by brothers Juan Manuel and Juan Marcos, is a lively bar and restaurant hidden in the winding streets of the *casco antiguo*. You may have to push your way through the throng of locals to get to the bar, but it's worth the trouble for the affordable and salty *panceta* *(€2)* or *chuletilla de cordero* *(lamb chop; €2.50)*, which go great with a glass of local Rioja *vino tinto* *(€0.70)*. For a full meal, try the 3-course lunch *menú* *(€14)* or an entrée *(€9-15)*; there are also plenty of vegetarian options *(€6)*.

🪧 Head west on C. Portales, then left onto C. Capitán Gallarza, then right onto C. San Agustín, and then left onto C. Albornoz. $ Entrees and tapas €2-15. ⏰ Open daily noon-4pm and 8pm-midnight.

EN ASCUAS — 💳♿🍸 SPANISH ❷

C. Hermanos Moroy, 22 — ☎941 24 68 67

The name En Ascuas literally "In the Embers," is a reference to the open flame in the kitchen that diners can see through a large glass pane in the back of the restaurant. This establishment is much more clean-cut and modern-looking than some of its neighbors but has no problem serving up traditional dishes like the savory *revuelto de hongos y jamón ibérico*, scrambled eggs with mushrooms and Iberian ham—don't let the runny texture scare you away *(€10.85)*. And, as befits any self-respecting restaurant in the heart of La Rioja, the wine selection is extensive.

🪧 Take C. Sagasta north from Paseo del Espolón, then left onto C. Hermanos Moroy. $ Entrees €8-15. Side dishes €4-7. ⏰ Open Tu-Su 1:30-3:30pm and 8:30-11:30pm.

LOS ROTOS — 🚫♿🍸 FAST FOOD ❶

C. San Juan, 14 — ☎941 23 65 67

This place's specialties are its namesake *rotos* *(€2.30)*—hollowed-out half-loaves of bread filled with scrambled eggs and just about anything you can think of: mushrooms, cod, Basque sausage, blood sausage, chicken, cheese, and more. These *rotos* are messy and wonderful, perfect for a late lunch or for a quick refueling stop before tearing up the nightlife.

🪧 From Pl. del Mercado, head south on C. Marqués de Vallejo, then left onto C. San Juan. $ €2-6. ⏰ Open Tu-Su noon-4pm and 6:30pm-1am.

NIGHTLIFE

Logroño's really not known for its club scene—to be honest, in most places it's not known at all. The main streets for nightlife are in the *casco antiguo:* **Calle de los Portales, Calle del Laurel, C. del San Agustín,** and **Calle de San Nicolás** tend to be the best for bar hopping, and there are a couple of places with older crowds along C. del Marqués de Murrieta.

JUAN Y PÍNCHAME

BAR

C. Laurel, 9 ☎678 58 96 33

This bar, whose name is a clever pun—*pinchos* are a type of tapas, and *Juan y Pínchame* is a classic joke (Question: "Juan and Pínchame are in a boat. Juan falls out. Who's left?" Answer: *"Pínchame,"* which means "stick me")—is a popular place for tapas in the afternoon and drinks at night. If you can push your way up to the bar, their specialty is a juicy *brocheta de langostino y piña*, a skewer with pineapple and prawns *(eight for €4).*

From C. Sagasta heading north, turn left at C. Hermanos Moroy, then left at C. del Capitán Gallarza, then right onto C. Laurel. $ Drinks and tapas €6-11. ⏰ Open Tu-Th 1-3:15pm and 8pm-12:30am, F-Su 1-3:15pm and 8-11:30pm.

ESSENTIALS

Practicalities

- **TOURIST OFFICES:** Logroño's **tourism office** offers information in English, French, and German and excellent (as well as necessary) maps of the city. Call for information about tours. *(C. Portales, 50 ☎941 27 33 53 🖥www.logroturismo.org. $ Tours €3 ⏰ Open Jul-Sep daily 10am-2pm and 5-8pm, Oct-Jun M-Sa 10am-2pm and 4:30-7:30pm, Su 10am-2pm.)*
- **CURRENCY EXCHANGE:** You can use any of the banks that line the Av. de La Rioja on the western edge of the Paseo del Espolón. *(⏰ Most open M-F 9am-2pm, though hours vary depending on the bank).*
- **LUGGAGE STORAGE:** This is available at the **bus station** ($ €2 ⏰ Open M-Sa 6am-11pm, Su 7am-11pm) and **train station** ($ €3 $ Open 24hr.).
- **POST OFFICE:** The **post office** or *correos* is four blocks west of the bus station on C. Pérez Galdós–don't forget to send everyone postcards (C. Pérez Galdós, 40. ⏰ Open M-F 8:30am-8:30pm, Sa 8:30am-2pm.)
- **POSTAL CODE:** 26001.

Emergency!

- **EMERGENCY NUMBERS:** ☎112. **Medical Emergency:** ☎061.
- **POLICE:** To get to the **local police station** take C. Sagasta toward the river and turn right at C. Ruavieja; the police station is on the left after 2 blocks *(☎092).*
- **MEDICAL SERVICES:** Go to **Hospital San Pedro** *(C. Piqueras, 98, on Pl. de San Pedro, ☎941 29 80 00.)*

Getting There

By Bus

The **bus station** *(Av. de España, 1 ☎941 23 59 83)* is a couple of blocks north of the train station. Buses from: **Barcelona** *($ €28. ⏰ 2½hr., 5 per day 8am-11pm.);* **Bilbao** *($ €13. ⏰ 2½hr.; M-F 5 per day 7:30am-8pm, Sa 4 per day 8:30am-8pm, Su 4 per day 8:30am-9pm.);* **Burgos** *($ €10. ⏰ 1¼hr.; M-F 7 per day 8:30am-9:30pm, Sa 5 per day 8:30am-7:45pm, Su 4 per day 2-7:45pm.);* **Madrid** *($ €16-21. ⏰ 4½hr.; M-Sa 13 per day 7am-1am, Su 18 per day 7am-1am.);* **Pamplona.** *($ €8. ⏰ 1¾hr.; M-F 8 per day 6:45am-8pm, Sa 7 per day 7:30am-8pm, Su 5 per day 10am-8pm.)*

By Train

The **train station** *(Pl. de Europa, ☎902 24 02 02)* is located on the south end of town, a 15min. walk from center. Daily RENFE Alvia trains *($ €56; if booked more than a week in advance €33.)* leave from **Madrid's** Atocha Station *(⏰ 3½hr.; M-F 6:30pm, Su 6:30pm.)* and goes back to Madrid. *(⏰ 3¼hr.; M-Sa 7:50am.)* Trains from: **Barcelona** *(⏰ 4hr., 5 per day, 7:30am-10:45pm. $ €40-64.);* **Bilbao** *(⏰ 2½hr., 7:45am and 3:30pm $ €21.);* **Burgos** *(⏰ 1¾hr., 3 per day,*

1:20-9am. $ *€19-21.)*; **Zaragoza** *(⏰ 2hr., 8 per day 3am-10:15pm.* $ *€12-22.)*

By Plane

Iberia *(☎902 40 05 00 💻www.iberia.com)* offers daily flights from **Madrid** *($ If purchased 6 days in advance €85. ⏰ 50min.; 8-9pm.)*, which arrive at **Aeropuerto de Logrono-Agoncillo** *(Carretera LO-20, 15km from city center ☎941 27 74 00)*.

Getting Around

Logroño is a great city to **walk:** the *casco antiguo* is almost entirely car-free, leaving it a pedestrian paradise. While it's nice to *callejear* ("meander through the streets," a wonderful word for which there's no accurate English equivalent) a bit sometimes, if you're in a rush to get somewhere or simply enjoy walking with purpose, make sure you plan your route beforehand, as many of the older streets are narrow and confusingly unmarked. For those interested in exploring parts of the city farther from the center or too lazy to walk to the train station, there is a **bus** system *(€0.60, 10-trip bonobús €4.52, 1-month bonobús €29)*. **Taxis** can be found at the **bus station** *(☎941 23 75 29)* or can be called: Radio-taxi *(☎941 22 21 22)* and Tele-taxi *(☎941 50 50 50)* are the main companies.

majorca *mallorca* ☎971

Since 7000 BCE, people have been using Majorca as an island pit stop in the Mediterranean. Whether it was the Romans, the Byzantines, the Arabs, or the Catalonians, it was always take, take, and more take. Majorca was convenient. It was the biggest island of the Balearics. It had a varied landscape. But over the past 9000 years or so, Majorca has taken a stand, and it isn't going to be pushed around any longer.

We're not going to suggest that Majorca is a spiteful up-and-comer. On the contrary, its rich, multicultural history contributes to the island culture today. Sights like the **Catedral** and **Castell de Bellver** are glowing reminders of all the people who were lucky enough to visit centuries ago, while museums like the **Fundacio Pilar i Joan Miro** suggest that even some of the most talented greats of our time proudly called Majorca home. This "island of calm," as famous Spanish poet Ruben Dario described it, now offers luxurious resorts, delicious local cuisine, abundant shopping options, and a thriving athletic culture centered around biking and aquatic sports. You can tan beside the turquoise waters of this summertime gem by day, and check out the clubs, bars, and restaurants around Palma's port all night. Majorca is mature—it wants to give you relaxation and fun, with some education along the way.

ORIENTATION

The city of Palma is organized around its major plazas. **Plaza Espanya** is the major transit center where the train and metro stations can be accessed and where many of the tour buses congregate. **Plaza Mayor** has some patio restaurants, street performers, and small kiosk shops, and is surrounded by small streets open only to foot traffic. **Calle San Miguel** and **Calle Sindicat** near the plaza are packed with small restaurants, cafes, and shops. **Plaza Rei Joan Carles I** is the center of the high-end, expensive shopping in Palma that extends onto **Avenida Jaime III, Calle Unio,** and **Passeig des Born.** The **Paseo Maritimo** curves around the port, where you'll find many of the most popular clubs and nightlife destinations.

ACCOMMODATIONS

While the city of Palma is definitely the center of the island, this center isn't necessarily catering to budget travel. If you're looking for cheaper rooms, inexpensive and thriving nightlife, and some beach time, the nearby town of **Arenal** is only a 25min. bus ride out of Palma on the Playa de Palma.

In Arenal

▨ HOSTAL TIERRAMAR
➥⊗((•))丫❄ HOSTAL ❸

C. Berlin, 9 ☎971 262 751 ▧www.hostaltierramar.com

One of the most popular accommodations in Arenal (and that's saying something—this whole town is packed with hostels), Hostal Tierramar knows how to provide a comfortable stay for the beach-minded. Enjoy sizable rooms with tiled floors and colorful sheets that light up when you open up your window to the ocean views. Your massive bathroom is the perfect place to scrub the sand and sunscreen from your body, and the first-floor cafeteria will give you the opportunity to get a book from the library, shoot some pool, or enjoy basic snacks and sandwiches 24hr. a day. At Tierramar, you're steps from the shining blue waters of the Playa de Palma—as well as a direct bus ride into the city (lines #15 and #25).

✈ *Take bus #21 from the airport to the last stop at Playa de Palma and walk back two blocks from the stop to C. Berlin.* ⓘ *Breakfast, sheets, towels included.* ⓢ *Singles €26-32; doubles €38-47; triples €57.* ⓠ *Reception 24hr.*

HOTEL LEBLON
➥⊗((•))丫⚘ BUDGET HOTEL ❷

C. Trasimero, 67 ☎971 490 200 ▧hotel-leblon@hotmail.com

Hotel Leblon would be an easy bet in a boxing match—it's a hotel-quality accommodation that keeps its prices competing in the budget ring, and shares a reception with the even cheaper **Sol de Mallorca.** The rose-colored sheets near your large closet and decorative art is just the beginning. Make your way down to the first-floor bar, colorfully decorated with liquors and syrups, and order up a cocktail *(€3.50)* or snack all day long. The pool out back is decorated with nautical tiles and overflowing with neon floatie toys, so hopefully you'll still have time to swim a lap or two after spending the day at the nearby Playa de Palma.

✈ *Take bus #21 from the airport to the last stop at Playa de Palma and walk back two blocks from the stop to C. Berlin, which intersects C. Trasimero.* ⓘ *Breakfast, sheets, and towels included. Pool available. Restaurant. Bike rentals €6.* ⓢ *Doubles €40; triples €45.* ⓠ *Reception 24hr.*

In Palma

▨ HOSTAL RITZI
⊕⊗((•))丫⚘ HOSTAL ❸

C. Apuntadores, 6 ☎971 714 610 ▧www.hostalritzi.com

Hostal Ritzi is a prime cut of convenience—you're steps from one of Palma's main plazas and paying a price that's more suited for a room in Arenal. This hostal totally embraces the bed-and-breakfast vibe: you'll get a warm welcome from the friendly staff, a spacious but homey room, and comfy green couches in the common area. Enjoy a full breakfast in the morning in the bright dining room or on the outdoor patio, and then make your way out onto the town.

✈ *C. Apuntadores branches off Plaza Reina.* ⓘ *Breakfast, sheets, and towels included.* ⓢ *Singles €30; doubles €55-70. Extra bed €20.* ⓠ *Reception 8:30am-midnight.*

SIGHTS
◉

▨ CASTELL DE BELLVER
HISTORICAL SITE, CASTLE, PRISON

C. Camilo Jose Cela, 17 ☎971 735 065

Every kid dreams of visiting a castle—especially one nestled up in the mountains with stone towers, a deep moat, and high ceilings. However, the Castell de Bellver didn't last as a castle for long. Although intended to be a royal residence for the Catholic kings when visiting the island, this structure has actually spent much of its history serving as a fortified, high-security prison. Exploring the grounds, you'll enjoy the best views of all of Majorca, the colorful tapestries and marble statues filling the rooms, and a fascinating exhibit about one of Bellver's most famous prisoners, Gaspar Melchor Jovellanos, the Enlightenment thinker locked up for simply being "different." While this Euro-Gothic sight may require quite the hike to arrive at the

majorca • sights

main gates (unless you take the bus which drops you at the doorstep), enjoy the exercise and climb the steps—we promise it's worth the trek.

Take bus #3 or #46 to Plaza Gomila and take C. Bellver to the top. Tour bus takes you directly to the sight. ℹ *Information in English and Spanish.* $ *€2.50, students under 18 €1.* ⏰ *Open June-Sept M-Sa 8:30am-8:30pm, Su 10am-5pm; Oct-May M-Sa 8am-7:30pm, Su 10am-5pm.*

FUNDACIO PILAR I JOAN MIRO MUSEUM

C. Saridakis, 29 ☎971 701 420 🖥miro.palma.cat

There are many people in this world who have a strong pride in their home town—how else would we end up with songs like *I Love LA* or *Cleveland Rocks?*—but not many people can turn that pride into something as fascinating and beautiful as the Fundacio Pilar. Creator Juan Miró spent his childhood summers in Majorca with his grandmother, escaped to the island during the Nazi invasion of France, and permanently moved to Palma in 1956. Even though he wasn't a resident until later in life, Miro still had an attachment to the capital and decided to donate his entire studio space and much of his collection to the city. Today, the Fundacio Pilar i Joan Miro not only holds about 2500 pieces by the artist, but also provides you with the chance to see his studios. You'll see easels and paintings in the *Taller Sert*, designed by exiled architect and close friend Josep Sert, as well as a large collection of original grafitti in the *San Boter*.

Take bus #3 or #46 to Marivent and then follow the signs up to the Fundacio. ℹ *Information in English and Spanish.* $ *€6, students €3, free on Sa.* ⏰ *Open May 16-Sept 15 T-Sa 10am-7pm, Su 10am-3pm; Sept 16-May 15 T-Sa 10am-6pm, Su 10am-3pm.*

PALACIO REAL DE LA ALMUDIANA PALACE

C. Palau Reyal ☎971 214 134 🖥www.patrimonionacional.es

Although this massive stone structure right on the shores of Majorca was originally constructed for Muslim royalty during the 10th century, Jaime II's arrival in Majorca marked a time for change. This first Catholic monarch of the island left a few remnants of the Arab constructions, but from the second he placed the cross-holding angel on top of *Torre de Angel*, it was clear that no one would be praying towards Mecca in this house. While many couples settle for the his-and-hers towels or coffee mugs, Spanish monarchs took things a step further—the Palacio Real has separate residences, orchards, and chapels for the Queen and King, all wonderfully decorated with pointed ceilings, colorful tapestries, and furniture. You can even wander through the original Arab baths used more for luxury than hygiene.

Take the steps near Plaza Reyna. Entrance is between the palace and the Catedral. ℹ *Information available in English and Spanish. Tours arranged based on demand.* $ *€3.20, students €2.30. Tours €4. Audio tours €2.50.* ⏰ *Open Apr-Sept M-F 10am-5:45pm, Sa 10am-1:15pm; Oct-Mar M-F 10am-1:15pm and 4-5:15pm, Sa 10am-1:15pm.*

FOOD

Majorca has quite the selection of international cuisine. Walking the streets of Palma, you'll come across many tapas bars and Spanish restaurants, but there are also tons of ethnic options. This island makes the most of its coastline—if you're looking for fresh seafood, just explore the larger restaurants on the **Paseo Maritimo** or leading up to **Plaza Reina.** You should also take advantage of the traditional Majorcan dishes. Fried *mallorqui* (fried offal, potatos, tomatos, and onions), vegetable *trumbet* (eggplant, peppers, potatos, tomatos, and onions), toasty *pa amb oli* (bread topped with tomato, oil, and salt with cheese, fish, or meats), and savory *sabrosada* (pork and pepper pâté) are some of the local specialities.

LA CUEVA TRADITIONAL [3]

C. Apuntadores, 5 ☎971 724 422

While **La Cueva** (the cave) lives up to its name with an undergound location and low ceilings, this bright, traditional destination wouldn't suit any stalagtites, pirates, or even Batman. La Cueva's menu is simple, with a long list of classic Spanish *tapas* served up at full *ración* sizes. You can see all your options sitting behind the bar, and the chef constantly cooks up more food to refill these deep-dish platters. Locals devour the *gambas al ajillo*, *(shrimp with garlic sauce; €12)* and massive platters of traditional *jamon jagubo* *(€14, large €22)*. You may have to fight your way through the crowd congregating outside the door, but it's worth the wait.

C. Apuntadores branches off Plaza Reina. $ Raciones €5-18. 🕐 Open M-Sa noon-midnight.

CAFE COTO INTERNATIONAL, MAJORCAN [2]

Plaza Drassana, 12 ☎636 096 126 www.bar-coto.com

Cafe Coto certainly knows how to be bold—the hot pink exterior, massive flowers growing up the gates, burning red interior walls, golden tables, and giant Frida Kahlo paintings certainly make a statement. However, the decor isn't the only thing making a statement at this cute patio-cafe. The international menu provides a wide array of homemade options to cure any craving. Indian dishes like the goat cheese with homemade mango chutney *(€6.50)* and Sri Lankan soups *(€5.50)* can transport you to anywhere on the globe. If you'd prefer some local flavor classic Mallorcan *pa amb olis* *(€6.50)* or a Spanish tapa tasting platters *(small €8; large €15)*. Freshly baked desserts like the warm apple strudel make the daily *menú* *(€10)* even more tempting.

From Plaza Reyna, take C. Apuntadores and make a left into the Plaza. $ Entrees €5.50-9.50. Salads €8.50. Sandwiches €3-4. Desserts €2-8. Menú of the day €10. 🕐 Open M-F 8am-1am, Sa-Su 9am-1am..

THE GUINESS HOUSE CAFE, BAR [2]

Parc de la Mar

Disclaimer: we understand that The Guiness House is innately touristy and that the menu isn't exactly creative, but the location and ambience make this spot one that you just can't skip. Located right on the waters of the Parc de la Mar with the city's best view of the Catedral, there's no better place to enjoy a summer afternoon snack. Busiest during the open hours of the Catedral, as visitors work up quite the appetite after gazing at Gaudi's glorious canopy, it also draws a crowd in summer evenings with open-air movies *(9pm July-Aug)*. For all you beer connoisseurs out there, The Guinness House lives up to its name with a lengthy list of international *cervesas* on tap or by the bottle *(€2.60-4.60)*, served up at the outdoor patio bar or the even larger tavern bar inside the restaurant.

On Parc de la Mar across from the Cathedral. i Outdoor movies available July-Aug. $ Sandwiches €4.85-5.90. Entrees €6.70-12.90 Salads €6.50-7.80. Pizzas €6.50. Burgers €4.75-7.25. 🕐 Open daily 8am-2am.

NIGHTLIFE

Around the streets of Palma, near the main plazas and city center, you'll come across a few late-night, loungey cafes and mellow bars, but the real nightlife is concentrated along the **Paseo Maritimo.** Take a walk along this pathway, checking out all those fancy yachts in the harbor as you go, and 10min. away from the Catedral, things will start to heat up.

MOJITO SOUL BAR

Paseo Maritimo, 27 www.mojitosoul.com

You may currently associate nature, envy, and marshmallow breakfast cereals with the color green, but one night out on the Paseo Maritimo and you may start to think of Mojito Soul every time you encounter that portion of the color wheel. That's because the entire place is lit by glowing green lights. The DJ spins a mix of soul and R and B hits to entertain the young, international crowd as they try to answer the eternal question—another daiquiri *(€8)* or another dance. While 75% of bars and clubs in Spain will tell you that they specialize in *mojitos* and *caipirinas*, here's a spot that actually deserves that accolade. You can try 7 varieties of each of these drinks *(€8)*, whether in their classic form or with a fruity twist like strawberry, peach, or passionfruit.

➜ On Paseo Maritimo on the inland side. $ Cocktails €8. ⏰ Open daily in summer 9pm-4am; in winter 10pm-3am.

GIBSON ♿🍸❄☁ BAR

Plaza Mercat, 18 ☎971 716 404

Unless you've spent quite a few years at bartending school, Gibson will likely be a learning experience. The lengthy menu (5 pages of whiskeys alone) lists drinks in varieties you never knew existed, but at least it features detailed explanations and histories at the bottom of each page. The house specialty dry martinis come in 14 styles, but the Gibson Dry is definitely the most popular, combining gin, vermouth, a small onion, and lemon zest *(€6.50)*. Cockails like the "bull shot" *(€7)* may be a test of testosterone levels, but you can also enjoy a simple caipirinha with or without alcohol *(€7)*. Gibson's open all day long, and we won't judge if you're looking for that 8am Bloody Mary *(€7)*, but you can also enjoy a simple coffee *(€1.50)* on the outdoor patio.

*➜ Plaza Mercat branches off C. Unio between Plaza Rei Joan Carles I and Plaza Weyler. **i** Non-smoking area available.$ Mixed Drinks €6-7. Beer €2. Coffee €1.50. ⏰ Open daily 8am-3am.*

MISTRAL 🍸❄☁ BAR, CLUB

Paseo Maritimo, 28

You'll have tons of club options along Paseo Maritimo, but Mistral isn't one to skip. You'll know just from walking by and scoping out the attractive locals on the outdoor patio that this is a crowd you want to be dancing against. The dark navy walls, accented by the two glistening, silver bars, may portray a **night sky,** but this doesn't signal bedtime—it signals a long night of groovin' and movin' to blasting mash-ups of commercial hits. Prismatic cocktails and colorful strobe lights will keep your energy up until the sun comes up to help you with a tan on your walk home.

➜ On Paseo Maritimo on the inland side. $ Beer €4. Mixed drinks €7. ⏰ Open daily 10pm-5am.

ESSENTIALS

The official language of Majorca is **Catalan,** not Spanish, and so the city's streets, plazas, and structures have Catalonian names. Luckily, almost everything is translated into Spanish, and often English as well.

Practicalities

- **TOURIST OFFICES:** There are 4 main tourist offices available in Palma. The **Majorca Tourist Information** service has two locations, the Head Office at Parc de las Estacions and the Casal Solleric Office at Passeig des Born, 27 (☎902 102 365 🖳palmainfo@a-palma.es.) The **Palma City Council** has also established two offices, one at **Placa de la Reina 2** *(☎971 712 216)* and one at the **Airport** *(☎971 789 556)*.
- **TOURS:** The **Town Council** runs walking tours from Plaça de Cort, next to the olive tree *(☎971 720 720 **i** Given in English and Spanish ⏰ M-Sa 9am-6pm)*. Other city tours are available from **Palma on Bike** *(⏰ 3hr. 30min.; M-Su 10am from Avenida Gabriel Roca, 15 and 10:30am from Avenida Antoni Maura, 10 $ €25.)* There are also **taxi tours.** *(➜ Look for designated signs on city cabs $ €30 per hr.)* The **tourist bus** picks up from 16 stops all over the city. *(⏰ Tours last 1hr. 20min. Leave every 20min. Mar-Oct 10am-8pm, Nov-Feb 10am-6pm. $ €13.)*
- **CURRENCY EXCHANGE:** There's a currency exchange office with an admittedly inconsistent schedule. *(Avenida d'Antoni Maura, 28 ⏰ Usually open in summer daily 10am-5pm; in winter M-F 10am-5pm.)*
- **INTERNET:** Free city Wi-Fi is available at Plaça Joan Carles I, the Parc de Llevant,

S'Escorxador, and the Cultural Centre Flassaders. It can be accessed in 30min. incremements by activating your computer's bluetooth. Many restaurants and cafes also offer Wi-Fi with more forgiving time limits. The **public library** also has Wi-Fi. *(Palau Reial, 18 ☎971 711 122 ⏰Open M 9:30am-2pm, T 4-8pm, W 9:30am-2pm, Th 4-8pm, F 9:30am-2pm.)*

- **POST OFFICE:** The **central post office** is located at C. Constitucion 6 (*☎902 197 197 🖥www.correos.es ⏰ Open M-F 8:30am-8:30pm, Sa 9:30am-2pm.)*

Emergency!

- **POLICE: Local police** can be found at C. Sant Fernan. *(☎971 225 500 🖥www.palmademallorca.es).* **National police** are at C. Ruiz de Alda, 8 *(☎971 225 200 🖥www.policia.es).*
- **HOSPITAL:** The **general hospital** is located at Plaza Hospital, 3. *(☎971 212 000 🖥www.gesma.org).*
- **LATE-NIGHT PHARMACY:** You'll find pharmacies all over the city, and a **24-hour pharmacy Bagur** at C. Aragon, 70 *(☎971 272 501).*

Getting There

By Plane

The **Palma de Mallorca Airport** *(☎971 789 000)* is located 11km southeast of Palma and runs flights from tons of international and domestic airlines including **Air Berlin** *(☎902 320 737 🖥www.airberlin.com),* **Easy Jet** *(☎08 712 882 236 🖥www.easyjet.com),* **Iberia** *(☎902 400 500 🖥www.iberia.com),* **Lufthansa** *(☎49 696 960 🖥www.lufthansa.com),* **Spanair** *(☎971 916 047 🖥www.spanair.com),* and **Vueling Airlines** *(☎807 001 717🖥www.vueling.com).* The **Aena** website *(🖥www.aena.es)* and **Amadeus** website *(🖥www.amadeus.net)* are particularly helpful in consolidating information from all the major airlines. As many of the flights are short and run very consistently, prices vary immensely depending on booking, day of the week, and time of day of the flight. The **Empresa Municipal de Transportes** runs an **airport bus line** (*$ €2 ℹ #1, every 12-15min. ⏰ M-F 6am-1:50am, Sa-Su 6am-1:10am)* taking your right into Palma, stopping along C. Gabriel Alomar, Porta de Camp, and Avenida Alexandre Rosello. You can use busline **#21** if you're staying in Arenal.

By Ferry

You can also travel to Mallorca on a boat *(general information Autoritat Portuària de Balears 🖥www.portsdebalears.com)* from the Spanish mainland or between Islands. **Acciona-Trasmediterranea** *(☎902 454 645 🖥www.trasmediterranea.es)* runs to Palma from **Barcelona** *(⏰ 7½hr., M-Th 1pm, 11pm, F-Su 11pm)* and **Valencia** *(⏰ 7hr., M-Sa 11:45am, Su 11:59pm)* on the mainland, as well as to **Ibiza** *(⏰ 4 hr., F, Su, M 7pm)* and **Menorca** *(⏰ 5.5hr., Su 5:30pm).* **Baleària Eurolínies Marítimes** *(☎902 160 180 🖥www.balearia.com)* runs to **Ibiza** *($ €52.20-65.40) ⏰ 3½hr., Sa-M 2:45am, 8pm, Tu, Th, F 12:30am, 8pm, W 12:30am, 2:45am, 8pm)* or **Formentera** *($ €52.20 ⏰ 4hr., M-Su 1:15pm).*

Getting Around

By Bus

Public buses within the city of Palma are run by the **Empresa Municipal de Transportes (EMT)** Urbanas de Palma de Mallorca *(C. Josep Anselm Clave, 5 ☎971 214 444).* There are 35 lines *($ €1.25, €8 for 10 rides)* that run M-Su from as early as 6am until as late as 2am. Lines **#1** and **#21** run to the **airport** *($ €2 ⏰ May-Oct 6am-1:50am, every 12min; Nov-Apr 6am-1:10am, every 15min)*, and line **#50** runs a circular route *(⏰ May-Oct 9:30am-7pm, Nov-Apr 10am-4:40pm; stops every 20min.).* Line **#41** is the overnight line *($€1⏰F-Sa 11:45pm-7am; every 15min).* Also useful are lines **#15** *($ €1.25⏰ Daily 5:45am-1:20am, every 10min)* and the faster **#25** *($ €1.25⏰ M-F 6:25am-9:25pm, Sa-Su 6:30am-9:30pm; every 10-13min)* to Playa de Palma, and lines **#3** *($ €1.25 ⏰ Daily 5:45am-12:35am, every 9-10min)* and **#46** *($ €1.25 ⏰ M-Sa 6:30am-11:10pm, Su 7:18am-11:30pm, every*

20-35min.) which travel along the port, stopping at major sights like Castell de Bellver and Fundacio Pilar i Joan Miro.

By Taxi

You can also take the city taxis *(⏰ M-F 9pm-7am and weekends $ €4 plus €1 per km)*, designated as available by a green light on the top of the car from **Taxi Palma Radio** *(☎971 755 440)* or **Radio Taxi** *(☎971 755 414)*. There are major taxi stops at **Plaza Weyler, Plaza Forti, Avenida Jaime III, Plaza Reina,** and **Passieg de Sagrera.**

To get to other parts of Majorca beyond Palma, **Transport de les Illes Balears (TIB)** *(☎900 177 777 🖳tib.caib.es)*, or TIB, runs 5 series of bus lines *(#100, #200, #300, #400, and #500)* from Palma that go clockwise around the island. They are notorious for running late, and their timetables vary significantly, but they are technically scheduled to begin running as early at 6am and until as late as 11pm. TIB also runs a Palma to **Pobles** train *(⏰ M-F 5:45am-11:15pm, Sa-Su 6:05am-11:15pm)* and a metro line between the **Estación Intermodal** and the **Estación UIB.** *(⏰ M-F every half hr. 6:30am-10:30pm; every 15 minutes 6:30am-7am, 8:30pm-10:30pm; Sa-Su every hour 6:30am-10pm, every 30 minutes 6:30am-7:30am, 9pm-10pm.)* Tren de Sóller runs the scenic "Western Highlights" route along the coast to **Soller** from **Plaça d'Espanya** *($ €10 ☎971 752 051 🖳www.trendesoller.com ⏰ 8am-7:30pm)*. enjoyed by tourists and locals alike.

By Bike

Palma is also a major center for cyclotourism, and getting around on a **bike** is extremely popular, whether on your own or in a guided tour. **Palma On Bike** *(Avenida Antoni Maura 10 and Avenida Gabriel Roca 15 ☎971 918 988 🖳www.palmaonbike.com$ Bike rental for 1-2 days €12 per day, 3-7 days €10 per day. Kayak rental doubles €50 per day, singles €30 per day. Rollerblades rental €10 per day)*,

stop worrying and love the nap

The afternoon nap is hardly an alien concept to the typical American college student, but out in the real world, dropping off for an hour or two in the middle of the day is a tough feat to pull off–if you live in the boring, nine-to-five United States, that is. Spain, on the other hand, has it all figured out: after waking up to a big bowl of *cafe con leche* and heading off to work for four or five hours, the Spanish come back home around 1pm for lunch, immediately followed by that most glorious of Iberian traditions, the *siesta.* The *siesta* doesn't have to be a nap; it's quite common instead to just tumbarse (lie down) on the sofa and slip into a dazed stupor in front of one of the popular game shows that daily grace the Spanish airwaves (or the Spanish-dubbed Los Simpson, whose afternoon broadcast consistently ranks among the top-rated programs). Yes, there are still another few hours of work in the afternoon, but the break helps divide and conquer the workday in a way that makes those last few hours between *siesta* and fiesta manageable.

ibiza ☎971

We won't tell mom and dad, but we know why you're making the trip to Ibiza. You want the whitest sands, the clearest waters, the hottest sun, and the sexiest clubs. This small, Mediterranean island has a rich history of settlement and exploration, but it's modern status is the real draw. You'll be wearing as little clothing at the beach as is acceptable, stuffing your face with the delicious selection of international eats, and reaping the benefits of the commercial tourist industry.

This is where the young and beautiful come to get tanner and more beautiful on their summer vactions. Take that summer designation seriously—this packed party scene turns into a quaint and empty town during the winter months, so work hard all year to save the cash for this trip. You'll be encountering pricey accommodations, ridiculous covers, and expensive *mojitos*, but memories (assuming you can remember all that goes down on this debauchery-filled island) are priceless. Test your limits and see how many nights straight you can go beaching by day and clubbing by night. You're in for a ride!

ORIENTATION

Ibiza City is not very large and can be traversed with just a short walk. The main avenues running across the city are **Avenida d'Isidor Macabich,** where you'll encounter the bus station, and **Avenida de España,** where you'll find a slew of different markets, restaurants, internet cafes, and small shops. The **Passeig Vara de Rei** and the **Plaza de Parque** both branch off Avenida de España and are frequented by all the city visitors. The commerical shopping area is most developed on and around **Avenida Bartolome Roselo,** and the most interesting restaurants line the port along **Avenida Andenes** and **Avenida de Santa Eularia del Riu.** The historical centers of Ibiza are the World Heritage sight of **d'Alt Vila** and the ruins of **Puig des Molins.**

ACCOMMODATIONS

Accommodations in Ibiza City are few and far between and generally pricey. If you're coming to the island to party, **Sant Antoni** may be your best bet. The hotels and hostals are less expensive, you're right on the beach, and you're in prime location to see some of the hottest clubs and the **Sunset Strip.** Also keep in mind that Ibiza is a highly seasonal island—summer prices will be significantly higher than anything in the winter (if the accommodation even stays open after September).

Sant Antoni

👍 HOTEL OROSOL 💳♿📶🍸❄🛁 HOTEL [3]

Cami General, 1 ☎971 340 712 💻www.orosolhotel.com

For these prices (especially if you're traveling with a group), the luxury you find at Hotel Orosol is unbelievable. This larger hotel is scooting its way up to 3-star status and is stacked with all those fine facilities that your hostel may be missing from all the hostel-hopping. Your massive room's red sheets, TV, and balcony are only some of the amenities—the full continental breakfast buffet, big pool (290m away), and bright, modern lobby add to the luxury. The welcoming receptionists will provide you with slews of information on local travel and give you tons of activity suggestions—need a bike? Want a discount club ticket? Care to visit Formentera? They'll organize it all for no additional cost. Just take it easy and relax. You're on vacation, remember?

➡ From the bus station, take Ramon y Cajal to the first intersection to the right. ***i*** *Breakfast, sheets, and towels included. Pool. Cafeteria. A/C €3-12. Laundry €7 wash, €4 dry.* [$] *Singles €26-53; doubles €40-92; triples €57-120; quads €70-172.* ⏰ *Reception 24hr.*

👍 HOSTAL VALENCIA
💳🚭📶🍸❄☀ HOSTAL [2]

C. Valencia, 23 ☎971 341 035 💻www.ibizahostalvalencia.com

Hostal Valencia looks more like a home than a hostal—and we're talking about a home that you're dying to own. From the comfy couches andwarm living room area to the full cafeteria-restaurant with orange-cushioned chairs and stocked bar to the porch-patio and lush garden, this is one little oasis that you won't want to leave. The forest-green sheets in your bedroom and small, yellow-tiled bathroom are pristinely clean and organized. Plus, the pool out back beckons. You can also find all the information necessary about Ibiza in the lobby, equipped with a whole kiosk of pamphlets and ideas to make your vacation much more interesting.

➡ *At the intersection of Carrer de Mosen and C. Valencia.* ℹ *Sheets and towels included. Pool. Cafeteria.* $ *Singles €25-70; doubles €40-80; triples €54-105.* ⏰ *Reception 24hr.*

HOSTAL MONTANA
💳🚭📶🍸 HOSTAL [2]

C. Roma, 8 ☎971 340 490 💻www.montanamarino.com

Hostal Montana knows how to help you make the most of your stay in San Antonio—the friendly staff will point out the best beaches, direct you to the pool at their sister-hostel, **Hostal Marino,** sell you discount tickets to the hottest clubs, or organize a ferry trip to Formentera. You'll enjoy your complimentary breakfast in the morning, but if that night of partying has you sleeping until the afternoon, you can always fight that hangover by grabbing a snack in the cafeteria-bar or wake yourself up with a game of foosball between *bocadillos.* The rooms will make you feel like you've scored a snazzy hotel room, as they come equipped with a mini-fridge (store the mixers), full closet (unpack the stilletos), small balcony (toast to the sunset), and clean, comfy beds (maybe get some—sleep, that is).

➡ *From the bus station, take C. Ramon y Cajal and make a left on C. Roma.* ℹ *Breakfast, sheets, towels, mini-fridge, and safe included.* $ *Singles €17-35; doubles €28-70; triples €42-105.* ⏰ *Reception 24hr.*

HOSTAL ROSALIA
💳🚭🍸☀ HOSTAL [2]

Carrer Santa Rosalia, 5 ☎971 340 709 💻www.hostalrosalia.com

This inexpensive accommodation is packed with partying beachgoers. The simple rooms with white walls and grey tiles get a nice splash of life from the colorful sheets and big windows. You can lounge around the pool and enjoy the TV in the cafeteria during the day, or take the short 10min. walk down to the beaches and port. And if the walk seems too long, Rosalia can get you there faster—the hostal also runs **Top Moto** next door.

➡ *Take Carrer del Progress to Carrer Santa Rosalia and turn left.* ℹ *Breakfast €3. Internet available on lobby computer. Pool.* $ *May-Oct singles €18-20; doubles €30-40; triples €45-60.* ⏰ *Reception 24hr.*

Ibiza City

👍 HOSTAL LAS NIEVES/JUANITO
💳🚭 HOSTAL [2]

C. Juan de Austria, 17/18 ☎971 190 819 💻www.hostalibiza.com

Located in the middle of the city center, a short walk from the historic d'Alt Villa and the history-making Playa d'en Bossa, this hostal pair is run out of the same reception on C. Juan de Austuria and gives you a bit of freedom in deciding how much you're going to spend. Simply put, Hostal Juanito is probably the best price you'll find in Ibiza city, but it isn't a point of luxury. You'll enjoy a spacious and clean room but will have to sleep through the heat with no A/C. Las Nieves provides some ventillation and the possibility of ensuite bathrooms, which ups the ante a bit. Either way, they both have the same best feature—the couple that owns the place is one of the nicest you'll encounter on the island, and they are ready to help you plan out your trip.

➡ *From the bus stop, take Avenida d'Isidor Macabich, turn right onto Avenida Ignac Wallis and left onto Juan de Austria.* $ *Nieves singles €30; doubles €60, with bath €75. Juanito singles €25; doubles €50.* ⏰ *Reception open daily 9am-1pm and 4-8pm.*

SIGHTS

The most historic part of Ibiza City is **d'Alt Vila** ("the Walled City"), a UNESCO World Heritage sight. Walking the small, winding streets (or rather climbing, as it's pretty steep), you can enjoy the major sights or follow one of the designated routes described in pamphlets available at the **information offices.** The **bastions** around d'Alt Vila are the perfect look-out points, and the **Baluarte des Porta Neu Sant Pere** holds a small museum exhibit explaining the construction of the city. Also, while the **Museum of Contemporary Art** is currently being renovated (as of summer 2010), the exhibits are available in the Ayuntamiento. Be sure to check of the **Catedral D'Eivissa,** which still rings the original bells from the 16th-century.

BEACHES

While it depends on how you divide it up, there are at least 50 distinct beaches surrounding the island of Ibiza. They all have their own character and pros and cons. You can endure the biggest crowds and enjoy the biggest parties at beaches closer to the city, or you can battle the bus schedule to reach Ibiza's nature reserves and smaller coves. Pick your poison, pick your pleasure. No matter what you choose, you'll be under that same Mediterranean sun, sipping the (essentially) same *mojitos*.

PLATJA DE SES SALINES ♿🍸 BEACH

10min. drive from Ibiza Town in the Salines Nature Reserve

There's a reason Platja de Ses Salines is one of Ibiza's most popular beaches. Here in the Salines Nature Reserve, you'll find clean, soft sands, and warm, clear waters. With barely any waves, you'll see tourists and locals wading out into the sea to test their skills at paddleball or just floating around on an inflatable tube. While Ses Salines is the perfect place to relax and work on that summer tan, it's also going to provide you with some of the biggest, most-established beach restaurants on the island. **The Jockey Club** and **Malibu** will serve cocktails right to your lounge chair, spray you with their mist machines, and have their DJs spinning hot tunes all day long.

Take Bus #11 from Ibiza City to Salines. ℹ *First aid available.* $ *Lounge chair and umbrella rentals €6-10.* ⏰ *Lifeguard on duty daily noon-7pm.*

CALA BASSA ♿ BEACH

Near Sant Antoni

If you say its name fast, "Cala Bassa" may remind you a touch of the *The Teenage Mutant Ninja Turtles*' "cowabunga!" While you can definitely enjoy pizza and sea creatures (and a life free of bad guys) while relaxing at this small cove getaway, there's way more to the Cala Bassa than any '80s cartoon can provide. Whether you want to leap off the rocky cliffs into the warm waters below, play some paddle ball right on the waveless shore, or enjoy the multi-tiered sand levels under the shade of the trees, you'll reap the benefits of smooth sand and clear waters. Cala Bassa is also perfect to test your wits at some water sports—**Ski Pormany** *(⏰ 11am-7pm, summers only)* offers waterskiing *(€20)*, banana-boating *(€10)*, and tubing *(€15)*, and **Pheonix Dive Center** *(☎971 806 374 🖥www.pheonixdive.de ⏰ 10am-6pm, summers only)* offers snorkling *(from €15)* and SCUBA *(€34)* adventures. Both companies work best with walk-ins, so just show up and hop in the water!

Take the #7 bus from Sant Antoni. ℹ *Showers and bathrooms available. No camping.* $ *Chair rentals €4.* ⏰ *Lifeguard on duty daily July-Sept 11am-7pm; Oct 1-15 noon-6pm; June 15-30 noon-6pm.*

PLATJA D'ES CAVALLET 🍸 BEACH

A short walk from Salines to the coast

Platja d'es Cavallet's free-spirited vibe stems from a few factors: groups of locals frequently make the switch from swimsuits to birthday suits, masseuses perform aggressive and artistic massages right on the sand, the few restaurants sprinkled along the beach (like the huge **Chiringay**) play mellower tunes than the average Ibizan beach-bar, and any tourists who arrive via public transit have just made the 30min. walk through the stunning Salines Nature Reserve to arrive at this peaceful paradise. Along the coast you'll find tons of rocky coves being settled by savvy locals looking for some private tanning and even pass by the 15th-century **Torre de ses Portes.**

↗ Take bus #11 from Ibiza City to Salines and then walk on the coast to D'es Cavallet. ℹ First aid available. Nudity permitted. ⏰ Lifeguards on duty daily 11am-7pm.

PLATJA D'EN BOSSA ♿🍸 BEACH

Lounging around Platja d'en Bossa you'll hear bottles popping, lighters clicking, and the repeated "Amigo, wanna come to (insert disco here) tonight?" of promoters offering free and discounted club tickets. While you may not get the pristine cleanliness of removed nature reserve beaches, you'll get lines of huge hotels, tall palm trees, and Ibiza's biggest seaside parties. Major beach bars like **Bora Bora** serve drinks and food all day before turning into raging discos after dark. If you go up one block from beach, you'll find tons of bars, pubs, supermarkets, internet cafes, gyms, and restaurants, making Platja d'en Bossa a tourist hub of total convenience.

↗ Take bus #14, summer bus #10B, or the discobus to Platja d'en Bossa. ℹ First aid, showers, and lockers available. Jet-ski and banana boat rentals. On-beach massages. $ Lockers €3 per 10hr. Lounge chairs €7.

FOOD

👍 BAR 43 TAPAS 🍸❄ INTERNATIONAL, OPEN LATE [2]

Avenida de Espana, 43 ☎971 300 992 💻www.ibiza-43.com

Some numbers hog all the attention: lucky (or unlucky) 13, fab 4, and sweet 16. But what ever happened to good old 43? Luckily, Bar 43 Tapas is here to boost this poor, neglected number's self-esteem by serving 43 varieties of international tapas to an equally international clientele. You can test your knowledge of international flags or chat with the owners about the decorations on the walls, all of which have been collected over the course of their world travels. These tapas are the perfect size for sharing, so grab a group to try some Spanish *albondigas* in mustard sauce *(€5)*, a Mexican *quesadilla* *(€4.50)*, a Greek salad *(€4.80)*, and some Indian chicken curry *(€6.50)*. You can add to the party by tasting one of their refreshing cocktails, like the fruity, tropical "Ibiza 43" that mixes rum, apricot brandy, various juices, and blackberry liqueur *(€7)*.

↗ Near the bus stop on Avenida de Espana. $ Tapas €4-6.50. ⏰ Open Tu-Sa 1-5pm and 8pm-1am.

👍 BON PROFIT ♿🍸❄ TRADITIONAL [2]

Plaza del Parque 5

If we learned anything from David and Goliath, *Stuart Little*, or *The Princess and the Pea*, it's that even the little guy can have a huge impact—and Bon Profit fits right in with those small-but-strong competitors. Located right on the Plaza del Parque, this classic Spanish restaurant may only cover a small space, but it serves up huge portions at shockingly low prices. You can enjoy a full plate of steaming *paella* *(€3.80)* for lunch any day of the week, or the selection of local fish like the specialty *dorada* *(€9.50)*. Even any selection off the lengthy wine list will only cost you €1.90 per glass. The friendly staff will serve you with a smile in this old-time establishment, where the plaster has been artistically removed from parts of the walls to uncover the warm brick below.

↗ On the Plaza del Parque, on the side closest to d'Alt Vila. ℹ No smoking. $ Entrees €3.80-10.90. Desserts €1.20-€2.70. ⏰ Open daily 1-3pm and 8-10pm.

BAR SAN JUAN 🍸❄ TRADITIONAL [3]

C. de Montgri, 8 ☎971 311 603

This Ibiza classic is a family establishment, passed down through three generations over the past 60 years. Just don't think that Bar San Juan is stuck in some outdated ways. You'll find a lengthy list of daily options every time you walk in to this small restaurant packed with chatty locals. It may not look too exciting from the outside, but the moment you walk in and see the massive portions passing under your nose, you'll understand why you're lost in the sound of bustling conversation and clinking glasses. On a menu that's all about choices, you'll find a slew of fresh options like dorada, salmon, sepia (€5-10.80), 6 different types of tortillas (€3.50-5), and a hefty mixed *paella* (€4.80).

⌖ From Passeig Vara de Rei, take either of the side streets to C. de Montgri. *i* Smoking and non-smoking areas available. Ⓢ Appetizers €4.50-8. Salads €3-6.50. Fish and meat €4-12. Desserts €1.80-2.50. Wine €1-1.70. ☼ Open M-Sa 1-3:30pm and 8:30-11:30pm.

NIGHTLIFE

Nightlife is Ibiza's pride and joy. Whether you're an Ibiza virgin or a proud veteran, the enormous, packed *discotecas* will never cease to shock and impress. While you need to be prepared for big covers and pricey drinks, you can find discounts from the street promoters in all the city centers and along the beaches as well as at many hostel receptions. The major clubs are generally located outside the cities, splashed all over the island, including **Eden** and **Es Paradis** in Sant Antoni, **Pacha** at the Ibiza port, and **Privilege** and **Amnesia** near San Rafael. But don't fret, as Ibiza has made club transport particularly convenient with the **discobus** (€3) which runs lines from midnight to 6:30am, dropping you right at the doors to the major clubs. There are also options for some less expensive partying. The **Sunset Cafes** and smaller clubs along **Calle Santa Anges** in Sant Antoni are some favorite spots, and there are also late night bars all over Ibiza City.

◈ SPACE
◆♥☼❋ CLUB

Playa d'en Bossa   ☎971 304 432 ◲www.spaceibiza.com

You may be wondering how they came up with the name Space. Maybe it's because this enormous club with over 4 dance floors, a bar around every corner, and various lounges will move the crowds to new spaces as the night gets busier and busier. Maybe it's because while you're dancing on the crowded dance floor among go-go girls and costumed performers on stilts, a little extra room would be desirable. Or maybe it's just because this club is out of this world. This top Ibiza disco is ready to party any night of the week, but you should make sure to check out the "We Love Sundays" parties and top DJ Carl Cox's hard techno beats every Tuesday.

⌖ Take the Discobus from the Ibiza port to Space, or bus #14 during the day to Playa d'en Bossa. Ⓢ Beer €10. Mixed drinks €13-17. ☼ Open M 10pm-6am, Tu 8pm-6am, W 10pm-6am, Th 8pm-6am, F-Sa 10pm-6am, Su 4pm-6am.

◈ EDEN
◆❋♆ CLUB

C. Salvador Espriu, 1   ☎971 340 212 ◲www.edenibiza.com

This is one debauchery-filled garden of Eden that could only have been created by the party gods—you've got massive flatscreens playing the hottest music videos, a giant warehouse-sized space, multiple levels of circular dance floors, and a VIP guest list stacked with some of the world's hottest DJs and celebs. Eden is all about temptation, and the glistening red apples all over the dance floor just remind you of all those things that you're dying to have, from that sexy dance partner across the room to those pricey spirits behind the bar. As major clubs on Ibiza go, every night is something special. For the past decade, Eden has created a name for itself with its "Judgement Sundays" of intense techno, and more recently, the "Wonderland" Fridays with world-class DJ sets that bring in stars like Lady Gaga. That apple's just sitting there—take a bite.

⌖ Take Disco Bus line #1 or #4 to Sant Antoni or take C. Ramon y Cajal to the rotund and follow C. Dr. Fleming. Ⓢ Cover €20-55. Beer €10. Mixed drinks €12. ☼ Open daily midnight-6am.

◈ ES PARADIS
◆❋♥ CLUB

C. Salvador Espriu, 2   ☎971 346 600 ◲www.esparadis.com

The title doesn't lie—you have found Ibiza's party paradise (and we doubt it was

ibiza • nightlife

hard, considering its ad posters absolutely blanket the island). Take one step inside this enormous pyramid of party glory and scope out the multiple levels of circular dancefloors and stages decorated with sparkling discoballs and spiraling vined terraces. The fog and strobe lights will get you lost in the line-up of house and electronic hits, and you'll dance until your feet are sore at Wednesday's "Clubland," whip out that leather for Tuesday's "Ibiza Rocks," bob your head along on the calmer Sunday "Jukebox," and then make use of Es Paradis' signature, deep dancefloor-gone-pool at the Monday and Friday "Fiesta del Agua" (pool fills up at 5am).

✳ *Discobus line #1 or #4 to Sant Antoni or take C. Ramon y Cajal to the rotund and follow C. Dr. Fleming.* ℹ *GLAS (gay, lesbian, and straight) night on Th.* Ⓢ *Cover €30-€45. Beer €6-7. Mixed drinks €11-12. Cocktail €12-13.* ⏲ *Open daily midnight-6am.*

CAFE DEL MAR
♥ ♿ Ψ ⌂ BAR

C. Vara de Rey, 27 ☎971 342 516 ✉www.cafedelmarmusic.com

There seems to be a striking similarity between the vibe in *Aladdin*'s "A Whole New World" and that in Cafe del Mar. This bar makes you feel like you're soaring through the clouds with its pillowed ceiling, white, pink, and blue decor, mellow tunes, and amorphous design. The cafe is a classic that's been around way longer than that street rat and his monkey friend (since 1980 to be exact). Head down on any summer night around sunset, and there's no doubt that you'll find an absolutely packed outdoor patio right on the water. Don't let all this talk of dreams and genies get you sleepy—while Cafe del Mar may be the perfect, laid-back alternative to the Ibiza club scene, it also is one of the island's most popular pre-clubbing spots.

✳ *Sunset Strip. Take Vara de Rey in Sant Antoni down to the water.* Ⓢ *Coffee €4-10. Beer €4.50-7.50. Wine €5.50. Liquors €5-15. Cocktails €10-11.* ⏲ *Open daily 5pm-1am.*

CAFE SAVANNAH
♥ ♿ Ψ ⌂ CAFE, BAR, CLUB

C. Balanzat, 38 ☎971 348 031 ✉www.savannahibiza.com

Coming to Ibiza, your priorities are likely partying, tanning, drinking, and eating—and Savannah can give you everything that you're looking for. This chic cafe-bar-club, right on Sant Antoni's sunset strip, is impossible to miss—from its hot pink drapes to its white globe lamps to its tiled, arching interior and pink bar. You can enjoy the large, beautifully presented portions off their menu, including international hits like Asian woks (€13-14), Spanish Iberian pork (€16), or the multicultural mini-burger combo (€13) with lamb-mint, beef-cheddar, and chicken-curry varieties for you to taste. Once you've filled up and watched the Ibiza sunset on the outdoor patio, the whole mood changes. The DJs' mellow tunes turn into commerical dance beats, and the club in back opens up to get you moving, whether hosting their notoriously popular pre-club parties (W-Sa), or holding their own until the early morning (M-Th, Sa).

✳ *Sunset Strip. Take Vara de Rey in Sant Antoni down to the water.* Ⓢ *Wine €4. Mixed drinks €8. Cocktails €9. Appetizers €8.50-10.50; entrees €13-22. Desserts €6.50-7.50.* ⏲ *Cafe open daily 11am-midnight. Bar open M-Th midnight-6am, Sa midnight-6am.*

SOUL CITY
◉ Ψ ❋ CLUB

C. Santa Agnes, 2 ☎971 340 509 ✉www.digitalibiza.com/soulcity

We're about to have your wallet jumping for joy—it's possible to party like crazy in Ibiza without dropping more on a cover than on your accommodation. Soul City will let you in for free, provide the hottest dance beats for free, and even project movies all over their flat-screen TVs and projection screens without asking for an additional dime. Ibiza's original, exclusive hip-hop and R and B club has DJs spinning songs that are insured to get you moving. Ironically, while this is supposedly a city, it's actually far smaller than many of Ibiza's school-sized discos. Think of it this way: pack the same amount of people into a much smaller space, and you have a steaming, sticky, overflowing dance floor of party animals.

✳ *Take Discobus line #1 or #4 to Sant Antoni and C. Santa Agnes runs down to the port.* ℹ *No cover.* Ⓢ *Beer €3-4. Spirits €5-6. Cocktails €7.* ☪ *Open daily 10pm-6am.*

ESSENTIALS

Practicalities

- **TOURIST OFFICES:** There are **information offices** (▣*www.ibiza.travel)* all around the island, including at the **port** *(C. Antoni Riquer 2* ☎*971 191 195* ☪ *Apr-Oct M-Sa 9:30am-6pm, Su 10am-1pm; Nov-Mar M-F 9:30am-3:30pm, Sa 9:30am-2:30pm.)* Another convenient location is at the **airport** *(*☎*971 809 118* ☪ *Open May-Oct M-F 9am-8pm, Sa 9am-7pm; Nov-Apr M-F 9am-3pm, Sa 8am-1pm).* There are multiple offices in Ibiza City, including at **Vara de Rey** *(Passeig Vara de Rey 1* ☎*971 301 900* ▣*info@ibiza.travel* ☪ *Open Apr-Oct M-Sa 9am-8pm, Su 9am-3pm; Nov-Mar M-F 9am-7pm, Sa 10am-6pm, Su 10am-2pm),* in **Dalt Vila** *(Plaza Catedal s/n* ☎*971 399 232* ☪ *Open June-Sept M-Sa 10am-2pm, 5pm-9pm, Su 10am-2pm; Oct-Mar M-Su 10am-3pm),* and at **Parc de la Pau** *(Avenida d'Isidor Macabich* ☪ *Open Apr-Oct M-Sa 10am-1:30pm, 5pm-8pm, Su 10am-2pm; Nov-Mar M-Sa 10am-2pm).* There are also offices in **Sant Anotoni** *(Passeig de Ses Fonts s/n* ☎*971 343 363* ☪ *Open May-Oct M-F 9:30am-8:30pm, Sa 9am-1pm, Su 9:30am-1:30pm; Oct-Apr M-F 9:30am-2:30pm, Sa 9:30am-1:30pm),* **Santa Eularia des Rui** *(C. Caria Riquer Wallis* ☎*971 330 728* ☪ *Open May-Oct M-F 9:30am-1:30pm, 5pm-7:30pm, Sa 9:30am-1:30pm; Nov-Apr M-F 9am-2pm, Sa 9am-1:30pm),* and beaches **Cala Llonga** *(*☪ *Open May-Oct daily 9:30am-2pm, 3:30pm-8pm)* and **Es Canar** *(*☪ *May-Oct daily 9:30am-2pm and 3:30-8pm).*

- **INTERNET:** You can get **Wi-Fi** access at the **public library** in the Espacio Cultural Can Ventosa *(C. Ignasio Wallis, 26* ☪ *Open M-F 8am-3pm; in summer Tu 8am-3pm),* or at **Telecentro** internet cafe *(Carrer de Castilla, 10* ☎*971 394 269* ☪ *daily 10am-11:30pm)* that offers internet for €1 per hour and printing and copying for €.20 per page.

- **LAUNDROMATS:** You can do your laundry at **Wash and Dry Ibiza** *(Avenida de Espana, 53* ☎*971 394 822),* which also has ironing services and internet access.

- **POST OFFICE:** The central **Post Office** of Ibiza City *(Avenida Isodor Macabich 67* ☎*971 399 769* ☪ *Open M-F 8:30am-8:30pm, Sa 9:30am-2pm)* also has an ATM, photocopy and fax services, and an Ebay desk.

Emergency!

- **EMERGENCY NUMBER:** ☎112.

- **POLICE: National** (☎091; 971 398 831). **Local** (☎092; 971 315 861 for Ibiza).

- **HOSPITALS: Can Misses** (☎971 397 000). **Red Cross Ibiza** (☎971 390 303).

- **LATE-NIGHT PHARMACIES: Pharmacies** around each city rotate being open 24hr. You can visit any pharmacy during the day, and they can give you the schedule of which pharmacies are next in line to stay open. Within Ibiza City, there are pharmacies all over, including at **Parque de la Pau,** at **Paseo Vara de Rey,** along **Avenida Espanya,** and three near the border of **D'alt Vila.**

Getting There

By Plane

The **Ibiza Airport**, Sant Jordi *(*☎*971 809 900),* is located 7km from Ibiza City and 5km from Sant Jordi. Over 50 airlines connect through the airport. There is also Wi-Fi access throughout the airport. From the airport, city bus line **#9** *(*Ⓢ *€3.20* ☪ *June and Sept only every 1hr. 30min., 7am-11:30pm)* runs to Sant Antoni, and **#10** *(*Ⓢ *€3.20* ☪ *Apr-Oct 6am-12am, every 20min., Nov-Mar 7am-11:30pm, every 30min)* and **#10B** *(*Ⓢ *€3.20* ☪ *July-Aug 12:30am-5:30am, every hour)* run to the Ibiza City. **Radiotaxi** *(*☎*971 800 080)* can take you by cab for €.90/km during the day and €1.10 over night, plus a €1.50 airport supplement

ibiza • essentials

fee. Cabs from the airport to Sant Antoni are generally €25-€30, and €15-€20 to Ibiza City. The Aena website (💻*www.aena.es*) and Amadeus website (💻*www.amadeus.net*) are particularly helpful in consolidating information from all the major airlines. As many of the flights are short and run very consistently, prices vary immensely depending on how far in advance you book, and the day of the week and time of day of the flight.

By Ferry

You can arrive via boat to Ibiza from the Spanish mainland or between other islands in the Mediterranean. **Acciona-Trasmediterranea** can take you from **Barcelona** (🕐 *8hr., Su-T, Th-Sa 1 per day at varying times froms 9:30am-10:30pm)*, **Valencia** (🕐 *4hr. 20min., F-Sa 5pm)*, and **Mallorca** (🕐 *3hr. 45min., M, F, Su 7pm)*. **Baleària Eurolínies Marítimes** can also take you from **Barcelona** (🕐 *8hr., M, W 10:30pm, F 10:30pm, 11pm, Su 11pm* 💲*€62.40)*, **Valencia** (🕐 *3-5hr., M, W 4:30pm, Tu, Sa 9pm, F, Su 4:30pm, 9pm* 💲 *€78)*, and **Mallorca** (🕐 *2-3hr., M-Sa 8am and 10am, Su 8am and 9am* 💲*€52.20-65.40)*, but also offers travel from **Fromentera** (🕐 *M-F 12 per day 7:30am-9pm, Sa-Su 17 per day 7:30am-9pm* 💲 *€23)*.

Getting Around

By Bus

Izabus is the main bus company for the city, running 34 lines to all different parts of the island. Lines **#9** (💲 *€3.20.*🕐 *June and Sept only every 1hr. 30min., 7am-11:30pm)*, **#10** (💲 *€3.20.* 🕐 *Apr-Oct every 20min., 6am-12am; Nov-Mar every 30min., 7am-11:30pm)*, and **#10B** (💲 *€3.20.* 🕐 *July-Aug every hr., 12:30am-5:30am)* run to the airport from Sant Antoni and Ibza City, respectively. Line **#0** (🕐 *Sept-June M-Sa every 15min., 7:30am-9am, 1:30pm-3:30pm, 7pm-8:30pm; July-Aug last leg runs until 2am)* circles the Ibiza City and **#3** (🕐 *June-Oct 15 every 30min., 7am-11:30pm; Oct 15-May every 30min., 7am-10:30pm)* runs between Ibiza and Sant Antoni. Fares and line schedules vary, but generally range between €1 and €2.50. The main **bus stop** in Ibiza City is located on Avenida d'Isidor Macabich, near the Pac de la Pau. As far as nightlife travel goes, the summer **Discobus** (☎*971 313 447* 💻*www.discobus.es)* runs 4 lines that stop at Ibiza's major clubs, including **Space, Pacha, Amnesia,** and **Privelege,** from approximately 12am-6:30am (💲 *€3)*.

By Taxi

There are also multiple **taxi companies** on the island, including Radio Taxi Ibiza (Ibiza City ☎971 398 483) and Radio Taxi Sant Antoni (☎*971 343 764)*. There are taxi points in Ibiza City along the **port,** near **Parque de la Pau,** off **Calle Galicia,** and off **Avenida Bartomeu Rossello.** You can rent a **motor scooter** (💲 *€38-€65 per day.)* or **bike** (💲 *€6-€10 per day)* from **Extra Rent A Car** in Ibiza City (*Avenida Santa Eulalia s/n* ☎*971 190 160* 💻*www. extrarent.com)*. **Top Moto** also rents scooters. (☎*971 344 266* 💲 *€24-29 per day.)*

sevilla   ☎95

ORIENTATION

Sevilla can be divided into a few loosely separated neighborhoods. While the areas of **Arenal** and **Santa Cruz** are decently designated and the canal provides a fairly obvious dividing line into Triana, knowing at which point you step into **El Centro** or **La Macarena** depends upon who you ask. Some locals will swear that a site is a devout member of El Centro, and others may describe the same area as being "nearby Plaza de Armas." Some friends from across the canal may strongly hold that they are Trianans, rather than Sevillaños. Most generally, the **Alcazar** and **Catedral** are the biggest historical landmarks in Santa Cruz, the **Alameda de Hercules** denotes La Macarena, and the dominant shopping trio of **Calle Sierpes, Calle Cuna,** and **Calle Velazquez Tetuan** hold strong in El Centro.

    The divisions aren't merely geographic—you'll quickly dub Santa Cruz as tourist-filled, El Centro as commercial, La Macarena as a mix of religious and reckless, and Triana as slow-paced and mellow. No matter what personality you prefer, you'll fit in anywhere in this welcoming capital city.

Santa Cruz

Santa Cruz can be divided into two main hubs: the transportation center and the cultural center. The **Prado de San Sebastian** is home to the main bus station and a metro stop, so you're likely to arrive at this large park when you first enter the area. The Prado is adjacent to the university and only a stone's throw away from the **Cathedral** and **Alcazar**, the main cultural centers of Santa Cruz. Surrounded by an array of small and slightly confusing streets inaccessible to any vehicle wider than a Vespa, this area definitely requires a map. Keep in mind that Santa Cruz is only a very small neighborhood of Sevilla, so you can walk across it, from the Cathedral to the **Plaza de Espana**, in under 20min. (assuming you're the fit traveler we know you are).

El Centro

El Centro (literally, "the center" for you stubborn anglophones) is the largest neighborhood in Sevilla and can be ambiguously designated as all areas that are not part of Santa Cruz, Triana, El Arenal, or Macarena. The heart of El Centro is the **Plaza de la Encarnación.** As El Centro happens to be the commercial focus of Sevilla, the three shopping streets of **Calle Cuna, Calle Sierpes**, and **Calle Velazquez Tetuan** are valuable landmarks to know when traversing this window-shopping haven. **Plaza Alfalfa** is the core of the local social scene, packed with bars and outdoor patios. A southern boundary for this neighborhood is the **Estación de Autobuses Plaza de Armas,** located along the canal, where you can find buses to neighboring province Cádiz.

La Macarena

The biggest landmarks to keep in mind for getting around La Macarena are the **Alameda de Hercules**, a center for eating, clubbing, and getting a drink, and **C. Feria**, a street lined with smaller shops and restaurants along with the occasional local bar. **C. Torneo** and **C. Resolana** border La Macarena and are major streets for bus routes and transport, and Torneo has quite a few hot clubs in its repitoire. Otherwise, the slew of convents and churches splashed all over La Macarena are useful landmarks for a personal pilgrimage to this area.

El Arenal and Triana

Sandwiching the canal between the **Puente de San Telmo** and **Puente de Triana** lie these two neighborhoods of Sevilla. On the northern side of the canal, El Arenal's main street is **Paseo de Cristobal Colon** along the canal, and its main center is the **Plaza de Armas,** located at the base of the Puente de Triana. Once making your way to the "other side of the tracks," per se, you'll find the neighborhood of Triana. While the main streets, **Avenida de la Republica Argentina** and **Calle San Jacinto** will be useful landmarks, the layout of Triana is generally much less confusing compared to the rest of Sevilla. **Calle Betis** along the water is home to some of the nicest seafood restaurants and best bars and clubs in Sevilla. **Calle de Salado** is another useful spot to check out, as it is lined with inexpensive, multi-cultural restaurants.

ACCOMMODATIONS

Santa Cruz

Santa Cruz is the most touristed region of Sevilla. The accommodations definitely reflect this fact, so you have tons of options when choosing where to stay. Because of this hostel-on-hostel competition, the hostels here are some of the best-priced and most conveniently located in Spain.

SAMAY SEVILLA HOSTAL

♦•((•))❊ HOSTAL ❶

Menendez Pelayo, 13   ☎955 215 668 ▥www.samayhostals.com

Probably one of the nicest hostels in the Santa Cruz region, Samay provides all the essentials at great rates. Upon entering the hostel, you'll be welcomed by an English-speaking staff member (or three) ready to help you to your room. While the patterned walls and loud furniture in the first-floor lobby are a little too retro for comfort, these minor decorative issues are worth overlooking. The rooms are comfortable and clean with ensuite bathrooms. They also offer an almost overwhelming slew of entertainment, including free walking tours, tapas tours, and flamenco and discoteca nights. Feel the comfort of Samay by relaxing on the top-floor terrace or making breakfast in the open kitchen. While the maximum stay is officially one week, some travelers report that if you flash a smile at the guy at the desk, he'll let you stay longer.

➜ 7min. from Prado de San Sebastian, on the left-hand side of the street if leaving the Prado. ℹ Lockers and towels included. $ 8-person dorm €15; 6-person €18; 4-person €20. ⏰ Reception 24hr.

HOSTAL FLORIDA 💳❄ HOSTAL ❹

Menendez Pelayo, 27 ☎954 422 557 💻www.hostalfloridasevilla.com

Although it has hostel in it's name, Hostal Florida would be much better described as a cheap hotel. While private rooms, TVs, and no bunk beds at all sound great on paper, the cramped bedrooms and total lack of common space eliminate the social feel of a backpackers' hostel. Such a sentiment is reflected in the staff as well: though friendly, they lack the energy and warmth seen at other local hostels. If you'd rather watch Spanish reruns on TV than imbibe in a pitcher of sangria with fellow travelers coming through Santa Cruz, then maybe this spot is for you.

➜ Located about a 10min. walk from Prado de San Sebastian, on the left-hand side of the street if leaving the Prado. ℹ Ensuite safes and bathrooms. $ Doubles and triples €45.

PICASSO BACKPACKER 💳📶❄ HOSTEL ❶

San Gregario, 1 ☎954 210 864 💻www.piramide.com

This smaller, inexpensive hostel is hidden in a small courtyard only meters from the Peurta de Jerez fountain and minutes from the Cathedral and Alcazar. It maintains an authentic Spanish feel with colorful Moorish-style tiles and greenery in the entryway but caters to foreign travelers. The older woman at the desk is extremely friendly and speaks clear English. The rooms are equipped with clean sheets, and the large windows and small balconies do wonders for the aesthetically minded. While Picasso "usually" offers Wi-Fi, some visitors complain that the service was shut down during their stay, without any specific date of return. Despite such complications, if you're looking for convenience, the location is hard to beat.

➜ If following the gaze of the statue at Puerta de Jerez, follow a small block and make a sharp right. The hostel is located in a small courtyard. ℹ Complimentary tea and coffee. Female-only housing available. $ 6-person dorms €10.50; doubles €44; triples €39; quads €33.

El Centro

👍 OASIS BACKPACKERS' HOSTEL 💳❄📶🍸 HOSTEL❷

Plaza de la Encarnacion 29 1-2. ☎954 293 777 💻www.hostelsoasis.com

If there was a competition to think of every possible accommodation a backpacker would request, Oasis could defeat even the neediest of travelers. From a roof-top pool (more of a pond, but in the Sevillian heat, any body of water is appreciated) to an in-hostel happy hour (2 beers, wines, sangrias, or shots for €2) to bike rentals and Spanish lessons, Oasis has it all. The rooms are the biggest seen in Sevilla with tons of additional shelving and space for those of you who are still working out the kinks of "light packing." The location also can't be beat: the Plaza de la Encarnacion is the center of El Centro, and Oasis is smack in the Plaza. While the hostel has three buildings of housing, try to get a room in the building with the reception because it houses the pool and the kitchen where breakfast is served.

➜ At the corner of Plaza de la Encarnacion. If looking at the more visible #29, turning right into the alley and the entrance is on the left-hand side where the alley curves. ℹ Pool, breakfast included 8am-11am daily. $ All rooms (4, 6, or 8-person) €20. ⏰ Reception 24hr.

HOSTEL NUEVO SUIZO 💳📶 HOSTEL❷

C. Azofaifo 7 ☎954 229 147 💻www.nuevosuizo.com

Located right off the main shopping streets of El Centro, Hostel Nuevo Suizo puts in a full effort to provide a classy establishment, from the skylight and stone columns in the entryway to the flowers resting on the pillows of each bed. By providing free breakfast, free Wi-Fi, a phone for free international calling, a terrace, and all the coffee and tea you can drink until you wet your pants or OD on caffeine (whichever comes first), this hostel brings the goods. But be mindful that Nuevo Suizo is a bit pricier than other local hostels, and they find ways to sneak the prices up a bit higher. While private suites range from €27-€31, even the public suites are €23-€25 for 2-3 people and €17 for 9 people. Keep in mind that the higher the floor, the higher the price because, as the girl at the desk explains, "you get the bonus of extra quiet."

In a small alley off C. las Sierpes right by C. Vargas Campos. $ *Private rooms €27-31. Public suites 2-3 people €23-€25, 9 people €17.* ⏰ *Reception 24hr.*

El Arenal and Triana

TRIANA BACKPACKERS — HOSTEL ❷

C. Rodrigo de Triana 69 ☎954 459 960 www.trianabackpackers.com

This peaceful, traditional looking hostel takes on the true Triana spirit—from the hammocks and jacuzzi on the terrace to the board games and couches in the lounge to the Spanish radio playing through the halls, it's the perfect place for a relaxing stay. You won't find the same hustle and bustle of other backpacker's hostels but rather a safe, pristinely-clean abode to just chill out. If you want to enjoy a walk, you're located just meters from the canal, or you could choose to just turn on the reading lamp at your bunk and lounge all evening. Mellow by no means implies boring—sign up for a 1.5h *(€5)* or 2.5h *(€6)* bike excursion to Cartuja or Italica, or head out for a free Flamenco show with your new hostel friends. The go-with-the-flow style has one drawback: the receptionists are sometimes missing from the desks and take their time coming back. But remember, patience is a virtue.

From Puente de Triana, take C. de San Jacinto and make a left onto Rodrigo de Triana; the hostel is on the left side of the street. i *Breakfast included. Female-only suites available.* $ *10-bed dorms €15-18; 6-bed dorms €16-19; 4-bed dorms €17-20. Doubles €50.* ⏰ *Reception 24hr.*

LA POSADA DE TRIANA S.L. — PENSIÓN ❹

C. Pages del Corro 53 ☎954 332 100 www.laposadadetriana.com

Within a recently-renovated 19th century building lies a small, welcoming hotel, La Posada de Triana. The friendly older woman at the desk will use her best English to greet you with a smile, and then lead you to your small, but colorfully decorated room equipped with artwork, closet space, a (very) compact bathroom, and your own fan. There aren't any bells and whistles, like breakfast or organized social events—just a simple place to sleep with a great location. You are going to be paying a heavier bill *(€23-30 per person)*, but at least there aren't any ridiculous charges for towels, sheets, credit card use, running water, or a hug (you know how some backpackers' hostels can get).

From Puente de Triana, take C. de San Jacinto, and make a right onto C. de Pages del Corro; the pensión is on the right side of the street. i *TV available.* $ *Singles €45; doubles €60; triples €70.* ⏰ *Reception 24hr.*

Outside the Center

CAMPING VILLSOM — CAMPSITE ❶

Madrid-Cadiz N-IV, exit 555 ☎954 720 828

If you're planning to visit Sevilla by trailor or tent, Camping Villsom is the closest campground to Sevilla. Equipped with clean bathrooms, a large pool, a TV room, and even ping-pong and mini-golf, you definitely won't get bored in the social, outdoor facility. The mini-mart and cafeteria can keep you fed with breakfast for only €2.40 and drinks for €1.20-€3.90. Only 25 minutes from Prado de San Sebastian, this is one way to find your natural roots and hone in on those lost Boy Scout skills.

➡ Take Bus 132 from Avenida de Portugal (25min, €1.35), M-F 7:15am-11:45pm every half hour; Sa-Su 7:45am-9:45pm 8 per day. ℹ Pool. Pets allowed. Mail service. $ €4.80 per person, €4.82 for spot, €5.05 per car, €5.24 for trailor. Minimum €15.60 per person. 🕐 24-hour security. Open year round.

ALBERGUE INTURJOVEN SEVILLA (HI) 🍴❄📶 HOSTEL [2]

C. Isaac Peral 2 ☎955 035 886 💻www.inturjoven.com

Located just 7 or 8 minutes from the Prado, Inturjoven provides open, modern, large spaces for a generally under-25 crowd. The large patios, snack rooms, all-you-can-eat buffet meals, and TV rooms makes this the perfect option for the high school or college-aged backpacker just looking to chill out and maybe open up a deck of cards at their hostel. The rooms are large and clean, although completely undecorated, and provide ample closet space. Price doesn't vary based on whether rooms have balconies or ensuite bathrooms, so do your best to score one of the nicer rooms.

➡ Take Bus 34 from C. del Cid to Isaac Peral Stop (about 7-8min, €1.20). ℹ Breakfast included. All other meals €8 buffet. Wifi €1 per hr, €6 per day. Laundry: €2.50 wash, €2 dry $ 25 years old and younger €22.50; 26 and older €28.50. €3.50 discount with HI card. 🕐 Reception 24hr.

SIGHTS 👁

With a history of violent battle, valient conquest, and devout relgion, Sevilla is bound to have quite a few sights worth seeing. Whether preserved or honored, the historic places all around this capital city are worth your time and energy. Even with this rich history, you'll find spicy hotspots for an evening out and perfect places to lounge.

Santa Cruz

Santa Cruz is the most historic portion of Sevilla, and it's got some sights to show for it. Join the other swarms of tourists checking out the most famous buildings, gardens, and establishments to take in all the Sevillian history.

✪ PLAZA DE ESPAÑA HISTORIC SITE, MONUMENT

Avda. Isabel la Católica

Constructed for the Iberian Exposition of 1929, you'd be shocked to see how well modern architecture can mock traditional Moorish style. Being a bit anachronistic is a common theme for the Plaza de España—George Lucas even filmed part of *Star Wars: Return of the Clones* on the bridges of the site. The Plaza was built as an apology to the nations of the world who had fallen to the violence of Spanish colonialism and takes on this request for forgiveness in full force—the plaza itself is constructed in the shape of a heart. The details of the Plaza are the perfect Spanish history study guide: the seating surrounding the main area is decorated with colorful, hand-made tiles, with each booth honoring one of the principal cities of Spain. All major Spanish leaders are preserved in statue form, so don't worry, you won't forget anyone important next Double Jeopardy round.

➡ Directly across Avenida de Portugal from the Prado of San Sebastian. $ Free. 🕐 Open daily 7am-11pm.

LA CATEDRAL CHURCH

Entrance by Pl. de la Virgen de los Reyes ☎954 214 971

This isn't just any old church. The Cathedral happens to be the world's largest Gothic building and the third-largest church, holding these literally huge distinctions with pride. The city restricts any construction project from exceeding 100m to ensure that the Jiralda Tower of the Cathedral remains the highest point in Sevilla. The church itself has a rich history of the Sevillian shift from Moorish to Catholic control. The tall, thin Jiralda Tower was mysteriously the only portion of the Islamic mosque to survive an earthquake in 1365. The stained-glass windows and gold-plated religious scenes lining the interior are worth checking out, as they have a Moorish-Catholic flare that traditional Renaissance churches lack. Watch out for the ambush of "religious" palm readers at the exit: they'll grab you, tell you how many kids you're bound to have, and then guilt you into tipping.

Located off Avenida de la Constitucion next to the Alcazar. $ €7.50, students €2. ⏰ Open July-Aug M-Sa 11am-5pm, Su 9:30am-4pm; Sept-June M-Sa 11am-5pm, Su 2:30pm-6pm.

THE ALCAZAR HISTORIC SIGHT, FORTRESS

Patio de Bandera ☎954 502 323 💻direccion@patronato-alcazarsevilla.es

Don't stress about getting your black tie back from the dry cleaners before visiting the Alcazar. While it does double as the summer palace for Spanish royalty, it also makes a great casual stop on any visit to Santa Cruz. After the Romans originally constructed the walls to protect the city, the Moors then expanded them into an all-out fortress to protect against enemy advances on Sevilla. Once the Catholics took over, they converted the fortress into a palace, somehow overcoming the irony of being peace-loving Christian monarchs residing in a Muslim establishment. Rich with honorary sites for icons such as Dona Maria de Padilla, the woman who threw boiling oil in her face to stop King Frederic from making moves on her (you'd think she would've just stopped showering), the Alacazar has a new story around every corner. The orange trees lining the outdoor plazas provide a picture-perfect splash of color.

Located off the back corner of La Catedral, off Plaza de Triunfo. $ €7.50, students free. ⏰ Open April-Sept M-Sa 9:30am-7pm; Oct-Mar daily 9:30am-5pm.

UNIVERSIDAD DE SEVILLA UNIVERSITY

C. San Fernando, 4 ☎954 551 000 💻http://www.us.es/

If every college in the world looked like this, we'd probably have far more productive youth. The *Universidad de Sevilla* is the second-largest building in all of Spain and uses every square inch to saturate you with impressive and breathtaking architecture. While the library and computers are only available to students and university personnel, the open stone courtyards lined with statues of religious and historic Spanish figures are the perfect place for some reading, writing, or a siesta. If you think you're too cool for school, consider that this university has quite the rebellious history. Originally built as a tobacco factory, the establishment once employed the "deadly sexy" Carmen, namesake of the traditional Sevillian song. And if you're interested in picking up some knowledge while spending time in Sevilla, the university provides a wide array of extension classes.

Down the block from Prado de San Sebastian. 3min. walk from Estacion de Prado. $ Free. ⏰ M-Sa 7am-9:45pm.

El Centro

MUSEO DEL BAILE FLAMENCO MUSEUM

Manuel Rojas Marcos 3 ☎954 340 311 💻www.museoflamenco.com

This museum is the one-stop shop for all things flamenco. Walking through the halls of this high-tech, automated museum, you'll be bombarded by movies, photography, and artifacts explaining the rich history of flamenco in Sevilla. Be sure to check out the dress worn during the opening ceremonies of the 1992 Barcelona Olympics for a piece of hip-shaking history. After you're done with the techy side of this museum's entertainment, look at the 300-year-old, underground Moorish gallery that holds classic flamenco photographs. The museum offers live flamenco performances in the evenings, and, if you're not too shy, try your hand at some dancing with the professionals and get your groove on, Sevillian style. The performers from the evening shows teach a quick, 20 minute class open to the public at 7:30pm M-Th.

From the Catedral, take C. Argote de Molina, turn left onto C. Estrella, and then turn left onto Manuel Rojas Marcos; the museum will be on the right. ℹ Exhibits in English and Spanish. $ €10, students €8. Flamenco performances M-Th €15, students €12; F-Sa €23/20. Flamenco classes €10. ⏰ Museum open daily 9:30am-7pm. Flamenco performances M-Th 7pm, F-Sa 7:30pm. Flamenco classes M-Th 6:30pm.

MUSEO DE BELLAS ARTES   MUSEUM

Plaza del Museo 9   ☎954 786 500 🖳www.museodeandalucia.es

The most user-friendly museum you'll ever encounter, the Museo de Bellas Artes is organized in such a way that you walk from room to room through a chronological journey of the history of Sevillian and Spanish art. Starting in the medieval period and progressing to the 20th century, the museum even devotes entire rooms to its favorite artists, including Murillo, Valdés Leal, and Zurbarán. The courtyards are also definitely worth exploring.

⚐ *At intersection of C. Alfonso XII and C. San Vicente.* *i* *Lockers available €1. Exhibitions rotated throughout the year.* Ⓢ *€1.50, free with EU passport.* ⚇ *Open Tu-Sa 9am-8:30pm, Su 9am-2:30pm.*

La Macarena

On paper, La Macarena may look like church upon church (with maybe a convent or basilica thrown in for variety), and that's just what you'll find. That's not to say that the religious history found in La Macarena is not unique at each of its sights. With some exploration, you'll come away with a much better understanding of **Semana Santa** and **Feria de Abril,** two of Sevilla's most important festivals.

BASÍLICA DE SAN LORENZO Y JESUS DE GRAN PODER   CHURCH

Plaza de San Lorenzo, 13   ☎954 915 686 🖳www.gran-poder.es

This church combo is one of the most ornate and impressive around. When facing the duo, the Basílica de San Lorenzo is on the left and is filled with golden artwork, glistening altars, and wall-covering frescos. The Basílica de Jesus de Gran Poder sticks to its name—it's one powerful place. Even the entirely marble, circular main room pales in comparison to the massive altar in the center. The tall golden statue of Jesus adorned with purple robes and carrying the cross is the main sight of this basilica. People from all over line up to pass behind the statue, showing reverence by kissing the ankle and saying a quick prayer—just make sure not to leave any lipstick stains!

⚐ *From Alameda, take C. Santa Ana and turn left onto C. Santa Clara; the Plaza and churches are on the right.* Ⓢ *Free.* ⚇ *Basilica open M-Th 8am-1:30pm and 6-9pm, F 7:30am-10pm, Sa-Su 8am-2pm and 6-9pm. Mass M-Th 9:30am, 10:30am, 12:30pm, 6:30pm, 7:30pm, 8:30pm; Sa 9:30am, 10:30am, 1:15pm, 7:30pm, 8:30pm; Su 9:30am, 11am, 12:30pm, 1:30pm, 7:30pm, 8:30pm.*

BASÍLICA LA MACARENA AND HEMANDAD DE LA MACARENA MUSEUM   CHURCH

C. Becker 1, 3   ☎954 901 800 🖳www.hermandaddelamacarena.es

Upon walking into the Basílica La Macarena, you will be immediately impressed by the highly ornate altars and stunning artwork decorating the ceiling. But let's be honest—if you've been traveling through La Macarena, you've seen a bunch of awe-inspiring churches at this point. What makes this one special is the history connected to this namesake of the neighborhood. Upon visiting the museum attached to the basilica, you'll learn all about the history of the **Semana Santa** (holy week) festivities in Sevilla. You'll hear tales of the **Hermandad,** or religious brotherhood, that has now become a main icon of this holy week. Perfectly preserved documents, books, tapestries, and ancient flags are great eye candy as you walk the museum halls. The massive, decorated floats once used during Semana Santa nearly 100 years ago will leave you with an appreciation for the magnitude and significance of the historic festival. You can also browse the crystal rosaries and bracelets being sold in the museum shop by the entrance.

⚐ *At the intersection of C. San Louis and C. Resolana; the entrance is on C. Resolana.* Ⓢ *Museum €5, under 16 €3. Basilica free.* ⚇ *Basilica open M-Sa 9am-2pm and 5-9pm, Su 9am-2pm and 5-9:30pm. Museum open daily 9am-1:30pm and 5-8:30pm. Mass M-F 9am, 11:30am, 8pm, 8:30pm; Sa 9am, 8pm; Su 10:15am, 12:15pm, 8pm.*

spain

CONVENTO SANTA PAULA MUSEUM, RELIGIOUS SITE

C. Santa Paula, 11 ☎954 536 330 💻www.santapaula.es

While you may feel like you're sneaking into the land of Oz when ringing the doorbell at the tiny, brown door toward the right corner of the convent, you'll soon be greeted by a slew of nuns and all feelings of rebellion will probably vanish (along with that dream of a scarecrow, tin man, and lion at your side). You can visit the small convent museum *(€3)* and browse the collection of artifacts stored in this 15th-century establishment. While none of the items are labeled, your own private nun will guide you through the three museum rooms, pointing out her favorite parts. She may have even helped to make the marmalade sold on the bottom floor. Pick up a bottle of any flavor you can imagine (what does an orange blossom even taste like?) *(small €3, large €4.35).*

⇄ Located near C. Siete Dolores, neighboring Plaza Santa Isabel and Iglesia San Marcos. $ Tour €3. Marmelade small €3, large €4.35. ⏰ Museum open T-Su 10am-1pm. Shop open T-Su 10am-1:30pm, 4:30-7pm.

El Arenal and Triana

👍 **PLAZA DE TOROS DE MAESTRANZA** ⊘♿ MONUMENT

Paseo de Cristóbal Colón, 12 ☎954 210 315 💻www.realmaestranza.com

Constructed between 1761 and 1881, Plaza de Toros de Maestranza is one of the oldest bullfighting rings in the world. The Maestranza offers a tours of the ring, stables, and museum (conducted in both English and Spanish) that will leave you feeling like a true master of the almost 300 years of bullfighting history. You can walk in right before the tours, conducted every 20min., and get in without a problem. The bullfights themselves, occurring on about 40 Sundays between April and October, are a true taste of Sevilla's culture. Aside from during the *Feria de Abril,* when the best matadors are in town, you're fine grabbing a ticket the day before or even hours before the fight.

⇄ Off Paseo de Cristóbal Colón between Plaza de Armas and Torre de Oro. $ Tours €6, students €4. Bullfights €25-150 depending on seat. ⏰ Museum open daily May-Oct 9:30am-8pm; Nov-Apr 9:30am-7pm. 40min. tours run every 20min. Bullfights select Su Apr-Oct 7pm, 7:30pm.

TORRE DE ORO 🎫♿ MUSEUM, VIEWS

Paseo de Cristóbal Colón s/n, near the intersection with Almirante Lobo ☎954 222 419

While it may no longer be filled with gold (sorry to burst your bubble), the Torre de Oro is still worth a visit. The now-maritime-museum can be covered in a maximum of 20min., at no cost with a student ID. But even if you come for some history, you'll stay for the views. Climb the spiraling marble steps to the top of the tour (yes, you should go all the way to the top) and you'll be able to see all of Triana to one side of the canal as well as great views of the Cathedral and Alcazar if looking toward Santa Cruz.

⇄ On the canal side of the street at the intersection of Cristóbal Colón and Almirante Lobo. i Cameras permitted. $ €2, students free. Automated tour free upon request. ⏰ Open Tu-F 9:30am-1:30pm, Sa-Su 10:30am-1:30pm.

Near Estación Plaza de Armas

👍 **CENTRO ANDALUZ DE ARTE CONTEMPORÁNEO MUSEUM** ⊘ MUSEUM

Avenida Américo Vespucio 2 ☎955 037 070 💻www.caac.es

Embedded into the grounds of **Monasterio de la Cartuja de Santa Maria de las Cuevas** lies this oasis of modern Sevillian art. And that's quite a pairing to have—the classic, Moorish-style monastery grounds provide a harsh contrast with the bright white walls and mutli-media art collection found in the hallways of the museum. From movies, to slideshows, to music, and even interactive pieces, you'll find some of the most creative, colorful, and shocking artwork on the Sevillian scene. Make an afternoon of the treck across the river and spend some time lunching in the monastery gardens after a bit of cultural exposure at the museum.

⚡About a 10 minute walk west from Estacion Plaza de Armas and then cross Puente de la Cartuja and make a right after crossing the bridge. *i* Tours available but must reserve a spot ☎955 037 096, educ.caac@juntdeandalucia.es. ⑤Museum admission €1.80, free on Tuesdays. ⏲Apr-Sept Tu-Fr 10am-9pm, Sa 11am-9pm, Su 10am-3pm. Tours Su 12:30pm.

THE GREAT OUTDOORS

PARQUE DOÑANA

Las Carretas, 10

● PARK

☎630 978 216 🖳www.donana-nature.com

One of the largest national parks in all of Europe, Parque Doñana provides you with a good dose of nature and a strong urge to purchase a pair of binoculars and the complete set of an *Indiana Jones* movie. The excursions led out of **El Rocío** can be described as "safari-lite"—bouncing around in the back of a 4x4, try to hold your camera steady enough to catch a photo or two (or 200). The park itself is bordered by three cities that proudly share rights to its territory (**Huelva**, **Cadiz**, and **Sevilla**) and is composed of three main ecosystems: **forest, marshland,** and **beach.** Such a variety of untouched natural conditions provides for the exciting diversity of flora and fauna found in the park. While the friendly tour guides will provide a disclaimer that they can't promise you'll see any animals (it's a national park, not a zoo), we'd be shocked if you went through a whole visit without getting sight of something with a heartbeat. There are eagles, horses, and red deer to name a few. And don't forget the swarms of pink flamingos (did you know they get their color from a shrimp-only diet? You'd know if you took the tour!). Doñana also offers free entrance for unguided hiking routes throughout the park, but we think the excursion services are worth the extra price—from diagrams to maps, your guide will have the knowledge to make sure you don't miss an inch of Parque Doñana. However, don't think it's all about nature—you'll hear myths and stories about of the park, too. Don't the tomb of **Duchess Doña Ana** and the park's 13th-century identity as a **hunting ground** pique your interest?

⚡From Estación Plaza de Armas, take a 1½hr. bus to Matalascañas (€6.61), and then take a 20min. bus to El Rocío/El Almonte (€1.17) and get off at the El Rocío stop. The visitor center for excursions to the park is to the left of the main church at El Rocío. *i* Tours led in Spanish. ⑤ Excursion through the park via van and bus €25 per schedule. ⏲ Excursions daily 8:30am and 5:30pm; 3-3½ hr. long.

FOOD

Santa Cruz

HORNO DE SAN BUENAVENTURA

28 Carlos Canal

🍴♿🅿☕ TRADITIONAL, CAFE ❷

☎954 221 829

Perfect for those exhausted by a day of travel in the Sevillian sun. Horno is located a hop, skip, and a jump (assuming all three of these are conducted with extensive force) away from the Cathedral and serves up a variety of perfect "cool down" foods at low prices. Utilize the overwhelming smell of the fresh bakery portion of the restaurant to help you ignore the line of pigs' legs hanging over the bar. The gazpacho *(€4.50)* is served chilled, with three large ice cubes floating atop this traditional tomato treat. If you're looking to further relieve the downpour of sweat streaming from your brow, try the wide selection of gelatos—the classic Málaga flavor of the region (actually rum-raisin) is the perfect sweet treat to end any meal. A historic relic originally established in 1385, Horno has had 5 different names and many more years of practice perfecting a wide selection of inexpensive dishes.

⚡ Located directly across Avenida de Constitución from the Cathedral, *i* Outdoor table, and bar seating available. ⑤ Tapas €2.25-€4.50. Sandwiches €3.50-€8.50. Ice cream €1.10. ⏲ Open daily 7:30am-11pm.

spain

TABERNA COLONIALES 🍴🍸❄ TRADITIONAL, TAPAS ❷

Plaza Cristo de Burgos, 19 ☎954 501 137 💻info@tabernacoloniales.es

The biggest complaint to make about Taberna Coloniales is that it's just too busy for its own good, but lucky for you they've expanded to two locations to ease the congestion. Even for lunch there's a chance that you'll need to wait for a table, but it's worth it. While most dishes—aside from the more expensive country bread platters or *tablas (€5.05-10.75)*—don't expect some tiny tapa to come out of the kitchen. Each helping is like a tapa on steroids, filling a whole face-sized plate. The *pollo con salsa de almendras (€2.50)* and the daily specials are both worth a try. Keep in mind that these waiters are pretty savvy: while they put bread on the table, it isn't free *(€1.70)*. If you're not going to eat it, ask them to take it away.

✈ Located across Avenida de Constitución from the Cathedral down Plaza Cristo de Burgos. $ Plates €1.55-€3.55. Tablas €5.05-10.75 ⏰ Open daily 1:30-4:30pm and 8:30pm-12:15am.

El Centro

✔ CONFITERIA LA CAMPAÑA 🍴☁ BAKERY ❶

C. Sierpes, 1-3 ☎954 223 570

If you've got a sweet tooth, we've found your kryptonite. La Campaña has been serving up desserts since 1885 and has definitely mastered the task. The staff, dressed in parlor-esque aprons with headbands for the women and striped vests and bowties for the men, welcomes you and indulges your cravings. Served since the restaurant's opening, the *cervantinas* and *ingleses* are classics you've got to try. The *ingleses (€2.20)*, their most popular dessert, provides a sweet flan-like flavor without the gooey texture. Not feeling so adventurous? La Campaña also sells meringues, éclairs, truffles, cakes, and tarts *(€1.80-2.20)*. If you're looking for a real meal (although we can't imagine why you'd turn down a couple different courses of dessert), La Campaña also serves some fancier savory items such as smoked salmon and fresh cheese sandwiches—in short, you're gonna want to use your get-out-of-diet free card to go *loco*.

✈ If walking from the Ayuntamiento down C. Sierpes, it will be on the right. $ All desserts €1.80-2.20. ⏰ Open daily in summer 8am-11pm; in fall, winter, and spring 8am-10pm.

✔ LA BODEGA DE LA ALFALFA 🍴♿🍸❄ TRADITIONAL, TAPAS ❷

C. Alfalfa, 4 ☎954 227 362

For those who want their food fast but also want to hang out, La Bodega offers the tastiest, most traditional tapas around, serving it before you can even pick out which barrel along the wall you'll use as a table. The restaurant, centered around a bar that serves up all its food and drinks, has some of the friendliest, most enthusiastic waiters around, ready to gush about their favorite traditional dishes. The *mambru carmelo (€2.10)*, made of a brie-like cheese topped with sugar and honey and then baked to carmelize the sugar, combines sweet and savory like you've never experienced before. The *bacaloa al estilo la viuda (€2.20)*, a house specialty seafood, will have you licking your plate to get every drop of the tomato sauce garnish (maybe use some bread to scoop it up for the sake of looking less savage). The regulars tend to order a side of olives and one of the beers on tap, so maybe try that if you're trying to live like the locals.

✈ Located right off Plaza de Alfalfa at the base of C. Alfalfa. $ Tapas €1.80-2.20. Entrees €5-9. ⏰ Open daily 2:30-4pm and 8pm-midnight.

EL RINCONCILLO 🍴🍸 TRADITIONAL, TAPAS ❶

C. Gerona 40-Alhóndiga, 2 ☎954 223 183 💻www.elrinconcillo.es

Opened in 1670, El Rinconcillo is the oldest tapas bar in Sevilla, and the tiled walls and warm lighting are clear relics of this historic past. Rinconcillo has definitely used its experience to get its staff in perfect working order—they serve so many people that they manage to keep tabs chalked on the bar without getting even a speck of white powder on their dressy uniforms. This place is even swanky enough for your senior prom (well, maybe a prom 25 years ago). Ask anyone for the house special and they'll tell you to try the *Pavia*—deep fried *bacaloa* served straight from the frier.

➔ Located on a tiny street behind Iglesia Santa Catalina if coming from the Plaza de Ponce de Leon. $ Tapas €1.80-2.80. ⏰ Open daily 1pm-1:30am.

HABANITA 💳♿🍸☂ INTERNATIONAL, VEGETARIAN [3]

C. Golfo 3 ☎606 716 456 💻www.habanita.es

Habanita represents the antithesis of typical Sevillian eating. While the secluded courtyard and mellow atmosphere could be a relaxing break from the party scene booming in nearby Plaza Alfalfa, the service is frustratingly slow and the prices continue to add up from the expensive courses and extra "service and bread" charge. We've yet to decide whether the combination of yucca, bolognese, cous cous, and ratatouille on one menu is a case of healthy variety or an identity crisis. While we'd suggest you save this option until you just can't even *look* at another tapa, we also recognize that the vegetarian and vegan distinctions on the menu will be extremely helpful to our more diet-specific travelers.

➔ Off the far right corner of Plaza Alfalfa when entering the plaza from C. Alfalfa. $ Half-portions €4.15-8.25. Cocktails €4.50-5.75. ⏰ Open daily 12:30-4:30pm and 8pm-12:30am.

La Macarena

👍 ESLAVA 💳🍸❄ TAPAS [2]

C. Eslava, 5 ☎954 906 568 💻rb@restauranteeslava.es

Although the restaurant's pricier options will probably burn a hole in your wallet before you finish your meal, you should definitely try the deliciious food at Eslava—even if it's only one plate of tapas. While it's filled to the brim in both the late afternoon and evening, try to squeeze your way through the crowd to place an order. All the ingredients are totally fresh, from the wide selection of raw shellfish *(half €6-8, full €12-17)* to the produce brought in straight from the owner's farm between June and October. Get your hands on those veggies by ordering the *strudel de verduras (€2.20)*. You'd be crazy to skip the over-easy egg served on top of a mushroom cake with mushroom sauce and honey *(€2.20)*—it won first prize for Sevilla's best tapa in 2010. Eslava is by no means a touristy establishment, but it rakes in locals and tourists alike.

➔ Take C. Santa Ana from the Alameda and turn left once you see C. Santa Clara. ℹ Bar and restaurant separate. $ Tapas €2.20. Drinks €1-2. ⏰ Bar open daily 12:30-4:30pm and 8pm-midnight. Restaurant open daily 1-4pm and 9-11pm.

CASA PACO 💳♿🍸❄☂ TRADITIONAL [2]

Alameda de Hércules, 23 ☎663 959 266

While Casa Paco serves an array of classic Sevillian dishes from *salmorejo (€2.50)*, a chilled soup similar to gazpacho, to *carrillada (€3.50)*, pig's cheek, its general ambience is a nice break from the typical dark, divey Sevillian tapas bar. The prices are a little higher than the competition nearby, but it's clearly worth it—the place is packed on any summer night starting at 9pm. Even the pharmacist next door promotes Casa Paco to her customers (after bagging your prescription, of course). Her favorite *revuelto de papas (€2.50)*, a Spanish-style egg and potato omelette, is a unique version of the classic Spanish tortilla.

➔ If coming from the Torneo, turn right off C. Santa Ana at the Alameda. $ Tapas €2.50-4. Entrees €7-12. Wine and beer €1.50-2.50. ⏰ Open daily 1:30-4:30pm and 8:30pm-midnight.

El Arenal and Triana

👍 FARO DE TRIANA 💳❄☂ TRADITIONAL, SEAFOOD, VIEWS [3]

Puente Isabel II (Puente de Triana) ☎954 336 192

You may get a bit discouraged walking down C. Betis and seeing restaurant after restaurant offering fresh seafood at painfully expensive prices. What's the backpacker to do? Faro de Triana may be your solution. While not cheap, Faro provides slightly lower prices without any loss of quality. You can keep it casual and still get the freshest fish around. Like most of the restaurants along the canal, Faro specializes in its fried *(½ portion €9, full €15)* and whole grilled *(€15-18)* fish options. The heaping half portions are large enough to fill you up and maybe even take you out of commission for your next meal. Even the location and seating options can't be beat: for great views and some A/C, eat at the bar; for a classier dining experience, try the lower dining room; and for some snacking along the canal, take your meal to the outdoor patio.

Immediately to the left once you cross Puente de Triana. $ Half portions €9, full €15-18. ⏰ Open M-Sa 8am-midnight. Open later on the weekends.

BLANCA PALOMA 🍴🍸❄ TAPAS, TRADITIONAL, SEAFOOD [2]

San Jacinto, 49 ☎605 816 187

Upon entering Blanca Paloma, you'll be immediately impressed by this clean, classy restuarant with a stunning wooden bar and charming red curtains. While Trianans love their larger fish platters, Blanca Paloma proves that they haven't neglected the tapas culture. You can still get top seafood—their eggplant stuffed with shrimp *(€2.10)* and shrimp with garlic *(½ portion €6, full €12)* are highly recommended—but you've also got the option to enjoy more classic tapas and meat dishes. While the staff will be happy to recommend their favorite dishes, just grab one of the many local regulars sitting at the bar, and they'll pour their hearts out on the best way to fill your belly.

At the intersection of San Jacinto and C. Pajes del Corro. On the farther right corner if coming from Puente de Triana. $ Tapas €1.80-3, ½ portions €5.40-9, full €9-15. ⏰ Open M-F 8:30am-4:30pm and 7pm-midnight, Sa 12:30-4:30pm and 8:30pm-12:30am, Su 8:30am-4:30pm and 7pm-midnight.

MERCADO DE TRIANA ♿❄ MARKETPLACE [2]

Intersection of San Jorge and Altozano

The cleanest, best organized, air-conditioned marketplace you'll find in Sevilla. Hop between vendors, checking out the freshest produce, meats, and pastries, and stop at the souveneir shop on your way out. **Bar La Muralla** *(Mercado de Triana 72 ☎954 344 302 ⏰ Open M-Sa 6:30am-3pm.)* in the back of the Mercado uses all the products offered in the marketplace to serve lunch and breakfast to its enthusiastic local customers. You'll get laughed at if you ask for a menu—they don't even have one! Just ask for a recommendation and they'll tell you about all the fresh products that have come in that day *(tapas €2.20-3, ½ portions €6)*. La Muralla is a particularly perfect place to grab a breakfast of *churros con chocolate* or a lunch to go.

On the right-hand side at the base of the Puente de Triana. ⏰ Open M-Sa 7:30am-3pm. Hours for specific vendors vary.

NIGHTLIFE

Santa Cruz

Not necessarily the party capital of Sevilla, Santa Cruz still has some nice spots to get your drink on, see a show, and enjoy some late-night tapas. Most of the hotspots retain their local flair despite the loads of tourists frequently this district. If you're looking for where the locals are spending their nights in the Santa Cruz area, make your way to **Plaza de Alfalfa** and the small surrounding streets. You'll find Sevillians dominating the outdoor patios of the bars and restaurants, snacking on *caracoles*, snails, and enjoying an inexpensive pitcher of sangria or tall glass of beer.

BAR ALFALFA 🍸 BAR

C. Candilejo, 1 ☎954 222 344 ✉baralfalfa@hotmail.com

When traveling to the locals' hotspot in Sevilla, Plaza de Alfalfa, you might as well go to the Plaza's namesake. While this small, wooden tavern keeps things traditional, offering only Spanish and Italian wines and liquors (sorry Tom Cruise, no cocktails) and specializing in classic *brusquettas* (locally made bread topped with different meat, seasoning, and vegetable combinations), it's by no means outdated. If you're willing to get adventurous and step out of the backpacker bubble to see what Sevilla's 20-somethings are up to (or maybe use this for an early pregame), get ready to test out your Spanish, listen to the local music, and chat over a glass of vino.

⚑ *Located right at the tip of Plaza Alfalfa, off C. Alfalfa.*Ⓢ *Drinks €1.60-€2.80, brusquetta €2.30-€2.90.* ⏲ *Open daily 9am-2:30am.*

ANTIGUEDADES
Ⓨ♨ BAR

Argote de Molina, 40   🖳www.tapearensevilla.com

Stepping into Antiguedades, you may be a little confused as to whether you're in a bar or a Halloween shop. With mannequins dressed as clowns draping the walls and fake bloodied hands and feet adorning the ceiling, let's hope you're a happy drunk who can get through the night without freaking out. And if the decor isn't enough to get you on your toes, maybe the Spanish covers of '80s American hits (Video le Mató la Estrella del Radio, anyone?), or mashups between classic Spanish songs and American hip hop will freak you out. The bar itself caters to a mix of mostly locals and some tourists, mostly popular for pre-dinner drinks around 5-9pm. While the cocktails are a bit pricey, they offer all the classics from *mojitos* to *caipiriñas* (a Barcelonian lemony, sweet drink). The pitcher of Sangria has a special splash of coconut rum and the perfect refreshing treat for 3-4 people to split.

⚑ *From Plaza Virgen de los Reyes, take Placentines to Argote de Molina and the bar will be on your left.* 𝒊 *Drinks discounted from 5-9pm.* Ⓢ *Wine and beer €2. Cocktails €6. Pitchers €12.* ⏲ *Open daily 5pm-3am.*

La Macarena and West

La Macarena and the area further west may be the best place to set out for an evening in Sevilla. You'll find everything from open patio dining to relaxed bars and classy clubs.

🏛 THEATRO ANTIQUE
🏖Ⓨ❄☀ CLUB

C. Matematicas Rey Pastor y Castro s/n   ☎954 462 207 🖳www.antiquetheatro.com

1200 square meters, a 1400 person capacity, 3 outdoor bars, *and* a swimming pool? We don't want to get you all flustered with the math, but the full magnitude of Theatro Antique can't even be comprehended without a visit. This upscale club is the place to see and be seen, catering to a few famous faces and thousands of trendsters looking for the snazziest evening around. You'll hear the booming music from all the way across the river, putting some of the smaller clubs along the Torneo to shame. In the summer, take relaxation to a whole new level by sitting around the pool on the Aqua Antique patio in your personal cabana, hanging with friends and sipping your overpriced *caipiriña* (€8). Antique continues to outperform even with it's schedule: it stays open so late that, upon leaving, you could stumble right over to a nearby breakfast joint for some *churros con chocolate*...and a giant cup of coffee.

⚑ *From the Alameda, take C. Calatrava and cross the bridge; the club is on the left.* Ⓢ *Beer €4. Sangria €6. Mojitos and caipirinas €8.* ⏲ *Open in summer Tu-Su midnight-7am; in winter Th-Sa midnight-7am.*

BODEGA VIZCAÍNO
◉Ⓨ BAR, LOCALS

C. Feria 27   ☎954 386 057

Even with only two guys behind the counter, Bodega Vizcaíno manages to cater to its overflowing, riotous clientele. Busiest with locals in their 20s and 30s around 9:30 pm, it's still completely packed for an afternoon drink. Grab a cold beer (€1.10) or local wine (€1-1.30) served straight out of the barrels resting behind the bar, or try a local specialty, the *Tinto de Verano*, a fruity drink offered with your choice of white, organge, or lemon liqueur (€1.10). If you're feeling really

adventurous, don't just snack on the complimentary green olives but order up some fresh, chilled *bacalao* like a local. Maybe you'll impress a Sevillian or two.
🪧 *Located near the intersection of C.Feria and C. Correduría.* [S] *Beer €1.10. Wine €1-1.30.* ⏰ *Open M-Sa 8am-11:30pm.*

JACKSON — CLUB

C. Relator 21

From the front door, Jackson may not look like much—it lurks in a dark corner with a cheesy icon as a sign—but don't pass judgement just yet. Walk down the slim hallway on any night of the week around 2am and you'll find a packed dance floor lined with colorful, patterned walls (which change multiple times a year for the sake of variety) booming with '80s funk. The bartenders joke about how the standard patron is what they describe as "pijippie," a combination of *pijos*, or trendy fashionistas, and a free spirited hippie youth, between the ages of 20 and 35. While they must advertise that they close at 3am, locals describe their schedule as "11pm through the rest of the week." So grab a beer *(€2-3)*, and rely on that next morning's latte to wake you up after a night of hip-shaking heaven.
🪧 *Off to the far left corner of the Alameda from El Centro; the bar is on the left.* [S] *Beer €2-3. Mixed drinks €6-7.* ⏰ *Open daily 11:30pm-3am.*

BOSQUE ANIMADO — BAR

Arias Montaro, 5 ☎954 916 862

Escape the noisy, crowded patios of the Alameda and experience the relief of entering into this fairy-tale cave setting—and it's GLBT-friendly to boot. The earth-toned walls, brass bar, and woody seating will provide you with a comfort and sense of secrecy that you haven't experienced since you built pillow forts out of your living room cushions. With your *cubata (€6)* in hand, grab any seat at the bar aside from the one at the corner—it's permanently occupied by a gnome statue, signature to Bosque Animado. Surrounded by a mix of 20- and 30-something tourists and locals, enjoy the mellow music early in the early evening, and hear the playlist shift to prep for the party around midnight. If you're in town at the right time, definitely don't miss Halloween in October and Carnivales in February.
🪧 *Located on the left-hand side of a small street branching off the Alameda between C. Recreo and C. Santa Ana.* [S] *Beer €1.50-2.50. Cocktails €6.* ⏰ *Open daily 4pm-2am.*

El Arenal and Triana

KUDÉTA CAFE CHILLOUT DISCOTECA (AKA BUDDHA) — CLUB

Plaza de la Legión ☎954 089 095 💻www.kudetasevilla.es

If you ask a local how to get to Kudéta, they'll likely shrug their shoulders. But if you drop the name Buddha, you'll get an immediate sly smirk—they've probably been there, and they've probably had some crazy nights. Kudéta is one of the largest clubs in all of Sevilla, packing its three stories so full that they even expand into the Centro Commercial during their busiest weekend hours. They know they'll fill up, so they have no problem offering prices far higher than much of their competition. While the 1st floor remains pretty mellow (how can you not be mellow with pictures of Siddhartha on every wall and silky pillows and drapes everywhere?), offering hookah and a selection of wines and beers, things get rowdy on the upstairs dance floor and outdoor terrace. Thursday nights are reserved for enormous study-abroad student parties of about 1000 visitors, so you'll probably fit in quite easily.
🪧 *Located within the Centro Comercial de Plaza de Armas, in the portion closest to Av. de la Expiración.* [S] *Bottles of beer €4. Cocktails €7.50.* ⏰ *Open in summer daily 3pm-6am; in winter M-W 3pm-4am (only lounge open), Th-Sa 3pm-6am, Su 3pm-4am (only lounge open).*

ISBILIYYA — BAR, CLUB

Paseo de Cristobal Colon, 2 ☎954 210 460

With a canalfront terrace absolutely packed on any summer night and a booming dance floor all year round, Isbiliyya may be Sevilla's greatest hotspot for GLBT nightlife. Cross the Puente de Triana and be welcomed by the friendly staff, as open and congenial as the crowds of locals (young and old) ready to meet and mingle. Enjoy the cafe during the evening, the bar a bit later (discounted drinks until 1am—beers are just €2 and mixed drinks €4), and the party until the early mornings. The combo of '80s dance and pop house music can't be beat. Did we mention the pride of Isbiliyya—every night at 1:30am the bar holds a drag show on its main stage, bringing out some of the most colorful and creative costumes that this city has ever seen. Grab a caipirina or mojito *(€3.50)* and enjoy the music, dance, and maybe even return that wink you get from the guy singing in the spotlight.

➜ Located on Paseo de Colon, right at the base of Puente de Triana. $ Beer €3. Cocktails €3.50. ⏰ Open daily 8pm-4am. Drag show daily 1:30am.

ARTS AND CULTURE 🎵

As the capital of **Andalucia,** Sevilla attracts the best and brightest on the artisic and cultural scene. Sevilla's got the money, the motivation, and the spirit of possibility flowing through the streets. Don't just think you're gonna find macarenas and castanets—Sevilla provides traditional flamenco, opera, dance, and performance, as well as a slew of avant-garde theaters and smaller concert halls to be enjoyed by young and old alike. The arts are by no means limited to velvet chairs and golf claps, though—scream your lungs out from the sidelines of a soccer match and try not to cover your eyes at the **Plaza de Toros.**

Theater

Theater culture in Sevilla caters to those looking for big, extravagant performances as well as smaller, private experiences. Apart from the listings below you can find indie and alternative concerts at **Sala Fun Club** *(Alameda de Hercules, 86 ☎954 218 064 💻www.funclubsevilla.com ⏰ Th-Sa 9:30-10pm),* or folk and blues shows at **Cafe Lisboa** *(Alhóndiga ☎983 291 615 ⏰ M-Sa 3pm-3am, Su 1pm-3am.)* or **El Hobbit.** *(C. Regina, 20 ⏰ Shows around 10pm, Th Jazz, Sa Folk)* If you want to catch a flick, **Avenida 5 Cines** *(C. Marques de Paradas 15)* shows international films with Spanish subtitles for €5.50, while **Cinesa** *(Plaza de la Legion, 8 ☎902 333 231)* in the mall at Plaza de Armas, shows flicks dubbed in Spanish *(€6.50)* and even 3D movies *(€9.50).*

TEATRO LOPE DE VEGA ◆ SANTA CRUZ

Av. María Luisa s/n ☎955 472 828 💻www.teatrolopedevega.org

Teatro Lope de Vega is the main theatrical stage in all of Sevilla, and it fits any stereotype you'd hold of a classic theater—red velvet chairs and curtains with golden trim. Run and orchestrated by the city government, this theater is located just behind the Universidad de Sevilla. Shows usually start around 9pm; depending on the performance, tickets can range from €4 to €45.

➜ Located off Parque Maria Luisa near the Universidad and the Plaza de España. $ Tickets €4-45. ⏰ Box office open Tu-Sa 11am-2pm and 6-9pm, Su 11am-2pm.

TEATRO DE LA MAESTRANZA ◆ ARENAL

Paseo de Colon 22 ☎954 223 344 💻www.teatromaestranza.com

Teatro de la Mestranza holds operas, flamenco shows, and dance and piano recitals for a classier, more formal crowd. Don't be troubled by the statue of the non-Spanish Mozart out front—the theater is merely thanking him for including the city of Sevilla in his *Marriage of Figueroa* through the character Barbaro.

➜ Located right next to the Plaza de Torros on Paseo de Colon. $ Tickets €17-39. ⏰ Open Th-F 8:30pm.

Flamenco

👍 TARDES DE FLAMENCO EN LA CASA DE LA MEMORIA ◆🍸☀ SANTA CRUZ

C. Ximenez de Enciso 28 ☎954 560 670 💻www.casadelamemoria.es

Hidden away in a small, tented garden plaza, Tardes de Flamenco knows how to set the scene and pack the house. The show is performed by four artists, all of whom couldn't be older than 25. Try not to scrape your chin on the floor when your jaw drops—these kids know their stuff. Running through two centuries of flamenco, they layer on the components, starting with just a guitar before adding in the male and female dancers one at a time. The dancers aren't the only ones getting their heart rate up—you'll get so sucked into the drama that you'll feel your chest pounding. Hands down the best deal for classic flamenco around. Buy tickets in advance and arrive at least 30min. early, as every show tends to sell out.

‡ C. Ximenez crosses C. Santa Maria la Blanca and extends into Plaza Alianza, right in between the Alcazar and Convento de la Encarnacion. [$] €15, students €13. ⏰ Daily shows at 9pm and 10:30pm. Arrive at least 30min. early to get a seat.

TABLAO EL ARENAL
🎫🍸 ARENAL

C. Rono, 7 ☎954 216 492 💻www.tablaoarenal.com

Tablao de Arenal requires an investment of time and money but has been rumored to host the very best classic Flamenco in town. If you don't want to take our word for it, even the 📰**New York Times** called it the best place in the world to experience flamenco. The show goes for about two hours and the prices range from €37-€72 depending on how much you want to be eating and drinking with the performance.

‡ Between the bullring and Hospital de Caridad. [$] Show and 1 drink €37. Show with tapas, drink, and dessert €59. Show with full dinner €72. ⏰ Shows daily 8pm and 10pm.

EL PATIO SEVILLANO
🎫🍸 ARENAL

Paseo de Cristobal Colón, 11A ☎954 214 120 💻www.elpatiosevillano.com

One of the oldest flamenco bars in town, El Patio Sevillano provides another classic Flamenco performance with a meal included at a steep price. Compared to Tablao de Arenal (whose prices are about the same), you're getting a shorter show (1½hr.) at a less famous establishment. That said, the colorful, cool, underground tiled dining room does set the tone for some traditional Spanish culture.

‡ On Cristobal Colón, only meters from the bull ring. [$] Show €37. Show with tapas €59. Show with full dinner €70. ⏰ Shows daily at 7pm and 9:30pm.

Festivals

SEMANA SANTA
SPRING

💻www.semana-santa.org

Semana Santa, or **Holy Week,** is the annual period between Palm Sunday and Easter Sunday, and thus the last week of Lent. During these seven days, all 57 religious brotherhoods of the city adorn hooded robes and guide two candlelit floats honoring Jesus and the Virgin Mary along the tiny, winding Sevillian streets.

the *botellón*

The *al fresco* method of Spanish socializing, the *botellón* has lately gotten a lot of negative attention from older generations of Spaniards. The word basically means a giant, public pregame, in which the youths of Spain buy cheap alcohol, bags of ice, and plastic cups and then drink in the street. Many people believe the tradition arose because of the steep drink prices in bars and the former lack of real open container laws in Spain. However, another possible cause is the Spanish custom of not inviting guests over to the home just to get wasted, which does seem to make pregaming a necessarily public activity. However, the *botellón*'s noisiness and (some would say) moral questionability have led the government to take extreme measures: some cities have considered passing laws forbidding any drink to be consumed in the street.

As they make their way to the Catedral, they grab the attention of around one million spectators year after year. You don't need to be a religious person to be awed by the history and picturesque spectacle that is Semana Santa. Hotels and hostels fill far in advance but are slightly less busy if you come during the first portion of the week, as Semana Santa culminates on **Good Friday.** If you're going to stay for the end of the week, you may also consider extending your trip until **Feria de Abril** (below)—you may be due for the shift from pious patron to partier. The tourist offices of the city are well-equipped to answer any questions about accommodations and dining during this busy time in Sevilla. You can also visit the museum at the **Basílica La Macarena** to learn more about the history of Semana Santa. *(C. Becker 1, 3 ☎954 901 800 🖥www.hermandaddelamacarena.es)*

FERIA DE ABRIL

Los Remedios District of Sevilla 🖥www.feriadesevilla.andalunet.com

Following the holy week of Semana Santa each year, Feria de Abril is the time for Sevilla to let its hair down and celebrate its rich culture and history. Started in 1847 as a **cattle-trade expo** in the Prado de San Sebastian, this week of festivities has made great strides ever since—the Feria today takes up one million sq. m of Sevillian territory! The celebrations take place in three main parts: the 15-block **Real de la Feria,** the colorful amusement park at **Calle de Infierno,** and the main entrance, or **Posada.** The Real is the heart of the Feria—the asphalt is covered in golden sand to match the bull ring, the sidewalks are lined with *casetas*, (canvas houses where you can spend the week drinking and eating with friends and family), and horse-drawn carriages and flamenco dancers pass through the streets. Each day, six bulls are set into the ring at **Plaza de Toros de la Maestranza** to face off against the most famous matadors Spain has to offer. Tickets go way in advance, so call the office for reservations. *(☎954 210 315)*

From the moment thousands of Chinese-style lanters light up the city in unison at midnight of the first night to when Sevilla cuts to black at the closing of the festivities at midnight on the last night, you are in for quite the treat. As far as suggestions for rooms, turn to the **information offices** throughout the city or the **kiosks** located on the Feria grounds. Special, direct buses run from the Prado and Charco de la Pava to the Real, and the C1, C2, and 41 bus lines stay running throughout the day *(€1.50)*. Both ends of Metro Line 1 are located smack in the middle of the excitement.

ESSENTIALS

Practicalities

- **TOURIST OFFICES:** The **Centro de Información de Sevilla Laredo** has extensive information for tourists in Sevilla. *(Pl. de San Francisco, 19 ☎954 595 288 🖥www.sevilla.org/turismo ⏰ Open M-F 9am-7:30pm, Sa-Su 10am-2pm.)* **Turnismo de la Provincia** also has tourist information and gives out special discounts at some of the newer and more popular restaurants in the area. *(Pl. del Turinfo, 1-3 ☎954 210 005 🖥www.tourismosevilla.org ⏰ Open daily 10:30am-2:30pm and 3:30-7:30pm.)*
- **LAUNDROMAT: Vera Tintoreria** provides self-service wash and dry at two different locations. *(☎954 534 495 for Aceituna 6; ☎954 541 148 for Menendez Pelayo, 11. $ Wash and dry €10. ⏰ Open M-F 9:30am-2pm and 5:30-8pm, Sa 10am-1:30pm.)*
- **INTERNET : Internetia** internet cafes offer Wi-Fi and computers. *(Menendez Pelayo 43-45 ☎954 534 003 $ €2.20 per hr.)*
- **POST OFFICE:** The main post office has a bank and also helps with international cell phones. *(Av. de la Constitución 32 ☎902 197 197 🖥www.correos.es.)*

Getting There

By Train

To get to Sevilla, your best option is to hop on a train. The main train station, Estación Santa Justa *(Av. de Kansas City ☎902 240 202)* offers luggage storage, car rentals, and an ATM. You can catch a train from the airport in Madrid to Sevilla via the **AVE** train *($ €80.70. ⏰ 2½hr., every 30min. daily 6:15am-11pm.)* or the **Alvia** train *($ €63.30. ⏰ 2hr. 45 min., 2 per day).*

By Bus

Take the C-1 bus to Prado de San Sebastian to get to the city center. If traveling by bus from the Estación Prado de San Sebastian, there are three major lines from which to choose: **Los Amarillos** *(☎902 210 317 💻www.touristbuses.es)*, **Alsina Graells** *(☎902 422 242 💻www.alsa.es)*, and **Transportes Comes** *(☎902 199 208 💻www.tgcomes.es)*.Estación Prado de San Sebastian also happens to be a stop on the city metro, a major local bus stop, and a tram stop. To purchase tickets to leave the city from the Estacion Prado, look for salesmen under yellow archways, behind the hustle and bustle of all the local buses on the street. The other major bus station in the southern part of the city, the Estación Plaza de Armas, receives every bus from **Portugal** and sends buses going to **Valencia, Salamanca, Leon,** and **Asturias.**

Getting Around

As far as getting around Sevilla goes, the only major restriction to walking is the temperature. The region itself is not very large and is easily manageable on foot. That being said, the city is well-equipped with buses, trams, a Metro line, and bike rentals. If you're not willing to withstand the heat (especially in those summer months), grab yourself a cold Fanta and hop on some public transit.

By Train

For booking regional travel by train, contact **Alsa** *(☎902 422 242 💻 www.alsa.es)* or **Damas** *(☎954 907 737 💻 www.damas-sa.es).*

By Bus

The **Tussam** buses blanket the city. *($ €1.20.)* The **C-3** and **C-4** buses, running every 10 min., are particularly helpful, as they circle the border of the city clockwise and counterclockwise, respectively.

By Metro

The **Metro** is also extremely useful. **Metro Line 1** *($ One-way €1.30, day pass €4.50. ⏰ M-Th 6:30am-11pm, F 6:30am-2am, Sa 7:30am-2am, Su 7:30am-11pm.)* ends in Ciudad Expo and Olivar de Quintos, making stops in Prado de San Sebastian, San Bernardo, Gran Plaza, and Parque de los Principales.

By Bike

As far as biking goes, you'll quickly notice that the locals are all about this mode of transport. You'll find lines of **Sevici** *(💻www.sevici.es)* bicycles around the city. Set up a year-long *($ €10.)* or week-long *($ €5.)* subscription at any kiosk with your credit card.

By Taxi

If you do decide to call a cab, **Radio Taxi** *(☎954 580 000)* and **Tele Taxi** *(☎954 622 222)* are the two lines recommended by city officials.

burgos ☎947

Burgos (pop. 180,000) has one of the most spectacular city entrances anywhere, and this breathtaking first impression accurately introduces this northern gem. After walking through the large and ornate **Arco de Santa María** to the mind-bogglingly massive **Catedral** on the Pl. del Rey San Fernando, it doesn't take much imagination to understand why this was a favorite seat and burial place of Castilian and Leonese royalty. Though the Catedral is undoubtedly Burgos's centerpiece, the city is filled with dozens of other churches, from the 9th-century *Castillo* up the hill to the medieval monasteries on the city's outskirts. In the evening, plazas fill with friends and families enjoying their *paseos*, and as the clock strikes midnight they buzz with partiers on their way to the bars along the Camino de Santiago and the *discotecas* in the shadow of the Catedral.

ORIENTATION

Burgos is a simple city, but the streets run in ridiculously complicated directions. Before traversing this area, pick up a map from the tourist office. The **bus station, post office, Museo de Burgos,** and **Monasterio de las Huelgas** are pretty much the only important things south of the east-west-running **Río Arlanzón**. Most of the *centro histórico* is to the north of the river, with the **Catedral** on the west end, the **Castillo** up the hill to the north, and various winding streets and **magnificent, open plazas** throughout the city. The **Plaza de España,** a hub for most city buses, is east of the centro, and the **train station** is outside of the city to the northeast.

ACCOMMODATIONS

HOSTAL CARRALES — HOSTAL ❷

C. Puente Gasset, 4 — ☎947 20 59 16 www.hostalcarrales.com

A couple of blocks from the *centro histórico* and about 15min. on foot from the bus station, this quiet *hostal* has basic rooms, full baths, and a very affectionate cat who lives in the reception (on a different floor from the rooms, allergy sufferers).

*Just on the north side of the river, between C. de Vitoria and Av. del Arlanzón, 4 blocks east of Pl. del Cid. **i** Private baths available. $ Singles €25-40; doubles €35-50. Reception 8am-11pm.*

CAMPING FUENTES BLANCAS — CAMPING ❶

Ctra. Burgos-Cartuja de Miraflores, Km. 3.5 — ☎947 48 60 16 www.campingburgos.com

Located in the Fuentes Blancas park a 10min. bus ride from the *centro*, Camping Fuentes Blancas is a beautiful municipal campsite. Campers can save money with this cheaper overnight option, and outdoorsy backpackers can explore the many hiking trails—they can even walk here along a scenic river from Burgos itself.

*#27 bus leaves from northwest side of Pl. de España and runs to Fuentes Blancas ("Camping" stop). 4 per day 9:30am-7:15pm, returns to Pl. de España 4 per day 9:45am-7:30pm. #26 bus runs Jun 29-Aug 31 and leaves from the same stop, 10 per day 11am-9pm, returns to Pl. de España 10 per day 11:15am-9:15pm. **i** Shop, restaurant, bar, lounge, pool, beach, mini-golf (€4), common showers. $ €4.65 per person, ages 2-10 €3.20, €3.72-7.55 per tent, €4.65 per car. Electricity €4. Bungalows with private bath €35-85. Open in summer daily 7am-midnight; in winter 8am-11pm.*

SIGHTS

Turn any corner in Burgos' *centro histórico* and you're likely to stumble across a 14th-century church or the building where Ferdinand and Isabella met with Columbus upon his return from his second voyage to the New World. (If *Let's Go* told you where it was, you wouldn't be able to stumble across it, now would you?) The **Catedral** is the city's main attraction, but Burgos has dozens of other sites that shouldn't be missed.

⚜ CATEDRAL DE BURGOS
Pl. del Rey San Fernando

⊛⊗ CHURCH

☎947 20 47 12 ▮www.catedraldeburgos.es

The **Catedral,** a UNESCO World Heritage site, is one of the most impressive churches in the world. Whether you first approach it from behind, by following the Camino de Santiago, or from the front via the magnificent Arch of Santa María, its incredible size and detailed stone carvings will blow your mind. What began in the early 13th century as a Romanesque church has been transformed over the intervening centuries into a Gothic marvel, and recent restorations (which some consider a bit excessive) have returned its original vivid colors and gilded finish. The Capilla de los Condestables is covered with incredible carvings in wood and stone; be sure to look up at the intricate skylight, and look to the right as you walk in for carved ▰**dragons.** Just off the stained-glass-enclosed upper cloister (built 1260-1280) is the ▰**Capilla de Santa Catalina,** whose walls are covered from floor to high ceiling with portraits of the clergy, and which houses documents such as the Visigothic Bible of Cardeña and **El Cid's** nuptial documents; **El Cid** himself is in the transept. The museum's extensive collection includes reliquaries containing the remains of many saints as well as an artist's rendition of a stunningly handsome El Cid that looks more like the cover of a romance novel than anything else.

⚐ *Take the Puente de Santa María bridge from the south side of the river; through the arch.* ⑨€5, *seniors €4, students €3, pilgrims €2.50, ages 7-14 €1.* ⌚ *Open in summer M 9:30am-6:30pm, Tu 9:30am-3pm and 3:30-6:30pm, W-Su 9:30am-6:30pm; in winter M 10am-6pm, Tu 10am-3pm and 3:30-6pm, W-Su 10am-6pm.*

⚜ MONASTERIO DE SANTA MARÍA LA REAL DE LAS HUELGAS
Compases de Huelgas

⊛⚭ CHURCH

☎947 20 16 30

Built in 1187 by King Alfonso VIII, the Monasterio de las Huelgas was a summer palace for Castilian kings and a Cistercian convent for princesses and nobles. Though the Cistercians preferred a no-frills attitude toward interior decorating, the monastery's royal status allowed it to break some of the order's strict rules against signs of opulence. The Romanesque cloister dates all the way back to the monastery's founding in the 12th century, and the colors on the ceiling of the Capilla de Santiago (which looks like it belongs more in the Alhambra of Granada than in a Castilian monastery) are original and from the 13th century. The museum contains the Pendón de las Navas de Tolosa, the Moors' flag captured by the re-conquering Castilians in 1212, which you can also see depicted on the far right of the huge 17th-century mural in the first room.

⚐ *Take the "Barrio del Pilar" bus (€0.85) from Pl. de España to Barrio de las Huelgas; or, walking (approx. 20min. from cathedral), follow Paseo de la Audiencia west along the river, then turn left across the bridge at Pl. de Castilla roundabout. Take a right along Av. de Palencia and a slight left onto Av. Monasterio de las Huelgas; monastery is at the end of the avenue.* ⑨ €5, *students, seniors, ages 5-16 €2.50, under 5 free.* ⌚ *Open Tu-Sa 10am-1pm and 3:45-5:30pm, Su 10:30am-2pm. Mandatory tours (1¼hr.) given in Spanish every 30min.*

FOOD ◖

Queso de Burgos and *morcilla* sausage are staples of the Burgalese kitchen and can be found throughout the *centro histórico,* mainly near the Catedral. For tapas, the C. San Lorenzo off the Plaza Mayor is overflowing with bars; the streets parallel to C. San Lorenzo are good for nightlife as well.

CERVECERÍA MORITO
C. Porcelos, 1

⊛⚭♈ BAR, RESTAURANT ❶

☎947 26 75 55

Even during the low season, the line for this *cervecería's* deliciously cheap fare runs out the door and around the block. Pair their sangria (*€1.50*) with the *ración of champiñones (mushrooms served with ham; €4),* or get adventurous and try something with *gulas* (baby eel).

burgos • food

✱ *From Pl. del Rey San Fernando (next to cathedral), follow C. de la Virgen de la Paloma 1 block, then right onto C. Porcelos.* Ⓢ *Raciones €1.50-6. Sandwiches €3-6. Beer €1. Sangria €1.50.* ☼ *Open daily noon-3:30pm and 7pm-midnight. Kitchen open 1-3:30pm and 7pm-midnight.*

LA TAPERÍA DEL CASINO
⊛☕♥☂ CAFE, RESTAURANT ❷

Pl. Mayor, 31 ☎947 27 81 56

Right on the Plaza Mayor, this place offers traditional Spanish food, from *paella* (€9-10) to *patatas bravas* (€2). There's a €0.40 surcharge to sit outside on the Plaza, but the shaded seating area is worth every cent. Make sure not to miss (or pay for) the free olives.

✱ *On the south side of the Pl. Mayor.* Ⓢ *Appetizers €1-2. Raciones €5.60-15.60. Salads €7.60-9.60. Sandwiches €3-4.10. Pizza €9.60. Menú del día €12.* ☼ *Open daily 9am-midnight.*

NIGHTLIFE

Locals start off the night with tapas and *tinto* in the crowded bars along **C. de San Lorenzo**, then head to the bars along **C. de San Juan** and **C. de la Puebla** for some liquid courage before hitting the **discotecas** on **C. del Huerto del Rey** and **C. de Fernán González** behind the Catedral.

EL BOSQUE ENCANTADO
⊛⊗♥ BAR, CLUB

C. de San Juan, 31 ☎947 26 12 66

For an undoubtedly unique (this bar is so funky *Let's Go* even uses a grammatically incorrect qualifier before "unique"!) experience, head to this bar along the busy C. de San Juan, where trance music floats around strangely placed dollhouses—yeah, we don't get it either. The establishment takes its name from the enormous fake tree that sits at the bar, illuminated by lighting reminiscent of a high school theater production. No matter how kitschy this bar may sound, it offers a great deal on beers and teas (€1.50-2.50).

✱ *On C. de San Juan west of C. Santander.* Ⓢ *Tea €1.50-2.50. Beer €2.* ☼ *Open M-W 5pm-midnight, Th 5pm-12:30am, F-Sa 5pm-4am.*

ESSENTIALS

Practicalities

- **TOURIST OFFICES:** The **tourist office** has excellent maps that are necessary for navigating the city's jumbled streets. *(Pl. Alonso Martínez, 7 ☎947 20 31 25 ▪www.turismocastillayleon.com* ☼ *Open Sep 16-Jun 30 M-Sa 9:30am-2pm and 4-7pm, Su 9:30am-5pm; Jul 1-Sep 15 daily 9am-8pm.)*

- **TOURS:** Contact the tourist office for guided tours of the *centro histórico.* *(12:15pm* Ⓢ *€10, ages 7-14 €3.)*

- **CURRENCY EXCHANGE: Banco Santander** offers currency exchange and ATMs. *(Pl. de Mío Cid, ☎902 24 24 24* ☼ *Open Apr-Sept M-F 8:30am-2pm; Oct-Mar M-F 8:30am-2pm, Sa 8:30am-1pm.)*

- **LUGGAGE STORAGE:** The bus station offers storage. *(C. Miranda, 4 ☎947 28 88 55* Ⓢ *€2 per day.)*

- **INTERNET ACCESS: Biblioteca del Teatro Principal** has 30min. free Wi-Fi. *(Paseo del Espolón ☎947 28 88 73* ☼ *Open July M-F 8:30am-2:30pm; Aug M-F 8:30am-9pm; Sept-June M-F 9am-9pm, Sa 9:30am-2pm.)*

- **POST OFFICE:** *(Pl. Conde de Castro ☎947 26 27 50* ☼ *Open M-F 8:30am-8:30pm, Sa 9:30am-4pm.)*

Emergency!

- **EMERGENCY NUMBERS:** ☎092.

- **POLICE:** *(Av. Cantabria ☎947 28 88 39)*

- **HOSPITALS/MEDICAL SERVICES: Hospital General Yagüe** *(Av. del Cid, 96 ☎947 28 18 00)*

Getting There

By Bus

The best way to get to Burgos is by bus; the bus station *(C. Miranda, 4 ☎947 28 88 55)* is 1 block south of the river and just across the bridge from the cathedral. Buses arrive from **Barcelona** *(⏰ 8hr., 5 per day 8:45am-11pm $ €35.),* **Bilbao** *(⏰ 2hr., 12 per day 6:30am-8:30pm $ €11.50.),* **Carrión de los Condes** *(⏰ 1¼hr., M-Sa 5:10pm $ €5.50.),* **León** *(⏰ 2hr., 3-4 per day 10:15am-9:15pm $ €14.),* **Logroño** *(⏰ 2hr., M-Sa 8 per day 9:30am-9:30pm, Su 4 per day 1-11:45pm $ €10.),* **Madrid** *(⏰ 3hr., M-Th, Sa 16 per day, F 24 per day, Su 17 per day 7am-12:30am $ €16.),* **Salamanca** *(⏰ 3-4hr., M-Sa 4-5 per day 9:30am-3:15am, Su 2 per day 9:30am-3:30pm $ €15-22.),* **San Sebastián** *(⏰ 3hr., 6-8 per day 7:40am-12:30am $ €15.50.),* **Santiago de Compostela** *(⏰ 7-9hr., 2 per day 2-11:15pm* $ €37-40.)

By Train

The new RENFE train station *(Av. Principe de Asturias ☎902 24 02 02)* is about 3mi. from the *centro histórico*. **Trains** arrive from **Barcelona** *(⏰ 6hr., 4 per day 9:20am-8:45pm $ €63-78.),* **Bilbao** *(⏰ 3hr., M-F 4 per day 8:55am-5:10pm, Sa 3 per day 8:55am-2pm, Su 3 per day 8:55am-5:10pm $ €13-19.),* **León** *(⏰ 2hr., 4 per day 1:12pm-12:14am $ €20-37.),* **Lisboa** *(⏰ 11hr., daily 4:30pm $ €61.),* **Logroño** *(⏰ 2hr., M 4 per day 7:36am-1:59am, Tu-Su 3 per day 4:06pm-1:59am $ €18-21.),* **Madrid** *(⏰ 2-4hr., M-F 6 per day 8am-5:30pm, Sa 4 per day 8am-4:10pm, Su 3 per day 8:am-4:10pm $ €25-40.),* **Pamplona** *(⏰ 2hr., daily 1:10pm $ €23.50.),* **Paris** *(⏰ 10hr., M-F, Su 7:47pm $ €150.),* **Salamanca** *(⏰ 2½hr., 3 per day 6:40am-12:35am $ €21-23.),* and **San Sebastián.** *(⏰ 3hr., 5 per day 8:42am-10:40pm $ €21-27.)*

By Air

The **Aeropuerto de Burgos-Villafría** *(☎902 40 47 04 💻www.aena.es)* is about 2½mi. outside the *centro;* **flights** arrive daily from **Barcelona.** *(⏰ 1½hr., 12:20pm. $ €62.)*

Getting Around

Burgos is a small city with an almost entirely pedestrian *centro histórico*, so the best way to get around is to **walk.** For sites outside the *centro*, the **bus** system *(€0.85)* is quick and easy to use; most buses run through the Pl. de España to the northeast of the *centro*. Buses #25 and #43 go from the Pl. de España to the RENFE station; bus #24 goes from the Pl. de España to the **airport.** For **taxis,** call Radio Taxi (☎947 27 77 77).

carrión de los condes ☎979

Carrión de los Condes (pop. 2,328) is a tiny *pueblo* in the province of Palencia, the heart of Castilla y León. It's the sort of place where you wake up to the sounds of church bells and roosters and spend the day meandering through the quiet streets under darting swallows and swooping storks. It is a mandatory stop—one of the most impressive—along the Camino de Santiago, and is renowned for its incredible Romanesque churches and the Renaissance cloister of San Zoilo across the river.

ORIENTATION

Rising above the surrounding plains and farmland, Carrión is located above its namesake Río Carrión, midway between Burgos and León. The **Camino de Santiago** runs est-west through the town and goes by most major sights, following the main roads and passing through the main plazas: C. de Santa Clara, Pl. Piña Merino (home to the bus stop), the beautiful Pl. de Santa María, C. de Santa María, Pl. Mayor (still "Plaza del Generalísimo" on many maps), and C. de Esteban Collantes, before heading across the river to the monastery of San Zoilo. Just follow the Camino up **C. Santa María** to get to the center of town from the bus stop. The northwest corner of town has several lovely churches but used to be the *judería* (Jewish quarter), hence the C. de Rabí Don Sem Tob. Interestingly, the Ermita de la Cruz was once the synagogue. Take note: on the tourist office's map and the map at the Pl. de Santa María, North is oriented about 45 degrees to the right.

ACCOMMODATIONS ⌂

PENSIÓN EL RESBALÓN ⊛⊗ PENSIÓN ❶

C. de Fernán Gómez, 19 ☎979 88 04 33

This *pensión* in the heart of the village offers little more than a bed, a window, and a lightbulb, but for these prices it's a steal. However, don't stay here if you're looking for a good night's sleep after a long day of pilgrimages or sightseeing—it's right next to the main nightlife street, and what the local youth may lack in numbers, they make up for in volume.

➤ From C. de Santa María heading toward the Pl. Mayor, turn right onto C. de Fernán Gómez. ℹ Shared bath. $ Singles €15; doubles €22; triples €27. ⏰ Reception 8am-11pm.

CAMPING EL EDÉN ⊛♿ CAMPING ❶

Parque Municipal ☎979 88 01 95

Sick of always having to take a bus or a 3mi. hike into town from the campsite? Not in Carrión: El Edén, right down by the river, is no more than a 2min. walk from the Pl. Mayor (though, to be fair, few things in this town are more than a 2min. walk from the Pl. Mayor).

➤ On the southwest side of town. Follow C. de Enrique Fuentes Quintana down from the Pl. Mayor, then left through the park. ℹ Shared bath. Restaurant and bar. $ €4 per person; €3.50-4 per tent; €4 per car. Electricity €3.50. ⏰ Reception 9am-10pm.

SIGHTS 👁

Though small in population and area, Carrión is full of historic religious buildings put up over the course of the last millennium. Many of them, such as Carrión's oldest church, the **Iglesia de Santa María del Camino** *($ Free. ⏰ Open in summer daily 9am-2pm and 4:30-6pm; in winter M-Sa 11am-1:30am and 6-9pm, Su noon-1:30pm.)*, lie on the Camino de Santiago, but a quick walk through town reveals churches, monasteries, and *ermitas* of all eras and architectural styles.

☑ REAL MONASTERIO DE SAN ZOILO ⊛⊗ CHURCH

C. de San Zoilo ☎979 88 00 50

Though the date of its founding is unknown, monks lived here as early as 948 CE. Throughout the Middle Ages it was a center of political and religious power, and a key point along the Camino de Santiago. The monastery features Romanesque elements dating to the 11th century and is perhaps best known for its glorious Renaissance cloister.

➤ Follow the well-marked Camino de Santiago: from the Pl. Mayor, head northwest on C. de Esteban Collantes, then left at C. de Piña Blasco, and across the bridge and to the right. $ €2, pilgrims and groups of over 20 people €1.50, ages 9 and under free. ⏰ Open daily 10:30am-2pm and 4:30-8pm.

FOOD 🍴

For standard but inexpensive meals, hit the bars near the bus stop and along the Pl. Mayor. Otherwise, get your grub on at eateries along the Camino.

RESTAURANTE LA CORTE ⊛♿🍸 CASTILIAN ❷

C. de Santa María, 34 ☎979 88 01 38 💻www.hostallacorte.com

Across from the Pl. de Santa María next to the affiliated *hostal*, this traditional Castilian restaurant has an affordable *menú* and a salty but filling *sopa castel-*

lana. Stop here for breakfast as early as 6am to try the *cafe*, *pan tostada*, and fresh orange juice *(€3)* before an early trip to the Camino.

➡ Up C. de Santa María 1 block from the bus stop. $ Entrees €6-17. Menú €10. Breakfast €3. 🕐 Open daily 6-10am, 1:30-4pm, and 7-11pm (closing times approximate).

BAR ABEL 🍸 BAR ❶

C. de Esteban Collantes, 15 ☎979 88 03 25

This welcoming bar is where locals come to hang out before their *siestas.* Don't worry, though: they won't make you feel left out, even though you're the only one who doesn't know that story about Don Ronaldo and the donkey.

➡ 2 blocks north of Pl Mayor, up C. de Esteban Collantes. $Menú €11, Sa-Su €17. 🕐 Open daily 1-3:30pm, F-Su also 8:30-10:30pm.

NIGHTLIFE

CAFETERÍA CARRIÓN 🍸 BAR, LOUNGE

C. de Esteban Collantes, 8

If this establishment's name were in English instead of Spanish, it would sound quite unappealing. Fortunately, the false cognate doesn't seem to drive away any of the locals. Most get their *cañas* and *kalimotxos* at the bar and take them out to the street, but some stay in the smoky and surprisingly large drinking space to play cards, *futbolín* (foosball) or *billar* (pool) before heading out to the *discotecas.*

➡ 1 block north of the Pl. Mayor on C. de Esteban Collantes. $ Beer €1.50. Kalimotxos €2.50. 🕐 Open M-Th 9am-1am, F-Sa 9am-2am.

ADARVE 🍸 CLUB

Pl. de los Regentes

If you can pick your way through the sometimes menacing crowd of *jóvenes* outside (approach from the Pl. Mayor rather than C. de Fernán Gómez, where the *botellones* and *lucha libre* tend to take place), this disco-pub is where Carrión's nightlife can be found. The party pours out onto the Plaza de los Regentes in front, and often down the adjacent streets. Watch out for flying bottles: smashing is the preferred method of glass disposal, as recycling hasn't completely caught on yet.

➡ From C. de Santa María, take C. de Fernán Gómez one block north, then left at Pl. de los Regentes. Or (the more dramatic route) from Pl. Mayor, go through the arch to the right of the Iglesia de Santiago, down the narrow alleyway past the museum, which leads right to the Pl. de los Regentes. $ Shots €1. Beer €1.50. 🕐 Open M-Th 10pm-2am, F-Sa 10pm-3:30am.

ESSENTIALS

Practicalities

- **TOURIST OFFICES:** For information and brochures on the area, head to the office across from the bus stop *(☎979 88 02 50 ➡ Across from the bus stop. 🕐 Open Sept-June Sa-Su 10am-2pm and 5:30-7:30pm; July-Aug daily 10am-3pm and 5-7:30pm.)* or in Pl. Mayor. (➡ In the Museo de Arte Contemporáneo. 🕐 Open Tu-Su 11am-2pm and 5-7pm.)
- **CURRENCY EXCHANGE: Banco Santander** *(Pl. Primer Marqués de Santillana, 4 🕐 Open M-F 8:30am-2:30pm.)*
- **INTERNET ACCESS: Cafetería Yadira** *(➡ Across from Bar España and the bus stop. $ €1 for 20min.)*
- **POST OFFICE:** *(C. José Antonio Girón ☎979 88 03 45 🕐 Open M-F 8:30am-2:30pm, Sa 9:30am-1pm).*

Emergency!

- **EMERGENCY NUMBER:** ☎092.

- **POLICE:** Police are located at the Ayuntamiento. *(Pl. Mayor ☎979 88 02 59)*
- **LATE-NIGHT PHARMACIES:** Pharmacies are located on Pl. Mayor *(Pl. Mayor, 14 ☎979 88 02 59)* and C. la Rúa *(C. la Rúa, 4 ☎979 88 03 33).*
- **MEDICAL SERVICES: Centro médico** *(Pl. Conde de Garay ☎979 88 02 45)*

Getting There

By Bus

Buses stop in front of Bar España in the town's eastern end, a 2min. walk up C. de Santa María from the Plaza Mayor. Buses arrive from **Bilbao** *(🕐 3½hr., M-Sa 9:15am $ €15.26.),* **Burgos** *(🕐 1¼hr., M-Sa 11:30am $ €5.36.),* **León** *(🕐 2hr., Su-F 3:15pm $ €8.49.),* and **San Sebastián.** *(🕐 5½hr., M-F 7:10am, Su 7:10am $ €13.89.)*

Getting Around

Walking is the easiest way to get around this small town. There is also a **taxi** stand at Pl. de Santa María (☎979 88 04 14).

león ☎987

León (pop. 165,000) is the last major city along the Camino de Santiago before the final stop of Santiago de Compostela itself. Though the old city retains vestiges of the Romans and the Middle Ages, the modern city that surrounds it has broad avenues and a cosmopolitan feel. The city's name (originally *Legio* in Latin, but changed over time to *León*) means "lion," and its inhabitants are appropriately proud of their city and identity, having been known to take down the occasional gazelle. The Roman walls still stand in part today, and the once heavily fortified city was a launching point for the knights of the *Reconquista.* The city is best known for its spectacular cathedral and its infamously boisterous nightlife.

ORIENTATION

León's **bus** station and RENFE **train** station are located on the west side of the Río Bernesga, while the rest of the city is to the east. **The Avenida Ordoño II** runs directly east from the river to the mainly pedestrian **casco antiguo,** where it goes through the **Plaza Santo Domingo** and becomes **Calle Ancha,** the *casco's* main street. To the north of C. Ancha is the walled part of the city, with the **Cathedral** and **Basílica de San Isidoro.** To the south is the **barrio húmedo** ("humid neighborhood") the main nightlife area, where the **Plaza Mayor** and **Plaza San Martín** can be found.

ACCOMMODATIONS

León has a fair number of inexpensive *hostals* and *pensiones* located between the old town and the river, especially around Av. de Roma, Av. de Ordoño II, and Av. de la República Argentina. They tend to fill up very quickly from June-Sept, so try to **reserve rooms in advance,** especially on weekends.

PENSIÓN BLANCA — B and B ❷

C. Villafranca, 2, 2A (3rd fl.) ☎987 25 19 91 www.pensionblanca.com

Large, brightly decorated rooms with high ceilings and clean wooden floors just steps from the main street between the river and the *casco antiguo.* Free breakfast and internet access keep guests happy, and daily newspapers will keep you up on current events in Spain and abroad.

Just off Av. de Ordoño II, 2 blocks from the river. i Breakfast included. Shared bath. Kitchen. Laundry €7. $ Singles €22, with bath €27; doubles €35, with bath €43; triples €55, extra bed €12. 🕐 Reception open daily 9am-11pm.

spain

HOSTAL OREJAS ✎♿ HOSTAL ❸

C. República Argentina, 28 ☎987 25 29 09 🖳www.hostal-orejas.es

Big, white rooms with large beds, private bathrooms, and cable TVs make this two-star *hostal* a pricier option but worth every penny. Make sure to book a room away from the seasonal construction directly across the street.

*# Entrance on C. Villafranca, 8. From Av. de Ordoño II heading toward casco antiguo, right onto C. Villafranca. **i** All rooms with private bath. Laundry service available. $ Singles €26-45; doubles €43-56; triples €53-69. Breakfast in restaurant €2.50; lunch and dinner €10. ⏰ Reception 24hr.*

SIGHTS

In addition to its Catedral—every Spanish city's mandatory sight—and the **Basílica de San Isidoro,** visitors to León can see the **Casa de Botines** *(at the far west end of C. Ancha, next to Pl. de Santo Domingo; now a bank),* one of Gaudí's few buildings outside of Cataluña, the **Convento de San Marcos,** a gorgeous palace on Pl. San Marcos converted into a luxury hotel, and several museums including the **Museo de León** *(Pl. Santo Domingo ⏰ Open Tu-Sa 10am-2pm and 4-7pm, July-Sept also Su 10am-2pm, €1.20, free weekends)* and the **Museo de Arte Contemporáneo.**

REAL COLEGIATA DE SAN ISIDORO ⊛⊗ CHURCH

Pl. de Santo Martino, 15 ☎987 87 61 61 🖳www.sanisidorodeleon.org

The *Basílica de San Isidoro* is beautiful inside and out, but the real attraction here is the **Panteón Real,** dating back to the 11th century and housing some of the original **Kings of Leon.** The museum upstairs has an impressive collection of reliquaries and other religious artwork and paraphernalia, while the tombs downstairs are the final resting places of 23 kings and queens, 12 *infantas,* and 9 counts, watched over by the 12th-century Romanesque paintings on the ceiling. While the basilica offers a guided tour, *Let's Go* recommends picking up a pamphlet at the information counter, giving yourself a tour, and saving a ton of time.

 # From C. Ancha, left onto C. del Cid to Pl. de San Isidoro. $ Basílica free. Museum €4, free Th afternoon. ⏰ Open July-Aug M-Sa 9am-8pm, Su 9am-2pm; Sept-June M-Sa 10am-1:30pm and 4-6:30pm, Su 10am-1:30pm. Hourly guided tours in Spanish.

FOOD

The *casco antiguo* is jam packed with restaurants, bars, and cafes, especially around the **Pl. Mayor** and **Pl. de San Martín.** Outside the *casco,* there are plenty of restaurants along **C. Renueva,** the pedestrian **C. Burgo Nuevo** and **Pl. Pícara Justina,** and along Av. de los Reyes Leoneses near MUSAC. In most Leonese bars, you'll receive some **free tapas** with your drink, so many just bar-hop instead of ordering a *menú*—three or four drinks can usually get you the equivalent of a full meal—and maybe a buzz.

RÚA NOVA ✎♿🍸 LEONESE ❷

C. Renueva, 17 ☎987 24 4 61

This lively bar and restaurant is on the restaurant-lined C. Renueva just two blocks from the basílica de San Isidoro and the *casco antiguo.* Leonese cuisine tends to be heavy on the pork, and Rúa Nova follows suit by serving a mean *ración* of *jamón asado* *(grilled ham; €8.10).*

 # From Pl. de Santo Domingo, follow Av. de Padre Isla 7 blocks, then turn right on C. Renueva. $ Menú €11. Entrees €8-16. ⏰ Open M 7:30pm-midnight, Tu-Sa 12:30-4pm and 7:30-midnight, Su 12:30-4pm.

EL VALENCIANO ✎♿🍸 DINER ❶

Pl. de Santo Domingo ☎987 23 71 39

Perfectly located on the Pl. Santo Domingo where Av. Ordoño II becomes C. Ancha, El Valenciano serves fresh orange juice *(€2)* that comes with a free churro—a perfect start to a day full of sightseeing. Be wary of the afternoon lines sweating it out for their share of ice cream.

꙰ *On the south side of Pl. de Santo Domingo.* Ⓢ *Coffee €1.20. Orange juice €2. Ice cream €1.60-3. Other food €3-9.* Ⓞ *Open daily 8am-midnight.*

NIGHTLIFE

León's best nightlife can be found in the casco antiguo, mainly around **Pl. San Martín** and **Pl. Mayor** in the neighborhood known as **el barrio húmedo** ("the wet neighborhood," for all the alcohol there) south of C. Ancha. The other side of C. Ancha tends to be a little more laid-back, but Spaniards do take a walk on the wild side around **Pl. Torres de Omaña**, **C. Cervantes**, and **C. del Cid**.

ESSENTIALS

Practicalities

- **TOURIST OFFICES:** The tourist office is hidden behind the Diputación on C. del Cid 1 block up C. Ancha toward the Catedral. *(C. del Cid, 1 ☎987 23 70 82* Ⓞ *Open Sept 16-June M-Sa 9:30am-2pm and 4-7pm, Su 9:30am-5pm; July-Sept 15 M-Sa 9am-8pm, Su 10am-8pm.)*

- **CURRENCY EXCHANGE: Banco Santander** *(Pl. de Santo Domingo ☎987 29 23 00* Ⓞ *Open Apr-Sept M-F 8:30am-2pm; Oct-Mar M-F 8:30am-2pm, Sa 8:30am-1pm.)*

- **LUGGAGE STORAGE:** Storage available at the RENFE train station *(€3)* and bus station *(€2).*

- **INTERNET ACCESS: Locutorio La Rua** *(C. Varillas, 3 ☎987 21 99 94* Ⓞ *Open M-F 9:30am-9:30pm, Sa 10:30am-2:30pm and 5:30-9pm.* Ⓢ *€1 per hr.)*

- **POST OFFICE:** *(Jardín de San Francisco ☎987 87 60 81,* Ⓞ *Open M-F 8:30am-8:30pm, Sa 9am-1pm).*

Emergency!

- **EMERGENCY NUMBER:** ☎112.

- **POLICE:** *(Paseo del Parque ☎987 25 55 00)*

- **HOSPITALS/MEDICAL SERVICES: Hospital San Juan de Dios** *(Av. San Ignacio de Loyola, 73 ☎987 23 25 00.)*

Getting There

By Bus

Buses arrive at the bus station *(Av. del Ingeniero Sáenz de Miera ☎987 21 10 00)* across the river from **Astorga** (Ⓞ *50min., M-F 17 per day 7am-10:30pm, Sa 8 per day 8:30am-7:30pm, Su 6 per day 11:50am-11:50pm.* Ⓢ *€3.30.),* **Barcelona** (Ⓞ *10hr., 3 per day 8:45am-10pm.* Ⓢ *€45.),* **Bilboa** (Ⓞ *5½hr., M-Sa at 9:15am.* Ⓢ *€23.75.),* **Burgos** (Ⓞ *2-3hr., M-Sa 4 per day 6:35am-5:25pm, Su 3 per day 6:35am-5:25pm.* Ⓢ *€13.85.),* **Logroño** (Ⓞ *4hr., 3 per day 4:35am-3:15pm.* Ⓢ *€16-19.),* **Madrid** (Ⓞ *3-4hr., M-F 18 per day 9am-12:30am, Sa-Su 14 per day 9am-11:30pm.* Ⓢ *€21-26.),* **San Sebastián** (Ⓞ *7hr., M-Sa at 7:40am.* Ⓢ *€28.47.),* and **Santiago de Compostela** (Ⓞ *6hr., daily at 8am.* Ⓢ *€26.41.).*

By Train

Trains arrive at the RENFE station *(C. Astorga ☎902 24 02 02),* also on the other side of the river, right next to the bus station, or at the FEVE station *(Av. del Padre Isla, 48 ☎987 22 59 19).* RENFE trains arrive from **Barcelona** (Ⓞ *8hr., 3 per day 9:20am-8:45pm.* Ⓢ *€68.),* **Bilbao** (Ⓞ *5hr., daily at 9:15am.* Ⓢ *€30.),* **Burgos** (Ⓞ *2hr., 4 per day 12:10pm-4am.* Ⓢ *€20-37.),* **Madrid** (Ⓞ *3-4hr., 9 per day 6:50am-10:30pm.* Ⓢ *€33-43.),* **San Sebastián** (Ⓞ *5hr., daily at 9am.* Ⓢ *€33.20.),* and **Santiago de Compostela.** (Ⓞ *8hr., daily at 9:25am.* Ⓢ *€31.40.)* FEVE trains arrive from **Bilbao** (Ⓞ *7hr., daily at 2:30pm.* Ⓢ *€22.).*

By Air

Flights arrive at León Airport 4mi. outside of the city from **Madrid** and **Barcelona**.

Getting Around

The easiest and cheapest way to get around is to **walk.** León has a **bus** system; bus #14 goes to the bus station, and #4 and #10 go to the RENFE train station. **Taxi stands** can be found at the Pl. Santo Domingo and along Av. Ordoño II, or call Radio Taxi *(☎987 26 14 15).*

astorga ☎987

Rising over the surrounding plain, Astorga (pop. 12,000) is the last major stop for Santiago-bound pilgrims before they hit the mountains like a caravan of steamrollers—or of tired pilgrims. Astorga has always been a crossroad: of silver-trading routes during Roman times, of pilgrimage trails during the Middle Ages, and of the A-6 and AP-71 today. The small old city is the renowned home of one of the few Gaudí buildings outside of Cataluña and also boasts a staggering rio of chocolate shops to square feet. In fact, Astorga may be the only city in Spain with more sweets shops than churches, and we bow down to its greatness. Those up to the challenge can try to eat one sugary treat from every store in town. C'mon. *Let's Go* double-dog dares you.

ORIENTATION

Astorga is a small city with Roman and medieval historic sights situated around the edges of its old city. The **Camino de Santiago** cuts through the center of town, passing the **Plaza de España,** the city's main square, at the eastern end and the **Plaza de Eduardo de Castro** at the northwest corner. The **bus station** *(Av. de las Murallas, 52 ☎987 61 91 00)* is just outside the northwest corner of the old city, and the **train station** *(Pl. de la Estación ☎987 84 21 22)* is about a 15min. walk to the northeast. Many accommodations are located a short walk west of the old city, about 15min. west of the bus station along **Av. de las Murallas,** which becomes **Av. de Ponferrada.**

ACCOMMODATIONS

Inexpensive lodging is tough to come by in Astorga: there's only one *hostal* and one *pensión* in the entire old city. However, there are three reasonably priced *hostales* and one *pensión* at the intersection of Av. de Ponferrada and the Carretera Madrid-Coruña, about a 15min. walk west of the historic center.

PENSIÓN GARCÍA PENSIÓN ❷
Bajada del Postigo, 3 ☎987 61 60 46

One of the only affordable accommodations in the old city itself, this *pensión* sits on a sloping street in the southeast corner of town, where several sights and much of the nightlife are located. The rooms have low but wide beds and are filled with the delicious aromas that waft up from the affiliated restaurant below.

From Pl. de España, take C. de la Bañeza (to right of Ayuntamiento); it's across from the playground. ***i*** *All rooms have shared bath. Make reservations in advance.* $ *Singles €20; doubles €30.* ⏰ *Reception 8am-midnight.*

HOSTAL SAN NARCISO HOSTAL ❷
Ctra. Madrid-Coruña, km 325 ☎987 61 53 70

About a 15min. walk from the old town, this hostal has huge rooms at very reasonable prices. Apparently, the builders were so set on making the rooms as big as possible for you that they made the walls as thin as they could to maximize living space, so you'd better hope your neighbors don't snore, smoke, or watch TV.

From the bus stop, take a right onto Av. de las Murallas, which passes through Pl. del Aljibe and becomes Av. de Ponferrada. Follow Av. de Ponferrada 5 blocks, then turn left before the gas station, and the hostal is across the street. $ *Singles €20, with bathroom €25; doubles €30, with bathroom €35.* ⏰ *Reception 24hr.*

SIGHTS

Most of Astorga's must-sees are located within the small old city, where monumental **Roman walls** still surround some of the town. The partially excavated Roman **forum** and **baths** are in the southeast corner, and the **Museo Romano** *(Pl. San Bartolomé ☎987 61 69 37 🕐 Open June-Sept Tu-Sa 10am-1:30pm and 4-6pm, Su 10am-1:30pm; Oct-May Tu-Sa 10am-1:30pm and 5-7:30pm, Su 10am-1:30pm. $ €2.50.)* is just a couple of blocks away by the **Plaza de España.** The monumental **Cathedral** and **Palacio Episcopal** are in the northwest corner.

PALACIO EPISCOPAL AND MUSEO DE LOS CAMINOS — HISTORICAL SITE

Pl. de Eduardo de Castro ☎987 61 68 82

From outside, the Palacio Episcopal (one of the few buildings outside of Cataluña designed by architect **Antoni Gaudí,** though those who have been to León probably think they're everywhere) looks like a quirky medieval castle perched above the Roman wall. The interior is magnificent, including an open floorplan, ceramic-lined arches and doorways, and seemingly weightless walls that are in places made more of glass than of stone. Since 1963 Gaudí's palace has housed the **Museo de los Caminos,** whose collection contains Paleolithic, Roman, and modern artifacts.

Just east of the Cathedral; from the bus station, cross the street, go through the small park and up the stairs, then turn left. $ €2.50, €4 entrada combinada available for Palacio Episcopal and Cathedral Museum (also €2.50). 🕐 Open Oct-May Tu-Sa 11am-2pm and 4-6pm, Su 11am-2pm; June-Sept 10am-2pm and 4-8pm, Su 10am-2pm.

FOOD

Astorga rose to prominence as the **chocolate capital of Spain** due to several factors: a cool, dry climate perfect for cocoa growth, an established network of trade routes, and, of course, the large local population of clergy and their notorious love of the sinful sweet. Since the 17th century, Astorga has been filled with chocolate factories (as many as 50 in 1914), and sweet shops line the streets of the old city today. Other local specialties are *cecina* (cured beef) and *Maragato* stew (chickpeas, potato, chorizo, cabbage, and various meats).

MUSEO DE CHOCOLATE — DESSERT, MUSEUM [1]

C. José María Goy, 5 ☎987 61 62 20

The Museo de Chocolate falls somewhere between the world's most delicious museum and the world's most informative desserterie. Redolent of fresh chocolate throughout, the museum is full of artifacts from Astorga's historic chocolate industry and ends with a *degustación:* free samples of **dozens of different types of chocolate.** And they're damn good, too: who would know chocolate better than a museum dedicated to it?

From Pl. de Eduardo de Castro (in front of Palacio Episcopal), head east 3 blocks along C. de los Sitios to Pl. Obispo Alcolea, then right onto C. José María Goy. $ €2, under 18 and over 65 €1, under 10 free. 🕐 Open May-Sep Tu-Sa 10:30am-2pm and 4:30-7pm, Su 11am-2pm; Oct-Apr Tu-Sa 10:30am-2pm and 4-6pm, Su 11am-2pm.

RESTAURANTE SERRANO — ASTORGAN [3]

C. Portería, 2 ☎987 617 866

This restaurant features *maragato* cuisine, the area's traditional home cookin'. The specialty is a *cecina con foie (cured beef with foie; €16)* that's big enough for at least 2 and best accompanied with plenty of bread to cut the overpowering richness.

Take C. Portería from Pl. de la Catedral. $ Menú €12. Entrees €8-18. 🕐 Open Tu-Su noon-4pm and 8-11pm.

NIGHTLIFE

Of the various things for which Astorga is known, nightlife cannot be considered one of them. What nightlife there is can be found on the east side of the old city, on **C. de Gabriel Franco** and **C. de Rodríguez de Cela.**

ESSENTIALS

Practicalities

- **TOURIST OFFICE: Oficina Municipal de Turismo** has detailed maps of the city and schedules for all major sights, buses, and trains. *(Pl. de Eduardo de Castro, 5 ☎987 61 82 22 💻www.ayuntamientodeastorga.com ➡ From bus station, cross the street, walk through the small park and up the stairs; go between the Cathedral (the massive building to the right) and the Palacio Episcopal (the massive building to the left), and left in front of Palacio Episcopal. The office is across the street. ⏰ Open Tu-Sa 10am-1:30pm and 4-6:30pm, Su 10am-1:30pm.*
- **TOURS: Ruta Romana** offers tours of Roman Astorga *($ €3.30. ⏰ 1¾hr., Tu-Sa 11am and 5pm, Su 11am.)* that leave from in front of the tourist office.
- **CURRENCY EXCHANGE AND ATMS: Banco Santander** is right down the street from the tourist office, Cathedral, and Palacio Episcopal. *(P. Obispo Alcolea, 10 ☎902 24 24 24 ➡ From Pl. de Eduardo de Castro follow C. de los Sitios east. ⏰ Open M-F 8:30am-2:30pm.)*
- **INTERNET ACESS: Ciberastor** offers internet access and printing. *(C. Manuel Gullón, 2 ☎987 61 80 17 💻 www.ciberastor.com ➡ From Pl. de España, take C. Pietro de Castro 1 block. $ Internet access €2 per hr. ⏰ Open daily 10am-2pm and 4-10pm.)*
- **POST OFFICE: Correos** *(C. Correos, 3 ☎987 61 54 42 ➡ From Pl. de Eduardo de Castro, follow C. de los Sitios east through Pl. Obispo Alcolea, and keep straight on C. de la Cruz for 3 blocks; the post office is on the left. ⏰ Open M-F 8:30am-2:30pm, Sa 9:30am-1pm.)*

Emergency!

- **POLICE:** ☎092.
- **MUNICIPAL POLICE: Policía Municipal** *(Pl. Arquitecto Gaudí, 6 ☎987 61 60 80 ➡ From Pl. de España, head northeast on C. Ovalle 1 block, then across the street, on the right.)*
- **MEDICAL SERVICES: Centro de Salud** *(C. de Alcalde Carro Verdejo, 11 ☎987 61 66 88 ➡ From bus station, turn right onto Av. de las Murallas, then turn right at the rotary onto C. de Alcalde Carro Verdejo.)*

Getting There

By Bus

ALSA runs **buses** from: **Bilbao** *($ €28.65. ⏰ 6½hr., daily 10:45am.)*, **Burgos** *($ €17.15. ⏰ 4hr.; M-Sa 4 per day 6:35am-5:25pm, Su 3 per day 6:35am-5:25pm.)*, **Barcelona** *($ €50. ⏰ 11-12hr., 4 per day 8:30am-8pm.)*, **Gijón** *($ €13. ⏰ 2½-3hr., 3 per day 8am-6:30pm.* **León** *($ €3.30. ⏰ 50min.; M-F 20 per day 6am-9:30pm, Sa 8 per day 7:30am-8:30pm, Su 6 per day 10:30am-8:30pm.)*, **Madrid** *($ €21-35. ⏰ 4-5hr.; M-F 10 per day 9:30am-12:30am, Sa-Su 8 per day 9:30am-12:30am.)*, **Santiago de Compostela** *($ €20. ⏰ 4-5hr., 5 per day 8am-11:15pm.)*, and **Sevilla** *($ €36. ⏰ 9½hr., daily 11:40pm.)*.

santiago de compostela ☎981

If you've made it to Santiago after finishing the Camino, congratulations. Kick back with some local *tinto* or white *albariño* and give those tired pilgrims' feet a rest. If you flew here, give your stiff neck a rest and *Let's Go* will keep the congratulations. Santiago de Compostela (pop. 94,000) has grown with the centuries as its colonnaded streets have swollen with pilgrims from around the world. The **Cathedral,** which houses the remains of the city's namesake **St. James,** is the main attraction, and much of the city—from the be-crossed almond cakes to the multilingual *menús*—is geared toward its visitors. There's more to the city than pilgrims, though: the nightlife buzzes with students from USC (Universidade de Santiago de Compostela, not its sunnier Californian counterpart), and every restaurant's window is full of octupi and giant, Hershey's-kiss-shaped cheeses. Though it's known for its pilgrims, and it certainly embraces that identity, Santiago has its own, quirky character hiding beneath each arch of the ancient old city.

ORIENTATION

As soon as you arrive in Santiago, be sure to get a **map,** since the streets are very poorly marked. The main streets of the old city are **Rúa do Franco, Rúa do Vilar,** and **Rúa Nova,** which run (with some name changes, at times) from the **Praza do Obradoiro** and the **Catedral de Santiago de Compostela,** the old city's hub, to the **Praza de Galicia,** which sits between the old and new parts of town. The **bus station** *(Pr. de Camilo Díaz Baliño ☎981 54 24 16 ⏰ Open daily 6am-10pm.)* is to the northeast of the old city. To get to Pr. de Galicia, take bus # 2 or #5 *($€0.90),* or head right on R. de Ánxel Casal, then left at the rotary onto R. da Pastoriza. Because this area is a living IQ test, this street subsequently turns into R. dos Basquiños, then R. de Santa Clara, and finally R. de San Roque. Next, turn left onto R. das Rodas which will turn into R. de Aller Ulloa, R. da Virxe da Cerca, R. da Ensinanza, and Fonte de Santo Antonio before reaching Pr. de Galicia. The **train station** *(R. de Hórreo ☎902 24 02 02)* is on the south end of the city; take bus #6 to get to Pr. de Galicia, or walk up the stairway across the parking lot from the main entrance and take R. do Hórreo uphill about 7 blocks.

ACCOMMODATIONS

HOSPEDAJE FONSECA — PENSIÓN [2]

R. de Fonseca, 1, 2nd fl. ☎646 93 77 65

The modern décor of this *pensión's* bright, high-ceilinged rooms contrasts with the ancient facade of the Cathedral, a literal stone's throw away across the street. These are just about the best prices you're going to find in the old city, and you couldn't dream of a better location.

➜ Take R. do Franco toward Pr. do Obradoiro, then turn right just before the Cathedral (1 block past little plaza) onto R. de Fonseca. Hospedaje Fonseca is on Rúa de Fonseca, not Praza de Fonseca or Travesa de Fonseca, which are all within 2 blocks of each other. ℹ All rooms have shared bath. $ Jul-Sept singles €20-22; doubles €35. Oct-Jun €15-18 per person. ⏰ Reception 8:30am-11pm.

HOSTAL PAZO DE AGRA — PENSIÓN [3]

R. da Caldeirería, 37 ☎981 58 90 45

The rooms are not quite as palatial as the "Agra" part of the name might suggest (Agra is the Taj Mahal's hometown), but feel free to address your subjects from your room's balcony over the old city. Or ignore the plebes and just bask in the view. The bathrooms are private, but for singles they're outside the room across a narrow hallway, so you'll still need to cover up after a shower.

➜ From Pr. de Galicia, take R. das Orfas into old city; it becomes R. da Caldeirería after 3 blocks, and the hostal is on the right after 1 more block. ℹ Private baths, but for singles are outside rooms. $ June-Sept singles €32; doubles €40. Oct-May singles €26; doubles €36. ⏰ Reception 24hr.

AS CANCELAS 🚗♿📶⏰ CAMPING [1]

R. do 25 de Xullo, 35 ☎981 58 02 66

Guests at this campsite can make the pilgrimage to Santiago de Compostela every day: the final 2km Camino runs just a couple blocks from the campsite toward the Cathedral, so guests can make the easiest and most brag-worthy part of the pilgrimage whenever they'd like. While As Cancelas is a campsite, it's hardly roughing it: there's a fancy restaurant and bar, and it's just a couple of blocks from a 5min. bus ride to the center of town.

 # Bus #4 (M-F every 30min., Sa-Su every hr.) runs from R. da Senra stop just west of Pr. de Galicia to As Cancelas. Or a 2km walk from old town north on R. de San Roque to Pr. da Paz to R. de San Caetano to Pr. de España, then right onto R. das Cancelas and right onto R. de 25 de Xullo. ***i*** *Supermarket, cafeteria, restaurant, pool, and laundry service available.* $ *Sept-June €5 per person, under 12 €2.90; €5 per car; €5 per tent; 4-person bungalow €49, 5-person €59. July-Aug €6.40 per person, under 12 €4.70; €6.70 per car; €6.70 per tent; 4-person bungalow €80, 5-person €96.* ⏰ *Reception 9:30am-11:30pm.*

SIGHTS

✓ CATEDRAL DE SANTIAGO DE COMPOSTELA AND MUSEUM CHURCH, MUSEUM

Pr. das Praterías ☎981 58 11 55 💻www.catedraldesantiago.es

Pilgrims have arrived at this site for more than a millenia, walking here by following the well-trodden Camino de Santiago in order to gain personal fulfillment and their **plenary indulgence** from the Church. The Cathedral's towers speckled with mosses, lichens, and flowers rise from the center of the city, making the enormous holy site look as though it has spent the last couple of centuries at the bottom of the nearby ocean. It has been above water the whole time, though (unless you count the frequent Galician rains), and the site has been a destination of pilgrims since the **relics of James the Apostle** were discovered here in the 9th century. Work on the ancient Romanesque cathedral began in 1075 and was completed in 1211, though the cloister was added during the Spanish Renaissance and most of the facades are 17th- to 18th-century Baroque. Today, pilgrims and tourists line up to **embrace the jewel-encrusted statue** of the Apostle and see the silver coffer that contains his remains. The *botafumeiro*, the massive silver-plated censer swung across the altar to disperse thick clouds of incense in the Cathedral's most famous spectacle, is usually used during the noon service, though the schedule varies and is not made public. The Cathedral's bells are older than the Cathedral itself, taken to Córdoba in 997 by invading Moors. Fortunately, the reconquering Christians had the last laugh when they took Córdoba in the 13th century and made their prisoners carry the bells all the way back to Santiago. The **museum** includes the peaceful cloister, the library (the books that line the shelves are ancient, but many of those on display are facsimiles), and the crypt. That funky smell in the crypt is caused by the humidity, not by human remains—or at least that's the official line.

 # Enter Cathedral on Pr. das Praterías; the museum entrance is inside on the left. $ *Cathedral free; museum €5, students, seniors and pilgrims €3.* ⏰ *Cathedral open daily 7am-9pm; museum open June-Sept M-Sa 10am-2pm and 4-8pm, Su 10am-2pm; Oct-May M-Sa 10am-1:30pm and 4-6:30pm, Su 10am-1:30pm.*

THE GREAT OUTDOORS

✓ CABO FINISTERRE (CABO FISTERRA) CAPE

For some pilgrims, walking from the Pyrenees (or beyond) to Santiago is just not enough. The route continues beyond the Cathedral and keeps going until there's not another foot of dry land left to walk at **Cape Finisterre**—literally "the end of the earth," once believed to be just that. The wind-battered cape sticks out into the Atlantic, reaching toward the New World from the infamous **Costa da Morte** ("Coast of Death"; Costa de la Muerte in Spanish), so called because of its jagged shores treacherous to seafarers and those made queasy by long, winding bus rides. The tiny town of **Fisterra,** once a trading hub at a nexus of sea routes, has narrow, winding alleys down to a lively port with restaurants lining the boardwalk and exhausted backpackers sunning themselves on the rocks.

It's a 45min. walk uphill along the road to the *faro* (lighthouse) at the end of the cape the very end of the Old World. Stunning views of the town, ocean, and nearby coastline are the prize that greets those who make it to the end of the trail, and the route runs past the ruins of an 18th-century fortress near the edge of town. 45min. in the other direction from Fisterra are the town's best beaches, though the water's usually chilly. To get there, walk the 3mi. along the road back to Santiago or take the bus and ask the driver to stop at the beaches. A 1hr. hike inland takes you up **Monte San Guillermo** home to several odd rituals. Pilgrims burn their clothes, couples having trouble conceiving make love on the bed-shaped fertility rocks, and weaklings and strong men alike move boulders by rolling **As Pedras Santas** (the round rocks move effortlessly when pushed in the right spot).

The **Albergue de Peregrinos** *(C. Real, 2 ☎981 74 07 81 🕐 Open Sept-May M-F 11am-2pm and 5-10pm, Jun-Aug 1-10pm)* has tourist information.

➤ The bus stop is near the Albergue de Peregrinos, a couple of blocks uphill from the water. 🕐 Buses €11.85; round-trip €21.70. ℹ Castromil/Monbus runs buses from Santiago to Fisterra. Last bus 7pm.

👍 O CASTRO DE BAROÑA — BEACH, RUINS

An hour's bus ride to the sea and another 30min. on a local bus down the coast takes you to **O Castro de Baroña,** a beautiful, out-of-the-way site that holds the ruins of a **5th-century Celtic fortress** and a small but pristine crescent beach. A rocky, overgrown trail leads out to a lonely promontory sticking out into the crashing waves, with the remains of the castle close to the bluff and high above the sea. All that remain of the 1500-year-old structures are their foundations and low walls, but the site is great to explore and enjoy the views of the sea and coast. Another path goes down to a quiet beach, whose cold but calm waters are protected by the cove. Clothing is *"prohibido,"* but many beachgoers remain bathing-suited, and hostility toward the clothed is limited. There's little there beyond the fort, beach, and a bar, but a 45min. walk or 5min. bus back toward Noia (to the left as you face the road from the bar) is Porto do Son, which has inexpensive restaurants and accommodations near the bus stop.

➤ To reach O Castro, you'll need to change buses in Noia. Castromil/Monbus runs buses from Santiago to and from Noia. (€3, round-trip €5.95). From Noia, Hefsel runs buses that stop at O Castro de Baroña (in front of Cafe-Bar O Castro) en route to Ribeira (€1.85) and return to Noia from the same stop. Check in the bar for the most up-to-date information and schedules, and take note of the last bus for each day. Be sure to tell the bus driver where you're going, as the stop for O Castro is easy to miss. From the bus stop, follow the signs to the fortress, downhill toward the water: at the fork with the two signs, the fortress is to the right, the beach to the left.

FOOD

👍 A TULLA — 💳🚭🍸☀ GALICIAN [2]

R. de Entrerrúas, 1 — ☎981 58 08 89

This is definitely the sort of place you have to know about in order to find—it's hidden down a crooked alley only a few feet wide—but those in the know just keep coming back. Pick just about anything off the handwritten menu (in Galego, of course), and it's bound to be delicious. Combine the *lentejas* (lentil stew; €3.50) with *chourizo á sidra* (spicy sausage cooked in cider; €4.50) to create one of the most delicious dishes in existence. They also have lots of vegetarian options, and a vegetarian *menú* (€10).

➤ In narrow alley between Rúa Nova and R. do Vilar, just toward Cathedral from Pr. do Toural on R. Nova, and just toward Cathedral from Municipal Tourist Office on R. do Vilar. $ Menú del día

€12, vegetarian menú €10. Soups/vegetables €3.50-7.50. Entrees €4.50-12.50. ⏰ *Open June-July M-Tu 1-4pm and 8:30pm-midnight, Th-Su 1-4pm and 8:30pm-midnight; Aug-May M-W 1-4pm, Th-Sa 1-4pm and 8:30pm-midnight, Su 1-4pm.*

👍 O DEZASEIS — 💳♿🍸 GALICIAN ❸

R. de San Pedro, 16 ☎981 56 48 80 💻www.dezaseis.com

If you're willing to shell out just a few more euro, you can get a serious step up in quality. This basement restaurant has an earthy stone-and-wood feel and delicious regional cuisine at very affordable prices. The classics like *tortilla española* (€5.40) are superb, and if you want a dish that Santiago himself would approve of, try the *vieira a galega* (a huge scallop served in its own shell, like the ones that line the Camino; €4.20). If you keep the shell, clean it, paint a cross on it, and sell it to a pilgrim, and the dish will nearly pay for itself.

➜ *Take R. da Virxe da Cerca along the edge of the old city, then turn onto R. de San Pedro away from old city.* $ *Menú del día €12. Raciones €3.50-13.50. Entrees €12-14.50.* ⏰ *Open M-Sa 2-4pm and 8pm-midnight.*

OBRADOIRO — 🚫🚭🍸☀ CAFE, BAR ❶

R. do Pombal, 44 ☎981 57 07 22

Pilgrims fill this bar and cafe for the daily €7 *menú*, which has huge portions and includes fresh bread and wine. With a patio for enjoying the rare but lovely Galician sun, this eatery offers one of the best-priced meals in town that isn't a kebab.

➜ *Just across the street from the Alameda (big park next to the old city); from Pr. de Galicia, follow R. da Senra to the left as you're facing the old city, then stay along the right side of the park down the hill.* $ *Menú del día €7.* ⏰ *Kitchen open daily 1-4pm and 8-10pm.*

NIGHTLIFE

Most of Santiago's nightlife is in the **old town** scattered around the **Cathedral,** but the area around the **Praza Roxa** has a more student-oriented scene.

CASA DAS CRECHAS — 🚫🚭🍸☀ BAR, LOUNGE, LIVE MUSIC ❶

Via Sacra, 3 ☎981 57 61 08 💻www.casadascrechas.com

Take a quick walk up the steps behind the Cathedral and descend into a Celtic witch's den that provides ample seating and beer. There are frequent jazz and Galician folk performances, so call ahead or check the website for the schedule; impromptu *foliadas* usually pop up on Wednesday evening, but you generally just have to be there when the right group of enthusiastic musicians comes in.

➜ *From Pr. da Quintana with the Cathedral to your left, head up the stairs and to the right, then left onto Via Sacra.* ⏰ *Open daily in summer noon-4am; in winter 4pm-3am.*

MODUS VIVENDI — 🚫🚭🍸 BAR, LOUNGE ❶

Pr. Feixóo, 1 ☎981 57 61 09 💻www.pubmodusvivendi.net

Welcome to the heart of Santiago's bohemia. Just about everyone will drop in at some point in the evening to mingle at the packed bar or push their way through to the more laid-back lounge. The trendy art and psychedelic lighting draw an eclectic crowd; the younger groups tend to gravitate to the back, so don't get scared off by all those graying male ponytails in front.

➜ *From Pr. da Quintana with the Cathedral to your left, head out to the far left corner of the plaza, then left onto R. da Conga, and bear left.* $ *Beer €2. Mixed drinks €4.50-6.* ⏰ *Open July-Sept M-W 6:30pm-3:30am, Th-Su 6:30pm-4:30am; Oct-June M-W 4:30pm-3am, Th-Su 6:30pm-4:30am.*

PUB TATOOINE — 🚫🚭🍸 CLUB, STAR WARS ❶

R. da República Argentina, 50

Far and away the most awesomely nerdy bar in town—if not along the entire Camino. Murals of stormtroopers and Darth Vader adorn this dark basement club, where clients are encouraged to show off their Jedi mind tricks and light sabers. Here, it's the cool kids who stand awkwardly against the wall.

From Pr. de Galicia, take R. do Doutor Teixeiro (follow street on right side of plaza with your back to old town) 2 blocks, then turn right onto R. da República Argentina. $ Beer €1.50-2. ⏰ Open Th-Sa midnight-5am.

ARTS AND CULTURE

Festivals

APÓSTOLO

Santiago de Compostela celebrates its patron saint's feast day for a full two weeks known as **Apóstolo,** kicking off the party about a week before **el Día de Santiago** (St. James' Day, July 25—especially holy when it falls on a Sunday, which will next be in 2021), the peak of the festivities. On the night of the 24th, **las Vísperas de Santiago,** fireworks and *gaitas* (traditional Galician-Celtic bagpipes) fill the Praza do Obradoiro in front of the Cathedral, while the *botafumeiro* (a giant incense-burner) swings within. July 25 is also Galicia Day (*Día de la Patria Galega*), and traditional music and dance fill the city.

⏰ *Apóstolo July 16-31; Día de Santiago July 25.*

Traditional Music and Dance

Thought bagpipes were limited to the British Isles and St. Patty's Day parades? Not so. The **gaita** is a traditional **Galician bagpipe,** left by the Celts during their migration, and it's just as irritating as its Highland cousin. Often heard on Santiago's streets, particularly around the **Pr. do Obradoiro** (the archway to the left of the Cathedral is a popular spot) and in the **Alameda** park, these badboys are inescapable during every major **festival.** Galician folk music's Celtic influences are obvious to the ear, and the best chance to dive into the Galician music scene is **Festival del Mundo Celta de Ortigueira** *(🖥www.festivaldeortigueira.com),* a massive folk festival held every July in tiny Ortigueira. Throughout July, the **Via Stellae Festival de Música** *(🖥www.viastellae.es)* takes place in Santiago and surrounding towns along the Camino; free music of all genres occurs at various venues throughout the city. **ARTERIA Noroeste** *(R. das Salvadas, 2A, Parque Vista Alegre ☎981 56 90 82 🖥www.arteria.com)* performs music that generally slides along the jazz-to-Galician-folk spectrum. To get to the performance space, take bus #4 toward Cancelas or bus #C2 or C4 toward Fontiñas.

Traditional **Galician dance** is loud and lively and also reflects its Celtic origins—it looks sort of like a castanet-filled combination between an Irish jig and Andalusian flamenco. Demonstrations can be seen at the **festivals,** and sometimes at the **Teatro Principal.** *(R. Nova, 21 ☎981 54 23 47)*

ESSENTIALS

Practicalities

- **TOURIST OFFICE: Oficina Municipal de Turismo** has maps and thorough information on accommodations, as well as a 24hr. interactive information screen outside. *(R. do Vilar, 63 ☎981 55 51 29 🖥www.santiagoturismo.com ⇆ On R. do Vilar 1 block toward Cathedral from Pr. do Toural. i English, French, German, Portuguese, Italian, Galego, and other languages spoken. ⏰ Open daily June-Sept 9am-9pm; Oct-May 9am-2pm and 4-7pm.)* **Oficina de Turismo de Galicia** has information on the rest of Galicia, and on festivals. *(R. do Vilar, 30 ☎981 58 40 81 🖥www.turgalicia.es ⇆ On R. do Vilar between Pr. do Toural and Cathedral, on opposite side of street from Municipal Tourism Office but closer to Cathedral. ⏰ Open M-F 10am-8pm, Sa 11am-2pm and 5-7pm, Su 11am-2pm.)* **Oficina del Xacobeo,** in the same building, provides information on the Camino de Santiago. *(R. do Vilar, 30 ☎981 58 40 81 ⏰ Open M-F 10am-8pm.)*
- **CURRENCY EXCHANGE:** Banco Santander has **Western Union** services and a 24hr. **ATM** outside, and cashes American Express Travelers Cheques commission-free. *(Pr. de Galicia, 1 ☎981 58 61 11 ⇆ On side of Pr. de Galicia to the right with your back to the old town. ⏰ Open Apr-Sep M-F 8:30am-2pm; Oct-Mar Sa 8:30am-1pm.)*

- **INTERNET ACCESS:** Ciber Nova 50 has fast computers and pay phones. *(R. Nova, 50 ☎981 56 41 33 ⇆ On R. Nova 1 block toward the Cathedral from Pr. do Toural. $ €0.45 for 12min., €2 per hour. ⏰ Open M-F 9am-midnight, Sa-Su 10am-midnight.)*
- **ENGLISH-LANGUAGE BOOKS:** Libraria Couceiro has several shelves of books in English. *(Pr. de Cervantes, 6 ☎981 56 58 12 💻www.librariacouceiro.com ⇆ From Pr. de Galicia take R. das Orfas into old city; it becomes R. da Caldeirería, then R. do Preguntoiro, and the bookstore is immediately to the left on Pr. de Cervantes. ⏰ Open M-F 10am-noon and 4-9pm, Sa 10am-noon and 5-9pm.)*
- **POST OFFICE:** Correos has a *Lista de Correos* and fax. *(R. das Orfas ☎981 58 12 52 💻www.correos.es ⇆ Take Cantón do Toural from Pr. do Toural 2 blocks to R. das Orfas. ⏰ Open M-F 8:30am-8:30pm, Sa 9am-2pm.)*

Emergency!

- **POLICE:** Policía Local. *(Pr. do Obradoiro, 1 ☎981 54 23 23 ⇆ On Pr. do Obradoiro across from Cathedral.)*
- **MEDICAL SERVICES:** **Hospital Clínico Universitario** has a public clinic across from the emergency room. *(Tr. da Choupana ☎981 95 00 00 ⇆ Take bus #1 from R. da Senra toward Hospital Clínico. ⏰ Clinic open M-Sa 3-8pm, Su 8am-8pm.)*
- **PHARMACY:** Farmacia R. Bescansa has been around since 1843—stop in to gawk at the classic 19th-century décor, even if you don't need anything. *(Pr. do Toural, 11 ☎981 58 59 40.)*

Getting There

By Bus

ALSA *(☎913 27 05 40)* runs buses from: **Astorga** *($ €20. ⏰ 5hr., 4 per day 4:15am-7:30pm.)*; **Barcelona** *($ €68.80. ⏰ 17hr., 3 per day 7am-8pm)*; **Bilbao** *($ €50-53. ⏰ 9-11hr., 4 per day 10:30am-1:45am.)*; **Burgos** *($ €37. ⏰ 8½hr., daily at 1:15pm.)*; **León** *($ €26.50. ⏰ 6hr., daily at 4:45pm)*; **Madrid** *($ €40-60. ⏰ 8-9hr.; M-Th 5 per day 7:30am-12:30am, F-Sa 4 per day 7:30am-12:30am.)*; and **Salamanca** *($ €29.20. ⏰ 6-7hr., M-F 3pm and 1:10am, Sa 5pm and 1:10am, Su 2 per day 3pm and 1:10am.)*.

By Train

RENFE trains arrive from: **A Coruña** *($ €5-15. ⏰ 40min., M-F 20 per day 5:45am-10:20pm, Sa 18 per day 6am-10pm, Su 17 per day 7am-10pm.)*; **Bilbao** *($ €44.90. ⏰ 11hr., daily at 9:15am.)*; **Burgos** *($ €40. ⏰ 8hr., daily at 12:11pm.)*; and **Madrid** *($ €49. ⏰ 7-9hr. M-Sa 2 per day 2:20-10:30pm, Su 2 per day 1:22-10:30pm.)*.

By Plane

Ryanair has inexpensive flights to Santiago's Lavacolla Airport *($ €2.50. ⏰ 30min. bus from bus station or city center.)* from: Alicante; Barcelona (El Prat); Barcelona (Reus); Madrid; Málaga; Frankfurt-Hahn; London-Stansted; and Rome. **Iberia** flies to Santiago from Bilbao, Sevilla, and Valencia.

Getting Around

Most of the old city is closed off to all but foot traffic, so the easiest way to get around is to **walk.** For those venturing farther afield, **buses** *(€0.90, €0.55 with bono)* are a good way to get around, though not particularly frequent on weekends. Bus #2 and #5 go to the bus station; bus #6 goes to the train station. **Freire** *(☎981 58 81 11)* runs buses *(30min., €2.50)* from R. do Doutor Teixeiro and the bus station to the airport. There are **taxi** stands at the bus and train stations and at Pr. de Galicia and Pr. Roxa. Otherwise, call Radio Taxi *(☎981 56 92 92)* or Eurotaxi *(☎670 53 51 54)*.

essentials

7

entrance requirements

- **PASSPORT:** Required for visitors from all countries except EU citizens who can show their national ID
- **VISA:** Required for those who wish to stay longer than 3 months
- **WORK PERMIT:** Required for all foreigners planning to work in Spain (see **Beyond Tourism**).

PLANNING YOUR TRIP
Time Differences
Spain is 1 hr. ahead of Greenwich Mean Time (GMT) and observes Daylight Savings Time. During the summer, from the end of March until the end of October, time is shifted forward one hour (GMT + 2). This means that it is 6 hours ahead of New York City, 9 hours ahead of Los Angeles, 1 hour ahead of the British Isles, 8 hours behind Sydney, and 10 hours behind New Zealand.

MONEY
Tipping and Bargaining
Native Spaniards rarely tip more than their spare change, even at expensive restaurants. However, if you make it clear that you're a tourist—especially an American—they might expect you to tip more. Don't feel like you have to tip, the servers' pay is almost never based on tips. No one will refuse your money, but you're a poor student so don't play the fool.

Bargaining is common and necessary in open-air and street markets. Especially if you are buying a number of things, like produce, you can probably get a better deal if you haggle. However, do not barter in malls or established shops.

Taxes
Spain has a 7-8% value added tax (IVA) on all means and accommodations. The prices listed in Let's Go include IVA unless otherwise mentioned. Retail goods bear a much higher 16% IVA, although the listed prices generally include this tax. Non-EU citizens who have stayed in the EU fewer than 180 days can claim back the tax paid on purchases at the airport. Ask the shop where you have made the purchase to supply you with a tax return form, but stores will only provide them for purchases of more than €50-100.

SAFETY AND HEALTH
General Advice
In any type of crisis, the most important thing to do is **stay calm.** Your country's embassy abroad is usually your best resource in an emergency; registering with that embassy upon arrival in the country is a good idea.

spain

Local Laws and Police

Travelers are not likely to break major laws unintentionally while visiting Spain. You can contact your embassy if arrested, although they often cannot do much to assist you beyond finding legal counsel. You should feel comfortable approaching the police, although few officers speak English. There are three types of police in Spain. The **Policía Nacional** wear blue or black uniforms and white shirts; they deal with crime investigation (including theft), guard government buildings, and protect dignitaries. The **Policía Local** wear blue uniforms, deal more with local issues, and report to the mayor or town hall in each municipality. The **Guardia Civil** wear olive green uniforms and are responsible for issues more relevant to travelers: customs, crowd control, and national security.

Drugs and Alcohol

Recreational drugs are illegal in Spain, and police take these laws seriously. The legal minimum drinking age is 16. Spain has the highest road mortality rates in Europe, and one of the highest rates of drunk driving deaths in Europe. Recently, Spanish officials have started setting up checkpoints on roads to test drivers' blood alcohol levels (BAC). Look for new cautionary signs on the highways that display how many Spaniards have died recently from drunk driving. Do not drive while intoxicated, and be cautious on the road.

Specific Concerns

Natural Disasters

Apart from the occasional mild earthquake evey 200 years, there is little to fear from nature in Spain. However, it is worth noting that if more than an inch of snow falls, many cities will shut down totally and driving will be incredibly slow, as Spanish drivers will be freaked from the weather conditions.

Terrorism

Basque terrorism concerns all travelers in Spain, with the active presence of a militant wing of Basque serparatists called the Euskadi Ta Askatasuna (ETA; Basque Homeland and Freedom). In March 2006, ETA declared a permanent cease-fire that officially ended in June 2007. ETA's attacks are generally targeted politically and are not considered random terrorist attacks that endanger regular civilians. The March 11, 2004 train bombings linked to al-Qaeda are viewed by Spaniards in the same way that Americans view September 11, and there is a monument in Madrid to those who died.

Pre-Departure Health

Matching a prescription to a foreign equivalent is not always easy, safe, or possible, so if you take **prescription drugs,** carry up-to-date prescriptions or a statement from your doctor stating the medications' trade names, manufacturers, chemical names, and dosages. Be sure to keep all medication with you in your carry-on luggage.

Pharmacists in Spain often speak very good English and can help you find common over-the-counter drugs. The names for such drugs in Spanish are also quite similar to those in English. One difference you will notice is that the Spanish are fond of effervescents, and often drugs are delivered in the powder form that you dissolve into water.

spain 101

CUSTOMS AND ETIQUETTE

Spaniards are generally polite and courteous to foreigners. Even if your Spanish is a little rusty, don't hesitate to speak in the native tongue–your efforts will be appreciated.

- **POPULATION:** 46.6 million
- **AUTONOMOUS REGIONS:** 17
- **REGIONAL LANGUAGES:** Catalan, Basque, and Galicia
- **KILOMETERS OF BEACHES:** Over 8,000
- **NUMBER OF OLIVE TREES:** Over 300 million
- **SPANIARDS INTERESTED IN BULLFIGHTING IN 1977:** 51%
- **SPANIARDS INTERESTED IN BULLFIGHTING IN 2006:** 27%

Taboos

Be aware that shorts and short skirts are not common in most parts of Spain, apart from the coasts. Wearing revealing clothing away from the beaches may garner unwanted attention or at the very least scream "I am a tourist!" Women with bare shoulders should carry a shawl to tour churches and monasteries, and it is considered disrespectful to wear shorts in these pious places.

Public Behavior

Spaniards tend to be very polite in mannerisms and social behavior, so in first encounters it's a good idea to be as formal as possible. Be sure to address those you meet as Señor (Mr.), Señora (Mrs.), or Señorita (Ms.), and don't be surprised if you get kissed on both cheeks in place of a handshake.

Tipping

Though a service charge is generally included in the check at bars and restaurants, an additional tip is common for good service: 5-10% will suffice. Taxi drivers and hotel porters will also expect small tips for their services.

FOOD AND DRINK

No immersion into Spanish culture would be complete without sampling the national cuisine, which is vibrant, varied, and inventive. Whether you're looking for a meal based on tradition or trendy culinary dishes, Spain is filled with epicurean delights. One dish all visitors are obligated to try at least once is *paella*, a quintessentially Spanish mix of rice, vegetables, seafood, and meat. Along with oranges, the Mediterranean city of Valencia is known for its sumptuous *paellas*. Spain's Mediterranean climate has played an important role in its culinary development; notably, its climate allows it to be the number one producer of olive oil in the world.

For a country smaller than the state of Texas, Spain has a large number of distinct regions, each with its own specialties. From the cold, tomato-based gazpacho soup in the hot southern climate of Andalucía, to calamar en su tinta (squid in its own ink) in northern País Vasco, each locality has a proud culinary tradition. One universal favorite are the ubiquitous tapas, or small, savory dishes served hot or cold, typically typically with drinks at bars. If you're looking for something other than plain vino (wine) or cerveza (beer) to go with your tapas, a delicious Spanish option is sangria, a red-wine punch made with fruit, seltzer, and sugar.

TURKEY

Turkey is a land like no other. There is something for everyone—foodies will love sampling Turkish *meze* and desserts, history buffs will wander in awe through Istanbul's palaces and places of worship, shopaholics will bargain-hunt in the immense bazaars and markets, party animals will dance their nights away in the clubs on İstiklal Avenue and in Ortaköy, hipsters will chatter their way through Beyoğlu's burgeoning art scene, the homesick will hobnob with expats in Cihangir, and idlers will rest inside the city's hamams. Take a ferry to the Asian side, at sunset. Learn about the city's history. Find your own best way to avoid a rakı hangover (a late-night çorba is a safe bet). Take a walk among the decrepit houses of Tarlabaşı or Fener. Pretend you're rich or beautiful at Reina or another prestigious club in Ortaköy. Spend a day down at the Princes' Islands, riding horse carriages or hiking up to a monastery. Voyage to Troy and Gallipoli, and mount your own assault where Agamemnon succeeded and Kitchener failed. Stay up all night and watch a sunrise over the misty Bosphorus. Whatever you want to do, Turkey is waiting.

greatest hits

- **BIKE PRINCES' ISLANDS:** Tour Heybeliada Island on two wheels, while enjoying its beaches, beer, and the beautiful vista of Istanbul (p. 1143).

- **GET STEAMED:** Head to Sofular Hamamı and experience a real Turkish bath (p. 1164).

- **EAT FRESH-OFF-THE-BOAT FISH:** Go to Sıdıka for grilled octopus. If that's too tentacle-y for your taste, get something else off their handwritten, chalkboard menu (p. 1159).

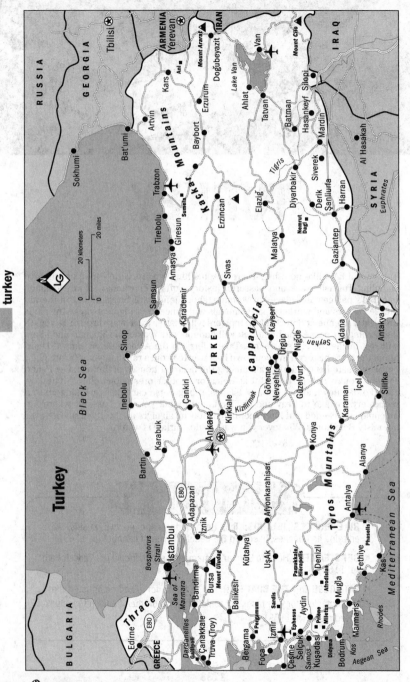

Turkey

istanbul ☎212, 216

ORIENTATION

Sultanahmet and Around

With the **Hagia Sophia** and other popular historical sights to its name, Sultanahmet is the center of Istanbul's tourism and the first stop for anyone who wants to explore the city. Sultanahmet proper is the area teeming with tourists around the **Blue Mosque**, where many of the budget accommodations and historical sights can be found. To the north there are the **Sirkeci** and **Eminönü** neighborhoods, home to the **Spice Bazaar**, bustling streets, and some decent eating options. The **Galata Bridge** above Eminönü connects the historic peninsula with **Karaköy** on the European side. The eastern tip of the peninsula is occupied by **Topkapı Palace** and the **Gülhane Park**, one of the few areas around that have greenery. To the west from Sultanahmet are **Çemberlitaş** and **Beyazıt Square**, home to nice tea places and cheap restaurants. Above Beyazıt is the **Grand Bazaar**, a maze-like area perfect for some shopping with your haggling. Below Beyazıt is the **Kumkapı** neighborhood, renowned for its fish restaurants.

Fener and Balat

Fener and Balat used to be a home to the Greek, Jewish, and Armenian minorities of Istanbul, but today they're populated mostly by poor Muslim migrants. It's a very dilapidated area, but doesn't feel unsafe. The fastest way to get here is by bus, but the prettiest is by ferry from Eminönü. The street plan is rather confusing, so use landmarks to navigate the area. **Vodina Cad.** runs parallel to the shore between Fener and Balat and has a number of local stores as well as the impressive, red-brick **Phanar Greek Orthodox College** (*Özel Fener Rum Lisesi*) some 300m inland from the Fener ferry jetty. The **Edirnekapı** neighborhood is a 15min. walk inland, close to the city walls, home to the mosaic-filled **Chora Church**. **Eyüp** is a neighborhood a few kilometers to the north of Balat, where you can find the **Eyüp Sultan Mosque** as well as the **Pierre Loti Cafe**.

Kadıköy, Moda, and Üsküdar

The Asian side of Istanbul tends to be more confusing for travelers, because it isn't laid out like most European cities. However, make your way through this disorienting part of town to discover the center of a lively alternative art scene, with an abundance of cafes and restaurants free from the hordes of tourists in other parts of the city. There are a few streets in historical **Kadıköy** whose location you should keep in mind. The **Söğütlüçeşme Cad.** runs from the ferry terminal inland and intersects with Kadıköy's important pedestrian street **Bahariye Cad.** This intersection is home to the well-known statue of a bull. Parallel to Bahariye Cad. is **Kadife Sok.**, the "bar street," where most of the local nightlife is located. Intersecting with Söğütlüçeşme near the ferry terminal is the **Güneşlibahçe Sok.**, where **Kadıköy Market** and many restaurants with live music can be found. **Moda** is a well-to-do residential area to the south of Kadıköy with some romantic beaches that people often use to watch the sunset. Within walking distance, Moda is also accessible by a nostalgic shoebox-of-a-**tram** that follows a circular route around Kadıköy into suburbia. **Üsküdar** is a rather sleepy historical neighborhood some kilometers north of Kadıköy that is home to a number of mosques. The easiest way to travel between Kadıköy and Üsküdar is to take public bus #12 or #12A.

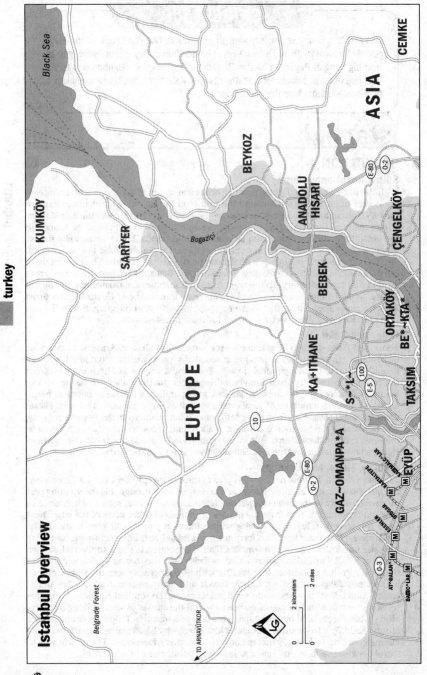

Istanbul Overview

Belgrade Forest

TO ARNAVÜTKOR

EUROPE

10

E-80

O-2

GAZ~OMANPA*A

SEBWAL^CLR

EYÜP

K^RATUTEPE

OTOGAR

S^LALAN*

BAĞC~LAR

M M M M M M

O-3

Black Sea

KUMKÖY

SARÎYER

Bogaziçi

BEYKOZ

ANADOLU HISARI

BEBEK

KA+ITHANE

S~*L~

E-5

100

TAKSIM

ORTAKÖY

BE*~KTA*

ÇENGELKÖY

ASIA

E-80

O-2

CEMKE

0   2 miles

0   2 kilometers

N

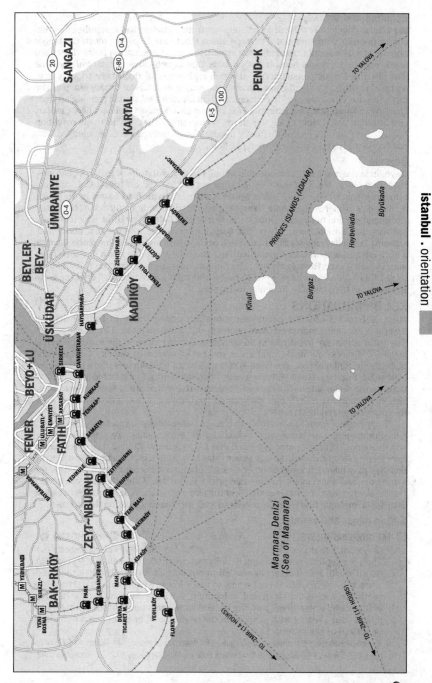

istanbul . orientation

SANGAZI
20
E-80
O-4
O-4

KARTAL

E-5 100

PEND~K

TO YALOVA →

ÜMRANIYE
O-4

BEYLER~
BEY~

ÜSKÜDAR

BOSTANCI

ERENKÖY

SUADIYE

GÖZTEPE

ZÜHTÜPAŞA

FENER YOLU

KADIKÖY

HAYDARPAŞA

Büyükada

Heybeliada

PRINCES ISLANDS (ADALAR)

Kınalı

Burgaz

TO YALOVA →

BEYO+LU

FENER

SIRKECI

CANKURTARAN

ÇANKURTARAN

FATİH M AKSARAY

M ULUBATL^

M EMNIYET

KUMKAPI

YENIKAPI

SAMATYA

YEDIKULE

ZEYT~NBURNU

ZEITINBURNU

NURPAŞA

YENI MAH.

BAKIRKÖY

TO YALOVA →

BATRAMPAŞA M

M YE+ILBA+I

KIRAZLI^

BAK~RKÖY

M PARK

ÇOBANÇE+ME

MAH.

ATAKÖY

YEN+
BOSNA

M

DÜNYA
TICARET M.

YE+ILKÖY

FLORYA

Marmara Denizi
(Sea of Marmara)

TO ~ZM~R (14 HOURS) →

TO ~ZM~R (14 HOURS) →

Beşiktaş and Ortaköy

Beşiktaş, a village a few local kilometers up from Kabataş, has a small pedestrian center popular with students. The **eagle statue** (there are two—we mean the bigger one), which is near the triangular **fish market,** is a good orientation point. There are a few expensive places here, but it's **Ortaköy** that is notorious as Istanbul's leading site of conspicuous consumption—the rich and powerful flock here to shop, eat, and party. Ortaköy's small center is near the water, around the **Ortaköy Mosque.** The city's famous clubs are mostly concentrated on **Muallim Naci,** a road running up from Ortaköy to **Kuruçeşme.** One main road (at various points called Dolmabahçe, Çirağan, and Muallim Naci) runs along the shore, connecting Kabataş with these neighborhoods. You can take one of the many buses, though the road is often clogged with traffic, so we suggest walking when possible.

Beyoğlu

Beyoğlu is the real heart of modern Istanbul, pulsing with tons of galleries, eateries, bars, and clubs. Many of these establishments are located off **İstiklal Cad.,** a throbbing promenade connecting **Taksim Square** in the north with **Tünel Square** in the south. A bit below Tünel is the **Galata Tower,** the most recognizable landmark of the entire European portion of the city. Don't confuse this with **Galatasaray Lisesi,** which is about halfway into İstiklal, near where **Yeni Çarşı** intersects the avenue. Just above Galatasaray is the **Nevizade Sokak,** where much of Beyoğlu's nightlife takes place. **Cihangir,** a bohemian neighborhood popular with expats, is between the **Alman Hastanesi** (German Hospital) and **Firuzağa Mosque.** The Sultanahmet tram doesn't run to İstiklal, so to get there, you can either go to Karaköy and take a funicular to Tünel, or go to Kabataş and then take the funicular to Taksim.

ACCOMMODATIONS

Most of Istanbul's budget accommodations are concentrated in **Sultanahmet,** but **Beyoğlu** is becoming more and more popular with travelers looking for cheap rooms. The main advantage to staying in Sultanahmet is being close to the major historical sights, while residing in Beyoğlu gives you easier access to the city's culture and nightlife. In Sultanahmet, boutique hotels and small guesthouses often provide the best value, but they usually fill up quickly. There are only a few suitable accommodations on the Asian side and in the more conservative districts like **Fatih** or **Fener,** while Beşiktaş is home to mostly upscale hotels. Avoid staying in hotels in the **Aksaray** area, the city's seedy red light district.

The prices of Istanbul's hostels can change faster than you can say "Çekoslovaky alılaştıramadıklarımızdanmışsınız" (which, by the way, means "are you one of those whom we couldn't have possibly turned into a Czechoslovak?"). All the prices quoted here were collected during the **high season** (Mar-May, Aug-Sept, Christmas-New Year's), but they may be much lower at other times. Not all hostels change their prices at the same time, and some maintain the same prices year-round. Often the deal you get depends on what kind of room is available at the moment, so the best way to find a **bargain** is to ask at multiple hostels in person, or to look for current prices on the internet.

Sultanahmet and Around

METROPOLIS HOSTEL — HOSTEL [2]

Akbıyık Cad. Terbıyık Sok. 24 — ☎212 518 1822 www.metropolishostel.com

Though skeptical of everything in Sultanahmet that's under than 400 years old, *Let's Go* still found an accommodation option that it can wholeheartedly recommend—Metropolis Hostel seems to really know what international travelers need. The rooms are clean and welcoming, the beds are comfortable (a rarity in the hostel scene here), and the terrace view beats much of the competition. Spend your evening with *nargile* on the rooftop bar, or join in on a pub crawl organized by the hostel.

[M]Sultanahmet. Near İshak Paşa Mosque. i Breakfast included. $ Dorms €14-17; all-female €17. Singles €37; doubles €54, with bath €66; triples €72; quads €72. Reception 24hr.

CORDIAL HOUSE

⚑ ♿ 📶 HOSTEL ❶

Peykhane Sk. 29   ☎212 518 0576 💻www.cordialhouse.com

One of the best budget options on the historical peninsula, this big hostel near *Çemberlitaş* is cheap, close to a tram stop, and very conveniently located for walking to both the Grand Bazaar and Sultanahmet. Since it has so many rooms, you might get a lower price even at a time when other hostels are still charging their high-season prices. It's not quite the social hotspot that hostels with terrace bars aspire to be, but if that aspect of hostel culture isn't too important to you, this is the place to stay.

✈ Ⓜ*Çemberlitaş. 50m south from the tram stop.* i *Breakfast €4.* ⑤ *Dorms €12; singles €24; doubles €30, with bath €60; triples with bath €70; quads with bath €80.* ⌚ *Reception 24hr.*

TULIP GUESTHOUSE

⚑Ⓧ📶❄ GUESTHOUSE ❷

Akbıyık Cad. Terbıyık Sok 15/2   ☎212 517 6509 💻www.tulipguesthouse.com

With a tiny kitchen in which to cook, cheerful and clean rooms, and an owner with a university education, this guesthouse offers better value than many bigger hostels. Twice a week there are community dinners prepared by the staff and the guests in the upstairs breakfast area, and there's a shower available in the basement for people who already checked out but are staying until the end of the day. Even the name reflects the management's desire to cater to the comfort of its guests—it was changed to "Tulip" after they realized it was more memorable than the original, unpronounceable one.

✈ Ⓜ*Sultanahmet. Near İshak Paşa Mosque.* i *Breakfast included. Bathrooms ensuite.* ⑤ *Dorms €10; singles €35; doubles €45; triples €55.* ⌚ *Guests get their own key.*

CHEERS HOSTEL

⚑Ⓧ📶 HOSTEL ❸

Alemdar Mahallesi Zeynep, Sultan Camii Sokak 21   ☎212 526 0200 💻www.cheershostel.com

Among the more expensive accommodations, Cheers Hostel offers great value for your money. The rooms are decorated with objects that could be mistaken for Ottoman relics by people not in the know, the showers are inside glass cubicles (not as common around here as you might think), and there's a killer view of Hagia Sophia from the terrace. The dorm beds have their own storage containers (most places only have safety boxes at the reception desk), but the dorms themselves aren't usually locked.

✈ *From* Ⓜ*Gülhane, continue up Divan Yolu, turn right after Zeynep Sultan Mosque, and continue for 30m.* i *Breakfast included. All doubles and triples with ensuite bath.* ⑤ *Dorms €16-20; doubles €60; triples €80.* ⌚ *Reception 24hr.*

NOBEL HOSTEL

⚑Ⓧ📶❄ HOSTEL ❷

Mimar Mehmet Aga 32   ☎212 516 3177 💻www.nobelhostel.com

Yet another good hostel that combines relatively low prices with acceptable quality. A vertigo-inducing staircase leads to the terrace upstairs that offers a great view of the Blue Mosque. Guests get a 15% discount in the restaurant downstairs, and a beer for just 4 TL upstairs. Here's a joke: Knock, knock. Who's there? Nobel. Nobel who? Nobel, so I rang. *Let's Go* doesn't know how long (if at all) the reception will find this joke funny.

✈ *From* Ⓜ*Sultanahmet, head down Akbıyık Cad.* i *Breakfast included.* ⑤ *Singles €30; doubles €40, with bath €50; triples €50, with bath €60.* ⌚ *Reception 24hr.*

ORIENT HOSTEL

⚑Ⓧ📶 ♈ HOSTEL ❷

Akbıyık Cad 13   ☎212 517 9493 💻www.orienthostel.com

Allegedly the first hostel in Turkey and one of the biggest ones in Istanbul, Orient Hostel is a safe bet for young travelers and offers a decent view of the sea from the terrace, a daily happy hour, and many common spaces in which to meet fellow backpackers. The rooms are small and reasonably clean, even if the stairs and the underground spaces can feel a bit musty. With a capacity of 152 guests, you're probably not going to get turned down when you show up fresh off the plane at 3am.

✈ *From* Ⓜ*Sultanahmet, walk past the Hagia Sophia; it's located in the middle of the hostel district.* i *HI member. Breakfast included. Happy hour beer 5TL.* ⑤ *Dorms €10-15; singles €30; doubles €40, with bath €55.* ⌚ *Reception 24hr.*

istanbul • accommodations

HOTEL ERENREL

💳🚭📶 HOSTEL ❶

Hoca Paşa Tayahatun Sk. 11 ☎212 527 3468 💻www.hotelerenler.com

A great choice for cheapskates who don't want to stay in a dorm, this hostel has single rooms that are half the price and half the size of what one tends to expect. The wireless connection is erratic, the English at the reception desk is intermittent, and the hostel is tucked away in a small street in Sirkeci that could look eerie at night—but hey, you get to stay in your own room for the price of an upscale kebab. The place isn't dirty or unsafe, so it can be used as a base for sleeping, because your waking hours will be spent in the magnificent streets of Istanbul.

➔ *[M]Gülhane. Follow the tram tracks north along the Gülhane Park walls. When the tram tracks turn left, keep to the right and continue for two blocks.* $ *Dorms €10; singles €13; doubles with bath €33.* ⏰ *Reception 24hr.*

Kadıköy, Moda, and Üsküdar

HUSH HOSTEL

💳🚭📶 HOSTEL ❶

Miralay Nazım Sok. 20, Kadiköy ☎216 330 9188 💻www.hushhostelistanbul.com

Decrepit but charming, this hostel housed within an Ottoman mansion seems to have a monopoly on budget accommodations in this area. The cracked paint and gloomy feel aren't for everybody, but the location next to Bar Street is great, and there's an art gallery downstairs. If you want to stay on the Asian side and close to all the nightlife, say no more than "hush."

➔ *From the bull statue, head south down Bahariye Cad. After passing the Süreyya Opera House,*

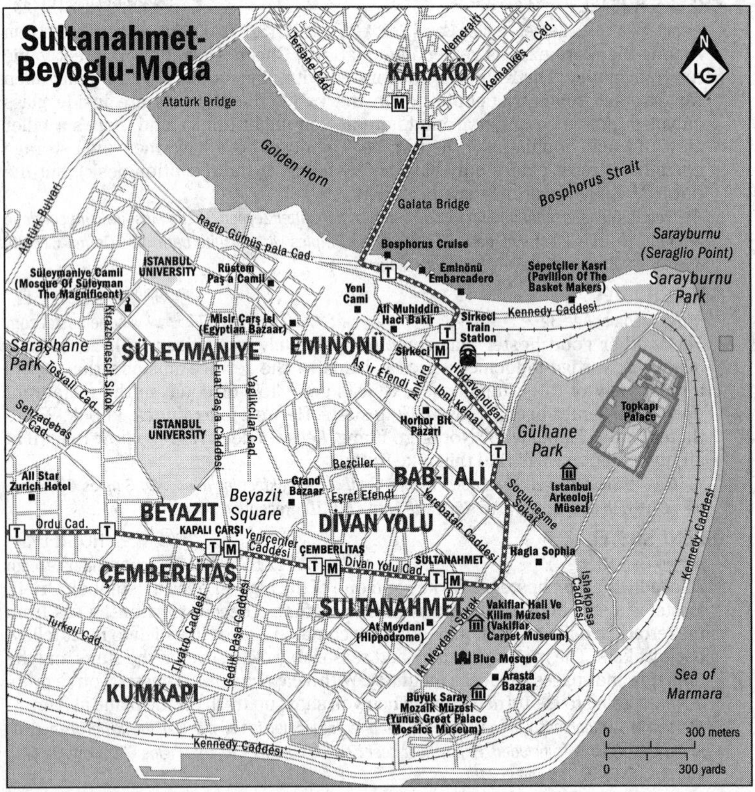

turn right, and then another right. The hostel will be on your left. $ *Dorms €11-12; doubles €34-38; triples €45; quads €52.* ⏰ *Guests get their own key.*

HOTEL GRAND AS 💳♿📶❄ HOTEL [4]

Nüzhetefendi Sok. 27, Kadiköy ☎216 346 9160 💻www.grandashotel.com

Despite the unfortunate name, this is one of the better options from among the cluster of hotels near the ferry terminal, which range from completely unmemorable to unforgettably terrible. You won't write home about this place, but at least the staff speaks some English and the rooms have ensuite bathrooms.

➡ *From the ferry terminal, head up Söğütlü Çeşme Cad. Turn left at Osmanağa Mosque, and it's two blocks ahead.* ℹ *Breakfast included.* $ *Singles 75TL; doubles 110TL; triples 140TL.* ⏰ *Reception 24hr.*

HUSH HOSTEL LOUNGE 💳🚭📶 HOSTEL [1]

Rıhtım Cad. Iskele Sok. 46, Kadiköy ☎216 450 4363 💻www.hushhostelistanbul.com

This very recent offshoot of the HUSH Hostel is a bit more expensive, a bit more modern, and a bit farther from everything interesting. The rooms are large and take the word "bare" to new extremes, but there are a couple of cool lounges downstairs that make up for it. The empty walls are slowly being populated by art that's left over from exhibitions at the other HUSH hostel, so the charisma of this place can only go up.

➡ *From the terminal that serves ferries from Eminönü, cross the street and head north. Instead of continuing on the bridge, turn right on Iskele Sok. and continue up the hill. It will be to your right.* ℹ *Breakfast included.* $ *Dorms €12-13; singles €33-35, with bath €44; doubles €34-38, with bath €50; triples €48-54, with bath €66; quads €60-64, with bath €72.* ⏰ *Reception 24hr.*

Beşiktaş and Ortaköy

HOTEL ÇIRAĞAN 💳📶 HOTEL [2]

Müvezzi Cad., Beşiktaş ☎212 260 0230 💻www.ciraganhotel.com

This is as close to budget accommodation as you can get in Beşiktaş and Ortaköy. If it weren't for some very tall trees, the hotel would have what could qualify as a "Bosphorus view" (the phrase that justifies unreasonably high prices in many establishments in Istanbul—its Sultanahmet equivalent is the "Blue Mosque view"). There is a pleasant restaurant on the sixth floor.

➡ *Take the ferry or bus to Beşiktaş. Walk down Çirağan toward Yıldız Park until you see Müvezzi on your left, just before the park walls start. The hotel is at the base of Müvezzi Cad. on the left. The Çirağan bus stop is very close to the hotel.* ℹ *Wi-Fi is available in the lobby and in the restaurant. The staff speak some English.* $ *Singles with bath 75TL; doubles with bath 95TL.* ⏰ *Reception 24hr.*

OTEL BEŞIKTAŞ 💳📶 HOTEL [2]

Ihlamurdere Cad. 19, Beşiktaş ☎212 261 0346

This locals-oriented hotel is right in the center of Beşiktaş, relatively close to the ferry terminal and the bus station. If you're an unmarried couple, you might have some trouble getting a room together, but if you act foreign enough you should be fine.

➡ *Take the ferry or bus to Beşiktaş. Walk inland on Ortabahçe Cad., which intersects with Dolmabahçe Cad. near the Naval Museum. After a few blocks, the hotel will be to your left.* ℹ *Little English spoken.* $ *Singles with bath 70TL; doubles 90TL.* ⏰ *Reception 24hr.*

Beyoğlu

👍 **RAPUNZEL GUESTHOUSE** 💳📶 HOSTEL [1]

Bereketzade Camii Sok. 3 ☎212 292 5034 💻www.rapunzelistanbul.com

This hostel is run by three charming people fresh out of university and very willing to give you advice on where to go and what to see in the city. What's more, every week they compile a list of concerts and events that might be of interest to travelers. The mattresses are orthopedic, and the location right below the Galata Tower is great, provided that you don't mind having to climb some steep slopes in the nearby streets. Rapunzel is quite new, so let's hope its owners never lose their current youthful enthusiasm.

⇆ [M]Tünel or [M]Karaköy. Get as close to Galata Tower as you can, then head down the hill on Camekan Sok. and take a right turn at the Berekzade Mosque; the hostel will be on right. ℹ Breakfast included. $ 4-bed dorms €16; singles with bath €40; doubles with bath €50. ⏰ Reception 24hr.

NEVERLAND HOSTEL 🌐 📶 HOSTEL [1]

Boğazkesen Cad. 96 ☎212 243 3177 🖥www.hostelneverland.com

With posters calling for the fall of neoliberalism, a giant yin and yang seat, and handpainted walls, this is one of the most charismatic hostels in the city. Its enactment of the word "alternative" is very thorough—few other places in Istanbul care about recycling paper and plastics and usually just leave it to the poor who make a living out of it. There are many pleasant common spaces, free tea and coffee from the kitchen, and a collective management that is set on creating an ecovillage one of these days. If you're nice, maybe they'll let you join.

⇆ [M]Tophane. Walk uphill on Boğazkesen Cad. for 5min. The hostel will be on your right. ℹ Breakfast included. $ Dorms €9-12; singles €20; doubles €28, with bath €34; triples €36. ⏰ Reception 24hr.

CHILL OUT CENGO HOSTEL 🌐 📶 HOSTEL [1]

Halas Sok. 3 ☎212 251 3148 🖥www.chillouthc.com

Perhaps the most atmospheric of the five Chill Out hostels in Beyoğlu, Cengo is also the biggest. It features some innovative interior design—the stairs to some of the attic rooms look like something you'd encounter in an obstacle course. The furniture in the common rooms is very pleasant to sit on, but you can also choose to sit on the indoor swing. If this one is full, you can try the **Chill Out Lya Hostel** *(Toprak Lüle Sok. 1 ☎212 244 7400)* or the **Chill Out Hostel Classic** *(Balyoz Sok. 3A ☎212 249 4784)*, which is closer to Tünel and a bit more impersonal. All five Chill Out hostels have crazily painted stairs and affordable prices.

⇆ From [M]Taksim, walk down İstiklal, turn right after the Ağa Camii mosque, and continue down Atif Yilmaz. Take the 2nd left, and the hostel's unmarked gate will be to your left. $ Dorms €15; singles €25; doubles €35. ⏰ Reception 24hr.

CHAMBERS OF THE BOHEME 💻 📶 HOSTEL [1]

Küçük Parmakkapı Sok. 11/13 ☎212 251 0931

Chambers of the Boheme has a great location for raiding bars in İstiklal, Çukurcuma, and Cihangir. The hostel's style is more old-fashioned than alternative, but it's nevertheless interesting: many private rooms, and even some of the dorm rooms, feature antique furniture. Guests get a 10% percent discount at the cafe on the ground level. Some website gave this place a "Best Hostel in Turkey" award in 2009, and the management equates this with winning an Oscar—we suggest you remain a bit skeptical.

⇆ From [M]Taksim, walk down İstiklal and take the 2nd left turn; the hostel will be to your left. ℹ Breakfast included. $ Dorms €15-18; 4-person family room €120. ⏰ Reception 24hr.

SOHO HOSTEL 💻 📶 HOSTEL [1]

Süslü Saksı Sok. 5 ☎212 251 5866

It's not the neatest of hostels (there isn't much space and the bathrooms can look a bit unappealing), but there's a sense of free-spiritedness to its color and common room. It's not one of the many bland, unmemorable hotels that clutter the streets in this area. Soho is one of the cheapest hostels near İstiklal Cad. and close to all the nightlife, so it can be a good base for sleeping and perhaps for connecting with similar-minded travelers.

⇆ [M]Taksim. From Taksim walk down İstiklal and take the fifth right turn (on İmam Adnan Sokak). Continue to the end and turn left, the hostel will be on your left side. $ Dorms €6-10; singles €20; doubles €34. ⏰ Reception 24hr.

SIGHTS

Princes' Islands *Kızıl Adalar*

Originally inhabited by monks and exiled aristocracy and later by wealthy merchants and writers, the Princes' Islands are today a popular escape spot for locals and tourists who want to take a break from Istanbul's busy streets. Of the nine islands, four have a daily ferry service to Istanbul, while the others are mostly uninhabited. Cars are not allowed on the islands, so people either walk, bike, or use *faytons* (horse-drawn carriages). These islands are not in the Caribbean—the paid beaches are often ugly, with limited sand, and overflowing with chaise lounges. If the traditional beach experience is what you're after, you'll be disappointed. However, there are fish restaurants, monasteries, forests, picnic areas, and hills overlooking the sea, so it's worth the daytrip if you're staying in Istanbul for at least a few days.

The easiest way to get to the islands is to take a **ferry** from Ⓜ Kabataş. Ferries may stop in Kadıköy before continuing to **Kiliada, Burgazada, Heybeliada,** and **Büyükada.** If you hop off at one island and then take a ferry to another one, you'll have to pay the fare again. The ferry system is mildly confusing because there are three kinds of ferries with separate schedules that leave from Ⓜ Kabataş—**IDO seabus, IDO passenger ferry,** and **Dentur Avrasya ferry.** The first two are operated by IDO, cost 2.5TL per ride, and can be paid for with Akbil, but each differ in their speed and routes. While the seabus may take you straight to Büyükada in 35 min., the passenger ferry may take up to 1½hr. by stopping at the smaller islands first. The Dentur Avrasya ferry (☎212 227 7894 Ⓢ *4TL one way, 6TL return ticket.)* leaves from behind the gas station and is faster than the passenger ferry. Free schedules are available at the ferry terminals—consult them so that you don't miss the last ferry home.

Büyükada *Prinkipo*

This is the largest and the most touristy of the islands. It can get unbearably crowded on weekends and during the summer, so your best bet is to visit midweek. The main attraction is the **Aya Yorgi Monastery** (☎216 382 3939 ⏰ *Open daily 9am-6pm.* Ⓢ *Free.),* located on top of a hill that offers a great view of the surrounding archipelago. To get here, first go to the Luna Park square *(fayton* costs 20TL, walking there should take about 30min.) and then walk up a very steep hill for about 20min. If you're into miracles, try the ascent without shoes while wishing something—word on the street is that the wish might come true after you reach the top (just don't wish for a pair of shoes). The monastery's church is rather new (it was built in 1906), but the interior is enthusiastically decorated with Christian imagery. The monastery used to function as a place for healing the mentally ill, who would spend their nights chained to the ground in front of Saint George's icon. Unfortunately, the chain rings were removed during a restoration some years ago. Nearby the church is the pleasant **Yücetepe Kir Gazinosu restaurant** (☎216 382 1333 🌐 *www.yucetepe.com),* where you can refuel after the hike. Other things to do here include visiting the **Princes' Islands Museum** (*Çinar Meydanı, due to open in 2010),* which will contain much more information about the islands than you'll ever need. There are three paid **beaches** (*15-25TL)* which run their own free shuttle boats from the docks, but don't set your expectations too high. A nice, if a bit barren spot for a **picnic** is the Dilburnu peninsula (*Piknik Alani* ☎216 382 4301 Ⓢ *3TL per person).* The authorities and entrepreneurs are working on transforming the island into the new Sultanahmet, but there are many sights which are still dilapidated and not accessible to the public, including the villa where Leon Trotsky spent four years of his exile (**Trocki Evi,** *down a steep cul-de-sac near Çankaya Cad. 59* and **Eşki Rum Yetimhanesi,** an abandoned orphanage on the hill opposite Aya Yorgi. As you exit the ferry, head left to the useful **tourist information** booth, where you can get free maps of the four major islands. Bike rental stores are scattered all over the village (Ⓢ *2.5-5TL per hr., 7.5-15TL per 24hr.),* while the *faytons* leave from above the clock tower square (Ⓢ *Tours 40TL-50TL).*

Heybeliada *Halki*

Heybeliada is the second-largest island and great for independent exploration. Unfortunately, many of the potentially interesting buildings are either blocked off by scary-looking soldiers holding guns or simply closed, so you'll have to do most of your sightseeing from afar. The most significant building here is the former **Greek Orthodox Theological Seminary** (now known as Özel Rum Lisesi) on top of the hill to the north of the docks. The building dates to 1896 and was built in the ruins of the former Haghia Triada Monastery. It served as an important Orthodox school (the current Patriarch Bartholomew I is an alum) until it was closed by the government in 1971. The Halki Seminary's closure remains a hot-button issue for the West, and its reopening is an important point in EU membership discussion. Another interesting sight is a Byzantine church dedicated to the **Blessed Virgin Kamariotissa** (marked as Aya Yorgi Monastery). It was the last church built before the Conquest, but since it is within the grounds of the off-limits **Naval School** (Deniz Lisesi), all one can see of it is the roof. A few blocks uphill from the center you can find the **house of İsmet İnönü** (the second president of Turkey), which now functions as a museum. The exhibits are only in Turkish and the museum isn't very well-known, which strongly contrasts the all-pervading fame of Atatürk, the first president. For swimming, there are some small beaches at the **Çam Limani Koyu**, attended mostly by the locals. One of the nicest places on the island is the **Akvaryum** *(☎535 294 4622 [$] 5TL.)*, a tiny pebbly beach amidst crags. It's very atmospheric and not well advertised, so you can come to have a little Robinson Crusoe moment here (unlike Robinson, you can sip on a 5TL beer). The beach is on the northwestern side of the island, close to Alman Koyu. From here, follow the road parallel to the northern shore until you reach a small wooden sign pointing you to the beach. A **biking** tour of the island *([$] 3-5TL per hr., 10-15TL per day, cheapest options near the fayton park)* can be very pleasant, provided that you're prepared to push the bike along on the steeper slopes. There are a number of *fayton* stands in the center *([$] Tours 25-35TL)*, and to the north of the ferry docks is a small **tourist information** booth.

Burgazada *Antigoni*

Rather unmarked by tourism, this is by far the most authentic of the three islands (the fourth major island is Kinaliada, generally agreed to be a boring landmass). There is no tourist office, so get your map in advance at one of the two bigger islands. There are two well-known fish restaurants, so head to **Barba Yani** *(☎215 381 2404 🖳www.burgazadabarbayani.com)* right at the docks, or **Kalpazankaya Restaurant** *(☎216 381 1504 🖳www.kalpazankaya.com)* on the opposite side of the island. Kalpazankaya is especially charismatic, with a great view of the sea and a small pebbly beach right below it (the drinks are cheaper at the beach than in the restaurant upstairs). A *fayton* will take you here for 20TL, or you can walk following the shore, which could take around 45min. Burgazada's main landmark is the **Hristos Manastiri** (Christ Monastery) which is on top of the central hill. Many trees on the island were destroyed in a forest fire in 2003, giving the walk up to the monastery one of the best views that the Princes' Islands offer. Unobstructed by trees, you can see three other islands (including the uninhabited **Kaşıkada,** the "Spoon Island") and Istanbul in the distance. In the town near the docks you can find the **Aya Yani Church** dating back to 1896 and the **Sait Faik Abasıyanık museum,** the former residence of this Turkish short story writer. There's a **bike rental** store to the south of the docks *([$] 5TL per hr., 15TL per day)*, while *faytons* wait to the north *([$] Tours 30-40TL)*.

Sultanahmet and Around

HAGIA SOPHIA — MUSEUM

Aya Sofya — ☎212 522 0989

In our cynical age of the internet, few things can truly impress. However, Hagia Sophia is an exception. Built as a Christian basilica in the 6th century, later converted into a mosque by the Ottomans, and finally turned into a museum 500 years later, this place has an overpowering aura that everyone who visits Istanbul should experience. Hagia Sophia had two predecessors that were destroyed—nothing remains from the first basilica, and the only remains from the second are the marble blocks depicting **12 lambs** (symbolizing the 12 apostles) near the entrance. Hagia Sophia is most famous for its **dome**—it seems to be suspended in the air, with no pillars cluttering the space in the middle. Notice the mosaics of the Archangel Gabriel and the Virgin Mary holding Jesus that can be seen in the semi-dome of the apse. The enormous **calligraphied medallions** were added during the building's stint as a mosque in the 19th century, and bear the names of Allah, Prophet Muhammad, the first four caliphs, and two of Muhammad's grandsons. When your neck starts hurting from staring up, walk up the stone ramp to the upper gallery. Here you can find the 13th-century **Deesis mosaic** depicting Jesus, Mary, and Joseph, and the **Loge of the Empress,** with a green stone marking the place where the empress used to watch the proceedings downstairs from her throne. Near the entrance is the sweating pillar, which can supposedly make your wish come true—just put in your thumb and rotate your hand 360 degrees.

From [M]Sultanahmet, walk south. $ 20TL, under 12 free. Guides from €40 per group. ⏰ Open Tu-Su 9am-7pm. Last entry 6pm.

TOPKAPI PALACE — PALACE

Topkapı Sarayı ☎212 512 0480 www.topkapisarayi.gov.tr/eng/indexalt.html

To do justice to this sprawling palace complex, you need to spend at least a few hours exploring what it has to offer. If that seems like too much, consider that some people had to spend their entire lives within its walls. The palace used to serve as the official residence for the sultans between the Conquest and 19th century, and today there are **four courtyards.** The First Courtyard contains the grounds outside of the Palace, including the **Archeological Museums** and **Hagia Eirene**. The Second Courtyard is known as the place where the **Divan meetings** took place and where legal decrees were discussed. The Third Courtyard is the real heart of the Palace—there's the **Privy Chamber** where the sultan used to receive foreign dignitaries, and the **Holy Relics Apartment** exhibiting some of Islam's most valued items—a sword, a cloak, a tooth, and other belongings of Prophet Muhammad. The Fourth Courtyard is a **small garden** with pavilions and kiosks. There's also the fascinating **Harem** where all the important women in the sultan's life used to dwell.

[M]Sultanahmet or [M]Gülhane. Enter the grounds down the hill from Hagia Sophia. i Audio tours 10TL. Guided group tours around €80. $ 20TL, with harem tour 35TL. ⏰ Open M 9am-6pm, W-Su 9am-6pm.

BASILICA CISTERN — CISTERN

Yerebatan Sarayı, Yerebatan Cad. 13 ☎212 522 1259 www.yerebatan.com

Much more atmospheric than its cousin Binbirdirek Cistern, this underground structure was built more than 1400 years ago under Emperor Justinian, the same guy who was responsible for Hagia Sophia. Even though it was once used to store water, today you can take a walk through its innards and listen to dripping water, feed the fish swarming underneath, or take invariably blurred photos of the beautifully lit columns. In the back of the cistern, there are two medusa heads forming the bases of two columns. These craniums were supposedly brought here from pagan Roman temples, but nobody seems to know why they are positioned upside-down and sideways, respectively.

[M]Sultanahmet. The entrance is across the street from Hagia Sophia, near the Million Stone. i Audio tours 5TL. $ 10TL. ⏰ Open daily 9am-7:30pm.

SULTANAHMET MOSQUE (BLUE MOSQUE) — MOSQUE

Sultanahmet Camii ☎212 518 1319

While people say Hagia Sophia is less remarkable on the outside than on the inside, the Blue Mosque is often said to have the opposite effect on visitors. Even if this tidbit were true, it wouldn't mean that much—the mosque's exterior is quite difficult to match. Some say that when the Blue Mosque was constructed in the early 17th century, its six impressive minarets caused an uproar, as the Haram Mosque in Mecca was the only place of worship with the same number. In what was quite a smart move, the sultan allegedly sent his architect to Mecca to build a seventh minaret

Unlike most countries in the world, Turkey bears the unique distinction of belonging to two continents. Straddling the line of both Europe and Asia, 97% of the country lies in Asia, while the remaining 3% lies in Europe. Though 3% may seem pretty insignificant, this latter percentage consists of Istanbul, the country's most recognizable and lively city. Simply because it's better known, Istanbul comes to define the whole country in the eyes of many outsiders. Yet, Turkey should perhaps be better described as "weast"—the crucible of West and East captured in a single noun. Over the centuries Greek warriors, Arab invaders, Crusaders, and Mongolian traders have all passed through or settled in the region, and their legacies live on today, bridging the old and new, the east and west, and ultimately embodying the "weast."

In particular, the city of Istanbul best illustrates this melting pot. It's simplest to think about the city as a historical core surrounded by modern, cosmopolitan growth. The southern shores of the Golden Horn peninsula are home to the city's historic districts – the old Sultan's palace, citadel, ancient religious sites like the Blue Mosque, and the tangy aromas of the Spice Bazaar. Beyond this core, rising residential buildings, tall offices and companies, and banks sketch a New York City skyline farther out on the western, European side of the city, while a mirroring layout of skyscrapers have also shot up on the Asian side. As a visitor, you can haggle for jewels and leather in the Grand Bazaar or peruse the designer shops at a modern-day mall. In addition to the intriguing combination of new and old seen in the physical architecture, this element of the "weast" is also embedded in the attitude of the people. There is crazy driving and a blatant lack of punctuality. Foreigners will undoubtedly be charged "tourist prices" in markets and bazaars, and might be surprised that the largest religious community is Islam.

Yet as the meeting point of west and east, Istanbul is also the place where common ground lurks beneath superficial differences. One commonality is the 500-year reign of the Ottoman Empire, which influenced the heritage of over 31 countries all over Europe, western Asia, and North Africa. In 1928, after the Empire's decline, Turkey's first president Mustafa Kemal wanted to model Turkey's relatively new nation on the West—Arabic script was discarded and replaced by the Latin alphabet, and turbans were banned. After such heavy influence from an Islamic empire, these changes set the stage for the many future identities within Turkey, yet also created controversy over how the nation should define itself.

The desire for a clear identity has continued to be a struggle for this relatively young nation, and Istanbul is the locus of this activity. In recent years, an explosion of creativity and renewed appreciation of Anatolian culture has swept the young generation. There are Turkish traditional jazz and rock fusion groups, mystic Sufi dancers, fashion designers using native cloths in distinct styles, and filmmakers earning recognition abroad. The "weast" is no longer just a blend of west and east, but rather a defining characteristic that can't be found anywhere else.

for their mosque. Decorated with the blue Iznik porcelain tiles responsible for the mosque's name, the dome is supported by four "elephant feet," enormous pillars 5m in diameter. Since the Blue Mosque is still in use, visitors have to enter through a separate entrance, keep to a designated area, and stay out during prayer times. ✠ ⓜSultanahmet. *i* No shoes or shorts allowed. Women must wear head covers. Ⓢ Free. ⌚ Open in summer M-Th 8:30am-12:30pm, 2-4:30pm, and 5:30-6:15pm; F 8:30am-noon and

2:30-6:15pm; Sa-Su 8:30am-12:30pm, 2-4:30pm, and 5:30-6:15pm.

ISTANBUL ARCHEOLOGY MUSEUMS

İstanbul Arkeoloji Müzeleri

MUSEUM

☎212 520 7740

Aside from the occasional schoolboy giggling at a nude statue, the atmosphere in this complex, which houses some of world's oldest artifacts within its three museums, is quite serene. The **Museum of Islamic Art** (i.e. the Tiled Kiosk) houses tiles and ceramics. The **Archeological Museum** is home to a collection of statues, sarcophagi, and the mummy of the Sidonian king Tabnit—who currently doesn't look too happy about the world's state of affairs. Finally, the **Museum of the Ancient Orient** holds the oldest preserved written international agreement, the Kadesh Peace Agreement, a treaty between the Hittites and Egyptians from 1258 BC.

⚐ Ⓜ*Sultanahmet or* Ⓜ*Gülhane; in the First Courtyard of Topkapı Palace.* Ⓢ *10TL.* ⚑ *Open Tu-Su 9am-7pm.*

SULTANAHMET SQUARE (HIPPODROME)

Sultanahmet Meydanı

(((•))) SQUARE

Very little remains from the Hippodrome (chariot racing stadium) that used to stand here, and what does remain was originally brought here from other places for adornment. The Greek **Serpent Column** (5th century BCE) was made from the melted shields of Persian soldiers in honor of Greek victory in the Battle of Plataea. The **Obelisk** (1490 BCE) was built by the Egyptian pharaoh Thutmose III. In fact, the only monument still around today that was actually constructed here is the **Walled Obelisk** that looks pretty decrepit (blame the Fourth Crusade—they took all the gilded plates off it). Speaking of old phallic monuments, don't miss the **Million Stone** right by Hagia Sophia—all distances in the Byzantine Empire used to be measured from this starting point; contrary to popular belief, the US hasn't always been the center of the universe. If you tire of historical monuments, Sultanahment Square is also a great place to people-watch.

⚐ Ⓜ*Sultanahmet; it's the square north from the Blue Mosque.*

LITTLE HAGIA SOPHIA

Küçük Aya Sofya

MOSQUE

☎212 458 0776

Older than its bigger sister, this charming mosque is a bit like Baby Taj Mahal in Agra, India—not quite the real deal, but worth a visit once you're done with all the big names. One of the first historical buildings built during Justinian's reign, Little Hagia Sophia has many architectural features similar to its counterpart, which it preceded by only a few years. After the Conquest, it took decades before it was converted into a mosque by the chief *eunuch* Hüseyin Ağa. After a long period of decay, it was finally restored a few years ago. It's located in a quiet neighborhood, so come here to have a tea in the garden nearby, or stop by on your way toward Kumkapi.

⚐ Ⓜ*Sultanahmet. From the Blue Mosque, walk down Küçük Aya Sofya Cad. for 5min.* Ⓢ *Free.*

GALATA BRIDGE

Galata Köprüsü

BRIDGE

Allegedly, the walk down this bridge isn't quite what it used to be before 1992, when the current structure replaced an earlier, iron version, but it still offers a great view of mosques and other landmarks on both the historical peninsula and the European side. Today, the upper level is populated by anglers with fishing rods catching fish in the Golden Horn, and the lower level is populated by ang...um, waiters catching tourists and making sure they eat at their overpriced seafood restaurants. Choose the upper level, and if you're hungry, try one of those famous fish sandwiches *(4TL)* that are sold on both sides.

⚐ Ⓜ*Eminönü or* Ⓜ*Karaköy.*

Fener and Balat

CHORA CHURCH

Kariye Müzesi, Kariye Camii Sok. 29, Edirnekapı

MUSEUM

☎212 631 9241

Chora Church requires some serious ceiling-gazing skills—the most beautiful

Byzantine mosaics and frescoes are on the domes. The church's history goes back to the fourth century, when Constantinople was so small that this church stood outside the city walls—hence the name *Chora*, meaning "countryside" in Old Greek. However, most of the mosaics date to the early 14th century, when the church was restored following an earthquake. A few decades after the Ottoman conquest in 1453, the building was converted into a mosque. Fortunately, the Christian images were not destroyed. Instead, they were covered over with plaster and wooden panels and stayed that way for over four centuries. In 1945 the mosque was converted into a museum and the artwork was restored and brought back into the daylight. The mosaics and frescoes depict various events in the busy lives of Virgin Mary and Jesus, which range from the Annunciation to Jesus healing the blind and paralyzed.

Bus to Edirnekapı. As you get off the bus, turn left and walk, then take the nearest right turn. Walk for 3 blocks, but before you reach the city walls, turn right and walk 2 blocks down the slope until you see the museum. If you're getting here from Fener or Balat, the walk takes around 15min. with a map and 45min. without one. [$] *15TL, Turkish students 10TL, under 12 free.* ⏰ *Open in summer M-Tu 9am-6pm, Th-Su 9am-6pm; in winter M-Tu 9am-4:30pm, Th-Su 9am-4:30pm.*

BULGARIAN ST. STEPHEN CHURCH — CHURCH

Sveti Stefan Kilisesi, Balat — ☎212 635 4432

What makes this church interesting is that it's got none of that stone-and-concrete nonsense. Instead, it's all made of iron parts that were manufactured in Vienna, sent down by boat on the Danube, and assembled here in 1898. Iron was in vogue back then (the church is just a few years younger than the Eiffel Tower), but it's not today—St. Stephen Church is one of the few surviving cast-iron churches in the world. Interestingly enough, it was built on the site of a previous wooden church, taking over as the new home of the Bulgarian Exarchate. The Exarchate was an autocephalous Orthodox church that seceded from the Ecumenical Patriarchate of Constantinople as a result of the increasing nationalist sentiment of ethnic Bulgarians in the Ottoman Empire during the 19th century. The Exarchate didn't last long. In 1913 it relocated to Sofia, and in 1915 it lost autonomy for three decades. However, even today St. Stephen Church remains important for the Bulgarian minority in Istanbul. Inside, the church is wonderfully decorated, and its internal structures are made completely out of iron.

Bus or ferry to Fener. The church is located in the park between Fener and Balat ferry jetties. If you're arriving by ferry at Fener, turn right and walk along the shore until you see the church across the road to the left. [$] *Free.* ⏰ *Open daily 8am-5pm.*

EYÜP SULTAN MOSQUE — MOSQUE

Eyüp Sultan Camii, Eyüp

This mosque is one of Islam's most important pilgrimage sites because it's the burial place of Ayyoub Al-Ansari (Eyüp Sultan in Turkish), a friend of Prophet Muhammad and the standard-bearer of Islam who died during the Muslim siege of Constantinople. The mosque was the first one built by the Ottomans after the Conquest, and the giant plane tree that grows in the mosque's courtyard was supposedly planted around that time. The mosque has a separate entrance for women, who generally pray in the upper gallery, but it should be possible for female tourists to enter through the main entrance provided that they stick to the usual mosque etiquette. The main attraction of the complex, however, is the **Tomb of Eyüp Sultan,** a wonderfully decorated burial site that's even more beautiful on the inside. Within the tomb you can find exhibited the footprint of Prophet Muhammad, a strange white object inside a glass display in the wall. The place is almost constantly full of believers showing their respect, so make sure to act accordingly. You'll see many young boys in curious white costumes—they are visiting the tomb as a part of their *sünnet*, the circumcision ritual that most Turkish boys have to undergo. Due to their religious significance, the mosque grounds became a popular burial place for government officials. When you're done with the tomb, go for a walk up the hill through the cemetery, preferably all the way to **Pierre Loti Cafe.**

Bus or ferry to Eyüp. Cross the road and head inland, following the 1 visible minaret of Eyüp Mosque. You'll have to pass through a long bazaar street and by a fountain. ℹ *Standard mosque etiquette applies.* $ *Free.* ⏰ *Mosque open in summer daily 4am-11pm. Tomb open in summer daily 9:30am-6:45pm.*

Kadıköy, Moda, and Üsküdar

ISTANBUL TOY MUSEUM — MUSEUM

Ömer Paşa Cad. Dr. Zeki Zeren Sok., Göztepe ☎216 359 4550 💻www.istanbultoymuseum.com

All right, it's no Hagia Sophia, but Istanbul's Toy Museum is unlike any other museum you'll visit in this city. This multi-story villa houses a collection of mostly European and American antique toys, the oldest dating back to 1817. Each room is dedicated to different kinds of toys, with music and lighting to complement the theme (the space exploration room has a particularly fierce disco flicker). The museum has got its share of kitsch, but there are many memorable exhibits. Come see what is supposedly the first Mickey Mouse toy (Performo Toy Company, 1926) and the first Mickey Mouse toy (Disney, appears in cartoons in 1928) standing side-by-side, throwing some suspicion on how Mr. Disney was inspired to create his world-famous mouse character. Bild Lilli, the German doll that inspired the creation of Barbie dolls, is here as well, alongside a rather hideous toy made by the Mattel toy company before it took up Barbies. The most interesting part of the collection is the army of 300 toy Nazi soldiers produced in Germany just before World War II. This exhibit proves that running a "toy museum" isn't just a frivolous waste of time, but instead a different way of documenting history. After all, children's toys often reflect adults' dreams.

Take the suburban train from Haydarpaşa Train Station to Göztepe (10min). After you leave the station, cross and walk down the street that faces the train exit. After the street turns right, take the nearest left turn and go straight. There are giant giraffe statues in front of the museum. $ *8TL, students 5TL.* ⏰ *Open daily 9:30am-6pm.*

MAIDEN TOWER — TOWER

Kız Kulesi, Üsküdar ☎216 342 4747 💻www.kizkulesi.com.tr

Maiden Tower is like a mountain—it looks more interesting from afar. Located on a tiny islet near the Asian side, it's been a legend-inspiring landmark for a few millennia. The oldest of the many legends by **Ovid** claims a nun named Hero from the temple of Aphrodite used to live here. She used to receive secret visits from **Leander,** the love of her life who would swim to her at night by following the light coming from the tower. One night a storm blew the light out, and as a result Leander got lost in the Bosphorus and drowned. When Hero found out, she threw herself from the tower. It's a nice story, but since the islet is within spitting distance of the Asian side, one cannot escape the impression that Mr. Leander must have had a very poor sense of direction. Legends aside, the first structure here was built by the Greeks around 400 BCE, but what you see today is a much more modern product of numerous reconstructions. The tower has served a variety of purposes over time, acting as a military center, a lighthouse, an infirmary, and, since 2000, a restaurant. Beautifully lit at night, the tower looks best from a ferry to Kadıköy after dark. If you decide to come here in person, you'll be able to climb the stairs to the top and enjoy the view of Istanbul's two sides. There's a restaurant in the base of the tower and a tiny cafe up on top, and neither is as ridiculously overpriced as you'd expect them to be.

To get here from Üsküdar's ferry terminal, walk around the huge construction site and then follow the shore south until you see the tower (15min). Shuttle boats run every 20min. or so from a pier to the south of the tower. There are hourly shuttle boats from Kabataş as well. $ *Tickets from Üsküdar 5TL, from Kabataş 7TL.* ⏰ *Shuttle boats run daily 9am-6:45pm.*

TURK BALLOON — BALLOON

Kadıköy Meydanı Deniz Otobüsleri İskelesi, Kadıköy ☎216 347 6703 💻www.turkbalon.net

Among the meager selection of tourist attractions on the Asian side of

Istanbul, this is perhaps the best known. With the capacity of 30 people, this big yellow balloon rises 200m into the air and allows you to experience Istanbul from a rather unusual perspective. The balloon doesn't move once it reaches its maximum height, but instead stays up for 15min. before descending. In the past couple of years, there have been problems with the availability of the balloon, and it wasn't operating at the time of writing. However, according to the staff, it should be back up soon. When you're in town, look up and search for a big yellow object in the sky that's not the sun to see if it's in service.

➔ *From the Kadıköy ferry terminal, head west along the shore; the balloon should be on top of a white building that resembles an anemone.* $ *20TL, students 15TL.* ⏰ *Open 9am-8pm; schedule dependent on weather.*

Beşiktaş and Ortaköy

DOLMABAHÇE PALACE — MUSEUM

Dolmabahçe Sarayı, Beşiktaş ☎212 236 9000 🖥www.millisaraylar.gov.tr

Topkapı may be the most historically significant of imperial palaces, but Dolmabahçe is probably the most impressive one. It was commissioned by Sultan Abdülmecid I, and upon completion in 1854, it replaced Topkapı as the official residence of the sultans. The palace is a real exercise in architectural and decorative overkill (think bear pelts, crystal chandeliers, and man-sized Japanese vases) and has 285 rooms, 43 salons, and six hamams. The most impressive part is the central **Ceremonial Hall,** which features the heaviest chandelier in Europe and which is still in use for special government events. During the tour you can also see the room where Mustafa Kemal Atatürk died on November 10, 1938—many clocks in the palace are set to five minutes after nine, the exact time of Atatürk's death. The place where the palace now stands was originally a bay—by the order of the sultans it was filled in with stones and turned into imperial gardens. Before the Conquest, the Byzantines had an enormous chain strung across the mouth of the Golden Horn to prevent enemy ships from entering it. It was in this former bay that Mehmet the Conqueror's ships started their journey on land (through Pera and Kasimpaşa) to circumvent this obstacle. The palace is a very popular tourist attraction, and the lines for tickets can be very long and very slow. Your best bet will be to come on a weekday early in the morning.

➔ *[M]Kabataş. The palace is a short walk northeast from Kabataş. Just walk parallel to the shore toward the Dolmabahçe Mosque and past it. To get here from Beşiktaş, you'll have to walk for approx. 7min. toward Kabataş down Dolmabahçe Cad.* ℹ *Guided tours are mandatory. Tours in Turkish or English, 40min., start every 15min. No photos.* $ *20TL, student with ISIC card 1TL.* ⏰ *Open Tu 9am-5:30pm, W 9am-5:30pm, F-Su 9am-5:30pm. Box office closes at 4pm.*

ORTAKÖY MOSQUE — MOSQUE

Büyük Mecidiye Camii, Ortaköy

This Ortaköy landmark was designed by the Balyans, the Armenian father-son tandem that contributed to the design of Dolmabahçe Palace. The inside is pretty, but you probably won't spend more than five minutes there. The mosque is best viewed from the outside—get a *kumpir* (potato stuffed with cheese and various other fillings—if there's one place in Istanbul where you should try this snack, it's here; 8TL) from one of the nearby stalls. Sit near the water and watch Ortaköy's beautiful and well-to-do youth promenade in front of the mosque and the Bosphorus.

➔ *Take the bus to Ortaköy. The mosque is right by the sea, to the east of the ferry terminal.* ℹ *Usual mosque etiquette (no shorts, women cover hair) applies.* $ *Free.* ⏰ *Open daily 4am-midnight.*

Beyoğlu

ISTANBUL MUSEUM OF MODERN ART — ♿❄ MUSEUM

Meclis-i Mebusan Cad. ☎212 334 7300 🖥www.istanbulmodern.org

Almost every corner in Beyoğlu has its own tiny gallery, but if there's one place for modern art, it's here. The upper floor hosts the permanent collection chronicling the development of modern art in Turkey over the past century, and the lower level hosts temporary exhibits by local and international artists. Even the staircase that connects these two floors is supposedly a work of art, one that "attacks" the "modernist logic" of "latently oppressive" sleek surfaces. There are a lot of big words on the explanatory signs, but many of the paintings, video projections, photographs, and installations are genuinely interesting. Don't miss the auto portrait gallery on the upper level, or the "False Ceiling" installation downstairs (it's a layer of books suspended from above, forming an artificial ceiling. Profound, isn't it?). For a schedule of the museum's frequent film screenings (mostly classics and modern Turkish films), check their website. Don't miss the awesome view of Istanbul Modern through the glass walls and from the museum's cafe.

⚑ From Ⓜ Tophane, walk in the direction of Kabataş, and after passing the Nusretiye Mosque, turn right and follow the signs. Ⓢ 8TL, students 3TL; Th free. 🕙 Open Tu-W 10am-6pm, Th 10am-8pm, F-Su 10am-6pm.

FOOD

Contrary to popular belief, food in Istanbul isn't all kebabs. Start your day with a generous Turkish breakfast plate (usually bread, cheese, olives, egg, tomatoes, cucumbers) or, even better, with *kaymak* (cream) and honey. If you don't have time for a breakfast, just grab a *simit* (Turkish bagel with sesame) from a street vendor. For lunch, pop into a *lokanta* to choose from among the ready dishes that are waiting for workers on their lunch breaks, or go to a restaurant and order a thin *pide*, the so-called "Turkish pizza." To combat your afternoon slump, find a patisserie and have a baklava, or any one of the many types of syrup-soaked pastries on sale. For dinner try a fish restaurant—if you don't want to spend too much money, just order some *meze* (vegetable or seafood appetizers) and share them among yourselves. At night, find a fast-food joint that sells *dürüms* (kebab wraps), *tantuni* (diced meat), or, if you're feeling frisky, *kokoreç* (chopped lamb intestines). Some of the nicest places to experience the authentic Turkish cuisine are small 🏠 homefood restaurants, so be on a lookout for those—they are generally not very well advertised. Few things are better than a late-night *çorba* (lentil soup), while *börek* (phyllo-dough pastry) is a choice breakfast staple. And these are just the basics—over time, you'll discover many more options. Oh, and let's not forget about *çay* (black tea), without which no Turkish meal can be complete.

Sultanahmet and Around

🏠 HOCAPAŞA PIDECISI
⚑ PIDE ❶

Hocapaşa Sok. 19 ☎ 212 512 0990

Don't let any of the mantis-like waiters around this well-known restaurant street direct you into their own place instead of this one—Hocapaşa Pidecisi is one of the few eateries here that isn't slowly turning into a tourist trap. With a menu only in Turkish, it serves excellent cheap *pides* to the locals who know their order by heart. There is more seating upstairs, but it's probably not the best option for taller travelers. Be on the lookout for other tourists—once they start coming here, everything is lost.

⚑ Ⓜ Sirkeci. Go south (up the slope), and then turn left on Hocapaşa street; the restaurant will be on your left. Ⓢ Pide 6-10TL. 🕙 Open daily 9am-9pm.

TARIHI SULTANAHMET KÖFTECISI SELIM USTA
● KÖFTE ❷

Divan Yolu Cad 12 ☎ 212 520 0566 🖳 www.sultanahmetkoftesi.com

Even with only two meat items on its 10-item menu, this place still manages to be one of Istanbul's most famous restaurants. Serving meatballs with vinegary bean salad since 1920, the restaurant attracts both tourists and the kind of Istanbul natives who would otherwise avoid Sultanahmet like a stinking toe. All three floors get wonderfully crowded, so give in to peer pressure and enjoy what locals and visitors alike agree is one of Istanbul's best offerings. While therere are a few imitators nearby, you'll know you are in the original if they only accept cash.

⚑ Ⓜ Sultanahmet. Ⓢ Bean salad 5TL. Köfte 10TL. 🕙 Open daily 11am-11pm.

BEREKET SOFRASI

♥ TURKISH ❶

Binbirdirek Mah. Peykhane Sk. 15/17   ☎212 518 7111 ▓www.bereketsofrasi.com

Foodwise, the real question in Sultanahmet isn't how to find an exhilarating restaurant, it's how to find a good, honest one. Berek Sofrası, a short walk from the center down Divan Yolu, is as authentic as they come and serves excellent *pide* and kebabs *(6-13TL)* to the locals for a local price. Tourists are welcome to eat here, but they aren't the main clientele. Have the *sütlaç (rice pudding; 3TL)* after a heavy meal.

✦ Ⓜ️*Çemberlitas. From the tram stop, head south 2 blocks.* Ⓢ *Entrees 6-13TL.* Ⓣ *Open daily 6:30am-11pm.*

ORIENT EXPRESS RESTAURANT

♥♿ ☙ TURKISH ❸

İstasyon Cd. 2 Gar İçi Sirkeci   ☎212 522 2280 ▓www.orientexpressrestaurant.com

When it's empty, this restaurant inside the Sirkeci train station seems like it's from a time when the century of electricity was merely beginning. The station was the last stop of the famous Orient Express, and the restaurant tries to imitate that cosmopolitan feel with waiters in bowties that speak French, German, and English. Don't just come to take a picture, however—sit down under the tall, arching ceiling and eat. Roast lamb shoulder *(25TL)* is the specialty, but appetizers such as *Imam Bayildi (10TL)* are good as well. Come when there aren't many people and let your imagination roam free. Then get on the Orient Express and solve a particularly convoluted murder case.

✦ Ⓜ️*Sirkeci. Enter the train station, and the restaurant is on your left.* Ⓢ *Entrees 16-25TL.* Ⓣ *Open daily 10:30am-10:30pm.*

HAMDI RESTAURANT

♥♿❄ TURKISH ❸

Tahmis Cad. Kalçın Sok.   ☎212 528 0390 ▓www.hamdirestorant.com.tr

With only a parking lot and some roads separating its building from the river, this restaurant is well-known for the view of Galata that it offers to the early birds who reserve the best seats. The food is traditional southeastern Turkish cuisine (kebabs) and worth the few extra liras. But even without a reservation, you can end up with some of the best seats—just sit one floor below the terrace, where there are fewer people, a great view, and the most potent A/C. Come for a dinner during the golden hour to see the entire town illuminated during sunset.

✦ Ⓜ️*Eminönü. Exit the station in the direction of Sultanahmet, turn right, continue until you see Hamdi on your left.* ℹ️ *Reservations are encouraged, but not necessary.* Ⓢ *Kebabs 16-22TL.* Ⓣ *Open daily 11am-11pm.*

YENI YILDIZ

♥☙♿ TURKISH, PIDE ❷

Cankurtaran Meydani 18   ☎212 518 1257

Down a crooked cobblestone path from Sultanahmet, this *pide* and kebab restaurant is a decent alternative to all of the tourist-filled eateries uphill. Originally owned by the late Erol Taş, a popular Turkish actor to whom much of the wall space is now devoted, this place offers expansive, colorful outdoor seating where you can eat, play backgammon, and smoke *nargile (hookah, 15TL)*. The restaurant is split into different parts as a result of alcohol licensing regulations, but don't let that confuse you. Come during the day and take a walk through the decrepit surrounding streets before enjoying this location's standard Turkish fare.

✦ Ⓜ️*Sultanahmet. From the hostel neighborhood, go south down the steps; it's 50m down the road on the right.* Ⓢ *Kebabs 10-15TL.* Ⓣ *Open daily 8am-midnight.*

PAŞAZADE RESTAURANT

♥ TURKISH ❸

Ibn-i Kemal Cad. 13   ☎212 513 3757 ▓www.pasazade.com

In certain pricey restaurants, you pay for an unbelievable view and cope with the usually mediocre food. In Paşazade, you don't get much of a view, which should be a good sign. Come to this restaurant to find tasty Ottoman dishes that you can't find on the street—no grilled kebabs here, just boiled or cooked food that is arranged in artistic-looking shapes. Try the *Mahmudiye (15TL)* with chicken, mashed potatoes, and fruit. This is one of the few places where you can get the upscale decor (candle and all) and not pay more than you'd like.

⚑ Ⓜ*Gülhane. Follow the tracks toward Sirkeci, turn left as soon as you can, and then turn right. Paşazade will be on your left.* Ⓢ *Entrees 13-23TL. Dessert 6-7.50TL.* ☒ *Open daily noon-11pm.*

SARNIÇ RESTAURANT
Soğukçeşme Sokağı   ☎212 512 4291 ▇www.sarnicrestaurant.com   TURKISH ❹

If you're a rich, elderly German tourist and you just happen to be reading a budget travel guide to amuse yourself, feel free to go to Sarnıç Restaurant. If you're a student and feel like eating inside a renovated water cistern from 1500 years ago (and are willing to shell out some serious dough for said experience), you should also eat here—and maybe pick up a mainstream hobby. With lit candles and acoustics worthy of a bat cave, an atmosphere like this is hard to imitate. If the cost of entrees *(25-57TL)* scares you but you still feel an urge to eat inside a centuries-old water cistern, there's an easy fix—have a hamburger in the cafe that's inside the Byzantine Cistern.

⚑ Ⓜ*Sultanahmet. Find it in the small street behind Hagia Sophia.* Ⓢ *Appetizers 20-35TL. Entrees 25-57TL. Desserts 16-22TL.* ☒ *Open daily 7:30-10:30pm.*

Fatih

ESKI KAFA
⊛(ᵗᵖ)⚘ CAFE, ORGANIC ❷

Atpazarı 11/A, Fatih   ☎212 533 4291 ▇www.eski-kafa.com

There aren't many items on the menu here, but every one is worth a try. Order the *gulaş (12TL)*, one of the Hungarian contributions to the greatness of the Ottoman Empire. All food here is organic, so the place is bound to be popular with all the yoga-lovin' hipsters who might happen across it. You can enjoy your cup of hibiscus tea either in the crammed interior or outside as you sit at one of the blocks of concrete that serves as a table.

⚑ *Take bus to Fatih. Leave the Fatih Mosque grounds through the southeastern exit. Turn left and walk for 3 blocks. Turn right into Atpazarı, and Eski Kafa will be to your right.* ⓘ *Free Wi-Fi.* Ⓢ *Meals 10-12TL. Desserts 4-7TL. Tea 1.50-4TL.* ☒ *Open daily 10am-11pm.*

SUR OCAKBAŞI
⊛(ᵗᵖ)⚘ TURKISH ❷

İtfaiye Cad. 19, Fatih   ☎212 533 8088 ▇www.surocakbasi.net

Apparently, Anthony Bourdain visited this place in 2009, and the food gave him an orgasm or something—so it's about time tourists started crowding this eatery. The specialty here is the *büryan kebab (11TL)* which is made from lamb back cooked in an underground pit. If one regional dish isn't enough for you, try the *bütün (7TL)*, a dessert made from ice cream and rice. The mascot of this restaurant is a nude, bewildered child standing inside a huge watermelon. Don't ask why.

⚑ *Take bus to Fatih. From the mosque walk, southeast until you reach the aqueduct. Walk along it, then turn left into Siirt Bazaar and go straight. The restaurant will be to your left.* ⓘ *Free Wi-Fi.* Ⓢ *Kebabs 10-17.50TL. Pide 11TL.* ☒ *Open daily 8am-1am.*

SELAM
⊛✳ TURKISH ❷

Fevzi Paşa Cad. 69, Fatih   ☎212 631 2595 ▇www.selam.com.tr

This multi-story chameleon of a restaurant offers something different on every floor: it serves sweets in the basement, fast food on the first floor, and kebabs and all that jazz on the second. As the quality of A/C varies by floor, choose where to dine based on what you feel like having as well as your preferred temperature. If you haven't tried it yet, order the *soslu manti (9-10TL)*, a handmade pasta with tiny bits of meat inside. Its preparation is a fascinating, machine-like process. Come in at the right time, and you'll see some of it take place inside the cubicle near the entrance.

⚑ *If you're walking northwest on Fevzi Paşa, Selam will be on your left, close to where the Fatih Mosque's walls end.* Ⓢ *Kebabs 11-18TL. Pide 6.50-10TL. Pastries 4.50-6.50TL.* ☒ *Open daily 11am-11pm.*

SARAY MUHALLEBICISI
(ᵗᵖ)✦✳ SWEETS ❶

Fevzi Paşa Cad. 1, Fatih   ☎212 521 0505 ▇www.saraymuhallebicisi.com

If you want to have a substance-induced state of altered consciousness in Fatih, your best bet will be to go for a sugar high. Take the elevator to the terrace on Saray's top floor, where you can feed on *kazandibis, muhallebis,* profiteroles, and baklava while taking in a view of the city. Sugar hangover? It's also a good spot for breakfast *(5-7TL).*

🍴 *Leave the Fatih Mosque grounds through the southeastern exit, turn right and walk to Fevzi Paşa. Saray will be right across the road.* 💲 *Desserts 5-6TL. Pastries 4.50-7.50TL. Sandwiches 6TL. Coffee 4TL.* 🕐 *Open daily 6am-1am.*

can't go back

The city of Istanbul has existed since 667 BCE, but not always as Istanbul. As a site of frequent conquest and springboard into the Middle East from Europe, this city has changed hands, religions, and names once every couple hundred years. Here is a etymological history so you can know why exactly, you can't go back to Constantinople.

- **BYZANTIUM:** This was the name of the original Greek settlement on the Bosphorous, derived from their King Byzas. This also was the adopted name of the Eastern Roman Empire, after the fall of the West in 395 AD—even though the city itself was known as Constantinople by then.

- **NEW ROME:** Okay, this one's cheating. Constantine might have named his new capital after himself, but apparently a lot of people gave it a more functional name—New Rome. You can still find this name on the inscription of the title of the Archbishop of Constantinople-New Rome.

- **CONSTANTINOPLE:** On May 11, 330, Emperor Constantine gave the city its classical name. This meaningful mouthful of a name made Constantinople the new capital of the Eastern Roman Empire. This name even lasted in Ottoman Turk times, called Kostantiniyye, and continued until the fall of the empire in 1923.

- **ISTANBUL:** This was the common name of the city since before the conquest in 1453 by the Turks. It was officially re-dubbed by Atatürk in 1923. The name change was expedited by the Turkish Postal Service by refusing to send packages marked with Constantinople as the destination.

KÖMÜR LOKANTASI
Fevzi Paşa Cad. 18

🍴🚻 LOKANTA ❶
☎212 521 9999 📧www.komurlokantasi.com

Kömür is one of the more pleasant *lokantas* spots, with four floors and a lot of busy waiters, but the food is nothing to write home about. If you're feeling important, go sit in the VIP lounge on the top floor, which looks quite similar to all the other floors—apart from the fact that it's VIP.

🍴 *If you're walking northwest on Fevzi Paşa, Kömür will be to your right, on the first corner after the mosque's walls end.* 💲 *Kebabs 7-12TL. Pilaf 3-5TL. Desserts 3-5.50TL.* 🕐 *Open daily 4am-11pm.*

Beyoğlu

🔳 **MANGAL KEYFI**
Öğüt Sok. 8

🍴 DÜRÜM ❶
☎212 245 1534

This charismatic, unpretentious place is attended mostly by young locals, but it's got better *dürüms* than you'll get at any touristy restaurant in Taksim. Try the excellent chicken *dürüm (4TL),* and have a cup of frothy *ayran* with it. It's surprising that this place is so cheap without being a dump. The dark red walls, the plethora of posters, and the nonstop rock music make eating here very agreeable.

🍴 *From Ⓜ Taksim, walk down İstiklal. Take a right onto Ağa Camii, then take the 2nd right onto Öğüt*

Sok; the restaurant will be to your left. $ *Dürüms 4-4.50TL. Kebabs 8-12TL. Ayran 1.50TL.* ⏰ *Open daily 8am-midnight.*

VAN KAHVALTI EVI 💳🌤 BREAKFAST [2]

Defterdar Yok. 52/A ☎212 293 6437

Cihangir is the best area in Beyoğlu for a lazy breakfast, probably because most of its inhabitants are a lazy lot (artists, expats, and the like), and Van Kahvaltı Evi offers the best deal, making excellent scrambled eggs with cheese and sausage *(8TL)* and mixed breakfast plates with varieties of cheese. Tea is served in big cups, but *Let's Go* recommends one of the organic fruit juices *(4TL)*. It's a simple place, but on weekend mornings it's hard to find an empty table.

➡ *From [M]Taksim, walk down Sıraselviler Cad.; this breakfast place is 1 block after the Firuzağa Mosque.* $ *Eggs 5-8TL. Breakfast plates 8-15TL. Coffee 3-4TL.* ⏰ *Open daily 7am-7pm.*

ZENCEFIL 💳📶 VEGETARIAN [2]

Kurabiye Sok. 8-10 ☎212 243 8234 💻www.zencefil.org

If you're vegetarian and have been navigating the kebab minefield that is Istanbul, you should definitely come to this Taksim eatery for a meal. Its "vegetable-oriented" menu changes according to season and tastes a cut above the standard at many restaurants that focus on meat. Zencefil cans its own vegetables, makes its own butter and bread, and even had its own homemade lemonade before this drink became a popular fare in the city's restaurants. Eating here isn't dirt-cheap, but it is worth your money.

➡ *[M]Taksim. Walk down İstiklal, take the 1st right and then the 1st left turn; walk straight until you see the restaurant on your right.* ℹ *Free Wi-Fi.* $ *Full entrees 11.50-13.50TL; small entrees 7.50-10.50TL. Lemonade 8TL.* ⏰ *Open M-Sa 8:30am-11:30pm.*

SOFYALI 9 💳🍸🌤 SEAFOOD, TURKISH [2]

Sofyalı Sok. 9 ☎212 245 0362 💻www.sofyali.com.tr

This is one of the best-known establishments in the Tünel area, and it's worth coming here for the *meze*. This Arabic specialty is on the expensive side, but you can always find some cheaper items in the daily-special section of the menu. Despite its poshness and reputation, the restaurant still has something of a *meyhane* feel, so don't hesitate to just come for *rakı* and some cheese.

➡ *[M]Tünel. Walk up İstiklal from Tünel, take the first left turn, walk to the end of the street and turn left. The restaurant will be to your left.* $ *Meze 2.50-10TL. Salads 8-11TL. Entrees 13-25TL. Desserts 5-7.50TL.* ⏰ *Open daily noon-11pm.*

KIVAHAN 💳📶 TRADITIONAL [2]

Galata Kulesi Meydanı 9 ☎212 292 9898 💻www.galatakivahan.com

Right in Galata Tower's backyard, this restaurant is almost a tourist trap, but the food is original enough to make it worth a visit. The recipes were collected from all over Turkey, and since the names on the menu aren't too familiar (where are the kebabs, Kivahan?), you'll probably just have to walk up to the counter and point at things you'd like to have. The portions are quite small, so if you're starving, get a street *dürüm* first.

➡ *[M]Tünel or [M]Karaköy. The restaurant is in the square right next to Galata Tower.* $ *Salads and meze 5-6TL. Vegetarian dishes 8-10TL. Entrees 10-20TL. Desserts 5TL. 10% service charge not included in price.* ⏰ *Open daily 9am-midnight.*

CEZAYIR 💳📶🍸🌤 TURKISH [4]

Hayriye Cad. 12 ☎212 245 9980 💻www.cezayir-istanbul.com

Cezayir is housed by an old Italian building that used to function as a school, and today the eatery is among Galatasaray's best known restaurants. The cuisine is Turkish, with a degree of innovation—the hallumi cheese with tomato pesto *(10TL)* and the grilled lamb tenderloin *(30.50TL)* are among the more popular dishes. If this place is too expensive for you, try the Cezayir Sokak nearby, a narrow, steep street with plenty of atmospheric, lesser-known restaurants.

➡ *[M]Taksim or [M]Tünel. From Galatasaray Lisesi, go down Yeni Çarşı and take the 1st left turn;*

the restaurant will be to your right. $ *Appetizers 10-18TL. Starters 17-36.50TL. Beer 8-13TL.* ⏰ *Open daily 9am-2am.*

EMINE ANA SOFRASI 🍴 TANTUNI ❶

Billurcu Sok. 5/A ☎212 292 8430

Kebab might be the default fast food in Istanbul, but leaving without trying *tantuni* (diced meat) would be a mistake—a grave one, at that. This visually unappealing eatery serves excellent and cheap *tantuni dürüms*, which taste far better than most of their kebab cousins. The only problem is that one *tantuni dürüm* is never enough, so you'll have to get two or three to be satisfied.

↗ *[M]Taksim. Billurcu Sok. is a small street off Kücükparmakkapı Sokak.* $ *Tantuni dürüm 4.5TL. Tantuni sandwich 5TL.* ⏰ *Open daily 11am-6am.*

KAFE ARA 🍴📶☀ CAFE ❷

Tosbağa Sok. 2 ☎212 245 4105

The cosmopolitan Kafe Ara is owned by Ara Güler, a respected Turkish photographer whose giant black-and-white photographs of Istanbul adorn the walls. If you come from 1-5pm, you might get to see the old man himself, now in his eighties, chilling in his shrine. The interior design is interesting, and ambient jazz music sets the mood. If you're hungry, try the Balkan *köfte (18TL)*, or just come for a coffee.

↗ *[M]Taksim or [M]Tünel. From Galatasaray Lisesi, go down Yeni Çarşı and take the 1st right.* $ *Breakfast buffet 15TL. Sunday brunch 22.50TL. Entrees 16-20TL. Desserts 7-10TL.* ⏰ *Open M-F 7:30am-midnight, Sa 10:30am-1am, Su 10am-midnight. Su brunch 10am-2pm.*

GALATA HOUSE 🍴🍸 GEORGIAN ❸

Galata Kulesi Sok. (61) 15 ☎212 245 1861 💻www.thegalatahouse.com

A former British jail, this building in Galata was restored by its architect owners and later converted into a restaurant. Apart from offering the (potential) thrill of eating in a former exercise yard, Galata House is also unique in Istanbul for serving Georgian and Russian cuisine. There aren't many tables, supposedly because the owners are against the industrialization of food consumption. A history lesson on Galata ("the Empire within an Empire") comes along with the menu.

↗ *[M]Tünel or [M]Karaköy. From Galata Tower, head down the hill on Galata Kulesi Sokak; the restaurant will be on your left.* $ *Entrees 17-23TL. Desserts 8-10TL.* ⏰ *Open daily noon-midnight. Kitchen open noon-11pm.*

Fener and Balat

FINDIK KABUĞUNDA KÖFTE 🍴📶 KÖFTE ❶

Mürsel Paşa Cad. 89, Balat ☎212 635 3310 💻www.findikkofte.com

It's surprising to find such a tourist-friendly restaurant with such reasonable prices in Balat. With a clean interior, free Wi-Fi, and a terrace offering a view of the Bulgarian St. Stephen Church and the Golden Horn, this spot makes for a great lunch. Try one of the three varieties of meatballs, the artichoke, or the saffron-tinged lentil soup.

↗ *Bus or ferry to Fener. From the ferry jetty, go inland, cross the road, turn right, and walk until you see the Bulgarian St. Stephen Church on the right. The restaurant is opposite the church.* $ *Köfte 6-7.50TL. Sides and salads 3TL. Desserts 3TL.* ⏰ *Open daily 9am-10pm.*

PIERRE LOTI CAFE 👁☀ CAFE ❶

Gümüşsuyu Balmumcu Sok. 5, Eyüp ☎212 581 2696

Positioned on top of a hill overlooking the Golden Horn, this used to be the favorite hangout place of Julien Viaud, the 19th-century French writer working under the penname Pierre Loti, whose detail-oriented style allegedly influenced the even more detail-oriented Marcel Proust. Viaud's first novel was based on his romantic adventures with a harem girl called Aziyade here in Istanbul. Come to this cafe to have some tea and enjoy the magnificent view—perhaps it will inspire you to write a blog post or something.

↗ *Bus or ferry to Eyüp. To get here from the Eyüp Sultan Mosque, you can either take a cable car (Piyerloti teleferik) or walk. It's a 15min. hike up the hill through the cemetery. The path begins with* *a flight of stairs to the side of the mosque. $ Tea 1.90TL. Coffee and soda 3.80TL. ⏰ Open daily 7am-midnight.*

MEKTEB-I CAFE
🍴 CAFE [1]

Vodina Cad. Akçin Sok. 3/A, Fener ☎535 953 1293

Quite close to the Fener ferry jetty, this small cafe seems like the intuitive place to have a tea or coffee before setting out to explore the neighborhood. It's pleasantly decorated, and the upper level with soft cushions and low ceilings is especially appealing. After you're done here, go find the castle-like Greek College.

 # Bus or ferry to Fener. From the ferry jetty, go inland, cross the road, turn right, and walk. Then take the first available left turn; the cafe will be on the corner to your left. $ Tea 2TL. Coffee 4TL. Toast 3TL. ⏰ Open daily 8am-8pm.

HALIÇ SOSYAL TESISI
TURKISH [2]

Abdülezel Paşa Cad., Kadir Has Üniversitesi Karşısı, Fener ☎212 444 1034 💻www.ibb.gov.tr

A government-run restaurant, this place exists as a result of the many attempts of the local authorities to turn Fener and Balat into a hip, gentrified place like Cihangir. The restaurant is clean, spacious, and reasonably priced. The fish or the chicken casserole *(10TL)* is worth the money, but the government is going to need to do a lot more to make this a tourist spot.

 # Bus or ferry to Fener. Head southeast along the shore (toward Sultanahmet) for some 300m. The restaurant is right by the water. $ Fish 10-18.5TL. Köfte 7.5-8.5TL. Desserts 4-5TL. ⏰ Open daily 8:30am-11pm.

Kadıköy, Moda, and Üsküdar

ÇIYA KEBAP
TURKISH [2]

Güneşlibahçe Sok. 48/B, Kadıköy ☎216 336 3013 💻www.ciya.com.tr

Arguably the best-known restaurant on the Asian side, Çiya has three branches right next to each other—two focus on kebabs, while the third one, Çiya Sofrası, has more vegetarian dishes. The daily offerings changed based on what's available, so if you're interested, check out the menu in advance on their website; otherwise, just stop by and pick something. Çiya's chef Musa Dagdeviren is celebrating one success after another with his obscure ingredients, and it's surprising that this doesn't translate into unbearably high prices. Sit outside and let the wind bring you the sound of live music coming from one of the less distinguished restaurants down the street.

 # Take the ferry to Kadıköy. It's a few blocks down from Kadıköy market. To get there from the ferry terminal, go on Söğütlüçeşme, turn right, and make a quick left. Walk up 2 blocks, then take a right and go straight until you see it. $ Kebabs 12-20TL. Salads 5-6TL. Desserts 5-6TL. ⏰ Open daily 10am-11pm.

ALI USTA
ICE CREAM [1]

Moda Cad. 264/A, Moda ☎216 414 1880

This small ice cream joint doesn't look like much, but the lines of locals that you can sometimes see here are a bit more telling. In fact, it's one of the best-known ice cream places in Istanbul. Get a scoop or two with some caramel sauce, chocolate chips, and chopped nuts on top, and set out for Moda's beaches.

 # The ferry to Kadıköy. Get off the nostalgic tram near Moda Cad. and walk down the street. Ali Usta is on the right side, close to where Moda forks. $ One scoop 2TL, 2 scoops 4TL, 3 scoops 6TL. ⏰ Open daily 8am-2am.

MEŞHUR MENEMENCI
🍴 MENEMEN [1]

Pavlonya Sok. 22, Kadıköy ☎216 336 6308

Preparing almost exclusively *menemen*—a popular scrambled egg dish—this tiny eatery is a great place to kick off your day. It's not exactly tourist central, but *Let's Go* likes its authenticity. The dishes are custom-made, so you can choose whether you want cheese, sausage, or chili inside your menemen (you want it all, by the way). Don't forget to use bread to wipe the pan clean—leaving any of it would be an act of barbarism.

Take the ferry to Kadıköy. Walk up Söğütlüçeşme, turn right immediately after Osmanağa Mosque, and walk straight. It will be on your right. $ Menemen 4-5TL. ⏰ Open daily 7am-8pm.

PIDE SUN — 🍴 PIDE ❶

Moda Cad. Şükran Apartmanı 97, Kadıköy ☎216 347 3155 💻www.pidesun.com

Pide Sun is an unassuming place that hits all the important points for an easy meal—it's cozy, cheap, and tasty. The *pides* here are so thin that even the most devoted pizza aficionados will be forced to suck up their pride and eat the *pides* the Turkish way, i.e. with utensils. It's easy to pass by the restaurant without noticing it, but the food is worth the extra time you'll spend searching for it.

Take the ferry to Kadıköy. Pide Sun is in the Kadıköy portion of Moda Cad., very close to a Migros supermarket. If you're walking from Kadıköy market, it will be to your left. $ Pides 7-10.50TL. ⏰ Open daily 11:30am-11pm.

İSKENDER İSKENDEROĞLU — 🍴 KEBAB ❸

Rıhtım Cad. PTT yanı, Kadıköy ☎216 336 0777 💻www.iskenderkebabi.com.tr

Who could have guessed that the famous İskender kebab was named not after a Turkish village but after a person? Well, it was. A century or so ago, Mr. Mehmet Oğlu İskender invented the dish in Bursa and later passed the recipe to his descendants. This restaurant is run by third- and fourth-generation İskenders who seem to be taking their legacy pretty seriously. The place itself is not very charismatic and the *İskender* kebabs are a bit overpriced, but it's a must-see for anyone who feels strongly about İskender kebabs or the İskender family pedigree. Next on the list: Mr. Döner and his grandchildren.

Take the ferry to Kadıköy. From the ferry terminal, head southwest on Faik Sözen; it will be on your left next to Benzin Cafe. $ İskender kebabs 18TL. Desserts 5-6TL. ⏰ Open daily 11:30am-10pm.

turkey

AGAPIA — 🍴 INTERNATIONAL ❷

Miralay Nazim Sok. 10, Kadıköy ☎216 418 3636

With a wonderfully atmospheric garden and creatively arranged dishes, this is one of the nicest dinner restaurants around. If you're not in the mood for international dishes like chicken fajitas *(9.50TL)* or grilled veal, come for a cocktail *(12TL)* complete with a funny-looking straw and umbrella. And if you order a dessert, much of the plate will be sprinkled with a layer of cocoa powder—which is a creative way of distracting you from how small the desserts look on their huge plates.

Take the ferry to Kadıköy. It's on the same street as HUSH Hostel. If you're walking down Bahariye from the bull statue, turn right just before the Süreyya Opera House and go straight. $ Entrees 9.50-14TL. Salads 7.50-11.50TL. Desserts 4.50-6TL. ⏰ Open daily 8am-2am.

KANAAT LOKANTASI — 🍴 LOKANTA ❷

Selmanipak Cad. 25, Üsküdar ☎216 553 3791

For some reason, this is one of the best-known restaurants in Üsküdar. The place looks like a very normal Ottoman *lokanta* and serves basic food to locals, but don't let that trick you into underestimating the bill at the end. The most impressive part of the restaurant is the dessert counter, so save some space for a *kazandibi* after your meal.

Take the ferry to Üsküdar. It's quite close to the ferry terminal. Cross the street and head toward Seyh Mosque. $ Meat entrees 7.50-13.50TL; vegetarian entrees 7.50-9TL. Pilaf 4.50TL. Desserts 5-7TL. ⏰ Open daily 6am-11pm.

MOLA YEMEKEVI — 🍴 TRADITIONAL ❶

Damacı Sok. 8/3, Kadıköy ☎216 348 6310

Small places like this are a good bet for travelers who want to see what food really tastes like in a Turkish home. Mola Yemekevi has a distinctly domestic feel due to its tiny kitchen, several child-made drawings pinned up on its walls, and an old Hi-Fi system playing CDs. Order something in the back and while they prepare it, go sit outside under the enthusiastically sprouting roof of climbing plants.

Take the ferry to Kadıköy. From Rexx Cinema go 1 block down Sakiz Gülü and turn left. The restaurant will be to your left, tucked into a small corner. $ Entrees 4.50-8TL. Soup 3TL. Salads 5-7TL. ⏰ Open daily 9am-9pm.

MODA TERAS 🍴♿🍸☀ INTERNATIONAL [4]

Mektep Sok. 1, Moda ☎216 338 7040 💻www.modateras.com.tr

The wedding albums at the entrance and the restaurant's motto (encouraging you to say your *romantik evet*, or proposals, here) may make this a bad choice for less than stable couples. Otherwise, Moda Teras is a pleasant place: the interior is trendy and the terrace overlooks the sea. There's a decent selection of international dishes, with one lonely kebab repping among all the Thai chickens and veal medallions. The prices are on the higher side, but if you don't want to dine here, you can always come for a cold drink sometime midday.

🚏 Take the ferry to Kadıköy. Go south on Moda Cad., go left when the road forks, then take another left and walk for 3min. $ Entrees 19-35TL. Desserts 8.50-13TL. Drinks 3.50-7.50TL. ⏰ Open M-F 10am-midnight; Sa breakfast buffet 10am-1pm, Su brunch 10:30am-2:30pm.

Beşiktaş and Ortaköy

👍 SIDIKA 🍴🍸 SEAFOOD [3]

Şair Nedim Cad. 38, Beşiktaş ☎212 259 7232 💻www.sidika.com.tr

Many seafood restaurants in Istanbul put candles on their tables, hire some *fasil* musicians, and then think they are entitled to charge a lot for mediocre food. Sıdıka, on the other hand, serves delicious fish dishes in a low-key, stylish environment. Let the energetic owner Sıdıka recommend a dish to you, or choose at random from the menu written on a blackboard. The *meze* are wonderful, but the house specialties are the grilled octopus *(8-12TL)* and the grilled fish in grape leaves *(16-20TL)*.

🚏 Take the ferry or bus to Beşiktaş. From the big eagle statue, walk down Şehit Asim, cross Ortabahçe Cad., and continue until you get to Şair Nedim. Turn right at Şair Nedim and continue up the road until you see the restaurant on your right side. ℹ Free Wi-Fi. $ Meze 3-10TL. Fish 14-20TL. Desserts 5-10TL. Rakı 9TL. ⏰ Open daily noon-2am.

PANDO KAYMAK ☀🍴 BREAKFAST [1]

Mumcu Bakkal Sok. 5, Beşiktaş ☎212 258 2616

This place has been open for over 100 years and is run by an elderly Bulgarian couple. Come here for bread with *kaymak* (cream) and honey, and have a cup of hot milk with it. It doesn't look like much at first, but Pando Kaymak is a very popular breakfast spot among students and expats.

🚏 Take the bus or ferry to Beşiktaş. Starting at the big eagle statue, walk in the opposite direction from the fish market. Pando Kaymak will be to your left (above the door it says "Kaymaklı kahvaltı burada"). $ Breakfast 5TL. ⏰ Open daily 8am-6pm.

THE HOUSE CAFE 🍴☀📶🍸 CAFE [3]

Salhane Sok. 1, Ortaköy ☎212 227 2699 💻www.thehousecafe.com.tr

The House Cafe has a number of locations throughout the city, but this is probably the best-known one. The food is westernized and comes in large portions, which makes it a popular hangout for well-to-do local students, and which also allows the chain to keep expanding like the Lernaean hydra. The interior was designed with quite some care, and late-night the cafe turns into a bar with DJ performances.

🚏 Take the bus to Ortaköy. The cafe is right by the Ortaköy ferry dock. ℹ Free Wi-Fi. $ Pizza 18.50-24TL. Burgers 25TL. Beer 10-13TL. Desserts 8.50-11TL. ⏰ Open daily 9am-1am. Kitchen closes earlier.

YEDI-SEKIZ HASANPAŞA FIRINI 🍴 BAKERY [2]

Şehit Asim Cad. 12, Beşiktaş ☎212 261 9766

This unpretentious bakery makes many kinds of tea cookies, great as an afternoon snack. You might have to communicate in sign language to indicate which of the freshly baked cookies you want, but they'll understand what you want fast enough. The store's name is "7-8" because Hasanpaşa, the Ottoman *paşa* who started it, didn't know how to write and made these two numbers his signature.

🚏 Take the bus or ferry to Beşiktaş. From the big eagle statue, walk down Şehit Asim; the store will be to your left. $ Tea cookies 14TL per kg., coconut-flavored 18TL per kg. ⏰ Open daily 8am-9:30pm.

NIGHTLIFE

Istanbul's bars and clubs are concentrated around **İstiklal Avenue,** so if you're staying in Sultanahmet, you should prepare yourself for a good amount of commuting. Sultanahmet does have a few bars, but these are generally looked down upon by the locals—that's why we listed a handful of *nargile* cafes instead. Another center of nighttime activity is **Muallim Naci Cad.,** the road running up from Ortaköy to Kuruçeşme, home to the city's most prestigious clubs. Note that during summer, many music venues close down and move to their summer locations (the famous **Babylon** is one of them). The English-laguage *Time Out Magazine* lists current performances as well as a very comprehensive list of GLBT-friendly bars and clubs. If you want to drink the infamous Turkish anise-flavored alcohol **rakı,** the best place to do so is a traditional *meyhane.* Whatever you do, don't fall for the **nighttime scams**—if a local speaking perfect English approaches you on the street and invites you for a beer after three lines of uninteresting dialogue, he's probably planning a scam of sorts on you (it usually involves you, an exorbitant bill, and coercion).

Sultanahmet and Around

▨ SETÜSTÜ ÇAY BAHÇESI

Gülhane Park

♥⚅ CAFE

On what is almost a cliff over the Bosphorus, this cafe offers an unbelievable, 180-degree view of the three parts of Istanbul and the water in between. With cascades upon cascades of small wooden tables, almost everyone gets Setüstü's best seats. The tea is pricy, but remember you're also paying for the monumental view. Make sure to order the heavy-looking stuffed potato *(10TL).* Especially suitable for couples and those people who catch more pics than the paparazzi.

⚐ Ⓜ*Gülhane. Enter the park and continue all the way to its back gate, then follow the signs.* Ⓢ *Tea for 1-3 people 6-17TL.*

CHEERS BAR

Akbıyık Cad. 20

●⚏⚅ BAR

💻www.cheerscafebar.com

One of the many drinking and socializing options on Akbıyık street, this bar has been around for a while and caters almost exclusively to tourists. The odds are it's right across the street from where you're staying, so unless you'd just rather stay on your hostel's terrace, come over for a beer and a bit of the old "Oh, you're from Australia? I'm from Austria!" thing. Your experience here really depends on whom you're with, as the bar itself is pretty standard.

⚐ Ⓜ*Sultanahmet. In the middle of the hostel neighborhood.* Ⓢ *Small beer 5TL; large beer 6TL. Entrees 7-10TL. Nargile 10TL.* ⏰ *Open daily 11am-2am.*

ERENLER NARGILE

Çorlulu Ali Paşa Medresesi

⚅ CAFE

☎212 511 8853

Çorlulu Ali Paşa Medresesi, a courtyard that formerly belonged to a *madrasa* (theological school), is famous among local students as the perfect place to come for a *nargile.* Erenler is the biggest of the three cafes here, and supplies visitors with waterpipes *(12TL)* and non-alcoholic drinks *(coffee and juice; 4TL).* With plentiful seating and a 24hr. courtyard, the entire place smells of sweet fumes. While there is indoor seating, these rooms seem to be dominated solely by Turkish men playing backgammon.

⚐ *From* Ⓜ*Beyazır, follow the tram tracks in the direction of Hagia Sophia; the entrance to the courtyard will be on your left.* Ⓢ *Nargile 12TL.* ⏰ *Open 24hr.*

GÜLHANE SUR CAFE

Soğukçeşme Sokağı 40/A

⚅ CAFE

☎212 528 0986 💻www.coskunbazaar.com

This small cafe on a historic cobblestone street between Hagia Sofia and Topkapı Palace is an excellent place to take a break from sightseeing. Have some tea or coffee while watching the other tourists trudge by and look at you enviously. To double their envy, order their *nargile (10TL).* The cafe is part of Coşkun Bazaar, a gift shop located right above it. Opposite the cafe is an unconventional "art exhibition" with paintings placed on the bare walls of a half-destroyed building, leading into a room that's full of stacked paintings—confused? So are we.

✦ *From* Ⓜ*Sultanahmet or* Ⓜ*Gülhane, find the small street behind Hagia Sophia and continue down the hill.* Ⓢ *Tea and coffee 2-5TL.* ⏰ *Open daily 9am-2am.*

Kadıköy, Moda, and Üsküdar

KÜP CAFE
✦ ✌ ⚐ GARDEN CAFE

Caferağa Mah. Güneşlibahçe Sok. 47, Kadıköy ☎216 347 8694 ▇www.kupcafe.com

It's difficult to find for those who aren't searching for it, but Küp's atmospheric courtyard has everything you need for a quiet night out. There's a jungle of vegetation, some mood lighting, and a lot of corners to sit in. Come here when you're fed up with looking at the skyline, not too excited about people-watching, and just want to have a beer and discuss the more important things in life.

✦ *Located toward the end of Güneşlibahçe Sok. If you're walking from Söğütlü Çeşme Cad., it will be on your left side.* Ⓢ *Tea 2-4TL. Beer 6TL. Entrees 8.50-15TL.* ⏰ *Open daily 9am-1am.*

KARGA
✦ ✌ ⚐ BAR

Kadife Sok. 16, Kadıköy ☎216 449 1726 ▇www.kargabar.org

One of the best known bars this side of the Bosphorus, Karga is so cool that it doesn't even need a name on its door. Thanks to its four stories, a garden, numerous balconies, and a top-floor art gallery, you can choose the decibel of your music and what kind of night you're going to have. Don't expect any Turkish music—Karga plays mostly alternative rock that fits its edgy atmosphere.

✦ *On the bar street. Walking from Rexx Cinema it will be on your right, an unmarked wooden door with a raven drawn above it.* Ⓢ *Beer 6TL. Cocktails 6-16TL. Rakı 7.50TL. Food 4-9.50TL.* ⏰ *Open Sept-June noon-2am.*

ARKAODA
✦ ✌ ⚐ BAR

Kadife Sok. 18, Kadıköy ☎216 418 0277 ▇www.arkaoda.com

With red lighting and three different levels, Arkaoda tries to embody the alternative spirit of the Asian side of Istanbul. Usually playing minimalistic techno, ambient drone, or freak folk, Arkaoda also has frequent live concerts and DJ nights with internationally acclaimed acts. Try one of their alcoholic coffees (7-10TL), which ingeniously manage to combine two vices at the same time.

✦ *Walking from Rexx Cinema it will be on your right. It has an unmarked wooden door right next to Karga.* Ⓢ *Tea 4TL. Beer 7.50TL. Rakı 8.50TL. Whiskey 16TL.* ⏰ *Open daily 2pm-2am.*

LIMAN KAHVESI
✦ ✌ ⚐ BAR

Kadife Sok. 37, Kadıköy ☎216 349 9818 ▇www.limankahvesi.com.tr

This place will make you feel like you're on a boat—or at least surrounded by them. The drinks counter is in the shape of a boat, the bookshelf on the second floor is modeled after a barge, and there's a massive ship hanging from the ceiling. On the wall there are yellowed instructions for putting on an inflatable vest as well as a brick of an old ship transmitter—just make sure their various shots don't make you seasick. Liman Kahvesi brings in weekly DJs, presumably spinning nautically inspired sets.

✦ *Toward the end of the bar street. Walking from Rexx Cinema it will be on your left.* Ⓢ *Beer 6TL. Rakı 8TL. Shots 9.50TL. Burgers and dürüms 8-9.5TL.* ⏰ *Open daily 10am-2am.*

Beşiktaş and Ortaköy

🔲 REINA
✦ ✌ ⚐ NIGHTCLUB, RESTAURANT

Muallim Naci Cad 44, Ortaköy ☎212 259 5919 ▇www.reina.com.tr

If you're going to wallow in excess, do it big time. Probably the most famous club in the city, Reina is where local and international social elite come to spend unchristian amounts of money. The club has six different restaurants (Chinese, sushi, kebabs, Mediterranean, fish, and international) and a dance floor in the middle, all with the Bosphorus Bridge looming as a backdrop. Reina also owns two boats that will transport you here from your hotel, if you happen to be one of the VIP guests. Not sure if you qualify as a VIP or not? Then you probably don't. However, there are ways to enjoy the club for very little money—come on a weekday and then spend the night nursing a beer or two.

➤ Take the bus to Ortaköy. Then walk down Muallim Naci until you see it to your right. **i** *Reservation for dinner required. Dress code is strictly enforced. Men need female company to enter the club.* $ *Cover F-Sa 50TL includes 1 drink. Beer 10TL. Cocktails 30TL.* ⏰ *Open daily for dinner 6pm-midnight. Club open daily midnight-4am.*

ANJELIQUE 💳🍸🍴 NIGHTCLUB, RESTAURANT

Salhane Sok. 5, Ortaköy ☎212 327 2844 💻www.istanbuldoors.com

Don't let the absence of cover charge at Anjelique on the weekends trick you: this is still one of the most prestigious clubs in the area. There are three floors, two restaurants (Asian and Mediterranean), and, during the club hours, two DJs at a time (one plays house, the other popular songs). The decor is stylish and simple (you won't find any of Reina's antlers-turned-lamps here) and the club's position over the Bosphorus is definitely an asset.

➤ Take the bus to Ortaköy. Anjelique is in a small street in the center of Ortaköy, opposite the Jazz Center and near a Hotel Radisson entrance. From the Ortaköy ferry jetty, head inland and take the first left, Anjelique will be to your left. **i** *Reservation for dinner required. Dress code strictly enforced. Men need female company to enter the club.* $ *No cover. Beer 13TL. Cocktails 30TL.* ⏰ *Open daily for dinner 6pm-midnight. Club open Tu-F midnight-4am.*

turkey

SUPPERCLUB 💳🍸 NIGHTCLUB, RESTAURANT

Muallim Naci Cad. 65, Ortaköy ☎212 261 1988 💻www.supperclub.com

This undeniably cool concept club has a number of branches in metropoles all over the world. There are no chairs; instead, there are huge beds covered with white satin. There is no menu either—if you order the surprise dinner *(80TL)*, the only thing you need to say before they bring it is whether you're vegetarian or not. The DJs are imported from the Netherlands and the club remains open till 7am, the latest among the Bosphorus' bling establishments. It is more compact than the other clubs, with the dancing section separated from the drinking section by a big glass wall.

➤ Take the bus to Ortaköy. Walk down Muallim Naci until you see it on your left. **i** *Reservation for dinner and club required. Dress code strictly enforced. Men need female company to enter the club.* $ *Cover F-Sa 35TL; includes 1 drink. Beer 10TL. Cocktails 30TL.* ⏰ *Open daily for dinner 8-11:30pm. Club 11:30pm-7am.*

JAZZ CENTER ISTANBUL 💳🍸 JAZZ CLUB

Salhane Sok. 10, Ortaköy ☎212 327 5050 💻www.istanbuljazz.com

If you're one of those people whose knees start to shake when they hear names like Mike Stern, Dave Weckl, or Stanley Clarke, you'll enjoy visiting this club. Outside of the summer months, the Jazz Center hosts jazz concerts five days a week, with two sets per night. The names that come to play here are relatively big, and so is the bill for food and alcohol at the end of the night. The small performance room gets crowded very easily, so come a bit earlier to catch a good spot.

➤ Take the bus to Ortaköy. From the Ortaköy ferry jetty head inland and take the 1st left; Jazz Center will be to your right. $ *Cover 15-50TL. Beer 15TL. Set menu 40-60TL. Entrees 25-36TL.* ⏰ *Open daily 7pm-4am. Music daily 9:30pm-midnight. Performances less frequent during the summer.*

Beyoğlu

👍 PAPILION INC. 💳📶🍸 BAR

Balo Sok. 31/4 ☎537 840 6359 💻papilioninc.blogspot.com

This place combines surprisingly cheap drinks with an elaborate decor (think aquariums, a crazy disco ball, and something that looks like a big spiderweb). It's run and manned by friendly young people, and you can choose between the louder lower level or the more intimate upper level with beanbags. If you're lucky, grab a seat on the coveted balcony.

➔ [M]Taksim. It's on the opposite side of the street as Araf. Find an unmarked black gate with two red alert lights (Machine Club), and then walk up the staircase that's to the left; Papilion is on the top floor. [$] Happy hour beers 2.50-3.50TL. Tequila 3TL. Beer 4-5TL. Vodka 5TL. ⏰ Open M-F noon-3am, Sa-Su noon-6am. Happy hour noon-9pm.

PEYOTE 💳📶🍸 LIVE MUSIC

Kameriye Sok. 4 ☎212 251 4398 🖥www.peyote.com.tr

Don't get discouraged by Peyote's first floor, which features some indifferent electronic music—the real places to be are the second floor (live music) and the third floor (a beer terrace). Peyote is a well-known venue where young bands perform before going big, and the place even has its own record label.

➔ [M]Taksim. Walk to Galatasaray, turn right onto Hamalbaşı Cad., and take the 4th right and walk until you see Peyote on the right. [$] Cover varies. Sausages 8TL. Beer 6TL. Shots 9TL. ⏰ Open daily noon-4am. Live music W, F, Sa at 11:30pm.

LIMONLU BAHÇE 💳📶🍸☀ CAFE

Yeni Çarşı Cad. 98 ☎212 252 1094 🖥www.limonlubahce.com

With its overgrown vegetation and apathetic-looking tortoises crawling amidst the table legs, this garden is great for an evening drink. The furniture and decor aren't glittering with newness, but perhaps that's part of its appeal. The food portions are big, so you can consider coming here for lunch when the prices are lowered by 10%. Fun game for erstwhile Pokemon fans: catch all the tortoises.

*➔ [M]Tünel or [M]Taksim. Walk to Galatasaray, go down the hill on Yeni Çarşı, and continue until you see its sign on the right. **i** Free Wi-Fi. [$] Entrees 13-23TL. Coffee 5-6TL. Beer 7.50TL. Cocktails 13-19TL. ⏰ Open daily 9am-midnight.*

LEB-I DERYA 💳📶🍸 RESTAURANT, BAR

Kumbaracı Yok. 57/6 ☎212 243 9555 🖥www.lebiderya.com

Leb-i Derya is a posh place, widely acknowledged as having one of the best views of Istanbul in the city. Its open terrace is quite nice, but if you want the best view, reserve the tiny upper terrace in advance as the spots here go quickly. The cuisine is Mediterranean and international, but the cheapest way to enjoy the place is to come for a drink. Don't get this branch confused with the other Leb-i Derya branch in the Richmond Hotel, where the view isn't half as interesting.

➔ [M]Tünel. Walking up İstiklal from Tünel take the 2nd right. Walk down the hill for a while, until you see Leb-i Derya to your right. [$] Beer 11-15TL. Cocktails 25-29TL. Entrees 32-40TL. Desserts 15-16TL. ⏰ Open M-F 4pm-2am, Sa 10am-3am, Su 10am-2am.

MOJO 💳🍸 LIVE MUSIC

Büyükparmakappı Sok. 26/1 ☎212 243 2927 🖥www.mojomusic.org

Bars on İstiklal tend to have a very limited understanding of what "live music" means (one jangly guitar and an annoying singer), so this edgy club hosting performances of local underground bands (pop rock, alternative rock) is a refreshing change. There is no seating on nights when cover is charged, so you'll have to either dance, stand, or pretend you're dancing. The club isn't very big and can get quite crowded, but that's the problem with most good clubs anyway.

➔ [M]Taksim. Walk down İstiklal and take the 3rd left turn. The club is toward the end of that street, on the right side. [$] Cover W 15TL, F 20TL, Sa 25TL. Beer 8-10TL. Vodka 10TL. ⏰ Open daily 10pm-4am. Live music M-Sa at midnight.

KIKI 💳🍸☀ BAR

Sıraselviler Cad. 42 ☎212 243 5373 🖥www.kiki.com.tr

A place popular with Cihangir dwellers, Kiki is known for its brunches and low-pressure atmosphere. The beer isn't cheap, but the price is similar to what many places in Cihangir charge. In the back there's a small garden good for talking and smoking (if a bar in Istanbul doesn't have an outdoor space for smoking, it's doomed), while indoors some dancing takes place between its narrow walls.

➔ From [M]Taksim, walk down Sıraselviler. After a few blocks, Kiki will be on the right. [$] Beer

10TL. Cocktails 20-22TL. ⏰ Open M-F 6pm-2am, Sa-Su 6pm-4am. Music W, F-Sa at 11:30pm.

ARAF 💵🍸 LIVE MUSIC

Balo Sok. 32 ☎212 244 8301 💻www.araf.com.tr

Some expats say Araf is an "Erasmus trap," attended mostly by exchange students and Turks who would like to hook up with them. On the other hand, the odds that you'll meet somebody who actually speaks English are quite high, which could be a refreshing change after every other place in Istanbul. The bands play loud world music, the drinks are relatively cheap, and the focus is on dancing.

🧭 ⓂTaksim. Walk down İstiklal toward Galatasaray, then turn right at Halkbank onto Balo Sokak. Continue down the street until you see Araf on the right. ℹ Live music M-Th and Su; DJ performances F-Sa. $ No cover. Beer 6TL. Rakı and shots 8TL. ⏰ Open M-F 5pm-2am, Sa-Su 5pm-3am.

ARTS AND CULTURE 🎵

Bathhouses

ÇEMBERLITAŞ HAMAMI 💵 HAMAM

Vezirhan Cad. 8, Çemberlitaş ☎212 522 7974 💻www.cemberlitashamami.com.tr

This is one of the well-known hamams frequented mostly by tourists, and everything here corresponds to that—it's clean, aesthetically pleasing, and on the expensive side. Built in 1584 and based on plans created by Mimar Sinan, this hamam offers all the basics from body scrubs and bubble washes *(55TL)* to facial masks *(12TL)* and head massages *(40TL)*. Your experience here depends on the crowds, so try to come in outside the rush hours (generally 4-8pm). If you plan to go to a hamam only once, this place is one of the top contenders. Yes, it's touristy, but visiting a hamam seems to be turning into a tourist activity anyway.

🧭 ⓂÇemberlitaş. The hamam is just across the street from the tram stop. ℹ Separate sections for men and women. $ Self-service 35TL; body scrub and bubble wash 55TL, with oil massage 95TL; facial mask 12TL; reflexology 40TL; Indian head massage 40TL. ⏰ Open daily 6am-midnight.

turkey

SOFULAR HAMAMI 🪙 HAMAM

Sofular Cad. 28, Fatih ☎212 521 3759

If a local, "authentic" experience is what you're after, consider going to the Sofular hamam in Fatih. Don't expect much English from the staff or too much polish in the changing rooms (it looks a bit like a hospital here), but once you enter the *hararet* (hot room) and lie down under its pleasant dome, all of these amenities will not matter. Instead of other tourists there will be old, local men with enormous bellies (or their female equivalents), and you'll pay about half the price charged by touristy hamams.

🧭 Take bus to Fatih. Head southeast down Fevzipaşa and turn right at Aslanhane. After 1 block get on the diagonal Sofular Cad. and continue down that street until you reach the hamam, which will be on the left near Sofular Mosque. ℹ Separate sections for men and women. $ Self-service 20TL; bath with massage 28TL, with scrub 28TL, with scrub and massage 36TL. ⏰ Open daily for women 8am-8pm, for men 6am-10:30pm.

CAĞALOĞLU HAMAMI 🪙 HAMAM

Cağaloğlu Hamamı Sok. 34, Cağaloğlu ☎212 522 2424 💻www.cagalogluhamami.com.tr

For some reason, somebody decided to list this hamam in a book called *1001 Things To Do Before You Die*, and the hamam has been unabashedly profiting from this citation ever since. With walls covered in photos of celebrities who have stopped by (yes, this includes Mr. Atatürk) and a few of Kate Moss engaging in some softcore posing, these guys surely know how to advertise themselves. If you keep in mind that few things that are well advertised in Sultanahmet live up to their image, your visit to this 270-year-old hamam could be very enjoyable.

🧭 ⓂSultanahmet. It's a few blocks down the street from the entrance of Basilica Cistern, on the right side. ℹ Separate sections for men and women. $ Self-service 38TL. Bath with scrub 57TL; with massage 62TL; with scrub and massage 75TL. Full service 95TL. ⏰ Open daily for women 8am-8pm; for men 8am-10pm.

TARIHI GALATASARAY HAMAMI
Turnacıbaşı Sok. 24, Galatasaray

❧ HAMAM

women ☎212 249 4342, men ☎212 252 4242
🖳www.galatasarayhamami.com

Another hamam focusing mostly on tourists. How do we know? Their brochure is filled with pictures of some pretty steamy heterosexual situations among young people, despite the fact that everyone who has been to a hamam before knows that genders have separate sections (an exception is the **Süleymaniye Hamamı,** near the Süleymaniye Mosque). This hamam is one of the priciest of the lot, but in exchange for its pricetag, it offers one of the loveliest interiors of all the local hamams. Not that you'll pay much attention to it when you're being massaged, but it's a nice touch.

❦ Ⓜ*Taksim. Walk down İstiklal from Taksim and turn left at Turnacıbaşı, near Halk Bank. It's at the end of the street.* *i* *Separate sections for men and women.* Ⓢ *Self-service 50TL. Bath with scrub 75TL; with massage 80TL; with scrub and massage 95TL. Full service 125TL.* ⏰ *Open daily for women 8am-9pm; for men 7am-10pm.*

BÜYÜK HAMAMI
Potinciler Sok 22, Kasımpaşa

❧ HAMAM

☎212 253 4229 🖳www.buyukhamam.net

Serving mostly locals, this is one of the biggest hamams in town (as you probably figured out by your fourth day in Turkey, *büyük* means "big"). Although this hamam is not frequented by tons of tourists, it still holds historic value similar to that of its more popular brethren—it is the brainchild of Mimar Sinan, built in 1533. While its walls could use a fresh coat of paint, its swimming pool on the roof (only for men) and its cheap prices make Büyük a decent choice.

❦ Ⓜ*Tünel. From Tünel go up İstiklal, then turn left at Kumbaracı Yokuşu. Go down the hill until you reach Bahriye. Cross the street, turn right and walk for 1 block. The hamam will on your left close to Kasımpaşa Mosque.* *i* *Separate sections for men and women.* Ⓢ *Self-service 17.5TL. Bath with massage 25TL; with scrub 22.5TL; with massage and scrub 30TL.* ⏰ *Open daily for women 8:30am-7:30pm; for men 5:30am-10:30pm.*

Dance Performances

HOCAPAŞA ART AND CULTURE CENTER
Hocapaşa Hamamı Sok. 5-9D

❧ SIRKECI

☎212 511 4626 🖳www.hodjapasha.com

Sema is a religious ceremony that has become a popular tourist attraction—and very few people seem to find this strange. This practice is performed by dervishes of the Mevlevi Sufi order, a branch of Islam which was founded by Rumi, a 13th-century poet. The highpoint of the event is the activity that so many tourist brochures present as quintessentially Turkish—the whirling of dervishes. This act focuses on the dancer's arms, one palm pointing to the sky, the other to the ground, symbolizing the channeling of spiritual energy from God to the Earth. Since the Galata Mevlevihanesi closed for restoration, the 15th-century hamam inside the Hocapaşa Center has become the safest bet to see whirling dervishes perform.

❦ Ⓜ*Sirkeci. After getting off the tram, walk north, away from the water. Take the 1st left after you pass the tram tracks; there will be signs pointing to the venue.* Ⓢ *Adults 40TL.* ⏰ *Performances last 1hr. and start M, W, F-Su 7:30pm. Box office open daily 10am-9pm.*

GALATA TOWER
Galata Kulesi

❧ BEYOĞLU

☎212 293 8180 🖳www.galatatower.net

If you're set on seeing belly dancing and other traditional dances in Istanbul, you're going to have a hard time finding something that's not expensive and touristy as hell. Dancing is usually packaged along with a set menu into a "Turkish night" that takes a few hours and can be thoroughly entertaining, provided that you're an overzealous European tourist. However, if you really want to experience it, head to the Galata Tower, another standard-bearer of Turkish culture. The tower dates back to the 14th century and allegedly served as a take-off point for Hezarfen Ahmet Çelebi, who is said to have used artificial wings to fly across the Bosphorus to Üsküdar sometime around 1630. If you don't want to come for the cultural night, you can take an elevator up during the day, even though the entry price is disproportionately high.

⇄ [M]Tünel or [M]Karaköy. From [M]Tünel, head down Galipdede Cad. until you see the tower on the right side. [$] 80€ per person; includes a set menu and unlimited local drinks. Entry during the day 10TL. ⏰ Shows 8pm-midnight. Galata Tower open daily 9am-4pm.

SHOPPING

Bazaars and Markets

GRAND BAZAAR — BEYAZIT

Kapalı Çarşı ☎212 519 1248 💻www.kapalicarsi.org.tr

No offense, but it is obligatory that you get lost here—this covered maze of 60 streets and 1200 shops is one of the largest bazaars in the world. It's been around for 550 years, first started in order to finance the conversion of Hagia Sophia into a mosque. Today, you can buy just about anything here, with the potential exceptions of love and happiness. With streets named after the specific trades that used to be centered in them (Fez-makers, slipper manufacturers, etc.), there is a central *bedesten* (market hall) where valuable jewelry and antiques are sold. We'll save you the trouble and won't recommend any specific shops within its walls—searching for particular places here is a harrowing experience.

⇄ [M]Beyazıt. From the tram station, head north. ⏰ Open M-Sa 8:30am-7pm.

SPICE BAZAAR — EMINÖNÜ

Mısır Çarşısı ☎212 455 5900

Also called the Egyptian Bazaar, this market is easier to navigate than the Grand Bazaar—its layout is in the shape of the letter "L." Finished in 1663, it was built to provide funds for the upkeep of the New Mosque. The bazaar sells what it's named after (that's spices, not Egyptians), but there also are containers of dried fruit, herbs, nuts, sweets, and trinkets. Some merchants get more creative than others—you'll come across glued balls of dried fruit and mystery nuts called "Turkish Viagra". Live on the edge and smell a heap of spices from close up to encounter a true Turkish sneeze.

⇄ [M]Eminönü. Right behind Yeni Cami, the New Mosque. ⏰ Open daily 8am-7:30pm.

ARASTA BAZAAR — SULTANAHMET

Arasta Çarşısı 107 ☎212 516 0733 💻www.arastabazaar.com

What's that? Your flight home's in four hours and you suddenly remember you forgot to buy an "I Love Turkey" T-shirt? Run to Arasta Bazaar, a conveniently located strip of shops right below the Blue Mosque. Apart from clothes, there's all kinds of souvenir stuff—fabrics, *nargile*, handmade pipes, tiles, and cheap bric-a-brac of all sorts. Here you can also find the small Great Palace Mosaic Museum showcasing a collection of old Byzantine mosaics.

⇄ [M]Sultanahmet. It's behind the Blue Mosque. ⏰ Bazaar open daily 9am-7pm. Museum open M 9:30am-5pm, W-Su 9:30am-5pm.

SALI PAZARI (TUESDAY MARKET) — KADIKÖY

Kent Meydanı, Tarihi Salı Pazarı ☎216 339 9819

Every Tuesday, this enormous marketplace in Kadiköy gets filled with locals selling and buying cheap clothes and fresh produce. Women outnumber men 10 to 1, but it's safe to assume that all genders are welcome. The bazaar is open on Fridays as well, but there tend to be fewer sellers. If your clothes have endured some wear and tear during your travels, come here to refill your supplies.

⇄ Walk down Söğütlü Çeşme Cad. away from the ferry terminal past the bull statue, and turn right onto Mahmut Baba Sok. There is a bus stop behind Wash Point, a carwash place. Get on the free shuttlebus that will take you to the bazaar. The ride takes 10min., and the shuttles leave approximately every 10min. ⏰ Open Tu, F 8am-7pm.

EKOLOJIK PAZARI — ŞIŞLI

Feriköy Halk Pazarı, Lala Şahin Sok., Bomonti Cad. ☎212 252 5255 💻www.bugday.org/eng

The idea of "organic food" is slowly starting to penetrate Turkish society, and

turkey

this market is proof. The first of its kind in Istanbul, Ekolojik Pazarı is organized by the Buğday Association and offers organic fruit, vegetables, and other food products.. A skeptic would say that all food in Turkey is organic, but here you can be sure that what you get qualifies as such.

✦ From Ⓜ️Osmanbey, get on the other side of the cemetery and continue down Ergenekon Cad. until you reach Lala Şahin Sok. It's in parking lot number 6. Ⓢ Prices vary. 🕐 Open Sa 8am-5pm.

TARLABAŞI PAZARI
TARLABAŞI

The streets around Tarlabaşı

First, we have to say that the Tarlabaşı neighborhood isn't the safest place to go if you look like a naive Western tourist. However, it's interesting for the same reason—this market is unlike the others we mention, offering low prices and a very authentic feel. It gets really crowded, so beware of pickpockets. Tarlabaşı, inhabited mostly by the Roma, Kurds, and African immigrants, is surprisingly close to Taksim, so it's not that hard to get back into a safer neighborhood.

✦ Ⓜ️Taksim. Walking down İstiklal, take a right onto Ağa Camii, then cross Tarlabaşı Bul. Continue down the hill until you hit the market, which sprawls across many streets of that neighborhood. Ⓢ Prices vary. 🕐 Open Su 10am-dusk.

Gifts

KARADENIZ ANTIK
GALATASARAY

Çukurcuma Cad. 55   ☎212 251 9605 📧www.karadenizantik.com

This is a good place to start your search for all kinds of old junk that gets lumped into the category of antiques. The objects on sale range from old gramophones and cameras to furniture and lamps to statuettes and vases. There are many other shops around, so make sure you compare prices elsewhere before buying here. The best places in Istanbul to buy antiques are here (on and around **Çukurcuma Cad.**), inside the **Grand Bazaar's** central bedesten, and in the huge **Horhor Flea Market** (Kırık Tulumba Sokak 13 ✦ Ⓜ️Aksaray). Just make sure you don't buy anything of real value—if it's more than 100 years old, taking it out of the country may be illegal.

✦ Ⓜ️Tophane. Walk up Boğazkesen Cad. until you reach Çukurcuma; turn right and continue straight until you see the shop to your right. Alternatively, walk down from Galatasaray. 🕐 Open daily 9am-7pm.

ASLIHAN PASAJI
GALATASARAY

Located on the street opposite of Yeni Çarşı

This passage off İstiklal is stacked with shops selling all kinds of used books, so come here to buy your copy of Dan Brown's *Da Vinci Sifresi* or Mario Puzo's *Vaftiz Babası* (or their English equivalents). Secondhand bookstores are often concentrated in clusters, so apart from this one, there's also the **Sahaflar Bazaar** (Ⓜ️Beyazıt) and the **Akmar Pasajı** (between Mühürdar Cad. and Neşet Ömer Sok).

✦ Ⓜ️Tünel or Ⓜ️Taksim. From Galatasaray walk on the street opposite to Yeni Çarşı and you'll see the passage to your right. 🕐 Open M-Sa 8am-8pm.

PAŞABAHÇE
🏷 TÜNEL

İstiklal Cad. 314   ☎212 244 0544 📧www.pasabahce.com

If you went through all the glass in the Grand Bazaar and didn't find anything to satisfy your high demands, try Paşabahçe. This well-known glass chain offers all kinds of practical and impractical glass products. While more expensive than similar items at the bazaars, these pieces are of higher quality and better design. If you've picked up a bit of the Turkish superstitious bug, you can get one of their enormous glass evil eyes to ward off bad luck.

✦ Ⓜ️Tünel. Walk up İstiklal until you see the store on your left, opposite the Dutch consulate. 🕐 Open daily 10am-8pm.

Practicalities

- **TOURIST OFFICES:** There are a number of offices in different districts, including **Sultanahmet** *(Divan Yolu Cad. 5 ☎212 518 1802 🕐 Open daily 9am-5pm.)*, **Beyoğlu** *(Hilton Hotel ☎212 233 0592 🕐 Open M-Sa 9am-5pm.)*, **Sirkeci** *(Sirkeci Train Station ☎212 511 5888 🕐 Open M-Sa 9:30am-5:30pm.)*, **Beşiktaş** *(Süleyman Seba Cad. ☎212 258 7760)*, **Atatürk International Airport** *(☎212 465 3151 🕐 Open daily 8am-11pm.)* and **Karaköy** *(Karaköy Liman Yolcu Sarayi ☎212 249 5776.)* All provide free maps, brochures, and information in English.
- **BUDGET TRAVEL OFFICES:** Some of the biggest low-cost carriers are **Pegasus Airlines** *(☎444 0737 💻www.flypgs.com)*, **Onur Air** *(☎212 663 2300 💻www.onurair.com.tr)*, and **SunExpress** *(☎232 444 0797)*, operating both domestic and international flights. Virtually every hostel has a partnership with tour companies that run affordable tours.
- **CURRENCY EXCHANGE:** Exchange bureaus are called *döviz* and can be found on İstiklal and around Divan Yolu. Among the better ones are **Klas Döviz** *(Sıraselviler Cad. 6/F ☎212 249 3550 🕐 Open daily 8:30am-10pm.)* and **Çetin Döviz** *(İstiklal Cad. 39 ☎212 252 6428 🕐 Open daily 9am-10pm.)*.
- **ATMS:** English-language **ATMs** (*bankamatik*) can be found on almost every corner. If your account is at a foreign bank, cash withdrawal will cost you extra (for precise amount, inquire at your bank). Most ATMs work with Turkish Lira. If you want to withdraw USD or Euros, try some of the banks around **Sirkeci Train Station.**
- **LUGGAGE STORAGE:** **24hr. luggage storage** (*Emanet Bagaj*), is available at the **Atatürk International Airport** *(☎212 465 3442 $ 15TL per day.)* and **Sirkeci Train Station** *(☎539 885 2105 $ 4-7TL for the first 4hr.; 0.50 TL per hr. thereafter, 96 hr. max.)*.
- **GLBT RESOURCES:** Istanbul's **GLBT resources** are rather decentralized, so your best bet will be an internet search. **Time Out Istanbul** magazine provides a good overview of the city's GLBT establishments. Some other organizations of interest are **Kaos GL** *(☎312 230 0358 💻www.news.kaosgl.com*, and **Lambda** *(☎212 245 7068 💻www.lambdaistanbul.org 🕐 Open M-Tu 5-7pm, F-Su 5-7pm.)*.
- **TICKET AGENCIES:** Tickets to most major cultural events are available through **Biletix.** *(☎216 556 9800 💻www.biletix.com)*
- **LAUNDROMAT:** Most hostels will do your laundry for a small fee. If you'd prefer a laundromat, some of the options are **Beybuz** *(Topçekenler Sok. 17 ☎212 249 5900 $ 2.25TL per kg, dry cleaning 10TL. 🕐 Open daily 9am-2:30am.)* and **Şık Çamaşır Yıkama** *(Güneşli Sok. 1/A ☎212 245 4375 $ 15TL per load. 🕐 Open 8am-8pm.)*.
- **INTERNET ACCESS:** **Sultanahmet Square** offers free Wi-Fi. **Beyoglu** has free Wi-Fi as well, but you'll need a cellphone to receive the access code. One of the best internet cafes in town is **Net Club** *(Büyükparmakkapı Sok. 8/6 $* 1.25TL per hr. 🕐 Open 24hr.) off İstiklal Avenue, but there are many others around Istiklal and a few near the Sultanahmet tram stop. In most cafes, expect to pay 2TL per hr.
- **POST OFFICES:** You can send letters and make calls at any of the many **PTT booths** around the city. There's a central post office in **Eminönü** *(Büyük Postahane Cad. 25 ☎212 511 3818)*, while some other offices are in **Taksim** *(Cumhuriyet Cad. 2 ☎212 292 3650)*, **Galatasaray** *(Tosbağa Sok. 22 ☎212 243 3343)*, and **Sultanahmet** *(Sultanahmet Meydanı ☎212 517 4966 🕐 Open daily 8:30am-12:30pm and 1:30-5:30pm.)*.

Emergency!

- **EMERGENCY NUMBER:** ☎112.

- **POLICE:** ☎155; 212 527 4503.
- **LATE-NIGHT PHARMACIES:** Pharmacies are called *eczane* in Turkish. Some stay open overnight (*nöbetci*) on a rotating basis, and the closed pharmacies will list the nearest open pharmacy on their doors. For a list of all open pharmacies, go to 🖥www.treczane.com.
- **HOSPITAL/MEDICAL SERVICES:** The best option for international travelers is to use a **private hospital.** They are clean, efficient, and have 24hr. emergency units and some English-speaking staff. Some of the options are **Alman Hastanesi** *(Sıraselviler Cad. 119 ☎212 293 2150 🖥www.almanhastanesi.com.tr [$] Consultation 160TL.)* and the **American Hospital** *(Güzelbahçe Sok. 20 ☎212 444 3777 🖥www.americanhospitalistanbul.com [$] Examinations 190TL.)* **Public hospitals** are generally crowded, confusing, and without English-speaking staff, but they are an option if you want to save money. The most conveniently located one is **Taksim Hastanesi.** *(Sıraselviler Cad. 112 ☎212 252 4300 🖥www.taksimhastanesi.com.tr.)*

Getting There

By Air

ATATÜRK INTERNATIONAL AIRPORT AIRPORT

İstanbul Atatürk Havalimanı, Yeşilköy ☎212 465 5555 🖥www.ataturkairport.com

The airport is 28km from central Istanbul and has an international and a domestic terminal. The easiest way to get from the airport to the center is to take the **metro** (LRT) and then the **tram.** At the airport, follow the "LRT" signs, get on the metro *([$] One jeton costs 1.50TL)*, and get off at Zeytinburnu. Here transfer to the tram going to [M]Kabataş, which passes through [M]Sultanahmet. You'll need to buy another 1.50TL *jeton* for the tram. You can also get off the metro at [M]Aksaray, but the transfer to the tram here isn't as convenient. Alternative ways of getting to and from the airport include the express **Havaş bus** *(☎212 465 4700 🖥www.havas.net [$] 10TL. ⏰ Around 40min., every 30min. 4am-1am.)* and **taxis.** *([$] Around 30TL for Sultanahmet, 35TL for Taksim.)* There is a **Lost and Found Office** *(☎212 465 5555, ext. 4690 ⏰ Open M-F 8am-5pm.)*, a **Tourist Information Office** *(In the international terminal ☎212 465 3451 ⏰ Open 9am-11pm.)*, and 24hr. **luggage storage.** *(☎212 465 3442 for the international terminal; 212 465 3000, ext. 2805 for the domestic terminal [$] 10-20TL per day.)* The airport serves almost 40 airlines, including Turkish Airlines *(☎212 444 0849)*, British Airways *(☎212 317 6600)*, and Air France *(☎212 465 5491)*.

🚏 Metro to Havalimanı. [$] Parking 7.50TL per hr., 9.75TL per 1-3hr. ⏰ Open 24hr.

SABIHA GÖKÇEN INTERNATIONAL AIRPORT AIRPORT

Sabiha Gökçen Uluslararası Havaalanı, Pendik ☎216 585 5000 🖥www.sgairport.com

Located on the Asian side of Istanbul, this airport is 40km from Kadiköy and 50km from Taksim. The best way to get to central Istanbul is to take the **Havaş bus.** *(☎555 985 1051 🖥www.havas.net [$] 13TL. ⏰ Around 1hr., every 30min. 4am-midnight.)* Alternatively, you can take the **public E10 bus** to Kadıköy *([$] 1.5TL. ⏰ 90min., every 10min.-1hr.)* and then transfer to a **ferry** to either Eminönü or Karaköy *([$] 1.50TL. ⏰ Around 20min.)* **Taxis** are rather expensive, charging around 75TL for the trip to Taksim. Among the facilities at the airport are **luggage storage** *([$] 10-20TL per day)*, a **lost and found office,** and a **PTT booth.**

🚏 Bus to Sabiha Gökçen. ⏰ Open 24hr.

By Bus

Bus travel is concentrated at the **Büyük İstanbul Otogarı,** *(☎212 658 0505 🖥www.otogaristanbul.com)* known simply as the "Otogar." The Zeytinburnu-Havalimanı metro line has a stop here, so to get to the center, take the metro to Aksaray and then walk to the Yusufpaşa tram stop. Many bus companies have free shuttle service *(ücretsiz servis)* between the Otogar and Taksim. Among the major bus companies are **Metro** *(☎212 444 3455 🖥www.metroturizm.com.tr)*, **Kamil Koç** *(☎212 658 2000 🖥www.kamilkoc.com.tr)*, and **Ulusoy** *(☎212 444 1888 🖥www.ulusoy.com.tr)*. Some of the most frequent bus routes go to: **Ankara** *([$] From 35TL. ⏰ 6-7hr.)*; **Edirne** *([$] From 10TL. ⏰ 2½ hr.)*; **Çanakkale** *([$] From*

35TL. 🕐 *6hr.); Izmir (*💲 *From 45TL.* 🕐 *8½hr.) often via Bursa. (*💲 *From 20TL.* 🕐 *3hr.)*

By Train

Sirkeci Train Station *(*☎*212 520 6575)* is the final stop for all trains from Europe. The Bosphorus express from **Bucharest.** *(*🕐 *20½hr., daily at 10pm.)* The Balkan Express goes to **Sofia** *(*🕐 *12½hr.)* and **Belgrad** *(*🕐 *21½hr., daily at 10pm.)* and the Dostluk/Filia Express goes to **Thessalonica.** *(*🕐 *13hr., daily at 8:30pm).* Trains from the Asian side terminate at **Haydarpaşa Train Station** *(*☎*216 336 4470).* Six different trains connect Istanbul with Ankara *(*💲 *Daytime tickets from 16TL, overnight 85TL.* 🕐 *8hr., 5 per day.)* Information about train schedules and routes can be found on 🖳www.tcdd.gov.tr.

By Ferry

Apart from local ferries, **IDO** *(*☎*212 444 4436* 🖳*www.ido.com.tr)* operates intercity ferries from Istanbul's **Yenikapı Ferry Terminal** to **Yalova** *(*💲 *14TL.* 🕐 *6-7 per day),* **Bandırma** *(*💲 *32TL* 🕐 *4-6 daily.),* and **Bursa.** *(*💲 *21TL.* 🕐 *4-6 daily.)* Over a dozen ferries per day on three different routes connect Yenikapı to **Bostancı.** To get to Yenikapı, take the suburban train from Sirkeci Train Station.

Getting Around

The public transportation network in Istanbul is very reliable and easy to navigate. This applies especially to ferries, trams, and trains, because they don't suffer from Istanbul's traffic congestion. Rides on all of the following (apart from the dolmuşes and the funiculars) have a flat rate of 1.50 TL, but it's cheaper if you use Akbil or another transit pass (see boxed text).

By Tram and Funicular

Tram: The tram line that runs from **Zeytinburnu** to **Kabataş** is excellent for transportation on the European side, stopping in **Aksaray, Sultanahmet,** and **Karaköy** *(*🕐 *Every 10min., 6am-midnight).* There are two nostalgic tram lines. One runs along **İstiklal Cad.,** connecting **Tünel** and **Taksim,** while the other follows a circular route in **Kadıköy** on the Asian side.

In addition to the trams, Istanbul is also connected by underground funiculars. Since there is no direct tram connection between Taksim and Sultanahmet, the funicular connecting Kabataş and Taksim *(*💲 *1 TL.)* is almost necessary for getting from one to the other. Another funicular connects **Karaköy** and **Tünel** *(*💲 *1 TL).*

By Metro

There's a metro line running from the **Atatürk International Airport** through **Büyük Otogar** to **Aksaray.** Ⓜ Aksaray is a 5min. walk away from the Yusufpaşa tram stop (there are signs showing the way). Another metro line runs from **Taksim** north to **4. Levent.** *(*🕐 *6am-midnight.)*

Two suburban trains complement the tram service. One line starts at **Sirkeci Train Station** and goes west through **Kumkapı and Yenikapı,** while the other starts at **Haydarpaşa Train Station** in Kadıköy and runs east through **Göztepe** and **Bostancı.** *(*🕐 *Every 20min., 5:30am-midnight.)*

By Ferry

Commuter ferries are the best way to get to the Asian side or to access some of the more distant neighborhoods. The most useful lines are **Eminönü-Kadıköy, Karaköy-Haydarpaşa-Kadıköy, Kabataş-Üsküdar, Eminönü-Üsküdar, Kadıköy-Beşiktaş, Kabataş-Kadıköy-Prince's Islands,** and the **Golden Horn line** (stops include **Üsküdar, Eminönü, Fener,** and **Eyüp**). *(*☎*212 444 4436* 🖳*www.ido.com.tr* 🕐 *Every 20min., consult website for departure times.)*

By Bus

There are many useful bus lines. See the table for a partial list of buses that connect major neighborhoods. For more specific information, contact IETT *(*☎*800 211 6068,* 🖳 *www.iett.gov.tr).*

The **dolmuş** is a shared minibus that runs on set routes, stopping every couple of blocks to take on and drop off passengers. The system is chaotic, but the destinations are always listed on the boards visible through the windows. Especially useful is the **Kadıköy-Taksim** dolmuş *(*💲 *5TL),* which leaves every 20min., even after ferries stop running.

BUS ROUTES	
Üsküdar-Kadıköy	12, 12A
Kadıköy-Taksim	110
Fatih-Taksim	87
Fatih-Eminönü	28, 31E, 32, 336E, 36KE, 37E, 38E, 90, 910
Fener-Taksim	55T
Fener-Eminönü	33ES, 36CE, 399B, 399C, 399D, 44B, 99, 99A
Beşiktaş-Taksim	110, 112, 129T, 25T, 40, 40T, 42T, 559C, DT1, DT2
Ortaköy-Taksim	40, 40T, 42T, DT1, DT2

By Taxi
The initial charge for cabs is 2.50TL, and every additional kilometer costs 1.40TL. The rates are the same for day and night. If you're taking a cab across the Bosphorus, you'll have to pay the bridge toll as well. Tipping is not necessary. Beware of common taxi scams like a "broken meter" or roundabout routes.

gallipoli and troy ☎212,217,286

Both Gallipoli and Troy are famous sites of war and worthwhile trips from Istanbul. The way **Homer** tells it, the Trojan War was actually pretty fun: Paris chooses the wrong goddess to receive his golden apple, Achilles is sensitive about his heel, and Odysseus outsmarts everyone in Troy with a **wooden horse,** only to get lost for ten years on his way home. These legends have little to do with what you'll see in the actual remains of Troy, but they do give it a mysterious spirit that draws crowds. Gallipoli, on the other hand, is the site of unambiguous tragedy—the military campaign that took place here in 1915 had over 400,000 casualties. The events became a defining event for some of the participating nations. It was the first independent military action for Australia and New Zealand and the moment of metaphorical birth for Turkey's national hero, **Kemal Atatürk.** Deceptively peaceful, the Gallipoli battlefields are among the most touching places you can find in Turkey. If you want to go to see Gallipoli and Troy, the easiest way to do it is by going to **Çanakkale**, a cheerful little seaside town on the Dardanelles. Çanakkale is no Istanbul, but maybe taking a short break from this metropolis is exactly what you need to appreciate it more fully.

ORIENTATION

In the middle of town is the **Cumhuriyet Meydanı Square.** Just a few steps south you can find the **Clock Tower** (1897), a good point of orientation. Restaurants and bars run in both directions along the shore, and a few hundred meters north from the jetty you can find the **wooden horse** that was used as a prop in the 2004 movie **Troy.** The naval museum and the Çanakkale fortress are 500 m south from the jetty. The **bus station** is a 10min. walk away from the center on Atatürk Cad., and the **dolmuş** stop is under a bridge over the Sarı River fifteen minutes away. The ruins of **Troy** are located 30km south of the town, while the **Gallipoli battlefields** are on Gallipoli peninsula across the Dardanelles strait from Çanakkale.

ACCOMMODATIONS

YELLOW ROSE PENSION — HOSTEL ❶

Kemalpaşa Mah. Aslan Abla Sok. 5 ☎286 217 3343 www.yellowrose.4mg.com

There's an Australian flag at the front door and jovial "G'day mate!" sign pointing you this way, so it's pretty obvious who the target customer group is at Yellow Rose Pension. This is one of the most appealing budget choices in the area—the rooms are clean, and many of them have fans. The reception desk also offers tours to Gallipoli and Troy *(60TL each)*.

From the Clock Tower head down Kemal Yeri Sok. and turn right onto the 2nd street. It will be to your left. i Breakfast included. $ Dorms 17TL; singles 25TL, with bath 30TL; doubles 40TL, with bath 50TL; triples 60TL, with bath 75TL; quads 80TL, with bath 100TL. Reception 24hr.

KONAK HOTEL HOTEL ②

Kemalpaşa Mah. Fetvane Sok. 12 ☎286 217 1150 www.konakhotelcanakkale.com

The amount of money that it takes to get a damp hostel room and a sleepy receptionist who spends most of his time in the hotel next door in Istanbul will get you much more in Çanakkale. Equipped with a minibar, A/C, and civilized-looking bathrooms, your lovely room might make you question going back to the bigger city. The prices here don't fluctuate with seasons, and it's one of the cheaper mid-range hotels in the area.

From the Clock Tower head down Fetvane Sok.; it will be on your right. [i] *Breakfast included.* $ *Singles €19; doubles with bath €36.* ⏰ *Reception 24hr.*

SIGHTS

GALLIPOLI BATTLEFIELDS

NATIONAL PARK

Almost one hundred years ago during WWI, the Gallipoli peninsula was the site of an eight-month-long military campaign that resulted in over 400,000 casualties and no military progress. These battlefields are now covered with shrubs and grass, but even today the soil here contains bones, pieces of shrapnel, and bullets. Cemeteries were built, monuments were erected, and the whole area is now a national park that commemorates the soldiers of this battle.

The objective for the **Allies** (British Empire, France) was to capture **Constantinople** (Istanbul) and thus knock the **Ottoman Empire** out of the war. They thought it would be an easy thing to do, but this takeover was actually very difficult. After failing to cross the **Dardanelles** by sea, the Allies decided to disembark on the Gallipoli peninsula and attack by land. Their progress was stalled early on, led to trench warfare, and ultimately ended with a withdrawal. This campaign has a special importance for the collective memory of Australians and New Zealanders because Gallipoli was the first major military operation for the Australia and New Zealand Armed Corps (ANZAC) since gaining independence. It was also important for Turkey, as the superhero lieutenant **Mustafa Kemal** made a name for himself as an extraordinarily capable leader in battle. This victory paved his way to becoming **Atatürk,** the father of modern Turkey.

The most commonly visited group of cemeteries and monuments lies near the **Anzac Cove,** the place where ANZAC forces disembarked. A few kilometers south is the **Kabatepe Museum** *(☎286 814 1297 $ 3TL, students 1.50TL ⏰ Open 9am-1pm, 2-6pm),* where you can see a gruesome collection of objects from the campaign, including a soldier's skull embedded with a bullet, old shoes with pieces of foot bones still inside them, artificial teeth, detached mandibles, unexploded hand grenades, and bullets that hit each other midair. There are also letters written by soldiers during the campaign. Look for a letter written by a certain William, who wrote to his mother and referred to one of the military skirmishes as "rather a hot job!" Make sure after visiting the museum to backtrack and find the walking trail to the left that leads to the **Lone Pine** cemetery, where almost 5000 soldiers who died in the span of a few days are buried. The pine standing in the center of the cemetery came from a seed that was produced by a pine tree in Australia, which in turn came from a cone that an Australian soldier sent from Gallipoli to his mother in 1915.

Continuing north up the road you will pass a number of cemeteries, including the Turkish **57th Regiment Cemetery.** In its graves are the people who received Atatürk's famous command: "Men, I'm not ordering you to attack. I'm ordering you to die. In the time it takes us to die, other forces and commanders can come and take our place." The soldiers obeyed the order, and in their honor, the Turkish army has never had a 57th regiment again.

Finally, a few kilometers up past some eroded trenches is **Chunuk Bair**, the only hill that the Allies captured during the whole campaign. Their success didn't last long, and the Turks regained the hill just a few days later.

$ *Free. Tours around 60TL.*

TROY — RUINS

Tevfikiye Köyü ☎286 283 0536

After visiting this place, many people complain that it's just a heap of stones. Perhaps there are a lot of stones, but these are some of the most interesting stones around. Troy wasn't just one city—the ruins go back to 2900 BCE and contain the remains of nine different cities, all built on top of another. Sundried mudbricks and trash from older periods weren't always removed but were actually paved over and used as foundation, creating the 15m mound on which the ruins are now located.

There are disputes about whether it was Troy VI or Troy VII that was the famed location of Homer's Iliad. Based on the signs of siege and fire that can be seen on the remnants of Troy VII, many believe this iteration was the subject of the myth. Troy VI seems to have been damaged by an earthquake, and even though there's no earthquake in Homer's version of the story, some think that the Trojan horse was in fact built to celebrate Poseidon, the god who possibly caused the earthquake that facilitated Troy's fall. These legends seem to be the main draw of the ruins today, and the tourist authorities know it—they recently built a big wooden horse near the entrance. Climb in and hope that the Trojans don't hear you sneeze.

Over the centuries, Troy was abandoned and forgotten. It was rediscovered for the Western world by German businessman Heinrich Schliemann in 1868, who excavated the ruins believing they were the site of the Homeric legend. More of a businessman than an archeologist, Schliemann believed Troy was only one city and destroyed many valuable buildings during the excavations. Notice the **Schliemann Trench**, which cuts through a number of settlement layers. Another subject on the list of grievances against this man is **Priam's Treasure**, a collection of valuable items that Schliemann found here, believing they originally belonged to the Trojan King Priam. Not only was he wrong about their origin (the artifacts come from Troy II, not Troy VII), but he smuggled the objects out of the Ottoman Empire. The ownership of Priam's Treasure remains problematic even today, as many of the objects were seized by the Russian Army after World War II and are now tucked away in the Pushkin Museum in Moscow, which refuses to return them to their country of origin.

Some of the more interesting heaps of stones include the Roman **Odeon** from Troy XI, where musical performances took place, the **sanctuary** dug into the remains of Troy VI and VII that was dedicated to unknown deities, and the **ramp** from Troy II close to where Schliemann discovered Priam's Treasure. Under a hideous white roof nearby, you can find the **megaron**, a house with a porch from the transitional period between Troy II and III. Down the hill, there's also a **water cave** that originated in the third millennium BCE and was associated with the god Kaskal.Kur (no, that's not a website).

Near Tevfikye village. Also known as Truva, or Troia. $ *15TL, ages 9 and under free.* ⏰ *Open daily in summer 8am-7:30pm, in winter 8am-5:30pm.*

FOOD

YALI HANI — CAFE ❶

Fetvane Sok. 28 ☎286 212 4926 www.yalihani.com

This is possibly the best down-to-earth hangout in town. Shaded by a huge wisteria tree and full of small wooden tables, this popular courtyard is an excellent place to come for some beer *(4TL)*, a few cigarettes or *nargile*, and friendly conversation. If you don't feel like sitting in the courtyard, there's always the darker, less spacious upper level.

From the Clock Tower continue down Fetvane Sok.; the courtyard will be to your right. $ *Beer 4TL. Nargile 7TL. Sandwiches 2-3TL. Tiramisu 3TL.* ⏰ *Open daily 11am-midnight.*

ESSENTIALS

Practicalities

- **TOURIST OFFICES:** The throbbing heart of all things practical is **Cumhuriyet Meydanı.** The **Tourism Information Office** has current schedules for ferries going to Eceabat and for dolmuşes going to Troy. *(☎286 217 1187. i Call ahead for schedules. ⏰ Open daily in summer 8:30am-7pm; in winter 8:30am-5:30pm.)*
- **TOURS:** There are a number of companies offering tours of Gallipoli and Troy, including **TJs Tours** *(☎286 814 3121)* and **Hassle Free Travel Agency** *(☎286 213 5969).*
- **CURRENCY EXCHANGE:** Use the **PTT booth** *(☎286 212 6981)* to exchange money, send postcards, and make phone calls.
- **ATMS:** Can be found mostly near the ferry jetty.
- **INTERNET:** There are no public wireless hotspots, but many cafes and hostels provide their own networks.
- **POST OFFICE:** The **Post Office** is 10min. away from Cumhuriyet Meydanı. *(İnönü Cad. 78 ☎286 217 1022 ⏰ Open daily 8am-7pm.)*

Emergency!

- **EMERGENCY NUMBER:** ☎112.
- **POLICE:** ☎155.

Getting There

By Bus

The intercity bus companies have their offices both in this square and inside the bus station *(☎286 217 5653).* There are numerous direct buses running from Istanbul to Çanakkale *($ 35TL ⏰ 6½hr., 5 per day)* operated by **Truva, Kamil Koç, Metro,** and **Ulusoy.** You can board these at the **Büyük Otogar**, but some of these companies have minibuses at **Taksim** that will take you to the *otogar.*

By Ferry

A more pleasant way to get to Çanakkale can be to take the **ferry** from Istanbul's Yenikapı Ferry Terminal (accessible by suburban train from Sirkeci) to **Bandırma** *(💻www.ido.com.tr $ 32TL ⏰ 2hr., 3 per day)* and then transfer to a Çanakkale-bound **bus.** *($ 20TL ⏰ 3hr.)* To get to Bandırma's bus station from the ferry terminal, take the **#8 bus** *(☎286 217 5653 $ 1.25TL ⏰ 20 min.)* that's 50m to the right of the terminal's exit.

By Plane

Turkish Airlines offers direct flights between the Atatürk International Airport and Çanakkale Airport. *(☎286 212 3366 ⇞ Transportation between the center and Çanakkale Airport is supplied by a shuttle bus. Airlines have office under the Anafartalar Hotel. i Call for exact shuttle times. $ Flights vary. Shuttles 2TL each way. ⏰ 1hr.; Tu, Th, Su at 4:15pm, return at 6:05pm.)*

Getting Around

In Çanakkale everything is within walking distance. To get from the bus station to the city center, leave through the main exit (there are silver letters saying *otogar* above it), turn left, and continue to the traffic light. Here, turn right and continue straight all the way to the ferry jetty. To get to the dolmuş stop from the jetty, walk inland toward the bus station, but instead of turning left at the second light, turn right and continue straight until you see a bridge (the dolmuşes stand is directly underneath). If circumstances require it, you can easily get a cab at Cumhuriyet Meydanı.

Troy

You can get around Troy with a guided tour or on your own. To get there by yourself, take a dolmuş from under the bridge. (*ℹ Call for weekend times. $ 4TL. ⏰ 40 min., weekdays hourly 9:30am-5:30pm, return hourly 7am-3pm.)*

Gallipoli

If you don't have your own transportation and don't want to take a tour, moving around Gallipoli on your own is a bit tricky. First, you'll need to take the ferry across the Dardanelles from Çanakkale to Eceabat. *($ 2TL. ⏰ 20min., hourly during the summer.)* In **Eceabat** you can hop on a dolmuş going to **Kabatepe** (they aren't too frequent and run primarily to connect with ferries that go from Kabatepe to **Gökceada** three times a day). The dolmuş will let you off at **Kabatepe Museum,** where you can walk to catch a dolmuş back. The distances are in kilometers and the area is hilly, so don't be too optimistic when estimating the time it will take you to cover most of the sites. Sometimes it's possible to arrange transport with guided tours or hire a taxi to drive you around, but these tend to be expensive for a student traveler.

essentials

entrance requirements

- **PASSPORT:** Required for citizens of all countries. Must be valid for 90 days after the period of intended stay.
- **VISA:** Citizens of Australia, Canada, Ireland, New Zealand, the UK and the US all require sticker visas which can be purchased at entry points (the fee varies based on nationality).
- **WORK PERMIT:** Required for all foreigners planning to work in Turkey.

PLANNING YOUR TRIP

Time Differences

Turkey is 2hr. ahead of Greenwich Mean Time (GMT), and it observes Daylight Saving Time. This means that they are 7hr. ahead of New York City, 10hr. ahead Los Angeles, 2hr. ahead of the British Isles, 7hr. behind Sydney, and 9hr. behind New Zealand.

MONEY

Tipping And Bargaining

In Turkey, you should tip 5-10% in fancier restaurants. Tips aren't expected in inexpensive restaurants, but will definitely be appreciated. It is not customary to tip taxi drivers, but often people will "round up" the fare. For example if the fare is 4.5TL, then passengers will give the driver 5TL. At hammams, attendants will line up to "bid you goodbye" when you leave, meaning that they expect tips—distribute 10-15% of the total cost amongst them. Porters generally expect a few liras, and generally if anyone ever helps you, they are likely to smile and ask for a *baksheesh*, or tip.

Bargaining in a street market or bazaar is life skill, but trying to get a cheaper price in an established shop can be considered disrespectful. The price tends to be more flexible in informal venues. If it's unclear whether bargaining is appropriate in a situation, hang back and watch someone else buy first. Be warned, merchants with any pride in their wares will refuse to sell to someone who has offended them in the negotiations, so don't lowball too much.

Taxes

In Turkey, there is a 10-20% VAT, known as the KDV, that is included in the price of most goods and services (including meals, lodging, and car rentals). Before you buy, check if the KDV is included in the price to avoid paying it twice. Theoretically, the KDV that you pay on your trip can be reclaimed at most points of departure, but this requires much persistence and hassle. An airport tax of $15 in Turkey is levied only on international travelers, but it is usually included in the cost of the ticket.

SAFETY AND HEALTH

General Advice

In any type of crisis, the most important thing to do is **stay calm.** Your country's embassy abroad is usually your best resource in an emergency; registering with that embassy upon arrival in the country is a good idea.

Local Laws and Police

The General Directorate of Security *(Emniyet Genel Müdüdlüğü)* is the civilian police force in Turkey. Police officers wear navy blue uniforms and caps. Police cars are blue and white and have "Polis" written on the side doors and hood. Police violence is a problem in Turkey, especially at protests and demonstrations, so exercise caution when near these event. According to Human Rights Watch, police routinely use firearms during arrests without exhausting non-violent means and also when there is not an apparent threat of death or injury. Always be respectful and compliant when dealing with the police, and make it clear that you are a tourist. Homosexuality is not illegal in Turkey, but GLBT travelers should exercise caution when traveling due to the conservative values embedded in Muslim-majority Turkish society.

Drugs and Alcohol

Turkey is a huge locus of drug trafficking coming in from Afghanistan and Iran into Europe. It is estimated that as much as 80% of heroin in Britain comes from Turkey. In recent years, the Interior Ministry has boasted a 149% increase in seizures of opium and opium derivatives, so the government takes drug trafficking very seriously. The Turkish government has adopted a harsh policy (including fines and jail time) against those caught with drugs. If caught, a meek "I didn't know it was illegal" will not suffice. Remember that you are subject to Turkey's laws while within its borders, not those of your home country. If you carry prescription drugs, have the prescription and if possible a note from the doctor. **Avoid public drunkenness.** Islam prohibits the consumption of alcohol, even though it is legal in Turkey. Do not drink during the holy month of Ramadan.

Specific Concerns

Natural Disasters

Located in one of the world's most seismically active areas, Turkey experiences frequent and occasionally large **earthquakes.** The most recent serious quake in 1999 wreaked an estimated US$3 billion worth of damage and caused nearly 45,000 casualties in Turkey. Earthquakes are unpredictable and can occur at any time of day. If a strong earthquake does occur, it will probably only last one or two minutes. Protect yourself by moving a sturdy doorway, table, or desk, and open a doorway to provide an escape route. In mountainous regions, landslides may follow quakes.

Terrorism

Terrorism is a serious concern for travelers to Turkey. A number of terrorist groups remain active, though mostly in southeastern Turkey, where the separatist Kurdistan Workers' Party (PKK) regularly attacks national security forces. *Let's Go* does not recommend travel in the southeastern provinces of Hakkari, Sirnak, Siirt, or Tunceli due to the instability and terrorism in these provinces. However, the PKK has bombed government and civilian targets in Ankara, Istanbul, Izmir and tourist resorts of the Mediterranean and Aegean. Bombs are normally planted in crowded areas in trashcans, outside banks, or on mini-buses and trains. Bombings occur a few times a year but are generally not deadly and target the police and the government.

Pre-Departure Health

Matching a prescription to a foreign equivalent is not always easy, safe, or possible, so if you take **prescription drugs,** carry up-to-date prescriptions or a statement from your doctor stating the medications' trade names, manufacturers, chemical names, and dosages. Be sure to keep all medication with you in your carry-on luggage.

Pharmacists often speak English reasonably well and can help you find common over-the-counter drugs like aspirin in the pharmacy.

Immunizations and Precautions

You should consult with your doctor before traveling to Turkey, and she or he may recommend getting Hepatitis A, typhoid, and rabies vaccinations, especially if you are traveling to rural areas.

Travelers over two years old should make sure that the following vaccines are up to date: MMR (for measles, mumps, and rubella); DTaP or Td (for diphtheria, tetanus, and pertussis); IPV (for polio); Hib (for *Haemophilus influenzae* B); and HepB (for Hepatitis B). For recommendations on immunizations and prophylaxis, check with a doctor and consult the **Centers for Disease Control and Prevention (CDC)** in the US or the equivalent in your home country. (☎+1-800-CDC-INFO/232-4636 🖳www.cdc.gov/travel)

Staying Healthy

Diseases and Environmental Hazards

In Turkey, be wary of food- and water-borne illnesses, like traveler's diarrhea, dysentery, cholera, Hepatitis A, Giardia, and typhoid fever. The best cure is prevention. Be sure that everything you eat is cooked properly. Never drink unbottled water unless you have treated it yourself. Bottled water is very cheap, and a large bottle typically sells for less than an American dollar. To purify your own water, bring it to a roiling boil or treat it with iodine tablets. Don't use untreated water even to brush your teeth, and don't open your mouth when in the shower. Ice cubes are just as dangerous as impure liquid water, so enjoy that gin and tonic off the rocks! Salads and uncooked vegetables (including lettuce) are chock full of untreated water. Other culprits include raw shellfish, unpasteurized milk and sauces containing raw eggs. Peel all fruits and vegetables yourself, and watch out for street food that may have been washed in dirty water.

turkey 101

CUSTOMS AND ETIQUETTE

When in Istanbul...

Visitors who've never traveled to a Muslim country before may be surprised by certain traditions. Public displays of affection are not as common or as widely accepted as in many other European countries, so even if you've found yourself a Turkish sweetheart (or brought one with you), keep your public canoodling to a minimum. Turkey's residents have a great deal of national pride, and insulting the Turkish nation, national flag, or founder Atatürk is both rude and illegal. Steer clear of touchy subjects; Islam is not an acceptable target for your latest rant or comedy routine. Turkish culture also places a high value on respect for elders. It is considered proper to make your greetings from eldest to youngest, regardless of how well you know each person.

At the Table

Invited to dine at someone's home? Welcome to a land of legendary hospitality. Show your gratitude by bringing a small gift, such as flowers or a dessert. Play it safe and don't bring a bottle of wine for your host. Because Turkey is mostly Muslim, many residents don't drink alcohol. Enjoy your meal, and make sure to let your host know how good it tastes. They'll be sure to keep loading up your plate, so bring a hearty appetite. If you're invited to dine out at a restaurant, bear in mind that the host always pays (although an offer to pay is customary).

Mosque Etiquette

Visitors are generally welcome in Istanbul's exquisite mosques, provided that they are courteous and respect local customs, but there are some mosques open only to Muslims. Remove your shoes before entering and wear modest clothing. Miniskirts, shorts, and tank tops are a definite no-no. Both men and women should make sure that their shoulders, upper arms, and thighs are completely covered. When entering, women will be provided with a headscarf to cover their hair—but feel free to bring your own to match your outfit! Remember that this is a place of worship, so speaking loudly or taking pictures will likely not be appreciated.

Body Language

Remember that body language isn't universal. Even something as simple as shaking your head might not mean what you expect. To say "yes," nod your head downward. "No" is nodding your head upwards, while shaking your head from side to side means that you don't understand. Making the "OK" sign with your hand has a much different meaning in Turkey, and is not appropriate for polite company. When you enter someone's home, take off your shoes and accept slippers if offered. Sitting cross-legged on the floor is common, but pay attention. Exposing the bottoms of your feet to another person is considered offensive, no matter how adorable your toesocks are. Blowing your nose is not something done in public, so take a quick trip to the bathroom instead.

FOOD AND DRINK

Fusion Food

With more than 2000 years of culinary history, Turkey has had plenty of opportunity to refine its palate. Fish, fresh eggplant, fragrant herbs, and local olive oil will please your stomach and maintain your waistline. Modern cuisine is a delicious blend of Balkan, Central Asian, and Middle Eastern specialties, from spicy kebabs of chicken and beef to *baklava*, a deliciously flaky pastry. *Doner kebabs* are one popular Turkish dish, consisting of lamb roasted to perfection on an upright spit. Meat-lovers will also enjoy *kofta*, balls of ground beef or lamb mixed with onions and spices. For lighter fare, order *dolma*, vine leaves stuffed with anything from spiced rice (*zeytinyagli dolma*) to eggplant (*patlican dolma*) to mussels (*midye dolma*).

Drink Up!

Caffeine-addicts should try a strong Turkish coffee on for size, then examine the dregs to test their skills at *kahve fali*, or coffee dreg fortune-telling. For less mystery and a stronger kick, sip *rakı*, an anise-flavored alcoholic drink often served with seafood. A common Turkish saying claims that if you want to get to know someone, you should either travel with them or drink *rakı* with them. If you're visiting Istanbul with friends, you can do both, and that effects of this famously strong drink will probably reveal more secrets about your friends than the *kahve fali* did earlier. Also called *aslan sütü* ("lion's milk"), *rakı* turns milky-white when diluted. Teetotalers can try another of Turkey's favorite drinks, *ayran*. An interesting mixture of yogurt, water, and salt, *aryan* is served chilled and provides the perfect concoction to accompany a steaming kebab.

ESSENTIALS

You don't have to be a rocket scientist to plan a good trip. (It might help, but it's not required.) You do, however, need to be well prepared, and that's what we can do for you. Essentials is the chapter that gives you all the nitty-gritty you need to know for your trip: the hard information gleaned from 50 years of collective wisdom (and that phone call to Marseille the other day that put us on hold for an hour). Planning your trip? Check. Staying safe and healthy? Check. The dirt on transportation? Check. We've also thrown in communications info, meteorological charts, and a ▩phrasebook, just for good measure. Plus, for overall trip-planning advice from what to pack (money and as little underwear as possible) to how to take a good passport photo (it's physically impossible; consider airbrushing), you can also check out the Essentials section of ▣www.letsgo.com.

We're not going to lie—this chapter is tough for us to write, and you might not find it as fun of a read as Discover Europe. But please, for the love of all that is good, read it! It's super helpful, and, most importantly, it means we didn't compile all this technical info and put it in one place for you (yes YOU) for nothing.

greatest hits

- **WE ARE ONE.** Poli Sci majors may think of the EU as a bureaucratic nightmare, but it's awesome for you—the Schengen Agreement allows you to move between most European countries without going through customs (p. 1180).

- **WE ARE ONE, PART TWO.** We have mixed feelings about the euro: on one hand, it's awfully convenient to have one currency for most of Europe. On the other hand, the exchange rate is just plain awful (p. 1180).

- **ONE-DOLLAR FLIGHTS.** Yes, it's true—budget airlines are a wonderful thing. We've compiled the continent's cheapest and most convenient (p. 1184).

- **WE AREN'T REALLY ONE.** As integrated as Europe becomes, they'll always speak some wildly different languages. This chapter has a phrasebook with the 10 biggest languages covered in this book (p. 1189). Can you say "Let's Go is awesome"? Can you say it in Hungarian?

planning your trip

DOCUMENTS AND FORMALITIES

You've got your visa, your invitation (if necessary; check individual countries' requirements), and your work permit, just like Let's Go told you to, and then you realize you've forgotten the most important thing: your passport. Well, we're not going to let that happen. **Don't forget your passport!**

Visas

EU citizens do not need a visa to globetrot through the many nations of Europe. Citizens of Australia, Canada, New Zealand, and the US do not need a visa for stays of up to 90 days, but this three-month period begins upon entry into any of the countries that belong to the EU's **freedom of movement** zone. For more information, see **One Europe** (below). Those staying longer than 90 days may purchase a visa at a European embassy or consulate.

Double-check entrance requirements at the nearest embassy or consulate of whatever countries you are visiting for up-to-date information before departure. US citizens can also consult ▧http://travel.state.gov.

Entering Europe to study requires a special visa. For more information, see the **Beyond Tourism** chapter.

one europe

The EU's policy of freedom of movement means that most border controls have been abolished and visa policies harmonized. Under this treaty, formally known as the Schengen Agreement, you're still required to carry a passport (or government-issued ID card for EU citizens) when crossing an internal border, but, once you've been admitted into one country, you're free to travel to other participating states. Most EU states are already members of Schengen (excluding Cyprus), as are Iceland and Norway.

Work Permits

Admittance to a country as a traveler does not include the right to work, which is authorized only by a work permit. For more information, see the **Beyond Tourism** chapter.

TIME DIFFERENCES

Most of Europe is on Central European Time, which is 1hr. ahead of Greenwich Mean Time (GMT) and observes Daylight Saving Time during the summer. This means that it is 6hr. ahead of New York City, 9hr. ahead of Los Angeles, 1hr. ahead of the British Isles, 8hr. behind Sydney, and 10hr. behind New Zealand. However, the UK, Ireland, and Portugal are on Western European Time (subtract 1hr. from Central European Time)—a.k.a. Greenwich Mean Time. In addition, Greece and Turkey (along with parts of Eastern Europe that *Let's Go* doesn't cover) are on Eastern European Time (add 1hr. to Central European Time).

money

GETTING MONEY FROM HOME

Stuff happens. When stuff happens, you might need some money. When you need some money, the easiest and cheapest solution is to have someone back home make a deposit to your bank account. Otherwise, consider one of the following options.

Wiring Money

Arranging a **bank money transfer** means asking a bank back home to wire money to a bank in Europe. This is the cheapest way to transfer cash, but it's also the slowest and most agonizing, usually taking several days or more. Note that some banks may only release your funds in local currency, potentially sticking you with a poor exchange rate; inquire about this in advance. Money transfer services like **Western Union** are faster and more convenient than bank transfers—but also much pricier. Western Union has many locations worldwide. To find one, visit ◪www.westernunion.com or call the appropriate number: in Australia ☎1800 173 833, in Canada and the US 800-325-6000, or in the UK 0800 735 1815. To wire money using a credit card in Canada and the US, call ☎800-CALL-CASH; in the UK, 0800 833 833. Money transfer services are also available to **American Express** cardholders and at selected **Thomas Cook** offices.

US State Department (US Citizens Only)

In serious emergencies only, the US State Department will forward money within hours to the nearest consular office, which will then disburse it according to instructions for a US$30 fee. If you wish to use this service, you must contact the Overseas Citizens Services division of the US State Department. (☎+1-202-501-4444, from US 888-407-4747)

TIPPING AND TAXES

Europe hasn't become totally homogenous yet; tipping etiquette still varies from country to country, as do tax laws. See **Essentials** in the relevant country chapter for details.

pins and atms

To use a debit or credit card to withdraw money from a cash machine (ATM) in Europe, you must have a four-digit Personal Identification Number (PIN). If your PIN is longer than four digits, ask your bank whether you can just use the first four or whether you'll need a new one. Credit cards don't usually come with PINs, so if you intend to hit up ATMs in Europe with a credit card to get cash advances, call your credit card company before leaving to request one.

Travelers with alphabetic rather than numeric PINs may also be thrown off by the absence of letters on European cash machines. Here are the corresponding numbers to use: 1 = QZ; 2 = ABC; 3 = DEF; 4 = GHI; 5 = JKL; 6 = MNO; 7 = PRS; 8 = TUV; 9 = WXY. Note that if you mistakenly punch the wrong code into the machine multiple (often three) times, it can swallow (gulp!) your card for good.

safety and health

GENERAL ADVICE

In any type of crisis, the most important thing to do is **stay calm.** Your country's embassy abroad is usually your best resource in an emergency; registering with that embassy upon arrival in the country is a good idea. The government offices listed in the **Travel Advisories** feature can provide information on the services they offer their citizens in case of emergencies abroad.

PRE-DEPARTURE HEALTH

Matching a prescription to a foreign equivalent is not always easy, safe, or possible, so if you take **prescription drugs,** carry up-to-date prescriptions or a statement from your doctor stating the medications' trade names, manufacturers, chemical names, and dosages. Be sure to keep all medication with you in your carry-on luggage.

Immunizations and Precautions

Travelers over two years old should make sure that the following vaccines are up to date: MMR (for measles, mumps, and rubella); DTaP or Td (for diphtheria, tetanus, and pertussis); IPV (for polio); Hib (for *Haemophilus influenzae* B); and HepB (for Hepatitis B). For recommendations on immunizations and prophylaxis, check with a doctor and consult the **Centers for Disease Control and Prevention (CDC)** in the US or the equivalent in your home country. (☎+1-800-CDC-INFO/232-4636 🖳www.cdc.gov/travel)

getting around

For information on how to get to Europe and save a bundle while doing so, check out the Essentials section of 🖳**www.letsgo.com.** (In case you can't tell, we think our website's the bomb.)

---

travel advisories

The following government offices provide travel information and advisories by telephone, by fax, or via the web:

- **AUSTRALIA: Department of Foreign Affairs and Trade** (☎+61 2 6261 1111 🖳www.dfat.gov.au)
- **CANADA: Department of Foreign Affairs and International Trade (DFAIT).** Call or visit the website for the free booklet *Bon Voyage...But.* (☎+1-800-267-8376 🖳www.dfait-maeci.gc.ca)
- **NEW ZEALAND: Ministry of Foreign Affairs** (☎+64 4 439 8000 🖳www.mfat.govt.nz)
- **UK: Foreign and Commonwealth Office** (☎+44 20 7008 1500 🖳www.fco.gov.uk)
- **US: Department of State** (☎888-407-4747 from the US, +1-202-501-4444 elsewhere 🖳http://travel.state.gov)

BY PLANE

Commercial Airlines

For small-scale travel on the continent, *Let's Go* suggests 🖳budget airlines (above) for budget travelers, but more traditional carriers have made efforts to keep up with the revolution. The **Star Alliance Europe Airpass** offers low economy-class fares for travel within Europe to 220 destinations in 45 countries. The pass is available to non-European passengers on Star Alliance carriers. (🖳www.staralliance.com) **EuropebyAir's** snazzy FlightPass also allows you to hop between hundreds of cities in Europe and North Africa. (☎+1-888-321-4737 🖳www.europebyair.com Ⓢ Most flights US$99.)

In addition, a number of European airlines offer discount coupon packets. Most are only available as tack-ons for transatlantic passengers, but some are standalone offers. Most must be purchased before departure, so research in advance. For example, **oneworld,** a coalition of 10 major international airlines, offers deals and cheap connections all over the world, including within Europe. *(🖳www.oneworld.com)*

budget airlines

The recent emergence of no-frills airlines has made hopscotching around Europe by air increasingly affordable. Though these flights often feature inconvenient hours or serve less popular regional airports, with ticket prices often dipping into single digits, it's never been faster or easier to jet across the continent. The following resources will be useful not only for crisscrossing countries but also for those ever-popular weekend trips to nearby international destinations.

- **BMIBABY:** Departures from multiple cities in the UK to Paris, Nice, and other cities in France. *(☎0871 224 0224 for the UK, +44 870 126 6726 elsewhere 🖳www.bmibaby.com)*
- **EASYJET:** London to cities in France. *(☎+44 871 244 2366, 10p per min. 🖳www.easyjet.com $ UK£50-150.)*
- **RYANAIR:** From Dublin, Glasgow, Liverpool, London, and Shannon to destinations in France. *(☎0818 30 30 30 for Ireland, 0871 246 0000 for the UK 🖳www.ryanair.com)*
- **STERLING:** The first Scandinavian-based budget airline connects Denmark, Norway, and Sweden to 47 European destinations. *(☎70 10 84 84 for Denmark, 0870 787 8038 for the UK 🖳www.sterling.dk)*
- **TRANSAVIA:** Short hops from Krakow to Paris. *(☎020 7365 4997 for the UK 🖳www.transavia.com $ From €49 one-way.)*
- **WIZZ AIR:** Has flights to major European cities. *(☎0904 475 9500 for the UK, 65p per min. 🖳www.wizzair.com)*

BY TRAIN

Trains in Europe are generally comfortable, convenient, and reasonably swift. Second-class compartments are great places to meet fellow travelers. Make sure you are on the correct car, as trains sometimes split at crossroads. Towns listed in parentheses on European train schedules require a train switch at the town listed immediately before the parentheses.

You can either buy a **railpass,** which allows you unlimited travel within a particular region for a given period of time, or rely on buying individual **point-to-point** tickets as you go. Almost all countries give students or youths (under 26, usually) direct discounts on regular domestic rail tickets, and many also sell a student or youth card that provides 20-50% off all fares for up to a year.

BY BUS

Though European trains and railpasses are extremely popular, in some cases buses prove a better option. Often cheaper than railpasses, **international bus passes** allow unlimited travel on a hop-on, hop-off basis between major European cities. **Busabout,** for instance, offers three interconnecting bus circuits covering 29 of Europe's best bus hubs. *(☎+44 8450 267 514 🖳www.busabout.com $ 1 circuit in high season starts at US$579, students US$549.)* **Eurolines,** meanwhile, is the largest operator of Europe-wide coach services. We get misty-eyed just thinking about their unlimited 15- and 30-day passes to 41 major European cities. *(🖳www.eurolines.com $ High season 15-day pass €345, 30-day pass €455; under 26 €290/375. Mid-season €240/330; under 26 €205/270. Low season €205/310; under 26 €175/240.)*

rail resources

- **WWW.RAILEUROPE.COM:** Info on rail travel and railpasses.

- **POINT-TO-POINT FARES AND SCHEDULES:** ■www.raileurope.com/us/rail/fares_schedules/index.htm allows you to calculate whether buying a railpass would save you money.

- **WWW.RAILSAVER.COM:** Uses your itinerary to calculate the best railpass for your trip.

- **WWW.RAILFANEUROPE.NET:** Links to rail servers throughout Europe.

keeping in touch

BY EMAIL AND INTERNET

Hello and welcome to the 21st century, where you can check your email in most major European cities, though sometimes you'll have to pay a few bucks or buy a drink for internet access. Although in some places it's possible to forge a remote link with your home server, in most cases this is a much slower (and thus more expensive) option than taking advantage of free **web-based email accounts** (e.g., ■www.gmail.com). **Internet cafes** and the occasional free internet terminal at a public library or university are listed in the **Practicalities** sections of cities that we cover.

Wireless hot spots make internet access possible in public and remote places. Unfortunately, they also pose security risks. Hot spots are public, open networks that use unencrypted, unsecured connections. They are susceptible to hacks and "packet sniffing"—the theft of passwords and other private information. To prevent problems, disable "ad hoc" mode, turn off file sharing and network discovery, encrypt your email, turn on your firewall, beware of phony networks, and watch for over-the-shoulder creeps.

BY TELEPHONE

Calling Home from Europe

Prepaid phone cards are a common and relatively inexpensive means of calling abroad. Each one comes with a Personal Identification Number (PIN) and a toll-free access number. You call the access number and then follow the directions for dialing your PIN. To purchase prepaid phone cards, check online for the best rates; ■www.callingcards.com is a good place to start. Online providers generally send your access number and PIN via email, with no actual "card" involved. You can also call home with prepaid phone cards purchased in Europe.

If you have internet access, your best—i.e., cheapest, most convenient, and most tech-savvy—bet is probably our good friend **Skype.** (■*www.skype.com)* You can even videochat if you have one of those new-fangled webcams. Calls to other Skype users are free; calls to landlines and mobiles worldwide start at US$0.021 per minute, depending on where you're calling.

Another option is a **calling card,** linked to a major national telecommunications service in your home country. Calls are billed collect or to your account. Cards generally come with instructions for dialing both domestically and internationally.

Placing a collect call through an international operator can be expensive but may be necessary in case of an emergency. You can frequently call collect without even possessing a company's calling card just by calling its access number and following the instructions.

Cellular Phones

The international standard for cell phones is **Global System for Mobile Communication (GSM)**. To make and receive calls in Europe, you will need a GSM-compatible phone and a **SIM (Subscriber Identity Module) card,** a country-specific, thumbnail-size chip that gives you a local phone number and plugs you into the local network. Many SIM cards are prepaid, and incoming calls are frequently free. You can buy additional cards or vouchers (usually available at convenience stores) to "top up" your phone. For more information on GSM phones, check out ▇www.telestial.com. Companies like **Cellular Abroad** (▇*www.cellularabroad.com*) and **OneSimCard** (▇*www.onesimcard.com*) rent cell phones and SIM cards that work in a variety of destinations around the world.

BY SNAIL MAIL

Sending Mail Home From Europe

Airmail is the best way to send mail home from Europe. **Aerogrammes,** printed sheets that fold into envelopes and travel via airmail, are available at post offices. Write "airmail" or *"par avion"* (or the equivalent in the local language) on the front. Most post offices will charge exorbitant fees or simply refuse to send aerogrammes with enclosures. Surface mail is by far the cheapest and slowest way to send mail. It takes one to two months to cross the Atlantic and one to three to cross the Pacific—good for heavy items you won't need for a while, like souvenirs that you've acquired along the way.

Sending Mail To Europe

In addition to the standard postage system whose rates are listed below, **Federal Express** handles express mail services from most countries to Europe. (☎*+1-800-463-3339* ▇*www.fedex.com*)

There are several ways to arrange pickup of letters sent to you while you are abroad. Mail can be sent via **Poste Restante** (General Delivery) to almost any city or town in Europe with a post office, but it is often not too reliable. Address Poste Restante letters like so:

Napoleon BONAPARTE
Poste Restante
City, Country

international calls

To call Europe from home or to call home from Europe, dial:

- **1. THE INTERNATIONAL DIALING PREFIX.** To call from Australia, dial ☎0011; Canada or the US, ☎011; Ireland, New Zealand, the UK, and most of Europe, ☎00.

- **2. THE COUNTRY CODE OF THE COUNTRY YOU WANT TO CALL.** To call Australia, dial ☎61; Canada or the US, ☎1; Ireland, ☎353; New Zealand, ☎64; the UK, ☎44.

- **3. THE CITY/AREA CODE.** *Let's Go* lists the city/area codes for cities and towns in Europe opposite the city or town name, next to a ☎, as well as in every phone number. If the first digit is a zero (e.g., ☎020 for Amsterdam), omit the zero when calling from abroad (e.g., dial ☎20 from Canada to reach Amsterdam).

- **4. THE LOCAL NUMBER.**

essentials

BACKPACKING
by the numbers:

117	photos snapped
41	gelato flavors (3 lbs gained)
23	miles walked (in the *right* direction)
6	buses missed
4	benches napped on
2½	hostel romances
1	Let's Go Travel Guide
0	REGRETS.

LET'S GO

www.letsgo.com

we'd rather be traveling, too.

The mail will go to a special desk in the central post office, unless you specify a post office by street address or postal code. It's best to use the largest post office, since mail may be sent there regardless. It is usually safer and quicker, though more expensive, to send mail express or registered. Bring your passport (or other photo ID) for pickup; there may be a small fee. If the clerks insist that there is nothing for you, ask them to check under your first name as well. *Let's Go* lists post offices in the **Practicalities** section for each city.

American Express has travel offices throughout the world that offer a free **Client Letter Service** (mail held up to 30 days and forwarded upon request) for cardholders who contact them in advance. Some offices provide these services to non-cardholders (especially AmEx Travelers Cheque holders), but call ahead to make sure. For a complete list of AmEx locations, call ☎+1-800-528-4800 or visit ▇www.americanexpress.com/travel.

climate

Europe is for lovers, historians, architects, beach bums, and... weather nerds? In fact, this smallest continent has quite the diverse climate. Southern Europe is well known for the warm weather surrounding the Mediterranean Sea, creatively named the Mediterranean climate. These areas have warm, wet winters and hot, dry summers. Northern Europe is marked by temperate forests, where cold arctic air in winter contrasts with hot summers. In between sits the exception: the mile-high Alps, where things are generally colder and wetter.

AVG. TEMP. (LOW/ HIGH), PRECIP.	JANUARY			APRIL			JULY			OCTOBER		
	°C	°F	mm	°C	°F	mm	°C	°F	mm	°C	°F	mm
Amsterdam	-1/4	30/39	68	4/13	39/55	49	13/22	55/72	77	7/14	45/57	72
Athens	6/13	43/55	62	11/20	52/68	23	23/33	73/91	6	15/24	59/75	51
Barcelona	6/13	43/55	31	11/18	52/64	43	21/28	70/82	27	15/21	59/70	86
Berlin	-3/2	27/36	46	4/13	39/55	42	14/24	57/75	73	6/13	43/55	49
Brussels	-1/4	30/39	66	5/14	41/57	60	12/23	54/73	95	7/15	45/59	83
Budapest	-4/1	25/34	37	7/17	45/63	45	16/28	61/82	56	7/16	45/61	5
Dublin	1/8	34/46	67	4/13	39/55	45	11/20	52/68	70	6/14	43/57	70
Istanbul	3/8	37/46	109	7/16	45/61	46	18/28	64/82	34	13/20	55/68	81
Lisbon	8/14	46/57	111	12/20	54/68	54	17/27	63/81	3	14/22	57/72	62
London	2/6	36/43	54	6/13	43/55	37	14/22	57/72	57	8/14	46/57	57
Madrid	2/9	36/48	39	7/18	45/64	48	17/31	63/88	11	10/19	50/66	53
Marseille	2/10	36/50	43	8/18	46/64	42	17/29	63/84	11	10/20	50/68	76
Naxos	10/15	50/59	91	13/20	55/68	19	22/27	72/81	2	18/24	64/75	45
Paris	1/6	34/43	56	6/16	43/61	42	15/25	59/77	59	8/16	46/61	50
Prague	-5/0	23/32	18	3/12	37/54	27	13/23	55/73	68	5/12	41/54	33
Rome	5/11	41/52	71	10/19	50/66	51	20/30	68/86	15	13/22	55/72	99
Venice	1/6	34/43	37	10/17	50/63	78	19/27	66/81	52	11/19	52/66	77
Vienna	-4/1	25/34	39	6/15	43/59	45	15/25	59/77	84	7/14	45/57	56

To convert from degrees Fahrenheit to degrees Celsius, subtract 32 and multiply by 5/9. To convert from Celsius to Fahrenheit, multiply by 9/5 and add 32.

°CELSIUS	-5	0	5	10	15	20	25	30	35	40
°FAHRENHEIT	23	32	41	50	59	68	77	86	95	104

measurements

Like the rest of the rational world, Europe uses the metric system. The basic unit of length is the meter (m), which is divided into 100 centimeters (cm) or 1000 millimeters (mm). One thousand meters make up one kilometer (km). Fluids are measured in liters (L), each divided into 1000 milliliters (mL). A liter of pure water weighs one kilogram (kg), the unit of mass that is divided into 1000 grams (g). One metric ton is 1000kg. Gallons in the US and those in Britain are not identical: one US gallon equals 0.83 Imperial gallons. Pub aficionados will note that an Imperial pint (20 oz.) is larger than its US counterpart (16 oz.).

MEASUREMENT CONVERSIONS	
1 inch (in.) = 25.4mm	1 millimeter (mm) = 0.039 in.
1 foot (ft.) = 0.305m	1 meter (m) = 3.28 ft.
1 yard (yd.) = 0.914m	1 meter (m) = 1.094 yd.
1 mile (mi.) = 1.609km	1 kilometer (km) = 0.621 mi.
1 ounce (oz.) = 28.35g	1 gram (g) = 0.035 oz.
1 pound (lb.) = 0.454kg	1 kilogram (kg) = 2.205 lb.
1 fluid ounce (fl. oz.) = 29.57mL	1 milliliter (mL) = 0.034 fl. oz.
1 gallon (gal.) = 3.785L	1 liter (L) = 0.264 gal.

language

PHRASEBOOK

ENGLISH	ITALIAN	FRENCH	SPANISH	PORTUGUESE	TURKISH
Hello	Buongiorno	Bonjour	Hola	Olá	Merhaba
Good-bye	Arrivederci	Au revoir	Adiós	Até logo	Iyi günler/Iyi akşamlar
Yes	Sì	Oui	Sí	Sim	Evet
No	No	Non	No	Não	Hayır
Please	Per favore	S'il vous plaît	Por favor	Por favor	Lütfen
Thank you	Grazie	Merci	Gracias	Obrigado/a	Teşekkur ederim
You're welcome	Prego	De rien	De nada	De nada	Bir şey değil
Sorry!	Mi scusi!	Désolé!	¡Perdón!	Desculpe!	Pardon!
My name is...	Mi chiamo...	Je m'appelle...	Me llamo...	O meu nome é...	Ismim...
How are you?	Come sta?	Comment êtes-vous?	¿Cómo estás?	Como você está?	Sen nasılsın?
I don't know.	Non lo so.	Je ne sais pas.	No sé.	Eu não sei.	Bilmiyorum.
I don't understand.	Non capisco.	Je ne comprends pas.	No entiendo.	Não entendo.	Anlamadım.
Could you repeat that?	Potrebbe ripetere?	Répétez, s'il vous plaît?	¿Puede repetirlo?	Você pode repetir?	Lütfen o tekrarla.
Do you speak English?	Parla inglese?	Parlez-vous anglais?	¿Hablas español?	Fala inglês?	İngilizce biliyor musun?
I don't speak ___.	Non parlo italiano.	Je ne parle pas français.	No hablo español.	Eu não falo português.	Turkçe okuyorum.
Why?	Perché?	Pourquoi?	¿Por qué?	Porque?	Neden?
Where is...?	Dov'è...?	Où est?	¿Dónde esta...?	Onde é..?	...nerede?
What time is it?	Che ore sono?	Quelle heure est-il?	Qué hora es?	Que horas são?	Saat kaç?
How much does this cost?	Quanto costa?	Combien ça coûte?	¿Cuánto cuesta esto?	Quanto custa?	Ne kadar bu bedeli do?
I am from the US.	Sono degli Stati Uniti.	Je suis des Etats-Unis.	Soy de los Estados Unidos.	Eu sou de os Estados Unidos.	Ben ABD geliyorum.

ENGLISH	ITALIAN	FRENCH	SPANISH	PORTUGUESE	TURKISH
I have a visa/ID.	Ho un visto/ carta d'identità.	J'ai un visa/de l'identification.	Tengo una visa/ identificación.	Eu tenho um visto.	Benim bir vizem/ ID var.
I have nothing to declare.	Non ho nulla da dichiarare.	Je n'ai rien à déclarer.	No tengo nada para declarar.	Não tenho nada a declarar.	Duyurmak için benim hiçbirşeyim yok.
I will be here for less than three months.	Sarò qui per meno di tré mesi.	Je serai ici pour moins de trois mois.	Estaré aquí por menos de tres meses.	Eu estarei aqui há menos de três meses.	Ben üçten az ay için burada olacağım.
One-way	Solo andata	Aller simple	Ida	Ida	Tek yön
Round-trip	Andata e ritorno	Aller-retour	Ida y vuelta	Ida e volta	Gidiş dönüş
Hotel/hostel	Albergo/ostello	Hôtel/auberge	Hotel/hostal	Hotel/albergue	Otel/pansiyon
I have a reservation.	Ho una prenotazione.	J'ai une réservation.	Tengo una reservación.	Tenho uma reserva feita.	Benim bir koşulum var.
Single/double room	Camera singola/ doppia	Chambre pour un/deux	Habitación simple/doble	Quarto individual/duplo	Tek/çift kişilik
I'd like...	Vorrei...	Je voudrais...	Me gustaría...	Gostaria...	Ben bir ...seveceğim.
Check, please!	Il conto, per favore!	L'addition, s'il vous plaît!	¡La cuenta, por favor!	A conta, por favor!	Hesap, lütfen.
I feel sick.	Mi sento male.	Je me sens malade.	Me siento mal.	Eu me sinto doente.	Ben hastayım.
Get a doctor!	Telefoni un dottore!	Va chercher un médecin!	¡Llama el médico!	Chamar um doutor!	Doktor ihtiyacim!
Hospital	Ospedale	Hôpital	Hospital	Hospital	Hastane
I lost my passport/luggage.	Ho perso il mio passaportol / miei bagagli.	J'ai perdu mon passeport/baggage.	Se perdió mi pasaporte/equipaje.	Eu perdi o meu passaporte/a minha bagagem.	Ben benim pasaportumu/ bagajımı kaybettim.
Help!	Aiuto!	Au secours!	¡Socorro!	Socorro!	Imdat!
Leave me alone!	Lasciami stare!/ Mollami!	Laissez-moi tranquille!	¡Déjame!	Deixe-me em paz!	Beni yalnız bırak!
Go away!	Vattene!	Allez-vous en!	¡Vete!	Vá embora!	Git başımdan!
Call the police!	Telefoni alla polizia!	Appelez les flics!	¡Llama la policia!	Chamar a polícia!	Polis çağırın!

ENGLISH	GERMAN	DUTCH	CZECH	HUNGARIAN	GREEK PRO-NUNCIATION
Hello	Hallo/Tag	Dag/Hallo	Dobrý den	Szervusz	yah sahs
Good-bye	Auf Wiedersehen!/Tschüss!	Tot ziens!	Nashledanou	Viszontlátásra	yah sahs
Yes	Ja	Ja	Ano	Igen	neh
No	Nein	Nee	Ne	Nem	oh-hee
Please	Bitte	Alstublieft	Prosím	Kérem	pah-rah-kah-LO
Thank you	Danke	Dank u wel	Děkuji	Köszönöm	Ef-hah-ree-STO
You're welcome	Bitte	Alstublieft	Prosím	Kérem	pah-rah-kah-LO
Sorry!	Es tut mir leid!	Sorry!	Promiňte!	Elnézést!	sig-NO-mee
My name is...	Ich bin...	Mijn naam is...	Mé jméno je...	A nevem...	meh LEH-neh
How are you?	Wie geht's (geht es Ihnen)?	Hoe gaat het?	Jak se máš?	Hogy vagy?	tee KAH-neh-teh
I don't know.	Ich weisse nicht/ Keine Ahnung.	Ik weet het niet/ Geen idee.	Nevím.	Nem tudom.	dthen KSER-o
I don't understand.	Ich verstehe nicht.	Ik begrijp het niet.	Nerozumím.	Nem értem.	dthen kah-tah-lah-VEH-no
Could you repeat that?	Können Sie wiederholen?	Kunt u dat herhalen?	Můžete opakovat, že?	Meg tudnád ismételni ezt?	bor-EE-teh na ep-an-a-LAH-vet-eh ahv-TO
Do you speak English?	Sprechen Sie Englisch?	Spreekt u Engels?	Mluví anglicky?	Beszél angolul?	mee-LAH-teh sng-lee-KAH
I don't speak ____.	Ich kann kein Deutsch.	Ik spreek geen Nederlands.	Nemluvím Česky.	Nem tudok (jól) magyarul.	dthen meel-AOH eh-lee-nee-KAH
Why?	Warum?	Waarom?	Proč?	Miért?	gee-ah-TEY
Where is...?	Wo ist...?	Waar is...?	Kde je...?	Hol van...?	poo EE-ne

ENGLISH	GERMAN	DUTCH	CZECH	HUNGARIAN	GREEK PRONUNCIATION
What time is it?	Wie spät ist es?	Hoe laat is het?	Kolik je hodin?	Hány óra van?	tee O-rah EE-neh?
How much does this cost?	Wie viel (kostet das)?	Wat kost het?	Kolik to stojí?	Mennyibe kerül?	PO-so kos-TI-dzeh ahv-TO?
I am from the US.	Ich bin von Amerika.	Ik ben uit de VS.	Já jsem ze Spojených států.	Én vagyok az Egyesült Államok.	EE-meh ap-OH tiss een-o-MEN-ess pol-ee-TEE-ess
I have a visa/ID.	Ich habe ein Visum/eine ID.	Ik heb een visum/ID.	Mám víza/ID.	Van egy vízumot.	EH-oh mia theh-OH-ray-sey/tahf-TOH-tay-ta
I have nothing to declare.	Ich habe nichts zu verzollen.	Ik heb niets aan te geven.	Nemám nic k proclení.	Nekem van egy azonosítója.	Dthen EH-oh TEE-poh-teh na day-LO-so
I will be here for less than three months.	Ich reste hier für weniger als drei Monate.	Ik blijf hier minder dan drie maanden.	I tady bude za méně než tři měsíce.	Én itt leszek kevesebb, mint három hónap.	Tha EE-meh eth-OH gee-ah lig-OH-teh-ro ap-OH treess MAY-ness
One-way	Einfache	Enkele reis	Jedním směrem	Csak oda	mon-OH-drom-OSS
Round-trip	Hin und zurück	Rondreis	Zpáteční	Oda-vissza	met ep-eess-tro-FACE
Hotel/hostel	Hotel/Herberge	Hotel/hostel	Hotel/ubytovna	Hotel/szálló	kse-no-dtho-HEE-o/ksen-OH-na
I have a reservation.	Ich habe eine Reservierung.	Ik heb een reservering.	Mám rezervaci.	Foglaltam asztalt.	EH-oh CAHN-ee KRA-tay-say
Single/double room	Einzelzimmer/ Doppelzimmer	Eenpersoonskamer / Tweepersoonskamer	Jednolůžkový/ dvoulůžkový pokoj	Egyágyas / kétágyas szoba	mo-NO-klin-oh/ DIE-klin-oh
I'd like...	Ich möchte...	Ik wil graag...	Prosím...	kérek...	THAH EE-the-lah
Check, please!	Die Rechnung, bitte!	Mag ik de rekening!	Paragon, prosím!	A számlát, kérem!	oh lo-ghah-ree-yah-SMOS, pah-rah-kah-LO
I feel sick.	Ich bin krank.	Ik ben ziek.	Je mi špatně.	Rosszul érzem magam.	EE-meh AH-rose-tose
Get a doctor!	Hol einen Arzt!	Haal een dokter!	Najít lékaře!	Orvost!	PAH-re-te HEN-ah yiah-TROH
Hospital	Krankenhaus	Ziekenhuis	Nemocnice	Orvos	no-so-ko-MEE-o
I lost my passport/luggage.	Ich habe mein Reisepass/ Gepäck verloren.	Ik heb mijn paspoort/bagage verloren.	Ztratil jsem pas/ zavazadla.	Elvesztettem az útlevelemet/ Elfelejtettem a poggyász.	EH-ah-sa toh dthaya-vah-tee-ri-o/vah-LEE-tsah moo
Help!	Hilfe!	Help!	Pomoc!	Segíts nekem!	vo-EE-thee-ah!
Leave me alone!	Verloren gehen!	Laat me met rust!	Nech mě být!	Hagyj békén!	a-FIS-te me EE-si-kho (m.)/ EE-si-khee (f.)
Go away!	Geh weg!	Ga weg!	Prosím odejděte!	Távozék!	FOO-geh
Call the police!	Ruf die Polizei!	Bel de politie!	Zavolejte policii!	Hívja a rendőrséget!	kah-LESS-ee teen stih-noh-MIH-ah

language · phrasebook

GREEK ALPHABET

In the epic historical rumble that was *Latin Vs. Greek: Conjugation of Terror CXXVI BCE*, Latin pretty much won out, and as a victory prize, its alphabet became used the world over. As a consolation prize, the Greek alphabet kept Greece. In case your travels find their way to this fair country, here's a guide to the font that's only slightly less cool-looking than Zapf Dingbats:

SYMBOL	NAME	PRONOUNCED	SYMBOL	NAME	PRONOUNCED
A α	alpha	*a* as in f**a**ther	N ν	nu	*n* as in **n**et
B β	beta	*v* as in **v**elvet	Ξ ξ	xi	*x* as in mi**x**
Γ γ	gamma	*y* or *g* as in **y**oga	O o	omicron	*o* as in r**o**w
Δ δ	delta	*th* as in **th**ere	Π π	pi	*p* as in **p**eace
E ε	epsilon	*e* as in j**e**t	P ρ	rho	*r* as in **r**oll
Z ζ	zeta	*z* as in **z**ebra	Σ σ/ς	sigma	*s* as in **s**ense
H η	eta	*ee* as in qu**ee**n	T τ	tau	*t* as in **t**ent
Θ θ	theta	*th* as in **th**ree	Y υ	upsilon	*ee* as in gr**ee**n
I ι	iota	*ee* as in tr**ee**	Φ φ	phi	*f* as in **f**og
K κ	kappa	*k* as in **k**ite	X χ	chi	*h* as in **h**orse
Λ λ	lambda	*l* as in **l**and	Ψ ψ	psi	*ps* as in oo**ps**
M μ	mu	*m* as in **m**oose	Ω ω	omega	*o* as in Let's G**o**

tell the world

Plan your next trip on our spiffy website, ▣www.letsgo.com. It features full book content, the latest travel info on your favorite destinations, and tons of interactive features: make your own itinerary, read blogs from our trusty Researcher-Writers, browse our photo library, watch exclusive videos, check out our newsletter, find travel deals, follow us on Facebook, and buy new guides. Plus, if this Essentials wasn't enough for you, we've got even more online. We're always updating and adding new features, so check back often!

essentials

BEYOND TOURISM

If you are reading this, then you are a member of an elite group—and we don't mean "the literate." You're a student preparing for a semester abroad. You're taking a gap year to save the trees, the whales, or the dates. You're an 80-year-old woman who has devoted her life to egg-laying platypuses and figuring out what the hell is up with that. In short, you're a traveler, not a tourist; like any good spy, you don't observe your surroundings—you become an active part of them.

Your mission, should you choose to accept it, is to study, volunteer, or work in Europe as laid out in the dossier—er, chapter—below. More general wisdom, including international organizations with a presence in many destinations and tips on how to pick the right program, is also accessible by logging onto the Beyond Tourism section of ▣www.letsgo.com. We leave the rest (when to go, whom to bring, and how many changes of underwear to pack) in your hands. This message will ✺self-destruct in five seconds. Good luck.

greatest hits

- **LET'S STUDY.** We're the student travel guide, so of course we're going to love study abroad. This chapter lists organizations that will help you pick a study-abroad program as well as Europe's best universities (p. 1194).

- **LET'S STUDY, OUTSIDE THE BOX.** If you want to be the next Indiana Jones, you can enroll in an archaeology field class in Athens. If you want to be the next winner of *So You Think You Can Dance,* you can sharpen your moves at Taller Flamenco School in Sevilla (p. 1198).

- **LET'S VOLUNTEER.** Till an organic farm with fellow WWOOFers in Italy or do some good for the community in Vienna (p. 1200).

- **LET'S WORK.** If you're going to pad your resume, why not do it in France? The jobs we list can also help you defray the cost of your travels (p. 1200).

studying

As you've doubtlessly already discovered from Googling "study abroad," becoming overwhelmed, questioning whether you want to go in the first place, and then calling your mom (yeah, we've been there), there are a ton of different study-abroad options out there. But don't worry! We're here to help. First, ask yourself what you want to get out of a study-abroad program. Are you looking for a basic language and culture course that will let you spend as much time as possible engaging with local, erm, language and culture? Or are you seeking university-level classes to count for college credit? Second, search certain study-abroad-specific websites like ▣**www.studyabroad.com**, ▣**www.goabroad.com**, and ▣**www.westudyabroad.com** for programs that meet your criteria. You can usually search by type of program, desired location, and focus of study. Once you've settled on a few favorites, research them as much as you can before making your decision—determine things like cost, duration, what kinds of students participate in the program, and what sorts of accommodations are provided.

visa information

If you're lucky enough to have an EU passport, stop reading and count your blessings. Non-EU citizens hoping to study abroad in the EU, on the other hand, must obtain a special student visa. The acquisition process can be complicated and requires more pieces of identification than you knew existed, but often if you study abroad with a program rather than enrolling directly, the program will help you with this process. For every country, the best and most up-to-date information can be obtained from your local consulate. Visa applications often have ▣**fees** attached to them that can range from $30 to $300.

UNIVERSITIES

OK, say you're a college student who wants to spend a semester abroad in the Netherlands at Heerhugowaard State. In addition to researching on your own as described above, your friendly neighborhood study-abroad office is an excellent place to get your bearings. Make sure that you're proficient in Dutch first, though: most university-level study-abroad programs are conducted in the local language (although many programs offer classes in English and lower-level language courses, too). Especially skilled speakers of Dutch (or whatever; you get the point) may find it cheaper to enroll directly in a university abroad, although getting college credit may be more difficult.

International Programs

AHA INTERNATIONAL

70 NW Couch St., Ste. 242, Portland, OR 97209 ☎800-654-2051 ▣www.ahastudyabroad.org
An affiliate of the University of Oregon, the ironically-named American Heritage Foundation will set you up to study abroad in major study-abroad destinations like Siena, London, Vienna, Berlin, and Athens.
⑨*Tuition $3730-14,300, depending on the destination and which term you take abroad.*

AMERICAN FIELD SERVICE

71 West 23rd Street, 17th Floor, New York City, NY 10010 ☎212-352-9810 ▣www.afs.org
Run by a network of volunteer organizations in over 50 countries, AFS runs high school exchange programs that send students all over Europe to live with host

beyond tourism

families and attend local schools full-time. Also, on their website, they offer a vision for the year 2020, so you know they're in it for the long haul.Contact the office in your home country for more details.

ℹ Prices and available spots vary over time; consult the website for up-to-date information. Scholarships available. ⏰ "School Programs" last for a trimester, semester, or year. Intensive and summer programs last for 1-3 months.

AMERICAN INSTITUTE FOR FOREIGN STUDY (AIFS)

River Plaza, 9 West Broad St., Stamford, CT 06902 ☎866-906-2437 🖥www.aifs.com

With programs in 17 different countries and over 50,000 participants each year, AIFS is one of the oldest and largest cultural exchange organizations out there. Better yet, it's open to both high school and college students. Destinations in Europe cover almost anywhere you'd possibly want to go: London, Berlin, Florence, Rome, Prague, and Paris, to name a few.

ℹ Scholarships available. $ Semester $13,495-16,495; summer $4995-10,995; prices depend on location and length.

ARCADIA UNIVERSITY

450 S. Easton Rd., Glenside, PA 19038 ☎866-927-2234 🖥www.arcadia.edu/abroad

Arcadia's program in each destination (destinations that include pretty much every major European country) has something unique to recommend it. For instance, Florence includes special design and intensive fashion design programs,the Toledo program fee includes a four-day field study in Morocco, and classes in Athens include field-study excursions to historical sites.

ℹ 2.7-3.0 min. GPA, depending on program. $ Semester $12,500-22,450; summer $2550-7600. Semester estimates do not include meal costs; summer estimate does not include room and board.

COUNCIL ON INTERNATIONAL EDUCATION EXCHANGE (CIEE)

300 Fore St., Portland ME 04101 ☎207-553-4000 🖥www.ciee.org

CIEE not only organizes study abroad programs for US high school and college students, but they also offer internships and teaching opportunities. They can whisk you away to places like London, Brussels, Prague, Naples, and Paris.

ℹ Scholarships available. $Semester $13,500-18,500; summer $3375-6400.

CULTURAL EXPERIENCES ABROAD (CEA)

2005 W. 14th St., Suite 113, Tempe, AZ 85281 ☎800-266-4441 🖥www.gowithcea.com

CEA offers summer, semester, or full-year programs in places like London, Paris, Grenoble, Aix-en-Provence, and Prague.

$Semester $10,995-16,595; 3-week summer program $4295.

EXPERIMENTIAL LEARNING INTERNATIONAL

1557 Ogden St., Denver, CO 80218 ☎303-321-8278 🖥www.eliabroad.org

A smaller study-abroad organization, ELI combines study programs with internships and other international goodies at campuses in Paris, Florence, and other spots.

$Semester $12,595-13,595; summer $1265-5335.

INSTITUTE FOR THE INTERNATIONAL EDUCATION OF STUDENTS

33 N. LaSalle St., 15th fl., Chicago, IL 60602 ☎800-995-2300 🖥www.iesabroad.org

A semester in Nantes? A summer in Barcelona? Or how about J-term in Rome? IES has opportunities for enrollment in courses at local universities, term-time and summer internships, "field study activities" (read: field trips), and language improvement. Homestays or apartment housing can be found through the institute.

$Semester $13,885-21,320; summer $6500-7340.

Local Programs

The following are just a few of literally thousands of local institutions of higher learning in Europe—culled from some of the continent's hottest study-abroad destinations. For more detail, check out Let's Go guides to specific countries.

EUROPEAN UNIVERSITY BARCELONA

Ganduxer 70, Barcelona, Spain   ☎+34 93 201 81 7 ◼www.euruni.edu

One of the world's top business schools just happens to be in Barcelona. Perfect for all those future world-dominators out there.

ⓈSemester approx. $7000.

LEIDEN UNIVERSITY (UNIVERSITEIT LEIDEN)

Rapenburg 70, Leiden, the Netherlands   ☎71 527 2727 ◼www.leidenuniv.nl

Oldest university in the Netherlands, dating back to 1575, with a campus in Amsterdam. Includes an observatory, medical center, and academy of performing arts. Part-time programs available.

LONDON SCHOOL OF ECONOMICS (LSE)

Houghton Street, London, WC2A 2AE, UK   ☎20 7405 7686 ◼www.lse.ac.uk

LSE accepts international students who have completed at least two years of undergraduate study for a year-long general course, running from October to July.

𝒊 Minimum GPA requirements vary by department. ⓈTuition £14,426.

UNIVERSIDAD EUROPEA DI MADRID

Madrid, Spain   ☎+34 911 421 015 ◼www.uem.es/en

One of the many institutions in this nation's capital, it even has programs for students over the age of 40. Some courses are offered in English.

Ⓢ4-week summer course €2950. Price includes housing and full board.

UNIVERSITÀ DI BOLOGNA

V. Zamboni 33, Bologna, Italy   ☎+39 051 208 8101 ◼www.eng.unibo.it

Take your pick of one of Bologna's five campuses, one each in Cesena, Forlì, Ravena, Rimini, and...Bologna! Luckily, no matter where you go, you can still say that you attend the super-cute-sounding "UniBo." The university offers a range of courses taught in English, including some classes created in partnership with other institutions of higher learning. You can also check out Bologna's summer school in Italian language and culture. With great generosity, the school offers free Italian-language instruction to non-Italian EU and other foreign students.

UNIVERSITY OF CAMBRIDGE

The Old Schools, Trinity Lane, Cambridge CB2 1TN, UK   ☎12 23 33 3308 ◼www.cam.ac.uk

Unlike your typical American university, Cambridge comprises 29 undergraduate colleges. Your college is where you eat, sleep, and have your "supervision"—Cambridge-speak for one-on-one or small group lessons with a professor. Lectures are optional, so you can sleep in and not even feel guilty about it.

ⓈFull year £15,000-19,000.

UNIVERSITY OF OXFORD

University Offices, Wellington Square, Oxford, OX1 2JD, UK   ☎18 65 27 0000 ◼www.ox.ac.uk

Like Cambridge, Oxford operates on the tutorial system and has 38 independent, self-governing colleges. (Sorry—Gryffindor isn't one of them, but the Great Hall in Harry Potter was based on Christ Church, one of the Oxford colleges.) Check individual college and departmental websites for more information.

ⓈFull year up to £19,700.

beyond tourism

LANGUAGE SCHOOLS

As renowned novelist Gustave Flaubert once said, "Language is a cracked kettle on which we beat out tunes for bears to dance to." While we at Let's Go have absolutely no clue what he is talking about, we do know that the following are good resources for learning any European language.

A2Z LANGUAGES

3219 E. Camelback Rd #806, Phoenix, AZ ☎888-417-1533 🖳www.a2zlanguages.com

France, Germany, Italy, Spain, Portugal, Austria, and Greece could be the place you master a new tongue if you study in one of A2Z's numerous programs, which vary from one location to the other. All sites service everyone from the complete beginner to the student hoping to master the language.

Ⓢ$890-5930, depending on program length, number of classes per week, choice of accommodations, and time of year.

AMERISPAN STUDY ABROAD

1334 Walnut St., 6th fl., Philadelphia, PA ☎800-879-6640 🖳www.amerispan.com

With a presence on Facebook, Twitter, YouTube, and Skype, Amerispan is not only invading all the newfangled social media, but also actually provides helpful information about a bunch of language schools in France, Germany, Italy, Spain, Portugal, Austria, and Greece.

Ⓢ$320-10,000, depending on program location, length, and choice of accommodations.

EUROCENTRES

Seestr. 247, CH-8038 Zürich, Switzerland ☎+41 044 485 50 40 🖳www.eurocentres.com

No matter how advanced a speaker you are, Eurocentres has classes for you studying the native language in France, Spain, Germany, and Italy. The schools all provide recreation rooms and free internet access and organize a variety of outings and social activities.

i 16+.

SPECIAL-INTEREST SCHOOLS

"But, wait!" we hear you cry, "What if I don't want to study the history and culture of Lisbon? What if I couldn't care less about fulfilling my home school's requirements?" If your tastes are more specific than what a typical university can offer, here's some information on just a handful of alternative schools in Europe.

THE AMERICAN SCHOOL OF CLASSICAL STUDIES AT ATHENS

Souidias 54, Athens 10676, Greece ☎21072 36 313 🖳www.ascsa.edu.gr

Since 1881, American graduate students and professors have flocked here to participate in ongoing excavations of ancient sites, including the ancient Athenian agora. A 6-week summer program allows undergraduates to work at its sites and others.

i Applicants selected based on academic achievement and previous fieldwork experience. Application deadline for summer digs set in Dec. of previous year Ⓢ Room and a small daily stipend are given to admitted volunteers who can provide their own travel arrangements.

APICIUS INTERNATIONAL SCHOOL OF HOSPITALITY

Florence, Italy ☎+39 055 265 81.35 🖳www.apicius.it

At Apicius' campus in Florence, aspiring chefs, sommeliers, bakers, or extreme foodies can study their hearts out, with one-, two-, and four-year professional programs. Amateurs can also indulge in less intense instruction that may include gastronomic walking tours or visits to local farms and markets.

ARCHAEOSPAIN

Rome, Italy ☎866-932-0003 🖳www.archaeospain.com

Check out the "ancient pottery dump" of Monte Testaccio in Rome. If that doesn't sound super-appealing, maybe knowing that the artifacts you'll be digging up date from the first to third centuries will make the excavation more exciting. Anyone 18+ is welcome, and academic credit is available.

CORDON BLEU PARIS CULINARY ARTS INSTITUTE
8 rue Léon Delhomme, Paris, France ☎+33 1 53 68 22 50 🖳www.cordonbleu.edu

There's no more prestigious training academy for the serious aspiring chef than the original Paris branch of the Cordon Bleu. Certificate and degree programs available. More tourist-friendly options include two- to four-hour workshops and short courses that range in length from two days to one week. Price of a one-day taste of Provence workshop? €175. Bragging rights? Priceless.

L'ÉCOLE DU LOUVRE
Palais du Louvre, porte Jaujard, Paris, France ☎+33 1 55 35 18 35 🖳www.ecoledulouvre.fr

Installed in the Louvre in 1882, the École du Louvre, dedicated to "making the Louvre into a living center of study," offers degree-granting undergraduate, graduate, and post-graduate classes in art history and museum studies, as well as evening and summer classes and an art auctioneer training program. Looking for less of a commitment? Every Monday, Tuesday, and Thursday from 6:30-7:45pm, the École organizes free lectures by academics, curators, and other museum professionals.

MOSAIC ART SCHOOL
Ravenna, Italy ☎+39 349 601 4566 🖳www.sira.it/mosaic/studio.htm

Want a little mo' saic in your life? Then consider taking a five-day class (open to all levels, who knew there were advanced mosaicists these days?) in Ravenna. You'll walk away having completed two original pieces of your own design.

TALLER FLAMENCO SCHOOL
C. Peral, 49, 1st floor, Sevilla, Spain ☎+34 954 56 42 34 🖳www.tallerflamenco.com

If you want to brush up on those sexy Spanish dances, the Flamenco School in Sevilla teaches you the moves to impress your future lovers.

volunteering

Got an itch to save the world? We at Let's Goget all types of itches, so we can commiserate. Most people who volunteer abroad do so on a short-term basis at organizations that make use of drop-in or once-a-week volunteers. Local or national volunteer centers are where you want to go for this: they'll marry your ideal interests to your ideal schedule to send you on a honeymoon to your ideal destination. Websites like 🖳www.volunteerabroad.com, 🖳www.servenet.org, 🖳www.worldvolunteerweb.org, and 🖳www.idealist.org also allow you to search for volunteer openings abroad. Just make sure you do your own research, too: for example, a six-week trip to the Galapagos to spot wild boobies may not be what you think it is.

Those looking for longer, more intensive volunteer opportunities usually choose to go through a parent organization that takes care of logistical details and often provides a group environment and support system—for a fee. There are twvo main types of organizations—religious and secular—although heathens are usually allowed to work for the former, and vice versa. Pay-to-volunteer programs might be a good idea for young travelers who are looking for more support and structure (such as pre-arranged transportation and housing) or anyone who would rather not deal with the uncertainty of creating a volunteer experience from scratch.

AMNESTY INTERNATIONAL
1 Easton St., London WC1X 0DW, UK ☎+44 20 74 13 55 00 🖳www.amnesty.org

One of the world's foremost human rights organizations. Contact the office in the country you want to volunteer in for info about paid positions and volunteer work. Internships are available, too.

EARTHWATCH

256 Banbury Rd., Oxford OX2 7DE, UK   ☎+44 1865 318 838 ▣www.earthwatch.org

This nonprofit takes on volunteers to help with fieldwork and data collection, helping to preserve Europe's cultural and archaeological heritage. Think summer camp meets service work, with volunteer opportunities like digging up ancient Roman artifacts in Tuscany and conducting wildlife research in the coastal waters of southwest Scotland.

Programs range 3-21 days.

GEOVISIONS

63 Whitfield St., Guilford, CT 06437   ☎203-453-5838 ▣www.geovisions.org

The fine folks at Geovisions let you volunteer in Austria, France, Germany, Italy, Spain, and Turkey. An example of one program, in Munich, is a homestay with a German family while teaching them English for 15hr. per week.

GLOBAL VOLUNTEERS

375 E. Little Canada Rd., St. Paul, MN 55117   ☎800-487-1074 ▣www.globalvolunteers.org

This American organization connects volunteers to multiple organizations in Europe, including in Budapest and Italy. Sometimes an initial fee must be paid to cover costs like food, housing, orientation, and medical insurance.

HABITAT FOR HUMANITY

121 Habitat St., Americus, GA 31209   ☎800-422-4828 ▣www.habitat.org

The grandaddy of them all, Habitat for Humanity keeps its international acclaim and name-brand appeal with destinations around the world. Volunteers build houses in over 83 countries, including Britain, Portugal, Ireland, the Netherlands, Germany, France, and Hungary.

Periods of involvement range from 2 weeks to 3 years.

INVOLVEMENT VOLUNTEERS

☎+61 3 9646 9392 ▣www.volunteering.org.au

Get down and dirty working in this global volunteering company's archaeological workcamp in Sicily or help the disabled community in Austria while living with a host family. More programs cut from the same cloth are available in Britain, France, Spain, Germany, Greece, and Turkey.

OXFAM INTERNATIONAL

226 Causeway St., 5th fl., Boston, MA 02114   ☎800-77-OXFAM ▣www.oxfam.org

Oxfam is dedicated to reducing poverty and injustice around the world, focusing in particular on basic human rights, income inequality, and arms reduction. They've got offices in Britain, Ireland, France, Germany, Belgium, the Netherlands, and Spain.

SERVICE CIVIL INTERNATIONAL

5474 Walnut Level Rd., Crozet, VA 22932   ☎434-336-3545 ▣www.sci-ivs.org

Legal residents of Canada and the US are assigned to workcamps in countries like Germany and Spain with tasks ranging from teaching English to farming. Sometimes, though, the assignments get kookier, like staffing an environmentally friendly youth festival near Bologna, Italy.

i 18+. *Programs last 2 weeks-1 year.*

UNITED PLANET

11 Arlington St., Boston, MA 02116   ☎800-292-2316 ▣www.unitedplanet.org

This international non-profit organizes "volunteer quests" in partnership with local programs in need of volunteers. Several such projects in Italy, Germany, and other European nations offer the opportunity to experience a high level of cultural immersion while doing community service.

volunteering

VOLUNTEERS FOR PEACE

1034 Tiffany Rd., Belmont VT 05730 ☎802-259-2759 🖳www.vfp.org

VFP hosts project directories for individuals, teenagers, and families that want to volunteer in various areas. It lists more than 70 volunteer opportunities in Italy alone. Accommodations are, mercifully, provided.

WORLD WIDE OPPORTUNITIES ON ORGANIC FARMS

🖳www.wwoof.org

"WWOOF-ing" involves an international network devoted to helping people create more sustainable lifestyles and has become increasingly popular in recent years. Volunteers work on a farm in exchange for free food, accommodation, and opportunities to learn first-hand about sustainable agriculture and organic farming techniques. In order to WWOOF, you must join the local WWOOF organization, which involves a small fee.

i Volunteers 18+. $Membership fees vary by country; membership for WWOOF Independents (countries without national organizations) £15 per year, joint membership for 2 £25. ⏰Duration and min. stay varies by project.

working

Nowhere does money grow on trees (though Let's Go Researcher-Writers aren't done looking), but there are still some pretty good opportunities to earn a living and travel at the same time. As with volunteering, work opportunities tend to fall into two categories. Some travelers want long-term jobs that allow them to integrate into a community, while others want short-term jobs to finance the next leg of their travels. (Really ambitious people want both.) **Transitions Abroad** (*🖳www.transitionsabroad.com*) helps potential worker-travelers of all persuasions with its up-to-date online listings for work over any time period. Those who might be skeptical about using this newfangled "World Wide Web" can also seek out classified ads in local newspapers (no joke), federally run employment offices, and American Chambers of Commerce.

more visa information

To work legally in any country as a non-citizen, more often than not you need a work permit or a work visa. Citizens of the EU may live and work in any EU country. For everyone else, a visit to your local consulate, a passport, and an official transcript of a job offer is a good start. Again, fees may apply, and they may be anywhere from $30 to $300. Make sure to start your visa application the moment you know you are working in Europe, as the process is long and arduous. First check with your employer or any contacts abroad about permits—usually they are easier to obtain from government organizations within the country in which you plan to work.

LONG-TERM WORK

If you're planning on spending a substantial amount of time (more than three months) working abroad, search for a job well in advance—they go like hotcakes at a dangerously understocked IHOP.

Teaching English

In almost all cases, you must have at least a bachelor's degree to be a full-fledged teacher, although college undergrads can often get summer positions teaching or tutoring. Many schools require teachers to have a **Teaching English as a Foreign Language**

(TEFL) certificate, or the regional equivalent. You may still be able to find a teaching job without one, but certified teachers often rake in more dough. However, the foreign-language-challenged don't have to give up their dream of teaching. Private schools usually hire native English speakers for English-immersion classrooms where the native language is not spoken. (Teachers in public schools will more likely work in both English and the local language.) Placement agencies or university fellowship programs are the best resources for finding teaching jobs. The alternatives are to contact schools directly or try your luck once you arrive at your destination. In the latter case, the best time to look is several weeks before the start of the school year (when no one else can stomach the thought of going back).

DAVE'S ESL CAFE

9018 Balboa Blvd. #512, Northridge, CA 💻www.eslcafe.com

A two-sided marketplace for ESL teachers and employers, Dave's ESL Cafe has listings around the globe. It's free for teachers, but there are fees for schools and recruiters. The "Job Links" link will lead you to help-wanted ads all over Europe. Plus, Dave is just a good-looking guy.

INTERNATIONAL SCHOOLS SERVICES

15 Roszel Rd., P.O. Box 5910, Princeton, NJ ☎609-452-0990 💻www.iss.edu

ISS hires teachers and administrators for more than 200 overseas schools. Candidates should have teaching experience and a bachelor's degree. Its American-school job openings are great if you don't speak the local language.

$ $185 application fee.

I-TO-I TEACH ENGLISH ABROAD

240 Commercial St., Suite 4A, Boston, MA ☎800-352-1793 💻www.onlinetefl.com

I-to-I sets you up with the proper TEFL courses you need and has job listings for after certification, including programs for academic purposes and business English.

$ Salary ranges $20-35 per hr., depending on qualifications and experience.

OXFORD SEMINARS

244 5th Ave., Ste. J262, New York City, NY 10001 ☎800-779-1779 💻www.oxfordseminars.com

If you want to teach English abroad but don't know "their" from "there" from "they're," Oxford might be the place to start. (Or middle school—zing.) Oxford offers TESOL/TESL/TEFL certification courses in the US and Canada and then helps to place its graduates at ESL teaching jobs around the world—as long as you've got a bachelor's degree to go along with your Oxford certification. The helpful website provides a ton of helpful information, including detailed explanations of how to obtain work visas for citizens of all different countries hoping to teach abroad.

$ TESOL/TESL/TEFL Teacher Training Certification Course $1095. 🕐 Courses generally take up 6 days over the course of 3 weeks. Check website for local course info.

US DEPARTMENT OF STATE

2201 C St. NW, Washington, DC 20520 ☎202-261-8200 💻www.state.gov/m/a/os

Leave it to Uncle Sam to monitor your every twitch and inhalation as you flirt naively with a freedom you'll never know. Er, that is, to link you to teaching opportunities in Europe. State's Office of Overseas Schools maintains a directory of international schools abroad and offers helpful info on how to pursue teaching jobs. Just try to act normal when the suits come knocking.

Au Pair Work

Au pairs are typically women (although sometimes men) aged 18-26 who work as live-in nannies, caring for children and doing light housework in exchange for room, board, and a meager spending allowance or stipend. (Well, "meager" isn't completely fair—sometimes it's just small.) One perk of the job is that it allows you to get to know a new country without large travel expenses. Drawbacks, however, can include long hours and, well, a meager spending allowance. Be warned: much of the au pair experience depends on the family with which you are placed.

AU PAIR CONNECT

🖳www.aupairconnect.com

Your basic pairing service. Au pairs can search for families by nationality as well as by country, so if you want to au pair in Belgium but only get along with Luxembourgers, you're in luck.

$ Free to register and search, $45 for 3 months for access to contact info.

CHILDCARE INTERNATIONAL

☎+44 20 89 06 31 16 🖳www.childint.co.uk

More of the same: an au pair and family dating service, essentially. France and the Netherlands are two big destinations.

GREAT AU PAIR

1329 Hwy. 395, Gardnerville, NV 89410 ☎775-215-5770 🖳www.greataupair.com

An easy-to-use, US-based organization that matches au pairs with families across the world. Make a profile and search for jobs. Also offers information on visas and immigration.

[i] You can search for jobs without a membership, but must register to access contact info. $ Free registration offers functional access to site. For full access, 30-day membership $60, 90-day membership $120. Criminal background checks $45-75.

SUNNY AU PAIRS

☎503-616-3026 🖳www.sunnyaupairs.com

This simple, convenient UK-based service connecting au pairs with families also provides testimonials from previous users.

$ Free to register as an au pair; membership for host families starts at £70 for 6 months.

Internships And Other Long-Term Work

CA EDUCATION PROGRAMS

112 E. Lincoln Ave., Fergus Falls, MN 56538 ☎218 739 3241 🖳www.communicatingforamerica.org/caep.html

Coordinates paid internships and other educational experiences with agricultural organizations. Jobs range from farming to wine-making and span the continent from France to the UK to Germany. College credit is also available.

EXPAT EXCHANGE

P.O. Box 67, Bernardsville, NJ 07924 ☎908-766-2733 🖳www.expatexchange.com

Expat Exchange is more of a discussion board for expats across the globe than a job site, but it does have job listings.

GLOBAL EXPERIENCES

🖳www.globalexperiences.com

Global Experiences arranges internships with companies in major cities like Milan, Dublin, and Sevilla. Programs include intensive language training, accommodation, emergency medical travel insurance, and full-time on-site support.

$ $6890-8990, depending on location and length of internship.

IAESTE

☎+44 20 73 89 4771 🖳www.iaeste.org

The International Association for the Exchange of Students for Technical Experience provides paid overseas internships to full-time university students studying in technical fields. If you're unsure whether you're studying in a "technical field," see the website for a detailed list of eligible disciplines. Most placements for 8-12 weeks during the summer, but some longer-term placements are also available.

Apply through your home country's IAESTE branch.

Ⓢ *$1000 program fee for placement.*

INTERNATIONAL COOPERATIVE EDUCATION

15 Spiros Way, Menlo Park, CA 94025 ☎650-323-4944 ▣www.icemenlo.com

Provides full-time paid internships (summer and semester) to US college students in a number of countries. Type-A workers rejoice: in addition to studying job-related vocabulary and current events, accepted students must write a five-page "paper of intent," a letter of introduction, a 10-page pre-departure paper, and a 15-page final report. So, uh, get to work.

i Applicants must be 18-30 years old. Ⓢ *Application fee $250. Placement fee $900; includes some housing, work authorization, and visa application fees. Salaries $300-2300 per month. $100 extra for students with non-US passports or students outside the US at the time of application. See website for details.* ⏰ *Internships run 2-3 months in the summer or for 1-2 college semesters.*

WORKAWAY

▣www.workaway.info

Workaway connects travelers with host families and organizations who offer room and board in exchange for a few hours of work per day *(generally 5hr. per day, 5 days per week)*. Lots of options to turn your man- or woman-power into a "vacation" of sorts at bed and breakfasts and farms in Europe.

Ⓢ *€18 for 2-year membership, €24 to sign up as a couple.* ⏰*No min. stay.*

SHORT-TERM WORK

Different countries have different kinds of odd jobs that can last a week, a month, or anything in between. One popular option is to work several hours a day at a hostel in exchange for free or discounted room and/or board. In some countries, though, this is illegal ("My bad, officer"), so double-check first. Most often, these short-term jobs are found by word of mouth or by expressing interest to the owner of a hostel or restaurant. Due to high turnover in the tourism industry, many places are eager for help, even if it is only temporary. *Let's Go* lists temporary jobs of this nature whenever possible as listings in our coverage of individual cities. In the meantime, some websites to try include ▣www.easyexpat.com, ▣www.backdoorjobs.com, ▣www.resortjobs.com, and/or ▣www.seasonworkers.com.

tell the world

If your friends are tired of hearing about that time you saved a baby orangutan in Indonesia, there's clearly only one thing to do: get new friends. Find them at our website, ▣www.letsgo.com, where you can post your study-, volunteer-, or work-abroad stories for other, more appreciative community members to read. There's also a Beyond Tourism section that elaborates on non-destination-specific volunteering, studying, and working opportunities. If you liked this chapter, you'll love it; if you didn't like this chapter, maybe you'll find the website's more general Beyond Tourism tips more likeable, you non-likey person.

INDEX

index

index

index

index

MAP INDEX

map index

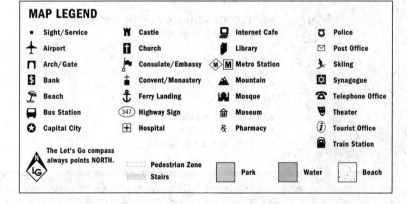

MAP LEGEND

- ■ Sight/Service
- ✈ Airport
- ⊓ Arch/Gate
- $ Bank
- 🏖 Beach
- 🚌 Bus Station
- ⊙ Capital City
- 🏰 Castle
- ✝ Church
- ⚑ Consulate/Embassy
- ⚓ Convent/Monastery
- ⚓ Ferry Landing
- (347) Highway Sign
- ✚ Hospital
- 💻 Internet Cafe
- 📖 Library
- Ⓜ M Metro Station
- 🔺 Mountain
- 🕌 Mosque
- 🏛 Museum
- ℞ Pharmacy
- 🛡 Police
- ✉ Post Office
- ⛷ Skiing
- ✡ Synagogue
- ☎ Telephone Office
- 🎭 Theater
- ⓘ Tourist Office
- 🚉 Train Station

The Let's Go compass always points NORTH.

⋯⋯ Pedestrian Zone
▨▨▨ Stairs

Park
Water
Beach

LET'S GO!

THE STUDENT TRAVEL GUIDE

These Let's Go guidebooks are available at bookstores and through online retailers:

EUROPE
Let's Go Amsterdam & Brussels, 1st ed.
Let's Go Berlin, Prague & Budapest, 2nd ed.
Let's Go France, 32nd ed.
Let's Go Europe 2011, 51st ed.
Let's Go European Riviera, 1st ed.
Let's Go Germany, 16th ed.
Let's Go Great Britain with Belfast and Dublin, 33rd ed.
Let's Go Greece, 10th ed.
Let's Go Istanbul, Athens & the Greek Islands, 1st ed.
Let's Go Italy, 31st ed.
Let's Go London, Oxford, Cambridge & Edinburgh,
    2nd ed.
Let's Go Madrid & Barcelona, 1st ed.
Let's Go Paris, 17th ed.
Let's Go Rome, Venice & Florence, 1st ed.
Let's Go Spain, Portugal & Morocco, 26th ed.
Let's Go Western Europe, 10th ed.

UNITED STATES
Let's Go Boston, 6th ed.
Let's Go New York City, 19th ed.
Let's Go Roadtripping USA, 4th ed.

MEXICO, CENTRAL & SOUTH AMERICA
Let's Go Buenos Aires, 2nd ed.
Let's Go Central America, 10th ed.
Let's Go Costa Rica, 5th ed.
Let's Go Costa Rica, Nicaragua & Panama, 1st ed.
Let's Go Guatemala & Belize, 1st ed.
Let's Go Yucatán Peninsula, 1st ed.

ASIA & THE MIDDLE EAST
Let's Go Israel, 5th ed.
Let's Go Thailand, 5th ed.

Exam and desk copies are available for study-abroad programs and resource centers.
Let's Go guidebooks are distributed to bookstores in the U.S. through Publishers Group West and through Publishers Group Canada in Canada.
For more information, email letsgo.info@perseusbooks.com.

ACKNOWLEDGMENTS

SARAH THANKS: Germany/BPB runs on Fun Pod. Bro-tastic Colleen(ie bear) for always being patient with her freshman Ed. Meagan for musicals "busting out all over" on the daily. Matt for his melodic Jamaican Patois. Daniel for the jajajas. Marykate for fielding questions despite disagreements on cuisine. Joey G for the bear hugs. Prod for solving multiple computer issues while jamming on the ukulele and sharing stories. Ashley, Nathaniel, and Joe for the inspiration and comedy, the best combination an employee could ask for. Everybody else at *Let's Go;* you're all incredible. My researchers for putting their best foot forward for this book. My friends who dealt with the antics and rain checks. Big sis' Becca, who's a trooper and a role model, and liltle sis' Nina, the light of my life. My parents for going the extra mile for me. And for feeding me, which is a full-time job.

TERESA THANKS: Veggie Planet pizzas and Petsi Pies coffee, Liza Flum's kitchen and bootleg TV and the rickety machines at the Central Square Y. I thank Joe Gaspard and my pod-mates for having my back, and my parents, bad music, and David Foster Wallace for getting me through. My uncle's 80s comic books and my grandpa's Chicago sundaes helped too.

MEAGAN THANKS: Matt for his unwavering dedication and fresh-to-deathness, even when *Rocky* ate my life; you're the best RM an Ed could ask for. Our RWs for their tireless work and adventurous spirits. DBarbs for MEdits and chop-busting. Marykate for calming my crazy. Sara and DChoi, who kept me rollin' on the RIVER. Joe for his marketing prowess, but mostly his smiles. Nathaniel for flawless editorial *and* ticket management. Ashley for teaching Meags how to make moves in the roughest times. I'm not really tryna forget Colleenie Bear and Sarah for making Fun Pod the best. Joey G. for hugs and *Glee.* Thanks to Betty White, Leslie Uggams, Cher, Meryl, Marge, and all the other deeves. HRST 2010 for Tater Tots and fishnet therapy. Matt and Chris for being so sweet when Maj had to edit. Here's to Billy Shakes, Ginny Woolf, and Jude Law. Thank you to Mrs. O'Brien and Nicole. Finally, thank you, mom, for your constant support.

BRONWEN THANKS: Ursula Brangwen. Lamont and Widener. Conor. The apartment is clean, and I miss you. Tarek and HubSummer, for getting me out of the office. Chris, for your commitment to ⬛Tanjore Tuesdays, the ⬛boat ikon, orange highlighter, and shots with silly names. You'll get your cannoli when you get it. Our RWs, who transported me to sunny beaches and moonlit *piazze* on rainy Cambridge days. Too many times I wanted to run off to the North End after reading your restaurant write-ups. Rossi and the Masthead team, for all their assists in the P1 and prod process. Mama MK. Hope this one's a winner. Sleep now? Most of all, my mom and dad. I am so lucky to have such wonderful parents. My week at home traversing California's golden hills with you guys was one of the best of the summer, closely rivaled by the week you came to Boston. To future travel together!

JONATHAN THANKS: In no particular order: Anna Boch, Marykate Jasper, the whole *Let's Go* office, Grace Sun, Michal Labik, Jocey Karlan, Mark Warren, Christa Hartsock, Elyssa Spitzer, my family, all the food establishments in Harvard Square, the Los Angeles Lakers, the Kevin & Bean radio show, Winthrop E-21, Winthrop G-42, Antoine Dodson, and coffee.

ANNA THANKS: In a very particular order: all the kick-ass RW's, Jonathan Rossi, Marykate Jasper, the Snuggie, Caturday, Iya Megre, honey-stung fried chicken, the Winthrop-Eliot Dramatic Society, Marcel Moran, friends-list, Lucy, Waffle, and Moustafa the smoothie guy in the T-stop.

JOE THANKS: the *Let's Go* office team and his RWs for their hard work. Special thanks go out to the Starbucks staff for keeping me well caffeinated, to Bolt Bus for taking me back to Dix Hills, to my brother and sisters for always being down to party, and to my mother for her continued support. The ladies of Harem Pod never failed to make me laugh, even when I was pulling my hair out. Lady Gaga should also be thanked for her part in keeping me happy; we could definitely have a bad romance.

CHRIS THANKS: 🔲**Bronwen,** for being the hardest-working person at LGHQ and an awesome person at the same time. Marykate, for remarkable patience in the face of an avalanche of questions. My RWs, for each bringing their own style and personality to this book, for being great at their jobs, and for a whole load of amity. DChoi and all of Prod land, for coming to the rescue countless times. *Let's Go Italy 1982,* for being totally baller. *Gazetta Football Italia,* for teaching me everything I know about this great country. Any product preceded by the letter G, for making everything so much easier. Kirkland House, for being so damn fine. Catan, for the settlers. Tanjore, for feeding me. No thanks to the Nepalese flag, the Social Security Administration, or any and all Florentine purse-snatchers. Finally, the most special thanks to Area 51, for three years of happiness; my family, for 22 years of the same; and PJ, for everything.

COLLEEN THANKS: My RWs for killer copy and staying in touch. Sarah for supering (and being super). FUN POD. Daniel for pep talks. Matt for letting me be Ari. Meg for Massachusetts and summer theater. Marykate for laying the smackdown at Crema. Nathaniel for hiring me. Joe for family dinners. Joe for marketing moves. Sara and Dan for fixing my lazy RIVER. Edward-Michael for treats on crebit. Trace for loving life and being a bestie. Iris for labbits. Aaron for tweeting at me and reminding me that my boyfriend is gay. Court and Cathy for being all-star Gato Girlz. Travis for that free drink (call me!). Unos for snack hours and karaoke. Winnie and Logan for SF. Katie for NYC. Mr. Cronin for my first Red Sox game. My proctees for being good. Brendy for buying great birthday presents. Mom for everything.

MATT THANKS: Our RWs, for their terrific work on the road. Meg, for being a friend, a grandma, a wordsmith and an Anglophile. Daniel, for his multilingual motivational speaking. Marykate, for answering my XV hourly questions. Colleen, for being the best. Colleen, for being not the worst. Sarah, for sharing my favorite corner of 67 Mt. Auburn. Ashley, for helping me lock it up by day and rip it up by night. Nathaniel and Sara, for all the late-night help and snack foods. Joe Molimock, for making marketing moves. DChoi, for his technological wizardry. Joe Gaspard, for assisting my caffeine addiction. Bronwen, for putting the number one in P1. Hasty Pudding Theatricals. Not floods. Anybody who brought me from homeless to Harvard. Elisandre, for starting the week off right. Drake. Snuggies. Bolt Bus. Mom, Dad, Rachel, Edna, and the rest of my family. And of course, Fun Pod: make big love, not war.

DIRECTOR OF PUBLISHING   Ashley R. Laporte

EXECUTIVE EDITOR   Nathaniel Rakich

PRODUCTION AND DESIGN DIRECTOR   Sara Plana

PUBLICITY AND MARKETING DIRECTOR   Joseph Molimock

MANAGING EDITORS   Charlotte Alter, Daniel C. Barbero, Marykate Jasper, Iya Megre

TECHNOLOGY PROJECT MANAGERS   Daniel J. Choi, C. Alexander Tremblay

PRODUCTION ASSOCIATES   Rebecca Cooper, Melissa Niu

FINANCIAL ASSOCIATE   Louis Caputo

DIRECTOR OF IT   Yasha Iravantchi

PRESIDENT   Meagan Hill

GENERAL MANAGER   Jim McKellar

LET'S GO
masthead

ABOUT LET'S GO

THE STUDENT TRAVEL GUIDE

Let's Go publishes the world's favorite student travel guides, written entirely by Harvard students. Armed with pens, notebooks, and a few changes of clothes stuffed into their backpacks, our student researchers go across continents, through time zones, and above expectations to seek out invaluable travel experiences for our readers. Because we are a completely student-run company, we have a unique perspective on how students travel, where they want to go, and what they're looking to do when they get there. If your dream is to grab a machete and forge through the jungles of Costa Rica, we can take you there. If you'd rather bask in the Riviera sun at a beachside cafe, we'll set you a table. In short, we write for readers who know that there's more to travel than tour buses. To keep up, visit our website, www.letsgo. com, where you can sign up to blog, post photos from your trips, and connect with the Let's Go community.

TRAVELING BEYOND TOURISM

We're on a mission to provide our readers with sharp, fresh coverage packed with socially responsible opportunities to go beyond tourism. Each guide's Beyond Tourism chapter shares ideas about responsible travel, study abroad, and how to give back to the places you visit while on the road. To help you gain a deeper connection with the places you travel, our fearless researchers scour the globe to give you the heads-up on both world-renowned and off-the-beaten-track opportunities. We've also opened our pages to respected writers and scholars to hear their takes on the countries and regions we cover, and asked travelers who have worked, studied, or volunteered abroad to contribute first-person accounts of their experiences.

FIFTY-ONE YEARS OF WISDOM

Let's Go has been on the road for 51 years and counting. We've grown a lot since publishing our first 20-page pamphlet to Europe in 1960, but five decades and 60 titles later, our witty, candid guides are still researched and written entirely by students on shoestring budgets who know that train strikes, stolen luggage, food poisoning, and marriage proposals are all part of a day's work. Meanwhile, we're still bringing readers fresh new features, such as a student-life section with advice on how and where to meet students from around the world; a revamped, user-friendly layout for our listings; and greater emphasis on the experiences that make travel abroad a rite of passage for readers of all ages. And, of course, this year's 16 titles—including five brand-new guides—are still brimming with editorial honesty, a commitment to students, and our irreverent style.

THE LET'S GO COMMUNITY

More than just a travel guide company, Let's Go is a community that reaches from our headquarters in Cambridge, MA, all across the globe. Our small staff of dedicated student editors, writers, and tech nerds comes together because of our shared passion for travel and our desire to help other travelers get the most out of their experience. We love it when our readers become part of the Let's Go community as well—when you travel, drop us a postcard (67 Mt. Auburn St., Cambridge, MA 02138, USA), send us an email (feedback@letsgo.com), or sign up on our website (www. letsgo.com) to tell us about your adventures and discoveries.

For more information, updated travel coverage, and news from our researcher team, visit us online at www.letsgo.com.

THANKS TO OUR SPONSORS

- **HOSTELS ALESSANDRO.** Alessandro Palace & Bar, Via Vicenza 42, 00185 Rome Italy. Alessandro Downtown, Via Carlo Cattaneo 23, 00185 Rome ITALY. ☎+39 06-4461958; info@hostelsalessandro.com

- **HOTEL ABACO.** 1 Via dei Banchi, Santa Maria Novella 50123 Florence, Italy. ☎39 055 2381919. ▆www.hotelabaco.it.

- **SMART HYDE PARK INN.** 48-49 Inverness Terrace, London, W2 3JA. ☎44 020 7229 0000.

- **SMART HYDE PARK VIEW.** 16 Leinster Terrace, London, W2 3EU. ☎44 020 7402 4101.

- **SMART HYDE PARK HOSTEL.** 2-6 Inverness Terrace, London, W2 3HU; ☎44 020 3355 1441.

- **SMART CAMDEN INN.** 55-57 Bayham Street, London, NW1 0AA; ☎44 020 7388 8900.

- **SMART RUSSELL SQUARE.** 70-72 Guilford Street, London, WC1N 1DF; ☎44 020 7833 8818.

- **SMART ROYAL BAYSWATER HOSTEL.** 121 Bayswater Road, London, W2 3JH; ☎44 020 7229 8888. ▆www.smartbackpackers.com.

- **CZECH INN.** ▆czech-inn.com.

- **MOSAIC HOUSE.** ▆mosaichouse.com.

- **MISS SOPHIE'S.** ▆miss-sophies.com.

- **SIR TOBYS.** ▆sirtobys.com.

- **THE PINK PALACE.** Corfu Island, Greece. ☎30 26610 53106 or 53104. ▆www.thepinkpalace.com.

- **HOTEL PAPA GERMANO.** Via Calatafimi 14/a, 00185 Rome ITALY. ☎+39 06-486919; info@hotelpapagermano.com. ▆www.hotelpapagermano.com.

- **HELTER SKELTER HOSTEL.** Kalkscheunenstr. 4-5, 10117 Berlin. ☎0049 0 30 280 44 99 7. ▆www.helterskelterhostel.com.

- **SUNFLOWER HOSTEL.** Helsingforser Str. 17, 10243 Berlin. ☎0049 0 30 440 44 250. ▆www.sunflower-hostel.de.

- **HEART OF GOLD HOSTEL.** Johannisstr. 11, 10117 Berlin. ☎0049 0 30 29 00 33 00. ▆www.heartofgold-hostel.de.

- **ODYSSEE GLOBETROTTER HOSTEL.** Grünberger Str. 23, 10243 Berlin. ☎0049 0 30 29 0000 81. ▆www.globetrotterhostel.de.

- **HOTEL HANSABLICK.** Flotowstr.6, 10555 Berlin, Germany. ☎49 030 390 48 00. ▆www.hansablick.de.

- **ALETTO KREUZBERG.** Tempelhofer Ufer 8/9, 10963 Berlin, Kreuzberg. ☎49 030 259 30 48 0. ▆www.aletto.de.

- **ALETTO SCHÖNEBERG.** Grunewaldstraße 33, 10823 Berlin, Schöneberg. ☎49 030 21 00 36 80. ▆www.aletto.de.

- **FIVE ELEMENTS HOSTEL.** Moselstr. 40, 60329 Frankfurt. ☎0049 0 69 24 00 58 85. ▆www.5elementshostel.de.

- **EASY PALACE CITY HOSTEL.** Mozartstr. 4, 80336 Munich. ☎0049 0 89 55 87 97 0. ▆www.easypalace.de.

- **PRAGUE CENTRAL HOSTELS.** ▆www.praguecentralhostels.com; ▆www.praguesquarehostel.com; ▆www.oldpraguehostel.com.

If you are interested in purchasing advertising space in a Let's Go publication, contact Edman & Company at ☎1-203-656-1000.

HELPING LET'S GO. If you want to share your discoveries, suggestions, or corrections, please drop us a line. We appreciate every piece of correspondence, whether a postcard, a 10-page email, or a coconut. Visit Let's Go at **www.letsgo.com** or send an email to:

feedback@letsgo.com, subject: "Let's Go Europe"

Address mail to:

Let's Go Europe, 67 Mount Auburn St., Cambridge, MA 02138, USA

In addition to the invaluable travel advice our readers share with us, many are kind enough to offer their services as researchers or editors. Unfortunately, our charter enables us to employ only currently enrolled Harvard students.

Maps © Let's Go and Avalon Travel
Design Support by Jane Musser, Sarah Juckniess, Tim McGrath

Distributed by Publishers Group West.
Printed in Canada by Friesens Corp.

ISBN-13: 978-1-59880-702-8
Fifty-first edition
10 9 8 7 6 5 4 3 2 1

Let's Go Europe is written by Let's Go Publications, 67 Mt. Auburn St., Cambridge, MA 02138, USA.

Let's Go® and the LG logo are trademarks of Let's Go, Inc.

quick reference

YOUR GUIDE TO LET'S GO ICONS

☎	Phone numbers	⊘	Not wheelchair-accessible	❄	Has A/C
▣	Websites	((•))	Has internet access	⇆	Directions
💳	Takes credit cards	⌂	Has outdoor seating	*i*	Other hard info
🚫	Cash only	▼	Is GLBT or GLBT-friendly	$	Prices
♿	Wheelchair-accessible	♈	Serves alcohol	⌚	Hours

IMPORTANT PHONE NUMBERS

EMERGENCY: ☎112			
Austria	☎113	Hungary	☎107
Belgium	☎101	Ireland	☎999
Great Britain	☎999	Italy	☎113
Czech Republic	☎158	Netherlands	☎911
France	☎17	Portugal	☎112
Germany	☎110	Spain	☎092
Greece	☎100	Turkey	☎155

USEFUL PHRASES

ENGLISH	FRENCH	GERMAN	ITALIAN	SPANISH
Hello/Hi	Bonjour/Salut	Hallo!/Tag	Ciao	Hola
Goodbye/Bye	Au revoir	Auf Wiedersehen/ Tschüss	Arrivederci/Ciao	Adios/Chao
Yes	Oui	Ja	Sì	Sí
No	Non	Nein	No	No
Sorry	Je suis désolé.	Es tut mir leid.	Scusa	Lo siento.
Thank you	Merci	Danke	Grazie	Gracias
Go away!	S'en aller!	Geh weg!	Andare via!	Vete!
Help!	Au secours!	Hilfe!	Aiuto!	Ayuda!
Call the police!	Appelez les flics!	Ruf die Polizei!	Chiamare la polizia!	Llamen a la policía
Get a doctor!	Cherchez un médecin!	Hol einen Arzt!	Avere un medico!	Llamen a un médic

TEMPERATURE CONVERSIONS

°CELSIUS	-5	0	5	10	15	20	25	30	35	40
°FAHRENHEIT	23	32	41	50	59	68	77	86	95	104

MEASUREMENT CONVERSIONS

1 inch (in.) = 25.4mm	1 millimeter (mm) = 0.039 in.
1 foot (ft.) = 0.305m	1 meter (m) = 3.28 ft.
1 mile (mi.) = 1.609km	1 kilometer (km) = 0.621 mi.
1 pound (lb.) = 0.454kg	1 kilogram (kg) = 2.205 lb.
1 gallon (gal.) = 3.785L	1 liter (L) = 0.264 gal.